ISBN 978-1-5281-4122-2
PIBN 10921310

# 1 MONTH OF
# FREE
# READING

## at

## www.ForgottenBooks.com

By purchasing this book you are
eligible for one month membership to
ForgottenBooks.com, giving you
unlimited access to our entire
collection of over 1,000,000 titles via
our web site and mobile apps.

To claim your free month visit:

www.forgottenbooks.com/free921310

English
Français
Deutsche
Italiano
Español
Português

# www.forgottenbooks.com

**Mythology** Photography **Fiction**
Fishing Christianity **Art** Cooking
Essays Buddhism Freemasonry
Medicine **Biology** Music **Ancient**
**Egypt** Evolution Carpentry Physics
Dance Geology **Mathematics** Fitness
Shakespeare **Folklore** Yoga Marketing
**Confidence** Immortality Biographies
Poetry **Psychology** Witchcraft
Electronics Chemistry History **Law**
Accounting **Philosophy** Anthropology
Alchemy Drama Quantum Mechanics
Atheism Sexual Health **Ancient History**
**Entrepreneurship** Languages Sport
Paleontology Needlework Islam
**Metaphysics** Investment Archaeology
Parenting Statistics Criminology
**Motivational**

# The Surveyor

## And Municipal and County Engineer.

# VOL. XIV.

JULY 1 TO DECEMBER 30. 1898.

London:

THE ST. BRIDE'S PRESS. Ltd.,

ST. BRIDE'S HOUSE, 24 BRIDE LANE,

FLEET STREET, E.C.

# he Surveyor

## And Municipal and County Engineer.

# VOL. XIV.

JULY 1 TO DECEMBER 30, 1898.

London:

THE ST. BRIDE'S PRESS, Ltd.,

ST. BRIDE'S HOUSE, 24 BRIDE LANE,

FLEET STREET, E.C.

# The Surveyor

### And Municipal and County Engineer.

—

# VOL. XIV.

## JULY 1 TO DECEMBER 30. 1898.

London:

THE ST. BRIDE'S PRESS, Ltd.,

ST. BRIDE'S HOUSE, 24 BRIDE LANE,

FLEET STREET, E.C.

# The Surveyor

## And Municipal and County Engineer.

# VOL. XIV.

## JULY 1 TO DECEMBER 30. 1898.

London:

THE ST. BRIDE'S PRESS, Ltd.,

ST. BRIDE'S HOUSE, 24 BRIDE LANE,

FLEET STREET, E.C.

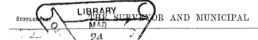
# INDEX.

# The Surveyor

## And Municipal and County Engineer.

| Vol. XIV., No. 337. | LONDON, JULY 1, 1898. | Weekly, Price 3d. |

## Minutes of Proceedings.

**Association of Municipal and County Engineers: The Annual Meeting.** The march of time has brought us once more to the annual meeting of the Association of Municipal and County Engineers—the great event in the history of the organisation and of municipal engineering from year to year. This year unusual interest attaches to the gathering, by reason of the fact that the association completes the first quarter of a century of its existence. In the full vigour of early manhood, therefore, and with the prospect of a useful and bright future, the organisation assembles in the historic capital of Scotland, where the members will find much that is interesting and instructive to occupy their time in the intervals of leisure which the compact and varied programme affords. In the programme itself, in fact, liberal provision is made for sight-seeing, and it gives an opportunity of visiting scenes and structures that have played an important part in Scottish history. In our last issue we gave a brief sketch of the main features of Edinburgh of to-day, and our readers can supply for themselves the pictures that fancy may suggest of the great figures that in the centuries that have passed moved on the stage of national life. A highly-satisfactory commencement was made yesterday, when the proceedings were opened under very favourable auspices. Probably many of the members had reached Edinburgh a day or two before the actual work began, and would no doubt have caught the vitalising spirit of the northern air, which would probably give them a real zest for work that combined both pleasure and profit. First in order of business came the annual report. This was of a very gratifying character, showing that substantial and satisfactory progress had been made during the twelve months. There is one painful fact that those annual gatherings invariably bring into prominence, and that is the gaps made by death in the ranks of the profession. In the year that has closed we have to deplore the death of half a dozen members whose faces were familiar at previous gatherings; and, in addition to them, the council had to record, with deep regret, their sense of the loss sustained through Sir Robert Rawlinson, who had been an honorary member of the association since its formation. Turning to more agreeable subjects, we note that the membership is increasing—slowly, it is true, but surely—and that the finances are in a flourishing condition. With reference to examinations—an important part of the work of the association—we observe with pleasure that the increase of candidates has been so great that the board of examiners have felt it incumbent upon them to make some new departures, which have been approved by the council. The new council will, we may be sure, worthily maintain the traditions of the office. The president, Mr. O. Claude Robson, the engineer to the Willesden Urban District Council, is a most acceptable and popular selection. Mr. W. Harpur, the borough engineer of Cardiff, now joins Messrs. J. Cooper and C. H. Lowe as vice-presidents, and he will, no doubt, do credit to the position. The additions to the ordinary members of the council are Mr. A. E. Collins and Mr. J. Price. Mr. Collins is the city engineer of Norwich, and we may say with regard to him that his great popularity has been considerably enhanced by the excellent meeting which he recently organised at Norwich. Mr. Price is the city surveyor of Birmingham, and it was inevitable that, sooner or later, he should be placed upon the council, and it is well that it should be sooner rather than later. The question of superannuation, which has been dealt with in our columns from time to time, was referred to in the report, and particulars were given of the action that had been taken with regard to the three Bills now before Parliament in which superannuation schemes are embodied. With a view to increasing the interest in the association in the Antipodes, the council have appointed Mr. R. W. Richards, the city surveyor of Sydney, corresponding secretary for Australasia, and there is every reason to believe that the appointment will be advantageous to the organisation.

The chief feature of the opening day's proceedings was, of course, the address of the president, who gave a most interesting, instructive and graphic sketch of the work of the municipal engineer. The work is certainly sufficiently varied to develop the versatility of those who aspire to the office, comprising as it does road-making and maintenance with concurrent bridge and viaduct work, tramways, sea and river walls, designing of sewerage and water systems, treatment of sewage, public lighting, erection of hospitals, public offices, free libraries, mortuaries, markets and buildings of all kinds incidental to municipal administration, to say nothing of the laying-out of public parks and pleasure grounds. Here, surely, is scope sufficient for ability and energy! Passing on from the general to the particular, Mr. Robson took up the interesting question of the purification of sewage by biological processes, and spoke of the valuable assistance rendered by the micro-organisms in tank and filter. The whole matter is still in the experimental stage, and hopes are centred upon the Royal Commission on the Treatment and Disposal of Sewage, which is the subject of comment in another column. Mr. Robson insisted upon the necessity for more careful consideration as regards the system to be adopted for the treatment of sewage. Public opinion and professional practice have undergone a change in this respect. Where there was a mere perfunctory examination of a stream in former years a duly-qualified staff of inspectors is now appointed, constant analyses are made, and riparian authorities are not allowed to evade their responsibilities. In the case of towns or districts situated upon sluggish streams an exceptionally high standard of purity is demanded, and Mr. Robson emphasised this very forcibly before passing on to sewer ventilation, which is still foremost among the difficulties in the path of the sanitary administrator. Closely related to it is the question of house drainage, and with regard to this it can scarcely be denied that if house drainage were more thoroughly and more effectively carried out there would be less necessity than there now is for the ventilation of sewers. A vast amount of the trouble that arises in connection with sewers is to be attributed to defective house drains. As Mr. Robson very truly observes, a systematic and efficient method of flushing house drains is an important factor in dealing with the ventilation of sewers. The maintenance of highways received attention from the president, and the substitution of wood paving for stone in all residential localities is alluded to as a necessity "in these neurotic days." The omnipresent microbe has now appeared upon the scene in connection with this particular form of paving, and an entirely new genus of bacteria, alleged to be injurious to human organism, has recently been discovered as emanating from imperfectly cleansed wood-paved roadways. The lesson drawn from this is the necessity for constantly and efficiently cleansing the streets and for using disinfectants in the work of watering them. Some eminently practical observations were made with regard to the need for watchfulness in the case of new buildings, to see that the stability of the structure is ensured and that due precautions are taken for the maintenance of health in the houses of the people  With regard to this it is almost superfluous to point out that too much attention cannot be paid to the efficient construction of the drainage, and the provision of requisite space around the dwellings in order that a free circulation of air may be secured. There can be no question that, great as have been the improvements of recent years and valuable as have been the by-laws framed in many districts, there is still room for advancement in both directions. Of all municipal works at present in progress or in contemplation, electric lighting monopolises the largest share of attention, and we quite agree with Mr. Robson that the almost universal action now taken by local authorities in the installation of electric light themselves, to the exclusion of monopolies, brings the question largely within the scope of the municipal engineer. The advantages possessed in many respects by electric light over any other form of artificial illumination is generally admitted, and it is gratifying to know that the financial success of most undertakings of municipal authorities seems to be fairly assured at the second or third year of working. The combination of the work incidental to the combustion of house refuse, with that appertaining to the generation of electrical energy, has been of late productive of no little discussion, and what Mr. Robson had to say with regard to it was worthy of attention. Some consideration was very properly given in the address to the state of the law with regard to public health, and he suggests the desirability of legislation in the direction of securing uniformity in the by-laws adopted, so that ignorance of the law could not be pleaded as an excuse for the neglect of obvious duty. The address was listened to with marked attention, and at its close Mr. Robson was cordially thanked.

A discussion was afterwards initiated by Mr. A. H. Campbell, Canterbury, on "Tar Macadam." Subsequently the members were entertained at luncheon, at the "Royal" hotel, by the Lord Provost and Corporation of Edinburgh. Later in the day papers were read on "Experiences of Edinburgh with Refuse Destructors," by Mr. John Young, Edinburgh; the "Conversion of Edinburgh, Leith and Portobello Horse-Tramway System into Cable Traction," by Mr. W. N. Colam, Edinburgh; "Notes on Sewer Ventilation as Applied to Water of Leith Intercepting Sewer," by Mr. Alex. Stewart, Edinburgh; and the "Housing of the Working Classes Act as Worked Out in Edinburgh," by Mr. Wm. Bruce, Edinburgh. Among the numerous papers which

will be read to-day are "Notes on the Bacterial Treatment of Sewage," by Mr. D. Cameron; "Electric Lighting of Edinburgh," by Mr. F. A. Newington, resident electrical engineer; and "Recent Extensions of Leith Docks," by Mr. Peter Whyte, docks superintendent. To-morrow, the concluding day of the meeting, will be largely devoted to sightseeing, the programme including a drive to Forth bridge.

\*          \*          \*

**The Royal Commission on Sewage Treatment and Disposal.** The Royal Commission for inquiry into the disposal and treatment of sewage have, we think, begun their work badly. They held two meetings last week, and at the first, at which they considered their mode of procedure, they decided that the proceedings would not be open to the public. We have no knowledge of the grounds upon which the decision was arrived at, but whatever they were they could not have been sufficient to justify the course adopted. It has ever been the policy of the Local Government Board to prefer darkness to light. Local government in its arteries, which spread their ramifications throughout the body politic of the nation, is illuminated by the transparent rays of the bright sun of public opinion, but in the main-spring of the arteries, the great heart centre at Whitehall, all is darkness. What passes within the walls of the central office we know not until it reaches the extremities of the system, where the pulse vibrates to the touch of local life. It was hoped that an exception would have been made in the case of the sewage commission, which might have been the medium by which much useful knowledge would have been disseminated upon a subject of vital importance to the health and well-being of the people, and upon which they are, we fear, wofully ignorant. The report of the commission will, no doubt, be available to the Press and the public at the close of the inquiry, but that is not enough. It will be impossible then to give more than a bare outline of the results arrived at. The exhaustive evidence will be sealed up within the lifeless pages of a Parliamentary blue-book, and available only for the industrious experts who will ponder over their discursive contents. Had the inquiry been open, how different would have been the result! From week to week, as the commission proceeded with their work, their labours would have been closely and studiously followed, stimulated by healthy and helpful opinion, and energised by critical observation which cannot now be secured. There is literally nothing to be said in favour of a hole-and-corner inquiry of the character now in progress. We cannot understand the commissioners favouring such a course. The chairman is the Earl of Iddesleigh, and the other commissioners who were present when the determination to sit with closed doors was arrived at were Sir Richard Thorne, K.C.B., Prof. Michael Foster, Prof. Wm. Ramsey, Major-General C. P. Carey, Dr. F. B. Russell, Colonel T. W. Harding, Mr. T. W. Killick and Mr. Chas. P. Cotton. The secretary is Mr. F. J. Willis. It is most unlikely that these gentlemen would have preferred a secret to an open tribunal. The strings in this matter were most likely pulled by the Local Government Board, and this is quite in harmony with their general dislike to publicity. The hearing of evidence has been commenced, for last week Mr. A. W. Adrian, C.B., assistant secretary of the Local Government Board, gave testimony as to the history and law of the subject under investigation so far as England is concerned, and he is being followed by witnesses from Scotland and Ireland. We trust that even yet it is not too late for the commission to reconsider the question of taking the public into their confidence and throwing the inquiry open to the Press. We know that many important and valuable experiments in sewage treatment and disposal have been made in recent years at a number of places, such as Exeter, Sutton, Oswestry and Winsford, and the engineering profession and the public would have followed with great interest accounts of the results obtained from the lips of the men whose discoveries have elevated matters of sanitation to the forefront of the scientific achievements of this wonderful century. We know that the attitude adopted by the Local Government Board towards the discoveries and the discoverers has not been invariably sympathetic. We mention these things merely to show what the public will lose through the present inquiry being conducted *januis clausis*. Some of the store of useful knowledge accumulated will, no doubt, itself be filtered out after the work of the commission is done; but will it serve the useful purpose it would have done had there been no concealment in the matter of the inquiry itself? We do not believe it, and for that reason we press for a reconsideration of the question by the commission.

\* \* \*

**Local Authorities and their Contractors.** The importance of ensuring the proper superintendence of contractors as regards precautions against accidents to the public is once more brought home to local authorities by the recent case of *Penny v. Wimbledon Urban District Council and Iles* (noted on p. 23). Short of actual superintendence, the council appear to have taken every means to secure proper safeguards. The work contracted for was the making-up of a road under sec. 150 of the Public Health Act, 1875, and by the terms of the contract the contractor was to provide all necessary watching, lighting and fencing. In the course of the preliminary process of clearing up the road sundry heaps of dirt and grass were formed, and these being left unlighted and unguarded, the plaintiff (an elderly lady), in passing along the road after nightfall, fell over one of these heaps and was injured. The council rather gave themselves away by proceeding to shut the stable door after the steed was stolen—in placing lights, or giving directions for lights being placed, on some of the other heaps. This action on their part, Mr. Justice Bruce, who tried the case, regarded as evidence that they not only had the power, but that they did, in fact, during the continuance of the contract, exercise the power, of directing lights to be placed as a warning to the public; thus negativing their contention that the contractor was an "independent contractor," over whom they had no control and for whose negligence they were not liable. Even apart from this, however, the case is, as the learned judge pointed out, practically indistinguishable from *Hardaker and Wife v. Idle District Council and Another* (noted pp. 95 and 217 of vol. ix.), in which the Court of Appeal held that the local authority, acting under the powers of the Public Health Act, could not, by employing a contractor, get rid of their own duty to other people, whatever that duty might be. A curious feature of the case is that the contractor, having paid into court £75 and the jury having returned a verdict for £50 only, the whole amount paid in will be returned to him—£25 as excess of damages and £50 on account of his costs (the balance whereof will be payable by the plaintiff)—while, on the other hand, the council, having denied liability and been found liable, will have to pay both their own and the plaintiff's costs, notwithstanding the superabundant payment into court by their co-defendant. This strikes us as in the highest degree inequitable, and we shall not be surprised if an attempt is made to get this portion of the judgment reviewed.

\* \* \*

**Municipal Electric Lighting at Coventry and Blackpool.** Attention may be called to the results of the municipal electric lighting system in Coventry. It will be seen from the following figures that very considerable progress has been made during the past twelve months. For the quarter ended December 31, 1897, the amount of electricity sold was 34,895 units against 25,685 units in 1896. The number of consumers had increased by twenty-eight, and there have been considerable extensions of the mains. Bringing the results more up to date the electricity supplied during the quarter ended March 31, 1898, was 35,690 units against 21,560 units in the corresponding period of the previous year. These results are all the more satisfactory because it was considered that there were special difficulties that would retard the progress of the municipal electricity works. The lighting accounts relating to Blackpool are almost as interesting as the tramway accounts to which we have previously referred. The total revenue for the year ended March 31st last was £12,837 and the expenditure was £7,152. A sum of £3,856 has been set aside for interest and sinking fund, this being at the substantial rate of 5¾ per cent., and there is then left the sum of £1,819 as representing the nett actual profit on the year's working. The profit on the previous year's working was £828, which is sufficient to show that substantial progress has been made. The units sold during that period have increased from 429,000 to 707,000, and the costs of production have been considerably decreased, being in fact 1·87d. against 2·61d. for the previous year, the total costs for the year ended 1897 being 2·42d. against 3·41d. for the previous year.

\* \* \*

**The Abuse of Power-Houses.** Mr. W. H. Preece, in the paper on this subject, which was read at the recent meeting of the Association of Municipal and County Engineers at Yarmouth, and is given in our present issue, was not a bit too strong in condemning some of the methods that have been adopted in designing and laying down electric lighting systems. There has been undoubtedly a want of foresight in predicting the growth of the electric industries, and there has been a want of economy in selecting suitable land upon which to erect electric lighting systems. While admitting these facts, however, it must not be forgotten that the supplying of electric energy was so totally different to gas and water that there was no experience whatever to guide the engineer when designing an electric system. There are many cases at the present moment in which municipal power-houses are much too small, and have been rather laid down with a view to meet the immediate demand than with any regard to future development. It would be very regrettable if, in the future expansion of electric work, municipalities did not consider the possible combination of lighting and tramway interests, and if these are kept carefully in view the previous mistakes of municipalities will be avoided. It is quite likely that the projected legislation on the subject of large power-houses for the purpose of distributing electrical energy over a large area will prove to be of great benefit to those large municipalities with such wide interests as in the case of Manchester, Glasgow and other large cities.

## PROPOSED PUBLIC BATHS AT BOLTON.

The Bolton Corporation propose spending the sum of £5,250 in the erection of public baths, on a site adjoining the branch public library in High-street. The building generally has been designed to harmonise with the free library adjoining, and will be of red brick with ornamental red terra-cotta dressings. In the basement there will be a boiler-house, coal-cellars, cistern-room, and an open gangway round three sides of the bath. The ground floor will contain a plunge or swimming bath, 75 ft. by 26 ft. It will have glazed-brick sides and a tiled bottom. The dressing-boxes number thirty-nine, and there is also an attendant's-room, besides soap and shower baths and conveniences. Circular staircases will lead to the gallery, which extends round three sides of the bath. The entrances are arranged so that they are controlled from the ticket office. The men's slipper baths—nineteen in number—are on the left of the entrance, there being a waiting-room close by, as well as needle and vapour baths. On the first floor of the building are the slipper and other baths for women. A caretaker's house and a laundry have also been provided. The architect is Mr. R. Knill Freeman, of Bolton.

# Association of Municipal and County Engineers.

## ANNUAL MEETING AT EDINBURGH.—I.

EDINBURGH: GENERAL VIEW OF THE CITY FROM THE CASTLE HILL.

Those who guide the policy of the Incorporated Association of Municipal and County Engineers have selected a picturesque and uniquely interesting spot in which to hold the twenty-fifth annual meeting. Judging from the opening proceedings yesterday, which we report as fully as circumstances would allow, from the admirably-arranged and comprehensive programme which was drawn up and from other factors in the case, this meeting promises to be unusually successful. It will be seen from the annual report, which we print below, that the council have a record of gratifying progress to place before the members, and this record will no doubt receive the appreciation it deserves. It will also be seen that Mr. Robson inaugurated his year of office by an able and comprehensive survey of municipal engineering and its responsibilities. To these and other matters, however, we refer at greater length in our editorial columns than we need do here.

What we may appropriately attempt here, as an introduction to our report of the proceedings proper, is a brief sketch of the renowned city in which municipal engineers are assembled, with special reference naturally to municipal development, of which it is in so many respects a splendid illustration in common with the great commercial city on the banks of the Clyde, some 40 miles away. Apart from municipal work, to attempt to sketch in our columns the history of such a city as the Scottish metropolis is neither necessary nor desirable, for such a record exists in many admirable forms and is easily accessible. Nor, indeed, would it be practicable, for to trace the history of Edinburgh is to a large extent to trace the history of Scotland, a task for the patient and voluminous industry of the historian, and not for the confined conditions which bind the journalist. It is, moreover, with the modern city that we are concerned, with its municipal progress, and more especially with that department of municipal work generally described as municipal engineering.

### EDINBURGH AND ITS MUNICIPAL WORK.

Whatever reasons may have influenced those who were responsible for the selection of Edinburgh as the scene of this year's annual meeting, there is no question as to the wisdom of that selection. It is true that for many the journey is somewhat long, but that is but a slight disadvantage in comparison with the attractions, professional and otherwise, which such a visit offers. The programme gives sufficient evidence of what has been found possible in regard to papers to be read and discussed, and to works and places of interest to be visited. Possibly not a few of those present may now be visiting for the first time a city which, on account of its quite exceptional associations—historical, literary and architectural—is numbered among those remarkable and favoured spots to which men travel as to a shrine. In the minds of Scotsmen, again, their capital city is peculiarly associated with some of the most remarkable events—often melancholy enough—of what for long was a stormy history, in the course of which they evolved national and individual characteristics

of singular strength and persistence. For centuries the history of Scotland was a record of struggles with a powerful and warlike neighbour, of unceasing efforts to make the best of comparatively poor resources, and of internal dissensions in which monarchs, nobles and people all figured, often amid scenes of the darkest tragedy. But the story, though often so fierce and sanguinary, is one upon which Scotsmen may look back with justifiable pride, and, as we have said, so peculiarly is the Scottish metropolis associated alike with some of the proudest and some of the most melancholy incidents of the country's history, that by Scotsmen it is regarded with a feeling amounting to almost religious veneration. To them it is to a large extent their Mecca, their holy city. To Sir Walter Scott it was ever "mine own romantic town." The romance, no doubt, was clear to his discerning eye, but that it is so clear to-day to Englishmen, and even to Scotsmen, how much is due to Sir Walter's imperishable pages, in which he cast a strange glamour over the history of his country from early mediæval times to the stirring days of "forty-five." The political importance of Edinburgh naturally declined after 1603, and still more after 1707, but the great literary outburst in the end of last century and the beginning of this gave it a period of rare social splendour, and it is to be hoped that it will continue to retain to a large degree that picturesque appearance and architectural beauty, the academic culture and refinement, the literary and artistic attributes, which have earned for it the title of "The Modern Athens."

### THE PAST AND THE PRESENT.

Famed alike for natural beauty and grandeur of situation, and for stately majesty of public buildings, Edinburgh has also a high reputation as a healthy and suitable place of residence for the leisured and wealthy. In the "Old Town," with its narrow streets, closes and wynds, the patriotic Scotsman and the antiquarian have almost unlimited scope for research and historical reminiscence. Every square foot of the ground may be said to be saturated with historic incident. The old Edinburgh of the historian is to a very large extent the Edinburgh of Queen Mary and her court. Round the chequered reign of that hapless queen much of the romance of Scottish history centres, and the fascinating picture of the intrigue, the chivalry and the rugged greatness of those days have invested Edinburgh with surpassing interest. The union, first of Crowns and then of Parliaments, which necessarily deprived Scotland of much of her independent interest and glory, has in the course of time fostered peace and prosperity within her borders. Of those results the metropolis has possibly had the largest share, though Glasgow, the commercial capital of the west, from her favoured maritime situation and the enterprise of her citizens and civic rulers, has made, and will continue to make, enormous progress in material prosperity and municipal government.

In the fifteenth century Edinburgh consisted simply of Castle Hill, Lawnmarket and High-street, with the closes and alleys leading therefrom, all being enclosed by the city wall. As it was practically impossible to extend the buildings along the surface, the only alternative, if further extension was desired, was to raise them into the air. Hence arose the celebrated "high lands" which still exist. The city wall, however, was extended in the beginning of the sixteenth century, as a result of the war scare associated with the disastrous Field of Flodden. The various points which form the sites of the old city gates are still designated by the name of ports—for example, Bristol Port and West Port. These old walls, protected with flanking towers and bulwarks, were erected under fear of warlike invasion; but, as they proved of little or no use, they were ultimately swept almost wholly away during the succeeding period of spirited civic extension. From time to time these city extensions have been promoted, and even during the last seventeen years the city has been twice extended, until to-day the superficial area is 8,804·38 acreas. Nor is the desire for this form of civic conquest by any means quenched, for in 1896 an abortive attempt was made to include Leith, Edinburgh's sea-

THE RIGHT HON. MITCHELL THOMSON,
Lord Provost of Edinburgh.

port, which has a population of about 80,000 souls. On behalf of the city it was contended that there was ample justification for the attempt, as a large section of the mercantile population of Leith reside in Edinburgh; and that as Leith and the adjacent burghs are benefitted by the common supplies of water, gas and tramways, there is thus to that extent and in other respects a community of interests which justifies the Edinburgh civic rulers in promoting amalgamation.

To-day the population of the city has reached 292,364. It is in a very real sense the metropolis of Scotland, the embodiment of everything distinctly national that remains since the Union of the Crown and Parliament with those of England; it is the principal seat of the administration of justice for the whole country; the meeting place of the supreme courts of the various Presbyterian bodies, the centre of scientific and literary activity, the seat of the greatest of the Scottish universities, and of many schools of the first rank. Every Scotsman has in Edinburgh a common bond of sympathy.

There are naturally fewer merchant princes than can be found in large manufacturing cities, but at the present time the city benefits from the princely benefactions of three munificent givers. These are Mr. Finlay, joint proprietor of *The Scotsman*, whose magnificent gift is the National Portrait Gallery, in Queen-street; Mr. McEwan, member of Parliament for the central division of the city, who has presented the splendid McEwan Hall; and Mr. Andrew Usher, whose noble donation was one of no less than £100,000 for the erection of a public hall for the cultivation of music. The site for this hall has not yet been decided upon.

EDINBURGH TO-DAY.

From probably every point of view from which Edinburgh can be observed, the most picturesque groupings, the most pleasing and novel effects, are presented to the eye. No one feature may approach the sublime, but no suggestion of meanness is ever present. The city is divided into three well-known and well-marked divisions. There is, first, the New Town, which has long been famed for the regularity of its streets and squares. This part of the city lies to the north of the valley separating Princes-street from the castle. The second division is the Old Town, to which our previous remarks on the subject of Edinburgh's historic interest specially apply. This part of the city is found between Princes-street and the Meadows. Finally, there is the third division, which consists of the south-side suburbs. The Castle, which is now undergoing certain additions and renovations, may justly be described as the central point of interest of the city, and next may be put Parliament-square, with the ancient cathedral of St. Giles' church in front and the law courts in the rear. We can only make a passing reference to the general public buildings of this splendid city, the exchanges, banks, insurance offices, post office, monuments, hospitals, the new medical buildings, the medical schools, the Museum of Science and Art, the Royal Institution, the Merchant Company's schools, the churches and theological colleges. An account of these would require a

paper for itself, and, after all, they are best appreciated when actually seen. To some of the most prominent features of the city we shall have an opportunity of further referring when dealing with the various points of the programme.

We may now refer more particularly to the city as it is found at the present day. As a rule the visitor is not long in Edinburgh before he finds himself in Princes-street, and there his attention is at once attracted by the irregular appearance of the buildings. Stately hotels are now occupying much of the frontage, though here and there low, antiquated buildings, not altogether swept away by the flood of "improvements," still remain to remind us of the Princes-street of the past. At the east end of this unique thoroughfare the North British Railway Company are erecting a station of magnificent proportions, and at the west end a vast hotel is shortly to be commenced by the Caledonian Railway Company in connection with their station.

Before proceeding to refer briefly to some of the more important public and municipal works of the city we may draw attention to the beautifully picturesque view which heads our report. In the foreground, conspicuous for their Ionic and Doric columns, are the Royal Institution, with its sculpture gallery, and the National Picture Gallery. Beyond the Scott monument, with its Gothic design, will at once be distinguished. One of the tall buildings on the opposite side of the road is the "Royal" hotel, the headquarters of the municipal engineers this week. The domed building beyond is the Register House, and opposite it are the fine buildings of the General Post Office. Further in the distance is the tall obelisk erected to the memory of the Edinburgh worthies transported for life for "speaking words tending to excite discord between king and people." In the distance rises the Calton Hill, crowned by the Nelson monument, with the unfinished model of the Parthenon immediately beyond it.

PUBLIC WORKS AND INSTITUTIONS.

The public works carried out in Edinburgh in recent years have been both numerous and extensive. The north viaduct, which connects the old town to the new, and which was widened in 1873-74, has just been rebuilt in magnificent style to a width of 75 ft. The street in continuation of this viaduct southwards as far as the iron church is also to be widened and rebuilt in a tasteful and handsome manner. In 1878 the old Royal infirmary was found to be inadequate for present day requirements, so it was converted into an isolation hospital, and in the following year a new Royal Infirmary was erected on a suitable site adjacent to the Meadows. This institution is not devoted exclusively to the benefit of the metropolis, but of the whole of Scotland, and is maintained by voluntary contributions. In the immediate neighbourhood the new medical school, erected some twenty years ago, forms a splendid palatial pile, to which only recently was added a stately range of buildings, the McEwan Hall, the princely gift from Mr. McEwan, M.P., to the university. The success of the isolation hospital above referred to has led to the erection of a suburban isolation hospital, which is estimated to cost £250,000, and will contain 600 beds. The Royal

MR. J. COOPER,
Burgh Engineer of Edinburgh.

infirmary possesses a magnificent convalescent home at Corstorphine, a village to the west of Edinburgh, where, facing the sun and sheltered from the inclement east winds, patients are restored to their wonted health and strength. In connection with the city hospital a similar convalescent home has been planted in a sheltered spot in Musselborough, to the east of Edinburgh. In 1887 the Free Libraries Act was adopted, and Mr. Carnegie came to the rescue with £50,000. As the free library is to be specially visited by the municipal engineers, we shall refer to it in greater detail in that connection. Branch free libraries are being provided in the suburbs and the outlying districts.

Though our paper has, for the purposes of this report, been considerably enlarged beyond the customary size, we still suffer from the limitations of space. Owing to this fact and to the magnitude of the subject with which we are attempting to deal, however imperfectly, in these introductory remarks, we are compelled to hold a portion of them over until next week, in order to proceed with the report of yesterday's proceedings. Next week we shall refer more particularly to municipal administration and municipal services, such as water, gas, lighting, sewerage, &c.

We have pleasure in presenting our readers this week with portraits [of Lord Provost Mitchell Thomson, who presides over the municipal affairs of the city with so much ability and dignity, of Mr. Cooper, the city engineer, who has taken so active a part in organising the present meeting, and of Mr. Morham, the city architect.

### THE BOROUGH ENGINEER.

Some particulars of Mr. Cooper's career will, no doubt, be acceptable to our readers. He received his education at Geddes Institution, Culcross, Dollar Academy and the Heriot-Watt College, Edinburgh, and after a term of practical experience in building construction entered the burgh engineer's office, Edinburgh, in 1871. This was immediately after the death of Mr. Charles Macpherson, and on the appointment of Mr. Thomas Fraser as burgh engineer. The office staff consisted at that period of some six assistants in all. After passing through the several grades of assistantship, he became principal assistant, which position he held until Mr. Fraser's last illness and death in 1881. Mr. Cooper was then appointed ad interim burgh-engineer, and shortly thereafter burgh engineer. To this appointment there was added, in 1886, that of master of works, the duties of which consist in advising the Dean of Guild Court and inspecting the erection and completion of all new houses and buildings. He was elected an Associate Member of the Institution of Civil Engineers in 1885. In 1889 he received the additional appointment, along with Mr. Beatson, burgh surveyor of Leith, of conjoint engineer to the Water of Leith Purification and Sewerage Commissioners, and in 1893 of corporation tramway engineer. During his term of office the following works, among others, have been carried out : I, The main outlet sewers in the suburbs of the city, which were formerly open burns or foul streams, have all been placed in culverts. The ordinary sewers of the city, many of them old and rudely formed, have been reconstructed, re-silled and repaired. The house drainage of the city has also been taken up, and reconstruction and repairs have been carried out for many years, at a cost to the owners of at least £10,000 per annum. At the present time there are few houses in Edinburgh which have not had their drainage and sanitary arrangements overhauled and certified. To these efforts Edinburgh no doubt owes its high place as a healthy place of residence.

The slums of the city were also vigorously taken up by Mr. Cooper's department, and a system of house-to-house inspection has been carried on for many years. The city improvement scheme of Sir James Russell was ultimately carried

MR. R. MORHAM.
City Architect.

through, with enormous benefit to the city. In 1884 the Powburn system of outlet sewerage was carried out, costing £40,000. In 1889 and following years a great scheme for the purification of the Water of Leith was conceived and carried out, a stretch of work, 7 miles in length, extending from Balerno to the sea, costing in all about £350,000. Edinburgh has also been forward in considering the question of the cremation of house refuse, and a destructor of ten cells has been in use for five years.

During recent years Mr. Cooper has been associated with Prof. Kennedy and the resident electrical engineer in the erection of electric lighting power stations. Their cost was £26,000. The conversion of nearly the whole of the horse tramway system to cable traction, which has been arranged by the corporation, has been entrusted to Mr. Colam, c.e., and Mr. Cooper jointly. This work will cost £756,300. His office staff (draughtsmen, inspectors, improvers and apprentices), which numbered six on his advent, is now sixty. He

has during his term of office been obliged to conduct certain sections of the work of sanitary inspection, especially in dealing with the slums of the city, and has been called upon to erect artisans' dwellings, as the city architect's hands were otherwise filled. He leads a loyal staff of assistants, several of whom have supported him throughout the last sixteen years of responsible public life. He has engineered several Parliamentary Bills through Parliament. Edinburgh has twice over extended its boundaries since his appointment At present there is on hand the tramway cable installation, an additional electric power station, dwellings for the poor, the promotion of[improvement schemes, and the ventilation of the Water of Leith system of sewerage.

## YESTERDAY'S PROCEEDINGS.

### RECEPTION AT THE CITY CHAMBERS.

The work of the day began as early as 10 o'clock, in the shape of a meeting of the council of the association at the Royal Hotel. Those who had made the journey no doubt congratulated themselves on the beautiful weather with which the opening of the proceedings, at all events, had been favoured. At 10.30 an adjournment was made to the City chambers, in the Council Chamber of which they were received by the Lord Provost, supported by Bailies Kinloch Anderson, Pollard, Robertson and Hay, Dean of Guild Millar, Treasurer McCrae, Judge Dunlop, Councillor Forbes Mackay, the town clerk and the city chamberlain. After the members of the association had been introduced by the burgh engineer, Mr. Cooper,

The LORD PROVOST, on behalf of the corporation and the city, said he had pleasure in giving them a hearty welcome to Edinburgh. It was extremely appropriate that they should have chosen Edinburgh for that meeting, for the city was at the present time executing important engineering works. He referred, of course, to that splendid work of Sir John Fowler and Sir Benjamin Baker at Queensferry. The Forth Bridge, which they would have an opportunity of visiting, was a work of world-wide renown. Then during the past two years they had taken down the old North Bridge, which connected the new town with the old. Its construction was looked upon as a great feat of skill, but it had served its time. They would agree that the new bridge was wide and beautiful. Like other cities, they had installed the electric light, and thought they had reason to be proud of its success, which was largely due to the fact that they had gained from the experience of others and to having an engineer of repute like Prof. Kennedy. Mr. Colam was to read a paper on the conversion of the tramways from horse to cable traction. He thought that their corporation was the first to purchase tramways from a company. They leased the tramways to the company on the principle that the company should pay a percentage on the capital expenditure of the corporation. The great beauty of the city influenced them in deciding against overhead wires. They had steep gradients, and their experience showed that the cable system would, as at San Francisco, work well in Edinburgh. The conversion would cost over £1,000,000. Municipal engineers had last visited Edinburgh in 1890, and he hoped that when they came again they would see the cable system successfully working. Mr. Cooper would take them to see the refuse destructor. He was sorry to say it had not been an unqualified success, and the visit might be beneficial by showing the mistakes that had been made. Baillie Pollard, convener of the Public Health Committee, was by his side, and that led him to say that they were at present erecting a large infectious diseases hospital on 150 acres of land in the vicinity of the city as a substitute for the old hospital in the centre of the town. Though only just begun, an inspection of the works and the plans would no doubt be of interest to them. The experience of all must be that these annual visits to centres of population had beneficial effects all over the country. The more they met the better for the general good of the people. He again bade them heartily welcome.

Mr. LEWIS ANGELL (West Ham), in the absence of Sir Alexander Binnie, the retiring president, whose public work prevented his attendance, expressed thanks for the cordial reception which had been accorded to them. The association had now been founded about a quarter of a century, and was no longer English but cosmopolitan. Its work was humanitarian.

### MEETING AT THE ROYAL HOTEL.

On returning to the Yellow-room of the Royal Hotel, Mr. Angell again took the chair, and the work of the general meeting began. The chairman called upon the secretary to read, first, the minutes of the last annual meeting, held in London, and afterwards the following

### ANNUAL REPORT OF THE COUNCIL :

In presenting the twenty-fifth annual report, the council are gratified to state that the progress of the association during the past year has been satisfactorily maintained.

### DISTRICT MEETINGS.

Since the last annual general meeting six district meetings have been held : At Rhayader, for the Birmingham waterworks, August 28th ; Sunderland, November 20, 1897 ; Westminster, February 18, 1898 ; Wimbledon, April 30th ; Harrogate, for the Bradford waterworks, June 4th ; Norwich and Great Yarmouth, June 10th and 11th.

### THE ROLL OF THE ASSOCIATION.

During the financial year ending April 30th last seventy-two new members, consisting of fifty-four ordinary members and eighteen graduates, have joined the association. One new honorary member—Monsieur Bechmann, chief engineer of Ponts et Chaussées, Paris—has been elected. Six members and one graduate have resigned. Sixteen names have been written off, and the council record with regret the deaths of Messrs. D. Bland, T. Higginson, D. C. Ottley, E. Rothwell, J. C. Stuart and W. S. Till.

The number on the roll of the association at the close of the year was ten honorary members, 732 ordinary members and ninety-two graduates, making a total of 834, being an addition equal to 5·4 per cent. on the numbers of the preceding year.

The council have transferred Messrs. G. Ball, H. W. Corrio, T. Hayward, G. T. Lynam and J. A. Settle from the class of graduates to that of members, these gentlemen having been elected to appointments qualifying them for this class under the articles of association.

The council have also to place on record with deep regret the death of Sir Robert Rawlinson, K.C.B., who has been an honorary member of this association since its formation. Sir Robert Rawlinson, who was chief inspector of the Local Government Board for many years, always showed a deep sympathy with, and a keen interest in, the work of this association.

### THE FINANCES.

The audited balance sheet and statement of accounts which accompanies this report shows a balance in hand on April 30th last of £255. The invested capital account of the association now stands at £750 7s. 4d., £250 having been invested to purchase £260 7s. 4d. India 2½ per cent. stock during the year. The statement of assets and liabilities shows the association to be in a highly satisfactory position.

### EXAMINATIONS.

A marked and gratifying increase is shown in this department of the association's work.

Since the last report two examinations have been carried out, the first of which was held at the Council House, Birmingham, on October 1st and 2nd, 1897. On this occasion twenty candidates were examined; eleven satisfied the examiners and were granted the association's certificate. The examiners were Messrs. Pritchard, Fowler, Lemon and Eayrs. The second examination was held on April the 1st and 2nd, 1898, at the Institution of Civil Engineers, Westminster, where the use of rooms was kindly granted by the council of that body.

On this occasion forty-six candidates were examined, of whom thirty satisfied the examiners and were granted the association's certificate. The examiners were Messrs. Fowler, Lemon, Lobley, May and Jones.

Arising out of the great increase of candidates for examination the council have had under consideration a report from the Board of Examiners submitting certain recommendations for the conduct of future examinations and have approved such report. To give effect to the same the council recommend the alteration of By-law 18, so as to give power to the council to enlarge the Board of Examiners and the number of examinations. The required alterations are set forth in the agenda notice of this meeting.

### THE NEW COUNCIL.

The ballot lists having been duly issued, the scrutineers reported the result of the voting as follows :—

PRESIDENT.—Mr. O. Claude Robson.
VICE-PRESIDENTS.—Messrs. J. Cooper, W. Harpur and C. H. Lowe.
ORDINARY MEMBERS OF COUNCIL.—Messrs. J. P. Barber, A. E. Collins, J. H. Cox, A. Creer, A. T. Davis, E. P. Hooley, E. G. Mawbey, J. Paton, S. S. Platt, J. Price, W. Weaver and T. H. Yabbicom.
GENERAL HONORARY SECRETARY.—Mr. Charles Jones.
HONORARY TREASURER.—Mr. Lewis Angell.

### PREMIUMS.

The council have awarded the association's premium of books value £10 to Mr. S. S. Platt, for his paper entitled "Some of the Municipal Works at Rochdale;" and the premium of books value of £5 to Mr. Blackshaw, for his paper entitled "Particulars of Some Municipal Engineering Works designed and carried out at Stafford."

### SUPERANNUATION.

A considerable amount of attention has been given by the council and its committees to the subject of superannuation, arising out of the considerations of three Bills now before Parliament. The Bills referred to are : 1, The Metropolitan Local Government Officers' Superannuation Amendment Bill; 2, the Local Authorities' Officers' Superannuation Bill; and 3, the Local Government (Ireland) Bill.

With regard to the first-mentioned Bill, the council took all available means by memorials and circulars to advance the measures and to protect the interests of the members of the association. In response to such efforts the council have received numerous promises of support from members of Parliament, and the Local Government Board have also promised to support the suggested scheme for superannuation as soon as they receive satisfactory assurance that the measures meet with the approval of the bulk of the local authorities affected by the Bills. With reference to the third of the above-named Bills, the council have had conference

with representatives of the county surveyors of Ireland and received from them a statement of their wishes as to alterations in the Bill necessary for the protection of their interests, and in the result the measure' has been materially amended on the lines desired by the Irish members of the association, and the council experience considerable gratification in recording the assistance thus afforded to their brethren across the channel.

### CORRESPONDING SECRETARY.

The council have appointed Mr. R. W. Richards, the city surveyor of Sydney, corresponding secretary for Australasia. Mr. Richards having evinced so strong an interest in the association, the council believe the appointment made will tend to benefit the association and to bring its advantages under the notice of many eligible officials in our Australian colonies.

### LOCAL GOVERNMENT BOARD JOINT EXAMINATIONS.

With respect to the joint committee on the question of the examination of sanitary inspectors, instituted by the Local Government Board, the council are pleased to report that satisfactory arrangements have lately been made by which the difficulties met with by the committee have been surmounted, and that shortly the final steps will be taken for the incorporation of the body thus formed.

On the motion of the CHAIRMAN, seconded by Mr. W. G Laws (Newcastle-on-Tyne), the annual report and the minutes of the last meeting were unanimously adopted. Then came the presentation of premiums. The first premium, of £10 in books, was awarded to Mr. S. S. Platt (Rochdale) for his paper

MR. S. S. PLATT, M.INST.C.E.,
Borough Engineer and Surveyor, Rochdale.
Awarded the First Premium.

on "Some of the Municipal Works of Rochdale," and the second premium, of books to the value of £5, to Mr. Blackshaw (Stafford) for his paper on "Particulars of Some Engineering Works designed and carried out at Stafford." Mr. Platt briefly replied, but Mr. Blackshaw was absent. Biographical notices of Mr. Platt and Mr. Blackshaw appeared in our issue of May 28, 1897, and July 2, 1897, respectively.

As will be seen from the programme, two notices of motion had been given, but the following motion, of which Mr. Weaver had given notice, was withdrawn :—

"That the resolution passed at the annual meeting, held at West Bromwich, July 13, 1893, directing that the attendances of the councillors at council and committee meetings be placed on the ballot lists be rescinded."

Mr. J. T. EAYRS had given notice to move :—

"That By-Law 18 be altered to read as follows : 18. Two (or more) examinations of candidates for certificates of competency in municipal engineering, surveying, building construction, sanitary science and municipal law, shall be held annually at such places and at such times as the council shall appoint.

"The board of examiners shall be not less than twelve in number, and shall be elected by and be members of the council, or such other members of the association as shall be leading men in their particular branch of the profession. Four (or more) of such board shall be selected by the council to carry out each examination, who, as 'acting examiners,' shall report to the council the names of those candidates who have satisfied them of their proficiency."

This motion was carried.

On the motion of MR. ANGELL, seconded by Mr. LEMON (Southampton), the various district secretaries were all re-elected, as were the auditors, Messrs. Savage and Lewis, and the scrutineers, Messrs. Silcock, Thomas and Clarson.

Mr. ANGELL then introduced the president-elect, Mr. O. Claude Robson, mentioning that the latter had received his first training in his (Mr. Angell's) office, whence he went to the post he had so long and honourably filled at Willesden.

Mr. ROBSON then took the chair amid loud and sustained applause.

Mr. ANGELL moved, and Mr. LOBLEY (Hanley) seconded, that a vote of thanks be awarded to the retiring president, both expressing regret that the onerous nature of Sir Alexander Binnie's duties had prevented his attendance.

The PRESIDENT, having explained that even that night Sir Alexander had a duty to perform, in the shape of attending the annual dinner of the London County Council, then proceeded to read his address, which was as follows:—

### PRESIDENT'S ADDRESS.

GENTLEMEN,—In addressing you upon this occasion my first and pleasing duty is to extend my heartfelt thanks to the council and members of this association for the high honour that I have received at their hands in being elected to the presidential chair for the ensuing year. It is a position of which I feel justly proud, and, although I may not hope to emulate the work of the eminent men who have preceded me, it will always be my earnest endeavour to enhance the interests of the association to the utmost of my power and steadily to maintain the high reputation it has gained in the past.

#### WORK OF THE MUNICIPAL ENGINEER.

The duties of the municipal engineer and surveyor are so varied, and embrace so many items of administrative and constructive work, that a large amount of time would be re-

MR. W. BLACKSHAW, ASSOC.M.INST.C.E.,
Borough Engineer and Surveyor, Stafford.
Awarded the Second Premium.

quired to deal with them in their entirety in this address, and I much fear the patience of my audience would be sorely tried were I to attempt so bold a measure. Some idea of the magnitude of these works may be obtained by reference to the last annual report of the Local Government Board. That report shows that since 1871 the local authorities have incurred upon the strength of their borrowing powers an indebtedness of over £150,000,000 for sanitary works and other improvements. This vast sum is in addition to, and quite independent of, the annual cost of works defrayed from current expenditure. The progress of sanitation since the constitution of the Local Government Board may also be fairly gauged by the figures in this report, the amount of the loans sanctioned to sanitary authorities by the Local Government Board, in 1871, being only £267,000, whilst, in 1896, the amount was upwards of £5,500,000.

The nature of these works for which the municipal engineer is responsible is varied, comprising road making and road maintenance with concurrent bridge and viaduct work, tramways, sea and river walls, design of sewerage and water systems, treatment of sewage, public lighting, erection of isolation hospitals, public offices, free libraries, mortuaries, markets and other buildings incidental to municipal administration, the laying out of public parks and pleasure grounds, fire brigade control and supervision of new buildings. In addition, the municipal engineer must advise on all Parliamentary promotions affecting his district, and have a fairly intimate knowledge of the various Acts now relating to public health. Upon the competency, energy and zeal displayed by the officials discharging these duties the comfort, convenience and health of the community largely depend, and the responsibility thus accepted is well known by those in this room to be no light one. It is, nevertheless, I believe, one that is taken up with enthusiasm by all of us. We feel that we are members of a grand profession, which

tends to the benefit of our fellow men, and I am glad to believe that this ever-present desire of the municipal engineer to further improvement in sanitary and kindred sciences is each year becoming more recognised and more appreciated by those whom we serve.

#### BIOLOGICAL PURIFICATION OF SEWAGE.

In the summary of duties before mentioned there are some matters that have been especially interesting to the municipal engineer during the preceding year, to which perhaps I may be allowed a brief reference. Among these that which has taken priority and has been most discussed is the now familiar subject of the purification of sewage by biological means, as exemplified by the septic tank—Mr. Dibdin's system—Colonel Ducat's filter and other methods. This very recent discovery of the valuable assistance rendered by the micro-organisms in tanks and filters must be deemed the more extraordinary if it be remembered that the much-condemned cesspools of olden days with filter tank attached evidently were adaptable, if they did not contain these natural media, for the breaking down and after oxidation of organic matter in the sewage to be treated, but presumably the generation, and, if I may so say, the intelligent nursing, of these minute organisms pent within the walls of tanks or filters was not then understood, and it is only quite recently that this system of nature has been adapted to the hygienic laws. The absence of sludge and the accompanying difficulty of its disposal in the neighbourhood of large towns is especially an important element in the system, and will in itself greatly tend to economise the expenditure upon sewage treatment.

Should the promise given in several of the experimental works prove as successful with a varying flow and every description of sewage, or in the more comprehensive scheme for Exeter as recently sanctioned by the Local Government Board, it will, indeed, be a long stride towards the solution of that difficult problem of the efficient treatment of sewage under all conditions. Especially will it be a boon to those towns discharging into rivers with a small catchment area and where land treatment is impossible by reason of great price or unsuitability of soil. With suitable land available, however, and at a moderate cost, it is probable that the rotation of Nature, as illustrated by the land treatment, from earth to plants, plants to animals, with return from animals to earth again, will in many places retain its early pre-eminence and the economy of Nature thereby be maintained.

The whole subject is now doubtless in a somewhat experimental stage, but will in all probability receive the earnest attention of the Royal Commission just formed for the consideration of the treatment of sewage, and whose report is awaited with so much interest and anxiety by municipal engineers. At the inquiry much valuable evidence will be received upon this important question, but, with all submission, it appears that beyond this some assistance might be rendered to the commission if experimental works were provided in the near neighbourhood of the metropolis, where the several systems of biological treatment could be panelled out and practically investigated and tested for a certain period of time under exactly similar circumstances as to character of sewage, extent of flow, climatic conditions and other situations of identity. With careful and intelligent daily supervision, investigation and systematic analyses, much valuable testimony might be gained for presentation to the commission. The cost of the construction of the necessary works need be but small, and should not stand in the way of what, I believe, would eventuate in most useful results.

#### A STANDARD OF POLLUTION.

The necessity for more careful consideration in the system to be adopted for the treatment of sewage is becoming each year intensified by the rapid increase of population, by the addition of legislation relating to river pollution and the more drastic supervision accorded by the river authorities with regard to sources of pollution. Where a mere perfunctory examination of a stream was accorded in former years a duly qualified staff of inspectors is now appointed, constant analyses are made, and the riparian authorities are kept closely up to the mark. Unfortunately, however, for many towns this mark is not a fixed one—i.e., no uniform standard is established as to the extent of impurity allowable in the effluent to be discharged into the stream. A distinction in the standard as between discharges above and below water intakes upon a river is understandable, but with similar tributaries to a parent stream, but supervised by a separate body of officials, it does appear incongruous that a varying standard of purity, or rather of impurity, should exist depending only on the individual opinion of the expert advising the particular river authority. A particular standard was certainly prepared by the Rivers Pollution Commission some years since, dealing more especially with the solids in suspension and solution and the albumenoid ammonia, but this is practically a dead letter, and no known standard is now available for many towns discharging into non-tidal waters.

Exceptional standards of purity are demanded in the case of those towns or districts that are situated upon sluggish streams possessing fiat declivities and shallow inclinations from the watershed, with a maximum amount of absorption and a minimum contribution of rainfall. The oxidation of the organic matter in the effluent is thus considerably diminished by the paucity of dilution from surface waters and by the sluggish character of the river's flow, casting especial burdens upon the towns thus situated where the population may be large and the volume of sewage altogether disproportionate to the natural flow of the stream into which it is discharged. In such cases as these a highly insanitary condition of affairs occurs, and of late much expensive litigation has ensued with regard thereto. To avoid this it is a point for consideration whether a more perfect if not more economical solution of the sewage difficulty would not be arrived at in various parts of the kingdom by the extension of the system of valley sewers or effluent channels, receiving contributions from the various towns *en route* to a final discharge into the sea, tidal river or parent stream as the case may be. The treatment of the sewage by each separate township with discharge of filtrate into the main valley conduit, or the conveyance of the combined bulk of crude sewage far away from habitations for treatment at the lower end of the valley, must be determined by the physical circumstances of the valley and questions of policy between the authorities. There are, however, at the present time some isolated schemes of this description, controlled by joint sewerage boards, which might with advantage to the general health and comfort of the public be more generally adopted in some densely-populated neighbourhoods by co-operation among the riparian authorities under the clauses of the Public Health Act relating to union of districts.

### SEWER VENTILATION.

Foremost still among the difficulties of sanitary administration is the over-troublesome question of the ventilation of sewers. This matter so closely affects the comfort of the people that I feel I may be excused for again referring to a question which has been so often discussed by the members of this association. Pamphlets and reports by the hundred have been written thereon, there has been abundant controversy, and yet we have advanced but little beyond the primitive methods of discharging the foul gases generated in the sewers by the open grids level with the surface of roadways. Numerous patents have been launched forth for the combustion or disinfection of the gases, but hitherto with no material result. Like many other patents, experiments upon a small scale were eminently satisfactory, which failed from various causes when applied to a comprehensive system extending over a large district.

In many towns the open grids have been augmented by the fixture of upcast iron shafts attached to houses and elsewhere, by which all odours offensive to the olfactory nerves are removed far above their sensitive action. The method adopted is a simple and inexpensive one, and although the efficacy of the shafts is by no means universally agreed upon, my own experience of the system, I must admit, has been most satisfactory. The complaints formerly made by residents have practically ceased in those districts where a perfect system has been available, and the life of the engineer has consequently been a more agreeable one during the summer months than was formerly the case. Doubtless, the success of the system largely depends upon local conditions and the position in which the shafts may be fixed. Some difficulty may also be experienced in obtaining the assent of all persons interested in the fixing of the shafts, but the promise to close the offending grid or grids near to the premises often secures the necessary permission. The action of these shafts is doubtless largely affected by climatic influences, a greater current being registered during strong winds, but, after a series of anemometrical readings for twelve months, I have found in no single instance a downward current apparent, whilst the upward current has averaged 30 cubic feet per minute, and has upon many days during the summer months, when the utility of the shafts is most required, amounted to 70 or 80 cubic feet. With a current of this rapidity much more success has been achieved in clearing the sewers of foul gases than would have been possible with the open grids.

### HOUSE DRAINAGE.

The necessity for these shafts as vents for the gases generated in the main sewers of a town would not, however, be so apparent were all the minor tributaries of a system of main sewerage laid with the same care as the public sewers under the control of the local authority. Given a carefully designed and constructed system of sewerage, it is only with the subsidence of flow in the sewers that objectionable gases will be generated, as no stagnation with putrefaction following should exist in the event of the sewer. The main cause of the odours in sewers so much complained of is, in my opinion, the foul contribution from faulty house drains, where the flushing administered by the occupiers is not sufficient to cleanse the drain and the intercepting syphon from deposit. A systematic and efficient system of flushing to the house drains, where necessary, is, therefore, an important factor in dealing with the ventilation of sewers, as by this work the possibility of the generation of *foul* gases is minimised by the sewers receiving a flow free from putrefaction. The flushing of the sewer itself is at times useless, as the malodorous contributions of the house drains are left untouched and the sewer itself may have been perfectly free from deposit prior to the application of flushing. The efficacy of this system of flushing to house drains, as connected with nuisances arising from ventilation, I have practically tested in my own district by meter barrow and special hose attached to water mains, and have found the results to be favourable in every way.

It is with bated breath that one dares to suggest the abolition of the syphons attached to the house drains, those miniature cesspools through whose putrefying media all drains must now discharge. Whilst at times they are useless for the purpose for which they are fixed, I am confident that at all times they are the source of emanations from the house drains. On the other hand, without them what multiplication to the area of ventilation would be accorded by the thousands of upcast shafts attached to the rear of the houses, and at the same time the atmospheric dilution of the sewer gases would be materially increased.

### MAINTENANCE OF HIGHWAYS.

The question of the maintenance of highways, although prosaic in character, is one that more closely affects the everyday life of the public than perhaps many other municipal works of a more apparently ingenious nature. During the middle ages and until well into the present century the greater part of the highways in town and country were much neglected, and it is only quite within comparatively recent years that the subject of formation and repair of all roads and footpaths has been more scientifically and intelligently administered both in the counties and boroughs of the kingdom. It is not much more than a century since that Palmer started the first mail coach, the "Tally Ho," which ran from London to Bristol. Before that time the mails were carried by post boys and were continually carried off by highwaymen. The mail coach certainly was a greater, though by no means complete, security. But this change made men look to their ways, and thus the main roads began to receive more attention, and in connection with this work we remember the honoured names of Metcalf, Telford and Macadam. The improvement effected in the main roads during the past twenty years, however, is due in a great measure to the higher standard of excellence demanded by the county authorities under the Highways and Locomotive Amendment Act, 1878, and the Local Government Act of 1888 prior to any contribution being made towards the repair of these roads, and in this respect doubtless the public have benefitted in the matter of comfort but somewhat suffered in the pocket by reason of the action thus taken by the county authorities. Another improving aspirant has, however, lately appeared upon the scene in the shape of the ubiquitous cyclist. The surface of a macadamised road that was considered satisfactory for ordinary vehicular traffic now proves utterly unfit for the pneumatic-tyred bicycle, and I believe it has been seriously contemplated in some localities where pleasure is perhaps more rampant than in others that an especially prepared track upon the public highway should be reserved for the cyclist. This may or may not be a necessity of the times, but should it be so by all principles of equity let "bicycles be taxed."

### WOOD PAVING.

Upon the merits of flint, slag, macadam, asphalte, brick, stone paving and hard and soft timber as materials for road repair I do not propose to dwell, as it is quite without the scope of this address and is a question that has received and will in the future still further receive detailed consideration by paper and discussion in the district meetings to be convened. Upon one point, however, it appears that but little controversy is likely to ensue, and that is the substitution of wood paving of some description for the stone paving in all residential localities, where the noiselessness of the former material is of necessity in these neurotic days. Upon macadamised roads undergoing excessive wear and tear, with the inconvenience of continuous repair, wood paving has been vastly extended during recent years, and has proved a measure of economy as well as comfort. The comparative advantages of hard and soft woods have respectively their advocates among men eminently fitted to judge, and it is possible that the battle of the timbers has yet to be fought out, not only upon the matter of durability, but also upon the important questions of noiselessness, liability to contraction and expansion and antiseptic qualities. The ever-popular microbe has also now appeared upon the scene with regard to this particular form of paving, and an entirely new genus of bacteria, alleged to be injurious to human organism, has been recently discovered as emanating from imperfectly cleansed wood-paved roadways. Unlike the septic tank or the aerobic microbe of the filter, these are of no advantage to humanity and must be exterminated. Thus, the necessity for constantly and efficiently cleansing the streets is intensified by this new discovery, and the use of disinfectants in combination with the watering of streets may become much more general.

A novel feature as affecting our highways has been recently introduced by the adoption of the Light Railways Act, 1896, by which powers are given for the construction of railways alongside or over public roads, ostensibly for facilitating the carriage of agricultural produce. During the present year of Parliament, however, these railways have been promulgated in more densely-populated quarters than it appears to many was contemplated by the promoters of the Act, and that what was intended as assistance to the farming interest is now developing into the acquisition of tramway facilities without compliance with the requirements of the Tramway Acts. It is an important question, closely affecting the suburbs of large towns, where these light railways may be introduced without the statutory consent of the road authority, and without any provision as to rate of speed, protection of public roads, restoration and maintenance of the same, purchase of undertaking by local authority and many other covenants now required by the Acts relating to the construction of tramways. The procedure for promotion is also totally distinct from that of tramway construction, although the work proposed to be carried out may be *de facto* the same. Should these promotions undertake the work hitherto associated with tramways every endeavour should be made to secure similar protection to local authorities to that provided in the Tramway Acts.

SUPERVISION OF NEW BUILDINGS.

The supervision of new buildings is possibly one of the most important of the duties of the municipal engineer in securing stability of buildings and in endeavouring to maintain health and ward off disease in the homes of the people. Provision is also made in the by-laws for the prevention from fire in all new buildings, and upon this matter it does appear that some additions are required in the present by-laws as generally adopted throughout the country, in order that better provision should be made for fireproof walls and floors in flats or buildings of the tenement class, now being so generally built in large towns. In the metropolis powers for prevention of spread of fire in these buildings already exist, but, except in private Acts, there is no authority that I am aware of outside the metropolis that can enforce this necessary provision, the corridors and staircases in many cases being of timber, thus adding enormously to the risks of the tenants in the upper floors of any high range of buildings. Endeavours should be made at least to secure powers in this direction by the construction of all corridors and staircases, with their enclosing walls, in incombustible material, as, I believe, is universal in Edinburgh, Glasgow and other large Scotch towns. To render the by-law absolutely satisfactory, fireproof floors or horizontal party walls should be rendered compulsory, being properly constructed according to a stringent specification embodied in the by-laws, so as to avoid a calamity similar to the deplorable accident that has recently occurred at Westminster. This case also seems to indicate the necessity of additional supervision as to the construction of floors and interior walls. The suggestion is possibly a matter that might be reasonably represented to the proper authorities by this association af.er careful deliberation.

Upon the sanitary aspect as relating to the supervision of new buildings too much attention cannot be paid to the efficient construction of the drainage, and the provision of requisite space around our dwellings in order that a free circulation of air may be secured. Upon the former question there is no doubt but that considerable improvement has been effected in recent years, and valuable additions and amendments have been made to the by-laws in some districts, ensuring additional precautionary measures where drains are laid under houses, and enforcing proper provision for inspection and testing of drains without the inconvenience caused by the disturbing of the ground as is now found necessary in cases of imperfect drainage. The water test as applied to drains, a simple thing in itself, but one largely affecting the efficiency of the house drain and consequently the health of the people, is also now almost universally adopted, although it would possibly be desirable that this description of test should be definitely fixed and ratified by reference in the by-laws. The maximum amount of air space as now provided, I think, will be agreed is but little enough, 25 ft. of ground being by no means too extensive an area for thorough ventilation in densely-inhabited neighbourhoods. Unfortunately, however, many of the smaller houses receive little more than half this extent of land in the rear of the house, so that with a rabbit-hutch and a chicken-run but little worthy of the name of garden remains. Every endeavour should therefore be made by the municipal engineer to enforce this necessary provision for sanitation to its utmost limits, as the health returns now so clearly point to the excess of sickness in crowded localities.

ELECTRIC LIGHTING.

Of all municipal works at present in progress and contemplated to a still greater extent in the future none show more general adoption in all parts of the kingdom than the installation of electric lighting plant, the provisional orders applied for during the present session being in excess of any previous year. The almost universal action now taken by local authorities in the installation of electric light themselves, to the exclusion of monopolies, brings the question largely within the scope of the duties of the municipal engineer, the highly-trained electrical engineer being an official of the corporation or town, together with his colleague the civil engineer and surveyor. In the first stages of the introduction of any scheme of electric lighting the latter officer is often actively engaged, more especially with regard to the sites for central and sub-stations, and the routes for the transmission and distribution of the electrical energy. This must be mv excuse for the few remarks I may have to make upon this prominent matter of municipal engineering interest.

The advantages in many ways of electric light over any other form of artificial light must be generally admitted, and the financial success of most undertakings by municipal authorities seems to be fairly assured after the second or third year of working. Thus it is to be anticipated that in the early future this system will, like many other municipal promotions of a similar character, become a relief to the burden of rating, and that the price will compare favourably

with that of any other description of lighting. At the outset in any new venture it is expected that the cost of supply to a limited number of customers must be greater in proportion than when the undertaking has been more generally adopted. This was the case in the early stages of gas supply, but, nevertheless, the better illumination and general superiority of gas was sufficient to practically eliminate the use of oil and candles where gas was available. In the same way, even supposing the cost of electric supply may exceed that of gas during the early years of installation, still its convenience and general utility is such that it cannot fail to become the popular illuminant, and that in the near future. The steady increase in demand for electric light is abundantly exemplified in the various installations throughout the country, where in so many instances the enlargement of the stations and plant are necessitated within two years, or even less, from completion of the work. In addition, therefore, to acquiring a site with special facilities for carriage of coal by. rail or water, or by both if possible, careful provision should be made by the municipal engineer for enlargement in the future and the buildings so erected as to admit of the most economical and ready means of adding thereto.

One great difficulty encountered in the general adoption of electric light in a residential neighbourhood, and especially where the property is of a small-class character, is the expense incidental to the wiring of premises. Endeavours have been made in several directions to remove the difficulty by instituting what is nominally called the free wiring of premises by companies formed for that purpose. This is a work, however, that would be better taken in hand by the municipal promoters themselves, and it does appear most desirable with this intent that borrowing powers should be accorded to local authorities similar to those now exercised for private improvement work, by which the payment of the cost of the work by the owner or occupier, as the case may be, could be spread over a term of years commensurate with the period of the loan. This would be but little felt by the owners of property, and would, I believe, conduce very largely to the extension of electric lighting in residential property tenanted by the middle and working classes.

The public lighting is at present almost entirely confined to arc lamps upon the main streets, the branch streets still being lighted by gas, an old friend that has stood us in good stead and in which considerable improvement with regard to public lighting has been effected during recent years. The introduction of the incandescent gas burner for public lighting has been introduced with- great effect in some districts where the lamps are not too far apart. With long intervals, however, this description of lighting does not appear to possess the same proportionate penetrating power as the ordinary burner. In my own district 400 lamps have been fitted experimentally with this description of burner with satisfactory results, both as to illumination and annual cost.

COMBINED UNDERTAKINGS.

The combination of the work incidental to combustion of house refuse with that appertaining to the generation of electrical energy is a subject that has resulted of late in a large amount of pamphleteering and discussion, and, although a matter of supreme interest to municipal engineers, is one upon which I dare not trust myself to enlarge on this occasion. Upon all sides, however, it must be admitted that by judicious design of the combined works in the first instance the utilisation of the caloric from the refuse furnaces must figure in some proportion as an assistance towards the generation of steam in connection with the electric lighting plant, and that outside the question of the value of the clinker for municipal work and the destruction of the useless refuse by combustion, every pound of steam thus generated should represent a saving in the expenditure incidental to the electric lighting work. Care, doubtless, should be taken in the disposition of the two departments, isolating them as far as is consistent with convenience and facilities for combined working, as the refuse tip and store with its attendant dust and dirt is not a too desirable neighbour to the engine-house of the electric lighting works. That the refuse, however, is generally of value for purposes of combustion there can be no doubt, and that it has for many years past unwisely been treated as a useless waste product in large towns has only recently become apparent.

The combination of other municipal works with an electric light installation is also possible in many ways for motive power, thus utilising the day load, which at times may in a measure be running to waste. In a minor degree this power could be most advantageously applied to motor cars or vans for the removal of house refuse, slopping and watering, and other work requiring mechanical power, provision being made for charging stations for this purpose at convenient localities within the area of supply. In this direction I believe considerable economy could be effected in a district with a large amount of cartage work, the cost of which often amounts to one of the heaviest items of administration in municipal work.

A somewhat important question as affecting electric lighting undertakings is the report of the Select Committee lately appointed to consider amendments to the electric lighting Acts that may be necessary to empower the Board of Trade to grant compulsory powers. Among other items in this report, recommendations are made that compulsory powers should be given to electric lighting undertakers for the com pulsory acquisition of land for a generating station outside their area of supply. This, doubtless, will prove of distinct advantage to those towns where the acquisition of site would involve excessive expenditure, but the advantage to the districts outside the area of supply and whose streets are to be broken up without any commensurate benefit received may not be so apparent. The matter is, however, in report stage only, and may hereafter be further heard of.

PUBLIC HEALTH LAW.

The law relating to public health, the study of which now forms part of the training of every municipal engineer, has been considerably extended since the original Act was passed in 1875. So numerous have been the subsequent Acts added to the statute book, and so varied the nature of the measures to which they refer, that the time has now arrived when great assistance would be rendered to municipal authorities, less litigation would be involved and the statutes themselves made much more clear if the Public Health Act, 1875, and the Acts incorporated therewith were consolidated in one General Act relating to matters connected with public health. In this could be included many useful measures now contained in private Acts, and which the Police and Sanitary Committee in their report to the House of Commons in 1897 have strongly recommended for inclusion in a public Bill. Opportunity might also be taken to secure desirable amendments to the existing Acts, notably in that ill-conceived clause 19 of the Public Health Acts Amendment Act of 1890, relating to combined drainage, which tends to the relief of owners' responsibilities at the cost of the rates.

Additional powers might likewise be conferred upon local authorities to make by-laws with regard to other matters than those mentioned in sec. 157 of the Public Health Act, 1875. In the latter case no authority is given over the question of more complete construction of roadways, the separate system of sewerage for foul and rain waters respectively, internal plastering to houses, plumbers' work, water supply (more especially with regard to locality and capacity of cisterns), and other matters upon which it is essential to obtain powers in connection with the healthy development of a town by construction of roads and erection of buildings.

There are also many other desirable amendments which, I believe, are now among the archives of the association, and were forwarded to the Local Government Board when I had the honour of presiding over the deliberations of the Parliamentary Committee, but which are of too detailed a character to refer to in this address. During the present session a Bill has been introduced into the House with a similar title to the Public Health Acts Amendment Act of 1890, in which many useful clauses have been introduced from private Acts of recent years. Unfortunately, however, I understand that this Bill has been withdrawn during the past few days. Like many former Amendment Acts, the principle of permissive legislation has been adopted in many cases where compulsory measures would possibly have been more desirable. That some powers to be conferred upon local authorities should be adoptive where the public health, or comfort or convenience of the majority are not concerned, is readily to be understood, but in all sanitary questions, or those relating to salubrious dwellings and convenient means of access thereto by roads or streets, it does seem that uniform legislation throughout the length and breadth of the country is in every way desirable. Being thus uniform, it becomes better known by all whom it concerns, and consequently there is not the same opportunity for the plea of ignorance by those who contravene the law and which is now so constantly the defence where powers are possessed in one district that are wanting, perhaps, in that immediately adjoining. A clause has been recently introduced into private Acts, as well as in the Bill before mentioned, which is of intense importance to municipal engineers throughout the kingdom, but especially to those appointed to districts where a large amount of building development is in progress. I allude to the granting of certificates by the surveyor to the local authority that, prior to occupation of all new houses, the premises are in every respect in accordance with the by-laws and requirements of the district for the time being in force, a most salutory clause and one that most surveyors would gladly adopt were proper and competent assistance rendered them for the close and constant supervision of buildings to ensure strict adherence to the by-laws in every particular. But what are the facts of the case? In many instances the surveyor, in addition to the many duties of his department, which necessitate a large amount of time spent in his office upon administrative work, has himself to supervise the erection of new buildings, and that perhaps over a district several square miles in extent with work in all directions. How is it possible under these circumstances for a satisfactory certificate to be granted, and is it fair under these circumstances to free the owner and builder from all liability and practically place the same upon the shoulders of the surveyor, and through him on his employers? Should such beneficial legislation for the property owners be enacted, by all means let it be accompanied by powers conferred upon local authorities to charge the owners and builders thus benifitted for the supervision of the buildings, by which means a sufficient number of qualified inspectors may be appointed to thoroughly supervise all building operations and thus to justify the granting of a bonâ-fide certificate. The question is of such moment to

public authorities and their engineers that earnest endeavours should be made to obtain general powers throughout the country to charge for supervision, without which the operations of any clause relating to the granting of certificates will be ineffective, and result in but little benefit to the public and an entirely new liability fraught with possible litigation to the certifying authority.

CONCLUSION.

Gentlemen, I am afraid I have somewhat overtaxed your patience in the few disjointed remarks I have made with regard to the works and duties appertaining to the office of the municipal engineer, but I look to the brotherhood which I hope exists in this association to condone any of my shortcomings. Mutual support was originally, as in most associations of this character, one of the main reasons for its constitution, and I sincerely trust that it may always be to the fore, so that in addition to the spread of professional knowledge we may also be ever ready to assist those of our profession who may at any time be in trouble or in need, thus training the heart as well as the intellect for the welfare of our professional brethren.

Mr. CHARLES JONES (Ealing) proposed a vote of thanks to the president for his address. He had seldom heard one so thoroughly utilitarian in character. It had touched upon questions in regard to which they all felt deeply, and it might well be submitted to the Local Government Board not to be pigeon-holed but to be acted upon.

Mr. J. PATTEN BARBER (Islington), in seconding the vote of thanks, said they had expected much, and had not been disappointed. He hoped they would all work towards giving practical shape to the very high aims and ideals so ably put before them. The powers of local authorities should be enlarged, and if extended in the directions suggested by the president, it would be for the general good.

The motion was carried unanimously, and after a brief acknowledgment by the president, the following paper was read :—

USE OF TARRED MACADAM IN THE CONSTRUCTION OF ROADWAYS IN URBAN DISTRICTS, AND COMPARATIVE CONSIDERATIONS.
By A. H. CAMPBELL, A.M.I.C.E.,
City Surveyor, Canterbury.

[Mr. Adam H. Campbell was elected city surveyor of Canterbury in 1893, succeeding Mr. Frank Baker, who is now borough engineer of Middlesbrough. He was formerly borough surveyor of Stratford-on-Avon, and antecedent to that was an assistant in the office of the borough engineer of Edinburgh ; Mr. Campbell was, indeed, the first assistant appointed by Mr. Cooper on his succeeding to the borch engineership of Edinburgh in 1882. Receiving his professional training as a civil engineer and architect in the office of a well-known firm of private practitioners in Edinburgh, Mr. Campbell became an assistant to a land surveyor in Perthshire, where he was engaged on several large surveys. Returning to Edinburgh in 1882, he remained as assistant to Mr. Cooper for seven years, works of main sewerage, street widenings, city extensions, clearance of slum areas, labourers' dwellings and tramways being the chief works of a constructive character undertaken. From the inside of the "Modern Athens" to the quiet of "Shakespeare's town" on the banks of the soft-flowing Avon appeared a remarkable translation ; but here was abundance of work to do and experience to gain. The treatment of the Stratford sewage question—peculiarly knotty as it turned out to be—the extension and amendment of the Stratford waterworks, the erection of the public lighting and gas destruction, the erection of public baths, the provision of new outfall sewerage works, new municipal buildings, abattoir drainage and labourers' dwellings, and the taking in hand of various items of street improvement works. When it is stated that the sum total of these works represents an expenditure of about £120,000, and that the erection of a lunatic asylum to cost £80,000 is also contemplated, it will be evident that this metropolitan city of England is determined to keep herself well abreast of the times.]

The committee of the last International Congress of Hygiene and Demography, held at Buda-Pesth, adopted the following resolution : " That the paving of streets should be smooth, and as far as practicable impervious, to facilitate cleansing and also to prevent contamination of the subsoil." With this resolution this association of municipal engineers and surveyors will no doubt heartily concur. It has served to suggest to the author a good text in the preparation of his paper. The text of the resolution comprehends in a sentence all the essentials of a good roadway. These may be briefly summarised under the following heads : (a) Durability ; (b) the minimum of noise ; and (c) the minimum of first cost (consistent with the foregoing).

The attainment of the first of these—viz., durability—is best realised by the adoption of granite sets, as may be witnessed more or less in all large cities, and nowhere to a greater proportionate extent than in the city where the association is now assembled. This kind of paving, however, is not smooth ; it is most noisy, the truism of " empty vehicles (not vessels) making the most sound " receiving abundant illustration on this form of road ; further, unless laid on a bed of concrete and jointed in pitch, it is not impervious, and the facility of cleansing is much impeded, due to the numerous joints wearing open and rounding off, holding the dirt and dust of roadways. It is moreover costly, probably nearly as costly in construction as wood pavement, and its only claim for use is its *durability*. Allied to this material for road formation is the use of blue brick setts for carriageways, which are having experimental trials in a few places. The attainment of the second head—*i.e.*, minimum of noise—is best realised by one or other of these descriptions of materials: (1) Gutta-percha; (2) compressed asphalte and concrete macadam; (3) wood paving; (4) macadam.

The first named is mentioned only as the ideal of noiselessness, and not as entering into comparison with any of the well-known materials of road construction. It is in a very experimental stage as yet, and has hardly come within the scope of practical consideration. It is to be seen in small short sections in Glasgow and at the entrance to Euston station, London.

Compressed asphalte, also concrete macadam, is clean, impervious, durable and saving for the clatter of horses' feet. May be described as comparatively noiseless. Involving, as asphalte does, the underlying bed of concrete, the first cost renders it prohibitory in all save large centres of population. It is, moreover, slippery and unsuited to inclined roads upon a hill.

Wood paving comes next in the fulfilment of the necessary conditions of the text. It is smooth; is probably the least noisy of any of the descriptions of hard pavement; it is of moderate durability; and if of the hard-wood description, practically impervious to moisture. Its first cost, however, and the unreasonably short periods allowed for repayment, render the general adoption of wood pavement in moderately-sized towns, or even in the suburban parts of large cities, very unlikely, if not prohibitory.

The class of town or urban district to which allusion is made is that of moderate size and limited financial resource, which are restricted therefore to the use of "macadam" in the construction of their highways.

As it is from moderately-sized towns or districts that so many members of this association come, the consideration of any *improved form of macadam paving* acquires special interest and importance; and there is no improved form of macadam which is so coming to the front, and demanding that attention which its merits unquestionably deserve, as that now going by the name of "Tarred Macadam." That is, a composition of any of the stones, gravel or clinkers commonly used in the making of macadam roads with a mixture of *tar*. It appears a simple enough composition, but its preparation and laying, so as to turn out a success, bristle with delicate detail.

When properly made and on roads suited for it this construction of road complies most nearly—compressed asphalte perhaps excepted—with the conditions laid down in the reso-

To its preparation, storage and laying the author has had special opportunity of study, the composition, as used by him, being prepared by the workmen in his department.

In tabular form there is here submitted an epitome of particulars of several streets laid by the author during the past three years. Besides the foregoing list, a number of lanes in Canterbury have been partially laid with this composition; and at the present time St. Margaret-street, about 700 ft. long, with a carriageway of only 12 ft. and in the centre of the city, having heavy vehicular traffic, is in process of laying. The preparation and laying embrace these details: (1) The nature of aggregate and its preparation; (2) the tar, its nature and treatment; (3) the mixing of these two together; (4) the storage; (5) the laying down upon the road; (6) the cost.

As regards the nature or description of the aggregate, the author has tried Kentish ragstone, surface-picked flints, pit gravel and Guernsey granite. The stone is prepared for the tar by burning in the open. It is laid out first of all in a flat bed about 12 in. thick and of rectangular plan; on this is spread a layer of coke and breeze about 3 in. to 4 in. thick, with a little wood to assist the fire; this is then overlaid so as to form a stack of stone of about 5 ft. in height from the ground; meantime, as the last addition of height is made, the fire of wood and coke has been kindled, and the fire is allowed to penetrate the stack. About 1½ chaldrons (54 bushels) of coke are consumed in a stack of 60 cube yards.

As regards the length and size of the stack of stone, this may be made endless by laying out the stack so as to describe a circle, thus following in the process of mixing a circular course, with certain obvious advantages. Other makers of tarred stone composition in the author's district arrange the stack in the form of a *cone*, close it up at the top, fire it in the centre, and allowing the fire to penetrate the mass leave the stack of stone untouched whilst this process of firing proceeds. This operation may take any time between seven and ten days: the stack is then opened up and the hot stone applied to the prepared tar.

In either of these methods of firing the stone a great deal of loss by disintegration occurs; the stone succumbing to the influence of fire, and tending to get reduced to a coarse-grained powder. Particularly so was this the case with a trial of granite exposed to fire, which quickly produced the condition above described. For this reason the author would much prefer the heating of the stone in an oven or kiln; the temperature would be more equable and the severe firing causing the disintegration described would be avoided.

On the subject of "heating" one or two remarks may be submitted. The author believes it to be the practice with some makers not to heat the stone at all, but, being sure that the stone is dry and free from moisture, apply it in the cold

| Name of Street. | Width of Carriageway. ft. in. | Nature of Traffic. | Date when laid. | Thickness, aggregate. | Cost per Superficial Yard. | Experience. |
|---|---|---|---|---|---|---|
| Stour-street ... | 8 2 | Heavy continuous traffic, three traction trains passing daily. | July, 1896. | 6-in. Kentish rag. | About 4s. 6d. | Failure; quite unable to support the constant action of the traction engine traffic. |
| Turnagain-lane (cul de sac) | 8 2 | Light van traffic ... | Nov., 1895. | 4 in. of gravel on the old natural road formation. | 3s. | Satisfactory. |
| Orange-street | 17 0 | Medium through traffic, carriers' waggons, carts and tradesmen's vans. | March, 1897. | 4 in. of gravel underlaid by 3 in. hard broken brick. | 4s. 6d. | Most satisfactory. |
| King-street ... | (1) 16 6 (2) 8 2 | Ditto ... ... | May, 1897. | 3 in. ditto ... | About 4s. | Moderately satisfactory; centre of way along horse track commenced to disintegrate, due to the tar being overboiled, and the material hardening or setting before using. |
| Guildhall-street | 15 9 | Heavy through traffic, omnibuses and general town traffic. | Sept. 1897. | 4 in. ditto ... | 4s. 6d. | Generally satisfactory; superficially softens on parts in sun heat, but otherwise is doing well. |

lutions set forth at the outset of this paper. It is a smooth and noiseless road, it is non-absorbent, it is cleanly in itself and easily kept clean, and its first cost is within the capacity of the most reasonably restricted finance of small towns and districts.

With all the advantages enumerated, it appears remarkable that tarred macadam has not been adopted except as yet on the most limited scale. It is true that tarred gravel or limestone footpaths have been in use for a great number of years and have now obtained a deservedly wide adoption, but the extension of this same composition, only of a larger gauge metal, to the construction of roadways has been most limited. As accounting for this, these reasons may be suggested—*viz.*, the failures which frequently attend a first trial; and uncertainty as to the properties and action of *tar*, and how it will unite with the aggregate which it is designed to incorporate.

The author can speak from personal experience of its failure and of its success too—failure where success was expected, and success where failure might be anticipated; and this as evidence of the fickle character of the composition.

but thoroughly dry state to the prepared tar. This condition of the stone, in the author's opinion, resembles the risk attached to laying the tarred mixture in position in cold instead of hot weather. The tar refuses to "work," the temperatures are so unequal, and when the sun (particularly the sun of the sunny South) beats upon such a road it is not improbable but that this defect will discover itself in the liquefied tar bubbling and spewing itself up over the surface. The proper or at least *best* condition of heating is to be obtained by the kiln, where the heat will be rather of the moderate *baking* than of the hot *roasting* sort.

The temperature of the stone when the tar is applied should be such as the palm of the hand can bear with comfort; if too hot the tar will be destroyed as a cohesive; if too cold the tar will go on too thickly, and under the rays of a hot sun will soften. The hot stone when ready to be mixed with the prepared tar is sifted through two gauges, graduated to 1 in. and to ½ in., giving three sizes of material—*viz.*, 1-in. to 2-in. gauge for the body material, ½-in. to 1-in. gauge for the intermediate or fining coat, and ¼-in. to ½-in. gauge for the skin or top dressing. These three sizes are laid in layers as follows—*viz.*, *3 in. to 4 in.* thick of the coarse, about ½ in. thick of the intermediate and the top dressing in the thinnest layer possible, with a view only to filling all interstices, thereafter a dressing of fine ¼-in. granite or limestone siftings is scattered broadcast and the traffic at once allowed on the road, working this top dressing in and assisting in the consolidation of the road formation. The weight of the roller employed by the author is nominally *10* tons, and each of the three layers is rolled separately.

Considerable importance is attached to the state of the weather at the time of laying, in the sun by preference and to assure a good result; if laid in a cold temperature and with any defects present in the composition, disappointment and possible failure will result. Weather being normal, any time between *May and September* (inclusive) may be regarded as suitable. One word as to wet weather—operations both of mixing and of laying should be suspended in time of "wet," where conducted in the open, as nothing so corrupts the composition as the presence of moisture.

In constructing a road of this tarred composition, the old surface is removed to a depth of 8 in. and re-made with a 4-in. thickness of dry, hard broken stone, furnace clinker or brick; this is rolled smooth and finished to the required camber of the road. The author's reasons for this underlying ballasting of dry material are two-fold: (1) To separate the tarred composition from any damp substratum; and (2) to economise in the thickness of tarred material.

Under the author's practice the tarred composition is only 4 in. thick (finished). This by itself would be an insufficient surface formation to bear the traffic and resist the damp, but underlaid by the dry ballasting of hard material, well rolled and perfectly grouted with cement or brushed with well-boiled tar, appears to answer the requirements for which it is introduced.

One sentence is necessary as to having the tarred mixture all in a fresh or "live" state when being laid, otherwise cracking and disintegration of the road will rapidly occur; also in keeping off all traffic during the progress of the work, not because the traffic in itself is an injury, but because of the dirt, dust and other matter foreign to the mixture being imported and destroying the binding together of the layers in one corporate mass. This hint is one to which the author attaches considerable importance, as the effects of this occurrence have been painfully present to his sight upon portions of two roads which he has laid down.

TAR.

The quality of the tar employed is no less important than the other details of the work. Some trading firms making this material use the refined or distilled tar, and excellent results are thus obtainable; but more commonly it is the ordinary gas tar that is used, at a cost of about 2d. per gallon. This tar should be as far as possible free from water, of a stiff dense consistency, any defects of this character having to be counteracted in the boiling operation; the lighter the tar the longer it must boil, so that all light oils are driven off.

The following pertinent observations on the subject of coal tar have been submitted by the author's friend and colleague (Mr. Sidney Harvey, F.I.C., public analyst).

"Coal tar is a by-product of extremely complex constitution, containing matters volatile at various temperatures.

"The effect of heat upon coal tar would be to volatilise certain principles therein, whereby the residue would be more viscid and tenacious than the original substance, while its melting or softening point will be proportionately raised.

"As the ultimate result of the continuous application of heat is coal tar *pitch*, it is desirable when coal tar is used in conjunction with road-making materials that the heat in question should be applied *long enough* to secure the most tenacious and difficultly fusible product, but *not pushed so far as to bring about a brittle nature to the pitch itself*, which latter would defeat the effect aimed at, which is to agglutinate the fragments of rock material with a watertight cement, which, while protecting the mineral from 'weathering,' would not yield to the heating action of the sun's rays."

In the author's practice the tar is boiled in 50-gallon coppers; it is brought to the boil and maintained so for a period varying from three to four hours; with good conditioned tar three hours' boiling is amply sufficient. To each 50 gallons of tar is added a small proportion of pitch (about half a bucketful), and these are boiled together. The author would not assert the necessity of introducing even this small proportion of pitch, but the cost is almost infinitesimal, and as a counteractive to bad quality of tar it is good and worth introducing.

The quantity of *tar* employed appears to vary with different makers, just as much as do the other details of this interesting work. It also varies with the season and with the consideration whether, when mixed, the material is to be at once laid or is to be stored in a heap. If the weather is cold and if the material is to be stored the less should be the quantity of tar used. Weather being hot, and material being laid down at once, a slightly greater proportion of tar may be used than under the reverse conditions. At the present season, with the material being laid soon after mixing, although a brief storage is found necessary, the following are the quantities of tar that are used—*viz.*:—

| | Gallons per cubic yard. |
|---|---|
| With the coarse (1-in. to 2-in. gauge) material ... | 8 |
| With intermediate (½-in. to 1-in. gauge) material | 10 |
| With fine sifted stone (¼-in. gauge) material ... | 12 |

From a return supplied to me by the foreman of works, the author submits the following statement giving the detail cost of the material. The stack of stone operated on for test contained 45 cubic yards; and the actual cost in preparing that quantity is:—

*Debit.*

| | £ | s. | d. |
|---|---|---|---|
| 45 cubic yards pit gravel, at 3s. 6d. ... ... | 7 | 17 | 6 |
| 79 gallons tar and cartage, at 2½d. per gallon ... | 0 | 16 | 5½ |
| 234 lb. of pitch, at 46s. 8d. per ton... ... ... | 0 | 4 | 10½ |
| 84 bushels of coke,* at 9s. 4d. per chaldron ... | 1 | 1 | 9½ |
| 30 „ breeze ... ... ... ... ... | 0 | 8 | 0 |
| Wages in preparing and mixing stone and tar ... | 7 | 18 | 7 |
| | £18 | 7 | 2½ |

*Credit.*

Actual product from the foregoing: 40 cubic yards of mixture costing £18 7s. 2½d., equal to 9s. 2d. per cubic yard.

This composition as above described, laid 4 in. to 4½ in. thick, finished in compressed condition, will work out at fully 1s. 6d. per super. yard for the mixture alone.

| | s. | d. | |
|---|---|---|---|
| To this... ... ... ... ... | 1 | 6 | per super. yard. |
| Add these items (estimated):— | | | |
| 1. Stripping road 8 in. thick ... | 0 | 9 | „ „ |
| 2. Broken brick ballasting ... ... | 0 | 10 | „ „ |
| 3. Applying the tarred material in three layers and finishing off... | 0 | 9 | „ „ |
| 4. Rolling road ... ... ... | 0 | 3 | „ „ |
| 5. Add contingencies 10 per cent.... | 0 | 5 | „ „ |
| Total ... ... ... | 4 | 6 | per super. yard |

The life of this description of road paving may be taken at seven years; so that, divided up over that term, the annual cost of a road so paved will work out at 7·7d. During this term it may become necessary to outlay certain small amounts in repairs so as to maintain the surface smooth, whole and impervious; this, estimated at 2d. per yard per annum, will give a grand total of 9·7d. per super. yard per annum for this description of roadway. This rate for a good street pavement in urban districts, for heavy vehicular traffic of the ordinary sort (that is excluding traction engine traffic, for which it is unsuited), is most moderate. Compare it with any of the other descriptions of paving; even than ordinary macadam it is rather *less*; and side by side with any of the improved harder pavements, *wood*, compressed asphalte or *setts* on concrete bed, it is incomparably less costly.

The author does not, however, suggest that this description of pavement should enter into competition with these superior materials of road construction; each and all of them—stone setts, wood, asphalte, tarred macadam and ordinary macadam—have their respective places; all, save tar macadam have had their field and play, and it is for a fair field, devoid of any favour, that the author presents to the association a plea on behalf of tar macadam. On the leading streets of smaller provincial towns, in the secondary and suburban thoroughfares of large towns, where in many cases stone or granite setts are used, of heavy cost, tarred macadam properly prepared and laid would form a welcome, valuable and economic substitute.

---

When the paper had been read a discussion was opened by Mr. SMITH SAVILLE (Darwen) and continued by Messrs. C. F. WIKE (Sheffield) and F. BAKER (Middlesbrough), after which an adjournment was made for luncheon given at the Royal Hotel on the invitation of the Lord Provost, magistrates and town council of the city. After luncheon the discussion of Mr. Campbell's paper was resumed by Mr. LEMON (Southampton), after whose speech it was decided to invite any further criticisms to be contributed in writing to the Transactions. Mr. YOUNG then summarised the chief points of his paper on "The Experience of Edinburgh with Refuse Destructors," and a discussion took place. Mr. COLAM next followed with a summary of his paper on "The Conversion of the Edinburgh, Leith and Portobello Horse Tramway System into Cable Traction," and a long discussion was closed by an admirable reply from the reader of the paper. The papers by Mr. STEWART and Mr. BRUCE, entitled respectively, "Notes on Sewer Ventilation as applied to the Water of Leith Intercepting Sewer" and "Housing of the Working Classes Act as worked out in Edinburgh," were also read and discussed. The paper by Mr. Bruce was as follows:—

## WORKING OF THE HOUSING OF THE WORKING CLASSES ACT (1890) IN EDINBURGH.

By WILLIAM BRUCE,
Graduate of the Association of Municipal and County Engineers and Member of the Sanitary Institute.

[Mr. Wm. Bruce was articled to a surveyor in Edinburgh, and acquired an experience in architectural and engineering work in his capacity as assistant to various private firms in that city. His early bent being for municipal engineering work, he sought to qualify himself in all the branches of the profession, and studied engineering, mechanics and sanitary science at the Heriot-Watt College. He entered

* Includes the coke consumed in the tar boiler.

the office of the burgh engineer of Edinburgh in January, 1892, at a time when the city was entering on a period of great municipal activity, and was fortunate in having the opportunity of participating in the various schemes about to be undertaken. The work on which Mr. Bruce has been principally engaged has been the designing and superintending of the construction of underground conveniences and public lavatories, the construction of new and the widening of existing streets

with relative works, the carrying out of the provisions of the Housing of the Working Classes Act, and city improvements generally. Mr. Bruce passed the examination of the Incorporated Association of Municipal and County Engineers in April, 1896, becoming a graduate of that body, and in July, 1897, was elected a member of the Sanitary Institute.]

The fair face of the city of Edinburgh has been so often extolled, its many advantages and beauties so often commented on and admired by strangers, that anyone not acquainted with the city might be led into the belief that in this favoured community there was no seamy side to life at all. Until recent years the changes and improvements ever taking place had for their object more the increasing of the beauty and convenience of the city at large than the promoting of the welfare or interest of any particular class. But as these changes and improvements were mostly effected on the older parts of the town, in our appreciation of what had been accomplished we were inclined to overlook the fact that all these clearances and street widenings must have been accompanied by a measure of inconvenience and hardship to a large number of persons.

It is said that by the improvement scheme promoted by Dr. Chambers, lord provost of the city some thirty years ago, that about 14,000 persons were removed from their houses. At that time many old landmarks were swept away; whole streets, closes and wynds obliterated to give place to what are now spacious and thriving thoroughfares.

The advantages and benefits of this scheme are acknowledged, and its good effects in bringing light and air into the midst of darkness and disease are visible to-day; but it is also a question if the present scarcity of small houses in Edinburgh, with the accompanying high rents, does not date from that same time. The improvements effected in more recent times, although not so extensive as the one just mentioned, have all brought with them their quota of hardship and discomfort to some poor people. The other causes—economic, social, or otherwise, which conduce to overcrowding and congestion in the poorer parts of all large cities—it is not within the province of this paper to discuss; but these causes have been active here as elsewhere, and in this city the facilities afforded by the closely-built and lofty tenements of the old town for crowding together a large number of persons on a small area are altogether exceptional, and for long have stood a constant menace to the whole city.

The clearing away of much of this old property, without making any suitable provision for those unhoused, only drove the poor into other quarters, and to meet the demand for small houses, tenements originally intended for and occupied by a class that could even lay claims to gentility, were sublet and subdivided until what was originally a house of five or six apartments became occupied by as many families. In these large blocks, with flat raised upon flat, this subdivision, as can be realised, resulted in much overcrowding, with all the attendant evils to health and morals.

A common feature, and, indeed, almost a rule in this class of tenement, is to have all the houses on one flat, to the extent sometimes of ten and more, entering from one common lobby running along the centre of the block, without any light but what is derived from one doorway communicating with the common stair, and with only the doubtful ventilation gained by the occasional opening of a house door. Into this lobby were compounded all the smells from the various houses, besides being the chosen position for the water-closet, sink and supply cistern common to several families.

Under conditions such as these, physical and moral degeneration is all that can be looked for or expected, and against this class of tenement the Public Health Committee have waged constant and unrelenting war, and have exercised their powers of compelling owners to introduce suitable sanitary accommodation and effect other improvements; but it was ultimately felt that something more drastic and

sweeping must be accomplished if the evils of this system of subdivision were to be successfully combated, and amelioration effected in the condition of the numerous class whose lot was cast in these congested and unhealthy areas.

With this object in view the Corporation of Edinburgh applied for, and obtained in the year 1893, a provisional order for a scheme under Part 1 of the Housing of the Working Classes Act, 1890. This scheme embraced ten areas situated in different parts of the city, ranging from about $\frac{1}{10}$th of an acre to about 2 acres in extent, the total areas scheduled amounting to about 6½ acres, with a population of nearly 10,000 persons. With the exception, perhaps, of individual properties here and there, all these areas have been acquired by the corporation, at a cost of about £70,000. In some cases these areas have been entirely reconstructed; others have been wholly or partially cleared of the whole properties, while some remain untouched as when first acquired. The actual number of persons unhoused by the corporation in carrying these improvements into effect was about 2,700.

It is unfortunate that, concurrently with the undertaking of the corporation, the North British Railway Company should have entered upon a large scheme for the enlargement and reconstruction of the Waverley station and approaching lines, which embraced the destruction of a great amount of property tenanted by the very class for whose betterment the corporation were labouring to improve; and that the additional evictions by the railway company of about 460 families caused great hardship and inconvenience among the labouring classes.

So great had the demand for small houses become that the corporation had not only to stay their hand in the work of clearing out the slums, but had to reinstate many families into their homes, and rehabilitate many houses that had been partly dismantled, in order to avoid any unnecessary suffering, and until such times as better housing accommodation could be provided.

While it is often too easy a matter to be able to put one's finger on the plague spots of a city and to effect sweeping clearances, it is only when the question of rehousing the displaced population arises that the real difficulty is confronted. Knowing the number of families to be accommodated, the first question is naturally, What class of house should be provided? To settle that they ought to be on the principle of cottage homes, flatted tenements, or anything else, does not sufficiently answer the question without first deciding what class of poor it is intended to cater for. There are some poor who only wish the conditions and opportunity to enable them to lead orderly and exemplary lives; while there are others (and these, unfortunately, constitute a large factor to be reckoned with) who can only be dragooned into order, and who would require that supervision be extended into the inmost arrangements and workings of their homes.

To the first may be entrusted a house with all sanitary conveniences private to itself; but for the second, who might not scruple to abuse any advantage or privilege, it might be better to have all sanitary appliances and such like under the control of a vigilant caretaker; and in any case, to bring these two classes together indiscriminately would result in injury and injustice to the one, with probably no counterbalancing advantage to the other. Up to the present time it may be said that anything the Edinburgh Corporation have done is for the benefit of what may be called the respectable poor, and it is to be hoped that they will yet do something to meet the requirements of that class whom we are inclined to regard as incorrigible and thriftless.

The sites selected for the erection of the new workmen's dwellings were two in number: One in Cowgate, in the centre of the city; the other at Tynecastle Meadows, a working-class suburb. Tynecastle Meadows was not an area scheduled under the Housing of the Working Classes Act, but the land had been acquired by the corporation, and it was thought that the erection of suitable houses here might relieve congestion elsewhere. In Cowgate there have been provided twenty-four houses of one apartment and thirty-two houses of two apartments, each house having its own water-closet and sink. At Tynecastle there have been provided—twenty-four houses of one apartment, sixteen houses of kitchen and bed-closet, and twenty-four houses of two apartments; and here the water-closets are common to two families. At Cowgate the area available for the new houses, after conceding a part of the ground to street widening, was so limited that space could not be afforded for washing-houses or bath-rooms, but from the immediate proximity of the public washing-houses and baths this was not considered a serious drawback; at Tynecastle, however, there is a wash-house and bath-room common to every four tenants.

The houses erected on both sites are in flatted tenements, on the balcony principle. The staircases are under cover, but have their entire fronts open to the outside air. In the Cowgate scheme each house is through-going from front to back, with the doors opening to the balconies and as far apart as planning will permit; all walls are plastered, with the internal angles rounded to prevent lodgment of dirt and to afford facilities for cleaning. Owing to the great difference in level between the ground at back and front of these tenements, it was found necessary to construct the entire ground floor as shops, which added to the cost and rather handicapped the scheme.

The cost of the two Cowgate blocks was £10,000, and the Tynecastle blocks about £8,700. Owing to the inequalities of level already referred to, the amount of excavation necessary and the retaining walls required before the site in Cowgate could be utilised, no charge for land is made against this scheme. At Tynecastle the land may be valued at £500, which makes the entire cost of this scheme £9,200 for land and building. The rentals for these corporation houses are: At Cowgate, houses of one apartment, 2s. 7d. per week; houses of two apartments, 4s. week. At Tynecastle, houses of one apartment, 2s. 4d. per week; houses of one apartment and bed-closet, 2s. 10d. per week; houses of two apartments, 3s. 3d. to 3s. 8d. per week. The tenant's proportion of local rates are included in these rentals, with the exception of poor and school rates, which run about 6d. in the £1; and it is estimated that after paying interest on capital, burdens and maintenance, the balance put into a sinking fund would pay off capital expenditure in about thirty-three years. These results are not much in excess of what is being paid in those dilapidated and insanitary houses already referred to. It may be quite possible to provide houses at a lower rent than those charged by adopting a different principle of construction, but we must not sacrifice any sanitary advantage to the question of cost.

Among sanitary authorities back-to-back houses stand condemned, but I believe that those who have studied the question will agree that through-going houses are less economical of space, and therefore more costly than back-to-back houses. This is especially the case if one and two roomed houses are mixed in one block; either the single-room house must be entered by a long lobby, or the room must be unnecessarily large; and when, as in Cowgate, each house of one and two apartments is provided with its own water-closet and sink, the effect on the cost becomes apparent. That houses with these advantages, however, are highly appreciated and much sought after is evident from the fact that for the corporation houses in Cowgate alone there are about twenty applicants every week seeking to be accommodated.

It may be generally accepted that for any housing scheme of the nature of those under consideration, supervision more or less stringent must be exercised if the property is to be prevented from entering on a downward course of dilapidation almost as soon as occupied. The amount of evil which a few unruly and worthless tenants can work is incalculable, and in all cases where the size of a scheme will permit, a resident caretaker should be provided. Fortunately, in some respects, but unfortunately in this, the schemes so far carried out in this city are small ones—too small to be burdened with the cost of a caretaker; but recognising the necessity for supervision, the corporation have handed over the factoring of those properties to the Edinburgh Social Union—a body whose object is to promote the welfare of the labouring classes, and to provide them with suitable and healthy houses at a low figure. The rents of the properties owned and factored by the social union are collected weekly by its lady members, who in many matters pertaining to household affairs exercise a wholesome influence over the tenants, or reprove any infringement of their rules with more tact and less offence than a man might be able to do.

Among the many applicants for these corporation houses no selection is made; each is accommodated as vacancies permit, but non-conformity with the rules, especially on the score of uncleanliness, is not tolerated unless amendment is made; and further, as showing the class of tenants occupying these houses, it may be of interest to state from information kindly supplied by the social union, that the weekly wages earned run from 7s. 6d. (in one case) up to 29s., the weekly average being 18s. to 22s.

In addition to the houses built by the corporation, the North British Railway Company have erected seventy-four houses to partly accommodate the working-class population displaced by them in the extension of their station. The social union have effected great reformation in remodelling and reconstructing several old tenements in the centre and crowded parts of the city, while there have also been several excellent examples of working men's houses provided by private agency; but these isolated examples of what can be done only serve by comparison to bring more into prominence how much yet remains to be accomplished.

Not satisfied with what they have recently undertaken, the Edinburgh Corporation have again, this year, applied for powers to deal with other seven areas under the Housing of the Working Classes Act, embracing an area of nearly 5 acres. Three of these areas are in Portobello, recently amalgamated with Edinburgh, and other four in the Stock-bridge district in the north-west of the city, and here we may shortly expect a new condition of things, and an important housing scheme for the poor of those parts.

But the field for improvement is a large one. Other areas and districts in the city are fast lapsing into a condition (if they have not already reached that stage) when only thorough and comprehensive treatment by our local authority can root out the evils hidden in their depths. The work can be surmounted if resolutely faced, and if spasmodic and intermittent efforts give place to something at once systematic and sustained; but its execution will be sufficient to tax the resources of our councillors, and will afford scope for the ingenuity of our municipal engineering department.

The remaining papers read yesterday we have been compelled to hold over, but they will be given in our next issue, together with a report of the discussions. The discussions on the papers of Mr. Campbell and Mr. Bruce will also be given, and a full account will appear of the annual dinner, which took place yesterday evening at the Royal Hotel. We may mention that ten new members and eighteen graduates were elected at the meeting yesterday morning.

## THE NEW PRESIDENT.

In the form of a special supplement we present to our readers what we believe will be admitted to be an excellent likeness of the new president, whose year of office can scarcely fail to be both successful and highly popular. The following details of his career will be of interest:—

Mr. Robson was educated at Lancing, and afterwards by private tutors. In 1863 he was articled to Mr. Lewis Angell, with whom he was engaged upon the main drainage of Portsmouth and other municipal works of that thriving seaport town. Subsequently he was employed on quantity work in Westminster, in connection with the Thames embankment, the London main drainage scheme, and other works of a varied character throughout the country, including the drainage of Clapham and Camberwell. Ultimately he was appointed assistant engineer to the West Ham Local Board, by whom a large number of municipal works were being carried out under Mr. Angell, with whom Mr. Robson was also engaged in schemes of drainage for other towns. At West Ham he remained until 1875, when he was appointed engineer to the Willesden Local Board. That body then represented a district with a population of 20,000, which has now increased to 100,000; a significant illustration of the extraordinary development of Greater London. Since 1875 Mr. Robson's professional life has been practically bound up with the growth of the district which he has done so much to regulate and promote, and he has carried out many and extensive works of drainage, bridge-making, road-making, recreation grounds and sewage treatment. When the local board was established, twenty-three years ago, the district was one of fields, streams, woods and vales, of country lanes, hedgerows and old manor houses. Lighting, well-kept roads, drainage and other amenities of a well-governed district were unknown. The board, however, set to work with a will. Plans and estimates for kerbing, channelling and lighting were drawn out, and at the present day Willesden is often cited as a model of municipal administration. Willesden is still to a large extent rural, especially in the northern parts, but the rural features are rapidly giving way to trim and well-arranged streets. The district is a purely residential one, the property erected being chiefly for the lower middle classes. About 1,200 houses are now erected each year. Willesden is well provided with open spaces. At Harlesden the authorities secured 26 acres of land, which was converted into a public park and recreation ground. The whole of Queen's Park, which is supported by the City Corporation, lies within the district. Three free libraries have been provided—at Kilburn, Harlesden and Willesden Green' respectively; and an infectious diseases hospital has been built. In 1885 the drainage of the Brent district was decided upon, at a cost of £33,000; two years later the erection of new offices in Dyne-road was decided upon, the cost being £8,500. From the few facts we have given of the progress of Willesden it will be seen that Mr. Robson's experience has been varied and extensive. When the association was first started, and before it was finally officered, Mr. Robson acted as hon. secretary in the correspondence that took place. After its constitution, of course, the first hon. secretary was Mr. Charles Jones, Ealing, who still holds office. In reference to the drainage of the Brent district, we should mention that during the past two years it has been extended, at a further cost of £60,000.

**Belem.**—The paragraph inserted in our last issue under "Foreign and Colonial" had reference to Belem in Brazil, and not to the suburb of Lisbon, which bears the same name.

**Lanchester.**—The contract for the construction of bacteria beds at Crayhead has been let to Mr. S. Walker, of Cockfield, Darlington, who submitted a tender amounting to £384. The engineer's estimate for the work was £380.

**British Association of Waterworks Engineers.**—Owing to the pressure on our space in reporting yesterday's proceedings at the annual meeting of municipal and county engineers at Edinburgh, we have been compelled to hold over the remainder of the report of the proceeding at the recent annual meeting of the British Association of Waterworks Engineers at Southampton.

**Curious Accident at Dover.**—An extraordinary accident, in which loss of life was narrowly averted, occurred on the Dover harbour works, on Monday. A steam crane, weighing 45 tons, was being employed to lift a smaller one, when both toppled over, one crushing through the custom house, where a number of officers were at work. The driver of the large crane managed to jump clear and thus save his life. The engines of both cranes were smashed, and other extensive damage was done. A chair in the custom house from which one of the officers had just moved was smashed.

# Association of Municipal and County Engineers.

## MEETINGS AT NORWICH AND YARMOUTH.—III.

In our last issue we gave, with numerous illustrations, the interesting paper read by Mr. Cockrill at the recent Yarmouth meeting. We now conclude our report, giving the paper contributed by Mr. Preece, and also notes of the discussions and of the visits to various works.

### DISCUSSION ON MR. COCKRILL'S PAPER.

Mr. E. G. MAWBEY (Leicester), in opening the discussion said that a man was known by his works, and in the splendid set of drawings exhibited on the walls there was evidence that they had a very able colleague. The town of Yarmouth was in the front rank of municipal enterprise. Mr. Cockrill seemed never to tire in giving information to his brother-engineers. The provision of sea water at the rate of 1½d. per 1,000 gallons was a great advantage. In regard to concrete footways, Mr. Cockrill was a pioneer of that form of paving. Of course, he had everything to his hand in the shingle beach, but he had utilised it in the best way, and could guarantee thirty years', if not fifty years', life, as had been mentioned.

Mr. COCKRILL remarked that some paving on the other side of the water had been laid in 1869.

Mr. MAWBEY, resuming, said that in regard to the question in Yarmouth of the destructor, he was surprised that more had not been said about the utilisation of waste heat. The refuse was, however, evidently of a very poor type. But in Leicester there was plenty of unburnt cinder left in the refuse, and they intended to utilise it to its fullest extent. Probably Mr. Cockrill would do so. He (Mr. Mawbey) had gone into the question, and proposed to utilise the waste heat for the purpose of generating energy for electric traction. There should be no difficulty in getting 3 horse-power per ton of refuse burnt per twenty-four hours. That was based on the assumption that 1 lb. of refuse evaporated 1 lb. of water, and allowing 30 lb. of water per indicated horse-power per hour. At Cambridge they obtained about 4½ horse-power per ton burnt per twenty-four hours. It was not desirable, however, to rush 10 to 20 tons of refuse a day through the destructor into the best plan was to thoroughly burn it, so as to avoid nuisance, and to so get the maximum amount of steam out of it. He would not allow more than 6 or 7 tons per cell per twenty-four hours; but they had adopted forced draught, and could get much more through if required. Roughly speaking, 5 cwt. of refuse per head per annum gave 25,000 tons of refuse per 100,000 of population. Before concluding he would like to call attention to a patent tile Mr. Cockrill had invented and largely used in connection with the admirable sanitary work he had carried out. He (the speaker) had a very good opinion of the invention, and would therefore like to bring it before the members. In the matter of electric lighting the town were certainly very well advised. They had acted very wisely in consulting Mr. Preece and his able son. At Leicester Mr. Cohen had advised the alternating current, and had found it very satisfactory. The Willans engines at Yarmouth were, no doubt, the ones to adopt.

Mr. LOBLEY (Hanley) said he had great pleasure in seconding the vote of thanks. He had known Mr. Cockrill for a great many years, but had not previously seen him in his own town. There were one or two points in connection with the paper to which he wished to refer, and he had one or two questions to ask. The problem of dust destruction was exercising people's minds at present. Like Mr. Cockrill, he also was troubled with bad foundations, not on account of subsoil water, but through undermining. He had four canal bridges which continually required to be raised, of course including the approaches. They found the sewers seriously interfered with, and experienced all sorts of trouble. He had been thinking of adopting a steel chimney, and he would like to have Mr. Cockrill's opinion about that. He wished to refer to one or two points in connection with the electric lighting. The number of lamps were given, but the size was not mentioned, but he understood they were of 8 candle-power. The number of arc lights, again, was given, but it was as well to have the size of the lamps mentioned. He believed that they were 11 ampères, while at Hanley they only had 8-ampère lamps. As to the Local Government Board not allowing a long period for the repayment of loans, Yarmouth was in good company. At Hanley the periods were ten, seventeen and twenty-five years. Possibly these short periods were not a bad thing. Engines and dynamos, like bicycles, became out of date. If they had not short periods they would have to put a certain sum on one side for a reserve. With short periods there was not the same reason for putting aside a reserve in addition to a sinking fund. If the ratepayers did not get an immediate profit they would do so later, when the loans were paid off, while other places would be still paying on them. He had great pleasure in seconding the vote of thanks.

Mr. E. J. SILCOCK (King's Lynn) called the attention of the members to the extremely low cost of the work carried out by Mr. Cockrill. It was no doubt a very great advantage to have shingle material at hand for making concrete, but Mr. Cockrill had made the fullest use of those materials

with the result that Yarmouth had secured splendid works at an extremely low cost. At the beginning of the paper it was stated that the 5-ft. sewer cost 33s. per yard run and the 3-ft. sewer 20s. per yard run without digging. They could see well that the work had been done by administration, and that it had been done at an extremely cheap rate. He had previously had an opportunity of visiting the works, and had been much struck by the way in which Mr. Cockrill handled his materials. In connection with the foundations for the destructor, Mr. Cockrill had certainly shown great courage in building a chimney 200 ft. high on such a site, and he hoped that he would be completely successful. It was most interesting to see the way in which the cylinders were being sunk. He (the speaker) had had some experience of bad foundations. At Lynn they were not all on the solid rock—(Mr. MAWBEY, "Hear, hear")—as Mr. Mawbey could bear out. He would like to know if 2,300 tons represented the absolute dead weight of the chimney, or if allowance had been made for wind pressure. As wind pressure would increase the pressure on the base he would like to know if the 2,300 tons would include that. In connection with the isolation hospital they would see much to admire, and he quite endorsed what Mr. Mawbey said in regard to the tiles. They were capital things, and he (Mr. Silcock) had himself used them. The hospital would be very much admired, especially when the cost was taken into consideration. With regard to the quantity of power from the destructor, Mr. Mawbey put the limit of the calorific value at 1 lb. of steam from 1 lb. of material. That was quite as high a result as had ever been obtained in practice, and quite as high as could be reckoned upon in going into the question of destructors. Those who talked about lighting towns from refuse destructors simply did not know anything of the subject.

Mr. HAYWARD (Sudbury) referred to the provision of sea water at 1½d. per 1,000 gallons and town water at 1s. per 1,000 gallons, and asked if sea water was conveyed to the town in the same way as other water. Having water carried 2 or 3 miles instead of 2 or 3 yards would seriously increase the cost. In his town they were able to get water from the service reservoir at 4½d. per 1,000 gallons.

Mr. BAKER (Middlesbrough) inquired as to the cost of labour per month for flushing sewers.

Mr. H. NETTLETON (Weston-super-Mare) asked if the sewers were self-cleansing, as flushing was not considered necessary in such a case unless for the purpose of cleansing the sides of the sewers.

The CHAIRMAN said there were one or two points to which he wished to refer. On page 3 of his paper Mr. Cockrill stated that he found that 3-in. and 4-in. pipes with delivery direct into the sewers will provide flush for 9-in. pipes, and that sewers up to 18 in. diameter could be kept clean with the larger sized valves. He would like to know the average head of discharge through these pipes. If there was a considerable head no doubt the flush would be sufficient, but not otherwise. Mr. Nettleton was perhaps under a misapprehension. The sewers were made self-cleansing by reason of the enormous amount of flushing done. The saving in road-way work by the use of sea water amounted to £500 per annum over a distance of 25 miles. He would like to know the exact way in which the saving was effected, whether it was due to the state in which the sea water kept the roads or to some other reason. In connection with the destructor it would be useful to know the cost of the chimney and also the length of the concrete blocks in the cylinder. The diameter of the cylinders and the thickness of the concrete blocks were given, but it would be useful also to know the length. Mr. Cockrill must have been extremely busy, and so complimented him on carrying out the work so well and so cheaply by administration. As to his paper, whatever he wrote was always practical and useful.

The vote of thanks was then unanimously awarded.

Mr. COCKRILL, in reply, said that with reference to waste heat he had for ten years been considering the question of destructors, and he had seen almost every destructor in the country and certainly the latest types. He was glad to observe Mr. Mawbey's reference to Cambridge, where the best that had yet been done in connection with destructors had been accomplished. They could not generate steam for electric lighting works, but if the company adopted a system of tramways they would put in two boilers from which to generate steam for electric traction. In regard to the chimney it was quite true that he had thought of a steel chimney, but as the Local Government Board would only grant a loan for five years he had abandoned the idea. The dead weight of the chimney was about 4½ tons per foot superficial, but the subsoil and gravel below would take 9 tons if not 11 tons per foot. There was then a good margin without giving the actual figures of wind pressure. Mr. Hayward had asked a question as to the distribution of sea water. The pipes were laid all over the town, but the hydrants were in such positions that the water-carts had a shorter distance to travel than in connection with the company's pipes. If the companies had reduced their charge to 6d. there would have•

been no sea-water scheme, but they refused. In reply to Mr. Baker he might mention that labour was cheap in that town, but it was apt to be inefficient. In reply to Mr. Nettleton he had to explain that the sewers were self-cleansing with the aid of the flushing. Mr. Eayrs had raised the question of the head of water discharged, which was from 20 to 30 ft. The advantage of using sea water on the roads was that it served to keep them moist and well together, but otherwise there was very little difference between sea water and that of the company. There was a saving of 30 per cent. in the cost of maintenance, and 1½d. per 1,000 gallons covered all charges, including those of capital and interest, the total inclusive annual cost since the extensions being about £600. Mr. Eayrs had inquired if the length of the cylinders used in the destructor foundations was about 24 ft. They would be built of rings of concrete and then filled up with concrete inside.

In the unavoidable absence of the author, through a business engagement, the following paper was then read by Mr. A. H. Preece.

## ON THE ABUSE OF POWER-HOUSES.

By W. H. PREECE, C.B., F.R.S.,
President of the Institution of Civil Engineers.

[Mr. William Henry Preece, C.B., F.R.S., engineer-in-chief to the General Post Office, was born in Wales in 1834. He was educated at King's College, London, and in 1852 entered the office of the late Mr. Edwin Clarke, M.I.C.E. The following year he secured an appointment under the Electric and International Telegraph Company, and in 1856 was appointed superintendent of that company's southern district. In 1860 he joined the staff of the London and South-Western Railway Company, and also acted as engineer to the Channel Islands Telegraph Company. In 1870 he was appointed divisional engineer to the General Post Office, and in 1877 electrician, whilst in 1892 he was promoted to his present position. Mr. Preece is the president of the Institution of Civil Engineers, and joint author with Mr. (now Sir James) Sivewright of a "Text-Book of Telegraphy," with Dr. Maier of "The Telephone," and with Mr. Stubbs of a "Manual of Telephony."]

There is a great tendency in the present day to multiply *power-houses*—or *central stations*, as they are more frequently called—unnecessarily. This arises from various causes.

1. From want of foresight in predicating the growth of electric industries.

2. Economy in selecting land we have rather than pay money for land more suitable by position, but which we have not.

3. The restriction of legislation in confining operations to a defined area.

4. The growth of other industries side by side, especially tramways and railways, worked by electric traction.

These causes have led to the original power-houses being designed too small and on space too confined, and to the subsequent construction of other power-houses, further afield and more extended; and even to the necessity of going to positions outside the original area secured by provisional order.

But worse than this, different industries have been promoted by rival and opposing interests. Trade competition and patent rights have led to the construction of power-houses side by side, until we see the absurdity of one installation being worked at night to supply energy for electric light, and another installation generating energy during the day for traction purposes being built practically on the same site; whereas not only can the power be generated conveniently and economically by the same plant, but the two energies can mutually assist each other, so as to reduce considerably the work cost per unit generated. This is what the author means by the abuse of power-houses. The man who causes two blades of grass to grow where one only grew before is called a benefactor, but the local authority which deliberately allows two power-houses to be built where only one is needed is a disturber of the peace.

It is very well affirmed by experience that the greater the plant, and the larger and more continuous the output, the cheaper is the cost of generation per unit. It may be said, roughly, that if a given plant, say 10,000 kilowatts, working at its maximum load, on the average three hours a day, produces electrical energy at 1d. a unit, it will do so at ¾d. per unit if it works six hours a day, ½d. per unit if it works twelve hours per day, and less than ¼d. per unit if it works twenty-four hours the day. Hence, concentration of power is distinctly financially desirable if it has the effect of lengthening the daily maximum output of the plant. One large station, conveniently built on the waterside, where coal can be delivered alongside, by rail or sea, at its cheapest; where water is abundant and available for condensing; where ashes, clinkers and dirt are easily barged away; where we have one control and one staff, is clearly the ideal power-house for economy. And it puts a stop to any cause of nuisance. The cartage of coal and rubbish does not impede traffic. Vapour clouds do not offend the eye, and apparent rain, in the form of condensed drops of water, does not damage one's garment or need the raising of umbrellas; vibration, noise and smells cease to be causes of vexation and litigation; additional chimneys do not disfigure the view. The question of securing a site is very much simplified. Hence comfort and convenience attest the value of the concentration of power plant in one locality.

In these days of high electrical pressure, whether continuous or alternating, the position of the power-house is not a matter of serious import. In the early days of the new electrical industry it was a question of economy of distribution to place the working plant in the centre of the area to be served, but now it is of little consequence where it is placed, within a limit of a few miles. The difficulty is a legal one, but even this has been considerably retrieved by the action of the recent joint committee of the Lords and Commons, who recommend that compulsory powers for purchase and for wayleaves for mains shall be allowed to those who find it necessary for public purposes to establish their power-house outside their own area of supply.

The whole tendency of recent legislation has been to favour local authorities, and to facilitate their acquisition or induce their acceptance of those municipal duties which include the conduct of industries which affect the whole community, like the supply of water, of light and of general locomotion. The success of the electric light industry in the hands of local authorities is beyond dispute, and some of our larger cities are now taking up vigorously and with great spirit the working of their tramways by electric traction. The ultimate success must be the same. These corporations, with their provisional orders and their electric light installations, have already the legal powers and the means to supply electrical energy. This is their right, and a valuable property it is to them. No one contests their right to do it, but there are corporations who have not yet acquired the working of the trams in their localities, but who have the right and the means to supply energy, and in these cases the right to supply energy to tramways is contested. If it were to succeed, and the tramway companies allowed in all cases to build and work their own power-houses, we should see the absurdity of two buildings existing where only one was needed, of two causes of nuisance perpetuated where none need exist, where the public would suffer from higher fares and the undertakers voluntarily accept the responsibility of generating their energy at a needless cost.

The supply of energy to work the tramways would enable the undertakers to reduce the price per unit to the electric light users by probably 1d., while they could at the same time supply the tramway company, if such exist, as cheaply as the company can make it themselves. Moreover, when the time arrives for the local authority to take over the tramways they would not be saddled with two power-houses.

There are other advantages in combining an electric light and a tramway plant. There is but one question of site, and but one management. There is only one set of boilers and one steam-pipe system, for the loss of energy by radiation from steam pipes is very large, and therefore of some consequence. There is, moreover, less reserve plant needed.

The author thinks this abuse of power-houses is a subject that well deserves the serious consideration of the Association of Municipal and County Engineers.

On concluding the reading of the paper Mr. Preece proceeded to draw attention to a few points in connection wit the Yarmouth electric light installation, especially in regard to the financial results.

### DISCUSSION.

Mr. MAWBEY said that he agreed that it would be unwise to allow any company to put down electric power stations for traction purposes in any town where a corporation had already a convenient central station for lighting, and that it was better for a corporation to undertake the working themselves, although it might not be in connection with lighting. With regard to the question of one station only, he had been advising a committee of the Leicester Corporation to utilise for electric traction the waste heat from several destructors, which, to save carting, had been erected in different districts, and it appeared to him that there could be no objection to using these destructors as power stations for that purpose. In supplying neighbouring manufactories from a destructor there was a considerable loss of power in transmission, consequently the horse-power generated at a destructor was of less value than the horse-power generated by the manufacturer himself at the place where it was to be used; but the power for electric traction must be transmitted under any system, therefore the power generated at the destructor would be of equal value for the work to be done to that produced by coal or any fuel at any other station. He would like to ask Mr. Preece if, provided there was one central distributing power station at one destructor or other place, he thought there was any objection to utilising other destructors in different districts, situated near the main tram lines, as supplementary power stations for electric traction by putting down simply an engine and dynamo at each place and supplying electric current into the cables at the nearest points, much in the same way as pumping water into a system of town mains at pumping stations in different parts of the town.

Mr. LOBLEY seconded the vote of thanks to Mr. Preece. He said the subject was one to which he had given a great deal of attention. He quite agreed with Mr. Preece that no authority having both traction and electric lighting should have more than one power station, excepting, of course, in very large cities. At Hanley they had first gone in for electric lighting and traction came later, the lines running through several towns. Every attempt to supply the tramways with current was met with opposition. Jealousy was aroused in the adjoining towns, and the idea had to be dropped. Since then they had another tramway company, and the corporation had been asked on what terms they would supply power, but the company would only pay a very small price,

He should like to have got 3d., as at Dover. He knew of no instance of the same engine supplying both light and tramways from the same mains at the same time. He had had opportunities of seeing combined arrangements in operation in other towns. The saving consisted in the buildings, chimney and boilers. At Dover they had separate generating plants entirely. Also at Havre, where the electric light company supplied the traction company with energy by meter. The advantage came in with respect to buildings, boilers, chimney-stack, stores of all kinds, and staff of electricians and workmen. There was also some advantage in respect to the reserve of engine power necessary, but in the above places this was not the case, as the lighting was from alternators.

The CHAIRMAN said he was quite agreed that there was a considerable waste of economy and energy in the construction of separate buildings for distribution and power. He had in his mind the case of a company which had been formed to supply energy for traction, industrial and electric lighting purposes, and there was no reason why various companies should not have energy from one central company or corporation rather than generate it themselves. In the case he had referred to the company were prepared to supply energy at 1d. per unit to local authorities and companies who could not generate it for themselves at the same rate.

A vote of thanks was then unanimously awarded, and Mr. PREECE, in briefly acknowledging, said he saw no objection to dust destructor stations in various parts of a town. They wanted to utilise waste steam. The paper did not necessarily apply to towns with over 60,000 or 80,000 inhabitants. Stations of 4,000 or 5,000 horse-power had been found by engineers to be the maximum. When it came to 8,000 or 10,000 they might just as well build two stations. There was no reason why the same plant should not be utilised one day for one object and another day for another object. The question of separate engines was not of great importance. The economy in combining lighting and power stations was in the building, the boilers and the use of one staff. Separate cables were necessary.

## VISITS TO WORKS.

When the discussion of Mr. Preece's paper had concluded the members left the town hall about 3 p.m., and proceeded in brakes to visit the various works referred to in the paper. These included the foundations for the destructor and chimney, the isolation hospital, which is being considerably extended, the recreation grounds, the beach gardens, the sea-water pumping stations, the electric lighting station, the new concrete quay wall at the fish wharf and the sewage pumping station. Special attention was given to the sinking of the cylinders to form the foundations of the destructor and the chimney and to the isolation hospital, where the tiles to which Mr. Mawbey had drawn attention were examined with much interest. The time, however, which could be devoted to the examination of the works was limited, as many of the party wished to return to their respective destinations the same evening, though not a few remained overnight. There was only one opinion in regard to the double meeting at Norwich and Yarmouth, and that was that it had been an unqualified success.

We have received from Mr. W. Bond, of 53 London-street, Norwich, a photograph of the group of municipal engineers taken at the recent meeting in that city. The portraits are excellent, and every detail comes out with remarkable clearness. The size of the photograph, copies of which can be obtained from Mr. Bond, is 11 in. by 9 in.

## ARBITRATIONS AND AWARDS.

In the Sheriff's Court, on Friday, Mr. West claimed from the London County Council a sum of £13,000 in respect of the compulsory purchase of a site fronting on Royal Mint-street, under the Tower bridge approach improvement scheme. In support of his claim, Sir Robert Reid called expert evidence to prove that land in the neighbourhood was worth £3 per foot. Mr. Edward Teween, who, in 1881, sold the property under the name to Mr. West, estimated its value at £2 per foot, and the whole site at £12,862. Alderman Sir Whittaker Ellis, Bart., placed the total value at £13,666. It was not fair, he said, to compare the price of land now in any part of London with its value at the beginning of the eighties. Land in London had appreciated in value by reason of the increased commercial power of gold, and, further, by the extraordinary developments that had been made commercially in the metropolis. He could recollect when he sold a site for £30,000 in Cornhill. That was a few years ago, comparatively. Now half of that site had been sold for £150,000. For the council expert evidence was called, which set out the value at a lower rate. The jury awarded £11,026.

At the Newington Sessions House, Mr. Loveland-Loveland and a special jury recently had before them the case of Marshall v. Wandsworth District Board of Works. This was a claim for compensation in respect of the acquirement of the leasehold premises, 151 Upper Richmond-road, Putney, occupied by the claimant, Mr. H. L. Marshall, job master, for the purposes of street improvements. The premises in question are held for an unexpired term of forty-five years. The carrying-out of the improvement scheme would necessitate the reconstruction of the claimant's premises, by which he would be deprived of certain accommodation. An adjoining shop, let by the claimant at 7s. per week, would be completely abolished, whilst the whole of the job master's premises would, it was alleged, be depreciated in value to a considerable extent through the loss of washing space, &c. Mr. Percy Henry Clarke, F.S.I., submitted plans, and estimated the reduction in value of the premises as a whole at £1,493; and other witnesses for the claimant were Mr. Daniel Watney, estimated loss £1,351; Mr. Samuel Walker, £1,392; and Mr. A. W. Taylor, £1,482. For the Wandsworth District Board of Works it was contended that the claim was exaggerated, and the witnesses called included Mr. Alex. R. Stenning, who estimated the fair amount of compensation at £623; Mr. W. Bennett Rogers, £638 4s.; Mr. G. H. Brougham Glasier, £634 13s. 6d.; and Mr. J. C. Radford, surveyor to the district board of works, £621. The jury awarded £1,200.

Mr. Troutbeck and a special jury, at the Guildhall, Westminster, recently heard the case of J. W. Downing v. London County Council, to determine the amount of compensation to be paid by the London County Council in respect of the leasehold interest in the premises, Nos. 1 and 3 Vincent-street, Pimlico, which are required for the Millbank Penitentiary site for working-class dwellings. Sir William Marriott, Q.C., and Mr. Lewis Coward were counsel for the claimant; and Mr. E. Morten and Mr. C. O. Fooks appeared on behalf of the county council. The jury, having viewed the premises, which were held on lease for an unexpired term of eleven years from June, 1898, at a ground rent of £10 per annum, Mr. B. I. Breach and Mr. E. F. B. Fuller gave evidence in support of the claim. Mr. Breach said he valued the property at £378. Mr. Fuller said both houses were in good repair and had modern drainage. Their productive power was 13s. per week. His valuation was £352. Sir William Marriott urged that, in addition to the value of the property, the value of the fixtures, £20, must also be given. On behalf of the council Mr. Glasier and Mr. Herbert Faber valued the property at £266 and £239 respectively. Mr. W. E. Horne also gave evidence, his figures amounting to £243. Ultimately the jury returned a verdict, including 10 per cent. for compulsory sale and the value of the fixtures, for £375. The offer under seal was for £300.

## WAKEFIELD ELECTRICITY WORKS.

### OPENING CEREMONY.

These new buildings, which have been erected by the Wakefield Corporation at Calder Vale, were formally opened on the 15th ult. They comprise boiler-house, engine-house, testing-room, workshop, stores and offices. The boiler-house contains two large Lancashire boilers built by Messrs. Spurr Inman, of Wakefield, each capable of evaporating 7,000 lb. of water per hour at 125 lb. pressure. They are fitted with mechanical stokers. In the engine-house there have been erected two slow-speed steam alternators made by Messrs. John Fowler & Co., of Leeds, each of 130 kilowatts maximum capacity, while a further set of plant of this size is now in the maker's shops and will be erected in due course. The engines are of the horizontal compound type, with the alternator built up on the fly-wheel. For the day-load business a small set of high-speed plant has been provided. By the aid of this plant the larger plant can be shut down during the period when the demand for electricity is small. This plant has been running since September in last year. All the switching apparatus has been fixed in a switch gallery in the engine-house, the main board being designed on the Lowrie Hall system of plug switches. The switchboard is divided into three parts, the centre portion dealing with the synchronising instruments, the left-hand portion with distributing circuits and the right-hand with the alternators. The distribution of electrical energy to all parts of the city is effected from one central point at the top of Westgate, where a large underground chamber has been built. Three high-pressure trunk mains connect this chamber with the generating works, and are here connected to the three large transformers which reduce the pressure from 2,000 to 200 volts for distribution to the surrounding streets. Branch high-tension mains are also taken from this sub-station to a few outlying transformers. The county buildings have already been dealt with in this way, and it is proposed to adopt a similar method for the St. John's district. The mains throughout, for both high and low pressure, are of the concentric pattern, with paper insulation between the conductors. The high-pressure mains are everywhere drawn into stoneware culverts, but the low-pressure ones are armoured with steel tapes and laid directly in the ground. Spare ways have been provided in the culverts to permit of the drawing in of additional high-pressure mains in the future without disturbing the surface of the pavements.

**Milksham.**—The district council have accepted the tender of Messrs. C. Cook & Sons, Milksham, amounting to £46, for the construction of a footpath at Sundridge-lane.

# Parliamentary Memoranda.

On Thursday, in the House of Lords, the Gainsborough Gas Bill and the Rhymney and Aber Valleys Gas and Water Bill were ordered for second reading, while the Rochdale Corporation Bill and the Thanet Gas Bill (Amendments) were read a third time and passed. The Locomotives on Highways Bill was also, after a short discussion, read a second time.

In the House of Commons the Blackburn Corporation (Tramways) Bill and the Middlesex County Council Bill were read a third time and passed. The Felixstowe and Walton Water Bill, the Filey Water and Gas Bill and the Newton Water Bill were read a second time and committed.

In the House of Lords, on Friday, the Matlock Urban District Council Bill was read a second time. The Todmorden Corporation Water Bill, Portsmouth Corporation Tramways Bill, Ilford Improvement Bill and the Carmarthen Improvement Bill were read a third time and passed.

In the House of Commons the following Bills were read a third time and passed: Higham and Hundred of Hoo Water Bill, Malden Water Bill, Mid-Kent Water Bill, Wey Valley Water Bill, Bolton, Turton and Westhoughton Extension Bill, Liverpool Corporation Bill and the Sheffield Corporation Bill.

In the House of Lords on Monday the following Bills were read a second time: The Coventry Corporation Gas Bill, Plymouth Corporation Bill, Bristol Tramways (Electrical Power, &c.) Bill, Bristol Tramways (Extensions) Bill, Middlesbrough Corporation (Gas) Bill, Drogheda Gas Bill and the Norwich Electric Tramways Bill. The Ferres Water Bill, Kew Bridge and Approaches Bill and Staines Reservoirs Joint Committee Bill were read a third time. The Rochdale Corporation Water Bill was also, after a brief discussion, read a third time and passed, while the Metropolis Management Acts Amendment (By-Laws) Bill passed through committee. The Floods Prevention Bill was read a third time and passed.

In the House of Commons the London County Council (General Powers) Bill, the Market Harborough Gas Bill, the Leyton Urban District Council and the London United Tramways Bill were read a third time and passed. The Blackpool and Fleetwood Tramroad (Tramways Extensions) Bill was ordered for a third reading, and the Hamilton Water Bill and the Kettering Water Bill were ordered for a third reading. The Bury Corporation Bill and the Carlisle Corporation Water Bill were read a second time and committed.

*The London Water Companies.*—The president of the Local Government Board, in reply to a question as to whether he intended to introduce early next season a Bill to ensure the supply by water companies of pure and wholesome water, and otherwise safeguard the interests of water consumers and, if so, whether the Bill would apply to all existing companies, said he was not in a position to make any statement as to the legislation the Government might propose next session or as to the scope and extent of the Bills they might introduce.

On Tuesday, in the House of Lords, the following Bills were read a second time: Blackburn Corporation (Tramways, &c.), Middlesex County Council, Windsor Dock (Cardiff), Higham and Hundred of Hoo Water, Bolton, Turton, and Westhoughton Extension, Liverpool Corporation, Sheffield Corporation, Mid-Kent Water, Wey Valley Water, Maldon Water, Burnley Corporation (Tramways, &c.), Cromer Gas, Glasgow Corporation (Sewage, &c.), Clacton-on-Sea Gas and Water, Leyton Urban District Council, and the London United Tramways Bills. The Heywood Corporation Water Bill and the Newcastle and Gateshead Water Bill were read a third time.

In the House of Commons, the Newhaven Harbour Bill was ordered for second reading. The Lords' amendments to the Nottingham Corporation Bill were considered and agreed to.

In the House of Commons, on Wednesday, the Thanet Gas Bill was considered, and the Belfast Harbour Bill, the Blackpool Improvement Bill, and the Sheringham Gas and Water Bill were ordered for third reading.

## PRIVATE BILLS IN COMMITTEE.

*Great Northern Railway Company and the London County Council and Islington Vestry.*—A House of Lords committee, presided over by Lord Heneage, passed on the 21st ult., the Bill promoted by the Great Northern Railway Company, which provides for the exceptionally large issue of £3,333,333 new capital and the construction of nearly 60 miles of new line, including widenings and duplications. This enormous outlay is rendered necessary by the altered conditions under which the system will have to be worked to meet the competition of the Great Central when the London extension of the old M.S. & L. Railway is completed. It is unnecessary to particularise the various projects embraced in this omnibus Bill, for only two parts of it were opposed—the construction of a couple of bridges over the river Ouse in Northamptonshire, which was contested by the River Ouse Navigation Commissioners, and new railways at Finsbury Park, which were objected to by the London County Council, because they meant the appropriation of 29 perches of the park, and by the Vestry of Islington, because they involved the construction of an additional bridge over a thoroughfare crowded with traffic. The case presented by the Ouse Navigation was soon disposed of. The committee took little time to decide that the company's proposal should be allowed to

stand. The London County Council agreed that the widening of the line at Finsbury Park was necessary, but contended that no part of the park should be taken unless there was urgent public necessity, and if any part were acquired the compensation should take the form of an equivalent area of ground, and should not be a money recompense, as provided by the Lands Clauses Act. Sir Henry Oakley, the late general manager of the railway, spoke of the congested state of the line there, stating that 850 trains passed through Finsbury Park station every day, and at busy times as many as fifty-four an hour. These were through trains which did not stop at the station. It was highly necessary that the company should increase the accommodation, and to do that they must acquire a small part of the park. There were no buildings there, and if he could take the land at night no one would miss it in the morning. The chairman, after a careful scrutiny of the plans, pointed out that the railway company had to the east a piece of land abutting on the park which they might give up in exchange. Mr. Balfour Browne, Q.C., one of the counsel for the promoters, admitted that by building a retaining wall they could give up a sufficient portion of the ground; and Mr. Freeman, Q.C., for the county council, accepted this proposal on the understanding that the company would plant and lay out the piece of ground so given in exchange. The committee were not favourably impressed by the representations of the Islington Vestry with regard to the bridge, so with the proviso indicated the Bill was allowed to proceed, and it was afterwards reported to the House with amendments.

*West Ham Corporation Bill.*—The Select Committee of the House of Commons on Police and Sanitary Regulations, under the presidency of Sir Stafford Northcote, took up on the 21st ult., the Bill promoted by the Corporation of West Ham, in which powers were sought to acquire and work the tramways within the borough, to execute works and acquire lands, to carry out street and building improvements, to obtain a reversion of powers of Lea Conservancy with respect to certain backwaters in the town, to enlarge the hospital and workhouse accommodation, &c. The Bill was opposed by the Corporation of London, the Essex County Council and the River Lea Conservancy. It appeared with respect to the tramways which were owned by the North Metropolitan Tramways Company that the date at which the council might purchase them, in accordance with the provisions of the Tramways Act of 1870, was the 10th of August of the present year, and as they had decided to purchase them it was necessary that they should come to Parliament for powers to work them and to introduce electric power. The council proposed to provide more efficient hospital accommodation for infectious diseases and to acquire further land for the purpose of a small-pox hospital. It was also deemed expedient to make additions to the workhouse at Leytonstone and the auxiliary workhouse in the parish of Leyton. With respect to the backwaters of the river Lea the council asked for authority to scour those streams, and to do so it was necessary to obtain permissive powers, because the jurisdiction really lay with the Lea Conservancy, who, for want of funds probably, had failed in their duty in this respect. The backwaters in question were Waterworks river, Channelsea river, City Mill river, Pudding Mill river, Three Mills river, Back river, Three Mills Back river, Three Mills Wall river, Meggs dock, Bow creek, Bow Back river, Abbey creek and a portion of the river Lea known as the River Lea Old river, and the outfall sewer. To enable them to carry out the various works they had in contemplation the corporation proposed to raise £250,000 in respect of the borough lunatic asylum at Chadwell Heath, £42,000 for town hall extensions, £106,000 for sewage at Plaistow, £34,500 for the Dagenham hospital, £24,000 for street improvements and £27,000 for a recreation ground. The population of West Ham had grown, it was stated, from 11,580 in 1831 to 274,000 last year, the borough was a perfect hive of industry, and its financial condition was most satisfactory, the price of its stocks standing very high indeed in the market. The opposition of the Corporation of London which related to the proposed acquisition of a portion of West Ham Park was first taken up. This park was vested in the Corporation of London as trustees for the inhabitants, and the part that the West Ham Council required for the purpose of their street improvements was a wedge-shaped strip, 405 yards in length at one end and running down to nothing. The council proposed that any purchase money that might be paid by them to the Corporation of London should be expended by the corporation in the purchase of other lands in West Ham. The corporation in the first place opposed the acquisition as not being urgently necessary, and submitted that if Parliament sanctioned the purchase they (the Corporation of London) should be allowed to spend the money where they chose. After hearing formal evidence the committee, at the suggestion of Mr. Littler, the leading counsel for the corporation, went out in the afternoon to view the locality in question and consequently did not proceed further with the Bill that day. After inspecting the portion of the park which the corporation proposed to appropriate for the widening of the road named the Portway, and hearing evidence as to the position taken up by the Corporation of London in the matter, the committee decided to allow the clauses relating to the acquisition to stand with a few minor amendments. The clauses relating to the acquisition of the tramways, and to the proposed borrowing powers for the buildings and improvements already indicated were approved, with modifications, to meet the views of the Local Government Board. The clauses providing for the devolution of certain powers from the River Lea Conservancy were struck out, the committee being of opinion that as regards the backwaters the Corporation of West Ham had, under the Drainage Act and under the authority transferred to them from the Dagenham Commissioners of Sewers, sufficient powers to cleanse the streams and prevent them from becoming a nuisance.

*Local Authorities and the Windsor Dock Bill.*—The Corporation of Cardiff and a number of local authorities have been greatly interested in the Windsor Dock Bill, which, after an inquiry which has lasted six weeks, was passed by a House of Commons committee, presided over by Mr. James Stewart, on Wednesday week. The Bill, which had the sympathy and support of the Cardiff Corporation, was the third attempt that had been made by the promoters to obtain powers to construct a new and commodious dock near the existing docks of the Taff Vale Railway Company at Penarth, Cardiff. Although not directly promoted by the Taff Vale, the Bill was advanced in the interest of that company, by whom the dock will be worked, and it was named after the chairman of that company, Lord Windsor, who was its chief supporter. It had to face most formidable opposition from the Cardiff Railway Company, formerly known as the Bute Docks Company, backed by the Marquis of Bute, the Barry Railway Company and various trading interests in South Wales. When the promoters first went to Parliament in 1896 the Bill was rejected owing to engineering difficulties and to the fact that such a large proportion of the mudlands was taken up. When they went to Parliament again in 1897 the evidence as to the necessity for the dock was stopped and the witnesses were sent away, and then the committee declared that they were not satisfied on the point and rejected the Bill. In the 1896 Bill it was proposed to take 112 acres of mudlands, in 1897 77 acres, but by the present Bill it was not proposed to acquire more than 17 acres. The part of the harbour which it was proposed to take up was the most shallow and was of little use for the anchoring of even small craft. The land required was mainly the property of Lord Windsor and the Taff Vale Company, but 63 acres of it was pasture land belonging to Lord Bute. The dock itself was to be 42½ acres in extent, with a lock 1,000 ft. long and 100 ft. wide—of such size and depth, in fact, as to accommodate the largest vessels afloat or likely to be built. About seventy witnesses altogether were examined in support of the Bill, and scores of pages of statistics were produced to show the enormous increase in the coal shipments from Cardiff, Penarth and Barry in recent years. The increase at the Bute docks since 1890 had been 11 per cent., at Barry 87 per cent. and at Penarth 93 per cent. All the docks were working at their full capacity now, and even after the extensions of the Bute and the Barry, which had been authorised by Parliament, were carried out there would, if the same rates of increase were continued, be 1,250,000 tons of coal brought annually to port seven years hence, or by the time which it would take to build the new dock, which could not be dealt with by the then existing accommodation. The new project, which was presented in a singularly complete form, had been devised by Sir Alexander Rendell, Sir Benjamin Baker and Mr. Sibbering, the engineer to the Taff Vale company. The committee were greatly aided in their deliberations by a beautifully-constructed model of the harbour, occupying on the table of the committee-room about 6 ft. square, which had been prepared in the Taff Vale offices under Mr. Sibbering's direction. The opposition to the scheme was concentrated on three points—(1) there was no necessity whatever for a fresh port at the dock of Cardiff; (2) that even if there were the Taff Vale company should not be allowed to make it, not even directly, still less indirectly, as was proposed; (3) that if the time should come when further extensions, beyond those already authorised, should become necessary not only would the extensions be made at Cardiff and Barry with greater propriety, but they could be done for a great deal less than half the money which the Windsor dock would cost. The outlay proposed on the new dock was £1,500,000, and Mr. John Aird, M.P., stated that his firm were prepared to carry out the work at that price. The committee in passing the Bill directed that clauses should be inserted giving the Cardiff Railway Company power to run their trains from the Glamorganshire collieries to the new dock.

*Leyton Urban District Council Bill.*—The House of Commons Committee on Police and Sanitary Regulations have concluded a lengthy inquiry into the Bill promoted by the Urban District Council of Leyton, in which they sought powers to work the tramways in that district for the time being owned by the North Metropolitan Tramways Company and the Lea Bridge, Leyton and Walthamstow Tramways Company, to transfer certain sewers from the Dagenham Commissioners of Sewers to the district council, and to carry out certain street and sanitary improvements. The counsel for the promoters were Mr. Beggallay, Q.C., Mr. Gerald Fitz-Gerald and Mr. Hutchinson; and the Dagenham Commissioners of Sewers, who opposed the transfer of the sewers, were represented by Mr. J. D. FitzGerald, Q.C. From the facts laid before the committee it appeared that the gross

rateable value of Leyton was £293,000; that the area of the district, which is situate immediately north of the borough of West Ham and separated from London by the river Lea, was 2,491 acres, and that the estimated population was 90,000. It was the largest urban district of the metropolis which had not yet been converted into a borough. It contained 15,300 houses, showing an average yearly increase since 1880 of 780. The public debt of the district was £190,000 and the general district rate was 3s. 4d. in the £1. There were 53 miles of streets dedicated to the public, 10 miles of which were accounted main roads. There were two systems of tramways running through the district, one belonging to the North Metropolitan Company, entering on the West Ham side and running through the northern part and the other near the East London waterworks, going over Lea bridge and running through the north-easterly part. As far as the North Metropolitan Company's tramways were concerned, the local authority had power to acquire part of them in August of the present year and the remainder in 1901; but, as regards the Lea Bridge Company's tramways, the period did not expire until 1902 and 1910. The council had already passed the resolutions necessary under the Tramways Act to enable them to acquire the undertakings. The powers sought by the council to work the tramways were not opposed, but the provisions relating to the transfer of the sewers were strongly opposed by the Dagenham Commissioners. They were identical with the clauses effecting a similar object which were inserted in the West Ham Act of 1888, which was warmly contested between the corporation and the Dagenham commissioners. The sewers under the jurisdiction of the commissioners were not, it may be well to explain, sewers in the ordinary acceptation of the term, dealing with the drainage of factories and so forth, but upon ditches and cuts used chiefly for the purpose of carrying off surplus land waters and providing in certain cases for irrigation. The commissioners had jurisdiction over such sewers for the levels of Havering, Dagenham, Ripple Barking, East Ham, West Ham, Leyton, Walthamstow, Bromley and East Marsh, but the body was popularly known as the Dagenham Commissioners. The sewers in the Leyton district were two in number, but it was one called the Leyton Level brook with which the local authority were chiefly concerned. The district council under the Public Health and Sanitary Acts had jurisdiction over the sewage and drainage within the district, but they did not manage these sewers, which were in such a state as to be a serious danger to public health, causing much suffering, in form of illness engendered by them being ulcerated throats and so forth. It was not alleged that the commissioners were personally responsible for this; it was the result of the system, and the only remedy was the transfer of these powers to the local authority, such as had been effected in the case of West Ham. The nuisance which had been going on had been the subject of litigation for more than twenty years. The commissioners who opposed the transfer, simply because they had a public duty to perform, obtained their authority under the following Acts: 23rd Henry VIII.; 3rd and 4th Edward VI., cap. 18; 13th Elizabeth, caps. 3 and 4; 1st William IV., cap. 22; 4th and 5th Vic., cap. 45; and 13th and 14th Vic., cap. 50. Their functions were to take charge of certain areas which were liable to be flooded either from sea or land, to deal with flooded districts and to tax the people for their own good. The commissioners might be proper persons to exercise powers in an agricultural district where there were low-lying marsh lands, but they ought not to have charge of sewers in a thickly-populated urban district such as Leyton. Under their control the Leyton brook had fallen into a dreadful state, the worst feature being that it was receiving the sewage effluent of a population of between 60,000 and 70,000 persons discharged into it from Walthamstow sewage works. Mr. Justice Chitty in the Court of Chancery, when he granted an injunction to Leyton against Walthamstow, found that the sewage effluent amounted to one-third of 2,000,000 gallons per day, and that it was such as to cause an intolerable nuisance. Evidence on these points was being given when the committee rose on Wednesday afternoon. Mr. William Dawson, surveyor to the Leyton District Council, stated that if the Bill passed the local authority would stop the nuisance, because they would at once remove the polluted matter and prevent it becoming a danger to the health of the public. Mr. W. W. Fairhead, an occupier of land adjoining the Leyton Level brook, stated that just before Christmas he went with his son and Dr. King Barry to inspect the brook, and saw the sewage matter from the Walthamstow farm flowing into the stream. Sister Murphy, lady superior of the St. Agnes Orphanage, Leyton, and Doctors A. F. Foskett and A. B. Bateley (the latter medical officer of health for the Leyton district) described the brook as very offensive and prejudicial to the health of persons living in the neighbourhood; sore throats, diarrhœa and even infectious diseases arising from it. Mr. W. C. Young, consulting chemist and analyst to the Lea Conservancy, who has had long experience in connection with the analyses of the water of sewage effluents, spoke as to repeated examinations which he had made of Leyton brook, which was in an excessively foul condition on account of the pollution by sewage matter which had not been subjected to any treatment to render it innocuous. It present disgraceful condition was due to the growth of foul vegetation, commonly called sewage fungus, which developed into sewage matter. This fungus in forty-eight hours might be fully developed, and it soon became decomposed and putrid. Mr. Lewis Angell, borough engineer of West Ham, stated that the result of the transfer of the jurisdiction of the Dagenham Commissioners of Sewers to the Corporation of West Ham had been most beneficial in that district. Things were going exceedingly smooth now. The West Ham Corporation had been able to mitigate the evil by carrying out diversions of the stream. Mr. C. G. Musgrave, a member of the district council of Leyton and of the Essex County Council, deplored the condition of the brook, and stated that the Dagenham Commissioners never did anything unless pressure was brought upon them. In his view the sanitary authority ought to have control over all the watercourses in the district. Nobody knew anything of the Dagenham Commissioners in Leyton; most of the people had never even heard of them. Why the commissioners should struggle to maintain their jurisdiction passed his comprehension. The fault for the existing state of things largely lay with the Walthamstow local authority for having laid out a sewage farm which was unsuitable to metropolitan conditions. They had tried to move the Local Government Board and the London County Council in the matter, but without success. At the close of the case for the promoters the committee consulted in private, and upon the public being readmitted the chairman announced that the majority had come to the conclusion that they were not prepared to transfer the jurisdiction of the commissioners to the Leyton District Council, and that part of the Bill would consequently be struck out. The clauses relating to the tramways were passed with certain modifications, and the remainder of the Bill was allowed to proceed with some slight amendments.

*Renfrew Borough and Harbour Extension Bill.*—A Select Committee of the House of Commons, presided over by Mr. Baldwin, has had under consideration for some days the Bill promoted by the Town Council of Renfrew for the extension of the limits of the burgh and the improvement of the harbour. The Bill was opposed by the Greenock Harbour Trust, the Clyde Navigation Trustees, the Corporation of Glasgow and the County Council of Renfrew. The Glasgow and South-Western Railway Company and the Glasgow and Renfrew District Railway Company had petitioned against the Bill, but no counsel appeared in support of their petitions. The inquiry is likely to prove a long one, for the promoters have in attendance a great number of witnesses interested in shipping and the coal, iron and steel industries of the Clyde, not merely from the Clyde, but from ports like Belfast, Cardiff, Hartlepool and Newcastle. The committee intimated that in accordance with the suggestion of Mr. Pember, Q.C., the leading counsel for the promoters, they would hear the case for the extension of the borough limits first, but before coming to a decision they would have the facts relating to both objects before them. Renfrew, it appeared, was a very old burgh, and much of its area was unbuilt upon; but in recent years it had witnessed a very remarkable development. The neighbouring towns on the Clyde had all developed towards the riverside, but Renfrew was at present debarred from development in that way by the limited extent of its river frontage, which was not more than about three-quarters of a mile. By the Bill it was proposed to incorporate the estate of Elderslie, belonging to Mr. Spiers, and thus to extend both the burgh and river frontage. By the passing of the Glasgow and Renfrew and District Bill of last year the district would be most materially benefitted. The Clyde Trustees, who were opposing the Bill, had purchased land in the district for the erection of wharves in connection with the timber trade. That only made it the more clear that the municipality ought, as a matter of precaution, to lay their hands on the territory over which the population would spread. Mr. Spiers was the owner of the whole of the riverside property proposed to be included in the burgh with the exception of a small piece of land 10 or 12 acres in extent in the possession of the Clyde Trust, which had been bought by the Corporation of Glasgow for the purpose of their sewage works. The Elderslie estate consisted of some 345 acres, more or less equally divided between the county of Renfrew and the county of Lanark; and Mr. Spiers, recognising the strength of the case for the Bill, consented to the inclusion of the estate within the burgh. The representatives of the county of Lanark had very fairly taken from the promoters a certain amount of money compensation in respect of their rights to them, but the county of Renfrew had dissented from such a settlement. The strongest opposition to the Bill came from the Clyde Navigation Trustees, who contended that there was no reason for either one part or the other of its provisions. They were hostile to the increase of the rateable value of the burgh by the incorporation of property belonging to them. Parliament, it was argued, had always recognised the great work done by the Clyde Navigation Trustees, and had steadily refused to allow that work to be hampered by the introduction of any other authority in the river. The trustees had made the Clyde what it was in its upper navigable reaches, and they ought to have the sole control of the river and its navigation. For that reason they asked Parliament to prevent the intrusion of the authority of the burgh of Renfrew into the jurisdiction of the river over the proposed extended burgh area. The Corporation of Glasgow objected to the Bill on the ground that as they had purchased a large piece of this land for the purpose of erect-

ing upon it important works dealing with sewage it was unfair now to place it under the jurisdiction of the burgh of Renfrew instead of their co-partners in the scheme—the County Council of Renfrew. The case for the extension of the dock was that the harbour of Renfrew was antiquated and unsuitable to existing conditions of shipping or commerce. The promoters had been considerably influenced in their present action by the passing of the Glasgow and Renfrew District Railway Bill last session. There was no question as to whether the railway would be made, because it had been taken over under a joint agreement between the Glasgow and South-Western and Caledonian Railway Companies. The promoters might be relied upon as being equally in earnest about the proposed dock. The scheme involved the construction of a dock basin about 15 acres in extent, fitted up with the most modern appliances, and with 35 acres of land for railway sidings and storage. The depth would be 20 ft. at low water and 31 ft. at high water. The estimated cost of land and works was £200,615, and borrowing powers were taken to the extent of £250,000. Mr. Charles Forman, C.E., Glasgow, explained at great length the principal features of the dock, in the laying out of which he had had the advice of Sir John Wolfe Barry. It was, he said, of vital importance to the success of the dock that there should be a basin to allow even the largest ships to go in without canting in the river, and the proposed basin would enable them to do this.

## THE SANITARY INSTITUTE.

THE FORTHCOMING ANNUAL CONGRESS.

The preliminary programme of the sixteenth congress of the Sanitary Institute, to be held in Birmingham from September 27th to October 1st, has now been issued. The president of the congress is Sir Joseph Fayrer, Bart., K.C.S.I., M.D., F.R.C.P., F.R.C.S. LL.D., Q.H.P., F.R.S. Dr. Christopher Childs, M.A., D.P.H., will deliver the lecture to the congress, and Dr. Alex. Hill, M.A., J.P., master of Downing College and Vice-Chancellor of Cambridge University, will deliver the popular lecture. Excursions to places of interest in connection with sanitation will be arranged for those attending the congress. A *conversazione* will be given by the Right Hon. the Lord Mayor (Councillor C. G. Beale), and a garden party, at the Botanical Gardens, Egbaston, will be given by members of the Sanitary Committee.

It appears from the programme that over 300 authorities, including several county councils, have already appointed delegates to the congress, and as there are also over 2,000 members and associates in the institute, there will probably be a large attendance in addition to the local members of the congress. In connection with the congress a health exhibition of apparatus and appliances relating to health and domestic use will be held as a practical illustration and carrying out of the principles and methods discussed at the meetings, which not only serves this purpose, but also an important one in diffusing sanitary knowledge among a large class who do not attend the other meetings of the congress.

The congress will include three general addresses and lectures, three sections meeting for two days each, dealing with (1) sanitary science and preventive medicine, presided over by Dr. Alfred Hill, M.D., F.R.S.,EDIN., F.I.C., M.O.H., Birmingham; (2) engineering and architecture, presided over by Mr. W. Honman, F.R.I.B.A.; (3) physics, chemistry and biology, presided over by Dr. G. Sims Woodhead, M.D., F.R.C.P., F.R.S.,EDIN. Five special conferences: Municipal representatives, presided over by Alderman W. Cook, chairman of the Health Committee, Birmingham City Council; medical officers of health, presided over by Dr. John C. McVail, M.D., D.P.H., F.R.S.,EDIN.; municipal and county engineers, presided over by Mr. T. de Courcy Meade, M.I.C.E.; sanitary inspectors, presided over by Mr. W. W. West, chief sanitary inspector, Walthamstow; domestic hygiene, presided over by Mrs. C. G. Beale (the lady mayoress).

The local arrangements are in the hands of an influential local committee presided over by the Right Hon. the Lord Mayor of Birmingham, with Prof. A. Bostock Hill, M.D., D.P.H., Mr. Bayley Marshall, M.I.C.E., and Mr. J. E. Willcox, A.M.I.C.E., as honorary secretaries.

## QUERIES AND REPLIES.

*Sketches accompanying Queries should be made separate on white paper in plain black-ink lines. Lettering or figures should be bold and plain.*

**198. Lead-lined Iron Pipes.**—" Waterworks Manager " writes : Referring to Query 193 in your issue of June 24th, I may state that Messrs. Edwin Walker & Co. are patentees and makers of lined pipes, either lead or iron. Their best pipe is lined with block tin throughout, and is made either with or without conducting material between the tin and iron covering. The tin-lined pipe has now been in use for some years, and has proved to be satisfactory.

We are obliged to our correspondent for the information conveyed. If he will, however, refer to Query 193 again he will see that the querist required particulars as to a lead-lined iron pipe and not a tin-lined iron or lead pipe, of which kind of pipe there are several manufacturers.

## THE "COTSWORTH" ARC LAMP.

### DEMONSTRATION AT TAGG'S ISLAND.

The well-known picnic party resort, Tagg's Island, Hampton Court, was the scene of an interesting function on the 20th ult., when over seventy press men and gentlemen interested in electric lighting, together with several of the fair sex, assembled at the invitation of Ʒr. Arthur Ormsby, of Ʒerton Park, Surrey, on behalf of the Cotsworth Arc Lamp and Electric Lighting Syndicate, to witness a practical demonstration of electric lighting by means of the "Cotsworth" arc lamp. This lamp, which is the invention of Ʒr. Haldane G. Cotsworth, claims for its *raison d'être* the overcoming of a disadvantage, common, more or less, to all arc lamps at present on the market—viz., unsteady regulation and consequent flickering of the light. Another feature of the "Cotsworth" arc lamp is that the regulation is independent of the main current, so that the light can be raised without altering the adjustment of the "feed." The mechanism of the lamp is certainly simple, especially the operation of trimming. A small knob at the side of the corona is pulled out, allowing two pistons and rods to gradually slide down ; the burnt-out carbons are then replaced by new ones, the globe is pushed up from the bottom and when in place it automatically locks itself. The whole of the operations require the use of one hand only, which is a great convenience should the lamp be located in an awkward position. The globe is cleaned by removing the ash tray at the bottom, but it has been found that if a steady arc is maintained little or no carbon dust is

deposited in the globe, practically the whole of the carbon being converted into $CO_2$.

The points in connection with the lamp were demonstrated to those present on Ʒonday, the whole of the island after 9.30 being illuminated by it, through the medium of current supplied by the "Immisch" Electric Launch Company, Limited. Prior to the demonstration there was a garden party, followed by a cold collation. Among those present were Sir John Campbell, Bart., Colonel Garnham, Ʒajor and Ʒrs. Baskerville, Ʒr. and Ʒrs. Logan, the Rev. Mr. Poynter, and Ʒr. and Ʒrs. Ormsby. Various toasts were proposed and honoured, among them, in addition to the usual loyal toasts, being "The' Cotsworth' Arc Lamp," proposed by the chairman and responded to by Ʒr. A. Ormsby and Ʒr. H. G. Cotsworth ; "The Press," " Ʒr. and Mrs. Ormsby," "The Chairman," " The Ladies," and " The Officials of the Syndicate." During the evening a selection of music was rendered.

We may mention that the syndicate has been formed with a capital of £35,000, divided into 35,000 ordinary shares of £1 each, and that a considerable amount of support is anticipated from local authorities who are carrying out electric lighting schemes.

The inventor of the "Cotsworth" arc lamp has been experimenting on different types of arc lamps for over two years at his private laboratory at Wimbledon, and claims that he has succeeded in perfecting an arc lamp for street lighting which will burn for forty hours with one trimming, and although it has two pairs of carbons has practically only one mechanism. These lamps are worked in series and work at 42 volts across the arc. When both pairs of carbons have burned out, or should the mechanism become damaged, an automatic cut-out placed in the base of the lamp-post short circuits or may be arranged to introduce an equivalent resistance in place of the extinguished lamp. When the carbons have been replenished the lamp is automatically cut into the circuit. We give an illustration of the "Cotsworth" arc lamp.

## THE TELEPHONE SERVICE.

### PARLIAƷENTARY INQUIRY.

Another meeting of the Select Committee on the telephone service was held on Thursday.

Ʒr. J. C. LAMB, C.B., second secretary of the post office, was re-examined with reference to the circumstances under which the areas of the National Telephone Company had been extended. He had not considered how far the extension of areas in the way it had been done might affect municipalities. It was not the policy at the time to entertain applications from municipalities, and that question was absent both from the mind of the Government and that of the Post Office. He was not aware that the effect of granting a large area round London for the National Telephone Company was to hamper the action both of the local authority and of the Post Office within that area.

Sir R. HUNTER, solicitor to the Post Office, was also recalled, and stated that he had carefully considered the legal aspect of the question of the National Telephone Company granting preferences. He did not think that the Postmaster-General, as the law stood, could interfere with the operations of the company in giving what might be considered undue favours or preferences. There were no statutory restrictions applicable to the company either in the licence or in the agreements which affected them. He did not think the Postmaster-General was bound by law against giving preferences, but rather by the principle which had guided the Post Office in the matter of telegraphs. On the suggestion of the chairman, Sir Robert promised to take the opinion of the law officers on the point. With regard to the agreement between the Post Office and the National Company in relation to the extension of areas, he was of opinion that the Postmaster-General was bound simply by the plain terms of the agreement and not by any assurances which might have been given outside the agreement.

Ʒr. LLOYD, town clerk of Huddersfield, also gave evidence in behalf of that corporation and also the Association of Municipal Associations, in favour of the municipalisation of the telephone service.

## MUNICIPALITIES FOR LONDON.

The vestries of Westminster, Bermondsey, Camberwell, Chelsea, Clerkenwell, Deptford, Fulham, Hammersmith, Hampstead, Islington, Kensington, Plumstead, Rotherhithe, St. James's, Piccadilly, St. Ʒartin-in-the Fields, Lambeth, Ʒarylebone, Ʒile End, Old Town, Paddington and St. George's, Hanover-square, were represented on Ʒonday at a conference, held at the Westminster Town Hall, to consider Sir Blundell Ʒaple's and Ʒr. Lough's Bills in reference to the proposed formation of municipalities in London. Lord Onslow presided.

In the discussion which followed Sir Blundell Ʒaple's explanation of the provisions of his Bill, objection was taken to its permissive character, and generally to too much power being left to the London County Council, who would veto some of the powers asked for by the new boroughs. Some of the speakers desired to have an appeal to the Local Government Board or the Privy Council. Ultimately it was agreed to refer the Bills to a committee, with instructions to draft a Bill embodying the best provisions of both, and also to introduce other provisions and report to the conference.

## CORRESPONDENCE.

**British Association of Waterworks Engineers.**—Mr. Edwd. T. Hildred, A.M.I.C.E., of Southampton, writes: In my reply to the discussion on the "Water Supply of Gosport," reported in last week's SURVEYOR, an inaccuracy has crept in, no doubt in the taking down of the shorthand notes, which I should be obliged if you will kindly correct in your next week's issue. I am reported to say "that in carrying out the Foxbury Well works, Gosport, great trouble had been occasioned by the invasion of *foul* water." We were troubled with foul air only during the execution of the heading works. For the above report to go uncorrected would be detrimental to the water company.

**The Westminster Building Accident.**—At the Old Bailey, on Thursday, before Ʒr. Justice Grantham, Ʒr. C. J. C. Pawley, the architect of Abbey Ʒansions, Westminster, who was found guilty of manslaughter by the coroner's jury, surrendered to his bail. Mr. Gill, for the Treasury, in the course of his remarks, said that the Treasury were not prepared to proceed with the prosecution. Mr. Justice Grantham, in summing up, said that he was of opinion that no liability attached to Ʒr. Pawley in any way, and that, practically, as there was no case against him, he would be acquitted. In the judge's opinion the accident was due to the striking the centring.

# Law Notes.

EDITED BY J. B. REIGNIER CONDER, 11 Old Jewry Chambers, E.C.,

Solicitor of the Supreme Court.

*The Editor will be pleased to answer any questions affecting the practice of engineers and surveyors to local authorities. Queries (which should be written legibly on foolscap paper one side only) should be addressed to "The Law Editor," at the Offices of* THE SURVEYOR. *Where possible, copies of local Acts or documents referred to should be enclosed. All explanatory diagrams must be drawn and lettered in black ink only. Correspondents who do not wish their names published should furnish a nom de plume.*

OBSTRUCTION ON HIGHWAY: PERSONAL INJURY; LIABILITY OF LOCAL AUTHORITY.—The case of *Penny v. The Wimbledon Urban District Council and Iles* (Queen's Bench Division, 16th June) affords an illustration of the principle that a local authority are liable for personal injury to individuals arising from the negligence of the contractor employed by the authority. A precedent is to be found in the case of *Hardaker and Wife v. Idle District Council and Another* (vol. ix., pp. 95, 217), where the injury was occasioned by a gas explosion which occurred in the course or the construction of a sewer. In the present case the accident was due to a heap of soil and grass left unprotected on a roadway, and over which the plaintiff, an elderly lady, fell, after dark, sustaining severe injuries. The road was being made up by the defendant Iles, as contractor for the council, under sec. 150 of the Public Health Act, 1875, and by the terms of the contract Iles was to provide all watching, lighting and fencing. A peculiarity of the case was that Iles had paid £75 into court, whereas the jury only gave the plaintiff £50 damages; so that the £75 came back to Iles again—*viz.*, £25 the overplus of damages and the £50 towards his costs. As regards the council, therefore, the question resolved itself into one of costs only, but in order to determine this it was necessary to consider whether they were liable for Iles' negligence, and thus properly made parties to the action. Mr. Justice Bruce, in giving judgment, after referring to the Idle case and also to *Pickering v. Smith* (10 C.B., N.S., 470) said: The district council employ the contractor to do the work upon the surface of a road which they know is being used by the public, and they must have known that the works which were to be executed would cause some obstruction to the traffic and some danger unless means were taken to give due warning to the public. The duty of affording protection to the public was in the circumstances incurred by the district council, and the district could not avoid the obligation of the duty by entering into a contract with Iles. The question remains — Can the defendants, the district council, avail themselves of the separate defence which is pleaded by Iles? The two defendants might, if they pleased, have joined in a defence of payment into court, which would have been available for both. But the district council have chosen to put in a separate defence. I cannot see in the circumstances that they can avail themselves of the payment into court by Iles. So far as their defence is concerned, it simply amounts to a denial of liability; but in that defence they have failed. The plaintiff is therefore entitled to judgment for £50 and costs. Of course, as the £50 has been obtained from the other defendant, Iles, the judgment against the district council will be confined to costs only.

COMBINED DRAINAGE: BY-LAW: PREMISES WITHIN THE SAME CERTILAGE: PUBLIC HEALTH ACT, 1875, SEC. 4.—An important decision bearing upon the subject of combined drainage, and involving the interpretation of a by-law, is that in *Blundell v. Prior* (Queen's Bench Division, 25th April). The by-law in question was as follows: "Every person who shall erect a new building shall provide in every main drain or other drain of such building which may directly communicate with any sewer or other means of drainage into which such drain may lawfully empty a suitable trap at a point as distant as may be practicable from such building and as near as may be practicable to the point at which such drain may be connected with such sewer or other means of drainage." The appellant had erected six houses, in two blocks of three each, in connection with which two passages were provided. One of these passages (which was closed at the ends) was at the back of the houses and parallel to the street on which they fronted; the other ran from that street to the back passage, between the third and fourth houses. The houses all belonged to the same owner, and all the tenants were entitled to use the passages; but each house had its own separate entrance, private yard, outbuildings and garden. There was a door at the end of the centre passage communicating with the street, to which each of the tenants had a key. The appellant provided for the drainage of the six houses by means of a pipe running down the centre passage and connected with the sewer in the street, with branches in the back passage, the separate drains of the several houses being connected with this pipe and its branches in the passages. In alleged compliance with the by-law he provided one trap in this pipe at the point where it came into the street and a short distance from its junction with the main sewer. The Birmingham Corporation (within whose district the property is situate) considered that the pipe fell within the definition of a "sewer," and that consequently the drain of each house ought

to have been trapped before its connection with the pipe. The magistrates adopted this view and convicted the appellant of an offence against the by-law, and the High Court have confirmed their decision. On behalf of the appellant it was contended that he had complied with the by-law, inasmuch as the common pipe in the passages was a "drain" within the meaning of the by-law. In support of this contention it was argued (*a*) that, even if the statutory definitions of "drain" and "sewer" were held to apply to the by-law, the houses were premises within the same curtilage, and therefore the pipe fell within the definition of a "drain"; (*b*) that, in any event, the pipe did not become a sewer until it began to be used as such, whereas the by-law related to something to be done anterior to such user; and (*c*) that, even if the pipe was a "sewer" within the Public Health Act, it might nevertheless be a "drain" within the by-law, the scope and intention of the latter being that there should be a trap above the junction of such a pipe with the main sewer. Mr. Justice Wills, in giving judgment, said: "I cannot persuade myself that there is any doubt that the justices were right in this case. The question in the case is what the expressions 'drain' and 'sewer' in the by-law mean. The definition in the Public Health Act, 1875, must govern this question. And under that definition a drain becomes a sewer as soon as it receives the drainage of two houses, unless those houses are within the same curtilage. It is argued that these six houses are within the same curtilage. On that point it is sufficient to say that the passages marked on the plan are passages and nothing else; and that whether you take the definitions referred to by Mathew J. in *St. Leonard (Shoreditch) Vestry v. Pilkrow* (L.R., 1895, 1 Q.B. 33) or, any of the tests suggested by Lord Esher M.R. or Lopes L.J. in the same case in the Court of Appeal (*L.R.*, 1895, 1 Q.B. 433), these passages do not satisfy the tests indicating what is a curtilage. Take the language of Mathew J. or of Lord Esher M.R. or of Lopes L.J. and apply it to the circumstances of this case, and it is clear that these passages do not fall within those tests. Therefore the common pipe is not within the definition of 'drain' and is within that of 'sewer.' We have to apply these definitions to the by-law, and I fail to see any difficulty in so doing. The by-law says that any person who shall erect a new building—and each of these houses is a new building—shall provide in any main drain or other drain which may directly communicate with any sewer, into which such drain may lawfully empty, a suitable trap. The pipe indicated by the dotted line is a sewer from the point at which it receives the drainage of two houses; and having regard to that I find no difficulty in applying the by-law. Mr. Lawson Walton says that the word 'sewer' in the by-law must mean the sewer in the street. But I fail to see why. True it would be impossible to make a communication between the most distant house and the sewer in the street without laying down the whole line of pipes. But that is no reason why when that line of pipes is laid down it should not be a sewer vested in the local authority. That being so the appellant must comply with the by-law."

**A Correction.**—We regret that, owing to a misunderstanding, it was erroneously stated in our last issue that Messrs. Joseph Place & Sons had removed from Halifax to Darwen. The announcement had reference not to the firm, but simply to a member of the firm. The works, as our readers are well aware, have always been at Darwen and never at Halifax.

**St. Saviour's Public Library.**—We have received the fourth annual report of the commissioners of this institution, for the year ended March 25th. The finances of the commissioners are reported to be in a highly satisfactory state, this being largely due to the careful and economical methods employed by the librarian, Mr. H. D. Roberts, in conducting their affairs.

**Belfast Deputations.**—A deputation from the Public Health Committee of the Belfast Corporation, consisting of Alderman Dr. Graham (chairman of the committee), Councillors Dr. Biggar, Dr. Brown, Dr. O'Connor, Gageby and John McCormick, with Mr. Munce, assistant surveyor, have been visiting various dust destructors in various parts of England, including Bradford, Leeds, Leyton and Shoreditch, with a view to the adoption of a system of dust destruction which would be adapted to the needs of Belfast. Another deputation, consisting of Aldermen O'Dempsey and Wm. McCormick and Councillor Taylor, with the city surveyor, Mr. J. C. Bretland, have been visiting various technical schools in Bradford, Sheffield, London and several places in the vicinity of the metropolis, Leicester, Birmingham, Manchester and Bolton.

# Municipal Work in Progress and Projected.

Some particulars of important works in progress or projected will be found in the paragraphs relating to Battersea, Bedford, Derby, Exeter, Godalming, Huddersfield, Hindley, Leigh and Lytham. Electric light activity still continues undiminished, as will be seen if one glances at the following paragraphs and notes the number of councils who have such schemes under consideration or in hand.

## METROPOLITAN AUTHORITIES.

### LONDON COUNTY COUNCIL.

The proceedings at Spring-gardens, on Tuesday, began with a somewhat hollow discussion on the report of the Finance Committee, which detailed the profits of the Works Department during the half-year ended 31st March. The matter was, however, soon disposed of, and the council were therefore able to reach the proposals of the Local Government and Taxation Committee with respect to certain by-laws as to street noises, &c. A lively debate broke out, but it was decided to receive the report and consider it in detail. This resulted in the first by-law being referred back by a vote of two to one. The rest of the proposals were then adjourned.

*Loans to Local Authorities.*—Upon the recommendation of the Finance Committee, it was agreed to lend the Islington Vestry £6,470 for laying-out the open space purchased from the London Corporation, at a cost of £16,000, and £15,500 for alterations and additions to the vestry offices; the Lambeth vestry £5,985 for wood paving works; the St. George's (Southwark) Vestry £4,025 for pipe sewer works; and the Shoreditch Vestry £4,585 for street improvements.

*The Works Department.*—The Finance Committee submitted the half-yearly statement of works executed during the half-year ended March 31st last. In this statement the committee showed what works were commenced under the late management and what under the present management. There were eleven works in all. Three of these were begun under the late management and before the reorganisation of the department. The final estimate for the latter amounted to £6,102, whilst the actual cost was £6,658, showing a balance of cost above final estimates of £556. The only loss was on one work—the Pimlico river fire station—on which there was a balance of cost above final estimate of £718, the final estimate being £990 and the actual cost £1,708. The other two works which had been executed for the Housing Committee showed a saving over final estimate of £162, making the balance of cost above estimate for the three works £556, as stated above. With regard to the eight other estimated works, the result appeared to be very satisfactory indeed, the final estimate for the works amounting to £23,021, whilst they had been executed at a cost of £17,846, showing the substantial balance of cost below estimate of £5,175. On jobbing works carried out during the half-year for the various committees, the schedule value of which was £15,055, there had been a saving of £2,033. Some discussion followed, and the report was then adopted.

*St. John's-street (Clerkenwell) Improvement.*—The Improvements Committee departed from their usual practice in authorising the Clerkenwell Vestry to set back the "Horse and Groom" public-house in St. John-street at the council's expense, and then recommending the council to confirm their action. The present case, however, was very exceptional, they stated, and would not be taken by them as forming a precedent. If they had waited for the council's instructions the opportunity for acquiring vacant land would have been lost and a new building would have been erected, and must have been acquired at great cost whenever the widening of the road was carried out. They would point out that in arranging for the setting back of the "Horse and Groom" public-house the council did not necessarily pledge itself to continue the improvement, and they thought it should be understood that the work was undertaken without prejudice to the question whether the widening of the whole of the narrow portion of St. John-street, if eventually carried out, either by the council or the vestry, should be considered a county or a local improvement. They added that the estimated nett cost of widening the whole of the narrow portion of St. John-street between Aylesbury-street and Albemarle-street was £59,000 if carried out under the ordinary conditions affecting street improvements, but they did not at present suggest that that work should be undertaken. They concluded by recommending the council to confirm their action. After discussion the report was approved.

*Proposed Purchase of Spitalfields Market.*—The Public Control Committee submitted a report recommending the council to include in one of the Bills in the next session of Parliament a clause empowering the council to acquire, by agreement or compulsorily, the freehold and other interests in Spitalfields market. It also recommended that the Public Control Committee should be authorised to negotiate, subject to the necessary Parliamentary power being obtained, for the purchase of the interests in the market. This report will be discussed at the next meeting of the council.

*Tenders.*—The following tenders were opened: For converting four beam engines at Crossness outfall into triple-expansion engines—J. Penn & Sons, Limited, Greenwich, £16,900; W. R. Renshaw & Co., Stoke, £17,900; B. Good-

fellow, Hyde, £20,684; United Ordnance and Engineering Company, Limited, Erith, £22,430; Fullerton, Hodgart & Barclay, Limited, Paisley, £25,000; Fleming & Ferguson, Limited, Paisley, £47,000. For the supply of compound pumping engines at Barking outfall—E. Chester & Co., 120 Bishopsgate-street Within, E.C., £6,134; W. R. Renshaw & Co., Stoke, £7,500; J. Cochrane, Barrhead, near Glasgow, £8,150; B. Goodfellow, Hyde, £10,216; Fullerton, Hodgart & Barclay, Limited, Paisley, £10,480; J. McNeil & Co., Govan, Glasgow, £11,525; Fleming & Ferguson, Limited, Paisley; £12,000; United Ordnance and Engineering Company, Limited, Erith, £12,840; J. Penn & Sons, Limited, Greenwich, £13,100; Clayton, Goodfellow & Co., Limited, Atlas Ironworks, Blackburn, £13,750.—The Main Drainage Committee reported that they had considered the tenders for the erection of a brick wall, with gates, along the north boundary of the Abbey Mills pumping station, and they recommended that the tender of Mr. J. Jackson, being the lowest, be accepted. The following were the tenders received: Messrs. J. Jackson, £518; G. Munday & Son, £560; and A. E. Symes, £625. The report was adopted.

## COURT OF COMMON COUNCIL.

A meeting of the court was held, on Thursday, under the presidency of the Lord Mayor. The Remembrancer reported that the Bill promoted by the corporation for the construction of a light railway from Deptford market to the South-Eastern Railway Company's line had passed both Houses of Parliament, and would probably shortly receive the royal assent. He suggested that the committee should be authorised to carry out the undertaking forthwith. The court agreed.—A report was brought up from the City Lands Committee asking for authority to spend £2,500 in carrying out certain works at the entrance to the Guildhall, in Basinghall-street. The new works will include a new entrance gateway, a path and carriage way, a new window and buttresses, a new building on the site of the Chamberlain's old parlour, and a new corridor connecting the library with the council chamber. The court unanimously approved of the recommendations of the committee.—The Improvements and Finance Committee recommended that the ground rents (£850 and £700) and reversion of St. Magnus House, Monument-street, should be offered for sale; and that arrangements should be made for acquiring the freehold interest in 124 Fenchurch-street for £23,500, the freehold interest in 82 Fleet-street for £11,800, and the sub-leasehold interest in 34 Basinghall-street for £350. The committee also submitted arrangements for acquiring the ground needed to widen the public way in front of 92 Gracechurch-street, it being proposed to pay £75 for the freehold interest and £500 for the leasehold interest. The court approved of these recommendations.

## VESTRIES AND DISTRICT BOARDS.

**Battersea.**—Last week, at a meeting of the vestry, the Baths and Wash-Houses Committee presented a report recommending the expenditure of £5,225, mainly for the purpose of sinking an artesian well for obtaining the necessary supply of water for the baths. The consideration of the matter, however, was adjourned for a week.

**Bermondsey.**—The vestry have resolved, on the recommendation of the Electric Lighting Committee, to erect a dust destructor in connection with the electric lighting station, subject to the passage of the Bill now before Parliament conferring power on the vestry to supply electrical energy.

**Hackney.**—A sum of £500 was, last week, contributed towards the cost of the construction of Carpenter's-road bridge and a proposed improvement in White Post-lane.—Representatives were appointed to attend the meetings of the Select Committee of the House of Commons and the Committee of the London County Council on the telephone service.—The Electric Light Committee were instructed to obtain from three electrical engineers their prices at which they would be prepared to advise the vestry to carry out the electric lighting undertaking.

**Lambeth.**—The South London Electric Supply Corporation, who some time ago acquired the Lambeth electric lighting provisional order, entered into an agreement with the Lambeth Vestry to erect a refuse destructor in conjunction with the projected electric light station, in order that at least a portion of the parish refuse might be disposed of by combustion in the destructor cells. The corporation have now submitted to the vestry for approval plans of the destructor which is proposed to be constructed by Messrs. Manlove, Alliott & Co., in Bengeworth-road, Loughborough Junction. As the agreement provided that the destructor should be "of the most approved sanitary type," the vestry were referred to that at Shoreditch, constructed by the same company. The Shoreditch destructor has been inspected by a committee appointed by the local authority, who report that it appears to be most efficient, and as a result of the examination and report the vestry have decided to approve the plans submitted on behalf of Messrs. Manlove, Alliott & Co.

**Newington.**—At last week's meeting of the vestry, a report was received from the Electric Lighting Committee, submitting the following tenders received for the supply and fixing of engines, generators and public lighting plant at the station in course of erection in Penrose-street—viz., Messrs. Sharp & Piper, £9,575; Messrs. Siemens Brothers & Co., Limited, £9,375; the Brush Electric Company, £9,090; Messrs. Johnson & Phillips, £8,975; Messrs. Crompton & Co., £8,802; Messrs. Fowler & Co., £5,200 (one section only). The report recommended that the tender of Messrs. Johnson & Phillips be accepted and the seal of the vestry affixed to the contract. The recommendation was adopted.

**Paddington.**—The Works Committee, at the vestry meeting last week, reported that they had caused plans to be prepared for the construction of a new steel-girder bridge, 45 ft. span, for Westbourne-terrace. The approximate cost would be about £4,500. It was decided to submit the plan to the London County Council for their approval, with an application for a contribution of two-thirds of the cost of the improvement.

**Plumstead.**—The Woolwich District Electric Light Company have been informed by the vestry that they intend to oppose any application for a provisional order to extend their supply to Plumstead.

**Shoreditch.**—Last week, at a meeting of the vestry, Mr. Kershaw moved that the charge for current to private consumers be reduced to 5d. per unit for the first two hours and 2d. per unit after, and that consumers have the option of being charged at a fixed rate of 4½d. per unit. This was agreed to; and it was also resolved to abolish the meter rents. The following recommendations were also agreed to: That the charge for current for motive power be reduced to 2d. per unit for all hours; that day users of current for light be charged on separate meters at 3½d. per unit; and that users of 50,000 units of current for motive power be charged at the rate of 4d. per unit for current for lighting purposes; users of 75,000 units for power, 3½d. for lighting; and users of 100,000 units for power, 3d. per unit for lighting purposes.

**St. Pancras.**—Two or three months ago, the St. Pancras Vestry were informed by their Electricity and Public Lighting Committee that the production of 437 electrical units had been traced as being due to the utilisation of the waste steam available at the refuse destructor, and it was suggested that in this direction the destructor might eventually become a source of profit to the parish. With this object in view the vestry instructed Mr. Sydney F. Baynes, the chief electrical engineer, to make a series of tests as to the possibility of using the steam in connection with the generation of electricity. Since then a number of tests have been carried out, but in consequence of the irregularity in the supply of steam it has been found impossible to rely upon it for generating purposes, and hence the experiments have had to be abandoned. A possible explanation of the lack of a constant supply of steam may be found in the fact that in two parts of the parish the collection and disposal of the refuse is being carried out by contract, and in this manner several of the cells are deprived of fuel and cannot be worked. It is, therefore, probable that on the expiration of the contract in question the interesting tests inaugurated by the chief electrical engineer will be resumed.

**Strand.**—At a meeting of the board of works, the Parliamentary Committee reported, with reference to Sir Blundell Maple's Municipal Corporation Bill, that they were not at present prepared to pass an opinion upon it. They had, therefore, adjourned further consideration thereof until the Government Bill on the same subject was introduced. Tenders for barging away refuse were opened; and that of Messrs. J. Shelbourne & Co., of Fenchurch-street, was accepted, at prices showing an increase of between £500 and £600 per annum in the aggregate on the present rates. The Wharf Committee were granted permission to enter into conditional contracts for the erection of a Horsfall refuse destructor on the board's Shot Tower wharf; but this course was adopted without prejudice to any negotiations between the board and the corporation. A letter was read from the Strand tradesmen asking that the streets might be more generously watered, and that, when precautions were necessary to prevent slipping, sand should be used instead of stones, on account of the damage caused by the latter to shop windows. The matter was referred to committee, as was a letter from the Holborn Board of Works asking the board to petition Parliament in favour of the appointment of a committee to inquire into the price of gas. After a short discussion on the procrastination of the London County Council in dealing with what they termed the insanitary area in the district, it was decided that a letter should be sent urging the council to push on with the work of improvement, as the present uncertain state of affairs was detrimental to the interests of traders in the affected area.

## PROVINCIAL AND GREATER LONDON AUTHORITIES.
### COUNTY COUNCILS.

**Derbyshire.**—Lord Waterpark, on behalf of the Derbyshire County Council, last week, conducted an inquiry at Swadlincote as to the necessity of the formation of a joint isolation hospital for the Swadlincote district, the Hartshorne and Seals districts, and the parishes of Drakelow, Rosliston, Walton, Cauldwell, Castle Gresley, Catton, Cotton-in-the-Elms, Linton and Lullington. All the places interested were represented, and there was a large attendance. It transpired that only Swadlincote, which had made no proper provision for infectious cases generally, was in favour of the scheme, which was objected to by the other places. Lord Waterpark expressed the hope that the report would be satisfactory, and the inquiry terminated.

## MUNICIPAL CORPORATIONS.

**Bedford.**—An inquiry was held recently, by the Local Government Board, in reference to a proposal of the council to borrow £5,400 for electric lighting extensions. Up to the present time £49,000 has been borrowed for electric lighting purposes. Sanction had been given to borrow £58,050, and therefore the corporation had still power to borrow a further sum of £6,950. The present loan was for the extension of the engine-room, with the necessary foundation, transformers, extra testing instruments, mains for public lighting, standards for lighting the market places, &c. This was necessary on account of increased demand and for the public lighting of the St. Cuthbert's glebe estate. The total number of lamps at present was 14,250 8 candle-power, exclusive of public lighting, and this scheme included sixty-five additional lamps for the St. Cuthbert's estate.

**Bolton.**—A change in the method of supplying electric energy in the central portion of the town is under contemplation. At present customers are supplied with alternating current; under the proposed scheme a continuous-current supply will be substituted. The matter is being considered by the General Purposes Committee as well as by the Electricity Committee.

**Cardiff.**—At a meeting of the Lighting Committee of the corporation, on the 21st ult., it was decided, on the recommendation of Mr. Appelbee, the electrical engineer, to reduce the charge for current for places of worship to 5d. per unit.

**Chester.**—The council have authorised the laying of arc mains and distributing mains for the supply of public and private electric lighting in George-street, St. Anne-street and adjoining streets, at an estimated cost, including street lamps, &c., of £1,260.

**Derby.**—A Local Government Board inquiry has been held by Colonel W. R. Slack, R.E., with respect to an application of the town council for sanction to borrow £20,000 for electric lighting purposes. £5,500 for the provision of a depot, £1,000 for the construction of a six-cell destructor, £2,300 for the purchase of land for purposes of street improvement, £1,098 for electric lighting purposes, £340 for market purposes, and £120 for the erection of a convenience.

**Exeter.**—Mr. W. A. Ducat, R.E., inspector of the Local Government Board, held an inquiry at the Guildhall, Exeter, on Thursday, relative to the application of the city council to borrow £7,000 for purposes of electric lighting. Of the £7,000 required, £1,104 was estimated extra expenditure on a boiler and steam alternator, £2,000 for new Killowutt steam alternator, steam and exhaust pipes, and feed-water heater, £2,800 for extension of mains, and £1,095 10s. for additional transformers, meters, &c., in connection with the above scheme of extension. Mr. Ducat subsequently inspected the electric light works.

**Godalming.**—The Local Government Board have refused to sanction the borrowing by the council of £15,000 for electric lighting purposes. As there was much opposition to the scheme, it is stated that the board thought it was doubtful whether it could prove remonerative, or even self-supporting, particularly in view of the smallness of the compulsory area. The council have to consider the letter, but the mayor has expressed an opinion that a poll of the residents will be taken.

**Huddersfield.**—Local Government Board sanction will shortly be asked for in connection with the borrowing of £14,140 for the purchase of land for cemetery purposes.

**Ipswich.**—The Electric Lighting Committee have been empowered to take the necessary steps to carry out the powers conferred on the council by the provisional order for the supply of electricity within the borough.

**Longton.**—Last week, Colonel W. R. Slack, R.E., an inspector of the Local Government Board, held a public inquiry at Longton with respect to an application of the town council for sanction to borrow a further sum of £3,500 for the purchase of property for the purpose of street improvements.

**Loughborough.**—It has been decided by the town council to make an application to the Local Government Board for sanction to borrow £2,500 for sewer extensions in the borough, £200 to defray the cost of the purchase of land to add to and improve the site acquired for a highway depot in Dead-lane, and £550 to defray the cost of fencing and laying-out the land acquired for the purpose of a pleasure ground in the Island House Park.

**Lynn.**—Major-General Crozier, Local Government Board inspector, held an inquiry at Lynn, last week, into the application made by the town council to the board for sanction to a loan of £2,500 to pay the cost for setting back various properties which were affected by the fire in High-street last Christmas. After evidence and some opposition, the inspector pointed out that the council should have taken steps to have had the inquiry held before the work was commenced. The fact of the buildings being partly put up on the new line made that inquiry rather a farce. If the board refused the loan they would throw a great burden on a lot of people who could not meet it or bear it, and who had had no voice in the matter at all. The mayor said the great idea of the corporation was not to do anything to prevent the people putting up their premises as soon as possible.

**Manchester.**—The River Committee of the City Council met, on Monday, Sir Bosdin Leech in the chair. The experts who have been requested to report upon the question of sewage treatment asked permission to put down two experimental filters at Davyhulme, one dealing with the system now in operation at Sutton, and the other demonstrating the septic system. The committee assented to the proposal, and referred the matter to a sub-committee to make the necessary arrangements.

**Middlesbrough.**—The new Cleveland borough lunatic asylum at Middlesbrough was formally opened, on Wednesday in last week. It has been built at a cost, exclusive of site, of £20,000, from plans by, and under the supervision of, Mr. Alfred J. Wood, of 22 Surrey-street, Victoria Embankment, W.C.

**Newport (Mon.).**—The Parliamentary Committee have recommended the purchase, for £5,350, of a site belonging to the Ecclesiastical Commissioners, near Careleon, and containing 53 acres, for the new borough lunatic asylum.

**Norwich.**—The town council having applied to the Local Government Board for sanction to borrow £5,700 for works of street improvement, an inquiry was held, on the 22nd ult., by Major-General D. Darley Crozier, R.E. Mr. A. E. Collins, the city engineer, was present at the proceedings, and explained the plans put before the inspector, and also as to the paving proposed to be laid down. A bridge on Station-road would be paved with soft wood. There being opposition to the use of granite paving, the corporation did not avail themselves of the amount granted for the purpose by the Local Government Board four years ago.

**Ripon.**—The tender of Messrs. Holmes & Co., Huddersfield, amounting to £1,275, has been accepted for the supply of a set of purifiers (14 ft. square) and for the erection of a shed for the same at the gasworks.

**Wakefield.**—The corporation electricity works at Calder Vale, which were opened a few days ago, have been laid down under the powers accorded to the corporation by their electric lighting provisional order granted in the year 1894. Mr. Robert Hammond was appointed consulting electrical engineer, and prepared plans and specifications of the works. The buildings comprise boiler-house, engine-house, testing-room, workshop, stores and offices.

**Walsall.**—Local Government Board sanction will shortly be applied for to a loan of £350 for the construction of an underground convenience. The plans have already been prepared by the borough surveyor. Application will also be made for sanction to a loan of £300 to defray the cost of purchasing property for road improvement purposes.

**Warrington.**—A Local Government Board inquiry has been held into an application of the corporation for sanction to borrow £31,933 for purposes of street improvement, £10,000 for the purchase of slot and other meters, and £700 for the purchase of a recreation ground.

**West Hartlepool.**—The erection of new municipal buildings is being contemplated by the council.

## URBAN DISTRICT COUNCILS.

**Balby-with-Hexthorpe.**—Mr. E. A. Sandford Fawcett held an inquiry, on the 17th ult., on behalf of the Local Government Board, concerning an application of the council for sanction to borrow £3,750 for works of private street improvement.

**Erith.**—The question of constructing a town pier has been referred to a committee for consideration.

**Crays.**—At the last meeting of the district council, the plans and estimates prepared by the surveyor to the council, Mr. Arthur C. James, for fencing the stoneyard site and erecting stables, cart-shed, stores, &c., at an estimated cost of £850, and for fencing and laying-out the recreation ground site, at a cost of £2,550, were approved, and it was decided to apply to the Local Government Board for permission to borrow the money.

**Hindley.**—Colonel C. H. Luard, R.N., Local Government Board inspector, held an inquiry, on Tuesday of last week, with reference to an application of the council for sanction to borrow £5,700 for works of private street improvements. Mr. Alfred Holden, the council's engineer, explained the plans, &c., which had been prepared by him, and also accompanied the inspector to view the various streets.

**Leigh.**—Mr. H. Hall, inspector of the Local Government Board, held an inquiry at Leigh, last week, into the application of the Leigh District Council for sanction to borrow £11,426 for works of street improvement and the improvement of main roads. The money would be spent in putting several main roads in the district into proper condition. The

council, it was stated, wish to commence the works as early as possible. Granite setts, grit setts and macadam are to be used for the roads. When the works are completed all the Leigh roads would, it was mentioned, be in excellent condition.

**Lytham.**—The Local Government Board have communicated their sanction to the expenditure of £10,000 upon a new scheme of sewerage for Lytham. It is over twelve months since the inquiry was held, and it is understood the delay has been occasioned by the opposition of the Preston Corporation, who feared the discharge from the outlet would have an injurious effect upon the Ribble channel. The Local Government Board have approved the scheme in its entirety.

**Matlock.**—The undertaking of the Matlock Cable Tramways Company, Limited, which has been presented to the urban district council by Sir G. Newnes, was, on Saturday, formally transferred to the council.

## RURAL DISTRICT COUNCILS.

**Ashford.**—The district council have instructed Messrs. Bailey-Denton, Son & Lawford, of Westminster, to advise them as to an efficient system of water supply for Willesborough, a populous suburb of Ashford, where the works of the South-Eastern Railway are situated.

**Billericay.**—The district council have resolved to apply to the Local Government Board for sanction to borrow £5,000 for a joint sewerage scheme for the parishes of Shenfield and Hutton. The scheme has been designed by Messrs. Bailey-Denton, Son & Lawford, of Westminster, and will be carried out immediately.

**Disley.**—On the 21st ult., an inquiry was held by Colonel A. G. Durnford, R.E., on behalf of the Local Government Board, into an application of the council for sanction to borrow an additional sum of £1,000 for works of sewerage and sewage disposal. The application was opposed by several ratepayers on the ground that sufficient care in the estimates had not been exercised and that the scheme was incomplete. Complaint was also made that property owners were being caused extra expense through having to take steps to prevent rain water from getting into the main sewer connections.

**Hatfield.**—The tender of Mr. John Maden, of Hatfield, has been accepted for the erection of a mortuary, for £335.

**Hunslet.**—The plans for the Temple Newsam drainage scheme were under the consideration of the council last week, and it was stated that the cost was estimated at £1,556.

**Nantwich.**—The council recently gave their consideration to plans prepared by the surveyor, Mr. Davenport, for certain water main extensions. The plans were eventually approved, it being decided to make the usual application to the Local Government Board for their sanction to the execution of the work, which is to cost £1,830.

**Woburn, Bucks.**—A detailed report has been submitted to the council for a scheme of water supply for the district of Wavenden, including Woburn Sands, by the engineers for the work, Messrs. D. Balfour & Son, civil engineers, London and Newcastle. This recommends a trial shaft being sunk about 100 ft. into the Lower Greensand, after which continuous pumping tests will be made for fourteen days at the rate of 10,000 gallons per hour. The site chosen is to the south of Woburn, on land belonging to the Duke of Bedford, and sufficiently far from the escarpment of the Lower Greensand to obtain a good supply. It is probable, if the quantity of water found will allow, that several neighbouring places may be supplied, but at present the supply is got from wells which are liable to pollution. The water will be pumped into an elevated tower on high land adjoining, from which it will gravitate in mains over the district. If the scheme is successful, Woburn Sands, with its almost Highland scenery, will have an excellent water supply.

## SCOTLAND AND IRELAND.

**Aberdeen.**—The question of the reconstruction of Regent bridge was under the consideration of the harbour board, at a meeting on, Monday of last week. On the recommendation of the Works Committee it was agreed to proceed with the erection of a new bridge, according to the plans of the harbour engineer, and approved by Mr. Wake, the consulting engineer. The estimated cost of the bridge is £49,740.—At a recent meeting of the district committee of the county council, a letter was read from Mr. William Dyack, burgh surveyor, stating that the town council were proposing to replace the existing aqueduct by cast-iron pipes along the Deeside-road between Aberdeen and Banchory. The first section they proposed laying was from Pitfodels to Cuiter, the pipes of which were to be 42 in. in diameter, and it was proposed to lay them on the side of the road, out of the macadamised track. He would be glad to have permission to have the road opened as soon as possible. It was remitted to the Roads Sub-Committee to consider and report.

**Edinburgh.**—At the meeting of the Edinburgh Town Council, on Tuesday, it was stated that it was expected all contracts for cabling the tramway would be completed in the spring of next year. The most important business transacted was, however, the decision to take no further action with the Fountainbridge improvement scheme, which would have involved an expenditure variously estimated at from

£51,000 to £100,000, after allowing for the subsequent letting of the spare land to be acquired. The settlement of the matter gave rise to a somewhat heated personal difference between the Lord Provost and Treasurer M'Crae, in which charges of "subterfuges and suppression" were freely bandied. The voting showed that the opinion of the council was decidedly with the Lord Provost. Apart from personalities, the main question appeared to be whether such an improvement as that contemplated should be carried out at once or deferred to some indefinite period. The council hesitated to apply for compulsory powers to compel the North British Railway to treat for the land that would have to be acquired, and preferred to wait, Micawber like, for something to turn up which would bring the company to them. There is a lingering hope that the company may in future want concessions, and the inference is that the council will then put the screw on. The improvement was generally admitted to be desirable, and it is not easy to see the morality or the logic of waiting to apply indirect compulsion rather than at once adopting the more dignified course of seeking Parliamentary powers. In the meantime the capital value of the company's property is daily increasing, and the council's delay will make far more costly the eventual effecting of an improvement which the burgh engineer has emphatically reported upon as a necessary one.

**Kirkcaldy.**—Recently, at a meeting of the town council, a report of Prof. Kennedy as to the proposed introduction of electric lighting and tramways was read. The proposal was to have two routes of tramways round the burgh, the upper being from West Bridge to Gallatown *via* the Public Park, Victoria-road and Rosslyn-street, the lower being from West Bridge, High-street and Sands-road, while an extra line would run up Whyte's-causeway and Wemysfield, to join the upper route. The total length of the route is 6½ miles. It was explained that the committee who had the matter in hand were anxious to give the council an opportunity of taking over the scheme, if they desired. If the council did not wish to take over the scheme, then it would be floated by a private company who had taken up the matter. The cost, he contemplated, would be at least £100,000. It was agreed to call a special meeting of the council to consider the matter and give their decision at the July meeting.

**Portsoy.**—A special meeting of the burgh commissioners was held recently, when it was resolved to relay about 4,600 yards of the gas mains within the burgh, the existing main pipes having been found on examination by an expert to be either in unsatisfactory condition or too small for the district served. It is understood that the board have accepted the offer of the Manchester Acetylene, Gas and Carbide Company to supply the requisite pipes, valves, syphons, generator, gasometer and standing meter, all complete. The plant to be put in for the generation of acetylene gas is expected to produce about ten times the quantity of gas which the old coal gas plant could have supplied. The works are to be proceeded with at once.

## ADVERTISEMENTS
Received too late for Classification.

### COUNTY BOROUGH OF WEST HAM.

*PRIVATE STREET WORKS.*

TO CONTRACTORS.

The Council hereby invite tenders for making-up the following streets:—

Freemantle-road.
Haslemere-road.
New-street, Plaistow.
Old-street, Plaistow.

Plans may be seen, and specification, form of tender and further particulars obtained, at the office of Mr. Lewis Angell, Borough Engineer, Town Hall, Stratford, E., upon payment of £1, which will be returned upon receipt of a bond-*fide* tender.

Tenders, endorsed "Tender for Private Street Works," to be sent to my office not later than 4 o'clock on Tuesday, the 26th July, 1898.

The Council do not bind themselves to accept the lowest or any tender.

The contractor will be required to enter into a bond, with two sureties, for the due performance of the contract, and no work will be ordered under the contract until such bond has been duly executed.

As regards all work to be done at the site or elsewhere within a radius of 20 miles from Charing Cross, the contractors will be bound by the contract to pay to all workmen (except a reasonable number of legally-bound apprentices) employed by them wages at rates not less, and to observe hours of labour not greater, than the rates and hours set out in the Council's list, and such rates of wages and hours of labour will be inserted in and form part of the contract by way of schedule.

(By order of the Council)
FRED. E. HILLEARY,
Town Clerk.
Town Hall, West Ham, E.
June 29, 1898.

### COUNTY BOROUGH OF WEST HAM.
TO WHEELWRIGHTS.

The Council hereby invite tenders for the supply of ten Slop Carts.

Form of tender, specification and further particulars obtained at the office of Mr. Lewis Angell, Borough Engineer, Town Hall, Stratford, E., upon payment of £1, which will be returned upon receipt of a bond-*fide* tender.

Tenders, endorsed "Tender for Slop Carts," to be sent to my office not later than 4 o'clock on Tuesday, July 26, 1898.

The Council do not bind themselves to accept the lowest or any tender.

The contractor will be required to enter into a bond, with two sureties, for the due performance of the contract, and no work will be ordered under the contract until such bond has been duly executed.

As regards all work to be done at the site or elsewhere within a radius of 20 miles from Charing Cross, the contractors will be bound by the contract to pay to all workmen (except a reasonable number of legally-bound apprentices) employed by them wages at rates not less, and to observe hours of labour not greater, than the rates and hours set out in the Council's list, and such rates of wages and hours of labour will be inserted in and form part of the contract by way of schedule.

(By order of the Council)
FRED. E. HILLEARY,
Town Clerk.
Town Hall, West Ham, E.
June 28, 1898.

### COUNTY BOROUGH OF WEST HAM.
TO BUILDERS AND CONTRACTORS.

The Council hereby invite tenders for the erection of twenty-nine Houses for the working-classes at Hermit-road, Plaistow.

Plans may be seen, and specification, form of tender and further particulars obtained, on and after Monday, July 11, 1898, at the office of Mr. Lewis Angell, Borough Engineer, Town Hall, Stratford, E., on the deposit of a £5 Bank of England note, which will be returned upon receipt of a bond-*fide* tender.

Tenders, endorsed "Tender for Artisans' Dwellings," to be sent to my office not later than 4 o'clock on Tuesday, July 26, 1898.

The Council do not bind themselves to accept the lowest or any tender.

The contractor will be required to enter into a bond, with two sureties, for the due performance of the contract, and no work will be ordered under the contract until such bond has been duly executed.

As regards all work to be done at the site or elsewhere within a radius of 20 miles from Charing Cross, the contractors will be bound by the contract to pay to all workmen (except a reasonable number of legally-bound apprentices) employed by them wages at rates not less, and to observe hours of labour not greater, than the rates and hours set out in the Council's list, and such rates of wages and hours of labour will be inserted in and form part of the contract by way of schedule.

(By order of the Council)
FRED. E. HILLEARY,
Town Clerk.
Town Hall, West Ham, E.
June 29, 1898.

### COUNTY BOROUGH OF WEST HAM.
TO SEWER CONTRACTORS.

The Council hereby invite tenders for the contruction of about 1,200 lineal yards of Sewers, 7 ft., 6 ft. and 3 ft. 6 in. diameter, together with Penstock Chambers, Manholes and other works.

Plans may be seen, and specification, form of tender and further particulars obtained, at the office of Mr. Lewis Angell, Borough Engineer, Town Hall, Stratford, E., on the deposit of a £5 Bank of England note, which will be returned on receipt of a bond-*fide* tender.

Tenders, endorsed "Tender for Sewers," to be sent to my office not later than 4 o'clock on Tuesday, 26th July, 1898.

The Council do not bind themselves to accept the lowest or any tender.

The contractor will be required to enter into a bond, with two sureties, for the due performance of the contract, and no work will be ordered under the contract until such bond has been duly executed.

As regards all work to be done at the site or elsewhere within a radius of 20 miles from Charing Cross, the contractors will be bound by the contract to pay to all workmen (except a reasonable number of legally-bound apprentices) employed by them wages at rates not less, and to observe hours of labour not greater, than the rates and hours set out in the Council's list, and such rates of wages and hours of labour will be inserted in and form part of the contract by way of schedule.

(By order of the Council)
FRED. E. HILLEARY,
Town Clerk.
Town Hall, West Ham, E.
June 29, 1898.

# Personal.

Mr. W. Cottam, surveyor to the Southwell Rural District Council, has had his salary increased by £20 per annum.

Southampton Borough Council have increased the salary of the assistant engineer, Mr. Killick, to £200 per annum.

Mr. William Walton has been appointed surveyor and inspector of nuisances to the Harpenden Urban District Council.

Mr. F. S. Whittell, surveyor to the Holmfirth Urban District Council, has been appointed surveyor to the Worksop Urban District Council.

Prof. Henry Robinson has been appointed by the town council of Hastings to prepare a report upon the local electric light company's undertaking.

Mr. Albert Nagel, B.SC.,EDINBURGH UNIVERSITY, of Newport, Dundee, has been appointed engineer and secretary to the Hartlepool Port and Harbour Commissioners.

Mr. O. T. Oldroyd, assistant in the office of Mr. S. W. Parker, engineer and surveyor to the Thornhill Urban District Council, has been appointed assistant in the city engineer's office, Hull.

Applications for the position of surveyor will shortly be invited by the Whitechapel District Board. The salary will commence at £400 and increase to £500. Six candidates will be selected for the final interview.

The Benwell and Fenham Urban District Council have instructed Mr. Harry W. Taylor, of St. Nicholas Chambers, Newcastle and Birmingham, to prepare a scheme of main sewerage for the Fenham portion of their district.

We learn that Mr. W. B. G. Bennett, the borough engineer of Southampton, has been appointed a vice-president of the municipal engineering section at the Birmingham congress of the Sanitary Institute, to be held in September next.

Mr. William Farrow, assistant in the office of the surveyor to the Kirkleatham Urban District Council, has been appointed temporary assistant in the office of Mr. James Diggle, surveyor to the Ashton-upon-Mersey Urban District Council.

About forty members of the Gloucestershire Engineering Society had a most enjoyable excursion to the Gloucester Corporation waterworks on the 18th ult. The president, Mr. R. Read (the city surveyor), gave a description of the works.

Mr. H. B. Longley, assistant in the office of Mr. G. T. Lynam, borough surveyor of Burton-on-Trent, was at the last meeting of the Coventry City Council appointed to fill the vacancy in the city engineer's department caused by the resignation of Mr. G. E. Jenkins.

It is reported that Mr. A. J. H. Carter, late clerk of works and chief assistant engineer for the Brighton Corporation, has been appointed clerk of works for the electric light installation in course of erection at Stockport. There were fifty-four applicants for the appointment.

At a meeting of the Gloucester City Council, held on Tuesday, it was unanimously resolved that Mr. E. W. A. Carter, who has for three years been an assistant in the office of the city surveyor, be appointed assistant surveyor. Mr. Carter served his articles with Mr. J. Fletcher Trew, of Gloucester and Bristol.

Mr. J. R. Monahan, Q.C., who has for a considerable period acted as law adviser to the Local Government Board, has been appointed permanent office in that department, at a salary of £1,200 a year, it is supposed as fourth commissioner. This creates a vacancy in the office of revising barrister for the co. Dublin, held by Mr. Monahan since 1884.

Mr. J. P. Greenwood, assistant surveyor to the Barry District Council, was, at a meeting on Thursday evening at Cadoxton, presented with a drawing-room clock and pair of ornamental bronzes to match on his departure from the district to take up the duties of deputy borough surveyor at Burnley. Mrs. Greenwood, also, was presented with a gold bracelet.

Sir Seymour Haden will preside at the twentieth annual meeting of the Church of England Burial, Funeral and Mourning Reform Association, to be held at 32 Wimpole-street on Wednesday. Among other resolutions will be one pointing out the desirability of the clergy enforcing the Christian obligation of carrying out the burial of the dead promptly, innocuously and inexpensively.

At a meeting of the Rothwell Urban District Council, on Wednesday of last week, Mr. John Pears was unanimously appointed surveyor to the council, in the place of Mr. W. Tuley, deceased. A member of the council stated that he thought Mr. Pears would be the right man in the right place. He had received an excellent training under the late Mr. Tuley, and was quite capable of performing the duties required.

We regret to say that in our last issue we erroneously stated that Mr. E. Clark had been appointed waterworks engineer to the East Westmoreland Rural District Council. We understand that Messrs. C. Watson & Son, of 3 St. Andrew's-place, Penrith, have for upwards of a quarter of a century been engineers to the council and to their predecessors, the rural sanitary authority. Mr. Clark was only appointed manager and collector of rates.

The Portmadoc and Tretfys School Board recently adopted the report and recommendations of Mr. J. D. Lewis, surveyor to the Portmadoc Urban District Council, respecting the drainage, water supply and ventilation of Tremadoc schools. It was at first proposed that the architect of the building should be appointed to carry out the works, but it was ultimately decided to ask Mr. Lewis to prepare the necessary drawings and carry out the work at once.

Through the kindness of Mr. E. Parry, engineer to the northern section of the Great Central Railway, the city engineer's department of the Nottingham Corporation, with a number of friends, on the afternoon of Saturday, the 18th of June, went over that portion of the line between East Leake and Annesley (a distance of over 18 miles), now rapidly nearing completion. Mr. Parry personally conducted the party, and placed an engine and trucks at their disposal. Stoppages were made at the various important works in progress, and a very enjoyable afternoon was spent.

At a recent ordinary meeting of the Middlesex County Council the Highways Committee presented a lengthy report dealing with the appointment of a county surveyor. For this post sixty-two applications were received, and of these five were disqualified in consequence of being under the specified age, and five others were disqualified as not being Members nor Associates of the Institution of Civil Engineers or Fellows of the Institute of Surveyors. Finally, the committee had interviewed four of them, and now recommended that Mr. H. T. Wakelam, of Hereford, be appointed, at a salary of £700 a year, rising to £850, and in the case of new buildings and new bridges where the contract price exceeds £1,000, the surveyor, when engaged by the council on these works, to be paid a commission, exclusive of quantity surveyor's fees, of 2½ per cent. Mr. Wakelam, it was added, was forty years of age, and since April, 1892, he had been county surveyor for Herefordshire. After a protest and an amendment against the principle of giving commission, the recommendation to appoint was carried by thirty-one to twenty. The subject of commission was, however, referred back to committee for further consideration.

## NEW COURT-HOUSE AND POLICE STATION AT HALIFAX.

The corner-stones have just been laid of the new court-house and police station which it is proposed to erect at Halifax. The plans show that the exterior of the building is Renaissance in style, freely treated. The court-house is in the centre of the block, and has open areas on two sides. In every department provision is made for conveniences and cloak-rooms. There is also an open parade ground, a part of which is under cover. A coach-house with four-stall stable is at the back. The magistrates will enter from Blackwall. Here, on the ground floor, are the magistrates' cloak-room, retiring-room and the lunacy-room. The entrance gives access to a wide staircase leading to the magistrates' retiring-rooms and the court-house. One of the rooms is large enough for use as a subsidiary court. The solicitors' entrance is also from Blackwall; but their rooms, as well as those for clients and witnesses, front to Ferguson-street, where will be the general public entrance. For the latter a large entrance hall is provided. The gaolers'-house and matron's apartments are provided on the ground floor. The police entrance is from Carlton-street, and leads into a large entrance hall. The police offices, which front to Harrison-road, are approached by a wide corridor. The charge-room and inquiry office are near the entrance hall, and the cells are placed round the parade ground, which is approached by a special corridor, with prisoners' lobby, search-room, &c. On the right of the entrance hall is a parade-room, and a staircase leads to the first floor, with policemen's lavatories and bath-rooms. The entrance to the warrant office is in Harrison-road, and this leads also to the rooms of the magistrates' clerk, the chief constable and his clerk on the first floor. The total estimated cost is between £13,000 and £14,000. The contractor is Mr. G. Charnock, and the architect is Mr. G. Buckley.

**Municipal Officers and their Patents.**—At a recent meeting of the Bombay Corporation, counsel's opinion as regards the legality or otherwise of municipal servants interesting themselves in patents of inventions by themselves or others utilised by the municipality was brought forward for consideration. After a short discussion the council decided that it was undesirable that municipal officers should be in any way interested in patents connected with the working of their departments.

## ASSOCIATION OF MUNICIPAL AND COUNTY ENGINEERS.

### ANNUAL MEETING AT EDINBURGH.

The following are the arrangements for to-day and to-morrow in connection with the annual meeting which is being held at Edinburgh.

To-ᴅᴀʏ.

10.30 a.m.—Papers and discussions. (7) " Notes on the bac-terial treatment of sewage," by D. Cameron. (8) " Two hours' test of a steam ram pumping plant," by J. B. Wilson, Cockermouth. (9) " Electric lighting of Edinburgh: The system adopted: Financial results," by Frank A. Newington, resident electrical engineer. (10) " Recent extensions of Leith docks," by Peter Whyte, docks superintendent.

1 p.m.—The members will be entertained to luncheon by Mr. W. N. Colam, engineer for the Edinburgh cable tram-ways.

2.50. p.m.—Brakes will be at the "Royal" hotel to convey the members to visit the following works :—

No. 1 Party.—1, Artisans' dwellings ; 2, electric light-ing works; 3, cable tramway power station, Tollcross ; 4, McEwen Hall·(organ, by Hope-Jones, will be played by Mr. J. H. Collinson, ᴍᴜѕ.ʙᴀᴄ., organist, St. Mary's Cathedral); 5, free library.

No. 2 Party.—1, Refuse destructor; 2, Chancelot mills; 3, cable tramway power station, Shrubhill; 4, Leith docks.

A charge of 2s. will be made to each member for brakes, &c.

To-ᴍᴏʀʀᴏᴡ.

No. 1 Party.

Visit the Forth bridge. Leave the "Royal" hotel, 9.30 a.m., in brakes for Forth bridge, go on bridge and under ; arriving back at 1 p.m.

No. 2 Party.

10 a.m.—Brakes will be at the "Royal" hotel to convey members to view the following places of interest : Scott Monument (immediately opposite "Royal" hotel), St. Giles' Cathedral, the Castle, Museum of Science and Art, Holyrood Palace, Burns' Monument and Calton Hill.

1 p.m.—Arrive back at "Royal" hotel.

A charge of 2s. will be made to each member for brakes.

C. Jᴏɴᴇѕ, ᴍ.ɪ.ᴄ.ᴇ.,　　Tʜᴏᴍᴀѕ Cᴏʟᴇ, ᴀ.ᴍ.ɪ.ᴄ.ᴇ., Secretary,
Hon. General Secretary.　　11 Victoria-street,
Westminster, S.W.

(Full details of trains were given in our last issue.)

## LONDON WATER SUPPLY COMMISSION.

The Royal Commission met again, on Monday, at the West-minster Town Hall, under the presidency of Lord Llandaff.

Mr. Jᴀᴍᴇѕ Bɪɢᴡᴏᴏᴅ, Parliamentary member for the Brent-ford division of Middlesex and chairman of the Parliamentary Committee of the Middlesex County Council, said the Middlesex County Council area was within the limits of supply of the New River, West Middlesex and Grand Junction companies, whilst the East London and several of the other companies had powers to supply in parts of Middlesex, but the power was not exercised. The population of Middlesex had increased from 320,000 in 1871 to 740,000 at the present moment. The general views of the county, and their desire to stand as a body separate and independent of London, both as regards rating and water supply, had been consistent throughout, and the county council had petitioned against the purchase Bills introduced by the London County Council. The council con-sidered it inexpedient and contrary to public policy that any outside authority should acquire the powers of any of the companies with reference to the supply of water within Middlesex, so as to be in any way empowered to control or interfere with that supply. The interests of such an authority might in many respects be antagonistic with those of Middle-sex. The county of Middlesex preferred to remain as it is, and protested against being made a party to the Welsh scheme and its consequences. Supposing that the scheme for the purchase of the undertakings of the metropolitan water companies were rejected, it was submitted that a power of control should be entrusted to a Government board, upon which local authorities interested should be represented in such a way as not to give any preponderating influence to one local authority over another. Witness believed that the constitution of such a board of control would probably be found to be a nearer approach to a solution of the London water question than purchase, seeing that it was very much to the interests of water consumers that efficient and eco-nomical control should be established, with a view to secure the following results: (1) Sufficient supply to all consumers, whether within or without the county of London ; (2) efficient and very stringent methods of preventing waste; (3) the primary right of the inhabitants of any district from which water is abstracted to a sufficient supply to meet their re-quirements; (4) more economical administration of the com-panies' affairs ; (5) the application of any dividends in excess of 10 per cent. on the paid up capital of any company to the

reduction of water rates　(6) an easy and simple method by application to a tribunal or officer who could without waste of time settle questions in dispute between any company and any water consumer; (7) the restriction and ultimate extinc-tion of back dividends; (8) the placing of the companies under regulations analogous to those under which the gas companies now carry on their undertakings. Another system of control which suggested itself was that the water com-panies supplying the inhabitants within the jurisdiction of county councils should be placed under some control from those councils within the districts of their jurisdiction.

Mr. E. J. Hᴀʟѕᴇʏ, chairman of the Surrey County Council, who also gave evidence, explained the attitude of his council upon the question of purchase. It was urged that if the water undertakings were taken away from the companies no settlement of the water question could be satisfactory which did not secure to the county of Surrey and its local authorities the control of the sources and distribution of water within the county.

---

**Wallasey.**—The district council have decided to purchase the Woodlands estate, adjoining Liscard Vale, and having a frontage to the Esplanade, for conversion into a public park. The estate contains 12,500 square yards, and the price given is £3,500.

**The Smoke Nuisance.**—At last week's meeting of the St. Olave's Board of Works, the clerk reported that he had, as instructed, written to the London, Brighton and South Coast Railway Company and the South-Eastern Railway Company complaining of the smoke nuisance from locomotives. The former company replied expressing some surprise that the board, in whose district trains had been running for so many years, had only now found it necessary to call attention to the fact that locomotives emitted smoke. The South-Eastern Railway Company replied that they were taking steps to prevent the nuisance.

---

## APPOINTMENTS VACANT.

*Advertisements which are received too late for classification cannot be included in these summaries until the following week.*

INSPECTOR OF NUISANCES.—July 4th.—St. Albans Rural District Council. £100.—Mr. R. W. Brabant, clerk to the council.

BUILDING INSPECTOR.—July 4th.—Corporation of Hanley. £100.—Mr. Joseph Lobley, borough engineer and surveyor.

DRAINAGE INSPECTOR.—July 4th.—Erith Urban District Council. £140.—Mr. Fred. Parish, clerk to the council.

INSPECTOR OF NUISANCES.—July 5th.—Ramsey Urban Dis-trict Council. £60.—Mr. Fred. R. Serjeant, clerk to the council.

SANITARY INSPECTOR.—July 5th.—Sefton Rural District Council. £100.—Mr. Harris P. Cleaver, clerk to the council.

FOREMAN FOR SEWERING WORK.—July 6th.—Vestry of Shoreditch. £3 3s.—The Vestry Surveyor.

BOROUGH SURVEYOR.—July 6th.—Bacup Town Council. £200.—Mr. Robert Hyde, town clerk.

SURVEYOR.—July 7th.—St. Mary Church (Devon) Urban District Council.—Mr. J. W. G. Wollen, clerk to the council.

TEMPORARY ASSISTANT SURVEYORS (Two).—July 8th.—Wallasey Urban District Council. £2 12s. 6d.—The Engineer and Surveyor to the Council.

CONSULTING ENGINEER AND SURVEYOR.— July 9th.—Hor-wich Urban District Council.— Mr. Peter Taberner, clerk to the council.

FOREMAN PAVIOR.—July 11th.—Norwich Corporation. £3.—Mr. Arthur E. Collins, ᴀ.ᴍ.ɪ.ᴄ.ᴇ., city engineer.

SANITARY INSPECTOR.—July 11th.—Plumstead Vestry. £104.—Mr. Edwin Hughes, vestry clerk.

ROAD FOREMEN (Two).—July 12th.—County Borough of Huddersfield. £100.—Mr. K. F. Campbell, ᴀ.ᴍ.ɪ.ᴄ.ᴇ., borough engineer and surveyor.

CHIEF ENGINEERING AND SURVEYING ASSISTANT.—July 12th.—County Borough of Huddersfield. £180.—Mr. K. F. Campbell, ᴀ.ᴍ.ɪ.ᴄ.ᴇ., borough engineer and surveyor.

ASSISTANT BUILDING AND DRAINAGE INSPECTOR.—July 12th.—County Borough of Huddersfield. £120.—Mr. K. F. Camp-bell, ᴀ.ᴍ.ɪ.ᴄ.ᴇ., borough engineer and surveyor.

CHIEF ROAD SURVEYOR FOR CITY ENGINEER AND SUR-VEYOR'S DEPARTMENT.—July 13th.—Corporation of Birming-ham. £300.—Mr. John Price, city engineer and surveyor.

CLERK OF WORKS.—July 13th.—County Borough of Sal-ford. £4 4s.—Mr. Samuel Brown, town clerk.

SURVEYOR OF HIGHWAYS.—July 13th.—Spilsby Rural Dis-trict Council. £200.—Mr. G. Beaumont Walker, clerk to the council.

CLERK OF WORKS.—July 16th.—Barnet Urban District Council.—Mr. H. W. Poole, clerk to the council.

WATERWORKS ENGINEER.—July 16th.—Lincoln Corpora-tion. £250.—Mr. H. K. Hellh, deputy town clerk.

BOROUGH ENGINEER.— July 22nd.— Corporation of Pietermaritzburg, Natal, South Africa. £800.—Messrs. Ford Brothers, 14 Southampton-street, Fitzroy-square, London, W.

CITY ENGINEER.—August 31st.—Corporation of Wellington, New Zealand. £800.—Agent-General for New Zealand, London.

## COMPETITIONS.

*Advertisements which are received too late for classification cannot be included in these summaries until the following week.*

WARRINGTON.—July 2nd.—Erection of a police station, court house, &c. £100, £50 and £25.—Mr. Thomas Longdin, borough engineer and surveyor.

EAST RIDING.—July 16th.—Extension of the county offices at Beverley and the erection of a new register office, for the county council. £30, £20 and £10.—Mr. John Bickersteth, county clerk, County Hall, Beverley.

## MUNICIPAL CONTRACTS OPEN.

*Advertisements which are received too late for classification cannot be included in these summaries until the following week.*

CHESTER-LE-STREET.—July 2nd.—Erection of an administrative block at the isolation hospital, for the rural district council.—Mr. W. T. Jones, architect, 7A North Bailey, Durham.

WOLVERHAMPTON.—July 2nd.—Construction of pipe sewers, manholes, lampholes, &c., in Melbourne-street, Ash-street and Green-lane, and about 200 manholes and lampholes in various parts of the borough. —Mr. J. W. Bradley, borough engineer and surveyor.

EVOY.—July 2nd.—Laying of a cast-iron outfall sewer, the provision and erection of iron storage tanks, pumping station, boiler-house, engines, boilers, pumps and other works in connection with the sewerage of the town, for the urban district council.—Messrs. Bailey, Denton, Son & Lawford, Palace Chambers, Westminster, London, S.W.

HARROW.—July 4th.—Supply of about 1,600 tons of 1½-in. or 2-in. handbroken granite and ¾in. granite chippings, for the urban district council.—Mr. T. Charles, surveyor to the council.

BELFAST.—July 4th.—Extension of the electric lighting station, Abercorn Basin, for the Harbour Commissioners.—Mr. G. F. L. Giles, harbour engineer.

WALSALL.—July 4th.—Construction of about 6,600 yards of 9-in. and 12-in. stoneware pipe sewers and 1,800 yards of 8-in. cast-iron hydraulic main in connection with the sewerage of the parish of Aldridge, for the rural district council.—Mr. J. Edward Willcox, Union Chambers, 63 Temple-row, Birmingham.

ASTON MANOR.—July 4th.—Alterations and additions to the administrative building at the infectious diseases hospital, Upper Witton, for the urban district council.—Mr. H. Richardson, A.M.I.C.E., engineer and surveyor to the council.

GLOUCESTER.—July 4th.—Erection of a public library and other buildings in connection with the technical schools in Brunswick-road, for the corporation.—Messrs. Waller & Son, 17 College-green, Gloucester.

CAERPHILLY.—July 4th.—Construction of about 8,500 lineal yards of 16-in., 18-in. and 21-in. stoneware and iron pipe sewers from Tenghenydd to Gwaun-y-bara sewage farm, for the urban district council.— Mr. A. O. Harpur, surveyor to the council.

BERMONDSEY.—July 4th.—Supply of 40,000 bricks.—Mr. Frank Sumner, vestry surveyor.

LONDON.—July 4th.—Construction of the superstructure of a lunatic asylum for 2,000 patients and staff at Horton, near Epsom, Surrey, for the county council.—The Clerk of the Asylum Committee of the County Council, 21 Whitehall-place, London, S.W.

SOUTHAMPTON.—July 5th.—Erection of a cart-shed at the wharf at Chapel.—Mr. W. B. G. Bennett, borough engineer.

BOOTLE.—July 5th.—Erection of an electric light station on land in Pine-grove.—Mr. J. A. Crowther, borough engineer.

FLEETWOOD.—July 6th.—Supply and delivery of a portable boiler and steam engine, for the urban district council.—Mr. Joseph Tildesley, clerk to the council.

HUDDERSFIELD.—July 6th.—Supply of 6 miles of cast-iron socket pipes of 12-in. diameter.—Mr. F. C. Lloyd, town clerk.

HOVE.—July 6th.—Road making and other works in Walsingham-road and the laying of asphalte paving in Queen's-gardens, from Grand-avenue to Palmeira-mews, a distance of about 870 yards.—Mr. H. H. Scott, town surveyor.

WAKEFIELD.—July 6th.—Wood paving and other works in Bond-street, Cliff-parade, College Grove-road, Eastmoor-road, Burton-street and Balne-lane.—Mr. Chas. Jas. Hudson, town clerk.

LONDON.—July 6th.—Erection of the first section of the proposed permanent North-Eastern Hospital, St. Anne's-road, Tottenham, for the Metropolitan Asylums Board.—Mr. T. Duncombe Mann, clerk to the board.

CARMARTHEN.—July 7th.—Supply of 530 yards of 6-in. cast-iron pipes, six 2½-in. fire hydrants and ten flanged and socketted junction pipes.— Mr. F. J. Finglah, borough surveyor.

KINGSTON-UPON-THAMES.— July 7th.— Construction of an underground concrete chamber for an electricity sub-station under the footway in Coombe-road.—Mr. Harold A. Winser, town clerk.

MAIDENHEAD.—July 11th.—Making-up of Ray Park-avenue.—Mr. Percy Johns, A.M.I.C.E., borough surveyor.

HORNSEY.—July 11th.—Erection of a fire engine station at Muswell Hill, for the urban district council.—Mr. E. J. Lovegrove, surveyor to the council.

LYMINGTON.—July 11th.—Erection of a small bridge near Winchelsea, in the parish of Brookenhurst, for the rural district council.—Mr. T. J. Fripp, surveyor to the council.

SOUTHAMPTON.—July 12th.—Supply and delivery of cast-iron pipes and special castings required during the ensuing twelve months, for the corporation.—Mr. W. Matthews, waterworks engineer.

HUDDERSFIELD.—July 13th.—Erection of an isolation block at the sanatorium, Mill-hill.—Mr. F. C. Lloyd, town clerk.

ST. HELENS.—July 13th.—Supply of various pumping plant to raise 1,500,000 gallons of water per day, for the corporation.—Mr. J. J. Lackland, A.M.I.C.E., water engineer.

TWICKENHAM.—July 13th.—Various sewering and road making works, for the urban district council.—Mr. G. B. Laffan, engineer and surveyor to the council.

WEST BRIDGFORD.—July 16th.—Laying of about 2,460 yards of 12-in. and 9-in. Hassell's pipe sewers, 15-in. iron pipe sewers and 9-in. surface-water drains, for the urban district council.—Mr. Wm. Pare, surveyor to the council.

NELSON.—July 16th.—Construction of two storage reservoirs in Ogden and Black Moss valleys about 4 miles from the town, for the corporation.—Messrs. Newton, 17 Cooper-street, Manchester.

SOUTH CROSLAND.—July 18th.—Construction of additional sewerage works, comprising the laying of over 1 mile of stoneware pipe sewers, varying in size from 6 in. to 9 in., for the urban district council.—Mr. W. H. Radford, Angel-row, Nottingham.

HONLEY.—July 18th.—Construction of 3½ miles of stoneware pipe sewers, varying in size from 15 in. to 7 in., for the urban district council.—Mr. W. H. Radford, Angel-row, Nottingham.

PORTSMOUTH.—July 19th.—Supply and fixing of cast-iron valve seatings to the pumps at the Eastney pumping station.—Mr. Alexander Hellard, town clerk.

LONDON.—July 19th.—Construction of underground conveniences in Fenchurch-street.—Sir J. B. Monckton, town clerk.

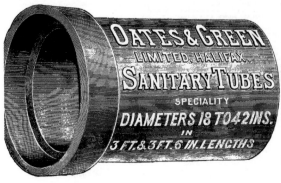

LEWES.—July 23rd.—Supply of 500 tons of 3-in. broken blue Guernsey, Cherbourg or Belgian granite, 100 tons of coarse granite screenings, 650 tons of broken surface-picked flints and 150 tons of Piddinghoe gravel.—Mr. Montague S. Blaker, town clerk.

WEST HAM.—July 26th.—Construction of about 1,500 lineal yards of sewers, 7 ft., 6 ft. and 3 ft. 6 in. diameter.—Mr. Lewis Angell, borough surveyor.

WEST HAM.—July 26th.—Making-up of Freemantle-road, Haslemere-road, New-street (Plaistow) and Old-street (Plaistow).—Mr. Lewis Angell, borough surveyor.

WEST HAM.—July 26th.—Erection of twenty-nine working-classes' dwellings in Hermit-road, Plaistow.—Mr. Lewis Angell, borough surveyor.

STRATFORD-ON-AVON.—Supply and delivery of about 130 tons of 5-in., 4-in. and 3-in. cast-iron pipes, together with special castings, for the rural district council.—Mr. J. E. Willcox, A.M.I.C.E., Union Chambers, Birmingham.

## TENDERS.

*ACCEPTED.*

BOURNEMOUTH.—For the supply of 220 yards of wrought-iron unclimbable fencing, &c., for the proposed new Boscombe pleasure grounds.—Mr. F. W. Lacey, M.I.C.E., borough engineer and surveyor:—

| | Fencing, per yard. | Extra for raking. | One pair Gates, 6 ft. high. | One pair Gates, 6 ft. high. | Single Gate. | Corner Post. |
|---|---|---|---|---|---|---|
| | s. d. | d. | £ s. d. | £ s. d. | £ s. d. | £ s. d. |
| Johnson Bros. & Co., Ld. ... | 15 9 | 0 6 | 27 10 0 | 26 0 0 | 24 0 0 | 9 10 0 |
| Taylor & Gardiner ... | 13 0 | 0 6 | 22 10 0 | 21 10 0 | 15 10 0 | 4 0 0 |
| F. Morton & Co., Ld. ... | 13 0 | 0 8 | 16 2 6 | 15 12 6 | 13 7 6 | 3 8 9 |
| Bayliss, Jones & Bayliss ... | 11 7 | 0 6 | 16 0 0 | 15 5 0 | 11 10 0 | 3 15 0 |
| Hill & Smith* | 11 0 | 0 4 | 14 15 0 | 14 5 0 | 10 10 0 | 3 3 0 |

BOURNEMOUTH.—For the supply of oak cleft fencing for the proposal new Boscombe pleasure grounds.—Mr. F. W. Lacey, M.I.C.E., borough engineer and surveyor:—

| | | | |
|---|---|---|---|
| Lunn Brothers, Brockenhurst ... | ... | ... | £114 |
| J. Stenning & Son, 11 Clement's-lane, E.C. ... | ... | ... | 114 |
| F. Ayles, Ringwood* ... | ... | ... | 94 |

HIGH WYCOMBE.—For various sewage outfall works.—Mr. T. J. Rushbrooke, borough surveyor:—

| | | | | |
|---|---|---|---|---|
| Meredith, Gloucester | ... | ... | ... | £5,309 |
| C. Ford, Harlesden | ... | ... | ... | 5,134 |
| Bentley & Loch, Leicester | ... | ... | ... | 4,602 |
| G. H. Gibson, Wycombe | ... | ... | ... | 4,217 |
| G. Bell, Tottenham | ... | ... | ... | 4,139 |
| Lee & Son, Wycombe | ... | ... | ... | 3,899 |

NORTH RIDING.—For the widening of the Leven county bridge, near Yarm, for the county council.—Mr. Walker Stead, A.M.I.C.E., county surveyor, Northallerton.

| | | | |
|---|---|---|---|
| A. Atkinson & Co., Yarm-road, Stockton | ... | ... | £998 |
| W. Blackburn, Broughton, Malton* | ... | ... | 760 |
| T. Pearson, Linthorpe, Middlesbrough... | ... | ... | 751 |

PLYMOUTH.—Erection of a chimney and fans at Prince Rock in connection with the new electricity works.—Mr. James Paton, borough engineer and surveyor:—

| | | | |
|---|---|---|---|
| Locking Joint Company, Reading | ... | ... | £3,998 |
| Finch, Plymouth | ... | ... | 2,905 |
| Skinner, Plymouth | ... | ... | 2,631 |
| Goddard, Massey & Warner, Traffic-street, Nottingham* | ... | 2,523 |
| Dart & Pollard, Paignton† | ... | ... | 2,170 |

† Withdrawn.

SUNBURY-ON-THAMES.—Accepted for the supply and delivery of various road materials, for the urban district council.—Mr. Harold F. Coales, surveyor to the council :—

Granite.—J. Mowlem & Co., Westminster, 11s. 1d. per ton at station ; 12s. 10d. at wharf.

Flints.—Wills & Packham, Sittingbourne, 7s. per yard at wharf.

Kerbing.—Blickfeldt & Co., 16 Water-lane, E.C., 1s. 4½d. per foot at station.

TEIGNMOUTH.—For the providing and laying of about 1,700 yards of 14-in. gas main, for the urban district council.—Mr. Chris. Jones, engineer and surveyor to the council :—

| | | | | |
|---|---|---|---|---|
| W. C. Woodward & Co., Gloucester | ... | ... | ... | £2,432 |
| J. Shaddock, Plymouth | ... | ... | ... | 2,337 |
| Rafarpe & Co., Barnstaple | ... | ... | ... | 2,291 |
| J. Dickson, Exeter | ... | ... | ... | 2,197 |
| W. J. Burden, Teignmouth | ... | ... | ... | 2,113 |
| J. Fisher, Plymouth | ... | ... | ... | 1,811 |
| Hawkins & Best, Teignmouth* | ... | ... | ... | 1,782 |
| Willey & Co., Exeter | ... | ... | ... | 1,760 |

## MEETINGS.

JULY.

2.—London Geological Field Class: Excursion to Sevenoaks.

## NOTICES.

THE SURVEYOR AND MUNICIPAL AND COUNTY ENGINEER may be ordered direct, through any of Messrs. Smith & Son's book-stalls, or of any newsagent in the United Kingdom. Applications to the Offices for single copies by post must in all cases be accompanied by stamps.

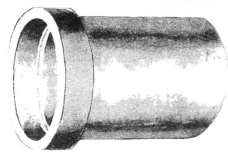

*The Prepaid Subscription (including postage) is as follows :*

|  | Twelve Months. | Six Months. | Three Months. |
|---|---|---|---|
| United Kingdom ... ... | 15s. | 7s. 6d. | 3s. 9d. |
| Continent, the Colonies, India, | | | |
| United States, &c. ... ... | 19s. | 9s. 6d. | 4s. 9d. |

The *International News Company, 83 and 85 Duane-street,
New York City; The Toronto News Company, Toronto; and
The Montreal News Company, Montreal,* have been appointed
agents in the United States and Canada for the sale of THE
SURVEYOR. *A thin paper edition is printed for circulation
abroad.*

EDITORIAL OFFICES:
ST. BRIDE'S HOUSE, 24 BRIDE-LANE, FLEET-STREET,
LONDON, E.C.

OFFICE FOR ADVERTISEMENTS:
13 NEW STREET HILL, FLEET STREET, LONDON, E.C.

PUBLISHING OFFICES:
13 NEW STREET HILL, FLEET STREET, LONDON, E.C.

## APPOINTMENTS OPEN.

### COUNTY BOROUGH OF HUDDERSFIELD.
TEMPORARY SURVEYING ASSISTANT.

Wanted, in the Borough Engineer's office, an experienced
Assistant, qualified to undertake the revision of the 1/2500
and 1/500 ordnance maps of the town.

He must have a thorough practical knowledge of trigonometry, levelling, surveying, and be a good draughtsman.

Salary at the rate of £120 per annum.

For further particulars please apply to the Borough Engineer.

Applications, in the handwriting of candidates, giving full
particulars of present and previous occupation, age, &c., accompanied by not more than four testimonials, endorsed
"Temporary Assistant," to be addressed to Mr. K. F. Campbell, A.M.INST.C.E., Borough Engineer and Surveyor, not later
than Tuesday, the 12th day of July.

Canvassing will disqualify.

(By order)
F. C. LLOYD,
Town Hall, Huddersfield.          Town Clerk.
June 22, 1898.

### SPILSBY RURAL DISTRICT COUNCIL.
APPOINTMENT OF SURVEYOR OF HIGHWAYS.

Applications are invited for the appointment of Surveyor
of Highways for the above district, which comprises 500 miles
of roads or thereabouts, at a salary of £200 a year, inclusive
of means of locomotion and all other expenses excepting
office accommodation, stationery and stamps.

The Council will provide a clerk.

The person elected must reside at Spilsby, be a good accountant, have a thorough knowledge of the management of
roads and must devote his whole time to the work.

He will be required to enter into a written agreement and
find a guarantee in the sum of £300 for the faithful discharge
of his duties, which will commence on the 1st day of October
next.

Application, in the handwriting of the candidate, with
copies of not more than three testimonials of recent date,
must be delivered at my office not later than Wednesday, the
13th day of July next, endorsed "Surveyor of Highways."

Preference will be given to candidates who are associate
members of the Institution of Civil Engineers or who have
obtained the certificate of competency granted by the
Incorporated Association of Municipal and County Engineers.

All canvassing prohibited, and any attempt to evade this
prohibition will disqualify.

(By order)
G. BEAUMONT WALKER,
Clerk to the Council.
Spilsby.
June 27, 1898.

### BOROUGH OF SHOREDITCH.
SUPERINTENDING FOREMAN.

An Experienced Foreman required to take control of certain
sewering work which the Vestry have resolved to carry out by
employing their own labour. Salary, 3 guineas per week.

The engagement will be a temporary one (not less than
three months), and preference will be given to candidates
who have held a similar position.

Applications, by letter, in own handwriting, stating age,
qualifications, and enclosing copies of at least two recent
testimonials, to be sent to the Surveyor, Town Hall, Old-
street, E.C., not later than Wednesday, 6th July, 1898, endorsed "Sewer Foreman."

## COUNTY BOROUGH OF HUDDERSFIELD.
### ROAD FOREMEN.

The Corporation require the services of Two Road Foremen. Applicants must have had previous experience in the repair and maintenance of macadamised roads and be thoroughly conversant with all kinds of paving, and must also be competent to set out and measure up works, and keep daily accounts of all labour and materials used.

The persons appointed must be prepared to reside within their respective districts.

Salary after the rate of £100 per annum.

Applications, in the handwriting of candidates, giving full particulars of present and previous occupation, age, &c., accompanied by three testimonials, endorsed "Road Foreman," to be addressed to Mr. K. F. Campbell, A.M.INST.C.E., Borough Engineer and Surveyor, Huddersfield, not later than Tuesday, the 12th day of July.

Canvassing will disqualify.

(By order)
    F. C. LLOYD,
    Town Clerk.

June 22, 1898.

## COUNTY BOROUGH OF HUDDERSFIELD.
### APPOINTMENT OF CHIEF ENGINEERING AND SURVEYING ASSISTANT.

The Corporation invite applications for the appointment of Chief Engineering and Surveying Assistant, at a salary of £180 per annum.

The person appointed must be thoroughly qualified to fulfil the duties of the office, particulars of which may be obtained on application to the Borough Engineer.

Application, in candidate's own handwriting, giving full particulars as to experience, age, &c., and accompanied by not more than four recent testimonials, to be addressed to Mr. K. F. Campbell, A.M.INST.C.E., Borough Engineer and Surveyor, not later than Tuesday, the 12th day of July, endorsed "Engineering Assistant."

Canvassing members of the Council is strictly prohibited, and will immediately disqualify any candidate.

(By order)
    F. C. LLOYD,
    Town Clerk.

Huddersfield.
June 22, 1898.

## COUNTY BOROUGH OF SALFORD.

Wanted, a Clerk of Works, with special knowledge of Buildings, Concrete Tanks, Cast-Iron Pipes, Valves, &c., to superintend the completion of the Salford sewage works. Salary, £4 4s. a week.

Applications, endorsed "Clerk of Works, Sewage Works," accompanied by not more than four recent testimonials, must be delivered to me not later than 3 p.m. on Wednesday, the 13th July next.

(By order)
    SAMUEL BROWN,
    Town Clerk.

Town Hall, Salford.
    June 24, 1898.

## URBAN DISTRICT OF WALLASEY.
### TEMPORARY SURVEYORS.

Wanted, in the Surveyor's Department, two thoroughly competent Surveyors and Levellers for about a three months' engagement, at £2 12s. 6d. each per week. Must be expeditious and accurate surveyors, and good draughtsmen.

Applications, stating age, qualifications and references, to be forwarded to the District Engineer and Surveyor, Public Offices, Egremont, Cheshire, not later than Friday, July 8, 1898.

(By order)
    H. W. COOK,
    Clerk and Solicitor.

Public Offices, Egremont, Cheshire.

## CITY OF NORWICH.

A thoroughly-experienced Foreman Pavior, accustomed to tramway construction, is required to act as Clerk of Works on the new tramways now being constructed. Wages, £3 per week. Engagement subject to one month's notice on either side.

Candidates must be capable of giving heights and regulating shapes of roads.

Applications, in writing, stating age and experience, must be sent to me not later than Monday, July 11th. Copies only of three testimonials may be sent to me.

ARTHUR E. COLLINS, ASSOC.M.INST.C.E.,
    City Engineer.

Guildhall, Norwich.
    June 24, 1898.

## THE CORPORATION OF BIRMINGHAM.

The Public Works Committee are prepared to receive applications for the appointment of Chief Road Surveyor in the city engineer and surveyor's department. Candidates, whose age must not exceed forty years, must be thoroughly qualified persons, having had active practical experience in the construction, scavenging and maintenance of roads and streets and of the various classes of pavement used therefor. They must also have had the management of large bodies of workmen, and be able to supervise the setting out and measuring up of works and preparation of estimates.

It will be a condition that the person appointed shall subscribe to the superannuation scheme, and shall devote the whole of his time to the duties of his office.

The salary will commence at £300 per annum, and rise by annual increments of £20 to £400 per annum. A horse and trap will be provided to help him to carry out his duties efficiently.

Applications, in the candidate's own handwriting, stating age, qualifications, present and past experience, together with not more than four recent testimonials, should be sent to the undersigned not later than noon on the 13th of July next.

Canvassing either directly or indirectly will be considered a disqualification.

JOHN PRICE,
City Engineer and Surveyor.
The Council House, Birmingham.
June 25, 1898.

## COUNTY BOROUGH OF HUDDERSFIELD.
### APPOINTMENT OF ASSISTANT BUILDING AND DRAINAGE INSPECTOR.

The Corporation invite applications for the appointment of Assistant Building and Drainage Inspector, at a salary of £120 per annum. Candidates must be between twenty-seven and forty years of age, and must have had previous similar experience. Statement of duties may be obtained on application to the Borough Engineer.

Written applications only, in candidate's handwriting, with particulars of present employment, experience, &c., and copies of not more than four recent testimonials, to be addressed to Mr. K. F. Campbell, A.M.INST.C.E., Borough Engineer and Surveyor, Huddersfield, on or before the 12th day of July, endorsed "Building Inspector."

Canvassing will disqualify.

(By order)
F. C. LLOYD,
Town Clerk.
Town Hall, Huddersfield.
June 22, 1898.

## CORPORATION OF PIETERMARITZBURG.
### BOROUGH ENGINEER.

Applications are invited for the appointment of Borough Engineer for the City and Borough of Pietermaritzburg, in the Colony of Natal, South Africa.

The gentleman appointed will be required to devote his whole time to the duties of his office. He must be a thoroughly competent engineer and surveyor, and must have had practical experience in a similar position.

The salary will be £800 per annum, without extras or allowances, and will be payable monthly. Offices, assistants, instruments and stationery will be provided by the corporation.

The city contains an area of 1,000 acres and the borough 27,000 acres. The population is 24,000 and the rateable value £2,250,000. There are 33 miles of streets in the city. Sewerage works, macadamising of roads, paving of footpaths, surface-drainage works, and additional water supply are either in progress or in immediate contemplation. The lighting of the city by electricity is now being proceeded with under the Borough Electrical Engineer.

Applications, stating the age and particulars as to experience of the applicant, &c., with original testimonials (which will be returned), must reach the undersigned not later than Wednesday, the 31st August, 1898, and be endorsed "Borough Engineer."

The appointment will be subject to passing an examination by a medical officer appointed by the corporation.

The appointment will be for three years, and thereafter terminable by three months' notice on either side.

The successful applicant will be required to take office as soon as possible after receipt of an intimation that the appointment has been conferred upon him.

Applicants residing in the United Kingdom are required to send their applications in duplicate to the London agents of the Corporation (Messrs. Ford Brothers, 14 Southampton-street, Fitzroy-square, London, W.) not later than 22nd July, 1898. A copy of the testimonials will be required in addition to the originals.

In the event of an applicant residing in the United Kingdom being selected the agent will be advised by cable, and will communicate with the gentleman appointed, who will be required to immediately proceed to Maritzburg; £50 will be allowed for passage from London; salary to commence from date of taking office in Maritzburg.

(By order)
STEPHEN STRANACK,
Town Clerk.
Town Office, Pietermaritzburg,
May 26, 1898.

ASSISTANT SURVEYOR.—There is a vacancy for an Assistant to the Surveyor of a very healthy urban district, where a thorough insight into the duties of the office can be obtained. No premium. A small salary of about 15s. weekly would be given. Applicants should be well educated and not under eighteen years of age.—Apply to " K.," Town Hall, Farnborough, Hants.

THREE ASSISTANT SURVEYORS required for service in the Surveyor-General's Department, West Coast of Africa; must be good levellers and draughtsmen, competent to design and superintend the erection of buildings and construction of roads, bridges and other public works, and to prepare plans and specifications. Commencing salary, £300 to £400 per annum, with free passages out and home.— Apply, by letter only, with copies (not originals) of testimonials, to W. SHELFORD, 35A Great George-street, Westminster, S.W.

## TENDERS WANTED.

MIDDLETON CORPORATION. The Middleton Corporation are prepared to receive tenders for Sewering, Draining, Paving, Curbing and Flagging Brewster-street from Rochdale-road to Church-street, and Church-street from Cheapside to Dawson-street. Quantities: About 157 yards of 9-in., 6-in. and 4-in. drains; 1,120 yards paving, 530 yards flagging and 330 yards curbing.

Plans, sections, details and specifications may be seen, and quantities obtained, on application to Mr. Welburn, Borough Surveyor, at his office, Town Hall, Middleton, any morning between 9 and 10 o'clock.

Sealed tenders, on forms supplied, fully priced out, must be delivered at my office, addressed to the Chairman of the Health and Surveyor's Committee, and endorsed " Street Works," not later than the 6th July, 1898.

The Corporation do not bind themselves to accept the lowest or any tender.

FREDERICK ENTWISTLE,
Town Clerk.
Town Hall, Middleton.
June 22, 1898.

BOROUGH OF MAIDENHEAD.

### PRIVATE STREET WORKS ACT, 1892.

#### TO ROAD CONTRACTORS AND OTHERS.

The Town Council of the Borough of Maidenhead is prepared to receive tenders for Putting in Order and Making Good a certain Street, called Ray Park-avenue, situated within the district.

The plans and specifications may be seen, and a form of tender and copy of the bill of quantities obtained, at the office of the undersigned, on the payment of the sum of £1 1s., which will be returned on receipt of a bona-fide tender.

Tenders, sealed and endorsed " Tender for Ray Park-avenue," must be delivered to me not later than 5 p.m. on Monday, the 11th day of July, 1898.

The Council do not undertake to accept the lowest or any tender.

(By order)
PERCY JOHNS, A.M.I.C.E.,
Borough Surveyor.
Guildhall, Maidenhead.
June 21, 1898.

BOROUGH OF LEWES.
TO STONE MERCHANTS, FARMERS, &c.

The Town Council of this Borough invite tenders for the supply of 500 tons of 2-in. Broken Blue Guernsey, Cherbourg or Belgian Granite, 100 tons of Coarse Granite Screenings, 650 tons of Broken Surface-Picked Flints and 150 tons of Piddinghoe Gravel.

Forms of tender and specification may be had, and any further information obtained, at the Borough Surveyor's office, Town Hall, Lewes.

Sealed tenders, endorsed " Tender for ———," must be left at my office on or before the 23rd July, 1898.

Power is reserved to reject the lowest or any tender.

(By order)
MONTAGUE S. BLAKER,
Town Clerk.
Town Clerk's Office, Lewes.
June 2, 1898.

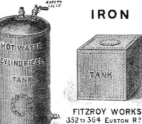

ASTON MANOR URBAN DISTRICT
COUNCIL.
TO CONTRACTORS.

The Council is prepared to receive tenders for certain Alterations and Additions to the Administrative Building at the Infectious Diseases Hospital, Upper Witton.

Plans and specification may be seen and bill of quantities obtained at the Surveyor's Offices, Council House, Aston Manor, after Monday, the 27th inst.

Tenders, under seal, endorsed "Hospital," and addressed to the Chairman of the Health Committee, Council House, Aston Manor, to be delivered on or before Monday, July 4, 1898, at noon.

The Council do not bind themselves to accept the lowest or any tender.

The contract to be entered into by the person whose tender is accepted will contain the clause adopted by the Council as to the standard rate of wages.

H. RICHARDSON, A.M.I.C.E.,
Engineer and Surveyor to the Council.
Surveyor's Department,
Council House, Aston Manor.
June 23, 1898.

TWICKENHAM URBAN DISTRICT
COUNCIL.
TO SEWER AND ROAD CONTRACTORS.

The Twickenham Urban District Council are prepared to receive separate tenders for the following works in the district of Twickenham :—

(1) The construction of about 1,400 ft. of 15-in., about 3,660 ft. of 12-in. and 1,070 ft. of 9-in. Stoneware Pipe Sewers, with manholes and other works, for the sewerage of Richmond-road and for the surface-water drainage of Orleansroad, Chapel-road, Montpelier-road, Richmond-road and Crow-road.

(2) The forming, making, levelling, sewering, paving, kerbing, channelling and making a New Street and branches therefrom, about 1,100 ft. in length and 40 ft. in width.

(3) The grubbing of banks, forming, widening, metalling, kerbing, paving and making-up of Turks-road and the construction of about 1,330 ft. of 12-in. and 1,210 ft. of 9-in. Stoneware Surface-Water Pipe Sewers, with manholes and other works, in The Avenue and Turks-road.

Forms of tender, on which tenders alone will be considered, can be obtained, and the drawings and specifications can be seen, at the office of Mr. G. B. Laffan, C.E., Engineer and Surveyor to the Council, Town Hall, Twickenham, between the hours of 10 a.m. and 5 p.m., and on Saturdays between 10 a.m. and 1 p.m.

Sealed and endorsed tenders, marked respectively "Richmond-road Sewers," "New-street" and Turks-road." must reach me not later than 4 o'clock in the afternoon of Wednesday, the 13th July next.

The Council do not bind themselves to accept the lowest or any tender.

(By order)
H. JASON SAUNDERS,
Clerk to the Council.
Town Hall, Twickenham.
June 24, 1898.

CITY OF WAKEFIELD.

*WOOD PAVING AND NEW CAUSEWAYS.*

TO CONTRACTORS.

The Council of the City of Wakefield are prepared to receive tenders for :—

(1) The providing and laying down of about 1,739 square yards of Australian Hardwood Paving in Bond-street and Cliff-parade, Wakefield.

(2) The construction of New Causeways, including the providing and laying of about 4,166 square yards of Elland Edge 3-in. Flags, 1,867 lineal yards of 12-in. by 8-in. Kerb stone, and 1,660 lineal yards of 8-in. Sett Channelling, 18 in. broad, and other work in connection therewith in College Grove-road, Eastmoor-road, Burton-street and Balne-lane, Wakefield.

The plans and specifications may be seen, and all further information obtained, at the office of the City Surveyor, Town Hall, Wakefield.

Tenders for all or any part of the works, under cover, addressed to the Town Clerk, Wakefield, and marked "Tender for Paving, &c.," to be delivered on or before Wednesday, July 6th next.

The Council do not pledge themselves to accept the lowest or any tender.

CHAS. JAS. HUDSON,
Town Clerk.
Town Hall, Wakefield.
June 24, 1898.

O. CLAUDE ROBSON, M.INST.C.E.,

President of the Incorporated Association of Municipal and County Engineers, 1898-9.

# The Surveyor

## And Municipal and County Engineer.

Vol. XIV., No. 338.     LONDON, JULY 8, 1898.     Weekly, Price 3d.

## Minutes of Proceedings.

**Appropriation of Electric Lighting Profits.**

A good deal has been said in these columns at different times as to what is a proper appropriation of profits derived from a municipal electric lighting scheme. The views that have been put forward have been in favour of giving some of the profits of a successful municipal scheme to the general ratepayer, who may not always be a consumer of electricity. A paper on "Appropriation of Profits and Repayment of Loans" was communicated by Bailie Wm. Maclay, convener of the Electricity Committee of the Glasgow Corporation, to the recent meeting of the Municipal Electrical Association, and the conclusions that the worthy bailie arrives at are somewhat antagonistic to the views which we have already put forward. In Glasgow it appears to be the custom of the corporation to allow each of the commercial departments to dispose of any surplus that may result from a successful year's business. They apparently recognise the fact that not one of these departments exists to make a profit, as is the case with a private commercial concern, but rather that it has been called into existence for the benefit of the community as a whole. In other words, whatever the profits that any of the famous Glasgow municipal departments make, it is not devoted to the relief of taxation. For example, the Electricity Committee last year in Glasgow had a profit of £18,000. In disposing of this surplus they first of all put aside £2,770 for depreciation on somewhat old plant, £1,500 was devoted to renewals of machinery, and £935 for probable renewals of ordinary plant and machinery. They also appropriated about £5,500 of the large surplus for ordinary depreciation of plant and machinery, making in all the sum of £10,705 for depreciation and renewals on the stations. It may be taken, therefore, that the ratepayers do not in any case directly benefit from the electricity works unless they are consumers, when, of course, there is an annual reduction in the charge of electricity; and there is, moreover, street lighting by electricity, which is supplied a good deal under cost price. Needless to say, the Glasgow methods are widely different from those which obtain in most parts of England, the general view taken on this side of the Border being that if, after supplying the consumer at moderate prices and providing the necessary fund for depreciation, renewals and sinking account, there is any profit it should be devoted to the reduction of rates. As we have already maintained in these columns, there is at the present moment a good deal to be urged in favour of such a course. It must not be forgotten that however much electric lighting may eventually become a universal illuminant, it is a light of luxury at the present time. In other words, the consumers of electricity, compared with the number of ratepayers, are in a very small minority. Take, for example, the case of Bristol, which was alluded to by Councillor Pearson when discussing the worthy bailie's paper. It was pointed out that the town

of Bristol has 50,000 ratepayers, and of this number only 1,000 are consumers of electricity, yet Bristol is one of the most successful electric lighting systems in the country, and has been in existence some few years. Therefore it is obvious that a considerable time must elapse before the benefits of electric light works are brought directly within the reach of the majority of the ratepayers. In starting electric light works the whole credit of the town's ratepayers is pledged, and in those towns in which the electric lighting works have not paid for two or three years it has been necessary to make a call upon the rates to meet the losses on the year's working. Consumers, as consumers, were not taxed because the works were running at a loss, and the whole of the ratepayers were called upon to find the necessary funds—a common experience in a municipality undertaking electric lighting. It is impossible that a ratepayer should be benefitted at the expense of the consumer, because the Electric Lighting Act clearly states that after a 5 per cent. profit has been made on the works the surplus shall be devoted to reducing the price of electricity, which is a sufficient safeguard against a consumer being unfairly treated. It is quite true that the matter may assume a different phase when electric lighting becomes more universal, and if it were possible to devote the surplus to carrying out extensions on a very large scale, with the ultimate idea of bringing electricity within the reach of all, then one might argue that it would be better to devote the surplus for such a purpose rather than hand it over to the ratepayers; but as things exist at the present moment it is certainly desirable that some return should be made to the ratepayer for the risk that he has undertaken. The question of repayment of loans is a very important one, and probably is much more keenly felt in the majority of English towns than it is in the case of Glasgow. The general rule is that a municipality borrowing money for electrical purposes shall repay the loan in a period of twenty-five years. There has been some variation of this in different towns. For example, Lancaster has permission to obtain a loan for a period of forty years, and Leeds Corporation have obtained their loan on similar terms; but Bailie Maclay distinctly stated in the discussion that in Glasgow the money for municipal developments is obtained by issuing stock, a good deal of which is interminable, and even if they raise money on stock which is terminable at a certain specified date when the term expires they simply obtain a fresh loan. Thus it will be seen that the conditions are very different to those which obtain in most English towns, and a comparison between Glasgow and an English city is rendered very difficult. Still, some reference was made to the case of Manchester by Bailie Maclay, who considered that the methods adopted in Manchester for appropriation of profits were distinctly inferior to those adopted in Glasgow; but an examination into the facts shows that Manchester is not only supplying

# The Surveyor

## And Municipal and County Engineer.

Vol. XIV., No. 338.  LONDON, JULY 8, 1898.  Weekly, Price 3d.

## Minutes of Proceedings.

**Appropriation of Electric Lighting Profits.**

A good deal has been said in these columns at different times as to what is a proper appropriation of profits derived from a municipal electric lighting scheme. The views that have been put forward have been in favour of giving some of the profits of a successful municipal scheme to the general ratepayer, who may not always be a consumer of electricity. A paper on "Appropriation of Profits and Repayment of Loans" was communicated by Bailie Wm. Maclay, convener of the Electricity Committee of the Glasgow Corporation, to the recent meeting of the Municipal Electrical Association, and the conclusions that the worthy bailie arrives at are somewhat antagonistic to the views which we have already put forward. In Glasgow it appears to be the custom of the corporation to allow each of the commercial departments to dispose of any surplus that may result from a successful year's business. They apparently recognise the fact that not one of these departments exists to make a profit, as is the case with a private commercial concern, but rather that it has been called into existence for the benefit of the community as a whole. In other words, whatever the profits that any of the famous Glasgow municipal departments make, it is not devoted to the relief of taxation. For example, the Electricity Committee last year in Glasgow had a profit of £18,000. In disposing of this surplus they first of all put aside £2,770 for depreciation on somewhat old plant, £1,500 was devoted to renewals of machinery, and £935 for probable renewals of ordinary plant and machinery. They also appropriated about £5,500 of the large surplus for ordinary depreciation of plant and machinery, making in all the sum of £10,705 for depreciation and renewals on the stations. It may be taken, therefore, that the ratepayers do not in any case directly benefit from the electricity works unless they are consumers, when, of course, there is an annual reduction in the charge of electricity; and there is, moreover, street lighting by electricity, which is supplied a good deal under cost price. Needless to say, the Glasgow methods are widely different from those which obtain in most parts of England, the general view taken on this side of the Border being that if, after supplying the consumer at moderate prices and providing the necessary fund for depreciation, renewals and sinking account, there is any profit it should be devoted to the reduction of rates. As we have already maintained in these columns, there is at the present moment a good deal to be urged in favour of such a course. It must not be forgotten that however much electric lighting may eventually become a universal illuminant, it is a light of luxury at the present time. In other words, the consumers of electricity, compared with the number of ratepayers, are in a very small minority. Take, for example, the case of Bristol, which was alluded to by Councillor Pearson when discussing the worthy bailie's paper. It was pointed out that the town of Bristol has 50,000 ratepayers, and of this number only 1,000 are consumers of electricity, yet Bristol is one of the most successful electric lighting systems in the country, and has been in existence some few years. Therefore it is obvious that a considerable time must elapse before the benefits of electric light works are brought directly within the reach of the majority of the ratepayers. In starting electric light works the whole credit of the town's ratepayers is pledged, and in those towns in which the electric lighting works have not paid for two or three years it has been necessary to make a call upon the rates to meet the losses on the year's working. Consumers, as consumers, were not taxed because the works were running at a loss, and the whole of the ratepayers were called upon to find the necessary funds—a common experience in a municipality undertaking electric lighting. It is impossible that a ratepayer should be benefitted at the expense of the consumer, because the Electric Lighting Act clearly states that after a 5 per cent. profit has been made on the works the surplus shall be devoted to reducing the price of electricity, which is a sufficient safeguard against a consumer being unfairly treated. It is quite true that the matter may assume a different phase when electric lighting becomes more universal, and if it were possible to devote the surplus to carrying out extensions on a very large scale, with the ultimate idea of bringing electricity within the reach of all, then one might argue that it would be better to devote the surplus for such a purpose rather than hand it over to the ratepayers; but as things exist at the present moment it is certainly desirable that some return should be made to the ratepayer for the risk that he has undertaken. The question of repayment of loans is a very important one, and probably is much more keenly felt in the majority of English towns than it is in the case of Glasgow. The general rule is that a municipality borrowing money for electrical purposes shall repay the loan in a period of twenty-five years. There has been some variation of this in different towns. For example, Lancaster has permission to obtain a loan for a period of forty years, and Leeds Corporation have obtained their loan on similar terms; but Bailie Maclay distinctly stated in the discussion that in Glasgow the money for municipal developments is obtained by issuing stock, a good deal of which is interminable, and even if they raise money on stock which is terminable at a certain specified date when the term expires they simply obtain a fresh loan. Thus it will be seen that the conditions are very different to those which obtain in most English towns, and a comparison between Glasgow and an English city is rendered very difficult. Still, some reference was made to the case of Manchester by Bailie Maclay, who considered that the methods adopted in Manchester for appropriation of profits were distinctly inferior to those adopted in Glasgow; but an examination into the facts shows that Manchester is not only supplying its electricity to consumers at a much lower price than the Glasgow municipal works, but it is, after putting heavy sums aside for depreciation and sinking fund, making a very considerable return to the ratepayers. Then, again, with regard to gas in Manchester, not only is the price charged a moderate one, but after paying off all the necessary charges the gas department is able to hand over no less a sum than £40,000 (per annum) to the city funds.

\*    \*    \*

**An Edinburgh Scheme.** It is a curious fact that the week which witnessed the visit of the Association of Municipal and County Engineers to the Scottish capital should have found the Edinburgh City Council occupied with the consideration of an imposing scheme of improvements upon which the "elders of the city" are not so unanimous as they were in the days of the old provost, "of ancient name and knightly fame and chivalrous degree," who roused his fellow-townsmen to guard the city after the fateful field of Flodden. The ranks of the elders are indeed very much divided, the Lord Provost being at the head of one contingent and the Treasurer the other. The present Lord Provost, unlike his grand old predecessor, who stirred the "burghers stout and true," is in this case the missionary of conciliation and peace; it is the Treasurer who calls to "fling the banner out once more." And, strange to relate, the cause of the divided counsels is a surfeit of riches. More than a year ago a local magnate, Mr. Usher, prompted by a desire to enhance the architectural beauties of the capital, and possibly by an ambition to perpetuate his name and fame in the public annals, handed over to the corporation a large sum of money to be devoted to the construction of a public hall, to be known as Usher Hall. The money was given on the condition that the corporation should find a site, and the finding of the site has been the difficulty. Even with the free gift of the structure itself, the question of site is a serious consideration. Various sites have been suggested, but at present there is a difference of opinion as to whether the hall should be erected on the canal basin at Port Hopetoun or on property at West Meadows. The first proposal was that it should be built on Castle-terrace; but that, as well as several other sites, which would have involved an expenditure of from £100,000 to £150,000, was abandoned on the ground of expense. In connection with the canal basin site there have been various difficulties. One of them was the unwillingness of the North British Railway Company to sell it. At first there was a belief that the company did not hold the property in absolute ownership, but this appears to have been ill-founded, and there is now no manner of doubt that they own the land in absolute fee. But there is another aspect of the scheme with regard to which there is diversity of opinion, and that is the utilisation of the area for the purpose of widening Fountainbridge-street and carrying out an eminently desirable public improvement in that locality. The question of application to Parliament for powers for that purpose was debated by the council at the last meeting. It is not disputed that if the canal basin could be obtained it would make an excellent site for the Usher Hall, and the other improvements contemplated would give the structure a splendid framework; but there is the refusal of the North British Railway Company to sell. The company have declared, through the voice of their general manager, that in no circumstances and on no conditions would they consent to part with the canal basin. As a matter of fact, they advance a strong argument for not parting with it. They are now making enormous additions to the Waverley station, but it becomes every day more apparent that by the time the station is completed it will be all too small for the expanding traffic, for which outlets will have to be sought in another direction. That other direction would naturally be

the site of the Port Hopetoun basin. The corporation can only obtain the basin by promoting a Bill in Parliament for powers of compulsory purchase, and while Parliament might be induced to pass the Bill for the contemplated Fountainbridge improvement scheme, it is most unlikely that it would deprive the railway company of such a valuable property for the mere erection of a hall. The Lord Provost admitted that it was not a pleasant thing to look at, to have the coal barges coming up and discharging their coal in that part of the town; neither was a railway goods station for that matter. Mr. Cooper, the burgh engineer, put the cost of the acquisition of Port Hopetoun and Port Hamilton at £150,000, and this included nothing for the closing of the canal. The Lord Provost added, in his speech at the last meeting of the council, that he would be quite pleased to acquire that ground, or any portion of it, but he was totally opposed to the city taking compulsory powers to obtain it, and he submitted a resolution to that effect. Treasurer M'Crae moved that application be made to Parliament in the ensuing session for powers to aquire the area for an improvement scheme, and that the Lord Provost's committee be instructed to enter into negotiations with that object in view. He described the Fountainbridge district as a discredit to the city, and commented upon its "lack of salubriousness" and the " air of decay " which, if not actually injurious to health, was not a healthy environment. A third motion was submitted to the meeting by Mr. Waterston in favour of the views of the ratepayers being ascertained, but this was defeated by forty votes to three. When the vote was taken upon the Lord Provost's resolution and the Treasurer's proposal the former was carried by thirty votes to twelve. Victory thus, for the present, lies with the Lord Provost. The alternative site for the Usher Hall, in West Meadows, seems to be very generally favoured. It may not be in all respects an ideal one, but it has its advantages. The building would be in an open space with Burntisland Links at hand; and economy and utility will probably outweigh other considerations.

\*    \*    \*

**District Surveyors and their Salaries.** Under the supervision of Mr. Heslop, county surveyor of Norfolk, the highways of that shire have reached a high degree of excellence. The chief credit must necessarily be due to the county surveyor, but that gentleman would probably be the first to acknowledge that the assistance which he has received from those subordinates who act in the capacity of district surveyors has been sufficiently great to call for special recognition from the county council in the shape of some additional remuneration. It is only just to that body to say that they also recognise the fact, but we cannot add that their recognition errs on the side of generosity. Very far from it. Each district surveyor who has served for three years or upwards to the satisfaction of the county surveyor is to receive an addition of £5 a year, which represents not quite 2s. a week. This decision was arrived at in preference to an amendment in favour of granting this small increase triennially until a maximum of £150 was reached. Each district surveyor has to keep a pony and trap, for which, we observe, Mr. Councillor Sapwell considers £25 an ample allowance. It appears that he has also heard of a gentleman who keeps a four-wheel carriage, a convertible car and a pony 14 hands high, the whole annual cost of these luxuries being only £28 3s. 4d., a fractional sum which smacks of a desire for minute accuracy. It may be that our experience of luxuries is not quite so extensive as we could desire, but we are certainly driven to the conclusion that Mr. Sapwell's friend must have a pronounced genius for doing things on the cheap. From the report of the discussion we observe also a general disposition to bring in the law of supply and demand by arguing that plenty of men could be obtained for the salaries now paid.

One of the most dangerous symptoms of the little knowledge against which we are proverbially warned is a disposition to drag into the affairs of daily life some cheap and shallow political economy. Nothing is more clearly indicative of a half-educated mental attitude, for it shows a hopeless misconception of the scope and object of what are generally known as the laws of political economy, which, like the so-called but equally misunderstood "laws of Nature," have been arrived at by thinkers simply as convenient formulæ or generalisations, and not as weapons to be thrown at the heads of our fellow-creatures. Only those who imagine vain things, and those whose thinking capacity is of the crudest, assume that the ordinary affairs of everyday life are or can be regulated in accordance with what they are pleased to think are "the laws of political economy"—a phrase to roll under the tongue—without reference to moral factors, which are the most powerful governing influences, no matter how much they may be hidden. We do not believe that such a view was ever taken by economists, and in any case it would scarcely be endorsed by the economists of the present day—more luminous and inspiriting, if less rigid, thinkers than their predecessors. The Norfolk councillors forget that, though remuneration is generally strictly limited, service is not, for the simple reason that in its highest form it can only be regulated by the conscientiousness of the worker and the self-respect which shows him that the adequate performance of his work is a duty which he owes to himself quite as much as to his employers. It is equally his duty to see that he is properly remunerated. These, we fear, are elementary and familiar truths, but it seems impossible to get them into the heads of many county councillors, or other councillors for that part of it. But there are two sides to every question, and the other side of this question of the district highway surveyors and their salaries has been very neatly and magnanimously expressed by our contemporary, The Eastern Daily Press, when it remarks that the district surveyors may comfort themselves with the thought that the reputation that the main roads of Norfolk have obtained will stand them in good stead when the chance offers itself of bettering their position elsewhere.

\* \* \*

**Public Health Law.** We referred very briefly last week to that portion of the address of the president of the Incorporated Association of Municipal and County Engineers which dealt with this subject. We should like, however, to add a word or two as to one suggestion made by Mr. Robson in the course of his remarks. After pointing out how greatly the law relating to public health has been extended since the passing of the Act of 1875, the president continued : "So numerous have been the subsequent Acts added to the statute-book, and so varied the nature of the measures to which they refer, that the time has now arrived when great assistance would be rendered to municipal authorities, less litigation would be involved, and the statutes themselves made much more clear, if the Public Health Act, 1875, and the Acts incorporated therewith were consolidated in one general Act relating to matters connected with public health." We cordially endorse these remarks, and should rejoice to see added to the statute-book a thoroughly well-drawn Public Health Consolidation Act, embodying the law at present distributed heterogeneously among a number of Acts and an infinitude of cases, with such amendments and additions as might be found desirable. The principle of consolidating legislation has been accepted in many instances—among other subjects thus dealt with may be mentioned arbitration, partnership, trustees and the sale of goods—with satisfactory results; and we do not hesitate to say that the subject of public health is ripe—and over-ripe—for similar treatment. We know not whether, amid the conflict

of party politics, the legislature will in the near future find either the time or the inclination for dealing with a subject which, great as is its importance, does not, we fear, appeal very loudly to the average elector. The first step in this direction, however, is undoubtedly to promote a more vigorous and united public opinion among those more intimately connected with matters pertaining to the public health. We trust, therefore, that this portion of the address will receive the attention and consideration which it undoubtedly merits, with a view to some concerted and practical action being taken. Mr. Robson indicated a few of the many matters which might, and should, be dealt with in such a consolidation Act—e.g., many useful police and sanitary measures now contained in private Acts, amendment of the "ill-conceived" 19th sec. of the Public Health Acts Amendment Act, 1890, additional extended powers of making by-laws, and so forth. Any such general Act should, of course, be compulsory in its entirety, and thus secure uniformity of practice throughout the kingdom, in lieu of the diversity at present fostered by the prevalent practice of permissive or adoptive legislation. It should also, in our opinion, either substantively re-enact—instead of merely incorporating by reference —or include in schedules appended, those clauses of the Towns Improvement and Towns Police Clauses Acts, 1847, which are incorporated with the Public Health Act, 1875. In short, it should, as far as reasonably practicable, comprise the entire law of public health up to date. Perhaps this is a "counsel of perfection," but, nevertheless, we believe it to be attainable.

\* \* \*

**Municipalities and Electric Lighting Companies.** The recent decision of the House of Commons to grant powers to the Marylebone Vestry for the supply of electrical energy within the parochial district has fluttered the dovecots of electric lighting shareholders, with the consequence that shares have been tumbling down with extraordinary rapidity. There has probably, since the commencement of the electrical industry, been no greater scare occasioned among investors than at present exists, but there is absolutely no reason why shareholders should have been so much agitated by the action of the Marylebone Vestry. We are not anxious to go into the question of the position of electric light companies in the various districts, but it might be mentioned that competition in electric light supply was clearly stated by Government officials to be desirable, and would, moreover, be encouraged. Indeed, this view has been carried out to such an extent that in most of the districts in London there is competition between electric lighting companies, but where two companies are supplying electricity in one area it is very unlikely that a vestry or a municipality would be given powers to come in and compete against the two existing companies. It is obvious that such a course would be risky, and the Board of Trade would, no doubt, with a view to protecting the interests of the ratepayers, decline to sanction any such scheme. Even in the district where only one company exists and powers are conferred upon a local authority to become suppliers of electricity, it by no means follows that the company will be starved out ; it will have the benefit of a riper experience, it will have an established business, and it ought to be able to supply electrical energy at the same price as the vestry.

## PROFESSIONAL PROVERBS.

For a Jerry Builder : A ditch of slime saves lime.

For a Parliamentary Agent : It is no use taking charts to Westminster.

For a Carpenter : Boards with a feather lock together.

For a Road Contractor : Those who live in workhouses should not break stones.

# Association of Municipal and County Engineers.

## ANNUAL MEETING AT EDINBURGH.—II.

VIEW OF EDINBURGH SHOWING NATIONAL GALLERY AND CASTLE.

Before resuming our report of the proceedings at Edinburgh we shall, as intimated in our last issue, give some further remarks in continuation of our sketch of the city and its municipal development.

#### GAS AND WATER SUPPLY.

The water supply of Edinburgh was at one time provided by private companies, but the inhabitants were dissatisfied with the service, and the works were transferred by compulsory sale to the corporation in 1869. The supply is derived from several sources, lying chiefly to the south of the city, but a splendid supply of spring water, which is stored in the reservoirs of Torduff and Clubbiedean, is obtained from the northern slopes of the Pentlands. A supply is also derived from the Moorfoot Hills. Public purposes, baths and ordinary domestic supplies consume something like 35 gallons per head per day, and taking into consideration the fact that not only is the city supplied, but the neighbouring villages also, it has been decided that a further supply is absolutely necessary. The head waters of the Tweed, from which a pure supply is available, are therefore being drawn upon, and at the present time a scheme which is expected to satisfy the requirements of the city for at least a quarter of a century to come, and which will be capable of further development and extension as occasion requires, is now in progress. The cost is estimated at £750,000. In connection with the water supply it might be mentioned that the public baths and wash-houses, which have been in use for several years, are so much appreciated that their extension and multiplication is demanded.

As in the case of the water supply, the gas supply for the city and neighbourhood was at first controlled by private companies, but in 1888 the corporation promoted a Bill for the acquisition of the undertakings, and as Leith and the adjacent burghs are supplied from the works, a joint commission, consisting of twenty-three representatives of the different authorities has been appointed for their management. When the electric light was introduced into Edinburgh four years ago, it was expected that the supply of gas in the city and its neighbourhood would diminish, but so far from that being the case, the output has gone on increasing, the existing works having been filled up with plant to their fullest capacity. They are situated in a densely-populated part of the city, and that fact, together with the appointment of a new engineer, has led the commissioners to seek a new site, on which an installation of the best kind may be erected and a modern plant utilised. A site near Granton, to the west of the city, has been acquired, and no time is being lost in taking steps to provide a gas installation of the best possible kind.

#### ELECTRIC LIGHTING—CABLE TRAMWAYS.

We have mentioned above that four years ago a scheme of electric lighting was promoted in Edinburgh, and a large central station in the immediate neighbourhood of railway sidings, with facilities for increasing the space for many years to come, was duly erected. So great has been the success of the scheme that to-day a new power station in a different part of the city and of greater magnitude is now in course of erection. Beginning with charges of 6d. per unit for lighting, $3\frac{1}{4}$d. for power, and £20 for each public lamp, the charges to-day are $3\frac{1}{4}$d. per unit for lighting, $1\frac{1}{4}$d. per unit for power, and £14 for each public lamp. The splendid lighting of the streets now always attracts the attention of visitors.

As in other cities, after the passing of the Act of 1870, a system of horse tramways was inaugurated by private companies. An efficient tramway service in towns of any size or importance is, of course, a necessity, and in 1893 the corporation acquired the horse tramways within the bounds of the city. In 1897 there was also acquired a system of cable tramways which had been laid down on the north side of the city where the gradients and slopes are excessive. This system has proved remarkably successful, and the corporation are now taking steps to acquire the section leading to Portobello, which in 1896 became part of the city in virtue of the extension scheme. It is true that the authorities of many other towns—after deliberating carefully, visiting other towns both at home and abroad, and anticipating a successful future for electricity—have either wholly or to a large extent adopted the system of the overhead trolley, but the Edinburgh authorities, after similar deliberation and close examination of other towns in this country and on the Continent, have decided that cable traction is the most suitable for Edinburgh with its many slopes and gradients.

At present the system is approaching completion. There will be in all four cable-power stations for the working of the lines. The road plant has been almost entirely renewed, and numerous extensions have been added. The cost of the whole work is estimated at £750,300. A contract has been entered into with a private firm for working the system for twenty-one years, the terms being that 7 per cent. be paid on the purchase price and an additional 7 per cent. paid on the capital expenditure of cabling. The maintenance of the whole system, roadwork, power stations and machinery, rests with the lessees, so that at the close of their contract the whole of the installation is to be handed over to the corporation in full equipment and working order, free of expense.

#### FIRE BRIGADE.

The Edinburgh municipal fire brigade was inaugurated in 1824, and was therefore the first in the country. It was called into existence after the great fire of that year, when one side of the High-street to the Tron* Church was burned down. Until about thirty years ago, however, the brigade was worked by auxiliary firemen, but since then the men have been more or less permanent, and are now almost entirely so. The present staff consists of fifty-one officers and

* We regret that, owing to a printer's error in our last issue, the word " Tron" was printed " Iron."

five auxiliary men. There are five steam fire-engines, tenders, &c., and the development and expansion of the city have impelled the corporation to build a central fire station.

This will have two steam fire-engines, two tenders and one fire-ladder always ready for immediate work, and accommodation will also be provided for the housing of the thirty officers and firemen and for the "firemaster." It will, of course, be equipped with the most modern appliances, including special arrangements for a speedy "turn out," and the cost is estimated at £35,000. All plant will be constructed and repaired in the workshops attached to the station, which will be lighted by electricity and heated by steam. Electric motors will be used throughout. The horsing of the engines will be on the American system, the horses being trained to take their places themselves. On ringing the alarm all doors will be opened automatically, and the first two engines will start to a fire within thirty seconds of the first alarm, the remainder following a few seconds later. The site of the new buildings is almost exactly in the centre of the city. A watch-tower, which will also be used for hose-drying purposes, will be provided, and it is proposed to build a sub-station in the Abbeyhill district, with a steam fire-engine and a permanent staff complete.

There are at present three district stations, with two steam fire-engines, and another steamer will shortly be obtained. The old station in the High-street will soon be discontinued. Since Mr. Pordage has become firemaster the brigade has been entirely remodelled, training better adapted to modern needs being given to the staff, and certain minor improvements adopted by the new firemaster, notably the use of aluminium in place of gun metal for all couplings, pipes and appliances. It will readily be gathered that nothing is being left undone to put the Edinburgh Fire Brigade on a thoroughly satisfactory and efficient basis, in conformity with the policy now consistently adopted in connection with the other departments of the municipal service.

### THE CITY SLUMS.

The question of dealing with the poor, more especially in regard to the housing problem, has always been an exceedingly troublesome one in Edinburgh, the poverty and consequent depression of the poorest classes being unusually great. This is by no means ascribed wholly to any peculiarly bad tendency in themselves, or to the evil influence of the insanitary surroundings and inadequate accommodation, but is probably very largely due to the absence of industrial activity in the city, of scope for employment and thus of healthy stimulus to exertion.

The tendency to erect flatted tenements of four, five and six storeys in height has more recently, on account of the

MR. THOMAS HUNTER, W.S.,
Town Clerk of Edinburgh.

demand for dwellings, led to the subdivision of such flats into separate houses, and has largely tended to dilapidation and the increase of insanitary conditions. About thirty years ago this state of affairs had reached so extreme a point that in 1867 an improvement scheme was promoted for the clearing out of numerous rookeries and the opening up of a number of new streets and thoroughfares, and the result was an immense advantage to the Old Town. The scheme was promoted when Dr. Robert Chambers was Lord Provost, and is known as Chambers' improvement scheme. The cost was something like £350,000.

But, while opening up areas for the admission of light and air to regions in which they were imperatively required, the expulsion of so many poor people from their homes without providing a corresponding amount of fresh accommodation served only to aggravate the overcrowding and the insanitary conditions of the remaining houses. This led to a more recent improvement scheme, which was inaugurated under the provisions of the Housing of the Working Classes Act, 1890, by Sir James A. Russell, when Lord Provost. In this case the authorities confined themselves to the absolute clearing out of dense squares and dilapidated buildings. Dozens of the old narrow " closes," from which daylight was almost absent, were abolished. The benefits of the scheme have

been incalculable, and districts in which formerly police supervision was incessantly required are now highly respectable. The Earl of Rosebery, for example, has acquired and renovated the old habitat of Lady Stair, and it now stands at the head of a court in which darkness and dilapidation were wont to reign supreme. But further improvements are still required before Edinburgh could be considered—if, indeed, such a consummation be possible—to be entirely free from slum life. Sir James Russell's scheme cost £80,000.

Some further details may be given of the work done in providing dwellings for the poor as a necessary complement of the merely negative work of clearing insanitary areas. The work has had to be done largely in co-operation with the North British Railway Company, who have made enormous clearances of working men's houses to carry out the enlargement of the Waverley Station. There are three schemes—by no means commensurate to the needs of the city, but sufficient to give the authorities the experience required for more extensive work in the future. On one of the cleared sites a scheme has been completed, at a cost of £10,000. Houses of one room and two rooms have been provided, and their administration is supervised by the Social Union, a body composed of citizens of good social position who have undertaken the work of seeking to ameliorate the condition of the poor. The scheme in question, it is gratifying to note, is regarded as satisfactory, both by the Social Union and by the occupants of the houses. The provision comprises some fifty-six houses, which are let at rents varying from 2s. 6d. to 4s. 3d. per week. Such rents, of course, are beyond the reach of those who have no regular means of livelihood, and a type of house suitable for the poorest inhabitants is still required. The problem is at the present moment receiving the earnest consideration of the authorities. Another scheme, by which some sixty-four houses have been provided, has been carried out in the suburbs at a cost of £9,000, and it is pleasant to be able to record that this scheme has also been highly successful, especially in regard to what must always be regarded as the primary test of such undertakings—the appreciation of those for whom the accommodation is designed. The North British Railway Company have also carried out a scheme which has provided over seventy one-room and two-room houses, at rentals varying from £6 to £10 per annum.

### SEWERAGE AND SEWAGE DISPOSAL.

Twenty years ago the sewers of Edinburgh, from the city boundaries towards the sea, were simply polluted open streams, giving off foul exhalations. One of these—the outlet from the Old Town—was, and still is, a feeder of the irrigated land known as Craigentinny Meadows. This system of irrigation, which has existed for the last 300 years, is still carried on. The exhalations from these meadows are considered to be noxious in the extreme, but the corporation have not yet ventured to acquire them. The fact that the public health has not been appreciably affected is largely attributed to the oxygenated atmosphere which proceeds from the sea, and serves to neutralise the evil effects of the emanations from the meadows. The south-west wind, again, has a tendency to carry the evil odours seawards. The irrigation of these meadows is carried on by a private owner for his own benefit, and whether the city will one day acquire them remains to be seen. The outlet sewers, of which there are four—two at Leith, one at Newhaven and one at Portobello—are now covered in and conducted to low-water mark, some 500 yards distant from the shore. Twenty years ago the condition of the house drains was very much an unknown quantity, but during the intervening period a system of persistent inspection has had the effect that there is to-day scarcely a house in Edinburgh that has not been overhauled and certified.

### MUNICIPAL ADMINISTRATION.

A very slight acquaintance with the municipal work of Edinburgh shows that, as regards some of the important services, it is governed by specially appointed commissioners, but it is at once obvious that, owing to the necessity of providing for the requirements of neighbouring places, some such form of administration was to a large extent unavoidable. As we have already indicated, one result of the existing state of affairs has been the fostering of a desire to amalgamate with Leith, far and away the most important of the surrounding places, and it is rumoured that the idea of municipal unification has by no means been abandoned by many of the leading civic administrators of Edinburgh. Their aim, in short, is to bring under one central administrative body the various departments of municipal work which are at present controlled by separate commissions, consisting of members representing not only Edinburgh, but also, in proportion to size and population, the outside burghs. If such a policy could be carried into effect the various departments in question would practically become executive committees of an expanded town council. That many important advantages would accrue can scarcely be gainsaid, but it will suffice to mention one or two of the most important. The collection of rates, which is at present carried out by several bodies, would be centralised under one management, and the same remark holds good with reference to the continual opening up of streets for the laying of mains in connection with the various services. Whatever objections may be urged and arguments advanced against the policy of unification and centralisation, the gain that would result in many directions is obvious, particularly in connection with the diminution of working expenses and the extinction of much of the friction that must necessarily prevail under the present system. That there is at present strong opposition to amalgamation cannot, of course, be denied, but everything points to the desirability and ultimate success of the policy. Several bodies of long-standing and exceptional privileges have already been abolished, the most important probably being the City Road Trust, to which was entrusted the paving of roads and streets. When it was found, two years ago, that further enlargement of the city boundaries was desirable the Bill that was promoted provided for the annexation of Leith, Portobello and a few small suburbs. As we have already mentioned, Leith succeeded in preserving its separate municipal existence, but the extension, which, of course, included Portobello, added considerably to the area of the city and increased the population by about 10,000.

A few miscellaneous but interesting facts may be added to those we have already given. The Edinburgh and District Water Trust was constituted in 1869, and consisted of representatives from the town councils of Edinburgh, Leith and Portobello; but, of course, the annexation of Portobello slightly altered the constitution of the trust. The Gas Trust consists of representatives from Edinburgh and Leith, and these two corporations join in forming a Purification Commission for the Water of Leith, the Edinburgh Corporation also taking part in the administration of Leith Harbour and participating in the administration of many activities which are not usually included among municipal functions. Among these matters, in the control of which the Edinburgh City Council have a voice, may be mentioned the University, which was founded by the corporation in 1582, the Calton Hill Observatory, the Veterinary College, Trinity College Hospital, and numerous charitable institutions. The Lord Provost, in addition to being Lord-Lieutenant of the County of the City of Edinburgh and Lord High Admiral of the Forth, occupies many philanthropic institutions. After the Lord Provost the most important office-bearer is the City Treasurer, who, like the former, is elected for a period of three years. The Dean of Guild is elected to the corporation by the guild brethren. We have said enough to prove to those who are not already aware of Edinburgh's splendid municipal record, that that record can, in many respects, compare favourably with that of any city in the world. The corporation have carried out one of the most successful electric lighting schemes in the country; they own the tramways, and an extensive system of markets—wholesale and retail of all kinds—from which a large revenue is drawn; they have established baths and wash-houses and free public libraries, and have erected artisans' dwellings. In addition to this, it should be remembered that the gas and water supplies have been virtually municipalised, though it has been found convenient to place them under the control of special trusts or commissioners, the Edinburgh City Council, however, taking the leading part in that control through the representatives nominated. Without transgressing the legitimate limits of municipal activity, the members of the Edinburgh City Council have shown themselves to be thoroughly alive to the duties and responsibilities of civic life. Special phases of municipal work in Edinburgh are dealt with in several of the papers read last week, notably in those of Mr. Young, Mr. Colam, Mr. Stewart, Mr. Bruce, Mr. Newington and Mr. Whyte.

CONCLUSION.

Our brief preliminary sketch of Edinburgh and its municipal development we must now bring to a close, though we recognise that the necessity of confining our remarks on so extensive and engrossing a subject within severe limits must render the treatment less effective than might otherwise be expected. Nevertheless, we part from the task with as much regret as the members of the Association no doubt parted from the beautiful city in which they had been sojourning. There is as little doubt that they carried away with them vivid and permanent impressions of the city and its many remarkable features—its beautiful public buildings, so placed on lofty terraces and otherwise as to give the best effect to their architectural features; the city's unique site—one of the chief causes of its peculiar characteristics—on hills separated by ravines, forming an outlying spur of the Pentlands, full of undulations and abrupt heights; and the rare beauty of the landscape, with the bold outline of the Castle as the central feature. Above all, there is the marked contrast between the New Town and the Old Town. The Edinburgh that so roused the enthusiasm of Scott was a city, the picturesque features of which were almost exclusively those associated with the Old Town, which, as we have already had occasion to mention, practically arose after Flodden. Accommodation was sought within the walls by crowding buildings on every available spot, displacing the earlier structures by lofty piles, from which often projected overhanging additions of timber. The slopes of the ridge along which the main street of the Old Town was formed were covered with picturesque alleys and closes, which contributed so much to the antique and peculiar aspect which the city still retained when Scott was in his prime, and when Sir David Wilkie, after wide experience of Continental art and cities, wrote:—

"What the tour of Europe was necessary to see elsewhere I now find congregated in this one city. Here are alike the

beauties of Prague and of Salzburg, here are the romantic sites of Orvieto and Tivoli, and here is all the magnificence of the admired bays of Geneva and Naples. Here, indeed, to the poetic fancy may be found realised the Roman Capitol and the Grecian Acropolis."

The resemblance between the distant view of Athens from the Ægean sea and that of Edinburgh from the Firth of Forth has often been admired, and in the abortive and uncompleted monument on the Calton Hill, which was intended to be at once a reproduction of the Parthenon and a memorial to Wellington and his comrades, there is a somewhat unfortunate indication of the extent to which the likeness has been present to the minds of the citizens, whose solicitude for preserving the beauty of their town is in general worthy of all respect. In two ways has that solicitude been shown in a marked degree—in a determination to discountenance industries which might injure the aspect of the city, and in a readiness to expend liberal sums of money in the erection of splendid public buildings. The Old Town is now merely the nucleus of the modern city, which has extended over the neighbouring heights northwards towards Leith, southwards and westwards towards the lower slopes of the Pentlands. On the whole, the improvements of the nineteenth century have not only retained and developed the quaint and picturesque features of the Old Town, but have added new features, in many cases equally picturesque, though of a different order, in the other parts of the city. The ridges on which it is built are connected by splendid bridges, beneath which run crowded thoroughfares; the valley between the Old and the New Town and the Castle is laid out in beautiful gardens, and on the lofty terraces stand out clearly splendid public buildings, built of the fine white freestone which abounds in the neighbourhood. In every respect the advance made by the city since the beginning of the century is, indeed, remarkable. In 1801 the population was 66,544; in 1871 it was 196,979; and to-day it is practically 300,000. But while a New Town has grown up, the Old has not been obliterated, and to-day they stand in vivid contrast, the former characterised by symmetry and careful design, and the latter by formless picturesqueness and by irregularity of site on the slopes of a ridge crowned by a massive and time-marked fortress. Here, indeed, we have a city which compares to advantage with the most picturesque and beautiful capitals of the world, and is even now as worthy of enthusiasm as when Sir Walter wrote:—

> Such dusky grandeur clothed the height
> Where the huge castle holds its state,
> And all the steep slope down,
> Whose ridgy back heaves to the sky,
> Piled deep and massy, close and high,
> Mine own romantic town.

## THURSDAY'S PROCEEDINGS

(continued).

In our last issue we were successful, largely owing to a liberal employment of telegraphic facilities, in reporting with considerable fulness the proceedings of the opening day of the annual meeting of the Incorporated Association of Municipal and County Engineers, which was this year held at Edinburgh on Thursday, Friday and Saturday of last week. It will thus be seen that the proceedings reported took place on the day immediately preceding the publication of our paper. A full account was given of the reception at the City Chambers, and also a clear outline of the general business of the day. Some of the day's functions—such as the luncheon and the annual dinner—will, of course, be dealt with more fully in subsequent pages. In addition to the president's address, two papers—those of Mr. Campbell and Mr. Bruce, dealing respectively with tar macadam and the housing of the working classes in Edinburgh—were given, though for obvious reasons it was impossible to give the discussions thereon. In continuing our report this week we give as many of the papers and discussions as space will permit of. The following is the list of those who were present at the meeting:—

PRESIDENT: Mr. O. Claude Robson, Willesden.

PAST-PRESIDENTS: Messrs. L. Angell, West Ham; J. Lemon, Southampton; C. Jones, Ealing; and J. Lobley, Hanley.

VICE-PRESIDENTS: Messrs. J. Cooper, Edinburgh; and W. Harpur, Cardiff.

MEMBERS OF COUNCIL: Messrs. J. Patten Barber, Islington; J. W. Cockrill, Great Yarmouth; A. E. Collins, Norwich; A. Creer, York; E. P. Hooley, Nottingham; J. Paton, Plymouth; J. S. Pickering, Nuneaton; S. S. Platt, Rochdale; J. Price, Birmingham; W. E. C. Thomas, Neath; T. W. Stainthorpe, Eston; and T. Cole, secretary.

MEMBERS: Messrs. T. Aitken, Cupar, Fife; C. F. J. Allin, Smethwick; J. A. Angell, Beckenham; W. Atkinson, Kiveton Park; F. Baker, Middlesbrough; B. Ball, Nelson; J. I. Barton, Isle of Wight; W. Beatson, Leith; G. Bell, Swansea; W. N. Blair, St. Pancras; J. H. Brett, Belfast; F. S. Button, Burnley; T. Caink, Worcester; K. F. Campbell, Stockton; H. J. Clarson, Tamworth; J. A. Crowther, Bootle; J. P. Dalton, Ryton-on-Tyne; H. Dearden, Dewsbury; E. Evans, Carnarvon; A. D. Greatorex, West Bromwich; J. Gregson, Padiham; T. Hunter, Leigh; E. W. Ingamells, Pokesdown; J. Pollard, Westminster; J. I. Landless, Brierfield; W. H. Leete, Bedford; J. L. Lumsden, Kirkcaldy; R. A. MacBrair, Lincoln; H. C. Marks, Carlisle; G. S. Matthews, Dorking; R. McKillop, Perth; N. Parr, Brentford; S. A. Pickering,

Oldham'; G. H. Pickles, Burnley; H. Richardson, Aston Manor; W. H. Savage, East Ham; N. Scorgie, Rotherhithe; T. Scott, Tadcaster; J. A. Settle, Heywood; J. E. Sharpe, Clitheroe; G. H. Shipton, Oldbury; J. S. Sinclair, Widnes; R. W. Smith-Saville, Darwen; J. P. Spencer, Newcastle-on-Tyne; S. Stallard, Maidstone; J. Standfield-Brun, Oyster-mouth; S. Stead, Harrogate; F. Sumner, Bermondsey; T. H. Tarbit, Loftus; R. J. Thomas, Aylesbury; A. J. Turnbull, Greenock; A. Ventris, Strand; C. F. Wike, Sheffield; J. B. Williams, Daventry; J. B. Wilson, Cockermouth; and F. S. Yates, Waterloo.

VISITORS.—Messrs. C. H. W. Biggs, London; W. Brown, London; Editor THE SURVEYOR, London; A. R. Finch; A. S. Jones, Finchampstead; O. J. Kirby; Councillor E. Mellor, Huddersfield; K. M'Kenzie; R. M. Reid, Stirling; and G. Watson, Leeds.

### NEW MEMBERS AND GRADUATES.

It will be remembered that last week we briefly stated that at the meeting of the council, held at the Royal Hotel, on Thursday morning, ten new members and eighteen graduates were elected. The following is the list :—

*As Members—*

Percy C. Dormer, surveyor to Urban District Council, Raunds, Northamptonshire; Francis J. Morris, borough surveyor, Grantham; Adam R. Paterson, burgh surveyor, Renfrow, N.B.; John E. Smales, surveyor to Urban District Council, Woodford, Essex; J. Standfield-Brun, surveyor to Urban District Council, Oystermouth; Acton A. Turriff, burgh surveyor, Elgin, N.B.; H. M. Whitehead, surveyor to Rural District Council, Cannock, Staffordshire; and Archibald Wilson, county surveyor, Dumbartonshire.

*For Transfer—*

William E. Y. Putman, borough surveyor, Morley.

*As Graduates—*

C. Adams, city surveyor's office, Birmingham; S. P. Andrews, Tottenham; H. S. R. Best, Beckenham; D. J. Bowe, borough engineer's office, Eastbourne; J. T. Briscoe, Enfield; T. O. Cudbird, Norwich; J. P. Dent, Nelson; W. A. Farnham, Westminster; E. E. Finch, town hall, Bermondsey; R. W. Fraser, town hall, Wolverhampton; R. Oakden, borough engineer's office, Stratford, E.; F. H. Parr, council offices, Mortlake; A. H. Quick, Newlands, S.E.; J. Spink, city surveyor's office, Manchester; W. F. Sutton, Birmingham; T. E. Tiffin, West Hartlepool; E. Willis, council offices, Kilburn; and F. Wilson, London.

The following is the

### DISCUSSION OF MR. CAMPBELL'S PAPER.

Mr. SMITH SAVILLE (Darwen) said he wished to thank Mr. Campbell for a paper which would be of very great interest to the members. Some years ago when he was using tar macadam he was accustomed to mix the hot tar with cold stone, and not heat the stone as was done by Mr. Campbell.

Mr. C. F. WIKE (Sheffield) said he had followed the paper with very great interest, as for the last ten years he had been laying a great deal of this kind of roadway. With respect to the burning of the material for the tar macadam they used in Sheffield a process used generally in the Midlands. Thus a good deal of time was saved, as the material could be made and dried perfectly in twenty-four hours. They had used different kinds of material for this work, but they found granite was unsatisfactory, because it was non-absorbent. Limestone and furnace slag—not clinker, which he thought would not be strong enough—had proved to be the best material. As to the life of the material, which Mr. Campbell put at seven years, he had made several tests with streets laid in Sheffield for ten years, and found the life and cost of the material to vary considerably, one costing 4d. per yard per annum, another 7½d., another 2½d., another 2d., another 9d. and another 7¾d. He had also had comparisons got out of the difference in the relative cost of tar macadam and granites. The cost of granite was 102d. per yard and of tar macadam 157d. per yard in a period of twenty years, consequently there was a saving on granite of 50 per cent. He thought Mr. Campbell had made a mistake as to the cost of this kind of paving, which he had given as 4s. 6d. per yard, including the foundations and stripping. The foundations would not be required every time.

Mr. CAMPBELL: Quite right, so much the better for tar macadam.

Mr. F. BAKER (Middlesbrough) considered that one of the chief points in the preparation of the material was the boiling of the tar, as it was important to obtain tar of the same consistency. He was glad to say he was able to get his tar boiled for him at a chemical works, and it was delivered through pipes, so it was always kept fine and delivered on the heaps of stones as required. Another important point was to get a good foundation. It was no use putting down a good tar macadam road unless there was a good sound foundation underneath it, and for this purpose he screened all the stone and got the dirt out of it. He used broken scoria, which was not equal to whinstone, but it was much cheaper, the difference in the two materials being 4s. 0d.—the whinstone costing 7s. 6d. and the scoria 3s. With respect to the heating of the stone he did not find it necessary, provided that the stone

was perfectly dry when the tar was run over it. It was necessary to keep the traffic off it while the road was being made, and for two or three days afterwards. He had splendid roads in Middlesbrough made in that way. The cost of material varied in every town, and, therefore, the figures given by Mr. Campbell were not of much practical value. He had laid many thousands of yards at 1s. 0d. per square yard, laid complete and rolled.

### THE LUNCHEON

On the conclusion of Mr. Baker's remarks the members adjourned to the saloon of the Royal Hotel, where they were most hospitably entertained at luncheon by the Lord Provost and the Corporation of Edinburgh. The Right Hon. Mitchell Thomson, Lord Provost, presided, and the "croupiers," as the vice-presidents are termed in Edinburgh, were Bailies Sloan and Kinloch Anderson, and Treasurer M'Crae. "The Treasurer," it may be noted, fills an honorary office, and is a member of the corporation—in Treasurer M'Crae's case an exceedingly active and able member to boot. Among other civic representatives present were Bailies Robertson, Mackenzie, Brand and Hay, Judge J. C. Dunlop and the Town Clerk (Mr. Thomas Hunter).

In proposing prosperity to the Association, coupled with the name of the President,

The LORD PROVOST said the Victorian era had been marked very specially in many ways, but he thought, if one read the signs of the times aright, he would acknowledge that a very important fact of the last fifty years was the enormous growth of sympathy between different classes of the community, and the recognition of the fact meant to all of them a call to do what they could for the moral and social benefit of the people. He felt sure that no association was better qualified to promote those interests than this association, because he knew that many of them were connected with the different corporations of their large cities, and to their hands was entrusted important work regarding sanitation and the care of public health. Had time permitted, information might have been given them in regard to the many questions that interested them in Edinburgh. He briefly mentioned the electric lighting department, under the convenership of Bailie Mackenzie; and the management of the roads, in charge of Judge Dunlop. Mr. Robson had told him that he thought Prince's-street would be a beautiful street if it were only all paved with wood. He agreed with that, but they must not blame them too much. They must remember that in Edinburgh they had to contend with very steep gradients, and horses had to be shod in such a manner as to enable them to protect themselves when going down the steep streets. The result was that the wood was very quickly torn up. Then, of course, he did not know whether in their cities they had a treasurer. They had one in Edinburgh, and a very good one he was. He took charge of the public purse, and naturally he had to see that they did not become extravagant. With time to save a little money, his lordship thought the result would be that they would wood-pave the other half of Prince's-street. They were Scotsmen there, and he dared say the visitors would be surprised on that account to know that, although they had expended very large sums indeed in recent years in Edinburgh, they had been putting their money on things that would pay them, and pay them well too. One of these was one to which he had alluded—the electric light —and in connection with their proceedings he could not forget that Mr. Newington was to read a paper to them. They had also had Mr. Manuelle, the representative of the tramway lessees, who were to pay them, he would not say a handsome return, but an adequate return on their money—it was 7 per cent.—and the City Treasurer was able to borrow the money at 2½ per cent. Taking everything into consideration, most of them would see that they had not made a bad bargain. In conclusion, he said it was the duty of every man connected with the profession to join the association and to do what he could for the benefit, not only of his own corporation but of the nation at large.

Mr. O. CLAUDE ROBSON, the president, in reply, acknowledged the kind reception and welcome of the Lord Provost and corporation, and in turn proposed the "Health of the Lord Provost"; and HIS LORDSHIP, in acknowledgment, hoped the next time the association visited Edinburgh they would be able to see the waterworks of the city. He mentioned also that they were to remove a blot on their city by moving the gas-works at the east end of the town to a site 3 or 4 miles away. They had selected a spot close by the seashore, where they would have accommodation for the immense amount of refuse that must necessarily come from gasworks.

Mr. J. C. DUNLOP also made a few remarks regarding city improvements, and pointed to the excellent drainage system which had been provided. If anything went wrong with the health of Edinburgh it would not, he said, be for the want of good sanitary provision.

### RESUMED DISCUSSION OF MR. CAMPBELL'S PAPER.

On resuming, after luncheon, the discussion of Mr. Campbell's paper,

Mr. J. LEMON (Southampton) said there was no doubt that the cyclist had much to do with the improvement of our highways. The members of the Works Committee at Southampton had taken to riding bicycles, and they had since made a great many complaints about the roads. Their surveyor of highways thought these complaints were very unreasonable, but the members of the committee were equal to the occasion, and they bought the surveyor a bicycle—(laughter). Since he had taken to riding a bicycle the surveyor had come to the conclusion that the roads which he considered so good were rather lumpy, and had gone in strongly for tar macadam. He must say there was nothing particularly new about tar macadam. He had seen it in various towns, and seen a great many failures. Everything depended upon the way in which the material was prepared, and he thought it a mistake to put it on new roads, though it could be used to advantage on old roads. In that case they did not require the very costly foundation referred to by Mr. Campbell. On an existing macadamised road a good tar macadam could be put down for 3s. per yard, and if that was done they were making a great improvement on the material. He wished to utter a word of warning with respect to the making of tar macadam roads. If they had no experience of the material they had much better put the work in the hands of a contractor—(no, no)—who had experience of it and would make it a success. The quality of the tar varied considerably even from the same gasworks, and there were many other details which made either for success or failure.

On the proposition of the PRESIDENT, a hearty vote of thanks was accorded to Mr. Campbell for his paper, and it was agreed that the author's reply should be forwarded to the secretary for inclusion in the "Proceedings" of the association.

The next paper was that of Mr. Young, on dust destructors in Edinburgh. On account of its length Mr. Young summarised the chief points of the paper, which was as follows :—

### EXPERIENCE OF EDINBURGH WITH REFUSE DESTRUCTORS.

By JOHN YOUNG, C.E., Edinburgh.

[Mr. John Young, C.E., of the burgh engineer's department, Edinburgh, was born and educated in Edinburgh, and studied the engineering sciences at Heriot-Watt College. He was trained as a surveyor with Messrs. Brown & Laurence, and Mr. R. Roberts, ordained surveyors, Edinburgh, and for six years was engaged in practical work as a surveyor and manager in the late firm of Messrs. W. & D. McGregor, contractors, London and Edinburgh. In 1886 he was appointed inspector of drainage in the burgh engineer's department, Edinburgh, and was afterwards promoted to the post of assistant engineer. Under the direction of Mr. John Cooper, ASSOC.M.INST.C.E., burgh engineer and master of works, he has carried out several drainage schemes and underground conveniences in the city; has also acted as resident engineer on (1) refuse disposal works, Powderhall; (2) central electric lighting station; (3) the conversion of Edinburgh Corporation tramways to the cable system of traction; and (4) Tollcross cable power station, which is now in course of completion. In 1893 Mr. Young was elected a Fellow of the Royal Scottish Society of Arts. He is also president of the East of Scotland Engineering Association and editor of its "Proceedings." He has contributed papers on engineering subjects to various societies, and made several tours of inquiry bearing on municipal work.]

MODE OF COLLECTION AND NATURE OF EDINBURGH REFUSE.

The population of the city of Edinburgh, with its extended boundaries and Portobello, is now 292,364, the area being 8,804·38 acres. The number of inhabited houses is about 61,622. Under the Edinburgh Municipal Acts penalties are enacted on "any person who accumulates within any enclosure, area, house, building, garret, cellar or other apartment any dung, soil, dirt, ashes, filth, or other offensive matter or thing." The ash-pit system is practically unknown here, and as the whole city is under the water-carriage system of sewage removal, and water-closets almost universal, very little fæcal matter finds its way into the refuse, which is consequently of poor manurial value to the farmer. The whole refuse becomes the property of the city, and the inhabitants are fairly regular in putting it out of their premises for removal. This they do in wooden buckets or iron receptacles, placed at the street kerb at night or early in the morning, but they must not empty their refuse on the street or allow it to blow about, or they are subject to a penalty. This is, however, a difficult matter to regulate. It is found that a large proportion is, however, emptied on the streets, and the

buckets are overturned by people who make a living by picking out materials which can be sold.

The refuse carts and waggons make a daily round of the whole streets of the city in the early morning and collect all the refuse put out, together with the street sweepings which the scavengers have collected on their various beats. The carts and waggons are covered over on the top to prevent the refuse being blown about while in transit to the depot or destructors. The carts have a capacity of about 73 cubic feet, with a weight of refuse carried of from 10 cwt. to 18 cwt., and the four-wheeled waggons a capacity of about 108 cubic feet, with a weight of refuse of from 15 cwt. to 23 cwt. The total amount of all kinds of house, shop, market, trade and slaughter-house refuse, street sweepings, slurry, road mud, and the heterogeneous compound known as police manure, collected in Edinburgh in one year is about 140,000 tons, made up as follows :—

100,000 tons of general city refuse.
40,000 tons of mud and street sweepings.

There are two tooms for street sweepings, road mud, &c., one being at Queensferry-road and the other at Powderhall. The refuse, which is despatched by railway to the country, is sent from the loading banks at Logie Green, Dundee-terrace, St. Leonard's and Meadowbank. A portion is also sent by canal-barge from Fountainbridge, and carted out of the city to an old quarry at Redhall. The principal tip in the country is at Clapperton Hall, 12 miles distant from Edinburgh to the west, where large natural hollows are being filled up. The portion of the Edinburgh refuse sent to the destructor is collected from that district of the city north of Queen-street, and amounts to nearly one-fourth of the total amount of refuse collected in Edinburgh. The area of the district is approximated in the different seasons, so as to yield as much refuse as the destructor will consume.

The quality of Edinburgh refuse sent to the destructor is very mixed, light in weight, bulky in measurement, very dry, and possessing a poor amount of cinders and carbonaceous substances, but contains a large amount of dusty and sandy matter. This is partly accounted for by the daily collection, the high-burning qualities of the coal used in the district, the habits of the citizens, the state of the weather and the admixture of street sweepings, which inevitably get mixed up in lifting refuse off the streets. From the following table a comparison may be drawn with ash-bin refuse as collected in London, and given in a report on "Dust Destructors" by the medical officer and engineer of the London County Council in 1893—viz.:—

| | London "ash-bin" refuse. | Average Edinburgh refuse. |
|---|---|---|
| Breeze, cinders and ashes ... | 64 per cent. | 25·5 per cent. |
| Fine dust ... ... ... | 19 ,, ,, | 37·0 ,, ,, |
| Paper, straw, organic matter, bottles, bones, tins, crockery, &c. | 17 ,, ,, | 37·5 ,, ,, |
| | 100 | 100 |

In regard to its bulky character, it is found by measurement that there are from 72 to 80 cubic feet to 1 ton, whereas it is said that there are only 40 cubic feet per ton in the ash-bin refuse of English towns. The former mode of disposal of the city refuse was by despatching to farmers as much as they could take, the surplus being carted and tipped in waste hollows, ravines and old quarries at Powderhall, Liberton dams and Redhall quarries.

RAPID DECLINE IN DEMAND BY FARMERS.

For the ten years from 1870 to 1880 the average amount of street refuse sold to farmers was 56,030 tons, and the average rate per ton obtained 2s. 0·203d. For the ten years from 1880 to 1890 the average amount sold was 63,827 tons, the average rate per ton being only 7·404d. The price per ton obtained for the refuse in 1870 was 2s. 9·661d., but this had fallen in 1890 to 3·477d., and ultimately nothing was got. The annual average revenue had decreased from £5,650 to £1,969, showing a falling away of £3,681 per year. The Cleaning Committee in the end of 1890 were thus brought face to face with an ever-decreasing demand for the refuse by farmers, and consequently a great drop in the revenue, the difficulties of finding suitable tips for the refuse, a marked diminution in its quality and manurial value, together with a considerable increase in the quantity of the refuse to be disposed of.

APPOINTMENT OF COMMITTEE OF INVESTIGATION IN 1890.
THE REPORT OF SAID COMMITTEE.

The town council, on August 11, 1890, adopted a motion by Councillor Sloan : " Remitting to the Cleaning and Lighting Committee, with powers to make further inquiry as to the best mode of disposal of the town's refuse." In due course a subcommittee was appointed which visited, between September 15 and 22, 1890, the towns of Newcastle-on-Tyne, York, Leeds, Bradford, Manchester, Birmingham and London, with the view of studying on the spot the methods of refuse disposal, and generally to ascertain the best scientific methods in operation, so far as to find as satisfactory and as permanent a solution as possible. After reviewing the situation of the refuse disposal question and the fall in the revenues derived therefrom, the report goes on to give important and statistical and other information bearing on the then current methods of refuse disposal as carried out by English corporations.

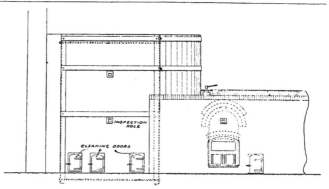

POWDERHALL REFUSE DESTRUCTOR (HORSFALL): DETAIL OF DUST CATCHER.
Elevation.

Very close attention was given in the report to the question of disposal by destructors, and a large number of these were visited and described. The conclusions arrived at in the report were as follows: That the question of diminished value and falling revenues in connection with the waste matters was neither so urgent nor important a matter as getting rid of them at all. That the English towns were more or less adopting the burning process, and the working of destructors was yielding satisfaction as regards sanitary and economic considerations. That the clinker and residual products are free of smells and innocuous, and can be used for filling up hollows for conversion into building sites and other lucrative purposes. That the time had now come for Edinburgh to deal with its refuse by means of destructors, as the mode of disposing of the city refuse was a failure. That there need be no apprehension on the part of the public as to nuisance or inconvenience arising therefrom. That with the adoption of destructors a real attempt could be made to classify the city's refuse into two distinct kinds; that these should be collected separately, that portion having no manurial value being sent to destructors. That, as the city had an area of 9 square miles, three or four divisions should be formed, each with provision for dealing with its own refuse. This report of the sub-committee was submitted to the Cleaning and Lighting Committee on January 30, 1891, and it was presented to the town council on February 17, 1891. The council approved generally of the report and recommitted to the Cleaning and Lighting Committee to bring up specific recommendations, and estimates for giving effect to the same. This was approved on a division on the minutes on March 3, 1891. On July 28, 1891, the Cleaning and Lighting Committee presented an interim report to the town council on the question of the disposal of city refuse, and submitted for general approval plans prepared by the burgh engineer, of a destructor and other necessary buildings for one district of the city—viz., the northern—the site which the committee had fixed upon at Powderhall being the most eligible in their opinion. The probable cost of the destructor was estimated at £3,000, and the buildings, &c., at £9,000. The committee asked power to obtain estimates and have the work started forthwith. In the report of the burgh engineer on the plans of the proposed Powderhall destructor, Mr. Cooper also recommended the dividing of the city into four districts, each district having a full equipment of destructor arrangements, with stabling and other accessories for the carting department, entailing a capital outlay of from £50,000 to £60,000. After mature consideration the town council, on September 8, 1891, approved the proposal to erect a destructor at Powderhall.

ERECTION OF DESTRUCTOR AT POWDERHALL.

In pursuance of the town council's instructions, working plans were prepared by the burgh engineer, for a branch cleansing depot with destructor at Powderhall. Stabling and cart sheds were provided for twenty horses, with overseer's house. Accommodation was also provided in a separate suite of buildings for a refuse destructor of ten cells, fume-cremators, boiler and flues, chimney shaft, roadways, weighing office, &c. The site of the works (about 1 acre in extent) belonged to the corporation, and was originally a sand quarry, which had been filled up with city refuse for some time. It was conveniently situated for the district, and allowed of all the cartage being downhill. The levels of the ground were very suitable, and allowed of the refuse being brought to the tipping or charging house at the level of the adjoining thoroughfare, with the clinkering floor on the next level some 15 ft. below, and the lowest level permitted of tipping the clinker and residue from a height of about 14 ft. The whole buildings were substantially built with stone in an ornate character, so as to obviate any unsightliness, and in a measure to disguise, as far as possible, their purpose. The ten cells of the destructor occupied the basement of the large building in the centre, with the tipping platform and charging floor on the floor above. The fume cremators, boiler and flues, and engine and dynamo room adjoined on the basement level. The buildings entirely enclosed the whole plant, and it was the intention from the first to conduct all the operations of disposing of the refuse within closed doors. The buildings were ventilated by a fan with air ducts to the various apartments, the foul air being conducted to ducts discharging into the ash-pits of the cells. The whole buildings of the destructor installation, and the stabling, &c., were lighted by electricity generated on the premises. The fires were lighted in the cells of the destructor on August 14, 1893, and preliminary firing and seasoning of the brickwork of the destructor, flues and chimney went on until September 11, 1893, when the works were formally opened by Lord Provost Sir James Russell and councillors. The works, including building and destructor, plant and machinery, were finished in eighteen months, and the cost was:—

| | | | |
|---|---|---|---|
| For buildings and other works... | ... | ... | £14,216 |
| For destructor plant and machinery | ... | ... | 3,866 |
| | | | |
| Total ... | ... | ... | £18,082 |

It was resolved to take specific offers and plans from two of the best-known firms of contractors for destructor plant, and Messrs. Manlove, Alliott & Co., and Messrs. Goddard, Massey & Warner, both of Nottingham, were invited to tender. It was found that Messrs. Manlove, Alliott & Co. had erected over 400 cells up to this time, and apparently were the leading firm and had the largest experience in the matter. The committee recommended the acceptance of their tender, notwithstanding that it was the higher of the two submitted. The legal contract entered into with Messrs. Manlove, Alliott & Co. provided that they were to erect and maintain for one year a ten-celled refuse destructor, plant, machinery and other appliances, at Powderhall, capable of each cell burning 8 tons per twenty-four hours, of the ordinary house refuse collected in Edinburgh. That the refuse so treated would be reduced in bulk to one-fourth of the original quantity, that the apparatus would effectually intercept all dust and consume all fumes, render these innocuous and cause no nuisance. The contractors were bound to exercise their best skill as specialists, so as to ensure the best results, to instruct the workmen in the process of burning. In default they were to forfeit the sum of £500, which was the penalty attached to any failure of their destructor appliances.

FRYER'S DESTRUCTOR OF TEN CELLS.

This ten-cell destructor was built by Messrs. Manlove, Alliott & Co., of Nottingham, in the summer of 1893. It was of the Fryer's patent back-to-back type, with live cells on each side, and formed a block of brickwork 36 ft. by 24 ft. by 12 ft. high. Each cell had a capacity of 126 cubic feet, with a fire-grate area of 25 square feet, a drying hearth behind this of 22 square feet area, covered over with a sloping reverberatory arch.

The cell possessed two new features over those previously erected, which were claimed as improvements at the time. First.—Instead of the back wall of the cell being taken up with the charging hopper on one side, and the exit opening to the main flue on the other, this wall was divided into two openings in connection with two down-take flues from the cell into the main flue. These openings were provided with flap doors, arranged so that by opening the front clinkering door of the cell the two back doors of the flues were closed all but an inch. It was hoped by this arrangement to prevent an inrush of cold air into the main flue when the clinkering door was opened. These flap doors were continually giving trouble by buckling up and refusing to work, so much so that they had to be done away with entirely. The *second* point of difference in this cell was the charging door, which was placed in the middle of the reverberatory arch, and was closed over with an iron sliding plate cover. This cover and its frame were also so affected by the heat that it frequently became red hot, and got distorted to such an extent that they would not cover the opening effectually. Many different expedients were tried without success to protect this door from the heat, but all these failed, with the result that the refuse lying on the top deck of the destructor smouldered and took fire, emitting very unpleasant smells in the charging-house. It was quite evident that the position of this charging door was badly placed, being almost immediately over the hottest part of the fire. Another cause of nuisance from bad smell in the charging-house was the extreme heat developed in the deck top of the destructor, which had the effect of communicating to the refuse lying thereon too much heat, and to such an extent that "cooking and stewing" of the refuse took place, and consequent nuisance resulted. The cells of this destructor were provided with rocking fire-bars, worked by hand levers from the front. The ash-pits were open and received the discharge from an exhausting fan, which was connected to the charging-house with the object of sucking away any noxious fumes generated therein.

At the beginning of the work a revolving screen was erected at one end of the charging-house. Attempts were made to screen some portion of the refuse, so as to obtain sufficient fuel for four of Jones' fume cremators, but the material obtained was both inadequate in quantity and quality for keeping the cremators up to anything like a proper temperature, and had to be dispensed with. Finally, gas breeze and coke had to be purchased and burned in the cremators. The cost of working the cremators was prohibitive, and quite out of proportion with any beneficial result, either in appreciable rise of temperature or cremation of the gases coming from the destructor. Beyond the cremators, placed side by side, was the bye-pass flue with large damper and the brick-seating of the multitubular boiler, 12 ft. long and 7 ft. diameter, with its damper behind. These both joined together and formed the main flue, 4 ft. by 7 ft., which curved round in a quadrant bend to the chimney. In the main flue were placed two wire screens for catching unburnt paper. These were made to slide into an underground pit for cleaning purposes, and answered their purpose very well. The chimney was built for natural draught, being 7 ft. 6 in.

diameter at the bottom and 6 ft. 6 in. diameter at the top, and 185 ft. high from ground level. It was provided with an internal lining and air-space all round for a height of 50 ft., and a dust-pit was placed in the bottom. A steam engine and shafting was also provided for driving the dynamo for electric lighting and the ventilating fan ; and a mortar mill is also placed outside for grinding clinker and making mortar, but there is no demand for it in Edinburgh.

As the work of erecting the Fryer's destructor installation had been carried out under the supervision of Mr. Cooper, burgh engineer, the burning of the refuse was also continued under his charge, with the view of ascertaining the capabilities of the destructor, and in order to determine whether the terms of the maker's contract had been fully implemented. Mr. Cooper reported to the Cleaning and Lighting Committee, in March, 1894, the result of the operations at the destructor for the period from January 17 to March 24, 1894, as follows :—

"(1) That the *amount of refuse* burned during the period was at the rate of 64 tons 5½ cwt. per day of twenty-four hours (three shifts of labour) for ten cells.

"(2) That the *cost per ton* of refuse burned, including labour, oil, wick, waste, gas cinders, arc lamp carbons and other sundries, and also taking into account the interest and sinking fund at 5 per cent. on £10,000 expenditure of capital outlay, the *cost per ton of refuse burned* worked out at 1s. 4·723d."

Mr. Cooper's report further comments on the nature of the refuse to be burned : "As regards Edinburgh refuse, our experience is that on the whole, owing to the amount of soft ash, road sweepings and sandy matter it contains, the furnaces are seriously hampered in their work. The first delivery of refuse in the morning, which is almost wholly house refuse, is, as a rule, of good quality for burning and clinkering. A large part of that delivered in the after part of the day, which is intermixed with road sweepings, is heavily charged with dust and sandy matter, which, as I have said, not only will not burn, but seriously chokes up the furnaces. It has also been found hopeless to obtain material out of the refuse for the cremator fuel. I think that were the same department and officers in charge of the burning who are in charge of the collection of the refuse, experience would speedily dictate the necessity for separating road sweepings, dust, &c., from the refuse delivered at the works, and the result would be a considerable improvement, both in the amount burned and in the nature of the clinker. As might also be expected, a number of improvements for more rapid combustion, for simplifying the labour in charging the furnaces, for fuller utilisation of waste heat, &c., have suggested themselves."

From time to time, as experience was gained, every effort was made to work the destructor up to this guaranteed efficiency, but without successful result. From several tests the following may be selected as what was accomplished :—

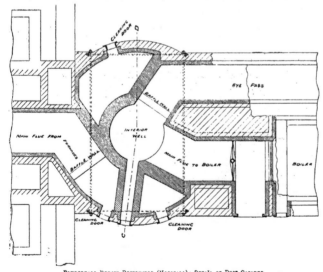

POWDERHALL REFUSE DESTRUCTOR (HORSFALL) : DETAIL OF DUST CATCHER.
Section through A B. (See diagram on page 47.)

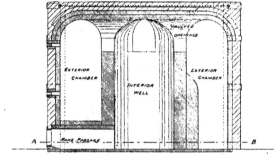

POWDERHALL REFUSE (HORSFALL) DESTRUCTOR: DETAIL OF DUST CATCHER.
Section through CD.   (See diagram on page 46.)

On October 4, 1893, 45½ tons burned in sixteen hours.
On ,, 24, ,, 60½ ,, ,, twenty-four hours.
For the period from January 18, 1894, to March 24, 1894, the average daily burning was at the rate of 64 tons 5¼ cwt. per twenty-four hours. For the first period, from August 14, 1893, to April 17, 1894, under the charge of the burgh engineer, the total amount of refuse burned at the Powderhall destructor was 10,868 tons. The men worked in three shifts of eight hours each, there being one engineer and three furnacemen to each shift for the period from September 30, 1893, to March 31, 1894, afterwards one engineer and four furnacemen per shift. For the period from April 18, 1894, to January, 1895, by order of the Cleaning and Lighting Committee, the destructor was handed over to the responsible officer of the cleaning department, who had full charge of the staff engaged in the collection, delivery, burning, and disposal of the refuse and clinker. The quantity of refuse delivered and consumed at the destructor during this period was 12,921 tons, being an average of 61¼ tons for ten cells in the twenty-four hours. The quantity of coke burned in the fume cremators was at the average rate of 2 tons per week.

SHORT HISTORY OF DESTRUCTOR ENDING IN LAW COURTS.

On November 12, 1894, after the destructor had been working for fourteen months, the corporation received notice of an action of interdict, at the instance of Alexander's trustees, on behalf of the proprietors of the adjoining property of Redbraes, situated on the opposite side of the North British Railway from the destructor. It was maintained that noxious fumes and gases, and offensive dust and charred paper, were disseminated over the Redbraes property from the destructor premises and the clinker bings, to the discomfort of the pursuers and their tenants, and damage to the trees and shrubs in the nursery grounds, causing them great discomfort and annoyance, and loss, injury and damage, and that the value of the property was being deteriorated. The corporation resolved to defend the action, and it was tried in the First Division of the Court of Session before Lord Stormouth Darling. The case was before the courts for ten days, between May 29 and July 24, 1895. There were thirty-four witnesses examined for the pursuers and twenty-eight for the defenders, and a large mass of very interesting and scientific evidence was given on both sides. The general purpose of the evidence went to prove that the destructor had been imperfectly worked from the beginning; that the temperatures obtained, on the whole, were too low, and the combustion defective for the peculiar nature of the refuse dealt with; that the fume cremators, although regularly in use, were inadequate for the destruction of the fumes, and the system did not sufficiently provide for the interception of the large amount of dust; and that, consequently, nuisance had resulted, and damage been occasioned to the adjoining nursery grounds of Redbraes.

The Lord Ordinary, in his interlocutor and opinion of July 31, 1895, found that the corporation had worked the destructor in such a manner as to create a nuisance, but that, as the remedial measures adopted since the raising of the action had to some extent abated the nuisance, it was reasonable that time should be allowed for making further improvements so as to remove, as far as possible, all just cause of complaint. He remitted to Mr. B. Hall Blyth, C.E., Edinburgh, to visit the premises from time to time, and, after conferring with Dr. Odling, Professor of Chemistry at Oxford, to report before the end of the year 1895 what change, if any, either in the apparatus itself or in the mode of working is, was necessary in order to prevent the escape of noxious gases or vapours, and the diffusion of noxious dust and other matters over the pursuers' said property. Finds the pursuers entitled to expenses, &c. Soon after the notice of the action by Alexander's trustees, and pending the beginning of the action and afterwards, the management of the destructor was again placed in the hands of the burgh engineer in January, 1895, by the corporation, and, as the consequence of his recommendations, a better mode of working was introduced, whereby the cells were charged and clinkered in rotation every two hours. Two experienced foremen were brought from Bradford to superintend and instruct the day and night shifts. Finer screens were put into the main flue to intercept the paper, and proper regulating of the dampers was insisted on. To prevent any nuisance from the watering of the clinker, a specially designed box was introduced by Mr. Cooper. This box was strongly made of sheet iron mounted on wheels. It had three sides and hinged top. It was wheeled in front of the ash-pit when a fire had to be clinkered, the clinkers were raked out of the cell into the box, the lid was closed and a hose turned on to the hot clinkers through holes in the side of the box. This entirely prevented any escape of sulphurous fumes into the clinkering-house, they being sucked into the ash-pit instead. This apparatus worked very well and anticipated all objections to the watering of the clinker. With the object of increasing the temperature in the cells, one of these was fitted with the steam air blast, and better combustion and clinker was obtained.

On December 23, 1895, Mr. B. H. Blyth and Dr. Odling reported to the court, after making visits to Powderhall destructor from time to time, as well as several destructors in England. In their opinion the nuisance complained of arose from three causes—viz.:—
(1) From imperfectly consumed noxious gases, and dust escaping from the chimney.
(2) From noxious fumes and dust being blown out of the clinkering chamber.
(3) From bad smells given off from the feeding chamber, owing to the refuse waiting for burning heating while lying on the top of the cells.

To obviate these they recommended that several alterations in the apparatus and mode of working be adopted—viz.:—
(1) That steam jets be introduced into all the cells, to assist combustion and raise temperature in main flue.
(2) That the cells be fitted with a front exhaust.
(3) That Boulnois and Brodie's charging trucks should be used on the top of the cells to prevent contact of refuse with heated top of destructor.
(4) That a large dust chamber be provided in main flue.
(5) That the clinker should not be watered, and a cooling platform be formed for laying down the hot clinker on outside the building.
(6) That more intelligent and experienced stokers should be employed in the working.

By the time the report was published, the corporation, at Mr. Cooper's instigation, had practically anticipated several of the recommendations made in Mr. Hall Blyth's report, notably with regard to the steam jets and the dust chamber. A complete system of forced blast was applied to the cells of the destructor. This consisted of closing up the fronts of all the ash-pits with brickwork, having doors for the removal of the dust falling through the fire-bars, and the provision of two steam jets with blowing nozzles into each cell. This result was fairly satisfactory at first, and a much greater combustion was got in the cells, and better clinker was obtained for a time. The only drawbacks experienced were the choking up of the blowing jets, the unsuitability of the rocking-bars for the proper admission and distribution of the forced blast, and the blowing out of the smoke and fumes from the cells, through the badly-fitting charging doors at the top. The increased heat obtained was very destructive to the brickwork of the cells, and a large proportion of dust was deposited in the flues. On the whole, this installation of forced blast rather emphasised than obviated the previous difficulties as to nuisance from dust, and the overheating of the refuse lying on the deck top of the destructor. Any benefit got from the forced blast in increased combustion was neutralised by the very light, sandy and dusty nature of the refuse, the greater portion of which could not be got to clinker in the fires. To prevent the dust escaping up the chimney, a pit was formed in the floor of the main flue near where it joined the chimney, and a water spray introduced for wetting the gases as they passed this point. This apparatus had the effect of arresting a fair quantity of dust and of cooling the gases before they entered the chimney. Under these somewhat improved conditions the burning of refuse was persevered in, and the amount consumed from May 15, 1895, to May 15, 1896 = 16,141 tons. The cost had, however, gone up to nearly 2s. 1d. per ton, including all charges, and this was felt to be excessive and could not be maintained.

As the recommendations of Mr. Hall Blyth involved considerable expenditure, and were calculated to make such radical changes in the construction of the destructor as regards the fitting up of charging trucks and the front exhaust from the cells, the corporation having met the rest of the proposals made, they lodged objections to these, which were duly answered by the pursuers. The reporter's recommendations being persisted in, the corporation ultimately resolved on the entire reconstruction of the Powderhall destructor on the most modern and approved system.

In August, 1896, an estimate was obtained from the Horsfall Refuse Syndicate, Leeds, and a legal contract was entered into on October 13, 1896, for the remodelling of Powderhall destructor on their improved system, with all special appliances necessary for the successful disposal of the refuse, to the entire satisfaction of Mr. Hall Blyth, c.e., or such other man of skill as the Court might appoint. The contract provided that each of the cells should consume 8 tons per twenty-four hours of the ordinary Edinburgh refuse, and that the residue would be reduced in bulk to at least one-fourth of its original quantity; and the temperature maintained would be 1,800 deg. Fahr. They were also bound to provide all other appliances for satisfying the terms of Mr. Hall Blyth's report to the Court as regards noxious fumes and dust. The work was to be entirely completed in twelve weeks, and maintained for one year after completion. In case of failure of any part of the contract a penalty of £500 was to be imposed. The work was completed in the end of January, 1897, and the burning of refuse again commenced under the new conditions, and has been in operation ever since, with the exception of a short period when sundry repairs were found necessary.

### RECONSTRUCTION OF FRYER'S DESTRUCTOR BY THE HORSFALL REFUSE SYNDICATE, LIMITED, LEEDS.

Under this scheme of reconstruction the whole of the old destructor cells were taken down to the under side of the fire-grate level, and ten entirely new cells built on the old foundations by the Horsfall Refuse Furnace Company, Leeds. The new destructor is much the same in outward appearance and size as the old Fryer's destructor, but has many new features, and special arrangements were adopted to meet the conditions imposed under the contract. The new Horsfall cell has a capacity of 165 cubic feet. The sloped fire-grate has an area of 25 square feet, and a curved drying hearth an area of 32½ square feet. A great change was made in the charging hole, which is in the form of a hopper, 3 ft. square and 3 ft. 3 in. deep, placed at back and common to two cells. This charging hopper has a flat bottom, and when filled up with refuse to the level of the deck top of the destructor it effectually seals up the openings at the back of the cells, but allows of the charging and moving forward of the refuse by the pokers. This form of hopper has prevented the refuse round the charging holes from taking fire as formerly. The altered position of these hoppers has also given a greater area for storage of refuse on the top of the destructor. The greatest change made, however, was in the front exhaust exit flue for the gases from the cell. This was placed at the top of the level reverberatory arch, but at the front of the cell instead of the back as formerly. This change has been entirely successful in its purpose, which was to make the gases, pneumatic fumes and vapours from the new charge of refuse on the drying hearth pass over the hottest part of the fire on the grate-bars before going into the branch flue from the cell to the main flue. The branch flues from the cells are taken over the top of the cell arch and, being about 12 ft. in length, these present a large area of very hot brickwork, which everything coming from the cell must encounter on its way to the main flue. The main flue was also very much decreased in size, and is now 4 ft. by 7 ft. 1 in.

Another important improvement was made in the construction of the deck top, so as to prevent heating of the refuse lying thereon and to obviate any "cooking and stewing" of the material. A layer of 3-in. agricultural drain tubes was laid all over the top of the destructor deck, this was covered with Portland cement concrete 6 in. thick. One end of these tubes was left open, and the other end connected to the down-take air shafts of the forced blast apparatus. By this means a continuous stream of cold air is sucked through the pipes, the refuse on the deck top being kept comparatively cool, and the former nuisance from nauseous smells in the charging

houses from the overheating of the refuse has been overcome. From previous experience in burning, and taking into account the peculiar nature of Edinburgh refuse, it was found necessary to provide a thoroughly effective system of forced blast to all the cells. For this purpose two main air ducts, each 2 ft. 6 in. by 4 ft. 9 in., were built under the cells between the ash-pit and the main flue. These air ducts are connected to two down-take air shafts in the charging-house, so that all the air used for the forced blast is taken from the vicinity of the destructor top, and assists materially in changing the atmosphere there. In each of these down-take air shafts is placed vertically a blowing trumpet 6 ft. 9 in. long, which at first had a steam jet 18 in. wide, but these have been replaced by three separate steam jets, each 2½ in. wide in each trumpet. From the forced blast air-duct cast-iron boxes are taken along each side of the cells at the level of the fire-bars. These boxes are 13 in. high, and are covered on the faces with two movable plates to each; the object of placing the boxes in this position being to prevent the clinkers in the fire adhering to the sides of the cell. It is well-known that where only brick sides are put into destructor cells a lot of labour is expended in cutting off the clinkers from the brick-work, which consequently needs frequent renewal. From the bottoms of these two cast-iron side boxes four connecting tubes are provided for the supply of the forced blast to the ash-pit below the fire-bars. These are controlled by sliding ports operated by handles from the front of the cells, for shutting off the blast when the cell is to be clinkered or a fresh charge of refuse put on the fire. The ash-pits are closed in front, and provided with airtight doors for the removal of the very fine dust which falls through the fire-bars. The original rocking fire-bars were put into the new cells, but these have all been replaced, with the exception of one cell (which still has the old rocking-bars) with V-shaped steel fire-bars 3 in. deep, with ¼ in. spaces between, riveted up in sections, and stretching the full length of the fire-grate. In the proper burning of refuse and the making of good clinker there is such a close relationship between the nature of the refuse burned, the form of the bar, the width of spaces between the same, and the pressure of the forced draught put on, that no satisfactory statement can be made about these without giving the records of a larger and more successful experience than has been had at Powderhall destructor. The cause for this has been largely due to several defects in various parts of the apparatus of the destructor, rather than in the type of destructor. For example, a very serious defect in the Horsfall furnace is to be found in the side boxes of the cells. The movable plates covering the faces of these boxes frequently crack, buckle up and get twisted out of shape, with the result that the leakage of the forced blast takes place directly into the cell and over the top of the fires, and the effect of the blast in the ash-pit is, to a large extent, lost, and, in some cases, entirely neutralised. It is obvious if ten side boxes for forced draught are connected to one of the air-ducts, and if even one of these has its plates defective and allows the forced blast to leak, the whole pressure in the ash-pits of the five cells on one side of the destructor is reduced. Again, these side plates are so situated and fixed that no single plate can be replaced until all the furnaces are damped down at the end of the week. The leakage of the forced blast into the cells above the fires forces fumes and smoke out at the hoppers, when the men are charging the cells, into the charging-house, frequently causing a temporary nuisance, and when clinkering the blast being cut off in the ash-pit, is only increased over the fires, a result the reverse of which should be the proper condition of things.

Turning now to the forced blast itself, even under an average condition of side boxes, the experience has been that not more than ⅛ in. of water column pressure is got in the ash-pits, and it need hardly be said that this pressure is entirely inadequate for the burning of refuse which has nearly double the quantity of ash, sand, and dusty matter and street sweepings in it, than that of an ash-pit town, or even of the refuse of London. The steam jet and blowing trumpet of the forced blast apparatus in this destructor were at first worked at a steam pressure of 35 lb. per square inch, but through corrosion in the steel lips of the jets the pressure was greatly reduced. The length of lips of the two jets was 36 in. at first, and these worked for one year, but the Horsfall company, in January of this year, put in six new steam jets of a total breadth of 15 in. with brass lips to the jets, and the steam pressure had to be raised to that of boiler pressure —viz., 75 lb. per square inch. This has been very hard work for the boiler, and it now remains to be found by what means the steam pressure can be reduced or economised, and a more effective forced blast given in the ash-pits; but it is doubtful if this result can be obtained until the side boxes are put on a more satisfactory basis as regards non-leakage into the cells.

Turning now from the destructor itself, the dust catcher and heat storage chamber deserves attention. This apparatus was specially designed and erected by the Horsfall company, so as to meet the conditions specified in the contract as to the interception of all dust coming from the destructor flue, and for the provision of a large chamber, highly heated, into which all the noxious fumes generated would be effectually cremated and destroyed. It consists of a large block of brickwork, 18 ft. in diameter and 13 ft. 7 in. high, situated at

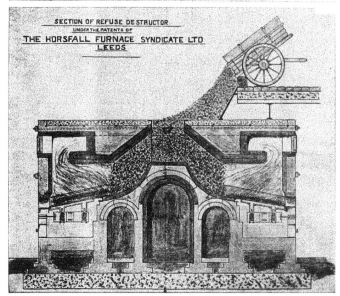

SECTION OF REFUSE DESTRUCTOR
UNDER THE PATENTS OF
THE HORSFALL FURNACE SYNDICATE LTD
LEEDS

POWDERHALL REFUSE DESTRUCTOR.

the one end and connected with the main flue of the destructor. The internal arrangement consists of a spiral flue traversing the entire circumference and winding upwards to the top of the chamber. There is an internal chamber, 5 ft. diameter and 12 ft. high, having a domed top, and communicating with the outer spiral flue by four ports at the top of its walls. In the floor of the outer spiral flue several dust traps are formed. These are provided with doors in the external wall of the chamber through which the dust deposited can be easily removed. From the bottom of the internal chamber there is an opening connected to the by-pass flue, and another opening and flue to the multitubular boiler, and, by arranging the dampers, the gases from the dust catcher may either be sent through the boiler tubes or passed through the by-pass flue.

Inspection holes are formed at different levels for looking into the chambers, from which the heat may be estimated and the clearness of the atmosphere inside noted. The large heat-storage capacity in this chamber, the long spiral circuit which the gases have to travel against the highly-heated brickwork, the baffling of the current and period of quiescence given to the gases, thereby relieving the pressure and promoting expansion, also favours their decomposition and provides effectually for the deposition of any dust they contain. This apparatus has given no trouble of any kind, requires no attention, except the weekly cleaning out, and has proved very successful for its purpose. The reservoir of heat, maintained at a steady temperature of from 1,500 deg. Fahr. to 1,800 deg. Fahr., is also very useful in keeping up steam in the boiler at an equable pressure for a long period. It is obvious, however, that the proper manipulation of the boiler damper and the by-pass flue damper are important elements in the successful working of this dust catcher and heat-storage chamber, so as to keep its temperature as near 1,800 deg. Fahr. as possible.

As the quality of the refuse varies from day to day, and even at different times of the day, and with the state of the weather and season of the year, difficulties are frequently experienced in keeping up the heat; but experience shows that by regulating these dampers properly, this may to a great extent be overcome. Too much care cannot be bestowed on the proper design and construction of these two dampers, so that they will at no time get out of order and always work perfectly. Cases have occurred where a by-pass damper has got twisted by excessive heat and remained standing open, resisting all attempts to close it without damping down the destructor, with the result that all the heat has leaked away, and the steam in the boiler had to be maintained by firing its furnace with coal. Again, should the damper fix itself in such a way as to close up the by-pass flue, all the

heat, and perhaps too much, must pass through the boiler on its way to the chimney. This is not unattended with serious risk which should not occur, and possibly a solution of the contingency is only to be found in providing a duplicate by-pass flue and damper.

The boiler setting and main flue were not reconstructed by the Horsfall company, with the exception of providing a coal furnace in front of the boiler and a cleaning opening for taking out dust cleaned from the tubes in front of the boiler. In the reconstruction scheme, however, another important adjunct was added by Mr. Cooper, in the form of a second dust deposition and expansion chamber in the main flue near the bottom of the chimney. It consists of an enlargement of the main flue from 4 ft. by 7 ft. to 10 ft. by 7 ft., but set at right angles thereto. It is provided with two fire-brick cross walls, 3 ft. high, forming the floor into three compartments. This chamber has been found very useful for depositing the dust and allowing the gases to expand and cool down before being discharged into the chimney.

The circular chimney is 185 ft. high above ground level, and lined with fire-brick to a height of 90 ft. It was provided with steel bands from the top to near the bottom, and thoroughly overhauled, and all cracks made good internally and externally in the beginning of this year. The cost of reconstruction of the Powderhall destructor on the Horsfall principle, and other incidental work, has been £1,500. After the Horsfall destructor had been working for about six months, a proper test, extending from June 28 to July 12, 1897, or twelve working days, was made for the satisfaction of the arbiter, Mr. B. Hall Blyth, C.E. The results obtained are given in the table on page 50—viz :—

Mr. Hall Blyth's report comments on the trials as follows : "The results show that during the first three days upwards of 80 tons of refuse were daily burned in the destructor, giving a residue of clinker of about 23¼ per cent. The average result during the whole period gives 7¼ tons of refuse per day, leaving 25 per cent. of clinker. During the first three days of the trial this refuse was properly selected, and the results fully come up to the terms of the specification. During the remainder of the trial considerable quantities of sand and dust were allowed to be mixed with the refuse, hence causing the diminution in quantity of the refuse burned. If the destructor is to continue to work satisfactorily instructions should be given to the inspector of cleaning that sand and dust should be carefully excluded from the refuse sent to the destructor for consumption."

At the start of the new Horsfall destructor in February, 1897, the corporation accepted an offer by the Horsfall Refuse Syndicate to dispose of the refuse at the rate of 1s. 4d. per ton. This they continued to do until May 13, 1897, when

## TABLE OF RESULTS OF TWO WEEKS' TEST OF TEN-CELL HORSFALL DESTRUCTOR, AT POWDERHALL, EDINBURGH.

### FROM JUNE 28 TO JULY 12, 1897.

#### FIRST WEEK.

| Date | Time | Weather | Refuse Weighed. | Number of Loads. | Remarks. | Refuse left on deck. | Total Refuse burned. | Clinker. | Clinker percentage to refuse. | Ashes (averaged). | Total Residuum. | Total Residuum percentage by weight to refuse. | Temp. Max. | Temp. Min. | Temp. Average. |
|---|---|---|---|---|---|---|---|---|---|---|---|---|---|---|---|
| | hours. | | tons cwt. qr. | | | cleaned with clear deck. tons cwt. qr. | tons cwt. qr. | tons cwt. qr. lb. | per cent. | tons cwt. qr. | tons cwt. qr. lb. | per cent. | Electric Pyrometer. deg. | deg. | deg. |
| June 28-29 | 24 | Dull, with showers | 84 10 0 | 120 | The refuse for the first three days was mainly composed of house refuse. For the remainder of the week a large percentage of street sweepings and sand was among the refuse delivered. | 3 0 0 | 81 10 0 | 19 0 0 0 | 25·31 | 1 13 0 0 | 20 13 0 0 | 23·33 | 1,816 | 1,242 | 1,264 |
| " 29-30 | 24 | Ditto | 81 0 2 | 119 | | 3 0 0 | 81 0 2 | 19 3 0 0 | 23·68 | 1 13 0 | 20 16 0 14 | 25·54 | 1,905 | 1,616 | 1,805 |
| " 30-July 1 | 24 | Clear, mist during night | 81 13 0 | 121 | | 3 0 0 | 79 13 0 | 19 3 0 14 | 24·05 | 1 13 0 | 20 16 0 14 | 26·12 | 1,903 | 1,525 | 1,781 |
| July 1-2 | 24 | Fair, strong west wind | 74 11 0 | 112 | | 5 0 0 | 74 11 0 | 19 19 1 14 | 26·79 | 1 13 0 | 21 12 1 14 | 28·99 | 1,850 | 1,688 | 1,769 |
| " 2-3 | 24 | Ditto | 69 3 0 | 102 | | 4 0 0 | 70 3 0 | 17 17 3 0 | 25·49 | 1 13 0 | 19 10 3 0 | 27·85 | 1,744 | 1,686 | 1,618 |
| " 3-4-5 (Sunday) | 24 | Fair, very strong west wind | 56 9 0 | 85 | | ... | 60 9 0 | 14 2 2 14 | 23·40 | 1 13 0 | 16 15 2 14 | 26·10 | Pyrometer broken. | | |
| Total loads | | | | 669 | Total burnt ... | ... | 447 5 2 | Total clinker, 109 6 2 14 | Average, 25·45 | Total ashes, 9 18 0 = 2·20 p.c. of total refuse. | Total residuum, 119 4 2 14 | Total, 26·55 | Average temperature, 1,671 deg. | | |
| | | | | | Average burned per 24 hours ... | | 74 10 3 | | | | | | | | |

Steam pressure on boiler, 75 lb. per square inch. On forced blast, 251 lb. per square inch.

#### SECOND WEEK.

| Date | Time | Weather | Refuse Weighed. | Number of Loads. | Remarks. | Started with clear deck. | Total Refuse burned. | Clinker. | Clinker percentage to refuse. | Ashes (averaged). | Total Residuum. | Total Residuum percentage by weight to refuse. | Temp. Max. | Temp. Min. | Temp. Average. |
|---|---|---|---|---|---|---|---|---|---|---|---|---|---|---|---|
| | hours. | | tons cwt. qr. | | | tons cwt. qr. | tons cwt. qr. | tons cwt. qr. lb. | per cent. | tons cwt. qr. | tons cwt. qr. lb. | per cent. | Davis Pyrometer. deg. | deg. | deg. |
| July 5-6 | 24 | Clear, strong west wind | 71 13 2 | 104 | The refuse sent to the destructor during this week had a large amount of street sweepings and sand mixed among the refuse. | 3 10 0 | 68 3 2 | 18 14 0 0 | 27·42 | 1 13 0 | 20 7 0 0 | 29·63 | 1,760 | 1,610 | 1,685 |
| " 6-7 | 24 | Showery, strong west wind | 71 18 2 | 108 | | 3 0 0 | 71 18 2 | 19 0 3 14 | 26·47 | 1 13 0 | 20 16 3 14 | 28·68 | 1,800 | 1,700 | 1,772 |
| " 7-8 | 24 | Showery, light west wind | 76 17 2 | 111 | | 2 0 0 | 77 17 2 | 18 3 0 14 | 23·34 | 1 13 0 | 19 16 2 14 | 25·55 | 1,800 | 1,600 | 1,735 |
| " 8-9 | 24 | Dull, strong N.W. wind | 73 5 0 | 120 | | 2 0 0 | 73 13 0 | 18 6 0 2 | 24·97 | 1 13 0 | 19 19 0 2 | 27·18 | 1,800 | 1,745 | 1,789 |
| " 9-10 | 24 | Clear, light west wind | 73 13 0 | 114 | | 6 0 0 and 6 11 0 in carts | 73 13 0 | 18 6 4 2 | 24·91 | 1 13 0 | 19 19 4 2 | 27·12 | 1,790 | 1,750 | 1,795 |
| " 10-12 | 16 & 8 calcu-lated* | Ditto | 61 0 0 | 86 | | | 75 13 2 | †20 0 1 0 | 26·51 | | 21 14 1 0 | 28·75 | | | 1,705 |
| Total loads | | | | 637 | Total burnt ... | | 440 11 2 | Total clinker, 112 12 3 2 | Average, 25·60 | Total ashes, 9 18 0 = 2·24 p.c. of total refuse. | Total residuum, 112 10 3 2 | Total, 27·82 | Average temperature, 1,757 deg. | | |
| | | | | | Average burned per 24 hours ... | | 73 8 2 | | | | | | | | |

Steam pressure on boiler, 75 lb. per square inch. On forced blast, 25 lb. to 35 lb. per square inch.

Edinburgh refuse measures 80 cubic feet to the ton. Edinburgh clinker measures 40 cubic feet to the ton (before being slaked).

\* Less 8 hours calculated. (60 tons 9 cwt. in 16 hours = 76 tons 13 cwt. 2 qr. in 24 hours.)

† 12 tons 6 cwt. 19 lb. in sixteen hours = 20 tons 1 cwt. 1 qr. in twenty-four hours.

NOTE.—The average over the whole trial of total residuum by weight being, say, 28 per cent. of the weight of refuse burned, the reduction of the bulk is 28 × $\frac{40}{80}$ = 14 per cent. of original bulk of refuse.

the rate was increased to 1s. 8d. per ton. At the beginning of October, 1897, the corporation took the burning of the refuse into their own hands, the services of the foreman of the Horsfall company being retained to superintend the work under the burgh engineer.

The staff and wages of the workmen are as follow—viz.: One manager, superintending and attending to boiler, engine and electric lighting, &c., £3 per week; one engineer, ditto, £2 2s. per week; seven stokers, charging the furnaces, 28s. each per week; six ditto, attending to fires and clinkering, 30s. each per week; three barrowmen, wheeling away clinker to cooling platform, 28s. each per week. There are also three men, at 25s. each per week, engaged in watering and wheeling away the cold clinker and dust from the cooling platform to the clinker bing. The men at the furnaces work in three shifts of eight hours each, disposed in the work of one shift as follows: Two men charging the cells, with the addition of one extra man on the night shift; two men attending and clinkering the fires; One barrowman wheeling clinker and ash from clinkering-house to cooling platform.

Work goes on continuously from 10 o'clock on Sunday night to 10 o'clock on the Saturday night following, the fires being damped down on Sunday. Flue cleaning is done weekly or fortnightly, as required, by the first shift beginning. The furnaces, until about three months ago, were charged and clinkered every one hour and twenty minutes. From the beginning of October, 1897, to the end of March, 1898, the average quantity of refuse burned per cell in twenty-four hours amounted to 7·3 tons. At this rate the average cost works out at 1s. 9·45d. per ton. With the object of burning the refuse more thoroughly, and trying to obtain a more satisfactory clinker, the furnaces are now charged and clinkered every two hours. It is found that the destructor could be worked with five men less under this arrangement, but the average amount of refuse burned is now reduced to 6 tons per cell per twenty-four hours. The average cost of burning at the present time is 1s. 9·23d. per ton. This amount only includes the wages of the manager, engineer, charging men, stokers and barrowmen, and the men employed in tipping the residue. No charge is included for maintenance, tools, repairs, &c., or for repayment of capital expenditure.

## DISCUSSION OF MR. YOUNG'S PAPER.

Mr. J. PATON (Plymouth) said it appeared to him that the Edinburgh Corporation had set up a very high standard with regard to the collection of refuse. If he was not mistaken, Mr. Young said that the dust was collected daily, a system which would add enormously to the cost of collection. He must say, however, that the corporation had been somewhat unfortunate in the erection of a destructor, and the figure of 1s. 9d. per ton for burning was somewhat alarming to him, because he had been accustomed to hear figures very much lower than that. He also understood that this 1s. 9d. per ton was without allowing for interest on capital and payments to sinking fund. It would, therefore, be of interest to know what was the actual cost of burning, including all charges. When they went before their committees or local authorities the first thing they wanted to know was the actual cost of the work.

Mr. C. JONES (Ealing) considered that Mr. Paton had put a very pertinent question when he said they wanted to know not only the cost of the burning but the total cost. Another point that was raised was the destruction of the road refuse as well as of the house refuse. It did not affect his district, but in many of the larger towns it would form a serious item in connection with the destruction of the refuse. With regard to the unfortunate position in which the Edinburgh Corporation found themselves some time ago, they must bear in mind that a destructor was a novelty. They knew that things went out of date rapidly in these fast-changing days; but, at the same time, they must give credit to those who went in front and made the way straight to those who came after them. They ought to feel thankful to those who took this up in the embryo stage. There were some striking features in the paper, and, perhaps, one of the most striking was the last clause of the report of the arbiters. It was to this effect: "That more intelligent and experienced stokers should be employed in the working." To himself that assumed the most important aspect of the whole affair. It was the intelligent working of the little details that went to make up the prosperity of the whole. It was his good fortune to visit Edinburgh, and, in company with Mr. Cooper and Mr. Laws, go over the destructor works, and, singularly enough, they arrived at the very same conclusion—that the principal difficulty in the whole thing was the fact that it was not intelligently worked. He was quite prepared to admit that he did not say as much as that before the judge, or whatever they called him in Scotland. What he wanted to say was this: A destructor was a valuable adjunct to every town, whether of the low-temperature type, of which he was supposed to be a great advocate, or of the high-temperature, which was just now flooding the market—but, of whichever type, it was the intelligent working of the destructor which made it a success. The question had been raised as to the working expenses. He must say that the expenditure per ton as given by Mr. Young staggered him. He had burnt at a low temperature, and whether he burnt off 6 or 7 tons per cell a day was of no

great moment, but he did get a splendid clinker; and the cost of burning was 1s. 6½d. as against 1s. 9d. Then at Edinburgh they had to add to the high figures the expenditure and permanent charges, which might be 5d., 6d. or 7d. per ton. That made all the difference as to the success of the thing. They might put up a high-temperature destructor, which might do a large amount of work, but if it was to be done at an excess of cost they had better fall back upon that which did not produce such startling effects, but gave them a result which was far more satisfactory so far as the Chancellor of the Exchequer was concerned. He must say that the charge put down was most extravagant. The utmost of his cost for the work was 1s. 6½d. per ton, and by the splendid clinker which he produced, and of which he had never an ounce to spare, using it for sewage tanks, artificial stone, &c., he reduced the cost to about 3½d. per ton. With respect to the various points that had been raised, he had only one thing to say, and, perhaps, somewhat outside the ordinary line. and that was to express his strong opinion to those who were going into this matter, to give very little heed to the destructor question beyond the fact of its being a destructor. From day to day, as his newspaper cuttings came in, he saw the tendency to mislead the economical members of their councils, and giving them the idea that they were going to get a marvellous lot of work out of nothing. In fact, they were going to light their towns by electricity out of the burning of the refuse, and the economical members of the council saw these fine things and wanted to know how it was their surveyor had not brought it before them. The member of the council was not behind the scenes as they were; did not know that the things which had been put before them had gone no further; that the thing upon which a company was to be founded had never had five minutes' action. Then they must take into consideration that the house refuse of certain districts was of a class which they could not match in other parts of England. These things were lost sight of. It was not said that the calorific value was so good that no other town in England could be compared with it. Only the previous day a newspaper cutting reported that the Vestry of Bermondsey had found that their refuse was infinitely better than the refuse of another place. Probably the next cutting would be that a town in the north, beginning with E, had a refuse which was infinitely better than places in the south beginning with S and B, and that they would have the town lighted with electric light, and electric cars running about the streets all from the burning of the house refuse. A destructor was a means of destroying house and road refuse, and there they had better leave it. If they put up electric light works, let them be independent and they might succeed, but if they depended upon the intermittent power to be obtained from the destructor, and the power must be intermittent, they would make a very big mistake, whatever the patentees of destructors, A, B and C, might say.

Mr. C. F. WIKE (Sheffield) said that, as he understood complaints were made in Edinburgh as to the nuisance caused by the destructor, he would say a few words as to how these things were worked up. Sheffield was not Edinburgh, neither was it rural nor very romantic, especially in the district where the destructor was constructed. Complaints had been made about certain works in the neighbourhood, and certain gentlemen, with a view to taking the wind out of the sails of the corporation, began to complain of the smoke from the destructor. The chairman allowed the complaints to go on for a time, and then the reply sent was a very simple one, that the destructor had not been working for a month (laughter). They were burning 10½ tons per cell per day to a certain extent at the expense of the fabric, and the residuum was 27 per cent.

Mr. MACKENZIE said he would like to support Mr. Jones' view that a destructor was a dust destroyer and not a wealth producer. They ought to insist, as sanitary engineers, that the refuse should be thoroughly destroyed. He was pleased that Edinburgh was prepared to pay the price to destroy its refuse thoroughly and completely.

Mr. J. PARKER (Hereford) said he could not quite agree with Mr. Jones' view as to the purpose of a destructor. There was a useful calorific value produced by the burning of the refuse, and he was of opinion that the heat should be utilised to produce steam for electric lighting or other purposes. He was struck by the high cost entailed by the burning of the refuse in Edinburgh, as the cost at Hereford was about 7d. per ton, and they obtained a large amount of clinker, which could be utilised for artificial blocks and other purposes. Mr. JONES wished to explain that he had been utilising the heat from his destructor in the production of steam for thirteen years.

Mr. W. HARPUR (Cardiff) asked whether they attributed their success in Edinburgh in getting rid of the nuisance which formerly existed to the alteration of the cell or the construction of the dust catcher, or a combination of both.

Mr. J. COOPER (Edinburgh) explained that their reason for bringing forward this paper was that they might gather up the experience of the country. They had experienced much criticism in Edinburgh in regard to the destructor, and no doubt quite justifiably. Latterly they had adopted a method which had put an end to the nuisance from the chimney, and the dust catcher had given them further help in dealing with the refuse without causing any nuisance. The other day, when Lord Kelvin was at the destructor, he told them he believed they could utilise the heat, and by converting it into steam obtain 300 horse-power. Lord Kelvin also told them that if they could utilise the steam in that way they might burn their refuse for nothing. He could only say they would be very glad to dispose of their refuse so cheaply. They were constantly being told in Edinburgh that Bermondsey and Shoreditch, and other places, were burning their refuse and lighting their districts with electric light from the power produced by the refuse. They had not investigated these things for themselves, and would be glad to hear the truth of them. There was no doubt in principle that the burning of the refuse was the right thing for large cities, and that the day would come when they would dispose of all their refuse in this way. They were getting rid of the greater part of their refuse in Edinburgh by dumping it into a big quarry, and that method of disposal was costing them 1s. 6d. per ton. That was an excessive price, and they could not tell what mischief they might be doing in poisoning the water springs in the neighbourhood. They had employed the Horsfall company to reconstruct the destructor because their specifications exactly met the requirements of the experts employed by the court of law, and they thought if the experts approved their methods they were safe in employing them. They had still to complete the year's maintenance agreed upon, and after that the corporation were left with the appliance to make the best and the worst of it. What they wanted to get at the bottom of was, how best and cheapest they could dispose of their house refuse, but they had not adopted Mr. Jones' method of making artificial stone and utilising the clinker so as to bring the cost down to 3¼d. per ton. They would be happy if they could do so. Mr. Jones was brought to Edinburgh when they were in the courts of law to deliver them, and he left them hopelessly in the hands of their enemies.

Bailie MACKENZIE (Edinburgh) remarked that, as one of the members of the town council, he came there to get a great deal of light on this question, one aspect of which he had studied for some time. They read in the daily newspapers, and sometimes in the technical journals, that in London they were able to destroy the refuse and get a good deal of power out of it, even making a profit out of it. Mr. Cooper had told them what had been said by Lord Kelvin, who was a great man, and sometimes spoke a deal of nonsense—(laughter)—and when the Shoreditch destructor was opened they heard of its value for electric lighting. He saw that the Shoreditch people had published their accounts for nine months' working, but he gathered they were in such a hopeless state of confusion that nobody could make head or tail of them. Mr. Hammond, a leading electrician, who laid himself out to analyse electric light accounts, examined these accounts, and admitted that they were very wonderful but not understandable—(laughter). When they in Edinburgh consulted an expert as to utilising the heat, he told them that if they put their electric light works at the destructor they might get 150 or 200 horse-power from the destructor, but as that was only a drop in the bucket to them they did not think the game was worth the candle. He hoped they would speak their minds freely and put down the humbug which was talked about of getting so much power from destructors.

Mr. A. E. COLLINS (Norwich) remarked that sufficient note had not been made of the fact that the large bulk of the Edinburgh refuse to its weight would much increase the cost of burning it. If they had refuse half the weight to that of other places, it would probably cost double as much to burn it. With respect to the nuisance from the Horsfall cell, he was surprised to hear there was a nuisance. In Norwich they had a small installation in the middle of the city, and they got absolutely no complaints at all—(Mr. Cooper: There are no complaints since the Horsfall system started). With reference to the power from the destructor when they got their winter refuse, they could get a useful horse-power from the cells, perhaps 80 to 100 horse-power for the two cells, but in the summer time, when they got a good deal of garden refuse, the horse-power was not much. Where a town collected all the refuse they could not rely upon it.

Mr. CAMPBELL (Canterbury) asked whether the diagram represented the cross-section of the destructor in use at Powderhall.

Mr. YOUNG said it exactly represented the destructor, with the exception that below the grate-bar there were two tubes carried down for the forced blast. They had side boxes along each side of the cell, and above the grate-bar they had two tubes fitted with valves. These side boxes were covered with plates, which occasionally buckled and the blast leaked directly into the cell. That was one of the disadvantages.

Mr. CAMPBELL said it seemed to him that a great deal of distillation of dry refuse must take place from the discharge into the hoppers, and that a good deal of vapour and foul odour would be given off.

On the proposition of the PRESIDENT, seconded by Mr. SMITH-SAVILLE (Darwen), a vote of thanks was then accorded to the author for his paper.

---

When the interesting and animated discussion of Mr. Young's paper had concluded, it was arranged that Mr. Colam, whose paper was the next to be taken, should also, on account of the amount of work to be got through in a limited time, briefly summarise the points. The following is the paper :—

## CONVERSION OF EDINBURGH, LEITH AND PORTOBELLO HORSE TRAMWAYS SYSTEMS INTO CABLE TRACTION.

### By WILLIAM NEWBY COLAM, M.I.C.E., M.I.M.E.

[Mr. William Newby Colam, M.INST.C.E., M.INST.M.E., a past-president of the Society of Engineers, served his time as civil engineer with Mr. Wilson W. Phipson, M.INST.C.E., London, and as mechanical engineer with Messrs. Maudslay, Sons & Field, of Westminster. Subsequently he was for over six years with a well-known firm of shipowners, being engaged during a part of that time in connection with the construction of floating docks, slip ways, &c. Mr. Colam, it seems, is not unacquainted with the trials attending shipwreck, so that his experiences with the sea have not been altogether without excitement. For the past seventeen years he has been principally engaged in tramway work, which he studied in the States, and has constructed over 40 miles of mechanically-worked lines, besides re-laying several miles of horse tramways in London. He is at present engaged upon a system of 41 miles of cable haulage in Edinburgh, as described in the following paper.]

The author regrets that the time given for the preparation of his paper has not been sufficient to enable him to deal with the subject in a more technical manner, but he hopes the practical results of working given will be of some use to the members.

On the occasion of your association's last visit to this city, in the year 1890, the author had the pleasure of submitting a paper explanatory of the construction and working of the Edinburgh Northern Cable Tramways, and on this occasion the author trusts it may be considered opportune to lay before the members the last eight years' experience in operating these lines, and to describe the conversion from horse to cable traction at present in hand within the Edinburgh boundaries, and also as about to be proceeded with in the Leith domain.

### EIGHT YEARS' EXPERIENCE.

In 1890 the cable system in Edinburgh was in its infancy, as the second line built had only been opened to the public in the month of February of that year, and the first line in January, 1888. The information available at that time as to the operating costs was not reliable, because the lines had not been at work long enough to ascertain how far the working costs would be increased after the lines and machinery

EDINBURGH: GENERAL VIEW OF THE SHRUBHILL CABLE POWER STATION FROM THE WEST.

had been in use for some years. This can now be given without any dubiety from the regular balance-sheets for the last ten and a half years up to the date when the Corporation of Edinburgh bought up the lines at a price which yielded a profit over the original cost of construction of about 30 per cent.

The conditions under which these lines have been compelled to operate cannot be considered conducive to the best financial results for either receipts or expenditure, for the following among other reasons :—

(1) The maximum speed was limited to 6 miles per hour when the system was inaugurated, mainly because it was something new, and has not since been raised because in the hilly district, perhaps, slow speed is not so noticeable.

(2) No Sunday traffic on tramways has been permitted.

(3) The routes are most exceptionally hilly.

(4) The ends of the routes are not built over, and lead nowhere in particular.

(5) The engines are high-pressure non-condensing, working at low pressure of steam.

(6) There are no economiser means of utilising the gases nor feed-water heaters.

(7) The whole managerial department was in London, which necessitated heavy travelling expenses.

Notwithstanding the unfair limitation in speed and other drawbacks, the results have been eminently satisfactory, as will be seen from the following statement (Table No. 1) made from a comparison of results in 1890 with the last year of the company's working in 1896.

TABLE No. 1.

| Year. | Motive Power. | Maintenance. | Total. | Car Miles. | Passengers |
|---|---|---|---|---|---|
| 1890 | £1,279 | £2,219 | £3,498 | 222,822 | 2,582,620 |
| 1896 | 1,180 | 2,710 | 3,890 | 376,725 | 3,715,989 |
| Increase ⎱ per cent. ⎰ | ... | 22·12 | 11·23 | 69·06 | 43·88 |
| Decrease ⎱ per cent. ⎰ | 7·74 | ... | ... | ... | ... |

NOTE.—The motive power, includes wages, coals, oil tar, waste, water, and engine-room requirements; maintenance is for road, cars and plant.

The tabulated results of No. 1 must be somewhat puzzling to the uninitiated in cable haulage, because, when analysed, they show that although the mileage has been increased 69·06 per cent., and the number of passengers carried increased 43·88 per cent., the cost of motive power, instead of being greater, happened to be less.

The reduction in cost of motive power has been due to improvements and a slight reduction in the price of coal, and the reason for no increase is that the loads up and down balanced on an average. These figures once more prove that cable haulage is able to enormously increase its car service, and so provide for the future without appreciable increase in its working expenses.

It will be observed from the returns of working that, whereas the number of passengers only increased 43·88 per cent., the car mileage increased 69·06 per cent. This is most important to note, because it points to a factor peculiar to cable haulage. It is directly in the interests of the management to improve the service of cars beyond even the requirements of the public, because, beyond the wages of the drivers and conductors, very little extra is incurred in placing each additional car on the line.

Even more satisfactory results than are shown in Table No. 1 were recorded on one of the cable lines during a week of greatly augmented traffic, and the author now presents these figures, believing them to show the most unique results for the conditions of operating which have ever been obtained in tramway practice in Great Britain. The ordinary weekly working expenses given in the table was arrived at by a division of the yearly certified accounts of fifty-two weeks, and the increased cost of operating was carefully checked during the week, and was mostly due to wages and gratuities given to the men and inspectors for close attention to their duties.

TABLE No. 2.

| Year 1893. | No. of Cars. | Mileage of Cars. | Passengers. | Tons hauled per Mile. | Cost per Ton per Mile in Pence. | Total receipts. | Total Ex-pences. |
|---|---|---|---|---|---|---|---|
| Show week, July 24th to 29th. | 47 | 3,395 | 112,663 | 7·14 | ·75 | £468 | £75 |
| Ordinary week. Average 4 weeks. | 36 | 2,514 | 27,541 | 5·75 | 1·11 | 114 | 67 |
| Increase per cent. | 31 | 35 | 309 | 24 | ... | 311 | 12 |
| Decrease per cent. | ... | ... | ... | ... | 33 | ... | ... |

Table 2 shows that with the same fares a cable tramway was able to increase its receipts 311 per cent. by a rise of working expenses of 12 per cent. only. That by quickening the service of cars by one and one-eighth minutes, when the traffic would warrant it, the working expenses per car mile run were reduced ¾d., and that the tons hauled per mile increased 24 per cent., and the cost of hauling a ton mile was reduced 33 per cent. *This is elasticity in the right direction, and the author is of opinion that local authorities and tramway companies too often make the mistake of not thoroughly arriving at sound conclusions as to the elasticity of a mode of traction in this direction when considering the initial cost of systems under scrutiny.*

The last return of the company's workings showed that the cost per car mile, including every charge possible, except. ing depreciation and interest on capital, was 5·2 pence, notwithstanding the restriction on speed and the severe hills, &c. The receipts per car mile had only been 10·13 pence, which was just about what the cost per car mile run has been on the horse system in Edinburgh. The foregoing facts conclusively prove that the lines have been a great success financially, and the fact of the Corporation of Edinburgh still favouring cable should be sufficient authority for the statement that mechanically they have met with public approval.

THE PRESENT SCHEME.

Having now brought the paper read before you in 1890 up to date, the author will lay before the members some particulars as to the big system of cable haulage which the Corporation of Edinburgh are nearing the completion of. The Corporation of Edinburgh have purchased all the tramways within the limits of the borough, and they have leased the working to a company for twenty-one years, the company agreeing as follows :—

(1) To pay interest of 7 per cent. upon the price paid by the corporation for old lines, and the same rate of interest upon all sums of mony expended by the corporation in converting to any form of mechanical traction they choose.

They also agree to set by each year a fixed sum of money sufficient to return the capital of the lessees, and to ensure the tramway lines and other works being left in a thoroughly good condition when the lease expires.

(2) To pay the cost of maintaining the tramway tracks and other works.

EDINBURGH: TOLLCROSS CABLE-POWER STATION, VIEW OF CHIMNEY.

(3) To reduce the hours of workmen as desired by the corporation.

(4) To pay 3 per cent. upon sums expended by corporation in reconstruction until the lines are finished.

The corporation by borrowing the necessary money for the purchase and construction of lines at 2¼ per cent., and by getting 7 per cent. from the lessees, will be able to write off the cost of the tramway system within the terms of the lease. The author thinks that the corporation is to be congratulated upon the arrangement made, and suggests that those who advocate municipal working of tramways might consider the Edinburgh arrangement worthy of favourable reflection.

Before entering upon descriptive matter, it may be of primary interest to give what the author believes to have been some of the corporation's reasons for adopting cable haulage in preference to other mechanical powers which have found favour elsewhere. First of all, it must be stated that the original lines were self-contained, there was in no measure the inducement for extending the system for the preservation of continuity. Secondly, the overhead wire system of electricity, which was the only other system reported as being anything like a financial success, was not entertained in Edinburgh because of its interference with the amenities of the city. Thirdly, because the contour of the city is peculiar in being exceptionally hilly, and where so many hills exist in a city it is of paramount importance that the speed ascending hills shall not be less than that attainable on level portions of the routes. Fourthly, the buildings limit line of the city is more markedly defined than in most cities. Fifthly, the cable system in Birmingham, London and Edinburgh had placed the fact beyond a doubt that the corporation could treat for a lessee with full knowledge of what would be an approximate working cost per car mile with the cable system, whereas by any other system which could be in any way considered no such reliable information was available, particularly from experience of operating under British Board of Trade regulations. Further, it is within the author's knowledge that eminent electrical opinion has been given that Edinburgh is not a suitable place for electrical traction in any form.

The diagram exhibited gives the tramways systems of Edinburgh, Portobello and Leith as at present cabled and being cabled, or about to be converted to cable haulage, and the subsequent table gives the miles of lines within these respective districts reduced to single track of tramway.

TABLE No. 3.

|  | Miles of Double Track. | Miles of Single Track. | Reduced to Miles of Single Track. |
|---|---|---|---|
| Edinburgh ... | 19·004 | ·700 | 38·708 |
| Portobello ... | 2·110 | ... | 4·220 |
| Leith ... | 2·165 | ·170 | 4·500 |
| Total ... | 23·279 | ·870 | 47·428 |

On the diagram the positions of power car-houses are indicated by circles. No. 1 is one of the new depots from which all the cables in the south-west and westerly districts are to be operated, and provision is here made for extensions in these districts. No. 2 depot is being constructed on a portion of the stable land of the horse tramways, and from here the whole Leith and south-east cables will be operated. No. 3 depot is to be a small depot principally for the storage of cars for the eastern district, but an engine is to be placed here to work the Portobello and Waterloo-place lines at higher speeds than would be convenient through the centre of Edinburgh. The old cable depot at Henderson-row will not be done away with, as it will be useful for extensions of the system on the northern districts.

EDINBURGH: TOLLCROSS CABLE-POWER STATION, SOUTH FRONT OF CAR SHEDS.

The diagram also indicates to a certain extent the various directions in which the tramway traffic can be worked. Throughout the system there will exist nearly all conditions of tramway operating which are to be met with in ordinary practice. For instance, the grades are as high as 1 in 11, there are right-angle branches, "S" junctions and compound triangular junctions to be worked. Single lines of track with passing places are not common, but at places are required. Cross traffic, where cables cross each other, have also to be dealt with. Bridges and cellars have already been crossed by the cable construction in Edinburgh, when clearances of 14in. only from the surfaces of the roads have been available, and lastly, an arrangement for crossing a swing-bridge in the Leith district has been designed. Arrangements are made by which the traffic can be returned or (short circuited) through turns out when the management considers it will be advisable during parts of the day to provide an augmented service of cars short of the terminus of the route, and such provision is also made for isolating a cable section where a block may occur.

The general speed of cars throughout the Edinburgh district is to be 8 miles per hour, but passing round important corners and over congested crossings the drivers of cars will not be able to acquire a higher speed than 4 miles per hour, and they will be able to go as much slower than 4 miles as may be required. Provision is being made to increase the maximum speeds when the Board of Trade may give permission. In the outlying district of Portobello it is expected that the Board of Trade will raise no objection to 0 miles.

SOME TECHNICAL DETAILS.

The permanent way will, perhaps, interest the members as much as anything on the cable tramways at their present stage of construction. The track rails are of the usual type

now common for tramways, and are 6½ in. deep, weighing 83 lb. to the yard run. The joint adopted by the Corporation of Edinburgh was quite new, as will be seen from the specimen produced. The two objects sought to be obtained are: Firstly, that the wheel in rolling along the tread of the rail shall not, in passing from one rail to the other, be left without a support, and thereby it is hoped that all chances of concussion due to break-joint will be abolished. Secondly, that by the arrangement of recessed nuts and flat cheese-headed bolts, the paving may be brought square up to the the edges of the rails, and the author submits these two improvements are of very considerable importance.

The tests of 42 to 44 tons per square inch for tensile, 15 to 20 per cent. on 8 in. for elongation, and 40 to 45 per cent. contraction called for in the specification was objected to by British manufacturers, but the engineers are pleased to report that the effort was made, and the tests were fully obtained, with the result that whereas 39 tons is rather hard and yet tough rails have been laid in the system.

The slot rails, a specimen of which is also shown, weighs 48 lb. per yard, and are made of a somewhat milder steel than the track rails, the tensile asked for being 39 tons to the square inch, with 15 per cent. elongation and a contraction of 30 per cent. The actual amount of metal appearing on the surface of the street in these slot rails is 1⅟₁₆ in. Against these rails also it will be observed that the paving setts can be placed right up to the edge of the rail without any chipping, and on a square bed, which is important. The Barrow Hæmatite Steel Company carried out one contract for rails and Messrs. Dick, Kerr & Co. the other

The points and crossings are all to be made of steel, and no facing points are used excepting when they cannot be avoided, such as at junctions. Trailing points for track and slot rails will work by springs, but where facing points are required the track points are connected underground to the slot points by levers in such a manner that, whichever way they are thrown over, there is a locking apparatus introduced to fix the slot correctly with the track points. The slot points are built up of cast and spring steel. The track points are made of cast steel, and track over slot and slot over track crossings are built up from the section of these rails, but the junctions of slot and slot are made of cast steel with renewable points.

The paving setts are granite of two qualities, as far as workmanship is concerned. Specimens of these two qualities are exhibited. Inside the track the setts are 3 in. wide by 5 in. deep, and the average length is about 6 in. Outside the track the setts are 6 in. deep by 3 in. wide. The better quality of setts are axed on top as well as square on ends and sides. The hatch covers, which are used in the track for obtaining access to the pulleys, are filled with granite setts specially dressed, and of the same size as other setts, so that in ordinary conditions they are almost imperceptible on the road surface. In the road construction a great deal of wood has been used, and this has chiefly been of the hard Australian qualities. In some cases the wood has been laid from curb to curb, including inside the tramway track.

The standard distance between the tramway tracks is 4 ft., but where the streets are narrow this has been reduced to 3 ft. At places where the streets are exceptionally wide, the tracks have been spread apart to give a distance between of 6 ft. and electric posts have been erected in the centre. The width of the slot is specified to be in no case more that ¼ in. The terminal pits for diverting the cables at the terminal of each route are not of the design described in the author's paper of 1890, but are so constructed that, regardless of whether the route ends on an incline upwards or downwards, the cars will proceed to the extreme end of the journey by means of the cable, and no gravitation whatever will be resorted to. This is attained by passing the cable around two large vertically-placed pulleys, one behind the other, and one slightly inclined. By this means, even in a heavy snowstorm, a car could proceed through the snow to its terminus and start out again without the tracks being cleared.

Where cables terminate in the middle of a route and meet other cables, the two cables are made to lap past each other by arrangement of large pulleys placed in a pit. At these places the cables are so arranged that the operation of releasing from one cable and taking the other is performed while the car is at a state of rest, and will not require more than fifteen seconds to accomplish the change over. The operation is practically automatic. The reduced maximum speeds of cables for passing round important main corners in streets is obtained by the introduction of auxiliary cables, which are worked off the axles of large pulleys kept in motion by the main cable, and the main cables are thus saved from a great deal of hard work, and their lives, consequently, will be materially lengthened.

The author feels sure that the following information as to the rate at which cable tramways have been laid in Edinburgh will be of interest to the members. There seems to be an idea existing that cable tramway tracks are very serious innovations for streets, because they require a tube construction beyond an ordinary tramway track. The following information will confute any such erroneous impression. During the first twelve months of the contract there were laid in the streets of Edinburgh a trifle over twenty miles of cable track. The greatest speed attained was during six consecutive days, when an average of 220 yards per day was attained on one section of new lines.  It will be seen that the amount of finished work during twelve months averages out to a little more than 112 yards per working day, which would be considered splendid work for an ordinary horse tramway line, where the traffic is such as in Edinburgh, and where the tramway service has to be maintained.  The contract for road and pit work was secured by Messrs. Dick, Kerr & Co., Limited.

The depot for the western district, No. 1 on diagram, is the most important, and, as some of the members may be visiting it, the author will briefly describe the construction and equipment which is intended for this depot.  The site is by no means an ideal one for the purpose, but by its adoption a miserable collection of houses has been removed and a great public improvement has been effected.  The buildings stand one block and a street back from the main road, and the communication between it and the main tramway is through a very narrow lane.  The principal materials used in the building are red stone and a fine quality of brick, the former being exclusively employed for the front elevations.  The buildings include engine-room, boiler-room, chimney 180 ft. high, pump-room, built-in water tanks to hold 40,000 gallons, turning-room, car-sheds for forty-three cars, cart-sheds and stable for three horses, stores for road work, and underground stores for oils, &c., lavatories, offices, &c.  The chief station for storing, painting and repairing cars is at No. 2 station, where the sheds are divided into sections, to isolate the cars in case of fire.  Total accommodation for the storing of 225 cars is being provided.

The engines are horizontal compound non-condensing, with cylinders placed side by side on separate cranks set at right angles.  There are three pairs of engines attached to the one line of main shafting.  Each main shaft is divided into sections, which can be connected by specially-arranged couplings forged on the shaft ends.  Two 14 ft. 6 in. diameter grooved pulleys are mounted in the line of shafting, so that any two of the three engines can be geared to work the two pulleys.  These pulleys are made for carrying thirty-two ropes of 1¾ in. diameter, and they will revolve at forty-five revolutions per minute.  The power of the engines will be transmitted to the counter shaft through pulleys 30 ft. diameter.  The high-pressure cylinders are 23 in. and the low-pressure cylinders are 40 in. diameter.  The stroke is 5 ft.  A premium of £5 per cent. has been offered as a bonus on the contract price of the engines for every 1 lb. of water per indicated horse-power consumed per hour less than the 20 lb. specified.  In like manner a deduction of £5 per cent. will be made, but should the consumption per indicated horse-power reach 23 lb. the engines may be rejected.  The engine-room is provided with two cranes to lift 2½ tons each.  Messrs. Dick, Kerr & Co., Limited, secured the contract for this portion of the work.

## THE BOILER-HOUSE.

This is placed immediately behind and considerably lower than the engine-room.  The coals taken in off the road have not far to be lifted into the bunkers over the boilers.  All the pipes to and from the boilers and engines pass underneath the engine-room floors without dipping, and do not appear at all in the engine-room, also the low level of boilers should also reduce the chance of priming through syphoning.

The boilers are cylindrical marine type, 10 ft. 6 in. by 12 ft., with superheater tubes on the top.  The gases from the fire enter a back combustion chamber, from which they pass to the front of the boiler through tubes into the smoke-box.  They are returned over the top of the boiler, passing on their way around superheater tubes into a second back chamber which directs the gases along the bottom of the boilers into the main flue.

Apparatus is provided for diverting the gases down the sides of the boilers, in case the superheater tube should require attention when the boiler is under steam.  The duty of these boilers is to evaporate not less than 9,000 lb. of water per hour at a boiler pressure of 160 lb.  There are four such boilers designed to work up to a pressure ultimately of 100 lb.  These boilers will not be worked to anything like their full capacity, and a large reserve will always be kept in hand.

The main steam piping is welded steel, and all in duplicate.  The feed pipes are in copper and are duplicated.  The boilers are fitted with "Vicars, mechanical stokers," supplied with coal from an overhead bunker running the full length of the boiler-house.  Coal is taken up with ropes to the bunkers in receptacles resembling contractors' steel waggons, which are so adapted that they are suitable either for use on the body of a cart through the streets or to form the tipping body of a tramway coal truck which will travel on rails over the top of the coal bunker.

There are two heaters, arranged so that they may be used together or separately.  These are of the "Brown-Berryman type," and each heater is capable of passing 1,600 gallons of water per hour.  The pumps are in duplicate, and are 8-in. double-vertical "Weir's type."  The arrangement of pipes from the pumps is to effect the following

### COMBINATION OF FEEDING:—

(a) All the boilers may be fed with hot water.
(b) All the boilers may be fed with cold water.
(c) Any number of boilers may be fed with hot or cold water,

(d) Any one boiler may be fed with hot and cold water.
(e) Any one boiler may be fed with hot or cold water.

Messrs. George Sinclair are the contractors for the work in connection with the boilers, &c.

At No. 2 depot the arrangements of boilers and machinery is much the same as at No. 1, only the boiler-house is not placed exactly in the same relative position to the engine-house, but has the advantage of being at the side of a railway, so that a siding has been made by which means coals can be lifted direct up into the bunkers instead of having to be brought in carts as at No. 1 depot.  At this depot all the smithy, repair, general machine, carpenter's and paint shops are placed.  At both depots the cars are brought in and taken out from the main road by auxiliary cables, and they are traversed into the repair shops or ordinary sidings by traversers, also worked by auxiliary cables.

The tension races are immediately at the back of the engine-rooms, and under car-shed floors.  This apparatus is similar in some respects to that described by the author in 1890, excepting that the pulleys on the main carriages are placed horizontally instead of vertically, and all the tension weights are arranged vertically upon the wall of the engine-room, so that the man in charge can observe at any moment the fluctuation of strains taking place upon any one line being driven from each station.  From No. 1 station there will be five cables driven, and the longest at present will be 21,000 ft., but these will all be capable of considerable extension.  The longest cable in the system at present is 34,500 ft.  The mode of driving the cables is somewhat as explained in the author's paper of 1890, but the grip pulley has the improved white metal jaw, which has given great satisfaction in the London cable tramways.  Each grip pulley can be thrown out of action without interfering with any other, by means of a coil clutch of powerful construction.

EDINBURGH : TOLLCROSS CABLE-POWER STATION, INTERIOR OF ENGINE-ROOM (ENGINES IN COURSE OF ERECTION).

Opposite each rope drive there will be an iron drum, with a spare cable for its respective route, ready at any moment to be run into the road.  At the side of the engine-room an engine and drum is provided for hauling out old cables, and it is estimated that the longest cable will be taken out and a new one put in within the space of one hour.

The gripper apparatus to be placed on the cars is an important feature of the arrangements made for cabling the Edinburgh extensions.  The gripper shown in the author's paper of 1890 would not meet all the requirements of the new lines where some cables have to be taken in the gripper to the left and others to the right of the direction in which the car is proceeding.  The new gripper also has to be able to pass over crossing cables.  The new gripper has been designed and tested on the lines of the existing cables, and can be seen by the members at the company's depot at Henderson-row.  The whole machinery is enclosed with a cast-iron box standing on the platform of the car, and occupying about the same space as is taken up on the car by an electric tramway standard.  The main improvements over the gripper of 1890 consists of provision by which the driver of the car standing in the front of the car can operate the gripper by his side or the one at the rear end of the car by a simple reversing of a lever.  It is by this means that the driver can cross over the cable running at right angles to his path.  He proceeds to a stopping point with the gripper attached to his main cable, he then by the one process lets go that cable in the front, and takes it in the rear gripper and proceeds over the crossing of the cable.  The operation takes only a few seconds and should be quite safe, because there is an automatic arrangement provided for stopping the car providing the driver should be forgetful or careless.  Another improvement is, that the portion of the gripper which works in the tube underground can be quickly detached from the car and dropped into the tube if anything should go wrong with it.  The attachment previously used direct on to the axles of the car was found in practice to have several drawbacks, and the new gripper is fixed to adjustable bars on the bogies, and the moving parts are enclosed so that there will be no fear of oil, &c., injuring

3²

wearing apparel. There are 125 cars being built on the bogie principle. The bogies are very light in construction, being made of $\frac{7}{16}$-in. pressed steel frames. The chief feature about them is that the wheels are on the axles outside the bearings, and that the wheel base is 3 ft. 9 in. and less than the gauge of 4 ft. 8$\frac{1}{2}$ in. This is contrary to customary practice, but the author has tried them very severely and finds them to answer admirably. The cars are designed to seat eighteen passengers inside and twenty-eight outside, and the only noticeable departure from ordinary practice is that the insides of the cars will be domed after the manner of railway carriages, instead of the type of roof common in tramway cars.

### FINANCIAL CONSIDERATIONS.

In concluding, I would specially invite the members, as advisers to their respective districts, to always insist upon arriving as far as possible at: Firstly, the saving which can be effected by any particular system over the whole period in which that system is intended to operate, before allowing the initial cost to have any influence upon the minds of their committees. Secondly, to compare (at least in a common-sense way) with existing systems the cost of repairs which are likely to result upon each individual system.

With regard to the first point, it is not generally recognised what amount of expenditure is justified in converting horse tramways to mechanical traction. What expenditure is warrantable upon introducing a system which can even only show a saving over the old system of 1d. per car mile run? We will take as an illustration a town system in which it is desired to have a good service of cars, such as 1,000 car miles per mile of double track per day, and experience shows this is to be quickly attained with cable haulage, which fosters, and can afford to foster, a tramway business in a way which no other system can.

One thousand car miles per mile of double track per day, with a mean car speed of 6 miles per hour (which is, of course, low), would require for a working day of seventeen

EDINBURGH: TOLLCROSS CABLE POWER, INTERIOR OF ENGINE-ROOM (ENGINES IN COURSE OF ERECTION).

hours an average interval between the cars of, say, two minutes, ten cars thus running on the mile of street length and performing 60 car miles per hour. This would give 365,000 car miles per mile of double track per annum, and 1d. per car mile saved would be in round figures £1,500 per mile of street per annum. That sum is sufficient to pay 5 per cent. interest on a capital of £30,000 per mile of street, and yet it is only 1d. saved per car mile. Cable haulage for such a service would be about 4d., and would probably be nearer 5d., per car mile cheaper than the present expenses for horse traction. And yet there are people who still hesitate, and some even refuse, to consider mechanical form of traction where the initial cost is high, and therefore never discover the extraordinary results and savings which may be effected in the future by the expenditure of additional capital at the right time.

With regard to the second point, the author would like to draw your attention to the class of figures which you have to guard against. In a paper lately read before the Institution of Civil Engineers, the costs of maintenance and repairs on an electric tramway line were given to four places of decimals as follows: For the maintenance and repairs of cars, with motors and everything complete, ·26725d. per car mile run. The author ventures to say that nobody will dispute that the cost of maintenance and repairs for heavy cars, with heavy motors and electrical machinery, must in the future cost far more to maintain than the ordinary horse car, and yet it can be most conclusively shown that the average cost of maintaining a horse car only in Edinburgh during eleven years has been ·51d. per car mile run, or twice the figure which is quoted for electrical maintenance.

Again, it was also stated that the cost of maintenance and repairs for lines, which would include the whole of the permanent way, rails, bonding, electric poles and wires, &c., was ·0088d. per car mile run. Experience shows that the average expense of maintaining the horse tracks alone in Edinburgh has been during eleven years ·64d. per car mile run,

or nearly seventy-three times the amounts given for maintaining electrical road and wires, &c. The author does not wish to infer that these figures are put forward to wilfully mislead, but he cannot too strongly warn those who are seeking for information, that a few such items in the cost of maintenance would make the difference between financial success and failure. The cost of maintenance can only be properly arrived at when the fullest data of working is available over an extended period of time.

The whole of the work is from the designs of the author and your vice-president, Mr. Cooper, who are superintending the carrying out of the work with the assistance of their respective staffs.

### DISCUSSION OF MR. COLAM'S PAPER.

Mr. BAKER (Middlesbrough) remarked that a private company was there putting down tramways extending for about 10 miles, on the electric trolley system. If any of the members who were seeking for information liked to visit Middlesbrough to see the system he would be only too pleased to give them any assistance and information in his possession.

Mr. COLLINS (Norwich) asked whether Mr. Colam had any experience with the cast-weld joint, and, if so, whether his experience was favourable.

Mr. PATON (Plymouth) proposed a vote of thanks to Mr. Colam. He said that the local circumstances must determine the authority as to the character and kind of tramway which would pay them best. He could quite conceive that with wide streets and a modern town a cable tramway could be laid at moderate cost; but in old towns, with narrow streets, where there was uncertainty as to the depth of drains, water and gas mains, &c., it was almost impossible to tell what would be the cost of installing a cable tramway. Personally he regarded the cable as the most perfect form of tramway haulage. It did not disfigure the streets, and with a little extra power at the central station almost any number of cars could be put on, while the proportion of expense in relation to income was not the constant figure it was with horse traction. In fact, the greater the number of cars the smaller in proportion was the cost of working. In Edinburgh it was put at 5d. a car mile. That, compared with horse traction, showed a considerable saving in working expenses. But it might so happen that in a town where they determined to lay down a cable tramway the initial cost would be such that they would never get a company to pay them 7 per cent on the capital outlay. The returns would not pay them to do so. That was a consideration, and materially affected the question of the term of repayment which would be allowed for the construction of the lines. If the Board of Trade would only allow them a term of twenty-one years, it became a serious question what would be the state of the lines on the expiration of the lease. In Plymouth the old system was horse traction, and the company made so bad a job of it that the corporation ultimately took it over. They were working it by horse traction, and a portion of it was being laid for electric traction. They considered at the time the cable, accumulator and overhead trolley, and after consideration the committee came to the conclusion that the overhead system was the best and cheapest for the town of Plymouth.

Mr. C. JONES (Ealing), in seconding the vote of thanks, said he should have liked some further information on this question, which was affecting some of their smaller towns and districts. They had been fighting a company for six days in the committee-rooms of the House of Commons, and had defeated them. An interesting point was raised by Dr. Siemens and Prof. Hopkinson in connection with the overhead and conduit system, and if anything could have been said as to those systems it would have been interesting to some of them, and perhaps have enabled them to reply to some of the questions which were sometimes asked them at their council meetings.

Bailie MACKENZIE (Edinburgh) said they had had this question of mechanical traction before the council for a considerable time. They did not enter into the cable system hastily. They looked round and found a number of companies who were very anxious to put their appliances and various systems of electric traction at the disposal of the corporation. They thought there was no question of underground electric traction worth looking at. Then, with regard to the overhead system, it was a very curious thing that, while in America they were throwing out the overhead trolley, in England they were adopting it. Was it the case that the mayor of Chicago had made an agreement with the different tramway companies that within a certain radius of the centre of the city there should be no overhead trolley? Was it the case that in Washington, Boston and New York they were throwing out the overhead trolley? It was very curious, and his own explanation was that many large syndicates with any amount of money behind them had made a raid upon the municipalities for working electric traction. With the knowledge of what had already been done in Edinburgh, and the uncertainty in connection with all forms of electric traction, they decided they would go in for cable traction, and they had seen no reason to regret it. He did not deny that the overhead trolley was a fairly good system, but they had yet to know that in a city where frequent stoppages must take place, and where the speed could not by the Board of Trade regulations be more than 8 miles an hour, the overhead trolley would be as successful as the cable traction had been.

Ir. J. LOBLEY (Hanley) considered the phrase car miles rather misleading, because there were cars of very different sizes. He had seen there, in Princes-street, single and double decked cars; therefore the cost per car mile was apt to be misleading unless the number of passengers was standardised. Bailie Mackenzie was wrong in saying that New York had thrown out the overhead system, because it had from the first consistently refused to allow the system to be introduced. In Hanley they were in the throes of a reconstruction, 2½ miles of streets being up for reconstructions and extensions. They had the overhead trolley system, and after the poles and wires had been up for twelve months he did not think any one took the slightest notice of them. Notwithstanding that, he would have preferred the cable system had it been possible. The roads were crooked, the gradients were severe, which was in favour of a cable, and they had a large number of canal bridges, the crowns of which were not more than 12 in., and which required to be constantly raised owing to undermining.

The vote of thanks having been adopted,

Ir. COLAM, replying seriatim to the questions, said that the first was whether he had experience of cast-weld joints. The objections to it were two-fold. That they could not, especially on curves, get rid of a certain amount of expansion and contraction of the rails. The greater objection was that they could not bring two portions of a rail together by a weld or cast-weld without changing the nature of the metal all round where the joint was made, and the consequence was that they increased the flat places and the knock on the wheel. Ir. Paton made some very pertinent remarks, and he (Ir. Colam) thoroughly agreed with him that every district required to be considered upon its merits and requirements, and the proper people to discuss that point were not engineers but local authorities. Edinburgh people said what they would not have, and then began to inquire what they would have. He knew many districts in the country which could not give better results than with one-horse cars. Ir, Lobley made a point about car miles being misleading. That was one of the disadvantages of an author not having an opportunity of reading his own paper. If he had read the paper they would have found that he gave ton miles as well as car miles. As to Ir. Lobley's remark as to getting accustomed to the overhead wires, he had found that himself. Living in a district where the overhead wires existed, they could get used to it to a certain extent. The difficulty was, if they had to live in a district where four roads met, there were so many guard wires and supports that the place became a perfect eyesore. Ir. Lobley also spoke of the bridge difficulty, and referred to the fact that they had only 12 in. cover. They had four cases of that kind in Edinburgh, and had got over them all right, and two they had been working for ten years. Bailie Mackenzie pertinently put the case against the overhead system in a nutshell. It was a little derogatory on their part to be taking a back seat to Chicago, New York and other cities, which were well known never to consider the amenities of their cities. That was, however, not an engineering question, but for the town councils to discuss. In America they were actually, where they were allowing the overhead wires to go up, introducing a clause into the agreement that the moment the town council were satisfied that they could find a conduit system which was economical they should have power to make them take the wires down and put in a conduit system.

The report will be continued in our next issue, beginning with Ir. Stewart's paper on "Sewer Ventilation as Applied to Water of Leith Intercepting Sewer."

## LONDON WATER SUPPLY CONMMISSION.

Lord Llandaff presided, on Monday, at a meeting of the above commission, held at the Guildhall, Westminster.

Ir. HOWARD MARTIN, chairman of the Water Committee of the Croydon Corporation, first gave evidence. The waterworks of Croydon were controlled by the corporation, and had involved a capital expenditure of £158,000. The corporation were now proposing to sink one or two additional wells, to provide for the growing population, which now numbered 120,000 and was increasing at the rate of 3,000 a year. The corporation supplied 94,000 and the Lambeth company supplied nearly 30,000. The corporation, as representing the inhabitants, submitted that, whatever change might be made in the present system of water supply in the metropolitan area, the borough of Croydon should not only be preserved in her present rights of water supply, but that the portion of the borough now supplied by the Lambeth company should be transferred to the corporation. The district in question could be much better supplied from Croydon than from Lambeth, and the present arrangement had many disadvantages. The acquisition of the undertakings of the water companies would not affect the borough of Croydon except with regard to the small part of the undertaking of the Lambeth company within the borough, and the corporation were of opinion that the question of the water supply of the area south of the river could be efficiently and satisfactorily dealt with by

placing it in the hands of the four county authorities exercising control over the area—namely, the county councils of London, Surrey and Kent, and the council of the county borough of Croydon, each exercising jurisdiction within their own area, and were not in favour of one authority being established for that area. The corporation were opposed to any combination of the different systems of supply now administered by the eight metropolitan water companies, in so far as this would result in either the Lambeth company or the Kent company being linked with any other company, and thus being enabled to supply water from their present sources of supply to any larger area than that already supplied by them.

Ir. T. H. WATSON, chairman of the Water Supply Committee of the Richmond Town Council, said that, having at present control of their own water supply, all that they desired was to be let alone. The water rate in the borough was only 11d., inclusive of all charges—a condition of things which was regarded as most satisfactory.

## THE HOUSING OF THE WORKING CLASSES.

A conference of the local authorities in the Parliamentary division of West Southwark, London, was held on Friday, at the Bridge House hotel, to consider the urgent necessity of providing additional workmen's dwellings in the locality. It was shown that since 1882 the number of persons displaced by demolitions and other causes was 3,050, and that fresh provision had been made for only 2,084. Other demolitions were now going on for which no adequate provision was being made. In the parish of Christ Church a few days ago there was only one house to let in the whole parish. In St. Saviour's 3,082 persons had been displaced by demolitions since 1891, and very little had been done in erecting new dwellings. In the course of the discussion which followed the overcrowding was declared to be increasing, and it was stated that the local authorities were not only powerless to deal with it under the present statutes, but even the London County Council could not be got to act, owing to their reluctance to interfere with private enterprise. The following resolution was subsequently carried : "That this meeting, being convinced of the great need of dwelling accommodation for the poorer classes in Southwark, urges the local authorities to take common action—(1) in endeavouring to obtain from the Corporation of the City of London, the railway and electric light companies, the ecclesiastical commissioners, and other land owners in the locality, facilities for the purchase of land on reasonable terms for the erection of dwellings; and (2) in impressing upon Parliament the necessity of assisting the London County Council in their efforts to provide further accommodation under the Housing of the Working Classes Acts without cost to the ratepayers, by an extension of the terms of years for repayment of loans and by the relaxation of the building conditions now imposed by the Home Office."

## NEATH IMPROVEMENTS.

### A DOUBLE CEREMONY.

Two interesting civic functions were performed at Neath, on Thursday, the new Victoria gardens and the new reservoir being opened with befitting ceremony. The gardens have been laid out in artistic style by Mr. Shaw, of Gowerton, at a cost of £1,400, upon plans drawn out by the borough surveyor, Mr. D. M. Jenkins. The total cost was about £2,800. The reservoir, which has been constructed by Mr. James Allan, of Cardiff, has a capacity of 25,000,000 gallons, and, in conjunction with the existing water supply, will prove more than sufficient for the inhabitants of the borough of Neath. The mayor, in his speech, submitted some interesting statistics. The reservoir, he said, was commenced in 1896, from plans and specifications drawn up by the borough surveyor, Mr. D. M. Jenkins. The site and plans were approved by experts, and the contract entrusted to Mr. James Allan, who had carried out the work most effectively. The reservoir was fed by three streams, and could supply 140,000 gallons per day in the driest weather. With the already-existing reservoir they had a total storage capacity of 41,000,000 gallons, sufficient to supply 20,000 people over a drought of 200 days.

**The City Streets.**—Mr. D. J. Ross, the chief engineer of the Public Health Department of the Corporation of the City of London, has been giving an interviewer his opinions on the crowded state of the City streets, and has also suggested three remedies—i.e., (1) the widening of the streets; (2) the adoption of means to get the heavy traffic out of the main streets by turning it into regular routes; (3) the crawling cab, touting for fares, should be got out of the way. Mr. Ross thinks the Central London Railway will help matters for a time, but that, as the congestion is chronic, it will soon become as bad as ever. No doubt if people in a hurry will make much use of the subway near the Bank, because of the extra labour of descending and ascending the steps, and for the same reason he does not regard an elevated railway as likely to be popular. In his opinion this should be the last resort.

## British Association of Waterworks Engineers.

### ANNUAL MEETING AT SOUTHAMPTON.—VI.

In our issue of the 24th ult. we gave the valuable and interesting paper, on "The Chemical and Bacterial Examination of Water," read by Dr. Frankland on the third day of the recent meeting. It was followed by a long and interesting discussion, of which we now give the substance.

#### DISCUSSION ON DR. FRANKLAND'S PAPER.

The CHAIRMAN, in opening the discussion, said he was sure that it required no words of his to introduce Dr. Frankland, who was already well known to them. They had derived much valuable information from the reading of his paper, the concluding remarks of which had particularly struck him. Dr. Frankland had gone to the root of the question. He had said that practically they were hunting for the specific germs, which, however, when found, were of very doubtful value, for the mischief was then done. They would go to a chemist with samples of water, and the chemist would be able to tell them whether the samples were of a polluted character or not. But the information was useless unless it was discovered what the water was polluted with. Dr. Frankland's advice and the light he had thrown on sand filtration should, in his opinion, be acknowledged by all engineers. He himself had been very much struck by the valuable and instructive figures which had been thrown on the screen, for they had enabled them to see at a glance the results of many years of labour. But there were, said the chairman in conclusion, many gentlemen fully qualified to go into the question, and he would first call upon Dr. Kemna.

Dr. KEMNA (Antwerp) remarked that he thought he had been called upon rather unexpectedly, and that it seemed to him that he was fast developing into a lecturer. The only thing he had to say was that he considered Dr. Frankland perfectly right in his opinions. But, he was perhaps better qualified to testify to the efficiency of sand filtration, because he contended that they were not so well acquainted with bad water as himself. He had, in Antwerp, a bad town to deal with; the pollution was great and all the conditions were unfavourable. In Belgium, he went on, they had a very high sense of personal freedom, and would not submit to any sanitary restrictions. The sewage of Brussels and Antwerp, he would point out, discharged into a river which was a mere ditch, and in his opinion Brussels was a place where such a thing should not have been permitted. The fact was that some of the rivers of Belgium were in a most awful state, being polluted to a very great extent. The water in his own works was analysed daily. Even the river was examined at various parts, and he made over 600 analyses monthly. Microbes, he added humorously, cost him 5s. per week for beef. He had an envious feeling when examining the figures which the London companies had to deal with, for they were really good, and the companies had, he thought, nothing to complain of. The results of the action of subsidence in water had interested him; personally, he had not always been able to obtain the same results, the latter generally differing according to the water. But London waters were not always satisfactory. One cubic centimetre of water should give under twenty microbes, and at Antwerp it was always under that figure. Great care was also taken in connection with the starting of the filters, and the first delivery was never taken into the reservoirs. Another point was the importance of regularity in working. The rate of filtration should always remain constant. It should be increased slowly each day, but he thought it best to allow a rest of twelve hours, in which time the deposit would form. Then it was possible to work at a very high speed indeed, although great shocks, he reminded them, should always be avoided. Filters should be separate and under proper regulation; their running should not be stopped at night, even although the consumption varied greatly. It was better to let water overflow than to interrupt the filtration, and he was sure that if engineers adopted that method they could obtain better results. In the case of entirely new filters months often elapsed before anything like satisfactory results were obtained, while it took two or three days to get good water after cleaning out the filters. Continuing, he mentioned that he did not consider that sand filtration was sufficient to produce a completely sterile water; in his opinion it was necessary to boil the water to make it thoroughly sterile. He had never yet found a water-filter in domestic use that was not leaking. They, therefore, were of no practical use. Statistics showed that cities supplied with filtered water had the lowest death rates. Engineers, said Dr. Kemna in closing his address, must remember that they had in their hands the lives of all their fellow-citizens.

Dr. A. ANGELL, county analyst of Southampton, remarked that he had felt it his duty to be present at the proceedings. He had had sufficient experience with water engineers to know that those gentlemen very often considered analysts something of a " bore ". But it was necessary, he thought, that water analyses should at all times be carried out in a methodical manner. Dr. Frankland's foes had brought up his own views on water analyses. If anybody, he continued, declared to him that he had discovered a pathogenic germ, —that was to say, a germ capable of transmitting any par-

ticular form of disease—he would be inclined to quarrel with him. With regard to the difficulties attending collection, they had already been spoken of by the learned lecturer. He warned them not to place a too-high value upon the bacteriological analyses of water. If water were submitted to a chemist they must look upon his figures as a diagnosis only. He had seen the water referred to by Dr. Kemna, and did not think there was anyone in England who would dare to face it.

Mr. CHARLES H. PRIESTLEY (Cardiff) said he thought he could bear out all that had been said by Dr. Frankland, and especially those remarks in regard to the subsidence of water in reservoirs. The character of the water obtained from large impounding reservoirs clearly showed the benefits to be derived from the practice. In regard to open or covered service reservoirs, he would, if it were not asking too much, like to know Dr. Frankland's opinion on that question. He himself had been told by a certain borough analyst that covered reservoirs were more preferable than open.

Mr. H. ASHTON HILL (Birmingham) said he did not rise to criticise the paper, as it was, in his opinion, incapable of criticism. He desired only to say a word or two. It was he who had suggested to Dr. Frankland that he should contribute his paper. They were, he told the doctor, a young association, and it was not everybody who recognised that they had justified their existence. Dr. Frankland had hesitated for a few moments and then consented. By doing so he had conferred a great favour upon him (the speaker), and he now trusted that the doctor would not regret his appearance before the association.

Mr. FRANCIS J. BANCROFT (Hull) remarked that they could not, of course, criticise a paper like Dr. Frankland's; in fact, they would have a difficulty in doing so. Water engineers, he continued, could not fail to notice how the bacteriological examination of water had lately been getting into popular demand, and it was therefore with the greatest pleasure that he had been enabled to hear the author's paper on the subject. Personally he had to deal with well water. Recently he had been making a study of the microbes which surrounded us, and when we dealt with questions of that magnitude we saw the importance of the subject. Then they asked what the value of a bacterial examination was, but that question could, he thought, be answered by the valuable figures they had seen on the screen. He held that the taking of samples of water for examination should be done by properly-qualified officials. He believed that typhoid fever could only be conveyed by fœcal matter in water, which when passing through a town was, of course, liable to become polluted. Microbes were, as they knew, more numerous in summer than in winter. After a brief reference to the case of chalk waters, Mr. Bancroft then went on to say that he also would be glad to have Dr. Frankland's idea concerning the relative advantages of open and covered service reservoirs, and whether there would be any gain in constructing a covered reservoir for a chalk supply. In Cardiff it was said that the water would be better if it were exposed to the light. Mr. Bancroft then brought his remarks to a close with a question as to the frequency with which the bacteriological examination of water should be conducted.

Mr. A. J. PRICE (Worcester) stated that he desired to put one question to the author. He was concerned with a river supply, but, unfortunately, was not in possession of a storage reservoir, and he wanted to know Dr. Frankland's suggestions for the elimination of the bacteria contained in the water. Everyone could not follow the examples set by the London companies. In many of the small towns the question of economy had to be taken into consideration, together with the difficulty of obtaining the necessary ground for the reception of reservoirs. Then, again, in conducting a river supply one was subject to floods. If they were going to impound water they would want something like twenty days' storage, and not only that, it meant increasing the pumping machinery.

Mr. WM. WATTS (Sheffield) could not help feeling that in such a discussion as the one they were engaged upon then sometimes " rushed where angels feared to tread." He thought also that many of the silent members knew as much about the subject of the discussion as those who took part in the debate. He came from a district where filtration was not introduced, for the reason that they took advantage of the gathering ground. By draining the swampy places, by ditching the streams, and by making some provision for watercourses, it was possible to exercise some control on the occasion of excessive floods, and he was sure that if they canvassed the ratepayers of their respective towns they would find that the latter were willing to pay a little more to carry out such schemes for the purification of their water. With regard to the bacteriological point of view, there were many opinions concerning it. But it was evident that filtration did a great amount of good, and he was glad that they had had such a man as Dr. Frankland to give them so much information on the subject. He had read the author's books and had argued out the matter.

Mr. HAMLET ROBERTS (Ipswich), in a reference to the

taking of samples of water for the purposes of analysis, considered that the cork should be replaced in the bottle before the latter was withdrawn from the water. He suggested the adoption of a special stopper.

Mr. ARTHUR BOWKER (Mid-Kent) submitted a question respecting the reduction of microbes in a certain well water.

Mr. O. WILLIAMS (Aberdare) also added a few remarks in regard to water filtration.

Mr. JOHN SHAW (Boston, Lincs.) next made a reference to the water supply of Antwerp. The source of the water there was the filthiest he knew, and the latter when passing over the filters was something like the colour of beer. After congratulating Dr. Kemna on producing such a clear liquid he went on to speak of the effect which variations in the number of organisms in his own water had upon him—generally, as they all knew, the most even-minded of men. Before starting sand filters to work his usual practice was to allow the water, after being run in, to stand for about three hours. The speed of working was then gradually increased. There was, he would mention, a limit of time at which a filter would work, because of the formation of matter upon its surface.

Dr. FRANKLAND, after thanking the members, then proceeded to reply to some of the questions raised. One of the

SOUTHAMPTON WATER WORKS

most important points which Dr. Kemna had emphasised in his remarks was that in regard to constancy in the rate of filtration. Then, again, he had spoken of the necessity of running the water to waste before putting the filters to work. That was not the practice in this country, although it should be. Dr. Kemna was wrong when he said that he (Dr. Frankland) had had no experience of bad water, because he had analysed Antwerp water himself. It was, he admitted, abominable stuff. Referring to the bacteriological examination of water, he had no hesitation in saying that the mere statement of the number of bacteria in water was of no use whatever. It threw no light on the subject, although, of course, the information itself possessed some value. The presence or absence of suspended matter in water made no difference in the numerical results. He was afraid that he was not in a position to reply to Mr. Priestley's question concerning the merits of open and covered reservoirs. Double filtration would, he thought, be a poor substitute for the improvement of water by storage. It was a mere makeshift. Other devices had also been resorted to, but they did not meet the case. During the period of storage pathogenic bacteria usually underwent destruction. He had shown, he remarked, that typhoid bacilli could be detected in some

waters a few days after introduction, but, on the other hand, in the case of well water, the bacilli were only found about thirty-three days after their introduction.

The proceedings then closed with the accordance of hearty votes of thanks to the town council of Southampton and the authorities of the Hartley College, for the facilities they had given the association to hold their meetings, and to Mr. Matthews for his duties as chairman.

VISIT TO SOUTHAMPTON WATERWORKS.

After luncheon the members left in brakes to visit the Southampton waterworks. En route a stoppage was made at the Red Lodge Rhododendron Nurseries, where the party were heartily welcomed by the owner, Mr. W. H. Rogers, one of Southampton's most popular ex-mayors. Perhaps the most remarkable feature of the gardens is the fact that seventy years ago their site was a mere waste of sand-pits. Now they show a wealth of colour from the blossoms of an infinite variety of rhododendrons and flowers of all hues, or are green with dense plantations of rare coniferous and other trees. A Sequoia gigantica—the giant tree of California—was noted with the more interest in connection with its rapid growth—70 ft. in thirty-five years; and an auraucaria which fronts Mr. Rogers' picturesquely thatched house was conspicuous as probably the most perfectly-grown of its kind in this country. Amid the most beautiful surroundings the visitors were photographed by Messrs. Chalkley Gould & Co., of Southampton, and in one of their excellent groups—reproduced in THE SURVEYOR of June 17th—the venerable owner of this English "Monperrat" may be descried modestly half-hidden in the shadow of the porch.

Not without reluctance the journey was continued to Otterbourne, where an examination was made of the wells, headings, pumping station and quarries, and especially interest was shown in the softening works with mechanical filtration. The following details of the arrangements had been prepared—

SOUTHAMPTON CORPORATION WATERWORKS,
1290-1898.

By WILLIAM MATTHEWS, M.INST.C.E.

The waterworks of Southampton have a history going back to a more remote date than can probably be ascribed to any other such undertaking in this country, it being recorded that on June 16, 1290 (Edward I.), one Nicholas de Shirlee granted to the Friars Minor the right to take water from a spring at Colwell (now called Spring-hill, Hill-lane) to Achard's bridge, and thence by the king's highway to their church in the town of Southampton. It is further recorded that upon the Feast of the Purification, 1310 (Edward II.), the friars granted the use of the water to the town. On October 3, 1420 (Henry V.), they conveyed to the mayor and community of Southampton all their rights and title in the springs, conduit and pipes, and the waterworks of the town have ever since, a period of 478 years, remained in their possession.

The original vaulted chambers covering the Colwell spring and one of the old water-houses (adjoining St. Peter's Church), to which the water flowed, may yet be seen. On June 1, 1515 (Henry VIII.), another spring at Lohery Mead (now Grosvenor-square) was presented to the town by John Flemynge. The water was led to a water-house (which until recently could be seen in Waterhouse-lane) and thence to the still existing house, which was quite close to it. From this water-house lead pipes conveyed the water to the town, and, together with sundry wells of a purely local character, including the Houndwell well, 1490 (Henry VIII.), constituted the water supply until 1803. The first Act of Parliament was obtained in 1747, followed by others in 1803 and 1810.

About 1804 the No. 1 reservoir was constructed. It collected surface water from the common by means of earthenware pipes, and a line of elm pipes conveyed the water to the town. This reservoir has been abandoned and the banks levelled down.

About 1811 the No. 2 reservoir and about 1832 the No. 3 reservoir was made on the common. They also collected the surface water, which was conveyed to the town by a line of 10-in. cast-iron pipes. They continued in regular use until 1852, after which, and until recently, the water was used only for road watering. They have now been converted into ornamental waters.

In 1838 the deep well on the common[*] was commenced, and the work carried on intermittently until 1883, when it was finally abandoned at a depth of 1,317 ft. (842 ft. in chalk), having involved an expenditure of £20,000 for a yield of only 130,000 gallons per day. The water from this well was, in 1887, used to supplement the supply for road watering by pumping into the No. 3 reservoir, a hydraulic engine actuated by the pressure in the 18-in. trunk main from the upper reservoir being used for the purpose.[†]

In 1851 a supply of water was obtained from the river Itchen at Mansbridge, the works comprising a brick and masonry lined subsiding reservoir (3,500,000 gallons), a pair of Cornish engines and three boilers; at the same time the two upper reservoirs, Nos. 4 and 5, on the common were constructed. The old supplies were then discontinued, and in 1865 the Mansbridge works were increased by the addition

---

* "Proceedings of the Institution of Civil Engineers," vol. xc.; and "Proceedings of the British Association," 1846 and 1882.
† "Proceedings of the International Congress of Hygiene," 1891, vol. vii.]

of a second engine and boiler house, containing a pair of coupled rotative engines and five Lancashire boilers. An additional boiler had meanwhile been added to the older plant.

In 1884 the water in the river Itchen had become so liable to pollution that it was determined to abandon that source and obtain a supply from wells sunk in the chalk at Otterbourne, to accomplish which an Act of Parliament was obtained in 1885. The works were put in hand at once, and completed by June, 1888.

These works* comprised two wells 100 ft. deep; a pumping station at a level of 90 ft. above ordnance datum, containing two compound steam engines and three boilers; a workshop; softening plant, consisting of two lime mills, two lime cylinders, a lime-storage tank, a mixer, a softening tank and thirteen Atkins disc filters; two limekilns; a railway siding; roadway; and seven cottages for the working staff. A 24-in. main was laid to the covered service reservoir which was erected on Otterbourne Hill, and thence a 16-in. main was laid to Swaythling, connecting the new to the then existing system of mains to the town and the reservoirs on the common. These works cost about £66,000.

In 1896 an additional engine-house was built, with space and foundations for two engines, and one engine was therein erected. A new shaft and well were sunk, and additions made to the softening plant by putting down two more lime cylinders and six filters; at the same time a lime store was built, the large lime-storage tank was done away with and replaced by a smaller one with mechanical agitators, and various alterations made to the softening plant generally, by which its output is increased to nearly 4,000,000 gallons per day and its efficiency and regularity much improved. The water is reduced in hardness from 18 deg. to 5 deg. or 6 deg., at a cost of about ½d. per 1,000 gallons for working expenses, while the repayment of principal and the interest comes to just about another ½d. per 1,000 gallons. The cost of the 1896 additional works was about £15,000.

At various times about 700 ft. of adits have been driven from the wells, at a level of about 33 ft. above ordnance datum, and a further length of 500 ft. is now being driven, as in the case of all the sub-aqueous work except the two original wells, without the aid of contractors. A contract has been let for the erection of two additional lime kilns.

In 1897 the two service reservoirs, Nos. 4 and 5, on the common were covered in, at a cost of £6,300, and an additional main, 24 in. diameter, laid from Otterbourne Hill reservoir to Swaythling, at a cost of £19,700.

Renewal of distribution mains goes on at the rate of about 3 miles per year. Deacon's waste-water meters are in use and have effected a reduction of consumption of over 30 gallons per head per day. All service pipes and outside step-cocks are maintained by the corporation, who also hire out meters, test and keep them in repair. The present annual consumption of water to a population of 77,500 is as follows:—

| | |
|---|---|
| Domestic supply ... ... ... ... ... | 749,000,000 |
| Public sanitary use, by meter ... ... ... | 36,000,000 |
| Softening works, cleansing reservoirs, &c. ... | 21,000,000 |
| Trade supply, by meter ... ... ... ... | 261,000,000 |
| Total ... ... ... ... | 1,067,000,000 |

* "Proceedings of the Institution of Civil Engineers," vols. xc. and cviii.; and "Proceedings of the Institution of Mechanical Engineers," 1893.

ANNUAL COST OF WATER SUPPLY.

| | Total. £ | s. | d. | Cost per 1,000 gallons. Pence. |
|---|---|---|---|---|
| Pumping, labour and materials... | 3,080 | 5 | 3 | ·693 |
| Softening " " | 1,101 | 10 | 8 | ·248 |
| Distribution " " | 2,145 | 3 | 5 | ·483 |
| Management, office, printing, &c. | 1,544 | 5 | 8 | ·348 |
| Collection of rates ... ... | 441 | 10 | 0 | ·099 |
| Rents, rates, taxes, &c. ... ... | 526 | 12 | 4 | ·119 |
| Total working expenses ... | 8,839 | 7 | 4 | 1·990 |
| Principal and interest ... ... | 9,484 | 10 | 11 | 2·135 |
| | £18,323 | 18 | 3 | 4·125 |

The receipts during the same period were: From meters, £9,208 10s.; and from a rate of 10d. in the £1 for domestic supply, £9,130 17s. 9d.

TABLE OF RESERVOIRS.

| Situation. | Date. | Description. | Height of water line above O.D. | Capacity. Gallons. |
|---|---|---|---|---|
| No. 1, Southampton Common... | 1804 | Circular, earthbanks* ... ... ... ... ... | 95 | 700,000 |
| No. 2, " " ... | 1811 | Rectangular, earthbanks† ... ... ... ... | 104 | 4,500,000 |
| No. 3, " " ... | 1832 | Quadrilateral, earthbanks† ... ... ... ... | 116 | |
| No. 4, " " ... | 1852 | Rectangular, earthbanks, brick-lined, covered with brick and concrete in 1897 ... ... ... ... | 190 | 5,000,000 |
| No. 5, " " ... | 1852 | | | |
| Otterbourne Hill ... ... | 1886 | Circular, covered, concrete and brick.... ... ... | 246 | 1,000,000 |
| Mansbridge, subsiding... ... | 1852 | Rectangular, sunk, brick-lined. ... ... ... | river level | 3,500,000 |

* Since dismantled and levelled. † Now used as ornamental waters.

## FOURTH DAY'S PROCEEDINGS.

### VISIT TO GOSPORT AND PORTSMOUTH WATERWORKS.

Papers and discussion had been eliminated from the programme of Friday, the fourth and last day of the meeting. At 9 a.m. members and visitors left the docks railway station for Fareham, whence they proceeded in brakes to the Foxbury works of the Gosport Waterworks Company. At this point an examination was made of the pumping station, well, headings and the brickwork tower, which appeared to be practically ready to receive the novel steel tank with which it is to be crowned. Full particulars of the works at Foxbury were, it will be remembered, given in Mr. Hildred's paper (The Surveyor, June 10th).

Thence the journey was resumed to the Havant and Bedhampton works of the Portsmouth Waterworks Company, where the remarkable feature is the extraordinary number and volume of the springs. They are briefly described in the following notes on

### BOROUGH OF PORTSMOUTH WATERWORKS.

By H. R. Smith,
Waterworks Engineer, Portsmouth.

Parliamentary powers for the supply of water to Portsmouth were first obtained in 1741, but nothing was accomplished until 1809, when the Farlington Waterworks Company constructed a pumping station and two reservoirs in Farlington Marshes, as well as the Drayton reservoir on the slope of Portsdown Hill, and commenced to supply water to Portsmouth in 1809. At the same time the Portsea Waterworks Company constructed works and supplied water from a well sunk at Landport, within the borough.

In 1840 these companies combined, and appear to have furnished Portsmouth with an intermittent and limited supply until the year 1857, when they were bought up by the present Borough of Portsmouth Waterworks Company, who, while making use of the Farlington springs, at once set about acquiring and utilising other and more voluminous springs at Havant, a course which had been strongly advocated in 1850 by the late Sir Robert Rawlinson.

The use of the well at Landport was abandoned and the Farlington works closed in 1860, when this company began

DETAILS OF PUMPING ENGINES AND BOILERS.

| Number and Type. | Date. | Size of Cylinders and Stroke. | Steam Pressure. | Revolutions per minute. | Indicated Horse-power. | Coal consumed per actual Horse-power per hour. | Water raised per twenty-four hours each Engine. | Lift without Friction. | Size of Pump Buckets and Stroke. | Number and Type of Boilers. | Size. | — |
|---|---|---|---|---|---|---|---|---|---|---|---|---|
| | | | lb | | | lb | Gallons. | Ft. | | | | |
| MANSBRIDGE. Two single-acting Cornish condensing ... ... ... | 1851 | 38½ in. × 8 ft. | 15 | 10 | 81 | 4·7 | 734,500 | 200 | 14¼ in. × 8 ft. | 3 Cornish<br>1 Lancashire | 5 ft. 6 in. × 26 ft.<br>8 ft. × 26 ft. | Iron<br>" |
| MANSBRIDGE. Two simple rotative beam condensing | 1865 | 40 in. × 8 ft. | 30 | 12½ | 90¾ | 4·9 | 1,530,000 | 200 | 18¾ in. × 8 ft. | 5 Lancashire | 7 ft. × 25 ft. | " |
| OTTERBOURNE. Two compound rotative Woolf beam condensing... ... | 1887 | High-pressure, 28½ in. × 4 ft. 9 in. low-pressure, 38¼ in. × 7 ft. | 60 | 18 | 125 | 1·7 | 2,000,000 | 220 | Low lift, 22 in. × 5 ft.; high lift, 19½ in. × 7 ft. | 3 Lancashire | 7 ft. × 28 ft. | Steel |
| One ditto ... ... | 1896 | | | | | | | | | | | |
| WELL ON COMMON. One two-cylinder horizontal hydraulic ... ... | 1887 | 8½ in. × 1 ft. 3 in. | Water 28 | 25 | — | — | 240,000 | 65 | No. 3, 6¼ in. × 1 ft. 6 in. | — | — | — |

to supply their water from the springs at Havant, the pumping station erected there being furnished with two beam engines, each of 90 indicated horse-power, and four Lancashire boilers; and the water from such station was pumped through a 20-in. main into the Drayton reservoir. In 1868 the third engine of the same type and power and two additional boilers were put down; also two high-service reservoirs were constructed on Portsdown Hill. In 1878 a fourth engine of 120 horse-power, together with additional boilers working at an increased pressure, were added, and an additional rising main of 24-in. diameter was laid to the high-service reservoirs above referred to.

The company continued to purchase additional land and springs at Havant and in the neighbourhood of Bedhampton, and in 1879, having overhauled and improved the house fittings, were able to introduce a constant service of supply, which has since been maintained throughout the whole of the company's district. In 1880, the Bedhampton springs having been acquired, a pumping station was erected there, and a compound Worthington engine of 300 indicated horse-power placed therein capable of lifting 4,500,000 gallons per diem to the service reservoirs at Farlington. This engine has recently been altered to a capacity of 7,000,000 gallons per diem, and there is sufficient space in the engine-house for an additional engine of at least the same power.

The two high-service reservoirs at Farlington are 150 ft. above the town of Portsmouth, and each contain 3,500,000 gallons. The Drayton old reservoir is 76 ft. above the town of Portsmouth, and contains 2,500,000 gallons. The three reservoirs are upon the chalk of Portsdown Hill, and constructed with a base of concrete upon the chalk, puddled clay upon the concrete and brickwork in cement upon the puddled clay. The Drayton reservoir is not in use, owing to its low elevation, and is kept in a state of repair for use in

**BOROUGH of PORTSMOUTH WATER WORKS.**

case of emergency. The mains from the reservoirs for the supply to the town and district consist of one 24-in., one 20-in., two 12-in. and one 10-in. The surface levels above ordnance datum throughout Portsmouth vary from 10 ft. to about 25 ft.

The springs at Havant and Bedhampton are of a remarkable character, both as to their volume, purity and permanence. Rising from the chalk, they are intercepted at their points of outbreak and either piped or surrounded by masonry banks, so as to form collecting basins and channels of great size; and, after being collected, the water is carried by gravitation into wells at the pumping stations. The arrangements are such that either pumping station can derive its supply from either set of springs, and any of the basins or channels could be temporarily cut out of the system for repairs or cleansing. The total yield of the company's springs at both places is estimated at about 15,000,000 gallons per diem, about 9,000,000 coming from those springs which have already been connected to the works. The average daily quantity of water pumped for the district is about 7,000,000 gallons, to an estimated population of 200,000 persons.

The company, in its anxiety to preserve the source of supply from any possible contamination, constructed a wall of puddled clay, carried down from the surface to the solid chalk or clay beds immediately over it, all round the collecting area at Havant; and the Hermitage stream, in its course from the northward, has been intercepted before it reaches the Bedhampton works and diverted through a 60-in. pipe, about three quarters of a mile in length, and made to discharge into tidal waters. Two fine cooling ponds, each holding about 350,000 gallons, have recently been erected at Havant works, and are well worthy of notice. The Farlington works were again brought into use a few years ago for the supply to the forts on Portsdown Hill and villages of

Waterlooville, Purbrook and Stakes on the northern slope of Portsdown Hill, a reservoir being constructed for that purpose near the "George Inn" at Portsdown, at an elevation of about 300 ft. above ordnance datum.

At the works luncheon on a most generous scale was provided by the directors of the Portsmouth company, and subsequently there were some brief speeches. In the absence of Colonel Charles L. Owen, the chairman of the directors, the visitors were cordially welcomed by the secretary, and Mr. SMITH then gave a clear and interesting review of the past and present position of the undertaking; the moral to be drawn from his remarks being that the local authority of Portsmouth had neglected a splendid opportunity when, some forty years ago, they had not sufficient foresight to municipalise the then existing works. They are probably regretting to this day that that they did not venture the £40,000, for which they could have secured the nucleus of an ample supply for their borough for, apparently, an indefinite time to come.

The members of the party afterwards drove to Southsea pier and returned to Southampton by boat. In the course of the various visits hearty votes of thanks were unanimously awarded for the cordial hospitality shown and for the courtesy of those who had so admirably acted as guides at the various places. These visits formed an excellent feature of a meeting, which was so eminently successful as to augur well for the future of the association.

Among those who attended the proceedings throughout was M. Victor J. Van Lint, of Brussels, the well-known civil engineer, who is prominently connected with our contemporary, *La Technologie Sanitaire.*

## QUERIES AND REPLIES.

*Sketches accompanying Queries should be made separate on white paper in plain black-ink lines. Lettering or figures should be bold and plain.*

**199. Hydro-Geology, Books on.** — "Aqua" writes: I should be greatly obliged if you or any of your readers would kindly give me the title, &c., of a book dealing with the subject of hydro-geology. The information that I particularly want is as to the strata in which water may usually be expected to be found, with some notes as to the quality and probable quantity to be expected.

Probably the best book on the subject of hydro-geology in relation to this country is "The Water Supply of England and Wales," price 10s., by Chas. E. De Rance, C.E., F.G.S., secretary of the British Association Underground Water Committee. Mr. De Rance is, we believe, the best authority in the kingdom on the subject, and shows what is the probable supply of water available in all the river basins of England and Wales, and what amount is required to satisfy the demands upon that supply. The book, we think, may be obtained from Mr. B. T. Batsford, engineering bookseller, &c., 94 High Holborn, London, W.C. "The Modern Practice of Sinking and Boring Wells, with Geological Considerations and Examples of Wells," by Ernest Spon, C.E., 10s. 6d. (E. & F. N. Spon), will also be found useful. The querist should also refer to an interesting paper, "A Consideration of Some of the Conditions requisite for Obtaining Underground Water Supplies," by Mr. George Hodson, M.I.C.E., which is published in vol. xix. of the "Proceedings of the Incorporated Association of Municipal and County Engineers." Books of a more elementary nature are Hughes' "Treatise on Waterworks for the Supply of Cities and Towns, with a description of the principal geological formations of England as influencing supplies of water," price 4s. 6d. (Crosby Lockwood & Son), and Swindell and Burnell's "Well Sinking," price 2s. (Crosby Lockwood & Son).

**200. Surveying, Book on, required.** — "A.J." writes: Will you kindly inform me which are the best books on surveying and plotting to scale for a beginner? I know a little about field work, but my knowledge is very meagre. Usill's "Practical Surveying," price 7s. 6d. (Crosby Lockwood & Son), and Andre's "Plan and Map Drawing," which includes instructions for the preparation of engineering, architectural and mechanical drawings, price 9s. (E. & F. N. Spon), will, we think, be found helpful. The querist is, however, advised to obtain tuition in geometry and building construction at one of the local classes in connection with the Science and Art Department if he desires to make sound progress in drawing to scale.

**Exmouth District Council.** — An Exmouth contemporary, in an editorial note, states: It was the habit of some persons to treat lightly Mr. Beswick's reiterated assertion that the duties of his department were more than one man could cope with. The new surveyor, Mr. Harding, had been in office just over a fortnight, when on Thursday, the 2nd ult., he stated that he should require assistance, and asked the council to allow him to take an articled pupil. This circumstance is an unexpected, and certainly a significant, corroboration of the late surveyor's oft-repeated contention as to the necessity of help being provided for him in the execution of his multifarious tasks.

# Principal Features of Electric Lighting Systems.—VI.

## DISTRIBUTION OF ENERGY.

The question of distributing electrical energy is probably more important than that of generation because it is the one section of an electrical supply system in which there is likely to be waste of energy. It need hardly be pointed out that any waste of energy that takes place in the distributing portion of a lighting system may mean all the difference between failure and success. It was pointed out in the first of these articles that in order to reduce waste in distributing electrical energy it is necessary to reduce the resistance of the conductors, and that in order to reduce the resistance of a conductor it is necessary to use a given size for a given current. Obviously there must be a limit to the size on the grounds of cost, and in the distribution of a given current there is a well-defined economical size of main to be adopted. In distributing electrical energy it is important that the lamps farthest from the point of generation should be as well lighted as those nearest to it, and this is a matter which calls for some care in apportioning the proper size of mains and also in regulating the electric-motive force, so that the lamps nearest the station will not be too bright and those farthest away will not be dull. The Board of Trade allow a certain variation in this respect, and a supplier may without let or hindrance supply a current or 96 volts to a lamp which is designed for 100 volts, and on the other hand it may be permitted to supply a 100-volt lamp with a current of 104 volts. When this provision was made it is more than likely that the exact results were not clearly realised, because if we examine for a moment the effects of this variation they are distinctly important from a consumer's point of view. For example, a 100-volt lamp which is being supplied with a current at 96 volts will be less bright than a lamp which is supplied with a current at a pressure of 100 volts. In other words, the consumer is not obtaining the amount of light that his lamps are designed to give. Then, again, if suppliers exercise their privilege of supplying a current at a voltage of 104 the effect is an increased brilliancy, but it cannot be said to tend to the prolonged existence of the lamp. The greatest trouble, however, from a lamp point of view, is when the variations are frequent, because it has been very conclusively proved that constant variations in the voltage have a very deleterious effect upon the life of a lamp. These, however, are matters that may be discussed in a subsequent article.

While dealing with the distribution of electrical energy, it may be interesting to point out that though the central electric lighting works provide the readiest and easiest means of supplying a great number of consumers, there are occasions when it would be better and cheaper for an establishment to have a lighting plant of its own. It is, however, only the circumstances of a particular case that can determine this point. When an establishment is depending for its lighting upon its own private plant it necessitates the employment of someone to look after that plant. In such a case it is necessary to consider the space taken up, which may vary in value according to the position of the establishment, and there is a greater danger of the supply suddenly ceasing that exists when the current is obtained from the public mains. Then, again, moving machinery is not always a desirable thing in many places. But, notwithstanding these drawbacks, there are undoubtedly cases where a supply can be obtained more cheaply from isolated plant than from public works. It was shown some time ago in the case of one well-known club in London that electricity obtained from a company at 7d. per unit would have cost £1,452 per annum, as against an annual cost of £894 for working private machinery. It is clear, however, that as the price of electricity is reduced—and this, of course, is happening on all sides—it becomes more difficult for the isolated plant to compete on the score of economy with the supply of electricity obtained from the public mains; and it is a significant fact that in Manchester, where for some years numerous small installations existed, many of these have been abandoned and electricity obtained from the corporation mains. In this case, of course, the price of electricity is very low, and can be, as a matter of fact, supplied to a consumer at a much cheaper rate than that at which he would be able to manufacture it for himself. We need scarcely enter into the why and the wherefore of its being possible, as a rule, in connection with a public supply to be able to deliver electricity at the consumer's house at a cheaper rate than he would be able to manufacture it himself. The chief factor is that a large system is able to employ larger engines and dynamos, which are vastly more economical than small ones and the cost of labour is very much minimised per unit by the fact that the labour is more constantly employed.

THE SYSTEMS OF DISTRIBUTION vary, of course, with the system of generation. A high-pressure alternating system, for example, naturally calls for some different method of distributing electrical energy to consumers than is necessary with a low-tension continuous-current system. In the former the high-pressure alternating current is carried through feeders laid underground to what are known as sub-stations, where the high-pressure alternating current is reduced or transformed to a condition in which it is safe to enter a consumer's house. The transformer may be said to consist of two windings of wire or other material, one of which is known as the primary and the other as the secondary. Describing it as simply and as briefly as possible, we may say that the secondary winding is interlaced or wrapped round the primary. The passage of an alternating current through the primary coil of a transformer sets up an effect in the secondary winding, and according to the amount and size of the winding so can the exact pressure of a current be regulated in the secondary winding of a transformer. Generally speaking, an alternating current station generates electricity at a pressure of 2,000 volts, and this passes to the transformer chamber or sub-station and is there transformed down to a current of 200 volts or 100 volts, and from thence distributed to the consumer. There are here and there in different parts of the country isolated instances in which the transformer is placed on the consumer's premises, but this only applies to some of the older systems, and the method has been altogether abandoned in the case of the more modern systems. A high-pressure continuous current is in some respects similar to the alternating system, in that high-pressure mains are taken to a sub-station where the current is transformed down to a condition suitable for lighting houses, but the means of transforming employed in this case differ very materially from the alternating-current transformer, and this difference is the main distinction between a high-pressure alternating and a high-pressure continuous current. The former is, by virtue of its peculiar nature, converted by means of stationary transformers, while the high-pressure continuous current needs some revolving mechanism. A high-pressure continuous converter is practically neither more nor less than a motor—which is driven by the agency of the high-pressure current—coupled direct to a low-pressure current machine, or the more modern form of a converter. The machine is provided with a double-wound armature, one end of which receives the high-pressure continuous current while the other end gives off the low-pressure current, which is then distributed.

A very important difference, however, arises in the management of these two systems, for in the case of the first it is possible to devise some automatic means of switching in and switching out the transformers, and no other attention beyond this function is necessary. In the case of the continuous-current machines, however, although there may be means of starting and stopping them automatically, it is obvious that having running machinery they should have a certain amount of supervision. As a matter of fact, the sub-stations in a high-pressure continuous current become, as it were, small generating stations, and are a great deal more inconvenient than in the high-pressure alternating sub-station system.

The simplest method of distributing an electrical current is the two-wire system, by which mains are taken from the generating station direct to the lamps, but the operation of such a system is very limited, and in dealing with a considerable area it is necessary to provide a little more complexity than is represented by a simple two-wire system. Even if a two-wire system pure and simple were adopted, which is extremely unlikely in any new installation, it would be necessary to employ what are termed "feeders," which are neither more nor less than specially heavy copper mains, designed to carry the whole of the current that is generated at the station to what are termed distributing points. The distributing points in this case may be copper or other metal bars, and from these bars distributing mains, which would be connected directly to the houses, would be taken off. This simple two-wire system was used in a good many instances in the early days of electric lighting, and, as a matter of fact, still exists in a few cases. The most notable municipal system laid down on this principle was at Bradford, and very considerable extensions were made on these lines before it was thought necessary to employ what was undoubtedly a more economical system of distributing electrical energy. The next step in the development of the two-wire system was the use of a third wire, from which the system became known as the three-wire system. The adding of another wire had a very remarkable effect on the economical distribution, and the results achieved by this have been so exceptional that in the next article it may be desirable to consider the advantages arising from the arrangement. Most low-pressure systems at present laid down are carried out on this principle, and it may be necessary before concluding this series of articles to consider one or two municipal systems in some detail.

**Weston-super-Mare.**—On Wednesday, the 15th ult., Mr. W. O. E. Meade-King, Local Government Board inspector, held an inquiry at the town hall in reference to an application made by the council for power to borrow £3,809 for market purposes. The clerk explained the scheme in detail, and also the estimated cost of carrying it out, the plans being produced and explained by Mr. Hans F. Price. There was no opposition, neither were there any questions forthcoming from any of those present in regard to structural matters.

# Municipal Work at Darwen.

## IMPORTANT LOCAL GOVERNMENT BOARD INQUIRY.

Major-General Crozier, R.E., an inspector of the Local Government Board, recently held an inquiry at Darwen relative to the application of the town council for sanction to borrow £48,170 for the following purposes : Electricity supply scheme, £30,000; electric lighting in streets, £800; refuse destructor, £6,870 ; public parks, £5,590 ; new road at Hollins-grove, £400 ; land for health depot, £800; land for highways, store yard, workshops, &c., £1,600; and sewage disposal works, £2,500.

### COMBINED ELECTRIC SUPPLY AND REFUSE DESTRUCTION.

This makes the fourth Local Government Board inquiry which has been held since the present borough engineer, Mr. W. R. W. Smith-Saville, A.M.I.C.E., took office less than two years ago, and shows the large amount of work which has been carried out since then. The work of the department has been rendered heavier by the desire of the corporation to proceed at once with an electricity supply scheme in conjunction with a refuse destructor. The consideration of an electrical supply scheme had been entered upon when Mr. Smith-Saville took up his duties, and a preliminary report had already been obtained from an engineer in private practice as to the desirability of carrying this out, but nothing farther was done for some months. Eventually, however, a provisional order was obtained, and it became necessary to proceed with the details of the scheme, so as to have the work completed within the time allowed by the order. Acting under the advice of the borough engineer, the corporation decided to have complete control of the whole scheme at every point. To do this effectually they decided to place the matter in the hands of the borough engineer and to appoint an electrical engineer whom they would subsequently require to manage the works, to collaborate with him in designing the scheme, and to act as resident engineer during the construction of the works. W. Stanley Clegg, of Burnley, received this appointment.

With the very awkwardly-shaped and almost precipitous site which was selected as being the best available in the position required, added to the complication caused by the works having to be worked in conjunction with a refuse destructor, resulted in the designing of the works to be an anxious one, not only so as to allow for a symmetrical arrangement capable of allowing considerable extension, but also so as to give the least possible chance for friction between the future management of two plants. Finally, however, it was decided that the two plants should each be complete in themselves but at the same time run parallel to each other, so that each may be extended in the most convenient manner possible without interference with the other ; whilst, at the same time, when the electricity supply works in the future require 'more power than possibly will be obtained from the destruction of the town's refuse independent boilers can be conveniently added, to be fired in the ordinary manner.

### TYPE OF REFUSE DESTRUCTOR.

The next important matter to determine was the type of refuse destructor which should be adopted, and with a view to this a deputation from the Electricity Supply and Health Committees visited the principal places where they were informed the heat from destructors was being best utilised. The committee visited Cambridge, Shoreditch, Leyton, Rochdale, Oldham, Bury and Hereford, and were well pleased with the various systems, but did not recommend any particular one, as the quotations received and the amount of steam which the various patentees were prepared to guarantee varied so much that it became almost an impossibility to determine which really was the most efficient and economical. The borough engineer therefore advised that he should prepare proper conditions and specifications, so that each could tender upon the same basis, for the purpose of affording a fair comparison, and this was carried out. In response to the advertisement six tenders and designs were received, and the order eventually was given to Messrs. Meldrum Brothers, of Manchester, to install two units on their system. Each unit will be entirely distinct from the other, and will consist of one continuous hearth, with the grate sub-divided into four compartments, into each of which will be fitted two of Messrs. Meldrum's patent blowers, for providing the forced draught. Each grate will be fired alternately, so that the newly-charged refuse is always adjoining that which is in an incandescent state. At the end of the hearth is a combustion chamber, for the settlement of dust and more complete destruction of any organic matter which may have escaped from the hearths, the hot gases next passing through the flues of an ordinary Lancashire boiler (30 ft. by 8 ft., one to each unit) in the ordinary manner, and subsequently through a regenerator, for heating air from which will be used in connection with the forced draught. The chimney will be 80 yards in height, and is placed in the centre between the two plants, and will be capable of being used by the electricity supply works when required.

The Darwen refuse averages about 40 tons per day, and in lieu of providing a complicated system of thermal or otherwise storage the engineer has deemed it better to have the cells rather in excess of the general requirements, the intention being to fire lightly during the period of light load at the electricity supply works and concentrate the bulk of the firing during the short period of heavy load, during which period it is anticipated that over 300 horse-power will be obtained from each of the two boilers. When complete it is believed that this will be the largest installation of refuse destruction, combined with Lancashire boilers for steam supply, in the kingdom, and it will be interesting to see how far the corporation have been justified in departing from the usual water-tube type of boiler used with refuse destruction.

### ELECTRICITY WORKS AND PLANT.

Although space is reserved in the electricity works for boilers, it is not, of course, intended to place any therein for some time, as it is thought that sufficient steam will be obtained from the refuse for the first two or three days. The electricity works will consist of the usual offices, with testing and store rooms, accumulator-room, generating-room, &c. The generating-room is 60 ft. in width, and will allow for two rows of direct-coupled steam dynamos, one end being constructed in a temporary manner, ready for extension. This room, however, will allow for space for 2,000 horse-power as it is now being built. The system of supply will be the three-wire low-tension continuous current (400 volts, with a 230-volt supply to consumers). The various contracts have been let subject to the sanction of the Local Government Board being obtained, and the following firms are the successful contractors : Steam dynamo, Siemens Brothers (with Belliss engines); steam and exhaust piping, John Spencer, Wednesbury ; switchboard and balancing apparatus, Thomas Partner, Wolverhampton ; accumulators, the Tudor Accumulator Company ; mains, the Callender Cable Company ; arc lamps and pillars, Lucy & Co., Oxford ; buildings and chimney, W. R. J. Whalley, Darwen.

The iron roof to generating-room, travelling crane, and iron buildings for refuse destructor, yet remain to be let, and will form another contract. It is anticipated that there will soon be a good demand for electricity, as many houses are already being wired in anticipation of the supply, and the corporation are acting in a very progressive manner by laying down about 4 miles of mains to commence with. A good load is also anticipated from the tramways, which will shortly be converted from steam to electricity and worked by the corporation. The town council have already, under the terms of their Act, given the local tramway company notice of their intention to purchase.

### OTHER WORKS.

The item for public parks is for their completion of the laying out of one of the parks and the construction of certain adjoining streets (conditional upon which some of the land was given by the lord of the manor), works in connection with a band-stand and meteorological station (already erected), being gifts in commemoration of the Diamond Jubilee, and an entrance lodge for the caretaker. The land for which power is sought to obtain for stables and health depot, and for highways, store-yard, workshops, sidings, &c., adjoins the electricity and destructor works, and the designs for these will next be proceeded with. It is also intended to erect public baths upon an adjoining site, and preliminary plans for these have already been got out.

The item for sewage disposal was for money overspent upon the works, and the inspector severely criticised the corporation in not having laid out the 17 acres of land for irrigation, as provided when the loan was sanctioned, in addition to the filters of polarite and coke which have been made and which are giving a very satisfactory effluent.

There was no opposition, and after the conclusion the inspector highly complimented the borough engineer upon the plans and details of the schemes which had been placed before him, and which have been carried out entirely by the regular staff in the office.

---

**Troon.**—The first annual visit of the Commissioners to the new waterworks, which were opened last year by the Duchess of Portland, took place recently. The commissioners and burgh officials met at the burgh buildings and walked down and inspected the new slaughter-house just erected at the north shore, at an approximate cost of £300. The building, which has all the latest sanitary appliances, was found in perfect order. It is to be opened on an early date. The party, accompanied by Mr. J. H. Turner, the Duke of Portland's factor, and Mr. Osborne, the contractor, then proceeded in brakes to the waterworks at the Glen, about 2 miles from Troon. Arrived there the reservoir, filters, &c., were minutely examined. The general opinion was that the filter from which the burgh is supplied should be covered over, thus preventing the accumulation of vegetable matter. There is at present an abundant supply of water, and the commissioners were convinced no fears need be entertained of scarcity.

# A Chapter in the History of Pottery.

## THE STORY OF TWYFORDS.

BIRD'S-EYE VIEW OF THE CLIFF VALE POTTERIES.

Never probably have romance and art been more beautifully woven together than in the history of pottery, the
handmaid of sanitary science. During the long march of
the centuries, from the days of the ancient Egyptians, the
potter's art has contributed to the happiness and comfort of
the peoples of every nation, and adorned the houses and
palaces of their kings and governors. It is as cosmopolitan
as the air we breathe, and it has ministered to the health of
the humblest as well as the greatest of the human family.
There is no barbarous race so rude as to know nothing of the
use of earthenware, and no people so civilised as to be able
to dispense with its services. The most useful ally of the
pioneer of sanitary science has been the potter, who has often
anticipated the want, and always responded to the call, for
his best inventions to improve the health of cities, towns and
villages, and given the best that ingenuity could suggest or
skill accomplish.

### CLIFFE VALE POTTERY AND ITS HISTORY.

From the pen of Mr. Joseph Hatton, published by the renowned
firm of art publishers, J. S. Virtue & Co., comes a handsome
work, superbly illustrated, tracing the development of work
in clay from days anterior to Tubal Cain and the artificers
in iron and brass to the present. It is a history of Twyfords
and of sanitary science, and he describes in graphic language
the works at Cliffe Vale, which are typical of the successful
application of pottery to the laws of health, which is the
foundation of the solid prosperity of that firm. In days when
the Wedgwoods were not, the name of Twyford was associated
with Staffordshire pottery, and Mr. Hatton tells how the first
Twyford and the first Astbury acquired, by assuming a guise
of stupidity and imbecility, the carefully-guarded secrets of
the Dutch potters, Elers, who established works at Bradwell
before 1700. Two hundred years later a descendant of the
first Twyford took to Staffordshire a colony of Scotchmen,
and their wives and families, for the purpose of manufacturing
a new variety of sanitary articles from the fire-clays of north
Staffordshire. Mr. T. W. Twyford, bent upon a great extension of manufactures in a line that was new to the
district, had gone to Scotland for potters already engaged
in a similar class of work to that which he intended to
introduce to Hanley. They had some experience of the
character of the articles contemplated, but they little
dreamed how far the development was destined to be carried.
The material to be used for the manufacture of the new

goods was nothing better than the old potters had used for
their pottingers, bread-dishes and milk-pans, but it was in
the character and the size of the pieces that the innovation
lay. His boldness staggered the new hands and was the
despair of the old ones, but after a period of experiment which
taxed his patience and perseverance to the utmost he achieved
a splendid success. From his experience in the manufacture
of large pieces of earthenware in connection with his sanitary
pottery, Mr. Twyford realised the possibility of utilising the
fire-clay of the district in the production and manufacture of
specialities in the shape of sanitary and culinary vessels,
sinks, cisterns and baths, of a size and strength which had
never hitherto been projected. The testing of the clays was
the most arduous part of the undertaking. Some having an
undue proportion of alkali or alkali earths would not stand
the fire; others having too great a percentage of silica, would
not stand the enamel; others were so much impregnated
with oxides of iron that they discoloured the enamel; and
others, again, contained impurities which rendered them useless for the purpose. It was not till towards the close of 1890
that the manufacture of porcelain enamel fire-clay goods was
begun in earnest. The manager of the new department more
than once gave up the enterprise in despair. Like the honest man
he was, he disliked the idea of taking his employer's money with
such poor results. After five years of unremitting toil and
anxiety, with very variable success, all difficulties were overcome, and out of the crude clays of the district were manufactured articles of enormous size and strength, with a dense, hard,
vitreous surface, equal in colour and smoothness to the finest
porcelain. Our space will not permit us to describe the
details of the elaborate process by which fire-clay goods are
made from the local fire-clays, the passage through the
"pulverising" mill, the watering-pan, the "pug" mill, the
forming, the pressing, the finishing, the drying and the
enamelling. The firing is the most critical stage in the existence of the newly-formed pottery. It proceeds very gently
at first and continues increasing in intensity for about twelve
days. At the end of that time the heat has to be intense
indeed to flux the glaze and finish off the goods. The time
occupied from first to last is at least eight weeks, and in the
case of failure in firing the work has to be done over again.

### SOMETHING ABOUT THE WORKS AND PROCESSES.

What impresses the visitor first about Cliff Vale works is
the stern air of business, and this impression continues to

the last. From the unshipping of the clays until they are despatched as finished goods by rail there is unvarying regularity of method. The works are spacious, occupying about 9 acres of ground. Twyfords for many years occupied three sites, but less than a dozen years ago the present proprietor concentrated all of them at Cliff Vale, where their position is unique for purposes of transport, bounded on one side by the Bridgewater canal and on the other by the North Staffordshire Railway. The buildings are all admirably adapted for the purposes they serve. Mr. Twyford's aim has always been to bring light, air and brightness into the occupations of those in his employment, and the men are naturally proud of the splendid shops they work in. It is worth noting that since Mr. Twyford has introduced the larger and superior class of sanitary ware, notably from the epoch of the "Unitas," the wages of sanitary potters have improved at least 50 per cent. The manufacture of sanitary pottery is really an art in itself. The old principle is revolutionised, for the historic method of throwing on the "potter's wheel" cannot be employed. All the pieces of this ware are made in moulds, and the preparation of these constitutes a special branch—modelling and mould-making. First comes the modelling of the article in clay, which must be done with the greatest care; hence the art of modelling and mould-making is rightly considered one in which technical and artistic training are very requisite. Next comes the division of the clay model into separate pieces, to enable plaster casts or models to be taken. These are termed "block moulds," and the working moulds are again cast in plaster of Paris, and must be properly fitted together with snips to keep them in position after the clay has been pressed into the moulds. The moulds being ready and the clay prepared the latter is conveyed by trolleys and lifts to the various potters' shops. These shops, which are built in proximity to the slip-house and the ovens, would well merit description, but it is impossible to do more here than to indicate their character. They are so arranged that the men work on each side of the shop with a drying stove heated by steam pipes in the centre, and in each shop, as far as possible, the men are engaged in the making of the same class of goods. Thus in the first shop "Twycliffe," "Deluge," "Unitas" and other basins are made. Another shop is devoted to tip-up basins—"Ideal," "Cardinal," "C. V." and other oval and round plug-basins—and so the process goes on. The "pressing," so named from the fact that the workmen have literally to press the clay firmly down in the moulds, also requires experience and dexterity, and later on comes the "fottling," which consists of trimming the edges with a knife and sponging out the marks and finally finishing with a piece of horn until the surface is perfectly smooth and no mark of any kind is left on the ware. The placing and the fixing come still later. To describe the "Bisque" ovens would require a chapter by itself, which would tell of many a success and many a failure. The visitor to Twyfords cannot fail to realise that "peace hath her triumphs no less renowned than war."

## A WATERTIGHT MANHOLE.

A manhole sewer invert which is claimed to be absolutely watertight has been patented by Mr. H. E. Stilgoe, borough engineer and surveyor of Dover. In the construction of sewers and drains in waterlogged ground it is now customary, in order to obtain watertight work with a minimum of pumping in carrying it out, to use iron pipes with turned and bored spigot and socket joints, and stoneware pipes with specially-designed joints. In this connection it has also been customary hitherto for the manhole inverts or bottoms to be constructed of brickwork, channel pipes or other materials

SECTIONAL PLAN

requiring the use of cement to make the structure watertight, so that pumping has to be resorted to when water is met with. The object aimed at by Mr. Stilgoe in his new "watertight" invert is its construction on sewers, &c., in waterlogged ground without any pumping whatsoever. As the cost of pumping has often been a heavy item it is obvious that if this object can be achieved a great saving must be effected. We append a few details of the invention.

The manhole as shown in the diagrams has the bottom or invert-piece constructed of cast iron, and connected to the flanged ends of cast-iron pipes with turned and bored spigot and socket joints. The flanged ends of the pipes are special

pieces which are faced for jointing, and are made either square or on the skew, according to the direction in which it is desired to lay the sewer. The pipes, having been laid up to the manhole, the invert-piece is lowered into place. A rubber ring or other suitable jointing material is placed between the facing ring on the pipe and the facing ring on the "invert"; the two are bolted together and the joint made after the same manner as the flanged joints of a water main

CROSS SECTION

valve. Pockets marked A on the diagram are constructed at the ends of the pipes and the invert-piece. The object of the pockets is that the insertion of the bolts and the bolting-up may all be done by a man standing inside the invert-piece, and in this connection it is pointed out that in the case of a very large quantity of water it would be a very difficult thing to screw up the lower bolts from the outside. When the joints are made the pockets are filled up with cement. The invert-pieces are made to any depth, according to the

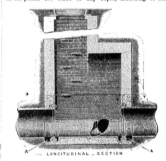

LONGITUDINAL SECTION

depth of the subsoil water, and can be set in concrete or not as desired. They are also made of stoneware or other suitable material, and arranged with various forms of joints for connection to stoneware drains and in one or more pieces. The invert level of the branch sewers may be at any desirable height above that of the main sewer.

The manufacturers are Messrs. Ham, Baker & Co., 13 Grosvenor-road, Westminster, S.W.

**Billing's Gas Burner Syndicate, Limited,** manufacturers of the patent non-mantle incandescent gas burner, ask us to state that, owing to the great demand for their patent burners, they have been compelled to remove from 17 Great Titchfield-street to more extensive premises, 180 Wardour-street, four doors from Oxford-street. London, W., and that with the increased facilities now at their disposal they will have no difficulty in promptly executing all orders.

**Rothes, Morayshire.**—The foundation-stone was recently laid of the new town hall. The architect is Mr. Pratt, of Elgin, whose plans were selected in competition. The hall measures about 70 ft. long by 35 ft. wide, and will accommodate 600 people. A circular crush-lobby gives entrance to the hall and adjoining ante-rooms. There will be a supper-room and refreshment-rooms on the ground floor, and ladies' cloak and retiring rooms. At the further end of the hall a small stage will be erected for theatrical and other entertainments, with a store-room underneath and dressing-rooms in the rear. The building is estimated to cost about £2,000.

# Parliamentary Memoranda.

In the House of Lords, on Thursday, the London County Council (General Powers) Bill was read a second time. The Northam Urban District Water Bill and the North Warwickshire Water Bill were read a third time and passed.

In the House of Commons, the Blackpool and Fleetwood Tramroad (Tramway Extensions) Bill, The Hamilton Water Bill and the Kettering Water Bill were read a third time and passed with amendments. The Lords' amendments to the Canals Protection (London) Bill were considered and agreed to.

*Parliament-street Widening.*—It was stated, in reply to questions, that it had not been possible to acquire the whole of the property between Parliament-street and King-street. It was hoped, however, that the acquirement would be carried out within the next three months.

On Friday, in the House of Lords, the Norwich City Water Bill, Gainsborough Gas Bill, Southend Water Bill, East Ham Improvement Bill, and Southwark and Vauxhall Water Bill were read a third time.

In the House of Commons, the Lords' amendments to the Kew Bridge Approaches Bill and the Staines Reservoirs Joint Committee Bill were considered and agreed to.

On Monday, in the House of Lords, the Newcastle-upon-Tyne Corporation Bill was read a third time and passed.

In the House of Commons, the Belfast Harbour Bill, the Blackpool Improvement Bill, The Sheringham Gas and Water Bill and the West Ham Corporation Bill were read a third time. The London County Corporation (Money) Bill and the Yeovil Corporation Bill were considered and ordered for third reading. The Newhaven Harbour Bill was read a second time.

*Petitions.*—Petitions were presented by many Irish members on both sides of the House, from various public bodies, praying the House to take steps to carry out the recommendations of the Royal Commission on the Financial Relations between Great Britain and Ireland.

In the House of Lords, on Tuesday, the Wishaw Water Bill, the Cranbrook District Water Bill, the Crawley and District Water Bill, and the East Ham Improvement Bill were read a third time and passed.

In the House of Commons, the Lords' amendments to the Ilford Improvement Bill were considered and agreed to.

On Wednesday, in the House of Commons, the Portsmouth Corporation Tramways Bill was read a second time. Consideration was given to the Local Government (Ireland) Bill and several new clauses were inserted.

## PRIVATE BILLS IN COMMITTEE.

*Forres Water Bill.*—This Bill, in which powers were sought by the Town Council of Forres to take over the local water undertaking with the consent of the water company, came before a committee of the House of Lords, presided over by Lord Heneage, last week. It was opposed by several land-owners, riparian owners and distillers, but when it came up it was announced that a settlement had been reached. The question at issue related to compensation water, and an agreement was arrived at by which, instead of 174,000 gallons of compensation water as proposed in the Bill, the petitioners would be allowed 250,000 gallons per day, three years being given for the construction of the necessary works. The measure afterwards went through the House unopposed.

*London County Council (Acton Sewage) Bill.*—The Bill promoted by the London County Council, to obtain powers to compel the Acton District Council to contribute towards the expenses of the metropolitan drainage scheme was passed by a committee of the House of Lords, last week. The Bill had previously gone through the Commons, where it was strongly opposed by the district council, who renewed their opposition in the Upper House. The principal witness in support of the measure was Sir Alexander Binnie, the engineer-in-chief to the London County Council, who explained that in former times the drainage of Acton went into the Stamford brook, which ran into the Thames, but by the Metropolitan Drainage Act this brook was converted into a sewer, which formed connection with the western branch of the low-level sewer. The Metropolitan Board of Works, in 1882, obtained an injunction to restrain the Acton local authority from passing any drainage through the Stamford brook to the metropolitan main drainage, and shortly afterwards the Acton local board carried out a drainage scheme of their own. Since that time no fresh houses had been connected with the old sewers, but the Acton board had never contributed to the cost of the main drainage. This cost, which had been equally borne by the whole metropolitan drainage area, had been £7,800,000, and the annual outlay in maintenance was £200,000. To go to the Acton district and cut off the drainage could hardly be done, but the county council considered that a proportionate payment should be made, such as had been made in the case of the other urban authorities outside the metropolitan area. The contention on behalf of the Acton council was that they had a right to discharge the surface water from the land into Stamford brook, and, having been deprived of that natural drainage by the conversion of the brook into a sewer, they should not be required to contribute to the cost of a sewage scheme in the management of which they had no voice. The

committee, in passing the preamble of the Bill, suggested that the counsel representing the parties should agree upon a clause as to the contribution to be made to the London County Council. The clause was afterwards drawn up and incorporated in the Bill, which was reported to the House.

*Electric Lighting Provisional Orders.*—A Bill to confirm provisional orders made by the Board of Trade, under the Electric Lighting Acts of 1882 and 1888, relating to Colne, Rochdale and St. Anne's-on-the-Sea, when before a House of Lords committee, presided over by Lord Brougham, was opposed by the County Council of Lancashire, so far as the order relating to Colne was concerned. It appeared that the corporation owned the gasworks of Colne, and manufactured 120,000,000 cubic feet of gas last year, and having spent £100,000 on the works, and having the land used for them fully occupied while the town was still growing, they decided to introduce electric light; and they got a provisional order from the Board of Trade in the model form. The Lancashire County Council now wanted a special clause inserted in the Bill to this effect: "Nothing in this order shall authorise the undertakers to interfere with or make use of any county or kindred bridge vested in the Lancashire County Council, except with the consent in writing of the said county council, and subject to such terms and conditions as they may impose." The county council, as a matter of fact, desired, if the corporation of Colne required to carry their wires along a bridge over a river under the jurisdiction of the county council, they should have an absolute veto in the matter. It was the first time the point had been raised, and the county council justified their action by stating that there were no less than fifty-four bridges which would be affected by similar orders this session, and, although this involved an alteration of the general law, it was necessary that some protection of the kind should be given. The committee passed the Bill and rejected the clause proposed by the county council.—A provisional order Bill, promoted by the Corporation of Leeds, was the subject of inquiry before the chairman of Ways and Means sitting in the Court of Referees in the House of Commons last week. The Yorkshire House-to-House Electricity Company sought to obtain a *locus standi* to be heard against the Bill on the ground, first, that it was an alteration of an Act of Parliament, and that it would be prejudicial to the company were the corporation to have power to go to individual shareholders and bargain with them in regard to giving up the right to take irredeemable stock and take redeemable stock in place of it as was proposed in the order before Parliament. The chairman intimated that the court had decided not to allow the company a *locus standi*.

*General Electric Power Distributing Bill.*—A very important Bill, promoted by the General Electric Power Distributing Company, has occupied for some days the attention of a committee of the House of Lords, presided over by the Earl of Northbrook. The measure, which embraced a scheme to supply electricity over a large area of the Midlands, of which Warsop was to be the centre, encountered very serious opposition, the corporations of Sheffield, Lincoln, Rotherham, Chesterfield, Doncaster, Nottingham and Ilkeston, and the urban district councils of Heanor, Long Eaton, Bakewell, Belper, Matlock Bath, Mexborough, North Darley, Swinton, Wath-upon-Dearne, Wombwell and Worksop being all arrayed against it. It appeared that from a generating station at Warsop it was intended to supply a district with an area of 2,000 square miles, and that the company intended to raise for this purpose capital amounting to £1,000,000. Seventy-two petitions were presented in favour of the scheme, by which it was hoped to supply electricity at a rate of 1¼d. per unit, and sometimes at 1d. per unit. Mr. Arnold Lupton, C.E., Professor of Coal Mining at Victoria University, Leeds, Mr. Emerson Bainbridge, M.P., Mr. A. D. Williamson, electrical engineer, and Mr. Acton, vice-chairman of the Nottingham Chamber of Commerce, spoke generally in support of the project. Mr. Bainbridge expressed the belief that the introduction of electric power into the district on the plans suggested would be of great benefit in cheapening the production of coal. He used electrical power in his own collieries, and was quite sure that it was much more economical than steam power. The general position taken up by the petitions against the Bill was that, while it might possibly be advantageous in some cases to create a central supply of electrical energy which would be distributed by the authorities, it could not be publicly advantageous for a foreign body to come in and break up their streets at will. Sheffield Corporation went a little further than most of the others, arguing that they could themselves supply electricity both for lighting and power at a very much cheaper rate than the company could. It was quite an easy thing, said the Sheffield people in effect, to take a large pair of compasses, and with one part laid on at a place like Warsop and the other part at a place 26 miles distant, and draw a circle and say they were going to supply the whole of that area; but Sheffield would rather be left out. To give the company power to compete against the municipalities would, it was argued, be most unfair. It was pointed out that, in the case of companies established in municipalities for purposes of gas and water, the corporation of those boroughs were precluded from competing, and if they desired to provide either commodity for the public good they had first to buy out the existing company. If, therefore, companies were protected in that manner, why should not the municipalities be protected too ? The counsel representing the various corporations opposing the Bill argued generally that they would welcome the Power Distributing Company if they could do what they suggested—supply cheaper electrical energy and deliver it at the borders of the municipalities at a less price than the corporations could do. But they had failed to produce satisfactory evidence upon this point, and the people objected to have energy thrust upon them for the purpose of distribution against their will. The mayor of Nottingham, Mr. E. H. Fraser, was very sceptical as to cheapness, but he said that if the company could produce electricity at their gates in bulk at a cheaper rate than it could be produced in Nottingham, for the corporation to distribute, they would be bound in the face of public opinion to adopt the scheme before the committee, but this the company were not prepared to do. Mr. Herbert Talbot, c.e., resident electrical engineer to the Corporation of Nottingham, and Mr. Arthur Browne, m.i.c.e., city engineer, declared that, even if coal were given to the General Power Distributing Company, they would not be able to supply electrical energy as cheaply as it could be supplied in Nottingham by the corporation. The committee, on Tuesday, passed the Bill, but considered that the local authorities should have greater power than they had now with respect to the placing of mains in their streets where the company desired to put them. It was decided that a proviso should be inserted in the Bill, to which the promoters had agreed, to the effect that the company should not supply electrical energy within the area of any borough the corporation of which should, within twelve months after notice from the company that the latter desired to supply electrical energy, undertake to receive from the company a supply of energy in bulk at a price and to a minimum amount not less than, failing agreement, should be determined by an arbitrator to be appointed by the presidents of the Institutions of Civil and Electrical Engineers. The committee thought, however, that some time limit should be inserted in the Bill, so that the price fixed by an arbitrator should be revised after the lapse of a certain period. Counsel representing the municipalities and other local authorities intimated that they would carry their opposition to the other House, and consequently would not oppose on clauses.

*Newcastle Corporation Bill.*—The Corporation of Newcastle had to fight very hard in the House of Lords, last week, for the Bill which they promoted in order to obtain powers to transfer about 10 acres of the town moor to the trustees of the Royal Infirmary for the purposes of the new hospital building. The Bill, which came before the Earl of Egerton's committee, was opposed by certain freemen, landowners and ratepayers, who contested the right of the corporation to sell land over which they had herbage rights without their unanimous consent. Mr. Pember and Mr. Hans B. Hamilton represented the corporation, and Mr. Balfour Browne, q.c., appeared on behalf of the petitioners. The present infirmary, it appeared, was altogether insufficient to meet the requirements of the rapidly-expanding town and district. It was built in the middle of last century, and since 1854 the corporation had been endeavouring to find a suitable site upon which to erect the new infirmary. It was most desirable that the hospital should be built according to modern ideas and in model form. A wealthy and philanthropic gentleman, Mr. John Hall, had offered to give £10,000 towards the erection of the new structure, and he had no opposition to offer to the proposed site, which was described as eminently suitable. Prof. G. H. Philipson, consulting physician to the hospital, and Dr. Haliburton Hume, the senior surgeon, gave evidence in support of the scheme. Mr. Riley Lord, who had been mayor of Newcastle in 1896, stated that during his term of office it had been thought desirable that something should be done to commemorate in a fitting manner the Queen's jubilee, and he suggested that the most appropriate thing would be to build a new infirmary, which had been required for a great number of years, and as it would cost £100,000 at least, an endeavour should be made to raise that sum by jubilee day. In jubilee week the amount had reached over £10,000. The present mayor, Mr. T. B. Sanderson, said the corporation, by a large majority, were in favour of the scheme. The existing site of the infirmary was granted on a long lease by the corporation to the governors at 2s. 6d. a year so long as it was maintained as an infirmary. Part of the present scheme was that the lease should be surrendered to the corporation, and a portion of the site was to be sold in order to buy 10 acres of land to replace that taken from the town moor and to defray the expenses of the present Bill. The old site so acquired by the corporation was very valuable, and part of it might be used to extend the cattle market. It seemed from the case presented on behalf of the opponents of the Bill that there was a conflict of opinion as to whether the present site or one at Losyes was the best. The freemen most strongly protested against the corporation handing over their rights in any part of the town moor without one penny of compensation, and if such a thing were sanctioned by the committee it would be absolutely, they argued, unprecedented in the history of Parliamentary legislation. After consultation, the committee decided to pass the Bill, subject to clauses being inserted by which, while the lease of the pre-

sent site should be surrendered, sufficient land should be retained on the same terms as now—namely, a rental of 2s. 6d. a year—to provide an accident ward and an out-patient's department or dispensary. The committee further decided that land equal in area and in grazing value should be purchased by the corporation under the Lands Clauses Acts, and that compensation for loss of convenience to the cowkeepers should be provided for either by money or additional land.

*Corporation Improvements at Leeds.*—A House of Commons committee, presided over by Colonel Gunter, has passed a Bill for the confirmation of Local Government provisional orders relating to various corporation improvements, among them being provisions with respect to the acquisition of property and the laying-out of new streets at Leeds. These were opposed by the Committee for the Execution of Charitable Uses in the City of Leeds. It appeared from the evidence that the principal object in view was the formation of a new street from Briggate to Vicar-lane, which would enable the council to get rid of the poorer property, which was a disgrace to one of the best and busiest parts of the town. The new street would form a junction with a thoroughfare which the corporation already had power to construct. Mr. Hewson, the Leeds city and waterworks engineer, explained that at first the intention had been to widen Kirkgate, where the traffic was extremely congested, but the cost of this rendered the project practically prohibitive, so that the new street had been laid out with a view to relieving that thoroughfare. The present scheme was the best that could be devised, having regard to the projected extensions between Vicar-lane and George-street on one side and Albion-place and Briggate on the other. The main objection against the Bill was that it was a proposal to take compulsory powers for admittedly far more land than was required, in order to hand it over to a commercial company for their benefit, in return for which the company agreed to pay all the costs except the paving of the streets.

*Wishaw Water Bill.*—A Bill promoted by the Commissioners of the Burgh of Wishaw was passed, on Tuesday, by a committee of the House of Lords, presided over by Lord Brougham. The Bill, which empowered the commissioners to provide an additional water supply, and to make and maintain new works, was opposed by the Earl of Home, Sir Edward Colebrook, Lord Newlands, Sir Charles Ross, Sir William Anstruther, and other property owners. The Corporation of Glasgow and the County Council of Lanark also petitioned against the Bill, but their opposition had been withdrawn. It appeared from the evidence given in support of the measure, that Wishaw was the centre of an industrial district with a large population. The present water supply, which was taken from the parish of Carluke, yielded 400,000 gallons a day, and the requirements of the burgh at the lowest computation were 570,000 gallons. The commissioners, in order to supplement the supply, had to supply carts, and adopt other means of distributing water from an old quarry, and they had to borrow water from the neighbouring burgh of Motherwell, who were good enough to help them in two dry seasons. After very careful consideration as to the proper sources of supply, they had been advised by engineers that it was prudent to go to the upper reaches of the Clyde, and they proposed to take the water from three streams running through Lord Hopetoun's property. The water they proposed to abstract could have no appreciable effect upon the Clyde, as the pipe they proposed to lay down would only be capable of carrying 1,500,000 gallons in twenty-four hours. That supply they calculated would be quite sufficient for Wishaw and the wants of its people for a considerable number of years to come. In order to meet the opposition of Lord Home, however, the commissioners proposed in the dry period, when there was less than 1,000,000 gallons flowing down from these streams, to take no water at all, but when there was an ample flow they proposed to take up to 3,000,000 gallons a day down to their reservoir at Wishaw, which would be capable of containing 45,000,000 gallons. Lord Hopetoun and Lord Belhaven spoke as to the deplorable state of Wishaw for want of water, and stated that there were numerous streams in the district from which it was proposed to take water. Engineering evidence as to the feasibility and reasonableness of the scheme was given by Mr. James Tait, c.e., Mr. W. R. Copeland, c.e., Glasgow, and Mr. George Horsley, water engineer. The committee passed the Bill on condition that a clause was inserted providing water compensation for the riparian owners.

*Drogheda Gas Bill.*—When the Drogheda Gas Bill came before the Standing Orders Committee of the House of Lords the promoters sought powers to add to the measure a provision embodying an agreement between the company and the corporation for the purchase of the undertaking. The committee dispensed with the standing orders and allowed the new provision to be added.

*Belfast Harbour Bill.*—The Belfast Harbour Bill, which recently went through the Lords, has now been passed by a committee of the Commons, presided over by Mr. J. W. Lowther, chairman of Ways and Means. The Bill empowers the Belfast Harbour Commissioners to improve the Victoria channel, and to construct additional docks and works at Belfast. It was explained by the secretary to the commissioners that, in order to satisfy the Corporation of Belfast, ample provision had been made that vessels having paid their dues should not again be charged for transhipment.

## For Assistants and Pupils.

### THE CONSTRUCTION OF ROADS AND STREETS.—XIV.

By WILLIAM H. MAXWELL, Assistant Engineer and Surveyor, Leyton Urban District Council.

ROAD MATERIALS AND CONSTRUCTION.

*Materials.*—The essential qualities of a good stone or "road metal" are hardness, toughness and power to resist the action of the weather. It should also possess strength to resist compression, and should when laid well unite with its own angles to form a compact surface not easily torn up by traffic, without the aid of much "*binding material.*" These qualities are not always to be found together in the same class of stone, but some of the best descriptions for the purpose are found among the igneous rocks, such as granite and trap-rock, or whinstone.

Whilst there are certain general tests which are useful in selecting stones for use as a road metal, yet the only satisfactory means of judging as to its suitability for the purpose is by making an experimental trial for a sufficient length of time upon a roadway with a known amount of traffic. The following preliminary tests are suggested by Mr. Boulnois[*]:—

1. Ascertain from local persons, such as masons, quarrymen and others, their opinion of the qualities of the stones in the neighbourhood.

2. Make a trial of the stone for *toughness* by setting a good stone-breaker to work upon a heap of the stone as quarried and carefully watching how much he can break in an hour.

3. Ascertain what power the stone has to resist abrasion, as by putting the broken metal into a revolving cylinder and then carefully noting by weight what the cubes lose by contact with each other, or press the stone against a grindstone with a uniform pressure and note the loss by such contact.

made use of owing to their cheapness in *first cost*, but, generally speaking, it will be better policy to obtain a superior material from a distance if there is much heavy traffic. Soft material should not be mixed with hard either for the construction or maintenance of a road, as one will obviously wear faster than the other and thus make the surface very uneven, unpleasant to ride over, and full of hollows which retain the wet and damage the road. The hard metal should be reserved for the surface coating.

A few of the most important materials will now be briefly described.

GRANITE[*] is a stone of a crystalline granular structure, occurring in large quantities in the older geological formations. It is an igneous rock, and probably is the product of the metamorphism of older sedimentary strata. It is found below the "primary" stratified rocks, but occurs in beds, veins and dykes, oftentimes injected from below through and over the adjacent strata; also in large masses gradually changing in character and passing into the surrounding rocks.

True granite consists of crystals of quartz and felspar[†] mixed with thin plates or scales of mica.

The *quartz* or silica occurs in hard glassy grey or colourless amorphous lumps.

The *felspar* is in the form of opaque crystals, of very irregular size, and of a white, grey, yellowish pink, red or reddish brown colour, which gives the tone to the mass.

The *mica* consists of small glistening scales, capable of being flaked off with the knife, and having a yellow or brownish-yellow, and sometimes dark grey or black, colour.

| Name of Quarry. | Colour of Stone. | Remarks. |
|---|---|---|
| **ENGLISH.** | | |
| Burdon Hill (Leicestershire) | Greenish | Road metal much used in Midlands. |
| Clee Hill (Shropshire) | —— | Used for road metal. |
| Grooby (Leicestershire) | Pink and green | Syenite. For paving setts and road metal. |
| Herm (near Guernsey) | Grey | Syenite. Fine grained, hard and durable; used chiefly for paving; apt to become slippery. |
| La Moye (Jersey) | Pink and grey | Syenite. For paving setts and road metal. |
| Markfield (Leicestershire) | Dark green | Do.          Do. |
| Mountsorrel (Leicestershire) | Pinkish brown | Syenite. Hard and durable; used chiefly for paving and road metal. |
| Portmadoc (Merionethshire) | —— | Syenite. For road metal. |
| **SCOTCH.** | | |
| Dancing Cairn (Aberdeenshire) | Usually grey; sometimes red | Buildings in Aberdeen. Used in London for curbs, paving, &c. |
| Tillyfourie (Aberdeenshire) | Bluish grey | Much used in London for paving and setts. |
| Tyrebagger (Aberdeenshire) | Grey | Do.          Do. |
| **IRISH.** | | |
| Dalkey (Dublin) | Grey | A good stone for building, road metal and paving setts. Hard to work. |
| Newry (Down) | Grey | A hard good stone for general building purposes; very durable; one of the best granites in Ireland. |

4. The power to resist compression may be easily ascertained by placing small cubes in a hydraulic press and noting under what pressures each cube will crush.

5. The effect of weather is not easily ascertained artificially, although it is suggested that a good test may be made by soaking the stones in a saturated solution of sulphate of soda, and then on exposure to the air, if soft, it is said the stone will disintegrate, as if under the action of thaw succeeding frost.

The specific gravity of a stone is no guide as to its fitness for a road metal.

Also, it is important to bear in mind that a stone should not be selected merely for its *high resistance to crushing stress*, but that *toughness* is an equally essential property for a good and durable material. This is illustrated by the following results of experiments made by Messrs. D. Kirkaldy & Son[†]:—

| | Crushed, steelyard dropped, lb. per square inch. |
|---|---|
| Common black *flint*, from chalk beds near Grays, Essex | 32,350 |
| Cherbourg stone (quartzite), containing about 93 per cent. of silica... | 31,719 |
| Guernsey granite (good average specimen) | 28,535 |

From the above it will be seen that the universally admitted best material (Guernsey granite) comes out lowest, and the worst material (flints) gives the highest result—indicating clearly that a high-crushing stress alone is no evidence of the durability of a stone for macadamising purposes.

Local stones not suitable for road making are frequently

The durability of the granite depends principally upon the quantity of quartz it contains, upon the nature and regular distribution of the felspar, upon the smallness of the quantity of mica, and upon the absence of iron in any form.

Potash felspar and lime felspar are those kinds occurring most frequently in granite—both kinds being sometimes found in the same stone. The potash felspar is the more liable to decay. "All granites are not suitable for road making. When a granite becomes weathered the felspar may decompose into kaolin or china (porcelain) clay.[‡] The commencement of this alteration is indicated under the microscope by the turbidity of the felspar. At the quarries it is often necessary to reject large quantities of stone for road purposes because of this change. All the toughness is gone out of it, and the quarrymen speak of it as 'dead.'"[§]

Mica readily decomposes, and its presence is therefore a source of weakness.

The granite should be close-grained. Large, dull crystals of felspar indicate weakness.

The above list of granite quarries[‖] indicate the districts in Great Britain and Ireland from which most of the road-making material is obtained:—

Granite is quarried by wedging for large blocks and by blasting for smaller pieces and road metal.

* "Municipal and Sanitary Engineers' Hand-Book."
† Vide *The Contract Journal*, November 25, 1891.

* From Latin, *granum* = grain.
† Also spelt *feldspar*.
‡ This is the case with the potash felspar, contained in large proportions in the Cornish and Devonshire granites.
§ "Municipal and Sanitary Engineers' Hand-Book," by Mr. H. Percy Boulnois.
‖ Abstracted from "Notes on Building Construction" (Rivington), vol. iii.

The *Scotch granites*, especially those from Aberdeen (grey) and Peterhead (red), are noted for their durability and beauty.

*Cornish and Devonshire granites* are not so good.

*Leicestershire granites*, generally syenites, are tough, hard and well suited for paving setts and road metal.

*Jersey and Guernsey granite* (syenitic) is hard, durable, used for paving, but apt to wear slippery.

The hardest and best stones for macadam are Guernsey granite and Penmaenmawr graywacké.[*] The crushing resistance of the latter is greatly in excess of granite, being equal to about 7½[†] tons per square inch. The maximum crushing resistances of inch cubes of various granites vary from 1 to 6 tons.[‡]

The *crushing resistances* of various granites are shown in the following table[§]:—

| Locality of Stone. | Pressure per sq. inch. | |
|---|---|---|
| | To fracture. | To crush. |
| Herm \| ... ... ... | 4·77 | 6·04 |
| Aberdeen (blue) ¦ ... ... | 4·13 | 4·64 |
| Heytor\| ... ... ... | 3·94 | 6·19 |
| Dartmoor\| ... ... ... | 3·52 | 5·48 |
| Peterhead (red)¦· ... ... | 2·88 | 4·88 |
| Peterhead (bluish grey)¦\|· ... | 2·86 | 4·36 |
| Penrhyn\| ... ... ... | 2·58 | 3·45 |
| Killiney (grey felspathic¶ ... | — | 4·31 |
| Ballyknocken (coarse grey)¶ ... | — | 1·43 |
| Ballybeg, Carlow (grey felspathic¶ | — | 3·17 |
| Aberdeen ... ¹ ... ... | — | 5·16 |
| Mountsorrel¹ ... ... ... | — | 5·74 |
| Bonaw, Inverary¹ ... ... | — | 4·87 |

The relative durability of granites, from experiments on stones laid down in 1830 at Limehouse so as to be exposed to the heavy traffic from the East and West India Docks, are given by Mr. Walker as follows²:—

| Name of stone. | Super. area. | Loss of weight per sq. foot. | Vertical wear. |
|---|---|---|---|
| | sq. feet. | lb. | inch. relative. |
| Guernsey granite ... | 4·73 | ·95 | ·060 | 1·000 |
| Herm granite... ... | 5·25 | 1·05 | ·075 | 1·190 |
| Budle whinstone ... | 6·34 | 1·22 | ·082 | 1·316 |
| Peterhead blue granite | 3·48 | 1·80 | ·131 | 2·080 |
| Heytor granite ... | 4·31 | 1·92 | ·141 | 2·238 |
| Aberdeen red granite | 5·38 | 2·14 | ·159 | 2·524 |
| Dartmoor granite ... | 4·50 | 2·78 | ·207 | 3·285 |
| Aberdeen blue granite | 4·82 | 3·06 | ·225 | 3·571 |

Mr. Walker has also proved that the relative wear of Guernsey and Aberdeen granite is as 1 to 6.

*Elvan* is a term used in Cornwall and Devon to denote certains veins of felspathic or porphyritic rock, usually of a whitish-brown colour, consisting of quartz and orthoclase (potash felspar). It occurs in dykes and veins proceeding from the granite, but differs from *true* granite in that it has no mica. It varies in texture, and is sometimes of a laminated nature ; it is durable and suited for road metal and building purposes.

*Gneiss* is " a crystalline rock, consisting like granite of quartz, felspar and mica, but having these materials, especially the mica, arranged in planes, so that it breaks rather easily into coarse slabs or flags. Hornblende sometimes takes the place of the mica, and it is then called *hornblendic* or syenitic gneiss. Similar varieties of related rocks are also called gneiss."³ In appearance and properties gneiss resembles granite, but is less strong and durable ; it is used for ordinary masonry in the neighbourhood where found, and, from its stratified nature, makes a good material for flagstones but not suitable for road metal.

**Neath.**—Mr. R. A. Browning, the gas manager, in his annual report, submitted to the quarterly meeting of the town council, stated that the profit for the year was £2,645, or about £350 less than in the previous year. The falling off was attributed to exceptional causes, such as a decrease in the consumption of gas owing to the mild winter, an increase in the coal bill owing to the higher price of coal, and extra expenditure on wear and tear account. The make of gas per ton of coal carbonised had, however, been larger, the leakage had been reduced, and in certain other respects the year's working had been satisfactory. The report was favourably received by the council.

---
[*] *Graywacké* = a conglomerate of grit rock, consisting of rounded pebbles and sand firmly united together. The term, derived from the *grauwacke* of German miners, was formerly applied in geology to different grits and shales of the Silurian series, but it is now seldom used.—Webster's " International Dictionary."
[†] Sir W. Fairbairn.
[¦] Mr. Mallet.
[§] Law and Clark on " Roads and Streets."
[¦] The table on *crushing resistance* is based upon data given by Sir John Burgoyne ; ¶ Prof. Hull ; ¹ and Sir W. Fairbairn.
¹ Law and Clark on " Roads and Streets."
² Webster's " International Dictionary."

---

## THE TELEPHONE SERVICE.

### FURTHER MEETINGS.

Mr. Hanbury presided at last week's meetings of the Select Committee dealing with the question of the telephone service.

Dr. COLQUHOUN, city treasurer of Glasgow, was called. He said that the telephone service in Glasgow was not now developed to anything like the extent which it ought to be in order to meet the needs of the community. It was practically confined to the business classes. The establishment of a municipal system would result in an immediate reduction of the charge to £5, and the service would be rendered more efficient. There would be a better staff, improved instruments, improved wires, and more attention to the wishes of the community. The number of public call-offices would be increased, they would be placed in all convenient centres, and the charge would be reduced to the lowest possible point. With this extended system there would be greater facilties for summoning the fire brigade and the police.

Mr. CHISHOLM, a member of the Glasgow Town Council, said that the service given to the corporation by the telephone company was very inefficient. One department of the corporation had presented no less than 200 complaints within eighteen months. There was great difficulty in getting connections made. The corporation, if they had a license, would at once establish a twin-wire system—the only effective system, as the telephone company admitted.

Sir JAMES A. RUSSELL, a former lord provost of Edinburgh and a member of the town council, stated that he had never met any telephone user in Edinburgh who was satisfied with the efficiency of the service. It would entail a grevious injury on the public if the present monopoly were maintained, even till 1911. The telephone was calculated to be of great general benefit, but at present it was not utilised to nearly the extent it ought to be, and would be with a proper service. While he preferred Government management to company monopoly, he believed that the municipality could and would work the telephones more efficiently and economically even than the Government. In present circumstances, with the National Company holding the field, he was of opinion that the best course was for the Postmaster-General to issue licenses to all municipalities who applied for them. This would not take away from the company any of the powers which they held under their present license.

Mr. R. CRANSTON, a member of the Edinburgh Town Council, and Mr. NICHOLSON, of Tunbridge Wells, also gave evidence.

Mr. A. C. MORTON, a member of the Court of Common Council, complained of the inefficiency and cost of the present service in London, and expressed the opinion that it was the worst in the kingdom. During the last two years, he admitted, the service in the City had improved, but, curiously enough, the complaints remained as frequent and bitter as ever.

Mr. Alderman GREEN, Norwich, also gave evidence, expressing the strong feeling in that city in favour of municipalisation. The view of the corporation was that they ought to have power either to work a service themselves or to hand it over to a responsible and accredited company under Parliamentary or municipal control.

Further evidence was taken on Tuesday, Mr. Hanbury presiding, as before.

Mr. LLOYD, town clerk of Huddersfield, spoke of the nature of the complaints made in his own town against the National Telephone Company, and referred to the general inefficiency of the service there.

Mr. HARCOURT E. CLARK, town clerk of Liverpool, also described the conditions existing in the latter city, and in the course of further evidence expressed the opinion that competition between the National Company and a corporation could not last. One of them would soon throw up the cards, and that one would not be the company. If a municipal service was to be of any use the municipality must have the whole concern and oust the company, either by purchase or otherwise.

---

## APOCRYPHAL WISDOM.

In the *Cornhill* for July appear some extracts " from an apocryphal wisdom book." Hear what the sage says to cyclists :—

" The inches of our gear are three score and ten, and though there be some so strong that they ride four score, yet is their speed but labour and sorrow at the day's end when they fetch their wind short upon a hill.

" Three things are plagues to a wheelman. yea, and a fourth is abominable : a boy which leadeth an unruly horse, and a swine which strayeth in the road, and a rash woman among traffic which regardeth not the right hand or the left ; *but the most grievous is a county council which scattereth heaps of stone in the highway and saith it is well mended.*

" Take heed unto thy riding in strange boroughs, and fall not into transgression of their by-laws, lest thou be worsted in striving with them that swear valiantly before the judgment-seat.

## For Assistants and Pupils.

### THE CONSTRUCTION OF ROADS AND STREETS.—XIV.

By WILLIAM H. MAXWELL, Assistant Engineer and Surveyor, Leyton Urban District Council.

ROAD MATERIALS AND CONSTRUCTION.

*Materials.*—The essential qualities of a good stone or " road metal" are hardness, toughness and power to resist the action of the weather. It should also possess strength to resist compression, and should when laid well unite with its own angles to form a compact surface not easily torn up by traffic, without the aid of much " *binding material.*" These qualities are not always to be found together in the same class of stone, but some of the best descriptions for the purpose are found among the igneous rocks, such as granite and trap-rock, or whinstone.

Whilst there are certain general tests which are useful in selecting stones for use as a road metal, yet the only satis-factory means of judging as to its suitability for the purpose is by making an experimental trial for a sufficient length of time upon a roadway with a known amount of traffic. The following preliminary tests are suggested by Mr. Boulnois[*] :—

1. Ascertain from local persons, such as masons, quarrymen and others, their opinion of the qualities of the stones in the neighbourhood.

2. Make a trial of the stone for *toughness* by setting a good stone-breaker to work upon a heap of the stone as quarried and carefully watching how much he can break in an hour.

3. Ascertain what power the stone has to resist abrasion, as by putting the broken metal into a revolving cylinder and then carefully noting by weight what the cubes lose by contact with each other, or press the stone against a grindstone and note the loss by such contact.

made use of owing to their cheapness in *first cost*, but, generally speaking, it will be better policy to obtain a superior material from a distance if there is much heavy traffic. Soft material should not be mixed with hard either for the construction or maintenance of a road, as one will obviously wear faster than the other and thus make the surface very uneven, unpleasant to ride over, and full of hollows which retain the wet and damage the road. The hard metal should be reserved for the surface coating.

A few of the most important materials will now be briefly described.

GRANITE[*] is a stone of a crystalline granular structure, occurring in large quantities in the older geological forma-tions. It is an igneous rock, and probably is the product of the metamorphism of older sedimentary strata. It is found below the "primary" stratified rocks, but occurs in beds, veins and dykes, oftentimes injected from below through and over the adjacent strata ; also in large masses gradually changing in character and passing into the surrounding rocks.

True granite consists of crystals of quartz and felspar[†] mixed with thin plates or scales of mica.

The *quartz* or silica occurs in hard glassy grey or colourless amorphous lumps.

The *felspar* is in the form of opaque crystals, of very irregular size, and of a white, grey, yellowish pink, red or reddish brown colour, which gives the tone to the mass.

The *mica* consists of small glistening scales, capable of being flaked off with the knife, and having a yellow or brownish-yellow, and sometimes dark grey or black, colour.

| Name of Quarry. | Colour of Stone. | Remarks. |
|---|---|---|
| **ENGLISH.** | | |
| Bardon Hill (Leicestershire) | Greenish | Road metal much used in Midlands. |
| Clee Hill (Shropshire) | — | Used for road metal. |
| Grooby (Leicestershire) | Pink and green | Syenite. For paving setts and road metal. |
| Herm (near Guernsey) | Grey | Syenite. Fine grained, hard and durable ; used chiefly for paving ; apt to become slippery. |
| La Moye (Jersey) | Pink and grey | Syenite. For paving setts and road metal. |
| Markfield (Leicestershire) | Dark green | Do.          Do. |
| Mountsorrel (Leicestershire) | Pinkish brown | Syenite. Hard and durable ; used chiefly for paving and road metal. |
| Portmadoc (Merionethshire) | — | Syenite. For road metal. |
| **SCOTCH.** | | |
| Dancing Cairn (Aberdeen-shire) | Usually grey ; sometimes red | Buildings in Aberdeen. Used in London for curbs, paving, &c. |
| Tillyfourie (Aberdeenshire) | Bluish grey | Much used in London for paving and setts. |
| Tyrebagger (Aberdeenshire) | Grey | Do.          Do. |
| **IRISH.** | | |
| Dalkey (Dublin) | Grey | A good stone for building, road metal and paving setts. Hard to work. |
| Newry (Down) | Grey | A hard good stone for general building purposes ; very durable ; one of the best granites in Ireland. |

4. The power to resist compression may be easily ascer-tained by placing small cubes in a hydraulic press and noting under what pressures each cube will crush.

5. The effect of weather is not easily ascertained artificially, although it is suggested that a good test may be made by soaking the stones in a saturated solution of sulphate of soda, and then on exposure to the air, if soft, it is said the stone will disintegrate, as if under the action of thaw succeeding frost.

The specific gravity of a stone is no guide as to its fitness for a road metal.

Also, it is important to bear in mind that a stone should not be selected merely for its *high resistance to crushing stress*, but that *toughness* is an equally essential property for a good and durable material. This is illustrated by the following results of experiments made by Messrs. D. Kirkaldy & Son[†] :—

| | Crushed, steelyard dropped, lb. per square inch. |
|---|---|
| Common black *flint*, from chalk beds near Grays, Essex ... ... | 32,350 |
| Cherbourg stone (quartzite), contain-ing about 93 per cent. of silica... | 31,719 |
| Guernsey granite (good average specimen) ... ... ... | 28,535 |

From the above it will be seen that the universally ad-mitted best material (Guernsey granite) comes out lowest, and the worst material (flints) gives the highest result—indi-cating clearly that a high-crushing stress alone is no evidence of the durability of a stone for macadamising purposes.

Local stones not suitable for road making are frequently

The durability of the granite depends principally upon the quantity of quartz it contains, upon the nature and regular distribution of the felspar, upon the smallness of the quantity of mica, and upon the absence of iron in any form.

Potash felspar and lime felspar are those kinds occurring most frequently in granite—both kinds being sometimes found in the same stone. The potash felspar is the more liable to decay. "All granites are not suitable for road making. When a granite becomes weathered the felspar may decompose into kaolin or china (porcelain) clay.[‡] The com-mencement of this alteration is indicated under the micro-scope by the turbidity of the felspar. At the quarries it is often necessary to reject large quantities of stone for road purposes because of this change. All the toughness is gone out of it, and the quarrymen speak of it as ' dead.' "[§]

Mica readily decomposes, and its presence is therefore a source of weakness.

The granite should be close-grained. Large, dull crystals of felspar indicate weakness.

The above list of granite quarries[‖] indicate the districts in Great Britain and Ireland from which most of the road-making material is obtained :—

Granite is quarried by wedging for large blocks and by blasting for smaller pieces and road metal.

* "Municipal and Sanitary Engineers' Hand-book."
† Vide *The Contract Journal*, November 25, 1891,

* From Latin, *granum*=grain.
† Also spelt *feldspar*.
‡ This is the case with the potash felspar, contained in large propor-tions in the Cornish and Devonshire granites.
§ "Municipal and Sanitary Engineers' Hand-book," by Mr. H. Percy Boulnois.
‖ Abstracted from "Notes on Building Construction " (Rivington), vol. iii.

The *Scotch granites*, especially those from Aberdeen (grey) and Peterhead (red), are noted for their durability and beauty.

*Cornish and Devonshire granites* are not so good.

*Leicestershire granites*, generally syenites, are tough, hard and well suited for paving setts and road metal.

*Jersey and Guernsey granite* (syenitic) is hard, durable, used for paving, but apt to wear slippery.

The hardest and best stones for macadam are Guernsey granite and Penmaenmawr graywacké.* The crushing resistance of the latter is greatly in excess of granite, being equal to about $7\frac{1}{2}$† tons per square inch. The maximum crushing resistances of inch cubes of various granites vary from 1 to 6 tons.‡

The *crushing resistances* of various granites are shown in the following table§:—

| Locality of Stone. | Pressure per sq. inch. | |
|---|---|---|
| | To fracture. | To crush. |
| Herm‖ ... ... ... ... | 4·77 | 6·34 |
| Aberdeen (blue)‖ ... ... | 4·13 | 4·64 |
| Heytor‖ ... ... ... | 3·94 | 6·19 |
| Dartmoor‖ ... ... ... | 3·52 | 5·48 |
| Potorhead (red)‖ ... ... | 2·88 | 4·88 |
| Peterhead (bluish grey)‖... | 2·96 | 4·36 |
| Penrhyn‖ ... ... ... | 2 58 | 3·45 |
| Killiney (grey felspathic¶ ... | — | 4·31 |
| Ballyknocken (coarse grey)¶ ... | — | 1·43 |
| Ballybeg, Carlow (grey felspathic¶ | — | 3·17 |
| Aberdeen ...[1] ... ... | — | 5·16 |
| Mountsorrel[1] ... ... | — | 5·74 |
| Bonaw, Inverary[1] ... ... | — | 4·87 |

The relative durability of granites, from experiments on stones laid down in 1830 at Limehouse so as to be exposed to the heavy traffic from the East and West India Docks, are given by Mr. Walker as follows[2]:—

| Name of stone. | Super. area. | Loss of weight per sq. foot. | Vertical wear. | |
|---|---|---|---|---|
| | sq. feet. | lb. | inch. | relative. |
| Guernsey granite ... | 4·73 | ·95 | ·060 | 1·000 |
| Herm granite... ... | 5·25 | 1·05 | ·075 | 1·190 |
| Budle whinstone ... | 6·34 | 1·22 | ·082 | 1·316 |
| Peterhead blue granite | 3·48 | 1·80 | ·131 | 2·080 |
| Heytor granite ... | 4·31 | 1·92 | ·141 | 2·238 |
| Aberdeen red granite | 5·38 | 2·14 | ·159 | 2 524 |
| Dartmoor granite ... | 4·50 | 2·78 | ·207 | 3·285 |
| Aberdeen blue granite | 4·82 | 3·06 | ·225 | 3·571 |

Mr. Walker has also proved that the relative wear of Guernsey and Aberdeen granite is as 1 to 6.

*Elvan* is a term used in Cornwall and Devon to denote certain veins of felspathic or porphyritic rock, usually of a whitish-brown colour, consisting of quartz and orthoclase (potash felspar). It occurs in dykes and veins proceeding from the granite, but differs from true granite in that it has no mica. It varies in texture, and is sometimes of a laminated nature; it is durable and suited for road metal and building purposes.

*Gneiss* is "a crystalline rock, consisting like granite of quartz, felspar and mica, but having these materials, especially the mica, arranged in planes, so that it breaks rather easily into coarse slabs or flags. Hornblende sometimes takes the place of the mica, and it is then called *hornblendic* or syenitic gneiss. Similar varieties of related rocks are also called gneiss."[3] In appearance and properties gneiss resembles granite, but is less strong and durable; it is used for ordinary masonry in the neighbourhood where found, and, from its stratified nature, makes a good material for flag-stones but not suitable for road metal.

**Neath.**—Mr. R. A. Browning, the gas manager, in his annual report, submitted to the quarterly meeting of the town council, stated that the profit for the year was £2,645, or about £350 less than in the previous year. The falling off was attributed to exceptional causes, such as a decrease in the consumption of gas owing to the mild winter, an increase in the coal bill owing to the higher price of coal, and extra expenditure on wear and tear account. The make of gas per ton of coal carbonised had, however, been larger, the leakage had been reduced, and in certain other respects the year's working had been satisfactory. The report was favourably received by the council.

* *Graywacké* = a conglomerate of grit rock, consisting of rounded pebbles and sand firmly united together. The term, derived from the *grauwacke* of German miners, was formerly applied in geology to different grits and slates of the Silurian series, but it is now seldom used.—Webster's "International Dictionary."
† Sir W. Fairbairn.
‡ Mr. Mallet.
§ Law and Clark on "Roads and Streets."
‖ The table on *crushing resistance* is based upon data given by Sir John Burgoyne; ¶ Prof. Hull; [1] and Sir W. Fairbairn.
[2] Law and Clark on "Roads and Streets."
[3] Webster's "International Dictionary."

## THE TELEPHONE SERVICE.

### FURTHER MEETINGS.

Mr. Hanbury presided at last week's meetings of the Select Committee dealing with the question of the telephone service.

Dr. COLQUHOUN, city treasurer of Glasgow, was called. He said that the telephone service in Glasgow was not now developed to anything like the extent which it ought to be in order to meet the needs of the community. It was practically confined to the business classes. The establishment of a municipal system would result in an immediate reduction of the charge to £5, and the service would be rendered more efficient. There would be a better staff, improved instruments, improved wires, and more attention to the wishes of the community. The number of public call-offices would be increased, they would be placed in all convenient centres, and the charge would be reduced to the lowest possible point. With this extended system there would be greater facilites for summoning the fire brigade and the police.

Mr. CHISHOLM, a member of the Glasgow Town Council, said that the service given to the corporation by the telephone company was very inefficient. One department of the corporation had presented no less than 200 complaints within eighteen months. There was great difficulty in getting connections made. The corporation, if they had a license, would at once establish a twin-wire system—the only effective system, as the telephone company admitted.

Sir JAMES A. RUSSELL, a former lord provost of Edinburgh and a member of the town council, stated that he had never met any telephone user in Edinburgh who was satisfied with the efficiency of the service. It would entail a grevious injury on the public if the present monopoly were maintained, even till 1911. The telephone was calculated to be of great general benefit, but at present it was not utilised to nearly the extent it ought to be, and would be with a proper service. While he preferred Government management to company monopoly, he believed that the municipality could and would work the telephones more efficiently and economically even than the Government. In present circumstances, with the National Company holding the field, he was of opinion that the best course was for the Postmaster-General to issue licenses to all municipalities who applied for them. This would not take away from the company any of the powers which they held under their present license.

Mr. R. CRANSTON, a member of the Edinburgh Town Council, and Mr. NICHOLSON, of Tunbridge Wells, also gave evidence.

Mr. A. C. MORTON, a member of the Court of Common Council, complained of the inefficiency and cost of the present service in London, and expressed the opinion that it was the worst in the kingdom. During the last two years, he admitted, the service in the City had improved, but, curiously enough, the complaints remained as frequent and bitter as ever.

Mr. Alderman GREEN, Norwich, also gave evidence, expressing the strong feeling in that city in favour of municipalisation. The view of the corporation was that they ought to have power either to work a service themselves or to hand it over to a responsible and accredited company under Parliamentary or municipal control.

Further evidence was taken on Tuesday, Mr. Hanbury presiding, as before.

Mr. LLOYD, town clerk of Huddersfield, spoke of the nature of the complaints made in his own town against the National Telephone Company, and referred to the general inefficiency of the service there.

Mr. HARCOURT E. CLARK, town clerk of Liverpool, also described the conditions existing in the latter city, and in the course of further evidence expressed the opinion that competition between the National Company and a corporation could not last. One of them would soon throw up the cards, and that one would not be the company. If a municipal service was to be of any use the municipality must have the whole concern and oust the company, either by purchase or otherwise.

## APOCRYPHAL WISDOM.

In the *Cornhill* for July appear some extracts "from an apocryphal wisdom book." Hear what the sage says to cyclists :—

"The inches of our gear are three score and ten, and though there be some so strong that they ride four score, yet is their speed but labour and sorrow at the day's end when they fetch their wind short upon a hill.

"Three things are plagues to a wheelman, yea, and a fourth is abominable: a boy which leadeth an unruly horse, and a swine which strayeth in the road, and a rash woman among traffic which regardeth not the right hand or the left; *but the most grievous is a county council which scattereth heaps of stone in the highway and saith it is well mended.*

"Take heed unto thy riding in strange boroughs, and fall not into transgression of their by-laws, lest thou be worsted in striving with them that swear valiantly before the judgment-seat.

# Law Notes.

EDITED BY J. B. REIGNIER CONDER, 11 Old Jewry Chambers, E.C.,

Solicitor of the Supreme Court.

*The Editor will be pleased to answer any questions affecting the practice of engineers and surveyors to local authorities. Queries (which should be written legibly on foolscap paper, one side only) should be addressed to "The Law Editor," at the Offices of THE*

SURVEYOR. *Where possible, copies of local Acts or documents referred to should be enclosed. All explanatory diagrams must be drawn and lettered in black ink only. Correspondents who do not wish their names published should furnish a nom de plume.*

BURIAL ACT, 1855, SEC. 9: SALE OF LAND FOR CEMETERY: ACTION BY VENDOR'S TENANT: DEROGATION FROM GRANT.—A curious action against a local authority was dismissed with costs on the 10th June (Toms v. Clacton Urban District Council, Chancery Division, Mr. Justice Romer). It appears that some short time since the council purchased certain land for the purpose of a cemetery, and the conveyance of the land contained a covenant by them not to use it for any other purpose without the vendor's consent. Upon certain adjoining land, also belonging to the vendor, and not included in the sale, stood a small cottage occupied by the plaintiff (who was the vendor's gardener) on a weekly tenancy. This cottage was within 100 yards of the proposed cemetery, and after the completion of the purchase the plaintiff commenced this action for an injunction to retrain the council from using the land purchased as a cemetery, basing his claim upon sec. 9 of the Burial Act, 1855. On the cross-examination of the plaintiff it was suggested that he was merely a dummy put forward by his employer, the vendor, with obvious motives. His prevarications in the witness-box called down repeated admonitions from the judge, who ultimately ordered him to leave the box. In giving judgment, his lordship said that the vendor had granted the land in order that every part of it should be used for the purposes of a cemetery. He then placed his gardener in a cottage near it for the purpose of bringing this action and preventing in effect any of it being so used. There was no doubt that the action in substance was the vendor's, and the costs of the action would have to be provided by him. He could not derogate from his own grant in this way. Even if for the purposes of a legal argument the plaintiff could be said to be a lessee or occupier, he was so after the vendor's grant and with the fullest notice, and it was monstrous to say that the plaintiff could be in a better position than his own grantor and could acquire a right which his own grantor could not. Other grounds could be stated for dismissing the action; but on the above ground alone the action failed. On the 18th June the case again came up for judgment as to whether the council were entitled to costs as between solicitor and client under the Public Authorities Protection Act, 1893, which point was also decided in favour of the council.

PUBLIC HEALTH (BUILDINGS IN STREETS) ACT, 1888: WATERWORKS CLAUSES ACT, 1847, SEC. 93.—The recent case of *The Grand Junction Waterworks Company* v. *The Hampton Urban District Council* (Chancery Division, Mr. Justice Stirling, 14th June) was an outcome of certain other proceedings between the company and the council, which are still pending. The company had claimed the right under their special Act of 1852 to erect, and had partly erected, an engine-house in contravention of the Public Health (Buildings in Streets) Act, 1888, which, it will be remembered, aims at securing uniformity of building line. The council took proceedings before the magistrate in respect of the alleged offence, and the magistrate decided against the company, who appealed to the Queen's Bench Divisional Court. Pending the hearing of the appeal the company commenced the present action, asking for a declaration that they were entitled to erect the proposed engine-house, or any other building they might think proper for the purposes of their undertaking, without the consent of the council. On behalf of the council it was argued that the Court had no jurisdiction to make such a declaration, and they also relied upon sec. 93 of the Waterworks Clauses Act, 1847, as precluding the company from any such exemption from the provisions of the Act of 1888. Mr. Justice Stirling considered that the Court had jurisdiction, but thought it ought to be exercised with the greatest care. He adopted the language of the Master of the Rolls (Sir George Jessel [in *Stannard* v. *Vestry of St. Giles, Camberwell*] L.R., 20 ch., D. 190), "where the legislature has pointed out a mode of proceeding before a magistrate it is not, as a general rule, for another court to interfere to stop that proceeding by injunction." His lordship desired to add that in contests between local authorities and private owners that rule ought to be adhered to very strictly. The legislature had provided a mode of obtaining a decision, and it would be a matter of regret if a more expensive method were resorted to in such cases. His lordship's own experience led him to believe that vestries and other local authorities were too ready to embark in costly litigation where there was no equivalent advantage to the public whom they represented, and he would be sorry, in cases where a cheap and speedy method of procedure was pointed out by the legislature, to see a more expensive one resorted to. The Court, therefore, in the exercise of its discretion, ought to be slow to restrain proceedings before a magistrate where that method of procedure was pointed out by the legislature. A

fortiori the Court ought to be slow, in the absence of special circumstances, to make a declaration in such a case as this. That brought his lordship to the question whether there were in this case any such special circumstances, and, in his judgment, there were not. He thought he ought not to interfere either by way of injunction or by making a declaration in accordance with the claim. The matter ought to be left to the tribunal pointed out by the legislature. The action must be dismissed with costs.

NEW STREET: METROPOLIS MANAGEMENT ACT, 1855, SEC. 105: METROPOLIS MANAGEMENT ACT, 1862, SEC. 75.—"The magistrate here had found that this was a 'new street.' It was a question of fact, which the Court could not review." We quote from the judgment of Mr. Justice Day in *Allen* v. *Fulham Vestry* (Queen's Bench Divisional Court, June 18th). This case affords another illustration of the well-established rule, to which we so frequently have occasion to refer in our replies to queries—*viz.*: That if there is any evidence to justify magistrates in finding that a street is a "new street" the High Court will not inquire into the sufficiency of that evidence, the question being one of fact for the magistrates to determine. The distinction between the inquiry, "Is there any evidence to justify the magistrates' finding?" and the inquiry, "Is the evidence sufficient?" is, perhaps, rather a fine one. But the meaning of the rule is sufficiently clear—*viz.*, that if there is evidence the Court will not attempt to appraise or weigh it, that being the magistrate's province. Although, therefore, no new principle is established by this case, it is worth while to note the facts upon which the magistrate's finding was based. The "new street" in question was a portion of Wandsworth Bridge-road, which road, together with the bridge to which it forms an approach, was made up by the Wandsworth Bridge Company in 1873, pursuant to the Wandsworth Bridge Act, 1864. The road then ran through agricultural land, and was bordered by market gardens. The Act provided that, when completed, the road should be a public highway repairable by the Fulham District Board of Works. That board, however, refused to take it over until 1876, when they received £1,750 from the company to complete it, and in the following year they made up the carriageway with flints rolled in over a hard core. From this time until 1897 the carriageway was annually repaired with granite, but no channelling or kerbing was done. There were no buildings on the land adjoining the road until 1890, when houses were erected on the east side; and in 1895 and 1896 houses were first built on the west side. In 1897 the Fulham Vestry passed a resolution that the road should be paved with wood blocks on a concrete foundation, at the expense of the frontagers. As already indicated, the magistrate decided in favour of the vestry on the main point that the street was a "new street," as well as on the minor point that wood paving was paving within the Act; and the High Court refused to interfere with his decision.

COMBINED DRAINAGE IN THE METROPOLIS: NUISANCE: RECOVERY OF COST OF REPAIR BY OWNER FROM LOCAL AUTHORITY: PUBLIC HEALTH (LONDON) ACT, 1891, SEC. 4 (SUB-SECS. 1 AND 4) AND SEC. 11 (SUB-SEC. 1).—In *Andrew* v. *St. Olave's Board of Works* (Queen's Bench Division, 29th March) the question for decision was whether the owner of two houses drained by a combined system, constructed without an order of the vestry, who has executed works thereto required by a nuisance notice served on him by the authority, can recover the cost thereof from the latter body. It may be within the recollection of some of our readers that a similar question arose in the case of *Florence* v. *Paddington Vestry* (W.N., 1895, 143; THE SURVEYOR, vol. viii., p. 461), and was answered by Mr. Justice Chitty in the affirmative. In the present case a similar decision was arrived at by the Queen's Bench Division of the High Court (Lord Russell of Killowen and Mr. Justice Mathew), reversing the judgment of the county court judge. The facts were as follows: The plaintiff was the owner of two houses, Nos. 5 and 6 Vine-street, Southwark, and two notices, one in respect of each house, were served on him by the defendants, under sec. 4 of the Public Health (London) Act, 1891. Each notice was addressed to the owner or occupier of the house to which it related, alleged that the drainage of the house was defective, and ordered the owner or occupier within fourteen days to remove the defective drain and redrain the house into the common sewer. The plaintiff, on receipt of the notices, consulted his surveyor, who, having opened the ground and found that the two houses were connected with the common sewer by a single pipe, endeavoured to find out whether the pipe had been laid under an order for combined drainage, and for that purpose searched the records of the defendants and of the Metropolitan Commissioners of Sewers. He found among the records of the latter body a plan for the combined drainage of houses described as Nos. 5 and 6 Vine-street. He then wrote to the defendants stating that he had discovered this plan, and that he would proceed to do the work, which he did. After the work had been done it was discovered that the plan did not refer to the plaintiff's houses, the numbering of the houses in the street having been since altered, and that the pipe was therefore a "sewer," for the maintenance of which the defendants were responsible. The Lord Chief Justice, in giving judgment, characterised the question as one of considerable difficulty, turning upon the construction of secs. 4 and 11 of the Act already referred to. Under sec. 4 (sub-sec. 4) the plaintiff was compelled to comply with the notices and repair the combined drain upon pain of becoming liable to the £10 penalty imposed by the the sub-section (*Gebbart* v. *Saunders*, *L.R.*, 1892, 2 Q.B., 452). Having thus, under stress of compulsion, done what the defendants were liable to do (*viz.*, repaired one of their sewers), the plaintiff was, on a well-known principle of the common law, entitled to recover the expenses to which he was put. Again, under sec. 11 the plaintiff was entitled to recover—the words "expenses incurred . . . . in carrying the order into effect" including the expenses of executing works in compliance with an abatement notice.

## QUERIES AND REPLIES.

OBSTRUCTIONS ON HIGHWAYS.—"Constant Reader" writes: Under what section of the Public Health or other Acts have an urban district council power to order private individuals, builders and others to remove building materials, kerb plant, &c., which are an obstruction to traffic over streets laid out by private persons, but which streets have not yet been properly made-up and dedicated under the Private Street Works Act, 1892? The streets are now well built up on both sides and subject to constant traffic.

By sec. 72 of the Highway Act, 1835, if any person shall lay any timber, stone, hay, straw, dung, manure, lime, soil, ashes, rubbish or other matter or thing whatsoever upon a highway, to the injury of such highway, or the injury, interruption or personal danger of any person travelling thereon, he shall for every such offence forfeit and pay a sum of 40s. over and above the damages occasioned thereby. By sec. 73 of the same Act if any timber, &c., &c. (as before), shall be laid upon any highway so as to be a nuisance, and shall not after notice given by the surveyor be removed, the surveyor may by order of a Justice remove and dispose of it; and if it does not realise enough to pay expenses the offender is liable to pay the difference. And by the Highway Act, 1864, sec. 51, if any person shall encroach by placing any dung, compost or other materials for dressing land, or any rubbish, on the side of any carriageway, within 15 ft. from the centre thereof, he is liable to a penalty of 40s. and the costs of removal. By sec. 144 of the Public Health Act, 1875, the urban authority is to become and have all the powers and duties of the surveyor of highways. Under sec. 73 of the 1835 Act (quoted above) the justices have jurisdiction to inquire whether the road in question is a highway or not. A "private" street may be a highway if thrown open to and used by the public, notwithstanding that it may not have been formally taken over by the authority.

BUILDING OVER SEWERS: NEW BUILDINGS.—"Stret" writes: In laying out a large estate for building plots plans have been submitted to the urban district council showing the line of road within 3 ft. of the centre line of a storm-overflow sewer, 39 in. diameter, 24 ft. deep. The authority refuse to accede to this distance. What powers have the authority to compel a fixed distance that may be reasonable and able to sustain in a court of law?

Under sec. 26 of the Public Health Act, 1875, any person who without the consent of the authority (1) causes any building to be newly erected over any sewer of an urban authority or (2) causes any vault, arch or cellar to be newly built or constructed under the carriageway of any street is liable to penalties; and the authority may demolish any building, &c., erected or constructed in contravention of this section. This appears to be the only enactment bearing on the subject. It is not quite clear from the query what is meant by "the line of road," and in the absence of a plan I cannot see that there is any contemplated contravention of the section.

PRIVATE STREET WORKS: SIDE STREET: PREMISES FRONTING, ADJOINING OR ABUTTING.—"T. H." writes: I shall be glad to know what you consider to be the owner's "frontage" to the street on the annexed sketch? Whether such frontage

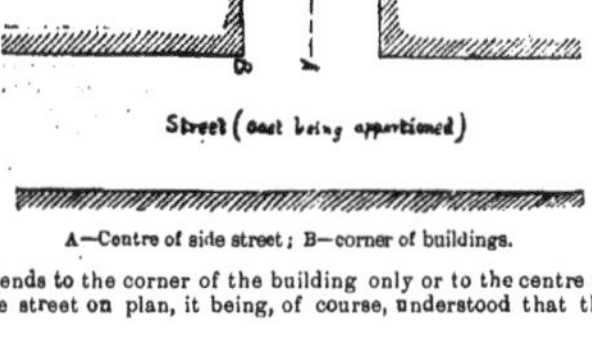


A—Centre of side street; B—corner of buildings.

extends to the corner of the building only or to the centre of side street on plan, it being, of course, understood that the land to the centre of the side street belongs to the owner of the buildings?

If the side street has been irrevocably dedicated to the public the owner of the soil thereof is not chargeable in respect of making-up the street into which it leads. (*Plumstead Board of Works* v. *British Land Company*, *L.R.*, 10, Q.B., 203.) In that event, therefore, the "frontage" would terminate at B, the corner of the building. If, however, the side street has been determinately reserved to the owners of the soil, and there has been no public dedication past recall, it falls within the description "premises adjoining or abutting" and can be included in the frontage (*Lord Northbrook* v. *Plumstead Board of Works*, *L.R.*, 7, Q.B., 183).

BY-LAWS: LAYING-OUT A NEW STREET.—"E." writes: Referring to the decision of the Appeal Court in *Smith* v. *Chorley Rural District Council* (C.A. [1897], 1 Q.B., 678), am I right in assuming that a council is entitled to determine the question as to whether a builder who is erecting buildings adjoining an old road is laying-out a new street or not, and that there is no appeal against their decision if it has been come to honestly and deliberately?

The precise point decided in this case was that where a local authority have in good faith refused to pass building plans on the ground that the erection of the proposed houses would amount to the laying-out of a new street of a width which is insufficient under their by-laws no action will lie for a *mandamus* to compel them to approve the plans. The action was tried before Mr. Justice Kennedy and a jury, and that learned judge left the question as to whether a new street was being laid out to the jury, who answered it in the negative. Upon further consideration and argument, however, the judge dismissed the action, considering that on technical grounds it would not lie. The Court of Appeal, in confirming this decision, expressed the opinion that the question ought not to have been left to the jury, it being for the local authority to determine. This view is not altogether reconcilable with former decisions, where (in the case of proceedings for infringement of by-laws) it has been held that this question is for the magistrates to determine (see *Taylor* v. *Metropolitan Board of Works*, *L.R.*, 2 Q.B., 213, *Regina* v. *Shiel*, 50 *L.T.* [N.S.], 590), subject to review by the High Court in the event of their being of opinion that there is no evidence to justify the magistrates' finding (*Williams* v. *Pouning*, 47 J.P., 490). It is doubtful how far *Smith* v. *Chorley Rural District Council* can be relied on as overruling these cases. It would, no doubt, shut out a landowner whose plans had been disapproved on the same grounds from bringing an action for a *mandamus*. But if he proceeded to build in defiance of the disapproval, and the authority summoned him for penalties it is questionable whether the Chorley case could be considered as ousting the jurisdiction of the magistrates to inquire and determine whether or not a new street is being laid out.

BUILDING BY-LAWS.—"Surveyor" writes: Has an urban authority power to require plans of additions to house erected before the constitution of the district and the adoption of the Model By-Laws to be submitted to them? A is erecting large additions to an existing residence, and refuses to deposit plans on the grounds that the by-laws do not apply, the house having been erected before the urban district was formed, and that additions to existing buildings are not "new buildings" within the meaning of the Act.

Yes, if the additions are such as to make the house a "new building"—which is a question of fact. "The question whether a building or not has been decided over and over again to be a question of fact; it is a question of degree. For instance, if a building were nearly all taken away and then rebuilt it would be a new building; on the other hand, it is clear that by a small addition of, say, a door, the building would not thereby become a new building. Between these two extreme cases there may be thousands of cases, and it would be impossible to give a definition in each particular case as to what is or is not a new building, and it must be left to the discretion of each judge to decide for himself what is a new building." (*Per* Chief Justice Coleridge in *James* v. *Wyvill*, 51 *L.T.* [N.S.], 237). The first sentence in the quotation means, I take it, "The question whether a given building is a new building or not has been decided, &c."

POWERS OF LOCAL AUTHORITY TO ENTER PREMISES: DANGEROUS STRUCTURES.—"Right" writes: (1) Has a surveyor or inspector any power to enter a yard which lies at the back of premises abutting a main street where there are two cottages, the whole belonging to same landlord, without asking permission of landlord or tenant? There is a door at end of passage by street which is shut at night time, but during the day is open. (2) The walls of side of passage marked dangerous are considered to be so by the surveyor. Has the surveyor power to serve notices on the owners calling upon them to take down and rebuild the walls under the Towns Improvement Clauses Act, incorporated in the Public Health Act, 1875? (3) Has a surveyor power to deal with dangerous buildings or walls on private property which endangers the lives of the occupiers or other persons?

(1) Sec. 305 of the Public Health Act, 1875, contains provisions enabling a local authority to obtain an order to enter any lands or premises for the purpose of making plans, surveying, measuring, taking levels, making, keeping in repair or examining works, ascertaining the course of sewers or drains, or ascertaining or fixing boundaries. An entrance may also be obtained for the purpose of examining drains and privies, as to nuisances and as to unsound meat, &c., under secs. 41, 102 and 119. (2) Notice can be given to the owners under sec. 75 of the Towns Improvement Clauses Act, 1847, to "take down, repair or secure" the walls. For form of notice *see* "The Municipal and Sanitary Engineers' Hand-Book," by H. Percy Boulnois (third edition), p. 236. (3) If dangerous to passengers or to the occupiers of neighbouring buildings the foregoing section would apply; but not apparently if merely dangerous to the occupiers of the building itself.

ERRATUM.—On page 23 *ante*, first column, line thirty-one from the bottom, for "*Blundell* v. *Prior*" read "*Blundell* v. *Price*."

**Ramsgate.**—Last week, the mayor formally opened an elaborate new pumping station at Whitehall in connection with the municipal waterworks. It has been erected under the superintendence of Mr. Valon, the borough engineer, and it is claimed to be the finest of its kind in southern England.

# Municipal Work in Progress and Projected.

Several large and important improvements are contemplated by the London County Council this week, as will be seen from our report of Tuesday's meeting. Extensive undertakings continue as numerous as ever in the provinces.

## METROPOLITAN AUTHORITIES.
### LONDON COUNTY COUNCIL.

Not a very large amount of administrative work was disposed of at the meeting of the county council, on Tuesday, most of the time being spent in considering the important report of the Improvements Committee dealing chiefly with the scheme for the construction of the proposed new street from Holborn to the Strand. Naturally this elicited a large amount of discussion, but ultimately a recommendation of the committee in favour of the construction of the new street was carried, together with a number of recommendations with reference to several minor improvements.

*The Holborn to Strand Improvement Scheme.*—The Finance Committee presented a report dealing with the subject of the projected street improvements, and stated that, from a financial point of view, the gross cost was an important matter. The amount in the case of the new street from Holborn to the Strand was as much as £4,562,500. When the improvement had been carried out, and the surplus lands had been let, and were therefore income-producing, the charge on the rates for interest and repayment was expected to be comparatively small; but during the early years, while the property was being acquired and the land was in process of being cleared, there would be a very considerable charge without any income from ground rents to assist. Mr. Campbell criticised at length the financial aspect of the case, and proposed that the report be not received. This motion was, however, rejected by a large majority. Mr. Shaw Lefevre then moved the reception of the main report of the Improvements Committee dealing with the county improvements, for which it is proposed to seek the necessary powers in the next session of Parliament. He pointed out that the six improvements contained in the report would run to a total cost of £1,100,000. The main improvement, however, was the Holborn to Strand thoroughfare, which was estimated to cost £774,000. He also pointed out that the improvement was not a new one, for, he said, it had occupied the attention of the council for many years past, and was a necessary complement to the schemes in the neighbourhood already approved by the council—the removal of Holywell-street, the widening of Southampton-row and the clearing of the Clare Market area. From whatever point of view the scheme was regarded—as a street improvement, as a great sanitary improvement involving the improvement of the whole district, or as an architectural improvement—it would add to the dignity and beauty of London. The report was received and a long discussion followed. Eventually the following recommendation of the committee was agreed to with only one dissentient: "That the council do apply to Parliament in the session of 1899 for powers to construct a new street and branch streets, 100 ft. wide, from Holborn to the Strand, and to carry out the subsidiary street improvements in general accordance with the scheme shown on the plan approved by the Improvements Committee on May 25, 1898." The following recommendations of the committee dealing with the scheme were also agreed to: "That the question of powers being sought to enable the council to lay tramways along the new streets be referred to the Highways Committee for consideration and report; that provision be made for the construction of a subway under the new streets (for mains, wires, &c.), and also for the planting of trees in the new thoroughfares; that provision be made in the Bill for part of the cost of the improvement to be dealt with on the same general principle as that embodied in the improvement charge sections of the London County Council (Tower-bridge Southern Approach) Act, 1895, but that a longer period than three years be allowed within which to judge of the effect of the improvement upon the surrounding property; that provision be made by scheme for rehousing within about a mile of their residences all the persons of the labouring class displaced who are dependent on fixed employment in the neighbourhood, and that adequate provision be made elsewhere for the remainder of the persons displaced; that provision be made as far as possible for rehousing the people previously to their being displaced; that if, on acquiring any property needed for the improvement, such property shall be proved to be insanitary, compensation shall be paid according to the rules laid down in the Housing of the Working Classes Acts, and not according to the Lands Clauses Consolidation Act, 1845."

*Other Street Improvements.*—The following further proposals of the Improvements Committee for street widening and improvement were also agreed to: The reconstruction of Cat and Mutton bridge, Shoreditch; the reconstruction of the swing bridge at Old Gravel lane; the widening of High-street, Kensington (estimated cost, £81,000); and the widening of Wandsworth-road between Vauxhall and Nine Elms-lane.

*Proposed Extension of the Embankment.*—The council approved the report of the Improvements Committee to the effect that they proposed later on to submit a scheme for the extension of the Embankment from the Victoria Tower garden to Lambeth bridge.

## METROPOLITAN ASYLUMS BOARD.

An ordinary meeting of the board was held, on Saturday, Sir E. H. Galsworthy, J.P., presiding. It was decided to accept the tender of Messrs. R. Ballard, Limited, for the execution of certain work in connection with the making-up of the internal roads, &c., of the Western hospital, at the sum of £669. On March 12th last Messrs. Burstall & Monkhouse were instructed to prepare plans and specifications for placing the heating arrangements of the South-Eastern hospital in satisfactory working order. It was now reported that Messrs. Burstall & Monkhouse estimated the total cost of the scheme at £8,832, of which £3,802 was for builders' work. After conference with the Hospital Committee, the Works Committee recommended that the scheme prepared should be adopted and transmitted to the Local Government Board for their sanction. This was agreed to.

## VESTRIES AND DISTRICT BOARDS.

**Bermondsey.**—At the vestry meeting, on Monday, seven tenders were opened for the supply of bricks, and were referred to the General Purposes Committee for consideration and report.—The Works Committee reported having had under consideration a statement as to certain of the vestry's workmen having executed private paving work on Bank Holiday and the previous Saturday afternoon. It was eventually resolved to make a rule that no workmen should be allowed to work for gain on any holiday granted by the vestry for which he is paid except he first receives permission to do so. Approval was given to a plan submitted by Messrs. Brown, Sons & Blomfield, on behalf of the Wilson Cooperage Company, for the erection of new sheds and workshops in Tanner-street.—The following tenders were received for fixing balance weights to the seven shoots at the wharf, East-lane : Messrs. Cripa & Son (accepted), £30 ; Waterfield & Hay, £49 10s.; and Strong & Collins, £125.

**Chelsea.**—The following resolution has been referred to the Works Committee : "That the vestry approach the chairman of the Ecclesiastical Commissioners, and the chairman of the London and North-Western Railway Company and others, asking them if they will provide some means of crossing the London and North-Western Railway at a central point in Allington-road, Kilburn-lane, to enable the residents of Queen's Park estate to visit Queen's Park without having to journey thereto by way of Salisbury-road and Chamberlayne Wood-road, viâ Harrow-road." The Works Committee have also been requested to give their consideration to a motion recommending: "That this vestry approach the London County Council with a view to seeking their assistance and co-operation in continuing and opening up Mozart-street into Third-avenue, Queen's Park."—At a meeting of the Works Committee the surveyor presented a report upon the desirability of constructing a lavatory in the Harrow-road, in place of the one at Wedlake-street, Kensal Town. The report stated that the only suitable spot that could be found was opposite the entrance to Fifth-avenue, Queen's Park, and he was strongly of opinion that if any lavatory was erected it should be at least 9 ft. high. One of less height could be erected at Fourth-avenue, but he did not think that would be a suitable place. The cost would be about £750, and the loss on working might vary from £150 to £200. It was decided not to carry out the work, but to instruct the surveyor to bring up plans for the erection of a lavatory in Harrow-road itself.

**Holborn.**—At a meeting of the district board of works, on Monday week, the Works Committee recommended that an underground convenience should be erected at the junction of Clerkenwell-road and Rosebery-avenue. Mr. Jacobs, who moved the adoption of the report, said that Holborn was the only parish in London which had not adopted these conveniences. The report was adopted.

**Islington.**—The vestry resolved, at the meeting on Friday, to authorise the clerk to affix the seal to the application to the Treasury for permission to raise a loan of £4,460 for the erection of a new chapel at Finchley cemetery.—The Works Committee asked for authority to instruct the vestry's solicitor to apply for an injunction to restrain the Hornsey Urban District Council from discharging water and sewage into the vestry's sewer in Stroud Green-road. It was resolved to lay two new pipe sewers, at a cost of £600.

**Marylebone.**—At the last meeting of the vestry, Mr. Brooke Hitching referred to the fact that the Bill to confirm the vestry's electric lighting provisional order was before a committee of the House of Commons. It was desirable that through the clerk every assistance should be given by way of evidence before the committee as to failures in the supply or as to complaints as to the quality of the light supplied by the Metropolitan Electric Supply Company, in order that the case of the vestry might be strengthened in view of the strong opposition anticipated at that stage.—The vestry referred to the Sanitary Committee a letter from the Sanitary Inspectors'

Association asking them to send their inspectors to the autumn meeting, to be held at Newcastle-on-Tyne on the 5th and 6th of August.—A motion by Mr. Down, seeking a reference to the Sanitary Committee to consider as to the advisability of every house in the parish being inspected once a year by the sanitary officers, was rejected.—Messrs. Greenwell & Co., solicitors to the vestry, wrote in regard to the smoke nuisance existing in the district. They stated that in view of the result of recent cases taken into court, they were strongly of opinion that any further proceedings would be futile, and that unless the nuisance materially increased the matter should, for the time being, be allowed to remain in abeyance. It was agreed to enter the letter on the minutes.

**Poplar.**—The Works Committee recommended "that the East India Dock-road from the boundary of the wood paving east of Poplar hospital to the foot of the incline to Barking-road bridge be paved with hard wood blocks on concrete foundation, and that the surveyor prepare specification and estimate." This was agreed to.

**Shoreditch.**—The Scavenging and Dusting Committee are considering the advisability of providing motor vans for the work of the department.—The most noteworthy feature of the vestry meeting, on Tuesday, was the announcement read by the vestry clerk of the intention of the Metropolitan Electric Supply Company to seek powers to enter into competition in electric lighting matters with the vestry's undertaking. The subject was felt to be of such importance that Mr. Kershaw, the chairman of the Lighting Committee, asked for the suspension of the by-laws in order to move a special resolution on the matter. Consent having been given, the speaker moved that the clerk should be requested to take immediate steps to oppose the application to be made by the company to the Board of Trade for a provisional order, and to oppose that of the County of London and Brush Provincial Electric Lighting Company, who proposed to obtain powers to lay their mains through Shoreditch. Mr. Kershaw declared that all the trouble arose from the report of the Joint Committee on the Supply of Electrical Energy, and he said that if the House of Commons was consistent it would grant powers to the first-mentioned company to compete with Shoreditch as it had to the Vestry of Marylebone to compete with the company. The resolution was adopted.—It was resolved, on the recommendation of the Works Committee, to invite tenders for the construction of an underground convenience in Hoxton-street, at an estimated cost of £1,750.—The special committee on the Workmen's Compensation Act reported having obtained quotations from four or five of the best accident insurance companies, and by far the lowest was that received from the Ocean Accident and Guarantee Corporation, who quoted a premium of 7s. 6d. per cent. on an estimated annual amount of salaries and wages of about £29,000, covering all officials and employees of the vestry, limiting official salaries to £100 each officer. This premium worked out at £108, and covered all risks under the Workmen's Compensation Act, 1897, the Employers' Liability Act and the Common Law. It appeared that the amount already paid in some years by the vestry to its employees on account of accidents was not largely exceeded by the amount of the above premium, the payment of which would relieve the vestry from such gratuities and at the same time protect the vestry from the risk of life pensions in respect of total disablement of £1 per week, involving a possible actuarial liability capitalised of £1,000 for each workman, which in case of an accident involving several persons would be a very heavy loss to the vestry if not covered by insurance. The committee recommended, and after some discussion the vestry resolved, to insure with the Ocean Corporation for one year, at a premium not exceeding 7s. 6d. per cent.—The vestry accepted the tender of Messrs. Pritchett & Gold for supplying a new storage battery for the electric light station, having a discharge capacity of 400 amperes for six hours, including allowance for the working of the existing battery, at the price of £1,062; and that of Messrs. Schooley & Son, for building a stokehole and fitting hot-water apparatus to the greenhouses in St. Leonard's churchyard, at the cost of £39.

**St. Pancras.**—At a meeting of this vestry, on Wednesday, the clerk reported the receipt of a letter from the Metropolitan Electric Supply Company intimating the intention of the company to apply to the Board of Trade for an electric lighting provisional order for the district of St. Pancras. The Baths and Wash-Houses Committee announced the receipt of a communication from the Local Government Board forwarding approval to the vestry raising a loan of £17,000 for the purchase of land in the Prince of Wales-road for the erection of baths and wash-houses. On the motion of Mr. E. M. Close, chairman of the Health Committee, it was resolved to ask the London County Council to provide for the rehousing of an additional number of persons to the 580 arranged for under the Churchway improvement scheme, since under the Act the council only intend to rehouse a little more than one-half of the population displaced. It was decided, on the recommendation of the Electricity and Public Lighting Committee, to insure the workmen in the employ of the department with the Scottish Employers' Liability and Insurance Company, at the rate of 12s. 6d. per cent. in wages for workmen and 4s. per cent. for the clerks. It was also resolved to transfer the boilers from the Regent's Park electric light works to the refuse destructor works, for the pur-

pose of raising steam by the use of the waste gases from six of the cells. The construction of two underground conveniences in Camden-road, in accordance with plans prepared by the engineer, Mr. W. N. Blair, was decided upon, the estimated cost being £2,550. It was also resolved to lay hard-wood paving in a portion of Fitzroy-street and Grafton-street, at an estimated cost of £250.

# PROVINCIAL AND GREATER LONDON AUTHORITIES.

## COUNTY COUNCILS.

**Somersetshire.**—The Sanitary Committee reported, at a meeting of the council on the 28th ult., that they had considered a report from the Long Ashton Rural District Council with regard to the alleged pollution of the stream at Long Ashton, and, in view of the conflicting statements in the reports of the rural district council and the medical officer of health for the city of Bristol, they recommended the county council to direct that an independent report upon the state of the stream be made. The consideration of the question was postponed till the next meeting of the council.

## MUNICIPAL CORPORATIONS.

**Bangor.**—On Tuesday, the 28th ult., Mr. W. O. E. Meade-King, Local Government Board inspector, held an inquiry concerning the application of the city council for power to borrow the sum of £2,500 for the erection of a new gasholder, £500 for a new scrubber-washer at the gasworks, and £300 for additional gasworks, and £150 for municipal offices' purposes.

**Bolton.**—A Local Government Board inquiry has been held by Colonel A. G. Durnford, R.E., respecting an application of the corporation for sanction to borrow £6,000 for market purposes and £10,000 for converting dry closets into water-closets in the cottage property of the town.

**Brighouse.**—At a recent meeting of the town council it was reported that the expenditure on the sewage scheme had amounted to £63,089.

**Bristol.**—The Finance Committee of the corporation recently held a special meeting to receive plans prepared by the city engineer for the new temporary council chamber, which the council had decided should be erected at a cost not exceeding £2,500. The plans, which embodied some alterations suggested by the committee at a previous meeting, were approved, instructions being given to proceed with the work.

**Bury.**—The contract for the erection of the new art gallery and public library has been let to Messrs. Thompson & Brierley, of Bury, the contract price being £21,259. The buildings will be erected from designs by Messrs. Woodhouse & Willoughby, of Manchester, which were selected in open competition.

**Cheltenham.**—On the 28th ult. Lieut.-Colonel Albert C. Smith, R.E., one of the inspectors of the Local Government Board, conducted an inquiry at the municipal offices into the matter of an application made by the town council for sanction to the raising of a loan of £283 for street improvements works in Henrietta-street.

**Eastbourne.**—At the monthly meeting of the town council, on Monday, the Duke of Devonshire, the mayor, announced his intention of presenting the town with a piece of land, of the value of between £5,000 and £6,000, as a memorial of his mayoralty, for the purpose of erecting upon it a technical institute and museum.

**Falmouth.**—On Monday of last week, at a meeting of the town council, it was almost unanimously resolved to adopt the report of a committee recommending the making of an application to the Local Government Board for sanction to the borrowing of £6,500 for the carrying out of waterworks extensions.

**Glossop.**—The town council have adopted a resolution recommending that an application be made to the Board of Trade for a provisional order for electric lighting.

**Grimsby.**—Last week the Public Lighting Sub-Committee met to consider the report of Prof. Kennedy on the electric lighting of the borough. The report dealt with the many details of the scheme, and the members decided to have another interview with Prof. Kennedy respecting the matter. It is stated that the question will be shortly brought before a full meeting of the Lighting Committee, and that it will be pushed forward as quickly as possible.

**Leamington.**—The Free Library Committee have recommended the town council to proceed at once with the erection of a building for the free public library and technical institute, that plans and specification should be invited from architects, and that £12,000 should be expended on the building, exclusive of the amount paid for the land and furnishing.

**Leeds.**—Steady progress is being made with the York-street insanitary area scheme. The sub-committee have just concluded negotiations for the purchase of a number of blocks of property, including three public-houses, and their proceedings have also been confirmed by the Sanitary Committee. The licensed properties are to be acquired on the understanding that they will not be pulled down for two or three years. With reference to the Camp Field insanitary area, a Local Government Board arbitrator has held an inquiry this week, and this arbitration will, it is stated, largely determine the future policy of the corporation. Subject to the approval of the city council, the Sanitary Committee have also decided to erect a latrine near the Corn Exchange, at a cost of £1,800.—At a meeting of the Highways Committee of the corporation, on Thursday, tenders to the extent of £43,924 were accepted in connection with the extension of the electric tramway system to Headingley, Chapeltown and Hunslet. The corporation had invited tenders for the supply of two engines and dynamos of about 7,000 horse-power, and for fifty new electric cars, which, it is anticipated, will be in use on the routes mentioned early next year. The committee accepted the tender of Messrs. Greenwood & Batley, of Leeds, for the engines and dynamos, at the sum of £15,586 ; that of Messrs. Dick, Kerr & Co., of Glasgow, for the fifty cars, at £468 10s. each ; and that of Mr. Isaac Gould, of Leeds, for the work in connection with the extension of the generating station at Crown Point, at £4,082, that sum including everything except smiths' and founders' work, which has been let to Messrs. Clayton, Son & Co., Limited, Hunslet, at £830.

Norwich.—The question of rebuilding the Three Holes bridge, at Upwell, at a cost of about £500, has been referred back.

Sheffield.—The corporation propose to construct a new bridge over the river Don at Ball-street. The bridge will be of arched steel girders on stone piers, and the plans and quantities have been prepared by Mr. Charles F. Wike, city engineer. The tender of Messrs. Braithwaite & Co., of Leeds, amounting to £9,087, has been accepted for the erection of the bridge.

Widnes.—Last year, Widnes held the world's record for cheap gas, the prices being 1s. 6d. and 1s. 8d. per 1,000 cubic feet, and the make of gas increased from 181,000,000 cubic feet to 202,000,000 cubic feet, while the number of consumers increased from 4,322 to 4,884. After defraying the cost of the public lighting of the borough, £1,457 14s., the nett profit on the gas undertaking was £2,073. From July 1st the price of gas will be reduced to 1s. 4d. and 1s. 6d. per 1,000 cubic feet, or about half as much as the gas consumers of Liverpool have to pay for their illumination.

## URBAN DISTRICT COUNCILS.

Barking.—On the 23rd ult., the Light Railway Commissioners held an inquiry with respect to an application of the district council for powers to construct a light railway connecting the town of Barking with the works of the Gas Light and Coke Company at Beckton. There was practically no opposition, and Lord Jersey stated that the commissioners would be very glad to recommend the Board of Trade to issue an order for the construction of the railway.

Chiswick.—The district council have decided to apply to the Local Government Board for sanction to a loan of £6,000, for the purchase of Homefields recreation ground and also for fencing-in and making-up the roads.

Colwyn Bay.—On Thursday, Mr. W. O. E. Meade-King held an inquiry, on behalf of the Local Government Board, with respect to an application of the district council for sanction to borrow £25,000 for the purchase of a town yard, £500 for the old promenade and sea wall, and £600 for sewerage extensions.

Leigh, Lancs.—Last week, Mr. H. Law, Local Government Board inspector, held an inquiry at Leigh with respect to the council's application to borrow £11,426 for works of main roads and private street improvements.—The council also have in hand schemes amounting to nearly £7,000 for improving Market-street, Bridge-street and Bradshaw-gate, in addition to gasworks extensions, the provision of electricity works, &c.

Llandudno.—The 6-mile drive around the Great Orme's Head has recently become the property of the district council, who have purchased it from a company for £12,000.

Morecambe.—An inquiry was held at the council office, Morecambe, last week, before Colonel W. Langton Coke, into an application of the council to borrow £2,122 for the purpose of private street improvements. The estimated population was stated to be 10,000, as against 6,476 at the last census. Those were the figures for permanent residents. The assessable value of the township was £541,500. Application had also been made a month ago for sanction to borrow £60,000 for sewerage purposes, but nothing has been heard of the application as yet. There was no opposition to the present application.

Newton Abbot.—Mr. Walter A. Ducat, an inspector of the Local Government Board, has held an inquiry concerning an application by the council for sanction to borrow £3,450 for the purposes of sewerage and sewage disposal and £1,550 for the purposes of public walks and pleasure grounds. Mr. Lewis Stevens, the surveyor, explained to the inspector how the amount of £5,000 was apportioned, and also stated the advantages of the council making the new road.

Pudsey.—Mr. A. Duckett, an inspector of the Local Government Board, held an inquiry last week respecting an application of the council for permission to borrow £4,900 for the purchase of land at Hough Tide and Troydale for the construction of sewerage disposal works.

Tipton.—The district council have unanimously decided not to entertain the question of purchasing the tramways in their district.

Urmston.—A Local Government Board inquiry has been held with reference to an application of the district council for sanction to a loan of £4,000 for street improvement works, including the flagging of the public footpaths. There was no opposition.

Weybridge.—The Local Government Board have sanctioned the application of the district council for a loan of £5,000 for the carrying out of a new surface-water drainage scheme and the formation of asphalte footways. The drainage scheme was designed by Mr. John T. Crawshaw, surveyor to the council, and it is proposed to carry out the whole of the works without the intervention of the contractor. It is interesting to note that only four weeks have elapsed between the holding of the inquiry and the receipt of the Local Government Board's sanction.

## RURAL DISTRICT COUNCILS.

Dorchester.—Mr. W. A. Ducat, an inspector of the Local Government Board, held an inquiry in the schoolroom, on Friday, at 11 o'clock, in respect of an application made by the council for leave to borrow £1,300 for the purpose of carrying out a system of water supply for the parish of Maiden Newton.

Sleaford.—It has been resolved by the council to purchase land at Great Hale for new waterworks. In a letter to the council the Local Government Board declined to grant a loan of £900 towards the cost of the works until they received information as to whether the site was the property of the rural district council or whether any provisional agreement was being entered into for the purchase.—It was resolved, before continuing the operations for supplying the parish of Anwby with water, to ascertain whether the principal owners were prepared to contribute towards the cost.

Winchester.—Mr. W. A. Ducat, on the 24th ult., held an inquiry, on behalf of the Local Government Board, relative to an application of the district council for sanction to borrow £1,300 for water supply works. Mr. F. W. Moger, surveyor to the Walsall Rural District Council, attended and gave evidence as to the present water supply, and explained the details of the proposed scheme, for which he is the engineer.

## SCOTLAND AND IRELAND.

Edinburgh.—At a meeting of the Gas Commission, held on the 27th ult., it was stated that in the consumption of gas during May there had been an increase of between 3,000,000 and 4,000,000 cubic feet, which, considering the season of the year, was regarded as quite satisfactory. The surplus for the year was £54,994, against a surplus last year of £40,570.

Glasgow.—Last week, at a meeting of the city council, it was decided by a large majority to proceed with the erection of baths in Whitevale-street, and to provide accommodation therein for Turkish baths. The cost would be between £300 and £400. The council also adopted the recommendation of a committee that the site of a proposed hall for Mount Florida, Langside and Shawlands should be at the junction of Pollokshaws-road and Langside-avenue, and that the amount to be spent in its erection should not exceed £8,000.—The Sub-Committee on Police Halls and Buildings recommended that a sum of £1,200 should be expended in reconstructing the staircase and providing improved retiring-room accommodation and additional exits for the Dixon Halls. The minutes were approved.

Limerick.—A committee of the corporation recently gave their consideration to letters from (1) Mr. H. Bickerdike, Montreal, proposing to introduce the "American electric trolley system" into the city on terms to be arranged ; (2) Mr. J. E. Palmer, Ballybrack, co. Dublin, applying for a lease for 150 years of the sole right to construct, equip, maintain and work electric tramways in the city, and proposing certain routes for which the lease is asked ; and (3) M. Zeitz, Hamburg, offering to supply cars, completely fitted out, for the overhead system of electric traffic.

## CORRESPONDENCE.

Weardale Sewerage.—Referring to an article in our issue of the 24th ult. on "Sewage Purification at Wolsingham," Mr. W. M. Egglestone, surveyor to the rural district council, writes : You say "We may mention that the Wolsingham sewage farm was laid out by Mr. Egglestone over twenty years ago, £1,800 being borrowed for the purpose." The £1,800 was borrowed for the sewerage works for the town of Wolsingham, 2,000 population, and the only expense incurred at the time the town was sewered was on the field—the fence separating the 5 acres of land. The total expenditure on the field then and since for underdraining, effluent outlet, &c., is covered by the £100 mentioned. Kindly correct this. The sewerage scheme for the town was laid out by me, and £1,800 was borrowed for the purpose, not for the sewage farm.

## ARBITRATIONS AND AWARDS.

On Tuesday, the 21st ult., Mr. James Green conducted an inquiry, at the Surveyors' Institution, Savoy-street, London, W.C., to determine the value of the property proposed to be included in the betterment area of the Strand improvement. The inquiry was conducted under the London County Council Improvement Act, 1897, which empowered the council to widen the Strand between the eastern end of the church-yard of the church of St. Mary-le-Strand and the western end of the churchyard of the church of St. Clement's Danes; and in connection therewith to take the lands, with the houses and the buildings thereon, situated between the two churches and Holywell-street and the Strand on the north and south respectively, and to remove the said houses and buildings to throw the site into the widened thoroughfare of the Strand. The improvement or betterment area under the Act includes the lands, all, or any part, of which fronts or abuts upon the northern side of Holywell-street. Several of the cases having been agreed upon, the case of 31 Newcastle-street, at the corner of Holywell-street, was brought forward. Mr. Bevan represented the owners, and Mr. Littleton the county council. Mr. Bevan stated that the house was at present let under a sub-lease to Mr. Russell as a refreshment-house. It was let on a lease for twenty-one years, expiring at Christmas, 1908, at £160 per year, but had been sublet for the remainder of the term, at £275 per annum. The premises were rated at £300 gross, or £250 nett; and the counsel contended that when the lease fell in the value would be at least £325 per annum. Mr. Galsworthy valued the property at £6,722. If it had been in possession he considered the value would have been £8,125. Mr. W. D. Beullie endorsed the valuation of Mr. Galsworthy; and Mr. B. J. Breach estimated the ultimate rental value at £350 and the property at £7,135. For the London County Council, Mr. Andrew Young, surveyor and valuer, was called. He considered £275 per annum was the rack-rental value of the property, and at twenty-two years' purchase he estimated the value at £6,050. Mr. Wilkinson agreed with Mr. Young's estimate. He thought £275 very full rent. The referee reserved his decision.

The Recorder, Sir Charles Hall, Q.C., M.P., and a special jury, sat at the Guildhall, on the 29th ult., to hear the case of the Trustees of the London Parochial Charities v. the Corporation of the City of London, a claim for compensation in respect of the freehold interest in premises known as No. 4A, Cheapside, which are required for the purposes of the widening of the west end of Cheapside. Mr. Edward Boyle, Q.C., and Mr. Reginald Neville appeared for the claimants; and Sir William Marriott, Q.C., and Mr. Rose-Innes represented the corporation. The property in question was let at a ground rent of £40 per annum for sixteen years from midsummer, 1898, and it was agreed, during the hearing, to be taken on the 3 per cent. tables, £500. It was admitted that the property would be worth about £500 per annum at the expiration of the existing lease in 1914, and the question for the jury was the proper basis upon which to capitalise that reversionary value. For the claimant, it was contended by Mr. Daniel Watney and Mr. G. A. Wilkinson that the £500 per annum receivable after the year 1914 should be valued on the 4 per cent. tables (13·4 years' purchase), or £6,700, which, with the customary addition of 10 per cent. for compulsory sale, brought the claim to a total of £7,924. On behalf of the corporation, Mr. Robert Vigers and Mr. Alexander Rose Stenning gave evidence to the effect that the reversionary rental of £500 in 1914 should be capitalised on the 5 per cent. tables (9·25 years' purchase), £4,255, showing a total of £5,626, including the usual 10 per cent. The jury awarded the claimants the sum of £6,850.

## NEW UNDERGROUND LAVATORIES AT BIRMINGHA ;

The construction of new underground lavatories, &c., in High-street (Bull Ring) and Corporation-street (Old square) has been commenced by the Public Works Committee of the Birmingham Corporation. The work will not be completed until about October. In each case there will be a department for ladies. The general plan of the subterranean areas is that of a triangle with the corners rounded off. The smaller end will be towards the upper part of the slope, and at this end will be the entrance to the ladies'-room. This department will contain six water-closets and an attendant's-room and lavatory. Hot and cold water will be provided. The men's department will communicate with the street at the wider end, with separate stairs for entrance and exit. Seven water-closets and other conveniences will be provided in this section, with two lavatories. The average depth of the floor below the street will be about 9 ft., and the area will be covered with glass prisms on the ground level, forming a "refuge." The entrances will be provided with ornamental iron railings, and upon the refuge triple street lamps. The interior of the lavatories will be faced with ivory-white glazed bricks, and the steps will be of hard York stone. The wood fittings will be of teak, and the divisions of polished rouge royal marble. The sanitary fittings will include closets, with syphonic discharge. A water-driven air-propeller will provide ventilation for both departments. In Corporation-street the lavatory is being constructed partly under the triangular refuge round which the tramcars pass and partly under the roadway of Corporation-street. The total cost of the two buildings will be about £4,000.

## NEW PUBLIC BATHS FOR EDINBURGH.

The plans of Mr. Robert Merham, the city architect of Edinburgh, for the new public baths at Saxe Coburg-place, Stockbridge, have been approved by the Dean of Guild Court. The building will be after the style of certain other baths at Dalry, and the cost is estimated at £15,000, a good part of which, however, has been swallowed up in securing the site. It occupies a vacant piece of ground on the north side of Saxe Coburg-place, between that thoroughfare and Glenogie-road. The nature of the levels and the narrowness of the site has made it a very difficult subject to treat. There is a fall of 30 ft. between the pavement at Saxe Coburg-place and the Glenogie-road level. The pond hall level will be 12 ft. above the Glenogie-road level. The swimming pond itself will measure 75 ft long by 35 ft. wide, the depth being, as usual, from 3 ft. to 7ft. Round the pond dressing-boxes will be provided for seventy-two swimmers. At the east end of the pond will be a gymnasium, and at the west end the officials' rooms and laundry. On the gallery floor will be situated thirty-two plunge baths and a club-room, and adjoining, just over the laundry, nine first-class bath-rooms. The boiler and steam apparatus will be placed at the east end of the building. Messrs Kinnear & Moodie, the contractors of the structure, have eighteen months in which to complete their contract.

**Cupar, Fife.**—The purchase of the gasworks by the town council is being discussed. A committee has been formed to obtain information on the matter.

# Personal.

Mr. A. S. Darby, of Great Lever, Bolton, has been appointed engineering assistant to Mr. S. S. Platt, borough surveyor, Rochdale.

The Ramsey Urban District Council have unanimously decided to increase the salary of their surveyor, Mr. D. Bell, by £30 per annum.

Mr. J. Boulton, of the borough surveyor's office, Burslem, has been appointed building inspector to the Swindon New Town Urban District Council.

Messrs. Treadwell & Martin, of Pall Mall, S.W., have been selected by the Metropolitan Asylums Board to act as architects of the Southern hospital.

Houses are springing up so rapidly in the Ilford district that the urban district council have decided to appoint an assistant surveyor to supervise their erection.

Mr. Sydney Perks, of 13 Waterloo-place, Pall Mall, S.W., has been elected by the council of the Royal Institute of British Architects a member of the Practice Committee of that body.

Mr. William Meredith, temporary clerk of works in the office of Mr. J. W. Bradley, borough surveyor of Wolverhampton, has been appointed divisional building inspector in the same office.

Mr. A. Saxon Snell, F.R.I.B.A., has been instructed by the West Ham Corporation to prepare plans for the erection of public swimming and private baths and other buildings in, Romford-road, Stratford, E.

Mr. Edward Wright, of the surveyor's offices, Wandsworth District Board of Works, has been appointed assistant draughtsman in the office of Mr. E. W. Dixon, water engineer to the Harrogate Corporation.

Mr. Walter H. Reading, chief drainage inspector in the office of Mr. J. W. Bradley, borough surveyor of Wolverhampton, has resigned, in order to enter upon private works as a contractor and sanitary expert.

Mr. James Watson, waterworks engineer to the Bradford Corporation, attended the summer excursion of the Bradford Society of Architects and Surveyors, which took place last week, to Harrogate, Pateley Bridge and Ramsgill.

Five candidates for the position of mechanical engineer at the Ponders End pumping station of the Enfield Urban District Council were interviewed on Thursday, at a meeting of that body, and Mr. A. J. Minty, of Chatham, was eventually appointed.

The London County Council, on Tuesday, decided to appoint Mr. Frederick William Hamilton, district surveyor for North Fulham, and Mr. Stanley Faithful Monier-Williams district surveyor for South Fulham. There were thirty-eight applicants.

At the parish church of Midhurst, on Thursday, a wedding was solemnised between Miss Ethel Mary Packham and Mr. Arthur Gordon Gibbs, surveyor to the Midhurst Rural District Council. Both the bride and bridegroom are well known in the town, and a large congregation of friends assembled to witness the ceremony.

Mr. Oliver E. Winter, surveyor to the Vestry of St. George-the-Martyr, Southwark, has been selected to fill the post of surveyor to the Poplar Board of Works, recently vacated by Mr. William Oxtoby on his appointment to the surveyorship of Camberwell. There were thirty-two applicants for the vacant position. The salary commences at £500 per annum.

Mr. Philip Edinger, surveyor to the Frome Urban District Council, met with a serious accident recently. Several ribs were broken on the left side, and a serious internal injury was also feared by the doctor who was summoned to attend Mr Edinger. We are glad to be able to state that Mr. Edinger, whose condition was at one time deemed to be very critical, is now progressing very favourably.

On Saturday, at a meeting of the Metropolitan Asylums Board, Mr. William Thomas Hatch was appointed as engineer, at a salary of £600 per annum. Mr. Hatch is thirty-six years of age, and was educated at Liverpool University and at Owens College, Manchester. For the last eleven and a half years he has held the appointment of general manager to the Empire Engineering Company, Manchester.

At the last meeting of the Harrogate Town Council Mr. W. Hoffman Wood, of Leeds and London, was presented with a testimonial and honorarium in recognition of the able manner in which he had prepared the quantities for the Royal baths, at a cost of over £70,000, without any extras on the contract. The presentation was made by the mayor, who referred in his address to the satisfactory completion of the undertaking, and was suitably acknowledged by Mr. Wood.

Last week, at a meeting of the Sunbury Urban District Council, it was proposed that the surveyor should be allowed an addition to his salary, at the rate of £12 10s. per quarter,

during the period of the sewerage connections. It was stated that it was the unanimous wish of the council that Mr. Coales should superintend the connections, and it was only fair that he should be paid for the extra work he was undertaking. The motion was unanimously adopted, a member remarking that the surveyor had always given them the greatest satisfaction.

The Leicestershire, Northamptonshire and Rutland Provincial Committee of the Surveyors' Institution had their summer excursion on Thursday, travelling over and inspecting the works of the new Great Central Railway. Luncheon was provided at East Leake. Mr. Woolley took the chair, and was supported by Messrs. E. K. and C. B. Fisher, H. H. Holloway and H. G. Coates (Market Harborough), G. Hodson (Loughborough), E. G. Mawbey (borough surveyor, Leicester), A. H. Walker (borough surveyor, Loughborough), A. T. Draper and J. Goodacre (Leicester), E. H. Holbeche and G. German (Ashby).

The Finance Committee of the Gloucester City Council have decided, upon the recommendation of the Improvement Committee, that in future the appointment of building inspector be distinct from that of assistant surveyor. They have unanimously recommended that Mr. E. W. A. Carter, who has for three years been an assistant in the office of the city surveyor, be appointed assistant surveyor, to discharge such of the duties of the surveyor's department as may be from time to time prescribed by the council or arranged by the city surveyor, at the salary of £125 a year, the appointment to be terminable by three calendar months' notice on either side.

Gloucester City Council last week received a letter from Mr. H. J. Weaver, stating that he had accepted an appointment as borough engineer and surveyor under the Corporation of King's Lynn, and asking if the corporation would accept one month's notice. A member, in supporting a resolution proposing the acceptance of the resignation, said Mr. Weaver had had opportunities of seeing the work of Mr. Weaver, and he considered they were losing a capable officer who had always performed his duty. The good wishes of the council would go with him.—The Streets Committee, it might be mentioned, also passed a resolution recording their appreciation of Mr. Weaver's services during his connection with the surveyor's department and congratulating him on his new appointment.

The will of Sir Robert Rawlinson, of Lancaster Lodge, the Boltons, West Brompton, formerly chief engineering inspector of the Local Government Board, who died on May 31st, aged eighty-eight years, leaving personal estate of the value of £82,838, has been proved. The testator made various personal bequests, and left his residuary estate in trust to pay the income thereof to Lady Rawlinson during her life, with power of appointment to her of one moiety of the residuary estate, and the other moiety of the residuary estate is to be held in trust to pay a legacy of £1,000 to the Institution of Civil Engineers, and, as to the ultimate remainder of this moiety, to pay the same to the trustees of St. Thomas's hospital for the general purposes of the hospital, which will thus receive, apparently, about £35,000.

The town of Sandwich is about to lose the services of its harbour master and borough engineer. Mr. A. J. Catt, says The Deal, Walmer and Sandwich Mercury, was appointed in 1890, and has carried out the duties of his various offices with great success and credit. He acted as clerk of the works during the construction of the waterworks, and gave entire satisfaction both to the corporation and to the contractors. As is well-known, besides the above offices he has acted as inspector of nuisances, collector of market tolls, manager of the gasworks, and in several other capacities. To say that in carrying out his many difficult and often delicate duties he has given everybody satisfaction would be to say that he is more than human, but those who are best qualified to judge can say with positive certainty that he has done so with conspicuous zeal and ability. Besides his strictly official duties, Mr. Catt has rendered great assistance in such matters as the regatta, the flower show, the jubilee celebration, and in many other matters pertaining to the honour and prosperity of the town. He will be greatly missed by his official superiors, who have found him a most willing and faithful servant, and those who have had more personal relations with him can testify that he is a staunch friend, ever ready to give a helping hand in a time of difficulty. The regrets felt at his leaving must be outweighed by the knowledge that he goes to take up a, financially, much more valuable appointment—that of harbour master and harbour engineer at New Shoreham. He was elected to this post out of 106 applicants, and, as the Corporation of Sandwich have consented to waive part of the three months' notice due to them under the terms of his appointment, he will commence his new duties in about a month's time. No man will better deserve the many good wishes for success and happiness which he will take with him.

## THE SANITARY INSTITUTE.

### EXAMINATIONS AT BELFAST.

At an examination in practical sanitary science, held in Belfast, on June 24th and 25th, the following two candidates presented themselves and were granted certificates : Mr. T. A. Gailey, B.E., B.A., 324 Woodstock-road, Belfast ; and Mr. W. H. Hargrave, Castle-street, Antrim. The following were the questions set for answer in writing : (1) What is meant by "specific gravity"? How is the "specific gravity" of any solid body determined? (2) Sketch and fully explain the principle of the syphon. (3) What is meant by "ground air"? How is its movement influenced? How does it affect the healthiness of a building site, and what steps may be taken to check its entry into a house? (4) State what constitutes a well-constructed open fire-grate, and of what materials it should be made. (5) Describe the manufacture of good bricks and the composition of lime mortar, cement mortar and concrete intended for drains and foundations. (6) describe and sketch a good form of water-closet, with its fittings and connections. What should be the diameter of the supply pipe and of the soil pipe, and what quantity of water is necessary to flush it? (7) In sinking a well for the supply of a town, what conditions would determine your selection of a site? What steps would you take to ascertain the quantity of water obtainable? (8) What do you understand by the "biological" treatment of sewage? Explain its action.

At an examination for sanitary inspectors, held on the same days, four candidates presented themselves, and two were certified, as regards their sanitary knowledge, competent to to discharge the duties of inspectors of nuisances. The following were the questions set for answer in writing : (1) Discuss the relative disinfectant powers of the following agents : Dry heat, superheated steam, saturated steam, Condy's fluid, carbolic acid, corrosive sublimate. (2) What is the definition of a cellar dwelling in the Public Health Act, 1875? State the conditions under which it is illegal to occupy an underground room as a dwelling, and name the penalties for breach of the provision of the above Act in this respect. (3) Explain the principles of natural and artificial ventilation, and show how you would apply each respectively in the case of (a) a cellar dwelling, and (b) an ordinary bedroom. (4) Under what circumstances are certain milk-sellers exempt from "registration"? To what points should you direct your attention when instructed to report upon dairies and upon cowsheds? State the diseases communicable to human beings by cows' milk. (5) Give a sketch plan and section of a dormitory for twenty persons, showing construction of floor and roof, thickness of walls and means of warming and ventilation. (6) How would you render the external wall of a building (south-western aspect) damp, rain and storm proof? Describe the methods usually adopted, and explain why. (7) When inspecting houses to what points would you direct your attention to ascertain whether the drainage is in proper condition. What are the methods generally employed for testing house drains? (8) What are the comparative advantages of the "dry" and "wet" method of sewage removal? Describe in detail one system of dry removal.

## APPROVAL OF PLANS.

### CONDITIONS ENFORCED AT GLOUCESTER.

The following are the conditions which are imposed at Gloucester in connection with plans passed by the Improvement Committee, subject to the approval of the council and to compliance with the by-laws now in force :—

1. *Notices.*—Two days' written notice must be given to me (*i.e.*, the city engineer) before commencing the work; one day's notice to inspect the house drains before they are covered up; two days' written notice of the completion of the building before the same is sold or inhabited, or the full penalty will be enforced.

2. *Concrete.*—The whole area or site of the building must be covered with a layer of good lime or cement concrete, 6 in. thick. This concrete is in addition to, and must be put in at the same time and connected with, the concrete foundations under the walls.

3. *Drains.*—The house drains must be of best stoneware glazed socketted pipes, 6 in. diameter with 4-in. branches to gullies and soil pipes, properly connected with the city sewers, and laid with a fall of not less than ¼ in. to each pipe. All joints must be yarned and made with the best Portland cement, and keen sand gauged one to one. All drains must be outside the building if possible and ventilated by 4-in. iron pipes, properly jointed, and carried up at least 2 ft. clear above the reof. When the house drains are obliged to be taken under the house they must take the shortest possible straight line, and be jointed in cement as above and entirely surrounded with good solid concrete, 6 in. thick. The necessity for taking drains under houses can be avoided by building in blocks of from one to eight houses ouch instead of in continuous rows. Not more than four small houses allowed on one drain and sewer connection. Where a block consists of less than four houses each block must have a separate

drain and sewer connection. The sewer connection and drain in the street will be laid by the corporation at the owner's expense.

4. *Sinks, Baths, Water-Closets and Rain-Water Pipes.*—All sink and bath wastes must discharge upon 6-in. glazed stoneware gullies in the open air outside the building. All inside water-closets must be built against an external wall, and the soil pipe, 4 in. diameter, fixed outside the building and carried up and ventilated the full size at least 2 ft. above the roof. Rain-water pipes, or the overflows from rain-water cisterns, must discharge upon 6-in. glazed stoneware gullies in the open air outside the building.

5. *City Water Supply.*—The city water must be laid on with proper pipes, fittings and flushing boxes to the water-closets in accordance with regulations.

6. *Party or Division Walls between Houses.*—All party or division walls between houses must be carried up, at least 9 in. thick, throughout the entire length of the houses to the underside of the roofing slates, and pointed so as to prevent the communication of fire from one house to another. All external or partly external walls must be at least 9 in. thick.

7. *Materials in Streets.*—No building materials are allowed to be deposited in streets.

## DOUGLAS BREAKWATER.

The faulty construction of Douglas breakwater, which, instead of being solid like the landing portion of the Queen's Pier, has an interior of rubble in the style of construction known as "pocket," and is also built on an artificial rubble mound, has long been a source of concern to the insular authorities, owing to subsidences which involve the middle length of the work, and make it feared that any great storm may breach it and throw the inner wall into the bay. Experts have reported on the state of the breakwater, and shown that it will take an expenditure of many thousands of pounds to avert the threatened danger and make it secure. The scheme for securing it has just been completed by Mr. Neville, the insular engineer. Arrangements have been made to use diamond drills, which have been used in the coal-boring operations in the north of the island. Special iron staging will be erected on the south side of the breakwater, and on this the boring apparatus will be placed and worked to cut holes through the cross-section of the breakwater. The borings will be about 3 in. in diameter. Through these iron bars the full diameter will be run and bolted on each side. The calculation is that in this way the walls can be secured from tumbling down, and the rebuilding of the middle portion of the structure avoided.

## VAUXHALL BRIDGE.

With the opening of the new temporary bridge at Vauxhall, shortly, the old structure may at once be closed and demolition commenced. According to a very interesting pamphlet written by Mr. H. W. Bridges, clerk of the Bridges Committee, and ordered to be printed by the authority of that committee, this was the first iron bridge across the Thames. It was begun in 1811, and was opened in 1816. It cost nearly £200,000. It was purchased by the Metropolitan Board of Works for £75,000, and was opened free to the public in 1879. The bridge was found to be inadequate to the traffic, it obstructed the waterway to an extent that was dangerous to navigation, and the scour of the river has had a serious effect on the foundations of the deep-water piers by washing the river bed away from them.

The new bridge will be the subject of two contracts. One will comprise the foundations and piers up to the level from which the arches spring. There is nothing to prevent this being proceeded with as soon as the old bridge has been got out of the way. But before the upper structure can be undertaken it will be necessary to obtain some modification of the Act by which the council are empowered to undertake the work. That Act requires that during the building of the bridge there shall be a clear headway of 18 ft. above high-water level. As it is to be a concrete bridge, it has been found impracticable to build it with this condition, and Parliament will next session be asked to reduce the stipulated headway to 16 ft. during the progress of the work. There will be no lowering of the arches of the bridge itself, but the alteration to be asked for is merely that the temporary staging may come down to within 16 ft. of the river level instead of 18 ft. There will be ample time to get this amended before it becomes necessary to take contracts for the building of the upper structure.

**Hammersmith.**—The following tenders for condensing plant have been accepted by the Vestry : Ledward evaporative condenser and tanks, T. Ledward & Co., £1,315 ; air pump. W. H. Allen & Co., £485 ; circulating pumps, W. H. Allen & Co., £300. The tenders that were sent in for pipe work were considered excessive by the Electric Lighting Committee, and none was recommended for acceptance. The committee will consider the matter further and report.

## PEPPERMINT OIL FROM A SEWAGE FARM.

Our contemporary, *The Chemist and Druggist*, on Saturday week published the following:—

Our news columns last week contained the curious announcement that the Sutton Urban District Council, having a quantity of peppermint oil to dispose of, had instructed their surveyor to sell it for the best price he could get. On seeing the item in print we wondered how the Sutton Council became possessed of the oil in question. We supposed they had bought a lot for testing drains, and were now wanting to realise a little profit on it. But if that were the case we thought it needed explanation that they should buy Mitcham oil for such work. So we charged them with being in possession of a certain drug—to wit, English oil of peppermint—and invited them to give any explanation in their power. We have to admit that the Sutton Urban District Council leave this court without a stain on their character. The surveyor, Mr. C. Chambers Smith, writes as follows: "It may probably be interesting to your readers to know that the Sutton Council cultivate the peppermint plant on their sewage farm, and obtain very satisfactory crops; about 4½ acres are under peppermint during the present season. The yield of oil from 2½ acres under cultivation last year was 61½ lb. The price realised from the oil just sold is 24s. 3d. per pound, the quality being considered excellent, and is of the kind known in the trade as Mitcham oil." We publish this explanation with much pleasure, and compliment the Sutton Council and their surveyor on their evident business smartness.

## APPOINTMENTS VACANT.

*Advertisements which are received too late for classification cannot be included in these summaries until the following week.*

TEMPORARY ASSISTANT SURVEYORS (Two).—July 8th.—Wallasey Urban District Council.  £2 12s. 6d.—The Engineer and Surveyor to the Council.

CONSULTING ENGINEER AND SURVEYOR.—July 9th.—Horwich Urban District Council.—Mr. Peter Taberner, clerk to the council.

FOREMAN PAVIOR.—July 11th.—Norwich Corporation. £3.—Mr. Arthur E. Collins, A.M.I.C.E., city engineer.

SANITARY INSPECTOR.—July 11th.—Plumstead Vestry. £104.—Mr. Edwin Hughes, vestry clerk.

ROAD FOREMEN (Two).—July 12th.—County Borough of Huddersfield. £100.—Mr. K. F. Campbell, A.M.I.C.E., borough engineer and surveyor.

CHIEF ENGINEERING AND SURVEYING ASSISTANT.—July 12th.—County Borough of Huddersfield. £180.—Mr. K. F. Campbell, A.M.I.C.E., borough engineer and surveyor.

BUILDING INSPECTOR.—July 12th.—Ilford Urban District Council. £120.—Mr. H. Shaw, A.M.I.C.E., surveyor to the council.

ASSISTANT BUILDING AND DRAINAGE INSPECTOR.—July 12th.—County Borough of Huddersfield. £120.—Mr. K. F. Campbell, A.M.I.C.E., borough engineer and surveyor.

CHIEF ROAD SURVEYOR FOR CITY ENGINEER AND SURVEYOR'S DEPARTMENT.—July 13th.—Corporation of Birmingham. £300.—Mr. John Price, city engineer and surveyor.

CLERK OF WORKS.—July 13th.—County Borough of Salford. £4 4s.—Mr. Samuel Brown, town clerk.

BOROUGH SURVEYOR, &c.—July 13th.—Borough of Sandwich. £120.—Mr. D. Baker, town clerk.

SURVEYOR OF HIGHWAYS.—July 13th.—Spilsby Rural District Council. £200.—Mr. G. Beaumont Walker, clerk to the council.

SECOND ASSISTANT BOROUGH SURVEYOR.—July 14th.—Corporation of Luton. £2.—Mr. Geo. Sell, town clerk.

CLERK OF WORKS.—July 16th.—Barnet Urban District Council.—Mr. H. W. Poole, clerk to the council.

WATERWORKS ENGINEER.—July 16th.—Lincoln Corporation. £250.—Mr. H. K. Helb, deputy town clerk.

INSPECTOR OF MAIN ROADS.—July 18th.—Glamorgan County Council. £85.—Mr. T. Mansel Franklin, county clerk, County Offices, Westgate-street, Cardiff.

HIGHWAY SURVEYOR, INSPECTOR OF NUISANCES, &c.—July 19th.—Newark Rural District Council. £155.—Mr. William Newton, clerk to the council.

BOROUGH ENGINEER. — July 22nd. — Corporation of Pietermaritzburg, Natal, South Africa. £800.—Messrs. Ford Brothers, 14 Southampton-street, Fitzroy-square, London, W.

CITY ENGINEER.—August 31st.—Corporation of Wellington, New Zealand. £800.—Agent-General for New Zealand, London.

## COMPETITIONS.

*Advertisements which are received too late for classification cannot be included in these summaries until the following week.*

EAST RIDING.—July 16th.—Extension of the county offices at Beverley and the erection of a new register office, for the county council. £30, £20 and £10.—Mr. John Bickersteth, county clerk, County Hall, Beverley.

## MUNICIPAL CONTRACTS OPEN.

*Advertisements which are received too late for classification cannot be included in these summaries until the following week.*

MAIDENHEAD.—July 11th.—Making-up of Ray Park-avenue.—Mr. Percy Johns, A.M.I.C.E., borough surveyor.

HORNSEY.—July 11th.—Erection of a fire engine station at Muswell Hill, for the urban district council.—Mr. E. J. Lovegrove, surveyor to the council.

LYMINGTON.—July 11th.—Erection of a small bridge near Winchelsea, in the parish of Brockenhurst, for the rural district council.—Mr. T. J. Fripp, surveyor to the council.

LEAMINGTON.—July 11th.—Supply of road stone for a period of twelve months.—Mr. W. de Normanville, borough engineer.

ST. PANCRAS.—July 12th.—Laying of cast-iron pipes between the Regent's canal and the King's-road electricity works.—Mr. C. H. F. Barrett, vestry clerk.

NANTWICH.—July 12th.—Construction of a precipitation tank, filter-bed and sludge strainer at the sewage outfall works, Gunnersclough, Barnton, for the rural district council.—Mr. Algernon Fletcher, clerk to the council.

SOUTHAMPTON.—July 12th.—Supply and delivery of cast-iron pipes and special castings required during the ensuing twelve months, for the corporation.—Mr. W. Matthews, waterworks engineer.

REIGATE.—July 12th.—Laying of pipe sewers in the districts known as South Park, Woodhatch, and the Nags Head, Earlswood.—Mr. W. H. Prescott, borough surveyor.

HUDDERSFIELD.—July 12th.—Erection of an isolation block at the sanatorium, Mill-hill.—Mr. F. C. Lloyd, town clerk.

ST. HELENS.—July 12th.—Supply of various pumping plant to raise 1,500,000 gallons of water per day, for the corporation.—Mr. J. J. Lackland, A.M.I.C.E., water engineer.

TWICKENHAM.—July 13th.—Various sewering and road making works, for the urban district council.—Mr. G. B. Laffan, engineer and surveyor to the council.

WORCESTER.—July 14th.—Erection of about 215 yards of stone coping along Croft-road.—Mr. T. Caink, A.M.I.C.E., city engineer.

ATHERTON.—July 14th.—Supply of a gas condenser, valves and connections, and the construction of a telescopic gasholder, 53 ft. in diameter, for the urban district council.—Mr. Daniel Schofield, clerk to the council.

STOKESLEY.—July 14th.—Re-erection of Raisdale bridge, in the township of Bilsdale, for the rural district council.—Mr. W. H. Dixon, surveyor to the council.

SWINTON.—July 15th.—Supply of 520 yards of cast-iron socket pipes of 6-in. diameter and other pipe castings, for the urban district council.—Mr. R. Fowler, engineer and surveyor to the council.

DARTFORD.—July 18th.—Making-up, &c., of Priory-lane, for the urban district council.—Mr. W. Harston, surveyor to the council.

WOODFORD.—July 16th.—Supply of 1,400 tons to 2,000 tons of broken Quennat or Guernsey granite, for the urban district council.—Mr. John A. Simpson, clerk to the council.

WEST BRIDGFORD.—July 16th.—Laying of about 2,460 yards of 12-in. and 9-in. Hassall's pipe sewers, 12-in. iron pipe sewers and 9-in. surface-water drains, for the urban district council.—Mr. Wm. Pare, surveyor to the council.

MANCHESTER.—July 16th.—Construction and erection of a wrought-iron bridge for carrying 30-in. cast-iron pipes over the river Tame at Broomstair, Hyde and Denton, for the corporation.—Secretary, Waterworks Office, Town Hall, Manchester.

NELSON.—July 16th.—Construction of two storage reservoirs in Ogden and Black Moss valleys about 4 miles from the town, for the corporation.—Messrs. Newton, 17 Cooper-street, Manchester.

SOUTH CROSLAND.—July 18th.—Construction of additional sewerage works, comprising the laying of over 1 mile of stoneware pipe sewers, varying in size from 6 in. to 9 in., for the urban district council.—Mr. W. H. Radford, Angel-row, Nottingham.

ILFORD.—July 18th.—Supply of a 15-ton combined compound steam road-roller, for the urban district council.—Mr. John W. Benton, clerk to the council.

HOWLEY.—July 18th.—Construction of 3½ miles of stoneware pipe sewers, varying in size from 15 in. to 7 in., for the urban district council.—Mr. W. H. Radford, Angel-row, Nottingham.

GREAT YARMOUTH.—July 19th.—Supply of one 150-kilowatt high-speed engine and alternator coupled direct and sundry additional steam and exhaust pipes.—Mr. A. H. Miller, town clerk.

LONDON.—July 19th.—Paving of the carriageway of John-street, Minories, with Australian hard wood.—The Engineer to the Corporation.

LONDON.—July 19th.—Construction of an underground convenience in Alderman's-walk.—The Engineer to the Corporation.

CROYDON.—July 19th.—Construction of 2,230 yards of 12-in. and 14-in. pipe sewers in the neighbourhood of London-road, Norbury, and for the construction of a covered concrete storage tank, near Norbury Manor farm.—Mr. E. Mawdesley, town clerk.

CROYDON.—July 19th.—Diversion of a portion of Long-lane.—Mr. E. Mawdesley, town clerk.

PORTSMOUTH.—July 19th.—Supply and fixing of cast-iron valve seatings to the pumps at the Eastney pumping station.—Mr. Alexander Hellard, town clerk.

LONDON.—July 19th.—Construction of underground conveniences in Fenchurch-street.—Sir J. B. Monckton, town clerk.

WORCESTER.—July 20th.—Various kerbing, channelling and paving works, for the county council.—Mr. J. H. Garrett, county road surveyor, Shire Hall, Worcester.

GRANGE-OVER-SANDS.—July 21st.—Erection of a new public hall and district council offices, for the urban district council.—Mr. John Hutton, architect, Kendal.

COLNE.—July 23rd.—Erection of technical schools and a public library in Albert-road.—Mr. Alfred Varley, town clerk.

LEWES.—July 23rd.—Supply of 500 tons of 2-in. broken blue Guernsey, Cherbourg or Belgian granite, 100 tons of coarse granite screenings, 550 tons of broken surface-picked flints and 150 tons of Piddinghoe gravel.—Mr. Montague S. Blaker, town clerk.

WEST HAM.—July 26th.—Construction of about 1,200 lineal yards of sewers, 7 ft., 6 ft. and 3 ft. 6 in. diameter.—Mr. Lewis Angell, borough surveyor.

WEST HAM.—July 26th.—Making-up of Freemantle-road, Haslemere-road, New-street (Plaistow) and Old-street (Plaistow).—Mr. Lewis Angell, borough surveyor.

BUCKLOW.—July 26th.—Construction of main sewers and outfall works for the township of Hale, for the rural district council.—Mr. Geo. Leigh, clerk to the council.

WEST HAM.—July 26th.—Erection of twenty-nine working-classes' dwellings in Hermit-road, Plaistow.—Mr. Lewis Angell, borough surveyor.

WEST HAM.—July 26th.—Supply of ten slop-carts.—Mr. Lewis Angell, borough surveyor.

BURY.—July 28th.—Erection of a manager's house at the sewage disposal works, Livesey Fields.—Mr. J. Cartwright, borough engineer.

BURY.—July 28th.—Erection of a model lodging-house in George-street and Foundry-street, off Rochdale-road.—Mr. J. Cartwright, borough engineer.

## TENDERS.

*ACCEPTED.*

BEESTON (Notts).—For re-drainage works at the residence of Mrs. Edmund Percy, West End, Beeston, Notts, for Major Hurst.—Mr. Charles Mason, c.e., consulting sanitary engineer:—
J. Down, Beeston; J. Hutchinson, Nottingham; W. Turner, Beeston,* £73; H. Vickers, Nottingham; W. Woodsend, Nottingham.

FULHAM.—For the making-up and paving of Narborough-street.—Mr. Charles Botterill, vestry surveyor:—
Roadway.—B. Nowell & Co., Kensington, £235; J. Mears, Fulham, £217; E. Parry, Fulham, £5·9: H. Greenham, Hammersmith, £275.
York Stone.—B. Nowell & Co., £105.
Victoria Stone.—Victoria Stone Company, Bishopgate-street, E.C., £136.
Imperial Stone.—Imperial Stone Company, East Greenwich, £119.

SOUTHAMPTON.—For various sewerage works.—Mr. W. B. G. Bennett, borough engineer:—
Western District Sewerage, Contract No. 3.

| | £ s. d. |
|---|---|
| S. Nichols, Southampton | £6,483 |
| M. W. Bull, Southampton | 5,690 |
| B. Cooke & Co., London | 5,175 |
| G. Bell, London | 5,144 |
| W. Jones, Neath | 5,046 |
| F. Orman, Southampton | 5,000 |
| W. H. Saunders & Co., Southampton* | 4,182 |

Diversion of Seware from Platform to Chapel.

| | £ s. d. |
|---|---|
| F. Orman, Southampton | £7,573 |
| H. W. Bull, Southampton | 7,500 |
| W. Jones, Neath | 6,903 |
| S. Nichols, Southampton | 6,834 |
| W. H. Saunders & Co., Southampton | 6,822 |
| B. Cooke & Co., London | 6,554 |
| G. Bell, London* | 6,491 |

## NOTICES.

THE SURVEYOR AND MUNICIPAL AND COUNTY ENGINEER may be ordered direct, through any of Messrs. Smith & Son's book-stalls, or of any newsagent in the United Kingdom. Applications to the Offices for single copies by post must in all cases be accompanied by stamps.

The Prepaid Subscription (including postage) is as follows :

| | Twelve Months. | Six Months. | Three Months. |
|---|---|---|---|
| United Kingdom | 15s. | 7s. 6d. | 3s. 9d. |
| Continent, the Colonies, India, | | | |
| United States, &c. | 19s. | 9s. 6d. | 4s. 9d. |

The International News Company, 83 and 85 Duane-street, New York City; The Toronto News Company, Toronto; and The Montreal News Company, Montreal, have been appointed agents in the United States and Canada for the sale of THE SURVEYOR. A thin paper edition is printed for circulation abroad.

EDITORIAL OFFICES :
ST. BRIDE'S HOUSE, 24 BRIDE-LANE, FLEET-STREET, LONDON, E.C.

OFFICE FOR ADVERTISEMENTS:
13 NEW STREET HILL, FLEET STREET, LONDON, E.C.

PUBLISHING OFFICES :
13 NEW STREET HILL, FLEET STREET, LONDON, E.C.

## APPOINTMENTS OPEN.

RURAL DISTRICT COUNCIL OF NEWARK. APPOINTMENT OF HIGHWAY SURVEYOR, INSPECTOR OF NUISANCES, CANAL BOATS INSPECTOR AND PETROLEUM INSPECTOR.

The Rural District Council of Newark invite applications for the above appointments.
There are twenty-five parishes in the district and 109 miles of roads.
The salary for the combined offices will be £155 per annum, and the person appointed must be fully qualified and competent to perform all the duties thereof, including the preparation of plans, &c., and will be required to devote the whole of his time to such duties.
Applications, in candidate's own handwriting, stating age, previous occupation, and accompanied by copies of not more than three recent testimonials, to be sent to me not later than Tuesday, the 19th day of July instant.
Canvassing the members of the Council, whether directly or indirectly, will be a disqualification.
The appointment will be made subject to the approval of the Local Government Board.

(By order)
WM. NEWTON,
Clerk.
Local Government Offices,
Middlegate, Newark.
July 6, 1898.

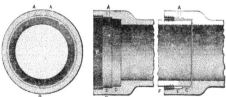

## PEPPERMINT OIL FROM A SEWAGE FARM.

Our contemporary, *The Chemist and Druggist*, on Saturday week published the following:—

Our news columns last week contained the curious announcement that the Sutton Urban District Council, having a quantity of peppermint oil to dispose of, had instructed their surveyor to sell it for the best price he could get. On seeing the item in print we wondered how the Sutton Council became possessed of the oil in question. We supposed they had bought a lot for testing drains, and were now wanting to realise a little profit on it. But if that were the case we thought it needed explanation that they should buy Mitcham oil for such work. So we charged them with being in possession of a certain drug—to wit, English oil of peppermint—and invited them to give any explanation in their power. We have to admit that the Sutton Urban District Council leave this court without a stain on their character. The surveyor, Mr. C. Chambers Smith, writes as follows: " It may probably be interesting to your readers to know that the Sutton Council cultivate the peppermint plant on their sewage farm, and obtain very satisfactory crops; about 4½ acres are under peppermint during the present season. The yield of oil from 2½ acres under cultivation last year was 61¼ lb. The price realised from the oil just sold is 24s. 3d. per pound, the quality being considered excellent, and is of the kind known in the trade as Mitcham oil." We publish this explanation with much pleasure, and compliment the Sutton Council and their surveyor on their evident business smartness.

## APPOINTMENTS VACANT.

*Advertisements which are received too late for classification cannot be included in these summaries until the following week.*

TEMPORARY ASSISTANT SURVEYORS (Two).—July 8th.—Wallasey Urban District Council. £2 12s. 6d.—The Engineer and Surveyor to the Council.

CONSULTING ENGINEER AND SURVEYOR.— July 9th.—Horwich Urban District Council.—Mr. Peter Taberner, clerk to the council.

FOREMAN PAVIOR.—July 11th.—Norwich Corporation. £3.—Mr. Arthur E. Collins, A.M.I.C.E., city engineer.

SANITARY INSPECTOR.— July 11th.— Plumstead Vestry. £104.—Mr. Edwin Hughes, vestry clerk.

ROAD FOREMEN (Two).—July 12th.—County Borough of Huddersfield. £100.—Mr. K. F. Campbell, A.M.I.C.E., borough engineer and surveyor.

CHIEF ENGINEERING AND SURVEYING ASSISTANT.—July 12th.—County Borough of Huddersfield. £180.—Mr. K. F. Campbell, A.M.I.C.E., borough engineer and surveyor.

BUILDING INSPECTOR.—July 12th.—Ilford Urban District Council. £120.—Mr. H. Shaw, A.M.I.C.E., surveyor to the council.

ASSISTANT BUILDING AND DRAINAGE INSPECTOR.—July 12th.—County Borough of Huddersfield. £120.—Mr. K. F. Campbell, A.M.I.C.E., borough engineer and surveyor.

CHIEF ROAD SURVEYOR FOR CITY ENGINEER AND SURVEYOR'S DEPARTMENT.—July 13th.—Corporation of Birmingham. £300.—Mr. John Price, city engineer and surveyor.

CLERK OF WORKS.—July 13th.—County Borough of Salford. £4 4s.—Mr. Samuel Brown, town clerk.

BOROUGH SURVEYOR, &c.—July 13th.— Borough of Sandwich. £120.—Mr. D. Baker, town clerk.

SURVEYOR OF HIGHWAYS.—July 13th.—Spilsby Rural District Council. £200.—Mr. G. Beaumont Walker, clerk to the council.

SECOND ASSISTANT BOROUGH SURVEYOR.—July 14th.—Corporation of Luton. £2.—Mr. Geo. Sell, town clerk.

CLERK OF WORKS.—July 16th.—Barnet Urban District Council.—Mr. H. W. Poole, clerk to the council.

WATERWORKS ENGINEER.—July 16th.—Lincoln Corporation. £250.—Mr. H. K. Kelb, deputy town clerk.

INSPECTOR OF MAIN ROADS.—July 18th.—Glamorgan County Council. £85.—Mr. T. Mansel Franklin, county clerk, County Offices, Westgate-street, Cardiff.

HIGHWAY SURVEYOR, INSPECTOR OF NUISANCES, &c.—July 19th.—Newark Rural District Council. £155.—Mr.· William Newton, clerk to the council.

BOROUGH ENGINEER. — July .22nd. — Corporation of Pietermaritzburg, Natal, South Africa. £800.—Messrs. Ford Brothers, 14 Southampton-street, Fitzroy-square, London, W.

CITY ENGINEER.—August 31st.—Corporation of Wellington, New Zealand. £800.—Agent-General for New Zealand, London.

## COMPETITIONS.

*Advertisements which are received too late for classification cannot be included in these summaries until the following week.*

EAST RIDING.—July 10th.—Extension of the county offices at Beverley and the erection of a new register office, for the county council. £30, £20 and £10. — Mr. John Bickersteth, county clerk, County Hall, Beverley.

## MUNICIPAL CONTRACTS OPEN.

*Advertisements which are received too late for classification cannot be included in these summaries until the following week.*

MAIDENHEAD.—July 11th.—Making-up of Ray Park-avenue.—Mr. Percy Johns, A.M.I.C.E., borough surveyor.

HORNSEY.—July 11th.—Erection of a fire engine station at Muswell Hill, for the urban district council.—Mr. E. J. Lovegrove, surveyor to the council.

LYMINGTON.—July 11th.—Erection of a small bridge near Winchelsea, in the parish of Brockenhurst, for the rural district council.—Mr. T. J. Fripp, surveyor to the council.

LEAMINGTON.—July 11th.—Supply of road stone for a period of twelve months.—Mr. W. de Normanville, borough engineer.

ST. PANCRAS.—July 12th.—Laying of cast-iron pipes between the Regent's canal and the King's-road electricity works.—Mr. C. H. F. Barrett, vestry clerk.

NANTWICH.—July 12th.—Construction of a precipitation tank, filterbed and sludge strainer at the sewage outfall works, Gunnersclough, Barnton, for the rural district council.—Mr. Algernon Fletcher, clerk to the council.

SOUTHAMPTON.—July 12th.—Supply and delivery of cast-iron pipes and special castings required during the ensuing twelve months, for the corporation.—Mr. W. Matthews, waterworks engineer.

REIGATE.—July 12th.—Laying of pipe sewers in the districts known as South Park, Woodhatch, and the Nags Head, Earlswood.—Mr. W. H. Prescott, borough surveyor.

HUDDERSFIELD.—July 12th.—Erection of an isolation block at the sanatorium, Mill-hill.—Mr. F. C. Lloyd, town clerk.

ST. HELENS.—July 12th.—Supply of various pumping plant to raise 1,500,000 gallons of water per day, for the corporation.—Mr. J. J. Lackland, A.M.I.C.E., water engineer.

TWICKENHAM.—July 13th.—Various sewering and road making works, for the urban district council.—Mr. G. B. Laffan, engineer and surveyor to the council.

WORCESTER.—July 14th.—Erection of about 215 yards of stone coping along Croft-road.—Mr. T. Caink, A.M.I.C.E., city engineer.

ATHERTON.—July 14th.—Supply of a gas condenser, valves and connections, and the construction of a telescopic gasholder, 53 ft. in diameter, for the urban district council.—Mr. Daniel Schofield, clerk to the council.

STOKESLEY.—July 14th.—Re-erection of Raisdale bridge, in the township of Bilsdale, for the rural district council.—Mr. W. H. Dixon, surveyor to the council.

SELBY.—July 15th.—Supply of 520 yards of cast-iron socket pipes of 6-in. diameter and other pipe castings, for the urban district council.—Mr. R. Fowler, engineer and surveyor to the council.

DARTFORD.—July 15th.—Making-up, &c., of Priory-lane, for the urban district council.—Mr. W. Harston, surveyor to the council.

WOODFORD.—July 16th.—Supply of 1,400 tons to 2,000 tons of broken Quenast or Guernsey granite, for the urban district council.—Mr. John A. Simpson, clerk to the council.

WEST BRIDGFORD.—July 16th.—Laying of about 2,460 yards of 12-in. and 9-in. Russell's pipe sewers, 12-in. iron pipe sewers and 9-in. surface-water drains, for the urban district council.—Mr. Wm. Pare, surveyor to the council.

MANCHESTER.—July 16th.—Construction and erection of a wrought-iron bridge for carrying 30-in. cast-iron pipes over the river Tame at Broomstair, Hyde and Denton, for the corporation.—Secretary, Waterworks Office, Town Hall, Manchester.

NELSON.—July 16th.—Construction of two storage reservoirs in Ogden and Black Moss valleys about 4 miles from the town, for the corporation.—Messrs. Newton, 17 Cooper-street, Manchester.

SOUTH CROXLAND.—July 18th.—Construction of additional sewerage works, comprising the laying of over 1 mile of stoneware pipe sewers, varying in size from 6 in. to 9 in., for the urban district council.—Mr. W. H. Radford, Angel-row, Nottingham.

ILFORD.—July 18th.—Supply of a 16-ton combined compound steam road-roller, for the urban district council.—Mr. John W. Benton, clerk to the council.

HOPLEY.—July 18th.—Construction of 3½ miles of stoneware pipe sewers, varying in size from 15 in. to 7 in., for the urban district council.—Mr. W. H. Radford, Angel-row, Nottingham.

GREAT YARMOUTH.—July 19th.—Supply of one 150-kilowatt high-speed engine and alternator coupled direct and sundry additional steam and exhaust pipes.—Mr. A. H. Miller, town clerk.

LONDON.—July 19th.—Paving of the carriageway of John-street, Minories, with Australian hard wood.—The Engineer to the Corporation.

LONDON.—July 19th.—Construction of an underground convenience in Alderman's-walk.—The Engineer to the Corporation.

CROYDON.—July 19th.—Construction of 2,230 yards of 9-in., 12-in. and 18-in. pipe sewers in the neighbourhood of London-road, Norbury, and for the construction of a covered concrete storage tank, near Norbury Manor farm.—Mr. E. Mawdesley, town clerk.

CROYDON.—July 19th.—Diversion of a portion of Long-lane.—Mr. E. Mawdesley, town clerk.

PORTSMOUTH.—July 19th.—Supply and fixing of cast-iron valve seatings to the pumps at the Eastney pumping station.—Mr. Alexander Hellard, town clerk.

LONDON.—July 19th.—Construction of underground conveniences in Fenchurch-street.—Sir J. B. Monckton, town clerk.

WORCESTER.—July 20th.—Various kerbing, channelling and paving works, for the county council.—Mr. J. H. Garrett, county road surveyor, Shire Hall, Worcester.

GRANGE-OVER-SANDS.—July 21st.—Erection of a new public hall and district council offices, for the urban district council.—Mr. John Hutton, architect, Kendal.

COLNE.—July 23rd.—Erection of technical schools and a public library in Albert-road.—Mr. Alfred Varley, town clerk.

LEWES.—July 23rd.—Supply of 600 tons of 2-in. broken blue Guernsey, Cherbourg or Belgian granite, 100 tons of coarse granite screenings, 650 tons of broken surface-picked flints and 150 tons of Piddinghoe gravel.—Mr. Montague S. Blaker, town clerk.

WEST HAM.—July 26th.—Construction of about 1,300 lineal yards of sewers, 7 ft., 6 ft. and 3 ft. 6 in. diameter.—Mr. Lewis Angell, borough surveyor.

WEST HAM.—July 26th.—Making-up of Freemantle-road, Haslemere-road, New-street (Plaistow) and Old-street (Plaistow).—Mr. Lewis Angell, borough surveyor.

BUCKLOW.—July 26th.—Construction of main sewers and outfall works for the township of Hale, for the rural district council.—Mr. Geo. Leigh, clerk to the council.

WEST HAM.—July 26th.—Erection of twenty-nine working-classes' dwellings in Hermit-road, Plaistow.—Mr. Lewis Angell, borough surveyor.

WEST HAM.—July 26th.—Supply of ten slop-carts.—Mr. Lewis Angell, borough surveyor.

BURY.—July 26th.—Erection of a manager's house at the sewage disposal works, Livesey Fields.—Mr. J. Cartwright, borough engineer.

BURY.—July 28th.—Erection of a model lodging-house in George-street and Foundry-street, off Rochdale-road.—Mr. J. Cartwright, borough engineer.

## TENDERS.

*ACCEPTED.*

BEESTON (Notts).—For re-drainage works at the residence of Mrs. Edmund Percy, West End, Beeston, Notts, for Major Hurst.—Mr. Charles Mason, c.e., consulting sanitary engineer:—
J. Down, Beeston ; J. Hutchinson, Nottingham ; W. Turner, Beeston,* £73 ; H. Vickers, Nottingham ; W. Woodsend, Nottingham.

FULHAM.—For the making-up and paving of Narborough-street.—Mr. Charles Botterill, vestry surveyor :—
Roadway.—B. Nowell & Co., Kensington, £135 ; J. Mears, Fulham, £317 ; E. Parry, Fulham, £309 ; H. Greenham, Hammersmith, £276.
York Stone.—B. Nowell & Co., £195.
Victoria Stone.—Victoria Stone Company, Bishopgate-street, E.C., £136.
Imperial Stone.—Imperial Stone Company, East Greenwich, £119.

SOUTHAMPTON.—For various sewerage works.—Mr. W. B. G. Bennett, borough engineer :—
Western District Sewerage, Contract No. 3.

| | | | | | | |
|---|---|---|---|---|---|---|
| S. Nichols, Southampton | ... | ... | ... | ... | ... | £6,485 |
| H. W. Bull, Southampton | ... | ... | ... | ... | ... | 5,286 |
| B. Cooke & Co., London | ... | ... | ... | ... | ... | 5,178 |
| G. Bell, London | ... | ... | ... | ... | ... | 5,143 |
| W. Jones, Neath | ... | ... | ... | ... | ... | 5,046 |
| F. Osman, Southampton | ... | ... | ... | ... | ... | 5,016 |
| W. H. Saunders & Co., Southampton* | ... | ... | ... | ... | 4,182 |

Diversion of Sewage from Platform to Chapel.

| | | | | | | |
|---|---|---|---|---|---|---|
| F. Osman, Southampton | ... | ... | ... | ... | ... | £7,773 |
| H. W. Bull, Southampton | ... | ... | ... | ... | ... | 7,509 |
| W. Jones, Neath | ... | ... | ... | ... | ... | 6,993 |
| S. Nichols, Southampton | ... | ... | ... | ... | ... | 6,824 |
| W. H. Saunders & Co., Southampton | ... | ... | ... | ... | 6,622 |
| B. Cooke & Co., London | ... | ... | ... | ... | ... | 6,554 |
| G. Bell, London* | ... | ... | ... | ... | ... | 6,491 |

## NOTICES.

THE SURVEYOR AND MUNICIPAL AND COUNTY ENGINEER may be ordered direct, through any of Messrs. Smith & Son's book-stalls, or of any newsagent in the United Kingdom. Applications to the Offices for single copies by post must in all cases be accompanied by stamps.

The Prepaid Subscription (including postage) is as follows ;

| | Twelve Months. | Six Months. | Three Months. |
|---|---|---|---|
| United Kingdom ... ... | 15s. ... | 7s. 6d. ... | 3s. 9d. |
| Continent, the Colonies, India, | | | |
| United States, &c. ... ... | 10s. ... | 9s. 6d. ... | 4s. 9d. |

The *International News Company, 83 and 85 Duane-street, New York City; The Toronto News Company, Toronto ; and The Montreal News Company, Montreal, have been appointed agents in the United States and Canada for the sale of THE SURVEYOR. A thin paper edition is printed for circulation abroad.*

EDITORIAL OFFICES :
ST. BRIDE'S HOUSE, 24 BRIDE-LANE, FLEET-STREET, LONDON, E.C.

OFFICE FOR ADVERTISEMENTS :
13 NEW STREET HILL, FLEET STREET, LONDON, E.C.

PUBLISHING OFFICES :
13 NEW STREET HILL, FLEET STREET, LONDON, E.C.

## APPOINTMENTS OPEN.

RURAL DISTRICT COUNCIL OF NEWARK. APPOINTMENT OF HIGHWAY SURVEYOR, INSPECTOR OF NUISANCES, CANAL BOATS INSPECTOR AND PETROLEUM INSPECTOR.

The Rural District Council of Newark invite applications for the above appointments.

There are twenty-five parishes in the district and 109 miles of roads.

The salary for the combined offices will be £155 per annum, and the person appointed must be fully qualified and competent to perform all the duties thereof, including the preparation of plans, &c., and will be required to devote the whole of his time to such duties.

Applications, in candidate's own handwriting, stating age, previous occupation, and accompanied by copies of not more than three recent testimonials, to be sent to me not later than Tuesday, the 19th day of July instant.

Canvassing the members of the Council, whether directly or indirectly, will be a disqualification.

The appointment will be made subject to the approval of the Local Government Board.

(By order)
WM. NEWTON,
Clerk.

Local Government Offices,
Middlegate, Newark.
July 6, 1898.

## BOROUGH OF SANDWICH.

### APPOINTMENT OF SURVEYOR, &c.

The Council invite applications from competent persons for the offices of Borough Surveyor, Harbour Master, Inspector of Nuisances and Collector of Coal Dues, and Haven Dues and Cattle Market Tolls, &c.

The person appointed will be required to devote his whole time to the performance of the duties comprised within the several offices, and he will be required to give security to such amount as may be fixed by the Council.

Annual salary, £120.

Applications, in handwriting of candidate, stating age, and accompanied by testimonials of recent date, not exceeding three in number, to be sent to me on or before Wednesday, the 13th inst., endorsed "Surveyor."

Further particulars may be obtained on application to the Town Clerk's office.

(By order)
D. BAKER,
Town Clerk.

Guildhall, Sandwich.
July 1, 1898.

## CORPORATION OF PIETERMARITZBURG.

### BOROUGH ENGINEER.

Applications are invited for the appointment of Borough Engineer for the City and Borough of Pietermaritzburg, in the Colony of Natal, South Africa.

The gentleman appointed will be required to devote his whole time to the duties of his office. He must be a thoroughly competent engineer and surveyor, and must have had practical experience in a similar position.

The salary will be £800 per annum, without extras or allowances, and will be payable monthly. Offices, assistants, instruments and stationery will be provided by the corporation.

The city contains an area of 1,000 acres and the borough 27,000 acres. The population is 24,000 and the rateable value £2,250,000. There are 33 miles of streets in the city. Sewerage works, macadamising of roads, paving of footpaths, surface-drainage works, and additional water supply are either in progress or in immediate contemplation. The lighting of the city by electricity is now being proceeded with under the Borough Electrical Engineer.

Applications, stating the age and particulars as to experience of the applicant, &c., with original testimonials (which will be returned), must reach the undersigned not later than Wednesday, the 31st August, 1898, and be endorsed "Borough Engineer."

The appointment will be subject to passing an examination by a medical officer appointed by the corporation.

The appointment will be for three years, and thereafter be terminable by three months' notice on either side.

The successful applicant will be required to take office as soon as possible after receipt of an intimation that the appointment has been conferred upon him.

Applicants residing in the United Kingdom are required to send their applications in duplicate to the London agents of the Corporation (Messrs. Ford Brothers, 14 Southampton-street, Fitzroy-square, London, W.) not later than 22nd July, 1898. A copy of the testimonials will be required in addition to the originals.

In the event of an applicant residing in the United Kingdom being selected the agent will be advised by cable, and will communicate with the gentleman appointed, who will be required to immediately proceed to Maritzburg; £50 will be allowed for passage from London; salary to commence from date of taking office in Maritzburg.

(By order)
STEPHEN STRANACK,
Town Clerk.

Town Office, Pietermaritzburg,
May 26, 1898.

## THE CORPORATION OF BIRMINGHAM.

The Public Works Committee are prepared to receive applications for the appointment of Chief Road Surveyor in the city engineer and surveyor's department. Candidates, whose age must not exceed forty years, must be thoroughly qualified persons, having had active practical experience in the construction, scavenging and maintenance of roads and streets and of the various classes of pavement used therefor. They must also have had the management of large bodies of workmen, and be able to supervise the setting out and measuring up of works and preparation of estimates.

It will be a condition that the person appointed shall subscribe to the superannuation scheme, and shall devote the whole of his time to the duties of his office.

The salary will commence at £300 per annum, and rise by annual increments of £20 to £400 per annum. A horse and trap will be provided to help him to carry out his duties efficiently.

Applications, in the candidate's own handwriting, stating age, qualifications, present and past experience, together with

not more than four recent testimonials, should be sent to the undersigned not later than noon on the 13th of July next.

Canvassing either directly or indirectly will be considered a disqualification.

JOHN PRICE,
City Engineer and Surveyor.

The Council House, Birmingham.
June 25, 1898.

## SPILSBY RURAL DISTRICT COUNCIL.
### APPOINTMENT OF SURVEYOR OF HIGHWAYS.

Applications are invited for the appointment of Surveyor of Highways for the above district, which comprises 500 miles of roads or thereabouts, at a salary of £200 a year, inclusive of means of locomotion and all other expenses excepting office accommodation, stationery and stamps.

The Council will provide a clerk.

The person elected must reside at Spilsby, be a good accountant, have a thorough knowledge of the management of roads and must devote his whole time to the work.

He will be required to enter into a written agreement and find a guarantee in the sum of £300 for the faithful discharge of his duties, which will commence on the 1st day of October next.

Application, in the handwriting of the candidate, with copies of not more than three testimonials of recent date, must be delivered at my office not later than Wednesday, the 13th day of July next, endorsed "Surveyor of Highways."

Preference will be given to candidates who are associate members of the Institution of Civil Engineers or who have obtained the certificate of competency granted by the Incorporated Association of Municipal and County Engineers.

All canvassing prohibited, and any attempt to evade this prohibition will disqualify.

(By order)
G. BEAUMONT WALKER,
Clerk to the Council.

Spilsby.
June 27, 1898.

CIVIL ENGINEER requires Junior Assistant or Improver. Must be accurate leveller and neat draughtsman; knowledge of building plans a recommendation. Commencing salary, 20s. to 30s. per week. Excellent opportunity of gaining experience in sewerage and water schemes, of which eight are now in hand.—Apply, enclosing copies of testimonials, to HARRY W. TAYLOR, A.M.I.C.E., St. Nicholas Chambers, Newcastle-on-Tyne.

## TENDERS WANTED.

COUNTY BOROUGH OF BURY.
The Sewage Committee of the Corporation of Bury are prepared to receive tenders for
(1) Brickwork,
(2) Stonework,
(3) Carpenter and Joiners' Work,
(4) Slaters' Work,
(5) Plumber and Glaziers' Work,
(6) Plasterer and Painters' Work,
required in the Erection of Manager's House at the Sewage Disposal Works, situated at Livesey Fields, within the borough.

On and after the 7th proximo, drawings may be seen and specification and bill of quantities, with form of tender, obtained on application at the office of Mr. J. Cartwright, the Borough Engineer, on payment of 20s. each for Nos. 1 and 3, and 10s. each for Nos. 2, 4, 5 and 6 specifications, which sum will be returned on receipt of a bonâ-fide tender.

Tenders, endorsed with the name of the work tendered for, must be delivered at my office on or before Thursday, the 28th prox.

JOHN HASLAM,
Town Clerk.

Corporation Offices, Bury.
June 29, 1898.

## SWINTON URBAN DISTRICT COUNCIL.
### TO PIPEFOUNDERS.

The above Council are prepared to receive tenders for making and delivering about 520 yards of Cast-Iron Socket Pipes of 6-in. diameter, and for other Pipe Castings.

Full particulars may be obtained on application to the undersigned.

Sealed tenders, endorsed "Tender for Pipes," must be delivered, free of charge, not later than 9 a.m., Friday, July 15, 1898.

The Council do not pledge themselves to accept the lowest or any tender.

(By order)
R. FOWLER,
Engineer and Surveyor to the Council.

Swinton (near Rotherham).
July 4, 1898.

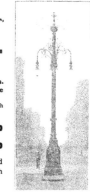

ILFORD URBAN DISTRICT COUNCIL.

TO ENGINEERS.

The Urban District Council of Ilford are prepared to receive tenders for a new 15-ton combined Compound Steam Road-Roller Traction and Hauling Engine, and a Portable Hand-Motion Stone-Breaker. State how soon delivery can be made.

Sealed tenders, endorsed "Tender for Steam Road-Roller," addressed to the Chairman, must be delivered to me here, on or before noon, on Tuesday, the 12th inst.

The Council do not bind themselves to accept the lowest or any tender.

JOHN W. BENTON,
Clerk to the Council.

Council Offices, Ilford.
July 1, 1898.

COUNTY BOROUGH OF WEST HAM.

*PRIVATE STREET WORKS.*

TO CONTRACTORS.

The Council hereby invite tenders for making-up the following streets:—

Freemantle-road.
Haslemere-road.
New-street, Plaistow.
Old-street, Plaistow.

Plans may be seen, and specification, form of tender and further particulars obtained, at the office of Mr. Lewis Angell, Borough Engineer, Town Hall, Stratford, E., upon payment of £1, which will be returned upon receipt of a *bonâ-fide* tender.

Tenders, endorsed "Tender for Private Street Works," to be sent to my office not later than 4 o'clock on Tuesday, the 26th July, 1898.

The Council do not bind themselves to accept the lowest or any tender.

The contractor will be required to enter into a bond, with two sureties, for the due performance of the contract, and no work will be ordered under the contract until such bond has been duly executed.

As regards all work to be done at the site or elsewhere within a radius of 20 miles from Charing Cross, the contractors will be bound by the contract to pay to all workmen (except a reasonable number of legally-bound apprentices) employed by them wages at rates not less, and to observe hours of labour not greater, than the rates and hours set out in the Council's list, and such rates of wages and hours of labour will be inserted in and form part of the contract by way of schedule.

(By order of the Council)
FRED. E. HILLEARY,
Town Clerk.

Town Hall, West Ham, E.
June 29, 1898.

URBAN DISTRICT COUNCIL OF DARTFORD.

TO CONTRACTORS AND OTHERS.

The Council invite tenders for the execution of the necessary works in connection with the Making-up of a certain street within their district, known as Priory-lane, and for laying Artificial Stone Footways in the said street, in accordance with plans, sections and specification, prepared by their surveyor, Mr. W. Hurston, and which may be seen at his office, High-street, Dartford.

Tenders, endorsed "Tender for Works—Priory-lane," must be delivered to me, the undersigned, at the address named below, not later than 12 o'clock noon, on Friday, July 15th inst.

Forms of tender may be obtained of the said surveyor on payment of £5, which will be returned to the person whose tender is accepted on execution of a contract and bond for ensuring the due carrying out of the works, and to the persons whose tenders are not accepted upon acceptance of the successful tender.

The person whose tender is accepted will also be required to provide two sureties to the bond to the satisfaction of the Council.

The contract will contain a clause providing that the wages paid to workmen employed in the execution of the works shall be those generally accepted as current for competent workmen for similar work in the district.

The Council do not bind themselves to accept the lowest or any tender.

(By order)
J. C. HAYWARD,
Clerk to the Council.

Sessions House, Dartford, Kent.
July 4, 1898.

COUNTY BOROUGH OF WEST HAM.

TO SEWER CONTRACTORS.

The Council hereby invite tenders for the contruction of about 1,200 lineal yards of Sewers, 7 ft., 6 ft. and 3 ft. 6 in. diameter, together with Penstock Chambers, Manholes and other works.

Plans may be seen, and specification, form of tender and further particulars obtained, at the office of Mr. Lewis Angell, Borough Engineer, Town Hall, Stratford, E., on the deposit of a £5 Bank of England note, which will be returned on receipt of a *bonâ-fide* tender.

Tenders, endorsed "Tender for Sewers," to be sent to my office not later than 4 o'clock on Tuesday, 26th July, 1898.

The Council do not bind themselves to accept the lowest or any tender.

The contractor will be required to enter into a bond, with two sureties, for the due performance of the contract, and no work will be ordered under the contract until such bond has been duly executed.

As regards all work to be done at the site or elsewhere within a radius of 20 miles from Charing Cross, the contractors will be bound by the contract to pay to all workmen (except a reasonable number of legally-bound apprentices) employed by them wages at rates not less, and to observe hours of labour not greater, than the rates and hours set out in the Council's list, and such rates of wages and hours of labour will be inserted in and form part of the contract by way of schedule.

(By order of the Council)
FRED. E. HILLEARY,
Town Clerk.
Town Hall, West Ham, E.
June 29, 1898.

## COUNTY BOROUGH OF WEST HAM.
### TO BUILDERS AND CONTRACTORS.

The Council hereby invite tenders for the erection of twenty-nine Houses for the working-classes at Hermit-road, Plaistow.

Plans may be seen, and specification, form of tender and further particulars obtained, on and after Monday, July 11, 1898, at the office of Mr. Lewis Angell, Borough Engineer, Town Hall, Stratford, E., on the deposit of a £5 Bank of England note, which will be returned upon receipt of a bonâ-fide tender.

Tenders, endorsed "Tender for Artisans' Dwellings," to be sent to my office not later than 4 o'clock on Tuesday, July 26, 1898.

The Council do not bind themselves to accept the lowest or any tender.

The contractor will be required to enter into a bond, with two sureties, for the due performance of the contract, and no work will be ordered under the contract until such bond has been duly executed.

As regards all work to be done at the site or elsewhere within a radius of 20 miles from Charing Cross, the contractors will be bound by the contract to pay to all workmen (except a reasonable number of legally-bound apprentices) employed by them wages at rates not less, and to observe hours of labour not greater, than the rates and hours set out in the Council's list, and such rates of wages and hours of labour will be inserted in and form part of the contract by way of schedule.

(By order of the Council)
FRED. E. HILLEARY,
Town Clerk.
Town Hall, West Ham, E.
June 29, 1898.

## COUNTY OF WORCESTER.
### WORKS OF KERBING, CHANNELLING AND PAVING.

The Highways and Bridges Committee of the County Council are prepared to receive tenders for the following Works of Kerbing, Channelling and Paving on Main Roads and Foot-paths:—namely :—

#### KERBING AND CHANNELLING.

2,790 yards on the Pershore-road, between Stirchley and Birmingham.

1,230 yards on the Bristol-road at Northfield.

#### BLUE BRICK PAVING.

1,885 square yards at Long-lane, near Blackheath.

2,912 square yards on the Pershore-road at the Cotteridge, Breedon and Stirchley.

8,415 square yards on the Alcester-road at Mosely and King's Heath.

4,894 square yards on the Warwick-road at Sparkhill and Greet.

2,317 square yards on the Warwick-road at Acock's Green.

1,010 square yards on the Bristol-road at Bournbrook.

Sealed tenders, properly endorsed, must be delivered or sent to the undersigned on or before Wednesday, July 20, 1898.

Detailed particulars, specifications and forms of tender will be forwarded on application to me.

The Committee do not bind themselves to accept the lowest or any tender.

J. H. GARRETT,
County Road Surveyor.
Shire Hall, Worcester.
July 1, 1898.

## COUNTY BOROUGH OF WEST HAM.
### TO WHEELWRIGHTS.

The Council hereby invite tenders for the supply of ten Slop Carts.

Form of tender, specification and further particulars obtained at the office of Mr. Lewis Angell, Borough Engineer, Town Hall, Stratford, E., upon payment of £1, which will be returned upon receipt of a bonâ-fide tender.

Tenders, endorsed "Tender for Slop Carts," to be sent to my office not later than 4 o'clock on Tuesday, July 26, 1898.

The Council do not bind themselves to accept the lowest or any tender.

The contractor will be required to enter into a bond, with two sureties, for the due performance of the contract, and no

work will be ordered under the contract until such bond has been duly executed.

As regards all work to be done at the site or elsewhere within a radius of 20 miles from Charing Cross, the contractors will be bound by the contract to pay to all workmen (except a reasonable number of legally-bound apprentices) employed by them wages at rates not less, and to observe hours of labour not greater, than the rates and hours set out in the Council's list, and such rates of wages and hours of labour will be inserted in and form part of the contract by way of schedule.

(By order of the Council)
FRED. E. HILLEARY,
Town Clerk.
Town Hall, West Ham, E.
June 28, 1898.

## BOROUGH OF MAIDENHEAD.

*PRIVATE STREET WORKS ACT, 1892.*

TO ROAD CONTRACTORS AND OTHERS.

The Town Council of the Borough of Maidenhead is prepared to receive tenders for Putting in Order and Making Good a certain Street, called Ray Park-avenue, situated within the district.

The plans and specifications may be seen, and a form of tender and copy of the bill of quantities obtained, at the office of the undersigned, on the payment of the sum of £1 1s., which will be returned on receipt of a *bona-fide* tender.

Tenders, sealed and endorsed "Tender for Ray Park-avenue," must be delivered to me not later than 5 p.m. on Monday, the 11th day of July, 1898.

The Council do not undertake to accept the lowest or any tender.

(By order)
PERCY JOHNS, A.M.I.C.E.,
Borough Surveyor.
Guildhall, Maidenhead.
June 21, 1898.

## BOROUGH OF LEWES.

TO STONE MERCHANTS, FARMERS, &c.

The Town Council of this Borough invite tenders for the supply of 500 tons of 2-in. Broken Blue Guernsey, Cherbourg or Belgian Granite, 100 tons of Coarse Granite Screenings, 650 tons of Broken Surface-Picked Flints and 150 tons of Piddinghoe Gravel.

Forms of tender and specification may be had, and any further information obtained, at the Borough Surveyor's office, Town Hall, Lewes.

Sealed tenders, endorsed "Tender for ———," must be left at my office on or before the 23rd July, 1898.

Power is reserved to reject the lowest or any tender.

(By order)
MONTAGUE S. BLAKER,
Town Clerk.
Town Clerk's Office, Lewes.
June 2, 1898.

# The Surveyor

## And Municipal and County Engineer.

Vol. XIV., No. 339.   LONDON, JULY 15, 1898.   Weekly, Price 3d.

## Minutes of Proceedings.

**By-Laws and the Liberty of the Subject.**
By-laws made by a local authority under the Public Health Act, 1875, and by-laws made by the council of a borough under the Municipal Corporations Act, 1882, for the prevention and suppression of nuisances, are void if repugnant to the laws of England. This is expressly provided, as to the former category, by sec. 182 of the first-mentioned Act, and as to the latter category, all the provisions of that Act are rendered applicable by sec. 187 thereof as amended by sec. 23 of the latter Act. The same rule would doubtless be applied in practice to by-laws made by a borough council for the good rule and government of the borough. But are by-laws void if unreasonable? Heretofore this has been supposed to be the case, and the courts have frequently disallowed them on that ground. From the recent decision in *Kruse* v. *Johnson* (noted this week under "Law Notes"), however, and from some remarks of the Lord Chief Justice in the course of his somewhat voluminous judgment in that case, it would appear that this principle is in danger. According to Lord Russell, if we understand him aright, just as the sovereign can do no wrong, so it is impossible for a by-law made by a local authority to be unreasonable. In support of this proposition the learned judge referred to the safeguards imposed by the procedure necessary to the passing of by-laws under sec. 23 of the Municipal Corporations Act, 1882—viz., the presence of two-thirds of the council on their being made, and the suspension of their operation until forty days after a copy has been fixed on the town hall and a sealed copy sent to the Secretary of State, with the advice of the Privy Council, having power to disallow them during that period. So far as the last requirement is concerned, it is to be observed that it has no application to by-laws for the prevention and suppression of nuisances, these being expressly excepted by sec. 187 of the Public Health Act, 1875, the operation of which is preserved by and rendered applicable to the section of the Act of 1882 above mentioned. This, however, by the way. In another part of his judgment Lord Russell admits that if by-laws "were found to be partial and unequal in their operation as between different classes, if they were manifestly unjust, if they disclosed bad faith, if they involved such oppressive or gratuitous interference with the rights of those subject to them as could find no justification in the minds of reasonable men, the Court might well say . . . . 'they are unreasonable and *ultra vires*.'" There may be much virtue in these "if's," but it is rather difficult to reconcile the admission that by-laws may be thus outrageously unreasonable with the assertion that the safeguards imposed are amply sufficient to secure their reasonableness.

The particular by-law under consideration in this case, we may remind our readers, was directed against street noises, and provided that "no person shall sound . . . . any musical instrument . . . . within 50 yards of any dwelling-house after being required by any constable, or by an inmate of such house, or by his or her servant, to desist." It will be observed that in order to constitute an offence under this by-law it is not necessary that any nuisance or annoyance shall have been caused. Now, there are not lacking precedents for holding that the absence of what we may call a "nuisance clause" from such a by-law makes it unreasonable and *ultra vires*, as being too wide. Not to multiply instances, it will suffice to refer to two cases. In *Munro* v. *Watson* (57 L.T. [N.S.], 366) the by-law was very similar in terms, providing that "every person who in any street shall sound or play upon any musical or noisy instrument, . . . . without having previously obtained a license in writing from the mayor, . . . . " should be liable to a penalty; and it was held to be unreasonable and invalid. Mr. Justice Cave said that "the town council have unfortunately gone far beyond the suppression of nuisances, and extended their by-law to all kinds of noises, whether nuisances or not, no discretion being given to the justices hearing the case, who must, if the by-law is good, inflict a fine . . . . however musical the sound may be." The clause providing for the mayor's license was regarded by the Court rather as an aggravation than as an extenuation of the unreasonableness, because it gave him "power to legalise a nuisance and stop a thing which is perfectly innocent." Again, in a more recent case, and one noted in our columns (vol. ix., p. 217). *Strickland* v. *Harper*, the by-law was as follows: "No person shall in any street or public place, or on land adjacent thereto, sing or recite any profane or obscene song or ballad, or use any profane or obscene language." This was held void, both for lack of the additional words "to the annoyance of the public," and also on account of the prohibition extending to land adjacent to a street, so that an offence would have been committed if a man sang a rowdy song on his own land with nobody within earshot to be scandalised. It is true that under such circumstances it would be impossible for him to be summoned, or if summoned to be convicted. But this consideration was not taken into account by the Court, which only shows how jealously even the slightest attempted infringement of the liberty of the subject has hitherto been guarded in the consideration of by-laws. Measured by the standard applied in these two cases (not to mention others), we think it will be admitted that the by-law in *Kruse* v. *Johnson* must be pronounced unreasonable. Nevertheless, a specially-constituted court of seven judges have by a majority of six to one upheld it. The dissenting judge, Mr. Justice Mathew, was of opinion that it is the duty of the Court to disallow any by-law which seeks to impose a restriction on personal liberty. Of course, in a sense, all by-laws, and all laws of any kind, impose a restriction on personal liberty. But we take it that the learned judge meant such a restriction as is not required for the protection of the liberty of others or the rights of the community, and we think it is to be regretted that his views did not prevail.

\* \* \*

**Municipal Engineers at Edinburgh.** In spite of the fact that in our last issue no fewer than eighteen pages were devoted to our report of the proceedings at the recent annual meeting of the Association of Municipal and County Engineers at Edinburgh, several papers and discussions had necessarily to be held over. These are now given in the present issue. Last week we reported the long and interesting discussion arising out of Mr. Young's paper on dust destructors. The most animated part of that discussion centred round the question of combining refuse destruction and electric lighting. Our own views on the subject have been repeatedly expressed. No one need object to utilising the heat from a destructor for the production of steam, but until the possibilities of combined schemes have been thoroughly tested exaggerated prophecies and assumptions as to what can be accomplished in this direction are certainly to be deprecated. As Mr. Jones pointed out, there is some danger at times of losing sight of what the primary purpose of a destructor must always be. Bailie Mackenzie did not mince matters either, and treated both Lord Kelvin and the famous Shoreditch experiments with an amount of daring irreverence which evoked equal laughter and admiration. It will be seen that the bailie also took a prominent part in the discussion which followed Mr. Colam's contribution to the proceedings — another instructive paper which served the purpose of bringing a much-debated question before the meeting. Bailie MacKenzie's remarks consisted of a vigorous defence of the cable system as opposed to the overhead trolley methods. Mr. Stewart's paper elicited a brief but interesting discussion, in the course of which Mr. Greatorex testified, from practical experience, to the same favourable results of the Reeves system which have been obtained at Edinburgh. The discussion of Mr. Bruce's paper on the housing of the working classes was characterised by practical unanimity on the part of the speakers in condemning one-room tenements, and certainly they would be difficult to justify in any circumstances or for any class of population. Mr. Hooley, as reported, seems to have made a remark which must have grated rather harshly on the feelings of those of his hearers who were on their native heath and whose guests the municipal engineers were for the time being. The remark in question appears to convey the opinion that Scotsmen generally are accustomed to herding together in one room. On the other hand, it is probable that Mr. Hooley merely expressed himself rather inadequately and meant to convey something much more restricted in its application. We take it, in short, that his remark had reference merely to the particular class of people — practically confined to the towns — who are accustomed to herd together in single rooms. We have accordingly punctuated the passage so as to convey this meaning, but it will be observed that the mere insertion of a comma after the word Scotsmen would give the sentence the very widest application. But surely the herding of families in single rooms is not confined to Scottish cities. Does Mr. Hooley maintain that such a state of affairs is unknown in English cities and towns? He is on safe ground, however, in protesting against any official encouragement being given to the tendency by the erection of one-room tenements by local authorities. In the case of Edinburgh the step may have been justified by special reasons of which we are not cognisant, but on general grounds we can only regard the erection of such tenements as a grave mistake and as constituting a domestic feature almost as objectionable as the so-called "concealed" beds, which, not many years ago, were so

prevalent in Scottish dwellings. They were simply unhealthy closets or recesses, which, we are glad to know, are now being severely discouraged. The longest, the most animated, and in many respects the most interesting, discussion of the meeting was that which arose out of Mr. Cameron's paper, but we refer to this separately in another paragraph. Brief discussions took place on the instructive papers read by Mr. Wilson and Mr. Whyte. Exceptional interest attached to Mr. Newington's able paper, on account of the remarkable success which has been achieved in Edinburgh in connection with municipal electric lighting, and appreciation of the fact was not absent in the discussion that followed. Next week we shall conclude our report with some notes and illustrations referring to the works and other places of interest visited on the Friday and Saturday.

\* \* \*

**Mr. Cameron's Paper.** It is a common assertion that a discussion is frequently more interesting than the paper on which it is based. There is often some truth in such a statement, but just as often a qualification is required. The probability is against the discussion being so useful or instructive as the paper, but it is certainly more likely to be lively and entertaining: A paper is generally prepared carefully beforehand; contributions to the discussions sometimes are—and sometimes are not. Several of the contributions to the discussion of Mr. Cameron's paper bear some evidence of having been carefully thought-out beforehand. The speeches of Mr. Lemon and Lieut.-Colonel Jones may be taken as representative of the views of those who regard with little favour the claims of the new "bacterial" systems of sewage purification. A critical discussion is useful in drawing attention to the weak points of a system, but the opposition to the new methods of sewage treatment err at times in being too extreme, and open even to the charge of prejudice. Nor can we attach so much importance as Mr. Lemon does to the question of patents, or make any hard-and-fast distinction between those bearing on the public health and any others. What encouragement is there for the inventor unless he derives some benefit, and if he happens to be an official surely his claim to benefit is as valid as that of any other patentee? Our report of the discussion shows that the new methods have plenty of defenders. We are frequently told that there is nothing new about them, but Mr. Campbell very neatly disposed of this assertion. Admitting that the main principles have long been familiar, it can scarcely be asserted that they were utilised or developed as they have been in recent years, or that they were so clearly described and explained. It is by no means certain, however, that the principles in question were formerly so well understood as they are at the present day, and the bacteriologists may reasonably protest against the somewhat unfair style of argument adopted by Lieut.-Colonel Jones and others, who systematically speak as if the former claimed to have *invented* bacteria. They do, however, claim, with some justice, to have *discovered* a great deal about them. It is not necessary to go very far back in the history of sewage disposal to learn that certain effects were formerly attributed to the operation of processes very different to those which are now accepted as a rational explanation. The recent decision of the Local Government Board was undoubtedly, to a certain extent, a triumph for the "septic" system and for bacterial methods generally. The insisting upon the passing of the effluent over land, at the rate of 1 acre for every 2,000 of the population, simply implies that the time is not considered to be ripe for dispensing with such a condition, and that bacteriology is not yet considered to be sufficiently definite in its conclusions or sufficiently reliable in the examination tests available either for sewage effluents or for water supplies, But there are many indications that bacteriologists. as Henry VIII. said of Cranmer ou a certain occasion, have got " the right sow by the ear."

       \*       \*

**Footpaths on Main Roads.** Probably the Derbyshire County Council little dreamt of discovering a hornets' nest when they began to tamper with the question of the payment for improvements in respect of footpaths on main roads. The question on the surface seems small, but little things are often fraught with very troublesome results. This has been the experience of the Derbyshire County Council. The county council are responsible for the maintenance of main roads and for permanent improvements to the footpaths. The work has hitherto been done by each of the urban authorities in its own district and then charged to the county council. That authority some time ago sent out a form of contract, to be signed by the urban councils, providing that when the sum expended on the improvement of footpaths, as distinct from the cost of maintenance, exceeds £50 the repayment by the county council shall be spread over a period of ten years. A number of the local authorities flatly refused to sign the document, which became a subject of indignant protest throughout the county. The authorities met in conference last week at the County Hall, Derby, where they swarmed about the ears of the county council in a way that must have been anything but pleasant. We gather from the proceedings that up to the present time the county council have given the urban authorities 60 per cent. of the money agreed to be expended upon main roads immediately the expenditure was incurred and the balance after the audit of the accounts of the various authorities. The effect of the new proposal is that when the sum expended exceeds £50 the whole of the repayments will be spread over the ten years. This seems a hard and arbitrary line to take. Parliament imposes upon county councils the duty and burden of paying for the footpaths upon main roads, but the urban authorities do the work and pay cash down for it. Upon what principle of justice should they have to wait ten years before getting their money back again? A resolution was submitted by Mr. Fitz-Herbert Wright, the chairman of the Alfreton Urban District Council, to the effect that the county council should be asked to increase the limit of £50 to £100, below which repayments should be made forthwith, and that where the expenditure is more than £100 the repayments should be made within three years instead of ten. It is reasonable that there should be some limit to the outlay in a matter of this kind. otherwise the county council might find themselves committed to a considerable expenditure, the extent of which they might not foresee, but Mr. Wright's compromise appears on the face of it to be fair. The resolution was agreed to, and a copy of it is to be sent to the county council. The assenting authorities were Alfreton, Ashbourne, Clay Cross, New Mills, Heage, Alvaston, Brampton and Walton, Long Eaton and Wirksworth, all of which were represented at the conference, in some cases by as many as three and four members. Several authorities have agreed to accept the contract proposed by the county council for one year. These are Ripley, Matlock Bridge, Swadlincote, Darley and Fairfield.

       \*       \*

**Rural Sanitation in Lincolnshire.** When recently investigating the causes of the prevalence of diphtheria in the rural district of Claypole, Dr. S. W. Wheaton, in accordance with the custom of the Local Government Board in conducting such inquiries, made an examination of the sanitary condition of the district. The result was to disclose a liberal share of those sanitary defects which may almost invariably be looked for, to a greater or less extent. in rural districts. A brief summary of the sanitary requirements will be a sufficient indication of the state of affairs. Sewers are practically non-existent, and thus, if liquid refuse from dwellings is to be disposed of without nuisance or danger to health, a proper system of sewers is necessary. The greater part of the sewage from the villages discharges into watercourses, ultimately finding its way into the river Witham. These highway " drains " frequently contain almost stagnant sewage and other offensive filth. and one discharges into the Witham at a point at which many of the inhabitants fetch water for drinking and cooking purposes. Something should obviously be done to prevent such a pollution of the watercourses. Connected with the latter by drains constructed of rubble or of agricultural pipes are catchpits, made of loose stones and not cemented, and into these catchpits slop-water is for the most part discharged. No time should be lost in having these removed and properly-trapped gullies substituted. There might also be considerable improvement in the system of excrement disposal, which is at present effected by means of vault privies so constructed and situated that they endanger the purity of the water furnished by many of the existing wells, which also leave a good deal to be desired in regard to construction. A supply of pure and wholesome water is another urgent requirement, the present sources being of very doubtful purity indeed. There is, as might be expected, a plentiful absence of facilities for isolation and disinfection, and the inspector suggests that for the purpose a combination might be effected with some neighbouring district council or councils. Probably the grossly unwholesome conditions, particularly as to house drainage, revealed in connection with many of the dwellings invaded by the disease go far to explain its prevalence. Liquid refuse was found accumulated in the neighbourhood of dwellings and escaping into the surrounding soil, untrapped pipes from catchpits were found communicating directly with the interiors of dwellings, and in other cases foul watercourses were in proximity to or actually passed under dwellings. An attempt was evidently made to attach some responsibility to the Grantham sewage farm, the effluent from which passes into the river Witham, but Dr. Wheaton could find nothing to substantiate the charge.

       \*       \*

**A Municipal Electric Lighting and Tramway Scheme.** Halifax Corporation have just completed one of the most important electrical systems in the country. The inhabitants of the town have had the advantage of a municipal lighting system for some three years. but the municipality have now completed a system of electric tramways which is operated by electricity obtained from the lighting works. It has, of course, been necessary to re-arrange the electric plant to some extent, but the alterations have consisted only in erecting continuous-current plant for supplying current to the tramway system and a battery of accumulators. The line is under 4 miles in length, but is remarkable in that the heaviest gradients in any town in this country are found there. It was said by cable experts that the only method of operating tramways in the steep streets of Halifax would be by cable, but the successful initiation and inauguration of an electrically-propelled system has falsified these views. It will be interesting to watch the future developments of the tramway and lighting system in Halifax, and to examine how far one operation will benefit the other. It is clear that the Electric Lighting Committee will obtain some immediate advantage, inasmuch as they have found a very huge consumer of electricity in the Tramway Committee, but how far this will affect the future price of electricity in the borough remains to be seen.

# Association of Municipal and County Engineers.

## ANNUAL MEETING AT EDINBURGH.—III.

EDINBURGH: THE FORTH BRIDGE.

Last week we carried our report of the proceedings to the end of the discussion of Mr. Colam's paper on the Edinburgh tramways. Of the first day's proceedings, which so far as papers and discussions were concerned were naturally much heavier than those of the two following days, there remain only Mr. Stewart's paper and the discussion thereof, the discussion of Mr. Bruce's paper (that paper having been given in our issue of July 1st), and the annual dinner. These we now proceed to give, continuing with the report of the second day's proceeding on Friday, July 1st.

### FIRST DAY'S PROCEEDINGS (continued),
(Thursday, June 30th).

After the discussion of Mr. Colam's paper the President called upon the reader of the following paper, which deals with a difficult and interesting problem in municipal engineering :—

NOTES ON SEWER VENTILATION AS APPLIED TO WATER OF LEITH INTERCEPTING SEWER.

By ALEX. STEWART, A.M.I.C.E.

[Mr. Alexander Stewart, ASSOC.M.INST.C.E., was educated at High School, Arbroath, and University College, Dundee. He commenced his professional training under Mr. W. G. Lamond, architect and surveyor, Arbroath, and after one year's service was articled to Mr. Alexander McCulloch, ASSOC.M.INST.C.E., Dundee, who retained him as an assistant on the expiry of his articles. While with Mr. McCulloch he gained much experience in the design of sewerage and waterworks and extensive warehouse buildings. He left Mr. McCulloch on receiving an engagement from Mr. Duncan Menzies, of Edinburgh, but was only a short period with the latter when he was appointed assistant to Mr. Cooper, burgh engineer of Edinburgh. This was in 1886. He has had a varied experience of the work of the department, and during the past seven years

has been principally engaged in designing and superintending the execution of large schemes of sewerage, road and bridge construction, and the carrying out of other city improvements under Mr. Cooper's supervision. He also holds the appointment, under the Edinburgh School Board, in Leith-walk Advanced Evening School of teacher of building construction, machine construction, and mechanical drawing, geometry, and the various art subjects. He was admitted a student of the Institution of Civil Engineers in 1886, and was elected an associate member in 1891.]

For a long series of years prior to 1889 the local authorities of Edinburgh had been extremely solicitous about the polluted condition of the river of Water of Leith. Forty or fifty years ago this river was full of fish life, but by the increase of population and dwelling-houses along its banks it had gradually become converted into an offensive and nauseous stream. In addition to this, seven or eight paper and other mills along the banks in the landward district had gradually added the noxious and soda-ley washings and other offensive matters from their several works. This resulted in the accumulation of high masses of froth at the several weirs, and, indeed, in certain states of the weather over the whole length of the river, which caused the stream to be unsightly and nauseous to a degree. The public authority first thought of repressive legal measures, but engineering forethought came to the rescue and devised a scheme which has been carried out to the letter, and which, while it has practically restored the stream to its former pristine purity, has also obviated any diminution of water supply to the several mills and works along the stream.

This scheme, which may be of interest to certain towns in England, consisted in the catching up by an intercepting sewer of the various sewage discharges on the way. It also intercepted the mill discharges, where these could safely be put into a conduit, where caustic soda was in use. Certain depositing ponds were constructed for eliminating the material, which had a tendency to collect in the inside of the pipes and so to obstruct the sewer. In order to supply a corresponding amount of water put into the sewer, two reservoirs were increased in storage capacity to the exact equivalent to the waste liquid abstracted from the sewer. This sewer extends from low-water mark at the Black Rocks, Leith, up for some 7 miles. Its total cost was about £350,000.

It has given general satisfaction, however, and fishes are again disporting themselves in the waters of the river. In the construction of this sewer street surface ventilators were introduced. Very soon, however, the hot discharges from distilleries and breweries, commingling with the sewage, gave off such nauseous smells that ventilator after ventilator had to be closed.

Instructions were given to the engineers to report on the best means of ventilating this sewer, because it was held that, although offensive smells were removed from the streets by the closing of the ventilators, there was still risk of sewer gases finding their way into the houses in the neighbourhood. The erection of tall shafts was considered, but on account of the undulating nature of Edinburgh, which would have necessitated the tops of the shafts being under the neighbouring houses, this scheme was abandoned. The engineers therefore considered the use of chemical agency in the destruction of these smells and gases. They opened communication with Reeves' Chemical Sanitation Company, Limited, formed three experimental manholes fitted for the introduction of their chemical apparatus, and watched the result. These manholes were situated in populous districts. They had, as explained, been closed because of the complaints of smells. The opening of the manholes and the application of the chemical apparatus was set agoing. During the months the experiment lasted frequent observations were taken of the results, and as no complaints were received and the experiment was so successful the engineers recommended the adoption of the system, and the commissioners entered into a contract for the supply and fixing of other fifty of these apparatus. The manholes have been altered, as shown on the accompanying diagram, so as to allow the apparatus to be placed in a recess clear of the manhole shaft. This arrangement gives free access to men entering or leaving the sewer. These apparatus have been fitted up and have been in operation during the past month, and from careful observations they seem to answer as successfully as the three experimental ones started last year.

It is probable that many of you are unacquainted with the details of this system, and a description may be interesting. Two chemical-ware vessels are placed in a recess formed in the manhole. The larger vessel contains a chemical mixture called by the proprietors " Reevozone," and the smaller vessel contains strong clear sulphuric acid. These chemicals are caused to mix continuously, meeting on the ware drip, the result of their mutual reaction being the formation of sulphurous acid gas, oxygen gas, permanganic acid and soda sulphate. These gases purify the foul air they come in contact with, whilst the oxidising solution falls into the sewer and has a beneficial effect on the sewage. The water supply for mixing the Reevozone is taken from the water main. Where it enters the manhole a drop stop-valve is fixed to the pipe, which when the pressure from the main ceases closes, and so entirely prevents air being sucked into the main. There is also another valve and a syphon of water about 3 ft. deep, which completely locks the pipes against any back pressure. Beyond the syphon a branch pipe with valve and spray is fitted, the discharge of the spray being thrown on to the three pots on which the chemicals fall after the gases are given off. The result of the water striking against the pots is that a fine spray or mist of the chemicals is produced, which in falling into the sewer purifies the gases coming up the shaft.

When the apparatus were first started a number of tests were made at the various manholes to determine the amount of air leaving or entering the sewer. The dates on which these tests were made were 30th and 31st May, 1898, and from the following table it will be noticed that the results give a curious condition of ventilation:—

*Observations and Readings of the Ventilation of the Sewers of Edinburgh and Leith on May 30 and 31, 1898.*

| Name of Street | Inlet, feet per minute. | Outlet, feet per minute. | Weight of Air at Road Surface, grains per cubic foot. | Weight of Air in Sewer, grains per cubic foot. |
|---|---|---|---|---|
| London-street, East End | — | 62 | 542·06 | 542·06 |
| London-street, Cochran-terrace... ... ... | — | 418 | 544·06 | 542·06 |
| Mansfield-place ... ... | — | 496 | 544·06 | 542·06 |
| Comely-bank ... ... | — | 186 | 551·36 | 545·53 |
| Great King-street ... | — | 837 | 536·16 | 542·06 |
| Donne-terrace ... ... | — | 3425 | 536·16 | 542·06 |
| Moray-place ... ... | 415 | — | 536·16 | 538·60 |
| Nelson-street ... ... | — | 789 | 532·84 | 536·33 |
| Dundonald-street ... | 310 | — | 537·45 | 537·45 |
| Great Stuart-street ... | — | 1317 | 535·16 | 534·00 |
| Randolph-crescent ... | 310 | — | 535·16 | 539·75 |
| Melville-street ... ... | — | 992 | 535·16 | 538·66 |
| Walker-street, opposite William-street ... | — | 372 | 532·84 | 538·66 |
| Walker-street ... ... | 930 | — | 535·16 | 538·66 |
| Chester-street ... ... | 992 | — | 535·16 | 536·30 |
| Rothesay-terrace ... | — | 744 | 535·16 | 536·30 |
| Palmerston-place ... | — | 186 | 535·16 | 536·30 |
| Eglinton-crescent ... | — | 372 | 535·16 | 532·80 |
| Comely-bank (West) ... | 186 | — | 551·36 | 545·53 |
| Raeburn-place ... ... | 737 | — | 546·89 | 545·53 |
| Deanhaugh-street ... | — | 446 | 544·36 | 539·75 |
| Ann-street ... ... ... | — | 1320 | 539·75 | 537·45 |

The lowest record is in East London-street (east end), which showed 62 cubic feet per minute leaving grating; and the highest is from the grating in Donne-terrace, which registered an outlet of 3,425 ft. per minute, pointing to the necessity for further ventilation of the adjoining sewer. At this time a slight smell was observed, which showed that the volume of gases was greater than the chemicals, as applied, were able to purify. Provision, however, has since been made to meet this extreme case also, as explained below. Undoubtedly the temperature of the trade refuse discharged into the sewers is one of the chief factors in producing this

extraordinary movement of air. Some time ago experiments were made on the temperature of the trade refuse discharged into the sewers, and the highest temperature reached was 135 deg. Fahr. When operations were being carried on in the intercepting sewer in James-place, Leith Links, which is 925 yards or thereby from mouth of outfall, on the 14th June, it was found that the temperature of the air in the sewer was as high as 75 deg., whilst that on the surface was only 60 deg. This shows the difficulties met with in dealing with sewer ventilation in a district where trade refuse is allowed to freely enter the sewers.

From the results given in the table above, and from other observations, Mr. Reeves suggested to the engineers that these results were produced by the wind and tidal action at the outfall, and proposed to cut off the gases at the highest point to which the tide rises in the sewer—viz., James-place, his idea being to purify and wash the whole of the gases in

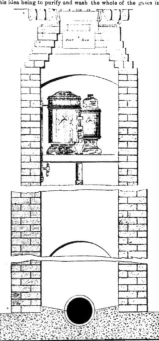

THE REEVES APPARATUS.

this length of sewer and prevent the gases above the tidal level being forced up into the city by the action of the tides. The process suggested is as follows: A chamber would be built at the highest point to which the tide rises. The air space above the sewage would be shut off by a floating trap, and the sewer air, displaced by the rising of the tide, washed through the chemicals as shown on the diagram, the purified air escaping through the gratings. Whilst the tide was ebbing and the sewage returning to its normal flow the air space would be filled with fresh air at each tide. He also suggested that a second purifying apparatus should be fixed at the base of the shaft nearest Leith Links. An experimental trap has been placed at the point suggested, and the tidal action on the air of the sewer is entirely removed, and the result of observation taken at the grating where the trap is situated shows that the inlet exactly corresponds to the vacuum caused by the lowering of the sewage.

The following is a statement of the cost of introducing the fifty-three apparatus:—

|  |  | £ s. d. |
|---|---|---|
| Three experimental apparatus at £15 | ... ... | 45 0 0 |
| Fifty apparatus, as per contract, at £10 | ... | 500 0 0 |
| Altering fifty-three manholes to suit apparatus, at £7 ... ... ... ... ... | | 371 0 0 |
| | Total cost ... ... ... | £916 0 0 |

The company have contracted to provide the necessary chemicals for manholes in series at the rate of £2 each per annum, and for detached manholes the charge is not to exceed £3 per annum. The company are under obligation to deliver chemicals here and maintain constantly a sufficient supply for three months in advance. Facilities will be afforded any gentlemen desirous of seeing the system in operation, and comparison may be made between manholes fitted up with apparatus and those which are not.

### DISCUSSION OF MR. STEWART'S PAPER.

Mr. J. LEMON (Southampton), in proposing a vote of thanks, said the paper raised a very important question as to how far manufacturers and others were to be allowed to discharge any noxious refuse into the public sewers. He had to deal with a case where the liquid refuse from breweries was about one-third of the total sewage, and he need not tell them that under such circumstances the sewage was very difficult to deal with. He was of opinion, and they took legal advice upon it, that the breweries and others who committed this

the whole time. Following those experiments he was induced to make some experiments with ventilation by means of shafts, and the results of his experience, which were published in THE SURVEYOR, showed that the system was a great mistake, the majority of the columns not acting at all. He persuaded the corporation to take down two of the columns and put in a similar apparatus to that on the low-level sewers, and they had no further complaints, thus proving that the system was a success.

Mr. BAKER (Middlesbrough) remarked that this question was of much importance to those of them who lived on tidal rivers. In Middlesbrough they were much troubled with complaints of smells from the sewers. He wished to know whether they had any galvanising works, the refuse of which passed into the sewers, and also whether, now they had adopted this arrangement, they kept the grids on the manholes closed or opened.

Mr. PICKERING (Nuneaton) said he noticed that it was necessary to utilise water from the water mains for the sewers. As a rule he thought those processes of ventilation

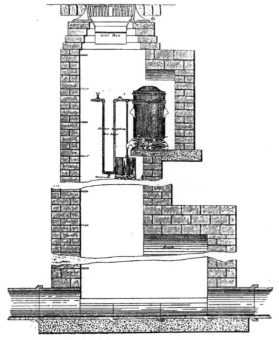

THE REEVES APPARATUS.

nuisance should be compelled to purify their refuse at their own works before sending it into the sewers. In Edinburgh the local authority had been put to the expense of £350,000 for the intercepting sewer which had been rendered necessary by paper mills and other manufactories, and he could not see the justice of the expenditure. With regard to smells from manholes, they sometimes had complaints of smells which only existed in the imagination of those who made the complaints. He had a case of a gentleman who made complaints about the manhole opposite his house, and who "gammoned" the Health Committee into putting in some charcoal trays. The charcoal trays were put in, but the charcoal did not arrive, and on the first opportunity he mentioned that the charcoal answered admirably, though there was not an ounce of charcoal in the manhole.

Mr. GREATOREX (West Bromwich) referred to a similar experiment which he was the first to carry out on the same system as at Edinburgh. About five years ago he introduced a system for the entire area of the low-level sewers, and, watching it continuously, he never had any complaints during

which required mechanical aid were not to be preferred if something could be got more simple and requiring less attention. At Nuneaton they were compelling the owners of all new streets to put up ventilating shafts, and found them very useful. They had a very offensive sewage to deal with, and by allowing the street grids to act as inlets and the shafts as outlets the nuisance was done away with. Another process which had been brought before them was the destruction of sewer gas by the consumption of coal gas. They had some of those gas destructors at work as an experiment, but they found that if the gas light went out the system of ventilation was made very much worse. He did not think there was an engineer who had put up these gas destructors who did not find them go out and leave the sewers unventilated.

Mr. PLATT (Rochdale) regarded it as somewhat strange that they had no power in Scotland to prevent refuse water being put into the sewers at so high a temperature. In England the highest temperature at which it could be discharged into the sewers was 110 deg. Sewer ventilation required human agency to adapt it to the climatic conditions, and on that account he did not think it possible to devise any automatic system which would be satisfactory.

Mr. SMITH-SAVILLE (Darwen) said he was once connected with a town where they had six times the ordinary flow of sewage, owing to brewery refuse. Consequently their complaints were very excessive, and they had to reconstruct their sewers and get a farm of 500 acres, at a cost of £250,000. Wherever they had a staple trade they could not rigidly enforce the law, and they frequently had water discharged into the sewers at 212 deg. He might say they had one of these sewer gas destructors, and it frequently went out, but they never had any complaints afterwards, though it was not working.

The PRESIDENT said that, without entering into the discussion, he could not help making some remarks as to ventilating by means of upcast shafts. He had ventilated upwards of 50 miles of sewers on that system with absolute and complete success. With respect to Keeling's gas destructor, he might add that if all these buildings had a better velocity with an ordinary shaft. It was very expensive and altogether unsatisfactory.

It was agreed that Mr. Stewart's reply to the points raised should be forwarded to the secretary for inclusion in the "Proceedings."

---

The first day's proceedings, so far as regards papers and discussions, concluded with Mr. Bruce's instructive paper on "Housing of the Working Classes Act as worked out in Edinburgh." The paper was given in our issue of July 1st. The following is the

## DISCUSSION OF MR. BRUCE'S PAPER.

Mr. C. JONES (Ealing), in proposing a vote of thanks to Mr. Bruce, said that as the question of the housing of the poor was a permanent one, the information contained in the paper was of importance to them. Mr. Bruce had done good service in bringing the question in so explicit a manner before them.

Mr. CAMPBELL (Canterbury), who remarked that he knew something of the social conditions of Edinburgh, wished to know if there were any restrictions as to the number of persons who should occupy these one and two room dwellings. He noticed that the cost worked out at £180 for the one-room tenement and £217 for the two-room tenement, which seemed a very high price for houses of such a small character. They were accustomed to get a three, four or five room dwelling for £200, cubing out at a cost of 4½d. per foot.

Mr. W. H. SAVAGE (East Ham) considered that it would be interesting to know how this scheme worked out financially, taking into consideration the cost of the area cleared, interest and sinking fund, &c., and whether the corporation were making the 7 per cent. interest of which they heard so much that morning. He objected to the one-room dwellings, as it did not seem a proper thing to have a family living and sleeping in a single room.

Mr. WIKE (Sheffield) wished to know whether these dwellings were approved by the working men. In Sheffield he was clearing 5 acres for artisans' dwellings, and they were spending £80,000 or £90,000 on a scheme to house 700. The fear was that if they put up these model dwellings they would not be occupied. Yorkshire men, and Lancashire men too, were averse to having a number of families under one roof, and preferred to have their own houses. Some time ago they built a number of cottages, which they were letting to pay 3½ to 4 per cent. When the plans were sent to the Local Government Board they were sent back because the Board said that the people in the bed-room would smell what was being cooked in the kitchens, and the answer they returned was that the people living in those houses would be very pleased to smell anything.

Mr. YABBICOM (Bristol) asked whether the author of the paper had included the whole of the expenses in connection with the purchase of the land or merely the building, as he considered the cost given rather high.

Mr. E. P. HOOLEY (Nottingham) said he would like the advocates for the erection of huge flats to go to Nottingham and look round there, as he believed the beautiful and artistic buildings put up there would serve as an example and warning to all of them. About twenty years ago the town, at a cost of £78,000, erected certain buildings. Two of the blocks had never had a single soul in them, and one of them had now been pulled down. These buildings might do for Scotsmen who were accustomed to living in one room, but they would not do for England, where the people would not be herded together in this fashion. When they considered that the Local Government Board were spending £200 a bed on lunatics, they ought not to object to their spending £200 to £300 on houses for sensible people to live in.

Mr. McBRAIN (Lincoln) said they had had a scheme before the Local Government Board for six months. After it had been in possession of the board for three months they returned it, saying that unless they made certain alterations they would not consider it. They insisted, among other things, on a fireplace in every bed-room, upon the dividing walls between the two houses being 9 in., that the street should be widened a further 5 ft., and the staircases of the houses ventilated. He objected to a good many of their requirements, and the local papers had taken the matter up

and criticised the Local Government Board's demands. He altered the plans to meet some of the requirements, though by no means all of them, and at last they sent down to say they would hold an inquiry, but it had not yet been held. There did not seem to be any disposition at the Local Government Board to help on the scheme, and he informed the Board that if all their requirements were insisted upon no doubt the corporation would reconsider their decision and not build the cottages at all.

Mr. PATON (Plymouth) said he considered the Local Government Board were perfectly right in insisting upon local authorities showing regard to and carrying out their own by-laws. The local authority should set an example in that respect, and they had no reason to object to the Local Government Board taking up that position. In Plymouth they were going to displace 800 or 1,000 people, and the Local Government Board compelled them to buy land in the outskirts of the town to build houses to accommodate these people. That did appear to act harshly upon the local authority if it was insisted upon to the letter. People were displaced from the densely-populated portion of the town, but they found artisans going to occupy the houses which were intended for the displaced population. In Plymouth they were clearing 3½ acres, with a population of 1,000 people. It was an old part of the town, with streets 18 ft. wide, and after pulling down the houses and widening the streets they could only provide for 500 people, so there would be nothing unreasonable in asking them to provide houses for the remaining 500 people in the suburbs. The houses were on two floors, and each floor was a separate tenement; and the only difference was that the tenant of the ground floor had access to the yard. For all practical purposes they were separate houses, and the price had cubed out at 4¼d. per foot. The rentals they were getting were not sufficient to pay interest on loans and sinking fund, and if that took place with a scheme on land purchased at £500 per acre, what was going to happen with property in the centre of the town bought at very much higher than its real value? With the 3½ acres the purchase of the property cost them £30,000, and they estimated that the scheme altogether would cost £70,000, and in that case there was bound to be a very considerable charge upon the rates. That presented a very awkward problem to a local authority. Why should corporations build houses and compete with the builders out of the pockets of the ratepayers? There was another question which affected the local authority. Where they had a considerable area dealt with in that way the tenants had a very considerable influence at municipal elections, and when candidates were canvassing for municipal honours they extorted all kinds of promises as to reduced rentals, &c.

Mr. TURNBULL (Greenock) said that they were the first authority in Scotland to adopt the Act. They had actually to pay for 3½ acres of land £126,000, and a further £75,000 in the erection of dwellings. They began with a rate on the owners of 3d. in the £1, and they found that, even at the present day, they were compelled to raise a rate of 5d. in the £1, notwithstanding the rentals they were receiving from the property.

The vote of thanks was then accorded to the author, and the meeting adjourned.

---

## THE ANNUAL DINNER.

In the evening the members of the association dined together in the Royal Hotel, under the chairmanship of Mr. O. Claude Robson, the president. The "croupiers" were Mr. John Cooper, the burgh engineer, and Mr. W. H. Harpur, Cardiff; and the company also included Bailies Pollard and Sloan, Dean of Guild Miller, Mr. Thomas Hunter (town clerk), and Mr. F. A. Newington, electrical engineer.

After the loyal toasts had been proposed by the PRESIDENT, Bailie SLOAN gave the toast of "Prosperity to the Association of Municipal and County Engineers." He thought they would be highly gratified, he said, to find with them that evening the father of the association—Mr. Louis Angell, West Ham—and it must be equally gratifying to him to find that the child which was born in 1873 had come into its manhood and was flourishing so well. He understood the association was making progress year by year. He was old enough, however, to remember when the questions of ventilation, drainage and water supply did not bulk so largely as they did now in the minds of the community; but he was afraid that the community had hardly realised their indebtedness to an association such as this for pressing on these matters, which had so much to do with reducing the sickness and death rate of their cities. In Edinburgh they were fortunate, indeed, in having such an esteemed burgh engineer as Mr. Cooper. As magistrates they were very pleased to meet with this association, and to know that they were not going to confine themselves only to England, but had come to Scotland, and also were trying to renovate Ireland.

The PRESIDENT, whose uprising was greeted with unanimous and continued applause, in responding to the toast said he could scarcely credit that it was only twenty-five years ago when he assisted in a very humble manner in the formation of the association. It then had a nucleus of some ten or twelve members, and he little thought that he should have had conferred upon him the distinguished position of president of an association with a roll of 900 members, many of whom represented important towns in the United Kingdom. It was increasing in numbers, and, he was glad to say, in prosperity, usefulness and influence. They were especially glad to find accessions to their ranks by the election, at the council meeting that morning, of several Scottish members. He hoped that after the Edinburgh meeting they should have a strong Scottish contingent to advance the fortunes of the association.   Another subject of congratulation was the large number of graduates that had been admitted during the year. He thought that showed the ever-increasing popularity of the examinations, which were perhaps the most useful work performed by the association. He thought, also, it gave evidence of the extraordinarily rapid strides that had been made in the education of the municipal engineer during the last thirty years. At the present time there was scarcely an office in the country that did not possess one or more graduates of the association who had passed the qualifying examination entitling them to practice as municipal engineers.   What a different state of affairs from thirty years ago.   In those days it was no uncommon thing when reference was made to a surveyor to hear asked what was his trade.   He believed even an ex-policeman was in those days considered eminently qualified for the office. (Laughter.) Recent legislation and the efforts of the association enabled him to say that there were now very few towns that did not possess a duly-qualified surveyor.   He trusted that the association's examination, so important to the profession generally, would extend, and that the day might come when no municipal engineer would be appointed without holding a qualifying certificate from the association.   He hoped by that time they would possess a royal charter. (Applause.) On the importance of organising district meetings, he remarked that some of the most interesting and instructive meetings were held in small towns, and it was not necessary to have particularly technical or abstruse papers read at them to ensure their success.   In small towns there could be seen works which were most interesting and instructive to members, and in this connection he recalled the statement made by the late Joseph Gordon, chief engineer to the London County Council—one of the best of men and ablest of engineers—that he never attended any single district meeting, however small, without coming away with some useful information which he had not possessed before.

Mr. J. Patten Barber (Islington) gave the toast of "The Municipal Institutions of the Country," remarking that perhaps he had been selected to propose it on the ground that those who looked on saw most of the game.   It might be supposed that he, as one who looked on, was in the best position for passing an opinion on the municipal institutions of the country.   Probably that which was dearest to a subject, next to the national government, was the government of the particular locality in which he lived.   He thought the principle upon which this was founded was distinctly a good one.   It had brought out some of the best men, and, as a proof that it had worked well, he noted that increasing powers were being given by the legislature to local authorities.   The time was when their energies were chiefly devoted to the making of roads and of sewers and drains, but they now devised wider schemes, whereby the intellectual and moral parts of men were improved. He believed that our municipal institutions were better to-day than ten years ago.   They were not yet perfect, perhaps, but they were increasing in ability, morality and straightforwardness.   It was to be regretted that politics should be brought into municipal elections and that sometimes local boards were arenas for political gerrymandering.   He could not help thinking it would be far better to select men who were noted for their integrity, ability and fairness, apart from whatever political party they might belong to.   In Edinburgh they had on the council some of the citizens of whom they might feel proudest.   He coupled the toast with the name of Bailie Pollard, convener of the Public Health Committee.   If he were a type of the Edinburgh citizen, that city must be a delightful place to live in (Applause).

Bailie Pollard, whose name was already familiar to municipal engineers in connection with his admirable monograph on the municipal government of Berlin, said he had felt particular pleasure in being introduced to Mr. Barber, as that gentleman came from a district where they once had a bailie's daughter.   All who could throw their memories back would agree that within the last thirty years enormous strides had been made in the condition of municipalities in this country. If they, for example, took Edinburgh, they would find that within that period very great improvements had been made. Thirty years ago the mortality of Edinburgh was 26 per 1,000. They were satisfied now with a mortality of 17 per 1,000, and they would be more satisfied if it were 14 per 1,000. A reduction like that in the death rate of a city with a population of 300,000 meant an enormous saving of life in the course of a year, and, if it was due to one think more than another, it was due in Edinburgh, as elsewhere, to sound sanitary engineering and to the work and brain of the men who were represented by the Association of Municipal Engineers. He agreed with Mr. Barber in his remarks about the introduction of party politics in municipal affairs, and he hoped that the elimination of the political element in municipal elections throughout Scotland would spread. He thought also it had more need to spread throughout England. He favoured the

sending more frequently of deputations from municipal departments. He would like to see introduced the practice of departments of sanitary and public health, of streets and buildings, or of street cleansing and lighting, sending forth on voyages of discovery to other cities and countries representative members, together with the permanent officials. That was a practice liberally followed on the Continent, and with immensely satisfactory results. He thought it was incumbent upon all of them, whether in the position of members of the corporation or of permanent officials, to have before them the ideal municipality, a municipality—if they were to take, for example, the one in which they were then situated—in which there would be no slaughter-houses within the municipal bounds; in which there would be no cattle markets, and consequently no cattle driven through the streets; in which there would be no cow byres or sheds; in which the milk supply would be all not town-fed milk, but country-fed; in which the scavengers would not be allowed to go about on wet days without overalls; a municipality in which there would be no house for the poorest people that the sunlight could not reach and that had not enough cubic space to provide a sufficient quantity of pure air for each individual; and a municipality in which every citizen, if he observed the ordinary laws of health, would have an equal chance with every other of living the whole length of his days. All the work which they would do, if they kept such an ideal before their eyes, would tend towards that end (Applause).

Mr. Charles Jones (Ealing) proposed the toast of "The Visitors," to which Mr. Hunter, the town clerk, replied, referring in his speech to the energy and ability of Mr. Cooper, the burgh engineer, who constantly helped them out of difficulties by his wonderful fertility of resource. Knowing, as he did, the work which Mr. Cooper was carrying out in Edinburgh, he rejoiced to think Mr. Cooper met at these municipal engineers' meetings others who occupied similar positions in other towns and who were able to interchange experiences with him.

Mr. Yabbicom (Bristol) having proposed the toast of "The Press," which was responded to by the editor of THE SURVEYOR,

Mr. Angell (West Ham) submitted "The Secretary." Mr. Cole, he said, had worked so devotedly in the interests of the association that they had come to regard him as one of themselves.   They now had members in all parts of the world—at Cape Town, Johannesburg, Hong Kong, Kurrachee, Penang, Sydney, Shanghai and other places abroad.   In addition to their corresponding secretaries, they had honorary district secretaries, and to all these gentlemen their cordial thanks were due.

Mr. Cole, who was warmly welcomed, responded.   He had been struck, he said, with the words of Bailie Pollard as to the value of visits of members of the association to one another's works, learning as they went from place to place, to the great benefit of the authorities they served.   In his travels in Sydney, Melbourne and elsewhere the association, as represented by him, was, he could assure them, most warmly received and welcomed.   Sydney, as an example, had actually sent their surveyor home to England to acquire facts of use to his municipality, and he thought this had not been altogether unconnected with his (the speaker's) visit to Sydney.   He could not sit down without offering his congratulations to the President, in whom he had had for many years a personal friend.   He hoped the association would go on and prosper, and would take its place among the foremost scientific societies of the day.

Mr. Pickering (Nuneaton) also briefly replied, explaining that he imagined he had been called upon as the youngest of the honorary district secretaries.   He had attended every meeting of the council, and would continue to do all he could for the association.

It should be added that there were connected with the dinner some local features which lent the charm of variety to the usual attractions of these annual functions.   On assembling the President and guests were played into the dining-room by a stalwart piper of the Royal Scots.   Hotch potch, Tay salmon and Scots' haggis were among the dishes included in the menu, the entry of the last also being honoured by the weird music of the pibroch.   Picturesque, too, was the perambulation of the room by the same stalwart piper, his halt by the President's chair, the ceremonious presentation to him by the President of a draught of "the wine of the country"— and the celerity with which the barley-brew was disposed of. By special request, "Cock o' the North" was one of the tunes which delighted the ears of those who love the pipes. Mr. James Galloway, the vocalist, was also an appreciated feature of the musical arrangements.

## SECOND DAY'S PROCEEDINGS

(Friday, July 1st.)

On the resumption of the proceedings on the second day the business of the meeting commenced with the reading by the secretary, in the absence of the author, of the following paper:—

NOTES ON BACTERIAL TREATMENT OF SEWAGE.
By Donald Cameron,
City Surveyor, Exeter.

It is but little more than a decade since Dr. Dupré predicted that the future methods of sewage disposal would be mainly biological. The statement received little attention at the time, except from those who thought fit to ridicule the opinion, and it must now be gratifying to the genial doctor to find the measure of success that has already attended this mode of rendering sewage innocuous, especially now that this form of treatment has obtained a nodding acquaintance with the Local Government Board, and that a Royal Commission has been appointed to inquire into the whole question. The appointment of this commission has, no doubt, been brought about by the advances in bacterial treatment and the study of the subject, particularly by medical men, in whose domain bacteriology properly lies.

In Britain the work done in gaining a knowledge of the best methods for the disposing of sewage has been confined to individual effort by individuals who could not be expected to combine all the experience or training necessary for providing the conditions required for the solution of the problem, and, with us, the law of the division of labour has not been prominent hitherto in dealing with this question. The American experiments have, the author thinks, shown nothing clearer than the necessity of combined qualified whole-time work in attacking a question of such extreme complexness. The published contributions to the subject in this country are very much like the oft-mentioned map of Africa of our school-days: each contribution forming, no doubt, a survey of part of the whole, but in each case very independent, extremely disconnected, and incomparable; and whether the blank spaces are marked "unknown" or not, they are there all the same, and this, in the author's opinion, is true of the work of each department into which the sewage question could be divided.

It has already, however, been demonstrated beyond a doubt that by bacterial treatment (a) domestic sewage can be rendered perfectly innocuous and as clear as spring water without the necessity for using a grain of chemicals, (b) that some of the foulest trade sewages in the country are equally amenable to this treatment. To gain any desired degree of purification, in both cases, is only a question of filtration, after the sewage has been dealt with so as to render filtration practicable. To gain this result the economy of the system, both in capital and revenue expenditure, is, after the experience of recent years, almost incredible, but more especially in the revenue expenditure. In the first place the cost of precipitation or use of chemicals is removed, and in the second this purification can be accomplished by a filtering material frequently to be obtained for the cost of removal.

Not the least of the advantages of the bacterial system is practically the removal of the sludge difficulty and the attendant expense. After one year and ten months' working at Exeter, and dealing with a flow averaging 54,000 gallons per day, the tank shows no sign of requiring the removal of the deposit, and the author is watching with interest how long it will be before any of it has to be removed, as he proposes to work it to its utmost limit. This tank deposit gives the same characteristics now that it showed from the first, that most peculiar to it being its finely divided condition.

For one year and eight months of working there was no provision for arresting the minute particles of the deposit coming away in the tank effluent, and which were deposited on the filter surfaces. There is now provided, at the end of the tank, a channel for the deposit of these particles, and, although not sufficiently long under observation, there is an apparent reduction in the number in the effluent. Obviously the freer from suspended matter the effluent is the more independent of attention the filter surfaces will be, and that is a condition worth attaining. It is a point gained if works require no attention for days, still more so when they can take care of themselves for weeks, and the author has no doubt it is possible to design works that will require no attention for years.

One of the most notable points observed in the Exeter tank has been the hitherto unrecognised energy stored in sewage, as evidenced by the production of marsh gas. With even the limited decomposition which the sewage undergoes the amount of gas evolved has not, the author thinks, been suspected. The large quantity of matter that must be converted into this condition explains some of the discrepancy shown by analysis.

The permeating power of the gas is another, to the author, new feature. The concrete arch of the tank is at no place less than 6 in. thick, that being again covered with 9 in. of soil; but the most delicate instruments fail to show any pressure in the tank, and it would appear as if it passed as easily through the concrete and as through an open pipe. Attempts to estimate the quantity evolved by drawing off into gasholders had therefore to be abandoned. Another way of estimating was tried. A metal cone of unit area, provided with an aspirating arrangement, was immersed in the liquid, and it was thought that absolute results could be obtained; but with quick variations, ranging from 130 c.cs. to 4,140 c.cs., it soon became apparent that only extended tests would give an estimate of the amount produced. We have thus continued its products the only constant characteristic of sewage—viz., its variableness.

The works and public path adjoining at Exeter have been lit with the gas and incandescent mantles. The author has not had more than ten such lights burning at one time, but it was apparent, even under the conditions of leakage already mentioned, that more than twice this number could be kept constantly alight, and this estimate was made during the cold,

wet weather of last winter. The gas is innocuous, and can only be detected ordinarily by applying a light.

The filters at Exeter have undergone another winter's work without any diminution in their powers of purification. As already mentioned, there were no means provided for preventing the humus from passing on to the filter surfaces, but, notwithstanding this, the depth of filtrant that has been scraped off since the filters were set to work is less than an average of 2 in. The greatest accumulation of humus takes place near the distributing channels or in the immediate vicinity of the outlet of supply pipes, and, curiously enough, the filters with the finest top layer have had less removed than those with coarser surfaces. While the life of a clinker filter must be a very long one, common sense tells us that the less straining it has to perform the longer that life will be and the less attention the filter will require.

The automatic gear upon which the efficiency of the filters depends has worked without a hitch, entirely dispensing with manual labour. Although the work of filtration at Exeter is apparently less than at other works, the costly washing of the filtrant is entirely dispensed with, and it is but false economy to provide works entailing heavy annual charges. When it is understood by local authorities that an engineer is justified in expending in capital outlay thirty times any maintenance charge that can thereby be saved present ideas will undergo a change.

The importance of having complete data of the sewage discharge of any district to be sewered—in which word may be included the disposal works—cannot be too strongly insisted upon. The engineer should have in graphic form the characteristic flows during dry weather and during different rates of rainfall. This is as necessary for setting that Cinderella of sewage schemes—the storm overflow, so essential and so much kept in the background—as it is for designing the works for disposal. The collection of the necessary data is a tedious operation, but without this one is working in the dark.

In concluding, the author would claim indulgence for these notes, thrown together, as they have been, when it was impossible to give them the thought and time that a paper for your association deserves.

## DISCUSSION OF MR. CAMERON'S PAPER.

Mr. GREATOREX (West Bromwich), in proposing a vote of thanks to Mr. Cameron for his paper, expressed regret that he was not present to take part in the discussion, because no doubt there were many members who would like to ask questions upon it. He was afraid he could not add anything new to what had already been brought out on the question, but he was in a position to tell them that he had prepared a scheme for dealing with the sewage of West Bromwich at the rate of about 2,000,000 gallons a day on the identical lines of those at Sutton. The scheme had been adopted by the council, who decided to have a portion of it put down and give it a trial for six months. Application was made to the Local Government Board about seven or eight months ago, and on the morning he left West Bromwich a letter was received from the Local Government Board sanctioning the scheme on certain conditions. The conditions were similar to those at Exeter, and provided that the effluent must be run over a certain area of land. The Board gave them seven years for the repayment of the loan, but if in the next three or four years the scheme was a success they would be prepared to increase the period for the repayment of the loan to the ordinary length of time granted for loans on sewage works. That decision appeared to be in the right direction, because it showed that the Local Government Board was taking up the question, and he thought the result of the inquiry by the Royal Commission would be to adopt biological treatment to a large extent. One very distinct point laid down by the Local Government Board was that there should be no outlet to the stream from the proposed filter-beds; and to make certain that there were no outlets he had to send a detailed drawing showing how the effluent would be taken from the filter. They could congratulate Mr. Cameron on having his large scheme sanctioned by the Local Government Board, even though the effluent had to be run on to the land. To his (Mr. Greatorex's) mind it did not matter if they had to run the effluent on the land, because it made the system doubly sure in its work. He hoped to be starting his works presently, and as soon as they were in a condition to make it worth while for the members to visit West Bromwich and see the system in operation, and dealing with sewage largely mixed with manufacturers' refuse, he would be pleased to arrange a visit.

Mr. J. LEMON (Southampton), who seconded the vote of thanks, said he should have much preferred that Mr. Cameron had been present, so that they might have discussed it more fully. The paper only gave a brief outline of what was being done at Exeter, and he did not think anyone could understand the working of the process unless he had seen the works in operation. He visited Exeter with the medical officer of his town, and by the kindness of Mr. Cameron they took samples of the effluent from the septic tank and from the filter; and the analyses showed that there was very little improvement from the septic tank, in fact, the sewage was rather worse than before, but there was a very decided improvement from the filters. Mr. Cameron stated that domestic sewage could be rendered perfectly innocuous and as clear as spring water without the necessity for using a grain of chemical. They all agreed with that statement; he thought they knew that years ago. He put in a filter in 1878 for dealing with domestic sewage, and after the sewage had passed through that filter it was put on to about 6 acres of land. That 6 acres of land was leased by the corporation to a man at so much an acre. He wrote a letter to the council complaining that he had contracted for sewage to be delivered on the land, and they were sending nothing but pure water. The result of the letter was that the corporation abandoned the filter and put the crude sewage on the land. There was no difficulty whatever with the proper treatment of domestic sewage in producing a clear effluent. When they came to the second statement, that some of the foulest trade sewages of the country were equally amenable to this treatment, he disputed it altogether. It was all very well to deal with domestic sewage, but if they had to deal with some of, the trade refuse which their friends in the Midlands had to. deal with it was a very different matter altogether. Trade refuse meant the use of chemicals, and the right sort of chemicals. He was pleased to hear that one town had appointed a chemist to be constantly on the works, to deal with the varying qualities of the sewage as it came down to the works. He hoped to see the day when there would be a chemist at every large sewage works which had to deal with difficult trade refuse, as he was certain that such an appointment would mean the saving of his salary in a very short period of time. He was not quite convinced about that. It appeared to him it was a question of area. If they worked out what was proposed to be done by that system they would find they could not do with less than an acre of land on which to filter 1,000,000 gallons of sewage. · Well, in a large town that was a big order ·and demanded a considerable expenditure of money. Then, again, if they had to pay Mr. Cameron or his syndicate 30 per cent. it still further increased the expenditure. The opinion he formed of Exeter was this—that to a certain extent it was a very small experiment, from which no definite results could be obtained. The septic tank was really their old friend the cesspool in another form. As regarded the filters, he thought they were beautifully designed, but he did not agree with the way in which they were working, because a filter required more rest if they were to get a good effluent. There was another point to which he wished to draw attention. Mr. Cameron stated that after a year and ten months' working, and dealing with a flow averaging 54,000 gallons a day, the tank showed no signs of requiring the removal of deposit, and he was watching with interest how long it would be before any of it had to be removed, as he proposed to work it to the utmost limit. Some of them had seen cesspools which had been in use for many years. He drained the oldest city in England—Winchester—and he found there cesspools which had been in existence for centuries, and which had never been emptied, thus showing that cesspools under these circumstances would go on for a very long period of time. He explained that in this way. When decomposition came on in these cesspools the particles of excreta were broken up into minute particles and passed away in the effluent by way of the overflow. Mr. Cameron himself seemed to have answered the question, for he said that for one year and eight months there was no provision for arresting the minute particles of the deposit which came away·in the tank effluent and were deposited on the filter surfaces. This was now provided for. If the minute particles passed away in the effluent, as he had no doubt they would, this septic tank would go on for a long time and not require emptying. Then as regarded the production of marsh gas. Was it a desirable thing that a sanitary engineer should manufacture marsh gas? He was afraid the days of electric lighting were going into the dim and distant future if the councils were going to light their towns with marsh gas. Mr. Cameron said he had put up ten lights. Well, if he could put up ten lights from those small works there was no reason why he should not light the city of Exeter with marsh gas. He had some discussion there, and one gentleman was unkind enough to call it the Exeter gasholder. · He was not calling it that, but he was not impressed with this manufacture of gas. It would be within recollection that one engineer went there and met with a serious accident. It all came to this, that unless they put the sewage on the land it was a question of area for filters. If they could have a very large area of filters they would not want the chemicals they had now. What they did as engineers in the precipitation processes was this. They wanted to deal with the sewage in a small cubic capacity in a very short space of time, and in order to do that they used chemicals to accelerate deposit. If they had time enough to allow it sewage would deposit itself, and they simply used chemicals to increase the rate at which it would deposit. That showed it was all a question of the area of the tank or the filter. He did not think the qualified assent of the Local Government Board proved anything. There were 20 acres of very suitable land at Exeter, and after the sewage was passed through the filters and the septic tank it was distributed on the 20 acres of land. · It appeared to him, looking at the surroundings, that the same result could be obtained by the land without the septic tank at all. He looked upon the system with very much doubt. He had spent very much time in travelling about the country and investigating these different sewage schemes from time to time. · There ·had been hun-

dreds ·of patents taken out for dealing with the sewage problem, and they had all settled the question. Speaking with an experience of thirty years, he asserted that the practical effect of many of these inventions had been to retard the proper solution of the disposal of sewage. They must look upon this matter with a certain amount of suspicion, especially when they knew it was a case of making money and £ s. d. for the inventors (Cries of "Oh !"). He would like to make it illegal for any man to take out a patent for anything affecting the public health, and then they would soon stop all these fads. He had been asked over and over again to be connected with these things, and had refused, because he thought what was done should be done without any self-interest whatever.

Mr. McBRAIR (Lincoln) expressed himself sorry that the paper did not give any figures as to,cost, and all through confused the septic tank with the bacterial treatment of sewage. As a matter of fact, sewage could be treated bacterially without the septic tank at all. Some months ago he laid down two bacterial filters, and they had been working for two months. In the working of these filters one serious point he had discovered was that the first quantity of sewage which came from the first or settling tank was bad, always discoloured and very foul. He had a theory of his own to account for this. It was the custom to put pipes for underdrainage at the bottom of the tanks, and these pipes got full of sewage which never received any treatment, but lay there and decomposed. With his tanks it was so bad that when his committee visited the works he had to run the sewage in the settling tank away, as it would never do to show them. It seemed to him that the only way to prevent that difficulty was by not underdraining the filter, or at least only underdraining 3 ft. or 4 ft. radiating from the valve, so that the whole of the sewage which went down must percolate through a large amount of coke before it went away. Then they were told they could obtain refuse ashes for these filters, but in his case he had to buy coke from the gas manager at 10s. per ton. Then they were told that the filters should have a rest on one day a week, and that they should make that rest day Sunday. But if they were to do that where was their sewage to go on Sunday ? It meant that they must have additional tanks other than those used for the ordinary flow of the sewage.

Mr. J. S. PICKERING (Nuneaton) thought it a step in the right direction that the Local Government Board had sanctioned the loan, though conditionally, for the West Bromwich works. He did not think it was clearly understood that the West Bromwich loan was for a large experiment; so the number of years for which it was granted was not a great matter. If it was a success the corporation would adopt the system, and then the Local Government Board would give the full term for the repayment of the loan. He could bear out what Mr. Cameron said as to foul trade sewage being amenable to the biological treatment. Notwithstanding that Mr. Lemon was sceptical, and he admitted he was sceptical six months ago, there was evidence that trade sewages could be treated in this way. He had one of the foulest trade sewages in the country to deal with, and some four or five months ago he laid down a filter of 100 yards square, composed of coke breeze, and every day since had been pouring crude sewage on the filter, without the use of any chemicals whatever, and he was quite sure that the results from that filter had greatly improved, and now were undoubtedly better than they were at the commencement. That was proof that manufacturers' refuses were to some degree amenable to this bacterial treatment. He was so satisfied with the result that he was going to try it on a larger scale. The conditions imposed by the Local Government Board might be necessary, but the absurdity of the thing was that whatever conditions they made they took no steps whatever to see that they were carried out. He wished to say he had an artificial filter composed of coke dust. He did not know what material was used in other towns, but he certainly did not think it necessary to go to the trouble and expense of getting coke breeze. He was convinced that the treatment could be equally well done with coke dust, a material which they were able to buy for 1s. a ton, as compared with the 7s. to 10s. charged for coke breeze. He had had filter-beds going for two years, and they were in as clean a condition as when first put in. Mr. McBrair always struck him that it was a weak point in these filters if they had a certain amount of underdrainage where no purification could take place. · He had come to the conclusion that if coarse material was put at the bottom of the filter it was not necessary to underdrain the filter. He formerly had the filter underdrained with 4-in. land pipes, and the invert pipe slightly below the floor of the filter was for half an inch a putrid mass and above it was quite clear, showing that the under material got no treatment whatever. The system at West Bromwich was not patented in any way, and all of them could try an experiment for themselves at very little cost indeed.

Colonel JONES, v.c., expressed his regret at Mr. Cameron's absence, because he was disappointed with the paper which he had put before the meeting. There was some truth in it, but that was all old, and what was not old was not true. They all knew that domestic sewage could be treated by filtration; they had always known it. And in the case of cesspools, they had ·always known ·that they produced the results put forward—marsh gas. They had always been accustomed to consider that it was very offensive, and the object of taking sewage away from the towns was that the marsh gas should not get into the houses. He would like to say something about the automatic process at Exeter, upon which alone it was patented, though it was true that Mr. Wynne Roberts, of Oswestry, had another plan of automatic transfer of the sewage from one filter-bed to another. The thing he complained of was that it was not justifiable to say there was a great saving in this automatic arrangement, because he preferred good, intelligent hand-labour in anything that had to do with sewage. Sewage had a way of clogging and choking up which upset all kinds of mechanical arrangement. He thought that would be found in time to be a bad arrangement in connection with this system, and at any rate it would not save much. As to the employing of these filters, Mr. Lemon very truly said they all knew of cesspools which did not require emptying, because they had overflows, or were in chalk or some other porous material, by which the matter got away unobserved. He had been waiting all along for this Exeter tank to be emptied. It was a matter of regret that the inspector of the Local Government Board did not say, "Kindly empty that tank and let me see it to-morrow morning." But instead of that the Local Government Board were content with the evidence given. At the sanitary congress at Leeds they were told that the tank, after a year's use, was a quarter full of sludge—the amount of humus was so many inches and the floating scum amounted to so many more inches. He put the two together, and made them 2 ft., while the tank was 8 ft. He was waiting to know how much more there was now, and when it was to be emptied. If the tank was calculated to dispose of one day's sewage, and it was a necessary part of the process that it should hold a day's sewage, when it was a quarter full of sludge there was only space for three-quarters of a day's sewage. His explanation was that if the tank was calculated to take the dry-weather sewage, whenever there was half an inch of rain in the twenty-four hours the particles of solid matter were carried away in the effluent and disposed of somehow or other, but they had not heard how. It was evident that these filter-beds could not dispose of the flood water. It might run off the surface of the filter-beds, and in some way the whole contents of the filter-beds might be washed out. He was sorry Mr. Cameron was not present, as he did not like to find fault with the paper in his absence. He must say he looked upon Mr. Cameron as a most honourable and upright man, and he had the highest opinion of the man, but he had the greatest suspicion when anything to do with sewage got into the hands of a company to make money of. He was sorry that they could not get public opinion sufficiently interested in any matters affecting sewage. They wanted their rivers purified, and to watch the results as practical men, but instead of that they said it was nothing to them. They left it to the chemists and the engineers. The public ought to take more pains, for the results of their apathy was that they were the victims of those speculative syndicates and money-making people. He was afraid of the effect of the paper being put before the association. In 1877 he was present at the annual meeting, when Mr. Webster brought forward the electrical system. He was never more astonished in his life than to find that a body of trained borough engineers, whose attention had been given to the treatment of sewage for years, received that as a message from Heaven and the solution of the whole thing. There was a kind of feeling going about now that this was something new, whereas bacteria had been working upon the sewage for millions of years. There was nothing new in it, not even the number of the bacteria, though they were to be cultivated, increased in numbers, and-bred to it. The only thing the advocates of this system put forward were the conditions which the late Mr. Bailey Denton and everybody insisted upon—that they should provide the most porous possible material as a filtering medium, and that the sewage should pass through it at a reasonable rate of speed, and that it should be intermittent in flow. The whole thing depended upon the flow of the sewage being intermittent.

Mr. CAMPBELL (Canterbury) said that in his innocence he went to Exeter to see the system, and he regretted that in Mr. Cameron's absence aspersions and suggestions of that kind had been brought forward. They might be correct, they might not be correct, but he had a more innocent mind than to suggest such things in connection with that paper. He went to Exeter with an unprejudiced mind, as a learner, and not as one who from thirty years' experience had learned to trust to land as the be-all and end-all of sewage purification. There were, no doubt, conditions in which Mr. Lemon's large experience of land had fulfilled all that was desired. Land was all right when they could get it sufficiently removed and isolated, but everyone had to meet the conditions of the towns where they work, and even admitting land was all Mr. Lemon had claimed it to be.

Mr. LEMON : I did not say a word against filtration. I am an advocate of filtration.

Mr. CAMPBELL, continuing, remarked that Colonel Jones had said so. His point was this, that the Local Government Board had made a great concession as to the amount of land in allowing 1 acre for every 2,000 of population. He returned from Exeter and constructed a tank at Canterbury similar to those Mr. Cameron had, and it had worked satis-

factorily for four months. If the Exeter tank and the Canterbury tank on the Exeter lines did produce a wonderfully clarified effluent from a very bad putrid sewage, then he claims that Mr. Cameron had done something. There might be noti   t new under the sun, but there were the developments o  .d practices, there was the reducing to a science, as Mr. Cameron and Mr. Dibdin were doing, of what on the land was an unknown, uncertain and an indefinite amount of purification of sewage. By these tanks they were able to define it and reduce it to the principles of a science.

Mr. SMITH-SAVILLE (Darwen) said that he had constructed a bacterial tank, as his authority was anxious to be free from sludge. They had never had any marsh gas from the tank, though the manager at the sewage works thought he was going to light his residence in that way. Although the tank had been going for three months, he found there was not much sludge in it, and, indeed, he was in a position to say it had reduced the sludge to one-fourth. Previously they produced 32 tons of sludge per 1,000,000 gallons; now he should put it at 8 tons of sludge per 1,000,000 gallons. The effluent from the tank had never been so good as to justify him in having it analysed. It was of a milky consistency, and there were slight particles in it. He allowed a fifteen hours' flow through the tank to enable it to clarify, and they then passed it through two coke filters. The filter took an hour to fill, rested two hours, then ran off and aërated for two hours. The effluent from the two filters was not very good—not so good as with the ordinary coke and sand filters. He had anticipated that the first lot of sewage would scarcely get treated; therefore he filled the bottom portion with 9 in. of coke dust, so as to aërate better. Though they had the fine coke at the bottom, they did not get an effluent such as he would be justified in sending into the river or that the Rivers Board would accept. The septic tank system was one which required very careful watching and could not be looked upon with too much caution. Whatever might be the case at Exeter, it did not appear suitable to their sewage at Darwen.

Mr. WISE (Sheffield) said he had not been to Exeter, but he had been to Sutton, and, with the consent of Mr. Smith, brought away their sewage works manager, and he was now at Sheffield. It might therefore interest them to have the result of the few experiments he had been making. The works consisted of thirty tanks, each holding 500,000 gallons. They had been for ten years using lime, and they make 1,000 tons of sludge a week. He took three of these tanks and filled one with slack and two with coke. He passed through the slack and coke tanks the crude sewage, and through the coke tank the sewage treated with lime. For a long time they got no good results whatever. He might say their sewage was very much mixed up with trade refuse, acids and vitriols. For several months they thought they were going to have a failure, but he was pleased to say now they were beginning to have a good effluent. They had abandoned the slack, which did not act, and as they were rather cramped for room, because the works were designed for a flow of 10,000,000 gallons and by the admission of surface water they often got 20,000,000 gallons, he had abandoned the use of two tanks, and was now using one, and by passing the effluent through a coke filter was getting very good results indeed.

The PRESIDENT thought it very gratifying that they should have had some record of this interesting process of sewage treatment and that it had provoked so interesting a discussion. Without wishing to enter into discussion, he considered there was one very important point they ought to get from Mr. Cameron, though it affected their councils more than anyone else—that was the cost. He did not wish to associate Mr. Cameron with £ s. d., but in reporting to their councils they would be required to say what it did mean over and above the actual construction of works. He did not himself perfectly understand what the 30 per cent. royalty commission meant. He had heard it stated that it meant 30 per cent. upon the whole of the constructive works, tanks and filters included. He could hardly credit that. He presumed it was not possible to patent an ordinary settling tank. The ironwork attaching to it might be patented, but the ordinary settling tank could not be patented any more than the microbes. Without insinuating any commercial interests, it would be very interesting if Mr. Cameron could give them the information which was essential in reporting to their councils on the matter.

On the close of the unusually-animated discussion which Mr. Cameron's paper had evoked the following contribution —of less general interest, perhaps, but full of the results of careful observation and sound reasoning—was read by the author :—

A TWO HOURS' TEST OF A STEAM RAM PUMPING PLANT.

By J. B. WILSON, A.M.I.C.E.,
Cockermouth.

[Mr. J. B. Wilson commenced his career in the office of Mr. Kendall, a civil engineer practising in Whitehaven, and was appointed, on the termination of his four years' apprenticeship, as chief assistant to that gentleman. He continued in this capacity for a further term of four years, after which he accepted the appointment of surveyor and water engineer to the Arlecdon and Frizington Urban District Council, with whom he remained three years. Mr. Wilson has held his present appointment under the Cockermouth Rural District Council since 1895,

[He holds the surveyor's certificate and diploma of the Sanitary Insti-
tute, together with the certificate of the Association of Municipal and
County Engineers, and is an Associate Member of the Institution of
Civil Engineers.]

The writer has repeatedly met during his professional
practice with both manufacturers and users of steam rams
whose views on the economical principles which govern the
design and proportion of these important adjuncts to public
water supply appeared to him to be at variance with well-
known laws of hydraulics.

In order, therefore, to try and elucidate the difficulties involved he has taken the liberty of bringing this subject
before the association, with a hope that discussion thereon
may lead to more improved methods of construction in the
future in country districts, where the experienced engineer is
not always available.

The two chief failings to which he would draw attention
are: (1) The adoption of a large-sized ram to a comparatively
small-sized main and suction pipe; (2) the laying of undulating rising mains without air valves or ventilation of any
kind.

Taking these questions in the order given: (1) The reason
assigned for this procedure is—"*there is nothing like having
plenty of size and weight.*" If weight is needed why not increase
the size of steam cylinder, that being the source from whence the
power is derived and not from the ram ? But if size is wanted,
what may be termed the "double" capacity of the ram
should be obtained by extending its length and not by increasing its diameter, as by so doing, if the capacity is
doubled, the load of resistance is also doubled, which is not
the case if it is extended, as the sectional area remains the
same.

The following tables give the results of a two hours' test
of a vertical pumping engine with two single-acting rams.
Table I. gives the load at seventeen revolutions per minute,
which is equal to a velocity of 1·41 ft. per second in the
main. Table II. gives the load at twenty-eight revolutions
per minute, equal to a velocity of 2·33 ft. per second. This
test could only be tried for about five minutes, as the 9-in.
suction pipe could not keep the two 12-in. rams supplied with
water, and the impact was so great that the speed had to be
reduced to seventeen revolutions, which was found to be the
maximum speed that the engine could be run with safety.
The proportions of the engine are as follows:—

Steam cylinder, 12 in. diameter, 15 in. stroke.
Rams, 12 in. diameter, 15 in. stroke.
Suction pipe, 9 in. diameter, 12 ft. lift from bottom of tank.
Rising main, very undulating, no air valves, 1 mile in length,
    8 in. diameter, 155 ft. rise to reservoir.

The suggested proportions of engine, given by way of
comparison, are as follows:—

Cylinders and rams, 2 ft. 6 in. stroke, 8 in. diameter.
Suction pipe and rising main, 8 in. diameter.

All other proportions same as in the first case : Delivery,
Table I., 180 gallons; Table II., 300 gallons per minute.

### TABLE I.

| Particulars and items of load. | 12-in. rams. lb. | 8-in. rams. lb. |
|---|---|---|
| Weight of column of water to be lifted $=62·4 \times ND^2H = W$ ... ... | 7596·88 | 3253·78 |
| Friction on piston $= W \times ·06$ ... ... | 455·78 | 200·22 |
| Friction of the water in the rising main excluding rams $= \dfrac{G^2 \times L}{(3d)^5}$ ... ... | 71·30 | 71·30 |
| Resistance due to contraction and fric- tion in suction pipe $= \left(\dfrac{G}{d^2 \times 13}\right)^2 =$ | 4·34 | 7·15 |
| Resistance due to valve, say ... ... | 4·00 | 4·00 |
| Total load of resistance ... ... | 8131·80 | 3536·45 |
| Which = per square inch of sec- tional area of ram ... ... | 71·12 | 71·27 |

The actual pressures registered by the gauge on the rising
main were, at rest 64 lb., working 78 lb. per square inch.

NOTE.—$n = 7,854$, D = diameter of main in feet, H head in
feet.
$d$ = diameter of main in inches, W = weight in lb.
G = number of gallons per minute.
L = length of pipe in feet.

### TABLE II.

| Particulars and items of load. | 12-in. rams. lb. | 8-in. rams. lb. |
|---|---|---|
| Weight of column of water to be lifted | 7596·88 | 3235·78 |
| Friction on piston ... ... ... | 455·78 | 200·22 |
| Friction of the water in the rising main, excluding rams ... ... | 195·93 | 195·93 |
| Resistance due to contraction and friction in suction pipe ... ... | 12·15 | 14·06 |
| Resistance due to valve, say ... ... | 4·00 | 4·00 |
| Total load of resistance ... ... | 8264·24 | 3667·99 |
| Which = per square inch of sec- tional area of rams ... ... | 73·13 | 73·36 |

The total pressure registered by the gauge on the rising
main was 100 lb. per square inch—to a round of 11,300 lb.
on the 12-in. rams. The 26 lb. excess pressure recorded, the
writer considers, is caused by " air lock " in the rising main
from want of proper air valves on the summits of the several
undulations.

This air lock is still further amplified by a continuous series
of blown joints, which take place usually on the up side of
the summits, rarely more than a few feet down on the rise
side and never in the bottom of the hollows. On summing
up the foregoing facts the writer is of opinion that they
prove beyond doubt that no ram should exceed in diameter
the suction and rising main to which it is connected, otherwise an economical loss takes place, which in the case before
us amounts to 125 per cent., or, inclusive of " air lock," 208
per cent. of waste over and above the necessary requirements to raise the water specified.

(2) As to the ventilation of rising mains on undulating
ground, no main should be laid, in such case, without suitable air valves, as an air lock ensues, causing an unnecessary
excess of pressure in the mains and reducing the flow. The
reason given for this arrangement was—" *the main works solid,
and therefore must be right* "—but the solidity is not always
experienced or there would be no blown joints.

The air valve recommended is a small air receiver cast on
the top of the main of the full diameter of the main, on
the summit of which a small brass air valve (ball valve) is
fixed, similar to the valves used on hot-water cylinders.
Through this valve the air is forced out under a slight
pressure, which steadies the upward flow of the water and
prevents waste. He has used these valves in barns filled
with hay with success. They were fitted on pressure tanks.

### DISCUSSION OF MR. WILSON'S PAPER.

Mr. A. E. COLLINS (Norwich) said he would like to propose
a vote of thanks to Mr. Wilson for these interesting records
of tests. They were as interesting as anything they had,
because they were actual records of facts. He did not quite
agree with all the deductions drawn by Mr. Wilson from his
tests. He agreed with Mr. Wilson as to increasing the suction pipes when running at high speeds. He was articled to
a firm of engineers who made their suction pipes the same
diameter as the plunger, but foere seemed to be a rule of
thumb with some of the smaller manufacturers to make them
only half the size. If they were running at high speeds they
must have plenty of space in the suction pipe. He scarcely
knew how Mr. Wilson had arrived at the friction on 12-in.
and 8-in. rams. It was all a question of the manner in which the
pistons were jacketed. He made it, instead of a difference
as between 455·78 lb. and 202·22 lb., a difference of two-
thirds. If they were going to reduce the size of the plunger
and get the displacement by increasing the speed, they would
increase the amount of friction by the amount of speed, and
thus get more friction with the smaller than the larger ones.

The PRESIDENT, in seconding the vote of thanks, expressed
his own personal thanks to Mr. Wilson for having given them
so interesting and useful a paper. It would, as Mr. Collins
said, serve as a valuable means of reference.

Then followed a clear and comprehensive description of

### THE ELECTRIC LIGHTING OF EDINBURGH.

By FRANK A. NEWINGTON,
Resident Electrical Engineer.

The Corporation of Edinburgh obtained, in 1891, a provisional order from the Board of Trade for the electric lighting of the city. The building of the station and the work of
laying the mains in the streets was commenced in May, 1894,
and the supply of electric energy was first commenced on
April 11, 1895. Prof. Kennedy is the consulting engineer
to the corporation.

#### GENERATING STATION.

The building is situated in Dewar-place and Torphichen-
street. It consists of the boiler-house and engine-room on
the ground floor, the coal store over the boiler-house and the
battery-room, meter testing-room and store over the engine-
room, the offices being at the south corner of the building.

#### BOILER-HOUSE.

The boiler-house is 152 ft. long by 46 ft. wide. This at

present contains thirteen boilers ; four others will be erected within the next three months. The boilers are of the dry-back type, 10 ft. 3 in. diameter by 12 ft. long, with two Purves flues 3 ft. 3 in. diameter, and 166 tubes of 2½ in. internal diameter. They are designed to evaporate 10,000 lb. of water per hour, the working pressure being 160 lb. per square inch.

The boilers are fitted with mechanical stokers of the coking type. Directly above the shells of the boilers superheaters are fixed, each of these consisting of two nests of zigzag tubes or coils 1½ in. diameter : there are twenty-six of those coils to each superheater. The coils are connected at both the back and front of the boiler to a cast-iron pipe, the steam from the boiler enters at the back pipe, then passes through the coils and leaves by the front pipe.

The gases, after leaving the furnace flues, enter a brick combustion chamber, pass through the tubes to the front of the boiler, over the top of the boiler around the superheater

EDINBURGH : NORTH FRONT AND END OF BOILER-HOUSE AND COAL STORE AT THE CENTRAL ELECTRIC LIGHTING STATION.

tubes, and then down each side of the boiler to the main flue. By these means the steam is superheated 40 deg. to 60 deg. Fahr.

FEED PUMPS.

There are two duplex steam pumps, having a maximum capacity of about 6,000 gallons per hour each, and three three-throw pumps driven through gearing by electric motors, each with a capacity of 4,500 gallons per hour. There are two ranges of feed-water pipes, and each boiler is fitted with two check valves. The feed water is measured by Kennedy water meters, and is heated by exhaust steam feed heaters. There are three electric motors in the pump-room for driving the shafting for the mechanical stokers.

The coal is delivered in railway trucks by a siding from the Caledonian Railway. At the east entrance to the boiler-house there is a hoist driven by an electric motor, which lifts the truck to the coal store level ; railway lines are fixed the whole length of the coal store, 8 ft. 6 in. above the floor level, and the trucks are drawn along these by means of an endless rope also driven by an electric motor. The coal is unloaded on to the coal store floor, and runs into hoppers fixed to the ceiling of the boiler-house, there being one hopper to each pair of boilers. Immediately below the hopper there is a measuring-box, holding 4 cwt. of coal, having slides at the top and bottom ; below this box are the shoots for leading the coal into the hoppers of the mechanical stokers. The slides in the measuring-box are arranged so that on opening the top one the measuring-box is filled with coal, this is then shut and the bottom one opened, a measured quantity of coal being delivered to the boiler each time. Ordinary counters are connected to the slides to indicate the number of times the slides are opened. This arrangement works admirably, saving a large amount of labour.

ENGINE-ROOM.

The engine-room consists of a building 102 ft. long by 98 ft. wide, divided down the centre by a row of columns, these carry the roof, which is in two spans. The machinery at present erected consists of :—

| | | |
|---|---|---|
| Two 100 i.h.p. engines coupled to two 60 kw. dynamos. | | |
| Two 250 i.h.p. | „ „ | two 155 kw. „ |
| Ten 360 i.h.p. | „ „ | ten 225 kw. „ |
| Two 150 i.h.p. | „ „ | two 84 kw. alternators. |
| Two 240 i.h.p. | „ „ | two 150 k.w. „ |

The engines are Willans' central valve type, running from 350 to 450 revolutions per minute, and are direct coupled to the dynamos and alternators. Both high and low tension systems of distribution are in use, the high-tension mains supplying the outlying parts of the city and the low-tension mains the more central part. The dynamos are two pole shunt-wound machines. The ten large machines are wound for a pressure of 460 volts, the four smaller machines for 230 volts. The four alternators are designed for 2,100 volts.

The engines and dynamos are bolted down to a solid block of concrete about 7 ft. thick. This is not in contact with the walls of the building, there being a space of about 3 ft. be-

tween them. The steam pipes form complete rings both in the boiler-house and engine-room, and the stop valves are so arranged that any section can be shut off without stopping more than one engine or boiler. The main steam pipes are 8 in. diameter, the straight lengths are of steel, with the flanges screwed and brazed on, the bends are of copper with steel flanges. The pipes are carried by rods from brackets fixed to the walls, thus allowing for expansion. The branch pipes to the engines are of copper. Four direct-coupled sets, of 300 kilowatt capacity, two for the low tension and two for the high, will be erected in about three months time. This new plant will fill up the station. The engines for these sets will be of the Bellias high-speed type.

SWITCHBOARDS.

The switchboards are arranged on a raised platform at the west end of the engine-room.

LOW-TENSION SWITCHBOARDS.

This is arranged for eighteen dynamos and nineteen feeders. The current from the dynamos is carried by cables laid in trenches under the engine-room floor to the switchboard, passing through fuses, automatic switches and ampere gauges to a common bar, to which the feeders are also connected. The feeders on leaving the switchboard are carried into a cellar below, and then run to various parts of the city. On starting an engine it is run up to its proper speed, which is regulated by the governor, the stop valve is opened out full, and all the regulation is done by the switchboard attendant by means of a resistance in the shunt winding of the dynamo.

HIGH-TENSION SWITCHBOARD.

This is arranged for seven alternators and seven circuits. Each alternator and circuit has a fuse and ammeter and two single pole switches. There are two omnibus bars, either of which can be connected to the inner conductor of the concentric mains by means of the circuit switches. The outer conductor is permanently connected to the machines, and is also connected to an earth plate in the station. There are seven Ferranti rectifiers for changing alternating currents to rectified currents for arc lamps, with the necessary switchboard for six circuits of arc lamps. Each rectifier is capable of lighting thirty-five to forty 12 ampere arc lamps in series. The rectified circuits are used to supply the outlying street lamps.

BATTERY-ROOM.

There are two batteries, one for the positive, the other for the negative side of the system ; each consists of 128 cells,

EDINBURGH : EAST END OF BOILER-HOUSE AT THE CENTRAL ELECTRIC LIGHTING STATION, SHOWING ELECTRIC COAL HOIST AND AUTOMATIC WEIGHING MACHINE FOR RAILWAY TRUCKS.

having a capacity of 850 ampere hours, at a discharge rate of 180 amperes. The batteries are always connected to the omnibus bars on the switchboard, but, as the pressure of the dynamos is not sufficient to charge all the cells at once, motor generators or boosters are used ; these are put in series with the dynamos, and are capable of increasing the pressure of the battery circuit 100 volts or so above the pressure of the dynamos. By this means the batteries are very conveniently worked, it being possible to charge them at any time. The cells are of the Crompton-Howell and Tudor types.

DISTRIBUTION: LOW-TENSION SYSTEM.

The system used is a three-wire network, with feeders at various points supplying it direct from the generation station.

FEEDERS.

There are at present sixteen pairs of conductors going out of the station. The points at which these feed into the distributing network are arranged according to the demand for energy in different parts of the city, the section of the conductors also varies for the same reason. From these feeding points pilot wires are brought back to the station and connected to voltmeters, which show the pressure of the supply at these points.

The feeders chiefly consist of bare copper strip, carried on insulators in concrete culverts; where it has not been possible to use this on account of there not being sufficient room between the pavements and the cellars of the houses, Siemens armoured cable has been laid down. One of the chief advantages of using culvert and copper strip lies in the ease with which the section of the conductor of any feeder can be increased as the load on that feeder increases. All that it is necessary to do is to add one or more extra strips of copper. The usual section of the copper strip is 1 in. wide by ¼ in. thick, and any number of these up to about six (or 1½ square inch section) can be used.

DISTRIBUTING MAINS.

The distributing mains in use are insulated with india-rubber, bitumen or paper. They are drawn into Doulton stoneware casing when laid under the pavement, or into cast-iron pipes under the roadway. The pressure between the two outer mains is 460 volts, or between either outer main and the middle wire 230 volts—that is, the pressure at the consumers' lamps is 230 volts. The distributing network of one district is connected to that of another district as much as possible, in order to insure an even pressure throughout the system.

HIGH-TENSION SYSTEM.

This is used for the outlying and scattered parts of the city. The conductors in all cases are concentric cables, insulated with paper impregnated with oil, and lead sheathed. These are laid in Doulton stoneware casing or in iron pipes. Armoured cable laid directly in the ground is also in use. The pressure of the high-tension mains is 2,100 volts, this is reduced to either 230 or 115 volts before entering the consumers' premises. The transformers for this purpose are contained in cast-iron watertight boxes, which are sunk under the pathway. The size of the transformers varies according to the number of consumers supplied by them. An extension of the high-tension mains is now being made to Portobello, about 5 miles distant from the generating station. Transformer sub-stations, with a low-tension distributing network, will be used.

PUBLIC LIGHTING.

There are now 608 arc lamps in use in the city, 441 of which are lighted from the low-tension mains and the remainder by the rectified circuits. The lamp-posts are placed 60 or 70 yards apart, except those in Prince's-street and Leith-walk, which are only about 45 yards apart. The lamps hang from a bracket projecting from the top of the posts, the centre of the lamps being 23 ft. from the pavement. The circuits for the arc lamps have been arranged so that alternate lamps are on different circuits, this allowing every other lamp to be switched out at midnight. The low-tension lamps are connected to the distributing mains, but the rectified lamps require separate conductors laid from the station for each circuit. These lamps are switched on and off at the station, but in the case of the low-tension lamps, the lamp trimmers go round to switch them on and off.

The public arc lighting is now being extended by the addition of 130 lamps. A site of about 3½ acres has recently been acquired by the corporation at the north-east end of the city, on which another generating station will be erected. Only a part of the ground will be built on at present, the buildings being designed for about 10,000 horse-power of machinery. The station when completed, however, will contain machinery of 40,000 to 50,000 horse-power.

FINANCIAL RESULTS.

When the supply was commenced on April 11, 1895, there were about twenty consumers connected to the mains, having an equivalent of 2,500 8 candle-power lamps and forty-six street arc lamps. At the completion of the first year's working on May 15, 1896, there were 507 consumers connected, having 53,250 8 candle-power lamps and 245 street arc lamps. On May 15, 1897, there were 900 consumers connected with 91,980 8 candle-power lamps and 471 street arc lamps, and on May 15, 1898, there were 1,630 consumers with 149,480 8 candle-power lamps and 556 street arc lamps.

During the last twelve months, therefore, an average of more than 1,100 8 candle-power lamps have been connected to the mains each week, and applications for a further 15,000 8 candle-power lamps have been received. The price per Board of Trade unit at first was 6d. for lighting, with discounts amounting to 25 per cent., according to the quantity used, and 3½d. for power and heating. This has been reduced each year as follows:—

| | | | | | | |
|---|---|---|---|---|---|---|
| Year 1895-6, | lighting | 6d. | per unit, | power | 3½d. | per unit. |
| ,, 1896-7, | ,, | 5d. | ,, | ,, | 3d. | ,, |
| ,, 1897-8, | ,, | 4d. | ,, | ,, | 2d. | ,, |
| ,, 1898-9, | ,, | 3½d. | ,, | ,, | 1½d. | ,, |

The public arc lamps, arc lamp-posts, and all cables, connections, &c., are supplied and erected by the Electric Lighting Department, who also trim the lamps and keep them in repair, for which the following charges have been made:—

| | | |
|---|---|---|
| Year 1895-6 ... ... ... | £20 | per lamp per annum. |
| ,, 1896-7 ... ... ... | £18 | ,, ,, |
| ,, 1897-8 ... ... ... | £16 | ,, ,, |
| ,, 1898-9 ... ... ... | £14 | ,, ,, |

The following are the units sold during each year:—

| | 1895-6. | 1896-7. | 1897-8. |
|---|---|---|---|
| Private lighting ... | 556,744 | 1,052,570 | 1,973,315 |
| Power ... ... ... | 13,914 | 47,727 | 86,654 |
| Public lighting ... ... | 331,043 | 621,276 | 834,660 |
| Total ... ... | 901,701 | 1,721,573 | 2,894,629 |

The capital expended on the undertaking now amounts to about £282,000.

A reserve fund has been commenced, £4,050 having been put aside for this purpose for the year ending May 15, 1897, and £4,000 for the year ending May 15, 1898. A considerable nett profit has been made each year, after paying all charges, including interest and sinking fund on the capital expenditure and the contributions to the reserve fund, in spite of the reduction in the price of energy.

EDINBURGH: INTERIOR OF ENGINE-ROOM AT THE CENTRAL ELECTRIC LIGHTING STATION (LOW-TENSION SIDE).

| Year. | Nett Profit. |
|---|---|
| 1895-6 ... ... | £2,976 |
| 1866-7 ... ... | £3,374 |
| 1897-8 ... ... | £2,000 to £3,000 (estimated, as the figures are not yet completed). |

The following table gives the works, cost and total costs per unit sold, for the years 1895-6 and 1896-7. The figures for the year 1897-8 are not quite ready yet. Works costs include fuel, oil, water, stores, wages and maintenance. Total costs include works costs, salaries, management, rent, taxes and insurance.

| | Works Costs. | Total Costs. |
|---|---|---|
| Year 1895-6 ... ... ... | ·92d. | 1·67d. |
| ,, 1896-7 ... ... ... | ·63d. | 1·13d. |

The growth of the undertaking has been extremely rapid and the results very satisfactory. This, I think, has been largely due to the policy which the corporation has adopted—namely, of extending the supply mains wherever there has been a demand for electric energy, and in reducing the price per unit as quickly as possible.

## DISCUSSION OF MR. NEWINGTON'S PAPER.

MR. J. PATTEN BARBER (Islington), in proposing a vote of thanks to Mr. Newington for his paper, said he wished they could show the same result in Islington as they did at Edinburgh. But he hoped before long they would be able to show a much better result than they did now. He thought the policy which Edinburgh had adopted, of laying mains wherever the demand justified it and reducing the price wherever they could, had brought about the excellent financial results which had been obtained. It distinctly showed the advantage of these undertakings being in the hands of the municipality. They were certainly hoping in Islington, which was not a rich parish by any means, that they would be able to show good sound financial results. At the present time they were not losing money, but were making a little money, and they would do much better if they were to make a plunge, as a company would do, and reduce the price of current at once. They could not do that at Islington, because they were dealing with money which was the money of the ratepayers, and the members of the board would not like to incur what would probably be a present loss. Anyway they had solved this problem—that the work of electric lighting could be done well by the municipality and done without losing money. He wished they could also say, as at Edinburgh, that it could not only be done economically but at a profit. It was very encouraging to come to Edinburgh and learn that the electric lighting was being so economically and well done by the municipality.

Mr. LEMON (Southampton), in seconding the vote of thanks, said he did not know that he had ever read a paper which gave so much information in a small space. He had had some experience in connection with electric lighting. He advocated that they should purchase the license of the then company, which they could have obtained for £50, and the council in their wisdom would not do so. The company went on and spent £21,000, and he again pressed that the council should purchase their works. They succeeded in purchasing them at par, and when he told them that the company were then paying 5 per cent. on their capital he considered they made a good bargain. They had had the works in hand two years, and were now laying out £60,000 in extensions. They were able to show a return of 7 per cent. upon the capital they had expended; but, of course, they were not able to show a return upon the capital during construction. They had also made considerable reduction in the price of the current to consumers. The company used to charge 7d. per unit. They had reduced it to 6d., with a heavy discount after a certain consumption, and they only charged 3d. per unit for power. The results of that reduction had been curious. There had been a great increase in the number of consumers and a large increase of revenue, which showed it was the right principle. Whenever there was any desire to take the electric light they had extended the mains in all directions. Mr. Barber had alluded to the difficulties which a local authority were met with in carrying out works of that description. They, of course, in their council had reactionaries and obstructionists, as most other authorities, and only the previous week they made a fierce attack upon the Electric Lighting Committee because they could not show a return upon the capital during construction. Then there was that bugbear the Local Government Board. When they had made an excellent purchase they applied to the Local Government Board for a loan, and they would not allow more than fifteen years for the repayment of the £21,000. He need not tell them that was a very heavy charge upon the undertaking, and, he considered, too heavy a charge. Notwithstanding that fact, they were able to pay that very heavy sinking fund, and interest upon capital and all expenses, and show a balance at the end of last year, though they had reduced the price of the current. That was a satisfactory result, but the results they had obtained were nothing compared to Edinburgh, and he congratulated them upon their energy and success in this matter.

Mr. C. JONES (Ealing) supported the vote of thanks, as he was much interested in this problem of electric lighting. There were one or two points which ought to be given in all these papers, for purposes of comparison. Mr. Lemon had told them that the Local Government Board allowed fifteen years for their loans; in Ealing they were allowed twenty-five years; and Mr. Barber would tell them that in Islington they were allowed forty-two years. When they attempted to make a comparison as to the probable success of an undertaking, it was important they should know how many years the loan was allowed for. Then it also affected them in another way. They would like to know the rate of interest or basis on which the loans were raised. In the case of Edinburgh they would probably have the information. In the case of Southampton they might be told the rate of interest which was being paid there. (Mr. Lemon: 2¾ per cent.) In Islington he thought it was 2½ per cent. (Mr. Barber: Under 3 per cent.) In Ealing it was 3¼ per cent. This information was necessary in order to get at a comparison of the success of these schemes. He had felt this very much. A gentleman got up in the council meeting and said, "Look at what they are doing somewhere or other," and it became necessary to explain the difference in the interest on capital and the difference in the term of years for the loan, whereas, if they had a table drawn out in which this information was given, it would very much assist them. Another point he wished to raise was the cost of material. For instance, when in Manchester a short time ago, he was informed that the cost of coal he would have said 12s. 9d. per ton. If he had been asked the price of coal he would have said 12s. 9d. per ton. Of course, this made a very material difference, and it would assist them very much if they could have this information and put a stop to the gentlemen who were so anxious to prove that the officers were making a fearful mistake, because in some other place where the expenses were 50 per cent. less they were making a profit. He would also like to ask if anyone had any experience of free wiring. They did it in connection with the installation in their churches, and the money was repaid in five or seven years at 4 per cent. interest. They charged the churches 4½d. per unit instead of 6d., and they were convenientcing their works and doing good to the community at large.

Mr. PARKER (Hereford) added his testimony as to the value of the paper. He came from a town which had got a provisional order, and, pending the appointment of an electrical engineer, it naturally fell upon the surveyor to do some portion of the preliminary work. He had availed himself of the knowledge of Mr. Lobley. He was certainly much struck with the great difference in the works cost at Edinburgh,

which was positively the lowest of any installation conducted by any corporation in the United Kingdom. Whereas the total works cost at Belfast was 4·01d. and Salford 12·57d., the total cost at Edinburgh was only 1·13d.; and while the actual works cost at Edinburgh, exclusive of management, &c., was only 0·62d., it ran up to 9·35d. at Salford. That was a very extraordinary difference in favour of Edinburgh.

Mr. LOBLEY (Hanley) remarked that the conductors of all electric lighting works looked with feelings of mingled envy and encouragement on Edinburgh. They could not help feeling some envy of the very good results that had been obtained, but at the same time they also felt very great encouragement. He proceeded in Hanley on the same lines as at Edinburgh, of extending the mains and reducing the price wherever possible. They had extended the mains in Hanley to a very considerable extent for a small town. He had not tho statistics at hand, but he believed they had more miles of mains and fewer customers than anywhere else, showing that they had increased the mains perhaps unduly, and they had reduced the price to such an extent that they made a small deficit. Mr. Lemon alluded to the period for loans granted by the Local Government Board. There seemed to be no rule. At Hanley their last application was only granted for seventeen years. Their first loan was for twenty-five years, another loan for ten years and the last for seventeen years. The question of a reserve mentioned in the paper, he took it, was in addition to the sinking fund. (Mr. Newington: Yes.) The question of a reserve fund depended entirely upon the period granted for the repayment of the loan. To say that Southampton, with a loan for fifteen years, must put on one side a reserve of 3 per cent. in addition to the sinking fund, and that Islington, with forty-two years loan, must only make the same reserve did not seem right or reasonable. There was no doubt that the charge of £14 per annum for the arc lamps, including trimming, carbon and all attendance was an exceedingly low charge. He saw that the customers' lamps in the centre of the city were supplied at 230 volts pressure, and he would like to have Mr. Newington's opinion as to these high-voltage lamps as compared with the ordinary low-voltage lamps.

Mr. KEEP also asked if there were any disadvantages in the use of 230 voltage circuits as compared with the usual 110 volts, and also whether the lamps could be maintained with an economical efficiency.

Mr. COLLINS (Norwich) asked whether Mr. Newington had any experience of explosions of gas. They had had such an explosion in Norwich, but it did not do any serious damage.

Mr. SMITH-SAVILLE (Darwen) asked how long the india-rubber insulation had been in use. They found in the town he was in last that it broke down within five years. He noticed that the india-rubber insulation was on the low-tension wires, and that the high tension had a paper insulation.

The PRESIDENT said he thought their thanks were due to Mr. Newington for the valuable paper he had contributed. He had seen many papers, but, as Mr. Lemon had said, he had never seen a paper with so much valuable information in so small a space.

Mr. NEWINGTON, in reply, said they had to repay the loan in thirty years, and the interest on capital, he believed, was from 2½ per cent. to 3 per cent., but he was not quite sure. The cost of the coal was 7s. 8d. per ton; it was small and not of very high heating value. As to free wiring, they had not done anything of the kind. They had not required it. The applications had been so numerous that they could hardly get along as it was. The reserve fund was over and above the sinking fund. It was limited by Act of Parliament to 10 per cent. The continuous-current lamps were 10 amperes, except in Princes-street, where they were 15 amperes. In other parts the rectified lamps were 15 amperes. The rectifiers were not thoroughly satisfactory—they wanted a lot of attention and care. The efficiency of the lamps were about 3½ watts per candle. Some lasted very well indeed, quite as well as the 110 volt lamps. There has not been any explosions of gas there, except when they were putting in the system, and then they had a case of gas accumulating and being lighted in a collar, or something of that kind. As to repairs of the india-rubber insulated cable, they had had a good deal of trouble with it, and were now using bitumen. For the high-tension mains they had paper insulation, and it answered very well indeed.

We are compelled to hold over Mr. Whyte's paper, which will be given next week, together with notes and illustrations in connection with the various municipal works and other places of interest visited on the Friday and Saturday of the meeting. We also wish to note that the name of Mr. T. H. Yabbicom, Bristol, should have been included among the members of the Council of the Association who attended the meeting.

**Rugby.**—Mr. W. G. Willcocks, Local Government Board inspector, held an inquiry at Rugby recently with reference to the application of the urban district council to borrow £2,650 for the purchase of land for sewage disposal purposes, £1,920 for a new fire engine station, £770 for an improved outfall sewer, and £2,500 towards the cost of erecting new public offices on the site of the "Shoulder of Mutton" inn, in the High-street, recently bequeathed to the council.

## LONDON WATER SUPPLY COMMISSION.

The Commission dealing with the question of the water supply of London sat again on Monday, Lord Llandaff presiding.

Mr. ANDREW JOHNSTON, chairman of the Essex County Council and member of the Staines Reservoir Committee, said that his council would prefer not to become a water authority at all if they could possibly avoid it; but in the event of the purchase by the London Council of the undertaking of the East London Company the only chance of efficient management would lie in the constitution of a metropolitan water authority for Essex under an Act of Parliament. This was provided for to some extent in the agreement between the London Council and the Essex Council, who desired to have as much of the wells and intakes of the East London Company as would afford a sufficient supply of water, not only for the present population of 295,000, but for the future population of the district. As a water consumer he was perfectly content with the present supply, and he felt certain that as the result of any change the consumers would have to pay more for their water in some shape or other.

Mr. WILLIAM IVEY, mayor of West Ham, stated that the question of the water supply of the county borough had been one of considerable anxiety to the corporation for some years past, and the various schemes which had been brought forward from time to time for dealing with the question of the future water supply for London and the suburbs had had the careful attention of the corporation and their officers. If the East London Waterworks Company's property were to be compulsorily acquired, looking to the magnitude of the area, the number of the population, and the vastness of their interest in the question, it would be most desirable that the Government itself should deal with the matter; but, failing that, if the interests of the water companies were acquired in any other way, the corporation considered that they ought to have conferred upon them similar powers and privileges to those contained in the proposed agreement between the London County Council and the Essex County Council. If the water companies were to be acquired by any local or municipal authority similar to the London County Council, steps would have to be taken for the protection of the outside authorities against any increase in the water rate. Speaking generally, the Corporation of West Ham were quite willing to consider the advisability of joining with any other outside authority in purchasing such parts of the sources of supply, reservoirs, pipes, mains, &c., as would be necessary for supplying West Ham or the adjoining districts.

Mr. W. K. MARRIOT, chairman of the Barking Urban District Council, said that, in the event of its being decided to allow local authorities to obtain a supply sufficient for their own requirements, his council would be prepared to acquire such supply or to purchase water in bulk at cost price and distribute it in the event of the London County Council buying out the East London Company.

Sir JOHN EVANS, vice-chairman of the Hertfordshire County Council, gave it as his opinion that the existing local authorities were the proper persons in whom the control of the water companies should be vested, and that the creation of any new board controlling the whole metropolitan water area would be a far less satisfactory solution of the question than the strengthening of the control which the local authorities of the districts supplied by the companies and the consumers of water already possess.

## QUERIES AND REPLIES.

*Sketches accompanying Queries should be made, separate on white paper in plain black-ink lines. Lettering of figures should be bold and plain.*

**201. Ordnance Maps and Scales : Meaning of Ordnance Datum.**—"Student" writes: Will you please state what are the scales of the ordnance maps in general use in this country? What is meant by ordnance datum, and where is it taken from? What is meant by a reduced level?

The following table shows the scales of the ordnance maps in general use in this country:—

| Natural Scale. | Inches to 1 Statute Mile. | Statute Miles to 1 in. | Chains to 1 in. | Remarks. |
|---|---|---|---|---|
| 1/2500 | 126·72 | 0·0079 | 0·631 | } Town maps. |
| 1/1056 | 60·00 | 0·016 | 1·3 | |
| 1/2500 | 25·344 | 0·0395 | 3·156 | } Parish maps of the United Kingdom. |
| 1/10560 | 6·00 | 0·16 | 13·3 | } County maps of the United Kingdom. |
| 1/63360 | 1·00 | 1·00 | 80·0 | } General map of the United Kingdom. |
| 1/253440 | 0·05 | 20·00 | 1600·0 | } Principal triangulation of United Kingdom. |

Datum is an imaginary line parallel with the horizon and equally with the lines of collimation. The ordnance datum

of this country is the approximate mean water at Liverpool. A reduced level is a calculated height above datum.

**202. Paint for Iron Cisterns : Kind Required.**—"Waterworks" writes: I shall be much obliged if you will kindly inform me the best and most suitable paint for using on the interior of large iron service reservoirs. I have a circular iron service reservoir of 100,000 gallons capacity, the sides of which are built up of wrought-iron sheets and the bottom of cast-iron plates, which need repainting. The paint used must be quick drying, to enable the work to be done expeditiously, non-poisonous and tasteless, so that no danger or nuisance is caused to consumers through the lack of either of these qualities.

For painting a service reservoir used for domestic water supply an oxide of iron paint must be used (as lead paints in any form will be dangerous). We advise the querist to write the Torbay Paint Company, 26 to 28 Billiter-street, London, E.C., or to Messrs. Young & Marten, Caledonian Works, Stratford, London, E., for prices of oxide of iron paints and inform them of the special requirements, which, we have no doubt, will be readily met.

## A NON-MANTLE INCANDESCENT GAS BURNER.

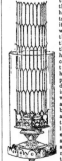

We give an illustration of what is described as a "non-mantle" incandescent gas burner (Billing's patent). For this invention it is claimed that, unlike the mantle system of gas lighting, the highest candle-power obtainable is extracted from the constituents of the gas itself without the use of any mantle, and we are told that the principle by which this result is achieved is the heating of the air so as to secure that the whole of the carbon of the gas is brought to the highest state of incandescence. To secure this result an Argand burner with two chimneys and a small expansion and heating chamber just below the burner proper are used. The air supply in being drawn down between the two chimneys is heated, and the expansion chamber, which is filled with filtering material, aids in heating the gas, which then combines rapidly with the heated air. The advantages claimed for this burner are that it provides an absolutely pure white light, without a greenish tint; that it effects a considerable saving in the consumption of gas; that it is not troublesome or difficult to manage; the illuminating power is considerably increased; that it gives a light of about 30 candle-power with a consumption of 5 cubic feet of gas per hour. The burner is provided by Billing's Burner Syndicate, Limited, 180 Wardour-street, W., where it can be seen in operation.

## WATER GAS.

The Public Control Committee of the London County Council have received a letter from the departmental committee of the Home Office which is considering the questions of the manufacture and supply of water gas, asking for the opinion of the council on the subject. The Public Control Committee now report that, having carefully considered the matter, they have come to the following conclusions, which they have communicated to the departmental committee:—(1) That considerable danger arises from the introduction of water gas in the process of the enrichment of water gas; (2) that non-carburetted and non-odorised water gas should not be allowed to be used under any conditions, since it is devoid of smell which would give warning of any escape of the gas; (3) that 25 per cent. should be the *maximum* amount of water gas allowed to be introduced in the enrichment of coal gas, the proportion of water gas being ascertained by determining the amount of carbonic oxide in the enriched coal gas (coal gas enriched to this extent would correspond in poisonous character to the Dowson gas which is already in use for heating purposes and for gas engines, and would exclude the use of carburetted water gas); (4) that when it is proposed to supply poisonous enriched gas to houses and the interior of buildings a proper inspection be made of the service pipes by a responsible officer appointed by the local or other suitable authority, who should certify that the pipes are in a sound condition and that there is no escape of gas, and that the cost of such inspection be borne by the gas company.

**Tunnel Explosion.**—Ten persons were killed on Monday evening by an explosion of gas in one of the tunnels in process of construction under Lake Erie in connection with the Cleveland city waterworks. The bodies are lying about 6,000 ft. inside the tunnel. A rescue party penetrated for a distance of about 5,000 ft., but were compelled to return.

# Parliamentary Memoranda.

On Thursday, in the House of Lords, the Seaham Harbour Bill, the Norwich Electric Tramways Bill and the Cardiff Corporation Bill were read a third time and passed.

In the House of Commons the London County Council (Money) Bill, the St. Thomas, Southwark, and St. Saviour, Southwark, Bill, the Yeovil Corporation Bill, and the Devon, Plymouth and Stoke Tramways Bill were read a third time. The Lords' amendments to the Southend Water Bill were agreed to.

In the House of Lords, on Friday, the Drogheda Gas Bill, the Cromer Gas Bill and the Wigan Corporation Bill were read a third time and passed.

In the House of Commons the Dundee Corporation Tramways Bill, as amended, was considered and ordered for third reading.

In the House of Lords, on Monday, the West Ham Corporation Bill was read a second time. The Chelsea Electricity Supply Bill, the Sheffield Corporation Bill and the Plymouth Corporation Bill were read a third time.

In the House of Commons the Lords' amendments to the following Bills were agreed to : Cranbrook District Water Bill, Crawley and District Water Bill, East Ham Improvement Bill and Wishaw Water Bill. The Liskeard Corporation Water Bill was read a third time, as were also the St. Helens Corporation Bill and the Renfrew Burgh and Harbour Extension Bill. The following Bills were read a second time : Newcastle and Gateshead Water Bill, Rochdale Corporation Water Bill and Todmorden Corporation Water Bill.

On Tuesday, in the House of Lords, the Higham and Hundred of Hoo Water Bill was read a third time.

In the House of Commons the Lords' amendments to the Norwich Electric Tramways Bill and the Cardiff Corporation Bill were agreed to. The Dundee Corporation Tramways Bill and the Keighley Corporation Bill were read a third time and passed.

On Wednesday, in the House of Commons, the Heywood Corporation Bill was ordered for second reading. The order for the second reading of the Superannuation (Metropolis) Bill was read and discharged and the Bill withdrawn.

*Local Government (Ireland) Bill.*—The House, sitting as a committee, have given further consideration to this measure during the past week. The debate was again adjourned on Wednesday.

## PRIVATE BILLS IN COMMITTEE.

*Stirling Gas Bill.*—The Bill promoted by the Stirling Gas Company for the purpose of obtaining statutory powers to supply gas in the burgh has for some days been under the consideration of a committee of the House of Commons presided over by Colonel Gunter. The Bill had been opposed in the Lords by the Corporation of Stirling, but, notwithstanding that opposition, the committee, who are presided over by the Duke of Richmond, passed it, and the corporation now removed their opposition in the Commons. It was the second Bill on the subject of gas legislation for Stirling which had occupied the attention of Parliament. The first Bill was introduced by the corporation to acquire the gas undertaking under an agreement with the gas company. That was opposed by certain ratepayers, and failed to pass the Lords. The question of purchase having been thus disposed of, the company wished to place themselves under Parliamentary control and to become a statutory company. The corporation were in the position of rival traders, as they had taken up and were pushing the supply of electric light. The effect of the new powers sought would be this : A statutory company conducted their business subject to penalties if the statutory conditions were not complied with. A non-statutory company had more freedom, no restrictions in price or quality of gas, and liberty as to expenditure ; but, on the other hand, they have no power to break up the streets. That power existed only on sufferance. The capital powers taken under the Bill amounted to £40,000, and of that amount £30,000 was taken as bearing interest at 10 per cent., and the balance of £10,000 at 5 per cent. The corporation contended that all the capital should be put on the 5 per cent. basis. The advantages to the public under the Bill, as stated by the witnesses called in support of it, were that they would be secured of gas of not less than 22-candle illuminating power, and as to price, it had been worked down to 3s. 4d. per 1,000 cubic feet, and from that the company did not propose to depart, but to provide against strikes and other emergencies. It was originally proposed to fix the standard price under the Bill at 3s. 8d., and in the other House, as the result of the evidence of one of the experts, they agreed to reduce the figure to 3s. 6d. It was further proposed that there should be a sliding scale, which would give the public an interest with the company in the success of the undertaking. The contention of Mr. Blennerhassett, on behalf of the corporation, was that the Bill should be amended in three particulars. First, with reference to capital, the corporation regarded it as excessive ; second, with reference to the standard price, it ought to be reduced ; and third, the corporation were anxious to preserve the rights of the ratepayers under the Burgh Gas (Scotland) Act until November next, so that the ratepayers, if they wished to do so, might decide as to putting the Act into force and buying up the gas company, or, if the gas company refused to be bought up, of starting a gas undertaking themselves. Where the gas company had not statutory powers the ratepayers had the powers of buying existing gasworks or of establishing gasworks of their own. There had been negotiations with regard to the acquisition and arbitration before Sheriff Lees as to the terms, and the question at issue was between a minimum of £61,000 odd and a maximum o £69,000 claimed by the company. A good deal of discussion took place on Monday, with a view to a settlement, and ultimately the Bill was passed with some modifications. Clauses were inserted providing that the capital should be £24,000 at 10 per cent., and £16,000 at 5 per cent., the expenditure on repairs to come out of the revenue. The standard price of gas was fixed at 3s. 4d., instead of 3s. 6d. as proposed, and the illuminating power at 25 candles.

*Keighley Corporation Bill.*—A Bill promoted by the Corporation of Keighley for powers to construct additional waterworks, to purchase land for the protection of the water, to make new streets, to carry out an important scheme of street improvements, and to extend the authority of the corporation in relation to various matters connected with the public health, was under the consideration of the committee of the House of Commons on Streets and Sanitary Regulations, on Tuesday. It appeared that under their Waterworks Extension and Improvement Act of 1869 the corporation were empowered to construct certain waterworks, and it was now considered expedient that the time limit of some of the works not yet completed should be extended, and that the corporation should be empowered to construct a reservoir in substitution for the Bully Trees reservoir, authorised by the Act of 1869. It was also deemed necessary to acquire lands within appropriated areas, for the purpose of preventing the pollution of the water. The new reservoir which it was now proposed to construct to be known as the New Bully Trees reservoir, situated in the parish of Haworth in the West Riding, was to be formed by means of an embankment, 196 yards in length, across Sladen brook at a point near South Bank bridge. The scheme embraced embankments, ways, wells, settling and other tanks, basins, gauges, filter-beds and so forth. Mr. W. H. Hopkinson, the borough engineer, and Mr. Fox, M.I.C.E., explained the nature of the works, stating that the difference between the scheme as now submitted and that of 1869 simply lay in the raising of the embankment 4 ft. or 5 ft., in order that the reservoir might hold more water. Some discussion took place in reference to what was known as the Harrogate clause, in which the county council were authorised to test the water in the reservoir in order to ascertain whether it was free from pollution by lead, but this was objected to by Alderman Brigg, on the ground that it was useless to test the water in the reservoir, seeing that the filtration process which purified the water took place after it left the reservoir. Every precaution was being taken that the water supplied to the consumer should be absolutely free from impurity. The committee passed the waterworks clauses. With regard to the street improvements within the borough, it was explained that they were urgently required in the interest of the public. The improvements included a new street commencing in Church Green and terminating at the entrance to Springfield mills in Oakworth-road, an alteration of the gradient of Westgate, and widenings in South-street, Cook-lane, Spring-street. Berry-lane, Marlow-street, Skipton-road, Lawkholme-lane, Brown-lane, Aireworth-street and Cornmill Bridge-street and a footbridge across the Midland railway in East-avenue. These improvements were sanctioned by the committee, who also approved clauses enabling the council to work the tramways by electric power, and the construction and maintenance of dynamos for the purpose of generating electricity. Provisions were also agreed to constituting the corporation the burial board of the borough, and empowering them to make better provision with reference to the sewers and drains in the borough, and to borrow £45,000 in respect of the additional waterworks and £205,000 for the purchase of land and the carrying out of the street improvements already described.

*St. Helens Corporation Bill.*—The House of Commons Committee on Police and Sanitary Regulations have passed the Omnibus Bill promoted by the Corporation of St. Helens for the acquisition of the tramways and for powers to carry out a number of improvements in the borough. With reference to the tramways, powers were sought to construct various new lines in or near the borough, to work them by electric power, to construct electric works, and to purchase the tramways within and without the borough owned by private companies. Very little difficulty was experienced in getting through the tramway clauses. The mayor of St. Helens stated that the corporation proposed to supply electric traction and to arrange for the carriage of goods as well as passengers at reasonable rates on the cars. The Bill contained provisions relating to extensions of time for street improvements and the compulsory acquisition of land. The improvements, he said, had long been necessary, but they had been postponed owing to depressed times. It was, however, intended to carry them out as soon as possible. Clauses were inserted in the measure allowing the corporation to lay mains outside the borough area for the purpose of supplying the outside districts with water, and for establishing a reserve fund in the place of the present depreciation fund. An important part of the Bill related to sanitary matters. It was explained on behalf of the corporation that it was proposed to establish a water-carriage system of closets. To this the Corporation of Warrington objected, on the ground that the sewage would flow into a certain brook through the borough of Warrington, and would be injurious to the health of the inhabitants of Warrington. The question of sewage had been one of much difficulty in St. Helens. Sir Edward Frankland having given evidence in support of the scheme, the committee sanctioned the clauses, but suspended their operation until the certificate of the Local Government Board was passed. The committee passed the Bill, which was afterwards reported to the House.

*Dundee and Aberdeen Corporations Tramway Bills.*—When the tramway Bills promoted by the Corporations of Dundee and Aberdeen, which had previously been passed by the House of Lords, came before a Commons committee, presided over by Mr. De Tatton Egerton, a serious blow was struck at the municipalisation of tramways. The two Scottish corporations, seeing the success which had attended the efforts of other corporations by the acquisition and working of tramways, entered into an arrangement with the existing companies to purchase the undertakings. The Bills to give effect to the purchase were opposed in the case of Dundee by the Caledonian and North British Railway companies and in the case of Aberdeen by the Great North of Scotland and Caledonian. The grounds of the opposition were that the tramway systems might become a burden upon the rates, and that it was unfair to allow corporations to use public funds to compete with private companies. To the surprise of the Corporation of Dundee, whose Bill was first considered, the committee decided to pass it on condition that the corporation maintained the fares at such a figure as would ensure the tramways showing a surplus on the balance-sheet to be annually prepared. In the event of a loss arising in the working in any year the amount was to be carried to a suspense debit balance to be met by an increase in the fares sufficient to cover the deficiency. The railway companies, as the largest ratepayers in the two towns, had strongly objected to being taxed to support a competition which would in certain parts cut into their carrying trade. The corporations contended that in consequence of this new proviso they would be unable to borrow money for tramway extension on such favourable terms as they would otherwise have been able to do. Sir James Thompson, the general manager of the Caledonian company, estimated that were the tramways taken over by the corporation there would be an annual deficit of £1,500, which, with £3,000 for renewals, would give a total deficiency of £4,500, which would have to be made up from the rates unless the receipts were increased. With regard to the Aberdeen case, Mr. Alexander Copland, manager of the Aberdeen Commercial Company, considered that the bargain proposed was most improvident, that it had been based upon a fool's valuation, and that it was altogether intolerable. Mr. John Fleming, chairman of the Tramway Committee of the Aberdeen Town Council, thought different, however. He held that the result of the acquisition would be accelerated speed, cheaper fares and extensions. Both Bills were passed with the stipulation with regard to fares already specified, and, as regards the Aberdeen Bill, some additional provisions were incorporated to meet the local circumstances.

*Manchester Carriage Tramways Company's Bill and the corporation opposition.*—A House of Lords committee, sitting under the presidency of the Earl of Northbrook, have had under consideration the Bill promoted by the Manchester Carriage and Tramway Company to obtain powers to work the tramways by electricity. The Bill provoked much opposition, among the petitioners against it being the Corporations of Manchester, Salford, Oldham and Eccles, and the district councils of Levenshulme, Heaton Norris, Moss-side, Stretford, Withington and Denton and Gorton. The company sought power to enable them to work their tramways by electricity, with the consent of the local authorities through whose areas they passed. The Manchester Carriage Company was a powerful body founded some years ago with the assent of all parties, and the characteristic feature of its operations was that there was a common service converging on the centre of Manchester from all the surrounding districts. In some parts the company were the owners of the tramways; in others they were simply the lessees. The leases expired at different times, and inasmuch as portions of the tramways were constructed at different dates, the period when the right of purchase could be exercised by the local authorities varied in different districts. Hence, unless something could be devised by which the common application of electrical traction to the whole system could be arranged, the public must suffer because there were, for example, tramways owned by the Corporation of Manchester and leased to the company, and the corporation had determined to adopt electric traction in regard to their lines, though they had sought the power to work by this method within their own area only. The Corporation of Manchester regarded the proposal as an interference with the city, which should not be sanctioned by Parliament. They had resisted successfully all attempts to give Parliamentary powers to companies to interfere with the streets of the city, and an electric supply

for tramway traction in the hands of a company would be particularly objectionable. Some of the tramway lines within the city belonged to the corporation and some to the company, but this anomaly would be put an end to by the corporation exercising their statutory powers of purchase which accrued as to a portion of the tramways on the 23rd July next, and as to the residue, with the exception of two short lengths, in Bradford and Crumpsall, in the year 1899. The corporation were authorised by provisional orders to supply electricity within the city, and they strongly objected to the introduction of a second electrical undertaking. They were also authorised to enter into agreements with local authorities adjacent to the city for the supply of electricity. Other district councils in the vicinity of Manchester had obtained provisional orders, which were confirmed by Parliament in the same session, for the supply of electricity within their respective districts. Moreover, the city council, at a meeting held on the 1st December, 1897, determined themselves to work, demand and take toils upon the tramways of the city at the expiration of the existing leases and to use electricity from their own electrical undertaking as the motive power. The objections of the other local authorities concerned were of a like character. As there was no evidence to show that either Manchester or Salford would give the company power to work these lines when the present arrangements expired, the committee found that the preamble, so far as the broad scheme was concerned, had not been proved. On the application of the agents of the Bill the committee made an exception in favour of clauses relating to the consolidation of the company's capital. To this part of the measure there was no opposition, so that unlike the rest of the Bill it went through.

*Folkestone Water Bill.*—The Bill promoted by the Folkestone Waterworks Company for powers to extend the limits of their supply, to construct additional waterworks, and to raise £250,000 additional capital, was passed by a House of Commons committee, presided over by Colonel Gunter, on Wednesday. The Bill, when before a committee of the House of Lords earlier in the session, had to face enormous opposition. The Corporations of Folkestone and Dover were arrayed against it, and quite a number of other petitioners. The Corporation of Folkestone opposed it, because for the purpose of acquiring the undertaking they were promoting a Bill of their own, which the Lords rejected. The Corporation of Dover were antagonistic because they feared that the new works which the company proposed to carry out would interfere with their supply, but as to this overwhelming expert evidence was adduced to show that there would be no interference. The Folkestone Corporation had threatened to continue their opposition in the Commons, but they had withdrawn their petition before the Bill came up for hearing. Several councillors opposed the measure, however, in their capacity as consumers of water, and some half-a-dozen other private petitioners, their principal objection being that the powers sought by the company were too extensive as regards the works they contemplated and the capital they proposed to raise. The chairman of the Folkestone Waterworks Company stated that the works proposed were sufficient to give Folkestone a constant supply of pure and wholesome water for the next fifteen or twenty years. Mr. C. J. Hawkesley, M.I.C.E., consulting engineer to the company, described the nature of the works by which the water was to be obtained from the chalk wells and pumped into the reservoir. He admitted, in cross-examination, that at certain periods of the year there had been some justification for complaints as to the purity of the water on account of there being a certain amount of vegetable growth through the supply being interrupted, but this would be obviated by the cementing of the reservoir and by the supply being made constant. While the water might have been short in quantity, and at times discoloured, it had never been unwholesome.

*Halifax Corporation Bill.*—The Bill promoted by the Corporation of Halifax for powers to construct additional water works, tramways and street widenings, and to amend certain provisions of the local Acts within the borough, was passed by a committee of the House of Commons, under the presidency of Colonel Gunter, on Thursday last. The principal object of the Bill, which had gone through the House of Lords earlier in the session, was to obtain an additional supply of water for the town, which had increased very considerably of late years, and was still increasing. The continuous growth of the population rendered the tramway extensions desirable. The committee found the preamble of the Bill proved.

**Compulsory Ventilation in Bombay.** — Under the Epidemic Diseases Act the Municipal Commissioner for the city of Bombay is now empowered to interfere in the constructive details of any house the use of which as a dwelling has been or may be prohibited under Clause 1 of a Government notification dated February 10 and March 5, 1897. He may require the owner thereof within not less that forty-eight hours to put in hand and diligently complete such structural alterations as may be prescribed. If within the stipulated time the order is not complied with the commissioner may have the work done and paid for out of the municipal fund, and shall recover the outlay in the same manner as is followed under the provisions of the City of Bombay Municipal Act, 1888.

# Law Notes.

EDITED BY J. B. REIGNIER CONDER, 11 Old Jewry Chambers, E.C.,

Solicitor of the Supreme Court.

*The Editor will be pleased to answer any questions affecting the practice of engineers and surveyors to local authorities. Queries (which should be written legibly on foolscap paper, one side only) should be addressed to "The Law Editor," at the Offices of* THE SURVEYOR. *Where possible, copies of local Acts or documents referred to should be enclosed. All explanatory diagrams must be drawn and lettered in black ink only. Correspondents who do not wish their names published should furnish a nom de plume.*

PUBLIC HEALTH ACT, 1875, SECS. 216 AND 269 : LOCAL IMPROVEMENT ACT: EXTENSION OF DISTRICT: HIGHWAY RATE.— In framing an order for the extension of the boundary of an urban district under the powers of the Local Government Act, 1894, a county council should carefully consider the provisions of any local Act affecting the district, and should take care that the order contains clauses either repealing or modifying any of such provisions which may be unworkable or inconvenient in the altered state of circumstances. For lack of such precautions with respect to an order of the Devonshire County Council, a complicated problem had to be unravelled by the Queen's Bench Divisional Court in *Hill* v. *Crediton Urban District Council.* The material facts were as follows : By the Crediton Improvement Act, 1836, provision was made for paving, lighting, watching, cleansing and otherwise improving the town of Crediton ; the limits of the town for the purposes of the Act were defined ; the commissioners appointed under the Act were empowered to assess a rate, under the name of the "Crediton Improvement Rate"; and the ratepayers within the limits of the Act were exonerated from contributing towards the repairs of the highways in the part of the parish beyond the limits of the Act, and the owners and occupiers of property in the latter part of the parish were exonerated from contributing towards the repair of highways within the limits of the Act. An appeal to quarter sessions was given against rates made under the Act, and it was provided that the quarter sessions might amend the same. Under the Public Health Act, 1875, the district within the limits of the Improvement Act became an urban district, and the commissioners under that Act became the urban authority for that district. At the time of the passing of the Local Government Act, 1894, the parish of Crediton was situate partly within the urban district of Crediton and partly within a rural sanitary district, and the several parts of the parish would (apart from any order under that Act) have become separate parishes under that Act. By an order, 1894, made by the Devonshire County Council and confirmed by the Local Government Board, under sec. 36 of the Local Government Act, 1894, and sec. 57 of the Local Government Act, 1888, the urban district of Crediton was, however, extended by the addition thereto of the part of the parish of Crediton formerly within the rural sanitary district, but the order did not repeal, extend or amend the Act of 1836. On September 22, 1896, the Crediton Urban District Council made a rate, which they termed "The Crediton Improvement Rate," on the tenants and occupiers of land and tithes in the town and parish of Crediton, within the limits of the Act of 1836. The appellant was rated in respect of property within the limits of that Act. The rate was levied to defray expenses to be incurred for the purposes of the Public Health Act, 1875, including the purposes for which rates were leviable under the Improvement Act ; and in part for the repairs of highways both within the limits of that Act and within the added portion of the district. The appellant appealed to quarter sessions, contending that the rule was bad. The quarter sessions held that they had power to amend the heading of the rate by expressing that it was made not only under the Crediton Improvement Act, but also under the Public Health Act, 1875, and they ordered it to be so amended, and held that, so amended, it was good. The High Court, however, while upholding the power of the quarter sessions to amend the rule, came to the conclusion that notwithstanding such amendment the rate was still bad. The judgment is too lengthy for reproduction, but it will suffice to give in outline the reasoning on which it was based. Within the area of the old local Act the council can, in exercise of the powers of that Act, make one rate for general purposes similar to those of the Public Health Acts, plus watching. Within the added area there is no such power, and no power to make any rate confined to that area. The only rate that can be made for expenses incurred within that area is a general rate, which must cover the whole of the enlarged district. Any expenses incurred for highways in the added area therefore must be paid for out of the rate for the whole district. But by the local Act the ratepayers of the old area are exempted from contributing to repair of highways in the added area, and *vice versâ.* Therefore, in making the rate, the highway expenses of the two areas should have been dealt with separately, and the rate in the pound of such respective areas modified accordingly. This, however, had not been done, and therefore the rate was bad. Such a mode of dealing with the rate would probably be found difficult, or at least inconvenient. But, as Mr. Justice Wills pointed out, the remedy for this state of things is to be found in a fresh order, either repealing or amending those sections of the local Act which clash with the present altered state of things

SALE OF LAND BY LOCAL AUTHORITY: RESTRICTIVE COVENANT: CONDITION OF PURCHASE.—An interesting point arose in the recent case of *Holford* v. *Urban District Council of Acton* (Chancery Division, Mr. Justice Stirling, June 18th). The council (or their predecessors) having acquired certain land, under their compulsory powers, for the purpose of street improvements, offered a portion thereof for re-sale by auction in lots in 1894. One of the conditions of sale provided that the purchasers of certain specified lots should in their conveyances enter into covenants with the vendors to erect within two years from the day of sale upon each of the lots bought by them a shop and dwelling-house of not less value than £650. One of these lots was bought by the plaintiff, who erected a shop and dwelling-house in compliance with the condition. Certain of the lots, however, were not sold, and the council had recently determined to erect upon these lots a fire-engine station, which was required for the purposes of their district; and the sanction of the Local Government Board had been obtained to the issue of a loan for the purpose of providing the necessary funds. The plaintiff asked for an injunction to restrain the council from erecting the proposed fire-engine station or any buildings other than shops and dwelling-houses of the value prescribed by the condition, his contention being that the council were themselves bound by the conditions subject to which the land was put up to auction. For the council it was argued, first, that the covenant was affirmative in form, and there was no negative stipulation not to erect upon the land any buildings other than shops or dwelling-houses, and, as no such negative stipulation could be implied, the defendants could not be restrained by injunction. Secondly, they contended that even if the covenant could be enforced as between the respective purchasers, it was not binding as against the defendants, inasmuch as it would be beyond their powers to subject the land in their hands to a restrictive condition which would have the effect of preventing them from dealing with it for the purposes of the requirements of their district. Mr. Justice Stirling came to the conclusion that, having regard to the authorities, no negative stipulation could be implied in the condition. That being so, the restrictive covenant could not be enforced against the defendants, and the action failed and must be dismissed, and (except as to a special direction on one point) with costs as between solicitor and client, pursuant to the powers of the Public Authorities Protection Act, 1893.

PUBLIC HEALTH ACT, 1875, SEC. 132 : EXPENSES INCURRED BY AUTHORITY IN MAINTAINING CHILD IN HOSPITAL : LIABILITY OF PARENT.—The above section, it will be remembered, provides as follows : "Any expenses incurred by a local authority in maintaining in a hospital, or in a temporary place for the reception of the sick (whether or not belonging to such authority), a patient who is not a pauper, shall be deemed to be a debt due from such patient to the local authority, and may be recovered from him at any time within six months after his discharge from such hospital or place of reception, or from his estate in the event of his dying in such hospital or place." In the case of a child patient, is his parent liable under this enactment to pay to the authority the expenses incurred by them in maintaining the child in the hospital ? One would have thought that it scarcely needed an appeal to the law to determine this question. Yet, in the recent case of *Hull Corporation* v. *Maclaren* (Queen's Bench Divisional Court, 20th May), the county court judge had given judgment against the father of a child who had been treated at a hospital belonging to the corporation for £6 7s. in respect of the child's maintenance. That judgment, however, has been reversed by the High Court. Mr. Justice Ridley said : I am of opinion that the decision of the learned county court judge cannot be upheld. It is clear from the note which the learned judge has supplied to us that he was under the impression that the liability for the maintenance of the child was cast on the father by the Public Health Act, 1875. But, from a perusal of sec. 132, on which the corporation relied, it is evident that such liability is cast on the "patient" only. The real question which should have been considered below was whether, apart from the statute, the parent had contracted, either expressly or by implication, to pay for the maintenance of his child in the hospital. But that question was not considered by the learned judge, nor are we entitled to consider it here, though I think it is clear that the parent did not agree to pay for the maintenance of the child. The real point was not considered : under the statute no such liability is cast on the parent. The appeal must succeed.

BY-LAW: VALIDITY: REASONABLENESS: RESTRICTION ON PERSONAL LIBERTY.—An important case in connection with the subject of by-laws is *Kruse v. Johnson* (Queen's Bench Divisional Court, 14th May), in which a specially-constituted court of seven judges pronounced the following by-law to be valid (Mr. Justice Mathew dissenting)—*viz.*: "No person shall sound any musical instrument within 50 yards of any dwelling-house after being required by any constable, or by an inmate of such house, or by his or her servant, to desist." The appellant, who had persisted in conducting an open-air religious service after having been required by a constable to desist, was convicted for playing the mandolin at an offence against the by-law. The appellant contended that the by-law was unreasonable and bad, because is made the mere fact of sounding an instrument an offence—without adding " to the annoyance of the public," or words to a similar effect. The Court, however, upheld the conviction on the somewhat novel ground that the by-laws of a public body cannot be other than reasonable, owing to the safeguards provided by statute law—*viz.*, the presence of two-thirds of the council to pass them, their exhibition for forty days at the town hall, and the postponement of their operation for forty days after the sending of a sealed copy to the Secretary of State—within which time the Queen, on the advice of the Privy Council, may disallow them. The dissenting judge thought, nevertheless, that it was the duty of the Court to disallow any by-law which seeks to impose a restriction on personal liberty (like the one in question), and there are undoubtedly precedents for this view (see, as instances, *Munro v. Watson*, 57 *L.T.* [N.S.], 366 ; *Strickland v. Hayes*, THE SURVEYOR, vol. ix., p. 217). From the point of view of local authorities the decision is a satisfactory one, establishing as it does more firmly than ever their *imperium in imperio* in matters regulated by by-laws. Whether it will be equally welcome to the general public is somewhat doubtful.

## QUERIES AND REPLIES.

COMBINED DRAIN: ALLEGED NUISANCE: LIABILITIES OF OWNER.—"H. M. F." writes : A row of labourers' houses are drained by a sewer which runs through the yards in the rear, and in each yard there is a gully trap and connection with this sewer. The houses all belong to the same owner, who has been served with a notice by the sanitary authority that a "nuisance exists by reason of defective drains, traps and connections," and requiring him "to provide proper drainage and ventilation to same, with suitable gully traps and disconnecting traps where necessary." The gully traps and connections were put down a few years since under the direction and supervision of the sanitary authority, and all appears to be working well, but it seems that the object of the sanitary authority is to try and force the owner to make a new "sewer" in the rear, as they call the present "sewer" a "drain," and allege that it is defective. They have not mentioned the word "sewer" in their notice, but they have verbally ordered the owner to open the present sewer for their inspection and testing. The owner has declined to do so, or to remake or repair the "sewer," but undertakes to do that part of it only which he states is a "drain"—*viz.*, from the commencement at the first house up to the point at which the drainage of the second house enters it—and he states that the remainder is a "sewer" to be repaired and maintained by the sanitary authorities from the above point onwards to its junction with the street sewer, which it joins by passing under a passage across the end of the row out to the street. The owner has also consented to make good any defective gully traps and connections with the "sewer" from the yards. The sanitary authorities are not satisfied with the proposals of the owner, and are proceeding against him by way of alleging "a nuisance by defective drains, traps and connections." (1) Is the owner bound to do anything more than he has consented to do, as above stated ? (2) Is he bound to open any part of the "sewer" for inspection and testing ? (3) In case of opening, repairing or remaking the "sewer," who would be responsible for restoring the yards and premises disturbed in the work ? (4) If the owner is summoned for "the existence of a nuisance," and an order made against him (so as to endeavour in this way to force him to reconstruct the "sewer"), what course should he adopt supposing he is right in his contention ?

(1) and (2) In my opinion he is not bound either to repair or to open any portion of the combined drain beyond the point where it becomes a "sewer." (3) The combined drain being (from the point where the drainage of the second house enters it) a "sewer" vested in the local authority, it is for them (not the owner) to open and repair it from that point. Any damage occasioned would be a matter for compensation under sec. 308 of the Public Health Act, 1875 ; or, in the event of damage arising by reason of the work being negligently done, an action would lie against the authority (*Brine v. Great Western Railway Company*, 31 *L.J.*, Q.B. 101). (4) He should oppose the summons before the magistrate on the ground that the "sewer" is repairable by the authority, and in the event of the decision going against him should apply to the magistrate to state a case for the opinion of the High Court. If the magistrate refuses, application should be made to the High Court for a *mandamus*.

BUILDING OPERATIONS: RESTORATION OF FOOTPATH.— "Municipal Surveyor" writes: I shall be obliged if you will allow your legal editor to give his opinion upon the following case : A builder applied for permission to erect a hoarding and occupy part of the footpath in a dedicated street in connection with repairs to a building, expressly stating that the footpath would not be interfered with. An undertaking was signed by the builder that if the paving was interfered with he would reinstate it to the satisfaction of the local authority and maintain it for twelve months, or, in default, authorising the local authority to do the work at his expense. A fee of 10s. was paid for the permit, this being returnable when the hoarding was removed, provided no damage had been done to the paving. When the return of the fee was applied for the path was examined, and it was found the flagging round a gantry door had been taken up, the gantry removed and a larger one fixed in a new position 2 ft. from the old, this being done without any notice or permission whatever. The builder gave the authority an order to reinstate the flagging round the new gantry frame, but they were not satisfied with this, and desired to proceed against the responsible party for enlarging and altering the position of the gantry without their consent. It is, however, stated that proceedings cannot be taken against either the owner, his architect, the contractor for the alterations or the sub-contractor who undertook the work connected with the gantry, but only against the man who actually did the work, as the offence is against the criminal law. The name of this man is certainly known, but the only evidence is that of his master, the sub-contractor, who told him to do the work and knows it was done, but did not actually see the man do it. An opinion is desired as to whether the corporation have any remedy against any person in this rather important case, and as to whether they would be justified in regarding the altered gantry as a new one, filling it up and flagging over it, and whether they could recover the expense of so doing from any of the parties.

There would, no doubt, be considerable difficulty in proving the criminal offence. The authority could, however, proceed against the builder for specific performance of his undertaking.

## THE TELEPHONE SERVICE.

At Tuesday's meeting of the Select Committee of the House of Commons dealing with this subject Mr. Hanbury again presided.

Mr. W. A. PREECE resumed his evidence and supplied statistics comparing the extent of the telephone service in Glasgow, Cologne, Liverpool and Hamburg. He found that Glasgow, with a population of 656,000, had 7,612 telephone instruments ; Cologne, with a population of 292,887, had 4,113 instruments ; Liverpool, with a population of 860,000, had 10,935 instruments ; and Hamburg, with a population of 573,792, had 13,561 instruments. As to London and Berlin, the population of London within the municipal area was 4,200,000, and there were 25,724 instruments, while in Berlin, with a population of 1,578,794, there were 36,620 instruments. In the course of further evidence he said that, however cheaply a municipality could establish a telephone system, the Post Office could always establish a cheaper one. The Post Office already had the powers, they had a monopoly, they had the buildings, the administration, the organisation and the experience, and they had a technical staff of the very highest skill and better fitted for looking after a telephone system than any staff in the world. The desire to hand over the telephone service to the municipalities was based on three assumptions. First, that the Post Office could not do the work properly and cheaply ; secondly, that the telephone company did not do the work properly ; and, thirdly, that the municipalities could do the work better and cheaply. All those three assumptions were wrong.

## CORRESPONDENCE.

**Lead-Lined Iron Pipes.**—Mr. Edwin C. Hiscox, secretary of the Sanitary Lead-lining and Pipe-bending Company, Limited, 55 Chancery-lane, writes : Referring to queries 193 and 198 in your issues of June 24th and July 1st, I beg to inform you that the whole of Messrs. Brighton & Jennings' interests in the lead-lined iron pipes and other patents have been acquired by this company, who have put down a very extensive plant at their works as above, and will, within the next fortnight, be prepared to execute orders, several being in hand already. With reference to your remark that you think the lead-lined pipes would have a very limited use, the members of this company have every reason to believe otherwise, as, in addition to the fact that the lead-lined pipes and patent joints are admittedly superior to any at present in use, work can be carried out with them at a cost of about 10 per cent. less than it would be if lead only was used.

**Municipal Opera Houses.**—In connection with the recent petition to the London County Council in favour of a municipal opera house, a deputation of musicians waited, on Monday, upon the General Purposes Committee of the council. Sir Alexander Mackenzie, principal of the Royal Academy of Music, who acted as spokesman, delivered an interesting address, in which he strongly advocated the scheme of an opera house partly owned by the municipality as an incentive to native talent and as a means of bringing the refining influence of operatic music within the reach of the masses.

# Municipal Work in Progress and Projected.

Considerable activity prevails among municipal authorities, both in the metropolis and in the provinces. The most important works mooted this week will be found under the paragraphs relating to Battersea, Bolton, Burnley, Leicester, Maldon, North Berwick and Warrington.

## METROPOLITAN AUTHORITIES.
### LONDON COUNTY COUNCIL.

The most notable feature of Tuesday's meeting of the council was the decision come to with respect to the purchase of the tramways. The matter has been under consideration for some time, and, on Tuesday, after some discussion, the council decided to buy up the undertaking and work it themselves. Mr. Benn, chairman of the Highways Committee, stated that the nett profit of the company was £85,000, and he believed that the council could work the lines as well as the company. The council also decided to insert a clause in one of their Bills to be promoted in the next session of Parliament for the purchase of the freehold and leasehold interests in Spitalfields market.

*Loans for Local Works.*—Upon the recommendation of the Finance Committee, it was agreed to lend the Hammersmith Vestry £15,500 for electric lighting purposes; the Islington Vestry £16,700 for similar purposes and £2,200 for street improvements; the Poplar District Board of Works £9,200 for paving works; the Stoke Newington Vestry £3,000 for wood paving; and the St. Pancras Vestry £21,590 for the purchase of a site for baths and the erection of conveniences.

*The Purchase of the Tramways.*—The Highways Committee presented a report recommending that the offer of the London Tramways Company to take a lease of their undertakings after they had been purchased by the council should not be entertained. The committee proposed at a later date to present a report with regard to the arrangements to be made for the efficient working of the lines after they had come into the possession of the council. The date named for the transfer was December 31st, and in the meantime the committee reported that they were negotiating the terms of the purchase. They recommended the council to authorise them to continue on the lines indicated in the report. Mr. Benn, chairman of the committee, in moving the adoption of the report said the company had expressed their willingness to pay £40,000 a year as rent for the lines if the council would agree to the present hours of labour being retained. For the buildings a rental of £17,000 was offered, and it was computed that the nett profit to the council for leasing would be £35,000 a year. He found that the nett profit of the company was £85,000 a year, which with £10,000 a year for incidental expenses, which were incurred by the company and would not be by the council, made £95,000. They had to assume that the council could work as well as the company, and that would mean that the working showed a gain of £60,000 over leasing. Some discussion followed, in the course of which Mr. B. L. Cohen, M.P., moved as an amendment to the proposal " that the committee should be authorised to negotiate for purchase, so that the council would become possessed of the whole of the lines on the last day of the present year; that the negotiations should be suspended; and that the Finance Committee should be, in the meantime, instructed to report on the financial part of the question." The amendment was, however, rejected and the report and recommendation finally approved.

*Light Railways Virtually Tramways.*—The Parliamentary Committee recommended that they should be authorised to take the necessary steps for supporting the objections to the London, Barnet, Edgware and Enfield Light Railways order, the committee contending that the so-called " light railway " was virtually a tramway, and that therefore it was necessary in the interests of the ratepayers that the provisions of the Tramways Act should apply. This was agreed to.

*Electric Lighting on the Embankment.*—Lord Russell asked whether tenders had been invited for the electric lighting of the Embankment; and if not, whether the chairman of the committee could hold out any hope of the work being undertaken at an early date. Mr. Benn said that tenders had not yet been invited, but he would call the attention of the Highways Committee to the matter.

*Proposed Purchase of Spitalfields Market.*—The Public Control Committee again submitted their report recommending the council to suspend the standing order which refuses to allow legislative proposals to be considered after the first meeting in June, the object being to enable a clause to be inserted in a Bill providing for the purchase of the leasehold and freehold interests in Spitalfields market. The recommendation of the committee was carried without opposition. The council then adopted another recommendation of the committee, to the effect that the Parliamentary committee be instructed to include in one of the Bills to be promoted by the council in the next session of Parliament a clause empowering the council to acquire by agreement or compulsorily the freehold and other interests in Spitalfields market.

*Proposed Clerkenwell Improvement.*—The Improvements Committee asked the council to approve their action in instructing the Clerkenwell Vestry, at the cost of the coun-cil, to set back the " Horse and Groom " public-house in St. John-street, on the understanding that the work was undertaken without prejudice as to whether the contemplated widening of St. John-street should be considered a metropolitan or a local improvement. Mr. Shaw-Lefevre asked to be allowed to withdraw the report, stating that a complicated legal question had arisen, and the council might perhaps be called upon by the proprietors of the house to buy the whole property. Colonel and Sheriff-Elect Probyn opposed, and moved that it should be referred back until after the committee had met the deputation from Clerkenwell Vestry. The recommendation of the committee was, however, rejected.

### COURT OF COMMON COUNCIL.

A meeting of the corporation was held, on Thursday, the lord mayor presiding. The town clerk read a petition soliciting the assistance of the lord mayor and corporation in the purchase as an open space of the estate at Hampstead formerly belonging to the late Sir Spencer Wells. It was believed that, if the assistance of the City could be invoked, the balance required towards the purchase money of £38,500 would soon be made up. The communication was referred to the Coal, Corn and Finance Committee for consideration.—The following resolution was approved : " That it be referred to the Central Markets Committee to consider and report to this court as to the practicability and advisability of so covering over, partially or otherwise, the northern end of the circular road way to the Great Western goods station as to increase the existing accommodation for vehicles without interfering with the present accommodation for railway access to the underground."—The town clerk laid before the court a letter which had been received by the lord mayor from the burgomaster of Cologne, who recently headed a deputation of German burgomasters to this country on a tour of inspection of our methods of dealing with street refuse. The burgomaster, who was entertained at luncheon at the Mansion House during the sojourn in London, thanked the lord mayor for the " complaisance " and readiness which the corporation had shown in facilitating their investigations. —It was decided to adopt a report from the Central Markets Committee recommending that the old fish market in Farringdon-street should be adapted for the purposes of the colonial and other meat trade, at an estimated cost of from £8,000 to £8,500.—Authority was given the Bridge House Estates Committee to carry out an improvement of Queen Elizabeth-street, at the southern approach to the Tower bridge, by giving up a portion of the vacant land to the St. Olave's District Board for widening the street and constructing a public convenience. The corporation would undertake the necessary repaving of the street and the maintenance of the southern approach to the bridge to the end of the parapet walls by the anchorage chains of the bridge. The court gave the necessary authority.—The court authorised the same committee to purchase the freehold of a block of premises at the rear of 25 and 26 Wood-street, belonging to the trustees of the Oxford University Chest, for £21,000.—Authority was given for the spending of £2,500 on the new entrance to the Guildhall in Basinghall-street.— The Port Sanitary Committee submitted a copy of an order issued by the Local Government Board assigning certain powers to the Port of London Sanitary Authority in respect of the docks and wharves in the port. The committee recommended that it should be referred to the committee to carry the order into execution. Authority was given.

### VESTRIES AND DISTRICT BOARDS.

**Battersea.**—At the vestry meeting, on Wednesday evening, the Finance Committee reported that the County of London and Brush Provincial Electric Lighting Company had given notice of appeal against the decision of Mr. Justice Jeune in the action of the vestry against the company for an injunction to restrain the latter from using pipes laid in Trinity-road without the permission of the vestry and for the removal of the pipes. It may be remembered that the injunction was granted, but was suspended for three months, with liberty to apply for a further suspension if required, to enable the company to make arrangements for carrying the wires in some other way than under the road. On the recommendation of the committe the vestry decided that in the event of no application being made to the Court for an extension of the suspension the solicitor should be instructed to take steps to oppose the application. It was resolved to apply to the Local Government Board for permission to borrow £5,300 for the sinking of two artesian wells at the baths, Latchmere-road, for which the tender of Messrs. Isler & Co., was recently accepted. On the proposal of the Baths Committee the vestry resolved to purchase land having a frontage in Battersea Park-road for the purpose of enlarging the public laundry and extending the public baths.—Mr. W. Lethbridge, on behalf of the Special Committee on Municipal Dwellings, moved that the county council should be asked to insert a clause in their General Powers Bill to authorise vestries and district boards to erect dwellings for the working classes under Part III. of the Housing of the Working

Classes Act. This was agreed to.—The Lighting Committee recommended the approval of provisional contracts for the acquisition of additional land for the erection of the proposed electric lighting station in accordance with the suggestions made by Prof. Kennedy and Mr. Samuel Peach. The recommendation was adopted. At the suggestion of the same committee the vestry decided to oppose notice given by the County of London and Brush Provincial Electric Lighting Company of intention to apply to the Board of Trade for an electric lighting provisional order. The Lighting Committee reported having had under consideration Bills promoted by companies in the present sessions of Parliament for the supply of electrical energy in bulk over large areas in parts of which provisional orders have already been granted to local authorities. The Bills also provide for the compulsory acquisition of land for the purpose of generating stations and the usual powers of a provisional order under the Electric Lighting Acts. The committee were of opinion that action should be taken by local authorities in opposition to the Bills. On the recommendation of the committee it was resolved (a) that communications be addressed to the borough members, urging them to strongly oppose the Bill of the General Power Distributing Company when before the House of Commons, and similar Bills, and, endeavour to secure the co-operation of other members of Parliament ; and (b) that a communication be addressed to the metropolitan vestries and district boards requesting them to ask their local members to oppose the Bills.

**Camberwell.**—At the vestry meeting on Wednesday the Plant and Scavenging Committee submitted a report by Mr. C. W. Tagg, clerk to the vestry, embodying a new scheme for the collection of house refuse in the parish. The proposal led to considerable discussion, and it was eventually decided not to receive the report, on the ground that it was the duty of Mr. W. Oxtoby, the recently-appointed surveyor, to devise a scheme for effectually dealing with the problem of collecting and disposing of the house refuse of the parish.—On the recommendation of the Finance Committee the vestry resolved to support the Metropolis Management Acts Amendment (By-Laws) Bill introduced by Lord Monkswell. The object of the Bill is to authorise the London County Council to make by-laws, under sec. 202 of the Metropolis Management Act, 1855, for the following purpose : " Requiring persons about to construct, reconstruct or alter drains in connection with buildings, to deposit with the sanitary authority of the district such plans, sections and particulars as may be necessary for the purpose of ascertaining whether such construction, or reconstruction or alteration, is in accordance with the statutory provisions relative thereto and with any by-laws made under the said section except as to alteration of drains in case of emergency."— The General Purposes Committee announced the receipt of notice from the Crystal Palace Electric Supply Company of intention to open Crystal Palace-parade for the purpose of laying electric light mains.—On the motion of Messrs. Ayers and Scott-Scott it was resolved to rescind a resolution, previously passed, for paving with granite pitching Hill-street and Peckham Park-road and to substitute wood-paving in place thereof, at a cost of £11,800. It was referred to the Finance Committee to make arrangements for obtaining a loan to that extent for the purpose of carrying out the work.—A letter was received from the Vestry of Battersea stating that it had been decided to take action with a view to the water supply being vested in the people of London, and asking for the views of the vestry on the subject.—The General Purposes Committee reported having had under consideration a reference from the vestry as to the schedule of wages and hours of labour attached to the forms of tender issued by the vestry, and had given instructions to the officers that this schedule of wages and hours of labour was to be revised from time to time, as might be rendered necessary, by any mutual agreement between employers and workmen. The committee, however, decided to take the paragraph back.

**Hampstead.**—On Thursday a tender was received from Messrs. Yerbury & Son for the construction of boiler and engine beds and for other works at the electric lighting station for £1,641. This, the only tender received, was referred to the Lighting Committee.

**Lambeth.**—On Thursday, a letter was received from the London County Council asking if the vestry were prepared to assist in defraying the cost of widening Camberwell New-road between Warner-road and Denmark-hill. Camberwell Vestry had offered to contribute £5,000. The General Purposes Committee, who had considered the matter, reported that, having regard to the fact that the vestry had already contributed one-half of the cost of Coldharbour-lane, they were of opinion that Lambeth should not again contribute towards the cost of another widening in the same portion of the parish boundary. The vestry concurred in the recommendation, declining to contribute to the scheme.—Messrs. A. & F. Manuelle had written to the General Purposes Committee announcing the completion of the vestry's orders for the supply of York stone, and asking whether they should continue to prepare stone in anticipation of the vestry's future requirements. In the opinion of the committee it was desirable that a certain quantity should be kept in stock, and on their recommendation the vestry decided to place an order

with Messrs. Manuelle for the supply of 20,000 ft. of stone, to be delivered as soon as ready.—The Wharf Committee reported that the Thames Conservancy were unable to consent to either of the amended embankment schemes submitted by the committee, and they had appointed a sub-committee to wait upon the commissioners in regard to the matter.—The County of London and Brush and Provincial Electric Lighting Company notified their intention to apply for an electric lighting provisional order to supply electricity in that part of Lambeth which lies to the north of Westminster Bridge-road. A second notice was given by the same company, stating that they intended to apply for powers to take their mains through Lambeth so as to connect the detached portion of Wandsworth with the main portion.—The following quotations as per van were received by the Wharf and Cleansing Committee for the supply of twelve new slop vans: Bristol Waggon Company, £39 ; Mr. Austin Rendell, Little Duke-street, S.E., £40 ; and Messrs. Glover & Sons, Eagle Works, Warwick, £42. The offer of the first-mentioned company was accepted.

**Limehouse.**—The Metropolitan Electric Supply Company intend to apply to the Board of Trade for an electric lighting provisional order.

**Newington.**—The following resolution has been adopted by the vestry : " That the tender of Messrs. Babcock & Wilcox, Limited, for the construction, supply and erection of boilers, pumps, steam and water mains, water tank, surface condenser, fuel economiser, ironwork, mechanical stokers, conveyer and elevator, for the sum of £9,348, be accepted, and the seal of the vestry affixed to the contract."

**Paddington.**—Last week the Works Committee reported that they, in conjunction with the surveyor, had further considered the subject of street cleansing, and, whilst admitting that the work in the parish is not perfect, they were, nevertheless, not prepared to recommend the vestry to make any material change in the system and method in force in carrying out such work. They had, however, instructed the surveyor to exercise the greatest diligence in the control of the sweepers and others, and to do everything in his power to cause the various thoroughfares in the parish to be maintained in a cleanly and decent condition.

**Strand.**—At a meeting of the board of works, held last week, attention was drawn to the nuisance caused on windy days by the vast quantities of loose paper constantly scattered about the streets, and it was suggested that some effort should be made to have this refuse collected and placed in receptacles, which might be cleared at stated periods. The matter was referred to committee.

**St. James, Westminster.**—The vestry last week considered letters from telephone subscribers calling attention to the inconvenience caused them owing to having been deprived of the use of the telephone in consequence of the Heddon-street fire, and stating that the company had informed them such disturbance could not possibly have arisen if the vestry would consent to the wires being placed underground, and asking the vestry to consider the subject favourably. As the attitude of the vestry in regard to the question has been either misunderstood or misrepresented, it was unanimously resolved to issue a pamphlet to the Press and the public setting forth clearly the exact position of affairs.—Mr. Watson, chairman of the Baths Committee, mentioned that it was intended to effect a great improvement at the baths. It was proposed, he said, either to remodel the existing buildings or to construct new baths that would be a credit to the parish.—Mr. T. Hensman Munsey, vestry clerk, read a letter from the county council stating in regard to the prevailing smoke nuisance, of which specified instances were cited, that if the vestry did not take effective measures to abate the evil the council would consider the question of taking proceedings in the matter, the expenses of which would have to be borne by the vestry. After discussion the letter was referred to the Health Committee with power to act.

**St. Marylebone.**—The vestry recently resolved to take no action in regard to the numerous applications received in response to advertisements for positions in the surveyor's department, leaving to the Works Committee, in conjunction with Mr. Waddington, the recently-appointed surveyor, the question of elaborating a further and improved scheme for dealing effectively with the requirements of the parish. As a result the vestry, last week, adopted a proposal to appoint a superintendent of cleansing, at a salary of £180 per annum rising to £230 ; a superintendent of sewers and drains, at £150 advancing to £200 ; and three district superintendents, at £150 each rising to £200 per annum. These positions, which will be advertised for, will be probationary for twelve months.—Mr. W. H. Garbutt, vestry clerk, read a petition drawing attention to the condition of the macadam roadway between Castle-street and Goodge-street, and asking for the substitution of wood paving. It was decided to inform the memorialists that the question would receive consideration later in the year when other streets were brought forward for discussion on the same subject.—On the motion of Dr. Snape it was resolved to adopt the report of the Sanitary and Sewers Committee recommending the construction of an underground convenience for both sexes in East-street, Marylebone-road, the cost being estimated at £2,000.—The secretary to the

Marylebone Cricket Club wrote asking what proportion of the cost the vestry would be prepared to contribute towards the urinal proposed to be erected on the new plot of ground adjoining Lord's cricket ground. The letter was referred to the Sanitary Committee.—It was resolved, on the recommendation of the Sanitary Committee, to inform Messrs. Bastin & Merryfield that the public urinal in Market-place would shortly be removed and replaced by a modern structure.

**Whitechapel.**—Letters have been received by the board from two electric lighting companies announcing their intention of applying for provisional orders to enable them to supply the district with electrical energy.

## MUNICIPAL CORPORATIONS.

**Bolton.**—The council have received Local Government Board sanction to the borrowing of £100,000 for gasworks purposes.

**Brighton.**—A meeting of the council was held, on Thursday, when the final arrangements were made in connection with the holding of an arbitration to assess the compensation to be paid in respect of certain lands required for the purposes of waterworks.

**Burnley.**—It is proposed to apply to the Local Government Board for sanction to borrow £10,000 for extensions of the electric supply undertaking.

**Bury.**—At a meeting of the town council, on Thursday, a sub-committee recommended the erection of public abattoirs, at a cost of £13,740, and that application be made to the Local Government Board for sanction to borrow the money. A long discussion ensued. The present slaughter-houses in Bury were stated to be in good sanitary condition, and the report was referred back for further consideration, the recommendation to be submitted to the council again in two months.

**Colchester.**—Colonel C. H. Luard, R.E., one of the Local Government Board inspectors, held an inquiry, on Tuesday of last week, as to the application of the Colchester Corporation for sanction to a loan of £500 for the improvement and widening of Maiden-road at its junction with Crouch-street. The borough surveyor, Mr. H. Goodyear, produced the plans and explained them.

**Croydon.**—The Local Government Board have refused to sanction a loan to cover the £1,000 payable under agreement to the British Thomson-Houston Company upon the taking over of the electric supply station by the corporation.

**Gateshead.**—It was last week reported that the Local Government Board had written to say they were glad to find that the questions, both of providing an efficient apparatus for disinfection and providing further suitable hospital accommodation, were under the consideration of the council. They requested to be informed of the decisions come to.

**Gloucester.**—A motion suggesting the appointment of a committee to consider the question of municipalising the tramways was brought up recently, but lost.

**Leamington.**—The tender of Mr. R. Bowen, of Leamington, at £897, has been accepted for the erection of a new engine-house at the Lillington pumping station.

**Leicester.**—An inquiry was conducted on Tuesday of last week, by Major-General H. Darley Crozier, R.E., into an application of the corporation for sanction to borrow £2,770 for the purchase of certain property for the purposes of public walks and pleasure grounds, and £26,077 to enable them to convert a portion of land, known as the Gilroes estate, into a cemetery.

**Longton.**—A deputation, appointed to inspect the coal filtration process now in use at the Wolverhampton sewage works, last week, reported that the filter effluent was clear and bright and apparently perfectly satisfactory, and the result, from a chemical point of view, was also most satisfactory. The analysis indicated 80 per cent. of purification upon the tank effluent. The approximate estimate of Mr. Garfield, the inventor of the process, of a coal filter to deal with 1,000,000 gallons of tank effluent per day was: Excavation, £630; coal, drains, carriers and valves, £2,200; and a royalty at 1s. per cubic yard, £417; total £3,247. It would probably be necessary to have brick walls for a permanent filter, and in that case this estimate would be very considerably increased. The Sewage Committee, having considered this report, recommended that the consideration of the adoption of any further system than that already decided upon be deferred until after the issue of the report of the Royal Commission on Sewage Disposal. This recommendation was confirmed.

**Ludlow.**—On Thursday, it was moved that application be made to the Board of Trade for a provisional order, under the Electric Lighting Acts of 1882 and 1888, to authorise the corporation to supply electricity for public and private purposes within the borough, and that the town clerk be authorised to instruct Parliamentary agents to take the necessary steps. It was stated that the council had endeavoured to obtain better terms from the gas company for the public lighting of the borough, but they still had to pay the same amount as individual consumers. The company had refused to sell the undertaking to the corporation. A letter was received from the Birmingham Installation Company saying they would be pleased to lease powers from the corporation for a period of seven years, or to themselves apply for the order and carry out the work, making an agreement to sell the undertaking to the council as a going concern in a certain time. The motion was unanimously agreed to.

**Newcastle.**—At last week's meeting of the town council, a member moved the adoption of the report of a special committee appointed to consider the desirability of the corporation undertaking the provision of electricity, recommending that the committee be authorised to negotiate as to terms upon which the electric lighting companies would transfer their undertakings to the corporation. In one case twenty-four years, and in the other case twenty-five years, had to elapse before the corporation could exercise their power of buying up the two companies compulsorily. If the companies were not agreeable the committee would have another scheme very shortly to put before the council. The adoption of the report would commit the council to nothing.

**North Berwick.**—At a recent meeting of this body a report on electric lighting for the town was submitted from Messrs. Burstall & Monkhouse, Westminster. The report showed the inadvisability of placing the electric light station at the present gasworks, and dealt with the extra capital and annual cost involved in putting it down at the site proposed for the new gasworks, and the minimum number of lamps required to make the scheme self-supporting. The system proposed was the low-tension current one. The capital cost for an installation of the size required was estimated at £7,600. It was agreed to have an early special meeting of the board to deal with the matter.

**Plymouth.**—The Finance Committee have held a special meeting to receive plans prepared by the city engineer for the new temporary council chamber, which the council had decided should be erected at a cost not exceeding £2,500. The plans, which embodied alterations suggested by the committee at a previous meeting, were approved, and instructions were given to proceed with the work.

## URBAN DISTRICT COUNCILS.

**Bedlington.**—At a recent conference between members of the council and the Tynemouth rural authorities it was decided to have a plan of a new stone bridge prepared, the structure at Bedlington being considered dangerous. A second plan, of an iron bridge to cost £2,700, will also be considered.

**Cowes, I.W.**—At last week's meeting of the council the following resolution of the Water Committee was approved : "That the committee having considered a report from the surveyor (Mr. John W. Webster) for improving the distribution of water and for providing a water tower, recommend the council to adopt the report and to apply to the Local Government Board to sanction a loan of £2,100 to carry out the work." The surveyor has also been instructed to prepare the necessary plans for a landing and pleasure pier on a site near the Prince's Green.

**East Ham.**—Central Park, the second public recreation ground which has been acquired by the council, was formally opened, on Tuesday of last week, by Mr. Thomas Leonan Knight, chairman, in the presence of several thousand local residents. The park comprises 25 acres, which have been purchased for £12,500.

**Enfield.**—A sub-committee appointed to consider the question of erecting public conveniences in Enfield Town on Thursday reported that they had had three schemes before them—one an underground one, costing £400; one for a convenience at the rear of the Market Cross, costing £80; and another, dealing with the north side of the Market-place costing £80.

## RURAL DISTRICT COUNCILS.

**Haltwhistle.**—The district council have engaged Mr. Harry W. Taylor, of St. Nicholas Chambers, Newcastle-on-Tyne, as their engineer for the preparation of a scheme of sewerage and sewage disposal for the west end of Haltwhistle.

**Hawarden.**—The council, at a meeting on Friday, received a report from a committee recommending the adoption of a scheme for dealing with the sewage of the district. The recommendation was adopted, and an engineer is to be called in to formulate a scheme. A communication was read from the inhabitants of Penyffordd calling attention to the need of a water supply for the village, and it was resolved that a deputation should wait on the Wrexham Waterworks Company in regard to the matter.

**Newport (Mon.)**—At a meeting last week a letter was read from the Local Government Board asking what was being done about the Edgmond drainage, and the clerk was instructed to reply that it would shortly be commenced, according to the surveyor's report.

# Personal.

Mr. W. Walden has been successful in obtaining the position of surveyor to the Christchurch Rural District Council.

Mr. G. E. Vint, of Sheffield, has been appointed surveyor and waterworks engineer to the Holmfirth Urban District Council.

Mr. Macdonald, resident waterworks engineer to the Newport Borough Council, has had his salary increased to £300 per annum.

At the last monthly meeting of the Aston Manor Urban District Council thé salary of Mr. G. H. Jack, assistant surveyor, was raised to £120 per annum.

By a large majority Wolverhampton Town Council, on Monday, decided to increase the salary of Mr. Woodward, the water engineer, from £350 to £450 per annum.

We have much pleasure in stating that Mr. T. B. Farrington, the borough surveyor of Conway, who has lately suffered from a severe illness, is now rapidly recovering.

Mr. W. S. Shell, of Consett, has been selected by the local authority to fill the post of surveyor, in succession to Mr. William Rippon, resigned. There were over 100 applicants.

Mr. Frederic Thomas Elliott, of Birkenshaw, near Leeds, has been appointed surveyor, waterworks manager and inspector of nuisances to the Eccleshill Urban District Council.

A marriage took place recently, at the parish church of Edenfield, between Miss Emily Chattwood, of Edenfield, and Mr. Edwin Percy Richards, son of Mr. E. Melville Richards, borough engineer and surveyor of Warwick.

☛ Mr. F. C. Keene, building inspector to the Bournemouth Corporation, has had his salary increased to £160 per annum. An assistant is also to be advertised for, at a salary of £2 per week, to assist him in the work of his office.

Sixty applications were received for the position of borough surveyor of Bacup. The General Works Committee have reduced the candidates to the following six: Mr. Benson, Salford; Mr. Bradley, Hull; Mr. J. S. Green, Haslingden; Mr. W. Holt, Heywood; Mr. Vickers, Blackburn; and Mr. Wood, Wakefield.

On Thursday, at a meeting of the Ealing Urban District Council, it was reported that nearly thirty applications for the post of principal assistant in the office of the surveyor had been received. Three candidates had been selected, and of these, Mr. Lobley, of Aberdeen, was recommended for appointment. This recommendation, after a short discussion, was adopted.

At the last monthly meeting of the Wednesbury Town Council the mayor moved that the salary of Mr. Scott, the borough surveyor, should be increased from £275 to £300 per annum. He spoke of the efficient manner in which Mr. Scott had performed his duties, and remarked that since he received the appointment the work had increased tremendously. The resolution was eventually adopted.

Mr. J. E. Jackson has lately severed his connection with the Horwich Urban District Council, with whom he has served as surveyor for the past nine years. He received his training with Messrs. Settle & Farmer, architects and surveyors, Ulverston, and subsequently was in the service of the Ulverston Local Board and the Ormskirk Board of Health. He has carried out a number of large and important works, including main road improvements and the formation of new streets.

Mr. Arthur Rhodes, deputy-manager at the Gaythorn gasworks of the Manchester Corporation, was the recipient of a handsome case of cutlery last week, on the occasion of his marriage with Miss Edith Cox, daughter of Mr. William Cox, contractor, Moss Side. The presentation, says a contemporary, which was from the officials and workmen, was made by the manager, Mr. John Merrell, who spoke in eulogistic terms of Mr. Rhodes, and wished him joy and happiness. Mr. Rhodes suitably replied.

We hear with regret of the death of Mr. John Mallinson, surveyor to the Skipton Urban District Council, which took place somewhat suddenly on Sunday night, at his residence. Mr. Mallinson had been ailing for some months, but so late as Friday last he was present in the council chamber and gave evidence at a Local Government Board inquiry there. The immediate cause of death was the breaking of a blood vessel. Mr. Mallinson, who had occupied the post of town surveyor at Skipton for nearly six years, was in his fiftieth year. He leaves a widow and large family to mourn his loss.

The Housing of the Working Classes Committee of the London County Council, on Tuesday, presented a report intimating that they had selected the following firms to submit competitive designs for the erection of dwellings on a portion of certain land known as the Millbank estate: Messrs. F. Armett, T. G. Bushell, R. H. Collins, H. F. T. Cooper, C. E. Cronk, H. W. Dobb, Ellison & Son, Gibson & Russell, G. S. Hill, F. Hooper, Howgate, Leeds & Keith, Joseph, Son & Smithem, Newman & Jacques, Rowland Plumbe, W.

H. Seth-Smith, Spalding & Cross, Waring & Nicholson, and R. Williams.

The officials of the Derby Corporation, accompanied by the mayor and a number of councillors, paid a visit to Castleton recently. Reserved carriages were provided for the party, and excellent arrangements were made for their comfort and enjoyment. A well-served dinner was provided, and the postprandial proceedings were rendered interesting by the presentation to Mr. W. A. H. Clarry, late assistant surveyor, of a gold watch, the gift of his late fellow-officials. The present was made by his worship the mayor, who expressed the hope that Mr. Clarry would give the same satisfaction to Sutton Coldfield as he had at Derby. The recipient suitably responded.

Mr. William Thomas Hatch, who, as we briefly announced last week, has been appointed engineer to the Metropolitan Asylums Board, is thirty-six years of age, and was educated at Liverpool University and at Owens College, Manchester. From 1876 to 1881 he was pupil to the Mersey Dock estate, of which Mr. G. F. Lyster was engineer. From 1882 to 1833 he was a Whitworth scholar and pupil to Sir W. Armstrong, Whitworth & Co., Manchester. In 1883 he was appointed works manager to Messrs. Follows & Bate, Limited, Gorton, and four years later he was appointed to his present position —viz., general manager to the Empire Engineering Company, Manchester.

At a dinner given, last week, to Mr. R. Read, the city surveyor of Gloucester, and his staff and others by Mr. H. J. Weaver, Mr. Read, after a reference to the latter gentleman's valuable assistance in his capacity of assistant surveyor, concluded a very eloquent speech by wishing him an easy struggle in life, coupled with health, and great success in his new undertaking. Mr. Weaver, who, as we have already announced, has accepted the post of borough engineer and surveyor under the King's Lynn Corporation, expressed his regret at having to leave Mr. Read, for whom it had always been a great pleasure to work, and said he hoped that he (Mr. Read) would continue to enjoy good health and prosperity and be enabled to fill the position of city surveyor of Gloucester for many years to come.

The following members of the Society of Engineers were among those who, on Wednesday, visited the London, Brighton and South Coast Railway locomotive works, the Brighton marine palace and pier works, Volk's electric railway and Rottingdean seashore electric tramroad: Mr. W. Worby Beaumont, president; Mr. A. T. Walmisley, past-president; Messrs. J. C. Fell and Charles Mason, vice-presidents; Messrs. George Burt, D. B. Butler, Percy Griffith and R. St. George Moore, members of council; F. W. Barclay, S. O. Cowper-Coles, T. F. Craddock, John Jones, N. Harker, Fred. Hovenden, E. Hulburd, R. J. G. Read, J. Waddington, W. G. Wales and Weatherburn; and Mr. G. A. Pryce Cuzson, secretary. Illustrated descriptions of the works inspected were, except in the case of those of the railway, given in our report of the annual meeting, in July, 1896, of the Association of Municipal and County Engineers.

We recently announced the resignation by Mr. E. J. Silcock of his appointment as borough engineer of King's Lynn in order to enter upon private practice. He has now opened offices at 10 Park-row, Leeds, as well as at King's-street, King's Lynn, and is therefore prepared to place himself at the disposal of those who wish to avail themselves of his services. Mr. Silcock still retains his appointment of engineer to the Lynn Harbour Conservators and the Lynn Corporation have retained him for the completion of the water supply and sewerage schemes now in hand, and he has also been entrusted with the designing and carrying out of a number of other schemes. Mr. Silcock has had twenty years' experience in Leeds and elsewhere in all the varied work of a municipal engineer and surveyor, and this, coupled with the ability and energy he is known to possess, will no doubt stand him in good stead in his future work.

Some time ago the Cannock Rural District Council appointed Mr. H. M. Whitehead to the dual offices of surveyor and sanitary inspector, at a salary of £300 per annum, subject to the sanction of the Local Government Board. At a recent meeting the board expressed themselves opposed to the appointment of one man to the two offices, and asked for the reason of the increase of salary paid to the sanitary officer, and for other information. The clerk was instructed to reply to these queries, and, on Friday, a letter was read from the Local Government Board to the effect that before further considering the appointment they would like to know how far the officer would be able to do the work over such an area, having regard to his work as surveyor. It was agreed that it should be pointed out that Mr. Whitehead had to cover the ground in carrying out his duties of surveyor, and that the combination of the offices had worked efficiently for the last three months.

**Warrington.**—Local Government Board sanction has been received to a proposal to borrow £4,750 for the purchase of gas meters.

## APPOINTMENTS VACANT.

*Advertisements which are received too late for classification cannot be included in these summaries until the following week.*

CLERK OF WORKS.—July 16th.—Barnet Urban District Council.—Mr. H. W. Poole, clerk to the council.

WATERWORKS ENGINEER.—July 16th.—Lincoln Corporation. £250.—Mr. H. K. Helb, deputy town clerk.

INSPECTOR OF MAIN ROADS.—July 18th.—Glamorgan County Council. £85.—Mr. T. Mansel Franklin, county clerk, County Offices, Westgate-street, Cardiff.

HIGHWAY SURVEYOR, INSPECTOR OF NUISANCES, &c.—July 19th.—Newark Rural District Council. £155.—Mr. William Newton, clerk to the council.

ASSISTANT INSPECTOR OF NUISANCES AND BUILDING INSPECTOR.—July 20th.—Clacton Urban District Council. 50s.—Mr. A. R. Robinson, clerk to the council.

INSPECTOR OF NUISANCES.—July 21st.—Aberdare Urban District Council. £91.—Mr. Thomas Phillips, clerk to the council.

SURVEYOR, INSPECTOR OF NUISANCES, SANITARY INSPECTOR AND WATER INSPECTOR.—July 21st.—Ashburton Urban District Council. £100.—Mr. R. E. Tucker, clerk to the council.

JUNIOR ENGINEERING ASSISTANT.—July 22nd.—Hull Corporation. £60.—Mr. F. J. Bancroft, water and gas engineer, Town Hall, Hull.

BOROUGH ENGINEER.—July 22nd.—Corporation of Pietermaritzburg, Natal, South Africa. £800.—Messrs. Ford Brothers, 14 Southampton-street, Fitzroy-square, London, W.

CHIEF SURVEYOR.—July 22nd.—Vestry of St. George-the-Martyr, Southwark. £300.—Mr. J. A. Johnson, vestry clerk.

ASSISTANT BUILDING INSPECTER.—July 23rd.—Corporation of Bournemouth. £104.—Mr. F. W. Lacey, M.I.C.E., borough engineer and surveyor.

BOROUGH ENGINEER AND SURVEYOR'S ASSISTANT.—July 23rd.—Corporation of Warrington. £100.—Mr. Thomas Longdin, borough engineer and surveyor.

ASSISTANT SURVEYOR AND INSPECTOR OF NUISANCES.—July 26th.—Uxbridge Rural District Council. £75.—Mr. Charles Woodbridge, clerk to the council.

JUNIOR ASSISTANT SURVEYOR.—July 27th.—County Borough of Middlesbrough. £80.—Mr. Frank Baker, borough engineer.

BUILDING INSPECTOR.—July 27th.—County Borough of Middlesbrough.—Mr. Frank Baker, borough engineer.

CITY ENGINEER.—August 31st.—Corporation of Wellington, New Zealand. £800.—Agent-General for New Zealand, London.

ENGINEERING ASSISTANT.—City of Canterbury. £2.—Mr. A. H. Campbell, city surveyor.

DISTRICT SURVEYOR.—Corporation of Sheffield.—Mr. Chas. F. Wike, M.I.C.E., city surveyor.

## COMPETITIONS.

*Advertisements which are received too late for classification cannot be included in these summaries until the following week.*

EAST RIDING.—July 16th.—Extension of the county offices at Beverley and the erection of a new register office, for the county council. £30, £20 and £10.—Mr. John Bickersteth, county clerk, County Hall, Beverley.

## MUNICIPAL CONTRACTS OPEN.

*Advertisements which are received too late for classification cannot be included in these summaries until the following week.*

SWINTON.—July 15th.—Supply of 520 yards of cast-iron socket pipes of 6-in. diameter and other pipe castings, for the urban district council.—Mr. R. Fowler, engineer and surveyor to the council.

DARTFORD.—July 16th.—Making-up, &c., of Priory-lane, for the urban district council.—Mr. W. Harston, surveyor to the council.

WEST BRIDGFORD.—July 16th.—Laying of about 3,160 yards of 12-in. and 9-in. Hassall's pipe sewers, 12-in. iron pipe sewers and 9-in. surface-water drains, for the urban district council.—Mr. Wm. Pace, surveyor to the council.

MANCHESTER.—July 16th.—Construction and erection of a wrought-iron bridge for carrying 30-in. cast-iron pipes over the river Tame at Broomstair, Hyde and Denton, for the corporation.—Secretary, Waterworks Office, Town Hall, Manchester.

WOODFORD.—July 16th.—Supply of 1,400 tons to 3,000 tons of broken Quenast or Guernsey granite, for the urban district council.—Mr. John A. Simpson, clerk to the council.

NELSON.—July 18th.—Construction of two storage reservoirs in Ogden and Black Moss valleys about 4 miles from the town, for the corporation.—Messrs. Newton, 17 Cooper-street, Manchester.

SOUTH CROSLAND.—July 18th.—Construction of additional sewerage works, comprising the laying of over 1 mile of stoneware pipe sewers, varying in size from 6 in. to 9 in., for the urban district council.—Mr. W. B. Radford, Angel-row, Nottingham.

ILFORD.—July 18th.—Supply of a 15-ton combined compound steam road-roller, for the urban district council.—Mr. John W. Benton, clerk to the council.

HORLEY.—July 18th.—Construction of 3½ miles of stoneware pipe sewers varying in size from 15 in. to 7 in., for the urban district council.—Mr. W. B. Radford, Angel-row, Nottingham.

GREAT YARMOUTH.—July 19th.—Supply of one 150-kilowatt high-speed engine and alternator coupled direct and sundry additional steam and exhaust pipes.—Mr. A. H. Miller, town clerk.

LONDON.—July 19th.—Paving of the carriageway of John-street, Minories, with Australian hard wood.—The Engineer to the Corporation.

LONDON.—July 19th.—Construction of an underground convenience in Alderman's-walk.—The Engineer to the Corporation.

CROYDON.—July 19th.—Construction of 2,350 yards of 9-in., 12-in. and 15-in. pipe sewers in the neighbourhood of London-road, Norbury, and for the construction of a covered concrete storage tank, near Norbury Manor farm.—Mr. E. Mawdesley, town clerk.

CROYDON.—July 19th.—Diversion of a portion of Long-lane.—Mr. E. Mawdesley, town clerk.

PORTSMOUTH.—July 19th.—Supply and fixing of cast-iron valve seatings to the pumps at the Eastney pumping station.—Mr. Alexander Hellard, town clerk.

LONDON.—July 19th.—Construction of underground conveniences in Fenchurch-street.—Sir J. B. Monckton, town clerk.

TOTTENHAM.—July 19th.—Making-up of Pemberton-road, Foyle-road and Shaftesbury-street, for the urban district council.—Mr. P. E. Murphy, engineer to the council.

NEW MILLS.—July 19th.—Construction of various sewers, &c., in connection with Contract No. 3 of the sewerage scheme, for the urban district council.—Messrs. Spinks & Beever, 9 Albert-square, Manchester.

LEWISHAM.—July 19th.—Enlargement of the committee-room at the lodge in the Sydenham recreation ground, for the district board of works.—The Surveyor to the Board.

LONDON.—July 19th.—Various works in connection with the concreting and asphalting of the arches beneath the Lambeth approach to Waterloo bridge, for the county council.—The Engineer to the Council, County Hall, Spring-gardens, London, S.W.

BROMLEY.—July 19th.—Works of sewering, levelling, paving, metalling, channelling and making-good the Avenue, Bickley, for the urban district council.—Mr. Fred. R. Norman, clerk to the council.

LIVERPOOL.—July 19th.—Construction of an open-air bath in Mansfield-street.—The Town Clerk.

HARTLEPOOL.—July 20th.—Paving of the footpaths at the cemetery with tar macadam, the approximate area being about 3,700 square yards.—Mr. H. C. Crummack, A.M.I.C.E., borough engineer.

CHELTENHAM.—July 20th.—Supply of 150 tons of iron water pipes and general road and sewer castings.—Mr. E. T. Brydges, town clerk.

WORCESTER.—July 20th.—Various kerbing, channelling and paving works, for the county council.—Mr. J. H. Garrett, county road surveyor, Shire Hall, Worcester.

GLANGE-OVER-SANDS.—July 21st.—Erection of a new public hall and district council offices, for the urban district council.—Mr. John Hutton, architect, Kendal.

LONDON.—July 21st.—Construction of a road and paths at the North-Western fever hospital, Haverstock-hill, N.W., for the Metropolitan Asylums Board.—Mr. T. Duncombe Mann, clerk to the board, Norfolk House, Norfolk-street, Strand, W.C.

SUTTON COLDFIELD.—July 21st.—Construction of 1,170 yards of 9-in. earthenware pipe sewer at Reddicap Hill.—Mr. W. A. H. Clarry, borough engineer and surveyor.

BURSLEM.—July 22nd.—Supply of 5,000 ft. of 6-in. granite edge kerb, 250 tons of granite pitchers, and 5,000 tons of granite spalls.—Mr. Francis J. C. May, A.M.I.C.E., borough engineer and surveyor.

SOUTH SHIELDS.—July 23rd.—Paving of 183 lineal yards of double line of steel-girder tramway.—Mr. S. S. Burgess, A.M.I.C.E., borough engineer.

MIDHURST.—July 23rd.—Supply of disinfectants, for the rural district council.—Mr. Edward Albery, clerk to the council.

COLNE.—July 23rd.—Erection of technical schools and a public library in Albert-road.—Mr. Alfred Varley, town clerk.

LEWES.—July 23rd.—Supply of 500 tons of 2-in. broken blue Guernsey, Cherbourg or Belgian granite, 100 tons of coarse granite screenings, 650 tons of broken surface-picked flints and 150 tons of Ridinghoe. gravel.—Mr. Montague S. Blaker, town clerk.

ISLINGTON.—July 25th.—Supply of eleven water-vans, four water-carts, forty-five sets of trunks and distributors for water-vans, thirty-five dust-vans and five sweeping machines.—Mr. J. Patten Barber, vestry surveyor.

CHELTENHAM.—July 25th.—Supply of stoneware pipes and cement for twelve months.—Mr. E. T. Brydges, town clerk.

NUNEATON.—July 25th.—Construction of filter-bed tanks and the laying and fixing of mains and other ironwork at the pumping station, Stockingford, for the urban district council.—Mr. J. S. Pickering, A.M.I.C.E., waterworks engineer.

GRESSEM.—July 26th.—Supply of six complete suits of firemen's uniform, for the urban district council.—Mr. S. Towlson, A.M.I.C.E., surveyor to the council.

EDMONTON.—July 26th.—Laying of about 1,850 ft. run of granite kerb in Park-road and Park-avenue, and 960 ft. run in Bury-street; about 365 yards super. of channelling and crossings in Park-road and Park-avenue; about 622 yards super. of asphalte in Park-road; about 704 yards super. of 2-in. indurated concrete slab paving in Park-avenue; and about 1,504 yards super. of 2-in. patent Victoria stone paving in Bury-street, for the urban district council.—Mr. G. Eades Bacon, M.I.C.E., surveyor to the council.

CRESSWELL.—July 26th.—Construction of about 1,200 ft. of 4 ft. diameter brick culvert, the laying of 2,500 ft. of granite kerb in Windmill-lane, and kerbing works in Park-lane and Eleanor-road, for the urban district council.—Mr. S. Towlson, A.M.I.C.E., surveyor to the council.

WILLESDEN.—July 26th.—Road-making and paving works in Pine-road, Cricklewood; Burrows-road, Kensal Rise; Harlesden-gardens, Harlesden; and West Ella-road, Harlesden, for the urban district council.—Mr. O. Claude Robson, M.I.C.E., engineer to the council.

HAYWARDS HEATH.—July 26th.—Supply of about 825 tons of granite, 6 tons of granite chippings and 30 tons of coarse gravel, for the urban district council.—Mr. Edward Waugh, clerk to the council.

BLYTH.—July 26th.—Sea defence works on the east foreshore, for the urban district council.—Mr. Arthur Rowlands, clerk to the council.

HULL.—July 26th.—Supply of cast-iron spigot and socket pipes and irregulars required during the year ending August 31, 1899.—Mr. F. J. Bancroft, gas and water engineer, Town Hall, Hull.

WEST HAM.—July 26th.—Construction of about 1,200 lineal yards of sewers, 7 ft., 6 ft. and 3 ft. 6 in. diameter.—Mr. Lewis Angell, borough surveyor.

WEST HAM.—July 26th.—Making-up of Freemantle-road, Hawkesmere-road, New-street (Plaistow) and Old-street (Plaistow).—Mr. Lewis Angell, borough surveyor.

BUCKLOW.—July 26th.—Construction of main sewers and outfall works for the townships of Hale, for the rural district council.—Mr. Geo. Leigh, clerk to the council.

WEST HAM.—July 26th.—Erection of twenty-nine working-classes' dwellings in Hermit-road, Plaistow.—Mr. Lewis Angell, borough surveyor.

WEST HAM.—July 26th.—Supply of ten slop-carts.—Mr. Lewis Angell, borough surveyor.

ABERDARE.—July 27th.—Supply and delivery of various cast-iron and steel work, including a light lattice girder footbridge of three spans (each 57 ft. in.), for the urban district council.—Mr. William Fox, M.I.C.E., engineer to the council, 5 Victoria-street, London, S.W.

# Personal.

Mr. W. Walden has been successful in obtaining the position of surveyor to the Christchurch Rural District Council.

Mr. G. E. Vint, of Sheffield, has been appointed surveyor and waterworks engineer to the Holmfirth Urban District Council.

Mr. Macdonald, resident waterworks engineer to the Newport Borough Council, has had his salary increased to £300 per annum.

At the last monthly meeting of the Aston Manor Urban District Council the salary of Mr. G. H. Jack, assistant surveyor, was raised to £120 per annum.

By a large majority Wolverhampton Town Council, on Monday, decided to increase the salary of Mr. Woodward, the water engineer, from £350 to £450 per annum.

We have much pleasure in stating that Mr. T. B. Farrington, the borough surveyor of Conway, who has lately suffered from a severe illness, is now rapidly recovering.

Mr. W. S. Shell, of Consett, has been selected by the local authority to fill the post of surveyor, in succession to Mr. William Rippon, resigned. There were over 100 applicants.

Mr. Frederic Thomas Elliott, of Birkenshaw, near Leeds, has been appointed surveyor, waterworks manager and inspector of nuisances to the Eccleshill Urban District Council.

A marriage took place recently, at the parish church of Edenfield, between Miss Emily Chattwood, of Edenfield, and Mr. Edwin Percy Richards, son of Mr. E. Melville Richards, borough engineer and surveyor of Warwick.

⚑ Mr. F. C. Keene, building inspector to the Bournemouth Corporation, has had his salary increased to £160 per annum. An assistant is also to be advertised for, at a salary of £2 per week, to assist him in the work of his office.

Sixty applications were received for the position of borough surveyor of Bacup. The General Works Committee have reduced the candidates to the following six : Mr. Benson, Salford ; Mr. Bradley, Hull ; Mr. J. S. Green, Haslingden ; Mr. W. Holt, Heywood ; Mr. Vickers, Blackburn ; and Mr. Wood, Wakefield.

On Thursday, at a meeting of the Ealing Urban District Council, it was reported that nearly thirty applications for the post of principal assistant in the office of the surveyor had been received. Three candidates had been selected, and of these, Mr. Lobley, of Aberdeen, was recommended for appointment. This recommendation, after a short discussion, was adopted.

At the last monthly meeting of the Wednesbury Town Council the mayor moved that the salary of Mr. Scott, the borough surveyor, should be increased from £275 to £300 per annum. He spoke of the efficient manner in which Mr. Scott had performed his duties, and remarked that since he received the appointment the work had increased tremendously. The resolution was eventually adopted.

Mr. J. E. Jackson has lately severed his connection with the Horwich Urban District Council, with whom he has served as surveyor for the past nine years. He received his training with Messrs. Settle & Farmer, architects and surveyors, Ulverston, and subsequently was in the service of the Ulverston Local Board and the Ormskirk Board of Health. He has carried out a number of large and important works, including main road improvements and the formation of new streets.

Mr. Arthur Rhodes, deputy-manager at the Gaythorn gasworks of the Manchester Corporation, was the recipient of a handsome case of cutlery last week, on the occasion of his marriage with Miss Edith Cox, daughter of Mr. William Cox, contractor, Moss Side. The presentation, says a contemporary, which was from the officials and workmen, was made by the manager, Mr. John Merrell, who spoke in eulogistic terms of Mr. Rhodes, and wished him joy and happiness. Mr. Rhodes suitably replied.

We hear with regret of the death of Mr. John Mallinson, surveyor to the Skipton Urban District Council, which took place somewhat suddenly on Sunday night, at his residence. Mr. Mallinson had been ailing for some months, but so late as Friday last he was present in the council chamber and gave evidence at a Local Government Board inquiry there. The immediate cause of death was the breaking of a blood vessel. Mr. Mallinson, who had occupied the post of town surveyor at Skipton for nearly six years, was in his fiftieth year. He leaves a widow and family to mourn his loss.

The Housing of the Working Classes Committee of the London County Council, on Tuesday, presented a report intimating that they had selected the following firms to submit competitive designs for the erection of dwellings on a portion of certain land known as the Millbank estate : Messrs. F. Arnett, T. G. Bushell, H. H. Collins, H. F. T. Cooper, C. E. Cronk, H. W. Dobb, Ellison & Son, Gibson & Russell, G. S. Hill, F. Hooper, Howgate, Leeds & Keith, Joseph, Son & Smithem, Newman & Jacques, Rowland Plumbe, W.

H. Seth-Smith, Spalding & Cross, Waring & Nicholson, and R. Williams.

The officials of the Derby Corporation, accompanied by the mayor and a number of councillors, paid a visit to Castleton recently. Reserved carriages were provided for the party, and excellent arrangements were made for their comfort and enjoyment. A well-served dinner was provided, and the postprandial proceedings were rendered interesting by the presentation to Mr. W. A. H. Clarry, late assistant surveyor, of a gold watch, the gift of his late fellow-officials. The present was made by his worship the mayor, who expressed the hope that Mr. Clarry would give the same satisfaction to Sutton Coldfield as he had at Derby. The recipient suitably responded.

Mr. William Thomas Hatch, who, as we briefly announced last week, has been appointed engineer to the Metropolitan Asylums Board, is thirty-six years of age, and was educated at Liverpool University and at Owens College, Manchester. From 1876 to 1881 he was pupil to the Mersey Dock estate, of which Mr. G. F. Lyster was engineer. From 1882 to 1883 he was a Whitworth scholar and pupil to Sir W. Armstrong, Whitworth & Co., Manchester. In 1883 he was appointed works manager to Messrs. Follows & Bate, Limited, Gorton, and four years later he was appointed to his present position —viz., general manager to the Empire Engineering Company, Manchester.

At a dinner given, last week, to Mr. R. Read, the city surveyor of Gloucester, and his staff and others by Mr. H. J. Weaver, Mr. Read, after a reference to the latter gentleman's valuable assistance in his capacity of assistant surveyor, concluded a very eloquent speech by wishing him an easy struggle in life, coupled with health, and great success in his new undertaking. Mr. Weaver, who, as we have already announced, has accepted the post of borough engineer and surveyor under the King's Lynn Corporation, expressed his regret at having to leave Mr. Read, for whom it had always been a great pleasure to work, and said he hoped that he (Mr. Read) would continue to enjoy good health and prosperity and be enabled to fill the position of city surveyor of Gloucester for many years to come.

The following members of the Society of Engineers were among those who, on Wednesday, visited the London, Brighton and South Coast Railway locomotive works, the Brighton marine palace and pier works, Volk's electric railway and Rottingdean seashore electric tramroad : Mr. W. Worby Beaumont, president ; Mr. A. T. Walmisley, past-president ; Messrs. J. C. Fell and Charles Mason, vice-presidents ; Messrs. George Burt, D. B. Butler, Percy Griffith and R. St. George Moore, members of council ; F. W. Barclay, S. O. Cowper-Coles, T. F. Craddock, John Jones, N. Harker, Fred. Hovenden, E. Hulburd, R. J. G. Read, J. Waddington, W. G. Wales and Weatherburn ; and Mr. G. A. Pryce Cuxson, secretary. Illustrated descriptions of the works inspected were, except in the case of those of the railway, given in our report of the annual meeting in July, 1896, of the Association of Municipal and County Engineers.

We recently announced the resignation by Mr. E. J. Silcock of his appointment as borough engineer of King's Lynn in order to enter upon private practice. He has now opened offices at 10 Park-row, Leeds, as well as at King's-street, King's Lynn, and is therefore prepared to place himself at the disposal of those who wish to avail themselves of his services. Mr. Silcock still retains his appointment of engineer to the Lynn Harbour Conservators and the Lynn Corporation have retained him for the completion of the water supply and sewerage schemes now in hand, and he has also been entrusted with the designing and carrying out of a number of other schemes. Mr. Silcock has had twenty years' experience in Leeds and elsewhere in all the varied work of a municipal engineer and surveyor, and this, coupled with the ability and energy he is known to possess, will no doubt stand him in good stead in his future work.

Some time ago the Cannock Rural District Council appointed Mr. H. M. Whitehead to the dual offices of surveyor and sanitary inspector, at a salary of £300 per annum, subject to the sanction of the Local Government Board. At a recent meeting the board expressed themselves opposed to the appointment of one man to the two offices, and asked for the reason of the increase of salary paid to the sanitary officer, and for other information. The clerk was instructed to reply to these queries, and, on Friday, a letter was read from the Local Government Board to the effect that before further considering the appointment they would like to know how far the officer would be able to do the work over such an area, having regard to his work as surveyor. It was agreed that it should be pointed out that Mr. Whitehead had to cover the ground in carrying out his duties of surveyor, and that the combination of the offices had worked efficiently for the last three months.

**Warrington.**—Local Government Board sanction has been received to a proposal to borrow £4,750 for the purchase of gas meters.

## APPOINTMENTS VACANT.

*Advertisements which are received too late for classification cannot be included in these summaries until the following week.*

CLERK OF WORKS.—July 16th.—Barnet Urban District Council.—Mr. H. W. Poole, clerk to the council.

WATERWORKS ENGINEER.—July 16th.—Lincoln Corporation. £250.—Mr. H. K. Helb, deputy town clerk.

INSPECTOR OF MAIN ROADS.—July 18th.—Glamorgan County Council. £85.—Mr. T. Mansel Franklin, county clerk, County Offices, Westgate-street, Cardiff.

HIGHWAY SURVEYOR, INSPECTOR OF NUISANCES, &c.—July 19th.—Newark Rural District Council. £155.—Mr. William Newton, clerk to the council.

ASSISTANT INSPECTOR OF NUISANCES AND BUILDING INSPECTOR.—July 20th.—Clacton Urban District Council. 50s.—Mr. A. R. Robinson, clerk to the council.

INSPECTOR OF NUISANCES.—July 21st.—Aberdare Urban District Council. £91.—Mr. Thomas Phillips, clerk to the council.

SURVEYOR, INSPECTOR OF NUISANCES, SANITARY INSPECTOR AND WATER INSPECTOR.—July 21st.—Ashburton Urban District Council. £100.—Mr. R. E. Tucker, clerk to the council.

JUNIOR ENGINEERING ASSISTANT.—July 22nd.—Hull Corporation. £80.—Mr. F. J. Bancroft, water and gas engineer, Town Hall, Hull.

BOROUGH ENGINEER. — July 22nd. — Corporation of Pietermaritzburg, Natal, South Africa. £800.—Messrs. Ford Brothers, 14 Southampton-street, Fitzroy-square, London, W.

CHIEF SURVEYOR.—July 22nd.—Vestry of St. George-the-Martyr, Southwark. £300.—Mr. J. A. Johnson, vestry clerk.

ASSISTANT BUILDINGS INSPECTOR.—July 23rd.—Corporation of Bournemouth. £104.—Mr. F. W. Lacey, M.I.C.E., borough engineer and surveyor.

BOROUGH ENGINEER AND SURVEYOR'S ASSISTANT.—July 23rd.—Corporation of Warrington. £100.—Mr. Thomas Longdin, borough engineer and surveyor.

ASSISTANT SURVEYOR AND INSPECTOR OF NUISANCES.—July 26th.—Uxbridge Rural District Council. £75.—Mr. Charles Woodbridge, clerk to the council.

JUNIOR ASSISTANT SURVEYOR.—July 27th.—County Borough of Middlesbrough. £80.—Mr. Frank Baker, borough engineer.

BUILDING INSPECTOR.—July 27th.—County Borough of Middlesbrough.—Mr. Frank Baker, borough engineer.

CITY ENGINEER.—August 31st.—Corporation of Wellington, New Zealand. £800.—Agent-General for New Zealand, London.

ENGINEERING ASSISTANT.—City of Canterbury. £2.—Mr. A. H. Campbell, city surveyor.

DISTRICT SURVEYOR.—Corporation of Sheffield.—Mr. Chas. F. Wike, M.I.C.E., city surveyor.

## COMPETITIONS.

*Advertisements which are received too late for classification cannot be included in these summaries until the following week.*

EAST RIDING.—July 16th.—Extension of the county offices at Beverley and the erection of a new register office, for the county council. £30, £20 and £10.—Mr. John Bickersteth, county clerk, County Hall, Beverley.

## MUNICIPAL CONTRACTS OPEN.

*Advertisements which are received too late for classification cannot be included in these summaries until the following week.*

SWINTON.—July 15th.—Supply of 520 yards of cast-iron socket pipes of 6-in. diameter and other pipe castings, for the urban district council.—Mr. R. Fowler, engineer and surveyor to the council.

DARTFORD.—July 15th.—Making-up, &c., of Priory-lane, for the urban district council.—Mr. W. Harston, surveyor to the council.

WEST BRIDGFORD.—July 16th.—Laying of about 2,460 yards of 12-in. and 9-in. Hassell's pipe sewers, 12-in. iron pipe sewers and 9-in. surface-water drains, for the urban district council.—Mr. Wm. Pare, surveyor to the council.

MANCHESTER.—July 16th.—Construction and erection of a wrought-iron bridge for carrying 30-in. cast-iron pipes over the river Tame at Broomstair, Hyde and Denton, for the corporation.—Secretary, Waterworks Office, Town Hall, Manchester.

WOODFORD.—July 16th.—Supply of 1,400 tons to 2,000 tons of broken Quenast or Guernsey granite, for the urban district council.—Mr. John A. Simpson, clerk to the council.

NELSON.—July 16th.—Construction of two storage reservoirs in Ogden and Black Moss valleys about 4 miles from the town, for the corporation.—Messrs. Newton, 17 Cooper-street, Manchester.

SOUTH CROSLAND.—July 18th.—Construction of additional sewerage works, comprising the laying of over 1 mile of stoneware pipe sewers, varying in size from 9 in. to 9 in., for the urban district council.—Mr. W. H. Radford, Angel-row, Nottingham.

LEEDS.—July 18th.—Supply of a 15-ton combined compound steam road-roller, for the urban district council.—Mr. John W. Benton, clerk to the council.

HORSLEY.—July 18th.—Construction of 3½ miles of stoneware pipe sewers, varying in size from 15 in. to 7 in., for the urban district council.—Mr. W. H. Radford, Angel-row, Nottingham.

GREAT YARMOUTH.—July 19th.—Supply of one 60-kilowatt high-speed engine and alternator coupled direct and sundry additional steam and exhaust pipes.—Mr. A. H. Miller, town clerk.

LONDON.—July 18th.—Paving of the carriageway of John-street, Minories, with Australian hard wood.—The Engineer to the Corporation.

LONDON.—July 19th.—Construction of an underground convenience in Alderman's-walk.—The Engineer to the Corporation.

CHERTSON.—July 19th.—Construction of 2,230 yards of 9-in., 12-in. and 15-in. pipe sewers in the neighbourhood of London-road, Norbury, and for the construction of a covered concrete storage tank, near Norbury Manor farm.—Mr. E. Mawsbery, town clerk.

CROYDON.—July 19th.—Diversion of a portion of Long-lane.—Mr. E. Mawsbery, town clerk.

PORTSMOUTH.—July 19th.—Supply and fixing of cast-iron valve seatings to the pumps at the Eastney pumping station.—Mr. Alexander Hellard, town clerk.

LONDON.—July 19th.—Construction of underground conveniences in Fenchurch-street.—Sir J. H. Monckton, town clerk.

TOTTENHAM.—July 19th.—Making-up of Pemberton-road, Foyle-road and Shaftesbury-street, for the urban district council.—Mr. P. E. Murphy, engineer to the council.

NEW MILLS.—July 19th.—Construction of various sewers, &c., in connection with Contract No. 3 of the sewerage scheme, for the urban district council.—Messrs. Spinks & Beever, 9 Albert-square, Manchester.

LEWISHAM.—July 19th.—Enlargement of the committee-room at the lodge in the Sydenham recreation ground, for the district board of works.—The Surveyor to the Board.

LONDON.—July 19th.—Various works in connection with the concreting and asphalting of the arches beneath the Lambeth approach to Waterloo bridge, for the county council.—The Engineer to the Council, County Hall, Spring-gardens, London, S.W.

BROMLEY.—July 19th.—Works of sewering, levelling, paving, metalling, channelling and making-good the Avenue, Beckley, for the urban district council.—Mr. Fred. H. Norman, clerk to the council.

LIVERPOOL.—July 19th.—Construction of an open-air bath in Mansfield-street.—The Town Clerk.

HARTLEPOOL.—July 20th.—Paving of the footpaths at the cemetery with tar macadam, the approximate area being about 3,700 square yards.—Mr. H. C. Crummack, A.M.I.C.E., borough engineer.

CHELTENHAM.—July 20th.—Supply of 150 tons of iron water pipes and general road and sewer castings.—Mr. E. T. Brydges, town clerk.

WORCESTER.—July 20th.—Various kerbing, channelling and paving works, for the county council.—Mr. J. H. Garrett, county road surveyor, Shire Hall, Worcester.

GRANGE-OVER-SANDS.—July 21st.—Erection of a new public hall and district council offices, for the urban district council.—Mr. John Hutton, architect, Kendal.

LONDON.—July 21st.—Construction of a road and paths at the North-Western fever hospital, Haverstock-hill, N.W., for the Metropolitan Asylums Board.—Mr. T. Duncombe Mann, clerk to the board, Norfolk House, Norfolk-street, Strand, W.C.

SUTTON COLDFIELD.—July 21st.—Construction of 1,170 yards of 9-in. earthenware pipe sewer at Reddicap Hill.—Mr. W. A. H. Clarry, borough engineer and surveyor.

BRIGHTON.—July 22nd.—Supply of 5,000 ft. of 6-in. granite edge kerb, 250 tons of granite pitchers, and 5,000 tons of granite spalls.—Mr. Francis J. C. May, M.I.C.E., borough engineer and surveyor.

SOUTH SHIELDS.—July 23rd.—Paving of 185 lineal yards of double line of steel-girder tramway.—Mr. S. S. Burgess, A.M.I.C.E., borough engineer.

MIDHURST.—July 23rd.—Supply of disinfectants, for the rural district council.—Mr. Edward Albery, clerk to the council.

COLNE.—July 23rd.—Erection of technical schools and a public library in Albert-road.—Mr. Alfred Varley, town clerk.

LEWES.—July 23rd.—Supply of 500 tons of 2-in. broken blue Guernsey, Cherbourg or Belgian granite, 100 tons of coarse granite screenings, 650 tons of broken surface-picked flints and 150 tons of Piddinghoe gravel.—Mr. Montague S. Blaker, town clerk.

ISLINGTON.—July 25th.—Supply of eleven water-vans, four water-carts, forty-five sets of trunks and distributors for water-vans, thirty-five dust-vans and five sweeping machines.—Mr. J. Patten Barber, vestry surveyor.

CHELTENHAM.—July 25th.—Supply of stoneware pipes and cement for twelve months.—Mr. E. T. Brydges, town clerk.

NUNEATON.—July 25th.—Construction of filter-bed tanks and the laying and fixing of mains and other ironwork at the pumping station, Stockingford, for the urban district council.—Mr. J. S. Pickering, A.M.I.C.E., waterworks engineer.

CHESHUNT.—July 25th.—Supply of six complete suits of firemen's uniforms, for the urban district council.—Mr. S. Towison, A.M.I.C.E., surveyor to the council.

EDMONTON.—July 26th.—Laying of about 1,850 ft. run of granite kerb in Park-road and Park-avenue, and 980 ft. run in Bury-street; about 365 yards super. of channelling and crossings in Park-road and Park-avenue; about 602 yards super. of asphalte in Park-road; about 700 yards super. of 2-in. indurated concrete slab paving in Park-avenue; and about 1,504 yards super. of 2-in. patent Victoria stone paving in Bury-street, for the urban district council.—Mr. G. Eades Eachus, A.M.I.C.E., surveyor to the council.

CHEQUENT.—July 26th.—Construction of about 1,200 ft. of 4 ft. diameter brick culvert, the laying of 2,600 ft. of granite kerb in Windmill-lane, and kerbing works in Park-lane and Eleanor-road, for the urban district council.—Mr. S. Towison, A.M.I.C.E., surveyor to the council.

WILLESDEN.—July 26th.—Road-making and paving works in Pine-road, Cricklewood; Burrows-road, Kensal Rise; Harlesden-gardens, Harlesden; and West Ella-road, Harlesden, for the urban district council.—Mr. O. Claude Robson, M.I.C.E., engineer to the council.

HAYWARDS HEATH.—July 26th.—Supply of about 875 tons of granite, 6 tons of granite chippings and 50 tons of coarse gravel, for the urban district council.—Mr. Edward Waugh, clerk to the council.

BUTE.—July 26th.—Sea defence works on the east foreshore, for the urban district council.—Mr. Arthur Rowlands, clerk to the council.

HULL.—July 26th.—Supply of cast-iron spigot and socket pipes and irregulars required during the year ending August 31, 1899.—Mr. F. J. Bancroft, gas and water engineer, Town Hall, Hull.

WEST HAM.—July 26th.—Construction of about 1,300 lineal yards of sewers, 7 ft., 6 ft. and 3 ft. 6 in. diameter.—Mr. Lewis Angell, borough surveyor.

WEST HAM.—July 26th.—Making-up of Freemantle-road, Haskmere-road, New-street (Plaistow) and Old-street (Plaistow).—Mr. Lewis Angell, borough surveyor.

BECKLOW.—July 26th.—Construction of main sewers and outfall works for the township of Hale, for the rural district council.—Mr. Geo. Leigh, clerk to the council.

WEST HAM.—July 26th.—Erection of twenty-nine working-classes' dwellings in Hermit-road, Plaistow.—Mr. Lewis Angell, borough surveyor.

WEST HAM.—July 26th.—Supply of ten slop-carts.—Mr. Lewis Angell, borough surveyor.

AMBRHAM.—July 27th.—Supply and delivery of various cast-iron and steel work, including a light lattice girder footbridge of three spans (each 57 ft. 6 in.), for the urban district council.—Mr. William Fox, M.I.C.E., engineer to the council, 5 Victoria-street, London, S.W.

WEST HARTLEPOOL.—July 27th.—Erection of an electric light station in Burn-road.—Mr. J. W. Brown, borough engineer.

BURY.—July 28th.—Erection of a manager's house at the sewage disposal works, Livesey Fields.—Mr. J. Cartwright, borough engineer.

BURY.—July 28th.—Erection of a model lodging-house in George-street and Foundry-street, off Rochdale-road.—Mr. J. Cartwright, borough engineer.

LONDON.—July 28th.—Erection of head office buildings on a site at the corner of Carmelite-street and the Victoria-embankment, for the Metropolitan Asylums Board.—Mr. T. Duncombe Mann, clerk to the board, Norfolk House, Norfolk-street, Strand, W.C.

GLASGOW.—July 28th.—Various works in connection with the erection of stable offices, &c., in the Queen's Park.—Mr. J. D. Marwick, town clerk.

TUNBRIDGE WELLS.—July 28th.—Supply of 500 tons of clean Cherbourg quartzite.—Mr. W. C. Cripps, town clerk.

CHERTOW.—August 1st.—Laying of 1,000 superficial yards of granite and cement concrete for footways in Bridge-street and Station-road, for the urban district council.—Mr. F. Feather, surveyor to the council.

WEMBLEY.—August 2nd.—Construction of the following streets, for the urban district council : Union-road, Copland-road, Montrose-crescent, Station-grove, Chaplin-road, Talbot-road, Napier-road, Stanley-avenue, Peel-road and Priory Park-road.—Mr. C. L. Whitehead, junr., engineer to the council.

SHOREDITCH.—August 3rd.—Construction of an underground convenience in Hoxton-street.—Mr. J. Rush Dixon, A.M.I.C.E., engineer and surveyor to the vestry.

## TENDERS.

*ACCEPTED.

EAST GRINSTEAD.—For the supply of 200 tons of 1½-in. broken granite, 160 tons of Kentish ragstone and 840 yards of hand-picked surface flints, for the urban district council.—Mr. R. Wilds, surveyor to the council :—

| FLINTS. | | | | Per yard. |
| --- | --- | --- | --- | --- |
| | | | | s. d. |
| T. & D. Scott, Warlingham | ... | ... | ... | 7 6 |
| W. Hudson, Brighton* | ... | ... | ... | 7 1 |

| RAGSTONE. | | Delivered to East Grinstead. | Delivered to Kingscote. |
| --- | --- | --- | --- |
| | | Per ton. | Per ton. |
| | | s. d. | s. d. |
| W. Arnold & Sons, East Peckham | ... | 8 7 | |
| Hall & Co., Redhill | ... | 8 5 | 8 5 |
| W. Hudson, Brighton | ... | 8 2 | 8 2 |
| J. S. Gabriel, Lambeth, S.E. | ... | 8 0 | 8 3 |
| W. H. Renested & Sons, Maidstone | ... | 7 11 | 8 0 |
| C. E. Mills, Maidstone* | ... | 7 9 | 7 11 |

| STEAM ROLLING. | | | Per day. |
| --- | --- | --- | --- |
| | | | £ s. d. |
| E. Mornement, junr., East Harling | ... | ... | 2 0 0 |
| C. D. Phillips, Newport, Mon. | ... | ... | 1 17 6 |
| Fry Brothers, Greenwich | ... | ... | 1 15 0 |
| G. G. Rutte & Co., Bromley-by-Bow, E. | ... | 1 15 0 |
| Eddison & De Mattos, Dorchester | ... | ... | 1 10 0 |
| E. Smith, Edenbridge | ... | ... | 1 8 0 |
| Chittenden & Simmons, West Malling | ... | 1 7 0 |
| J. Ellis & Co., Maidstone | ... | ... | 1 7 0 |
| The Exors, of late A. Foster, East Grinstead* | ... | 1 7 0 |
| A. J. Ward, Egham | ... | ... | 1 6 6 |

GRANITE.

Guernsey Granite.—R. L. & J. Fennings, London bridge, 15s. 8d.; W. Griffiths, Bishopsgate-street Without, E.C., 14s. 9d.; A. & F. Manuelle, Gracechurch-street, E.C., 14s. 6d.; J. Mowlem & Co., Westminster, S.W., 13s. 8d. per ton.

Leicestershire Granite.—The Mountsorrel Granite Company, Loughborough, 14s. 9d. 14s., The Enderby and Stoney Stanton Granite Company, Leicester, 13s. 9d.; W. Hudson, Brighton, 13s. 8d.; Hall & Co., Redhill, 13s. 9d.; the Whitwick Granite Company, Leicester, 13s. 1d.; the Narborough and Enderby Granite Company, Leicester, 13s. 1d. per ton.

Leicestershire (second quality) Granite.—Hall & Co., Redhill, 12s. 2d. per ton.

Cherbourg Granite.—The Cherbourg Quartzite Company, Mark-lane, E.C., 13s. 4d., 11s. 11d., per ton.

Belgian Granite.—Watts, Powell & Co., Mark-lane, E.C., 13s. per ton.

Quenast Granite.—C. M. Manuelle, Lime-street, E.C.,* 13s. per ton.

LEEDS.—Accepted for the erection of an underground convenience in Duncan-street, opposite the corn exchange.—Mr. Thos. Hewson, M.I.C.E., city engineer :—

| Bricklayer and Mason's Work.—Schofield, Son & Co., Leeds, £1,239. |
| --- |
| Ornamental Iron Railings.—Walter MacFarlane & Co., Glasgow, £106. |
| Plumbing—Adams & Co., Leeds, £303. |
| Ventilating Fans.—J. H. Pickup & Co., Bury, £31. |
| Pavement Lights.—St. Pancras Ironworks Company, £49. |
| Flooring.—Diespeker & Co., £51. |
| Electric Lighting.—W. Wharam, Leeds, £31. |

RUNCORN.—For the extension of the sewerage works in the parish of Frodsham Lordship, for the rural district council.—Mr. William Diggle, surveyor to the council :—

| Winnard & Weston, Chester | ... | ... | ... | ... | £1,780 |
| --- | --- | --- | --- | --- | --- |
| Sace & Randel, Widnes | ... | ... | ... | ... | 1,819 |
| J. Taylor, Garston, Liverpool | ... | ... | ... | 1,076 |
| J. Rowland, Sandiway, Northwich | ... | ... | ... | 996 |
| H. N. Davison, Manchester | ... | ... | ... | 997 |
| J. E. Jones, Patricroft | ... | ... | ... | ... | 996 |
| F. T. Bennin, Warrington* | ... | ... | ... | ... | 932 |

WEDNESBURY.—For reinstating certain roads in the borough damaged by mining operations.—Mr. E. M. Scott, borough engineer and surveyor :—

| F. J. Smith, Wednesbury | ... | ... | ... | ... | £248 |
| --- | --- | --- | --- | --- | --- |
| J. W. Fereday, Wednesbury* | ... | ... | ... | ... | 188 |

WEDNESBURY.—For the erection of a fire station and other buildings on land in High Bullen.—Mr. E. Martin Scott, borough engineer and surveyor :—

| W. H. Mallin, Wednesbury | ... | ... | ... | ... | £965 |
| --- | --- | --- | --- | --- | --- |
| J. Dallow, Blackheath | ... | ... | ... | ... | 950 |
| G. Williamson, Wednesbury | ... | ... | ... | 903 |
| W. T. Lees, Darlaston | ... | ... | ... | ... | 900 |
| G. Summerhill, Wednesbury | ... | ... | ... | 895 |
| J. Holloway, Wednesbury* | ... | ... | ... | ... | 850 |
| W. Ginder, Walsall | ... | ... | ... | ... | 835 |

WHITBY.—For the construction of a new bridge at Iburndale, for the rural district council.—Mr. George Buchannan, clerk to the council :—

| C. Firth, Scarborough | ... | ... | ... | ... | £850 |
| --- | --- | --- | --- | --- | --- |
| Atkinson & Co., Stockton-on-Tees | ... | ... | ... | 758 |
| A. Palframan, Whitby | ... | ... | ... | ... | 673 |
| C. Winterburn, Whitby | ... | ... | ... | ... | 652 |
| W. Blackburn, Broughton, Malton | ... | ... | ... | 649 |
| Robinson Harland, Cleveland-terrace, Whitby* | ... | ... | 618 |

## NOTICES.

THE SURVEYOR AND MUNICIPAL AND COUNTY ENGINEER may be ordered direct, through any of Messrs. Smith & Son's book-stalls, or of any newsagent in the United Kingdom. Applications to the Offices for single copies by post must in all cases be accompanied by stamps.

The Prepaid Subscription (including postage) is as follows :

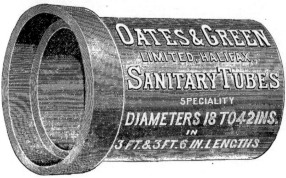

|  | Twelve Months. | Six Months. | Three Months. |
|---|---|---|---|
| United Kingdom ... ... | 15s. | 7s. 6d. | 3s. 9d. |
| Continent. the Colonies, India. |  |  |  |
| United States, &c. ... | 19s. | 9s. 6d. | 4s. 9d. |

*The International News Company, 83 and 85 Duane-street, New York City; The Toronto News Company, Toronto; and The Montreal News Company, Montreal, have been appointed agents in the United States and Canada for the sale of THE SURVEYOR. A thin paper edition is printed for circulation abroad.*

EDITORIAL OFFICES :
ST. BRIDE'S HOUSE, 24 BRIDE-LANE, FLEET-STREET, LONDON, E.C.

OFFICE FOR ADVERTISEMENTS :
13 NEW STREET HILL, FLEET STREET, LONDON, E.C.

PUBLISHING OFFICES :
13 NEW STREET HILL, FLEET STREET, LONDON, E.C.

## APPOINTMENTS OPEN.

RURAL DISTRICT COUNCIL OF NEWARK.
APPOINTMENT OF HIGHWAY SURVEYOR, INSPECTOR OF NUISANCES, CANAL BOATS INSPECTOR AND PETROLEUM INSPECTOR.

The Rural District Council of Newark invite applications for the above appointments.

There are twenty-five parishes in the district and 100 miles of roads.

The salary for the combined offices will be £155 per annum, and the person appointed must be fully qualified and competent to perform all the duties thereof, including the preparation of plans, &c., and will be required to devote the whole of his time to such duties.

Applications, in candidate's own handwriting, stating age, previous occupation, and accompanied by copies of not more than three recent testimonials, to be sent to me not later than Tuesday, the 19th day of July instant.

Canvassing the members of the Council, whether directly or indirectly, will be a disqualification.

The appointment will be made subject to the approval of the Local Government Board.

(By order)
WM. NEWTON,
Clerk.
Local Government Offices, .
Middlegate, Newark.
July 6, 1898.

COUNTY BOROUGH OF MIDDLESBROUGH.
The Streets Committee are prepared to receive applications for the position of Junior Assistant in the Borough Surveyor's department.

Applicants must have had some experience in surveying, levelling, architectural drawing and the working of the Model By-Laws. Salary, £90 per annum.

Also for the position of Building Inspector.

Applicants must have had some experience in the carrying out of the Model By-Laws of the Local Government Board.

Applications for each appointment, stating age, experience, and accompanied by copies of three recent testimonials, to be sent to the undersigned not later than the 27th day of July, 1898.

Applicants for the office of Building Inspector are to state the salary required.

Canvassing any member of the Corporation will be deemed a disqualification.
FRANK BAKER, C.F , F.G.S.,
Borough Engineer.
Municipal Buildings, Middlesbrough.

BOROUGH OF BURTON-UPON-TRENT.
Wanted, immediately, in the Borough Surveyor's office, an Architectural Assistant, well up in specifications, quantities and estimates for general building work.

The engagement will be terminable by one month's notice on either side, but the person appointed must undertake to hold the position two years if required. Salary, £130 per annum.

Applications, stating age and experience and earliest date when disengaged, together with copies of three recent testimonials, must be sent to the undersigned not later than Wednesday, the 20th inst.
G. T. LYNAM,
Borough Surveyor.
Town Hall, Burton-upon-Trent.
July 13, 1898.

VESTRY OF ST. GEORGE-THE-MARTYR,
SOUTHWARK.
TO SURVEYORS.

The Vestry of the parish of St. George-the-Martyr, Southwark, require the services of a fully-qualified Surveyor. Age, thirty to forty-five years. Salary, £300 per annum, rising by annual increments of £25 to a maximum of £450 per annum.

Forms of application, conditions of appointment and list of duties can be had on application at the Vestry offices.

Applications, endorsed "Surveyor," to be sent to me not later than 12 o'clock noon on Friday, 22nd day of July, 1898.

Canvassing the members of the Vestry, directly or indirectly, will be a disqualification.

                            J. A. JOHNSON,
                               Vestry Clerk.

Vestry Hall, 81 Borough-road, S.E.
    July 13, 1898.

## CITY OF SHEFFIELD.

Wanted, in the office of the City Surveyor, a District Surveyor for the Eastern District of the City, to take charge of the street and sewer work (including many miles of paved streets), also tramway maintenance and construction.

Applicants must have had good experience of similar work.

Apply, stating qualifications, age, references and salary required, to Mr. Charles F. Wike, M.INST.C.E., City Surveyor's Office. Town Hall, Sheffield.
    July 8, 1898.

## CITY OF CANTERBURY.
### ENGINEERING ASSISTANT.

Wanted, at once, an Engineering Assistant—temporary engagement in first instance—for a term of three months, or thereabouts, in the office of the City Surveyor. Well up in sewer construction, tanks and outfall works. Salary, £3 per month.—Apply, stating age and experience, with references or copy of testimonials, to the City Surveyor, Tudor Chambers, High-street, Canterbury.

REQUIRED, a representative of gentlemanly appearance and address, who has had experience in waiting upon corporation and vestry surveyor and other municipal officials. No orders taken.—Address, "Concessions," Box 2,033, Sell's Advertising Offices, London.

## TENDERS WANTED.

## HAYWARDS HEATH URBAN DISTRICT COUNCIL.
### TENDERS FOR MATERIALS.

The above Council invite tenders for the supply of about 825 tons of Granite, broken to 1½-in. ring ; 6 tons of Granite Chippings, ¾ size ; and 50 tons of Coarse Gravel.

The whole to be delivered, carriage paid, to Haywards Heath railway station, at such times and in such quantities as the Surveyor may direct.

Tenders, on forms to be obtained of me, must be sent to me on or before the 26th day of July instant, endorsed "Tender for Materials."

A 28-lb. sample of granite to be delivered, carriage paid, to the railway station, Haywards Heath, on or before the 26th inst.

The contractors will, if the Council so order, be required to find security for the due performance of the contract.

                (By order)

                    EDWARD WAUGH,
                             Clerk.

Haywards Heath.
    July 11, 1898.

## CHESHUNT URBAN DISTRICT COUNCIL.

The above Council are prepared to receive tenders at per suit for about six complete suits of Fireman's Uniform.

Particulars may be obtained upon application being made to Mr. S. Towison, A.M.I.C.E., Surveyor to the Council.

Tenders to be sent addressed

              The Chairman,
                 Cheshunt Urban District Council,
                     St. Mary's Hall,
                        Cheshunt, Herts,

by Monday, July 25th.

                A. COLLINGWOOD LEE,
                           Clerk.

Cheshunt.
    July, 1898.

## CHESHUNT URBAN DISTRICT COUNCIL.
### TO CONTRACTORS.

The above Council are prepared to receive tenders for the construction of about 1,200 ft. of 4-ft. diameter Brick Culvert, and for laying 2,500 ft. of Granite Kerb in Windmill-lane ; also for Kerbing in Park-lane and Eleanor-road, and for 1,200 yards each of Kerb and Channel in the main road.

Plans and specifications may be seen on and after Monday, July 18th. Tenders, on the form to be obtained, are to be sent addressed

              The Chairman,
                 Cheshunt Urban District Council,
                     St. Mary's Hall,
                        Cheshunt, Herts,

by Monday, July 26th.

The Council are not bound to accept the lowest or any tender.

                A. COLLINGWOOD LEE,
                           Clerk.

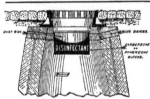

## NUNEATON AND CHILVERS COTON URBAN DISTRICT COUNCIL.

### CONSTRUCTION OF FILTER-BED TANKS.

Tenders are invited for the Construction of Filter-Bed Tanks, and the Laying and Fixing of the Mains and other Ironwork connected therewith, near the Council's pumping station, Stockingford.

Plans and specification may be seen, and bill of quantities obtained, at the office of the undersigned, to whom sealed tenders, endorsed "Filters," are to be sent on or before Monday, July 25, 1898.

The lowest or any tender will not necessarily be accepted.

J. S. PICKERING, ASSOC.M.INST.C.E.,
Waterworks Engineer.

Council Offices, Nuneaton.
July 9, 1898.

## WILLESDEN DISTRICT COUNCIL.

### TO ROAD CONTRACTORS.

The Willesden District Council are prepared to receive tenders for the execution of certain Road-making and Paving works in the following roads—viz.,—

Pine-road, Cricklewood.
Burrows-road, Kensal Rise.
Harlesden-gardens, Harlesden.
West Ella-road, Harlesden.

Plans and specification may be seen and all further particulars obtained on and after Monday, July 18, 1898, upon application to Mr. O. Claude Robson, M.INST.C.E., Engineer to the Council, Public Offices, Dyne-road, Kilburn, N.W.

The tenders, upon printed forms and endorsed "Private Streets," to be delivered at the offices of the Council not later than 4 p.m. on Tuesday, July 26, 1898.

The Council do not bind themselves to accept the lowest or any tender.

(By order)
STANLEY W. BALL,
Clerk to the Council.

Public Offices, Dyne-road, Kilburn, N.W.
July 13, 1898.

## CHEPSTOW URBAN DISTRICT COUNCIL.

### FOOTWAYS, &c., CONSTRUCTION.

The above Council invite tenders for the laying of 1,000 yards super., or thereabouts, of Granite and Cement Concrete, for Footways in Bridge-street and Station-road.

Plans may be seen and specification, with bill of quantities and form of tender, obtained on application at the Surveyor's Office, Chepstow.

Tenders, endorsed "Tender for Footways, &c., Construction," and addressed to the Chairman of the Council, to be delivered at the Council Offices not later than 12 o'clock noon on Monday, August, 1, 1898.

The lowest or any tender will not necessarily be accepted.

F. FEATHER,
Town Surveyor.

Council Offices, Chepstow.
July, 1898.

## COUNTY BOROUGH OF BRIGHTON.

### TO CONTRACTORS AND OTHERS.

Notice is hereby given that the Council of the said County Borough will receive tenders from such persons as may be willing to enter into a contract for the supply of 5,000 ft. run of 6-in. Granite Edge Kerb, 250 tons of Granite Pitchers, and 5,000 tons of Granite Spalls, Elvan Whinstone, or other hard stone suitable for breaking up for road macadam.

The specification and form of tender may be obtained at the office of the Borough Engineer and Surveyor, Mr. Francis J. C. May, M.INST.C.E., at the Town Hall, Brighton.

Sealed tenders, addressed to me and endorsed "Tenders for Granite," must be left at my office, at the Town Hall, before 10 o'clock in the forenoon on Friday, the 22nd day of July, 1898.

The Council reserve to themselves the right to reject the lowest or any tender, and to accept any tender as to part only of the quantity of material offered to be supplied.

FRANCIS J. TILLSTONE,
Town Clerk.

Town Hall, Brighton.
July 8, 1898.

## MIDHURST RURAL DISTRICT COUNCIL, SUSSEX.

The Council are desirous of receiving tenders for the Supply of Disinfectants, to be delivered at the offices of the Council.

Further particulars may be obtained upon application to the undersigned, to whom tenders must be delivered on or before the 23rd instant.

The Council do not bind themselves to accept the lowest or any tender.

EDWIN ALBERY,
Clerk to the Council.

District Council Offices, Midhurst.
July 5, 1898.

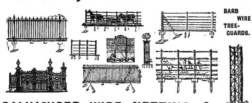

## BOROUGH OF SUTTON COLDFIELD.

The Corporation invite tenders for the construction of 1,170 yards, or thereabouts, of 9-in. Earthenware Pipe Sewer, with Manholes and Lampholes complete, at Reddicap Hill.

Plans, sections, specifications and conditions of contract may be inspected on application to the undersigned at his offices, Town Hall, Sutton Coldfield, where forms of tender may be obtained.

Sealed tenders, endorsed "Reddicap Hill Sewer," must be deposited with the Town Clerk, T. V. Holbeche, Esq., at his offices in Coleshill-street, on or before Thursday, 21st inst.

The Corporation do not bind themselves to accept the lowest or any tender.

W. A. H. CLARRY,
Borough Engineer and Surveyor.

Town Hall, Sutton Coldfield.
July 8, 1898.

## TO CONTRACTORS.

### SEA DEFENCE WORKS AT RHYL.

The Rhyl Urban District Council invite tenders for Works of Sea Defence on the East Foreshore.

Plans and description of the works may be seen at the Town Surveyor's office.

The Council do not bind themselves to accept the lowest or any tender.

The tenders, sealed and endorsed "Sea Defence," may be delivered to me on or before 10 a.m. on Tuesday, the 26th instant, at the Council Offices, Clwyd-street.

Approved security will be required.

ARTHUR ROWLANDS,
Clerk to the Council.

## VESTRY OF ST. MARY, ISLINGTON.

The Vestry is prepared to receive tenders for the supply of eleven Water-Vans, four Water-Carts, forty-five sets of Trunks and Distributors for Water-Vans, thirty-five Dust-Vans and five Sweeping Machines.

Conditions and specifications can be seen, and forms of tender obtained, upon application to the Chief Surveyor, Mr. J. Patten Barber, at the Vestry Hall, Upper-street, Islington, N., between the hours of 10 and 12 noon, and the deposit of 2 guineas, which amount will be returned upon the receipt of a *bond-fide* tender which is not withdrawn, and the return of the whole of the documents issued.

Tenders, endorsed "Tender for the Supply of Water-Vans,

&c.," must be delivered at the Vestry Hall not later than 4 p.m. on the 25th inst.

WM. F. DEWEY,
Vestry Clerk.

Vestry Hall, Upper-street, Islington, N.
July 13, 1898.

## BOROUGH OF SHOREDITCH.

### PROPOSED UNDERGROUND CONVENIENCE.

#### TO SANITARY ENGINEERS.

The Shoreditch Vestry invite tenders for the whole of the works required in the Construction and Completion of an Underground Public Convenience in Hoxton-street, opposite the workhouse infirmary.

The plans and specification can be seen at the offices of Mr. J. Rush Dixon, A.M.INST.C.E., Engineer and Surveyor, or to the Vestry Town Hall, Old-street, E.C., from whom also tender forms and a copy of the instructions to contractors may be obtained on payment of a deposit of £5, which will be returned after the contract has been decided by the Vestry in the case of *bond-fide* tenders having been received.

Tenders, sealed and endorsed "Underground Convenience," must be sent to the undersigned by 4 p.m. on Wednesday, August 3rd next.

Security must be given to enter into a bond for £500 for the due performance of the contract, and the contractor whose tender is accepted must be prepared to pay the trade union rate of wages and observe the hours of labour in force at the time of tendering.

The Vestry do not undertake to accept the lowest or any tender.

(By order)
H. MANSFIELD ROBINSON,
Solicitor and Clerk.

Town Hall, Old-street, E.C.
July, 1898.

## BOROUGH OF LEWES.

### TO STONE MERCHANTS, FARMERS, &c.

The Town Council of this Borough invite tenders for the supply of 500 tons of 2-in. Broken Blue Guernsey, Cherbourg or Belgian Granite, 100 tons of Coarse Granite Screenings, 650 tons of Broken Surface-Picked Flints and 150 tons of Piddinghoe Gravel.

Forms of tender and specification may be had, and any further information obtained, at the Borough Surveyor's office, Town Hall, Lewes.

Sealed tenders, endorsed "Tender for ———." must be left at my office on or before the 23rd July, 1898.

Power is reserved to reject the lowest or any tender.

(By order)

MONTAGUE S. BLAKER,
Town Clerk.

Town Clerk's Office, Lewes.
June 2, 1898.

## COUNTY BOROUGH OF WEST HAM.
### TO SEWER CONTRACTORS.

The Council hereby invite tenders for the contraction of about 1,200 lineal yards of Sewers, 7 ft., 6 ft. and 3 ft. 6 in. diameter, together with Penstock Chambers, Manholes and other works.

Plans may be seen, and specification, form of tender and further particulars obtained, at the office of Mr. Lewis Angell, Borough Engineer, Town Hall, Stratford, E., on the deposit of a £5 Bank of England note, which will be returned on receipt of a bona-fide tender.

Tenders, endorsed "Tender for Sewers," to be sent to my office not later than 4 o'clock on Tuesday, 26th July, 1898.

The Council do not bind themselves to accept the lowest or any tender.

The contractor will be required to enter into a bond, with two sureties, for the due performance of the contract, and no work will be ordered under the contract until such bond has been duly executed.

As regards all work to be done at the site or elsewhere within a radius of 20 miles from Charing Cross, the contractors will be bound by the contract to pay to all workmen (except a reasonable number of legally-bound apprentices) employed by them wages at rates not less, and to observe hours of labour not greater, than the rates and hours set out in the Council's list, and such rates of wages and hours of labour will be inserted in and form part of the contract by way of schedule.

(By order of the Council)

FRED. E. HILLEARY,
Town Clerk.

Town Hall, West Ham, E.
June 29, 1898.

## COUNTY BOROUGH OF WEST HAM.
### PRIVATE STREET WORKS.
### TO CONTRACTORS.

The Council hereby invite tenders for making-up the following streets:—

Freemantle-road.
Haslemere-road.
New-street, Plaistow.
Old-street, Plaistow.

Plans may be seen, and specification, form of tender and further particulars obtained, at the office of Mr. Lewis Angell, Borough Engineer, Town Hall, Stratford, E., upon payment of £1, which will be returned upon receipt of a bona-fide tender.

Tenders, endorsed "Tender for Private Street Works," to be sent to my office not later than 4 o'clock on Tuesday, the 26th July, 1898.

The Council do not bind themselves to accept the lowest or any tender.

The contractor will be required to enter into a bond, with two sureties, for the due performance of the contract, and no work will be ordered under the contract until such bond has been duly executed.

As regards all work to be done at the site or elsewhere within a radius of 20 miles from Charing Cross, the contractors will be bound by the contract to pay to all workmen (except a reasonable number of legally-bound apprentices) employed by them wages at rates not less, and to observe hours of labour not greater, than the rates and hours set out in the Council's list, and such rates of wages and hours of labour will be inserted in and form part of the contract by way of schedule.

(By order of the Council)

FRED. E. HILLEARY,
Town Clerk.

Town Hall, West Ham, E.
June 29, 1898.

## COUNTY BOROUGH OF WEST HAM.
### TO BUILDERS AND CONTRACTORS.

The Council hereby invite tenders for the erection of twenty-nine Houses for the working-classes at Hermit-road, Plaistow.

Plans may be seen, and specification, form of tender and further particulars obtained, on and after Monday, July 11, 1898, at the office of Mr. Lewis Angell, Borough Engineer, Town Hall, Stratford, E., on the deposit of a £5 Bank of England note, which will be returned upon receipt of a *bona-fide* tender.

Tenders, endorsed "Tender for Artisans' Dwellings," to be sent to my office not later than 4 o'clock on Tuesday, July 26, 1898.

The Council do not bind themselves to accept the lowest or any tender.

The contractor will be required to enter into a bond, with two sureties, for the due performance of the contract, and no work will be ordered under the contract until such bond has been duly executed.

As regards all work to be done at the site or elsewhere within a radius of 20 miles from Charing Cross, the contractors will be bound by the contract to pay to all workmen (except a reasonable number of legally-bound apprentices) employed by them wages at rates not less, and to observe hours of labour not greater, than the rates and hours set out in the Council's list, and such rates of wages and hours of labour will be inserted in and form part of the contract by way of schedule.

(By order of the Council)
FRED. E. HILLEARY,
Town Clerk.
Town Hall, West Ham, E.
June 29, 1898.

### COUNTY BOROUGH OF WEST HAM.
TO WHEELWRIGHTS.

The Council hereby invite tenders for the supply of ten Slop Carts.

Form of tender, specification and further particulars obtained at the office of Mr. Lewis Angell, Borough Engineer, Town Hall, Stratford, E., upon payment of £1, which will be returned upon receipt of a *bona-fide* tender.

Tenders, endorsed "Tender for Slop Carts," to be sent to my office not later than 4 o'clock on Tuesday, July 26, 1898.

The Council do not bind themselves to accept the lowest or any tender.

The contractor will be required to enter into a bond, with two sureties, for the due performance of the contract, and no work will be ordered under the contract until such bond has been duly executed.

As regards all work to be done at the site or elsewhere within a radius of 20 miles from Charing Cross, the contractors will be bound by the contract to pay to all workmen (except a reasonable number of legally-bound apprentices) employed by them wages at rates not less, and to observe hours of labour not greater, than the rates and hours set out in the Council's list, and such rates of wages and hours of labour will be inserted in and form part of the contract by way of schedule.

(By order of the Council)
FRED. E. HILLEARY,
Town Clerk.
Town Hall, West Ham, E.
June 28, 1898.

### COUNTY OF WORCESTER.
WORKS OF KERBING, CHANNELLING AND PAVING.

The Highways and Bridges Committee of the County Council are prepared to receive tenders for the following Works of Kerbing, Channelling and Paving on Main Roads and Footpaths—namely :—

KERBING AND CHANNELLING.

2,790 yards on the Pershore-road, between Stirchley and Birmingham.

1,230 yards on the Bristol-road at Northfield.

BLUE BRICK PAVING.

1,885 square yards at Long-lane, near Blackheath.

2,912 square yards on the Pershore-road at the Cotteridge, Breedon and Stirchley.

8,415 square yards on the Alcester-road at Mosely and King's Heath.

4,894 square yards on the Warwick-road at Sparkhill and Greet.

2,317 square yards on the Warwick-road at Acock's Green.

1,010 square yards on the Bristol-road at Bournbrook.

Sealed tenders, properly endorsed, must be delivered or sent to the undersigned on or before Wednesday, July 20, 1898.

Detailed particulars, specifications and forms of tender will be forwarded on application to me.

The Committee do not bind themselves to accept the lowest or any tender.

J. H. GARRETT,
County Road Surveyor.
Shire Hall, Worcester.
July 1, 1898.

# The Surveyor

### And Municipal and County Engineer.

Vol. XIV., No. 340.    LONDON, JULY 22, 1898.    Weekly, Price 3d.

## Minutes of Proceedings.

**Professional Qualifications.** In the United States the evil of insufficient professional qualifications is probably more troublesome than it is in this country, where, indeed, there is reason to believe that cases at all serious are becoming fewer and fewer every day. After all, it must in the long run be a question of the survival of the fittest. Even the smaller local authorities seem now to realise the importance—we might even say necessity—of appointing thoroughly efficient men to official posts. It is to be regretted that they do not always see equally well the importance of paying adequate salaries. Unfortunately, it is in connection with municipal work that the evil is most acutely felt in the United States, and no one requires to be told that this state of affairs is distinctly traceable to the vicious system of making official appointments the spoil of unscrupulous office-seekers and party politicians, instead of appointing capable permanent officials. One wonders how long such a pernicious practice will be tolerated in a country so advanced and enlightened in other respects. Our able American contemporary, *Municipal Engineering*, which recently discussed this question in its different bearings, cited the case of a thoroughly efficient city engineer, of education and experience, who had to make way for a successor with no training or experience as an engineer, and with only a little experience in surveying, picked up in the intervals of other occupations. The displaced official has been the chief factor in securing for the city a comprehensive scheme of sewerage, which has already been partly carried out under his supervision, and has carried out other municipal works in a thoroughly satisfactory way. It has been pertinently pointed out that, though no one imagines that the new official can possibly do the work as intelligently as his predecessor, the fact is not sufficiently realised that his lack of training and experience may entail upon the city in the future practically unlimited loss and inconvenience through bad designs, defective construction and inadequate precautions. This is what is meant by the oft-repeated remark that in certain positions some men would be dear at any price. People are apt to overlook or minimise the responsible nature of certain duties, and the potentiality of vast losses which one man would incur and another avert. To no profession do such considerations apply more forcibly than to that of the municipal engineer. Many kinds of work can be carried out satisfactorily by people of no special capacity or training, but municipal engineering is emphatically one of the professions which can be efficiently followed only by the expert few, if the ratepayers are to be saved from great and needless expense arising directly out of neglect, bad work or misdirected effort. Our transatlantic contemporary is undoubtedly right in demanding the restriction of such offices to those whose competence has been proved by the adoption of some valid test. The prominent qualifications which go to the making of a successful engineer are much the same as those necessary in all the other higher professions—natural aptitude and intelligence, education, training and experience, with, of course, the requisite energy and perseverance. It is frequently asserted that thoroughly competent and even eminent engineers may exist on the strength of natural aptitude alone, and we are triumphantly referred to certain great names of the past, when applied science was in its infancy. In those days the argument may have possessed considerable force, but circumstances alter cases. The vast developments of engineering involve the necessity of mastering so extensive a preliminary groundwork that a certain amount of systematic training and instruction is absolutely imperative. In addition, some test is required to indicate, more or less accurately, whether the instruction has been intelligently assimilated. Apart from the actual execution of work, the test which suggests itself is that of examination—by no means a perfect test, but probably the most convenient and practicable to be had. It is admittedly easy to exaggerate the utility and function of written examinations, and to make them the sole test of fitness for public appointments, irrespective of other considerations, would, in our opinion, be a policy of questionable judgment. Within reasonable limits, however, the examination test, written and oral, is not only justifiable, but commendable and necessary, especially for young members of a difficult and responsible profession. Many men of sound and even brilliant parts would not distinguish themselves greatly under examination, but no fairly-educated man who really understands his work should have any difficulty in passing a reasonable examination with tolerable credit. This is the test which our contemporary advocates as a remedy, to some extent, for the evils which are at present found in connection with municipal life in the United States. In support of the argument the work of the Incorporated Association of Municipal and County Engineers in this country is referred to in terms of commendation, as the following passage will show:—

The British Association of Municipal and County Engineers inaugurated some time ago a series of voluntary pass examinations, which have developed into an institution of considerable value, notwithstanding the pronounced opinions of many prominent men that the work would be useless in elevating the standard of this branch of the profession. The examination is now styled one of "candidates for the offices of municipal engineers and surveyors to district councils," is carried outby the association, and is entirely voluntary. An evidence of its popularity is the fact that the twenty-fifth of the series, held April 1st and 2nd, was taken by forty-nine men. The examination consisted of one day of written work and one day of oral, and was conducted by live members of the Institution of Civil Engineers. It included engineering as applied to municipal work, building construction, sanitary science, and municipal and local government law. Some cities and county councils in Great Britain and Ireland conduct elaborate examinations of candidates for such positions, but most of them, including all the smaller corporations, do not take the trouble or incur the expense. The tendency in favour of such examinations, however. The corporation officers are rapidly gaining confidence in the examination as conducted by the association, and a candidate for a position who has passed them in many cases has a long lead over his competitors. The tendency is strongly in favour of the method of procedure described, and, while the whole scheme is entirely voluntary, public opinion is rapidly raising it to the authority of law.

\* \* \*

**Electrical Competition: Companies and Local Authorities.** The principle of municipal ownership has recently received a somewhat rude shock. A Parliamentary committee have declared in favour of what we may term the revolutionary doctrine of competition in municipal boroughs. The matter has arisen more directly in connection with electric lighting, and, carried to its logical issue, the result of the committee's decision is that where a municipal electric lighting scheme already exists it is open to an electric lighting company to enter into the district and without the sanction of the local authority undertake the supply of electricity. It need hardly be pointed out that if such a principle is accepted by the House of Commons it will seriously jeopardise the security of capital. It is true that it cuts two ways, and it is as unfair for an electric lighting company to be permitted to go into a district where a municipal scheme exists as it is for a local authority to enter into competition with an electric lighting company already existing, assuming always that the service is organised and worked in the interests of the consumer. It cannot be seriously maintained that any local authorities owning electric lighting works have been neglectful of the consumer's interests. On the contrary, we have frequently pointed out that the consumer has been generally well treated, even if the ratepayer has suffered. The new principle laid down by the Parliamentary committee arose out of the scheme that had been brought forward by the General Power Distributing Company and the Midland Power Distributing Company. The objects of these companies' Bills were to obtain powers to generate electricity on a large scale and distribute it to the various towns within their area of supply.

In considering these matters on a former occasion we concluded that, if certain provisions were made to safeguard the interests of municipalities, it might under some circumstances be to the advantage of a local authority to work in conjunction with the power-distributing companies. We sketched an arrangement by which a municipality might extend its supply of electricity by buying from the large companies in bulk and distributing to the consumers as required, but the clauses suggested by the committee go very materially beyond that. Not only are powers given to supply local authorities in bulk, but, in addition, this company may enter into a district and compete with the local authority in supplying electrical energy to the larger consumers—that is, to those taking 10,000 Board of Trade units and upwards. In other words, if these measures are passed by Parliament as they stand the large power companies will be able to enter a borough and compete in supplying electricity to everybody, with the exception of the small consumer; and in order that a municipality may retain the power of supplying to the small consumer it must engage itself to purchase electricity in bulk from the company, otherwise it will be open to this company to compete in supplying electricity to everybody. The matter is of the utmost importance so far as municipalities are concerned, and, although only a few of the large towns are concerned at the moment, it is absolutely necessary that they should take immediate steps to combine in order to resist the principle of the measure when it comes before the House of Commons in complete form. The property of ratepayers is threatened, and unless vigorous measures are taken the whole future of municipal electric supply is jeopardised.

Although we have thus been compelled to make some severe remarks on the question of competition in those towns affected by the large power-distributing companies' Bills, certain proposals have originated in London which are just as much opposed to the principle of fair trading as those already alluded to. The Marylebone Vestry sought powers to supply electricity in their district, although the Metropolitan Company had had powers for some time. In this case the matter is probably not very serious so far as it affects the Metropolitan Company, because Marylebone forms only one small portion of the area over which this company have powers, but, at the same time, the principle involved is one of the utmost importance, and after due consideration it is not surprising that the Bill of the Marylebone Vestry should have been rejected. The Electric Lighting Act clearly states that " the grant of authority to any undertakers to supply electricity within any area, whether granted by license or by means of a provisional order, shall not in any way restrict granting of a license to any other local authority or to any other person within the same area." That practically means that under some circumstances competition may be permitted in districts; but up to the present, with the exception of two or three London districts, competition has not been expressly encouraged by the Board of Trade. If a company in a provincial town had spent a large sum of money upon establishing a system of electric light, and the local authority after business had been established for some years were to undertake a similar supply, it is clear that the interests of the company would be very seriously interfered with. The same may be said of a corporation undertaking a supply. Hitherto, if local authorities have not undertaken a supply themselves but have left it to a company to carry out, the recognised policy has been for the former to purchase outright the business and plant of the company; and we must confess that such a course savours more of equity than does the decision to grant competitive powers.

\* \* \*

**The Sewage Disposal Commission.** We are informed that the Royal Commission on Sewage Treatment and Disposal have given much consideration to the question of throwing the sittings open to the Press, but they have come to the conclusion that the purpose of the inquiry would be obstructed and retarded rather than fostered and quickened by the publication of the proceedings during its progress. The Commission think that outside criticism upon sections of the evidence before the whole is presented in a complete form would be embarrassing and not helpful. Another reason which has influenced them in their decision in favour of " closed doors " is the fact that undue publicity would possibly be given to the projects and nostrums of certain theorists before their value had been tested. If these are the best arguments that can be advanced in support of a secret investigation their weakness is transparent, for, supposing the evidence were criticised, what possible harm can healthy criticism do? Its effect would, on the contrary, be beneficial, because it would bring to light before it was too late new facts which would probably otherwise escape consideration. The Commission need not be afraid of any advertisement that might be given to crude and imperfectly-developed theories, inasmuch as their defects as well as their virtues would become manifest, and no public authorities would be likely to take them up before the result of the inquiry became known. It is pointed out, on behalf of the Commission, that in excluding the Press they are acting in accordance with precedent which was only departed from in the case of the Water Commission on account of the exceptional circumstances that were under investigation. Even so, but if the precedent is bad why should it be perpetuated? We still think that the Commission have made a great mistake, and that much of the good that would have attended their labours will be lost.

Last week the Commission held three sittings. The members present on each occasion were Lord Iddesleigh (chairman), Sir Richard Thorne, General Carey, Prof. Ramsay, Prof. Michael Foster, Mr. Cotton, Dr. Russell, Colonel Hardy and Mr. Killick. Mr. F. J. Willis, the secretary, was also in attendance. Evidence was given with regard to public health legislation in Ireland and Scotland and to the existing state of the law in those countries by Mr. Dean, who represented the Irish Local Government Board, and Mr. Murray, on behalf of the Local Government Board for Scotland. Then came testimony from the three rivers boards which have been endowed with exceptional powers to cope with river pollution in the populous manufacturing districts of Lancashire and Yorkshire. These are the Mersey and Irwell, the Ribble and the West Riding Joint Committees, which during their brief history—they are essentially modern authorities, the Mersey and Irwell having only been established about seven years—have done a great work in the purification of the streams under their jurisdiction. The witnesses examined with reference to that work were Mr. Tatton, the chief inspector for the Mersey and Irwell, and Mr. Scudder, assistant to Sir Henry Roscoe; Mr. Naylor, inspector for the Ribble Joint Committee; and Dr. Maclean Wilson and Mr. Trevor Edwards for the West Riding Rivers Joint Committee. Their testimony related to the steps that had been taken to compel manufacturers to deal with their refuse in such a manner that it would not pollute the rivers upon which their works are situated. Before the boards were constituted the rivers were so polluted as to be a constant and serious danger to health in thickly-populated districts, and while much remains to be done many of the more flagrant nuisances have been abated. Practically the same course is followed in each case. The inspectors examine the condition of the streams and recommend to the boards what works they consider necessary. Their reports are considered, and offenders against the public health are served with notices; but before compulsory steps are taken manufacturers are allowed an opportunity of stating their case and of appealing to the Local Government Board, whose decision has to be given within three months. After hearing this evidence the Commission adjourned till the autumn. They came to the conclusion that it would be useless to hold further sittings until then, owing to the difficulty of getting witnesses to attend during the months of August and September.

*          *          *

**Yellow Fever and Sanitation.** The operations in Cuba have naturally drawn increased attention to the question of yellow fever and the close connection which, in common with plague, cholera and typhoid fever, can be found between its prevalence and insanitary conditions. Its origin has been traced, with some plausibility, to the slave trade, the accompanying filth of which was not the least of its horrors. Apart from that theory, the endemic influence to which the disease can undoubtedly be attributed is effluvial or miasmatic, from the harbour mud or from the bilge-water of a ship that had lain in the harbour or from the alluvial foundations of houses nearest to the beach. It is rarely found beyond a certain range of latitude, or to any extent in ports which are in a satisfactory sanitary condition. On shore the disease seems to follow much the same laws as cholera and typhoid fever, in that it is an exogenous or soil infection, a fermentation of filth in the ground, with a seasonal activity closely following the movements of the subsoil water. When imported to Spain, for example, it has clung to alluvial soil, and has spread after the fashion of a soil-borne infection rather than by personal contagion; and it has been clear that no epidemic is likely to be established in a distant port unless a material quantity of the specially-poisonous harbour filth should be carried in ships' bilges,

and unless the conditions favourable to its increase and diffusion by fermentation should exist in the new soil. Where harbours are most tideless, the soil most alluvial, and the movements of the subsoil water most extensive, the specific putrefaction or fermentation, when introduced into the harbour, will spread farthest on shore, being aided or encouraged always by the abundance of other organic matter met with at particular spots, such as the foundations of houses. Like typhus, now practically extirpated in this country, yellow fever is essentially a filth disease. Herein comes in its close connection with sanitation and with sanitary engineering in the endemic seats of the disease in the West Indies, Guiana, Brazil, Central America and the United States ports on the Gulf of Mexico. The disease has practically vanished from the Atlantic ports of the Union, and has become rare in such harbours as Port Royal, Jamaica. The Brazilian ports, where it was last developed, are now the most active centres of the fever. The case is so far peculiar that the harbour bottom, the adjoining mudbanks and mangrove swamps, and even the sea-water itself, are apt to retain the specific taint, especially where the cleansing action of the tides is slight. But there is reason to believe that the specific taint in the soil is everywhere slowly disappearing, now that it is no longer reinforced by fresh supplies year after year. The great object, indeed, is to secure a clean soil, and thus the bearing of proper sewerage and drainage upon a satisfactory solution of the question will be obvious to our readers. Such paltry matters have never received much attention from the Spaniard or the Cuban, and the island has in a liberal degree all the conditions, natural and acquired, for the propagation of the scourge. There will be a splendid field in Havana, and in Cuba generally, when affairs are more settled for many forms of activity, and sanitary engineering should certainly be one of them. But what about the sanitary condition of New Orleans, Mobile and other Gulf cities of the United States, where people might be expected to know better ?

*          *          *

**Electric Lighting in Bethnal Green.** Although the company which applied to the Bethnal Green Vestry for permission to introduce electric lighting into the district would have carried out the work satisfactorily, it is, nevertheless, a matter for congratulation that the vestry have resolved to keep the power in their own hands; and to show that immediate action is intended the vestry have sought the advice of Prof. Henry Robinson, who recommends the putting down of plant which will supply 5,000 lamps of 16 candle power. This will entail a capital expenditure of £33,000, exclusive of land; £4,000 will be spent upon buildings, £10,500 on mains, £2,400 on house connections and £11,500 for machinery. We must frankly confess that we should have been better pleased if Prof. Robinson had recommended a larger scheme. It is true that a larger system would not have shown an immediate profit, upon which considerable stress is laid in the report, but it cannot be too widely known that some of the most successful municipal schemes in the country are those which showed a loss during the first two or three years, this loss being occasioned by the large capital expended with a view to meet future requirements. Prof. Robinson expresses an opinion that the Bethnal Green undertaking will be at once remunerative, and he estimates the profit at £200 at the end of the first year, at £300 at the end of the second, and at £1,010 at the end of the third year. The price to private consumers will be 6d. for the first year and 5d. afterwards. Some system of street lighting is contemplated in the report, and there is no reason to think that the scheme will not be completely successful, but it is to be regretted that more consideration has not been paid to the future development of lighting in the district.

# Association of Municipal and County Engineers.

## ANNUAL MEETING AT EDINBURGH.—IV.

EDINBURGH: HOLYROOD PALACE.

Last week we were compelled to hold over the instructive paper read by Mr. Whyte at the recent meeting on the subject of the Leith docks. This completed the series of papers and discussions, the remainder of the time being devoted to visits to various municipal works and other places of interest which are so plentiful in the Scottish metropolis. These visits we are describing at such length as may seem necessary, but it will, of course, be remembered that many of the works visited have been described in considerable detail in some of the papers read and discussed before the meeting.

### SECOND DAY'S PROCEEDINGS (continued),
(Friday, July 1st).

Mr. Whyte's paper was as follows :—

NOTES ON LEITH DOCKS AND NEW WORKS NOW IN PROGRESS.

By PETER WHYTE, M.INST.C.E.

[Mr. Peter Whyte was born about half a century ago at Invermay, near Perth. He received his education at Perth Academy, and was subsequently apprenticed to a firm of surveyors in the city. In this employment he acquired the rudiments of the profession of his adoption. Having attracted the notice of Mr. Hugh H. Maclure, a leading civil engineer of Glasgow, he was induced to join the staff under that gentleman. With him he remained two years and acquired most valuable experience. On the initiation of the Bute docks scheme at Cardiff, in 1866, Mr. Whyte received an appointment, and for eight years was actively engaged on work connected with the construction of wet and graving docks and their equipment, with warehouse accommodation, and with hydraulic machinery and other requisite appliances. In 1875 he was appointed chief assistant to the general manager of the docks, and thus, in addition to being acting engineer, he had extensive expe-

rience in matters relating to the management of docks, including the maintenance and working of machinery, the working of local traffic, discharging and loading cargoes, &c. Mr. Whyte was elected to the combined office of superintendent of harbour and docks and acting engineer to the Dock Commission of Leith in 1883. He has, in the course of his experience, designed and carried out several large works of sewerage and gas and water supply, and laid out some miles of streets. He is a Member of the Institution of Civil Engineers and a Fellow of the Royal Scottish Society of Arts, to which he recently contributed a paper on "Hydraulic Machinery."]

Leith is one of the oldest seaports in Scotland, and, notwithstanding the tendency of all old things to decay, it still remains one of the most flourishing ports in the empire. It is first mentioned in historical records in the year 1128, but its authentic history as a port dates from 1329, in which year King Robert the Bruce granted a charter of the harbour and mills of Leith to the City of Edinburgh. This charter and other royal charters granted in subsequent centuries, and Acts of Parliament too numerous to mention from 1788 onwards, have constituted from time to time the authority and the limits of the jurisdiction of the commissioners for the harbour and docks of Leith, and define the port as extending from Wardie on the west to "Figgate Burn" on the east, a distance of 3½ miles along the south shore and extending northwards to the middle of the Firth of Forth.

It would be, doubtless, interesting to follow the history of the port from the time of its first being granted to the City of Edinburgh to the present time, to follow its course during the five centuries under which it remained as a vassal of Edinburgh, and to consider the somewhat intemperate and interminable series of conflicts which subsisted between the "City of Palaces and Towers" and their plucky little vassal by the sea. This would not be quite within the line of thought of a body of men of the engineering profession, whose associations and occupation are more concerned with matter-of-fact everyday work, so the author will come to times not yet remote and more practical, if less interesting.

Until the beginning of the present century the whole accommodation for shipping at Leith consisted of the harbour, formed in the bed of the Water of Leith, a small stream rising in the Pentlands, and which, after a course of some 12 or 14 miles, here joins the Firth of Forth. Along the banks of this water for nearly half a mile quay walls have been constructed, at which the vessels were discharged, the depth of water alongside these quays being about 12 ft. at high-water neap tides and 16 ft. at high-water spring tides. The harbour was dry at low water, the bottom of it at its lowest part being about the level of low water of ordinary spring tides. The entrance to this harbour was not then protected by piers, and great difficulty was experienced by navigators in reaching the harbour owing to the long stretch of sands and the continued shifting of the outlet of the river towards low-water line outside. Like many other ports there was a bar at Leith, respecting which Lord Jeffrey gave vent to his pent-up feelings when delayed for want of water :—

> In deep profound surpassing far
> I blest the Edinburgh bar;
> But, muttering oaths between my teeth,
> I cursed the shallow bar at Leith.

This was the position of the harbour at the close of the last century. The trade being then considerable, and the accommodation admittedly inadequate, the Lord Provost, magistrates and council of Edinburgh (in whom the harbour was then vested), after having discussed a number of impracticable and fanciful schemes proposed by amateur engineers (fortunately all of which were rejected), wisely agreed to consult the eminent engineer John Rennie, and on his advice in the year 1799 obtained Parliamentary powers for, and subsequently carried out from his designs and under his direction, the first docks at Leith, now known as the East and West Old Docks.

These docks, the former opened in 1806 and the latter in 1817, cost, with their adjoining quays, graving dock and other works incidental to their completion, upwards of £300,000, a very large sum, having regard to the trade at that date. Each dock is 750 ft. long, 300 ft. wide, and they are entered by a lock 150 ft. long, 35 ft. wide and with a depth on the sill of 17½ ft. at high-water springs. At the time of their construction they were able to accommodate 180 vessels of the class then frequenting the port. The docks are still in excellent condition and still largely used for the smaller class of vessels.

Having regard to the trade at that period and to the size of vessel, these docks were a gigantic undertaking, and here the author would like to say what he had said elsewhere before, that notwithstanding the severe criticism and comments which have been made regarding the management of the harbour by the City of Edinburgh in the past, that the corporation of that time deserves the very greatest credit for having initiated and undertaken works of such magnitude at that period, works which remain a tribute to their enterprise and sagacity, and also may be said to have laid the foundation of the prosperity and the future development of the port.

About the year 1835 the finances of the City of Edinburgh became embarrassed. The corporation had borrowed large sums of money, applied, among other purposes, to the construction of the docks, of which sums about £260,000 was due to the Government practically on the security of the dock rates. The trade had considerably increased. Continued allegations were made that surplus revenues were being applied for civic and municipal purposes, and not for the improvement of the harbour as required by the Acts of 1799 and 1826.

An inquiry was instituted by the Government, and a result of this inquiry and of certain negotiations was that the municipal and the mercantile and maritime affairs of Edinburgh and Leith were wholly separated and dissevered. By an Act of Parliament passed in 1838 the harbour and docks were vested in eleven commissioners, of whom three were appointed by the Town Council of Edinburgh, three by the Town Council of Leith, and five by the Lords of the Treasury ; and it was specially enacted that no member of either town council could be elected a commissioner for the harbour and docks, restrictions which exists at the present time, having been confirmed in successive Acts of Parliament. The commissioners are incorporated under the whole property and revenues of the harbour and docks, subject to an annual payment of £7,680 per annum, of which £2,000 was due to the ministers of the city, and which was commuted in 1871 by a payment of £40,000. Of the remaining sum £3,180 was due to the "creditors of the City of Edinburgh," £2,300 to the University of Edinburgh, and these were commuted in 1896 by a payment of £190,000, so that the financial tie which bound the docks to the city for the sixty years since the municipal tie was broken is now also dissolved.

Shortly after the constitution of the commission in 1838 the question of the improvement of the harbour and docks was again under consideration, and the commissioners resolved to consult some of the leading civil engineers of the day. They accordingly obtained reports from Sir William Cubitt and Mr. James Walker, the latter of whom in 1839 recommended the extension of the pier to points very near their present limits, and proposed to dredge the entrance channel so as to give a depth of 12 ft. at low-water spring tides. Only within recent years this depth has been obtained and a further depth of 5 ft. will shortly be inaugurated.

Several years elapsed before any practical steps were taken to extend the accommodation, but ultimately the consent of the Treasury was obtained in 1847 to a plan by Mr. James Meadows Rendel, C.E., London, being adopted. This led to the construction of the Victoria dock and the extension of the piers now existing, the dock being opened for traffic in July, 1852. This dock is 750 ft. long, 300 ft. wide and 33 ft. deep. The entrance is 60 ft. wide, and the sill is 6 ft. lower than the sill of the old dock, so that it will be seen that a great advance was made in the character of the accommodation due to the development of steamer tonnage in the previous years.

The trade of the port continued to augment after the opening of the Victoria dock, and the commissioners resolved to provide still further accommodation. Hitherto the docks were all on the west side of the entrance channel and har-

hour. Acting on the advice of Sir Alexander Meadows Rendel, the commissioners now resolved to construct a new dock on the east sands. The works were commenced in 1859 and in 1865 the Albert dock was opened. This dock is 1,100 ft. long, 450 ft. wide and 35 ft. deep, and is entered through a lock 350 ft. long and 60 ft. wide, with the sill 2 ft. lower than the Victoria dock and 8 ft. lower than the old docks. The available depth of water on the sill is at springs about 26 ft. and at neaps about 22 ft. It may be interesting here to note that it was at this dock that hydraulic appliances were first used in Scotland in working the dock gates and machinery.

The dock gates are constructed of yellow pine trussed beams, 21 in. square, with greenheart heel and mitre posts, and greenheart planking below the water-line and pine planking above. They are moved by chains working on barrels fixed in the masonry and actuated by hydraulic engines, fixed in pits under the coping.

No sooner was the Albert dock opened than it became apparent that further dock accommodation would be required, and the construction of the Edinburgh dock was therefore undertaken. This dock lies to the east of the Albert dock, with which it is in communication and from which it is entered by a passage 95 ft. wide at coping level. The dock is 1,500 ft. long, 650 ft. wide, with a jetty 1,000 ft. long and 250 ft. wide in the centre. The dock is 35 ft. deep, the same as the Albert dock, and was opened in July, 1881. The cost of these two docks was upwards of £650,000.

The docks are well equipped with sheds, cranes, rails, &c. For the protection of goods when discharged there are sheds varying from 60 ft. to 80 ft. in width, and some are being extended to a width of 120 ft. at the present time. The sheds cover an area of over 13 acres, and they are all floored with whinstone setts or granolithic pavement. There are altogether forty-six hand, hydraulic and steam cranes, fixed and movable cranes varying from 1 ton to 65 tons power, the latter being a steam crane for lifting boilers and heavy machinery on board vessels. On the top of the jib of this crane an auxiliary jib was recently constructed rising considerably higher, with a power of 18 tons, worked from the intermediate shaft of the machinery, for masting vessels.

#### COAL SHIPMENT.

The facilities for coal shipping consist of one steam coal crane, two hydraulic coaling cranes and three hydraulic coal hoists, all of modern type and construction. A peculiarity of the coal hoist is that there is only one cylinder and ram, the tipping of the waggon, usually done by a separate ram, being in this case effected by a chain fixed to the front of the cradle, which holds it at the required level for the shoot, and the waggon being tipped up by the lifting ram being raised to the height necessary to give the angle to discharge the coal from the waggon. The tipping cradle is hinged at the centre, and consequently when tipped a space is left between the front of the cradle and the butt end of the sheet. This space would allow the coal to fall between the cradle and the shoot, but this is prevented by an ingenious arrangement in which by a parallel motion a small subsidiary shoot, level with the floor of the waggon, is projected forward as the cradle rises and thus effectively "bridges over the gulf."

#### BRIDGES.

Communication between the two systems of docks on the east and west sides of the harbour is maintained by four bridges, two of which are swing bridges and two bascule bridges. The largest of the swing bridges is 120 ft. clear span, and was erected in 1874, at a cost of over £32,000. The bridge is constructed of main braced girders, and carries two lines of railway and roadway, with a footway on each side. The bridge is 215 ft. long and weighs upwards of 700 tons. It turns on a central hydraulic ram, 60 in. diameter, and is swung by two rams, each 14 in. diameter, with multiplying sheaves and chains. At the time of its construction it was the largest swing bridge in the kingdom, but it is now surpassed by two or three others, notably by the bridge at Connah's quay, which is 140 ft. span, and by the Manchester canal bridge at Trafford-road, which, although less span, weighs over 1,800 tons.

#### GRAVING DOCKS.

The accommodation for the repairs of vessels consists of six graving docks, respectively 382 ft., 338 ft., 300 ft., 266 ft., 180 ft. and 174 ft. in length. The latter has been in existence since the old docks were opened, is still in excellent condition and is very useful for the repairs of small vessels and steam trawlers. The largest graving dock, known as the Prince of Wales dock, was opened in 1860 and cost £60,000. The water is pumped from all these graving docks by turbine or centrifugal pumps of such power that the docks can be emptied in about two hours.

#### SHIPBUILDING AND SHIP REPAIRS.

Shipbuilding has a history at Leith. It was inaugurated by James IV., who formed a dockyard at Newhaven (then called " Our Lady's Port of Grace "), and in 1511 ordered the building of the *Great Michael*, a war vessel 240 ft. long 36 ft. beam, and which " within the walls " was 10 ft. thick, with massive sides of oak. The building of this vessel is said to have " wasted all the woods in Fife (except Falkland Wood), besides timber that came from Norway." This vessel " had 300 mariners, six score gunners, 1,000 men of war, besides captain, skippers and quartermasters." The *Great Michael* was afterwards sold or presented to Louis XIII.

The patent slip for the repair of vessels was invented at Leith by Messrs Morton & Co., a firm still in existence; and Messrs. Menzies & Co., who built the renowned *Sirius*, the pioneer of Atlantic steam navigation, in 1837, have occupied premises at the harbour for over 100 years. There are several other shipbuilding and repairing yards, the largest being that of Messrs. Ramage & Ferguson, who have acquired distinction as the builders of some of the finest steam yachts afloat.

### TRADE AND FINANCE.

The cost of the harbour and docks up to the present time has been over £2,000,000, and the amount of the existing debt is £436,000. The revenue last year was £106,000, of which over £10,000 was derived from rents of ground, warehouses, feu duties, &c. The number of vessels arriving at the port during the year was 6,046, with an aggregate tonnage of 1,814,435 nett register tons, of which 5,215 vessels of 1,678,784 tons were steamers. The total imports and exports were over 2,500,000 tons, of which fully one-half arrived at or was despatched from the ship's side direct in railway waggons, rails being laid on every quay in direct communication with the Caledonian and North British Railways, thus affording rapid and efficient means of transit to all parts of the country.

Goods imported and exported are of great number and variety, there being upwards of 400 classified articles and probably an equal number unclassified. The rates on vessels vary from 2d. per register ton on all coasting vessels to 5d. for Continental, 7d. for Baltic and 10d. for American and eastern vessels. But there are important concessions in all cases after two or three voyages of a vessel in any one year, and all vessels pay only 2d. per ton after eight voyages. The rates on goods vary from 1d. per ton on coal to 8d. per ton on grain, flour, timber, hemp, flax, &c.

### LIGHTING AND WATER SUPPLY.

Water is supplied to the vessels and works by the Edinburgh and district water trust, by arrangements with the commissioners. The latter body obtain the water in "bulk" and distribute it to the vessels and collect the charges thereof. The commissioners have water mains on every quay, the aggregate length of mains over 3 in. diameter being about 6 miles. The quantity of water used is about 55,000,000 gallons per annum. There are also about 6 miles of gas mains, and the lighting by gas necessitates the use of about 430 large Bray and other lamps, and the consumption of about 7,000,000 cubic feet of gas per annum in addition to 60 electric 10 ampere arc lamps. The plant supplying the current for the electric light is situated at the west end of Victoria dock, and of it there will probably be a considerable extension in the near future, in view of the completion of the new dock works now in progress.

### NEW WORKS.

The new dock works now in course of construction necessitated the reclamation of an area of about 80 acres of the foreshore lying to the north or seaward side of the Albert dock. This reclamation was effected by a sea wall of somewhat unusual design. It consists of a mound of hand-packed rubble stone, 30 ft. wide at the base and 9 ft. at the top, the sea face of which is covered with large classified blocks, each 6 ft long and 4 ft. wide. The whole of the wall is laid on the surface of the sand, which is dry at low water of spring tides, and the face of the wall has a slope of about ¾ to 1. A row of pine sheet piling was driven down to the clay along the back of the wall, and a row of greenheart sheet piling was driven to a depth of 8 ft. into the sand at the toe of the wall. The result was that the sand between these rows of piling became quite firm, and some small stone being spread over it made it resemble a road. The laying of the large concrete toe blocks, each weighing about 14 tons, was thus easily and expeditiously accomplished. Above the sheet piling the wall is backed with clay puddle up to high-water line, to make the sea wall "watertight," so that it became a cofferdam to exclude the water from the reclaimed area. The clay puddle was kept in position by a backing of dry stone, earth, sand, &c. The wall is surmounted by a parapet constructed of six to one cement concrete *in situ*, carried up to 15 ft. above high-water ordinary springs. The wall was completed in 1896 and has stood through the gales of two winters quite satisfactorily.

The dock now being constructed within the reclaimed area, from which the water was excluded in June, 1896, is 1,100 ft. long, 550 ft. wide and 40 ft. deep. The length can easily be increased to 2,000 ft. at small expense in the future. The dock is being surrounded with walls of solid masonry, set in cement mortar and carried down into the boulder clay 4 ft. below the bottom of the dock. The walls are 20 ft. thick at the base and 9 ft. at the top. The face is formed of squared stones close-jointed and with a batter of ½ in. per foot. The back sets off 3 ft. at 11 ft. from the top, and again 4 ft. at 19 ft. below coping. From this point to the bottom the back of the wall is vertical. The walls are all finished with granite coping, 3 ft. wide in the dock and 4 ft. wide in the lock and basin, and all 1 ft. 6 in. thick. The dock will be entered by a lock 350 ft. long between the sills, 70 ft. wide and 38 ft. deep from coping to sill. This will give a depth of water over the sill at ordinary springs of 30 ft. 6 in., and at neaps of about

25 ft. 6 in.; at equinoctial springs the depth over the sill will rise to about 33 ft.

The lock walls are being constructed of masonry similar to the dock walls. The invert is of cement concrete, gauged six to one, and is to be covered with squared whinstone, 12 in. thick. All the hollow quoins, sills, roller-path stones and sluice stones are of Aberdeen granite. The culverts are each 6 ft. high and 4 ft. wide, and the sluices are to be of greenheart timber and to be raised and lowered by direct-acting hydraulic rams fixed to the masonry of the wall. A stop groove of granite is constructed on each side of the sluices, so that by inserting dummy paddles temporarily the sluices can easily be examined or repaired if necessary. The dock gates are being constructed on the flotation principle, wholly of steel and fine Yorkshire iron, with greenheart sills and heel and mitre posts. Each pair of gates, with the requisite pivots and roller paths, will weigh about 292 tons. The gates will be opened and closed by direct-acting pistons, with a piston rod attached to a horizontal lever on the top of the gate. This lever is hinged to the anchor block of the gate at one end and the other end is fixed to a bracket on the top of the gate.

A passage, 60 ft. wide and 36 ft. deep, will form a communication between the new dock and the Albert dock. The construction is similar to the entrance lock. It will be fitted with a single pair of gates also of the flotation type, but the machines for opening and closing will be fixed on the back of the walls, and will actuate the gates by means of chains passing over pulleys at the heel post. The value of this passage will be obvious, as, besides enabling vessels to pass from one dock to another, it provides practically a duplicate entrance from the harbour to the whole system of the docks on the east side of the harbour, a point of manifest importance in the working of the traffic.

Across this passage a swing bridge has been constructed. The bridge is on the skew, and is 132½ ft. long over all, 28½ ft. wide, and has two lines of roadway and rails and a footpath on each side. This bridge is formed of two mild steel plate main girders with cross girders, and with the roadway of timber. It weighs 350 tons and is carried on a central hydraulic pivot. The tail end is carried on two rollers travelling on a segment laid in the masonry. The turning of the bridge is effected by a pair of hydraulic rams with multiplying sheaves, with chains attached to a quadrant under the bridge, one for opening and one for closing the bridge. A similar bridge is now under contract to be placed across the entrance lock, Albert dock, so as to afford an additional means of communication to the south side of the new dock.

It is expected that the dock will be opened for traffic by the end of the year 1900. The equipment is not yet decided upon, but it may be assumed that the sheds, cranes and other appliances will be of the best construction and highest efficiency, so as to place Leith in the front rank of modern, as it was for many years in the front rank of ancient ports.

### DISCUSSION OF MR. WHYTE'S PAPER.

Mr. W. H. HARPUR (Cardiff) said he had pleasure in proposing a vote of thanks to Mr. Whyte, who, many years ago, was at Cardiff. Most of them were not interested in the construction of docks, but it did come within the purview of many municipal engineers to erect sea walls, and the illustration given in the paper would be of very great value to them.

Mr. J. PATTEN BARBER (Islington), who seconded the vote of thanks, said the portion of the paper which interested him was the wall which had been constructed for the purpose of reclaiming some of the foreshore. He thought fairly might describe that wall as of novel construction. It was ingenious and daring. He used the word advisedly, and he hoped its meaning would not be misunderstood. He did not say reckless—it was daring, it was bold. He should like to know with what Mr. Whyte had protected the sheet piling. It looked somewhat like concrete bag work. He should also like to know whether there had been any indication of these stones, or whatever they might be, being rolled away by the flood tides. And were the concrete blocks, forming the toe of the wall, constructed in the open? The boldest part of the construction seemed to be the formation of the heart of the wall in dry rubble. With this clay puddle being put in at the back any excess of water in the heart of the wall with a full tide might have had a tendency to break up the concrete face with hydrostatic pressure. It was a bold piece of work, but, as Mr. Whyte had told them, the result had been successful, and they need not criticise a bold piece of work when the result had been absolutely successful. It was a very ingenious piece of work, and he felt perfectly confident that no one but a man who knew what he was doing would have had the courage to adopt that method of construction. He particularly wished to draw attention to the way in which the foundation of the wall was prepared for laying the toe of the wall upon the sand. He once had occasion to design a retaining wall which was to be 60 ft. high, and the foundation was somewhat similar to the sands on which this embankment or wall had been constructed, and he intended, had the wall been constructed, to have placed hard-burnt clinker on the soft foundation to have made it somewhat harder than it was, and to have assisted in consolidating the clay and prevent spewing by the weight of the wall upon it.

The vote of thanks having been accorded,

Mr. WHYTE, in reply, said he wished to say a word in

reference to the question raised by Mr. Barber. They were rough stones laid at the toe of the wall, and not one of them had shown the slightest sign of movement at any time. The object was to prevent the backwash washing away the sand. As to the boldness of the design, it was not arrived at in one day. A smaller wall was built on the same design, and as they got on perhaps they got bolder. The object of the sheet piling was to keep the sand in place, without that they could not get the sand firm enough to have the blocks laid. Then he recommended sheet piling, and that overcame all their difficulties, and the foundations became so strong that they could drive trucks along it.

### LUNCHEON.

At the close of the indoor business of the meeting the members were entertained to luncheon by Mr. W. N. Colam, the engineer for the Edinburgh cable tramways.

After the toast of "The Queen" had been submitted by Mr. Colam, who occupied the chair,

Mr. JAMES LAW (Edinburgh) gave "The Lord Provost and Magistrates of the City." He did not know, he said, a body of men more able or more disinterested than those who composed the Corporation of Edinburgh. For his own part he wondered how busy men found time to do so much public work. He noticed that in connection with all the leading departments of municipal work in Edinburgh the conveners of committees always placed the greatest reliance on the wisdom and judgment of their skilled advisers. He was speaking to a company of skilled engineers, who were the advisers to municipal corporations, and when they went back to their own spheres of work they would, he hoped, impress upon their councils the great advantage which the City of Edinburgh derived from, and the implicit faith it placed in, the wisdom and skill of its trained engineers and specialists (Applause).

Bailie ROBERTSON, in responding, after commenting upon the beauties of Edinburgh, alluded to its industries, and remarked upon the fact that a good deal of the printing trade had recently gone from Edinburgh to London. He was very pleased to know, however, that one of their leading and most important newspapers in the country had acquired a site for new printing premises, which he was sure, from all he had heard, would be second to none in the kingdom. He had no doubt that, should any of the gentlemen present be back in Edinburgh in a year or two, they could not do better than visit these printing premises, which, he felt sure, would be superior to anything in the country.

Mr. COLAM, in proposing the toast of "The Association," said municipal engineers had to be a great deal more than engineers—they had to be diplomats, and if they were not he was afraid they would not have a very happy time. They had in Edinburgh, in charge of a department in which municipal engineers were interested, a gentleman who was almost aggressive in his desire to get information. He referred to Bailie Mackenzie, convener of the Electric Lighting Committee. They wanted more Bailie Mackenzies in their municipal life. If they had more bailies and aldermen at these meetings they would find that these gentlemen, instead of grumbling at the absence of their officials, would be the first to propose that the expense of the members should be paid. He was convinced that what he was saying was correct, and he hoped that members of the association would use their persuasive powers to bring this desirable state of matters to pass (Applause). They had just been speaking about that powerful organ, The Scotsman, which represented the Press power of the country, and he would like to say that Mr. Law, in making the great changes he was about to carry out, had recognised the importance of picking up all the information he could, and at the present moment he had even spared his right hand to go to America, in order to bring back the latest information to make the great enterprise a success.

The PRESIDENT of the association acknowledged the toast, and preposed the "Health of Mr. Cooper" (burgh engineer of Edinburgh), who, he said, had been the mainspring of the success of their gathering in Edinburgh.

Mr. COOPER having briefly acknowledged the toast, the PRESIDENT gave "The Chairman," and spoke of his eminence as an engineer. Mr. Colam, he said, was a recognised authority on tramway work—the highest authority in the world, in fact, upon cable traction.

The CHAIRMAN, in reply, said that the association would probably arrange another visit to Edinburgh when the cable system was in full operation, and the corporation would then, he had no doubt, be only too glad to receive the members. The proceedings then terminated.

A special word of recognition is due to the menu card of the luncheon, characteristic in its indication of the completeness with which everything Mr. Colam does is carried through in every detail. The card bore, embossed, the arms of the city, was illustrated with an excellent portrait of the Lord Provost and with a view of the National Gallery and Castle, and was tastefully printed.

### VISITS OF INSPECTION.

In the afternoon the members were divided into two parties, for the purpose of visiting a number of the municipal and other features of the city. The programme arranged for one section included the following visits:—

### THE ARTISANS' DWELLINGS.

Those inspected are situated in a central and crowded part of the city, on one of the areas dealt with by the corporation under the Housing of the Working Classes Act. The buildings have a frontage to Cowgate of 150 ft., and are substantially built in Binny stone with red stone dressing. The entrance to the houses is from a high-level street—High School-yards—on the southern front. The houses are planned on the balcony principle, to give each an entrance direct to the outside air. The two tenements together

EDINBURGH: SOUTH FRONT OF TENEMENTS AT HIGH SCHOOL-YARDS.

accommodate fifty-six families, and provision is made so that the blocks can be extended at any future time. Mr. W. Bruce, of the burgh engineer's department, and several lady members of the Social Union, referred to in a recent SURVEYOR (page 41), communicated a number of other particulars as to the construction and management of the dwellings. Our readers have already had an opportunity of perusing the paper read by Mr. Bruce before the meeting, and also the discussion thereon. The paper was given in our

EDINBURGH: WEST FRONT OF TENEMENTS AT TYNECASTLE.

issue of July 1st and the discussion last week. We give two illustrations representing respectively tenements at Tynecastle meadows, a working-class suburb, and at Cowgate, in the centre of the city. It will be seen that the latter were the tenements visited.

### THE ELECTRIC LIGHTING STATION.

The central electric lighting station is in Torphichen-street, in the west end of the city. It is a handsome building in stone, built in the Italian Renaissance style from designs by Mr. John Cooper, the burgh engineer. This large station was completed in April, 1895, and now is entirely fitted up with its machinery for generating electricity for lighting and power, all to the design and arrangement of Prof. A. B. W. Kennedy, of Westminster. The boiler-house is 150 ft. by 45 ft., with the coal store above of the same size, the coal being fed into automatic stokers in front of the powerful boilers, of which there will be seventeen. The engine-room is 100 ft. by 89 ft., in two sections—high-tension side and low-tension side. The engines are of the Willans & Robinson type, with Siemens' dynamos and Ferranti alternators. The switchboard occupies the whole length of the engine-room on one end, over which are the battery-rooms, meter-testing rooms, stores, &c. Owing to the extraordinary success of the electric lighting in Edinburgh, the present station is rapidly becoming too small, and a beginning is soon to be made of the construction at McDonald-road of another station, which will be on a scale equal to, if not greater than, the present central station. Mr. F. Newington, the resident electrical engineer, acted as cicerone to the visitors

Full particulars of the works will, of course, be found in Mr. Newington's paper, which, together with the discussion, ap-

EDINBURGH: WEST FRONT OF CENTRAL ELECTRIC LIGHTING STATION (ENGINE ROOMS, &c.).

peared in our last issue. We give another illustration of the works in addition to the three given last week.

THE TOLLCROSS CABLE TRAMWAY POWER STATION.

This cable power station, now in the course of completion, is situated at Tollcross, on an area of ground about an acre in extent, which was previously cleared under the improvement scheme. The group of buildings will form a complete depot, providing the necessary power and accommodation for driving five lines of cables operating the Braid Hills, Circular, Prince's-street, Murrayfield and Gorgie routes of tramways, soon to be placed under the cable system of traction. The buildings comprise the following, *viz.*,—

*The boiler house*, 104 ft. by 40 ft., containing four large boilers of the marine dry back type, with superheaters above and the flues under the floor, two feedwater heaters and a Calvert's economiser.

*The chimney* is also placed here, and rises to a height of 175 ft. Coal storage is also provided above the boilers, the coal being fed automatically into mechanical stokers.

*The engine and hauling machinery rooms* are 103 ft. by 89 ft. by 40 ft. high. Two powerful travelling cranes traverse the width of these rooms, for raising and setting the heavy machinery. The machinery foundations are very substantially built of brick and cement, and vary from 10 ft. to 15 ft. in depth below the floor.

*Engines and Machinery*.—There will be three pairs of compound engines, each capable of developing 900 horse-power at 160 lb. steam pressure. The first motion shaft will have two pulleys of 14 ft. diameter, driving two pulleys of 30 ft. diameter on the second motion shaft by means of thirty-two cotton ropes of 1½ in. diameter. This second shaft will drive the grip and deflecting pulleys for the five lines of cables. Clutches are also provided for putting these in and out of gear. There will also be five large rope drums for running the new ropes into the lines when changing.

*Tension Races-Room*.—Beyond the engine-room on the basement is the tension races-room, 160 ft. by 89 ft., where the machinery for maintaining an equable tension on the cables will be placed; and beyond this, again, under the street in front of the building, is the depot road pit, 96 ft. by 19 ft., containing twenty pulleys of from 8 ft. to 11 ft. diameter for diverting the cables into the subway (120 ft. by 5 ft.) which runs out to Earl Grey-street pit.

*Cable Cellar*.—At right angles to the tension races-room, also in the basement, is placed the cellar for storing the old cables. This is provided with a large rope drum, engine and machinery, for drawing the ropes out of the lines when those have to be changed.

*Pump and Tank Rooms, &c.*—At the side of the engine-room are the pump and tank rooms, for water storage, lavatories, engineers' offices, carsheds, &c.

*Car Sheds and Storage of Cars*.—The front part of the buildings is wholly set apart for the storage of about sixty cars. These cars will be elevated above the floors on open gantries, for the convenience of getting at the grippers and brakes and making any adjustments required. The cars enter the depot by an inclined plane on to a movable platform or traverser which runs the whole length of the car sheds, and are readily stored in the byes. Behind the car sheds are placed the stable, store-rooms and smithy and mechanics' shop.

*Design and Cost*.—The buildings have been substantially constructed of stone and brick, with iron and glass roofs, and are practically fireproof. The design of the front elevation to the new street and to Ponton-street is treated in a free interpretation of late Victorian Gothic work built in Corsehill stone. The cost of the buildings will be about £44,000.

*Contractors*.—The contractors are Mr. Colin MacAndrew, of Edinburgh, for the whole buildings; Messrs. Dick Kerr & Co., Limited, Kilmarnock, for the engines, hauling machinery and other plant; and Mr. George Sinclair, Leith, for the boilers, piping, pumps, &c.

*Engineers*.—The whole buildings and machinery are from the designs of Mr. W. N. Colam, C.E., and Mr. John Cooper, burgh engineer, engineers to the corporation for the cabling of the tramways. Mr. Colam accompanied the party of inspection and courteously replied to all the questions raised on the spot. Some illustrations of the cable power station at Tollcross and that at Shrubhill were given in our issue of July 8th, in connection with Mr. Colam's paper and the discussion arising out of it.

M'EWAN HALL.

At the M'Ewan Hall the following description was given of this magnificent feature of Edinburgh's architectural acquisitions:—

No doubt you are aware that this beautiful building was erected at the expense of Mr. William M'Ewan, member of Parliament for the central division of the city, and generously given by him to the University of Edinburgh for use as a graduation and concert hall. No doubt you are also aware that the building was designed by Dr. Robert Rowand Anderson, R.S.A., the eminent architect of the new medical school adjoining the hall.

The building is designed in the Early Italian Renaissance style of architecture, and has taken about nine years to erect and complete. The plans and sections laid out for your inspection are working drawings used during the erection. Considerable care had to be exercised in the setting out of the building, but I am glad to say the work was so accurately done that when the columns were built and tested on top of caps the variations of the distances from centre to centre did not exceed ⅛ in. The semicircular shape of the building is after the plan of the ancient Greek theatre, and is seated for 2,600 comfortably. The dimensions of the hall internally are: On the large diameter, 106 ft.; the smaller diameter, about 66 ft. The diameter over the galleries is 134 ft., the height being 90 ft. to the dome light. The depth of the galleries is about 14 ft. The outer wall, which is 3 ft. 6 in. thick, is about 64 ft. high, and is strengthened with massive buttresses placed radially behind the large pillars you see supporting the dome. The dome rises about 38 ft. above the cornice, and is surmounted by an ornamental lantern 30 ft. in height. The total height from the street level to the top of lantern is about 130 ft.

*Construction of Dome*.—The roof is constructed of mild steel of an equal quality to that used in the Forth bridge. There are twenty-two massive lattice girders in the circle, attached at their tops to a heavy steel ring enclosing the circular light at the apex. The girders radiate from this ring so that the foot of a girder rests directly over the centre of one of the stone columns. The backs of the girders are kept about 2 in. clear of the stone work, to allow for expansion, and their feet are set upon turned steel rollers fitted in cast-iron bed-plates resting upon the stone caps of the pillars. The wall of the clerestory, which you see is pierced with circular lights thirteen in number and about 7 ft. in diameter, is supported on the outside by strong flying buttresses, which are intended to convey to the vertical buttresses any lateral pressure that can take place. I may mention a fact which will show the high quality of this roof work. When the steel work was completed, and previous to the removal of the supporting staging, we had a fine silk cord stretched across the hall and under the steel work, and by the use of vertical gauging-rods between this cord and the under side of the central steel ring it was found, when the wedges were removed, that the sinking of the structure was less than ⅛ in. The total weight of steel used in the construction amounts to about 200 tons. Externally the steel framework is covered with boarding and lead. Those of you who care to mount the stairs up to the roof will see one of the finest pieces of lead work in Edinburgh, or, I may venture to say, in the country. The lead used weighs 8 lb. to the superficial foot, and there is altogether about 140 tons of it on the roofs. The ceiling which you see is of boarding ½ in. thick, in very narrow widths and bent to the required curves. The red stone columns are 28 ft. in height from base to cap and 2 ft. 2 in. in diameter at the neck. We calculated that the weight to be sustained by each column at the under side of the cap amounts to slightly over 80 tons.

The two galleries are fitted with continuous benches in yellow pine wood stained, the balustrades in front being in oak. In the lower balustrade you will notice that each bay or division has a panel in the centre; on these panels are carved the monogram and crest of the donor, the arms of the university and the city. On the panel above the centre doorway is carved the words Jacobus VI., that genial monarch being the founder of the university. On one side is the date 1584, being the year of the foundation of the university; on the other side is the date 1894, the year in which that particular portion of the work was executed, and probably some sanguine spirit really expected the building to be finished and opened in that year! While speaking about the galleries it may be interesting to some of you if I point out the rather clever way the stairs are arranged. In each of the two round towers projecting from the outer wall are constructed two stairs, one within the other, somewhat like a screw with a double thread. One of the stairs enters from the street and gives access to the upper gallery only, the other stair entering from the wide corridor and giving access only to the lower gallery, the idea being to prevent the occupants of the two galleries meeting until out in the street.

The whole of the area is done up in oak, the floor being laid with what is known as block flooring in walnut and oak panels laid on concrete. The flaps of the seats in the raised portion of the area are a Canadian production, and are made of five thicknesses of "Ouram" wood glued together transversely under enormous pressure. The flaps are very strong and yet very light. The platform and senate stalls and the screen behind are also constructed in oak. In the basement floor you will find provision made for storing hats and cloaks. The walls are lined with white glazed bricks, giving the place a light and cleanly appearance. In the centre of the basement is the store-room, where is stored the movable gallery which on the occasion of an orchestral concert is fitted up over the fixed platform and senate stalls. Behind this store are placed the steam batteries, the ventilating fans and engine, and also the electrically-driven machinery belonging to the organ. Our engineer, Mr. Mitchell, will explain this machinery to those of you who care to go below.

*Warming and Ventilating.*—The warming is by low-pressure steam, the fresh air being drawn in by a pair of 48-inch Blackman fans and sent over the steam pipes in the battery chambers, passing into the hall through a number of ducts under the floor and in the walls, the warm fresh air being thus well distributed throughout the place. When empty the hall can be heated direct from the steam batteries by opening panels in the front of the platform. On the few occasions the hall has been used we have been able to keep the place quite fresh and comfortable and without the temperature varying more than one degree during the two or three hours each function lasted.

*Electric Lighting.*—Before arriving at the present arrangement of the lamps a number of experiments were made, first with arc lamps, then with the incandescent lamps which were finally adopted. As you see, a large pendant hangs in the centre of the dome, carrying thirty-nine lamps having 6,400 candle-power. Above the cornice and hid from view are placed 260 lamps of 16 candle-power each, and in each of the galleries are thirty-nine lamps of 32 candle-power each, giving within the hall a total illuminating power equivalent to 13,120 candles. The whole artificial illumination connected with the hall amounts to the equivalent of about 18,000 candle-power. The whole installation is found to be very successful.

*Decoration.*—The painted decoration of the interior was entrusted to Mr. W. M. Palin, of London, a clever young artist who worked like a slave for three years in producing the beautiful pictures you see around you. The whole of the figure work is painted on canvas fixed to the wood or plaster surfaces with white lead. The scheme of decoration on the dome is a series of symbolical figures typical of the various faculties in the university. Beginning at the left side, the figures are named Astronomy, Mathematics, Poetry, History, Divinity, Philosophy, Medicine, Oratory, Jurisprudence, Fine Arts, Music, Biology and Physics. In the spandril above the arch over the platform you observe a large painting, called the Temple of Fame. There are over eighty figures in the picture, representing students and philosophers working their way up to Fame. In the centre you will notice three goddesses, seated, named Science, Art and Literature. Underneath the Temple of Fame are four large wall panels. The panel on the right has a figure representing Minerva seated upon a throne receiving a gift of the building; on the left of the goddess is a portrait of the donor, Mr. M'Ewan. On the left the composition represents "Fame crowning Success." The whole of the painted decoration is allowed by competent critics to be well worthy of the clever artist who designed and carried out the work. On the grand staircase ceiling, which was decorated by Messrs. Reid & Downie, of Edinburgh, are painted the arms of the trustees of the hall and the high officials of the university. In the centre, on the north, are the arms of the donor; on the left those of Sir W. Turner, Lord Balfour and Sir William Muir; and on the right those of the late Mr. John Christison, the late principal, Sir Alexander Grant, and Mr. A. J. Balfour, the present chancellor. On the south side of the ceiling are the arms of the late Lord President Inglis and of the present Lord President Robertson, the whole work forming a piece of very rich colouring.

*Organ.*—The organ is by the Hope Jones Electric Organ Company, Birkenhead, and is thought to be the finest in the country. It contains over 2,400 speaking pipes, and the cable connecting the console with the speaking parts of the organ contains over 1,500 wires. The bellows are placed in the basement and are driven by a 10 horse-power electric motor. The cases were designed by Dr. Rowand Anderson, and executed by Mr. James Slater, of Edinburgh, and are made in oak. I regret that I am unable to describe in detail the working of this magnificent instrument, but through the courtesy of Mr. Collinson you will shortly hear its fine tones and be able to judge for yourselves of its high qualities. The cost of the organ, with its cases and the alterations on the building necessary for its accommodation, amounted to nearly £10,000. The cost of the decoration was also about £10,000, and the total sum paid by Mr. M'Ewan towards the balance of the cost of site and expenditure on the hull amounts to little less than £115,000. We do well to call it a princely gift.

As mentioned in the above description, Mr. J. H. Collinson, MUS.BAC.OXON., the organist of St. Mary's cathedral, delighted the visitors with selections calculated to bring out in harmonious contrast the enormous power and the extreme delicacy of the organ. Votes of thanks, moved by the president of the association, were accorded with general enthusiasm.

The day's visits of the section concluded with an inspection of

THE EDINBURGH PUBLIC LIBRARY.

This building is situated in George IV. bridge, and is the outcome of a gift of £50,000 to the city of Edinburgh through the munificence of Mr. Andrew Carnegie, of Pittsburgh. It is a first-class and highly-equipped library, possessing large reading-rooms, boys' and girls' lending library and a general library, and a very valuable reference department in which there is also a collection of valuable antique books and manuscripts. The planning of the building, the arrangements for the storing of the books, and the mode of working the lending department, have all been carefully arranged, and the library may be considered to be a model of its kind. It is under the direction of Mr. Morrison, the city librarian, who was unwearying in his explanation to the visitors of its main features. The buildings are in the French Renaissance style, from designs by Mr. G. Washington Browne, A.R.S.A.

The second section of the members were at the same time visiting the following:—

THE POWDERHALL REFUSE DISPOSAL WORKS.

This establishment is in the northern district of the city, and consists of stabling and other accommodation for twenty-two horses and all the carts, sweeping machines and other appliances of a branch cleansing depot. Here is also placed

EDINBURGH : GENERAL VIEW OF THE POWDERHALL REFUSE
DESTRUCTOR BUILDINGS FROM THE NORTH.

the refuse destructor of ten cells recently reconstructed on the Horsfall principle, together with the boiler and engine for the electric lighting plant. The whole operations of burning the refuse are conducted inside the buildings, so that all risk of nuisance may as far as possible be obviated. The chimney is 185 ft. high. The buildings are substantially constructed, Hailes stone and red Dumfriesshire stone being freely used. The whole of the buildings are in the Scottish

EDINBURGH : POWDERHALL REFUSE DESTRUCTOR WORKS, EAST
FRONT OF STABLING, ETC., TOWARDS BROUGHTON-ROAD.

Baronial style, from designs by Mr. John Cooper, the burgh engineer. We need not refer to them further in detail, as they were fully dealt with in the paper by Mr. Young, already given in THE SURVEYOR of July 8th, together with discussion and several illustrations. This week we give two general views of the works.

THE CHANCELOT ROLLER FLOUR MILLS.

This very large establishment is situated in the north of

EDINBURGH: THE CHANCELOT ROLLER FLOUR MILLS.

Edinburgh, and is one of the largest flour mills in Scotland. The plant and machinery is on the roller system, from the design of Mr. Henry Simon, Manchester, and possesses all the most modern features in the various processes. The buildings are erected in the French Renaissance style, are very substantial, and practically fireproof. The silo house is 137 ft. long by 34 ft. wide by 70 ft. high. The mill proper is 103 ft. 6 in. by 34 ft. and is five storeys high. The warehouse, 189 ft. long by 53 ft. wide, is six storeys in height and has a capacity for storing 50,000 sacks of flour. Its treatment is the Roman Corinthian order of architecture. The engine-room is a very fine one, being decorated in characteristic style emblematic of the trade. The central tower, rising to a conspicuous height, is a prominent landmark for miles round. It contains the large water tank for the Grinnell automatic sprinkler fire-extinction apparatus. There are two boilers, and the main engine, of 600 indicated horse-power, is by D. Stewart & Company, Limited, Glasgow. The ponds, situated to the west end of the building, contain 1,000,000 gallons of water for condensing and feedwater purposes. The mill was opened in 1894, and belongs to the Scottish Co-operative Wholesale Society, Limited, to whom we are indebted for the accompanying illustration.

THE SHRUBHILL CABLE TRAMWAY POWER STATION.

This station is situated at the present Horse Tramway Central Depot in Leith-walk. The engine-room, boiler-house, coal store and tension races-room are very similar in plan to those described in the previous account of the Tollcross power station. The notable features of this station are, however, the very large provision which is being made for storage of the cars—150 of them will be housed here. The whole buildings, when completed, will cover an area of 6·65 acres. The joint engineers for the corporation are Mr. W. J. Colam and Mr. John Cooper, the burgh engineer. A general view of this station was given in our issue of July 8th, together with views of the Tollcross station, in connection with Mr. Colam's paper.

THE LEITH DOCKS.

The Leith docks, although only second in importance to Scotland, are continually being improved and extended under the able supervision of Mr. Peter Whyte, M.I.C.E., the dock engineer and superintendent. At the present time a very large new dock is being constructed, and tidal locks are to be formed connecting the new dock with the Albert dock and the harbour. The reclamation wall is already built, and the foundations for the locks and dock gates are proceeding. The whole machinery will be operated by hydraulic power. The dock works quay walls, railways and other works will occupy the next few years in completion. Very complete details of the recent extension of the docks will be found in the able paper read by Mr. Whyte and given in the present issue.

The following list of the books, selected by Mr. Platt in connection with the premium of £10 awarded by the association, may be of interest: Published by Spon—Tudsbery's "Water-works," Hood's "Warming Buildings," Boulnois' "Municipal Engineers' Hand-Book," and Codrington's "Roads"; published by Crosby Lockwood & Co.—Burton's "Water Supply," Simm's "Tunnelling," and Clark's "Tramways"; published by Engineering—Dawson's "Electric Tramways; published by Longman & Co.—Mill's "Railway Construction; and Baker's "Masonry Construction," published by Chapman & Hall for Wiley & Sons. Of course it will readily be understood that, as every municipal engineer is probably in possession of an extensive professional library, some difficulty must necessarily be experienced in making a selection on such an occasion. We may also mention that four of the books—those by Hood, Boulnois, Codrington and Clark—were chosen to take the place of previous editions.

SOME MEMBERS OF COUNCIL.

On former occasions we have published supplement sheets containing portraits of the majority of the members of the council of the association. A number, however, still remained to be given, and some of these we present this week in the form of a special supplement, among the portraits being those of the two new members elected this year, Mr. Price and Mr. Collins, and the two members elected last year for the first time, Mr. Paton and Mr. Yabbicom. Except in the cases of Mr. Lemon and Mr. Price, biographies have already been given in our columns in connection with various district meetings. That of Mr. Paton was given in our issue of May 23, 1895; Mr. Yabbicom, October 2, 1896; and Mr. Collins, June 17, 1898. We append brief biographical notices of Mr. Lemon and Mr. Price.

MR. JAMES LEMON.

Mr. James Lemon, M.INST.C.E., after going through the usual term of pupilage and filling minor offices, was appointed in the year 1859 assistant in the office of the late Sir Joseph Bazalgette. This was at the commencement of the metropolitan main drainage scheme, and he thus had an opportunity of gaining experience on the most important drainage works in the country. In the year 1866 he was elected by public competition to the office of borough engineer and surveyor of Southampton. After twelve years' service he resigned and went into private practice, the corporation retaining his services as consulting engineer for three years. In 1883 the water supply of the borough was attracting a good deal of attention, and it was well known. Mr. Lemon took strong views in favour of the entire abandonment of the supply from the river Itchen and the adoption of a new supply from the chalk at Otterbourne (afterwards carried out). He was asked to become a candidate for the largest ward in the borough, and was elected without opposition. In 1889 he was also elected a member of the Hauts County Council, and served on that body for six years. In November, 1891, he was unanimously elected mayor of the borough, which position he held for two years. He is a partner in the firm of Messrs. Lemon & Blizard, civil engineers and surveyors, practising at Westminster and Southampton. He is also a member of the Institution of Civil Engineers; a fellow of the Royal Institute of British Architects, the Surveyors' Institution, the Geological Society, the Sanitary Institute, and the Meteorological Society; a member of the council of the Sanitary Institute and one of the examiners of that body, and also of the Incorporated Association of Municipal and County Engineers. As our readers well know, Mr. Lemon was one of the founders of the latter association. He acted as its first vice-president and in 1870 was elected president. He is actively engaged in designing and carrying out public works in various towns, but still finds time to attend to the duties of the various bodies of which he is a member.

### MR. JOHN PRICE.

Mr. John Price was educated at Manchester Grammar School and at the Victoria University, obtaining the Ashbury Exhibition at the university for civil engineering. In 1871 he entered the office of Mr. Hartley Watson, of Manchester, as articled pupil, and three years later was given charge of the construction of the Hollinwood branch of the Lancashire and Yorkshire Railway, as engineer to the contractor, Mr. James Evans. In 1876 he entered the office of Mr. Arthur Jacob, B.A., M.I.C.E., then consulting engineer to the Burrow-in-Furness Corporation, and was engaged upon the designs for the main drainage works of that town. On Mr. Jacob's appointment to Salford, Mr. Price was appointed resident engineer on these and other works, involving an expenditure of about £20,000. In 1878 he was elected to the appointment of engineer and surveyor to the Barton Sanitary Authority, which post he held until 1884, when he was appointed engineer and surveyor to the Toxteth Park Local Board. During this period he superintended the construction of main drainage works and works of sewage disposal costing nearly £50,000, and prepared plans for private street works estimated to cost nearly £40,000, the greater portion of which were carried out under his superintendence. He also acted during this period as consulting surveyor to four different highway authorities in connection with the Ship Canal Bill, 1883-4. On the extension of the boundaries of the city of Liverpool, whereby the district of four important urban districts councils, including Toxteth Park, were added to the city, Mr. Price was offered the appointment of assistant city engineer, at a salary of £550 per annum. This position he held till July, 1896, when he was appointed city surveyor of Birmingham, and deputy engineer to the Tame and Rea Drainage Board, at a combined salary of £800 per annum. On the death of the late Mr. W. S. Till, in the earlier part of this year, he resigned his appointment with the drainage board, and was appointed city engineer and surveyor of Birmingham, at a salary of £1,000 per annum. Mr. Price, we may mention, besides being a member of the council of the Incorporated Association of Municipal and County Engineers, is a member of the Institution of Civil Engineers, a fellow of the Surveyors' Institution, and a vice-president of the Municipal Officers' Association.

Next week we shall conclude our report of this interesting annual meeting, giving some illustrations in connection with the visits made on Saturday, July 2nd, the third day of the meeting.

## IMPERMEABLE CAPPED SOCKETS.

We give some illustrations of patented joinders or impermeable capped sockets, which have been brought out by the well-known sanitary engineering firm of George Jennings,

Fig. 1.—Joinder on Pipe Eye.    Fig. 2.—Joinder on Junction.    Fig. 3.—Sectional View.

Lambeth Palace-road, S.E., and the South-Western Pottery Works, Parkstone, Dorset. A few particulars of these joinders or socket will, no doubt, be of interest to our readers. They are intended for introduction into lines of stoneware pipe sewers, for the purpose of facilitating future connections and when required. It is considered to be especially valuable in the sewering of new roads in connection with building estates, as it can be introduced freely, without risk, wherever a future connection is likely to be required, and has no detailed supervision is necessary to ensure complete security. The cap or cover of the socket being formed, together with the pipe on junction, in one piece of highly-vitrified glazed stoneware, it is claimed that leakage of any kind, either from without or from within, is absolutely impossible, whilst its removal, which can be speedily and safely accomplished by any bricklayer or handy pipelayer, leaves the open socket in readiness for the continuity of the branch drain. A few sharp blows upon a fine-edged chisel at the cutting groove are all that is necessary to ensure a clean fracture at this point. Further details as to sizes, prices, &c., may, of course, be obtained from the makers.

## ACETYLENE GAS.

### DEMONSTRATION AT EARL'S COURT.

On Thursday a number of Press representatives were invited by the Acetylene Gas Light, Power and Calcium Carbide Company, Limited, to view a large-scale installation of acetylene gas at the Earl's Court exhibition.

Gradually "the new illuminant" has been developed and made of practical use since Sir Humphry Davy discovered it some sixty years ago. In 1859 Berthelot named it "acetylene," but the difficulty of producing calcium carbide on a large scale stood in the way of progress until Moissan in France, and Willson in America, simultaneously hit upon the method of coke and lime fusion by the heat of the electric arc. Now there are about a score of manufactories of carbide in different countries, and it is promised that the gas will soon be the cheapest artificial light in the market. Its photometric value as an illuminant is given as fifteen times that of coal gas, and it is stated to be cool and comparatively free from noxious vapours.

As seen at Earl's Court the production of acetylene by the new process seemed an easy matter. There were generators suited for a multiplicity of objects—from a cycle lamp to a street lamp, from a portable hand lamp to a lighthouse. In the generator is placed the calcium carbide, and the dripping of water upon it forms the gas ready for use. Apparently there was no danger in the operation. Calcium carbide itself will not burn on a fire, nor will it emit light if hammered. It becomes effective only by the action of the hydrogen of the water.

The installation at Earl's Court represents more than 12,000 candle-power, and includes a search-light which on clear nights has been seen from Epsom Downs. We understand that acetylene has not yet been tried here by a local authority, though in Hungary and North Italy towns are lighted with it, so that there is chance of distinction for a pioneer municipal engineer who likes to test it for street lighting and for the enrichment of coal gas. The address of the company is St. Olave's House, Ironmonger-lane, E.C.

## DISCHARGING WORKMEN.

### THE QUESTION OF NOTICE.

A case of considerable interest to surveyors and to local authorities was heard at the Horsham County Court, before his honour Judge Martineau, on Tuesday. Mr. Renwick, surveyor to the Horsham Urban District Council, was sued by a man named Buck for 18s., in lieu of a week's notice. Plaintiff said he had been in the employ of the council for over three years, and that a week or two ago the defendant dismissed him at a minute's notice, paying him his money up to that time and telling him he should not require his services further. He was paid 18s. per week, and he claimed that own in lieu of notice, which he should have given had he left his employment. Mr. Renwick stated that the plaintiff was a labourer and was paid by the day and quarter. Plaintiff was dissatisfied over an odd hour, and he told him to finish up. All such employees as the plaintiff were engaged by the day, though they were paid by the week as a matter of convenience. The engineers at the sewage and water works were permanent employees, because they were always required, but the others were engaged by the day, because a change in the weather or other unforeseen circumstances would render their services unnecessary. He had discharged many men at a moment's notice, and many men had left their work at similar notice. His honour said he had nothing to do with what was right or wrong as to the dismissal, but to do what was legal. There was a very common notion on the part of people that they were entitled to a week's notice, but the custom of the trade had to be considered in all cases. Agricultural labourers were engaged by the day, and consequently could be discharged at a minute's notice if their work was unsatisfactory and for many other reasons. He was satisfied that plaintiff was engaged by the day, and therefore gave judgment for the defendant.

**King's Norton.**—The council have decided to apply to the Local Government Board for sanction to borrow £6,372 for the execution of various works of sewerage.

# Some Annual Municipal Engineering Records.

## DUDLEY : NEW SOUTH WALES : NEWCASTLE.

An annual report of the work carried ont by the borough surveyor's department, and "of the expenditure incurred in repairing, lighting, watering and maintaining the respective roads and streets, also of other public works in the borough, for the year ended 25th March, 1898," has been presented by Mr. John Gammage, borough surveyor of Dudley.

The total length of roads and streets in the borough is 44 miles. Four new streets have been constructed during the year, and this has increased the total length by 482 yards. The total area of the roads and streets macadamised was 93,550 square yards; of this area 54,137 square yards were macadamised with Rowley stone and 39,413 square yards with cinders. The amount of materials used in the repair and maintenance of the roads was: Rowley macadam, 3,382 tons (342 tons of which were broken from old setts); broken cinders, 2,626 cubic yards; sand, 250 tons; ashes and cinder chippings, 3,754 loads; and water, 9,512 loads (equal to 2,405,800 gallons). The cost of maintaining the whole of the roads and streets was £5,519, including £976 for interest on loans and repayment of principal on works of footway paving. This amount is equal to about £125 per mile.

The cost of lighting, repairing, extinguishing, &c., the 804 lamps in the borough was £2,361, an average of about £2 18s. 8d. per lamp per annum. The cost of the water used for watering the roads and streets, and for supplying fountain urinals, &c., was £132. The following is a list of carts and machines used by the department in the work of cleansing and maintaining the several roads and streets: Nine water-carts, two vans, twelve mud-carts, four ordinary carts, two sweeping machines, three road scrapers and one steam roller.

The report proceeds to give details of several improvements and new works which were either completed during the year or which are at present in hand. Eighty-two notices and plans were received and approved for the erection of 123 houses, one theatre, one school, five workshops and thirty-three other buildings and additions.

In conclusion, Mr. Gammage points out that the traffic, a greater portion of which is through traffic, is yearly increasing, thus necessitating more repairs and consequently a greater expenditure. He considers that next year an increased amount for maintenance will have to be provided. "It will be seen," he says, "that the expenditure for the year has been £300 more than last year, but the cost per mile is only equal to the cost of the year 1894 and less than that of 1896. The average cost per mile for the last five years has been £123 12s. 7d."

\* \* \*

Much information of a highly interesting nature is, we find, contained in the report for 1896 of the Department of Public Works of New South Wales, and the following details selected by us from the publication may assist our readers to form an idea of the manner in which the public moneys of the colony are being expended. Briefly, the gross expenditure for the year amounted to over £1,772,485, this sum being made up as follows: Establishment, £56,220; railway construction, £208,154; tramway construction, £6,562; harbours and rivers, £246,502; dredge service, £108,434; water supply, £28,972; roads and bridges, £776,400; sewerage, £133,816. The report of the engineer-in-chief for railway and tramway construction shows that no new lines were completed or opened for traffic during the year, but that three new lines of the "Pioneer" class were in course of construction. As the weather remained favourable, no floods or heavy seas being experienced, very fair progress was made with the various works for the improvement, maintenance and convenience of navigation. The ever-pressing work of protection against floods, to which most of the rivers are so liable, occupied the attention of the department, and a considerable amount of work was carried out in this direction on the Richmond river and its tributaries, the Macleay river, and the Hunter river and its tributaries. Excellent results were obtained from the dredging operations, while the cost of them bore satisfactory comparison with previous years. Signal success more especially attended the use of the sand-pump dredges at Sydney and Newcastle. The reclamations effected by them formed a very valuable asset, which, states the report, if realised on at an opportune time, would far more than repay the outlay on the work. As a consequence, the work of converting grab dredges into the much more efficient and economical sand-pump dredges was vigorously proceeded with at the Fitzroy Dock establishment.

During the year 123 new bridges were completed, aggregating 10,218 ft. in length, made up of 296 timber beam spans, seven timber truss spans, and four iron spans, the total cost being £70,492. As one instance of the valuable work accomplished in the direction of conserving water, mention is made of a weir which was built on the Macquarie river at a point 3 miles above the township of Warren. This weir throws back and retains the water for a distance of about 11 miles, and is estimated to impound something like 172,000,000 gallons. It would be impossible, the report observes, to overrate the supreme importance to the colony of the question of water conservation, as the development and settlement of th.

country were absolutely dependent upon securing a permanent and regular supply of water.

Generally, the year with which the report deals was a good one for road work, the rainfall being normal, and there being no flood of any magnitude. The total roads mileage under the direct or indirect charge of the department had grown at the end of the year to 38,951 miles 76 chains, being an increase over the preceding year of 2,181 miles 50 chains. In addition to purely roads formation there were constructed 7 miles 36 chains of culverts, and 7,079 rods of fencing were erected. The bridges of 20-ft. span and over, for the maintenance of which the branch is responsible, numbered 2,722, having 7,655 spans, and an aggregate length of 260,519 ft., or 49 miles 27½ chains. The culverts totalled 31,073, with an aggregate length of 461,578 ft., or 57 miles 33½ chains. The average number of men employed by the roads branch during the year was 9,876, of whom 1,488 were directly employed by the branch, while 8,388 were contractors and their workmen.

With regard to the repairs and maintenance of bridges, which now demand a large and yearly-increasing expenditure, the assistant engineer suggests, as settlement advances in the colony, replacing timber structures, so far as practicable, by bridges of a more permanent character, and thus reducing the annual cost of repairs and maintenance. He points out that, in consequence of the improvement effected of late years to the surface of the roads and the cutting down of grades, the bridges are now required to bear the strain of much heavier loads than they were estimated to sustain at the time they were built. In the opinion of the department there is something to be said in favour of this contention. At the same time, they think they should not lose sight of the fact that in New South Wales they possess the best timber in the world for bridge building. It appears to Mr. Robert Hickson, the under-secretary for public works and commissioner for roads, who is responsible for this report, that the policy of the country should be to use this material—which with careful pricking has a life of from thirty to forty years—as largely as possible. There were cases, no doubt, where it would be more economical to the long run to erect iron, or, better still, stone bridges, but he feels satisfied that for many years to come it would be found more advantageous to use timber in the construction of a large proportion of the bridges. In travelling through the country one could not help remarking how bad the roads were in the vicinity of the towns, and how a long length of good road was spoilt by a few miles of bad road lying within a municipality. Under existing conditions Mr. Hickson sees no prospect of improving this state of affairs, inasmuch as to become incorporated, the areas of the municipalities had to be of considerable size; consequently municipal councils were obliged to take over a road mileage quite beyond their means to maintain. It seemed to him that councils should be responsible only for those lengths of roads that lay within the inhabited portions of the municipalities. Attention is drawn in the report to the urgent need of legislation in the matter of width of tyres. The heavy loads borne on waggons having narrow tyres cut up the roads to an excessive degree, and consequently entailed on the department a large expenditure for repairs.

During the year there was an expenditure of £132,816 in connection with the sewerage schemes for the metropolis, Newcastle and its suburbs, and some three or four country towns. The northern and southern metropolitan systems, which include the areas of the city of Sydney and of the municipalities of Redfern, Darlington, Waterloo, Alexandria, Paddington, Woollahra and Waverley were completed with the exception of some small areas lying around the foreshores of the harbour, the sewage from which would have to be lifted to the gravitation sewers. Work in connection with the western suburbs scheme was urgently pressed forward, and the extension of the main eastern branch sewer was almost completed. This extension provided for the drainage of a large area of Petersham, Leichhardt and Annandale. The main northern sewer was extended to Balmain. The sewage farm in connection with the western suburbs system was being prepared, and a good deal of work was being done in the levelling of the sandhills to form filter-beds for the reception of the sewage.

From January, 1895, to June, 1896, over 99 miles of new water mains, 28 miles of sewers (5½ miles being transferred from the Government) and 4½ miles of storm-water channels were laid by the metropolitan board, making a total of 891 miles of water mains, 230 miles of sewers and 14½ miles of storm-water channels now under their control. The capital cost of the water and sewerage works combined stood, on June 30, 1896, at £5,565,704. The gross revenue for the eighteen months was £250,843, and the working expenses £67,799, absorbing £26·09 per cent. of the gross revenue and leaving a nett revenue of £192,043, or a return of £3·46 per cent. on the capital debt of the board. The average daily supply of water was 16,645,014 gallons, and the estimated number of persons supplied was 408,282. Among other improvements, some important works were carried out at the pumping station for the purpose of increasing the supply and improving the quality of the water.

Mr. Hickson concludes his valuable report with a reference to the magnitude of the business of his department. It will, he says, be readily understood that the economical disbursement of a sum of £1,772,485, which was the amount expended during the year, demands the exercise of incessant vigilance and intelligent supervision. During the year 46,798 vouchers were examined and checked to the minutest detail before being forwarded to the treasury for payment, 65,771 letters and other documents were received and recorded, 11,855 letters were written and despatched, and 5,061 contracts were entered into, being at the rate of about seventeen contracts per working day. Finally, he bears testimony to the energy and zeal displayed by all the officers, and to the satisfactory manner in which the work of the department had been performed.

Special reports were included in the body of the volume from the following, among other officials: Messrs. H. Deane, engineer in chief for railway construction; C. W. Darley, engineer in chief for public works; H. R. Carleton, principal assistant engineer for harbours and rivers; J. Davis, engineer for sewerage construction; E. M. de Burgh, assistant engineer for bridges; H. G. McKinney, principal assistant engineer; J. B. Benson, board engineer; and Percy Scarr, principal assistant road engineer.

The value of the report is greatly enhanced by the addition of some admirable plans, map and views illustrative of works in progress or completed. We may mention specially the two views which give an excellent idea of the great outfall sewer across the Arncliffe sewage farm. The sewer is in triplicate, and the carrier is built on concrete arches of 50-ft. span springing from concrete piers.

\* \* \*

In his annual report to the Town Improvement and Sanitary Committees of the Newcastle Corporation the city engineer, Mr. W. G. Laws, shows that the expenditure on the account of the first-named committee was £22,220, as against an estimate of £22,800. Sewering cost £8,917, flagging and paving £11,921, and special improvements £1,382. The 1898-9 estimates for these items are respectively £7,480, £13,130 and £1,270, totalling £21,880. The Sanitary Committee, by original and and supplementary estimates, had a sum of £44,284 allowed for their year's work, the actual cost being £43,919, made up as follows: Roads, £10,768; street watering, £1,164; scavenging (including the removal of box ashes), £11,450; ash-pit cleansing (including the removal of tub ashes), £11,857; sanitary work, £6,583; destructor (working), £924; special improvements, £1,173. The total sum which it is estimated will be required for the current year is £47,005. There is an excess of expenditure over original estimates of £2,317. Extra expenditure on road metal, increases in the number of horses and carts, and street watering practically account for the difference.

The general particulars furnished show that the city has now 170¼ miles of sewers and drains of all sizes, and 179½ miles of streets. Scavenging exceeded the original estimate of £10,660 by £790, having actually cost £11,450. The cost of scavenging, Mr. Laws says, is increasing rather more rapidly than the population. Seven years ago it was 1s. per head, while now it costs just under 1s. 1d. per head. The public ask for more, the workmen ask for more, and the committee properly enough seems inclined to give more, so that this work may rise in cost still further. At the same time, it seems to him that Newcastle compares very favourably with other towns of similar size, both in the cleanliness of the streets and the cost of keeping them so.

The amount of refuse disposed of has been: Sent by rail as manure, 17,006 tons; sent by rail to deposit, 8,232 tons; sent by barge to sea, 23,787 tons; deposited in tips within the city, 51,073 tons; burnt at refuse destructor, Byker, 20,478 tons—total, 120,576 tons. These were collected at a nett cost of £28,732, or 4s. 9½d. per ton. The amount dealt with per house is 76·1 cwt., at a cost of 18s. 1½d.; per head of the population the amount is 10·8 cwt., at a cost of 2s. 7d. At Byker destructor the 22,715 tons burnt cost £795 17s. 5d. 8·41d. per ton burnt, slightly less again than last year. Adding to this cost interest on capital at 4 per cent. and rent of site, the total cost was just 11½d. per ton. The cost of sending refuse to sea from Mitford-street was £1,742 for 23,787 tons; 1s. 5½d. per ton, or, adding interest at 4 per cent., 1s. 6½d. "Is it proper once more to point out," he asks, "what would be the saving to the rates if a destructor, instead of a refuse wharf, were established at Mitford-street? Without reckoning the difference in cost of the downhill lead as against the uphill lead to Byker, there would be a saving of 9½d. upon 24,000 tons, equal to £950 per annum."

Under the head of relief labour no expenditure had been required during the past year. As to the water supply, Mr. Laws says: The season has not commenced so favourably as last year, as the company's reservoirs have never been full; but, on the other hand, there has been what is rather unusual, an increase in the month of May, so that the deficiency, which was 600,000,000 at the end of March, has been reduced to 300,000,000 early in May, leaving the stock at the end of the first week in May, though 200,000,000 less than last year,

yet just about the usual average for the date. On the whole, then, unless there be drought during the summer (of which there is no present sign), we may hope to have no scarcity. Since 1860 the sum of £1,844,269 has been spent on improvements in the way of sewering, paving, &c. With a population of 223,000, and a rateable value of £1,116,307, the expenditure of the two committees last year worked out to 6s. 4d. per head, or 1s. 3·2d. in the £1. The number of inhabited houses in the city is 31,710.

## QUERIES AND REPLIES.

*Sketches accompanying Queries should be made, separate on white paper in plain black-ink lines. Lettering or figures should be bold and plain.*

**203. Ditch: Interpretation of Width.**—"E. R." writes: Will you please help me to solve the following—viz., What will be the width across the top of a ditch, the depth of which is to be 4 ft., the width at the bottom to be 3 ft., and the sides having a batter of 1 to 1?

As each side is to have a batter or slope of 1 to 1—that is, for each foot of rise the side slopes back 1 ft.—there will be for each side having a 4-ft. rise a total batter of 4 ft. The bottom width being 3 ft., the top width of the ditch therefore will be: 3 ft. + 4 ft. + 4 ft. = 11 ft.

**204. Hydraulic Mean Depth, Meaning of.**—"Perplexed" writes: I shall be glad if you will explain the meaning of the term "hydraulic mean depth of sewer."

Hydraulic mean depth, or radius, is the sectional area of the sewage flow divided by the wetted perimeter. The wetted perimeter is the length of the inner surface of a pipe, measured at right angles to the flow, which is in contact with the water flowing through the pipe. Thus, in the case of a 24-in. diameter pipe running full, the hydraulic mean depth will be

$$\frac{2 \text{ ft.} \times 2 \text{ ft.} \times \cdot7854}{6\cdot2832} = \frac{3\cdot1416}{6\cdot2832} = \cdot5 \text{ ft.}$$

For a 6-in. diameter pipe the hydraulic mean depth will be

$$\frac{\cdot5 \text{ ft.} \times \cdot5 \text{ ft.} \times \cdot7854}{1\cdot5708} = \frac{\cdot196350}{1\cdot5708} = \cdot125 \text{ ft.}$$

In all cases where a circular sewer runs full or half full the hydraulic mean depth is equal to one-fourth the diameter.

## LONDON WATER SUPPLY COMMISSION.

The Royal Commission met on Monday, at the Guildhall, Westminster, under the presidency of Lord Llandaff.

Mr. ALLEN STONEHAM, Local Government Board arbitrator appointed under the Metropolis Water Act, 1871, to audit the accounts of the London water companies, having explained his system, expressed the opinion that his powers were sufficiently wide to enable him to make a very satisfactory audit. He could not suggest any further powers with which he could be usefully entrusted.

Mr. REGINALD E. MIDDLETON, engineer of many of the New River Company's works, and joint engineer with Mr. Hunter of the Staines reservoirs, expressed a decided opinion that purchase of the water companies by any body whatsoever would be financially inexpedient in the interests of the consumers, who would be placed in a much worse position than at present. He did not mean to deny that the revenue would ultimately meet the charges, but that time would be very far distant. Whether the companies continued in existence, or whether purchase took place, some further capital expenditure on additional water supply would be necessary.

**The Inventor of the Bunsen Burner.**—The Bunsen burner is so closely related to ancient history that it must be quite a surprise to many people to hear of its inventor being alive and in active practice as professor of chemistry at the University of Heidelberg. Dr. Bunsen has just been presented with the Royal Albert Medal of the Society of Arts, in connection with which the council has published the following little eulogy: Among the numerous and important scientific discoveries which have made the name of Bunsen famous, perhaps the most striking is that in which he was associated with his distinguished colleague, Professor Kirchhoff—viz., spectrum analysis, a discovery which has shed a new and unexpected light on the composition of terrestial matter, and has enabled us to obtain a knowledge of the chemical composition of sun and stars. The contributions which Bunsen has made in the application of chemistry and physics to the arts and manufactures are of the utmost value, and their importance may be measured by two out of many instances. The Bunsen battery was, until the introduction of the dynamo, the cheapest source of electricity, the Bunsen gas burner, by which a non-luminous, smokeless but, highly heated flame is obtained, is not only still indispensable in all laboratory work, but issued for heating purposes in thousands of houses and factories, and for illumination, by the incandescent system, in millions of lamps.

# Parliamentary Memoranda.

On Thursday, in the House of Lords, the London County Council (Money) Bill was read a second time, while the London County Council (Acton Sewage) Bill was given a third reading.

In the House of Commons the Lords' amendments to the Cromer Gas Bill, the Drogheda Gas Bill and the Wigan Corporation Bill were agreed to. The Bacup Corporation Water Bill and the Dover Harbour Bill were each read a third time.

In the House of Lords on Friday the Renfrew Burgh and Harbour Extension Bill and the Devonport, Plymouth and Stoke Tramways Bill were read a second time. The Tottenham and Edmonton Gas Bill, the Dublin Port and Docks Bill, and the Matlock Urban District Council Bill were read a third time.

In the House of Commons the Lords' amendments to the Sheffield Corporation Bill and the Plymouth Corporation Bill were agreed to. The Halifax Corporation Bill, the Stirling Gas Bill and the Paignton Improvement Bill were read a third time.

In the House of Lords on Monday the St. Helen's Corporation Bill and the Keighley Corporation Bill were each read a second time. The following Bills were read a third time and passed : London Building Act (1894) Amendment Bill, Plymouth and Stonehouse Gas Bill, Bristol Tramways (Electrical Power, &c.) Bill, Coventry Corporation Gas Bill, Bristol Tramways (Extensions) Bill and Blackburn Corporation (Tramways, &c.) Bill.

In the House of Commons the following private Bills, which came down from the Lords, were read the third time : Aberdeen Corporation (Tramways) Bill and Folkestone Water Bill. The following, which also came from the Lords, were ordered for third reading : Felixstowe and Walton Water Bill and Newtown Water Bill. The following, also from the Lords, were read the second time : Heywood Corporation Water Bill, Newcastle-npon-Tyne Corporation Bill and Seaham Harbour Bill. The Local Government (Ireland) Bill, after a short debate, was read a third time.

On Tuesday, in the House of Lords, the Paignton Improvement Bill was read a second time, while the Middlesbrough Corporation (Gas) Bill and the Leyton Urban District Council Bill were read a third time. The Local Government (Ireland) Bill, which had been passed by the Commons, was brought up and read a first time.

In the House of Commons the Newhaven Harbour Bill was ordered for third reading. The Lords' amendments to the London County Council (Acton Sewage) Bill were considered and agreed to.

In the House of Commons on Wednesday the Metropolitan Electric Supply Bill was read a second time.

## PRIVATE BILLS IN COMMITTEE.

*London and South-Western Railway Bill and the London County Council and Lambeth Vestry.*—The House of Commons committee, over which Mr. De Tatton Egerton presided, cut away an important part of the London and South-Western Railway Bill when it was before them last week. The Bill when it passed the House of Lords earlier in the session embodied a scheme for the enlargement of Waterloo railway station by the compulsory acquisition of land extending between the Lower Marsh on the north and Waterloo-road on the west. Since the Bill had left the Lords the company had found that the cost would be so great, having regard to the attitude of the southern frontagers of Lower Marsh and the acquisition of properties in an easterly direction, that they had been compelled for the present to modify the scheme. It had been reduced to something like half its original proportions, so far as the additional area proposed to be acquired was concerned. The London County Council had offered no opposition to the Bill in the Lords, because the measure as presented had included provision for street improvements in which the council acquiesced. Now that the Bill had been so mutilated by the change of policy on the part of the company the advantage to the public would be so insignificant that the council felt bound to oppose the measure. They asked that Parliament should not sanction such an incomplete scheme, but compel the promoters to take it back and bring forward a more perfect proposal next session. The Lambeth Vestry also opposed the Bill on the ground that it did not sufficiently provide for the housing of the poorer classes, whose dwellings would be disturbed. The committee found that the preamble had not been proved so far as the enlargement of Waterloo station was concerned.

*Chelsea Electric Supply Bill.*—A House of Lords committee, presided over by the Earl of Northbrook, passed on Wednesday week a Bill promoted by the Chelsea Electricity Supply Company, Limited, in which powers were sought to acquire additional lands and erect generating stations. The Bill was opposed by the London County Council, the Chelsea Vestry, the Earl of Cadogan and the Rev. W. H. Webb-Peploe, and the lessees and occupiers of houses in Flood-street, Chelsea. This, it was explained, was one of the Bills which led to the appointment of the joint committee on electrical energy which has been recently sitting under the presidency of Lord Cross. That committee, in their report, recommended that

in special circumstances electricity supply companies should be allowed to acquire land compulsorily, and it was contended that special circumstances existed in this case. The company, who had a capital of some £260,000, and were supplying with electricity nearly 100,000 8 candle-power lamps—an increase upon last year's supply of 20 per cent.—had reached the limits of the capacity of the generating station, and it had become necessary for them to provide further accommodation. They came to Parliament for compulsory powers because they had been threatened with an injunction, and they felt that without Parliamentary powers they would be blackmailed, first, by having to pay an exorbitant price for land which they required, and, second, by being taken into the Court of Chancery and prevented from carrying on their work. The objections raised by the various petitioners against the Bill related mostly to minor points. The county council, on the ground that some of the mains were in close proximity to the main sewers, claimed to have the power to supervise and control the lighting of the vestries. The Chelsea Vestry complained of gritty emanations and smoke from the chimney shaft and of vibration and noise, and suggested that the company should establish its large generating station outside London. Lord Cadogan's objection was that his property in the neighbourhood would be injuriously affected. The committee passed the Bill, but inserted a clause giving persons within a certain area of the company's works some compensation for any proved damage which might be done by the company's works to their houses.

*Devonport Borough Extension Bill.*—A Bill promoted by the Corporation of Devonport for the extension of the boundaries of the borough has been the subject of a spirited contest before a committee of the House of Commons presided over by Colonel Gunter. The opposition to the Bill came from the Parish Council of St. Budeaux, who objected to being annexed to Devonport. Mr. Balfour Browne, Q.C., who appeared for the St. Budeaux opposition, explained very fully the precedents bearing upon the case. If good reason for annexation were shown then Parliament should agree to it, but if the area taken in dissented Parliament ought not to assent unless strong grounds were brought forward in favour of the annexation. If they formed absolutely part of one community, if the streets were continuous, if their interests were the same, and if St. Budeaux were really a suburb of Devonport and the area was in an unsanitary condition, Parliament might well override their non-assent and pass the scheme. St. Budeaux was absolutely separated from Devonport by an arm of the sea, which was a good natural and physical boundary, and physical boundaries had before stood in the way of annexation. Having cited the cases of Leamington, Wigan and Plymouth, Mr. Browne went on to observe that people were not like flocks of sheep, to be driven into places to which they did not wish to go; and why should the people of St. Budeaux be driven into Devonport against their will. The districts were different in many ways, and St. Budeaux could manage the place better, more cheaply, and more to their own satisfaction, than Devonport could. It would not be local self-government if the committee put them within the jurisdiction of Devonport. If it had been proved that St. Budeaux was a hot bed of disease and a pest, then there might be some reason for the scheme; but St. Budeaux was not the pest, Devonport was the pest. What Devonport wanted was simply to tax St. Budeaux. St. Budeaux had applied to the county council for urban powers, and their decision was awaiting the result of this Bill. The St. Budeaux scheme was better and cheaper than that proposed by the Corporation of Devonport. St. Budeaux was not only separated from Devonport by an arm of the sea, but it was separated by an intense longing to remain divided. The eloquence of the learned counsel was in vain. The committee passed the Bill, but they gave a concession as to rating.

*Tynemouth Corporation Water Bill.*—The Corporation of Tynemouth had to fight for their water Bill in the Lords, and the fight was renewed before Colonel Gunter's committee in the Commons last week. Powers were sought in the Bill to obtain additional water, to construct additional waterworks and to borrow £430,000. The corporation had to face the opposition of their former opponents, the County Council of Northumberland. The county council championed the cause of the authorities of the district north of Tynemouth, which had a population of 5,000 inhabitants and ought to have a pre-emption for the water. As the corporation had taken all the water from the Font some provision ought to be made for those who were living on a day-to-day supply. The corporation ought to be required to supply the surplus water at a certain price to be fixed, if necessary, by arbitration. Mr. Horatio Adamson, the town clerk of Tynemouth, in his evidence in support of the Bill stated that the corporation expected to obtain 2,500,000 gallons per day as the result of the construction of the additional works provided for in the Bill, and they required 1,500,000 gallons for their own purposes. The surplus they proposed to sell, he presumed, at a profit. The owners who opposed the project, including Earl Percy, would be compensated for any fishing rights they might have. Lord Percy, it appeared, regarded the storage, capacity of the reservoirs as insufficient. Mr. J. F. Smillie, who had been borough surveyor of Tynemouth since 1888, stated that it was absolutely essential that a new supply should be obtained. After obtaining the supply of water from the Font the corporation would abandon that at Whitby as soon as possible, although a spring yielding 90,000 gallons might still be used for street watering if necessary. The anticipated supply from the Font was 3,670,000 gallons per day, which would be sufficient to meet the whole requirements of the district for many years to come. The works now contemplated would convey only 2,500,000 gallons from the Font, and the surplus would thus be only 1,000,000 gallons a day. In a report which he had presented to the corporation he had said that between the northern limits of the borough there was in the district through which the gravitation main would pass a population of 40,000 without a reliable supply of water, and there was no obligation upon the Newcastle company, which now supplied that district, to continue to supply. Mr. G. Richardson Strachan, civil engineer, partner of Mr. Mansergh, also gave evidence, stating that the promoters would not run any risk of a polluted supply. It had been suggested that the rich Tynemouth Corporation might buy out the poor millowners and so take all the water, but in that case any person interested would have the right to apply for a mandamus to compel them to give the compensation water. The committee last week passed the Bill, subject to the insertion of clauses giving the district north of Tynemouth facilities for obtaining water and protecting the fishing rights of the owners of the streams feeding the proposed reservoir.

*Plymouth Corporation Bill.*—The Bill promoted by the Corporation of Plymouth went through the Lords with practically no opposition. The Bill conferred upon the corporation a variety of powers, among them being authority to use certain lands as a site for an electric generating station. Mr. J. Ellis, the town clerk, gave formal evidence before Lord Morley's committee in support of the measure. There was some discussion with reference to a clause providing that the corporation might appropriate and use for the purpose of the Act any lands within the borough for the time being vested in them as a municipal or sanitary authority which were not wanted for the purpose for which such lands were originally acquired, but that the corporation should not create or permit the creation of a nuisance on any of these lands. This had reference to the proposed generating station, and the town clerk explained that the works would not be constructed except on such lands as were described in the schedule. The Bill was ordered to be reported with amendments to the House.

*Central Electrical Supply Company's Bill.*—The Bill promoted by the Central Electrical Supply Company for power to construct a generating station on the Regent's canal at Northbank, St. John's Wood, adjoining the proposed terminus of the Great Central Railway, was thrown out by Lord Northbrook's House of Lords committee on Friday week. The Bill had to face four sets of opponents—the Great Central Railway Company, the London County Council and the Vestry of St. Marylebone—but it was the opposition of the Great Central Railway Company that was fatal to the measure. The main object which the promoters had in view in seeking powers to establish a generating station was to supply electrical energy in bulk to the Westminster and the St. James's and Pall Mall Electric Lighting Companies, the current being brought at high pressure to the area of supply under conditions laid down in the report of the recent Joint Committee on Electrical Energy. It was stated by Captain Bax and Mr. T. Dobson, general manager and engineer respectively of the Westminster Electric Supply Association, gave evidence as to the difficulty of finding a site for the generating station within the area of supply and the advantageous character of the proposed site. It appeared from the evidence of Mr. William Pollitt, the general manager of the Great Central Railway, that Parliamentary powers to purchase the site proposed by the Central Electrical Supply Company had been granted to his company by their Act of 1893. A serious mistake was made in allowing the power to lapse, but it was unintentional, and it was owing to the press of other matters that it had escaped attention. The committee held that the balance of public advantage in this case rested with the railway company, but the chairman intimated that when the next Bill in the list, the Great Central Railway Bill, came before them the committee would be prepared to consider a clause securing that, should it be decided to establish the generating station on the other side of the north bank away from the Regent's canal, the railway company should give the electrical company facilities for the use of the canal and provide siding accommodation.

*Metropolitan Electric Supply Company's Bill.*—The Bill promoted by the Metropolitan Electric Supply Company authorising the company to use lands acquired by them in the parishes of Acton and Willesden for the establishment of a large generating station, to convey the current into their district by means of cables leading along the Grand Junction canal, has been passed by a committee of the House of Lords, presided over by Lord Northbrook. The current is to be brought at high pressure to the areas of supply under conditions laid down in the report of the recent Joint Committee on Electrical Energy. The operations of the committee were limited to their present area and to their maintaining existing conditions.

*Coventry and Middlesbrough Corporation Gas Bills.*—The House of Lords committee presided over by Lord Morley have passed the Bill promoted by the Corporation of Coventry for powers to borrow £250,000 for the construction of additions to the gasworks, and that promoted by the Corporation of Middlesbrough for authority to borrow £130,000 for the purpose of enlarging their gasworks. In neither case was any opposition offered, and as the Bills had already been passed by the House of Commons the two corporations will be able to carry out the additions.

*Middlesex County Council Bill.*—The Bill promoted by the Middlesex County Council to make more effectual provision for preventing the pollution and obstruction of the streams in the county of Middlesex, and to confer further powers on the county council for that purpose; to give to the county council powers in relation to making loans to local authorities, main roads and other matters, and to enlarge in some respects the powers of district councils in the county, came before a House of Lords committee presided over by Lord Ribblesdale, on Monday of last week. When the measure was before the House of Commons Committee on Police and Sanitary Regulations the facts were very fully explained in our columns, and it is only necessary now to deal briefly with the principal features of the scheme which came before the county council have in view. In the Commons the Bill was opposed by the Thames Conservancy, the Grand Junction Canal Company, the North Metropolitan Railway and Canal Company, the London County Council, the Hanwell Urban District Council, the Tottenham Urban District Council and the Vestry of St. Mary's, Islington, but of these opponents only the Grand Junction Canal Company and the North Metropolitan Railway and Canal Company were represented in the Lords. There were, however, two new sets of opponents who now sought special concessions—Messrs. Curtis and Harvey and Earl Percy. The Middlesex County Council were again represented by Mr. Worsley Taylor, Q.C., and Lord Robert Cecil, who championed it so successfully in the other House. Mr. Pember, Q.C., and Mr. F. W. Pember appeared for the North Metropolitan and Mr. Balfour Browne, Q.C., and Mr. G. A. R. FitzGerald for the Grand Junction Company. Mr. Lewis Coward appeared on behalf of Messrs. Curtis and Harvey, and Mr. Claude Bagnalley, Q.C., and Mr. A. V. Frere for Earl Percy. Both Messrs. Curtis and Harvey and Earl Percy, who were riparian owners of certain streams which came within the scope of the Bill, claimed exemption from its provisions on the ground that they kept the Duke of Northumberland's river and the other streams over which they exercised riparian rights absolutely free from pollution. Mr. Littler, the chairman of the Middlesex County Council, expressed his willingness that they should be exempted so long as they kept the streams free from pollution, and this opposition was thus disposed of quite early in the proceedings. The only remaining contest, therefore, was with the two canal companies. With reference to the Brent, whose polluted condition throughout its entire course is notorious, powers were sought—in addition to general authority to prohibit pollution and to execute work, such as the deepening, enlargement and improvement of the river—to compel the North Metropolitan and Grand Junction Canal Companies to discharge out of the Brent reservoir, of which they are the owners, into that portion of the river Brent immediately below that reservoir, regularly throughout every twenty-four hours, a quantity of water not exceeding 4,000,000 gallons and not less than 3,000,000 gallons. The clause providing for this came up in the modified form in which it had passed the Commons. In substance it placed the council in the position and endowed them with all the powers of riparian owners, and gave general powers to the canal companies to agree with the council as to the sending of water down the Brent, which would provide that if the council succeeded in establishing in a court of law the right of riparian owners to compel the canal companies to send down compensation water under sec. 37 of the Act of 1793, the amount of compensation water should be fixed at 3,000,000 gallons per day, or such quantity as required. The county council contended that by the statute named they had the right to the whole of the water which was intercepted by the canal companies at the Brent reservoir, but they were willing to give up three-fourths of it to the companies. If in the legal proceedings the council were unsuccessful in establishing this point, then they would be entitled to so much water as they might require up to 3,000,000 gallons per day at an agreed price, or, in the case of difference, at a price to be settled by arbitration. They maintained that the canal companies were doing what Parliament never allowed any company or corporation to do—they were impounding the whole of the water in a dry time from the catchment area, taking it away and giving no compensation. Then when the time came when they could impound no more with safety to their embankments and their works generally they pulled up their sluices, but, instead of letting the water escape gradually, they opened them all at once and let the water go in a torrent. When the flood came it broke down the banks and tore up the bottom of the river, scooping out holes in one place and depositing shoals in another, and between the sewage deposited and the holes scooped out, the river in the summer months was simply stagnant pools and festering masses of sewage. Mr. R. D. M. Littler, Q.C., C.B., as chairman of the county council, described the general scope and explained the provisions of the Bill. As regards the canal companies or any local authorities who had the control of the streams, there was, he said, not the slightest intention to do anything unreasonable. Mr. Littler emphasised the three evils experienced with regard to the streams of Middlesex. The first was the danger of ordinary pollution from sewage; the second the danger, arising from their circuitous route, of the rivers being choked up; and the third, the special difficulties arising from the exclusive ownership of the Brent reservoir being vested in the North Metropolitan and Grand Junction Railway and Canal Companies. That was why the county council sought to be endowed with the rights of riparian owners. Some local authorities—Willesden, for example—had done a great deal to remedy the present condition of the streams. That authority had spent £100,000 in improvements. Mr. Montague Sharpe, the deputy-lieutenant of Middlesex, and Mr. James Bigwood, member of Parliament for, Brentford, gave evidence as to the wretched state of the Brent. Mr. Oliver Claude Robson, M.I.C.E., surveyor to the Willesden District Council, described the result of his inspection of the Brent, which for months at a time was simply a series of foul pools, and Mr. Charles Jones, M.I.C.E., surveyor to the Ealing District Council, told briefly the opinion he had formed from examinations he had made, and spoke as to the dangerous flooding of the river by the opening of the sluices at the reservoir. The canal companies again made a strong protest against clause 8 of the Bill, under which the council sought to be put in the position of riparian owners in regard to instituting and maintaining actions against the canal companies for the purpose of enforcing the powers given under the Act. On Tuesday, the committee passed the Bill, subject to amendments, to which the promoters acceded, defining more clearly the position the council was to assume as riparian owners.

*Paignton District Council Bill.*—The House of Commons Committee on Police and Sanitary Regulations, who have been exclusively occupied with Bills promoted by corporations and county authorities during the session, have now concluded their labours. The last measure they dealt with was the Bill conferring powers upon the Urban District Council of Paignton with reference to the purchase and laying-out of lands for recreation grounds, and to making better provision for the improvement of the public health in the local government district. It was shown that in this popular seaside resort, with its rapidly-increasing population, it was expedient in the interest of the health and prosperity of the district that the council should be empowered to purchase a piece of marshy land, and reclaim and lay it out as a recreation ground. By an ancient custom, ratified by a time-honoured enactment, all persons "resiant" and dwelling in the counties of Devon and Cornwall may remove sand from any place under the full sea-mark for the bettering of their land and the increase of their tillage, with the result that considerable quantities of sea sand, shingle and gravel were removed every year from the seashore at Paignton and disposed of for profit. So serious had the evil become, both as regard, beach sands and foreshore and encroachments from the sea, that the corporation now sought powers to restrict the removal of the sand. It was also considered expedient that the maritime boundary of the district should be defined, and that the corporation should be invested with further powers over the seashore. Further powers were also required, in order to enable the council to make better provision with regard to the building of streets and sanitary matters. For the purchase and laying-out of the recreation ground by the council it was estimated that an expenditure of £3,000 would be necessary, and in connection with this and the other improvements contemplated it was proposed to borrow £10,000. The committee declared in their decision that in some respects the Bill gave powers relating to police and sanitary regulations in excess of the provisions or powers of the general law, but in most cases they were made in accordance with recent precedent. In the case of certain clauses inflicting a penalty on washing house-fronts save in prescribed hours, regulations as to bicycles and powers to grant gratuities to officers and servants, they were amended upon the evidence given as to local necessity. The clause relating to restricting the removal of sand was allowed for the same reason. With these modifications the Bill was passed and reported to the House.

*Burnley Corporation Tramways Bill.*—Burnley and District Tramways Company struggled gallantly, but struggled in vain, before a committee of the House of Lords last week to prevent the Corporation of Burnley from getting the Bill empowering them to work the local tramways, which they had obtained authority to purchase, by electricity or any mechanical power, to effect street improvements and to erect a crematerium. The Bill was originally opposed by the Nelson Corporation and the district councils of Brierfield and Padiham, but as they had agreed to purchase the tramways in their respective districts and lease them to the Burnley Corporation their opposition had been withdrawn. This left the tramway company the only petitioners against the measure. Evidence in support of the Bill was given by the town clerk of Burnley, the former borough surveyor (Mr. Button) and Councillor Burrows. Mr. Button stated that the total length of the system was 7 miles, and of this the corporation proposed to acquire 5 miles. The present system was very defective,

both as to the permanent way and the service generally. More passing places were required and the fares needed revision. In consequence of the insufficient service rival lines of omnibuses had been established on some of the routes. Mr. Button admitted that the scheme of the corporation would not provide for a continuous system in the borough and outside, which would certainly be preferable to a disjointed service. The committee passed the Bill after hearing the argument of Mr. Worsley Taylor, Q.C., on behalf of the company that they were in a better position to work the system satisfactorily than the corporation would be.

*Rhymney and Aber Valleys Gas and Water Bill.*—The question of the water supply of the Rhymney valley was very thoroughly discussed last week before the committee of the House of Lords presided over by Lord Clinton. The Bill was promoted for the purpose of obtaining powers to incorporate a company which is being established for the purpose of acquiring the undertakings of the Rhymney Valley Gas and Water Company, the new Tredegar Gas and Water Company, Limited, and the Caerphilly Gas Light, Coke and Water Company, the gasworks of the Rhymney Gas Company, Limited, and the waterworks of the Rhymney Iron Company, Limited, to construct new gasworks, and to supply gas and water within the limits prescribed. . The local district councils within whose area of jurisdiction the new company proposed to operate took a watchful interest in the proceedings, but did not oppose the Bill, which was petitioned against by the Rhymney Iron Company only. Mr. Rees, engineer to several district councils in the neighbourhood of the Rhymney valley and engineer to the promoters, stated in his evidence that all the local authorities concerned were now in favour of the scheme as well as the landowners—the Marquis of Bute, Lord Worcester, Lord Tredegar and Lord Windsor. As far as the Rhymney Iron Company were concerned, their works were in part dismantled and the machinery had been removed. If they did not desire to sell their reservoir they might keep it, and the promoters would give them 180,000 gallons of water which would come from the brook upon which the reservoir was situated, and that would place them in a better position than they were in at present. Mr. Hill, waterworks engineer, who made an exhaustive examination of the catchment area, described the supply which the works would yield as being amply sufficient for the district and the limestone formation as good. There would be no difficulty whatever in the matter of the construction of the reservoirs. Upon this point his testimony was confirmed by the evidence of Mr. Stephenson, M.I.C.E., who said the formation was sufficiently watertight for reservoir purposes. Dr. Redwood, the Rhymney medical officer of health, gave evidence as to the unsatisfactory condition of the water, to which illness had been clearly traceable. Many local witnesses were called, who spoke as to the necessity for a more efficient supply of water. Sir Henry Taylor, the chairman of the iron company, explained that the company had not opposed the Bill in the Commons because they had hoped that the negotiations in progress would have been satisfactory. They were prepared to sell the undertaking, but not on arbitration terms. The company claimed to be the judges of what was reasonable. Mr. Strong, a member of the Geological Survey of London and of the geological survey of the district, expressed the belief that the reservoirs would not hold water on account of the fissures and swallow-holes. At the close of the case it was announced that at last an understanding had been arrived at with the iron company. The promoters undertook that unless more than 25,000 gallons came down the stream they would not take any of it away. The compensation water was to be the first charge upon them, and the purchase of the iron company's works was to be deemed compulsory under the Lands Clauses Act. The committee passed the Bill with a clause to the effect just indicated.

## UXBRIDGE NEW SEWERAGE WORKS.

### OPENING CEREMONY.

The new sewage purification works of the Uxbridge Urban District Council, the effluent from which finally enters the Thames, were formally opened on the 9th inst. by Sir Fredk. Dixon Hartland, M.P., in the presence of the council and their engineer, Mr. C. Nicholson Lailey, of Westminster. The sewage is pumped into the precipitation tanks after treatment with ferozone, and then flows on to the filter-beds containing a layer of the well-known filtering material—polarite. The effluent was found to be of a high degree of purity and several of the visitors did not hesitate to taste it. Sir Fredk. Dixon Hartland, as chairman of the Thames Conservancy, congratulated the council upon the improvements effected. It may be mentioned that the sewage of Uxbridge was formerly treated in covered tanks without the use of chemicals and then passed through coke filters, but the results were so unsatisfactory that another system was adopted.

**Millar's Karri and Jarrah Forests, Limited.**—The returns from Australia are just to hand, and give the total output of both karri and jarrah for the half-year ended 30th June as 33,371 loads. This is a record, and is considerably in excess of the output for the corresponding period of last year.

# For Assistants and Pupils.

## THE CONSTRUCTION OF ROADS AND STREETS.—XV.

By WILLIAM H. MAXWELL, Assistant Engineer and Surveyor, Leyton Urban District Council.

ROAD MATERIALS AND CONSTRUCTION
*(continued).*

SYENITE AND SYENITIC GRANITE.—*Syenite* is named from Syene, in Upper Egypt, where the rock is found.

*True syenite* consists of quartz, felspar and hornblende.

*Syenitic granite* consists of quartz, felspar, mica and hornblende.

*Hornblende* is an important mineral, occurring in great variety in composition and appearance, and is a silicate of magnesia, iron, lime and alumina, and often containing other substances. In *syenite* it takes the place of the mica of ordinary granite, whilst in *syenitic granite* it forms the fourth constituent, added to those of true granite. The commoner varieties of hornblende are dark green and black—these forming a large portion of the mass of greenstone (also known as *trap* or *whinstone.*) The mineral is hard and tough, and crystallises in prisms.

"The syenitic granites are on the whole tougher and more compact than the ordinary granites, take a fine polish and are exceedingly durable."[*] The darker colours are found to be the most durable.[†]

"Syenite occurs at Malvern and Charnwood Forest. It appears that both granite and syenite occur at Mountsorrel. The rock is of a pink colour, and has been worked also at Grooby (Leicestershire.) Bardon Hill is composed of it."[‡]

TRAP ROCKS.—"Trap "[§] is an old term indefinitely applied to any eruptive rock, and is rather loosely used to designate various dark-coloured, heavy *igneous* rocks, including especially the felspathic-augitic rocks, basalt, dolerite, amygdaloid, &c., but including also some kinds of diorite.[||]

*Greenstone,* also known as *trap* or *whinstone,* consists of felspar and hornblende; it sometimes has a granular crystalline structure, the grains being much finer than in granite, and at times so compact as to be without apparent grains. The colour is usually dark green, but varies. Greenstone is compact, hard, tough and durable, and splits up into small blocks, so that it is well suited for paving setts and road metal, but not for use in large masonry works.

Three varieties in common use may be mentioned—Penmaenmawr, Bardon Hill and Whinstone. *Penmaenmawr* stone, near Caernarvon, is a felstone occurring as an intrusive mass in the Cambrian (Lower Silurian) rocks near Conway.[¶] It is easily split by cutting a fine line with an axe in the direction required, and then giving the stone a few smart taps with a hammer.[1] *Bardon Hill* stone (Leicestershire) is largely used in the Midlands as a road metal. *Whinstone* is found in Wigtownshire, near Selkirk, in Kincardineshire, near Haddington, near Edinburgh, at Falkirk, in Perthshire, Fifeshire, Inverness, Ross and other places in Scotland.[2]

BASALT[3] is "a rock of igneous origin, consisting of augite and triclinic felspar, with grains of magnetic or titanic iron, and also bottle-green particles of olivine frequently disseminated. It is usually of a greenish-black colour, or of some dull-brown shade or black. It constitutes immense beds in some regions, and also occurs in veins or dykes cutting through other rocks. It has often a prismatic structure, as at the Giants' Causeway in Ireland, where the columns are as regular as if the work of art. It is a very tough and heavy rock, and is one of the best materials for macadamising roads"[4]; also it affords great resistance to crushing and is well adapted for crushing, &c.

*Rowley Rag,* a basalt found at Rowley Regis (Staffordshire), is columnar, and was considered by Jukes to be a lava flow during the cone period. It is used as a road metal, for paving setts, and for the manufacture of artificial stone. The material is also found in Armagh, Antrim and Londonderry.

*Great Ayton stone*[5] is largely used in the north of England for repairing macadam roads. This is a basaltic rock obtained from Great Ayton, Cookfield and other places along the north of England dykes. The stone has a specific gravity of about 2·7, and is composed[6] chiefly of silica, alumina, ferric and ferrous oxide, lime and magnesia.

CLAY SLATE.—Clay slate is a primary stratified rock of considerable hardness and density, but is no use for road making, as they crumble upon exposure and make a good deal of mud.

[*] Page's "Practical Geology."
[†] "Municipal Engineers' Hand-Book," by H. Percy Boulnois.
[‡] Woodward's " Geology of England and Wales."
[§] [*Trap,* Sw. *trapp;* akin to *trappa* = stairs; so called because the rocks of this class often occur in large, tabular masses, rising above one another like steps.
[||] Webster's "International Dictionary of the English Language."
[1] Woodward's " Geology of England and Wales."
[1] Seddon.
[2] " Notes on Building Construction," vol. iii. (Rivington).
[3] Latin, *basaltes* (an African word), a dark and hard species of marble found in Ethiopia.
[4] Webster's "International Dictionary."
[5] " Proceedings of the Association of Municipal and County Engineers," vol. xiii., p. 98.
[6] *Quarterly Journal of the Geological Society,* May, 1884.

LIMESTONE.—The name *limestone* is applied to rocks consisting chiefly of calcium carbonate or carbonate of lime. There is, however, considerable difference both as regards chemical composition and physical characteristics even among stones of the same class. Limestone is a stratified rock, of sedimentary origin, and occurs in geological formations of all ages, the beds oftentimes being of enormous thickness.

Limestones are classified by the engineer according to their physical characteristics as follows: Marbles, compact limestone, granular limestone, shelly limestone and magnesian limestone.

*Marble* is the name given to any limestone which is sufficiently hard and compact to take a line polish. It generally consists of pure calcium carbonate. " In the absence of better material marble may be used for road metal and paving setts, but it is brittle and not adapted to withstand a heavy traffic. Roads made with it are greasy in wet weather and dusty when dry."[*]

*Compact Limestone.*—This consists of calcium carbonate, either pure or mixed with sand and clay. It has a dull earthy appearance, and is grayish blue, black or mottled in colour. Some of the carboniferous limestones, the Lias limestone and Kentish Rag (cretaceous system) are of the compact class. *Kentish Rag* occurs in the Greensand formation, and is found in the central part of Kent in the neighbourhood of the towns of Sevenoaks, Maidstone, Lenham and others. Ragstone is suitable for paving setts and curbs, and is used for road metal, but makes a dusty road in dry weather. In respect to this stone Mr. Francis J. C. May, M.I.C.E., observes† that " Kentish Rag is one of the oldest and one of the very best of building stones. There are several large quarries in the neighbourhood of Maidstone, which form one of its staple industries. It is a very useful stone for road metal, and is largely used on roads of moderate traffic and where the subsoil is dry. Its use is also valuable on hills in conjunction with flints. Indeed, a road made of rag and flints, in the proportion of two of rag to one of flints, will last longer and wear better than a road made of either material separately."

Compact limestone in Torquay has been found to be " well fitted for forming good smooth roads when not required to carry excessive traffic."[‡]

*Granular Limestone.*—This "consists of carbonate of lime in grains, which are in general shells or fragments of shells, cemented together by some compound of lime, silica and alumina, and often mixed with a greater or less quantity of sand. . . . In many cases it is so soft when first quarried that it can be cut with a knife and hardens by exposure to the air."[§] This stone affords some of the principal building stones of this country—as the *Oolites,* including Portland, Bath and Caen stone—but is of no use as a road metal.

*Quenast* is a limestone from Belgium. At first sight it may be mistaken for granite, but it is softer than granite and does not wear so well. In colour it is a brownish grey.

*Shelly limestone* consists (a) of small shells cemented together and showing no crystals on fracture, as—*e.g.,* Purbeck stone—(b) of shells breaking with a highly crystalline fracture, as Hopton Wood stone. *Purbeck* stone (Oolitic) is of a brownish-grey colour, is much used for paving and is durable, but wears slippery. *Hopton Wood* stone (Derbyshire) is a carboniferous limestone, of a grey colour, is fine grained, compact, weathers well and is used for paving, steps, &c. It has been used for paving part of Abingdon-street, London.

*Magnesian limestone* is composed of carbonates of lime and magnesia, with a small quantity of silica, iron and alumina. "When the magnesia is present in the proportion of one molecule of carbonate of magnesia to one molecule of carbonate of lime the stone is called a *Dolomite.*"[||] Bolsover Moor and Mansfield stone are magnesian limestones. The stone has been very largely used for building purposes, including the Houses of Parliament. " In Britain it is found in the New Red Sandstone formation immediately above the coal."[¶]

Limestone, as largely obtained from Skipton and Clithero, is used in many Yorkshire and Lancashire towns, but is not in any way equal to granite or basalt for road construction. Its power of resistance to crushing force is much less, and it is very sensitive to atmospheric changes. Its general use is probably accounted for by its cheapness of first cost.[1] Mr.

[*] " Notes on Building Construction," vol. iii.
[†] " Proceedings of the Association of Municipal and County Engineers," vol. xiv., p. 120.
[‡] " Proceedings of the Association of Municipal and County Engineers," vol. xi., p. 105.
[§] Rankine's " Civil Engineering."
[||] " Notes on Building Construction," vol. iii.
[¶] Rankine's " Civil Engineering."
[1] " Proceedings of the Association of Municipal and County Engineers," vol. xiii.

James Hall, borough surveyor of Stockton (1881), states[*] that "limestone alone is a very unsuitable material from its great affinity for water, which causes it in dry weather to crumble to dust. When mixed with whinstone, flints or other compact material, it is useful in causing the whole to bind quickly, and is therefore often used in roads of steep gradients, where it is difficult to get the stones bedded." More than one-half the roads in Ireland are repaired with limestone or limestone gravel, according to Mr. Dorman (county surveyor of Armagh), makes an excellent road. The white or grey limestone, he observes, is very inferior and wears rapidly.[†] Mr. H. P. Boulnois, in his valuable "Municipal Engineers' Hand-Book," writes on the use of limestone as a road metal as follows: "Many hundreds of miles of roadways in this country are made with limestone; they often make an excellent surface, as they possess a considerable power of binding together, but weather and very heavy traffic affect them considerably, as they all have a strong affinity for water; their very power of thus cementing themselves together causes a quantity of dust in dry and mud in wet weather."

Mr. Molesworth gives the crushing strain per square inch of "compact limestone" as 7,700 lb.; whilst the average of six tests made by D. Kirkaldy & Sons on the "dark limestone," largely sold as road material by the Buxton Lime $F_{1r}m_{8}$ Company, gives a crushing strain of 19,349 lb. per square inch.

SANDSTONE is a stratified rock, found in every geological formation above the primary rocks, but the best kinds on the whole are those which belong to the coal formation.[‡] In composition it usually consists of grains of quartz, cemented together by silica, carbonates of lime and magnesia, alumina and oxide of iron. The stone in which the cementing material is nearly pure silica is the most durable, and that containing much alumina is the weakest. As a rule the weathering qualities of the stone are entirely dependent upon the cementing material, but where the grains are of carbonate of lime instead of quartz, and the cementing matter is silica, the grains are the first to fail. Sandstone is found of various colours, as white, yellow, brown, red and blue of many shades —usually depending upon the presence of iron. The stone is very largely used for building, flagging, &c. Prof. Rankine observes that it "is in general porous and capable of absorbing much water; but it is comparatively little injured by moisture, unless when built with its layers set on edge, in which case the expansion of water in freezing between the layers makes them split or 'scale' off from the surface of the stone. When it is built 'on its natural bed' any water which may penetrate between the edges of the layers has room readily to expand or escape."

"Some of the harder sandstones are used for setts and also for road metal, but they are inferior to the tougher materials, and roads metalled with them are muddy in wet and very dusty in dry weather."[§]

Prof. Anstead, in writing on roads, considered sandstone to be better than limestone, and hard limestone better than slate, while basalts and granites, he further stated, are exceedingly good or exceedingly bad, according to the proportion of alkaline earths (especially soda) which they contain.

Some of the principal varieties of sandstone in general use are :—

*Bramley Fall* (Leeds), originally a fairly coarse-grained sandstone of the Millstone Grit formation, of considerable strength and durability, and very extensively used for heavy engineering work. The old Bramley Fall quarries have now almost ceased to be worked, but a good deal of similar stone is now sold under the same name although quarried elsewhere.

*Yorkshire stone* comes from the coal measures and Millstone Grit series and the New Red Sandstone formation. It is used for heavy engineering work, and for flagging and landings; the best stone for the latter use comes from near Bradford and Halifax.‖

*Scotgate Ash.*—Used for landings, steps, setts, paving and building.

*Mansfield stone* is a siliceous dolomite occurring in the Permian system, between the New Red Sandstone and the carboniferous series.‖ It is an important building stone.

*Craigleith stone* is a very durable sandstone, consisting of quartz grains, siliceous cementing material and mica.

*Brandon Hill stone* (Gloucestershire) is largely used for paving the streets of Bristol.

*Pennant stone* (Fish Ponds, Bristol) is a good and durable sandstone, largely used for paving, &c.

FLINTS.—These are "found in nodules or as pebbles scattered through the chalk strata and in beds of gravel, apparently left after the washing away of the chalk."[¶] The surface-picked flints are superior to quarry flints, and if tough make good roads, but they are too brittle for very heavy traffic. Mr. Ellice Clark, speaking at a meeting of municipal engineers held at Bristol, gave it as his experience that roads repaired with *flints* required no binding material.

---

[*] *Ibid*, vol. vii.
[†] *Ibid*, vol. xviii.
[‡] Prof. Rankine's "Civil Engineering."
[§] Wray.
[‖] "Notes on Building Construction," vol. iii.
[¶] Prof. Rankine.

## VENTILATION OF SEWERS.

### REPORT BY SIR A. R. BINNIE.

The following is the text of the report prepared by Sir A. R. Binnie, engineer to the London County Council, as to the result of a conference of engineers and surveyors of the several vestries and district boards of the metropolis on the ventilation of sewers :—

In accordance with the instructions of the committee, I issued two circular letters to the engineers and surveyors of the various vestries and district boards in the county, inviting them to a conference on the subject of the ventilation of sewers, with a view to some uniform system being adopted, if possible, for dealing with complaints of offensive emanations from gratings connected with both local and main sewers. In response to the invitation, a meeting was held at the County Hall on Friday, 25th February, at which upwards of forty of the gentlemen invited were present. A list of those who signed the attendance book, together with the names of the districts represented by them, is appended hereto. The discussion on the subject of the ventilation of sewers occupied a period of over two hours, and resulted in the following resolutions being passed :—

(1) That the closing of sewer ventilators in response to complaints increases the general evil, the diminution of which is to be attained by the multiplication of the ventilators at regular frequent intervals.

(2) That in connection with any interceptor hereafter fixed on a main house drain it is advisable to carry up a ventilating pipe from the sewer side of the interceptor, up the front, side or back of the house, to the satisfaction of the local sanitary authority, and that the outlet drain from the interceptor shall not be flap-trapped in sewer unless required by the local sanitary authority.

(3) That pipe ventilators up buildings, or otherwise, where possible, should always be adopted, in addition to surface ventilation. It will be observed that the general result of the conference has confirmed the action of the committee and the council in recent years, and that the remedy for sewer emanations is to be looked for from the maintenance of more frequent ventilating openings, both at the street level and by means of pipes carried up houses and other buildings. I would suggest that, as the meeting was a very representative one, this report be printed, and that copies be sent to each member of the council and to the engineers and surveyors of the district boards and vestries in the metropolis.

## SANITARY WORKS AT DUMBARTON.

Mr. David Dunbar, county and district sanitary inspector, Dumbarton, has submitted his seventh annual report on the sanitary condition of the county and of the work carried out in his department during 1897. There were 1,717 nuisances dealt with, of which 923 were in the eastern district and 794 in the western district, showing an increase of 410 in the eastern district and 220 in the western district. There were 4,889 inspections made for the detection and removal of nuisances, 356 to dairies and cow sheds, 965 investigating the causes of infectious disease, and sixty-eight to factories and workshops, in addition to special inspections made as to the erection of lamps in the lighting districts in the parish of West Kilpatrick, and house-to-house inspections in consequence of outbreaks of measles and whooping cough in various parts of the county. The report proceeds to detail the work done in each of the districts of the county. In the eastern district a drainage scheme has been adopted for Duntocher village, whereby the sewage will be conveyed to a point in Duntocher burn, near the river Clyde, a distance of fully 1½ miles from the village. The sizes of the sewers range from 6 in. to 15 in. in diameter, and are provided with manholes and lampholes in suitable positions. The work is expected to be completed in about six months.

**Cost of the Maidstone Epidemic.**—According to the official balance-sheet, issued on Wednesday week, a sum of nearly £45,000 was spent in connection with the recent typhoid epidemic at Maidstone. The doctors' fees alone absorbed £5,200.

**Church Sanitary Association.** — The Rev. A. Robins rector of Holy Trinity, Windsor, recently presided at the Westminster Palace hotel, over the sixth annual meeting of this association, of which the Archbishop of York is president. He said that the association sought, by means of the Church's institutions in every parish, to prevent overcrowding and to provide better conditions of life for the poor, many of whom lived in places where the elementary decencies of civilisation could not be observed. He moved a resolution asking the association to seek by all means at its disposal to impress the Church with a sense of its duty and responsibility in calling upon the Government to deal drastically—i.e., by compulsory legislation—with insanitary areas, which were fruitful of physical and moral disease, and death. This was seconded and agreed to. A resolution suggesting the desirability of placing all shelter for the poor under official control was also passed.

# Law Notes.

EDITED BY J. B. REIGNIER CONDER, 11 Old Jewry Chambers, E.C.,

Solicitor of the Supreme Court.

*The Editor will be pleased to answer any questions affecting the practice of engineers and surveyors to local authorities. Queries (which should be written legibly on foolscap paper, one side only) should be addressed to "The Law Editor," at the Offices of* THE SURVEYOR. *Where possible, copies of local Acts or documents referred to should be enclosed. All explanatory diagrams must be drawn and lettered in black ink only. Correspondents who do not wish their names published should furnish a nom de plume.*

## QUERIES AND REPLIES.

BY-LAWS: ALTERATIONS AND ADDITIONS TO OLD BUILDINGS: WHAT IS A "NEW BUILDING"?—Mr. G. William Lacey, borough surveyor, Saffron Walden, writes: The by-law's in force prior to 1895, when model building by-laws were adopted, contained no reference whatever to the structure of new buildings, air space or ventilation, but only as regarded the construction of the drainage, water-closets and privies, cesspools and ash-pits. They provided for the inspection before occupation of all new houses and buildings, but did not compel the deposit of plans, simply strongly recommending that it should be done. The new by-laws with respect

to the alteration of buildings provide that "where any building has been erected in accordance with the requirements of any by-laws made by the sanitary authority under the Public Health Acts, and in force at the time of such erection, no person shall alter such building in such a way that the same as altered would, if at first so constructed, have contravened such by-laws," and also "every person who hall intend to alter a building, in regard to any matter as to which a by-law was in force when such building was erected, shall give to the sanitary authority notice in writing, &c., and shall deliver complete plans and sections, &c." It seems to me that under these circumstances—and, if so, it is very regrettable—that a person has, practically, a free hand in altering a building erected previous to the adoption of the new by-laws, and that the council is quite powerless to compel the deposit of plans or to regulate the building in any way. I should like your opinion on this. There is then the question of what is comprised in the term "alteration of a building." It has been held, I think, that an addition is an alteration, and I should esteem your views and information on the following case, as sketch. The new addition in question is of considerable size and is of one storey, and has communication by one door to the existing premises.

The whole question is whether the proposed alterations and additions amount to the erection of a new building. If they do, then the new by-laws are applicable; but if they do not, then the new by-laws are not applicable, there is in so far as to prevent such alterations as would contravene the old by-laws (see Public Health Acts Amendment Act, 1890, sec. 23, sub-sec. (4)). By sec. 159 of the Public Health Act, 1875, the re-erecting of any building pulled down to or below the ground floor, or the conversion into a dwelling-house of a building not originally constructed as such, or the conversion into more than one dwelling-house of a building originally constructed as one dwelling-house, shall be considered the erection of a new building. These, however, are only "samples" of "new buildings," the definition not being exhaustive. The question is a "question of fact" for the decision of the magistrate in each particular case. (*James v. Wyvill*, 51 L.T. [N.S.], 237; 48 J.P., 728.) See some observations on this subject in THE SURVEYOR for 20th May last, p. 526.

CELLARS UNDER PAVEMENTS.—"Constant Reader" writes: Will you kindly inform me in your next issue under what sections of the Public Health Acts an urban district council have power to refuse passing a plan of a shop and dwelling-house by reason of a hatchway being shown on the footpath giving access to the cellar under the shop

This is a somewhat doubtful point. By sec. 149 of the Public Health Act, 1875, "all streets . . . . repairable by the inhabitants at large . . . , and the pavements, stones and other materials thereof . . . , shall vest in and be under the control of the urban authority," and "any person who without the consent of the urban authority wilfully displaces or takes up . . . , the pavement . . . , in any street . . . , is liable to penalties; and by sec. 26 of the same Act any person who without such consent "causes any vault, arch or cellar to be newly built or constructed under the carriageway of any street " incurs penalties. The latter section, however, refers to the carriageway only, and has no reference to the footpath. Then by sec. 73 of the Towns Improvement Clauses Act, 1847 (which section is incorporated with the Public Health Act, 1875), "when any opening is made in any pavement or footpath . . . , as an entrance into any vault or cellar, a door or covering shall be made by the occupier for owner, see sec. 160 of the 1875 Act) of such vault or cellar of iron or such other materials, and in such manner as he "causes" direct, and such door or covering shall from time to time be kept in good repair by the occupier (or owner) of such vault or cellar;" and by sec. 35 of the Public Health Acts Amendment Act, 1890, "all vaults, arches and cellars under any street, and all cellar-heads, gratings, lights and coal-holes in the surface of any street . . . , shall be kept in good condition and repair by the owners or occupiers of the same, or of the houses or buildings to which the same respectively belong." In "The Municipal and Sanitary Engineers' Hand-Book," by H. Percy Boulnois (third edition, p. 221), it is stated that it is generally assumed that the powers conferred by sec. 149 of the Act of 1875 enable the authority to prevent the construction of

cellars under the footpath without their consent. I am not aware, however, of any decision on this point; and it is characteristic of the hazy condition in which important questions are frequently left by legislation that we have side by side on the statute-book, on the one hand, the absolute prohibition of an act—*viz.*, the taking up, &c., of a pavement—and, on the other hand, certain regulations which presuppose the legality of the prohibited act.

DUTIES OF OFFICER OF LOCAL AUTHORITY.—"A. T. A." writes: A. holds the office of inspector of nuisances, district and highway surveyor to an urban council, and has received the instruction of his committee to prepare a design for laying-out of the recreation ground, which plans have been approved by the council. Other works are now contemplated, such as public library, new offices, &c., and these he has also received instructions to prepare the drawings for. *Can this work be said to belong to the surveyor's department, with no addition to his salary, or can the surveyor make a legal claim for fee? If so, what claim should he make, and should it be made as soon as the drawings are approved and before the work is begun, or after the works are completed, which may be a few years' distant? In any case, would not the original drawings be the property of the surveyor?*

An urban authority has power, under sec. 189 of the Public Health Act, 1875, to make regulations with respect to the duties of their officers. A specimen of such regulations is given in "The Municipal and Sanitary Engineers' Hand-book," by H. Percy Boulnois (third edition, pp. 14, *et. seq.*), among which is included "(18) To prepare all plans, drawings and estimates required, and to superintend the execution of all improvements." And on page 25, in a "Table showing some of the duties of a town surveyor," is included "Landscape gardening—recreation grounds;" and, again, on page 6, among the duties of a town surveyor, are enumerated: "(7) As architect for the construction of . . . , municipal offices . . . , cemetery chapels . . . , and other similar work," and "(8) As landscape gardener for the laying-out of public recreation grounds . . . ," If in A.'s case there are any "regulations" he would be bound by them; if none, the presumption would be that his duties were the usual ones, and unless extra remuneration was expressly stipulated for beforehand he could not claim it. Assuming that the plans are made in pursuance of his duties, they would be the property of the authority in the absence of express stipulation to the contrary.

BUILDING ESTATE: LAYING-OUT STREETS.—"Surveyor" writes: A piece of land is to be laid-out within this district for building purposes, and the architect for the estate has submitted a plan and section for the laying-out of one street only, although boards are placed at different points in the land stating that such land is to be let for building purposes. Could not the council insist, under the enclosed by-laws, upon the owner submitting plans and sections of the whole estate, so as to enable them (the council) to fix the levels, &c., of the streets and sewers of such estate?

The by-laws provide that every person who shall intend to lay-out a street shall give to the authority notice of such intention, and deliver plans and sections (No. 85); and shall, before beginning to lay-out such street, give notice to the surveyor of the date on which he will begin to lay-out such street (No. 87). There is nothing, so far as I can see, in the by-laws requiring an owner to submit plans of a building estate as a whole; but, of course, he would have to submit plans of each street before laying it out.

PRIVATE STREET WORKS: SIDE STREET: PREMISES FRONTING, ADJOINING OR ABUTTING.—"Frontage" writes: Referring to your answer to the above in this week's SURVEYOR, will you kindly inform me who is liable for the cost of the apportionment between A and B? (1) Should it be charged to the rates? Or (2), should the cost of the side street abutment be thrown over the whole of the street being apportioned?

Sec. 150 of the Public Health Act, 1875, does not (as does sec. 77 of the Metropolis management Act, 1862) expressly make the frontagers liable for the intersections of streets. The point does not seem to have been decided, but it would appear that the cost of paving intersections should be borne by the rates under sec 210 of the Public Health Act, 1875.

## Town Hall Destroyed.

—The town hall of Pietermaritzburg, where the sittings of the Legislative Council of Natal are held, was totally destroyed by fire last week. The damage is estimated at £60,000.

## Ventilation of the "Fram."

—The new expedition to the North Pole under the leadership of Otto Sverdrup, captain of the *Fram* during Dr. Nansen's expedition, left Christiana in that now historic craft on Friday, the 24th ult. Considerable alterations have been effected in the vessel. Special provision has been made for the ventilation of the saloon, the system of the well-known ventilating engineers, Messrs. R. Boyle & Sons, London and Glasgow, having been adopted for the purpose. As altered the ventilators are fixed on the flush deck, so that the wind can reach them freely and unobstructedly while blowing from any quarter. We may mention that the "Boyle" system of ventilation was originally designed for the *Fram*.

# Municipal Work in Progress and Projected.

It will be seen from our reports this week that, in the provinces at all events, plenty of activity prevails among local authorities, and in this connection we may draw special attention to the paragraphs referring to Blackpool, Burnley, Liverpool, Bolton, Burton, Leamington, Epsom, Hornsey, Horsham and Wimbledon. Of the metropolitan authorities the London County Council have decided to carry out several extensive improvements, and the Islington Vestry are pushing forward arrangements in connection with important electric lighting extensions.

## METROPOLITAN AUTHORITIES.

### LONDON COUNTY COUNCIL.

The chief matters which occupied the attention of the county council on Tuesday were the proposed new by-laws and the report of the Asylums Committee recommending that the Works Department should carry out the erection of the superstructure of the Horton asylum. With respect to the first-mentioned matter, the by-law for abating the nuisance caused by street cries was rejected, but the one for abating the nuisance caused by "noisy animals" was accepted, as was also the one relating to street betting. The proposal of the Asylums Committee was strongly supported, chiefly by the testimony of Mr. Howell Williams, who declared, as the result of a recent visit to the Belvedere establishment, that it is by no means fully employed. An amendment to refer the matter to the Finance Committee was defeated, together with a proposal to give the work to the lowest tenderer. Several other important matters were considered by the council, the chief of which are given below.
*Loans to Local Authorities.*—Upon the recommendation of the Finance Committee, it was agreed to lend the Bethnal Green Vestry £20,500 for the redemption of compulsory church rates; the Hackney Vestry £2,190 for electric lighting and other works; the Hampstead Vestry £39,980 for electric lighting; the Islington Vestry £9,600 for street improvements, and £23,840 for electric lighting works; the St. Pancras Vestry £16,560 for various works; the Shoreditch Vestry £11,340 for electric lighting; and the Wandsworth District Board of Works £11,600 for paving works.
*A Big Job for the Works Department.*—Last March the manager of the Works Department offered to erect the asylum which is it is proposed to build at Horton, near Epsom, for £284,445. The architect's estimate being, however, only £281,400, it was decided to invite tenders for the work. Three tenders were received in response to the advertisements, the lowest being £296,675, submitted by Messrs. Kirk & Randall. The Asylums Committee now brought up a report recommending that the work be done by the Works Department. Some discussion followed, but ultimately, on a show of hands, it was decided to adopt the recommendation of the committee.
*A Costly Asylum.*—The Asylums Committee reported that the sum of £350,000, specified as the cost of the Heath asylum, Bexley, would be exceeded.
*More Thames Tunnels.*—The Bridges Committee reported that two tenders had been received for the construction of the proposed Thames tunnel which is to connect Greenwich with Millwall. One was for £119,732 and the other for £155,000. The chief engineer, Sir Alexander R. Binnie, estimated that the work ought only to cost £83,175, and had been asked if he would himself construct the tunnel for that amount. He had consented to do so if an allowance was made for the cost of the necessary plant, which would approximately outlay the outlay to £100,000. The committee therefore recommend that the tunnel should be constructed by Sir A. R. Binnie. The council, however, opposed the proposal, and the chairman of the committee withdrew the report.—The same committee also reported that they were considering a scheme for constructing a tunnel under the Thames to connect Rotherhithe with Shadwell. In order to enable the committee to report fully to the council upon the subject, it was necessary that borings should be made to ascertain the nature of the ground through which it had been suggested the tunnel should be constructed. The committee therefore recommended that the council should sanction an expenditure of £1,400 for that purpose. This was agreed to.
*Proposed Tramways Department.*—The Highways Committee reported that, in view of the probable development of the council's policy as regarded the working of the tramways which it might in the future acquire, they were of opinion that it was expedient that a tramways department of the council should be established for the purpose of dealing with all matters relative to tramways acquired, or to be acquired, by the council. The committee further stated that, in accordance with the resolution of the council, they were endeavouring to arrange for the transfer to the council by agreement on January 1st next of the whole of the system of the London Tramways Company beyond the 2½ miles already purchased by the council. They submitted a recommendation for the establishment of a department for the administration of the tramways. The consideration of the report was postponed.
*Proposed Widening of Lothbury.*—The Improvements Committee reported that the City Corporation had asked the council to contribute part of the cost of widening that por-

tion of Lothbury between Old Jewry and Princes-street. The present width varies from 30 ft. to 33 ft., and the proposal of the corporation is to increase this to 60 ft. by acquiring about 2,905 square feet of land from the trustees of the Bank of England, who are about to let the property on building lease. The estimated cost of the land is £72,625, to which must be added the cost of the paving works—viz., £1,500—making a total of £74,500. The cost of widening the road to 50 ft. only is estimated at £47,500. The committee stated that they understood that the corporation contemplated at some future time continuing the improvement by setting back the northern side of Gresham-street between Coleman-street and Basinghall-street and the southern side between Old Jewry and No. 54 Gresham-street, which was almost opposite Basinghall-street. One of the principal objects of the improvement was to provide an alternative route by way of Old Jewry for the vehicles, principally omnibuses, which at present used Princes-street. Old Jewry was at present less than 30 ft. wide, and apparently it was not proposed to widen that thoroughfare. This being so, it did not appear to the committee that, if the improvement was carried out, Old Jewry could well be utilised as an alternative to the Princes-street route. They were also unable to learn that there was any intention on the part of the corporation to undertake the widening of Gresham-street throughout, and they could not therefore see that the widening of the small portion of Lothbury in question would in itself constitute an improvement of such general importance to the through traffic in London as to justify the council in contributing towards the cost. Holding this view, they felt that they had no alternative but to recommend "that the City Corporation be informed that the council do not see their way to contribute to the cost of the proposed widening of Lothbury between Old Jewry and Princes-street, as, in the opinion of the council, the improvement, as at present contemplated, is one which, if effected, should be undertaken by and at the cost of the City authorities." The consideration of the report was adjourned, owing to the late hour when the council reached it.
*The Proposed Transfer of Powers.*—After a short discussion the council decided to postpone until the autumn the consideration of the report of the Local Government and Taxation Committee on the transfer of powers from the council to the local authorities.
*Tenders.*—On the chairman reading over the list of tenders for various public works it was discovered that no tenders had been sent in for the erection of Hedsor Buildings and Laleham Buildings, in connection with the Bethnal Green improvement scheme. The following tenders were opened: (a) For paving works in certain streets, Bethnal Green improvement scheme—Trinidad Lake Asphalte Paving Company, £6,359; W. Griffiths, £6,738; Val de Travers Asphalte Paving Company, Limited, £6,964; W. Wadey, £7,344; Brunswick Rock Asphalte Paving Company, £7,550; Bradshaw & Co., £7,653. (b) For making borings required in connection with the proposed Rotherhithe tunnel—S. F. Baker & Son, £1,126; T. Docwra & Son, £1,179; J. Mowlem & Co., £1,210. (c) For repairs to arches of the Lambeth approach to Waterloo bridge—Brunswick Rock Asphalte Paving Company, £8,978; Trinidad Lake Asphalte Paving Company, £12,854; Val de Travers Asphalte Paving Company, Limited, £13,107; Bradshaw & Co., £13,917. (d) For the demolition of the old bridge at Vauxhall, and for the partial construction of the new bridge—Pethick Brothers, £166,568; Kirk & Randall, £174,499; J. S. Pearson & Son, Limited, £177,236.

### METROPOLITAN ASYLUMS BOARD.

Sir Edwin H. Goldsworthy presided on Saturday at a meeting of the managers at County Hall, Spring-gardens. The clerk read a letter from the Local Government Board stating that they had under consideration a further letter relative to the managers' proposal to obtain tenders for the erection of the new head office without advertising, and that they did not feel justified in assenting to a departure from their regulations. A letter was received from the department sanctioning the expenditure of £11,223 0s. 3d. in respect of the provision and maintenance of ambulances and ambulance stations and other outlay connected therewith during the half-year ended March 26th. It was agreed to engage Sir J. Whittaker Ellis to act as valuer in connection with the proposed purchase of some property at Sutton belonging to the South Metropolitan School District Board.— A resolution of the Works Committee recommending the provision of a greenhouse at the Park hospital was adopted. Among the tenders accepted were the following: Fuller's Manufacturing Company, for the supply of roller blinds to the Western hospital; Ballard (Limited), for £127, for re-making a road at the same hospital; Messrs. Armstrong & Co., 116 Queen Victoria-street, for £267, for improving the drying accommodation at the same institution; and Mr. T. Knight (of Sidcup), for £378, for the erection of a destructor at the Gore Farm hospital.—The Works Committee recommended that the tender of Messrs. McCormick & Sons, of Northampton-street, for the partial reconstruction of the North-Eastern hospital, at the sum of £113,642, should be.

accepted. The architect's revised estimate was £115,000. Messrs. McCormick's tender was accepted.

## VESTRIES AND DISTRICT BOARDS.

**Bermondsey.**—On Monday the Baths Committee reported to the vestry the receipt of a specification from the surveyor for work in connection with the renovation of the laundry. The committee recommended that tenders should be invited for carrying out the work, and that they should be authorised to act in the matter. An amendment was moved that the surveyor should be instructed to undertake the work, but on a division this was rejected by thirty-two votes to twenty-five, and the original recommendation adopted.—Mr. Layman, on behalf of the Works Committee, moved the adoption of the report relating to the Workmen's Compensation Act. The committee pointed out that there were three courses open to the vestry. One was to cover the risk by insurance, the second was to submit an alternative scheme to the Registrar of Friendly Societies, and the third was for the vestry to take the risk until some experience had been gained of the working of the Act. The committee recommended the vestry to adopt the last-mentioned course. In supporting this Mr. Layman stated that the insurance companies asked for high premiums, amounting to as much as 20s. per cent., and that in taking up the risk the companies required the insurance of all the vestry's employees, whether comprised within the scope of the Act or otherwise. It was best to continue as hitherto, and for the vestry to take its own risk. After some discussion the recommendation of the committee was unanimously adopted.—The General Purposes Committee reported the receipt of a letter from the London County Council, stating that they had had under consideration a letter from the Strand District Board of Works calling attention to the necessity for regulating the methods of advertising by the electric light and other similar devices, and asking the council whether they could not obtain the prohibition of advertising by means of search or flash lights thrown on the public highways. The council asked whether the vestry knew of any such advertisements in its district, and whether it considered it desirable that some by-law should be made for the regulation generally of these advertisements. On the recommendation of the committee it was resolved to inform the council that flash-light advertisements were occasionally shown in the parish, and that some by-law should be made for their regulation.—The Electric Lighting Committee reported the decision of the House of Commons committee in regard to the Bill to confirm the vestry's electric lighting provisional order. On the recommendation of the committee it was decided to submit a clause for insertion in the Bill consenting to purchase by agreement, or at a price to be fixed by an arbitrator appointed by the Board of Trade, the distributing mains in the parish laid by the London Electric Supply Corporation, such purchase to be completed before the vestry commenced to supply electricity. Mr. Cox, chairman of the Electric Lighting Committee, expressed the hope that the clause drafted to that effect would meet the wishes of the House of Commons committee, and that the provisional order would be confirmed. The cost of purchase was estimated at about £5,000.—The following tenders were received for the supply of bricks, at per 1,000: West Brothers, £2 per 1,000, delivered alongside the vestry's wharf, East-lane; Smeed, Dean & Co., £2, less 2½ per cent., delivered at the same wharf; Tucker & Son, £2, £2 10s. and £2 18s. respectively per 1,000, delivered in trucks at Mint-street station; C. Burley, £1 19s., at the vestry wharf; the Weldon and Corby Brick Company, £1 17s., at Mint-street station; and Wakeley Brothers, £2 5s., at the vestry depot, Spa-road. The General Purposes Committee recommended the acceptance of the tender of the Weldon and Corby Brick Company, at £1 17s. per 1,000, the bricks to be supplied as required. The recommendation was agreed to.

**Clerkenwell.**—On Thursday, at a meeting of the vestry, the Works Committee reported that their attention had been called to the bad condition of the carriageway of Clerkenwell-green, and having inspected it were of opinion that it was in need of repair; at the same time, they thought that a great improvement would be effected and the cost lessened if two large portions in the centre were paved with York paving or asphalte, and planted with trees. The estimated cost of the work, including the re-dressing and re-laying of the carriageway, was £975, and they (the committee) begged to recommend that the work be carried out. The report was adopted.

**Hackney.**—At last week's meeting of the vestry, the General Purposes Committee reported that, in their opinion, it was desirable that the wood paving of Dalston-lane should, as an experiment, be done by the vestry, without the intervention of a contractor. They recommended that this course be adopted, the conditions of employment and rates of wages to be the same as those which the vestry would require a contractor to observe were the work carried out by contract. The recommendation was agreed to.

**Hampstead.**—The Free and Open Spaces Committee have resolved to recommend the vestry, at its next meeting, to contribute £10,000 to the Hampstead Heath Extension Fund for securing the Golder's-hill estate, of over 36 acres, as an addition to Hampstead Heath. About £40,000 is required for the purpose, towards which nearly £12,000 has already been secured by private subscription.

**Islington.**—At the vestry meeting, on Friday, Mr. Fuller

asked the chairman of the Electric Lighting Committee whether it was a fact that the committee were in the habit of granting to those who had been less than twelve months in the employ of the vestry holidays for which the vestry had to pay; and, secondly, by whose authority such permission was given. Mr. Quayle replied in the affirmative to the first question, and stated that the vestry gave the necessary authority in January of last year. The matter then dropped.—The Parliamentary Committee further reported having considered the question of establishing a fund against fire and other insurances, and had been furnished in connection with the matter with a return giving particulars of the vestry's existing fire and guarantee insurances. Being, however, of opinion that the vestry were not empowered by law either to create or to contribute to such a fund, the committee recommended that the consideration of the matter should be deferred until the introduction of the Bill for the reform of the local government of London, which would, in all probability, afford an opportunity for the local authorities to acquire the necessary powers to establish or contribute towards such a fund. The recommendation was unanimously adopted.—At the suggestion of the Electric Lighting Committee it was resolved to borrow £72,000 for the extension of the electricity works. In this connection the committee pointed out that they had instructed the architect to draw up plans, &c., for a considerable extension. The electrical engineer estimated that the increased boiler and engine house accommodation would be sufficient to contain the whole of the additional machinery required for about seven years, and he advised that plant, to the extent of 3,000 horse-power, should be placed on order forthwith, two engines and dynamos of 1,000 horse-power each, to be erected within twelve months, and the third to be erected within two years. The estimated cost is as follows: Six boilers and fittings, £8,400; three 1,000 horse-power engines, £16,500; three 600 kilowatt alternators, £15,000; steam and exhaust pipes, pumps, heaters, injectors, switch gear, regulators, connections and contingencies, £9,000; and estimate for building extensions, £22,500; being a total of £71,400.—The Works Committee submitted a scheme prepared by the chief surveyor for relieving the sewers of the Strand Green-road district, in order to prevent the flooding of the Crouch Hill station during periods of heavy rainfall. It was resolved to submit the scheme to the county council for approval.—The same committee reported having considered returns obtained from the contractors for supplying horses and drivers for watering roads of the rates of wages paid to their employees. On the recommendation of the committee it was resolved to instruct the vestry clerk to give notice to Messrs. G. Malin & Son, Messrs. W. King & Son, and Mr. W. Watson that they were not paying the trade union rate of wages, of 24s. per week, and that unless they did so, and observed the conditions as to hours of labour in accordance with their contract, the vestry would enforce the penalty provided for them.—The following tenders were accepted by the Works Committee for the supply of horse forage during July: Messrs. D. N. Howell & Co., Sufferance wharf, Belvedere-road, S.E., 100 qrs. of oats, equal to sample No. 1, at 16s. 9d. per qr.; Mr. G. W. Steap, 58 New Corn Exchange, E.C., 1½ tons of mill bran, at 115s. per ton; Mr. Geo. Rose, Little Halling-bury, seven loads of hay, at 75s. per load; twelve loads of straw, at 33s. per load; and seven loads of mixture, at 77s. 6d. per load; Messrs. Turner, Byrne & Co., Cumberland hay market, N.W., seven loads of clover, at 87s. 6d. per load.—On the motion of Mr. Dove, as amended by Mr. Mills, the vestry passed a resolution that provision should be speedily made for the adequate accommodation of the stuff by obtaining a site for the erection of municipal buildings and referring the question to the General Purposes Committee for consideration and report.

**Kensington.**—The Works and Sanitary Committee last week reported having given consideration to the result of the conference of engineers and surveyors of the several vestries and district boards in the metropolis on the subject of sewer ventilation. The Main Drainage Committee recommended that the council be requested to adopt the remedy for sewer emanations advocated by the conference in respect of the Counter's creek sewer in the parish, numerous complaints having been received from parishioners and the sanitary inspectors of offensive smells from sewer ventilators in streets in the line of the said sewer; also that the surveyor be requested to report to the committee as to any practicable action which might be taken by the vestry to give effect in this parish to the third recommendation of the conference. This, it may be remembered, was as follows: (3) That pipe ventilators on buildings, or otherwise, when possible, should always be adopted, in addition to surface ventilators." The recommendations were agreed to.

**Marylebone.**—The vestry resolved at the meeting held on Thursday that in the advertisements to be issued for the positions of district superintendents and superintendents of cleansing and of sewers and drains it should be stipulated that no pensions would be granted at the expiration of service.—On the recommendation of the Sanitary Committee it was resolved to accept the offer of Messrs. Mead & Co. to remove the manure from the stables in the parish by way of experiment for three months and at the rates of charge to owners mentioned in the report of the medical officer of health.—The same committee stated, with regard to the reference, to consider and report if Part II. of the Housing of the Working Classes Act could and ought to be applied in the parish, that they did not see their way to recommend the vestry to take any action in the matter at the present time. The consideration of the report was adjourned.—It was mentioned that the preamble of the Bill promoted by the Metropolitan Electric Supply Company for the acquisition of land for the erection of a generating station at Willesden had been passed. So far as Marylebone was concerned the vestry had been successful in securing the insertion of a clause which upheld the vestry's agreement with the company of the 1st October, 1889, and which bound the company to maintain the generating stations in South-street and Rathbone-place.—The vestry referred to the Sanitary Committee a letter from the county council threatening to take proceedings, at the cost of the vestry, should the latter not take effective steps to abate the smoke nuisance. In this connection Mr. Brook-Hitching stated that the Court of Common Council had had to take proceedings against the county council for the same offence in regard to their river steamers. The very people who complained were themselves guilty of the same nuisance.—The vestry postponed the consideration of the following notice of motion by Mr. T. W. Baker : " That, having regard to the increased liability of the vestry in the employment of their labour coming under the Workmen's Compensation Act, it be referred to the Parliamentary committee to bring up a report as to how many of the workmen come under the Act, and the advisability of insurance or otherwise, and at what rate it can be effected."

**Newington.**—On Wednesday the Roads and Depot Committee recommended that they should be empowered to accept a tender, if necessary, during the recess for the erection of the proposed flats in Manor-place, in accordance with plans and specification prepared by the architect, Mr. Plumb; The recommendation was adopted.—The Lighting Committee recommended that the vestry should undertake by direct labour, under the supervision of the surveyor, the removal and relaying of pavement and excavation of trenches in connection with the laying of the electric light mains. The recommendation was carried.—The committee also recommended, and the vestry decided, that the National Telephone Company should be permitted to lay in the same trenches as those made for the electric light mains their telephone pipes and cables, under the supervision of the vestry's consulting engineers, on condition that the company should bear a moiety of the expense of taking up and relaying the footpaths and excavating the trenches.

**Plumstead.**—It is reported that the vestry, who are themselves considering the question of applying for a provisional order for an electric supply, have received notice from the Woolwich District Electric Light Company of their intention to apply for powers to light Plumstead with electricity. The vestry have decided to oppose the granting of the order.

**Poplar.**—The district board of works have decided to repave a portion of East India Dock-road with hard wood, at an estimated cost of £420.

**Shoreditch.**—At the vestry meeting on Tuesday the Finance Committee recommended that application should be made to the county council for a loan of £10,653 at 2¾ per cent, for engineering works in connection with the baths and wash-houses. The vestry clerk pointed out that the county council had raised the rate of interest on loans exceeding £10,000 to 3 per cent. In that connection the clerk mentioned that he had been in communication with the Public Works and Loans Commissioners, who had offered to advance the amount of the loan at 2¾ per cent. An amendment was accordingly moved and carried referring the recommendation back to the committee for further consideration.—A letter was read from the county council in reference to the nuisance arising from peat litter manure, and asking for the vestry's views on the subject. The communication was referred to the Public Health Committee.—A further letter from the county council was read enclosing copy of a resolution passed by the council proposing to obtain powers for the reconstruction of the Cat and Mutton bridge on condition of the Hackney Vestry contributing £5,000 and the Shoreditch Vestry £17,000 towards the cost of the work. The subject was referred to the Works Committee.—A petition was submitted asking the vestry to pave Old-street with wood, and this was also relegated to the Works Committee. —Tenders were received and opened by the chairman of the vestry for the supply of boilers and transformers in connection with the electric light station. In view of the long vacation, it was unanimously resolved to authorise the Lighting Committee to accept tenders and report their action to the vestry. The committee were also empowered to have specifications prepared and tenders invited and dealt with for the extension of the boiler-house and battery-room at the electricity works.—In reply to representations made by the county council on the subject of the smoke nuisance, the Public Health Committee recommended that a reply should be sent stating that the vestry were taking proceedings to abate the evil. The recommendation was, however, referred back to the committee, in order that an explanation might be forwarded to the county council of the difficulty experienced in enforcing the law in the police courts.—On the motion of

Mr. Winkler the Works Committee were authorised to invite tenders for reconstructing a portion of the Britannia-street sewer.

**St. George-in-the-East.**—At a meeting of the vestry on Thursday the Finance Committee recommended, that a memorial be sent to the London County Council in favour of a communication between Rotherhithe and Wapping, and asking that a deputation from the vestry might be received on the subject. Mr. Jacobs moved the adoption of the report, and referred to the importance of the subject. Notwithstanding the Tower bridge, there was still, he said, a need for further facilities of communication. The London County Council were practically pledged in the matter, though the committee was unable to decide in favour of either a tunnel or a bridge. Mr. C. Barratt seconded and the motion was agreed to.

**St. Pancras.**—The vestry last week adopted a recommendation of the Works Committee that the carriageway in front of the North London Hospital for Consumption, in Grafton-street, be repaved with hard wood grouted in pitch, at a cost of £250.—On the recommendation of the Baths Committee it was resolved to authorise the vestry clerk to complete the purchase of freehold and leasehold interests in Bayham-place, for the extension and improvement of the laundry in King-street.—The Baths and Wash-Houses Committee asked for authority to invite tenders from well engineers for the sinking of a well at the King-street baths in accordance with a specification prepared by the borough engineer. After some discussion the vestry gave the desired permission. The Baths Committee also recommended that applications should be invited, by advertisement, from architects who have had experience in the designing and carrying out of public baths and wash-houses and are willing to submit designs for the new baths in the Prince of Wales-road, and that six firms be selected therefrom to compete; that the architect of the design placed first in order of merit be asked to carry out the work at the usual charges approved by the Royal Institute of British Architects; and that a premium of £50 be awarded to each of the five unsuccessful architects; and that a professional assessor should be appointed, at a fee of 100 guineas, to report and advise the committee on the designs that would be received. The recommendations were adopted.—Dr. Smith, for the Electric Lighting Committee, reported that they had, in consequence of complaints received respecting the alternate extinction of the arc lamps at midnight, viewed after midnight the localities complained of. It was found generally that the thoroughfares were sufficiently well lighted when half the lamps were extinguished, with the exception of two or three places which cannot be improved unless the whole of the lamps are kept in lighting till daylight. The committee deemed it sufficiently important that these special places should be lighted, and had given instructions for the whole of the lamps throughout the parish to be left in lighting throughout the night.—The Highways Committee recommended that advertisements should be issued inviting tenders for the supply of hard wood paving blocks, required at a later period for the repaving of Guildford-street and Midland-road, in order that merchants might be enabled to arrange for the importation of the material when it became necessary for the work to be put in hand. The recommendation was adopted.— The following tenders were considered for the supply of condensing plant and steam pipes for the Regent's Park electric light station : Meehan & Sons, £5,000 : Klein Engineering Co., Limited, £4,875 ; W. Gailes & Co., £4,306 10s. 10d. ; John Fraser & Son, £4,155 14s. 4d. ; T. Ledward & Co. (informal), £3,097 ; Fairbrother & Co. (informal), £3,231. The tender of Messrs. John Fraser & Son, of Millwall, was accepted.

**St. Saviour's.**—Last week, at a meeting of the district board of works, the surveyor intimated that the wood paving of Borough High-street had been completed in eight days. It was done at the rate of 30,000 blocks daily.—It was also reported that final arrangements had been made with the London County Council for the improvement of Bear-lane.

## PROVINCIAL AND GREATER LONDON AUTHORITIES.

### COUNTY COUNCILS.

**Derbyshire.**—At their meeting on the 6th inst. the county council adopted a report of the Asylum Committee recommending that £39,990 be expended on extensions at the asylum.

**Essex.**—At a meeting of the county council on the 5th inst. Dr. Thresh, the medical officer of health, reported that he had received a letter from Halstead, saying that some pollution of the river Colne had occurred, and that all the fish were being poisoned. Upon investigation he found that a gasometer tank belonging to a private firm had been pumped out into the river and had caused the mischief. The gentleman responsible assured him that he had no idea that it would have any deleterious effect. No doubt no liquor of this character would be again discharged into the river from these works. The committee reported that they had " directed a letter to be written to Messrs. S. Courtauld & Co., Limited, stating that they considered the matter a serious one, and that it must not occur again."

**West Riding.**—The county council adopted, at their meeting on the 13th inst., the following resolution: That the Finance Committee apply to the Local Government Board for sanction to the borrowing of £43,600 for the purchase of the Storthes estate, comprising 629 acres, on which to build a new asylum, and for incidental expenses, the period of repayment suggested being thirty years.

## MUNICIPAL CORPORATIONS.

**Accrington.**—The town council recently approved the action of the Legal and Parliamentary Committee, who, having considered a letter from the Local Government Board declining to sanction a loan for the construction of a main sewer for the Baxenden district, because of the unsatisfactory state of the effluent produced at the Accrington and Church joint outfall sewerage works, passed a resolution placing upon record its opinion that the joint sewerage board ought forthwith to proceed with the construction of further filter-beds, and ought also to enter into negotiations for the purchase of land for filtration purposes. The Health Committee considered a communication from the Local Government Board emphasising the necessity for an infectious diseases hospital other than the present small-pox hospital, and the town clerk was instructed to reply that the refusal of the Local Government Board to sanction a loan for the Baxenden sewer had placed the corporation in a great difficulty, inasmuch as until that sewer was constructed there was no outlet for the sewage from the site already secured for an infectious diseases hospital.

**Bath.**—On the 12th inst., at a meeting of the Rivers Pollution Prevention and Floods Committee, it was reported that a letter had been sent to the Local Government Board, asking whether sanction might be given for a practical scheme—namely, for sewage collection—leaving the question of disposal until it was seen whether the Exeter experiment with the septic system was successful. The board wrote that they could not entertain this proposal. The committee agreed to leave further action until the matter came before the town council.

**Birmingham.**—The question of the class of workmen's dwellings to be erected on the land in Milk-street, which was cleared by the corporation of that city some time ago, was considered on Tuesday week by the joint committee, composed of members of the Improvement and Health Committees. The plans were approved, and it was decided that a report should be presented at the next council meeting recommending the approval of the plans prepared by Mr. Tart, the manager of the improvement department. The rent of the houses will work out at an average of about 1s. 6d. per room.

**Bolton.**—Approval has been given to the recommendations of the electrical engineer (Mr. Arthur Ellis) for extensions of the electric lighting plant and a change from the present alternating current to the continuous current for the central part of the town. The cost for extensions on the alternating-current principle was estimated at £16,830, and for the introduction of the continuous current the engineer says £21,576 is required.

**Bournemouth.**—On the 6th inst. the following tenders for an electrical installation at the pier, the pleasure grounds and the winter gardens, were received: The Walsall Electrical Company, Limited, £2,605; Leonard G. Tate, £2,997; Siemens Brothers & Co., Limited, £2,192; Crompton & Co., Limited, £2,097; Johnson & Phillips, £2,083; Brush Electrical Engineering Company, £1,598; R. Algar & Sons, £1,867; Cash Robinson & Co., £1,784 1s. 4d. A letter from the secretary of the Local Government Board was read, stating that the board would not be prepared to further consider the applications for sanction to borrow £1,600 and £900 until the council had decided whether or not they could generate their own electricity.

**Brighton.**—The council recently adopted the report of a committee, stating that they (the committee) had tried to find the best reflector for the electric lamps, and recommended one which their men at the electricity works could make for about 6s. each. They thought it advisable to spend £282 in putting in a radiator in connection with the old chimney shaft. It would save the shaft from the tremendous heat, which had caused it to crack.

**Bristol.**—The site at the back of the council-house, Bristol, is being cleared for the erection of the temporary council chamber, the cost of which is to be limited by resolution of the council to £2,500. The building is to be erected under the supervision of the city engineer, Mr. T. H. Yabbicom.

**Burnley.**—The town council have instructed the Finance Committee to apply to the Local Government Board for sanction to the borrowing of £50,140 for the purchase of property, and for extending the gas and electric light works.

**Burton.**—It has been resolved to apply to the Local Government Board for sanction to borrow £50,140 for the execution of various works, chiefly in connection with the gas and electric light undertakings.

**Cambridge.**—On account of the rise in the price of wood blocks the town council have decided to apply to the Local Government Board for permission to increase their proposed loan for paving works from £15,000 to £17,260.

**Chesterfield.**—It was announced, at a meeting of the town council last week, that it had been decided to reduce the price of gas for power purposes to 2s. 6d. per 1,000 cubic feet.

**Colne.**—On Wednesday of last week, at Colne, a Local Government Board inquiry was held into an application of the Borough of Colne for sanction to a loan of £24,400 for works of private street improvement and £4,200 for the erection of stables in Spring-lane.

**Devonport.**—The council at a recent meeting gave their consideration to a report of Prof. Kennedy on the proposed light and power station.

**Dudley.**—The desirability of purchasing the gasworks is under the consideration of a committee of the town council.

**Durham.**—A committee has been appointed by the town council to prepare a report on the lighting of the city by incandescent lamps or electricity.

**Evesham.**—Mr. P. H. Fletcher, manager of the corporation gasworks, has submitted a report to the Gas Committee giving details of improvements and extensions, estimated to cost £2,270, which he considers will be necessary in the near future if the consumption of gas continues to increase. Consideration of the report has been deferred.

**Hereford.**—The council have decided to adopt the recommendation of a committee that application should be made for powers to borrow the necessary money to purchase a site for electricity works.

**Hove.**—The town council have accepted the tender of Messrs. J. Parsons & Sons, Hove, at £1,227, for road-making and other works in Walsingham-road, and that of the same firm, at £203, for laying asphalte paving in Queen's-gardens, from Grand-avenue to Palmeira-mews (a distance of about 870 yards).

**Leamington.**—Last week the council adopted a series of recommendations recently drawn up by the Technical Instruction and Free Library Committee with reference to the proposed new free library and technical institute for the borough. It is proposed that £12,000 shall be spent on the new building, exclusive of land and furnishing, the work of design to be thrown open to competition—the first premium to be awarded the accepted design, the author to have the privilege of carrying out the work; the second premium to be 50 guineas.

**Liverpool.**—The members of the city council have resolved to provide themselves with a new council chamber at the lowest possible cost, and accepted at their last meeting the proposal of Sir Thomas Hughes to make alterations in the present chamber, at an estimated cost of £8,000, rather than erect an entirely new council-house on the site of St. George's church, at a probable cost of £60,000.

**Ludlow.**—The corporation decided at a recent meeting to apply for a provisional order for the supply of electricity in the borough. It was stated that the £300 a year at present paid to the gas company would pay the interest on the loan that would be necessary in connection with the installation of electric light.

**Manchester.**—The special Tramways Committee of the Manchester Corporation met on Friday. It was decided to visit Liverpool for the purpose of inspecting some electric trams. The Liverpool Corporation contemplate employing electricity as the motive power for the tramway system of that city, and the cars, which are of different patterns, have been sent there by their respective makers for experimental purposes. The Manchester committee, having regard to the future use of electricity for the tramways here, decided to take advantage of the opportunity of seeing the new cars at work.

**Oldham.**—The annual inspection of the gasworks by the corporation Gas Committee was made last week. At the Hollinwood station the new retorts attracted attention, and at the Higginshaw works a coke elevator and screener that have recently been put into use.

**Ryde.**—The formal opening of an organ erected in the town hall at a cost of £1,000 took place on Monday of last week.

**Scarborough.**—A committee having considered the question of a suitable site for the refuse destructor, and the borough engineer having submitted a report upon the matter, it has been resolved that the town clerk be instructed to write to the Office of Woods inquiring if they will allow the corporation to take a long lease of the land comprising about 7 acres adjoining the Scarborough and Whitby railway, on the Crown's Northstead estate, for a site for a refuse destructor, and, if so, upon what terms.

**Woodstock.**—A fire camp and review, promoted by the National Fire Brigades Union, will be held from August 20th to the 24th in Blenheim Park, the estate of the Duke of Marlborough.

**Worthing.**—An inspector of the Local Government Board last week held an inquiry with respect to the application of the town council for sanction to borrow £762 for street improvement works.

## URBAN DISTRICT COUNCILS.

**Aston Manor.**—The tender of Mr. W. Cotterill, Aston Manor, has been accepted for painting and decorating the council offices and free library.

**Bakewell.**—The council recently took possession of the undertaking of the Bakewell Gas Light Company, which they purchased at a cost of £11,522, and of this sum £1,200 was paid to the Duke of Rutland for his reversionary interest and freehold. At a special meeting of the council, on Thursday evening, a cheque was signed for £10,350. The original capital of the company was £1,500, in 300 shares, and by this transfer the shareholders receive about £34 per share.

**Bognor.**—The district council have under consideration the advisability of lighting the esplanade and pier with electricity.

**Bromsgrove.**—On Friday Mr. W. O. E. Meade-King, M.I.C.E., held an inquiry at the town hall, Bromsgrove, touching the application of the urban district council for sanction to borrow £1,200 for purposes of street improvement and £600 for the purchase of land for purposes of public walks and pleasure grounds. The surveyor, Mr. R. H. Nowell, attended the proceedings. No opposition was offered.

**Castleton.**—Mr. H. Percy Boulnois, engineering inspector of the Local Government Board, attended at the council offices recently to make inquiries respecting the council's application to borrow £2,250 to pay for additional land required for sewage works. Mr. Clayton (principal assistant to Mr. J. Diggle, the engineer for the sewage works scheme) explained the plans and proposals.

**Chesterton.**—It was stated, at the last monthly meeting of this body, that the Sewerage Committee had given their consideration to the question of dealing with the smells emanating from the manholes, and had asked the surveyor to prepare plans showing where ventilating shafts were desirable. They had come to the conclusion that they would for the present authorise eight shafts to be erected in different points of the system, where the surveyor had advised the smells were most pungent. If, after those shafts had had been fixed, there were still manholes which were offensive, then the committee would take them also into consideration and put up further shafts. For the present, however, they believed eight would be sufficient to obviate the smells complained of. It was decided to erect the shafts.

**Epsom.**—The Local Government Board have held an inquiry into an application of the council for sanction to borrow £440 for works of sewerage and £3,400 for the purposes of a recreation ground.—The district council, who were recently fined in respect of the pollution of the Hogg's Mill river, have applied to the Local Government Board for sanction to a loan of £17,000 for the drainage of Ewell.

**Erdington.**—On Wednesday of last week Mr. W. O. E. Meade-King, inspector of the Local Government Board, held an inquiry at the council offices, Erdington, in reference to an application by the council for sanction to borrow £3,000 for works of surface-water drainage, £1,321 for purpose of sewerage, and £424 for the purchase of land, and a cottage for purposes of a refuse tip. Mr. W. Ashford, clerk to the council, in supporting the application, said, in reference to the last-named sum, the council, under pressure of the Local Government Board, the county council and the medical officer, had undertaken the removal of house refuse and the emptying of ash-pits, but one of the principal difficulties in the carrying out of that work was the obtaining of proper tips and convenient wharf accommodation on the canal.

**Grange-over-Sands.**—The council have adopted plans, and are making application to the Local Government Board for powers to borrow £10,000 to carry out certain improvements which have been under consideration for three and a half years. It is proposed that the sewage which now drains upon the foreshore at various points shall be collected and carried beyond the river along the railway embankment, outside which will be erected a promenade. The new sea wall will reclaim 5¾ acres of land, which will probably be used as a recreation ground.

**Halesowen.**—A Local Government Board inquiry was held on Thursday with respect to an application of the district council for permission to borrow upwards of £1,150 for completing works of sewerage at Hasbury, Halesowen and Hawne.

**Handsworth.**—At the last monthly meeting of the council a letter was received from the Board of Trade stating that they had consented to the use of steam on the South Staffordshire tramways for a further period of six months. By a small majority the council decided to erect a public convenience in the Stafford-road. A few months ago a similar convenience in this road was demolished by order of the council.

**Hoylake and West Kirby.**—Recently, at a meeting of the General Purposes Committee of the council, consideration was given to a scheme for the improvement of the Hoyle lake. In the course of the discussion it was explained that in the original scheme provision was made for the expenditure of about £5,000 for dredging purposes, while the scheme itself involved an expenditure of £13,500. It was further stated that the sum of about £800 per annum would also be required for dredging purposes in addition to the expenditure of £5,000, and that this would involve the payment of £1,000 to £1,400 a year as the result of the adoption of the original scheme. Numerous resolutions and amendments were proposed at the meeting, but it was eventually decided to call another meeting of the ratepayers to place before them the present position of the original scheme.

**Horsham.**—The council, at a recent meeting, adopted the report of a committee recommending an application to the Board of Trade for a license to supply electricity within the urban district, at an estimated cost of a little over £10,000.

**Leyton.**—The council have accepted the following tenders for the extension of the electric lighting plant: Accumulators—The Hart Secondary Battery Syndicate, £1,480; Switchboards—The General Electric Company, £150; Cables —The Western Electric Company (schedule prices).

## RURAL DISTRICT COUNCILS.

**Croydon.**—The district council, at a recent meeting, resolved to apply to the Local Government Board for sanction to a loan of £14,000 for the purpose of the drainage of Coulsdon, to include £1,300 for Sanderstead, and also to provide for the drainage of Russell-hill schools and Cane-hill asylum.

**Hartley Witney, Hants.**—Mr. Herbert H. Law, C.E., one of the inspectors of the Local Government Board, held an inquiry on the 12th inst., in reply to the application of the council to borrow £5,500 for works of sewerage and sewage disposal. The scheme was unopposed. After the inquiry the inspector proceeded to view the site proposed for sewage disposal, which is on the septic tank system. The engineers for the scheme are Messrs. Fairbank & Son, civil engineers, of York and Westminster, S.W.

**Wantage.**—The tender of Mr. W. A. Wheeler, at £154, has been accepted for the carrying out of certain sewerage works.

## SCOTLAND AND IRELAND.

**Aberdeen.**—The annual inspection of the waterworks took place on the 5th inst. Lord Provost Mearns and the members of the town council drove to Invercannie and made the usual investigation of the works, giving particular attention to the parts of the aqueduct where sewage matter has been found to percolate.—A new swimming bath was last week formally opened by the Lord Provost. The pond measures 90 ft. in length by 35 ft. in breadth. The depth of water at the shallow end is 3 ft. 6 in., gradually deepening to 7 ft. 6 in. at the other end. The pond, which should prove a useful adjunct to the bathing station at all seasons—and, it is to be hoped, also a profitable convenience—is situated in an underground building, the walls of which are of concrete, lined with cement inside. The cost of the station, including the original building, up to date is estimated at £12,000. Mr. John Rust, the city architect, designed the alterations.

**Peebles.**—The town council have offered to take over the gas undertaking, giving the shareholders 10 per cent. annuities on their holdings for thirty-five years, after which the council will buy up the concern at £157 10s. per £100 value of stock, the burgh to pay the cost of the transfer.

---

**Holborn Public Library.**—We have received the sixth annual report of the commissioners of this institution, the affairs of which, judging from the contents of the pamphlet, are in a highly satisfactory condition.

**Business Announcement.**—We have been informed that, finding it necessary to have larger premises, Messrs. Hall Brothers, wholesale manufacturers of electrical apparatus, 18 Fenchurch-buildings, Fenchurch-street, E.C., have removed to 156 Upper Thames-street and 21 Bush-lane, Cannon-street, E.C.

**From the Editor.**—We may occasionally have to return to contributors manuscripts which circumstances prevent our using. It is not a congenial task, and one is anxious to soften it as much as may be by some courteous formula. The *Referee* of India gives the following sample of the courtesies of Chinese editors, and we quote it with the request that it may be understood, though somewhat long for every-day use, to accompany our own "declined with thanks": "Illustrious Brother of the Sun and Moon.—Behold thy servant prostrate before thy feet. I kowtow to thee, and beg that of thy graciousness thou mayest grant that I may speak and live. Thy honoured manuscript has deigned to cast the light of its august countenance upon us. With raptures we have perused it. By the bones of my ancestors, never have I encountered such with such pathos, such lofty thought! With fear and trembling I return the writing. Were I to publish the treasure you send me, the Emperor would order that it should be made the standard, and that none be published except such as equalled it. Knowing literature as I do, and that it would be impossible in ten thousand years to equal what you have done, I send your writing back. Ten thousand times I crave your pardon. Behold my head is at your feet. Do what you will.—Your servant's servant,—THE EDITOR."

# Personal.

Mr. Robert Dryden has been appointed burgh surveyor of Dalkeith.

Lancaster Corporation have selected Mr. J. Fisher, of Lancaster, to fill the post of building inspector.

Mr. C. H. Broadbent, of Otley, has been appointed surveyor and sanitary inspector to the Guiseley District Council.

Out of twenty-six applicants, Mr. J. W. Garbutt, of Barnsley, has been appointed surveyor to the Farsley Urban District Council.

Mr. Diggle, assistant surveyor of Heywood, has been appointed district surveyor for Moseley by the urban district council.

Romford Urban District Council have increased the salary of Mr. Herbert T. Ridge, their assistant surveyor, by £15 per annum.

Mr. S. Donald, gas analyst to the Dundee Corporation Gas Committee, has been granted an increase of salary of £25 per annum.

Mr. H. Riley, surveyor and water engineer to the Gainsborough Urban District Council, has had his salary increased by £50 per annum.

Mr. W. Ryle Wright, the borough engineer of Burnley, will shortly visit the United States for the purpose, it is reported, of picking up new ideas on matters concerning his profession.

Mr. H. W. Corrie, surveyor to the Neston and Parkgate Urban District Council, has resigned his post in order to take up a similar appointment under the Lower Bebington Urban District Council.

Brightlingsea Urban District Council have adopted a report recommending the engagement of Mr. H. Goodyear, surveyor to the Colchester Town Council, as consulting engineer in connection with the waterworks.

Mr. Byrom, the chairman of the Bury Corporation Gas Committee, at a recent meeting of the town council, stated that Mr. Simmonds, the new gas manager, had put the works in good order and was showing marked ability.

Mr. Herbert S. Goodall, formerly a pupil of Mr. W. Wing, F.I.A.S., of Caversham, Reading, has been appointed assistant to the surveyor of the urban district of Farnborough. Twenty applications for the post were received.

At a recent meeting of the town council of Bridgwater it was unanimously resolved to increase the salary of the borough engineer, Mr. Francis Pherr, to £280. Further annual increases of £10 are also to be granted, bringing up the amount to £300.

In our reference last week to Mr. Macdonald that gentleman was inadvertently described as the resident waterworks engineer to the Newport Borough Council. Mr. Macdonald, of course, holds the position of manager. Mr. N. Holloway is the resident engineer.

We regret to announce the sudden death, at the Golden Lion Hotel, Ipswich, of Mr. Walter Horne, who for some years was borough surveyor and waterworks engineer of Worthing. At the time of his decease he was representing Messrs. Haan, Baker & Co., engineers, 13 Grosvenor-road, Westminster.

A deputation of six members of the Corporation of York and the borough engineer (Mr. A. Creer) have been visiting Southampton to inspect the new drainage works and refuse destructors. After visiting the municipal buildings they were shown over the various works by the borough engineer, Mr. W. B. G. Bennett.

At last week's meeting of the South Bank Urban District Council a letter was read from Mr. Poole tendering his resignation as surveyor and inspector of nuisances, owing to having accepted a superior position under the Sefton Urban District Council. The resignation was accepted, and it was agreed to advertise for a qualified surveyor at an open salary.

Mr. John Mallinson, who is at present chief assistant to Mr. O. J. Kirby, borough engineer and surveyor of Batley, has been appointed town surveyor of Skipton, in succession to his late father, Mr. Thomas Mallinson. The deceased gentleman's name was, we find, incorrectly given in our last issue as Mr. John Mallinson. We regret the error, which, however, did not originate with us.

At a meeting of the Norfolk County Council, on the 2nd inst., the county surveyor, Mr. Heslop, applied for some remuneration in respect of the surveillance of works carried out at the asylum during the last two years, and necessitating an expenditure of £7,000. Some discussion followed, but it was eventually decided to refer the matter to the Finance and General Purposes Committee.

In moving the acceptance of the resignation of Mr. Oliver Winter, the surveyor to the Vestry of St. George-the-Martyr, last week, a member of that body remarked that if they had dealt more liberally with Mr. Winter they might have retained his valuable services. But, he added, St. George's vestrymen did not appreciate brains. The chairman and several others spoke eulogistically of Mr. Winter's services.

The first business transacted at Thursday's meeting of the Itchen Urban District Council was the appointment of a surveyor. The committee who had been elected at the last meeting to bring up a report upon the thirty-three applications received had selected three candidates, who were present, to be interviewed by the board. Eventually Mr. Thomas G. Collingwood was appointed, at a salary of £125 per annum.

Ill health has, we learn, compelled Mr. F. Harman Lewis, the borough electrical engineer of Wolverhampton, to send in his resignation. Mr. Lewis commenced his duties under the corporation in May, 1893, at a salary of £300 per annum. Last week the resignation was accepted by the council with regret, but upon the recommendation of the Lighting Committee it was decided to retain his services as consulting engineer, at a salary of £150 per annum.

Mr. William Thomas Olive, who was for ten years chief assistant to the city surveyor of Manchester, and afterwards for five years resident engineer on the Manchester sewerage scheme recently completed, and which was designed by him, is at present on a visit to Manchester. He left England for Cape Colony in 1895, and has there successfully carried out a great scheme for the sewerage of the city of Cape Town, involving an expenditure of £300,000. Mr. Olive returns to the Cape in August.

On Saturday last, by kind permission of Mr. Edward Parry, of Nottingham, the staff of the borough engineer and surveyor of Leicester, and the members of the Leicester Society of Architects, were conveyed over the section of the new Great Central Railway from Aylestone to East Leake and back, by engine and waggons placed at their disposal by the contractor, Mr. H. Lovatt. The resident engineer, Mr. G. B. Chalcraft, accompanied the party and gave a description of the works. On the motion of Mr. Alderman Sawday, seconded by Mr. E. George Mawbey, a hearty vote of thanks was accorded Mr. Chalcraft and Mr. Lovatt for the pleasure afforded.

At the Warrington Town Hall, on Friday, Mr. Herbert W Longdin was presented with a gold watch, subscribed for by the officials of the corporation and friends. Mr. Longdin, it may be mentioned, is leaving the town to take up the duties of assistant surveyor to the Heston and Isleworth Urban District Council. The mayor, in making the presentation, spoke in eulogistic terms of the professional capabilities of Mr. Longdin and of the valuable services rendered by him to the corporation. He and the whole of the members of the corporation could not help regretting that they were losing the services of so valuable an official. They at the same time wished him every success in his new sphere.

The mayor of Gloucester presided over an interesting ceremony last week, when Mr. H. J. Weaver, the assistant city surveyor, was presented with a handsome eight-day clock, bearing the following inscription : " Presented to Mr. H. J. Weaver by members of the corporation, officials and staff of the city of Gloucester, on his appointment as borough engineer of King's Lynn." The mayor, in the course of an address, congratulated Mr. Weaver upon his new appointment, and also upon his pluck and perseverance in endeavouring to improve his position. He (the mayor) did not believe in young men sticking to one post or in one office all their days, waiting for the shoes to drop off the older feet, so that they might drop into their shoes. They should keep looking around and see the advertisements which were from time to time inserted in the newspapers which were especially adapted for their work, and so benefit themselves.

We much regret to announce the death of Mr. Hudson Reah, who for the past twenty years has filled the important position of borough surveyor and water engineer to the Preston Corporation. Mr. Reah, we learn, returned from the Isle of Man on Friday, and proceeded immediately to Alston. After tea, at his residence, Garstang-road, he complained of feeling unwell, and at 8 o'clock he had a paralytic seizure, from which death resulted about 10.30 on Saturday night. Mr. Reah, previous to being appointed borough surveyor of Preston in 1878, held a similar office at Darlington. Here he succeeded Mr. R. N. Hunter, who resigned on commencing business in the town. Mr. Reah was appointed at the same time that Mr. Hamer was chosen town clerk. The deceased gentleman carried out with great ability some very important works, the chief being the construction of a sewage farm at Freckleton, which cost about £130,000, and at the time of his death he was supervising works at Alston in connection with the extension of the Preston water supply by the building of a large reservoir. This latter undertaking, it is expected, will also cost over £100,000. The responsibilities of directing the expenditure of such large amounts Mr. Reah discharged with abilities which quite justified the choice of the council in selecting him, and his sudden death has brought forth expressions of regret from all hands. Mr. Reah, who was fifty-eight years of age, leaves a widow, a son and several daughters.

## NEW OPEN SPACE FOR EAST HAM.

### OPENING OF THE CENTRAL PARK.

On Tuesday, the 5th inst., Councillor Knight, J.P., chairman of the East Ham Urban District Council, performed the ceremony of opening the new Central Park in White Horse-lane. The following are a few particulars with respect to the park: In 1896 the district council purchased 17 acres of freehold land, with Ranclliffe House and various buildings, from Colonel Burgess, for £8,500. Part of the land was pasture and part arable—some of the latter being held on lease with other land by Mr. W. Hollington, and a small part with a barn by Mr. J. G. Hollington. In one case the lease expired a few months ago, and in the other it happened that the barn was burnt down, and, as it was no longer needed, an arrangement was made to divide the insurance money and take possession of the land. Subsequently Colonel Burgess proposed to develop the adjoining land for building purposes, and it was thought desirable to acquire, if possible, further land for the park while it was to be had, and negotiations for that purpose resulted in the council purchasing from Colonel Burgess 8 acres more for £4,000, making the area of the park 25 acres and the total cost of the land £12,500. The shape of the land adapts itself to useful development, and the plans for laying it out, prepared by the council's surveyor, Mr. W. H. Savage, provide for a large area of grass, where cricket, football and other games can be played, besides affording full scope for the children. A corner for young children is to be set apart. There will be four entrances, so as to provide for the several parts of the ward. The whole of the northern boundary is to be laid out as flower gardens, facing the south—the whole length of the walks therein being nearly 1 mile, and in the midst of this there is to be a handsome band-stand, surrounded by a large circular open space, planted with acacias, where people can be seated to hear the music. Near this a shelter is to be provided. The total length of roads and walks is very considerable. The plans also provide for an open-air bath, 90 ft. by 30 ft., properly screened ; the erection of a lodge for the gardener, greenhouse and frames, and the fencing of the site. The total estimated cost of the work mentioned is £4,200. The Local Government Board have sanctioned loans for the purchase of the land and for laying-out, &c. The latter work was only commenced a few months ago, and so far as it has progressed has cost £1,675, and there is every reason to expect that the amount provided will not be exceeded.

Councillor Knight, in declaring the park open for the public for ever, said that one parish in which his work laid, with a population of 70,000 (about the same as East Ham), had not a square foot of ground belonging to the people, and, what was more, could not get it. East Ham, with its 3,500 acres, had acres and acres of open spaces, yet Lime-house, with 5,000 acres, had not a foot, and it could not be disputed that futurity would thank the East Ham Council for taking steps to secure these open spaces for healthful purposes.

Lord Teynham, deputy-chairman of the Metropolitan Public Gardens Association, proposed, on behalf of the public, a vote of thanks to the district council for acquiring the park, and this was carried.

Councillor Murty proposed a vote of thanks to the surveyor and his assistants, including the workmen. In their surveyor, he said, they had a good officer, and the acquisition of this land was a pet scheme of his. He had also shown good judgment in the laying-out of the grounds and in the smartness with which they had been got ready, yet his other work had not been neglected.

The vote having been carried,

Mr. Savage, the surveyor, thanked them sincerely on behalf of himself and his ever-ready and willing assistants, Messrs. O. Anstead and J. E. Birch. A look round would show that the gardens were a credit to the gardener, Mr. Lucas. The workmen also had evidently given a fair day's work for a fair day's money. Among his multifarious duties nothing had given him greater pleasure than the acquisition of open spaces in the neighbourhood, and they were all pleased that Lord Teynham had that day honoured them with his presence and encouraged them in their work. They all knew and recognised the great and good work done by the Metropolitan Gardens Association in and around London, thus transforming London, once so ugly, into one of the handsomest cities in the world.

A number of other votes of thanks were passed and the proceedings concluded.

**Lead-lined Iron Pipes.**—In the letter we published last week with the above heading the patentees' names should have been Brighton & Venning, not Brighton & Jennings as printed. The works are at Creworne Wharf, Lots-road, Chelsea, S.W., 55 Chancery-lane merely the registered offices of the company.

**An Award.**—Messrs. Joseph Place & Sons, Limited, the well-known sanitary pipe, glazed brick and fire brick manufacturers, have, we understand, been awarded the first prize (a silver medal) at the Royal Lancashire Agricultural Show in the competition open to all England for the best collection of feeding-troughs for cattle.

## SOME RECENT PUBLICATIONS.

### SOME PERIODICALS.

The July number of The Architectural Review (1s.) has, as usual, some special features of remarkable excellence. The coloured chromotype supplement plate illustrating the open-air pulpit at Vitré, Brittany, is a highly artistic production. There is also a sixteen-page supplement constituting the third series illustrative of architecture and design at the Royal Academy. Mention should also be made of the admirable supplement portrait of the late Sir E. Burne-Jones. Among other articles, not only dealt with by able writers but well and profusely illustrated, we may mention "Fountains and Water Treatment," "The Church of St. Mary-the-Virgin, Oxford," "Abyssinian Churches" and "The Life and Work of Welby Pugin."—The July issue of Cassier's Magazine, like that of the previous month, cannot be commended to the notice of our readers as being strong in subjects of municipal engineering interest, the entire issue being given up to articles on battleships and the other forms of tremendous war engines which constitute the modern navy. At present every one is more or less interested in the subject, especially as recent operations in Cuba and the Phillipines will probably compel experts to modify considerably a good many of the opinions hitherto held.—In Brick (Chicago) for July we observe an illustrated article on sewer-pipe joints in England, in the course of which descriptions are given of all the well-known patents of this class, such as the Stanford joint, Doulton's joint, Hassall's double-lined joint, Green's "tru-invert" pipe joint, Button's "secure" joint, Sykes' patent joint, Place's "lock" joint, Ames & Crosta's joint and others. Another article gives an interesting account of the extensive sewer-pipe works and-potteries of Red Wing, Minnesota, and there is, of course, the usual variety of current information in regard to the great brick industry of the United States.—In Baily's (1s.) for July a good deal of attention is given to cricket, as is only natural at this time of year. The customary portrait and biography is that of the Hon. Alfred Lyttleton, M.P., who in his time was one of the very finest exponents of the game. Other articles deal with jockeyship, fishing, the turf in various aspects, and other branches of field sports.—In Knowledge for July (6d.) articles on "The Karkinokosm, or World of Crustacea," "A Classic Legacy of Agriculture," "The Petroleum Industry" and "Botanical Studies" are continued, and there is the usual well-illustrated treatment of other scientific subjects.—The July number of the American Monthly Review of Reviews (New York) is naturally very much monopolised by the war, and municipal questions are, for once, conspicuous by their entire absence. There are appreciative notices of Mr. Gladstone, and some cordial reference to the better feeling and understanding which have been growing up of late between England and the United States. —Our American contemporary, The Sanitarian (New York), is more medical than engineering, but is full of interesting reading to those who follow the sanitary developments of the day.—From Messrs. Cassell & Co., Limited, we have received Chums (6d.) and Work (6d.). Among other subjects dealt with in the latter we observe electro-magnets, foundry core-boxes, perspective drawing, photographic lenses and weighing machines.—The Quarry (6d.) has an able editorial on the new state of affairs with regard to compensation to workmen, and there is an interesting illustrated description of the celebrated Clee Hill quarries in Shropshire.—The Builders' Merchant has much useful matter within the province with which it deals.—We have also received The Indian Engineer, Building Industries (Glasgow, 6d.), The Sanitary Inspectors' Journal (6d.), The Journal of the Society of the Estate Clerks of Works, The Analyst (1s.) and The Surveyor (Sydney).

## SOUTHPORT GASWORKS.

### A YEAR'S RESULTS.

Mr. John Booth, manager of the Southport Corporation gasworks, stated, in his report for the year ended March 31st, submitted at a meeting of the town council last week, that the total quantity of gas made during the year was 368,694,000 cubic feet, or a decrease of 0·2 per cent. as compared with the previous year. This is only the second time during the period of forty-eight years over which the history of the works extends that there has been a falling off in the make of gas, and it is attributed to the substitution of the electric light for gas for private lighting and to the mildness of the winter months. The revenue from gas sold for purposes other than lighting had increased by £2,677, but this gas had been sold at practically cost price, and in view of the decreased consumption of profitable gas it had not been possible to maintain the profits of previous years. Compared with 1896-7, the nett profit for the year showed a decrease of £2,322 15s. 2d. Among the causes of the falling off there were mentioned the abolition of meter rents (equal to about £1,300 per annum), the large expenditure out of revenue for the relaying and enlargement of mains, and the falling off in revenue from residuals. Having regard to these circumstances, Mr. Booth expressed the opinion that the results of the year's working must be considered satisfactory.

## THE TELEPHONE SERVICE.

Another meeting of the Select Committee of the House of Commons appointed to inquire into the working of the telephone service was held on Friday, under the presidency of Mr. Hanbury.

Mr. JAMES STAATS FORBES, chairman of the National Telephone Company, was called. He stated that before he signed the 1892 agreement he had a verbal promise given him by Mr. Goschen and Sir James Ferguson, and later on by Mr. Arnold Morley, that the right accorded to the Post Office by the agreement to grant competing licenses would only be used in the event of the company so conducting itself as to make competition a necessity. There was, however, no record of this important verbal agreement. As to the company, they were free to compete with the Post Office when and where they like. Thus if a new telephone area were created, and the postal authorities decided to establish an exchange of their own, the company would not be debarred from competing in that area. When the 1892 agreement was signed it was also verbally understood that the company should buy up all the existing licenses, and so leave the Post Office with only one telephone authority to deal with when the licenses expired in 1911. With regard to the suggestion that the company were in the habit of according preferential treatment to certain of their subscribers, Mr. Forbes said that they possessed a free hand to compete as they wished in the matter. They were a commercial company, and this was one of the weapons with which they might have to fight. They had never exercised this power, still they proposed to reserve all their rights, as cases might arise when the exercise of them would be necessary. The company would, however, be prepared to enter into an undertaking to supply every reputable applicant able to give proper security with a telephone, providing that a similar obligation was imposed on any competitor they might be called upon to face. The company were in the habit of compelling all their subscribers to enter into an agreement to allow the company to erect wires over their houses. This was a necessity, especially in face of the fact that some corporations refused way-leaves over or under public roads. If sufficient compensation were given them, however, they might be induced to give up this plan. He also reminded the committee that local authorities possessed certain powers with regard to the breaking up of streets, which the company did not, and could not obtain. He thought that if competition were allowed, these rights should be accorded to the National Company.

The committee met again on Tuesday.

Mr. FORBES confirmed a previous statement that the company would not have entered into the temporary agreement of 1892 unless they had received an assurance that the Postmaster-General would consider any reasonable proposition the company made in regard to the extension of areas. The question of competition in areas was another vital point. He would not say that he objected to the granting of licenses to municipalities on the ground that it would be a breach of faith on the part of the Government; it would not be consistent with equity. Replying to other questions, Mr. Forbes said he was strongly opposed to competition in the interests of the public. He believed the Post Office were the only body who could give an effective service to the country, and personally he should be opposed to giving powers to municipalities to set up such a service. In 1904 the Government would probably be forced to come to terms of some kind with the National Company, or to take over the whole concern or to compete, although he should be sorry to see that course adopted, because to have two separate systems in the same area would be a great waste of energy and cause great inconvenience to the telephone subscribers, half of whom would be in one service and half in another.

## THE SANITARY INSTITUTE.

EXAMINATIONS AT CARDIFF.

At an examination in practical sanitary science, held in Cardiff, on the 8th and 9th inst., the following two candidates presented themselves and were granted certificates: Mr. J. E. Jarvis, 14 Lipson-vale, Plymouth, and Mr. W. J. Tamlyn, The Parade, Minehead, Somerset. The following were the questions set for answer in writing:—

(1) Define motion, velocity, force, matter and pressure. (2) What is the action of waters of varying composition on lead pipes? What is the best method of dealing with the distribution of water known to take up lead? What quantity of lead in water is considered objectionable? And how would you ascertain its presence? (3) Define the expression "degrees of hardness," as applied to potable waters. How would you estimate the hardness of water? (4) What considerations would govern your selection of a site for an impounding reservoir in a mountainous district? How would you proceed to ascertain the quantity of water available for supply? (5) What are the constituents of Portland cement, and from what does it derive its hydraulicity? What is the setting of the cement due to? How would you proceed to test a sample of cement? (6) Under what conditions is carbon-monoxide gas sometimes found in the air of inhabited places? What is known about the physiological effects of this gas on human beings? (7) What process would you recommend for dealing with the sewage from an ordinary town previous to its discharge into a brook, the flow of which is twenty times that of the dry-weather flow of the sewage? (8) Give the substance of the London County Council by-laws in reference to the construction of new water-closets. How far do the same by-laws apply to the alteration of existing water closets?

At an examination for sanitary inspectors, held on the same days, forty candidates presented themselves, and thirty were certified, as regards their sanitary knowledge, competent to discharge the duties of inspectors of nuisances. The following were the questions set for answer in writing:—

(1) Define a "canal boat." State when such boats may be used as dwellings, and give the usual regulations applicable to them. (2) What powers have sanitary authorities for regulating dairies and cowsheds? State briefly the provisions of the regulations usually enforced. (3) What head of water is sufficient for testing stoneware socket-jointed pipes, and what time should elapse between making the joint (Portland cement) and applying the test? (4) Give detailed directions for disinfecting the surfaces of a room, with an area of 2,500 cubic feet, by means of (a) a liquid disinfectant, and (b) a gaseous disinfectant. (5) Describe the method you would use, and the instruments you would employ, if asked to make a complete and detailed report upon an ordinary house as to (a) the ventilation, (b) the drainage, (c) the sanitary appliances, and (d) the general sanitary condition. (6) What are the nuisances that are likely to arise from the carrying on of the business of a fat melter? How may they be obviated? (7) State the relative advantages and disadvantages of a combined and separate system of dealing with the sewage and rainfall of an urban district. (8) What statutory provisions relating to an adequate pure supply of water to premises are in force (a) under the Public Health Act, 1875, and (b) under the Public Health (London) Act, 1891?

## SEWAGE DISPOSAL IN DARWEN.

Recently, at a meeting of the General Purposes Committee of the Darwen Corporation, a letter was read from the Local Government Board with reference to the report made by their inspector, General Crozier, after the inquiry held by him with regard to the application of the town council for sanction to borrow £6,670 for a refuse destructor and £2,500 for works of sewage and sewerage disposal, and complaining of departures from the original scheme at the sewage works without their consent. The letter also states that the board will not be prepared to further consider the application now before them until they have been furnished with an undertaking, in the form of a resolution, that, in addition to the system of chemical treatment and artificial filtration of the sewage adopted, the land at the sewage works will be used as originally intended. Further, the board will not be prepared to agree to the omission of sludge-presses unless they are satisfied that other suitable means for the disposal of the sludge will be adopted. The committee resolved that application be made to the board that they approve of coke filters, and it was respectfully submitted that in fire out of twelve filters where coke had been used it had proved as effective as polarite. With regard to sludge presses, the council had under consideration the question of deciding on suitable means for disposing of the sewage, and for that purpose are making experiments, and in due course a scheme will be submitted to the board. The town council further undertake that the whole of the 17 acres of land available shall be prepared, and at all times utilised for the treatment of the sewage effluent by downward filtration, and for this purpose the borough engineer be directed to prepare plans of estimate, with a view to applying to the board for their sanction to borrow the amount required.

## APPOINTMENTS VACANT.

BOROUGH ENGINEER. — July 22nd. — Corporation of Pietermaritzburg, Natal, South Africa. £800.—Messrs. Ford Brothers, 14 Southampton-street, Fitzroy-square, London, W.

ASSISTANT BUILDINGS INSPECTOR.—July 23rd.—Corporation of Bournemouth. £104.—Mr. F. W. Lacey, M.I.C.E., borough engineer and surveyor.

YARD FOREMAN AND STOREKEEPER.—July 23rd.—Vestry of St. Matthew, Bethnal Green. £2.—Mr. F. W. Barratt, surveyor to the vestry.

BOROUGH ENGINEER AND SURVEYOR'S ASSISTANT.—July 23rd.—Corporation of Warrington. £100.—Mr. Thomas Loughlin, borough engineer and surveyor.

SURVEYOR, INSPECTOR OF NUISANCES AND NEW BUILDINGS. —July 25th.—Birkenshaw Urban District Council. 30s.—Mr. W. Haigh, J.P., chairman of the council.

ASSISTANT PLUMBING INSPECTOR.—July 25th.—Corporation of Birmingham.—Mr. E. Antony Lees, secretary to the Water Committee, 44 Broad-street, Birmingham.

Assistant Surveyor and Inspector of Nuisances.—July 26th.—Uxbridge Rural District Council. £75.—Mr. Charles Woodbridge, clerk to the council.

Sewage Works Manager.—July 27th.—Yeadon Urban District Council.—Mr. Clifton Lund, surveyor to the council.

Junior Assistant Surveyor.—July 27th.—County Borough of Middlesbrough. £80.—Mr. Frank Baker, borough engineer.

Building Inspector.—July 27th.—County Borough of Middlesbrough.—Mr. Frank Baker, borough engineer.

County Surveyor.—August 1st.—Herefordshire County Council. £400.—The County Clerk, Shirehall, Hereford.

Borough Engineer and Surveyor's Assistant.—August 1st.—Corporation of Warrington. £100.—Mr. Thos. Longdin, borough engineer and surveyor.

Surveyor and Inspector of Nuisances.—August 1st.—Shildon and East Thickley Urban District Council. £120.—Mr. J. T. Proud, clerk to the council.

Superintendent of House Refuse Removal.—August 1st.—Handsworth Urban District Council. £2 5s.—Mr. E. Kenworthy, A.M.I.C.E., surveyor to the council.

Assistant Inspector of Nuisances, Water Inspector and Surveyor.—August 5th.—Conway Rural District Council. £100.—Mr. T. E. Parry, clerk to the council.

City Engineer.—August 31st.—Corporation of Wellington, New Zealand. £800.—Agent-General for New Zealand, London.

## MUNICIPAL CONTRACTS OPEN.

*Advertisements which are received too late for classification cannot be included in these summaries until the following week.*

Brighton.—July 22nd.—Supply of 5,000 ft. of 6-in. granite edge kerb, 250 tons of granite pitchers, and 5,000 tons of granite spalls.—Mr. Francis J. C. May, M.I.C.E., borough engineer and surveyor.

South Shields.—July 23rd.—Paving of 185 lineal yards of double line of steel-girder tramway.—Mr. S. S. Burgess, A.M.I.C.E., borough engineer.

Midhurst.—July 23rd.—Supply of disinfectants, for the rural district council.—Mr. Edward Albery, clerk to the council.

Colne.—July 23rd.—Erection of technical schools and a public library in Albert-road.—Mr. Alfred Varley, town clerk.

Lewes.—July 23rd.—Supply of 500 tons of 2-in. broken blue Guernsey, Cherbourg or Belgian granite, 100 tons of coarse granite screenings, 650 tons of broken surface-picked flints and 150 tons of Piddinghoe, gravel.—Mr. Montague S. Blaker, town clerk.

Islington.—July 25th.—Supply of eleven water-vans, four water-carts, forty-five sets of trunks and distributors for water-vans, thirty-five dust-vans and five sweeping machines.—Mr. J. Patten Barber, vestry surveyor.

Cheltenham.—July 25th.—Supply of stoneware pipes and cement for twelve months.—Mr. E. T. Brydges, town clerk.

Nuneaton.—July 25th.—Construction of filter-bed tanks and the laying and fixing of mains and other ironwork at the pumping station, Stockingford, for the urban district council.—Mr. J. S. Pickering, A.M.I.C.E., waterworks engineer.

Morley.—July 25th.—Levelling, paving, kerbing and flagging of Auty-square, Wordsworth-square and Charles-street.—Mr. W. E. Putman, A.M.I.C.E., borough engineer and surveyor.

Southend-on-Sea.—July 25th.—Making-up of Manor-road, Seaford-road, Clifton Drive, Station-road and Elmer-avenue.—Mr. Alfred Fidler, A.M.I.C.E., borough surveyor.

Clerkenwell.—July 25th.—Paving of a portion of the footway of Colney Hatch-lane with tar paving, for the vestry.—Mr. R. E. Paget, clerk to the vestry.

Cheshunt.—July 25th.—Supply of six complete suits of firemen's uniform, for the urban district council.—Mr. S. Towlson, A.M.I.C.E., surveyor to the council.

Edmonton.—July 26th.—Laying of about 1,850 ft. run of granite kerb in Park-road and Park-avenue, and 980 ft. run in Bury-street; about 365 yards super. of channelling and crossings in Park-road and Park-avenue; about 692 yards super. of asphalte in Park-road; about 704 yards super. of 2-in. indurated concrete slab paving in Park-avenue; and about 1,504 yards super. of 2-in. patent Victoria stone paving in Bury-street, for the urban district council.—Mr. G. Eades Eachus, M.I.C.E., surveyor to the council.

Cheshunt.—July 26th.—Construction of about 1,200 ft. of 4 ft. diameter brick culvert, the laying of 2,500 ft. of granite kerb in Windmill-lane, and kerbing works in Park-lane and Eleanor-road, for the urban district council.—Mr. S. Towlson, A.M.I.C.E., surveyor to the council.

Willesden.—July 26th.—Road-making and paving works in Pine-road, Cricklewood; Burrows-road, Kensal Rise; Harlesden-gardens, Harlesden; and West Ella-road, Harlesden, for the urban district council.—Mr. O. Claude Robson, M.I.C.E., engineer to the council.

Haywards Heath.—July 26th.—Supply of about 825 tons of granite, 6 tons of granite chippings and 50 tons of coarse gravel, for the urban district council.—Mr. Edward Waugh, clerk to the council.

Rhyl.—July 26th.—Sea defence works on the east foreshore, for the urban district council.—Mr. Arthur Rowlands, clerk to the council.

Hull.—July 26th.—Supply of cast-iron spigot and socket pipes and irregulars required during the year ending August 31, 1899.—Mr. F. J. Bancroft, gas and water engineer, Town Hall, Hull.

West Ham.—July 26th.—Construction of about 1,200 lineal yards of sewers, 7 ft., 6 ft. and 3 ft. 6 in. diameter.—Mr. Lewis Angell, borough surveyor.

West Ham.—July 26th.—Making-up of Freemantle-road, Haslemere-road, New-street (Plaistow) and Old-street (Plaistow).—Mr. Lewis Angell, borough surveyor.

Bucklow.—July 26th.—Construction of main sewers and outfall works for the township of Hale, for the rural district council.—Mr. Geo. Leigh, clerk to the council.

West Ham.—July 26th.—Erection of twenty-nine working-classes' dwellings in Hermit-road, Plaistow.—Mr. Lewis Angell, borough surveyor.

West Ham.—July 26th.—Supply of ten slop-carts.—Mr. Lewis Angell, borough surveyor.

Ilford.—July 26th.—Construction of a section of sewer to be laid in Ilford-lane and Natal-road, for the urban district council.—Mr. Herbert Shaw, A.M.I.C.E., surveyor to the council.

Barking Town.—July 26th.—(1) The supply and fixing of about 100 flushing cisterns to water-closets on various properties in the district, and (2) the erection of about 150 yards of pole and space fencing in Tanner-street, for the urban district council.—Mr. E. H. Lister, clerk to the council.

Ilford.—July 28th.—Erection of an underground latrine in The Broadway, for the urban district council.—Mr. Herbert Shaw, A.M.I.C.E., surveyor to the council.

Southall-Norwood.—July 26th.—Various works at the sewage farm, Wyke Green, Isleworth, for the urban district council.—Mr. Howard R. Felkin, engineer and surveyor to the council.

Wallasey.—July 27th.—Supply of a 10-ton compound steam roller, for the urban district council.—Mr. W. H. Travers, engineer and surveyor to the council.

St. George-the-Martyr.—July 27th.—Construction of a ladies' lavatory at the rear of the public library buildings in the Borough-road.—Mr. Oliver E. Winter, vestry surveyor.

Salford.—July 27th.—Supply of the concrete work and ironwork in connection with an elevated circular tank at the sewage works.—Mr. Samuel Brown, town clerk.

Aberdare.—July 27th.—Supply and delivery of various cast-iron and steel work, including a light lattice girder footbridge of three spans (each 57 ft. 6 in.), for the urban district council.—Mr. William Fox, M.I.C.E., engineer to the council, 5 Victoria-street, London, S.W.

Hackney.—July 27th.—Supply of materials required for wood paving work proposed to be executed in Dalston-lane from Graham-road to Pembury-road, for the vestry.—Mr. E. J. Lovegrove, chief surveyor to the vestry.

West Hartlepool.—July 27th.—Erection of an electric light station in Burn-road.—Mr. J. W. Brown, borough engineer.

Ashton-in-Makerfield.—July 27th.—(1) Supply of 250 tons of 12-in. socketted iron water pipes and a small quantity of 4-in. by 6-in. pipes; (2) supply of sluice and air valves, valve covers and specials; (3) laying of 2,274 lineal yards of 12-in. water main; (4) enlargement of filter-beds; and (5) supply of 1,200 lineal yards of 18-in. stoneware socketted pipes, for the urban district council.—Mr. John W. Liversedge, surveyor to the council.

St. George-in-the-East.—July 27th.—Supply of 300 tons of 3-in. by 7-in. Aberdeen granite pitchings, and 30 tons of 5-in. by 7-in. Guernsey granite pitchings, for the vestry.—Mr. H. Thompson, clerk to the vestry.

Bury.—July 28th.—Erection of a manager's house at the sewage disposal works, Livesey Fields.—Mr. J. Cartwright, borough engineer.

Bury.—July 28th.—Erection of a model lodging-house in George-street and Foundry-street, off Rochdale-road.—Mr. J. Cartwright, borough engineer.

Hambledon.—July 28th.—Construction of two coarse filter-beds for dealing with the storm-water flow and other works at the sewage outfall, Cranleigh, for the rural district council.—Mr. E. L. Luun, surveyor to the council, 36 High-street, Guildford.

London.—July 28th.—Erection of head office buildings on a site at the corner of Carmelite-street and the Victoria-embankment, for the Metropolitan Asylums Board.—Mr. T. Duncombe Mann, clerk to the board, Norfolk House, Norfolk-street, Strand, W.C.

Worcestershire.—July 28th.—Rebuilding of Eastham bridge, situated over the river Teme, in the parishes of Eastham and Lindridge, for the county council.—Mr. J. H. Garrett, county surveyor, Shirehall, Worcester.

Clerkenwell.—July 28th.—Re-dressing and re-laying of the carriage-way paving of Margaret-street, part of Warner-street and part of Clerkenwell Green, for the vestry.—Mr. R. E. Paget, clerk to the vestry.

Glasgow.—July 28th.—Various works in connection with the erection of stable offices, &c., in the Queen's Park.—Mr. J. D. Marwick, town clerk.

Cardiff.—July 28th.—Alterations at the chief inspector's house and additions to the covered shed at the waterworks depot, Trade-street, Penarth-road, for the corporation.—Mr. C. H. Priestly, waterworks engineer, Town Hall, Cardiff.

Leeds.—July 28th.—Extension of Kirkgate market roof and the building of new fish shops and a boundary wall.—The City Engineer.

Tunbridge Wells.—July 28th.—Supply of 500 tons of clean Cherbourg quartzite.—Mr. W. C. Cripps, town clerk.

Wimbledon.—July 29th.—Making-up of Ridgway-gardens and Edge-hill (section 2), for the urban district council.—Mr. W. H. Whitfield, clerk to the council.

Burton-upon-Trent.—July 29th.—Construction and erection of a new retort-house at the gasworks, for the corporation.—Mr. F. L. Ramsden, engineer, Gas and Electric Light Works, Burton-upon-Trent.

Hunstanton.—July 30th.—Construction of a telescopic gasholder, for the urban district council.—Mr. J. S. B. Glasier, clerk to the council.

Kettering.—July 30th.—Erection of a green-house, 30 ft. long by 12 ft. wide, in the cemetery, for the urban district council.—Mr. Thos. R. Smith, surveyor to the council.

Great Harwood.—July 30th.—Erection of a block of offices in Police-street, for the urban district council.—Mr. R. Chippendale, clerk to the council.

St. Thomas-the-Apostle (near Exeter).—July 30th.—Supply and fixing of the gas engines and centrifugal pumps required in connection with the new sewage outfall works, for the urban district council.—Mr. S. Churchward, surveyor to the council.

Leyland.—July 30th.—Construction of precipitation tanks, filters, reservoir, engine and boiler house, conduits, subsoil drainage, &c., for the urban district council.—Mr. William Wrennall, 9 Harrington-street, Liverpool.

Chepstow.—August 1st.—Laying of 1,000 superficial yards of granite and cement concrete for footways in Bridge-street and Station-road, for the urban district council.—Mr. F. Feather, surveyor to the council.

Ryde.—August 2nd.—Supply and delivery, and also laying, of about 1,650 yards of 4-in. and 120 yards of 3-in. cast-iron pipes.—Mr. C. Mathew, borough engineer.

Wandsworth.—August 2nd.—Providing and laying of about 14,000 superficial yards of wood block paving (creosoted deal) in Richmond-road, Putney, for the district board of works.—Mr. Henry George Hills, clerk to the board.

Wembley.—August 2nd.—Construction of the following streets, for the urban district council: Union-road, Copland-road, Montrose-crescent, Station-grove, Chaplin-road, Talbot-road, Napier-road, Stanley-avenue, Peel-road and Priory Park-road.—Mr. C. L. Whitehead, junr., engineer to the council.

Penzance.—August 2nd.—Laying of between 500 and 600 super. yards of Jarrahdale jarrah wood paving in St. Clare-street.—Mr. George H. Small, borough surveyor.

Shoreditch.—August 3rd.—Construction of an underground convenience in Hoxton-street.—Mr. J. Rush Dixon, A.M.I.C.E., engineer and surveyor to the vestry.

Aldershot.—August 3rd.—Works of metalling, kerbing, channelling, paving, &c., in St. Michael's-road, St. George's-road and St. Joseph's-road, for the urban district council.—Mr. W. E. Foster, clerk to the council.

Hampton Wick.—August 3rd.—Laying of about 1,000 yards of limestone tar paving, for the urban district council.—Mr. J. Nixon Horsfield, surveyor to the council.

ILKESTON.—August 4th.—Supply of a new pumping engine, for the Little Hallam pumping station.—Mr. H. J. Kilford, borough surveyor and water engineer.

SKIPTON.—August 4th.—Providing and laying of about 2,000 lineal yards of 3-in. cast-iron pipes and for the construction of a covered service reservoir and conduit, for the rural district council.—Mr. A. Rodwell, engineer and surveyor to the council.

ASHTON-IN-MAKERFIELD.—August 4th.—Supply and delivery of 250 tons of 2-in. best hand-broken granite macadam and 50 tons of ½-in. clean sharp granite chippings, for the urban district council.—Mr. John W. Liversedge, surveyor to the council.

BRADFORD.—August 4th.—Supply of cast-iron cylinders, valves, upstand pipes, deck and floor plates, girders, headstocks and other appliances required for the outlet towers of Gouthwaite reservoir.—Mr. James Watson, M.I.C.E., waterworks engineer, Town Hall, Bradford.

SLOUGH.—August 6th.—Making-up works in the streets known as Chalvey Vale, for the urban district council.—Mr. G. H. Charsley, clerk to the council.

CHAPEL-EN-LE-FRITH.—August 10th.—Construction of a concrete service reservoir, and the providing and laying of about 1½ miles of cast-iron mains for the water supply of the township of Bamford, for the rural district council.—Mr. J. Burton Boycott, clerk to the council.

WREXHAM.—August 10th.—Erection of a bridge over the river Gwenfro, at a place called Stryt y bidden, in the township of Broughton, for the urban district council.—Mr. John Strachan, surveyor to the council, Crispin Lodge, Wrexham.

## TENDERS.

*ACCEPTED.

ASTON MANOR.—For alterations and additions to the administrative building at the infectious diseases hospital, Upper Witton, for the urban district council.—Mr. H. Richardson, A.M.I.C.E., engineer and surveyor to the council:—

| | | | | | |
|---|---|---|---|---|---|
| R. M. Hughes, Birmingham | ... | ... | ... | ... | £2,110 |
| J. E. Moorhouse, Handsworth | ... | ... | ... | 2,062 |
| W. & A. Heaps, Birmingham | ... | ... | ... | 1,968 |
| Reeves & Son, Birmingham | ... | ... | ... | 1,910 |
| W. Hopkins, Birmingham* | ... | ... | ... | 1,833 |

CAERPHILLY.—For the construction of about 8,500 lineal yards of 15-in., 18-in. and 21-in. stoneware and iron pipe sewers from Tenghenydd to Gwaun-y-bara sewage farm, for the urban district council.—Mr. A. O. Harpur, surveyor to the council:—

| | | | | | |
|---|---|---|---|---|---|
| A. Harper & H. Agland, Senghenydd, Glamorgan | | | £16,520 |
| Monk & Newell, Liverpool | ... | ... | ... | 15,833 |
| G. Rutter, Barry | ... | ... | ... | ... | 15,538 |
| W. Jones, Neath | ... | ... | ... | ... | 15,340 |
| R. & J. Mathias, Pontypridd | ... | ... | ... | 13,901 |
| T. Taylor, Pontypridd | ... | ... | ... | 13,991 |
| W. E. Willis | ... | ... | ... | ... | 13,804 |
| E. Powell, Pontypridd | ... | ... | ... | 13,707 |
| J. Howell, Caerphilly | ... | ... | ... | 13,472 |
| A. S. Morgan & Co., Newport | ... | ... | ... | 12,333 |
| Barnes, Chaplin & Co., Cardiff | ... | ... | 12,245 |
| Parfitt & Monk, Newport | ... | ... | ... | 11,903 |
| T. Rossiter, Caerphilly | ... | ... | ... | 11,758 |
| E. Page, Cardiff | ... | ... | ... | ... | 11,650 |
| | Engineer's estimate, £12,437. | | | | |

BOOTLE.—For the erection of an electric light station on land in Pine-grove.—Mr. J. A. Crowther, borough engineer:—

| | | | | | |
|---|---|---|---|---|---|
| J. Corkill, Liverpool | ... | ... | ... | ... | £7,361 |
| Hughes & Stirling, Bootle | ... | ... | ... | 7,150 |
| J. Paterson & Son, Liverpool | ... | ... | ... | 7,067 |
| P. Tyson, Liverpool | ... | ... | ... | 7,000 |
| S. Webster, Bootle | ... | ... | ... | ... | 6,559 |
| W. Musker, Bootle* | ... | ... | ... | ... | 6,398 |

CAVERSHAM.—Accepted for the making-up of Champion-road, for the urban district council.—Mr. W. R. Locke, surveyor to the council:—

Piggott's-road.

| | | | | |
|---|---|---|---|---|
| F. Talbot, Reading | ... | ... | ... | £229 |

Champion-road.

| | | | | |
|---|---|---|---|---|
| F. Talbot, Reading | ... | ... | ... | 190 |

CHURCH.—For paving, kerbing, &c., works in Blackburn-road, for the urban district council.—The Surveyor to the Council:—

| | | | | | |
|---|---|---|---|---|---|
| Chadwick Brothers, Blackburn | ... | ... | ... | £1,220 |
| J. Moore, Accrington | ... | ... | ... | 1,581 |
| W. H. Bury, Oswaldtwistle | ... | ... | ... | 1,903 |
| G. Adams, Oswaldtwistle* | ... | ... | ... | 828 |
| Exors. of A. Broadley, Great Harwood | ... | ... | 594 |
| T. Horrocks, Liverpool | ... | ... | ... | 572 |
| A. Lord, Accrington (flagging only) | ... | ... | 81 |

LEAMINGTON.—For the supply of road stone for a period of twelve months.—Mr. W. de Normanville, borough engineer:—

| | Spalls. Per ton. s. d. | Hand-broken, 2-in. gauge. Per ton. s. d. |
|---|---|---|
| Clee Hill Dhu Stone Company* | — | 11 1 |
| Clee Hill Granite Company* | — | 11 1 |
| Narborough and Enderby Granite Quarries Company* | — | 8 8 |
| W. A. Jadkins* | 5 6 | — |
| Mountsorrel Granite Company, Limited | 7 0 | — |
| W. Bussano & Co. | 7 7 | 9 7 |
| H. J. Ross | — | 8 6 |
| Enderby and Stoney Stanton Granite Company, Limited | 6 4 | 9 0 |
| C. Abell | 6 0 | 7 0 |

MAIDENHEAD.—For the making-up of Ray Park-avenue.—Mr. Percy Johns, A.M.I.C.E., borough surveyor:—

| | | | | | |
|---|---|---|---|---|---|
| F. Talbot, Caversham-road, Reading | ... | ... | £192 |
| T. Free & Son, Maidenhead* | ... | ... | ... | 441 |

STOWMARKET.—For the laying of about 517 lineal yards of 9-in. and 12-in. stoneware pipe sewers and about 47 yards of 6-in., 17 yards of 9-in., 1,016 yards of 12-in. and 307 yards of 24-in. cast-iron pipe sewers, for the urban district council.—Messrs. Pollard & Tingle, 31 Old Queen-street, Westminster, London, S.W.:—

| | | | | | |
|---|---|---|---|---|---|
| Thomas & Edge, Woolwich, S.E. | ... | ... | £7,591 |
| B. Plummer, Rattlesden, Suffolk | ... | ... | 6,802 |
| M. S. Kitteringham, Cheshunt, Herts. | ... | ... | 6,101 |
| H. Roberts, West Bromwich, staffs.* | ... | ... | 5,504 |
| A. Coe, Ipswich, Suffolk | ... | ... | ... | 4,708 |
| J. Moran & Son, Harwich, Essex | ... | ... | 4,177 |

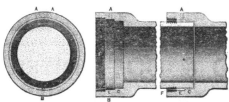

REIGATE.—For the execution of certain paving works.—Mr. Clair J. Grece, town clerk :—

**Tar Paving.**

| | Per yard super. |
|---|---|
| | s. d. |
| W. G. Cloke, Rye-lane, Peckham | 3 6 |
| W. H. Bensted & Son, Maidstone* | 3 3 |
| G. S. Faulkner, Reigate | 2 0 |
| W. R. Constable & Co., Kentish Town, N.W. | 2 0 |
| J. Smart, Victoria-street, Westminster | 2 0 |
| A. C. W. Hobman & Co., Cliftonville, South Bermondsey | 2 0 |
| Pitt & Son, Reigate | 2 0 |
| T. Andrew, Redhill | 1 11 |
| D. March, Bromley | 1 10 |

**Artificial Stone Paving.**

| | |
|---|---|
| Jones Annealed Concrete Company, Middlesbrough, Yorks. | 5 6 |
| Imperial Stone Company, Greenwich* | 5 4 |
| D. Pitt & Son, Reigate | 5 0 |
| Josiah Smart, Victoria-street, Westminster | 4 9 |
| Adamant Stone and Paving Company, Old Broad-street, E.C. | 4 6 |

## NOTICES.

THE SURVEYOR AND MUNICIPAL AND COUNTY ENGINEER may be ordered direct, through any of Messrs. Smith & Son's book-stalls, or of any newsagent in the United Kingdom. Applications to the Offices for single copies by post must in all cases be accompanied by stamps.

The Prepaid Subscription (including postage) is as follows :

| | Twelve Months. | Six Months. | Three Months. |
|---|---|---|---|
| United Kingdom | 15s. | 7s. 6d. | 3s. 9d. |
| Continent, the Colonies, India, United States, &c. | 19s. | 9s. 6d. | 4s. 9d. |

The International News Company, 83 and 85 Duane-street, New York City; The Toronto News Company, Toronto; and The Montreal News Company, Montreal, have been appointed agents in the United States and Canada for the sale of THE SURVEYOR. A thin paper edition is printed for circulation abroad.

EDITORIAL OFFICES :
ST. BRIDE'S HOUSE, 24 BRIDE-LANE, FLEET-STREET, LONDON, E.C.

OFFICE FOR ADVERTISEMENTS :
13 NEW STREET HILL, FLEET STREET, LONDON, E.C.

PUBLISHING OFFICES :
13 NEW STREET HILL, FLEET STREET, LONDON, E.C.

## APPOINTMENTS OPEN.

### SUNDERLAND BOROUGH ASYLUM DRAINAGE WORK.

The Committee require the services of a competent Clerk of Works, to supervise the above drainage work.

It is essential that the candidate should be intimately acquainted and have had a considerable experience in seeing large systems of domestic drainage work carried out.

Applications, stating age, qualifications, works carried out and salary required, together with copies of three recent testimonials, to be sent to me not later than Saturday, July 30th next.

JOHN LITTLE,
Sanitary Engineer.
Viaduct Chambers, Carlisle.
July 16, 1898.

### HEREFORDSHIRE COUNTY COUNCIL.
COUNTY SURVEYOR.

The Roads and Bridges Committee of the above Council are prepared to receive applications for the office of County Surveyor, which must be lodged with the Clerk of the Council by the 1st August. The person appointed (who must not be more than forty years of age) will be required to devote his whole time to the duties, and to supervise county buildings, bridges and about 500 miles of main road, at present repaired by highway authorities under contract. Salary, £400, to include travelling expenses. An office provided.

Particulars as to duties, &c., will be forwarded on application to the Clerk to the Council, Shirehall, Hereford.

Canvassing members of the Committee or Council will be considered a disqualification.

### COUNTY BOROUGH OF MIDDLESBROUGH.

The Streets Committee are prepared to receive applications for the position of Junior Assistant in the Borough Surveyor's department.

Applicants must have had some experience in surveying, levelling, architectural drawing and the working of the Model By-Laws. Salary, £80 per annum.

Also for the position of Building Inspector.

Applicants must have had some experience in the carrying out of the Model By-Laws of the Local Government Board.

Applications for each appointment, stating age, experience,

and accompanied by copies of three recent testimonials, to be sent to the undersigned not later than the 27th day of July, 1898.

Applicants for the office of Building Inspector are to state the salary required.

Canvassing any member of the Corporation will be deemed a disqualification.

·FRANK BAKER, C.E., F.G.S.,
Borough Engineer.

Municipal Buildings, Middlesbrough.

### BOROUGH OF WARRINGTON.

Wanted, in the Borough Engineer and Surveyor's office, an assistant accustomed to surveying, levelling and the general routine of a municipal surveyor's office. Salary, £100 per annum.

Applications, stating age, experience and qualifications, and accompanied by not more than three recent testimonials, to be delivered at my office not later than Monday, the 1st day of August, endorsed "Assistant."

Canvassing members of the Council is strictly prohibited, and will disqualify any candidate.

THOS. LONGDIN,
Borough Engineer and Surveyor.

Town Hall, Warrington.
July 11, 1898.

### SHILDON AND EAST THICKLEY URBAN DISTRICT COUNCIL.
#### SURVEYOR AND INSPECTOR.

Notice is hereby given that the above Council will, on Tuesday, the 9th August, proceed to the appointment of a Surveyor and Inspector of Nuisances for their district. The appointment as inspector will be subject to the approval and regulations of the Local Government Board. Salary, £120 per annum—viz., £80 as inspector and £40 as surveyor. The person appointed must reside within the district and devote his whole time to the duties of his office (no private work being allowed).

Applications, in candidate's handwriting, stating age and present occupation, accompanied by copies of three recent testimonials, to be sent to me on or before the 1st August. Canvassing disqualifies.

J. T. PROUD,
Clerk to the Council.

Bishop Auckland.
July 20, 1898.

### CITY OF SHEFFIELD.

Wanted, in the office of the City Surveyor, a District Surveyor for the Eastern District of the City, to take charge of the street and sewer work (including many miles of paved streets), also tramway maintenance and construction.

Applicants must have had good experience of similar work.

Apply, stating qualifications, age, references and salary required, to Mr. Charles F. Wike, M.INST.C.E., City Surveyor's Office, Town Hall, Sheffield.

July 8, 1898.

### WANTED. — Draughtsman, for about three
months' work, required. Surveyor and plan buildings; bring ordnance to date.—Apply, writing only, stating experience and salary required, Francis Parr, A.M.I.C.E., Borough Engineer, Bridgwater.

### ARCHITECTURAL ASSISTANT.—Required, a
competent Architectural Assistant, with good knowledge of ironwork, construction, details, quantities and estimates, for the surveyor's office in a county borough. Salary, £120 a year.—Applications, stating age, qualifications, references, &c., accompanied by copies of not more than three recent testimonials, to be sent in at once, addressed Box 78, Office of THE SURVEYOR, 24 Bride-lane, Fleet-street, E.C.

## TENDERS WANTED.

### SLOUGH URBAN DISTRICT COUNCIL.
#### STREET WORKS.

The above Council are prepared to receive tenders for Making-up the Streets known as Chalvey Vale (under the Private Streets Works Act, 1892), consisting of about 1,200 yards of Kerbing and Channelling, 2,200 super.yards Foot.way and 4,400 super. yards of Flint Roadway, &c.

Plans, sections and amended specification may be seen, and schedule of quantities obtained, at the office of the Surveyor to the Council, No. 1 Mackenzie-street, Slough, between the hours of 10 a.m. and 4 p.m., upon payment of a deposit of 1 guinea, which will be returned on the receipt of a bona fide tender on the prescribed form.

Tenders, addressed to the "Chairman of the Council," daly sealed, to be delivered at the Office of the Council, No. 1 Mackenzie-street, Slough, not later than Saturday, the 6th day of August next, endorsed "Street Works."

REIGATE.—For the execution of certain paving works.—Mr. Clair J. Grece, town clerk:—

Tar Paving.

| | Per yard super. |
|---|---|
| | s. d. |
| W. G. Cloke, Rye-lane, Peckham ... ... ... ... | 3 6 |
| W. H. Bensted & Son, Maidstone* ... ... ... | 3 3 |
| G. S. Faulkner, Reigate ... ... ... ... | 2 0 |
| W. R. Constable & Co., Kentish Town, N.W. ... ... | 2 0 |
| J. Smart, Victoria-street, Westminster ... ... | 2 0 |
| A. C. W. Hobman & Co., Cliftonville, South Bermondsey ... | 2 0 |
| Pitt & Son, Reigate ... ... ... ... ... | 2 0 |
| T. Andrew, Redhill ... ... ... ... ... | 1 11 |
| D. March, Bromley ... ... ... ... ... | 1 10 |

Artificial Stone Paving.

| | | |
|---|---|---|
| Jones Annealed Concrete Company, Middlesbrough, Yorks. | 5 | 6 |
| Imperial Stone Company, Greenwich* | 5 | 4 |
| D. Pitt & Son, Reigate | 5 | 0 |
| Josiah Smart, Victoria-street, Westminster | 4 | 9 |
| Adamant Stone and Paving Company, Old Broad-street, E.C. | 4 | 6 |

## NOTICES.

THE SURVEYOR AND MUNICIPAL AND COUNTY ENGINEER *may be ordered direct, through any of Messrs. Smith & Son's book-stalls, or of any newsagent in the United Kingdom. Applications to the Offices for single copies by post must in all cases be accompanied by stamps.*

*The Prepaid Subscription (including postage) is as follows :*

| | Twelve Months. | Six Months. | Three Months. |
|---|---|---|---|
| United Kingdom ... ... | 15s. | 7s. 6d. | 3s. 9d. |
| Continent, the Colonies, India, | | | |
| United States, &c. ... ... | 19s. | 9s. 6d. | 4s. 9d. |

*The International News Company, 83 and 85 Duane-street, New York City; The Toronto News Company, Toronto; and The Montreal News Company, Montreal, have been appointed agents in the United States and Canada for the sale of* THE SURVEYOR. *A thin paper edition is printed for circulation abroad.*

EDITORIAL OFFICES:
ST. BRIDE'S HOUSE, 24 BRIDE-LANE, FLEET-STREET, LONDON, E.C.

OFFICE FOR ADVERTISEMENTS:
13 NEW STREET HILL, FLEET STREET, LONDON, E.C.

PUBLISHING OFFICES:
13 NEW STREET HILL, FLEET STREET, LONDON, E.C.

and accompanied by copies of three recent testimonials, to be sent to the undersigned not later than the 27th day of July, 1898.

Applicants for the office of Building Inspector are to state the salary required.

Canvassing any member of the Corporation will be deemed a disqualification.

FRANK BAKER, c.e., f.g.s.,
Borough Engineer.

Municipal Buildings, Middlesbrough.

## BOROUGH OF WARRINGTON.

Wanted, in the Borough Engineer and Surveyor's office, an assistant accustomed to surveying, levelling and the general routine of a municipal surveyor's office. Salary, £100 per annum.

Applications, stating age, experience and qualifications, and accompanied by not more than three recent testimonials, to be delivered at my office not later than Monday, the 1st day of August, endorsed "Assistant."

Canvassing members of the Council is strictly prohibited, and will disqualify any candidate.

THOS. LONGDIN,
Borough Engineer and Surveyor.

Town Hall, Warrington.
July 11, 1898.

## SHILDON AND EAST THICKLEY URBAN DISTRICT COUNCIL.

### SURVEYOR AND INSPECTOR.

Notice is hereby given that the above Council will, on Tuesday, the 9th August, proceed to the appointment of a Surveyor and Inspector of Nuisances for their district. The appointment as inspector will be subject to the approval and regulations of the Local Government Board. Salary, £120 per annum—viz., £80 as inspector and £40 as surveyor. The person appointed must reside within the district and devote his whole time to the duties of his office (no private work being allowed).

Applications, in candidate's handwriting, stating age and present occupation, accompanied by copies of three recent testimonials, to be sent to me on or before the 1st August.

Canvassing disqualifies.

J. T. PROUD,
Clerk to the Council.

Bishop Auckland.
July 20, 1898.

## CITY OF SHEFFIELD.

Wanted, in the office of the City Surveyor, a District Surveyor for the Eastern District of the City, to take charge of the street and sewer work (including many miles of paved streets), also tramway maintenance and construction.

Applicants must have had good experience of similar work.

Apply, stating qualifications, age, references and salary required, to Mr. Charles F. Wike, m.inst.c.e., City Surveyor's Office, Town Hall, Sheffield.

July 8, 1898.

WANTED. — Draughtsman, for about three months' work, required. Surveyor and plan buildings; bring ordnance to date.—Apply, writing only, stating experience and salary required, Francis Parr, a.m.i.c.e., Borough Engineer, Bridgwater.

ARCHITECTURAL ASSISTANT.—Required, a competent Architectural Assistant, with good knowledge of ironwork, construction, details, quantities and estimates, for the surveyor's office in a county borough. Salary, £120 a year.—Applications, stating age, qualifications, references, &c., accompanied by copies of not more than three recent testimonials, to be sent in at once, addressed Box 78, Office of The Surveyor, 24 Bride-lane, Fleet-street, E.C.

## TENDERS WANTED.

## SLOUGH URBAN DISTRICT COUNCIL.

### STREET WORKS.

The above Council are prepared to receive tenders for Making-up the Streets known as Chalvey Vale (under the Private Streets Works Act, 1892), consisting of about 1,200 yards of Kerbing and Channelling, 2,299 super. yards Foot-way and 4,400 super. yards of Flint Roadway, &c.

Plans, sections and amended specification may be seen, and schedule of quantities obtained, at the office of the Surveyor to the Council, No. 1 Mackenzie-street, Slough, between the hours of 10 a.m. and 4 p.m., upon payment of a deposit of 1 guinea, which will be returned on the receipt of a bonâ fide tender on the prescribed form.

Tenders, addressed to the "Chairman of the Council," duly sealed, to be delivered at the Office of the Council, No. 1 Mackenzie-street, Slough, not later than Saturday, the 6th day of August next, endorsed "Street Works."

The Council do not bind themselves to accept the lowest or any tender.

G. H. CHARSLEY,
Clerk to the Council.

11 Mackenzie-street, Slough.
July, 1898.

A LDERSHOT URBAN DISTRICT COUNCIL.
TO ROAD CONTRACTORS AND OTHERS.
The Aldershot Urban District Council are prepared to receive tenders for the Metalling, Kerbing, Channelling, Paving, &c., of the following new streets:—

St. Michael's-road,
St. George's-road,
St. Joseph's-road.

Plans and specifications may be seen, and forms of tender obtained, by applying at the office of the Surveyor to the Council, No. 126 Victoria-road, Aldershot.
Sureties will be required.
Tenders, endorsed "Tenders for New Streets," are to be delivered in a sealed envelope at my office not later than 9 a.m. on Wednesday, the 3rd day of August next.
The Council do not bind themselves to accept the lowest or any tender.

(By order)
W. E. FOSTER,
Clerk to the Council.

126 Victoria-road.
July 12, 1898.

W ANDSWORTH DISTRICT BOARD OF
WORKS.
TO WOOD PAVING CONTRACTORS AND OTHERS.
The Board of Works for the Wandsworth District are prepared to receive tenders for providing and laying, complete, in Upper Richmond-road, Putney, about 14,000 superficial yards of Wood Block Paving (creosoted deal) on 6 in. of cement concrete, including the breaking-up and carting to the parish depot (a distance of under 1 mile) of the present macadam and all superfluous earth and rubbish.
The specification and plan may be seen, and forms of tender obtained, at the Surveyor's office, No. 153 High-street, Putney, S.W., between the hours of 10 and 4 (Saturdays, 10 till 1).

Tenders are to be delivered, under seal, at the offices of the Board, East-hill, Wandsworth, endorsed "Wood Paving," on or before Tuesday, August 2nd next, and must contain the names and addresses of two responsible persons to join the contractor in a contract for the due execution thereof.
No tender will be received unless it is made upon one of the printed forms provided for the purpose.
The Board do not pledge themselves to accept the lowest or any tender.
(By order of the Board of Works for the Wandsworth District)

HENRY GEORGE HILLS,
Clerk to the Board.

East-hill, Wandsworth, S.W.
July 20, 1898.

B OROUGH OF SOUTHEND-ON-SEA.
TO ROAD CONTRACTORS AND OTHERS.
The Corporation invite tenders for Street Works in the making-up of the following streets:—

Manor-road,
Seaforth-road,
Clifton-drive,
Station-road,
Elmer-avenue.
} West Cliff.

Plans, sections and specifications may be seen, and bills of quantities and forms of tender obtained, on and after Monday, the 25th July (on payment of £1 1s. in respect of each street, which will be returned on receipt of a bonâ-fide tender), upon application to Mr. Alfred Fidler, ASSOC.M.INST.C.E., Borough Surveyor, Clarence-road, Southend.
No tender will be considered unless made on the prescribed form, and there must be a separate tender for each street.
Sealed tenders, endorsed with the name of the street, and marked "Tender for Private Street Works," to be delivered at my office before 10 o'clock in the morning of Thursday, the 4th August.
The Corporation will not be bound to accept the lowest or any tender.

(By order)
WILLIAM H. SNOW,
Town Clerk.

Southend-on-Sea.
July 20, 1898.

MR. J. LEMON, Southampton
*(Past-President).*

MR. T. H. YABBICOM,
City Engineer, Bristol.

MR. J. PRICE,
City Surveyor, Birmingham.

Incorporated
Association of
Municipal and County
Engineers.

SOME MEMBERS OF THE
COUNCIL.

MR. A. E. COLLINS,
City Engineer, Norwich.

MR. J. PATON,
Borough Engineer, Plymouth.

# The Surveyor

## And Municipal and County Engineer.

Vol. XIV., No. 341.　　　LONDON, JULY 29, 1898.　　　Weekly, Price 3d.

## Minutes of Proceedings.

**Protection of Water Supplies.** The withdrawal by Mr. Chaplin of the clauses which had been prepared by the Local Government Board with the object of securing the protection of sources of water supply, and of punishing companies who failed to exercise the powers conferred upon them by Parliament to provide a constant supply of pure and wholesome water within the areas they undertake to serve, may be accepted as an indication that the Government do not contemplate any action in the matter during the present session. The purpose which the president of the Local Government Board had in view was in every respect commendable, but, as we pointed out in these columns some weeks ago, the method by which he proposed to proceed was open to very damaging criticism. As a matter of fact, the objections raised, although not insurmountable, were so strong and so very generally expressed—not openly, of course, but through the channels which are invariably used when Ministers desire to test the opinion of Parliament upon a question before it comes up for debate—that it was considered advisable to proceed no further with the clauses. The method of procedure was unquestionably bad. The Bill selected for bringing the question before the House—the Higham and Hundred of Hoo Water Bill—was of the simplest possible character, consisting of some five clauses only, devised to amend a previous Act of the company, but not to confer additional powers of any kind. The clauses submitted by the President of the Local Government Board were, on the other hand, of a far-reaching character, affecting an infinite variety of interests. The little company had probably failed in its duty, but not to a greater extent than scores of other companies had done in various parts of the country. Why, therefore, should it be selected for punishment, while larger and more powerful offenders were allowed to go scot-free? No reason could be advanced. It looked as if the company had been selected by reason of its very weakness. The clauses were to be inserted in all water Bills that came hereafter before the House. This would undoubtedly have provided the public with safeguards for the future, but against the companies that had already got their powers there was no remedy whatever. It might be assumed that in course of time every company would come to Parliament at one period or another for additional powers, and thus be brought within the scope of the new provisions, but could any process be slower, more clumsy and ineffectual? Surely the proper, regular and equitable course would have been to introduce a public Act to amend the Waterworks Clauses Act.

Strong as these objections were, they by no means exhausted the indictment against the clauses. Serious questions of principle, public policy and Parliamentary procedure were raised. The clauses were in direct contravention of the principle acted upon every session by the House of Commons in appointing the Select Committee on Police and Sanitary Regulations. That principle is that no amendment of the general law shall be allowed by a private Bill without previous inquiry by the committee with respect to the reasons which would justify the amendment and the conditions under which it should be allowed to take place. This, of course, struck the weak spot in the proposed method of procedure. No argument could be adduced in support of inserting the clauses in the particular Bill chosen which would not apply with much greater force to every water company's undertaking in the kingdom. Another weapon which the opponents to the clauses were able to handle effectively was that they were an attempt to override the decisions of the several select committees to whom the Higham and Hundred of Hoo and other water Bills of the session were referred. These committees, we may remark, had before them the recommendations of the Local Government Board upon which the clauses were based, but declined to adopt them for the reason that they were in violation of the well-known and well-understood principle of Parliament which we have already explained. The clauses, moreover, were in themselves a serious breach of the Standing Orders of Parliament, and would have plunged the Bills affected into serious Standing Order difficulties during their future progress. The opponents did not forget to show that the clauses were illogical and capricious in application, inasmuch as while it was intended to bring them into operation in the case of one of the very smallest water companies—supplying a sparsely-populated rural district getting its supply from wells sunk upwards of 150 ft. in the chalk-beds of Kent, a supply which, although not so large as required, was reasonably pure—there were large undertakings, both in the metropolis and in the country, obtaining their water under conditions of great complexity, which involved risk of pollution, that would not be brought within the operation of the clauses until they happened to be promoting a Bill in Parliament, possibly a quarter of a century hence. The clauses were, furthermore, condemned as impracticable, ineffectual, vexatious and dangerous—impracticable and ineffectual because they did not ensure that the samples of water taken for purposes of analyses were the same as the water to be supplied to the consumer; vexatious and dangerous because they would lead to great conflict of jurisdiction between water companies and local authorities while conferring no commensurate benefit upon the consumer. The sampling of water for purposes of analysis raises the question of the much-debated Harrogate clause, which was objected to, in the case of several Bills this session, because of its sheer inefficiency. It provides for samples of water taken from the reservoirs being tested, whereas the filtration works of the company or local authority concerned are usually established, or to be established, to deal with the water after it has left the reservoir and before it reaches the con-

# The Surveyor

## And Municipal and County Engineer.

Vol. XIV., No. 341.    LONDON, JULY 29, 1898.    Weekly, Price 3d.

## Minutes of Proceedings.

**Protection of Water Supplies.**

The withdrawal by Mr. Chaplin of the clauses which had been prepared by the Local Government Board with the object of securing the protection of sources of water supply, and of punishing companies who failed to exercise the powers conferred upon them by Parliament to provide a constant supply of pure and wholesome water within the areas they undertake to serve, may be accepted as an indication that the Government do not contemplate any action in the matter during the present session. The purpose which the president of the Local Government Board had in view was in every respect commendable, but, as we pointed out in these columns some weeks ago, the method by which he proposed to proceed was open to very damaging criticism. As a matter of fact, the objections raised, although not insurmountable, were so strong and so very generally expressed—not openly, of course, but through the channels which are invariably used when Ministers desire to test the opinion of Parliament upon a question before it comes up for debate—that it was considered advisable to proceed no further with the clauses. The method of procedure was unquestionably bad. The Bill selected for bringing the question before the House—the Higham and Hundred of Hoo Water Bill—was of the simplest possible character, consisting of some five clauses only, devised to amend a previous Act of the company, but not to confer additional powers of any kind. The clauses submitted by the President of the Local Government Board were, on the other hand, of a far-reaching character, affecting an infinite variety of interests. The little company had probably failed in its duty, but not to a greater extent than scores of other companies had done in various parts of the country. Why, therefore, should it be selected for punishment, while larger and more powerful offenders were allowed to go scot-free? No reason could be advanced. It looked as if the company had been selected by reason of its very weakness. The clauses were to be inserted in all water Bills that came hereafter before the House. This would undoubtedly have provided the public with safeguards for that, against the companies that had already got their powers there was no remedy whatever. It might be assumed that in course of time every company would come to Parliament at one period or another for additional powers, and thus be brought within the scope of the new provisions, but could any process be slower, more clumsy and ineffectual? Surely the proper, regular and equitable course would have been to introduce a public Act to amend the Waterworks Clauses Act.

Strong as these objections were, they by no means exhausted the indictment against the clauses. Serious questions of principle, public policy and Parliamentary procedure were raised. The clauses were in direct contravention of the principle acted upon every session by the House of Commons in appointing the Select Committee on Police and Sanitary Regulations. That principle is that no amendment of the general law shall be allowed by a private Bill without previous inquiry by the committee with respect to the reasons which would justify the amendment and the conditions under which it should be allowed to take place. This, of course, struck the weak spot in the proposed method of procedure. No argument could be adduced in support of inserting the clauses in the particular Bill chosen which would not apply with much greater force to every water company's undertaking in the kingdom. Another weapon which the opponents to the clauses were able to handle effectively was that they were an attempt to override the decisions of the several select committees to whom the Higham and Hundred of Hoo and other water Bills of the session were referred. These committees, we may remark, had before them the recommendations of the Local Government Board upon which the clauses were based, but declined to adopt them for the reason that they were in violation of the well-known and well-understood principle of Parliament which we have already explained. The clauses, moreover, were in themselves a serious breach of the Standing Orders of Parliament, and would have plunged the Bills affected into serious Standing Order difficulties during their future progress. The opponents did not forget to show that the clauses were illogical and capricious in application, inasmuch as while it was intended to bring them into operation in the case of one of the very smallest water companies—supplying a sparsely-populated rural district getting its supply from wells sunk upwards of 150 ft. in the chalk-beds of Kent, a supply which, although not so large as required, was reasonably pure—there were large undertakings, both in the metropolis and in the country, obtaining their water under conditions of great complexity, which involved risk of pollution, that would not be brought within the operation of the clauses until they happened to be promoting a Bill in Parliament, possibly a quarter of a century hence. The clauses were, furthermore, condemned as impracticable, ineffectual, vexatious and dangerous—impracticable and ineffectual because they did not ensure that the samples of water taken for purposes of analyses were the same as the water to be supplied to the consumer; vexatious and dangerous because they would lead to great conflict of jurisdiction between water companies and local authorities while conferring no commensurate benefit upon the consumer. The sampling of water for purposes of analysis raises the question of the much-debated Harrogate clause, which was objected to, in the case of several Bills this session, because of its sheer inefficiency. It provides for samples of water taken from the reservoirs being tested, whereas the filtration works of the company or local authority concerned are usually established, or to be established, to deal with the water after it has left the reservoir and before it reaches the consumer. The consumer himself was not required to take a sample of water and submit it for analysis by a competent person.

The tribunal itself which was to impose the penalty was taken exception to as being incompetent to deal with matters of such a highly-specialised character. For that reason its decisions would fail to inspire confidence. Above and beyond this it was maintained that, while water supply companies and authorities were to be penalised for failure to provide a supply of pure and wholesome water, the failure itself might arise from circumstances entirely beyond their control, inasmuch as no power was given them to prevent the pollution of the sources over which they had no jurisdiction. These are all very weighty arguments, and we are ourselves inclined to doubt whether the clauses would not have had a tendency to weaken the sense of responsibility which medical officers of health now feel in the discharge of this most essential part of their functions. While every precaution ought certainly to be taken to see that water is kept free from pollution, it is manifestly undesirable that power should be placed in the hands of consumers, grossly ignorant in the majority of cases of technical details, to raise a scare as to the water supply of any particular place. The cases of Maidstone and King's Lynn are scandalous instances of the results of neglecting clear and obvious precautions, and they show the absolute necessity for Parliament stepping in and insisting with a strong hand that the public health shall be protected; but there is a danger which might become a very serious and damaging thing to a health resort were the feelings of an ignorant populace stirred up, possibly for some interested purpose, against a particular water service. A matter so delicate as the impeachment of the water supply ought only to be possible on the trained judgment of an expert and not by the expression of irresponsible opinion. By the withdrawal of Mr. Chaplin's clauses the way is clear for the introduction of a Bill next year to amend the Waterworks Clauses Act, and it is to be hoped that meanwhile the best advice will be sought in the framing of a measure which, while securing the object in view, will not be open to the objections which have proved fatal to the present proposals.

\* \* \*

**A Voice from the Local Government Board.** Not the least interesting item in the last issue of *The Journal of State Medicine* is the report—apparently verbatim as regards some of the speeches—of the recent annual dinner of the Royal Institute of Public Health, of which somewhat pompously-named body our contemporary, whose title, consistently enough, is also of the high-sounding order, is the official organ. Our excuse for allowing some weeks to elapse before referring to this function is that those who control the affairs of the institute seem to be somewhat chary of issuing invitations to the Press apart from the big dailies, none of which, so far as we are aware, reported the proceedings at any length. Our reason for referring to the matter at all is to be found in the fact that the institute had secured the presence of the Parliamentary Secretary to the Local Governmet Board, and Mr. T. W. Russell not only spoke at considerable length, but explained with tolerable clearness the attitude of the Local Government Board with regard to one or two important and troublesome questions of local government. For this many people will be duly grateful, and we therefore consider it desirable to bring the right honourable gentleman's remarks to the attention of our readers, who might otherwise have remained in ignorance of something which they will no doubt be glad to know. We wish to explain, however, that by the foregoing remark we have no intention of suggesting that the perusal of the *Journal of State Medicine* is confined to those connected with the body of which it is the official organ, but that is by the way. No branch of municipal and sanitary engineering is more important than water supply. Tius Mr. T. W. Russell, as reported—

> They had the misfortune in Maidstone to have a serious epidemic, by which a number of lives—he could not say precisely how many—were lost. So far as anything could be proved in this world—though it had been held to be open to dispute whether Napoleon Bonaparte ever existed—it was proved that that epidemic was due to the water supply. There had been similar epidemics in King's Lynn and other towns, all due to the same cause.

This declaration, coming as it does with all the weight of official position, is the more interesting from the fact that we have been assured, on more or less competent authority, that the Maidstone epidemic was chiefly, if not wholly, due to defective drainage and sewerage. That such sanitary defects will lower the vitality of a community and render the members of it more susceptible to an epidemic needs no demonstration at this time of day; but it is quite another thing to imply that but for the existence of the defects referred to there would have been no epidemic, and that the outbreak was not directly attributable to a polluted water supply. The presence of the specific virus of typhoid fever in the Maidstone water supply may not have been so conclusively proved as it might have been, but there was absolutely no question as to gross pollution of certain sources with organic matter of the most offensive character, and the probability is that when the bacteriological examination was made the specific pollution had passed away after having done its deadly work. Bacteriologists have still much to do, but one thing they have done—they have proved to demonstration the existence of specific microbes, though we hope they will be able by and by to tell us better what to do with them now that they have been found. It has also been proved with tolerable certainty that the typhoid bacillus is water-borne, and that, while it seems to find a congenial habitat in certain soils, especially polluted soils, there is no reason to believe that it can be transmitted aerially. Yet that is what the theory of defective drainage and sewerage comes to. Are we to assume, then, that bacteriology is unreliable in its methods and conclusions? Lowered vitality, resulting from insanitary conditions, is bound to make an epidemic worse than it would otherwise have been; but that remark would hold good of any infectious or contagious disease, and it by no means follows that the absence of such conditions would have prevented the Maidstone epidemic. If the virus of typhoid finds its way into a water supply, and there are no means of arresting it—and such means, in the shape of filters, for example, were notoriously absent at Maidstone—an outbreak is inevitable. It has been asserted that houses in which the sanitary arrangements were satisfactory escaped the disease; but that is a somewhat loose statement, the accuracy of which it would be very difficult to verify. Nor do we remember such an assertion in any of the responsible reports published in connection with the outbreak. On the other hand, it was recognised that the incidence of the epidemic corresponded closely with the part of the town served with water from the polluted sources, the remainder of the town practically escaping unless through secondary causes. Judging from the remarks of Mr. T. W. Russell, it is quite evident that the opponents of the water supply theory have not converted the Local Government Board. On another phase of the water supply question Mr. Russell is reported to have expressed himself thus:

> The Local Government Board, a body which was pretty well abused, being in possession of the facts he had stated, thought that the opportunity arose this session, when no fewer than twenty-one Water Bills were before the House of Commons, of trying to do a stroke of business on behalf of the public health. The Board proposed to insert clauses in those Bills which would have helped to secure that the water to be supplied was pure water. But the House of Commons arose in its might, and the clauses had to be withdrawn. The House of Commons was all in favour of public health. It was all in favour of pure water, but it wanted to have the clauses in the shape of a public Bill, and the clauses had to

go. He fully believed that if the President of the Local Government Board were to introduce those identical clauses in a public Bill next session there would still be great opposition to them.

In a separate article we have endeavoured—not unsuccessfully we hope—to show that the House of Commons was quite justified in arising in its might and demanding the withdrawal of the clauses in the form in which they were introduced. It is not necessary to anticipate what will happen if the clauses are introduced in the form of a public Bill. When such a Bill has been actually rejected it will be time enough then to consider the position. Like Mr. Russell, we hope "that the question would be pressed, so that those who undertook to supply the public with pure water should carry out the undertaking." Now for sewage disposal. In the reported words of Mr. Russell,—

It was a question of exceeding difficulty. Let them take the case of large towns like Manchester and Liverpool. This question had become the greatest problem they had to face. The responsible authorities of such towns had a tremendous interest in the public health of their localities, and the large towns approached the Local Government Board and asked privileges of it; but the board was bound by Act of Parliament, and gave them the stereotyped reply: "Sewage must go through land." The answer the board received was either that land was so costly that it became an intolerable tax, or that it could not be had at all, or that it was not suitable. That was an awkward position for a public authority, but it was the position of a large number of great towns at that moment. They went to the Local Government Board, therefore, and pleaded for alternative processes. The board being, as he had said, bound by Act of Parliament, had to take refuge, as every department had to do, in a Royal Commission.

Mr. Russell omitted to mention that the Royal Commission proceeds to sit *in camera*, a detail in regard to which we have already had occasion to express some opinions.

\* \* \*

**Urban District Councils and their Surveyors.** In another column we give some particulars of the common-sense and enlightened manner in which the Cirencester Urban District Council have recently dealt with the representations of their surveyor in regard to his duties and emoluments. Having filled the combined position of surveyor, sanitary inspector and rate collector since 1895, Mr. Hibbert naturally concluded that he was justified in asking for an increase of salary, and also thought the time appropriate for asking relief from a portion of his work, on the ground that his duties as surveyor and inspector had largely increased. The reasonable spirit in which the General Purposes Committee and the council generally approached the question is worthy of all praise, especially as such an attitude is by no means so common as could be desired. The first consideration was the manner in which the surveyor had acquitted himself in the past. From the report of the committee we learn that he had not only discharged his duties generally to the satisfaction of the committees, but had prepared plans of sewerage and drainage works, street improvement works and bath renovation, and had carried through, satisfactorily all of those works that had so far been executed. For the extra work undertaken in connection with the preparation of a new scheme of surface-water drainage a special fee was awarded. Though such considerations alone might justify an increase of salary, the committee were only doing their duty in inquiring as to the rates of remuneration in similar cases elsewhere. The result was a recommendation in favour of a substantial increase of salary, and the manner in which the committee and the council recognised the facts of the case is worthy of all praise, though we regret to observe that there were two dissentients, who, while admitting the surveyor's claims, would have reduced any recognition to such grudging limits as to make it worse than none at all. Not the least important of the council's decisions was that of relieving Mr. Hibbert of a portion of his duties by placing the col-

lection of the rates in other hands, having regard to heavier responsibilities owing to the transference of the waterworks, the increase of work generally, and the expected further increase through the execution of the surface-water drainage works. Of the wisdom and expediency of such a decision there can be no question. Unless under very exceptional circumstances the combination of the duties of rate collector with those of surveyor to a local authority is quite indefensible. There is no doubt, however, that the practice is much less common than formerly.

\* \* \*

**Sanitary Work in Cuba.** In speaking last week of the close connection between yellow fever and sanitation we remarked that among other forms of activity there was plenty of scope for sanitary engineering in Cuba if the towns and cities are to be made decently habitable. The fact that yellow fever and the various deadly malarial fevers prevail almost exclusively in the towns is too significant to permit of any but one conclusion. A recent writer, in dealing with the future of the island generally, has touched incidentally on the question of sanitation, particularly with reference to drainage and water supply. Such sewers as do exist are described as being built without the most elementary knowledge—horrible contrivances in which the congested filth of years breeds disease and vile odours. Provision for flushing is unknown, and to the abominable condition of the towns is traced the prevalence of fevers, small-pox and dysentery in the island. These diseases are uncommon on the isolated estates, and in the opinion of many they might be largely eliminated from the island by giving attention to the most ordinary rules of sanitation. As to water supply, that of Havana is said to be fairly good, but in most other towns there is little besides the rain water stored during the wet season in great stone cisterns beneath the houses. This state of affairs seems to be more the fault of the executive than of inability on the part of the people to appreciate the advantages of a good water supply. Taxes may be raised for works or for coal to keep pumps going, but the money has been known to be actually banked to the credit of the officials, or the coal bought and then resold for their benefit. The matter is all the more deplorable from the fact that excellent springs abound in most places and small rivers of good water are fairly common.

\* \* \*

**The Edinburgh Meeting.** It will be observed that we this week conclude our report of the recent annual meeting of the Incorporated Association of Municipal and County Engineers with some notes on the visits of inspection which took place on the third day of the meeting. Of the conspicuous features of the meeting and its general success we need not now speak at any length, as we have dealt with the subject in some closing remarks at the end of our report. The more purely social functions—which are practically inevitable on such occasions—were as successful as any others, and this gratifying circumstance may to a large extent be attributed to the fact that the hospitable reception accorded to the visitors left nothing to be desired. At the dinner and luncheons the Lord Provost and other members of the town council expressed the most cordial sentiments, and throughout the meeting showed the liveliest interest in the proceedings, conspicuous in this respect being Bailie Mackenzie, who took an effective part in more than one discussion. Nor was appreciation of municipal engineers and their work confined to councillors. In another column we quote from the representative Scottish daily paper an extract which clearly indicates the appreciative attitude of the Press. The meeting will be a pleasant reminiscence for all who attended it.

# Association of Municipal and County Engineers.

## ANNUAL MEETING AT EDINBURGH.—V.

EDINBURGH : ST. GILES' CATHEDRAL.

With this instalment we conclude our report of the annual meeting with an account of the proceedings of the third and last day, the earlier portion of which was devoted to the purposes of the meeting in the shape of visits to various places of interest in continuation of those paid on the previous day.

### THIRD DAY'S PROCEEDINGS

(Saturday, July 2nd).

### VISITS OF INSPECTION.

On Saturday, the third and last day of the meeting, two parties were again formed, one of them visiting

#### THE FORTH BRIDGE.

The drive to this wonderful engineering triumph is one of the most pleasant in the district, skirting as it does the grounds of Dalmeny, the seat of the Earl of Rosebery. Of the bridge itself, the connecting link between the southern and northern portions of the North British Railway system, nothing can now be said that has not already been written. A few sternly practical notes may, however, be recalled to mind. Old as was the cantilever principle, it had previously been introduced only in works of comparatively small dimensions, but in the case of the Forth structure the engineers had to construct a bridge 30 fathoms above high-water mark, and crossing two channels, each a third of a mile in width. Had it not been for the intervening island of Inchgarvie, on which the northern central pier partly rests, the project would have been impracticable. The extreme length of the bridge, including the approach viaduct, is 2,765 yards, and the actual length of the cantilever portion 1,780 yards. The weight of the Siemens' rolled steel used in it is 51,000 tons, the extreme height of the steel structure above the mean water level is over 370 ft., the rail level above high water is 156¼ ft. About 8,000,000 rivets were used in the bridge, and 32 miles of bent plates in the tubes. Allowance is made for contraction and expansion to the extent of 1 in. per 100 ft. over the whole bridge. The wind pressure allowed for was 56 lb. per square foot of area, amounting in the aggregate to about 7,700 tons of lateral pressure on the cantilever portion of the bridge. When it is necessary to paint the iron work about 25 acres of surface has to be gone over. The total cost, not including the railway approaches, was nearly £2,500,000. The work was commenced in April, 1883, and the bridge was opened for traffic in March, 1890. In the meantime some 4,000 men had been employed on it. It is, of course, the work of Sir John Fowler and Sir Benjamin Baker, Sir William Arrol being the contractor. In

our illustration (see succeeding page) are shown, for comparison, the two other famous bridges for which Sir William Arrol was the contractor. For the use of the block we are indebted to our contemporary, The Scots Pictorial. The Tay bridge, which carries the North British Railway across the next estuary, is longer than the Forth bridge, but does not rival it in height. In this last respect the wonderful work which the municipal engineers inspected with such interest may at present claim to be the greatest bridge in the world.

#### THE SCOTT MONUMENT.

While the first party were at the Forth bridge the remainder of the members were afforded an opportunity of seeing some of the chief architectural features of Edinburgh. First on the list was the Scott Monument, but time did not permit of an ascent to its platforms. It was erected in 1840-44, after a design by the ill-fated George M. Kemp, at a cost of £15,650. Its Gothic spire, rising from four grand arches, reaches a height of 200 ft. Beneath these is a sitting statue of Scott, by Steell, and in various niches are thirty-two statuettes of characters in the novelist's works.

#### ST. GILES' CATHEDRAL,

which was next visited, dates historically from the ninth century, but architecturally has no extant feature of later date than the fourteenth century. It became a cathedral in 1633, on the creation of the short-lived bishopric of Edinburgh. Its most remarkable feature is its crown-shaped spire, and among the noteworthy incidents associated with it are the preaching of John Knox, the hurling of Jenny Geddes' stool at the head of the Dean of Edinburgh, the swearing of the Solemn League and Covenant, and the imprisonment within it of Covenanters captured at the battle of Rullion Green. Renovations and restorations in 1829-32, 1872-73, 1879 and 1883, have left the building a somewhat perplexing, though highly interesting, study for the ecclesiologist.

#### THE CASTLE,

already shown in more than one of the views we have given of Edinburgh, crowns a precipitous rock which rises to an altitude of 445 ft. above the sea-level. Here, though a passing heavy shower of rain for the moment damped the ardour of the exploring engineers, all of interest was conscientiously explained and inspected. Under the long vaulted archway surmounted by an old state prison—which of old held the Earl of Argyle and many another illustrious captive—they passed; the Parliament Hall was duly exploited; in the Crown-room they saw and listened to the story of the discovery of the ancient regalia of Scotland; the tiny St. Margaret's chapel—

a Norman edifice—the oldest existing building in Edinburgh and the only portion of the castle of earlier date than the fifteenth century, was visited ; famous old Mons Meg received its share of attention ; and there was enjoyed the glorious view over "long miles of masonry," and the

Far landscapes where the sea
Smiles on in softest witchery.

### HOLYROOD.

The Museum of Science and Art was to have been visited,

gateway of the western front. Then the historical apartments of Holyrood Palace were visited ; and here were seen the picture gallery, hung with about 100 ill-painted and imaginary portraits of Scottish kings, and Queen Mary's apartments, with the vestibule once stained with the blood of Rizzio. An illustration of the Palace was given in our last issue.

### THE CALTON HILL.

The return from Holyrood was made by way of the Burns

SIR WM. ARROL'S THREE BRIDGES—FORTH, TAY AND TOWER.

but as time did not permit the party drove next to Holyrood, where the ruins of the abbey chapel were first seen. Practically all that remains of it now is a fragment of the ancient nave and of a wall built by the early reformers across the east end to adapt it to the forms of Protestant worship. The most noticeable portions are the exquisite Norman cloister doorway, on the south side ; the richly-sculptured arcade which ornaments the face of the tower ; and the Decorated

Monument and the base of Calton Hill. There was no time to ascend the latter, but probably its main features were already familiar to those who had been fortunate enough to be in Edinburgh during the whole period of the meeting. The Calton and Castle hills, and Arthur's Seat, and the precipitous Salisbury Crag in its foreground, are natural objects which dominate the city and fill the eye from almost any point of view. Nor is it possible to overlook the towering monument to Nelson, which tops the Calton Hill, nor that picturesque "folly" which was intended to be a reproduction of the Parthenon at Athens, but which never got nearer completion than the twelve columns, with their basement and architrave, which were sufficient to absorb some £16,000. The Calton Hill, and the return thence by Prince's-street, were the last incidents of a meeting which will be memorable in the history of the association's foregatherings.

### CONCLUSION.

A few general remarks before closing this report of the annual meeting of 1898. First, on a point which was so much the subject of general comment that it remains uppermost in

EDINBURGH : THE SCOTT MONUMENT.

the mind. We refer to the conspicuous distinction achieved by the new president of the association, Mr. O. Claude Robson. As an engineer Mr. Robson's name was widely known and honoured; it came as something of a revelation to find him a ready and cultivated public speaker, and altogether an admirable chairman, whether presiding over a professional conference or a social function. The association could not have been happier in their choice.

Secondly, with regard to another element which made for the unqualified success of the annual meeting. Mr. Cooper, the burgh engineer, may not be recalled to memory by this allusion, since his share in ensuring this success may not have been so obvious. He is the most modest of men. But it is to him we refer, for to him is due the lion's share of credit for his unobtrusive labour, his forethought, his never-failing courtesy, his thorough grasp of every detail of Edinburgh's municipal works. Personally, we shall not soon forget the prompt and able assistance rendered to us both by Mr. Cooper and by the chief members of his loyal staff.

Another matter which was on all men's minds was the absence of any municipal buildings adequate to the civic life of Edinburgh or in keeping with her wonderful natural beauty and imposing architectural features. Time was when the authorities beguiled architects into a great competition for an effective city hall, which was never built; and presumably the opportunity has passed, for the present municipal buildings are being extended. The work is in the competent hands of Mr. Morham, the city architect, who may be trusted to carry out artistically all that he has been empowered to do. But we imagine Edinburgh will still retain the peculiarity of having for its finest buildings only educational institutions, and for its civic headquarters a makeshift structure unworthy of the splendid possibilities of the site it will cover.

Finally, as to the general success of the meeting. Of this there can be no question. There were grave doubts as to whether the numbers of papers to be read would not have necessitated the squeezing out altogether of some of them, or at least of the discussions upon them. But, thanks in great measure to the tact of the president and to the businesslike directness of the remarks of nearly all the speakers, the work

was got through, and practically the whole programme was carried out as arranged.

### THE SCOTSMAN ON MUNICIPAL ENGINEERS.

The following eloquent and pertinent remarks, which appeared in our able and influential Scottish contemporary, are certainly worth quoting, and will be perused with pleasure by our readers :—

"Year by year the tale of peripatetic congresses grows apace, and the months of July, August and September have become as much the set season of their sittings as May is the season for the meetings of evangelists in Exeter Hall. Ill-natured critics, and those labouring under the burden of a hospitality ungraciously rendered, have at times asked whether knowledge is really increased by all this going to and fro upon the earth. They have marked the disproportion between the armies of science and the numbers of the camp-followers whom they bring in their train, and hinted that meetings of sections and presidential addresses merely serve as a pretext for picnics, banquets and excursions. Whatever ground there may be in general for such churlish grumblings, they are singularly inappropriate in regard to such an association as that of Municipal and County Engineers, which is holding its annual sittings in Edinburgh at present. For most men of science these annual gatherings are at best an opportunity for the interchange of ideas and the communication of results obtained. Where they meet is a matter of indifference, and is generally determined by circumstances which have little connection with the main object of the meeting. On the other hand, to such an association as that of the Municipal and County Engineers the place of meeting is all-important. Their work is practical : it can only be learned by experience, and by seeing what has actually been done in different places. Description is unprofitable compared with actual inspection, and their yearly peregrinations from place to place give the members of the association an opportunity of learning much whereof their knowledge would otherwise be at best meagre and imperfect. The calling that they pursue can hardly be said to be in its infancy. Rome had its municipal engineers, and to this day it enjoys the fruits of their labours. But if not in its infancy, it is certainly in its youth. The growth of our cities, the demands that their inhabitants make for more

EDINBURGH : THE BURNS MONUMENT.

water, more light, better means of communication, and better sanitary conditions, have brought new problems, which are still being worked out and which can best be worked out by bringing to bear upon them all the experience that is available. Failure in this sense is often as valuable as success, and in both respects Edinburgh has its lessons for those who have selected it as their place of meeting. In the majority of the subjects which come before them for discussion the general public takes but a languid interest, though it is acutely critical as to the results achieved. It cares little how its refuse is disposed of as long as it is disposed of. It is not concerned with the relative merits of low-tension or high-tension currents as long as the resultant light is cheap and bright; it cares not how sewers are ventilated as long as they are well ventilated. Perhaps, too, after all this is the safest and most logical position, and by giving free discretion to those who serve it, while scanning carefully the results achieved, it will be best served. Poets may dream of ideal cities, but under modern circumstances it is the municipal engineer who must realise their ideals."

## SOME MEMBERS OF THE COUNCIL.

We this week present another supplement sheet containing portraits of members of the council, thus completing the series. With three exceptions, biographical notices have already appeared in our columns. We append those not previously given :—

### MR. G. R. W. WHEELER.

Mr. G. R. W. Wheeler, ASSOC.M.INST.C.E., was educated at a private school at Sutton. After serving his articles with an architect and surveyor, he was successful in obtaining a position under the Kensington Vestry as assistant surveyor. In 1882 he was appointed surveyor to the Westminster Vestry, which post he still occupies. During the time he has been at Westminster Mr. Wheeler has carried out many miles of wood and asphalte paving and several large sewerage works. He has also designed new stables for the vestry, as well as a mortuary, &c. Mr. Wheeler was elected an associate member of the Institution of Civil Engineers in 1883.

### MR. J. W. M. SMITH.

Mr. J. W. M. Smith received his education at a private school near Liverpool, and subsequently at Liverpool College. He served his articles in the engineer's office of the Mersey Docks and Harbour Board, afterwards acting as an assistant in that office. In 1872 he was unanimously elected borough surveyor of Wrexham, and this position he holds at the present time. Besides the many works of drainage extensions and town improvements, Mr. Smith has supervised the laying-out of the new cemetery, the new cattle markets and the borough offices, art school, &c. In conjunction with Lieut.-Colonel Jones, V.C., he has also had charge of the designing and carrying out of the reconstruction and extension of the sewage disposal works, including the laying-out of a new sewage farm. Mr. Smith became a member of the Incorporated Association of Municipal and County Engineers soon after its formation, and has been honorary district secretary for North Wales for several years.

### MR. JOHN COOK.

Mr. John Cook, ASSOC.M.INST.C.E., commenced his professional career in 1874, in the office of the then Local Board of Health, Darwen. He there served articles with Mr. William Stubbs, ASSOC.M.INST.C.E., now borough and water engineer of Blackburn, and was afterwards engaged as chief assistant. In 1884 he was appointed chief assistant to Mr. J. Cartwright, M.INST.C.E., borough and water engineer of the county borough of Bury, which position he held until 1890, when he was appointed to the position he now holds—viz., borough surveyor and water engineer of Lancaster. During the time he was at Darwen and Bury many important schemes were designed and carried out by him, including sewage works, reservoirs, bridges, culverts, railways, &c. At Lancaster he has successfully carried out extensive street improvements, the construction of tramways, new fire station, electric light installation, infectious diseases hospital, extension and re-modelling of baths and wash-houses, astronomical observatory, and extensions to waterworks. At the present time is constructing by administration a large storage and service reservoir, besides several large street improvements and new buildings.

## THE TELEPHONE SERVICE.

Mr. Hanbury again presided at a meeting of the Select Committee of the House of Commons, held on Thursday.

Sir COURTENAY BOYLE, secretary to the Board of Trade, who first gave evidence in regard to the working of the provisional order system under the Electric Lighting Acts of 1882 and 1888, said he saw no objection to giving municipalities powers to supply a telephone under provisional orders, just as they supplied electric light. The procedure was very simple and the cost very slight. Before the principles of procedure were laid down the opposition to orders was very decided, but now it was not serious at all.

Sir R. HUNTER, solicitor to the Post Office, considered that if provisional orders were granted for supplying a telephone service the privileges of the Post Office would be trenched upon. The licensing authority should be the Postmaster. General, and not the Board of Trade. The procedure in regard to the granting of the provisional order should be conducted by the Post Office.

Mr. GAINE, general manager to the National Telephone Company, the next witness, pointed out that in granting licenses to municipalities a difficulty would occur in giving trunk-line communication to the new exchange areas. The Post Office would probably have to spend £250,000, without a shilling of revenue from it, in laying down junction wires between the new exchanges and the nearest trunk-wire terminal stations.

Mr. GOSCHEN, First Lord of the Admiralty, referred, in the course of his evidence, to a portion of a speech of his in the House of Commons on March 29, 1892, which, he thought, stated his policy regarding the competition of municipalities very clearly. It ran : "Therefore all the licensees have been warned that the Government have retained the power in their own hands, and it will not be against either the spirit or the letter of the license if we establish trunk lines. But I do think it would be against the spirit of the license if we were to take the local arrangements entirely into our hands. during the continuance of that license, to the detriment of those who on the faith of that license have been extending their system up to the present moment." His recollection and interpretation of that passage would be that if immediately after the signing of the agreement they had entered into competition with the company it would have been against the policy they intended. But, on the other hand, their discretion was not tied in any way, though that point should not be pressed too far. The Post Office must retain entire discretion, and he did not think it would be against the agreement to raise such competition as was clearly contemplated both in the agreement and in the Treasury minute. But he thought it would have been a surprise to the company, and they would have considered it as hard usage, if the moment after signing the agreement competition had been established against them throughout the country. That would not have prevented competition in any particular locality. They reserved competition in particular areas as a power for themselves and for succeeding Governments. But the idea at the moment was that taking over the trunk lines was not to establish competition immediately, as they had enough on their hands with the trunk wires. The Treasury minute was later than his speech, and therefore a more formal embodiment of the Government's policy, but it seemed to him conclusive as to the intention of the latter. Continuing, he thought it was impossible that he could have given Mr. Forbes (the chairman of the National Company) any assurance that the policy so enunciated would be departed from, and he could not think, he said in closing his evidence, that the granting by the Post Office of a license to a municipality would now be an evasion of the spirit of the agreement.

Mr. GAINE, recalled on Friday, submitted, in the course of his evidence, that it was essential in justice to his company that there should be an appeal against the absolute veto of the local authority. Municipalities would have way-leave powers, and they could deny them to the company. That was not competition. In the event of licenses being granted, he said it would be most unjust if the period during which they should run were extended beyond the period of the company's license—namely, 1911. They asked to be placed on a footing of absolute equality, nothing more. In the course o further evidence witness expressed the opinion that the telephone service had been laid down on quite wrong principles the price should be according to user and not subscription. Such a system would, he thought, do a great deal to popularise the service. If licenses were taken up by municipalities in competition with the company, and the business was conducted at a loss, it would not be fair that Parliament should allow that loss to be thrown on £2 per cent. of the ratepayers who would get no return whatever for the expenditure incurred. On the other hand, if municipalities conducted the business at a profit, it would be almost impossible for the State to resume possession of the telephones at any future time. No Government would be strong enough to take away the service from the municipalities if they were working it at a profit.

## SANITATION IN COLOMBO.

According to Indian Engineering, it is claimed that the Health Department of the Colombo Municipality have removed the foulest defect in the sanitation of Colombo, and have, at a minimum of cost and annoyance, substituted a regular and reliable service for the removal and disposal of night-soil. The acceptance of the service is optional, and it is a tribute to its efficiency that it has been practically adopted universally. It offends no race or caste prejudice, and it has been organised without adding to the rates. The public latrines are no longer a nuisance to passers-by. The depots, now under efficient control, are open to inspection at any time and are absolutely free of offence. The only serious failure has been caused by the cinerators. The municipal engineer to whom the work of erection was entrusted has not as yet succeeded in providing a method for the speedy destruction of refuse. Mean. while burial with deodorants and disinfectants is still continued, and, under constant supervision works well.

**Eastleigh.**—At a recent meeting of the district council the clerk said he had the pleasure of reporting that he had received the sanction of the Local Government Board to the erection of new offices, and that they had not insisted upon the alterations which were recently the subject of discussion. The board sanctioned the borrowing of the sum of £3,600 for the purpose of erecting offices, and of £1,400 for the provision of a fire station, stabling, and storage accommodation, &c., the money to be borrowed for a period of thirty years.

# Comparative Reports of General Practice.

## XXV.—INCANDESCENT GAS LIGHTING : ALDERSHOT REPORT.

In presenting a report recently to the Roads and Lighting Committee of the Aldershot Urban District Council on the lighting of the district, Mr. Nelson F. Dennis, surveyor to that body, incorporated some interesting information on incandescent gas lighting which he had gleaned as the result of inquiries as to the experience of other districts in this direction. The detailed replies are given below. In the course of his general report Mr. Dennis says:—

The public street lighting is done by 285 lamps, supplied with gas on the average meter system, there being eleven lamps per meter for the area supplied by the gas and water companies, and in The Avenue eleven lamps are supplied by the Government, there being a meter to each lamp. The lighting, extinguishing and repairs are performed under a contract with a man who employs three others to assist him in the work, the gas company supplying gas only, at the rate of 2s. 9d. per 1,000 cubic feet, bearing a discount of 10 per cent. The average number of hours each lamp is alight throughout the year is about 2,300, and the average cost per lamp per annum upon the present system is: Gas, £2 0s. 10d.; lighting, extinguishing and repairs, 13s. 1d.; total, £2 13s. 11d. The painting of lanterns and columns produces a further average expenditure of 9d. per lamp per annum.

I believe it will be admitted that the lighting of the streets generally, and the main business thoroughfares particularly, is unsatisfactory, which, however, cannot be said to be due to a depreciation in the quality of the gas supplied, the test indicating the illuminating power to be slightly in excess of the standard—viz., 15 candle-power—but to the fact that of late years, through the advent of many devices for improved lighting, the mind has gradually become accustomed to things more brilliant, and what was considered sufficient a few years ago has by degrees become inadequate for present purposes.

### THE QUESTION OF MANTLES.

Your committee have taken measures to improve the lighting by the adoption of a new type of lantern and by experimenting in the past with the incandescent burner, which experiments, owing to the abnormal breakage of mantles, had to be discontinued as, I am informed, an absolute failure. I cannot help thinking that that failure was due, in a great measure, to preventable causes. Holding that view, I ascertained from the engineers and surveyors of several towns their experience with regard to incandescent lighting. In some districts it has not gone beyond the experimental stage, but in others, such as Croydon, Eastbourne, Surbiton and Teddington, it is superseding the flat-flame burner, whilst at St. Mary Abbotts, Kensington, 350 incandescent burners are in use. It appears that about six mantles per lamp per annum are required on an average. The number, however, varies in different towns, governed, doubtless, to a great extent by local conditions and circumstances varying in each, there-fore I do not consider that the average experience in that respect would be a fair criterion upon which to base an estimate. There are several agencies at work which tend to destroy the mantles, among others natural decay—which very seldom happens—vibration caused by traffic, insufficient care on the part of the men in lighting and cleaning, and excessive draughts. There are several appliances which, by their adoption, are said to diminish the destruction of mantles by vibration, but of those I do not at present intend to speak. Great care by the lamplighters is necessary in dealing with the incandescent lamp. This was fully demonstrated at Hornsey, where the saving in mantles, when the lighting and extinguishing was performed by men accustomed to the work, amounted to 160 per cent. Many mantles are broken in lighting and extinguishing the lamps upon the ordinary ring and hook system, and to avoid this I suggest that an alteration be made to the lever by slightly loosening it so as to work freely, and by attaching a small lead weight to the end of each chain, the mere process of lifting one weight by the lighting rod will suffice to set the lever in motion. This, I believe, would save some of the time that would otherwise be occupied in fishing for the ring, and would obviate the breakages caused by unnecessary jerks. Notwithstanding the additional care and attention a system of incandescent gas lighting of necessity demands, it appears from the returns I have received, and from which much valuable information may be obtained, that one man can control from seventy to 100 lamps. It would not, therefore, were a general scheme of incandescent lighting adopted for the district, be necessary to increase the number of lamplighters beyond that which at present exists.

I have tested the consumption of gas and the candle-power of the burner in use for street lighting, and the following table gives the results as compared with similar tests made with the "C" Welsbach burner:—

| Burner. | Gas consumed. | Candle-Power. | | |
| --- | --- | --- | --- | --- |
| | | Flat Flame. | Side Flame. | Average. |
| Burner in use | 5·06 | 13·5 | 11·2 | 12·3 |
| "C" Welsbach burner | 3·50, including by-pass during day | | | 33 |

Upon the consumption of gas a saving per lamp per annum would result in a money value of 8s. 7d., which would no doubt be absorbed by the charges for renewals, but the lighting efficiency would be increased considerably. In obtaining the above results the incandescent burner was so regulated to consume the quantity of gas stated, and I consider it desirable that all such burners should be tested and regulated before being fixed, in order to prevent the passage of gas in excess of what would be necessary for perfect incandescence. An excess of gas has the effect of blackening the mantles.

I beg to recommend that your committee authorise me to make experiments with a view to ascertain the best methods and appliances to be adopted for incandescent lighting, keeping in view the desirability of reducing to a minimum the cost of chimney, stick and mantle renewals. I would further recommend for the purpose the purchase of three of Marriage's patent street lanterns and burners, three of the anti-vibration patent street lanterns and burners, three of the anti-vibration patent spring burners, three of Gloyne's new patent anti-vibration springs for fitting to burners and one double Clay's patent shock-proof, &c., fittings, supplied by Messrs. H. Greene & Son.*

---

The following are the detailed replies received in answer to the queries addressed to various towns:—

### ASTON MANOR.

At Aston Manor incandescent gas lighting is in the experimental stage, only two large Bray's lamps being fitted with the burners. The Anti-Vibration Incandescent Gas Lighting Company, of 12 and 14 Westgate-arcade, Bradford, have fitted up the two lamps with their burners and mantles (three in each lamp) at their own expense, and with the understanding, that, when called upon, they shall replace the old burners and leave the lamps as before. No special means have been adopted for lighting and extinguishing the burners, and as yet it is impossible to say how many burners can be controlled by one man. No special lanterns have been adopted for the lamps.

### BECKENHAM.

In this district thirty-nine lamps are fitted with incandescent burners (twenty-eight with bulb burners and eleven with ordinary burners). Seven others were fixed fifteen months ago and the remainder in March last, all being fitted with by-passes. It is impossible to give the number of burners capable of being controlled by one man, as the greater part of the lamps are being attended to by the gas company. The average number of mantles used on the eight lamps under the control of the council for the six months ended September 25th last was three-and-a-half per lamp, and the total number of hours each lamp is alight is about 3,848. In one or two cases special lanterns have been used, but it is found that the ordinary 14-in. lantern is quite suitable. Since last March twenty-eight lamps have been taken in hand by the gas company, who make the same charge for cleaning and lighting as for the other lamps in the district. They also charge 10s. per lamp per annum to cover the cost of the mantles, &c., plus the cost of gas actually consumed as ascertained by the meter. For the ordinary street lighting a fixed inclusive sum per annum is paid to the gas company, so the cost of the incandescent lighting cannot be compared until a full year under the present arrangement has been completed.

### BOURNEMOUTH.

Sixty-two lamps are fitted with incandescent burners in this borough. This system of lighting has, however, only been adopted for about twelve months. The "C" by-pass burner, with metal chimney and glass bulb, is used to enable the lighting and extinguishing to be effectually carried out, and seventy burners are controlled (lighted, cleaned and extinguished) by one man. The burners require taking apart and cleaning very frequently, and it is estimated that five mantles are found necessary for each lamp per annum. Along the main roads each lamp is alight for about 2,000 hours per annum. No special lanterns have been adopted for incandescent lighting, and the gas company do not undertake the lighting and extinguishing of the lamps. The company only supply the gas, and the saving in gas almost pays for the mantles.

### CANTERBURY.

No particulars as to incandescent gas lighting were received from this borough, as the mantles had not been in use sufficiently long to take notice of the results.

### CROYDON.

At Croydon there are 850 lamps fitted with incandescent burners. This system of lighting has only been adopted for about twelve months, but it gives great satisfaction, and

---

* It should be remembered that since this report was written the Incandescent Gas Light Company, Limited, have placed upon the market a new and improved incandescent gas burner, of which some details were given in our issue of May 20th.—Ed. THE SURVEYOR.

will, no doubt, be extended into most of the roads where the electric light is not used. The Croydon Gas Company provide the ordinary gas lamps and keep them in repair, light and extinguish them, at the rate of £3 6s. 6d. per lamp per annum. For the incandescent lamps they provide everything in the same way at the cost of 4s. 3d. extra each lamp per annum.

### EASTBOURNE.

About 350 lamps are fitted with incandescent burners at this seaside resort. This system of lighting has been in use since 1894, and is at present being extended. No special method is adopted for lighting and extinguishing the burners, except that a bent nail is fixed in the ordinary torch. As regards control, one man is able to attend to the same number of incandescent lamps as to the ordinary lamps. Occasionally a little difficulty is experienced with the mantles, but Mr. R. M. Gloyne, the borough surveyor, has patented and introduced a spring which effectually prevents damage by vibration, and which the corporation have adopted after long trial. Each lamp is alight for 3,600 hours during the year, and no special lanterns have been adopted for use with the mantles. The gas company do not undertake the lighting and extinguishing of the lamps, they only supply the gas. All the incandescent burners before being fitted are regulated to 3¼ cubic feet per hour.

### GLOUCESTER.

At Gloucester sixteen lamps are fitted with incandescent burners, and these have been in use for two years. No special means have been adopted for lighting and extinguishing the lamps, the ordinary by-pass burner being used. The number of lamps one man is able to control depends very largely upon circumstances, such as distance apart, or whether the positions are very exposed, as at the corner of streets, &c. Some difficulty is very often experienced with the mantles, and the life of the mantles is very uncertain. Two mantles, even in one lamp, will frequently have lives very disproportionate. The average number of mantles used per lamp per annum is, however, about six. The number of lanterns has been adopted for the incandescent lamps, but the gas company are experimenting with special lanterns having anti-vibrators fixed to the burners. The lighting and extinguishing of the ordinary lamps is carried out by the gas company, but the corporation maintain the incandescent lamps. There is at present a dual payment, and a fair comparison of the charges cannot, therefore, be made. If maintained under contract a comparison would be in favour of the incandescent system, if the illuminating power is considered. The average hourly consumption is about 4·25 cubic feet per burner, including the gas burnt during the day by the by-pass. Magnesium carbides used on the tubes beneath the mantles are found to lengthen the life of the mantles.

### HALIFAX.

The incandescent system of gas lighting in this borough is only in the experimental stage, and consequently no particulars are forthcoming. Twenty lamps have been under trial for about six months, but it has not yet been definitely decided to extend the system.

### HORNSEY

is another of the authorities who are at present only experimenting with the incandescent gas lighting system. About 100 lamps are fitted with the burners, the "C" burner with by-pass lever and chain and the Incandescent Gas Company's suspension frame being used. At present the lighting is in sections only, and no definite particulars can be given with reference to the number of lamps one man is able to control. Recent results show that the average life of the mantles is about fifty-two days. During the year each burner is alight for about 3,940 hours, and the lighting, extinguishing, cleaning, &c., is done by the district council's own staff. The lanterns in use for this system of lighting is the "Hornsey Council" lantern—a lantern built to the council's own design by Messrs. Pontifex & Co.

### KETTERING.

At this town six lamps were fitted up for trial and used from November 10, 1894, to January 26, 1895, and then replaced with ordinary lamps. Three lamps were also tried from January 26 to April 6, 1895, the consumption of gas being measured. In the first trial one lamp consumed 2,100 cubic feet of gas against an average of 2,486 cubic feet for ordinary lamps, and in the second trial the three lamps averaged 1,666 cubic feet against 1,772 cubic feet for ordinary lamps. Only one lamp had a special lantern, but this did not seem to give any advantage. The lamps were found to be quite as easy to light as the ordinary lamps, the by-pass being used. They took, however, much longer to clean, more care being necessary. The lamps were discontinued after these trials, as, owing to the rapid deterioration of light, the frequent necessary repairs and the small saving of gas, they were not considered satisfactory.

### KENSINGTON

has 350 gas lamps fitted with incandescent burners, these having been in use for about four years. The by-pass is adopted for the lighting and extinguishing of the lamps, which are alight for about 3,800 hours in each year. One man is able to take charge of 100 lamps, but no difficulty is

experienced with the mantles. The average life of each mantle is about 400 hours. In the wide streets of the parish a special lantern is used for the incandescent lamps. The gas company do not undertake the lighting, extinguishing, &c., of the lamps, that work being done by the vestry's own staff. The gas is supplied by the company by the average meter system—one meter to twenty lamps.

### KING'S NORTON.

At this town the incandescent system of gas lighting has been in use for about three years, the number of lamps at present fitted with the burners being 109. No special means of any kind have been adopted for lighting and extinguishing the lamps, and one man is able to control about twenty-seven incandescent lamps and thirty ordinary lamps. Under ordinary circumstances no difficulty is experienced with the mantles, eight of which are found necessary for each in the course of twelve months. During winter the lamps are alight for about fourteen hours per day, and during the summer for about six hours per day. This gives an average for the whole year of about ten hours per day. No special lanterns have been adopted for the incandescent gas lamps. The district council carry out the lighting of the lamps themselves. The consumption of gas by the old burners was 10 cubic feet per hour, but by the incandescent burner it is 3¼ cubic feet per hour.

### SURBITON.

All the lamps in this district are fitted with incandescent gas burners. A portion of them have been in use for about twelve months, but the whole of them were fitted with the burners about six months ago. Each lamp is fitted with a by-pass for extinguishing and lighting. The number of lamps controlled by one man is not known, as the gas company carry out the work of lighting and extinguishing. It is, however, believed to be about 100. No difficulty is experienced with the mantles beyond frequent renewals. The lamps are in use each day during the year from sunset to sunrise. Messrs. Sugg & Co.'s "Kensington" pattern improved lantern is adopted for use on the incandescent lamps. An arrangement has been entered into with the gas company whereby they extinguish and light the lamps for £3 5s. 6d. per lamp per annum, including all charges for cleaning, maintenance, &c.

### TEDDINGTON.

At Teddington all the lamps are fitted with the incandescent gas burners, but this system of lighting has only been in use for about twelve months. The lighting, extinguishing and cleaning is in the hands of the gas company, and four men are engaged to do the work in eighty minutes. No great difficulty is experienced with the mantles. The exact number of mantles used per lamp per annum is not known, but it is believed to average about from four to six. The lamps are alight for 3,636 hours each year, but no special mantles have been adopted for the lamps. The gas company undertake to supply the incandescent burners complete for 15s. 6d. each, and light, clean, extinguish and repair the lanterns, and supply the gas for the sum of £3 8s. 6d. per lamp per annum. The Lighting Committee of the district council, when considering the question of incandescent lighting, reduced the number of hours over 4,000, which, together with the saving in gas consumed by the new burner, effected a yearly saving of £103.

### WIMBLEDON

has no lamps fitted with the incandescent burners. Certain lamps were some time ago fitted with the burners by the gas company as an experiment, and their quotation for supplying gas and lighting from sunset to sunrise, including the cleaning and repairing of the lanterns, and the supply of the mantles, burners, &c., was £4 5s. per lamp per annum.

## LAMBETH VESTRY AND CONTRACTORS.

### THE KENNINGTON ROAD BATHS.

At a meeting of the Lambeth Vestry, on Thursday, Mr. F. S. Price gave notice of motion that a committee of five members be appointed to report generally upon the question of the Kennington-road baths and particularly on the following points: (1) The dates of the contracts and the dates respectively at which the various works were to be finished. (2) Whether there have been any breaches of the "time" clauses; and, if so, whether notice has been given to the contractors that the penalties would be enforced. (3) The architect having advised the Baths Committee that the breaches of the contract be waived, to ascertain fully his reasons for such advice. (4) If the penalties were enforced, what saving of public money would be effected. (5) How it was that the commissioners did not detect at the outset the omission by the architect from the specifications of any provision for boilers, machinery and other work, involving an additional outlay of over £8,500. (6) The date at which the omission first came to the knowledge of the commissioners, and their reasons for withholding it from the vestry. (7) The commissioners having come to the vestry for approval of the original estimate for building, why they did not adopt the same course with respect to the artesian well and the electric lighting.

# The Water Supply of Ramsgate.

## EXTENSIVE IMPROVEMENTS.

A large company assembled; on the 28th ult., to witness the opening ceremony in connection with the new pumping station, which has been erected at Whitehall to the design and under the supervision of the borough engineer, Mr. W. A. McIntosh Valon, and Mr. Arthur Valon.

### THE NEW PUMPING STATION.

The building forming the new pumping station is in three divisions, the centre or main building being 63 ft. by 59 ft. by 25 ft. high. This, says *The East Kent Times*, is lined throughout with glazed bricks, and has an iron roof supported in the centre with cast-iron columns. The flooring is composed of a tessellated pavement laid on concrete, the borough arms being tastefully worked in colours at the central entrance. The main building covers the machinery, which consists of an engine 50 horse-power nominal working up to 90 horse-power. On the ground floor there has been placed a condenser. The air is withdrawn by a vacuum pump, and the vacuum thus made is kept steadily at 27 lb. on the square inch. This improvement abolishes the necessity of using the jet condenser worked by the engine itself, while at the same time it saves the loss of at least 60,000 gallons of fresh water per day. All the valves controlling the main supply pipes leading to the reservoirs are here brought under cover, and the foreman in charge has within range of his vision the whole of the machinery for raising the water, as well as the valves controlling its issue from the pumps to the reservoirs. It may be mentioned that the ventilation of the building is made as nearly perfect as possible by the insertion of a water-driven fan in one of the ornamental outlets of the building.

### THE BOILER-HOUSE.

Adjoining the main building and directly connected with it is the boiler-house, 35 ft. by 59 ft. 6 in. by 16 ft. In this two Lancashire boilers, 30 ft. long by 7 ft. 6 in. in diameter, have been set, the working pressure being 80 lb. These boilers are worked alternately. In the front of the boilers iron plates have been laid down, to form easy shovelling spaces for the fuel. In the flat roof, immediately over the boilers, has been inserted a water-driven fan, the water for driving being taken from the pumping main in the same way as for the main building. On the opposite side of the main building is the smiths' and engineers' shop, 26 ft. by 15 ft. by 16 ft., the stores 13 ft. 6 in. by 15 ft. by 16 ft., and the office 13 ft. 6 in. by 15 ft. by 16 ft. These are of convenient size, joined to and entered from the main building, the front view of which is shown, as well as may be from a photograph, in our illustration. The outside of the building is made presentable by the use of grey terra-cotta, the design of which not only adds beauty, but gives strength to the buildings. The sloping roofs are covered with red tiles and the flat roofs with zinc. For the comfort of the men, at a short distance from the main building have been erected a bath-room and lavatory. In the execution of this work it was necessary to build over and cover in the then existing engine-house before interfering with it. This made the work difficult and somewhat hazardous, as any accident of such a kind as would have stopped the working of the machinery would have meant the stoppage of the supply of water to the town and the district. We are indebted to the proprietors of *The East Kent Times* for the accompanying illustration of the building. The contractors were Messrs. Paramor.

# BRISTOL ELECTRIC LIGHTING.

## IMPORTANT EXTENSIONS.

Extensive preparations have been, and are being, made at the Bristol Corporation electrical station, Templebacks, to supply the power that will shortly be required to light the main thoroughfares beyond the present bounds, and to cope with the ever-increasing demands from private individuals for electrical force. The building, according to *The Bristol Times*, has been extended about two-thirds of its original size—about 80 ft. in all—in the direction of Temple Meads, so that now there is a fine engine-room, 210 ft. long. Being a continuance of the original structure, both the design and the material employed are similar. The walls are of pressed Cattybrook bricks, the lower portion of the street

wall being of granite. The walls and bases and the plant rest upon piles driven to a depth of 44 ft., and the new chimney stack stands upon an immense mass of concrete and granite. The work, of a very substantial character, has been done by Mr. C. A. Hayes, to the design of Mr. Henry Williams.

The capacity of the engine-room is rather more than doubled, and machinery of very much larger size has been ordered. In the boiler-house have been placed five additional Lancashire boilers, the whole number now being twelve. The new portion of the boiler-house is a few feet wider than the original portion, hence room has been provided for laying down economisers, which enable gases to pass from the boiler flues to be used for heating water, and thus effect considerable saving. The boilers are fed with coal from the bunkers by means of elevators, conveyers and screws, with this important alteration, that the apparatus is driven by electrical motors instead of by small engines. The latter are not so economical as motors, consequently the result in greater cleanliness will prevail in the boiler-room. The feed and other pumps here are also worked by electrical motors, instead of steam as formerly. Indeed, the whole of the plant now put down, with the exception of the main engines, is worked by electrical motors, thus enabling the larger engines, with much higher efficiency than smaller ones, to

RAMSGATE WATERWORKS: PUMPING STATION AT WHITEHALL.

be used. The coal bunkers have been very much increased, the new ones alone having a capacity rather more than double that of the former ones. On the roof of the bunkers have been placed two capacious tanks, one for the storage of softened water, for use in the boilers, and the other for the storage of ordinary water, to be employed in keeping cool certain parts of the engines. Along the top of the coal bunkers the coal tramway has also been extended.

In the engine-room have been put down two large steam alternators, each of which is capable of supplying electricity sufficient for 14,000 incandescent lamps, and another similar engine is on order and will be delivered before the winter—for which the department is fully equipped—for the extended street lighting. One additional dynamo is already fixed and is ready for running, another is complete at the works of the manufacturer and ready for testing, and a third is to be delivered within the next two months. Before the winter comes there will be between 4,000 and 5,000 horse-power of engines in the engine-room. Of this plant the present street lighting only needs 100 horse-power to be used at any one time, and the additional street lighting, for which cables are being laid, will require another 200 horse-power. It will be seen, therefore, that the street lamps make a very small demand upon the total resources of the station. The condensing plant has been trebled in capacity. Up to within the last month or two there has only been one condenser, capable of dealing with the exhaust steam from rather more than 2,000 horse-power engines. A circulating pump for use in connection with the same is electrically driven. Although considerable plant has been recently added—and there is more to come—room will yet remain for some more boilers and another 14,000-light steam alternator; but the business is growing so rapidly that before long it may be found prudent to further increase the plant.

# New Ladies' Bath at Sheffield.

NEW LADIES' BATH AT SHEFFIELD: INTERIOR OF THE BUILDING.

Mrs. Franklin, the mayoress of Sheffield, on the 13th ult., opened a new public bath, which has been erected for ladies at the Glossop-road baths.

The baths building, which included two swimming baths, Turkish bath, &c., were purchased by the corporation in 1895. Very extensive repairs were found necessary, as both swimming baths were leaky, the second-class bath leaking at the rate of about 6 in. per day. This work was at once taken in

NEW LADIES' BATH AT SHEFFIELD: EXTERIOR OF THE BUILDING.

hand, at a cost of about £3,500 for structural work and alterations and £1,800 for new boiler heating apparatus and engineering work. Subsequently the town council decided to erect a new bath for ladies. This was much needed, as there was no such bath in the city, and the only accommodation in

this respect was provided by reserving the gentlemen's bath on one or two days each week. Mr. C. F. Wike, the city surveyor, who had planned and carried out the alterations to the old baths, was accordingly instructed to design a ladies' swimming bath to be built on the site of the old second-class bath and bath saloon, and the building shown in the illustration is the result. The builder's contract was £5,129 and the heating contract £500, but the latter sum does not include boilers or laundry apparatus, which were included in the contract for the old bath alterations. The new ladies' swimming bath is 75 ft. by 25 ft., and varies in depth from 3 ft. 3 in. to 5 ft. 6 in. Thirty-five dressing boxes are provided, together with ten slipper baths.

The contractor for the alterations and the erection of the new bath was Mr. George Webster, of Sheffield, and the heating and engineering throughout has been entrusted to Messrs. Bradford & Co., of Salford.

## MANCHESTER STEAM USERS' ASSOCIATION.

We have received a copy of a memorandum prepared by Mr. Stromeyer, chief engineer to this body, and read at the recent annual meeting. The useful advice to boiler attendants which was issued in the beginning of the year is here reprinted, with the addition of a few practical remarks on the best method of cleaning boilers and economisers, fuller explanations of the injury caused to boilers by incrustation and grease, and an appeal to steam users to spare their boilers by using less oil in their cylinders. Some interesting comparisons are given as to the costs of explosions of boilers other than those approved by the association. That body, we learn, is still in the proud position of having had only one explosion out of the 6,000 boilers entrusted to its care. It is pointed out that of 215 persons killed or injured during the last five years, the large proportion of about one in thirteen were boiler owners or their sons or managers, and steam users are urged, for their own personal safety, to insist on having their boilers properly inspected. The memorandum also refers to the average cost of explosions distributed over the entire number of boilers in the United Kingdom, the calculation being made in view of the increased liabilities imposed upon factory owners by the Workmen's Compensation Act, which came into force on the 1st inst. Mr. Stromeyer also gives an appreciative notice of the career of his predecessor, the late Mr. Lavington E. Fletcher, with special reference to his services to steam users and engineers and the estimation in which those services are held.

# The Sterilisation of Water.

THE VAILLARD AND DESMAROUX APPARATUS.

There is no sanitary problem more important to-day than the provision for domestic, and especially for potable, purposes of water which shall be as nearly as possible absolutely pure from a bacteriological point of view. Indeed, this may without hesitation be described as quite the most important and most pressing sanitary problem of the day; and in support of this statement it is only necessary to recall the typhoid outbreaks of last year—essentially water-borne epidemics. Generally speaking, the question of a pure water supply resolves itself into two broad divisions—the prevention of pollution at the original sources, whether watersheds or wells, and, in the second place, the treatment of the water when stored or on delivery. It is with the latter phase of the question that we are at present concerned. Hitherto the treatment has been practically confined to filtration, but not a few competent authorities have grave doubts as to the ultimate efficacy of the process, whether adopted on a large scale at waterworks with sand and gravel as the filtering media or on a small scale in the shape of domestic filtration. The latter, indeed, may be purely mischievous unless the most scrupulous care is experienced, not only in the choice of a filtering apparatus, but also in keeping it in proper order. Our readers do not require to be told what the results are likely to be if objectionable matter is allowed to accumulate on the filter. Boiling, again, has long been recommended to the householder as an infallible remedy, but it has the obvious objection of quite destroying the flavour of the water.

To overcome the last-named as well as other serious difficulties was the object of MM. Vaillard and Desmaroux in designing the apparatus in connection with which we give two illustrations, one representing the elevation of the apparatus in two sizes, a small-size apparatus being seen at the extreme left of the larger one. Our second illustration is a diagram of an installation of the apparatus adapted to the requirements of a town of 40,000 inhabitants. Such installations, we believe, have been fixed at Tsaritsine in Russia and Manaos in Brazil. It will thus be seen that the inventors have aimed at producing an apparatus both on a comparatively large scale in connection with municipal and other waterworks, and on a smaller scale for the purposes of hotels, asylums, hospitals, barracks, camps, private houses and various industries, and the process should certainly receive attention from authorities, officials, and others interested.

To ensure the complete destruction of all organisms the water is heated to a temperature of 230 degrees to 239 degrees, the heating, however, being done in a closed vessel, so that none of the natural gases are evolved, the salts are not deposited, and the water leaves the apparatus only a degree or two higher in temperature than it enters. There is also the additional security that the cooling of the water takes place out of all contact with the air, so that no contamination can arise from that source. The following were the conditions which the inventors set themselves to fulfil as essential to a satisfactory solution of the problem of supplying potable sterilised water: (1) The water is to be bacteriologically pure; (2) the flavour, salts and limpidity are to be preserved; (3) the water is to be emitted cold; (4) large quantities must be obtainable at a moderate cost; (5) the plant must be inexpensive, so that it may be of general utility.

The sterilising apparatus consists essentially of two parts—the heater and the cooler. In the former the water, which has passed through the cooler on its way from the supply is heated, as already stated, to a temperature several degrees above the boiling point. Thus the water leaves the heater effectually sterilised, and it then passes into the cooler, which is arranged on a somewhat novel principle. It consists of a double spiral of pipes, one series of which carries the cold water from the source to the heater, while the other series conveys the hot water from the heater to the outlet. The apparatus can be made to deliver from 2 to 500 gallons per hour, and hence it can be adapted to all requirements, from those of a town of several thousand inhabitants to those of a single household.

In connection with the water supply of a district it is suggested that a central station might be constructed, where the requisite number of sterilisers could be sufficiently worked by a common heating arrangement. It is further suggested that use might be made of the waste heat from pumping engines. As a temporary expedient for checking an epidemic traceable to an impure water supply, it is pointed out that with a very slight expenditure of time, trouble or money, sterilising apparatus might be placed in public positions at various points about the town. The inhabitants could then fetch their water from the nearest steriliser or a municipal service could be instituted for its distribution.

But equally important is the supply of pure water to public institutions, such as hospitals, hotels, asylums, barracks, &c., and it is pointed out that the addition to the expense of the water supply per head would be quite negligible in comparison with the greatly-increased safety of the inmates. In hospitals the sterilisors could be run in connection with heating chambers, which are necessary for the now universa antiseptic treatment, and by a simple arrangement could be made to deliver both hot and cold sterilised water. We are informed that the apparatus is now in use in several French hospitals, including the sanatorium of St. Trojan, and that it has also been fitted at Netley hospital. Assuming that the results are as satisfactory as we have reason to believe they are, the advantages of such an apparatus in connection with hotels, asylums, barracks, camps, military expeditions, prisons, factories, colleges and schools are obvious enough. Finally, even if the system is not adopted for public purposes, the householder, who should always be solicitous for the health of his family, may take the matter into his own hands by making use of the small form of apparatus. For this a small petroleum lamp or gas flame is quite sufficient, so that after the first outlay the expense is small.

There are, of course, a large number of industries in which the use of bacteriologically pure water should be regarded as absolutely necessary. Among these we may mention the manufacture of artificial ice and of malt liquors. In conclusion we may briefly summarise the advantages claimed by the inventors for the apparatus. They point out that it combines simplicity with small initial cost and slight cost of maintenance; that it can be manufactured from a small size, suitable for domestic purposes, to supply 20 litres per hour to one large enough for supplying a small town for ordinary purposes; that it is portable, and will give from any

## KIRKBY-IN-ASHFIELD WATER SUPPLY.

### LOCAL GOVERNMENT BOARD INQUIRY.

Major-General H. Darley Crozier, R.E., conducted an inquiry on Wednesday of last week, on behalf of the Local Government Board, with reference to an application of the Kirkby-in-Ashfield Urban District Council for sanction to borrow £9,200 for the purposes of water supply.

Mr. G. H. Hibbert, clerk to the council, made a statement, from which it appeared that the district, which had now a population of 9,000, had grown very rapidly of late years, and was being supplied with water from the Sutton-in-Ashfield council's waterworks, for which they were paying 10d. per 1,000 gallons. The supply had been extremely intermittent, and on that account, as well as on the ground of its unsatisfactory quality caused through the extension of the works, they asked for sanction to borrow money to erect their own works. The loan would provide £1,000 for compensation to the Sutton authority and contingencies, £1,280 13s. for rising main and service main, £1,200 for the reservoir, £1,500 for the sinking of a well and lining the same, £2,000 for duplicate pumping machinery, and £1,000 for pumping station, engine-house, &c. The engineer, Mr. W. H. Radford, estimated that by having their own works the council would save £917 a year. At present they were paying Sutton

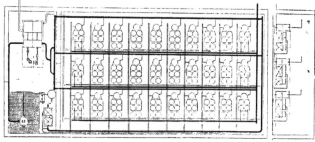

PLAN OF INSTALLATION FOR A TOWN OF 40,000 INHABITANTS.

ordinary river water, in the course of a few minutes, a constant supply of pure cold water at the rate of 1,000 litres per hour; that wood, coal or liquid fuel can be used for the apparatus, the consumption of coal for an apparatus of the size indicated being only a few pounds per hour; that coal, gas, petroleum or steam can be used to operate the fixed machinery; and that in all public institutions having steam-circulating pipes for heating purposes it would simply be necessary to connect the loop to these pipes and fix the apparatus wherever desired. An apparatus for which so many advantages can be claimed certainly merits investigation on the part of those interested in the important question of the purity of water supplies.

The apparatus has certainly found a large amount of favour in France. For more than eighteen months it has been fixed at the Sanatorium de St. Trojan (Ile d'Oleron) and we understand that it has given entire satisfaction. Since its adoption at the Chateaudun barracks typhoid fever has almost entirely disappeared, and the apparatus is also in use at a number of other barracks, as well as at Cherbourg in connection with the French navy. An apparatus has also been fixed at the residence of Baron Rothschild, Chantilly, and negotiations are in progress for installations in the towns of Castres, Carcassone, Cannes, Toulouse, Beziers, and elsewhere.

The address of the company is the Water Sterilisation Syndicate, Limited, 152 Winchester House, E.C., and we may also mention that an apparatus has recently been on view at the Sanitary Institute, Margaret-street, W., where it has been inspected by a number of medical men, engineers and others.

**York.**—The city council have received a report from the town clerk stating that he had received from the Local Government Board sanction to borrow £1,805 for street improvements in Skeldergate, Barker-hill and Spurriergate; £354 for the purchase of old cottages in Beetham, and laying-out the ground adjoining the Abbey walls; and £5,036 for carrying out improvements in Parliament-street, Healington-road, South-bank and other streets.—It is proposed to accept the tender of Messrs. Parker & Sharp, contractors, York, at the sum of £7,174, for the erection of the electric lighting station. The Electric Lighting Committee have had before them the question of adapting the dynamos and instruments for use afterwards for electric traction. The extra cost will be £274, and the committee ask for instructions of the council.

£1,420 for water. The medical officer, Dr. Mackenzie, strongly supported the scheme, and stated that epidemics of typhoid fever were indirectly due to the intermittent supply from Sutton, the people having gone to some of the old wells for water. There was no opposition to the scheme.

## ROYAL INSTITUTE OF PUBLIC HEALTH.

### THE CONGRESS AT DUBLIN.

The preliminary programme of the congress to be held by the Royal Institute of Public Health in Dublin, from the 18th to the 23rd August, has been issued. Particulars of the congress have at various times been published in our columns, but the programme gives some additional information. The presidential address will be delivered by Sir Charles A. Cameron, M.D., in the Examination Hall, Trinity College, on Thursday, the 18th of August, at 12 o'clock. Among the subjects selected for discussion the following will be of most interest to municipal engineers: The water supply of urban and rural populations, the pollution of rivers and the treatment of sewage, Irish health resorts, climate in relation to hospital sites, the designing and construction of hospitals, designs for lunatic asylums, heating and ventilation of public buildings, housing of the working classes, construction of refuse destructors, subsoil in relation to sites of dwellings, housing of the working classes (including the very poor), municipalisation of tramways and public lighting, prevention of hideous hoardings and structures in the streets of the city, the terminable leasehold system in regard to municipal sanitation, the extension of towns as a means of promoting public health and the housing of the poor.

In addition to the papers and discussions it is proposed that inspection shall be made of the principal buildings in connection with the Public Health Department of the corporation, and their workings explained to the delegates. Large public works and institutions throughout the city will also be visited, and there will be visits to the scientific departments in and around the city. The Health Exhibition of the congress will be held, by kind permission of the Senate, in the Royal University Buildings, 18th to 27th August. Full information concerning this department will be furnished on application to the hon. secretary, Mr. G. Ross, M.A., C.E., 61 Dawson-street, Dublin.

## CORRESPONDENCE.

**Sewer Ventilation.**—Mr. Edward Pitts, secretary of Webb's Engineering Company, Limited, 52 Queen Victoria-street, E.C., writes : 'In your report of the annual meeting of the Association of Municipal and County Engineers, held at Edinburgh, published in your issue of the 15th inst., Mr. Pickering, of Nuneaton, makes the following statement : "Another process which had been brought before them was the destruction of sewer gas by the consumption of coal gas. They had some of these gas destructors at work as an experiment, but, they found that if the gas light went out the system of ventilation was made very much worse. He did not think there was an engineer who had put up these gas destructors who did not find them go out and leave the sewers unventilated." As Mr. Pickering does not give the name of the apparatus to which he refers, I must ask you to kindly get him to do this, as we are interested in a sewer gas extractor and destructor which has been in use a considerable time and has received the approval of many of the leading engineers of this country. We have received testimonials from many engineers of most important towns, and wherever our apparatus has been tried it has given entire satisfaction ; in no case has it been known to fail in the manner Mr. Pickering mentions. We have never supplied our destructors to Nuneaton, therefore we do not think Mr. Pickering has had the opportunity of testing our method, which is the only one of its kind on the market at the present time that I am aware of, and as this statement, appearing as it does in your valuable paper, will come under the notice of most of the engineers in this country, and is calculated to do us a serious injury, we must ask you to be good enough to get Mr. Pickering to name the apparatus he talks of, otherwise undoubtedly it will be thought that he refers to Webb's patent sewer gas extractor and destructor, which is the property of this company. I do not doubt for a moment that Mr. Pickering speaks truthfully and in perfect good faith, and does *not* refer to our destructors ; but, as I have before mentioned, I have no knowledge of any other apparatus of a similar description on the market, and see no reason why he should not give the name of the apparatus in question, or the name of the maker or makers. I enclose for your perusal a circular containing some of the testimonials which we have received, which will bear out my letter. You are at perfect liberty to apply to any of the gentlemen whose names are attached as to the genuineness of these testimonials, or I shall be pleased to show you the originals at this office.

[We insert Mr. Pitt's letter with pleasure, but we must point out that it would be rather out of place for us to approach Mr. Pickering in the matter, as that gentleman is himself the sole judge of what he should say on the subject, and may not consider that he is under any obligation to add to his remarks. The letter, of course, speaks for itself. The names to which Mr. Pitt refers in his last sentence include those of some well-known municipal engineers, and no assurance is required as to the genuineness of the testimonials.—Ed. The Surveyor.]

**Illuminating Gas from Sewage Sludge.**—Mr. Edward A. Harman, Corporation Gasworks, Huddersfield, writes : At the recent annual conference of the Association of Municipal and County Engineers in Edinburgh, Mr. Cameron read a paper upon the above subject. As bearing somewhat indirectly upon it, permit me to state that I made some experiments with sludge from the corporation sewage works of this town some twelve months since, with a view to ascertaining whether there were sufficient gases existing in the sludge to make it worth while carbonising. I had a whole week's test, the result of which was as follows :—

*Summary of Tests.*

| Date, 1897. | Gas made per Cubic feet per ton | Illuminating Power. Candles. | Moisture. Per cent. |
|---|---|---|---|
| June 11th | 3,680 | 11 | 63 |
| „  14th | 3,680 | 12 | 40 |
| „  „ | 3,920 | 15 | 40 |
| „  15th | 5,360, 6,000 | 16·1 | 35 |
| „  16th | 5,360, 5,120 | 16·3 | 35 |
| „  „ | 5,440, 5,760 | 16·74 | 27 |
| „  17th | 5,600, 5,840 | 16·1 | 27 |
| „  „ | 6,320, 6,560 | 14·7 | 27 |
| „  „ | 7,200, 6,000 | 7·6 | 25 |
| „  18th | 5,200, 5,520 | 8·4 | 25 |
| „  „ | 5,680, 5,120 | 8·2 | 25 |
| Average  … | 5,440 | 12·02 | 33 |

It will be apparent that, as only 5,440 cubic feet of gas of an illuminating power of 12·02 candles was obtainable per ton on an average, it was not economical to do anything with the refuse, with the present prices of coal ; but in cases of emergency it would be worth further consideration. The average moisture in the material was 33 per cent.; and there was the further serious objection that the sludge contained large quantities of minute organisms. It occurs to me that these tests may have some slight interest, although upon different lines from those indicated in Edinburgh. Needless to add, such treatment of sludge is a perfect destructor.

## ARBITRATIONS AND AWARDS.

On Thursday Mr. Shaw, Q.C., M.P., as overman in the arbitration between the city of Perth and Mr. Rollo, of Rodney Lodge, in regard to compensation for loss and damage sustained by the latter through the erection of a new bridge at Perth, issued his final decision. The sum claimed by Mr. Rollo was £20,000, but on the hearing of the case in Edinburgh, a month ago, Mr. Shaw awarded claim at £3,785. The commissioners and Mr. Rollo appealed against the decision, but on again hearing parties' agents the overman adhered to his former findings.

On Tuesday, at the Guildhall, Westminster, Mr. Troutbeck and a special jury heard the case of Roberts v. The London County Council, a claim for about £33,000 as compensation in respect of the freehold interest in the premises Nos. 268, 270 and 271 Strand, which have been acquired by the London County Council for the purposes of the Strand improvement. The premises Nos. 270 and 271 are in the occupation of Mr. Nutt, at £650 a year, on lease for twenty-one years from 1888 ; while No. 268 is at present vacant, the front being let as an advertising station at £130 a year. It appeared that Mr. Nutt had to expend about £1,000 on the premises as one of the conditions of the lease, and it was submitted, on behalf of the claimant, that the present rental value on the premises 270-271 Strand is £900 a year. Sir J. Whittaker Ellis valued the property Nos. 270 and 271 for the term of the lease at £6,500, and in reversion (deferred twelve years on the 3 per cent. table) at £15,700 ; and No. 268 at £310 a year (on the 5 per cent. table), £7,750; a total of £29,950, to which he added 10 per cent. for compulsory sale, making £32,945, to which one year's rent of No. 268 had to be added as a *solatium* for the interference with the letting of the property subsequent to the date of the notice to treat. On behalf of the London County Council the rental in the lease of Nos. 270-271 was stated to be full, and the reversionary rental as not more than £700, while the rental of No. 268 was estimated at £200. From this there was a deduction for repairs, and the total valuations averaged £21,600. The jury awarded the claimant the sum of £25,850, plus one year's rent of No. 268, making a total of £26,100.

## STOCKPORT SEWERAGE WORKS.

In the presence of a number of members of the Stockport Corporation, a trial was recently made of the engines and pumps just completed at the sewage outfall works, now almost completed, on the Cheadle side of the river at Heaton Mersey. For the past four years, says *The Manchester Guardian,* the work of constructing a main intercepting sewer has been in progress. It is equal to 7 ft. diameter through the town, and runs to a depth of 60 ft. in the red sandstone rock, crossing under the river three times, twice by inverted syphons. A peculiar difficulty was met with in a number of tunnels, 5 ft. to 6 ft. square, formed many years ago for the purpose of conveying water from the upper reaches of the river to the mills in the valley, and which crossed the route of the sewer at almost the same level. For the purpose of treating the sewage to be conveyed by this sewer the corporation purchased 95 acres of land, of which 60 acres are now under construction into filtration areas of 5 or 6 acres each, for the purposes of intermittent filtration after the sewage has passed through the tanks and been treated with lime for purification and precipitation. There are eight tanks, each covering an area of 120 ft. by 60 ft.

#### THE MACHINERY.

It is necessary to raise the sewage from the sewer to the tanks, and the machinery for this purpose, which was set in motion last week as a trial, comprises two boilers constructed by Mr. T. Oldham, Heaton Norris, and capable of a pressure of 200 lb. to the square inch, and a pair of horizontal compound double-crank jet-condensing engines and pumps, erected by Mr. J. H. Gwynne, of London, known as the "Invincible," and each pump capable of lifting 18,000 gallons per minute 19 ft. high, having a 27-in. suction.

Mr. A. M. Fowler, the engineer, under whose direction the works have been carried out at a cost so far of some £140,000, expressed satisfaction with the working of the machinery. He said there had been great difficulty in obtaining a supply of water for the engines for condensing purposes and for general use on the sewage outfall works. A well sunk 25 ft. failed to yield sufficient supply. A borehole was then carried to a depth of 240 ft. into the red sandstone and produced 5,000 gallons per hour, and the problem of lifting the water to the top of the buildings without placing machinery outside the main structure was solved by pneumatic action. The borehole was sealed at the top, having been lined with iron pipe, and a small pipe, 3 in. diameter, was put down inside the larger pipes and the water forced up. The air engine which effects this result will also be used for pressing the mud and for other purposes. Messrs. Hughes & Lancaster, of Westminster, put down this apparatus, which is said to be novel in this district. The engineer further expressed strong hopes of being able to produce a satisfactory effluent.

# Parliamentary Memoranda.

On Thursday, in the House of Lords, the Southampton Gas Bill and the Maldon Water Bill were each read a third time and passed.

*The Local Government (Ireland) Bill.*—This Bill was read a second time, after a three hours' debate and without a division. Lord Ashbourne, in moving the reading, expressed an earnest hope that all classes and all interests in Ireland would loyally combine to work out its provisions to the best of their ability. That hope was strengthened, among other things, by the desire shown by many of the loading and experienced country gentlemen who had long taken part in the administration of the grand jury system, and he sincerely trusted that the proposals embodied in the Bill would be found to operate with fairness and justness to all concerned.

In the House of Commons the Lords' amendments to the Matlock Urban District Council Bill and the Tottenham and Edmonton Gas Bill were agreed to. The following Bills from the Lords were read the third time: Felixstowe and Walton Water Bill and the Newton Water Bill. The Chelsea Electric Supply Bill was read a second time.

In the House of Lords on Friday the Clacton-on-Sea Gas and Water Bill was read a third time and passed.

In the House of Commons the Lords' amendments to the following Bills were agreed to: Blackburn Corporation (Tramways, &c.) Bill, Bristol Tramways (Electrical Power, &c.) Bill, Bristol Tramways (Extensions) Bill, and Plymouth and Stonehouse Gas Bill. The Newhaven Harbour Bill was read the third time (Queen's consent, on behalf of the Crown to be signified).

On Monday the House of Lords met at 3 o'clock, to hear the Royal assent given by commission to several Bills which had passed both Houses. When the Speaker and the House of Commons appeared at the bar the Royal assent was given to the following private Acts: The Local Government Board's Provisional Orders Confirmation (Nos. 4 to 12) Acts, Gas Orders Confirmation (No. 1 and 2) Acts, Edinburgh Improvement Scheme Provisional Order Confirmation Act, Local Government Board (Ireland) Provisional Orders Confirmation (No. 3) Act, Leith Burgh Provisional Order Confirmation Act, Electric Lighting Orders Confirmation (Nos. 6, 10, 11 and 14) Acts, Pier and Harbour Orders Confirmation (No. 1) Act, Local Government Board's Provisional Orders Confirmation (Gas) Act, Local Government Board's Provisional Orders Confirmation (Housing of the Working Classes) Act, Aberdeen Corporation (Tramways) Act, Staines Reservoirs Act, Belfast Harbour Act, Blackpool Improvement Act, Sheringham Gas and Water Act, Carmarthen Improvement Act, Northern Urban District Water Act, North Warwickshire Water Act, Gainsborough Gas Act, Southend Waterworks Act, Southwark and Vauxhall Water Act, Yeovil Corporation Act, Ilford Improvement Act, Cranbrook District Water Act, Crawley and District Water Act, East Ham Improvement Act, Wishaw Water (Additional Supply) Act, Liskeard Corporation Act, Norwich Electric Tramways Act, Cardiff Corporation Act, Dundee Corporation (Tramways) Act, Cromer Gas Act, Droghedn (Corporation) Gas Act, Dover Harbour Act, London Building Act, 1894 (Amendment) Act, Plymouth Corporation Act, Stirling Gas Act, London County Council (Acton Sewage) Act, Halifax Corporation Act, Folkestone Water Act, City of Norwich Waterworks Act, Blackpool and Fleetwood Tramroad Act, Hamilton Water Act, Kettering Water Act, Kew Bridge Act, Bacup Corporation Water Act, Higham and Hundred of Hoo Water (Amendment) Act, Dublin Southern District Tramways Act, Newtock Urban District Council Act, Tottenham and Edmonton Gas Act, Felixstowe and Walton Water Act, Newtown Water Act, Blackburn Corporation (Tramways, &c.) Act, Bristol Tramways (Electrical Power, &c.) Act, Bristol Tramways (Extensions) Act, Plymouth and Stonehouse Gas Act, and the Newhaven and Seaford Sea Defences Act. The ordinary business was then proceeded with. The Burnley Corporation (Tramways, &c.) Bill was read the third time. The House then went into committee on the Local Government (Ireland) Bill. After considerable discussion, the Bill, with several amendments, was reported to the House, and yesterday was fixed for the report stage.

In the House of Commons the Clontarf and Hill of Howth Tramroad Bill and the Tynemouth Corporation Water Bill were read the third time and passed with amendments. The Electric Lighting Provisional Orders (No. 12) Bill was considered, and also read the third time and passed.

On Tuesday, in the House of Lords, the Liverpool Corporation Bill, the London County Council (Money) Bill and the Middlesex County Council Bill were read the third time. Lord Windsor intimated that he did not intend to proceed with the Public Libraries Bill, which was down for second reading.

In the House of Commons the Newhaven and Seaford Water Bill was considered, with amendments, and ordered to be read the third time. The Electric Lighting Provisional Orders (Nos. 7 and 8) Bills were read a second time and committed, and the Lords' amendments to the Locomotives on Highways Bill were considered and agreed to. Mr. Hanbury introduced a new Bill to transfer to the commissioners of the township of Kingstown certain roads and lands now vested in the Commissioners of Kingstown Harbour, and for other purposes. The Bill was read a first time.

On Wednesday, in the House of Commons, the Buckie (Clury) Harbour Bill was read a third time and passed, with amendments, together with the Pier and Harbour Provisional Orders (No. 2) Bill, the Tramways Orders Confirmation (No. 2) Bill and the Water Orders Confirmation Bill. The Electric Lighting Provisional Orders (No. 5) Bill and the Tramways Orders Confirmation (No. 1) Bill, as amended, were considered and ordered to be read the third time yesterday.

### PRIVATE BILLS IN COMMITTEE.

*London United Tramways Bill*—When the Bill promoted by the London United Tramways Company recently came before a committee of the House of Lords, presided over by Lord Ribblesdale, the London County Council did not appear as opponents. The negotiations that had taken place with that authority had resulted in an understanding by which both the overhead and underground systems of electric traction were to be tested side by side, and thus the council were satisfied. The Bill was presented in the modified form in which it had passed the Commons. It provided that the company should be empowered to extend their existing lines from Kew bridge to Hounslow, through Brentford, along the Chiswick high road, and from Brentford along the Boston road to Hanwell, and to introduce electricity throughout the whole of the system. The Bill was again opposed by the Middlesex County Council, but the point in dispute related to the contributions of the company to local authorities in respect of the maintenance of roads. The committee passed the Bill, but decided that any contributions received by the local authorities from the company should be handed over to the Middlesex County Council. In the case of Chiswick it was decided that an apportionment should be agreed upon between the district council and the county council.

*Marylebone and Bermondsey Electric Lighting Bills.*—Underlying the Bills promoted by the vestries of Marylebone and Bermondsey for the confirmation of the provisional orders granted by the Board of Trade to enable them to undertake the supply of electricity within their district was an important principle which the House of Commons Committee presided over by Sir A. F. Godson have decided against the vestries. Incidentally, the decision arrived at implies a censure on the Board of Trade. Not long ago the principle itself was raised in the House of Commons by Mr. Cripps, Q.C., the member for Stroud, who severely condemned the Board of Trade for authorising indiscriminate competition, by granting two or more provisional orders to companies and local authorities operating within the same area. Companies are at present in existence which have obtained powers to supply the districts in question with electricity mainly for the purpose of lighting, and now the vestries came forward with provisional orders empowering them to establish competitive services. The Board of Trade had passed the provisional orders, and Mr. Cripps characterised this as in substance expropriation without compensation, and declared it to be a serious and dangerous infringement of the recognised principle of security that every man should be compensated before his property, and particularly property guaranteed by an Act of Parliament, could be attacked or depreciated. Mr. Ritchie, in defending the department of which he is the ministerial head, had no hesitation in saying that, had the Board of Trade not acted as they did, they would not have met the approval of Parliament. How far he was right will be seen from the sequel. The Bill of the Marylebone Vestry was opposed before the committee by the Metropolitan Electric Supply Corporation, who at present supply the district with electricity. Mr. Worsley Taylor, Q.C., the counsel for the promoters, put the issue very clearly before the committee. There were two questions to consider—whether there should be an alternative system of supply by somebody, and whether that somebody should be the local authority. He urged, of course, the value of competition, which would secure an advantage to the consumer and a regulation price, as well as the additional advantage of a different system. The vestry had received applications from two companies to obtain their sanction to supply electricity, but they thought it better to undertake the supply themselves. Mr. T. Brooke Hitching, L.C.C., chairman of the Electric Lighting Committee of the Marylebone Vestry, who gave evidence in support of the Bill, stated that he considered competition would lead to a better light and lower price. Mr. Balfour Browne, Q.C., on behalf of the company, who had expended £320,000 on their electric system in the district, contended that a report of Sir F. Marindeu and a letter of the Board of Trade proved that they had never contemplated the competition of a local authority with an established company. In the case of two rival companies the board had advised that these should not be of the same system. In the case of gas and water companies Parliament had distinctly refused to allow the local authority to take powers unless they purchased the rights of the company in possession. The company had a capital of £782,500, and if the committee granted powers to the vestry the result would be that at the end of forty-two years the undertaking would be of no value. Sir John Lubbock, M.P, called on behalf of the opponents, expressed the opinion that there had been an understanding that the agreement with the vestry would secure them against competition from the local authority. Mr. F. Bailey, managing director of the company, and Mr. R. Hammond, consulting electrical engineer, gave evidence to the same effect. The committee decided that they would not confirm the provisional order. The Bermondsey case differed from the Marylebone in this respect. The opposing company—the London Electric Supply Corporation—had not supplied a single unit of electrical energy within their area, although they had been established in 1889. The main trunk had been laid, but this had been done for the supply of the district beyond the parish. The vestry had applied for the electric light to be furnished to their public buildings, the town hall and the public library, without success, and they had, therefore, determined to undertake a separate supply. Mr. Robert Stewart Bain, the managing director of the company, stated that since 1892 they had not had a single demand for the supply of electric light in Bermondsey. Of the 3,000,000 or 4,000,000 lamps which they supplied only 1,462 were in Bermondsey. The committee, after consultation, suggested that the order should be withdrawn, as the point raised in it was not ripe for discussion. They were of opinion that the local authority should consider the question in the light of purchase. They thought that if by an original order, or by purchase, any local authority became the sole power for electric lighting in their district they should not be interfered with by competitors from the granting of a provisional order to any company in the district. Mr. Littler, Q.C., who represented the vestry, intimated that they would like to take the view of the company as to purchase and get the order, so as to save expense. Mr. Pembroke Stephens, Q.C., stated, on behalf of the company, that if an agreement as to the purchase of the works was arrived at the vestry could get an unopposed order next year. There the matter rests. After giving the Bermondsey Vestry and the London Electric Corporation an opportunity for negotiation, Sir A. F. Godson's committee resumed consideration on Thursday of the Bill to confirm the provisional order in the case of Bermondsey. The committee had suggested that the order should be withdrawn until next session, but they were willing to postpone the question, so that the vestry might consider the advisability of acquiring the company's undertaking by purchase. They had laid down that a local authority, becoming by purchase or otherwise the sole electric lighting authority in a district, should be protected from competition. On Thursday Mr. Littler, Q.C., on behalf of the vestry, offered to insert a clause in the Bill by which that authority would only be able to exercise the powers conferred upon them after acquiring by purchase the mains and works already laid down by the company, the terms to be fixed by arbitration, and the company's powers of supply to altogether cease on the completion of the purchase. Mr. Pembroke Stephens, for the company, argued that the matter should not be allowed to proceed further. • After listening to the arguments advanced and deliberating in private, the committee decided to confirm the order with the additional clause submitted.

*Newhaven and Seaford Water Bill.*—When the session began there were two Bills before Parliament in which powers were sought to supply Newhaven and Seaford with water. The first, and in some respects the more important of the two, never reached the committee stage. It was defeated on technical objections, taken as to non-compliance with standing orders. It provided for the constitution and incorporation of a water board for the urban districts of Newhaven and Seaford and the rural district of Newhaven Union, for the transfer to the board of the undertaking of the Newhaven and Seaford Water Company, Limited, for the construction of additional waterworks and supply of water within the prescribed limits, and for powers to raise £93,000. This Bill was promoted by the three local authorities named, but objection was raised to it by the Newhaven and Seaford Water Company, Limited, on the ground that the opinion of the ratepayers had not been taken with regard to the scheme, and the objection was fatal. The other Bill was submitted by the Newhaven and Seaford Water Company, who came to Parliament for powers to dissolve the present company and re-incorporate it, with powers to construct additional waterworks and supply water within extended limits, and to raise £25,000 new capital. This measure was very vigorously opposed before a House of Commons committee, presided over by Sir A. F. Godson, on Monday by the urban district councils of Newhaven and Seaford. The company, it appeared, had promoted a similar Bill last year, but it had been rejected on the strength of expert evidence, called on behalf of the district councils, to prove that a new well which they proposed to sink in the chalk beds would not yield a sufficient supply of pure and wholesome water to meet the requirements of the district. Since last year, however, the company had under the statutory powers they already possessed purchased the site for the new well, at the place proposed in last year's Bill, constructed the well, and had found that it yielded an abundant supply of excellent water. Up to the last two years the company had been drawing 220,000 gallons a day, but since the new well had been sunk they had proved that they could draw up to 700,000 gallons. They had stopped up the old Farmhouse

well, to which exception had been taken, so that it should not contaminate the new source of supply. The new well had been sunk at a cost of £11,000. The company, while fairly prosperous, had not paid exceptionally large dividends. For the first two years after its establishment in 1881 it had paid no dividend, but after that time the dividends went on increasing until it paid 6 per cent. The average dividend paid since the waterworks started was 3 per cent. It was contended by the opposing councils that the site of the new well was objectionable by reason of its proximity to the sea; that, like the existing Farmhouse well, the water would in time become impure by reason of the excess of saline, and that a sufficient supply could not be depended upon. The district councils sought the insertion of a clause in the Bill to compel the company to agree to the purchase of the undertaking by the proposed water board, to which reference has already been made, the price, failing agreement, to be fixed by an arbitrator. The clause stipulated, however, that no compensation should be given to the company for any works they might construct after July, 1897, thus debarring the company from the recoupment of their outlay in connection with the construction of the new works. Mr. Robert Lamb, the chairman of the Newhaven and Seaford Water Company, sketched the history of the company, and stated that the authorised capital amounted to £30,000. They had still £7,400 of the capital they were authorised to raise unissued. Mr. F. T. Courtney, M.I.C.E., Mr. Hawkesley, M.I.C.E., Prof. Boyd Dawkins, and Mr. Whitaker, the well-known geologist, gave evidence to the effect that the site selected was the best that could possibly be chosen to supply Newhaven on the one side and Seaford on the other, that the water from the new well was absolutely pure, that the well was capable of supplying from 1,000,000 to 2,000,000 gallons per day, and that there was no danger of an inflow of salt water so long as they did not over-pump. The district councils brought forward a large amount of engineering evidence, with a view to showing that the new well sunk by the company at Poverty Bottom was, by reason of its proximity to the sea, liable to be contaminated by salt water. Among the witnesses called were Mr. Archibald Millar, M.I.C.E., Mr. Henry Rolfe, M.I.C.E., and Mr. E. S. Burstall, M.I.C.E., who had all inspected the well and the site of the new reservoir, and they declared that it was inevitable that some time or other—it might be years or it might be months—when the sea level was reached by the pumping operations that the promoters should come in contact with salt water. The committee passed the Bill, but inserted a clause providing that the local authorities might acquire the undertaking by compulsory purchase at a price to be fixed by an arbitrator. It was provided, however, that the arbitrator should take into consideration the works executed under the Bill and under the former statutory powers of the company.

*London County Council General Powers Bill.*—The London County Council encountered a good deal of opposition in connection with the promotion of their General Powers Bill, an omnibus measure, providing for a variety of improvements. The improvements contemplated included the construction of a new street in continuation of Roehampton-street, Westminster, the widening of York-road, Battersea, and the Albert Embankment, and the reconstruction of the Rosemary Branch bridge of the Regent's canal. The petitioners against the Bill, when it came the other day before a committee of the House of Lords, presided over by Lord Ribblesdale, were the Wandsworth District Board of Works, the South London Tramways Company, and Mr. R. R. Fairbairn and other watermen. Sir Alexander Binnie, the chief engineer to the London County Council, stated that all the improvements proposed in the Bill were very necessary in the public interest. The Bill was passed, but clauses were inserted giving protection to various interests, particularly those of the tramway company.

*Portsmouth Corporation Tramway Bill.*—The Bill promoted by the Corporation of Portsmouth for the acquisition of the tramway system of the town was passed by a committee of the House of Commons, presided over by the chairman of Ways and Means, on Tuesday. After a comparatively smooth passage through the Lords the measure was threatened with serious opposition in the Commons. This opposition was led by Mr. A. W. White, the chief promoter of the Cosham Light Railway. He objected to a clause extending the powers of the Portsmouth Town Council over the Cosham section of the line for seven years beyond the period when the Cosham Parish Council could acquire it at valuation. This clause was inserted to protect the interests of the ratepayers of Portsmouth, who will incur an expenditure of some thousands of pounds in the equipment of the line for electric traction, and it was considered to be manifestly unfair that almost immediately after the completion of this work the Cosham Parish Council should have the right to step in and take possession at the price of old metal. Rather than this, the corporation were determined that if the opposition were not withdrawn the electrical equipment of the Cosham line should not be proceeded with. Mr. White's real object was to force the hands of the corporation, so that they would have to give him a connection at Cosham between their system and the light railway, and also to give him many powers over their lines to North End. The corporation had no objection to make arrangements with the Light Railway Company later on, but they declined to be bound hand and foot to the adaptation of their system to the light railway. Mr. White, having failed to obtain the support of the Fareham Rural District Council, withdrew his opposition almost at the last moment, and the Bill went through.

*Gas Light and Coke Company's Bill and London County Council.*—The Bill promoted by the Gas Light and Coke Company for the conversion and consolidation of their capital had again to face the opposition of the London County Council before a select committee of the House of Lords presided over by the Earl of Camperdown, an opposition which it will be remembered was unsuccessful in the Lower House. The company in the Bill sought powers to consolidate and convert the existing stock into 4 per cent. consolidated preference stock, 3½ per cent. maximum stock, ordinary stock with a standard rate of dividend of 4 per cent and 3 per cent. consolidated debenture stock. The county council in their petition raised the question of the price of gas charged by the company to North London consumers as compared with that fixed by the South Metropolitan Gas Company and other companies in the south of London. It was explained, on behalf of the promoters, that the proposed conversion would make the stock a tangible and useful investment stock for small holders, readily realisable and marketable. By fixing the price to be charged for gas and applying the sliding scale in regard to dividends, Parliament had made the consumer predominant partner with the company in any economy secured in the production of gas. The sliding scale had operated enormously to the advantage of the consumer, by cheapening gas. Were the price raised the company would be obliged to decrease the dividend; were the price lowered the dividend could be increased above the 10 per cent. fixed in their Act. The company, with a standard price of 3s. 9d., were now charging 3s. per 1,000 cubic feet, and the last dividend was 12½ per cent. Before the company was compelled to fix the price at 3s., and thereby come under the penalty of smaller dividends imposed by the sliding scale, the stock stood in the market at £312, and it now stood at about £275. Anybody who went into the market and bought £100 of stock therefore had to pay roughly about £300 for it. It was almost unintelligible to the small investor, whom it was especially desirable to encourage, to become a holder in gas undertakings, that after paying £300 he received a certificate for only £100 of stock. The object of the Bill was to convert the stock by exactly correlative and proportionate conversion into a stock bearing a lower rate of dividend, and therefore commanding a smaller proportionate price in the market. There were at present fifteen different descriptions of gas light and coke stock on the market, and it was proposed to convert them into three descriptions of stock and a debenture stock. The operation of the sliding scale as to the price of gas would remain unchanged, and the position of the 280,000 consumers would not be affected one atom. Mr. J. W. Field, secretary and general manager of the company, stated that they wanted to get rid of the anomaly of being charged with having 12½ per cent. stock when really the investor buying shares under the auction clauses received only 4 per cent.; and they desired to get rid of the cumbrous nature of their capital account. On behalf of the County Council it was argued that the company were really asking to be allowed to put £1,800,000, or thereabout, into their pockets. Mr. H. E. Haward, comptroller of the London County Council, stated that he thought the proposed conversion would enhance the saleable value of the stock. It appeared to him that the sole object of the promoters was to make the stock more marketable, and therefore increase its price. Should the county council acquire the undertaking, the stock exchange value would indirectly affect the award of an arbitrator when fixing the purchase price. The committee passed the Bill, but inserted a clause to the effect that in the event of purchase by a public or local authority the market prices of the stock should not be taken into consideration by the arbitrator.

*Renfrew Burgh and Harbour Extension Bill.*—The House of Lords have wrecked the Bill promoted by the Corporation of Renfrew for the extension of the burgh and harbour. A committee of the House of Commons gave the measure, which provided for a considerable extension of the burgh area along the Clyde and the construction of a commodious new dock, fifteen days' patient consideration, deciding that the council should be allowed to construct the dock, but limiting the extension of the burgh to the property to be acquired for dock purposes. The Lords' Committee presided over by the Earl of Kintore threw out the Bill after four days' hearing. Some of the most powerful interests on the Clydeside came forward to oppose the measure. At the head of them was the Clyde Trust, who objected to it, as they had objected to Kilpatrick dock scheme last year, because they saw in it an attempt to subvert their authority and to put an end to their monopoly in matters affecting the navigation of the river. The Corporation of Glasgow, the Greenock Harbour Trustees, the Cart Navigation Trust, the Glasgow and South-Western Railway Company, were all hostile to the Bill. It was explained on behalf of the promoters that the burgh extension portion of the Bill might be said to have dropped, because the Committee of the House of Commons had only allowed such an extension of the burgh as was necessary to enable the dock to be enlarged, with a fair margin round it for sidings and so forth, so that the dock might be within the limits of the burgh. The Bill was therefore practically one for the

extension of the harbour. The dock was to have an area of 15 or 16 acres of water and 1,300 or 1,400 yards of quayage, furnished with all modern appliances for dealing expeditiously with the coal and iron traffic, which it was believed would form the staple trade. The corporation would also have 35 acres of land for sidings and storage a matter of very considerable importance in connection with such a project. The estimated cost of the work was rather over £200,000, and the borrowing powers were £250,000. Mr. Forman, C.E., and Sir John Wolff Barry laid the engineering details of the scheme before the committee, but Mr. Forman's evidence only took an hour and a half, whereas he sat in the witness chair two and a half days in the other House. Mr. Harper, the joint town clerk of Renfrew, gave the committee the most positive assurance that the Bill was promoted by the Corporation of Renfrew alone and that the dock would be constructed and managed by them. The petitions of the Clyde Trustees and the Corporation of Glasgow were based on the theory that they had a monopoly in the dock accommodation of the Clyde for 20 miles, and that, having regard to their enormous outlay in improving the navigation, their rights ought not to be encroached upon by rivals. Lord Provost Richmond explained what the Clyde Trust had done for the river, claiming that they had been the making of it, and insisted that the new dock would seriously injure the Trust. It was not needed, inasmuch as the facilities afforded for the traffic at the existing docks were ample. Since the Kilpatrick dock scheme was thrown out last year the new Prince's dock, constructed at great cost, had been completed and opened. The Clyde Trust, he said, had 100 acres of land at Shield Hall admirably suited for dock accommodation when it should be required. They had £5,000,000 or £6,000,000 outstanding to the public, and he was of opinion that if this dock were made their bonds would be seriously affected. It was probable that if a dock were made at Renfrew it would take away part of the trade of Glasgow; but that did not prove that a dock at Renfrew was required. He firmly maintained that no outside authority should be allowed to put down a dock on territory under the jurisdiction of the Clyde Trustees. Mr. John Ure, the deputy-chairman of the trustees, declared that, so far from the harbour being congested, it was capable of doing a great deal more work than it was doing now. The Earl of Kintore, in giving the decision of the committee on Friday, said they had given the measure earnest consideration, and were unanimously of opinion that it should not be allowed to proceed.

*Rochdale Corporation Water Bill.*—After disposing of the Bury Corporation Bill, Colonel Gunter's House of Commons committee took up the measure promoted by the Corporation of Rochdale for the acquisition of the Todmorden waterworks, in pursuance of their agreement with the waterworks company for authority to construct additional works and for power to borrow £450,000 for the purposes of the undertaking. The Todmorden Corporation, the West Riding of Yorkshire County Council, the West Riding Rivers Board, the Corporation of Dewsbury and the Littleborough District Council petitioned against the Bill in the other House, but now the only opposing corporation was Littleborough. It was explained that new waterworks had become a matter of urgency in Rochdale, whose population had now increased to 107,000, and whose water service was 1,952,000 gallons per day. To meet the requirements of the town and district it was proposed to acquire the reservoir of the Todmorden Waterworks Company at Ramsden Clough, which had the storage capacity of 104,000,000, and was capable of yielding a supply of 450,000 gallons after allowing for compensation water. The capacity of the present Rochdale reservoir was 2,000,000 gallons per day, which would probably be equal to the demand for two or three years, but it was estimated that by the year 1906 not less than 2,500,000 gallons would be required to supply the town and district. Messrs. Molesworth, manufacturers, whose water supply was affected by the scheme, obtained a clause providing that, should their mills be injured by the diversion of water as the result of the new project, their property should be acquired by the corporation at valuation price. Littleborough District Council were anxious to impose such conditions upon the promoters as would entitle the smaller authority to establish a water supply of their own at some future time.

**Opening of Highgate Wood.**—The Duchess of Albany on Saturday visited Highgate, for the purpose of formally opening the Queen's Wood, which has hitherto been known as Churchyard Bottom Wood, but has received its new name in commemoration of the fact that the money required for its purchase was raised in the year of her Majesty's diamond jubilee. The wood, which forms a portion of the primæval forest of Middlesex, comprises 52 acres, and has been purchased from the Ecclesiastical Commissioners for the sum of £25,000, towards which the Hornsey Urban District Council contributed £10,000, the Middlesex County Council £5,500, the Islington Vestry £2,000, and the St. Pancras Vestry £1,000. The wood has been enclosed with a 6-ft. iron fence, and all the paths have lately been re-made. Two other pieces of land have been added to it, and a lodge and refreshment pavilion are in course of erection. The wood will be under the control of the Hornsey Urban District Council.

# For Assistants and Pupils.

## THE CONSTRUCTION OF ROADS AND STREETS.—XVI.

By WILLIAM H. MAXWELL, Assistant Engineer and Surveyor, Leyton Urban District Council.

ROAD MATERIALS AND CONSTRUCTION
*(continued).*

GRAVEL.—Gravel consists of small loose stones which have become rounded and worn by the action of water. It is found in alluvial deposits, drift, sea beaches and river beds, both recent and ancient. If free from large quantities of earthy matter and of a flinty nature it may be used for roads of very light traffic, but will require constant attention to maintain a good surface. Owing to the smooth character of the stones it is difficult to roll in, and often may be seen to move forward in a wavelike manner in front of a steam roller even when considerable quantities of binding material are used. There is no advantage therefore in using "double-screened" gravel, as the fine stuff or "hoggin" screened out must invariably be again added in the form of a "*binding material*" before the surface can be consolidated. Gravel surfaces, especially if subjected to much traffic, are seriously affected by wet weather and frost; also during the processes of scraping and scavenging large quantities of road material are unavoidably carted away.

The general remarks of Sir H. Parnell in his valuable "Treatise on Roads" will be of interest. He says: "With respect to the subject generally of road materials, it may be observed that the best descriptions consist of basalt, granite, quartz, syenite and porphyry rocks." The *whinstones* found in different parts of the United Kingdom, Guernsey *granite*, Mountsorrel and Hartshill stone of Leicestershire, and the *pebbles* of Shropshire, Staffordshire and Warwickshire are among the best of the stones now commonly in use. The *whinstone* stones will make smooth roads, being of a slaty and argillaceous structure, but are rapidly destroyed when wet by the pressure of wheels, and occasion great expense in scraping and constantly laying on new coatings. *Limestone* is defective in the same respect. It wears rapidly away when wet, and therefore when the traffic is very great it is an expensive material. *Sandstone* is much too weak for the surface of a road; it will never make a hard one, but it is very well adapted to the purpose of a foundation pavement. *Flints* vary very much in quality as a road material. The hardest of them are nearly as good as the best limestone, but the softer kinds are quickly crushed by the wheels of carriages and make heavy and dirty roads. *Gravel*, when it consists of pebbles of the hard sorts of stones, is a good material, particularly when the pebbles are so large as to admit of their being broken; but when it consists of limestone, sandstone or flint it is a very bad one, for it wears so rapidly that the crust of a road made with it always consists of a large portion of the earthy matter to which it is reduced. This prevents the gravel from becoming consolidated, and renders a road made with it extremely defective with respect to that perfect hardness which it ought to have."

"*Coefficients of quality*" for various road materials have been obtained by the engineers of the French Administration des Ponts et Chaussées'. The quality was assumed to be in inverse proportion to the quantity consumed on a length of road with the same traffic, and measurements of traffic and wear were systematically made to arrive at correct results. These processes requiring great care and considerable time, direct experiments on resistance to crushing and to rubbing and collision have also been made on 673 samples of road materials of all kinds. The coefficients obtained by these experiments, which were found to agree fairly well with those arrived at by actual wear in the roads, are summarised in the following table. The coefficient 20 is equivalent to 'excellent,' 10 to 'sufficiently good,' and 5 to 'bad.' "†

| Material. | Coefficient of Wear. | Coefficient of Crushing. |
|---|---|---|
| Basalt ... ... | 12·5 to 24·2 | 12·1 to 16·00 |
| Porphyry ... ... | 14·1 to 22·9 | 8·3 to 16·3 |
| Gneiss ... ... | 10·3 to 19 | 13·4 to 14·8 |
| Granite ... ... | 7·3 to 18 | 7·7 to 15·8 |
| Syenite ... ... | 11·6 to 12·7 | 12·4 to 13·00 |
| Slag ... ... | 14·5 to 15·3 | 7·2 to 11·1 |
| Quartzite ... ... | 13·8 to 30 | 12·3 to 21·6 |
| Quartzose sandstone | 14·3 to 26·2 | 9·9 to 16·6 |
| Quartz ... ... | 12·9 to 17·8 | 12·3 to 13·2 |
| Silex ... ... | 9·8 to 21·3 | 14·2 to 17·6 |
| Chalk flints ... ... | 3·5 to 16·8 | 17·8 to 25·5 |
| Limestone ... ... | 6·6 to 15·7 | 6·5 to 13·5 |

The breaking of stone for road metal is either effected by

* *Porphyry* is a term used somewhat loosely to designate a rock consisting of a fine-grained base (usually feldspathic) which crystals, as of feldspar or quartz, are disseminated. There are red, purple and green varieties which are highly esteemed as marbles.—Webster's "International Dictionary."
† "Encyclopædia Britannica," art. "Roads and Streets."

hand or by *machine*. Hand-broken stone makes the best roadways, as machines crush the material and do not turn it out in fairly uniform and cubical pieces as required for road coatings. There are also large quantities of small stuff, that separated by the revolving screen being, however, frequently used as "binding." The tendency of stone-breaking machines is to deliver large quantities of material of a very irregular pyramidal form, a difficulty which has not yet been overcome. Long, thin or flaky pieces of stone may pass several times through a machine before being broken fit for road material. The cost of breaking a hard tough-stone by machine is about 1s. per ton, whilst the same work performed by manual labour costs from 2s. to 2s. 6d. per ton.* Prof. Rankine states that "the stone-breaking machine of Messrs. Blake breaks stone into cubes of about 1½ in. in the side, with an expenditure of power at the rate of from 1 horse-power to 1½ horse-power for each cubic yard broken per hour." Mr. A. M. Fowler speaks of have found great difficulty in making good roads with a steam roller and stones broken by Blake's machine, as they were not sufficiently cubical, although they did very well for the bottom.†

The wear and tear of stone-breaking machines is very considerable, and, in a case described‡ by Mr. Arthur Jacob, B.A., M.I.C.E., the actual repairs cost £124 in twelve months, representing 62½ per cent. of the original price of the machine.

"A good stone-breaker will break 2 cubic yards of hard limestone to the ordinary gauge in a day, and some men will break more. Hard silicoous stones and igneous rocks can only be broken at a rate of 1½ or of 1 cubic yard per day. Of some of the toughest, such as Guernsey granite, a man can only break on an average half a cubic yard per day. River gravel, field stones, or flints, which are already of a small size, can be broken at the rate of 3 or 4 cubic yards per day."§

As 55 per cent. of broken road metal is solid the weight of a cubic yard can be calculated as follows:—

$$W \times 27 \times ·55 = \text{weight of a cubic yard broken for road metal,}$$

W being the weight of a cubic foot of the stone.

Mr. D. Kinnear Clark, M.I.C.E., gives the following rules‖:

(*a*) *To find the area of surface that can be covered by 1 ton of broken granite, when the thickness of the layer is given:* divide 32 by the thickness of the layer, in inches, *unrolled*; or, divide 24 by the thickness of the layer, in inches, when *rolled*. The quotient is the area in square yards.

(*b*) *To find the area of surface that can be covered by 1 cubic yard of broken granite, when the thickness of the layer is given:* When the metal is *not* rolled, divide 36 by the thickness in inches; the quotient is the number of square yards that can be covered. When the metal is *rolled*, divide 27 by the final thickness, in inches, to give the required quotient.

The specific gravity of granites vary from 2·60 to 3·00, the volume of *a ton* equals from 12 to 14 cubic feet, and the weight of a cubic yard of solid granite is from 1·93 to 2·25 tons, or about 2 tons on the average. A cubic foot equals about 1½ cwt.

Granite absorbs on an average 10 lb. (a gallon) of water per cubic yard, or about 1/10th of its weight.

Various opinions have been entertained as to the proper size to which stones should be broken for road metal. Ordinarily the stone is reduced, by means of a steel-faced hammer, to pieces approximating to a cubicle shape and weighing not more than 6 oz.,¶ which is the average weight of a cube of stone measuring 1·6 in. on its side.

Mr. Boulnois states[1] that "an old method of ganging used to be 'such a size as the stone-breaker could put in his mouth,' but this was a *varying gauge* and unsatisfactory to all persons concerned, and 'to pass all ways through a ring of 2½ in. internal diameter' is now the size very often adopted."

Telford specified road metal to be such that the largest piece should pass through a ring 2½ in. diameter, a mode of ganging which is certainly more convenient in practice than that of weighing, and has therefore become general.

In connection with the subject of the size or weight of materials to be used, the observations of Mr. E. B. Ellice-Clark, M.I.C.E., made at a meeting of municipal engineers at Hanley, in 1886, will be of interest:—

"Some difference of opinion exists as to the sizes to which stone should be reduced for metalling a road. There is a prevailing opinion that all stones should be broken to pass a

* The actual prices must, of course, vary with the nature of the stone and the value of the labour.
† "Proceedings of the Association of Municipal and County Engineers," vol. i., p. 167.
‡ "Proceedings of the Association of Municipal and County Engineers," vol. ii., p. 82.
§ "The Maintenance of Macadamised Roads," by T. Codrington.
‖ *Vide* "Roads and Streets," by Law and Clark.
¶ Mr. Macadam required his road inspectors to carry a small pair of scales to test the weight of stones to be used upon his roads.
[1] "Municipal Engineers' Hand-Book."
[2] *Vide* "Proceedings of the Association of Municipal and County Engineers," vol. xii.

gauge of 1½ in. The writer ventures to express the opinion that this is an error. All the hardest stone, like granite, trap, rock, basalt, the Devonshire dolerite and similar rocks, should be broken to a smaller gauge than flints and the hardest limestone, which in their turn should be broken smaller than such materials as Kentish rag and stones of a similar character. The method of specifying the dimensions of stone should be abandoned for the weight test. Macadam says : 'Every piece of stone put on to a road which exceeds 1 in. in any of its dimensions is mischievous,' and in most of his specifications he insists on no stone weighing more than 6 oz. Parnell adopts 2½ in.* for the largest dimensions. To within the past few years the latter size was very generally adopted, irrespective of the quality of the material. It has been the fashion now for upwards of half a century, when repairing roads with granite and the harder rocks, to have the stones broken as uniformly as possible. The results of this are that, though the general surface may be in good repair, the road will be full of small rises and depressions, the surfaces of which are also rough, stones rising abruptly above the general surface of the road. It is this which causes granite macadam roads to be so unsuitable for light-springed vehicles, and as cyclists use. The author has recently been led to investigate the cause of complaints arising from cyclists when travelling over what was apparently a well-kept road, and he has come to the conclusion that it is of as much importance to have stones of different sizes as it is to have a maximum size. The proportion of different sizes requires yet to be determined. So far as his investigations have gone, he gives the following as closely approximating upon the proper proportions of sizes :—

|  | Maximum Weight. | Minimum Weight. |
|---|---|---|
|  | oz. | oz. |
| Granite and similar rocks ... | 3½ | ½ |
| Flints and similar stones ... | 5 | ¾ |
| Limestones and similar stones ... | 6 | 1 |

One-half of the total quantity to be of the maximum weight, one-eighth of the minimum weight, the remaining three-eighths to be composed of stones varying between the maximum and minimum. This brings us to the question of *binding materials.* A road formed of different-sized stones will require no binding materials. In a former paper on this subject, published ten years ago, the author stated his conviction that the 'decadence of modern roads commenced with the using of binding material,' the introduction of which was coincident with the use of stones broken to a uniform size. Longer experience has confirmed this, and, though in practice he is compelled to use materials to bind (?) roads, he does so very sparingly, and only because of the inability to obtain materials broken to various sizes in sufficient quantity. If the demand is, however, generally set up for proportions of different-sized stones, the necessary quantities will soon find their way into the market."

Mr. Thomas Codrington writes† : " The stone for a *new road* should pass a 2½-in. ring ; for *repairs* 2½-in. or 2-in. ring. . . . Broken road material contains 55 per cent. solid stone to 45 per cent. of void space. Specimens of good road surfaces weigh from 93 per cent. to 95 per cent. of the weight of the solid stone of which they are made. In the coating of a well-maintained road the proportion of stones of various sizes varies, but generally from one-third to one-half is found to consist of detritus under ¾-in. in diameter, and there is a very constant proportion of about one-fifth of mud and detritus under ⅟₁₀ in. in diameter. This appears to be the amount necessary to fill the voids between the fragments of stone when compacted together. In an ill-kept road, from which the mud is not removed, the proportion of detritus is much higher, and mud may constitute nearly one-half of the coating. In proportion, as the detritus and mud are kept down to the minimum by constant removal from the surface, so will the road be able to resist the action of wet and frost and the wear of the traffic."

*Construction.*—Generally speaking, there are three classes of macadamised roads—*viz.*,—

(1) Roads as constructed by Mr. Macadam, consisting simply of a coating of broken stone laid upon the natural ground.

(2) Roads as constructed by Mr. Telford, with the distinguished feature of a " *pitched foundation* " upon which to lay the " *metalling.*"

(3) Roads having a *concrete foundation*, as used by Sir J. Macneill, on the Highgate Archway (London) road.

The class of road, quality and thickness of materials, to be adopted in any particular situation will necessarily depend upon the circumstances of the case, and the amount and nature of the traffic accommodated must also be kept prominently in mind in determining upon the details of its construction. There can be no model type of road which can be fitly adopted universally. For a park or pleasure garden it will generally be sufficient to form the roads or drives by simply shaping the earth to a curved contour and covering it with 3 in. or 4 in. of fine gravel, hand rolled ; for an ordinary country road, with a comparatively small amount of traffic, a

* " Treatise on Roads."
† *Vide* " Encyclopædia Britannica," art. " Roads and Streets."

coating of about 9 in. of broken stone, laid upon the natural ground properly shaped, will be adequate; whilst for main roads between large towns and all roads having a considerable amount of traffic a solid pitched foundation with a good coating of about 9 in. of broken granite will be necessary, in order that the road may be as hard and durable as possible, so that loads may be conveyed over it with a minimum expenditure of traction power, which should be the main object to be aimed at in all road-making operations.

## ELECTRIC LIGHTING AT BURY ST. EDMUNDS.

### INQUIRY BY THE LOCAL GOVERNMENT BOARD.

Mr. H. Percy Boulnois recently held an inquiry, on behalf of the Local Government Board, with reference to an application of the Bury St. Edmunds Town Council for sanction to a loan of £20,000 for electric lighting purposes. Mr. J. C. Smith, the borough surveyor, and Mr. Medhurst, the electrical engineer, attended in support of the application.

In opening the inquiry, Mr. Blofeld, who appeared on behalf of the town council, said that in October, 1895, the council appointed a committee, composed of the leading business men of position and capacity in the town, to consider the subject of electrically lighting the town. One of the first steps taken was to visit Bedford, and the committee were so pleased with the system of electric lighting there that they instructed the engineer of those works, Mr. Medhurst, to prepare a scheme for Bury. Mr. Medhurst did so, and the learned counsel went on to summarise the principal points of the scheme. The charge for the light was to be 6d. per unit, which would make it cheaper than gas at 3s. 6d., which the people of the town were paying. The estimated consumption in the first instance was 80,000 units, which would bring in a revenue of £2,000; and the engineer was careful to point out that the revenue would increase in a much greater ratio than the working expenses.

In 1896 application was made for a provisional order, which was obtained in due time without any objection being raised with regard to it by any inhabitant, a fact upon which counsel commented strongly. Reading over the sections of this order, Mr. Blofeld stopped to make an explanation of public importance. Many persons were under the impression, he said, that if they did not live within the area to be compulsorily lighted by such an order they could not obtain the light, and would therefore derive no benefit from it. But that was a mistake. If any six owners or occupiers in any street or part of a street within the whole district applied for the electric light the undertakers were bound to supply it. On December 14, 1897, the council passed a resolution to apply to the Local Government Board to borrow £20,000 in order to carry out the scheme finally approved and adopted. So far as this affected public lighting, the facts were that there were now 323 gas lamps, which cost the town £583 a year, including a calculation for interest on the £2,500 advanced to the gas company, and that under the electric lighting system there would be six arc lamps and 420 incandescent lamps, which would cost £498. As a matter of fact, Mr. Blofeld said, the lighting of the town was at present very insufficient.

After evidence had been given by several members of the council,

Mr. MEDHURST was called, and explained his scheme at some length. Upon the calculation that 80,000 units could be produced at 3d. per unit and sold at 6d., the estimate showed a nett profit of £229 10s. This allowed for £1,100 expenditure on interest and sinking fund, and £510 receipts on the public lighting service, plus 75 per cent. for interest on the £2,500. Witness instanced a number of towns in which electric lighting schemes were carried on at a gross profit.

Mr. EGERTON SAYER, distributing electrical engineer to the Hampstead Vestry, was also examined with regard to the cost of the proposed scheme at Bury. He gave figures in detail which differed materially from those of Mr. Medhurst, making out that the total annual cost of lighting the town by electricity would be something like £1,587. The actual increase of expenditure, as compared with the old system, would be at least £800 a year in the opinion of this witness. In cross-examination, Mr. Sayer modified some of his figures. He accepted Mr. Blofeld's interrogatory statement that there were two authorities upon the point—Mr. Preece and Mr. Arthur Wright. Mr. Medhurst might have adopted the views of the first-named expert ; witness himself took the authority of Mr. Wright, believing that he was right.

Several other minor witnesses were examined and the inquiry closed.

**Sheffield.**—A statement has been prepared showing the cost of the site, erection and furnishing of the new town hall. This shows that the site, which consists of 6,412 square yards, was purchased for £49,000, the cost of erection was £110,032 10s. 7d., and the cost of furnishing £22,196 4s. 10d., making a total of £181,228 15s. 5d. This is £12,110 15s. 5d. in excess of the money that the corporation have power to borrow for the town hall, and the Improvement Committee now recommend that the city council apply to the Local Government Board for their sanction to the borrowing of £12,000, the balance of £110 15s. 5d. to be raised out of the borough rate.

# Law Notes.

EDITED BY J. B. REIGNIER CONDER, 11 Old Jewry Chambers, E.C.,
Solicitor of the Supreme Court.

*The Editor will be pleased to answer any questions affecting the practice of engineers and surveyors to local authorities. Queries (which should be written legibly on foolscap paper, one side only) should be addressed to "The Law Editor," at the Offices of THE*

*SURVEYOR. Where possible, copies of local Acts or documents referred to should be enclosed. All explanatory diagrams must be drawn and lettered in black ink only. Correspondents who do not wish their names published should furnish a nom de plume.*

TRAMWAY COMPANY: LEASE FROM LOCAL AUTHORITY: COVENANT TO INDEMNIFY FROM "ALL EXPENSES WHATEVER": LIABILITY FOR RATES AND TAXES.—The decision of the House of Lords in the Scotch appeal case of *Glasgow Corporation v. Glasgow Tramway and Omnibus Company* (11th July) turned upon the construction of a clause in the lease of certain tramways from the corporation to the company, providing that the latter should "pay to the corporation the expenses of borrowing, management, &c," and that "this provision shall be construed so as to keep the corporation free from all expenses whatever in connection with the said tramways." The question was, Did this clause render the company liable, as between themselves and the corporation, to pay rates and taxes, local and imperial, which, apart from special contract, would ultimately fall upon the latter as "actual proprietors" of the tramways, by virtue of sec. 6 of the Valuation Act, 1854? It would appear that the company themselves had until recently considered that they were so liable, since during the term of twenty-three years granted by the lease they had paid the rates and taxes, and had not deducted the amounts thereof from the rent paid by them to the corporation. They now, however, sought to recover the sums so paid, amounting to £14,246, and the Court below gave judgment in their favour. In reversing that judgment and allowing the appeal of the corporation the House interpreted the clause in question in its widest sense. Lord Watson, in the course of a lengthy judgment, said that in his opinion the provision ought to be construed in connection with the whole stipulations of the lease so far as these related to the considerations passing between the corporation and the company. Viewed in that light, the general scheme of the lease was that the obligation of constructing the tramways was to rest upon the corporation, it being in the contemplation of both parties that the corporation was to raise money for that purpose by borrowing upon its own credit. On the other hand, the company undertook the whole cost of maintenance and repair during the period of their tenure; and they agreed to pay 3 per cent. per annum on the gross sum from time to time expended by the corporation on capital account, the interest falling due upon the money from time to time borrowed by the corporation on capital account, and interest on the expenses incurred by the corporation and by the board of police in obtaining statutory power of construction in the year 1870, or incident to the execution of the lease. The substance of the scheme, as embodied in these stipulations, appeared to have been that no pecuniary obligation was to attach to the corporation beyond that of borrowing funds in order to pay for the construction of the tramways; and that the company during the currency of their right were to relieve the corporation of all other outlays connected with or incident to the performance of the obligation to construct, or incident to their position as proprietors of that which they had constructed. Continuing, his lordship said: "I have had no difficulty in coming to the conclusion that payment of assessments, whether imperial or local, levied from the owner in respect of a tramway or other erection *in solo* is an expense connected with such tramway or erection. But for the construction of the tramway no such liability would have arisen. I am, for these reasons, of opinion that the first plea is well founded, and that the company are suing for a sum of which they were bound by their lease to relieve the corporation." Other pleas raised by the corporation were that the only right of recovery given to the company was to deduct the rates from their rent, a remedy which they had failed to pursue and therefore lost; and that, even assuming that they had the alternative remedy of an action, their claim was barred by "taciturnity and *morn*." Upon these pleas, however, no decision was pronounced, there being no necessity for it.

---

## QUERIES AND REPLIES.

SURVEYOR TO RURAL DISTRICT COUNCIL.—"C." writes: Can a rural district council legally claim the fees and profits which may accrue on a patent *proposed* to be brought out by their surveyor whilst in their service? The terms of his appointment are: To devote the whole of his time to the duties of the office, perform all work required to be done as engineer and surveyor in respect of sewerage and waterworks and other works directed by the council, the commission thereon to be paid to the council, and that he be not allowed private practice, but be at liberty to take one pupil. If the claim is legal, would another person's name used for the registry of the patent meet the difficulty, as no part of the time devoted to the surveyor's official duties has been used in the preparation of the subject of the patent?

Assuming that there is nothing in the agreement affecting the question except the clause quoted, the council clearly can have no such claim.

PUBLIC HEALTH ACT, 1875, SEC. 150.—"C. I. W." writes: The street shown on the accompanying sketch is now being made up under sec. 150 of the Public Health Act, 1875. Abutting on this street are two streets, 36 ft. wide, marked A and B (which have not been taken over by the authority), and a right-of-way, 5 ft. wide, marked C, which leads to the

backs of houses abutting on the street in question and another street parallel with it, which is repairable by the inhabitants at large. In apportioning the expenses, can the cost of paving, &c, of the intersections of the streets and right-of-way, marked A, B and C, be charged on the whole of the owners of houses and land abutting on the street now being made up? If not, please say who would be liable.

The above section does not (as does sec. 77 of the Metropolis Management Act, 1862) expressly authorize the authority to charge the frontagers with the expenses of paving the street, "including the cost of paving at the points of intersection of streets." It is, therefore, doubtful whether in an urban district the cost of paving the intersections is recoverable from the frontagers. If not recoverable from the frontagers, these expenses must presumably be defrayed as provided by sec. 216 of the Public Health Act, 1875. As to whether the owners of the soil of the streets A and B and footpath C are liable to contribute to the cost of making-up the street, it would appear that they are not so liable if A, B and C have been irrevocably dedicated to the public (see *Plumstead Board of Works v. British Land Company, L.R.* 10, Q.B. 203). This case, however, was decided under the Metropolitan Act and not under the Public Health Act.

---

APPORTIONMENT OF PRIVATE STREET WORKS.—"A. B." writes: How should the costs of private street works be apportioned (1) when the works are carried as far as line A in

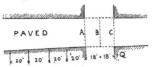

sketch, (2) when carried to B, (3) when carried to C? Also, would property situated at Q be liable for any of the cost in any of the above three cases?
(1) In this case the owners of premises fronting on that portion of the street which has been made up should be charged. (2) and (3) See reply to "C. I. W."

---

**Bath.**—Messrs. Henry Spackman and Henry Williams, who were asked to act as arbitrators in a dispute between the corporation and Mr. H. P. Tanner, the owner of property to be demolished in connection with the London-street improvement, recently wrote stating that their award was ready, the fees amounting to £52 8s. 3d. The value of the property is £1,075. A committee, thinking the charges too high, declined to take up this award, leaving it to Mr. Tanner, who had claimed £1,600 against 1,000 guineas offered.—The clerk was instructed, on the recommendation of the sub-committee, to take steps to get the tramway company to repair the tram lines and area in Cheap-street.—The city surveyor had reported to the sub-committee respecting the drainage at Upper Hedgemead, and an additional outlay of £60 was recommended in connection with this work. This was agreed to.

# Municipal Work in Progress and Projected.

Both the London County Council and the Court of Common Council have this week decided to carry out a number of extensive improvements. News of other important works projected will be found in the paragraphs relating to Blackpool, Douglas (Isle of Man), Halifax, Mansfield, Sunderland, Widnes, Wallasey, Leicester, Paisley and Scunthorpe.

## METROPOLITAN AUTHORITIES.

### LONDON COUNTY COUNCIL.

Following the custom of his predecessors, Mr. T. McKinnon Wood, at the outset of the proceedings on Tuesday, delivered his annual address on the work of the council during the past year. This was soon concluded, however, and the council proceeded to dispose of an agenda which filled eighty pages. Mr. Benn carried his proposal for establishing a department for the administration of the council's tramways, an amendment favouring delay being promptly rejected by seventy-five votes to thirty-five. Several improvement schemes which have been awaiting the decision of the council for some time were also dealt with on Tuesday, the council in every case except one deciding in favour of having them carried out. A number of other important matters were disposed of, the chief of which will be found below, and the council adjourned for the summer recess till Tuesday, the 4th October.

*Loans to Local Authorities.*—Upon the recommendation of the Finance Committee it was agreed to lend the Bermondsey Vestry £4,000 for paving works, the Newington Vestry £5,000 for various works at the parish depot, the Shoreditch Vestry £10,650 for engineering works at the baths and washhouses, and the Wandsworth District Board of Works £1,800 for underground conveniences.

*Widening of Fleet-street.*—The Improvements Committee reported that they had received a letter from the City Corporation stating that, as an opportunity is now presented for continuing the widening of Fleet-street by setting back the premises Nos. 19 and 20 (Gosling's bank), they are prepared to arrange, as opportunity occurs, for the widening of that portion of the thoroughfare between Falcon-court (opposite St. Dunstan's church) and the City boundary (opposite Bell-yard) provided the council will agree to contribute in the same proportion as in the case of the part of Fleet-street between Ludgate-circus and Salisbury-court—viz., one-half. The plan submitted by the City authorities shows that the width of Fleet-street between Falcon-court and the City boundary varies from 53 ft. to 56 ft., and it is proposed to increase this to a uniform width of about 60 ft. by adding to the public way a strip of land having a length of about 400 ft. and a maximum width in the centre of 5 ft., and tapering to a point at either end. The committee were advised by the council's valuer that, assuming that the land will be obtained at about the same price per foot as that paid for land acquired for the widening of other portions of Fleet-street, the cost will work out at about £36,000, but, as this is merely an empirical estimate, they think that £40,000 should be taken as the basis of the council's contribution, which should be limited to one-half of the nett cost, not exceeding £20,000. They therefore recommended " that the council do contribute, on the usual conditions, one-half of the nett cost of setting back the southern side of Fleet-street between Falcon-court and the City boundary, as shown upon the plan submitted by the City Corporation, such contribution not to exceed the sum of £20,000." The recommendation of the committee was agreed to.

*Extension of Hampstead Heath.*—On the recommendation of the Parks Committee it was unanimously agreed to contribute £12,000 towards the purchase of the Golder's Hill estate as an addition to Hampstead Heath.

*Proposed Widening of Lothbury.*—The Improvements Committee again brought up their report, full particulars of which appeared in our last issue, recommending that the council should inform the City corporation that they could not see their way to contribute towards the above improvement, as in their opinion it should be undertaken at the cost of the City authorities. Some discussion followed, in which Mr. Henry Clarke moved an amendment, that the matter should be referred back for further consideration, as he thought the work might be done for £40,000, and all the corporation were asking for was a contribution of £20,000. The amendment was, however, lost and the recommendation of the committee agreed to.

*New Relief Sewer.*—On the recommendation of the Main Drainage Committee it was agreed to spend £125,000 on the construction of a new relief sewer from Gainsborough-road, Hackney Wick, to the Abbey Mills pumping station, the work to be carried out by the Works Department.

*Additional Tramway Stabling at Lea Bridge.*—The Highways Committee were authorised to spend £20,000 for the erection by the North Metropolitan Tramway Company of additional stabling and other buildings at Lea Bridge.

*Additional Office Accommodation.*—A report was presented by the Establishment Committee recommending the council to purchase land and to erect new offices in Warwick-street,

Pall Mall, at a cost of £25,000. The recommendation was adopted.

*Proposed Tramways Department.*—The Highways Committee recommended the council to agree to the formation of a tramways department, and to instruct the General Purposes Committee to confer and report upon the organisation of the department, and to advise the council upon the question of what salary should be assigned to the chief officer of that department. A long and animated discussion ensued, during which it was casually stated that it was the intention of some of the members of the Highways Committee to offer a salary of £1,500 a year. Mr. Benn, the chairman of the committee, deprecated the action of members in stating facts which were only known to the committee. Whatever salary was recommended, the council would have the opportunity of approving or condemning it, and no appointment would be made without the sanction of the council. The recommendation of the committee was, upon a division, carried by seventy-five to thirty-five.

*Tenders.*—The Main Drainage Committee recommended that the tender of the Safety Concentric Wiring Company, Limited, amounting to £4,990, for the supply and erection of the engines, dynamos, accumulators, &c., required for the electric light installation at Crossness outfall, be accepted ; that the tenders of Messrs. J. H. Pickup & Co., Limited, amounting to £2,713, for the supply and erection of the wiring, lamps and fittings required for the electric light installation at Crossness outfall be accepted ; that the tender of Messrs. John Penn & Sons, Limited, amounting to £16,900, for converting four beam engines at the Crossness outfall into triple-expansion engines be accepted ; that the tender of Mr. John Cochrane, amounting to £8,150, for the supply and erection of the compound pumping engines required in connection with the sludge-settling channels at the Barking outfall be accepted ; that the tender of the Brunswick Rock Asphalte Company, amounting to £3,978 13s. 7d., for repairing the tops of the arches of Waterloo bridge approaches be accepted ; that the council accept the tender of Messrs. Baker & Son, amounting to £1,126 8s., for making borings in the line of the proposed Rotherhithe tunnel ; and that the estimate of £170,000, submitted by the Finance Committee for the building of that portion of new Vauxhall bridge up to springing level be approved, and that the tender of Messrs. Pethick Brothers for the work, amounting to £165,435 1s. 6d., be accepted. The recommendations were adopted.

## COURT OF COMMON COUNCIL.

The corporation met on Thursday, under the presidency of the Lord Mayor. An influential deputation attended, representing persons in business in Crutchedfriars and the neighbourhood, and suggested that, having reference to the large vacant site stretching from Fenchurch-street to Crutchedfriars, opportunity might be taken of improving the communication by connecting the streets with a broad public thoroughfare. The memorial was referred to a committee to consider.—The Finance and Improvements Committee submitted for approval a plan for continuing the improvement of Fleet-street by making it 60 ft. wide westward of St. Dunstan's church to the City boundary. They recommended that, on the London County Council signifying their intention of contributing half the nett cost of carrying out that section of the improvement, notice be served to acquire the ground needed in front of Messrs. Gosling's bank, and that they (the committee) be authorised to take the necessary steps for setting back the other premises as opportunities occurred. The report was carried.—It was announced by the Finance and Improvement Committee that a claim for the freehold interest in No. 4A Cheapside had been settled by a jury for £6,850.—The court approved of schemes for making London-wall and Blomfield-street (between Tower Chambers, Moorgate-street, and Blomfield House) 50 ft. and 60 ft. wide, at estimated costs respectively of £44,000 and £93,500. In the opinion of the committee the 50 ft. widening should be adopted, but they recommended that before any action was taken by the corporation in the matter the views of the London County Council should be ascertained as to the alternative lines of improvement, and that the council should be asked to co-operate with the corporation by contributing half the nett cost of the scheme which in their opinion it would be most desirable to carry out.—The Streets Committee, in a report on a new automatic hydrant designed with the object of reducing the expenses of checking the quantity of water consumed for watering and washing streets, recommended that, before the adoption of the system generally, an experiment with the hydrants should be tried in Cheapside, King William-street and Lower Thames-street, at an estimated cost of about £220. This was carried.—A report was brought up from the City Lands Committee enclosing a letter from the Home Secretary conveying the terms upon which the Government would be ready to co-operate in the scheme for the rebuilding of the sessions-house, Old Bailey. The letter stated that the Government would be ready to hand over to the corporation the male wing of Newgate prison in consideration of the sum of £40,000. The report was agreed to.—It was decided to spend £530 in fitting improved dust-shoots to the dwellings in Corporation Buildings, Farringdon-road, to replace those condemned by the sanitary authorities.—The Streets Committee were authorised to take the necessary steps for converting the present underground convenience in Farringdon-street into a latrine for women, the structure in New Bridge-street being unsuitable for adaptation for both sexes.—The tender of Mr. W. Shurmur, of £1,197, for the construction of an underground convenience in Alderman's-walk, Bishopsgate, was accepted.—The court, having accepted a tender of the Improved Wood Company, Limited, for £942, for paving the carriageway of John-street, Minories, then adjourned for the summer vacation.

## VESTRIES AND DISTRICT BOARDS.

**Battersea.**—On Wednesday the vestry resolved to apply to the county council for sanction to borrow £8,541 for the purchase of additional property in connection with the site for the electric light station, and to the same authority for permission to borrow £35,000 for the erection of new baths and wash-houses. It was resolved that the contract should be carried out by the Works Department as soon as the necessary sanction had been obtained.—The Finance Committee further reported having considered a letter from the Battersea Trades and Labour Council as follows : " That, having regard to the recent serious and fatal accidents that have taken place on buildings in course of erection and altera- tion, this council is of opinion that improvement is greatly needed in the method of inspection of such buildings, and as steps to such improvement begs to ask the London County Council to adopt the following suggested regulations with regard to district surveyors : (1) That all district surveyors should devote the whole of their time to the duties of district surveying; (2) that they should be paid a salary by the London County Council, and that all building fees (if con- tinued) should be paid to the council direct; (3) that an office be provided for the district surveyor at the local vestry hall or offices, so that he may be brought into closer touch with the local authorities." On the recommendation of the committee the vestry decided to adopt the resolutions and to forward copies to the London County Council and to the vestries and district boards. The House Committee recom- mended, and the vestry resolved, to procure six screw-tip vans (not painted) for the dust department from the Bristol Waggon and Carriage Works Company, at the price of £40 each.—The Health Committee announced that they had con- ferred with the Baths Committee as to the suitability of the land adjoining the baths, Latchmere-road, as a site for the proposed mortuary and coroner's court, and they recom- mended that the necessary steps be taken to erect the build- ing upon the site in question. This was agreed to.—The Works Committee had had under consideration the question as to the arrangements to be made for cutting the hard wood blocks recently ordered. The committee suggested that the arrangements should be carried out at the dust depôt in accordance with a plan prepared by Mr. Pilditch, their vestry surveyor, at a cost of £200. This was agreed to without dis- cussion, and it was decided to accept, at £108 10s., the tender of Messrs. T. Robinson & Son for the execution of the work, exclusive of the cost of shafting and belting.—A letter was read from Mr. H. G. Hills, clerk to the Wandsworth District Board of Works, forwarding copy of resolutions passed by that board on the subject of the telephone service, and ask- ing the vestry if they concurred in those views to pass similar resolutions. The resolutions, which were referred to the Finance Committee, were as follows: (1) That having regard to the opinions expressed by Mr. J. W. Benn on the 16th and 21st June, 1898, before the Select Committee of the House Commons appointed to inquire into the telephone service, and their divergence from those expressed by the repre- sentatives of the local authorities, and particularly by the representatives of this board, at the conference held on the 14th June, 1898, on this subject, and on behalf of whom Mr. Benn was giving evidence, this board thinks it of importance to record its views as follows : (a) That the telephone service is already of so great public importance and is calculated to become of such general use and benefit that it ought to be exclusively exercised by Government, and for the reason (among others) that it is essential for a successful service that it be under one and the same supreme and exclusive authority for the whole country ; (b) that it is not desirable that the telephone service should be undertaken by the London County Council and the other local authorities, whether in competition with or after purchase from the National Tele- phone Company; (c) that the Post Office should not under- take a distinct telephone service in competition with the National Telephone Company, but, on terms to be arrived at by arbitration or other means mutually agreed, should take over the undertaking and property of the company.

**Camberwell.**—The vestry on Wednesday devoted some three hours to the consideration of recommendations of the Plant and Scavenging Committee in favour of acquiring various sites and properties in order to provide depot and stabling accommodation, the purchase prices amounting to a total of about £23,000. It was eventually decided to em- power the chairman of the vestry (Mr. Cousins), the vestry clerk (Mr. C. W. Tagg) and others to carry out the negotia- tions necessary to complete the purchase of the sites and properties.—The Finance Committee reported having had under consideration the Workmen's Compensation Act, that

they had received circulars from companies, quoting pre- miums for the insurance of the vestry workmen's, and that a communication had been received from the vestry of St. Margaret, Westminster, suggesting the establishment of a mutual insurance fund among local authorities. The com- mittee recommended that the vestry of St. Margaret and St. John, Westminster, be informed that the vestry is in accord with its suggestion and would be pleased to take part in any conference, and that at present the vestry take no action in insuring against accidents until it has seen how the Act works. These recommendations were adopted.—It was resolved to inform the county council that the vestry con- sidered it advisable that the generating station of the County of London and Brush Company for the supply of electricity in Camberwell should be located in the parish, and not at Wandsworth.—The consideration of the following recom- mendations of the General Purposes Committee was post- poned : (a) That the work of wood-paving the north and east sides of Camberwell-green, Grove-lane (Church-street to Daneville-road), Church-street, Peckham High-street and Queen's-road, Peckham, to Pomeroy-street, and also certain portions of Havil-street and Southampton-street, be carried out by the vestry workmen, under the direction of the sur- veyor ; (b) that tenders be obtained for the supply of wood blocks for this work; (c) that a special clerk of works be engaged by the surveyor to supervise the work.—The lowest tenders of the following were accepted for tar-paving works, the first prices being for streets and the second for tar- paving in trenches : A. C. W. Hobman, 2s. and 2s.; J. Smart, 1s. 11½d. and 2s. 6d.; Brunswick Rock Asphalte Company, 2s. 9d., and 3s. 6d.; and W. G. Cloke, 3s. 3d. and 3s. 6d. Tenders from the following were accepted for the supply of fodder : A. C. Taylor, Rathbone & Son, H. S. Shipten, Taylor & Son, and Hood & Moore's Stores, Limited.

**Kensington.**—Last week the clerk submitted to the vestry a letter from the clerk to the London County Council, stating that the council would apply to Parliament in the session of 1899 for powers to carry out the improvement in Kensington High-street, subject to a contribution by the vestry of one- third of the nett cost, and that they were in negotiation with the Vestry of St. Margaret and St. John, Westminster, with reference to a contribution from that body. A discussion arose on the communication, and the question of whether the vestry should contribute one-third of the cost was brought up by a member. Mr. Robinson remarked that the vestry had already decided that they should contribute, and the question dropped.

**Lambeth.**—On the suggestion of the General Purposes Committee the vestry resolved, at their meeting on Thurs- day, to hire a steam roller from Messrs. Aveling & Porter, Rochester, with a view to purchasing it at the end of three months, at a cost of £378.—The same committee reported that during the quarter ending Lady Day last it was found necessary to buy 51 tons of Portland cement from Messrs. Francis & Co., in consequence of Messrs. Wakeley Brothers, the contractors for the cement, failing to deliver; and from Messrs. Wakeley's account was deducted the sum of £21 14s. 3d., the difference between Messrs. Francis' price and their contract price. Having reconsidered the matter, the vestry decided to forego half the difference and only de- duct £10 17s. 2d.—Mr. Farmer announced for the Wharf and Cleansing Committee that the Thames Conservancy Commis- sioners had fixed the 12th October for the deputation from the vestry to wait upon them in regard to the scheme for embanking the Thames at the vestry wharf. As the delay would cause considerable inconvenience the surveyor, Mr. J. P. Norrington, had written to the commissioners asking for an earlier appointment before the commencement of the re- cess.—It was decided to apply to the county council for a loan of £4,000 for wood paving purposes.—The Finance Committee submitted the accounts of the South London Electric Supply Corporation, and in doing so the committee recommended that the Board of Trade should be requested to hold an official inquiry into the circumstances of the transfer of the vestry's provisional order to Mr. Sax, and into the means employed to secure the transfer. A heated discussion ensued, it being stated that members of the vestry, whose names were not mentioned, had been bribed to vote for the transfer to the extent of the payment of a total of £1,000. The resolution was eventually carried unanimously, the name of the Local Government Board being added as an alternative to the Board of Trade as the authority to conduct the suggested investiga- tion.—On the motion of Mr. Quick it was decided to appoint a committee to inquire into and report upon the condition of the tramways belonging to the South London Tramways Company.

**Lee.**—Last week the Carlton surveyor was instructed by the district board of works to obtain at an early date from the vestries and district boards of the metropolis particulars of the cost of purchase of horses, carts, harness and other incidental details, and the opinion of such authorities as to whether the result of carrying out works by direct employ- ment of the vestry's or board's own staff and plant is desirable or otherwise, such information when received to be tabulated and submitted to the committee.

**Lewisham.**—At a meeting of the district board of works last week, Mr. W. H. Dawson drew attention to the serious complaints which had been made in regard to emanations at Catford-hill, Perry-hill and other places in the district from the London County Council's new sewer, and stating that during the last few days living in those neighbourhoods in comfort had been impossible for this reason. It was decided immediately to call the attention of the London County Council, as a matter of urgency, to serious nuisances and great danger to health arising from emanations from the council's sewer at Catford-hill and Perry-hill, and that the council be requested to take steps for the immediate abatement of the nuisance, and that to assist towards this result the board withdraw its objection to ventilating shafts in the locality, provided the pattern and situation were approved by the surveyor, and that the council be requested to close the surface sewers forthwith and to provide shafts where necessary in the district.

**Mile End.**—At a meeting of the vestry last week, the Dusting, Cleansing and Watering Committee reported that they recently visited the vestry's land at Edmonton on which is deposited the house refuse which cannot otherwise at present be disposed of; that they found the same burning in several places, which in their opinion was the result of spontaneous combustion; that they were strongly of opinion that all the material which is at present being carried to Edmonton ought to be destroyed within or near the hamlet; that if this course were adopted it would result in an annual saving, and not make the board liable to a charge of causing a nuisance from burning; and that the committee were of opinion that if no better site could be found it would be advantageous to erect a modern destructor upon the present depot at Devonshire-street if the freehold of the land could be acquired. They therefore resolved that authority be given to them to negotiate terms upon which a suitable site can be acquired. The recommendation was unanimously agreed to.

**Rotherhithe.**—On Tuesday of last week, at a meeting of the vestry, Mr. Vezey, on behalf of the deputation which waited upon the Bridges Committee of the London County Council with reference to the projected Rotherhithe tunnel, stated the committee promised that all possible speed should be made in the construction of the tunnel. The surveyor stated that shafts were already being sunk, and Mr. Glanville added that the council had that day voted £1,400 for experimental works.—The vestry accepted the tenders of Messrs. J. H. Pickup & Co., amounting to £79 and £178 respectively, for providing additional ventilation in the council chamber and for installing the electric light at the town hall. The vestry had already made arrangements with the London Electric Supply Corporation for bringing a main up to the town hall, along Lower-road, and for supplying the current.

**St. James, Westminster.**—The vestry on Thursday received a deputation, introduced by Mr. Arthur Newton, asking that the vestry would again consider the question of granting permission to the National Telephone Company to place its telephone cables underground in the parish. Mr. Newton stated that the company could undertake the work without serious interference with the traffic, and that the company would be prepared to pay for the concession. The deputation having retired, the vestry proceeded to consider a report of the Works Committee recommending that the application of the National Telephone Company for sanction to lay mains to distributing stations in a number of streets in the parish, especially in consequence of the inconvenience caused to subscribers through the recent fire in Heddon-street, should not be granted. After considerable discussion the vestry adopted an amendment, moved by Mr. Mitchell, referring the recommendation back to the committee for further consideration and report.—On the recommendation of the General Purposes Committee it was decided to invite tenders from local firms for the repair, cleansing and re-painting of the whole of the vestry hall.—The committee further stated that they had considered a letter from the Vestry of St. Margaret and St. John, Westminster, stating, with reference to the Workmen's Compensation Act, 1897, that, having regard to the excessive rates of premium quoted by some of the assurance offices, they were desirous of suggesting whether it might not be found mutually advantageous if local authorities in combination were to form an assurance fund from which claims could be met, and asking the vestry's opinion on the subject, with a View to a meeting of representatives of concurring authorities being called to consider the matter. On the recommendation of the committee the vestry decided to appoint representatives to attend the conference.—A letter was read from the Battersea Vestry stating that they had addressed a communication to the London County Council asking them to insert a clause in their next General Powers Bill empowering the local authorities to erect dwellings under Part 3 of the Housing of the Working Classes Act.—The vestry referred to committee a letter from the Works Committee of the Islington Vestry, stating that they had under consideration the Metropolis Management Acts Amendment (By-laws) Bill, which authorises the London County Council to make by-laws relating to the construction and laying of drains, inquiring if the vestry were of opinion that the council should have such powers, and asking what action the vestry were taking in the matter.

**St. Marylebone.**—The vestry, at their meeting on Thursday, considered a letter from Messrs. Greenwell & Co., their solicitors, informing them of the non-confirmation of the electric lighting provisional order granted by the Board of Trade. On the motion of Mr. J. Brook-Hitching, it was resolved to refer the question to the Electric Lighting Committee for report and to make a further inquiry as to the present position of the vestry. The proposer of the motion stated that, although failure had been the result in that instance, it did not follow that failure would result on subsequent occasions. It was desirable, he said, that if not by Parliamentary aid, at least by purchase, the vestry should obtain possession of the undertaking for lighting the parish.—The vestry also referred to the Electric Lighting Committee a letter from the county council asking for support in opposing the Metropolitan Electric Supply Company's Bill. The council intimated its intention to seek the insertion of a clause to empower the local authorities to combine for the purchase, at a date to be fixed, of the works proposed by the Bill, and for them to be worked for their mutual benefit.—The Metropolitan Electric Supply Company wrote asking whether the vestry would be prepared to entertain a proposal to light the whole of the streets in the parish by electricity. The letter was also entrusted to the Electric Lighting Committee for consideration and report.—Dr. Snape moved the adoption of the report of the Sanitary Committee, stating that the committee did not see their way to recommend any steps being taken at present under Part 2 of the Housing of the Working Classes Act. After some discussion the report was adopted.—The Works Committee recommended the acceptance of the tender of Messrs. Burt, Boulton & Haywood for the supply of a large quantity of Swedish yellow deal blocks at £6 18s. 9d. per 1,000. The relative merits of deal blocks and hard wood were discussed at some length, but eventually the recommendation was referred back to the committee for further consideration.—Mr. W. H. Garbutt, vestry clerk, read letters from the Battersea Vestry suggesting that the vestries should have powers to act under Part 3 of the Housing of the Working Classes Act, and asking them whether the vestry would be prepared to assist in the promotion of a Bill to deal with the London water supply. The letters were referred to the Parliamentary Committee.

## PROVINCIAL AND GREATER LONDON AUTHORITIES.

### COUNTY COUNCILS.

**Herefordshire.**—At a meeting of the council on the 9th inst. it was resolved, on the recommendation of the Asylum Committee, to enlarge the asylum by 150 beds.

**Norfolk.**—The county council have decided to offer no opposition to the light railway which it is proposed to construct from Trowse, Norwich, to Beeles vid Lodden.

### MUNICIPAL CORPORATIONS.

**Blackpool.**—At a recent meeting of the town council letters were submitted from the Local Government Board consenting to the adoption of the overhead trolley system of electric traction on the corporation tramways, and as to the department's sanction to the borrowing by the corporation of an additional £40,000 for electric lighting extension in the borough. A member, who moved the adoption of the proceedings of the Electric Lighting and Tramways Committee, said that in addition to the £40,000 sanction had been obtained for the borrowing of a further sum of £9,400, which was applied for at the same time. They had already spent £4,000 on motors and other things, so that, whatever system was adopted, this amount of money had been expended. In answer to a question, he said they were not adopting any system at present, and the committee were determined to have the whole scheme before them shortly, with explanations from the engineer.—A report has been issued by the corporation of the deputation's visit to Dymchurch, near Hythe, and Cromer, concerning the system of groynes erected there by Mr. Case. It is intended to widen 3 miles of Blackpool promenade, and Mr. Case says the front ought to be groyned in order to prevent the sea wall being undermined. The deputation report favourably of what they saw, and recommend an experiment on North Shore works, which have just been completed at a cost of over £100,000.—On Thursday Colonel Luard held a Local Government Board inquiry into an application of the corporation for sanction to borrow £5,000 for a new sewer outlet at the Gynn, £4,781 for private street improvements and £671 for public street improvements. It was stated that the new sewer outlet was rendered necessary by the great increase of property at North Shore. There was no objection.

**Douglas, Isle of Man.**—Negotiations have passed between the town council and the Isle of Man Tramways and Electric Power Company with regard to the Upper Douglas cable tramway. The chairman of the company had stated that, if the council would take a section over at the amount it cost the company, the latter would pay a fixed sum of £1,500 per annum for the Douglas Bay section in addition to the 15 per cent. on the gross receipts now payable to the council. At the last meeting of the town council Councillor Chadwick proposed that the offer should be referred to a committee, but after some discussion it was decided that it should not be entertained.—The Tynwald Court sat at Douglas on Tuesday of last week to inquire into the petition of the town council to borrow £16,000 for the purposes of building a row of artisans' dwellings, improving the infectious diseases hospital and purchasing property for street improvements. The committee took a quantity of evidence, and it is understood will report in favour of the applicants, except that they will probably insist on the artisans' dwellings being erected in a locality other than that chosen by the council.

**Halifax.**—A Local Government Board inquiry has been held by Mr. Herbert H. Law, M.I.C.E., respecting an application of the corporation for sanction to borrow £88,987 for various purposes, including street improvements and works in connection with the Birks Hall estate and £19,940 for the erection of a new police court and station.—The Tramways Committee of the corporation on Thursday resolved to extend the electric tramways to Salterhebble and Skircoat Green on one side of the town and to Boothtown on the other. It is also proposed to construct a line up Warley-road, to connect the terminus at King's Cross with that at Highroad Well.

**Kidderminster.**—At the monthly meeting of the town council on the 20th inst., the Drainage and Waterworks Committee reported that, it being found impossible to maintain a constant water supply during the summer months owing to a diminished supply in the wells, they were unanimously of opinion that it was imperative that an additional supply should be obtained without delay. They recommended therefore that a new well and borehole be made in the gardens at the rear of the cottages in the New-road, and that they be empowered to obtain estimates and accept tenders for the work. After a long debate the report was adopted.—It was decided to carry out the widening of the Sutton-road at its junction with the Stourport-road according to plans prepared by Mr. Shepherd, the surveyor.

**Leeds.**—The Highways Committee of the city council have decided upon further extensions of their tramway service. Lines are to be laid down from Wellington-road along Armley-road to the bottom of Branch-road, Armley; also from Meanwood-road along Cambridge-road and Woodhouse-street, across Hyde Park-corner, down Victoria-road and on Cardigan-lane. Parliamentary powers have already been obtained for carrying out these extensions.

**Leicester.**—At a special meeting of the town council on Tuesday the report of the Highway and Sewerage Committee, which recommended the adoption of a scheme of new tributary sewers for the borough, and that an application be made to the Local Government Board for sanction to a loan of £30,299 for executing the first section of the scheme, was adopted with only one dissentient. Another recommendation of the committee, to the effect that an arrangement be entered into with Messrs. H. L. Powys-Keck and S. Harris for an improvement of Evington-road from Mere-road to the brook, and that an application be made to the Local Government Board for sanction to a loan of £3,433 in connection therewith, was also adopted. It was further agreed that an arrangement should be made with the Great Central Railway Company with respect to the improvement of Bridge-street and Bath-lane, and that an application should be made to the Local Government Board for sanction to a loan of £2,200 for sewerage and paving works in Newark-street.—On the recommendation of the Sanitary Committee it was decided to accept the tender of Messrs. J. E. Johnson & Son for erecting the new isolation hospital at Gilroes, at a cost of £48,381. It was explained that the architect's estimate was £54,000, but, owing to alterations made in the plans by the Local Government Board and an increase in wages, it was thought that that sum would be largely exceeded.—The Parks and Recreation Grounds Committe recommended that the council should purchase 20 acres of land at the junction of Saffronlane and Knighton-lane from the trustees of the estate of Colonel Craddock, at £500 per acre, for the purpose of a recreation ground. The recommendation was referred back to the committee for further consideration. — The Lunatic Asylum Committe submitted for the approval of the council a contract with Messrs. Moss & Son for works in connection with the asylum, at the sum of £58,716. The contract was approved.

**Lichfield.**—The Streets and Highways Committee of the corporation have decided to experiment with an acetylene lamp for street lighting.

**Liverpool.**—Colonel Marsh, R.E., held an inquiry last week on behalf of the Local Government Board, with reference to an application of the corporation for sanction to borrow £100,000 for the extension of the museum and the erection of the new technical institute.

**Macclesfield.**—Mr. Eaton, chairman of the Gas Committee, commenting on the results of the past year's working of the gas undertaking, at the last monthly meeting of the town council, said the profit, amounting to £2,626, was, with two exceptions, the largest amount of profit made during the last thirteen years. In one of the exceptional years referred to the gas was being sold at 3s. per 1,000 cubic feet, and in the other at 2s. 10d. per 1,000 cubic feet, while in the past year the price had been 2s 6d., the lowest price ever reached since the acquisition of the works by the corporation. The prepayment meters were now clearly beginning to be a source of profit. During the past year the amount received from them had been £2,391, and at a rough calculation £270

of that was profit. Thanks to the increasing popularity of gas for cooking purposes, the consumption of gas in the midsummer quarter continued to increase, the year 1896-7 showing an increase for that quarter of 23 per cent. over the corresponding quarter of the previous year, while during the year recently ended the increase had been at the rate of 25 per cent.

**Madron.**—Colonel W. R. Slacke, R.E., conducted an inquiry recently, on behalf of the Local Government Board, into an application of the council to borrow £724 for works of water supply and £130 for works of sewerage. Mr. Martin, of Exeter, who gave details of the first scheme, stated that the source of the supply was a spring at Tregonnah, whence the water was taken in 3-in. pipes to a reservoir of 100,000 gallons capacity overlooking Tolcarne, and thence in 5-in. pipes to the town, where stand pipes would be provided. There would be no house-to-house supply.

**Manchester.**—The Special Tramways Committee of the Manchester Corporation have resolved to pay a visit to Liverpool, in order to inspect twelve samples of electric tram cars. The cars are stated to have been obtained at Liverpool for the purpose of being tried.

**Mansfield.**—The application of the town council for sanction to borrow £15,900 for sewerage and sewage disposal works was the subject of a Local Government Board inquiry conducted last week by Major-General H. D. Crozier, R.E.

**Sunderland.**—On the 13th inst. an inquiry was held, on behalf of the Local Government Board, with reference to the application of the town council for sanction to borrow £26,000 for electric light extensions and £25,650 under the Housing of the Working Classes Act, 1890. Mr. F. M. Bowey, the town clerk, explained that the deficiency on the corporation electric lighting scheme, for the first year of £642 and for the second year of £982, had been this year converted into a nett profit of £164 or more. They asked that the loans might be for a period not shorter than thirty years. In the case of the other application it was proposed to entirely demolish and sweep away an extensive area of insanitary property, which Mr. Rounthwaite, the borough engineer, characterised as a menace to public safety, and to erect model dwellings on the vacant site thus provided.

**Widnes.**—A Local Government Board inquiry has been held concerning an application of the corporation for sanction to borrow £8,041 for the proposed extension of the infectious diseases hospital at Crow Woods.

## URBAN DISTRICT COUNCILS.

**Broadstairs.**—The council have received notices from the Isle of Thanet Light Railway and also from the County of London and Brush Provincial Electric Light Company of their intention to apply for powers to supply electric energy in Broadstairs and St. Peter's. The Lighting Committee have been requested to act in the matter.

**Scunthorpe.**—The district council have appointed Messrs. Stevenson & Birstall, of London, engineers for their new gas and water works. The tender of Messrs. Vivian's Boring and Exploration Company, Whitehaven, for sinking the bore the required size and depth has been accepted, the amount being £4,495. A Bill is to be promoted in the next session of Parliament by the council authorising them to manufacture and supply gas, and conferring on them powers with respect to the supply of water and for other purposes. Messrs. Timmins, whose scheme the council have adopted, was the next lowest tender to that of Messrs. Vivian's.— The contract for kerbing, channelling, metalling, asphalte paving, and other works necessary for the construction of six new streets to be taken over by the council, has been let to Mr. George Holiday for £1,088.

**Swindon New Town.**—Mr. E. A. Sandford Fawcett, Local Government Board inspector, held a public inquiry on Thursday concerning the application of the district council for sanction to borrow £4,650 for works of private street improvement and £3,300 for channelling all public streets at present not channelled. Among those who attended the inquiry were Mr. H. J. Hamp, the surveyor, and Mr. J. N. Jefferies, the assistant surveyor. After receiving particulars, supplied by the surveyor and the clerk, the inspector inspected the streets included in the scheme.

**Tunstall.**—Two communications from the Potteries Extension Tramways Company were read at a recent meeting of the district council. The first announced the company's intention to apply to the Board of Trade to prolong the time limited for the completion of the work authorised under their order of 1896 to February 7, 1899, and the clerk was instructed to inform the company that the council were prepared to consent to the extension asked for, but that any further application would be most strenuously opposed. In their second letter the company stated that they proposed to apply to the Board of Trade for a provisional order authorising them to supply electrical energy for the lighting of Tunstall. The council decided to oppose the application.

**Wallasey.**—A Local Government Board inquiry was held on the 20th inst. with respect to an application of the district council for power to borrow £14,130 for public works, pleasure grounds and other purposes. Mr. H. D. Cook, clerk to the council, detailed the various schemes.

## SCOTLAND AND IRELAND.

**Alloa.**—The burgh commissioners last week gave their consideration to the question of applying for a provisional order for electric lighting. A motion to make the application was eventually carried by eight votes to three.

**Annan.**—It is reported that at a recent meeting of the Burgh Commission a committee was appointed to draw up a report with regard to the electric lighting of Annan. It was proposed either to use the old water mill, situated about a mile up on the river Annan, which was burned down a few years ago, or to use the old cotton mill in Port-street, which is also driven by water-power. When the report came up, however, it was agreed to let it lie on the table in the mean-time.

**Belfast.**—A new electric lighting station is being erected for the corporation in East Bridge-street. It will contain an engine-room to accommodate engines and dynamos to the extent of about 5,000 horse-power, and a boiler-house. At the west end are the public offices, battery, and test-rooms and store-rooms, while the general offices for the staff are situated upstairs. The whole scheme was designed by Mr. Victor A. H. M'Cowen, electrical engineer to the corporation, and the work has been carried out by Messrs. J. & W. Stewart.

**Clontarf.**—On the 7th inst. an inspector of the Local Government Board held an inquiry with reference to an application of the commissioners for sanction to a loan of £450 for the purpose of constructing a main sewer and water main in Seafield-avenue, Dollymount. It is intended to place the proposed main through some 400 yards of the road. The district is a very rising one, and many new houses are being built. Formal evidence was given, and there being no opposition the proceedings terminated.

**Dumfries.**—New public baths and wash-houses, which have been presented to the town by a lady resident, were formally handed over by her to the town council on the 14th inst. The building, which has been erected in the Greensands Park, contains ten separate washing apartments, with laundry-room, eight plunge baths, and two spray, shower and wave baths. It has been built from the plans of Mr. Barbour, Dumfries, and the cost will approximate to £4,000.—Mr. G. Malam, gas manager, in his report, states that the amount of gas made was 72,783,000 cubic feet, or 9,953 cubic feet per ton of coal and oil, as against 70,034,000 cubic feet, or 10,140 cubic feet per ton, in the preceding year. The gas sold was 64,735,200 cubic feet, as against 64,477,000 cubic feet, and the unaccounted-for gas was 11·06 per cent. The scrubbing plant is being increased to 1,000,000 cubic feet per day. In Mr. Malam's opinion additional holder capacity is urgently needed, while a great increase in coal storage would be very desirable.

**Dundee.**—At a recent meeting of the Gas Committee of the Dundee Town Council, a report was submitted by the electrical engineer with regard to the proposed extension of the electric lighting area of the city. After consideration, the committee agreed to recommend the erection of twenty-seven lamps, at an estimated cost of £838, the running cost being £550 per annum.

**Edinburgh.**—On the representation of the resident engineer, the Electric Lighting Committee of the Edinburgh Town Council have recommended an extension of the low-tension continuous-current mains to Balcarres-street, the usual guarantee being given. The probable cost is £1,600. It has also been agreed to recommend acceptance of an offer for new offices, stores and other buildings at the corporation's electric lighting station in Dewar-place to somewhat over £6,000. The Board of Trade have formally intimated to the solicitors of the Edinburgh Street Tramways Company their approval of the agreement for the sale of the Portobello lines to the city of Edinburgh.—The town council have approved a proposal to offer £65,000 to the North British Railway Company for Port Hopetoun, as a site upon which to erect the proposed Usher hall.

**Elgin.**—The question of the price of gas was the subject of a wordy discussion at a recent meeting of the town council. It was proposed that the rate be continued at 4s. 7d. per 1,000 cubic feet, as at present, but an amendment was moved in favour of fixing the price at 4s. 2d. per 1,000 cubic feet. On being put to the vote the original motion was, however, carried.

**Glasgow.**—In consequence of Messrs. Goddard, Massey & Warner, Nottingham, declining to proceed with their contract to supply the laundry machinery required at Ruchill hospital in terms of the specification, the next lowest offer, that of Messrs. D. & J. Tullis, Kilbowie, amounting to £3,690, has been accepted, and the Nottingham firm have been notified that the corporation hold them liable for £807, the difference being the amount of their contract and the one which has now been accepted.

**Gourock.**—At the last monthly meeting of the burgh commission, on the 19th inst., a letter was read from the H. B. Electric Light Company, London, stating that they intend to apply to the Board of Trade for an order to supply the burgh with electric light. It was agreed to instruct the town clerk to acknowledge the receipt of the letter and to intimate that the commissioners would oppose the application.

**Greenock.**—At the last monthly meeting of the police board a letter was submitted from the North British Supply Company, Limited, intimating their intention to again apply for a provisional order for the burgh of Greenock on or before 21st December. The letter was remitted for consideration.

**Inverness.**—A meeting of the town council was held on the 18th inst. for the purpose of considering a report on the subject of the introduction of the electric light into the burgh. The sub-committee recommended that before approaching the community to ascertain whether or not they desired electric light to be introduced by the corporation, a report on the approximate cost of introduction and the cost at which the light could be supplied to the consumers should be got from a competent authority. The recommendation was adopted.

**Paisley.**—In connection with the offer of the British Electric Traction Company to run the Paisley tramways by means of the trolley system, it is stated, says a contemporary, that a section of the town council have raised the proposal that they should approach the Glasgow Corporation to see if they would be willing to lease the burgh streets from the council and work the tramways as a part of their system, in the same way as is done at Pollokshaws, Govan, and other places adjoining the city.

**Perth.**—At a recent meeting of the Waterworks Committee it was agreed to recommend that the building to be erected in connection with the waterworks extensions should be sufficient to accommodate two engines. The estimates are understood to have warranted the committee in coming to this decision.—The Perth District Committee of the county council, at their last quarterly meeting, had under consideration the estimates of Mr. Scott, the surveyor, for the erection of the proposed bridge across the May at Forteviot. The clerk intimated that the estimates were £650 for a bridge to carry extraordinary traffic and £450 for ordinary traffic. Some discussion followed, and ultimately it was agreed by a large majority to erect the bridge for extraordinary traffic.

**Queenstown.**—New salt-water baths have just been erected at Queenstown by Mr. D. Forde, from the designs of Mr. D. J. Coakley, C.E. There are four entrances to the building, the main entrance being at the west end. The men's bath, which is at the westward end of the main building, is 70 ft. long by 40 ft. wide. It is surrounded by a balcony on all sides, and, in addition to which, on the north side are dressing-rooms. The bath, which has a graduated floor, is over 9 ft. deep at its western end. Steps are erected at each angle for the use of the bathers. The women's bath, at the eastern end of the building, is 50 ft. long and 40 ft. wide. The baths will be refilled at every tide.

**Shandon.**—The hydropathic baths at this town were lately completely gutted by fire. The building included Turkish, swimming, and a general suite of ladies' and gentlemen's baths. The damage is estimated at between £3,000 and £4,000.

**Tain.**—The price of gas is to be reduced by the gas commissioners from 6s. 8d. to 6s. 3d. per 1,000 cubic feet. This makes a total reduction of 4s. 10d. per 1,000 cubic feet since the gas undertaking was acquired by the town council, six years ago.

## FOREIGN AND COLONIAL.

**Singapore.**—The municipal commissioners have decided to light the town with oil on the termination of the gas company's contract in December next, until they are able to take up the lighting of the town by gas or electricity.

**St Helier, Jersey.**—The municipality have accepted the tender of the Horsfall Furnace Syndicate, Limited, for a refuse destructor with accessories complete for steam-raising.

**Berlin.**—The municipality have resolved, reports *The Building News*, to construct a system of underground electric tramways, 25 to 30 kilometres long, and costing from 40,000,000 marks to 80,000,000 marks.

# Personal.

Southampton Borough Council have increased the salary of Mr. Lee, their electrical engineer, from £180 to £210 per annum.

The Sandwich Town Council, sitting as a committee, last week appointed Mr. Charles J. Conquest to the post of borough surveyor.

Messrs. Sands & Walker, of Nottingham, have been instructed by the Bingham Rural District Council to prepare a scheme of sewerage and sewage disposal for their district.

Mr. John H. Fraser, private street works assistant on the staff of the borough surveyor of Wolverhampton, Mr. J. W. Bradley, has been appointed engineering assistant to the borough surveyor of Burton-on-Trent.

At the last meeting of the Chesterfield Rural District Council it was resolved "that the resolution passed at the last meeting, increasing the highway surveyors' salaries by £30 and £20 respectively, be rescinded."

The Water and Sewers Committee of the Swansea Corporation last week appointed Mr. Barnett, of Pateley Bridge, resident engineer of the Cray water supply scheme, in succession to Mr. Smallpiece, at a salary of £450 per annum.

Mr. Arthur W. Ward has been appointed chief assistant to Mr. O. J. Kirby, borough engineer of Batley. Mr. Ward served his articles with Mr. S. Stead, borough surveyor of Harrogate, and was an assistant with him up to twelve months ago.

Last week Mr. W. Swain, of Sowerby Bridge, was appointed drainage and building inspector under the Bath Corporation, in succession to Mr. Craven, who has been appointed assistant sanitary inspector. There were twenty-three candidates for the post.

Mr. W. M. Jameson, surveyor to the South Hornsey Urban District Council, was last week appointed surveyor to the Whitechapel District Board of Works, in succession to Mr. J. P. Waddington, who has accepted the surveyorship to the St. Marylebone Vestry.

At the invitation of Mr. Samuel W. Johnson, who is president of the Institution of Mechanical Engineers, the members of that institution attended a reception and garden party at the Nottingham Castle and Museum yesterday. During the day visits were paid to a number of works in the city.

Mr. E. J. Scown, of the borough engineer's office, Plymouth, Mr. J. McArthur, Southampton, and Mr. W. S. Douthwaite, Lancaster, have been appointed chief engineering assistant, temporary assistant and building inspector respectively in the office of Mr. K. F. Campbell, borough engineer and surveyor of Huddersfield.

Mr. William Green, senr., superintendent of the Lighting Department of the Birmingham Corporation, having retired under the provisions of the superannuation scheme, the Public Works Committee have temporarily appointed Mr. William Green, junr., who has been assistant superintendent for the past twenty years, in his place.

At a meeting of the Roads and Bridges Committee of the Glamorgan County Council on Thursday seventy-six applications were received for the post of road inspector. The following five applicants were selected to appear before a future meeting: Alexander Mark, Bridgend; Thomas Oakley, Aberdare; Joseph Rees, Penygraig; Harry T. Jones, Clydach; and David Williams, Aberdare.

Mr. Vincent Turner has been appointed assistant to the water engineer of the Wakefield Corporation. He is an old Mason Engineering College student, and has been articled for three years to the borough surveyor of Wolverhampton. During this period he has qualified for the studentship of the Institution of Civil Engineers, the Surveyors' Institution, and as a graduate of the Institution of Mechanical Engineers.

It is reported that the General Purposes Committee of the Batley Corporation have agreed to allow Mr. O. J. Kirby, the borough surveyor, to act as expert adviser and engineer to the Manufacturers' Committee in connection with the preparation of some scheme for dealing with trade effluents, in response to the demand from the West Riding Rivers Board. It is stated that Mr. Kirby will prepare plans and submit them to the committee at once.

Mr. Buckley, road surveyor to the Birmingham Corporation, who for some time has been in failing health, recently expressed a desire to retire under the superannuation scheme. The Public Works Committee have accepted his resignation, and have decided to advertise for an experienced road surveyor to take his place, at a salary of £300 per annum, rising by annual increments of £20 to £400. Mr. Buckley's salary was £500 per annum.

Upwards of twenty employees of the Batley Corporation held their annual outing last week to Holmfirth. A char-a-banc was requisitioned, and a start made about 8 o'clock, the outward journey being made by way of Berry Brow, Hurley and Brockholes. Lunch was served at the Commercial Inn,

and afterwards the party, under the guidance of Mr. Barrowclough, the water engineer, paid a visit to the extensive waterworks owned by the corporation. The Bilberry reservoir was also visited during the day. After dinner a hearty vote of thanks was passed to Mr. Barrowclough. The return journey was by way of Lockwood and Huddersfield.

At the last meeting of the Harpenden Urban District Council a letter was read from the Local Government Board regarding the appointment of Mr. William Walton as surveyor and inspector of nuisance stating that they observed, from the answers to queries put by them, that Mr. Walton was to be allowed to continue in business as an architect. If this was the case he should enter into an undertaking with the council to provide that he would wholly abstain, in private business, from engaging in any works arising out of, or connected in any way with, the duties of his office of inspector. The council agreed to reply confirming to these requirements.

On Thursday the Cirencester Urban District Council had under consideration a report of the Streets and General Purposes Committee in regard to the salary of Mr. T. Hibbert, the surveyor. Up to the present, it seems, Mr. Hibbert has been receiving £185 yearly, although at the time of his appointment it was recognised that that amount would necessitate a revision after a time. During the period of his appointment Mr. Hibbert has prepared plans of and executed sewerage and drainage works, street improvement works and bath renovation, and has in every case satisfied the committee charged with the execution of each particular work. In the opinion of the committee the time had come when Mr. Hibbert should be relieved of some portion of his work, and that relief, they considered, could be best afforded by placing the collection of the rates (until now one of Mr. Hibbert's duties) in other hands. The report, which included the recommendation for the advancement of the salary to £225 per annum, was eventually adopted, the chairman remarking that it was evident, from inquiries they had made as to the rates of payment in other places, the present salary was not adequate remuneration.

On the occasion of Mr. Blackman's leaving Aberdeen to fill the position of electrical engineer to the Poplar District Board of Works, he was on Friday, in the offices of the Aberdeen electricity works, Cotton-street, made the recipient of a complete set of ivory dessert knives and forks in a handsome walnut case. Among those present were Mr. Alexander Smith, manager of the gas department, and Mr. J. A. Bell, the newly-appointed city electrician. Mr. Smith, in making the presentation, remarked that he felt both glad and sorry—glad that Mr. Blackman had secured a better appointment, but, on the other hand, sorry to lose Mr. Blackman as electrical engineer to the Corporation of Aberdeen. He felt sure that they would all follow Mr. Blackman's future with the greatest possible interest. He took advantage of the opportunity afforded to welcome Mr. Bell, and trusted that they would all get along harmoniously together. Mr. Smith then formally handed over the present to Mr. Blackman with the hope that both he and Mrs. Blackman would long be spared to use and enjoy it. Mr. Blackman thanked the company heartily, not only for the handsome gift, but also for the expressions of goodwill which accompanied it. He felt sure that he had the entire sympathy and goodwill of the staff, as had been evinced on many occasions. In concluding, he trusted that if any of those present had occasion to visit London they would not leave the city without paying him a visit. Mr. Bell in a few remarks thanked those present for the way they had received the kind sentiment that had been expressed by Mr. Smith. He said that this was perhaps the only known instance where the new city electrician had had the opportunity of seeing the send-off of his predecessor.

**Bootle.**—The town council have accepted the tender of Mr. Walter Musker, of Bootle, to carry out an electric lighting station at Pine-grove, for the sum of £6,598.—Electric lighting charges will shortly be fixed on a sliding scale.

**Birkenhead.**—Good progress is reported as being made with the scheme for providing a municipal tramway service on the overhead trolley system. At a recent meeting the Special Tramways Committee brought up a list of routes, and it was arranged to schedule these in next session's application for a tramways provisional order.

**Bournemouth.**—At a meeting of the town council on the 20th inst. the Roads Committee reported that they had considered the following tenders for making-up Alington and Heron Court roads, Portman-place and St. John's-avenue: Messrs. Grounds & Newton, £401; and Mr. George Troke, £409. They recommended that the lowest tender be accepted, and this was agreed to. The same committee reported that a letter had been received from the Local Government Board sanctioning a loan of £480 for the works in the above roads, and another stating that the board were not prepared to sanction a loan of £500 for the continuation of Bradley-road,

## ASSOCIATION OF MUNICIPAL AND COUNTY ENGINEERS.

### IRISH DISTRICT MEETING AT CORK.

The following are the arrangements for the above meeting, which will be held on Friday and Saturday, August 5th and 6th :—

FRIDAY, AUGUST 5TH.

11.30 a.m.—The members will be received in the council chamber, Municipal Buildings, by the Right Worshipful P. H. Meade, Esq., Mayor of Cork. Reading of the minutes.

12 noon.—The following papers will be read and discussed : (1) " Restoration of Municipal Buildings and Description of Cork Waterworks, with means adopted for checking Waste of Water," by Mr. H. A. Cutler, city engineer, Cork ; (2) " Description of Cork Electric Tramways," by Mr. Hevily Griffin, A.M.I.C.E., resident engineer for the contractor for permanent way ; and (3) " Main Roads under County Councils," by Mr. R. H. Dorman, county surveyor, Armagh.

2 p.m.—Luncheon, which will kindly be provided by the mayor.

3 p.m.—Visit to Cork Electric Tramway and Lighting Company's central station and other works in course of construction in the city.

4.30 p.m.—Special train (Cork and Muskerry Light Railway) to visit Blarney and St. Anne's, where tea will be provided by Mr. R. Bertie, J.P., chairman of the company. The engineer for the railway, Mr. W. H. Hill, will accompany the members. On returning to Cork the members will dine together at the Imperial Hotel, at 7.30 o'clock. Dinner tickets 5s. each (wines extra).

SATURDAY, AUGUST 6TH.

*Visit to Queenstown Waterworks.*

10 a.m.—The members will meet at the Municipal Buildings and drive to Tippotstown, site of head works. Messrs. Kirkby & Doran, the engineers, will explain the scheme on the ground.

1 p.m.—Leave Queenstown Junction for Queenstown.

1.30 p.m.—Luncheon at Queen's Hotel, Queenstown, provided by the local members.

2.30 p.m.—Start on board American tender for a cruise round Cork harbour and visit harbour works ; and also Cork, Blackrock and Passage Railway extension to Crosshaven. Messrs. James Price, M.I.C.E., harbour engineer, and S. Perry, engineer to the railway company, will accompany the members. Afternoon tea will be provided by Mrs. Kirkby, at Miramar, Queenstown, where the steamer will touch during the afternoon.

Hotels recommended — Imperial, Victoria, Métropole, Moore's and Turner's.

Train and boat services—Leave Euston, 8.45 p.m. *viâ* Holyhead. Arrive Cork, 10.35 a.m. Leave Paddington, Tuesdays, Thursdays and Saturdays, 4.30 p.m., for New Milford. Arrive Cork, 9 a.m.

R. H. DORMAN, M.I.C.E.,　　THOMAS COLE, A.M.I.C.E., *Secretary,*
*Hon. Sec. Irish District,*　　11 Victoria-street,
Armagh.　　　　　　　　Westminster, S.W.

## LONDON WATER SUPPLY COMMISSION.

The Royal Commission on the London Water Supply, presided over by Lord Llandaff, hold their thirty-first sitting at the Guildhall, Westminster, on Monday.

Mr. REGINALD S. MIDDLETON, assistant commissioner to Lord Balfour's commission and one of the engineers of the Thames reservoir scheme, who was called at the close of the previous meeting, continued his evidence. Dealing first with the probable increase of the population of London and its effect upon the purity of the water of the Thames, he said that the population of greater London in 1891, which amounted to 5,732,950, was 500,795 in excess of the population supplied by the eight water companies ; but he had taken the larger figure as the basis of his calculations, and with an estimated rate of increase of 18·2 per cent. per annum the population would not amount in 1931 to 11,250,000. He had satisfied himself—and in this respect he was supported by the calculations of Sir Benjamin Baker and Mr. Deacon—that it would be possible to obtain from the Thames something more than 400,000,000 gallons a day without depleting the river to such an extent as to reduce the flow over Teddington weir below 200,000,000 gallons a day. If local authorities of Middlesex and Hertfordshire and elsewhere supplied their respective districts from wells, it would not have any appreciable effect on the river Thames. This, he said, in reply to a question, is also true of the river Lea. He did not agree with the evidence of other witnesses that pumping from the wells in the Lea valley would have a very sensible effect. Replying to further questions, the witness went on to say that Lord Balfour's commission did not express or imply any insistence upon Staines as the only site for storage reservoirs when they gave a preference to the scheme laid before them by Messrs. Hunter & Fraser. They merely expressed their approval of reservoirs of this type situated in the Thames valley as near

to the intakes of the companies as possible. Moreover, the conditions which no doubt influenced Messrs. Hunter & Fraser to place their intakes above Bell weir—namely, that Staines, Sunbury and other villages on the banks of the Thames drained into cesspools—no longer existed, for Sunbury, Weybridge, Walton and Hampton had all instituted sewage disposal works, or were constructing them, and consequently they were equally suitable with Staines as sites for storage reservoirs. Moreover, so far from the increasing population of the Thames valley having had a deteriorating effect on the raw Thames water as found at Hampton, the reverse appeared to be the case, and there had been a notable decrease in the organic impurity of the Thames at the point where it was utilised for the water supply of London. This was borne out by the latest report of the Rivers Pollution Commission, and also by Sir E. Frankland's annual reports on the metropolitan water supply. The witness then handed in a series of tables and calculations for the purpose of showing that it was possible to obtain within a certain area adjacent to the metropolis 645,000,000 gallons of water a day, which was sufficient to enable the companies to go on supplying London with water for a long period, and that therefore, when they had the materials at hand, it was unnecessary to go to Wales. In further cross-examination witness said he thought that further wells could be sunk in the chalk basin of the Thames to produce at least 190,000,000 gallons a day, probably more. He considered that a storage of 1,802,000,000 gallons was necessary to satisfy the conditions laid down by Lord Balfour's commission in order to provide for the present average supply of 130,000,000 gallons a day.

Mr. PEMBER pointed out that the cubical capacity of the Staines reservoirs must not be measured by the 30,000,000 gallons a day which they were authorised by Parliament to supply, as they were capable of supplying 54,000,000 a day, and even more. The London County Council estimates for the Welsh supply had been compared with the known cost of the Thirlmere and Vyrnwy supplies, and with the estimated cost of the Elan valley supply, and it was believed that the expenditure incurred in providing, in addition to the existing supply, a further supply of 123,500,000 gallons daily from Wales would be about £21,000,000, while the cost of the Thames reservoirs storage scheme to supply a like amount would be little more than £5,000,000, to which would have to be added a further sum of £500,000 for the pipe line from Hampton, or other place of drawing the supply, into the districts of the companies.

The commission adjourned until the beginning of November.

## LAMBETH VESTRY AND THE SMOKE NUISANCE.

With regard to complaints made by the London County Council as to the smoke nuisance in Lambeth, the Sanitary Committee, at the meeting of the vestry on Thursday, submitted a lengthy report on the subject by the medical officer of health, who had had the question under consideration from the beginning of the year and prior to representations made by the county council. During the course of his inspections the medical officer found that in all cases patent appliances were in use in connection with the different boilers and furnaces—*e.g.,* Ellis & Eaves' forced or induced draughts, rocking bars, patent grids (opening and shutting automatically or otherwise), steam jets, mechanical stokers, split bridges, &c., so that every reasonable precaution appears to have been taken in connection with the construction of the furnaces and boilers themselves. With reference to the question of coal, the medical officer stated that in all cases the excuse offered is the inability of the various firms to obtain the best Welsh steam or smokeless coal, owing to the South Wales strike, and there is no doubt but that the use of second-class (and inferior) coal has recently increased the smoke nuisance in Lambeth, as elsewhere. It is a matter for the vestry to decide as to whether this excuse shall be considered a valid one in the future, or whether written notice should not be sent to the various Lambeth firms to the effect that after a certain period (say three months) this excuse will not be accepted by the vestry. Having regard to all the circumstances of the case, the vestry decided, on the recommendation of the Sanitary Committee, that the evidence submitted did not warrant any further legal proceedings being taken in the matter.

**New Weir on the Upper Thames.**—The Thames Conservators have decided to construct a new deep weir on the upper Thames at Sonning, near Reading.

**Berlin Pavements.**—It appears, from some statistics furnished by the United States consul at Berlin respecting the carriage pavements of that city, that wood pavement does not find much favour there. The area of pavements is 6,500,405 square yards, and of this area a little less than 7¼ per cent. has stone pavements, about 25 per cent. asphalte, and a fraction over 1 per cent. wood. The consul states that the proportion of asphalte is steadily increasing. The soil consists of coarse gritty sand, forming apparently an excellent foundation for the heavy 8-in. layer of gravel and cement, over which the 2-in. covering of asphalte is spread.

## NEW FORTS AT DOVER.

### DETAILS OF THE CONTRACTS.

For the protection of the great national harbour now being constructed at Dover by Messrs. Pearson & Son, the Government have decided to construct three powerful forts, and contracts have now been signed and sealed. All the forts will be on the cliffs. The one at the eastern end of the harbour will be at Langdon, and known as Langdon fort, the contract for this having been secured by Messrs. Johnson, of 66 Watling-street, London. The other two will be at Western Heights, the contractors for these being Messrs. Patrick, of Point Pleasant, Wandsworth. The forts are to be erected simultaneously, and the contractors are under very heavy penalties—something like £6 a day—to complete them within eighteen months from date.

The forts are to be armed with the most modern guns. At Langdon fort there will be two 9-in. B.L. wire guns, besides 6-in. B.L. quick-firers, all erected on barbette mountings. The tender of the successful contractor for this fort was 15 per cent. above schedule. It is estimated that 9,000 yards of concrete will be used at the Langdon fort alone, with a thick splinter-proof centre.

The construction of the two forts at the Western Heights by Messrs. Patrick will be a very difficult operation, on account of the awkward position of the sites for conveying material, and to overcome the difficulty a road will have to be cut through the Ropewalk meadow and a bridge thrown across the trenches.

It is stipulated that the three forts shall be erected before the turret at the Admiralty pier, containing two 80-ton guns, is dismantled, so that there is a prospect apparently of at least another eighteen months or two years before the extension of the Admiralty pier, in connection with the construction of the harbour, can be gone on with. This delay will be particularly felt in regard to the commercial harbour, which suffers so much from the want of the protection which the extension of the Admiralty pier will provide.

The contractors for the eastern fort have been granted office accommodation at the hospital building of the disused convict prison, which is situated close by.

## APPOINTMENTS VACANT.

*Advertisements which are received too late for classification cannot be included in these summaries until the following week.*

County Surveyor.—August 1st.—Herefordshire County Council. £400.—The County Clerk, Shirehall, Hereford.

Borough Engineer and Surveyor's Assistant.—August 1st.—Corporation of Warrington. £100.—Mr. Thos. Longdin, borough engineer and surveyor.

Surveyor and Inspector of Nuisances.—August 1st.—Shildon and East Thickley Urban District Council. £120.—Mr. J. T. Proud, clerk to the council.

Superintendent of House Refuse Removal.—August 1st.—Handsworth Urban District Council. £2 5s.—Mr. E. Kenworthy, A.M.I.C.E., surveyor to the council.

Inspector of Nuisances.—August 1st.—Failsworth Urban District Council. £90.—Mr. H. C. Broome, clerk to the council.

Junior Assistant Electrical Engineer.—August 2nd.—Wolverhampton Corporation. £80.—Mr. Horatio Brevitt, town clerk.

Clerk of Works.—August 2nd.—Kettering Urban District Council. £3.—Mr. Thomas R. Smith, surveyor to the council.

Clerks for City Engineer's Office (Two).—August 3rd.—Hull Corporation. £65 and £40.—Mr. A. E. White, city engineer.

Assistant Inspector of Nuisances, Water Inspector and Surveyor.—August 5th.—Conway Rural District Council. £100.—Mr. T. E. Parry, clerk to the council.

Clerks of Works (Two).—August 6th.—Edmonton Urban District Council. £3 3s.—Mr. G. Eedes Eachus, M.I.C.E., engineer and surveyor to the council.

Surveyor and Inspector.—August 5th.—Street Urban District Council. £90.—Mr. S. Thompson Clothier, clerk to the council.

Inspector of Nuisances.—August 15th.—Highworth and Swindon Rural District Council. £120.—Mr. John P. Kirby, clerk to the council.

Architectural Assistant.— August 19th.— Beckenham Urban District Council. £3 3s.—Mr. J. A. Angell, surveyor to the council.

City Engineer.—August 31st.—Corporation of Wellington, New Zealand. £800.—Agent-General for New Zealand, London.

## COMPETITIONS.

*Advertisements which are received too late for classification cannot be included in these summaries until the following week.*

Plymouth.—September 24th.—Erection of shops and dwelling-houses fronting Tavistock-street. £250.—Mr. J. H. Ellis, town clerk.

## MUNICIPAL CONTRACTS OPEN.

*Advertisements which are received too late for classification cannot be included in these summaries until the following week.*

Wimbledon.—July 29th.—Making-up of Ridgway-gardens and Edge-hill (section 2), for the urban district council.—Mr. W. H. Whitfield, clerk to the council.

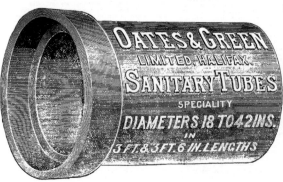

BURTON-UPON-TRENT.—July 29th.—Construction and erection of a new retort-house at the gasworks, for the corporation.—Mr. F. L. Ramsden, engineer, Gas and Electric Light Works, Burton-upon-Trent.

HUNSTANTON.—July 30th.—Construction of a telescopic gasholder, for the urban district council.—Mr. J. S. B. Glasier, clerk to the council.

KETTERING.—July 30th.—Erection of a green-house, 30 ft. long by 12 ft. wide, in the cemetery, for the urban district council.—Mr. Thos. R. Smith, surveyor to the council.

GREAT HARWOOD.—July 30th.—Erection of a block of offices in Police-street, for the urban district council.—Mr. R. Chippendale, clerk to the council.

ST. THOMAS-THE-APOSTLE (near Exeter).—July 30th.—Supply and fixing of the gas engines and centrifugal pumps required in connection with the new sewage outfall works, for the urban district council.—Mr. S. Churchward, surveyor to the council.

LEYLAND.—July 30th.—Construction of precipitation tanks, filters, reservoir, engine and boiler house, conduits, subsoil drainage, &c., for the urban district council.—Mr. William Wrennall, 9 Harrington-street, Liverpool.

WHITSTABLE.—August 1st.—Supply of about 300 tons of granite or quartzite chippings, 400 ft. run of 10-in. by 5-in. granite kerbing, 400 ft. run of 10-in. by 5-in. granite channelling, and Portland cement, for the urban district council.—Mr. Alfred Goldfinch, surveyor to the council.

CLERSTON.—August 1st.—Laying of 1,000 superficial yards of granite and cement concrete for footways in Bridge-street and Station-road, for the urban district council.—Mr. F. Feather, surveyor to the council.

RYDE.—August 2nd.—Supply and delivery, and also laying, of about 1,050 yards of 4-in. and 120 yards of 3-in. cast-iron pipes.—Mr. C. Mathew, borough engineer.

WANDSWORTH.—August 2nd.—Providing and laying of about 14,000 superficial yards of wood block paving (creosoted deal) in Richmond-road, Putney, for the district board of works.—Mr. Henry George Hills, clerk to the board.

WEMBLEY.—August 2nd.—Construction of the following streets, for the urban district council : Union-road, Copland-road, Montrose-crescent, Station-grove, Chaplin-road, Talbot-road, Napier-road, Stanley-avenue, Peel-road and Priory Park-road.—Mr. C. L. Whitehead, junr., engineer to the council.

BRIGHTON.—August 2nd.—Alterations and additions to the gentlemen's cloak-room, and lavatory at the Royal Pavilion.—Mr. Francis J. C. May, M.I.C.E., borough engineer and surveyor.

TOTTENHAM.—August 2nd.—Construction of 12-in. and 9-in. sewers in Fairview-road, South Tottenham, for the urban district council.—Mr. P. E. Murphy, engineer to the council.

PENZANCE.—August 2nd.—Laying of between 500 and 600 super. yards of Jarrahdale jarrah wood paving in St. Clare-street.—Mr. George H. Snull, borough surveyor.

SHOREDITCH.—August 3rd.—Construction of an underground convenience in Hoxton-street.—Mr. J. Rush Dixon, A.M.I.C.E., engineer and surveyor to the vestry.

NEWMARKET.—August 3rd.—Supply of 1,500 tons of best broken Leicestershire granite metalling, for the urban district council.—Mr. S. J. Ennion, clerk to the council.

ALDERSHOT.—August 3rd.—Works of metalling, kerbing, channelling, paving, &c., in St. Michael's-road, St. George's-road and St. Joseph's-road, for the urban district council.—Mr. W. E. Foster, clerk to the council.

HAMPTON WICK.—August 3rd.—Laying of about 1,000 yards of limestone tar paving, for the urban district council.—Mr. J. Nixon Horsfield, surveyor to the council.

DONCASTER.—August 3rd.—Erection of an isolation hospital adjoining Common-lane, Balby.—Mr. William H. R. Crabtree, borough surveyor.

HUDDERSFIELD.—August 4th.—Supply and delivery of not less than 3,000 tons of granite setts.—Mr. F. C. Lloyd, town clerk.

ILKESTON.—August 4th.—Supply of a new pumping engine, for the Little Hallam pumping station.—Mr. H. J. Kilford, borough surveyor and water engineer.

SKIPTON.—August 4th.—Providing and laying of about 2,000 lineal yards of 3-in. cast-iron pipes and for the construction of a covered service reservoir and conduit, for the rural district council.—Mr. A. Rowell, engineer and surveyor to the council.

ASHTON-IN-MAKERFIELD.—August 4th.—Supply and delivery of 250 tons of 2-in. best hand-broken granite macadam, and 50 tons of 2-in. clean, sharp granite chippings, for the urban district council.—Mr. John W. Liversedge, surveyor to the council.

BRADFORD.—August 4th.—Supply of cast-iron cylinders, valves, upstand pipes, deck and floor plates, girders, head-stocks and other appliances required for the outlet towers of Gouthwaite reservoir.—Mr. James Watson, M.I.C.E., waterworks engineer, Town Hall, Bradford.

WAKEFIELD.—August 4th.—Supply of about 1,500 tons of Guernsey granite or Openaë stone, for the urban district council.—Mr. William Blewitt, clerk to the council.

SLOUGH.—August 6th.—Supply of 4,300 tons of 2-in. broken clean field flints and about 600 tons of 1-in. machine-broken and hand-broken granite, for the urban district council.—Mr. W. W. Cooper, surveyor to the council.

NEWTON-IN-MAKERFIELD.—August 6th.—Making-up Portland, Alpine, Peel, Nelson, Water and Brookfield-streets and Bradleigh-road, for the urban district council.—Mr. W. W. Shirley, clerk to the council.

PERTH.—August 6th.—Extension of the quay at the harbour.—Mr. William MacLeish, town clerk.

GUILDFORD.—August 8th.—Construction of certain surface-water drains, including new works of drainage in connection therewith.—Mr. C. G. Mason, borough surveyor.

ABERGAVENNY.—August 8th.—Erection of a footbridge and the construction of a culvert at the Old Mill, Cwmyoy Lower, for the rural district council.—Mr. John Gill, surveyor to the council.

RADNAM.—August 8th.—Supply of 40s yards of 2-in. cast-iron pipes, for the urban district council.—Mr. J. Gregson, A.M.I.C.E., engineer and surveyor to the council.

CHAPEL-EN-LE-FRITH.—August 10th.—Construction of a concrete service reservoir, and the providing and laying of about 1¼ miles of cast-iron mains for the water supply of the township of Bamford, for the rural district council.—Mr. J. Burton Boycott, clerk to the council.

WREXHAM.—August 10th.—Erection of a bridge over the river Gwenfro, at a place called Syrys y bidden, in the township of Broughton, for the urban district council.—Mr. John Strachan, surveyor to the council.—Mr. Crispan Lodge, Wrexham.

HORSLEY.—August 13th.—Laying and jointing of about 6,150 yards of 3-in. cast-iron pipes, also fixing and walling-in of about twenty valves and hydrants for the Templenewsam and Thorpe Stapleton water supply for the rural district council.—Mr. W. B. Pinder, clerk to the council.

GLOUCESTER.—August 13th.—Erection of an infectious diseases hospital at Over.—Mr. Geo. Sheffield Blakeway, town clerk.

SHOREDITCH.—August 15th.—Erection of a new battery-room, boiler-house and extension of offices at the electricity supply station, Coronet-street.—Mr. H. Mansfield Robinson, vestry clerk.

BEXHILL.—August 15th.—Erection of boundary walls, the railing, kerbing, paving and channelling of footpaths, and other works opposite the town hall, for the urban district council.—Mr. George Ball, A.M.I.C.E., surveyor to the council.

WOLVERHAMPTON.—August 16th.—Supply of cast-iron, wrought-iron and steel work required for structural and other purposes at the swimming bath and assembly hall to be erected in Bath-place.—Mr. J. W. Bradley, borough surveyor.

ROTHERHAM.—August 23rd.—Construction of sewers, outfall works, and other works connected therewith, for the corporation.—Mr. R. E. W. Berrington, Bank Buildings, Wolverhampton.

HOYLAKE AND WEST KIRBY.—Supply of about 2,500 lineal yards of standards and railing for promenades, for the urban district council.—Mr. Thomas Foster, engineer to the council.

## TENDERS.

*ACCEPTED.

ALVASTON.—For various pipe-laying works for the water supply of the town, for the urban district council.—Mr. J. Edward Willcox, Union Chambers, 63 Temple-row, Birmingham :—

| | | | |
|---|---|---|---|
| J. G. Fincher & Co., Stratford-on-Avon | ... | ... | £1,260 |
| W. H. Smith & Son, Bristol | ... | ... | 1,044 |
| J. Mackay, Smethwick | ... | ... | 969 |
| W. Jowett, Hemsworth, near Wakefield | ... | ... | 980 |
| H. Shardlow, Nottingham | ... | ... | 850 |
| J. Roberts, Stratford-on-Avon | ... | ... | 785 |
| T. Vale, Stourport | ... | ... | 748 |
| Batchelor & Snowdon, Cardiff | ... | ... | 741 |
| B. Law, Chester-road, Erdington | ... | ... | 735 |
| J. W. Lord, Henly-in-Arden* | ... | ... | 640 |

ALVASTON.—For the supply of cast-iron water pipes in connection with the water supply of the town, for the urban district council.—Mr. J. Edward Willcox, Union Chambers, 63 Temple-row, Birmingham :—

Stanton Ironworks Company, Limited, near Nottingham, £883.
Sheepbridge Coal and Iron Company, Chesterfield, £862.
J. & S. Roberts, West Bromwich,* £587.
H. R. Merton & Co., Metal Exchange Buildings, London (agents for R. D. Wood & Co., Philadelphia).—3-in., £5 17s. 3d. per ton; 4-in., £5 14s. 3d. per ton; 5-in., £5 16s. 3d. per ton. Specials of ordinary shapes and sizes, £9 7s. 6d. per ton; flanged specials, including facing and boring, £14 7s. 6d. per ton.

BOURNEMOUTH.—For making-up Alington and Heron Court roads, Portman-place and St. John's-avenue.—Mr. F. W. Lacey, M.I.C.E., borough engineer and surveyor :—

| | | | |
|---|---|---|---|
| G. Troke | ... | ... | £409 |
| Grounds & Newton* | ... | ... | 401 |

BROMLEY.—For works of sewering, levelling, paving, metalling, channelling and making-good The Avenue, Bickley, for the urban district council.—Mr. Fred. H. Norman, clerk to the council :—

| | | | |
|---|---|---|---|
| R. Ballard, Limited, Kilburn | ... | ... | £1,326 |
| E. Peill & Son, Bromley | ... | ... | 1,326 |
| Mowlem & Co., Westminster | ... | ... | 1,196 |

HARROW.—Accepted for the supply of about 1,500 tons of 1¼-in. or 2-in. hand-broken granite and ¾-in. granite chippings, for the urban district council.—Mr. T. Charles, surveyor to the council :—

1¾-in. Hand-Broken Granite (per ton).—The Clee Hill Dhu Stone Company, Ludlow, Salop, 11s. 6d.

¾-in. Granite Chippings (per ton).—The Clee Hill Dhu Stone Company, Ludlow, Salop, 11s. 7½d.

1½-in. Hand-Broken Granite (per ton).—W. H. Murray & Co., King William-street, E.C., 10s. 9d.

ILFORD.—For the supply of sludge-pressing machinery, oil engines and other apparatus at the outfall works, Loxford-lane, for the urban district council.—Messrs. John Taylor, Sons & Santo Crimp, 27 Great George-street, London, S.W.—

| | | | |
|---|---|---|---|
| J. Wolstenholme, Radcliffe, Lancs. | ... | ... | £1,460 |
| S. B. Johnson & Co., Stratford, E.* | ... | ... | 1,248 |
| Goddard, Massey & Warner, Nottingham | ... | ... | 1,167 |
| T. C. Williams & Sons, Reading | ... | ... | 1,069 |

KEIGHLEY.—Accepted for the erection of twelve artisans' dwellings in Lawkholme-lane.—Mr. W. H. Hopkinson, A.M.I.C.E., borough engineer :—

Masons' Work.—J. W. Fishburn, Silsden, near Keighley, £1,498.
Joiners' Work.—F. Driver, Keighley, £600.
Plumbers' Work.—J. Harrison, Keighley, £85.
Slaters' Work.—W. Thornton, Keighley, £143.
Plasterers' Work.—J. King, Keighley, £176.

LEICESTER.—For the erection of thirty-eight butchers' stalls at the general market.—Mr. E. George Mawbey, borough surveyor :—

| | | | |
|---|---|---|---|
| J. E. Johnson & Son, Leicester | ... | ... | £326 |
| F. H. Stevens, Leicester | ... | ... | 308 |
| W. T. Burbidge, Leicester | ... | ... | 300 |
| Hardington & Elliott, Leicester | ... | ... | 287 |
| Gretton, Leicester | ... | ... | 286 |
| J. C. Kellet, Leicester | ... | ... | 276 |
| T. G. Cross, Leicester | ... | ... | 275 |
| T. Herbert, Leicester | ... | ... | 236 |
| W. Gimson & Sons, Leicester | ... | ... | 232 |
| D. Gadd, Leicester | ... | ... | 226 |
| F. Neal, Leicester | ... | ... | 220 |
| Tyers & Yates, Leicester* | ... | ... | 205 |

LONDON.—For the erection of the first section of the proposed permanent North-Eastern Hospital, St. Anne's-road, Tottenham, for the Metropolitan Asylums Board.—Mr. T. Duncombe Mann, clerk to the board :—

| | | | |
|---|---|---|---|
| Martin, Wells & Co., Vauxhall | ... | ... | £139,725 |
| Leslie & Co., Limited, Kensington-square | ... | ... | 121,145 |
| W. Johnson & Co., Limited, Wandsworth Common | ... | ... | 111,340 |
| Spencer, Santo & Co., Limited, Westminster | ... | ... | 114,975 |
| McCormick & Sons, Northampton-street, N.* | ... | ... | 113,942 |

## NOTICES.

THE SURVEYOR AND MUNICIPAL AND COUNTY ENGINEER *may be ordered direct, through any of Messrs. Smith & Son's book-stalls, or of any newsagent in the United Kingdom. Applications to the Offices for single copies by post must in all cases be accompanied by stamps.*

*The Prepaid Subscription (including postage) is as follows :*

|  | Twelve Months. | Six Months. | Three Months. |
|---|---|---|---|
| United Kingdom | 15s. | 7s. 6d. | 3s. 9d. |
| Continent, the Colonies, India, United States, &c. | 19s. | 9s. 6d. | 4s. 9d. |

*The International News Company, 83 and 85 Duane-street, New York City; The Toronto News Company, Toronto; and The Montreal News Company, Montreal, have been appointed agents in the United States and Canada for the sale of THE SURVEYOR. A thin paper edition is printed for circulation abroad.*

EDITORIAL OFFICES :
ST. BRIDE'S HOUSE, 24 BRIDE-LANE, FLEET-STREET, LONDON, E.C.

OFFICE FOR ADVERTISEMENTS :
13 NEW STREET HILL, FLEET STREET, LONDON, E.C.

PUBLISHING OFFICES :
13 NEW STREET HILL, FLEET STREET, LONDON, E.C.

## APPOINTMENTS OPEN.

BECKENHAM URBAN DISTRICT COUNCIL.
ARCHITECTURAL ASSISTANT.

Required, temporarily, in the Surveyor's office, Beckenham, an experienced Architectural Draughtsman. One having experience of swimming baths and technical institutes preferred. Salary, £3 3s. per week.

Applications, stating age and experience, accompanied by not more than three testimonials, to be sent to Mr. J. A. Angell, Surveyor, Council Offices, Beckenham, Kent, by Friday, August 19th.

EDMONTON URBAN DISTRICT COUNCIL.
CLERK OF WORKS.

The Edmonton Urban District Council invite applications for the appointment of Two Clerks of Works for certain Private Street Improvement Works in their district.

The appointment will be for a period of about six months, and candidates must be prepared to enter upon the duties within one week after notice from the Council's Engineer.

The salary will be 3 guineas per week, and the persons appointed will be required to devote their whole time to the duties of the office.

Applications, with copies of not more than three recent testimonials, to be sent to Mr. G. Eedes Eschus, M.INST.C.E., Engineer and Surveyor to the Council, Town Hall, Edmonton, on or before the 6th day of August, 1898.

Canvassing will disqualify.

(By order),
WM. FRANCIS PAYNE,
Clerk.

Town Hall, Edmonton.
July 22, 1898.

ARCHITECTURAL ASSISTANT.—Required, a competent Architectural Assistant, with good knowledge of ironwork, construction, details, quantities and estimates, for the surveyor's office in a county borough. Salary, £120 a year.—Applications, stating age, qualifications, references, &c., accompanied by copies of not more than three recent testimonials, to be sent in at once, addressed Box 78, Office of THE SURVEYOR, 24 Bride-lane, Fleet-street, E.C.

## COMPETITION.

VESTRY OF ST. PANCRAS.
TO BATHS ARCHITECTS.

The Vestry of St. Pancras invite applications from Architects who have had experience in designing and supervising the construction of public baths and wash-houses, and are willing to submit designs for the Vestry's new baths in the northern part of the parish. From those sending applications six will be selected to compete. A professional assessor will be appointed to report and advise on the designs sent in. The architect of the design placed first in order of merit will be asked to carry out the work at the usual institute charges, and the five unsuccessful architects will be awarded a premium of £50 each. The several designs sent in will become the property of the Vestry.

Applications to be sent to the undersigned not later than the 25th August, 1898.

C. H. F. BARRETT,
Vestry Clerk.

Vestry Hall, Pancras-road, N.W.

## TENDERS WANTED.

COUNTY BOROUGH OF WOLVERHAMPTON.
NEW BATHS.—CONTRACT No. 7.

The Parks and Baths Committee invite tenders for Cast-Iron, Wrought-Iron and Steel Work required for structural and other purposes in Swimming Bath and Assembly Hall to be erected in Bath-place, Wolverhampton.

Drawings may be seen, and specification, bill of quantities and form of tender obtained, on application at the offices of the undersigned.

Sealed tenders, endorsed "Tender for Iron and Steel Work for Bath, &c.," and addressed to the Chairman of the Parks and Baths Committee, must be delivered at the Town Clerk's office not later than 9 o'clock a.m. on Tuesday, August 16, 1895.

The contractor will be required to enter into an undertaking to pay not less than the minimum standard rate of wages of the district and to observe certain hours of labour in accordance with the resolution of the Town Council.

The lowest or any tender will not necessarily be accepted.

J. W. BRADLEY, C.E.,
Borough Surveyor.

Town Hall, Wolverhampton.
July, 1895.

THE URBAN DISTRICT COUNCIL OF HOYLAKE AND WEST KIRBY are prepared to receive designs and tenders for about 2,500 lineal yards of Standards and Railing for Promenades.

Particulars may be had upon application to the undersigned.

THOMAS FOSTER
Engineer.

Public Offices, Hoylake, Cheshire.
July 20, 1895.

BOROUGH OF RYDE.
TO PIPE FOUNDERS AND LAYERS.

The Corporation of the Borough of Ryde invite tenders for the Supply and Delivery at Ryde, and also for Laying about 1,650 yards of 4-in. and 120 yards of 3-in. Cast-Iron Pipes, with Valves, Hydrants and other Castings.

Specifications and forms of tender may be had and any further information may be obtained, on payment of 1 guinea, which will be returned on receipt of a bona-fide tender, from Mr. C. Mathew, Borough Engineer, Town Hall.

Sealed tenders, endorsed "Tender for Pipes" or "Tender for Pipe-laying," must be delivered, free of charge, to the Town Clerk, Town Hall, Ryde, not later than Tuesday, 2nd August.

The Corporation do not bind themselves to accept the lowest or any tender.

CHAS. G. VINCENT,
Town Clerk.

Ryde.
July 18, 1895.

BOROUGH OF ROTHERHAM.

SEWERAGE AND SEWAGE DISPOSAL WORKS.

CONTRACTS Nos. 1 AND 2.

The Corporation of Rotherham is prepared to receive tenders from competent persons for the Construction of Sewers, Outfall Works and other work connected therewith.

The drawings may be seen, and copies of the specification, bill of quantities and form of tender may be obtained from the Engineer, Mr. R. E. W. Berrington, Bank Buildings, Wolverhampton, on and after Thursday, July 25th next, on payment of 3 guineas, which will be returned on receipt of a bona-fide tender.

The contractor must not pay less than the standard rate of wages paid in the district, and must observe the proper conditions of labour, and no sub-contracting will be allowed except by permission of the Corporation.

Sealed tenders, addressed to me and endorsed "Tender for Sewerage Works: Contract No. 1 or 2," as the case may be, are to be delivered at my office, Town Hall, Rotherham, at or before noon on Tuesday, August 23rd next.

The Corporation does not bind itself to accept the lowest or any tender.

H. H. HICKMOTT,
Town Clerk.

Town Clerk's Office, Rotherham.
July 12, 1895.

BOROUGH OF GUILDFORD.
SURFACE-WATER DRAINAGE.

The Town Council are prepared to receive tenders for the reconstruction of certain Surface-Water Drains within the borough, including new works of drainage in connection therewith.

A specification, containing bill of quantities, form of tender and general conditions of contract, may be obtained on application to Mr. C. G. Mason, C.E., the Borough Surveyor, at his

MR. THOMAS COLE, Westminster
(Secretary).

MR. G. B. LAFFAN, TWICKENHAM
(Hon. Secretary of the Home Counties' District).

MR. G. R. W. WHEELER, Westminster
(Hon. Secretary of the Metropolitan District).

Incorporated
Association of
Municipal and County
Engineers.

SOME MEMBERS OF THE
COUNCIL.

MR. J. W. M. SMITH, Wrexham
(Hon. Secretary of the North Wales District).

MR. J. COOK, Lancaster
(Hon. Secretary of the Lancashire and Cheshire
District).

MR. J. S. PICKERING, Nuneaton.
(Hon. Secretary of the Midland Counties' District).

MR. J. W. COCKRILL, Great Yarmouth
(Hon. Secretary of the Eastern Counties'
District).

## TENDERS WANTED.

COUNTY BOROUGH OF WOLVERHAMPTON.
NEW BATHS.—CONTRACT No. 7.

The Parks and Baths Committee invite tenders for Cast-Iron, Wrought-Iron and Steel Work required for structural and other purposes in Swimming Bath and Assembly Hall to be erected in Bath-place, Wolverhampton.

Drawings may be seen, and specification, bill of quantities and form of tender obtained, on application at the offices of the undersigned.

Sealed tenders, endorsed "Tender for Iron and Steel Work for Bath, &c.," and addressed to the Chairman of the Parks and Baths Committee, must be delivered at the Town Clerk's office not later than 9 o'clock a.m. on Tuesday, August 16, 1898.

The contractor will be required to enter into an undertaking to pay not less than the minimum standard rate of wages of the district and to observe certain hours of labour in accordance with the resolution of the Town Council.

The lowest or any tender will not necessarily be accepted.
                              J. W. BRADLEY, C.E.,
                                        Borough Surveyor.
Town Hall, Wolverhampton.
    July, 1898.

THE URBAN DISTRICT COUNCIL OF HOYLAKE AND WEST KIRBY are prepared to receive designs and tenders for about 2,500 lineal yards of Standards and Railing for Promenades.

Particulars may be had upon application to the undersigned.
                              THOMAS FOSTER,
                                        Engineer.
Public Offices, Hoylake, Cheshire.
    July 20, 1898.

BOROUGH OF RYDE.
TO PIPE FOUNDERS AND LAYERS.

The Corporation of the Borough of Ryde invite tenders for the Supply and Delivery at Ryde, and also for Laying, about 1,650 yards of 4-in. and 120 yards of 3-in. Cast-Iron Pipes, with Valves, Hydrants and other Castings.

Specifications and forms of tender may be had and any further information may be obtained, on payment of 1 guinea, which will be returned on receipt of a bonâ-fide tender, from Mr. C. Mathew, Borough Engineer, Town Hall.

Sealed tenders, endorsed "Tender for Pipes" or "Tender for Pipe-laying," must be delivered, free of charge, to the

Town Clerk, Town Hall, Ryde, not later than Tuesday, 2nd August.

The Corporation do not bind themselves to accept the lowest or any tender.
                              CHAS. G. VINCENT,
                                        Town Clerk.
    Ryde.
    July 18, 1898.

BOROUGH OF OTHERHAM.

SEWERAGE AND SEWAGE DISPOSAL WORKS.

CONTRACTS No. 1 AND 2.

The Corporation of Rotherham is prepared to receive tenders from competent persons for the Construction of Sewers, Outfall Works and other work connected therewith.

The drawings may be seen, and copies of the specification, bill of quantities and form of tender may be obtained from the Engineer, Mr. R. E. W. Berrington, Bank Buildings, Wolverhampton, on and after Thursday, July 28th, on payment of 5 guineas, which will be returned on receipt of a bonâ-fide tender.

The contractor must pay not less than the rate of wages paid in the district, and observe proper conditions of labour, and not sublet without allowed, except by permission of ...

Sealed tenders, addressed ...
Sewerage Works, Contract ...
are to be delivered at ...
or before noon on Tuesday ...

The Corporation do ...
or any ...

MR. THOMAS COLE, Westminster
(Secretary).

MR. G. B. LAFFAN, TWICKENHAM
(Hon. Secretary of the Home Counties' District).

## Incorporated Association of Municipal and County Engineers.

### SOME MEMBERS OF THE COUNCIL.

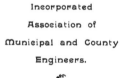

G. R. W. WHEELER, WESTMINSTER
Secretary of the Metropolitan District).

MR. J. W. M. SMITH, Wrexham
(Hon. Secretary of the North Wales District).

Lancaster
Lancashire and Cheshire
District.

MR. J. W. COCKRILL, Great Yarmouth
(Hon. Secretary of the Eastern Counties' District).

MR. J. S. PICKERING, Nuneaton.
(Hon. Secretary of the Midland Counties' District).

## TENDERS WANTED.

COUNTY BOROUGH OF WOLVERHAMPTON.
NEW BATHS.—CONTRACT No. 7.

The Parks and Baths Committee invite tenders for Cast-Iron, Wrought-Iron and Steel Work required for structural and other purposes in Swimming Bath and Assembly Hall to be erected in Bath-place, Wolverhampton.

Drawings may be seen, and specification, bill of quantities and form of tender obtained, on application at the offices of the undersigned.

Sealed tenders, endorsed "Tender for Iron and Steel Work for Bath, &c.," and addressed to the Chairman of the Parks and Baths Committee, must be delivered at the Town Clerk's office not later than 9 o'clock a.m. on Tuesday, August 16, 1898.

The contractor will be required to enter into an undertaking to pay not less than the minimum standard rate of wages of the district and to observe certain hours of labour in accordance with the resolution of the Town Council.

The lowest or any tender will not necessarily be accepted.
J. W. BRADLEY, C.E.,
Borough Surveyor.

Town Hall, Wolverhampton.
July, 1898.

THE URBAN DISTRICT COUNCIL OF HOYLAKE AND WEST KIRBY are prepared to receive designs and tenders for about 2,500 lineal yards of Standards and Railing for Promenades.

Particulars may be had upon application to the undersigned.
THOMAS FOSTER,
Engineer.

Public Offices, Hoylake, Cheshire.
July 20, 1898.

BOROUGH OF RYDE.
TO PIPE FOUNDERS AND LAYERS.

The Corporation of the Borough of Ryde invite tenders for the Supply and Delivery at Ryde, and also for Laying, about 1,650 yards of 4-in. and 120 yards of 3-in. Cast-Iron Pipes, with Valves, Hydrants and other Castings.

Specifications and forms of tender may be had and any further information may be obtained, on payment of 1 guinea, which will be returned on receipt of a bonâ-fide tender, from Mr. C. Mathew, Borough Engineer, Town Hall,

Sealed tenders, endorsed "Tender for Pipes" or "Tender for Pipe-laying," must be delivered, free of charge, to the Town Clerk, Town Hall, Ryde, not later than Tuesday, 2nd August.

The Corporation do not bind themselves to accept the lowest or any tender.
CHAS. G. VINCENT,
Town Clerk.

Ryde.
July 18, 1898.

BOROUGH OF ROTHERHAM.

SEWERAGE AND SEWAGE DISPOSAL WORKS.

CONTRACTS No. 1 AND 2.

The Corporation of Rotherham is prepared to receive tenders from competent persons for the Construction of Sewers, Outfall Works and other work connected therewith.

The drawings may be seen, and copies of the specification, bill of quantities and form of tender may be obtained from the Engineer, Mr. R. E. W. Berrington, Bank Buildings, Wolverhampton, on and after Thursday, July 28th next, on payment of 5 guineas, which will be returned on receipt of a bonâ-fide tender.

The contractor must not pay less than the standard rate of wages paid in the district, and must observe the proper conditions of labour, and no sub-contracting will be allowed except by permission of the Corporation.

Sealed tenders, addressed to me and endorsed "Tender for Sewerage Works, Contract No. 1 or 2," as the case may be, are to be delivered at my office, Town Hall, Rotherham, at or before noon on Tuesday, August 23rd next.

The Corporation does not bind itself to accept the lowest or any tender.
H. H. HICKMOTT,
Town Clerk.

Town Clerk's Office, Rotherham.
July 12, 1898.

BOROUGH OF GUILDFORD.
SURFACE-WATER DRAINAGE.

The Town Council are prepared to receive tenders for the reconstruction of certain Surface-Water Drains within the borough, including new works of drainage in connection therewith.

A specification, containing bill of quantities, form of tender and general conditions of contract, may be obtained on application to Mr. C. G. Mason, C.E., the Borough Surveyor, at his

Mr. Thomas Cole, Westminster
(Secretary).

Mr. G. B. Laffan, Twickenham
(Hon. Secretary of the Home Counties' District).

Mr. G. R. W. Wheeler, Westminster
(Hon. Secretary of the Metropolitan District).

Incorporated
Association of
Municipal and County
Engineers.

❧

SOME MEMBERS OF THE
COUNCIL.

Mr. J. W. M. Smith, Wrexham
(Hon. Secretary of the North Wales District).

Mr. J. Cook, Lancaster
(Hon. Secretary of the Lancashire and Cheshire
District).

Mr. J. S. Pickering, Nuneaton.
(Hon. Secretary of the Midland Counties' District).

Mr. J. W. Cockrill, Great Yarmouth
(Hon. Secretary of the ... District).

# The Surveyor

## And Municipal and County Engineer.

Vol. XIV., No. 342.     LONDON, AUGUST 5, 1898.     Weekly, Price 3d.

## Minutes of Proceedings.

**The Telephone Inquiry.**

The labours of the Select Committee appointed to inquire into the question of the acquisition of the telephone service by municipalities are drawing to a close, and it may be of some interest to sum up the most important facts tendered in evidence. The scope of the inquiry has been fairly wide. It will be remembered that the committee were instructed to ascertain whether the telephone service is or is likely to become of such general benefit as to justify its being undertaken by municipal authorities, regard being had to local finance; and, if so, whether they should have power to undertake such service in the districts of other local authorities outside the area of their own jurisdiction, and what powers, duties and obligations ought to be conferred or imposed upon such local authorities. The beginning of the inquiry was marked by full and exhaustive evidence, given by General Post Office officials, as to the exact position of the telephone company in its relation to that department. It is hardly necessary to say that under a decision of the High Court the Postmaster-General was held to have complete control over telephones and that no system could be carried on without special license granted by him. A very important point was established in the evidence given on behalf of the Post Office in reference to the question of competition. There is little doubt that former Postmasters-General—the late Mr. Raikes in particular—contemplated competition in various parts of the country, and though to a great extent limited by their official position, direct encouragement was given to competition by granting licenses to other companies than the National Telephone Company; but whatever faults may be laid to the door of the National Telephone Company, it has been able to show marked ability for absorbing all and every competitor. Although in a sense the telephone company has been under the direction of the Post Office, and has been even termed in some quarters an unofficial department of the Post Office, it has been unmistakeably set forth that without the consent of the local authority no company had any right whatever to lay telephone wires between an exchange and a subscriber's house, and even the authority of the Postmaster-General could not override the powers vested in the representatives of the ratepayers. Sir Robert Hunter, solicitor to the General Post Office, in giving evidence before the committee defined the present position of municipalities with regard to telephony. First of all a corporation must obtain a license from the Postmaster-General, and with authority to exercise his right of way-leave could take up its own streets, but without that license a corporation could not so act. In the case of a municipality carrying on business or seeking to extend the telephone outside its own district; in some other borough for example, it would be in the same position as the National Telephone Company now occupies—it would have to obtain permission to go into the borough, and, if granted, it would be compelled to go to the road authority for permission to take up the road; and if that were refused it would have to go to the magistrates. Within its own area a corporation would to a certain extent adjudicate on its own account.

The evidence of Mr. Lamb, who has had charge of the telephone and telegraph departments of the General Post Office, seems to be clearly directed against a municipal scheme of any sort. He considered that it was undesirable in the public interests that a private company should have a monopoly; but, on the other hand, he was firmly convinced that the establishment in one town of competing services of telephones would not be in the interests of the public; and he concluded his statements by declaring that the whole thing should be in the hands of the General Post Office. The point raised by Mr. Lamb against competition certainly receives some corroboration from the fact that a good deal of inconvenience has attended the competition in various towns of the country between the National Telephone Company and the General Post Office. In these places subscribers to one system have been compelled to become subscribers to the other in order to keep up a continuity of their business connections. There seems to have been a good many applications on the part of local authorities for licenses to operate telephone systems in their own localities, but in every case the Post Office seems to have considered itself justified in not granting the request, although admitting in the towns of Glasgow, Tunbridge Wells and Manchester, from which corporations applications were received that the telephone service was defective. No doubt the Post Office officials have been acting under the impression that some immediate action would have been taken by the Government, and probably little fault can be found with them for the view they have taken. The official view of Mr. Lamb may be briefly set forward—that he would not permit a municipality to start a system where none existed, and he would not give sanction to enable a municipality to buy out the existing service of the company. Considering the clear and specific nature of the subject set before the committee. there seems to have been in the course of the inquiry some drifting away from the real question at issue, and the questions put to witnesses seem to suggest that the Post Office in dealing with the National Telephone Company had been inclined to favour them to a greater extent than they ought to have done, and when Sir James Fergusson, who was Postmaster-General from December, 1891, to August, 1892, was examined an attempt was made to show that the Post Office had given greater facilities to the National Telephone Company for extending their areas than they were altogether justified in doing. But that phase of the matter is not of very great moment from the municipal point of view. In a subsequent issue we shall have occasion to make some further reference to the evidence given before the inquiry.

\*     \*     \*

**The Responsibilities of Employers : A New Phase.** We have heard a great deal lately about the Workmen's Compensation Act and the onerous nature of the liabilities to which the employers of labour are thereby subjected. It is not our intention to enter upon the discussion at the present moment, but the prominence given to it seems naturally to recall attention to certain responsibilities of employers in other directions which have not received so much notice. In the month of January last an application of a somewhat novel character was made to Mr. Justice Stirling upon interlocutory motion in an action of *Chase v. the London County Council and Others.* A note of the application appeared in our "Law Notes" column (vol. xiii., p. 238), and we do not hesitate to say that the case was one of very considerable interest and importance to local authorities and their contractors, and, indeed, to all large employers of labour. Let us briefly remind our readers of the facts. The London County Council, in the exercise of their statutory powers and duties, proposed to erect an asylum for pauper lunatics. For this purpose they acquired an estate and entered into a contract with Messrs. Leslie & Co. (their co-defendants in the action) for the construction of the foundations of the proposed building. The carrying out of the works necessarily involved the employment of large numbers of workmen, who were imported from a distance, and left to make their own arrangements as to lodging and sleeping accommodation. The plaintiff was the owner of farm lands adjoining the estate, and according to his account these workmen had been guilty of almost every conceivable act of trespass and nuisance upon his property, breaking down his fences for firewood, treading down his crops, sleeping in his barns, using his hay, chasing his cattle, and committing acts of indecency. The plaintiff sought to fix the responsibility for this state of things upon the council and their contractors, alleging that they had failed to provide proper accommodation for the men and had neglected to fence off the road by which they went to and from the works. He therefore asked for an injunction restraining the council and the contractors from collecting together " large numbers of disorderly persons " without providing by means of fences or walls for the protection of his land. No injunction was granted, but it is significant that liberty was reserved to the plaintiff to renew his application in the event of any further contract being entered into by the council for the erection of the asylum. Even more significant are some observations made by the learned judge, which serve to show how nicely the scales were balanced. We quote from the report of the judgment :—

Looking at all the circumstances of the case, his lordship thought he ought not to interfere by way of interlocutory injunction. Although he had come to that conclusion, he thought the matter required serious consideration on the part of the county council; even if the possibility of their being held legally liable for what had happened be left out of consideration, still they might reasonably be expected, as owners of this property, on which they were erecting extensive buildings, to take care to minimise the inconvenience caused to neighbouring owners and occupiers by the presence of so large a body of men under imperfect control. There was one step which his lordship would point out that the county council might possibly take. The proposed asylum must at some time necessarily be fenced off. It would be very reasonable if the fences were erected before the building was proceeded with, so that they might be used for the purpose of preventing these trespasses.

It is an old-established principle that " if a person collects together a crowd of people to the annoyance of his neighbours that is a nuisance for which he is liable," but so far as we are aware the doctrine has never been applied to a set of circumstances such as those we are now considering. Indeed, Mr. Justice Stirling expressly stated that in his opinion the plaintiff's claim went considerably beyond the doctrine itself, although at the same time he " was not prepared to say that the claim was not to some extent well founded." The *dictum* is attributable to Lord Tenterden, and was pronounced in the case of *The King* v. *Moore* (3 B. and Act, 184). In that case the defendant was the owner of shooting grounds —both for target and pigeon shooting—and disorderly crowds collected outside the grounds to shoot at those pigeons which escaped, causing a great noise and disturbance and doing mischief by the shot. He was indicted for a nuisance, and found guilty, and the verdict was upheld by the Court of King's Bench. There are obvious differences between that case and the London County Council case. Nevertheless, having regard to the qualifications subject to which the injunction was refused in the latter and to the judge's observations which we have quoted, too much reliance should not be placed upon those distinctions. At all events it would seem that in future contractors for works necessitating the assemblage of large numbers of workpeople at a distance from their homes must either take precautions to secure the proper accommodation and orderly conduct of the latter or face the possibility of litigation with its attendant anxieties and expense. We think that this is a factor in the responsibilities of employers which has hitherto hardly, if at all, entered into their calculations ; and we venture to suggest that it deserves serious consideration.

\*     \*     \*

**Local Authorities and Officials.** In our last issue we had occasion to comment very favourably on the manner in which the Chesterton Urban District Council had dealt with their surveyor in regard to remuneration. It is to be regretted, however, that the opportunities of speaking thus favourably, whether in connection with remuneration or in other respects, are not so common as might be desired, especially among the smaller authorities. There is, for example, the question of municipal appointments and the abuses which sometimes attend them. This week we publish a communication on the subject from a Scottish contributor. The contribution is a signed one, and thus it should be understood that we do not identify ourselves with everything our contributor says. But while a few of his statements seem to us a little too extreme and somewhat too sweeping in their application, the evils of which he complains undoubtedly do prevail to a very serious extent, though certainly not to the same extent as formerly. Nor do we think that in the appointments of municipal engineers there is so much to object to as in the case of some other classes of municipal officials. This remark, of course, refers more particularly to the higher appointments, for in the cities and large towns public opinion must of necessity have a stronger and more steadying effect. On the force of public opinion the ultimate reliance must be placed, and if that fails so much the worse. Unhappily, cases still occur from time to time of an appointment being advertised and a man with some local claims being selected in preference to other candidates whose qualifications may be immensely superior, and who have been put to needless trouble and expense. An authority may have good ground to think that a man on the spot may best suit their requirements, but in that case to advertise the appointment as open to public competition is a farce and a fraud. But reviewing the appointments that have been made for some years back in towns of any importance the majority have probably been made on *bonâ-fide* lines, with the object of getting the best man available, no matter where he hails from. Unfortunately, the remark does not apply to the smaller authorities ; but for our part we have certainly waged unceasing war against the abuses, and will continue to do so. We fear, however, that it is scarcely practicable to adopt our correspondent's suggestion and take the power of appointing municipal officials away from the authorities concerned and hand it over to certain professional bodies, however eminent. The central government would probably look with little favour upon such a policy, the authorities concerned would oppose it tooth and nail, and it is doubtful if the professional bodies referred to would welcome their new responsibility. No doubt these bodies would be better judges of professional competence, but is it quite certain that they would not in turn be susceptible to undue influence? On the other hand, the authorities would have nothing to lose and everything to gain by seeking the advice of one or more eminent professional men to help them in their task of selection. The question, however, is one in regard to which we would gladly welcome the opinions of readers, many of whom are so directly interested in it.

\* \* \*

**Provisional Orders in 1898.** This week we give the concluding instalment of our reports of the proceedings in connection with Private Bills in Committee. At the beginning of the year we made arrangements to publish these reports in a comprehensive and accurate form, and as the information thus brought together is not to be found elsewhere in anything like adequate shape, we have no doubt that it has proved both interesting and valuable to many classes of our readers. It will be observed that we are also giving a complete list of Provisional Orders for 1898, and this also should prove of value to contractors, engineers and others, especially as the results of the various applications are given. That local authorities, as well as companies, are eager to avail themselves of the facilities for obtaining powers to execute new public works and extend old ones under Provisional Orders is fully demonstrated by the annually increasing volume of Orders issued by the Board of Trade. This year the number is greater than it has ever been, and it testifies to the very remarkable activity of local authorities in the enlargement of their sphere of operations and influence. The cause of the growing popularity of the Provisional Order is not difficult to understand. The process is both less complicated and less costly than a Parliamentary Bill. With simplicity and economy on its side, it is extremely likely that procedure by Provisional Order will be far more generally adopted in the near future than it is now. Lord Balfour of Burleigh, the Secretary for Scotland, who has given a large amount of attention to the question, stated in his evidence before the Select Committee on Private Bill Procedure a few weeks ago that he looked to an extension of the Provisional Order system as a means of relief from the congestion of business in the Parliamentary committee-rooms. Whether the relief comes from that quarter or not, it is quite certain that Provisional Orders are an important part of the machinery of the State, and many of our readers will be interested in the results of the work done through their instrumentality during the session.

\* \* \*

**The True Function of the Dust Destructor: Testimony from Edinburgh.** We have frequently expressed keen appreciation of the economic and sanitary value of dust destructors, but we have failed to share the cheery optimism which has characterised many of the statements made by the advocates for the incineration of dust. One of the essential facts to be remembered in considering a dust destructor scheme is the variation of local conditions, and the necessity of this is abundantly illustrated in Mr. Young's recent paper before the Incorporated Association of Municipal and County Engineers at Edinburgh. How widely different are the components that go to make up towns' refuse is clearly demonstrated by an analysis of London and Edinburgh refuse. In the case of the former breeze,

cinders and ashes, or what we may term fair burnable matter, forms 64 per cent. of the whole, but in the case of Edinburgh it forms less than 26 per cent. Probably one of the most valuable lessons to be drawn from the Edinburgh experience is the legal one, and if Mr. Young had done no more than summarise the view of the Scotch Courts on dust destructors constituting nuisance he would have rendered a valuable service to the association. It is clear that unless great skill is exercised dust destructors may become an intolerable nuisance to surrounding property, and it is equally clear that the Courts would not be slow to grant injunctions. The main grounds of the action brought against the Edinburgh Corporation were the escape of noxious gases and vapours and the diffusion of noxious dust and other matter over contiguous property. Probably inefficient working was mainly responsible for the early troubles, and it is clear that as much skill is necessary in burning refuse as in burning coal. A discussion on dust destructors inevitably concludes with one question, Is the system worth combining with an electric lighting scheme? It was not surprising, therefore, that in discussing Mr. Young's paper the question was clearly raised as to the value of destructors for raising steam to run lighting plant. The subject has been always an alluring one to the town councillor, but we have pointed out more than once the limited assistance which can be rendered to an electricity works by any scheme of dust destruction. It is quite true that steam can be raised by such means, and it ought to be utilised, if it is possible to do so, with economy, but it is obvious that when a combined scheme is undertaken there is more difficulty in securing suitable sites, and if an electric lighting system in a town develops, as it ought to do, the total horse-power developed from that towns' refuse would form a small proportion of the total horse-power required to run the electric lighting plant. Moreover, it should never be forgotten that the cost of fuel in modern electricity works is one of the smallest items in the cost of production.

\* \* \*

**An Appointment at Erith.** In our correspondence columns we print, with the omission of some passages that did not seem desirable to reproduce, a letter from a correspondent who was a candidate recently for an appointment under the Erith Urban District Council. The office was described as that of building and drainage inspector, but the duties will practically be those of assistant surveyor. To this responsible post the council have appointed a carpenter, who was formerly a member of the body, and is about fifty years of age. Though, no doubt, a very estimable person, his qualifications can scarcely be those which are required in such an office, or equal to those of his chief opponent, Mr. Jennings, who was, indeed, the only suitable selected candidate. The salary was not excessive, but it was sufficient to satisfy many an able young man on the threshold of his professional career. How it came that three out of four selected candidates were respectively a bricklayer, a carpenter and joiner, and a builder, we must leave our readers to conjecture. Our correspondent's letter comes as a striking confirmation of the strictures made elsewhere in the present issue as to the objectionable manner in which many appointments are made by the smaller authorities. The matter calls for no further comment from us, as the action of the council stands condemned on the face of it; but some good may be done by publicity, in gradually evolving a better and more determined public opinion in these matters. We cannot but condemn the feeble action of the chairman, who gave the casting vote in favour of the local candidate simply on that ground alone. It is satisfactory to note, from the cutting enclosed by our correspondent, that this gross piece of jobbery has been severely condemned by the local press.

# The Bacterio-Chemical Study of Sewage.

## THE SLUDGE QUESTION.

In view of the attention which the sewage disposal question has of late been receiving, and the extreme divergences of opinion which have arisen in connection with recent developments, the following paper, recently read before the Institution of Civil Engineers of Ireland, will no doubt be of interest to our readers:—

RECENT ADVANCES IN THE BACTERIO-CHEMICAL STUDY OF SEWAGE AND POLLUTED WATERS. SEWAGE SLUDGES.

By W. E. ADENEY, D.SC., F.I.C.,

Curator in the Royal University, Dublin.

In a paper under the above title, which I had the honour of reading before the members of this institution,[*] I described and detailed the results of a research which I had made on the changes which the common bacteria of nature bring about in the *soluble* organic matters of polluted waters. Among other things I gave experimental data to show that the polluting matters in a foul water may be divided into two classes—*viz.*, (1) unfermented organic matter, and (2) ammonium compounds. I also showed that, under aerobic conditions, the common bacteria of nature bring about the purification of polluted waters by two successive and sharply-defined stages of chemical change. During the first stage the unfermented organic matters alone suffer change, and they are completely broken down, their carbon and nitrogen being almost entirely converted into carbon dioxide and ammonia respectively; a small quantity only of organic matter remaining as such, and that in a highly-changed or oxidised form. During the second stage the ammonium compounds are oxidised to nitrous and nitric acids, and finally completely to nitric acid. The altered organic matters, resulting from the first stage of change, playing the important *rôle*, in the second stage of change, of determining the complete oxidation of the ammonia to *nitric* acid. In the complete absence of these altered organic matters it should be remembered that nitrifying bacteria carry the oxidation of ammonia only to nitrous acid and no further.

Another important conclusion, which I showed could be drawn from the experimental results which I described to you, was, that there is a simple quantitative relationship between—(1) the quantities of polluting matters present in a sewage; (2) the products of the complete fermentation of these matters; and (3) the volume of atmospheric oxygen consumed during the formation of the products; and that it is quite possible to accurately determine the quantities of polluting matters in a sewage; the organic matters in terms of carbon dioxide and ammonia formed, and of the volume of oxygen consumed, during the first stage of their fermentation; and the ammonium compounds in terms of the nitric acid formed, and of the oxygen consumed, during their complete nitrification.

I suggested in my first paper that the two stages of change here referred to should be designated by the terms "bacteriolysis" and "nitrification." I have, however, given reasons, in a paper more recently published,[*] for preferring to denote them by the terms "carbon oxidation" and "nitrogen oxidation, or nitrification," respectively. With these introductory remarks I may pass on to the subject of this paper—the solid matters of sewage, or sewage sludges. And I propose to limit the consideration of this subject to the question—how these matters can be treated in sewage works so as to prevent "after-putrefaction" being set up in them; not by the application of antiseptics, but by furnishing to them the conditions necessary for their slow combustion by means of bacteria, or, in other words, by furnishing the necessary conditions for their aerobic fermentation.

### PRECIPITATION BY MANGANESE COMPOUNDS.

It may at once be stated that it is quite possible and practically easy to ensure the conditions I refer to in sewage sludges if we use suitable substances in the process known as clarification in purification works; such compounds are those of the element manganese. The marked efficiency of the compounds of this element in sewage precipitation or clarification has been admitted by a number of observers, among whom I may mention Prof. Hartley, F.R.S., Mr. Slater and the late Mr. Macdonald Graham; but the true explanation of the cause of this efficiency has, so far as I know, only recently been discovered.

I was led to this discovery quite by accident. During some of my earlier work on sewage, some years ago, I made an experiment to ascertain whether sewage, after treatment with an excess of a neutral solution of permanganate of potash, would suffer, without further treatment, "after-putrefaction." This experiment was conducted in a large glass vessel in the

laboratory with about 2 gallons of sewage; a neutral water solution of permanganate of potash was added slowly to the sewage until it remained for some time pink in colour. The permanganate was of course decomposed—hydrated peroxide of manganese, a brown insoluble body, being precipitated in big flakes. On keeping this vessel with its contents undisturbed for two or three days, I found the sewage did undergo putrefaction, but I noticed in addition a change which was quite unlooked for. It was a change in the composition of the precipitated peroxide of manganese, which was indicated by a gradual change which took place in its colour, from dark brown to yellowish-white. In a few days the change was complete, and the well-known brown colour of the peroxide had completely given way to a yellowish-white, except by powerful re-agents.

Now, such a change as here indicated was entirely unlooked for, because the peroxide of manganese happens to be one of the most stable oxides known, and one of the most difficult to reduce under ordinary conditions. On examination of the yellowish-white substance it proved to be manganese carbonate, with not a trace of peroxide left in it. It was evident from this that the change which the peroxide had undergone was one of reduction, and then of conversion into manganous carbonate. I need scarcely point out that the reduction of a higher oxide of manganese, such as the precipitated peroxide, to the form of manganous oxide under the conditions described was the more surprising since the lower or manganous oxide is so unstable that, even when kept under water, it is rapidly oxidised to the form of peroxide.

With the general chemical characters of the peroxide of manganese in mind, it was impossible to avoid the conclusion that its reduction to manganous carbonate was due to some, at least, of the organisms which were abundantly present in the sewage in which it was immersed, and that the decomposition was probably analogous in character to that which Gayon and Dupetit have shown nitre to undergo when it is present in waters containing organic matters and the other constituents requisite for the growth of bacteria.

It will be remembered that I explained in my previous paper that these observers regard the decomposition of nitre under these conditions as a fermentation, consisting of a direct oxidation of the organic carbon at the expense of the available oxygen of the nitre, and that the decomposition may be expressed by the three following equations:—

$$
\begin{align}
(1) \quad & 4KNO_3 = 2N_2 + 2K_2O + 5O_2 \\
(2) \quad & 5C + 5O_2 = 5CO_2 \\
(3) \quad & 2K_2O + 2CO_2 = 2K_2CO_3
\end{align}
$$

If the decomposition of the peroxide above described be regarded as analogous in character, then it should be reduced to manganous oxide, MnO, and oxygen. The latter should combine with organic carbon to form carbon dioxide, while the former should combine with the carbon dioxide formed during the fermentation and form manganous carbonate, which is, I may remark, a stable substance, thus:—

$$
\begin{align}
(1) \quad & 2MnO_2 = 2MnO + O_2 \\
(2) \quad & C + O_2 = CO_2 \\
(3) \quad & MnO + CO_2 = MnCO_3
\end{align}
$$

These reactions will be found on calculation to give rise to a considerable quantity of heat, and constitute, therefore, a source of considerable energy to the organisms.

The question, however, whether the reduction of the peroxide was, or was not, due to organisms was capable of being settled by direct experiment; and my friend and colleague, Dr. E. J. M'Weeney, Professor of Pathology and Bacteriology in the Catholic University School of Medicine, very kindly undertook to make some direct experiments on the subject for me. He immersed some freshly precipitated peroxide of manganese in carefully sterilised nutrient liquid media. No growth of organisms occurred and no reduction of the peroxide was obtained. When, however, he seeded the nutrient media with some particles of manganous carbonate, previously obtained by the reduction of the peroxide in sewage, a rapid and abundant growth and development of living organisms took place in the media; and at the same time it was noticed that the brown colour of the peroxide immersed therein was gradually and completely changed into a yellowish-white substance, which I found on examination to be manganous carbonate.

We may therefore take it for granted that the organisms ordinarily to be found in sewage are capable of reducing peroxide of manganese, and in doing so effect an oxidation of the organic matter at the expense of part of the oxygen combined with the manganese, forming first carbon dioxide, and then manganous carbonate. Here, then, we have the key to the explanation of the observed efficiency of manganese compounds for the treatment of sewage. Having thus arrived at the explanation of the nature and cause of the chemical changes which peroxide of manganese undergoes when immersed in ordinary water-carried sewage, it was necessary to determine whether a similar series of changes are obtained

---

[*] "Transactions of Institution of Civil Engineers of Ireland," vol. xxv., p. 45. Reprinted in *Engineering*, vol. lxi., pp. 728-730, and 702-704 (1896).

[*] "The Course and Nature of Fermentative Changes in Natural and Polluted Waters, and in Artificial Solutions, as indicated by the Composition of the Dissolved Gases," (part iv.). "Transactions of the Royal Dublin Society," vol. vi., No. 11, 1897.

when the peroxide is mixed with the solid organic matters of sewage.

PEROXIDE OF MACANESE—EFFECT ON SOLID ORGANIC SEWAGE MATTERS.

Fortunately I had an opportunity of testing this point soon after my original experiment, on a somewhat large scale, at some purification works, where manganate of soda was being employed for treating the sewage.  At the works referred to the heavier portions of the solid matter in suspension in the sewage was first separated by mechanical subsidence ; the sewage was then mixed with a water solution of manganate of soda ; the peroxide, which afterwards separated out, was allowed to subside, together with matters which remained in suspension in the sewage, to the bottom of the tank in which the operation was conducted.  It was finally drawn off from the tank in the ordinary form of sludge.  I obtained several hundredweights of this sludge, and first drained it on a gravel bed, and, when of sufficient consistence, I made it up into a large heap, and left it exposed to the air in a covered shed.  After about three months' time I found the interior portions of the heap still wet and of a clay-like consistence ; they had assumed a grey colour, and only those portions of the heap immediately exposed to the air had retained the original brown colour of the peroxide.  There was a complete absence of offensive odour in every part of the heap ; any odour that was noticed resembled that of ordinary cultivated garden soil.

From the change of colour and from the absence of offensive odour in the interior portions of the heap it was fair to conclude that the peroxide had suffered a change in composition, and had exerted an influence, both similar in character to those which obtained when the peroxide was simply immersed in the liquid sewage.  To gain, however, positive proof of this a careful examination of portions of the interior part of the heap was made.  Some of the portions were air-dried, and submitted to chemical analysis with the the following results* :—

|  |  |  |  | Percentage. |
|---|---|---|---|---|
| Insoluble mineral matter | ... | ... | ... | 16·66 |
| Moisture | ... | ... | ... | 15·68 |
| Organic matter | ... | ... | ... | 8·35 |
| MnO | ... | ... | ... | ... | 24·60 |
| CaO | ... | ... | ... | ... | 2·7 |
| Fe₂O₃ } |  |  |  |  |
| Al₂O₃ } | ... | ... | ... | 10·06 |
| CO₂ | ... | ... | ... | ... | 18·98 |
| Other bases | ... | ... | ... | 2·705 |
| Other acids | ... | ... | ... | 0·96 |
|  |  |  |  | 100·895 |

NOTE.—The wet sludge contained ·014 per cent. ammonia; no nitrites, nor nitrates, were present in it.

These results show that the manganese was present in the interior parts of the heap as manganous carbonate ; a careful examination was made for peroxide of manganese, but with negative results.  Sulphides and other products of putrefactive fermentation were also tested for, but no indication of their presence was obtained.

The organic matters which remained in the heap of sludge after the peroxide had been thus completely changed into manganous carbonate were next examined, and they were found to be of very great interest.  A special analysis of some air-dried portions of the sludge showed that they (the air-dried portions) contained 4·7 per cent. of organic carbon and 0·07 of organic nitrogen.  These organic matters were further found to be practically completely soluble in a water solution of sodium carbonate, and they then formed dark brown solutions precisely similar in colour and in chemical characters to those brown organic matters which are always present in cultivated soils, and which are known under the name of humus.

The fermentative properties of these organic matters were next examined by the methods which I described in my first paper.  An experiment was first made to ascertain whether the organic matters in the interior portions of the heap had been completely fermented, or whether there still remained any in an unfermented condition.  For this experiment some pieces, about 40 grammes in weight, were detached from interior parts of the heap, and while still in the wet condition were mixed with 2 litres of good tap water, and then preserved in bottles out of contact with air, as described in my first paper, for twenty-one days.  On analysing the dissolved gases and the inorganic nitrogen compounds in the water before and after keeping for the twenty-one days indications of a considerable fermentation were found, as was, of course, anticipated.  The whole of the dissolved oxygen of the water had been consumed, and a large volume of carbon dioxide had been formed ; but, inasmuch as no appreciable increase in the amount of ammonia originally present was detected, and the water remained perfectly free from offensive odour, it appeared evident that practically all the organic matters in the pieces of sludge employed for the experiment had previously suffered a first stage fermentation, or carbon oxidation, as I prefer to call this stage or fermentation.

It was fair to conclude, therefore, that the organic matters

* See " Scientific Proceedings," Royal Dublin Society, vol. viii. (N.S.), part IV., p. 247, 1895.

originally present in the sludge had suffered as complete a change as the peroxide, and that the changes in these two constituents of the sludge heap had been coincident, the organic matters undergoing a slow combustion or carbon oxidation, the peroxide supplying the oxygen required for such fermentation, and suffering a consequent reduction, and a final conversion into manganous carbonate.  The organic matters in the fermented sludge were subjected, however, to further experiment, to ascertain whether they possessed the characteristic properties of fermented organic matters.  For this purpose an extract of them was made by means of a solution of carbonate of soda, and the fermented properties of the extract were carefully studied.

The details and results of experiments with this extract have already been published,* and I need only repeat here the main results obtained.  The organic matters in question were found to possess all the properties characteristic of fermented organic matters, and described in my first communication to this institution.  For example, when solutions of them were kept out of contact with air they were found to undergo fermentative change, but very slowly.  When, however, the same solutions were mixed with ammonium compounds the latter were readily oxidised to nitric acid in their presence.

I have, perhaps, quoted sufficient evidence to show that peroxide of manganese when mixed in sufficient quantity with the solid organic matters to be found in sewage may perform the part of an oxygen carrier to the organisms also present in the sewage, and enable them to effect a complete carbon oxidation of those organic matters, changing them into the inoffensive forms of matter—carbon dioxide, water, ammonia and humus.  The question which, no doubt, will be regarded as an important one by the members of this institution is, Can manganese compounds be obtained at a sufficiently cheap rate to render their employment possible in the treatment of sewage on the large scale ?

IS THE USE OF MANGANESE COMPOUNDS PRACTICABLE ?

I am glad to be in a position to state that this question has been taken up by my friend, Mr. T. A. Shegog, F.I.C., director of technical instruction under the Monmouthshire County Council, and formerly a student and assistant chemist in the Royal College of Science, Dublin.  I am glad, also, to be able to state that Mr. Shegog has been most successful.  He is now manufacturing a crude manganese sewage precipitant which he can sell at as low a price as any of the good precipitants in the market.  I have, myself, had an opportunity of examining the efficiency of his precipitant in the treatment of sewage at some small purification works, and can testify that it has proved successful in completely deodorising the sludges obtained at the works, and in promoting a healthy fermentation also in the soluble organic matters of the sewage treated to an extent quite beyond my anticipations.  But it is only fair to Mr. Shegog that the description of the manufacture of his precipitant, and details as to its efficiency in sewage treatment, should be left to himself.

This paper completes the subject which I first had the honour of bringing before the notice of the members of this institution in 1896, and I trust I have given sufficient evidence to show that the purification of sewage is simply a matter of modified aerobic bacterial fermentation—that is, bacterial fermentation under the condition of an ample supply of oxygen in the free state or in certain forms of combination, such as nitre and peroxide of manganese; and that this statement holds good for the solid organic matters of sewage, as well as for those in solution ; and that, further, it is quite possible to provide on a large scale the supply of oxygen requisite for the aerobic fermentation of both soluble and insoluble forms of organic matters in sewage.

So far as regards the cost of making provision for the necessary oxygen supply, I showed in my first paper how this could be accurately calculated for the organic matters in solution in any sewage, from data easily obtainable by the methods of examination I had employed in my studies.  I trust it will not be long before Mr. Shegog will be in a position to give us an estimate of the cost of providing an oxygen supply on a large scale for the aerobic fermentation of the insoluble, or solid, forms of organic matters in sewage sludges.

Rhyl.—The council were recently informed that the General Purposes Committee had considered a proposal to introduce electric light and electric tramways into Rhyl, and after discussion it was resolved to ask Mr. Buddicomb to submit a more detailed scheme for the consideration of the council.—The town clerk said he had received several notices of intention to apply to the Board of Trade for provisional orders to supply Rhyl with electric light.  One was from the solicitors representing Mr. Buddicomb, and another from "The Rhyl Electricity Company," who, on inquiry being made, turned out to be the British Insulated Wire Company, Limited, whose offices are at Prescot.  The other applicants were the United Electric and Traction Company.  The consideration of the several applications was deferred pending the receipt of Mr. Buddicomb's detailed scheme.

* See " Transactions of the Royal Dublin Society," vol. vi., No. xi., 1897, before referred to.

# Municipal Electric Tramways.

The success which municipalities have achieved in the working of electric lighting undertakings has no doubt had considerable influence on the question of corporation electric tramways. To some extent there is considerable relationship between the electric lighting and the working of an electric tramway in a town, because within certain limits the works that have been put down for lighting may be used also for the purpose of supplying electrical energy for working the local tramway system. The unmistakable tendency of provincial boroughs to-day is towards combined schemes of lighting and tramways. Such an arrangement permits of the generating plant for both purposes being supervised by the same staff; and it obviously decreases the capital cost of the tramway system, where it is possible to house the tramway plant in the same building as that used for electric lighting. In most of the large boroughs the local authorities have quite made up their minds as to the desirability of working tramways themselves, and it is hardly necessary to point out that the towns of Glasgow, Manchester, Sheffield, Leeds, Dover, Plymouth and Liverpool have decided to equip tramway lines with electrical apparatus or they have already completed some such scheme.

THE OVERHEAD WIRE AND CONDUIT SYSTEMS.

It is interesting to point out that in the whole of the tramway schemes of this country, whether in the hands of local authorities or joint-stock companies, the overhead wire system is the only one that is being adopted. It may, then, be taken for granted that the objections about which one has heard so much are not considered insuperable. Moreover, the lines at Bristol and Leeds have probably done much to eradicate the natural prejudices of members of local authorities against the suspended wire. The position of affairs there clearly indicate that of all electrical systems the overhead wire seems to be the only one that can at the present moment be safely adopted. Neither the conduit system nor the accumulator system have been yet sufficiently developed to be able to compete under average conditions with the overhead system. It is perfectly true that the conduit system is a workable one, and the same may, with perhaps more limitations, be said of the accumulator system; but having disposed of the æsthetic objections to the suspended wire, the question narrows itself down to one of initial cost, and that has been the determining factor in the minds of municipalities.

In the present state of tramway practice the conduit system may be said to cost from £10,000 to £20,000 per mile of track, while the overhead system would cost something between £2,000 and £10,000 per mile. In Berlin the price per mile of the electric conduit system is given by the company as £6,450, while the overhead electric system cost £2,400. The Union Electric Company of that city state that the conduit costs about four times as much as the overhead. The great house of Messrs. Siemens & Halske state that the conduit will cost from £4,000 to £5,000 more than the overhead per mile of double track. The complete equipment of the overhead line in Brussels is £5,410 for the overhead and £9,800 for the conduit per mile of track. In Buda-Pesth, where the conduit system has been developed to an enormous extent the average cost per mile is two-and-a-half times that of the overhead system. In the estimates that have been recently submitted to the Liverpool Corporation, Mr. Pearson, the American electrical engineer, who has had great experience in laying down both systems of tramways, states that the estimate for 1 mile of straight track for the overhead trolley would be £5,822, while for 1 mile of straight track of the slotted conduit system the initial cost would be £9,648. But it is not only in the initial cost that the conduit system compares somewhat unfavourably with the overhead wire system. The question of maintenance is a very important one, and experience suggests that, while the maintenance of the overhead system might be £60 per year per mile of track, that figure would be increased to £180 per year for maintaining each mile of an underground conduit system.

CLOSED CONDUIT AND ACCUMULATOR SYSTEMS.

It will be seen, therefore, that from the financial aspect the conduit system is for most towns hopelessly out of court and the so-called closed conduit systems are still more out of consideration, because in all probability the initial cost would be higher than the slotted conduit and the maintenance charges would be particularly heavy. Apart from the question of £ s. d., an open slot in the middle of the street is not a very desirable thing. Under some circumstances it might prove positively dangerous, and wherever the system was adopted it would be necessary to have the slot so narrow that it would cause great difficulties in working.

The accumulator system has undoubted merits, the chief being that it permits the cars to be self-contained and it does not necessitate any special construction of track. Moreover, it permits the car to be absolutely independent of a central power-house, which is practically the heart of an overhead or a conduit system. Still there are undoubted objections to this system. It cannot at the present moment be maintained that it is particularly efficient, and, what is more important than all, it has not yet been established that the system has reached a stage where the maintenance charges can be said to have approached a reasonable limit for such

undertakings, and before there is any development in the direction of self-contained electric cars it will be necessary to have more experience and more figures at one's disposal before they can be conscientiously recommended.

COST OF THE OVERHEAD WIRE SYSTEM.

Quite recently there has been, especially in a daily contemporary, considerable agitation as to what it really costs to work an overhead tramway system. It has been maintained for a long time that the average cost should be about 6d. per car mile. There are many examples of the cost being much lower than 6d. and few cases where it has been higher. The Brussels lines equipped with the overhead electric system cost 4½d.; Dresden, which possesses two systems of electric tramways, cost in one case 6d. per car mile and in the other 3·86d.; Remscheid electric lines cost 4d. per car mile, and, to quote as an instance from America, the railroad commissioners of the State of Connecticut showed in some recent figures that the average cost per car mile on nine electric tramways was 5½d.

It may with some reason be urged that these figures have very little significance in this country, because they probably do not represent the conditions that generally obtain here. It is not, however, a matter of great difficulty to secure returns from the lines that have been working for some time in the United Kingdom. On the old electric tramway line of Leeds, which was put up when practically very little was known about the economical working of tramways, the cost for every car mile run was about 5½d.; but, to come to more recent examples, we can quote that of Bristol, where electricity has been employed on difficult sections of the Bristol Tramway Company's lines, sections, moreover, that hitherto were impossible for horses to work, yet the cost per car mile has been shown to be no more than 5½d. This is an interesting example, because one has an opportunity of comparing that figure with what the horse lines cost in the same city, and from last year's report we find that the horse lines have cost 9½d. per car mile. At Coventry the economical nature of an electric tramway service has been amply demonstrated, and the curious part about this is that previous to the institution of the electric system there tramway systems of any description had been complete failures and two companies had gone into liquidation in their attempts to provide the people of Coventry with a tramway service. The electric tramway company of that city has not only been able to declare a dividend of 8 per cent., notwithstanding that the line passes through sparsely-populated districts, but has been able to demonstrate that the cost of working the line is not more than 6d. per car mile.

We can give a still more favourable illustration in the case of the Dover Corporation tramways, which have been for the past four or five months worked on the overhead wire system. The borough engineer says that the cost per car mile is only 5½d.; and this is very important, because the conditions prevailing in Dover are not altogether ideal ones for the economical working of an electric tramway system, as the corporation buy the necessary electrical energy to work their service from the local electric lighting company, and the charge made for energy is, if not excessive, a good deal more than it would cost the corporation if they manufactured it themselves.

Therefore, out of the few electric systems at present in use in this country, it can be shown that on four lines at least the total cost of working is under 6d., a state of things that ought to demonstrate that electricity is certainly the most economical agent for tramways, because it can be said from figures that are open to everybody that the horse lines of this country average 9d. per car mile, while those lines rarely cost less than 11d. and in some cases more. Some recent figures relating to the comparative cost of various systems of traction in Paris are interesting, and they show us that horses cost 8·55d.; accumulators, 8·83d.; steam locomotives, 5·39d.; and the overhead trolley system, 4·62d. per car mile. These figures ought to be convincing, because the overhead system in Paris has certainly not had particularly fair play.

It is interesting to note the relation of tramways to the population in some of the chief American cities, some European and those in the United Kingdom. They will, at any rate, show that there is considerable room for extending the tramway systems, and thus make them more popular vehicles than they have proved to be in the past.

RATIO OF TRAMWAY MILEAGE TO POPULATION.

*American.*

| Town. | Population. | Miles of Track. | Population per Mile of Track. |
|---|---|---|---|
| New York | 1,851,060 | 458 | 4,042 |
| Chicago | 1,700,000 | 595 | 2,857 |
| Philadelphia | 1,047,000 | 462 | 2,266 |
| Brooklyn | 1,053,393 | 393 | 2,680 |
| St. Louis | 644,000 | 335 | 1,922 |
| Baltimore | 613,965 | 225 | 2,728 |
| Boston and Suburbs | 782,839 | 290 | 2,700 |
| Cleveland | 368,895 | 269 | 1,371 |
| Buffalo | 360,000 | 143 | 2,517 |
| Detroit | 280,000 | 202 | 1,386 |

| Town. | | | Population. | Miles of Track. | Population per Mile of Track. |
|---|---|---|---|---|---|
| *Continental.* | | | | | |
| Berlin | ... | ... | 1,860,000 | 180 | 10,000 |
| Paris | ... | ... | 2,500,000 | 184 | 13,587 |
| *Great 3ritain and Ireland.* | | | | | |
| Glasgow | ... | ... | 840,000 | 73 | 11,507 |
| Liverpool | ... | ... | 600,000 | 60 | 10,000 |
| Manchester | ... | ... | 520,000 | 50 | 10,400 |
| Bradford | ... | ... | 216,400 | 21 | 10,304 |
| Bristol | ... | ... | 221,600 | 18 | 12,311 |
| Cardiff District | ... | ... | 129,000 | 2·33 | 55,364 |
| Leicester | ... | ... | 174,000 | 9 | 19,411 |
| Newcastle and Gosforth | | ... | 186,300 | 13 | 14,330 |
| Nottingham | ... | ... | 213,900 | 10·25 | 20,868 |
| Sheffield | ... | ... | 324,300 | 9 | 36,033 |
| Sunderland | ... | ... | 131,000 | 5 | 26,200 |
| Aberdeen | ... | ... | 109,800 | 10·25 | 10,712 |
| Dundee | ... | ... | 153,000 | 7·25 | 21,103 |
| Edinburgh | ... | ... | 256,400 | 13·5 | 19,000 |
| Belfast | ... | ... | 256,000 | 20 | 14,800 |

## CORRESPONDENCE.

**Strange Doings at Erith.**—Mr. A. H. Jennings, surveyor to the Carshalton Urban District Council, writes: I am reluctantly compelled to draw your attention to the result of an appointment which is deserving of publicity through your valuable paper. The advertisement ran as follows: "The Urban District Council of Erith require an inspector to superintend the laying of private drains and connections to the sewers of the council, and to inspect the construction of new buildings and generally assist the surveyor. He must have a practical knowledge of works of drainage, the construction of buildings, the preparation of plans, and be fully competent to keep all books and accounts connected with the office of surveyor. Salary, £140." The applicants, I understood, numbered nearly 150, and a selection of six was made to interview the council and to " produce original testimonials with specimens of plans and draining work." Being a selected candidate, I made my appearance at the appointed time, and found my chances more favourable than expected, two being absent. Meeting my fellow-candidates, I soon found, to my surprise, that their respective callings were as follows: (1) Bricklayers' foreman, (2) bricklayer, (3) carpenter (a former member of the council), but, unfortunately, out of work. The monotony of waiting an hour and a half was broken by mutual conversation, chiefly on the laws of sanitation, but when an attempt of mine to advance the cause of smoke, air and water for the testing of drains was derided I held my tongue and spoke nothing. At last we were summoned before the council. I produced my qualifications, original testimonials, and specimen drawings of street work, sewers and drains; also copy regulations for private house connections to main sewers in this district (the supervision of which has been one of my chief duties), when I was catechised by the apparent supporters of the local man on such questions as these: Had I ever used a trowel? Could I lay bricks? Had I experience with jerry builders? and similar questions. On the local carpenter being called a second time my hopes vanished, for it was soon announced that he had been successful, although I was informed the voting between him and myself were equal, the chairman giving his casting vote in the carpenter's favour because he was a local man. My cause for complaint is the misleading advertisement, which tempts so many experienced and qualified men to waste their valuable time in applying for an appointment when the result is practically known beforehand. Why should not the Council of Erith advertise locally if a local man, even if devoid of experience, is intended to be appointed against all comers of whatever qualifications they may possess. If the Erith Council had been wise they would have left the appointment to the engineer of their sewerage scheme, or even the surveyor. This scheme, I understood, costs nearly £100,000, and its success depends largely upon the manner in which the private house drains are connected. Time will prove the folly of such a procedure. Yet this is a council, I presume, pledged to study the interests of their ratepayers and uninterested devotion to the public service. I enclose herewith the local paper, marked, giving particulars of the appointment, and editorial comments in stronger and more eloquent terms than words of mine have described.

**Illuminating Gas from Sewage Sludge.**—Mr. Edward A. Harman, engineer and manager of the Huddersfield Corporation gasworks, writes: Will you kindly permit me to supplement my letter to you last week upon the above subject. The sewage sludge, containing an average moisture of 33 per cent., naturally involved serious loss of heat in the retorts. It was difficult to wholly carbonise the material *per se.* When drawing a retort, although the outside of the material appeared to be carbonised, it was noticeable there was still a quantity of gas left in it. At the conclusion of the regular tests I tried a small portion mixed with half coal, and was satisfied that further experiments in that direction would undoubtedly yield vastly improved results. Although

sewage sludge would not be economical to carbonise ordinarily for gas manufacture, yet in cases of emergency, when coal stocks were short, some such system might be worked temporarily with considerable advantage, especially upon works where an oil gas plant is available for maintaining the illuminating power to the required standard. If ordinary gas coal is considered as yielding approximately 10,000 cubic feet of gas per ton of 16 candle-power, a multiple of 160,000 cubic feet is obtained. With the sewage sludge experiments, as published in your last week's issue, the material yielded 5,440 cubic feet of 12·92 candles, which gives a multiple of 70,284 cubic feet, or only 44 per cent. of that obtained from coal. Drying the material apparently had prejudicial effects, evaporating the oils contained in it. I understand the residue "dust" left in the retort after carbonising is valuable for filtration purpose. Singularly enough, the laboratory tests led one to anticipate very much better results. There was evidently a serious decomposition of gas in the retort, due possibly to the outside of the material being first carbonised and the gases evolving from the inner cone having to force their passage through the incandescent coke. When making the experiments it seemed most desirable that the material should be stirred up in some manner during the process of carbonising, and Yeadon's revolving retort suggested itself as being suitable for such purpose. The variableness of the composition of sewage sludge is a characteristic feature of it, and this is clearly demonstrated in the results indicated last week both as to quantity and quality of the gas made.

**Urban District Councils and their Surveyors.**—Mr. T. Hibbert, surveyor to the Cirencester Urban District Council, writes: In your account of the report of the Street and General Purposes Committee respecting my increase of salary and relief from duties of rate collector, which appeared in the columns of THE SURVEYOR issued on Friday last, the 29th ult., there is an important omission. The report of the committee, which was adopted by the council, not only carries with it an increase of salary to £225 per annum as from the 24th June last, but it also ensures further annual increments of £10, £10 and £5, which will bring up the total to £230 a year with the advent of June 24, 1901. In these days, when, as you put it, dealing with applications for increases of salary in a reasonable spirit is all too rare, and lest my council's considerate dealing with me should be wrongly understood, to the possible detriment of any other surveyor who may be supporting a similar application with a reference to your account of my increase, it would seem to be due to my council and myself that the full effect of the adoption of the committee's report should be published, hence my troubling you with this communication.

**Gas Cremators.**—"Acme" writes: I would like to be placed in communication with any one who can furnish me with information regarding any method by which fumes or gases of a nauseous nature are destroyed by any form of cremator.

[Communications, addressed to "Cremator" at the offices of this paper, will be forwarded to our correspondent.—Ed. THE SURVEYOR.

## MANCHESTER SEWAGE DIFFICULTY.

At a meeting of the Rivers Committee of the Manchester Corporation, on the 25th ult., the financial position of the committee was one of the subjects brought under consideration. Recently the Finance Committee called the attention of the Rivers Committee to the heavy adverse balance which exists in connection with the sewage works and scheme, and to the fact that the deficiency has greatly increased during the present year. It was stated that, as the result of an interview with the authorities of the Local Government Board, that body were prepared to grant borrowing powers as a means of obtaining money to pay off the committee's liabilities if a provisional order was obtained for the purchase for sewage treatment purposes of 213 acres of land at Flixton, an area which was scheduled in 1893. The committee decided to resume their powers in the next Parliamentary session, with a view to obtaining the consent of the Local Government Board to borrowing powers. The present liabilities of the Rivers Committee amount to between £60,000 and £80,000, and without some course being taken the whole amount would require to be found out of the city rates. It is probable that powers for borrowing from £100,000 to £150,000 will be obtained.

**London's Water Supply.**—The water examiners in their report on the composition and quality of the water supplied to London during the month ended June 30th state that all the 182 samples of water collected by them from the mains of the London water companies taking their supply from the Thames and Lea were found to be clear, bright and well filtered.

**Tenders Wanted.**—The Secretary of State for Foreign Affairs has received a despatch from Her Majesty's consul at Genoa, stating that tenders are invited by the municipality of Spezzia for the supply of 2,500 tons of gas coal for the gas works at that place. A copy of the conditions of the contract may be examined at the commercial department of the Foreign Office any day between the hours of 11 a.m. and 5 p.m.

# The Appointing of Municipal Engineers and Surveyors.

### By ALEXANDER MACLACHLAN, Assoc.M.Inst.C.E.

It is believed by many members of the engineering profession that municipal engineers and surveyors are the best paid in the profession. Thus, when vacancies occur in this department of engineering, there are large numbers of applicants, and the competition is very keen, and canvassing, although confessedly counted a disqualification, is, nevertheless, carried on to a great extent. So much is this the case that the art of applying for municipal appointments, with all the canvassing and procuring and getting-up of the requisite number of testimonials, has become one of the fine arts, a knowledge of which, it is said, is positively essential in these degenerate days to obtain situations. On the other hand, it is well known that when a vacancy occurs in the official municipal staff in many cases the man has already been chosen for the place, and the place for the man, even before an advertisement has been inserted in the papers. The situation is advertised merely to allow the chosen one an opportunity of applying with the public for a situation already given him. This is done to try and deceive the public into the belief that it is a bonâ-fide advertisement of an open and free competition to all properly and duly qualified to occupy an important and responsible public appointment. But the public are not so easily deceived, and pretty well know to whom the situation will be given. "Send in your application, apply, and we will secure you the appointment," say the two or three knowing ones of brief authority and influence. So he whom they delight to honour hies him home, wrestles through the composition and writing of a hypocritical mockery of an application, and gets it printed with the so-called testimonials procured from people who know little or nothing about him or are utterly incapable of judging of his fitness. So he gets the place, and into the power of the knowing ones at the same time. These knowing ones ever after this annex that man's services to themselves, to serve their own little ends—for did not they get him the appointment? Thus he is robbed of his liberty of action, and becomes but a tool in their hands to do their work—dirty and mean enough work at the best—and to further their own little schemes and plans; and this all to the prejudice of the public interests.

There are few public appointments into which more enters the elements of influence and favour than into municipal appointments; and the appointing of a municipal engineer is in this respect not a whit behind even the appointment of a city or town clerk.

It is a very difficult thing for even able experts to judge of a man's suitability and fitness for a high public appointment. It is strange and extraordinary that men who commonly compose our town or county councils, corporations, magistracies, &c., should be allowed by the public to decide the appointments of men entrusted with the engineering, building and sanitation of our large cities and towns. One would be apt to think that it would be a safer and wiser plan to give the adjudication of such appointments to judges specially fitted by their recognised high attainments and abilities and great and extensive practice in their particular professions. Such learned institutions or associations as the Institution of Civil Engineers, the Royal Institute of British Architects, or the Incorporated Association of Municipal and County Engineers, the Surveyors' Institution, the Sanitary Institute, &c., contain any number of experts highly qualified in their respective professions for selecting from among applicants the most suitable candidates for the several municipal situations.

The days are gone now when simply masons, joiners or plumbers, with nothing more to recommend them but the goodwill of their magisterial acquaintances, can be allowed to occupy the highly important and responsible positions of municipal or county engineers. But time was when such things were permitted and encouraged, and freely and openly practised; and appointments were given by friend to friend, irrespective of ability, fitness, experience or knowledge. Consequently, in town and county, to put it very mildly, things were in a bad way, a very bad way indeed, for many long years to come. Mistakes were made, money was misspent in useless works, or even in mischievous and dangerous works; and, what is far more important than the misspending of money, neglect, culpable neglect, was shown, especially in regard to drainage and water supply, or the want of them, resulting in disease and death to many of the unsuspecting inhabitants of city, town and village.

The duties of the municipal engineer are exceedingly varied and difficult, and they are becoming more and more so every day. Besides being an expert in a few professions, such as that of a surveyor, architect, civil, mechanical, hydraulic and sanitary engineer, he must now be not unacquainted with that profession which deals with that subtle, mysterious and wonderful something called electricity, in order to supply the illuminant of the day, or at least to work in harmony with the electrical expert chosen for that purpose. Those informed on all the particular details of knowledge and the great experience and sagacity required to fill such onerous and responsible positions as modern municipal engineers, surveyors, architects, &c., will hardly admit that a baker, tailor, fishmonger and carter—for such are the bulk of our magistrates—are altogether fitted to judge as to who should give us electric light, gas, water, tramway, cable or electric cars, streets, roads, sewers, bridges, public buildings, city or town halls, municipal buildings, hospitals, universities, destructors and what not. The baker, tailor, fishmonger and carter may be all very good at their respective trades, and even possess a certain amount of experience and knowledge of municipal affairs, and know how to work elections and speak at meetings—rowdy and noisy enough at times—but they are hardly the clever, discerning, well-informed, educated and good gentlemen that an honest and conscientious public should have to decide its environment and conduct and control its affairs.

According to sec. 140 of the London Building Act, 1894, applicants for district surveyorships require to send with their applications certificates of the Royal Institute of British Architects that they are competent to perform such duties. This is all very well as far as it goes, but particular fitness of candidates for particular appointments might well be given over to the Royal Institute of British Architects to settle or determine. It is becoming common to stipulate that candidates for civil, mechanical or electrical engineering appointments must be either members or associate members of the Institutions of Civil, Mechanical or Electrical Engineers. This is an excellent stipulation, but these appointments also might well be delegated to committees of these august and learned bodies to adjudicate.

Therefore it can hardly be considered out of the way to say that the judging of the proficiency of applicants for filling public appointments, as indicated, should be entrusted to experts in the particular professions required to be known and practised by the successful competitors. It is to be hoped that this will become in the future the general order of the day, and not the exception, so that the public interests may be safeguarded and the most efficient and able men be chosen to fill public appointments.

---

## LIVERPOOL SEWAGE FARM.

The following communication recently appeared in a Liverpool contemporary, under the signature of Sigmund Stein: I took the opportunity, on the occasion of my inspection of the Liverpool Corporation sewage farms in West Derby and Walton respecting their suitability for the growing of sugar beetroot, of investigating the work of this filtering method. Through the kindness of our city engineer, Mr. J. A. Brodie, and Mr. Cooper, I received for analysis samples (taken the same time) of the original sewage of the West Derby sewage farm, and also of the drained and filtered water (sent into the brook), and I publish now the result of my analysis. The same is very satisfactory, and gives great credit to our city engineer and his staff. The drained water is nearly pure, and the organic oxidisable matters which cause putrefaction have been extracted to the greatest part and have been absorbed by the soil. I may mention that I planted experimentally sugar beetroot on the corporation sewage farms in Walton and West Derby, and the result of this experiment will be published in due course.

ANALYSIS OF (IN 100,000 PARTS) THE SEWAGE.

| | Original | Drained |
|---|---|---|
| Dry substance... ... ... ... | 132·73 | 92·16 |
| Organic substance ... ... ... | 37·19 | 16·84 |
| Organic nitrogen ... ... ... | 5·86 | ·56 |
| Ammonia ... ... ... ... | 14·26 | 1·13 |
| Nitric Acid ... ... ... | ·09 | 6·27 |
| Phosphoric Acid ($P_2 O_5$) ... ... | ·87 | ·05 |
| Sulphuric Acid ($SO_3$) ... ... | 7·14 | 6·23 |
| Chlorine ... ... ... ... | 42·44 | 17·58 |
| Potassium ... ... ... | 7·62 | 1·17 |
| Sodium ... ... ... ... | 32·10 | 13·64 |
| Lime ... ... ... ... | 13·47 | 14·21 |

---

**Wolverhampton.**—An inquiry was held recently respecting an application of the council for permission to borrow a sum of £1,855 for the purpose of laying-out an "open space" above the vaults of the hall. The inquiry was held by Mr. W. O. E. Meade-King, on behalf of the Local Government Board.

**New Bridge at Keswick.**—A new steel-rope suspension bridge, of 90 ft. span, has just been opened at Keswick. The bridge is erected over the river Greta, and is for the convenience of the public in gaining access to the Fitz park from that part of the town. The bridge was designed and supplied by Mr. Louis Harper, A.M.I.C.E., of Aberdeen.

# The Telephone Service.

The Select Committee of the House of Commons, which is engaged in an inquiry into the Telephone Service, held two more sittings last week.

Mr. ROBERT GIBSON, Lord Mayor of Manchester, was called. He said he wished to contradict the statement made by Mr. Gaine, manager of the National Telephone Company, that the negotiations between the Manchester Corporation and the neighbouring local authorities as to the working of the electric tramways had completely broken down. So far from that being the fact, the arrangements were in a most satisfactory position. The Manchester Corporation had entered into a special agreement with the National Telephone Company as to the granting of underground way-leaves, but there was nothing at all in the agreement which could create a monopoly for the company. He considered that the whole of the telephone service should be in the hands of the Post Office.

Mr. LAMB, second secretary to the Post Office, was recalled, and invited by the chairman to give any objections there might be, from the Post Office point of view, to the granting of municipal licenses. Witness said that the opinions which he expressed were his own, and not those of the present Postmaster-General. While it was impossible not to sympathise to a certain extent with the Glasgow Corporation, he could not agree with the remedies proposed by that body. He was sure that the granting of municipal licenses would strengthen the hands of the company, because, as a general principle of competition, the municipal system would fail, and if that happened the company would have a greater claim for goodwill in case of purchase. But supposing that the municipal system did not fail, then, having proved themselves proper authorities for administering the telephone service, the municipalities must retain the administration for all time; and it became at once a question whether Parliament was to rescind its decision placing the telephone service in the hands of the Post Office. The corporations would not be willing to accept licenses terminating in 1911; and in any case their licenses would strike at the root of any development of the telephone system in the rural districts. If the most profitable part of the telephone business were to be handed over to the municipalities, no one would undertake the cost of establishing the telephones in the country areas. Hitherto the municipalities had adopted a very courteous and friendly attitude towards the Post Office in the matter of way-leaves, but the position would be completely changed when the municipalities became the competitors of the Post Office. Then, under any system of municipal licenses, the difficulties of administration at the Post Office must be greatly increased. There would be innumerable managers to settle with and much more work in auditing the accounts. The municipalities would not give any trunk system, such as the Post Office gave. As to terminals, it would be absurd to expect efficient and harmonious working between the different municipal exchanges in the country. The tendency would be to retard the trunk-wire system. The want of harmonious working between local exchanges would be the greatest obstacle to a truly national service, and the granting of municipal licenses would encourage further inroads on the monopoly of the Postmaster-General in regard to every new telegraphic invention. As to the question of telephone licenses being granted by the Board of Trade under provisional orders, just as electric lighting orders were granted, he thought there was no analogy between the two cases. Electric lighting was the business of no Government department, while the telephone service was the business of the Post Office. It was not reasonable that the Board of Trade should govern the discretion of the Treasury and the Post Office as to supply and price. Then as to the Post Office itself granting provisional orders, it was erroneous to suppose that the National Telephone Company was the mere licensee of the Postmaster-General. In reply to a question, witness said he was not in favour of any competition with the Post Office or by municipalities. He would leave the telephone service in the hands of the company until 1911 without any competition as long as they gave a fairly good service.

Sir S. JOHNSON, town clerk of Nottingham, and one of the four representatives delegated by the Association of Municipal Corporations on this question, was next called. The association, he said, was almost unanimously in favour of a Post Office telephone system, and, failing that, they desired to have municipal licenses. Nottingham, however, had not applied for and did not desire to have a license, as it looked forward to the time when the whole service would be taken over by the State. Nottingham had a very good service provided by the company, but it left out large areas which no one but the State would undertake to serve. The town council had an agreement with the company as to way-leaves, but nothing was provided by the company as to rates or preferences. Sufficient protection was afforded by the fact that the agreement could be terminated at twelve months' notice.

Mr. JOHN GAVEY, second assistant engineer to the Post Office, next gave evidence, describing the toll system of working the telephones which was established in Switzerland, and which he had inspected this year and reported upon to the Post Office.

Mr. A. D. PROVAND, M.P., was called and questioned by Mr. CAWLEY, who called witness's attention to the following question and answer which occurred in the course of Mr. Forbes's evidence : " But you remarked the other day that nobody would be foolish enough, and no body of subscribers would be foolish enough, to start a company in the present tenure ?—Only on the same principles which were developed by the Manchester Company—getting hold of people's money on mistaken pretensions, I will not apply a harder term to it, ending in failure and being bought up." Witness said that statement was intended to cast reflection on him and those who co-operated with him in connection with the Manchester Company. He characterised the statement as simply a calumnious falsehood. It had been made to the committee by Mr. Forbes, and he claimed to be heard in reply to it. He was not going to be defamed in that way. He went on to say that after the Mutual Company started they compelled the National Company to lower their rates. They refused to sell to the National Company because that company refused to carry out their policy of a double-wire system. He and his friends went into the telephone business as reformers, and they brought about extraordinary reforms. The Duke of Marlborough started the new company in London, and they sold to that company because they agreed to their terms. In cross-examination witness denied the statement of Mr. Forbes that the telephone service in this country was better developed than anywhere else. In Germany, Switzerland, Holland, and Norway and Sweden, there were much better services than in England, and the number of telephones in proportion to population was enormously larger. The only way to break down a monopoly was to have different systems, though one first-rate service would be the ideal. That, however, was not obtainable except by competition. In Manchester, for instance, they had to begin with a very bad and expensive service, but by competition they were able to get a much better one. He would prefer to see the service in the hands of the municipalities rather than in the hands of the Post Office. The Post Office would have to spend more capital, and, as far as he could see, their rates would be much higher. The Post Office had only the General Post Office buildings in towns, whereas the municipalities had ready to hand a number of buildings which they might make use of for laying down a telephone service. In the next place, he thought that if the telephones were in the hands of municipalities the management would be much better. No one could get any redress from the Post Office. Rural districts could be better served by local bodies than by the Post Office. Even a local company would be better than the Post Office.

Mr. SINCLAIR, engineer to the National Telephone Company, then gave evidence to show that the average initial cost to the company of setting up an exchange was £57 per subscriber, and that over a series of years this amount became reduced to between £38 and £40. It was absolutely impossible to establish an exchange at rates varying from £12 to £24, as had been suggested. In his opinion, if the company were to start de novo to give such a service as they were now giving it could not be done under £51 per subscriber. In reply to Mr. Bartley and the chairman, witness said that he did consider two rival systems in one area detrimental to the public using the telephones. He was aware that the National Telephone Company went to certain places where there was a Post Office system, but at the time they did so the company was an ordinary licensee, and there were twelve others in the country. He did not think the company were under any obligation to the Post Office to supply a particular type of telephone, but they were under a strong obligation to supply the best they could find. He could not say whether the Post Office had any power to prevent the company using any instrument. If it was the fact that the company was the only licensee that could establish a single-wire system, it was not their practice to do so. They had not put up a single wire for many years.

Mr. LAMB, second secretary to the Post Office, was then recalled, and said, in answer to the chairman, that the wires between exchanges were not the property of the company, but were laid by the Post Office and used by the company at a rental. The earliest of these wires was handed over in September, 1896. Having mentioned various places in the country in which wires were also leased, witness went on to say that the leases had not yet been actually executed, and the arrangement rested on correspondence at present. Formal agreements had been drafted but not settled. He thought the correspondence bound the Post Office. As the agreements were drafted the leases were for the remainder of the term under the license, with power to the Post Office to terminate in 1904, or at any time when the company was taken over, if it should be taken over. He was not able to say from memory whether that point had been absolutely settled, but it was in the draft agreement. The general terms and conditions of the draft agreement were intended to be applicable to all cases, but no doubt certain particulars would have to be settled in each case. The draft agreement had not yet been submitted to the company, and the regulation of the use of these wires rested at present on the correspondence. The company had been paying rent for these wires.

Sir Robert Hunter, solicitor to the Post Office, was also questioned on the same point, and the committee then adjourned.

## ELECTRIC LIGHTING OF MORLEY.

### NEW CORPORATION WORKS OPENED.

The new electric lighting works erected by the Corporation of Morley from the plans of Mr. Hammond, at a cost of £21,219, were recently opened by the chairman of the Electric Lighting Committee.

The generating works are situated in the Corporation-street, between the new public baths and the corporation depot. The buildings, which were designed by the late borough surveyor (Mr. M. H. Sykes), are placed on the south side of the land reserved for the generating works, and are so arranged that a considerable area of land is reserved for future extensions. The total area of the site consists of 4,132 square yards. The engine-house is 40 ft. wide by 38 ft. long, with switch-room at one end. At a height of 20 ft. an overhead travelling crane runs along steel rails the full length of the engine-house. The test-room is conveniently situated at the east side of the switch-room, the floors of which rooms are laid with wood-block flooring. The accumulator-room, 40 ft. by 12 ft. 6 in., is placed over the switch-room and test-room, and is approached by a staircase near the main entrance. The boiler-house is placed parallel with the engine-house, on the west side thereof, and is 68 ft. long by 48 ft. wide. Along the west side of the boiler-house are placed the coal bunkers, 10 ft. wide, and the pump-room, 10 ft. by 12 ft. At present there are two Lancashire boilers, 30 ft. by 8 ft. diameter, and accommodation is provided for two others of equal size. The offices are situated over the work and store-rooms, and are approached by two staircases, one being from the main entrance-hall and the other being a spiral staircase from the boiler-house to the chief engineer's private office. The contracts for the buildings have been carried out by local firms, as follows: Building and masons' work—Messrs. Newton & Asquith; joiners' work—Mr. D. Marsden; plumbers' work—Mr. Firth; plasterers' work—Mr. Wilson; slaters' work—Messrs. D. Thornton & Sons; painters' work—Mr. W. Lawton. The two main engines are made by Messrs. Pollit & Wigzell, of Sowerby Bridge. They are of the horizontal compound non-condensing type, with cylinders 14 in. and 23½ in. diameter, 30 in. stroke, running at a speed of 100 revolutions per minute with a working pressure of 130 lb. per square inch. The two alternators are the Electric Construction Company's fly-wheel machines. The exciting current for the alternators is supplied by a separate direct-current plant. It may be mentioned that for some three months past the works have been in operation successfully.

The system adopted is the high-pressure alternating, with a pressure of 200 volts at the consumers' terminals. It should be explained that Morley is a somewhat scattered town, and the high-pressure alternating system, perhaps, offered the readiest facilities for adequately meeting the future demands. The two Lancashire boilers are each capable of evaporating 7,000 lb. of water per hour at 125 lb. pressure. The most interesting feature about the boiler-house is that the mechanical coal stokers are actuated by an electric motor. The generating plant is entirely in accordance with modern ideas, and the principal machines are combined with the engine fly-wheel. We have already referred briefly to the two sets of 120 kilowatt fly-wheel alternators and to the direct current exciting plant of 30 kilowatts capacity which is provided to excite the field magnets of the alternators. There is also a motor alternator, to which further reference will be made. The cylinders of the two main engines are arranged side by side with the alternators running between them. The diameter over the poles of the alternators is 13 ft. and the weight of the fly-wheel, including the field magnets which it carries, is 10 tons. What makes the system of special interest is the provision of accumulators which will no doubt exercise a marked economy in the operation of the plant. The battery of accumulators comprises fifty-seven cells of the Chloride Company's manufacture, and is capable of giving a discharge of 250 amperes for two hours, or 100 amperes for six hours, or 70 amperes for ten hours, with a terminal electro-motive force of 1,000 volts. The battery is charged by means of the exciting plant referred to, and is then utilised to drain the motor alternator which will supply the whole of the current required during the daytime. When necessary the battery will also supply current for exciting the field magnets of the large alternators. There are two switchboards, one of which is devoted to the alternator and feeder circuits, the other being exclusively used for the exciters, batteries and the motor alternator.

The mains consist of concentric conductors, each one insulated by a di-electric of bituminised fibre, the outer di-electric being sheathed with a very heavy covering of lead, and finished by a yarn braid, and compounded. These cables are drawn into stoneware ducts or pipes. The high-pressure mains are connected to six sub-stations, whence current is distributed to consumers. At these sub-stations are arranged the necessary transformers which convert the high-pressure current into a low one suitable for distribution to the consumers.

The street lighting is on a small scale and is mainly experimental. The lamp columns carry an arc lamp and two incandescent lamps, switching gear being provided in the base of the column for the purpose of extinguishing the arc and putting on the incandescents, which is done at midnight. A small transformer is also placed in each lamp-post, for the purpose of reducing the pressure of the current to that necessary for the arc.

The Morley Corporation are to be congratulated upon the completion of the works, which represent the very latest practice in the generation and distribution of electricity.

## COMBINED DRAINAGE.

### REPORT TO THE LAMBETH VESTRY.

Mr. J. P. Norrington, surveyor to the Lambeth Vestry, has presented a report to that body on the subject of combined drainage. He begins by remarking, that while under circumstances combined drainage may be accepted, in most cases it is advisable that each property should have a separate drain communicating directly with the sewer in the road. Mr. Norrington then continues as follows:—

The method of construction I advocate is that every property should have a manhole at the back to receive the branch drains, and a manhole in the front to facilitate ready access to the syphon and the connection to the sewer. All the drains to be laid in a perfectly straight line and surrounded with 6 in. of concrete. In this way every part of a drain is immediately under control, and should any impediment to the flow or stoppage arise it can be cleared by rods; also, the main line from manhole to manhole can even be examined by means of lights, should any defect be suspected. The possibility of a defect arising in this main line, when laid in the manner described, is so very remote as hardly to entitle it to consideration in connection with this question.

In years past the construction of drains has been carried out in such an inferior manner that an objection has arisen to the passage of drains underneath a dwelling, and a person letting or selling a property likes to be able to say that the drains do not pass under it. It is also possible that such a statement enables a slightly-increased price or rent to be obtained for the dwelling. Combined drainage, by saving a number of connections to the main sewer, in many cases is cheaper in construction than the system of providing a separate drain to each house.

#### CONDITIONS FOR COMBINED DRAINS.

The vestry is, in my opinion, justified in meeting the above-mentioned objections to drains passing under houses, and in sanctioning a method that will lessen the original cost of building, provided that the following conditions can be complied with in the construction of the combined drain or sewer:—

(1) That the drain be laid in a passage at the back of the houses. The said passage either to open to a side street or to a passage at the flank of the houses leading to the street in front.

(2) That the drain be laid under precisely the same conditions as a main sewer.

(3) That the number of manholes provided to the main drain shall be ample for the purposes of access, examination, cleansing and flushing.

(4) That there shall be a clear space or passage, 5 ft. wide, between buildings for this sewer to pass with, with an undertaking on the part of the owners not at any time to build over the said space or passage. This arrangement will permit of the reconstruction of the sewer without difficulty at any future time, should it be necessary.

(5) That the owners undertake the future paving, cleansing and maintenance of the said passage, which should be kept closed by means of doors or gates with spring locks.

(6) That each house should have a separate manhole and an interceptor between the manhole and the combined drain or sewer.

The provision of the clear space or passage overcomes the great difficulties and delay frequently caused by an owner or tenant refusing to allow his property to be entered, on the ground that he has not created the obstruction or that he is not going to have his premises pulled up for the benefit of others, &c. If a passageway is insisted on it affords an opportunity of removing the dust, &c., without carrying it through the houses. Subject to the above conditions, I see no objection to the vestry undertaking the permanent maintenance of such a combined drain or sewer.

The principle of accepting the maintenance of the combined drain as a sewer is carried out in many other districts, in some cases without the safeguards for ready access, &c., which I consider necessary and reasonable. As to the question of the number of houses which should discharge into a combined drain, I see no reason to impose any limit to the number, provided that the capacity of the sewer is sufficient. The greater the number of properties discharging into a sewer the more constant is the flow, and the more frequently and completely will it be flushed. It is manifest that the rainfall from twenty roofs and yards would be more beneficial to such a drain than the rainfall of only a few properties.

# Provisional Orders for 1898.

### REMARKABLE ACTIVITY AMONG LOCAL AUTHORITIES.

In another column we have some remarks on the subject of provisional orders generally, but with special reference to the following details, which we have been at considerable pains to procure and which will no doubt be serviceable. Whilst there has been an increase in the total number of provisional orders, it is in electric undertakings that this mode of procedure has found most general acceptation. In the present year thirteen applications for tramway provisional orders, representing a capital expenditure of £412,230, have been made, and of these nine have been granted. Eleven applications were made for gas provisional orders, representing an outlay of about £250,000, and of these nine have been granted. Applications for water provisional orders numbered seven, representing an expenditure of about £120,000, and six of them have been granted. The applications for electric lighting provisional orders were no less than eighty-four in number, and the capital represented was £2,148,670. Of the orders applied for, sixty-seven have been granted. Leaving the present session out of consideration, it appears that since the passing of the Electric Lighting Acts of 1882 and 1890 580 orders have been applied for, 3s0 of the applications have been granted by the Board of Trade and 387 confirmed by Parliament. The orders which have been dealt with during the present session are as follows :—

TRAMWAY PROVISIONAL ORDERS.

*Blackpool, St. Anne's and Lytham Tramways.*—To authorise the Blackpool, St. Anne's and Lytham Tramways Company to construct additional tramways and to apply certain provisions of the Acts of 1893 and 1896. Length of new line, 55 chains ; estimated cost, £4,830. Granted.

*Carlisle Tramways.*—To authorise the construction of tramways in and near the city of Carlisle to be worked by electrical or any power. Length, 7 miles 14 chains ; cost, £36,750. Granted.

*East Ham Urban Council Tramways.*—To authorise the urban district council to construct tramways to be worked by electrical or any power. Length, 3 miles 58 chains ; cost, £49,107. Granted.

*Eccleshill Urban Council Tramways.*—To authorise the urban district council to construct tramways to be worked by electrical or any power, and to confer running powers over the Bradford Corporation tramways. Length, 42 chains ; cost, £2,900. Granted.

*Great Crosby Tramways.*—To authorise the urban district council to construct tramways to be worked by electrical or any power, and to provide for the transfer of powers with the consent of the Board of Trade. Length, 2 miles 22 chains ; cost £14,635. Granted.

*Highgate and Finchley Tramways.*—To authorise the construction of tramways in the parishes or districts of St. Mary, Islington, Hornsey and Finchley, to be worked by mechanical or other power, and to enter into running and working agreements. Length, 3 miles 79 chains ; cost, £34,052. Refused on the ground that the consent of the local authorities had not been obtained.

*Huddersfield Corporation Tramways.*—To authorise the Huddersfield Corporation to construct additional tramways and to enter into working agreements with the Linthwaite District Council. Length, 2 miles 52 chains ; cost, £15,277. Granted.

*Linthwaite Tramways.*—To authorise the Linthwaite Urban District Council to construct a tramway in their district to be worked by electrical or any power and to enter into agreements with the Corporation of Huddersfield. Length, 2 miles 91 chains ; cost, £17,928. Granted.

*Liverpool Corporation Tramways Extension.*—To authorise the corporation to construct additional tramways in the city and to apply certain provisions of the order of 1883 and the Act of 1897. Length, 15 miles 36 chains ; cost, £159,000. Granted.

*Llandudno Urban District Council Tramways.*—To authorise the Llandudno Urban District Council to construct a tramway in their district to be worked by electrical or any power. Length, 2 miles 65 chains ; cost, £21,243. Refused on account of the council having failed to obtain the consent of certain property owners.

*North Staffordshire Tramways.*—To authorise the construction of tramways in Stoke-upon-Trent, Newcastle-under-Lyme, Hanley, Fenton and adjoining places to be worked by electrical or any power, and to vary sec. 43 of the Tramways Act of 1870 as to the purchase of tramways by the local authority. Length, 5 miles 37 chains ; cost, £30,000. Refused on account of the company having failed to obtain the consent of the local authorities.

*Oxford Tramways Extension.*—To authorise the construction of an additional tramway in the City of Oxford and to provide for the purchase of the tramways by the local authority. Length, 63 chains ; cost, £3,670. Granted.

*Waterloo-with-Seaforth Tramways.*—To authorise the Urban District Council to construct tramways to be worked by electrical or any power and to transfer the undertaking with the consent of the Board of Trade. Length, 1 mile 53 chains ; cost, £10,119. Granted.

*West Hartlepool Tramways.*—To authorise the General Electric Tramways Company, Limited, to construct additional tramways in the borough of West Hartlepool to be worked by electrical or any power. Length, 22 chains ; cost, £1,800. Granted.

*Woolwich and South-East London Tramways.*—To authorise the construction of tramways in Woolwich and Plumstead to be worked by electrical or any power. Length, 2 miles 36 chains ; cost, £10,910. Refused on the ground that the consent of the local authority had not been obtained.

GAS PROVISIONAL ORDERS.

*Budleigh Salterton Gas.*—To empower the Budleigh Salterton Gas Company, Limited, to maintain and continue the gasworks ; to construct new works ; to raise capital by shares, original £3,000, additional £10,000, by loan £5,500 ; proposed standard price per 1,000 cubic feet, 5s. Granted.

*Cannock Gas.*—To empower Cannock, Hednesford and District Gas Company, Limited, to maintain and continue gasworks ; to raise capital by shares, original £10,000, additional £10,000, by loan £12,500 ; proposed standard price, 3s.6 Granted.

*Churwell Gas.*—To empower the Churwell Gaslight Company to maintain and continue gasworks ; to raise capital by shares, original £3,075, additional £2,925, by loan £1,500 ; proposed standard price, 4s. 2d. Refused on account of the Morley authority having obtained powers by a Bill passed this session to acquire the Churwell undertaking.

*Coatbridge Gas.*—To empower the Coatbridge Gas Company to raise additional capital, £25,000 by shares, £6,250 by loan. Granted.

*Coalwall Gas.*—To empower the Coalwall Gas Company, Limited, to maintain and continue the gasworks ; to raise capital by shares, original £5,000, additional £5,000, by loan £2,500 ; proposed standard price, 6s. Granted.

*Crossgates, Halton and Seacroft Gas.*—To empower the Crossgates, Halton and Seacroft Gas Company, Limited, to maintain, continue and extend the gasworks ; to raise capital by shares, original £10,000, additional £2,000, by loan £3,000 ; proposed standard price, 4s. Granted.

*Freshwater Gas.*—To empower the Freshwater Gas Company, Limited, to construct, maintain and extend the gasworks ; to raise capital, £12,000 by shares, £3,000 by loan ; proposed maximum price, 5s. Refused in consequence of opposition by the local authority.

*Great Marlow Gas.*—To empower the Great Marlow Gas Company, Limited, to maintain and continue the gasworks and extend the area of supply ; to raise capital by shares, original £9,000, additional £21,000, by loan £7,500 ; proposed standard price, 4s. 8d. Granted.

*King's Lynn Gas.*—To empower the King's Lynn Gas Company to raise £8,000 capital and to construct additional works. Granted.

*Slough Gas.*—To empower the Slough Gas and Coke Company to acquire additional land and to construct new works. Granted.

*Whitchurch (Salop) Gas.*—To empower the Whitchurch (Salop) Gas Company, Limited, to maintain and continue gasworks ; to raise capital by shares, original £20,500, additional £9,500, by loan £7,500 ; proposed maximum price, 5s. Granted.

WATER PROVISIONAL ORDERS.

*Broughton-in-Furness Water.*—To empower the Broughton-in-Furness Water Company, Limited, to construct and maintain the waterworks and extend the supply ; to raise capital, £1,700 by shares, £437 by loan. Granted.

*Ightham and Wrotham Water.*—To empower C. G. Hale to construct and maintain waterworks and to supply Ightham and Wrotham with water. Refused in consequence of opposition by the local authority.

*Borough of Portsmouth Water.*—To empower the Portsmouth Waterworks Company to raise additional capital, £4,500 by shares and £15,000 by loan. Granted.

*Ross Water.*—To empower the undertakings of the Ross waterworks to raise additional capital, £5,000 by shares and £1,250 by loan. Granted.

*St. Neot's Water.*—To empower the St. Neot's Water Company to construct and maintain waterworks, and to raise additional capital, £3,000 by shares and £750 by loan. Granted.

*South Hayling Water.*—To empower the South Hayling Water Company, Limited, to construct and maintain waterworks and extend the limits of supply. Granted.

*Wrexham Water.*—To empower the Wrexham Waterworks Company to raise additional capital, £10,000 by shares and £10,000 by loan. Granted.

ELECTRIC LIGHTING PROVISIONAL ORDERS.

*Airdrie Burgh Electric Lighting Order.*—To authorise the provost, magistrates and council of Airdrie to supply electricity within that burgh ; to raise £10,000 capital. Granted.

*Aldershot Electric Lighting Order.*—To authorise the Aldershot Urban District Council to supply electricity ; to raise £18,000 capital. Granted.

*Aston Manor Electric Lighting Order.*—To authorise the

pondence. The company had been paying rent for these wires.

Sir Robert Hunter, solicitor to the Post Office, was also questioned on the same point, and the committee then adjourned.

## ELECTRIC LIGHTING OF MORLEY.

### NEW CORPORATION WORKS OPENED.

The new electric lighting works erected by the Corporation of Morley from the plans of Mr. Hammond, at a cost of £21,219, were recently 'opened by the chairman of the Electric Lighting Committee.

The generating works are situated in the Corporation-street, between the new public baths and the corporation depot. The buildings, which were designed by the late borough surveyor (Mr. M. H. Sykes), are placed on the south side of the land reserved for the generating works, and are so arranged that a considerable area of land is reserved for future extensions. The total area of the site consists of 4,132 square yards. The engine-house is 40 ft. wide by 38 ft. long, with switch-room at one end. At a height of 20 ft. an overhead travelling crane runs along steel rails the full length of the engine-house. The test-room is conveniently situated at the east side of the switch-room, the floors of which rooms are laid with wood-block flooring. The accumulator-room, 40 ft. by 12 ft. 6 in., is placed over the switch-room and test-room, and is approached by a staircase near the main entrance. The boiler-house is placed parallel with the engine-house, on the west side thereof, and is 68 ft. long by 48 ft. wide. Along the west side of the boiler-house are placed the coal bunkers, 10 ft. wide, and the pump-room, 10 ft. by 12 ft. At present there are two Lancashire boilers, 30 ft. by 8 ft. diameter, and accommodation is provided for two others of equal size. The offices are situated over the work and store-rooms, and are approached by two staircases, one being from the main entrance-hall and the other being a spiral staircase from the boiler-house to the chief engineer's private office. The contracts for the buildings have been carried out by local firms, as follows: Building and masons' work—Messrs. Newton & Asquith; joiners' work—Mr. D. Marsden; plumbers' work— Mr. Firth; plasterers' work—Mr. Wilson; slaters' work— Messrs. D. Thornton & Sons; painters' work—Mr. W. Lawton. The two main engines are made by Messrs. Pollit & Wigzell, of Sowerby Bridge. They are of the horizontal compound non-condensing type, with cylinders 14 in. and 23½ in. diameter, 30 in. stroke, running at a speed of 100 revolutions per minute with a working pressure of 130 lb. per square inch. The two alternators are the Electric Construction Company's fly-wheel machines. The exciting current for the alternators is supplied by a separate directcurrent plant. It may be mentioned that for some three months past the works have been in operation successfully.

The system adopted is the high-pressure alternating, with a pressure of 200 volts at the consumers' terminals. It should be explained that Morley is a somewhat scattered town, and the high-pressure alternating system, perhaps, offered the readiest facilities for adequately meeting the future demands. The two Lancashire boilers are each capable of evaporating 7,000 lb. of water per hour at 125 lb. pressure. The most interesting feature about the boiler-house is that the mechanical coal stokers are actuated by an electric motor. The generating plant is entirely in accordance with modern ideas, and the principal machines are combined with the engine fly-wheel. We have already referred briefly to the two sets of 120 kilowatt fly-wheel alternators and to the direct current exciting plant of 30 kilowatts capacity which is provided to excite the field magnets of the alternators. There is also a motor alternator, to which further reference will be made. The cylinders of the two main engines are arranged side by side with the alternators running between them. The diameter over the poles of the alternators is 13 ft. and the weight of the fly-wheel, including the field magnets which it carries, is 10 tons. What makes the system of special interest is the provision of accumulators which will no doubt exercise a marked economy in the operation of the plant. The battery of accumulators comprises fifty-seven cells of the Chloride Company's manufacture, and is capable of giving a discharge of 250 amperes for two hours, or 100 amperes for six hours, or 70 amperes for ten hours, with a terminal electromotive force of 1,000 volts. The battery is charged by means of the exciting plant referred to, and is then utilised to drain the motor alternator which will supply the whole of the current required during the daytime. When necessary the battery will also supply current for exciting the field magnets of the large alternators. There are two switchboards, one of which is devoted to the alternator and feeder circuits, the other being exclusively used for the exciters, batteries and the motor alternator.

The mains consist of concentric conductors, each one insulated by a di-electric of bituminised fibre, the outer di-electric being sheathed with a very heavy covering of lead, and finished by a yarn braid, and compounded. These cables are drawn into stoneware ducts or pipes. The high-pressure mains are connected to six sub-stations, whence current is distributed to consumers. At these sub-stations are arranged the necessary transformers which convert the high-pressure current into a low one suitable for distribution to the consumers.

The street lighting is on a small scale and is mainly experimental. The lamp columns carry an arc lamp and two incandescent lamps, switching gear being provided in the base of the column for the purpose of extinguishing the arc and putting on the incandescents, which is done at midnight. A small transformer is also placed in each lamp-post, for the purpose of reducing the pressure of the current to that necessary for the arc.

The Morley Corporation are to be congratulated upon the completion of the works, which represent the very latest practice in the generation and distribution of electricity.

## COMBINED DRAINAGE.

### REPORT TO THE LAMBETH VESTRY.

Mr. J. P. Norrington, surveyor to the Lambeth Vestry, has presented a report to that body on the subject of combined drainage. He begins by remarking, that while under circumstances combined drainage may be accepted, in most cases it is advisable that each property should have a separate drain communicating directly with the sewer in the road. Mr. Norrington then continues as follows:—

The method of construction I advocate is that every property should have a manhole at the back to receive the branch drains, and a manhole in the front to facilitate ready access to the syphon and the connection to the sewer. All the drains to be laid in a perfectly straight line and surrounded with 6 in. of concrete. In this way every part of a drain is immediately under control, and should any impediment to the flow or stoppage arise it can be cleared by rods; also, the main line from manhole to manhole can even be examined by means of lights, should any defect be suspected. The possibility of a defect arising in this main line, when laid in the manner described, is so very remote as hardly to entitle it to consideration in connection with this question.

In years past the construction of drains has been carried out in such an inferior manner that an objection has arisen to the passage of drains underneath a dwelling, and a person letting or selling a property likes to be able to say that the drains do not pass under it. It is also possible that such a statement enables a slightly-increased price or rent to be obtained for the dwelling. Combined drainage, by saving a number of connections to the main sewer, in many cases is cheaper in construction than the system of providing a separate drain to each house.

#### CONDITIONS FOR COMBINED DRAINS.

The vestry is, in my opinion, justified in meeting the abovementioned objections to drains passing under houses, and in sanctioning a method that will lessen the original cost of building, provided that the following conditions can be complied with in the construction of the combined drain or sewer :—

(1) That the drain be laid in a passage at the back of the houses. The said passage either to open to a side street or to a passage at the flank of the houses leading to the street in front.

(2) That the drain be laid under precisely the same conditions as a main sewer.

(3) That the number of manholes provided to the main drain shall be ample for the purposes of access, examination, cleansing and flushing.

(4) That there shall be a clear space or passage, 5 ft. wide, between buildings for this sewer to pass under, with an undertaking on the part of the owners not at any time to build over the said space or passage. This arrangement will permit of the reconstruction of the sewer without difficulty at any future time, should it be necessary.

(5) That the owners undertake the future paving, cleansing and maintenance of the said passage, which should be kept closed by means of doors or gates with spring locks.

(6) That each house should have a separate manhole and an interceptor between the manhole and the combined drain or sewer.

The provision of the clear space or passage overcomes the great difficulties and delay frequently caused by an owner or tenant refusing to allow his property to be entered, on the ground that he has not created the obstruction or that he is not going to have his premises pulled up for the benefit of others, &c. If a passageway is insisted on it affords an opportunity of removing the dust, &c., without carrying it through the houses. Subject to the above conditions, I see no objection to the vestry undertaking the permanent maintenance of such a combined drain or sewer.

The principle of accepting the maintenance of the combined drain as a sewer is carried out in many other districts, in some cases without the safeguards for ready access, &c., which I consider necessary and reasonable. As to the question of the number of houses which should discharge into a combined drain, I see no reason to impose any limit to the number, provided that the capacity of the sewer is sufficient. The greater the number of properties discharging into a sewer the more constant is the flow, and the more frequently and completely will it be flushed. It is manifest that the rainfall from twenty roofs and yards would be more beneficial to such a drain than the rainfall of only a few properties.

# Provisional Orders for 1898.

## REMARKABLE ACTIVITY AMONG LOCAL AUTHORITIES.

In another column we have some remarks on the subject of provisional orders generally, but with special reference to the forthcoming details, which we have been at considerable pains to procure and which will no doubt be serviceable. Whilst there has been an increase in the total number of provisional orders, it is in electric undertakings that this mode of procedure has found most general acceptance. In the present year thirteen applications for tramway provisional orders, representing a capital expenditure of £412,230, have been made, and of these nine have been granted. Eleven applications were made for gas provisional orders, representing an outlay of about £250,000, and of these nine have been granted. Applications for water provisional orders numbered seven, representing an expenditure of about £120,000, and six of them have been granted. The applications for electric lighting provisional orders were no less than eighty-four in number, and the capital represented was £2,148,670. Of the orders applied for, sixty-seven have been granted. Leaving the present session out of consideration, it appears that since the passing of the Electric Lighting Acts of 1882 and 1890 560 orders have been applied for, 3s0 of them have been granted by the Board of Trade and 387 confirmed by Parliament. The orders which have been dealt with during the present session are as follows :—

### TRAMWAY PROVISIONAL ORDERS.

*Blackpool, St. Anne's and Lytham Tramways.*—To authorise the Blackpool, St. Anne's and Lytham Tramways Company to construct additional tramways and to apply certain provisions of the Acts of 1893 and 1896. Length of new line, 55 chains ; estimated cost, £4,830. Granted.

*Carlisle Tramways.*—To authorise the construction of tramways in and near the city of Carlisle to be worked by electrical or any power. Length, 7 miles 14 chains ; cost, £36,750. Granted.

*East Ham Urban Council Tramways.*—To authorise the urban district council to construct tramways to be worked by electrical or any power. Length, 3 miles 58 chains ; cost, £49,107. Granted.

*Eccleshill Urban Council Tramways.*—To authorise the urban district council to construct tramways to be worked by electrical or any power, and to confer running powers over the Bradford Corporation tramways. Length, 42 chains ; cost, £2,900. Granted.

*Great Crosby Tramways.*—To authorise the urban district council to construct tramways to be worked by electrical or any power, and to provide for the transfer of powers with the consent of the Board of Trade. Length, 2 miles 22 chains : cost £14,635. Granted.

*Highgate and Finchley Tramways.*—To authorise the construction of tramways in the parishes or districts of St. Mary, Islington, Hornsey and Finchley, to be worked by mechanical or other power, and to enter into running and working agreements. Length, 3 miles 79 chains ; cost, £34,052. Refused on the ground that the consent of the local authorities had not been obtained.

*Huddersfield Corporation Tramways.*—To authorise the Huddersfield Corporation to construct additional tramways and to enter into working agreements with the Linthwaite District Council. Length, 2 miles 52 chains ; cost, £15,277. Granted.

*Linthwaite Tramways.*—To authorise the Linthwaite Urban District Council to construct a tramway in their district to be worked by electrical or any power and to enter into agreements with the Corporation of Huddersfield. Length, 2 miles 91 chains ; cost, £17,928. Granted.

*Liverpool Corporation Tramways Extension.*—To authorise the corporation to construct additional tramways in the city and to apply certain provisions of the order of 1883 and the Act of 1897. Length, 15 miles 36 chains ; cost, £159,000. Granted.

*Llandudno Urban District Council Tramways.*—To authorise the Llandudno Urban District Council to construct a tramway in their district to be worked by electrical or any power. Length, 2 miles 65 chains ; cost, £21,343. Refused on account of the council having failed to obtain the consent of certain property owners.

*North Staffordshire Tramways.*—To authorise the construction of tramways in Stoke-upon-Trent, Newcastle-under-Lyme, Hanley, Fenton and adjoining places to be worked by electrical or any power, and to vary sec. 43 of the Tramways Act of 1870 as to the purchase of tramways by the local authority. Length, 5 miles 37 chains ; cost, £90,000. Refused on account of the company having failed to obtain the consent of the local authorities.

*Oxford Tramways Extension.*—To authorise the construction of an additional tramway in the City of Oxford and to provide for the purchase of the tramways by the local authority. Length, 63 chains ; cost, £3,070. Granted.

*Waterloo-with-Seaforth Tramways.*—To authorise the Urban District Council to construct tramways to be worked by electrical or any power and to transfer the undertaking with the consent of the Board of Trade. Length, 1 mile 53 chains ; cost, £10,119. Granted.

*West Hartlepool Tramways.*—To authorise the General Electric Tramways Company, Limited, to construct additional tramways in the borough of West Hartlepool to be worked by electrical or any power. Length, 22 chains ; cost, £1,800. Granted.

*Woolwich and South-East London Tramways.*—To authorise the construction of tramways in Woolwich and Plumstead to be worked by electrical or any power. Length, 2 miles 36 chains ; cost, £10,910. Refused on the ground that the consent of the local authority had not been obtained.

### GAS PROVISIONAL ORDERS.

*Budleigh Salterton Gas.*—To empower the Budleigh Salterton Gas Company, Limited, to maintain and continue the gasworks ; to construct new works ; to raise capital by shares, original £3,005, additional £10,000, by loan £5,500 ; proposed standard price per 1,000 cubic feet, 5s. Granted.

*Cannock Gas.*—To empower Cannock, Hednesford and District Gas Company, Limited, to maintain and continue gasworks ; to raise capital by shares, original £10,000, additional £10,000, by loan £12,500 ; proposed standard price, 5s. Granted.

*Churwell Gas.*—To empower the Churwell Gaslight Company to maintain and continue gasworks ; to raise capital by shares, original £3,075, additional £2,925, by loan £1,500 ; proposed standard price, 4s. 2d. Refused on account of the Morley authority having obtained powers by a Bill passed this session to acquire the Churwell undertaking.

*Coatbridge Gas.*—To empower the Coatbridge Gas Company to raise additional capital, £25,000 by shares, £6,250 by loan. Granted.

*Coalvall Gas.*—To empower the Coalvall Gas Company, Limited, to maintain and continue the gasworks ; to raise capital by shares, original £5,000, additional £5,000, by loan £2,500 ; proposed standard price, 6s. Granted.

*Crossgates, Halton and Seacroft Gas.*—To empower the Crossgates, Halton and Seacroft Gas Company, Limited, to maintain, continue and extend the gasworks ; to raise capital by shares, original £10,000, additional £2,000, by loan £3,000 ; proposed standard price, 4s. Granted.

*Freshwater Gas.*—To empower the Freshwater Gas Company, Limited, to construct, maintain and extend the gasworks ; to raise capital, £12,000 by shares, £3,000 by loan ; proposed maximum price, 5s. Refused in consequence of opposition by the local authority.

*Great Marlow Gas.*—To empower the Great Marlow Gas Company, Limited, to maintain and continue the gasworks and extend the area of supply ; to raise capital by shares, original £9,000, additional £21,000, by loan £7,300 ; proposed standard price, 4s. 8d. Granted.

*King's Lynn Gas.*—To empower the King's Lynn Gas Company to raise £8,000 capital and to construct additional works. Granted.

*Slough Gas.*—To empower the Slough Gas and Coke Company to acquire additional land and to construct new works. Granted.

*Whitchurch (Salop) Gas.*—To empower the Whitchurch (Salop) Gas Company, Limited, to maintain and continue gasworks ; to raise capital by shares, original £20,500, additional £9,500, by loan £7,500 ; proposed maximum price, 5s. Granted.

### WATER PROVISIONAL ORDERS.

*Broughton-in-Furness Water.*—To empower the Broughton-in-Furness Water Company, Limited, to construct and maintain the waterworks and extend the supply ; to raise capital, £1,700 by shares, £437 by loan. Granted.

*Ightham and Wrotham Water.*—To empower C. G. Hale to construct and maintain waterworks and to supply Ightham and Wrotham with water. Refused in consequence of opposition by the local authority.

*Borough of Portsmouth Water.*—To empower the Portsmouth Waterworks Company to raise additional capital, £4,500 by shares and £15,000 by loan. Granted.

*Ross Water.*—To empower the undertakings of the Ross waterworks to raise additional capital, £5,000 by shares and £1,250 by loan. Granted.

*St. Neot's Water.*—To empower the St. Neot's Water Company to construct and maintain waterworks, and to raise additional capital, £3,000 by shares and £750 by loan. Granted.

*South Hayling Water.*—To empower the South Hayling Water Company, Limited, to construct and maintain waterworks and extend the limits of supply. Granted.

*Wrexham Water.*—To empower the Wrexham Waterworks Company to raise additional capital, £10,000 by shares and £10,000 by loan. Granted.

### ELECTRIC LIGHTING PROVISIONAL ORDERS.

*Airdrie Burgh Electric Lighting Order.*—To authorise the provost, magistrates and council of the burgh of Airdrie to supply electricity within that burgh ; to raise £10,000 capital. Granted.

*Aldershot Electric Lighting Order.*—To authorise the Aldershot Urban District Council to supply electricity ; to raise £18,000 capital. Granted.

*Aston Manor Electric Lighting Order.*—To authorise the

Aston Manor Urban District Council to supply electricity; to raise £10,000 capital. Granted.

*Barnes Electric Lighting Order.*—To authorise Barnes Urban District Council to supply electricity; to raise £20,000 capital. Granted.

*Batley Electric Lighting Order.*—To authorise the mayor, aldermen and burgesses of Batley to supply electricity; to raise £25,000 capital. Granted.

*Bermondsey Electric Lighting Order.* — To authorise the Vestry of Bermondsey to supply electricity within the parish; to raise £15,000 capital. Granted.

*Bermondsey, Rotherhithe, Greenwich and Lewisham Electric Lighting Order.*—To authorise the County of London and Brush Provincial Electric Lighting Company, Limited, to supply electricity in the parishes named; to raise £25,000 capital. With regard to Bermondsey, preference was given by the Board of Trade to the application received from the local authority. With regard to the other districts, the promoters failed to produce the consents of the local authorities or to satisfy the board that they should be dispensed with. The board therefore refused to grant the order.

*Bethnal Green, Poplar and Whitechapel Electric Lighting Order.*—To authorise the County of London and Brush Provincial Electric Lighting Company to supply electricity; to raise £25,000 capital. Refused on account of the promoters failing to produce the consents of the local authorities.

*Birkdale Electric Lighting Order.*—To authorise the Birkdale Urban District Council to supply electricity within their district; to raise £20,000 capital. Granted.

*Bolton Electric Lighting Order.*—To authorise the mayor, aldermen and burgesses of Bolton to supply electricity within the borough and townships of Astley Bridge, Heaton, Smith Hills, Darcy Lever, Breightmet, Lostock, Deane-over-Hulton, Middle Hulton, Tonge and Great Lever; to raise £15,000 capital. Granted.

*Brechin Electric Lighting Order.*—To authorise the provost and councillors of the Royal Burgh of Brechin to supply electricity; to raise £10,000. Granted.

*Bridgwater Corporation Electric Lighting Order.*—To authorise the mayor, aldermen and burgesses of Bridgwater to supply electricity within that borough; to raise £17,500 capital. Granted.

*Burslem Electric Lighting Order.*—To authorise the mayor, aldermen and burgesses of Burslem to supply electricity within the borough; to raise £22,000 capital. Granted.

*Chelmsford Rural District Electric Lighting Order.*—To authorise the Chelmsford Electric Supply Company, Limited, to supply electricity within the parishes of Writtle, Great Baddow, Bromfield, Springfield and Widford within the Chelmsford rural district; to raise £600 capital. Granted.

*Chichester Corporation Electric Lighting Order.*—To authorise the mayor, aldermen and citizens of Chichester to supply electricity within the city; to raise £25,000. Granted.

*Chislehurst Electric Lighting Order.*—To authorise the Chislehurst Electric Supply Company, Limited, to supply electricity within a portion of the parish of Chislehurst; to raise £15,000. Granted.

*Chorley Corporation Electric Lighting Order.*—To authorise the mayor, aldermen and burgesses of Chorley to supply electricity within the borough; to raise £12,000. Granted.

*Colne Corporation Electric Lighting Order.*—To authorise the mayor, aldermen and burgesses of Colne to supply electricity; to raise £10,000. Granted.

*Crewe Electric Lighting Order.*—To empower the mayor, aldermen and burgesses of Crewe to supply electricity; to raise £25,000. Granted.

*Darlington Electric Lighting Order.*—To extend the area within which the Corporation of Darlington may supply electricity, under the Darlington Electric Lighting Order, 1890; to raise £10,000 additional capital. Granted.

*Dartford Electric Lighting Order.*—To authorise the Dartford Urban Council to supply electricity within the borough; to raise £7,000. Granted.

*Doncaster Corporation Electric Lighting Order.*—To authorise the mayor, aldermen and burgesses to supply electricity; to raise £60,000. Granted.

*East Ham Electric Lighting Order.*—To authorise the district council to supply electricity; to raise £12,650. Granted.

*East Stonehouse Electric Lighting Order.*—To authorise the East Stonehouse Urban Council to supply electricity; to raise £15,000. Granted.

*Gravesend Electric Lighting Order.*—To authorise the mayor, aldermen and burgesses to supply electricity; to raise £18,920. Granted.

*Greenock, Port Glasgow and Gourock Electric Lighting Order.* —To authorise the North British Electrical Supply Company, Limited, to supply electricity in Port Glasgow and Gourock; to raise £50,000 capital. Refused on account of the promoters having failed to produce the consents of the local authorities.

*Hamilton Electric Lighting Order.*—To authorise the provost, magistrates and councillors to supply electricity; to raise £10,000 capital. Granted.

*Hastings Corporation Electric Lighting Order.*—To authorise the mayor, aldermen and burgesses of Hastings to supply electricity; to raise £275,000. Granted.

*Hereford Electric Lighting Orders.*—To authorise the mayor, aldermen, and burgesses of Hastings to supply electricity; to raise £24,196 capital. Granted.

*Holborn and St. Giles Electric Lighting Order.*—To authorise the County of London and Brush Provisional Electric Lighting Company, Limited, to supply electricity within a portion of the Holborn district, the district of St. Giles' and the extra parochial places of Lincoln's Inn, Gray's Inn, Staple Inn and Furnival's Inn; to raise £25,000. Order granted in respect of part of the district.

*Holborn District Electric Lighting Order.*—To authorise the Charing Cross and Strand Electricity Supply Corporation, Limited, to supply electricity within a portion of the Holborn district; to raise £30,000. Order granted in respect of part of the district and part of St. Giles district, the remaining portion of the districts applied for being included in the Holborn and St. Giles electric lighting order.

*Hornsey Electric Lighting Order.*—To authorise the Hornsey Urban District Council to supply electricity; to raise £35,000 capital. Granted.

*Hove (Alderington) Electric Lighting Order.*—To authorise Hove Urban District Council to supply electricity; to raise £30,000. Granted.

*Ilford Electric Lighting Order.*—To authorise the Ilford Urban District Council to supply electricity; to raise £10,000. Granted.

*King's Norton Electric Lighting Order.*—To authorise King's Norton Rural District Council to supply electricity within the parishes of King's Norton and Northfield; to raise £20,000. Granted.

*Kingswinford Electric Lighting Order.*—To authorise the district council to supply electricity; to raise £12,500. Granted.

*Leatherhead Electric Lighting Order.*—To authorise the district council to supply electricity; to raise £8,000. Granted.

*Leigh-on-Sea Electric Lighting Order.*—To authorise the district council to supply electricity; to raise £18,500. Granted.

*Lewes Corporation Electric Lighting Order.*—To authorise the mayor, aldermen and burgesses to supply electricity; to raise £16,000. Granted.

*Lewisham District Electric Lighting Order.*—To authorise the Lewisham Board of Works to supply electricity; to raise £45,000 capital. Refused on account of certain requirements of the [Electric Lighting Act, 1882, and the Board of Trade rules not having been complied with.

*Lewisham Electric Lighting Order.*—To authorise the Great Western Electric Light and Power Company, Limited, to supply electricity; to raise £50,000. Refused on account of promoters failing to produce the consent of the local authority.

*Lowestoft Electric Lighting Order.*—To authorise the mayor, aldermen and burgesses to supply electricity; to raise £20,000 capital. Granted.

*Maidenhead Electric Lighting Order.*—To authorise the corporation to supply electricity; to raise £15,000. Granted.

*Margam Electric Lighting Order.*—To authorise the district council to supply electricity; to raise £10,000. Granted.

*Melton Mowbray Electric Lighting Order.*—To authorise the Melton Mowbray Electric Light Company, Limited, to supply electricity in Melton Mowbray and the parishes of Sysonby, Welby, Eye Kettleby, Burton Layars and Thorpe Arnold; to raise £10,000. Granted.

*Middlesbrough Electric Lighting Order.*—To authorise the corporation to supply electricity; to raise £50,000. Granted.

*Midland Electric Power Distribution Order.*—To authorise the Midland Electric Corporation for Power Distribution, Limited, to supply electricity; granted in respect of the borough of Wednesbury, and in the urban districts of Bilston, Coseley and Darlaston; Heath Town, Rowley Regis, Sedgley, Short Heath, Tipton, Wednesfield, and Willenhall, and the rural district of Walsall; to raise £200,000. Granted.

*Mitchellstown Electric Lighting Order.*—To authorise the Mitchellstown guardians to supply electricity in the town; to raise £900. Refused on account of ratepayers' objections.

*Montrose Electric Lighting Order.*—To authorise the corporation to supply electricity; to raise £10,000. Granted.

*Norwich Extension Electric Lighting Order.*—To authorise Norwich Electricity Company, Limited, to supply electricity in the town and adjoining parishes; to raise £2,000. Granted.

*Nuneaton Electric Lighting Order.*—To authorise the Nuneaton Electric Company, Limited, to supply electricity within portions of the parishes of Nuneaton and Chilvers Coton; to raise £6,500. Granted.

*Oldbury Electric Lighting Order.*—To authorise the district council to supply electricity; to raise £24,000. Granted.

*Ossett Electric Lighting Order.*—To authorise the corporation to supply electricity; to raise £10,000. Granted.

*Partick Electric Lighting Order.*—To authorise the Kelvinside Electricity Company, Limited, to supply electricity; to raise £33,694. Refused on account of failure to produce the consent of the local authority.

*Penarth Electric Lighting Order.*—To authorise the Penarth Electric Lighting Company, Limited, to supply electricity; to raise £25,000. Granted.

*Perth Electric Lighting Order.*—To authorise the Perth Commissioners to supply electricity; to raise £25,000. Granted.

*Peterborough Electric Lighting Order.*—To authorise the Peterborough Electric Light and Power Company, Limited, to supply electricity; to raise £25,000. Refused on account of the promoters failing to produce the consent of the local authority.

*Prescot District Electric Lighting Order.*—To authorise the British Insulated Wire Company, Limited, to supply electricity within the urban district of Huyton-with-Roby; to raise £7,500. Granted.

*Preston (Extensions) Electric Lighting Order.*—To authorise the National Electric Supply Company, Limited, to supply electricity within the Fulwood urban district and part of Preston rural district; to raise £2,000. Granted.

*Ramsgate Electric Lighting Order.*—To authorise the Electric Supply Corporation, Limited, to supply electricity in Ramsgate; to raise £15,770. Refused on account of promoters failing to produce the consent of the local authority.

*Raunarsh Electric Lighting Order.*—To authorise the district council to supply electricity; to raise £2,000. Granted.

*Rochdale Electric Lighting Order.*—To authorise the corporation to supply electricity; to raise £22,000. Granted.

*Rotherham Corporation Electric Lighting Order.*—To authorise the corporation to supply electricity; to raise £30,000. Granted.

*Rothbay Electric Lighting Order.*—To authorise the magistrates and town council to supply electricity; to raise £7,000. Granted.

*Royal Leamington Spa Electric Lighting Order.*—To authorise the corporation to supply electricity; to raise £50,000. Application was refused; and a similar application by the Midland Electric Light and Power Company was withdrawn.

*Ryde Electric Lighting Order.*— To authorise the Ryde Electric Light and Power Company, Limited, to supply electricity; to raise £25,000 capital. Refused.

*St. Alban's Electric Lighting Order.*—To authorise the corporation to supply electricity; to raise £13,800. Granted.

*St. Anne's-on-the-Sea Electric Lighting Order.*—To authorise the district council to supply electricity; to raise £10,000. Granted.

*St. Giles District Electric Lighting Order.*—To authorise the Charing Cross and Strand Electricity Supply Corporation, Limited, to supply electricity in St. Giles parish. Granted.

*St. Marylebone Electric Lighting Order.*—To authorise the Vestry of St. Marylebone to supply electricity; to raise £75,000. This order was granted by the Board of Trade, but the Bill providing for its confirmation was subsequently rejected by Parliament. Another order to authorise the county of London and Brush Provincial Electric Lighting Company, Limited, to supply electricity within the parish of St. Marylebone and to raise £100,000 was refused.

*Shrewsbury Electric Lighting Order.*—To authorise the corporation to supply electricity; to raise £24,000. Granted.

*Smethwick Electric Lighting Order.*—To authorise the district council to supply electricity; to raise £28,500. Granted.

*Stoke-upon-Trent Electric Lighting Order.*—To authorise the corporation to supply electricity; to raise £20,000. Granted.

*Warrington Electric Lighting Order.*—To authorise the corporation to supply electricity; to raise £17,500. Granted.

*West Bromwich Electric Lighting Order.*—To authorise the corporation to supply electricity; to raise £20,000. Granted.

*Westgate-on-Sea Electric Lighting Order.*—To authorise the Isle of Thanet District Council to supply electricity; to raise £10,000. Refused on account of objections from the ratepayers.

*Weston-super-Mare Electric Lighting Order.*—To authorise the Weston-super-Mare Electric Light and Power Syndicate to supply electricity; to raise £25,000. Refused on account of failure to produce the consent of the local authority.

*Weymouth and Melcombe Regis Electric Lighting Order.*—To authorise the corporation to supply electricity; to raise £30,000. Granted.

*Whishton Electric Lighting Order.*—To authorise the Whishton Rural District Council to supply electricity; to raise £5,000. Granted.

*Willesden Electric Lighting Order.*—To authorise the Willesden Urban District Council to supply electricity; to raise £46,000. Granted.

## DARTFORD ROADS.

In compliance with the request of the Dartford Rural District Council, Mr. J. Hookins, the surveyor, recently presented a report on the maintenance of the highways under his control. The cost of the work, in his opinion, was governed by the following considerations—viz., the weight of traffic passing over the roads, the existence of, and the facilities for, obtaing good hard stone in the several parishes within the district, the local cost of manual and horse labour, and the standard of repair to which the inhabitants of each particular district require them to be kept.

### TRAFFIC.

The Dartford district, it may be mentioned, is the first rural district out of the metropolitan area on the south-eastern side; its roads reach to within 9 miles of London bridge, and in that part the traffic is of a semi-metropolitan character, and has greatly increased since the Woolwich free ferry was opened. Its roads adjoin and partially surround the urban districts of Dartford, Erith and Bexley, which contain a population of upwards of 40,000. The coal, manure and mercantile traffic to and from these towns over the roads is immense, more especially from Dartford and Erith. There is also a very heavy traffic to and from the paper and flour mills on the river Darenth; and the carriage of coal to the West Kent gasworks at Crayford, Mr. Hookin is informed,

reaches to over 4,000 tons per annum. Then a very heavy traffic arises from the wharves on the river Thames and Dartford creek, and from the numerous railway stations and sidings in the district. Several traction engines are kept within the district, and numerous others are constantly passing through, and the repairs arising from the crushing and destructive power of these machines alone to the macadam roads forms no inconsiderable item in the cost of the repairs. Undoubtedly the traffic in the district is as heavy as, if not heavier than, in any of the rural districts surrounding London.

### MAINTENANCE.

The absence of any hard rock in the district suitable for road-making must, with an ever-increasing traffic, dobar the council from maintaining their roads at a comparatively low cost. They have in about seven or eight of their eighteen parishes an appreciable quantity of flints picked from the land; these have to be carted for miles to the other parts of the district at great expense in horse labour, so much so that it is found more economical to use granite in many places. Considerable sections of the roads have to be coated with the hardest imported granite to sustain the traffic over them, and the surveyor points out that it therefore costs upwards of £500 per mile to granite a road, which in many cases has to be renewed every third or fourth year. He adds that the cost of horse and manual labour is undoubtedly from 30 to 40 per cent. higher in the Dartford district, in comparison with the cost in many of the rural districts in other counties and in Wales.

Mr. Hookins thinks that the roads are as well maintained and have as good a surface as any roads in the kingdom. One thing contributing to that has been the use of the steam roller; the authority was one of the first in the country to adopt rolling the whole of the material throughout the rural roads of the district. Although the average cost, inelusive of horse and manual labour, is from £4 to £5 per mile, this luxury has been vastly appreciated by the inhabitants of the district.

If the expense of repairs in some hundreds of inexpensive districts in England and Wales are added to, or pooled with, the cost of a comparatively few expensive districts like the semi-suburban and market-garden districts of Dartford, an average of the whole must, Mr. Hookins considers, palpably be valueless as a comparison. For example, if nine provincial towns spending £100 per mile on their roads and one London vestry spending £600 are taken, these together would give an average of £150 per mile, and would be most misleading to the general public, who only look at the result of the averaging without examining the method by which it has been obtained. This could be of no practical use whatever as a basis for proving that one was economical and the other extravagant. It would be most unfair, Mr. Hookins adds, to assert that the district was not economically managed without taking into account the foregoing considerations. The law of averages cannot possibly apply to the cost of road maintenance as any true guide without the law of local circumstances being coupled therewith.

## HOUSING OF THE WORKING CLASSES.

A conference convened by the Bermondsey Vestry was held at the Town hall, Spa-road, Bermondsey, on the 15th ult. for the consideration of the question of overcrowding and the housing of the working-classes. Delegates were sent from twenty-eight of the London vestries and district boards. Mr. W. W. Tyler, chairman of the Bermondsey Vestry, was elected chairman of the conference. As the result of a very lengthy discussion, in which it was contended that the mere enforcement of the by-laws with respect to houses let in lodgings or the provision of cheap railway fares would not effectually remedy overcrowding, the conference agreed to the following motion : " That the London County Council be asked to exercise their power under part 3 of the Housing of the Working Classes Act, to provide accommodation within the county of London where required." The conference also passed a resolution calling upon the London County Council " to insert a clause in their General Powers Bill of 1899 to enable metropolitan vestries and district boards to erect municipal dwellings under part 3 of the Housing of the Working Classes Act, 1890." Other resolutions agreed to expressed the opinion that the London County Council ought to contribute to the cost of the dwellings erected by the local authorities, that the management and retention of such dwellings should be permanently vested in the local authority, and that, in view of the heavy cost of land in London, the local authorities should not be compelled to repay the cost of such land out of the income from the dwellings, and that the period for borrowing for buildings should be extended to 100 years.

**Hexham.**—At the last monthly meeting of the district council the Hospital Committee presented a report recommending that the clerk be instructed to make application to the Local Government Board for permission to erect a permanent general hospital, with accommodation for small-pox patients, on the ground belonging to the guardians at the workhouse. The report was adopted.

# Parliamentary Memoranda.

On Thursday, in the House of Lords, the London County Council (General Powers) Bill, the Devonport, Plymouth and Stoke Tramways Bill (now the Devonport and District Tramways Bill), the Mid-Kent Water Bill and the Middlesex County Council Bill were read a third time and passed. Lord Balfour moved the second reading of the Rivers Pollution Prevention (Border County Councils) (No. 2) Bill, and explained that its object was to empower county councils to appoint joint committees for the purposes of preventing the pollution of a river where the river ran through portions of Scotland and Ireland. The Bill was read a second time. The Local Government (Ireland) Bill was then considered on report. On the motion of Lord Dunraven, clause 19, relating to ancient monuments, was struck out and a new clause substituted providing inter alia that a county council might prosecute for any penalty under sec. 6 of the Ancient Monuments Protection Act, 1882. Lord Inchiquin moved to insert in clause 27 a new subsection, having practically the same object as the amendment moved in committee by Lord Londonderry and then negatived—viz., to extend the 25 per cent. limit imposed on the extra expenditure to be incurred by district councils upon roads to various other branches of expenditure by those bodies. Lord Ashbourne strongly opposed the amendment, and after some further discussion the amendment was negatived by thirty-six votes to fifteen. Several other amendments were proposed by Irish peers, but most of them, after discussion, were not pressed; and, the report stage having been completed, the third reading of the Bill was fixed for the following day.

In the House of Commons the Lords' amendments to the Clacton-on-Sea Gas and Water Bill, the Maldon Water Bill and the Southampton Gas Bill were considered and agreed to; while the Paisley Corporation (Loans) Bill, the Electric Lighting Provisional Orders (No. 5) Bill and the Tramways Orders Confirmation (No. 1) Bill were read a third time and passed with amendments. The Kingstown Harbour Roads Transfer Bill was also read a second time.

On Friday, in the House of Lords, the Glasgow Corporation (Sewage, &c.,) Bill and the Aber Valleys Gas and Water Bill were read the third time and passed. After the insertion of some drafting amendments, the Local Government (Ireland) Bill was also read the third time and passed.

In the House of Commons the Lords' amendments to the Burnley Corporation (Tramways, &c.) Bill, the Ipswich Dock Commission Bill and the Usk Valley Railway Bill were considered and agreed to. The Manchester Carriage and Tramways Company Bill was read the third time and passed, without amendment; while the Newhaven and Seaford Water Bill was read the third time and passed with amendments. The Electric Lighting Provisional Order (No. 15) Bill was also read a second time and committed. On Saturday, in the House of Commons, the Kingstown Harbour Roads Transfer Bill was considered in committee and reported, without amendments, to the House.

On Monday, in the House of Lords, the Rivers Pollution Prevention (Border County Council) (No. 2) Bill was read the third time and passed.

In the House of Commons the Lords' amendments to the Sheffield Corporation Bill, the London County Council (General Powers) Bill, the London County Council (Money) Bill and the Mid-Kent Water. Bill were considered and agreed to. The Portsmouth Corporation Tramways Bill was read a third time and passed with amendments; while the following Bills, ordered to lie upon the table, were considered and afterwards, the standing orders having been suspended, were read the third time: The Carlisle Corporation Water Bill, the Filey Water and Gas Bill, the Forres Water Bill, the Newcastle-upon-Tyne Corporation Bill, and the Newcastle and Gateshead Water Bill. The Tramways Orders Confirmation (No. 3) Bill, as amended, was also considered, and afterwards read the third time and passed with an amendment.

On Tuesday the House of Lords met at 3 o'clock to hear the Royal assent given by commission to certain Bills. The Speaker and the House of Commons having appeared at the bar, the Royal Commission was read and the Royal assent duly given to the following Bills: The Rivers Pollution Prevention (Border Councils) Act, the Electric Lighting Orders Confirmation (Nos. 9 and 13) Acts, the Pier and Harbour Orders Confirmation (No. 2) Act, the Tramways Orders Confirmation (No. 2) Act, the Water Orders Confirmation Act, the Coventry Corporation Gas Act, the Leyton Urban District Council Act, the Middlesbrough Corporation (Gas) Act, the Tynemouth Corporation (Water) Act, the Dublin Port and Docks Act, the Clontarf and Hill of Howth Tramroad Act, the Clacton Gas and Water Act, the Maldon Water Act, the Southampton Gas Act, the Paisley Corporation (Loans) Act, the Burnley Corporation (Tramways, &c.) Act and the Ipswich Dock Act. The ordinary business of the House was then proceeded with. The Keighley Corporation Bill, the Wey Valley Water Bill, the Paignton Improvement Bill, the London United Tramways Bill, and, after the standing orders had been dispensed with, the St. Helen's Corporation Bill were read a third time and passed.

In the House of Commons the Chelsea Electricity Supply Bill, the Heywood Corporation Water Bill, the Metropolitan, Electric Supply Bill, the Rochdale Corporation Water Bill and the Todmorden Corporation Water Bill were considered and afterwards, the standing orders having been suspended, read the third time and passed with amendments. The Lords' amendments to the Local Government Provisional Orders (No. 13) Bill and the Metropolitan Common Scheme (East Sheen) Provisional Order Bill were considered and agreed to.

On Wednesday, in the House of Commons, the Seaham Harbour Bill and the Wath-upon-Dearne Urban District Council Bill were read a third time and passed with amendments. The Lords' amendments to the Local Government (Ireland) Bill were considered. On the amendment giving to the Galway Town Improvement Commissioners the same powers in Galway as were possessed by the mayor and corporation of a county borough, the Speaker ruled that the Lords' amendment was a breach of the privileges of the House, inasmuch as it created a new rating authority. The motion that the House agree with the amendment was consequently not put. On the first of the Lords' amendments creating two-member constituencies for district councils the Attorney-General moved that the House should agree with the Lords' amendment. A long debate followed, but the motion was carried on a division by 115 to 64, and the Lords' amendment was accordingly agreed to. The other Lords' amendments were, with some slight modifications, also agreed to.

## PRIVATE BILLS IN COMMITTEE.

*Bury Corporation Water Bill.*—The Bill promoted by the Corporation of Bury for the purpose of enabling them to purchase lands for the purposes of their water undertaking; to obtain land for a public library, an art gallery and an infectious diseases hospital; and to borrow money to the amount of £275,000, was passed last week by a committee of the House of Commons, presided over by Colonel Gunter. The opposition, although still strong, was less formidable than when the measure was before Lord Poltimore's House of Lords committee in May last. The Lancashire County Council, then foremost among the opponents, had been conciliated. The present opposition, which was directed to the waterworks clauses, emanated from the Bury Rural District Council and several other neighbouring authorities, who contended that the proposed power to make additional changes on the outside districts for water supply was contrary to public policy, unjustifiable and inequitable. From the evidence of the town clerk of Bury, Mr. J. Haslam, and the engineer of the corporation, Mr. J. Cartwright, it appeared that in 1872 the Bury Commissioners purchased the undertakings of the Bury and Radcliffe Waterworks Company, and the Haslingden and Rawtenstall Waterworks Company for £237,000; and in 1876, when the borough was incorporated, the corporation took the works over. The revenue from the combined undertakings in 1874 was £18,538 and last year £37,966. The corporation had spent £277,941 on the waterworks since they acquired them. They supplied 61,000 out of 62,000 in the borough of Bury, and 97,000 out of 140,000 inhabitants in the outside districts of Haslingden, Rawtenstall, Ramsbottom, Radcliffe, Whitefield, Prestwich and Little Lever, together with the area under the jurisdiction of the Bury Rural District Council. Out of a total revenue of £35,000 in respect of waterworks and meters the borough of Bury contributed £15,000. The charges varied, the minimum being at Prestwich, where they had as competitors the Corporation of Manchester, and they had to make the same charges as that body. The revenue from Prestwich was £1,174, but if they charged what they were entitled to charge it would have been £250 a year more. Except in one or two years, when they made a slight profit, the water undertaking had been a loss to the town council, no less than £70,000 having been charged on the borough rate in and since 1872. The outside districts had made no contribution towards the deficit. One of the objects of the Bill was to redress that inequality by entitling the corporation to claim from the outside districts a fair contribution, but the primary object was to acquire the watersheds, where pollution took place. The corporation desired to treat all alike, and had no intention of making a profit out of the water supply. Any surplus would go in the reduction of prices. The area of supply was about 18 miles long by 4 miles broad, and some of the houses were 850 ft. above sea level. Mr. Cartwright's evidence related mainly to the necessity for increasing the supply and purifying the water. For the latter purpose it was essential that the corporation should be armed with the means of protecting the sources of supply. They were prepared to meet the requirements of the Local Government Board in the matter by establishing filtration areas, which would involve an additional expenditure of some £30,000 or £40,000. The committee, in passing the Bill, accepted the proposal made by Mr. Pembroke Stephens, Q.C., who (with Mr. Pope, Q.C., and Mr. Lloyd) appeared for the promoters, with reference to a sinking fund, but intimated that in allowing the measure to proceed they did not prejudice any future action that might be taken by the outside local authorities. They considered that no maximum was needed, as it was just as much to the interest of Bury to keep down the price as it was to that of the outside local authorities.

*Rochdale Corporation Water Bill.*—The spirited antagonism offered by the District Council of Littleborough to the Bill promoted by the Corporation of Rochdale for the acquisition of the Todmorden waterworks, in pursuance of their agreement with the waterworks company of that Yorkshire town for authority to construct additional works and to borrow £450,000, failed to influence Colonel Gunter's House of Commons committee in favour of the smaller local authority. The Bill was passed without consideration of any kind to the claim of Littleborough that the Todmorden undertaking should be reserved for their use when they took in hand a waterworks scheme for the supply of the district under their jurisdiction. Rochdale Corporation will now have at their command a service which will be sufficient for their requirements for many years to come.

*London Electric Bills.*—Three electric Bills affecting the metropolis were under the consideration of Parliamentary committees last week. Two of them, which had already passed the Lords, were dealt with by a House of Commons committee presided over by Mr. Brynmde Jones, and the third was under the consideration of a Lords committee presided over by Lord Pirbright. The first taken up by Mr. Brynmde Jones was the measure promoted by the Metropolitan Electric Supply Company to enable them to establish a large station for the generation of electricity at Willesden and to bring the current into the company's area of supply by a conduit laid along the Grand Junction canal. The Bill was opposed by the St. Giles District Board of Works and the London County Council. The company proposed to avail themselves of the recommendations of the joint committee which had during the session considered various measures before Parliament relating to electricity. The company started with a capital of £250,000, but that had been increased to £1,000,000. The amount they had spent on works was £782,500, and there were five generating stations—one at Sardinia-street, one at Rathbone-place, one at Manchester-square, one at Amberley-road and one at Whitehall. It was impossible to enlarge the present works, so a new site—and a very excellent one it was—had been found at Willesden. It would enable the company to get their mains into their district of supply without breaking up any streets or roads, inasmuch as they would be laid along the footpath of the Grand Junction canal. The cost of the site was £12,500 and that of the works and the mains £400,000. The St. Giles Board of Works were apprehensive that the new generating station would be substituted for the one already existing in the district, and there would then be no generating station for them to acquire if they wished to buy the undertaking in their district—only cables, wires and mains. They asked that the company should be placed under obligation to continue the existing generating station, but Mr. Balfour Browne, Q.C., on behalf of the promoters, pointed out that this would put the company under an obligation to which they were not liable now, inasmuch as they could abandon their station to-morrow if they liked. Moreover, it must not be assumed that the St. Giles board had a right to buy the Sardinia-street station, for that station supplied the Strand and Holborn districts as well. Mr. Worsley Taylor, Q.C., for the London County Council, asked for the insertion of clauses which would enable the county council to purchase the undertaking at the expiration of the statutory period of forty-two years. Were the Bill passed in the form submitted it would render the right of purchase which the local authorities had under the existing law absolutely inoperative. At present each separate parish had the right to purchase so much of the undertaking as was situated within its limits, but distributing mains without a generating station would be useless. The county council, it was urged, had ample means and the staff necessary for the purpose of carrying on a large electrical undertaking. The committee passed the measure and imposed no obligation upon the promoters with regard to purchase. The Bill promoted by the Chelsea Electricity Supply Company, Limited, to authorise them to compulsorily acquire lands in their district on which to erect a generating station next came before the committee. There were two opponents, Mr. H. C. Pennell, represented by Mr. Dowen Rowlands, and the London Assurance Company, represented by Mr. Pembroke Stephens, Q.C., who submitted that property owned by them would be injuriously affected by the erection of the works contemplated. The principal purpose which the company had in view was to obtain compulsory powers for the acquisition of land, in order that they might be free from actions for creating a nuisance should they conduct their business with proper care—that is to say, they sought no immunity from actions if they failed to conduct their business with due and necessary precautions. The London County Council and other local authorities had opposed the Bill in the other House, but they did not press their objections in the Commons. The company had originally a generating station at Cadogan-gardens, but they were obliged, in consequence of an injunction having been obtained by a gentleman in the neighbourhood, to remove it to Flood-street, where it now stands. It was proposed to extend this station, and the consideration at first mentioned in connection with one portion of the land was £200, but the owner insisted that, instead of buying the small piece they

required, the company must purchase a much larger area, which he valued at £30,000. This was more than the resources of the company would justify them in acquiring, so they declined the offer. The owner, Mr. Holland, thereupon endeavoured to obtain an injunction to restrain the company from carrying on their business on the ground that they were causing a nuisance by vibration. An inspection, in pursuance of an order by the High Court of Justice, was made in February. Sir F. Bramwell acting for the company and Mr. Swinburne for Mr. Holland, and the conclusion arrived at was that there was no vibration at all. Mr. Frank King, the engineer-in-chief to the company, declared that the demand for electricity had lately been increasing so rapidly in Chelsea that unless they obtained possession of the proposed site almost immediately they would be unable to fulfil their obligations. The company had taken great pains, and had, in fact, altered their machinery more than once in order to avoid vibration. The foundations had been so prepared that whatever vibration was caused by the machinery was deadened in the foundations and not communicated to the surrounding ground. The ground was first levelled and a concrete bed laid, and on that was placed a thick layer of hair felt, upon which again was a foundation about 12 ft. in depth of solid concrete. Upon this the engine rests. Mr. Pembroke Stephens, on behalf of the London Assurance Company, explained that what that corporation complained of was that if the Bill passed and the company did anything amounting to a nuisance the petitioners would have no redress, because in the present Bill the nuisance clause was got rid of. Mr. Bowen Rowlands, on behalf of Mr. Chollmondelly Pennell, asked the committee to insert a clause which would reserve to him the right of obtaining from the company compensation for any damage which he might prove he had sustained. The company passed the Bill, and inserted a clause giving a certain amount of protection. The Bill investigated by Lord Pirbright's committee provided for the confirmation of two provisional orders, relating to the district of High Holborn and St. Giles. The first order gave the County of London and Brush Provincial Electric Lighting Company power to supply electrical energy within the area to the west of Gray's Inn-road and north of High Holborn, including Lincoln's Inn, Gray's Inn, Staple Inn and Furnival's Inn, and the second empowered the Charing Cross and Strand Electricity Supply Corporation to supply electrical energy to the area south of New Oxford-street and High Holborn. The Bill was opposed by the Metropolitan Electric Supply Company on the ground that as they already supplied the district with electricity, and as no complaint had been made against their service, their territory ought not to be invaded by new companies. Competition, they argued, would not benefit the consumer. The promoters of the two orders included in the Bill argued, on the other hand, that it would. Mr. Edward Seal, secretary of the Brush Company, stated that they were supplying light at an average of 4·47 per unit, whereas the Metropolitan Company's average was about 6d. They were paying a dividend at the rate of about 7 per cent., and had no difficulty in getting capital. Mr. W. H. Patchett, engineer-in-chief to this company, said that in the Strand and St. Martin's district there was competition which, he thought, was good for both companies, and had assuredly benefitted the public by several reductions in price. Counsel for the Metropolitan Company argued that competition within this district ought not to be sanctioned by Parliament. They had spent large sums of money, and had in every way done their best for the public. There was nothing in the nature of electricity which differentiated it from gas, and open competition with gas companies had only led to bad gas, high price and public inconvenience. The company passed the Bill confirming the orders.

*Windsor Dock Bill.*—The House of Lords have wrecked the Windsor Dock Bill, just as they wrecked the Renfrew Burgh and Harbour Extension Bill. In the Commons Prof. Stuart's Committee gave eighteen days to the consideration of the project for the construction of the splendid new dock at Penarth, to rival the finest basins of the Cardiff and Barry companies; but the labour was useless, for all that the Commons committee did the Lords have undone. The Bill was in everything but name the project of the Taff Vale Railway Company, and it had the support and sympathy of the Corporation of Cardiff and many of the local authorities of South Wales, who saw in it the possibility of increased advantages to the public, greater facilities for the shipment of mineral produce and more economical charges. It is useless to speculate on the reasons which influenced Lord Welby's committee in their decision to throw out the Bill. The powerful interests experienced by the Marquis of Bute were simply too strong for the Taff, who, however, made out an excellent case for additional dock accommodation in the neighbourhood of Cardiff.

**Stockport.**—At a meeting of the Stockport Electric Lighting Committee, held recently, it was reported that the public supply for street lighting would be available at the beginning of November, and that tradesmen would also be supplied than under specially-advantageous arrangements. The committee will also enter specially for the supply of electric power in manufacturing processes. The inauguration of an electric tramway system is under consideration.

# For Assistants and Pupils.

## THE CONSTRUCTION OF ROADS AND STREETS.—XVII.

By WILLIAM H. MAXWELL, Assistant Engineer and Surveyor, Leyton Urban District Council.

ROAD MATERIALS AND CONSTRUCTION
(continued).

*Macadam's Plan of Construction.*—Although considerable credit is due to Mr. Macadam for the general improvements he effected in roads under his charge by means of the adoption of the practice of putting " broken stone upon a road which should unite by its own angles so as to form a solid hard surface," yet he appears to have entertained some very erroneous notions in respect to the proper construction of *new roads.* He has stated

" That a foundation of bottoming of large stones is unnecessary and injurious on any kind of subsoil."

" That the maximum strength or depth of metal requisite for any road is only 10 in."

" That the duration only, and not the condition, of a road depends upon the quality and nature of the material used."

" That free stone will make as good a road as any other kind of stone."

. " That it is no matter whether the substratum be soft or hard." In fact, that he " should rather prefer a soft one to a hard one," or even a bog, " if it was not such a bog as would not allow a man to walk over it."

. These ideas are, of course, entirely at variance with the first principles of science and with universal experience. It was thought that when the road materials rested upon a soft and yielding bed they were less likely to be crushed by the passage of heavy traffic over them than when the foundation was hard and solid.

The *foundation,* however, of a road must be looked upon as its most essential part, and "the outer surface (or broken stone coating) should be regarded merely as a covering to protect the *actual working road beneath,* which should be sufficiently firm

In respect to this class of road Sir H. Parnell observes that " experience has fully established their unfitness for roads of great traffic in comparison with those made with a proper foundation. The reason is very obvious, for if a coating of small broken stones be laid on the natural soil the weight of carriage wheels passing over it forces the lower course of the stones into the soil, while the soil is forced up into the interstices between them ; the clean body of stones first laid on to make the road is thus converted into a mixed body of stones and earth, and, consequently, the surface of the road cannot but be very imperfect as to hardness. It is necessarily heavy in wet weather, on account of the mud the earth makes on its surface, and, in warm weather, on account of a quantity of dry dirt. A road made on this plan will require, for two or three years after it is said to be finished, the expenditure of large sums in new materials to bring it into anything like even an imperfectly consolidated state ; and, after all that can be done, such a road will always run heavy, and break up after several frosts ; for, as the natural soil on which such a road is laid is always more or less damp and wet, it will necessarily keep the body of materials of which the road is made damp and wet ; in consequence of which the surface of the road will wear down quickly. Hard frosts will penetrate through the materials into the under soil, and when thaws take place break up the whole surface."

Although this form of construction has been very largely adopted throughout the country, it is only suitable for minor roads with a small amount of traffic.

*Telford's Plan of Construction.*—The most prominent feature of this mode of construction, as has already been said, is the use of a solid " *pitched foundation.*" A specification of Telford's, describing the manner of forming a road of

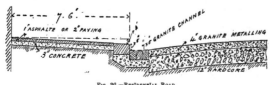

FIG. 26.—RESIDENTIAL ROAD.

and substantial to support the whole of the traffic to be carrried over it."[*] In short, the function of the road metalling is to take the *wear,* and that of the foundation to carry the *weight* of the traffic.

In forming roads wholly of broken stone the ground must be first prepared by levelling its irregularities and forming the surface to the intended contour of the finished roadway. Should the subsoil be of a soft, wet and retentive nature, it must be efficiently drained by means of cross drains, laid in the manner already described, at frequent intervals across the roadway, and discharging into deep side ditches, to be cut on each side of the road to a sufficient depth below the formation surface. In the case of a very soft or boggy ground, layers of faggots or brushwood are also frequently laid with advantage over its surface, and upon these the materials are spread. If the tract over which the road is to be formed consists of newly-made ground, as in the case of embankments, it should first be consolidated by punning or rolling. The ground surface having been properly prepared, the broken stone is spread uniformly over the road, by means of a shovel and rake, in successive layers of about 3 in. in depth, allowing, in the absence of a steam roller, time between the layers for their proper consolidation by the traffic. The total thickness of coating which will be required will necessarily depend upon the nature and extent of the traffic and upon the firmness or otherwise of the bed upon which it is laid. From 6 in. to 12 in. is the usual thickness, varying according to circumstances. Over the stone when laid " *binding material,*" consisting of fine gravel, sand or road scrapings, is frequently spread, with a view of assisting the consolidation of the road metal and of making the traffic easier over the new surface. Its use was strongly objected to by McAdam, and although at the present time it is very generally used by surveyors, it should be dispensed with wherever possible, and only used in the least possible quantities at any time. Telford usually covered a newly-metalled surface with about 1½ in. of gravel as a " binding," but this is now rendered unnecessary, the use of the steam roller for effectually and quickly consolidating fresh-laid road metal having become so general.

this kind of 30 ft. in width, taken from a contract for making a part of the Holyhead road, has been given at length

The method of laying down the foundation, also the objects and merits justly claimed for it, are best set forth in Mr. Telford's own words[*] : " This foundation is a regular close pavement of stones, carefully set by hand, and varying in height from 8 in. to 6 in., so to suit the curvature of the road ; these stones are all set on edge, but with the flat one lowest, so that each shall rest perfectly firm. The interstices are then pinned with small stones, and care is taken that no stone shall be broader than 4 in. or 5 in., as the upper stratum does not bind upon them so well when they much exceed that breadth. The pavement thus constructed is quite firm and immovable, and forms a complete separation between the top stratum of broken stones and the retentive soil below. Any water which may percolate through the surface is received among the stones of the pavement, and runs from them into the next leading or cross drain, and there escapes."

" The different parts of the Holyhead road, which have been newly made with a strong bottoming of stone pavement, place beyond all question the advantage of this mode of construction ; the strength and hardness of the surface admit of carriages being drawn over it with the least possible distress to horses. The surface materials, by being on a dry bed and not mixed with the subsoil, become perfectly fastened together in a solid mass, and receive no other injury by carriages passing over them than the mere perpendicular pressure of the wheels ; whereas, when the materials lie on earth, the earth that necessarily mixes with them is affected by wet and frost ; the mass is always more or less loose, and the passing of carriages produces motion among all the pieces of stone, which, causing their rubbing together, wears them on all sides, and hence the more rapid decay of them when thus laid on earth than when laid on a bottoming of rough stone pavement. As the materials wear out less rapidly on such a road the expense of keeping it in repair is proportionably reduced. The expense of scraping and removing the drift is not only diminished,

---

* " The Construction of Roads and Streets," by Law and Clark.

* First report of Mr. Telford on the Holyhead road, May, 1824 ; also sixth report, May 23, 1820.

but with Hartshill stone, Guernsey granite, or other stone equally hard, is nearly altogether avoided."

In a roadway of 30 ft. in width, constructed after Telford's plan, a convexity or rise of 6 in. was obtained at the crown, the convexity of 4 ft. from the centre being ½ in., at 9 ft., 2 in., and at 15 ft., 6 in., thus giving the form of a flat ellipse.

The stone employed for the foundation may be such as would not be suitable for other purposes, as metalling, building retaining walls, &c., and may therefore frequently be obtained locally for this purpose. Chalk may be used to form the foundation if kept sufficiently deep to be entirely out of the reach of frost. Mr. M'Neill states[*] that "sandstone, limestone or schistus, or such as can be had in the neighbourhood, that will bear weight and not decompose by the atmosphere."

The "bottoming" being thus properly performed, a coating of about 6 in. or 9 in. in depth, of some hard and tough road metal, such as Guernsey granite or whinstone, should then be uniformly laid down, and rolled in in layers by the aid of the

foundation is thoroughly set. When this has taken place a top covering of broken stone is laid on 3 in. in depth, forming a solid road throughout.

In respect to the laying on of the first coat of stone, Mr. Thomas Hughes observes[*] that " the beneficial effect arising from the practice of laying on the gravel exactly at the proper time—i.e., just before the concrete has become quite hard—is that the lower stones, pressed by their own weight and by those above them, sink partially into the concrete, and thus remain fixed in a matrix from which they could not easily be dislodged. The lower pebbles being thus fixed, and their rolling motion consequently prevented, an immediate tendency to bind is communicated to the rest of the material; a fact which must be evident if we consider that the state called binding, or rather that produced by the binding, is nothing more than the solidity arising from the complete fixing and wedging of every part of the covering, so that the pebbles no longer possess the power of moving about and rubbing against each other."

This form of construction was applied by Mr. Charles Pen-

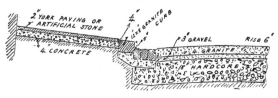

FIG. 27.—BUSINESS ROAD.

steam roller or consolidated by the traffic, the surface being well attended to during the process, and all hollows or ruts which may appear being at once filled in with road metal. If the road material is, as it should be, in angular cubical pieces, so that their angles may interlock with each other, no binding material will be required.

In and about the metropolis the *foundation* of a macadamised road is usually formed of " *hard core*," a term which is applied to a heterogeneous mixture consisting of broken stone brick rubbish, clinker, broken pottery and various other hard materials. In the north of England, and generally in towns situated near blast furnaces, the foundation is formed of *slag*. The thickness of the hard-core foundation will depend upon the nature of the subsoil, upon the amount of traffic, and also upon the nature of the material used, but 12 in. may be regarded as the minimum thickness, and this should be consolidated by rolling to about 9 in., all hollow places being at once filled in and made level.

Upon this a 5-in. layer of Thames ballast or gravel should be uniformly spread and consolidated to about 3 in. in depth. Then, to receive and withstand the wear and tear of the traffic, a 6-in. coating of broken Guernsey granite should be laid down in two layers and well rolled. About ½ in. of sharp sand is frequently scattered over the surface, and the whole consolidated by rolling and watering. In London a road constructed after the above manner would cost about 6s. per square yard.

For ordinary *country* roads the ground should be excavated in the usual manner to an approximate circular segment, and the foundation formed of rough stones, flints, &c., to a thickness of at least 12 in., and covered with a 6-in. coating of broken flints. Binding material is not generally used, and steam rolling in many country districts is almost unknown, the new metalling being left to be gradually worked in by the traffic, assisted by occasional attention to the raking in of ruts and hollows appearing on the surface.

*Roads with Concrete Foundations.*—Roads have been constructed with *concrete foundations* and have proved very successful, but the process is too expensive for general application, and has therefore not been very extensively adopted, except in special situations, where the traffic is very great, or where the road is intended to be paved with granite, wood or asphalte. Mr. Henry Law, C.E., states[†] that " one of the principal advantages attending the employment of concrete as a foundation for roads is that a good and solid road may be made with materials such as round pebbly gravel, which, on any other mode of application, would be ill-suited to the purpose, and would form a very imperfect road."

The concrete for the foundation may consist of good clean gravel, containing a little sand, mixed with hydraulic lime in the proportion of four or six parts of the former to one of the latter. The mixture being thoroughly well incorporated, is at once wheeled into position, spread over the roadway to a depth of 6 in., trimmed and spread to the form of the roadway surface. Upon this, just before the concrete has become hard, a layer of broken stone or gravel, 3 in. in thickness, is laid, the traffic not being allowed upon the surface until the

fold to the Brixton and Walworth roads with marked success, also in Southwark-street a 12-in. bed of lias lime concrete was put down, and Mr. M'Neill suggested this plan for use upon the Highgate Archway-road. The circumstances leading to its adoption upon the latter road are interesting as well as instructive, owing to the difficulties to be overcome, and will therefore be briefly described.

## ELECTRIC LIGHT PROVISIONAL ORDERS.

### LOCAL AUTHORITIES AND COMPANIES.

The electric lighting industry in the United Kingdom has always been hindered rather than fostered by the Acts which relate to it. One notorious electric lighting Act practically strangled it at birth, and retarded developments for something like ten years. To-day, says *The Pall Mall Gazette*, the struggle is between companies holding provisional orders to supply electricity and municipal corporations anxious to control so important a supply. The corporations and vestries which have gone in for electric lighting have, almost without exception, done wisely and well up to now, and, owing to the encouraging example of the pioneer bodies in this movement, some £6,000,000 of rates are at present invested in electric lighting ventures. As a rule there has been an absence of competition, even rival companies holding provisional orders for the same district preferring to map out limits for themselves instead of indulging in cut-throat antagonism; and the tendency of the Board of Trade has been to restrict the number of provisional orders for one district, so as to prevent ruinous competition. A committee of the House of Lords, however, has just decided in favour of granting concurrent powers to companies to trade in districts already monopolised by local authorities. Whether such competition would succeed is beyond the point, as numerous applications for the purpose have already been received. The decision is likely to fall very heavily on the authorities, because, whereas in the opposite case, when a local authority sought powers to work in competition with a company, it has always been a point of honour for the authority to buy out the company first (sometimes at a very high price), the present rule does not make it incumbent on the company to buy out the authority, and exposes an authority which is already at work to the risk of a purely fictitious competition on the part of companies formed solely for the purpose of being bought off. Such a state of things would not be fair to the authorities, nor could it be tolerated by the ratepayers, whose money they would have to squander.

**St. Helens.**—The corporation have been informed that the Local Government Board have sanctioned the borrowing of £17,500 for proposed improved lighting arrangements of the borough. The Electric Lighting and Traction Committee have instructed the borough surveyor to prepare plans for the concentration of the whole of the electric plant, both for lighting and traction purposes, at the Boundary-road site.

[*] Evidence of Mr. M'Neill before a Select Committee of the House of Commons in May, 1830.
[†] "Roads and Streets," by Law and Clark.

[*] *Vide* " The Practice of Making and Repairing Roads."

# Law Notes.

EDITED BY J. B. REIGNIER CONDER, 11 Old Jewry Chambers, E.C.,

Solicitor of the Supreme Court.

*The Editor will be pleased to answer any questions affecting the practice of engineers and surveyors to local authorities. Queries (which should be written legibly on foolscap paper, one side only) should be addressed to "The Law Editor," at the Offices of THE SURVEYOR. Where possible, copies of local Acts or documents referred to should be enclosed. All explanatory diagrams must be drawn and lettered in black ink only. Correspondents who do not wish their names published should furnish a nom de plume.*

## QUERIES AND REPLIES.

CELLAR OPENING ON FOOTWAY. — "Barrelway" writes: Will you be good enough to inform me if an urban council have the power to refuse to allow a barrelway in connection with a cellar being built in and opening on the footpath.

If by a "barrelway" is meant something comprised within the opening, I do not think the council can object so long as sec. 73 of the Towns Improvement Clauses Act, 1847, is complied with, but if it means something extending over the pavement, I think the council can refuse to allow it.

CONVERSION OF PRIVIES INTO WATER-CLOSETS: HOUSE DRAINS: CONNECTION WITH SEWERS.—" Kumbo " writes: Our sanitary inspector has served several owners with notices to abate a nuisance on their property by converting privies into water-closets. Plans have been deposited for the drainage of the same. I have taken objection to the way they wish to carry out the work, see Plan No. 1, and have recom-

PLAN No. 1.

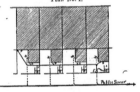

Public Sewer

PLAN No. 2.

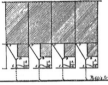

Public Sewer

A—Water-closets.
B—Yard and area gullies.
C—Kitchen sinks.
D—Rain-water pipes.
E—Syphon traps.
F—Ventilators.
............ Existing drains.
———— New drains.
———— Public sewer.

mended them to connect to the existing drains, as per Plan No. 2, also to have " a window built in an external wall, 2 ft. long by 1 ft. wide, exclusive of the frame," and " to provide constant means of ventilation by at least one air brick built in an external wall." The owners object to do the work as requested. One owner has four houses and intends executing the drainage as shown on Plan No. 1, contending that we have no by-laws applicable to old houses, and can connect the drains as they choose, so long as they abate the nuisance, submit a plan showing the mode of connection and due notice of their intention to carry out the work. You will observe by the dotted lines that each house has a separate connection to the public sewer. We have adopted the Public Health Acts Amendment Act, 1890, but have made no by-laws applicable to the drainage of old buildings. These houses have been built twenty-five years. (1) Are they old houses within the meaning of the term *old houses*? (2) Can we compel them to connect each house into the existing drain? (3) Can we compel a window and an air brick? (4) If the owners have power to do as they propose, will *all* of the drainage systems (as shown), or any of them, become *sewers* vested in the council to cleanse and maintain? And, further, they propose to remove the gullies and refix them, leave all the disused drains in and simply stop the end of each drain up. (5) Have we power to compel them to remove all the disused drains and to stop up the junction at the point of connection with the public sewer?

(1) The term "old houses," in connection with by-laws, I understand to mean houses erected before the by-laws were in force. But the point is immaterial in the case under consideration. So far as I

gather from the statements in the query, what has happened is this The local authority have served certain notices under sec. 41 of the Public Health Act, 1875, requiring the conversion of privies upon certain premises into water-closets, and the owners have thereupon given notices to the authority under sec. 21 of the same Act of their intention to empty their drains into the public sewer. Both these sections apply to both old and new houses. (2) "Existing sewer" I presume is meant. This is a difficult question. The section (sec. 21) is general in its terms, and allows the owner of "any premises" to cause "his drains" to empty into the sewers on the conditions therein specified, one of them being that he shall comply with the regulations of the authority. The regulations are in the entire discretion of the authority (Lumley's "Public Health Acts," p. 52, fifth edition), and presumably, therefore, a regulation requiring each house to be separately drained would not be *ultra vires*. So far as I am aware, however, the point has not been decided in any reported case. There is no express regulation to this effect in the printed "Regulations" which accompany the query, but the provision that "the whole arrangement of the drainage of the buildings must be approved by the surveyor" is very wide, and would appear *prima facie* to empower him to veto the proposed combined drainage scheme. (3) There is a regulation to this effect, but it is doubtful whether it is not *ultra vires*, as this can hardly be said to have reference to "the mode in which the communications between such drains and sewers are to be made. (4) The combined drain would become a sewer vested in the authority and repairable by them—*i.e.*, assuming all the houses connected with it to belong to the same owner—if they belong to two or more owners then sec. 19 of the Public Health Act, 1890, applies. (5) I think the general clause in the regulations, that the whole arrangement must be approved by the surveyor, would cover this.

# A GRASPING CORPORATION.

The people of Glasgow have for years been regarded by such portions of the rest of the world as knew anything about them as most patient slaves of the most advanced type of town councildom. The corporation, we are informed, says *The Railway World*, manage everything for the people that can possibly be managed municipally, and it attempts to manage some things which could be better done by private enterprise. The officials would even like to regulate in detail the life of the individual, and who knows but we shall find them starting, say, co-operative stores, for the alleged good of the community. But at present the corporation are seized with a new and high ambition. The plain man would have thought that the addition four years ago to the multifarious duties of the town council of working the tramways in the city would have been enough to satiate the municipal maw for ten or twenty years. But the appetite grows with what it feeds upon. The proposals recently made by a company to build an electric light railway from Glasgow to Paisley, which would run on the high road and the tramway system of the two towns, has been strenuously rejected by the Glasgow Corporation so far as the part of the line within their area is concerned. Not only so, but this militant town council have approached the local authority of the county of Renfrew, through whose district most of the proposed light railway would run, and have succeeded in persuading a committee of that authority that they also should oppose the scheme.

But more remains behind. These Glasgow town councillors have actually persuaded the presumably mild and innocent rural committee to support the preposterous proposal that the Corporation of Glasgow should themselves build a tramway through Renfrewshire to Paisley. It seems that the town council contemplate applying next year to Parliament for power to build and work the line, and that they had been spurred on to that course by the promotion of the scheme now before the Light Railway Commissioners. It is hardly necessary to point out that such a proposal is absurd. If it was granted we should soon have town councils all over the country going beyond their functions as the governing bodies of towns and operating inter-urban tramways through rural districts. It required a Glasgow town council's audacity to conceive such a scheme, and it will be very surprising if Parliament grants it. A few weeks ago a case occurred in Parliament which is probably the nearest approach up till now to the Glasgow proposal, but which is a very mild affair in comparison. The Corporation of Burnley are promoting a tramways Bill in the present session, and among its proposals is one to enable the corporation to take a lease of some short lengths of tramways which lie beyond the borough boundary, but form an integral portion of the tramways of Burnley. The committee of the House of Commons before whom the Bill came sanctioned this proposal, but in their report to the House they specially mentioned that they only did so in view of the peculiar circumstances of the locality, and this although there was no appearance in opposition to the Bill. There should not he much doubt as to what course a Parliamentary committee will take when an unblushing town council asks powers to build and work 4 or 5 miles of tramway along a county road into a town in another county.

# Municipal Work in Progress and Projected.

This week we are able to give very little news with respect to projected works in the metropolis as the majority of the local authorities have adjourned their meetings for the summer recess. In the provinces, however, several extensive works are projected, notably at Bristol, Chorley, Lincoln, Barry and Taunton.

## METROPOLITAN AUTHORITIES.
### METROPOLITAN ASYLUMS BOARD.

An ordinary meeting of the above body was held at the County Hall, Spring-gardens, London, S.W., on Saturday. A letter was read from the Local Government Board forwarding a copy of a notice which Dr. Farquharson, M.P., had placed on the order book of the House of Commons asking for a return showing the actual cost of each of the managers' hospitals in comparison with the original estimate. The managers' observations thereon were asked.—The North-Western Hospital Committee reported that they had issued advertisements for tenders for the work of making-up, &c., the main road of the hospital in accordance with a plan and specification prepared by Messrs. Pennington & Son, architects. They recommended that the tender of R. Ballard, Limited, for making-up the main road, &c., and repairing paths, &c., at the North-Western hospital, at the sum of £643, should be accepted. The architect's estimate for the work was £1,080. After some slight discussion with reference to the disparity between the architect's estimate and Messrs. Ballard's tender the recommendation was adopted. The following is a list of the tenders received : Messrs. Ballard, Limited, Childs Hill, N., £643 ; Mr. Ephraim Hollingsworth, Hendon, £996 10s.; Messrs. C. W. Killingback & Co., Camden Town, £997 ; Mr. Thomas Adams, Green-lanes goods station, Great Eastern Railway, £1,035 ; Mr. William Griffiths, Bishopsgate-street Without, £1,040 ; Mr. George Bell, Tottenham, N., £1,079 ; Mr. Robert Jackson, 92 Upper Tollington-park, N., £1,187 ; Mr. A. J. Cole, Notting Hill, W., £1,215 7s. 6d.; and Messrs. B. Newell & Co., Kensington, £1,286.—The board accepted without discussion the tender of Messrs. John Shillitoe & Son, of Bury St. Edmunds, for the erection of the new band office buildings, at the sum of £47,532, in accordance with plans and specification prepared by Mr. E. T. Hall, architect. The following is a list of the tenders received : Messrs. John Shillitoe & Son, Bury St. Edmunds, £47,532 ; Messrs. Foster & Dicksee, Rugby and London, £48,980 ; Messrs. W. Pattison & Sons, Parliament-street, S.W., £51,243 ; Messrs. Leslie & Co., Limited, Kensington-square, W., £54,043 ; Messrs. E. Lawrance & Sons, May-road, City-road, £54,127 ; Mr. B. E. Nightingale, Albert Works, S.W., £54,827 ; and Mr. Henry Lovatt, Wolverhampton, not priced. The architect's revised estimate was £46,328.—The tender was accepted of the India-Rubber, Gutta-Percha and Telegraph Works Company, Limited, of Silvertown, E., for the supply of dynamos and engines required in connection with the proposed electric lighting installation at the Northern hospital, at the sum of £1,705 for dynamos and engines and £71 for the spare armature. The consulting engineer's revised estimate was £1,900. —The board accepted the tender of Messrs. Taylor & Sons, of Marsden, Yorks, for the supply of boilers, at the sum of £725, in connection with the proposed electric light installation at the Northern hospital. The consulting engineer's revised estimate (including the cost of certain mechanical stokers, tenders for which are still under consideration) was £1,000.—A recommendation by the Darenth Asylum and Schools Committee "that steps be at once taken to insure the managers against claims for compensation under the Workmen's Compensation Act, 1897, for injuries received in the performance of their duties by workmen in the board's service," was, after discussion, referred to the Finance Committee for consideration and report.— After considering several other matters the board adjourned till the 10th September.

### VESTRIES AND DISTRICT BOARDS.

St. Marylebone.—The vestry on the 28th ult. reversed its previous decision in regard to the wood paving of Maida-vale. It was resolved to authorise the Works Committee to obtain and submit tenders for the supply of hard wood blocks for the paving of Maida-vale, and to accept the tender of Messrs. Burt, Boulton & Haywood for the Swedish yellow deal blocks for the paving of three other streets, provided that the firm would supply 250,000 blocks at the same price per 1,000 (£6 18s. 9d.) as that contained in their tender for 750,000 blocks that was rejected at the previous meeting.—The Sanitary Committee were authorised to invite tenders for the construction of an underground convenience in East-street and to bring the proposals before the vestry for consideration. Mr. C. Warren moved that it be referred to the Sanitary and Sewers Committee to consider and report on the practicability of providing free accommodation for women, the same as now supplied to men, in the underground conveniences in the parish. This was rejected.—On the motion of Mr. J. M. Butler it was resolved to refer to the Works Committee to consider and report as to the desirability of the surveyor annually inspecting the coal plates on the public footways in the parish, with a view to compelling the owners to substitute new plates for all those found defective. The Baths Committee were empowered to make inquiries as to the cost of providing plant at the baths and wash-houses to enable the vestry to generate electricity for the lighting of those buildings, and the surveyor was instructed to prepare a specification and invite tenders for improving the ventilation of the wash-houses.—The tender of Messrs. Wright & Adams, of 84 Seymour-place, amounting to £71 5s., was accepted for the annual cleaning and other work at the court-house.

## PROVINCIAL AND GREATER LONDON AUTHORITIES.
### COUNTY COUNCILS.

Berkshire.—At the last quarterly meeting of the county council, after a lengthy discussion, the following resolution was adopted : That it be referred to the Highways Committee to prepare a report to the council dealing with the extent to which steam-rolling might be adopted upon the country roads, or some of them, together with the cost thereof.

Middlesex.—At a meeting on the 26th ult. it was resolved to inform the Ecclesiastical Commissioners that the county council were not prepared to increase beyond £1,000 the price offered for the site for the proposed court-house at Enfield. It was resolved, on the recommendation of the Finance Committee, to apply to the Local Government Board for consent to borrow £55,000 for the purchase of the Napsbury site, St. Albans, for the purpose of an additional county asylum ; the period of repayment to be extended over thirty years or such further period as the board might be disposed to sanction. In connection with this matter the Asylums Committee reported that by their directions Dr. Gardiner Hill and Mr. Roland Plumbe had inspected and reported upon some asylums in Scotland and in the north of England. This joint report would be very valuable to the committee in connection with the consideration of the question of the kind of asylum to be provided for Middlesex. The committee hoped after the vacation to be in a position to submit preliminary sketches of the proposed new asylum.—The Asylum Committee were authorised to expend £530 in providing a cow-house with iron partitions for the asylum at Wandsworth.—It was resolved to inform the Bucks County Council that the council would be prepared to contribute a sum not exceeding £1,000 in respect of a bridge costing £3,500, or more, subject to the plans being approved by the council and to a satisfactory arrangement being made as to future maintenance. The proposed bridge is to be built over the Colne between West Drayton and Iver. The Highways Committee recommended that Turkey-street bridge, Enfield Wash, should be widened in accordance with the plans submitted, so as to provide a roadway of 27 ft. and one footpath of 6 ft.; and that the county surveyor be instructed to prepare drawings and specifications, and to invite tenders by advertisement, for carrying out the work. These recommendations were adopted.—It was decided to take no action in respect of the insurance of the roadmen under the Workmen's Compensation Act. In discussing this question the Highways Committee stated that the only reason why insurance would be necessary would be in connection with the work of steam rolling, but that this particular work on the main roads repaired by the county council was done by a contractor, whose contract provided "that the contractor shall take all responsibility for any accident or damage that may happen or be done consequent upon the use of the roller." It is to be noted that the council's roadmen work in gangs at the same spot, but not actually *with* the steam rollers.—On the recommendation of the Technical Education Committee it was resolved to approve the plans submitted showing the proposed alterations necessary to adapt the Yeast House premises, adjoining the Tottenham Polytechnic, for the purposes of a plumbers' and carpenters' shop, and the second floor of the Tottenham Polytechnic main building for the purposes of chemical and physical laboratories ; and to instruct the county surveyor to prepare working drawings and specifications, and to procure tenders for the execution of the work, from five firms approved by the committee.—The Finance Committee reported that the county surveyor had submitted a specification of external and internal painting and repairs required to be done at the Guildhall. Tenders had been obtained for the work from the following firms for the undermentioned amounts : Woodward & Co., £330; Putman & Fotheringham, £325; A. Porter, £246; Phillips & Son, £238; and Higgs & Hill, Limited, £224. The tender of Messrs. Higgs & Hill, Limited, was accepted.

Shropshire.—At the quarterly meeting of the county council, on the 23rd inst., the Roads and Bridges Committee reported that they had had under their consideration an application from Clun district council for a grant towards the erection of a bridge over the river Oney at Whitcote, on the road leading from Norbury to Craven Arms. The total cost would be £455, and the committee recommended a grant of one-third of that amount, the local council to provide one-third, and the remainder to be raised by public subscription. It was recommended that the council should, if possible, enter into agreements with Wellington, Ellesmere and Whitchurch for the repair of the main roads in those districts by the three separate authorities, at a cost of £75 per mile. The committee had appointed a sub-committee to consider the desirability of insuring the men employed with the steam rollers on the county road, so as to meet liabilities which may arise under the Workmen's Compensation Act. It was estimated that £2,836 would be needed to meet the expenses of the main roads for the quarter. The report was adopted without discussion.—The Local Government Committee's report stated that a memorial had been submitted to them by the Wellington Rural District Council requesting the Board of Trade to use their influence with the Great Western Railway Company to do away with four level crossings over their railway between Wellington and Oakengates, and substitute bridges or subways. The committee recommended that the council support the memorial. The report was adopted.—The Visiting Committee to the Salop and Montgomery Lunatic Asylum presented a report, which stated that the surveyor had prepared an estimate for connecting the asylum drains with the new system of sewerage for the borough, and the cost would be about £500. The asylum was reported to be much overcrowded. There was accommodation for 811 patients, and it was suggested that the buildings should be enlarged so as to accommodate 1,000. The county surveyor had the matter in hand, and the committee would report further upon the subject at the next council meeting. The report was adopted.

**Warwickshire.**—The County Roads and Bridges Committee reported at the last quarterly meeting of the county council that, having received a petition from the Foleshill Rural District Council " showing that the canal bridge on the main road from Coventry to Bell Green, known as the navigation bridge, 12 ft. wide, is dangerous both to vehicle and pedestrian traffic, owing to the steepness of the approaches and of the narrowness of the bridge, that the bridge is very largely used, that the canal company are willing to erect a bridge 36 ft. wide for the sum of £500, that until the bridge is reconstructed the tramway company are debarred from carrying their line to Bell Green, which is a great disadvantage to the neighbourhood, and asking the council to pay a proportion of the £600. They recommended that the council do undertake to contribute one moiety of the cost of widening and improving the bridge, such contribution not to exceed the sum of £250." The report was adopted.—The County Buildings Committee recommended that the portico at the judge's house be restored, at a cost not to exceed £70; and that the tender of Mr. John Webb for the erection of the sub-police station in Lorzells-road, Aston Manor, at the price of £2,222, be accepted. This report was also adopted.

**West Sussex.**—Acting on a report from the county surveyor as to the advisability of having a depot for stores at Horsham, the Roads and Bridges Committee, at the last meeting of the county council, recommended that a plot of 2 roods 14 poles of land, situated at the back of Upper New-street, be leased for twenty-six years, at an annual rental of £3; and also that a shed and fences be erected on the land and other necessary works carried out, at an estimated cost of £325. The recommendation was agreed to.

## MUNICIPAL CORPORATIONS.

**Birmingham.**—The Baths and Parks Committee, accompanied by the lord mayor, made their annual inspection on Saturday week of the parks and recreation grounds of the city. They left the council house at 2 o'clock, and drove by way of Calthorpe-park, Cannon-hill, Queen's-park, Harborne, Summerfield-park, Burbary-street-gardens, Aston-park, Adderley-park, Victoria-park, Small Heath, Palsall Heath-park, &c., thence to Village Green House, Moseley, the residence of the chairman of committee, where they were entertained to tea.—Last week an inquiry was held at the council house by Mr. W. O. E. Meade-King, Local Government Board inspector, relative to an application of the corporation for sanction to borrow £5,000 for sewerage works.

**Bradford.**—The council recently decided to light the street lamps at Frisinghall by electricity. The district has up to the present been lighted by the Shipley Gas Light Company, who charge a much higher price than the corporation do. The corporation have been greatly pressed to make some arrangement with the Shipley company, but have failed to do so, and in the alternative have determined to extend the electric cables to these places by degrees.—The corporation have concluded terms with Colonel Maude for the purchase of his manorial rights over Baildon Moor. The property includes Shipley Glen and Baildon Green, the total area being 770 acres, comprising charming woodland scenery, which is to be preserved for recreative purposes.

**Bristol.**—At a recent meeting of the Sanitary Committee of the corporation the assistant clerk reported that sanction had been received from the Local Government Board to loans of £10,000 for wood paving and £266 for repairing a sewer in Redcross-street.

**Cardiff.**—At a recent meeting of the Public Works Committee of the Cardiff Town Council, held at the town hall, a letter was read from the Local Government Board stating that the draft by-laws relating to new streets and buildings were still under consideration. It is now nearly

ten years since the first draft of these by-laws was submitted to the board at Whitehall, and, owing to the delay in their consideration and the necessary amendments that were subsequently required, this extraordinary delay has taken place.

**Chorley.**—At the monthly meeting of the town council, on Thursday, Mr. Stone, in moving the adoption of the minutes of the Sewage Works Committee, reported that a deputation had waited upon the Local Government Board with respect to their insistance on land irrigation of the effluent after treatment by precipitation before they would grant the loan of £6,500 for sewage disposal, and stated that Sir Hugh Owen had, in response to the deputation, consented to reconsider the question.

**Conway.**—New municipal buildings are in course of erection at Conway, from plans by Mr. R. Davies, of Bangor. The contractors are Messrs. Thorp & Son, of Llandudno. The gangways have been completed the repair of the town walls. Gangways have been provided between Upper Gate and the Conway river in seven places, and the promenade along the existing portion of the walls is complete.

**Dudley.**—At the Board of Trade offices, Whitehall, Sir T. Courtenay Boyle, secretary to that board, who was accompanied by Mr. Hopwood, C.B. (secretary of the Railway Department), Sir Francis Marindin, Sir Thomas Blomefield, Mr. A. T. Thring and Mr. H. A. Steward (secretary to the Light Railway Commissioners), recently held an inquiry in regard to the objections raised by the Dudley Town Council to the confirmation of the order made by the Light Railway Commissioners authorising the construction of certain lines by the British Electric Traction Company.

**Godalming.**—The town council have resolved to purchase the Frith Hill, Godalming and Farncombe Water Company, and a committee have been formed to arrange all formalities, and, if necessary, to promote a Bill in Parliament for the acquisition of the undertaking. According to the terms agreed upon in the negotiations, the corporation's liability in purchasing the concern will be £67,250, involving £2,858 8s. 7¾d. yearly. The annual repayment of the borough's existing loans is equivalent to a rate of 2s. 1½d. in the £1.

**Haslingden.**—The town council had before them on the 20th ult. a report of the Parks Committee recommending that a plan and estimate be adopted for the laying-out of Whitecroft as a park. After some discussion the report was, however, referred back on the ground that the estimate of £4,000 was more than had been thought would be required, and the scheme provided simply for roads and fences, and only £250 for planting, while there was no provision for greenhouses and a caretaker's house.

**Hastings.**—The town council have decided to give the incandescent gas lighting a trial in the Hollington district, where there are no public lamps at present. Being approached on the matter, the gas company offered to supply gas, maintain the mantles and chimneys, and light and extinguish the lamps, at £3 7s. 8d. per lamp per annum, being the same price as charged for ordinary single-burner lamps, such price, however, to be subject to revision at the end of each year. The council have resolved to have thirty-four lamps lighted in the district on these terms.

**Lincoln.**—On Friday week Mr. P. Gordon Smith, architect to the Local Government Board, and Major-General H. D. Crozier, R.E., one of the inspectors of the Local Government Board, held an inquiry into the application of the town council for sanction to borrow £6,500 for the erection of houses at New Boultham, under the provisions of Part III. of the Housing of the Working Classes Act, 1890, and £1,944 for works of street improvement. The proposals were explained by Mr. H. K. Hebb, the deputy town clerk, and Mr. McBrair, the city surveyor.

**Mansfield.**—At the monthly meeting of the town council, on the 22nd ult., it was resolved that the seal of the council be affixed to a petition against the General Powers Distributing Bill.—A recommendation by the Free Library Committee that a scheme proposed by the Pleasley Hill Committee for the formation of a branch library be adopted was confirmed.

**Maldon.**—Colonel W. R. Slacke, R.E., an inspector to the Local Government Board, held an inquiry recently, as to the application of the council to borrow £724 for works of water supply for Tolcarne, £1,425 for works of water supply and £1,301 for works of sewerage for Heamoor.—The district council have unanimously decided to request the Local Government Board to hold their inquiry into the Purley water supply scheme as early as possible, so that the work might be commenced in the autumn, when labour would be more plentiful and cheaper than in the spring.

**Newcastle.**—The Town Improvement Committee of the Newcastle Corporation met recently, when plans were submitted on behalf of Mr. Watson-Armstrong for laying into streets 45 acres of land at North Heaton, in the neighbourhood of Chillingham-road. It is proposed to build from 600 to 800 houses. Mr. F. W. Rich, of Newcastle-on-Tyne, is the architect. The committee passed the plans.

**Northwich.**—At a recent meeting of the council a letter was read from the clerk to the county council, stating that the Main Roads Committee had recommended the council to make the following contributions to the Northwich authority towards bridging the river Dane and providing an alternative route from London-road to the lower portion of Witton, thus avoiding one of the most treacherous of the subsiding roads in the district : To hand over the present Northwich town girder bridge, estimated to be of the value of £1,000 ; to contribute one-third the cost of removing and refixing it, and the like proportion of the cost of constructing the proposed new road, exclusive of the cost of acquiring any land necessary to do so. The county council also agreed to maintain and repair in perpetuity the structure of the bridge when erected.

**Otley.**—Mr. H. Percy Boulnois, recently conducted an inquiry, on behalf of the Local Government Board, into an application of this authority for sanction to borrow £600 for works of sewerage in respect of certain houses which it is proposed to erect.

**Penarth.**—The Board of Trade have granted a provisional order authorising the supply of electricity by the Penarth Electric Lighting Company, Limited. The company have scheduled an extensive list of streets for the compulsory area in which mains must be laid within two years. Provision is made in the order for the acquisition of the undertaking by the council after a period of fifteen years.

**Plymouth.**—A letter from Mr. B. Priestley Shires, on behalf of the architects of Plymouth, was read at the last meeting of the Special Works Committee of the Plymouth Corporation. It intimated that they were unanimously agreed that their objections to the terms of the competition in connection with the Tavistock-road improvement scheme were reasonable, and were of considerable importance to them professionally. They therefore requested the committee to reconsider and adopt at least the general principle underlying the suggestions they had put forward. Under the circumstances the committee recommend the council to make it an open competition, on the conditions originally laid down for the competition restricted to Plymouth architects.

**Portishead.**—An inquiry was recently conducted by Mr. W. O. E. Meade-King, on behalf of the Local Government Board, in reference to an application of the council for sanction to borrow £3,000 for purposes of sewerage.

**Richmond, Yorks.**—In reply to an application from the corporation to the Local Government Board for the approval of the sale of certain corporate lands, the transfer of a certain amount of 2¾ per cent. consolidated stock, and of the appropriation of the sums realised to defray the cost of the erection of a farmhouse and buildings, Mr. G. W. Wilcocks held an inquiry at Richmond town hall last week.

**Ripley.**—Mr. A. S. E. Fawcett, inspector of the Local Government Board, held an inquiry in the town hall, Ripley, recently, with reference to the application of the council to obtain leave to borrow £1,000 for extension of the mains for water supply and for sewerage purposes. No opposition was offered. It was stated, that owing to the growth of the town, it had been found necessary to extend the water mains and provide additional facilities for sewerage. The surveyor submitted plans of the sewerage scheme. The proceedings having terminated, the inspector visited the localities which had formed the subject of inquiry.

**Ryde.**—Consideration was recently given to a proposal to appoint a committee "to consider the subject of the introduction of electricity into the town of Ryde, with power to employ a consulting engineer to advise fully on the subject and to bring up a report at an early date." It was urged that, as it had been decided to light the town by electricity, it was the duty of the corporation to ascertain the best means of doing it. It was eventually decided to appoint the committee.

**Salford.**—The following resolution has been adopted by the council : "That the council be recommended to purchase the land abutting on the westerly end of Great Cheetham-street East, containing about 21,683 square yards, as a grass playground for the district, at 3d. per square yard and twenty-five years' purchase, and that the requisite application be made to the Local Government Board for sanction to borrow the purchase money."

**Southampton.**—It was reported, at a recent meeting of the town council, that Mr. W. H. Brothers, secretary to the British Association of Waterworks Engineers, had forwarded a resolution passed by the association during their recent visit to Southampton, thanking the mayor and corporation for the courteous and hospitable welcome accorded to the members, and for the many facilities and conveniences placed at their disposal.—A letter was read from the Local Government Board acknowledging the receipt of their letter of the 15th inst., with reference to the scheme of the Town Council of Southampton for the provision of artisans' dwellings. The board consented to the deviation from the scheme, for the execution of which they had sanctioned a loan of £14,500 on the 28th January, and asked that that sanction might be returned with a detailed estimate of the cost of the new scheme. The board acknowledged the new scheme as providing accommodation for 186 persons, and they expected the town council to submit at an early date proposals on the housing of sixty-four more persons, to make up the 250 referred to in Article 111 (5) (b) of the provisional order of 1895. The communication was referred to the Housing of the Working Classes

Committee.—The corporation recently took over the whole tram and 'bus system in the borough. The cost has yet to be fixed, and arbitration to this end is going on between the company and the corporation. In six months' time it is proposed to abolish horse traction and use only electricity.—Colonel A. G. Durnford, Local Government Board inspector, has held an inquiry for the purpose of hearing evidence on behalf of an application made by the Southampton Town Council for sanction to borrow £2,500 for technical instruction purposes.

**Tamworth.**—On Friday Colonel J. T. Marsh, R.E., held an inquiry, on behalf of the Local Government Board, respecting an application of the town council for an order sanctioning an improvement scheme under the Housing of the Working Classes Act, 1890, which involves the demolition of Bradbury-square. The town clerk and the borough surveyor explained the scheme, and the inspector subsequently visited the area involved.

**Taunton.**—At a special meeting of the council, held lately, the Electric Lighting Committee recommended the acceptance of a tender, amounting to £4,456, for the carrying out of certain works, subject to the sanction of the Local Government Board to the proposed loan of £11,500, but with power for the committee to arrange with the tenderers to at once carry out urgent works included in the tender, and also for the committee to proceed with the sub-station and a portion of the mains to supply the Staplegrove and Rowbarton districts, the whole of such urgent works amounting to about £2,000. The committee also recommended the acceptance of a tender, amounting to £1,325, for electric arc lighting. Both recommendations were adopted.

**Tiverton.**—The result of the year's working of the gas undertaking is a profit of £198, which makes a total profit of £2,347 realised since the corporation acquired the works, three years ago. The gas produced last year amounted to 25,000,000 cubic feet, of which 6·22 per cent. was lost by leakage. Of the total capital of £20,000, £968 remains unspent, and is to be used to provide a new gasholder. The manager is well pleased with the increased number of stoves on hire, and he expects a great development in this department from the reduction in the price of gas for cooking to 3s. 6d. per 1,000 cubic feet.

## URBAN DISTRICT COUNCILS.

**Abergele and Pensarn.**—The district council have applied to the Local Government Board for sanction to a loan of £3,500 for the carrying out of a promenade and other improvements.

**Barry.**—At a meeting of the Finance Committee of the district council last week a communication was read from the Local Government Board giving power to borrow £4,321 for roads around Romilly Park and £1,180 for the drainage of the same. It was decided to borrow an additional sum of £13,000 for public works in the district.

**Clayton.**—On Saturday week a new open space, know as Victoria Park, was formally opened to the public, thereby bringing to its consummation a project started in commemoration of the Queen's diamond jubilee. The ground which has been utilised for the purpose was formerly the villinge green, and was practically vested in the overseers, from whom it has been transferred to the district council. The park forms a square, with buildings on every side, in Greenwell-row, Green Side, Riva Syke and Co-operation-road. It has been surrounded with iron railings, and very nearly laid out in grass plots, flower-beds and walks. At the upper end is a terrace, in front of which the principle flower-bed—a large one of circular shape—has been formed. The area of the park is about 2½ acres, and the expenditure upon it is estimated at about £1,150.

**Coalville.**—A motion in favour of steps being taken to purchase the Ibstock gasworks was submitted at the last fortnightly meeting of the district council. The motion was not, however, seconded, and so fell to the ground.

**Enfield.**—A letter was read at the last meeting of the district council from the medical officer of health to the Hackney Vestry, asking if the council had decided to join in the conference to be held at the House of Commons on the question of the pollution of the river Lea and a main drainage scheme for the Lea valley. The more united the districts were in the neighbourhood of the river the better prospect there would be of the Government taking some action to alter the present condition of the river. It was decided to reply that a deputation would attend the conference.

**Finchley.**—The North London Electricity Company have written to the district council, stating that they intended to apply to the Board of Trade and to Parliament in the ensuing session for a provisional order authorising them to supply electricity within the area of the council. The letter has been referred to the Highways Committee.

**Friern Barnet.**—The district council have appointed a committee to inquire and report as to the erection of cottages under the Housing of the Working Classes Act.

**Hexham.**—Mr. W. A. Ducat on the 20th ult. conducted an inquiry, on behalf of the Local Government Board, with reference to an application of the district council for sanction to borrow £896 for water supply works. Mr. W. Pruddah, clerk to the council, and Mr. R. T. Surtees, surveyor to the council, explained the proposed works. There was no opposition to the application, and it was stated that the council themselves were perfectly unanimous upon it.

**Holme Cultram.**—The district council have been making inquiries, with a view to the lighting of the streets of Silloth, on the Solway, with acetylene gas. The British Illuminating Gas Company, in reply to these inquiries, state that they can supply street lamps, with generators, at £6 16s. each, and are prepared to send one on approval free of charge. The council have decided to obtain a lamp on trial, but as it will be impossible, whatever the result of the trial, to get acetylene gas lamps erected in the streets in time for the coming lighting season, it has been agreed to ask the North British Railway Company, who own the gasworks at Silloth, to light the town with coal gas, as usual, during the coming winter.

**Hornsey.**—At a recent meeting of the district council tenders were opened for the erection of a new fire station at Muswell Hill, as follows: Wilmott & Sons, £1,295; Chessum, £1,241; Houghton & Sons, £1,217; Smith & Son, £1,130; and Irwin, £1,102. The lowest tender was accepted.

**Prestatyn.**—The district council have resolved to apply to the Local Government Board for sanction to a loan of £3,000 for the purpose of drainage and general improvements.

**Rounds.**—The district council have purchased by public auction, for £700, a site in the High-street on which to erect municipal buildings.

**Saltburn.**—At a recent special meeting of the district council the clerk reported that Mr. Carrick, whose tender for the work required in the laying-out of the new cemetery was accepted at the last meeting, had withdrawn his tender, as he had found that he had left out £400 for drainage. This occasioned much discussion, but as the additional sum did not bring the amount of Mr. Carrick's tender up to the next highest it was agreed to allow the tender to be amended.

**South Hornsey.**—At a recent meeting the district council unanimously adopted a resolution in favour of the establishment of a public library in the district. Some months ago a poll of the ratepayers was taken, and the result showed a large majority in favour of the library.

**Surbiton.**—A meeting of this council was held on the 11th inst., when it was stated that the arrangements for obtaining an electric lighting provisional order had been completed.—A committee reported having visited the sewage farm, when the surveyor explained his proposals for preventing the effluent from the filtering beds percolating through the present earth and clay division, so that separate cleansing might be possible. They carefully considered two suggestions made by the surveyor, and agreed that division walls would be the most effective and permanent barrier between the upper and lower beds. They therefore recommended, as an experiment, that dwarf concrete walls be built between certain of the beds, and that tenders be invited for the work.

**Tottenham.**—The district council have appointed a committee to consider the question of erecting municipal buildings.

**Wimbledon.**—The surveyor, Mr. C. H. Cooper, has submitted an estimate showing that the cost of erecting the new infectious diseases hospital in accordance with the plans approved by the Local Government Board would be £17,000.

**Wilmslow.**—At a meeting of the district council on Monday week the clerk reported that the Local Government Board had refused to sanction the application of the council for permission to borrow for six years the sum of £600, which was needed for road improvements in the district. They would only allow the council to borrow for three years.

**Withington.**—Colonel Smith, R.E., Local Government Board inspector, recently held an inquiry at the Withington town hall into an application of the council for power to borrow £3,118 for works of private street improvement and £177 for works of sewerage. The surveyor informed the inspector that the sewering had become necessary owing to the attention of the council having been drawn by the Mersey and Irwell Joint Committee to the fact that the present sewer, which was made before the urban council was constituted, was connected with the storm-water overflow and allowed the sewage to pass into the river Mersey, causing pollution. The main sewer ran along Barlow Moor-road, and by means of the proposed works they would be able to divert the sewage into that. The inspector promised to report to the Local Government Board in due course. There was no opposition.

## RURAL DISTRICT COUNCILS.

**Barrow-on-Soar.**—The Local Government Board have given notice that they will hold an inquiry with respect to an application of the council for sanction to a loan of £3,000 for sewerage works in the parish of Barkby.

**Blackwell.**—In respect to the pollution of a stream at Blackwell, complaints of which had been made by the Duke of Devonshire's agent, a letter from the Hucknall Huthwaite Urban District Council was read at the last fortnightly meeting of the district council, stating that they were engaged on

a sewage scheme for the whole district, which they hoped would remedy any pollution they were at present responsible for. The medical officer presented an analytical report on samples of water taken from various places in the course of the stream. It was decided to communicate the result of the medical officer's report to the Hucknall council, and to state that the South Normanton representatives were to meet the surveyor and investigate the matter.

**Feckenham.**—At a recent meeting of the council the chairman reported that the deputation who inspected the new system of coal filtration of sewage at Malvern were perfectly satisfied with its operation, and recommended the same system to be adopted at Astwood Bank. The clerk was instructed to procure plans and estimates for two coal filters.

**Helston.**—Colonel A. G. Durnford, R.E., has held an inquiry, on behalf of the Local Government Board, respecting an application of the council for sanction to borrow £500 for sewerage works in the west end of the parish of Landewednack. Several ratepayers opposed the scheme.

**Kingsbridge.**—At the last meeting of this authority the Admiralty wrote offering £200 towards making a new road and sea wall between Inner and Outer Hope, which had been before the council for several years. It was agreed to commence the work as soon as possible, the tender of Mr. George Hooper, for £401, being accepted.

**Richmond, Yorks.**—The district council have engaged Mr. Harry W. Taylor, of St. Nicholas Chambers, Newcastle, to report upon the best means of supplying the village of Middleton Tyas with water. In consequence of the prolonged drought most of the springs and wells are dry.

**Southmolton.**—At a recent meeting of the district council it was reported that three tenders had been received for the erection of a new bridge at Town Moor Water, Worlington—viz., Mr. F. A. Hooper, Chittlehampton, £36 10s.; Mr. F. Hill, Chawleigh, £43; and Mr. W. Amory, Chumleigh, £49. It was resolved to accept the tender of Mr. Hooper.

## SCOTLAND AND IRELAND.

**Arbroath.**—At a meeting of the Public Health Committee, on Friday week, a letter was read from the Local Government Board enclosing a copy of a petition signed by a number of residents in Arbroath complaining of the insufficiency of the water supply. The clerk was instructed to reply that the commissioners were at present engaged in attempting to augment the water supply of the burgh.

**Belfast.**—The tender of Messrs. J. & W. Stewart, Adelaide-street, Belfast, has been accepted by the harbour commissioners for the extension of the electric lighting station at Abercorn basin.

**Dundee.**—A joint meeting of the Works Committee and the Gas Committee was held on Friday, week when the burgh engineer submitted a report as to a proposal to widen Ferry-road at a point opposite the gasworks, and to construct a foot-path, 10 ft. wide, to the east between Ferry-road and Dock-street. Objection was taken to the width of the footpath, several members being of opinion that it ought to be made very much wider; but ultimately it was agreed to recommend the council in terms of the engineer's report. The cost to each department is estimated at fully £1,700.

**Edinburgh.**—From a financial, and indeed from every, point of view the electric light has been, says a contemporary, a remarkable success in Edinburgh. It is under the management of the corporation, and that management has been excellent. The light is supplied at an unusually low rate, and despite this there is a profit to the community. During the year ended May 13, 1898, the report for which has now been issued, the total output was, for private lighting power 2,059,763 units, an increase over the previous year of nearly 90 per cent., and for public lighting 834,660, making a total of 2,894,423 Board of Trade units. The income from private lighting and power has been £30,024 4s. 2d., and from public lighting £7,993 5s., in all £38,017 9s. 2d. The total expenditure, including interest and sinking fund, has been £30,368 1s. 11d., leaving a nett profit of £7,649 7s. 3d. Of this sum £4,000 is to be put to reserve, leaving £3,649 7s. 3d. available as a contribution to the rates.

**Glasgow.**—The Water Sub-Committee of the corporation considered on Saturday week the tenders submitted for the supply of 1,000 tons of pipes. Offers were sent in by four Glasgow and two Philadelphia firms, the prices by local firms ranging from £5,960 upwards, and American £4,437. It was stated that the tenders by the American firms were for 12-ft. lengths, instead of 9-ft., as specified. The committee, in view of the great difference in the offers of the local and the American firms, which amounts to £670 per 1,000 tons, agreed to re-advertise for further offers, alternatively for 9-ft. and 12-ft. lengths.

# Personal.

Mr. Harrison, who for the past five years has been assistant borough engineer at Newport, has been appointed surveyor to the St. George's Vestry, Southwark.

Mr. Alfred Wilson, of Sidmouth, has been appointed surveyor, inspector of nuisances, sanitary inspector and water inspector to the Ashburton Urban District Council.

The salary of Mr. H. J. Ridge, assistant surveyor to the Romford Urban District Council, was, at a meeting of the council on the 18th ult., increased by £15 per annum.

Mr. Thomas A. Busbridge, surveyor to the Chesterfield Rural District Council, has resigned his position in order to take up a similar one under the Spilsby Rural District Council.

Mr. William Plant, of the borough engineer's department, Stafford, has been appointed assistant in the sewerage department of the Leicester Corporation, at a salary of £2 2s. per week.

On the 30th ult. Mr. F. J. Whittaker, highway surveyor to the Peterborough Rural District Council, was unanimously appointed to the additional office of building surveyor to the council.

At an adjourned meeting of the Roads Committee of the Glamorgan County Council, held recently, Mr. Alexander Mark, of Bridgend, was appointed road surveyor for the Bridgend district.

Mr. Alfred Clibbens, of the city surveyor's office, Bristol, has been appointed surveying assistant in the office of Mr. E. G. Mawbey, borough engineer and surveyor of Leicester, at a salary of £2 5s. per week.

At the quarterly meeting of the Wolverhampton Town Council, on Tuesday a recommendation in favour of increasing the salary of Mr. J. Garfield, the manager of the Barnhurst sewerage works, was adopted after a short discussion.

Mr. John Hunt Hedley, of the firm of Messrs. Thos. F. Hedley & Sons, of Sunderland and Westminster, has been placed by the Board of Trade on the list of surveyors and umpires from which selections are made by the board for appointment in cases of disputed compensation for land, &c.

At the last meeting of the Lancashire County Council it was decided to appoint Mr. William Harold Radford to the office of county bridgemaster, at a salary of £1,000 per annum, with travelling expenses. It was also decided to appoint Mr. William Higginson Schofield, the senior district surveyor, county surveyor, at a salary of £500 per annum.

The sixty-five years' age limit has been reached by Mr. E. D. Goddard, superintendent in the Birmingham Gas Department, but at last week's meeting of the city council the Gas Committee were authorised to retain the services of Mr. Goddard till October next year. Mr. Alderman Pollack explained that Mr. Goddard will then have been connected with the gas undertaking for forty years.

Among the proposals to be brought forward at the Keighley Town Council meeting on Tuesday, are the increase of the salary of Mr. Hopkinson, borough engineer, from £300 to £350, with an honorarium of £50 for extra services rendered in connection with the Bill now before Parliament, the increase of the salary of Mr. Joseph Smith, water superintendent, from £90 to £100, and the fixing of the salary of Mr. Wharfe, assistant sanitary inspector, at £78.

Mr. Alfred J. Hope has been appointed superintendent of the Effingham-street works of the Sheffield United Gas Company. Mr. Hope was for three years a pupil to Mr. F. W. Stevenson when that gentleman held the position of engineer and manager to the Chester Gas Company, and he afterwards acted for two years as assistant to Mr. Robert Hunter, who succeeded Mr. Stevenson at Chester. He was then appointed chief assistant at the Halifax Corporation gasworks, under Mr. Thos. Holgate, a post he has held for the past eight years. He will take up his new duties on 1st September.

Dr. H. McLean Wilson recently read a paper before the Bristol Medical Association, at their meeting in Edinburgh, on "River Pollution." Dealing with the question whether the present laws relating to river pollution were sufficient, he referred to the Act of 1876 and to the Bill at present before Parliament. With regard to the former, he held that it was far from sufficient, and he then proceeded to point out what he considered the weak points of the new Bill. The most important omission, he thought, was that there was no prohibition of new pollution. It would be a mistake if the Bill were permitted to pass. In conclusion, he expressed himself as opposed to the standard of purity.

The Local Government Board do not like the idea of a dual appointment of chief sanitary inspector and surveyor. The board stated, says London, that since the arrangement by which the late chief sanitary inspector of Stoke Newington held also the office of surveyor was assented to, their experience had led them to the conclusion that the combination of the two offices was objectionable in a district such as Stoke Newington, as leading to neglect of the duties of the office of sanitary inspector. They asked the vestry to reconsider the matter, with a view to separate officers being appointed. The vestry, however, are quite satisfied with themselves, and have politely informed the Whitehall authorities that they desire the continuance of the old-fashioned arrangement.

At the last meeting of the Middlesex County Council the Highways Committee submitted the following letter from Mr. Henry T. Wakelam, who was recently appointed county surveyor: "Will you kindly ask your committee, at their next meeting, to allow me the privilege of taking pupils into the offices at the Guildhall after I take up my duties there as county surveyor. The committee will be aware that it is an almost general custom throughout the country for engineers and surveyors to take pupils, and I trust your committee will give me the right of having not more than two pupils in the office at a time. They would be trained chiefly in the general drawing office, and the county would reap the benefit of their services, they being solely engaged in the work of the county." On the recommendation of the committee the council resolved to permit the new surveyor, who will take up his duties in October, to have two pupils.

A meeting of the Newark Rural District Council was held on Tuesday, for the purpose of electing a new surveyor to fill the vacancy caused by the resignation of Mr. Tom Vickers. The report of the committee appointed to consider the applications stated that they had had before them applications from a large number of qualified persons for the post of highway surveyor and inspector of nuisances, and after careful consideration had selected the following three candidates in the order named: Mr. Cecil Stewart Hodges, of Nottingham; Mr. Goddard, of Ware; and Mr. Ralph Oakden, of West Ham. The chairman said there were about forty-five candidates, but the majority of them were urban men, who had not been used to country life and country traffic. The committee had therefore selected the above, any of whom they considered eligible for the appointment. The applications were then read. Each of the candidates attended, and answered such questions as the council desired to put. The council then voted by ballot, nine votes being recorded for Mr. Oakden, seven for Mr. Hodges and one for Mr. Goddard. Mr. Oakden was therefore declared elected.

At the quarterly meeting of the Roads and Bridges Committee of the West Sussex County Council, on the 8th ult., the county surveyor laid before the committee a request that the subject of the assistance in his department might be considered, and stated that since he was appointed a stone quarry had been acquired and worked by the county, footpath repairs had been extensively carried out, and upwards of 1 mile of kerb had been laid, a steam roller with a stone-breaker had been purchased, and a second roller with haulage tackle, &c., had been ordered and would be delivered for use in August of this year; also, that it was necessary that these extra works should have additional superintendence to ensure efficient and economical working, and at present only one assistant, at 25s. per week, was appointed for both office and outdoor assistance. He recommended that the present assistant be allowed a substantial increase to cover everything, including out-of-pocket expenses, that he be employed more out of doors in general supervision, and that some clerical assistance be allowed. The committee decided to recommend the council "that the surveyor be allowed a sum of £2 a week for an assistant, to cover all out-of-pocket expenses, also that he be allowed a sum of 5s. a week for clerical assistance in his office, such allowances to commence as from July 23, 1898, when the present allowance of 25s. per week should cease." The recommendation has since been adopted by the council.

**Southport.**—The Health Committee of the corporation have resolved to revive their recommendation for the erection of a town's destructor as now a matter of urgency.

**Runcorn.**—Runcorn possesses considerable advantages for the production of electric light, and the council have had the subject under consideration for years without result. Their hands are now being forced, notice having been given by the Electrical Power Distribution Company, London, of their intention to apply to the Board of Trade for a provisional order to supply electricity within the district. Believing such power should be vested in the council, the committee have decided to make application accordingly.

**Sewage Purification at Leigh.**—At a meeting of the Leigh and Atherton Joint Sewerage Board on the 20th ult., Monday week was fixed as the date for commencing to receive and treat the sewage of the two districts at the new works, which are now practically completed. The expenditure up to date on the works is nearly £55,000, and loans to the amount of £64,088 have been sanctioned. The farm contains 233 acres, and £18,888 has been borrowed for land and buildings, £17,400 for sewage, and £27,800 for outfall works. The sewage will be treated by chemical filtration, and the works are claimed to be among the most complete and best equipped in the country.

## ASSOCIATION OF MUNICIPAL AND COUNTY ENGINEERS.

### IRISH DISTRICT MEETING AT CORK.

The following are the arrangements for the above meeting, which will be held to-day and to-morrow :—

To-day.

11.30 a.m.—The members will be received in the council chamber, Municipal Buildings, by the Right Worshipful P. H. Meade, Esq., Mayor of Cork. Reading of the minutes.

12 noon.—The following papers will be read and discussed : (1) " Restoration of Municipal Buildings and Description of Cork Waterworks, with means adopted for checking Waste of Water," by Mr. H. A. Cutler, city engineer, Cork; (2) "Description of Cork Electric Tramways," by Mr. Beverly Griffin, A.M.I.C.E., resident engineer for the contractor for permanent way; and (3) "Main Roads under County Councils," by Mr. R. H. Dorman, county surveyor, Armagh.

2 p.m.—Luncheon, which will kindly be provided by the mayor.

3 p.m.—Visit to Cork Electric Tramway and Lighting Company's central station and other works in course of construction in the city.

4.30 p.m.—Special train (Cork and Muskerry Light Railway) to visit Blarney and St. Anne's, where tea will be provided by Mr. R. Bertie, J.P., chairman of the company. The engineer for the railway, Mr. W. H. Hill, will accompany the members. On returning to Cork the members will dine together at the Imperial Hotel, at 7.30 o'clock. Dinner tickets 5s. each (wines extra).

To-morrow.

*Visit to Queenstown Waterworks.*

10 a.m.—The members will meet at the Municipal Buildings and drive to Tippotstown, site of head works. Messrs. Kirkby & Doran, the engineers, will explain the scheme on the ground.

1 p.m.—Leave Queenstown Junction for Queenstown.

1.30 p.m.—Luncheon at Queen's Hotel, Queenstown, provided by the local members.

2.30 p.m.—Start on board American tender for a cruise round Cork harbour and visit harbour works; and also Cork, Blackrock and Passage Railway extension to Crosshaven. Messrs. James Price, M.I.C.E., harbour engineer, and S. Perry, engineer to the railway company, will accompany the members. Afternoon tea will be provided by Mrs. Kirkby, at Miramar, Queenstown, where the steamer will touch during the afternoon.

R. H. DORMAN, M.I.C.E.,          THOMAS COLE, A.M.I.C.E., *Secretary*,
Hon. Sec. Irish District,          11 Victoria-street,
Armagh.          Westminster, S.W.

## ELECTRIC LIGHT AT SALFORD.

### PROPOSAL TO BORROW £33,000.

Lieut.-Colonel Albert C. Smith, representing the Local Government Board, held an inquiry into an application by the Salford Corporation for power to borrow £33,000 for purposes of electric lighting and £2,220 for the construction of storm-water overflows on the main intercepting sewer at Hough-lane, Springfield-lane and Regent-road.

From the opening statement of the town clerk (Mr. S. Brown) and the evidence of the borough treasurer (Mr. J. E. Elliott), the electrical engineer (Mr. C. L. Turner) and the chairman of the Electricity Committee of the corporation (Mr. Haworth), it appeared that £57,770 has been already borrowed for the purposes of the electric installation, and that of the £33,000 now sought to be borrowed £10,000 is required for land for a large new generating station at Strawberry-hill, Pendleton, £10,700 for electrical mains and £11,300 for three battery sub-stations in the different districts of the borough, together with accumulators and the necessary machinery for charging and discharging the accumulators.

In illustration of the urgent necessity for the provision of land for a new station, figures were given showing the great increase in the demand for the current. In the quarter ended June, 1897, the amount of current sold was 11,513 units; in the quarter ended September, 1897, it was 16,234 units; in the quarter ended December, 1897, it was 67,876 units; in the quarter ended March, 1898, it was 80,595 units; and during the quarter ended June last it was 43,944 units, or getting on for four times the quantity sold in the corresponding quarter of last year. The demand was still increasing, and if one of the battery sub-stations was not completed by the coming winter the Electricity Committee would be in a fix. The witnesses said they expected to have in the coming winter new customers for 20,000 8 candle-power lamps; applications had been received for motive power equal to about 2,000 horse-power, and motive power equal to about 6,000 horse-power would be required to drive the tramcars by electricity.

With regard to the £2,200 required for storm-water overflows, Mr. J. Corbett, the borough engineer, stated that on the intercepting sewer by which the sewage of the borough was carried to the sewage works at Mode Wheel there are at present three storm overflows. The additional overflows now proposed to be constructed were for a part of the sewer that was in the most populous part of the borough. At that point there was 4½ miles of intercepting sewer without any overflow to the main sewer, although there was some small overflow to the individual sewers. Frequent complaints had been made about the flooding of the district, and it was felt that something ought to be done to remove all cause of complaint.

At the conclusion of the inquiry the inspector visited the sites of the proposed works, and also accepted an invitation by Alderman Jenkins, on behalf of the River Conservancy Committee, to visit the sewage works at Mode Wheel.

## APPOINTMENTS VACANT.

*Advertisements which are received too late for classification cannot be included in these summaries until the following week.*

CLERKS OF WORKS (Two).—August 6th.—Edmonton Urban District Council. £3 3s.—Mr. G. Eedes Eachus, M.I.C.E., engineer and surveyor to the council.

SURVEYOR AND INSPECTOR.—August 5th.—Street Urban District Council. £90.—Mr. S. Thompson Clothier, clerk to the council.

SURVEYOR.—August 8th.—Yardley Rural District Council. £250.—Mr. F. L. Thompson, clerk to the council.

CLERK OF WORKS.—August 8th.—Corporation of Chepping Wycombe. £3.—Mr. T. J. Rushbrooke, borough surveyor.

INSPECTOR OF NUISANCES.—August 8th.—Corporation of Eastbourne. £104.—The Town Clerk.

SURVEYOR.—August 9th.—Cleckheaton Urban District Council. £150.—Mr. J. Armitage, clerk to the council.

DRAUGHTSMAN AND ASSISTANT FOR GAS ENGINEER'S OFFICE.—August 10th.—Corporation of Halifax. £2 10s.—Mr. Thos. Holgate, gas engineer and manager.

ASSISTANT BOROUGH ENGINEER AND SURVEYOR.—August 11th.—County borough of Newport, Mon. £150.—Mr. Albert A. Newman, town clerk.

BUILDING ASSISTANT FOR THE WORKS DEPARTMENT.—August 13th.—London County Council. £300.—Mr. C. J. Stewart, clerk to the council, County Hall, Spring-gardens, London, S.W.

ENGINEERING ASSISTANT FOR WORKS DEPARTMENT.—August 13th.—London County Council. £300.—Mr. C. J. Stewart, county clerk, County Hall, Spring-gardens, London, S.W.

QUANTITY TAKER FOR THE WORKS DEPARTMENT.—August 13th.—London County Council. £3 10s.—Mr. C. J. Stewart, county clerk, County Hall, Spring-gardens, London, S.W.

GENERAL FOREMAN OF WORKS.—August 15th.—Corporation of the City of Canterbury. £2 2s.—Mr. A. H. Campbell, city surveyor.

INSPECTOR OF NUISANCES.—August 15th.—Highworth and Swindon Rural District Council. £120.—Mr. John P. Kirby, clerk to the council.

SURVEYOR AND INSPECTOR OF NUISANCES.—August 17th.—South Hornsey Urban District Council. £250.—Mr. Edward B. Bennett, clerk to the council.

INSPECTOR OF SEWERS. — August 18th.—Corporation of Coventry. £2.—Mr. J. E. Swindlehurst, city engineer and surveyor.

ARCHITECTURAL ASSISTANT.— August 19th.—Beckenham Urban District Council. £3 3s.—Mr. J. A. Angell, surveyor to the council.

CIVIL ENGINEERING ASSISTANT.—August 23rd.—Corporation of the City of Hull. £85.—Mr. A. E. White, city engineer.

CITY ENGINEER.—August 31st.—Corporation of Wellington, New Zealand. £800.—Agent-General for New Zealand, London.

## COMPETITIONS.

*Advertisements which are received too late for classification cannot be included in these summaries until the following week.*

ST. PANCRAS.—August 25th.—Erection of public baths and washhouses.—Mr. C. H. J. Barrett, vestry clerk.

PLYMOUTH.—September 24th.—Erection of shops and dwellinghouses fronting Tavistock-street. £250.—Mr. J. H. Ellis, town clerk.

## MUNICIPAL CONTRACTS OPEN.

*Advertisements which are received too late for classification cannot be included in these summaries until the following week.*

SLOUGH.—August 6th.—Supply of 4,300 tons of 2-in. broken clean field flints and about 500 tons of 1½-in. machine-broken and hand-broken granite, for the urban district council.—Mr. W. W. Cooper, surveyor to the council.

NEWTON-IN-MAKERFIELD.—August 6th.—Making-up Forland, Alpine, Peel, Nelson, Water and Brookfield-streets and Bradleigh-road, for the urban district council.—Mr. W. W. Shirley, clerk to the council.

PERTH.—August 6th.—Extension of the quay at the harbour.—Mr. William MacLeish, town clerk.

SLOUGH.—August 6th.—Making-up works in the streets known as

CHALVEY VALE, for the urban district council.—Mr. G. H. Charsley, clerk to the council.

GUILDFORD.—August 8th.—Construction of certain surface-water drains, including new works of drainage in connection therewith.—Mr. C. G. Mason, borough surveyor.

WORSBOROUGH (NEAR BARNSLEY).—August 8th.—Conversion of an engine-house in furnace yard into a dwelling-house, for the urban district council.—Mr. J. Whitaker, surveyor to the council.

DROMLINGTON (Yorks.).—August 8th.—Levelling, channelling, kerbing and flagging of about 480 lineal yards of causeway on the Leeds and Whitehall-road, for the urban district council.—Mr. Henry Roberts, surveyor to the council.

ABERGAVENNY.—August 8th.—Erection of a footbridge and the construction of a culvert at the Old Mill, Cwmyoy Lower, for the rural district council.—Mr. John Gill, surveyor to the council.

PADIHAM.—August 8th.—Supply of 408 yards of 24-in. cast-iron pipes, for the urban district council.—Mr. J. Gregson, A.M.I.C.E., engineer and surveyor to the council.

KNIGHTLEY.—August 8th.—Paving, flagging, kerbing, &c., of Back Aireworth-street.—Mr. W. H. Hopkinson, borough surveyor.

BRIDGWATER.—August 9th.—Construction of about 587 lineal yards of sanitary pipe sewer in Washington-terrace and Washington-gardens.—The Borough Surveyor.

CHERTSEY.—August 9th.—Making-up of an accommodation road between Long Cross and Chobham-road, for the rural district council.—Mr. Arthur W. Smith, surveyor to the council.

BENFIELDSIDE (Durham).—August 10th.—Formation of a portion of new streets at Blackhill, for the urban district council.—Mr. John Dixon, surveyor to the council.

GLAMORGANSHIRE.—August 10th.—Improvement of Gellifaelog bridge, for the county council.—Mr. T. Mansel Franklen, clerk to the council, County Offices, Cardiff.

BILSTON.—August 10th.—Erection of a superintendent engineer's house at the Bratch waterworks, for the urban district council.—Mr. John Wassell, clerk to the council.

CHAPEL-EN-LE-FRITH.—August 10th.—Construction of a concrete service reservoir, and the providing and laying of about 1½ miles of cast-iron mains for the water supply of the township of Bamford, for the rural district council.—Mr. J. Burton Boycott, clerk to the council.

NEW MILLS.—August 10th.—Supply and delivery of 1,280 yards of 3-in. turned and bored cast-iron mains and 600 yards of 2-in. turned and bored mains, for the urban district council.—Mr. Joseph Pollitt, clerk to the council.

GLAMORGANSHIRE.—August 10th.—Supply and delivery of a 10-ton steam roller, for the county council.—Mr. T. Mansel Franklen, county clerk, County Hall, Cardiff.

WREXHAM.—August 10th.—Erection of a bridge over the river Gwenfro, at a place called Stryt y bidden, in the township of Broughton, for the urban district council.—Mr. John Strachan, surveyor to the council, Crispin Lodge, Wrexham.

THORNHILL (Yorks.)—August 13th.—Supply of flushing valves, manhole and lamphole covers, &c., for the urban district council.—Mr. S. W. Parker, surveyor to the council.

HUNSLET.—August 13th.—Laying and jointing of about 6,150 yards of 3-in. cast-iron pipes, also fixing and walling-in of about twenty valves and hydrants for the Templenewsam and Thorpe Stapleton water supply, for the rural district council.—Mr. W. B. Pinder, clerk to the council.

DEWSBURY.—August 13th.—Excavators' work required in the construction of a tank at the gasworks, Savile Town.—Mr. H. Dearden, A.M.I.C.E., borough surveyor.

SHEFFIELD.—August 13th.—Extension of car sheds, consisting of two-span steel roof, car pits, stores, boundary wall, latrines, footmat, &c., house, &c., at Tinsley.—Mr. Charles F. Wike, city surveyor.

HASTINGS.—August 13th.—Supply of 120,000 9-in. by 3-in. by 14 in. jarrah wood paving blocks.—Mr. P. H. Palmer, M.I.C.E., borough engineer.

GLOUCESTER.—August 13th.—Erection of an infectious diseases hospital at Over.—Mr. Geo. Sheffield Blakeway, town clerk.

SHOREDITCH.—August 15th.—Erection of a new battery-room, boiler-house and extension of offices at the electricity supply station, Coronet-street.—Mr. H. Mansfield Robinson, vestry clerk.

BEXHILL.—August 15th.—Erection of boundary walls, the railing, kerbing, paving and channelling of footpaths, and other works opposite the town hall, for the urban district council.—Mr. George Ball, A.M.I.C.E., surveyor to the council.

ROMSEY.—August 15th.—Erection of a concrete retaining wall in the Abbey.—The Borough Surveyor.

PEMBROKE.—August 15th.—Erection of buildings and foundations in connection with the township electric light works, for the commissioners.—Mr. Robert Hammond, 64 Victoria-street, London, S.W.

WOLVERHAMPTON.—August 15th.—Supply of cast-iron, wrought-iron and steel work required for structural and other purposes at the swimming bath and assembly hall to be erected in Bath-place.—Mr. J. W. Bradley, borough surveyor.

ILKESTON.—August 15th.—Construction of a new filter-bed at the Little Hallam works.—Mr. H. J. Kilford, borough surveyor.

HAMPTON.—August 20th.—Supply and delivery of a 10-ton steam roller, for the urban district council.—Mr. John Kemp, A.M.I.C.E., surveyor to the council.

OXFORD.—August 22nd.—Supply and laying of cast-iron and stone-ware pipe carriers, brick and concrete work in manholes and distributing chambers, land drainage, embanking, road making and other works on land adjoining the corporation sewage farm.—Mr. R. Bacon, town clerk.

TEDDINGTON.—August 22nd.—Making-up of Clarence-road, for the urban district council.—Mr. M. Hainsworth, surveyor to the council.

CARSHALTON.—August 23rd.—Widening of High-street, for the urban district council.—Mr. W. W. Gale, A.M.I.C.E., surveyor to the council.

STEVENAGE.—August 22nd.—Supply of 500 tons of 1½-in. broken Guernsey, Leicester or other granite, for the urban district council.—Mr. William Onslow Times, clerk to the council.

CARSHALTON.—August 23rd.—Supply of 200 tons of broken 1-in. Quenast or Guernsey granite and 620 yards of hand-picked flints, for the urban district council.—Mr. W. W. Gale, A.M.I.C.E., surveyor to the council.

ILFORD.—August 23rd.—Construction of an underground latrine in The Broadway, for the urban district council.—Mr. Herbert Shaw, A.M.I.C.E., surveyor to the council.

ROTHERHAM.—August 23rd.—Construction of sewers, outfall works, and other works connected therewith, for the corporation.—Mr. R. E. W. Berrington, Bank Buildings, Wolverhampton.

HOYLAKE AND WEST KIRBY.—Supply of about 2,500 lineal yards of standards and railing for promenades, for the urban district council.—Mr. Thomas Foster, engineer to the council.

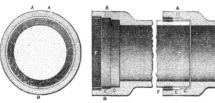

## TENDERS.

*ACCEPTED.

BERMONDSEY.—For the supply of 40,000 bricks.—Mr. Frank Sumner, vestry surveyor:—
At per 1,000, delivered alongside, vestry's wharf, East-lane.—West Brothers, £2; Smeed, Dean & Co., £2 (2½ per cent. off) ; C. Burley, £1 19s.
At per 1,000, delivered in trucks at Mint-street station.—Tucker & Son, £2 18s., £2 10s., £2 ; Weldon & Corby Brick Company,* £1 17s.
At per 1,000, delivered at the vestry's depot, Spa-road.—Wakeley Brothers, £2 5s.

LEICESTER.—For the erection and completion of a new isolation hospital for the borough, consisting of administrative block, five fever pavilions, two isolation blocks, discharging blocks, laundry, mortuary, porter's lodge, &c.—Mr. James Bell, town clerk :—

| | |
|---|---:|
| E. Fox, Leicester ... ... ... ... ... | £57,639 |
| H. Herbert & Sons, Leicester ... ... ... | 54,851 |
| Hardington & Elliott, Leicester ... ... | 52,753 |
| T. Herbert, Leicester ... ... ... ... | 51,338 |
| W. M. Sharp, Leicester ... ... ... | 50,945 |
| Clark & Garrett, Leicester ... ... ... | 50,008 |
| Merredew & Wort, Stevenage, Herts. ... | 49,350 |
| J. E. Johnson & Son, Leicester* ... ... | 48,381 |

DARTFORD.—For the making-up, &c., of Priory-lane, for the urban district council.—Mr. W. Harston, surveyor to the council :—

| | |
|---|---:|
| Mowlem & Co., London ... ... ... | £210 |
| T. Adams, Wood Green N. ... ... ... | 196 |
| Kent Road Company, Gravesend* ... ... | 195 |

SOUTHAMPTON.—For the erection of a cart-shed at the wharf at Chapel.—Mr. W. B. G. Bennett, borough engineer :—

| | |
|---|---:|
| G. Webb & Co., Southampton ... ... ... | £587 |
| H. W, Bull, Southampton ... ... ... | 587 |
| Jenkins & Sons, Southampton ... ... | 574 |
| S. Nichols, Southampton ... ... ... | 483 |
| J. Nichol, Southampton ... ... ... | 462 |
| F. Osman, Southampton* ... ... ... | 444 |

## NOTICES.

THE SURVEYOR AND MUNICIPAL AND COUNTY ENGINEER may be ordered direct, through any of Messrs. Smith & Son's book-stalls, or of any newsagent in the United Kingdom. Applications to the Offices for single copies by post must in all cases be accompanied by stamps.

The Prepaid Subscription (including postage) is as follows :—

| | Twelve Months. | Six Months. | Three Months. |
|---|---|---|---|
| United Kingdom ... ... | 15s. | 7s. 6d. | 3s. 9d. |
| Continent, the Colonies, India, United States, &c. ... ... | 19s. | 9s. 6d. | 4s. 9d. |

The International News Company, 83 and 85 Duane-street, New York City; The Toronto News Company, Toronto ; and The Montreal News Company, Montreal, have been appointed agents in the United States and Canada for the sale of THE SURVEYOR. A thin paper edition is printed for circulation abroad.

EDITORIAL OFFICES:
ST. BRIDE'S HOUSE, 24 BRIDE-LANE, FLEET-STREET, LONDON, E.C.

OFFICE FOR ADVERTISEMENTS:
13 NEW STREET HILL, FLEET STREET, LONDON, E.C.

PUBLISHING OFFICES:
13 NEW STREET HILL, FLEET STREET, LONDON, E.C.

## APPOINTMENTS OPEN.

CITY OF HULL.
The Corporation require a Civil Engineering Assistant in the City Engineer's office, at £85 per annum.
It is essential that candidates should be quick and neat draughtsmen.
Applications, stating name, experience and qualifications, are to be delivered to the undersigned on or before Tuesday, the 23rd August.
Testimonials need not be sent in the first instance.
(By order)
A. E. WHITE,
City Engineer.
Town Hall, Hull.
. July 30, 1898.

DISTRICT OF SOUTH HORNSEY.
SURVEYOR AND INSPECTOR OF NUISANCES.
The District Council invite applications for the appointment of a Surveyor and Inspector of Nuisances.
The district comprises an area of 230 acres, a population of 17,200 and about 2,430 houses, and is fully developed.
The duties will be those ordinarily required from a surveyor and inspector of nuisances to an urban sanitary authority.
All applicants must satisfy the Council that they are ac-

quainted with the duties of those offices, and must hold the certificate of the Sanitary Institute.

The salary will be as Surveyor £175, per annum, with residence; and as Inspector of Nuisances, £75 per annum, making together £250 a year.

Applications, endorsed "Surveyorship," stating age and qualifications, with particulars of previous experience, and enclosing copies of not more than three recent testimonials, must be received here not later than 5 o'clock p.m. on the 17th of August next.

Personal canvassing will be deemed a disqualification.

EDWARD B. BENNETT,
Clerk to the District Council.
Offices, Milton-road, South Hornsey, London, N.
July 28, 1898.

## COUNTY BOROUGH OF NEWPORT.
### ASSISTANT BOROUGH ENGINEER.

The Corporation require the services of an experienced Assistant Borough Engineer and Surveyor (not more than thirty-five years of age), at a salary commencing at £150 and rising by yearly advances of £10 to £250. List of duties may be obtained from the Borough Engineer, Newport.

Applications, stating age, qualifications and experience, accompanied by not more than three recent testimonials, must be sent to my office, endorsed "Assistant Borough Engineer," not later than 10 a.m. on the 11th August next.

Canvassing strictly prohibited.

ALBERT A. NEWMAN,
Town Clerk.
Town Hall, Newport.
July 30, 1898.

## CITY OF COVENTRY.
### INSPECTOR OF SEWERS.

The Corporation of Coventry are prepared to receive applications from qualified persons for the position of Inspector of Sewers.

The person appointed will require to have had experience in the construction of brick and pipe sewers and the maintenance of the same, and will be required to take charge of the staff engaged in the general supervision and maintenance of the sewerage system.

The candidate appointed will act under the immediate direction of the City Engineer, his hours will be the same as those of the working staff, and he will be required to keep all the books necessary.

Wages will be at the rate of £2 per week.

Applications, in candidate's own handwriting, stating age (which must be between thirty and forty-five years), experience, past and present employment, accompanied by copies of not more than three recent testimonials and endorsed "Inspector of Sewers," to be sent to the undersigned on or before Thursday, the 18th August.

Canvassing, directly or indirectly, will be considered a disqualification.

J. E. SWINDLEHURST,
City Engineer and Surveyor.
St. Mary's Hall. Coventry.
July 29, 1898.

## CITY OF CANTERBURY.
### GENERAL FOREMAN OF WORKS.

Required, by the Corporation of the City of Canterbury, a thoroughly experienced and qualified Foreman of Works and Workmen, to work under the immediate direction of the City Surveyor. He must be accustomed to the handling of large staffs of men, and well up in road and street pavement works; also in sewer and drain construction. Hours, 6 a.m. to 6 p.m. and 1½ hours off. Wages, 42s. per week.

Applications, in candidate's own handwriting, stating age, and giving full details of experience, present and past situations, and enclosing copies of three testimonials of recent date, to be addressed to the undersigned not later than Monday, 15th August next.

Canvassing members of Council will disqualify.

A. H. CAMPBELL,
City Surveyor.
Canterbury.

THE LONDON COUNTY COUNCIL invite applications for employment as Quantity Taker in the Building Branch of the Works Department.

Candidates must have had considerable experience in the taking off of quantities and ordering materials for large jobs. Salary, £3 10s. per week.

The person appointed will be required to give his whole time and energies to the service of the Council.

Applications must be made on forms to be obtained by sending a stamped addressed foolscap envelope to the London County Council Works Department, Belvedere-road, Lambeth, S.E.

The latest time for receiving applications is 10 o'clock a.m. on Saturday, 13th August.

C. J. STEWART,
Clerk of the Council.
July 28, 1898.

---

THE LONDON COUNTY COUNCIL is pre-
pared to receive applications for employment as an
Assistant in the Engineering Branch of the Works Department, at a commencing salary of £300 per annum (no pension
attached).

Candidates must have had considerable experience in the
actual carrying out of engineering works and in the management of men.

The person appointed will require to give his whole time
and energies to the service of the Council.

Applications must be on forms to be obtained by sending a
stamped addressed foolscap envelope to the London County
Council Works Department, Belvedere-road, Lambeth, S.E.

The latest time for receiving applications is 11 o'clock a.m.
on Saturday, the 13th August.

C. J. STEWART,
Clerk to the Council.

July 28, 1898.

THE LONDON COUNTY COUNCIL is pre-
pared to receive applications for employment as Assistant in the Building Branch of the Works Department, at
a salary of £300 per annum (no pension attached).

Candidates must have had experience in the actual carrying
out of large building operations, and have a thorough knowledge of the different trades and materials.

The person appointed will be required to give his whole
time and energies to the service of the Council.

Applications must be on forms to be obtained, by sending
a stamped addressed foolscap envelope to the London County
Council Works Department, Belvedere-road, Lambeth, S.E.

The latest time for receiving applications is 10 o'clock a.m.
on Saturday, the 13th August.

C. J. STEWART,
Clerk to the Council.

July 28, 1898.

BECKENHAM URBAN DISTRICT COUNCIL.
ARCHITECTURAL ASSISTANT.
Required, temporarily, in the Surveyor's office, Beckenham,
an experienced Architectural Draughtsman. One having ex-
perience of swimming baths and technical institutes preferred.
Salary, £3 3s. per week.

Applications, stating age and experience, accompanied by
not more than three testimonials, to be sent to Mr. J. A.
Angell, Surveyor, Council Offices, Beckenham, Kent, by
Friday, August 19th.

## TENDERS WANTED.

NEWTON-IN-MAKERFIELD URBAN
DISTRICT COUNCIL.
TO CONTRACTORS FOR STREET-MAKING.

The above Council invite tenders for the Materials and
Labour required in Excavating and Making the following
Private Streets within their district—viz., Portland, Alpine,
Peel, Nelson, Water and Brookfield-streets and Bradleigh-
road—according to plans, sections and specifications prepared
by the Council's surveyor.

Tenderers are requested to forward alternative tenders for
each street—i.e. (a) for paving the roadway with setts and
(b) for macadamising the roadway.

Quantities for the work and any further particulars required may be obtained on application to the Surveyor, at his
office, Town Hall, Earlestown, between the hours of 9 a.m.
and 5.30 p.m.

Tenders, endorsed "Streets," addressed to the Chairman of
the Highways Committee, to be delivered at my office not
later than 10 a.m. on Saturday, the 6th of August, 1898.

The Council do not bind themselves to accept the lowest or
any tender.

W. W. SHIRLEY,
Clerk to the Council.

Town Hall, Earlestown, Newton-le-Willows.
July 21, 1898.

THE URBAN DISTRICT COUNCIL OF
HOYLAKE AND WEST KIRBY are prepared to re-
ceive designs and tenders for about 2,500 lineal yards of
Standards and Railing for Promenades.

Particulars may be had upon application to the undersigned.

THOMAS FOSTER,
Engineer.

Public Offices, Hoylake, Cheshire.
July 20, 1898.

# The Surveyor

## And Municipal and County Engineer.

Vol. XIV., No. 343.   LONDON, AUGUST 12, 1898.   Weekly, Price 3d.

## Minutes of Proceedings.

**Extraordinary Traffic.**

It is curious how sometimes language, apparently the most precise and simple, will reveal latent ambiguities and difficulties in its application to actual facts. Acts of Parliament, unfortunately, are not always marked either by simplicity or precision of language, but at first sight one would say that the meaning of sec. 23 of the Highways and Locomotives (Amendment) Act, 1878, is so clear that he who runs may read. And yet (to mention one only of the points on which questions productive of litigation have arisen under this section), when a local authority have to proceed to recover expenses of extraordinary traffic, it is in many cases by no means an easy matter to determine who is the person "by whose order such weight or traffic has been conducted." This question cropped up in the early days of the Act, and in several cases it was held that either the employer or his contractor could be proceeded against, whilst in one instance the owner of traction engines who let them to move manure for a farmer was held to be liable. On the other hand there are cases reported in which, original contractors having employed sub-contractors, it was held that the latter alone were liable, being under no obligation to do the carting in any particular manner. Yet, again, in another instance a contractor who sub-contracted with three owners of traction engines was held to be the person "by whose order the traffic had been conducted. In a recent case, which went to the House of Lords, the traffic consisted of the carriage by means of traction engines of materials for additions to a mansion house. No contractor was employed, the owner of the house himself ordering the materials at a price inclusive of delivery, but without giving any special directions either as to the mode of delivery or the route to be taken. The Divisional Court of Queen's Bench held that the owner was liable ; but this decision was reversed in the Court of Appeal, Lord Justice Lopes, however, dissenting. (*Lord Gerard v. Kent County Council*, noted at p. 216 of vol. xi. of THE SURVEYOR). The decision was arrived at upon consideration of the fact that the dealer who supplied the goods was not a mere servant, and that the mode in which he was to carry out his contract was left entirely to his own discretion. The dissenting judge, on the other hand, wished to read "by whose order" as meaning " in consequence of whose order," and pointed out the difficulties that might arise in the case of a person employing a number of different tradesmen whose aggregate traffic might cause damage, though it would be impossible to bring home that damage to either of them individually.

This decision of the Court of Appeal was confirmed by the House of Lords. Lord Herschell's judgment is very instructive. He disposes of Lord Justice Lopes' suggested reading by " the simple answer . . . that is not what the statute has said " ; and with regard to the imagined difficulties in the case of a person employing a number of tradesmen, he shows that the adoption of that reading would lead to equal difficulties in the converse case. " You might have a man in business conducting a large traffic . . . and the several persons for whom he was building houses . . . having only ordered an amount of goods, the carriage of which would not lead to extraordinary traffic, they would be under no liability." In a still more recent case, contractors for the building of a lunatic asylum employed a sub-contractor to haul materials. The sub-contractor agreed to supply carts and horses as and when required, to provide workmen, to unload the materials from railway trucks, and to haul them to such place on the works as should be pointed out by the contractor, receiving from the latter such assistance as should be necessary, and only to use such roads as should be pointed out to him. Moreover, the sub-contractor was to employ no cart or traction engine which the contractor should certify to be improper for the service. It was held by the Court of Appeal that the contractor was not liable (*Pethick v. County Council of Dorset*, noted in this issue). In this case the Court expressly followed *Lord Gerard v. Kent County Council*. It will be seen, however, that Pethick's case goes considerably further in the direction of the immunity of the person who is in reality the prime mover, or *causa causans*, of the traffic. In the course of the judgment already referred to Lord Herschell said, " If the person sought to be charged has had nothing to do with the conduct of the traffic, or the mode in which it is to be conducted, *and has had no power to give orders in relation to it*, then I think it is impossible to say that it was by his order that the traffic was conducted." Now, in Pethick's case the contractor undoubtedly had "power to give orders in relation to the traffic," under the terms of his contract with the sub-contractor. This, indeed, seems to have been fully recognised by the Court, but nevertheless it was held that, not having in fact exercised that power, the contractor was not liable. Altogether it cannot be said that any very definite rule can be deduced from the decided cases. In each instance the decision turned upon the facts, and in no two instances were the facts precisely identical. Speaking generally, however, and without attempting to draw any hard and fast line, we think it may be inferred that where the person who actually conducts the traffic is not a mere servant, and has no special directions, but is left to his own discretion as to how he will carry out his contract, he alone is the responsible person and not the party who employs him, and this notwithstanding that the latter may have reserved to himself full powers of supervision and discretion, provided he has not in fact exercised that right. It may be observed in passing that, whoever is liable, the liability ceases on his death, proceedings under this section being in the nature of a personal tort and incapable of being taken against his executor.

The question of what is "extraordinary traffic" within the meaning of the section mentioned above has been equally fruitful in litigation. Traffic arising out of a recognised industry in a district has been held not to be "extraordinary traffic," though greater than the other traffic and not continuous. Yet a case is reported in which the cartage of stone along a road not adapted for heavy traffic was held to be "extraordinary traffic," although stone quarrying was a recognised business in the neighbourhood. In one of the earlier reported cases the carting of building materials along a road generally used for agricultural traffic was held not to be extraordinary traffic. This decision, however, was disapproved in a subsequent case which went to the Court of Appeal (*Hill* v. *Thomas*, L.R. [1893] 2 Q.B., 233), and in which Lord Justice Bowen gave the following definition, or rather explanation, of the meaning of the term "extraordinary traffic":—

Extraordinary traffic is really a carriage of articles over the road, at either one or more times, which is so exceptional in the quality or quantity of articles carried, or in the mode or time of user of the road, as substantially to alter and increase the burden imposed by ordinary traffic on the road, and to cause damage and expense thereby beyond what is common.

This may be regarded as the authoritative judicial declaration on the question, and, though difficulties may arise in its application to exceptional sets of circumstances, it affords valuable guidance in ordinary cases. As a rule it is easier to determine whether traffic is extraordinary than it is to decide against whom proceedings should be taken to recover expenses in respect thereof. The answer to the latter question may, as we have seen, depend to a great extent upon the terms of certain contracts, the contents of which are unknown to the local authority.

  &ast;   &ast;   &ast;

**The Telephone Inquiry.** Some additional comments may be made on the evidence at this inquiry in continuation of the remarks given in our last issue. The most direct evidence given was that of Mr. A. R. Bennett, whom we may describe as the "corporation expert," and who was probably the chief technical witness brought against the existing *régime*. While the evidence given by this witness was chiefly of a technical nature, his conclusions are that a municipality would be able to provide a much cheaper service than is being furnished at the present time by the National Telephone Company. The estimate he made for the Glasgow Corporation was for £5 5s. per subscriber, which he reckoned would enable the corporation to get a return for its capital outlay, and he thought that careful management of the local authorities throughout the country might even improve upon that amount. A local authority had no expensive board of directors to pay, and it was free from many other charges which a company would have to meet. This witness disagreed entirely with the views of the Post Office officials on the subject of competition, and he declared that it would be in the best interests of the public to permit competition in any given areas, but he would not commit himself to the opinion that local authorities would be the best competitors. He maintained, however, that local management was a very essential feature in telephones, and whether that local management came from a municipality or a local company did not, in his opinion, affect the matter much; what was wanted was a knowledge of the local requirements."

It was not until the inquiry had been in progress for some time that the views of prominent members of municipalities and local governing authorities were put forward, and perhaps the most important evidence adduced on the question of municipal control was that contributed by Mr. Benn on

behalf of the London County Council. From this it appears that the County Council have ascertained whether the telephone users of London were satisfied with the existing service, and in 1895, out of 2,500 subscribers communicated with, 1,305 were generally dissatisfied. They had just lately been sending round to ascertain what was the present position of those persons who were then complaining, and so far they had succeeded in dealing with 561 cases. They found that there were eight persons now satisfied with the service, fifty-three had changed their address, thirty-six had discontinued through dissatisfaction, and 235 were still dissatisfied for various reasons. The general summary of complaints was as follows: General inefficiency, 65 ; delay in getting connection, 213 ; indistinctness, 189; ringing-off before conversation was finished,196; and failure to get connection on account of being engaged, 217. This is undoubtedly a black list, but it is nevertheless satisfactory to notice that Mr. Benn has somewhat moderated his opinion on the subject of a municipally-worked telephone scheme by saying that if the Post Office will enter into the matter on the basis of honest and thorough competition there will be no necessity for the London County Council to take up this work. Failing that, he considers the County Council would do very much better for London than the National Telephone Company, and he based his contention on the fact that they had greater advantages with regard to way-leaves, fire stations and other places being open to them which would not be available to the National Telephone Company, and therefore they could manage a system altogether more efficiently and cheaply. Coming to actual figures, he calculated that they would be able to reduce the present telephone charges down to £10 per subscriber during the first five years, and reduce it to £9 afterwards. It seemed to be established, however, that special legislation would be necessary, apart from the question of granting a telephone license to the County Council, for, as things stood at present, it would be within the rights of any vestry to refuse to grant the County Council powers to take up its streets ; and, therefore, it would be necessary to go to Parliament for powers having special reference to this phase of the subject. It will be remembered that we have endeavoured to demonstrate that the telephone service is one which must necessarily serve only a limited section of the community. Mr. Benn, however, does not agree with this view, for he considers that a telephone service cannot be described as meeting the needs of a small class, because it must be evident that if the telephone is a necessary adjunct to commercial and business firms then the advantages which result in increased business must extend to the carmen and warehousemen. It would seem, however, that whatever benefits employées of a firm might get from the telephone being used by their employers, they might have to pay a direct tax for the purpose of providing a cheaper telephone system, from which they obtain no direct benefit. The figures advanced by the London County Council through its engineer are scarcely as reliable as one would have expected, and certainly differ very materially from ascertained figures of actual working.

The best evidence, however, from the municipal point of view, was that contributed by various members of the Glasgow municipality, and Dr. Colquhoun, a member of the Glasgow Town Council, considered that it was both desirable and, in fact, necessary that the corporation should take the telephone service up. In his opinion the telephone in Glasgow had not been developed, and had been confined merely to the large businesses and manufacturers. They had received between 4,000 and 5,000 applications from prospective users, and these were from all classes of the community. He voiced the opinion of the town council when he said that the municipality would be able to give a much more efficient service both to the corporation itself and to the general public. These opinions were corroborated by Mr. Colville, Mr. Nichol, Mr. Chisholm and other members of the town council. There was a point of considerable importance raised in the examination of the Scottish witnesses with reference to the profits made out of operating a system. It was their opinion that the scheme should not be carried on for the purpose of relieving the general taxation, but that the system should be carried on for the public good, and that any profits made should go in reducing telephone charges. We have already dealt with this peculiar Scottish view of things, and we need hardly reiterate what seems to be self-evident. If the ratepayers are responsible for the initial capital expended some return should be made to them, and a direct return cannot be made to all unless it be by reducing taxation, because the users of the telephone will be small compared with the total number of ratepayers. In the present issue we report the concluding proceedings of the inquiry and summarise the main findings of the committee. We shall take an early opportunity of commenting upon these. In the meantime we need only say that not only will they be received with more than usual interest by local authorities, but that they will probably tend to force the Government to declare whether the State should undertake the telephone system or whether powers should be granted to local authorites.

\*        \*        \*

**The Cork Meeting.**    The Cork meeting of municipal engineers was a great success, and in some respects it was even remarkably successful. It is true that a larger attendance might have been expected, but the limited number of members who put in an appearance can no doubt be accounted for in various ways. The distance was too great for many English members to travel, especially as they had gone in considerable strength to Edinburgh a month before to attend the annual meeting. It might have been thought, however, that the meeting would have attracted more than actually put in an appearance, especially as the programme was obviously of unusual interest. According to the last published list of members the Irish contingent number thirty-six, and this being the case the comparatively small number who attended was rather disappointing, though, perhaps, the unpromising outlook at the last moment as to the weather may have deterred some from carrying out their intention of being present. However that may be, we believe we are correct in asserting that the number of members who attended fell considerably short of the number who had written accepting. This, unfortunately, is by no means an uncommon experience for district secretaries, but it is certainly one to be avoided if possible. It can only be avoided by the exercise of a little consideration on the part of the members themselves. It is scarcely fair to those organising a meeting to send an acceptance unless one is tolerably sure of being able to attend, but if an acceptance be sent every effort should be made to be present. The council of the association are sometimes adversely criticised on the score of shortcomings, but the members should not forget that they themselves have duties. The loss, however, was to those who were absent, for, apart from rather bad weather on Friday, the meeting was equally pleasurable and profitable. The Irish reputation for hospitality was more than maintained, and in this respect the genial mayor, Mr. P. H. Meade, whose portrait we give in another column, led the way in a fashion that was beyond praise. Members of the town council and others evinced the liveliest interest in the proceedings, and a genuine appreciation of the work of municipal engineers which was equally gratifying to the visitors and creditable to themselves. As for the proceedings, the interest which the papers of Mr. Cutler, Mr. Griffin and Mr. Dorman excited can easily be gauged from the discussions, of which we give a full report. Special attention was attracted by Mr. Cutler's ability in dealing with the defective construction of the municipal buildings and with the waste of water, and due credit should be given to Mr. Griffin for the obliging and energetic manner in which he came to the aid of the meeting by contributing a paper at very short notice. The visits, like the papers, were instructive and interesting, and will receive due attention in our next issue. All who took part in the function, whether or not they were connected with the association or the town council, seemed animated by feelings which might almost be described as enthusiastic, and neither on Friday nor Saturday was there a single jarring note.

\*        \*        \*

**A Carnarvon Rural District.**    Complaints of outbreaks of infectious disease and of general sanitary shortcomings in the area administered by the Bettws-y-Coed Rural District Council led, in the natural course of things, to an inquiry by a medical inspector of the Local Government Board. From Dr. Wheaton's report, which has now been issued, we learn that the district is mostly mountainous and uncultivated, that the people are resident in villages, and that the chief sanitary defect is probably in connection with the water supply, though it is far from being the only defect. In very few of the villages is the supply at all satisfactory, either as to quality or to quantity. As a rule it is taken from the rivers and streams, which are often subject to very gross forms of pollution, and there is no attempt at storage or filtration. This state of affairs is the more surprising when we find Dr. Wheaton pointing out that the district abounds in lakes, the water of which is in nearly all cases free from risk of pollution, and which are situated at a high level, thus forming natural reservoirs from which the district could be supplied by gravitation without difficulty. He adds that the quickly-flowing nature of the streams can hardly allow of any purification of them by subsidence, and that filth entering above the intakes must be very quickly conveyed to the latter, with serious risk to the health of the consumers. We have recently had occasion to speak at some length of the pressing necessity for some legal machinery which would compel local authorities to fulfil their obligations to provide adequate water supplies in rural districts. One Local Government Board report after another confirms the pressing nature of the problem. In regard also to sewerage and to excrement and refuse disposal, an unsatisfactory condition of things exists in these Carnarvonshire villages. Dr. Wheaton leaves no doubt as to where the responsibility lies. The medical officer has from time to time drawn the attention of the council to the urgent sanitary needs of the district, but—" hitherto his recommendations have not been carried out." The inspector of nuisances seems to carry out his work intelligently and conscientiously, especially in reporting nuisances, but—" he receives no encouragement from the council." We may remark, in passing, that inspector of nuisances, inspector of sewers and supervisor of waterworks is a somewhat singular combination of offices, and should command something more than £60 a year, especially when the holder devotes the whole of his time to his duties. There is no accommodation for the reception of cases of infectious disease. " It is evident," remarks the inspector, "that the action taken by the district council for the sanitary improvement of their district has been almost nil." The county council have granted their application for the conversion of the parish into an urban district. Possibly this administrative promotion may act as a stimulus to the members, but their record as a rural district inspires no great hopes for the future.

**Seaford.**—At a special meeting of the district council on the 2nd inst. a resolution was adopted recommending that the necessary steps be taken to purchase the undertaking of the water company.

# Association of Municipal and County Engineers.

## IRISH DISTRICT MEETING AT CORK.—I.

CORK : ST. PATRICK'S QUAY FROM ST. PATRICK'S BRIDGE.

The "beautiful citie of Cork"—to use Spenser's phrase—was the scene of an Irish district meeting on Friday and Saturday, the fourth meeting of the kind, as the president remarked, that had ever been held in Ireland, the last having been that at Londonderry, in August, 1895. The third town in importance and commercial prosperity in Ireland, Cork is looked upon as the capital of the South. Even to those who

THE RIGHT WORSHIPFUL P. H. MEADE,
Mayor of Cork.

have never visited Ireland the name of the river on which the city stands should be familiar from the famous lyric in which Father Prout immortalised

The bells of Shandon,
That sound so grand on
The pleasant waters
Of the river Lee.

In the city itself, to say nothing of the surrounding country, the visitor finds in Cork certain elements of the picturesque. The streets are tolerably spacious, but somewhat irregular in their formation. This is attributed to the fact that the town was originally built on the banks of the streams which separated islands that are now united as one. These channels were gradually arched over, some as recently as the beginning of the present century, and roadways formed over them. The resulting state of affairs is that the river now divides into two parts just above Cork, and after passing it reunites and swells out into the harbour of Queenstown. The town, of course, has long extended beyond the limits of the islands, and the two branches of the river practically divide the city into three parts, the intercommunication between these being carried on by means of eight bridges, the chief of which are St. Patrick's and Parnell bridges. The want of regularity in the streets extends to the buildings, though in the case of the latter it might be better to speak of want of uniformity, both in style and in colour. In one part of the town the building stone is reddish-brown in colour, in another it is of a cold grey tint. Other structures, again, are of brick, sometimes whitewashed and sometimes coloured, and many of them are protected from the weather by slate of a very dark colour.

The diversity finds very concentrated expression in the steeple of Shandon church, two sides of which are built of limestone and the other two of red sandstone.

The origin of the city is traced back to the foundation of the cathedral by St. Fin Barre, the patron saint of Cork, early in the seventh century. A more effective settlement was made by the Danes in the beginning of the eleventh century, from which point the real foundation of the place may be said to date. Little or nothing, however, is on record until Anglo-Norman days. The city had a somewhat eventful record during Stuart and Jacobite times, and until last century was surrounded with a wall. When the troublous periods mentioned had passed away the walls were destroyed and the inhabitants settled down to the development of trade, with the results that we have already indicated.

The north and south branches of the river are lined with fine quays of cut limestone. The city is rich in churches, both Roman Catholic and Anglican. The foundation-stone of the new cathedral was laid in 1865. The other Protestant churches, as a rule, are not very imposing externally, but some of the Roman Catholic places of worship are magnificent structures, ranking among the finest modern ecclesiastical edifices in Ireland. A brief reference may here be made to the most prominent public buildings. The Court House is an elegant Grecian structure, with a Corinthian portico, about 30 ft. in height. The Corn Exchange and some of the principal banks are handsome buildings of cut limestone. On a portion of the Corn Exchange site the Municipal Buildings, containing the mayor's office, council chamber and the offices

MR. A. McCARTHY,
Town Clerk of Cork.

of the various departments, have been erected. This structure we need not further refer to, as it is dealt with in Mr. Cutler's paper. The Commercial Buildings and the Chamber of Commerce may also be mentioned as prominent structures. The Custom House is built at the junction of the two branches of the river.

CORK : MUNICIPAL BUILDINGS.

Among educational, charitable and other institutions mention may be made of the Queen's College, a fine structure in the Tudor-Gothic style, and of the Crawford Municipal Schools of Science and Art. The latter edifice was opened by the Prince and Princess of Wales during their visit to Ireland in 1885. The site of the old Custom House was granted by the Crown to the corporation for the erection of the building, which was the gift of Mr. William H. Crawford. The Cork District Lunatic Asylum occupies a fine position on the brow of a hill on the western suburb, and a fine view of the building was obtained by the members on Friday when travelling on the Cork and Muskerry Light Railway.

A few words may be said as to the trade of the city and its commercial activity. The merchants have the advantages of the double waterway on which to ship their goods for conveyance to all ports of the United Kingdom. Queenstown, again, acts as a convenient port of transhipment, and thus the exports of the city find their way to every part of the globe. Butter-making is the chief industry, not only in the county but in the province of Munster, but the exports embrace cattle, pigs, dairy produce and generally all kinds of provisions. Among the industries are the manufacture of tweed and other kinds of woollen goods, leather and agricultural implements, flax and hemp spinning, iron founding, brewing, distilling and chemical works.

We may appropriately conclude this brief preliminary sketch of the city by a few facts as to its municipal history and position. The corporation — which now consists of a mayor, sheriff, fourteen aldermen and forty-two councillors — is of very ancient date. At first the place was a borough by prescription. Its oldest charter was one granted by King John, when Earl of Morton, and acting as Viceroy of Ireland, during the reign of his father, Henry II. The principal charter, however, is that of James I. The population of the city is 97,281, its rateable value £234,507, and its area 46,080 acres. The corporation maintain the water supply, the markets, the Crawford School of Science and Art and the Public Library.

## FRIDAY'S PROCEEDINGS.

As was expected, the attendance consisted for the most part of members located in Ireland. Owing to the distance it was scarcely likely that many members from England would be able to attend, especially as so many had travelled to Edinburgh a month before to attend the annual meeting. The proceedings began at 11.30 on Friday, when the members were cordially received in the Council Chamber, Municipal Buildings, by the Right Worshipful Mayor, Mr. P. H. Meade, who was accompanied by the town clerk, Mr. A. McCarthy. Among those present were the following :—

PRESIDENT: O. Claude Robson, London.
MEMBERS OF COUNCIL: R. H. Dorman, Armagh; J. Cook, Lancaster; and T. Cole, London, secretary.
MEMBERS: G. R. Andrews, London; A. G. McBeath, Sale, England; C. Bottorill, Pulham; M. Buckley, Drumcondra; H. A. Cutler, city engineer, Cork; M. J. Fleming, Waterford; J. Horan, county surveyor, Limerick; S. A. Kirkby, M.A.,CANTAB, county surveyor, Cork (South); R. W. Longfield,

county surveyor, Donegal; A. O. Lyons, county surveyor, Cork (east) ; J. Morgan, Portardawe; J. Smith, county surveyor, Galway; and H. Dawkin Williams, Bridgend, Wales.

VISITORS: C. H. W. Biggs, London; C. G. Doran. Queenstown Waterworks; Beverley Griffin, resident engineer to contractor for permanent way of Cork Electric Tramways; W. H. Hill, Cork ; W. H. Hill, junr., engineer Cork and Muskerry Light Railway; M. J. McMullen, Cork; C. H. Mery, secretary and resident engineer to Cork Electric Tramways and Lighting Company; W. Paton, London; R. T. Perry, Blackrock and Passage Railway, Cork; and H. S. Ridings, Dulwich, London.

The MAYOR, in extending a hearty welcome to the visitors on behalf of the citizens of Cork, said he believed that was their first visit to the city in their organised representative capacity, but he only re-echoed the wishes of the people of Cork, without distinction, when he said that he hoped they might often have the pleasure of meeting them again. As a body, he need not say that they represented a class of professional gentlemen, the importance of whose work it would not be easy to over-estimate. In their hands he might say that the health and happiness of vast bodies of their citizens rested. Town councillors, he was quite aware, were not the most angelic or lovable of beings at times. Perhaps they had an undue sense of their own importance, and that made them rather obstreperous at times, but the very worst of them would never think of questioning the opinion of their engineers, who used their high position with a most conscientious regard for the welfare of the people. He hoped to meet them again in Cork, and he was confident that in no part of the United Kingdom could they depend upon a more cordial welcome than in that ancient city of Cork.

His worship then vacated the chair, which was taken by

The PRESIDENT, who, on behalf of the Incorporated Association of Municipal and County Engineers, thanked the mayor very heartily for the kind reception accorded on that occasion. Hitherto their meetings had been held in the sister kingdoms of England and Scotland. That was only the fourth meeting held in Ireland, the previous meetings having been held in Dublin, Belfast and Derry. Notwithstanding the few visits the Association had paid to that country, he was sure they would all be pleased to know that the Association numbered about 900 members, including nearly the whole of the Irish surveyors—a body of gentlemen of whom they were justly proud, and who did honour to the Association. He thanked his worship for giving them that opportunity of meeting their Irish brethren in somewhat greater numbers than they could do on the other side of the Irish Channel. He was sure the meeting would prove both interesting and instructive to the members, and that incidentally it would prove beneficial to those whom they served in various parts of the country.

Mr. R. H. DORMAN, the hon. secretary for the Irish district, then read the minutes of the last district meeting, which were duly adopted and signed. The meeting next proceeded to elect an hon. district secretary.

Mr. H. A. CUTLER (Cork) said he had great pleasure in proposing that Mr. R. H. Dorman, Armagh, be re-elected to the position for the coming year. He was sure he had discharged his duties up to the present to the greatest satisfaction of everybody, and from what he had seen of Mr. Dorman's ability in organising that meeting he was certain they could not have a better district secretary.

Mr. S. A. Kireby (Cork) said he had the greatest pleasure in seconding the proposition. For many years Mr. Dorman had taken the greatest interest in the Association, and, in fact, with everything connected with the progress of the work they had at heart.

The motion, having been put to the meeting, was adopted unanimously, and

The President, addressing Mr. Dorman, said he had very great pleasure in stating that he had been re-elected hon. secretary for the Irish district for the succeeding year, and personally he was only too glad to find that Mr. Dorman was willing to take office again. He was sure the association was to be congratulated on having such a district secretary.

Mr. Dorman thanked them for the honour they had done him in re-electing him to the office of hon. secretary for the Irish district. He was the oldest member of the association in Ireland, and would certainly do his best to forward its interests in future.

The next business on the agenda was the reading and discussion of papers, the following being the first one taken:—

## RESTORATION OF MUNICIPAL BUILDINGS AND DESCRIPTION OF CORK WATERWORKS.

By Henry A. Cutler, Assoc.M.Inst.C.E.,
City Engineer.

[Mr. Henry A. Cutler began his professional career in 1877 with a firm of contractors, for whom he acted as agent on the Cinderford waterworks and the Chiswick sewage outfall works. From 1879 to 1882 he was articled to Mr. A. T. Walmisley, M.I.C.E., of Westminster, engineer to the Dover Harbour Board, and was subsequently employed for four years as assistant to Mr. W. H. Fox, borough engineer of Barrow-in-Furness. On leaving that town Mr. Cutler returned to the office of Mr. A. T. Walmisley, as chief assistant, with whom he remained for two years, at the time joining the staff of the late Mr. Joseph Gordon, M.I.C.E., then borough engineer of Leicester, and afterwards chief engineer to the London County Council. This appointment was vacated when Mr. Cutler was selected for the post of borough engineer of Rawtenstall, in which capacity he served for seven years. In 1896 the city engineership of Cork became vacant under circumstances which need not now be recalled, and the corporation decided to adopt the course—as unusual one, so far as municipal engineers are concerned—of selecting the new official as the result of a stringent competitive examination. Mr. Cutler came out of the ordeal in brilliant fashion at the head of the list, with no fewer than 76 per cent. of marks, and was immediately appointed to the vacant office. Those who attended the meeting last week had abundant opportunities of observing how well the policy of the corporation has been justified, and how readily they themselves appreciate the fact. Mr. Cutler was awarded a "Millar" prize by the Institution of Civil Engineers for a student paper on "The Stability of Voussoir Arches," and is one of the authors of Cutler and Edges' "Curve Tables."]

For many years the Corporation of Cork had under consideration the question of municipal buildings, as great inconvenience was experienced through having the various departments located in different parts of the city. In the year 1889 the town council decided to purchase the Corn Exchange, and by alterations and additions, which were completed in 1891, to make the building suitable for the requirements of the city. The old Corn Exchange, with a slight modification of the front elevation, occupies the central portion of the new building, the wings on the east and west sides being entirely new. The roof of the old building was removed, and an upper floor, carrying the council chamber and other offices, constructed on girders and columns over the ground floor, which is now used as a vestibule. Before the work was completed serious settlements occurred in both wings, and within a very short time after completion the openings had to be braced and various temporary measures adopted to prevent accidents occurring.

In 1896 the author was instructed to report to the town council on the present state of the buildings and on the work necessary for their restoration, together with an estimate of the cost. On surveying the buildings the concrete foundations of the wings were found to have insufficient spread and to be too thin for the weight they carried, as evidenced by the longitudinal cracks in the concrete under the walls; they

were also laid practically on the surface of the ground, without more than about 6 in. of excavation. The foundations of the old walls to which the new work was bonded were on a bed of gravel 17 ft. below the floor line, and the ground above the gravel consisted of about 10 ft. of slob, or blue mud, surmounted by about 6 ft. of filling.

The walls of the new wings, which were rough rubble plastered externally with cement, were found to have sunk about 6 in. in the middle of their length, the ends being suspended from the old walls to which they were bonded. Large and dangerous cracks were found in all the new work, some of the relieving arches had dropped out, and the floors and roofs had followed the sinking of the walls. Some of the old walls were cracked with the extra weight caused by the new walls being bonded in to them. The two central columns in the vestibule supporting the girders under the council chamber had sunk about 1 in. and were considerably overloaded, while the girders which they were supporting were strained to their elastic limit, and the joists of the council chamber floor were only about half the necessary strength.

After carefully considering the cost, the author reported to the council that it would not only be considerably cheaper to underpin the walls and raise the floors and roof than to pull down and rebuild, but that the work could be done without turning the officers out of the building. The estimated cost of underpinning and restoring the building to its original condition, including the erection of six cast-iron stanchions to support the defective girders over the vestibule and the forming of two new offices and two new strong-rooms, was £2,000, and the actual cost of the work has been little, if anything, over the estimate. In deciding to underpin the defective building the only doubt in the mind of the author was whether the pumping of the water with which the ground was charged would cause further settlements before the foundations could be put in, and it was only by the exercise of the greatest care that failure was avoided. Before the walls were underpinned all the openings were temporarily braced with timber, and the walls were further supported by half-timber raking shores properly footed and secured by oak keys inserted right through the walls.

The underpinning was done in lengths of about 9 ft., with cement concrete mixed in the proportion of six to one, one 9-ft. pier being built under the centre of the length of each wall before any other holes were sunk. When a central pier was completed holes were sunk for piers on each side simultaneously, leaving a space of about 9 ft. between the piers, thus leaving alternate bays standing on the original foundation. Had it been found necessary, it was intended to afterwards excavate the bays between the alternate piers, thus making a continuous foundation; but the piers appear to be amply sufficient. In making the excavations the ground was first cleared to the underside of the original foundations, and two trenches cut at right angles to the walls about 6 ft. apart, deep enough to get steel needles under the concrete. The needles were 12-in. by 6-in. rolled joists 12 ft. long, supported at their ends by half timbers about 10 ft. long, laid in trenches cut parallel to the walls. When the half-timber sleepers and needles had been placed in position and wedged up, the ground was excavated on one side of the wall only for the length of the intended pier, about 3 ft. 6 in. wide, and 5 ft. below the underside of the old concrete. The ground under the walls was then excavated as far back only as the width of the footing. The excavation below the point described was cut to the exact dimensions of the intended pier, so that the concrete could be brought up without any casing, the extra width at the top being only necessary for the access of the men and for casting out the excavated earth. When the excavations had been carried to a depth within 2 ft. of the gravel the work was stopped until low water, as the ground was fairly dry down to that point, but if the work was carried any further without the precaution mentioned the bottom was found to burst up and cause a delay of two or three tides, besides involving extra pumping and endangering the building. Before the excavation was proceeded with sufficient materials were gauged and mixed dry to form a bed of concrete over the bottom of the hole about 3 ft. thick, and about an hour before low water the remaining 2 ft. was excavated, the concrete mixed with a small quantity of water and deposited before the tide had risen appreciably. The filling of the needles was reached, then a pier was formed between the needles within about 4 in. of the underside of the old foundation, the space being packed tight with concrete when the lower portion had properly set. By making the space as small as consistent with proper filling no appreciable shrinkage occurred and the ramming could be done more effectually. When the central pier had set for about three days the needles were removed and the side spaces packed with concrete in the same manner as the central portion, thus completing the pier.

The foundations for the stanchions in the vestibule were formed with concrete, and were carried to the same depth as the piers for underpinning. The height from the finished concrete foundations to the underside of the girders was 1¼ in. greater than the length of the stanchions, and when the stanchions were put in position they were wedged up tight to the underside of the girders by driving iron wedges between the concrete and the base plates; a bank of clay was then formed all round, about 3 in. from the edge of the hare stanchion, and the space grouted with neat cement. When the grout had set, the iron wedges were drawn and the holes filled with cement. By the method adopted part of the load on the girders was at once transferred to the stanchions, the cost of a stone template was saved, and a thoroughly uniform bed was obtained. The base plates had two holes, 2 in. in diameter, cast close to the web of the stanchion, which allowed free vent for the air when the grout was poured in from the outside of the base plate, and showed when the grout filled the space by its rising in the holes. Two of the stanchions are embedded in the walls of two new rooms formed in the vestibule, while four are encased in concrete, with stone caps and bases, and finished in imitation of the two columns previously existing.

The joists of the council chamber floor, which had a span of 26 ft., were of the ordinary width of 12 in. apart, and had a scantling only of 12 in. by 2 in., and had sagged in the centre about 2½ in. By fixing rolled-steel girders under the

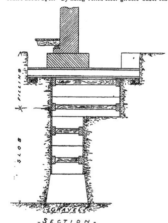

- S E C T I O N -

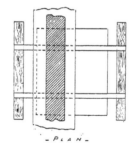

- P L A N -

CORK : UNDERPINNING OF MUNICIPAL BUILDINGS.

joists, so as to divide the span into two, the necessary strength was obtained, and wedges could be used for taking the sag out of the floor. When the foundations were considered secure the building was considered secure the floors and roof were jacked up to their original position. All loose plaster was stripped from the walls inside and out, the jambs of openings were taken down, plumbed and rebuilt ,cills and heads were set level, defective arches rebuilt loose and shattered walling taken out and rebuilt, and all cracks stopped and filled with cement grout. A large quantity of new plaster, ing had to be executed, and most of the windows, doors, frames and linings had to be taken out and partly renewed and repaired ; but any detailed description of such work would not be of interest and is not worth describing.

DESCRIPTION OF THE CORK WATERWORKS, AND MEANS ADOPTED FOR CHECKING WASTE.

The city of Cork is supplied with water from two resor-

voirs situated above the city, and into which the water is pumped from the river Lee. The upper, or high-level, reservoir has a capacity of 721,500 gallons, and supplies water to 17,760 persons, whilst the low-level reservoir has a capacity of 3,404,000 gallons, and supplies water to 68,529 persons, making a sum total of 86,289 persons who use the city water for domestic purposes. Like other commercial towns, a large quantity of water is also used for trade purposes, most of which is taken from the city mains.

The power required for pumping is derived from the following steam engines and turbines—viz., one horizontal low-pressure condensing engine, capable of delivering 68,596 gallons per hour to the low-level reservoir and 22,066 gallons per hour to the high-level reservoir ; two beam engines, each capable of delivering 55,501 gallons per hour to the low-level reservoir one Cornish engine, capable of delivering 69,228 gallons per hour to the low-level reservoir ; two "New American" turbines, capable of delivering jointly 56,982 gallons per hour to the low-level reservoir and 24,102 gallons per hour to the high-level reservoir ; and one old turbine, capable of delivering 46,818 gallons per hour to the low-level reservoir. Summarising the foregoing figures, the total pumping capacity of the plant is as follows :—

*Steam Plant.*

|  | | | | Low-level. Gallons. | High-lev Gallons. |
|---|---|---|---|---|---|
| Horizontal engine | ... | ... | ... | 68,569 | 22,066 |
| Two beam engines | ... | ... | ... | 111,002 | — |
| Cornish engine | ... | ... | ... | 69,228 | — |

*Water Plant.*

| Two "New American" turbines | ... | 56,982 | 24,102 |
|---|---|---|---|
| One old turbine | ... | ... | 46,818 | — |
| | | | |
| Hourly delivery from all machinery | 352,599 | 50,168 |

With the exception of the two "New American" turbines, the whole of the foregoing pumping plant is wasteful and obsolete. The coal consumed per horse-power hour by the steam plant varies between 5·5 lb. and 6·5 lb., and the efficiency of the old turbines is considerably below that which can be obtained from a well-designed turbine of the present day. At the present time two other "New American" turbines are being erected, of the same power as the present ones, and when completed it will be possible to pump the whole of the water for the city supply by water-power, except for two or three months in the year, when the quantity of water flowing down the river is insufficient to work all the turbines. After the erection of the new turbines it will be a matter of calculation as to whether the annual repayment of principal, with interest, necessary for the erection of new steam plant will be less than the saving which modern machinery could effect, and this can only be determined from data now being obtained as to the actual average horse-power hours lost by the water plant per annum in consequence of insufficiency of water for driving.

The water of the river Lee at the intake is a good potable water, containing only 4·5 deg. of hardness, and is an excellent water for domestic purposes, besides which it does not attack lead pipes. In times of heavy rainfall large quantities of peat and decayed vegetable matter are brought down the river, causing great discoloration and deposits in the reservoirs, water mains and services, but at the present time plans are being prepared for the erection of filters, which, when completed, will no doubt relieve the minds of the consumers from the uneasiness always felt when drinking water is discoloured. A large sum of money was expended by the corporation, about sixteen years, ago in constructing a filter tunnel along the bank of the Lee, but as the quantity of water obtained is totally inadequate to the requirements of the city, the bulk of the water has to be pumped direct from the river.

In 1895 the corporation were advised that an underground river was flowing through the valley of the Lee, from which a pure supply might be obtained by pumping from wells sunk into the gravel beneath an overlying impervious stratum. Trial borings were sunk and cross-sections of the valley obtained, which showed about 16 ft. of impervious earth, with coarse gravel beneath, overlying the old red sandstone rock. The gravel varied in thickness from nil at the sides to 70 ft. near the centre of the valley.

On being supplied with the data obtained, the author reported to the corporation on the scheme, but could not recommend its adoption, as the area of the valley of the Lee. which is apparently the catchment area of the underground reservoir, would only be large enough to supply 2,000,000 gallons per day, assuming a percolation of 4 in. per annum, whereas the consumption at the time of reporting was over 6,000,000 daily. It is probable that to some extent the river Lee may also feed the underground reservoir through fissures or changes in the overlying stratum, but as it was reported that the borings showed the impervious bed in which the river Lee flows to be practically uniform, and that the water in the bore-holes rose above the level of the river at a time when its discharge was above the normal, one would not be safe in making any such assumption. Had the data obtained led to the supposition that sufficient water for the supply of the city could be obtained, the cone of depression at the wells caused by pumping such a large quantity would no doubt have lowered the water level to 50 ft. or 60 ft. below the surface, which would have added considerably to the present cost of pumping. The new works and machinery necessary would also have entailed a large expenditure, and would have required a boldness bordering on the reckless to advocate such a scheme with such a supply as that at present obtainable.

The daily quantity of water supplied through the water mains to the city for all purposes in 1896 had reached the enormous quantity of 71 gallons per head, with the result that the higher portions of the city were entirely without water except during the night and early morning. The pressure in many of the mains was so small as to be totally inadequate for the extinction of fires, and the pumping plant was taxed to its utmost capacity. Early in 1897, under the author's directions, the most strenuous exertions were made to prevent the waste of water, with the result that at the end of the year the water supplied to the city for all purposes had been reduced to 48 gallons per head.

The area of supply of the high-level mains being comparatively small, the Deacon meter system was introduced, with very satisfactory results, but owing to the large first cost, and the difficulty of dividing the low-level system up into small areas of control, the system was not introduced in the low-level supply area except in three sub-districts. As no regulations with regard to pipes and fittings were in force, and no sort of control had been exercised over the laying of house services, house-to-house tests at night by stethoscoping the stop-cocks was impossible, for very few stop-cocks were in existence except inside the dwellings.

The means adopted for checking the waste were as follows. An adequate staff of inspectors was engaged during the day in inspecting house services and serving notices. Two turn-cocks, with an intimate knowledge of the mains, valves and hydrants, were sent out during the day to stethoscope the valves and hydrants, and to report at the office any from which a noise was heard. The noisy valves were located on a plan of the water mains prepared for the purpose (no plan having previously existed), and a rough tracing made of all the mains supplied through each, together with the valves on the branch mains, and between 12 p.m. and 4 a.m., a small staff was sent out to locate the defects causing the noises. Before trying to locate the cause of a noise in a valve it was again sounded, as in some cases it was found to have ceased altogether at night when the consumption was at a minimum; but if it still existed all the branch mains were shut off, and if the noise was then heard the defect was known to be confined to the particular main controlled by the valve, but if not, the branch valves were opened one after the other until the noise again occurred, when the main in which the defect existed became known. Having located the defect within the limit of a particular main, the surface of the ground immediately over the main was sounded every 2 or 3 yards with a stethoscope, until the exact position of the defect was located.

In many instances noises have been found at hydrants without the valves on the mains they were attached to being affected, which, as a rule, indicates a leak within a short distance of the hydrant, and is easily located with the stethoscope. With Deacon meters it is possible to tell the quantity of water at any time flowing through the mains they control, either separately or collectively, which is no doubt a much more refined test than the rough-and-ready method of sounding the valves, but at the same time it is of very little use without the stethoscope to locate defects. The stethoscope is a most valuable instrument in the hands of a man experienced in its use, and will locate a leak as definitely as if it could be seen.

The principal difficulties now encountered in reducing the waste still further occur through the total inadequacy of the service pipes and house fittings to withstand the increased pressure in the mains, and it is only by rigorously enforcing the waterworks regulations recently passed by the Cork Town Council that any headway can be made. In some districts, where the pressure was excessive, a great reduction of waste has been made by the use of pressure-reducing valves on the mains, as it has been found that fittings which were previously always out of repair give considerably less trouble.

In writing this paper for the association I feel that it is only a makeshift, but pressure of work and the short time I have held office in Cork must be my excuse for any shortcomings.

### DISCUSSION OF MR. CUTLER'S PAPER.

Mr. W. H. HILL (Cork) said he would have been delighted to have made some remarks if he had had the least idea that he would have been called upon, for he came simply as a visitor. He might say, however, that he was connected with these municipal buildings before Mr. Cutler came to Cork. He knew a great deal about them at one time, and he almost thought it hopeless to attempt any restoration at all, the walls were in such a damaged state. Mr. Cutler and his gang, however, set to work patiently, and he was glad to say that it was carried out, as described by Mr. Cutler, efficiently and well, though at one time it appeared to him (Mr. Hill) to be hopeless. From his observation he could say that it was a good job, and he did not think they were going to have any further subsidence, as all the foundations now rested on the gravel bed. The entire building was now not only perfectly secure, but was a homogeneous building.

Mr. J. COOK (Lancashire) said he would like to ask Mr. Cutler the number of men he put on each shift for detecting waste. That might be of interest and value to the members

of the Association. Before his time Lancaster was in a very similar position, but the Deacon meters were utilised and the great waste was checked. He thought Mr. Cutler had done very well in using pressure-reducing valves, and he would like to know of what make they were. He thought Mr. Cutler had given them a very able paper.

Mr. S. A. KIRKBY (Cork) said he was hardly able to offer much criticism upon the subject under discussion, because he had not had the pleasure of seeing the work in progress. He had seen the buildings before Mr. Cutler took them in hand, he had seen them since, and they all felt a degree of security in them now that they did not feel previously. As regarded the actual work itself, he was not really competent to say anything. He knew that the whole of Cork was built more or less on treacherous ground, and that in dealing with heavy buildings great care had to be taken. He thought, therefore, that it was highly creditable to Mr. Cutler that, without any previous information of the quagmires prevalent there, the work should have been carried out without the slightest hitch. Mr. Cutler was very lucky indeed not to have had a similar experience to what he (the speaker) had in constructing the Youghal bridge, where they came upon a strata of quicksand, which caused the cylinders to sink down sometimes 16 ft. or 18 ft. at a run. He was afraid he could not say what would have become of that building if Mr. Cutler had met with such a catastrophe. He liked the citizens of Cork were much pleased with Mr. Cutler's work.

Mr. M. J. FLEMING (Waterford) was compelled to say that the consumption of water in Cork was enormously expensive. The present consumption of water was 48 gallons per head, and in Waterford, with a constant supply at high pressure, their consumption was only at the rate of 24 gallons, though

CORK: ST. FIN BARRE'S CATHEDRAL.

altogether, including water sold, it would perhaps be at the rate of 27 gallons per head. In regard to the economising of water and the checking of waste, he approved of the Deacon meters very much. He had had some of them lately in Waterford, and by their means he had managed to reduce very considerably the waste in districts where it occurred from leaking pipes. He believed these meters were well worth using in all towns supplying water under high pressure.

The PRESIDENT proposed a cordial vote of thanks to Mr. Cutler for the interesting paper he had given them. The papers on both subjects—the clever bit of underpinning of the building and the ingenious checking of waste water—showed his good judgment. He thought it was not only creditable and gratifying to Mr. Cutler himself but to the corporation whom he served.

Mr. BUCKLEY (Drumcondra) had great pleasure in seconding the vote of thanks to Mr. Cutler. He had listened with great interest to both papers, and he was only sorry he did not see the work before it was commenced. He had, however, seen it when it was finished, and found it most interesting.

The vote of thanks having been unanimously agreed to, Mr. CUTLER, in acknowledging the vote of thanks and replying upon the discussion, said that in regard to the first paper Mr. Kirkley had made some remarks to the effect that he (Mr. Cutler) had had no previous knowledge of the ground. It was the case that he did not know from personal knowledge, but from inquiry, that the foundations of the old building went down to the bed of gravel, to which he had underpinned the new structure. Knowing that the old building stood well on the gravel, of course he was safe in going down to the old underpinning. Mr. Cook had asked as to the number of men he had put on each shift in checking waste water, but that depended upon what they were doing. If they used Deacon meters the number of men employed depended upon the number of mains served off one meter. In some cases the area supplied off a Deacon meter was rather too large. If they were testing by the noise in the valves, three men only were necessary. The pressure-reducing valves were manufactured by the Palatine Engineering Company.

The following paper was then read :—

## CORK ELECTRIC TRAMWAYS.

By Beverley Griffin, Assoc.M.Inst.C.E.

[Mr. Beverley Griffin has been associated with public works since 1872, when he became resident engineer on the Great Northern Railway from Louth to Lincoln, the late Mr. J. H. Tolmie, M.I.C.E., being chief engineer. He held the position until after the opening of the line in 1877. In 1878 he was engaged by Mr. John Addy, M.I.C.E., in connection with the Peterborough sewerage works. In 1881 Messrs. Water, Smith & Watson, contractors, appointed him their constructive engineer on the works of the railway from Cirencester to Andover. Mr. Griffin was next engaged upon the Halesowen (Dingle) viaduct, a steel structure over 100 ft. in height, at the completion of which much satisfaction was expressed by the Board of Trade and Mr. Griffin's employers. Having reconstructed the East and West Junction Railway, Mr. Griffin was afterwards engaged by the late Mr. Charles Liddell, C.E., in 1886, to build the Metropolitan Railway between Harrow and Rickmansworth, acting in the capacity of engineer and contractor. He received much praise for his indefatigable exertion. Several light railways opening up in Ireland in 1889, Mr. W. M. Murphy asked him to undertake the construction for him of the South Clare Railway. The exceptional character of those works gave him much responsibility, and he well deserved the praise he received on their completion. In 1893, by request of the directors of the company, he undertook the building of the Henley-in-Arden Railway, and, acting again as engineer and contractor, finished the work (which had been commenced by the late Mr. Brassey) to the complete satisfaction of his directors and the Great Western Railway—by whom the line is worked. Whilst at Henley-in-Arden he carried out the waterworks and main drainage of the place, and also all the house connections for the local authority. Then in 1896 Mr. Griffin was sent for by the Vale of Glamorgan Railway (Sir James Szlumper, M.I.C.E., chief engineer), to complete the Bridgend section. Those works were of a heavy character, but almost before their completion Mr. Murphy again requisitioned his services to carry out the Cork Electric Tramways—now completed.

It is worthy of note that the Cork Electric Tramways and Lighting Company, Limited, incorporated by order in council, 1897, is the first company in the British Isles supplying electricity for traction and lighting from one central station. The tramways are for the most part single lines with passing places. The length of the track is 11 miles. There are 1¾ miles of track beyond the city boundary on the Douglas road, and this portion is laid with sleepers. The sleepers are rectangular, creosoted, 6 ft. long, 9 in. wide and 4½ in. thick, and there are eleven to each pair of 30-ft. rails. The rails are fastened down to the sleepers by thirty dog spikes and fourteen fang bolts and clips. The steepest grade is 1 in 14, and the sharpest curve is 27 ft. radius.

The passing places are 3 chains in length, and the space between each pair of rails is 4 ft. 6 in.; but when centre poles are used the space between the tracks is 6 ft. 6 in. The gauge is 2 ft. 11½ in., and was determined with a view to the probable use of the tramway for conveying the trucks of the Muskerry Light Railway Company to and from the quays and, for interchange of traffic with the Cork and Passage Company. The Muskerry Company's gauge is 3 ft., and that of the Cork and Passage Company is being converted from 5-ft. 3-in. to a 3-ft. gauge.

The rails are of the girder type, of steel, weighing 83 lb. per yard, and are of American manufacture. They are 30 ft. long, 6½ in. deep, and are slotted for the tie-bars, and drilled for the fish-bolts and electrical bonding. The fish-plates are of steel, 26 in. long, weighing 56 lb. per pair, and the outer plate is the larger, giving support to the rail head. The tie-bars are of wrought iron, 2 in. by ⅜ in., weighing 10½ lb., double-nutted at both ends, placed at 8-ft. centres and 3 ft. from the ends of the rails. The points are of chilled steel, and were supplied by Messrs. Miller & Co., of Edinburgh, and Messrs. Dick Kerr & Co., London.

The crossings are built up as the work proceeds, and the rails are cut and scarfed for this purpose by one of Hill & Son's cold-steel cutting saws. The scarf is held to the crossing rail by special made fish-plates forged to suit, and a plate, 6 ft. long by 1 ft. 6 in. by ¾ in., is placed beneath and bolted up to the rail flange with ten bolts, 2½ in. by ¾ in. The crossing is completed by cutting a groove through the head of the crossing rail. The rails are laid upon a continuous bed of Portland cement concrete (five to one), 6 in. deep and 7 ft. wide. The roadway between the rails, and 18 in. outside each rail, is paved with Welsh granite setts, 6 in. deep and 3½ in. wide, laid on a ½-in. bed of sand, and grouted with Portland cement mortar (three to one), well swept into the joints.

The city of Cork is built on an island formed by two branches of the river Lee. The tramway has to cross the river twice, first by Parnell swivel bridge, a steel structure, and again on Patrick's bridge, which is of stone. At both points the track is double, and in order to facilitate the running of the cars two short tracks of single line have been laid along Marlborough-street and Robert-street, thus giving an up and down way. These streets have been laid throughout with wood block paving, laid on Portland cement concrete, 6 in. thick, and a double junction formed at each end of the streets to be used in case of obstruction in either street.

The power station is conveniently situated near the Cork and Passage Railway terminus. The site upon which the station is built was once a slob, and to obtain a foundation 137 pitch pine piles, 12 in. by 12 in., were driven 37 ft. below the surface level of the street, at 5-ft. centres, placed zigzag, and upon these concrete (six to one) was laid. The walls are of 18-in. brickwork, with pilasters for carrying the overhead gantry crane, carried up at 10 ft. intervals. An additional pile was driven under each pilaster.

The station is 100 ft. long by 104 ft., and consists of engine and boiler rooms, with battery-room. The plant comprises three tandem horizontal compound condensing McIntosh & Seymour engines, directly coupled to 220 kilowatt generators, running 150 revolutions per minute. The Wheeler standard condensers have each a capacity of from 8,000 lb. to 12,000 lb. steam per hour. The three boilers by Babcock & Wilcox have each 2,531 square feet of heating surface, and capable of evaporating 8,000 lb. of water per hour. There is also an auxiliary heater, combined hot well and filter tank, and duplicate set of Edmiston filters. Compound feed-water pumps are in the engine-room. The condensing water will be taken from the river. A tank, 20 ft. by 11 ft. by 8 ft., will be erected outside the building, holding a reserve of 10,000 gallons, for use in the event of the city supply, which serves the boilers, being shut off. The battery-room contains 256 Tudor cells, capable of discharging 110 amperes for seven hours. The booster for regulating the charge of the cells is situate in the engine-room. The switchboard consists of a combination of

Cork Electric Tramways: Power-House.

tramway and lighting panels, the same machines being interchangeable in either service. The engine-beds are of six to to one Portland cement concrete, 8 ft. in depth, laid upon ninety-six pitch pine piles, 12 in. by 12 in., driven at 5-ft. centres.

The chimney is of steel, and was built by Messrs. Keeler & Co., of Williamsport, Pa. The height is 130 ft., and the diameter at base is 12 ft., curving in to 7 ft. 6 in. at 12 ft. above ground, and finishing 7 ft. 6 in. at top. The stack is built of rivetted plates, 4 ft. 6 in. in height, three plates forming a course. They are $\frac{7}{16}$ in. thick at bottom, decreasing $\frac{1}{16}$ in. for every 32 ft., and finishing ¼ in. thick. The breeching nozzle, 6 ft. wide and 7 ft. high, connecting the brick flue is reinforced by the addition of a 2-ft. 6-in. angle iron, forming an arch up the sides and over the top of the nozzle. The stack is lined with 4½-in. radial fire-bricks, set in fire-clay. A water guard is fixed at the top of the chimney, made of 3-in. angle iron, turned down to cover the brick lining. The base plate is of cast iron, 2 in. thick and 15 ft. diameter, in eight parts, strongly ribbed and joined by 1½-in. bolts. The base, 21 ft. square, is of Portland cement concrete (six to one), and built upon a foundation of twenty-five pitch pine piles, 12 in.

CORK ELECTRIC TRAMWAYS: INTERIOR OF POWER-HOUSE.

by 12 in., and anchor bolts, 14 ft. long by 2½ in. diameter, were placed in position before the concreting commenced. The advantages claimed for the steel shaft are saving of time in the erection and cost in the structure. The time occupied in erecting was about five weeks, and the brick lining occupied twenty days. The saving in cost over a brick stack was about 25 per cent.

The electrical equipment is of the trolley type, overhead construction, carried on the pole-bracket system. The poles are built in three sections of 5-in., 6-in. and 7-in. best tubular steel, made by overlapping joints, shrunk together while hot. The double-bracket pole, placed in the streets where double tracks are laid, will carry an arc lamp besides the trolley wires; the single-bracket pole the trolley wires only. The poles are placed about 120 ft. apart where the line is straight. The cars (eighteen in number) are built to carry twenty passengers inside and twenty-four outside, and will be electrically lighted. The car-shed, 125 ft. long by 70 ft., built on ground adjoining the power station, will contain pits for inspection and cleaning the cars, and a repair shop. The rails are efficiently bonded with two Chicago bonds to each joint, and also cross-bonded at short intervals. Where the track approaches Parnell swivel bridge the rail ends will be held in a casting, acting as a kerb to both sides of the opening portion. The kerb will be bolted down to the structure, and prevent lateral motion or jumping when the cars enter or leave the bridge. Span wires will only be used in one or two instances, where there are double curves in the street. A tramway station has been laid out at Father Mathew's statue, in Patrick-street, where four lines of track have been laid with double cross-over roads, and here the cars can meet for interchange of passengers.

### DISCUSSION OF MR. GRIFFIN'S PAPER.

Mr. CUTLER said he was sure they were all very much indebted to Mr. Griffin for his very able paper, more especially as he had filled up a gap at the last moment. He would like to make a remark in regard to the tramways, although he was interested in them as city engineer of Cork. He considered the paving of the tramway to be a question very worthy of discussion—as to whether the setts should be bound up with cement and sand, or with pitch and gravel. From his own point of view, and from the point of view of the tramways, he thought that pitch was far preferable to cement. When cement and sand were used it was necessary to keep traffic off for some time if they wanted it to set properly. As traffic became considerably congested there was no place that could be protected long enough to allow the gravel to set. The result was that the joints were broken, the setts became uneven, and in the long run it cost the tramway company two or three times as much as if the setts had been bound with pitch. Another serious question was whether a tramway should be laid upon a public road with sleepers. They knew it was cheaper, but the result was the breaking up of the surface within a very short time, probably to take the sleepers out to renew them, thus having the roadway in a constantly broken state. He thought those points were worthy of discussion, and he would like to hear the views of other gentlemen in regard to them.

Mr. R. H. DORMAN (Armagh) said he differed entirely from

Mr. Cutler in regard to grouting. His experience had been chiefly in the south, and particularly in London, where, as a rule, grouting was done with cement and sand. He knew that in the North of England pitch and gravel were customary. If they had a perfectly solid foundation beneath he thought the grouting with cement and sand was the best thing. Of course, if it was not given time to set, and there was a subsidence, it would not set afterwards. He thought Mr. Cutler was right in regard to wooden cross-sleepers. He observed that the gauge of the tramway was 2 ft. 11½ in., and that of the Muskerry and Cork and Passage lines was 3 ft., and he would like to know why the ½ in. difference existed.

Mr. J. W. WARDLE (Longton) said that in regard to the wooden sleepers he could corroborate what Mr. Cutler had said. The North Staffordshire tramway was laid some years ago on wooden sleepers, heavy locomotive engines of 10 or 12 tons had to pass over the line, and its history was that it got into a wretched condition. Ultimately it was decided to relay the line, and little by little it was done with girder rails. That was carried out three years ago, and after two years they were again in a shaky condition, for every time a locomotive passed over the line a longitudinal vibration was set up. It is now in almost as bad a condition as it was under the old Vignolles system. The setts of the North Staffordshire Company were originally laid with cement, and when they took up a portion of the pavement they found that there had been no cohesion whatever between the cement grouting and the setts.

Mr. J. BUCKLEY (Drumcondra) said he was very glad to hear a strong opinion expressed against the sleepers. In his district—a township adjoining the city of Dublin—the Dublin United Tramway Company proposed to lay part of the tramway in wooden sleepers. In reporting to his board he opposed that course, and they asked the company to lay down setts in the centre of the road. He was glad to say, that so far as he was aware—the draft order had not been finally issued—he had been the means of saving the tramway company from the expense of having to relay their tramway in a very short time.

Mr. S. A. KIRKBY (Cork) said he had listened to the paper read by Mr. Griffin with very great pleasure. He thought the question of a tramway on sleepers, either longitudinal or transverse, was not one that would commend itself to the experience of anyone, but in country districts it was often a question of expenditure only—a question of cutting down expense to the lowest minimum. It was often the only thing to do. In this case of the Cork tramways, when the order was first sought, the question was very carefully gone into by the Finance Committee of the Grand Jury. It was shown to them that if this part of the tramway was not laid on sleepers that it would make such a difference in cost as to prevent the promoters from going on with the project, if concrete foundations and granite setts were insisted upon. With regard to their endurance of heavy wear and tear, they had an example in the Muskerry tramway. A portion of it was laid on transverse sleepers, sunk some 12½ in. or 18 in. below the surface. They put blocks on each sleeper. That plan had stood the test of time very well, and he himself had been very much surprised to see what little packing it had required. The traffic on the line was in excess of that of any tramway he had seen elsewhere. There was often a passenger train of thirteen carriages, and a luggage train of eight or ten carriages heavily freighted, moving over it. Where economy was essential he thought transverse sleepers well packed and bound might be safely used. That was the experience that had come within his range in the matter.

The PRESIDENT proposed a hearty vote of thanks to Mr. Griffin for his interesting paper. It teemed with useful information to the engineer who was in any way connected with tramway matters, and he was sure it would be a very valuable addition to the "Proceedings."

Mr. COOK (Lancaster), in seconding the proposition, said he thought the question of sleepers was a very important one.

The vote of thanks having been unanimously accorded, Mr. GRIFFIN, in replying, said that Mr. Cutler drew attention to the grouting in pitch *versus* cement. For speed there was not the slightest doubt that pitch grouting would be preferable. There was a serious difficulty in this case, because in laying the tramway through streets in which there was great traffic they had to turn the traffic on almost before the work was properly set, and the only thing they did to protect it was to lay a sort of carpet of sand upon the surface. In regard to the sleepers on the country roads, the life of the sleepers, of course, depended upon the quality of the timber and creosoting. In places where the traffic would be squeezed into a very narrow space, the tramway took the same form as in the city—concrete foundations and setts. Mr. Dorman had asked why the gauge of the tram line was 2 ft. 11½ in., while that of the light railway was 3 ft. Before commencing the tramway, and whilst discussing the gauge, he made some experiments with the assistance of Mr. Hill, engineer to the Muskerry railway, whether it was possible to work the tracks of the Muskerry line on the tramway. They came to the conclusion that it was, by adjusting the guage. They found that in order that the flange of the Muskerry trucks should get a good grip on the surface of the tramway rails, the distance between the inner surface of the tramway rails should be slightly less than that on the Muskerry line. They tried a truck on the tramway, and they would have no hesitation in taking those trucks through the city in the same way as they took their own. He had seen sleepers taken out sound after they had been in ten years, and when well ballasted with gravel and sand he thought they would last quite as long as was reasonable.

The third and last paper was the following :—

## MAIN ROADS UNDER COUNTY COUNCILS IN IRELAND.

By R. H. DORMAN, M.INST.C.E.,
County Surveyor, Armagh.

[A portrait and biography of Mr. Dorman appeared in our issue of September 5, 1895.]

The present meeting of the Association of Municipal and County Engineers in Cork appears to the author to be a fitting opportunity for referring to the future management of county works in Ireland. It is unnecessary for the author to refer to the good work done under the grand jury system in Ireland during the past sixty years. The network of roads, maintained with efficiency and economy, which cover the face of the country are a record of the signal success attained by grand juries in this respect. But, in order to demonstrate the economy and saving effected under the grand jury system, I would like to refer to an extract taken from some information recently compiled by Mr. Wilson, county surveyor of Fermanagh : "Shortly after the Grand Jury Act was passed, and when the office of county surveyor was instituted in 1834, there were 13,191 miles of road under contract in Ireland, at an annual cost of £228,316, or an average cost of £17 8s. per mile. In 1895 there were 53,064 miles of roads under contract in Ireland, at an annual cost of £660,532, or only an average cost of £12 9s. per mile. Had the average cost remained as it was in 1834, then the cost of the roads in Ireland in 1895 would have been £918,007, or £257,475 more than it actually was. Now, not taking into account the increase in the cost of labour between 1834, when a labourer was 6d. a day, and 1895, when a labourer was 2s. a day, it may be fairly argued that the institution of county surveyor and the grand jury system in Ireland has saved the country something like £257,475 per annum. This is enhanced when it is remembered that before county surveyors were appointed the main and post roads were largely, if not altogether, maintained by the Board of Public Works, or by the turnpike system, whereas both of these systems have now been abolished, and the roads are altogether maintained by the grand juries, from which it appears that, in spite of the more expensive roads having been thrown on the grand juries, still, after the appointment of the present system, there has been a considerable decrease in the average cost of the maintenance of public roads." Notwithstanding this statement, there is yet no doubt that for many years past the grand jury system has laboured under many difficulties. Among other disadvantages the Act contained no powers for the purchase of any plant, such as steam rollers, stone-breakers, &c., and the want of these had seriously impeded other progress being made in the conditions of road maintenance, and has rendered some changes in the laws, at any rate in this respect, imperative.

But it is not to dwell on the past that I have commenced

this paper—our thoughts are with the future and with the probable changes which may result under the new *régime*. A glance at the new Bill and the schedule attached show that the general arrangements proposed for the carrying out of works, &c., follow very closely on the lines contained in the Grand Jury Act. In one important particular, however, the procedure is quite new. I refer to sec. 8, part 1, of the Bill, which commences as follows : (1) One-half of the maintenance, enlargement or improvement of any main roads shall be levied off the administrative county, and the other off the county districts in which the road is situate ; (2) every road, the maintenance of which at the passing of this Act is levied partly off the county at large and partly off any barony, shall be a main road until it ceases so to be as hereinafter provided, and the enactments respecting main roads shall be repealed ; (3) the council of each county may, upon the report of the county surveyor, make a general statement declaring what roads in the county shall be main roads, and any roads not mentioned in such declaration shall cease to be a main road, and at any time after the end of five years the council may, if they think fit, reconsider the declaration and make a new declaration, and so on, at intervals of not less than five years, &c.

The first thing to note in connection with these clauses is that the enactments with regard to mail-car roads shall cease. The absurdity of the law requiring the cost of maintenance of any road over which a mail-cart passed to be levied off the county at large is too apparent to merit discussion. I will only mention that in my county of Armagh the cost of maintenance of mail-car roads has in recent years varied

CORK : SCHOOL OF ART AND FREE LIBRARY.

from £12 per mile to £480 per mile, and in exceptional cases the cost has gone up to £900 per mile. For instance, only last year over 2 miles of the main road from Armagh to Castleblayney was made up at a cost of £960 per mile, and half the cost of this work was levied off the county at large, because a light car carrying a mail bag passed over it twice a day.

I believe that one or more grand juries, already anticipating this change in the law, have assumed the section of the Act dealing with main roads to be obsolete, and made a declaration to the effect that all roads, whether post roads or not, should be repaired entirely at the cost of the baronies in which they were situated.

Adverting now to clause 3. There is no doubt that this clause will lead to much discussion by every county council in Ireland, and it will be interesting to note the declarations which will be made respecting main roads in each county. It appears to me that the two chief elements which should decide whether a road should be declared a main road or not are (1) the cost of maintenance ; (2) is the road one of the main arteries of the country over which the general public are accustomed to travel for divers purposes ? Considering these elements conjointly we may have (a) leading roads connecting important towns and villages, and costing a high rate to maintain ; (b) unimportant roads, with little traffic over them, used chiefly by the local farmers, and some of them open at one end only ; (c) several intermediate classes—for instance, important cross roads leading from one main artery to another, or roads which in the ordinary sense of the term would be considered main or leading roads, but which do not connect any towns or important villages, and over which there is little traffic, or we may have roads carrying heavy traffic leading to railway stations, mines or similar places, and terminating there.

So many circumstances and conditions will have to be considered in different cases that it will probably be impossible for any county council or county surveyor to lay down any hard-and-fast rule. I will, however, for a moment consider the case of the co. Armagh. In this county the roads are classed as first, second, third and fourth class. The cost of the first class for the past twelve months averaged £41 16s. per mile, the second class £15 5s. per mile, the third class £9 5s. per mile, and the fourth class £5 6s. per mile. Now for this county I would suggest, but do not propose, that a road which is a main artery of the county over which the general public travel for diverse purposes, and which has for the previous three years cost on the average £24 per mile per annum to repair, should be termed a main road, and the expense of maintaining same should be levied half off the county at large.  It may be noticed that the sum of £24 per mile is equivalent to 57·5 per cent. of the average cost of the existing first-class roads in co. Armagh.

It is quite possible that some county councils may decide to declare all county roads main roads, and other councils may refuse to declare any roads main roads, but I consider that either of these views of the question would be unreasonable.  If all roads in the county were declared main roads a large number of by-roads used exclusively for local traffic would be included, and it would be unfair to make the expense of repairing these roads a charge on the county at large, because the number of by-roads in different baronies is not proportional to the area, or to the valuation of the baronies—the proportion of by-roads under contract in some baronies being much greater than in others.  On the other hand, if no roads were declared main roads the cost of maintaining important roads would in some cases be an unfair tax on the district through which the road, or part of a road, passed.  For instance, we may have a road carrying heavy traffic connecting two important towns, say, 10 or 15 miles apart, but passing for part of its way through a poor district, or through a district which did not participate or benefit largely in the traffic passing over the roads.  It would be manifestly unfair that these districts should pay the whole cost of maintaining such roads, the traffic over which they did not benefit by, or only to a limited extent.   Finally, I think it will be conceded that a proportion of the roads in every county should be declared main roads, but it will require much discrimination on the part of each county council to decide what roads should be included in the declaration.

Turning now to the consideration of footpaths by the sides of main roads.  It was for several years, subsequent to the passing of the Local Government Act of 1888, a vexed question in England whether footpaths should be considered as part of a road or not, but it appears to have been ultimately decided that the whole space from quick to quick formed part of the road, and that therefore the footpaths should be included in the cost of maintaining the roads of which they form part.  In Ireland, although the practice of dealing with footpaths on the sides of mail roads seems to vary, I believe it has been decided that the footpath does not form part of the road under the Grand Jury Act, and sec. 52 of the Act seems to favour this view.  As it is not intended to repeal that portion of sec. 52 referring to the matter, it will be interesting to note how the question will eventually be decided in this country.  I am personally rather in favour of footpaths being included as part of the road, and it is certainly desirable that the road and footpath by the side of it should be included in the one contract.

As regards the future maintenance of roads in this country —that is, whether they should be maintained under the contract system or by the county surveyor's own staff—I think the general opinion among county surveyors is that the most economical method of maintaining the by-roads is under the contract system, but that for the main roads contracts should only be entered into for the supplying of material, and that the rest of the work should be carried out by the surveyor's own staff.  I was for a long time in favour of the contract system, but I have in recent years completely changed my opinion.  In the co. Armagh, when presentments are now given into the county surveyor's hands to execute, the amount of the presentment is lodged to a particular account in the bank, and the county surveyor is authorised to draw on this account for the amount of the presentment.  My experience of this method of working is that I can, with ready money in my own hands, carry out contracts, no matter whether they be for maintenance works or special works, for main roads or by-roads, for at least 25 per cent. less than under the contract system.  I do not suggest, however, that county councils should refuse to accept any tenders for works in the first instance.  I would rather suggest that they should accept tenders for all contracts except the main roads, and I am strongly of opinion that these roads should be maintained strictly by the county surveyor's own staff.  This arrangement would no doubt necessitate an increase in the county surveyor's staff, but the better results which would be obtained would far more than repay the cost of the extra staff.   I would leave it an open question whether the county surveyor should raise his own material, or whether a contract should be entered into for it.  This can only be determined by local conditions.  I would then, if I had all the main roads in a county in my own hands, arrange as follows :—

(1)  As regards materials, I would enter into a contract for the requisite quantity of material if I could obtain it at a reasonable price, if not I would raise and break it myself.  My experience, however, is that I can usually obtain it by contract nearly as cheaply as I could put it out myself.

(2)  Consolidation of material.  I would, as a rule, roll in about 75 per cent. of all the material put out on the main roads, but on good hard roads I would roll in as much as 90 per cent.  I would leave the purchase of as many steam rollers as could be conveniently kept at work all the year round, but in some counties it might be more convenient for the present to hire the rollers as required.

(3)  Surface work.  I would divide the county up into districts, and I would appoint a foreman to each district.  I would put a sufficient number of men under him for the proper surfacing of the roads, and I would hold each foreman responsible for the proper care of the roads in his district.  Each foreman and surfaceman would be registered, and I would divide the men into two grades—first and second.  The first grade I would term the permanent class, and the second grade probationary or temporary.  I would recommend the county council to provide an old-age pension for men who have served satisfactorily in the first grade for a number of years.

(4)  Horse brooms and horse scrapers.  I would provide these in the neighbourhood of towns, where the traffic is heavy, also in country districts where long stretches of level roads exist, but in hilly districts they are troublesome to work, and the roads could be more easily attended to with hand scrapers.

(5)  I would keep an assistant at the head office, who would be responsible for the accuracy of all pay-sheets and time-sheets.  I would arrange for all sheets to reach the head office on each alternate Friday morning, when they would be inspected, and cheques issued by the county surveyor and forwarded to the assistants for the amounts.  The assistants would then distribute the amounts among the different foremen.

In conclusion, I would only point out that the conditions under which traffic is being conducted in this country has to some extent changed during recent years, and further changes in this respect are imminent.  The tourist traffic in Ireland is being rapidly developed, and myriads of cyclists are inundating the country ; that hydra-headed monster, the traction engine, is making its appearance particularly in the north of Ireland, and we may look forward at no distant date to see the light carts of this country superseded by a heavier class and perhaps by motor cars.  These changes will not be viewed with favour or appreciation by the people of this country at first, but for its proper development and progress they are inevitable, and the authorities who have control of the roads should be prepared for this.  I would here refer to the necessity for the authorities in Ireland together framing, if they have power, a set of by-laws for the conduct of traction engines, which would apply all over the country.  Much annoyance and inconvenience will be caused to owners of traction

Cork :  City Court House.

engines if a different set of by-laws is framed for each county, and it would be for the benefit of all concerned if one set of by-laws could be framed applicable to the whole country at large.

I stated in the first part of this paper that the roads in Ireland had been maintained with efficiency and economy in the past, but the majority of our roads are only strong enough for light traffic, and would be quickly squeezed out of shape by the passing of a traction engine or other heavy motor over them in wet weather ; further, many of our roads are not properly surfaced, this work being done generally at irregular intervals and in a slovenly manner.  The main roads in England are rapidly improving and being brought to a high state of perfection, and if we in Ireland are to keep pace with the present rate of progress in England we shall have to pay more attention to the strengthening and to the surfacing of our roads.

## DISCUSSION OF MR. DORMAN'S PAPER.

The President trusted they would hear from some of the county surveyors on the very interesting paper that had been read by Mr. Dorman.

Mr. A. O. Lyons, county surveyor, East Riding, co. Cork, having briefly proposed the accordance of a vote of thanks to the author, said the subject he (Mr. Dorman) had taken in hand was very large.  The new Bill brought into Parliament would very much alter the system of keeping up public works in Ireland, but it would involve a great deal of trouble on the county surveyors until things got into shape. The questions raised in the paper were so numerous and important that he would not occupy their time in entering into a discussion at that stage.

Mr. JOHN HORAN (Limerick) seconded the vote of thanks. The paper was a most interesting one, and came very opportunely, but it dealt with such a big subject that it would be wrong to keep them to-day to discuss it on its merits and at length. Mr. Dorman was in favour of putting one-half of the maintenance of the main roads on the county at large. With that he disagreed, and his experience in Limerick would lead him to put the whole of the maintenance on the county at large. He had had no experience of any other county. Mr. Dorman had mentioned what he thought was a very excessive cost incurred in the making of roads that required strengthening. He referred to the road from Armagh to Castleblayney, which he stated was made up at a cost of £960 per mile. County surveyors knew where labour was cheap, and he thought a very respectable new road could have been made for that sum. As regarded the declaring of what roads were main roads, he thought the county council would not trouble themselves very much on that point, and it would rest in the hands of the county surveyors to say what were main roads and what were not. He would be against asking important assistants to become pay clerks. He would like assistants to be professional men, and if eventually the roads were put in the hands of the county surveyors they ought to be paid for those men by the county councils. He was sorry to hear Mr. Dorman speak disrespectfully of the traction engine. He thought it was better than the old 2½-in. tyre, that cut into their roads so much. He was greatly in favour of the steam roller, and could quote a case where he introduced it and considerably improved an important road. It was a nice point that Mr. Dorman made about the by-laws for traction engines. There should be no difficulty with the new bodies in bringing it about, for those bodies would be subject to the control of the Local Government Board, and there should be no difficulty in forming proper by-laws for use throughout the country. He had no doubt they would wonder why the county surveyor viewed with apprehension the introduction of a popular form of government. The immediate result would be to place in the hands of the board of guardians what was previously done by grand juries. Of course they, as loyal men, would do their best to work under them, and they could only hope that the new bodies would rise to a sense of the increased responsibilities placed upon them.

Mr. H. A. CUTLER, city engineer of Cork, said he had no knowledge of the county roads in the country, but their cost surprised him. He would ask Mr. Dorman how many men per mile he considered fair on those roads. It would be useful information to himself, not having had experience of that class of road. What length of road would he put under a good foreman, and would he require him to keep a horse ? Or what form of locomotion would he recommend ? He should have some means of getting round his district.

Mr. R. W. LONGFIELD (Donegal) remarked that they all looked forward with a considerable amount of apprehension and curiosity to see what the new bodies would do. He thought that in the North of Ireland there would be a considerable amount of friction between the district and county councils. There would be a large amount of trouble on the whole, and a deal of odium would be thrown on the county surveyor. Regarding traction engines, he know one road personally in the north of Donegal where the engine had done a great deal of good. It broke up the road first by putting on a good deal of stuff, and subsequently turned it into an excellent highway. In Donegal a great deal of harm had been done by the extreme narrowness of the tyres of the cars. He believed that a law existed in France compelling those vehicles to have tyres not less than 4 in. wide, and it would, he thought, be a very good thing if such a law could be brought into force in Ireland. He quite agreed with Mr. Dorman in saying that in Ireland they would have to improve very much to keep pace with the tourist traffic—and especially bicycles.

Mr. S. A. KIRKBY (East Riding, Cork) said he would like, for his own information, to ask Mr. Dorman what power the county councils would in future have to frame regulations for traction engines or any heavy engines. None of the existing by-laws dealt with the case, and the last Act passed by Parliament specially exempted Ireland from its operation. He himself had considerable difficulty in dealing with traction engines, locomotives and goods trains having gone over the public roads. Their legal advisers had not yet been able to find a satisfactory way to enable grand juries to make proper regulations for that traffic. As regarded the contract system and the carrying out of works by the county surveyor, he could say that he agreed with Mr. Dorman. He had had experience with both, and he had to say that he preferred the contract system. It was, according to his experience, more economical, and from the selfish point of view more satisfactory to the surveyor.

Mr. DORMAN, in reply, first thanked those present for the vote of thanks they had been good enough to pass him for his paper. Mr. Horan, he continued, had asked with regard

to the main road from Armagh to Castleblayney. The expense was entirely for making-up. The road got into a bad state. The actual cost of the road in future would be about 10s. per perch, or £106 per mile. Mr. Horan objected to the assistant at the head office dealing with the pay-sheets. Perhaps he did not understand what he (the speaker) meant. He thought it always wise to keep the youngest assistant at the head office in order that he might learn his business. While he was there he might as well undertake the care of the pay-sheets. Mr. Cutler had asked him about the number of men on a road, but he could not make an estimate. Mr. Kirkby had referred to certain by-laws being framed, but he could not reply to the question he had asked. He (Mr. Kirkby) preferred the contract system, and he was quite right if he could get a sufficient number of good contractors. The worst thing in connection with the grand jury system was the practice of accepting the lowest tender. Nothing had given him more trouble than accepting the tenders of rotten contractors. Not only did the men themselves give trouble, but so did their securities. He found that by taking the main roads into his own hands, and working them with his own staff, he could save 25 per cent.

The PRESIDENT said that in putting the vote of thanks he had to say that the paper of Mr. Dorman would prove a valuable appendix to the one he had already written and included in their " Proceedings," and which he had seen more than once quoted as an authority. There was one matter he would like to ask Mr. Dorman with regard to the cost of roads. That was so low that it made the mouths of them in the metropolis water, and he would ask Mr. Dorman if the £24 per mile included the whole of the roads of the country or merely the roads in the hands of the county surveyor. He presumed there were other roads maintained by local authority. With regard to cyclists, he supposed they were having the same trouble as they in the neighbourhood of London were. The motor-car and cyclists had caused a considerable increase, and he would be glad to know if that question was as troublesome in Ireland in the matter of costs.

The vote of thanks having been passed with acclamation, the sitting then closed.

This concluded the proceedings so far as regards the reading and discussion of papers. The remainder of the meeting will be dealt with in our next issue.

## PARLIAMENTARY MEMORANDA.

On Thursday, in the House of Lords, the West Ham Corporation Bill was read a third time and passed.

In the House of Commons the Lords' amendments were considered to the Bolton, Turton and Westhoughton Extension Bill, Glasgow Corporation (Sewage, &c.) Bill, and Rhymney and Aber Valleys Gas and Water Bill. The Bills were ordered for third reading.

In the House of Lords on Friday their lordships agreed with the Commons' amendments to the Lords' amendments to the Local Government (Ireland) Bill.

In the House of Commons the Lords' amendments to the following Bills were considered, and the Bills ordered for third reading: Liverpool Corporation Bill and the Middlesex County Council Bill.

On Monday, in the House of Lords, the Kingstown Harbour Roads Transfer Bill passed through committee without amendment.

In the House of Commons a member asked the Secretary of the Treasury whether his attention had been drawn to the publication in full detail in the Press of the report of the Telephone Committee. He wished to know whether steps would not be taken to prevent newspapers publishing confidential documents which certainly ought not to appear. Mr. Hanbury, in his reply, said that every possible step had been taken to ascertain how the filching of the paper occurred, but hitherto without success. He could only say that in his opinion, and in the opinion of the committee, the practice complained of was becoming absolutely intolerable.

In the House of Lords on Tuesday the Kingstown Harbour Roads Transfer Bill, the Metropolitan Commons Bill and the Public Loans Bill were read a third time and passed.

In the House of Commons the report from the Select Committee on Telephones was brought up and read.

**Shanklin.**—On the 29th ult. Prince Hermann of Saxe-Weimar performed the ceremony of the installation of an auxiliary water supply for the district of Shanklin. Owing to the rapid growth of the place there has been danger of inconvenience owing to the want of an adequate supply of water, but it is now believed that a constant supply of pure water is assured.

**An Annual Outing.**—An enjoyable excursion to Margate was last week made by the employees of Messrs. Young & Marten, of Stratford, E. An excellent dinner, presided over by the general manager, Mr. E. Montague Edwards, was served at the Terrace Hotel, and at the subsequent proceedings Mr. Edwards, in responding to the toast of his health, said he trusted that he might be spared in health and strength to be present at many future gatherings of the kind. ¶

# New Sewerage Scheme at Exmouth.

## SANITATION AT THE SEASIDE.

Mr. H. H. Law, Local Government Board inspector, recently held an inquiry at the Town Hall, Exmouth—a popular Devonshire seaside resort—relative to an application from the urban district council to borrow £34,500 for the new sewerage works. The proceedings were watched by several members of the council and a large number of ratepayers.

In opening the case for the council, Mr. Adams, the clerk, informed the inspector that the population of Exmouth was 10,000 and the annual assessable value £54,000, while the outstanding loans amounted to £13,396.

Several owners and occupiers of property who opposed the scheme were represented by Mr. Beal, of Exeter; Mr. H. Adams opposed, on behalf of Mr. Carter, the erection of the pumping station; and the Rev. O. Reichel appeared to offer some suggestions relative to the conditions on which the loan should be issued.

Evidence was first given by Mr. Strahan, assistant to Mr. Mansergh, of Westminster, the engineer who prepared the scheme. He described the existing condition of affairs, which resulted in flooding during storms, causing the sewage to make its appearance. Withycombe, which had recently been added to Exmouth, was innocent of sewerage. The essential feature of the projected scheme was to have a high-level sewer, starting at the present outlet, skirting round two of the hills, cutting through Withycombe, and at such a level that the sewage, whatever the state of the tide or however great the rainfall, would discharge clear out, although it would be, of course, under pressure. He proposed to erect a pumping station to take the sewage from the Exeter-road low-level area to the high-level sewer for the purpose of discharge. The pumping station would take the sewage and such portion of the roof water as he could not exclude. The existing system of sewerage, he believed, did its work comfortably in its early stages, but as the town grew the amount of the sewage to be discharged became overpowering. He proposed to have the existing system to deal with an area which contained 5,000 people. The experiment should, he thought, be made as to whether, when the demands made upon it was thus restricted, the old system would revert to its old efficiency. He had no doubt that it would, as the sewer would not be overburdened, as it had been hitherto. The scheme proposed to discharge the sewage into deep water 160 yards from the present point of discharge. Provision had been made to meet a possible increase of the population to 20,000. The high-level sewer would be capable of discharging 8,500,000 gallons of sewage every twenty-four hours, and assuming the full amount of sewage, 600,000 gallons, was present, there would be provision for dealing with twelve times that maximum. He described in detail the pumping station, which, he said, had been so arranged that no one would be able to see the sewage in its progress from the low to the high level. In the pumping station even all that would be open to view would be a large engine and two small ones. Anyone objecting to such a station would be alarming himself about nothing. A site for the pumping station had not yet been obtained, and he understood that if difficulties were thrown in the way a provisional order would be applied for to get the land necessary. There would be no abandonment of an existing work on which a debt still remained. He had made arrangements to utilise all existing sewers, although their use would be in some instances altered. For instance, the Exeter-road sewer, which now dealt with sewage and storm water, would under the new circumstances be used for storm water only. Dealing with the discharge, he said the sewage would never be tide-locked during neap tide, but it would be for two hours at the outside during spring tide. The advantage of the outlet at the present point was that if the time should come when Exmouth was very rich the sewage could be carried out still further to Oroombo Point.

In answer to Mr. Beal, the witness said he had been told that the land at the marsh had been laid out for building sites, and that there would be a difficulty in getting it. He did not know that until he came there, but he should have thought that the owners would have given them the land, because until the pumping station was erected it was no good for building purposes. Asked as to what was his opinion of the value of the land, the witness said that that was one of the things of which he knew nothing. Whenever a pumping station was to be put down in a marsh it was always stated that it was to be used as a building site. As an engineer he might say it was possible to put the pumping station on the other side of the railway line, but it would be unreasonable to do so. It would have to be taken to a much lower level and would cost a great deal more money. The pumping station would look like a respectable laundry, and as for the sewage, they would not see it or smell it. Continuing, he said the cost of working and maintenance of the scheme would be £300 a year. The annual repayment of the loan would be £1,706, and that would be covered by a rate of 10½d. in the £1. but he preferred to put it at 11d. in the £1, because the cost of the scheme might grow a little in working it

out. In answer to Mr. H. Adams, who said he appeared for Mr. Carter, the owner of the land, Mr. Strahan said the capacity for the pumping station would allow for a large increase of population.

Mr. Orchard, of Exeter-road, objected to the scheme as being too elaborate and costly. He did not question that it would be effective, but in view of the fact that Exeter, with 40,000 inhabitants, had recently applied for and obtained a loan of £40,000 to work their sewage on the septic system, it appeared to him that they at Exmouth perhaps might adopt that, or an alternative scheme at a less cost, to provide for the sewage of 10,000 inhabitants, or less than one-fourth of the population of Exeter.

Mr. S. Tupman, Exeter-road, also objected to the scheme on the ground of its costly character.

Mr. Ponsford, also of Exeter-road, opposed the proposed site of the pumping station on the ground that it would depreciate the value of the property by one-half. He thought the station should be placed further north.

Dr. Kemp, medical officer of health, said he considered the scheme would meet the wants of the district, but he should have liked to see the sewage of Littleham included. At present it contaminated the scheme. He said he should also prefer the outfall to be in the deep water at Orcombe point, but Mr. Strahan pointed out that that would cost £9,000 extra.

The Rev. O. Reichel said the district was not purely urban, but embraced a large agricultural area. There were 500 acres of houses, and another 500 acres of land in Withycombe parish which might be built upon. No provision was made in the present scheme for Littleham parish. The Exmouth District Council could really be acting as a purveyor of sewage discharge, and the charge should be borne by those who benefited by it. He also thought that the repayment of the loan should be by instalments and not on the annuity system.

Mr. Carter pointed out that the whole of the land in the rural portion only paid a quarter of the district rate. In other words, out of a 1s. 3d. rate the urban wards paid £2,900 and the rural wards only £527.

Mr. C. J. Ross raised the question of whether, seeing the extensive building operations going on towards the east, it would not be better, while the scheme was under consideration, to carry the sewage right out to Orcombe Point.

Mr. Pratt said the necessity for the works did not arise in the rural districts.

The inspector pointed out that his board did not grant a special drainage district except under very special circumstances. They all knew that the rates on land was one quarter what they were on houses, and if any works were carried out in the rural districts the people in the urban portion would have to pay four times the amount that the rural population paid. Therefore both sides of the question had to be considered.

Mr. Pratt protested against land at so low a level as the site in question being built upon.

A ratepayer asked whether, if the loan was sanctioned, the scheme would be carried out as submitted, and not deviated from, as was the case in the previous instance.

The inspector said if the scheme was sanctioned it would be a very irregular thing to deviate from it, and if on being proceeded with it was found that something else had to be done for which more money was wanted one of the first questions asked would be, "Has it been carried out in accordance with the conditions sanctioned by the Local Government Board?" Of course they had to rely to a great extent upon the good faith of the authorities concerned.

## PUBLIC SLAUGHTER-HOUSES FOR LONDON.

The Public Health Committee of the London County Council have issued a report as to the desirability of establishing public slaughter-houses throughout London. The committee think that every effort should be made to render the places self-supporting, but that it would be futile at present to attempt to submit estimates, as so much will depend upon the locality of the sites, the circumstances of the trade and the character of the buildings. They propose to transmit their opinions on the matter to the Local Government Board, with an intimation that the council are prepared to accept such responsibilities as may be necessary to give effect in London to the recommendations of the Royal Commission on Tuberculosis, and to ask the Local Government Board whether they will include in any legislation introduced by them in connection with the commission's report the provisions which will be necessary for this purpose.

Royston.—A loan of £250 for the purchase of lamps and the extension of street lighting by the district council has been sanctioned by the Local Government Board.

# Comparative Reports of General Practice.

## XXVI.—REFUSE DESTRUCTORS : TIVERTON REPORT.—I.

For several years past the disposal of house refuse at Tiverton has been a question of ever-increasing difficulty, mainly on account of the absence of suitable places in close proximity to the town for tipping the rubbish where it will not be likely to create a nuisance. It was decided to inquire into the method of burning, and after a general report from the borough surveyor, Mr. J. Siddalls, it was decided that a sub-committee, consisting of Councillors Barrons, Pleass and Deering, should visit and report upon the refuse destructors adopted in various towns. The guiding considerations in the selection of the towns to be visited were : (1) The type of destructor furnace in use, one or more installations of each of the systems in operation being seen ; and (2) the character of the locality. In selecting a town an endeavour was made to ascertain the merits of the system under various conditions as to population, nature of district, whether residential or manufacturing, and the different descriptions of town refuse. These considerations are pointed out in the course of the report, which concludes with the general findings of the deputation. After a general description of the construction and working of a destructor, the report proceeds to deal with the various places visited. These were Bath, Winchester, Hornsey, Leyton, Shoreditch, Cambridge, Loughborough, Bradford, Rochdale, Farnworth and Oldham. The report continues thus :—

### BATH (Population 52,000).

We found eight cells of the "Perfectus" type in use, the makers being Messrs. Goddard, Massey & Warner, of Nottingham. Eight cells are worked in winter and six in summer ; but in the winter more cells are wanted, and two additional ones are to be erected of the same type. During this, the winter season, the cells are worked by four men by day and three by night. The installation was erected in 1895, and cost, including roadways and buildings, £11,000. The superintendent, Mr. J. Barter, tells us that the plant has worked continuously since its erection, without any trouble, and has cost very little in repairs.

The refuse is brought up an inclined roadway and shot on to the platform at the top of the furnaces, the tins and iron utensils are picked out and put to a heap to be taken away, and the rest is fed into hoppers, which when full are discharged into the furnace below by pulling a lever releasing the bottom of the hopper, after which the process is repeated. The clinker is sifted, the fine ash is made into mortar and sold, and there is a good demand for it. The rough clinker is broken fine in a mill and made up with cement into paving stones, kerb and channel blocks, which are used in the streets of the city or elsewhere.

The motive power is provided by steam raised in a boiler from the waste heat of the furnace, and is much more than enough to drive the 20 horse-power engine required. The amount of refuse destroyed per week is 240 tons, which is equal to 5 tons per cell per day of twenty-four hours. The cost of burning is 8d. per ton, without reckoning anything for interest of capital or allowing for value of steam raised or clinkers made. The chimney is 165 ft. high, and we could detect nothing but a slight vapour leaving the top and discernable for a very short distance. There are many houses in the immediate locality of the works the occupants of which have never complained respecting the destructor, and just opposite is a public park and recreation ground.

### WINCHESTER (Population 20,000).

The destructor here is of the "Fryer" type of two cells, one cell erected fourteen and the other seven years ago by Messrs. Manlove, Alliott & Co., of Nottingham. Meldrum steam-blowers were added six months ago, and the opinion of the superintendent, Mr. H. Lamb, is that "they can now do about double the work, and make a better clinker." The furnace bars are kept in a better state by the moisture of the steam, and therefore last longer, but the brick lining suffers from the greater heat. There is a better combustion, and therefore greater efficiency in the disposal of the refuse.

Although the steam blast is very effective, it would, in our judgment, be an objectionable feature, owing to the noise made by it. This, however, is not unavoidable, for we found at other places a powerful blast being used with very little noise. Eighty to 100 tons a week are burned ; the large tins and iron pans are sorted out and buried, but the small tins are put through the furnace, and the solder melted out into the clinker. The furnace bars are worked every day and night, except that the men are only in attendance six hours each Sunday ; for the remainder of the week two men are at work by day and one by night.

The works are on the outskirts of the city, but there are many good houses close by, and a building estate is being laid out adjoining the site of the works, and we were assured there were no complaints, except a few as to smoke before the blowers were put in. The destructor has been erected at the sewage outfall, and the waste heat is used for assisting in raising steam for pumping the sewage to the farm, which is situated about ¾ mile away ; this is effected by means of a

Green's economiser fixed in the hot-air line, which saves about 30 per cent. of the coal bill as compared with former costs.

The chimney of the pumping station has been utilised and is 80 ft. high ; we could see nothing but a small quantity of light-coloured smoke coming from it. There is a good demand for the ashes at 1s. 6d. per load and for the clinker at 2s. per load ; what is not sold is made up by hand into paving stones. The clinker here is of very hard quality.

### HORNSEY (Population 70,000).

The destructor works are at the central depot, and we were very much interested here in observing the completeness of the stabling, repairing shops, mortuary, public disinfector and other municipal works, which were shown to us by the council's engineer, Mr. E. J. Lovegrove. The destructor is of the "Perfectus" type (similar to that at Bath), and there are twelve cells working every day except Sunday, when the fires are banked up until Monday morning. There is no forced draught, the furnaces easily disposing of the present quantity of refuse. With the increase of the population it may become necessary to add forced draught.

The repairs to the furnaces up to the present have been very small, only one new set of furnace-bars having been fixed to the first six cells erected. The works are in the midst of a populous district, houses being built right up to the walls surrounding the works. There are good houses not 20 yards from the chimney stack, which is 217ft. in height, and the entrance is in the High-street of the town, but no complaints are made on account of the destructor.

The clinker is a fairly good one, although not so hard as at Winchester. It is used for making slabs under pressure, which cost 1s. 9d. per superficial yard to make, including cement and allowing for value of clinker. A new hydraulic machine is being erected for pressing the slabs, when the cost will be reduced to 1s. 3d. per yard. No granite is used with the clinker, and the blocks are extremely hard, well finished and of even texture.

There is a great demand for clinker ; when they have any to sell, which is seldom, 2s. a load is charged. It is used by the authority for many purposes besides making paving slabs, for instance as hard core for foundation of new streets, bottom course for concrete or other paving, and a scheme for workmen's dwellings is in course of erection, the whole of the brickwork of which is being built with clinker mortar and the foundations constructed with clinker concrete ; indeed, the demand for the clinker for their own purposes is so great that they cannot provide anything like enough for their own requirements.

Mr. Lovegrove informed us that, after allowing for repairs, interest and repayment of capital and crediting value of clinker (2s. per load), the total cost of disposal works out at 1s. 8d. to 1s. 10d. per ton of refuse destroyed. The waste heat is utilised to raise steam in a multitubular boiler, and a 12 horse-power nominal engine provides power for a variety of purposes in connection with the sanitary depot.

### LEYTON (Population 90,000).

The furnace in use here is the "Beaman & Deas ;" makers, The Beaman & Deas Syndicate, of Warrington. There are eight cells, but it has only been found necessary up to the present to work four of them, and these are worked continuously for five days per week. The furnaces have been at work since October, 1896, and cost £7,000, including the chimney stack, which is 150 ft. high and cost £1,100.

The town refuse destroyed weekly amounts to 195 tons, but 135 tons of pressed sewage sludge are also mixed with the refuse and burnt with it, the residue being a hard clinker 25 to 30 per cent. of the original bulk, which has all been sold up to the present time. The destructor has been erected at the sewage works, and is close to a large board school, and within 100 yards of a fever hospital for fifty patients, and 200 yards from other good properties.

We were informed by the borough surveyor, Mr. W. Dawson, that the authorities at the hospital used to complain of smells from the sewage works, owing to the pressed sludge being deposited near it ; but since the erection of the destructor, and the burning therewith of the sewage sludge, these complaints have ceased and none have been made regarding the destructor itself. This is, so far as we have been able to discover, the only destructor in England burning pressed sludge ; the sludge is mixed with the refuse on a platform above the cells, in the proportions indicated above, and each cell disposes of 15 to 17 tons per twenty-four hours.

The feeding is done at the top, down a sloping hearth to the grate. The outlet to the flues is at the opposite end to the feed opening, so that all the gases must pass over the hottest part of the fire. Forced draught from a fan is introduced under the grate and passes into the furnace between the bars, the heated gases pass from the furnace through a combustion chamber, in which a temperature of 2,000 deg. Fahr. is maintained.

The clinkering is done at the side, by which arrangement whatever cold air may rush into the furnace when the door

is opened passes over the hot fire and into the combustion chamber, instead of over the partially burnt materials on the feeding hearth. The heated gases are passed through two "Babcock & Wilcox" tubular boilers, each ninety-six horse-power nominal, and thence to the chimney stack, and the steam raised is utilised for driving dynamo, fans for air blast, pumps for sewage, sludge presses and mixing machinery. There is a 45 horse-power engine at the sewage works, and two 12 horse-power for the other operations carried on.

The water evaporated by the burning of the refuse is ½ lb. for every pound of the mixed refuse. Taking into account the fact that the furnace is burning sewage sludge (which is always in a wet, pasty condition) as well as domestic refuse, this we consider a very satisfactory result. We were much struck with the cleanly condition of the works and plant, and the entire absence of offensive smells, even though the destructor and the sewage works were so closely connected with each other.

### SHOREDITCH (Population 124,000).

We included this most interesting installation in our inspection, mainly on account of the fact that the waste heat is utilised for the supply of electricity to the district. The furnaces are of the "Fryer" type, with modifications under Wood & Brodie's patents; makers, Messrs. Manlove, Alliott & Co. There are twelve cells and six "Babcock & Wilcox" boilers (one boiler between each pair of cells). Forced-air draught is used, driven by powerful fans worked by an electric motor, the fumes from the refuse being drawn through the fan and sent through the hottest part of the fire. Steam draught is provided for, but has not been regularly used, the fan blast having been found more efficient.

The fine ash from the furnaces meets with a ready sale for making mortar, but no use is made of the clinker on the premises, and there is such a large quantity produced that the supply is much in excess of the demand, the district being practically all built over, no new streets are being laid out, and there is every likelihood of this becoming shortly a real difficulty; and this having been realised, steps are being taken to dispose of the clinker.

One hundred tons of refuse are destroyed daily, it being delivered at the ground level, and tipped into huge tanks which are raised in a lift when full to the level of the top of the furnaces, over which the tanks run on rails and discharge their contents as required into the cells. These appliances are known as "Boulnois & Brodie's" patent refuse storing and charging apparatus.

In addition to the cells, there is under each boiler a smaller furnace, the object of which we were able to observe. We fortunately happened to pay our visit to the works at the moment of the highest load at the electricity works, just as it was getting dark, when unaided the cells are not sufficient for raising the full quantity of steam. During the day the more inflammable parts of the refuse—paper, boards and other dry material—are kept back, and at the time of the highest load these are used in the furnaces under the boilers to raise steam rapidly for a short time; and while we were there everybody was at work at the highest tension to keep things going, and we were all the more grateful to the courteous manager, Mr. C. Newton Russell, for giving us so much of his time and taking such pains to give us detailed explanations of the whole process.

The chimney stack is 150 ft. high, and, although we visited the works at a time when everything was at the greatest strain, we could detect nothing proceeding from the chimney but a light brown smoke, which entirely disappeared within a few yards; and Mr. Russell told us there had been no complaints since the works started, seven months ago. The works are in the midst of a densely-populated part of London, and although the general surroundings are such as to lead one to suppose the inhabitants would not be very hypercritical, yet no doubt if there was any serious cause of complaint it would have been made before now.

The furnaces are worked continually, night and day, all the week round, and waste heat is all utilised for driving the electric light machinery, the system being high-tension direct-current on the Oxford transformer method. The refuse is not quite sufficient to provide the whole of the power required, some coal having to be provided for Sundays, when the refuse runs short, and on other occasions during excessive demand; but the system demonstrates what valuable use can be made of the refuse in circumstances similar to Shoreditch, where there is a dense population on a small area, or, in other words, an enormous quantity of refuse to be disposed of and a confined area to be lighted.

### CAMBRIDGE (Population 36,983).

Here the destructor is of the "Fryer" type, modified, as at Shoreditch, under Wood & Brodie's patents (Messrs. Manlove, Alliott & Co.), and consists of six cells, four of which are in use and two kept as reserve. The destructor was erected in 1894, but as it was included in the general contract for pumping station, which it adjoins, the cost cannot be given.

The refuse is brought up an inclined roadway and tipped into trucks, each having five compartments (each compartment holding just enough for one charge), and there are two charging trucks to each cell. This trucks run on rails on the top of the furnaces, and the compartments are successively brought over the charging opening of the furnace, and the contents fall into the cell. The truck system appears to work

very well indeed, and the manager, Mr. J. Mitten, strongly recommends it. It is a very cleanly method of storing and charging the refuse, but it has this objection, which, however, does not apply at Cambridge, that extra height must be allowed for the depth of the charging truck. This apparatus is the invention of Mr. H. Percy Boulnois, formerly city engineer of Liverpool.

Forced-air draught is provided, which is arranged to be practically noiseless and to which there can, as here applied, be no objection. The average temperature according to test obtained in the furnace is 1,600 deg. Fahr., but this has frequently been exceeded. Cast iron, we were told, had been melted in the furnaces, when the temperature must have been 2,400 deg.

The chimney stack is 175 ft. high. As the waste heat is utilised to supply engines for pumping the sewage from the outfall to the farm, 2 miles away, the furnaces have to be worked continuously and every day in the week. There are two engines, each of 80 horse-power nominal, but in an emergency enough steam can be generated with the four cells to give 170 indicated horse-power; 140 tons a week are disposed of in the four working cells; one man is sufficient to attend to the feeding, the truck system requiring very little manual labour, and two men are engaged in drawing out the clinker, which falls into a box at the front of the furnace, the advantage of this being that the heat of the clinker is retained within the furnace and the quantity reduced to 20 per cent.

The men work in twelve-hour shifts and did not appear to be overworked. The cost of burning is said to be from 7½d. to 10d. per ton. The clinker is used for making roads, and some is sold at 1s. per load; most of it, however, is being used at the works, in filling up, levelling and forming new roads. The locality of the works is away from the city and in open country, but there was nothing coming from the chimney but a light, thin, almost imperceptible smoke or steam; indeed, considering that all the refuse of the city is brought here and the whole of the sewage is being pumped, the beautifully clean condition of the whole of the works is quite wonderful and the complete result excellent.

### LOUGHBOROUGH (Population 20,000).

The destructor has been constructed by Messrs. Coltman & Sons, of Loughborough, and is the only one of its kind at present at work. It is erected at the sewage outfall, some distance outside the town, and as it is used for pumping it has to work continuously. The furnace consists of one cell only, having a reverberatory arch of fire-clay blocks, over which is set a boiler of the water-tube type. The cell is fed down a slope at the back, the clinkering doors being at the front, and there is a powerful steam and air draught driven by a fan.

This single cell disposes of 80 tons per week, and one man feeds and clinkers for eight hours, the furnace being worked in three shifts, each man being paid 21s. per week. The destructor is a compact arrangement, but it is considerably larger than we should require, and Mr. Coltman recommends a size capable of destroying 5 tons a day. The boiler supplies steam for driving sewage pumping plant, consisting of three centrifugal pumps, lifting the whole of the sewage of the town 25 ft., also for a small electric lighting plant for the works. The cost of the chimney stack, which is 80 ft. high, was £250, and the destructor plant, including boiler, £1,000.

As this plant is away in the open country no cause of nuisance arises, but we saw no reason why any such should happen even if it was erected in proximity to dwellings. A peculiar feature of this furnace consists in the bars of the grate, which are Perret's patent dust fuel bars, the bottom edges of which rest in a trough of water, the life of the bars being thereby prolonged, so that only six new bars have been required since the furnace was erected in September, 1896. Repairs and renewals have cost only £10 since commencing work.

### BRADFORD (Population 230,000).

There are several refuse destructors in various parts of the town of Bradford. The one we visited is the one most recently erected, and the furnaces adopted are those of the "Horsfall" type, the present installation having taken the place of furnaces of older makers which were in use up to five months ago. There are twelve cells in all, four of which we were able to inspect while in course of construction.

The cells are fixed back to back, and the firing apertures are at the top. The refuse first passes over a drying hearth at the back of the fire, which is so formed that the rubbish is gradually dried and falls on to the hearth, the gases passing from the refuse over the hottest part of the fire. The clinkering doors are at the front of the furnace, and a special feature of the furnace is the forced draught of steam and air, by means of which a high temperature is secured in the furnaces.

It appears from an exhaustive test (extending over six days) in October last by the manager, Mr. McTaggart, that the temperature of the gases in the main flue was 1,800 deg. (maximum 2,100 deg., minimum 1,700 deg.) Fahr., and at the foot of chimney, after (passing through the boiler) 900 deg. Fahr. and ·72¾ lb. of water was evaporated per pound of refuse burnt, giving as a result 81 indicated horse-power hours per ton of refuse burnt. The percentage of clinker and ash was 30·3.

There is a novel provision in these furnaces for reducing the wear and tear on the sides of the furnaces. Iron side boxes are built in to the wall, and the steam draught is forced through these boxes and from thence into the ash-pit below the grate-bars. By this plan two useful objects are attained—the sides of the furnace are slightly cooled, and the steam and air draught is warmed before reaching the fires.

As the installation has only been at work here for a short period, we were not able to elicit any experience obtained on the subject of repairs. The chimney stack is 160 ft. high, and we could perceive no sign of anything obnoxious proceeding therefrom. The troublesome question of the disposal of the old tins, &c., is here satisfactorily settled. They are sent away in truck loads to a firm of manufacturing chemists at Halifax.

The waste heat is utilised for driving mortar mills and grinding the clinker, which is very hard, and is used for road foundations and making concrete, for all of which purposes the clinker is in great demand. The works are also lighted by electricity, and an artificial manure plant is driven by the heat of the furnaces. The refuse at Bradford is of a difficult kind to dispose of, being unscreened midden or privy refuse, mixed with ordinary household waste.

ROCHDALE (Population 73,000).

The furnaces in use here are of the "Meldrum" type. The grates are each 9 ft. wide and 5 ft. in depth, divided in their width in the ash-pit only by a division wall, on which rests a cast-iron division tee, with its thin edge level with the top of the fire-bars. This divides each grate into two, and as each portion contains its own blowers it is independent of the other, the object being that while one side of the fire is at a high temperature the other may be clinkered or fresh charged with fuel, the gases given off from the freshly-charged refuse being drawn over the hot part of the fire and cremated in the furnace itself. There is also a large combustion chamber immediately behind the furnace cells, the high temperature of which completes the cremation of the products of combustion.

Two Lancashire boilers, 30 ft. long by 8 ft. in diameter, are fixed one to each cell, and the steam pressure is 120 lb. per square inch. During a recent test by the manager, Mr. F. W. Brookman, the temperature in the combustion chamber was found to reach 1,988 degs. Fahr. The water evaporated per pound of refuse was 1·64 lb., with feed water at 52 deg. Fahr., and the percentage of clinker, &c., 36. A temperature much higher than that named has frequently been reached and maintained for long periods, when the copper test pieces of "Siemens" pyrometer have been quickly melted.

The feeding is done entirely from the front, the carts being tipped on to the floor of the destructor building. The cells are also clinkered at the front, and we considered that the two operations being carried on so close together rather tended to confusion. Except as to the point last mentioned, however, we cannot do other than acknowledge the good results obtained, the clinker being of a hard quality, and the combustion so far as we could discover was perfect. The steam jet blowers provided are not of the "silent" kind, though the noise was not enough to be objectionable.

The tub or pail system of collecting excreta is in use in Rochdale, and the quantity collected is about 10,000 tons a year, while 16,000 tons of ashes are burnt in the destructor. When the excreta arrives in special vans at the works it is first dried, and afterwards ground fine and sold for £5 10s. per ton, at which price the manure finds a ready sale. The waste heat from the destructor is utilised for driving mortar and clinker mills, for generating electricity for lighting the works and offices, chopping and crushing the food for forty-two horses, and for running the artificial manure plant.

FARNWORTH.

We visited this town to inspect a new type of destructor, known as the "Bennett-Pythian," but we found that, owing to an accident to the drainage, the furnaces were partially flooded and were not in working order. The special feature of this furnace is the movable grate. There are three cells side by side, and in these three cells are two travelling grates, each of which fills one cell, and are movable together from end to end of the furnace. When the furnace is in full work one of the cells is in the highest state of combustion, one end cell is empty and the other end cell is being clinkered, after which it is charged with fresh refuse and the grate moved over so that the last charged cell comes into the hot middle cell, while the late contents of that cell have been moved into the previously empty cell for clinkering.

The waste heat is utilised to raise steam in a water-tube boiler erected over the cells. Owing to the fact that we could not see this furnace in operation, we were unable to form any judgment on its merits. The destructor is the private property of its patentees, Messrs. Ham, Baker & Co., who are burning town refuse in it. It is the only one of its kind at present erected, but it has been adopted at South-ampton, where a destructor of this type is now being built.

OLDHAM (Population 147,000).

The destructor is of the "Horsfall" type, six cells erected in 1891 in one series and four erected in 1895 in another, the whole having forced blast. That to the four cells is of the ordinary type and rather noisy, while the six older cells have been newly fitted with the "silent" blast, which works very satisfactorily. The general description of the furnaces is similar to that at Bradford. The waste heat, passing through two Lancashire boilers, raises steam to a pressure of 140 lb., which is used for supplementing the power at the electric lighting station, for mortar grinding and driving machinery at the corporation workshops. The furnaces are fired by hand from behind. Both Mr. Pickering, the borough surveyor, and Mr. Jessop, the manager, prefer this to the hopper charging system, the refuse being more evenly distributed over the fire.

No repairs have up to the present been required to the four cells erected in 1895, but from the appearance of the crown of the furnaces we think such will soon be wanted. The chimney is 120 ft. high, but the day we visited the works the fog was very thick, and it was impossible to see whether anything was coming out of the top. The works are situate about 400 yards from a middle-class residential district, comprising houses rented at about £18 a year, and we were told no complaints had ever been received.

GENERAL CONCLUSIONS.

In the course of our inspection, the deputation say in conclusion, we have seen quite enough to convince us that the destructor is a cleanly and economical method for the disposal of household and other refuse, and we are unanimously of opinion that, properly worked, no nuisance need arise from it. As to the best type of furnace for the requirements of this town we cannot at present speak in such positive terms, most of those we saw possessing some feature of which we approved.

We would recommend that the following firms be invited to submit proposals and prices for the erection of a destructor suitable for the requirements of this town, and we shall then be able to weigh the relative advantages of the various types of furnaces with the prices submitted: The Beaman & Deas Syndicate, Messrs. Coltman & Son, Messrs. Goddard, Massey & Varner, the Horsfall Furnace Company and Messrs. Manlove, Alliott & Co.

We cannot, we think, more usefully close our report than by recapitulating in a condensed form the information we have detailed in the previous pages. The types we inspected were: The "Perfectus," at Bath and Hornsey; the "Fryer," at Vinchester, Shoreditch and Cambridge; the "Beaman & Deas," at Leyton; the "Horsfall," at Bradford and Oldham; the "Bennett-Pythian," at Farnworth; the "Meldrum," at Rochdale; and the "Coltman," at Loughborough. We found forced draught in operation at every place except Hornsey and at Bath, where there are very high chimneys. The effect of the forced draught is to increase the temperature, and enables the refuse to be disposed of more quickly with less possibility of complaint, but the wear and tear is no doubt greater.

The quantity of clinker produced varies from 25 per cent. to 35 per cent. in weight of the refuse burnt. The clinker is ground for mortar, and it is admirably adapted for making concrete or concrete slabs, which, if made under great pressure (as at Hornsey), would be very valuable for paving. We found at each place we visited that the old tins were practically indestructible, and steps had to be taken to remove them. The waste heat was utilised at every place we visited for pumping, electric lighting, clinker crushing, mortar grinding or driving machinery.

On this point, while we strongly deprecate the extravagant ideas which have been industriously circulated in some quarters that there is such an enormous amount of energy lying dormant in town refuse, sufficient, for example, as to ensure enough power for the whole of the electric lighting of a town, we still consider that the power which may be reasonably expected from the burning refuse is a valuable item, and may be turned to extremely useful purpose if the system is adopted at Tiverton.

On the question of cost we cannot at present give exact particulars, but we estimate approximately that a destructor sufficient for Tiverton may be erected for £560; cost of chimney, say, 120 ft. high, £200; purchase of land, £200; buildings, which need not be of an expensive character, £300; machinery, boiler, &c., £200; contingencies, £100; total, £1,500.

We consider that two men in the daytime and one at night will be sufficient for three days a week to work the destructor and the machinery, which will amount to per annum, say, £80; interest and repayment of £1,500 in twenty years, £100; repairs, say, £30; total, £210. The value of power for mortar-grinding, stone-breaking, sale of clinker, or value of same if utilised for concrete slabs, may safely be taken at per annum, £100; leaving a balance of £110. From this should be deducted the present cost of carting away and burying the refuse after the ashes have been sifted from it, and the rent of refuse tips, say, £55. Leaving nett cost to the borough of the destructor plant at £55 per year, which sum we consider as a small amount to pay for the undoubted advantages accruing to the public health of the town by the prompt destruction of the refuse.

**Torquay.**—A recommendation of the Roads Committee was last week adopted, giving permission to the National Telephone Company to place certain of their wires underground, on condition that the company pay a way-leave of 1s. per sub. per annum, and provide and equip complete a number of fire alarms in various parts of the borough.

## QUERIES AND REPLIES.

*Sketches accompanying Queries should be made, separate on white paper in plain black-ink lines. Lettering or figures should be bold and plain.*

**205. Tar Boiling, Fumes from: Alleged Damage to Fruit Crops.**—"T." writes: The occupier of a large garden adjoining a place used for mixing and preparing material for tar paving alleges that the fumes from the tar have destroyed his crop of fruit and generally damaged the vegetation. Will you please inform me whether the fumes from boiling tar have any ill-effect on vegetation, and whether complaints of the kind are common?

We do not remember having heard of a similar complaint to that put forward, wherein the fumes from boiling tar are alleged to have injuriously affected vegetation. We do not think such fumes given off are poisonous *per se.* There may, however, be local circumstances affecting the present case, such as very close proximity of the fruit trees to the tar-boiling apparatus, which are not present in most cases. We should be much obliged if those of our readers who have had similar experience will communicate with us on the subject for the benefit of other surveyors.

**206. Sludge-pressing Machinery, Makers of.**—"R. D." writes: Could you inform me the names and addresses of any firms you know of who make a speciality of sludge-pressing machinery? Also makers of a reliable lime-mixing machine?

The following firms are of well-known repute as manufacturers of sludge presses and lime-mixing machines: Goddard, Massey & Warner, Nottingham; Manlove, Alliott & Co., Limited, Nottingham; John Wolstenholme, Albert Works, Radcliffe, Manchester; and S. B. Johnson & Co., Stratford, London, E.

**207. Civil Engineers, Examinations for.**—"Darius" writes: I shall be pleased if you will inform me the difference in the meaning of the letters "A.M.I.C.E." and "M.I.C.E." Also I wish to know what steps I should have to take to obtain the letters "C.E." or any of the foregoing letters. Are there any examinations to pass, and, if so, what fees are to be paid?

The letters referred to designate the two classes of membership of the Institution of Civil Engineers, the former denoting "associate member" and the latter "member" of the institution. We described in our reply to Query 154, in our issue of February 25th last, the character of the examinations in connection with the institution, to which reply the querist should refer. The Incorporated Association of Municipal and County Engineers also hold examinations for young civil engineers under local authorities. Particulars of the subjects of these examinations may be obtained from the secretary, Mr. Thomas Cole, 11 Victoria-street, Westminster, S.W.

**208. Books for Civil Engineers Recommended.**—"Cortaber" writes: I should esteem it a favour if you would recommend me the best works for civil engineers on the following subjects—*viz.*, (1) Masonry, (2) brickwork, (3) quantities, (4) calculation of earthwork quantities, (5) construction of works in concrete, (6) tunnelling for sewers.

The following books are recommended as being thoroughly good in their several subjects :—

(1) *Masonry :* Baker's "Masonry Construction" (American), (price 21s. nett, B. T. Batsford) ; Purchase's "Practical Masonry " (price 7s. 6d., Crosby Lockwood & Son).

(2) *Brickwork :* Hammond's "Rudiments of Practical Bricklaying" (price 1s. 6d.) ; Walker's "Principles of Bricklaying, Cutting and Setting" (price 1s. 6d., both published by Crosby Lockwood & Son).

(3) *Quantities :* Banister Fletcher's "Quantities" (price 7s. 6d., B. T. Batsford) ; Dobson and Tarn's "Guide to Measuring and Valuing Artificer's Work" (price 7s. 6d., Crosby Lockwood & Son) ; Leaning's "Quantity Surveying" (price 15s., E. & F. N. Spon).

(4) *Calculation of Earthwork Quantities :* Bidder's "Tables showing the Contents of Excavations, Area of Slopes, &c." (price 3s. 6d., Vacher & Sons) ; Trautwine's "Method of Calculating Cubic Contents of Excavations and Embankments by the Aid of Diagrams" (price 8s. 6d., E. & F. N. Spon) ; Cunningham's "Earthwork Tables" (price 10s. 6d., E. & F. N. Spon).

(5) *Concrete :* Sutcliffe's "Concrete: Its Nature and Uses" (price 7s. 6d., Crosby Lockwood & Son) ; Potter's "Concrete: Its Use in Building" (2 vols., price 7s. 6d., B. T. Batsford) ; Newman's "Notes on Concrete and Works in Concrete" (price 6s., E. & F. N. Spon).

(6) *Tunnelling for Sewers :* Simm's "Practical Tunnelling : Explaining in Detail, Setting-out the Works, Shaft-sinking and Heading-driving, Ranging the Lines and Levelling Underground" (price 42s., Crosby Lockwood & Son).

Any of the books are obtainable at discount prices from Mr. B. T. Batsford, engineering and technical publisher and bookseller, 94 High Holborn, London, W.C.

**209. Sewage Farming : Fungus from Subsoil Drains.**—"Puzzled" writes: Three months ago about 15 acres of land were underdrained and laid out for sewage irrigation, the drain pipes being 4 in. in diameter, laid 3 ft. 6 in. below the surface of the ground, the drains being about 40 ft. apart.

The sewage, about 200,000 gallons per day, before it is put on the land is treated with aluminoferric. The effluent from the drains at the outfall is quite clear, but we are greatly troubled with fungus growing in the pipes. This fungus is discharged at the outfall into a small brook, where it lodges and proves most objectionable. Can any surveyor who has had a similar experience suggest a remedy for this growth in the drain pipes and outfall pipes?

The difficulty experienced by the querist is a rather common one, and can only be effectually counteracted by the construction of filters of coke or burnt ballast at the outfall. These should be constructed so as to be used intermittently.

## THE SANITARY INSTITUTE.

### LIVERPOOL EXAMINATIONS.

At an examination in practical sanitary science, held at Liverpool on July 29th and 30th, five candidates presented themselves. Of these the following were granted certificates: Mr. H. E. Bellamy, Municipal Buildings, Truro; Mr. T. Graham, 20 Alfred-road, Birkenhead; and Mr. T. Summers, M.I.C.E., 32 Craigmillar Park, Edinburgh. The following were the questions set to be answered: (1) On what does the velocity of a liquid issuing from an orifice depend? What is the effect of bends and branches in pipes upon the flow of the liquid? (2) Define the terms "porosity," "capillarity," "absorptivity" and "permeability." (3) State in detail the method adopted by public water companies for the purification of water from springs, rivers, &c. Explain fully the action of such filter-beds, and how the water should be stored after filtration and before delivery. (4) Describe the method of coating cast-iron pipes for water supply with Dr. Angus Smith's composition. Give the proportions of materials used. (5) What do you understand by the terms "wetted perimeter" and "hydraulic mean depth"? What would be the flow in a rectangular aqueduct of brickwork, 10 ft. wide, flowing 5 ft. deep, with a fall of 9 in. per mile? (6) State what you know as to the proper construction of a furnace with boiler for steam raising, which has to consume the smoke produced from the combustible used in it. What are the different kinds of fuel used in steam boilers, and what are the main characteristics of each? (7) Describe the steps you would take, and the instruments you would use, to test the amount and regularity of the fall in a main drain. (8) Describe in detail the procedure for discovering and dealing with unsound food.

An examination for inspector of nuisances was held on the same day. Sixty-four candidates presented themselves, and thirty-seven will receive certificates. The questions set were as follows: (1) What is the best position for an underground soft-water cistern in a country house? How should it be constructed? Show by sketches how you would deal with the overflow therefrom. (2) Describe a good form of slop sink, stating the sizes of flush pipe and outlet, and the method of trapping the same. Under what conditions may the waste from a slop sink be connected to a vertical soil pipe? (3) Mention the various kinds of joints made in connecting lengths of lead soil pipe. State which variety you prefer, with the reasons for your selection. (4) Describe the conditions under which privies should be allowed, and give a sketch plan of one you would recommend. (5) State the statute law providing for the abatement of smoke nuisance. (6) A bedroom of about 3,000 cubic feet of area has been occupied by a patient suffering from small-pox. Describe in detail how the room and its contents may be efficiently disinfected. (7) Describe briefly the construction of three kinds of roof covering, and illustrate by sketches. State the advantages and disadvantages of each from a sanitary point of view. (8) What powers have sanitary authorities, and under what Acts, for dealing with milk alleged to be unwholesome or adulterated?

---

**The True Function of the Sanitary Engineer in India.**—Judging from what Mr. Jones, the sanitary engineer to the Government of Madras, has been directed to do, the work of the sanitary engineer in this country should, says *Indian Engineering,* be confined to investigations, opinions and reports, conjoined with the preparation and submission of estimates and reports. That is, the functions of such an officer should be more "consultative" than *executive.* In other words, a sanitary engineer is not an executive engineer.

**Manchester.**—The Manchester Corporation have decided to borrow £6,000 for purposes of tramway extension in the city, and an application into the matter was held recently at the town hall by Sir Francis Marindin, an inspector of the Board of Trade. The application was not opposed. It was explained that the money asked for was needed to defray the cost of constructing tram lines in Cross-street, Chorlton-road, Ashton New-road, Moss-lane East (two lines), Wilmslow-road, Denmark-road and Greenheys-lane. These were found to be necessary additions for the convenience of the city. The amount originally borrowed on account of the tramways of the city was £169,362, and all this had been repaid with the exception of £21,907,

# Law Notes.

Edited by J. B. REIGNIER CONDER, 11 Old Jewry Chambers, E.C.,

Solicitor of the Supreme Court.

*The Editor will be pleased to answer any questions affecting the practice of engineers and surveyors to local authorities. Queries (which should be written legibly on foolscap paper, one side only) should be addressed to "The Law Editor," at the Offices of THE SURVEYOR. Where possible, copies of local Acts or documents referred to should be enclosed. All explanatory diagrams must be drawn and lettered in black ink only. Correspondents who do not wish their names published should furnish a nom de plume.*

BETTERMENT: TOTTENHAM COURT-ROAD IMPROVEMENT.—A curious point anent the principle of betterment was raised in *The Oxford (Limited) v. The London County Council* (Chancery Division, Mr. Justice North). Under one of the local Acts of last session applicable to the metropolis the Council have power to make certain improvements in the Tottenham Court-road, and the Act contains a "betterment" clause. The Oxford Music Hall has its principal entrance in Oxford-street some little distance from the Tottenham Court-road. The plaintiff company, however (the owners of the music hall), recently purchased a house, which when the improvements are carried out will front on to the Tottenham Court-road. This house communicates, by an entrance and an exit on the ground floor, with the hall. The council contended that the house had in effect thus become part and parcel of the music hall, and that the entire hall, as thus added to, must be considered as fronting on the road and liable to the contribution provided for by the "betterment" clauses. The company did not dispute that the house itself was liable to contribute, but contended that it should be treated as a separate building, and not as forming part of the hall. Mr. Justice North decided in favour of the council. He said the fallacy of the plaintiff's contention was that he treated the various properties that together went to make up the music hall separately. He (the learned judge) thought that the house, together with the building behind it, to which it gave entrance, must be taken as one messuage; and it was not disputed that the house did front on the Tottenham Court-road.

HIGHWAY: GREEN SWARD ADJOINING CARRIAGE ROAD: RIGHT OF OWNER OF SOIL TO ERECT POSTS.—An important question in connection with highway law was raised in the case of *Dawson v. Hendon Urban District Council* (Chancery Division, Mr. Justice North). In front of Mill Hill Grammar School is a strip of green sward. On the grass, near the public carriage road, there is a row of very fine elms, between which and the road there is a post and rail fence that has existed as long as the memory of the oldest inhabitants. Traversing the green sward is a gravel paths, used by the public, who have access to it at either end through openings in the post and rail fence. The space between the trees and the wall of the school premises is crossed by paths or roads giving access to the latter. The plaintiffs (who are the trustees of the school), in order to prevent the carts of tradesmen going to the school from spoiling the grass, have recently put up posts (four in one place, three in another) to keep such carts off the green sward. The council considered this an unlawful interference with the highway, and took the posts up. The plaintiffs reinstated them, whereupon the council again took them up and removed them to premises of their own. The plaintiffs then brought this action, asking for a mandatory injunction to the council to restore the posts and not to interfere with them when replaced. The present application was made upon motion for an interim injunction until the trial of the action. The plaintiffs contended that they were the absolute owners of the strip of land within the post and rail fence, subject only to a public right of way for foot passengers over the gravelled portion thereof. The council, on the other hand, claimed that the entire strip, green sward and all, was a highway. The Court declined to make an order on the motion, being of opinion that it was better for both parties that the posts should not be replaced until the questions between them shall be finally decided at the trial; but the council gave an undertaking to abide by any order the Court may make at the trial as to restoring the injured turf. The final decision will probably turn very largely on the nature of the evidence as to public use forthcoming at the trial.

EXTRAORDINARY TRAFFIC: HIGHWAYS AND LOCOMOTIVES (AMENDMENT) ACT, 1878, SEC. 23.—Another most important contribution to the decisions under the above section is afforded by the case of *Pethick and Others v. County Council of Dorset* (Court of Appeal, 28th July), in which the vexed question as to the meaning of the expression "person by whose order" extraordinary traffic is conducted was again the subject of judicial consideration. The traffic consisted in the hauling of building materials for the erection of the Dorset county lunatic asylum under the following circumstances. First of all the Visiting Committee of the asylum entered into a contract with Messrs. Pethick for the erection by the latter of the asylum, for the sum of £52,000, by which contract they agreed to indemnify the committee from all claims in respect of extraordinary traffic. Messrs. Pethick then entered into a sub-contract with one John Trenchard for the hauling of the materials, whereby Trenchard undertook to supply carts and horses as and when required by Pethick, to provide skilled workmen, to unload the materials from the railway trucks, and to haul them to such place on the works as should be pointed out by Pethick, receiving from the latter such assistance as should be necessary, and using only such roads as should be pointed out to him. The sub-contract also provided that Trenchard was not to employ any person to whom Pethick should object, and that no cart or traction engine should be used which Pethick or his foreman should certify to be improper for the service; and, further, that Trenchard should indemnify Pethick against all extraordinary traffic claims. Trenchard performed the hauling in accordance with this contract, and damage to the extent of £231 was thereby done to certain roads. The council summoned Pethick for this amount, and the magistrates made an order for payment against him. The Queen's Bench Divisional Court quashed the magistrates' order, and the council appealed to the Court of Appeal, but without success. Mr. Justice A. L. Smith said it was clear that Pethick gave no order to Trenchard other than was to be found in the sub-contract. Therefore, if that contract did not constitute an "order" within the meaning of the section Pethick could not be made liable. There had been a great amount of litigation on that section, and there were numerous authorities which showed a considerable conflict of opinion; but the House of Lords had put a construction upon the section, which was binding on this Court, in the case of *Kent County Council v. Lord Gerard* (1897, A.C., 633, THE SURVEYOR, vol. xi., p. 215). Now, by whose order had this extraordinary traffic been conducted? He had no doubt that it had been conducted by the order of Trenchard, and that he might have been made liable. But it was argued that even if that were so Pethick had ordered it to be conducted. It was said that power was reserved to Pethick under the contract to say what carts should be used. He was not satisfied that that was the meaning of the contract; but, even if it were so, if he merely had the power to give orders as to what carts should be used, but did not give such orders, he was not within the Act. Reliance was also laid on the clause providing that no cart or engine should be used which Pethick might think improper for the service. In his opinion those words referred to the fitness of any cart or engine for the work, and did not refer to the contingency of the roads being cut up. Lord Justice Rigby was of the same opinion. The House of Lords had laid it down that it was not sufficient to show that the traffic had been conducted at the instance of the person sought to be made liable, or for his benefit. He thought that the control which the contract gave Pethick over the work to be done by Trenchard was much less than was suggested in argument. And the question was not whether orders might have been given by Pethick, but whether they were given. Lord Justice Vaughan Williams agreed, but he desired to base his judgment on this—that the case did not state sufficient to fix Pethick with liability. There was nothing to indicate how much of the damage was caused by excessive weight of particular parcels, or what was the nature of the extraordinary traffic in question. If it had been shown that the damage had been caused entirely by the total amount of the traffic carried, as distinguished from excessive weight of particular parcels, he should unhesitatingly say that the extraordinary traffic had been conducted by the order of Pethick. He thought that that would clearly follow from the case of *Kent County Council v. Vidler* (1895, 1 Q.B., 448). But the facts of the case did not permit him to say that the extraordinary traffic which had caused the damage consisted solely and entirely of the total amount of the traffic. On this ground he thought that Pethick could not be held to be responsible.

## QUERIES AND REPLIES.

COMBINED DRAIN.—"J. T." writes: Referring to the answer given "H. M. F." in the "Queries and Replies" column of this week's SURVEYOR (p. 104) respecting the drainage of a row of labourers' houses, is not the drain a "drain" even beyond where the drainage of the second house enters it, seeing all the houses belong to the same owner, provided the local authority have adopted Part III. of the Public Health Act (Amendment Acts), 1890? This being the case, is not the local authority noting within its rights in asking the owner to do all they have asked him? I shall be glad if you will kindly give me a reply. I find your paper a great help in studying municipal engineering, especially the "Law Notes."

Sec. 19 of the Public Health Act (Amendment Act), 1890, only applies to two or more houses belonging to different owners. It is for the very reason that these houses belong to the *same* owner, that the combined system is a sewer, even if Part III. of the Act has been adopted. The premises are evidently not within the same curtilage, as it is clear from " H. M. F.'s " statement that each house has a separate yard.

By-Laws: New Street.—"New Street" writes: Has a council power to compel an owner depositing plans for the erection of four houses, as per sketch, to set back and give up (not enclose) the area of land indicated by the letters A in order to make provision for a 36 ft. road as required by the council's by-laws? This plan is the commencement of building operations on an estate recently sold with only a 17 ft. road to it, the front being called building land and the back allotments, and the person purchasing this particular plot does it with an expressed (verbal) condition that he can build up to the limit of such land. He, however, sets back his building-line, but intends to enclose the whole area. Can you give me recent decisions on such a point ?

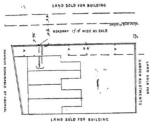

LAND SOLD FOR BUILDING

ROADWAY 17'·6" WIDE AS SOLD

LAND SOLD FOR BUILDING

If a "new street" is being laid out the council can insist upon its being of the width required by the by-laws. The question whether or not a " new street " is being laid out is a question of fact for the magistrates to determine, and if there is any evidence upon which they can find that the street is a new street the High Court will not inquire into the sufficiency of the evidence. See our note of the case of *Allen* v. *Fulham Vestry* (p. 70 *ante*). In *Taylor* v. *Metropolitan Board of Works* (L.R. 2, Q.B. 213), which is a leading case on this subject, Mr. Justice Blackburn said : " I do not think that if a person merely puts up a hoarding or leaves the way without any fence, or leaves the old fence untouched while he is building, he can be said to have laid out the road, but as soon as he begins to put up fences, and marks out the boundary, which he intends to be the permanent boundary between his building and the road, then he may be said to have begun to lay out the road for the forming of the street; and this also is a question of fact for the magistrate." This and various other cases are noted in Lumley's " Public Health Acts," fifth edition, pp. 206 *et seq.*

## SEWAGE DISPOSAL AT HYDE.

The Sewage Works Committee last week recommended that, having regard to the fact that the Local Government Board would not pass any scheme of artificial filtration unless it also embraced one of subsequent filtration through land, plans of a scheme for automatic filters and land filtration, at an estimated cost of £5,500, be adopted, and that the town clerk be instructed to make application to the Local Government Board for sanction to the loan. A member, in submitting the minutes for adoption, said the estimated expenditure included the purchase of automatic filters, the building of a filter-house, the erection of a pump for the washing-out of the filters, and the underdraining of 10½ acres of land, which was to be laid out in 1 acre plots for the purpose of land filtration. They intended to take the solid matter from the sewage by means of the automatic filters and then turn it upon the land, but he was not prepared to say that even then they would be able to give satisfaction to the Mersey and Irwell Committee. A lengthy discussion ensued, the opinion being expressed that, pending the report of the Royal Commission, the scheme should not be proceeded with. The mayor said that the matter had been forced forward owing to a magisterial resolution. Ultimately the resolution was referred back to the committee for further consideration.

**Dundee.**—On Thursday, at a meeting of the town council, a long discussion took place on a report prepared by the burgh engineer for the extension of the esplanade. In the report it was suggested that the sea wall should be extended westwards in a straight line, and, it was pointed out that the result of this would be a reclamation from the foreshore of 132 acres. This, with the 31½ acres already reclaimed, would give a total of 163 acres. The works were estimated to cost £35,840. The proposals of the burgh engineer were criticised at some length by a member, who urged that the sea wall should be continued further westward than was proposed at present, and he indicated a scheme for the extension whereby the work could be undertaken for £17,000. The proposals were favourably considered by several other members, and it was eventually decided that both plans should be circulated among the members of the board and discussed at a meeting of the Works Committee, to which all the members of the council would be invited.

## THE TELEPHONE SERVICE.

Mr. Hanbury again occupied the chair at a meeting of the Select Committee, held on Thursday.

Sir William Harcourt, who first gave evidence, expressed surprise at a statement made by Mr. Lamb to the effect that he (Mr. Lamb) was able to say that both Mr. Goschen and himself (the speaker) were of opinion that if licenses were given to corporations it should be on condition that the corporations purchased the local system of the company. He took no direct part in the details of the arrangements about the telephones, but he found that in March, 1893, the question was discussed between the Postmaster-General, Mr. Arnold Morley, and himself, when certain proposals were put forward by the National Telephone Company. Those proposals appeared to have been two—first, the constitution of large areas, each comprising several towns; and secondly, an undertaking on the part of the Postmaster-General not to grant licenses to municipalities or other local authorities. After some discussion on the matter—which, he need hardly say, he did not bear in his memory, nor, even if he did, would he think it proper to state confidential communications between heads of departments—they came to a formal and deliberate decision, which was communicated to the telephone company. The result of the discussion of those two proposals between Mr. Arnold Morley and himself was contained in a letter addressed to the National Telephone Company and dated, he thought, March 13th, 1893, in which they expressed their determination to decline to accept either of those proposals, and stated distinctly that it was impossible to restrict the freedom of the Postmaster-General in any way to grant licenses—a question which they considered had been closed by the arrangement of August 11th, 1892. That letter certainly did not say anything about its being a condition for the working of licenses by corporations that they should purchase the local system of the National Telephone Company. The committee would, he supposed, obtain that letter from the Post Office, but the words which he had taken from that letter were that "it was impossible to restrict the freedom of the Postmaster-General in any way." What Mr. Lamb had stated as his opinion was not, in point of fact, his opinion. His opinion was set forth in the letter. He certainly did not think it necessary to impose such a condition. What he had stated was the conclusion they arrived at formally and officially on the matter.

Mr. Goschen was examined with regard to Mr. Lamb's statement. What he believed happened, though his memory was not at all clear on the subject, was this. In the course of the debate he (the speaker) used some phrases which he thought had been before the committee with reference to municipalities being willing to undertake the telephone business themselves, and he said he saw nothing contrary to the Government policy in such a proposal. He understood that after the conclusion of the debate in the House of Commons the then Postmaster-General, Sir James Fergusson, expressed his surprise at what he had said, and that Mr. Lamb, who was sitting under the gallery at the time, also was impressed, because this had not formed the subject of discussion at all. He understood that he then said to Sir James Fergusson, "I presume that if municipalities are to undertake the business then they will have to pay for it." Sir James Fergusson's memory was clear upon that point and Mr. Lamb's also, perfectly clear. He certainly could not set his memory in the negative against it, and he assumed, therefore, that he said it.

Mr. Lamb, recalled, said he would like to make an apology—a very sincere and heartfelt apology—to Sir W. Harcourt and Mr. Goschen for bringing their names into the matter. He ought not to have mentioned a confidential communication. He thought he could offer a defence which would appeal to their generosity, if not to their judgment, but he preferred to leave it there, and to say how very sorry he was he should have mentioned a thing which they did not intend to be mentioned to the public. Mr. Lamb then proceeded to read the correspondence referred to which passed between the Post Office and the National Telephone Company previous to the agreement of 1896.

The committee met again on Friday to consider their report, and on Tuesday brought their deliberations to a close. They unanimously adopted, with some amendments, Mr. Hanbury's draft, and at the outset expressed the opinion that the telephone service (1) was not at present of general benefit, either in the United Kingdom at large, or even in these limited portions of it where exchanges existed ; (2) was not likely to become of general benefit, either in the country as a whole, or in existing or future exchange areas, so long as the present practical monopoly in the hands of a private company continued ; and (3) as it had already become of much more general benefit in other countries, affording less scope for its development than was afforded by the greater density of population, and the greater wealth and commercial activity of the United Kingdom, so it was fitted to become in this country, if worked solely or mainly with a view to the public interest, a valuable instrument in further developing the trade and social life of the nation, towards which new means of communication had always hitherto so largely contributed.

# Municipal Work in Progress and Projected.

Owing to the summer recess there is naturally a dearth of news in regard to municipal work on the part of metropolitan authorities. It will be seen, however, that there is plenty of information as to the doings of provincial authorities.

## METROPOLITAN AUTHORITIES.
### VESTRIES AND DISTRICT BOARDS.

**Fulham.**—The vestry have decided to pave King's-road with wood, at an estimated cost of £5,880.

**Greenwich.**—At last week's meeting of the board of works the Greenwich Committee recommended, and it was agreed, that the engineer be authorised to expend a further sum of £100 in the execution of the work of relaying and making good a sewer in Dinsdale-road.—The St. Paul (Deptford) Committee recommended that so much of the granite cube paving forming the boundary of the Broadway, and extending from Church-street to the western boundary of the London and County Bank premises, as is repairable by the board be taken up and the stones redressed and relaid at an estimated cost of £200. This was agreed to. The tender of Messrs. Mowlem & Co., for £1,811, was accepted for paving as a new street that portion of Trundley's-road, Deptford, extending from Rolt-street to Neckar bridge.—A letter from the London County Council stated that, as the council were about to adjourn for the summer recess, the Bridges Committee were unable to fix an earlier date than September 28th, at 3 o'clock, when they would be prepared to receive a deputation from the board on the subject of a tunnel between Rotherhithe and Shadwell. The consideration of the matter was deferred until the next meeting of the board.

**Islington.**—The vestry, on the 5th inst., referred to the Public Health Committee for consideration a letter from the London County Council on the subject of establishing a bacteriological laboratory.—It was decided to refer to the Works Committee for consideration and report a letter received from the Batterses Vestry on the subject of the powers of district surveyors, and the desirability of those gentlemen being in the direct employ of the county council.—Mr. W. F. Dewey, the vestry clerk, read a letter from the Batterses Vestry notifying the application made by the latter to the county council in favour of powers being conferred upon local authorities to erect artisans dwellings under part iii. of the Housing of the Working Classes Act. The vestry asked that Islington should take a similar step, but it was resolved to take no action in the matter.—The Vestry of St. Margaret and St. John, Westminster, wrote, in reference to the Workmen's Compensation Act, that, owing to the vacation the present was an inopportune time for holding the proposed conference to consider the question of a mutual scheme of insurance for the metropolitan local authorities. The letter was referred to the General Purposes Committee.—The vestry clerk reported the receipt of approval of the Treasury to the borrowing of £4,460 for the erection of a chapel at the cemetery.— In reply to Mr. Tomkins, Mr. Gordon, chairman of the Electric Lighting Committee, stated that smoke-consuming devices were being fixed at the electric light station, and that the committee had not censed the contract for Welsh coal, but that the contractors gave notice as long ago as the beginning of April that they could not supply that class of coal, owing to the strike. On the presentation of the estimate for the lighting rate for the ensuing half-year, Mr. James submitted that a reduction should be made in the charge for public lighting, he contending that the electric light works did not in reality yield any profits, but that the apparently satisfactory position was due to the excessive sum of £40 per lamp per annum charged for public lighting. In reply, Mr. Fearnhead stated that the Electric Lighting Committee would, no doubt, lower the price at an early date. It was further mentioned that the question of a refuse destructor was under the consideration of a committee.—On the recommendation of the Parliamentary Committee, it was decided to convene a conference in the autumn to consider the subject of the reform of the local government of the metropolis, and particularly the provisions of the Metropolis Management Act Amendment Bill, introduced by Mr. Thomas Lough, M.P. The committee further stated that in connection with the question of the suggested establishment of a fund against fire and other insurances, they had considered the advisability of insuring the whole of the several fire risks of the vestry with one of the leading fire insurance companies, with a view to the saving of trouble and expense, and that after considering the quotations of several of the leading offices, they had accepted that of the Commercial Union Assurance Company, which had undertaken the whole of the insurances at an annual premium of £283 1s. 9d., and had agreed to allow a commission of 15 per cent. on regularly appointed agent, thereby further lessening the cost to the vestry.—The Works Committee recommended that a portion of Holloway-road should be paved with hardwood, at a cost of £6,500. The Works Committee further reported having considered the Metropolitan Management Acts Amendment (By-Laws) Bill, introduced into the House of Lords by Lord Monkswell, presumably at the instigation of the London County Council, whereby it is proposed to extend the powers of the council,

under sec. 202 of the Metropolis Management Act, 1855, to enable the council to make by-laws for the following purpose: "Requiring persons about to construct, reconstruct, or alter drains in connection with buildings, to deposit with the sanitary authority of the district such plans, sections and particulars as may be necessary for the purpose of ascertaining whether such construction, reconstruction, or alteration is in accordance with the statutory provisions relative thereto, and with any by-laws made under the said section." Whilst agreeing that powers to make such by-laws should be obtained, the Works Committee expressed the opinion that they should be granted to the local authorities rather than to the London County Council.—The following tenders were accepted for the supply of horse forage during August : Mr. Geo. Rose, Little Hollingbury, seven loads of hay, at 75s. per load, and twelve loads of straw, at 36s. per load : Messrs. Gingell, Son & Co., Whitechapel High-street, E., seven loads of clover, at 97s. per load, and seven loads of mixture, at 82s. per load ; Messrs. Pattison & Co., 123 High-street, E., 140 quarters of oats, equal to sample No. 1, at 16s. 10d. per quarter ; and Mr. G. W. Stemp, 58 New Corn Exchange, E.C., 1½ tons of mill bran, at 115s. per ton.

**Lambeth.**—At a meeting of the vestry on the 4th inst. Mr. Baldwin moved the appointment of a Special Committee, composed of the chairman of each Standing Committee and two members from each ward, to consider the advisability of erecting a town hall for the parish of Lambeth, to fix the site thereof, and to obtain designs and estimates for the same. An amendment to this motion, proposed on behalf of Mr. Corbin, was moved and eventually carried appointing a Special Committee to consider the possibility of increasing the vestry office accommodation on the present site, or the necessity of erecting a town hall for the parish.—A letter was read from Messrs. William Webb & Co. intimating that the application to the Light Railway Commissioners for an order authorising a light railway from Herne Hill to Farnborough would not be proceeded with.—It was resolved to forward to the county council a copy of a report of the Sanitary Committee, stating that the vestry did not consider it advisable to include street litter within the provisions of the council's by-laws, prescribing the hours of removal of offensive matter and the construction of the carts for conveying such material.—The surveyor had reported to the Sewers Committee the receipt from the county council of a plan and application by Messrs. Lapthorne & Co., on behalf of Messrs. Atkinson & Co., for permission to erect a warehouse at Messrs. Atkinson & Co.'s premises, Addington-street, to abut upon Sapphire-place at the rear. It appears that Sapphire-place is only 5 ft. wide, and it was proposed to erect buildings fronting it at a height of 27 ft. The vestry decided to ask the county council to disapprove the plan.—The Wharf and Cleansing Committee reported having considered the question of partially covering the dust-vans while engaged in the clearance of dust, and that they had directed the surveyor to inquire of the surveyors to the various metropolitan local authorities whether, in their opinion, it was advisable to fit the vans with revolving iron covers. The majority of the answers received were against the iron covers, and the committee therefore directed the surveyor to fit a van with circular iron stays, to which an ordinary canvas cover can be attached, so that one-half of the van may be covered while the men are filling the van from the side nearest the pavement. The committee inspected the van which had been fitted in accordance with their instructions, and they recommended the vestry to sanction the whole of the vans engaged in the removal of dust being so fitted, at a cost of about 30s. per van. This was agreed to.—Last February the vestry sanctioned the purchase of four news and distributors, who, in response to advertisements, the following tenders were received by the Wharf and Cleansing Committee, who, owing to the winter being practically over, allowed the matter to remain in abeyance : Four-wheel machines—W. Smith & Son, Barnard's Castle, £42 10s. each ; Glover & Son, Warwick, £44 ; Wadsworth & Son, Halifax, £57 10s. and £60. Two-wheel machines—James Mell\ug, New Broad-street, E.C., £29 ; W. Smith & Son, £31 ; Glover & Son, £32 ; Bristol Waggon Company, Bristol. £35 ; Wadsworth & Son, £42 10s. and £34 10s. The Wharf Com. mittee stated that they had again considered these tenders and tried to obtain sample machines from the makers for inspection, but were unsuccessful, and recommended the vestry to order one two-wheeled sand distributor from Messrs. Glover & Co. (the makers of the machine now in use), at a price of £32. The committee further recommended that, if this machine gave satisfaction, the order for the other three machines should be given to the same company. These recommendations were adopted.—At the suggestion of the Wharf Committee, the vestry accepted the tender of Messrs. Guerrier, Marshall & Co., of 40 York-road, S.E., for the supply of 100 quarters of oats, to weigh not less than 38 lb. per imperial bushel, at 15s. 6d. per quarter of 304 lb. The other firms who tendered were : A. & W. Aste, Old Barge House Wharf, Blackfriars, 15s. 3d. per quarter ; C. & J. Denny, 37 Belvedere-road, 16s. 1½d. per quarter ; E. Rathbone & Son, 19 Newington-causeway, 16s. 6d. per quarter ; J. Husband &

Co., Acorn Wharf, Wapping, 16s. 9d. per quarter; D. N. Howell & Co., Belvedere-road, S.E., 15s. 9d. per quarter; H. Passmore & Co., 33 Mark-lane, S.E., 16s. 3d. per quarter; A. Keevil, Brixton Granaries, S.W., 15s. 9d. per quarter; Gould Brothers, Stratford, 16s. 9d. per quarter; S. H. Wells & Son, 61 Millbank-street, S.W., 17s. per quarter; G. W. Stemp, 39 Seething-lane, 17s. 3d. per quarter; and W. A. Pattison & Co., 123 High-street, Borough, 16s. 8d. per quarter.

**Marylebone.**—At the meeting on the 4th inst. the surveyor was empowered to accept a tender for the ventilation of the wash-houses. A letter was read from the county council stating the proposal of the council to apply for Parliamentary powers to establish a bacteriological laboratory and appoint experts, or make arrangements whereby medical officers could obtain the examination by a competent bacteriologist of material from suspected cases of infectious disease, with a view to aiding in the diagnosis. As the council asked for the views of the vestry, it was resolved to refer the letter to the Sanitary Committee for consideration.—The question of wood paving was again brought forward, consequent upon the difficulty of obtaining early deliveries of both soft and hard wood blocks, and, on the suggestion of Mr. Dennis, the Works Committee were authorised to enter into contracts for supplies so as to be ready to commence the work in the spring. It was resolved, on the recommendation of the Sanitary Committee, to inform the Vestry of Clerkenwell, in reply to their letter in favour of drainage plans of new buildings being submitted to local authorities before the commencement of the work, that the practice is already in operation in Marylebone.—The same committee reported in regard to the reference as to the desirability and practicability of constructing an underground public convenience in Marylebone-road by Edgware-road, that the large number of gas and water mains on the site appeared to render the construction of a convenience impracticable.—On the motion of Mr. Morris, it was resolved to instruct the surveyor to prepare a report on the respective merits of hard and soft wood blocks for paving purposes.—It was decided to accept the tender of Mr. Frank Saunders for scraping down, preparing for and painting the public urinals, externally and internally, with two coats of paint, for the sum of £34 17s. 6d.; that of Mr. George Smith, of 6 Henry-street, St. John's Wood, for painting railings of Paddington-street and St. John's Grounds, and the greenhouses and frames in St. John's Ground, for the sum of £108; and that of Messrs. Thorpe & Salter, amounting to £102, for the substitution of Maskelyne automatic penny-in-the-slot locks for the existing registering locks to the water-closets at the public conveniences.

**St. James, Westminster.**—The Public Health Committee recommended that underground conveniences for both sexes should be built in Broad-street, and that the Health Committee should obtain plans and estimates for carrying out the work. The recommendation was adopted.—The Parliamentary Committee reported that they had considered a letter from the Vestry of Battersea, stating that they had decided to take action with a view to the water supply being vested in the people of London, and that, before deciding as to the steps to be taken in the matter, they would like to have the opinions of the various metropolitan local authorities on the subject. On the recommendation of the Parliamentary Committee, the vestry resolved to inform the Battersea Vestry that they were not prepared to express any opinion on the subject at the present time.—It was also resolved to take no action in regard to the request of the Islington Vestry for an expression of opinion on the subject of the Metropolis Management Acts Amendment (By-Laws) Bill, which proposes to authorise the county council to make by-laws relating to the construction and laying of drains.—The General Purposes Committee reported having considered a letter referred to them from the Vestry of Battersea, stating that they had addressed a letter to the London County Council, asking them to insert a clause in their next General Powers Bill, empowering the local authorities to erect dwellings under part iii. of the Housing of the Working Classes Act, 1890. On the recommendation of the committee it was resolved to inform the Battersea Vestry that the vestry concurred with their action.—A long discussion took place on the report of the Works Committee, in reference to the request of the National Telephone Company to place its wires underground. The committee recommended that, subject to the submission of an amended plan for laying its wires underground, and to the omission of a condition in regard to future extensions, the vestry should grant the application on the company agreeing to pay an annual rental of 7s. 6d. in lieu of the 5s. offered for each separate exchange subscriber's line. An amendment, moved by Mr. Cheney, was eventually carried by thirteen votes to seven votes, agreeing to call a conference of adjoining local authorities in order to discuss their respective action in the matter.—Among the letters received was one from the Vestry of Clerkenwell, drawing attention to the fact that, with respect to new buildings erected to plans approved by the district surveyor or the county council, application is frequently made to the vestry, after the building is up, to modify the by-laws relating to water-closets, soil pipes, &c., it being found difficult or impossible to comply with them. The Clerkenwell Vestry suggested that it might be advantageous if the attention of builders were drawn, through the county council, to the necessity of making application to the

local authority before commencing to build, submitting details as to proposed drains, &c., and asked the vestry to co-operate in the matter. The letter was referred to committee. —A communication was also received from the Battersea Vestry stating that they have had under consideration the recent serious accidents which have taken place on buildings in course of erection and alteration, and have informed the county council that they are of opinion (1) that all district surveyors should devote the whole of their time to the duties of district surveying, (2) that they should be paid a salary by the county council, and that all building fees (if continued) should be paid to the council direct, and (3), that an office should be provided for the district surveyor at the local vestry hall, so that he may be brought into closer touch with the local authorities.—The following tenders were opened for cleansing, painting and other work at the vestry hall: S. & S. Dunn, 31 Brewer-street, £430; H. & E. Lee, Warwick-street, £445; G. Fosley, King-street, Regent-street, £467; Johnson & Manners, Great Pulteney-street, £469 10s.; G. A. Row, York-street, St. James'-square, £488; C. W. Knight, Marlborough-mews, £495; R. & J. Shires, £496; H. Faulkner & Co., Jermyn-street, £497; and Bywaters, King-street, Regent-street, £545. The tender of Messrs. S. & S. Dunn was accepted.

# PROVINCIAL AND GREATER LONDON AUTHORITIES.
## COUNTY COUNCILS.

**Brighton.**—The Pavilion Committee on Friday submitted tenders received for carrying out certain alterations and additions to the gentlemen's cloak-room and lavatory at the Pavilion, and recommended the acceptance of that of Mr. V. P. Freeman, of Kensington-street, Brighton, to perform the work for the sum of £320. The recommendation was adopted.

**Cheshire.**—Sanction was on Thursday given to the expenditure of £1,202 for the making of roads in connection with the extension of the county asylum at Upton. A statement showed that the complete extension would probably cost £90,197.—The medical officer, in a report on the alleged pollution of the river Weaver, stated that there could be no doubt of the river being polluted, or that it gave off an effluvium. A large amount of the pollution appeared to be brought in with the Leighton brook, which received much of its pollution from Crewe. The Nantwich urban district was still putting its sewage into the river Weaver. It was resolved to call the attention of the Town Council of Crewe and the Urban Council of Nantwich to the complaint, and to request them to prevent the pollution.

**Northumberland.**—The county surveyor, Mr. H. S. Kynnersly, has received a communication stating that the Earl of Tankerville has consented to make a gift of the land necessary for the improvement of Turvelaw bridge.

**Surrey.**—The county lunatic asylum at Brookwood being overcrowded, the county council have authorised the extension of the building, so as to provide for 350 additional patients. The council have also authorised the purchase of the Netherne House estate, near Coulsdon, containing 153 acres, as a site for another asylum. The new asylum will cost £250,000.

## MUNICIPAL CORPORATIONS.

**Bideford.**—Colonel Durnford, R.E., recently held an inquiry, on behalf of the Local Government Board, relative to an application of the town council for power to borrow £1,050 for diverting and culverting a "hill" adjoining the town marshes, filling in the original trench and constructing a road across it, the improvement reclaiming about 4 or 5 acres of land for the use of the public. In 1896 permission was granted to borrow £1,500 for the culvert, but the lowest estimate was £1,836. It was considered best to proceed with the work, which with engineer's fees, &c., ran up to £2,112. There were, in addition, maintenance money £208, cost of roadway £200, and incidental £29, or a total of £2,500. Mr. G. B. Latham, representing Mr. Baldwin Latham, in explaining the proposals, said that the original contract was for a rubble stone culvert. There was some difficulty with regard to the stone; brick and concrete were substituted. Instead of a 12-in. stone culvert they had brick and concrete of 14 in., thus compensating for the change. Owing to the unsatisfactory nature of the ground, it was found necessary to increase the excavation and place a bed of concrete 1 ft. in depth and 8 ft. in width, which considerably enlarged the expense. At the conclusion of the inquiry the inspector paid a visit to the river bank and culvert.—The town clerk last week decided to apply to the Local Government Board for sanction to borrow £250 for removing some old boat steps at the end of the quay and sloping the face in unison with the remainder of the river bank. Plans for the alteration were submitted by the borough surveyor.—It was also decided to apply for a further sum of £260 to complete the filling of the Pill.

**Bournemouth.**—The council have decided to petition the county council to declare Winborne, Holdenhurst, Queen's and Lansdowne roads main roads, and it is thought that in case of refusal the town council's case for making Bournemouth a county borough will be strengthened. The tender of Messrs. Macfarlane has been accepted for electric light standards. The council have refused to take the drainage of a portion of the Branksome urban district, and have refused to entertain a proposal to make the fever hospital free.

**Bristol.**—The town council have adopted a recommendation of the Docks Committee in favour of going to Parliament for powers to construct a new lock and other works at Portishead dock, so as to provide accommodation for the largest classes of steamers afloat or building. The estimated outlay is £350,000. An amendment to the effect that the dockisation of the river Avon was defeated by forty-one votes to twenty-one.

**Cardiff.**—Mr. R. H. Bucknell, Local Government Board inspector, attended at the town hall, Cardiff, last week, for the purpose of inquiring into an application by the corporation for the sanction of the board for borrowing the sum of £14,500 for the purpose of establishing a fish market on the eastern side of Working-street, £6,220 for the alteration of Roath market, and £2,965 for street improvements in Llandaff-road and Leckwith-road. Formal evidence was given for the corporation. There was no opposition, and the inspector will report the application in due course to the Local Government Board.

**Cheltenham.**—The following will shortly be discussed by the council : " That, whereas the present distribution of the fund available for technical instruction in Cheltenham secures quite inadequate results for the money spent, this council is of opinion that the time has arrived when steps should be taken to establish a school of technical instruction under the control of the Corporation of Cheltenham, and hereby requests the Technical Education Committee to forthwith consider and prepare a scheme for the establishment of such school."

**Coventry.**—The first instalment of the electric lamps which are to illuminate the principal streets of Coventry has been erected, and was for the first time lit up on the 20th ult. It is an arc light of 2,000 candle-power, and is fixed on an ornamental post in the centre of the crossing refuge which is being laid down at the corner of Eaton-road and Warwick-road. The light is 20 ft. from the ground, and the post is to be neatly painted, so that when completed the erection will add in some degree to the appearance of the road in question. It is the first of forty lights of the same power which are to be fixed in a line from the station to the top of Bishop-street, and from Fleet-street to Jordan Well, at distances of from 70 to 80 yards apart. The other parts will be of the same height as the one at the Eaton-road corner, but will be of an overhung type, the arc lamps being suspended from a curved bracket and hanging 2 ft. lower. The lights will be all of the same illuminating power.

**Darlington.**—It has been decided to proceed with Prof. Kennedy's scheme of electric lighting, at a cost of £25,000.

**Douglas.**—Prof. Fleming has, at the request of the corporation, presented a report with regard to the lighting of Douglas by electricity. His report is in favour of such lighting by the corporation, and he adduces the following grounds: The profits accruing go to the ratepayers, monopolies of the kind should be in the ratepayers' hands, private consumers will be sure of fair treatment, the prospects for electric lighting in Douglas are encouraging, and the extra expenditure produces a superior illumination, of which the public get the benefit. The estimated cost is in the neighbourhood of £30,000.

**Gloucester.**—At the last quarterly meeting of the city council, the chairman of the Markets Committee having referred to the suggestion that a wholesale fruit market should be established, it was resolved that a sub-committee be appointed to consider and report as to the advisability of establishing a market or auction for the sale of fruit and other agricultural produce.

**Halifax.**—The Improvements Committee have decided to recommend the corporation to consider the construction of a road 60 ft. wide, from Queen's-road, via Shroggs-park, to Ovenden Cross, at an approximate cost of £130,000, conditional upon the free grant of the required land by all the owners, and that the borough engineer be instructed to prepare detailed plans and estimates.

**Heywood.**—Last week, at Heywood, Colonel Hepper, a Local Government Board inspector, held an inquiry relative to the application of the town council for powers to borrow £10,000 for the purposes of the gas undertaking. The money is required for land, new store-room and stables at the gasworks, and for new mains and penny-in-the-slot gas meters. It was explained that a large demand was anticipated for this kind of meter.

**Hull.**—The Works Committee, at a recent meeting, accepted the tender of Mr. Brumby Robinson, amounting to £656 9s. 5d., for the channelling and paving of Smeaton-street and Silvester-street. Mr. J. Sangwin's tender for the same work in connection with Beverley-road—namely, £147—and Elm. terrace, amounting to £363, were also accepted.

**Leeds.**—The following resolution has been adopted by the council : " That the corporation, in pursuance of sec. 59 of the Leeds Electric Supply Order, 1891, do give notice in writing to the Yorkshire House-to-House Electricity Com-

pany, Limited (being the undertakers for the purpose of the said order), requiring them forthwith to sell to the corporation their undertaking upon the terms contained in sub-sec. 1 of the said sec. 59."

**Liverpool.**—The Insanitary Property Committee of the corporation met on the 29th ult. A resolution was adopted instructing the city surveyor to report as to the suitability of land belonging to the committee, situate between Dryden-street, Rachel-street and Virgil-street, for the erection thereon by the committee of dwellings suitable for the accommodation of persons who have been dispossessed through the demolition of insanitary property, the dwellings to be similar in character to those erected from the designs of the building surveyor in Gildart's-gardens and Fore-street. The surveyor was also instructed to report as to the probable cost of and income from such dwellings, and whether they should be erected by contractors or by the corporation. The committee further resolved to request the surveyor to make a report as to whether the committee had any land in the south end of the city suitable for similar houses.—At a recent meeting of the Tramways Committee a report of the manager, with respect to establishing a central belt omnibus route between Netherfield-road North and Princes-road, was approved, and the following resolution was passed : " That the question of continuing the present tramway service from Princes Park gates along existing lines in Princes-road, Catherine-street, Leece-street and Renshaw-street during the relaying of the lines in Upper Warwick-street, be referred to the chairman, Councillor Rutherford, the city engineer and the manager."

**Ludlow.**—At the last monthly meeting of the council a letter was read from the Local Government Board denying that they had sanctioned the borrowing of money by the Town Council of Exeter in respect of their scheme for treating the sewage of the city by the septic tank system alone, and repeating that so far as the Ludlow scheme was concerned the board would not be satisfied with the provision of less land than that which they were originally prepared to accept—viz., 7 acres.

**Ramsgate.**—The following has been adopted : " That the council do offer three premiums—viz., £50, £20 and £10 for competitive designs for dealing with the surplus land belonging to the corporation under and in front of the Paragon Gardens."

**Rotherham.**—On the recommendation of the Gas Committee, the town council, at their last quarterly meeting, accepted the tender of Messrs. W. Thornton & Son, for £2,325, for the conversion of an existing gasholder tank into a tar and liquor storage well, and also for the putting in of foundations for new purifiers, &c., in connection with the gasworks extensions.

**Salford.**—The council, without discussion, last week passed a resolution authorising an application to borrow £38,500 for the purchase of the infantry barracks site in Regent-road, and also adopted a proposal to apply for power to borrow £2,500 to cover the balance of the cost of completing the erection and fitting-up of the spinning and weaving department at the Royal Technical Institute.

**Scarborough.**—All hope of having the marine drive round Scarborough Castle Hill finished next year, according to contract, has been practically abandoned. One-third of the wall is not yet completed, and it is doubtful whether half the length of foundation will be laid before the winter. In these circumstances the town council will apply to Parliament next session for a provisional order to extend their borrowing powers for twelve months from the 12th August next year.

**Southend.**—We hear that a plan for converting the unsightly mud foreshore at Southend into a sand parade has been submitted for approval. The proposal is to fill in the space—which is at present useless for sea or land purposes—to above high-water mark, so as to be available at all times of the tide. It is stated there are no engineering difficulties to overcome, and little more than unskilled labour would be necessary, so that the cost would be small for making one of the finest seaside promenades in the kingdom.

**St. Helens.**—On Friday, at the St. Helens town hall, Colonel A. J. Hepper, D.S.O., R.E., held an inquiry, on behalf of the Local Government Board, into the application by the corporation for the sanction of the board to the borrowing of £2,500 for the construction of a storm-water overflow in Liverpool-road, £5,000 for the construction of a subway in Church-street and Ormskirk-street, and £900 for works of paving. At the close of the inquiry the town clerk thanked the inspector for his attention, after which the inspector proceeded to visit the sites of the works mentioned.

**Swansea.**—A singular condition of things has come to light respecting a decision of the corporation to enlarge one of their storm outlets on the foreshore. The enlargement was deemed necessary on account of the constant flooding during wet seasons of Wellington and other streets, but when the workmen engaged under the present contract were digging up the old pipes it was found that a wreck that occurred at the spot many years ago had dislodged one of them, with the result that the intervening space had become completely filled up with sand. Several copper bolts from the wreck have been picked up around the pipe.

**Taunton.**—Mr. H. H. Law, Local Government Board inspector, has held an inquiry with reference to an application from the town council for sanction to borrow £11,500 for purposes of electric lighting. Evidence in support of the application was given by the mayor and others, and opposition was offered by Mr. C. P. Clarke, for the gas company, Mr. C. Smith and Mr. J. Standfast.

**Wolverhampton.**—The Lighting Committee on Thursday recommended that the tender of Messrs. Callender's Construction and Cable Company, Limited, for the supply and laying of mains, at an estimated cost of £898 12s. 1d., and also that the tender of Messrs. Willcock & Co., amounting to £379, for the construction of a new sub-station adjoining the Exchange Hall, be accepted. The recommendations were adopted.—In pursuance of a report presented to and adopted by the council on the 14th March last the Sewerage Committee were empowered to carry out the various sewerage works therein enumerated, at a total estimated cost of £4,561.

**Worthing.**—At the suggestion of the mayor the surveyor was last week requested to submit specifications and estimates for paving the carriageway in Chapel-road, adjoining the town hall, with wood blocks or cork pavement.

**Wrexham.**—On Thursday Mr. W. A. Ducat, Local Government Board inspector, held an inquiry at the Guildhall, Wrexham, respecting an application by the Wrexham Town Council for sanction to borrow £1,250 for the purposes of street improvement. Evidence in support of the application was given by the mayor, the borough surveyor, Mr. J. W. M. Smith, the assistant town clerk, Mr. J. W. Rogers and Mr. Councillor Charles Davies. Mr. Llewellyn Adams, clerk to the Denbighshire County Council, attended on behalf of that body to watch their interests, one of the streets proposed to be improved being a county main road. There was no opposition to the proposed loan.

## URBAN DISTRICT COUNCILS.

**Aldershot.**—The district council have accepted the tender of Mr. Thomas Turner, of Blackwater, Hants, amounting to £1,306, for the making-up, &c., of St. Michael's-road, St. George's-road and St. Joseph's-road.

**Corton.**—The district council having purchased a plot of land for a cemetery for the district, the ceremony of cutting the first sod was performed on Thursday afternoon by Mr. W. T. Showell, chairman of the Cemetery Committee. In addition to the members of the council and a number of invited guests, there was a large gathering of residents of the district. The land, which is known as Waterhouse Farm, is 17 acres in extent, and has been purchased for £4,800.

**Heaton Norris.**—At a meeting of the district council recently it was unanimously decided to apply to the Board of Trade for a provisional order for the purpose of supplying and lighting the district with electricity. It was stated that an agreement had been come to with the Manchester Corporation for the supply at the same cost to consumers as it was used in Manchester.—Further complaints were made as to what was described as the horrible condition of Black brook, alleged to be polluted from the Reddish district, and to be so serious as to hourly menace the health of people living in the locality. The attention of the Reddish council had been repeatedly drawn to the matter, but nothing had been done, and the chief engineer to the Mersey and Irwell Joint Committee, replying to the Heaton Norris council's letter, now wrote that the pollution ought to have been stopped long ago. Numerous letters from householders, and a strong complaint from the medical officer, were read, and the council decided to take legal proceedings against the Reddish urban authority if steps were not immediately taken to remedy the nuisance.

**Horsforth.**—At a recent meeting of the district council a letter was read from Messrs. North & Son, solicitors to the waterworks company, informing the council that they were unwilling sellers, but they would sell at the terms sanctioned by Parliament and no other. They did not believe in the exclusion of 10 per cent. compensation for compulsory purchase. After a lengthy discussion it was proposed that the council should purchase the works on the company's terms. It would, it was urged, bring an end to these unseemly wrangles. The water company were now supplying better water than recently. When the motion was put no one voted against it, and the chairman declared it carried. The proposal is now to be placed before the ratepayers for them to vote upon it. The council consider that the purchase will be the best way out of a serious difficulty, but they expect strong opposition from the ratepayers when the time for the poll arrives.

**Levenshulme.**—At the last monthly meeting of this body the proceedings of the General Purposes Committee, which were adopted, contained the following resolution: "That the clerk be and is hereby directed to write to the Local Government Board informing them that at recent inquiries held in this council's district manholes were not required on the surface drains, and, further, that the council cannot see the utility of placing manholes on the surface drains, and that if their present demands were insisted upon it would have the effect of preventing this council from carrying out private

street improvement."—On the recommendation of the General Purposes Committee the council passed a resolution to grant £50 to the Technical Instruction Committee of the district for technical instruction purposes during the coming winter session.—A Local Government Board inquiry was held on Wednesday week by Colonel A. J. Hepper, an inspector of the Local Government Board, into the subject-matter of an application by the council for permission to borrow £4,434 for main road improvements and to defray the cost of a recreation ground for the district.

**Moss Side.**—A Board of Trade inquiry was held on Thursday into the subject-matter of an application made by the district council for permission to borrow £13,000 to meet the cost of tramway extensions now in progress in the district. There was no opposition to the application. The £13,000 is needed to meet the cost of extensions of the tramway lines along the following roads in the district: Withington-road, Raby-street, Moss-lane East, Princess-road, Denmark-road and Upper Lloyd-street. The work is already in progress, and will be completed in about three months hence.

**St. Anne's-on-the-Sea.**—The council last week decided to assemble at an early date for the purpose of adopting a scheme for having the town lighted by electricity, Royal assent having been given to the provisional order.

**Stretford.**—The council at a recent special meeting decided by resolution that notice should be given to the Manchester Carriage and Tramways Company, that directly the statutory term of the lease of twenty-one years expired, it was the intention of the council to purchase the tramways in the district. A resolution was also passed proposing in the next session of Parliament to promote a Bill empowering the council to work the tramways by mechanical power, including electrical haulage, and that it was their intention to use the necessary cars and other plant. Also to give the council power to borrow money for relaying the lines and adapting them for electrical haulage, and work the system singly or in conjunction with other local authorities.

**Swinton and Pendlebury.**—Recent minutes of the General Purposes Committee, which were approved, stated that a communication had been received from the Local Government Board setting forth that with regard to the council's application for sanction to borrow the sum of £7,470 for works of private street improvements the board had considered the further representations of the council on the subject, but they adhered to the decision conveyed in their letter of May 6th last withholding their sanction until the council acquired more land for sewage purification purposes.—It has been announced that a report has been received from the Mersey and Irwell Joint Committee as to the effluents from the council's sewage works, classing the effluent from the Swinton works among "good effluents," and that from the Pendlebury works among "fair effluents."

**Yeadon.**—At a meeting of the council on Wednesday week a letter was read from Messrs. Bond, Barwick & Peake, solicitors, stating that their clients, the Misses Stansfield, of Esholt Hall, would not sell the site of the present sewage works, nor would they on any account whatever allow a destructor to be erected there. The works had been such a constant nuisance, and were in such an unsuitable position, that the owners did not feel disposed to give any facilities for their extension, and reserved their rights to require them to the closed if the present condition of affairs continued. The letter went on to say that the Misses Stansfield were prepared to sell or lease 20 acres of land adjoining the river for disposal works, the price to be, if purchased, £250 per acre, and if leased £7 per acre, and they would grant an easement for the continuation of the sewer down to such land. It was resolved to hold a special meeting of the council in committee to discuss the proposals.

## RURAL DISTRICT COUNCILS.

**Orsett.**—Colonel C. H. Luard, R.E., Local Government Board inspector, held an inquiry last week into an application of the council to borrow £6,000 for the improvement of the roads in Little Thurrock and Chadwell St. Mary.

**Pershore.**—The General Purposes Committee last week recommended that an application should be made to the Local Government Board to postpone dealing with the question of the sewerage and water supply of Pershore until after the report of the Royal Commission. The minutes were adopted.

**St. Faiths.**—A letter has been received by the council from Mr. Collins, the city engineer of Norwich, intimating the city's willingness to accept the offer of the district council for the repair of Sandy-lane, Hellesdon, at a cost not exceeding £250, to be borne in equal shares.

**Aberdeen.**—At a recent meeting of the town council the Finance Committee reported that if the fish market wharf were extended into the waterway, along Market quay, for the extension of the market the additional cost would be about £6,850. The committee again recommended the adoption of the Market-street site as the most suitable. The matter was remitted back to the committee.

## Personal.

Mr. James Arthur, inspector of cleansing to the Dundee Corporation, has had his salary increased to £300 per annum.

Crewe Town Council have decided to raise the salary of Mr. George Eaton-Shore, the borough surveyor, from £300 to £350 per annum.

A proposal to increase the salary of the manager of the Barnhurst sewage works of the Volverhampton Town Council to £150 has been approved.

Mr. William Higginson Schofield, senior district surveyor to the Lancashire County Council, has been appointed county surveyor under the same authority, at a salary of £500 a year, with travelling expenses.

A letter has been received by the Itchen Urban District Council from Mr. Collingwood, the newly-appointed surveyor, stating that he would be prepared to enter upon his duties on Wednesday next, the 17th inst.

At the last meeting of the Sudbury Town Council it was resolved that a substantial honorarium should be granted to the borough engineer, Mr. T. W. A. Hayward, for extra services rendered in connection with the waterworks.

Mr. H. P. Maybury, surveyor to the Malvern Urban District Council, presided recently at a dinner given in connection with an outing of the town employees to Weston-super-Mare. The proceedings passed off very successfully.

Mr. H. M. Bairstow, late assistant and formerly articled pupil to Mr. Robert Hunter, of the Chester gasworks, has been appointed assistant manager at the corporation gasworks, Darwen, in succession to Mr. H. Davies, who has been appointed assistant at Colne.

Mr. D. M. Price, of Ferndale, who has for the past twelve months held the post of assistant surveyor and sanitary inspector at Blaenau Festiniog, has, out of the forty-nine applicants, been appointed sanitary inspector to the Upton-upon-Severn Rural District Council, Worcestershire.

At a special meeting of the Audenshaw Urban District Council, on the 3rd inst., the scheme designed by Mr. J. P. Wilkinson, A.M.I.C.E., of Arcade Chambers, St. Mary's Gate, Manchester, for the sewerage of the district, was unanimously approved and adopted. The estimated cost is £14,500.

The resignation is announced of Mr. J. E. Stewart, the electrical engineer for the borough of Derby. Mr. Stewart has obtained another appointment, and the Electric Lighting Committee recommend that a successor to him should be advertised for, at a salary of £350, with the right to take two pupils.

Wolverhampton Town Council have selected Mr. Charles E. C. Shawfield to fill the post of borough electrical engineer, at an annual salary of £200. The appointment, which was unanimously agreed to, was strongly urged, the sound character of Mr. Shawfield's past services being specially referred to.

The County Council of Lancashire on Thursday adopted the report of a Special Committee recommending the appointment, as county bridgemaster, of Mr. William Harold Radford. Mr. Radford, who succeeds his father, will be allowed a salary of £1,000 per annum, with the addition of travelling expenses and staff.

On Thursday, at a meeting of the Cheshire County Council, Mr. William Holland, surveyor of the Wirral district of the council, was appointed as assistant county surveyor. The appointment was made chiefly for the purpose of supervising and verifying the work done on the main roads, which the various urban councils and municipal boroughs have retained in their own hands.

Some discussion was recently given by the Saddleworth (Yorks) Rural District Council to a proposal to advertise for a surveyor to supervise the roads, and take charge of all the main roads and parish highways in the district, to superintend the execution of repairs on the roads and highways under the direction of the council, and prepare such plans and estimates as might be required by the council.

At a meeting of the Neston and Parkgate Urban District Council, held on Wednesday of last week, Mr. J. Bourne was unanimously appointed to fill the office of surveyor and inspector of nuisances for the district, the present surveyor, Mr. H. W. Corrie, having accepted an appointment under the Lower Bebbington District Council, Mr. Bourne resigning a similar position under the Little Woolton Council in favour of the Neston vacancy.

Mr. Frederick J. Wool, A.M.I.C.E., has been appointed county surveyor for East Sussex, in succession to Mr. Henry Card, and will take up his duties on October 1st. The salary is £400 per annum, with allowances for clerks, &c., and there were eighty-one candidates. Those were reduced to four, who were interviewed by a sub-committee. Mr. Wool, the successful one of the four, is thirty-five years of age, and is at present a district surveyor under the Lancashire County Council.

The Waterworks Committee of Lincoln Corporation have resolved by a large majority to recommend the council to appoint Mr. J. H. Teague to the vacant post of waterworks engineer, at a salary of £250 per annum. The appointment has been confirmed by a meeting of the council in committee. Mr. Teague is a son of the late Mr. Teague, who filled the position worthily for a great many years. He has been superintending the department since his father's death. He has already been in the employment of the corporation for more than a quarter of a century, and he is practically acquainted with every branch of the work.

Preston Town Council, at a recent meeting, passed the following resolution : " That this council receives with very deep regret the announcement of the death of Mr. Hudson Reah, C.E., who for twenty years held the office of borough surveyor, and for seventeen years was engineer and steward to the corporation, during which time he ably carried out important works ; and this council desires to place on record their high appreciation of the valuable services rendered by him, and that the mayor be requested to convey to Mrs. Reah this expression of the sincere sympathy and condolence of the council with her and her family in their bereavement."

Seventy-eight applications for the appointment of building inspector having been received by the Gloucester City Council, a sub-committee were recently appointed to consider the qualifications of the applicants and select not less than six for the consideration of the Improvement Committee. The six applicants subsequently attended before the committee, and were questioned as to their qualifications and experience. After throwing out all the applications except two—namely, Mr. Philip Lewis, of Gloucester, and Mr. E. A. Newton, of Clapham Junction—a show of hands was taken, which showed a majority in favour of Mr. Newton. The committee were recommended to appoint Mr. Newton, at a salary of £2 2s. a week, the appointment to be determinable by a month's notice on either side.

At a meeting of the St. Mary Church Urban District Council, held on Thursday, Mr. Wm. Stringfellow, A.M.I.C.E., surveyor to the Eastleigh (Hants) Urban District Council, was appointed to the vacant post of surveyor. Mr. Stringfellow, who holds the certificate of the Association of Municipal and County Engineers, has an excellent record. After serving four years in the office of the Southampton surveyor, he acted as chief assistant for three years to the borough surveyor and water engineer of Cheltenham, Mr. Joseph Hall, who was formerly surveyor of Torquay. Mr. Stringfellow successively acted as surveyor at East Stonehouse (the chairman of which, Mr. W. W. Blight, gives him an excellent testimonial), East Cowes, and Eastbigh, and from the latter place he came direct to St. Mary Church.

Mr. H. T. Wakelam, the newly-appointed county surveyor of Middlesex, received his professional training through the ordinary routine of pupilage with the late Mr. Benjamin Baker, borough engineer, of Wolverhampton, with whom he gained an excellent all-round experience. On the expiration of his articles in February, 1879, he was appointed assistant under Mr. Baker, holding that office about two years, and was then unanimously elected, from seventy-nine candidates, assistant borough surveyor of the seaport town of King's Lynn. During the seven years spent with Mr. Baker he was continually engaged in the preparation of plans, surveys, &c., and in the supervision of the works carried out. After his election by the Town Council of King's Lynn in February, 1881, he was appointed to superintend the new sewage scheme for that town under Mr. W. H. Wheeler, M.I.C.E., and he was also engaged upon the ordinary work of the borough, and in the supervision of the town hall and other buildings. As surveyor at King's Lynn he remained about two years, being then elected in May, 1883, from 110 candidates, borough and water engineer for the Town Council of Oswestry. During five years at Oswestry he was engaged in the management of the borough public buildings, markets, waterworks, &c., and in the latter part of his time there he acted as resident engineer of the new water storage reservoir. In 1888 he was elected, from 131 candidates, engineer and surveyor of the rapidly-increasing district of Garston, Liverpool. Mr. Wakelam left the Garston district in 1892 upon being appointed county surveyor by the Herefordshire County Council, which office he held prior to his appointment in Middlesex.

London Municipalities.—A meeting of the conference of representatives of the metropolitan vestries concurring in the proposal for the establishment of municipalities in London was held on Friday, at the Westminster Town Hall, to receive a report from the committee appointed by the conference on Monday, June 27th, upon the following reference : " That the draft Bill of Sir J. Blundell Maple, Bart., M.P., L.C.C., and the Bill introduced by Mr. Thomas Lough, M.P., be referred to a committee for consideration, with authority to bring up a draft Bill embodying the best provisions of both, as also to introduce other provisions and to report to the conference ; and that Sir Blundell Maple be invited to attend the meetings of the committee."

## LAMBETH VESTRY AND THE KENNINGTON BATHS.

### LETTER FROM THE ARCHITECT.

In a recent issue (see THE SURVEYOR, p. 157) reference was made to the notice of motion given by Mr. F. S. Price in favour of the appointment by the Vestry of Lambeth of a committee of five members to report generally upon the question of the new baths in Kennington-road, and particularly upon several points mentioned by Mr. Price. The attention of the architect (Mr. A. Hessell Tiltman) having been drawn to the matter, that gentleman has addressed the following letter to Mr. H. J. Smith, the vestry clerk :—

" It is the case that the estimate of £55,000 made in the commissioners' report of March 25th, 1895, correctly included my current estimate for the new baths in the Kennington-road. This estimate (as did every estimate submitted by me to the commissioners) included the approximate cost of boilers, machinery and fittings necessary for the working of the establishment, with the exception of the plant for the junction of the electric current for lighting purposes then contemplated to be taken from the adjoining company's supply.

' It is also a fact that when the tenders were invited for the ordinary builder's work, the boilers, machinery and general engineering work was not included in the specification and quantities supplied. These, as they must necessarily be tendered for upon their own specification and quantities, were intentionally left out by me in accordance with my invariable practice for the past few years.

" This separation of tenders for two such differing classes of work is the only reasonable and fair way of dealing with such contracts, having regard to the interest of the rate-payers, and the increasing importance and cost of the various engineering installations involved. It was also more especially necessary, as within the last five or six years public authorities have almost universally determined to have the benefit of public competition for the engineering as well as for the structural portion of the work. Even the amounts of such engineering contracts could not be included as a provision in the main and structural contract, as this course would have involved the payment twice over for the quantities.

" There has been no intentional reticence or concealment in the matter. Until very recently I have been entirely under the impression that the commissioners knew of the separation of tenders ; but my letters, although showing clearly that this impression was in my mind, still do not convey in themselves sufficient knowledge of the intention of the commissioners, and I am confident from this and other incidents that they never so understood it."

On the motion of Mr. Price, the vestry last week decided to refer the letter to the Baths Committee for report.

## NEW COUNTY HALL FOR DURHAM.

The members of the Durham County Council on the 25th ult. formally took possession of a new county hall, which will add to the architectural beauties of the city, while at the same time affording accommodation under one roof for the many departments of the council's work.

The structure, which occupies a site in Old Elvet, has cost a sum approaching £30,000. The façade is a handsome one, dominated by a domed tower over the main entrance, which is approached by an imposing flight of steps. The building is an exception among the other public edifices of the city, in the fact that Ruabon red terra-cotta has been used instead of stone in the execution of the architect's designs. This course, though provoking some criticism, has effected a saving of about £3,000. Around the entire length of the hall, which has a frontage of over 200 ft., runs a splendid balustrade. In the centre is the main entrance, through an elaborately enriched archway, approached by a fine flight of Mansfield stone steps, some 30 ft. in width. The grille is richly wrought in hammered iron, after passing which is seen the grand staircase. Its steps are of marble, while the balustrade is of terra-cotta, and the supporting columns of polished white Parian. Upon the ground floor are the council chamber and committee-rooms and the offices of the county clerk. The council chamber is a handsome and convenient apartment. Around the walls are marble columns, panels and carving, and each of the windows is filled with stained glass, representing the arms of the county and of a number of the different boroughs in the Palatinate. Accommodation is provided for 100 members, in addition to the officers and press. The architects were Messrs. H. Barnes & F. Coates, of Sunderland and Hartlepool, and the contractors Messrs. D. & J. Ranken, Sunderland.

## APPOINTMENTS VACANT.

*Advertisements which are received too late for classification cannot be included in these summaries until the following week.*

BUILDING ASSISTANT FOR THE WORKS DEPARTMENT.—August 13th.—London County Council. £300.—Mr. C. J. Stewart, clerk to the council, County Hall, Spring-gardens, London, S.W.

QUANTITY TAKER FOR THE WORKS DEPARTMENT.—August 13th.—London County Council. £3 10s.—Mr. C. J. Stewart, county clerk, County Hall, Spring-gardens, London, S.W.

GENERAL FOREMAN OF WORKS.—August 15th.—Corporation of the City of Canterbury. £2 2s.—Mr. A. H. Campbell, city surveyor.

INSPECTOR OF NUISANCES.—August 15th.—Highworth and Swindon Rural District Council. £120.—Mr. John P. Kirby, clerk to the council.

SURVEYOR AND INSPECTOR OF NUISANCES.—August 17th.—South Hornsey Urban District Council. £250.—Mr. Edward B. Bennett, clerk to the council.

INSPECTOR OF SEWERS. — August 18th.—Corporation of Coventry. £2.—Mr. J. E. Swindlehurst, city engineer and surveyor.

SURVEYOR.—August 18th.—Carmarthen Town Council. £180.—Mr. J. H. Bodoel Roberts, town clerk.

QUANTITY SURVEYOR.—August 19th.—Aylesbury Urban District Council.—Mr. J. H. Bradford, surveyor to the council.

ARCHITECTURAL ASSISTANT.— August 19th.— Beckenham Urban District Council. £3 3s.—Mr. J. A. Angell, surveyor to the council.

SECOND ENGINEERING ASSISTANT.—August 22nd.—Edmonton Urban District Council.—Mr. Wm. Francis Payne.

CLERK OF WORKS.—August 22nd.—London County Council. £5 5s.—Mr. R. W. Partridge, clerk of the Asylums Committee.

CIVIL ENGINEERING ASSISTANT.—August 23rd.—Corporation of the City of Hull. £85.—Mr. A. E. White, city engineer.

ENGINEERING ASSISTANT.—August 27th.— Burton-upon-Trent Corporation.—Mr. George T. Lynam, borough engineer and surveyor.

ELECTRICAL ENGINEER.—August 27th.—Corporation of Ashton-under-Lyne. £250.—Chairman, Electricity Committee.

INSPECTOR OF NUISANCES AND SURVEYOR.—September 6th.—Little Woolton Urban District Council. £110.—Mr. Percy Dobell, clerk to the council.

CONSULTING ENGINEER.—Buckley Urban District Council. —Mr. G. H. Simon, clerk to the council.

PRIVATE STREET WORKS ASSISTANT.—County Borough of Wolverhampton. £2 5s.—Mr. J. W. Bradley, borough engineer and surveyor.

## COMPETITIONS.

*Advertisements which are received too late for classification cannot be included in these summaries until the following week.*

ST. PANCRAS.—August 25th.—Erection of public baths and wash-houses.—Mr. C. H. J. Barrett, vestry clerk.

PLYMOUTH.—September 24th.—Erection of shops and dwelling-houses fronting Tavistock-street. £250.—Mr. J. H. Ellis, town clerk.

WIVENHOE.—September 19th.—Works of drainage and water supply, for the urban district council.—Mr. C. W. Denton, clerk.

REIGATE.—October 6th.—Erection of municipal buildings, fire station, public offices, &c.—Mr. Clair J. Grece, town clerk.

## MUNICIPAL CONTRACTS OPEN.

*Advertisements which are received too late for classification cannot be included in these summaries until the following week.*

THORNHILL (Yorks).—August 13th.—Supply of flushing valves, manhole and lamphole covers, &c., for the urban district council.— Mr. S. W. Parker, surveyor to the council.

HEPSLEY.—August 13th.—Laying and jointing of about 6,150 yard of 3-in. cast-iron pipes, also fixing and walling-in of about twenty valves and hydrants for the Templenewsam and Thorpe Stapleton water supply, for the rural district council.—Mr. W. B. Pinder, clerk to the council.

DEWSBURY.—August 13th.—Excavators' work required in the construction of a tank at the gasworks, Savile Town.—Mr. H. Dearden, M.I.C.E., borough surveyor.

WARE.—August 13th.—Execution of sewerage works at Stanstead Abbots, for the rural district council.—Mr. G. H. Gisby, clerk.

SPENNYMOOR.—August 13th.—Kerbing, cement and tar paving, for the urban district council.—Mr. T. Badcock, clerk.

PENISTONE.—August 15th.—Sewerage, pier, road and other works.— Mr. William Spinks, 30 Park-row, Leeds.

WASHINGTON.—August 15th.—Supply of 500 yards of 2¼-in. hose piping.—Mr. Thomas Longden, borough surveyor.

BIRKENHEAD.—August 15th.—Painting.—Mr. Alfred Gill, town clerk.

SHEFFIELD.—August 15th.—Extension of car sheds, consisting of two-span steel roof, car pits, stores, boundary wall, latrines, foreman's house, &c., at Tinsley.—Mr. Charles F. Wike, city surveyor.

HASTINGS.—August 15th.—Supply of 120,000 9-in. by 3-in. by 4-in. jarrah wood paving blocks.—Mr. P. H. Palmer, M.I.C.E., borough engineer.

GLOUCESTER.—August 15th.—Erection of an infectious diseases hospital at Over.—Mr. Geo. Sheffield Blakeway, town clerk.

SHOREDITCH.—August 15th.—Erection of a new battery-room, boiler-house and extension of offices at the electricity supply station, corner-street.—Mr. B. Mansfield Robinson, vestry clerk.

IRONHILL.—August 15th.—Erection of boundary walls, the railing kerbing, paving and channelling of footpaths, and other works opposite the town hall, for the urban district council.—Mr. George Ball, A.M.I.C.E., surveyor to the council.

ROMSEY.—August 16th.—Erection of a concrete retaining wall in the Abbey.—Mr. the Borough Surveyor.

PENROSE.—August 16th.—Erection of buildings and foundations in connection with the township electric light works, for the commissioners.—Mr. Robert Hammond, 64 Victoria-street, London, S.W

WOLVERHAMPTON.—August 16th.—Supply of cast-iron, wrought-iron and steel work required for structural and other purposes at the swimming bath and assembly hall to be erected in Bath-place.—Mr. J. W. Bradley, borough surveyor.

CROSLEY.—August 16th.—Supply of gas meters.—Mr. J. Mills, town clerk.

SWINTON.—August 16th.—Erection of cells, &c., and alterations to police office, for the county of Lancaster.—Mr. H. Littler, architect, County Offices, Preston.

SOYLAND.—August 16th.—Supply of street materials.—Mr. John Wadsworth, surveyor.

HALIFAX.—August 16th.—Laying of about 400 yards super. of setting at King's Cross, for the rural district council.—Mr. F. Gordon, Clifton, Brighouse.

CROSLEY.—August 16th.—Supply of cast-iron mains.—Mr. J. Mills, town clerk.

BIRKENHEAD. — August 17th.—Sewering, kerbing and levelling Osborne-road.—Mr. Charles Brownridge, borough surveyor.

SHIPLEY.—August 17th.—Construction of sewage works, for the urban district council.—Mr. M. Paterson, 36 Manor-road, Bradford.

ILKESTON.—August 18th.—Construction of a new filter-bed at the Little Hallam works.—Mr. H. J. Kilford, borough surveyor.

BARNSTAPLE.—August 18th.—Construction of concrete impounding sewer, for the urban district council.—Mr. Frank W. Chanter, engineer.

BIRKENHEAD.—August 19th.—Sinking a bore-hole in connection with proposed pumping station.—Mr. W. A. Richardson, water engineer.

MANCHESTER.—August 19th.—Construction of seven public urinals. The City Surveyor.

COSSART.—August 20th.—Kerbing, channelling, cementing and macadamising works.—Mr. William S. Shell, surveyor to the urban district council.

TONBRIDGE.—August 20th.—Supply of 1,000 tons of best quality 2 in. broken quartzite, Guernsey granite, &c.—Mr. A. H. Neve, junr., clerk to the urban district council.

RUGBY.—August 20th.—Works of street making and sewer construction, for the rural district council.—Mr. T. W. Willard, surveyor.

SOUTHBOROUGH.—August 20th.—Street works, for the urban district council.—Mr. Philip Hanmer, clerk.

HAMPTON.—August 20th.—Supply and delivery of a 10-ton steam roller, for the urban district council.—Mr. John Kemp, A.M.I.C.E., surveyor to the council.

OXFORD.—August 22nd.—Supply and laying of cast-iron and stoneware pipe carriers, brick and concrete work in manholes and distributing chambers, land drainage, embanking, road making and other works on land adjoining the corporation sewage farm.—Mr. R. Bacon, town clerk.

TEDDINGTON.—August 22nd.—Making-up of Clarence-road, for the urban district council.—Mr. M. Hainsworth, surveyor to the council.

STEVENAGE.—August 22nd.—Supply of 500 tons of 1½-in. broken Guernsey, Leicester or other granite, for the urban district council.— Mr. William Onslow Times, clerk to the council.

LITHERLAND.—August 22nd.—Flagging works, for the urban district council.—Mr. W. B. Garton, surveyor.

GLASGOW.—August 22nd.—Supply of rails and fish-plates.—Mr. John Young, tramways manager.

WILMSLOW.—August 22nd.—Construction of about 1,300 yards of 15-in. and 12-in. earthenware pipe sewers, &c., for the urban district council. —Mr. John Bowden, 14 Ridgefield, Manchester.

MILTON.—August 23rd.—Supply of road materials, for the urban district council.—Mr. A. B. Acworth, surveyor.

WALTHAMSTOW.—August 23rd.—Erection of public baths, for the urban district council.—Mr. E. J. Cowen, clerk to the council.

TORQUAY.—August 23rd.—Repair of the masonry apron and foreshore at the Haldon breakwater.—Mr. Henry A. Garrett, A.M.I.C.E., harbour engineer.

TYNEMOUTH.—August 23rd.—Paving works.—Mr. John F. Smellie, borough surveyor.

GOOLE.—August 23rd.—Paving with hard wood about 3,750 square yards of roadway, for the urban district council.—Mr. Geo. England, clerk.

BUCKLOW.—August 23rd.—Works of levelling, paving, metalling, channelling and making good a street at Hale, for the rural district council.—Mr. J. M'Kenzie, surveyor.

CARSHALTON.—August 23rd.—Supply of 200 tons of broken 1-in. Quenast or Guernsey granite and 620 yards of hand-picked flints, for the urban district council.—Mr. W. W. Gale, A.M.I.C.E., surveyor to the council.

ISLEAM.—August 23rd.—Construction of an underground latrine in The Broadway, for the urban district council.—Mr. Herbert Shaw, A.M.I.C.E., surveyor to the council.

ROTHERHAM.—August 23rd.—Construction of sewers, outfall works, and other works connected therewith, for the corporation.—Mr. R. N. W. Berrington, Bank Buildings, Wolverhampton.

CARSHALTON.—August 23rd.—Widening of High-street, for the urban district council.—Mr. W. W. Gale, A.M.I.C.E., surveyor to the council.

WOKING.—August 24th.—Supply of sludge-pressing machinery, steam engines and other apparatus, for the urban district council.—Mr. R. Mossop, clerk.

HALIFAX.—August 24th.—Excavation and formation of tramway track.—Mr. Edward R. S. Escott, borough engineer.

TREFOR.—August 24th.—Flagging, paving and other works.—Mr. V. W. Leithwaite, surveyor to the urban district council.

HALIFAX.—August 24th.—Supply of steel rails, points, crossings, fish-plates, &c., for about 5 miles of tramway.—Mr. Edward R. S. Escott, borough engineer.

NELSON.—August 24th.—Supply of cast-iron pipes, special castings, valves, &c., for the Water Committee.—Mr. J. Hartley, waterworks manager.

SHOREDITCH.—August 24th.—Construction of about 333 lineal feet of 18-in. pipe sewer in Britannia-street (City-road end), for the vestry.— Mr. J. Rush Dixon, A.M.I.C.E., engineer and surveyor to the vestry.

CARLISLE.—August 24th.—Laying of socket-jointed sewer pipe from Moorville to Knowefield Gates, for the rural district council.

HALIFAX.—August 24th.—Supply of best Portland cement for tramway works.—Mr. Edward R. S. Escott, borough engineer.

HULL.—August 25th.—Supply and erection of electric lighting plant. —Mr. A. S. Barnard, city electrical engineer.

HACKNEY.—August 25th.—Supply and delivery of Portland cement required for works of wood paving.—Mr. James Lovegrove, chief surveyor.

TUNBRIDGE WELLS.—August 25th.—Supply of edge kerbing.—Mr. W. C. Cripps, town clerk.

SPRINGFIELD.—August 25th.—Erection of technical college at Greenterrace.—Mr. F. M. Howey, town clerk.

DARWEN.—August 25th.—Erection and construction of iron and steel buildings in connection with a refuse destructor.—Mr. Charles Costeker, town clerk.

HAWORTH.—August 25th.—Conversion of stone gasholder into a tar and liquor tank, for the urban district council.—Mr. W. Robertshaw, clerk.

MORLEY.—August 25th.—Construction of brick culverts, together with manholes, storm-water overflow and other works.—Mr. W. E. Putman, borough engineer and surveyor.

WILMSLOW. — August 26th. — Sewering, kerbing, metalling and channelling.—Mr. William Cobbett, town clerk.

MORLEY.—August 26th.—Manufacture, delivery and erection of a steel girder bridge, to carry cast-iron pipes.—Mr. W. E. Putman, borough engineer and surveyor.

NELSON.—August 27th.—Supply of 550 lineal yards of wrought-iron unclimbable fencing.—Mr. B. Hall, borough engineer.

CLEATON MOOR.—August 28th.—Providing and laying 3,000 superficial yards of asphalte at the Market-place, for the urban district council.— Mr. R. Robertson, surveyor.

WIMBLEDON.—August 25th.—Supply of pipework, for the urban district council.—Mr. A. H. Preece, 39 Victoria-street, S.W.

SHEFFIELD.—August 29th.—Construction and erection of additional buildings in connection with the destructor at Attercliffe.—Mr. Charles F. Wike, city surveyor.

BURTON-UPON-TRENT.—August 31st.—Supply, construction and erection of foundations, arches, fire-brick work and furnace brickwork for retorts.—Mr. F. L. Ramsden, manager and engineer.

NORWICH.—September 3rd.—Making-up of roads.—Mr. Arthur K. Collins, city engineer.

NORWICH.—September 3rd.—Making-up of Mousehold-street, Cavalry-street, Anchor-street, Wadlonone-street and Tracey-road.—Mr. Arthur E. Collins, A.M.I.C.E., city engineer.

DERBY.—September 5th.—Construction of a covered service reservoir at Littleover.—Mr. H. F. Gadsby, town clerk.

ROCHDALE.—September 6th.—Electric lighting plant.—Mr. James Leach, town clerk.

ALDERSHOT.—September 6th.—Supply of 2,000 tons of granite (more or less), for the urban district council.—Mr. W. E. Foster, clerk.

ALDERSHOT.—September 6th.—Supply and delivery of a Morrison's scarifier, for the urban district council.—Mr. W. E. Foster, clerk.

ALDERSHOT.—September 7th.—Metalling Albert-street, West End, for the urban district council.—Mr. W. E. Foster, clerk.

BIRMINGHAM.—September 13th.—Construction of aqueducts.—Mr. E. O. Smith, town clerk.

MALDENS AND COOMBE.—Supply of road materials, for the urban district council.—Mr. Thomas V. H. Davison.

SWANAGE.—Main sewerage and works connected therewith.—Messrs. Newman & Cocks, 3 Thomas-street, Ryde.

---

## TENDERS.

*ACCEPTED.

CARMARTHEN.—For the supply of 530 yards of 6-in. cast-iron pipes, 42 2½-in. fire hydrants and ten flanged and socketted junction pipes. —Mr. F. J. Finglah, borough surveyor :—

| The Isca Foundry Company, Newport | £225 |
| J. Mackwan, Glasgow | 221 |
| The Old Foundry Company, Carmarthen | 219 |
| H. Baker-borough & Sons, Brighouse, Yorks | 216 |
| J. Davies, Carmarthen | 209 |
| T. Spittle, Limited, Newport | 207 |
| The Stanton Ironworks Company, Nottingham* | 147 |

ILFORD.—For the construction of a section of sewer to be laid in Ilford-lane and Natal-road, for the urban district council.—Mr. Herbert Shaw, A.M.I.C.E., surveyor to the council :—

W. Gibbs & Co., Ilford ;* Glenny, Barking ; D. T. Jackson, Barking ; J. Jackson, Forest Gate ; G. Bell, Tottenham ; Wilson, Border & Co., Canning Town ; and J. Adams & Co.

LEICESTER.—For the extension of the borough lunatic asylum.—Mr. G. T. Hine, F.R.I.B.A., architect, Parliament-street, London :—

| J. E. Johnson & Son, Leicester | £71,846 |
| J. C. Kellett & Son, Leicester | 65,950 |
| Parnell & Sons, Rugby | 65,055 |
| T. Herbert, Leicester | 62,800 |
| Moss & Son, Loughborough* | 58,716 |
| Herbert & Sons, Leicester (withdrawn) | 57,092 |

LEWES.—For the supply of 600 tons of 2-in. broken blue Guernsey, Cherbourg or Belgian granite, 100 tons of coarse granite screenings, 650 tons of broken surface-picked flints and 150 tons of Piddinghoe gravel.—Mr. Montague S. Baker, town clerk :—

H. L. Cooper, Mark-lane, E.C.—Monmarte granite, 11s. per ton ; Monmarte screenings, 10s. 3d. per ton ; Cherbourg granite, 11s. 9d. per ton ; Cherbourg screenings, 11s. 3d. per ton.
J. Runnalls, Penzance.—Penlee granite, 11s. 8d. per ton ; Penlee screenings, 6s. 6d. per ton.
A. & F. Manuelle, London.—Guernsey granite, 12s. 7d. per ton ; Sommerfeld screenings, 6s. 10d. per ton.
L. Sommerfeld, Great Tower-street, E.C.—Guernsey granite, 12s. 9d. per ton ; Guernsey screenings, 6s. 9d. per ton.
W. Griffiths, London, E.C.—Guernsey granite, 12s. 9d. per ton ; Guernsey screenings, 10s. 4d. per ton.
R. L. & J. Feinings, Wellington Chambers, S.E.—Blue Guernsey granite, 13s. 6d. per ton ; blue Guernsey screenings, 10s. 9d. per ton.
Fry Brothers, Greenwich.—Blue Guernsey granite, 12s. 9d. per ton ; Blue Guernsey screenings, 10s. 3d. per ton.
J. Nowlson & Co., Westminster, S.W.—Guernsey granite, 11s. 11d. per ton* ; Guernsey screenings, 8s. 11d. per ton.*
E. Smith, Edenbridge.—Flints, 9s. per ton.
W. Hudson, Brighton.—Flints, 8s. 9d. per ton.
T. F. Smith, Lewes.—Flints, 7s. 6d. per ton.
R. Brown, Lewes.—Flints, 7s. 6d. per ton.* Delivered on streets as required.

SOUTH SHIELDS.—For building boundary walling, with palisading and entrance gates, at the North Marine Park.—Mr. S. E. Burgess, A.M.I.C.E., borough engineer :—

| S. Sheriff, South Shields | £611 |
| Thornton & Co., South Shields | 501 |
| H. H. Partridge, South Shields* | 475 |
| J. Foster, South Shields | 1s |

SOUTH SHIELDS.—For painting work at the North and South Marine Parks.—Mr. S. E. Burgess, A.M.I.C.E., borough engineer :—

W. Laidler, South Shields* ...

SOUTH SHIELDS.—For painting work at the West Park.—Mr. S. E. Burgess, A.M.I.C.E., borough engineer :—

| C. Thompson, South Shields | £** |
| T. Dalton, junr., South Shields | ** |
| W. Laidler, South Shields* | ** |

SOUTH SHIELDS.—For the laying of 185 lineal yards of double-line steel girder tramway, electrical bonding and paving therete.—Mr. S. E. Burgess, A.M.I.C.E., borough engineer :—

| | |
|---|---|
| Laing, Wharton & Down, London | £2,377 |
| Thornton & Co., South Shields | 1,313 |
| G. E. Simpson, Newcastle | 1,001 |
| A. Brunton & Son, Edinburgh* | 660 |

SOUTH SHIELDS.—For repaying works at the Market-place.—Mr. S. E. Burgess, A.M.I.C.E., borough engineer :—

| | Aberdeen. | Norway. |
|---|---|---|
| M. D. Young, Hexham | £1,056 | £1,056 |
| G. E. Simpson, Newcastle | 784 | 784 |
| Thornton & Co., South Shields* | 732 | 716 |

SOUTH SHIELDS.—For wood paving works in St. Hilda's School-road.—Mr. S. E. Burgess, A.M.I.C.E., borough engineer :—

| | |
|---|---|
| M. D. Young, Hexham | £160 |
| G. E. Simpson, Newcastle | 115 |
| Thornton & Co., South Shields* | 86 |

ST. GEORGE-IN-THE-EAST.—For the supply of 300 tons of 3-in. by 7-in. Aberdeen granite pitchings, and 30 tons of 5-in. by 7-in. Guernsey granite pitchings, for the vestry.—Mr. H. Thompson, clerk to the vestry :—

| | Guernsey. | | Aberdeen. | |
|---|---|---|---|---|
| | Per ton. | | Per ton. | |
| | s. | d. | s. | d. |
| W. Gibbs, Limehouse, E. | 37 | 6 | 36 | 0 |
| Mowlem & Co., Westminster, S.W. | 37 | 0 | 36 | 6 |
| A. & F. Manuelle, Gracechurch-street, E.C. | 36 | 6 | 34 | 6 |
| W. Griffiths, Bishopgate-street Without, E.C. | 37 | 0 | 35 | 6 |
| Samuel Juckett & Sons, King's Cross, N.* | 39 | 6 | 32 | 6 |
| R. L. & J. Jennings, London-bridge, S.E. | 27 | 0 | | |

SWINTON.—For the supply of 520 yards of cast-iron socket pipes of 6-in. diameter and other pipe castings, for the urban district council.—Mr. R. Fowler, engineer and surveyor to the council :—

| | 4-in. Pipes. | | | 6-in. Pipes. | | |
|---|---|---|---|---|---|---|
| | Per ton. | | | Per ton. | | |
| | £ | s. | d. | £ | s. | d. |
| J. & S. Roberts, West Bromwich | 5 | 13 | 0 | 5 | 8 | 9 |
| J. Lees, Manchester | 5 | 15 | 0 | 5 | 10 | 0 |
| Stanton Ironworks Company, near Nottingham | 5 | 12 | 6 | 5 | 10 | 0 |
| J. B. Cooring, Glasgow | 5 | 12 | 6 | 5 | 9 | 6 |
| E. & W. H. Haley, Bradford | 5 | 10 | 0 | 5 | 5 | 0 |
| J. Ritchie, Middlesbrough | 5 | 3 | 9 | 5 | 2 | 0 |
| Sheepbridge Coal & Iron Company, Chesterfield* | 5 | 0 | 0 | 4 | 15 | 0 |

TUNBRIDGE WELLS.—For the supply of 500 tons of clean Cherbourg quartzite.—Mr. W. C. Cripps, town clerk :—

Mountsorrel Granite Company (Mountsorrel granite).—15s. per ton.
Mountsorrel Granite Company (Stoney Stanton granite).—14s. 9d. per ton.
L. Somerfeld, 14s. 5d. per ton.
Kent Road Maintenance Company.*—14s. per ton.
J. Runnalls (Penlee stone).—13s. per ton.

WALSALL.—For the construction of about 6,500 yards of 9-in. and 12-in. stoneware pipe sewers and 1,800 yards of 8-in. cast-iron hydraulic main in connection with the sewerage of the parish of Ald-ridge, for. the rural district council.—Mr. J. Edward Willcox, Union Chambers, 65 Temple-row, Birmingham :—

| | |
|---|---|
| J. Biggs, Birmingham | £6,603 |
| R. Holloway, Wolverhampton | 5,600 |
| J. Ford & Hudson, Coalville | 5,479 |
| J. Ford, junr., Coalville | 5,479 |
| Carroll, Lewis & Martin, Birmingham | 4,793 |
| G. Low, Kidderminster | 4,670 |
| J. Mackay, Smethwick | 4,488 |
| T. Vale, Stourport* | 4,295 |

WEST HAM.—For the making-up of Freemantle-road, Haslemere-road, New-street (Plaistow) and Old-street (Plaistow).—Mr. Lewis Angell, borough engineer :—

| | |
|---|---|
| R. Ballard, Limited, Kilburn | £4,125 |
| B. W. Glenny, Colchester | 3,962 |
| J. Jackson, Plaistow* | 3,746 |
| W. Griffiths, Bishopgate-street Without, E.C. | 3,701 |
| T. Adams, Wood Green | 3,684 |
| G. Bell, Tottenham | 3,640 |

WEST HAM.—For the construction of the northern and southern in-tercepting sewer.—Mr. Lewis Angell, M.I.C.E., borough engineer :—

| | |
|---|---|
| R. Ballard, Limited, Kilburn | £29,709 |
| W. Neave & Son, Paddington | 23,834 |
| B. Cook & Co., Westminster | 23,281 |
| R. Jackson, Finsbury Park | 22,638 |
| T. Adams, Wood Green | 22,432 |
| J. Jackson, Plaistow | 20,330 |
| C. W. Killingback & Co., Camden Town | 19,991 |
| Pedrith & Co., Finsbury Park | 19,976 |
| G. Bell, Tottenham | 18,800 |
| Clift Ford, Harlesden* | 17,715 |

WEST HAM.—For the supply of ten slop-carts.—Mr. Lewis Angell, M.I.C.E., borough engineer :—

| | |
|---|---|
| Barrows & Co., Limited, Banbury | £201 |
| E. & H. Hora, Limited, Peckham-road | 200 |
| W. Constable & Son, Paddington Green | 200 |
| E. H. Bayley & Co., Limited, Newington Causeway | 220 |
| W. Smith & Sons, Barnard Castle | 195 |
| W. Glover & Son, Limited, Warwick* | 189 |

## MEETINGS.

### AUGUST.

15.—Institution of Sanitary Engineers : Council meeting at 5 p.m., and special general meeting at 7 p.m. Offices of the Institute, 63 and 64 Chancery-lane, E.C.

## NOTICES.

THE SURVEYOR AND MUNICIPAL AND COUNTY ENGINEER may be ordered direct, through any of Messrs. Smith & Son's book-stalls, or of any newsagent in the United Kingdom. Applications to the Offices for single copies by post must in all cases be accompanied by stamps.

The Prepaid Subscription (including postage) is as follows :

| | Twelve Months. | Six Months. | Three Months. |
|---|---|---|---|
| United Kingdom | 16s. | 7s. 6d. | 3s. 9d. |
| Continent, the Colonies, India, United States, &c. | 19s. | 9s. 6d. | 4s. 9d. |

The International News Company, 83 and 85 Duane-street New York City; The Toronto News Company, Toronto; and The Montreal News Company, Montreal, have been appointed agents in the United States and Canada for the sale of THE SURVEYOR. A thin paper edition is printed for circulation abroad.

---

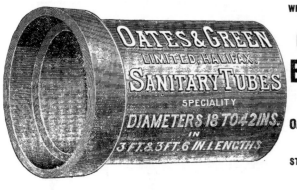

EDITORIAL OFFICES:
ST. BRIDE'S HOUSE, 24 BRIDE-LANE, FLEET-STREET,
LONDON, E.C.

OFFICE FOR ADVERTISEMENTS:
13 NEW STREET HILL, FLEET STREET, LONDON, E.C.

PUBLISHING OFFICES:
13 NEW STREET HILL, FLEET STREET, LONDON, E.C.

## APPOINTMENTS OPEN.

CITY OF HULL.
The Corporation require a Civil Engineering Assistant in the City Engineer's office, at £85 per annum.
It is essential that candidates should be quick and neat draughtsmen.
Applications, stating age, experience and qualifications, are to be delivered to the undersigned on or before Tuesday, the 23rd August.
Testimonials need not be sent in the first instance.
(By order)
A. E. WHITE,
City Engineer.
Town Hall, Hull.
July 30. 1898.

BUCKLEY URBAN DISTRICT, FLINTSHIRE.
The Council of the above district are desirous of engaging an Engineer, to consult on the question of sewage and sewage disposal for the whole district, and to make a report to the Council thereon (excluding plans, details, &c.), for a fixed fee.
Applications should be sent at once to the undersigned.
G. H. SIMON,
Clerk to the Council.
August 9, 1898.

BOROUGH OF BURTON-UPON-TRENT.
Wanted, in the Borough Engineer's Office, for about twelve months, an Assistant accustomed to Main Sewerage Work. Salary at the rate of £130 per annum.
Applications, stating age, experience and how soon disengaged, accompanied by copies of three recent testimonials, must be lodged with me not later than Saturday, the 27th inst.
GEORGE G. LYNAM,
Borough Engineer and Surveyor.
Town Hall, Burton-on-Trent.
August 10, 1898.

LITTLE WOOLTON URBAN DISTRICT
COUNCIL.
INSPECTOR OF NUISANCES AND SURVEYOR.
Applications are invited for the appointment of Inspector of Nuisances and Surveyor for the urban district of Little Woolton, which comprises an area of 1,387 acres, with a population at the last census of 1,131.
The appointment is an annual one, and will be subject to confirmation by the Local Government Board.
The person appointed must be between the ages of twenty-five and forty-five years, and will be required to reside in the district and to devote the whole of his time to the duties of the office.
As inspector he will be required to make thorough periodical inspections of the district, and to perform all duties prescribed by the Public Health and Sanitary Acts and by the Local Government Board; also to prepare all notices, and keep all necessary and usual books and accounts relating to the office.
As surveyor he must be well acquainted with the making of streets, roads and footpaths, the taking of levels and surveys, the management of a sewage farm, the construction and management of sewers and drains, the value of labour and materials (including measuring such materials), and the preparation of plans, specifications and estimates, including the keeping of all books and accounts prescribed by the Local Government Board, and he must generally carry out the instructions of the Council from time to time given.
Preference will be given to candidates holding the certificate of the Sanitary Institute.
The person appointed will be required to commence his duties on the 1st day of November next, and to find an approved guarantee, in the sum of £100, for the faithful discharge of his duties.
The salary will be £110 per annum, and will be apportioned as follows—viz., £50 per annum as inspector and the residue as surveyor.
Sealed applications, in candidate's own handwriting, endorsed "Inspector," stating age, present and previous occupations, and accompanied by copies of not more than three recent testimonials, to be addressed to the undersigned at the undermentioned address, so as to be received not later than Tuesday, the 6th day of September instant.
Canvassing members of the Council, either directly or indirectly, will disqualify a candidate.
PERCY DOBELL,
Clerk to the Council.
5 Castle-street, Liverpool.
August 8, 1898.

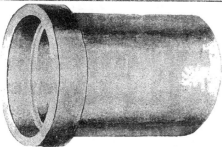

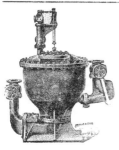

DISTRICT OF SOUTH HORNSEY.
SURVEYOR AND INSPECTOR OF NUISANCES.

The District Council invite applications for the appointment of a Surveyor and Inspector of Nuisances.

The district comprises an area of 230 acres, a population of 17,200 and about 2,430 houses, and is fully developed.

The duties will be those ordinarily required from a surveyor and inspector of nuisances to an urban sanitary authority.

All applicants must satisfy the Council that they are acquainted with the duties of those offices, and must hold the certificate of the Sanitary Institute.

The salary will be as Surveyor £175, per annum, with residence; and as Inspector of Nuisances, £75 per annum, making together £250 a year.

Applications, endorsed "Surveyorship," stating age and qualifications, with particulars of previous experience, and enclosing copies of not more than three recent testimonials, must be received here not later than 5 o'clock p.m. on the 17th of August next.

Personal canvassing will be deemed a disqualification.

EDWARD B. BENNETT,
Clerk to the District Council.

Offices, Milton-road, South Hornsey, London, N.
July 28, 1898.

EDMONTON URBAN DISTRICT COUNCIL.
SECOND ENGINEERING ASSISTANT.

The Edmonton Urban District Council invite applications for the appointment of Second Engineering Assistant in the engineer's office.

The person appointed must have had previous experience in levelling and making surveys and other duties connected with a municipal engineer's office.

The salary will commence at £60 per annum, paid monthly.

Applications, accompanied by not more than three testimonials, to be sent to G. Eedes Eschus, Esq., Town Hall, Edmonton, on or before Monday, August 22nd.

Canvassing will disqualify.

(By order)
WM. FRANCIS PAYNE,
Clerk.

Town Hall, Lower Edmonton.
August 10, 1898.

COUNTY BOROUGH of WOLVERHAMPTON.
Wanted, at once, Private Street Works Assistant, experienced in sewerage and street construction, apportionments, &c. Salary, £2 per week, rising to £2 5s. at the expiration of six months' approved service.—Applications only, in the first instance, to the undersigned.
J. W. BRADLEY, C.E.,
Borough Engineer and Surveyor.
Town Hall, Wolverhampton.
August 4, 1898.

AYLESBURY URBAN DISTRICT COUNCIL.
QUANTITY SURVEYOR.

Applications are invited for the position of Quantity Surveyor, for a few weeks, to assist in taking-off quantities for a sewage disposal scheme.

Candidates must be quick and accurate, and have had experience in similar work.

Applications, in candidate's own handwriting, stating age, experience, qualifications, salary required, and when at liberty, accompanied by not more than three copies of recent testimonials, must be received not later than 10 o'clock a.m. on Friday, August 19th inst., and endorsed "Quantity Surveyor."

J. H. BRADFORD,
Surveyor to the Council.
Surveyor's Offices, Aylesbury.
August 9, 1898.

## COMPETITION.

BOROUGH OF REIGATE.
TO ARCHITECTS.

The Council of the Borough of Reigate invite Competitive Designs for the Erection of Municipal Buildings, Fire Station, Police Offices, &c.

Three premiums are offered, and the conditions of competition, together with a lithographed plan of the site, can be obtained on application to the Borough Surveyor.

All drawings to be addressed to the undersigned, and delivered at my office, 84 Station-road, Redhill, not later than Thursday, the 6th October next.

Given under my hand this 8th day of August, 1898.

(By order)
CLAIRE J. GRECE,
Town Clerk.

## TENDERS WANTED.

**CITY OF NORWICH.**
PRIVATE STREET WORKS.

Tenders are invited for making-up Monschold-street, Cavalry-street, Anchor-street, Wodehouse-street and Stracey-road.

The specifications, plans and sections may be seen, and the bills of quantities and forms of tender obtained, on application at my office.

Tenders, on the forms supplied, accompanied by priced-out bills of quantities, enclosed in sealed envelopes, endorsed "Private Streets," and addressed to the Chairman of the Executive Committee, must be delivered at my office not later than September 3, 1898.

The Corporation does not bind itself to accept the lowest or any tender.

ARTHUR E. COLLINS, A.M.I.C.E.,
City Engineer.

Guildhall, Norwich.
August 2, 1898.

**HAMPTON URBAN DISTRICT COUNCIL.**
STEAM ROAD-ROLLER.

The above Council invite tenders for the supply and delivery of a 10-ton Steam Roller at Hampton, Middlesex.

Tenders, including specification and other particulars, to be sent to the undersigned not later than Wednesday, the 20th day of August, 1898.

Conditions and instructions may be obtained on application in writing.

The lowest or any tender will not necessarily be accepted.

(By order)
JOHN KEMP, Assoc.M.Inst.C.E.,
Surveyor.

Council Offices,
High-street, Hampton-on-Thames.
July 30, 1898.

**TO CONTRACTORS.**
SWANAGE SEWERAGE.

Persons desirous of tendering for the Main Sewerage of Swanage, including the construction of about 221 yards of 27-in. iron outfall sewer, 970 yards of 27-in. and 30-in. rock concrete, and 3,932 yards of 9-in., 12-in. and 15-in. stoneware pipe sewers, with the requisite valve chamber, manholes, lampholes, ventilation shafts, flushing tanks and works connected therewith, are requested to communicate with the Engineers, Messrs. Francis Newman & Cooke, 5 St. Thomas'-street, Ryde, who will supply information as to quantities, time for tendering, &c.

Ryde.
August 10, 1898.

**ALDERSHOT URBAN DISTRICT COUNCIL.**
SCARIFIER.

The above Council are prepared to receive tenders for the supply and delivery at Aldershot of a Scarifier of the type known as Morrison's. The scarifier must be capable of being attached to and worked by a 10-ton steam roller. A separate price is required for the work of fixing, &c., to the steam rollers. The contractor must give a full description of the machine with his tenders. Full particulars may be obtained of the Surveyor.

Tenders, to be endorsed "Scarifier," are to be delivered at my office not later than the 6th day of September.

The Council do not bind themselves to accept the lowest or any tender.

The contractor must state when he will undertake the delivery. This is important.

(By order of the Council)
W. E. FOSTER,
Clerk.

Aldershot.
August 5, 1898.

**ALDERSHOT URBAN DISTRICT COUNCIL.**

Tenders are hereby invited by the above-named Council for a supply of 2,000 Tons of Granite (more or less) of approved quality, at per ton, in such quantities as the Council may direct.

Samples of the material tendered for, broken to pass through 1½-in. and 2-in. rings, must be forwarded to the Council's Surveyor, at the Council's Offices, Aldershot.

Tenders must state separate prices for the materials broken to the sizes named.

Further particulars may be obtained on application to the Council Surveyor, at the offices aforesaid.

Tenders, endorsed "Tenders for Granite," to be sent to me

at the offices aforesaid not later than Tuesday, the 6th day of September, 1898.

The Council do not bind themselves to accept the lowest or any other tender.

W. E. FOSTER, Clerk.

Aldershot.

August 5, 1898.

# ALDERSHOT URBAN DISTRICT COUNCIL.
TO ROAD CONTRACTORS AND OTHERS.

The Aldershot Urban District Council are prepared to receive tenders for the Metalling, &c., of :—

Albert-street, West End, Aldershot.

Plans and specifications may be seen, and forms of tender obtained, by applying at the office of the Surveyor to the Council, 126 Victoria-road, Aldershot.

Sureties will be required.

Tenders, endorsed "Tenders for New Streets," are to be delivered in a sealed envelope at my office not later than 9 a.m. on Wednesday, the 7th day of September next.

The Council do not bind themselves to accept the lowest or any tender.

(By order)

W. B. FOSTER,
Clerk to the Council.

126 Victoria-road.

August 5, 1898.

# BIRMINGHAM CORPORATION WATER.

*ELAN SUPPLY.—CONTRACT No. 12.—AQUEDUCT.*

TO CONTRACTORS.

The Corporation of Birmingham are prepared to receive tenders from competent persons willing to enter into a contract for the construction of about 17¼ miles of the Aqueduct from Cleobury Mortimer, in the county of Salop, to Hagley, in the county of Worcester. The contract consists principally of providing and laying two lines of cast-iron pipes and laying only two lines of steel pipes, 41 in. in diameter.

The drawings may be seen, and specification and bills of quantities obtained, at the office of the Engineer, Mr. James Mansergh, 5 Victoria-street, Westminster, on and after the 16th inst., on the deposit of cheque or bank note for £20, which will be returned on receipt of a *bonâ-fide* tender with the bills of quantities fully priced out.

Early application for particulars is necessary, as only a limited number will be given out, and none after the 3rd day of September next.

The contractor will be required to undertake not to pay less than the minimum standard rate of wages current in the district in which the works are situate.

Sealed tenders, addressed to me, and endorsed "Tender for Aqueduct, Contract No. 12," are to be delivered at my office (post paid) at or before noon of Tuesday, the 13th day of September next.

The Corporation do not bind themselves to accept the lowest or any tender.

(Signed)

EDWARD ORFORD SMITH,
Town Clerk.

Town Clerk's Office,
Council House, Birmingham.
August, 1898.

# BOROUGH OF DERBY.

*DERBY CORPORATION WATERWORKS.*

CONSTRUCTION OF COVERED SERVICE RESERVOIR.

The Corporation of Derby are prepared to receive tenders for the construction of a Covered Service Reservoir at Littleover, near Derby.

Drawings may be inspected, and copies of the specification and forms of tender may be obtained, on payment of £2 2s., to be returned if a *bonâ-fide* tender be made, on application at the office of the Borough Surveyor, Babington-lane, Derby, and at the office of Messrs. T. & C. Hawksley, civil engineers, 30 Great George-street, Westminster, S.W., on and after Monday, the 25th instant.

Tenders, on the prescribed form, must be delivered with the specification (enclosed in a sealed envelope, endorsed "Derby Corporation Waterworks—Contract No. 2—Tender for Covered Service Reservoir," and addressed to the undersigned), at the Town Hall, Derby, on or before 12 noon on Monday, the 5th day of September next.

The lowest or any tender will not necessarily be accepted.

H. F. GADSBY,
Town Clerk.

Town Hall, Derby.

August 4, 1898.

# The Surveyor

## And Municipal and County Engineer.

Vol. XIV., No. 344.     LONDON, AUGUST 19, 1898.     Weekly, Price 3d.

## Minutes of Proceedings.

**Combined Drainage.** It is a trite observation that the law relating to the subject of combined drainage is in anything but a satisfactory state. Nevertheless, at the risk of wearisome iteration, we venture (à propos of a recent contribution to the numerous cases which, like satellites, are grouped round the statutory definitions of a "drain" and a "sewer") to call attention to some of the anomalies which characterise this subject. To begin with, there is the illogical lack of uniformity in the several definitions applicable to the metropolitan area and to the rest of the kingdom. Under the Public Health Act, 1875, the term "drain" is applicable to a drain used for the drainage of one building only or premises within the same curtilage, and made for communicating with a cesspool, sewer, &c.; while the term "sewer" includes all sewers and drains except "drains" as previously defined, and except drains under the control of a road authority not being a local authority under the Act. Under the Metropolis Management Act, 1855, however, the definition of a "drain" is more extensive, including (in addition to drains as above defined) a drain for draining any group or block of houses by a combined operation under the order of any vestry or district board. Then there is the enigmatical sec. 19 of the Public Health Acts Amendment Act, 1890, extending the meaning of the term "drain" "for the purposes of this section" to a drain used for the drainage of two or more houses belonging to different owners. The purposes of the section are proceedings under sec. 41 of the 1875 Act, which can only be set on foot on the application of a person stating that a drain is a nuisance or injurious to health. And it has been held that, apart from any nuisance, the general liability of the authority to repair a combined drain in repair is not affected by this enactment. Thus it may be said that combined drains to which this section is applicable are "drains" for some purposes and "sewers" for others, which only makes the confusion more confounded. Among the many questions which have from time to time arisen in connection with these various definitions is one which was raised with reference to the drainage of some property at West Cowes—viz., whether, where a sewer is intersected by a cesspool, the latter forms part of the sewer. The question arose under the following circumstances: A number of houses were built having drains leading into a line of 6-in. pipes, intersected by a pit or cesspool, whence the pipes passed under the land of a neighbouring owner. The latter cut off the pipes, with the result that the sewage flowed back and caused a nuisance. The local authority required the owner of the houses to abate the nuisance by cleansing the cesspool. He, however, contended that the cesspool was part of the line of pipes which admittedly constituted a "sewer," and that it was therefore vested in and repairable by the authority; and he brought an action for an injunction to restrain the authority

from causing the nuisance. It was held, however, that the cesspool formed no part of the sewer, and that therefore the action could not be maintained (*Meader v. West Cowes Local Board* [1892], 3 ch., 218). In that case be it noted it was the local authority who contended—and successfully—for the exclusion of the cesspool from the limits of the definition of a "sewer," although apparently it formed an integral part of the drainage system. In the more recent case previously alluded to, however, in which the facts were somewhat more complicated, we find the authority unsuccessfully contending for a contrary view. In this instance thirty-five houses at Tottenham were drained into a series of small cesspools, from which a conduit of stoneware pipes conducted the overflow into a larger cesspool 500 ft. distant. One of the by-laws of the district provided that a person constructing a cesspool should not construct it so that it should have, by drain or otherwise, any outlet into or means of communication with any sewer. The authority (very naturally, it must be admitted) considered that the line of pipes formed a "sewer," and that the owner of the houses had committed a breach of the by-law by connecting the small cesspools with it. It was held, however, that no breach of the by-law had been committed (*Button v. Tottenham Urban District Council*, noted at p. 571 of vol. xiii. of THE SURVEYOR). It will be seen at once that this decision goes far beyond that in the West Cowes case. The latter merely decided that a cesspool is no part of a sewer. The Tottenham case may be said in effect to decide that a drain which would otherwise, according to the definition, be a sewer is not a sewer when cesspools are interposed between it and the houses, the drainage of which it receives. This is a somewhat startling specimen of judicial "interpretation" of legislative enactments, amounting in fact to a very substantial addition to the definition of a drain and a corresponding curtailment of the definition of a sewer. The fact is that the legal distinction between a drain and a sewer is based upon a false principle. The test to be applied should be not whether the conduit receives the drainage of one or more than one house, but whether it is in fact an entirely private construction or a portion of the public system. Is there any reason in the nature of things why, if two houses are drained by one drain, it should be repaired at the expense of the ratepayers, whilst if drained by separate drains the owner should be liable for their repair? Again, why in the metropolis if a builder smuggles in a combined drain without an order of the vestry, should it be a "sewer," whilst if constructed by order it is a "drain"? Much litigation, it may be observed, has arisen from this last provision in consequence of the difficulty that frequently occurs in the case of old drainage systems in showing whether or not any such order was obtained. The difficulties to which this false principle have given rise in practice have been to a certain extent recognised by the legislature in sec. 19 of the 1890 Act, already referred to. But this enactment applies only in those districts in which Part iii. of the Act has been adopted—it has, as we have seen, been the subject of judicial decisions, tending to deprive it of any practical value, and when all is said and done, it has no application to the numerous cases in which groups of houses belong to the same owner. It is surely time that these discredited definitions were repealed and fresh ones substituted based on sounder principles and practical experience.

\* \* \*

**Fences Adjoining Highways.** The owner of land adjoining a highway is not in general bound to fence it from the highway. But if he does erect a fence, is he bound to keep it in good repair? He must, no doubt, maintain it in such a condition that it will not be a nuisance to persons using the highway. But this answer is, after all, an inconclusive one, since the question remains, What amounts to a nuisance? Is it a nuisance if the fence (though perfectly stable while untouched) is so slight or so rotten that if a passenger, pausing to rest or to admire the view, leans against or sits upon it it gives away? In short, must the fence be substantial and sound enough, not only not to fall of its own accord but to serve for a seat or a support? Suppose, for instance, a child looks upon it as a suitable structure for the practice of gymnastics, and in the course of his evolutions it breaks down and the youthful gymnast is injured, is the landowner liable in damages? We imagine that there is not a landowner in the kingdom who would not until recently have received such a suggestion with a scornful smile. But the decision of the Court of Appeal in the recent case of *Harrold* v. *Watney* (noted in this issue) is one more instance of the surprises that the law has in store for the man who presumes to judge a legal question by his own intuitive notions of what is right and fitting. In that case a small boy of the tender age of four climbed a fence adjoining the highway, in order to look at some children playing on the other side. The fence broke, and the boy fell and was injured. Well, of course, the child had no business on the fence, which was not constructed to be climbed but to separate the defendant's land from the street. Moreover, not only was the climbing a purely voluntary act on his part (and *volenti non fit injuria*) but it was an act of trespass. All these considerations were urged on behalf of the landowner, but they were urged in vain, and he was mulcted in damages to the tune of £45. The Court held, in substance, that the fact of the fence breaking down was evidence of its being in such a condition as to be a nuisance. Lord Justice Vaughan Williams put it that the probability of such an accident ought to have been present to the mind of the defendant as the result of leaving the fence in a dangerous condition; that he ought, in fact, to have taken into account the well-known proclivities of children, who are just as much entitled to use a highway as their more staid and less agile elders. But Lord Justice Smith goes a step further than this, and lays it down that if a person passing along a highway feels tired and leans against a fence and it comes down he has a right of action.

In short, it is hardly going too far to say that, if this decision is to stand, a landowner must in future deliberately consider every possible use to which his fence may be put, whether by adults or by children passing along the highway, and must take care that it is so constructed as not to involve the risk of injury to persons so using it. How far this doctrine would be followed in every possible case that can be imagined may, indeed, be considered doubtful. Take, for instance, the case of a short-sighted man sitting down on the top of a wall on which broken glass has been fixed. Has he a right of action? Again, take the case of a fence which will sustain the weight of a single individual—or even, say, half

a dozen at a time—but which succumbs to the pressure of a crowd. Is the landowner liable then? This decision, it seems to us, goes a great deal further than any previous case in the direction of the liability of the landowner, and is hardly reconcileable with some earlier decisions. For example, in *Gibson* v. *Plumstead Burial Board* (noted in THE SURVEYOR, vol. xi., p. 425) the landowner had erected a spiked iron fence adjoining the highway, and the plaintiff's horse stumbled and fell on the spikes and was injured. Judgment having been entered for the defendant (the landowner), the Court of Appeal refused an application for a new trial. The plaintiff contended that the mere fact of the accident was evidence of a nuisance, but this contention was brushed aside by the Court as untenable, the Master of the Rolls giving it as his opinion that "no man of sense could say that this fence was a nuisance." It is difficult to see what evidence of nuisance there was in *Harrold* v. *Watney*, beyond the mere fact of the accident; and, in fact, the Court appear in that case to have adopted the very argument pronounced to be "untenable" in *Gibson* v. *Plumstead Burial Board*. We understand that the decision has caused quite a flutter in the dovecotes of the landowners, and we do not wonder at it.

\* \* \*

**More Rural Sanitation.** In the end of last year Dr. Reece was instructed by the Local Government Board to inquire into the sanitary circumstances of Aldbrough, in the jurisdiction of the Skirlaugh (Yorks) Rural District Council. The inspector's investigations left no room for doubt that the cases of enteric fever which had occurred were due to the water supply, which is derived from shallow wells, varying from 10 ft. to 20 ft. in depth and dry-steined. These wells are often placed near to the dwelling-houses, in proximity to privies and ash-pits. The inspector also notes that the order in which the houses were successively attacked followed the direction in which the underground water might be expected to travel from the first house invaded. The general sanitary needs of the village may be gauged from the inspector's recommendations. These may be briefly summarised. (1) Each house should be provided with an adequate water supply, and, pending that, the existing wells should be safeguarded from pollution, wells irremediably polluted being permanently closed. (2) The village should without delay be provided with efficient means of sewerage. (3) Attention should be given to the defective construction of the privies and ash-pits in the district. These should be so constructed and managed as to prevent the admission of rain or ground water and the leakage of filth into the surrounding soil. Dryness of contents, together with their frequent removal, are objects which should be kept in view in the alteration of all privies and the construction of new ones. (4) The district council are recommended to undertake without delay the duty of removing privy contents and house refuse at frequent and regular intervals, either by their own staff or by contractors, under sec. 42 of the Public Health Act, 1875. (5) Thorough and systematic inspection for the discovery of nuisances is also essential. And (6) the adoption and enforcement of a new series of by-laws, based upon the model series issued by the Local Government Board. Finally (7), the council are recommended seriously to consider the desirability of providing sufficient and proper hospital accommodation for infectious diseases occurring in the district. Similar authorities should observe that it is not necessary that the accommodation provided in the first instance should be on a large and costly scale, but that it is essential that it should be ready beforehand, in order that the first person attacked may be promptly isolated with a view to prevent the further spread of the disease.

**An Appointment at Street.** In our issue of the 5th inst. we had to draw attention to a singular appointment made by the Erith Urban District Council. Before many days have elapsed we find ourselves confronted with a similar piece of jobbery on the part of the Street (Somerset) Urban District Council. The office of surveyor and inspector became vacant through the resignation of Mr. Collingwood, in regard to which event the chairman expressed the feeling of regret which the council felt at losing Mr. Collingwood's services, and thanked that gentleman for the efficient and courteous manner in which he had carried out his duties. For the vacancy there were twenty-four applicants, which were reduced to three, among whom was a local man, who was also an ex-councillor and a tradesman. These enlightened administrators of Street evidently felt themselves in something of a quandary in the matter, for they wrote to the Local Government Board and to a weekly paper to find out whether it was necessary that a member of the council, applying for the offices of surveyor and inspector, should first retire and pay the statutory fine. The paper in question considered that it was not necessary to retire, but the Local Government Board merely acknowledged the letter. This would seem to indicate disgust, and, if so, it is not surprising. The astute councillor who aspired to be an official solved the problem by resigning and paying the fine of £1 fixed by the council. This showed a pleasing confidence in the ultimate success of his candidature. The confidence was not misplaced, for he was elected by a large majority. The salary for the combined office is not a large one, but a district council would find it cheaper in the long run to pay more and get a properly trained and qualified official. This a tradesman cannot be. We observe that one of the councillors who voted for the local man bears the same Christian name. Are they relatives?

\* \* \*

**Leicester and Loughborough: A Question of Water Supply.** Many of our readers will read with keen attention the account we print in another column of certain negotiations — unfortunately so far abortive — which have recently taken place between the municipal authorities of Leicester and Loughborough in connection with water supply. Obviously the question is one of the utmost importance for the towns and districts involved, and next year it may produce one of the biggest Parliamentary fights of the session. The negotiations appear to resolve themselves into two stages, and in each stage the issues seem clearly enough defined. At first the question was whether Loughborough should retain possession of certain sources of supply and provide Leicester with a certain quantity of water on terms to be agreed upon, or whether the sources of supply should be surrendered to Leicester, the latter town then to supply the former with the quantity of water required on terms to be arranged. Loughborough, not unnaturally, preferred the former course, and this brings us to what we may call the second stage of the negotiations—namely, the rate at which Loughborough should supply to Leicester the water required by that town. Leicester wanted it at 2½d. per 1,000 gallons, but the Loughborough sub-committee were not authorised to agree to less than 3d. The lower rate, however, was ultimately agreed to, but when the fact was communicated to the Leicester representatives a somewhat evasive answer was returned to the effect that they thought the first proposal was final and that they were negotiating for a supply from another source. It is not easy to resist the conclusion that the present position of the Leicester Corporation in the matter is somewhat capricious and illogical, but for the full facts our readers may be referred to the report in

another column and to the able statement of Councillor Cartwright.

\* \* \*

**Two Important Letters.** In our correspondence columns will be found two letters, important in themselves and dealing with important subjects. Last week a correspondent drew attention to certain difficulties in connection with fungoid growth in subsoil drains, and invited suggestions from other surveyors with some details of their experience. The letter of Mr. H. H. Humphreys, which appears this week, will be read with very great interest, for, as he remarks, the subject is of considerable importance to those who are concerned with sewage purification works. We join with Mr. Humphreys in hoping that others will contribute to the correspondence he has started, and thus give their brother officials the benefit of their experience and suggestions. Needless to say, our columns are at the service of those who may wish to make an effort to come to some definite conclusions on a subject which is none too clearly understood in some of its bearings. The second letter to which we have referred is that from Mr. Edward A. Harman, Corporation Gasworks, Huddersfield, on the subject of the flash point of petroleum as affecting gas authorities. The interest of the question for gas authorities is stated by Mr. Harman under two heads—(1) the number of gasworks enriching gas with petroleum, in some form or other, render regulations regarding petroleum an important consideration for gas authorities; and (2) the increase of carburetted water-gas plants has created a demand for petroleum which formerly did not exist. Mr. Harman also makes the noteworthy remark that the extension of the " penny-in-the-slot meters " for small consumers is perhaps the best competitor against petroleum lamps. We have no doubt that both letters will receive from our readers the attention they deserve.

\* \*

**The Cork Meeting: Next District Meeting.** We this week conclude our report of the interesting two day's meeting at Cork a fortnight ago. As will be seen, only the round of visits on Friday and Saturday remained to be dealt with, and our report will easily demonstrate what excellent material for such a meeting was afforded in Cork, Queenstown and the neighbourhood. The particulars of the Cork and Muskerry Light Railway will be read with interest. We are told that the future will find narrow-gauge railways running along country roads in England for the conveyance of both passengers and agricultural produce, but the prospect seems far from realisation. At Cork the locomotive on the roadside does not produce any unpleasant impression. We also give some interesting information respecting the Queenstown waterworks, together with a special supplement sheet of illustrations, and we have endeavoured to indicate the importance and advantages of the Cork and Queenstown harbour and the increasingly important part it will play in the future, especially in connection with Transatlantic mails and passengers. From the programme we give in another column it will be observed that a midland counties district meeting has been arranged at Bilston, where the chief features of interest will be the waterworks, the technical school and Spring Vale furnaces.

## PROFESSIONAL PROVERBS.

*For a Scavenging Contractor:* All is not sold that litters.

*For a Designer of Roofs:* Where there's a weight there's a stay.

*For a Bricklayer's Labourer:* Spare the lime and spoil the mortar.

# Association of Municipal and County Engineers.

## IRISH DISTRICT MEETING AT CORK.—II.

QUEENSTOWN HARBOUR.

In our last issue we reported fully the greater part of the first day's proceedings of this highly-interesting two days' meeting. It will be remembered that we completed our report of all the papers and discussions, giving a number of illustrations. The remainder of the proceedings, both on Friday and Saturday, consisted of visits to various works and places of interest, and a few notes on these will be not unacceptable.

### FIRST DAY'S PROCEEDINGS
(Friday, August 5th).

When the sitting in the Council Chamber concluded with the discussion of Mr. Dorman's paper, the members adjourned to the Victoria Hotel at 2 o'clock, where they were entertained to an excellent luncheon, on the invitation of the mayor. Among others present, in addition to those who were present at the earlier sitting, were: Aldermen W. T. Hungerford, G. S. Crowley and P. J. Madden; Councillors E. Hall, R. M. Keatinge, A. O'Driscoll, W. H. Bible, Mr. A. M'Carthy (town clerk), Mr. D. F. Giltinan (mayor's secretary) and Mr. R. K. Mills (manager Clyde Shipping Company). After luncheon, which was excellently served,

The MAYOR proposed the toast of the "Incorporated Association of Municipal and County Engineers," coupling with it the name of its distinguished president, Mr. Robson. The aim of the Association, which had on its roll nearly 1,000 members, scattered throughout the kingdom and the colonies, was to raise the tone of the great profession with which it was connected, and at the present time, when they saw such progress and improvement in sanitary science and engineering generally, it was peculiarly gratifying to welcome the Association to Cork.

The PRESIDENT, in responding, thanked his worship for the kind way in which he had proposed the health of the Association, and the gentlemen present for the reception they had given the toast. It had been a pleasure to all of them to visit this old city of Cork, and meet many of its genial and kind-hearted representatives, some of whom, perhaps, they had had the pleasure of meeting before. During their twenty-five years' existence he thought they had been most hospitably entertained by most of the towns of the kingdom, and he felt sure, from the programme that had been prepared for the present occasion, this visit to Cork would be one of the most happy reminiscences of their existence. The primary reason for the holding of those meetings was the diffusion of professional knowledge and the gaining of additional experience by intercommunication of ideas, the reading of papers and discussions such as they had that day, and by conversation at the tea table and elsewhere. During the past thirty years the duties of municipal engineers had enormously increased, and not alone did the health of the community depend upon municipal engineers, but also, what was of equal importance to many, the judicious expenditure of public money. The 900 members of their Association represented something like 16,000,000 people. They were very grateful to all who aided them in organising that meeting, and they thanked them very heartily for receiving them so hospitably in the city of Cork. Before resuming his seat he proposed in felicitous terms the health of the Mayor and Municipality of Cork. He congratu-

lated the corporation upon Mr. Cutler's appointment by examination. In the old days these appointments were a question of interest and local influence, and merit often came second. Well, the city of Cork had taken a noteworthy initiative, and appointed the most capable man they could got to the position. In this way Cork virtue would have its own reward, and he hoped its example would be followed by many other towns.

The MAYOR, in reply, said he was very much obliged to the president of the Association for the way he had referred to him (the mayor) and his colleagues. He could do very little himself were it not for the almost priceless services of the officials. He joined with them in paying a tribute to their present city engineer, under whose able administration he was sure the city would prosper.

After luncheon the visitors drove, in those conveyances peculiar to Ireland, to the Cork Electric Tramway and Lighting Company's central station in Albert-street and other works in course of construction in the city. The secretary and resident engineer to the company is Mr. C. H. Merz. It will be remembered that the station and the tramways were described and illustrated in our last issue in connection with the paper of Mr. Beverley Griffin, who has been in special charge of the tramways. Needless to say, the works were examined by the visitors with the keenest interest. The inspection being over, they re-entered the cars in order to proceed to the terminus of the Cork and Muskerry Light Railway, where a special train was in waiting to convey them to St. Anne's. In addition to the mayor, the town clerk and some members of the council, the visitors were accompanied by the genial and courteous resident engineer, Mr. W. H. Hill, junr., and the traffic manager, Mr. Wilson. For part of this journey the party had an opportunity of gazing upon many points of interest, and of seeing a locomotive railway, albeit a narrow-gauge one, running along the side of a country road. Before following the wanderings of the visitors further we may give some particulars of this highly-interesting undertaking. For the information and other assistance we have to express our cordial thanks to Mr. Hill.

### THE CORK AND MUSKERRY LIGHT RAILWAY COMPANY.

The Cork and Muskerry Light Railway was completed in 1888, and an extension to Donoughmore was subsequently constructed, the total length of the system being 27 miles. The railway is of the 3-ft. gauge, and for the first 4 miles from Cork the track has been formed at the south side of the Carrigrohane-road, where there is a considerable amount of vehicular traffic. The rails in the portion within the municipal boundary are flush with the surface of the road, and the space between them, as well as a margin 18 in. wide at each side, is paved with stone setts, so that the entire width of the road is available for ordinary traffic. The greater part of the tramway in the county has been formed on a tram track, raised about 8 in. over the level of the road. This is a good arrangement where the public road is sufficiently wide to admit of its adoption.

The permanent way consists of steel rails, 30-ft. lengths, weighing 50 lb. to the yard, and laid on transverse timber creosoted sleepers, 6 ft. by 8 in. by 4 in., eleven sleepers being set under each rail. In the straight portions of the line three sleepers are sole-plated for every rail, and every second sleeper is thus treated in some of the curved portions. The rail is secured with two mushroom-headed faug-bolts at each plated sleeper and with dog spikes elsewhere. Wrought-iron tie-rods have been used to keep the line to gauge on the curves, but sole-plates and faug-bolts make a more permanent job, and are now being used instead of tie-rods. The joints are made with heavy angle fish-plates, 18 in. long, secured to the rails with four bolts and nuts. The ruling gradient is 1 in 58 and the quickest curve about 5 chains. As regards station buildings, these are for the most part constructed of galvanised iron, supported upon timber framing,

VIEW ON THE CORK AND MUSKERRY LIGHT RAILWAY.
Transfer of Milk Cans to the Train for Cork.

and lined internally with timber sheeting, but the dwelling-houses have in all cases been formed of masonry with slate roofs. The station yard at the Cork terminus is reclaimed slob land, and some difficulty has been experienced with the foundations for some of the buildings, as the gravel stratum is at a great depth beneath the surface, and piling would be costly.

The station master's house is the only masonry structure in the Cork yard. It was built about two years ago under the supervision of Mr. W. H. Hill, junr., C.E., resident engineer. The footways have practically been constructed upon the surface of the ground, which has only been excavated sufficiently to give a horizontal leaning surface. They are formed of cement concrete, and are *very wide at the base* and bound together with old railway irons, which are well bonded at the corners.

On arriving at St. Anne's the visitors were met by the chairman of the Cork and Muskerry Light Railway Company, Mr. Richard Barter, J.P., who conducted them to his beautifully-situated residence, where they were entertained to tea and in every way hospitably received. Mr. Barter is a many-sided man, who interests himself in many things, and cultivates not a few elegant and cultured tastes. His guests could have spent much more time than was practicable in examining his valuable collection of historial antiquities,

RESIDENCE OF MR. R. BARTER, J.P.,
Chairman of the Cork and Muskerry Light Railway Co.

not the least interesting of which were those relating to Napoleon I., especially during his exile at St. Helena, where he was attended by Surgeon O'Meara, and where his relations with the governor, Sir Hudson Lowe, were so unfortunate. Mr. Barter is known far and wide in Ireland as a remarkably successful breeder of cattle and sheep, and ample evidence of this is forthcoming in the trophies and certificates innumerable with which some of the rooms in the house are adorned. He conducted his guests over the grounds of his model farm, when they had an opportunity of seeing the splendid herds for the breeding of which Mr. Barter is

so renowned. A man of Mr. Barter's calibre must be of value through the example he sets his neighbours. If the example does not bear fruit it ought to. In this case it is certainly not Mr. Barter's fault. An opportunity was also afforded of inspecting the well-known and beautifully appointed hydropathic establishment, which is the property of Mr. Barter, the baths attracting special attention. We may mention that this establishment was founded by Dr. Barter in 1843 and was the first in the United Kingdom. Mr. Barter is specially to be commended for the manner in which he utilises the water-power on his estate.

The party then re-entered the train and proceeded to Blarney in order to inspect the famous castle, grounds and the celebrated Blarney stone. This classic spot is known to every tourist, so we need not descant upon it further. It will be remembered that it was the subject of the celebrated lines—

Statues gracing this noble place in—
All heathen gods and nymphs so fair;
Bold Neptune, Cæsar and Nebuchadnezzar,
All standing naked in the open air.

When finished with Blarney Castle and its stone, the party returned to Cork, and at half past eight sat down to an excellent and well-served dinner in the Imperial Hotel, the

BLARNEY CASTLE.

proceedings being kept up with great heartiness until a late hour. Toasts were conspicuous by their absence, but not so songs and recitations.

## SECOND DAY'S PROCEEDINGS
(Saturday, August 6th).

The second day's proceedings consisted solely of visits, and highly interesting and enjoyable they were, the chief points being Queenstown waterworks, the harbour, and the Cork, Blackrock and Passage Railway Extension to Crosshaven. Assembling at the Municipal Buildings, the members drove in brakes to Tibbotstown, the site of the head works, being accompanied by the engineers for the scheme, Messrs. Kirkby & Doran, and by the resident engineer. We may here give a brief account of these works, which are illustrated in our special supplement.

### QUEENSTOWN WATERWORKS.

In a special supplement sheet we give some diagrams illustrating the system of waterworks now in course of construction for Cork Town Commissioners. The catchment area from which the storage reservoir will be supplied is some 800 acres in extent, and is chiefly moorland and pasturage, very little being under cultivation at any time, so that there is no danger of the water being polluted from any source. There are very few inhabited houses in the district, and these are sufficiently remote not to affect the water within the catchment area. A sparkling stream of pure water rushes down the valley, and during rainy weather it swells up to a very respectable volume, owing to the quick declivity of the land, which scarcely retains 10 per cent. of the water that falls upon it. There are a great many springs within the valley coming through the Old Red Sandstone rock, which underlies the whole area.

The storage reservoir is being constructed to contain some 37,000,000 gallons of water, and with the filtration and clear water tanks occupies a space of 16 acres. This quantity of water represents 180 days' supply for the population of Queenstown and of Haulbowline and Spike Islands, for which provision will also be made. The island of Haulbowline contains a very commodious floating basin and a splendid dry dock, in which H.M.S. *Howe* and H.M.S. *Black Prince* were lately docked, and is now being provided with the necessary workshops and machinery for the building and repairing of vessels. The works on this island have been carried out by the Admiralty for the purpose of providing accommodation for her Majesty's vessels when they visit the harbour for shelter, stores or repairs. The Admiralty are negotiating

MR. S. A. KIRKBY, M.A.,
County Surveyor of Cork (South).

with the Town Commissioners for a copious supply of water to the islands for troops and dockyard, and the commissioners have made ample provision in their new system of water supply to meet the requirements.

The storage reservoir is some 7½ miles to the north of Queenstown and at an elevation of 110 ft. above the service reservoir at Carrignafoy, near Queenstown, into which it is delivered through a cast-iron main pipe of 9 in. in diameter. From the service reservoir the supply for Haulbowline will be conveyed in a special main, extending for a distance of 2 miles to the foreshore, where it is proposed to carry it upon the harbour bottom, for a distance of 550 yards, to the quay at Haulbowline, and thence to a large tank already constructed on the highest point of the island. As will be seen by the section showing the extensions to Haulbowline and Spike the depth at which this main will be laid will in some parts exceed 12 fathoms. The engineers purpose using cast-iron pipes, with ball and socket joints of special design, for the submerged portion of this work, or flexible steel pipes. The reservoir at Tibbotstown will be formed by a concrete masonry dam of some 400 ft. in length, extending across the valley, below which will be constructed the filtration and clear-water tanks as shown in our supplement. The water face of the dam will have an elevation of 57 ft. and a foundation of 16 ft., making a total height of 53 ft. The width of the dam at the bottom will be 37·1 ft. and at the top 8 ft. The elevation of the front will form an arcade of nineteen arches, which will

MR. C. G. DORAN,
Joint Engineer with Mr. Kirkby for the Queenstown Waterworks.

have rather a handsome effect when viewed from the road which leads up the valley. The trench for the foundation of the dam is excavated into the Old Red Sandstone for a depth of 9 ft. It was necessary to sink to this depth to secure an impervious rock to build the dam upon, as the portion through which the excavation was made, though sufficiently strong for the purpose of a foundation, was of a rather open description that would not resist percolation.

The cost of the whole of the works when carried out will not exceed £20,000. The amount of the contract at present

being proceeded with is £14,000. Mr. Michael Connors, Youghal, is the contractor.

The engineers for the works are Messrs. S. A. Kirkby, M.A., CANTAB. and C. G. Doran, Queenstown, and the resident engineer is Mr. H. V. Potter. Mr. Kirkby is a graduate of Cambridge and a Whitworth scholar, was assistant to Sir John Fowler, Bart., and obtained a county surveyorship in Ireland in open competition. He has constructed many large works, such as the Youghal bridge—the largest in Ireland—the Kinsale western bridge, both over wide tidal rivers, the sea wall at Youghal, the Kanturk railway, the Youghal and Middleton waterworks and other undertakings.

During the drive the beauty and variety of the scenery along the route afforded much pleasure to the visitors. The was lies partly along the river Lee for about 6 miles, and then quitting that pleasant stream winds gently upwards among some tree-clad hills for some 5 miles further, until it reaches the valley dividing the townlands of Tibbotstown and Cloneen, where the storage reservoir, filtration and clear-water tanks are being constructed. Among other things which called forth the favourable comments of the visitors were the excellent selection of a site for the reservoir, the general planning of the scheme, the low cost, and the fine quality of the sand to be used for the filter-beds.

Leaving Tibbotstown the visitors drove through a most attractive stretch of country to Queenstown, and at the Queen's Hotel were met by Mr. J. Long, chairman of the town commissioners; Mr. J. H. Campbell, J.P., town clerk, and Mr. A. M'Carthy, town clerk, Cork, representing the mayor of that town. At the Queen's Hotel an excellent luncheon was provided by the local members of the Association, Mr. Kirkby occupying the chair and Mr. Dorman the vice-chair. When justice had been done to it Mr. ROBSON, in proposing the health of Messrs. Kirkby, Cutler and Dorman, referred

MR. H. V. POTTER,
Resident Engineer, Queenstown Waterworks.

to the right royal welcome they had received both at Cork and at Queenstown. He dwelt upon the proverbial hospitality of the Irish people, and paid a warm tribute to the part taken in organising the meeting by Messrs. Cutler and Dorman, and thanked Mr. Kirkby for what he had shown them that morning in connection with the Tibbotstown waterworks The toasts were duly acknowledged, and then followed "Prosperity to Queenstown," coupled with the names of Mr. Long, chairman of the Town Commissioners, and Mr. J. H. Campbell town clerk.

After visits to some spots of interest in the immediate neighbourhood, the visitors went on board the tender, *America,* at the deep-water quay to make a cruise round the harbour. Some details of this remarkable harbour may here be given.

### QUEENSTOWN HARBOUR.

Queenstown harbour, which is practically Cork harbour, is an example of the successful treatment of a port by dredging alone without training walls. At present the principal engineering work is dredging, and the new plant in use for this work is a good example of modern practice in this direction. The harbour is one of the most capacious and secure in the British Islands, containing a vast water area, and affording safe anchorage and shelter for the largest class of vessels at all times. Nearer to New York by 350 miles than Southampton, it is easy of access and especially advantageous as a rendezvous for the fleet and for vessels of commerce. At Queenstown there are quays, landing piers, boat harbours and a deep-water quay immediately outside the terminus of the Great Southern and Western Railway, giving 24 ft. at low-water spring tides, with much deeper water a short distance from the quay. Here are found the largest Government transports for the embarkation and disembarkation of troops, and here also take place the landing and embarking of the American mails and passengers. The large and commodious custom examining-room forms a part of the station buildings. Powerful tenders, luxuriously appointed and lighted by electricity, convey passengers to and from the

Transatlantic steamers, which call there regularly on their outward and homeward voyages.

There is a large Government dockyard in the harbour, capable of accommodating some of the largest vessels in her Majesty's navy, and further expenditure is being incurred. There is extensive dry dock accommodation and facilities for ship-building and ship-repairing on the river at Passage West and Rushbrook, and at Gridiron Works at Carrigaloe. A very large amount of money has been expended in deepening and improving the river channel from Horsehead to Cork, a distance of about 5½ miles, and in providing deep-water quay accommodation at Cork for vessels of a large draft of water. We have already referred to the dredging operations and the powerful plant provided. There is a depth of 14 ft. at low-water spring tides in the channel from Horsehead to Cork, with a rise at ordinary spring tides of 12¾ ft. and 10 ft. at neap tides, affording a depth of nearly 27 ft. at ordinary high-water spring tides and 24 ft. at high-water neap tides. The work at present in progress will give an additional depth of 2 ft. for a width of 350 ft.

The quayage and wharfage at Cork is considerable. At the Victoria Wharf there is 19 ft. 6 in. at low-water spring tides, and vessels with a draught of 23 ft. can lie afloat at all times of the tide at the South Deep Water Quay. At the north side of the river there is a deep water quay affording 19 ft. 6 in. of water at all states of the tide, and vessels lying thereat can discharge cargo by hydraulic machinery into the trucks of the Great Southern and Western Railway Company, thus enabling it to be transported rapidly direct from the vessel into the interior of the country. Owing to the increased facilities and accommodation afforded to shipping the trade of the port has for some years shown a substantial increase. Landing piers for passenger steamers have been erected and maintained by the commissioners at several places within their jurisdiction. Powerful cranes and other machinery, with a lifting power varying from 5 tons to 20 tons, have been provided within the port.

The most important matter in connection with the work of the Harbour Commissioners is the dredging of the river, and a comparison between the present state of the channel and what it was in former days is of interest. In 1824 there was practically no water in the channel at low tide, for in that year a contract was entered into to dredge it to the depth of 2 ft. at low water. In 1867 what was known as "the 11-ft. cut" was commenced, and that was completed in 1872. In 1874 the late engineer, Mr. Philip Barry, recommended the board to give a minimum depth of 14 ft. at low water spring tides, from Horsehead up to Cork quays, and at the same time to widen the channel to 300 ft., the width at the time being 180 ft. to 200 ft. The recommendation was adopted, and for the purpose a new dredger and two hopper barges were procured at a cost of £37,460. The work was begun in 1877, and, with the exception of some widening, was completed in 1883, when the plant purchased for the work was sold for £20,000.

In 1894 it was further decided, also on the recommendation of Mr. Barry, that in consequence of the increased size of the vessels coming up the river and using the deep water quays at Cork, the time had arrived for a further improvement in the depth and width of the channel—in short, that it should not in any part be less than 350 ft. wide, and that there should be a uniform depth of 16 ft. at low-water spring tides. The commissioners obtained for the work a new and powerful dredger, at a cost of £16,500, and two 1,200-ton hopper barges, at a cost of £24,000 for the two, both dredger and hoppers being supplied by Messrs. Fleming & Ferguson, of Paisley. We understand that the machinery has proved in every way satisfactory, the dredger easily lifting 350 tons per hour, even under unfavourable conditions. In favourable ground it has sometimes lifted as much as 600 tons in an hour, and the hoppers have on several occasions taken as much as 1,300 to 1,400 tons of mud to sea in one trip. Mr. Jas. Price, M.I.C.E., the harbour engineer, in his report for the year ended July 31, 1897, also endorses the wisdom of purchasing the new dredging plant. It is expected that the work of dredging the full depth and width now decided on the entire 5½ miles of channel between Passage and Cork will take about three to four years. The advantage will be a much wider channel, with a uniform depth of 29 ft. at high-water spring tides, which will enable the largest modern cargo steamers likely to be chartered for this port to come up to the deep-water quays at Cork, where they will be able to lie afloat even in low water.

To the particulars given above we may add that the Cork Harbour Commissioners are the port authority under a local statute passed in the reign of George IV. and under subsequent enactments. The city is about 16 miles distant by water from the seaward limits of the port—Roche's Point lighthouse at the entrance to the harbour. From that point to the entrance to Cork harbour both harbour and river are thoroughly well lighted by a series of leading lights. The value of the harbour is enhanced by the efficiency of the service between Queenstown and London via Holyhead for the conveyance of mails and passengers.

The tender made a brief stop at Haulbowline to admit of an inspection of the docks on the island, the basin constructed mainly by convict labour receiving special attention and admiration, as did also the spacious outer dock. All the works and structures were inspected with evident interest and curiosity. Leaving Haulbowline, the tender steamed round the harbour and up the East Ferry river. Returning to the harbour the boat was steered towards Crosshaven. At that popular resort the party disembarked in order to visit, under the guidance of the engineer, Mr. Perry, the extension of the Cork, Blackrock and Passage Railway to Crosshaven. Cork was reached again in the evening, after a most enjoyable and instructive day. We cannot conclude without again expressing our sense of the credit due to those who had organised the meeting, and to the mayor and others who gave it such hearty support and the members so cordial a welcome.

## TRADE EFFLUENTS AT RAVENSTHORPE.

At a recent meeting of the Ravensthorpe Urban District Council a deputation representing the manufacturers of the town waited upon the council to see what could be done in assisting them to deal with their trade effluents. Mr. Kaye said the manufacturers proposed to put down settling tanks and getting rid of the solids, and they asked whether the council could take the liquid sewage. It was pointed out that the interests of the manufacturers and those of the general community were identical, and that being so it was pleaded that the council ought to give them what assistance they could in the matter. Mr. Balme suggested that a better scheme would be to deliver the solids and everything on the council's sewage farm, and let the council deal with it; but it was mentioned that a preferable plan would be for each manufacturer to treat his own sewage and pass the effluent on to the council to treat. The chairman remarked that the council intended putting down a few settling tanks, and that the job would be a costly one; but it was replied that these were for the treatment of domestic sewage only. The difficulties of the question were discussed, and it was incidentally mentioned that the manufacturers in the Colne valley had declined to move in the matter, whereupon it was suggested that in that event it would be useless for the manufacturers of the Calder valley to do anything. The deputation were satisfied that the council's disposition was to favourably consider the question, and it was understood that expert advice would be taken as to the ways and means. The deputation then withdrew.

## DERBY'S WATER SUPPLY.

An important report was recently presented to the Derby Town Council by the Waterworks Committee. It stated that, referring to previous orders authorising the expenditure of £33,700 on waterworks purposes, the committee had modified their proposals and at the same time extended them. Instead of providing permanent engines, for which £17,500 was previously voted, it had been decided that temporary engines should be provided, at a cost of £2,000, with connections, to cost a further £1,500. It was also decided that the construction of the filter tunnels, estimated to cost £31,900, should be proceeded with forthwith. The council were therefore recommended to grant £31,900 for this purpose, and to approve the proposals mentioned above, at a cost of £17,500. The committee had given their careful attention to the question of further water supply, and had come to the conclusion that the promotion of a Bill for the supply of Derby from the upper waters of the river Derwent could be no longer deferred. They had information that several other towns had decided to promote Bills with the object of securing the upper waters of the Derwent. They were strongly of opinion that any such action should be strenuously opposed, and such opinion was shared by the County Council of Derbyshire, with whom the committee had been in consultation on the question, and where support in opposition to the schemes of other towns could be reckoned upon. The report and its recommendations, together with a resolution empowering the committee to promote a Bill in Parliament to enable the corporation to obtain an additional water supply from the upper waters of the Derwent, were eventually adopted.

**Greenock.**—At a recent private meeting of the Police Board a Sub-Committee on Electricity reported as to the best method of carrying out a scheme for the proposed installation of electric lighting. A deputation, it was stated, had visited Glasgow, Edinburgh and Leith, inspected the electric light stations and obtained information as to the procedure adopted, and the general system of electric lighting in the various places. At Edinburgh it was reported that the original capital expended was about £143,000, and that it had been arranged to proceed with the erection of a new electric lighting station in another part of the city, at a cost of about £200,000. The gasworks had not suffered from the competition; the Gas Trust had had a much larger surplus during the past year than in any previous year, and they were about to expend £500,000 in erecting an extension. At Leith they were proceeding with a station, to cost about £28,000, and at Glasgow the corporation, in view of the great demand for lighting and power, had resolved to erect new installations at Port Dundas and Old Pollokshaws-road.

# Leicester Water Supply.

## LOUGHBOROUGH AND THE BLACKBROOK.

At the monthly meeting of the Loughborough Town Council last week a special report was presented by the Water Committee on the negotiations with the Leicester Corporation with reference to the Blackbrook water supply. The report was as follows :—

"In November last your committee discussed the desirability of communicating with the Leicester Corporation with reference to the informal proposal which had been made that the question of a supplementary supply to Leicester from the Blackbrook watershed should be taken into consideration before settling the plans for the construction of the proposed new storage reservoir. A sub-committee was appointed to meet representatives of the Leicester Corporation to discuss the question, and, after being advised by their engineers (Messrs. G. & F. W. Hodson), met a sub-committee representing the Corporation of Leicester on the 3rd of February. The representatives of your committee were advised that if the whole of the works sanctioned by Parliament were carried out, including a reservoir having a capacity of 506,000,000 gallons, the Loughborough Corporation would for many years be able to spare at least one-half of the total available supply (2,000,000 gallons per day) from the Blackbrook watershed, and they offered to sell to the Leicester Water Committee, for a period of fifty years, the whole of such surplus water, the water to be delivered unfiltered through a meter, or meters, at Nanpantan, from whence it could be gravitated on to the filters belonging to the Leicester Corporation at Swithland, and the price they asked was 4d. per 1,000 gallons. Alderman Wood, on behalf of his committee, made counter proposals :—

"(a) For the acquisition by Leicester of the Blackbrook rights, Loughborough to utilise its other sources of supply, and Leicester guaranteeing, after such utilisation, to supply at cost price all further requirements of Loughborough, if any; and

"(b) That Leicester should take over all the sources of water supply at present acquired by or available to Loughborough, Leicester to supply the Loughborough water area with filtered water to the full extent of its requirements at 4d. per 1,000 gallons.

Your committee did not feel justified in accepting either of these proposals, and "A further conference was held at Loughborough on the 4th of April, at which Alderman Wood raised a preliminary discussion as to the terms on which any offer of a price should be based, and it was mutually agreed that the supply should be on the basis of a guaranteed minimum supply by Loughborough of 1,000,000 gallons per day, with a minimum guaranteed take by Leicester of 1,250,000 gallons per day, if available, the supply to commence in 1905. Alderman Wood stated that, considering the cost to Leicester of the works which would be necessary to enable them to avail themselves of the supply to be afforded under the proposed arrangement, the maximum price per 1,000 gallons which his committee authorised him to offer was 2½d. per 1,000 gallons. This offer was not at the time accepted, and after considerable discussion further negotiations were deferred. Negotiations were resumed on the 5th of May by the chairman and vice-chairman of each Water Committee. No agreement as to price was then arrived at, but it was arranged that a formal communication from Loughborough should be sent to Leicester. On the 13th of May the chairman of your committee wrote to Alderman Wood, stating that the sub-committee would recommend the acceptance of 3d. per 1,000 gallons on the terms arranged—namely, Loughborough Corporation agree to supply Leicester Corporation, commencing in 1905, or somewhat earlier if preferred, either at Blackbrook or Nanpantan, a guaranteed minimum quantity of 1,000,000 gallons per day, or 90,000,000 gallons per quarter, of unfiltered water (which, reckoning 16½ gallons per head per day, is equal to a supply for a population of 60,000 persons), such minimum to be guaranteed for a period of twenty years, and thereafter the whole of the surplus water for fifty years if desired, Leicester guaranteeing to take 1,250,000 gallons per day if and so long as that surplus quantity is available, and to have the right to terminate the agreement by notice as soon as such surplus water is less than 500,000 gallons per day. This offer was considered at a special meeting of the Leicester Water Committee on the 6th of June, and a reply was received to the effect that the committee had reluctantly come to the conclusion that they were unable to accept the offer.

"The sub-committee did not feel justified in accepting any less price before consulting the Water Committee, and on the 14th of June reported to the Water Committee the result of their negotiations up to that date. After a long discussion it was resolved, subject to the necessary confirmation of the council, that the sub-committee be authorised to accept 2½d. per 1,000 gallons for water on the terms and conditions set out in the letter addressed by the chairman (Councillor Cartwright) to Alderman Wood, dated the 13th of May. Councillor Cartwright at once communicated with Alderman Wood, intimating that his committee had resolved to recommend the acceptance of the offer which had been made on behalf of the Leicester Water Committee to purchase at 2½d. per 1,000 gallons on the terms and conditions mentioned in his (Councillor Cartwright's) letter of the 13th of May, and asking for a letter confirming these terms, and suggesting whether, previous to reporting to their respective councils, it would not be better for their respective town clerks to settle a provisional agreement. On the 16th of June Alderman Wood acknowledged the receipt of this letter, and promised to report it to the Water Committee at their next meeting, to be held on the following Monday, the 21st of June, when it should have their careful consideration. In his letter Alderman Wood stated that his Water Committee at their last meeting, when they had the offer of 3d. per 1,000 gallons under consideration, deemed that a final offer, and had since entered into negotiations for another source of water, and were entirely free to treat elsewhere if they found it to their advantage to do so, the provisional offer of his sub-committee having been declined, but at the same time his committee would give the revised offer the consideration it deserved. On the 27th of July, no definite reply having been received, your committee communicated with the town clerk of Leicester, asking for the decision of the committee on the matter, to which Mr. Bell replied that his committee had entered into negotiations for another source of water supply, and had therefore not come to any resolution on the amended offer that the Loughborough Committee were good enough to submit, but of course they could not ask them (the Loughborough Water Committee) to remain bound by their offer. At the same time his committee instructed him to express their very high appreciation of the kindness and consideration that the Loughborough Water Committee had shown throughout the matter."

Councillor Jas. Cartwright, the chairman of the Water Committee, in moving the adoption of the report, said that it was not necessary to enter into more detail than was there given as to the efforts of the committee to arrive at an arrangement with the Corporation of Leicester for the sale of their surplus water. The committee had recognised the fact that it would be advantageous to Loughborough, by relieving the burgesses of some part of the initial burden of the expenditure on the proposed new reservoir, if arrangements could be made with Leicester which were equally advantageous to them. It would be observed by the report that the negotiations had not to the present terminated in such an arrangement being made, and they would have gathered from other sources that the Corporation of Leicester were proposing to take steps to obtain a supply from another watershed. At one time the negotiations certainly pointed to a mutually satisfactory arrangement being arrived at. Without taking the council through the details of the negotiations, they would have noticed that

#### THE ONLY DIFFERENCE

between the two committees was on the question of the price of the water to be taken. They would be in a position to supply Leicester before the time at which they desired Loughborough to be ready to supplement the present sources of supply, and the quantity they were prepared to absolutely guarantee would be equal to supplying an additional population of 60,000, reckoning 16½ gallons per head per diem, which was the amount recognised as necessary by Leicester. The terms were so arranged that it would have been to the advantage of Loughborough to make the best possible use of their resources to enable them to supply the Corporation of Leicester with as much surplus water as the watershed would produce. This would not be less than 1,250,000 gallons, and probably considerably more. Therefore it was clear that Leicester would obtain full advantage from this watershed under arrangement with Loughborough, subject to Loughborough's needs, as if they were to obtain possession of the property and the rights for which Loughborough had had to fight and pay. That was a great point between the two corporations. Was Loughborough to part with the absolute

#### POSSESSION OF THE PROPERTY

and allow Leicester to supply them, or were they to retain possession and supply Leicester? Acting on the feeling of the council in the past, and, he believed, now, the committee considered that they ought not to part with the possession of the property (Hear, hear). Their offer to Leicester, in short, was to sell them the whole surplus water for fifty years. On the question of price the committee had not looked at these negotiations otherwise than with the desire to arrive at arrangements that would be equitable to both sides. They had an article to sell which Leicester wanted to buy. Water, like many other articles, had a market value, and if they considered that value they found that, particularly in the Midlands, it was constantly increasing, and the committee felt justified in endeavouring to get from Leicester its full market value. As the cost of water went now, 2½d. per 1,000 gallons, which was the price at which it had been offered to Leicester, not only in the opinion of the water committee but of their professional advisers, was a very reasonable price. If they carried out the proposed works at

Blackbrook—and they would do so at an exceptionally low cost, cheaper than any other town could—and if they utilised every drop of water Blackbrook supplied, it would cost them within a decimal of 2d. per 1,000 gallons. Perhaps he would be expected to say a word about

ALDERMAN WOOD'S STATEMENT,

which appeared in *The Leicester Daily Post* on Friday last. At first that statement as to the price on which Loughborough were willing to sell appeared to be accurate, but he observed that Alderman Wood failed to add that he, on behalf of Leicester, was the first to name the price of 2½d. per 1,000. At that time the Loughborough sub-committee, who were acting with professional advice throughout, to whom the offer was made, were of opinion that without further instructions they could not take less than 3d. The Water Committee then authorised them to accept the offer of 2½d., and this was done at once, but a reply was received to the effect that the provisional offer of the sub-committee having been declined, negotiations had been entered into for another supply. It was, therefore, rather singular to read Alderman Wood's statement of the reasons against purchasing from Loughborough. The facts were known to the Leicester sub-committee, and had not altered. He did not think it devolved upon him to say what might be said on the assumed increase of population or the capital expenditure. But he would point out that against the so-called charge on the Revenue Department of £75,000 paid for water there would be receipts for the sale by the Corporation of Leicester of the water, when filtered, at a price of from 6d. to 10d. per 1,000 gallons. That water the corporation would buy from Loughborough unfiltered at 2½d. per 1,000 gallons, and the cost of filtration, on the amount quoted by Leicester, was less than 1d. per 1,000. The Water Committee throughout these negotiations had endeavoured to meet the Leicester authority in every possible way consistent with the protection of the interests of the Loughborough inhabitants, and that had been duly acknowledged at meetings between representatives of the two boroughs. The town clerk of Leicester had also received the instructions of his committee to express their appreciation of the consideration shown by the Loughborough committee throughout. At the last meeting of the Water Committee it was decided that it was absolutely necessary and desirable that they should now commence to carry out the works at Blackbrook, and they had given instructions for the matter to be brought before the council. He would present a report probably at the next meeting, and would be able then to justify, both to the council and the public, the step the committee proposed to take.

Councillor CLIFFORD seconded the adoption of the report, and it was agreed to without further discussion.

## LOUGHBOROUGH BATHS.

OPENING CEREMONY.

On the 10th inst. the Marquis of Granby, in the presence of a large and representative gathering, performed the opening ceremony in connection with the new baths which have been presented to the town of Loughborough. The buildings occupy a commanding position at the end of the Queen's Jubilee Park, and have a south-east aspect. The building is faced externally with local red-pressed bricks, with Ruabon terra-cotta dressings, the roofs being covered with grey slates. The principal entrance is about the centre of the front elevation, through a vestibule having panelled ceiling and divided from the inner hall by a lead light glazed screen. From this hall access is obtained to the large swimming bath, corridors leading to the private slipper baths, the office being conveniently arranged on the left of entrance. The private slipper baths, nine in number—four first-class to the left and five second-class to the right—are arranged to the front of the building, the roof of which is a lean-to, abutting on the swimming bath outer wall. These baths are divided by pitch pine partitions, each having a separate window and ventilating Tobin tube box, the material of the baths being cast-iron white-glazed enamel. They are fitted with hot and cold water valves. At the end of the first-class baths is the laundry and ironing rooms, whilst at the end of the second-class is an emergency exit and a staircase leading to the spectators' gallery of the large bath.

THE SWIMMING BATH.

This has a water area of 80 ft. by 30 ft., with depth varying from 6 ft. to 3½ ft. It is surrounded by a cement concrete path, having coloured concrete kerb, and there are thirty dressing boxes off pitch pine, running the entire length of one side and end. The size of the hall is 94 ft. by 42 ft. The walls are lined with glazed bricks to form a dado, and coloured with duresco above, having an open pitch pine roof, supported by light iron principals, surmounted by a lantern light. The bath is lined throughout with white-glazed bricks, having at intervals lines of blue-glazed bricks. Access to the bath is obtained at either end by step-ladders. A large diving stage has been erected at the deep end, and at the other end, over the dressing boxes, is the gallery capable of accommodating 150 persons. At the east end of the swimming bath are the soap and spray baths, having dressing-room and lavatories, all of which are lined with glazed bricks,

and with similar concrete flooring to the large bath. To the rear is the boiler-house, which has an octagonal chimney stack of 60 ft.

The woodwork throughout the building is of specially-selected pitch pine, varnished; the walls are furnished in duresco, and the whole lighted by gas brackets and star pendants. The laundry has been fitted with three large wash-tubs, each having hot and cold water supply, connected direct with steam from the boiler. There is a large revolving washing machine, with wringer attached, and also a hydro extractor. There are sliding drying-houses in the ironing-room, of which live are provided with necessary heating and ventilating apparatus. Steam for the heating is generated by a 20 horse-power Cornish boiler, passed through an instrument attached to the circulating main, capable of displacing 10,000 gallons of water per hour. The boiler is also capable of heating the whole of the water in the baths (upwards of 75,000 gallons) to a uniform temperature of 75 deg. in ten hours. This is the time required to fill the bath from the 4-in. town water supply, which enters at the shallow end. The copper spray pipe at the shallow end is capable of sending a flow of cold water one-third the length of the bath, and will be used for clearing off the scum from the surface of the water, which will flow through the overflow gratings arranged for the purpose at the opposite end. The water supply for slipper baths is obtained from a 400-gallon cold and 300-gallon hot galvanised iron tanks fixed in the laundry. The water of the latter is circulated and heated under similar arrangements as described for the large bath.

## GLASGOW SEWAGE SCHEME.

The sub-committee of the Glasgow Corporation appointed to visit different cities and towns in England, and inspect the arrangements in use for the treatment of sewage and the disposal, have issued their report. Among other places visited were London, Manchester and Salford. As an outcome of their investigations the deputation are impelled to the conclusion that in the design of the new sewage works at Dalmuir and Braehead it is imperative to continue the use of methods where experience has proved practicable on a large scale, and there seems no room for doubt that chemical precipitation alone is the means to adopt, and the most economical and satisfactory method of disposing of the sewage is to send it to sea. While implying no disparagement to the efficiency of the methods in use at Dalmarnock—which are the only possible means available under the circumstances—the deputation are satisfied that these methods cannot be advantageously applied at Dalmuir or at Braehead, where the volumes of sewage to be ultimately treated are so much larger that it would be hopeless to look for a market for any form of pressed sludge, no matter how high might be its estimation among agriculturists. The initial volume of sewage to be treated at Dalmuir is estimated at 27,000,000 gallons of dry-weather flow per day, which will ultimately be increased to about 48,000,000. Supposing the works at Dalmuir and Braehead to be in operation, the combined daily product of sewage would not for some time exceed 1,200 tons a day, the ultimate quantity being about 2,300 tons. Two barges would for years suffice for the removal of the whole sludge, though eventually a third would require to be added, and the sub-committee have little doubt that the sludge can be disposed of in this manner more economically than by pressing. The sub-committee think that no time should now be lost in commencing the undertaking.

## NEW LUNATIC ASYLUM.

The foundation-stone of an asylum for the county borough of West Ham, which has a population of about 260,000, was laid by Alderman Ivey, the mayor, at Chadwell Heath, Essex, on the 3rd inst. The buildings, which will cover more than 10 acres, and have some 90 acres of surrounding land, will accommodate 800 patients in addition to the staff. The administration block is placed centrally, the front portion being occupied on the ground floor by the chief medical officer's, steward's and clerk's offices, board-room, dispensary, library, &c. The museum and laboratories and assistant medical officer's rooms are on the first floor. At the back are the waiting-room, matron's apartments, recreation hall, rooms for male and female attendants, kitchen, bakery, general stores, laundry, boiler, engine-house and workshops, &c. The foundations have been put in by Messrs. Gregar & Son, of Stratford, at a cost of about £16,000. Messrs. Leslie & Co., of Kensington, have the contract for the superstructure—£210,000. In addition to the main buildings there will be a medical officer's residence, together with steward's, chief attendants' and married attendants' houses, isolation block, mortuary, lodges and chapel to accommodate 550 adults. The total cost is estimated at about £300,000. The architect is Mr. Lewis Angell, F.R.I.B.A., the borough engineer.

**Perth.**—A letter was read from Lord Rosebery, at a recent meeting of the town council, stating that he will visit Perth on October 26th, to open the Sandeman public library.

# Institution of Mechanical Engineers.

## MEETING AT DERBY.

Although primarily intended to promote the practice of mechanical engineering, and to facilitate the interchange of ideas relating to improvements in various branches of mechanical science, the meetings of the Institution of Mechanical Engineers, and especially the summer meetings, are by no means limited to these objects.

The session which has recently been held at Derby included social functions, which, no doubt, proved highly satisfactory not only to representatives of various branches of the engineering profession present, but also to those more directly representing municipal institutions.

Papers were read and discussed bearing on the subjects of aluminium manufacture, water softening, purification and narrow-gauge railways. The two latter subjects, possessing a distinct interest to those concerned in local government, will be again mentioned in dealing with visits made in connection with the meeting.

By the courtesy of the Midland Railway Company a special saloon train was placed at the disposal of members, so that they were enabled conveniently and comfortably to pay a large number of visits to neighbouring places of professional interest. The object of the following notes is not so much to enter into a chronological detailed description of the various works, as to place before our readers such facts and comments as may be likely to prove of interest.

### WATER SOFTENING AND PURIFYING.

At the pumping station of the new waterworks of the Joint Water Committee of the Swadlincote and Ashby Urban District Councils there is an extremely compact installation of the Archbutt-Deeley softening and purifying plant. The apparatus is very simple, and consists of four cast-iron tanks, each of 30,000 gallons, above which a chemical treating-house contains the necessary mixing apparatus. The process is expeditious and in every way under the most perfect control. Several novel features are incorporated in the apparatus, such as the use of injectors for mixing lime water, for mixing the lime water with water to be treated, and for stirring up previous deposit to aid clarification. The water is further clarified and its natural qualities are restored by an ingenious process of recarbonation. Drawn from the Trent gravel, the water contains not only lime and other salts, but a considerable quantity of iron, which renders it unfit for general distribution before treatment. The iron is completely removed, and general hardness reduced from 22 deg. to 8·5 deg., at an inclusive cost of 0·8d. per 1,000 gallons. At present the output is 540,000 gallons daily, but this could be readily increased if desired. Water on leaving the softening tanks is delivered into another tank, from whence it is pumped into a service reservoir at Woodville, having a capacity of 1,000,000 gallons, from which it is decanted into distributing pipes. It is somewhat unfortunate that the pumping machinery in the adjoining engine-house should have been laid down on so small a scale, as owing to the popular demand, especially by manufacturers, for softened water, the maximum duty has already been very nearly reached. The whole of the machinery was furnished by Messrs. Taugyes, of Birmingham, and the softening plant by Messrs. Mather & Platt, of Salford.

### WATER SUPPLY OF DERBY, LEICESTER, &c.

#### PROPOSALS FOR A JOINT SCHEME.

Considerable attention is now being devoted to the question of water supply, not only in Derby and Leicester but elsewhere in the district. At Derby an organised system of water supply has existed since the year 1691, and these works remained without material alteration until 1848, when the first instalment of the present works was commenced at Little Eaton. Further additions have been made from time to time, the chief source of supply being the river Derwent. It has recently been recommended by the Waterworks Committee that further sums be expended in the provision of temporary engines and connections, in the extension of filter tunnels and in the enlargement of the service reservoir at Littleover. Beyond these recommendations the committee have come to the conclusion that the promotion of a Bill for the supply of Derby from the upper Derwent can no longer be deferred.

It happens that several other towns, including Leicester, Nottingham and Sheffield, would also like to participate in such a scheme, a wish which does not appear to meet with approval from the Derby Corporation. The claims of Sheffield particularly are strongly resented, because the watersheds of the Peak do not run towards Sheffield in any way. It seems probable that municipal and other authorities in the counties of Derby, Leicester and Nottingham may ultimately join their forces in promoting a suggested scheme, at a cost of some £3,000,000, for the supply of about 14,000,000 gallons of water daily. The upper Derwent water is most abundant and of excellent quality, and has an average hardness of about 2 deg. Such a scheme would be a great boon to many districts, but when it is borne in mind that the total distance to be traversed from the Derwent and Leicester is not less than 66 miles it will be seen that the co-operation of a large number of local councils will first have to be secured.

#### WATER SUPPLY OF LEICESTER.

By the authorities at Leicester the inauguration of such a scheme is recognised to be of paramount importance. For years past the population of the town has been rapidly increasing, and, in spite of extensions of the waterworks, scarcity of supplies have been experienced during the past five years. The construction of the Swithland reservoir, recently opened, it was hoped would remove all anxiety for many years, but this belief has not been realised. We had an excellent opportunity of inspecting the new works at Swithland, which include a storage reservoir of 490,000,000 gallons, and six filter-beds, having a total area of 88,644 square feet, and a filtering capacity of about 2,750,000 gallons daily. The beds are furnished with modern type sand washers, constructed by Messrs. Hunter & English, of London. In the pumping station two 140 indicated horse-power triple-expansion pumping engines of marine type have been erected by Messrs. Easton, Anderson & Goolden, of Erith. From the filtered-water tank the water is pumped through a 20-in. main into the Hall Gates service reservoir, a distance of about 2¼ miles. Speaking generally, the whole of the works have been excellently conceived and carried out, but it is open to question whether the depth of the storage reservoir might not with advantage be greater, so as to reduce proportionate loss by evaporation. Including the cost of land, &c., the outlay involved at Swithland was upwards of £317,000, and there are not wanting in Leicester those who regard with amazement the recent announcement that the town council contemplate a further source of water supply, at a cost expected to involve some £800,000.

A good deal of the disquietude and foreboding evinced is probably due to the fact that for reasons of policy the council thought it best to keep their intentions private until the matter came on for final decision and action. There is no doubt, however, that the progress of the town must be largely influenced by the abundance and quality of the water supply, and on the extent to which it complies with the special requirements of local industries. As usual, there are advocates of further temporary measures, who regard themselves as being under no debt to "posterity," but it is to be hoped the corporation will not be deterred from carrying through their bold and public-spirited scheme on the lines contemplated.

### NARROW-GAUGE RAILWAYS.

Narrow-gauge railways are more or less in the same condition as motor vehicles; they are talked about but not extensively used. Comparatively few engineers realise either their capabilities or the saving that can be effected by their adoption. By the aid of these little railways materials may be carried with a minimum expenditure of power and money, and this fact is not only proved by results obtained at Festiniog, Daijerling, Caen and elsewhere, but by the admirable experimental line, which, by the courtesy of Sir Arthur P. Heywood, was open to examination by members of the institution at Duffield Bank, Derby. Here a branch line rises in one-third of a mile to a height of 80 ft., passing a two-third circle curve of 25 ft. radius, and having a 1 in 10 gradient. The main line, half a mile in length, is arranged in the form of a figure 8, so that runs of any length may be made for experimental purposes. Although the gauge is only 15 in., both the passenger, goods and mineral vehicles are roomy, and on the occasion of our visit about 120 persons were conveyed in one train. It has been also proved that an annual traffic of 50,000 tons of minerals may be dealt with on a single line 3 miles in length, with one locomotive. A similar system, 4½ miles in length, has been in successful operation for over two years to connect Eaton Hall with the Great Western Railway. In this case the traffic is about 7,000 tons annually, and, including interest on a total outlay of £5,893 and allowance for depreciation, the cost per ton mile is less than 1s., a charge which would be reduced by one-half if the traffic were four times increased.

### SOME NOTES ON DERBY AND LEICESTER.

It would, perhaps, partake of the nature of exaggeration to say that the town of Derby is divided into two portions, the first being the Midland Railway works and offices, where the inhabitants work by day, and the second the houses where they rest at night. Nevertheless, it is a fact that the company's premises, covering an area of over 200 acres, resemble a fair-sized town, and noticeably in the arrangements for the supply of water, gas and electricity. Water used in the works and supplied to locomotives is pumped from the river Derwent and treated to the extent of 360,000 gallons daily by the Archbutt-Deeley process, which not only removes hardness but also precipitates foreign matter and about 98 per cent. of the bacteria present.

Gas is required on an extensive scale, and the old gasworks adjoining the locomotive works were purchased from the corporation in 1875, and have since been enlarged to meet with increasing demands. In 1897 about 133,000,000 cubic feet of gas were made and supplied to stations, sidings and signals in the Derby neighbourhood. Oil gas for carriage lighting is also made at the Midland works from shale oil, by the Pintsch process; 1 gallon of oil will produce about 75 cubic feet of gas, which is used at a pressure of 150 lb., and has an illuminating power of 45 candle-power for 5 ft. consumption per hour. Similar processes are well known, but might be more generally used in rural districts than at present is the case.

The Midland Railway electric lighting station is of considerable extent. From it several large buildings are lighted, extending over an area of 1,560 ft. by 1,020 ft., and the total number of lamps in operation consists of 2,175 of 16 candle-power, 348 of 8 candle-power and a number of arc lights.

The streets of Derby are efficiently lighted by electricity, and supplies are also available to private consumers for light, power, cooking, &c. Designed by Messrs. Bramwell & Harris, of Westminster, the corporation electric light station was opened in 1893. In the engine-room are fourteen combined engines and dynamos, and another combined machine of 1,000 indicated horse-power is shortly to be in operation. There are also four engines and exciters. Twenty-two centres in the town are fitted with sub-distributing transformer boxes, where the current is transformed from 2,000 volts to 100 or 200 volts. Two independent mains are applied alternately to arc lamps used for street lighting.

Nottingham also possesses excellent arrangements for electric lighting, designed and carried out in 1894 under the supervision of Mr. H. Talbot, electrical engineer to the corporation. The number of lamps connected to the mains is equivalent to 40,000 of 8 candle-power, and there are upwards of 500 private consumers. Observant visitors from London cannot fail to notice with humiliation that even in second-rate provincial centres are more ready to adopt scientific and other improvements than the miscellaneous assortment of governing bodies controlling the welfare of the metropolis. Not only are the important subjects of water supply, lighting plant and means of locomotion more adequately considered, but such towns are apparently more mindful of educational responsibilities. For their size both Derby and Nottingham are well supplied with educational and other institutions. In Derby there is an excellent public library, museum and art gallery, and a municipal technical college, both being under control of the corporation.

Nottingham Castle, adapted by the corporation in 1878 as a public museum and art gallery, is well-known; and University College, opened in 1881, was erected at a cost of nearly £80,000, and is one of the finest piles of public buildings in the provinces. It comprises, in addition to the college, excellent technical schools and a natural history museum. The east block of the college is occupied by the central free public libraries and reading-rooms. During the meetings of the institution a large number of visits were made to engineering works, of which space forbids detailed mention. In conclusion, it may be mentioned that the Derby meeting has proved to be one of the most successful in the history of the Institution of Mechanical Engineers.

## THE HOUSING PROBLEM IN BIRMINGHAM.

### THE MILK-STREET SCHEME.

The Improvements Committee of the Birmingham City Council recently presented a report to the council, in which they state that the question of the erection of houses in Milk-street suitable for the labouring classes has been under consideration both by a sub-committee, formed of members of the Improvement and Health Committees, and by the two committees jointly. The action taken in the past by the Improvement Committee to provide dwellings, and also the course now being pursued by the Health Committee in the closing of the insanitary dwellings, were discussed, and it was recognised that a suitable houses were not erected by private enterprise in the place of those taken down, a duty had devolved upon the council to carry out the intention of the Acts of Parliament to provide some accommodation for the class of persons displaced in the interest of public health, and this view was strengthened by the scarcity of the class of building referred to. It was therefore decided to formulate a scheme for the erection of labourers' dwellings.

WORK IN OTHER TOWNS.

The Corporation of Liverpool having recently erected artisans' and labourers' dwellings of several types, the sub-committee visited that city. It was found that in 1885 and 1892 large blocks of flats were erected four and five storeys high, occupied chiefly by persons of the artisan class. In 1897 dual houses were erected; but the rents were hardly within the reach of the labouring classes. This fact was recognised by the authorities, and experiments have just been made in "Gildart's Gardens" to provide dwellings for the labouring classes. Those dwellings are erected at right angles to the street, in terraces 112 ft. in length, the distance between the fronts of the houses being 30 ft. The houses are arranged in blocks of three storeys in height, the ground-storey tenements being entered directly from the street level, and the upper tenements from a common balcony running along the rear of the houses at the level of the first

floor, a staircase being provided from such balcony for each pair of tenements on the third storey. The dwellings erected by the Corporation of Manchester, the Wharncliff dwellings, London, and several blocks of dwellings in Bristol have also been visited, but the sub-committee considered that none of the dwellings inspected were suitable for labourers' dwellings in Birmingham.

DETAILS OF CONSTRUCTION.

The manager was instructed to prepare and submit sketch plans of through houses, and also of several types of houses designed in two and three storeys. These plans were laid before the members of the joint committee, who came to the unanimous conclusion that the dwellings shown upon the plans will provide healthy and suitable dwellings for the class for which they are intended. The plans have been placed before the architect of the Local Government Board, who expresses the opinion that they could not be more economically designed, and that they comply with the requirements of his board. The Public Works Committee and the medical officer of health have also approved them. Representatives of the Trades Council have seen the plans and discussed the merits of them at a friendly conference, but, although no general agreement was arrived at, nothing took place to justify the altering of the plans or the committee's recommendations in regard to the same.

The tenements are arranged in four terraces, and comprise twenty-four, containing living-room, averaging 13 ft. by 14 ft., bed-room, averaging 12 ft. 2 in. by 9 ft.; and twenty-eight, comprising living-room, averaging 13 ft. 4 in. by 14 ft., bed-room, averaging 8 ft. 2 in. by 14 ft., bed-room, 9 ft. by 9 ft. The plans also provide on the ground floor one tenement, consisting of a shop, with living-room and two bed-rooms, and another with shop, living-room and one bed-room, and on the first floor two dwellings, each containing living-room, with three bed-rooms. Each tenement is provided with a water-closet, approached from a small verandah (open to the air) at the rear of the dwelling, and a scullery, containing copper, coal-bunk and sink. To use the site to the best advantage the design provides for five artisans' dwellings, each containing living-room, 14 ft. 6 in. by 12 ft. 4 in., bed-room, 11 ft. 2 in. by 12 ft. 6 in., bed-room, with a floor space of 84 ft. 9 in. Each house is provided with a water-closet and scullery accommodation.

THE FINANCIAL QUESTION.

The rent suggested to be charged is 1s. 6d. per week per living-room; or, for the first type of dwelling described, 3s. per week, for the second 4s. 6d., and for the through houses 5s. per week. These rents, after paying interest and sinking fund on the outlay now proposed, will leave a margin sufficient to pay a ground rent on the land of 2½d. per yard. The estimated cost of building, including paving, &c., is £8,975; road-making, £146; contingencies, £897; land, at 5s. per yard (4,030 yards), £1,007; total, £11,025. The estimated annual statement will be : Interest and sinking fund on £11,025, £441; estimated rental, £659 2s., from which must be deducted the outgoings, £219 14s., leaving a total of £439 8s. The cost of the Milk-street site was £6,000. Deducting the £1,007 charged to the houses from this sum leaves £4,993 to be provided for. The interest and sinking fund will amount to £199, and this annual payment from the rates must be considered as the city's payment for the sanitary improvements thus made. At the end of the period for which the money is borrowed the property, kept in good repair, will fall in unencumbered, and at present rents will yield a clear income of £400 for ever.

It is a matter of deep regret that many of the houses inhabited by the poorer classes are not in the state of repair they should be, and that infectious diseases claim the majority of their victims from those houses. The committee feel that the scheme submitted will be a step in the direction of lessening this loss of life, and safeguarding the health and lives of the community at large. They therefore urge that the temporary debit balance of the cost of the land can fairly be charged to the rate as a sanitary improvement, and trust that the council will see their way to approve the proposed scheme and to authorise them to make an application to the Local Government Board for their consent to the erection of the houses and the borrowing of £10,100 for the purpose.

West Bromwich.—The Sewerage Committee have recommended that tenders be obtained for the construction of bacteria-beds at the sewage farm. An application is to be made to the Local Government Board for sanction to borrow the necessary money—£1,500.

American Competition.—The Water Committee of the Glasgow Corporation, at a meeting on Monday, considered the new offers for 1,000 tons of cast-iron piping. It was reported that a Philadelphia firm was the lowest offerer and that a local firm came next, the total difference in the price being £800. It may be remembered that when the offers were opened on the first occasion there was a difference of between £600 and £700. The committee was pretty equally divided as to what firm should receive the contract, it being pointed out that it would be unfair to use the American lenders to bring down the prices of the home pipes. It was ultimately agreed to remit the matter for further consideration.

# Comparative Reports of General Practice.

## XXVI.—REFUSE DESTRUCTORS : TIVERTON REPORT.—II.

### Aston Manor (Population 80,000).

Mr. H. Richardson has charge of the works at Aston Manor, where some 350 tons of refuse are disposed of weekly, at a cost of 1s. per ton. The destructor, which has eight cells, works every day, the percentage of clinker produced being from 20 to 30 per cent. It was erected in 1890, and its cells each destroy 8 tons of refuse in a day of twenty-four hours. The makers were Messrs. Manlove, Alliott & Co. The neighbourhood is both a residential and manufacturing one. The houses are 60 yards from the destructor works, which are situated in Chester-street. The chimney shaft is 140 ft. in height, and was erected at a cost of £1,200; £6,500 was spent on the erection of the works. No complaints of any kind have been received. Waste heat is used in connection with the forced draught.

### Bath (Population 54,000).

At this town, where the works are managed by Mr. Joseph Barter, 240 tons of refuse are dealt with during a week; the number of working days is six, but seven are occasionally worked. The cost of working is 8d. per ton, there being eight cells to the destructor. Clinker is never weighed. Each cell of the destructor, which was put down by Messrs. Goddard, Massey & Warner in February, 1895, destroys from 5 to 8 tons of refuse daily. The neighbourhood is mainly residential, and several houses are on the site of the destructor; forty others are in course of erection within a distance of 300 yards. The destructor and chimney cost £5,426; the height of the latter is 165 ft. Complaints regarding the works have been received, but have been found to be groundless. A 20 horse-power engine, employed to drive a mortar mill, utilises the waste heat.

### Batley (Population 30,000).

The engineer in charge here is Mr. J. Lindley. With the exception of Sunday, work is carried on every day and 110 tons of refuse are destroyed, at a cost of about 1s. 7d. per ton. The amount of clinker remaining averages 25 per cent. The cells of the destructor number six, and each destroys from 3 to 4 tons of matter daily. The works were laid down in 1888 by Messrs. Manlove, Alliott & Co. They are situated in a valley and at a distance of 200 yards from houses, which stand on both hillsides. The district is both a manufacturing and residential one. The costs of the destructor and chimney were respectively £2,230 and £416, the height of the chimney being 60 ft. What complaints have been received have been proved to be untrue. Waste heat is used for generating steam for pumping and for driving two mortar mills.

### Birmingham (Population 505,772).

Mr. William Holt, engineer. The destructor is always at work, and destroys 1,875 tons of refuse weekly, at a cost of 11d. per ton; 30 per cent. of clinker remains. The cells, each of which deals with from 5 to 6 tons per twenty-four hours, number fifty. The destructor was built chiefly from Mr. Holt's own designs, and is situated in a manufacturing district from 50 to 100 yards distant from houses. There appear from the report to be three chimney stacks, one being 260 ft. and the others each 160 ft. high. No complaints have been received in regard to the working. The waste heat is utilised in the generation of steam.

### Blackburn (Population 131,000).

Mr. William Stubbs is responsible for the works at Blackburn, where one-third of the refuse collected is destroyed. Work is carried on every day, and the clinker resulting amounts to 15 per cent. There are eight cells to the destructor, which was erected in 1891 by Messrs. Manlove, Alliott & Co., and each deals with 6 tons of refuse daily. The district is, of course, a manufacturing one, and the works are situated on the fringe of a populous district 100 yards away from houses; £2,600 was spent in erecting the chimney stack, which is 300 ft. in height. The cost of the destructor was £8,500. There have been no complaints. Waste heat is used for generating steam.

### Blackpool (Population 40,300).

The engineer in this case is Mr. A. Jasper Anderson. Some 600 tons of refuse are weekly disposed of, work being done on every day with the exception of Sunday. The cost of working, it seems, is 2s. 1·27d. per ton, and the amount of clinker remaining averages 25 per cent. There are twelve cells to the destructor, which was laid down by the Horsfall Furnace Syndicate in 1895. Each cell is capable of destroying 10 tons of refuse per twenty-four hours. The works, which deal with the refuse of a residential population, are in the centre of the town, although 400 yards from houses. The chimney stack is 116 ft. in height. The works, including the stack, cost £5,572. Complaints have been made regarding the working of the destructor, although not lately. The waste heat is employed in working an engine, which provides the forced draught for the furnaces.

### Bolton (Population 121,433).

Engineer, Mr. W. H. Brockbank. The destructor does not work on Saturday afternoons and Sundays. It disposes of 264 tons of refuse weekly, and the cost of the working is covered by the mortar sales. Clinker to the amount of 33 per cent. usually remains. There are eight cells to the works, which were erected in 1880 by Messrs. Manlove, Alliott & Co. Each cell destroys 6 tons of refuse daily. The district is a manufacturing one, and the destructor works occupy a position in the centre of a populous district, houses being within 50 yards; £4,300 was expended on the erection of the buildings and chimney stack. The latter is 180 ft. in height. Only a few trivial complaints have been made regarding the working. Waste heat is utilised in the mortar making, already referred to.

### Bournemouth (Population 54,798).

Mr. F. W. Lacey is responsible for the affairs of the destructor here. Some 225 tons of matter are destroyed weekly, the work being carried on every day. The cost, including labour and repairs, works out at 9d. per ton, and 25 per cent. of clinker generally remains. There are six cells to the destructor, which was erected in 1887 (enlarged in 1891) by Messrs. Manlove, Alliott & Co.; each cell deals with 5 tons of refuse daily. The destructor is a residential one, and the works are surrounded by houses. A sum of £3,171 was spent in connection with the buildings and chimney stack, the latter being 140 ft. high. No complaints have been made. The waste heat in this case is utilised for drying the stone used in tar paving.

### Bradford (Population 230,000).

These works, which are controlled by Mr. J. H. Cox, destroy 322 tons of refuse every week, the period of working extending from Sunday midnight to Saturday noon. The clinker remaining totals 30·3 per cent. There are six cells to the destructor, which was erected in September, 1897, by the Horsfall Furnace Syndicate, and each cell deals with 9·13 tons of refuse every twenty-four hours. The district, according to the report, is a manufacturing one, and houses stand within 150 yards of the destructor works. The latter cost £1,200 to build and the chimney stack £850. The stack is 160 ft. in height. No complaints have been received. A mortar mill and crusher are driven by the waste heat.

### Balstol (Population 318,000).

Mr. T. H. Yabbicom acts as engineer of these works. The latter deal with 686 tons of matter in a week of six days, at a cost of 1s. per ton. Clinker resulting amounts to 25 per cent. Each cell of the destructor (there are sixteen) deals with 7½ tons of matter. The works were erected in 1892 by Messrs. Manlove, Alliott & Co., and are situated in a manufacturing part of the city, within 150 yards of houses. The district, it may be mentioned, is as much residential as manufacturing in character. A sum of £10,729 was spent in erecting the destructor buildings, while the chimney, which is 180 ft. in height, cost £1,689. Only two complaints regarding dust have been made, and for some time none other has been received. The waste heat drives a 40 horse-power tubular boiler, working a stone crusher, mortar pans and sawing machinery.

### Burslem (Population 360,000).

Mr. F. Bettamy is the manager at Burslem. Some 100 tons of refuse are weekly disposed of, at a cost of 1s. 5d. per ton, the works running every day with the exception of Sunday; 35 per cent. of clinker remains. There are four cells, each capable of dealing with 4 tons of refuse, attached to the destructor, which was laid down in 1889 by Messrs. Manlove, Alliott & Co. The district is a manufacturing one, although the works are situated in the open country, houses being 500 yards distant. A sum of £2,410 was expended upon the erection of the buildings. The chimney stack is 80 ft. high, but it was not built with the destructor. Nothing in the nature of a complaint has been received. Fans connected to cells are driven by the waste heat.

### Burton-upon-Trent (Population 50,000).

The engineer in charge at this town is Mr. George T. Lynam. The works, running every day except Sunday, destroy some 192 tons of refuse, at a cost of 1s. 8d. per ton, they leaving 40 per cent. of clinker. The cells number eight, and each deals with 8 tons of stuff daily. Messrs. Manlove, Alliott & Co. were the contractors for the works, which were erected in 1890. The buildings are situated in a manufacturing district only 100 yards from a large number of houses, and cost £4,800 to build; £600 was spent upon the chimney, which is 144 ft. high. One or two complaints have been made respecting the smell emanating from the works. Those, however, were received at least two years ago. A hospital disinfector was formerly supplied with the waste heat from the destructor, but it is now utilised in connection with mortar mills.

### Cambridge (Population 36,983).

Mr. E. Wareham Harry officiates at the Cambridge works, which at the present time destroy 145 tons of refuse weekly. There is no Sunday working. The work costs some 1s. 2d. per ton, and from 25 to 30 per cent. of clinker remains. The destructor was erected in 1895 by Messrs. Manlove, Alliott &

Co. (with Wood & Brodie's patents), and has six cells, each capable of dealing with from 10 to 12 tons of matter daily. Cambridge is a university town and has no manufactures. The works are situated by the river Cam, adjoining the gasworks, and 100 yards from any residence. Their cost was included in the main drainage scheme. The chimney, it may be stated, is 175 ft. in height. There have been no complaints. Sewage pumping is carried out with the waste heat, except on Sundays, when coal is used.

CHELTENHAM (Population 49,000).

The engineer at Cheltenham is Mr. Joseph Hull. Refuse consumed during the course of a week amounts to 200 tons, work being carried on every day. The cost is put down at 10d. per ton, but the percentage of clinker remaining is not known. Eight cells are attached to the destructor (erected in 1890), and each deals with 4½ tons per twenty-four hours. Messrs. Manlove, Alliott & Co. were the builders. The district is a residential one, and the nearest houses are a quarter of a mile distant from the works. The latter cost £5,700 to erect, £800 being spent on the chimney stack, which has a height of 160 ft. There have been no complaints. Electric lighting and disinfecting are carried on with the heat resulting from the works.

DERBY (Population 103,000).

Mr. W. H. Clarry, engineer. In a week of seven working days 280 tons of refuse are dealt with, 33 per cent. of clinker resulting. The works cost (apparently) £500 per annum to maintain, but this does not include repairs. Cells, to the number of six, each consume 7 tons of refuse every twenty-four hours. Messrs. Manlove, Alliott & Co. were also in this case the contractors, and carried out the work of erection in 1882. The refuse is that of a residential district, the works being situated 1 mile from the centre of the town and one quarter of a mile from any houses. One cottage, however, stands 700 ft. away. The destructor buildings cost £9,244, and the chimney stack, which is 160 ft. in height, £300. Occasionally complaints are received. The waste heat is utilised in working elevators, &c.

DEWSBURY (Population 30,000).

The engineer in charge here is Mr. Henry Dearden. Working every day, with the exception of Sunday, some 140 tons of refuse are destroyed, at a cost of 1s. 8⅜d. per ton. The clinker remaining amounts to 32 per cent. There are two cells to the destructor, which was erected in September, 1895, by Messrs. Beaman & Deas. The daily capacity of the works is 15 tons. Houses and business premises surround the buildings, which are situated in a manufacturing district. The chimney stack has a height of 90 ft. No complaints have been received. Forced draught and a feed-water pump are driven by the waste heat.

EASTBOURNE (Population 43,000).

Mr. R. M. Gloyne acts as engineer in this town, where the destructor, working every day, deals with 180 tons of refuse, at a cost of 1s. 4d. per ton, and leaving 27 per cent. of clinker. There are six cells in the works, which were laid down in 1891 by Messrs. Manlove, Alliott & Co., and each cell destroys 5 tons of matter every twenty-four hours. The neighbourhood wherein the works are placed is on the outskirts of the town (which itself is of a residential character) and 100 yards distant from houses. The buildings cost £3,984 to erect and the chimney £845. The latter is 140 ft. high. Complaints are not frequent and usually only received on the occasion of high winds. Steam for working sewer ejectors is generated from the waste heat.

HAMPSTEAD (Population 77,000).

Mr. Charles H. Lowe superintends the work of destruction at Hampstead, where from 250 to 300 tons of matter are dealt with, at a cost of 1s. 4d. per ton. Of clinker there remains 16 per cent. and of fine ash 8 per cent. Each cell destroys 6 tons daily. Messrs. Manlove, Alliott & Co. were the builders of the destructor works, which occupy a position on the Grand Junction canal in a residential neighbourhood. Some recently-built workmen's cottages adjoin the buildings, the nearest being 20 ft. away; £3,235 was expended on the erection of the works. The chimney stack is 120 ft. in height. No complaints have been made regarding the working. Waste steam is not utilised.

HANDSWORTH (Population 43,000).

Mr. S. Henworth has charge of the Handsworth destructor works, which at present destroy 400 tons of refuse weekly. A new eight-cell destructor is now being erected by Messrs. Goddard, Massey & Warner, and each cell is expected to have a capacity of from 8 to 10 tons per day. The neighbourhood which the buildings will be situated in is of a residential character, the nearest house being 150 yards distant. A sum of £6,200 is being expended on the destructor and shaft. The latter will have a height of 200 ft. No complaints are anticipated.

**Glasgow Corporation and the Telephone.**—The Special Committee on Telephones appointed by the Glasgow Corporation met on Tuesday for the first time since the issue of the report of the House of Commons Select Committee. It was decided to renew the application to the Postmaster-General for a telephone license for the municipality, and to appoint a deputation to wait on the Duke of Norfolk and Mr. Hanbury at the earliest convenient date to press the application.

## SEWAGE DISPOSAL AT SWINDON.

### NEW TANKS.

On the 3rd inst. the new sewage tanks, which have been constructed at the Old Swindon District Council's sewage farm, were formally opened. The tanks have been built in order to deal more effectively with the sewage and to make the effluent as pure as possible before it enters the river Rae, the Thames Conservancy Board having forced the council to do this. The work of constructing the tanks was commenced last September, and was almost completed by the end of the year, but there has been delay owing to the scarcity of coke breeze—a large quantity of which was required. Each of the filters will hold 33,000 gallons of sewage and 100 tons of coke breeze. There are three of these tanks. The tanks are constructed of concrete, and the system adopted is really a modification of Dibden's process — precipitation, biological treatment and broad irrigation.

The tanks have been constructed under the supervision of Mr. F. Redman, engineer, of Swindon, who worked out the idea of this system some thirteen years ago. In the filter-beds the water passes through automatic valves—quite a new invention. Mr. Redman does not think there is another system like it in the West of England. The work has been most satisfactorily carried out by Messrs. W. H. Smith & Son, contractors, of Clifton, Bristol. The cost has been £1,300, in addition to which a further sum of £800 has been spent on the construction of a storm-water overflow sewer.

## ARBITRATIONS AND AWARDS.

The following report has been issued by the umpire appointed to determine the sum to be paid by the Southampton Corporation in respect of the borough tramways : " I award and determine that in case the Court shall be of opinion that the arbitrators and umpire appointed as aforesaid should treat the undertaking of the company as defined by the Act of 1897, as an undertaking which the tramways company only enjoyed subject to the contingency of being compelled to part therewith under the terms of sec. 43 of the Tramways Act, 1870, the price to be paid under the Act of 1897 as aforesaid, is the sum of £51,505. I award and determine that if the Court shall be of opinion that the said arbitrators and umpire should treat the undertaking of the company as defined as aforesaid as an undertaking which the tramways company enjoyed free from all obligations to part therewith, other than the obligation created by the Act of 1897 itself, the price to be paid under the Act of 1897, as aforesaid, is the sum of £109,963."

## VAUXHALL TEMPORARY BRIDGE.

The temporary bridge which has been erected across the Thames, between Vauxhall and Pimlico, was to have been opened during the present week. It has been constructed to last ten years, for the first five of which it will take the place of the old Vauxhall bridge, which is to be knocked down and rebuilt, and during the remaining period it will be used for the traffic which will be diverted while Lambeth bridge is being reconstructed. It is not proposed to close Vauxhall bridge until next week, the officials of the London County Council being desirous of watching the working of the temporary bridge for at least a week, in order to be certain that it will be capable of taking the traffic of the old bridge. Providing no hitch occurs Vauxhall bridge will be closed on the 26th inst., and a fortnight later its demolition will be commenced. The new bridge crosses the Thames immediately in front of the Tate Gallery.

## PARLIAMENTARY MEMORANDA.

On Friday in the House of Lords the Royal assent was given in the usual form to the Local Government (Ireland) Act.

Parliament, following the reading of the Queen's speech was declared duly prorogued until Saturday, the 29th of October next.

*Local Government in Ireland.*—The Queen's speech stated that her Majesty had seen with much gratification that an important measure for assimilating the local institutions of Ireland to those of England and Scotland had during the year been added to the statute-book. Her Majesty trusted that that valuable reform would tend to strengthen the bond which united the people of Great Britain and Ireland, and to strengthen their common affection to the fundamental institutions of the realm.

**Worthing.**—The town council have approved of the recommendation of the Electric Lighting Committee that Messrs. Burstall & Monkhouse prepare a complete electric lighting scheme and attend the Local Government Board inquiry, and afterwards supervise the carrying out of the undertaking if sanctioned.

## CORRESPONDENCE.

**Fungoid Growth in Subsoil Drains.**—Mr. H. H. Humphreys, Willesden Green, writes : The inquiry of "Puzzled" on the above matter has opened a subject which is, I think, of some considerable importance to those of us who are interested in the success of sewage purification works. The description given by "Puzzled" reminds me of an experience I had when engineer to one of the district councils on this side of London, an experience which, I may add, has since been supplemented in other districts. As the former case was the most pronounced I have ever seen of flocculent growth, it afforded ample opportunity for the study of the matter by experimental treatment. To enable me to give the conclusions arrived at, as to its prevention or elimination, it will be needful to briefly state the condition of the farm on which the growth took place. It must, however, be clearly understood that the conclusions I arrived at result from my own observation, the authority I was then under regarding an analyst as a superfluous luxury. The purification works had been laid down some ten or twelve years prior to my appointment, and the land was divided into a series of beds approximately level on a longitudinal section, and with a slope of about 1 in 30 from the sides towards the centre. Under the centre of each bed there was a 4-in. agricultural drain pipe, about 700 ft. long and at a depth varying from 2 ft. to 3 ft. 6 in. The soil of the farm was heavy clay, with a small admixture of stone ballast, which, however, did not in any way tend to lighten the ground. Each end of the effluent pipe was sealed, the upper being simply a stunt end in the ground, and at the outfall a tide flap was fixed, abortive for the purpose it was intended to serve, but effectual in preventing aeration of the pipe. Over the pipes 1 ft. or 18 in. of burnt ballast had been put and covered with clay and soil. From the effluent pipes large pieces of opaque flock were continually discharged into the river, rendering the appearance of the water milky, by their being broken up, but collecting together again on the first rough substance they met with in the river bottom and forming a long grey fur or flock. The Thames Conservancy was at the time I speak of bringing a steadily-increasing pressure to bear on the riparian authorities along the river, with a view to better purification being effected, and, after an adverse report by the conservators' inspector on our effluent, I was instructed to take whatever steps were possible to obtain a better result. I had the effluent drains opened out in places, the tide flaps removed and the upper ends of the drains aerated. Not only did this effect a general improvement in the effluent, but it diminished at once the quantity of flock, and led me to conclude that it was principally an anaerobic growth. This was further confirmed by stripping the ballast from the pipes, the interstices being full of fungus. Physically the fungus was of a sticky nature, and under a microscope showed practically no sign of a coherent structural growth, and had very little in common with the characteristic sewage fungus which is generally found in badly-ventilated sewers and manholes. I noted with much interest that when the river bed obtained no fresh supplies of fungus from the effluent pipes, that which had already collected on the gravel developed a green colour, showing itself capable of producing chlorophyl, which I have never heard of a real sewage fungus doing. Ultimately the flock on the river bed appeared to develop into silkweed, and it seems to me to be at least possible that both growths have a common origin, but that one is the protoplastic and anaerobic from the other. I am by no means sure that the nature of a soil heavily charged with iron has not an appreciable effect on the growth. From a conversation I had recently with Prof. Kenwood it would appear that he holds this view too. I have noted that the growth is more pronounced in recently drained land, owing presumably to their being room in the interstices of the imperfectly filled trench for the growth to take place, as was the case with the burnt ballast filling mentioned above. It is certain that as the land becomes tightened down the growth become less. I do not think that it is possible to entirely do away with the fungus, and, as far as my observation has led me, I am of opinion that the subsoil drains should have very careful aeration, and that the better the trenches are filled over the drains the less the growth will be. I do not think that percolation through a horizontal filter of coke breeze is the best way of getting rid of the flock. This course presupposes that additional fall is available near the outfall, which is not usually the case. Further, I have found that a vertical sliding screen, covered either with cocoanut matting or perforated zinc (preferably the latter), and placed in the outfall carrier, is much better for the retention of the flock than is a coke or clinker filter, where the very nature of the flock chokes the pores and in a short time the filtering media are rendered inoperative. In venturing to write somewhat *in extenso* I am hoping that a correspondence may be started with a view to throw light on a subject which is imperfectly understood by many of us, and possibly we may, by comparing notes, arrive at a definite conclusion as to the harmfulness or otherwise of a familiar and at least suspicious component of effluents from newly underdrained clay soils.

**Gas Authorities and the Flash Point of Petroleum.**—Mr. Edward A. Harmon, Corporation Gasworks, Huddersfield, writes : Perhaps one of the most important questions with which the engineering world is intimately concerned at the present moment, directly or indirectly, is that relating to the control of the petroleum trade, concerning which the Select Committee on Petroleum have recently concluded their labours. The recommendations of the committee, as presented in the report to the House of Commons by the chairman, the Right. Hon. Jesse Collings, have already been clearly set forth. The whole issue seems to turn upon the desirability or otherwise of increasing the flash point to 100 deg. (Abel close test). Such a large increase in the flash point as 37 per cent. must necessarily increase the cost of petroleum to the consumer very considerably. Proof is wanting that the flash point is the chief danger. Inferior lamp reservoirs and defective wicks are responsible for not a few of the accidents, if not actually for the bulk of them. The principal points requiring consideration are proper restrictions and regulations for the storage of petroleum. With so many gasworks enriching gas with petroleum in some form or other, regulations regarding petroleum have of course become an important consideration for gas authorities. The increase of carburetted water-gas plants has created a demand for petroleum which formerly did not exist. The extension of the "penny-in-slot" meters for small consumers, and the advantageous terms on which these are offered, is perhaps the best competitor for petroleum lamps. It is a question whether such dangerous articles as lamps have proved to be, in case of excitement, should be allowed to be available for regular use, except under restrictions. Undoubtedly the agitation for raising the flash point was commenced with a view of bestowing an equivalent to a bounty on Scotch oil, the trade of which has been on a downward course for years. When the subject is considered impartially on its merits and demerits, it is very doubtful whether the present flash point is undesirable. With the experiments in progress for the utilisation of liquid fuel for locomotives, &c., the question of reducing the facilities for obtaining it becomes a serious one. The public was recently agitated concerning the extensions of carburetted water-gas plants upon gasworks. This bogey has been practically disposed of, and probably in a few years' time the one alleging the various lamp explosions to the flash point will also disappear as many another has in the past. Increase the flash point to a maximum, and a drunken man in a fit of fury can at once neutralise all the provisions made for safety by using the lamp as a missile. The summary of the recommendations of the Select Committee on the subject as published appears to cover the whole of the important items involved.

## QUERIES AND REPLIES.

*Sketches accompanying Queries should be made separate on white paper, in plain black-ink lines. Lettering or figures should be bold and plain.*

**210. Sewer Ventilation.**—"Borough Surveyor" writes : There appears to be a difference of opinion by the inhabitants of this town, for which I am borough engineer and surveyor, as to the cause of typhoid fever. Of course, the idea held by many is that it is caused by bad water, which is a well-known cause; but may I ask if, in your opinion, typhoid fever may be caused by improper sewer ventilation, such as rain-water fall pipes being connected directly with the sewer, where the hopper heads or inlets from rain water from the roof are in close proximity with bed-room windows, which latter, for a great portion of the day, and, during summer months, all night, are left open ?

There can be no doubt, in our opinion, that there is a close connection between the influence of sewer gas from ill-ventilated or improperly-constructed house drains and sewers and typhoid fever, and we are strongly of opinion that the conditions described by the querist are highly favourable to the development of typhoid in the inmates of houses where such improper methods of drainage and sewer ventilation exist, whilst it is now generally admitted that putrid gases from sewers and drains cannot be held to spontaneously generate typhoid fever, there is no doubt that sewer gas is a strongly-predisposing cause in that it lowers the vitality of the human system and renders it readily susceptible to the entrance of the specific germ which produces typhoid in the human being. Instances of outbreaks of enteric (or typhoid fever) arising from sewer gas poisoning are numerous, such as those at Worthing in 1865, at Croydon in 1875, at Melton Mowbray in 1880, and at York in 1884, and in the sporadic cases occurring from time to time in almost every sanitary district in the kingdom. It is a noteworthy fact that in almost every instance defects in house drainage and the entry of sewer gas or drain air into the dwellings, or otherwise defective sanitary construction, have been found. The subject is one which is open to considerable controversy, as there is much difference of opinion among the numerous observers, but the broad fact that insanitary conditions are a strongly-predisposing cause to outbreaks of typhoid fever should not be lost sight of. Roechling's "Sewer Gas and its Influence upon Health" (Biggs & Co., 5s.) will be found useful to those who desire to further study the subject.

## Some Recent Publications.

SOME SHORT NOTICES.

St. Botolph, Aldgate: The Story of a City Parish Church, by A. G. B. Atkinson, M.A. (Grant Richards), is a more pretentious publication than either of those already noticed. The title-page states that it has been "compiled from the record-books and other ancient documents," and considerable care has evidently been bestowed on the production of an agreeably-written and valuable historical work. Want of space precludes us from referring to more than a few of the numerous interesting facts recorded of an important city parish, identified in mediæval times with the gate through which access to the city was obtained from the east. We find here mentioned that as early as the thirteenth century tolls for the repair of the roads were levied upon all vehicles entering and leaving the city, and that at a subsequent period the wealthy were exempted from payment; but the principal adjacent street was not paved until 1503, and the thoroughfares "without Aldgate, in the suburbs of London," were paved with stones, in accordance with Acts of Parliament passed in 1571 and 1581. In 1374 Aldgate had a notable tenant in the person of Geoffrey Chaucer, the father of English poetry, who obtained a lease for life from the city authorities of "the whole of the dwelling-house above the gate of Aldgate." The gate itself was demolished in 1606, when many Roman coins were found under it, and another built on the same site, at a cost of £4,000, was taken down in 1761 and the materials sold to Ebenezer Mussell for £117 10s. For full particulars of these and a multitude of equally-interesting events we must refer our readers to the detailed records interwoven in pleasant narrative form in a well-printed volume.

Uniform with the hand-books in "Bell's Cathedral Series," and similar in appearance, is a publication of the same firm, entitled The Church of St. Martin, Canterbury: An Illustrated Account of its History and Fabric, by the Rev. C. F. Routledge, M.A., F.S.A., Hon. Canon of Canterbury. This attractive little volume refers to several historical incidents of absorbing interest, and contains numerous fine illustrations of the places and objects described. The text is well and carefully written. A judicious arrangement has been adopted with regard to the various subjects treated, and accuracy in matters of detail appears to be a predominant feature. Canon Routledge quotes the words of an antiquarian authority, to the effect that "it is every day more true that people want history in guide-books. The tourist is a much better-informed person than he used to be, and desires to be still more so." St. Martin's church occupies a unique position as regards both its history and structure, and no more desirable companion than the work before us can be recommended to the intelligent visitor who wishes for full and reliable information respecting a venerable edifice that may be regarded as being the one remaining building that could certainly be associated with St. Augustine's preaching; the one spot that without doubt felt his personal presence, whatever we may think of the more or less strong claims put forth on behalf of Ebb's Fleet, Richborough Castle, the ruins of St. Pancras, or the site of Canterbury Cathedral.

The Cathedral Church of Hereford: A Description of its Fabric and a Brief History of the Episcopal See, by A. Hugh Fisher (G. Bell & Sons, 1s. 6d.), is one of a series of monographs designed to supply visitors to the great English cathedrals with accurate and well-illustrated guide-books at popular prices. We are told by the editors, Messrs. Gleeson White and E. F. Strange, in the general preface, that the aim of each writer has been to produce a work compiled with sufficient knowledge and scholarship to be of value to the student of archæology and history, and yet not too technical, in language for the use of an ordinary visitor or tourist. A careful examination of the book convinces us that Mr. Fisher has accomplished this purpose in a very efficient manner, and the volume is handsome in appearance, choicely printed on good paper, and copiously illustrated with excellent reproductions of photographs and artistic sketches.

The Hand-Book of Eastbourne, published by the Chamber of Commerce in that town, is a handsomely-printed and beautifully-illustrated practical guide to a favourite watering place.

Travel and Entertainment is the title of a small guide-book, containing the tariffs of the Midland Railway hotels, in addition to useful local information.

OLD ENGLISH LIFE.

Life in an Old English Town; A History of Coventry from the Earliest Times, by Mary Dormer Harris (Swann Sonnenschein & Co., Limited, 4s. 6d.), necessarily proceeds on somewhat different lines from the last-mentioned work. It forms a volume of the "Social England Series," which, we are told in the editorial preface, "rests upon the conviction that it is possible to make a successful attempt to give an account, not merely of politics and wars, but also of religion, commerce, art, literature, law, science, agriculture, and all that follows from their inclusion, and that without a due knowledge of the last we have no real explanation of any of the number." Surely not very intelligible writing for a writer who assumes a responsible position in developing new sources of enlightenment and instruction. If the main object in compiling this book has been "to describe some leading features of English social life," as exemplified in the local annals and municipal enactments of a historic town, on the author's own testimony the selection does not appear to be a happy one, for we read: "So far was Coventry from the great centres of the national life that there is little to connect the place in the early part of its history with the history of the kingdom." York, Winchester, Bristol or Chester would appear to offer superior advantages in this respect. We may question whether it is quite correct to affirm that "there is hardly any subject on which ordinary folk, especially members of large communities, are so ignorant as local government." Evidently, in the author's estimation, Coventry is an exceptional town, and possesses many novel features apart from the Godiva processions. In the concluding chapter, headed "Old Coventry of the Present Day," we see it stated that "Coventry is well worth a whole day's visit, though the day may be an easy one, as all the principal buildings lie very near together, and are practically always open," a course which is not without its risks, but is certainly of advantage to the visitor who has little time to waste on unearthing sacristans or other caretakers. Again, it is stated that "either the powers that be have little leisure to think of tourists, or they must be men of singular enlightenment, for I know of no place which can be seen so freely and cheaply, where lingering over a charming effect, a loss, inscription or painted window may be done with such pleasure, because interruption is so rare." Yes, indeed, "this is a condition of things tourists ought to be thankful for," and no wonder that this piece of seasonable advice is added : "The sightseer ought to have an opera (?) glass." The book, however, is full of interesting details.

THE METROPOLIS AND ITS INHABITANTS.

London and Londoners, by Rosalind Pritchard, professes to give adequate information as to "what to see, what to know, what to do, where to shop," in addition to "practical hints." We are informed that "in placing a new guide to London before the public the aim of the editor has been to enable the stranger visiting the metropolis for the first time, or the provincial making his annual and fleeting stay, to get at the root of the matter as speedily and with as little labour to himself as may be." We fear that the authoress is not at all times the best pioneer to the uninitiated visitor "who may be actuated by the laudable desire to probe the matter to the root," whatever that may mean. The twelve chapters devoted to "What to See" give a very superficial description of the ordinary London sights, and matters of detail are frequently treated in a most unsatisfactory manner; as, for instance, in the list given of the principal pictures in the National Gallery, only two of Turner's pictures are mentioned, and these not by any means the most important. The first chapter of "What to Know" commences with the announcement "that the Queen now rarely resides in London." Evidently the "stranger" in his first visit, or the "provincial" on his annual sojourn, are assumed to be unacquainted with Truth. We find the Royal College of Music described among the "Learned Societies," and hearers. Audie and W. H. Smith & Son mentioned among the "Public Libraries," and in doubtful connection with the word "free." "Macmillan and Blackwood" are omitted from the list of magazines, and The Edinburgh and Church Quarterly from the reviews. Lunatic asylums are not included with hospitals in the chapter headed "London Charities," but somewhat unaccountably introduced into that containing a list of the names of eminent medical men. The portion of the book comprised in "What to Do" is devoted to a description of the theatres, places of amusement and varieties of sport available. Here we see "Ascot Races," "Fourth of June at Eton" and "Henley Regatta" classed as "Red-Letter Days in London." Twenty-two pages are given up to an account of various packs of hounds, and more space is allotted to the Romney Marsh Harriers or the Walthampton Beagles than to cycling or football; but then we are assured by the writer that "beagling is a favourite sport in England," and apparently a "Greenlander" is informed that "these hounds hunt the hare and it is usual to follow beagles on foot." The questionable proceedings of gun clubs are not recognised in this volume. The commercial element enters so largely into "Where to Shop" as to render criticism superfluous; and why the Royal Pier Hotel, Ryde, and the Hotel Metropole, Folkestone, should receive more notice than the Hotel Cecil or the Coburg is not very clear from a utilitarian point of view. We are compelled to omit reference to some debateable matters in the summary of the "London Way of 'Smart' Society" and the information contained in "Practical Hints," but we note the significant announcement that, 'as nothing is more evanescent than the passing whims of smart society, and the unwritten code by which the 'best people' steer their course. 'London and Londoners' will be carefully revised and brought up to date each year."

Jarrahdale Jarrah.—The Sydenham, with 952 loads, and the steamer Orestes, with 804 loads of Jarrahdale jarrah on board, have arrived in London to the order of the agents of McLean Brothers & Rigg, Limited, 1 Fenchurch-avenue, E.C.

# Law Notes.

Edited by J. B. REIGNIER CONDER, 11 Old Jewry Chambers, E.C.,

Solicitor of the Supreme Court.

*The Editor will be pleased to answer any questions affecting the practice of engineers and surveyors to local authorities. Queries (which should be written legibly on foolscap paper, one side only) should be addressed to " The Law Editor," at the Offices of The*

*Surveyor. Where possible, copies of local Acts or documents referred to should be enclosed. All explanatory diagrams must be drawn and lettered in black ink only. Correspondents who do not wish their names published should furnish a nom de plume.*

Highway: Defective Fence: Liability of Landowner for Personal Injury.—The case of *Harrold* v. *Watney* (Court of Appeal) is of more interest perhaps to landowners than to highway authorities. It is, nevertheless, indirectly interesting to the latter, and, moreover, the point decided is so novel and the decision so important that a brief note of the case will, we think, be acceptable to our readers. The defendant was the owner of a piece of waste land adjoining South-street, Wandsworth, and separated from the highway by a wooden fence belonging to him. The plaintiff, a boy of four years of age, was clambering up the fence (in order to look at some children playing on the other side) when the fence gave way, and the boy fell, sustaining considerable injuries. The action was tried before Mr. Justice Ridley and a jury. The jury assessed the damages at £45, but the learned judge, being of opinion that the defendant was not legally liable, entered judgment in his favour. That decision, however, has been reversed by the Court of Appeal. On behalf of the plaintiff it was contended that the defendant was bound to keep the fence in a safe condition; that its dangerous state amounted to a nuisance, for the consequences of which he was liable; and that it made no difference that the boy, in climbing the fence, was committing a trespass. For the defendant, on the other hand, it was argued that, in order to give a right of action for nuisance in such a case as this, it must be shown that the injuries were the result of an involuntary act on the part of the plaintiff, whereas the climbing of the fence was a purely voluntary act. Lord Justice Vaughan Williams, in the course of his judgment, said that the test of liability was this: Was that which the child did something which ought to have been present to the mind of the defendant as to the probable result of leaving the fence in a dangerous condition? If the defendant answered, " No grown-up person would have thought of climbing the fence," the reply was "The Queen's highway was not intended for grown-up people only, and a defective fence is very likely to cause injury to children using the highway." We think this decision will be rather a startling one to landowners.

Sewerage Works: Application for Mandamus: Metropolis Management Act, 1855, sec. 69: Metropolis Management Act, 1862, sec. 45.—The Court of Appeal have discharged a rule absolute for a mandamus granted by the Queen's Bench Divisional Court in the recent case of *Regina* v. *Vestry of St. Mary, Islington* (2nd August). The rule was made on the application of one James Williams, on behalf of the Midland, Great Eastern, and Tottenham and Hampstead Junction Railway Companies, and directed the vestry to prepare a scheme of such sewers, or such diversions or alterations of sewers and works, as it might be necessary to construct for effectually draining their parish or district, and to submit a plan of the proposed sewer or sewers to the County Council. The facts of the case are briefly as follows : Part of the railway of the Tottenham and Hampstead Junction Railway Company, which passed through a cutting between Hornsey-road station and Crouch Hill station, was frequently flooded. The overflow came from a sewer which had been originally built in 1865 by the Tottenham and Hampstead Junction Railway Company, but was now vested in the vestry, and which ran along and underneath the 6-ft. way of the railway for about half a mile. The sewer consisted of a brick culvert, with manholes and ventilation gratings, and in times of heavy rains the water flooded the line to the depth sometimes of 6 ft., thus stopping or delaying the traffic. The overflow from the sewer, which took place every year from 1882 down to the present time, was caused during heavy rains by the insufficiency of another sewer vested in the vestry (into which the sewer in question ran) to carry off the sewage, and this insufficiency was alleged to be due to the vestry allowing the Hornsey District Council to send their sewage into it, which dammed back the sewage coming from the sewer in question. In 1889 the vestry submitted a scheme for a new sewer to the London County Council, but the latter had not sanctioned the scheme. Lord Justice A. L. Smith, in the course of his judgment, referring to this scheme, said there was no suggestion that that was an improper plan, or that it was not made *bona fide*. But there was a difficulty in fitting in the plan with the main drainage scheme, and the facts showed that the vestry were not in a position to carry out a scheme for carrying off the overflow. A correspondence took place between the vestry and the London County Council, which had been going on ever since. It seemed to him to be clear on the facts that the vestry had done their best to carry out their statutory duties, and that on that ground a mandamus ought not to be granted. There was another ground on which he thought

their judgment might be based. A mandamus ought not to be granted unless there had been a demand and a refusal. No doubt there had been—a demand of some sort here—a demand to construct a sewer—but he could not find that there had been a refusal of any demand which had been made. The mandamus, however, which was asked for, and for which a rule was granted, was a mandamus to prepare a scheme for effectually draining the district. He did not see the slightest evidence that a demand had ever been made on the vestry to prepare such a scheme. He thought that the appeal ought to be allowed. Lord Justice Rigby was of the same opinion. He did not think there was any ground for saying that the vestry had tried to evade their duty, but, on the contrary, he came to the conclusion that they had from the first been anxious to do their duty, and to do it in the right way, and that the plan which they had submitted was a reasonable plan. Further, he thought that the terms of the rule for a mandamus differed so much from the terms of the demand which had been made on the vestry that on that ground they ought to refuse to make the mandamus absolute. Lord Justice Vaughan Williams agreed in the result, but he did so reluctantly. He agreed because his brethren were of opinion on the evidence that the vestry had honestly applied themselves to the performance of their duty of draining their district. He would not disagree with that conclusion of fact. But he should be sorry to have to say that in his opinion the mandamus ought not to go because of any irregularity in the form of the application. The substance of the complaint of the railway companies was that the vestry had not properly performed their statutory duty of effectually draining their district. He desired to disavow basing his judgment on the ground that there had been no demand on the vestry to take the preliminary step of submitting plans to the County Council.

## QUERIES AND REPLIES.

Private Streets: Public Health Act, 1875, sec. 150.—Mr. Fred. Rayner, Newhaven Urban District Council, writes : My council decided to make-up and take over a certain road, according to sec. 150 of Public Health Act, 1875, and to charge the separate owners with the cost. A question now arises as to who is liable for the passages marked A on rough

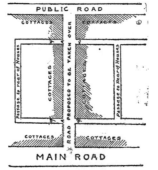

sketch herewith which are right-of-ways only to the back entrances of the houses, and are so mentioned in the deeds of conveyance. This road has only been opened about four years. I shall be glad to receive this information as to whether the frontages of these passages to the road should be paid by the original owner of the estate or by the various freeholders of the houses in the said road.

It was decided in *Jewett* v. *Idle Local Board* (67 L.T. [N.S.], 928) that the definition of a " street " contained in sec. 4 of the Act must be read into sec. 150. That definition includes any alley or passage, whether a thoroughfare or not. And in *Tyzler* v. *Gildhem Corporation* (L.R., 4 Ch., D. 305) it was held that the latter section extends to streets which are in all respects private and over which the public have no right. These passages are therefore " streets " within secs. 160, and the owners of the premises " fronting, adjoining or abutting " thereon (*i.e.*, the various cottages and also the land at the backs of the passages) are liable for the cost of making them up.

HOARDINGS SET UP DURING THE PROGRESS OF BUILDINGS.—
"C. S." inquires: Under sec. 34 of the Public Health Acts
Amendment Act, 1890, can the urban sanitary authority require *notice* to be given (at the office of their clerk or surveyor) by builders and others for leave to erect hourdings
*before erecting same?* In other words, is the existence of any
hoarding on the public highway *illegal without the urban
authority's consent has first been applied for and obtained?*
If not so, how is the machinery of the Act to be set in motion
and applied? The giving of notice is not required in so
many words, but inferentially is there not strong presumption of the necessity of such notice being required? If any
cases decided upon this clause please quote.

In the metropolis a license from the vestry has to be obtained before
a hoarding is erected, under sec. 122 of the Metropolis Management
Act, 1855. There is, however, no corresponding provision in the Public
Health Acts Amendment Act, 1890, nor in the sections of the Towns
Improvement Clauses Act, 1847, which are applicable in districts where
the Act of 1890 has not been adopted. "A householder may put up
hoards temporarily during repairs, although they may to some extent
obstruct the highway" (Glen's "Highways"). The authority given
by Mr. Glen for this statement is the case of *Fisher* v. *Prowse* (2 B. and
S. 770). That case, however, was decided in 1862, and in districts in
which the Act of 1890 is in force the principle deduced from the decision must be considered as subject to any modification or qualification effected by sec. 34 of that Act. The section provides that every
person intending to build, or take down any building, or to alter or
repair the outward part of any building in any street or court, shall
*before beginning the same,* unless the urban authority otherwise consent
in writing, cause close-boarded hoards or fences, *to the satisfaction of
the urban authority,* to be put up. Although, therefore, there is nothing
(apparently) making it compulsory on a builder to give notice to the
authority before erecting a hoarding, or to obtain their *permission* to
erect it, he must obviously obtain their *approval* of the hoarding before
beginning his building or alterations. Practically I should think this
gives the authority sufficient control, because it would be less trouble
to a builder to consult the authority beforehand as to the construction
of the hoarding than to have to alter it to meet their views after he
has put it up.

MATERIALS FOR REPAIR OF HIGHWAY: HIGHWAY ACT,
1835, SECS. 51 AND 53.—"Surveyor" writes: Is it necessary
to give a month's notice to owners and occupiers of land
adjoining brooks and rivers when they refuse permission to
go through their lands to the brooks for the purpose of obtaining road material?

Sec. 51 of the Highway Act, 1835, empowers the surveyor of highways to take material for repairing the highway from any waste land
or common ground, river or brook, so that he does not interrupt the
course of the river, &c., or damage buildings, &c.; and likewise to
gather stones lying upon any land without making satisfaction for the
materials, but making satisfaction for damage; but no stones, &c., are
to be gathered without the consent of the owner of the lands or the
license of two justices. Sec. 53 provides that the surveyor is not to
take material from enclosed lands until he has given one month's
written notice to the owner to appear before two justices to show
cause why a license to take the material should not be granted. The
term "enclosed lands" in this section includes all lands (whether
actually fenced or not) in the exclusive occupation of one or more
person or persons for agricultural purposes (4 and 5 Vic., c. 51). Sec. 51
appears to place rivers and brooks in the same category with waste
land and commons. In the case of a river or brook flowing through
private land, however, it would seem that sec. 53 must apply ; but I
have not been able to find any case dealing with this point, and the
text-book writers (Pratt and Glen) ignore it altogether, although they
annotate the sections literally. If actual access can be obtained to the
river or brook in question, I think the surveyor would be justified in
disregarding the owners' refusal and leaving them to make the question. But if it is physically impossible or difficult to get through the
lands without the owners' consent, the better plan would be to give
notice under sec. 53.

HOUSE DRAINS: COMMUNICATION WITH SEWERS.—Mr. F. W.
Mager, district surveyor to the Rural District Council of
Walsall, writes : In preparing regulations under 38 and 39
Vic., cap. 55, would it be *ultra vires* to insert clauses : (*a*) Requiring cement joints throughout the whole length of drain
proposed to be connected with the sewer; (*b*) requiring an
inspection chamber in connection with the "interceptor"?
These two clauses might be considered to come more properly
under building by-laws, but are not expressly mentioned in
the code as adopted in my district; but may it not be argued,
as regards (u), infiltration of ground water (in my case a
matter of extreme importance) is prevented, and (*b*) interceptors may be inspected if necessary and the "ventilation"
difficulty reduced.

I presume sec. 21 of the Act is referred to, which empowers an owner
to cause his drains to empty into the sewers on giving notice and complying with the regulations of the authority "in respect of the mode in
which the communications between such drains and sewers are to be
made." It seems to me that both the suggested clauses go somewhat
beyond regulations as to the mode of communication, and would more
properly be the subject of building by-laws.

SURVEYOR TO DISTRICT COUNCIL.—"Assistant" writes:
Would you be so good as to inform me if a surveyor to an
urban district council or rural district council has any legal
power to act in connection with his duties without consulting his council, and, if so, by what enactment?

The surveyor is the servant of the council, and is bound to act under
their directions. They can, of course, if they please, give him a
general authority to act in regard to his ordinary duties without consulting them at every step, and they may (under sec. 189 of the Public
Health Act, 1875) make regulations with respect to the duties and
conduct of their officers." But their authority is paramount, and he
has no independent power.

BUILDING BY-LAWS.—"F. J. W." writes: Where building
by-laws have been recently adopted, do they apply to buildings incomplete at the date they come into force?

The power of making by-laws under the Public Health Act, 1875, applies only to new buildings. What is a "new building" within the
meaning of the Act is a question of fact for the magistrates in each

case (*James* v. *Wyvill*, 51 L.T. [N.S.], 237). A building in an advanced
stage would be hardly likely to be held to be a new building, but one
in a very early stage might perhaps be so considered.

BUILDING LINE.—"Lino" writes: Will you kindly inform
me from what Act or Acts of Parliament the power to
define building lines (frontage) for buildings about to be
erected in district where by-laws are in force? And would
there be any difference in these powers in a rural and urban
district?

See the Public Health (Buildings in Streets) Act, 1888, sec. 3, which,
however, only applies to urban districts.

## ARBITRATIONS AND AWARDS.

On the 29th and the 30th ult., at the Westminster Palace
Hotel, London, Mr. Samuel Jackson, F.S.I., sat as arbitrator
in regard to a claim made by Sir John Ramsden against the
Huddersfield Corporation, with reference to the compulsory
purchase of land under the Corporation Act, 1897. It was
stated that substantially the whole of Huddersfield belonged
to Sir John Ramsden, and he now claimed for certain of his
land being taken for sanitary purposes by the corporation,
and also for certain other land of his which was injuriously
affected by the corporation having power to build dust destructors and things of that kind. The whole area of the
land to be taken, which was situate on both banks of the
river Elne, was 34,000 square yards. It was very advantageously situate, being near to Huddersfield station, and the
land adjacent was occupied by woollen mills, dye works,
chemical and machine works, and so on, and that it was land
that was very valuable for building sites. Coal had been
worked in the neighbourhood, but borings had been taken,
and it would be agreed that there was no coal
now left, so that there would be no interference with building operations. For the corporation, Mr. Kenneth Findlater
Campbell, the borough surveyor, said the land in question
could certainly not be utilised for building purposes without
an elevation of its level. In his opinion the land was admirably adapted for tipping purposes, and nothing else. The
arbitrator reserved his award.

## GLASGOW ELECTRIC LIGHTING.

The Electricity Committee of the corporation have considered certain recommendations by Mr. Chamen, the en-
gincer, as to charges, and adopted the following: (1) That
all consumers of current, whether for lighting or motive
power, during the year which commenced on June 1st last,
should have the option of continuing to be charged in accordance with the demand indicator system, which has been in
operation for the last two years, or of being charged a fixed
rate per annum of 8 candle-power lamp, or its equivalent,
fitted up in the premises, spreading this charge uniformly
over each month in the year, with an additional rate of so
much per unit (over and above the fixed charge) for each
unit consumed as recorded on the meter; (2) that in the case
of the demand indicator system, the initial charge should remain at 6d. per unit for the first hour, with 2¼d. per unit
thereafter to the 100-volt consumers, and 2d. per unit thereafter to the 200 and 250 volt consumers; (3) that, under the
alternative method of charging to be given to the consumers,
the fixed rate should be 4s. 6d. per lamp per annum, with
2¼d. per unit additional to the 100-volt consumers, and 2d.
per unit to the 200 and 250 volt consumers; and (4) that, to
all consumers who take a supply for more than the equivalent
of seven hours each day at full load for twelve months, the
initial charge in the case of the demand indicator system,
and the fixed charge of 4s. 6d. per lamp in the case of tho
alternative system, should be remitted.

## PROPOSED NEW BRIDGE OVER THE THAMES.

A movement is on foot in Twickenham and other places
having for its object the erection of a new bridge across the
Thames opposite that town. At present Twickenham is
practically deprived of any enjoyment to be derived from
walking alongside the Thames, as nearly all the river frontages are in private hands, and the Surrey shore opposite can
only be reached by means of a ferry. It was proposed at
first that a footbridge should be erected similar to the one at
Toddington, the cost of which is estimated at about £7,500.
It was proposed to carry this bridge over Eel Pie Island,
where a large hotel is about to be built. Others, however,
deemed this a half measure, holding that what was wanted
was a stone bridge for horses and carriages, which would
bring Kingston, the only market town in the neighbourhood,
1½ miles nearer to Twickenham than it is at the present time.
The movement has now assumed definite shape, as the
Twickenham District Council have taken the matter in hand,
and have appointed a committee to approach the Middlesex
County Council, the Surrey County Council, the Earl of
Dysart, and any other authorities or persons concerned, with
a view of constructing a carriageway bridge over the Thames
at the point mentioned. Such a bridge, it is believed, would
cost about £90,000.

# Municipal Work in Progress and Projected.

This being the autumn recess, matters municipal are in the metropolis quiescent, but it is not so in the provinces, to judge from the information to hand in regard to Bristol, Bury, Halifax, Newcastle and other towns. The activity in connection with electric lighting and tramways continues in undiminished vigour.

## METROPOLITAN AUTHORITIES.
### VESTRIES AND DISTRICT BOARDS.

**Poplar.**—The Local Government Board have received a petition objecting to the application of the vestry for sanction to borrow £9,000 for the establishment of baths, &c., on the Isle of Dogs.

**Whitechapel.**—It is stated, says a local contemporary, that the electric lighting question at Whitechapel has not been allowed to slumber. A meeting of the committee has been held, and it is probable that an effort will be made to induce Mr. Wright, the electrical engineer to the Brighton Corporation, who possesses perhaps the most successful municipal installation in the kingdom, to give part of his time to carrying out the Whitechapel installation, at a salary approaching £600 per annum.

## PROVINCIAL AND GREATER LONDON AUTHORITIES.
### COUNTY COUNCILS.

**Bucks.**—Correspondence has taken place with the Middlesex County Council in reference to bridging the river Colne between Iver and West Drayton, which is partly in Bucks and partly in Middlesex, and the Middlesex County Council have intimated that they will be prepared to contribute a sum not exceeding £1,000, subject to the plans being approved by the Middlesex County Council and to a satisfactory arrangement being made as to its future maintenance. The Bucks County Council is requested to undertake also to provide a sum not exceeding £1,000, subject to the plans and the arrangements for future maintenance being approved by this council, and provided the remainder of the cost of the bridge and approaches can be raised locally. The Middlesex County Council estimate that a suitable bridge would cost £3,500.

**East Riding.**—The council will shortly give their consideration to the following resolution: "That a more convenient bridge, of modern structure, is desirable in the place of the existing dangerous and obsolete structure known as Hull bridge, which is totally unfit to meet the requirements of the present traffic, and that the county council be pleased to take into favourable consideration the erection in its place of a modern iron swing bridge, which would be more suitable both for the road and river traffic."—Upon the recommendation of a committee, it was last week decided to accept the plans of Mr. B. S. Jacobs, of Hull, for a new register office and additional accommodation for the clerk of the council, the inspector of weights and measures and the caretaker. The estimated cost of the work amounts to £3,826.

### MUNICIPAL CORPORATIONS.

**Birkenhead.**—At a recent meeting of the town council a member, in moving the adoption of the minutes of the Gas, Water and Electrical Committee, referred to the report of the resident electrical engineer upon the proposed extension of the electric light supply to Bidston and Noctorum. He gave two reasons for the preparation of the report—viz., first, that the residents had memorialised the committee not once but several times, and that they had entered into an agreement to use the light if it was brought to them; secondly, the electric light could be extended in the district without any loss, or a very small loss, in the first year, and in subsequent years the profit would be very considerable. The minutes were passed.

**Blackburn.**—Eight designs and estimates for a new conservatory in Corporation Park, varying in price from £967 to £3,646, exclusive of mason's work and brickwork, have been under the consideration of the council. Two designs have been selected, and a final choice will shortly be made. The amounts of the selected designs amount to respectively £1,400 and £2,100.

**Bournemouth.**—The council have accepted tenders for carrying out a scheme for lighting the lower pleasure gardens, pier and winter gardens by electricity, and it was decided to hold a special meeting to consider the desirability of applying for a provisional order empowering the corporation to adopt a scheme for lighting the town generally. We understand that the accepted tenders were those of the Brush Electrical Engineering Company (£1,598) and Siemen Brothers & Co. (£1,135).

**Bristol.**—The town council have adopted a recommendation of the Docks Committee in favour of applying for powers to construct a new lock and other works at Portishead dock, so as to provide accommodation for the largest classes of steamers afloat or building. The estimated outlay is £350,000.

An amendment to the effect that the "dockisation" of the river Avon was the best scheme was defeated by forty-one votes to twenty-one votes.

**Bury.**—The Electric Lighting Committee last week recommended that the following tenders be accepted, subject to the approval of the Local Government Board being obtained to the proposed loan for electric lighting—viz., Messrs. Davey Brothers, Sheffield, for the boilers, &c.; the Callendar Cable and Construction Company, for the mains, &c.; and Messrs. Fowler & Co., Leeds, for plant, &c. The tenders, with the cost of the engineer, clerk of the works, &c., amounted to £19,439 15s., exclusive of the cost of buildings, which is estimated at £2,500, making a total of £21,939 15s. The loan for which permission has been applied for is £20,000, which, with the sum of £2,500 in the hands of the gas company, £22,500, which will leave £560 for contingencies. The report was adopted.

**Canterbury.**—A Local Government Board inquiry, with regard to the application of the town council for power to borrow £70,000 for the purchase of the Stone House estate and the erection of a lunatic asylum, was held by Lieut.-Colonel Albert C. Smith, R.E., at the Guildhall, Canterbury, on Friday.

**Deal.**—The mayor of Deal has written a letter with a view to qualifying the somewhat exaggerated paragraphs appearing in some of the morning papers in regard to the encroachment of the sea. His worship says that about eight years back they spent some thousands of pounds in erecting a sea-defence wall at the north part of the town, and also decided to erect certain groynes during the present summer. They have asked the Local Government Board for the necessary powers, but as they have not succeeded in getting the requisite Government inquiry they are proceeding with the work without delay. The mayor points out that these measures are only precautionary, and there is not the slightest danger at this season of any inundation.

**Derby.**—Colonel W. R. Slacke, one of the Local Government Board inspectors, held an inquiry at the Town Hall, Derby, on Tuesday, for the purpose of considering the advisability of borrowing £310 for street improvements; £150 was required for the improvement of a portion of East-street and £160 for London-road. The necessity of these improvements had been already admitted by the board. The inspector intimated that he would report to the Local Government Board in due course.

**Godalming.**—The town council have resolved to purchase the Frith Hill, Godalming and Farncombe Water Company, and a committee have been formed to arrange all formalities, and, if necessary, to promote a Bill in Parliament for the acquisition of the undertaking. According to the terms agreed upon in the negotiations, the corporation's liability in purchasing the concern will be £67,257.

**Halifax.**—The town council are about to extend the electric tram system by constructing new lines, at an estimated cost of £31,000, and also to purchase four new tramcars, at a cost of about £500 each.

**Hastings.**—At the meeting of the town council on Friday the question of providing a lift to the East Hill will be discussed. The East Cliff is one of the chief beauties of Hastings, and leads to Ecclesbourne and Fairlight Glens, but many are debarred from visiting these spots on account of the wearisome climb to the summit of the hill.

**Ilkeston.**—In proposing the adoption of the General Works Committee's minutes last week, a member said that it was absolutely necessary to provide a duplicate engine at the water works, at a cost of £1,500 to £2,000, to prevent a water famine in case of a breakdown of the present engine; also a new filter-bed, at a cost of £600 or £700; and also a 12-in. main from Bath-street main to the Shipley reservoir, at a cost of £1,300 or £1,400. These works were absolutely imperative. The minutes were adopted.

**Leeds.**—Some little time, according to a Leeds journal, must elapse before Eccup reservoir can fulfil its proper functions. Meanwhile, however, a fair amount of progress has been made with the task of filling it. The water, in fact, has reached a depth of 17 ft. without any leak being discernible. This was reported last week to the Leeds Corporation Waterworks Committee. The present storage of water in the corporation reservoirs, by the way, is equivalent to fifty-nine and a half days' supply, as compared with forty-seven and a half days' supply last year at this time. Another satisfactory statement made to the committee had reference to Harehills reservoir, which not only is now completed, but will in all probability be filled before the committee hold their next monthly meeting. It is expected to prove a very useful addition to the water supply of the growing districts of Northern Leeds. The work in connection with the Headingley pumping station is also advancing. A second engine is being taken down, and will shortly be replaced by one of a new and improved type. On the watershed, too, the committee are prosecuting a progressive policy. With a view to avoiding all possibility of contamination, they recently secured an order for the closing of a graveyard at Fewston, and now they are applying to the Home Office to close Holy Trinity churchyard at West End, Blubberhouses.

**Leicester.**—The scheme of the borough engineer, Mr. E. G. Mawbey, for the laying of 34 miles of new tributary sewers, has been adopted by the council. About 29 miles of these are to replace old brick sewers. The estimated cost of the whole scheme is £128,300, and the work is to be carried out in four sections, the first of which (estimated to cost £30,229) is to be proceeded with as soon as the sanction of the Local Government Board is obtained. The old sewers have been thoroughly examined by the sinking of no less than 1,436 trial holes.

**Liverpool.**—A contemporary states that the scheme whereby various parts of Liverpool are to be supplied with open air baths is progressing satisfactorily. The one at Gore-street is now practically completed, and will be opened within the next few days; and it is expected that the baths at Mansfield-street and Green-lane, the work of constructing which is to proceed at once, will be in readiness for next season.

**Lowestoft.**—A quarterly meeting of this body was held last week, when it was reported that at a meeting of the Joint Sanitary and General Purposes Committee the surveyor reported that he had examined No. 1 Smith's-marsh, with reference to providing a site for a destructor and electric light station, and had come across hard material about 4 ft. below the surface, and, generally speaking, the subsoil was very much better that at the site next Hervey-street, and he submitted plan of his proposed arrangement of the destructor buildings. It was moved that the committee recommend that the destructor and electric light station be erected on the north-west corner of No. 1 Smith's-marsh, as shown by the plan submitted by the surveyor. The report was adopted by the council.—The town clerk had formally announced to the members of the General Purposes Committee that the Bill confirming the provisional order granted by the Board of Trade for the electric lighting of the borough had received the Royal assent; and the committee recommended that "the order be put in operation by the council itself, and that it be referred to this committee to obtain a scheme for lighting the town by electricity, with all details, estimates and tenders, and report thereon to the council, with a view to an application being made to the Local Government Board for their sanction to a loan for carrying out the works." The report was formally adopted.

**Nelson.**—An inquiry will shortly be held by the Local Government Board respecting an application of the town council for sanction to borrow £20,000 for private street works.—To satisfy the requirements of the Ribble Joint Committee, the sub-committee dealing with the matter have been given authority to make an extension of 4,000 yards of filtration area at the sewage works.

**Newark.**—On the 5th inst. the new waterworks at Farnsfield, which have been erected by the Newark Corporation, were formally opened by the mayor, Councillor Milthorp. A special train ran from Newark at 12.30 p.m., conveying the members of the corporation and a number of burgesses. On arriving at the works, which adjoin the Midland line at Farnsfield, the party were shown over the works under the guidance of the engineer, Mr. Rofe. Proceeding to the engine-house, the mayor started one of the magnificent beam engines, Mr. Doubleday, chairman of the Waterworks Committee, starting the other, amidst cheers. The works are of an extensive character.

**Newcastle.**—The Newcastle Town Council on Friday sanctioned the expenditure of £84,000 as an instalment towards carrying out improvements on the quay. It is to cover the cost of erection of a range of sheds from the milk market to the Swirle, together with railways, cranes, lifts, &c., and the rebuilding of the quay at the Rotterdam and London wharves, and the 80-ton crane berth. This is part of a scheme, which has already been approved by the Finance Committee, to increase the width of the quay at the milk market, to provide double-tier sheds from the milk market to the Swirle and from the grain warehouse to the Ouseburn, with the necessary cranes, &c. The whole scheme is to cost £234,000. In the discussion it was pointed out that many large merchants had to have about 75 per cent. of their goods sent to Hull, Grimsby and Hartlepool, because there was not adequate facilities for the steamers to go to the Tyne.

**Oldham.**—A committee of the council recently resolved: "That the council be recommended to authorise and direct this committee to take all the necessary proceedings to promote in the next session of Parliament a Bill for the purpose of authorising and enabling the corporation, subject to existing leases, to work any tramways for the time being belonging to them either by electric, animal or other power, and to place and run carriages thereon, and to take tolls, rates and charges in respect of the use of such carriages, or to lease the said tramways if the council should determine to do so; to construct and lay down additional tramways within the municipal borough, and in case any of the townships within the Parliamentary borough should desire the council so to do, to enable the corporation to enter into agree-

ments with the authorities thereof to lease, work and use any tramways for the time being situate or to be constructed in all or any of the townships, or to supply electric or other power to enable such authorities to work and use their respective tramways." The town clerk was instructed to write the authorities within the Parliamentary borough to obtain their views on the matters mentioned in the resolution referring to their respective districts.

**Ossett.**—On the 8th inst. it was decided to carry out certain extensions of the drainage of the Gawthorn portion of the borough, in accordance with plans prepared by Mr. S. Wood. Application was ordered to be made to the Local Government Board for sanction to the borrowing of £4,000 for the purpose. Instructions were also given for the erection of stabling and sheds on a site in Bank-street, at a cost of £600, and an application to the Local Government Board for sanction to a loan for hospital purposes.

**Richmond (Yorks).**—The corporation have referred to a committee the consideration of the desirability of pulling down the existing town hall and of building a new and more adequate group of municipal buildings.

**Scarborough.**—At the town council meeting on Monday week the chairman of the Fire Brigade Committee announced, somewhat to the astonishment of his colleagues, that the fire-extinguishing appliances of Scarborough were only worthy of a village. Another councillor contradicted this with emphasis, declaring that all the sensation that had arisen had occurred through the unhappy Queen-street fire fatality.

**Sunderland.**—The special sub-committee appointed to consider the question of fire-extinguishing appliances intend to recommend the council to purchase two fire engines, one to discharge 450 gallons per minute through a 1¾-in. jet, and the other to discharge 450 gallons per minute through a 1½-in. jet; and also to purchase a 50 ft. fire escape.

**Wolverhampton.**—On Monday afternoon a meeting of the Building Committee of the proposed new free library for Wolverhampton was held at the town hall. Over twenty tenders for the erection of the building were received; but, on opening them, it was found that they were at "a somewhat larger sum than the committee anticipated." Several members of the committee were absent on their holidays, and it was decided to defer the consideration of the tenders.

## URBAN DISTRICT COUNCILS.

**Audenshaw.**—The council have approved and adopted the proposals of Mr. J. P. Wilkinson, A.M.I.C.E., Manchester, for the sewerage of the district. The estimated cost is £14,500.

**Castleford.**—A formal resolution has been passed by the council sanctioning a loan of £2,000 for the purchase of land required for the enlargement of the cemetery, £1,550 to be borne by Castleford and £450 by Glass Houghton. A proposal to utilise the old water supply for flushing the sewers and watering the streets has been referred to the Special Water Committee for consideration.

**Clacton.**—Instructions have been given for the making. up of the East Marine Parade with a total frontage of 2,573 ft. The estimated cost is £2,300. The surveyor has reported that the sea-water mains have been laid, and that the whole scheme would probably be in working order shortly.

**Ilfracombe.**—It has been resolved by the council to purchase a field, at a cost of £1,200, for purposes of a sports ground.—Alternative schemes of drainage, one costing £20,000 and the other £30,000, have been submitted by Mr. Mansergh, and will shortly be discussed by the council.

**Knaresborough.**—Application is shortly to be made by the council to the Local Government Board for power to obtain a loan of £2,000 for the erection of a new gas purifier. house, and to purchase a set of four purifiers and an exhauster.

**Leigh.**—On Tuesday of last week Mr. W. O. E. Meade. King, inspector of the Local Government Board, held an inquiry at the Town Hall, Leigh, into the application of the Leigh District Council for sanction to borrow £25,000 for gasworks extensions and £10,500 for purposes of electric lighting In regard to electric lighting it was stated that it was proposed to erect works on the gasworks land, and they would save the cost of boilers and chimney stacks by using these for the gasworks extensions. They intended to put sufficient plant down to supply electrical energy for five years, and from a canvass taken in the district they anticipated making the electric works a paying concern even during the first year of their existence.

**Llandudno.**—Mr. Walter Ducat held an inquiry, on the 2nd inst., at Llandudno respecting an application by the district council to the Local Government Board to sanction loans of £2,350 for water undertaking, £1,400 for street improvements, £550 for the provision of shelters on the promenade, £750 for sewerage works and £225 for the erection of a fire station at Craigydon. The engineer, Mr. E. Paley Stephenson, in explaining the water extension, said that it was proposed to raise 20,000 gallons, the motive power being a gas engine. It would serve a district of 100 houses, but the scheme provided for 550. The capacity for the proposed reservoir would be 50,000 gallons. Mr. Humphreys, the surveyor of the Mostyn estate, said that he was present to give every facility for the carrying out of the scheme.

**Mountain Ash.**—Mr. Robert H. Bicknell recently held an inquiry, on behalf of the Local Government Board, into the application of the urban district council to borrow £20,700 for the purpose of carrying out a sewerage scheme for the Abercynon portion of the district.

**Skipton.**—The council have been in negotiation for some time past with the proprietors of the Skipton gasworks, with the view of purchasing the undertaking for the benefit of the town. At a private meeting of the gas company, a few days ago, the council's offer to buy was refused. The company, at the same meeting, decided to call up its capital and to exercise its borrowing powers under the Act of 1863.

**Stourport.**—At a meeting of this council, held on the 3rd inst., the Sanitary Committee reported that they had consulted Mr. J. E. Willcox, C.E., of Birmingham, on the question of dealing with part of the sewage of Upper Mitton. They recommended the council to instruct Mr. Willcox to prepare a complete scheme for the drainage of the part of the district referred to, such scheme to be so arranged as to form part of a future comprehensive scheme for the whole of the district. The report was adopted.

**Teignmouth.**—A recent report from the manager, Mr. C. Jones, stated that while during the last quarter 12 tons less coal had been carbonised than in the corresponding period of 1897, there had been an increase of 288,000 cubic feet in the sales of gas. This was attributed to the relaying of mains and the consequent reduction in leakage.—Sanction has been given to borrow £200 to complete the purchase of the ground for the erection of a new gasholder.—Application has been made to the Public Works Loan Board to obtain a loan of £3,820 for gas purposes.

**Urmston.**—It was last week reported that the Local Government Board sanction had been received to the borrowing of £4,400 for flagging and kerbing public footpaths in the district.

**Wimbledon.**—On the 3rd inst. a Local Government Board inquiry was held as to the establishment of a dust destructor at the electric lighting works, similar to that at Leyton, for erecting which a loan of £5,000 is to be raised. It was argued that to burn the sewage sludge, instead of putting it on the land, as at present, would be a waste; but the advocates of the scheme pointed out that about £400 a year would be saved for coal to drive the dynamos.

**Withington.**—The Main Drainage Committee last week reported having received a letter from the farm manager, stating that recent bad effluents complained of by the Mersey and Irwell Joint Committee were probably due to the sinking of a short length of a 6-in. drain, which had allowed unfiltered sewage to get into the outfall.—The council have decided to purchase machinery, at a cost of £1,500, for the manufacture of concrete flags at the refuse destructor in Barlow Moor-road. It is expected that they will shortly be able to lay flags in the various highways of the district.

## RURAL DISTRICT COUNCILS.

**Chelmsford.**—At a recent meeting of this authority Dr. Thresh stated that he had received a written complaint about the stench arising from the river Wid at Writtle Bridge. He found that the river there was in a really foul condition, and it appeared to be due to sewage entering from a ditch in Lawford-lane. No time should be lost in proceeding with the sewerage of the village, for the council were taking a serious responsibility by the delay. There were many grossly insanitary conditions in the village, which could only be remedied by laying down a system of sewers. Things were now getting so bad that the council could no longer afford to ignore them.

**Chipping Sodbury (Glos.).**—Having been instructed by the council to prepare a scheme for the sewerage and sewage disposal of the town, Mr. Walter L. le Maitre, of Victoria-street, Westminster, has submitted plans and estimates for the work, and they have been referred to the parish council for consideration.

**Feckenham.**—The council have instructed Mr. J. E. Willcox, C.E., of Birmingham, to report upon the question of sewage disposal and to prepare plans for filter-beds in connection with their existing sewage disposal works at Astwood Bank.

**Howden (East Riding).**—At the last monthly meeting of the council a novel application was made on behalf of the cyclists in the Howden district for permission to make, through the main street of that town, a cycle track. It was pointed out that, on account of the large boulders in the street—which is paved with the material known as "petrified kidneys"—cyclists found it very inconvenient in riding over them, and they had requested him to make that application in order that a small track might be made on the side of the road, they (the cyclists) giving an undertaking to pay the cost of laying and maintaining it. After some slight discussion the council unanimously agreed to the proposed innovation.

**Richmond, Yorks.**—The council have engaged Mr. H. W. Taylor, of St. Nicholas Chambers, Newcastle, and Birmingham, to report upon the best means of supplying the village of Middleton Tyas with water. In consequence of the prolonged drought most of the wells and springs are dry.

**Stratford-on-Avon.**—At the last meeting of the council Mr. J. E. Willcox, C.E., of Birmingham, attended and submitted a scheme for sewage disposal works at Snitterfield. The scheme was duly adopted and instructions given to enter into negotiation for acquiring the necessary land.

**Thrapston.**—The council having applied to the Local Government Board for sanction to borrow £1,000 for the purpose of erecting a bridge over the Nene at Ringstead, Colonel Luard, C.E., attended at the Temperance Hall, Ringstead, on Thursday morning to hold an inquiry into the circumstances of the application. After formal evidence had been given the inquiry closed, the inspector having intimated that he had already visited the site of the bridge.

## SCOTLAND AND IRELAND.

**Aberdeen.**—The Waterton and Dyce Sub-Committee of Aberdeen District Committee, appointed to carry out the new Parkhill waterworks, held yesterday their sixth, and probably final, visitation of the works prior to the formal turning on of the water. The committee expressed themselves perfectly satisfied with the works. Water from the new source has been supplied to Bucksburn during the past week or ten days.

**Dumfries.**—At a meeting of the Dumfries Town Council on Wednesday a letter was read from Mr. Andrew Carnegie offering £10,000 for the erection of a library, provided that the Free Libraries Act was adopted by Dumfries and Maxwelltown. Mr. and Miss McKie, of the Mote House, Dumfries, have given a free site for the purpose of the library building.

**Dundalk.**—A special meeting of the town commissioners was held recently for the purpose of considering the report of the committee appointed to arrange details of agreement with the Dundalk Electric Tramway Company, Limited, for lighting the town of Dundalk with electricity and for the handing over to them of powers under provisional order for electric lighting, on the basis that the company would recoup the commissioners the expense of obtaining same. After hearing the report of the committee, it was decided to approve of the draft deed of agreement as submitted, on condition that the tramway company complete the contract of agreement on or before the 5th of October next.

**Johnstone.**—A deputation from this authority who visited Rouen and Havre to witness the electric tramways at work, to guide them in their decision whether they should support the Electric Traction Company to put down a system from Johnstone to Glasgow, returned to town on Saturday week. It is reported that the system is perfectly applicable to Johnstone, and that the deputation are in favour of the scheme.

**Stirling.**—The Police Commissioners had before them last week a minute of the Lighting Committee, recommending that the negotiations in connection with the scheme for the electric lighting of the town by water power should cease. The minute was adopted, and it was remitted back to the committee to carry out their previous instructions in connection with Prof. Kennedy's steam-power scheme.

**Stranraer.**—The contract for the repairing of the principal streets of Stranraer with granite setts has been let to Mr. Charles Macandrew, Ayr, the cost of which will be £2,323.

# Personal.

Mr. Thomas Sopwith, M.I.C.E., has died at Lismore, N.B., from the result of an accident while out shooting.

Mr. W. H. Owen, surveyor to the Ellesmere Rural District Council, has had his salary increased by £10 per annum.

Cheltenham Town Council have raised the salary of Mr. Kilgar, the borough electrical engineer, from £300 to £350.

Mr. Herbert Vickers, of Bolton, has been appointed by the Wolverhampton Corporation as junior assistant to the borough electrical engineer.

The Aberdeen City Council have confirmed the appointment of Mr. J. A. Bell, as city electrical engineer, at a commencing salary of £225 per annum.

Mr. A. E. Freeman, of Uxbridge, was on Friday selected by the local authority of the latter town to fill the post of assistant surveyor and inspector of nuisances.

It is understood that Mr. R. Ll. Jones, surveyor to the Carnarvon Town Council, has resigned, and that a successor will be appointed at a salary of £180 per annum.

Mr. Thomas Smith, works manager on the granite and wood paving works, Wolverhampton, has been appointed works manager on the new tramway works, Norwich.

The death has taken place, at the age of sixty-seven, of Mr. John George Dawson, the surveyor to the Kingston Rural District Council. He was a member of the Surveyors' Institution.

Mr. Arthur Smith, who is at present surveyor to the Chertsey Urban District Council, has been appointed surveyor to the Yeadon Rural District Council, at a salary of £250 per annum.

At a meeting of the Greenock Police Board, held recently, it was agreed, on the recommendation of a sub-committee on electricity, to advertise for a resident electrical engineer, at a salary not exceeding £300 per annum.

At a meeting of the Finance Committee of Dundee Harbour Board, on Monday week, it was agreed to grant an increase of £100 to the salary of Mr. G. C. Buchanan, harbour engineer, thus raising it to £500.

Mr. Isaac Thomas Hawkins, the deputy-director of Public Works at Lagos, arrived at Liverpool last week on board one of the West African liners. Mr. Hawkins, it will be remembered, was formerly engineer and surveyor to the Langport (Somerset) Rural District Council.

Mr. R. Lindon, of Plymouth, who for two years has been an assistant surveyor under Mr. J. Paton, borough engineer of Plymouth, was on Tuesday evening unanimously elected sanitary inspector and highway surveyor of Tavistock Urban District Council, at a salary of £100 a year. There were eighteen candidates.

The deputy-mayor of Wolverhampton, Mr. Alderman Craddock, J.P., Mr. Alderman Saunders, J.P., and the borough engineer, Mr. J. W. Bradley, are attending the Iron and Steel Institute congress at Stockholm. They will also visit Copenhagen,' St. Petersburg, Moscow, Nigni Novgorod, Hamburg, Kiel and other German towns.

Out of about 100 candidates, Mr. R. O. Wynne-Roberts, borough surveyor and water engineer of Oswestry, has been selected to fill the post of city engineer of Cape Town. Mr. Wynne-Roberts' salary will commence at £800 per annum, and he will also be allowed first-class expenses. He will leave England in about three months' time.

The County Council of Bucks on Thursday adopted a report recommending the raising of the salary of Mr. R. J. Thomas, the county surveyor, from £500 to £600 per annum. The amount allowed to him for office and travelling expenses was also increased to £300 per annum, while it was further resolved to provide his office in the county hall rent free.

Mr. A. S. Barnard, the borough electrical engineer of Hull, was married on Wednesday, 10th inst., at Platt Chapel, Manchester, to Miss Muriel Marles-Thomas, B.A., youngest daughter of the late Rev. Wm. Thomas (Gwillym Marles), of Llandyssul. The ceremony was performed by Rev. J. C. Street, of Shrewsbury. The happy couple afterwards left for North Wales.

At Kirkham parish church recently the remains were interred of the late Mr. E. H. Hargreaves, who died on the previous Saturday at his residence, Poulton-street. He was sixty-five years of age. For a period he was surveyor to the Kirkham Urban Council, but retired on the grounds of ill health about two years ago. A widow, three sons and two daughters survive.

The Ambleside (Lake Windermere) Urban District Council have engaged Mr. Harry W. Taylor, A.M.I.C.E., of St. Nicholas Chambers, Newcastle-on-Tyne and Birmingham, as their engineer for the preparation of a scheme of sewerage and sewage disposal for their district. Pumping will have to be resorted to to raise the sewage from the low-lying portions of the district.

The Sewerage, Water and Fire Brigade Committee of the Lymington Town Council, reporting on a proposal to appoint a water engineer, on Thursday submitted the following names, and recommended the selection of one of the gentlemen mentioned : Mr. T. Hawksley, Mr. Wm. Fox, Messrs. Taylor, Sons & Santo Crimp, Mr. James Mansergh, Mr. Baldwin Latham, Mr. Wm. Jeffery, Mr. S. H. Terry and Mr. J. M. Hood.

On the recommendation of the Parliamentary and Finance Committee the Matlock Urban District Council have sanctioned an honorarium of £25 to Mr. Albert M. Clarke, their surveyor, for additional work performed by him as engineer for the Matlock sewage scheme included in the Matlock Parliamentary Bill. Sir Edward Frankland, K.C.B., F.R.S., Reigate, Surrey, and Mr. George Chatterton, M.I.C.E., of Westminster, supported the scheme.

Mr. John Richmond, of Dunbar, has been appointed manager of the Kilkenny gasworks. Mr. Richmond was trained under his father, at the Whitburn gasworks, West Lothian, and he became manager there at the age of seventeen. Seven years afterwards he was appointed manager at Dunbar. The Dunbar Gas Commissioners offered Mr. Richmond an increase in salary of £20 to remain with them, and on the offer being declined they voted him an honorarium.

It is stated that it is not yet determined who is to succeed Mr. W. D. Bowden in the surveyorship to the St. Mary Church Urban District Council. As we last week stated, Mr. Stringfellow was selected to fill the post, but since the time of the appointment he has received from the Eastleigh Urban District Council an offer which has induced him to decline the Mary Church position. The council will, therefore, be called upon to select another of the candidates, who numbered about two dozen.

In our reference of last week to Mr. Henry T. Wakelam, the county surveyor of Herefordshire, we stated that he served his articles with Mr. Benjamin Baker, borough engineer of Wolverhampton. The latter gentleman, however, had no connection with Wolverhampton, but was the engineer and surveyor of the adjoining town of Willenhall, and architect to the local school board. Our information, we may mention, was derived from a local paper, which, we assumed, had verified its statements.

At a recent meeting of the Marylebone Vestry the duties of the superintendent of cleansing, superintendent of sewers and drains, and district superintendents, were approved of as follows : That the superintendent of cleansing be responsible to the surveyor as regards the whole parish for the washing and sweeping of roads and cleansing of footpaths, the removal of the dirt and slop therefrom, and for the street watering, as well as for the removal of snow. That for the whole parish the construction, maintenance and flushing of sewers and urinals, and the construction of drains, so far as laid by vestry, be allocated specially to the superintendent of sewers and drains, that officer to be responsible to the surveyor for those works ; and that for the construction and maintenance of macadam, flint and paved carriageways and footways, and supervision of hoards, public lamps, &c., the parish be divided into three districts, and that the district superintendent for each shall have authority and responsibility, under the surveyor, for all such works and matters in his district.

We last week announced the appointment of a surveyor to the East Sussex County Council. Some particulars of the voting will be of interest as showing the closeness of the contest and the uncertainty attending such elections. The Roads and Bridges Committee interviewed the following four selected candidates : Mr. A. Dryland, A.M.I.C.E., assistant surveyor, county of Kent; Mr. C. Lawgreen, surveyor of Croydon Rural District Council; Mr. F. S. Morris, assistant-surveyor, county of Stafford ; and Mr. F. J. Wood, A.M.I.C.E., assistant surveyor, county of Lancaster, there having been originally eighty-one candidates. The four gentlemen above-named were interviewed in the order given, and upon the names being put to the vote Mr. Dryland obtained ten and Mr. Wood ten, there being twenty members present. The chairman declined to decide the matter by giving a casting vote, but stated he had voted for Mr. Dryland, and if he did exercise his right would have to do so in his favour. He remained firm in his refusal to give a second vote, and, after considerable discussion upon the merits of the respective candidates and upon the position caused by the equality of votes, it was resolved to try the effect of taking another vote, when Mr. Wood obtained eleven to Mr. Dryland's nine, and was therefore declared elected.

**Edinburgh.**—On the recommendation of the Lord Provost's Committee, it was recently resolved that the present contractors for the cabling of the tramways be employed to carry out the work of cabling the Portobello and Joppa section at the same rates as under their existing contracts.

## ASSOCIATION OF MUNICIPAL AND COUNTY ENGINEERS.

### EXAMINATIONS.

The attention of candidates is drawn to the fact that the entrance fee is £2 2s., instead of £1 1s., and the sitting fee as before (£2 2s.), and that it is absolutely necessary that the prescribed form, duly filled up, should be deposited with the secretary, together with the entrance fee, on or before March 5th or September 5th, as the case may be.

### MIDLAND DISTRICT MEETING AT BILSTON.

A meeting of the members of the midland district will be held on Saturday, September 17th, at Bilston. The following are the arrangements:—

11 a.m.— The members will be received in the council chamber, Town Hall, by the chairman (Councillor R. A. Harper, J.P.) and other members of the council. Minutes of Stafford and Rhyader meetings. Election of hon. district secretary.

11.30 a.m.—Leave for a visit to the Spring Vale furnaces, arriving about 11.40 a.m., where, by the kind permission of Sir Alfred Hickman, the process of steel manufacture will be witnessed. A short descriptive paper will be given.

12.30 p.m.—Leave in brakes, kindly provided by Councillor J. W. Sankey, chairman of the Water and Baths Committee, for a visit to the waterworks covered service reservoir (which will be specially emptied for the inspection of the members), arriving about 12.45.

1.15 p.m.—Leave in brakes for the Rinley Arms Hotel, arriving about 2 p.m., where a light luncheon will be provided by Councillor R. A. Harper, J.P., chairman of the council.

3 p.m.—Leave in brakes for a visit to the Bilston waterworks pumping station, arriving about 3.30 p.m.

4.15 p.m.—Leave in brakes for the Technical School, Bilston, arriving about 5 p.m.

6 p.m.—Dinner at the Technical School. Tickets, 3s. 6d. each (exclusive of wine).

Arrangements will be made for any members desirous of doing so to inspect the public baths and the public market.

Mr. C. L. N. Wilson, the water engineer and surveyor to the Bilston Council, will give a descriptive paper of the works. As the paper will be in the hands of members intimating their intention to attend some days before the meeting, it will be taken as read.

Among the hotels at Bilston may be mentioned the Pipe Hall, Globe and Great Western.

Wolverhampton is within 2½ miles and Birmingham 10½ miles, and there is a good service of trains from these towns. The Great Western station at Bilston is the nearest to the Town Hall.

Any member desirous of introducing a visitor (other than members of the public authority where the meeting is held) to the meeting must submit the name and address of such visitor to the president on the form to be obtained from the secretary. The ticket signed by the member introducing the visitor must be in the hands of the hon. district secretary at least four days before the date of the meeting, after which date no application can be entertained.

J. S. PICKERING, A.M.I.C.E.,          THOS. COLE, A.M.I.C.E.,
Hon. District Secretary.                    Secretary.
Council Office, Nuneaton.

## NEW BATHS FOR GLASGOW.

After a short discussion the City Council of Glasgow last week adopted the report of their engineer on the nature and cost of the amended plans of the proposed Whitevale baths and wash-houses. The report was as follows: " The sketch plans now produced show two swimming ponds—one, 75 ft. by 40 ft., for males, and one, 50 ft. by 25 ft., for females—fourteen second-class hot baths for males on street floor, and thirty-one first-class hot baths for males on first floor; eight hot baths for females. Gymnasium in connection with large pond, 44 ft. by 24 ft. Turkish baths, to accommodate eight persons, with first and second hot-rooms, shampooing-room, plunge bath, cooling-room, &c. Wash-house, with accommodation for sixty-six washers, eight water-driven hydro-extractors, waiting-room, workshop, &c., wash-house entering from East John-street. Private wash-house for washing towels. Apartment for library, 50 ft. by 22 ft., on the first floor fronting Whitevale-street, with separate entrance. Superintendent's house on third floor, and entering by library stair. The front to East John-street has the boiler-house and wash-house entrances, with two floors above, containing six houses of two apartments. I have gone into the question of the probable cost of this establishment along with Mr. John G. Atchison, measurer, and beg to report that the building will cost about £23,000 and the necessary machinery about £5,000; from this there falls to be deducted the sum of £1,200 which has been allocated towards the expense of the reading-room from the Rankin bequest fund."

## OPENING OF BARTON WATERWORKS.

Mr. W. H. Sissons on the 27th ult. performed the ceremony of opening the new waterworks which have been constructed at Barton. A large number of persons witnessed the proceedings. The works consist of a well, 120 ft. deep, with a bore which goes to a further depth of 25 ft. There is a set of double pumps, capable of pumping 12,000 gallons per hour, and the softening tank has a capacity of 23,000 gallons. The adoption of water softening for the treatment of waters derived from chalk, lime and sandstone formations is, in the opinion of Mr. E. T. Hildred, the engineer consulted by the contractors of the filtering and softening plant, becoming very general. At Barton, he thinks, the experiment is a signal success. Messrs. Atkins' system is the one selected. The storage tank, which has been newly concreted by Mr. J. W. Briggs, contractor, of Barton, is capable of holding 120,000 gallons. The rest of the buildings consist of boiler-house, engine, pumping and filtering houses, foreman's house, board-room and the necessary outbuildings. All the works have been inspected, tested and pronounced satisfactory by Mr. Hildred. The hardness of the water as it issues from the well is 23·6, and at the first test of softening this was reduced to 9 00, which at once makes it an ideal water for domestic use. The company, however, hope to still further reduce the hardness.

At a luncheon which followed the opening of the works Mr. Hildred, in responding to the health of " The Engineers," congratulated the company on their pluck in putting down at the outset such a splendid system of softening and filtering. The speaker then went on to speak of the advantages of soft water over hard, and showed how it was possible by the use of soft water to effect a great saving, both in the manufactory and in the house.

## APPOINTMENTS VACANT.

*Advertisements which are received too late for classification cannot be included in these summaries until the following week.*

QUANTITY SURVEYOR.—August 19th.—Aylesbury Urban District Council.—Mr. J. H. Bradford, surveyor to the council.

ARCHITECTURAL ASSISTANT.— August 19th.— Beckenham Urban District Council. £3 3s.—Mr. J. A. Angell, surveyor to the council.

SECOND ENGINEERING ASSISTANT.—August 22nd.—Edmonton Urban District Council.— Mr. Wm. Francis Payne.

CLERK OF WORKS.—August 22nd.—London County Council. £5 5s.—Mr. R. W. Partridge, clerk of the Asylums Committee.

DEPOT SUPERINTENDENT.—August 22nd.— Corporation of Dewsbury.—Mr. G. Trevelyan, clerk.

CIVIL ENGINEERING ASSISTANT.—August 23rd.—Corporation of the City of Hull. £85.—Mr. A. E. White, city engineer.

ELECTRICAL ENGINEER.—August 24th.—Watford Urban District Council. £150.—Mr. H. Morten Turner, clerk.

ARCHITECTURAL ASSISTANT.—August 24th.—Corporation of Halifax. £3 3s.—The Borough Engineer.

CLERK OF WORKS.—August 25th.—Corporation of Leicester. £3 3s.—Mr. James Bell, town clerk.

SURVEYOR.—August 25th.—Aysgarth Rural District Council. £100.—Mr. W. E. M. Winn, clerk, Askrigg, R.S.O., Yorkshire.

DRAUGHTSMAN.— August 26th.— Corporation of Bacup. 30s.—Mr. Francis Wood, borough engineer.

CLERK OF WORKS.—August 27th.—Vestry of St. Matthew, Bethnal Green. £4 4s.—Mr. F. W. Barratt, surveyor.

ELECTRICAL ENGINEER.—August 27th.—Corporation of Ashton-under-Lyne. £250.—Chairman, Electricity Committee.

DISTRICT SURVEYOR.— August 29th. — Cheshire County Council. £200.—Mr. Reginald Potts, clerk.

SENIOR ASSISTANT.—August 30th.—West Hartlepool Corporation. £75.—Mr. J. W. Brown, borough engineer.

ELECTRICAL ENGINEER AND MANAGER.—August 31st.—Corporation of Derby. £350.—Mr. H. F. Gadsby, town clerk.

SURVEYOR OF HIGHWAYS.—August 31st. — Chesterfield Rural District Council. £160.—Mr. George Shaw, clerk.

BUILDING INSPECTOR.—September 2nd.—Southend-on-Sea Corporation. £125.—Mr. William H. Snow, clerk.

SUPERINTENDENT OF SEWERS AND DRAINS.—September 5th. Vestry of St. Marylebone. £150.—Mr. W. H. Garbutt, clerk.

SUPERINTENDENT OF CLEANSING.—September 5th.—Vestry of St. Marylebone. £180.—Mr. W. H. Garbutt, clerk.

DISTRICT SUPERINTENDENT.—September 5th.—Vestry of St. Marylebone. £150.—Mr. W. H. Garbutt, clerk.

INSPECTOR OF NUISANCES AND SURVEYOR.—September 6th.—Little Woolton Urban District Council. £110.—Mr. Percy Dobell, clerk to the council.

CLERK OF WORKS.—Metropolitan Asylums Board. £3 3s. —Offices, Norfolk House, Norfolk-street, Strand, W.C.

## COMPETITIONS.

*Advertisements which are received too late for classification cannot be included in these summaries until the following week.*

ST. PANCRAS.—August 25th.—Erection of public baths and wash-houses.—Mr. C. H. J. Barrett, vestry clerk.

PLYMOUTH.—September 24th.—Erection of shops and dwelling-houses fronting Tavistock-street. £250.—Mr. J. H. Ellis, town clerk.

WIVENHOE.—September 29th.—Works of drainage and water supply, for the urban district council.—Mr. C. W. Denton, clerk.

REIGATE.—October 6th.—Erection of municipal buildings, fire station, public offices, &c.—Mr. Clair J. Grece, town clerk.

## MUNICIPAL CONTRACTS OPEN.

*Advertisements which are received too late for classification cannot be included in these summaries until the following week.*

MANCHESTER.—August 19th.—Construction of seven public urinals.—The City Surveyor.

BIRKENHEAD.—August 19th.—Sinking a bore-hole in connection with proposed pumping station.—Mr. W. A. Richardson, water engineer.

COSSETT.—August 20th.—Kerbing, channelling, cementing and macadamising works.—Mr. William R. Shell, surveyor to the urban district council.

TONBRIDGE.—August 20th.—Supply of 1,000 tons of best quality 2 in. broken quartzite, Guernsey granite, &c.—Mr. A. H. Neve, junr., clerk to the urban district council.

RUGBY.—August 20th.—Works of street making and sewer construction, for the rural district council.—Mr. T. W. Willard, surveyor.

SOUTHBOROUGH.—August 20th.—Street works, for the urban district council.—Mr. Philip Ranner, clerk.

HAMPTON.—August 20th.—Supply and delivery of a 10-ton steam roller, for the urban district council.—Mr. John Kemp, A.M.I.C.E., surveyor to the council.

OXFORD.—August 22nd.—Supply and laying of cast-iron and stone-ware pipe carriers, brick and concrete work in manholes and distributing chambers, land drainage, embanking, road making and other works on land adjoining the corporation sewage farm.—Mr. R. Bacon, town clerk.

TEDDINGTON.—August 22nd.—Making-up of Clarence-road, for the urban district council.—Mr. M. Hainsworth, surveyor to the council.

STEVENAGE.—August 22nd.—Supply of 500 tons of 1½-in. broken Guernsey, Leicester or other granite, for the urban district council.—Mr. William Onslow Times, clerk to the council.

LITHERLAND.—August 22nd.—Paving works, for the urban district council.—Mr. W. B. Garton, surveyor.

GLASGOW.—August 22nd.—Supply of rails and flash-plates.—Mr. John Young, tramways engineer.

ROCHFORD.—August 22nd.—Repairs and alterations in connection with the construction of a filter tank and outfall, for the rural district council.—Mr. Frederick Greggson, clerk, Alexandra-street, Southend.

BRANDON AND BYSHOTTLES.—August 22nd.—Supplying and fixing engine and pumping machinery, for the urban district council.—Mr. Richard Gardner, surveyor.

WILMSLOW.—August 22nd.—Construction of about 1,300 yards of 15-in. and 12-in. earthenware pipe sewers, &c., for the urban district council.—Mr. John Bowden, 14 Ridgefield, Manchester.

MILTON.—August 23rd.—Supply of road materials, for the urban district council.—Mr. A. B. Acworth, surveyor.

WALTHAMSTOW.—August 23rd.—Erection of public baths, for the urban district council.—Mr. E. J. Gowen, clerk to the council.

TORQUAY.—August 23rd.—Repair of the masonry apron and foreshore at the Haldon breakwater.—Mr. Henry A. Garrett, A.M.I.C.E., harbour engineer.

TYNEMOUTH.—August 23rd.—Paving works.—Mr. John F. Smellie, borough surveyor.

GOOLE.—August 23rd.—Paving with hard wood about 3,750 square yards of roadway, for the urban district council.—Mr. Geo. England, clerk.

BUCKLOW.—August 23rd.—Works of levelling, paving, metalling, channelling and making good a street at Hale, for the rural district council.—Mr. J. M'Kenzie, surveyor.

BUCKLOW.—August 23rd.—Levelling, paving, metalling, channelling, &c.—Mr. J. M. D. M'Kenzie, surveyor to the rural district council.

CARSHALTON.—August 23rd.—Supply of 200 tons of broken 1-in. Quenast or Guernsey granite and 850 yards of hand-picked flints, for the urban district council.—Mr. W. W. Gale, A.M.I.C.E., surveyor to the council.

ILFORD.—August 23rd.—Construction of an underground latrine in The Broadway, for the urban district council.—Mr. Herbert Shaw, A.M.I.C.E., surveyor to the council.

PENRITH.—August 23rd.—Supply of new steam boiler, for the urban district council.—Mr. E. Shaul, gas manager.

MIDDLESBROUGH.—August 23rd.—Work required in the erection of retort-house, &c., at the corporation gasworks.—Mr. David Terrace, gas manager.

ROTHERHAM.—August 23rd.—Construction of sewers, outfall works, and other works connected therewith, for the urban district council.—Mr. R. E. W. Berrington, Bank Buildings, Wolverhampton.

CARSHALTON.—August 23rd.—Widening of High-street, for the urban district council.—Mr. W. W. Gale, A.M.I.C.E., surveyor to the council.

WOKING.—August 24th.—Supply of sludge-pressing machinery, steam engines and other apparatus, for the urban district council.—Mr. R. Mossop, clerk.

HALIFAX.—August 24th.—Excavation and formation of tramway track.—Mr. Edward R. S. Escott, borough engineer.

TURTON.—August 24th.—Flagging, paving and other works.—Mr. V. W. Laithwaite, surveyor to the urban district council.

HALIFAX.—August 24th.—Supply of steel rails, points, crossings, fish-plates, &c., for about 5 miles of tramway.—Mr. Edward R. S. Escott, borough engineer.

NELSON.—August 24th.—Supply of cast-iron pipes, special castings, valves, &c., for the Water Committee.—Mr. J. Hartley, waterworks manager.

SHOREDITCH.—August 24th.—Construction of about 333 lineal feet of 18-in. pipe sewer in Britannia-street (City-road end), for the vestry.—Mr. J. Rush Dixon, A.M.I.C.E., engineer and surveyor to the vestry.

CARLISLE.—August 24th.—Laying of socket-jointed sewer pipe from Moorville to Knowefield Gates, for the rural district council.

HALIFAX.—August 24th.—Supply of best Portland cement for tramway works.—Mr. Edward R. S. Escott, borough engineer.

HALIFAX.—August 24th.—Erection of various works in connection with certain additions to the borough hospital.—Mr. E. R. S. Escott, engineer.

PEMBERTON.—August 24th.—Construction of about 1 mile of 9-in. sewer.—Mr. Paul Partington, clerk.

HULL.—August 25th.—Supply and erection of electric lighting plant.—Mr. A. S. Barnard, city electrical engineer.

HACKNEY.—August 25th.—Supply and delivery of Portland cement required for works of wood paving.—Mr. James Lovegrove, chief surveyor.

TUNBRIDGE WELLS.—August 25th.—Supply of edge kerbing.—Mr. W. C. Cripps, town clerk.

SUNDERLAND.—August 25th.—Erection of technical college at Greenterrace.—Mr. F. M. Bowey, town clerk.

DARWEN.—August 25th.—Erection and construction of iron and steel buildings in connection with a refuse destructor.—Mr. Charles Cooteker, town clerk.

MALDEN AND COOMBS.—August 26th.—Erection of proposed public buildings at New Malden, for the urban district council.—Mr. Thomas V. Herbert Davison, architect, New Malden.

MAIDENHEAD.—August 26th.—Works of drainage.—Mr. John Kiek, clerk.

HAWORTH.—August 26th.—Conversion of stone gasholder into a tar and liquor tank, for the urban district council.—Mr. W. Robertshaw, clerk.

MOSLEY.—August 26th.—Construction of brick culverts, together with manholes, storm-water overflow and other works.—Mr. W. Putman, borough engineer and surveyor.

WILMSLOW.—August 26th.—Sewering, kerbing, metalling and channelling.—Mr. William Cobbett, town clerk.

MOSLEY.—August 26th.—Manufacture, delivery and erection of a steel girder bridge, to carry cast-iron pipes.—Mr. W. E. Putman, borough engineer and surveyor.

HALIFAX.—August 27th.—Supply and erection of retort-house fittings.—Mr. Thomas Holgate, gas engineer.

BLACKPOOL.—August 27th.—Supply of three-lift gasholder.—Mr. John Chew, engineer and manager.

NELSON.—August 27th.—Erection of 550 lineal yards of wrought-iron unclimbable fencing.—Mr. R. Ball, borough engineer.

CLEATOR MOOR.—August 28th.—Providing and laying 3,000 superficial yards of asphalte at the Market-place, for the urban district council.—Mr. R. Robertson, surveyor.

EAST HAM.—August 29th.—Supply of about 6,000 ft. run 12-in. by 8-in. and about 10,000 ft. of 12-in. by 8-in. granite curb, for the urban district council.—Mr. C. E. Wilson, clerk.

EAST HAM.—August 29th.—Supply of about 1,000 yards of best lilac Guernsey and about 1,000 yards of other kinds of broken granite, for the urban district council.—Mr. C. E. Wilson, clerk.

EAST HAM.—August 29th.—Supply of 10-ton steam roller and a scarifier, for the urban district council.—Mr. C. E. Wilson, clerk.

WIMBLEDON.—August 29th.—Supply of pipework, for the urban district council.—Mr. A. H. Preece, 39 Victoria-street, S.W.

SHEFFIELD.—August 29th.—Construction and erection of additional buildings in connection with the destructor at Attercliffe.—Mr. Charles F. Wike, city surveyor.

SOUTHPORT.—August 29th.—Supply and delivery of granite cubes.—Mr. R. P. Hirst, borough surveyor.

DEVONPORT.—August 29th.—Erection of convenience at Northcorner quay.—Mr. John F. Burns, borough surveyor.

BARNET.—August 30th.—Construction of new sewers, for the urban district council.—Mr. H. W. Mansbridge, surveyor.

WATFORD.—August 31st.—Supply and delivery of electricity meters and main cut-outs, for the urban district council.—Mr. H. Barnum Turner, clerk.

KING'S LYNN.—August 31st.—Construction of sewers in the south drainage district of the borough.—Mr. E. J. Silcock, borough engineer.

WILLASEY.—August 31st.—Supply of wrought-iron railings and gates, for the urban district council.—Mr. H. W. Cook, clerk.

BURTON-UPON-TRENT.—August 31st.—Supply, construction and erection of foundations, arches, fire-brick work and furnace brickwork for retorts.—Mr. F. L. Ramsden, manager and engineer.

CIRENCESTER.—September 1st.—Construction of a system of surface-water drainage, for the urban district council.—Mr. Thomas Hibbert, surveyor.

WEST HAM.—September 2nd.—Erection of museum at Stratford.—Mr. Fred. E. Hilleary, town clerk.

WELLS.—September 3rd.—Erection of public hall and post office buildings.—Mr. R. L. Foster, town clerk.

NORWICH.—September 3rd.—Making-up of Mousehold-street, Cavalry-street, Anchor-street, Wadehouse-street and Tracey-road.—Mr. Arthur E. Collins, A.M.I.C.E., city engineer.

DERBY.—September 5th.—Construction of a covered service reservoir at Littleover.—Mr. H. F. Gadsby, town clerk.

DEVONPORT.—September 5th.—Construction of drainage culvert.—Mr. John F. Burns, borough surveyor.

BUXTON.—September 6th.—Supply and erection of electric lighting plant, for the urban district council.—Clerk.

SHEFFIELD.—September 6th.—Extension of car-shed.—Mr. Henry Sayer, town clerk.

ROCHDALE.—September 6th.—Electric lighting plant.—Mr. James Leach, town clerk.

ALDERSHOT.—September 6th.—Supply of 2,000 tons of granite (more or less), for the urban district council.—Mr. W. E. Foster, clerk.

ALDERSHOT.—September 6th.—Supply and delivery of a Morrison's scarifier, for the urban district council.—Mr. W. E. Foster, clerk.

ALDERSHOT.—September 7th.—Metalling Albert-street, West End, for the urban district council.—Mr. W. E. Foster, clerk.

EDINBURGH.—September 7th.—Work in connection with Portobello public baths.—Mr. R. Morham, city superintendent of works.

WEYBRIDGE.—September 7th.—Supply and delivery of various materials, for the urban district council.—Mr. G. Wheeler, clerk.

SOUTHEND-ON-SEA.—September 8th.—Making-up of roads.—Mr. William H. Snow, town clerk.

BANGOR.—September 8th.—Supply and erection of electric lighting plant.—Mr. R. Hughes Pritchard, town clerk.

BIRMINGHAM.—September 13th.—Construction of aqueduct.—Mr. E. O. Smith, town clerk.

NOTTINGHAM.—September 17th.—Construction of new sewer.—Mr. Arthur Brown, city engineer.

EDINBURGH.—October 17th.—For various works in connection with gasholder tank at Granton.—Mr. James M'G. Jack, clerk to the commissioners.

HOGSLEY.—September 19th.—Sewering, levelling, paving, metalling, channelling and making good certain roads, for the urban district council.—Mr. F. D. Askey, clerk.

CARRICKNACROSS.—Construction of waterworks, for the board of guardians, acting as the rural sanitary authority.—Mr. John Phelan, clerk of the union.

CUCKFIELD.—Supplying and laying 1,800 superficial yards of tar paving in Station-road, for the urban district council.—Mr. Edward Waugh, clerk.

## TENDERS.

*ACCEPTED.

ASHTON-IN-MAKERFIELD.—For the supply and delivery of 250 tons of 2-in. best, hand-broken granite macadam and 50 tons of ½-in. clean sharp granite chippings, for the urban district council.—Mr. John W. Liversedge, surveyor to the council:—

| | 3-in. Macadam. Per ton. | ½-in. Chippings. Per ton. |
|---|---|---|
| | s. d. | s. d. |
| Clee Hill Granite Company, Ludlow | 12 6 | 10 2 |
| Mountsorrel Granite Co., Mountsorrel... | 12 3 | 11 0 |
| J. J. Lee, Manchester... | 10 10 | 9 2 |
| L, Copper, Leeds | 10 8 | 8 2 |
| Threlkeld Granite Company, Keswick... | 10 5 | |
| Ceiriog Granite Company... | 9 7 | 8 10 |
| Pwllheli Granite Company, Liverpool | 9 3 | |
| Brundritt & Co., Liverpool | 9 0 | 6 9 |
| Darbishires, Limited, Penmaenmawr* | 8 9 | 6 0 |

For the supply of 12-in. Cast-Iron Pipes, &c.

| | | | |
|---|---|---|---|
| Newton, Chambers & Co., near Sheffield, | | | £1,490 |
| Stanton Ironworks Company, near Nottingham | | | 1,411 |
| Stavely Coal & Iron Company, near Chesterfield ... | | | 1,406 |
| Thompson & Co., Wigan ... | | | 1,404 |
| Cochrane & Co., Dudley* | | | 1,375 |
| Merton & Co. (on behalf of Wood & Co., Philadelphia) ... | | | 1,368 |

BANBURY.—For the repairing of the stonework of parapet, walls and roof at the town hall.—Mr. N. H. Dawson, borough surveyor :—

| | | |
|---|---|---|
| S. Orchard & Son, Banbury | | £37 |
| J. S. Kimberley, Banbury* | | 31 |

BRIGHTON.—For alterations and additions to the gentlemen's cloak-room and lavatory at the Royal Pavilion.—Mr. Francis J. C. May, M.I.C.E., borough engineer and surveyor :—

| | | |
|---|---|---|
| Satten & Evershed, Brighton | | £346 |
| T. E. Nye, Brighton | | 333 |
| V. P. Freeman, Brighton* | | 320 |

BURTON-UPON-TRENT.—For the construction and erection of a new retort-house at the gasworks, for the corporation.—Mr. F. L. Ramsden, engineer, Gas and Electric Light Works, Burton-upon-Trent :—
Building.—J. T. Barlow, Burton-upon-Trent,* £2,398.
Wrought-Iron Roof.—Gough & Felgate, Burton-upon-Trent,* £589.

BURY.—For the erection of a manager's house at the sewage disposal works, Livesey Fields.—Mr. J. Cartwright, borough engineer :—
Bricklayers' and Stonemasons' Work.—J. Comfort, Bury.
Carpenter and Joiner.—J. Inman, Bury.
Slater.—J. Kay & Sons, Bury.
Plumber and Glazier.—Jackson & Co., Bury.
Painter and Plasterer.—J. Ramsden, Bury.

DONCASTER. — For the erection of an isolation hospital adjoining Common-lane, Balby.—Mr. William H. R. Crabtree, borough surveyor :—
W. Johnson, Doncaster.*

GUILDFORD.—For the construction of certain surface-water drains, including new works of drainage in connection therewith.—Mr. C. G. Mason, borough surveyor :—

| | | |
|---|---|---|
| Pedrette & Co., Finsbury... | | £6,224 |
| G. A. Franks, Guildford .. | | 5,074 |
| Streeter Brothers, Godalming* ... | | 4,325 |

RICHMOND (Surrey).—For the construction of about 600 yards of 15-in. stoneware pipe sewer from Sheen-road to Parkshot.—Mr. J. H. Brierley, borough surveyor :—

| | | |
|---|---|---|
| T. Adams, Wood Green, N. | | £1,407 |
| Killingback & Co., James-street, Camden Town, N.W... | | 1,157 |
| E. Parry, Chesilton-road, Fulham* ... | | 1,127 |

SKIPTON.—For providing and laying of about 3,000 lineal yards of 3-in. cast-iron pipes, and for the construction of a covered service reservoir and conduit, for the rural district council.—Mr. A. Rodwell, engineer and surveyor to the council :—

| | | |
|---|---|---|
| T. Rowland, Sandiway, Northwich | | £800 |
| Hartley & Pickles, Gargrave | | 888 |
| J. & M. Hawley, Colne | | 848 |
| T. Young & Co., Gullingworth, Bradford | | 811 |
| T. Kassel, Hawes | | 704 |
| G. H. Mason, Skipton | | 696 |
| H. Wilson, Great Horton, Bradford | | 684 |
| G. Dougill, Aygarth, R.S.O.* | | 680 |
| Sheepbridge Coal and Iron Company, Chesterfield (pipes only)... | | 196 |

WEST BRIDGFORD.—For the laying of about 2,460 yards of 12-in. and 9-in. Hassell's pipe sewers, 12-in. iron pipe sewers and 9-in. sur. face-water drains, for the urban district council.—Mr. Wm. Pare, surveyor to the council :—

| | | |
|---|---|---|
| Bower Brothers, West Bridgford, Notts | | £3,041 |
| Cope & Raynor, West Bridgford, Notts | | 3,035 |
| Barry, Radcliffe | | 2,955 |
| R. Peck, Chesterfield | | 2,124 |

WORSBOROUGH (near Barnsley).—For the conversion of an engine. house in furnace yard into a dwelling-house, for the urban district council.—Mr. J. Whitaker, surveyor to the council :—

| | | |
|---|---|---|
| W. Barrow, Barnsley | | £155 |
| Higham & Son, Barnsley | | 115 |
| W. Bigram, Barnsley | | 113 |
| Turton & Field, Barnsley | | 108 |
| Porter & Son, Barnsley* | | 95 |

## NOTICES.

THE SURVEYOR AND MUNICIPAL AND COUNTY ENGINEER may be ordered direct, through any of Messrs. Smith & Son's book-stalls, or of any newsagent in the United Kingdom. Applications to the Offices for single copies by post must in all cases be accompanied by stamps.

The Prepaid Subscription (including postage) is as follows :—

| | Twelve Months. | Six Months. | Three Months. |
|---|---|---|---|
| United Kingdom | 14s. | 7s. | 3s. 9d. |
| Continent, the Colonies, India, | | | |
| United States, &c. ... | 19s. | 9s. 6d. | 4s. 9d. |

The International News Company, 83 and 85 Duane-street New York City; The Toronto News Company, Toronto; and The Montreal News Company, Montreal, have been appointed agents in the United States and Canada for the sale of THE SURVEYOR. A thin paper edition is printed for circulation abroad.

EDITORIAL OFFICES:
ST. BRIDE'S HOUSE, 24 BRIDE-LANE, FLEET-STREET, LONDON, E.C.
OFFICE FOR ADVERTISEMENTS:
13 NEW STREET HILL, FLEET STREET, LONDON, E.C.
PUBLISHING OFFICES:
13 NEW STREET HILL, FLEET STREET, LONDON, E.C.

## APPOINTMENTS OPEN.

BOROUGH OF BURTON-UPON-TRENT.
TEMPORARY ASSISTANT IN BOROUGH ENGINEER'S OFFICE.

The advertisement appearing in last week's SURVEYOR is hereby cancelled, other arrangements in the staff having been made.

G. T. LYNAM,
Borough Engineer and Surveyor.
Town Hall, Burton-upon-Trent.
August 17, 1898.

BOROUGH OF SOUTHEND-ON-SEA.
BUILDINGS INSPECTOR.

The Corporation invite applications for the appointment of a Buildings Inspector, at a salary of £125 per annum.

The person appointed will be required to supervise the erection of new buildings, and to see that the by-laws in force within the borough with respect to new streets and buildings are complied with, and it is essential that he should be practically acquainted with building construction and have a thorough knowledge of the Model By-Laws of the Local Government Board, under the Public Health Act, 1875.

Applications to be made in writing, accompanied by copies of not more than three recent testimonials (which will not be returned), stating age, qualifications, experience and where at present engaged, to be delivered at my office before 10 o'clock a.m. on Friday, the 2nd September.

Canvassing members of the Town Council will be a disqualification.

(By order)
WILLIAM H. SNOW,
Town Clerk.
Southend-on-Sea.
August 16, 1898.

VESTRY OF ST. MARYLEBONE.
APPOINTMENT OF SUPERINTENDENT OF SEWERS AND DRAINS.

Notice is hereby given that the Surveyor to the Vestry is authorised to engage the services of a person competent to superintend the construction, maintenance and cleansing of all public sewers and urinals, and the construction of drains, so far as laid by the Vestry, within the parish of St. Marylebone. When the duties of the office have been performed for a period of twelve months in a manner satisfactory to the Surveyor the person engaged will be submitted to the Vestry for appointment. He will be required to reside in the parish and to devote the whole of his time to the duties of the office. The salary will be at the rate of £150 per annum, rising by annual increments of £10 to £200, the grant of such annual increments to be dependent upon the efficient and satisfactory discharge of the duties of the office, and the appointment will be made upon the understanding that no pension or retiring allowance will attach thereto.

Applications, in candidate's own handwriting, stating age (which must not be less than thirty nor more than forty-five years), with copies of three testimonials (only) of recent date, to be forwarded to J. Paget Waddington, C.E., Surveyor to the Vestry, at the Court House, Marylebone-lane, W., endorsed "Application for Superintendentship of Sewers and Drains," on or before Monday, September 5th proximo.

(By order)
W. H. GARBUTT,
Vestry Clerk.
August, 1898.

VESTRY OF ST. MARYLEBONE.
APPOINTMENT OF DISTRICT SUPERINTENDENTS.

Notice is hereby given that the Surveyor to the Vestry is authorised to engage the services of three persons (one for each of the three districts into which the parish is divided) competent to superintend the execution of all macadam, flint and paved carriageway and footway works, and to undertake the supervision of all hoardings, public lamps, &c., within the district to which each may be appointed. When the duties of the office have been performed for a period of twelve months in a manner satisfactory to the Surveyor each person engaged will be submitted to the Vestry for appointment. He will be required to reside in the parish and to devote the whole of his time to the duties of the office.

The salary will be at the rate of £150 per annum, rising by annual increments of £10 to £200, the grant of such annual increments to be dependent upon the efficient and satisfactory discharge of the duties of the office, and the appointment will be made upon the understanding that no pension or retiring allowances will attach thereto.

Applications, in candidate's own handwriting, stating age (which must not be less than thirty nor more than forty-five years), with copies of three testimonials (only) of recent date, to be forwarded to J. Paget Waddington, C.E., Surveyor to the Vestry, at the Court House, Marylebone-lane, W., endorsed "Application for District Superintendentship," on or before Monday, September 5th proximo.

(By order)

W. H. GARBUTT,
Vestry Clerk.

August, 1898.

### BOROUGH OF WEST HARTLEPOOL.

JUNIOR ASSISTANT.

Wanted, in the Borough Engineer's Department, a Junior Assistant, who has been thoroughly trained in the duties of a borough engineer's office. He must be a good draughtsman and surveyor, and have architectural ability. Salary, £78 per year.

Applications, stating age, present employment, and accompanied by copies of three recent testimonials, and addressed to the "Chairman of the Works Committee," endorsed "Junior Assistant," are to be delivered at this office on or before 4 p.m. on the 30th inst.

(By order)

J. W. BROWN,
Borough Engineer.

Borough Engineer's Office, West Hartlepool.
August 11, 1898.

### VESTRY OF ST. MARYLEBONE.

APPOINTMENT OF SUPERINTENDENT OF CLEANSING.

Notice is hereby given that the Surveyor to the Vestry is authorised to engage the services of a person competent to discharge the duties of superintending the street cleansing, washing, watering, snow removal, &c., of the parish of St. Marylebone. A horse and trap will be available for use by the person engaged, in order that he may be enabled to efficiently discharge the duties of the office. When such duties have been performed for a period of twelve months in a manner satisfactory to the Surveyor the person engaged will be submitted to the Vestry for appointment. He will be required to reside in the parish and to devote the whole of his time to the duties of the office.

The salary will be at the rate of £180 per annum, rising by annual increments of £10 to £230, the grant of such annual increments to be dependent upon the efficient and satisfactory discharge of the duties of the office, and the appointment will be made upon the understanding that no pension or retiring allowance will attach thereto.

Applications, in candidate's own handwriting, stating age (which must not be less than thirty nor more than forty-five years), with copies of three testimonials (only) of recent date, to be forwarded to J. Paget Waddington, C.E., Surveyor to the Vestry, at the Court House, Marylebone-lane, W., endorsed "Application for Cleansing Superintendentship," on or before Monday, September 5th proximo.

(By order)

W. H. GARBUTT,
Vestry Clerk.

August, 1898.

### RURAL DISTRICT COUNCIL OF CHESTERFIELD.

This Council is prepared to receive applications for the office of a Surveyor of Highways for the northern district of their jurisdiction, the area of which is 32,927 acres, with a population in 1891 of about 36,580 people and about 126 miles of highways.

The salary to be paid will be after the rate of £160 per annum, rising £10 per annum until the sum of £200 is reached, which sum will include everything (stationery and postages excepted).

The person appointed must be competent to take levels, prepare plans, estimates and bills of quantities of any works required to be done, and must personally see to the carrying out of the same. He must also be competent to keep all books and accounts required under the Acts, obey all orders of the Council and other road authorities, and devote his whole time to the duties of his office.

The person appointed will be required to reside at Eckington or Staveley.

Security in the sum of £200, with an approved guarantee society, for the due performance of the duties will be required, and the appointment will be terminable by three calendar months' notice on either side.

Applications, stating age (which must not exceed forty-five) and previous occupation, accompanied by three testimonials of recent date, to be sent to me on or before the 31st instant. Canvassing is strictly prohibited. Only third-class railway fare (return) will be allowed to selected candidates. No allowance for hotel or other expenses.

(By order)

GEORGE SHAW,
Clerk.

Union Offices, Chesterfield.
August 17, 1898.

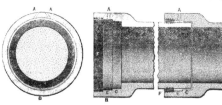

CITY OF HULL.

The Corporation require a Civil Engineering Assistant in the City Engineer's office, at £85 per annum.

It is essential that candidates should be quick and neat draughtsmen.

Applications, stating age, experience and qualifications, are to be delivered to the undersigned on or before Tuesday, the 23rd August.

Testimonials need not be sent in the first instance.

(By order)
A. E. WHITE,
City Engineer.

Town Hall, Hull.
July 30, 1898.

## TENDERS WANTED.

CITY OF NOTTINGHAM.
TO CONTRACTORS.

The Stoke Farm Committee of the City Council is prepared to receive tenders for the Construction of a new Sewer in Lenton Boulevard, together with all appurtenant works.

The works required consist of the construction of about :—
1,760 yards Brick and Concrete Main Sewer, 9 ft. wide and 7 ft. 3 in. high.
40 yards 4 ft. 6 in. diameter Brick Barrel Sewer.
16 yards 5 ft. diameter Brick Barrel Sewer.
146 yards 3-ft. 6-in. by 2-ft. 4-in. Egg-Shaped Brick Sewer.
55 yards 3-ft. by 2-ft. Egg-Shaped Brick Sewer.
24 yards 15 in. diameter Pipe Sewer.
550 yards 12 in. diameter Pipe Sewer.
80 yards 9 in. diameter Pipe Sewer and other appurtenant works.

Drawings may be seen, and specification, bills of quantities and forms of tender obtained, at my office, on payment of a deposit of 3 guineas, which will be returned on receipt of a bond-fide tender and the copy of the specification.

Sealed tenders, endorsed "New Sewer, Lenton Boulevard," are to be sent to the Town Clerk on or before Saturday, the 17th September, 1898.

The lowest or any tender will not necessarily be accepted, and tenders will only be accepted from persons who conform to the conditions of contract as regards paying the local standard rate of wages, &c.

(By order)
ARTHUR BROWN, M.Inst.c.e.,
City Engineer.

Guildhall, Nottingham.
August 16, 1898.

WALLASEY URBAN DISTRICT COUNCIL.
WROUGHT-IRON RAILINGS.

The Wallasey Urban District Council are prepared to receive tenders for the supply of Wrought-Iron Railings and Gates for the fencing-in of extended Cemetery.

Specification, forms of tender and further particulars may be obtained on application to Mr. W. H. Travers, District Engineer and Surveyor, Public Offices, Egremont, Cheshire, at which place tenders are to be delivered not later than Wednesday, the 31st instant, in sealed envelope, endorsed "Cemetery Railings," and addressed to the Chairman of the Health Committee.

The Council do not bind themselves to accept the lowest or any tender.

(By order)
H. W. COOK,
Clerk to the Council.

Public Offices, Egremont, Cheshire.
August 16, 1898.

CARRICKMACROSS UNION.
NOTICE TO CONTRACTORS.

The Board of Guardians of the above Union, acting as the rural sanitary authority, will, at their meeting to be held at 2 o'clock p.m. on Tuesday, 6th September, 1898, be prepared to consider tenders for the construction of works to supply the town of Carrickmacross with water, in accordance with plans and specification prepared by P. F. Comber and the late W. G. Strype, MEMBS.INST.C.E., 19 Lower Leeson-street, Dublin, which can be seen at the office of Mr. J. H. Blackader, solicitor, Carrickmacross, between the hours of 11 a.m. and 3 o'clock p.m. daily.

The works comprise the supply and laying of 102 tons or thereabouts of Cast-Iron Water Mains; the construction of a Pumping House, with duplicate sets of oil engines and three-throw gun-metal plunger force pumps, each set of pumping

plant being capable of delivering 90 gallons per minute to a height of 200 ft.; and the construction of a Service Reservoir, to contain 100,000 gallons or thereabouts.

Printed copies of the specification and form of tender may be obtained from Mr. Blackader on payment of £2 sterling from each competitor, which will be returned on the receipt of a *bond-fide* tender.

Tenders to be addressed to the undersigned, and endorsed "Tender for Waterworks," naming solvent sureties.

The Guardians do not bind themselves to accept the lowest or any tender.

(By order)
JOHN PHELAN,
Clerk of the Union and Executive
Sanitary Officer.

Board-room, Carrickmacross.
    August 16, 1898.

### ALDERSHOT URBAN DISTRICT COUNCIL.
SCARIFIER.

The above Council are prepared to receive tenders for the supply and delivery at Aldershot of a Scarifier of the type known as Morrison's. The scarifier must be capable of being attached to and worked by a 19-ton steam roller. A separate price is required for the work of fixing, &c., to the steam rollers. The contractor must give a full description of the machine with his tenders. Full particulars may be obtained of the Surveyor.

Tenders, to be endorsed "Scarifier," are to be delivered at my office not later than the 6th day of September.

The Council do not bind themselves to accept the lowest or any tender.

The contractor must state when he will undertake the delivery. This is important.

(By order of the Council)
W. E. FOSTER,
Clerk.

Aldershot.
    August 5, 1898.

### ALDERSHOT URBAN DISTRICT COUNCIL.
TO ROAD CONTRACTORS AND OTHERS.

The Aldershot Urban District Council are prepared to receive tenders for the Metalling, &c., of :—

Albert-street, West End, Aldershot.

Plans and specifications may be seen, and forms of tender obtained, by applying at the office of the Surveyor to the Council, 126 Victoria-road, Aldershot.

Sureties will be required.

Tenders, endorsed "Tenders for New Streets," are to be delivered in a sealed envelope at my office not later than 9 a.m. on Wednesday, the 7th day of September next.

The Council do not bind themselves to accept the lowest or any tender.

(By order)
W. B. FOSTER,
Clerk to the Council.

126 Victoria-road.
    August 5, 1898.

### CITY OF SHEFFIELD.

*TO IRONFOUNDERS AND OTHERS.*

EXTENSION OF TINSLEY CAR-SHED.

The Tramway Committee invite tenders for Iron Roof, Columns, &c., in connection with the extension of the above car-shed.

Plans and specifications may be seen, and quantities obtained, at the office of Mr. Charles F. Wike, c.f., city surveyor, Town Hall, Sheffield, after Thursday, the 18th inst., on payment of 1 guinea, which will be returned on receipt of a *bond-fide* tender.

Tenders, endorsed "Ironwork, Car-Shed," to be sent in not later than Monday, the 5th September, 1898, addressed "Chairman and Members of the Tramways Committee, City Surveyor's Office, Town Hall, Sheffield."

The contract will comprise the fair wages and conditions of labour clause which has been adopted by the Sheffield Corporation, particulars of which will appear in the specification.

The Committee do not bind themselves to accept the lowest or any tender.

(By order)
(Signed) HENRY SAYER,
Town Clerk.

Town Clerk's Office, Town Hall, Sheffield.
    August 15th, 1898.

### BOROUGH OF SOUTHEND-ON-SEA.
TO ROAD CONTRACTORS AND OTHERS.

The Corporation invite tenders for Street Works in the making-up of the following streets :—

Hadleigh-road.
Wickford-road.
Canewdon-road (eastern portion of).

Plans, sections and specifications may be seen, and bills of quantities and forms of tender obtained, on and after Monday, August 22nd (on payment of £1 1s. in respect of each street, which will be returned on receipt of a *bond-fide*

tender), upon application to Mr. Alfred Fidler, ASSOC.M.INST.C.E., Borough Surveyor, Clarence-road, Southend.

No tender will be considered unless made on the prescribed form, and there must be a separate tender for each street.

Sealed tenders, endorsed with the name of the street, and marked "Tender for Private Street Works," to be delivered at my office before 10 o'clock in the morning of Thursday, September 8th.

The Corporation will not be bound to accept the lowest or any tender.

(By order)
WILLIAM H. SNOW,
Town Clerk.

Southend-on-Sea.
August 16, 1898.

EAST HAM URBAN DISTRICT COUNCIL.
SUPPLY OF BROKEN GRANITE.

The above-named Council invite tenders for the supply of about 1,000 yards of Best Blue Guernsey and about 1,000 yards of other kinds of Broken Granite.

Particulars and form of tender may be obtained of Mr. W. H. Savage, the Council's Surveyor, at the Public Offices, East Ham.

Tenders to be sent in on or before 5 o'clock on Monday, August 29, 1898.

So far as is practicable in connection with this contract the person or persons whose tender is accepted will be required to pay such rates of wages and observe such hours of labour as are recognised by the trades unions, and also to supply the Council with the schedule rate of wages adopted by his or their firm.

C. E. WILSON,
Clerk to the Council.

Public Offices, East Ham, E.
August 17, 1898.

EAST HAM URBAN DISTRICT COUNCIL.
SUPPLY OF GRANITE CURB.

The above-named Council invite tenders for the supply of about 6,000 ft. run 12-in. by 8-in., also about 10,000 ft. run 12-in. by 6-in. Granite Curb.

Particulars and form of tender may be obtained of Mr. W. H. Savage, the Council's Surveyor, at the Public Offices, East Ham. Tenders to be sent in on or before 5 o'clock on Monday, August 29, 1898.

So far as it is practicable in connection with this contract

the person or persons whose tender is accepted will be required to pay such rates of wages and observe such hours of labour as are recognised by the trades unions, and also to supply the Council with the schedule rate of wages adopted by his or their firm.

C. E. WILSON,
Clerk to the Council.

Public Offices, East Ham, E.
August 17, 1898.

HORNSEY URBAN DISTRICT COUNCIL.
TO ROAD AND SEWER CONTRACTORS.

The Hornsey Urban District Council are prepared to receive tenders for Sewering, Levelling, Paving, Metalling, Channelling and Making-good the following Roads and Portions of Roads, all situate within the district of Hornsey—viz.,

(1) Barrington-road (third section),
(2) Harefield-road, and
(3) Hampden-road (second section).

Plans and specifications may be seen, and forms of tender and all information obtained, on application to Mr. E. J. Lovegrove, Engineer to the Council, at the offices mentioned below, on any morning (on or after Monday, the 29th inst.) between the hours of 10 and 12 o'clock, on a sum of £2 being deposited with the Clerk to the Council, which sum will be retained by the Council and deemed to be forfeited if a bond-fide tender is not made by the depositor.

If a tender is made which is not accepted the sum deposited will be returned, and if a tender is accepted such sum will be retained by the Council until the contract has been executed by the depositor, and will be forfeited in the event of his or his sureties failing or neglecting to execute such contract or the bond accompanying it within seven days after he or they respectively shall have been requested to execute them.

No tender will be considered except on the prescribed form.

Sealed and endorsed tenders are to be deposited in the tender-box in my department not later than 4 o'clock p.m. on Monday, the 19th day of September next.

The Council reserve to themselves the right to decline all or any, or any portion, of the tenders so sent in.

(By order)
F. D. ASKEY,
Clerk to the District Council.

Offices; Southwood-lane, Highgate, N.
August 15, 1898.

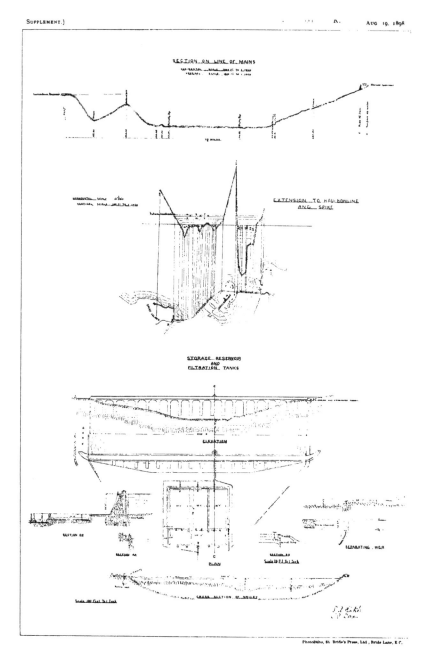

SECTION ON LINE OF MAINS

EXTENSION TO HAULBOWLINE
AND SPIKE

STORAGE RESERVOIR
AND
FILTRATION TANKS

ELEVATION

SECTION CC

SECTION AA

SEPARATING WEIR

PLAN

Scale 20 Ft To 1 Inch

CROSS SECTION OF VALLEY

Scale 100 Feet To 1 Inch

PhotoLitho. St. Bride's Press, Ltd , Bride Lane, E C.

ASSOCIATION OF MUNICIPAL AND COUNTY ENGINEERS. CORK MEETING
QUEENSTOWN WATERWORKS.

# The Surveyor

## And Municipal and County Engineer.

Vol. XIV., No. 345.     LONDON, AUGUST 26, 1898.     Weekly, Price 3d.

## Minutes of Proceedings.

**Protection of Water Supplies.** Some time ago Dr. Bruce Low submitted a report to the Local Government Board with respect to complaints regarding the Bury water supply. The chief remedies indicated were the protection of the watersheds and filtration. Bury Corporation, however, were even then formulating a scheme, though it appears to have been at first considered that the prevention of pollution by the acquisition of the watersheds, which were the subject of complaint, would render filtration unnecessary. The question of the pollution of gathering grounds of water supply has given much anxiety to many local authorities, and the thriving and enterprising borough of Bury has certainly been perplexed by a water problem which has greatly taxed its energies and resources. During the session which has just come to a close a Bill aiming chiefly at the improvement of the water service of the borough has occupied the attention of both Houses of Parliament. In May last a committee of the House of Lords was engaged in the investigation of the merits of a scheme which was evidently matured after most careful inquiry on the part of highly competent experts. That House had to deal with very powerful opposition, and the petitions lodged in the House of Commons were in themselves evidence enough of the vigilance and activity of property owners and rival authorities, who conceived, rightly or wrongly, that their interests were menaced. The Bill itself was of what is known as the "omnibus" type—that is to say, it embraced other subjects than water. From Dr. Bruce Low's report it appears that the water supply of Bury is obtained from six gathering grounds, five of which are situated at distances varying from 2 to 10 miles from the borough, the sixth lying on the outskirts, though almost altogether within the boundary of the town. Dr. Low's communication to the Local Government Board dealt exhaustively with each of the gathering grounds, and showed the areas of collecting reservoirs and the capacity of the springs. As a matter of historical interest, we may remark that the waterworks, which now belong to the Bury Corporation, were originally the property of two companies—the Radcliffe and Bury Waterworks Company and the Haslingden and Rawtenstall Waterworks Company. As time went on Bury, the most important centre of that energetic manufacturing district, acquired predominating influence, and at various times powers were given for the construction of additional works. At the present time the gathering grounds of the Bury Corporation consist in great part of high-lying moorlands, sparsely populated except in some places. The collecting reservoirs have been constructed in most instances by throwing dams across valleys, the people resident upon the gathering grounds being chiefly occupied with agricultural pursuits. The water is not filtered before delivery to the consumers, but it passes through a copper-wire gauze screen, in some cases,

before entering the mains. The gathering grounds, which, as already stated, are six in number, are Calf Hey, 872 acres; Holden Wood, 1,313 acres; Hampton or Clow Bridge, 1,303 acres; Clough Bottom, 736 acres; Harden Clough or Shuttleworth, 206 acres; and Gin Hall, 202 acres. The Bury Corporation were of opinion that the carrying out of the regular and systematic flushing of the mains and gradual replacement of the old, encrusted and corroded pipes with modern ones, properly prepared against internal encrustation, would result in a total cessation of the complaints that have hitherto been frequent. The corporation were advised that the construction of filter-beds would entail an expenditure almost beyond their present resources without giving absolute security against water-borne disease. There can be no doubt that the corporation have done their very best to provide an ample and pure supply of water, but the difficulties with which they have had to contend have been of no ordinary magnitude. As would be observed from the reports we recently published of the Private Bill proceedings, the corporation decided not to rely upon the mere acquisition of watersheds for the prevention of pollution, but to adopt a system of filtration. They have certainly done well, not only in grappling promptly with the problem, but in making an effort to meet the requirements of the Local Government Board, though this involves considerable additional expenditure.

**Overdoing It.** We regret to find ourselves provided this week with more than one cause for grumbling. One of those causes is found set forth in the paragraph elicited by the stupendous—and in the case of one clause offensive—list of duties drawn up in connection with the appointment of borough surveyor in a small Welsh town. Another cause will be found in connection with a list of questions sent to municipal engineers in order that they might supply gratuitous information to another borough. Now, we freely admit that this custom, within certain limits, has long been a recognised one, and has undoubtedly prevailed to a considerable extent. Municipal engineers have always been glad to help one another, and in no way is this more conclusively shown than in connection with the gratuitous work that is given in organising the district meetings of the Association and in the preparation of papers. Banded together, as the great majority of them undoubtedly are, especially those in the more prominent positions, in a strong Association, it is not to be expected that the spirit of co-operation will stop short at meetings of that Association. If a municipal engineer be suddenly called upon to carry out a new scheme in a branch of work in which professional practice varies considerably, it is obvious that the experience of other towns in the same direction must be of considerable assistance to him in framing a report on

times of necessity only upon the New River Company. On the other hand were are told that five companies can be drawn upon—by purchase. If so, we should certainly advise the company to be liberal in the matter. To our mind the only likely solution of the problem is the bringing of the whole water supply of the metropolis under proper public control.

\* \* \*

**Duties of a Borough Surveyor.**

We have received a copy of a portentous list of duties which was drawn up recently for the behoof of candidates for an appointment as borough surveyor in a small Welsh town. Every one knows, of course, that it is customary on these occasions for such a list of duties to be drawn up, but is it too much to expect that some glimmerings of a conscience should be shown in drafting the document? Here is a small Welsh town, and yet they want accomplishments in their borough surveyor which would stamp him as an engineer of very remarkable capabilities indeed. If it were an appointment to which a salary of something between £500 and £1,000 a year were attached there might be less to be said. but nothing like this salary is found in connection with the municipal surveyorship of an insignificant Welsh borough, even though a county town. As our readers have an opportunity of perusing the document for themselves, we need not refer to the clauses in detail. To this, however, we wish to make one exception. The phenomenal accomplishments which are expected in return for a trifling salary are bad enough, but one particular clause is so grossly offensive in its terms that no one could without loss of self-respect enter upon an office to which such a condition attached. We refer to clause 5, in which, after stating that the surveyor will be required to prepare all surveys, plans and estimates of new works and alterations (Parliamentary and otherwise) required by the corporation, the extraordinary condition is added that "should the surveyor be found incapable of properly doing any particular work required of him the council or any committee may employ another surveyor and deduct the cost from any salary that may be due to him, the council or committee to be the sole judge of any matter arising out of this clause." What next? We certainly sympathise with an official who is under agreement to accept the decision of people who can, apparently without blushing, draft or endorse a clause like this.

**Typhoid in Camborne.**

The sanitary condition of rural and semi-rural districts is evidently a source of no small tribulation to the medical department of the Local Government Board. One of the reports recently issued by the Local Government Board is that by Dr. R. Bruce Low on an outbreak of enteric fever in the Camborne urban district and in portions of the adjoining rural districts of Redruth and Helston. Briefly put, the matter is this. In December of last year a sudden outbreak of enteric fever appeared simultaneously in the three adjacent parishes of Camborne, Illogan and Crowan, situate in three separate sanitary districts. Altogether 165 attacks, with twelve deaths, were recorded in about six weeks. The only condition common to the three localities was that of water supply, derived from the same source—the Camborne Water Company's waterworks. This company's supply immediately previous to the outbreak came from Roswyn, where some springs are piped to a service tank, and where, to augment the supply, water from a brook was piped to the same tank. Within the catchment area of this brook there occurred, in October and November, 1897, in a single cottage four cases of enteric fever, the discharges from which fouled a pond close to the dwelling. In wet

weather the pond in question overflows, and the water therefrom runs down the hill in a channel to the above-mentioned brook, entering it 100 yards above the pipe leading from the brook to the service tank. In mid-November the rainfall was excessive, and by the flood thus caused the fever poison emanating from the infected cottage was no doubt swept into the Roswyn supply. After the brook water was shut off from the service tank, and after the service tank had been scrubbed out and cleansed and the water mains well flushed, the outbreak came suddenly to an end. The inspector's own summing up is that the general sanitary condition of Camborne, as well as of parts of Crowan, is far from being satisfactory.

**Death of Mr. Ashmead.**

It is with deep regret that we record the death, on Tuesday, of Mr. Frederick Ashmead, formerly borough engineer of Bristol and a past-president of the Incorporated Association of Municipal and County Engineers. After serving his articles with the late Mr. Underwood, a civil engineer and architect, he was one of the resident engineers during the construction of the South Wales Railway, being in charge of the Neath section. Mr. Ashmead returned to Bristol in 1851, when he was appointed deputy borough engineer, Mr. Armstrong then filling the post of borough engineer. On the death of the latter Mr. Ashmead was appointed borough engineer, a post he held with credit to himself and benefit to his native city until 1894, when ill-health compelled him to retire, and he was appointed consulting engineer, being succeeded as borough engineer by Mr. T. H. Yabbicom. The main drainage works of Bristol, which are inseparably connected with Mr. Ashmead's name, were begun in 1855 and completed in 1874, at a cost of £168,000. The deceased gentleman was president of the Incorporated Association of Municipal and County Engineers in 1877-78, when the annual meeting was held at Bristol.

\* \* \*

**The Dublin Congress.**

In another column we give some notes of the proceedings at the Health Congress at Dublin, which constituted the annual conference of the Royal Institute of Public Health. However interesting the papers and discussions may have been for medical officers and for those sanitarians who are accustomed to look at sanitary questions chiefly from the medical side, we cannot find that there was a great deal that was distinctly interesting to the municipal and sanitary engineer. In this respect the Sanitary Institute generally contrive to prepare a much better programme. There were some suggestive passages in the opening address of Sir Charles Cameron. In the engineering and building construction section papers were read on such subjects as the designing and construction of refuse destructors, hidden dangers in the sites of dwelling-houses and, the subsoil in relation to sites for dwellings. In the municipal and Parliamentary sections the topics of discussion included the housing of the working classes, and the municipalisation of tramways and public lighting. If likely to be of sufficient interest to our readers, we shall give abstracts of some of these.

## PROFESSIONAL PROVERBS.

For *Members of Local Authorities :* Take care of the houses and the towns will take care of themselves.

For a *Householder :* When the workmen come in at the door comfort flies out of the window.

For a *Constructor of Roofs :* There's many a slip 'twixt rafter and hip.

the subject and in supporting such recommendations as he may decide to lay before his council. Such assistance is naturally most serviceable to the younger members of the profession; as they grow older and more experienced they become more and more able to dispense with it. But it does not follow that because municipal engineers are prepared to give a certain amount of gratuitous assistance to one another, from the strong feeling of *esprit de corps* that prevails among them, they should be called upon to dispense it to all and sundry, or, at all events, to other classes of officials. This, as we have before now had occasion to point out, is carrying altruism too far in these days, when competition is so severe and when professional knowledge and skill cannot always find remunerative scope for their exercise. When the method of obtaining knowledge by a circular of questions is resorted to among municipal engineers it is recognised as desirable to keep the questions within reasonable limits, both as to number and scope, so as not to trench too much on the time and attention of those to whom they are addressed. So far as concerns the list of questions we print this week in another column, this wise discretion seems to have been thrown to the winds, and we leave our readers to calculate for themselves the length of time that would be absorbed in giving adequate replies to such an interminable string of questions. The gravest feature of the case, however, in our opinion, is that the circular has been issued, not by a municipal engineer, but by a medical officer of health. Now, the erection of a refuse destructor is no doubt partly a sanitary question, but surely it is to a much greater extent an engineering question, and, whether or not it be combined with an electric lighting scheme, it lies much more within the province of the municipal engineer than of the medical officer of health. This is probably how the great majority of municipal engineers will look at the question, and for that and other reasons will very likely decline to act as so many consulting engineers without fee. Simply because they are generally prepared to stretch a point to assist a brother engineer, it does not follow that they should be called upon to do the same for all and sundry, especially when the application is the outcome of a clear invasion of the municipal engineer's province by another official.

\* \* \*

**Public Health Work in Edinburgh.** Municipal engineers who attended the recent annual meeting at Edinburgh, and those who followed our report of it, are familiar with the name of Baillie Pollard as one who has always taken an enlightened interest in public health work. He has now brought out a well-printed and illustrated pamphlet giving an historical sketch of the development of public health in Edinburgh, and a description of its culminating achievement in the erection of the new hospital at Colinton Mains. In Edinburgh, as elsewhere, the growth of the movement was tardy and intermittent, and the energising effect of outbreaks of disease was apt to be temporary, even though the severity of the outbreak was aggravated by the peculiar construction of the high houses, a result of the walling in of the town. Baillie Pollard sketches the sanitary history of the city from the fifteenth century. Peculiarly interesting it is, and we regret that we cannot do more than make a passing reference to it here. Something may be said as to the water supply, as its imperfect nature had much to do with the former condition of the city. In 1621 the sunk wells were augmented by the introduction of a supply from the near Pentlands at Comiston. Powers were granted for the construction of a 3-in. pipe, but the supply continued very unsatisfactory until the completion of the reservoir on Castle Hill sixty years later. By means of this reservoir an equable—and except in times of great drought a fairly constant—supply was maintained. Further supplies from Comiston

were introduced in 1722, and again in 1785, while in 1790 the Swanston area was tapped, and in 1821 the Edinburgh Water Company introduced the Crawley water. No further increase was made till the Moorfoot scheme of 1870 gave the inhabitants the supply upon which they must subsist until the completion of the Talla scheme four or five years hence. But for the spread of the city beyond the city walls to the south and over the fields lying on the north side of the Nor' loch, an improved water supply would have availed little in the interest of public health. The dwellers in the lofty tenements in the Old Town, having to carry all their water, used as little as possible. About 100 years ago the city was considered one of the filthiest in the United Kingdom, and earned opprobrious words both from Smollett and from Samuel Johnson. Better conditions, however, gradually supervened; but the century was sixty years old before typhus was stamped out. A new municipal and sanitary era was inaugurated for Edinburgh by the appointment in 1863 of a medical officer of health in the person of Dr. (now Sir) Henry D. Littlejohn, who began his work by a remarkable report on the sanitary condition of Edinburgh. Not only describing the existing state of affairs, but suggesting improvements and remedies, he sharply awoke the citizens to a sense of their sanitary dangers and civic duties. A succession of able and conscientious lord provosts—especially Chambers and Russell—assisted in the work, and the result was the series of extensive improvement and other schemes of which we gave an account in connection with the recent annual meeting. One of the greatest of the works is the new hospital for infectious diseases, on which no less than £250,000 sterling will be spent. The main object of Baillie Pollard's excellent publication is to give a full description of this great work, and those who are interested in hospital construction should certainly procure a copy of the book, for it comprises an exhaustive series of plans. It is published by T. & A. Constable, Edinburgh University Press. We should mention that the architect of the new building is Mr. Robert Morham, superintendent of public works.

\* \* \*

**East London Water Supply.** A final settlement of this irritating question seems as far off as ever. As soon as a drought of more than average duration sets in the East-End is threatened with its periodical water famine, and the continuous supply is suddenly cut off. The contradictory statements that find their way into the Press require a considerable amount of sifting on the part of anyone who wishes to do justice to both sides. A few years ago the East London Water Company confidently asserted that if they were allowed to carry out certain works they would be able to cope with any emergency that might arise. Now comes a drought—bad enough to be sure, but by no means so severe as many that have been experienced in the past—and the company are quite unable to cope with it satisfactorily, from the consumer's point of view at all events. We are told that their calculations did not contemplate such a drought as this, and that they are now carrying out additional works for which powers were obtained last year. If the calculations were too modest a scale, the company must accept the responsibility for the consequences. A six hours' supply is a peculiarly dangerous state of affairs in the East-End. There remains the point that only one company has been inconvenienced by the drought, and we are told that the East London Company suffers from the fact that another company has priority of claim upon the Lea water. This, in our opinion, is simply a condemnation of the source, and should make a good many people think again of Wales. There remains the question of supplementary supplies from other companies. On the one side we are told that the East London Company can draw in times of necessity only upon the New River Company. On the other hand were are told that five companies can be drawn upon—by purchase. If so, we should certainly advise the company to be liberal in the matter. To our mind the only likely solution of the problem is the bringing of the whole water supply of the metropolis under proper public control.

\* \* \*

**Duties of a Borough Surveyor.** We have received a copy of a portentous list of duties which was drawn up recently for the behoof of candidates for an appointment as borough surveyor in a small Welsh town. Everyone knows, of course, that it is customary on these occasions for such a list of duties to be drawn up, but is it too much to expect that some glimmerings of a conscience should be shown in drafting the document? Here is a small Welsh town, and yet they want accomplishments in their borough surveyor which would stamp him as an engineer of very remarkable capabilities indeed. If it were an appointment to which a salary of something between £500 and £1,000 a year were attached there might be less to be said, but nothing like this salary is found in connection with the municipal surveyorship of an insignificant Welsh borough, even though a county town. As our readers have an opportunity of perusing the document for themselves, we need not refer to the clauses in detail. To this, however, we wish to make one exception. The phenomenal accomplishments which are expected in return for a trifling salary are bad enough, but one particular clause is so grossly offensive in its terms that no one could without loss of self-respect enter upon an office to which such a condition attached. We refer to clause 5, in which, after stating that the surveyor will be required to prepare all surveys, plans and estimates of new works and alterations (Parliamentary and otherwise) required by the corporation, the extraordinary condition is added that "should the surveyor be found incapable of properly doing any particular work required of him the council or any committee may employ another surveyor and deduct the cost from any salary that may be due to him, the council or committee to be the sole judge of any matter arising out of this clause." What next? We certainly sympathise with an official who is under agreement to accept the decision of people who can, apparently without blushing, draft or endorse a clause like this.

\* \* \*

**Typhoid in Camborne.** The sanitary condition of rural and semi-rural districts is evidently a source of no small tribulation to the medical department of the Local Government Board. One of the reports recently issued by the Local Government Board is that by Dr. R. Bruce Low on an outbreak of enteric fever in the Camborne urban district and in portions of the adjoining rural districts of Redruth and Helston. Briefly put, the matter is this. In December of last year a sudden outbreak of enteric fever appeared simultaneously in the three adjacent parishes of Camborne, Illogan and Crowan, situate in three separate sanitary districts. Altogether 165 attacks, with twelve deaths, were recorded in about six weeks. The only condition common to the three localities was that of water supply, derived from the same source—the Camborne Water Company's waterworks. This company's supply immediately previous to the outbreak came from Boswyn, where some springs are piped to a service tank, and where, to augment the supply, water from a brook was piped to the same tank. Within the catchment area of this brook there occurred, in October and November, 1897, in a single cottage four cases of enteric fever, the discharges from which fouled a pond close to the dwelling. In wet weather the pond in question overflows, and the water therefrom runs down the hill in a channel to the above-mentioned brook, entering it 100 yards above the pipe leading from the brook to the service tank. In mid-November the rainfall was excessive, and by the flood thus caused the fever poison emanating from the infected cottage was no doubt swept into the Boswyn supply. After the brook water was shut off from the service tank, and after the service tank had been scrubbed out and cleansed and the water mains well flushed, the outbreak came suddenly to an end. The inspector's final summing up is that the general sanitary condition of Camborne, as well as of parts of Crowan, is far from being satisfactory.

\* \* \*

**Death of Mr. Ashmead.** It is with deep regret that we record the death, on Tuesday, of Mr. Frederick Ashmead, formerly borough engineer of Bristol and a past-president of the Incorporated Association of Municipal and County Engineers. After serving his articles with the late Mr. Underwood, a civil engineer and architect, he was one of the resident engineers during the construction of the South Wales Railway, being in charge of the Neath section. Mr. Ashmead returned to Bristol in 1851, when he was appointed deputy borough engineer, Mr. Armstrong then filling the post of borough engineer. On the death of the latter Mr. Ashmead was appointed borough engineer, a post he held with credit to himself and benefit to his native city until 1894, when ill-health compelled him to retire, and he was appointed consulting engineer, being succeeded as borough engineer by Mr. T. H. Yabbicom. The main drainage works of Bristol, which are inseparably connected with Mr. Ashmead's name, were begun in 1855 and completed in 1874, at a cost of £163,000. The deceased gentleman was president of the Incorporated Association of Municipal and County Engineers in 1877-78, when the annual meeting was held at Bristol.

\* \* \*

**The Dublin Congress.** In another column we give some notes of the proceedings at the Health Congress at Dublin, which constituted the annual conference of the Royal Institute of Public Health. However interesting the papers and discussions may have been for medical officers and for those sanitarians who are accustomed to look at sanitary questions chiefly from the medical side, we cannot find that there was a great deal that was distinctly interesting to the municipal and sanitary engineer. In this respect the Sanitary Institute generally contrive to prepare a much better programme. There were some suggestive passages in the opening address of Sir Charles Cameron. In the engineering and building construction section papers were read on such subjects as the designing and construction of refuse destructors, hidden dangers in the sites of dwelling-houses and, the subsoil in relation to sites for dwellings. In the municipal and Parliamentary sections the topics of discussion included the housing of the working classes, and the municipalisation of tramways and public lighting. If likely to be of sufficient interest to our readers, we shall give abstracts of some of these.

## PROFESSIONAL PROVERBS.

*For Members of Local Authorities:* Take care of the houses and the towns will take care of themselves.

*For a Householder:* When the workmen come in at the door comfort flies out of the window.

*For a Constructor of Roofs:* There's many a slip 'twixt rafter and hip.

# Royal Institute of Public Health.

## ANNUAL CONGRESS AT DUBLIN.—I.

The annual congress of the Royal Institute of Public Health, which this year was arranged to be held at Dublin, was formally opened on Thursday, when the delegates and visitors were received by the Lord Mayor of Dublin, the president of the congress and the executive committee, in the examination hall of Trinity College.

The proceeding were opened by Prof. William Smith, M.D., the president of the institute, who in a brief address introduced Sir Charles Cameron as the president of the congress. Sir Charles Cameron then delivered his

### PRESIDENTIAL ADDRESS.

The PRESIDENT opened his address by expressing his warmest thanks to the institute for the honour which they had conferred upon him in selecting him to preside at the congress. He next welcomed, on behalf of the Reception Committee of the congress, the visitors who had come from England, Scotland, Wales and the Irish provinces to take part in the proceedings of the congress. Touching on the questions which would come under discussion at the conferences, the president referred to

#### HIGH DEATH RATES IN TOWNS.

The aggregation of a large number of people upon a limited area operates, he said, injuriously upon their health and lessens the mean duration of their lives. Many years ago Doctor—now Sir William—Gairdner, of Glasgow, pointed out that, whilst the death rate in England was 15 per 1,000 persons living on every square mile, it rose as the density of population increased until it became 27 and upwards when the population came to be 2,900 per square mile. The death rates in purely rural districts have not been very largely reduced since the beginning of the present century; in the towns the case has been different. Before the system of national registration of deaths was adopted there existed the means of closely approximating the death rates in towns. The causes which raise the urban death rates so much above the rural ones are numerous and perhaps not fully discovered. The causes of the enormous difference between the bills of mortality of the healthiest and least healthy of the towns have not been fully investigated. The contagion of the fevers must clearly be more readily conveyed from the sick to the sound in towns, owing to the closer contact of the people. The town atmosphere is less pure than the air of the country; its soils are generally contaminated with filth. In its narrow streets and courts the direct sunlight—so necessary to maintain the purity of the air—and thorough ventilation are wanting. The effete matter from dwellings and workshops and the sweepings of the streets are sometimes allowed to accumulate and to pollute the air by their noisome exhalations. Many of the occupations of the townspeople are of a more or less unhealthy nature, and the majority of them are sedentary. The outdoor life of the farmer and agricultural labourer is obviously more healthy than that of the town bakers, shoemakers, tailors, mill-workers, &c. The death rate in Ireland is for the whole country very low. In the ten years ended in 1896 it was only 18. In the same period the rate in Hungary was 35·6 and in Austria 30. The low rate in Ireland is largely due to the circumstance that by far the larger portion of the population reside in the open country. The urban bills of mortality are very high. In the decade ended in 1897 the death rate was 24·65 per 1,000 in the twenty-three largest towns. Their zymotic death rate was 2·64. There is therefore a great difference between town and country death rates in Ireland.

#### PUBLIC HEALTH IN DUBLIN.

As this congress is meeting in Dublin, it seems fitting that some account of the sanitary state of the city should be given to it. Thirty-two years ago the sanitary staff of Dublin consisted of one whole man (an inspector of nuisances) and a small part of another man (the secretary to the Markets Committee). At present the staff consists of a superintendent medical officer of health, who holds also the positions of public analyst and executive sanitary officer, fifteen district medical officers of health, who hold that position ex-officio as poor law medical officers, a sanitary engineer, a superintendent and assistant superintendent of sanitary sub-officers (i.e., nuisance inspectors), twenty-three sanitary sub-officers, three inspectors of dairies, three food inspectors, an inspector of slaughter-houses, two inspectors (one a lady), under the provisions of the Shop Hours Act, and about a dozen persons, exclusive of whitewashers and charwomen engaged in disinfection operations and the removal of fever patients to hospital. The disinfecting premises have recently been improved and enlarged at a cost of £2,000, and a large isolated house, the property of the corporation, has been fitted up, at a cost of £500, as a refuge for persons whose dwellings are undergoing disinfection. The estimated expense of the sanitary department, exclusive of the cost of making and maintaining sewers, was, in 1897, £23,607. Salaries and wages amounted to £9,068 10s.; £1,040 was, however, received as a Parliamentary grant in aid of the salaries of the sanitary officers,

and a considerable revenue is derived from the baths and wash-houses and other sources. Loans for the following purposes have been sanctioned, and all but a small portion obtained and expended: For clearing unhealthy areas (on which the Dublin Artisans' Dwellings Company have since erected houses), £54,200; artisans' and labourers' dwellings, £137,323; new streets, by which slums were cleared away, £116,000; public abattoir, £16,700; baths and wash-houses, £12,500; improvement in disinfection house, £2,000; a refuge for persons whose houses are being disinfected, £500; a mortuary, £200; open spaces, £2,900; offices for sanitary department and city laboratory, £10,000; underground sanitary accommodation, £2,200—£354,523. For the following purposes, which also tend to improve the public health, loans have been sanctioned and nearly altogether obtained: Sewers and works connected with them, £62,107; works in connection with public and domestic scavenging, £34,050; paving, flagging and concreting, £421,988; fish and vegetable markets, £98,800; "private improvement" expenses, £12,628. All these make a total of £984,096. For another great sanitary improvement—namely, the main drainage of the city—a loan of £350,000 has been sanctioned and is being expended. Lastly, if we add the cost of the improved supply of water to the city—namely, £720,000—we have a grand total of £2,054,096 expended on purposes all of which tend to improve the health and comfort of the citizens. When the main drainage and sewage precipitation scheme is completed —probably in about two years more—the Liffey will no longer be polluted, and the sewage, now impounded for many hours daily, will flow uninterruptedly through the sewers. He hardly ventured to claim that the large sum of money expended in sanitary works in Dublin and the exertions of the sanitary department of the corporation had been the chief means by which the reductions in the death rate had been effected. He had, however, no doubt that if the sanitary staff still consisted of only one individual and part of another there would be much more fever in Dublin than there had been for some years past.

#### HOUSING OF THE POOR.

The improvement in the viability of the working classes which has taken place within the last thirty years is to some extent due to the better dwellings provided for them. Owing to the benevolence of the late Mr. Peabody, Lord Iveagh and other philanthropists, a considerable number of healthful dwellings have been built for artisans and labourers. A still larger number have been erected by companies, some of which have been founded on semi-philanthropic semi-commercial lines. In this city and its suburbs the Dublin Artisans' Dwellings Company own dwellings occupied by 2,194 families, who pay from 1s. 9d. to 12s. per week. This company is now constructing 188 additional dwellings. The City and Suburban Artisans' Dwellings Company have provided dwellings for 284 families, who pay from 2s. 6d. to 6s. per week; the Industrial Tenement Company own a block of buildings in which there are forty-six separate tenements, let at from 2s. to 4s. per week. Many employers of labour, such as railway companies, brewers, distillers, &c., have erected improved dwellings for their employees. Fourteen years ago he suggested to the corporation the desirability of putting in force the provisions of the Housing of the Working Classes Act. The suggestion was acted upon, and at the present time the corporation have provided 375 separate dwellings. Whilst much has been accomplished in the way of providing proper dwellings for artisans and the better class of unskilled workers, practically nothing has been done to improve the miserable state of the homes of the very poor. It is in the wretched homes of these poorest of the poor that the seeds of fever are developed as in a hotbed. Their dwellings are a peril to the whole community, for their inmates carry contagious matter into the streets, shops, factories and other places. It is the dwellings of the very poor that demand nearly all the attention of the sanitary inspector. He finds it almost an impossibility to get their owners, who are nearly as poor as their tenants, to keep them in even moderately good condition. Since 1879 more than 3,000 houses have been detenanted and closed in Dublin on account of their insanitary condition; of these not one-half have been rebuilt or rendered fit for human occupation. He is convinced that the ordinary landlords of tenement houses, the majority of whom are leaseholders only or yearly tenants, cannot provide proper dwellings at from 1s to 2s. per week, the rent which the very poor can only afford. Dwellings so low rented can only be provided by the municipality or by philanthropic societies and individuals. An attempt is now being made to raise a sum of money sufficient to erect a block of tenements which it is proposed to let at from 1s. 6d. to 2s. per week.

#### MUNICIPAL AUTHORITIES AND LOANS FOR ARTISANS' DWELLINGS.

The borrowing powers of municipal authorities are limited to a sum equivalent to two years' valuation of the town for rateable purposes. Thus, if a town were valued at £1,000,000 its governing body would be empowered to borrow £2,000,000. When this restriction was placed upon civic authorities the money borrowed by them was expended nearly, if not altogether, on what might be termed unproductive works, such as the paving, sewering and lighting of the thoroughfares, &c. It seemed to him to be unreasonable that the money expended by urban authorities in providing artisans' dwellings, baths and wash-houses, abattoirs and markets, from which revenues are derived, should be included in the amount authorised to be borrowed. Mortgages on these buildings as well as the security of the rates is required by the Treasury for loans granted in connection with them. It is evident that as the loans for the erection of artisans' dwellings are to be placed in the same category as loans for sewers and other non-revenue producing works, the power of municipal authorities to provide dwellings for the working classes must be extremely limited. It is to be hoped that this disability will soon be removed. The market value of the artisans' dwellings in the possession of the sanitary authorities should be ascertained, and the sum found added to the amount allowed to be borrowed on the two years' rateable valuation system. Thus, if a corporation could borrow £1,000,000 for unproductive purposes, and that it possessed artisans' dwellings valued at £100,000, then their borrowing powers should be extended to £1,000,000.

### THE WATER CARRIAGE OF FILTH.

When, in 1879, the Department of Public Health was placed under his direction he commenced to wage a determined war against the system of storing filth in pits, which had prevailed in Dublin for centuries, exclusively in the poorer quarters of the city and partially in the other districts. To this storage of filth must be ascribed the polluted condition of the soil, which still has not yet been got rid of. It was no easy task to induce or compel the owners of houses to adopt the water-carriage system of filth removal, but the task has practically been accomplished. Unfortunately, the occupants of the tenement houses too often do not take proper care of the improved sanitary conveniences supplied for their use, and the landlords complain that they are constantly called upon to repair injuries to the sanitary arrangements due to the action or carelessness of their tenants. The Public Health Act provides that in the case of two or more houses having sanitary accommodation in common the tenants can be collectively proceeded against for the abuse of the sanitary arrangements. The law should be made to apply to single houses inhabited by two or more families. In this connection he would like to express his strong opinion that every separate dwelling should be supplied with sanitary arrangements for its exclusive use. Those which are used in common by several families will never be kept in proper order.

### PREVALENCE OF TYPHOID FEVER IN DUBLIN.

The mortality caused by typhoid fever is greater in Dublin than in nearly every other town in the United Kingdom. In Ireland, Belfast alone has a higher death-rate from this disease. On the other hand, diphtheria is very much less fatal in Dublin than in the English towns. He had come to the conclusion that both diseases have, to a great extent, a telluric origin; they seem to be in some way intimately connected with the soil. If, then, they take both and regard them as semi-malarial, Dublin will not occupy a worse position than the English towns. The deaths from enteric fever and diphtheria combined were in 1887-96 in the ratio of 55 per 100,000 persons living in Dublin and 60 per 100,000 in London. In 1897 the rate was 54 in Dublin and 64 in London. In 1896 the mean diphtheria rate alone was 50 per 100,000 in London, Wales, Essex, Kent and Worcestershire; in Dublin diphtheria and enteric fever combined caused 44 deaths per 100,000 inhabitants. Dublin has a supply of water of great purity; its street sewers can compare favourably with those of other towns; and the plumbers' work in its houses is as good as it is in the great majority of towns. Why, then, should there be so much enteric fever in Dublin? He had long been of opinion that the micro-organisms of this disease have an abiding place in its soils, which for so long a period were polluted by leakage from the filth receptacles and defective sewers of former times. He believed that, under certain conditions to which he had often referred in papers and reports, these malignant organisms escape from the soil into the atmosphere, from which they pass through various media into the bodies of human beings. That there is a connection between enteric fever and the soil is shown by the results of observations of the distribution of more than 4,000 cases of the disease in Dublin. Where gravel forms the site of streets there is far more typhoid fever than in districts which rest upon the stiff boulder clay. This is clearly owing to the fact that the "bacillus typhosus," which is aerobian—that is, requires oxygen—can get it more freely in the loose gravels than in the stiff clays. In the gravel, too, there is a much greater space for the development and movement of the bacilli. It has long been assumed that the soil of Dublin lying nearest to the river was always waterlogged, and it was suggested that the drainage of this soil and its subsoil might lesson the prevalence of enteric fever. A few years ago he caused a number of wells to be sunk in the ground near the river and at the higher parts of the city. Long-continued observations

of the height of the ground, or subsoil water in those wells, proved that in the higher the water came to within 4 ft. or 5 ft. of the surface of the ground, whilst near the river the water remained at from 12 ft. to 18 ft. from the surface. It seems strange that the surface of that part of the city from 50 ft. to 70 ft. above the level of the river at high water should be only 4 ft. or 5 ft. above that continuous sheet of subterranean water termed subsoil or ground water, whilst the low-lying districts have from 12 ft. to 18 ft. of dry soil. The explanation is, after all, a simple one. The low-lying districts rest on gravel, which permits the rain to sink into it very deeply, whilst the high grounds are stiff clays, which retain the water. When a soil becomes infected by the *materies morbi* of typhoid fever it is difficult to eradicate it. The recent experiments of Dr. Sidney Martin, recorded in the supplement to the annual report of the English Local Government for 1896.97, show that typhoid bacilli put into soil multiply in it and ramify throughout it; at the expiration of 105 days they were quite lively. These experiments and the investigations of other scientists, especially of Dr. Porter, of Stockport, clearly prove that typhoid bacilli can live and multiply in soils containing organic matter. He felt satisfied that they are to be found in the soils of Dublin and other places. Now that the pollution of the soil in Dublin has almost ceased, we may expect that the *pabulum* of the typhoid organism will gradually be used up, with consequent diminution of the amount of enteric fever.

### CONCLUSION.

The president then concluded his address, stating that, although a great improvement has taken place in the state of public health in these countries and most parts of Europe, a further improvement is required and is obtainable. So long as two or three out of every thousand of the population perish annually from diseases which are termed "preventable," so long must the efforts of the sanitary reformers and professors of preventive medicine be continued. They required, perhaps, some additions to and amendments of our sanitary laws, but what is most required is the thorough enforcement of the laws, such as they are, and they confer great powers upon the sanitary authorities. The notification of infective diseases and the laws relating to disinfection should be strictly enforced. The proper isolation of fever patients should be provided for. The speedy and complete removal of filth from houses and towns should be secured. Healthy dwellings and cheap baths and wash-houses for the most dependent classes of the community should be multiplied. The "unhealthy occupations" should be rendered innocuous, or, at least, less unhealthy. The injurious emanations from certain kinds of work should be prevented or reduced to a minimum. These are only some of the measures required in order to assimilate our towns as nearly as possible to that ideal City of Hygiea which Richardson has described.

Soon after the conclusion of the above address the Health Exhibition, which occupies the principal chambers of the Royal University Buildings, Earlsfort-terrace, was opened by his Excellency the Lord-Lieutenant. The ceremony was conducted in the ladies' waiting-room, and afterwards the Lord-Lieutenant and the other members of the viceregal party were conducted through the exhibition by Sir Charles Cameron and the members of the Exhibition Committee. Following this, the luncheon given by the high sheriff to the institute took place in the examination ball. Upwards of 600 persons partook of the lunch, during which the Royal Irish Constabulary band performed a selection of music. Among the toasts honoured were "Her Majesty the Queen," "The Members of and Delegates to the Congress," "The High Sheriff of the City of Dublin," and "The Lord Mayor and Members of the Dublin Corporation." The proceedings then terminated, and the remainder of the day was spent in inspecting the Health Exhibition.

The following day, Friday, was chiefly devoted to the meetings of the several sections of the congress, when the president of each respective section delivered his presidential address. In the afternoon, by the kind invitation of Sir Christopher and Lady Nixon, a large number of the members joined a garden party in the grounds of Roebuck Park, Clonskeagh, and in the evening a ball was given by the lord mayor at the Mansion House, when a very numerous and distinguished company attended.

On Saturday the various sections resumed their meetings, and in the afternoon a garden party was given by Alderman Meade and Mrs. Meade at St. Michael's, Ailesbury-road. This was followed in the evening by a banquet at the Royal College of Surgeons, at which the Lord-Lieutenant was present.

Monday was entirely devoted to excursions to different places of interest within a short distance of the city. A party of 150 travelled to Rathdrum, co. Wicklow, and from there drove to the historic and beautiful neighbourhood of Glendalough. On their return through Bray they, with many others, availed themselves of an invitation by Sir Henry and Lady Cochrane to a garden party. Another party travelled to Belfast, where they were received by the local committee of the congress, driven to various places of interest, and entertained at luncheon by the lord mayor. The party returned to Dublin by special train in the evening.

On Tuesday, the last day of the congress, the various sections concluded their meetings, after which a general meeting of the congress was held in the Examination Hall. In the afternoon visits were paid to Lucan and Maynooth, and in the evening the popular lecture to the congress was delivered in the theatre of the Royal Dublin Society by the Right Rev. Monsignor Molloy, D.D., D.SC., on "Wireless Telegraphy," Signor Marconi's own and most recently perfected apparatus being kindly lent for the occasion.

Next week we will publish abstracts of some of the more important papers likely to interest our readers.

## INFORMATION WANTED.

The following portentous list of questions was recently addressed by a medical officer to municipal engineers. We have some general remarks on the subject in our editorial column. The questions were :—
(1) Name of city or town. (2) Population. (3) Rateable value. (4) Type of destructor and name of maker or patentee. (5) Area of land provided for destructor. (6) Total number of cells. (7) Number used at one time. (8) Is a fume cremator used ? (9) Height of chimney in feet. (10) Total gross capital outlay—(a) land, (b) works, (c) appurtenances, (d) total. (11) Total working expenses—(a) fuel, (b) wages, (c) repairs and renewals, (d) any other expenses, (e) total. (12) What sum is written off annually as depreciation on plant ? (13) Products of destructor. (14) Amount and value of (a) clinkers, (b) mortar, (c) of any other product. (15) What use is made of steam generated ? (16) How are clinkers disposed of ? (17) Cost of burning per annum. (18) Percentage of capital outlay and interest. (19) Working expenses and depreciation. (20) Total gross cost. (21) Less value of products. (22) Total nett cost of burning. (23) Number of loads disposed of by destructor—(a) during day, (b) during night, (c) total annually. (24) Number of men required to work destructor—(a) by day, (b) by night. (25) Total cost per load of collecting refuse and carting it to destructor. (26) Nature of refuse carted. (27) Average weight of a load of refuse. (28) If all refuse is not disposed of by destructor, what is done with remainder ? (29) At what intervals and on what system (daily, weekly, &c.) is refuse collected ? (30) Do you burn in the destructor the following—(a) privy midden contents, (b) market refuse, (c) trade refuse. (31) Is any charge made for collecting the latter ; if so, what ? (32) What distance is destructor from centre of town ? (33) Approximate distance of destructor from nearest group of houses. (34) Have complaints ever been received of the following nuisances in connection with the destructor ?—(a) carting offensive refuse to it ? (b) deposit of refuse at it ? (c) fumes or smells ? (d) dust from refuse or chimney ? (e) depreciation of land, &c., in vicinity ? (f) any other cause ? (35) In the event of any complaints, what have been respectively the results of investigation and attempted remedies ? (36) Do you consider that there are any genuine objections to the placing of a modern destructor in the central part of the town ? (37) What do you estimate as the calorific value of your average refuse ? (38) What horse-power per cell do you estimate you could obtain on an average by burning house refuse. (39) Have you an electric lighting installation—(a) combined with, (b) separate from, the refuse destructor ? (40) Was your destructor combined with the electric lighting scheme from the commencement or has it been added since ? (41) Is any fuel besides refuse used for generating steam for this purpose; if so, in what approximate quantities. (42) On what system (high or low tension) is your electric lighting worked ? (43) Do you use accumulators or thermal storage in your system ? If so, please state —(a) capital outlay, (b) working expenses, (c) depreciation. (44) What is the cost per ton of the most generally used steam coal in your town ? (45) Can you state what the cost per unit is using coal as a fuel and what it is using house refuse as fuel ? (46) Are you of opinion, that all things considered, the raising of steam for electric lighting purposes by burning house refuse is advisable. Were there any serious objections to the system that you are aware of ?

## THE DRAINAGE OF DORCHESTER.

The report of the Dorchester Town Council in committee on the surveyor's report relative to the borough drainage and extension schemes has been received. The committee are of opinion that Mr. Hunt's report, with the accompanying plans and sections, is of a most careful and complete character except in regard to the method of treatment to be adopted in dealing with the sewage at the outfall, which question, for good reasons, Mr. Hunt has reserved for further consideration, having regard to the scientific investigations upon the subject which are now taking place and the great difficulty of arriving at the present time at a satisfactory conclusion as to the method of treatment best adapted for Dorchester. The surveyor's scheme, so far as he has propounded it, both as regards the drainage and extension of the borough, appears to meet the requirements of the town, subject to a slight addition of area at the sewage outfall, which the committee have explained to the surveyor.

## MARKET IMPROVEMENTS AT ILFRACOMBE

### PROPOSED EXPENDITURE OF £5,000.

Mr. H. Percy Boulnois, M.I.C.E., recently conducted an inquiry, on behalf of the Local Government Board, with reference to an application of the Ilfracombe Urban District Council for sanction to borrow £5,000 for market purposes. The application was opposed by a number of owners of property included in the improvement.

Mr. FFINCH, who appeared on behalf of the council, in opening the inquiry referred to the growth of Ilfracombe, which made the proposed work necessary. He related the circumstances connected with the exchange of sites with the Wesleyan trustees, one of the conditions upon which this was obtained being the making of a road 24 ft. wide on the west side of the market so far as the chapel extends. He referred to the purchase of the land for market extension in 1887 by the old local board, and remarked that the cost of the old market, erected in 1862, had been entirely met, but there was a balance of £1,094 due on the additional land purchased in 1887 for £1,400. The council intended making a 22-ft. road the entire length of the west side of the building, in accordance with sec. 166 of the Public Health Act, as an approach road. The entire cost would be about £5,000. It being mentioned that the council's by-laws insisted upon new roads being made 36 ft. wide, Mr. Ffinch stated that the road would not be a new road, strictly speaking, but only an approach to the market.

Mr. O. M. PROUSE, surveyor to the council, explained the plans in detail. He said that the area of the old market was 8,300 square feet, but it had been reduced to 5,800 ft. by the erection of the chapel on a portion of the site. The plans provided for a space of 14,000ft., including 2,280ft. in balcony accommodation. His total estimate was £5,014, which the council appeared to think excessive. The plans provided for lavatories, &c., and the building would be in two flats, instead of four as originally. The new buildings would be higher than the old, but he did not think that they would shut out light and air from the opposite property. Witness concluded by explaining the original agreement with the owners of the Wildersdale property as to making the road 36 ft. wide.

Mr. H. BRAUND, chairman of the council, stated that the exchange of sites was approved by the ratepayers and sanctioned by the Local Government Board. That involved the making of a road one-third of the distance, and the council thought it better to continue it the whole length. If the Wildersdale owners renewed their offer to give up 12 ft. of land the council might make the road the full width.

Several owners of property next gave evidence, opposing the scheme on various grounds, chiefly that of expense.

Mr. BRAUND, at the request of the inspector, was again called, and gave evidence as to the necessity of the new market during the summer months. He said that under existing circumstances it was impossible to widen Market-street, because of the position of the chapel. If they attempted it, all they could do would be to make a kind of "square," which would not be advantageous. The council considered that the approach road on the west side would relieve the traffic and thereby be beneficial to the Market-street property. He was sure the council had no wish to injure anybody and would willingly modify their scheme to meet any real grievance.

The inspector then closed the inquiry, remarking that he would report to the board in due course.

## LONDON'S STREETS.

Past finding out are the ways of vestry paving committees. After all these years of experiment they have not yet decided upon one uniform kind of paving for London streets. The consequence is that in a comparatively short drive one may come upon wood, macadam, asphalte and granite setts. Nor do they seem able to agree upon a definite plan of campaign, so as to avoid having two parallel main thoroughfares "up" at the same time. At the present moment, when the Strand is absolutely impassable, half Holborn is in the hands of the excavators, and we should not be surprised if an excuse were found to dig up the Embankment also. To such vagaries we have grown accustomed. But at least it might have been expected that the Strand authorities, having decided to re-pave, would have chosen the most lasting wood for the purpose. Years ago a small portion of the roadway was laid with some species of Australian wood. The experiment answered admirably. Will it be believed then (asks The Globe) that the Strand Vestry has actually reverted to the use of the old creosoted deal blocks, which under the wear and tear of skidded omnibus wheels cannot last more than a couple of years, when all the present discomfort will have to be repeated ? There is no excuse for this reactionary measure, for there are now three or four large companies in London engaged in the supply of the durable Australian woods and able to furnish any quantity of the necessary blocks. One feels almost inclined to echo the witticism of Sydney Smith, and say if only the vestrymen would lay their heads together the thing would be done. Meanwhile we sincerely commend the action of the Strand to other paving authorities as an example of how not to do it.

# Comparative Reports of General Practice.

## XXVI.—REFUSE DESTRUCTORS : TIVERTON REPORT.—III.

HastInos (Population 58,000).

In the case of these works, which are under the super-intendence of Mr. P. H. Palmer, no definite figure is supplied concerning the weekly capacity of the destructor. The latter, however, is working every day, refuse being destroyed at a cost of 1s. 6¾d. per ton. Some 15 per cent. of clinker is produced by the cells, each of which deal with 9 tons of matter daily. Messrs. Manlove, Alliott & Co. were the builders of the works, which are situated in a residential neighbourhood a quarter of a mile from houses. The contract price was £4,000. The chimney stack is 130 ft. high. Complaints, it seems, are only received when the fume chambers are not working. Waste heat is used to pump water for street purposes, and also to drive sewage pumps; the coal bill of the latter previously amounted to £200 yearly.

Hereford (Population 22,000).

The destructor, which is to be under the superintendence of Mr. J. Parker, is expected to dispose of 50 tons of refuse weekly, 33 per cent. of clinker remaining. It will work daily. There will be four cells, which will each be capable of consuming 7 tons of matter in twenty-four hours. Messrs. Meldrum Brothers are the contractors for the work, which is being carried out in a residential neighbourhood, but half a mile from populous parts and adjoining the sewage outfall works. The chimney stack, which is 40 ft. in height, was erected with the sewage works. The works will cost £700, and it is proposed to generate steam to drive sewage pumps (which cost £200 annually in coal) with the waste heat.

Hornsey (Population 70,000).

Mr. E. J. Lovegrove has charge of the destructor here. From 250 to 350 tons of refuse is dealt with every week, the works running every day. As to cost, the men are paid 1s. for every 25 cwt. burnt; clinker remaining amounts to 25 per cent. There are twelve cells attached to the destructor, six being erected in 1889 and six since. Each destroy 8 tons of matter daily. The contractors were Messrs. Goddard, Massey & Warner. The works are in a residential quarter, and in the midst of houses and a thickly-populated district. They are, it may be mentioned, very near the open filtering-beds of the New River Company; the total cost was £9,623, that of the chimney stack (217 ft. in height) being £2,750. No complaints have been made in regard to the destructor, the waste heat from which is utilised in driving a mortar mill, sawing and drilling machinery, a clinker crusher and slab-making machinery.

Hull (Population 225,000).

The engineer managing the works at Hull is Mr. A. E. Whyte. Some 250 large loads of refuse are dealt with every week, at a cost of 1s. 1·2d. per ton; the destructor runs every day and leaves 33 per cent. of clinker. Fourteen tons of matter are consumed by each cell (there are six). The works were erected by Messrs. Manlove, Alliott & Co. in a manufacturing district and within built up area, 60 yards from houses. Their cost was £2,268; that of the chimney, which is 180 ft., was £932. Formerly there were complaints regarding charred paper coming from the works, but none have been made as to smell. Waste heat is not made use of.

Hyde (Population 32,000).

Mr. J. Mitchell is the engineer at Hyde. Working every day, with the exception of Sunday, over 130 tons of matter is dealt with at a cost of 2s. per ton. There are four cells to the destructor, which was erected in June, 1893, by Messrs. Goddard, Massey & Warner, and each cell destroys from 5 to 6 tons of matter daily. The town is of a manufacturing character, the works being situated near the centre, close to the sewage works and 250 yards from houses built since the erection of the destructor. A sum of £4,656 was spent upon the carrying out of the works. The cost of the chimney shaft was included with that of the buildings; the shaft has a height of 180 ft. No complaints have been made. Waste heat is used to drive a mortar mill.

Leyton (Population 90,000).

At Leyton, where 190 tons of house refuse and 135 tons of pressed sludge are destroyed every week at a cost of 1s. 7d. per ton, Mr. William Dawson is engineer. Work is carried on for five days (of twenty-four hours) in the week, and from 25 to 30 per cent. of clinker, which is subsequently sold, remains. There are eight cells to the destructor, but only four work. Messrs. Beaman & Deas were the builders of the works, which commenced working in October, 1896; each cell deals with from 15 to 17 tons per twenty-four hours. Leyton is a residential district, and the destructor is situated some 200 yards from good property. The sewage works, a large board school and a fever hospital also adjoin the buildings. The latter cost £7,000, and the chimney stack, which is 150 ft. high, £1,100. No complaints have been made. The waste heat in this case drives two 96 horse-power Babcock & Wilcox boilers, attached to a dynamo, fans, sewage pumps, sludge presses and mixing machinery.

Liverpool.

The refuse destroyed here amounts to 930 tons weekly. The cost per ton is 1s. to 1s. 3d., and the clinker remaining usually amounts to 17 to 18 per cent. of clinker and from 8 to 9 per cent. of fine ash. There are thirty-two cells in the destructor, which was completed in 1893 by Messrs. Manlove, Alliott & Co. The district is a manufacturing one. The cost of the destructor and chimney shaft (which is 170 ft. in height) was £12,143.

Loughborough (Population 20,000).

Mr. O. A. Walker supervises the work of refuse destruction at Loughborough, where from 60 tons to 80 tons of matter are weekly dealt with, work being carried on every day. Labour in connection with the work is paid for at the rate of 9½d. per ton. Clinker remaining amounts to 24 per cent. There is one cell, which deals with from 15 tons to 20 tons of refuse daily; the buildings were put down in 1895 by Messrs. Coltman & Sons. This town is also largely interested in manufactures. The destructor occupies a position adjoining the sewage farm—a mile from the town. Its erection cost £1,100; the chimney, the height of which is 80 ft., cost £303. It was only on the occasions of fish offal being destroyed that complaints were made; this particular refuse is now, however, only burnt at night. Sewage pumps are driven by the waste heat.

Longton (Population 36,240).

The engineer here is Mr. J. W. Wardle. Two hundred and twenty tons of matter are weekly dealt with, at a cost of from 10d. to 11d. per ton, the works running every day, and from 25 to 30 per cent. of clinker usually remains. The destructor has six cells, each with a capacity of 6½ tons per twenty-four hours; the buildings were completed in 1896. Messrs. Manlove, Alliott & Co. and Messrs. Goddard, Massey & Warner were the contractors. The works are situated in a manufacturing district, the nearest houses being 150 ft. distant. A sum of £6,840 was spent upon their erection; the chimney stack cost £1,000 and is 150 ft. in height. Steam is generated by the waste heat, and used in connection with the forced draught and for driving a mortar mill.

Newcastle-upon-Tyne (Population 218,000).

Engineer, Mr. George Laws. Working every day, these works destroy 400 tons of refuse in a week at a cost of 8½d. per ton. The clinker resulting amounts to between 25 and 30 per cent. There are twelve cells (each having a capacity of 8 tons per twenty-four hours) to the destructor, which was constructed in the years 1886 and 1891 by respectively Messrs. Manlove, Alliott & Co. and Messrs. Goddard, Massey & Warner. The district is both manufacturing and residential in character, the works, on which £7,000 were spent, being situated in a quarter 100 yards from houses. Complaints concerning the working have been very few in number, and all without foundation. The chimney shaft in this case is 150 ft. high. Nothing is done with the waste heat.

Nottingham (Population 235,000).

The engineer here is Mr. Arthur Brown. Refuse destruction is carried on every day, and 200 tons are dealt with every week, 20 per cent. of clinker remaining. There are five cells to the works, which were erected in 1882 by Messrs. Manlove, Alliott & Co. Each cell has a capacity per twenty-four hours of 8 tons. The destructor buildings occupy a position 200 yards from houses, and in a district of both a residential and manufacturing character. Their cost was £6,000; that of the chimney, which is 150 ft. in height, being £1,401. There have been no complaints. The waste heat is employed in connection with electric lighting and for working an elevator and mortar mill.

Oldham (Population 147,000).

Mr. S. A. Pickering has charge at this town, where, working every day with the exception of Sunday, some 500 tons of matter is dealt with at a cost of 9½d. per ton. Clinker remaining usually amounts to 33 per cent. There are ten cells, each with a capacity of 8 tons. The works were erected in the years 1891 and 1895 by the Horsfall Furnace Syndicate. Oldham is a populous manufacturing town, and houses face the destructor buildings, which have cost £4,000 to erect. The chimney shaft, which is 120 ft. in height, cost £527. No complaints have been made regarding the works, the waste from which is used to generate steam for blast furnaces and for the electric light and workshops.

Rochdale (Population 73,000).

The engineer responsible for the work of destruction at Rochdale is Mr. F. W. Brookman. Refuse dealt with totals 600 tons weekly, work being carried on daily with the exception of Saturday afternoon and Sunday. The cost per ton is 10d., and 35 per cent. of clinker is left. There are two large cells to the destructor, and each has a capacity of 1 ton per hour. The works were erected in 1894 by Messrs. Meldrum Brothers, their position being close to the centre of the town which is a manufacturing one. The neighbourhood, it is said, is one of the healthiest in the borough, in spite of its low-lying character. A sum of £1,000 was spent upon the chimney shaft. Some complaints, it appears, have been made regarding the destruction of excreta, but they have not been very frequent. In the case of the ordinary refuse there have not been any. Waste heat is utilised in connection with a manure factory, mortar mills, electric light, &c.

ROYTON (Population 14,500).

At Royton Mr. Thomas Bleasdale has charge of the destructor. Working every day except Sunday, 78 tons of refuse is destroyed weekly, at a cost of 10½d. per ton. About 45 per cent. of clinker is left. Each cell of the destructor (there are four) consumes 43 tons of matter. The works were laid down in 1893 by Messrs. Goddard, Massey & Warner. They occupy a site a quarter of a mile from houses. The district is a manufacturing one; £4,500 was spent upon the buildings, while the chimney, which is 210 ft. in height, cost £900. No complaints have been received. Steam is raised from the waste heat to press sludge.

SHOREDITCH (Population 124,000).

Mr. J. Rush Dixon superintends the Shoreditch works, which deal with 450 tons of refuse weekly, working day and night. Clinker remaining amounts to 30 per cent. There are twelve cells, each with a capacity of 10 tons per twenty-four hours. Messrs. Manlove, Alliott & Co. were the contractors for the works, which are situated in the centre of a densely-populated manufacturing district and only 25 ft. from houses. The chimney stack is 150 ft. high and cost £2,700; the works cost £17,800. With the exception of some informal complaints in reference to dust caused by the removal of clinker, no trouble has been experienced. As is well known, electric lighting is carried on by means of the waste heat.

WARRINGTON (Population 62,000).

The works here are in the hands of Mr. James Deas, and destroy 250 tons of refuse every week. Work is carried on every day except Saturday and Sunday. The cost per ton is 7¾d., and 25 per cent. of clinker remains from the working. There were originally three cells, each capable of dealing with 15 tons of refuse in a day of twenty-four hours, but two more were, at the time of the compilation of the report, in course of erection by Messrs. Beanum & Deas. The works stand 50 yards from houses and outside the borough, which deals largely with manufacture. They cost £3,964 to build, while £480 was spent upon the chimney stack, which is 120 ft. in height. There have been no complaints. The waste heat generates steam to drive fans and machinery for evaporating excreta. It is intended to shortly use it for the supply of electricity.

WHITECHAPEL (Population 78,676).

Mr. J. Paget Waddington has charge here. The works destroy 520 tons of refuse weekly, at a cost of 1s. 10d. per ton, and work every day with the exception of Sunday. They leave 25 per cent. of clinker. Sixteen cells are attached to the destructor, and each destroys from 6 tons to 8 tons daily. Eight were erected in 1886 and the remainder in 1893 by Messrs. Manlove, Alliott & Co. The neighbourhood is both a manufacturing and residential one, the works being in the centre of the town; £8,400 was spent upon the works and £2,000 upon the chimney, which is 180 ft. high. Some years ago there were some complaints regarding the dust from the shaft. Nothing is done with the heat from the destructor.

WINCHESTER (Population 20,000).

Mr. William Gamon, engineer. The works, running every day, deal with 180 tons of matter weekly, at a cost of 7d. per ton. Each cell, of which there are two, deals with ten loads. The contractors were Messrs. Manlove, Alliott & Co. and Messrs. Goddard, Massey & Co. The works were erected in the years 1885 and 1892. They adjoin the sewage pumping station. The district is a residential one; £746 was spent upon the works. There have been no complaints. Two Meldrum blowers and one Green's economiser are worked by the waste heat.

WOOLWICH (Population, 41,314).

Working every day with the exception of Sunday, the works in this district, where Mr. H. O. Thomas is engineer, deal with 180 tons of refuse weekly. Clinker remaining totals 25 per cent. There are six cells in the works, which were erected in 1893 by Messrs. Manlove, Alliott & Co., and are situated in a residential neighbourhood. The cost of erection was £5,000, the cost of the chimney, the height of which is 160 ft., being included in that sum. There have been no complaints. Heat is not utilised.

**Limerick.**—A special meeting of the corporation was held on Thursday week to consider a scheme for the laying down of a line of electric tramway. The scheme, subject to certain modifications, has met the requirements of the Board of Works, who, a few days since, sent down a special engineer to hold an inquiry into the project. Mr. H. D. Connor attended at the inquiry and explained the details of the scheme, which was being promoted by a number of wealthy Dublin gentlemen. The cost of the line of tramways which it was now proposed to make was estimated at £67,000.

## MACADAMISED TRAM ROADS AT SHEFFIELD.

### A REPORT FROM THE CITY SURVEYOR.

The city surveyor of Sheffield has reported to the Tramways Committee on the question of using macadam on streets where tram rails are to be laid. He says:—

"In accordance with the request of your committee, I now give reasons for so strongly condemning the adoption of the system of constructing the tramways in suburban roads, with macadam on each side of the rail and macadam in the middle, or with macadam only as was suggested at the last committee. The chief advantages are: (1) The impossibility of keeping an even surface to the road where macadam and rails join. This is difficult in the case of macadam and setts, but it would be far worse if the setts were abandoned, because (a) the rails and macadam are of very different degrees of hardness, (b) it is scarcely possible to make a good joint between the two, (c) the vibration of the rails would soon shake the macadam loose. (2) The road would have to be constantly under repair, causing additional expense, as well as inconvenience to frontages along the routes. (3) The macadam between the rails could not be satisfactorily rolled and would always be loose. It would be difficult to put down on account of the setts or rails. (4) It would soon wear hollow and hold water. (5) On gradients this hollow would in times of rain act as a watercourse and the macadam would gradually be washed away. (6) The track could not be properly cleansed, and it would be nearly impossible to keep the rails free from mud in wet weather. This is much more important with electric traction than with horses, and the rails would wear much quicker.

"Before giving my opinion to the committee I was quite conversant with the methods of construction adopted in nearly all the large towns of England, but I thought the members might like to have the opinions of the different surveyors. I have therefore written to them and obtained a large number of replies. Generally the replies are most unfavourable, and my opinion is unaltered. Many of the surveyors speak of macadam paving for tramways in the most unfavourable terms, and I feel certain if the system is adopted it will prove a costly failure. In view of the above facts, I feel bound to say I cannot take the responsibility of advising the committee to lay rails without paving of some description for the full distance between the rails and 18 in. beyond. In all cases where the roads are narrow I think it would be advisable and economical to pave them across from kerb to kerb. It is argued that when the electric trams are running they will practically monopolise the track. If this is the case the objections to paving on the grounds of slipperiness and noise practically disappear."

The report has been adopted.

## MAIDSTONE WATER SUPPLY.

The mayor of Maidstone stated on Monday that he did not believe there was any cause for alarm in regard to the water supply of the town. Undoubtedly there was a scarcity of water, but there was no danger of anything like a water famine. It was only necessary that people should be economical. At the present time there were, he said, 3,000 persons outside the borough drinking water from one of the springs at Farleigh which were cut off during the typhoid epidemic last year on the recommendation of the medical officer of health. Ewell spring was not one of those which were proved to be contaminated, and the town council were about to consider the advisability of asking the water company to restore the supply derived from it. He was satisfied that the water company could not increase their supply by taking additional water from the Mid-Kent company. At present the Maidstone company could only get about 3,000 gallons per hour from their neighbours, or a total of 60,000 or 70,000 gallons per day, whereas they originally guaranteed 100,000 gallons per day. The manager of the Maidstone waterworks (Mr. Ware) stated that the Ewell spring has been analysed fortnightly by Dr. Gregory, the company's analyst, during the past year, and it has maintained a uniform standard of purity. Barming lunatic sylum has been supplied from the spring throughout the year; also the inhabitants of Barming parish and East and West Farleigh.

**The City Surveyor and the Highwayman.**—A city surveyor has strange functions thrust upon him in Klondike and the adjacent territories. We quote the following from *The Vancouver World*: "Soapy" Smith, of Skagway, the confidence man who has been trying to terrorise Skagwayaians for a long time, has been shot by Frank Reid, city surveyor. Even a dead highwayman possesses a pecuniary value in the eyes of those who cater to the seekers for a new sensation. In proof of this C. O. Venu and Herbert Savage, who are now in Victoria, purpose leaving for the north by the next steamer sailing, their mission being to obtain by purchase, if not otherwise, the body of "Soapy" Smith. A Victoria doctor accompanies the two prime movers in the enterprise, to superintend the embalming of the desperado's remains, and the plan is to exhibit the body in all the chief cities and towns of the West.

# Municipal Work at Hexham.

Hexham is pleasantly situated on the south bank of the river Tyne, about a mile below the junction of the North and South Tyne, amidst beautiful scenery and surroundings of great interest. It is shut in by hills on three sides, the old abbey church, with its Roman tomb, recently removed from the foundations of the abbey, standing up above the houses with what appears to have been an old castle or keep, and the Meet Hall close by, whilst in the near neighbourhood are the Roman antiquities, such as the Roman road, part of the Roman wall, remains of Roman bridges, villas, baths, &c. There are also Dilston Castle, too, with its historical associations and connection with the unfortunate last Earl of Derwentwater, Queen Margaret's cave, which is said to have sheltered the unfortunate queen and her son, and many other places of historical note.

## WATER SUPPLY.

It is not surprising that a town so pleasantly situated, so rich in historical associations, with its now excellent water supply and drainage, is so rapidly becoming a popular health resort. A few years ago it was a rarity to see a new building, but during the last three years streets have been laid out and terraces of semi-detached houses and villas rapidly pushed forward. During the past year, owing to the rapid extension in the west and south parts of the town on account of the development of new building estates, the urban district council and their surveyor have had an exceptionally busy time. The water supply to the town has been entirely divided into a "high and low service, to supply the high and low parts respectively. The water before the last alterations were completed was collected from the well-known Ladle springs, at a distance of 8 miles, into Hexhamshire and delivered into a high-service reservoir, from whence it was delivered to the consumers, the water being of such purity that no filtration was necessary. This supply was obtained in 1888, and previous to that the water had been collected from a gathering ground of uncertain yield and indifferent quality into a storage reservoir. It was then filtered and delivered from a service reservoir. These latter works had been well

Mr. R. J. SURTEES,
Surveyor to the Hexham Urban District Council.

constructed and are in excellent condition, but owing to the new service reservoir being at a considerable higher level they could not be utilised, whilst the severe strain on the fittings in the lower parts of the town was the cause of much waste. To remedy this, the council in 1896 decided to adopt the new high-service reservoir for the higher reaches only, and bring the old one into use to supply the lower parts of the town. This has necessitated the laying of several thousand yards of new water mains and extensive alterations to the connections. Previous to this the original supply to the storage was cut off and the reservoir filled with the overflow coming from the springs. The chief difficulty in utilising the old reservoir was to get the lower service filled and the overflow to pass from the high service into the storage for the use, if required, of the lower parts of the town, for any overflow from the low service means a waste of water. However, this was got over by a simple and novel arrangement fixed to the main connecting the two reservoirs, and specially designed for the purpose by Mr. Surtees.

As soon as the lower reservoir is filled this comes into operation, closes the main valve, and causes the overflow to pass from the high reservoir into the storage. Altogether, the works carried out have reduced the pressure on the lower parts of the town to the extent of reducing the waste of water by 1,300 gallons per hour, whilst all parts of the town have now a constant supply. The new scheme was formally opened by Mr. Alderman Stainthorpe, who had been its chief advocate, and who spoke in high terms of the manner in its engineering had been carried out. The old source of supply has

not been wasted, but has been brought down to the town for street watering, sewer flushing and trade purposes.

## SEWERAGE AND OTHER WORKS.

Very extensive sewerage works have also been carried out, both in extensions, storm-water and relief sewers. The work of carrying the main outfall sewer along under the railway, which had to be tunnelled through what was virtually a quicksand, was both difficult and dangerous, and it speaks well for those employed on the works that no accident of any kind occurred during the progress of the works.

The cattle market has been cemented throughout, and the private streets improvements carried out in the west and of the town can only be fully appreciated by those who reside in that part. Pleasure grounds, too, have received attention, and the works carried out on the Seal and Tyne Green are a step in the right direction. The whole of the works have been carried out from plans prepared by the surveyor, Mr. R. T. Surtees, and several of the schemes have been completed without the aid of a contractor. Nor are the council yet finished, for it is only a short time since a Local Government Board inquiry was held to obtain borrowing powers for carrying out the repaving of several public and private streets, whilst works of sewage disposal and an infectious diseases hospital are in preparation, and sanction will shortly be asked for the erection of public slaughter-houses. The council appear therefore to be making great efforts to bring the town up to a high standard of sanitary efficiency.

Mr. Richard T. Surtees, who has recently been so busily engaged on these schemes of water supply, sewerage and private streets improvements in the district to which he is surveyor, received his education at Sir Arthur Middleton's school at Belsay, finishing at the Durham College of Science, Newcastle-on-Tyne. He served articles with his father, Mr. J. Surtees, at the expiration of which he was engaged in the Consett and Blackhill district, where he gained a valuable experience in sewering, street works, &c. He was afterwards engaged at the construction of the Newcastle and Gateshead Water Company's new reservoirs at Hallington, at the conclusion of which he was appointed, out of eighty-six applicants, surveyor and inspector for the borough of Morpeth, and in May, 1894, he was appointed surveyor to the Hexham Local Board of Health out of seventy-three applicants.

## THE POLLUTION OF THE RIVER LEA.

The deputation to the President of the Local Government Board, which was postponed from the 30th ult., has now been abandoned until after the holidays. The memorialists base their case on facts, that the condition of the river Lea, as it passes through Hackney, has for many years given rise to complaints, and that analyses have shown the water to be highly polluted. It is pointed out that the districts of Walthamstow and Leyton, with an estimated population of 120,000, send the whole of their sewage after treatment into the river. The same complaint, in a mitigated degree, applies to West Ham. The result is that from Tottenham to the Thames the Lea is little better than an open sewer. The Government inquired into the matter in 1886. The select committee then recommended that the sewage should be dealt with in the same way as it was in the case of the Thames by the Metropolitan Board of Works. The local authorities now ask that another committee may be appointed, and that legislation should be initiated adequate to deal with the existing evils.

## THE PROTECTION OF FORESHORES.

On Friday, at the usual meeting of the Hastings Town Council, a committee reported that their attention had been called to the fact that it was contemplated by the contractor for the new Crowhurst, Sidley and Bexhill Railway to remove beach for the purposes of the works from the foreshore at Glyne Gap, and that in view of the probable serious consequences which would be likely to result thereby they had given instructions for a communication to be addressed to the Board of Trade on the subject. A reply had since been received from the board stating that they would be prepared to consider an application from the council for the making and issuing of an order to prohibit the removal of the materials, and the committee therefore recommended the adoption of that course by the council. The report was approved.

**Morecambe.**—At the last monthly meeting of the district council letters were read from the Local Government Board consenting to the council borrowing the sum of £3,540 for works of water supply. The board further wrote stating that, before deciding upon the application of the council to borrow £1,590 for street improvements, they would hold a public inquiry into the matter.

# The St. Helens Borough Sanatorium.

## AN EXTENSION OPENED.

An extension of the St. Helens borough sanatorium at Peasley Vale was some little time ago formally opened by the mayor, Alderman R. Pilkington, in the presence of a large company. Some fourteen years ago the institution was this apartment a full view of each ward is obtained by means of a small window on either side provided for this purpose. An extra one-bed ward for acute cases also opens off the hall, the doors being of such a size as to allow a bed being wheeled

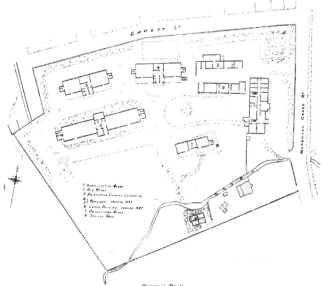

GENERAL PLAN.

wholly contained in an old house, consisting of seven rooms and a kitchen, standing on about 4 acres of land. At various subsequent periods it was found necessary to provide additional accommodation for patients, until at last in 1897 the council decided to proceed with the erection of a large pavilion and an observation block of two wards, with a kitchen to each pavilion. They also decided upon a large increase to the administrative block, adding fifteen additional bed-rooms, nurses' dining and sitting rooms, servants' dining-room, store-rooms and dispensary, and enlarging the laundry accommodation by erecting new drying-closets and ironing-room.

These buildings, which have just been completed, have been erected on the most modern principles. They are built of brick, with Ruabon terra-cotta facings throughout, and, although devoid of any elaborate ornamentations, are well constructed and of good appearance. Each pavilion is provided with a glass verandah in front, the floors of which are formed with Stuart's granolithic cement paving, the patients being thus enabled to sit outside in the warm weather. Internally they are plastered with Robinson's cement, all corners being rounded off, both on the floor and ceiling, in order to prevent accumulation of dust. All windows open at the top for ventilation, and each of the large wards is provided with one fireplace and two double stoves. The bath-rooms and water-closets are at the extreme end of each ward, and open into a passage which provides for through ventilation. They contain in separate rooms one bath, one water-closet and slop-water basin, and three wash hand-basins. The floors of all the wards, &c., are paved in oak with wood blocks. The entrance hall is lighted by means of a glass dome, and contains two small closets for coal and stores. It is paved with marble mosaic, with the St. Helens coat of arms, in colours, in the centre. The kitchen, opening out from the hall, is provided with hot and cold water, kitchen range and all necessary requisites. From

in from either of the wards. The observation block is fitted in all respects similarly to the large pavilion, the only difference being that no bath-room is provided, the bath being on wheels; it is kept outside and taken to the patient when required. The two large pavilion wards are each 72 ft. long by 26 ft. wide; each ward accommodates twelve beds, or a total of twenty-four beds; and these, together with the wards of the observation block, which provide four beds, have an area of 156 square feet per bed and a cubical air space of 2,029 ft

LARGE PAVILION.

per patient. The total number of patients that can now be accommodated in the hospital is about seventy.

The sewage of the whole of the wards is specially dealt with, being treated with aluminoferric, and conducted over the brook into tanks 12 ft. long, 8 ft. wide and 6 ft. deep. After lying in a state of quiescence for about twelve hours it is then allowed to flow into filter-beds formed of coke breeze, 2 ft. deep, covered with gravel, 6 in. deep, after which the effluent is allowed to run into the brook. The storm water is passed direct into the brook by separate drains.

The cost of the last contract has been £6,389, a wall in front and a porch being extras to the contract to the amount of £207. Thus the total amount spent upon the whole building up to the present time has been £14,120, including £2,654, the cost of the purchase of house, land and sundry alterations. Of this amount the sum of £1,300 has been set aside and paid off out of sinking funds provided for that purpose. The contractors for the various works in the contract just completed were as follows: Erection of buildings, Messrs. Whittaker & Woods, St. Helens; stove in wards, Messrs. J. Cooper & Sons, Liverpool; wood block flooring, Messrs. Geary, Walker & Co., London; mosaic pavement, Messrs. Diespeker & Co., London; furniture for wards, Mr. C. W. House, Crewe. The whole of the works since 1884 have been designed and carried out by Mr. George J. C. Broom, M.I.C.E., the borough engineer. Mr. Henry Helms, Liverpool, was the clerk of works.

## DUTIES OF A BOROUGH SURVEYOR.

### AN EXTRAORDINARY DOCUMENT.

The following extraordinary list of duties was drawn up in connection with a recent vacancy in Carnarvon. The document is, we hope, unique, and deserves to be given in full:—

The borough surveyor is to devote the whole of his time to the execution of all duties usually and properly performed by a borough surveyor, including those falling under the undermentioned heads, and not at any time during his appointment to undertake private practice.

(1) Surveyor of highways.

(2) The construction, repair and maintenance of public roads, bridges, sewers, waterworks and appurtenant works, and such other works or buildings as may be required by the corporation.

The repair and maintenance of the guildhall, markets, public slaughter-houses, institute, Anglesey ferry, park, and all other corporate buildings and property and appurtenant works.

(3) The execution of private improvement works by order of the council, and apportionment of the cost thereof.

(4) Advising committees on the requisite works of sewerage, road-making, town improvement, private improvement, sanitary improvement, and the like, and supervision of the execution of such works.

(5) The making of all surveys, plans and estimates of new works and alterations (Parliamentary and otherwise) required by the corporation, structural gas plant excepted. Should the surveyor be found incapable of properly doing any particular work required of him, the council or any committee may employ another surveyor and deduct the cost from any salary which may be due to him. The council or committee to be the sole judge of any matter arising under this clause.

(6) The examination of plans of new streets and buildings and other private works, and the supervision of such works, so as to secure compliance with by-laws, statutes and regulations.

(7) To enforce the provisions of all borough by-laws and of the Public Health Acts, or of any Acts incorporated therewith, not included within the purview of the inspector of nuisances' duties as set forth in the printed list.

(8) Special reports of any proposed railway, tramway and similar works, and periodical reports on matters in progress.

(9) The execution of the council's powers as to house numbering, street naming and similar matters.

(10) To keep at the corporation office in an orderly manner duplicates of all plans of new streets, buildings or other works submitted for approval of committee, and make an index of same for ready reference.

(11) To keep and index in a similar manner all other plans made for or belonging to the corporation.

(12) To mark and show on one general plan of the borough all new streets, buildings, sewers, drains, water mains and services, as soon as such streets, buildings, &c., are completed.

(13) The supervision of the watering of streets and the flushing of sewers. To keep a record of the last mentioned.

(14) To attend all council meetings. To convene and attend the meetings, and transact the business (other than financial) of the following committees: The Highway and Town Improvement, Sanitary and Water, the Park, the Ferry and Aber Bridge, &c., and such other committees as may be required of him. To see that all orders of the said committees are carried out. To keep the minutes of the said committees, and see to the printing of same for monthly council meetings.

(15) To attend daily at his office in the Guildhall from 8 to 10 a.m. and from 5 to 6 p.m.

(16) To record all complaints received and report the action taken thereon. To keep all such books as may be necessary with regard to workmen, stores, works and plans; particularly to keep a book showing as to works ordered by committee to be carried out, the date of order, the estimated and the actual cost of work, and the date of completion of same.

(17) To submit all his books from time to time to the committees, and to the borough accountant as required.

(18) The personal supervision of workmen employed by the corporation (except the scavengers). To arrange and superintend their work so as to secure efficiency and economy, and to see that they commence and leave work at the proper time. With the approval of the committee having charge of the works, to appoint and discharge workmen. To suspend immediately any workman (artisan or labourer) who shall be seen to enter any public-house during working hours (except when on duty), and to report such suspension to committee.

(19) The personal supervision of contractors, horses, carts, tools, implements and stores. To prepare contracts and contractor's bonds.

(20) The surveyor shall from time to time submit to the proper committee for their sanction and approval a list of all materials or work which may be required in his department. In emergencies the same may be ordered upon the sanction of the chairman.

(21) The proper fulfilment of contracts for works and materials. To give orders for all work and materials sanctioned, on the prescribed form, and see that invoices are received with goods supplied and for work done. To check, allocate, certify and hand over bills to the accountant as received, and attach invoices thereto. To see that all bills are passed through committee and handed over to the accountant within three months from completion of order.

(22) To keep an accurate account in a book of all works executed for or materials supplied to private parties, and to hand the same weekly to the accountant. No work to be done or materials to be supplied except on written order given by the party requiring same.

(23) To keep a stock-book, debiting value of goods received and crediting goods as and when given out. The stock-book to be balanced half-yearly and compared with actual stock in hand.

(24) A separate inventory of horses, carts, tools and like articles to be kept and dealt with in the same manner.

(25) To keep a list of streets, roads, and lanes repairable by the council.

(26) To prepare annual estimates under the required heads, and lay the same before committees in the month of February in each year, preparatory to the making of rates, so far as such estimates may relate to matters under his charge.

(27) To direct the workmen employed in his department to send in their weekly time-sheets made out in sufficient detail and receipted. To check and certify the correctness of the time-sheets, and hand same over to the accountant on Friday mornings, together with a properly allocated pay-sheet made up therefrom. To see that separate time-sheets of the prescribed form are sent in for work done on main roads, and to see that particulars of all materials supplied for main roads are given on the back thereof weekly.

(28) To inspect and report monthly to the Finance Committee upon the water meters in use.

(29) To be responsible for supplying punctually to the accountant information as to parties using water from town mains for various purposes (including domestic purposes) not already charged for such use.

(30) To see that no connection with water main is made or renewed for any purpose (domestic purposes included) until an agreement to pay rent is signed by the party requiring the same. To inform such party that an agreement is necessary.

(31) To attend and give evidence when and where required for and on behalf of the corporation in any action or legal proceedings.

(32) Together with all subservient duties and any other or further duties imposed by statute or by the council.

Note.—The appointment to be terminable by one month's notice on either side.

## QUERIES AND REPLIES.

*Sketches accompanying Queries should be made separate on white paper, in plain black-ink lines. Lettering or figures should be bold and plain.*

**211. Natural Philosophy: Engineers' Pocket-Book: Books Recommended.**—"Inquirer" writes: Could you inform me if there is a (1) work published on natural philosophy suitable for civil engineering students? (2) Also, which engineers' pocket-book would you recommend?

(1) Ganot's "Physics," price 15s. (Longmans), and Ganot's "Natural Philosophy," price 7s. 6d. (Longmans), will be found to meet the requirements of the querist. (2) Trautwine's "Civil Engineers' Pocket-Book," price 21s., is, in our opinion, although an American publication, the best of its kind. It is published by E. & F. N. Spon. Kempe's "Civil Engineers' Year-Book," price 8s. (Crosby Lockwood & Son) is also a useful book.

**Suspension Bridges,** made of iron chains, were first built in China 2,000 years ago.

**Bricks.**—Bricks, burnt, were used in the earliest times of human civilisation. They were introduced into England by the Romans. It has been calculated that ninety bricks per annum are used for each inhabitant of England.

# The Telephone Inquiry.

## THE COMMITTEE'S REPORT.

The report of the Select Committee on Telephones, which was published last week, is a lengthy one, as, no doubt, every one expected. We may, however, give a few extracts from it, especially those bearing upon the granting of licenses to local authorities. The principal questions the committee dealt with were :—

I. Is the telephone service now, or is it calculated to become, of general benefit ? II. Is the Post Office in any way hindered by legal agreement or by good faith from competing itself or through licensees with the National Telephone Company in exchange areas. III. Ought competition to take place, and should municipal and other local authorities be empowered to undertake a telephone service ; and, if so, upon what terms ?

The report opens with a condemnation of the present system as not, nor likely to, become a general benefit either to the country as a whole or to the areas in which exchanges exist so long as the present monopoly should continue. It is considered, however, that under a different system, worked mainly with a view to the public interest, the telephone service might become a valuable instrument in further developing the trade and social life of the nation. The company's monopoly is emphatically condemned, and the right to competition is established. Then come the following interesting facts in connection with the granting of licenses to local authorities :—

### MUNICIPAL COMPETITION.

The right to compete being thus made clear, we had next to consider whether competition was expedient ; and, if so, whether local authorities should be empowered to undertake a telephone service.

Competition appears to be both expedient and necessary, in order, firstly, to extend and popularise the service, and, next, to avoid a danger which is by no means remote, if no alternative system is in operation, that a purchase of the company's undertaking at an inflated price may be forced upon the Government of the day.

Competition by a local authority must differ in many ways from competition by a private company, and requires special provision to meet the special conditions of the case.

In areas where the company have already an exchange, municipal competition, if permitted, should be conducted, so far as possible, on equal terms. It would be plainly unfair to concede to the new licensee a position of general advantage over that possessed by the elder competitor.

The peculiar advantages, however, already possessed by the company themselves constitute the principal difficulty in the way of formulating such an equality of treatment. The duration of its license, the power to give preferential rates (a power which when exercised by the predecessor of the company is alleged to have driven the Post Office from the field at Plymouth), the absence of a maximum rate, the power to refuse service, and the consequent power to require concessions of overhead wayleaves, its numerous exchanges, and the power to make other areas pay for reduced rates in areas where competition exists ; these are advantages which together outbalance the special advantage which would be possessed by a local authority as licensee—the right to give to itself and refuse to its rival permission to lay wires under its own public streets.

### CONDITIONS FOR LOCAL AUTHORITIES.

A local authority must also submit to conditions to which the company is not subjected.

Among these conditions are the following :—

(1) The system (unlike that of the company) must be one of double wires, and be erected in accordance with the regulations of the Post Office. The Post Office should insist upon uniformity of system so far as the differing conditions of different localities may permit.

(2) A maximum rate should be imposed, and no opportunity be afforded to local authorities to carry on the service with a view to lighten the burden of local taxation.

(3) It must give a service to all alike on equal terms.

A royalty should be paid to the Post Office, which should be 10 per cent. on the gross receipts, and be the same in all respects as that paid by the company.

Although there appears no reason in equity why a new licensee should not be conceded a term equal to that originally conceded to the company, there may be reasons of public convenience why all licenses alike should lapse to the Post Office at the same date.

Where two systems compete in the same area, the first in the field has a further advantage. But your committee believe that, the areas being so large, in every area large sources of supply remain untapped. Under a more popular scheme of service this supply may be very considerable. The company is itself in vigorous competition in several areas with its licensor, the Post Office, which is almost every case was the first to occupy the ground. While the profits of the company in such areas are probably large, it is satisfactory

to learn that, in spite of the hampering restraints till lately imposed by the Treasury and of the necessity a public body is under to give no preferences, the local profits of the department have not been inconsiderable.

A difficulty arises in holding the balance equally between the local authority and the company from the fact that, while it seems generally admitted to be desirable in the public interest that all licenses should terminate in 1911, it is not possible to secure this and at the same time leave to the local authorities adequate time to recoup themselves for their outlay.

### THE POST OFFICE AND LOCAL AUTHORITIES.

The opinion has been strongly urged that, as between the company and the local authorities, the most equitable course would be that the Post Office, in licensing a local authority, should undertake to buy its plant at a fair valuation in 1911, if the license were terminated at that date ; but that, owing to the length of time which the company has had for recouping its outlay, it is not necessary to apply the same condition to it.

It has also been urged that it would be unfair to the company that the Post Office should agree to purchase the property of the local authority and remain in the future, as it is now, under no obligation to purchase that of the company in the same area.

It would be unjust to the taxpayer that the Post Office should undertake to purchase in 1911 two sets of plant and buildings, which might be to a great extent superfluous.

While, however, a portion of the plant and buildings of the two competitors may be superfluous or obsolete in 1911, much will probably be found useful and as good as the Post Office could purchase elsewhere.

On the whole, your committee think it would be fair as between its competing licensees that the Post Office should agree to take off their hands in 1911, at the then value, without any compensation for goodwill or future profits, so much of the plant and buildings as it might consider suitable for the actual requirements of its own local service. Should the total quantity so considered to be suitable exceed the amount necessary for such requirements, due regard should be had, in purchasing the quantity actually required, to the fact that the local authority had been allowed a shorter period of license than the company in which to recoup its expenditure.

At the same time your committee are strongly of opinion that the Post Office should remain, as it is now, under no obligation to purchase any plant or buildings in any area where a local authority and the company are not in bona fide competition or are not working together under the sanction of the Post Office.

The possibility of amalgamation is then discussed as bearing upon equality of treatment and the ultimate transfer of an undertaking to the Post Office. Then come the following interesting remarks on

### LICENSES AND FINANCE.

Your committee would recommend that, if licenses are to be granted to local authorities, the precedent of the Electric Lighting Act of 1882 should be followed, and provisional orders, containing borrowing powers, should be made by the Post Office for the installation of a telephone service, as they are now made by the Board of Trade where wayleaves and other powers are required for electric lighting purposes.

From the point of view of local finance your committee are of opinion that a telephone service would be as successful as has been the supply of gas, water, tramways and electric light by local authorities. Much, of course, depends in this case, as in those, upon the cost of constructing the service, and in all cases the local authority is perhaps the best judge of what is likely to be successful or not. It seems clear to your committee that a local authority should be able to construct a system at a price below that which, from various causes, the company have spent upon theirs, and this opinion is confirmed by the fact that the probable cost of such a service in the hands of the Glasgow Corporation is based not upon estimates alone, but on tenders actually received.

So far, therefore, as the legal or equitable rights of the company or the financial or other interests of the locality are concerned, your committee see no reason why licenses should not be granted to local authorities.

Although, as stated in evidence by Mr. Gaine, 95 per cent. of the telephonic messages are local, yet a local telephone service must differ in some important respects from a local service for supplying gas, water or electric light. It is not, like them, purely local and isolated, but it forms part of a national system, the general efficiency of which largely depends upon its uniformity and the equal facilities afforded for communication everywhere. The council of the Association of Municipal Corporations by a small majority, and a conference of representatives of London local authorities unanimously, preferred the competition of the Post Office to that of local authorities. At the meeting of the council of the Association of Municipal Corporations there were no representatives of Scotch municipalities, the two largest of which have applied for licenses.

The report concludes with some arguments in favour of

### A POST OFFICE SERVICE.

A more general competition than the local authorities appear likely to undertake is a necessity :—

(1) Individual traders and others have a right to object to the service of a public necessity becoming a private monopoly where the monopolist has the power to distinguish between competitors in the same trade and the same district, a result which is not possible when the service is in public hands.

(2) A service so important to the trade of the country should not depend on the present precarious wayleave rights of the company ; and the necessary general wayleave powers over the whole country can only be entrusted to a public department.

(3) The taxpayers have a right to be protected against purchasing as a monopoly a system which was never intended to become such, and as to which the most complete rights of competition were reserved ; and more especially against being placed in a position in which they may be forced to purchase such a monopoly at a price still further inflated by the necessity of immediate purchase.

On reviewing the whole of the evidence, your committee is strongly of opinion that general, immediate and effective competition by either the Post Office or the local authority is necessary, and consider that a really efficient Post Office service affords the best means for securing such competition. We further consider that, when in an existing area in which there is an exchange the local authority demands a competing service, the Post Office ought either to start an efficient telephone system itself or grant a license to the local authority to do so.

With regard to areas in which there is no exchange and districts which are not areas, we think some provision should be made beyond what is now offered by the National Telephone Company for giving a service when there is a reasonable local demand. In such cases the Post Office should either start a service of its own, subject to proper regulations, or should grant licenses to the local authorities to do so.

Your committee, in thus recommending a Post Office service, assume that it will constitute a real and active competition, and that concessions to the company not required by the agreement will cease. Such a competition should, in their opinion, be carried on by a distinct and separate branch of the department, and in future be conducted under strictly businesslike conditions and by a staff specially qualified for such a duty.

## MANCHESTER SEWAGE DISPOSAL.

### THE CITY SURVEYOR'S REPORT.

The city surveyor of Manchester has submitted his annual report on the treatment of sewage. Details of expenditure for the year ending December 31st last are given in tabulated statements under the following headings : (1) Sewage precipitation, (2) sludge-pressing and disposal, (3) filtration, (4) coal supply, (5) sundries and incidental expenses, (6) summary of annual cost of treatment. The nett cost of the work for the year has been £19,089 9s. 7d., as against £15,780 5s. 0½d. for the year 1896. These sums are exclusive of interest and repayment of capital, and are equivalent to £2 11s. 9d. and £2 14s. 3d. respectively per 1,000,000 gallons of sewage treated. A summary of the cost of treating the sewage for the year 1897 shows a reduction of 2s. 0½d. per 1,000,000 gallons on the cost of treatment for the year 1896.

### PRECIPITATION.

The volume of sewage delivered and treated during the year was 7,373,917,000 gallons, as against 5,818,200,000 gallons for 1896, being an increase of 1,555,717,000, or 26·7 per cent. on the preceding year. The estimated population contributing to the sewerage system has increased from 400,360 on January 1st, 1897, to 512,500 on December 31st, 1897, being an increase of 112,140, or 28 per cent. The increase of population contributing to the sewerage system during the year 1897 has exceeded the increase during the year 1896 by 49,780, or 79·8 per cent. The daily average flow of sewage was 20,426,363 gallons, that for 1896 being 15,896,721 gallons, showing an increase at the rate of 4,529,642 gallons per day, or 28·5 per cent. The average daily flow of sewage treated per head has ranged from a minimum of 39·3 gallons per head for the month ending May 19th to 50 gallons per head for the month ending December 1st. The average amount of wet sludge precipitated has been 21·16 tons per 1,000,000 gallons, as against 21·84 tons for the previous year, yielding 7 tons 12 cwt. of pressed cake per 1,000,000 gallons, as compared with 7 tons 18·4 cwt. for the year 1896.

### SEWAGE PURIFICATION.

The proportion of chemicals used during the year was less than in the preceding year. When the sewage is diluted by large quantities of storm water it has been customary to sus-

pend treatment during the flush, as the chemicals have but little effect in increasing the purity of effluent at such times, owing to the rapidity with which the water passes through the tanks, and to the extremely attenuated condition of flocculent organic matter which it is the function of the precipitant to carry down. When it is necessary to allow a portion of the storm water to pass directly by way of the storm overflow into the canal, the addition of chemicals would only increase the amount of suspended matter in the sewage. Treatment was stopped on account of storm water on twenty-one occasions during the year for a total period of 128 hours.

### RESULT OF CHEMICAL TREATMENT.

The result of chemical treatment and precipitation are shown in a series of tables containing the result of the analyses made at various times. On no occasion did the oxygen absorption come within the requirements of the Mersey and Irwell Joint Committee, and the albuminoid ammonia was below the grain per gallon in only a few instances.

### FILTRATION.

Land filters have been at work as far as practicable during the year. Experiments have been continued with the coke and cinder filters which were constructed at the end of 1895 under the advice of Sir Henry Roscoe. As in 1896, the cinder filter has throughout given better results than the coke, both as regards the percentage, reduction of impurity effected and in non-putrescibility. The results obtained from the experimental coal filters are equal to or even better than those obtained from the cinder filter. During the year an experimental red sand and a burnt clay filter have also been tried, and likewise an automatic self-cleansing filter.

### MISCELLANEOUS EXPERIMENTS.

Various experiments have been made during the year in connection with the settlement of solids in suspension in the sewage without the addition of chemicals, the exposure of the effluent to the air and the passing of air through the effluent. Tests have also been made to ascertain the effect of the effluent on the water in the Ship canal and the effect of the admixture of acid and water with the effluent. In all cases the effluent contains the larger amount of impurity than the canal water, although in most cases, unless diluted by rain, the amount of impurity in the Ship canal above Barton locks is sufficient to cause putrefaction of incubation. The putrefaction which takes place in a mixture of Ship canal water and tank effluent is generally greater in amount than in either taken separately. The experiments also showed that although it is possible to sterilise the effluent by the addition of a small quantity of acid, yet if a sterilised effluent be mixed with Ship canal water the effect of the acid is largely destroyed and putrefaction again occurs. If an acidified sample of tank effluent be mixed with tap water the sterilising effect of acid appears to be maintained. When the Ship canal water is largely diluted by rain putrefaction does not, as a rule, take place in the mixture of effluent and canal water. Sea salt has been added to samples of tank effluent, with the result that a large quantity is found to be necessary to prevent putrefaction taking place.

## NEW CENTRAL SANITARY DEPOT FOR LEEDS.

The new central sanitary depot, upon which the Leeds Corporation are spending over £30,000, is nearing completion, and will be formally opened early next month. The situation of the premises is very convenient. The site is in Dock-street, to the south of Leeds bridge. Stabling accommodation is here provided for 168 horses. Commodious offices, store-rooms and sheds for the many vehicles that are used in the scavenging and water-cleansing department are also being built. At present the only stables the Sanitary Committee can call their own are a few wooden structures in Black Bull-street. Over 100 of the 150 horses belonging to the department have therefore to be sent to private stables. The land on which the new depot is built has cost about £20,000, whilst the buildings will necessitate an expenditure of about £13,000. The whole of the land, however, is not being used for the purposes of the depot. About 1,000 yards are being utilised to widen Dock-street and the other thoroughfares bounding the site. The Sanitary Committee are also credited with £8,000 for their old site at Crown Point, which has been demolished to make room for the electrical generating station. In addition, the committee have received £1,000 for their old buildings and appliances. It may be taken, therefore, that the nett cost of the new depot and of the land which is being used for the widening of the adjoining streets does not greatly exceed £20,000. For this sum the committee obtain commodious offices for their officials, stables for their horses, shelter for their vehicles, and a capital centre for carrying on the important work which devolves upon the street cleansing and scavenging departments.

**Enniskillen.**—A proposal to erect artisans' dwellings on a plot of vacant land at Forthill is being considered by the Town Improvement Committee.

# For Assistants and Pupils.

## THE CONSTRUCTION OF ROADS AND STREETS.—XVIII.

By WILLIAM H. MAXWELL, Assistant Engineer and Surveyor, Leyton Urban District Council.

### ROAD MATERIALS AND CONSTRUCTION
#### (continued).

The *Highgate Archway-road*, about 1½ miles in length, was originally made by a private company, at great expense, owing to the nature of the subsoil, which consisted of sand, clay and gravel. An unsuccessful attempt having been made to form a tunnel through the hill, open cutting was resorted to, and the roadway made by laying large quantities of gravel and sand upon the natural soil and thickly coating the same with broken flint and gravel. The result, however, not being satisfactory, the road was discarded by much of the traffic, and the company, being naturally anxious to improve its condition, among other schemes took up the road material and covered the subsoil with pieces of waste tin, upon which were placed gravel, flints and broken stone, but without attaining the desired success.

The road continued in a very bad state for some considerable time, as may be seen from Mr. Telford's annual reports to the Parliamentary Commissioners, until in 1829 an arrangement was made by the commissioners with the Highgate Archway Company for taking the road under their management; whereupon it was re-formed and put into proper repair. "In order to accomplish this," writes Sir Henry Parnell,[*] several experiments were tried, by draining the surface and subsoil, and by laying on a thick coating of broken granite; but from the wet and elastic nature of the subsoil the hardest stones were rapidly worn away by the wheels of carriages, but much more by the friction of the stones themselves against each other; for, in a very short time they were found to become as round and as smooth as gravel pebbles, even at the bottom of the whole mass of road materials. It was therefore evident that to form a perfect road, which might be kept in repair at a moderate expense, it was necessary to establish a dry and solid foundation for the surface broken stones; but as no stones could be obtained for making a foundation of pavement but at a very great expense, a composition of Roman cement and gravel was suggested by Mr. M'Neill, and this on a trial was found to answer effectually.

The foundation was formed of concrete, consisting of Roman cement, washed gravel and sand, mixed in the proportion of one cement to eight of gravel. In forming the bed of the road "there were four drains formed longitudinally, and there were secondary drains running from these to the side channel drains, and those again to drains outside the footpaths, covered with brick, and they all communicated with each other, and discharged the water into proper outlets."[*] The cross drains occurred at intervals of 30 yards, and the intermediate small drains every 10 yards under the cement. Mr. M'Neill also stated that this special drainage was rendered necessary through the nature of the ground—the road being cut through a clay soil, with high banks on each side, so that all the surface water descending from the slopes and Highgate Hill came down and rested in the hollows of the subsoil.

"On the prepared centre of 6 yards in width, after it had been properly levelled, the cement was laid on, mixing it first in a box with water, gravel and sand in certain proportions"[*] as above. The concrete, when in position, was found to have set in a quarter of an hour, and "in about four minutes after being laid a triangular piece of wood, sheeted with iron, was indented into it, so as to leave a track or channel at every 4 in. for the broken stones to lie and fasten in."[†] "This triangular indent had an inclination of fully 2 in. from the centre to the sides; so that if water came through the broken stones it ran off the cemented mass into the longitudinal drains."

Quite recently some concrete blocks about 12 in. by 6 in. by 4 in. were met with in the course of excavations in this road. They occurred at a depth of about 2 ft. 6 in., and are now to be seen in the museum of the Hornsey District Council—the authority now responsible for the maintenance

of that portion of the road north of the "Arch."[*] These blocks and slabs, and also faggots, it is stated by a very old resident, were used in the foundations upon soft and treacherous ground.

The foundation stone of the "Arch,"[†] was laid on October 31, 1812, but it was not until the early part of 1830 that Mr. McNeill had completed the laying-in of his concrete foundation and other improvements, and the road thus brought into a satisfactory condition.

The road appears to have been liberally encumbered with "toll gates" from its formation to within a comparatively recent date. The old toll gate in the year 1825 was in the line with the then "Archway" tavern, but some years later was shifted northwards to a point between the "Archway" tavern and the Archway, just north of the Whittington almshouses. This gate finally disappeared in the year 1879 or 1880. The amount of the toll levied was 6d. for horses and 1d. for foot passengers. Another gate crossed the Archway-road, near the "Woodman" public-house, just north of Southwood-lane, and was removed some twenty-five years ago. Within the Hornsey district, opposite the Manor farm, a further gate existed, which, however, was removed in 1863.

As regards the *present experience* of the maintenance of this important highway, Mr. E. J. Lovegrove, A.M.I.C.E., engineer and surveyor to the Hornsey District Council, states that "speaking of the road generally, it is a difficult one to keep in repair, having regard to the peculiar class of traffic and also to the fact that there is a considerable amount of movement in the road itself."[‡]

In an excellent paper, read at Blaydon-on-Tyne before the Association of Municipal and County Engineers, Mr. James Hall observes that "the only objection to a road formed with a concrete bottoming is its first cost, which precludes its general use. In towns, however, where it is considered desirable to have a broken-stone road, a better foundation could not be obtained; one of its great disadvantages is that, becoming a compact mass after setting, the weight is evenly distributed over the whole surface of the roadway, thus preventing, to a very large extent, an uneven surface, which is often found in roads where the traffic is heavy. Concrete

| | Pinned Foundations. | | | Broken Stones. | | Concrete. | |
|---|---|---|---|---|---|---|---|
| | Pinning. | Covering. | Metal. | Under. | Upper. | Concrete. | Metal, &c. |
| Country roads ... | 6 in. | 3 in. | 4 in. | 9 in. | 4 in. | 4 in. | 3 in. |
| Suburban roads... | 9 in. | 3 in. | 5 in. | 9 in. | 6 in. | 6 in. | 5 in. |
| Town streets ... | 9 in. | 6 in. | 5 in. | 15 in. | 6 in. | 10 in. | 5 in. |

can be made both with lime, lias lime, and cement; the latter is preferable. When a concrete foundation is to be used, great judgment should be exercised in the proper time the metal should be spread. Some engineers say that the concrete must be allowed to get thoroughly set, then covered with a thin coating of fine gravel (pit gravel preferred), and the required thickness of metal then spread; while others consider it better to spead the metal upon a thin coating of gravel before the concrete is set, and roll the surface until the metal has partly embedded itself in the concrete. I am strongly of opinion that the latter plan is the better. The road, however, must not be open for traffic until the concrete is quite hard, and until after the first coating of metal has been covered with a thin coat of finely-broken material."[§]

The above *thicknesses of foundation and metalling* of broken-stone roads have also been suggested by Mr. Hall.

**Kirkcaldy.**—The scheme for the introduction of electric lighting and traction into Kirkcaldy has now assumed an aspect that points to a private company taking it in hand. It is stated on good authority that the town council will not take up the scheme, but they will be urgently requested to support the local company in preference to any outside combination. Several leading gentlemen in the district are doing their utmost to forward the movement and bring it to a successful issue.

---

   * *Vide* "A Treatise on Roads."
   † Evidence of Mr. M'Neill before a Select Committee of the House of Commons, in May, 1830.

   * The portion below the Arch is in the Islington district.
   † The Arch was of itself a substantial-looking stone structure, but disfigured by a number of ugly brick arches, built across it for the purpose of conveying the Hornsey-lane over the Archway-road cutting.
   ‡ I am also indebted to Mr. Lovegrove for the above particulars in reference to the toll gates and concrete blocks.
   § "Proceedings of the Association of Municipal and County Engineers," vol. vii.

# Law Notes.

EDITED BY J. B. REIGNIER CONDER, 11 Old Jewry Chambers, E.C.,

Solicitor of the Supreme Court.

*The Editor will be pleased to answer any questions affecting the practice of engineers and surveyors to local authorities. Queries (which should be written legibly on foolscap paper, one side only) should be addressed to "The Law Editor," at the Offices of THE SURVEYOR. Where possible, copies of local Acts or documents referred to should be enclosed. All explanatory diagrams must be drawn and lettered in black ink only. Correspondents who do not wish their names published should furnish a nom de plume.*

OBSTRUCTION OF STREET BY LOCAL AUTHORITY UNDER STATUTORY POWERS: DAMAGE TO GOODWILL OF BUSINESS: LIABILITY: LONDON COUNTY COUNCIL ACTS, 1891 AND 1894. —Rather a novel point was raised in the recent case of *Martin v. London County Council* (Queen's Bench Division, Mr. Justice Kennedy, July 30th and 31st and August 6th). The plaintiff was a greengrocer carrying on business in Wellington-street, Deptford. In 1897 the council, in exercise of their statutory powers, proceeded to construct a new road, cutting Wellington-street diagonally. The usual accompaniments of a work of this kind (in the shape of the blocking-up of Wellington-street and the adjacent thoroughfares and the general chaotic condition of the neighbourhood) had, according to the plaintiff's account, such a disastrous effect upon his business that, after incurring extra expense and labour in getting goods to his shop and thence to his customers, he had ultimately to relinquish the business and quit the premises. He therefore sought to recover damages against the council on two grounds—viz., (1) That they had obstructed the approaches to the street at more points and in a greater degree than was necessary; and (2) that there had been unreasonable delay in the conduct of the works. After somewhat lengthy arguments on both sides, judgment was given in favour of the council. The learned judge, after pointing out that the council were not only bound to enter on a portion of Wellington-street in order to carry out the works, but that they were invested with very large statutory powers, continued: They were a public body who had to carry out important works for the public good, and great discretion was entrusted to them with regard to stopping up particular streets and regulating and stopping traffic. It was at least arguable that, assuming that they did nothing in bad faith and that what was done was for the purposes of improvements, no action would lie for mere delay or for the extent to which the street was blocked. But there must always be the reservation that if they did certain classes of damage to the person or property through negligence or want of reasonable care they might in certain circumstances be held liable. For instance, if in the present case they had carelessly left heaps without lights, they would be answerable. But in the present case the complaint was that at a street called Wellington-street, at the other end of the street to that in which the plaintiff's house was, they blocked up more of the road than they need have. It was also said they were two months longer over the work than they ought to have been. The plaintiff said he was prepared to prove that he had suffered damage by reason of the loss of customers through foot passengers being disheartened in going down the street, and that although there was a roundabout way by which they could go to his shop they would not do so. It was not contended that the obstruction continued after the making of, or for other purpose than, the improvements. It was not like the case of *Wilkes v. Hungerford Market* (2 Biny., N.C. 281), where the hoarding was afterwards kept up unnecessarily. The plaintiff, who became the leaseholder of the shop after the passing of the Act of 1891, admitted that the most serious injury he suffered was from the destruction of certain premises for the purposes of improvement of a district from which he had previously drawn large custom. The fair result of the cases was that if a private person were injured by works of this description, if they were in the manner, or to the extent, unauthorised or unreasonable, the injured person would have a claim if, and only if, he proved that, by reason of that which was not authorised by the statute, he had been injured specially, directly and substantially. By specially was meant an injury not merely common to anyone living in that neighbourhood. That the injury must be direct was shown by the judgment of Mr. Justice Brett in the case of *Benjamin v. Storr*. The plaintiff must show an injury special to himself as distinct from the public generally. Was the loss of some custom by the plaintiff a direct injury within the definition? In his opinion it was not. The house itself was in no way obstructed. There was always access to the shop, although by a roundabout way. The house in itself was not rendered less commodious for trading or less healthy for occupation. The injury was not direct in a sense in which the cases had treated it. The case of *Wilkes v. Hungerford Market* could no longer be treated as an authority, having regard to the observations of Lord Chelmsford in *Ricket v. Metropolitan Railway Company* (L.R. 2, E. and I.A. 175), and Mr. Justice Willes in *Beckett v. Midland Railway Company* (L.R. 3, C.P. 97). The present case was not one under such circumstances as gave a right of action, and there must be judgment for the defendants, with costs, except the costs of the special jury.

## QUERIES AND REPLIES.

HOUSE DRAINAGE: OPEN DITCH: NUISANCE.—"Surveyor" writes: The owner of some cottages a few years ago was allowed to discharge the sewage from the same into an open ditch at the side of the highway. This has become a nuisance. Will you kindly inform me in your next issue whether my

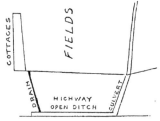

council can compel the owner to pipe and cover in the ditch, or disconnect and carry the sewage elsewhere. The accompanying diagram will explain. I may add that this case occurs in a village.

There are several points to be considered in connection with this case. First of all, the question arises whether the open ditch is (1) a drain, (2) a sewer, or (3) merely a watercourse. Unless the cottages are "premises within the same curtilage" it cannot be a "drain." Even if the cottages are within the same curtilage I do not think it would be held to be a drain, as it was evidently not "made merely for the purpose of communicating" from the premises with a cesspool or sewer (see the definition of a "drain," sec. 4, Public Health Act, 1875). But is it a sewer? In *Reg. v. Godmanchester Local Board* (L.R., 1 Q. B., 328) a stream supplied by the drainage—natural and artificial—of cultivated land and receiving the drainage of two or three houses was held not to be a sewer within the meaning of the Public Health Act, 1848. But in *Wheatcroft v. Matlock Local Board* (52 L.T. [N.S.], 356), where the sewage of certain houses drained into a sewer, and, after passing through the sewer, was for a period of some years allowed to fall into an open watercourse, it was held that the watercourse was a "sewer." And in *Kirkheaton Local Board v. Beaumont* (52 J. P., 68) several houses drained into a road drain and, the latter into a ditch in a field belonging to the owner of the houses which ditch became a nuisance. The owner, upon being summoned, contended that the ditch was a sewer vested in the local board and that it was their duty to cover it up; and the justices refused to make an order against him, as he was not the person by whose act default or sufferance the nuisance arose. It was held, upon appeal, that the justices were right. The facts in that case are somewhat similar to those in the present case, except that in the latter the ditch is not on the houseowner's own land. I am inclined, therefore, to think that this ditch would be held to be a sewer, in which case the council could not compel the owner to pipe and cover it in. They could, however, proceed under sec. 24 of the Public Health Act, 1875. If the ditch is neither a drain nor a sewer, but only a watercourse, then sec. 69 of the same Act would apply.

## WELLINGTON NEW SEWAGE SCHEME.

On Friday the sewage works, just completed at a cost of some thousands of pounds, at Admaston, for treating the sewage from Wellington, were utilised for the first time. The scheme is very comprehensive and obviates the causes of complaints which have been made from time to time by the inhabitants of the town as well as those living at Admaston, where the sewage matter formerly mingled in the water of a brook running close to the highway. After chemical treatment in a tank constructed on the Ivo's principle, the liquid elements separated from the grosser matter will run over a large area of land, and after irrigating it will pass purified into a brook. At the invitation of Mr. Clift, the members and officials partook of tea in a tent, and congratulatory speeches were made.

**Paris and Its Water Supply.**—In addition to the inconveniences of the excessive heat, it is announced that unless rain falls heavily within a day or two the inhabitants of the French capital will be reduced to drinking Seine water. It appears that, notwithstanding the extremely large number of millions of francs which have been spent some years ago to supply the city with the pure water of the Avre, in addition to that they already received from the Dhuys and the Vanne, the reservoirs are almost empty.

# Municipal Work in Progress and Projected.

This week we are able to publish particulars of several important schemes which are being carried out by local authorities, notably at Bristol, Cheltenham, Abercarn, Birkdale, Bredbury, Castle Donington, Armagh, Crewe, Maidstone, Manchester, Newport (Mon.), Preston, Salford and South Shields. Electric supply schemes, it will be seen, are still engaging the attention of many of the authorities.

## METROPOLITAN AUTHORITIES.
### VESTRIES AND DISTRICT BOARDS.

**Hackney.**—On Monday a special meeting of the General Purposes Committee of the vestry was held "to consider the action of the East London Waterworks Company in discontinuing the 'constant' supply system in favour of a daily service of six hours." Mr. W. Sheean, in the course of a prolonged discussion, moved that the clerk be instructed to write to the company stating that the vestry were determined to continue watering the roads and also to supply water to the inhabitants. He further suggested that a committee of five be appointed to carry out the necessary arrangements. The resolution having been seconded, the chairman advocated the formation of a sub-committee to approach the East London Waterworks Company with a view of securing a written promise that the directors would pay all expenses incurred in sending the water round the district in carts. It was eventually decided that a sub-committee should be formed to devise measures by which the supply of the East London Water Company could be appreciably augmented.

**Hampstead.**—The Hampstead Vestry at their last meeting received a letter from the London County Council suggesting that the positions of fire-alarms should be indicated by painting the nearest lamp-post a bright red colour. It so happens that the vestry had already adopted this colour for the lamp-post nearest to the 4-mile radius boundary, and in carrying out the suggestion of the council Mr. C. H. Lowe, the surveyor, had to give instructions for the colour of the radius lamp-posts to be altered. Now Hampstead has lamp-posts of three distinct colours. Those nearest to fire-alarms are painted red, those nearest to the radius boundary blue, and the ordinary lamp-posts are painted white.

**Stoke Newington.**—The vestry have received notices from several electric lighting companies intimating their intention to apply to the Board of Trade for provisional orders for the supply of electric energy within the parish. The vestry have notified the companies to the effect that they are in possession of a provisional order, noted that they are taking steps to exercise their powers, and will oppose the application of the companies.

**Wandsworth.**—Last week the General Purposes Committee reported to the board of works that, after taking time to consider their judgment, the Court of Appeal, consisting of the Master of the Rolls, Lord Justice Chitty and Lord Justice Collins, have unanimously reversed the decision of Mr. Justice Kekewich, who had granted an injunction, upon the application of the Southwark and Vauxhall Water Company, restraining the board from lowering the footpath in West Hill-road, Wandsworth, so as to make the water main there more liable to frost or to be otherwise prejudicially affected. As this is a matter of great importance to local authorities, the committee recommended that the judgment of the Court of Appeal be printed and a copy forwarded to each member of the board and to each vestry and district board in the metropolis. This was agreed to.

**Whitechapel.**—On the recommendation of the Electric Lighting Committee, the board of works decided, last week, to request the member of Parliament for the Whitechapel division to oppose the General Power Distributing Companies' Bill now before Parliament, and Bills of a similar nature which seek to give power to companies to supply electrical energy in bulk over large areas in parts of which provisional orders have already been granted to local authorities.

## PROVINCIAL AND GREATER LONDON AUTHORITIES.
### COUNTY COUNCILS.

**Kesteven.**—At a meeting of the county council on the 10th inst., the Asylum Visiting Committee reported that the total cost of the new asylum was as follows: Cost of building, as estimated by architect, £92,000; cost of furnishing, £15,000; laying-out grounds, architect's and other commissions, &c., £18,000; total, £125,000. The Finance Committee recommended that application again be made to the Local Government Board for their sanction to the application of the sum of £4,963 18s. 10d., being the balance of capital moneys in the hands of the county council, towards the cost of the erection of the county asylum, and that the board be furnished with the Visiting Committee's estimate of the cost with the plans and sections of the new asylum, and any other information required by them. They further recommended that application be made for the Local Government

Board's sanction to the borrowing by the county council of a sum not exceeding £120,000 for the cost of the erection of the county asylum. The recommendations were adopted.

**Wigtownshire.** — A meeting of the road board of the county council was held at Stranraer last week. The meeting was convened for the purpose of considering the recommendations of the Upper District Committee with regard to the erection of new bridges over the Soleburn, on the main road between Stranraer and Kirkcolm, and over the Pultanton at Greenfield, in the parish of Leswalt, near Stranraer. Plans were submitted by Mr. Tait, the road surveyor for the Upper District, for the construction of a new bridge over the Soleburn, and it was resolved to pull down the present structure, which has become dangerous for heavy traffic, and erect a bridge with stone abutments and wings and a brick arch, at an estimated cost of £340. It was also agreed to construct a new bridge over the Pultanton at Greenfield, with stone abutments and wing walls, spanning the water with steel and iron beams and girders, the cost estimated by the surveyor being £143.

## MUNICIPAL CORPORATIONS.

**Bath.**—At last week's meeting of the Bath Surveying Committee it was agreed, on the request of the Baths Committee, to pay £500 towards the cost of the Abbey-avenue, which this committee had already paved with destructor blocks. The whole cost was £1,950.

**Bournemouth.**—A lively inquiry was held on Tuesday by Mr. A. E. Sandford Fawcett, Local Government Board inspector, respecting an application of the town council for sanction to borrow £1,000 to transform the course of the stream in the well-known lower pleasure gardens into an ornamental watercourse, with islet grottos, ferneries, weirs and a rustic bridge. The proposal is looked upon with great disfavour by many ratepayers, who offered strenuous opposition. The decision of the Local Government Board is awaited with considerable interest.—A special meeting of the town council is to be held shortly to consider the desirability of applying for a provisional order empowering them to adopt a scheme for lighting the town by electricity.

**Bristol.**—The sub-committee of the sanitary authority have received the report of Mr. Santo Crimp, Westminster, on the disposal of the sewage of the city. The scheme is very comprehensive, and deals with the whole question of sewage disposal. It provides for an outfall near Dunball Island, which has been chosen after a long series of experiments, and tanks constructed at Avonmouth for storage, so that the discharge may be effected at suitable states of the tide. A new sewer will be constructed following the course of the river on the Gloucestershire side, and a pumping station provided somewhere near the Clift House estate, so as to lift the sewage into the outfall sewer, whence it will be conveyed to the Bristol Channel. It is contemplated to extend the sewer up the valley of the Avon, and it has been suggested that it might be utilised for accommodating outlying districts, if satisfactory arrangements can be concluded with the local authorities. The whole of the sewage now discharging into the Avon will be collected at a point near Clift House, and lifted by pumps into the new outfall sewer. The cost of the scheme will be between £300,000 and £400,000, and in its conception allowance has been made for the growth of the population for many years to come.

**Bury.**—The town council have accepted tenders for electric light works amounting in the aggregate to £22,500, subject to the usual approval of the Local Government Board.

**Carlisle.**—It is reported that the profits of the corporation's gas and water undertakings for the past year amount to £9,088 and £6,050 respectively. The gas profits are £875 less than the previous year, owing chiefly to the increased price of coal, but the nett amount to be handed over to the relief of the rates will be larger, owing to the falling in of the gas loan of 1887, in respect of which £1,225 was charged against the account last year. The nett amounts which went in relief of rates last year were £5,757 on the gas account and £3,069 on the water account.

**Carnarvon.**—The town council have resolved to oppose an application, which is to be made by Edmundson's Electricity Supply Company, Limited, for a provisional order empowering them to supply electricity within the borough.

**Cheltenham.**—Colonel J. T. Marsh, R.E., Local Government Board inspector, held an inquiry at Cheltenham, on the 12th inst., into an application by the Cheltenham Town Council for sanction to borrow £13,410 for purposes of sewerage and sewage disposal, and for the appointment of an inspector to make an inquiry into the matter of certain works of sewerage and sewage disposal, which the said council propose to construct without the limits of the borough, and into certain objections which have been received thereto. Mr. Hall, borough surveyor, stated that in 1896 he reported on the state of the sewer from the Arle tank to the Barn farm. He found the pipes unjointed and the gradients irregular. Roots had penetrated the joints, reducing the carrying capacity of the sewer by two-thirds. Complaints had been made by the tenant of the farm of the diminution in the supply of sewage, and compensation had been granted him. The improvements proposed would increase the carrying capacity to 1,350 gallons per minute. Similar facts were cited in connection with other parts of the scheme. The inspector afterwards visited the districts affected.

**Crewe.**—The provisional order applied for by the town council to provide a generating station and to supply the borough with electric light has been granted. The cost of the scheme is estimated at about £25,000. Prof. Hopkinson has been called into consultation, and has advised the corporation as to a suitable site for the electric lighting plant in the south ward.

**Deal.**—The Corporation of Deal have had under their consideration for some time the question of the sea encroachment, and they have now decided to proceed with new works of sea defence near Sandown Castle, at the north end of Deal. The surveyor to the corporation stated that unless these works of defence were undertaken at once the encroachment of the sea would undermine the existing wall and cause it to collapse. The urgency of the matter was also emphasised by the town clerk, who said that he had visited the spot, and the state of things so alarmed him that he had written to the Board of Trade pointing out that the whole of Deal was likely to be submerged if the wall went. The sea wall was much damaged by the heavy gale of several months ago, which carried away the shingle to such a depth as to leave the foundations exposed.

**Derby.**—Last week an inquiry was held by Colonel Slacke, on behalf of the Local Government Board, with reference to an application of the town council for sanction to borrow £310 for purposes of street improvements.

**Dorchester.**—The following has been adopted by the council : " That the surveyor be instructed to draw up a report on the water supply of the borough, dealing with the additional requirements through the proposed extension of the borough, the waste of water and necessary storage."

**Falmouth.**—A committee have presented a report to the town council in favour of purchasing both the gas and water undertakings, and a special meeting is to be called to consider the matter ; meanwhile the committee have been asked to make a recommendation in regard to the employment of an expert.

**Hastings.**—The town council, at a meeting on Friday adopted the following resolution : " That this council, being of opinion that the erection of a lift to the East Hill should prove a much-needed public improvement and supply a greatly-felt public want, respectfully invites the Rev. W. Sayer-Milward to give his consent to the construction of the same by the corporation, if found practicable."—It was reported that the sanction of the Local Government Board had been received to the supplying of the parish of Ore with water.

**Hyde.**—The Sewage Works Committee recommended, at a recent meeting of the town council, that, having regard to the fact that the Local Government Board would not pass any scheme of artificial filtration unless it also embraced one of subsequent filtration through land, plans of a scheme for automatic filters and land filtration, at an estimated cost of £5,500, be adopted, and that the town clerk be instructed to make application to the Local Government Board for sanction to the loan. It was stated that the estimated expenditure included the purchase of automatic filters, the building of a filter-house, the erection of a pump for the washing out of the filters, and the underdraining of 10¼ acres of land, which was to be laid out in 1-acre plots for the purpose of land filtration. The committee intended to take the solid matter from the sewage by means of the automatic filters, and then turn it upon the land, but they were not prepared to say that even then they would be able to give satisfaction to the Mersey and Irwell Committee. A lengthy discussion ensued, the opinion being expressed that, pending the report of the Royal Commission, the scheme should not be proceeded with. Ultimately the resolution was referred back to the committee for further consideration.

**Liverpool.**—The Tramways Committee of the corporation have adopted a resolution that the council be recommended to authorise the Tramways Committee to take steps to have plans, sections and estimates prepared to continue the overhead electric traction tramways from the termination of the experimental line at the Dingle to the end of Aigburth-road, and also for an extension of the experimental line from the Prince's Park gates along Croxteth-road to Ledge-lane, in accordance with the lines as authorised by the Tramways Provisional Order of this session.

**Lowestoft.**—On the recommendation of a committee, the town council have decided to proceed under its electric lighting provisional order, and have instructed the committee to have a scheme, with estimates, prepared, with a view to application being made to the Local Government Board for sanction to a loan for carrying out the works.

**Maidstone.**—Application will shortly be made by the Local Government Board for sanction to borrow £6,050 for the reconstruction of the old brick sewers in the borough in accordance with plans prepared by the surveyor.

**Manchester.**—An inquiry was held on Tuesday, at the Manchester Town Hall, to consider the application of the corporation for power to borrow £27,500 for the alteration and enlargement of Monsall hospital. Mr. W. W. E. Fletcher conducted the inquiry, on behalf of the Local Government Board. No opposition was offered, and the inspector hinted that there would probably be no difficulty in the matter. The great stumbling-block, at first sight, was the small-pox question, but if the corporation intended to provide separate accommodation elsewhere probably no difficulty would arise.

**Mansfield.**—At the last meeting of the town council tenders for the making-up and forming of Quarry-lane were considered from nine firms, and it was resolved that the tender of Mr. W. A. Vallance be accepted, at the sum of £1,249.

**Newport.**—On Thursday Mr. H. Percy Boulnois, Local Government Board inspector, held an inquiry at the Newport Guildhall respecting an application by the corporation for sanction to borrow £8,300 for the purposes of water supply. It was explained that the original loan was £10,000, which was increased to £12,000 without an inquiry. During the progress of the works it was found necessary to make certain alterations and additions, bringing the total estimated expenditure up to £20,201. Mr. Baldwin Latham produced a plan showing the works originally contemplated and the portions already executed. He stated that the Local Government Board insisted upon the source of supply being carried 2 miles further on. This entailed considerable increased cost, in consequence of the nature of the strata met with. Blasting had to be resorted to, and enormous quantities of water were met with, occasioning the use of as many as six light engines being employed in pumping. The work had been pushed on most expeditiously, but although the contract was first fixed to be carried out in nine months, then increased to twelve months, it had now been over two years in progress. So it would be seen how the extra cost arose.

**North Shields.**—On Wednesday of last week Mr. Robert H. Bicknell, Local Government Board inspector, held an inquiry at the town hall, North Shields, in reference to the application of the corporation for sanction to borrow £3,000 for the construction of the Northumberland Dock-road and £300 for the improvement of the Tiger stairs. It was explained that for many years the road had been out of repair, and it had been strongly urged upon the council that it should be reinstated and put in proper order. The road went from Hay Hole in a westerly direction for a distance of 1,400 yards to Howdon, close to the western boundary of the borough.

**Portsmouth.**—A singular mishap occurred in Portsmouth harbour on Wednesday. A working party are engaged in widening the entrance between basins No. 4 and 5, and in order to keep the water back a large dam has been erected. This yielded to the pressure of water and flooded the works, the men fortunately escaping. The undertaking will be considerably delayed, as some time must elapse before the dam can be reconstructed and the water pumped out.

**Preston.**—The town council are considering the offer of the Lancashire County Council to purchase, on certain conditions, a piece of land for £16,000 for the purpose of erecting a new sessions house for the Preston Quarter Sessional Division.

**Salford.**—A Local Government Board inquiry was held recently with respect to an application by the Salford Corporation for power to borrow £33,000 for purposes of electric lighting and £2,200 for the construction of storm water overflows on the main intercepting sewer at Hough-lane, Springfield-lane and Regent-road. Mr. J. Corbett, the borough engineer, stated that on the intercepting sewer by which the sewage of the borough was carried to the sewage works at Mode Wheel there are at present three storm overflows. The additional overflows now proposed to be constructed were for a part of the sewer that was in the most populous part of the borough. At that point there were 4½ miles of intercepting sewer without any overflow to the main sewer, although there were some small overflows to the individual sewers. Frequent complaint had been made about the flooding of the district, and it was felt that something ought to be done to remove all cause of complaint.

**Southport.**—At a recent meeting of the town council a resolution was proposed to the effect " that a first-class expert be engaged to report upon the gas estate, with instructions to recommend to the council any improvements which, in his opinion, would be likely to result in an increased profit." After some discussion the matter was referred to to the Gas Committee for consideration.

**South Shields.**—At the last meeting of the town council Alderman Rennoldson moved the adoption of the Electric Lighting Committee's report, and stated that the demand for the light was still increasing. The committee had decided to go in for a further extension of the plant at the station, and asked the council to instruct the town clerk to apply to the Local Government Board for their sanction to the borrowing by the council of the sum of £20,000 for the purpose of providing the additional plant. The committee's report was adopted.

**Stamford.**—Another scheme for the sewerage of the

borough was recently laid before the town council in committee by Mr. J. B. Everard, of Leicester. The council resolved to have the report printed and circulated amongst the members and the local Press, but pledged themselves to no definite decision. The total cost of the proposed works would amount to about £47,000 and the annual expenditure to £540.

**Stratford-upon-Avon.**—The Gas Committee reported at the last meeting of the town council that the profit from the gas undertaking for the past year showed an increase of £352, as compared with the previous year, and that this sum had been handed over in reduction of the rates.

**Tonbridge.**—A considerable amount of consternation was caused in Tonbridge recently by the sudden plunging of the town into darkness just before 8 o'clock. The extinction of the gas occurred just when the streets were most busily thronged and the business of the town in full swing. For about six minutes the business portion of the town was in absolute darkness, and much inconvenience was caused at the station in connection with the working of the signals. The sudden defection of the gas was due either to an accident to a pipe in the gas-holder or to negligence in allowing a water syphon to become filled, thus shutting off the supply. With great promptitude the manager of the gasworks caused a fresh holder to be turned on, and in a short time the town was again in its normal condition.

## URBAN DISTRICT COUNCILS.

**Abercarn.**—Colonel J. T. Marsh, R.E., recently held an inquiry, on behalf of the Local Government Board, relative to an application of the district council for sanction to borrow £8,150 for water supply purposes.

**Acton.**—A Local Government Board inquiry has been held respecting an application of the district council for sanction to borrow £1,161 for street improvements and £905 for public library purposes.

**Belper.**—During the past few months negotiations have been proceeding between the urban district council and Mr. J. B. Marsden-Smedley, J.P., proprietor of the Dethick estate, for the acquisition of a water supply. It will serve the villages of Holloway, Crich, South Wingfield, Pentrich, and probably others. The population is about 7,000, and provision has to be made for 60,000 to 70,000 gallons per day. Mr. Firth, C.E., of Baslow, is the engineer concerned, and he has gauged two springs on the Dethick estate, which yield about 200,000 gallons per diem. The agreement was laid before a special meeting of the Belper Council recently, and received the seal of the authority.

**Birkdale.**—Colonel Luard, Local Government Board inspector, held an inquiry on Saturday at the Birkdale town hall in respect to an application made by the urban district council for sanction to borrow £7,435 for the following works—viz., street improvements, £4,250; sewer extension, £630; caretaker's lodge at the Victoria Park, £575; fire brigade station, £500, and gas mains extension, £1,500.—The plans and estimates were prepared by Mr. F. C. Hodgkinson, engineer and surveyor to the authority, and official sanction was received on Thursday.

**Bolsover.**—Under pressure from the Derbyshire County Council, this authority decided at a recent meeting to write to Mr. W. H. Wagstaffe, of Chesterfield, asking his terms for preparing a scheme for sewerage and sewage disposal for the district.

**Bredbury and Romiley.**—A Local Government Board inquiry was held on the 12th inst. by Mr. W. O. E. Meade-King with reference to an application of the council for sanction to borrow £7,250 for sewerage and sewage disposal works.

**Chiswick.**—During the past few weeks considerable improvements have been made at the pumping station. The roads leading to it, which were practically a mud pond, have been paved, and the ground surrounding the station has been tastefully laid-out in flower beds. The embankment facing the Thames has also been improved, and all that is wanted now are a few seats and permission to the public to use the embankment. The whole work reflects great credit on the surveyor, Mr. Arthur Ramsden, and also on those members of the council who have championed the improvement.

**Colwyn Bay.**—The inauguration of electrically lighting the new promenade took place here on Tuesday night. The promenade was opened on Jubilee Day; the drinking fountain presented to the town as a jubilee gift was subsequently dedicated to public use, and the council afterwards decided to instal electric light. As an outcome, twenty-four arc lamps have been erected. Great interest was centered in the inauguration, the proceedings being preceded by a banquet, given by the contractors, at the Imperial Hotel. The company afterwards adjourned to the promenade, where the ceremony of switching on the electric light was performed by Mrs. Herbert Roberts, who was presented by the chairman with a silver key for the purpose, suitably engraved.

**Failsworth.**—The district council have decided to take steps to obtain powers for lighting the district with electricity. At present the district is lighted with gas supplied by the Oldham Corporation.

**Farsley.**—The contract for the construction of a sewerage system at Farsley, and of outfall work at Rodley, for the council, has been let to Mr. William Brigg, Shipley Fields, Frizinghall. The amount of the contract is about £12,000. The scheme will include three trunk sewers—viz., the Old Road, New-street, and the Valley sewers, which will finally unite at Bagley, and thence proceed in one larger main trunk to the outfall works at Rodley. The works are to be completed by the end of September, 1899. A commencement has already been made with the work at Bagley.

**Itchin.**—The district council have decided to apply to the Local Government Board for sanction to a loan to cover the cost of purchasing 250 gas lamps. Mr. S. W. Dunkin, the manager of the Southampton Gas Company, attended the meeting of the committee appointed to consider the matter, and advised as to the mode of lighting to be adopted.

**Longridge.**—An application is to be made to the Local Government Board for sanction to borrow a further sum of £850 for the extension of the main sewer.

**Maidstone.**—The district council have received a communication from the gas company stating that the directors in the course of a few weeks, hope to be in a position to make a definite proposal for lighting the streets with incandescent lamps.

**Tottenham.**—Colonel Durnford recently held an inquiry, on behalf of the Local Government Board, relative to an application of the district council for permission to borrow £1,400 for paving work in Green-lanes and £300 for sewering Fairview-road.

**Wortley.**—A Local Government Board inquiry was held last week respecting an application of the district council for sanction to borrow £4,500 for purposes of sewerage and sewage disposal at Pilley, in the township of Tankersley.

## RURAL DISTRICT COUNCILS.

**Castle Donington.** — On the 17th inst. Colonel W. R. Slacke, R.E., one of the inspectors of the Local Government Board, held an inquiry at Castle Donington into an application by the rural district council for sanction to borrow £6,500 for works of sewerage and sewage disposal. At present there is no system whatever, and the raw sewage finds its way down open dykes and eventually into the Trent. The engineer, Mr. Herbert Walker, of Nottingham, explained the scheme, which consists of a system of gravitating sewers, a pumping station at the outfall works, "Cosham" precipitation tanks, and subsequent land treatment.

**Keynsham.**—A Local Government Board inquiry will shortly be held with reference to an application of the district council for sanction to borrow £450 for water supply works in the parish of Whitchurch.

**Yeovil.**—A letter was read last week from the Local Government Board with reference to an application by the district council to invest them with the powers of sec. 104 of the Public Health Act, 1875, in regard to the proposed new road between Norton and Stoke, and for sanction to borrow £250 for the purpose of carrying out the work. Before deciding the application the board stated that they would direct that a local inquiry should be held at as early a date as possible.

## SCOTLAND AND IRELAND.

**Armagh.**—At a special meeting of the town commissioners, on the 18th inst., the town clerk submitted a copy of the provisional order which has been granted to the town commissioners, acting as the urban sanitary authority, in connection with the new system of sewerage which it is proposed to construct for the city at a cost of £12,000. The provisional order empowers the commissioners to enforce the provisions of the Land Clauses Act to enable them to acquire otherwise than by agreement the lands required for the purpose of the scheme. Three years have been allowed for carrying out the work.

**Arbroath.**—A report having at the instance of the Police Commission been submitted to the board by Mr. M'Culloch, Edinburgh and Dundee, engineer on the Colt Loan extension works, on the position of the water supply, in which Mr. M'Culloch recommended the commissioners to proceed with the present scheme until the first 200 yards adit is finished, and that future action should be determined by the result, the board have now agreed, by a majority of ten to seven, to continue the adit as against an amendment to abandon the work in favour of a gravitation scheme.

**Glasgow.**—The Special Committee on Telephones, appointed by the corporation, meet on Tuesday week, for the first time since the issue of the report of the House of Commons Select Committee. It was decided to renew the application to the Postmaster-General for a telephone license for the municipality and to appoint a deputation to wait on the Duke of Norfolk and Mr. Hanbury at the earliest convenient date to press the application.

## FOREIGN AND COLONIAL.

**St. Helier's.**—The municipality have accepted the tender of the Horsfall Furnace Syndicate, Limited, for a refuse destructor, with accessories complete for steam raising.

# Personal.

Mr. W. J. Petch, surveyor to the Rawmarsh Urban District Council, has had his salary increased.

Greenock Town Council have adopted the report of a committee recommending the appointment of a resident electrical engineer, at a salary of £300 per annum.

Dorchester Town Council have approved the attendance of the borough surveyor, Mr. G. J. Hunt, at the forthcoming meeting of the Sanitary Institute at Birmingham.

It was last week proposed and agreed that the salary of Mr. Richard Whitbread, surveyor to the Urban District Council of Carlton, should be increased by £20 per annum.

After a short discussion, at their last week's meeting, the Wenlock Town Council decided to form a committee to report upon the question of appointing an assistant surveyor.

Bexley Heath Urban District Council have agreed, upon the recommendation of the General Purposes Committee, to appoint Mr. E. R. Boulter as assistant and consultive surveyor.

Ninety-nine applications have been received by the Belper Urban District Council for the post of working engineer to the waterworks department. A committee is at present preparing a selected list of names.

Mr. C. Heslop, son of Mr. Heslop, surveyor to the Auckland Rural District Council, has been appointed surveyor and inspector of nuisances to the Shildon Urban District Council. There were thirty applications for the post.

Mr. Clifton Lund, who is at present surveyor to the Yeadon Urban District Council, has been selected to fill the post of surveyor to the Cleckheaton Urban District Council. His salary will commence at £150 per annum.

At a recent meeting of the Wareham Town Council a resolution was passed regretting the surveyor's determination to resign his office, and resolving to advertise for a successor to fill the vacancy. Mr. G. Hobbs is the present official.

On Tuesday, at a meeting of the Basford Rural District Council, Mr. S. Maylan was appointed inspector of nuisances and surveyor for the whole of the district, at a salary of £300 a year, and Mr. Windows was appointed his assistant, at £80 per annum.

We understand that about three weeks ago the Sudbury Corporation unanimously voted Mr. T. W. A. Hayward, their borough engineer, an honorarium of 10 guineas and also presented him with a bicycle. We now learn that at their last meeting they further decided to increase his salary by £50 per annum.

At the last monthly meeting of the Chesterfield Town Council, Mr. Busbridge, surveyor to the northern portion of the district, submitted his resignation by September 15th. The resignation was accepted, and it was decided to advertise at once and try and meet Mr. Busbridge, though the council, it was remarked, were entitled to three months' notice.

We learn with regret of the death of Mr. Joseph Towers, surveyor to the Urban District Council of Thame, Oxfordshire, which took place, after a rather protracted illness, on Thursday week. Mr. Towers, who was fifty years of age, had held his office since April, 1895. The funeral took place on Saturday afternoon, at the parish churchyard. The council were represented by the chairman, Mr. E. G. Bryer.

Mr. J. E. Stewart, the borough electrical engineer of Derby, having resigned that position, a new engineer at £350 is to be appointed. Mr. Stewart has asked to be relieved of his duties in a few weeks' time, so that he may proceed to his new position, which is stated to be in America. The appointment was subject to three months' notice, but there seems to be a feeling in the council that he should be released if a new man can be appointed, so as to have a week or so with him before he leaves.

A committee of the Cheshire Town Council recently recommended the appointment of Mr. William Holland (at present surveyor of the Wirrall district) to assist the county surveyor generally in the performance of his duties, and in particular in the inspection of the main roads in the municipal boroughs and urban districts, and the work connected with the maintenance, repair and improvement thereof. It was recommended that he should be paid £275 per annum (his present salary), with allowance for travelling expenses. The report was adopted.

The Lewes Corporation's consulting engineer, Mr. F. J. Warden Stevens, has received further instructions in connection with the electric lighting of the borough, the provisional order now having been obtained. Mr. Stevens has also been requested to prepare a scheme of electric tramways for Port Louis, Mauritius. At Queenstown the scheme of electric lighting prepared by Mr. Stevens has been approved by the commissioners, while at Fleet, Hants, where a local company intend to establish works for the supply of electricity, Mr. Stevens has been retained as consulting engineer.

At a meeting of the Lodden and Clavering (Norfolk) Rural District Council, held in the early part of the week, consideration was given to the question of the appointment of a surveyor and inspector of nuisances for the Lodden district. The candidates in attendance were Mr. T. Jelfs, Birmingham; Mr. C. W. Pritchard, Sheffield; and Mr. W. J. Vessoy, South Lowestoft. The testimonials of each candidate were placed before the council, and ultimately Mr. Pritchard was elected by a unanimous vote. Mr. Pritchard thanked the council for the confidence they had placed in him, and agreed to commence his duties that day month.

At a recent meeting of the Weybridge Urban District Council the question of remunerating the surveyor, Mr. John S. Crawshaw, for extra services rendered by him in preparing plans and specifications for private street and other works, was taken into consideration, and it was resolved that a sum of 60 guineas be paid to Mr. Crawshaw for the work he had done up to the present time. A member, in moving the adoption of the report of the committee dealing with the matter, said, in the course of his remarks, that although he did not wish to lavish too much praise on the surveyor, he might say that what Mr. Crawshaw valued more than the money was the knowledge that he possessed the respect and confidence of his employers.

The Edinburgh and District Lunacy Board, after some consideration, recently appointed Mr. Hippolyte J. Blanc, R.S.A., to be architect for the new asylum at Bangour. They also awarded the following premiums: First premium (£250) to Messrs. M'Arthy & Watson, Edinburgh; second premium (£200), Mr. William Eaglesham, Ayr; third premium (£150), Messrs. Thomson & Sandilands, Glasgow; fourth premium (£100), Messrs. M'Gibbon & Ross, Edinburgh. Under the conditions and instructions to architects it was provided that whatever architect was placed first by the assessor should receive the appointment, and that among the other competitors there should be distributed in addition four money awards in the order of merit.

The report of a special committee appointed to consider the question of the salaries of the surveyors of highways to the Chesterfield Rural District Council was presented at the last monthly meeting of the latter body. It had been unanimously resolved by the committee to recommend the council to raise the salary of Mr. Robinson, the southern surveyor, from £150 to £160 per annum, and to give him a rise of £5 a year up to a maximum of £170. Mr. Busbridge, the northern surveyor, having resigned, it had been decided to recommend that his successor should be offered £160 to start with. The council, however, eventually adopted an amendment that the surveyors, instead of working up to £170, should have their salaries raised to £200 per annum at yearly increases of £10.

A number of gentlemen, including several members of the town council, the town clerk, borough treasurer and electrical engineer, assembled on Tuesday at the Newport (Mon.) Town Hall, for the purpose of saying good-bye to Mr. A. Harrison, the assistant borough engineer, and presenting him with a handsome silver tea and coffee service, subscribed for by his brother officials, fifty in number. The presentation was duly made by the deputy mayor, while two other gentlemen each added a few phrases expressing their personal liking for the recipient and an earnest hope for his future welfare. Mr. Harrison, much touched at the evidence of cordiality and appreciation, briefly and simply thanked the contributories and the members of the corporation. Mr. Harrison leaves Uskside in a few days to take up his new duties.

## A STEAM-PRESSURE REDUCING VALVE.

The "Foster" steam-pressure reducing valve has been introduced as an improvement for reducing and regulating steam pressures. If a demand for more steam be made upon it, the valve, we are told, instantly opens wider and supplies that demand, but maintains a uniform reduced pressure. It is added that it can also open full bore, if necessary, and yet prevent the reduced pressure rising above that at which the valve is adjusted. The following are represented as its chief features: (1) A compensating spring movement, exerting a uniform power on diaphragms, without regard to the opening of the valve; (2) unvarying tightness; (3) absence of friction; (4) absence of noise; (5) a patent balanced valve which ensures steam-tight seats regardless of pressure or temperature; (6) parts all metallic, without rubber, &c.; and (7) absence of pistons, stuffing boxes and drip. The makers are Messrs. W. H. Bailey & Co., Limited, Albion Works, Salford, who claim that the valve can be fixed anywhere either on sea or land.

Cnosall.—The district council at their next meeting will consider the question of widening the road near the Anchor Inn.

## ASSOCIATION OF MUNICIPAL AND COUNTY ENGINEERS.

### VOLUNTARY PASS EXAMINATION.

Notice is hereby given that the twenty-sixth examination for candidates for the offices of engineer and surveyor to municipal corporations and district councils will be held at the Technical School, Princess-street, Manchester, on Friday and Saturday, September 30 and October 1, 1898. Application forms, duly filled in by intending candidates, together with entrance fee of £2 2s., must be in the hands of the secretary on or before the 5th September.

MIDLAND DISTRICT MEETING AT BILSTON.

A meeting of the members of the midland district will be held on Saturday, September 17th, at Bilston. The following are the arrangements :—

11 a.m.— The members will be received in the council chamber, Town Hall, by the chairman (Councillor R. A. Harper, J.P.) and other members of the council. Minutes of Stafford and Rhyader meetings. Election of hon. district secretary.

11.30 a.m.—Leave in brakes, kindly provided by Councillor J. W. Sankey, chairman of the Water and Baths Committee, for a visit to the Spring Vale furnaces, arriving about 11.40 a.m., where, by the kind permission of Sir Alfred Hickman, the process of steel manufacture will be witnessed. A short descriptive paper will be given.

12.30 p.m.—Leave in brakes for a visit to the waterworks covered service reservoir (which will be specially emptied for the inspection of the members), arriving about 12.45.

1.15 p.m.—Leave in brakes for the Hinley Arms Hotel, arriving about 2 p.m., where a light luncheon will be provided by Councillor R. A. Harper, J.P., chairman of the council.

3 p.m.—Leave in brakes for a visit to the Bilston waterworks pumping station, arriving about 3.30 p.m.

4.15 p.m.—Leave in brakes for the Technical School, Bilston, arriving about 5 p.m.

6 p.m.—Dinner at the Technical School. Tickets, 3s. 6d. each (exclusive of wine).

Arrangements will be made for any members desirous of doing so to inspect the public baths and the public market. Mr. C. L. N. Wilson, the water engineer and surveyor to the Bilston Council, will give a descriptive paper of the works. As the paper will be in the hands of members intimating their intention to attend some days before the meeting, it will be taken as read.

Among the hotels at Bilston may be mentioned the Pipe Hall, Globe and Great Western.

Wolverhampton is within 2½ miles and Birmingham 10½ miles, and there is a good service of trains from these towns. The Great Western station at Bilston is the nearest to the Town Hall.

| | |
|---|---|
| J. S. PICKERING, A.M.I.C.E., | THOS. COLE, A.M.I.C.E., |
| Hon. District Secretary, | Secretary, |
| Council Offices, Nuneaton. | 11 Victoria-street, S.W |

## APPOINTMENTS VACANT.

*Advertisements which are received too late for classification cannot be included in these summaries until the following week.*

DRAUGHTSMAN.— August 26th.— Corporation of Bacup. 30s.—Mr. Francis Wood, borough engineer.

CLERK OF WORKS.—August 27th.—Vestry of St. Matthew, Bethnal Green. £4 4s.—Mr. F. W. Barratt, surveyor.

ELECTRICAL ENGINEER.—August 27th.—Corporation of Ashton-under-Lyne. £250.—Chairman, Electricity Committee.

DISTRICT SURVEYOR.— August 29th.— Cheshire County Council. £200.—Mr. Reginald Potts, clerk.

SENIOR ASSISTANT.—August 30th.—West Hartlepool Corporation. £78.—Mr. J. W. Brown, borough engineer.

ELECTRICAL ENGINEER AND MANAGER.—August 31st.— Corporation of Derby. £350.—Mr. H. F. Gadsby, town clerk.

SURVEYOR OF HIGHWAYS.— August 31st. — Chesterfield Rural District Council. £160.—Mr. George Shaw, clerk.

DISTRICT SURVEYORS (Two).—August 31st.—Lancashire County Council. £200.—Mr. Fred. C. Hulton, county clerk, County Offices, Preston.

ELECTRICAL ENGINEER.—August 31st.—Greenock Board of Police. £300.—Mr. Collin MacCullock, town clerk.

DISTRICT MAIN ROAD SURVEYOR.—August 31st.—Hertfordshire County Council.—Mr. Urban A. Smith, county surveyor, 41 Parliament-street. London, S.W.

BUILDING INSPECTOR.—September 2nd.—Southend-on-Sea Corporation. £125.—Mr. William H. Snow, clerk.

CLERK FOR SURVEYOR'S DEPARTMENT.—September 3rd.— Staines Rural District Council. £52.—Mr. G. W. Manning, surveyor to the council.

ASSISTANT SANITARY INSPECTOR.—September 3rd.—Blaby Rural District Council. £1 10s.—Mr. B. A. Shires, clerk to the council, Alliance Chambers, Municipal-square, Leicester.

SUPERINTENDENT OF SEWERS AND DRAINS.—September 5th. Vestry of St. Marylebone. £150.—Mr. W. H. Garbutt, clerk.

SUPERINTENDENT OF CLEANSING.—September 5th.—Vestry of St. Marylebone. £180.—Mr. W. H. Garbutt, clerk.

DISTRICT SUPERINTENDENT.—September 5th.—Vestry of St. Marylebone. £150.—Mr. W. H. Garbutt, clerk.

INSPECTOR OF NUISANCES AND SURVEYOR.—September 6th.— Little Woolton Urban District Council. £110.—Mr. Percy Dobell, clerk to the council.

CLERK OF WORKS.—September 6th.—Aldershot Urban District Council.—Mr. Nelson F. Dennis, surveyor.

SURVEYOR AND INSPECTOR OF NUISANCES.—September 6th. —Chertsey Urban District Council. £160.—Mr. T. E. Harland Chaldecott, clerk to the council.

BOROUGH SURVEYOR AND SANITARY INSPECTOR.—September 17th.—Borough of Oswestry. £200.—Mr. J. Parry Jones, town clerk.

DISTRICT SUPERINTENDENTS (TWO OR THREE). — The British Electric Traction Company. £300 to £350.—Mr. G. Stevens, secretary to the company.

CLERK OF WORKS.—Metropolitan Asylums Board. £3 3s. —Offices, Norfolk House, Norfolk-street, Strand, W.C.

## COMPETITIONS.

*Advertisements which are received too late for classification cannot be included in these summaries until the following week.*

WITHERNSEA.—September 29th.—Works of drainage and water supply, for the urban district council.—Mr. C. W. Denton, clerk.

REIGATE.—October 6th.—Erection of municipal buildings, fire station, public offices, &c.—Mr. Clair J. Grece, town clerk.

GUERNSEY.—December 23rd.—Sewerage and sewage disposal scheme for the No. 1 and 2 wards of the district. £50, £30 and £20.—Mr. T. E. Harland Chaldecott, clerk to the council.

## MUNICIPAL CONTRACTS OPEN.

*Advertisements which are received too late for classification cannot be included in these summaries until the following week.*

HAWORTH.—August 26th.—Conversion of stone gasholder into a tar and liquor tank, for the urban district council.—Mr. W. Robertshaw, clerk.

MORLEY.—August 26th.—Construction of brick culverts, together with manholes, storm-water overflow and other works.—Mr. W. E. Putman, borough engineer and surveyor.

MALDENS AND COOMBE.—August 26th.—Erection of proposed public buildings at New Malden, for the urban district council.—Mr. Thomas V. Herbert Davison, architect, New Malden.

MORLEY.—August 26th.—Manufacture, delivery and erection of a steel girder bridge, to carry cast-iron pipes.—Mr. W. E. Putman, borough engineer and surveyor.

HALIFAX.—August 27th.—Supply and erection of retort-house fittings. —Mr. Thomas Holgate, gas engineer.

BLACKPOOL.—August 27th.—Erection of three-lift gasholder.—Mr. John Chew, engineer and manager.

NELSON.—August 27th.—Supply of 550 lineal yards of wrought-iron unclimbable fencing.—Mr. B. Ball, borough engineer.

CLEATON MOOR.—August 29th.—Providing and laying 3,000 superficial yards of asphalte at the Market-place, for the urban district council.— Mr. R. Robertson, surveyor.

EAST HAM.—August 29th.—Supply of about 6,000 ft. run 12-in. by 6-in. and about 10,000 ft. of 12-in. by 6-in. granite curb, for the urban district council.—Mr. C. E. Wilson, clerk.

EAST HAM.—August 29th.—Supply of about 1,000 yards of best blue Guernsey and about 1,000 yards of other kinds of broken granite, for the urban district council.—Mr. C. E. Wilson, clerk.

EAST HAM.—August 29th.—Supply of 10-ton steam roller and a scarifier, for the urban district council.—Mr. C. E. Wilson, clerk.

WIMBLEDON.—August 29th.—Supply of pipework, for the urban district council.—Mr. A. H. Preece, 39 Victoria-street, S.W.

SHEFFIELD.—August 29th.—Construction and erection of additional buildings in connection with the destructor at Attercliffe.—Mr. Charles F. Wike, city surveyor.

SOUTHPORT.—August 29th.—Erection of convenience at Northcorner quay.—Mr. John F. Burns, borough surveyor.

BARNET.—August 30th.—Construction of new sewers, for the urban district council.—Mr. H. W. Mansbridge, surveyor.

FARNHAM.—August 30th.—Supply of forage for twelve months from September 19th, for the urban district council.—Mr. L. W. Case, surveyor to the council.

WALSALL.—August 31st.—Painting and other works at the Science and Art Institute, Bradford-place.—The Borough Surveyor.

BIRKENHEAD.—August 31st.—Flagging, paving, channelling and sewering of various passages in the borough.—Mr. Charles Brownridge, A.M.I.C.E., borough engineer and surveyor.

SELBY.—August 31st.—Laying-out, levelling, draining, &c., about 2 acres of land as a public park, for the urban district council.—Mr. Bruce Mc. G. Gray, A.M.I.C.E., town surveyor.

BELFAST.—August 31st.—Supply of 370 lengths of cast-iron pipes of 12 in. diameter.—Sir Samuel Black, town clerk.

WATFORD.—August 31st.—Supply and delivery of electricity meters and main cut-outs, for the urban district council.—Mr. H. Morten Turner, clerk.

KING'S LYNN.—August 31st.—Construction of sewers in the south drainage district of the borough.—Mr. E. J. Silcock, borough engineer.

WALLASEY.—August 31st.—Supply of wrought-iron railings and gates, for the urban district council.—Mr. H. W. Cook, surveyor.

BURTON-UPON-TRENT.—August 31st.—Supply, construction and erection of foundations, arches, fire-brick work and furnace brickwork for retorts.—Mr. F. L. Ramsden, manager and engineer.

Salford.—September 1st.—Painting of the town hall at Broughton.—Mr. Samuel Brown, town clerk.

Romford.—September 1st.—Construction of a cottage, stable, stall and cart shed at the town yard, Market-place, for the urban district council.—Mr. George Bailey, clerk to the council.

Cirencester.—September 1st.—Construction of a system of surface-water drainage, for the urban district council.—Mr. Thomas Hibbert, surveyor.

West Ham.—September 2nd.—Erection of museum at Stratford.—Mr. Fred. E. Hilleary, town clerk.

Wells.—September 3rd.—Erection of public hall and post office buildings.—Mr. R. L. Foster, town clerk.

Tenbury.—September 3rd.—Building of a retaining wall, about 200 ft. long by 12 ft. high, at the side of Kyre brook, for the rural district council.—Mr. R. W. Jarvis, surveyor to the council.

Tonbridge.—September 3rd.—Erection of a proposed new technical institute and free library, for the urban district council.—Mr. A. H. Neve, junr., clerk to the council.

Lewisham.—September 3rd.—Formation of a new exit, &c., at the public baths at Ladywell, for the vestry.—Mr. Edward H. Oxenham, clerk to the vestry.

Norwich.—September 3rd.—Making-up of Mousehold-street, Cavalry-street, Anchor-street, Wadehouse-street and Tracey-road.—Mr. Arthur E. Collins, A.M.I.C.E., city engineer.

Derby.—September 5th.—Construction of a covered service reservoir at Littleover.—Mr. H. F. Gadsby, town clerk.

Devonport.—September 5th.—Construction of drainage culvert.—Mr. John F. Burns, borough surveyor.

Buxton.—September 5th.—Supply and erection of electric lighting plant, for the urban district council.—Clerk.

Sheffield.—September 5th.— Extension of car-shed.—Mr. Henry Sayer, town clerk.

Rochdale.—September 6th.—Electric lighting plant.—Mr. James Leach, town clerk.

Aldershot.—September 6th.—Supply of 2,000 tons of granite (more or less), for the urban district council.—Mr. W. E. Foster, clerk.

Aldershot.—September 6th.—Supply and delivery of a Morrison's scarifier, for the urban district council.—Mr. W. E. Foster, clerk.

Hull.—September 6th.—Supply of four steel Lancashire boilers, 30 ft. by 8 ft., with mechanical stokers.—Mr. A. E. White, city engineer.

Diss.—September 6th.—Supply of about 250 tons of Belgian granite, for the urban district council.—Mr. Henry O. Lyus, clerk to the council.

Weybridge.—September 7th.—Supply of stoneware pipes, gullies, Bristol blue pennant kerbing, prepared limestone or granite for tar paving, Thames ballast, Portland cement, and gas tar, for the urban district council.—Mr. John S. Crawshaw, surveyor to the council.

Grays.—September 7th.—Supply of 1,000 tons of granite and quartzite, for the urban district council.—Mr. Arthur C. James, surveyor to the council.

Derby.—September 7th.—Erection of a boundary wall at the Nottingham-road cemetery extension.—Mr. John Ward, borough surveyor.

King's Lynn.—September 7th.—Supply of electric lighting plant, &c.—Mr. T. G. Archer, town clerk.

Aldershot.—September 7th.—Metalling Albert-street, West End, for the urban district council.—Mr. W. E. Foster, clerk.

Edinburgh.—September 7th.—Work in connection with Portobello public baths.—Mr. R. Morham, city superintendent of works.

Weybridge.—September 7th.—Supply and delivery of various materials, for the urban district council.—Mr. G. Wheeler, clerk.

Southend-on-Sea.—September 8th.—Making-up of roads.—Mr. William H. Snow, town clerk.

Lancashire.—September 10th.—Repair of Read old bridge crossing the Sabden brook in the townships of Whalley and Read, for the county council.—Mr. W. Harold Radford, county bridge-master, 19 Brazenose-street, Manchester.

Wimbledon.—September 10th.—Supply of forage for the six months ending March 31, 1899, for the urban district council.—Mr. W. H. Whitfield, clerk to the council.

Bury St. Edmunds.—September 10th.—Erection of buildings, chimney shaft, &c., for the electric light station.—Mr. J. Campbell Smith, borough surveyor.

Ramsgate.—September 10th.—Erection of buildings to be used as offices for the gas and water department.—Mr. W. A. Hubbard, town clerk.

Bangor.—September 10th.—Supply and erection of electric lighting plant.—Mr. R. Hughes Pritchard, town clerk.

Birmingham.—September 13th.—Construction of aqueduct.—Mr. E. O. Smith, town clerk.

Hastings.—September 13th.—Supply of about 1,797 tons of 16-in., 169 tons of 10-in. and 84 tons of 6-in. cast-iron water pipes and about 35 tons of irregulars.—Mr. R. H. Palmer, M.I.C.E., borough engineer.

Dover.—September 13th.—Erection of a workshop, &c., adjoining the car sheds at Maxton.—Mr. Henry E. Stilgoe, A.M.I.C.E., borough engineer.

Weston-super-Mare.—September 13th.—Alterations and additions to the Knightstone baths, for the urban district council.—Mr. Sydney C. Smith, clerk to the council.

St. Luke.—September 14th.—Construction of an underground sanitary convenience in Old-street, for the vestry.—The Surveyor to the Vestry.

St. Luke.—September 14th.—Paving of Golden-lane and part of Banner-street with jarrah wood and part of Peartree-street with granite, for the vestry.—The Surveyor to the Vestry.

Epping.—September 14th.—Erection of a new ward at the isolation hospital at Theydon Garnon, for the rural district council.—Mr. R. D. Trotter, clerk to the council.

Nottingham.—September 17th.—Construction of new sewer.—Mr. Arthur Brown, city engineer.

Edinburgh.—October 17th.—For various works in connection with gasholder tank at Granton.—Mr. James M'G. Jack, clerk to the commissioners.

Hornsey.—September 19th.—Sewering, levelling, paving, metalling, channelling and making good certain roads, for the urban district council.—Mr. F. D. Askey, clerk.

Swanage.—September 19th.—Completion of the main sewerage of the district, for the urban district council.—Messrs. Francis Newman & Cocks, 5 St. Thomas-street, Ryde.

Lytham.—September 19th.—Construction of about 900 yards of 3-ft. diameter brick sewer, about 1,500 yards of 24-in. and 18-in. pipe sewer, and concrete and storage tanks, together with sea embankment, roadway and other contingent works, for the urban district council.—Messrs. Newton, 17 Cooper-street, Manchester.

Witney.—September 26th.—Main drainage of Eynsham, for the rural district council.—Mr. Nicholas Lailey, A.M.I.C.E., 16 Great George-street, London, S.W.

Hull.—September 30th.—Supply of forty-five electric motor cars, twenty trail cars, two sprinkler cars and two traversing platforms.—Mr. A. E. White, city engineer.

# TENDERS.

*Accepted.

BRIGHTON.—For the supply of 5,000 ft. of 6-in. granite edge kerb, 250 tons of granite pitchers and 5,000 tons of granite spalls.—Mr. Francis J. C. May, M.I.C.E., borough engineer and surveyor:—

| | Description of granite. | Curb at per foot run. s. d. | Pitchers at per ton. £ s. d. | Spalls at per ton. s. d. |
|---|---|---|---|---|
| Blichfeldt & Co., 16 Water-lane, Great Tower-street, E.C. ... | Norwegian | 1 11 | 1 19 0 | — |
| Cherbourg Quartzite Company, 24 Mark-lane, E.C. ... ... | Cherbourg | — | — | 10 0 |
| J. Goodchild & Co., 118 Fenchurch-street, E.C. ... ... | Norway | 1 5½ | 1 11 6 | — |
| W. Griffiths, 35 Hamilton House, Bishopsgate-street, E.C. ... | Guernsey | 1 6 | 1 17 0 | 10 10 |
| A. Hill, Marple Bridge *vid* Stockport ... ... ... ... | Norwegian | 1 9 | 1 19 0 | 11 0 |
| W. Hudson, Terminus Gates, Brighton ... ... ... | Norwegian | 1 10½ | 1 17 9 | — |
| Kent Road Maintenance Co., The Crescent, Gravesend ... | Cherbourg | — | 1 12 6 | 9 8 |
| London Basalt Stone Company, Victoria Wharves, Cardiff... | Basalt | — | — | 12 6 |
| A. & F. Manuelle, 57 Gracechurch-street, E.C. ... ... | Guernsey | 1 4½ | 1 15 3 | 10 3 |
| A. & F. Manuelle, 57 Gracechurch-street, E.C. ... ... | Norway | 1 4 | 1 10 0 | — |
| J. Mowlem & Co., Grosvenor Wharf, S.W. ... ... ... | Guernsey | 1 6 | 1 16 6 | 10 8 |
| A. Robinson, Annalong, co. Down ... ... ... ... | Irish | 0 11 | — | — |
| J. Runnalls, The Penlee Elvan Quarries, Penzance ... ... | Penlee, Penolva | — | — | 9 6 |
| L. Sommerfeld, 2 Fowkes Buildings, Great Tower-street, E.C. | Scotch Whinstone | — | — | 10 0 |
| E. J. Van Praagh & Co., 6 East India-avenue, E.C. ... ... | Norwegian | 1 8½ | 1 19 0 | — |

The tender of A. & F. Manuelle accepted for 180 tons of ordinary dressed Guernsey granite pitchers at £1 9s. 6d. per ton, 70 tons best dressed ditto at £1 15s. 3d. per ton, 5,000 ft. run of Guernsey granite edge curb at 1s. 4½d per foot and 4,000 tons of Guernsey granite spalls at 10s. 3d. per ton. The tender of the Kent Road Maintenance Company accepted for 1,000 tons Cherbourg quartzite spalls at 9s. 8d. per ton and for 100 tons of French quartzite pitchers at £1 12s. 6d. per ton.

CHARTHAM.—For carrying out drainage and other works for the Lunacy Commissioners, of Chartham Asylum, Kent.—Mr. W. J. Jennings, architect, Canterbury:—

| | |
|---|---|
| Martin, Ramsgate ... ... ... ... ... ... ... | £22,180 |
| Paramor & Sons, Margate ... ... ... ... ... ... | 21,500 |
| Pryor & Sons, Maidstone ... ... ... ... ... ... | 21,000 |
| Keeler, Dover ... ... ... ... ... ... ... ... | 19,434 |
| Hill, Maidenhead ... ... ... ... ... ... ... ... | 19,056 |
| Wise, Deal ... ... ... ... ... ... ... ... ... | 18,392 |
| Saunders & Co., Southampton* ... ... ... ... ... | 17,300 |

CHELTENHAM.—For the supply of 150 tons of iron water pipes and general road and sewer castings.—Mr. E. T. Brydges, town clerk:—

| | Per Ton. Straight. £ s. d. | Special £ s. d. |
|---|---|---|
| R. D. Wood & Co., Philadelphia, U.S.A. (3 in.) ... | 5 12 6 | 9 5 0 (ordinary) |
| R. D. Wood & Co., Philadelphia, U.S.A. (4 in.) ... | 5 7 6 | — |
| R. D. Wood & Co., Philadelphia, U.S.A. (6 in.) ... | 5 3 6 | 14 5 0 (flanged) |
| McNeal Pipe Foundry Co., Philadelphia, U.S.A. | 5 8 0 | — |
| R. McLaren & Co., Eglington Foundry, Glasgow | 6 12 6 | 12 0 0 |
| T. Spittle, Limited, Newport, Mon. ... ... ... | 5 14 0 | 9 10 0 (1s. extra at Tewkesbury) |
| Stanton Ironworks Company, Stanton-by-Dale, near Nottingham (3 in.) ... ... ... ... | 6 7 6 | — |
| Stanton Ironworks Company, Stanton-by-Dale, near Nottingham (4 in.)* ... ... ... ... | 5 10 0 | 9 10 0 |
| Stanton Ironworks Company, Stanton-by-Dale, near Nottingham (6 in.) ... ... ... ... | 5 12 6 | — (1s. 8d. extra at Tewkesbury.) |

Castings.

| | Gully Grates and Frames. | Gully Grates only. | Manhole Covers and Frames. | Manhole Covers only. |
|---|---|---|---|---|
| | each s. d. | each s. d. | each s. d. | each s. d. |
| Hardy & Padmore, Ltd., Worcester | 7 9 | 2 10 | 42 3 | 15 0 |
| Tingle Brothers, Cinderford ... ... | 7 6 | 2 9 | 39 6 | — |
| | per cwt. | per cwt. | per cwt. | per cwt. |
| Teague, Chew & Fleming, Cinderford | 9 6 | 9 6 | 9 6 | 9 6 |
| | each | each | each | each |
| E. White, Redditch ... ... ... | 8 0 | 3 0 | 42 6 | — |
| A. & W. Longsdon, Poole ... ... | 7 0 | 2 6 | 35 0 | 35 0 |
| J. Needham, Stockport* ... ... | 6 0 | 2 9 | 33 9 | 33 9 |
| Meats & Co., Limited, Cheltenham | 8 0 | 4 3 | 38 6 | 6 9 per cwt. |

| | Manhole Buckets, galvanised sheet iron. each s. d. | Hydrant Covers. each s. d. | Stop Tap Boxes. each s. d. | Street Name Plates. per letter d. |
|---|---|---|---|---|
| Hardy & Padmore, Ltd., Worcester | 14 0 | 6 9 | 2 3 | 3½ |
| Tingle Brothers, Cinderford... ... | — | 5 6 | 1 9 | 6 |
| Teague, Chew & Fleming, Cinderford | — | 4 6 | 1 9 | 4 |
| E. White, Redditch ... ... ... | 45 0 | 4 3 | 1 3 | 3 |
| A. & W. Longsdon, Poole ... ... | 7 0 | 4 6 | 1 6 | 3 |
| J. Needham, Stockport* ... ... | 7 0 | 4 3 | 1 3 | 3 |
| Meats & Co., Ltd., Cheltenham ... | 23 6 | 4 6 | 1 7 | 7 |

CHELTENHAM.—For the supply of stoneware pipes and cement for twelve months.—Mr. E. T. Brydges, town clerk:—

Stoneware Pipes.

G. Skey & Co., Limited, Tamworth, 25 per cent. discount of Midland list.
H. Tugby & Co., Moira, near Ashby-de-la-Zouch, 22½ per cent. discount of Midland list.
Midland Stoneware Pipe Co., Limited, Polesworth, 33⅓ per cent. discount of Midland list.
Doulton & Co., Lambeth, 15 and 7½ per cent. discount of Midland list.
H. R. Mansfield, Church Gresley, 20 per cent. discount of Midland list.
Gibbs & Canning, Limited, Tamworth, 27½ per cent. discount of Midland list.

**Glasgow.**—It is stated that the Statute Labour Committee have received a letter from Messrs. M'Clure, Naismith & Brodie, solicitors, on behalf of Messrs. Stewart & M'Donald, refusing the corporation's offer of £5,000 for ground for the proposed improvement of the corner of Buchanan-street and Argyle-street on the west side, the reason assigned being that the price was totally inadequate. The ground required consists of 70 yards, and Messrs. Stewart & M'Donald wanted £130 per yard.—A sub-committee of the Statute Labour Committee, appointed to consider complaints by shopkeepers occupying premises under and near to the Caledonian railway bridge crossing Argyle-street as to the annoyance and inconvenience caused by the noise of the traffic passing under the bridge, recommended that the portion of Argyle-street under the railway bridge and for 15 ft. on either side thereof be paved with wood, and that the material to be used be Jarrahdale—the probable cost to the Tramways Department being £233 and to the Statute Labour Department £260. The sub-committee further agreed to recommend that the remaining portion of said street east of the bridge to Jamaciastreet, a length of 92 ft., be restored with granite. The minute was adopted.

## NOTICES.

The Surveyor and Municipal and County Engineer *may be ordered direct, through any of Messrs. Smith & Son's book-stalls, or of any newsagent in the United Kingdom. Applications to the Offices for single copies by post must in all cases be accompanied by stamps.*
*The Prepaid Subscription (including postage) is as follows :*

|  | Twelve Months. | Six Months. | Three Months. |
|---|---|---|---|
| United Kingdom ... ... | 15s. | 7s. 6d. | 3s. 9d. |
| Continent, the Colonies, India, | | | |
| United States, &c. ... ... | 19s. | 9s. 6d. | 4s. 9d. |

*The International News Company, 83 and 85 Duane-street New York City; The Toronto News Company, Toronto; and The Montreal News Company, Montreal, have been appointed agents in the United States and Canada for the sale of* The Surveyor. *A thin paper edition is printed for circulation abroad.*

EDITORIAL OFFICES :
ST. BRIDE'S HOUSE, 24 BRIDE-LANE, FLEET-STREET, LONDON, E.C.

OFFICE FOR ADVERTISEMENTS :
13 NEW STREET HILL, FLEET STREET, LONDON, E.C.

PUBLISHING OFFICES :
13 NEW STREET HILL, FLEET STREET, LONDON, E.C.

## APPOINTMENTS OPEN.

### HERTFORDSHIRE COUNTY COUNCIL.
DISTRICT MAIN ROAD SURVEYORS.
Applications are invited for District Main Road Surveyorships in the county of Hertford. The persons appointed will act under the instructions of the County Surveyor, and will have charge of a district comprising about 120 miles of rural main roads. Applicants must be cyclists and not more than thirty-five years of age. Particulars of duties and terms of appointment, &c., may be obtained on applying by letter to the undersigned.
Applications to be sent in not later than Wednesday, the 31st inst.
URBAN A. SMITH, c.e.,
County Surveyor of Highways.
41 Parliament-street, Westminster, S.W.
August 22, 1898.

### BOROUGH OF WEST HARTLEPOOL.
JUNIOR ASSISTANT.
Wanted, in the Borough Engineer's Department, a Junior Assistant, who has been thoroughly trained in the duties of a borough engineer's office. He must be a good draughtsman and surveyor, and have architectural ability. Salary, £78 per year.
Applications, stating age, present employment, and accompanied by copies of three recent testimonials, and addressed to the "Chairman of the Works Committee," endorsed "Junior Assistant," are to be delivered at this office on or before 4 p.m. on the 30th inst.
(By order)
J. W. BROWN,
Borough Engineer.
Borough Engineer's Office, West Hartlepool.
August 11, 1898.

### BOROUGH OF SOUTHEND-ON-SEA.
BUILDINGS INSPECTOR.
The Corporation invite applications for the appointment of a Buildings Inspector, at a salary of £135 per annum.
The person appointed will be required to supervise the erection of new buildings, and to see that the by-laws in force within the borough with respect to new streets and buildings are complied with, and it is essential that he should be practically acquainted with building construction and have a thorough knowledge of the Model By-Laws of the Local Government Board, under the Public Health Act, 1875.

Applications to be made in writing, accompanied by copies of not more than three recent testimonials (which will not be returned), stating age, qualifications, experience and where at present engaged, to be delivered at my office before 10 o'clock a.m. on Friday, the 2nd September.
Canvassing members of the Town Council will be a disqualification.
(By order)
WILLIAM H. SNOW,
Town Clerk.
Southend-on-Sea.
August 16, 1898.

### VESTRY OF ST. MARYLEBONE.
APPOINTMENT OF SUPERINTENDENT OF CLEANSING.
Notice is hereby given that the Surveyor to the Vestry is authorised to engage the services of a person competent to discharge the duties of superintending the street cleansing, washing, watering, snow removal, &c., of the parish of St. Marylebone. A horse and trap will be available for use by the person engaged, in order that he may be enabled to efficiently discharge the duties of the office. When such duties have been performed for a period of twelve months in a manner satisfactory to the Surveyor the person engaged will be submitted to the Vestry for appointment. He will be required to reside in the parish and to devote the whole of his time to the duties of the office.
The salary will be at the rate of £180 per annum, rising by annual increments of £10 to £230, the grant of such annual increments to be dependent upon the efficient and satisfactory discharge of the duties of the office, and the appointment will be made upon the understanding that no pension or retiring allowance will attach thereto.
Applications, in candidate's own handwriting, stating age (which must not be less than thirty nor more than forty-five years), with copies of three testimonials (only) of recent date, to be forwarded to J. Paget Waddington, c.e., Surveyor to the Vestry, at the Court House, Marylebone-lane, W., endorsed "Application for Cleansing Superintendentship," or or before Monday, September 5th proximo.
(By order)
W. H. GARBUTT,
Vestry Clerk.
August, 1898.

### VESTRY OF ST. MARYLEBONE.
APPOINTMENT OF DISTRICT SUPERINTENDENTS.
Notice is hereby given that the Surveyor to the Vestry is authorised to engage the services of three persons (one for each of the three districts into which the parish is divided) competent to superintend the execution of all macadam, flint and paved carriageway and footway works, and to undertake the supervision of all hoardings, public lamps, &c., within the district to which each may be appointed. When the duties of the office have been performed for a period of twelve months in a manner satisfactory to the Surveyor each person engaged will be submitted to the Vestry for appointment. He will be required to reside in the parish and to devote the whole of his time to the duties of the office.
The salary will be at the rate of £150 per annum, rising by annual increments of £10 to £200, the grant of such annual increments to be dependent upon the efficient and satisfactory discharge of the duties of the office, and the appointment will be made upon the understanding that no pension or retiring allowances will attach thereto.
Applications, in candidate's own handwriting, stating age (which must not be less than thirty nor more than forty-five years), with copies of three testimonials (only) of recent date, to be forwarded to J. Paget Waddington, c.e., Surveyor to the Vestry, at the Court House, Marylebone-lane, W., endorsed "Application for District Superintendentship," on or before Monday, September 5th proximo.
(By order)
W. H. GARBUTT,
Vestry Clerk.
August, 1898.

### VESTRY OF ST. MARYLEBONE.
APPOINTMENT OF SUPERINTENDENT OF SEWERS AND DRAINS.
Notice is hereby given that the Surveyor to the Vestry is authorised to engage the services of a person competent to superintend the construction, maintenance and cleansing of all public sewers and urinals, and the construction of drains, so far as laid by the Vestry, within the parish of St. Marylebone. When the duties of the office have been performed for a period of twelve months in a manner satisfactory to the Surveyor the person engaged will be submitted to the Vestry for appointment. He will be required to reside in the parish and to devote the whole of his time to the duties of the office.
The salary will be at the rate of £150 per annum, rising by annual increments of £10 to £200, the grant of such annual increments to be dependent upon the efficient and satisfactory discharge of the duties of the office, and the appointment will be made upon the understanding that no pension or retiring allowance will attach thereto.
Applications, in candidate's own handwriting, stating age

(which, must not be less than thirty nor more than forty-five years), with copies of three testimonials (only) of recent date, to be forwarded to J. Paget Waddington, C.E., Surveyor to the Vestry, at the Court House, Marylebone-lane, W., endorsed "Application for Superintendentship of Sewers and Drains," on or before Monday, September 5th proximo.

(By order)
W. H. GARBUTT,
Vestry Clerk.

August, 1898.

## TO LOCAL GOVERNMENT OFFICIALS.

The British Electrical Traction Company, Limited, is prepared to appoint two or three additional District Superintendents. The essential qualifications are a knowledge of the district in which the candidates reside and ability to negotiate with local authorities. Some knowledge of tramway work is desirable but not absolutely necessary. Salary, £300 to £350 per annum, according to qualifications and position.

Applications (which will be treated confidentially) to be made in writing on foolscap paper, enclosed in an envelope endorsed "District Superintendent," and stating age, full particulars of past experience and the districts in which the applicants have influence, to be sent to the undersigned.

GEO. STEVENS,
Secretary.

Donington House, Norfolk-street,
Strand, W.C.

## RURAL DISTRICT COUNCIL OF CHESTERFIELD.

This Council is prepared to receive applications for the office of a Surveyor of Highways for the northern district of their jurisdiction, the area of which is 32,921 acres, with a population in 1891 of about 36,589 people and about 126 miles of highways.

The salary to be paid will be after the rate of £160 per annum, rising £10 per annum until the sum of £200 is reached, which sum will include everything (stationery and postages excepted).

The person appointed must be competent to take levels, prepare plans, estimates and bills of quantities of any works required to be done, and must personally see to the carrying out of the same. He must also be competent to keep all books and accounts required under the Acts, obey all orders of the Council and other road authorities, and devote his whole time to the duties of his office.

The person appointed will be required to reside at Eckington or Staveley.

Security in the sum of £200, with an approved guarantee society, for the due performance of the duties will be required, and the appointment will be terminable by three calendar months' notice on either side.

Applications, stating age (which must not exceed forty-five)

and previous occupation, accompanied by three testimonials of recent date, to be sent to me on or before the 31st instant.

Canvassing is strictly prohibited. Only third-class railway fare (return) will be allowed to selected candidates. No allowance for hotel or other expenses.

(By order)
GEORGE SHAW,
Clerk.

Union Offices, Chesterfield.
August 17, 1898.

## BOROUGH OF OSWESTRY.
### APPOINTMENT OF SURVEYOR AND SANITARY INSPECTOR.

The Town Council of this borough require the services of a Surveyor and Sanitary Inspector, who must be thoroughly conversant with water and sewerage works, and who shall devote the whole of his time to the duties of his office. He will be permitted to take one pupil only.

Salary, £200 per annum.

Personal canvass will be deemed a disqualification.

Applications, accompanied with recent testimonials and endorsed "Surveyor," to be sent to me on or before 17th September next.

J. PARRY JONES,
Town Clerk.

Oswestry.
August 22, 1898.

## CHERTSEY URBAN DISTRICT COUNCIL.
### APPOINTMENT OF SURVEYOR AND INSPECTOR OF NUISANCES.

The Council invite applications for the appointment of Surveyor and Inspector of Nuisances for their district, at a combined salary of £160 per annum, payable monthly.

The person appointed must be between twenty-seven and forty years of age, will be required to devote his whole time to the duties of the office, and to reside in the district. He must be thoroughly competent and have had practical experience in a similar position.

The successful applicant will be required to take office in one month from date of appointment, which shall be determined by two months' notice on either side.

Sealed applications, endorsed "Surveyor and Inspector," stating the age, qualifications and experience, accompanied by copies of not more than three recent testimonials, must reach the undersigned by noon on Tuesday, the 6th day of September next.

Canvassing, directly or indirectly, will be a disqualification. A list of duties and further particulars may be obtained from me.

T. E. HARLAND CHALDECOTT,
Clerk to the Council.

Chertsey.
August 24, 1898.

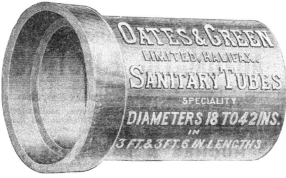

LANCASHIRE COUNTY COUNCIL.
TO CIVIL ENGINEERS AND SURVEYORS.

The Lancashire County Council require the services of two competent persons to act as District Surveyors of Main and Secondary Roads, under the supervision of the County Surveyor.

The gentlemen appointed will be required to devote the whole of their time to the duties of the office.

The initial salary will be at the rate of £200 per annum, with such travelling expenses as are fixed by the Council.

The appointment will be made subject to termination by three months' notice on either side.

Applications, in candidate's own writing, stating age (which must not exceed thirty-five years) and past experience, and accompanied by copies of not more than three recent testimonials, to be addressed to the undersigned, County Offices, Preston, marked "Main Road Surveyor," not later than Wednesday, the 31st day of August, 1898.

Personal canvassing will be considered a disqualification.
FRED. C. HULTON,
Clerk of the County Council.
Preston.
August 10, 1898.

ALDERSHOT URBAN DISTRICT COUNCIL.
CLERK OF WORKS.

A temporary Clerk of Works is required in connection with new street works. Preference will be given to an applicant having a good knowledge of road work and concrete paving.

Applications, stating experience, salary required, and accompanied by three testimonials, to be delivered not later than Tuesday, the 6th day of September.
NELSON F. DENNIS, A.M.I.C.E.,
Surveyor.
Aldershot.

## COMPETITION.

CHERTSEY URBAN DISTRICT COUNCIL.

*COMPETITION FOR SEWERAGE SCHEMES.*

TO ENGINEERS.

The Chertsey Urban District Council invite competitive plans for the Sewerage and Treatment of Sewage from the Nos. 1 and 2 Wards of their district, showing separate and joint schemes for such wards.

The following premiums are offered: First, £50; second, £30; third, £20.

Plans, details and estimates of cost to be signed by a *nom-de-plume.*

The names and addresses of competitors to be sealed in an envelope endorsed with the *nom-de-plume* adopted.

Plans of the suggested areas may be seen and other particulars (printed or written) obtained, on application up to the 28th day of October next, from the Surveyor to the Council, Mr. Arthur W. Smith, Eastworth-road, Chertsey. Plans and other documents should be delivered free to the undersigned by the 23rd day of December next.

Competitors must not approach or consult members of the Council.

(By order)
T. E. HARLAND CHALDECOTT,
Clerk to the Council.
Chertsey.
August 26, 1898.

## TENDERS WANTED.

ALDERSHOT URBAN DISTRICT COUNCIL.

Tenders are hereby invited by the above-named Council for a supply of 2,000 Tons of Granite (more or less) of approved quality, at per ton, in such quantities as the Council may direct.

Samples of the material tendered for, broken to pass through 1½-in. and 2-in. rings, must be forwarded to the Council's Surveyor, at the Council's Offices, Aldershot.

Tenders must state separate prices for the materials broken to the sizes named.

Further particulars may be obtained on application to the Council Surveyor, at the offices aforesaid.

Tenders, endorsed "Tenders for Granite," to be sent to me at the offices aforesaid not later than Tuesday, the 6th day of September, 1898.

The Council do not bind themselves to accept the lowest or any other tender.
W. E. FOSTER,
Clerk.
Aldershot.
August 5, 1898.

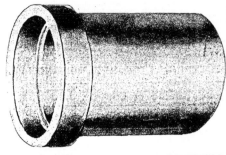

## SWANAGE URBAN DISTRICT COUNCIL.
### TO SEWERAGE CONTRACTORS.

The Urban District Council of Swanage, in the county of Dorset, are prepared to receive tenders for the completion of the Main Sewerage of the district, including about 221 yards of 27-in. Iron Outfall Sewer, 976 yards of 27-in. and 30-in., and 3,900 yards of 9-in., 12-in. and 15-in. Pipe Sewers, with requisite arrangements for flushing, inspection and ventilation.

Drawings and specification may be seen at the offices of the Council, Town Hall, Swanage, and of the Engineers, 5 St. Thomas-street, Ryde, of whom copies of the quantities may be obtained on the deposit of 1 guinea, to be returned on receipt of a bonâ-fide tender. The tenders to be delivered by noon on Monday, September 19, 1898.

FRANCIS NEWMAN & COCKS,
Engineers.

## BOROUGH OF DERBY.

### DERBY CORPORATION WATERWORKS.

CONSTRUCTION OF COVERED SERVICE RESERVOIR.

The Corporation of Derby are prepared to receive tenders for the construction of a Covered Service Reservoir at Littleover, near Derby.

Drawings may be inspected, and copies of the specification and forms of tender may be obtained, on payment of £2 2s., to be returned if a bonâ-fide tender be made, on application at the office of the Borough Surveyor, Babington-lane, Derby, and at the office of Messrs. T. & C. Hawksley, civil engineers, 30 Great George-street, Westminster, S.W., on and after Monday, the 25th instant.

Tenders, on the prescribed form, must be delivered with the specification (enclosed in a sealed envelope, endorsed "Derby Corporation Waterworks—Contract No. 2—Tender for Covered Service Reservoir," and addressed to the undersigned), at the Town Hall, Derby, on or before 12 noon on Monday, the 5th day of September next.

The lowest or any tender will not necessarily be accepted.

H. F. GADSBY,
Town Clerk.

Town Hall, Derby.
August 4, 1898.

## ST. LUKE (MIDDLESEX) VESTRY.
### PAVING WORKS.

Tenders are invited for Paving Golden-lane and part of Banner-street with jarrah wood and part of Peartree-street with new granite.

The plans, specifications and conditions of contract may be seen and forms of tender may be had any day save Saturday from 11 to 5 o'clock, and on Saturdays from 11 to 1 o'clock, on application to the Surveyor's department.

Tenders must be made on the official form and marked outside "Paving Works," and be delivered before noon on the 14th September, 1898.

(By order)
G. W. PRESTON,
Clerk to the Vestry.

Vestry Clerk's Office,
St. Luke's Vestry Hall, City-road, E.C.
August 20, 1898.

## WEYBRIDGE URBAN DISTRICT COUNCIL.

The above-named Council are prepared to receive tenders for the supply and delivery of the following Materials —viz.:—

(1) Stoneware Pipes and Gulleys from the London, Leicestershire or Dorsetshire districts.
(2) Bristol Blue Pennant Kerbing.
(3) Prepared Limestone or Granite for Tar Paving.
(4) Thames Ballast.
(5) Portland Cement.
(6) Gas Tar.

Particulars and form of tender can be obtained from Mr. John S. Crawshaw, Surveyor to the Council, on and after August 22, 1898, on a deposit of 10s. 6d., which will be returned on receipt of a bonâ-fide tender.

Tenders, duly sealed and endorsed tender for ——, to be sent to the undersigned not later than 5 p.m. on September 7, 1898.

The Council do not bind themselves to accept the lowest or any tender.

(By order)
GEO. WHEELER,
Clerk to the Council.

Council Offices, Weybridge.
July 30, 1898.

LANCASHIRE COUNTY COUNCIL.
TO CIVIL ENGINEERS AND SURVEYORS.

The Lancashire County Council require the services of two competent persons to act as District Surveyors of Main and Secondary Roads, under the supervision of the County Surveyor.

The gentlemen appointed will be required to devote the whole of their time to the duties of the office.

The initial salary will be at the rate of £200 per annum, with such travelling expenses as are fixed by the Council. The appointment will be made subject to termination by three months' notice on either side.

Applications, in candidate's own writing, stating age (which must not exceed thirty-five years) and past experience, and accompanied by copies of not more than three recent testimonials, to be addressed to the undersigned, County Offices, Preston, marked "Main Road Surveyor," not later than Wednesday, the 31st day of August, 1898. Personal canvassing will be considered a disqualification.
FRED. C. HULTON,
Clerk of the County Council.

Preston.
August 10, 1898.

ALDERSHOT URBAN DISTRICT COUNCIL.
CLERK OF WORKS.

A temporary Clerk of Works is required in connection with new street works. Preference will be given to an applicant having a good knowledge of road work and concrete paving.

Applications, stating experience, salary required, and accompanied by three testimonials, to be delivered not later than Tuesday, the 6th day of September.
NELSON F. DENNIS, A.M.I.C.E.,
Surveyor.
Aldershot.

## COMPETITION.

CHERTSEY URBAN DISTRICT COUNCIL.

*COMPETITION FOR SEWERAGE SCHEMES.*

TO ENGINEERS.

The Chertsey Urban District Council invite competitive plans for the Sewerage and Treatment of Sewage from the Nos. 1 and 2 Wards of their district, showing separate and joint schemes for such wards.

The following premiums are offered: First, £50; second, £30; third, £20.

Plans, details and estimates of cost to be signed by a *nom-de-plume*.

The names and addresses of competitors to be sealed in an envelope endorsed with the *nom-de-plume* adopted.

Plans of the suggested areas may be seen and other particulars (printed or written) obtained, on application up to the 28th day of October next, from the Surveyor to the Council, Mr. Arthur W. Smith, Eastworth-road, Chertsey. Plans and other documents should be delivered free to the undersigned by the 23rd day of December next.

Competitors must not approach or consult members of the Council.
(By order)
T. E. HARLAND CHALDECOTT,
Clerk to the Council.
Chertsey.
August 26, 1898.

## TENDERS WANTED.

ALDERSHOT URBAN DISTRICT COUNCIL.

Tenders are hereby invited by the above-named Council for a supply of 2,000 Tons of Granite (more or less) of approved quality, at per ton, in such quantities as the Council may direct.

Samples of the material tendered for, broken to pass through 1¼-in. and 2-in. rings, must be forwarded to the Council's Surveyor, at the Council's Offices, Aldershot.

Tenders must state separate prices for the materials broken to the sizes named.

Further particulars may be obtained on application to the Council Surveyor, at the offices aforesaid.

Tenders, endorsed "Tenders for Granite," to be sent to me at the offices aforesaid not later than Tuesday, the 6th day of September, 1898.

The Council do not bind themselves to accept the lowest or any other tender.
W. E. FOSTER,
Clerk.
Aldershot.
August 5, 1898.

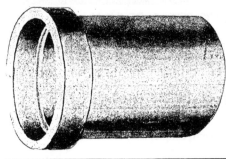

SWANAGE URBAN DISTRICT COUNCIL.
TO SEWERAGE CONTRACTORS.

The Urban District Council of Swanage, in the county of Dorset, are prepared to receive tenders for the completion of the Main Sewerage of the district, including about 221 yards of 27-in. Iron Outfall Sewer, 976 yards of 27-in. and 30-in., and 3,900 yards of 9-in., 12-in. and 15-in. Pipe Sewers, with requisite arrangements for flushing, inspection and ventilation.

Drawings and specification may be seen at the offices of the Council, Town Hall, Swanage, and of the Engineers, 5 St. Thomas-street, Ryde, of whom copies of the quantities may be obtained on the deposit of 1 guinea, to be returned on receipt of a bonâ-fide tender. The tenders to be delivered by noon on Monday, September 19, 1898.

FRANCIS NEWMAN & COCKS,
Engineers.

BOROUGH OF DERBY.

DERBY CORPORATION WATERWORKS.

CONSTRUCTION OF COVERED SERVICE RESERVOIR.

The Corporation of Derby are prepared to receive tenders for the construction of a Covered Service Reservoir at Little-over, near Derby.

Drawings may be inspected, and copies of the specification and forms of tender may be obtained, on payment of £2 2s., to be returned if a bonâ-fide tender be made, on application at the office of the Borough Surveyor, Babington-lane, Derby, and at the office of Messrs. T. & C. Hawksley, civil engineers, 30 Great George-street, Westminster, S.W., on and after Monday, the 25th instant.

Tenders, on the prescribed form, must be delivered with the specification (enclosed in a sealed envelope, endorsed "Derby Corporation Waterworks—Contract No. 2—Tender for Covered Service Reservoir," and addressed to the undersigned), at the Town Hall, Derby, on or before 12 noon on Monday, the 5th day of September next.

The lowest or any tender will not necessarily be accepted.

H. F. GADSBY,
Town Clerk.

Town Hall, Derby,
August 4, 1898.

ST. LUKE (MIDDLESEX) VESTRY.
PAVING WORKS.

Tenders are invited for Paving Golden-lane and part of Banner-street with jarrah wood and part of Peartree-street with new granite.

The plans, specifications and conditions of contract may be seen and forms of tender may be had any day save Saturday from 11 to 5 o'clock, and on Saturdays from 11 to 1 o'clock, on application to the Surveyor's department.

Tenders must be made on the official form and marked outside " Paving Works," and be delivered before noon on the 14th September, 1898.

(By order)
G. W. PRESTON,
Clerk to the Vestry.

Vestry Clerk's Office,
St. Luke's Vestry Hall, City-road, E.C.
August 20, 1898.

WEYBRIDGE URBAN DISTRICT COUNCIL.

The above-named Council are prepared to receive tenders for the supply and delivery of the following Materials —viz.:—

(1) Stoneware Pipes and Gulleys from the London, Leicestershire or Dorsetshire districts.
(2) Bristol Blue Pennant Kerbing.
(3) Prepared Limestone or Granite for Tar Paving.
(4) Thames Ballast.
(5) Portland Cement.
(6) Gas Tar.

Particulars and form of tender can be obtained from Mr. John S. Crawshaw, Surveyor to the Council, on and after August 22, 1898, on a deposit of 10s. 6d., which will be returned on receipt of a bonâ-fide tender.

Tenders, duly signed and endorsed tender for ————, to be sent to the undersigned not later than 5 p.m. on September 7, 1898.

The Council do not bind themselves to accept the lowest or any tender.

(By order)
GEO. WHEELER,
Clerk to the Council.

Council Offices, Weybridge.
July 30, 1898.

## BIRMINGHAM CORPORATION WATER.

*ELAN SUPPLY.—CONTRACT No. 12.—AQUEDUCT.*

### TO CONTRACTORS.

The Corporation of Birmingham are prepared to receive tenders from competent persons willing to enter into a contract for the construction of about 17¼ miles of the Aqueduct from Cleobury Mortimer, in the county of Salop, to Hagley, in the county of Worcester. The contract consists principally of providing and laying two lines of cast-iron pipes and laying only two lines of steel pipes, 41 in. in diameter.

The drawings may be seen, and specification and bills of quantities obtained, at the office of the Engineer, Mr. James Mansergh, 5 Victoria-street, Westminster, on and after the 15th inst., on the deposit of cheque or bank note for £20, which will be returned on receipt of a *bonâ-fide* tender with the bills of quantities fully priced out.

Early application for particulars is necessary, as only a limited number will be given out, and none after the 3rd day of September next.

The contractor will be required to undertake not to pay less than the minimum standard rate of wages current in the district in which the works are situate.

Sealed tenders, addressed to me, and endorsed " Tender for Aqueduct, Contract No. 12," are to be delivered at my office (post paid) at or before noon of Tuesday, the 13th day of September next.

The Corporation do not bind themselves to accept the lowest or any tender.

(Signed)
EDWARD ORFORD SMITH,
Town Clerk.

Town Clerk's Office,
Council House, Birmingham.
August, 1898.

## ST. LUKE (MIDDLESEX) VESTRY.
### CONSTRUCTION OF UNDERGROUND SANITARY CONVENIENCE.

Tenders are invited for the construction of an Underground Sanitary Convenience in Old-street, near its intersection by City-road, in accordance with the plans, specification, &c., and bill of quantities prepared by the Surveyor to the Vestry and Mr. H. Williams Mellor, quantity surveyor, respectively.

These may be seen, and forms of tender and bill of quantities had, any day except Saturday from 11 to 5 o'clock, and on Saturdays from 11 to 1 o'clock, on application to the Surveyor's department.

Tenders must be upon the official form only, properly filled up and signed, and marked outside " Sanitary Convenience," and must be delivered before noon on 14th September next.

(By order)
GEORGE WHITEHEAD PRESTON,
Vestry Clerk.

Vestry Clerk's Office,
St. Luke's Vestry Hall, City-road, E.C.
August 20, 1898.

## URBAN DISTRICT COUNCIL OF LYTHAM.
### SEWERAGE AND SEWAGE DISPOSAL.

The Urban District Council of Lytham invite tenders for the Construction of about 900 yards of 3-ft. diameter Brick Outfall Sewer, about 1,500 yards of 24-in. and 18-in. Pipe Sewers, the Construction of Concrete Storage Tanks, together with sea embankment, roadway, and other contingent works.

Plans may be seen and specifications, quantities and forms of tender obtained at the office of the Engineers, Messrs. Newton, 17 Cooper-street, Manchester, on depositing £2,

which will be repaid on receipt of a *bonâ-fide* tender and the documents supplied.

The lowest or any tender will not necessarily be accepted.

Sealed tenders, endorsed " Tender for Sewerage," to be delivered at these offices not later than noon on the 19th September, 1898.

CHAS. A. MYERS,
Clerk to the Council.
August 23, 1898.

## CIRENCESTER SURFACE-WATER DRAINAGE WORKS.

The Cirencester Urban District Council are prepared to receive tenders for the construction of a system of Surface-Water Drains in a portion of their district.

The drawings and specification may be seen at my office, where copies of the quantities and forms of tender can be obtained on payment of £1 1s., returnable if a *bonâ-fide* tender be made.

Sealed tenders, which must be on the proper form and endorsed " Tender for Surface-Water Drainage Works," must be delivered at my office on or before Thursday, the 1st day of September, 1898.

The Council do not bind themselves to accept the lowest or any tender.

(By order of the Council)
THOMAS HIBBERT,
Surveyor.

Cirencester.
August 10, 1898.

## DISS URBAN DISTRICT COUNCIL invite
tenders for the supply of about 250 tons Belgian Granite, broken and screened to a size 1¼ in., to be delivered at Diss railway station at such times and in such quantities as may be required.

Sealed tenders, with samples of the granite, to be sent to the Clerk of the Council, Market-place, Diss, endorsed " Tender for Granite," by 6th September next.

The Council do not bind themselves to accept the lowest or any tender.

HENRY O. LYUS,
Clerk.

Diss.
August 22, 1898.

## BOROUGH OF SOUTHEND-ON-SEA.
### TO ROAD CONTRACTORS AND OTHERS.

The Corporation invite tenders for Street Works in the making-up of the following streets :—

Hadleigh-road.
Wickford-road.
Canewdon-road (eastern portion of).

Plans, sections and specifications may be seen, and bills of quantities and forms of tender obtained, on and after Monday, August 22nd (on payment of £1 1s. in respect of each street, which will be returned on receipt of a *bonâ-fide* tender), upon application to Mr. Alfred Fidler, ASSOC.M.INST.C.E., Borough Surveyor, Clarence-road, Southend.

No tender will be considered unless made on the prescribed form, and there must be a separate tender for each street.

Sealed tenders, endorsed with the name of the street, and marked " Tender for Private Street Works," to be delivered at my office before 10 o'clock in the morning of Thursday, September 8th.

The Corporation will not be bound to accept the lowest or any tender.

(By order)
WILLIAM H. SNOW,
Town Clerk.

Southend-on-Sea.
August 16, 1898.

# CITY OF SHEFFIELD.

*TO IRONFOUNDERS AND OTHERS.*

EXTENSION OF TINSLEY CAR-SHED.

The Tramway Committee invite tenders for Iron Roof, Columns, &c., in connection with the extension of the above car-shed.

Plans and specifications may be seen, and quantities obtained, at the office of Mr. Charles F. Wike, C.E., city surveyor, Town Hall, Sheffield, after Thursday, the 18th inst., on payment of 1 guinea, which will be returned on receipt of a *bond-fide* tender.

Tenders, endorsed "Ironwork, Car-Shed," to be sent in not later than Monday, the 5th September, 1898, addressed "Chairman and Members of the Tramways Committee, City Surveyor's Office, Town Hall, Sheffield."

The contract will comprise the fair wages and conditions of labour clause which has been adopted by the Sheffield Corporation, particulars of which will appear in the specification.

The Committee do not bind themselves to accept the lowest or any tender.

(By order)
(Signed) HENRY SAYER,
Town Clerk.

Town Clerk's Office, Town Hall, Sheffield.
August 15th, 1898.

# ALDERSHOT URBAN DISTRICT COUNCIL.

TO ROAD CONTRACTORS AND OTHERS.

The Aldershot Urban District Council are prepared to receive tenders for the Metalling, &c., of :—
Albert-street, West End, Aldershot.

Plans and specifications may be seen, and forms of tender obtained, by applying at the office of the Surveyor to the Council, 126 Victoria-road, Aldershot.

Sureties will be required.

Tenders, endorsed "Tenders for New Streets," are to be delivered in a sealed envelope at my office not later than 9 a.m. on Wednesday, the 7th day of September next.

The Council do not bind themselves to accept the lowest or any tender.

(By order)
W. B. FOSTER,
Clerk to the Council.

126 Victoria-road.
August 5, 1898.

# ALDERSHOT URBAN DISTRICT COUNCIL.

SCARIFIER.

The above Council are prepared to receive tenders for the supply and delivery at Aldershot of a Scarifier of the type known as Morrison's. The scarifier must be capable of being attached to and worked by a 19-ton steam roller. A separate price is required for the work of fixing, &c., to the steam rollers. The contractor must give a full description of the machine with his tenders. Full particulars may be obtained of the Surveyor.

Tenders, to be endorsed "Scarifier," are to be delivered at my office not later than the 6th day of September.

The Council do not bind themselves to accept the lowest or any tender.

The contractor must state when he will undertake the delivery. This is important.

(By order of the Council)
W. E. FOSTER,
Clerk.

Aldershot.
August 5, 1898.

# CITY OF NOTTINGHAM.

TO CONTRACTORS.

The Stoke Farm Committee of the City Council is prepared to receive tenders for the Construction of a new Sewer in Lenton Boulevard, together with all appurtenant works.

The works required consist of the construction of about :—
1,750 yards Brick and Concrete Main Sewer, 9 ft. wide and 7 ft. 3 in. high.
40 yards 4 ft. 6 in. diameter Brick Barrel Sewer.
16 yards 6 ft. diameter Brick Barrel Sewer.
146 yards 3-ft. 6-in. by 2-ft. 4-in. Egg-Shaped Brick Sewer.
55 yards 3-ft. by 2-ft. Egg-Shaped Brick Sewer.
24 yards 15 in. diameter Pipe Sewer.
550 yards 12 in. diameter Pipe Sewer.
80 yards 9 in. diameter Pipe Sewer and other appurtenant works.

Drawings may be seen, and specification, bills of quantities and forms of tender obtained, at my office, on payment of a deposit of 3 guineas, which will be returned on receipt of a *bond-fide* tender and the copy of the specification.

Sealed tenders, endorsed "New Sewer, Lenton Boulevard," are to be sent to the Town Clerk on or before Saturday, the 17th September, 1898.

The lowest or any tender will not necessarily be accepted, and tenders will only be accepted from persons who conform to the conditions of contract as regards paying the local standard rate of wages, &c.

(By order)
ARTHUR BROWN, M.INST.C.E.,
City Engineer.

Guildhall, Nottingham.
August 16, 1898.

# CARRICKMACROSS UNION.

NOTICE TO CONTRACTORS.

The Board of Guardians of the above Union, acting as the rural sanitary authority, will, at their meeting to be held at 2 o'clock p.m. on Tuesday, 6th September, 1898, be prepared to consider tenders for the construction of works to supply the town of Carrickmacross with water, in accordance with plans and specification prepared by P. F. Comber and the late W. G. Strype, MEMBS.INST.C.E., 19 Lower Lesson-street, Dublin, which can be seen at the office of Mr. J. H. Blackader, solicitor, Carrickmacross, between the hours of 11 a.m. and 3 o'clock p.m. daily.

The works comprise the supply and laying of 102 tons or thereabouts of Cast-Iron Water Mains; the construction of a Pumping House, with duplicate sets of oil engines and three-throw gun-metal plunger force pumps, each set of pumping plant being capable of delivering 90 gallons per minute to a height of 200 ft.; and the construction of a Service Reservoir, to contain 100,000 gallons or thereabouts.

Printed copies of the specification and form of tender may

be obtained from Mr. Blackader on payment of £2 sterling from each competitor, which will be returned on the receipt of a *bonâ-fide* tender.

Tenders to be addressed to the undersigned, and endorsed "Tender for Waterworks," naming solvent sureties.

The Guardians do not bind themselves to accept the lowest or any tender.

(By order)
JOHN PHELAN,
Clerk of the Union and Executive
Sanitary Officer.

Board-room, Carrickmacross.
August 16, 1898.

### SALE BY AUCTION.

By Order of the Corporation.

TO CONTRACTORS, BUILDERS AND OTHERS.

EASTBOURNE.

Mr. GEORGE S. JINMAN has been favoured with instructions to sell by public auction, at the Depot, Fort-road, "The Crumbles," on Wednesday and Thursday, September 21 and 22, the valuable

CONTRACTORS' PLANT AND MATERIALS, consisting of a large quantity of Pitch Pine, baulk and other Timber, Sleepers, a Pile Engine, Iron Shutters, ditto Piping, Tramway Metals, Zinc Water-Tanks, a 7-Ton Travelling Hand Crane, Centring, a large quantity of Bolts, Manhole Steps, Cut Nails, a 20 Horse-Power Boiler (Portable), a Gantry with Travelling Platform, ½-yard Wooden Side Tip-Waggons, Revolving Iron ditto, a Steam Winch, 2 Wooden Chests, Wheelbarrows, Picks, Shovels, Iron Chains, Crowbars, a 2-Ton Travelling Steam Crane (4-ft. 8½-in. Guage), Galvanised Buckets, a quantity of Thigh and Knee Boots, Sledge Hammers, 3 Large Wooden Sheds, Hurricane Lamps, Ducks, 4 Sail Cloths, and a large quantity of miscellaneous effects.

Sale to *commence* at 11 o'clock precisely each day. The whole may be viewed prior to days of sale, and catalogues obtained of the borough engineer, R. M. Gloyne, Esq., the Town Hall, or of the auctioneer, at his Auction and Estate Offices, 4 Grove-road, Eastbourne.

# The Surveyor

## And Municipal and County Engineer.

Vol. XIV., No. 346.     LONDON, SEPTEMBER 2, 1898.     Weekly, Price 3d.

## Minutes of Proceedings.

**The Maidstone Report.**

The report of the Local Government Board inspectors who were appointed to inquire into the Maidstone typhoid epidemic of last year has been awaited with no small interest. It has now been issued, and it is not too much to say that it entirely confirms the conclusions to which the great majority of reasonable and thoughtful people who had no pet theory to bolster up had felt themselves bound to arrive. The inspectors were Mr. J. S. Davy, Dr. Theodore Thomson, and Mr. G. W. Willcocks, M.I.C.E., who opened their inquiry at Maidstone on January 31st, the proceedings lasting eight days. Much of the report is occupied by narrating in considerable detail the history of the epidemic, but to this we need only briefly refer, as we dealt with it fully at the time of the outbreak, and also in our account of the proceedings during the inquiry. It will be remembered that the epidemic began in September and lasted for about four months. Up to January 20, 1898, there had been a total of 1,681 cases in the borough, exclusive of 107 notifications by the Kent Lunatic Asylum at Barming There were also twenty cases in the Maidstone Union Workhouse, which is situated outside the borough, while a number of persons were attacked in rural parishes which adjoin Maidstone and are supplied with water by the Maidstone Water Company. The most interesting part of the report is to be found in the concluding comments. Naturally the first question of importance is to ascertain the immediate cause of the outbreak. Here is the decision to which the inspectors have come :—

> On a review of the whole of the epidemic, we have no hesitation in coming to the conclusion that the epidemic was caused by the pollution of the water supplied by the Maidstone Company from their Farleigh sources. It is true that there is abundant testimony to show that grave insanitary defects exist in the construction of some of the sewers and of many house drains and water-closets within the borough; while one of the expert witnesses, Dr. Corfield, said that, in his opinion, these defects were sufficient to account for the epidemic. But the sudden and simultaneous outbreak of fever over a wide area, and the rapidity with which the epidemic grew, cannot be accounted for by the existence of defective conditions of sewerage and drainage. Further, the facts as to the local incidence of the disease are not consistent with the theory that these conditions had anything to do with its origin. The old brick barrel sewers are almost all in the lower part of the town, which was comparatively free from attack, and the hand-flushed and defective house drains are distributed pretty equally over the whole town, whereas the cases of typhoid fever were confined to the Farleigh area of water supply to an extent which quite precludes the possibility of mere chance.

This deliverance does not lend much support to the abortive attempts that were made in certain quarters to explain to the public that the outbreak was due, not partially but *wholly*, to defects of drainage and sewerage. Our own point of view has more than once been placed before our readers without ambiguity. In our issue of the 19th inst. we expressed the opinion, in reply to a correspondent,

that "there is a close connection between the influence of sewer gas from ill-ventilated or improperly-constructed house drains and sewers and typhoid fever," but at the same time we pointed out that, "whilst it is now generally admitted that putrid gases from sewers and drains cannot be held to generate typhoid fever spontaneously, there is no doubt that sewer gas is a strongly predisposing cause, in that it lowers the vitality of the human system and renders it readily susceptible to the entrance of the specific germ which produces typhoid in the human being." We also added that "the broad fact that insanitary conditions are a strongly predisposing cause to outbreaks of typhoid fever should not be lost sight of." Were the sanitary defects of Maidstone so acute and so widely spread as to produce such a wholesale lowering of the vitality of the community that but for the existence of these evils there would have been no epidemic? The remarks of the inspectors in regard to the incidence of the outbreak should be a sufficient answer to such a contention, though it may readily be admitted that the sanitary defects intensified the disease. But however strongly exposure to the influence of sewer gas may predispose towards disease, it has not been proved that it is a medium for the transmission of the specific typhoid bacillus. On the other hand it has been proved with tolerable certainty that water is such a medium. On behalf of the water company it was objected that the evidence, strongly as it pointed to the pollution of the Farleigh water supply, was circumstantial and established grounds for suspicion only, but it was supplemented by other facts which appeared to the inspectors to leave no room for doubt. They, however, accept the contention of the company so far as regards a limited number of cases. They remark :—

> We are of opinion that many of the typhoid cases in the borough were due to defects of drainage and sewerage, with consequent pollution of the soil underlying the town. The responsibility for the existence of these insanitary conditions lies with the town council, whose duty it was to take steps that would lead to effective remedy of these defects. This duty they have in large measure neglected, notwithstanding that for many years the medical officer of health has repeatedly warned them of the risk to which the inhabitants of the town were exposed by the continuance of these insanitary conditions.

Before concluding their report the inspectors draw attention to a very important point, so important, indeed, that we may be justified in quoting the whole passage :—

> The history of the epidemic appears to us to raise the question as to how far the regulations of the Board relating to the duties of medical officers of health and the statutes which regulate the powers and obligations of private water companies are sufficient to ensure a reasonable amount of protection to the public health. The general order of the Board of 1891 p escribes that the medical officer of health "shall inform himself as far as may be practicable respecting all influences affecting or threatening to affect injuriously the public health within the district." This regulation might be held to make it the duty of the medical officer to visit and inspect the works of a private water company supplying

water to his district, even though the works were situate outside it, as is the case at Maidstone. This, however, was not the construction put upon the regulation by Mr. M. A. Adams, the medical officer for Maidstone, and as a matter of fact he had never seen the sources of the water supply furnished to the Farleigh area. He pointed out with considerable force that he had no legal right of access to the works, and as to taking samples of the water. Yet sec. 7 of the Public Health (Water) Act, 1878, imposes upon rural sanitary authorities the duty of taking such steps as may be necessary to ascertain the condition of the water supply within their district. It must be stated, however, that it did not appear that any application to inspect the works or to take samples of the springs separately was ever made to the directors of the water company by either of the sanitary authorities concerned.

The moral of the preceding paragraph is that the whole question of water supplies, whether controlled by local authorities or by private companies, requires attention from the Government, in order that it may be placed upon such a basis as will ensure freedom from gross pollution and a reasonable amount of protection to consumers. The last sentence of the paragraph indicates that responsibility was not monopolised by the company, but that a certain share is to be attributed to the sanitary authorities. When the epidemic began we had occasion to point out that the ratepayers were by no means free from blame, as they had vetoed the acquisition of the supply by the corporation when an excellent opportunity for purchasing had presented itself. We are waiting with considerable interest for some signs of a movement in favour of municipalisation. If there are any insuperable obstacles or serious objections we should be glad to hear of them.

\* \* \*

**Some Municipal Engineering Questions.** In the last annual report submitted to the Nuneaton and Chilvers Coton Urban District Council, Mr. Pickering, the engineer and surveyor to that body, discusses in a general and interesting way some of the more troublesome questions which confront municipal engineers. We observe that Mr. Pickering seems to be more fortunate than many of his brethren in connection with the inspection of new buildings and drains, inasmuch as he finds a general willingness on the part of builders to carry out the requirements of the council and to remedy any irregularities pointed out. In this connection we may mention that the council in March last adopted new regulations and instructions setting forth their requirements in regard to building and drainage operations. Mr. Pickering repeats the familiar warning against entrusting drainage work to incompetent workmen or unskilled labourers, and he suggests that no one should be allowed to carry out drainage work without a proper certificate of competency from the council or some other recognised authority. The necessity for such a provision, however, does not seem to be very great in Nuneaton, for the rare occurrence of blocked drains is cited as a proof of the care that is exercised in their construction. A more serious problem in Nuneaton is the removal and disposal of night-soil. The bulk of it has to be carted, at the expense of the council, a considerable distance from the town and deposited on agricultural land. The refuse from dry ash-pits is of no manurial value, and consequently there is no return against the expense of its removal. Mr. Pickering considers, however, that the refuse has some value as fuel for steam-raising, and that the question is almost ripe for consideration as to whether it could not be utilised for the purpose with advantage. It is surprising to find that so many loads of night-soil can be removed with so few complaints; but no matter how carefully the work is carried out, the privy system can never, in a town like Nuneaton, be otherwise than objectionable and insanitary, and the sooner a new system is substituted the better. In speaking of team labour Mr. Pickering incidentally condemns the hiring system, the chief of a number of disadvantages being that the drivers are not directly under the control of the council. At Nuneaton the main roads have for

six years been maintained under an agreement with the county council, and it is satisfactory to learn that the arrangement has worked to the advantage of both bodies, no complaints having been made by the county surveyor. In order to obtain control of the whole of the public roads, arrangements are made with the various railway companies for the council to repair the roads over their bridges at a fixed annual charge. In speaking of another vexed question, the ventilation of sewers, Mr. Pickering, after quoting the resolutions passed at the conference of metropolitan officials some time ago, remarks that the main point, upon which there appears to be a tolerably unanimous opinion, is that the openings to sewers for ventilation should be increased rather than diminished, the position of the openings and whether provided by pipes up houses or shafts in the streets to be decided according to circumstances. It is considered that in Nuneaton ventilating shafts have had the effect of checking the diseases attributable to emanations from sewers. The system is admitted to be by no means an ideal one; but while open to many objections, the provision of a sufficient number of shafts as outlets for foul air and openings for fresh air is considered to be the most efficacious system at present devised. Mr. Pickering also deals at some length with the questions of sewage disposal and water supply in the district. The extension of the sewage works is temporarily arrested, owing to the demands of the Local Government Board in regard to land. These the council are not prepared to meet, because of the unreasonable cost, while, in Mr. Pickering's opinion, artificial filtration would solve the difficulty. In connection with the water supply it should be noted that the service has now been municipalised.

\* \* \*

**Work of the Metropolitan Asylums Board.** The Metropolitan Asylums Board was created by the Metropolitan Poor Act of 1867 to provide accommodation for the imbecile and for those suffering from infectious diseases. Previously there was no adequate provision for these purposes. Those who wish to gain an idea of the nature and scope of the vast work that is now being done by this body can do so by glancing at the report of the Statistical Committee for 1897. The severely statistical character of such a report may repel many, but the volume has abundant interest for those who can interpret statistics intelligently. The Board now own and manage ten fever hospitals accommodating 4,000 patients, four imbecile asylums with 6,000 inmates, hospital ships and a convalescent hospital at Darenth for the treatment of 1,500 small-pox cases, and there is an ambulance service for the whole of London. Among other activities of the Board are the training ship *Exmouth*, in which 600 boys from workhouses are educated and trained for the navy, the mercantile marine and the army, and schools for the teaching of 400 imbecile children. Since 1890 provision has been made in connection with infectious diseases for other than pauper patients, and diphtheria cases were first admitted in 1888. The total staff at the hospitals now number about 2,000, practically treble the number in 1890, a significant indication of the enormous expansion of the work of the board in recent years. The expenditure last year amounted to £665,393. In the report reference is made to the decision of the Local Government Board to give the Metropolitan Asylums Board charge of certain classes of Poor Law children. Our periodical reports of the meetings of the board give an idea of the vast amount of building and other contract work which has to be done by this important body. Particulars have already been given in our columns of the splendid block of offices which the Board have decided to erect on the Thames embankment. The report is supplemented by a number of maps showing the incidence of the various diseases and embodying other information.

**Sanitary Work in Essex.**

The summary of the reports of the district medical officers of health presented annually by Dr. Thresh, county medical officer of Essex, always contains interesting and instructive matter. In the summary for last year he comments upon the fact that certain districts, Barking and Epping for example, have large death rates, 21·2 and 19·5 respectively, while others have an extremely low mortality, the rates in Leyton and Walthamstow, for instance, being 12·1 and 11·9 respectively; and there is little doubt that this is very largely due to the care taken in sanitary matters during the development of the districts in question, while the exercise of the same care in future cannot fail to ensure a continuance of satisfactory sanitary conditions. No one is likely to dispute the remark of Dr. Thresh that the prevention of overcrowding of houses on space, the provision of adequate sewerage, and efficient public scavenging, will ensure the preservation of the soil from such pollution as ultimately fosters disease; while the neglect of those precautions, on the other hand, must lead to soil pollution, the effect of which on the death rate must ultimately make itself felt. We observe that the mortality from typhoid and similar fevers continues to be excessive, especially in the urban districts, and more particularly in the districts bordering on the Thames. The recurrence of this phenomenon year after year in connection with the Thames district points undoubtedly to the existence of some condition favourable to the presence of typhoid fever. The discharge of London sewage into the river at Barking is mentioned as a possible cause, and others might be suggested, but Dr. Thresh considers that none are at present capable of proof. The section of the report referring to sanitary administration is extremely interesting. As might be expected, Dr. Thresh gives the necessary attention to water supply, especially in connection with an anticipated decrease below ordnance datum of the level of the water in the chalk wells. Some remarks on combined drainage, the working of the destructor at Leyton, and the taking of specimens of drinking water, sewage effluents, &c., for purposes of examination, will repay perusal.

*　*　*

**Another "Appointment."**

It has been our painful duty of late to give some remarkable examples of the singular principles—or want of principles—which animate the members of many of the smaller local authorities in appointing officials, and especially surveyors. The cases of Erith and Street were bad enough, but they almost pale into insignificance in comparison with a recent appointment by a rural district council in Devonshire, the details of which have just reached us. Though we have every belief in the perfect good faith of our correspondent, the circumstances are so extraordinary and so difficult to credit that we hesitate to mention the name of the district. With this reservation we shall give the story as it reaches us. The rural district council in question advertised for a surveyor of highways, asking the applicants to name the salary they wanted. Three were selected, and out of these a youth, about twenty-three years of age, and a relative of a prominent member of the council, was appointed by a large majority, the unsuccessful candidates being informed unofficially by the chairman and other members that the successful man had paid a large sum to the retiring surveyor on the understanding that he should succeed him, and that this had great weight with the council. Why, O why? Apart from that and his extreme youth, is the successful candidate otherwise competent? The district in question, we may mention, has lately earned some notoriety through its insanitary condition, the result of ignoring the recommendations of the medical officer of health. It is possible that we may have occasion to return to the subject.

**The East-End Water Question.**

The weather during the past week has certainly been variable, but there has been no rain to speak of and thus no relief from that quarter for the tension in the East-End of London. In fact, the company have been credited with the intention of still further reducing the supply—to be precise, of giving only a three hours' instead of a six hours' supply. This extreme step, however, has apparently been arrested by the intervention of the Local Government Board. Neither the company nor the Local Government Board have shown themselves capable of learning from past experience or of forecasting the necessities of the future in this particular matter. The officials of the company have been at considerable pains to reply to assertions that they could obtain sufficient water from five other companies if they were willing to pay for it. The contention is that the only company from which assistance can really be obtained is the New River Company, and that this source is being tapped to the fullest extent. It is not denied that there are connections with the systems of other companies, but we are asked to digest the explanation that the mains through which the supplementary water would have to pass are too small to take it. But surely this is quite a new defence, for has not the trouble arisen from the fact that there is not sufficient storage of water to pass a continuous supply through the mains? We fear that the company and their officials will have to try again.

*　*　*

**Water Supply in New York.**

It is certainly an anomaly to find that the first city in the United States in population, commerce and manufactures should be the lowest of thirty of the principal cities in regard to an adequate water supply. The need of an additional water supply is pressing in Brooklyn, and is expected to become so in Manhattan. A recent writer on the subject says that what is wanted is a gravitation supply, which shall have an ample watershed free from pollution, with sufficient head to supply the highest buildings. It should be within the State of New York and duplicate existing sources, so that if one source failed it would be supplemented by the other. Such a supply, we are told, can be found in the Catskill Mountains, in the southern part of which there is a clear, cold trout-stream supply, from a sparsely-settled hardwood forest district known to every fisherman, with ample volume and an elevation to afford an adequate head to reach the highest buildings, at a distance and at a cost much less than in the case of the Adirondacks, or the Great Lakes, or any other available supply.

*　*　*

**Dr. John Hopkinson.**

The Alps—that happy hunting ground of those who feel the irresistible fascination of mountaineering to such an extent as to despise its dangers—has claimed many victims, but seldom one so distinguished as Dr. John Hopkinson, equally eminent as a man of science and as a practical electrician. His tragic death, in company with two daughters and a son, will come as a shock to many municipal engineers, to whom he was well known in connection with some of the extensive municipal schemes of electric lighting and traction for which the deceased gentleman acted as engineer. The electric lighting of Manchester and the electric tramways at Leeds are only two among many such schemes. It is not too much to say that his career as a civil engineer was as brilliant and as completely successful as the academic distinction he achieved in early life. To all appearance he had many years of active work still before him, and his undisputed eminence, together with the tragic circumstances of his death, intensifies the feelings of regret with which the news of the event has been received.

# The Designing and Construction of Refuse Destructors.

By FRANK LESLIE WATSON, Assoc.M.Inst.C.E.*

In the design and construction of a successful and economical refuse destructor plant the following are the principal points which must be borne in mind :—

A. It must never be forgotten that the primary object of a refuse destructor is, as its name implies, to destroy refuse, and to destroy that refuse as completely as possible and without the production of any description of nuisance. By the term to destroy refuse in this connection is implied a practically absolute chemical separation of the combustible portions of the refuse (such as the carbon, phosphates and nitrates which are found in cinders and in animal and vegetable matter) from the non-combustible portions (which are chiefly mineral), and includes the complete oxidation of the former class, and the fusion and agglomeration so far as is possible into hard clinker of the latter parts. It must be regretfully admitted that in a very large number of destructors these important objects are only attained to a very limited extent.

In order to insure a perfect result :—

(1) A high temperature must be attained; 1,300 deg. Fahr. is admissible, but 1,600 deg. to 1,800 deg. Fahr. is better. It is not sufficient to impart the desired temperature to the furnace gases after they leave the furnaces. Such devices as Mr. Jones's patent fume cremator (intended for this purpose) have done good service in their day in preventing the abominable emanations from the chimneys of old-fashioned low-temperature destructors; but at the best such a device as a fume cremator is only useful in securing perfect oxidation of the gases and vapours distilled from the refuse, while giving no assistance whatever towards completing tho other and equally necessary part of the process—namely, the reduction to innocuous clinker of the solid refuse itself. For this purpose it is essential that a high temperature must be kept up in the furnace itself as well as in the flue.

(2) Having provided means for securing a high temperature in the furnaces and the flues, such arrangements must be made as will secure that the whole of the refuse and the whole of the products of combustion or distillation must be subjected to this high temperature, in presence of sufficient air and for a sufficient length of time to insure complete oxidation of all combustible substances.

(3) It is also necessary that the products of combustion passing up the chimney must be as free as possible from solid matter such as dust, which, although they may be so perfectly burnt as to be free from any taint of putrefaction, yet their mechanical effect upon the leaves of trees and plants, upon the lungs of persons and animals, and upon clothing and furniture, are such as to become an intolerable nuisance, and a nuisance which has been proved in more than one instance to be actionable at law.

B. The destructor must be so designed as to involve the least possible expense in its working. To this end the handling of the refuse should be reduced as much as possible, though it must be borne in mind that the adoption of cumbrous and complicated mechanical feeding arrangements has hitherto been found to give no relief in the matter of labour; in fact, it has even involved additional labour, while at the same time such machinery is frequently very costly both in construction and in upkeep and working charges. It must always be borne in mind that machinery working in the presence of large quantities of dusty and dirty material deteriorates very rapidly, and any machinery which is required about a destructor, particularly electrical machinery, must be so arranged as to be as nearly as possible boxed in and protected from dust. The author would mention as an instance the Shoreditch combined electrical lighting and destructor plant, where, according to the abstract of accounts published in *The Electrical Review* of May 27, 1898, a large proportion of the total current produced appears to have been used on the works in driving fans, lifting machinery, &c. The author believes that this excessive expenditure of energy is due in a large measure to the extra resistance caused by the impossibility of keeping switches, brushes, &c., in proper order in presence of dust and dirt. In order to ensure economy, the safest points to bear in mind are that the refuse should be brought in the collecting carts as near as possible to the charging holes of the furnaces, and the tipping arrangements should be such that a minimum of work is involved in properly charging the furnaces. It must also be remembered that considerable judgment is required in working a fire, and that judgment is not usually a faculty possessed by machinery. In order to obviate any difficulty in separating clinker from unburnt matter, and in order to insure as nearly as possible a continuous process in the furnaces, they should be fed at one end of the grate and clinkered at the other, and the arrangements at the clinkering end should again be such as to involve the least possible labour in removing the clinker and to avoid altogether the necessity for breaking it up in order to get it through small openings.

(C) In these days people are not content with getting rid of the refuse in an inoffensive manner. It has been demonstrated that large quantities of heat are available from the combustion of refuse, and therefore it has become necessary that this heat should be utilised, and at present almost the only practicable method of utilising the heat is in the evaporation of water. When it has been shown that in practical use 8 tons of refuse will raise as much steam as 1 ton of good coal burnt under good conditions, and that it will raise that steam to the highest working pressures ordinarily adopted, there can be no doubt as to the advisability of providing sufficient boiler room and arranging a suitable use for the available power. In order to secure the best results the boilers must be placed near enough to the cells to prevent any important loss of heat by radiation, but they must not be placed near enough to interfere with perfect combustion of the gases, which is generally not completed until after they have left the furnaces and traversed a certain length of flue to insure proper mixing. It must be borne in mind that, even in boiler firing with coal, any contact of the gases with comparatively cool cross tubes, &c., before they are perfectly oxidised will check the combustion and cause smoke, and it is obviously useless to mix any further oxygen with such unburnt gases after they have dropped below their natural temperature of combustion or "flashing point." It may here be mentioned that water-tube boilers are the most readily adapted to the requirements of a destructor station, although very good results have been obtained with other types, particularly Lancashire boilers. The comparative safety of water-tube boilers from explosion, and their general handiness and convenience, render them particularly adapted for working where the labour employed is not of a highly cultivated order, and generally in connection with these plants it is best to remember that, whatever apparatus is provided, it will probably have to be worked by stokers.

(D) The solid matters resulting from the combustion of the refuse—e.g., clinkers from off the grates and fine ashes from underneath them—must be made use of for two reasons. First, if they are not made use of they must be carted away and tipped to waste at a further cost. Second, they may be made a valuable source of revenue. It must not be forgotten that we have here another powerful argument in favour of high temperature destructors, the clinker from which will be completely fused, and will therefore be of a hard and sharp nature, in contra-distinction to the clinker from low temperature destructors, which is soft, friable and totally useless, and frequently even putrescible. It is no uncommon thing for such half-burnt clinker to take fire again after being tipped into a heap, and thus to occasion serious nuisance. Assuming, however, that the clinker is going to be of a hard and useful character, we shall require machines for breaking it up, grinding it, and mixing it with lime, &c., to form mortar, and these machines must be powerful, massive and durable. Having thus briefly sketched the requirements of a destructor plant, the author will proceed to give some details of the manner in which these objects have been attained in one or two plants in the design and construction of which he has been concerned.

This purpose will perhaps be best served by a brief description of the plants in question.

### THE POWDERHALL DESTRUCTOR, EDINBURGH.

This is a ten-cell plant. It was originally of the Fryer type, having been constructed in the year 1893. The working of the destructor, however, gave rise to serious complaint from the neighbours, culminating in an action for nuisance by the proprietors of the neighbouring estate of Redbraes, on which were situated some nursery gardens. It was held by the High Court at Edinburgh that a serious nuisance had been established, and the corporation were condemned in damages and costs. The costs, owing to the very large number of expert witnesses called on both sides, were extremely heavy. The Court appointed Mr. Benjamin Hall Blyth, the eminent civil engineer of Edinburgh and Westminster, to confer with Prof. William Odling, of Oxford, and to report to the Court as to the practicability of remodelling the destructor in order to prevent a recurrence of the nuisance. Mr. Blyth inspected the most important destructors in England, and his report to the Court was to the effect that if the type of destructor in use at Oldham and at Leeds were adopted the nuisance would be abated. Thereupon the author's firm made an offer to the corporation to take upon their shoulders the whole responsibility of the alteration and to guarantee that all the causes of complaint should be removed. A formal contract was entered into, Mr. Hall Blyth being retained as referee, and the contractors bound themselves to fulfil all their obligations to his entire satisfaction. It so happened that the grates of the old furnace were of practically the same dimensions as those of the Horsfall standard cell, and therefore the furnaces were only pulled down to the level of the grate bars, the foundations and ash-pit walling being left in place. After the heavy expenses to which the corporation had already been put, there was a natural desire to economise as far as

* A paper read in the Engineering and Building Construction Section of the Congress of the Royal Institute of Public Health recently held at Dublin.

possible in the alterations, and therefore some of the old ironwork, including the clinkering doors, was made to do duty over again. These clinkering doors are of a somewhat awkward pattern. They swing upwards on hinges, and are provided with balance weights, working into recesses in the furnace fronts. The hinges give a good deal of trouble from sticking, and, although the doors have the advantage of providing an opening right across the grate for the removal of clinker, they have the great disadvantage that the amount of opening is fixed—that is to say, they must be either wide open or shut—and when they are wide open the hot baffle plate at the back of the door reflects great heat on to the arms, hands and faces of the workmen. With the exception of these and some other minor details the furnaces as reconstructed are of the Horsfall standard pattern. They are built in a double row, back to buck, five cells on each side. Each pair of cells communicates at the back with a feed hole 2 ft. square, common to the pair of cells. The feed hole has a flat table at the bottom, and the refuse is pushed over the edge of this table by means of a three-pronged fork. It falls down on to the sloping drying hearth of the furnace. The sides of the furnace flare out sideways from the feeding end down to the grate, so that when the refuse is once pushed over the edge of the table at the bottom of the feed hole it cannot possibly stick. In this manner somewhere about a cubic yard of refuse is fed in at one operation on to the drying hearth. The operation of feeding takes place a few minutes after the operation of clinkering, the red fire on the grate being given a short period to brighten up under the action of the blast before the fresh refuse is drawn on. The stoker on the clinkering floor pulls the refuse forward from the drying hearth on to the grate bars and spreads it evenly over the grate. It should be mentioned that the drying hearth is paved with fire-brick, and is kept hot by being in close proximity to the main flue. It is found that 6 ft. is the maximum length of grate which can be conveniently worked by the men. It is also found that making the grates 5 ft. wide insures the handiest and most economical disposition of the labour; therefore each grate is 5 ft. wide by 6 ft. long, or 30 square feet in area. The grate bars in the Edinburgh destructor are of wrought iron, rivetted together in slabs of four. Each bar is of a tapered section, ½ in. thick at the top and ⁷⁄₁₆ in. at the bottom edge. The distance pieces or washers between the bars are cast from the bars themselves, and inverted so that the air space between the bars is ⁷⁄₁₆ in. wide. They are made in 6 ft. lengths. There is thus no joint in the middle of the grate for the firing tools to get caught in. Each furnace is provided with hollow cast-iron sides, having removable plates next to the fire. The air from the forced draught apparatus is introduced into these boxes, which communicate for that purpose with a blast flue common to each row of cells. The boxes are closed above the grate. They communicate with the ash-pit by openings controlled by valves. The valves are operated by handles placed below the clinkering door. These side boxes serve a double purpose—first, the air is heated, and, second, the brickwork of the furnaces is protected from the erosive action of the clinker, which in ordinary brick-lined furnaces adheres to the brickwork and brings away small particles of the same at every time of clinkering, so that the furnace sides become rapidly eaten away. Ordinary iron plates will not stand the heat, but this difficulty is completely avoided by the side-box arrangement alluded to. The blast flues are placed one on each side of the main flue, so that any heat which is given up by conduction from the sides of the main flue is communicated to the air, and finds its way back to the furnaces, to assist in promoting rapid combustion. Each blast flue communicates at its outer end with a vertical flue, in which is placed the forced draught apparatus. This consists of a large steam-jet blower of an improved and patented design, a row of adjustable flat jets being placed so as to introduce a powerful current of air in a cast-iron trumpet, also of a flat shape. The use of these steam jets saves a good deal of expense and trouble in keeping an engine and fan in running order, and they require no skill and attention, besides which the steam is of considerable assistance in raising the temperature in the cells. The flues are arranged according to Horsfall's well-known patent. The whole of the products of combustion pass out of the furnaces at the front end through openings in the arch immediately above the clinkering door. It will thus be observed that the gases pass away at the clinkering or hot end of the furnaces, in contra-distinction to the Fryer destructor, in which the gases pass away at the feeding or cold end of the furnaces. The front flue arrangement insures that any vapours given off by the green refuse in drying shall be mixed with the hot flames from the blazing refuse, and the furnace crown and cross tines are thus raised to a rod or white heat, the bricks retaining their high temperature even after the fires are freshly charged, and thus ensuring that at all times and in all states of the fires the gases are perfectly consumed. The cross lines run back over the top of the cell, the two flues from each pair of cells meeting at a point over the centre of the main flue and communicating therewith by a vertical passage. On looking into the main flue of one of these destructors bright blue flames can always be seen descending through these passages. In order to be visible at that point the flame must be at least 25 ft. long, and persons who are familiar with furnace work will realise that the production of a bright flame

25 ft. long from ordinary house refuse, mixed with decaying fish and other matter of the most abominable description, is no mean achievement. It is found that when a considerable number, say six cells or more, are combined in one block the mixing of the gases from the various furnaces insures a very steady and very high temperature in the main flue, and it is therefore always found advisable to construct the furnaces in blocks in this manner rather than to divide them up and put boilers between them. At Edinburgh the main flue communicates immediately with a large dust-depositing chamber, circular in form, and of somewhat peculiar construction. The gases pass first into the outer cavity, swing round this, enter the inner cavity or well at the top, and leave it at the bottom. Various baffles are provided in the outer cavity. The swirling action thus produced causes any small quantity of dust which the gases may contain to be deposited within this chamber. The exigencies of space were the cause of the dust-catcher being placed between the cells and the boiler, which doubtless causes some loss of heat. The boiler is the original boiler belonging to the old destructor. It is of the multitubular type, and is not nearly large enough to use the whole of the heat from the cells. It, however, produces steam for forced draught apparatus and for driving a mortar mill and an electric light plant, which provides light for the destructor-house and a range of stables and superintendent's house belonging to the cleansing department.

The effect of the alterations carried out by the author's firm was that all causes of complaint were entirely removed to the satisfaction of the referee.

The tipping arrangements are as originally designed. There is a tipping-floor on each side of the row of cells, and the refuse is tipped from the carts on to the furnace top in close proximity to the feed-holes. To prevent stewing of the refuse on top of the cells, the charging floor is honeycombed with drain pipes, communicating with the forced draught apparatus, whereby fresh air is continually drawn through the pipes.

### THE DESTRUCTOR AT BRADFORD.

We may now proceed to a brief description of the twelve-cell destructor at Hammerton-street, Bradford. In this case, as in the case last described, there was originally a Fryer destructor. It had, however, been fitted some years ago with Horsfall's forced-draught apparatus, and it worked with fair success until it was considered by the corporation to be worn out. The contract for reconstructing the furnaces was then entrusted to the author's firm. The destructor consisted of two blocks of six cells each, with a pair of multitubular boilers and a chimney between the two blocks. Each block of cells has a passage through one boiler and an alternative passage direct to the chimney. These cells were ordered by the corporation to be completely removed to the ground level, and the new cells were constructed entirely with new material and according to improved designs prepared under the immediate supervision of the author. The flues are arranged exactly as described in the case of the Edinburgh destructor, the dimensions of the cross flues being slightly enlarged, in the light of more recent experience. The dimensions of the charging holes and feeding table were also slightly altered for the same reasons, in order to insure a greater facility in charging. Observations having been made with regard to parts of the old destructor, which had failed after years of service, the new one was constructed with much heavier end walls and with far more massive stays. It is tied together by means of heavy rolled-steel joints 8 in. by 4 in. and tie rods 1¼ in. diameter, swelled to 1⅜ in. to receive the nuts, and there are two steel channels, 12 in. by 3 in., running the whole length of the block of cells over each furnace front. It was found that the ordinary cast-iron washer blocks through which the tie rods pass and which hold the channels in position were liable to give way under expansion of the furnaces. Cast-steel washer blocks were therefore substituted, and very heavy spring steel washers were placed under the nuts, in order to allow a certain limited freedom of movement. These improvements have been quite effectual. The side boxes were also improved by placing the controlling valves in the neck of the boxes and cutting off the supply of air at the point of junction with the blast flue, the openings from the side boxes in the ashpit being always left open. The blast is controlled by large swinging valves placed in cast-iron boxes built into the arch of the blast flue and bolted up to the side boxes. The movable plates which close the front of the boxes are of an improved pattern, held in place with spring wedges, and after nearly twelve months of continuous hard work not one of these plates has shown the smallest sign of either burning or cracking. The clinkering doors are also of an improved design. They are constructed similarly to the doors usually employed on plate furnaces, being hollow castings with a space at the back, which is filled up with fire-bricks. The door is balanced by a solid cast balance weight provided with a handle, and is suspended by a wire rope passing over two pulleys. Although the door weighs 5 cwt. and the balance weight the same, there is not the slightest difficulty in opening or closing it with one hand. The ashpit doors and flue doors are very carefully designed and fitted up, the faces of the doors and frames being planed and the pin holes drilled with the door in position, thus insuring a perfect close fit. They are held by lever catches working on wedge-shaped faces. The boilers belonging to this plant were not disturbed, and they are, like the Edinburgh boilers, of the multitubular type and not half large enough to take up the whole of the heat. They supply steam, however, for the forced draught apparatus, which is of the same pattern as at Edinburgh, for a large quantity of clinker-grinding and mortar-mixing machinery, for the electric lighting of the works and manager's house and office, and for certain fish-drying pans belonging to a private enterprise. The corporation contemplate putting down more boilers and machinery, to utilise the heat from the destructor. The results of the building of the new cells have been as follows : The capacity of the destructor, which was formerly 7½ tons per cell per twenty-four hours, has been increased up to 10 tons per cell per twenty-four hours, and since the men have been used to the cells a further increase up to 11 tons has taken place. This is without any increase in the number of men employed. The cost of labour has been reduced from 7¼d. to 8d. per ton under the old system to just over 5d. under the new system. This is by several pence the lowest authenticated cost of labour in the world. The temperature in the cells and fines has been very largely increased, and the smoke from the chimney has been reduced to an absolutely inappreciable quantity ; in fact, it requires a remarkably clear state of the atmosphere to be able to distinguish anything from the chimney top at all, although no dust-catcher is in use and the chimney is quite close to the cells. At Hammerton-street an ingenious arrangement of overhead railway, carrying a swinging truck into which the clinkers are pulled direct from the furnaces, has been applied to both of the blocks of cells. This is the invention of Mr. Cox, the city engineer, and Mr. McTaggart, the superintendent of the cleansing department. Improved machinery for dealing with the clinker has also been introduced, and it is a fact that since the new cells were got to work there has not been the slightest difficulty in disposing of every ounce of clinker, fine ash and fine dust produced at a profit, either in the shape of mixed mortar or of ground ballast for making plaster, concrete, &c. At the present time machinery is on order for the manufacture of artificial stone from the clinker.

### THE NORWICH DESTRUCTOR.

This is a two-cell plant, erected at the New Mills sewage pumping station of the Norwich Corporation. It was put down specifically for the purpose of raising steam, tenders having been invited upon the basis of specifying the quantity of steam to be raised instead of specifying the number of cells required. The destructor is of the single-row type, but is fed from the top, this design having been adopted to suit an existing building which it was desired to utilise. The boiler is of the Babcock & Wilcox type, of 735 square feet of heating surface. It is placed as close as possible to the pair of cells, and communicates directly with the chimney. It supplies steam for driving air compressors for Shone's patent sewage-lifting machinery. The working pressure is 120 lb. per square inch. The main features of the furnaces are precisely the same as those at Bradford. The feeding arrangements are somewhat different, there being no room to make an inclined approach roadway for carts to tip on to the top of the furnaces, as is the case at Edinburgh and Bradford. There is a pit provided below the ground level. In this pit several hopper waggons run on rails. They are brought up to the tipping beam and the carts tip into them. The bodies of the hopper waggons are then lifted off the wheels by a travelling crane and conveyed to the charging holes of the furnaces. The doors in the bottom are opened and the refuse dropped on to the drying hearth. These two furnaces, on their official trial by the city engineer of Norwich, were found to burn 30 tons of refuse per twenty-four hours, or 15 tons per cell per twenty-four hours. They evaporated over 2,400 lb. of water per hour from cold river feed to a steam pressure of 120 lb. per square inch. These results are largely in excess of the maker's guarantee. The general results obtained from this plant have been of a highly satisfactory character.*

At this point a brief description of the plant which is about to be erected for the Pembroke Township Commissioners, co. Dublin, in connection with their electric lighting station, may not be out of place. The general scheme of the plant has been arranged to suit the electric lighting plans of Mr. Robert Hammond, the consulting engineer of the commissioners. The destructor will consist of two cells of the same size as those at Norwich, and a Babcock & Wilcox boiler also of the same size. The boiler will be capable of withstanding a working pressure of 150 lb. per square inch, the proposed working pressure of the electric light boilers being 140 lb. The furnaces will be of the back-fed type, obviating the necessity of tipping the refuse on the top of the furnaces and saving 6 ft. in the height of tipping platform, and consequently reducing the slope of the inclined road. The tipping platform and building of the destructor are to be large enough for a plant of double the size, which will probably soon become necessary. When that time arrives all that will be required will be to add two cells and another boiler of the same size. For all this provision is made in the original scheme. The tipping platform is so arranged that the coal for the

electric light boilers will be tipped from it exactly where it is required, and the space under the tipping platform will form on one side coal bunkers and on the other side a cable store. The destructor, in addition to relieving the commissioners of a large quantity of objectionable refuse, will provide some 80 horse-power in aid of the electric light station and in reduction of the coal bill. This will be the first high-temperature destructor to be erected in Ireland, and it will also be the first destructor in Ireland combined with a public electric lighting plant. The Commissioners of Pembroke Township are therefore to be congratulated upon their foresight in becoming the pioneers of the sanitary disposal and economical utilisation of town refuse in Ireland.

## ARBITRATIONS AND AWARDS.

The arbitration case of Yates v. The Leigh District Council has been concluded, before Mr. J. W. Fair, F.S.I., as arbitrator. The claim was for £11,500, for the acquisition by the council of the Market-street premises, trade interest, &c., of Mr. Yates, a pork butcher. Mr. Bradbury represented the council and Mr. Edward Boyle, Q.C., appeared for the plaintiff. Mr. Yates deposed that he did a large wholesale and country business by means of carts. The business profits were put down at £1,500 per year nett. Messrs. G. Needham & Brody, pork butchers, of Manchester, also gave evidence. For the council, Mr. J. H. Stephen valued the property at £2,683 12s., with one and a half years' purchase on the nett profits. Mr. John Cross, Manchester, valued the premises at £110 per annum, and deducting £8, or 7½ per cent., for repairs and insurance, the nett annual value was £102, which at twenty-two years' purchase would produce £2,244. Adding £247 for fixtures and 10 per cent. for compulsory sale, or £249 2s., his total valuation for land, buildings and fixtures came to £2,740 2s. He did not consider the loss by trade disturbance a serious one, and one and a half years' purchase would be, in his opinion, full compensation on Mr. Yates' retail business. Other evidence having been given, the award was reserved.

Mr. Ambrose, Q.C., M.P., recently sat at Manchester as arbitrator in the case of Danby's Trustees v. The Leigh District Council. The claim was for £13,000, for the acquisition by the council of the shop and premises 24 Market-street for purposes of street improvement, the claim including the value of the land, buildings, stock-in-trade, goodwill, and damages for injury to trade by compulsory removal, &c. Mr. Edward Boyle, Q.C., and Mr. J. C. Calvert appeared for the claimants and Mr. J. K. Bradbury for the district council. Mr. W. Wilson, Manchester, was called on behalf of the claimants, and said he valued the land, buildings and fixtures at £7,973. The nett profits of the business were stated to be £1,200 per annum, although no account books had been kept, and the accountants on both sides had not been able to complete what examination they could make of the existing books. The stock was valued at £3,850, and witness considered a loss of 40 per cent. would accrue in realising it. Mr. T. T. Wainwright, Liverpool; Colonel Bridgeford, Manchester ; and Mr. G. Heaton, Leigh and Wigan, also gave evidence, supporting the statements made by Mr. Wilson. On behalf of the district council, Mr. J. H. Stephen valued the land and buildings at £4,529, and considered that in addition one and a half years' purchase on the nett profits ought to be allowed for trade disturbance and any depreciation that might accrue in removing the stock. Mr. John Cross, F.S.I., fixed the nett annual value of the premises at £178 2s., and this at twenty-two years' purchase gave a total value of the freehold of £3,918 4s. Then he reckoned £389 13s. for the fixtures, and added 10 per cent. for forced sale (£430 15s.), making a total of £4,738 12s. Mr. Thomas R. Greenough, Leigh, said that he considered £8 per yard would be a fair price for the land on which Mr. Danby's property stood, and £188 3s. 6d. was a fair gross rental for the premises. He valued the property and fixtures at £4,760 8s. The case then closed, the award being reserved.

## QUERIES AND REPLIES.

*Sketches accompanying Queries should be made separate on white paper, in plain black-ink lines. Lettering or figures should be bold and plain.*

### 212. Institution of Civil Engineers' Examinations: Model Answers to Questions.—"Pupil" writes : Will you kindly inform me if there are any model questions and answers issued in connection with the students' examinations (Institution of Civil Engineers), and, if so, where can I obtain same?

We are not aware of any book having been published giving model answers to questions set at these examinations.

**Tenders Wanted.**—The Secretary of State for Foreign Affairs has received a dispatch from her Majesty's Consul-General at Hamburg stating that tenders are invited by the City of Hamburg for supplying 1,000,000 kilog., or about 19,692 cwt., of Portland cement for the use of the Hamburg engineering department.

* It will be remembered that we published some illustrations of this destructor in our issue of June 17th, in connection with the recent district meeting of the Association of Municipal and County Engineers at Norwich.—Ed. THE SURVEYOR.

# Royal Institute of Public Health.

## ANNUAL CONGRESS AT DUBLIN.—II.

In our last issue we gave a brief outline of the proceedings of this congress and the chief passages of Sir Charles Cameron's address. The remainder of our report will consist of a summary of the sectional proceedings. Some of the most important papers touching on municipal engineering will, however, be dealt with separately. It will be seen that in another column we give the paper on "Dust Destructors" contributed by Mr. Watson to the Engineering and Building Section.

## SECTION OF PREVENTIVE MEDICINE AND VITAL STATISTICS.

The business of this section, of which Dr. T. W. Grimshaw, C.B., the Registrar-General, was chairman, was opened by Dr. R. B. Mahon, F.R.C.S.E., Ballinrobe, who read a paper on the causes and management of outbreaks of typhus fever occurring in rural sanitary districts. This was followed by papers on "The Prevention of Measles in Rural Districts," by Dr. Patrick Letters, Valentia Island ; "The Control of Infectious Diseases, with special reference to Measles and Whooping Cough," by Dr. William Berry, J.P., Wigan ; "The Notification of Measles," by Dr. J. Wright-Mason ; "The Present Day Methods and Appliances for the Suppression of Scarlatina, Small-Pox, Diphtheria, and Typhus Fever in Rural and Urban Sanitary Districts having populations of 5,000 and under," by Dr. J. T. Kelly, Enniscorthy ; and "The Duties of the Community with regard to Tuberculosis," by Dr. Joseph O'Carroll. The section then adjourned till the following day.

On the members re-assembling on Saturday (the 20th ult.), the Registrar-General, president of the section, delivered an address on "The Relations between Preventive Medicine and Vital Statistics." The following papers were then read : "The Increase of Lunacy in Ireland," by Mr. Wm. Corbett, M.P. ; "A Few Causes of the Increase of Insanity in Ireland," by Mr. J. W. Tate ; and "The Treatment of Infectious Diseases in General Hospitals," by Sir Wm. Stokes. Papers having been read by Drs. T. Laffan, J. B. Storey, A. H. Jacob and J. Knox Denham, treating of puerperal fever, ophthalmia and bacteriology, the section again adjourned.

Re-assembling on the following Tuesday, Prof. Smith, president of the Royal Institute of Public Health, read a paper on "The Vital Statistics of Dublin in Comparison with those of London." A number of resolutions were then adopted, after which Dr. J. A. Morehead introduced a discussion on the subject of workhouse hospital reform. Miss Rose M. Barrett next read a paper on "Some Aspects of Child Life." At 12 o'clock the section concluded their meeting, the remaining papers on the programme being taken as read. These were as follows : "Defective Infant Life," by Mr. Walter Bernard, F.R.C.P.I. ; "Popular Education in the Laws of Health," by Dr. Anthony Roche ; "Administrative Aspect of the Marking of Meat," by Mr. R. Sydney Marsden, F.R.C.P.I.,ENG. ; "Defect in Door-Bin System," by Dr. G. B. White ; "Real Improvement in Sanitation for the Working Classes," by Dr. T. Laffan ; "Exhibition—Photographs in Omagh," by Dr. Walter Bernard ; "Observations made in the Anthropological Laboratory of Trinity College, Dublin," by Prof. Cunningham, M.D., F.R.S., and Dr. Charles R. Browne ; and "Slaughter-Houses," by Dr. C. E. Moore, M.D.

## CHEMISTRY AND METEROLOGY SECTION.

The section devoted to chemistry and meteorology met under the presidency of Dr. John Williams Moore, F.R.C.P.I.

The PRESIDENT, in his opening address, dealt with the climatology of the city of Dublin and the scenery of the country. Dublin comprised an area with the municipal boundary of 3,733 acres, containing, in 1891, 25,764 inhabited houses and a population of 245,001. But these figures by no means represented what may be called "Greater Dublin," or the Dublin registration district. This consists not only of the city proper, but also of the populous suburban districts of Rathmines, Donnybrook, Blackrock, Kingstown, Clontarf, Howth, Coolock, Drumcondra, Finglas, Glasnevin and Palmerston. The population of this "Greater Dublin" was, in 1891, 349,594 ; and its extent is 24,093 statute acres. At the present time a costly and extensive system of main drainage was in process of construction, and would, no doubt, have a highly beneficial effect upon the health of the city, especially in respect of the prevalence of and fatality from filth diseases. Dublin was a handsome and in parts a picturesque city, and it was well supplied with "lungs" in the splendid squares on both north and south sides of the Liffey. The grave defect, which does much to neutralise the beneficial effect of the situation and surroundings of the capital upon public health was the housing of the poorer classes. All sanitary reformers agree that the housing of the poor was one of the most pressing questions of the day in Dublin. Much had been done of late years to abate the crying evil of the Dublin tenement-houses—witness the splendid work of the Dublin Artisans' Dwellings Company, of the Corporation of Dublin, and last, but not least, of the Guinness Trust, which had given living expression to the philanthropy and princely munificence of the

Right Hon. Lord Iveagh, K.P. A further movement was on foot at present to provide sanitary accommodation on very reasonable terms for even the very poor among the industrious and sober classes of the population. Having dealt with the mean temperature, the rainfall and relative humidity, the president said the climate of Dublin was in the fullest sense an insular one, free from extremes of heat and cold except on very rare occasions, and characterised by a moderate rainfall (about 28 in.) annually. He concluded his address by describing some of the natural beauties of Ireland, which he said, was in truth a land of poetry and romance.

### KINGSTOWN AS A HEALTH RESORT.

Dr. J. BYRNE POWER, Kingstown, read a paper on "Kingstown as a Health Resort." The climate of that town was, he said, considerably milder than that of the Phœnix Park. This difference was remarkable, and showed the modifying influence of sea temperature upon places in immediate proximity to the coast. During the winter months the mean temperature of Kingstown was equal to that of Ventnor. The rainfall at Kingstown was very low, and during the winter months was considerably less than that at any station on the south coast of England, being little more than half that at Penzance. These comparisons showed the superiority of the climate of Kingstown in these respects to some of the most favoured English health resorts. As regards sanitary conditions of life in Kingstown, he had to state that the Vartry water supply was excellent in quality, and the sewerage of the township had gradually been extended. The central sewers were now good, and when the works at the West Pier outfall have been completed by the Drainage Board he thought that there would be little to complain of. Thus they found all that the physical and sanitary conditions of life at Kingstown were favourable. But the general death rate was very high for a place enjoying all the natural advantages of Kingstown, the rate for last year being 22·3, and the birth rate comparatively low, that for last year being 21·2. A statement of the following facts might be sufficient to prove the deplorable insanitary condition of the township up to the year 1866. In that year Kingstown was visited by an epidemic of cholera, which in about four months carried off 127 lives. In 1871 the pure Vartry water was turned on to the township, and from that time to the present Kingstown had been free from any serious epidemic, though frequently exposed to infection from the city. Then if they examined the annual zymotic death rate for the past eighteen years they would find that the average annual number of such deaths for the last ten years had diminished by nearly one half. Towards the close of 1886 the present system of domestic scavenging was first established, and to this alone could he attribute this most marked decrease in their zymotic death rate. He found that the average zymotic rate in Kingstown for the last five years was less than half that of the total for twenty-one of the principal towns in Ireland, excepting the large cities of Dublin and Belfast, and considerably below that for the adjoining townships of Blackrock and Rathmines. All this had been accomplished, although he had hitherto failed to induce the sanitary authority to adopt the Infectious Diseases Notification Act or to provide the township with a small hospital for infectious diseases. If those two means were adopted he had no doubt that the zymotic death rate could be reduced as low as that at any English health resort.

One of the honorary secretaries then read a paper, by Mr. J. E. Cullum, Valentia Observatory, on "The Climatology of Valentia Island." This was followed by papers on "Valentia as a Health Resort," by Dr. Patrick Letters, and "Some Meteorological and other Statistics in Connection with the National Hospital for Consumption for Ireland," by Dr. B. H. Steede, M.D., and the section adjourned.

Resuming business on Saturday, Prof. J. C. Thresh, M.D., medical officer of health to the Essex County Council, read a paper on "The Protection of Urban and Rural Water Supplies." This was followed by a paper by Dr. Edgar Flinn, entitled "Some Points in the Supply of Water to Villages in Ireland." Dr. Flinn maintained that sanitary authorities should be especially careful as to the manner in which the contracts for supplying villages with drinking water were carried out, as frequently, through inexperience or incompetence on the one hand on the part of a contractor, and from lack of skilled supervision on the other, the supply was often scanty and defective in every particular.

Mr. FRANCIS HYNDMAN, B.SC.LONDON, read a paper on "The Commercial Production of Cold Sterilised Water." This process was described and illustrated in our issue of July 29th. In the course of the discussion which followed,

Prof. MACWERNEY said a great deal of false confidence in the purity of water was produced by the habit of relying on analyses of samples sent to experts living at a distance from the source of supply. He believed that nothing could compensate for the want of personal inspection of the source of supply by the expert. Samples taken from the Liffey, for example, at one time of the twenty-four hours might differ very much from samples taken at another hour, and the condition of the weather at the time at which the sample was taken would also make a difference. The analysis should be made by an expert who had himself collected the sample at the source from which it was obtained, and who could judge the possibility of pollution to which the well or other source was exposed. He did not think it necessary to sterilise water for drinking purposes. The great object should be to keep pathogenic germs out of a water supply, and the only way to accomplish that was to select a collecting ground which would not be exposed to contamination from manure, sewage, &c.

The following resolution was, on the motion of Prof. Thresh, unanimously adopted : "That legislation is urgently needed for securing the supervision of all public water supplies, in order to ensure the provision of pure and wholesome water ; and, further, that it is desirable that sanitary authorities should be empowered to make by-laws with reference to the construction and protection of private wells, and to enable them to close all wells yielding a water liable to dangerous pollution." It was resolved to send a copy of the foregoing resolution to the Local Government Board.

Dr. W. ADENEY, F.L.C., read a paper on "The Determination of the Polluting Power of Drainage Waters by Bacterio-Chemical Methods."

Prof. MACWEENEY read a paper entitled "A Plea for the More Complete Biological Examination of Water Supply." He began by pointing out the several advantages and drawbacks of the various methods of water analysis. Notwithstanding the high degree of accuracy to which chemical methods had been brought, they left us in the dark as to the origin and nature of polluting organic matters. Turning to the bacteriological analysis, he said it certainly gave expression to the extent and character of the water pollution in a most decisive manner. Great care had, however, to be exercised in collecting samples, and the analysis had to be proceeded with at once. The analysis required to be extended to the totality of the micro-organisms present. The expert should in every case visit the source of supply and collect personally, not only the water sample, but also specimens of the various gelatinous or filamentous growths or incrustations which might be found close to the water. Such growths presented the great advantage of representing the average condition of the water. The microscopic side of water analysis deserved more attention than had hitherto been paid to it. The determination of the degree to which contamination of a stream had taken place—whether by sewage or refuse water from factories—could be accurately estimated by this microscopic, or, as he preferred to call it, biological method. In conclusion, the author referred to a series of algæ, fungi and protozoa which he had obtained from the river Liffey between O'Connell and Grattan bridges, and which afforded a capital illustration of the fauna and flora of a most gravely polluted river. He hoped soon to be in a position to publish lists of the several low forms of animal and vegetable life that characterised pure and variously contaminated waters, and hoped thereby to enable an estimate of the real character of such waters to be arrived at with greater accuracy than was heretofore possible.

Prof. TICHBORNE read a paper on "The Adulteration of Foods and Drugs," and the section adjourned until the Tuesday following.

Resuming on Tuesday, Mr. ROBERT J. DOWNS, president of the Pharmaceutical Society of Ireland, read a paper entitled "Legislation Relative to the Sale of Poisons." At the conclusion of the discussion which followed the president proposed that the recommendations embodied in Mr. Downs' paper should be forwarded to the general meeting of the congress. This was unanimously agreed to.

Mr. RICHARD M. BARRINGTON, M.A., LL.B., then submitted some meteorological tables embodying the results of observations taken at Fassaroe, Bray, co. Wicklow, for thirty-four years (since 1864), and the proceedings of the section closed.

MUNICIPAL AND PARLIAMENTARY SECTION.

The above section conducted their deliberations under the presidency of the Right Hon. Alderman Meade.

Sir CHARLES CAMERON, as president of the congress, said that he had great pleasure in installing the Right Hon. Alderman Meade as president of that section. Alderman Meade was chairman of the Reception Committee, and for many months past he had taken an active part in making arrangements for receiving the members and delegates of the congress. He was sure that they were all prepared to listen to Alderman Meade's address.

Alderman MEADE then delivered his presidential address. He said it was with very great pleasure that he availed himself of the invitation of the Royal Institute of Public Health to open the municipal and Parliamentary section. Although the other departments of the congress devoted themselves to important points of the general question of public health, its establishment and safeguarding lay almost entirely in the hands of Parliament and the municipalities. Parliament could make laws for its maintenance, while to see them effectively carried out was one of the chief functions of the municipal and other corporate bodies. First in order in the programme of this section was placed the

HOUSING OF THE WORKING CLASSES,

but especially of the very poor members of those classes.

He was glad that a distinction had been drawn. Owing to the congested area of Dublin, this work was there surrounded with difficulties and expense unknown in modern centres of industry in England or Scotland. Might he be permitted to quote an instance being at present carried out by the corporation to illustrate the difficulties they had to contend with ? In the month of August, 1893, the Public Health Committee reported to the council that a certain district, called the Bride's-alley area, should be acquired, the site cleared and dwellings erected, which the council approved. All necessary steps were taken, an inquiry held by the Local Government Board inspector, and the scheme approved and sanction given to the obtaining of a loan in February, 1896. The area of the site was 3 acres. Now, the cost so far—and they have not yet, after five years, got possession of the whole of the site—had been : Cost of site, £32,000 ; clearing and levelling site, £1,500 ; legal expenses and costs, £3,000 = £36,500. This, he thought, would show that it was impossible for the corporation to clear sites and erect healthy dwellings without a serious loss to the corporate fund. But he was of opinion that such works were works of great practical utility and for the advancement and improvement of the public health, and should not be charged to the Artisans' Dwellings Act, but to the expenditure under the Public Health Act ; and that when sites were cleared by the corporation they should be allowed to get the site valued as a building site and offered to private companies or individuals for building dwellings on same suitable for artisans or labourers, to be let at moderate rents, the plans to be submitted to and approved by the corporation, or that the corporation itself might be empowered to build, when he had no doubt but that a fair return would be obtained for the amount expended. But the housing of the very poor would require more enterprise and energy ; there philanthropy, public or private, must come in. One great problem, then, which faced the promoters of public health was how were healthy dwellings to be provided for the very poor at 1s. or 1s. 3d. per week. Sir Charles Cameron, their distinguished officer of health, had started a scheme by which it was hoped it would be shown that, if a site be provided and no taxes charged, a block of dwellings could be erected, according to plans prepared by their city architect, Mr. J. C. M'Carthy, providing comfortable dwellings which could be let a 1s. 3d. per week, pay for all maintenance, collection of rents, &c., and allow 2½ per cent. on the capital sunk. He earnestly commended the scheme to the philanthropic members of the congress. Now, in addition to the desirability of existing private benevolence in that vital matter, he thought the sanitary authority ought to be empowered, if it was not already, to provide for that work free sites and exemption from local taxes. That could not be considered a new burden on the ratepayers, for it was merely a better way of spending the rates. If the classes he was referring to were not helped in that way in the struggle to earn, and were kept in their present miserable and unsanitary dwellings, where they were liable to be affected with disease and rendered unable to work, they must be supported in poor-houses, hospitals or refuges, or assisted by the many charitable organisations in the city at a much greater cost than if his recommendation were adopted, and their great object, public health, would be endangered. Now, if thus provided for, the very poor among the working classes, and if the health authorities put in force the ample powers at their disposal to compel landlords receiving fair rents to keep their premises in order, the question of the housing of the working classes seemed within measurable distance of solution. While on that subject he alluded to the insufficient number of public libraries and technical schools in Dublin, and he expressed a hope that the corporation, under the new Local Government Bill, would provide at least four additional libraries, with proper equipments, reading and assembly rooms, and also proper technical schools, one at each side of the city, suitable to the public requirements as understood and adequate for this city of 255,000 inhabitants. The next item of the programme was

THE MUNICIPALISATION OF TRAMWAYS AND PUBLIC LIGHTING.

There was no doubt as to the advisability of that ; the provision of public wants should not be in the hands of private individuals. As to tramways, lighting, water supply, &c., one great reason for their being in the hands of the municipality was that there would be only one authority with power over the public streets. Now, in Dublin or any great city the divided authority results in the roadways being continually cut up. The corporation scarcely closed an opening for water or sewer purposes when the gas company does it for a supply from their mains. The city engineer had had scarcely time to finish his portion of the street and remove the débris when the tramway company bring on to the thoroughfare material for the purpose of repairing their portion, and at present many citizens complained of the divided authority that has several leading streets in an almost impassable condition. Public lighting as to gas would have been in the hands of the corporation many years since but that several leading citizens opposed the corporation of the day and prevented them getting power from Parliament to purchase from the gas company, and at such a price as would have before that paid off the capital required, paid the interest on the capital, and would now be contributing a large annual sum in aid of the rates. Electric lighting, he was glad to say, was in the hands of the corporation, but at present, owing to the small area supplied, the price charged was high. Yet, as application was about to be made for a very extensive addition to the works and also for liberty to supply electricity for motive and other purposes than lighting, he had no doubt that in Dublin they would have the same result as in other large cities (Edinburgh, for example), and be able to supply the citizens with electric lighting and power at a very low price without any charge on the rates, and that that great source of revenue would be kept in trust for the people in the hands of their representatives. When tramways were first introduced into the city the corporation of the day thought it was a great advantage to secure cheap fares and easy travelling through the city, to have so many miles of the streets paved and maintained by the tramway company, and gave concessions and rights of way to the company almost amounting to a monopoly. At that time, of course, the value of the concession was not known, but now that the application of electricity to the haulage of these carriages had become a commercial success, the corporation being hampered by the rights conceded to the tramway company, had only been able to arrange with the company for a moderate rental for a term of years, when the lines and the right to use them would revert to the corporation. As a citizen of Dublin he could refer with pride to their unequalled supply of pure water, which was given, not only to their own citizens, but to the inhabitants of the surrounding townships (except Rathmines), and at the cheapest rate in the whole kingdom. The next item was hideous hoardings, which subject would be treated by his friend, Dr. Drew. The latter would show the intimate connection between sanitation, or rather insanitation, and the terminable leaseholds in towns. It was obvious that those owners of house property whose leases were running out or about to expire would not, if they could avoid it, lay out money in the sanitation of what would shortly be other people's premises. Nowadays there was more necessity for providing harmless recreation for the people than formerly. There was a field for municipal work. In Glasgow, the second city of the empire in population and enterprise, the corporation owned and managed eight concert halls. In Manchester the swimming baths were used during the winter months as gymnasia and concert halls. He hoped they would soon be able to boast that they had done something in that way in Dublin. The next item—the

EXTENSION OF TOWNS

as a means of promoting public health—was one that, as a public health reformer and member of a municipal body, interested him most. On the recommendations in very many cases, and with the approval of Parliament, the chief cities and towns in England and Scotland—in Ireland they had the case of Belfast—had been extended, and the outlying districts added to the towns. There in Dublin the city had provided for the artisan who worked inside and outside its boundaries dwellings and model lodging-houses, at a cost of over £200,000. All the hospitals except one were in the city, and their support was largely contributed out of the city rates. Technical schools, swimming baths, public libraries, &c., were open to the residents of the townships and the working classes employed there, as well as to the city ratepayers. So glaring had been that injustice, that in 1879 a Royal Commission was held, and a unanimous recommendation was made to include the townships only separated by a few canal bridges from the city. But now, nearly twenty years after, they remained still cut off, enjoying all the benefits of the city, but congesting its population into the unparalleled and unhealthy overcrowding of sixty-four persons to the acre, a state of things unknown in any other city in the kingdom. How the city in such a condition preserved even its present moderate death rate would be a puzzle were they not acquainted with the efficient and vigilant working of the Public Health Department. It would, perhaps (continued the speaker), be interesting to review a part of what the corporation of Dublin had effected in the last half-century. The new corporation (so soon to be called the old) repaved the city, constructed the unrivalled waterworks, reconstructed and built many miles of main sewers, cleaned spaces, erected artisans' dwellings, opened people's parks, swimming baths, public libraries, electric power stations, and were at present constructing a great system of main drainage, all those costing not less than £2,000,000. He trusted their visitors would be enabled to see those works and judge of the manner of their execution. In concluding, he could not fail to express his belief that the progress of the congress and of their section would be productive of much good, that it would promote the interests of public health, especially in those matters in which Parliament and municipal action could be effective, and, not least of all, that by the happy combination of all creeds and classes, comprising many visitors from the sister isles, it would knit them all closer together in the common effort to make the public health better and life all round for all classes more useful and more pleasant.

Sir CHARLES CAMERON, in proposing a vote of thanks to Alderman Meade for the admirable address he had delivered, said he might divide sanitarians into two classes—first, critical sanitarians who never themselves did anything to further sanitation, but were always ready to criticise the action of those who were actively engaged in the work. Then

there were practical sanitarians, among whom he counted their friend, Alderman Meade. Alderman Meade had referred in his address to the very important subject of the housing of the poor. He (Sir Charles) claimed to have originated the term "housing of the very poor."

Mr. R. P. CARTEN, q.c., in seconding the resolution, said he had listened with very great interest to the thoroughly practical and able address that Alderman Meade had given. During his short experience as a divisional magistrate in Dublin the importance of the housing of the very poor had been brought home to him in a very special manner. Having regard to the mode of housing the very poor in Dublin, and their singular want of anything in the nature of amusements, there was very little alternative but the public-house. It was his opinion, based on his experience as a magistrate, that at the bottom of all misery, and at the bottom of nearly all crime, was this evil of drink. He hoped before the meeting of the section terminated that some practical suggestion would be made that would enable projects for the better housing of the poor to be carried out.

The resolution was carried unanimously.

Alderman MEADE returned thanks, and remarked that if the corporation decided to forego all taxes on houses devoted to the very poor it would go far to remove a difficulty in the way of constructing these houses. He hoped one of the first advantages to be derived under the new Bill would be to enable the corporation to devote funds for the purpose of providing proper houses for the very poor.

THE HOUSING OF THE WORKING CLASSES, INCLUDING THE
VERY POOR.

Sir CHARLES CAMERON said that he had been invited to open the discussion on the housing of the working classes, including the very poor. As much of the subject had been dealt with in the presidential address, and as the president of the congress had gone largely into it on the previous day, very few observations were required from him now to initiate the discussion of the subject. He was altogether in sympathy with the workers in their desire to have decent, comfortable homes, but it should be borne in mind that the artisan who had from 35s. to 40s. a week was able to pay rent for a fairly decent cottage or tenement. He had never been very much in favour of providing out of the funds of public boards for dwellings for those who could pay 3s. 6d. or more a week. The people to be considered were those who could not pay more than 1s. to 2s. per week, and he thought that it was the duty of their members of Parliament to keep pressing on the legislature until it passed a law to provide decent dwellings for such people. That subject was, he thought, among the first problems in sanitation.

Sir WILLIAM PINK thought that the housing of the very poor required very careful consideration. It was an expensive matter, but one that should be tackled; and, on the other hand, they would make a saving in the cost of hospitals if they had healthy sanitary dwellings.

Sir T. W. RUSSELL, M.P., Parliamentary secretary to the Local Government Board, remarked that he knew the city of Dublin, and he had learnt a good deal on the question of the housing of the working classes in England on the Local Government Board. He thought that the city of Dublin differed largely from the circumstances of any other city in the three kingdoms. It was not alone that these tenement houses were of the worst and the poorest character, but to his own knowledge they were largely in the hands of small house-jobbers, who bought at the lowest rate possible and charged naturally the highest rent they could get. He confessed that he did not share Sir Charles Cameron's squeamishness in dealing with those gentlemen. They had gone into this business, they had made their investment deliberately, and he should be very much inclined to tell them when they bought this property they bought the responsibility, and he would strongly advise the corporation to insist upon these houses, so far as it was possible to do it, being put into habitable order. These were things that should be insisted upon. Dublin was blessed with a pure, admirable, wholesome water supply. Householders had no excuse on that ground, and therefore the corporation ought to insist upon their doing what was plainly their duty. As to the requirements of sanitation, he would say the same thing. He was delighted to know that the corporation after many years' struggle had at last tackled the main drainage question. He knew ratepayers' associations and municipal bodies rarely agreed. He was delighted that the Dublin Corporation had had at last the courage to get a thorough system of main drainage. Much had been done in recent years, but, as regards the drainage of the tenement-houses, the corporation should see that they were put into a sanitary condition. The people who had these houses were responsible for them in the ordinary way. English and Scottish representatives who were present there that day could have no idea of the difficulties that beset the local authorities of Dublin and other Irish cities. It was not the same question. The class of people were poorer; everything was worse rather than better. So far as Dublin was concerned the position was different from any English city or town by the poverty of the people and by the want of work. The want of work was not due to strikes, but absolute want of work. In the country much had been done by the south and west, so far as the agricultural labourers' cottages were concerned. He hoped that the

Dublin Corporation would not be bothering their heads about the ratepayers' associations. He would advise the corporation to give these ratepayers' associations a wide berth, and he trusted that they would take up this question of the houses for the very poor of the city.

Alderman Sir Robert Sexton thought there was no doubt that the housing of the extreme poor was the most important consideration that they had to deal with in the City of Dublin. He did not attach any importance to the question of return, but the corporation should do what it could to provide comfortable dwellings for those who could not afford more than 1s. to 2s. a week rent. He was strongly in favour of anything that could be done towards the carrying out of that work, but the difficulty that they had was the large number of tenement houses in the City of Dublin. He thought if they could raise sufficient money for the housing of the very poor it would be one of the greatest benefits that could be conferred on the sanitary arrangements of the City of Dublin. The corporation were in favour of carrying out the suggestions of the Public Health Department, but some things could not be done right away, and they should remember that this was a very large question. He hoped that one of the outcomes of that congress would be that this subject would be taken up energetically. If they got the corporation to make a grant of the site for this purpose, he thought that would be as much as they could ask them to do, for the corporation, they should remember, had recently carried out works that involved a large expenditure of money for the benefit of the citizens and the interests of the city generally. He hoped that the philanthropic public would be awakened to an interest in the matter.

Mr. John Byrne (Dublin) said that Sir Charles Cameron, under the auspices of the corporation, had made a beginning in the way of providing healthy dwellings for the very poor, having cleared a site on which to erect houses to be let at 1s. to 1s. 6d. a week. He had heard complaints from working men as to the uniformity of style in the new houses erected for them, and there were also complaints as to the distance these houses were from their work. It might be worth the while of the corporation to consider whether the corporation might not provide dwellings for the very poor by entering into possession of the houses where the very poor now lived, and putting them into sanitary repair, thus providing houses in the centre of the districts in which employment was to be found. Mr. Russell had made a sweeping charge against owners of tenement-houses. He (Mr. Byrne) was not a tenement-house owner, but he knew that several owners had gone to great expense in putting their houses in fair tenantable repair, only to find in a very short time that the appliances were misused by the tenants, the water pipes broken, and the sewers blocked by foreign matter. The rent, in fact, was only a sort of insurance against the exorbitant sums they were called upon to pay for the repairs they were forced by the sanitary authorities to make.

Colonel Whitney (Liverpool) endorsed the views expressed by Sir Charles Cameron, but said they should be very careful how they carried out the idea, as he found from experience that many people who had no right to these houses were admitted as tenants. He believed in doing away with workhouses, as it was his opinion if they gave the very poor decent houses to live in and helped them with outdoor relief that the condition of the poor would be very greatly improved.

Bailie Dick, chairman of the Health Committee, Glasgow, described the work of the Glasgow Corporation in housing the poor, and said their great difficulty was how to provide accommodation for the poorest of the poor. The income from houses rented to such a class would not pay the outlay, and he was afraid the only way to overcome that was to make the ratepayers provide the deficit out of the rates.

Dr. Shelton Daly (Manchester), Mr. W. S. Brown, J.P. (Edinburgh), Dr. Niven (medical officer, Manchester), Mr. Batley (chairman of the Building Committee, Leeds), Mr. Henry A. Cutler (city engineer, Cork), Mr. John Lindsay (solicitor to the Glasgow Corporation), Mr. W. R. Cooney (Enniskillen), Mr. J. Howes, J.P. (St. Luke's, London), Mr. W. J. Robinson (Londonderry), and Mr. William Field, M.P., also added some remarks.

Alderman Meade then reviewed the various points made by the speakers, and expressed the hope that the very interesting discussion might be productive of good by marking the inauguration of schemes for housing the very poor.

TERMINABLE LEASEHOLD SYSTEM.

Mr. William Field, M.P., then read an interesting paper on "The Terminable Leasehold System in Regard to Municipal Sanitation," in the course of which he reviewed the relations existing between ground landlords and their tenants. As a rule, he said, the ground landlord took over absolutely the houses built by the tenant. The absence of security for the tenant was a direct incentive to carelessness in everything, particularly sanitation. The present system discouraged enterprise and thrift among working classes and prevented the operation of building societies. It encouraged jerry building and maintained badly-constructed houses. All the sanitary defects which the system gave rise to could be very easily changed if occupation meant ownership. The terminable leasehold system was the father of slums and the progenitor of disease. Rent was to the ground

landlord the prime necessity. Health and sanitation and human comfort were seldom considered in opposition to rent, and it was next to impossible to expect that a middleman or a house jobber, or an experimenting agent, or a holder of premises with a lease nearly expired, would lay out money for the benefit of the ground landlord, who seldom had any regard whatever for the health of the inhabitants.

Mr. J. S. Baxter, barrister-at-law, Belfast, also read a paper on the same subject, and dealt with the legal aspect of the question.

Mr. John Byrne and Mr. Linsay having spoken, the section then adjourned until the following day.

## ELECTRIC LIGHTING AT KIRKCALDY.

The town clerk of Kirkcaldy has just issued the minutes of the joint committee of the town council and the promoters of the local company on the subject of tramways and electric light for the burgh. A long letter has also been issued by the clerk to the members of the council. The minutes contain a further interesting report from Prof. Kennedy recommending a limited tramway route. The length of the line is just under 3 miles, and the total cost of the whole undertaking is estimated at £80,000. The committee, after examining the figures, did not see their way to make any recommendation to the town council in regard to the proposed scheme, but resolved to lay before the town council an abstract of the figures. In his letter to the members of council the town clerk strongly recommends them not to take up at the present time a combined scheme of tramways and electric lighting, but to consent to private companies taking up the scheme. He further expresses the opinion that an application for a combined scheme of electric lighting and tramways is incompetent. In the first place, by the rules of Parliament powers for electric lighting can only be obtained by a provisional order under the Electric Lighting Act, and not by an Act of Parliament. In the second place, electric lighting and tramways are, by the public legislation of this country, two separate things, and a town council, as local authority, are entitled to purchase either scheme without purchasing the other. He, however, thinks it necessary for the town council, in the case of the electric lighting, to apply for powers at once, more especially seeing the Edmundson Company have already given the statutory notice that they intend to apply for such an order.

## CYCLISTS AND THE ROADS.

Mr. Charles H. Lowe, surveyor to the Hampstead Vestry, says, in his annual report to that body: "The condition of the roads in Hampstead is good. The standard of excellence, however, which the cyclist has set up has not been attained, and, with the wear and tear caused by the incessant heavy traffic over the main roads, it is hardly possible for it to be, and to make special provision for bicyclists is impracticable. What it might have been had the machine been known to our forefathers can only be surmised. Probably a carriageway, two footways and a cycle track would have formed the ordinary highway repairable by the inhabitants at large. The nearest approach to the ideal, from the cyclist's point of view, is the wood-paved carriageway, and, now that the experimental stage in the use of jarrah and other similar hard woods has been passed, the only thing standing in the way of their more general adoption for paving purposes is the initial cost. The supply of the material is practically unlimited, and with the cost reduced—and it is reasonable to expect that this will be effected by the competition in the trade—there is no reason why jarrah should not be used in paving the more important streets, such as are now coated with the best quality broken granite." Referring to motor cars, Mr. Lowe says: "If ever the day does come which shall see the highways taken possession of by the horseless carriage, that same day will witness the difficulty of maintaining a smooth surface surmounted, for every wheel will have a rubber tyre, and the decrease in the number of horses pounding the roads with their hoofs will be so marked that the destroying agents in the roadway will be reduced to a minimum."

**London Tramways.**—An extraordinary general meeting of The London Tramways Company, Limited, was held at the company's offices on Monday, when resolutions passed at a previous extraordinary general meeting were confirmed. The resolutions agreed to the sale of the company's undertaking to the London County Council for £850,000, apart from a short length of 2½ miles and the Lawson-street depot, for which they were to receive a further sum of £22,872.

**Bursting of a Reservoir.**—An alarming accident happened late on Monday night at Blackley, near Manchester. A large reservoir, covering an acre of ground and 20 ft. deep, suddenly gave way, and in ten minutes the vast body of water had emptied itself. The roads were rendered impassable, and the gas and water mains were damaged, and the adjoining roadways washed away. Fortunately there were no lives lost. The water was carried in flood down the river Irk.

# Comparative Reports of General Practice.

## XXVIII.—TRAMWAY TRACTION : BLACKPOOL REPORT.—I.

On February 14, 1898, the members of the Blackpool Corporation Electric Lighting and Tramways Committee, together with Mr. Robert C. Quin, borough electrical and tramway engineer and Mr. John Lancaster, general manager of the corporation tramways, were instructed by resolution to visit the Continent in order to inspect the various systems of electric traction in operation, and they subsequently submitted a report.

The report begins by recounting the history of electric traction in Blackpool. In 1885 the corporation laid down a tramway from Cooker-street to the end of the Promenade at South Shore, and leased the running powers over the same for a period of seven years to the Blackpool Electric Tramways Company, Limited. At the expiration of this period —viz., in September, 1892—the corporation, having obtained Parliamentary powers in this behalf, purchased the company's undertaking and plant for the sum of £15,587, including expenses of purchase. In addition to this sum the corporation had expended £13,435 in the construction of the permanent way, upon which, of course, they received interest from the company during the continuance of the agreement.

It was found essential, however, on the completion of the purchase to relay part of the conduit, and to replace and repair part of the plant and machinery which had just been taken over, the cost of this work being placed against maintenance account. Notwithstanding further expenditure during 1893-94, the conduit still failed to give satisfaction, as also did the general plant, and the running of the cars continued to be very uncertain owing to breakdowns. The Electric Lighting and Tramways Committee therefore went very closely into the causes of the failure, and instructed their then engineer, Mr. John Hesketh, to furnish a report on the various systems of electric traction in use in England and on the Continent. This report, dated November 17, 1893, gave full details of the conduit, overhead, accumulator and other systems then in use.

The committee, recognising the strong objection which would then be taken if a recommendation were made to adopt the overhead system, decided to make a strong effort to put the conduit and the whole of the plant in a condition likely to ensure satisfactory working. During the winters of 1894-96 the whole of the conduit along the promenade was therefore re-laid on a new principle, at a nett cost of £6,754, and the eight old cars purchased from the company were repaired and repainted and the armatures rewound, at an additional expenditure of £1,721, all of which went to capital account. In spite of this large expenditure on the conduit, supplemented as it was by a further expenditure out of the maintenance account of £340 during 1895-96, and of £886 during 1896-97 for repairs, &c.—the trouble increased rather than decreased, and it was felt that some radical change in the system was necessary if the tramways were to be made reliable and popular and capable of yielding the handsome revenue which it was in their power to do.

The committee then instructed Mr. Quin, their borough electrical engineer, to take charge of the electrical portion of the tramways and to report on the position of affairs. On the 19th August, 1897, this report was submitted to and considered by the committee, who ultimately came to the decision that it was useless endeavouring any longer to patch up a system which the conditions obtaining in Blackpool conclusively proved to be unsuitable, and they thereupon recommended the council to abandon the conduit system and substitute for it the overhead trolley system.

The council by a majority accepted the committee's recommendations, and application was forthwith made to the Board of Trade for permission to convert the system and to borrow the moneys incidental thereto. The Board of Trade deputed Major Cardew, R.E., to hold an inquiry in the matter, and this took place on November 30, 1897. At the inquiry considerable opposition was manifested by a section of the townspeople to the corporation's proposals, unsightliness of the overhead line and danger from falling wires during gales, &c., being alleged.

On December 23, 1897, the corporation received a communication stating that the Board of Trade did not see their way to grant the permission asked for, and suggesting the use of accumulators instead of the overhead system. To this the corporation replied asking where accumulators were successfully used for traction purposes, and were referred to Hanover and Paris among other places on the Continent.

To thoroughly acquaint themselves with the various systems of electric traction, so that they might arrive at an irrevocable decision, the committee subsequently deemed it desirable that a visit should be made to the Continent to inspect the accumulator systems indicated by the Board of Trade, as has already been stated, and the council duly sanctioned this visit. The deputation accordingly left Blackpool on Wednesday morning, the 2nd February, and travelled, viâ London, Queenborough and Flushing, to Hamburg, arriving at the latter city on the evening of the Thursday following.

### HAMBURG.

The city of Hamburg is the Liverpool of the Continent, has a population of over 700,000, is generally flat, has wide well-laid streets, and an extensive system of canals and inland lakes. There are three tramway companies at work—viz., the Hamburger Strassen Eisenbahn Gesellchaft, Hamburger Altona and Hamburger Trambahn Gesellchaft. The first-named company possess 700 tram cars, the second fifty, and the third thirty-five.

The overhead system of electric traction is used throughout the city, being mostly upon what is known as the "span wire," that is to say, steel columns are erected on each side of the street and a steel wire is strung between the two carrying the overhead electrical conductor. At portions of the route. where the roads are wide, centre posts of ornamental construction are used. The general scheme is very similar for the whole of the companies—as a matter of fact, for a portion of the line all three companies run over the same route. Previous to the adoption of the overhead system, in March, 1894, horses to the number of 2,600 were used. With the exception of one or two smaller lines, horse traction has now been entirely superseded by overhead.

The first impression obtained of the working of these cars was decidedly favourable, and the deputation marvelled at the speed and the smooth travel which were everywhere apparent. There was no jolting over points or crossings, nothing to indicate that there was motion but the hum of the wheels and the hum of the trolley as the car pursued its 14 miles per hour journey through the town.

The general appearance of the cars also is pleasing. They are throughout of the single-deck type, carrying from twenty-nine to thirty-nine passengers, lightly painted and brilliantly lit after dusk. Five 16 candle-power lamps are used inside each car, one on the rear platform and four on the roof, two being at each end, making ten lamps in all. The roof lights are placed in coloured lanterns, to indicate the route of the car. Generally these routes radiate from the Rathaus Markt, or Town Hall-square, and standing in this place the cars were timed and found to pass every half minute in the same direction. In fact, never less than six cars were in sight at one time.

The span-wire system of carrying the overhead conductor, though somewhat unsightly where junctions and corners occur, is one which certainly is suited to the city of Hamburg, as in wide thoroughfares trees are planted which almost hide from view the steel posts, and in narrow thoroughfares no posts are used, the wires being supported from rosettes attached to houses on each side of the street.

As the system of working by each of these companies is almost identical, the deputation confined their inquiries principally to the largest company—viz., the Hamburger Strassen Eisenbahn Gesellchaft. They were first conducted over the generating station, which supplies current both for the lighting of the town and for the cars of all three companies. This station was formerly the property of the municipality, but was some time ago transferred to a company distinct from any of the tramway companies.

At this central station are installed six engines, five of which are each coupled direct to two dynamos, the other engine to one dynamo. Each set is capable of generating 500 units per hour. Two of the sets work at a pressure of 250 to 300 volts for lighting, the other four sets working at a pressure of from 500 to 600 volts for traction purposes. Arrangements are made upon the switchboard, however, for placing the dynamos of the lighting sets in series with one another and using the whole of the plants for the power supply if necessary. During the daytime, the lighting load being small, it is taken by motor-driven dynamos from the tramway supply. The engines are of the triple expansion condensing type, running at a speed of 100 revolutions per minute, and working at a steam pressure of 160 lb. Welsh coal is used in the boilers.

From this station twenty-six feeders radiate to different points of the overhead line, at which points meters are placed for the registration of the current. The largest company take current to the extent of some 600,000 units per month, or, roughly, three times as many units as the Blackpool trams in one year. The tramway company pay 12½ pfennigs, or 1½d., per unit, of which sum the lighting company pay 2·5 pfennigs, or ·3d., to the municipality. In addition to this indirect tax, the tramway company also pay a further sum of 1 pfennig for every ticket issued. This is probably the reason why they do not, as in some other cases, issue short stage tickets, but invariably issue the ticket for the whole journey.

At present this company have 120 miles of tram road, principally double track, working on the overhead system of traction. The gauge of the track is the usual standard, 1·435 metres or 4 ft. 8½ in. There are car depots at numerous points of the line. Their principal depot, at Falkenreid, is not only a car shed but also a manufactory.

Starting to build their own cars, they now construct cars

for other companies. At the present time their output of new cars averages ten per week, and when the deputation visited these premises the company were executing an order for 150 cars for Berlin. Not only are tram cars manufactured at these premises, but uniforms also for the drivers and conductors. The undertaking is certainly an example of remarkable enterprise and capable management, the arrangements being everything that could be desired.

The deputation were also interested in the museum attached to the works, which contained a remarkable historical collection of tramway roads and tramway appliances, commencing with the earliest form of tramroad in use in Hamburg in 1866 to the very latest pattern. The original consisted of a longitudinal wooden sleeper with a bogie rail spiked on; the latest pattern is a remarkably good sample of rolled-steel rail weighing 106 lb. per yard and having a tread of 2¼ in. The joint of this rail is not of the usual butt type, but is a half-and-half lapped one, having a longitudinal cut 10 in. in length. The fish-plate on the outside of the rail extends halfway under the bottom flange, and is 2 ft. 10 in. in length, secured by six ⅞ in. bolts. The gauge ties consist of an I section girder 4 in. deep, which passes under the rails and is fitted with two substantial and adjustable chairs. The rails are laid throughout on a concrete bed 10 in. deep.

Except at crossing points the depth of the groove is 1¼ in., but at crossing points it gradually tapers up until its depth is ¾ in. This system of road construction accounts for the remarkably smooth working of the cars. The tread of the wheel is the same width as the tread of the rail. When the wheels are passing over a joint of the rails they do not sink into the cavity of a butt joint, but of necessity pass smoothly over, there being a continual surface. Again, the flange of the wheel, projecting approximately 1 in. beyond the tread of the wheel, does not touch the bottom of the groove except at crossing places. In such places the tread of the rail is not, of course, continuous, but the groove is necessarily so; hence the flange is made to ride in the groove of the rail, and thus smooth running is ensured.

From the public point of view, and also from the tramway company's, this system of road construction is greatly to be commended, seeing the great influence this smooth running must naturally have upon the comfort of the passengers and upon the upkeep of the cars and their equipment. A novel method of paving the road adjacent to the rails is also adopted. On each side of the tramway rail there are laid longitudinal setts 9 in. wide, 21 in. long and 6 in. deep. These setts are tapered on the side farthest from the rail, for ease in removing. This arrangement certainly appeared to wear well, and has the advantage that only one line of setts has to be removed when alterations or repairs are being made to the rail.

The general service during the early hours of the morning and the late hours of the night is maintained by the cars before mentioned carrying from twenty-nine to thirty-nine passengers, but during the busier portions of the day trailer cars are attached. These trailer cars are used for smokers. About 750,000 car miles are run by these motor cars, and about 400,000 by the trailer cars per month. The weight of the small motor car is approximately 6½ tons, and of the larger car 11 tons—the latter ones having bogie trucks and being somewhat more strongly constructed. These weights are inclusive of passengers. The motors and equipment generally are of the Thomson-Houston type, similar to those now being installed on our own cars. Although this system has been in use since 1894, there have been no accidents connected with the electrical part of the system.

Financially, as well as electrically, the system under notice is a highly successful one. The cost per car mile amounts to 1·526d., that is rather over 1½d., trailers being counted separately in these car miles. This figure includes the repair of trucks, motors and gearing, overhead line and cost of current. About ·8 of a unit is taken per car mile. Accumulators are not now used in Hamburg for traction purposes. Some few years ago they were experimented with, but abandoned.

BERLIN.

The next place at which information was sought was the city of Berlin, the capital of Germany. In this city there are three companies working by means of electrical traction —*viz.*, Grosse Berliner Pferde Eisenbahn Gesellschaft, Siemens & Halske (Behren Strasse-Treptow), and Berlin Charlottenburger Strassenbahn Gesellschaft.

The first named is the largest electric tramway company at work on the Continent, and possesses 250 miles of tramroad, mainly double. This is worked on the span wire and bracket system of overhead support, combined with accumulators. About 12½ miles of this line have no overhead conductors, but, with the exception of 1,100 yards of conduit system, the cars are propelled by storage batteries contained in them. The current is taken from the municipal lighting station, the charge for the same being 10 pfennigs, or 1·2d., per unit, until 2,000,000 units are consumed in one year, above 2,000,000 the charge is 9 pfennigs. Five hundred cars are equipped for working on the overhead and accumulator lines. They carry forty passengers, and weigh 10 tons complete. Another 500 cars have no batteries installed, being equipped for the overhead and conduit line solely. These carry thirty passengers, and weigh 7 tons. The equipment of the cars and the overhead line was carried out by the Union Elektricitäts Gesellschaft, Berlin (the German Thomson-Houston Company), and they started with 8 kilometres (5 miles) of line in the spring of 1896. The conduit system is of the usual rail-slot type, having two insulated conductors working at a difference of potential of 500 volts. The slot is nominally 3 centimetres, or 1$\frac{3}{16}$ in.; but at points and crossing places, as will be readily understood, it approaches nearly double this width. In one particular respect it resembles the Blackpool system—It had failed, and is now about to be abandoned.

The overhead conductor is 8 millimetres, or ⅓ in., in diameter. The trolley is of the Thomson-Houston type, and the working pressure of the line is nominally 500 volts, working up to 560 volts. There are fifty feeding points provided, and, what is of more moment, there have been no accidents due to the system. The energy taken per car mile is ·8 of a unit. The gauge of the line is the usual standard one of 4 ft. 8½ in. The speed inside the city, including stoppages, is 7½ miles per hour, outside the city 12½ miles. The maximum gradient is 5 per cent., and is about 220 yards long. The accumulators in the cars arranged on this system are placed under the seats. They are charged while running from the overhead line. There are two types of battery at present in use—the Hagen and the Majert. The weight of accumulators on each car is 3 tons, and they cost £300 per car. The cost of the upkeep of these batteries was given to the deputation as rather more than ¾d. per car mile; but there is also a very considerable increase in the cost of maintenance of the cars and trucks due to the carrying of these accumulators. These items approximately work out to about £75 per car per annum. The life of the plates of the accumulators is given as not exceeding two years, and their efficiency—*i.e.*, the percentage of energy returned by the cells—at about 65 per cent.

The deputation were introduced by the manager of the company to Herr Schmidt, the Continental agent of Hagener Akkumulatoren Fabrik Gesellschaft, from whom much interesting information was obtained. With the object of securing a reliable statement, questions as to the cost, &c., of these batteries were put to him in writing, and answers similarly in writing were requested. At a further interview with Herr Schmidt the deputation were informed that these questions had been transmitted to his company's English house (The Tudor Accumulator Company, Limited, Manchester and London), who would give the replies. These questions and their answers will be dealt with in the conclusions.

The deputation next visited Messrs. Siemens & Halske, who are the proprietors of one of the tramway services and the constructors of the remaining one. The Behren Strasse-Treptow tramway system is combined overhead and conduit, 4½ miles being overhead and 1⅓ miles conduit, and commenced working in 1896. The gauge is of the usual standard and the line double. The maximum speed inside the town is 6 miles and outside 10 miles. There are thirty-seven motor cars, carrying forty-two passengers each and weighing, exclusive of passengers, 9⅓ tons, together with forty-five trailer cars, carrying forty passengers, and weighing 4 tons each. The equipment is of the usual Siemens & Halske type.

The current in this case, as with the larger company, is taken from the municipal lighting station. The overhead system has the usual rail return, but in the case of the conduit both conductors are insulated and connected to the overhead system by means of what is known as a "one to one transformer." The slot of the conduit is placed in one of the rails, and the dimensions given above for the slot of the great Berlin tramway company's conduit apply equally to this. The conduit is similar in construction to that in use at Buda-Pesth, also put down by Siemens & Halske, but is not viewed with favour either by the municipal authorities or by those working it.

In connection with the fares charged by the two companies just mentioned, the deputation were informed that when the concessions to run into Berlin were under negotiation the municipality insisted on the companies charging the same fares in the city as in the environs. To this the companies objected, pointing out that the cost of running by the conduit or accumulator system, which the municipality desired, was considerably greater than the cost of running by the overhead system, so that they were not in a position to meet this request. The municipality agreeing to this statement, after assuring themselves of its accuracy, the fares were accordingly fixed at a rate of 25 per cent. higher in the city, where the conduit and accumulator system were used, than outside, where the overhead system was employed. The effect of this arrangement is that the two companies are practically subsidised by the municipality, so far as the city lines are concerned. This subsidy could doubtless be discontinued if a cheaper system of working were adopted.

The Berlin-Charlottenburg tramway service was opened on the 1st October, 1897. There are 6¼ miles of track, the cars being worked entirely by accumulators, which are placed under the seats. These accumulators are of the "Schäfer-Heinemann" type, manufactured by the Watt Akkumulatoren Werke. At present twenty-eight cars are in use, carrying forty-two passengers, and weighing complete 23 tons. Accumulators are charged at night at the Charlottenburg terminus, six hours being occupied in this operation. Each car runs its 75 miles journey daily with this charge. There are 180 cells, coupled in two series of ninety, and having thirteen plates each cell. The weight of the cells is approximately 8 tons, and the initial outlay £750 per car. The cost of up-keep was given as 1·15d. per car mile; but, in addition to this, the wear on the road is very great and quite apparent, though it is too early to estimate what this will cost. There has only been one accident up to the present, and, fortunately, that happened when the car was in the shed, although it may not always occur under these circumstances. It was due to a short circuit in the battery, and resulted in the burning of a portion of the seating.

In an interview with the deputation subsequently held with the makers of these cells the opinion was expressed by the makers that the weight of the Charlottenburg cars could be reduced by altering the construction of the cars to 16 tons, and that upon this basis the Blackpool cars with batteries would weigh 23 tons. This company would not enter into a contract for supplying accumulators on any but the system adopted at Charlottenburg—that is to say, not on the short journey charging principle—as they contended the life of cells was greatly affected thereby.

DRESDEN.

From Berlin the deputation travelled to Dresden, and interviewed there the Dresdener Strassenbahn Gesellschaft. This company has altogether rather more than 13½ miles of line, 5 of which are overhead entirely, 5 miles combined overhead and accumulators, and approximately 3½ overhead and conduit. The gauge is standard, the track principally double, the speed inside the town about 6 or 8 miles, outside about 12 miles, per hour. The maximum gradient is extremely slight, being only 2¼ per cent. Current is taken from the municipal lighting station, for which a charge of 1·23d. per unit is made. Twenty cars are used for overhead only, each carrying thirty-six passengers and weighing complete 8 tons. Seventy cars, each weighing 10 tons, working on the combined overhead, conduit and accumulator systems. The equipment of the line is by Siemens & Halske.

The conduit system is somewhat similar to those already described, being of the slotted-rail type, having an opening 3 centimetres normal width, and working at a pressure of 500 volts, with two conductors, both insulated. It has been in operation for eighteen months, but is suffering from a complaint to which conduit systems appear to be liable—that of failure. The expression of opinion given by the tramway manager was far from favourable to conduit systems in general and his own in particular. The overhead conductor is supported by span wires, the gauge of the conductor 10 millimetres in diameter, working at the usual pressure of 500 volts. The energy taken per car mile is approximately three-quarters of a unit, and about 2,500,000 car miles are run yearly. On the combined accumulator and overhead systems each car is equipped with 200 Hagen cells, placed under the seats, each cell containing three plates, and 200 cells weigh 2 tons. The cost of installing these batteries amounted to £275 per car, and the makers have given a guarantee that the costs of repairs to the batteries themselves shall not exceed £45 per car per annum.

Although these cells have been in use only eighteen months, the deputation were informed that the greater part of the plates had already been replaced, and that it was expected that the whole of them would have been replaced within a period of two years from the commencement. The managing director also informed the deputation that from tests which had been taken of the efficiency of the cells it had been found that the ampere hour efficiency was 70 per cent.—i.e., neglecting the difference between charging and discharging pressure, the actual current value returned from the cells was 70 per cent. His opinion was strongly in favour of overhead, but the municipal authorities would not allow overhead construction in the centre of the town. The deputation were also informed that the overhead lines were owned by the municipality, the tramway company paying a rent for their use.

**Spennymoor.**—A Local Government Board inquiry has been held into an application of the district council for sanction to borrow £3,000 for the erection of an isolation hospital. After the plans and specifications of the scheme had been fully considered the inspector said that he thought that it would take nearly another £1,000 to complete the scheme. There was no opposition.

**On the Value of Roads.**—In his wonderfully suggestive discourse on "The Day of Roads," Horace Bushnell elaborated the idea that roads are the best evidence of civilisation. "If a people have no roads they are savages. Or, if you inquire after commerce, look at the roads ; for roads are the ducts of trade. If you wish to know whether society is stagnant, learning scholastic, religion a dead formality, you may learn something by going into universities and libraries ; something also by the work that is doing on cathedrals and churches or in them ; but quite as much by looking at the roads. For if there is any motion in society, the road, which is the symbol of motion, will indicate the fact. . . So if there is any kind of advancement going on, if new ideas are abroad, new hopes rising, then you will see it by the roads that are building. . . Nothing makes an inroad without making a road. All creative action, whether in government, industry, thought or religion creates roads."

## MAIDSTONE WATER SUPPLY.

At a meeting in committee of the Maidstone Town Council, last week, the question of supplementing the water supply of the borough was discussed at considerable length, a proposal being put forward to the effect that the water company should be asked to revert to the use of certain of their Farleigh springs, said to be capable of yielding some 2,000,000 gallons per week. In view of the fact that the typhoid epidemic of last year originated from the Farleigh water and that the whole of the springs were more or less condemned by experts, the proposal raised an angry protest, and the opinion was expressed that a riot would ensue if any portion of the suspected supply were restored. The opposition was strengthened by the report of Mr. M. A. Adams, medical officer of health, in regard to certain samples of the water now under examination. One of these samples he had no hesitation in saying was very bad. Looking to what occurred last year, and bearing in mind that the whole of the Farleigh water was derived from surface springs, it was impossible not to regard it with suspicion. Eventually a resolution was passed that the Ewell water should not again be turned on for the use of the town, a rider being added requesting the inhabitants of the borough to use their best endeavours to prevent any waste of their present supply. One or two members of the council contended that the Maidstone Company could further augment the quantity of water at their command by entering into an agreement with the Mid-Kent Company, which up to the present they had declined to do. On behalf of the Maidstone Company it was pleaded that they were already taking all the water their neighbours could supply. Not being satisfied with this assurance, the council appointed a deputation to meet the chairman and directors of the Mid-Kent Company on the subject. The action of the corporation is generally approved by the townspeople.

The intermittent supply of water to the inhabitants within the area of the company was resumed on Saturday, and is likely to be continued for some time to come, owing to the small amount of water which the company are able to obtain in consequence of the serious drought. The present shortness of water, the company officials contend, has been greatly exaggerated. They declare that they are able to meet every reasonable demand, but it is pointed out that the company cannot provide for watering lawns during the dry weather. The springs and gathering beds are being examined daily, and while the hoppers are about all the sources of supply will be protected.

## HALIFAX WATERWORKS.

### THE WALSHAW DEAN SCHEME.

At a meeting of the Waterworks Committee of the Halifax Corporation, held on the 23rd ult., it was unanimously decided to recommend the council to proceed with the Walshaw Dean reservoir extensions. Therefore the time has now come for the corporation to decide whether they will or will not carry forward the great waterworks scheme which is to cost the town from £150,000 to £200,000.

The members of the council, on the occasion of a visit to the site of the proposed works last month, were informed that the bottom reservoir would have a top water area of 21 acres and a capacity of 126,000,000 gallons. The length of the embankment would be 230 yards, its greatest height 76 ft., and the greatest depth of water 70 ft. The quantity of material that would be used in the construction of the embankment was 110,000 cubic yards. The middle reservoir will have a top water area of 46 acres and a capacity of 350,000,000 gallons. The length of the embankment would be 340 yards, and its height 74 ft. The greatest depth of water would be 68 ft., and the quantity of material in the embankment 182,000 cubic yards. The upper reservoir would have a top water area of 27 acres and a capacity of 164,000,000 gallons. The length of the embankment would be 230 yards, its height 74 ft., the greatest depth of water 66 ft., and the quantity of material used in the construction of the embankment 200,000 cubic yards. The total capacity would be almost equal to that of Widdop, and the amount of compensation would also be about the same. In the case of Walshaw Dean, however, the compensation would be continuous, at the rate of 1,430,000 gallons per day, leaving 2,500,000 gallons per day for distribution. The average rainfall was about 45 in. Of this 10 in. goes for compensation, 17 in. is lost by absorption, evaporation and leakage, leaving 18 in. for the supply of Halifax for distribution.

**Scottish Plumbers' Congress.**—The ninth annual Scottish Congress of the Association for the National Registration of Plumbers opened in Glasgow on Thursday week, and its proceedings extended over the Friday and Saturday. The delegates, who numbered about 300, comprised representatives of employers and employed in the plumbing trade, as well as many members of municipalities and other public men interested in sanitary science.

# Some Annual Municipal Engineering Records.

## WARWICKSHIRE : NOTTINGHAM : ECCLES.

Mr. Willmot, county surveyor of Warwickshire, has recently submitted his seventh annual report of the work carried out in his department during the past year. The report is more than usually interesting and instructive, since it contains a table showing the working expenses of three steam rollers for a period of five years. The nett cost of the roads directly maintained by the council during 1897-98 has been £21,103 11s., as against an estimated expenditure of £21,000. About £406 has also been expended on improvements. When this sum is deducted, the average rate of expenditure per mile for ordinary maintenance has been £45 2s., "the lowest rate per mile since the first year the council undertook the direct control of the roads." The mileage of main roads under the direct control of the council is 457; the amount expended upon day labour, including inspectors' salaries, has been £5,563 8s. 8d., or deducting the amounts paid for railway fares and lodgings, £5,494 1s. 1d., which is equal to an average rate of wages of 15s. 6¼d. per week, the average number of men working full time being 119. The cost of materials, including stone-breaking, has been £9,893 19s. 8d., or 46 per cent. of the total expenditure. The total quantity purchased was 30,351 tons, the average price being 6s. 5d. per ton. The council have had at work during the year three steam rollers, the nett cost of which, after deducting £3 15s. received for hire of rollers, has been £303 6s. 10d. In addition to the 14,950 tons of stone put down by the council's own rollers, a further quantity of 4,106 tons was consolidated by hired rollers, at a cost of £161 15s., or 9½d. per ton. This makes a total of 19,056 tons consolidated by steam rolling, which is practically the whole of the stone put on the roads during the year in the three districts in which the rollers have been at work. The three steam rollers have now been at work for five years, during which time careful accounts have been kept of the annual expense of working them and of the quantity of stone they have consolidated. These accounts have enabled Mr. Willmott to prepare a statement, which gives the cost of working them during that period, the quantity of stone consolidated, and other details. It is shown that on the average each of the three rollers has each year spent eight days in travelling and nineteen days in cleaning and repairs, has been stopped by frost fifteen days, has been in dock sixty days, and 211 days at work on roads. The total cost of working of each roller per year has been £120 16s. 6d., £63 0s. 6d. has been expended on engine-drivers' and flagmen's wages, and fuel and sundries are responsible for £38 19s. 9d. Each roller has used 3 3 cwt. of coal per day, at a cost of 2s. 7d. The repairs of each roller each year have cost £18 16s. 3d., and its average cost per day at work has been 11s. Each roller has consolidated 5,660 tons of stone in each of the five years, or 27 tons per day, at a cost of 5¹d. per ton. The cost of watering during the period covered by the return was £1,020, or 2 9d. per ton, and if this is added to the cost of rolling in the stone—namely, 5¹d.—the total cost of consolidation has been 8d. per ton. The foregoing calculations are turned to good account by the fact of a comparison between them and those for District No. 4, which includes the Leamington and Wellesbourne road, the Stratford and Edgehill road, and the Warwick and Banbury road, where only horse rollers have been used. About 7,500 tons of stone have been consolidated by horse rollers, at a total cost of £375 0s. 5d., including watering, which gives an increase of 11½d. per ton as against 8d. per ton, the cost of steam rolling. "This shows," Mr. Willmot adds, "that horse rolling cannot be recommended on the score of economy."

\* \* \*

The town council of Nottingham have received the report of the General Works and Highways Committee for the year. Expenditure in connection with public works, it appears, amounted to over £37,738. The number of new buildings passed during the last four years was : For the year ended March 31, 1895, 929; 1896, 1,051; 1897, 2,110; and 1898, 1,859. The buildings, plant, tools, &c., under the charge of the committee had been maintained in good repair. The number of loads of material weighed over the various public weighing machines during the last four years were : 1894-95, 52,421; 1895-96, 51,521; 1896-97, 53,755; and 1897-98, 56,528. During the past year 43,327 streets were scavenged, from which 26,844 loads of refuse were removed. The total mileage of streets scavenged was 0,751, or an average length per day of 18·49 miles, and the daily average of men employed on this work was 37·55. The street gulleys had been frequently emptied and the refuse carted away. During the year street watering was necessary on 148 days, and 20,487 loads of water were distributed over 23,855 streets. The streets in the busy parts of the city, and in some of the poorer districts, were disinfected during the hot weather by adding to the water used for watering a strong but nonpoisonous disinfectant. The sanding of the principal streets of the city had been regularly carried out, and the following material was used for this purpose : Sand gravel, 1,168 tons 14 cwt. 1 qr.; boulder gravel and dust, 209 tons 11 cwt. 3 qr.;

and sand, fifty-nine loads. The public sewerage works had been maintained in good repair, the sewers had been flushed at frequent intervals, and the ventilation shafts cleaned and any repairs required executed. The report embodies a list of the streets flushed, cleansed and repaired, also those in which general repairs to paving and macadam had been carried out, those upon which the steam rollers had been used, and others where repairs to flagging, kerbing, brick paving and asphalting had been executed.

During the year repairs of the cost of new sewering and paving works in twenty-nine streets had been made, necessitating the preparation and making of 147 separate apportionments for service on owners of property, agents and others. The total number of apportionments, old materials and other notices served in connection with private works during the year was 356. Various other works, of kerbing, flagging, brick paving, concreting, granite paving, house drainage connections, and other sundry works, independently of the works done under the Public Health Act, by notice, had been carried out at the request and on the signature of 774 owners and others to pay the cost of the same. The repairs and reinstatements of paving, flagging, asphalting, concreting, &c., disturbed by gas, water and electric lighting connections were carried out by the committee's workmen, and the costs charged to the respective committees, and during the year various repairs over 2,054 gas, 1,235 water and 139 electric tracks had been done. The amount of wages paid through the weekly wages sheets of the committee to men employed on private improvement and sundry works to be re-charged amounted to £12,444. The report also gives details of the various works carried out and the special works for other committees, including those consequent upon the new Great Central and Great Northern lines entering the city.

\* \* \*

Much interesting information is contained in the last annual statement of Mr. Arthur C. Turley, the borough surveyor of Eccles, a large amount of useful and valuable work having apparently been carried out since the issue of the previous report. The area of the borough is 2,008 statute acres, while the roads have a total length of nearly 38 miles. Of main roads there are about 4½ miles, of secondary roads over 3½ miles, and of other roads about 30 miles. Proposed dwelling-houses, for which plans have been approved, numbered 296, and other buildings down for erection total sixty-nine. Of new streets seven were contemplated. Some 197 certificates of habitation were granted in respect of dwelling-houses, and the following inspections attended to : In connection with foundations, sixty-seven; damp-proof courses, ninety-seven; new drains, 240. Carefully-compiled statements of the sewering, paving, kerbing and flagging of public and private streets are also included in Mr. Turley's report; in addition to which there is a short description of a 3-ft. by 2-ft. egg-shaped sewer, which has been completed and set to work. The sewer has throughout its entire length been constructed in tunnel, its invert being formed with Doulton's stoneware invert blocks. The sides are constructed with Staffordshire blue bricks, and the arch with a 4½-in. ring of pressed engineering bricks. At the summit an overflow weir has been fixed, and is so arranged that when the 18-in. shallow main from Eccles is flowing more than two-thirds full the excess flow can pass over the weir into the new sewer. This arrangement is expected to prevent the backing-up of sewage in the branch drains during floods.

**Downham (Norfolk).**—In consequence of a dispute between the district council and the local gas company, the town streets have lately been unlighted. The company demand 42s. per annum per street lamp, the lamps not to be lighted for five nights at each full moon. The council is willing to pay the price, but strike against the off nights.

**Sutherland.**—The county council met last week, when a communication was read from the Congested Districts Board intimating a grant of £600 towards the construction of the proposed pier at Droman on condition that the balance of £200 is locally contributed. Considerable discussion took place regarding the condition of Embo village, which was stated as disgraceful. The Congested Districts Board wrote that before considering any representation it was necessary they should know what the county council desired them to do and what had already been done or contemplated by the local authorities. The Local Government Board drew attention to the medical officer's report regarding the grossly insanitary condition of the village, and the sanitary inspector's statement that the inhabitants suffered to a greater extent last year than for a good many past seasons for want of a water supply. The committee replied that they had found it impossible to supply water within their statutory powers. The case required legislation or other exceptional treatment.

# Law Notes.

EDITED BY J. B. REIGNIER CONDER, 11 Old Jewry Chambers, E.C.,

Solicitor of the Supreme Court.

*The Editor will be pleased to answer any questions affecting the practice of engineers and surveyors to local authorities. Queries (which should be written legibly on foolscap paper, one side only) should be addressed to "The Law Editor," at the Offices of THE*

SURVEYOR. *Where possible, copies of local Acts or documents referred to should be enclosed. All explanatory diagrams must be drawn and lettered in black ink only. Correspondents who do not wish their names published should furnish a nom de plume.*

METROPOLIS LOCAL MANAGEMENT ACT, 1855, SEC. 98: POWERS OF VESTRY TO LOWER SURFACE OF STREET: LIABILITY AS TO PIPES OF WATER COMPANY.—The above section, it will be remembered, provides as follows : " It shall be lawful for every vestry and district board from time to time to cause all, or any, of the streets within their parish or district, or any thereof respectively, to be paved or repaired when and as often, and in such form and manner, and with such materials as such vestry or board think fit, and to cause the ground or soil thereof to be raised or lowered, and the course of the channels running in, into, or through the same to be turned or altered, in such manner as they think proper, and to alter the position of any mains or pipes in or under such street, such alteration to be made subject to the approval of the engineer of the company to which such mains or pipes belong." Does this enactment impose an obligation on a vestry or district board, in the event of their lowering the surface of a street, to relay the pipes of a water company at a sufficient depth to prevent their being injured by traffic, frost, &c.? In the recent case of *Southwark and Vauxhall Water Company* v. *Wandsworth District Board* (Court of Appeal, 8th August), the board contemplated lowering certain footpaths to such an extent as to leave only a few inches of soil above the company's mains, and an injunction was granted by Mr. Justice Kekewich restraining the defendants from altering the position of such mains by placing them in a position in which they would be more liable to injury than they originally were. The Court of Appeal, however, have reversed that decision. The Master of the Rolls, after pointing out that the words of the section are "it shall be lawful," &c., that the board had not in any way disturbed or injured the pipes, and that the company had failed to show that the section imposed a duty on the board to lower the pipes, continued : " Underlying the plaintiffs' contention is the assumption that they are entitled to have a certain amount of soil over their pipes. I can find no warrant for this assumption ; and, as the defendants are clearly empowered by sec. 98 to remove the soil above the pipes, I see no ground for saying that the additional powers conferred upon them of lowering the plaintiffs' pipes imposes the duty of lowering them in order to protect them from injury. The plaintiffs pay nothing for the privilege of laying their pipes down in a public park or road, and they run the risk of having it made higher or lower by the road authorities under their statutory powers. This conclusion is strengthened by sec. 61 of the Towns Improvement Act, 1847 (10 and 11 Vic., c. 34), which is *in pari materia*, and which empowers the Improvement Commissioners to raise or lower pipes ' if they deem it necessary so to do,' No duty to do so is cast upon them. Sec. 98 of the Metropolitan Management Act, although not quite so clearly worded, has in my opinion, the same meaning." Lord Justice Chitty said : " I am unable to find in the section any express or implied duty cast upon the road authority, when they exercise their power of altering the level of the road, whether by raising or lowering it, to exercise at their own expense their power of altering the position of the pipes for the benefit of the company owning the pipes, much less any duty to place the pipes at a depth below the now surface corresponding with the depth at which they stood below the old surface. I think that no such duty is imposed upon the appellants. The real question is on whom the expense of altering the position of the pipes is to fall. It appears to me that it falls on the company. They are, under no statutory obligation as to the particular depth at which their pipes are to be placed from the surface of the road ; it is for them to place them at such a depth as will protect the water from freezing. As between the road authority and the company, I think that the road authority is paramount. They are entrusted with the powers over the street, not for their own profit as a statutory body, but for the benefit of the public using the street as a highway. The statutory undertaking of the water company is vested in them with a view to their own profit as a company, and for the purpose of affording a supply of water to the consumers of water within their district. Where the road authority alters the level of the street sec. 98 does not afford any means of ascertaining the point at which the supposed duty of the road authority begins in reference to the distance from the surface at which the pipes are to be left, subject only to this qualification—that where the position of the pipes themselves is altered the approval of the company's engineer is required in relation to the position where the pipes are to be relaid." Lord Justice Collins read a judgment to the same effect. The following cases were referred to in the course of the arguments: *Julius* v. *Bishop of Oxford* (5 App. C., 214, see pp. 223 and 224) ; *The Gas Light and Coke Company* v. *Vestry of St.*

*Mary Abbotts* (15 Q.B.D., 1) ; and *Geddis* v. *Proprietors of the Bann Reservoir* (3 App. C., 430).

## ELECTRIC LIGHT AT NEWBURY.

Newbury Town Council, at a recent meeting, spent several hours discussing the comparative merits of gas and electricity. Notice had been given by the Great Western Electric Light and Power Company and the United Electric Light and Power Company of their intention to apply for provisional orders to supply the town, and Mr. Offor, of the Municipal Electric Supply Company, proposed to purchase the provisional order obtained eight years ago by the corporation, paying all the expenses which had been incurred, taking over the lighting of the town, and the option of purchase by the corporation at the end of ten years, plus 6s. 8d. in the £1. The charge suggested was £2 10s. to £3 10s. for public lamps, and private consumers at 5d. per unit after the first hour at 8d., equal to 2s. per 1,000 ft. of gas. The price in Newbury is now 4s. 2d. per 1,000, and the corporation are the owners of the gas works. The Gas Committee recommended the council to decline the offer and to instruct the town clerk to oppose all applications for power to supply electricity. The general opinion seemed to be that it would be suicidal to allow an electric lighting company to come as a competitor with the gas, although it was argued that electricity was much dearer, and the option of purchase could not be supplied at the price named. The mayor considered that if they could get for 2s. what now cost them 4s. it was their duty to get it. The council obtained their order eight years ago, and no steps have been taken to carry out its conditions, the reply being that no one has ever applied for electricity. It was, however, realised that if half a dozen burgesses did make application they must supply it, or allow someone else to do it. The council adopted the committee's recommendation.

## SANITARY MANUFACTURES.

Messrs. Morrison, Ingram & Co., Limited, have just completed important additions, which have been in hand for nearly twelve months, at their Midway Pottery Works, Swadlincote, Derbyshire, and we understand that these extensions and the equipment of the works with up-to-date machinery will enable the firm to double this branch of their business. The patterns have been all practically remodelled and a great number of new designs added. Recent experiments have been made with the object of demonstrating that "Densitas" eune clay is well adapted for the manufacture of sanitary vessels. It is a clean, compact body of great strength and with a small degree of porosity, and the manufacturers are confident that it will occupy an important position in the future, owing to the fact that it forms a suitable substitute for iron in a variety of articles.

**North-Eastern Sanitary Inspectors' Association.**—The report of this body for the year ended June 30th last appears to be in every way satisfactory, the receipts to date now amounting to £25,800.

**Nuneaton.**—The district council have adopted the report of the Sewerage Committee recommending that application be made to the Local Government Board for sanction to borrow £4,000 for two precipitation tanks, two new sludge presses and rams, air compressor and other machinery, and the building of a new press-house.

**Huntly.**—On Wednesday of last week a new reservoir, which has been constructed at Craighead, about 2 miles from the town, was formally opened. The reservoir is 100 ft. long by 25 ft. wide and 10 ft. deep, and has a storage capacity of 220,000 gallons. The storage in the two reservoirs is now ample to ensure Huntly of an abundant supply of excellent water for many years to come. Having provided an additional reservoir, the commissioners have now turned their attention to laying additional piping between the reservoirs and the burgh to supplement the existing main, and a new main has been laid. The contractor, Mr. J. Hunter Clark, Elgin, has executed the undertaking in a manner entirely satisfactory to all concerned. The extension of the works, which has been carried out at a cost of somewhat under £2,000, was designed by Mr. James Barron, c.e., Aberdeen. The new supply was also turned on last week.

## Some Recent Publications.

THE MUNICIPAL AND SANITARY ENGINEER'S VADE-MECUM.

There has just been issued the third edition, revised and enlarged, of the MUNICIPAL AND SANITARY ENGINEERS' HAND-BOOK, by Mr. H. Percy Boulnois, M.I.C.E. (E. & F. N. Spon, Limited, 125 Strand. Price, 15s.) The fact that a third edition has been called for speaks for itself, but it cannot be called surprising. Though no longer in office as a municipal engineer, Mr. Boulnois had reached the very summit of the profession when he resigned his Liverpool appointment, and there is probably no one whom municipal engineers would more readily accept as an authority on the work and details of their profession. The author's remark in his brief preface, that the book appears to be of some use, errs on the side of modesty, for it is not too much to say that the book has from the first been recognised as indispensable to municipal and sanitary engineers, and especially to young members of the profession, and to those preparing for the examinations of the Incorporated Association of Municipal and County Engineers and other bodies. The municipal engineer who was unacquainted with the book or of whose professional library it did not form a part would probably be regarded as a phenomenon, and it is sure to be included in any list of books recommended for certain examinations. Special text-books, of course, deal exhaustively with special subjects, but as a general hand-book for the municipal engineer this work stands alone. The exhaustion of the previous edition is not the only imperative reason that calls for a third edition. In no direction is there more rapid and effective advance than in municipal and sanitary engineering, and a hand-book which aims at being authoritative must from time to time incorporate new developments. In this new edition the author has "made such alterations and additions as appear to be necessary, owing to the growth of municipal engineering."

It seems to us that the work involved in bringing out the new addition is much more extensive than the quoted words would imply, and thus we need offer no excuse for glancing more or less fully at the contents of the volume. Nowadays the engineer has to specialise, like everyone else, and probably none more so than he. Municipal and sanitary engineering has long been a recognised department, and probably in no branch of engineering has the specialising tendency been so slightly marked. Owing to the multifarious nature of his duties and the variety of the qualifications demanded from him, the municipal engineer approaches most nearly to the idea conveyed by the term engineer as understood in former days. What his duties and qualifications are can best be gleaned from Mr. Boulnois' book.

The first chapter deals with the position of the town surveyor generally. He came into existence practically with the Towns Improvement Clauses Act, 1847, though there had been similar previous appointments, notably in the case of Liverpool, where in 1842 surveyors had been appointed under the Liverpool Building Act. The office was confirmed under the Public Health Act, 1848, and the Public Health Act, 1875, but under the latter statutes surveyors may be removed at the pleasure and the discretion of the urban authority, which was not the case under the statute of 1847. Mr. Boulnois, in his first chapter, goes very fully into the whole question of the appointment of surveyors to local authorities as regulated by statute, and in the course of his remarks has occasion to notice not a few anomalies. One of these is the use of the word surveyor when that of engineer would be much more appropriate. The one exception to this is the city of Liverpool, where special provision exists for the appointment of an engineer. An even more glaring anomaly, however, is the inadequate protection in regard to tenure of office which the surveyor enjoys as compared with the medical officer and sanitary inspector. This is an abuse against which we have long waged war in these columns and which we still hope to see rectified. Had space permitted we would gladly have quoted the remarkable list of duties as given in this work which a municipal surveyor may at any time be called upon to undertake. Mr. Boulnois also refers to the question of superannuation, and lays down clearly the broad principles by which it should be regulated. The second chapter deals with the customary procedure in connection with the actual appointment of a surveyor, and a typical example of a "list of duties" is quoted. How many men seeking appointments in private life are confronted with such a formidable document? The clear manner in which Mr. Boulnois discusses such questions as that of allowing the surveyor a limited amount of private practice, and the necessity of some adequate test of capability, will not escape attention. The morality or otherwise of canvassing is also referred to, and young members of the profession should read, mark and inwardly digest the hints to candidates which are set forth by so experienced a municipal engineer as the author of this standard hand-book. In the third chapter the duties of the town surveyor are discussed in further detail, and the author gives the remarkable table in which these duties are so vividly set forth.

In subsequent chapters the various branches of work are dealt with separately, street work, of course, occupying a large share of attention. In the brief space at our disposal we cannot do more than make a passing reference to some of the more important matters and points dealt with. After a discussion on the general principles of traffic as regulated by the requirements of particular localities, separate chapters are devoted to macadamised roads, road metal and breaking, road-rolling, pitched pavements, wood paving, compressed asphalte roadways, footpaths, and curbing and channelling. The limitations of macadam and tar macadam roadways in urban and suburban districts are clearly pointed out, and then in discussing road metal and breaking, the superiority of hand over machine broken materials is pointed out, and Mr. Ellice-Clark's objection to binding materials are quoted. In his next chapter, however, Mr. Boulnois has occasion to discuss the use of road-rollers, and in doing so he makes it clear that a certain amount of some sort of binding material is absolutely necessary. From time to time we have published comparative reports on road-rolling, and these have shown conclusively that the great majority of surveyors are in favour of the practice. Mr. Boulnois describes it as a necessity at the present day. A chapter is devoted to the use of granite setts, which are regarded as often absolutely necessary for slow heavy traffic, though their objectionable features are fully recognised. The remarkable development of wood paving in recent years is traced in the chapter devoted to the subject. Undoubtedly the advantages of certain classes of wood paving far outweigh the disadvantages. "There is no doubt," says Mr. Boulnois, "that the best wood pavement is that which can be constructed in the simplest manner, as, for instance, jarrah or karri blocks, 4 in. or 5 in. deep, laid to a close joint upon a Portland cement concrete bed, the blocks being well grouted in with pitch or some description of bituminous mixture."

With the discussion of compressed asphalte roadways, the slipperiness of which is duly noted, Mr. Boulnois completes this branch of the subject, and then passes on to deal with footways, the various materials and methods being duly passed in review. A separate chapter, clearly illustrated, is devoted to curbing and channelling, and then the author proceeds to deal with such important matters as street lighting, street naming and numbering, the breaking up of streets and scavenging. In treating on street lighting Mr. Boulnois refers to the marked developments of recent years in connection with electric lighting and the incandescent gas burner, and gives a clear account of his experience in Liverpool. The chapter on the opening up of streets is one which municipal engineers could read only with sympathetic interest. Obstructions in streets, the improvement of private streets, and new streets and buildings are important subjects which all obtain adequate attention, the difficulty surrounding the definition of "a new building" receiving full discussion. In the chapter on scavenging reference is made to destructors, a subject which Mr. Boulnois has made his own, and then come chapters on sewerage and sewage disposal. That on sewerage is accompanied by some necessary illustrations, and in that on sewage disposal a wonderful amount of information on a difficult and much-debated question is given in a small space. Another subject which has excited a good deal of controversy is that of sewer ventilation, and Mr. Boulnois discusses it fully and impartially.

The remaining chapters deal respectively with public conveniences, artisans' and labourers' dwellings, defects in dwelling-houses, house drainage, public pleasure grounds and street trees, public abattoirs, markets, cemeteries and mortuaries, borrowing under the Local Government Board and contracts. We can only mention these subjects, but we have said enough to indicate the wonderful scope of the book. What is equally remarkable is the amount of compression that has been brought to bear without omitting any desirable information. The book thus becomes a veritable *multum in parvo*, in which the municipal engineer will find the essentials of the almost bewildering number of subjects he must master. The arrangement is admirable throughout, and the points are presented with great clearness and conciseness. The book gives one a good idea of what manner of man the municipal engineer is expected to be, and what qualifications are required of him. Mr. Boulnois has provided him with a model hand-book. We would suggest, however, that in future additional chapters might be added on water supply and tramway traction. These matters are often in the hands of specialists, but the municipal engineer is frequently called upon to deal with them. The information on dust destructors and on the bacterial methods of sewage disposal might also be somewhat amplified. In his brief preface Mr. Boulnois mentions that the various legal references have been scrutinised and revised by Mr. J. B. Reignier Conder, the able writer of the "Law Notes" in THE SURVEYOR, and that gentleman is thanked by Mr. Boulnois for the manner in which he has performed the task. It has certainly been admirably performed.

STAGE AND THEATRE CONSTRUCTION.

As a supplement to his monumental work, MODERN OPERA HOUSES AND THEATRES, which is being issued in instalments, Mr. Edwin O. Sachs, the well-known architect, has produced an interesting work, entitled: STAGE CONSTRUCTION:

Examples of Modern Stages, selected from Playhouses recently erected in Europe, with Descriptive and Critical Text." The publisher is Mr. B. T. Batsford, Holborn. Stage mechanism, as now understood, is practically a development of the last twenty years, and Mr. Sachs had a clear field for the production of a standard technical work on the subject. It is obvious that he has seized his opportunity and has studied his subject with conscientious thoroughness and in exhaustive detail. The credit for initiating and carrying on the movement for the improvement of scenic representation by the development of mechanical appliances is practically monopolised by Austria and Germany, England having taken little or no part in the movement. This valuable work of Mr. Sachs, however, will no doubt give an impetus to the movement in this country. There is, no doubt, almost indefinite scope for improvements in stage mechanism, and a tendency in that direction is almost inevitable. It may be doubted, however, if elaborate mounting can have otherwise than a deleterious effect upon the spirit and genius of acting, for, after all, the play and its interpretations are the things. The work comprises ninety pages of text, grand folio size, interspersed with 170 valuable original illustrations, reproduced by the most improved and artistic processes from diagrams, drawings, sketches and photographs, for the most part specially prepared on the spot, together with six plates from engineers' working drawings to a large scale, the whole printed on fine paper.

The second volume of the great work on "Modern Opera Houses and Theatres" is divided into two parts, the first comprising examples from France, Italy, Monaco and Spain, and the second consisting of examples representing Austria, Germany, Great Britain, Greece, Holland, Roumania and Switzerland. Incidentally Mr. Sachs points out the difference in the sentiments with which the theatre is regarded in this country and those which prevail in some Continental countries. In England the theatre, despite the pathetic appeals of certain eminent actor-managers, is persistently regarded as a place simply and solely for entertainment, rather than for instruction. Amusement is looked upon as its raison d'être ; to its elevating influence, of which we are occasionally told, the average playgoer is sublimely indifferent. In Austria and Germany, again, the theatre is undoubtedly regarded as an educational institution, and until similar sentiments prevail in this country it will be, useless in our opinion, to talk of municipal or other subsidised theatres, over which a mild agitation occasionally arises. The prevailing sentiments of a country affect also the architectural features of its theatres. In England the indifference to architecture is sometimes painfully obvious in the exteriors of the theatres ; in France, Austria and Germany the aim is to make them temples and palaces of art. This large-sized and beautifully-produced work will be indispensable to every student of the subject.

### SOME SHORT NOTICES.

THE TOURIST GUIDE TO THE CONTINENT, by Percy Lindley, issued under the auspices of the Great Eastern Railway Company at the moderate price of 6d., is a carefully compiled and exceedingly well-illustrated hand-book, which will be found extremely useful to persons making brief visits to the various countries therein described. A pamphlet issued by the same company, entitled ROYAL MAIL ROADS TO HOLLAND, contains short practical notes of travel and some pretty coloured views of scenery.

LESSONS FROM FIRE AND PANIC forms No. 9 of the publications of the British Fire-prevention Committee. It is a reprint of the thoughtful paper contributed by Mr. Blashill to the proceedings of a meeting of the Surveyors' Institution, held at Manchester, the council of that body having courteously permitted its publication in this form. The substance of it was given in our columns at the time of the meeting, and we therefore need not further refer to it. The paper certainly deserves attention from all who are interested in the subject.

MY HOME AND HOUSEHOLD COMPENDIUM, by I. W. Jarvis and W. J. Woods (London : Simpkin, Marshall & Co.), is a book of 128 pages, on somewhat novel lines. It has practical chapters on hiring houses and apartments, fire, burglary, life and accident insurances, and the making of wills. But the larger portion of it consists of ruled pages, conveniently arranged for the easy making of an inventory of one's household effects, preceded by an explanation of how to make the inventory. The precise person who has sufficient industry to utilise the book will find it admirably adapted to its purpose.

An interesting and well-printed pamphlet has been issued from the office of the British Fire Prevention Committee, entitled "How to Build 'Fireproof.'" It is written by Mr. Francis C. Moore, who is one of the leading insurance authorities on the subject in the United States and is prominently connected with the New York Building Department. In the pamphlet a summary is given of various suggestions as to methods of erecting "fireproof" buildings. This summary has been prepared in America, and the whole of the questions dealt with has particular reference to the constructional practice in the United States. This fact, however, in no way lessens the value of the pamphlet for the metropolis and the other great centres of the empire, for with slight modifications it applies equally to the buildings of all countries. Attention should be especially drawn to

the interesting remarks on the effect of rust on ironwork, and the advisability of making part of the coverings movable, to allow of periodical examination.

Messrs. Ward, Lock & Co., Limited, have issued an entirely new edition of their pictorial and descriptive GUIDE TO THE ISLE OF WIGHT. "That beautiful island, which he who once sees never forgets," as Sir Walter Scott wrote, is one of the most delightful holiday resorts in the kingdom, and with equal truth it may be said that every inch of it is so well worth traversing that the visitor with limited time may find its attractions embarrassing him by their number and claims. How shall he portion them out so as to compass the best of them ? This hand-book is the reply. With it excursions can be made methodically, with the minimum of trouble and expense. With tradition and history ready for reference, with a map, over seventy illustrations and crisply-written description, the guide is a remarkable shillingsworth. ILFRACOMBE, BARNSTAPLE AND NORTH-WEST DEVON is the title of another of the same publishers' shilling series. Here, again, is a district of wonderful appeal to the invalid, the tired townsman, the lover of nature, the student of old-time places and folk-lore. In this hand-book it is admirably treated from all these points of view.

## BELPER SEWERAGE SCHEME COMPETITION.

At a recent meeting of the Belper Urban District Council a report was presented by a committee appointed to examine the competitive plans received for the carrying out of a sewerage scheme. A premium had been offered, and the plans dealt with the sewage of outside and inside the district. Those dealing with the sewage in the former manner would be certain to raise strenuous opposition from both public bodies and private individuals. One of the competitors placed his works opposite to the new foundry of Mr. Smedly, but with this one exception the whole of the plans favoured land near the Belper goods station and on the other side of the river Derwent. The committee felt that the proper place for dealing with the sewage was on the west side of the river. With regard to the treatment, it was felt that until there had been visits to other works, and the different processes had been seen in operation, it would not be wise to proceed, and it was felt that the results of the Royal Commission on Sewage Disposal would be to modify the present requirement of the Local Government Board with regard to the area of land needed for filtration purposes. It had been decided to ask Major Tulloch, lately the chief inspector to the Local Government Board, to act as assessor, and he consented to do so on payment of 100 guineas and expenses. There will be no opposition from Mr. Strutt, who is the owner of the land proposed to be taken.

## CORRESPONDENCE.

**Municipal Engineers and Medical Officers of Health.—** " A Borough Engineer" writes : I quite agree with what you say in your last week's leader respecting the encroaching by medical officers upon work properly belonging to the municipal engineer. I have had experience of this objectionable practice myself, and I put my foot down on it at once, and I would strongly recommend all municipal engineers to do likewise. This officious interference with the department of the borough engineer is, I regret to say, at times attempted by other officials besides the medical officer of health—viz., by the town clerk, sanitary inspector, and even the borough accountant. Let the cobbler stick to his last. Speaking for myself, I am fully occupied in looking properly after the work in my own department, and I take it that if the other officials named stuck to the legitimate duties of their own departments, as they should do, they would have no spare time to interfere with the work of a brother-official. My advice to municipal engineers is this : Don't answer queries sent by post upon any matter which comes within the scope of municipal engineering unless such queries come from a borough engineer. If this advice is taken all round the objectionable practice referred to will soon cease.

**Threatening a Municipal Engineer.**—The water engineer to the Bombay Municipality lately received a letter, ostensibly written by a Mahommedan, stating (according to Indian Engineering) that if the meter system is adopted he will be cut to pieces. The correspondent further states that the system is being forced on the city so that he (the water engineer) may obtain a big commission from some firm of manufacturers in England.

**An Outing.**—Mr. W. P. Butterfield, of the Shipley galvanising tank and cistern works, gave his employees an outing to Southport on the 20th ult. Dinner was partaken of at the Hoghton Arms Hotel, when about thirty sat down. Various places of interest were subsequently visited, and, following an excellent tea, which was served at 6 o'clock, a hearty vote of thanks was accorded Mr. Butterfield for his generosity.

# Municipal Work in Progress and Projected.

Most of the metropolitan authorities are still in recess, and consequently there is very little news forthcoming with respect to projected works. From the provinces, too, comparatively little news has come to hand, but we have some information relative to extensive works which are being carried out at Epsom, Retford, Ampthill, Bridgend, Garston, Leytonn, Birkenhead and Burnley.

## METROPOLITAN AUTHORITIES.

### VESTRIES AND DISTRICT BOARDS.

**Hampstead.**—At a recent meeting of the vestry a memorial was received from the Hampstead Art Society, signed by several prominent artists, urging the erection of an art gallery as an addition to the central public library in the Finchley-road. The matter was referred to the Public Libraries Committee.—The Lighting Committee have just received a report from Mr. A. P. Johnson, the vestry clerk, on the electric lighting undertaking in the parish for the year ended Lady Day last. The total amount of capital expended up to that date was £100,176, of which £2,246 had been repaid. The ordinary expenditure had been much less than in any corresponding period, chiefly owing to the decreased amount of coal consumed and a drop in the expenditure for repairs of machinery. The report states that the policy initiated by the vestry at the opening of the central electric lighting station, and adhered to ever since, of laying mains wherever possible for private consumers, was bearing good fruit, and must continue to do so in the future to an ever-increasing amount. Nearly every street of importance had been wired, and the vestry were therefore able to face with confidence the threatened competition from outside companies, even if, as appears most doubtful, those companies obtain the powers which they seek. The total income for the twelve months was £15,930. The nett profit, after meeting current expenses and interest and repaying a portion of the loan, was £3,905 3s. This represented 4 per cent. on the capital expended, but, assuming that as a private company the amount paid for repayment of principal of loans is equivalent to a contribution to a sinking fund, the dividend would have been declared on £6,885, or nearly 7 per cent. These figures must be welcome to the vestry's customers, as in the event of the nett profit reaching 5 per cent. the price of the current must be reduced by the vestry under the terms of their provisional order.

**St. Pancras.**—The vestry have notified that the portion of Euston-road from Gower-street to Cardington-street, now paved with stone, will be closed for six weeks for the purpose of relaying it with wood.

## PROVINCIAL AND GREATER LONDON AUTHORITIES.

### COUNTY COUNCILS.

**Kent.**—A committee recently reported that the asylum cemetery at Barming was full, and asked permission for steps being taken to enclose an additional 2 acres of asylum land adjoining the present cemetery.—The committee also recommended that the tender of Messrs. Simpson & Co., of Pimlico, S.W., for £1,223, exclusive of builders' work, which would be carried out by the asylum staff, be accepted for the purpose of completing the heating on the male side of the old building, and for the heating of the whole of the male side of the additional building.—In connection with the Cartham extension, the committee had accepted the tender of Messrs. Saunders & Co., of Southampton, for £17,300. The report was adopted.

### MUNICIPAL CORPORATIONS.

**Aberavon.**—A special meeting of the Markets Committee of the town council was held on Tuesday of last week, to consider the advisability of extending the markets. The committee subsequently inspected the site of the proposed extension. Upon returning, two schemes were submitted : (1) Forming a portion of the cattle market into an arcade, running from Water-street to Church-street ; (2) covering in the whole of the cattle market, and carrying it out on the principle of the present market. After considerable discussion it was moved that the whole of the cattle market be covered in, with the exception of the portion now occupied by the fire brigade station and the portion of land intervening between the station and Church-street to the width of the building. This was seconded and carried. It was agreed, on the motion of the mayor, that the cost not exceed £5,000.

**Berwick.**—A Local Government Board inquiry will shortly be held with respect to an application of the town council for sanction to borrow a sum of £8,000 for the erection of a new police station.

**Birkenhead.**—A Local Government Board inquiry was last week held by Colonel W. R. Slacke into an application of the town council for sanction to borrow £10,000 for the purposes of street improvements, £740 for widening Rock-lane railway bridge, and £280 for sewerage works.

**Bootle.**—Colonel W. R. Slacke, R.E., last week held an inquiry, on behalf of the Local Government Board, with reference to an application of the town council for permission to borrow £15,351 for the erection of a technical school.

**Bradford.**—At a meeting of the Watch and Fire Brigade Committee of the Bradford Corporation, on Tuesday, it was decided to recommend the council to purchase a site opposite St. James's Church, Nelson-street, for the purpose of erecting a new fire station. The site belongs to Messrs. Murgatroyd & Lister, and the price of the land is, it is stated, £2 10s. a yard, the total cost amounting to £11,000. It is estimated that the whole cost of the new station will be £20,000.

**Brighton.**—The Lighting Committee have resolved that an electricity main be laid in Harrington-road, at a cost of £150; in Elm-grove from the west end to Bonchurch-road and in Bonchurch-road, at a cost of £275; and that the fourteen street lamps on the route of the mains be lighted by electricity instead of gas.

**Bristol.**—At a recent town's meeting, held under the presidency of the mayor, a resolution was unanimously adopted in favour of the promotion of a Bill in the next session of Parliament to make provision for the prevention of floods in the city.

**Burnley.**—On Tuesday, on behalf of the Local Government Board, an inquiry was held at Burnley by Major-General Crozier into an application by the corporation for sanction to borrow £15,060. This comprised £5,250 for the construction of the two Yorkshire-street subways under the Leeds and Liverpool canal, £300 for the construction of a footpath along Springfield-road, £4,310 for purposes of public walks and pleasure grounds, £3,100 for the purchase of land for street improvements, and £1,300 for the purchase of land for slaughter-house purposes. With regard to the subways under the canal, the town clerk explained that the total cost was £7,242, but £2,000 of this sum had been previously sanctioned by the Local Government Board. The estimated cost was £5,000, but a subsidence of the embankment whilst the work was in operation, and the consequent delay of the canal traffic, had rendered the corporation liable for unexpected payments to the canal company by way of compensation. The subsidence at one time became so serious that it was feared the whole of the canal would break through the works, but happily this was avoided. There was no opposition to the application.

**Canterbury.**—The town council have asked the Local Government Board to sanction a loan of £70,000 for the provision of a lunatic asylum. In the course of the Local Government Board inquiry the medical superintendent of the Kent County Asylum at Chatham said that the increase of lunacy in Kent is about sixty cases a year, and it was also shown by statistics that in the county generally lunacy has increased nearly threefold in forty years.

**Eccles.**—Notice is given in Monday's *Gazette* that the corporation intend to make a lease, by way of supplemental lease, to the Manchester Carriage and Tramway Company of all the tramways within the borough of Eccles belonging to the corporation for the period from the 31st March, 1899, to the 27th April, 1901, at the annual rent of £900. A general description is given of the covenants and conditions contained in the original lease which by reference are incorporated in the proposed lease.

**Grimsby.**—The Public Lighting Committee on Friday week decided to recommend the town council to carry out an installation of the electric light in the town, including the supply of current to the tramway company for electric traction, at a total cost of about £40,000. The tramway company's present lease expires in two years' time, and to enable them to reconstruct their line and accept current from the corporation, they required an extended lease of twenty-one years. To this there was some objection, but eventually the whole of the recommendations were adopted.

**Haslingden.**—The town council have adopted the Lighting Committee's recommendation to select a site at the town's yard for the purpose of electric lighting works. The suggested area of supply has also been approved, and an electrical engineer will be engaged to advise upon the several matters connected with the application for a provisional order. The council will, of course, oppose the application for powers proposed to be made by the Electrical Power Distribution Company.

**Haverfordwest.**—The town council held a special meeting last week to decide as to whether a certain scheme for the supplying of water by gravitation should be proceeded with or abandoned. The exhaustive report of Mr. Horace B. Woodward, F.R.S., F.G.S., of London, who thoroughly examined the springs near Little Newcastle, was again considered. This report stated that "the area which contributes the water to the springs must be considerably over a quarter of a square mile; but estimating only of this amount of area taking the average amount of rainfall at 45 in., and allowing liberally for evaporation and absorption, making allowance also for the Hotwells springs for the supply of the village, the stream might confidently be expected to yield on an average not less than 150,000 gallons of water per day. After discussion it was decided to abandon the scheme and proceed with another.

**Huddersfield.**—At the last meeting of the town council it was resolved to make an application to the Board of Trade for sanction to the borrowing of £7,454 for the construction of the Oat-lane tramway.

**Leominster.**—Mr. Herbert H. Law, Local Government Board inspector, attended at the town hall on Friday to inquire into an application of the corporation to borrow £300 for depot purposes.

**Lowestoft.**—It was reported at last week's meeting of the town council that sanction had been received from the Local Government Board to the borrowing of the sum of £5,000 for works of sea defence for the south beach.

**Manchester.**—The lord mayor has convened a meeting of ratepayers for Tuesday, to adopt resolutions in reference to the promotion by the city council of a Bill to enable the corporation to work tramways in the districts adjoining the city, and to authorise the making of agreements with local authorities for the working of the tramways by animal, mechanical or other power.

**Nelson.**—At their last meeting the town council approved of the borough surveyor's plans, &c., for an extension of the filter-beds at the sewage works. The filters, which are to be on the bacteriological system, are 1 acre in extent, and are to be commenced at once.

**Pwllheli.**—The town council have resolved to consider the advisability of lighting the town by means of electricity rather than gas.

**Retford.**—It is understood that the Local Government Board have sanctioned the borrowing of £40,000 for the execution of drainage works in the town.

**Richmond, Surrey.** — The island opposite Petersham Meadows, known as "Glover's Island," is in the market. It is in the very centre of the beautiful landscape view from Richmond Hill, and the corporation are anxious that it should not pass into hands which might possibly use it as a gigantic advertising medium, or in some other way calculated to destroy the amenities of the district. The owner has given the corporation the option of purchase, prior to the day of sale on September 21st, at £4,000. The corporation do not feel justified in expending so large a sum on a somewhat unproductive purchase, but if a substantial contribution is obtained from the public the island will be acquired in the interest of the public. The mayor of Richmond appeals for subscriptions.

**Scarborough.**—Mr. Robert Bicknell, Local Government Board inspector, held an inquiry recently respecting an application of the town council for sanction to borrow £620 for the purchase of certain property for the purposes of a police station and £127 for the acquirement of land for the purposes of public walks and pleasure grounds.

**Taunton.**—On the 23rd inst., at a special meeting of the council, the Main Drainage Committee, with a view to remedying the flooding of Station-road, which takes place on the occasion of heavy storms, recommended the council to carry a 3-ft. sewer from the Royal Mail Inn to the present manhole in Jarvis's field, and also to have the storm overflow in Jarvis's field examined and cleaned out if necessary. A member proposed an alternative scheme in the shape of the extension of the storm overflow, and after considerable discussion the matter was adjourned to next month. The Emergency Committee recommended the acceptance of the tender of Mr. T. Moggridge for the erection of the new technical institute in Corporation-street, and this was adopted. The amount was £1,851. The meeting was marked by a series of very lively personalities.

**Wednesbury.**—The work of extinguishing the subterranean fire is now being carried on satisfactorily. Two pit shafts, 40 ft. deep, are being sunk, and it is proposed to make roads and remove the seam of burning coal, and to fill up the cavities with black sand.

## URBAN DISTRICT COUNCILS.

**Ampthill.**—A letter was recently read from the Local Government Board, stating with reference to the application of the Ampthill Urban District Council for sanction to borrow the sum of £6,100 for purposes of sewage and sewage disposal, the Local Government Board proposed to cause an investigation to be made of the nature of the soil and the subsoil of the two alternative sites which had been proposed for the sewage farm as soon as the present crops were off the ground. The council were also requested to cause trial pipes to be sunk on each site as soon as the crops had been carted, and inform the board when this had been done.

**Basford.**—A letter last week was read from the Local Government Board as to the recent inquiry held at Gotham into the request of the council for permission to borrow £1,500 for waterworks at that place. The scheme was said to be generally satisfactory, but it was desirable that the reservoir should be situated below Weldon spring, in order to

avoid any possibility of subsidence through mining operations. A request was made that the plans should be amended in that respect.—The West Bridgford Urban District Council wrote intimating their intention to construct reservoir and surface works, and for that purpose to take land in the parish of Colwick, also in the city of Nottingham, and also in the parish of West Bridgford. It was decided to oppose the action of the council.

**Bridgend.**—At a meeting of the Urban District Council, last week, the clerk reported that notice had been received of an intended Local Government Board inquiry into the application of the Penybont Main Sewerage Board for a loan of £30,000 to cover the cost of the proposed sewerage scheme for the urban district of Bridgend and Newcastle Higher, Yniswdre, and St. Bride's Minor, in the Penybont rural district. The inquiry will be held at the town hall, Bridgend, on September 1st.

**Garston.**—On behalf of the Local Government Board, Colonel W. R. Slacke, R.E., has held an inquiry into an application of the district council for sanction to borrow £25,000 for the erection of a refuse destructor and electric light station in Garston Old-road, Grassendale. Strong opposition was offered to the proposed site of the destructor, and the inquiry was adjourned.

**Castleton.**—At a special meeting of the Castleton District Council, on Tuesday evening, the draft order of the proposed light railway from Middleton to Rochdale was considered. The proposed line, if constructed, will pass through the village of Castleton. It was decided that the clerk should inform the Secretary of the Board of Trade of the clauses which were considered necessary for the protection of the interests of the village of Castleton.

**Croston.**—The Local Government Board last week granted permission for the raising of a loan for the purpose of executing a scheme of sewerage and sewage disposal prepared by Mr. W. Naylor, A.M.I.C.E., of Preston. The district is exceedingly flat, and the sewage is to be raised at various points by means of a compressed air system of lifting. The treatment at the outfall is by precipitation and filtration through land.

**Heaton Norris.**—The clerk, at the last monthly meeting of the district council, read a letter from the Local Government Board drawing attention to the proposal of the council to borrow £4,100 for the purchase of land for sewage disposal. The council were reminded that the board had not yet received plans and estimates and other information asked for in February last. The clerk said this was the fourth letter received since February, and the matter was becoming urgent. The chairman suggested that the clerk should write in reply, stating that the matter was in hand and would have immediate attention. The Local Government Board could not reasonably complain of the delay of the council. The council had had to wait a good deal for them in times gone by, and, indeed, they were waiting now.

**Horsham.**—The district council have decided to apply to the Board of Trade for a provisional order authorising the council to undertake the electric light supply of the town, in accordance with the report and estimate prepared by Mr. Hartayne.

**Kirkburton.**—The scheme of Mr. T. Aird Murray, of Sheffield, for the disposal of the town's sewage has been accepted by the council. They have also decided to appoint Mr. Murray to act as engineer in connection with the works.

**Ledbury.**—The council having applied to the Local Government Board for permission to borrow £3,200 for purposes of sewerage and sewage disposal, Mr. Herbert H. Law held an inquiry on the 18th ult. on behalf of the board. Mr. Berrington, Wolverhampton, the engineer, and Mr. J. Ellis, surveyor to the urban council, were present at the inquiry. No opposition was raised to the scheme.

**Leigh.**—Authority was on Tuesday given for an application to be made to the Local Government Board for their sanction to the issue of leases of the surplus lands required under the street improvement scheme, upon which £87,000 is being spent. It was stated that the resolution was necessary, because if they did not get the sanction of the Local Government Board the lands would have to be sold outright.—The clerk announced that as the result of recent arbitrations in regard to the acquisition by the council of land required for street improvement, the trustees of Mr. Danby had been awarded £7,140; Mr. Yates, £6,482; Mr. C. Guest, £907 6s. 3d.; total, £14,535 6s. 3d. It was resolved that application be made to the Local Government Board for sanction to borrow the money.

**Leyton.**—Last week, at the Leyton town hall, Colonel Albert C. Smith conducted a Local Government Board inquiry into the application of the council for sanction to borrow £5,000 for purposes of electric lighting, £1,030 for works of private street improvement, £680 for works of sewerage, and £110 for the provision of a urinal at the junction of Woodhouse and Harrow roads. There was no opposition to any of the proposals, and the proceedings were not of a lengthened character.

**Maryport.**—The district having for years past ineffectually striven to prevent the pollution of the river Derwent, from which it draws its water supply, by sewerage from Keswick and other places, Mr. Ross, at a recent meeting of the council, raised the question of obtaining a pure supply. Workington and Cockermouth are considering the question of bringing down an additional supply from Crummock lake, and it is thought Maryport ought to consider whether they would not join these two authorities and obtain an unlimited supply of water from an absolutely unpolluted source. The question was referred to a committee of the whole council.

**Oswaldtwistle.**—The Local Government Board have sanctioned the borrowing by the district council of a sum of £3,276 for purposes connected with the gas undertaking.

**Rhyl.**—The district council are about completing the first section of the Western Promenade extension. The work is being undertaken in front of the old winter gardens, which are now laid out for building sites. The work, which will cost several thousands of pounds, is undertaken by the council without a contractor, Mr. Robert Hughes, the surveyor, being the engineer. The works consist of a sea defence wall, with a promenade, carriageway and parapet on the land side. At the completion of these works it is expected that the sea defences and the erection of a promenade at the Marine-drive will be undertaken, and for which the Local Government Board have sanctioned a loan. A Birmingham firm have applied to the council for permission to lay down an electric tramway from the Grand Pavilion along the sea front, a distance of 4 miles, to Prestatyn.

**Romford.**—At the next meeting of the district council a resolution will be submitted to the effect that the council apply to the Local Government Board for permission to borrow an additional £1,000 for the public baths.

**Royton.**—Local Government Board sanction has been received to the borrowing by the district council of £19,605 and £2,324 for purposes of sewerage and sewage disposal and £1,445 for the completion of the destructor.

**Rugby.**—At the last meeting of the district council a letter was read from Edmundson's Electricity Corporation, stating that they understood that the council had decided to obtain a provisional order for electric lighting, and then to lease their powers to some company if necessary. They expressed a willingness to take such transfer instead of obtaining an order direct. The letter was referred to the General Purposes Committee. Mr. Seabroke formally gave notice that on that day six weeks he would move a resolution to the effect that the council take certain steps to obtain a provisional order for public lighting.

**Skipton.**—The district council on Thursday week received a report giving the conclusions of the sub-committee negotiating for the purchase of the Skipton Gas Company's undertaking. It appeared that the committee had called in Mr. John Waugh, of Bradford, to advise them generally as to the condition of the company's plant, and Mr. Waugh's report was appended, but its contents were not divulged. The price offered by the committee for the gasworks was £30,000, but this offer was refused, and the directors intimated that the company were unwilling sellers of their undertaking. The council decided to hold a special meeting to go into the whole question and determine what course to pursue.

**Sowerby Bridge.**—An inspector of the Local Government Board recently conducted an inquiry respecting an application of the district council for permission to borrow the sum of £8,800 for gasworks purposes and also for supplying gas to the Luddenfoot district.

**Staines.**—A committee of the council have recommended the institution of an application to the Local Government Board for sanction to borrow £2,560 to cover the cost of making-up certain roads.

**Stroud.**—Sir John Dorrington, Bart., M.P., has generously offered to present to the town a piece of land for the purpose of a recreation ground. At present the town lacks this necessary provision.

**Sunbury.**—Mr. Walter A. Ducat, an inspector of the Local Government Board, on the 19th ult. held an inquiry respecting an application of the district council for permission to borrow £4,000 for sewerage and sewage disposal works.

**Tipton.**—A Local Government Board inquiry was held on Tuesday respecting an application of the district council for sanction to borrow £4,500 for the laying-out of the new Victoria Park.

**Tong.**—The council's new sewage disposal works, which have been constructed from plans by Mr. John Drake, of Queensbury, are rapidly approaching completion. The contractor is Mr. F. Robinson, of Thornton. The cost of the works will be over £7,000.

**Watford.**—The district council have instructed the clerk to make an application to the Public Works Loan Commissioners for a loan of £21,000 in connection with the electric lighting works.

**Wigston.**—The district council have decided not to entertain the offer of the directors of the Great Wigston Gas Company to sell their undertaking to the council for £52,500.

**Wirksworth.**—A monthly meeting of the urban district council was held on Monday night, when the surveyor reported that he had inspected a natural gorge situate on the north of Gilkin, which could be made into a storage reservoir capable of holding 3,000,000 gallons of water, and which could supply the low-level district in times of scarcity.

**Worksop.**—The Sanitary Committee presented a report at last week's meeting of the district council recommending that a provisional order should be applied for in connection with the Electric Lighting Bill. The chairman pointed out that now was the time to decide the question. If they decided upon applying for a provisional order they would have to spend £200, and probably £10,000 more on the electric lighting system. The report of the committee was carried, and a special meeting of the council will be called in a month's time to consider the whole question.

## RURAL DISTRICT COUNCILS.

**Barrow-on-Soar.**—On the 18th ult. Colonel W. R. Slacke, R.E., held an inquiry, on behalf of the Local Government Board, into an application of the council for sanction to borrow £3,100 for purposes of sewerage and sewage disposal for the township of Barkby. No opposition was offered to the scheme, which was explained by Mr. W. H. Simpson.

**East Grinstead.**—The Roads and Bridges Committee at a recent meeting reported that the tender of Mr. P. Edwards for the erection of Harts-lane bridge, Hartfield, for £475, had been accepted, and that they had given instructions for the erection of a notice board diverting the traffic while the bridge was being constructed.

**Epsom.**—An inspector of the Local Government Board has held an inquiry respecting an application of the district council for sanction to borrow the sum of £22,000 for purposes of sewerage and sewage disposal.

**Hendon.**—A letter from the Metropolitan Drinking Fountain and Cattle Trough Association was read at a recent meeting of the district council, asking if the council would consent to undertake the maintenance of the Tooke memorial fountain in London-road, Pinner, as the association was in debt to the extent of £6,000. The clerk was instructed to write and ascertain the annual cost of maintenance.

**Llanelly.**—At a meeting of the council on Thursday the clerk reported the receipt of fourteen tenders for laying pipes from Llanelly reservoir to Llwynhendy.

**Ringstead.**—An inquiry has been held, on behalf of the Local Government Board, respecting an application of the district council for sanction to borrow £1,000 to cover the cost of erecting a bridge over the river Nene.

## SCOTLAND AND IRELAND.

**Aberdeen.**—An important event in the municipal history of Aberdeen took place on Friday, when the local tramways were taken over by the corporation, by whom they will in future be worked. The occasion was marked by an interesting celebration, in which the members of the town council and representatives of all the other public boards in the city took part.

**Belfast.**—Preparations are now being made for the formal opening of the new electric light station at the Albert bridge, which will be performed by Earl Cadogan, K.G., Lord Lieutenant of Ireland. The actual date of the ceremony has not yet been fixed, but it will take place about the 18th inst.

**Glasgow.**—At the last meeting of the corporation Bailie Maclay, in moving the approval of the minutes of the Electricity Committee, stated that they were now making rapid progress with the new works at Port Dundas. He was happy to say that all the plant, engines and dynamos under order were likely to be completed within the contract time. Their difficulty would now be in hurrying on the erection of the works to receive the plant. As regards the new works in Pollokshaw's-road, they hoped to begin operations there at a very early date.—The Tramways Committee have been in conference with Lanarkshire and Renfrewshire representatives on the question of extending the tramway system to Cambuslang and Rutherglen and to Paisley. It is understood that the proposals made by the committee have been favourably entertained.

**Greenock.**—At a recent meeting the police board considered the proposed erection of an electric lighting station. The minutes of the Law and Finance Committee contained the report of the deputation appointed by the Electric Lighting Committee to visit various towns in connection with the proposed electric lighting. The deputation visited Edinburgh, Leith and Glasgow, inspected the electric light stations, and, after carefully considering the information obtained and the advice given, they recommended that the board should appoint a resident engineer, who should prepare a design of the works and report thereon and on the area of supply. The sub-committee also considered the terms of the notice from the North British Electricity Supply Company, Limited, and recommended that the company should be informed that the board would oppose their application for a provisional order to supply electricity in Greenock, as the board were taking active steps to introduce the electric light. The report was adopted.

# Personal.

Mr. J. A. Bell, the newly-appointed burgh electrical engineer of Aberdeen, was formally installed in office on the 10th ult.

Mr. T. De Courcey Meade, the city surveyor of Manchester, is, we regret to hear, seriously ill. Mr. J. P. Wilkinson is acting during his absence.

Mr. J. E. Benton, of Sheffield, has been appointed an assistant in the Works Department of the London County Council, at a salary of £3 10s. per week.

The position of assistant to Mr. A. B. Mountain, the borough electrical engineer of Huddersfield, recently vacated by Mr. C. R. Brown, has been filled by the promotion of Mr. J. W. Turner.

A marriage took place on Wednesday of last week between Miss Miller, the youngest daughter of the late Mr. John Miller, of Reigate, and Mr. J. Herbert Norris, borough surveyor of Godalming.

Mr. F. J. Hopwood, surveyor and inspector of nuisances to the Shildon and East Thickley Urban District Council, has been appointed to the vacant position of highway and building surveyor, &c., to the Wealdstone Urban District Council.

On Monday of last week, at a meeting of the select committee dealing with the appointment of a surveyor for the Carnarvon Town Council, six of the fifty applicants for the position were selected to appear before the council at a future date.

The Holywell Rural District Council have appointed, out of seventeen applicants, Mr. John Meirion Williams, a son of Mr. David Williams, county surveyor of Flintshire, as surveyor of the roads in Holywell district, the post having become vacant by the resignation of Mr. Judd through ill-health.

At the forthcoming meeting of the British Association at Bristol Mr. W. M. Acworth, a member of the Metropolitan Asylums Board, will read a paper on "Rectification of Municipal Boundaries," while papers will be read on "Municipal Enterprise," by Mr. Cannan, and "Municipalities and Electric Supply," by Mr. George Pearson.

At a meeting of the Ilford Urban District Council, held last week, the Works Committee reported that they had interviewed four of the five selected candidates for the post of surveyor's assistant, and that they had unanimously resolved that Mr. Samuel Turner, of Birmingham, be appointed, at a salary of £120 per annum. Mr. Turner is understood to have commenced his duties on Monday.

For greater convenience in his private practice as a consulting civil and mechanical engineer, Mr. William Fairley, whose only offices were until recently at Mortlake, S.W., has now taken offices at 53 Victoria-street, Westminster, S.W. Communications may also be addressed to Mr. Fairley at the offices of the Main Sewerage Board, Mortlake. As our readers are aware, Mr. Fairley is engineer to that body.

The death has taken place at Annan, Dumfriesshire, of Mr. James Galletly, junr., road surveyor. Mr. Galletly suffered from an internal complaint, and had been in failing health for some time. He was in his early manhood, and of an active, genial disposition. He was a young man of considerable promise, and was very highly respected by those in the different districts of which he had charge. He leaves a widow and two children.

At the first general meeting of the Enfield Urban District Council since their adjournment Mr. R. Collins, the surveyor to the council, reported that Mr. Yates, the buildings inspector, was too ill to resume his duties. Mr. Collins asked that arrangements should be made for the efficient discharge of the inspector's duties. It was decided to give Mr. Yates a month's salary in lieu of notice, and to advertise for a building inspector at a salary of £150 rising to £200.

Consideration was given last week by the Cromer Protection Commissioners to the appointment of an engineer to superintend the construction of sea defence works. Out of a large number of applicants four were selected to meet the commissioners — viz., Mr. Webster, 39 Victoria-street, Westminster; Mr. Douglas, 15 Victoria-street, Westminster, son of Sir N. Douglas, and an engineer to the Board of Trade, Trinity House, and the Lifeboat Institution; Mr. Moore; and Mr. Mayo. Mr. Douglas was elected, the terms being 100 guineas for the preparation of Parliamentary work, to be merged into the 5 per cent. commission if the work was proceeded with.

On Thursday, at the monthly meeting of the Preston Town Council, a memorial addressed by certain ratepayers of the borough objecting to a recommendation of a special committee "that a sum of £500 be voted in recognition of the late borough surveyor's (Mr. Hudson Real) services for the benefit of the widow and daughters" was read by the town clerk. The memorialists stated that they were advised that the granting of £500 or any other sum out of the public rates

would be illegal, and if any money were allocated for the purposes proposed they would reserve to themselves the right to adopt such legal proceedings as they might be advised. The memorial was received in silence. In a discussion which subsequently ensued the council adopted a suggestion that counsel's opinion should be taken on the matter.

At a meeting of the Barnstaple Town Council, held last week, a member of that body brought forward the question of appointing a full-time surveyor. They were really without a surveyor, and had been so for a very long time, and he ventured to say that the position of the town in that matter was unique, as he doubted whether they could find another corporation like Barnstaple without the assistance and aid of a recognised borough surveyor. It was a disgrace to the town, and the sooner a properly-qualified official was appointed the better. He had nothing to say against the present town officials, the foreman of works and sanitary inspector, but in the interests of a progressive town they required a perfectly competent surveyor, to whom they could appeal for advice and assistance in any matter which might be brought forward, and he would move that the usual steps be taken to carry this into effect. Eventually it was agreed that the matter should be considered at an early date by the council in committee.

A letter was, last week, received by the Chertsey Urban District Council from Mr. A. W. Smith, the surveyor, stating that, as he had been appointed to a more lucrative position in the Midlands, he desired to resign his present post under the council. Two or three members expressed their regret at Mr. Smith's resignation, and it was decided to discuss matters with him after the meeting. The council subsequently went into committee on the question, which they seriously considered. They recommended the council that, in consideration of the surveyor not leaving until October 31st, he be paid for such a period outside the usual month at the rate of £250 per annum, and that his resignation be accepted subject to this arrangement. They further recommended the council to at once advertise for a person to fill the joint offices of surveyor and inspector, the salary to be the same at which Mr. Smith commenced — namely, £160 per annum. On the committee resolving back into council the whole of the recommendations were approved. Particulars of the appointment will be found in our advertising columns.

The daily papers at the beginning of the week contained the announcement that Dr. John Hopkinson, the well-known electrician, of 5 Victoria-street, London, S.W., with a son and two daughters perished together on Saturday morning in one of the most terrible mountain accidents of recent times. Dr. Hopkinson was a practised mountaineer, having quite recently ascended the Matterhorn and the Dent Blanche with his son in a tour through Zermatt. It appears that he started with his son and two daughters from Arolla to ascend the Petite Dent de Veisivi, one of the striking points dominating Evolena, in the Val d'Hérens, running south from the Rhone Valley at Sion. As they started late they were not expected back till about 7 o'clock in the evening. The time for their return passed, and as they did not appear two search parties were despatched, and a third party early in the morning. At daybreak one of the search parties discovered Dr. Hopkinson and his children roped together and all dead on a moraine at the foot of the highest cliffs. Dr. Hopkinson was the eldest son of Alderman Hopkinson, an ex-mayor of Manchester, and was a brother of Prof. Alfred Hopkinson, who lately resigned his seat in Parliament for the Cricklade Division of Wilts to become principal of Owens College. Dr. Hopkinson was educated at Lindow-grove School and Queenwood College, and in his sixteenth year went to Owens College. He afterwards went up to Trinity College, Cambridge, and was Senior Wrangler and first Smith's prizeman in 1871, being appointed fellow and tutor of his college. While at Cambridge he obtained the D.Sc. of London University. He paid special attention to lighthouse machinery, in which he introduced many improvements, particularly the group flashing apparatus. After residing in Birmingham for some years as engineer to Messrs. Chance & Co., he removed to London and practised as an engineer. He took up electrical engineering, and was soon recognised as one of the foremost men in the profession. He presented valuable papers to the Royal Society on electrostatics and magnetism, and he also read papers on technical subjects before the Institutions of Civil Engineers and Electrical Engineers. In 1890 one of the Royal Society's medals was awarded to him, and he was also elected president of the Institution of Electrical Engineers. He was Professor of Electrical Engineering at King's College, London. Dr. Hopkinson has carried out extensive electric tramway schemes in Leeds and other northern towns, and for many years acted as consulting engineer to the Birmingham Corporation. On the 3rd September last he was also appointed consulting engineer for the electric tramways in course of construction at Liverpool. The experimental line ordered for construction under his superintendence is now nearly complete and will be opened in October.

## ASSOCIATION OF MUNICIPAL AND COUNTY ENGINEERS.

VOLUNTARY PASS EXAMINATION.

Notice is hereby given that the twenty-sixth examination for candidates for the offices of engineer and surveyor to municipal corporations and district councils will be held at the Technical School, Princess-street, Manchester, on Friday and Saturday, September 30 and October 1, 1898. Application forms, duly filled in by intending candidates, together with entrance fee of £2 2s., must be in the hands of the secretary on or before the 5th inst.

### MIDLAND DISTRICT MEETING AT BILSTON.

A meeting of the members of the midland district will be held on Saturday, the 17th inst., at Bilston. The following are the arrangements:—

11 a.m.— The members will be received in the council chamber, Town Hall, by the chairman (Councillor R. A. Harper, J.P.) and other members of the council. Minutes of Stafford and Rhyader meetings. Election of hon. district secretary.

11.30 a.m.—Leave in brakes, kindly provided by Councillor J. W. Sankey, chairman of the Water and Baths Committee, for a visit to the Spring Vale furnaces, arriving about 11.40 a.m., where, by the kind permission of Sir Alfred Hickman, the process of steel manufacture will be witnessed. A short descriptive paper will be given.

12.30 p.m.—Leave in brakes for a visit to the waterworks covered service reservoir (which will be specially emptied for the inspection of the members), arriving about 12.45.

1.15 p.m.—Leave in brakes for the Hinley Arms Hotel, arriving about 2 p.m., where a light luncheon will be provided by Councillor R. A. Harper, J.P., chairman of the council.

3 p.m.—Leave in brakes for a visit to the Bilston waterworks pumping station, arriving about 3.30 p.m.

4.15 p.m.—Leave in brakes for the Technical School, Bilston, arriving about 5 p.m.

6 p.m.—Dinner at the Technical School. Tickets, 3s. 6d. each (exclusive of wine).

Arrangements will be made for any members desirous of doing so to inspect the public baths and the public market.

· Mr. C. L. N. Wilson, the water engineer and surveyor to the Bilston Council, will give a descriptive paper of the works. As the paper will be in the hands of members intimating their intention to attend some days before the meeting, it will be taken as read.

Among the hotels at Bilston may be mentioned the Pipe Hall, Globe and Great Western.

Wolverhampton is within 2½ miles and Birmingham 10½ miles, and there is a good service of trains from these towns. The Great Western station at Bilston is the nearest to the Town Hall.

J. S. PICKERING, A.M.I.C.E.,          THOS. COLE, A.M.I.C.E.,
    Hon. District Secretary,                 Secretary,
    Council Offices, Nuneaton.    11 Victoria-street, S.W

## SLOP-WATER CLOSETS.

DECISION OF THE LOCAL GOVERNMENT BOARD.
IMPORTANT TEST CASE.

Some time ago the Lincoln Corporation gave notice to an owner of property to take out several Duckett's slop-water closets and to substitute closets which entailed the use of corporation water. It was alleged that the existing closets were not sufficient water-closets and insanitary. The owner declined to comply with the notice, and the corporation therefore carried out the work, charging £17 as the cost thereof, payment of which was refused by the owner, and an appeal was made by him to the Local Government Board. A local inquiry was held in March last, and evidence taken by the inspector. The decision of the Local Government Board has now been given, and an order made that the owner be not called upon to pay the charges of the corporation or any portion thereof, and that the corporation pay the Local Government Board's costs in the matter. The effect of this decision is that slop-water closets are recognised by the Local Government Board as being sufficient water-closets, and may therefore be used as such. We understand that the closets referred to were Duckett's well-known patent arrangement "B."

## APPOINTMENTS VACANT.

*Advertisements which are received too late for classification cannot be included in these summaries until the following week.*

BUILDING INSPECTOR.—September 2nd.—Southend-on-Sea Corporation. £125.—Mr. William H. Snow, clerk.

CLERK FOR SURVEYOR'S DEPARTMENT.—September 3rd.—Staines Rural District Council. £52.—Mr. G. W. Manning, surveyor to the council.

ASSISTANT SANITARY INSPECTOR.—September 3rd.—Blaby Rural District Council. £1 10s.—Mr. B. A. Shires, clerk to the council, Alliance Chambers, Municipal-square, Leicester.

SUPERINTENDENT OF SEWERS AND DRAINS.—September 5th. Vestry of St. Marylebone. £150.—Mr. W. H. Garbutt, clerk.

SUPERINTENDENT OF CLEANSING.—September 5th.— Vestry of St. Marylebone. £180.—Mr. W. H. Garbutt, clerk.

DISTRICT SUPERINTENDENT.—September 5th.—Vestry of St. Marylebone. £150.—Mr. W. H. Garbutt, clerk.

INSPECTOR OF NUISANCES AND SURVEYOR.—September 6th.—Little Woolton Urban District Council. £110.—Mr. Percy Dobell, clerk to the council.

CLERK OF WORKS.—September 6th.—Aldershot Urban District Council.—Mr. Nelson F. Dennis, surveyor.

SURVEYOR AND INSPECTOR OF NUISANCES.—September 6th. —Chertsey Urban District Council. £160.—Mr. T. E. Harland Chaldecott, clerk to the council.

BUILDING INSPECTOR.—September 6th.—Enfield Urban District Council. £150.—Mr. T. W. Scott, clerk to the council.

CLERK OF WORKS.—September 6th.—Stoke-upon-Trent Corporation. £2 10s.—Mr. Wm. Bowen, borough engineer.

TEMPORARY ASSISTANT OF SEWERAGE WORKS.—September 8th.—Cannock Urban District Council. 30s.—Mr. W. Blackshaw, A.M.I.C.E., engineer and surveyor to the council.

INSPECTOR OF NUISANCES.—September 12th.—Northfleet Urban District Council. £80.—Messrs. Sharland & Hatten, clerks, Court House, Gravesend.

THIRD ASSISTANT TO ENGINEER AND SURVEYOR.—September 12th.—Leigh Urban District Council. £70.—Mr. Tom Hunter, engineer and surveyor to the council.

ELECTRICAL ENGINEER. — September 20th. — Willesden Urban District Council. £400.—Mr. O. Claude Robson, M.I.C.E., engineer and surveyor to the council.

BOROUGH SURVEYOR AND SANITARY INSPECTOR.—September 17th.—Borough of Oswestry. £200.—Mr. J. Parry Jones, town clerk.

DISTRICT SUPERINTENDENTS (TWO OR THREE). — The British Electric Traction Company. £300 to £350.—Mr. G. Stevens, secretary to the company.

CLERK OF WORKS.—Metropolitan Asylums Board. £3 3s. —Offices, Norfolk House, Norfolk-street, Strand, W.C.

## COMPETITIONS.

*Advertisements which are received too late for classification cannot be included in these summaries until the following week.*

PLYMOUTH.—September 24th.—Erection of shops and dwelling-houses fronting Tavistock-road. £250.—Mr. J. H. Ellis, town clerk.

WIVENHOE.—September 29th.—Works of drainage and water supply, for the urban district council.—Mr. C. W. Denton, clerk.

REIGATE.—October 6th.—Erection of municipal buildings, fire station, public offices, &c.—Mr. Clair J. Grece, town clerk.

CHERTSEY.—December 23rd.—Sewerage and sewage disposal scheme for the No. 1 and 2 wards of the district. £50, £30 and £20.—Mr. T. E. Harland Chaldecott, clerk to the council.

## MUNICIPAL CONTRACTS OPEN.

*Advertisements which are received too late for classification cannot be included in these summaries until the following week.*

WEST HAM.—September 2nd.—Erection of museum at Stratford.—Mr. Fred. E. Hilleary, town clerk.

WELLS.—September 3rd.—Erection of public hall and post office buildings.—Mr. R. L. Foster, town clerk.

TENBURY.—September 3rd.—Building of a retaining wall, about 200 ft. long by 12 ft. high, at the side of Kyre brook, for the rural district council.—Mr. R. W. Jarvis, surveyor to the council.

TONBRIDGE.—September 3rd.—Erection of a proposed new technical institute and free library, for the urban district council.—Mr. H. Neve, junr., clerk to the council.

LEWISHAM.—September 3rd.—Formation of a new exit, &c., at the public baths at Ladywell, for the vestry.—Mr. Edward M. Oxenham, clerk to the vestry.

NORWICH.—September 3rd.—Making-up of Mousehold-street, Cavalry-street, Anchor-street, Wadehouse-street and Tracey-road.—Mr. Arthur E. Collins, A.M.I.C.E., city engineer.

DERBY.—September 5th.—Construction of a covered service reservoir at Littleover.—Mr. H. F. Gadsby, town clerk.

DEVONPORT.—September 5th.—Construction of drainage culvert.—Mr. John F. Burns, borough surveyor.

BRIXTON.—September 5th.—Supply and erection of electric lighting plant, for the urban district council.—Clerk.

SHEFFIELD.—September 5th.— Extension of car-shed.—Mr. Henry Sayer, town clerk.

ROCHDALE.—September 6th.—Electric lighting plant.—Mr. James Leach, town clerk.

ALDERSHOT.—September 6th.—Supply of 2,000 tons of granite (more or less), for the urban district council.—Mr. W. E. Foster, clerk.

ALDERSHOT.—September 6th.—Supply and delivery of a Morrison's scarifier, for the urban district council.—Mr. W. E. Foster, clerk.

HULL.—September 6th.—Supply of four steel Lancashire boilers, 30 ft. by 8 ft., with mechanical stokers.—Mr. A. E. White, city engineer.

DISS.—September 6th.—Supply of about 250 tons of Belgian granite, for the urban district council.—Mr. Henry O. Lyus, clerk to the council.

MALLING.—September 6th.—Extension of the sewerage system, for the rural district council.—Mr. Henry Robinson, 13 Victoria-street, London, S.W.

UXBRIDGE.—September 6th.—Construction of a catchment chamber at the sewage works, Cowley Mill-road, for the urban district council. —Mr. W. Garner, clerk to the council.

Carshalton.—September 6th.—Supply of about 345 ft. of 18-in. cast-iron socket and spigot pipes in 12-ft. lengths, for the urban district council.—Mr. S. Willis Gale, A.M.I.C.E., surveyor to the council.

Halifax.—September 7th.—Slating of the purifying-house and retort-house at the gasworks, for the corporation.—Mr. Thomas Holgate, gas engineer.

Tamworth.—September 7th.—Supply of about 300 tons of broken granite, for the rural district council.—Mr. Henry J. Clarson, surveyor to the council.

Weybridge.—September 7th.—Supply of stoneware pipes, gullies, Bristol blue pennant curbing, prepared limestone or granite for tar paving, Thames ballast, Portland cement, and gas tar, for the urban district council.—Mr. John S. Crawshaw, surveyor to the council.

Grays.—September 7th.—Supply of 1,000 tons of granite and quartzite, for the urban district council.—Mr. Arthur C. James, surveyor to the council.

Derby.—September 7th.—Erection of a boundary wall at the Nottingham-road cemetery extension.—Mr. John Ward, borough surveyor.

King's Lynn.—September 7th.—Supply of electric lighting plant, &c.—Mr. T. G. Archer, town clerk.

Aldershot.—September 7th.—Metalling Albert-street, West End, for the urban district council.—Mr. W. E. Foster, clerk.

Edinburgh.—September 7th.—Work in connection with Portobello public baths.—Mr. R. Morham, city superintendent of works.

Weybridge.—September 7th.—Supply and delivery of various materials, for the urban district council.—Mr. G. Wheeler, clerk.

Southend-on-Sea.—September 8th.—Making-up of roads.—Mr. William H. Snow, town clerk.

Cannock.—September 8th.—Supply of about 3,300 yards of Wirksworth kerb, 270 yards of setts and 20,000 yards of 5-in. blue Staffordshire channel blocks, for the urban district council.—Mr. W. Blackshaw, engineer and surveyor to the council.

Southend-on-Sea.—September 8th.—Making-up of Claremont-road.—Mr. Alfred Fidler, A.M.I.C.E., borough surveyor.

Llandovery.—September 9th.—Erection of a highway bridge over the river Cothi at Pontbrenllwyd ford, near Pumpsaint, for the rural district council.—The Clerk to the Council.

Cromer.—September 10th.—Erection of a public convenience, with accommodation for both sexes, on the sea front, for the urban district council.—Mr. A. F. Scott, surveyor to the council.

Nottingham.—September 10th.—Sinking of two bore-holes, each 32 in. diameter, in the parish of Broughton.—Sir Samuel G. Johnson, town clerk.

Lancashire.—September 10th.—Repair of Read old bridge crossing the Sabden brook in the townships of Whalley and Read, for the county council.—Mr. W. Harold Radford, county bridge-master, 19 Brazenose-street, Manchester.

Wimbledon.—September 10th.—Supply of forage for the six months ending March 31, 1899, for the urban district council.—Mr. W. H. Whitfield, clerk to the council.

Bury St. Edmunds.—September 10th.—Erection of buildings, chimney shaft, &c., for the electric light station.—Mr. J. Campbell Smith, borough surveyor.

Ramsgate.—September 10th.—Erection of buildings to be used as offices for the gas and water department.—Mr. W. A. Hubbard, town clerk.

Bangor.—September 10th.—Supply and erection of electric lighting plant.—Mr. R. Hughes Pritchard, town clerk.

Cardiff.—September 12th.—Erection of three new pavilions, lodge and contingent works in connection with the extension of the sanatorium.—Mr. W. Harpur, M.I.C.E., borough engineer.

Glasgow.—September 12th.—Erection of a bridge over the river Kelvin, opposite Montgomerie-street, North Kelvinside.—Mr. John Lindsay, interim clerk, City Chambers, Glasgow.

Blackburn.—September 12th.—Alteration of the slaughter-houses.—Mr. William Stubbs, A.M.I.C.E., borough and water engineer.

St. Pancras.—September 12th.—Supply of about 140,000 jarrah or karri wood paving blocks for repaving Guildford-street and Midland-road, for the vestry.—Mr. Wm. N. Blair, engineer and surveyor to the vestry.

Bexley.—September 12th.—Supply of materials, stores, cartage, team labour, removal of dust and steam rolling, for the urban district council.—Mr. Tom Vickers, surveyor to the council.

Ilford.—September 12th.—Various works at Valentine's, the site of the public park, for the urban district council.—Mr. H. Shaw, A.M.I.C.E., surveyor to the council.

Torquay.—September 13th.—Supply of about 300 tons of Portland cement.—Mr. Henry A. Garrett, A.M.I.C.E., borough surveyor.

Rugby.—September 13th.—Construction of about 170 yards of main outfall sewer at the sewage farm, New Bilton, for the urban district council.—Mr. D. G. Macdonald, A.M.I.C.E., surveyor to the council.

North Riding.—September 13th.—Rebuilding, &c., of Tanton bridge, near Stokesley.—Mr. Walter Stead, M.I.C.E., county surveyor, Northallerton.

Birmingham.—September 13th.—Construction of aqueduct.—Mr. E. O. Smith, town clerk.

Hastings.—September 13th.—Supply of about 1,707 tons of 16-in., 169 tons of 10-in. and 84 tons of 6-in. cast-iron water pipes and about 35 tons of irregulars.—Mr. R. H. Palmer, M.I.C.E., borough engineer.

Dover.—September 13th.—Erection of a workshop, &c., adjoining the car sheds at Maxton.—Mr. Henry E. Stilgoe, A.M.I.C.E., borough engineer.

Weston-super-Mare.—September 13th.—Alterations and additions to the Knightstone baths, for the urban district council.—Mr. Sydney C. Smith, clerk to the council.

St. Luke.—September 14th.—Construction of an underground sanitary convenience in Old-street, for the vestry.—The Surveyor to the Vestry.

St. Luke.—September 14th.—Paving of Golden-lane and part of Banner-street with jarrah wood and part of Peartree-street with granite, for the vestry.—The Surveyor to the Vestry.

Epping.—September 14th.—Erection of a new ward at the isolation hospital at Theydon Garnon, for the rural district council.—Mr. R. D. Trotter, clerk to the council.

Plumstead.—September 14th.—Paving works in White Hart-lane, for the vestry.—Mr. W. C. Gow, surveyor to the vestry.

Nottingham.—September 17th.—Construction of new sewer.—Mr. Arthur Brown, city engineer.

Edinburgh.—October 17th.—For various works in connection with gasholder tank at Granton.—Mr. James M'G. Jack, clerk to the commissioners.

Staines.—September 17th.—Making-up of Sidney-road, Bremer-road, Farnell-road and Billet-road, for the urban district council.—Mr. E. J. Barrett, A.M.I.C.E., surveyor to the council.

Staines.—September 17th.—Supply and delivery of about 200 tons of 1½-in. hand-broken Guernsey granite, for the urban district council.—Mr. E. J. Barrett, A.M.I.C.E., surveyor to the council.

Loughborough.—September 17th.—Construction of a new filter-bed at Nanpantan.—Mr. A. H. Walker, A.M.I.C.E., borough engineer and waterworks manager.

Walton-on-Naze.—September 17th.—Sewering, curbing, channelling, paving and metalling works in Station-road, for the urban district council.—Mr. H. W. Gladwell, surveyor to the council.

Wimbledon.—September 19th.—Making-up of Ashley-road, Caxton-road, Clarence-road, Edith-road, Effra-road (section I) and Hamilton-mews, for the urban district council.—Mr. W. H. Whitfield, clerk to the council.

Hornsey.—September 19th.—Sewering, levelling, paving, metalling, channelling and making good certain roads, for the urban district council.—Mr. F. D. Askey, clerk.

Swanage.—September 19th.—Completion of the main sewerage of the district, for the urban district council.—Messrs. Francis Newman & Cocks, 5 St. Thomas-street, Ryde.

Lytham.—September 19th.—Construction of about 900 yards of 3-ft. diameter brick sewer, about 1,600 yards of 24-in. and 18-in. pipe sewer, and concrete and storage tanks, together with sea embankment, roadway and other contingent works, for the urban district council.—Messrs. Newton, 17 Cooper-street, Manchester.

Leeds.—September 20th.—Supply of (a) poles and (b) trolley wire and attachments in connection with the extension of the electric tramway systems.—The City Engineer.

Barking Town.—September 20th.—Supply of a 6 or 10 ton steam road-roller adaptable for traction, for the urban district council.—Mr. E. H. Lister, clerk to the council.

East Sussex.—September 23rd.—Erection of two temporary buildings for 100 patients at the county lunatic asylum.—Mr. Henry Card, county surveyor, County Hall, Lewes.

Beckenham.—September 26th.—Widening of Croydon-road and East End-road, for the urban district council.—Mr. John A. Angell, surveyor to the council.

Beckenham.—September 26th.—Erection of about 200 cast-iron ventilating columns, 13 ft. 6 in. high, on concrete beds, together with the laying of 9-in. stoneware pipe connections to the main sewers, &c., for the urban district council.—Mr. John A. Angell, surveyor to the council.

Witney.—September 26th.—Main drainage of Eynsham, for the rural district council.—Mr. Nicholas Lailey, A.M.I.C.E., 16 Great George-street, London, S.W.

Hastings.—September 27th.—Excavating and steining two wells, about 270 ft. deep, at Brede.—Mr. D. H. Palmer, M.I.C.E., borough engineer.

Hastings.—September 27th.—Construction of two covered service reservoirs (each 1,500,000 gallons capacity) at Ore.—Mr. P. H. Palmer, M.I.C.E., borough engineer.

Bexhill.—September 28th.—Supply of various electric light plant, for the urban district council.—Mr. A. H. Preece, A.M.I.C.E., 30 Victoria-street, London, S.W.

Hull.—September 30th.—Supply of forty-five electric motor cars, twenty trail cars, two sprinkler cars and two traversing platforms.—Mr. A. E. White, city engineer.

# TENDERS.

*Accepted.

BARNSTAPLE.—For the construction of a concrete impounding sewer, for the urban district council.—Mr. Frank W. Chanter, engineer to the council:—

| | |
|---|---|
| W. C. Shaddick, Plymouth | £1,591 |
| W. Slee, Barnstaple | 1,315 |

BOURNEMOUTH.—For the supply of two material and slop tip-carts.—Mr. F. W. Lacey, M.I.C.E., borough engineer and surveyor:—

| | |
|---|---|
| Gloucester Railway Carriage and Waggon Company, Limited | £50 |
| Austin & Sons | 35 |
| W. Glover & Sons | 35 |
| Bristol Waggon and Carriage Works, Limited | 34 |
| W. Smith & Sons | 29 |
| J. Smith & Sons, Limited* | 26 |

CARSHALTON.—For the supply of 400 cubic yards of hand-picked surface flints delivered at various depots within the district, for the urban district council.—Mr. W. W. Gale, A.M.I.C.E., surveyor to the council:—

| | Per ton. s. d. |
|---|---|
| W. Hudson, Brighton | 7 6 and 8 6 |
| J. C. Forsdick, Wallington | — 8 6 |
| E. Smith, Crockham Hill, Edenbridge* | — 7 9 |

CARSHALTON.—For the supply of 200 tons of broken 1-in. Quenast or Guernsey granite and 620 yards of hand-picked flints, for the urban district council.—Mr. W. W. Gale, A.M.I.C.E., surveyor to the council:—

| | | Per ton. s. | d. |
|---|---|---|---|
| R. F. & J. Fennings, London-bridge, S.E. | (Guernsey) | 15 | 6 |
| A. & F. Manuelle, 57 Gracechurch-street, E.C. | (Guernsey) | 14 | 8 |
| W. Griffiths, Bishopsgate-street Without, E.C. | (Guernsey) | 14 | 3 |
| J. Mowlem & Co., Millbank, Westminster, S.W. | (Guernsey) | 14 | 1 |
| Cherbourg Quartzite Company, 20 Mark-lane, E.C. | (Quartzite) | 13 | 3 |
| C. M. Manuelle, 12 Lime-street, E.C.* | (Quenast) | 12 | 3 |
| Narborough Granite Company, Narborough | (Leicester) | 11 | 4 |
| Wentwick Granite Company, Coalville | (Leicester) | 11 | 4 |

CARSHALTON.—For the widening of High-street, for the urban district council.—Mr. W. W. Gale, A.M.I.C.E., surveyor to the council:—

| | |
|---|---|
| R. Ballard & Co., Limited, Child's Hill, Kilburn | £587 |
| S. Kavanagh, Surbiton Hill | 555 |
| W. Jouner, Sutton | 538 |

On account of the difference between the surveyor's estimate and the lowest tender, the council decided to do the work departmentally.

CHEPSTOW.—For the laying of 1,000 superficial yards of granite and cement concrete for footways in Bridge-street and Station-road, for the urban district council.—Mr. F. Feather, surveyor to the council:—

| | |
|---|---|
| E. R. Gyles & Co., Manchester | £263 |
| Patent Victoria Stone Company, Leicester | 242 |
| A. Lawson & Co., Newport, Mon. | 240 |
| G. Walker & Co., Birmingham | [illegible] |
| H. C. Parfitt, Newport, Mon.* | [illegible] |

Surveyor's estimate, £213.

HUNSTANTON.—For the construction of a telescopic gasholder, for the urban district council.—Mr. J. S. B. Glasier, clerk to the council:—

| | |
|---|---|
| Ashmore, Benson, Pease & Co., Stockton | £1,067 |
| R. Dempster, Elland, Yorks | 1,062 |
| C. W. Walker, Donnington, Newport | [illegible] |
| Porter & Co., Lincoln | 949 |
| Westwood & Wright, Brierly Hill, Staffs. | 907 |
| A. Holmes & Co., Huddersfield* | 895 |

PEMBERTON.—For the construction of about 1 mile of 9-in. sewer.—
Mr. Paul Partington, clerk :—

| | | | | | |
|---|---|---|---|---|---|
| W. Winnard, Wigan ... | ... | ... | ... | ... | £989 |
| E. Cheetham, Pendleton ... | ... | ... | ... | ... | 800 |
| W. Gaskell & Son, Wigan ... | ... | ... | ... | ... | 743 |
| P. Hitchen & Son, Orrell | ... | ... | ... | ... | 716 |
| J. Prescott, Wigan ... | ... | ... | ... | ... | 679 |
| J. J. Blackburn, Hurniston... | ... | ... | ... | ... | 655 |
| T. Kearsley, Leigh ... | ... | ... | ... | ... | 652 |
| J. Fairhurst, Pemberton* ... | ... | ... | ... | ... | 580 |

CHORLEY.—Accepted for the supply of cast-iron mains.—Mr. J. Mills,
town clerk :—

Mains, 3 in., 4 in., 5 in. and 6 in.—The Sheepbridge Coal and Iron Company, Limited, Chesterfield.
Mains, 9 in. and 20 in.—The Stanton Iron Company, Limited, Nottingham.

PORTSMOUTH.—For the supply and fixing of cast-iron valve seatings
to the pumps at the Easthey pumping station.— Mr. Alexander
Hellard, town clerk :—

| | | | | | |
|---|---|---|---|---|---|
| Horn & Sons, London | ... | ... | ... | ... | £260 |
| McKinlay & Co., Landport... | ... | ... | ... | ... | 260 |
| Vosper & Co., Portsmouth ... | ... | ... | ... | ... | 248 |
| Davis & Sons, Landport | ... | ... | ... | ... | 205 |
| J. Sherveli, Landport | ... | ... | ... | ... | 179 |
| Tingle Brothers, Oinderford* | ... | ... | ... | ... | 165 |

SPENNYMOOR.—For curbing, cement and tar paving, for the urban
district council.—Mr. T. Badcock, clerk :—

Section I.

| | | | | | |
|---|---|---|---|---|---|
| Hobbs & Elenor, Stockton-on-Tees | ... | ... | ... | ... | £470 |
| J. Carrish, Durham ... | ... | ... | ... | ... | 319 |
| J. Manners, Coundon, Bishop Auckland* | ... | ... | ... | 284 |

Section II.

| | | | | | |
|---|---|---|---|---|---|
| Hobbs & Elenor, Stockton ... | ... | ... | ... | ... | 38s |
| J. Manners, Coundon | ... | ... | ... | ... | 297 |
| J. Carrish, Durham* ... | ... | ... | ... | ... | 272 |

TURTON.—For flagging, paving and other works.—Mr. V. W. Laith-
waite, surveyor to the urban district council :—
J. E. Jackson, Horwich.
Jones's Annealed Concrete Company, Middlesbrough.
W. Pollitt, Bolton.*

---

## NOTICES.

THE SURVEYOR AND MUNICIPAL AND COUNTY ENGINEER
*may be ordered direct, through any of Messrs. Smith & Son's
book-stalls, or of any newsagent in the United Kingdom.
Applications to the Offices for single copies by post must in all
cases be accompanied by stamps.*
*The Prepaid Subscription (including postage) is as follows :*

| | Twelve Months. | Six Months. | Three Months. |
|---|---|---|---|
| United Kingdom ... | 16s. | 7s. 6d. | 3s. 9d. |
| Continent, the Colonies, India, | | | |
| United States, &c. ... | 19s. | 9s. 6d. | 4s. 9d. |

*The International News Company, 83 and 85 Duane-street
New York City; The Toronto News Company, Toronto; and
The Montreal News Company, Montreal, have been appointed
agents in the United States and Canada for the sale of THE
SURVEYOR AND MUNICIPAL AND COUNTY ENGINEER. A thin
paper edition is printed for circulation abroad.*

EDITORIAL OFFICES :—
24 BRIDE-LANE, FLEET-STREET, LONDON, E.C.
ADVERTISEMENT AND PUBLISHING OFFICES :—
13 NEW STREET-HILL, FLEET-STREET, LONDON, E.C.

---

## APPOINTMENTS OPEN.

LEIGH URBAN DISTRICT COUNCIL.
Wanted, a Third Assistant in the office of the Engineer
and Surveyor. Must be a good draughtsman, surveyor and
leveller, and have been trained in a municipal office. Salary,
£70 per annum.
Applications, stating age and qualifications, together with
copies of three recent testimonials, will be received by the
undersigned up to 12th September, 1898.
TOM HUNTER,
Engineer and Surveyor.
Leigh, Lancashire.

WILLESDEN DISTRICT COUNCIL.
ELECTRICAL ENGINEER.
The Willesden District Council require the services of an
Electrical Engineer for the design of an electric lighting
installation, and the ultimate management and maintenance
of the same after completion.
He shall be resident in the district, and shall devote the
whole of his time to the duties of his office. The salary will
be £400 per annum, with office, assistants and supply of all
office materials.
All further particulars may be obtained upon application
to Mr. O. Claude Robson, M.INST.C.E., Engineer to the Council, Public Offices, Dyne-road, Kilburn, N.W., on and after
September 6, 1898.
Applications, endorsed " Electric Lighting Engineer,"
stating age and enclosing not more than three recent testimonials (copies only, which will not be returned), to be
addressed to the undersigned, and delivered not later than
4 p.m. on September 20, 1898.
Personal canvassing is strictly prohibited and will dis-
qualify the candidate.
(By order)
STANLEY W. BALL,
Clerk to the Council.
Public Offices, Dyne-road, Kilburn, N.W.
September 1, 1898.

CANNOCK URBAN DISTRICT COUNCIL.
SEWERAGE WORKS ASSISTANT.
Wanted, at once, in the Engineer and Surveyor's depart-
ment for six months, an Assistant, thoroughly competent to
take sewerage sections, plot same, prepare plans, and a good
draughtsman.
Salary, 30s. per week.
Application, stating age, experience and how soon dis-
engaged, accompanied by copies of three recent testimonials,
endorsed " Assistant," must be lodged with me not later than
Thursday, the 8th September, 1898.
W. BLACKSHAW, A.M.I.C.E.,
Engineer and Surveyor.
Council Offices, Cannock.
August 29, 1898.

URBAN DISTRICT COUNCIL OF ENFIELD.
BUILDING INSPECTOR.
The Council invite applications for the appointment of
Building Inspector, at a salary of £150 a year, rising £10
annually on the 29th September to a maximum of £200.
Candidates must be between sixty and seventy years of age,
must have had experience in building operations, and be
qualified to act as draughtsman if required.
Applications, in candidate's own handwriting, on forms
which can be obtained at this office, accompanied by copies
only of three recent testimonials, to be sent to me not later
than noon on Tuesday, the 6th day of September next.
Selected candidates will have notice to attend the meeting
at which the appointment will be made.
(By order)
T. W. SCOTT,
Clerk.
Court House, Enfield.
August 25, 1898.

BOROUGH OF OSWESTRY.
APPOINTMENT OF SURVEYOR AND SANITARY
INSPECTOR.
The Town Council of this borough require the services of
a Surveyor and Sanitary Inspector, who must be thoroughly
conversant with water and sewerage works, and who shall
devote the whole of his time to the duties of his office. He
will be permitted to take private practice.
Salary, £200 per annum.
Personal canvass will be deemed a disqualification.
Applications, accompanied with recent testimonials and
endorsed " Surveyor," to be sent to me on or before 17th
September next.
J. PARRY JONES,
Town Clerk.
Oswestry.
August 22, 1898.

CHERTSEY URBAN DISTRICT COUNCIL.
APPOINTMENT OF SURVEYOR AND INSPECTOR
OF NUISANCES.
The Council invite applications for the appointment of
Surveyor and Inspector of Nuisances for their district, at a
combined salary of £160 per annum, payable monthly.
The person appointed must be between twenty-seven and
forty years of age, will be required to devote his whole time
to the duties of the office, and to reside in the district. He
must be thoroughly competent and have had practical experience in a similar position.
The successful applicant will be required to take office in
one month from date of appointment, which shall be determined by two months' notice on either side.
Sealed applications, endorsed " Surveyor and Inspector,"
stating the age, qualifications and experience, accompanied
by copies of, not more than three recent testimonials, must
reach the undersigned by noon on Tuesday, the 6th day of
September next.
Canvassing, directly or indirectly, will be a disqualification.
A list of duties and further particulars may be obtained
from me.
T. E. HARLAND CHALDECOTT,
Clerk to the Council.
Chertsey.
August 24, 1898.

---

## COMPETITION.

CHERTSEY URBAN DISTRICT COUNCIL.

*COMPETITION FOR SEWERAGE SCHEMES.*

TO ENGINEERS.
The Chertsey Urban District Council invite competitive
plans for the Sewerage and Treatment of Sewage from the
Nos. 1 and 2 Wards of their district, showing separate and
joint schemes for such wards.
The following premiums are offered : First, £50 ; second,
£30 ; third, £20.
Plans, details and estimates of cost to be signed by a *nom-
de-plume.*

The names and addresses of competitors to be sealed in an envelope endorsed with the *nom-de-plume* adopted.

Plans of the suggested arena may be seen and other particulars (printed or written) obtained, on application up to the 28th day of October next, from the Surveyor to the Council, Mr. Arthur W. Smith, Eastworth-road, Chertsey. Plans and other documents should be delivered free to the undersigned by the 23rd day of December next.

Competitors must not approach or consult members of the Council.

(By order)
T. E. HARLAND CHALDECOTT,
Clerk to the Council.
Chertsey.
August 26, 1898.

## TENDERS WANTED.

STAINES URBAN DISTRICT COUNCIL.
TO ROAD CONTRACTORS.

The above Council invite tenders for the making-up of the following streets—*viz.*,—

Sidney-road.
Bremer-road.
Farnell-road.
Billet-road.

Plans and sections may be seen, and specifications, bills of quantities and forms of tender obtained (on payment of £1 1s. in respect of each street, which will be returned on receipt of a *bond-fide* tender), upon application to Mr. E. J. Barrett, ASSOC.M.INST.C.E., Surveyor, Town Hall, Staines, on and after Monday, 5th September, between the hours of 10 a.m. and 1 p.m.

No tender will be considered unless made on the prescribed form and accompanied by the bill of quantities and schedule of prices properly filled in. A separate tender must be submitted for each street.

Sealed tenders, endorsed with the name of the street, to be delivered at my office not later than Saturday, 17th September.

The Council do not bind themselves to accept the lowest or any tender.

JOHN ANTHONY ENGALL,
Clerk to the Council.
Clarence-street, Staines.
August 31, 1898.

THE ILFORD URBAN DISTRICT COUNCIL hereby give notice that they are prepared to receive tenders for the following works at Valentine's, Ilford, the site of the Public Park :—

For Cleansing, Levelling, &c., the Lake, Making Roads and Footpaths through Grounds (including getting gravel), Making Catch-Pit.

Specification and plan may be seen, and form of tender and schedule obtained, on application to Mr. H. Shaw, A.M.I.C.E., Surveyor to the Council, at his offices, 7 Cranbrook-road, Ilford, on and after Monday next, during the usual office hours.

Sealed tenders, addressed to the Chairman, must be delivered to me here by 9 a.m., Monday, the 12th day of September next.

The Council do not bind themselves to accept the lowest tender, while the successful applicant must be prepared to commence the works forthwith.

JOHN. W. BENTON,
Clerk.
Council Offices, Ilford.
September 1, 1898.

STAINES URBAN DISTRICT COUNCIL.
GRANITE MACADAM.

The above Council invite tenders for the supply and delivery at Staines of about 200 tons of 1¾-in. Hand-Broken Guernsey Granite.

Particulars and forms of tender may be obtained upon application to Mr. E. J. Barrett, Surveyor, Town Hall, Staines. No tender will be considered unless made on the prescribed form.

Sealed tenders, endorsed "Tender for Granite," to be delivered at my office not later than Saturday, 17th September.

The Council do not bind themselves to accept the lowest or any tender.

JOHN ANTHONY ENGALL,
Clerk to the Council.
Clarence-street, Staines.
August 31, 1898.

PLUMSTEAD VESTRY.
NOTICE TO CONTRACTORS.

The Plumstead Vestry invite tenders for Paving the Roadway of part of White Hart-lane, including its continuation north of the South-Eastern Railway, with Granite Patching.

The person or firm whose tender is accepted will, in the case of all workmen to be employed by him or them, be re-

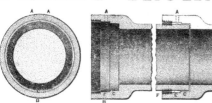

quired to pay wages at rates not less, and to observe hours of labour not greater, than the rates and hours set out in the Vestry's list (such rates of wages and hours of labour will be inserted in a schedule, and form part of the contract), and will also be required to enter into a formal contract and bond with two approved sureties for the due performance of the contract.

Plans may be seen, and form of tender, specification and approximate quantities, and lists of wages and hours of labour, may be obtained on application to Mr. W. C. Gow, c.r., Surveyor to the Vestry, on and after Monday, the 5th September, 1898, on deposit of £2, which sum will be returned on receipt of a *bond-fide* tender, provided such tender is not subsequently withdrawn.

The Vestry does not bind itself to accept the lowest or any tender.

Sealed tenders, properly filled in, must be sent to me at the Vestry Hall on or before Wednesday, the 14th September, not later than 4 p.m., in envelope, marked "Tender for Paving."

(By order)
EDWIN HUGHES,
Vestry Clerk.

Vestry Hall, Maxey-road, Plumstead.
August 29, 1898.

## SWANAGE URBAN DISTRICT COUNCIL.
### TO SEWERAGE CONTRACTORS.

The Urban District Council of Swanage, in the county of Dorset, are prepared to receive tenders for the completion of the Main Sewerage of the district, including about 221 yards of 27-in. Iron Outfall Sewer, 976 yards of 27-in. and 30-in., and 3,900 yards of 9-in., 12-in. and 15-in. Pipe Sewers, with requisite arrangements for flushing, inspection and ventilation.

Drawings and specification may be seen at the offices of the Council, Town Hall, Swanage, and of the Engineers, 5 St. Thomas-street, Ryde, of whom copies of the quantities may be obtained on the deposit of 1 guinea, to be returned on receipt of a *bond-fide* tender. The tenders to be delivered by noon on Monday, September 19, 1898.

FRANCIS NEWMAN & COCKS,
Engineers.

## ST. LUKE (MIDDLESEX) VESTRY.
### CONSTRUCTION OF UNDERGROUND SANITARY CONVENIENCE.

Tenders are invited for the construction of an Underground Sanitary Convenience in Old-street, near its intersection with City-road, in accordance with the plans, specification, &c., and bill of quantities prepared by the Surveyor to the Vestry and Mr. H. Williams Mellor, quantity surveyor, respectively.

These may be seen, and forms of tender and bill of quantities had, any day except Saturday from 11 to 5 o'clock, and on Saturdays from 11 to 1 o'clock, on application to the Surveyor's department.

Tenders must be upon the official form only, properly filled up and signed, and marked outside "Sanitary Convenience," and must be delivered before noon on 14th September next.

(By order)
GEORGE WHITEHEAD PRESTON,
Vestry Clerk.

Vestry Clerk's Office,
St. Luke's Vestry Hall, City-road, E.C.
August 20, 1898.

## WITNEY RURAL DISTRICT COUNCIL.
### EYNSHAM MAIN DRAINAGE.

The Rural District Council are prepared to receive tenders, under the advice of their Engineer, from contractors for the execution of this work.

The plans and specifications can be seen, and information obtained, upon application to Mr. Nicholson Lailey, F.G.S., ASSOC.M.INST.C.E., the Council's Engineer, at his chambers, 16 Great George-street, Westminster, between the hours of 10 and 4 o'clock on and after September 12th next.

Sealed tenders, endorsed "Eynsham Main Drainage," are to be delivered at my offices at Witney not later than 6 o'clock p.m. on Monday, September 26th.

The Council do not pledge themselves to accept the lowest or any tender.

A copy of the plans and specification are also deposited at the offices of Mr. W. George Eaton, Surveyor to the Council, Witney, and information can be obtained upon the dates and times before named.

The Engineer will give due notice to persons proposing to tender of the date and time that he or his chief assistant will attend at Eynsham in order to explain the nature of the proposed undertaking.

(By order)
N. JOHN G. RAVENOR, Solicitor,
Clerk to the Rural District Council.
Witney.
August 15, 1898.

### BEXLEY URBAN DISTRICT COUNCIL.

TENDERS FOR MATERIALS, STORES, CARTAGE, TEAM LABOUR, REMOVAL OF DUST AND STEAM ROLLING.

The General Purposes Committee invite tenders for the following materials and materials, &c., within the Bexley district during twelve months ending September 30, 1809 :—

(A).—MATERIALS AND STORES.

1.—Broken granite, furnace slag, flints, rag stone, gravel, &c.
2.—Granite and limestone curb, channelling and sett paving.
3.—Lime, Portland cement, sand, and drain pipes, &c.
4.—Pitch, illuminating oil, disinfectants, lamp glasses, lamp wick, brushes, castings, &c.

(B).—TEAM LABOUR, DUSTING, &c.

1.—Collection of dust and house refuse.
2.—Hire of horses, carts and drivers for cartage of materials, day cartage, slopping, horsing water vans, sewage-vans, &c.

(C).—STEAM ROAD-ROLLING.

The hire of a steam road-roller in the district, at per day.

Specifications, conditions of contract and forms of tender, containing full particulars, may be obtained on application to Mr. Tom Vickers, C.E., Surveyor, Public Hall, Bexley Heath, on receipt of a stamped addressed foolscap envelope, such application stating the section—(a), (b) or (c)—required.

Tenders, distinctly endorsed on the outside cover "Tenders for ————," as the case may be, are to be addressed to me, the undersigned, not later than Monday, September 12, 1898.

The Council do not bind themselves to accept the lowest or any tender.

The Council reserve to themselves the right to accept a tender for a period of either six or twelve months.

THOS. G. BAYNES,
Clerk.
Council Offices, Bexley Heath.
August 23, 1898.

### BOROUGH OF SOUTHEND-ON-SEA.

TO ROAD CONTRACTORS AND OTHERS.

The Corporation invite tenders for Street Works in the making-up of Claremont-road.

Plans, sections and specifications may be seen, and bills of quantities and forms of tender obtained, on and after Tuesday, the 30th August (on payment of £1 1s., which will be returned on receipt of a bonâ-fide tender). upon application to Mr. Alfred Fidler, ASSOC.M.INST.C.E., Borough Surveyor, Clarence-road, Southend.

No tender will be considered unless made on the prescribed form.

Sealed tenders, endorsed with the name of the street and marked " Tender for Private Street Works," to be delivered at my office before 10 o'clock in the morning of Thursday the 8th September.

The Corporation wil not be bound to accept the lowest or any tender.

(By order)
WILLIAM H. SNOW,
Town Clerk.
Southend-on-Sea.
August 26, 1898.

### CARRICKMACROSS UNION.

NOTICE TO CONTRACTORS.

The Board of Guardians of the above Union, acting as the rural sanitary authority, will, at their meeting to be held at 2 o'clock p.m. on Tuesday, 6th September, 1898, be prepared to consider tenders for the construction of works to supply the town of Carrickmacross with water, in accordance with plans and specification prepared by P. F. Comber and the late W. G. Strype, MEMB.INST.C.E., 19 Lower Leeson-street, Dublin, which can be seen at the office of Mr. J. H. Blackader, solicitor, Carrickmacross, between the hours of 11 a.m. and 3 o'clock p.m. daily.

The works comprise the supply and laying of 102 tons or thereabouts of Cast-Iron Water Mains; the construction of a Pumping House, with duplicate sets of oil engines and three-throw gun-metal plunger force pumps, each set of pumping plant being capable of delivering 90 gallons per minute to a height of 200 ft.; and the construction of a Service Reservoir, to contain 100,000 gallons or thereabouts.

Printed copies of the specification and form of tender may be obtained from Mr. Blackader on payment of £2 sterling

from each competitor, which will be returned on the receipt of a bonâ-fide tender.
Tenders to be addressed to the undersigned, and endorsed "Tender for Waterworks," naming solvent sureties.
The Guardians do not bind themselves to accept the lowest or any tender.

(By order)
JOHN PHELAN,
Clerk of the Union and Executive
Sanitary Officer.
Board-room, Carrickmacross.
August 16, 1898.

## BOROUGH OF LOUGHBOROUGH.

### NANPANTAN RESERVOIR.

### NEW FILTER-BED.

Persons desirous of tendering for the Construction of a new Filter-Bed, with appurtenant works, at Nanpantan are requested to send in their names and addresses to the undersigned.
Plans may be inspected and bills of quantities, &c., obtained as below on deposit of cheque for £3 3s., which will be refunded on receipt of a bonâ-fide tender and return of the documents.
Sealed tenders are to be sent in, endorsed "Tender for Filter-Bed," on the forms supplied, addressed to the Town Clerk, Town Hall, Loughborough, on or before 17th September, 1898.
Contractors tendering must guarantee to pay not less than the standard rate of wages.
The Corporation reserve the rights to accept or reject any tender.

A. H. WALKER, A.M.I.C.E.,
Borough Engineer and Waterworks Manager.
Municipal Offices, Ashby-road, Loughborough.
August 30, 1898.

## BECKENHAM URBAN DISTRICT COUNCIL.
### TO CONTRACTORS.

The Beckenham Urban District Council invite tenders for Widening Croydon-road and Elmers End-road. The works comprise the widening of Croydon-road for about 800 lineal feet and of Elmers End-road for 150 lineal feet, together with the formation of new footways. In connection therewith the following works are necessary—viz., about 800 lineal feet 9-in. pipe sewer, 700 lineal feet 9-in. pipe surface-water drain, with manholes, gullies, &c., 110 lineal feet concrete retaining wall about 4 ft. high, 1,000 lineal feet curb and channelling, making-up roadways, &c.
Plans and sections may be seen, and bills of quantities, specifications and forms of tender obtained, on application to Mr. John A. Angell, Surveyor, on or after September 7th, on deposit of £1, which will be returned on receipt of a bonâ-fide tender.
A clause will be inserted in the contract providing that the contractor shall pay to the workmen employed in the execution of the work the wages generally accepted as current for workmen engaged on similar work in the district.
Tenders, duly sealed and endorsed "Tender for Widening Croydon and Elmers End Roads," to reach undersigned not later than 4 p.m., Monday, September 26, 1898.
The Council do not bind themselves to accept the lowest or any tender.

(By order)
F. STEVENS,
Clerk to the Council.
August 30, 1898.

## BECKENHAM URBAN DISTRICT COUNCIL.
### TO CONTRACTORS.

The Beckenham Urban District Council invite tenders for Erecting about 200 Cast-Iron Ventilating Columns, 13 ft. 6 in. high, on concrete beds, together with the laying of 9-in. Stoneware Pipe Connections to the main sewers, &c.
Plans and sections may be seen, and bills of quantities, specifications and forms of tenders obtained, on application to Mr. John A. Angell, Surveyor, on or after September 7th, on deposit of £1, which will be returned on the receipt of a bonâ-fide tender.
A clause will be inserted in the contract providing that the contractor shall pay to the workmen employed in the execution of the work the wages generally accepted as current for workmen engaged on similar work in the district.
Tenders, duly sealed and endorsed "Tender for Erection of Ventilating Columns," to reach undersigned not later than 4 p.m. Monday, September 26, 1898.
The Council do not bind themselves to accept the lowest or any tender.

(By order)
F. STEVENS,
Clerk to the Council.
August 30, 1898.

# The Surveyor

### And Municipal and County Engineer.

| Vol. XIV., No. 347. | LONDON, SEPTEMBER 9, 1898. | Weekly, Price 3d. |

## Minutes of Proceedings.

**Carnarvon Water Supply.** A report from Dr. Wheaton on the water supply of Carnarvon has just been issued by the Local Government Board. From it we learn that for some years past the unsatisfactory nature of the supply, more particularly its liability to pollution by liquid refuse from a certain village, has been before the Board. Three years ago it was shown in a similar report that the water supply was subject to pollution, not only from this, but from other sources, including foecal matter from privies and liquid matter from cesspools pertaining to various dwellings in the upper part of the valley, from which the supply is derived. The offending village of Rhyd-ddu is situated in the districts of the Gwyrfai and Glaslyn Rural Councils, who have in vain been urged to deal with the sewerage of the village so as to prevent the pollution of the river Gwyrfai, and the Carnarvon Town Council contend that unless that is done they themselves can do nothing. It was under these conditions that Dr. Wheaton was instructed to make an inspection of the gathering ground and report on the conditions of the water supply generally. The supply is derived from the river Gwyrfai, the valley of which is one of a number that run in a westerly direction from the Snowdonian range towards the Menai Straits. The valleys are nearly parallel, and each contains one or more lakes. On the north the Gwyrfai valley is bounded by hills from 1,000 to 2,000 ft. in height and on the south by a range of nearly equal height. At the head of the valley the steep western slopes of Snowdon form a deep hollow and there is formed a sharply-defined watershed lying midway between the villages of Rhyd-ddu and Beddgelert, the head of the valley being about 3 miles wide. In the valley are two lakes, Llyn-y-Gader being situated about the middle and Llyn Quellyn at a lower level. From the upper lake the Gwyrfai issues as a large stream, and after a course of nearly 3 miles passes the village of Rhyd-ddu and falls into Lake Quellyn, at which point the valley is not more than 1¼ miles in width, the lake being about 1 mile in length and ¾ mile at its greatest breadth. From it the Gwyrfai issues as a fair-sized river, and after a course of about 12 miles falls into the sea at the southern extremity of the Menai Straits, 4 miles south of Carnarvon. The intake for the supply of the borough is ½ mile below Lake Quellyn and about 6½ miles from the town. At the intake a dam has been constructed across the stream, and the water thus held up flows through twelve copper gauze screens, or strainers, directly into an iron pipe, by which it is conveyed to a reservoir 2¼ miles from the town. This reservoir has a capacity of 2,780,000 gallons, and from it the town is supplied by gravitation. There is no filtration, and the supply is a constant one, there being few storage cisterns in the borough. In 1891 the population was 9,804 persons, living in 2,154 houses. There are no large manufactories or businesses re-

quiring a large quantity of water in the town, but during the summer months the supply has been at times inadequate, this being attributed in part to corrosion and consequent narrowing of the calibre of the smaller mains, in part to leakages from mains, and to waste from taps in dwellings and from stand-pipes in courts. The corporation have therefore decided to provide an increased storage, by means of an additional reservoir. The present water supply was inaugurated in 1865, when the town council were authorised by Act of Parliament to take water from the Gwyrfai. At that time the water was obtained from the river at a point much nearer to Carnarvon than the present intake. Finding that the water was polluted by the drainage of a particular village, the corporation consulted Mr. Baldwin Latham, who advised the removal of the intake to its present position, and a provisional order for the purpose was obtained in 1879. The town council are in a more or less helpless condition, from the fact that they have absolutely no control over Lake Quellyn or any portion of the area from which the water is derived. The whole of the valley on both sides of the river above the intake, including Lake Quellyn and extending to a short distance above the upper end of that lake, is under the control of the Gwyrfai Rural District Council. From that point the river forms the boundary between the two rural districts—Glaslyn on the north and Gwyrfai on the south. The troublesome village of Rhyd-ddu stands on both sides of the river, about ¾ mile above Lake Quellyn. and is therefore partly in one rural district and partly in the other.

After a description of the watershed and the works, the report goes on to deal with the specific forms of pollution. The valley above the intake is occupied by farms, which are generally situated on streams falling into the Gwyrfai, and these streams have a tendency to receive all sorts of refuse, liquid or solid, from the farm. We need not go into all the details of the definite instances of pollution, both of river and lake, given by Dr. Wheaton. Really serious danger exists in connection with a quarry on the shores of Lake Quellyn, as a very large number of men are there employed, and a case of enteric fever would entail no small risk to those consuming the water. The worst pollution, however, undoubtedly comes from the village of Rhyd-ddu, and this deserves some attention. The whole of the liquid refuse from this village, which consists of thirty-nine dwellings and has a population of about 150 persons, is discharged into the river either directly—the refuse being thrown from the dwellings on to the river banks—or indirectly, by means of rubble drains or surface channels on the roadside. The village is not sewered, and, though steps have lately been taken to prevent foecal matter being thrown into the stream, a certain amount undoubtedly does still find its way there, being thrown from the bucket privies which are in use in the village. The dwellings on the south of the stream are without receptacles for storing refuse, which are consequently heaped on the banks of the river. "There can be no doubt," says the inspector, "that the sanitary circumstances of this village are such as to form a serious danger to the consumers of the water from the Gwyrfai river, and there would be grave risk to such consumers should enteric fever or cholera at any time break out in this village." All the circumstances point to a joint scheme of sewerage as the solution of the difficulty, so far as this village is concerned, and the two district councils are incurring a serious responsibility in thus neglecting their obvious duties in the matter. In comparison with the lower, the higher lake may be regarded as practically free from pollution, though not absolutely so. The inspector, in concluding his report, recognises that the work of preventing pollution of the Carnarvon water supply is by no means easy, involving as it does the exercise of constant vigilance over a very large area. He recommends the following steps for the purpose:—

(1) The thorough sewerage of the village of Rhyd-ddu, and the disposal of the sewage in such a manner as to avoid any risk of pollution of the river. (2) The scavenging of this village at frequent and regular intervals, in order to put an end to the throwing of the contents of pail closets, of privies, or of household refuse, into the stream. (3) Frequent inspection of all farms and dwellings upon the gathering ground. The disposition of all liquid refuse from dwellings, farmyards, manure heaps, and the like, in such fashion that these matters shall not foul streams. The prevention, as far as possible, of manuring of land in the immediate neighbourhood of the lakes and streams. (4) The provision of movable receptacle for fæcal matter for all dwellings upon the gathering ground, in order to prevent the direct fouling of streams by fæcal matter. Strict attention to be directed to the method of disposal of contents of such movable receptacles. (5) The diversion of all water ·passing through Glan-r-afon quarry from the river above the intake. (6) The diversion of all surface water from the main roads from the river.

It is pointed out that the last two measures would require engineering works of considerable difficulty. Filtration has also been recommended as a precautionary measure, but Dr. Wheaton doubts if filtration, as ordinarily carried out, could, in the present circumstances of the Carnarvon water supply, be trusted to secure a ·uniformly wholesome water. The case of Carnarvon is another addition to the already long list of cases which point to the necessity for more effective intervention on the part of the central government in connection with public water supplies.

\* \* \*

**Charging for Electricity on the Brighton System.** There can be little doubt that the Brighton or Maximum Demand Indicator System more than any other, with the exception of the Manchester system, takes into consideration the peculiar conditions prevailing in the supply of electricity. Unfortunately, there is a difficulty in making the lay mind understand the principle of the system, and it is no exaggeration to say that comparatively few consumers on a municipal system have any practical appreciation of the value of the Demand Indicator from their point of view. The one predominant fact in the supply of electricity is that the cost of producing it depends rather upon the way in which it is supplied than upon the amount actually supplied. That is due mainly to the fact that storage of electricity on a large scale is not yet practicable. Consequently, if the consumer has to be supplied at any time, it is necessary to run a certain amount of plant which may not always be doing a fair amount of work. The chief cost of an electric lighting station is the standing-by costs, or those incurred in getting the plant ready to supply. As a matter of fact, the stand-by charges are almost three times as high as the running costs, which include coal, water, and stores, repairs, &c., and therefore any system which will reduce the standing-by costs provides at once a means of cheapening electricity. The Brighton system is based on this principle. It first charges

every consumer a certain proportion of the standing-by costs, and when these costs have been met the consumer obtains his electricity at the lowest possible price based upon the running charges. It follows that such a system would benefit a consumer who used a few lamps for a long period rather than a consumer who used a large number of lamps for a short period. The tendency of the system, therefore, is to prevent a consumer from being extravagant in the number of lamps he uses ; in other words, it tends to diminish the burning of more lamps at one time than is actually required. ' The usual method is to charge a certain sum per unit for the first hour in which the lamps are in use. This figure varies in different towns, but in most cases it is 6d., and beyond the first hour or two hours, or. whatever may be the time basis employed, the consumer obtains his electricity in many cases at 50 per cent. of the price charged during the first hour. The following tables, taken from a recent report by Mr. Rider, the borough electrical engineer of Plymouth, will probably make the economy of the system clear.

A customer with 100 16 candle-power lamps fixed. Each 16 candle-power lamp consumes ·06 units per hour. Meters at end of quarter indicate that 350 units have been used, and that the maximum number of lamps burning at any one time has been sixty.

|  | £ | s. | d. |
|---|---|---|---|
| Then sixty lamps × ·06 unit × ninety-one hours per quarter = 327·6 units at 8d. ... ... ... | 10 | 18 | 4 |
| Balance of 22·4 units at 3d.... ... ... ... | 0 | 5 | 7 |
|  | 11 | 3 | 11 |

If this same customer by careful management had never more than fifty lamps burning at one time, but had consumed the same total quantity, then his account would have been :—

|  | £ | s. | d. |
|---|---|---|---|
| Fifty lamps × ·06 units × ninety-one hours per quarter = 273 units at 8d.... ... ... ... | 9 | 2 | 0 |
| Balance of 77 units at 3d. ... ... ... | 0 | 19 | 3 |
|  | 10 | 1 | 3 |

In others words, this is £1 2s. 8d. less for the same quantity of electricity, because the amount of plant called into use at the works to supply him was less in proportion.

\* \* \*

**The East-End Water Question.** We regret to have to record that our anticipation, expressed last week, that the interposition of the Local Government Board would prevent the further reduction of the intermittent supply from the East London Water Company has not been borne out. On the very morning after we went to press the announcement appeared that the company were compelled to further reduce the supply, that is to say, from six hours to four, two in the morning and two in the afternoon. We referred last week to the contention of the company and their officials that they could not take supplementary supplies from other companies, because the mains at Blackwall and elsewhere, through which the water would have to be taken, were too small to admit it. Hitherto it has always been thought to be a question of inadequate storage capacity and of mains without any water to pass through them except during certain hours of the day. The new contention certainly calls for some further elucidation. The suggestion from the Local Government Board as the result of Major-General Scott's investigation was that the New River Company should have a supply from another company with whose mains communication either existed or could be made, and that in this way the New River Company could spare more of the Lea water for the use of the East London Company. The limit of this assistance has now been reached, and it certainly does not amount to much. Another contention on the part of the company is that there must be excessive waste on the part of consumers, because even the restricted supply has been at the rate of 26 gallons per head. But how much of that goes to those who are supplied by meter for trade purposes and how much is left for the consumer either to consume or to waste ? If one ventures to point out that other companies do not complain of waste, we are told that there are storage cisterns in the districts they supply. If there are no storage cisterns in the district supplied by the East London Water Company it is not the fault of the consumers and they have no right to suffer. But they will evidently suffer still more unless ruin comes to their assistance and to that of the benighted company. In our opinion three conclusions are inevitable after this latest drought: (1) The company have so far failed to provide adequate storage; (2) the Lea can no longer be relied upon as a source of supply, at all events for two companies; and (3) public control cannot too soon be brought about. The morning papers of Wednesday announced that even the four hours' service, which began on Saturday, was in many parts of the district a dismal failure. The pressure was inadequate, the water was discoloured, and in many parts none could be obtained at all fit for use. Yesterday the outlook was worse than ever. In another column we quote a spirited letter addressed by the Shoreditch Vestry to the Local Government Board.

\* 　　\* 　　\*

**Free Electric Wiring.** We have at various times made some reference in these columns to the development of free wiring throughout the country, and it has been conclusively proved in Taunton, Blackpool, West Hartlepool, Worcester and St. Leonards that a judicious use of the system is a material aid in the development of an electrical supply business Although the term "free wiring" is somewhat of a misnomer, the system provides an easy means of enabling the poorer classes of consumers to avail themselves of the benefits of electric lighting; but though the wiring and fittings are, so far as regards initial expenditure, free to the consumer, he has to pay a slightly enhanced price on the usual charges for electricity that prevail in the community. It has been pointed out that the system lends itself to some abuse in the fact that all free-wiring systems at the present time are introduced and carried out by companies who work in conjunction with the municipal authorities. In the course of a discussion at a recent meeting of the Portsmouth Town Council free wiring received a somewhat severe check, at all events so far as that town is concerned. There appears to have been a feeling that the system might to some extent interfere with the legitimate business of local tradesmen, and it was thought that it was scarcely the duty of a corporation to join hands with a company, even when certain advantages were offered to consumers. There may be something to be urged in favour of this view of the matter, but free wiring gives such unmistakable advantages that it would be regretted if the principle were entirely rejected. The easiest solution of the difficulty—and it applies as much to other towns as to Portsmouth—is for the municipality to undertake some hiring system of wiring and fittings much in the same manner that the Bradford corporation hire out electric motors. As far as the consumer is concerned, he would in all probability be treated better by a municipality than in the case of a company working in conjunction with a corporation. It cannot be too widely known, however, that in the towns to which allusion has been made a distinct success has followed the introduction of the free wiring system.

\* 　　\* 　　\*

**The Recent Dublin Congress.** As the proceedings of the recent congress went on it was seen that not a few of the papers and discussions possessed more direct interest for municipal engineers than one might have gathered from the opening proceedings and the special conferences, which seemed to be largely monopolised by medical officers of health and sanitary inspectors. This week we give the third instalment of our report, summarising those addresses, papers and discussions most likely to attract our readers. In our last issue there was some interesting matter in reference to such subjects as the housing of the working classes, the extension of towns, and the municipalisation of tramways, water supplies and public lighting. The discussion initiated by Sir Charles Cameron served a distinctly useful purpose in drawing attention to the class for whom municipal authorities should primarily, if not exclusively, provide housing accommodation. The subject is one we have frequently discussed in these columns, but we may again express the opinion that the provision of such accommodation by municipalities for classes who can afford to find it for themselves in the ordinary way is economically wrong, is likely to do more harm than good, and had much better be left to private enterprise; in short, it is to go beyond the legitimate limits of municipal activity and enter upon a policy of Socialism, the ultimate effects of which must undoubtedly be mischievous. An the other hand, an attempt to solve the problem of housing accommodation for the very poor is called for in the interests of the public health and general well-being of the community. In our continuation of the report this week there is further and more detailed discussion of the subjects referred to above. The section of the proceedings with which our readers are most concerned is that which was devoted to the discussion of engineering and building construction topics—of course as bearing upon the central idea of the public health. Some of the papers in this section we have, therefore, dealt with separately. The paper of Mr. Watson was a useful summary of the dust destructor question, and that of Mr. Kaye Parry, which appears this week, will be read with interest on account of its defence of Dr. Bailey Denton as a pioneer of sewage treatment on biological lines. We expect to finish our report of the proceedings in our next issue.

\* 　　\* 　　\*

**The British Association at Bristol.** The destruction of the fine Colston Hall caused no small inconvenience to the recent Trades Union Congress, and has compelled the members of the British Association to carry on their meeting this week in less commodious and suitable premises than they would otherwise have had. We may mention that this is the third meeting in Bristol, the first having been held in 1836, and the second forty years later—in 1875—when the office of president was filled by an eminent engineer in the person of the late Sir John Hawkshaw. On the present occasion the president is Sir William Crookes, one of the most distinguished of English chemists. The proceedings generally are expected to show no falling off in interest and value, and we observe that a larger number of papers than usual will have a special and direct interest for municipal engineers. Especially is this the case in section G. (mechanical science), over which, as our readers will observe with pleasure, Sir John Wolfe Barry presides. The following are among the papers to be read in this section: "The Hiring of Electric Motors to Local Authorities and to Small Industries as carried out at Bradford," by Mr. Gibbings, borough electrical engineer of Bradford; "Corrosion of Gas and Water Pipes by Earth Currents," by Prof. Fleming; "A Description of the Bristol Municipal Electrical Works," by Mr. Proctor, borough electrical engineer; "Scheme for Improvement of Severn Waterway to Birmingham," by Mr. Marten, chief engineer to the Severn Commissioners; and "The Conditions Necessary for the Successful Treatment of Sewage by Bacteria," by Mr. Dibdin. In section F. (economical science and statistics) Mr. G. Cannon will read a paper on "Municipal Enterprise," and Mr. G. Pearson one on "Electrical Enterprise and Municipalities." To some of the papers mentioned we shall refer further in our next issue.

# Royal Institute of Public Health.

## ANNUAL CONGRESS AT DUBLIN.—III.

On the Saturday the discussion on the paper "The Terminable Leasehold System in regard to Municipal Sanitation" was resumed, in the Municipal and Parliamentary Section, by Mr. Alexander Bruce, of the Caithness County Council.

Alderman MEADE said that this was a question that ought to be dealt with, but it was yet hardly ripe. It was a large question which involved much consideration. The discussion was useful, and would tend to make the subject ripe for practical consideration.

This concluded the discussion.

TRAMWAYS, PUBLIC LIGHTING AND WATER SUPPLY.

The CHAIRMAN said he was certain that everybody would be interested in the subject which would be raised in the next paper. It was an important subject for consideration at the present time.

Mr. EDWARD CUMING, B.L., then read a paper on "The Municipalisation of Tramways, Public Lighting and Water Supply." Nothing in modern life, he said, differed so much from ancient and mediæval times as the position taken up and the province filled by municipal authorities and organisations. What was it that came home to most people living in a town like Dublin, Glasgow or Belfast, or that affected their life and happiness most? First, their earnings and their food, but after those such matters as local bodies dealt with affecting the life and interests and well-being of the community. The legislature had of late given over to the local bodies a vast amount of power, and power involved duty. The water question came home to everyone. Artificial lighting had become a municipal question, and tramways soon would be. Without water in lavish abundance no modern drainage could be practically carried out effectively. It was impracticable for any public body to carry on any business that did not affect all the members of its community, and if it should attempt such a task, those favoured to the exclusion of others would be regarded as getting undue advantage. Water, gas and cheap tramways were important to everyone. Dublin was a case in point. For many reasons Dublin was a town that it would always be difficult to keep in good health. In Belfast the gas company were bought up by the town council, and that had been an admirable purchase. The constant complaints about the London water companies showed the danger of having the water supply in the hands of a private individual. The real advantage of having the supply of water, gas and the providing of tramways carried on by the local government of towns was that the governing body did not need to make a profit for a body of shareholders. The local authority would be satisfied with a moderate rate of interest, and with a small sinking fund to pay off the moneys invested in the construction; and having at their disposal the rates of the town, they could borrow money at a very low rate of interest. They could also for a time disregard profit altogether, and carry on part of the water, gas and tramways at an actual loss, if such a course were found beneficial to the general interests of the community. A trading company could not venture on doing that. But it was plain that many of the labouring classes in large towns now resided in most unhealthy places, in order to be near their work and the places where they were employed, and who could live farther away if they were provided with the means of cheap travelling backwards and forwards. They could be brought at a very small expense—such expense as would just keep the local government free from loss. Such fares would not pay a trading company at all. It would in many cases be more convenient for a governing body to incur a loss in the working of part of the tramway rather than take compulsorily the areas inhabited and crowded, and which should not be so used and crowded. The value of areas when they were to be taken seemed often to rise to a most alarming amount, and they had many instances of that even in Dublin.

Dr. CHARLES PORTER, medical officer of health to the County Borough of Stockport, read a paper on "The Supervision by Sanitary Authorities of Public Water Services in the Hands of Private Companies." He said the terrible power for evil of specifically polluted water as a vehicle of disease had been repeatedly demonstrated during the past half-century by the four cholera epidemics during that time, and the fearful visitation of Hamburgh in 1892, as well as by the numerous outbreaks of enteric fever from Guildford and Terling in 1867 to the recent experiences of Worthing, the Tees Valley, Maidstone, King's Lynn and Cambourne (Cornwall). It would, therefore, perhaps be scarcely credible to many who had not before had their attention directed to the fact that at the end of the nineteenth century, and in spite of their boasted advances in sanitary science, local authorities in England and Ireland, whose districts were served by private water companies, possessed no executive powers whatever for the protection of their water supply. They had no right of entry upon the gathering grounds or waterworks, no right to take samples for examination, and no right to satisfy themselves that the processes of purification adopted left no room for entry to the distributing mains of matters of a noxious nature. Complaint to the central health authority when evil had resulted was oftentimes tedious and unsatisfactory in its results, and at best resembled the policy of locking the stable door when the horse was stolen. That defect in their sanitary legislation was the more remarkable inasmuch as the Public Health Acts conferred upon sanitary authorities and their officers adequate powers of entry and inspection as regards the premises and articles sold by vendors of bread, flesh, fish and other eatables; while, as regarded milk, the Infectious Diseases Prevention Act extended the right of inspection of dairies, cow-sheds, &c., possessed by the medical officer of health within his district to dairies, cow-sheds, &c., entirely outside his district where circumstances rendered desirable such inquiry. Much of the existing indifference and inattention to questions of purity of water supply and of proper watchful insistence that such supplies should be adequately guarded from pollution were due to the unfortunate fact that by the great majority of people all requirements of water were thought to have been met if in a sample of water taken from their taps a chemist failed to find evidence of pollution. Such a faith, however, ignored the fallibility of chemical methods as well as the fact that pollutions were frequently intermittent in their occurrence, and that polluted material was not necessarily diffused uniformly throughout the whole body of water which it entered. In other words, with an intermittent pollution a source of water supply that was innocuous now might be highly dangerous a few hours hence. In short, as the late Sir George Buchanan said, in his annual report for 1889, as medical officer of the Local Government Board, "unless the chemist is well acquainted with the origin and liabilities of the water he is examining he is not justified in speaking of a water as 'safe' or 'wholesome' if it contain any trace whatever of organic matter; hardly, indeed, if it contains none of such matter appreciable by his very delicate methods. The chemist can, in brief, tell us of impurity and hazard, but not of purity and safety. For information about these we must go, with the aid of what the chemist has been able to tell us, in search of the conditions surrounding watercourses and affecting water services." If pollutions of water were actually *seen to occur*, any form of examination was superfluous, and "as neither bacteriology nor chemistry can be depended upon to prove that a water is free from all dangerous pollutions, such examinations are, in many cases, quite useless." Bacteriology had, however, a most important application in regard to the filtration of water, as it afforded the only reliable method of gauging the efficient performance of that process. Under the Waterworks Clauses Act, 1847, the sum of £5 and a daily penalty of £1 for a continuing offence was forfeitable *to the proprietors* of a water undertaking by any person who bathed in, or caused any animal to enter, any stream, reservoir, aqueduct or other part of a waterworks, or who fouled the water thereof by washing in it clothes, wool or skins, or by allowing any water from a sink, drain, sewer or other foul source to enter therein. But too frequently these salutary provisions were not enforced by commercial companies, and it was therefore very necessary and important that, in addition to water companies, *the sanitary authority of the district served* should have power to recover in a summary manner much heavier penalties than those referred to. The powers required by sanitary authorities included the following: (1) To investigate the *pedigree* of their water supply—*i.e.*, the cleanliness and purity of its sources; (2) to recover summarily deterrent penalties for causing or allowing pollutions; (3) to test and inquire as to the means and efficiency of the purification methods adopted—*e.g.*, the action of each individual filter; and (4) to ascertain the state of the distributing mains under certain conditions—*e.g.*, possibility of pollution through defective joints or pipes. In December, 1897, the Stockport Corporation resolved to petition the president of the Local Government Board to initiate legislation on the lines indicated above, and at the same time induced the influential Association of Municipal Corporations, as well as a number of other towns supplied by private water companies, to adopt and forward to Mr. Chaplin a similar resolution. Moreover, in November, 1897, Sir Richard Thorne Thorne, K.C.B., chief medical officer to the Local Government Board, publicly recorded his emphatic agreement "that the water companies should be held responsible for the quality of water they supplied." It was, therefore, not surprising that on June 23rd last Mr. Chaplin moved to make applicable to twenty-one Water Bills before the House certain clauses protecting consumers from shortcomings on the part of the water authorities: (1) By empowering an officer authorised by the local authority to enter, inquire and take samples on the premises of the water authority; (2) by allowing consumers, on a justice's order, and after reasonable notice to the water company, to take a similar course; and (3) by enacting heavy penalties for failure to fulfil existing obligations to provide a pure and wholesome supply of water. Mr. Chaplin also proposed : (4) To invest the water authorities with sufficient powers to protect themselves from pollution of the sources from which they draw their supply. In asking the House to support him in the matter Mr. Chaplin truly said that it was a question directly affecting the public health, that there was nothing in the clauses to which reasonable objection could be taken, and that it had been impossible, owing to pressure of business, to introduce those clauses in a public Bill. The opposition offered to his proposals, nominally on the ground that those alterations should be made by a public Bill applicable to the country at large, was, however, of such a nature that Mr. Chaplin had to withdraw them. Here the matter at present rested, except that Mr. Chaplin had since stated, in reply to Mr. Marks, M.P., that no decision had been arrived at as to the introduction next session of a public Bill embodying those proposals. It had recently been suggested—he believed by Dr. Thresh—that as water companies in the past stepped in and supplied a pressing public want, it was not altogether reasonable to maintain that their operations should now be subjected to supervision in the interests of public health. But even assuming that such undertakings, instead of being autocratic and highly remunerative monopolies, were purely philanthropic in origin and object, the frequent and repeated failure of their promoters to make a righteous choice between dividends and disease, with the resulting terrible epidemics of which they had recently heard so much, completely refuted such special pleading. "The need of this reform cannot be denied," were the words addressed by Mr. Chaplin to the House of Commons; and convinced that it was one of the most pressing sanitary questions of the day, he desired to enlist the sympathy and powerful influence of that institute towards its speedy and satisfactory solution, and ventured, with confidence, to invite the congress to strengthen the hands of the president of the Local Government Board in his enlightened desire to deal with it.

The above two papers were discussed together.

Mr. JOHN BYANE (Dublin) said nothing caused so much dissatisfaction or inconvenience as to have the roadways of the streets cut up by the tramways and gas companies. The people of Dublin had the experience of, say, the gas company tearing up the streets and turning them into muddy banks, inconveniencing the residents along the line of the excavation, and in a week afterwards, when the road was restored to its former state, they had the tramway coming in and excavating, and bringing the thoroughfare back to the same state in which the gas company had it. It involved much expenditure of the rates to put the roadways into the condition they ought to be, when first one company and again another were done with them. If there were no other reasons than that, he thought that there were strong reasons indeed for the public bodies having the charge of carrying out those under takings. There were also other considerations. When the waterworks were first introduced the rate was 1s. 3d. in the £1, 1s. for water and 3d. for the fire brigade. That, consequent on the repayment of the loan, and the disappearance of the charge for interest and the extension of the water system, and the revenue derived from the use of the water by breweries and other big institutions, had been reduced to 6d. In a year or two it would be reduced to 4d., and again to 2d., and would eventually disappear. He thought that if the corporation had the control of the gas and the tramways they would be able in the same way to reduce the rates, and the revenue derived from the tramways would be applied to a reduction of the rates. Those two reasons were, he thought, very strong.

Alderman HIGHMARSH (Gateshead) said he was also in favour of the municipalisation of the several systems.

Mr. T. W. RUSSELL, M.P., thought a good deal might be said on both sides on the general question of the municipalisation of the interests mentioned. He agreed that it was very largely a matter for each locality. He held the view that there would be difficulties in the way of laying down a general principle. If they laid down a general principle, where were they to stop? They would, he thought, find localities where it would be of the highest importance for municipalities to have municipalisation of all these matters, but as regarded all districts, he thought that the public bodies should have the control and the administration of the water. On the general question he thought that the section should not arrive at a conclusion fixing a hard-and-fast rule. The municipalisation of water was a matter of the greatest importance in this country. Look at what happened at Maidstone, where hundreds of people died of an epidemic due to the defective water supply. Owing to that outbreak the president of the Local Government Board proposed to introduce clauses into twenty-one Bills before Parliament which would make the companies responsible for the condition of the water they supplied; but the companies were so powerful that in the House of Commons the Government proposals were defeated. He disregarded those private interests in Parliament, believing that the public interest should be supreme.

Alderman MEANE mentioned that Dr. Porter had handed him a resolution which he desired to propose. He thought the section were agreed as to the importance of the municipal control of the water supply, and he would at that stage submit to them Dr. Porter's resolution, which was as follows:— "That this congress of the Royal Institute of Public Health hereby records its warm appreciation of the enlightened efforts of the Right Hon. H. Chaplin, M.P., president of the Local Government Board, to protect the consumers of water

supplied by water companies, and venture to express the earnest hope that during the forthcoming session the Government will introduce a public Bill embodying the proposals submitted by Mr. Chaplin to the House of Commons on June 23rd last."

The resolution was unanimously adopted.

Mr. WORMSLEY, chairman of the Sanitary Committee of the Leeds Town Council, advocated the municipalisation of tramways and gas. The citizens should not, he said, allow the highways to be taken over and profit made out of them by a private company. He thought that all municipalities should take the tramways into their own hands, and in that way they would help the rates and have lower tram fares. An important consideration was that areas would be acquired cheaply outside for the erection of cottages for workmen, who could be brought to the city for their work at a cheap rate.

Mr. R. JONES, of the Dublin Town Council, said they were not so backward in Dublin as some of their English friends might suppose. They had the water supply in their hands, and if they had not the gas they had the electric light, which was a more valuable asset than the gas company, and now, owing to the provisions for electric traction, they had been able to exact terms from the tramway company for the use of the streets. They were getting a rent of £10,000 a year for way-leave, and they had also gained a good deal in taxes, because the taxation on the property of the tramway company had gone up. A main drainage scheme was also in progress.

After Mr. J. Howes, of St. Luke's Vestry; Mr. Taylor, of Barnsley; Mr. Whitney, of Liverpool; and Mr. Batley, of Leeds, had also spoken,

Alderman MEADE said that he took it that the congress agreed as to the advisability of the municipalisation of tramways and public lighting. They had heard that the Leeds Corporation had the gas supply in their hands, and were able to supply the gas at 2s. 2d. per 1,000 cubic feet, and made a profit of £250,000, which went to the rates. In Dublin they had to pay 3s. 5d. per 1,000 cubic feet for gas, and got nothing to relieve the rates. Figures like that he regarded as more important than any amount of discussion. In Belfast, where the gasworks were under the corporation, the price was 2s. 4d. per 1,000 cubic feet for the same quality of gas as they were getting in Dublin, and there was, in addition, a large revenue in relief of the rates. Mr. Jones had told them very fairly the situation in Dublin as regarded the tramways. But the Dublin Corporation embraced a large number of members, for whom he might speak, whose opinion was that the management of the tramways, public lighting and water supply ought to lie in the hands of the corporation, in the interests of all classes of inhabitants. He took it that the congress was in favour of the municipalisation of the tramways and public lighting, as well as the water supply.

HIDEOUS HOARDINGS.

Mr. R. P. CARTON, Q.C., read a paper on "The Prevention of Hideous Hoardings and Structures in the Streets." He said that the advertising stations were one of the most hideous and objectionable institutions of the time. It prevailed to a great extent in Dublin, and the advertising station, whether hoarding or otherwise, was unsightly in itself. He thought that the corporation should be empowered to exercise supervision over advertising.

After some discussion, Alderman MEADE said he hoped that the corporation would have control over public bill posting, so that they might exercise the same supervision as was exercised over pictures in shop windows. In regard to newspaper placards in the streets, they had appealed to the chief commissioner of police to prosecute in some cases, but that gentleman replied that he had no power. The corporation were now taking steps to obtain such power through the Privy Council.

THE EXTENSION OF TOWNS.

Mr. RICHARD JONES, of the Dublin Town Council, read a paper entitled "The Extension of Towns in Connection with the Public Health." He said the subject which he had been requested to bring before the congress was suggested by the recent movement in that city to provide dwellings for the very poor. One of the most difficult problems presented to those having charge of the public health of great cities was the overcrowding of the poorest of the population within very limited areas, and under conditions which rendered it almost impossible to provide for proper sanitation. There was no city in the empire which had felt this difficulty more keenly than Dublin, and yet, in spite of a combination of circumstances well calculated to daunt even the most courageous, more had been done during the latter quarter of this century in Dublin (having regard to its resources) to ameliorate that great evil than in any other municipality of the kingdom. The natural tendency of the labouring population to drift into the towns during periods of agricultural depression was felt more or less in every centre of industry. There the conditions were chronic. There had been for several decades a steady influx into the city of unskilled labourers in search of employment, who, having come so far, had no means to go further, and so settled down to face a precarious existence with hundreds of others who had preceded them in the same path. Dublin was a very old city, and was formerly a very gay one. Its area was within very circumscribed limits, and its population was crowded together in a manner wholly unknown in any other city of the kingdom. All around its limits it was completely surrounded by a number of growing townships which had themselves unlimited areas for expansion, and at the same time, under present conditions, completely blocked any expansion of the city. The municipality during the past twenty years had cleared, at the public expense, congested areas, some of which they had in turn rented to an artisan dwelling company, who had provided at moderate rents suitable dwellings for their working classes—other sites they had built upon themselves—but the number of new dwellings fell far short of providing homes for the dispossessed, and the fact remained that whilst some quarters of the city had been improved and relieved the remaining portions were in a still worse condition than formerly. Their municipal council now found themselves in face of a nearly depleted exchequer, the limits of their borrowing power being almost reached; and being prevented from going outside their own limits to find sites for working men's dwellings, their efforts to further the advancement of sanitation were seriously hampered. Within the city the vast population was composed of the working classes, the poor and the destitute, whose taxable capacity had long been reached, and who were cooped within narrow limits which they dared not pass. Outside the city resided the wealthy merchants, the manufacturers and the public officials, who drew their wealth and their large salaries from the toiling masses of the municipality, who escaped a large portion of their responsibilities by living beyond its limits, and who by their very situation as dwellers in independent townships not only contributed to the poverty of the city, but actually offered effectual barriers to any great scheme for its improvement. It might seem a sweeping statement, but he was convinced that nearly all the dangers from which the public health of Dublin had suffered might be traced to the insanitary conditions under which a great portion of the people were obliged to live. He said obliged—for the fact was those people would gladly welcome the opportunity of removing to more healthy houses were such provided for them. The rents they at present paid were usually exorbitant, and it was not too much to say that to its owners the tenement property of Dublin was the most lucrative in the city. The extension of Dublin to its natural expansive area would at once place the municipality in a position to grapple with that great problem in an effectual manner. In cities where development was accompanied by expansive growth much moral evil was avoided, and every possibility was afforded for the advancement of the science of modern hygiene. Drainage could be undertaken and carried out more completely, and streets made wide and spacious to permit of the enjoyment of light and air. Open spaces could be provided, and playgrounds for the children, and sites upon which dwellings suitable to the requirements and the dignity of the working classes could be erected. The care and advancement of the public health was a noble work; it meant, especially for those who were unable to live apart from the scene of their daily work, the making of life more worth living for. It brought immediate relief to thousands who had not the power of themselves to alter the conditions which surrounded them, and gave added security to the lives of those who were better able to take care of themselves. To considerations of such paramount importance all artificial restrictions must give way. Men and women, to be strong and healthy, required pure air and the light of heaven. Cities to be clean and healthy must have room to grow.

Some discussion followed, in the course of which a delegate inquired what were the difficulties in the way of the extension of the Dublin city boundaries.

Alderman MEADE said they had been trying to extend the boundaries and take in the wealthy and prosperous townships, which were divided only by a canal from the city. It was a monetary difficulty that stood in the way.

Mr. CHATTERTON, consulting engineer to the Dublin Corporation, said the corporation had gone to great expense over the main drainage system, which they expected to have completed within two years' time. It was a dangerous thing to predict, but he had no hesitation in saying that when the drainage system was carried out, the salt water would come up as far as O'Connell Bridge, the Liffey in Dublin would be totally transformed. Rathmines and Pembroke had already carried out a system of drainage which was excellent. The difficulty would be to provide drainage for Drumcondra and Clontarf. The corporation in designing their system was fully alive to that, and they would be able to intercept the sewage in those districts, whether they were part of the borough or not.

Sir ROBERT SEXTON said that unless the corporation extended their boundaries he did not see how they would be able to carry out sanitary improvements properly or provide for the housing of the working classes.

Mr. JOHN BYRNE said that circumstances had hitherto prevented the townships from receiving this amalgamation scheme with favour, but he thought that under the new Local Government Act, which would bring into operation new constituencies and new sets of representatives for every one of these townships and for Dublin, things might lead to an accommodation of circumstances between the two bodies which would effect everything desired.

Alderman MEADE pointed out that the question had been dealt with in England and Scotland in the way suggested in the paper. That system had been taken as a matter of course in the large cities throughout England and Scotland, and if there were small bodies outside those cities they were brought in on fair terms. In Dublin there had been no extension of the city during the past fifty years. The boundaries fifty years ago were the boundaries to-day. During those fifty years the townships had grown up and were built up to the city borders. If those townships were brought into the area of Dublin, one government for the whole district would be more economical, and would afford more time and more means for attending to the interests of public health in providing for the needs of a larger area. In inaugurating their great system of main drainage they were providing for such an area as could take the drainage of all the townships into it. There were two townships which had provided drainage for themselves. That was a system which was in force twenty-five years ago, while the corporation had adopted a system of precipitation, and would discharge nothing into the estuary of the river except clarified water. The whole of the river within the city up to Kingsbridge would be a clear stream. As a member of the corporation, he wished to state that it was their intention, at the earliest possible moment they considered it prudent, to go for the extension of the boundaries of the City of Dublin, not only in the interests of the city, but in the interests of the surrounding townships.

Mr. JOHN BYRNE read a paper entitled "Is Reform of the Work-House System in Ireland. Desirable?" A long discussion followed, and the conference adjourned until the following Tuesday.

On Tuesday the meeting was opened by Prof. Carroll, of the Royal Albert Model Farm, Glasnevin, who read a paper on "The Milk Supply of Towns."

Mrs. TOLLERTON, secretary to the Philanthropic Reform Association and the Police-aided Children's Clothing Society, Dublin, read a paper on "Dublin Tenement Houses," in the course of which she said that statistics obtained by the Police-aided Children's Clothing Society showed that over 75 per cent. of tenement occupants lived in one room. Some time ago she was in a room in which the space was portioned out as follows: The woman who rented it had a small bed at the end opposite to the fireplace. Along the wall to her right were two beds, with the heads close together, occupied by permanent lodgers—four people—viz., two of each sex. In one corner was a ragged mattress and correspondingly ragged heap of bed-clothes that served at night as the sleeping place of a man, his wife and three children, who were temporary lodgers. That corner was a Cave of Adullam, where those in distress and debt and in arrear of rent found a temporary refuge. The lodgers paid the room-keeper 4s. a week, and she cooked for them. The "irregulars" paid 6d. a night, always in advance. If the money was not forthcoming admittance was rigorously denied, and the ragged mattress was exchanged for a hall or landing. These social conditions were so common as to be accepted as a matter of course. A room and small closet would be regularly occupied by seven or eight persons of different sex and family; a front drawing-room would house three families, a small back kitchen two—with several individuals in each family. She would ask serious consideration for one remedy for this—namely, inducing the well-to-do artisan to live in the suburbs. Side by side with overcrowding was the indescribably dirty condition in which tenement houses were kept. The children had a form of sore eyes that was the direct result of dirt. The habits of the people were very discouraging to landlords. She was certain many of the evils she was familiar with could be prevented if well-to-do citizens fully recognised their duty to the slums and did it. No doubt areas had been cleared and numbers of houses detenanted. But where did the people go that were turned out? Some went as lodgers into rooms already crowded, others to tenements as bad as those from which they had been evicted. New buildings should have separate entrances to each dwelling.

At 12 o'clock the conference closed, and the following papers, which were included in the programme, were taken as read : "The Existing Sanitary Law; its Possibilities," by Mr. R. J. Kelly, barrister-at-law; "A Few Remarks on Real Sanitation," by Mr. T. Laffan, chairman of the urban sanitary authority, Cashel; "The Necessity for Municipal Ambulances for Removing Accident Cases and Cases of Sudden Illness for the Streets of Dublin," by Mr. G. Jameson Johnston, M.A., M.B., F.R.C.S.I.; and "Public Health Acts (Ireland), 1878, from an Engineering Standpoint," by Mr. R. W. Walsh, township surveyor, Dalkey.

## The Forthcoming Congress at Birmingham.

The Sanitary Institute have issued a programme of the arrangements of the annual autumn congress, which this year is to be held at Birmingham from the 27th September to the 1st October. A full list of the arrangements has already appeared in our columns, so it is unnecessary to give them again. We may mention, however, that a very useful map of the centre of Birmingham is presented with the programme, which gives a list of public buildings (including the congress buildings), hotels, clubs, restaurants, &c. This information should be especially useful to those persons who intend to be present at the congress and who are unacquainted with the ins and outs of the city.

# Notes on the Design and Erection of Architectural Ironwork.

By HENRY A. CUTLER, A.M.I.C.E., City Engineer, Cork.*

During the last few decades considerable changes have taken place, not only in the design but in the details of construction of public buildings and business premises. The changes have no doubt been principally brought about by the enormous value of land in cities and towns, the increased demand for window space, and the necessity for so-called fireproof construction. The great prices demanded for building sites make it incumbent upon architects to provide the largest amount of accommodation in the smallest possible space, which means increasing the height of buildings and diminishing the walls and piers to the smallest possible limits. The demand for window space considerably diminishes the area of the external walls of buildings, and necessitates the use of other material than brick and stone to ensure stability. The demand is brought about partly by the close packing of buildings and their increased height, partly because the buildings principally referred to are used for business purposes only (in which case abundance of light is necessary), and partly by the requirements of sanitary science. The demand for fireproof construction makes in necessary to use non-inflammable material wherever possible, and in many cases calls forth considerable ingenuity of design to prevent the spread of fire from one part of the building to another.

The great development which has taken place in the manufacture of iron, and the consequent lowering of its cost, has made possible the many changes in construction necessitated by the changes in design, and has left the architect free and untrammelled by the want of a suitable material. Many of the most important buildings of to-day are virtually iron structures clothed with brick, stone or other building material, and not only require architectural skill in their design but the scientific knowledge of the engineer to construct the framework on which the design is hung. The materials principally used for the framework of buildings are cast iron, wrought iron and steel, the determination of which material to use in any particular case depending upon the skill of the designer, the cost, and other circumstances of the particular case under consideration. As a general rule it may be taken that cast iron is not the most suitable material where it would be subject to transverse stress or tension, but that it is the most suitable material in direct compression within certain limits. Wrought iron and steel may be used under any kind of stress, but where strength only is to be considered it is possible to use lighter sections, with steel on account of its greater strength. In using girders of small depth in proportion to the span the flexibility as well as the strength must be determined; and there may occur cases where very little advantage would be obtained by the use of steel, as a heavier section might have to be used than required for strength to prevent undue deflection. The ultimate strength of iron and steel varies considerably, but the figures in the following table may be taken in ordinary practice :—

|  | Tensile Strength. Per square inch. | Crushing Strength. Per square inch. | Clearing Strength. |
|---|---|---|---|
| Cast iron ... | 7 tons | 36 tons | 8 tons |
| Wrought iron ... | 22 ,, | 16 ,, | 20 ,, |
| Steel ... | 32 ,, | 30 ,, | 24 ,, |

The working stresses should in no case exceed one-fourth of the ultimate strength, and in the case of stanchions for warehouses or supporting machinery, or where shocks may be expected, a larger factor of safety should be used. The safe bearing stress to which materials may be subjected may be taken as follows :—

|  |  |  |  |  | Per square inch. |
|---|---|---|---|---|---|
| Cast iron | ... | ... | ... | ... | 8 tons |
| Wrought iron | ... | ... | ... | ... | 5 ,, |
| Steel | ... | ... | ... | ... | 7½ ,, |
| Brickwork in mortar | ... | ... | ... | ⅜ cwt. |
| Brickwork in cement | ... | ... | ... | ¾ cwt. |

The most general sections for pillars are the hollow circular column. The hollow square column, the "H" section and modifications of the same, the cruciform section, the solid circular section, and the solid square section, all of which can be manufactured in either cast iron, wrought iron or steel. In designing pillars the form of section is not always of moment, and it becomes a question which section will be the most economical. To save preliminary calculations in such cases, the author has calculated the strength of a hollow column 10 in. in diameter with metal 1 in. thick, and compared the same with the calculated strength of pillars of the sections previously mentioned, designing them with the same length, area of section and (except in the case of the solid round and square sections), the same thickness of metal, so that the weight of metal would be the same in each case. The results of the investigation are given in the following table of relative strengths, the calculations being made on the assumption that the pillars are of cast iron rounded at both ends. The arbitrary value of 100 was given to the hollow column, to which the values for other sections are related according to their strength.

| Section. | Relative Strength. | Section. | Relative Strength. |
|---|---|---|---|
| ○ | 100 | ╬ | 25 |
| □ | 65 | ● | 23.3 |
| I | 51 | ■ | 23 |

If the pillars were of wrought iron or steel, the relative strengths would be in the same order as for cast iron, and would vary but little from the values given in the tables for cast iron. Although the hollow round and hollow square columns prove to give a far more economical distribution of metal than any other section, it must not be forgotten that it is impossible to properly calibrate the thickness of metal in castings of such sections, that they may be badly cored in their manufacture, giving more metal on one side than another, and that the unequal thickness considerably lessens the strength of the column.

The author is of opinion that a considerably larger factor of safety should be used with castings which it is impossible to measure and examine in every part than would be necessary with other sections. Pillars may fail by the crushing of the material of which they are made, which occurs with pillars that are short compared with their radius of gyration, by flexure, which occurs with long pillars, or by a combination of both; but no hard-and-fast line can be drawn between failure by crushing and failure by flexure. With short pillars the material which has the greatest unit-crushing strength will give the most economical results as regards weight, but in pillars failing by flexure the strength depends upon the modulus of elasticity of the material.

From the foregoing remarks it will be seen that the length of a pillar may have a great deal to do with the selection of the material of which it should be made, for which purpose the following table may be of assistance, as it gives the different material in order of strength for different proportions of pillars. As an instance of the use of the table for a pillar, the length of which divided by the radius of gyration is between the limits of 1 and 50, the greatest unit strength would be obtained from cast iron, steel coming second, and wrought iron third.

PILLARS WITH ENDS ROUNDED.

| Length divided by radius of gyration. | Materials in order of Strength. | | |
|---|---|---|---|
| 1 to 50 | Cast Iron | Steel | Wrought Iron |
| 50 to 60 | Steel | Cast Iron | Wrought Iron |
| 60 to 300 | Steel | Wrought Iron | Cast Iron |

PILLARS WITH ENDS FIXED.

| Length divided by radius of Gyration. | Materials in order of Strength. | | |
|---|---|---|---|
| 1 to 80 | Cast Iron | Steel | Wrought Iron |
| 80 to 100 | Steel | Cast Iron | Wrought Iron |
| 100 to 300 | Steel | Wrought Iron | Cast Iron |

When pillars carry girders mistakes are often made in designing the seats, and it cannot be too strongly urged that the loads transmitted to pillars should be carried as near the centre of gravity of the section as possible. The provision of girder seats far too large for the weight to be carried is a common error, and frequently is a source of danger, because the deflection of the girders carried cause all the weight to be thrown on the outside of the seat, and removes the centre of gravity of the load considerably away from the centre of the pillar, a condition for which it has never been calculated. In designing the seat for a girder it is only necessary to have sufficient bearing area to prevent the safe bearing stress of the material of which the girder or the seat is made being exceeded, calculating, of course, on the safe bearing stress for the weaker material.

In the erection of ironwork care should be taken that girders are properly secured to stanchions or other girders which they intersect, and in most cases it is better to make use of the ends of the girders for fastening rather than securing the flanges to their seats. It is also better practice to depend upon the clearing strength of bolts and rivets than to put them in direct tension and allow the load to be suspended from heads and nuts. In designing the ironwork for a building it is also a matter for consideration as to what extent the framing will be required to brace the structure besides supporting vertical loads, because where lateral security is required it will be necessary to properly anchor the bases of the pillars, and in some cases make use of diagonal bracing.

In fixing the sizes of bolts to be used in securing one pillar above another and securing girders to cast-iron pillars it is

* A paper read in the Engineering and Building Construction Section at the Dublin Congress of the Royal Institute of Public Health.

better to err on the side of safety, and it may be laid down as a rule that 1¼-in. bolts are the smallest that should be used, except with small girders or in special cases. In bedding girders on iron seating a strip of lead may be used, but where a girder or pillar is supported upon a stone-template the safe unit stress is small in comparison, and some material with considerably less resistance to crushing should be used between the surfaces. As the strength of a stanchion largely depends upon the way in which it is fixed, a doubt often exists in the mind of the designer as to what assumption shall be made in calculating its strength; that is to say, whether he shall consider both ends to be rounded, one end fixed and one rounded, or both ends fixed, the relative strength of pillars fixed in the ways described being one, two and three respectively. Even when one is warranted in assuming fixity of one end or both, careless workmanship will often upset all his calculations.

In calculating pillars with flat bases, but supporting other stanchions or girders subject to a variable load, the author assumes one end to be fixed and the other rounded, but stanchions carried on others he assumes to have both ends rounded. The only cases in which he would consider both ends to be fixed are where both ends of the pillar are flat, and where the load supported is constant and evenly distributed. For bedding a pillar the best plan, perhaps, is to make the vertical distances between the stone template and the load which the pillar is to support about 1½ in. greater than the length of the pillar. Then wedge the pillar up to its position by driving iron wedges between the template and the base of the pillar, grouting the space with neat cement. If pillars are bedded in the way described it is unnecessary to machine-face the base, but holes about 2 in. in diameter should be left in the base plate as near to the centre of the pillar as possible, so that the grout which is poured in from the outside between a raised mound of clay and the base will rise in the grout holes and indicate when the space is properly filled. The top of a cast-iron pillar supporting another should be machined-faced.

Wherever ironwork is used in a building it should be covered with fire-resisting material, so as to protect the supporting framework of the structure as long as possible from the influences of heat. Many kinds of fireproof flooring are in the market, but the author would give preference to floors where the whole of the ironwork is properly protected from fire by some suitable covering.

## CREMATION OF SEWAGE.

The following letter from the Archdeacon of Gloucester on the above subject appeared in Friday's issue of *The Times* :—

"The profane were wont to call the ex-Parliamentary the ' silly season'; not a very appropriate term, unless all wisdom be concentrated on politics and none on the social welfare of the country. Let me ask your help in promoting such welfare in one momentous direction—the disposal of sewage. There are few evils, in my opinion, more pressing or even scandalous than the pollution of rivers. Water is one of God's most precious gifts (poor East London will testify to this). To turn a fair river into a foul drain seems to me not only a hideous blunder but a hideous crime. Will you let me open a correspondence on the cremation of sewage, for our pest may thus be turned even to our advantage? I plead for the erection of huge furnaces at the outfalls of our drains. No doubt they would require lofty chimneys and chemical ingredients to neutralise the noisome gases; but this, surely, cannot be beyond the reach of science. In these furnaces the solid matter would be burnt and form artificial manure; the liquids, being properly filtered and deodorised, might then be allowed to flow away. Let us sum up our present position. Our beautiful West Riding rivers are only awaiting their time for being turned into foul channels of manufacturing centres. ' Sabrina fair ' is rapidly becoming ' Sabrina foul,' to the great discomfiture of the salmon. Limpid Thames is condemned to bear the ignoble burden of London sewage. Have we not heard of a huge sewage island being piled up on the borders of Essex? Have not the oyster sellers been half ruined by sewers disgorging themselves near the oyster-beds of Kent? Have we not tried the 'Ealing Styx'— the Brent? Fifty-seven years ago my father had his kitchen garden surrounded by that pretty river at Hanwell. I am now staying on the coast of South Hampshire. A nice little trout stream empties itself past the village into the sea. Up the stream trout are caught abundantly, below the houses large fish are caught, but ought not to be eaten, for a disgusting freight of sewage is carried to the sea, and Oceanus has to dispose of accumulated poison as best he may. Shame to say, it is the same story for all our watering-places. Could the Chancellor of the Exchequer use a cool million better than to establish by grants (repayable, if you will) crematories for all our great towns and cities? Now, what are the palliatives on which we place our reliance? Miserable subterfuges indeed—sewage farms. At first we heard much of the enrichment, now we hear of the poisoning, of the soil. At best it is the spread of noisome exhalations over fair fields instead of fair rivers. I do not envy the olfactory senses of the man who walks anywhere near the sewage farm. The huge sewage marsh at Saltley, near Birmingham,

had to be thickly covered by masses of sand and gravel, I suppose to be in their turn as much poisoned as the stratum which lies below them. No doubt we must come to cremation sooner or later; but why not sooner than later? I throw out this suggestion, to be taken up, I trust, by practical and scientific men. I am sure he will be a public benefactor who can turn a curse into a blessing."

## THE HOUSING OF THE WORKING CLASSES.

### AN EXTENSIVE SCHEME.

The largest scheme for the provision of working-class dwellings as yet undertaken by the London County Council, known as the Boundary-street, Whitechapel, scheme, is now nearing completion. There will be in all twenty-three separate blocks of buildings on the area, the first of which was commenced in 1894. The number of persons displaced from the area was 5,719. The council was required by the scheme to provide accommodation for not fewer than 4,700 persons, of which number 144 were to be accommodated on the Goldsmith-row site, acquired for that purpose. On the Boundary-street area, however, dwelling accommodation has been planned for 5,380 persons, which, with the 144 rehoused on the other site, makes a total of 5,524 persons rehoused, or only 195 fewer than the number displaced and 824 more than the scheme requires. In addition to this, eighteen shops and seventy-seven workshops have been provided. The 5,524 persons will be rehoused in 1,069 tenements, making an average of 5·168 persons per tenement. There are 601 tenements entirely self-contained. In the first half of the area the living-rooms average 144 square feet and the bed-rooms 96 square feet, while in the latter buildings these sizes were increased to 160 and 110 square feet respectively. Every habitable room on the area is provided with a 45° angle of light horizontally and vertically, and the buildings are so arranged that nearly every room commands an open outlook. The entrance avenue and the circus are 60 ft. wide and the principal streets 50 ft. There are on the area three public gardens, well laid out, of an aggregate area of nearly three-quarters of an acre. There is clothes-washing accommodation in two blocks only, it being provided in a well-equipped central laundry, behind which is a small annexe containing twelve hot and cold slipper baths and a cold shower bath, and over the laundry are two club-rooms for the use of the tenants. A bakery and an estate workshop are now in course of construction. The buildings as a whole have been designed within the financial requirements of the Treasury, the interest on the capital being calculated at 3 per cent., and the sinking fund for land and buildings for terms varying from fifty-two to sixty years. The rents charged are somewhat higher than those charged by the Peabody and Guinness trustees.

## A NEW BATH FOR LIVERPOOL.

The mayor of Liverpool, on the 26th ult., performed the opening ceremony in connection with a new open-air bath which the corporation have erected in a thoroughfare known as Gore-street. The bath, situated immediately behind St. Matthew's church, Hill-street, occupies the site of about fifty dwelling-houses which were demolished some time ago as insanitary. Together with the gymnasium it covers an area of about 1,100 square yards. The gymnasium, which will be provided with the usual youths' gymnastic apparatus, is 44 ft. long, with an average width of 40 ft. Adjoining is a small bath, 6 ft. by 5 ft., supplied with hot and cold water, in which the lads may wash before entering the bath or using the gymnasium. Around the bath, which is only 3 ft. 6 in. deep at the greatest depth, are situated covered dressing-sheds. The water in the bath is fresh water from the mains, and there is a drinking fountain for the use of the children. All the buildings are structures of red brick with terra-cotta dressings. Mr. W. R. Court, the engineer and superintendent of the baths, designed the buildings. Messrs. L. Marr & Son, Liverpool, were the contractors.

**Classes for Engineers, Surveyors, &c.**—We have received from King's College, London, and the City of London College syllabuses of their classes for engineering, architecture, building construction, &c., for the 1898-99 session. Full particulars of these and other classes can be obtained upon application at the respective colleges.

**Pneumatic Street-cleaning Machines.** — Pneumatic street-cleaning machines have now been in use in Indianapolis for several years, says *The Engineering Record*, and have recently done much work in Columbus. It has been found that one machine, with driver and operator and one or two two-horse waggons to haul away the sweepings, can clean 6 miles of 40-ft. paved street in ten hours. Both the mayor and the Board of Public Works of Indianapolis have commended the character of the work in their annual reports, and one particular advantage of this system of cleaning which experience has demonstrated is its efficiency in cold weather, when sprinkling is impracticable.

# Progress in Sewage Purification.

By W. KAYE PARRY, M.A., A.M.I.C.E.*

From time to time the world is startled by the announcement that some wonderful discovery has been made which is calculated to revolutionise existing methods of manufacture, to open up new industries, or to afford facilities hitherto unobtainable for achieving some desirable result. It often happens, after the first burst of applause has died away, some critic comes forward to question either the value or the originality of the alleged discovery. While we should be careful not to disparage the labours of those who have achieved success in a field of research in which others have toiled without any apparent result, we are quite entitled to satisfy ourselves that if praise be accorded it is well merited, and that the alleged discovery is really a step in advance which will promote the cause of science or the well-being of the community. We have heard a great deal within the last year or two about the advances which have been made in sewage purification, and it is, therefore, well worth considering in what these advances really consist, and by whose labours and researches they have been brought about.

## PRINCIPLE OF THE DORTMUND TANKS.

At the congress of the Sanitary Institute at Leeds, in 1897, one of the papers read on the subject of sewage purification included a description of the circular deep tanks in use in Dortmund, in Germany, and the author of the paper distributed lithographed copies of the drawing of these tanks to the audience, apparently under the impression that they were a novelty. All engineers who are conversant with the literature of sewage purification were aware that these tanks had been fully described in Mr. Santo Crimp's admirable work on sewage disposal works, published in 1890, and that they were no longer a novelty; but comparatively few persons are aware that even before these tanks had been either designed or constructed the same principle had been applied to the clarification of sewage.

In May, 1895, Mr. W. H. Hartland, of Glasgow, took out a patent for the purification of water and sewage, which embraces among other features a type of tank which embodies the same principle as the Dortmund tank. In the words of the patentee: "The process consists mainly of settlement, but under somewhat peculiar conditions, or what I will term equilibrio subsidence under which the full effect of the laws of gravity may be obtained in freeing a liquid from suspended impurity."

The form of tank which Mr. Hartland patented differs from that used at Dortmund. He used a rectangular tank, sunk to a considerable depth below the level of the sewer invert. This tank was provided with two vertical shafts or pipes, fixed at the opposite ends and carried up to the level of the sewer invert. The tank was worked continuously, and, owing to the depth to which it was sunk, the liquid in it was under pressure resulting from the head of water in the vertical pipes. The sewage flowed down one of the vertical pipes into the tank, and after passing along its entire length it again flowed up to the surface by the second pipe, passing out of the tank at the same level as it entered it, while the sludge was periodically drawn off from the bottom. But in both the Hartland and the Dortmund tanks the principle is identical—that is to say, the liquid containing the suspended matter is first made to flow in a downward direction to a considerable depth, and before it can escape it is compelled to rise again to the original level, leaving behind it the finely-divided particles of suspended matter which will not rise with the liquid.

In the year 1887 the author of this paper made the acquaintance of Mr. Hartland, and by arrangement with the latter a trial apparatus, having model tanks constructed in accordance with Hartland's patents, was erected in Kingstown, co. Dublin, and a series of practical tests was undertaken by the author. These experiments were described in a paper read before the Institution of Civil Engineers of Ireland, on December 5, 1888, and the paper will be found in the "Transactions" of the Institution.

When the author read the description of the Dortmund tanks in Mr. Santo Crimp's work he at once recognised their value from his own experience of the results arrived at by the Hartland tanks, and as the form of tank used at Dortmund was somewhat more simple than that adopted by Hartland, while the principle of both was identical. The author constructed Dortmund tanks for the sewage purification works at Dundrum, which were designed in 1891, and described at the congress of the Royal Institute of Public Health held in Dublin, in 1892. The paper will be found in The Journal of State Medicine, vol. I., October, 1892. When, therefore, in 1897 this principle was put forward as a new departure in sewage treatment it was, as a matter of fact, more than twelve years old.

## THE WORK OF MR. BAILEY DENTON.

It would be wise for all those who take up the question of sewage purification to make themselves conversant with its history. If they were to do so they would find that there were clever chemists and able engineers engaged upon this problem when many of us were still in our cradles, and that,

although they did not recognise the labours of aerobic organisms or give us a true explanation of the action which takes place in a filter, they had a very practical acquaintance, not only with the difficulties of the sewage question, but with the lines upon which it would be possible to deal with it successfully. Take, for example, the valuable series of reports published by the late Dr. Angus Smith, how many of our more modern chemists take the trouble to peruse them or to study his experiments on aëration ?

But in the present short paper the writer desires to allude more particularly to the labours and the writings of the late Mr. Bailey Denton, whose first work on land drainage was published in the year 1854, and who from that time until his death contributed a series of most valuable additions to the literature of sewage treatment. Nor were his exertions confined to literary productions, for, as all engineers know, he designed and carried out a great number of extensive sewage disposal works, to the principles underlying which the writer desires particularly to draw attention. In 1880 a brochure appeared from the pen of Mr. Bailey Denton, entitled "Ten Years' Experience in Works of Intermittent Downward Filtration." This little book is worthy of more attention than it has received at the hands of some recent writers.

At present we are expected to accept the so-called bacterial filters as the real solution of the sewage problem. We cannot take up a professional journal without hearing something about them, and about those who are trumpeting forth their virtues and who claim credit for having originated them. Time alone can show whether these filters really constitute the best and most economical means of purifying sewage. Into this controversy the writer does not at present intend to enter, but it is worth while to stop and ask whether these bacterial filters are really new, and in what respect do they differ essentially from the land filters the use of which Mr. Bailey Denton advocated?

The latter selected land of an open, porous character; he prepared the surface carefully and divided it up into a number of plots, each plot was surrounded by a bank, and was as level as a croquet ground or a lawn tennis court. These plots were all carefully and thoroughly underdrained to a depth of 6 ft. by a series of herring-bone drains, connected with a central drain by which the filtrate was conveyed away. The sewage was turned on to each plot alternately, and it was allowed to filter through the porous land until it reached the under drains, each plot was allowed an interval of rest after it had been working for a certain number of hours. According to Mr. Bailey Denton's own words, the process was one of filtration in a downward direction carried on intermittently. It is most important to remember that he lays the greatest stress on the absolute necessity for the intervals of rest. He writes as follows: "In speaking of intermittent filtration . . . . I refer to the concentration of sewage, at regular intervals, on as few acres of land as will absorb and cleanse it without preventing the production of vegetation."

In the process just described, the land, after being levelled, was ploughed, so as to make a series of ridges and furrows; the sewage flowed along the furrows and the crops were planted in the ridges. All these works were the outcome of the researches of Dr. Frankland, who had reported that " an acre of suitably-constituted soil, well and deeply underdrained, with its surface levelled and divided into four equal plots, each of which in succession would receive the sewage of six hours, would cleanse the sewage of 3,300 persons." These words were written in 1870, and Mr. Bailey Denton promptly put these theories to the test, and in 1880 he was able to give the world his experience and to show that substantially Dr. Frankland was absolutely correct, for although, as a matter of precaution, he very wisely kept on the safe side by preparing land enough to enable him to allow an acre of land to every 1,100 persons, instead of 3,300, yet he states distinctly "although he had acted thus cautiously in designing the first work of the kind, there was no intention to discredit the conclusions come to by the Rivers Pollution Commissioners as to the cleansing capability of suitably-constituted soil," and the evidence submitted in his book fully bears out Dr. Frankland's views. Thus, in 1870, although bacteriology as applied to sewage treatment was an unborn science, and no one had ever heard of the benevolent bacillus, yet sewage was successfully purified on exactly the same lines as those the merits of which are now so loudly proclaimed.

In 1887 the author, following Mr. Bailey Denton, laid out 3 acres of land on Dr. Frankland's principles for the purification of the sewage of the Rathdown Union Workhouse, at Loughlinstown, co. Dublin. These plans were approved of by the chief engineering inspector of the Local Government Board for Ireland, Mr. Charles P. Cotton, who is now presiding over this section. These works were described by the writer at a meeting of the Institution of Civil Engineers of Ireland, in April, 1892. The land was divided into plots,

* A paper read at the recent Dublin congress of the Royal Institute of Public Health.

levelled and underdrained, as recommended by Dr. Frank land, and the sewage of the workhouse has been filtered through these land filters ever since.

These filters have been in use for the last ten years, so that the writer can now adopt Mr. Bailey Denton's language, and write of his ten years' experience of intermittent downward filtration, and from a recent visit he is pleased to be able to state that they are still giving satisfaction and producing an effluent which can safely be discharged into the river. No doubt modern artificial filters are capable of dealing with a larger volume of sewage than the land filters, but on the other hand, they will not grow crops, whereas Mr. Bailey Denton aimed at "cleansing the sewage without preventing the production of vegetation."

### THE QUESTION OF COST.

As regards the relative cost, Mr. Dibdin tells us that the cost of making a burnt-clay filter at Sutton, with an area of one-tenth of an acre, was "less that £100." So that the cost of preparing an acre of land for the purpose would in this case have been about £1,000, exclusive of the purchase of the land. But Mr. Santo Crimp informs us in his paper on the main drainage of London that the bacterial filter, about an acre in extent, constructed at Barking, cost about £2,000, the breeze and cinders being acquired on exceptionally favourable forms.

Mr. de Courcy Meade tells us that he estimates that the cost of constructing bacterial filters for Manchester would be at the rate of £5,500 per acre, exclusive of the purchase of the land. Mr. Bailey Denton states that the total cost of preparing 40 acres of land at Merthyr Tydfil for intermittent downward filtration, including under drains, surface formation, construction of tanks and conduits, distributing chambers, roads, fencing, engineer's fees and clerk of works, was £3,300, which is equal to £82 10s. per acre.

Now, according to Dr. Frankland, an acre of suitable land thus prepared would take the sewage of 3,300 persons, and this may be put down at 132,000 gallons a day, whereas, according to Mr. Dibdin, the artificial filter of 1 acre would deal successfully with 1,000,000 gallons per day, but Mr. de Courcy Meade only allowed 600,000 gallons to the acre. That is to say, following Mr. Dibdin's figures, an artificial filter of 1 acre is more effective than a land filter in the ratio of 1 to 7·57. If therefore we multiply £82 10s. by 7·57, we find that the cost of preparing land enough to deal with 1,000,000 gallons a day would be £624 10s. 6d., against £1,000 for an acre of artificial filter according to Mr. Dibdin's figures for Sutton, or £2,000 according to Mr. Santo Crimp's figures for Barking, or £9,166 according to Mr. de Courcy Meade's estimate for Manchester. These figures are instructive, and throw a side light on the progress of sewage purification since 1870.

But if sewage purification by filtration be not a novelty, the writer ventures to state that successful sewage purification without filtration either through land or artificial filters is absolutely a new departure, and those who have any doubt as to the practicability of these methods are invited to visit the criminal lunatic asylum at Dundrum, co. Dublin, or the metropolitan police barracks, Chapelizod, co. Dublin.

## TELEPHONE WIRES.

### KENSINGTON VESTRY REGULATIONS.

In his report on the work carried out by his department during the year ended March last Mr. William Weaver, surveyor to the Vestry of St. Mary Abbotts, Kensington, refers to an application of the National Telephone Company for permission to lay underground wires in a large number of streets in the parish. The application was referred to Mr. Weaver, and he subsequently reported that he was of opinion that the laying of telephone mains in the streets of the metropolis should be dealt with by Parliament, in order that the rights and duties of the company and of the local authorities respectively should be settled by statute. On the other hand (continued Mr. Weaver), if the vestry were inclined to give the assent applied for, it should only be accorded under a formal agreement embodying certain conditions. The vestry, after considerable debate and after taking legal advice, granted the application subject to an agreement being entered into containing the following provisions:—

(a) That one month's notice be given to the vestry by the company prior to the commencement of work in any street, and that such notice be accompanied by a plan showing the position in the roadway or footpath of the proposed pipe and the position of all inspection or other boxes.

(b) That detail drawings of all boxes be submitted for the approval of the vestry prior to their insertion in the public way.

(c) That three days' notice of the actual commencement of work in any street in accordance with the plans to be approved as aforesaid be given to the vestry's surveyor.

(d) That the pipes be laid in such positions and at such depths as the vestry's surveyor may direct, and that the public way be reinstated to his satisfaction, the surfaces being made good by the vestry at the cost of the company, the charges for such work being at the same rates as are levied upon the gas and water companies.

(e) That the vestry be under no liability for damage, other than wilful damage, to the property of the company arising from the execution by the vestry or their contractors of any work in the roads or footpaths, and the company to indemnify the vestry against any claims which may be made in consequence of the execution of the company's works or the subsidence of their trenches.

(f) That the company do alter the position of any pipe or box, free of cost, at the request of the vestry.

(g) That the company do pay to the vestry all costs and expenses entailed by the examination of the plans of the company by the vestry's surveyor, or by the supervision of their work and of the restoration and repair of the highways.

(h) That the company do pay to the vestry a rental of 1s. per annum in respect of each 100 lineal yards of pipe laid, such rental to be irrespective of any rating or assessment to the parochial rates.

(i) That the company do pay the vestry's solicitor's charges for the preparation of an agreement embodying the foregoing conditions.

## SANITARY WORK IN MANCHESTER.

### A YEAR'S RECORD.

The report of the Sanitary Committee of the Manchester Corporation for the year states that the large number of 42,806 complaints of nuisances have been dealt with, and the twenty-eight district and four smoke nuisance inspectors have made 73,539 inspections of various kinds, and have applied smoke and water tests with the view of discovering any defects which migh exist in the drainage at 2,266 houses. The notices which have been served for the abatement of nuisances of various kinds number 12,888, and 427 magistrates' summonses have been issued under the direction of the committee for non-observance of such notices. There are 1,396 lodging-houses registered under the by-laws made under sec. 90 of the Public Health Act, and in the course of the year 1,864 day and 413 night visits were made to these houses, with the result that fifty-six persons were reported to the committee for infringements. Great efforts have been made to mitigate the nuisance arising from the emission of black smoke from the chimneys of works, &c., and special attention has been given to the works in the newly-incorporated districts, with the result that a very great diminution of the nuisance has been effected. The new underground lavatories have been opened—one in South-street and the other in Great Bridgwater-street—which will supply a much-felt need in those neighbourhoods. Two House Drainage Department have re-drained no fewer that 5,905 dwelling-houses and 274 business premises, public buildings, &c., during the year. The cost of this work amounted to £29,359.

## STOCKPORT WATER SUPPLY.

### PROPOSED MUNICIPALISATION.

At a special meeting of the Stockport Town Council, Mr. Alderman Lees, the chairman of the Finance Committee, formally moved a resolution suggesting the desirability of acquiring the undertaking of the Stockport District Waterworks Company. The subject (continued Alderman Lees) had been before the corporation on various occasions during the last forty years, the financial question having up to now debarred them from acquiring the works. He had no hesitation, having given the matter great consideration for several years, in asking the council to take it up earnestly with a view to purchase. The object of giving municipal corporations more control was to promote the health, good government and well-being of the people, and it could not be denied that water was one of the first necessities of life. From a sanitary point of view it was important that a corporation should have control of the water supply, and Government were now most favourable to the transfer of these water undertakings to the municipal authority. Other members spoke in support of the motion, the vice-chairman of the committee remarking that with the example of Maidstone before them—the epidemic there being attributed to the quality of the water—they had to remember that their first duty was to preserve as far as possible the health of the people. The resolution was passed unanimously, and a committee were subsequently appointed to open negotiations with the company.

---

**Illinois Roads.**—If, as Bushnell the philosopher says, roads are indicative of a people, what is indicated by the roads of Illinois? The Arkansas traveller's roof is suggested, says *Good Roads*. In fair weather it needed no repairs; in foul weather it could not get none.

**A Lioness in a Sewer.**—When a young African lioness, just arrived from abroad, was being taken to the Onion Fair at Birmingham it suddenly escaped from its van. Finally it ran into a main sewer (says *The Rambler*), but as it could not be found the panic in the neighbourhood was extraordinary. The people locked themselves in their houses, and men went about with pitchforks, revolvers and guns till the animal was traced to its lair.

# Comparative Reports of General Practice.

## XXVIII.—TRAMWAY TRACTION : BLACKPOOL REPORT.—II.

### LEIPZIG.

The deputation next visited the tramway system of the Grosse Leipziger Strassenbahn Gesellschaft, which was opened at the end of 1896. It is throughout on the overhead span-wire system, the track being of standard gauge and double, 74 miles in length. The maximum gradient is 3 per cent., and the sharpest curve 50 ft. radius. One hundred and eighty-five cars are in use of the single-deck type, each carrying thirty passengers. The only batteries in use are at the central station. The usual pressure is 500 volts, and there are installed four dynamos of a total capacity of 1,450 kilowatts.

The system is a remarkably good one, and in many respects is similar to that in Hamburg; but in the construction of the track, or rather of the curves, there is one feature which is worthy of imitation. The curve at the corner of a street, instead of being at one uniform radius, really consists of two short curves, with a straight portion of line connecting them. This straight portion approaches within 2 ft. of the corner, the obvious advantage for tramway purposes being that one bogie is always on the straight, and therefore the tendency to leave the line is very slight.

### HANOVER.

Hanover being one of the places mentioned by the Board of Trade, the deputation were especially interested in the system in operation there; the more so that they had been advised from other sources that accumulators were working very satisfactorily in Hanover.

The tramway system is worked by the Hannoverische Strassenbahn Gesellschaft. There are in all 147 miles of tramroad, principally double and of standard gauge. The speed inside the town is about 7½ miles per hour and outside about 18 miles. There are no gradients worth speaking of. A little over a mile on the outskirts of the town is worked by the overhead system only, there being nine cars used in this service, each carrying thirty-two passengers and weighing 5½ tons. There are, in addition, 216 cars fitted for the overhead and accumulator system; sixteen of these carry thirty-two passengers, and weigh 8½ tons; 100 carry thirty-six, and weigh 10 tons; the remainder carry thirty-six, and weigh 11½ tons, it having been found advisable to strengthen the trucks on account of the extra weight. Approximately 63 miles are overhead line and 84 miles are worked by accumulators. About 10 miles of this latter reute are worked by cars which do not run along the portion of track fed by the overhead line, but are charged at two stations *en route*.

The accumulators are placed beneath the seats, and each car is fitted with 208 cells of the Hagen type, having three plates in each cell. The weight of these cells is approximately 2 tons, and the cost per car £200. On the question of the life of these cells no very definite information could be obtained. The deputation were informed that a good plate might last two years, a bad plate would probably go in a month; but the average life ought to be taken as anything between one and two years. Although this type of battery has been in use for a period of three years, the company could not give the cost of its upkeep. There have been three or four accidents due to the short circuiting of the batteries, but no personal injuries resulted therefrom. One piece of information, however, regarding the efficiency of the cells was obtainable—*viz.*, the energy taken from the dynamos to drive the different classes of cars 1 mile, and they are as follows: Without accumulators ·68 units, with accumulators 1·37 units with light cars and 1·50 units with heavy cars.

On the car route worked solely by accumulators there are placed two charging stations, at one of which a twenty-five minutes' charge is given, at the other a six to eight minutes' charge. The total length of the journey is a little short of 10 miles, and occupies about forty-five minutes, while the period of charging, as will be seen, occupies from thirty-one to thirty-three minutes. This of necessity increases the number of cars essential to maintain the service, as at each station there are cars always charging. The overhead system is chiefly on the span-wire principle, but there are in places side brackets and centre posts. These posts are of lattice girder construction, and did not appear to the deputation as ornamental. The gauge of the trolley wire is 8 millimetres. The overhead line and car equipments were originally constructed by Siemens & Halske some six years since, but this class of work is now almost entirely done by the tramway company themselves. There have been several accidents due to the breakage of the wire, resulting in the death of five or six horses, but there has been no loss of human life. The trolley is the usual under-running bar of Siemens & Halske, very similar to that in use on the Isle of Man tramways.

### COLOGNE.

From Hanover the deputation journeyed to Paris, breaking the journey to Cologne. They were struck by the narrowness of the streets in which double lines of tramways were laid, and by the steep gradients up which the cars run apparently with great ease. The wires invariably are supported by span wires attached to the houses, as also are the arc lamps for lighting the streets. Time limits and the lateness of the hour did not permit of further investigation, the deputation continuing their journey by the night train to Paris.

### PARIS.

The first tramway system visited was that belonging to the Compagnie de Tramway de Paris du Départment de la Seine. It was one of the very latest construction, having, in fact, been only opened for service on the Saturday preceding the deputation's visit.

There are two lines of tramway, one of which, running from Aubervilliers to Place de la Republique, has approximately a mile of overhead conductor and 3¼ miles of track worked by accumulators. The other line runs from Pantin to Place de la Republique, and has approximately a mile of overhead line and about 3 miles worked by accumulators. About 500 yards of the track is single, the rest double. The whole is of the standard gauge. The speed inside the town is about 8½ miles per hour, and about 16 miles outside. The maximum gradient is 3¼ per cent., and is only of short length. There are thirty tramcars of the double-deck type, carrying fifty-five passengers, and weighing complete 14 tons. This is the first tramway company as yet met on the Continent having double-decked cars. The accumulators are placed in an iron containing case slung underneath the cars between the bogies. The cells are made by the Societè Anonyme pour le Travail Electrique des Metaun, and each car has 224 cells, each containing seven plates. The weight of the cells, exclusive of containing case, is 4 tons, and the cost £275. They are partly charged from the overhead trolley when running, and completely re-charged at night. The overhead line is on the span-wire system, the gauge of the conductors 8 millimetres, the trolley of the Thomson-Houston type, and the working pressure 500 volts.

The second system is one also belonging to the Compagnie de Tramway de Paris du Départment de la Seine, and runs from the Madeleine to the Pont de Neuilly, a distance of 3¾ miles. It is entirely on the accumulator system, and the track is double throughout. The heaviest gradient is about 4½ per cent. and the length about 120 yards. The speed in the centre of the town is about 8 miles and outside about 11 miles. It was opened in 1892, and was then equipped with Laurent-Cely cells. At the end of last year Hagen cells were installed. There are thirty-eight cars in use of the double-deck type, carrying fifty-two passengers each. The weight of car, motors and passengers is 14 tons, of accumulators 3·6 tons. There are 200 cells, each having five plates, and are fixed under the seats. The cells are charged at a feeding point (Puteaux), at which place a fifteen minutes' charge is given. The cost of the batteries per car is given as about £300, and a double journey is run with one charge; and the cost of repairs to the batteries at about 3·2d. per car mile.

### BRUSSELS.

The next stopping-place of the deputation was Brussels. The tramway system in this city is worked by the Compagnie des Tramways Bruxellois. The electrical network comprises the following lines—the line round the upper Boulevards, which is 3 miles long, and a double track, was opened on 1st May, 1894. The line from Place Stephanie to Uccle, 2¼ miles, double track, was opened at the same time. The line from Gare du Midi to Uccle, 2¾ miles long, double track, was opened on the 29th October, 1896. All these lines are on the overhead trolley system. The line from l'Impasse du Parc to Bois de la Cambre through the street called la Loi and the Boulevard Militaire was opened in May, 1897. This line is about 4 miles long, double track, part of it (1·18 miles) is fitted with an underground conduit and the remainder with overhead wires. The line from Schaerbeek to Bois de la Cambre has a total length of 5 miles, double track, and is equipped throughout on the conduit system, being opened in September, 1897. The whole of the electrical network now in use in Brussels is about 17¼ miles of double track.

The electricity is taken from the company's own station in Rue Brogniez. The generating plant originally installed consisted of three Babcock & Willcox boilers, five tandem compound engines by McIntosh & Seymour, each of 180 horse-power, working at a pressure of 130 lb.; and five belt-driven dynamos of Brown's "Oerliken" type, each of 100 kilowatts capacity. In 1897 two more boilers of similar make and size and two tandem compound steam engines (Corliss-Bonjour) of 750 horse-power, running at 150 revolutions per minute were installed. These machines are coupled direct to two special 400 kilowatts dynamos of the Thomson-Houston type. There are also two steam engines of the same type as last of 400 horse-power, coupled direct to two Thomson-Houston dynamos of 225 kilowatts each. The later engines are of the condensing type, condensing water being brought from La Senne by an underground aqueduct 330 yards long at a mean depth of about 22 ft. below the ground. The switchboard is of the usual panel type, the feed to the conduit being entirely separate from that to the overhead lines.

The feeding cables are of the lead-covered type, the overhead lines Thomson-Houston pattern, partly bracket posts and partly span-wire system. This overhead line is divided into sections of about 550 yards, each section being joined to the feeding cables. The lines of the underground system of traction are provided with conduits of the Berlin type, laid down by the German Thomson-Houston Company. The cost of the conduit per mile of single track complete was stated to be £12,800 (200,000 frs. per kilometre), as against £3,200 the cost of the overhead line, including permanent way. The conduit is placed under one of the rails; the groove for the plough is 1 3/16 in. normally, and is formed by the space between two Haarmann rails of about 54 lb. yer yard. The depth of the conduit from the ground level is 25 in. The skeleton of the conduit is made up of frames 4 ft. apart, the intervening space being filled up by concrete or brickwork. Sumps and syphon outlets to the sewers are placed about every 45 yards. The conduit contains two insulated conductors of I-shaped iron weighing 19 lb. per yard. These conducting irons are supported at about every 5 yards by insulators, and the electrical circuit is completed at the junctions of the irons by copper bonds. The cost of working the conduit is said to be about ¼d. per car mile more than the overhead. This, of course, does not take into account the additional cost of the installation.

The are 100 cars fitted for electrical working, weighing from 6½ to 7 tons each and carrying twenty-eight to thirty passengers. The equipment is of the usual Thomson-Houston type. The average speed, including stoppages, is 7½ miles per hour. The gradients are extremely heavy, being in some instances as much as 1 in 16 and for a length of 1,100 yards. The cars are fitted with Westinghouse air brakes.

OSTEND.

The deputation next visited Ostend. Here experiments are being made in accumulator traction by la Societe Anonyme de Railways Economiques de Liège-Tersing et Extensions. The length of track is 3¾ miles, double, of metre gauge, and the general car equipment other than batteries was by the Westinghouse Electrical Company. At present only five single-deck cars are fitted. The cars carry forty passengers and weigh 10½ tons. They are equipped with 108 new type Julien cells, 3½ tons weight, placed under the seats. Each car runs five hours with one charge. They are partially re-charged at the end of every one or two journeys, and are completely re-charged at night, from two to three hours being so occupied. They were installed last July, and worked for four months. No electrical tramcars are run in the winter in Ostend. The cost of these cells was about £250 per car, and the life of the cells is given, by the makers, as from two to three years. The cost of the repairs of the cells per car mile was given at about 8d. The deputation were also much interested in viewing the remains of three other different types of accumulators which have been experimented with on this line within the last year. The condition of these cells was extremely bad.

GENERAL.

Before advancing to the conclusions, the deputation would like to record the great impression made upon their minds by the conditions under which electric tramways are worked on the Continent. Instead of being, as in England, looked upon with suspicion, if not disfavour, they are allowed great latitude, and their progress is fostered by the authorities, so that the public appear to have found electric tramways essential to their welfare by reason of the ease and expedition transit from place to place, without discomfort or noise. Stopping places are declared and cars stop at these places only, resulting in a punctual and prompt service. The outcome of these conditions, then, is that tramways serve the cities on the Continent just as railways serve the districts in England; or, in other words, they are street railways rather than tramways.

## DARTFORD ROADS.

### URBAN DISTRICT COUNCIL REPORT.

Mr. William Harston, surveyor to the Dartford Urban District Council, has, in accordance with a request of the latter authority, submitted a report dealing with the cost of maintaining the highways (other than main roads) of his district. The local taxation returns, published by the Local Government Board, did not, it seems, contain any statement as to the cost of maintaining such roads in urban districts, and Mr. Harston has been unable to find that any figures are published upon which a comparison could be based, a fact which he suggests might possibly be due to the difference in the incidence of account in urban and rural districts. In the absence of any published information on the subject, Mr. Harston has therefore submitted to the surveyors of several corporate and urban authorities a series of queries with reference thereto. In comparing the expense involved in one district with another, Mr. Harston thinks it is necessary that the circumstances obtaining in each particular case should be taken into consideration, as the varying cost of materials, the expense of horse and manual labour, and the nature and extent of the traffic in each district are important factors, without which no proper comparison can be made.

In Dartford they laboured under an initial disadvantage arising from the absence of any quarries in the locality yielding stone suitable for road maintenance. With the exception of flints, which were unsuited for roads subjected to heavy traffic, the whole of the material required was imported into the district, and, owing to the expense of railway carriage, it was found more economical to utilise Guernsey granite than to obtain a somewhat inferior English stone which might otherwise serve the purpose. The cost of manual labour in the district, too, exceeded that in the majority of corporate towns and urban districts further remote from London. This could be seen from the return which was lately laid before the council when the subject of sick pay was under their consideration. The traffic also was quite exceptional for a town of the size; but it should be borne in mind that it was a busy and rapidly-increasing industrial centre, and that, although its population was but 14,000, it was distant only 15 miles from the metropolis, and was in close proximity to Erith, Woolwich and Plumstead, and adjoined the urban district of Bexley. Then at Stone, Crayford, Swanscombe and other so-called rural parishes in its vicinity important manufacturing industries were pursued; indeed, Dartford might be said to be one of the links in the long chain of manufacturing towns extending from the metropolis along the banks of the Thames. Further, it should not be forgotten that the cartage of supplies to the City of London Asylum at Stone and the Metropolitan Asylums Board's institutions at Darenth helped in an appreciable degree to increase the weight of traffic passing over the district roads.

TRAFFIC.

Another exceptional source of traffic arose from the fact that the produce of the market gardens and fruit farms in that part of Kent was almost exclusively forwarded to Covent Garden by road, while the cartage of manure from the wharves on Dartford Creek to the agricultural parishes in the neighbourhood and of raw materials and manufactured articles to and from the numerous factories situated in the town and its vicinity was very considerable. The extensive building operations now in progress in Dartford and the adjacent parishes also added largely to the wear and tear to which the roads were subjected, and when it was remembered how extensively traction engines were now employed in and around the district it was easy to understand that the traffic was very heavy, not only on the main roads, but on those which had to be maintained exclusively at the expense of the general district ratepayers. As an instance of the nature of repairs which were now necessary as compared with that requisite in former years, Mr. Harston points out that it has been found expedient to use granite for the repair of several thoroughfares all of which until a few years ago were entirely repaired with flints. In conclusion, the report states that, deducting the expense of sweeping, to say nothing of the cost of slopping, the average cost of maintaining the highways under the control of the council was about £46 per mile. That compared very favourably with the returns alluded to in the report, but any thorough comparison was difficult, owing to the fact that the larger proportion of the engineers to whom communications had been addressed had been unable to supply any information as to the cost per mile involved.

## BURY ELECTRIC LIGHTING.

The minutes of the Electric Lighting Committee of the Bury Town Council last week contained a report of the borough engineer and the electrical engineer as to the manner in which the electric light works had increased their scope. The report showed that, whilst in March, 1897, forty-one consumers used 2,481 lamps, in August, 1898, 101 consumers used 6,788 lamps. To the latter figures must be added a further 1,725 for which applications have already been received, making a total of 8,513, leaving a balance of 1,487 to make up the full complement of 10,000 8 candle-power lamps, the estimated total capacity of the present plant. The borrowing powers, £30,000, were almost exhausted, as there had been expended up to the end of July last over £28,000, while authority had been given to spend another £4,000 on mains. The committee resolved that plans and estimates for an extension of the plant at the electricity works be prepared, and that the town clerk make application to the Local Government Board for power to borrow the sum of £20,000 to carry out the necessary works; and, further, that arc lamps be substituted for the present gas lamps in Moss-street, Market-street, Silver-street, Broad-street, Bolton-street, Haymarket-street, Fleet-street, Rock-street, Stanley-street, and Water-street to the Swan Hotel. The council confirmed these minutes.

**National Registration of Plumbers.**—A public meeting will be held in the Mayor's Parlour, Manchester, on the 19th inst., at which the lord mayor will distribute the prizes, certificates and bronze medal of the Plumbers' Company awarded in connection with the recent exhibition of plumbers' work at Manchester. The meeting will be a large and influential one, and several prominent men are expected to be present. The programme will include a lecture on "The Registration of Plumbers and Domestic Sanitation," by Dr. Mansel-Howe, of London.

# Some Annual Municipal Engineering Records.

## JOHANNESBURG.

From the last annual report of Mr. Charles Aburrow relating to the Public Works Department of the Stadsraad, Johannesburg, we learn that at the end of last year the total area controlled by the municipal authorities was 4·56 English square miles, the length of roads and streets being over 130 miles, an increase of about 4½ miles on the previous year. Some 9,376 lineal yards of macadam were laid in various thoroughfares, while re-metalling to the amount of 4,305 lineal yards was carried out. The stone and binding used totalled respectively 107,971 and 18,009 loads. In Johannesburg there are 14,707 lineal yards of kerb, and of gutters: Freestone (2 ft. 6 in. wide), 908 lineal yards; asphalte (2 ft. 11 in. wide), 9,702 lineal yards; freestone (4 ft. wide), 1,261 lineal yards; and asphalte (4 ft. 5 in. wide), 4,144 lineal yards. There are 926 superficial yards of freestone and 6,637 superficial yards of asphalte crossings, while there are 37 superficial yards of freestone cart entrances. Of asphalte entrances there are 1,609 superficial yards. The number of loads of material used in the construction of tar macadam crossings (of which there are 2,012 superficial yards) was 841, or 408 cubic yards; of footpaths, some 9,360 lineal yards were formed.

In connection with drainage it might be mentioned that at the end of the year there were 133 catchpits. Stone crushing is carried on, but the stone from the crushers is irregular in shape and often requires sorting before being taken on to the roads. Two new steam road-rollers, supplied by Messrs. J. Fowler & Co., of Leeds, England, commenced work early in September, after having been passed by the Government boiler inspector, and have both given satisfaction. The total length of tramways within the jurisdiction of the council at the end of 1896 was 10 miles. A sum of £74,196 was derived from the working of the system, the mileage run being 474,711. For purposes of street watering about 35,815,760 gallons of water were used. Some 5½ miles of gas mains and branches were laid in various streets during the year, so that the total length of mains is now nearly 25 miles; 225,000 cubic feet of gas can be stored, the two gasholders having a capacity of 160,000 and 65,000 cubic feet respectively. The quantity manufactured was 31,120,700 cubic feet, the average price charged being a fraction over 18s. 8½d. per 1,000 ft. Over 53 miles of overhead wires were fixed, out of which Messrs. Siemens & Halske erected 26 miles.

The total length of streets containing electric mains is now nearly 25½ miles, representing about 87 miles of wires. There are approximately 21,000 8 candle-power lamps connected, in addition to eight arc lamps for the use of private consumers. The number of units generated was 639,592, being an increase of 234,230 over the previous year, and the current was distributed as follows: Private consumers, 365,111; public lighting, 91,754; public lighting (Doornfontein), 4,767; used on works, 26,416; unaccounted for, being the difference between station meters and consumers' meters, by transformer losses and loss in mains, &c., 131,544. During 1897 the average price per unit obtained was a fraction under 1s. 5d. Of public lamps there are forty-two arc lamps of 2,000 nominal candle-power, 130 incandescent lamps of 35 candle-power, 131 incandescent lamps of (mostly) 16 candle-power, three gas lamps of three lights and 446 others of one light. Lamps therefore total 752. The following additional plant, &c., has been put down during the year: One 45-kilowatt alternator, with switchboard; one overhead travelling crane in old engine-house; four 100 horse-power "Sterling" water-tube boilers, and a "Worthington" feed-pump; one wrought-iron delivery, 150 ft. high and 6 ft. 6 in. diameter; two 200 horse-power "Turner" compound horizontal condensing engines; two 120-kilowatt "Three-phase" generators (self-excited), with switchboards complete; one switchboard, 36 ft. long, containing generator and circuit boards for the three-phase plant, with instruments and synchronising gear; one new wood and iron engine-house, 60 ft. 6 in. by 47 ft.; extension to boiler-house, 60 ft. 6 in. by 36 ft.; and one small electrical testing-room.

In connection with rainfall, the report states that in January the amount recorded in Joubert's Park amounted to 9·71 in., and at Doornfontein, 8·87 in. Rain fell on seventeen days. During the whole of the year there was rain on eighty days, the total amount registered in Joubert's Park being 28·98 in. and at Doornfontein 27·825 in. The average for eight years has been 28·867 in., the average number of days on which rain fell during the same period being eighty-three.

Mention is also made in the report of the erection, at a cost of £13,167, of a " compound " for the sanitary department. The contract included the provision of offices (six rooms, with overhanging verandah); men's quarters (twenty-two rooms, reading-room, dining-room, kitchen, pantry, scullery, three bath-rooms and verandah); workshops (harness maker's rooms, wheelwright and carpenter's shop, farriery, shed for shoeing mules, smithy, cart-shed and tinsmith's-room); general store, 100 ft. by 30 ft.; forage store, 116 ft. by 40 ft., which includes mealie store, engine-room and shed; four

blocks of stabling for mules (400), each measuring 192 ft. by 32 ft. 6 in.; stabling for twenty horses, harness-room, stable-boys'-room, cleaning-room and general harness-room; kafir compounds for day and night boys, consisting of forty-four sleeping compartments, each 24 ft. by 14 ft., two kitchens, two wash-houses and latrines, &c.; water trough, 100 ft. long, sentry-box and sanitary arrangements for white men. The whole of the ground was fenced in with corrugated-iron fencing, 8 ft. high, secured to wooden uprights and rails, with two pairs of sliding gates. A similar fence was also fixed, 5 ft. high, within the enclosure for the purpose of forming a paddock. The buildings were completed and handed over by the contractors at the end of May. In April tenders were invited for a 6 brake horse-power petroleum engine, for driving the contractors' plant. The accepted tender was for £160, exclusive of the cost of gearing, &c., which was arranged by the Sanitary Department.

Slop-pumping, with the exception of the irrigation works at the outfall site, is carried out by the Public Works Department. The scheme consists of two "aprons," constructed of freestone bedded on concrete, with strong iron gratings and catch-pits, over which the slop waggons discharge their contents. From the pits the slop water passes through iron gratings into duplicate tanks, each capable of holding 5,000 gallons. The tanks are constructed of brickwork in cement, with a cement-rendered face; the bottoms are formed with cement concrete with rendered surface, while the top of the tanks are finished off with stone coping. Strong wire screens are fixed across the centre of each tank and round the sumps, for preventing other than liquid matter going into the suction pipe. The slop water from the tanks is lifted by means of two 14-in. by 6½-in. by 10-in. "Worthington" duplex steam pumps, through 11,937 ft. of 6-in. and 4,809 ft. of 5-in. wrought-iron piping, with a vertical lift of 190 ft., and is discharged on to a portion of the farm Waterval, which adjoins the ground used for a depositing site. It is lifted through the 6-in. piping only, and then allowed to run on the ground through the 5-in. pipes by gravitation.

In September and October advertisements were issued inviting tenders for the erection of refuse destructors, and twenty offers were received. The merits of each offer were thoroughly gone into; four of them were selected as most suitable for the requirements of the town, and letters were sent to each of those chosen asking for further particulars with regard to the working, &c. Upon receipt of these particulars, and after further consideration by the council, it was decided not to accept any of the tenders, but to wait until a suitable piece of ground had been selected, so that each tenderer could go into the question on a sound basis. This conclusion was arrived at chiefly on account of the great difference in the estimation and cost of foundations, &c.

The usual printed conditions relating to cellar openings under footpaths had to be altered, in consequence of the owners of property making use of the cellar openings for purposes other than lighting and handing in of goods, so that this clause in the conditions now reads: "No openings will be allowed under a public footpath unless the whole of the outer wall running parallel with the street is built with a batten of one horizontal to three vertical, and no excavation under a footpath will be permitted of a greater aggregate length than one-half the frontage of the building. All plans for new buildings must in future show the correct level of the stand as well as the street level adjoining same, also full particulars of all columns, posts and girders or breastsummers, giving calculations of the different weights they are to carry." The paving of public footpaths is not done at the expense of the Stadsraad, but a fair amount of this work has been done by private owners of property. In the case of verandahs, balconies and other projections over a public footpath the paving is compulsory, as well as in cases of cellar openings under a footpath. Several kinds of paving have been laid in the town—viz., tar macadam, asphalte, granolithic, concrete, slate, tiles, &c. During 1897 about 5,300 lineal yards of granolithic paving was laid in public footpaths. In most cases the kerbing is of freestone, but as a trial this department has allowed some kerbing to be formed with a granolithic composition.

For five months, from 1st June to the end of October, Mr. Aburrow was absent on leave, during which time he visited a number of large towns in England, and also several towns in Germany, Holland and France, inspecting refuse destructors, different sewerage systems and sewage disposal works, road paving and construction, and the various tramway systems. He wishes to place on record his best thanks to the different engineers and representatives of the municipalities or companies who afforded him the above opportunities; and, in conclusion, he has also much pleasure in expressing his satisfaction with the manner in which his staff generally carried out their duties. He especially wishes to record his appreciation of the services of his chief assistant, Mr. Andrews, who acted very ably during his absence.

# Municipal Work at Brentford.

## THE NEW VESTRY HALL AND FIRE STATION.

In the Supplement we publish this week will be found a reproduction of a perspective drawing of the

NEW VESTRY HALL

which the Brentford Urban District Council propose to erect on the corner piece of land facing St. Paul's-road and the Half Acre. The designs have been prepared by Mr. Howell Parr, the surveyor to the council, and the hall, when erected, will undoubtedly prove an ornament to the district and a striking feature in the thoroughfare.

The accommodation provided in the building will be as follows: Basement plan—soup kitchen, 20 ft. by 30 ft., lift, heating-chamber, strong-room, stores, water-closets and lavatory, and necessary passages. Ground plan—large hall, 83 ft. by 35 ft. with platform, four retiring-rooms, offices, &c., and a separate entrance to platform, vestry-room, 32 ft. by 20 ft., collectors' office, overseers' office, staircase and corridors. First-floor plan—committee-room, 32 ft. by 20 ft., clerk's office, overseer's office, and two rooms for the caretaker. The upper portion of the hall has a balcony, two retiring-rooms, lavatory, &c.

In describing the external features of the building we should say that the main feature was the tower. This tower is a stately structure, well proportioned and elegant in its simplicity. It rises square for two storeys, with window openings to the collector's-room on the ground floor and the clerk's office on the first floor, with the Middlesex arms modelled above. From the second storey it breaks on to an octagon, the corners or spandrils being filled in with ornamental scrolls and projecting angle pilasters. The octagon contains eight small openings and is roofed with a small lead-covered dome, terminated with a suitable circular spirelet.

The elevation to Half Acre is set back from the present line of frontage a distance of 15 ft. on the south corner and 10 ft. at the principal entrance. This entrance has a semicircular arch with projecting voussoirs and keystone, with modelled spandrils and filled in with ornamental wrought-iron gates. There are double pilasters, at the sides with cornices and large fascia and with a panel inscribed "Vestry Hall." Above is a window, with pilasters and circular pediment in character with the design. The principal part of this elevation slightly projects from the other part of the building, and has octagonal corner ornaments from the plinth to the terminal. The centre portion has a massive semi-circular arch window to the lower storey, with projecting voussoirs and keystone, &c., in character with the principal entrance; surmounting this is a deep-moulded string and modelled panelling, with three segmental gauged arch windows to the upper storey; above this is an ornamental gable with the Middlesex arms modelled between two coffin-shaped pilasters, the whole surmounted by circular pediment with bossed terminal.

The elevation to the St. Paul's-road, again, is extremely simple yet most effective. At the side of the corner tower is the side entrance to the main corridor, with three-stepped staircase, windows and ornamental parapet above. The end elevation to the large hall faces the St. Paul's-road, and is treated in a suitable manner to harmonise with the rest of the design. The main feature is an ornamental gable with projecting octagonal features on the angles. The centre has a long, large window, with a semi-circular head as before, with a very effective deep-moulded string with scrolls—the gable, as with the others, is surmounted with a circular pediment and terminal.

The material proposed to be used in the construction of the edifice is best pressed red bricks, with red Mansfield stone or dark terra-cotta dressings. The estimated cost of the building is £7,000.

In the supplement will also be found a reproduction of a photo of another welcome addition to the public buildings of Brentford.

THE NEW FIRE STATION.

This building was opened on the 22nd February by Mr. J. Dorey, J.P., chairman of the district council, who was duly presented with a silver key by Mr. Nowell Parr, the surveyor to the council and architect of the building. The occasion was marked by much ceremony, a procession, comprising representatives from all the neighbouring fire services (each contingent being accompanied with the fire engine from their district), being the chief feature of the day's function. Of course the usual banquet took place in the evening to celebrate the opening of the station.

Most of our readers would be interested with a description of the building, so we publish the following official description: The front elevation is surmounted by two gables filled in with ornamental Patra bricks, and separated from the middle storey by moulded string courses. This middle storey composes three windows, lighting the firemen's recreation-room, which have deep moulded reveals and semi-circular arches, with projecting voussoirs and four label mouldings. These openings are filled in with moulded wooden frames, following the arch lines, and glazed with ornamental ob-

soured glass, two of the windows have octagonal oriels with ornamental wrought-iron railings, the tail of the oriels terminating in the keystone of the large arches spanning the opening to the engine-house. These arches have likewise projecting voussoirs and label mouldings. The sides of these openings have moulded projecting pilasters with caps and bases; a moulded plinth runs round the entire building. These openings are filled in with patent doors hung fourfold, fitted with Messrs. Shand, Mason & Co.'s quick opening and closing gear. On the east side is provided a large drill yard, with an escape projection and hose tower. The material employed in facing is red pressed bricks and red terra-cotta, the latter supplied by Messrs. Doulton & Co., of Lambeth. The accommodation provided is as follows: Large engine-room, 31 ft. by 25 ft.; workshop, cellar, watch-room; firemen's recreation-room, 31 ft. by 18 ft.; officers'-room and store-room, &c. Caretaker's apartments consist of living-room, kitchen, and two bed-rooms, &c. The fire-alarms, fire-ball and other electrical apparatus have been fitted by Messrs. Stuart & Moore, of Ealing.

On the occasion of the opening of the fire station a local paper published the following remarks about Mr. Nowell Parr, the town surveyor: "To enlarge upon the qualifications of Mr. Parr for the task he has so successfully undertaken is unnecessary. Mr. Parr's professional abilities have been long adequately recognised in Brentford. In accomplishing the material realisation of his ideas of the necessities of the town for a new fire station Mr. Parr has added yet another laurel to the wreath of public approval which he had already acquired by the skilful works designed and carried out in the course of his duties in Brentford and elsewhere. Mr. Parr's connection with the town began when he had achieved professional distinction, and his career in Brentford has fully justified the judicious selection of the council in making him the man of their choice. The handsome public baths, the new mortuary, and the less striking, but not less useful, series of works in connection with the drainage of the town form a fitting prelude to his latest architectural achievement—the new fire station—which we trust will by no means be the last service he is to render to the town."

---

## PLYMOUTH WATERWORKS.

### THE BURRATOR RESERVOIR.

On the 21st inst. the Corporation of Plymouth celebrate their annual "Fyshynge Feaste" and the completion of the Burrator reservoir. This reservoir has been constructed by the corporation. Its main embankment is the third largest stone dam in the country, and is the only one constructed of granite. The engineers for the scheme are Mr. James Mansergh, engineer, of Victoria-street, and Mr. Edward Sandeman, of Plymouth. The waterworks of the Plymouth Corporation are believed to be the oldest waterworks established by a municipality which have been continuously in the ownership and under the control of the municipality since their inception. London, as a municipality, commenced the construction of waterworks before Plymouth, but London has parted with its waterworks undertakings as a municipality, and is now supplied entirely by companies. The Plymouth waterworks have the further additional interest in that they were constructed by Sir Francis Drake, the great navigator, under powers obtained in the reign of Queen Elizabeth, the Act of Parliament showing on its face that they were designed at that day not merely for a local but also for an imperial purpose—viz., "the deepening of the Plymouth harbour, supplying her Majesty's ships of war, and also for the purpose of extinguishing fires in the town occasioned by the assaults of foreign Powers." The Fyshynge Feaste is an ancient ceremony, which has been continuously observed for upwards of three centuries, and the only two toasts then drunk, and these being drunk in silence, are: (1) "To the pious memory of Sir Francis Drake" (this is drunk in water taken from the works); and (2) "May the descendants of him who brought us water never want wine." On this occasion, in celebration of the construction of the great dam, there will be, in addition to the usual Fyshynge Feaste, a banquet in the Guildhall after the event, to which most of the notables in Devon and the adjoining county will be invited. The last stone of the dam will be laid on the 21st inst.

---

**Peterborough.**—The new electric light works for the town have been started, so far as the foundations are concerned, on a site in the Albert-place Meadow, adjoining both the river Nene and the Great Northern Railway. At present, however, the full plans for the superstructure, by Mr. J. C. Gill, the borough electrical engineer, are not quite completed. The scheme, nevertheless, having been generally approved by the Local Government Board, it only remains for the engineer's plans to be passed by the corporation and the construction thrown open to competition by tender.

# Law Notes.

### Edited by J. B. REIGNIER CONDER, 11 Old Jewry Chambers, E.C.,
#### Solicitor of the Supreme Court.

*The Editor will be pleased to answer any questions affecting the practice of engineers and surveyors to local authorities. Queries (which should be written legibly on foolscap paper, one side only) should be addressed to "The Law Editor," at the Offices of The*

*Surveyor. Where possible, copies of local Acts or documents referred to should be enclosed. All explanatory diagrams must be drawn and lettered in black ink only. Correspondents who do not wish their names published should furnish a nom de plume.*

## QUERIES AND REPLIES.

COMBINED DRAIN.—" Rflong " writes: A is an unoccupied house, and the water-closet from B is connected to drain A B, passing through hall of B. B was lately sold, and is to be pulled down shortly. The sanitary state of A has been condemned. Can the sanitary authority insist on the owner of A making a new piped drain to connect from his water-closet

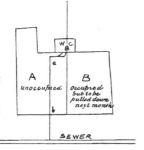

into street sewer, the house being unoccupied and for sale; and can the owner of A prevent the sewage from B's water-closet passing through his (A's) drain. A and B were lately the property of the same owner.

As the drain is made for the drainage of two houses it is a " sewer " vested in the authority, subject to the qualification effected by sec. 19 of the Public Health Acts (Amendment) Act, 1890, if part iii. of that Act has been adopted in the district. That section, however, has been held not to relieve local authorities of their general liability to repair combined drains, the powers thereby conferred being only applicable where there is an actual nuisance (*Travis v. Mayor of Hastings*, TAX SURVEYOR, vol. xi., p. 267). Apparently there is an actual nuisance in this case, but it is not stated whether part iii. of the Act has been adopted, nor when the houses ceased to be the property of the same owner. Assuming either that part iii. of the Act has not been adopted or (if it has been adopted) that the houses belonged to the same owner at the passing of the Act, the authority cannot, in my opinion, compel the owner of A to make a new drain, nor can A prevent sewage from B passing through the drain. It has never been decided whether the section applies where two houses belonged to the same owner at the time of the passing of the Act and the ownership has since been severed. But in a case under the Metropolis Management Acts it was held that when a drain which originally drained two houses was disconnected from one of them, it nevertheless remained a sewer, on the principle once a sewer always a sewer " (*Verity of St. Leonard, Shoreditch, v. Paclen*, TAX SURVEYOR, vol. xi., p. 266). On the same principle it would seem, that if two houses belonged to the same owner at the passing of the Act of 1890, the " sewer " would not cease to be such on the severance of the ownership.

DRINKING TROUGHS IN STREETS.—" Dacio " writes: In the urban district of X there are placed on the sides of some of the principal streets opposite public-houses drinking troughs for horses. These troughs are placed by, and are the property of, and maintained by, owners of these houses, the idea being an attraction for custom to house. The water from these troughs either leaks from or runs over on to the highway and causes a continual stream, being a nuisance to foot passengers and damage to highway. Can the urban district council demand the removal of these troughs or what steps can they take?

This is rather a difficult question. Under sec. 72 of the Highway Act, 1835, penalties are imposed on any person wilfully destroying or injuring the surface of any highway, or suffering any filth or other offensive matter to flow thereon. But it has been held that rain dripping from a railway bridge are not within this section, and it is doubtful whether it is applicable to the case stated in the query. Anything, however, which obstructs the passage of a highway or renders it less commodious is an indictable offence at common law, and the offender is liable to fine or imprisonment, or both, and the nuisance, if continuing, is to be abated. The owners of these troughs might therefore, it is presumed, be indicted for the nuisance caused by the overflow of the water. As regards the removal of the troughs, however, the question would arise whether they were erected before or after the dedication of the highway. In the former case it would seem that they could not be removed.

BREAKING-UP STREETS: HOARDINGS.—Mr. Frederick J. Raynor, town surveyor, Newhaven, writes: (1) What powers have any council to make builders and others pay a deposit before opening up a road for drainage, &c., such sum to be

repaid when road is made up to the satisfaction of the surveyor? (2) What powers have any council to make a like charge for hoardings, &c., on footpaths, or charge a fee, not to be returned, while the hoardings and scaffoldings, &c., are on the footways?

There appears to be no express powers for either of these purposes in any of the Public Health Acts, but such powers are frequently inserted in local Improvement Acts. As regards (1), sec. 149 of the Public Health Act, 1875, prohibits the breaking-up of streets without the consent of the urban authority, but it is doubtful whether this section applies to opening the road for drainage or other legitimate purpose, the words used being " wilfully displaces or takes up or . . . injures." Assuming, however, that it does so apply, it is presumed that the authority could legally make their consent conditional upon the payment of a deposit. At all events I believe in practice this is very frequently done. As regards (2), the hoarding has to be erected to the satisfaction of the authority (see Towns Improvement Clauses Act, 1847, sec. 80, and Public Health Acts Amendment Act, 1890, sec. 34). This would seem to give the authority power indirectly to require a fee, as in the case of a person who objected to pay a fee they would probably not expedite matters very much, and their " satisfaction " would not be very readily obtained.

BY-LAWS: NEW STREET.—" Surveyor " writes: V shows a piece of vacant land abutting upon three back streets, 15 ft. wide, but these back streets have been dedicated to the public. Our by-laws state every person who shall lay out a new street shall be intended for use as otherwise shall as a carriage road and shall not exceed in length 100 ft. and so lay out such street that the width thereof shall be 24 ft. at

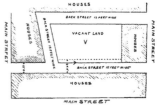

least. Question. As these streets were laid out before the local board was formed, but paved and dedicated after the formation of the local board, can houses be built on the vacant land to come to the line of the back street marked A, or must they be set back 24 ft. according to the by-law?

It will be a question of fact for the magistrate to decide, when building commences, whether " new streets " are being formed; and, if there is any evidence to justify them in finding such to be the case, the High Court will not inquire into its sufficiency. (*Reg. v. Staff, 50 L.T. [N.S.], 590*). Inasmuch as there are already houses on one side of each street (and as in two of them on both sides), I think it is very doubtful whether the building of houses on the vacant land would be held to be the laying-out of a new street.

## BIRKENHEAD ELECTRICAL EXTENSIONS.

Mr. William Bates, the electrical engineer to the Birkenhead Corporation, recently drew attention to the lack of reserve power at the central electrical generating station, and was requested by the Electrical Committee to prepare a report on the plant therein and as to further extensions which may be necessary. In the report since presented he suggests that tenders for the supply and erection of a further 150-unit steam dynamo should be asked for at the earliest possible date. As to the proposed extension, provision is made to meet all demands for the next two years, at a cost of £13,343. A list of thirty-two streets is given for the laying of distributing mains, and it is recommended that provision should be made for service cables, &c., for 150 fresh consumers. The borrowing powers of the corporation for electricity supply are £41,500. At present there is an excess over that authorised outlay on the cost of the existing works of £1,512 2s. 9d. In order to cover this excess and carry out the proposed extension, the committee have resolved to apply to the Local Government Board for power to borrow a sum of £15,000.

Thakeham.—Local Government Board sanction is reported to have been received to a loan of £600 for the construction of the Hardham Arches.

## THE ADMISSION OF DAYLIGHT TO BUILDINGS.

When daylight enters a room through ordinary glass, only a portion of it is available for the purpose of lighting up the room. This is, of course, due to refraction, and it is with this object of properly utilising this principle that the "Luxfer" prisms have been designed. They consist of plates of glass having the outer surface plain and the inner surface moulded into semi-prisms. The object kept consistently in view is that in passing through the prisms the natural light would be so refracted as to travel horizontally into the interior of a room, diffusing light to every part of it.

Fig. 1.—Prism Light.

To accomplish this under the varied conditions where windows open on a wide or a narrow street, facing low or lofty buildings, a variety of prisms are necessary, and success in getting desired results depends on the proper calculation of the degree of refraction needed and the proper installation of a prism having a corresponding refracting angle. This, of course, implies scientific treatment, and we understand that the necessary data were obtained only after a long series of careful and expensive experiments.

The practical utilisation of these prisms has been worked out in connection with a system of electro-glazing, the ordinary lead glazing not being considered strong enough to support prisms in a window where the action of the wind and weather would affect them. The prisms, after being ground to a templet, are laid in a frame with a small ribbon of

Fig. 2.—Prism for Sidewalk.

copper surrounding each prism. The whole sheet is immersed in an electric bath, and cemented together with a deposit of copper by a new patent electrolytic process. The object is to make a window strong and elastic, water and weather tight, and the whole construction durable, strong and neat, the metal network being so very small as to shut out a minimum amount of light. The completed frame of prism lights is commonly inserted in the transom frame or window sash in place of the sheet of plate-glass. Where the window frame is set under a deep reveal, or where the light from the sky is obstructed by very high buildings opposite the premises to be lighted, it may be necessary to set the

prism lights in an independent frame set flush with the building line or in an iron frame extending out over the window opening similar to a canopy.

To light a basement, the ceiling of which is on a level with the street, the light will, of course, be taken through the footway of the street. The prisms for this purpose must necessarily be extremely heavy, so that when fixed in iron frames or cement they will be capable of carrying any load that a footway can reasonably be expected to bear. The prisms are cut with reflecting angles on the pendant prisms, so that the light striking the surface of the footway is refracted into the basement. In lighting basements in which the light requires to be carried a considerable distance to reach the rear of the apartment, a curtain, consisting of prisms of various angles glazed together, is used, and this receives the light from the sidewalk prisms and refracts it in the proper direction so as to diffuse it throughout the basement. The first of our two illustrations represents a prism light for ordinary windows, or for fixing as outside canopies. The second illustration shows the prism light for footways in connection with the lighting of basements. In this country these prisms have been fixed among other places at St. George's Cathedral, Southwark, and the new Birkbeck Bank, while orders are in hand for a number of banks and private houses. Originating in America they had, of course, been used in a large number of places both in Canada and the United States. Having been fitted in the engine-room of the new municipal buildings at Toronto, the architect found them very satisfactory in diffusing light. The address of the company is the British Luxfer Prism Syndicate, Limited, 16 Hill-street, Finsbury, E.C., where an admirable show of prisms is on view.

## A MUNICIPAL FAMILY HOME AT GLASGOW.

### AN INTERESTING EXPERIMENT.

The proposal of the Glasgow Corporation to provide a good home and tender parental care for the widowed and fatherless was much laughed at when it was put forward; but the municipal philanthropists had their way, and the home has been open for over two years. The latest accounts of the Improvement Trust have just been issued, says a correspondent of The Pall Mall Gazette, and it is possible to estimate the value of the work which has been done. The home was built to accommodate widowers of the labouring class who had been left with young children, and widows similarly burdened; and the aim of the promoters was to protect the children and see them properly cared for rather than to help the adults. The home was built on part of a slum area which had been cleared, and provides 160 rooms, each of which is intended to accommodate one adult and three children. At present it is only a little more than half full, and under these circumstances it does not pay. The home is not open to all comers; applicants for rooms must submit to an official investigation of their character, and if they do not satisfy the committee that they are perfectly well-behaved persons they cannot enjoy the advantages of the system or obtain them for their children. The home therefore does not meet the worst cases of child neglect, and the least-fortunate children are denied the benefit of its care.

The home is well built, but it is too large, and its size adds to the difficulties in the way of good management. Each woman pays 3s. 6d. for her room, men pay 1s. more, and the rent is increased in ratio to the number of children. The children are fed and looked after at the rate of 1s. 10d. per week for one, and 4s. for three; and the adults are able to obtain good and substantial meals at low prices—2½d. for breakfast, 4d. for dinner, and 3d. for tea. The servants clean the men's rooms, and the women must look after their own; but while they are out at work their children are taken care of by the staff. Those of school age are sent to school; the infants are tended in the nursery, and those able to run about are provided for in recreation-rooms. The adults have a big dining-room, and a recreation and smoke room, where they may read the papers and play dominoes and draughts; and the home is heated throughout with steam pipes, is lighted by electricity, and is even provided with lifts. Its first cost was £13,000. In the last financial year the revenue was £1,607, including £737 for rent, £308 for the board of children, and £561 for food sold; the expenditure was £2,108, leaving a deficit of £501.

The amiable experiment is not intended as a charity, but last year the tenants did not repay the city for the advantages they received. The housing of the two sexes under one roof, though on separate floors, is productive of difficulties occasionally; and, though entertainments are provided for the tenants and they are are not allowed to take spirituous liquors into the home, some of them have had to be turned out for bad conduct. Moreover, the promoters made no allowances for sickness, and were rather perplexed when an outbreak of measles came to add to their troubles. In short, this illustration of municipal philanthropy is losing money, and it is questionable whether the benefits it offers to a very small number of citizens are adequate return for the outlay and the risks. Municipal Socialists can hardly be encouraged by the result to venture much further in this direction.

# Some Recent Publications.

A TEXT-BOOK ON MAGNETISM AND ELECTRICITY.

THE FIRST PRINCIPLES OF ELECTRICITY AND MAGNETISM, by Mr. C. H. W. Biggs, editor of *The Electrical Engineer* (London: Biggs & Co.), is a book which has aroused a good deal of opposition, and has been subjected to much criticism by those who follow the orthodox school of thought. It is somewhat difficult to deal with it quite fairly, because, while much that it contains is useful and valuable, Mr. Biggs so often goes out of his way to invite slashing criticism by the contentious matter so freely introduced. If one were to proceed on a basis of comparison with existing works, the book before us might suffer in a way it hardly deserves, and it is best to take it alone and by itself. When we bear in mind that there has been published a library of books that cover almost exactly the same ground, it will be evident that the reviewer is in rather a different position to the teacher or lecturer who may be asked by a student to recommend a work for study. In the former case we have a specific book before us, in the latter a suitable selection has to be made, bearing in mind the mental capacity of the student, his object in study, and the amount he is prepared to expend in literature. We have often been tempted to write at length on this latter question, for as lecturer and as practising engineer the present writer has had frequently to name a work for students' use. From this point of view there is much to be said in favour of Mr. Biggs' book. It is couched in simple language, indeed it is a reprint of a series of written lectures to elementary students which appeared in *The Electrical Engineer*, commencing in the issue for September 7, 1894, under the title of "City and Guilds of London Institute. Electric Lighting and Power Transmission. Preliminary Examination. Lecture I. (Specially contributed)."

We have here the key to the position ; the style, scope and intention of the book are readily understood from this. The preface states that "this book is intended for beginners in practical work," but the title is misleading, inasmuch as the City and Guilds examinations are technical and "Electricity and Magnetism" is a science subject under the Science and Art Departmental examinations. We see, therefore, that Mr. Biggs has revised and corrected, as well as extended, matter which was prepared for beginners in applied electrical science, intending to proceed to an examination in which success would come to those who had most carefully followed a published syllabus. If it be admitted that such a book—as that must be which is useful to the student with this intent—can be prepared and fairly reviewed, then we think that Mr. Biggs has succeeded. The preliminary grade student ought to face his paper without any qualms if he has read the book before us ; and having said this, we have little more to say. Few writers have set themselves the same limited task. To understand Mr. Biggs' position we cannot do better than turn to one of his earlier ventures—his "First Principles of Electrical Engineering." We read in the preface that he "did not know, nor much care, if there was a want to supply," although the formula of most writers is that their productions supply a want. His "Notes," to use a well-defined theological term, were the *circuits*—inductive, conductive and magnetic—and getting "rid of abstract mathematical jargon which seldom leads anywhere," putting in its place "physical conceptions which may be handled without much fear of getting off the track." The value of the book before us and of the one we have cited lies in the first of these two points —that the student who realises that all effects proceed from causes by action through a medium, and that such actions are cyclic, has got something worth having from a book, even if Philistines may cavil at the manner of expression and re. viewers of the orthodox school brand the author as unorthodox, or even heterodox. We must confess that the second point is inadequately met by Mr. Biggs in his latest work. Examples might be multiplied almost indefinitely, but we will take one which is of most importance. In dealing with resistance it is stated that "Prof. Ohm proved .... with

steady continuous currents not only that $C = \frac{E}{R}$, but that $C = \frac{E}{R}$,

and this connection between current pressure and resistance is known as Ohm's law." To find this corollary of Ohm's law given *as* Ohm's law is disappointing after all the work of the British Association Committee on Ohm's law and all Prof. Oliver J. Lodge has said on the subject. Ohm arrived on the scene at a time when physicists were unacquainted with the conception of "resistance" as a physical entity. Take friction. We know that air friction varies with velocity, being proportional to velocity for low values and increasing faster than proportionality would indicate with rising magnitudes for velocity. One cannot therefore write a *general law* in simple terms. What Ohm did was to prove and to define the general law that resistance was independent of the current in the conductor having such resistance. That is, that

$R = \frac{E}{C}$ and R is constant for all values of C, provided the

physical state of the conductor remain unchanged. Here is a "physical conception" which should have been made quite clear. Unfortunately, it is left wrapped up in a corollary which is not the general law Ohm so magnificently elaborated.

Immediately following this section is one on "Resistance or Capacity," suggesting the use of *capacity* as the reciprocal of resistance and attributing the term to Mr. Sprague. "If Mr. Sprague's suggestion ever takes root, the term 'conductivity' might be used instead of capacity." Lord Kelvin has done much to popularise the use of this conception of the reciprocal of resistance, but his term "mho" never found favour generally outside of Glasgow University and White's workshop. Suppose it did, one ought to talk of "resistance" and "conductance," leaving "resistivity" and "conductivity" for the specific values of R and $\frac{1}{R}$

Those of our readers who are anxious to begin the study of applied electricity and have time to work out numerical examples would find Mr. Biggs' book useful. General readers or students of electricity and magnetism have abundant choice of works better suited to their respective requirements.

SOME PERIODICALS.

The *Architectural Review* is making quite a feature of special supplement illustrations. In the September issue we observe, in the form of a tasteful photogravure plate, the second of a series of illustrations entitled "Coming-down London." The subject is Holywell-street, Strand, otherwise known to fame as "Booksellers'-row," to say nothing of a more questionable title to fame, or rather notoriety. This thoroughfare is certainly one of the most familiar landmarks in London, but there is no question, from the point of view of street improvements, of the expediency and necessity of the removal of the block of buildings which form its southern side. These photogravure plates are exceedingly pleasing to the eye. There is also a double supplement plate representing Stowell Park, designed by John Belcher for the Earl of Eldon. The work of this architect is the subject of an appreciative article by Charles G. Harper, and Esther Wood writes on "The Work of Edgar Wilson." Those interested in architecture, either professionally or otherwise, cannot fail to find both letterpress and illustrations to their taste, so we need not refer specially to the other contents, which certainly show no falling away either in variety or in merit.—In *The Engineering Magazine* for September it is not surprising to find at least two articles on naval subjects by well-known authorities. After recent events such contributions will be plentiful for time to come. The number, however, has more than one article which might be attentively read by municipal engineers. We naturally mention first that entitled "Bacterial Processes of Sewage Purification," by the well - known American civil engineer, Mr. Rudolph Hering, but we shall refer to this separately in our next issue. Among the other contents are the following articles: "European and American Bridge Construction," reviewing the extension of modern methods and materials to wide spans; "The Comparative Cost of Steam and Water Power;" "The Underground Railways of London," an account of the development of rapid transit in the metropolis; and "The Application of Alternating Currents to Electric Traction," a comparison of local power stations with distant natural sources. There is the usual engineering index in addition to the review of the engineering press.—With these exceptions all the articles in *Cassier's Magazine* for September relate to naval subjects. Of the three exceptions one article deals with diamond-mining in South Africa, another with the cyanide process of treating gold ores, and the third is entitled "General Distribution from Electric Central Stations by Alternating Currents," and constitutes a review of alternating current applications.— The *American Monthly Review of Reviews* is naturally this month, as for some time past, largely monopolised by the Spanish-American war. In normal times our contemporary has always shown a deep interest in matters municipal, as might be expected in a periodical edited by Dr. Albert Shaw. No doubt we shall now, "when the war is o'er," see a return to this commendable policy.—That genuine sportsman and accomplished writer, Sir Herbert Maxwell, is the subject of the portrait and biographical sketch in this month's *Baily*. Articles on chargers, the revised laws of billiards, cricket centuries, public school cricket and other subjects will suit the tastes of the many readers of our green-covered contemporary. In connection with the article on chargers there is a tasteful portrait of Lord Roberts on his Arab charger. The serial by Major Arthur Griffiths is continued. —From Cassell & Co., Limited, we have received *Work* and *Chums*. In the former we observe useful information on artistic ironwork, dynamo and electric motor design, processes for determining the hardness of water, and other matters.—*Knowledge* is almost exclusively occupied with natural history, astronomy and botany. There is a pleasant literary flavour about the article on "The Astronomy of the 'Canterbury Tales.'"—We have also to acknowledge the *Quarry, The Indian Engineer* and *The Analyst*.

**Oban.**—The new municipal buildings in Oban are to be formally opened next week by Lord Strathcona and Mount Royal. The function will include a luncheon, to which a number of local notabilities will be invited.

# Municipal Work in Progress and Projected.

The paragraphs relating to Berwick, Bolton, Nelson, Cardiff, Salford, Guiseley, Redditch, Ashford, Bridgend and Ilford comprise the chief news that has come to hand this week relative to the progress of municipal works in the provinces. It will be observed that one or two of the vestries have resumed their deliberations.

## METROPOLITAN AUTHORITIES.

### VESTRIES AND DISTRICT BOARDS.

**Rotherhithe.**—The vestry, at a meeting on Tuesday, discussed a resolution passed by the Battersea Vestry in favour of metropolitan vestries and district boards having the power of erecting dwellings for the working classes, and asking the London County Council to insert a clause giving this power in their next General Powers Bill. Mr. Beasley said it was agreed at the Bermondsey conference that it was necessary in some cases and advisable in all that local authorities should possess this power, and he moved that the vestry concur with the Battersea resolution. Mr. Brown seconded. Mr. Mortimer moved as an amendment that no action should be taken, and said it was very undesirable that local authorities should saddle themselves with the enormous expenditure which the erection of workmen's dwelling would involve. This was a matter for the London County Council. Mr. Moss seconded the amendment, which was agreed to.—At the next meeting of the vestry Mr. R. L. Stuart will move that application be made to the Local Government Board for the transfer to the vestry of the powers, duties and liabilities of the Commissioners for Baths and Wash-houses and the Commissioners for Public Libraries.

**St. George-the-Martyr.**—At the meeting of the vestry on Tuesday, a letter was read from the Chief Commissioner of Police stating that the whole of the metropolitan vestries and local authorities were being approached with a view of obtaining their co-operation to lessen the present congested state of the traffic in the streets of the metropolis. The owners of the omnibuses and the great carrying companies were desirous of facilitating this object, and wished their vehicles to keep as nearly as possible to the near-side; but they pointed out that, owing to the watering of the roads, horses driven at the sides were liable to slip. It had been suggested that to get over this difficulty the streets might be cleaned and watered at night, and the opinions of the vestries were asked as to this. It was hoped that all the arrangements would be made, and the experiments as to the value of the various methods to lessen the congestion of the traffic tried before the commencement of the next London season. The matter was referred to a committee to report.

**St. Pancras.**—The vestry on Wednesday voted £1,000 towards the purchase of the Golder's Hill estate as an addition to Hampstead Heath. It is stated that between £2,000 and £3,000 has yet to be raised.

## PROVINCIAL AND GREATER LONDON AUTHORITIES.

### COUNTY COUNCILS.

**Montgomeryshire.**—The county council have decided to carry out certain alterations at the police stations at Welshpool, Montgomery and Llanfyllin.

### MUNICIPAL CORPORATIONS.

**Barnsley.**—The Local Government Board have sanctioned the borrowing by the town council of £950 towards the cost of repairing Sheffield-road between the Griffin Inn and Beechfield.

**Barrow.**—A letter has been received from the Local Government Board in reference to the council's application for sanction to borrow £5,000 for purposes of sewage disposal at Syston. The board are of opinion that a storage tank should be provided at the pumping station for the night flow of sewage, instead of pumping it both day and night, as proposed; further, that an additional filter should be provided, so as to bring the rate of filtration to a maximum of 300 gallons per square yard.

**Berwick.**—On the 30th ult. an inspector of the Local Government Board held an inquiry into the application of the town council for sanction to borrow £8,000 for the erection of a stable and lock-up.

**Bishop's Castle.**—An inspector of the Local Government Board last week held an inquiry respecting an application of the corporation for sanction to a loan of £1,600 for lining a reservoir at Mees Gwyn, in Shropshire, as it had developed such numerous leaks as to become useless. Mr. E. S. Cobbold, consulting engineer to the corporation, stated that it was proposed to line the reservoir with a layer of cement concrete 6 in. thick, with a core of Callender's pure bitumen sheeting. He considered it hopeless, in such fissured strata, to expect a watertight reservoir unless it was lined throughout, and after careful consideration he had decided to adopt concrete, with a bitumen core, as being the most simple, economical and efficient method of carrying out the work. There was no opposition to the application.

**Bolton.**—A discussion took place at Wednesday's meeting of the town council in reference to the purchase of land by the Electricity Committee for the extension of the works in Spa-road. The extension has been rendered necessary in view of the proposal to run the trams by electricity, and for the purpose of laying down the necessary plant to supply the areas recently added to the borough, borrowing powers for this purpose having been acquired to the extent of £250,000.—The council sanctioned a proposal by the Sanitary Committee to borrow £20,000 for the purpose of removing insanitary and obstructive dwellings.

**Bradford.**—The mayor of Bradford recently formally opened the new line of electric tramways at Great Horton, and at a luncheon, held subsequently at the town hall, Mr. C. R. Rindley proposed the health of the city surveyor (Mr. J. H. Cox), the city electrical engineer (Mr. Gibbins), the deputy surveyor (Mr. Dawson), and the deputy electrical engineer (Mr. Dalton).

**Brighton.**—At a further outlay of nearly £100,000, the corporation have recently acquired and developed the waterworks at Aldrington and Shoreham, and Brighton now not only supplies water to the 30,000 inhabitants of the sister town of Hove, but at a reduced rate to an extended district stretching along the coast for about 12 miles from Shoreham to Rottingdean. The results of last year's working, published in an agenda of the town council, show nett profits to the amount of over £8,500, almost all of which is to be allotted to the relief of the rates. The sum transferred is equivalent to a rate of fully 3d. in the £1.

**Bury.**—The monthly meeting of the town council was held on Thursday. On the Health Committee's minutes another discussion took place on the abattoir question. The Abattoirs Sub-Committee reported an interview with the representatives of the Bury Co-operative Society, who are constructing an abattoir of their own, for the purpose of trying to arrange some method of avoiding the threatened difficulty, but no arrangement was come to. The Co-operative Society had subsequently resolved, at a crowded meeting of members, to proceed with their own abattoir, and had formally applied to the Health Committee for a licence. This the Health Committee had refused to grant, in face of the fact that the corporation themselves intended erecting public abattoirs in which all the slaughtering of animals must be done. It was at this stage that the council considered the matter on Thursday, and although an amendment was proposed that the question of the license be referred back, the amendment was lost, the minutes being carried by twenty-one votes to seven.

**Cardiff.**—Mr. H. Percy Boulnois held an inquiry at the town hall, Cardiff, on Saturday morning, on behalf of the Local Government Board, regarding an application made by the town council for the loan of £34,200 for the purpose of paving Bate-terrace, Adam-street and part of the Penarth-road with hard wood, and also a number of streets, crossings, and the re-laying of footways of certain streets. Evidence in support of the application was given by the mayor and the deputy borough engineer. There was no objection, and Mr. Boulnois stated that he would report the matter in due course, after which the town clerk would receive a communication.

**Colchester.**—The work of laying the cables for the electric light at Colchester by the contractors (Messrs. Siemens Brothers, of London) is proceeding apace, and already over half of the area proposed to be lighted has been attended to. It is anticipated that the work will be completed by the 29th inst., when the laying of the cables connecting the business establishments and houses requiring the light with the mains will be commenced. It is stated that up to the present there have been numerous applications for the light, every day seeing a fresh batch of orders.

**Crewe.**—The borough surveyor on Wednesday reported that on the 3rd August, on account of a heavy rainfall, the sewers became overcharged, causing damage to both outfalls and flooding the banks of the Valley and Leighton brooks. The lake in the Queen's Park became full of storm water mixed with the contents of the sewer, and there was a thick yellow scum on the surface, destructive of all vegetable substances coming in contact with it.

**Deal.**—At a recent meeting of the town council the town clerk stated that the Board of Trade had given the corporation permission to proceed with the sea defence works at North Deal. The town clerk added that he had written an urgent letter to the Board of Trade, in which he stated that the council could not allow the north part of Deal to be washed away, and that they proposed to proceed with the work on Monday. A Board of Trade inquiry with reference to the proposed works was to have been held this week.

**Eccles.**—Some discussion arose on Monday respecting the desirability of adopting a resolution of the General Purposes Committee wherein the opinion was expressed that it is inexpedient at present to carry out the scheme of improvement of the area bounded by Church-street, Barton-street and

St. James-street. The minutes were at length approved by eleven votes to nine.

**Halifax.**—On Wednesday, at the usual meeting of the town council, the Waterworks Committee presented a minute proposing that after the close of the present municipal year one water-closet and one bath in dwelling-houses should be supplied free of charge; also that no charge should be made for service pipes for the supply of water to dwelling-houses, and that water for warming apparatus in churches and chapels should be supplied free of charge.

**Keighley.**—At last week's meeting of the town council the Gasworks Committee reported that they had requested the town clerk to give the necessary one month's notice for a special meeting of the council, to be held on the 27th inst., to consider and determine upon the expediency of an application to the Board of Trade on or before the 21st December next for a provisional order authorising the council to put down an installation and supply electricity for public and private purposes within the borough; they further asked the council to authorise them (if such application is determined upon) to take such steps and call in such advice as they may deem necessary in connection with the obtaining of such order. The necessary powers were given.

**Littlehampton.**—Application will shortly be made to the Local Government Board for sanction to a loan of £1,250 for works of auxiliary water supply.

**Liverpool.**—At a recent meeting of the Finance Committee of the corporation a report from the city surveyor as to the condition of the roof of the large ball-room at the town hall was approved, and it was decided, if necessary, to have the roof and ceiling reconstructed, at a cost not exceeding £3,000. It is understood that a serious development of dry rot was discovered in the roof, though, unfortunately, this was not ascertained until the work of redecorating the present ceiling was well in hand. The extra outlay is in addition to the £8,000 already voted for certain alterations and redecorating of the town hall. It was hoped that the work originally sanctioned would be completed at the beginning of September, but the reconstruction of the ball-room ceiling will keep the place in the hands of the workmen for some two or three months longer.

**Manchester.**—At a meeting of the Rivers Committee of the Manchester Corporation, on Monday, a letter was read from Mr. F. J. Willis, the secretary of the Royal Commission on Sewage Disposal, who desired to know whether the committee would permit some members of the commission to visit the Davyhulme works on the 4th of October next. The request was at once acceded to. So far as could be gathered, it does not appear that the members of the commission will hold anything in the nature of a formal inquiry. They only desire to see for themselves what method the Manchester Corporation have adopted in the treatment of their sewage.

**Nelson.**—On Wednesday of last week a Local Government Board inquiry was held by Major-General Crozier into the application of the town council for sanction to a loan of £40,000 for the extension of the gasworks and gas mains and £20,000 for the purpose of private street improvements. The inspector, accompanied by the borough surveyor, afterwards visited the gasworks, the sewage disposal works, and the streets included in the application.

**Ramsgate.**—The corporation have decided to widen the Elms in accordance with the plans and specifications prepared by the borough surveyor, at an estimated cost of £430.

**Rawtenstall.**—A local newspaper states that at a recent meeting of the General Purposes Committee of the town council it was decided to promote a Bill in Parliament to empower them to provide a new water supply for the borough.

**Salford.**—The Local Government Board have given their sanction to the borrowing of £33,000 by the Salford Corporation for electric lighting purposes. Of the sum named £23,000 is for the establishment of three battery sub-stations and £10,000 for the land for new generating stations. The board have also signified their approval of the use of the basement of the Pendleton town hall and the subways around the women's second-class baths at Broughton for the purposes of the Salford Electric Lighting Order, 1890.

**Southsea.**—Some time ago complaint was made by Government authorities that the electric light cables interfered with the working of the service of the telephone in the neighbourhood, and it was apprehended that considerable alterations would have to be made in the system of lighting. It has transpired, however, after a long delay, that a Government expert has reported that the fault rests with the telephone and not with the electric light apparatus.

**Torquay.**—At last week's meeting of the town council the Harbour Committee submitted a couple of recommendations respecting the repair of the Haldon pier, which they requested to be allowed to carry out, in consequence of the excessive amount of the tenders. The recommendations were then adopted, and the Harbour Committee afterwards met to arrange for the work being undertaken forthwith.

**Warrington.**—Tuesday's minutes of the Rivers Committee stated that the borough surveyor had been instructed to report upon the condition of the channel in the Mersey, which

the Manchester Ship Canal Company were required to dredge and to keep dredged. A member pointed out that this had been done in consequence of complaints that the dredging of the river was not being maintained as it ought to be. The committee wished to have these complaints verified by the borough surveyor before moving in the matter.

## URBAN DISTRICT COUNCILS.

**Altrincham.**—In reference to a complaint of the Mersey and Irwell Joint Committee as to the unsatisfactory quality of the effluent from the sewage farm at Sinderland, it was on Tuesday stated that the escape of sewage into the effluent pipes had arisen through some pipes giving way in the land recently levelled and drained, and the clerk was instructed to write the Joint Committee accordingly.

**Ashford.**—An inquiry was recently held by an inspector of the Local Government Board concerning an application of the council for sanction to borrow a sum of £14,000 for the purposes of alterations, extensions and improvements at the gasworks. The present works, it was stated, were hardly large enough for the size of the town. The maximum output was 220,000 cubic feet of gas a day, which was only equal to the consumption at the present time. The consumers last winter complained that the pressure was not high enough. The new works would comprise a new retort-house, forty-eight new retorts with regenerative furnaces, and a telescopic gas-holder capable of storing 140,000 cubic feet of gas. The works, if these alterations and extensions were carried out, could then produce 330,000 cubic feet a day. An application to borrow £2,785 for the purchase of a recreation ground was also made the subject of inquiry. Mr. W. Terrill, the surveyor to the council, gave evidence respecting the position of the land.

**Balby.**—The district council have instructed their surveyor to prepare plans as soon as possible for the improvement of Queen-street, Carr-hill and St. John's-road.

**Bridgend.**—The inquiry, instituted by the Local Government Board into the application of the Penybont Main Sewerage Board for leave to borrow £30,000 for the purpose of carrying out a drainage scheme for Bridgend and the surrounding district, was held at the town hall, Bridgend, on Thursday, the inspector being Mr. H. Percy Boulnois. The scheme, it was stated, provided for the outfall sewer to be 1,400 yards below low water-mark. At a certain point the line of pipes went into the parish of Coity Lower, which was not to be drained by this scheme. Precautions had been taken at various points in the pipes to intercept rags, &c. Allowance had been made for an increase of the population of the district in thirty years of 12,000. The only store water which would get into the sewers would be rain water and slop water. About 915,000 gallons of sewage per day would pass through the pipes.

**Brierley Hill.**—The district council have under consideration the desirability of carrying out deep drainage works, embracing the construction of 7 miles of mains, outfall works, &c. If they join with other outlying districts it is estimated that the works will take several years to complete.—The council on Monday decided to erect a fire station, stores, stables, &c., including a caretaker's house, at a cost of £600. The site of the proposed buildings is being purchased at the rate of 9s. 1½d. per yard.

**Denton.**—A letter was, on Monday, read from the Board of Trade, stating that they had extended the time for the completion of the Oldham, Ashton and Hyde electric tramways to the 12th February, 1899, and that the company had made out a case for a single "decker" car. It was resolved, that, whilst having no further observation to offer on the subject, the committee were of opinion that cars with outside seats were best adapted for the requirements of the district, and the clerk was instructed to ask the Hyde Corporation, the Ashton Corporation and the Audenshaw District Council what action they were taking.

**Epping.**—A Local Government Board inquiry was held on Wednesday of last week respecting an application of the town council for sanction to borrow a sum of £6,000 for the execution of certain works of sewerage and sewage disposal.

**Guiseley.**—On Wednesday of last week a deputation from the Yeadon Urban District Council asked to be allowed to have the New Scarborough sewage connected with the Guiseley disposal works forthwith. The council said they could not accede to the request without the sanction of the Local Government Board, but promised to push the matter forward. Mr. Johnson (Messrs. Preston & Johnson) submitted plans of proposed alterations and additions to the disposal works, also of several new sewers in different parts of Guiseley. The cost, including land, he estimated at £5,230, and he advised the council to ask for borrowing powers for £5,500. This was agreed to.

**Ilford.**—On Tuesday of last week Colonel Coke, an inspector of the Local Government Board, held an inquiry into the application of the council for permission to borrow £16,000 for a public park and recreation ground, £750 for the purchase of a steam roller and stone-crushing machine, and £500 for the fixing of hydrants. The proceedings were of a formal character.

**Newmarket.**—A letter was, last week, read from the Board of Trade with reference to the proposed laying down of an electric light installation. A letter was also received from an electric lighting company giving notice of their intention to lay mains for the distribution of energy in several thoroughfares.

**Portishead.**—There was last week presented to the council a report on the Portishead sewerage works, stating that during the past month most satisfactory progress had been made. Owing to unfavourable weather the outfall was not finished, although some additional work had been done. It was hoped that the outfall would be finished in a few days. The water and gas pipes had been laid to the engine - house. The machinery had been erected and put in working order, and it was expected that the whole of the machinery would be shortly finished. The whole of the compressed-air pipes, valves and other fittings had been subjected to the prescribed test for leakage, and a few small leaks were discovered, but a second test showed that the leaks were insignificant.

**Redditch.**—On Wednesday of last week Mr. R. H. Bicknell, Local Government Board inspector, held an inquiry at the district council offices into the proposal of the council to borrow £14,200 for the purposes of the recently-adopted electric lighting scheme and other public improvements, including £11,000 for electric lighting, £700 for street improvements, and £2,500 for purchasing land for electric lighting works and other purposes.

**Shipley.**—The council have decided, upon the recommendation of the Electric Lighting Committee, to accept the tender of Messrs. Cole, Marchant & Morley, of Bradford, for the supply of a 45 horse-power engine, dynamo, motor and pumps for £1,225 10s., for the pumping station at the sewage works. A special meeting of the council is to be held on October 4th, to consider the question of electric lighting for the district, with the view of applying for a provisional order.

## RURAL DISTRICT COUNCILS.

**Belper.**—It is reported that the council have issued a circular suggesting a conference of representatives from all the councils in Derbyshire, with a view to the formation of a Derbyshire District Councils' Association, to confer with some or all the authorities which may promote Bills for obtaining water from the Peak district of Derbyshire in the ensuing or subsequent sessions of Parliament.

**Chard.**—A committee has been instructed by the district council to visit the Sutton sewage works, with the view of acquiring information concerning the septic tank system of sewage treatment.

**Darlington.**—On Monday, at a meeting of this authority, the Hurworth Parish Council complained of the pollution of the Tees at Croft by the Corporation of Darlington fouling the Skerne, which emptied into the Tees, by sewage. It was decided to ask the county council to take action.—The surveyor reported the finding of a water supply at Aycliffe.

**East Ashford.**—It was recently reported that the engineer's estimate for the provision of a constant house-to-house water supply at Willesborough and for the drainage of the parish amounted to £16,800, this estimate being based on a supply of water for a population of 10,000 persons. It was further reported that the engineer had been requested to modify his figures on a calculation for a population of 5,000, and that the parish council were considering the advisability of a private company being formed to provide a supply of water. The Ashford Urban District Council had been asked if they could supply water to the houses on the freehold estate and at South Willesborough. The reply to the latter request was to the effect that at Ashford there was barely sufficient water for the requirements of the town at present.

**Great Ouseburn, Yorks.**—The council have instructed Messrs. Fairbank & Son, of York and Westminster, to prepare a scheme of sewerage and sewage disposal for Aldborough and Boroughbridge in their union. They have also instructed the same engineers to inspect the sewerage and sewage disposal works of Acomb, York, and to report on the best method of disposing of the sewage of that place.

**Hollingborne.**—Mr. W. O. E. Meade-King, Local Government Board inspector, held an inquiry at the public hall, Sutton Valence, with reference to the application of the rural district council for power to borrow £500 for the purpose of extending the Sutton Valence waterworks. It is now proposed to increase the present supply by lengthening the headings. It is also proposed to raise the reservoir and extend the mains.

**Market Bosworth.**—The Finance Committee have decided to recommend the district council to apply to the Local Government Board for sanction to an additional loan of £848 for the Ibstock sewerage scheme.

**Mutford and Lothingland.**—On the 24th ult. an inquiry was held by Mr. Samuel Walter Wheaton, M.D., an inspector of the Local Government Board, into an application of the council for powers to borrow £2,700 for the purpose of constructing an isolation hospital for the district. Mr. A. Smith, surveyor, and Mr. Clarke, architect, were among those present.

**Pontefract.**—At a recent meeting of this authority a letter was read from Mr. Waugh, engineer to the Ferrybridge and Brotherton proposed drainage scheme, stating that the Local Government Board were pressing for some progress to be reported, and adding that they would not countenance the septic system without the acquisition of land. The clerk said he would write and ask for the matter to be pressed forward. The clerk read a further letter from the Local Government Board stating that all property owners within the statutory distance of the public sewers were liable to be required to connect with the drains at their own expense.

## SCOTLAND AND IRELAND.

**Aberdeen.**—At a meeting of the Gas Committee of the town council, held on the 30th ult., it was resolved to recommend that the price of gas be reduced 1d. per 1,000 cubic feet—namely, from 3s. 2d. to 3s. 1d. The committee considered the statement of accounts—already published—very satisfactory, and although the estimates showed a large surplus, which would admit of a further reduction than that proposed, they resolved to adopt the suggestion of the convener not to make the reduction more than 1d. meantime.

**Dundee.**—The Gas Committee of the town council last week resolved to recommend the council to extend the electric lighting plant, at a cost of some £3,000, with the object of making a further demand for current.

**Glasgow.**—The Water Committee of the Glasgow Corporation met on Monday and decided to accept the offer of Messrs. Robert MacLaren & Co., Glasgow, for the supply of 995 tons of cast-iron water pipes. It will be remembered that at first six tenders were received for the supply of 1,000 tons of piping, the two lowest—£4,282 and £4,965—being from America, and the lowest local tender being £5,641. It was afterwards found, however, that the American offers were for pipes in 12 ft. lengths, in place of 9 ft. as advertised, and it was agreed to re-issue new specifications. This resulted in Messrs. R. D. Wood & Co., Philadelphia, offering to supply 995 tons for £4,892 1s., while the tender of Messrs. R. MacLaren & Co. was £4,958 7s. 4d., a difference of £66 7s. 4d. in favour of the former, or 1s. 4d. per ton less. On the engineer stating that in view of the slight difference it was not worth while placing the order out of the country, the committee accepted the offer of the local firm.

**Leith.**—The ceremony of laying the last brick on the top of the new chimney in connection with the electric lighting station, now in course of erection at Junction-street, was performed on Friday week by Bailey Manclark, convener of the Electrical Lighting Committee of the town council. Among those present were Mr. W. Bryson, electrical engineer for the corporation, and Mr. H. Simpson, architect. Bailie Manclark was presented, on behalf of the builders, Messrs. Kinnear, Moodie & Co., with a silver trowel. The chimney is 155 ft. in. height, 18 ft. in diameter at the base, and 12 ft. in diameter at the top, with an internal diameter of 8 ft. 3 in. at the bottom and 9 ft. 3 in. at the top. There is an internal shaft of firebrick to the height of 100 ft., built entirely independent of the outer walls of the chimney, having a space of 10 ft. all round.

**Naas.**—An inquiry was held recently by Mr. Charles P. Cotton, chief engineering inspector to the Local Government Board, into the necessity for a water supply for the town of Naas, the Naas Board of Guardians, acting as the rural sanitary authority, having applied for a loan of £4,000 for the purposes of the scheme. Among those present was Mr. Francis Bergin, B.E., engineer to the board. Evidence was given by Dr. Smyth as to the necessity of a proper water supply to the town, as the present means of supply by public pumps—two of which were condemned—was dangerous to public health. The source for the proposed supply is an historic well near the town which had been closed for many years, but was reopened two years ago. Other evidence was submitted by Mr. Bergin, who said the supply from the well would be abundant and good, and that seventeen fountains would be erected in the town, and the inquiry closed.

**Paisley.**—In connection with the proposals by the British Electric Traction Company to establish a system of electric traction for a tramway car service throughout Paisley, the town council have met in conference with representatives of the company and had their scheme definitely detailed. This has created a favourable impression. Meantime the council have agreed to meet with Glasgow Corporation Tramways Committee, to learn what they would propose doing in the same direction. Thereafter Paisley Council will come to a decision as to which scheme to support.

## FOREIGN AND COLONIAL.

**New York.**—A contemporary states that some consternation has been caused by a rumour that the safety of the Brooklyn bridge is imperilled by the tremendously increased strain that it has had to bear since the trolley cars have been permitted to cross it. A careful examination shows that, owing to the buckling of a steel truss, the bridge has sagged sufficiently to justify some anxiety. The accident has caused the huge structure to groan and vibrate unpleasantly, but it is believed that there is no actual danger.

# Personal.

Mr. Benjamin Milnes, of Wakefield, has been appointed junior assistant in the office of Mr. J. W. Brown, the borough engineer of West Hartlepool.

Blackpool Town Council have adopted a resolution of the Tramways Committee recommending the increasing of the salary of the tramway manager from £156 to £180 per annum.

Eleven applications have been received for the post of surveyor and inspector of nuisances to the Yeadon Urban District Council, and the following three have been asked to meet the council next Wednesday : Mr. W. A. Sharman, Pontefract ; Mr. N. Houlden, Yeadon ; and Mr. J. W. Llorsfield, Leeds.

We are informed that Mr. F. J. Edge, chief engineering assistant to the city surveyor of Manchester, is performing the duties of the latter gentleman during his (the city surveyor's) absence through illness. Our paragraph of last week mentioning Mr. J. P. Wilkinson as being in charge was therefore incorrect.

At last week's meeting of the Torquay Town Council, on the recommendation of the Water Committee, Mr. A. S. Rendell, of Newton Abbot, was appointed the corporation's arbitrator to settle the disputed compensation respecting the purchase of parts of Middle Westcott and Ballaton farms, in connection with the acquisition of the watershed.

At Tuesday's meeting of the Carnarvon Town Council it was reported that there were thirty-one applications for the post of borough surveyor, and voting took place upon the three qualified candidates selected : Messrs. R. W. Davies, Newtown ; E. Hall, Pwllheli ; and D. R. Parry, Carnarvon. Upon a division, a majority was found for Mr. Hall.

We learn that Mr. Edgar A. Ashcroft, having severed his connection with the Sulphide Corporation (Ashcroft's process), Limited, is now open to be consulted on all matters connected with metallurgy, mines and minerals, electrical, chemical and general engineering. Mr. Ashcroft is, for the present, occupying offices at 13 Victoria-street, Westminster, S.W.

Consideration was, at the last meeting of the Dublin City Council, given to the appointment of an assistant superintendent of cleansing. The candidates were as follows : Messrs. John J. Gahan, Matthew Rigney, Francis Purcell, Daniel Kavanagh and Francis Richard. In the final poll Mr. Purcell received thirty-two votes and Mr. Gahan sixteen. Mr. Purcell was therefore declared elected.

The Tramways Committee of the Devonport Town Council have appointed Mr. C. H. Chadwell to act as engineer to undertake the preparation of plans and sections, and do all the work necessary for obtaining Parliamentary powers for tramways from the existing borough boundary near Camel's Head bridge to the London and South-Western Railway station at St. Budeaux, for a fee of 4 per cent. on the estimated cost of the work, inclusive of all travelling and other expenses.

On Thursday morning several members of the Edinburgh and Leith Gas Commission and Mr. Herring, engineer, left by the East Coast express for Harwich and the Continent. These gentlemen constitute a deputation from the commission who are to visit a number of the chief towns on the Continent to inspect the gasworks, in view of the erection of new gasworks for Edinburgh and Leith at Granton. They were to cross on Thursday night from Harwich to Amsterdam, and among other cities it is proposed to visit are Copenhagen, Berlin, Vienna, Paris and Brussels.

The South Hornsey Urban District Council proceeded on Wednesday to fill up the office of surveyor and inspector of nuisances, rendered vacant by the appointment of Mr. W. Jameson, the late surveyor, to Whitechapel. There were seventy-two applicants for the post, of which the following were selected to attend before the council : Mr. W. T. Brown (Willesden), Mr. H. Hills (Shoreditch), Mr. W. Loveday (Mile End), Mr. J. Smith (Islington), Mr. E. F. Spurrell (St. Giles). The final selection was between Mr. Loveday and Mr. Spurrell, and the former gentleman was ultimately appointed. Mr. Loveday has been for many years assistant surveyor at Mile End.

On Monday, at the monthly meeting of the Carnoustie Town Council, the clerk submitted a letter from Mr. William Cumming resigning his appointments of burgh surveyor and sanitary inspector, he having accepted another situation at a higher salary. Mr. Cumming thanked the members of commission for the uniform courtesy and consideration he had received from all during the five years he had served them. Provost Colquhoun expressed his regret at Mr. Cumming's departure, but in view of the considerable advantage Mr. Cumming was to receive he was sure that, speaking for the commissioners, they had pleasure in hearing of his success. It was decided to advertise for a successor to Mr. Cumming at a salary of £100 per year.

Minutes of the Town Hall Committee of the Manchester Corporation, submitted at Wednesday's meeting of the council, referred to the resignation of Mr. Gibbons, chief architect in the city surveyor's department. The lord mayor stated that he and Sir John Harwood had seen Mr. Gibbons and endeavoured to dissuade him from persisting in his resignation, but Mr. Gibbons was still determined to resign his position. That being so, he did not think that anything more could be said in the matter. Sir John Harwood, remarked Mr. Gibbons, had been in the town hall for twenty-two years, and during that time he had been under various surveyors. Mr. Gibbons had given every satisfaction. He was a very civil, obliging, and capable man—qualities which did not always go together. He was very sorry indeed that a man who had spent the best days of his life in their service should wish to leave them.

The funeral of Dr. John Hopkinson and his three children, who, as we announced in our last issue, lost their lives on the Dent Veisivi, was held on Friday morning at Territet. The four bodies were brought to Territet on Thursday night and placed in the English church. The coffins were covered with flowers, and many of the wreaths had been sent from England. One was forwarded by the Institute of Electrical Engineers, and the British Vice-Consul at Lausanne sent another. At a special meeting of the council of the Institution of Electrical Engineers, held on the 31st ult., the following resolution was passed unanimously : " That the council of the Institution of Electrical Engineers do hereby place on record this expression of their sincere sorrow and deep regret for the great and irreparable loss sustained by the institute through the untimely and calamitous death of Dr. John Hopkinson, F.R.S., past-president of the Institution of Electrical Engineers, major commanding the Corps of Electrical Engineers, Royal Engineers (volunteers), and Professor of Electrical Engineering in King's College, London." It was further decided that, subject to its being consonant with the wish of the family, the members of the council should attend the funeral as representatives of the institution, but owing to the alteration in the arrangements it was impossible for them to do so.

The members of the Birmingham and Manchester Association of Students of the Institution of Civil Engineers, accompanied by Mr. T. C. Vaudrey, president of the Birmingham association, paid a highly-successful visit on Friday and Saturday to the Elan Valley, to inspect the waterworks of the Birmingham Corporation, which are now in progress of construction. The journey to this remote spot in Mid-Wales is a tedious one, but it was made in comfort, as the Great Western Railway kindly ran a special saloon through for the party. Mr. James Mansergh, the engineer, who is a vice-president of the Institution of Civil Engineers, personally conducted the party by a special train about 10 miles up the valley as far as the top reservoir, and explained all the details of this vast scheme in a very lucid and interesting manner to the students. On the return journey Mr. Mansergh generously provided luncheon in the offices near the model village, which, with its public buildings, was afterwards visited under the guidance of the village superintendent. The men having just stopped work, the municipal canteen was seen in full working order. The weather throughout was glorious, and, thanks to the kindness of Mr. Mansergh, Mr. Yourdi, resident engineer, and other assistants, who met the party at the various points of interest, the visit proved a most enjoyable and instructive one. The respective honorary secretaries, Messrs. Henry C. Adams, city surveyor's office, Birmingham, and P. F. Story, city surveyor's office, Manchester, had charge of the organisation of the trip, and Mr. Fisher, Lion Hotel, Rhayader, catered for the party.

## SUNDERLAND TRAMWAYS.

Mr. J. F. C. Snell, the borough electrical engineer of Sunderland, in concluding a report upon the question of electric traction, says : " I strongly recommend the adoption of the overhead trolley wire system, on the ground that it is the cheapest in construction and working expenses, and affords the best facilities to the public and ratepayers as regards minimum fares with quick and reliable service. A certain amount of opposition may arise from the alleged unsightliness of the overhead wires, but past experience proves that this opposition is entirely removed as soon as the increased advantages of this system are brought home to the public. The corporation have their own electric lighting station, and it must be borne in mind that the same station, with certain additions of plant, will serve both for lighting and traction, reducing the cost of management and wages and materially helping in the reduction of the general engineering costs of both concerns, and the combination of the two systems will materially increase the prosperity of not only the tramways scheme, but also the electric light undertaking."

Epsom.—Local Government Board sanction have been received by the council to borrow £440 for sewerage extensions in Mill and Bridge roads.

## ASSOCIATION OF MUNICIPAL AND COUNTY ENGINEERS.

### NEW MEMBERS.

At a meeting of the council, held on Saturday, the following gentlemen were elected

*As Members :—*

Eugene O'Neill Clarke, county surveyor, Leitrim.

Ernest Charles Cooper, surveyor to Urban District Council, Shanklin, Isle of Wight.

R. P. Hirst, borough surveyor, Southport.

Sydney Howard, surveyor to Urban District Council, Bradford-on-Avon.

Charles Booth Jones, county surveyor, Sligo.

C. J. Mulvany, county surveyor, Roscommon.

A. H. Walker, borough surveyor, Loughborough.

Messrs. Reginald Brown, vestry surveyor, Stoke Newington, and James H. Norris, borough surveyor, Godalming, were transferred to the class of " Members."

THOMAS COLE,
11 Victoria-street,                    *Secretary.*
Westminster, S.W.

MIDLAND DISTRICT MEETING AT BILSTON.

A meeting of the members of the midland district will be held on Saturday, the 17th inst., at Bilston. The following are the arrangements :—

11 a.m.— The members will be received in the council chamber, Town Hall, by the chairman (Councillor R. A. Harper, J.P.) and other members of the council. Minutes of Stafford and Rhyader meetings. Election of hon. district secretary.

11.30 a.m.—Leave in brakes, kindly provided by Councillor J. W. Sankey, chairman of the Water and Baths Committee, for a visit to the Spring Vale furnaces, arriving about 11.40 a.m., where, by the kind permission of Sir Alfred Hickman, the process of steel manufacture will be witnessed. A short descriptive paper will be given.

12.30 p.m.—Leave in brakes for a visit to the waterworks covered service reservoir (which will be specially emptied for the inspection of the members), arriving about 12.45.

1.15 p.m.—Leave in brakes for the Hinley Arms Hotel, arriving about 2 p.m., where a light luncheon will be provided by Councillor R. A. Harper, J.P., chairman of the council.

3 p.m.—Leave in brakes for a visit to the Bilston waterworks pumping station, arriving about 3.30 p.m.

4.15 p.m.—Leave in brakes for the Technical School, Bilston, arriving about 5 p.m.

6 p.m.—Dinner at the Technical School. Tickets, 3s. 6d. each (exclusive of wine).

Arrangements will be made for any members desirous of doing so to inspect the public baths and the public-market.

Mr. C. L. N. Wilson, the water engineer and surveyor to the Bilston Council, will give a descriptive paper of the works. As the paper will be in the hands of members intimating their intention to attend some days before the meeting, it will be taken as read.

Among the hotels at Bilston may be mentioned the Pipe Hall, Globe and Great Western.

Wolverhampton is within 2¼ miles and Birmingham 10¼ miles, and there is a good service of trains from these towns. The Great Western station at Bilston is the nearest to the Town Hall.

J. S. PICKERING, A.M.I.C.E.,           THOS. COLE, A.M.I.C.E.,
    *Hon. District Secretary,*                    *Secretary,*
    Council Offices, Nuneaton.   11 Victoria-street, S.W

## EAST LONDON WATER SUPPLY.

SHOREDITCH VESTRY AND THE LOCAL GOVERNMENT BOARD.

On Wednesday, in accordance with the decision of the Shoreditch Vestry, Mr. H. M. Robinson, the vestry clerk, forwarded a reply to the secretary of the Local Government Board, Sir Hugh Owen, with regard to the communication of the board in which it was alleged that a great deal of waste of water by residents was going on. The letter, after stating that the board's communication has been considered, continues : " This vestry emphatically declines to insult the intelligence of the water consumers of this district by urging them, as suggested, not to waste water which they do not get for twenty hours out of the twenty-four, or to assist your board in thus trying to shift some of the blame on to the wretched victims of it. The only waste of water known to this vestry is that caused by the leaky and defective pipes and mains of the company, which was animadverted upon by a metropolitan police magistrate on the recent occasion of the flooding of Commercial-road. To assume, because the company allege that they pump so many gallons of water to each consumer into their mains, that such a quantity ever reaches such consumer to be wasted by him is to confess a faith in the condition of the company's mains that would be

rudely shaken if your board would cause a test to be made of them by raising the pressure therein to 100 lb. per square inch, as provided by the New River Company. The vestry also desire to take this opportunity of informing you that public opinion in this district is beginning, after contemplation of the history of the water question, to have very considerable doubts as to the disinterestedness or intelligence of the Government in their dealings with this matter." After referring to evidence given as to the storage capacity and resources of the water company to some length, the letter concludes : " The storage reservoirs referred to have now been constructed, but the famine continues, and appears this year likely to be worse than any heretofore, and such a result has shaken public confidence in this district in the authorities who have so far dealt with this question, as in the case of the telephone monopoly. The vestry propose, therefore, as a last resource, to appeal to the Railway and Canal Commissioners for a fresh consideration of the circumstances by them."

## WATER SUPPLY IN ABERDEENSHIRE.

### NEW WORKS AT WATERTON.

The new waterworks for the supply of Dyce, Bucksburn, Bankhead and Stoneywood, or what is known as the Waterton district, have now been completed, and will be formally opened to-morrow. The new scheme owes its origin to the scarcity of water both in Waterton and Dyce. To remedy this the Aberdeen District Committee resolved to introduce, if possible, a new water supply, which would be adequate not only for the present wants of these villages, but also for the requirements of future years. Mr. J. D. Watson, the county engineer, was accordingly instructed to report on this question ; and his report was submitted to the committee in the autumn of 1896. In the spring of 1897 the District Committee adopted the plans, which have since been carried into effect.

The source of the new supply is a spring near the kennels at Parkhill House ; but, with a view to future requirements, two other springs, also on the Parkhill property, one situated at Aryburn and another at Toddhill, have also been acquired. These, however, will not be requisitioned for many a long year to come ; and in the meantime the water of the spring situated near the kennels, which by analysis has been shown to be of excellent quality, and from its softness suitable for drinking, cooking and washing purposes, will be collected in an intake cistern. In the driest season of the year the yield from this spring is 200,000 gallons every twenty-four hours ; and, allowing 20 gallons per day to every one of the 5,000 inhabitants of the district supplied, it will thus be seen that the spring will be sufficient until the present population of the district has been doubled. The water is brought from the intake through a 7-in. cast-iron pipe to a point on the Goval burn near Parkhill railway station, whence it is pumped by a pair of horizontal double-acting pumps driven by two vortex turbine wheels up to a high-level cistern about 200 ft. higher than the pumping station, and nearly 2 miles distant. The cistern into which all the water is pumped is near the Dyce quarries, and from this point it gravitates to the Standing Stones reservoir in a 6-in. cast-iron pipe, nearly 1 mile in length, for the supply of Bucksburn and Bankhead. The Dyce water supply is also carried from the high-level cistern to Dyce reservoir in a pipe 3 in. in diameter.

**March.**—The Local Government Board have sanctioned the application of the district council for permission to borrow £2,600 for the provision of additional market accommodation. The buildings will comprise a corn exchange, offices and a clock tower, and will be erected in the Market-place.

## APPOINTMENTS VACANT.

*Advertisements which are received too late for classification cannot be included in these summaries until the following week.*

INSPECTOR OF NUISANCES.—September 12th.—Northfleet Urban District Council. £80.—Messrs. Sharland & Hatten, clerks, Court House, Gravesend.

THIRD ASSISTANT TO ENGINEER AND SURVEYOR.—September 12th.—Leigh Urban District Council. £70.—Mr. Tom Hunter, engineer and surveyor to the council.

CLERK OF WORKS.—September 13th.—Wetherby Rural District Council.—Mr. E. H. Coates, clerk to the council.

CHIEF ENGINEERING AND SURVEYING ASSISTANT.—September 16th.—Leyton Urban District Council. £130.—Mr. William Dawson, M.I.C.E., engineer and surveyor to the council.

BOROUGH SURVEYOR AND SANITARY INSPECTOR.—September 17th.—Borough of Oswestry. £200.—Mr. J. Parry Jones, town clerk.

ENGINEERING ASSISTANT.—September 17th.—Ilfracombe Urban District Council.—Mr. O. M. Prouse, engineer and surveyor to the council.

ELECTRICAL ENGINEER. — September 20th. — Willesden Urban District Council. £400.—Mr. O. Claude Robson, M.I.C.E., engineer and surveyor to the council.

TEMPORARY ASSISTANT.—September 20th.—Llantrisant and Llantwit Fadre Rural District Council.—Mr. Gomer S. Morgan, surveyor to the council, Pontyclun.

SECRETARY AND CITY MANAGER—September 21st.—York Waterworks Company. £300 with house.—The Directors of the Company, Lendal Hill, York.

DISTRICT SUPERINTENDENTS (TWO OR THREE).—The British Electric Traction Company. £300 to £350.—Mr. G. Stevens, secretary to the company.

CLERK OF WORKS.—Metropolitan Asylums Board. £3 3s.—Offices, Norfolk House, Norfolk-street, Strand, W.C.

## COMPETITIONS.

*Advertisements which are received too late for classification cannot be included in these summaries until the following week.*

PLYMOUTH.—September 24th.—Erection of shops and dwelling-houses fronting Tavistock-road. £250.—Mr. J. H. Ellis, town clerk.

WIVENHOE.—September 29th.—Works of drainage and water supply, for the urban district council.—Mr. C. W. Denton, clerk.

REIGATE.—October 6th.—Erection of municipal buildings, fire station, public offices, &c.—Mr. Clair J. Grece, town clerk.

ASHTON.—December 1st.—Extension of the covered market, at a cost not to exceed £6,000. £21.—The Borough Surveyor.

CHERTSEY.—December 23rd.—Sewerage and sewage disposal scheme for the No. 1 and 2 wards of the district. £50, £30 and £20.—Mr. T. E. Harland Chaldecott, clerk to the council.

## MUNICIPAL CONTRACTS OPEN.

*Advertisements which are received too late for classification cannot be included in these summaries until the following week.*

LLANDOVERY.—September 9th.—Erection of a highway bridge over the river Cothi at Pontbrenllwyd ford, near Pumpsaint, for the rural district council.—The Clerk to the Council.

CROMER.—September 10th.—Erection of a public convenience, with accommodation for both sexes, on the sea front, for the urban district council.—Mr. A. F. Scott, surveyor to the council.

NOTTINGHAM.—September 10th.—Sinking of two bore-holes, each 32 in. diameter, in the parish of Broughton.—Sir Samuel G. Johnson, town clerk.

LANCASHIRE.—September 10th.—Repair of Read old bridge crossing the Sabien brook in the townships of Whalley and Read, for the county council.—Mr. W. Harold Radford, county bridge-master, 19 Brazennose-street, Manchester.

WIMBLEDON.—September 10th.—Supply of forage for the six months ending March 31, 1899, for the urban district council.—Mr. W. H. Whitfield, clerk to the council.

BURY ST. EDMUNDS.—September 10th.—Erection of buildings, chimney shaft, &c., for the electric light station.—Mr. J. Campbell Smith, borough surveyor.

RAMSGATE.—September 10th.—Erection of buildings to be used as offices for the gas and water department.—Mr. W. A. Hubbard, town clerk.

BANGOR.—September 10th.—Supply and erection of electric lighting plant.—Mr. R. Hughes Pritchard, town clerk.

CARDIFF.—September 12th.—Erection of three new pavilions, lodge and contingent works in connection with the extension of the sanatorium.—Mr. W. Harpur, M.I.C.E., borough engineer.

GLASGOW.—September 12th.—Erection of a bridge over the river Kelvin, opposite Montgomerie-street, North Kelvinside.—Mr. John Lindsay, interim clerk, City Chambers, Glasgow.

BLACKBURN.—September 13th.—Alteration of the slaughter-houses.—Mr. William Stubbs, A.M.I.C.E., borough and water engineer.

ST. PANCRAS.—September 13th.—Supply of about 140,000 jarrah or karri wood paving blocks for repaving Guildford-street and Midland-road, for the vestry.—Mr. Wm. N. Blair, engineer and surveyor to the vestry.

BEXLEY.—September 12th.—Supply of materials, stores, cartage, team labour, removal of dust and steam rolling, for the urban district council.—Mr. Tom Vickers, surveyor to the council.

ILFORD.—September 13th.—Various works at Valentine's, the site of the public park, for the urban district council.—Mr. H. Shaw, A.M.I.C.E., surveyor to the council.

TORQUAY.—September 13th.—Supply of about 300 tons of Portland cement.—Mr. Henry A. Garrett, A.M.I.C.E., borough surveyor.

RUGBY.—September 13th.—Construction of about 170 yards of main outfall sewer at the sewage farm, New Bilton, for the urban district council.—Mr. D. G. Macdonald, A.M.I.C.E., surveyor to the council.

NORTH RIDING.—September 13th.—Rebuilding, &c., of Tanton bridge, near Stokesley.—Mr. Walter Stead, M.I.C.E., county surveyor, Northallerton.

BIRMINGHAM.—September 13th.—Construction of aqueducts.—Mr. E. O. Smith, town clerk.

PONTYPOOL.—September 13th.—Erection of offices, &c., at Pontymoile, Pontypool, for the urban district council.—Mr. Thomas Williams, clerk to the council, Albion-road, Pontypool.

RUSHDEN.—September 13th.—Painting, &c., work at the waterworks pumping station at Wymington and at the isolation hospital, for the urban district council.—Mr. W. B. Madin, town surveyor.

HASTINGS.—September 13th.—Supply of about 1,707 tons of 16-in., 1060 tons of 10-in. and 44 tons of 6-in. cast-iron water pipes and about 35 tons of irregulars.—Mr. R. H. Palmer, M.I.C.E., borough engineer.

DOVER.—September 13th.—Erection of a workshop, &c., adjoining the car sheds at Maxton.—Mr. Henry E. Stilgoe, A.M.I.C.E., borough engineer.

WESTON-SUPER-MARE.—September 13th.—Alterations and additions to the Knightstone baths, for the urban district council.—Mr. Sydney C. Smith, clerk to the council.

ECCLES.—September 13th.—Supply of various provender during the half-year ending 25th March, 1899.—Mr. Geo. Wm. Bailey, town clerk.

GREENWICH.—September 14th.—Supply of corn, straw and fodder, for the district board of works.—Mr. J. Spencer, clerk to the board.

ST. LUKE.—September 14th.—Construction of an underground sanitary convenience in Old-street, for the vestry.—The Surveyor to the Vestry.

GREENWICH.—September 14th.—Footway paving works in Deptford-street, Fergus-street and a portion of Gibson-street, for the district board of works.—Mr. J. Spencer, clerk to the board.

GREENWICH.—September 14th.—Demolition of Nos. 50 and 50A, Douglas-street, Deptford, for the district board of works.—Mr. J. Spencer, clerk to the board.

ST. LUKE.—September 14th.—Paving of Golden-lane and part of Banner-street with jarrah wood and part of Peartree-street with granite, for the vestry.—The Surveyor to the Vestry.

EPSOM.—September 14th.—Erection of a new ward at the isolation hospital at Theydon Garnon, for the rural district council.—Mr. R. D. Trotter, clerk to the council.

HALIFAX.—September 14th.—Supply of 6-in. granite setts, 2,000 tons of 6-in. Lancashire setts and 2,500 yards of wood blocks.—Mr. Edward R. S. Escott, borough engineer.

PLUMSTEAD.—September 14th.—Paving works in White Hart-lane, for the vestry.—Mr. W. C. Gow, surveyor to the vestry.

GLASGOW.—September 15th.—Various alterations at Strathbungo police station.—Mr. John Lindsay, clerk, City Chambers, Glasgow.

NEWTON-IN-MAKERFIELD.—September 16th.—Supply of various road materials for one year commencing 1st October, for the urban district council.—Mr. W. W. Shirley, clerk to the council.

WHITLEY.—September 16th.—Widening of the road from Marine-avenue to St. Paul's church and the road from Park-road, Front-street, to the south end of Whitley-road, for the urban district council.—Mr. J. F. Spencer, Newcastle-on-Tyne.

DALTON-IN-FURNESS.—September 16th.—Sewering works in parts of Victoria-street and Back Diversion-road, for the urban district council.—Mr. J. Tyson, clerk to the council.

ROTHBURY.—September 17th.—Supply of a 12-ton steam roller, one sleeping-van and one water-cart, for the rural district council.—Mr. James Wood, surveyor to the council.

KERSHAM.—September 17th.—Building of a new bridge, altering course of brook, and other works connected therewith, at the boundary of Bengeworth and Badsey parishes, for the urban district council.—Mr. Edward Wadams, clerk to the council.

NOTTINGHAM.—September 17th.—Construction of new sewer.—Mr. Arthur Brown, city engineer.

AMBERLEY.—September 17th.—Supply for one year of electricity meters, house fuse-boxes and house service cables.—Mr. J. Alex. Bell, city electrical engineer.

STAINES.—September 17th.—Making-up of Sidney-road, Bremer-road, Farnell-road and Billet-road, for the urban district council.—Mr. E. J. Barrett, A.M.I.C.E., surveyor to the council.

STAINES.—September 17th.—Supply and delivery of about 200 tons of 1½-in. hand-broken Guernsey granite, for the urban district council.—Mr. E. J. Barrett, A.M.I.C.E., surveyor to the council.

DOWNPATRICK.—September 17th.—Improvement of the storage reservoir at Tanraghmore.—The County Surveyor, Downpatrick.

LOUGHBOROUGH.—September 17th.—Construction of a new filter-bed at Nanpanton.—Mr. A. H. Walker, A.M.I.C.E., borough engineer and waterworks manager.

WALTON-ON-NAZE.—September 17th.—Sewering, curbing, channelling, paving and metalling works in Station-road, for the urban district council.—Mr. H. W. Gladwell, surveyor to the council.

WIMBLEDON.—September 19th.—Making-up of Ashley-road, Caxton-road, Clarence-road, Edith-road, Effra-road (section 4) and Hamilton-mews, for the urban district council.—Mr. W. H. Whitfield, clerk to the council.

BURNHAM-ON-CROUCH.—September 19th.—Public lighting of the town for one year from 29th September, for the urban district council.—Mr. E. Dilliway, clerk to the council.

CAMBERWELL.—September 19th.—Painting of the exteriors of Camberwell and Dulwich baths, for the vestry.—The Clerk to the Vestry.

WEST RIDING.—September 19th.—Erection of a farm residence at the asylum at Menston.—Mr. J. Vickers Edwards, county surveyor, County Hall, Wakefield.

GLOUCESTER.—September 19th.—Erection of new electricity works.—Mr. George Sheffield Blakeway, town clerk.

HORNSEY.—September 19th.—Sewering, levelling, paving, metalling, channelling and making good certain roads, for the urban district council.—Mr. F. D. Askey, clerk.

HULL.—September 19th.—Construction of engine foundations and setting of economiser and four boilers at the Springhead pumping station.—Mr. F. J. Bancroft, water and gas engineer, Town Hall, Hull.

LYTHAM.—September 19th.—Completion of the main sewerage of the district, for the urban district council.—Messrs. Francis Newman & Cocks, 3 St. Thomas-street, Ryde.

LYTHAM.—September 19th.—Construction of about 900 yards of 3-ft. diameter brick sewer, about 1,500 yards of 24-in. and 18-in. pipe sewer, and concrete and storage tanks, together with sea embankment, road-way and other contingent works, for the urban district council.—Messrs. Newton, 17 Cooper-street, Manchester.

WAKEFIELD.—September 19th.—Construction of a cast-iron water-tank, to hold 18,000 gallons, at Woolley-edge in the township of Crigglestone, for the rural district council.—Mr. Frank Massie, A.M.I.C.E., engineer and surveyor to the council.

PADDINGTON.—September 19th.—Supply of about 500 cubic yards of fine crushed Thames shingle, for the vestry.—Mr. Frank Delbridge, surveyor to the vestry.

AMBLE.—September 19th.—Supply of 100 tons of broken whinstone, for the urban district council.—Mr. W. Gibson, surveyor to the council.

TORQUAY.—September 19th.—Supply of meters and arc lamp carbons for twelve months from 1st October.—Mr. P. Storey, borough electrical engineer.

LIVERPOOL.—September 20th.—Alterations at the Steble-street public wash-house, for the corporation.—Mr. W. R. Court, engineer and chief superintendent, Cornwallis-street Baths, Liverpool.

LONDON.—September 20th.—Construction of underground conveniences at Queenhitho.—The City Engineer, Guildhall, E.C.

LEEDS.—September 20th.—Supply of (a) poles and (b) trolley wire and attachments in connection with the extension of the electric tramway systems.—The City Engineer.

AMBLE.—September 20th.—Excavating, levelling and paving works in Albert-street, Dock-lane and Middleton-street Back-lane, for the urban district council.—Mr. W. Gibson, surveyor to the council.

BUCKLOW.—September 20th.—Repaving of certain boulder pavements and channels in Carrington, Partington and Warburton, for the rural district council.—Mr. Joseph Burgess, surveyor, Tabley, Knutsford.

GOSPORT AND ALVERSTOKE.—September 20th.—Supply of various materials during the year ending 30th September, 1899, for the urban district council.—Mr. H. Frost, surveyor to the council.

BARKING TOWN.—September 20th.—Supply of a 8 or 10 ton steam road-roller adaptable for traction, for the urban district council.—Mr. E. H. Lister, clerk to the council.

BRADFORD.—September 21st.—Supply of about 150,000 jarrah or karri wood paving blocks.—Mr. J. H. Cox, borough engineer.

KAMINGTON.—September 21st.—Waterworks for Wingate Mill, Wingate-lane and Hugh Wheatley Hill, for the rural district council.—Messrs. D. Balfour & Son, 3 St. Nicholas-buildings, Newcastle-on-Tyne.

## ASSOCIATION OF MUNICIPAL AND COUNTY ENGINEERS.

### NEW MEMBERS.

At a meeting of the council, held on Saturday, the following gentlemen were elected

*As Members:*—

Eugene O'Neill Clarke, county surveyor, Leitrim.

Ernest Charles Cooper, surveyor to Urban District Council, Shanklin, Isle of Wight.

R. P. Hirst, borough surveyor, Southport.

Sydney Howard, surveyor to Urban District Council, Bradford-on-Avon.

Charles Booth Jones, county surveyor, Sligo.

C. J. Mulvany, county surveyor, Roscommon.

A. H. Walker, borough surveyor, Loughborough.

Messrs. Reginald Brown, vestry surveyor, Stoke Newington, and James H. Norris, borough surveyor, Godalming, were transferred to the class of "Members."

THOMAS COLE,
11 Victoria-street, *Secretary.*
Westminster, S.W.

### MIDLAND DISTRICT MEETING AT BILSTON.

A meeting of the members of the midland district will be held on Saturday, the 17th inst., at Bilston. The following are the arrangements:—

11 a.m.— The members will be received in the council chamber, Town Hall, by the chairman (Councillor R. A. Harper, J.P.) and other members of the council. Minutes of Stafford and Rhyader meetings. Election of hon. district secretary.

11.30 a.m.—Leave in brakes, kindly provided by Councillor J. W. Sankey, chairman of the Water and Baths Committee, for a visit to the Spring Vale furnaces, arriving about 11.40 a.m., where, by the kind permission of Sir Alfred Hickman, the process of steel manufacture will be witnessed. A short descriptive paper will be given.

12.30 p.m.—Leave in brakes for a visit to the waterworks covered service reservoir (which will be specially emptied for the inspection of the members), arriving about 12.45.

1.15 p.m.—Leave in brakes for the Hinley Arms Hotel, arriving about 2 p.m., where a light luncheon will be provided by Councillor R. A. Harper, J.P., chairman of the council.

3 p.m.—Leave in brakes for a visit to the Bilston waterworks pumping station, arriving about 3.30 p.m.

4.15 p.m.—Leave in brakes for the Technical School, Bilston, arriving about 5 p.m.

6 p.m.—Dinner at the Technical School. Tickets, 3s. 6d. each (exclusive of wine).

Arrangements will be made for any members desirous of doing so to inspect the public baths and live meat-market.

Mr. C. L. N. Wilson, the water engineer and surveyor to the Bilston Council, will give a descriptive paper of the works. As the paper will be in the hands of members intimating their intention to attend some days before the meeting, it will be taken as read.

Among the hotels at Bilston may be mentioned the Pipe Hall, Globe and Great Western.

Wolverhampton is within 2½ miles and Birmingham 10½ miles, and there is a good service of trains from these towns. The Great Western station at Bilston is the nearest to the Town Hall.

J. S. PICKERING, A.M.I.C.E.,    THOS. COLE, A.M.I.C.E.,
*Hon. District Secretary,*    *Secretary,*
Council Offices, Nuneaton.    11 Victoria-street, S.W

## EAST LONDON WATER SUPPLY.

SHOREDITCH VESTRY AND THE LOCAL GOVERNMENT BOARD.

On Wednesday, in accordance with the decision of the Shoreditch Vestry, Mr. H. M. Robinson, the vestry clerk, forwarded a reply to the secretary of the Local Government Board, Sir Hugh Owen, with regard to the communication of the board in which it was alleged that a great deal of waste of water by residents was going on. The letter, after stating that the board's communication has been considered, continues: "This vestry emphatically declines to insult the intelligence of the water consumers in this district by urging them, as suggested, not to waste water which they do not get for twenty hours out of the twenty-four, or to assist your board in this trying to shift some of the blame on to the wretched victims of it. The only waste of water known to this vestry is that caused by the leaky and defective pipes and mains of the company, which was animadverted upon by a metropolitan police magistrate on the recent occasion of the flooding of Commercial-road. To assume, because the company allege that they pump so many gallons of water to each consumer into their mains, that such a quantity ever reaches such consumer to be wasted by him is to confess a faith in the condition of the company's mains that would be

rudely shaken if your board would cause a test to be made of them by raising the pressure therein to 100 lb. per square inch, as provided by the New River Company. The vestry also desire to take this opportunity of informing you that public opinion in this district is beginning, after contemplation of the history of the water question, to have very considerable doubts as to the disinterestedness or intelligence of the Government in their dealings with this matter." After referring to evidence given as to the storage capacity and resources of the water company to some length, the letter concludes: "The storage reservoirs referred to have now been constructed, but the famine continues, and appears this year likely to be worse than any heretofore, and such a result has shaken public confidence in this district in the authorities who have so far dealt with this question, as in the case of the telephone monopoly. The vestry propose, therefore, as a last resource, to appeal to the Railway and Canal Commissioners for a fresh consideration of the circumstances by them."

## WATER SUPPLY IN ABERDEENSHIRE.

NEW WORKS AT WATERTON.

The new waterworks for the supply of Dyce, Bucksburn, Bankhead and Stoneywood, or what is known as the Waterton district, have now been completed, and will be formally opened to-morrow. The new scheme owes its origin to the scarcity of water both in Waterton and Dyce. To remedy this the Aberdeen District Committee resolved to introduce, if possible, a new water supply, which would be adequate not only for the present wants of these villages, but also for the requirements of future years. Mr. J. D. Watson, the county engineer, was accordingly instructed to report on this question; and his report was submitted to the committee in the autumn of 1896. In the spring of 1897 the District Committee adopted the plans, which have since been carried into effect.

The source of the new supply is a spring near the kennels at Parkhill House; but, with a view to future requirements, two other springs, also on the Parkhill property, one situated at Aryburn and another at Toddhill, have also been acquired. These, however, will not be requisitioned for many a long year to come; and in the meantime the water of the spring situated near the kennels, which by analysis has been shown to be of excellent quality, and from its softness suitable for drinking, cooking and washing purposes, will be collected in an intake cistern. In the driest season of the year the yield from this spring is 200,000 gallons every twenty-four hours; and, allowing 20 gallons per day to every one of the 5,000 inhabitants of the district supplied, it will thus be seen that the spring will be sufficient until the present population of the district has been doubled. The water is brought from the intake through a 7-in. cast-iron pipe to a point on the Goval burn near Parkhill railway station, whence it is pumped by a pair of horizontal double-acting pumps driven by two vortex turbine wheels up to a high-level cistern about 200 ft. higher than the pumping station, and nearly 2 miles distant. The cistern into which all the water is pumped is near the Dyce quarries, and from this point it gravitates to the Standing Stones reservoir in a 6-in. cast-iron pipe, nearly 1 mile in length, for the supply of Bucksburn and Bankhead. The Dyce water supply is also carried from the high-level cistern to Dyce reservoir in a pipe 3 in. in diameter.

March.—The Local Government Board have sanctioned the application of the district council for permission to borrow £2,600 for the provision of additional market accommodation. The buildings will comprise a corn exchange, offices and a clock tower, and will be erected in the Market-place.

## APPOINTMENTS VACANT.

*Advertisements which are received too late for classification cannot be included in these summaries until the following week.*

INSPECTOR OF NUISANCES.—September 12th.—Northfleet Urban District Council. £80.—Messrs. Sharland & Hatten, clerks, Court House, Gravesend.

THIRD ASSISTANT TO ENGINEER AND SURVEYOR.—September 12th.—Leigh Urban District Council. £70.—Mr. Tom Hunter, engineer and surveyor to the council.

CLERK OF WORKS.—September 13th.—Wetherby Rural District Council.—Mr. E. H. Coates, clerk to the council.

CHIEF ENGINEERING AND SURVEYING ASSISTANT.—September 16th.—Leyton Urban District Council. £130.—Mr. William Dawson, M.I.C.E., engineer and surveyor to the council.

BOROUGH SURVEYOR AND SANITARY INSPECTOR.—September 17th.—Borough of Oswestry. £200.—Mr. J. Parry Jones, town clerk.

ENGINEERING ASSISTANT.—September 17th.—Ilfracombe Urban District Council.—Mr. O. M. Prouse, engineer and surveyor to the council.

ELECTRICAL ENGINEER. — September 20th. — Willesden Urban District Council. £400.—Mr. O. Claude Robson, M.I.C.E., engineer and surveyor to the council.

TEMPORARY ASSISTANT.—September 20th.—Llantrisant and Llantwit Fadre Rural District Council.—Mr. Gomer S. Morgan, surveyor to the council, Pontyclun.

SECRETARY AND CITY MANAGER—September 21st.—York Waterworks Company. £300 with house.—The Directors of the Company, Lendal Hill, York.

DISTRICT SUPERINTENDENTS (TWO OR THREE). — The British Electric Traction Company. £300 to £350.—Mr. G. Stevens, secretary to the company.

CLERK OF WORKS.—Metropolitan Asylums Board. £3 3s. —Offices, Norfolk House, Norfolk-street, Strand, W.C.

## COMPETITIONS.

*Advertisements which are received too late for classification cannot be included in these summaries until the following week.*

PLYMOUTH.—September 24th.—Erection of shops and dwelling-houses fronting Tavistock-road. £250.—Mr. J. H. Ellis, town clerk.

WIVENHOE.—September 29th.—Works of drainage and water supply, for the urban district council.—Mr. C. W. Denton, clerk.

REIGATE.—October 6th.—Erection of municipal buildings, fire station, public offices, &c.—Mr. Clair J. Grece, town clerk.

ABENLOW.—December 1st.—Extension of the covered market, at a cost not to exceed £9,000. £21.—The Borough Surveyor.

CHERTSEY.—December 23rd.—Sewerage and sewage disposal scheme for the No. 1 and 2 wards of the district. £50, £30 and £20.—Mr. T. E. Harland Chaldecott, clerk to the council.

## MUNICIPAL CONTRACTS OPEN.

*Advertisements which are received too late for classification cannot be included in these summaries until the following week.*

LLANDOVERY.—September 9th.—Erection of a highway bridge over the river Cothi at Pontoewllwyd ford, near Pumpsaint, for the rural district council.—The Clerk to the Council.

CROMER.—September 10th.—Erection of a public convenience, with accommodation for both sexes, on the sea front, for the urban district council.—Mr. A. F. Scott, surveyor to the council.

NOTTINGHAM.—September 10th.—Sinking of two bore-holes, each 32 in. diameter, in the parish of Bingham.—Sir Samuel G. Johnson, town clerk.

LANCASTER.—September 10th.—Repair of Read old bridge crossing the Sabden brook in the townships of Whalley and Read, for the county council.—Mr. W. Harold Radford, county bridge-master, 19 Brazenose-street, Manchester.

WIMBLEDON.—September 10th.—Supply of forage for the six months ending March 31, 1899, for the urban district council.—Mr. W. H. Whitfield, clerk to the council.

BURY ST. EDMUNDS.— September 10th. — Erection of buildings, chimney shaft, &c., for the electric light station.—Mr. J. Campbell Smith, borough surveyor.

RAMSGATE.—September 10th.—Erection of buildings to be used as offices for the gas and water department.—Mr. W. A. Hubbard, town clerk.

BANGOR.—September 10th.—Supply and erection of electric lighting plant.—Mr. R. Hughes Pritchard, town clerk.

CARDIFF.—September 12th.—Erection of three new pavilions, lodge and contingent works in connection with the extension of the sanatorium.—Mr. W. Harpur, M.I.C.E., borough engineer.

GLASGOW.—September 12th.—Erection of a bridge over the river Kelvin, opposite Montgomerie-street, North Kelvinside.—Mr. John Lindsay, interim clerk, City Chambers, Glasgow.

BLACKBURN.—September 12th.—Alteration of the slaughter-houses.— Mr. William Stubbs, A.M.I.C.E., borough and water engineer.

ST. PANCRAS.—September 12th.—Supply of about 140,000 jarrah or karri wood paving blocks for repaving Guilford-street and Midland-road, for the vestry.—Mr. Wm. N. Blair, engineer and surveyor to the vestry.

BEXLEY.—September 12th.—Supply of materials, stores, cartage, team labour, removal of dust and steam rolling, for the urban district council.—Mr. Tom Vickers, surveyor to the council.

ILFORD.—September 12th.—Various works at Valentine's, the site of the public park, for the urban district council.—Mr. H. Shaw, A.M.I.C.E., surveyor to the council.

TORQUAY.—September 13th.—Supply of about 300 tons of Portland cement.—Mr. Henry A. Garrett, A.M.I.C.E., borough surveyor.

RUGBY.—September 13th.—Construction of about 170 yards of main outfall sewer at the sewage farm, New Bilton, for the urban district council.—Mr. D. G. Macdonald, A.M.I.C.E., surveyor to the council.

NORTH RIDING.—September 13th.—Rebuilding, &c., of Tanton bridge, near Stokesley.—Mr. Walter Stead, M.I.C.E., county surveyor, Northallerton.

BIRMINGHAM.—September 13th.—Construction of aqueduct.—Mr. E. O. Smith, town clerk.

PANTEG.—September 13th.—Erection of offices, &c., at Pontymoile, Pontypool, for the urban district council.—Mr. Thomas Williams, clerk to the council, Albion-road, Pontypool.

ROSSBORO.—September 13th.—Painting, &c., work at the waterworks pumping station at Wymington and at the isolation hospital, for the urban district council.—Mr. W. B. Madin, town surveyor.

HASTINGS.—September 13th.—Supply of about 1,707 tons of 14-in., 100 tons of 10-in. and 84 tons of 6-in. cast-iron water pipes and about 38 tons of irregulars.—Mr. R. H. Palmer, M.I.C.E., borough engineer.

DOVER.—September 13th.—Erection of a workshop, &c., adjoining the car sheds at Maxton.—Mr. Henry K. Stilgoe, A.M.I.C.E., borough engineer.

WESTON-SUPER-MARE.—September 13th.—Alterations and additions to the Knightstone baths, for the urban district council.—Mr. Sydney C. Smith, clerk to the council.

ECCLES.—September 13th.—Supply of various provender during the half-year ending 25th March, 1899.—Mr. Geo. Wm. Bailey, town clerk.

GREENWICH.—September 13th.—Supply of corn, straw and fodder, for the district board of works.—Mr. J. Spencer, clerk to the board.

ST. LUKE.—September 14th.—Construction of an underground sanitary convenience in Old-street, for the vestry.—The Surveyor to the vestry.

GREENWICH.—September 14th.—Footway paving works in Deptford-street, Fergus-street and a portion of Gibson-street, for the district board of works.—Mr. J. Spencer, clerk to the board.

GREENWICH.—September 14th.—Demolition of Nos. 50 and 50A Douglas-street, Deptford, for the district board of works.—Mr. J. Spencer, clerk to the board.

ST. LUKE.—September 14th.—Paving of Golden-lane and part of Banner-street with jarrah wood and part of Peartree-street with granite, for the vestry.—The Surveyor to the vestry.

EPPING.—September 14th.—Erection of a new ward at the isolation hospital at Theydon Garnon, for the rural district council.—Mr. R. D. Trotter, clerk to the council.

HALIFAX.—September 14th.—Supply of 1,000 tons of 6-in. granite setts, 2,000 tons of 6-in. Lancashire setts and 2,500 yards of wood blocks.— Mr. Edward R. S. Escott, borough engineer.

PLUMSTEAD.—September 14th.—Paving works in White Hart-lane, for the vestry.—Mr. W. C. Gow, surveyor to the vestry.

GLASGOW.—September 15th.—Various alterations at Strathbungo police station.—Mr. John Lindsay, clerk, City Chambers, Glasgow.

NEWTON-IN-MAKERFIELD.—September 16th.—Supply of various road materials for one year commencing 1st October, for the urban district council.—Mr. W. W. Shirley, clerk to the council.

WHITLEY.—September 16th.—Widening of the road from Marine-avenue to St. Paul's church and the road from Park-road, Front-street, to the south end of Whitley-road, for the urban district council.—Mr. J. P. Spencer, Newcastle-on-Tyne.

DALTON-IN-FURNESS.—September 16th.—Sewering works in parts of Victoria-street and Back Ulverston-road, for the urban district council. —Mr. J. Tyson, clerk to the council.

ROTHBURY.—September 17th.—Supply of a 12-ton steam roller, one sleeping-van and one water-cart, for the rural district council.—Mr. James Wood, surveyor to the council.

EVESHAM.—September 17th.—Building of a new bridge, altering course of brook, and other works connected therewith, at the boundary of Bengeworth and Hadsey parishes, for the urban district council.— Mr. Edward Wadams, clerk to the council.

NOTTINGHAM.—September 17th.—Construction of new sewer.—Mr. Arthur Brown, city engineer.

ABERDEEN.—September 17th.—Supply for one year of electricity meters, house fuse-boxes and house service cables.—Mr. J. Alex. Bell, city electrical engineer.

STAINES.—September 17th.—Making-up of Sidney-road, Bremer-road, Farnell-road and Billet-road, for the urban district council.—Mr. E. J. Barrett, A.M.I.C.E., surveyor to the council.

STAINES.—September 17th.—Supply and delivery of about 200 tons of 1½-in. hand-broken Guernsey granite, for the urban district council.— Mr. E. J. Barrett, A.M.I.C.E., surveyor to the council.

DOWNPATRICK.—September 17th.—Improvement of the storage reservoir at Tannaghmore.—The County Surveyor, Downpatrick.

LONGBENTON.—September 17th.—Construction of a new filter-bed at Nanpantan.—Mr. A. H. Walker, A.M.I.C.E., borough engineer and waterworks manager.

WALTON-ON-NAZE.—September 17th.—Sewering, curbing, channelling, paving and metalling works in Station-road, for the urban district council.—Mr. H. W. Gladwell, surveyor to the council.

WIMBLEDON.—September 19th.—Making-up of Ashley-road, Caxton-road, Clarence-road, Edith-road, Effra-road (section 2) and Hamilton-mews, for the urban district council.—Mr. W. H. Whitfield, clerk to the council.

BURNHAM-ON-CROUCH.—September 19th.—Public lighting of the town for one year from 29th September, for the urban district council.—Mr. E. Dilliway, clerk to the council.

CAMBERWELL.—September 19th.—Painting of the exteriors of Camberwell and Dulwich baths, for the vestry.—The Clerk to the Vestry.

WEST RIDING.—September 19th.—Erection of a farm residence at the asylum at Menston.—Mr. J. Vickers Edwards, county surveyor, County Hall, Wakefield.

GLOUCESTER.—September 19th.—Erection of new electricity works.— Mr. George Sheffield Blakeway, town clerk.

HORNSEY.—September 19th.—Sewering, levelling, paving, metalling, channelling and making good certain roads, for the urban district council.—Mr. F. D. Askley, clerk.

HULL.—September 19th.—Construction of engine foundations and setting of economiser and four boilers at the Springhead pumping station.—Mr. F. J. Bancroft, water and gas engineer, Town Hall, Hull.

SWANAGE.—September 19th.—Completion of the main sewerage of the district, for the urban district council.—Messrs. Francis Newman & Cocks, 5 St. Thomas-street, Ryde.

LYTHAM.—September 19th.—Construction of about 900 yards of 9-ft. diameter brick sewer, about 1,500 yards of 24-in. and 18-in. pipe sewer, and concrete and storage tanks, together with sea embankment, road-way and other contingent works, for the urban district council.—Messrs. Newton, 17 Cooper-street, Manchester.

WAKEFIELD.— September 19th.—Construction of a cast-iron water-tank, to hold 18,000 gallons, at Woolley-edge in the township of Crigglestone, for the rural district council.—Mr. Frank Massie, A.M.I.C.E., engineer and surveyor to the council.

PADDINGTON.—September 19th.—Supply of about 500 cubic yards of fine crushed Thames shingle, for the vestry.—Mr. Frank Delbridge, surveyor to the vestry.

AMBLE.—September 19th.—Supply of 100 tons of broken whinstone, for the urban district council.—Mr. W. Gibson, surveyor to the council.

TORQUAY.—September 19th.—Supply of meters and are lamp carbons for twelve months from 1st October.—Mr. P. Storey, borough electrical engineer.

LIVERPOOL.—September 20th.—Alterations at the Steble-street public wash-house, for the corporation.—Mr. W. R. Court, engineer and chief superintendent, Cornwallis-street Baths, Liverpool.

LONDON.— September 20th. — Construction of underground conveniences at Queenhithe.—The City Engineer, Guildhall, E.C.

LEEDS.—September 20th.—Supply of (a) poles and (b) trolley wire and attachments in connection with the extension of the electric tramway systems.—The City Engineer.

AMBLE.—September 20th.—Excavating, levelling and paving works in Albert-street black-lane and Middleton-street black-lane, for the urban district council.—Mr. W. Gibson, surveyor to the council.

BUCKLOW.—September 20th.—Renewing of certain boulder pavements and channels in Carrington, Partington and Warburton, for the rural district council.—Mr. Joseph Burgess, highway surveyor, Tabley, Knutsford.

GOSPORT AND ALVERSTOKE.—September 20th.—Supply of various materials during the year ending 30th September, 1899, for the urban district council.—Mr. R. Frost, surveyor to the council.

BARKING TOWN.—September 20th.—Supply of a 6 or 10 ton steam road-roller adaptable for traction, for the urban district council.—Mr. E. H. Lister, clerk to the council.

BRADFORD.—September 21st.—Supply of about 150,000 jarrah or karri wood paving blocks.—Mr. J. H. Cox, borough engineer.

KIRKHOUSE.—September 21st.—Water supply works for Wingate Mill, Wingate-lane and High Wheatley Hill, for the rural district council.— Messrs. D. Balfour & Son, 3 St. Nicholas-buildings, Newcastle-on-Tyne.

Leek.—September 21st.—Erection of a science and art school and county silk school, for the urban district council.—Mr. Chas. Henshaw, clerk to the council.

Hull.—September 21st.—Supply of steel roofs and sundry iron and steel work for the tramway power station.—Mr. A. E. White, city engineer.

Hoyland.—September 22nd.—Construction of about 73 yards of 15-in., 1,690 yards of 12-in. and 1,766 yards of 9-in. pipe sewers, in connection with the King-street and Platts Common sewerage, for the urban district council.—Mr. William Farrington, A.M.I.C.E., engineer and surveyor to the council.

Blaydon-on-Tyne.— September 22nd. — Erection of new public offices and a technical school, for the urban district council.—Mr. H. Dalton, clerk to the council.

East Sussex.—September 23rd.—Erection of two temporary buildings for 100 patients at the county lunatic asylum.—Mr. Henry Card, county surveyor, County Hall, Lewes.

Willenhall.—September 24th.—Supply of various stores and materials during the six months ending March 31, 1899, for the urban district council.—Mr. Chas. J. Jenkin, town surveyor.

Beckenham.—September 26th.—Widening of Croydon-road and East End-road, for the urban district council.—Mr. John A. Angell, surveyor to the council.

Beckenham.—September 26th.—Erection of about 200 cast-iron ventilating columns, 13 ft. 6 in. high, on concrete beds, together with the laying of 9-in. stoneware pipe connections to the main sewers, &c., for the urban district council.—Mr. John A. Angell, surveyor to the council.

Witney.—September 26th.—Main drainage of Eynsham, for the rural district council.—Mr. Nicholas Lailey, A.M.I.C.E., 16 Great George-street, London, S.W.

Hastings.— September 27th.—Excavating and steining two wells, about 270 ft. deep, at Brede.— Mr. D. H. Palmer, M.I.C.E., borough engineer.

Hastings.—September 27th.—Construction of two covered service reservoirs (each 1,600,000 gallons capacity) at Ore.—Mr. P. H. Palmer, M.I.C.E., borough engineer.

Bexhill.—September 28th.—Supply of various electric light plant, for the urban district council.—Mr. A. H. Preece, A.M.I.C.E., 39 Victoria-street, London, S.W.

Hull.—September 30th.—Supply of forty-five electric motor cars, twenty trail cars, two sprinkler cars and two traversing platforms.—Mr. A. E. White, city engineer.

Ramsgate.—October 5th.—Erection of a refuse destructor.—Mr. T. G. Taylor, borough surveyor.

Southampton.—October 11th.—Supply and fixing of three high-pressure Lancashire boilers, economisers, calorifiers, radiators, steam and hot-water mains, and all necessary pumps, valves, &c., required for the extension of the heat and power generating plant at the county lunatic asylum at Knowle, Fareham.—Mr. W. J. Taylor, county surveyor, The Castle, Winchester.

Edinburgh. — October 17th. — Various works in connection with gasholder tank at Granton.—Mr. James M'G. Jack, clerk to the commissioners.

## TENDERS.

*ACCEPTED.

Birkenhead.—For the sinking of a bore-hole in connection with proposed pumping station.—Mr. W. A. Richardson, water engineer:
E. Timmis & Sons, Runcorn ; J. Wilson, Runcorn ; J. Smalley, Hull ; T. Matthews, Manchester ; J. Wilding, Parbold, Wigan ; Chapman, Salford.*

Darwen.—Accepted for the erection and construction of iron and steel buildings in connection with a refuse destructor.—Mr. Charles Costeker, town clerk :—
E. Wood & Co., Limited, Manchester.

Farnham.—For the supply of forage for twelve months from September 12th, for the urban district council.—Mr. L. W. Cass, surveyor to the council :—
W. Ball, near Alton*  ...   ...   ...   ...   ...   £52

Nelson.—Accepted for the supply of 550 lineal yards of wrought-iron unclimable fencing.—Mr. B. Ball, borough engineer :—
W. Walton, Newtown Iron Warehouse, Bromley.

Southborough.—For various street works, for the urban district council.—Mr. Philip Ranmer, clerk :—

| | £ s. d. |
|---|---|
| W. A. Locke, High Brooms ... ... ... ... ... | £3,087 |
| J. Jarvis, Tunbridge Wells ... ... ... ... | 3,000 |
| W. Wadey, Stoke Newington ... ... ... ... | 2,700 |
| W. H. Wheeler, Southwark ... ... ... ... | 2,429 |
| T. Hallett, Tunbridge Wells ... ... ... | 2,387 |
| T. Free & Sons, Maidenhead* ... ... ... ... | 2,368 |

Tonbridge.—Accepted for the supply of 1,000 tons of best quality 2-in. broken quartzite, Guernsey granite, &c.—Mr. A. H. Neve, Junr., clerk to the urban district council :—
C. M. Mannelle, 12 Lime-street, E.C., 13s. 6d. per ton.

## MEETINGS.

SEPTEMBER.

19.—Plumbers' Company : Public meeting at Manchester, for the distribution of prizes awarded in connection with the recent exhibition of plumbers' work at Manchester.
27, 28, 29 and 30.—The Sanitary Institute: Annual Autumn Congress at Birmingham.

OCTOBER.
1.—The Sanitary Institute: Annual Autumn Congress at Birmingham.

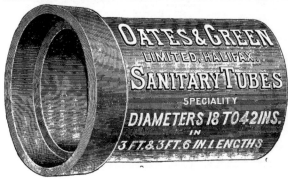

## NOTICES.

THE SURVEYOR AND MUNICIPAL AND COUNTY ENGINEER *may be ordered direct, through any of Messrs. Smith & Son's book-stalls, or of any newsagent in the United Kingdom. Applications to the Offices for single copies by post must in all cases be accompanied by stamps.*

*The Prepaid Subscription (including postage) is as follows :*

|  | Twelve Months. | Six Months. | Three Months. |
|---|---|---|---|
| United Kingdom | 15s. | 7s. 6d. | 3s. 9d. |
| Continent, the Colonies, India, United States, &c. | 19s. | 9s. 6d. | 4s. 9d. |

*The International News Company, 83 and 85 Duane-street New York City; The Toronto News Company, Toronto; and The Montreal News Company, Montreal, have been appointed agents in the United States and Canada for the sale of* THE SURVEYOR AND MUNICIPAL AND COUNTY ENGINEER. *A thin paper edition is printed for circulation abroad.*

EDITORIAL OFFICES :—
24 BRIDE-LANE, FLEET-STREET, LONDON, E.C.
ADVERTISEMENT AND PUBLISHING OFFICES :—
13 NEW STREET-HILL, FLEET-STREET, LONDON, E.C.

## THE SURVEYORS' INSTITUTION.

*(Incorporated by Royal Charter.)*

TEMPORARY ADDRESS—
SAVOY-STREET, VICTORIA-EMBANKMENT, W.C.

### EXAMINATIONS, 1899.

PRELIMINARY EXAMINATION.

Notice is given that the Preliminary Examination for the admission of Students will be held on the 18th and 19th of January next.

It is proposed to examine candidates from the counties of Lancashire, Cheshire, Yorkshire, Durham, Cumberland, Westmoreland and Northumberland at Manchester. Candidates from other counties in England and Wales will be examined in London.

Irish candidates will be examined in Dublin.

PROFESSIONAL EXAMINATIONS.

Notice is also given that the Annual Professional Examinations for Land Agents, Valuers and Building Surveyors (held under the provisions of the Charter), qualifying for the Fellowship and Associateship of the Institution, will commence on the 20th of March next.

English candidates for the Professional Examinations will be examined in London.

Irish candidates will be examined in Dublin.

Particulars as to subjects, course of examination, prizes and scholarships can be obtained of the Secretary.

All applications for the Professional Examinations, Divs. II., III., IV. and V., must be sent in before the 31st of October, and applications for the Students' Preliminary Examination before the 30th of November. The necessary entry forms for the various Examinations can be obtained of the Secretary.

## APPOINTMENTS OPEN.

ILFRACOMBE URBAN DISTRICT COUNCIL.
WANTED IMMEDIATELY,
Engineering Assistant (fully qualified), to devote the whole of his time for a period of not less than three months. Must have had varied experience in the construction of sewers, and in the preparation of plans, estimates, specifications, &c., in connection with the same. State salary required, which will be paid monthly.

Apply, by letter, on or before Saturday, September 17, 1898, stating experience and enclosing copies of recent testimonials to

O. M. PROUSE,
Engineer and Surveyor.
Town Hall, Ilfracombe.
September 6, 1898.

WILLESDEN DISTRICT COUNCIL.
ELECTRICAL ENGINEER.
The Willesden District Council require the services of an Electrical Engineer for the design of an electric lighting installation, and the ultimate management and maintenance of the same after completion.

He shall be resident in the district, and shall devote the whole of his time to the duties of his office. The salary will be £400 per annum, with office, assistants and supply of all office materials.

All further particulars may be obtained upon application to Mr. O. Claude Robson, M.INST.C.E., Engineer to the Council, Public Offices, Dyne-road, Kilburn, N.W., on and after September 6, 1898.

Applications, endorsed " Electric Lighting Engineer," stating age and enclosing not more than three recent testimonials (copies only, which will not be returned), to be ddressed to the undersigned, and delivered not later than p.m. on September 20, 1898.

Personal canvassing is strictly prohibited and will disqualify the candidate.

(By order)
STANLEY W. BALL,
Clerk to the Council.

Public Offices, Dyne-road, Kilburn, N.W.
September 1, 1898.

LEYTON URBAN DISTRICT COUNCIL.
The Council invite applications for the appointment of Chief Engineering and Surveying Assistant. He must be an accurate and expeditious draughtsman, surveyor and leveller, and possess a good knowledge of drainage and sewerage works, designing and building construction; be capable of preparing estimates, and must be conversant with the Model By-Laws of the Local Government Board. Salary, commencing at £130 per annum, rising by yearly increments of £10 to a maximum of £200 per annum.

Applications, giving full particulars as to experience, age, present and previous occupation, &c., and accompanied by copies of four recent testimonials, to be addressed to Mr. William Dawson, M.INST.C.E., Town Hall, Leyton, not later than Friday, the 16th inst.

Canvassing members of the Council will disqualify any candidate.

(By order)
R. VINCENT,
Clerk.

September 6, 1898.

LEIGH URBAN DISTRICT COUNCIL.
Wanted, a Third Assistant in the office of the Engineer and Surveyor. Must be a good draughtsman, surveyor and leveller, and have been trained in a municipal office. Salary, £70 per annum.

Applications, stating age and qualifications, together with copies of three recent testimonials, will be received by the undersigned up to 12th September, 1898.

TOM HUNTER,
Engineer and Surveyor.
Leigh, Lancashire.

LLANTRISANT AND LLANTWIT FARDRE RURAL DISTRICT COUNCIL.
Wanted, at once, as Temporary Assistant in Surveyor's office, a man who has had experience in the preparation of plans for water and sewerage.

Applications (accompanied by copies of three recent testimonials), stating age, qualifications and salary required, to be sent to the undersigned on or before Tuesday, the 20th inst.
GOMER S. MORGAN.

Surveyor's Office, Pontyclun.

TO PARENTS AND GUARDIANS.
CIVIL ENGINEERING PUPIL.
The Borough Engineer and Surveyor of the County Borough of Brighton has a vacancy for an Articled Pupil.— Apply to Mr. Francis J. C. May, M.INST.C.E., F.S.I., Town Hall, Brighton.

YORK WATERWORKS COMPANY.
Wanted, a Secretary and City Manager. One having had previous experience in a waterworks office preferred. Salary, £300 a year with house.

Application, with not more than three testimonials, to be forwarded by the 21st September instant, addressed to the Directors of the York Waterworks Company, Lendal Hill, York.

ARCHITECTURAL ASSISTANT.
Required, immediately, in a District Surveyor's office, adjacent to London, a thoroughly competent Architectural Assistant, capable of preparing designs for public buildings from sketches, working drawings and specifications. Weekly salary, 3½ guineas.—Qualifications, stating age, together with testimonials, to be sent to " X," office of THE SURVEYOR, 24 Bride-lane, Fleet-street, London, E.C.

TENDERS WANTED.

CITY OF LONDONDERRY, TO WIT.
The Corporation of Londonderry invite proposals for the Purchase of their Steam Road-roller, which can be inspected, at any time up to date of tendering, in the shed in Victoria Market.

The Corporation also invite tenders for Supplying a New 10-ton Compound Steam Road-roller. Contractors to set out in tender a full description of roller to be tendered for, with date at which it is proposed to be delivered in Londonderry.

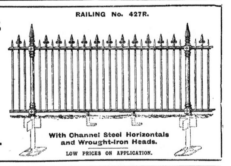

Tenders, endorsed "Tender for Steam Roller," to be lodged with me at my office, situate in the Guildhall, Londonderry, not later than Saturday, the 24th day of September instant. Dated this 6th day of September, 1898.

(By order of the Corporation)
R. NEWMAN CHAMBERS, Knt.,
Town Clerk.

## WILLENHALL URBAN DISTRICT COUNCIL.

The above Council desire tenders for the undermentioned Supplies during the six months ending March 31, 1899 :—

| | |
|---|---|
| Portland Cement. | Lime. |
| 2¼-in. Basalt or Granite. | 4-in. cubes Basalt or Granite. |
| Cast Iron Work. | Disinfecting Powders. |
| Disinfecting Fluids. | Machine Oil. |
| Cylinder Oil (Marine). | Lamp Oil. |
| Petroleum Jelly. | Aluminoferric Cake. |
| Stoneware Pipes. | Coal. |
| Coke. | Gas Tar. |
| Cotton Waste. | Scavenger Brooms. |
| Paving Bricks. | Steel Picks. |
| Steel Shovels. | 8 vo. Printed Notices. |

Drawing Materials.

Specification may be seen and form of tender and further particulars as to minimum quantity, &c., may be obtained on application at the Town Surveyor's office.

Sealed tenders, endorsed "Supplies," together with samples where required, to be sent to me on or before Saturday, September 24, 1898.

The Council do not bind themselves to accept the lowest or any tender.

(Signed) CHAS. J. JENKIN, C.E.,
Town Surveyor.

Council Offices, Willenhall.
September 7, 1898.

## COUNTY BOROUGH OF HALIFAX.

The Tramways Committee of the Halifax Corporation are prepared to receive tenders for the Supply of 1,000 tons of 6-in. Granite Setts, 2,000 tons of 6-in. Lancashire Setts, and 2,500 yards of Wood Blocks.

Specifications may be seen and forms of tender obtained on application to Mr. Edward R. S. Escott, C.E., Borough Engineer, Town Hall, Halifax.

Tenders, properly endorsed, must be sent to the under signed on or before Wednesday, 14th September, 1898.

The person whose tender is accepted will be required to observe the fair contracts clauses adopted by the Corporation.

The Committee do not bind themselves to accept the lowest or any tender.

(By order)
KEIGHLEY WALTON,
Town Clerk.

## CITY OF GLOUCESTER.

*NEW BUILDINGS FOR ELECTRICITY WORKS.*

TO BUILDERS AND CONTRACTORS.

The Corporation of Gloucester invite tenders for the Erection of the New Buildings in connection with the above.

Plans and specification may be seen at the office of Mr. Harry A. Dancey, 26 Clarence-street, Gloucester, between 10 a.m. and 5 p.m., after Monday, 5th September next.

The quantities are being prepared by Mr. Dancey, and may be obtained from him on payment of a charge of £2 2s., which will be returned on receipt of a bond-fide tender.

The Committee do not pledge themselves to accept the lowest or any tender.

Tenders, endorsed "Tender for Electricity Works," to be delivered at the Town Clerk's office, Guildhall, Gloucester, before 11 o'clock on Monday, the 19th September, 1898.

(By order)
GEO. SHEFFIELD BLAKEWAY,
Town Clerk.

Guildhall, Gloucester.
August 30, 1898.

## ROTHBURY RURAL DISTRICT COUNCIL.

The above Council invite tenders for the supply and delivery of a 12-ton Steam Roller at Rothbury, Northumberland; also for a Sleeping-Van, with furniture and bedding for three men ; also one Water-Cart, to hold 200 gallons, with pump and spreaders all complete.

Tenders, including specification and other particulars, to be sent to the undersigned not later than Saturday, the 17th day of September, 1898.

JAMES WOOD,
Surveyor.

September 5, 1898.

# COUNTY OF SOUTHAMPTON.

## COUNTY LUNATIC ASYLUM, KNOWLE, NEAR FAREHAM.

### EXTENSIONS, &c.—CONTRACT No. 3.

#### TO STEAM AND HOT-WATER ENGINEERS.

Persons desirous of tendering for the supply and fixing of three high-pressure Lancashire Boilers, Economisers, Calorifiers, Radiators, Steam and Hot-Water Mains, together with all the necessary Pumps, Valves, &c., required in the centralisation and increase of the heat and power generating plant at the County Lunatic Asylum, Knowle, Fareham, may obtain copies of plans and specification of the scheme and any other information on application at the office of Mr. W. J. Taylor, County Surveyor, The Castle, Winchester, on and after September 12th, between the hours of 9 a.m. and 5 p.m., Saturdays between 9 a.m and 1 p.m. A deposit of one £10 Bank of England note will be required for each set of plans and specification. The deposit will be refunded on the return of the plans and specification together with a bona-fide tender.

Tenders, strictly in accordance with forms supplied by the County Surveyor, to be delivered to me on or before October 11th next.

The Committee of Visitors do not bind themselves to accept the lowest or any tender.

JOHN R. WYATT,
Clerk to the Committee of Visitors.

Knowle.
August 31, 1898.

# BECKENHAM URBAN DISTRICT COUNCIL.
## TO CONTRACTORS.

The Beckenham Urban District Council invite tenders for Widening Croydon-road and Elmers End-road. The works comprise the widening of Croydon-road for about 800 lineal feet and of Elmers End-road for 150 lineal feet, together with the formation of new footways. In connection therewith the following works are necessary—viz., about 800 lineal feet 9-in. pipe sewer, 700 lineal feet 9-in. pipe surface-water drain, with manholes, gullies, &c., 110 lineal feet concrete retaining wall about 4 ft. high, 1,000 lineal feet curb and channelling, making-up roadways, &c.

Plans and sections may be seen, and bills of quantities, specifications and forms of tender obtained, on application to Mr. John A. Angell, Surveyor, on or after September 7th, on deposit of £1, which will be returned on receipt of a bona-fide tender.

A clause will be inserted in the contract providing that the contractor shall pay to the workmen employed in the execution of the work the wages generally accepted as current for workmen engaged on similar work in the district.

Tenders, duly sealed and endorsed "Tender for Widening Croydon and Elmers End Roads," to reach undersigned not later than 4 p.m., Monday, September 26, 1898.

The Council do not bind themselves to accept the lowest or any tender.

(By order)
F. STEVENS,
Clerk to the Council.

August 30, 1898.

# BECKENHAM URBAN DISTRICT COUNCIL.
## TO CONTRACTORS.

The Beckenham Urban District Council invite tenders for Erecting about 200 Cast-Iron Ventilating Columns, 13 ft. 6 in. high, on concrete beds, together with the laying of 9-in. Stoneware Pipe Connections to the main sewers, &c.

Plans and sections may be seen, and bills of quantities, specifications and forms of tender obtained, on application to Mr. John A. Angell, Surveyor, on or after September 7th, on deposit of £1, which will be returned on the receipt of a bona-fide tender.

A clause will be inserted in the contract providing that the contractor shall pay to the workmen employed in the execution of the work the wages generally accepted as current for workmen engaged on similar work in the district.

Tenders, duly sealed and endorsed "Tender for Erection of Ventilating Columns," to reach undersigned not later than 4 p.m. Monday, September 26, 1898.

The Council do not bind themselves to accept the lowest or any tender.

(By order)
F. STEVENS,
Clerk to the Council.

August 30, 1898.

THE PROPOSED VESTRY HALL.

THE NEW FIRE STATION.

# MUNICIPAL WORK AT BRENTFORD.

COUNTY OF SOUTHAMPTON.

COUNTY LUNATIC ASYLUM, KNOWLE, NEAR FAREHAM.

*EXTENSIONS, &c.—CONTRACT No. 3.*

TO STEAM AND HOT-WATER ENGINEERS.

Persons desirous of tendering for the supply and fixing of three high-pressure Lancashire Boilers, Economisers, Calorifiers, Radiators, Steam and Hot-Water Mains, together with all the necessary Pumps, Valves, &c., required in the centralisation and increase of the heat and power generating plant at the County Lunatic Asylum, Knowle, Fareham, may obtain copies of plans and specification of the scheme and any other information on application at the office of Mr. W. J. Taylor, County Surveyor, The Castle, Winchester, on and after September 12th, between the hours of 9 a.m. and 5 p.m., Saturdays between 9 a.m and 1 p.m. A deposit of one £10 Bank of England note will be required for each set of plans and specification. The deposit will be refunded on the return of the plans and specification together with a *bonâ-fide* tender.

Tenders, strictly in accordance with forms supplied by the County Surveyor, to be delivered to me on or before October 11th next.

The Committee of Visitors do not bind themselves to accept the lowest or any tender.

JOHN R. WYATT,
Clerk to the Committee of Visitors.

Knowle.
August 31, 1898.

---

BECKENHAM URBAN DISTRICT COUNCIL.
TO CONTRACTORS.

The Beckenham Urban District Council invite tenders for Widening Croydon-road and Elmers End-road. The works comprise the widening of Croydon-road for about 800 lineal feet and of Elmers End-road for 150 lineal feet, together with the formation of new footways. In connection therewith the following works are necessary—viz., about 800 lineal feet 9-in. pipe sewer, 700 lineal feet 9-in. pipe surface-water drain, with manholes, gullies, &c., 110 lineal feet concrete retaining wall about 4 ft. high, 1,000 lineal feet curb and channelling, making-up roadways, &c.

Plans and sections may be seen, and bills of quantities, specifications and forms of tender obtained, on application to Mr. John A. Angell, Surveyor, on or after September 7th, on deposit of £1, which will be returned on receipt of a *bonâ-fide* tender.

A clause will be inserted in the contract providing that the contractor shall pay to the workmen employed in the execution of the work the wages generally accepted as current for workmen engaged on similar work in the district.

Tenders, duly sealed and endorsed "Tender for Widening Croydon and Elmers End Roads," to reach undersigned not later than 4 p.m., Monday, September 26, 1898.

The Council do not bind themselves to accept the lowest or any tender.

(By order)
F. STEVENS,
Clerk to the Council.

August 30, 1898.

---

BECKENHAM URBAN DISTRICT COUNCIL.
TO CONTRACTORS.

The Beckenham Urban District Council invite tenders for Erecting about 200 Cast-Iron Ventilating Columns, 13 ft. 6 in. high, on concrete beds, together with the laying of 9-in. Stoneware Pipe Connections to the main sewers, &c.

Plans and sections may be seen, and bills of quantities, specifications and forms of tenders obtained, on application to Mr. John A. Angell, Surveyor, on or after September 7th, on deposit of £1, which will be returned on the receipt of a *bonâ-fide* tender.

A clause will be inserted in the contract providing that the contractor shall pay to the workmen employed in the execution of the work the wages generally accepted as current for workmen engaged on similar work in the district.

Tenders, duly sealed and endorsed "Tender for Erection of Ventilating Columns," to reach undersigned not later than 4 p.m. Monday, September 26, 1898.

The Council do not bind themselves to accept the lowest or any tender.

(By order)
F. STEVENS,
Clerk to the Council.

August 30, 1898.

THE PROPOSED VESTRY HALL.

THE NEW FIRE STATION.

# MUNICIPAL WORK AT BRENTFORD.

# The Surveyor

## And Municipal and County Engineer.

Vol. XIV., No. 348.　　LONDON, SEPTEMBER 16, 1898.　　Weekly, Price 3d.

## Minutes of Proceedings.

**The Bacteriology of Crude Sewage.** It is possible that within a very few years we shall be able, by the aid of bacteriology, to arrive at a fairly reliable estimation of the character of and of the part played by bacteria in sewage, and to classify these organisms in the same manner as we do other, but larger, organisms in the animal and vegetable kingdoms. The report on the bacteriological examination of London crude sewage recently presented to the County Council by Dr. Frank Clowes, chemist to the Council, advances our knowledge in considerable measure in this respect. It appears that the Council decided, several months ago, to construct experimental filters of coke for the treatment of crude sewage, and appointed Dr. Houston as a bacteriologist to co-operate with Dr. Clowes in an investigation into bacterial filtration. Although the London County Council are somewhat belated in their experiments in the construction of crude sewage bacteria filters—numerous smaller authorities having successfully adopted such filters long before the Council arrived at a determination to do so, and in one case, that of Sutton, Surrey, such a filter was constructed as early as November, 1896—nevertheless the council's experiments will be followed with considerable interest by engineers and chemists from a scientific point of view. Smaller authorities, with remarkably few exceptions, are unable to maintain a staff of chemists and bacteriologists, and although sufficient is known to prove that the bacteria filter destroys the sludge by the action of aerobic organisms, and that in like manner by the aid of anaerobic organisms, sludge is liquefied in the equally well-known septic tank process, yet the *rationale* of the process in either case has not yet been demonstrated to such a degree as to satisfy the scientific mind of the engineer. For the reason that the investigations will be conducted under such conditions and by men of such high repute in their profession, the results will be, when published, most welcome and valuable. Some remarkably good work in the study of bacteria in sewage, chiefly as regards their presence and characteristics, has been carried out by Mr. Jordan, and is embodied in the report of the State Board of Health of Massachusetts (1888-90, Part II.); by Sir Henry Roscoe and Mr. Lund, published in "The Transactions of the Royal Society, 1892"; and by Mr. J. Parry Laws and Dr. Andrewes for the London County Council, published as a separate report in 1894, under the title of "Micro-Organisms of Sewage"; but apart from those, little systematic work has been done. Moreover, that which has been published is not sufficient from a practical point of view.

The present report by Dr. Clowes is preliminary, we learn, to a bacteriological study of the filter itself and of "the filtrates," or filtered sewage, which discharged as an effluent from the coke filter, and really a bacteriological study of the raw sewage as to gain a knowledge of the number and kind of bacteria therein. The new coke filter had been in action up to June last, when this report was presented, for about seven weeks, and was considered to be rapidly maturing or arriving at a period when it furnishes its best results. The methods employed in the examination of the sewage as described in the report certainly deserve notice, but to the ordinary reader it may be of greater interest to learn that Barking sewage contains on an average nearly 4,000,000 and Crossness sewage 3,500,000 bacteria per cubic centimetre (= ·00176 pint), and that waste matters from manufactories, which are discharged in large quantities into the London sewers and yet may be regarded as foreign to sewage, do not inhibit the growth of the sewage bacteria to any marked extent. We should have been glad to have had some information as to the extent to which sewage when first discharged into the sewers is charged with bacteria, but are disappointed to be told that such is not known; in other words, we conclude that experiments have not been conducted to ascertain their presence and condition. It cannot therefore be said, we learn, that there is either an increase or decrease in the number of spores during the passage of the sewage to the outfalls. It is possible that the original spores germinate into cells in the sewers, but as the struggle for existence between the different species increases they possibly again form spores. In future reports it is anticipated that it will be possible to explain whether the conditions prevailing in the biological filters lead to an increase or a decrease in the number of spores. Some bacteriologists hold that bacteria proceed to sporulation chiefly or solely when the cells have attained their highest development, while others assert, we learn, that bacteria change from a transitory "growth form" to a "persistent spore form," in order to avoid extinction when the conditions for their growth are unfavourable. Some particulars are given as to the number of liquefying bacteria found in the sewage, these being always very great. The rapidity with which they multiply may be gathered from the statement that the multiplication is so rapid as to liquefy the gelatine and "flood" a plate before it is ready for counting.

Aerobic putrefaction is at work, we gather, on the sewage in transit through the sewers, and this is accompanied and followed by a decomposition produced by facultative anaerobes. As to the volatile products evolved during the process of aerobic putrefaction, these are carbonic acid, ammonia, &c., while the gases which are given off during the anaerobic decomposition of organic matter are hydrogen, marsh gas, sulphuretted hydrogen, &c. "Speaking generally," Dr. Clowes writes, "it may be said that there is less nuisance, and perhaps less danger, attending aerobic than anaerobic putrefaction, and if the two processes are equally efficacious in splitting up the various and complex kinds of organic matter present in the sewage into their elementary and innocuous constituents, then preference must be given to the aerobic process." The report is illustrated with photographs of some of the bacteria found in London crude sewage, and contains a lengthy table showing the results of the bacteriological examinations. Speaking generally, we believe that the report will be found of considerable value, and will assist to a better understanding of the life history of bacteria and of the part which they play in the changes which sewage undergoes. We shall, however, await with interest the promised further report on the subject.

\* \* \*

**An American Engineer on Bacterial Sewage Purification.** In the September number of *The Engineering Magazine* Mr. Rudolph Hering, the well-known American civil engineer, has an article on "Bacterial Processes of Sewage Purification." So far as regards the septic tank and the Dibdin experiments at Sutton the article is merely a repetition of information that has long been familiar to those who follow the subject in this country. Mr. Hering quotes from the reports of Mr. Dibdin and from a description of the Sutton experiments which has been given by Mr. C. Chambers Smith, the engineer and surveyor to the Sutton Urban District Council. In connection with the septic tank Mr. Hering quotes from a French periodical an account which appeared about seventeen years ago of a contrivance that certainly seems like an anticipation of the principle of the septic tank—that is to say, the liquefaction of crude sewage by the operation of anaerobic organisms. Mr. Hering's conclusions will be of interest to many of our readers. He considers that the bacterial process will be satisfactory if the sewage is previously freed from suspended matters, and if there is not enough poisonous matter in the sewage to destroy the useful bacteria. The difficulties which he anticipates in the Sutton process lie in the possible gradual filling up of the filters with slowly-oxidisable vegetable matter not strained out by the screens, on the ground that it is difficult to operate economically a strainer fine enough to keep out fibrous vegetable material. Mr. Hering goes on to say that at Leeds it was found that the sludging up of the beds was one of the chief difficulties, and that a permanent relation between the length of time during which the retained fibrous sewage matter is removed by oxidation and the amount of sewage that can be permanently filtered per square yard of filter area has not yet been discovered. He does not find that the cost of construction and of annual operation has been definitely determined, and he considers that sufficient time has not elapsed to give results which can be permanently relied upon. His general position is eminently cautious. While admitting that the Exeter and Sutton experiments are not only interesting, but promise to improve the present methods of sewage disposal where suitable land for slow filtration is not available, he considers it judicious to remark that the improvement may not be so great as the promoters anticipate. The following passage is worth quoting:—

It appears that with a limited amount of land permanent success in purifying sewage can be accomplished only by a prior separation of the suspended and dissolved organic matter. Organic matter in solution can be thoroughly purified by aerobic bacteria, and in large quantities per acre in properly-devised filters of sand, coke breeze, or similar porous and permanent material, operated intermittently. Undoubtedly, also, some fine fibrous or globular nitrogenous matter may also be removed by this relatively rapid process. But the organic matter in suspension requires a preliminary separate treatment, either, first, by a system of chemical precipitation, or, secondly, by a system of liquefaction as accomplished in the septic tank, by which the quantity of sludge is at least very greatly reduced, or, thirdly, by a preliminary very fine screening, with a subsequent liquefaction the remaining suspended matter in a so-called bacteria Whether the first, second or third method will prethe future depends largely on the question of cost of

obtaining satisfactory result which may be ascertained from the experience now being g ied.

\* \* \*

**Hampstead Vestry Electricity Accounts.** The scently published accounts of the ectric lighting department of the estry of St. John, Hampstead, eveal a very interesting state of affairs, and it is evident that the works now form a most impor nt branch of the administration of the vestry. I considering these accounts there is one very import t point to be remembered, and that is that the expenditure on mains when compared with the cos of other portions of the system is exceedingly ; but the vestry very early adopted the cours of laying electric lighting mains in almost every oad in the parish. This policy, which was initiad at the opening of the station, is now bearing uit, and future consumers will be connected up to e existing mains without much additional expens As evidence of the increase in the number of onsumers, it is only necessary to mention that ti outlay on their meters is very much in excess o the two preceding fifteen months. The capital e penditure for the year is £16,845, which now brin the total capital expenditure to £100,176. In a se there is a difficulty in comparing the results of the past year's accounts with what has gone befo , because the two previous accounts each cover a pe od of fifteen months. In spite of that fact, howev , the receipts for the past twelve months stand a the substantial figure of £8,081, as against £5, 7 being an increase of £2,823, or nearly 54 p cent. Another way of comparing the figures is ike the average income per quarter, and this duri g the fifteen months ended March, 1897, was £2,685 while the average income per quarter during the t lve months ended March, 1898, was £3,982. Notwithstanding the considerable addition to income the expenditure during the past twelve months oes not differ very materially from that incurred uring the previous fifteen months. The coal bill which usually forms the heaviest item of expendi re. amounts to £3,330, as against £3,100 for the pr e ing fifteen months, and this, considering the outp , is a highly satisfactory figure. The real interest hese electricity accounts, however, is the nett profi on the undertaking after discharging the interest d principal of loans and providing for all debts. ter making due credit for these items the nett profits no less than £3,905—a most gratifying result. Th re is one statement in the accounts that we cannot gree with, although it is one that has been acce ed occasionally in the conduct of municipal electricity works. It is held that repayment of the pr cipal of loans is equivalent to a contribution a sinking fund; but although this might be a ir way of looking at the matter when comparing t economy of the undertaking with that of a pra e company, it is to be hoped that the vestry ill not act upon that assumption when dealing ith future profits. We hold the strongest possibl pinion that a sinking fund or a reserve fund shold be built up out of the early profits of an underta ng, in order to meet the improvements in electric machinery that might take place almost at an period. The following table illustrates the rate progress made by the undertaking since 1895:—

| Items of Income and Expenditure. | Fifteen month to Christmas, 1895. | Fifteen months to Lady Day, 1897. | Twelve months to Lady Day, 1898. |
|---|---|---|---|
| Sale of current ... | £3,432 | £11,583 | £14,238 |
| Public lighting ... | 1,030 | 1,470 | 1,145 |
| Rental of meters ... | 142 | 365 | 531 |
| Sundry receipts ... | 3 | 8 | 16 |
| | £4,607 | £13,426 | £15,930 |

In order to cope with he development of the undertaking, the vestry hve been for some time negotiating for a loan of £51,500, which, it is expected, will more than met the expenditure to Lady Day. From that we may conclude that in the natural expansion of the business fr h capital will very shortly be necessary.

* * *

**The British Association Meeting.**

As we antici<sub></sub> e the proceedings at this yea<sup></sup> 'ting of direct interest to our r d s were practically confined t tl papers indicated in our last issue as set dow.. fo eading in the sections devoted respectively to ec nical Science and to Economic Science and ra tics. In the former the president, Sir John W fe Barry, delivered an able address of c ne engineering interest but with comparatively lit reference to municipal work. On Thursda i his section, a paper was contributed by Messr D i in and Thudichum on the conditions necessar fo he successful treatment of sewage bacteria, an tl we shall deal with separately. On Monday M red Gibbings, president of the Municipal E r l Association, discoursed on the application o. h electric motor to small industrial purpose: M. H. Faraday Proctor, city electrical enginer, escribed the Bristol electric lighting under s ; and Prof. Sylvanus Thompson and Mr. Mile contributed a paper on electric traction by su contacts. On Tuesday, practically the closing l iy f the sectional proceedings, Prof. Fleming calle ention to the electrolytic corrosion of gas ar we r pipes by the earth currents from electric rail w y nd tramways. Of even greater interest from m icipal point of view were Monday's proceeding the Economic Science and Statistics section. T e nportant question of the legitimate scope of r nicipal undertakings received opportune discus n. In these columns we have in general fa ou d the municipalisation of those great public e ices which are of the nature of a monopoly; b t e have pointed out that in the case of the tel i , for example, the conditions call rather for S t han for municipal control. Mr. Pearson's pa er "Municipalities as Traders" we are printin s ately in full, and a selection of other paper l e found summarised in a general report.

* * *

**Restrictions upon Officials.**

It would b 'a to say where the placing of ur sing and tyrannical restriction u n local government officials o l end if some people had their way. It can ea ly be believed, however, that a proposal such t tl of which we hear from Lambeth would be. d by any body of reasonable men, but it has. b y enough, been taken seriously by the vario r ropolitan local government employees' associa vho are watching results with a view to n such action as may be deemed necessary and le. It is said that a member of the Lambet o d of Guardians proposes to bring forward r ions with the amiable object of abolishing t l sent system of granting testimonials. He d e o provide that the heads of departments not give testimonials to their subordinates n that the board should not grant testimonials t ff rs and servants seeking other situations while i n the employ. ment of the guardians. This n man, however, is agreea b jle that in such case ters, signed b the chairman and countersig d y the clerk might be sent to the authorit l ing a vacancy. It will at once be obvious ho ɪ just the working of such a system might be many applicants; but the chief feature of the oposals is that they appear so needless. As we ha said, we should be surprised if they were adopted e her at Lambeth or elsewhere; but when proposals, en if objectionable, are adopted by one authority er bodies show a tendency to take them up. T matter should therefore be watched in the interes of local government officials, who have quite er gh burdens to

bear. We may have occasion to say something when it is actually brought up, and when we have perused the text of the resolutions, the arguments by which they are supposed to be supported, and the objections raised to the present system.

* * *

**Threatened Litigation in Electric Lighting.**

The officials of many corporations employing an alternating current system of electric lighting have been recently somewhat perturbed by threats of proceedings in regard to transformers. The facts may be briefly stated. A syndicate, headed by Mr. Martin Rucker, has purchased some old transformer patents of Zipernowski and Deri, and it is apparently the amiable intention of this syndicate to levy a tax upon a portion of the electrical industry. The extraordinary feature of this threatened attack is that the patents upon which the actions are based have been in existence for over thirteen years, and up to the present time no attempt whatever has been made to demonstrate the validity of the alleged inventions. It is quite true that the existence of the patents was well known to most electrical engineers, but it was never expected that action would have been taken, because it was generally felt that anticipation could be easily set up. The most important of the patents owned by Mr. Rucker is dated March 16th, and the second April 27th, of the year 1885, and in a few months the expiration of the patents is due. It is hardly necessary at the present moment to go into this patent question in any detail, but it is satisfactory to find that the municipalities using transformers are combining together with a view to resist the claims of the transformer syndicate, and it will be interesting to watch developments.

* * *

**The Bilston Meeting.**

Midland Counties district meetings are invariably successful, whether in regard to numbers or to general interest, and we have every reason to believe that to-morrow's meeting will be no exception to the rule. Mr. Pickering, the district secretary, and Mr. Wilson, the water engineer and surveyor to the council, have been very energetic in making arrangements well in advance, and the result is a strong and interesting programme. The comprehensive and profusely illustrated paper to be contributed by Mr. Wilson will probably be found to cover practically the whole field of municipal engineering work in the district, not only in regard to those numerous undertakings for which Mr. Wilson has been directly responsible, but also in connection with those works for which Mr. Baldwin Latham is acting as consulting engineer. The water supply works will figure prominently in both paper and visits. The municipal activity of Bilston is nothing new to our readers, descriptions and illustrations having previously appeared in our columns in connection with the baths, the technical school and other works. Only good weather should be wanted to make the meeting a complete success.

**York.**—At a recent meeting of the shareholders of the City of York Tramways Company, the chairman, Mr. J. Kincaid, said that the directors were a little disappointed that the negotiations with the corporation in regard to the adoption of electric power on the tramways had not yet resulted in anything definite. He attended a meeting of the committee of the corporation some months ago, and had a long conversation with them with reference to the carrying out of the power that Parliament had granted to the company for applying electric traction, but up to the present time nothing had been done, and the company did not know what the ideas of the corporation on the matter were. That was unfortunate for the company, and certainly it was unfortunate for the public, because the better the tramway service the better the public were satisfied. The company were at present unable to make any change, but if they knew the plans of the corporation they would be able to carry out the traffic better and also the repairs to the road.

constituents, then preference must be given to the aerobic process." The report is illustrated with photographs of some of the bacteria found in London crude sewage, and contains a lengthy table showing the results of the bacteriological examinations. Speaking generally, we believe that the report will be found of considerable value, and will assist to a better understanding of the life history of bacteria and of the part which they play in the changes which sewage undergoes. We shall, however, await with interest the promised further report on the subject.

\* \* \*

**An American Engineer on Bacterial Sewage Purification.** In the September number of *The Engineering Magazine* Mr. Rudolph Hering, the well-known American civil engineer, has an article on "Bacterial Processes of Sewage Purification.' So far as regards the septic tank and the Dibdin experiments at Sutton the article is merely a repetition of information that has long been familiar to those who follow the subject in this country. Mr. Hering quotes from the reports of Mr. Dibdin and from a description of the Sutton experiments which has been given by Mr. C. Chambers Smith, the engineer and surveyor to the Sutton Urban District Council. In connection with the septic tank Mr. Hering quotes from a French periodical an account which appeared about seventeen years ago of a contrivance that certainly seems like an anticipation of the principle of the septic tank—that is to say, the liquefaction of crude sewage by the operation of anaerobic organisms. Mr. Hering's conclusions will be of interest to many of our readers. He considers that the bacterial process will be satisfactory if the sewage is previously freed from suspended matters, and if there is not enough poisonous matter in the sewage to destroy the useful bacteria. The difficulties which he anticipates in the Sutton process lie in the possible gradual filling up of the filters with slowly-oxidisable vegetable matter not strained out by the screens, on the ground that it is difficult to operate economically a strainer fine enough to keep out fibrous vegetable material. Mr. Hering goes on to say that at Leeds it was found that the sludging up of the beds was one of the chief difficulties, and that a permanent relation between the length of time during which the retained fibrous sewage matter is removed by oxidation and the amount of sewage that can be permanently filtered per square yard of filter area has not yet been discovered. He does not find that the cost of construction and of annual operation has been definitely determined, and he considers that sufficient time has not elapsed to give results which can be permanently relied upon. His general position is eminently cautious. While admitting that the Exeter and Sutton experiments are not only interesting, but promise to improve the present methods of sewage disposal where suitable land for slow filtration is not available, he considers it judicious to remark that the improvement may not be so great as the promoters anticipate. The following passage is worth quoting :—

It appears that with a limited amount of land permanent success in purifying sewage can be accomplished only by a prior separation of the suspended and dissolved organic matter. Organic matter in solution can be thoroughly purified by aerobic bacteria, and in large quantities per acre in properly-devised filters of sand, coke breeze, or similar porous and permanent material, operated intermittently. Undoubtedly, also, some fine fibrous or globular nitrogenous matter may also be removed by this relatively rapid process. But the organic matter in suspension requires a preliminary separate treatment, either, first, by a system of chemical precipitation, or, secondly, by a system of liquefaction as accomplished in the septic tank, by which the quantity of sludge is at least very greatly reduced, or, thirdly, by a preliminary very fine screening, with a subsequent liquefaction of the remaining suspended matter in a so-called bacteria tank. Whether the first, second or third method will prevail in the future depends largely on the question of cost of

obtaining satisfactory results, which may be ascertained from the experience now being gained.

\* \* \*

**Hampstead Vestry Electricity Accounts.** The recently published accounts of the electric lighting department of the Vestry of St. John, Hampstead, reveal a very interesting state of affairs, and it is evident that the works now form a most important branch of the administration of the vestry. In considering these accounts there is one very important point to be remembered, and that is that the expenditure on mains when compared with the cost of other portions of the system is exceedingly high; but the vestry very early adopted the course of laying electric lighting mains in almost every road in the parish. This policy, which was initiated at the opening of the station, is now bearing fruit, and future consumers will be connected up to the existing mains without much additional expense. As evidence of the increase in the number of consumers, it is only necessary to mention that the outlay on their meters is very much in excess of the two preceding fifteen months. The capital expenditure for the year is £16,845, which now brings the total capital expenditure to £100,176. In a sense there is a difficulty in comparing the results of the past year's accounts with what has gone before, because the two previous accounts each cover a period of fifteen months. In spite of that fact, however, the receipts for the past twelve months stand at the substantial figure of £8,081, as against £5,257, being an increase of £2,823, or nearly 54 per cent. Another way of comparing the figures is to take the average income per quarter, and this during the fifteen months ended March, 1897, was £2,685, while the average income per quarter during the twelve months ended March, 1898, was £3,982. Notwithstanding the considerable addition to income, the expenditure during the past twelve months does not differ very materially from that incurred during the previous fifteen months. The coal bill, which usually forms the heaviest item of expenditure, amounts to £3,330, as against £3,100 for the preceding fifteen months, and this, considering the output, is a highly satisfactory figure. The real interest in these electricity accounts, however, is the nett profit on the undertaking after discharging the interest and principal of loans and providing for all debts. After making due credit for these items the nett profit is no less than £3,905—a most gratifying result. There is one statement in the accounts that we cannot agree with, although it is one that has been accepted occasionally in the conduct of municipal electricity works. It is held that repayment of the principal of loans is equivalent to a contribution to a sinking fund; but although this might be a fair way of looking at the matter when comparing the economy of the undertaking with that of a private company, it is to be hoped that the vestry will not act upon that assumption when dealing with future profits. We hold the strongest possible opinion that a sinking fund or a reserve fund should be built up out of the early profits of an undertaking, in order to meet the improvements in electrical machinery that might take place almost at any period. The following table illustrates the rate of progress made by the undertaking since 1895 :—

| Items of Income and Expenditure. | Fifteen months to Christmas, 1896. | Fifteen months to Lady Day, 1897. | Twelve months to Lady Day, 1898. |
|---|---|---|---|
| Sale of current ... | £3,432 | £11,583 | £14,238 |
| Public lighting ... | 1,030 | 1,470 | 1,145 |
| Rental of meters ... | 142 | 365 | 531 |
| Sundry receipts ... | 3 | 8 | 16 |
|  | £4,607 | £13,426 | £15,930 |

In order to cope with the development of the undertaking, the vestry have been for some time negotiating for a loan of £51,500, which, it is expected, will more than meet the expenditure to Lady Day. From that we may conclude that in the natural expansion of the business fresh capital will very shortly be necessary.

\* \* \*

**The British Association Meeting.** As we anticipated, the proceedings at this year's meeting of direct interest to our readers were practically confined to the papers indicated in our last issue as set down for reading in the sections devoted respectively to Mechanical Science and to Economic Science and Statistics. In the former the president, Sir John Wolfe Barry, delivered an able address of general engineering interest but with comparatively little reference to municipal work. On Thursday, in this section, a paper was contributed by Messrs. Dibdin and Thudichum on the conditions necessary for the successful treatment of sewage bacteria, and this we shall deal with separately. On Monday Mr. Alfred Gibbings, president of the Municipal Electrical Association, discoursed on the application of the electric motor to small industrial purposes; Mr. H. Faraday Proctor, city electrical engineer, described the Bristol electric lighting undertaking; and Prof. Sylvanus Thompson and Mr. Miles contributed a paper on electric traction by surface contacts. On Tuesday, practically the closing day of the sectional proceedings, Prof. Fleming called attention to the electrolytic corrosion of gas and water pipes by the earth currents from electric railways and tramways. Of even greater interest from a municipal point of view were Monday's proceedings in the Economic Science and Statistics section. The important question of the legitimate scope of municipal undertakings received opportune discussion. In these columns we have in general favoured the municipalisation of those great public services which are of the nature of a monopoly; but we have pointed out that in the case of the telephone, for example, the conditions call rather for State than for municipal control. Mr. Pearson's paper on "Municipalities as Traders" we are printing separately in full, and a selection of other papers will be found summarised in a general report.

\* \* \*

**Restrictions upon Officials.** It would be hard to say where the placing of harassing and tyrannical restrictions upon local government officials would end if some people had their way. It can scarcely be believed, however, that a proposal such as that of which we hear from Lambeth would be adopted by any body of reasonable men, but it has, rightly enough, been taken seriously by the various metropolitan local government employees' associations, who are watching results with a view to taking such action as may be deemed necessary and desirable. It is said that a member of the Lambeth Board of Guardians proposes to bring forward resolutions with the amiable object of abolishing the present system of granting testimonials. He desires to provide that the heads of departments should not give testimonials to their subordinates, and that the board should not grant testimonials to officers and servants seeking other situations while still in the employment of the guardians. This gentleman, however, is agreeable that in such cases letters, signed by the chairman and countersigned by the clerk, might be sent to the authority filling a vacancy. It will at once be obvious how unjust the working of a system might be to many applicants; but the chief feature of the proposals is that they appear so needless. As we have said, we should be surprised if they were adopted either at Lambeth or elsewhere; but when proposals, even if objectionable, are adopted by one authority other bodies show a tendency to take them up. The matter should therefore be watched in the interests of local government officials, who have quite enough burdens to bear. We may have occasion to say something when it is actually brought up, and when we have perused the text of the resolutions, the arguments by which they are supposed to be supported, and the objections raised to the present system.

\* \* \*

**Threatened Litigation in Electric Lighting.** The officials of many corporations employing an alternating current system of electric lighting have been recently somewhat perturbed by threats of proceedings in regard to transformers. The facts may be briefly stated. A syndicate, headed by Mr. Martin Rucker, has purchased some old transformer patents of Zipernowski and Deri, and it is apparently the amiable intention of this syndicate to levy a tax upon a portion of the electrical industry. The extraordinary feature of this threatened attack is that the patents upon which the actions are based have been in existence for over thirteen years, and up to the present time no attempt whatever has been made to demonstrate the validity of the alleged inventions. It is quite true that the existence of the patents was well known to most electrical engineers, but it was never expected that action would have been taken, because it was generally felt that anticipation could be easily set up. The most important of the patents owned by Mr. Rucker is dated March 16th, and the second April 27th, of the year 1885, and in a few months the expiration of the patents is due. It is hardly necessary at the present moment to go into the patent question in any detail, but it is satisfactory to find that the municipalities using transformers are combining together with a view to resist the claims of the transformer syndicate, and it will be interesting to watch developments.

\* \* \*

**The Bilston Meeting.** Midland Counties district meetings are invariably successful, whether in regard to numbers or to general interest, and we have every reason to believe that to-morrow's meeting will be no exception to the rule. Mr. Pickering, the district secretary, and Mr. Wilson, the water engineer and surveyor to the council, have been very energetic in making arrangements well in advance, and the result is a strong and interesting programme. The comprehensive and profusely illustrated paper to be contributed by Mr. Wilson will probably be found to cover practically the whole field of municipal engineering work in the district, not only in regard to those numerous undertakings for which Mr. Wilson has been directly responsible, but also in connection with those works for which Mr. Baldwin Latham is acting as consulting engineer. The water supply works will figure prominently in both paper and visits. The municipal activity of Bilston is nothing new to our readers, descriptions and illustrations having previously appeared in our columns in connection with the baths, the technical school and other works. Only good weather should be wanted to make the meeting a complete success.

**York.**—At a recent meeting of the shareholders of the City of York Tramways Company, the chairman, Mr. J. Kincaid, said that the directors were a little disappointed that the negotiations with the corporation in regard to the adoption of electric power on the tramways had not yet resulted in anything definite. He attended a meeting of the committee of the corporation some months ago, and had a long conversation with them with reference to the carrying out of the power that Parliament had granted to the company for applying electric traction, but up to the present time nothing had been done, and the company did not know what the ideas of the corporation on the matter were. That was unfortunate for the company, and certainly it was unfortunate for the public, because the better the tramway service the better the public were satisfied. The company were at present unable to make any change, but if they knew the plans of the corporation they would be able to carry out the traffic better and also the repairs to the road.

# Royal Institute of Public Health.

## ANNUAL CONGRESS AT DUBLIN.—IV.

As the proceedings of the Engineering and Building Construction Section are of special interest to our readers, we have given some of the most important papers separately. The proceedings opened with an excellent address by Mr. Charles P. Cotton, M.I.C.E., chief engineering inspector of the Local Government Board for Ireland. As it constitutes a review of sanitary legislation, we give it at some length.

### SANITARY LEGISLATION IN IRELAND.

The PRESIDENT said he proposed to take for the subject of his address the effect and result of recent sanitary legislation in Ireland. In talking of recent sanitary legislation he meant to refer to the period since the passing of the Public Health Act, 1875, followed by the Public Health (Ireland) Act, 1878. Before that time there were various sanitary Acts in existence, but they dealt more with the removal of nuisances and the prevention of diseases than with the necessity of, and provisions for, the efficient carrying out of sanitary structural works. The Public Health (Ireland) Act, 1874, effected a considerable change in sanitary law, but it was left for the Public Health (Ireland) Act, 1878, to sweep away all existing legislation on the subject in that country, and to make a fresh start by re-enacting the most useful parts of the previous Acts, with amendments and considerable additions. Since then several Acts relating to the same subject matters had been passed, to which he would allude so far as they dealt with sanitary engineering and building construction. The most important of those Acts were the Public Health Acts Amendment Act, 1890, the Housing of the Working Classes Act, 1890, the Labourers' (Ireland) Acts, and the Public Health (Ireland) Act, 1896.

### THE IRISH ACT OF 1878

followed very closely the lines of the English Act of 1875, but in some respects there were differences between them, to which he proposed to direct their attention. The most important point in which the Irish Act differed from the Act of 1875 was the power given to every sanitary authority by the section dealing with the "Power to Purchase Lands" to acquire compulsorily sources of water supply and water rights for the purpose of supplying their district with water for drinking and domestic purposes. This was effected by the provision in the section dealing with "Regulations as to Purchase of Land," that, under the term "Lands," there should be included "any land covered with water, or any water, or right to take or convey water." This enabled a provisional order to be made, giving compulsory power of purchase of streams, springs and lakes, but it should be noted that it was *only* operative for obtaining a supply of water for "*drinking and domestic purposes*." Such power could not, he believed, be given by a provisional order in England when the acquisition of water rights, otherwise than by agreement, could only be got by a private Act. Local Water Acts had been obtained in some few cases in Ireland, but, generally speaking, sanitary authorities hesitated to incur the responsibility and risk of proceeding for a private Act, whereas they had largely availed themselves of the cheaper procedure by provisional orders. In connection with the acquisition of property for sanitary purposes, and the putting in force of the powers of the Lands Clauses Acts with respect to the purchase and taking of land otherwise than by agreement, he mentioned the great simplification in procedure which had been recently effected by the Public Health (Ireland) Act, 1896, sec. 8 of which enacts that for the purpose of taking lands compulsorily by purchase under the Public Health (Ireland) Acts, 1878 to 1890, the provisions of the Lands Clauses Acts shall be amended by the provisions of the second schedule of the Housing of the Working Classes Act, 1890. The practical result of this was, that on the lodgment of plans, &c., with the Local Government Board an arbitrator was appointed, who held *one* sitting to hear and examine into claims, and then made his award, which was *final*. To anyone who had had experience of the cumbrous and costly process of putting the Lands Clauses Acts into operation it would be at once clear how short, sharp and decisive the new procedure was. He might appear to dwell unnecessarily on that technical detail, but he deemed it of great importance that it should be generally understood by sanitary authorities in Ireland how much less expensive and less uncertain, and at the same time more speedy and economical, was the new process of obtaining, compulsorily, property required for carrying out the purposes of the Public Health Acts. The power to make by-laws respecting new buildings, &c., was in England confined to *urban* authorities, but by sec. 41 of the Irish Act such by-laws could also be made by any *rural* sanitary authority. The importance of that was evident when it was considered how many towns in Ireland were, as regards sanitary matters, under the jurisdiction of rural authorities—*e.g.*, Tipperary, with a population of 7,000, Omagh, Strabane, Dungannon, Castlebar, Mullingar, and many others. He regretted that that most useful provision was not more availed of by the rural authorities; indeed, he doubted if many of them were aware

that they possessed any such power. Another and rather important difference between the two Acts was connected with the areas and incidence of taxation for "special expenses" incurred for sanitary purposes by rural sanitary authorities. In England the *contributory* place on which such expenses were charged was the parish where there was no special drainage district. The contributory area in Ireland might be an electoral division, a dispensary district, a townland, or (with the consent and by order of the Local Government Board) a portion of a townland. In England the rate to meet special expenses was payable by the occupier, but in Ireland it was levied "as part of the poor rate." Subsequent to 1878 several Acts had been passed dealing with matters relating to public health; but not having reference to works of construction, he therefore passed them by. The Public Health Acts Amendment Act, 1890, contained some useful additional provisions as to sewers, house drains, public conveniences, building by-laws, &c. Two years ago the Public Health (Ireland) Act, 1896, was passed. This Act contained some important provisions, supplementing previous Acts. Among them he might mention the power of the Local Government Board to invest a rural authority with urban powers for any particular purpose of the Public Health Acts. Power was also given to a certain number of ratepayers to require water rates to be levied for water taken into the house, which related to a certain extent the general rates. Also increased powers were given as to markets. In dealing with a defaulting sanitary authority the Local Government Board were given power, if necessary, to carry out works to remedy the default, at the cost of the sanitary authority. Power was also given to sanitary authorities to combine together for the purpose of executing and maintaining any works that might be for the benefit of their respective districts. The Open Spaces Act, 1887, gave great facilities to sanitary authorities to provide open spaces for the use of the inhabitants of the respective sanitary districts for "exercise and recreation."

### THE WORK OF SANITARY AUTHORITIES.

From the enactments for purposes of public health Mr. Cotton turned to what had been done in that country since the passing of the Act of 1878, and was now being done, by their sanitary authorities. He said that in the year 1879, the year in which he became first engineering inspector of the Local Government Board for Ireland, loans to the amount of £124,454 were sanctioned under the Public Health Act. In the year 1897 loans were sanctioned to the amount of £203,386, of which £12,840 was for dwellings for the working classes in municipal towns.* The total amount of sanitary loans sanctioned in Ireland had been £3,858,452, exclusive of Labourers (Ireland) Acts loans, or inclusive of those loans, £5,767,763. Of course sanction to many loans had been sought for, which had had to be refused, principally on account of non-compliance with legal requirements, for dispensing with which the Local Government Board had absolutely no power. Such cases occurred in proposed sewage works which would involve the pollution of rivers and insufficiency of the available margin of borrowing powers. The Labourers (Ireland) Acts for providing improved house accommodation for the labouring classes had been in operation since 1884. The number of houses definitely authorised since that time had been 15,748, and loans to the amount of £1,909,311 had been sanctioned for their erection, and over 13,000 had been completed and were tenanted. At least three rooms—a living-room and two bed-rooms—were required in each house, and proper sanitary accommodation, the average rent being 1s. per week for the house and half acre of land. There could be no doubt as to the good effected by the erection of those houses in educating the class for whom they were provided in habits of neatness and comfort in their surroundings, before almost unknown to them, and the improved dwellings must also be attended with a general improvement in health.

### WATER SUPPLIES.

Previous to 1878 waterworks for the supply of the larger districts—Dublin, Belfast, Londonderry, Cork, Limerick and Waterford—had been constructed under local Acts, but since that time it had been found necessary to increase those supplies, not so much from increase of population (except in the case of Belfast) as from increased consumption per head. The Varity works, which supplied Dublin and its suburban townships (except Rathmines), had been fully described in the "Transactions of the Institution of Civil Engineers." Quite recently a supplemental reservoir of 1,200,000,000 gallons capacity, and the duplication of the mains to the service reservoirs at Stillorgan, had been undertaken. The Belfast water supply, for a population of over 300,000 persons, had been about 11,333,000 gallons daily, and was now being increased by water to be taken from the Mourne mountains,

---

* The loans to municipal authorities for this purpose up to 1800 were administered by the Commissioners of Public Works. Since that date they have been under the control of the Local Government Board.

45 miles away, so that an additional quantity of, at first, 10,000,000 gallons daily might be got, to be ultimately increased to 30,000,000. These works were estimated to cost £1,500,000. The new additional reservoirs near Newcastle would contain 3,000,000,000 gallons. The Londonderry supply, which in 1878 was given by a reservoir containing only 85,000,000 gallons, was added to in 1883 by a second reservoir of 50,000,000 gallons, and last year the construction of a third reservoir, to hold over 80,000,000, had been authorised. Limerick, which in 1878 depended wholly on small works of a private company, had now a copious supply pumped up by turbines from the river Shannon at Doonass Falls, 10 miles above the city. Others of the larger towns, which twenty years ago depended on surface wells, unprotected streams or canals, had now been provided with new and good supplies—the property rights having been compulsorily acquired, and the works having been carried out under the Public Health Act—*e.g.*, Athlone, Ballymena, Bangor, Carlow, Clonmel, Cavan, Dungarvan, Fermoy, Larne, Lisburn, Lurgan, Maryborough, Queenstown, Sligo, Tipperary and Youghal. In country districts great benefits had been conferred on isolated places by the rural authorities providing small but pure supplies of water where nothing of the kind was previously available. This applied especially to cases in which national schools had been established without any regard to a supply of good drinking water being available. Before passing away from the subject of waterworks it might be interesting to mention the construction of the service tanks at Athlone and Tipperary, both of which were circular in form and constructed of steel plates. The Athlone tank was 45 ft. in diameter and 24 ft. high, holding over 235,000 gallons. The Tipperary tank was 55 ft. in diameter and 22 ft. high, holding 325,000 gallons. In both cases they were economical as to first cost, and in the case of Athlone the adoption of that form of tank was attended with an increase to the working head, an addition which was most desirable. The tanks were from the designs of the late Mr. Strype and Mr. Coucher, but the idea was taken from numerous service tanks of a similar design constructed by his friend, Mr. Cecil West Darley, municipal and harbour engineer-in-chief of Sydney, New South Wales, who had put up some of those tanks of a capacity of 1,500,000 gallons. Water mains, although coated with Dr. Angus Smith's composition, were subject to incrustation resulting from corrosion or the deposit of peaty matter. That was now frequently removed by scraping. The water main from the reservoir to the town of Omagh was an interesting example. That main got so filled with a deposit of peaty matter that its delivery was reduced to one-third what it should be, and no supply was given to the higher parts of the town. A loan was applied for, in order to lay a second and larger main at considerable cost (about £3,000). The sanitary authority, however, were induced to have scraping tried, and at a comparatively trifling cost (£53) the main was thoroughly cleaned and its original delivering power fully restored.*

### SEWERAGE.

A sewerage scheme of considerable magnitude was now being carried out in that city (Dublin). Hitherto the internal drainage was all discharged into the river Liffey, along its entire length through the city. The corporation were now carrying an intercepting sewer along each side of the river, the contents of which will be taken to precipitation tanks at the Pigeon House Fort, whence the sludge will be taken by specially-constructed vessels to be discharged at sea. In Belfast a similar intercepting system had been carried out. The contents were pumped up into a reservoir, where the sewage was stored until such time as the tide current was setting to the north-east, when it was discharged and at once carried out to sea. That that had been successful was evident from the fact that recently salmon trout had been caught in the Lagan. Owing to the fact that the large towns in Ireland were situated on tidal rivers, the discharge of their sewage had been direct into the tideway, and no schemes of sewage disposal otherwise had been carried out except on a very small scale. Recently the local authorities of the city of Armagh and the town of Lisburn had arranged for the purchase of land for sewage disposal works, but the particular plan to be adopted had not in either case been yet definitely settled on. No doubt other towns would be forced to follow suit. As they were aware, a Royal Commission had been appointed to inquire and report: "(1) What method or methods of treating and disposing of sewage (including any liquid from any factory or manufacturing process) may properly be adopted consistently with due regard for the requirements of the existing law, for the protection of the public health, and for the economical and efficient discharge of the duties of local authorities; and if more than one method may be so adopted, by what rules, in relation to the nature or volume of sewage, or the population to be served, or other varying circumstances or requirements, should the particular method of treatment and the disposal to be adopted be determined; and (2) to make any recommendations which may be deemed desirable with reference to the treatment and disposal of sewage." The Royal Commission held sittings in July and August, and would resume them after the holidays. With such a wide reference the final result could not be expected for some considerable time. Under the Public Health Acts many structural works were authorised which were not so directly connected with the question of health as were those of sewerage and water supply. Such were street paving, gas works and electric lighting, public clocks, slaughter-houses, mortuaries, burial grounds, scavenging plant, baths and wash-houses, rubbish depots, hospitals, disinfecting chambers, street improvements, public sanitary conveniences, &c. He need not go into those in detail, but he would like to direct attention to one item, which he thought might be attended with considerable benefit to the health of inhabitants, especially of the children resident in the poorer parts, the courts and alleys of towns. He referred to the replacing of footpaths of gravel, or more often of mud, by neat concrete footways which let the rain water run off and became dry at once. The cost was small, quite incommensurate with the benefit.

### THE HOUSING OF THE WORKING CLASSES ACT, 1890,

like its Public Health predecessors, swept away all previous legislation on its subject and replaced them with a concise code dealing with the clearing of unhealthy *areas* in a town, the removal of unhealthy *houses*, and the erection of dwelling-houses for the working classes. Part I., practically a re-enactment with amendments of the Artisans Dwellings Act, 1875, enabled an urban authority to apply for compulsory powers of purchase and clearance of areas which had been represented by the medical officer of health to be unfit for habitation, or dangerous or injurious to the health of the inhabitants. The repealed Act of 1875 had been put in force by the urban authorities of Cork, Dublin and Belfast, but owing to the cumbrous machinery of the Lands Clauses Act, to which he had already alluded, the result financially was far different from what was anticipated. He supposed this was found generally to be the case, as for the purposes of that part of the Act there was then provided the much more simple, more speedy and more economic procedure of the "second schedule," which he had already referred to as being now so happily applied to the Public Health (Ireland) Acts generally. That part of the Act had recently been put in force in Dublin, Belfast, Limerick and Lurgan. Part II. had not, as far as he knew, been yet acted upon by any sanitary authority in Ireland. Part III. enabled any urban sanitary authority to erect dwellings for the working classes on any land which they might acquire for the purpose, or (with the consent of the Treasury) on any land already in their possession. The operation of that part of the Act was restricted in Ireland to urban authorities, because the same object was achieved in rural districts in a more workable manner by the Labourers (Ireland) Acts. It also applied to municipal authorities who were not sanitary authorities. The provisions of the Public Health Act applied to loans for the purpose of that part of the Act, as also do the provisions for the compulsory acquisition of land. Urban authorities had erected, or were erecting, dwellings under that part of the Act in Cashel, Dublin, Waterford, Wicklow, Thurles, Kells, Kilkenny, Limerick, Newry, Pembroke township and Wexford, and the town commissioners of Longford, Middleton, Mullingar, and other town commissioners who were not sanitary authorities, had also availed themselves of their powers under that Act. Intimately connected with the carrying out of sanitary works was

### THE PROVISION OF WAYS AND MEANS.

When sanitary authorities got sanction to borrow it was open to them to do so from any source that offered. In Ireland, with but one or two exceptions, recourse was, until recently, always had to the Commissioners of Public Works in Ireland, who, acting with the consent of the Treasury, had power to lend, up to a limit of fifty years for repayment, money to carry out purposes of the Public Health (Ireland) Acts. Until recently the minimum rate of interest charged by the Board of Works was 3½ per cent. for a term of thirty-five years, and more for periods of forty and fifty years. By the Public Health Acts Amendment Act, 1890, power was given to urban authorities, with the consent of the Local Government Board, to consolidate their sanitary debts, and to effect future borrowing for sanitary purposes by the issue of stock. That had been availed of by many towns with considerable relief to the present ratepayers. Be it *post hoc* only, or perhaps *propter hoc*, the Treasury rates of interest had been recently greatly reduced and loans for sanitary purposes were now advanced by the Board of Works at rates of 2¾ per cent. for thirty years and under, 3 per cent. up to forty years, and 3¼ per cent. up to the limit of fifty years. A great deal of sanitary improvement in Ireland depended on the consent of the ratepayers of the area of rural sanitary districts to be charged with the expenses thereof. In villages and small towns the cost of sewers and of a proper supply of water would be beyond the resources of the inhabitants, and therefore the expense had to be charged on a larger area than that which was built on. That was not so unfair as it might at first sight appear to be, for the people of the country district within a certain distance of a town who frequent and use it for its shops, markets, fairs, schools and places of worship, could not, or at all events *should not*, be indifferent to its sanitation and the avoidance of epidemics. It might not be always right that the taxation should be equal throughout the area, and the Public Health Act provided for differ-

* See paper by Mr. J. H. H. Swiney, M.I.C.E., "Transactions of the Institution of Civil Engineers of Ireland, 1887."

ential rating being fixed for different portions of the area of charge in such proportions as the sanitary authority might think fit, subject to appeal to the Local Government Board. He might, perhaps, be expected to say something of the new order of things, in connection with public health, under the Local Government (Ireland) Act, 1898, when it comes into operation. He had not closely studied the measure, but he understood that beyond the changes of designation and constitutions of the local authorities there would be absolutely no alteration in the procedure for carrying-out structural works under the sanitary laws.

Mr. W. KAYE PARRY proposed a vote of thanks to Mr. Cotton for his address. He said that the most important Royal Commission that had sat for a long time, as far as civil engineers were concerned, was the commission dealing with the question of sewage purification. They were gratified to have Mr. Cotton as their representative on that commission. They knew that his presence would be an element of strength, justice and impartiality on the commission.

The motion was carried.

Mr. FRANK LESLIE WATSON, A.M.I.C.E., read a paper on "The Designing and Construction of Refuse Destructors," which we published in full in our issue of the 2nd inst.

## SITES AND SOILS.

Mr. EDWARD MAGENNIS, M.D., read a paper on "Hidden Dangers in the Sites of Dwelling-Houses." In the course of the paper he stated that the houses in many of their towns, especially in their large towns and cities, were erected upon sites that were simply the hiding places of sewers, upon mounds that contained the remains of their ancestors, on locations that had been the reservoirs of all filth, decaying animal and vegetable matter, street sweepings, and other most objectionable materials. In winter the heat of the building and the aspirating action of fires must tend to draw noxious gases in large quantities through the surface of the soil, and thus engender disease if preventive measures be not adopted. They knew that among the many evils attributed to insanitary sites were reckoned typhoid, cholera, yellow fever, dysentery, rheumatism, and the numerous respiratory diseases so common in their climate. England in twenty-two years of continuous war lost 79,700 lives; in one year of cholera, one of the most preventable diseases, the death roll number was 144,860. He considered that, as conservators of the public health, it was their duty to combat these preventable diseases. In the sites of their dwelling-houses the subtle enemies might be everywhere; they must be sought out, assailed and conquered, and for that purpose he would suggest the use of three weapons. The first was effective drainage, the second was that the entire site of the house within the external walls should be covered with an impervious layer, and the third that an horizontal damp-roof course should be inserted in the walls slightly above the level of the ground adjoining. In concluding, he said that it was scarcely too bold to assert that if, with the means which science had placed at their disposal, they had a thoroughly organised action and a generous measure of Governmental support, death would be no longer the grim spectre that smote the young and old indiscriminately, but rather the gradual decay of the forces of nature, and disease, its shadow, would brood less frequently over the land.

Mr. JAMES DILLON, past-president of the Institution of Civil Engineers of Ireland, read a paper, entitled "The Subsoil in Relation to Sites for Dwellings." Mr. Dillon opened his paper by giving the general character of subsoils and their present conditions on which the majority of the dwellings and towns in Ireland were built, and the nature of the works best calculated to improve their present conditions, and the order in which such works should be carried out. He then proceeded to indicate some of the principles to be observed when selecting or trying to improve proposed sites for towns and dwellings, and concluded by stating that the Local Government Board for Ireland and their able officers, including their president, had rendered valuable services to the people of that country, pointing out to them their present defective sanitary conditions, while at the same time assisting them to obtain loans on easy terms for sanitary work. Parliament having sanctioned that year a new Local Government Act for Ireland, they must all hope that each district council and county council would try without delay to carry out the suggestions of the Local Government Board in the directions he indicated, as they would have ample legal powers to do so.

The section then adjourned until the following day.

## SEWAGE DISPOSAL IN TROPICAL CLIMATES.

On resuming business on the Saturday, Mr. J. Desmond McCarthy, M.P., formerly administrator of the Gold Coast, read a paper on "The Disposal of Sewage in Tropical Climates." The paper dealt principally with the district of Lagos and the Gold Coast. Referring to the former place, he said that a great danger was created by the storage of sewage matter in house pits and down in the loose sand. That system contributed largely to the high death rate which prevailed. Water was contained in wells, from which the people drew their drinking supply, but these wells became contaminated by the passage of sewage matter through the soil. He made an analysis of the contents of twelve of these wells, and found the water seriously contaminated. Having

given the matter a good deal of consideration, he recommended that in order to get rid of the dangers arising from that contamination that the soil should be cleansed by abolishing the numerous house pits; and with regard to the wells he suggested that every well sunk should be allowed a drainage area of 100 yards; that instead of deep wells covered pump wells should be provided, that they should be prevented from leakage by the use of cement, and that a space around each of them should be bricked and cemented. The improvements, however, were not carried out, and the wells were still in an unprotected state. With regard to the proposed abolition of the house pits, the natives had an insuperable objection to such a measure. Some details were then given with regard to drainage matters and water supply in the Gold Coast district, which, it was stated, were in an unsatisfactory condition. Among the sources of nuisance which he mentioned as characteristic of the towns of this region was the wandering through the streets of thousands of swine. This constituted an objectionable feature, and was a continuous source of nuisance.

Mr. J. C. BRETLAND, city engineer of Belfast, read a paper entitled "Descriptive Notes on the Albert Bridge, Belfast." The paper was one which Mr. Bretland read in October, 1896, before the Belfast Mechanical and Engineering Association.

Mr. W. KAYE PARRY read a paper on "Progress in Sewage Purification," which we published in our last issue.

## STREET MAKING AND HYGIENE.

Mr. EDWARD GLOVER next read a paper on "The Hygienic Aspects of Street-making." In the course of the paper he said that in slums they found "matter out of place" in all degrees of saturation, age and pulverisation. In most of the ancient laneways they travelled, as on a switchback, over various catchment areas and land-locked lakelets, unable to discharge themselves into some misplaced lazy gulley, which, like a tank overflow, rose high and dry above water-level. In places not under the charge of the corporation or other authority they found the slums repeated, while as regards the new streets or roads of enterprising builders many of them were only jerry-made, mere "dirt" roads, which involved reconstruction in the future. No private owner should be allowed to make a street and then hand it over to a public authority. The authority should do the work, and the cost be assessed on the proper area or individuals. Streets served as open spaces as well as for lines of communication, and in the case of new ones their location, alignment and minimum width should be carefully considered. From the traffic point of view the travelling surface of a street should be as clean and smooth as possible. Omitting altogether the kind of materials used in forming a surface, it was therefore evident that (1) it should be impossible for water to lodge on the top or at the bottom of the crust, and (2) the crust should be watertight and of sufficient strength. Street surfaces not kept clean, or which held lodgments of even clean water, wore away very quickly under traffic, while any crust which allowed water to leak through became bumpy, irregular and uneven, in spite of the greatest care in maintenance. Water close underneath the crust was, as a general rule, a greater enemy to a road surface than water lodging on top. In producing and maintaining a proper carriageway along their streets they easily saw that the requirements for health and traffic were the same. Surface cleanliness was necessary for both, and it was hard to say whether scavenging conduced more to longevity for human life or road life. The same might be said in relation to ground water-level in the subsoil. It was known how great a factor the soil was in the spread of many diseases, and nothing influenced the ground in that way more than water. So, too, a wet subsoil made a good street surface impossible. Although a certain amount of moisture was necessary for street surfaces, yet over 90 per cent. of their wear and tear was due to the influence of water. He did not know if street-making and maintenance were included in the curriculum for sanitary or health officers; if not, they should be, and with as much reason as ventilation, light and allied subjects. Drainage for the efficiency and conservation of a street surface, of whatever materials constructed, should not only prevent water lodging, but also make it flow off quickly. Surface water should be compelled to remove itself automatically by proper grading and levels into gullies in the water tables or side channels. Even upon the flattest ground there should be no difficulty in obtaining the necessary falls, cross and longitudinal, because they could be worked out of the thickness of the crust itself. To prevent too much winding or distortion of the surface, and too great a height of footpath kerbing, the position and number of the gulleys required accurate consideration. As regards subsoil drainage, they had to consider it in two aspects—(1) as regards water coming from an area outside the ground covered by the street, and (2) as regards local water percolating down through a leaky crust. In the former case the water to travel laterally underground should be under pressure as coming from higher ground, or else the street should be over or upon an underground basin whose lowest point of discharge was too high. Ordinary intercepting drains outside the street area, or lowering the overflow of the basin, would prevent a wet subsoil and lower the line of saturation to any required level in those cases. Secondly, as regards water percolating through a leaky crust, they should see that intercepting drains or lowering an overflow would not cure it. Of course frequen~t~ minor intermediate drains would tend towards a cure, bu they were practically impossible in street work. Local water travelled at a very small lateral angle, and it was therefore hard to catch it. There could be no doubt that local water leaking into the soil was the chief factor in raising the "ground water-level" in most places. Water tight street surfaces would prevent much mischief, considering how large was the area of a town which its streets occupy. All houses should have eaves gutters discharging into drains, and footpaths should have a good fall to the channels and be watertight also. Those necessities were evident if they examined the weeping and damp-sodden walls of basements and areas, which were only too common. He had two cases in his mind where basements became unusable from water oozing through the walls from near ceiling level to the floor. Several remedies were tried and failed until the footpath was made watertight, when the evil disappeared. A footpath should act as an external dump-course, extending beyond wall face at ground level to save the part below. Much could be said about the materials employed in street-making, as well as their undoubted influence on public health, apart from proper workmanship. But probably it was not necessary in a general review to enter into such details. The choice of materials for any particular street was chiefly a question of first cost, and the public should be educated to pay for the proper article. In the near future, however, they might afford, at small expense, to have clean, smooth and noiseless streets. Electricity, motor cars and rubber tyres seemed to point that way. If so, the new era would add to the span of human life.

The meeting then adjourned until the following Tuesday.

At the commencement of the meeting on the Tuesday the chairman called upon Dr. McElligott to read his paper on "An Improved Method of Exhausting the Steam and Fumes from Wash-Houses, Sculleries, &c."

THE SEPTIC TANK SYSTEM.

Mr. R. H. DORMAN, M.I.C.E., town surveyor of Armagh, read a paper on "Some Experiments with the Septic Tank System of Sewage Treatment." After the first publication of Mr. Donald Cameron's experiments, Mr. Dorman said, he himself put down a small tank and filter-bed on his own premises, and, following on Mr. Cameron's lines, he found he was able to get a clear, bright effluent. He then advised the Portadown Commissioners to construct experimental filters in connection with an existing covered tank, and two small filters were constructed. With a filtering material only 3 ft. 3 in. deep, and with only a fall of 4 ft. between the tank overflow and the winter level of the river Corcrain, into which the filtrate discharged, satisfactory results were obtained, and had continued for some time. After some early defects had been remedied, the sewage passed through the tank normally, only requiring to be regulated occasionally by the town sergeant. No choking had taken place recently, the action being precisely that proceeding in the tank at Exeter, and no trouble being experienced in the working of it. The sewage due to a population of about 3,000 persons passed through the tank, but, the water supply being limited, not more than about 18,000 gallons of sewage passed through per day. Occasionally the tank got congested, but it was easily rectified by diverting the sewage into a by-channel for a few days, when the tank returned to its normal state of activity. The filtrate was, as a rule, faintly coloured and had a slight smell on discharge. Nevertheless, the results obtained by this simple and inexpensive process were regarded as wonderful. Nearly all the solid matter in the crude sewage was thrown into solution in the septic tank, and only occasional particles of solid matter were apparent to the eye as the effluent passed down the trough to the filter beds. After passing through these all colour had almost entirely disappeared and only a few very small particles remained in the filtrate. The author of the paper was convinced by these results that if the filters at Portadown had been of the same dimensions as those at Exeter equally good results would have been obtained. They could not obtain a depth of 5 ft. at Portadown, but it was proposed to extend the number of filters by adding a series of secondary filters composed of fine clinker, and experiments already made in this direction entitled them to anticipate the best results. For the reasons stated the filtrate at Portadown and the degree of purification there obtained would hardly compare with the results at Exeter, or with those obtainable with good chemical processes, but from these experiments the author had arrived at the following conclusions: (1) That the cost of installation compared favourably with the cost of any other system yet known; (2) the working expenses were small, and by adopting Mr. Cameron's alternating gear they could be reduced to a minimun; (3) no sludge was left to be dealt with, and the small quantity of deposit that accumulated at the bottom of the tank only needed to be removed about once in twelve months; and (4) there appeared to be no secondary decomposition set up after the filtrate was discharged into the river. It was, he thought, difficult to decide between the septic tank system and the Sutton (Dibdin's) process for dealing with sewage, but for the treatment of ordinary domestic sewage, or that from any district not overloaded with chemicals, he knew of no system of chemical treatment yet applied which would com-

pare favourably with this and one or two other biological processes. Some forms of sewage might perhaps be too strong for the organisms found in the septic tank to deal with. The author had had no practical experience with the septic treatment of sewage overloaded with chemicals, such as that resulting from Manchester, Wolverhampton, Wednesbury and similar places, and he would like to hear an expression of opinion from any one who had tried to treat sewage of that character by this or the Sutton process. But it appeared to him that as Mr. D. Cameron availed himself to the fullest extent of the anaerobic as well as of the aerobic micro-organisms he had more power at his disposal than was obtained by the Sutton process.

The reading of the paper was followed by a long discussion, and the conference then closed, the remaining papers on the programme being taken as read—viz., "Sanitary Work of the Romans in Lincoln," by Dr. W. O'Neill, M.R.C.P., London, &c., and "Notes on the Design and Erection of Architectural Ironwork," by Mr. H. A. Cutler, city engineer, Cork. The last-named paper, it will be remembered, was published in full in our last issue. A paper, entitled "The Laying and Jointing of Sewer Pipes," by Mr. R. H. Dorman, town surveyor, Armagh, which was also included in the programme, was read before the conference of Sanitary Inspectors.

This concludes our report of the proceedings of the congress. Certain special conferences, such as those of municipal representatives, medical officers and sanitary inspectors, together with a variety of other functions incidental to such occasions, were held, but do not call for any lengthy report in our columns. More than one of the papers we have given in abbreviated form were well worth printing in full, but space and other considerations rendered this impracticable.

## THE SEWERAGE OF DOUGLAS.

The report of Mr. Mansergh on the above question was circulated among the members of the Douglas Town Council last week. Mr. Mansergh states that he has been furnished with reports on the sewerage of the town by Mr. Stevenson (the engineer carrying out the work), Mr. Fox, Mr. Taylor, and Mr. Cregeen. From a discussion which has taken place with the Drainage Committee, it was evident there were many opinions on the schemes before them; and the effect of these reports and opinions on the mind is confusing. He is not surprised that the members of the corporation had a difficulty in deciding which advice was right. But the problem presented is really not serious. It is only necessary to realise one or two simple physical facts—the elevations of the town and the levels of the tide. Speaking broadly, the low-lying lands are as fully built on as they are likely to be; but there are several basements which are at much lower levels than the surface of the streets. If these basements are drained directly into the sewers a gravitation system would cause them to be flooded periodically. The proper method is to divide the town into the high and low level system of sewers —as is being done by Mr. Stevenson. There are no special circumstances to justify the council in departing from this obvious and natural method. The manner in which the low-lying basements are drained is, indeed, a sorry state of things, but to transfer the onus of dealing with the basements from the public authority to the householder would be a serious mistake. It would be possible to sewer the low-level area by gravitation if a tank were provided and a separate outfall made. On the score of expense this method could not be entertained. Regarding the method of lifting the sewage from the low-level into the high-level, he thinks that an automatic apparatus, for which the power is generated at a distance from the pump, is well suited to Douglas. The "lift" proposed to be used for this purpose is a new invention, but seems to Mr. Mansergh well suited for the conditions of Douglas. It was therefore apparent that the plans of Mr. Stevenson commended themselves to him, as they are laid out on the lines he had indicated. As to the cost of the work, Mr. Mansergh says it "will exceed what was at first contemplated, yet it must be faced. I do not see how the cost is to be reduced if the work is to be thoroughly done, and it is false economy to do less than is really required by the conditions."

## QUERIES AND REPLIES.

*Sketches accompanying Queries should be made separate on white paper, in plain black-ink lines. Lettering or figures should be bold and plain.*

213. Velocity and Discharge of Sewers, Book on.— "Kutterite" writes: Can you inform me if there is published any comprehensive table of sewer discharges and velocities for both circular and egg-shaped sewers flowing at different depths, similar to those in Latham's "Sanitary Engineering," but worked out by Kutters formula. Is it generally considered that Crimp's formula is as reliable as Kutter's?

One of the best and most reliable books is Crimp and Bruge's "Tables and Diagrams for use in Designing Sewers and Water Mains" (Price 10s. 6d. Biggs & Co.). The two tables give results approximating very closely to those resulting from Kutter's formula, and the formula used is, in our opinion, quite as reliable as Kutter's.

# The British Association.

## SOME PAPERS ON MUNICIPAL WORK.

The greatest congress of the year so far as science is concerned opened on Wednesday of last week and continued well into the present week. We have elsewhere indicated the scope of the proceedings so far as municipal work, and especially municipal engineering, is concerned. Two of the papers—those of Mr. Didbin and Mr. Pearson—we are giving separately, and therefore all that remains for us to do here is to summarise some of the other papers likely to interest our readers. It would, of course, be impracticable to print them in full. On Monday the papers and discussions in the

### ECONOMIC SCIENCE AND STATISTICS SECTION.

were devoted almost exclusively to municipal matters, which, though not directly relating to engineering, touched upon it closely enough to call for some notice. Mr. Pearson led off with the paper on "Municipal Trading," which we print elsewhere.

### A PROFIT IN AID OF RATES.

Mr. EDWIN CANNAN, M.A., followed with a paper, entitled "Ought Municipal Enterprises to yield a Profit in Aid of Rates?" Municipalities, he said, had been likened by an ex-Cabinet Minister, who had had a unique municipal experience, to joint-stock companies, the ratepayers being the shareholders. If the parallel were exact, there could scarcely be any question about the propriety of municipal enterprises yielding a profit, since to make a profit was the object of the existence of a joint-stock company. How far, then, did a municipality resemble a joint-stock company? In form the two bodies were very much alike, the management of both being committed to an elected council or directorate, and the ordinary members only interfering on rare occasions directly, though the citizens or burgesses exercised far more influence on the decisions of the representatives than the shareholders. But the basis of membership was very different. In the company it was ownership of a fraction of the homogeneous capital of the company, each fraction being exactly the same as every other fraction of the same magnitude. In the municipality it was connection with particular objects which had for the most part an individuality of their own, which were not in the possession of the municipality, but only subject to its claim for rates, and which were re-valued from time to time, so that they need not continue to bear the same proportion to the whole of the rateable property. The business of both the company and the municipality was economic work for the benefit of their members, but the company performed services for outsiders and distributed profits in money dividends to its shareholders, while in performing its ordinary functions the municipality provided commodities or services for its members directly, and consequently had no opportunity of making profits to be divided among them in money dividends. As far as municipal enterprises were concerned, however, the position of the municipality resembled that of the company much more nearly. Municipal enterprise was distinguished from ordinary municipal work by the fact that the commodities or services which it provided were supposed not to accrue to the citizens approximately in proportion to the rateable value of the property with which they were connected, so that it was considered necessary to charge for them by methods and standards different from those which regulated the levying of rates. By hypothesis, then, the business was no longer a merely "mutual" one, in which each member received direct benefit in proportion to his share, but a business like that of an ordinary company. The municipality ought to be allowed to make a profit, for the same reasons as a company is allowed—(a) in order that it may have some inducement to undertake the enterprise, which it would not have if it must take all risk of loss and no chance of gain; (b) in order to secure efficient management; and (c) in order that the economic proportion in the production of different commodities might not be disturbed. The arguments against profit-making in municipal enterprise seemed to be founded on an antiquated socialism or on a false analogy, either from co-operative institutions or from ordinary municipal work. That there might be cases in which it was not economically desirable that the highest possible profit should be made was probable, but these cases were far less frequent than was supposed, and since, when they occurred, the damage must be much greater to the locality than to the country in general, and also be tolerably obvious, there seemed no need to restrict the freedom of the locality.

### RECTIFICATION OF MUNICIPAL FRONTIERS.

Mr. W. M. ACWORTH next read a paper on the "Rectification of Municipal Frontiers." The title, he said, was intended to apply not literally but metaphorically, and he had no idea of expressing or encouraging others to express opinions on the abstract question of municipal socialism versus private enterprise. His only object was to invite consideration of certain recent developments in the life of our great towns, which must, as it seemed to him, tend in the long run to an important readjustment of frontier between

private and municipal enterprise. Gas and water supply had long been regarded, on the ground of their general necessity, as natural subjects for municipal ownership. Oddly enough, however, it was reserved for a commercial company—the South Metropolitan—to make gas really available in the poorest house, by the adoption of the penny-in-the-slot system. But with the rapid advance of rival methods of lighting, petroleum, electricity, and now perhaps acetylene, coal-gas was much less a general necessity of life than it was. Simultaneously there had been a rapid advance in the use of coal-gas as a source of power. In America they were building gas engines of 700 and, he believed, of as much as 1,000 horse-power. Now it would hardly be argued that the supply of gas as a source of power on a wholesale scale was a natural function of the municipality. There was no special reason why the credits of the ratepayers should be pledged to enable a capitalist to procure the power for his mills at a cheaper rate. Now, putting the matter from another point of view, would it be contended that municipal management, with its inevitable rapidity and slowness of methods, was better fitted than private enterprise to supply gas-power in competition with power derived from other sources. On the advantages of a municipal supply of gas for lighting purposes there was no need to dwell. But even here it must be admitted that there had been found a corresponding disadvantage in the natural reluctance of corporations already possessing profitable gas undertakings to admit electric light, either in their own hands or in the hands of private promoters, to compete with their own gas supply. The supply of water was a natural subject for public ownership. Even in America, where, in well-justified despair of municipal management, the great city of Philadelphia had recently sold its gasworks to a trading company, no one suggested that public water supply should be placed on a commercial basis. Nor need the question be argued here. For all that, the question of delimitation of frontier, not between private and municipal ownership, but between the rights of different local authorities, arose in this matter also, and seemed likely to become more pressing in the near future. But it was not by water that the boundaries of municipal enterprise were likely to be undermined. Their process would be rather one which their friends in the adjacent Physics section were accustomed to term electrolysis. Let him notice in the first place a possible new extension of municipal functions. A House of Commons Committee had just reported that competition in telephone service was desirable in the public interest, and that they saw no reason why, in any place where the Post Office did not compete with the National Telephone Company, licenses should not be granted to the local authority. They further expressed the opinion that "from the point of view of local finance a telephone service would, as far as could be seen, had been the supply of gas, water, tramways and electric light by local authorities." So, as the Corporations of Edinburgh and Glasgow had already applied for telephone licenses, and as the Post Office was hardly likely to incur the odium of entering into competition with the National Telephone Company merely in order to keep the corporations out, we should probably see the experiment of municipal telephones tried on a considerable scale ere long. Electric lighting, he pointed out, had from the outset been a mixed service, in the hands here of a company and there of a municipal corporation, subject to this—that the corporation had always been given the refusal before the company was admitted. Theoretically, competition was contemplated almost from the outset, for the Electric Lighting Act of 1888 expressly provided that "the grant of authority to any undertakers to supply electricity within any area by license or provisional order shall not in any way hinder or restrict the granting of a license or provisional order to the local authority, or to any company or person within the same area." But in practice what competition there had been had been of companies inter se. Last session, however, saw a change. Two local authorities sought, and one of them obtained, statutory power to compete within their district with companies in possession of the field. He pointed out that the accepted tramway policy of the country was also rapidly being dissolved by electrolytic action. This policy, now nearly thirty years old, provided that, while the veto of the local authority on construction by a company was paramount, any municipality could lay down, and of late years could also work, tramways of its own. In conclusion, he submitted that the ever-increasing complication of civilisation, and the ever-increasing specialisation of science, coupled with the ever-increasing inter-dependence of independently-organised local government districts, all tended towards a re-adjustment of the boundaries of direct municipal activity, and that the re-adjustment was likely to be on the whole in the direction of extending, rather than restricting, the public functions allotted within the municipal area to commercial enterprise.

All three papers were discussed together, the discussion being opened by

Mr. ɪᴀᴄᴅᴏɴᴀʟᴅ, who said that information on these subjects which had come to them from America should be received with caution. With regard to Mr. Cannan's paper, what he felt was that a clear line should be drawn between municipal undertakings and municipal enterprise, and he ventured to suggest that an approach towards such a distinction should be attempted. He did not know that it would be an altogether successful attempt to divide municipal antipathies into two great divisions, the first to correspond with the enterprise in which the individual use was still a more permanent feature than social activities. It had been suggested that an attempt should be made to divide the activities into those in which the individual use was still paramount, and consequently ought to be charged. It was distinctly his view that a charge upon private enterprise could legitimately be made. The other division was that in which social use or social efficiency was the more prominent feature than individual use. He was glad that Mr. Acworth had referred to the telephone system, because he was assured that they were all agreed that municipal telephone services would be a great mistake.

Mr. Gᴇᴏʀɢᴇ Iʟᴇs (of Montreal), describing electrical traction in that city, said that experience proved that the larger the receipts were, point to point, the larger was the proportion of the taxes paid on the gross receipts. It might be instructing to them to know, as a matter of comparison, that the receipts from the Bristol tramway lines, he was told, amounted to about £250 per day, whereas the receipts in Montreal, with a population one-sixth the size of Bristol, ran to no less than $4,000, or about £800, a day, and that notwithstanding a long and severe winter. He was absolutely sure that municipal government would never be anything like so efficient, intelligent and safe a system as that which prevailed in Montreal at the present moment, at least not in his country.

Major Cʀᴀɪɢɪʀ (of the Board of Agriculture) could not agree with Mr. Cannan's analysis of a joint-stock company and a municipal corporation. He failed, indeed, to see any analogy at all, and for this reason : He became a member of a joint-stock company because it pleased him to do so, and because he bought stock, bnt he did not become a sufferer from the rates in a municipality by any action of his own, at least he need not necessarily do so.

Mr. Scᴏᴛᴛ, of Toronto, expressed concurrence with the distinction between work of common benefit and that of which the use was in the discretion of individuals. In Canada they had adopted the principle of private enterprise subject to comprehensive municipal control. The telephones were used, like the tramways, to contribute to the rates, though disputes had arisen, and the municipalities declined to undertake any burden in respect of them. On the whole, municipal management had been found less satisfactory than that of commercial companies. In New York and elsewhere the underground trolley was found the most effective, and was displacing the cable, and it was felt that the overground system was doomed.

Mr. F. Tʜᴏᴍᴘsᴏɴ said that at Croydon they had water and electric lighting in the hands of the municipality, and expected to make a profit by the latter.

Mr. R. A. Hᴏᴏᴘᴇʀ suggested there should be a limit of profit to be made by municipal enterprise. The profit should be as low as possible, because if they made it too large the consumer of the commodity would be to some extent damnified. For instance, if in the case of water he paid for it on too great a scale he paid too much and a margin went to the alleviation of those who did not use water at all by reason of having their own private wells.

Mr. Cʜᴀʀʟᴇs Tʜᴏᴍᴀs (deputy-chairman of the Midland Railway Company) said that in his view there was much to be desired in the supervision of labour under the municipalities, and contended that those employed in municipal work were allowed to waste their time, and were of nothing like the same value as similar employees who served private contractors. If municipalities were to become great manufacturers or great employers of labour, the difficulty connected with labour would be inevitably increased.

Mr. R. C. Mɪʟʟᴀʀ observed that the subject was a very wide one, and it seemed to him that it would be very difficult to deduce general propositions applicable to all the questions raised. Gas, water, telephones and electrical traction all interfered with streets, and no doubt one of the most important reasons why municipalities wished to have these matters in their own hands was that if they had one department looking after the streets, that department could more effectually control the up-keep of the streets, if central organisation also had to do with the things that used the streets. Then he agreed that water was a proper subject for municipal monopoly, mainly because the whole community derived advantage from the use of water. The community suffered if the individual did not use the water. The growth of municipal debts proved the progress municipalities had made in England.

Mr. Pᴇᴀʀsᴏɴ, in replying on the discussion, said that in the matter of large enterprises, where it became a question of company v. corporation, the side which had the most credit would get the money cheapest. For instance, if the corporation had promoted the tramways at Bristol it could have raised the money at 2¼, 2½ or 3 per cent., whereas the

cost to the company was 5¼ or 5½ per cent. When he heard one of his colleagues in the reading of the papers say that the corporation had not the command or ability which a company possessed, he naturally asked himself who were advising the Bristol Corporation in its electrical undertaking. He claimed that, man for man, the employees of the corporation were equal to the employees of any company. Speaking from a considerable experience, he denied that there was anything to fear from the action of the working classes in bringing pressure to bear upon corporations to raise the rate of wages of the employees, and he heard with amazement that councillors had been compelled to wink at the shirking of work. People who shirked their work would very soon hear of it. When it was suggested that employees of the Bristol Corporation should have their wages increased to £1 a week he had no hesitation in voting for the proposal. Now, in his view, they had more to fear from the combinations of the masters than from the combinations of working men. The question which corporations had specially to consider was the cheapest way of getting an article they wanted the people to have into the hands of the public.

Mr. Cᴀɴɴᴀɴ and Mr. Acᴡᴏʀᴛʜ also replied on the discussion.

## ECONOMIC AND SOCIAL INFLUENCES OF ELECTRIC TRACTION.

Prof. S. P. Tʜᴏᴍᴘsᴏɴ read a paper on this subject. He said that no one could doubt that important effects were being produced upon the prosperity and habits of those communities who had adopted electric tramways, by reason of the cheap and rapid conveyance which had been secured. Even the introduction of horse tramways thirty years ago produced marked social and economic effects, and much more was this true of the better organised and more expeditious mode of travelling when electric power was used for propulsion. He first realised the importance of these effects in 1893, when travelling in the United States, and when revisiting Pittsburg he found what changes the introduction of electric tramways had wrought in that city. Formerly the vast bodies of artisans lived near the factories, crowded together in tenement houses in narrow streets. The advent of the electric cars changed all this, and the outlying districts became populous with delightful rows of little semi-detached workmen's villas. The uniform charge for riding was 5 cents (2½d.), but now men purchased tickets for several rides at a cheaper rate. The fare might seem high to us, but it was not considered so in Pittsburg, and it must be considered that while in the engineering circles men worked harder and for somewhat longer hours, the wages, whether for skilled or unskilled labour, was about double those paid in England. Pittsburg was no solitary example, for in every large American and Canadian town something of the same kind was going on. In the city of Boston electric cars had long superseded horse cars; indeed, if a return were made, 29,000 horses would be required to do the work at present done by electricity. The gain in the cleanliness of the streets and public health in the absence of these 29,000 horses must be very great. The reader gave a detailed description of the system as it obtains in Toronto, and went on to say that the Province of Ontario had already over 900 miles of electric tramways, while in all Europe there was a total of only 700 miles. When he visited Toronto in 1884 it had a very complete system of horse tramways; in 1897 he saw no horse tramways, but a fine network of electric tramways on the most modern lines. It was found in Toronto that electric transit prevented the congestion of the population in certain districts and the creation of slums. It enabled working people and others of small means to find good and cheap house accommodation in open suburban districts, with rapid conveyance to and from their work at a reasonable cost. It tended to develop the departmental store system and concentrate the retail sale in the business centre, at the expense of smaller storekeepers. It largely increased the value of real estate in the suburban and outlying districts, and consequently detracted from that of house property in the immediate region. Under strict municipal control it ensured fair wages and just treatment to a large class of working men. On the whole it conduced greatly to the advantage of Toronto as a place of residence, and the physical and moral well-being of the population. Among interesting developments of the electric car system he might mention the open cars in summer, and cars in winter electrically lighted.

The Right Hon. G. Sʜᴀᴡ-Lᴇғᴇᴠʀᴇ thanked Prof. Sylvanus Thompson for his extremely able paper. It showed how very much we were behind in these matters in the old country as compared with Canada and many parts of America. He hoped that the principle of electric traction would some day, and sooner rather than later, be introduced into some cities in England. At all events the experiment might very well be made. The reader of the paper did not say whether the electric tramways were the property of the city or of the companies. He presumed they had been constructed by the different companies—(Prof. Thompson : That is so)—and he supposed the author quoted that for the purpose of demonstrating the expediency of such enterprises being undertaken by the corporation, but he (Mr. Lefevre) was rather in favour of the municipalisation of such concerns. In the case of London he had himself advised this—that where the county council took over the tramways they should, for a period at all events, be left for management in the hands of the companies. He was afraid there was no chance of the principle of electric traction being applied in London for some time, but he thought the results obtained elsewhere had shown them that it would prove a factor in settling the problem of the housing of the working classes.

Mr. Scott thanked Mr. Thompson for the manner in which he had treated the city of Toronto. He was amazed at the accurate and full information which Mr. Thompson possessed on the subject.

Mr. Acworth thought the paper should be read at the market cross of every corporation in the kingdom. He thought, however, it would be difficult to adopt the principle in England, because of the speed at which the cars travelled and of the fares charged. England would be handicapped in such a competition.

Mr. R. C Millar would like to be informed wherein lay the superiority of electricity over the cable system.

Mr. Iles (Toronto) also thanked Prof. Thompson for his address, and Mr. Thompson briefly replied on the discussion.

This concludes the proceedings of the section so far as they are within our scope. Next week we shall deal in a similar way with certain papers read in the Mechanical Science section, including that of Mr. Dibdin, which we expect to give at considerable length. Only in the two sections in question were papers read to which we can appropriately refer.

## THE DISPOSAL OF SEWAGE.

### CONFERENCE AT SALFORD.

On Monday, at the Salford Town Hall, a meeting of representatives of local authorities in the Irwell watershed was held to consider the question of sewage disposal by land treatment. The meeting, which was attended by a large number of representatives of various bodies, was called by the River Irwell Conservancy Committee of the Salford Corporation. The Mayor of Salford presided.

At the opening of the proceedings a letter was read from the town clerk of Manchester tendering the thanks of the Rivers Committee of his corporation for the invitation to attend the conference, and adding: "They, however, feel that Manchester is in a somewhat exceptional position, as they have already given an undertaking in reference to the subject which renders it undesirable at the present time for them to take part in the meeting which you have convened."

After a statement in regard to the business of the meeting, the following resolution was moved: "That this conference of local authorities in the Irwell watershed gladly recognises the great advance made during recent years in efficient and economical means of sewage disposal, affording methods alternative to that of filtration through vast areas of costly land plus artificial filters, &c., demanded by the Local Government Board, and is of opinion that not only are the board's requirements needlessly expensive and embarrassing to most sanitary authorities, but to some are economically and to others physically impossible." A brief discussion ensued upon the motion, which was subsequently put to the meeting and carried. The following was then adopted: "That it be recommended that an association be formed of the local authorities within the Irwell watershed, to be composed of two representatives of each authority, to fully consider and report upon the following matters—namely: (a) The requirements of the Local Government Board with respect to filtration of sewage effluent through land. (b) The rights of manufacturers to turn trade liquids and refuse into the public sewers. (c) The standard of purity of effluent required by the Mersey and Irwell Joint Committee. And that each authority be required to contribute towards the incidental expenses pro rata according to population."

Mr. Brown, the town clerk of Salford, expressed astonishment at certain remarks which had been made in the course of the meeting. It had been said, for example, that in certain places the Local Government Board had refused to sanction loans for other purposes because the local authorities declined to carry out their wishes in regard to land filtration. The thing was preposterous. But they had no power to do it, and they could be compelled by mandamus to cease withholding their sanction. Another matter he desired to mention was this—that in certain circumstances they had no need to go to the Local Government Board for power to borrow money for sewage purposes. All authorities who had "land, works, or other property for the purposes of the disposal of sewage," had no need to go to the Local Government Board —that board had nothing to do with the matter in any shape or form. Such authorities might borrow to the extent of two-thirds of the annual assessable value of their districts, and that was more than any local authority would ever want. The Local Government Board admitted that he was right in this contention, and Mr. Fletcher Moulton, although he hesitated at first, also accepted his view. The Bank of England, through their solicitors, had also looked into the matter, and were lending money to the corporation in the full conviction that his view was correct.

A vote of thanks to the mayor for presiding and to the Salford authorities for calling the meeting brought the proceedings to an end.

## CREMATION OF SEWAGE.

The letter of the Archdeacon of Gloucester on the cremation of sewage published in our last issue has elicited the following from a correspondent of The Times:—

"Archdeacon Sheringham, in his letter, hits the nail on the head when he says that the turning of fair streams into open sewers. Various landowners and farmers, for the sake of individual gain, have from time to time either sold their land to the Cheltenham Corporation or allowed it to be used for irrigation purposes, whilst their neighbours, and especially the poorer classes, have, without compensation, had the air which they breathe polluted, and in some cases their water supply contaminated. And this, forsooth, is done by the sanitary authority of a town calling itself a health resort! There are, no doubt, other towns worse than Cheltenham, and it seems certain that, if Parliament much longer allows corporations and manufacturers to go on acquiring as it were prescriptive rights to pollute the fields and streams of England, the evil will have grown beyond control. In the meantime Archdeacon Sheringham has done a public service by calling the attention of our legislators to it."

"There are many of us who would prefer that the attention of Parliament should be directed more to the social welfare of the people and less to political quackery."

## A CLEVER SURVEYING INSTRUMENT.

The Ziegler-Hager tacheograph is a clever surveying instrument to which the attention of our readers may be drawn, for though it has been in use for several years on the Continent, it does not seem to be so well known here as its merits entitle it to be. It is remarkably simple, both in theory and manipulation. It is the universal tacheograph of Victor von Ziegler, a well-known writer on geodesy, and of C. Hager, scientific instrument maker, Luxemburg. The instrument, which is constructed in various forms for special purposes, belongs to the class of plane table theodolites. Its chief merits are that horizontal distances and vertical heights are read off at the same time, that there are no calculations, that the instrument checks itself, and that the operations require very little time and skill.

The three levelling screws of the table fit into grooves of the tripod stand, which is of the now usual construction, both firm and light, and provided with a screw and with a strong spiral spring, by which means the table is secured to the tripod. The instrument is neatly and carefully finished, and there appears to be no delicate parts likely to get out of order. The staff is made of triangular section, and is hinged in the middle, so that it can be folded up to form a prismatic bar. The centimetre divisions will then be on the inside faces, and thus not exposed to any wear. These instruments have found great favour with surveyors and mining engineers in Luxemburg, France and Germany, as being both accurate and convenient. Our surveying and engineering readers who desire further information on the subject will find it in an illustrated article in our contemporary, Engineering, for May 6, 1898.

## PROPOSED HARBOUR AT LOWESTOFT.

The East Anglian Daily Times states that, with a view to avoiding, if possible, the great outlay for protection works on the Denes at Lowestoft, a suggestion which was made some sixty years ago has been revived at Lowestoft—namely, the making of a harbour of refuge on the Denes, and the provision of wharves, docks, warehouses, &c. Lowestoft boat-owners, in common with the residents generally, have realised with serious concern the denuding of their beaches and the possible permanent flooding of the Denes. Now, after a lapse of sixty years, a suggestion has been made that the Denes belonging to the corporation south of the model yacht pond should be offered to a railway or other company, with a view to the construction of a new harbour, with docks, wharves, &c. A memorial on the subject has been prepared for presentation to the town council.

**Irish Local Authorities.**—The Local Government Board for Ireland have intimated to several public bodies in the south of Ireland that they are not disposed to sanction the carrying out of new works until the new Local Government Act for that country comes into operation next March.

# Municipalities as Traders.

### By G. A. PEARSON.*

In writing this paper I have felt that this meeting does not require from mo a long explanation of my own municipal dogmas, but would prefer that I should review the present position of municipalities as traders and the progress made in municipal trading; and I am inclined to think that that course will best serve as a peg on which to hang the discussion to-day. We are long distant from the so-called "good old times," when it could be said "if each man swept his own doorstep the village would be clean."

Individual performances of cleansing duties such as these, to say nothing of the still more important duty of sewage disposal, has long since ceased to be possible, and, further, the days when citizens "paid their scot and bore their lot" have also long passed, and the performance of duties at the public expense which were formerly looked upon as the duties of the private individual has been accepted as reasonable and proper; and, proceeding one step further, the public provision of a water supply, and also of the supply of light, and, lastly, of a cheap, frequent and regular mode of locomotion, has become so common as to cease to surprise, and now the suggestion of a dweller in any city providing his own separate system of cleansing, sewage disposal, water supply or light would be regarded as a stupid waste of a private energy.

## MUNICIPAL ACTIVITIES.

Drainage was first recognised as a public duty forced on municipalities by the density of the population, to be followed by a public system of cleansing; but, at a comparatively recent date, a municipal water supply was looked upon as a first step in a downward course leading to the pit of socialism: but few at the present time regard it in this light. The provision of light at a more recent date stood in the same position, but the advocates of the purchase of the gas and electric light undertakings form a majority of municipal councils at the present time; but to-day the man who publicly advocates the provision of a tram system by a corporation is called "very advanced" in his views, to say the least, and by the older members of the corporation he would be looked upon as really a dangerous man, leading a confiding public to the abyss of municipal socialism. Personally I have no dread of a name, and any scheme bearing on the face of it the impress of common sense would not be rejected by me because its opponents called it by a disagreeable title, and to hear a scheme in which I am interested called "socialistic" has no terrors for me.

Let us consider for one moment the growth of municipal trading, which will be best seen from the growth of municipal indebtedness, by means of which municipal trading has been rendered financially possible. The loans to municipalities outstanding in the year 1875 amounted to £92,820,100. These outstanding loans had grown in the year 1895 to £235,335,049, an increase of £142,514,949, being an increase at the rate of 153·5 per cent. in the twenty years. The National Debt was in the year 1875 £768,945,757, and it had decreased in the year 1895 to £656,998,941, or a decrease of £111,946,816 in the twenty years. It will be seen from these figures that the increase of local indebtedness exceeds the decrease in the national indebtedness by £30,568,133. Local indebtedness represents loans due in respect of:—

| | |
|---|---|
| Waterworks ... ... ... ... | £43,970,490 |
| Harbours, piers, docks and quays ... | 32,777,992 |
| Highways, street improvements and turnpike roads ... ... ... ... ... | 30,143,979 |
| Sewage and sewage disposal ... ... ... | 23,734,738 |
| Schools ... ... ... ... ... | 22,970,555 |
| Gas works ... ... ... ... | 16,931,943 |
| Poor law purposes ... ... ... | 7,773,504 |
| Markets ... ... ... ... | 5,775,076 |
| Parks, pleasure grounds, commons and open spaces ... ... ... ... | 5,051,092 |
| Public buildings... ... ... ... | 4,958,954 |
| Artisans' dwellings, improvements ... ... | 4,351,532 |

There is also a long list of loans in respect of other public works, in respect of each of which a debt approaching £4,000,000 now exists, the list being too long for quotation here. The figures I have read show the extent to which public funds have been used by local authorities in municipal trading. Taking gas, water, dock works, as three of the largest classes of municipal trading concerns, we find that the debt now existing (not the sum originally raised, which would, of course, be much larger, the present reduced figures being brought about by the operation of the sinking fund arrangement made in respect of each of these loans) shows the indebtedness at £93,680,425, being about £860,325 more than the total local indebtedness in the year 1875.

The foregoing figures show the great growth in municipal trading, by showing in some degree the growth of the municipal capital invested in it during the last twenty years; and these figures do not remain stationary. I have been unable to obtain the report of the Local Government Board for this year, but I have, by the courtesy of the secretary of the Local Government Board, obtained the figures of the national

and local indebtedness for the year ending 1896. The National Debt has sunk to £648,474,143, as against £656,998,941 in the year 1895, a decrease of about £8,000,000 in the year, whilst the local indebtedness has grown to £243,200,862 as against £235,335,049 in the year 1895, being an increase of about the same amount.

The electric light figures are very instructive, and show the growth of municipal trading in electric current. Up to the year ended March, 1895, £1,378,818 only had been invested in these undertakings by local authorities, whilst I find, from the tables published in Lightning, that fifty local authorities own their electrical undertakings, and from the figures there given I estimate the capital invested up to the year ended March, 1897, at £4,000,000, and think by this time this sum must have grown to nearly £6,000,000.

## EXTENSION OF MUNICIPAL TRADING.

Having shown the growth of municipal trading as evidenced by the growth of the capital account, let us consider for one moment the extent to which it may be extended to the advantage of the public. I think that municipal trading should be confined to the provision of those necessities of civilisation which are so large as to be beyond the power of individual effort to supply and which do not form part of any Government department. The effort of the individual will generally produce more economically than either a company or local authority, but as between a company and a local authority there is, economically speaking, very little to choose and corporations can claim to be free from the misappropriations of capital which appear to be incident to the formation of so many of the companies which from time to time come under our notice; and therefore the cheapness of the price of money when raised on the credit of a local authority as against the dearness of money when raised by a company must always enable a local authority to trade on a smaller gross profit than a company, and therefore requires less to be abstracted from the pocket of the consumers to secure success to the undertaking, whatever it may be. I am therefore of opinion that the supply of water, gas, electrical energy and trams should be in the hands of the local authority. Cleansing, ashing and watering should also be done without the aid of a contractor; but I would not suggest, except under exceptional circumstances, that all municipal works, such as erection of buildings and other matters of that kind, should be undertaken by the municipality, but where for any reason whatever, and there are many reasons I know, there is a lack of outside competition, then these works can be done generally more economically and always better than by a contractor.

There is another point which has to be considered—viz., the formation of "rings" and "trusts," formed with the object of keeping up prices to artificial levels. The only way to meet combinations such as these is for local authorities to face the position and do the work themselves. On the other side of this question is to be found the question of labour. Local authorities popularly elected are liable to pressure from without, to which the directors of public companies and private individuals are relatively free. Working men have votes, and will use them to serve their own ends precisely to the same extent as other people, and labour questions raised just before a November election put the independence of a candidate for a seat in the council to a severe test; but this, in my opinion, is a "nettle to be grasped" by a straight refusal on the part of the candidate. It is seldom, when this is done, that the labour combination is successful.

I cannot claim a very long experience in the management of large bodies of men, having only had a few years' experience as a member of the Sanitary Committee of Bristol. This department pays about £2,000 per week in wages; but the experience I have had as a member of that committee shows me that a position of absolute neutrality in respect of all trade combinations, and the acceptance of the services of any competent workman, whether unionist or not, extorts a respect even from those who may be violent partisans either on the one side or the other.

## THE TELEPHONE AND MUNICIPAL TRADING.

There remains one other enterprise which appears likely to be placed within the reach of any enterprising municipality. I refer to the telephone. The recent report appears to contemplate municipalities undertaking this work. Personally I would rather be without it. I have no more faith in a municipal telephone than a municipal telegraph or municipal post office. In my opinion telephonic communication should be provided by the Imperial Government and not by the municipalities. If this is done, we can do without the competition in telephone supply, of which we have lately heard so much, and the sooner this is done the better. If it is long delayed it will have developed into a large undertaking, with a large goodwill built upon the basis of the grants made by municipalities of the use of the public street at a nominal

---

* A paper read before Section F (Economic Science and Statistics) of the British Association.

cost, or, perhaps, at no cost at all to the company. If we are to have the nuisance of underground telephone wires, and the still greater nuisance of overhead wires, the quicker the better it will be for the Government to secure from that nuisance some profit for the public who have to submit to it. The longer the present companies live the tighter will they fix themselves on the public shoulders, and the more expensive it will be to remove them, as removed they must be, sooner or later, at any costs.

There is one other question now being prominently raised, and it is discussed in the recently-issued report of the Telephone Committee—viz., ought municipalities to trade for a profit. In my opinion they ought. Speaking as a municipal man, I should have very little inducement to trade at all but for the hope of success with its usual accompaniment profit. Birmingham trades, Manchester and other towns trade, at a profit, and I fail to see why they should not—subject only to the condition that they do so on the same lines as ordinary individuals and companies, and that they do not secure a profit by charging at a higher rate than would be charged by a company. Take the case of Bristol as an example, and I think ours is a fair sample of the average of cases of the kind. We have in Bristol 60,000 ratepayers and under 1,000 users of the electric light. The luxury of private lighting to the few is rendered possible by pledging the credit of the many, and why should not the many reap some benefit from the risk they run, to say nothing of the actual loss which attended the early years of our undertaking, which was paid out of the rates levied upon them. I think Parliament will be wise not to put such restriction as to profit-making as are shadowed forth by the report of the Telephone Committee. They may well leave the question of the amount of the profit to be settled by the natural law of supply and demand. The moment a municipality charges more for an article than it is worth will be the moment the public refuse it.

If we review the result of municipal trading, I think its advocates (of which I am one) have little to fear. Birmingham, Manchester, Glasgow and other large towns have shown a very good lead, which it remains for others only to follow. Failures are very seldom reported, and, having regard to the "fierce light" which surrounds all municipal trading, I think the fact that few failures are reported is caused by the fact that there are few failures to report. There is one other risk which it is impossible to omit to notice. There may be dishonesty in the official, or, still worse, there may be dishonesty in the council, but I think the risk is small in each case. So far as officials are concerned, business-like regulation may be made which, if powerless to actually prevent fraud, will most assuredly detect it, and I think the personal character and position of the members of the various representative bodies, coupled with the fact that more than one or two must be "in it" to secure success, will prevent any serious malpractices by the representatives, even if they were so minded.

## THE PRINCIPLE OF THE SEPTIC TANK.

In our editorial columns this week we refer to an interesting article on "The Bacterial Processes of Sewage Purification," by Mr. Rudolph Hering, the well-known American civil engineer, which appears in the current issue of The Engineering Magazine. In the course of our remarks we mention that Mr. Hering quotes from a French periodical an account of a contrivance that seems to him to be an anticipation of the principle of the septic tank, which hostile critics have described as being merely the principle of the cesspool. We here publish that part of the article referred to in full, as no doubt it will be of considerable interest to many of our readers:—

In a French periodical, Cosmos-les Mondes (December, 1881, p. 622, and January, 1882, p. 97), there is an article on the Mouras automatic scavenger, which is described as being a "mysterious contrivance" that has been used for twenty years. It consists of a vault, hermetically closed by a hydraulic seal. "By a mysterious operation, and one which reveals an entirely novel principle, it rapidly transforms all" the excrementatious matter which "it receives into a homogeneous fluid, only slightly turbid, and holding all the solid matters in suspension in the form of scarcely-visible filaments." The vault is self-emptying and continuous in its working. "The liquid which escapes while it contains all the organic and inorganic elements of the fæces, is almost devoid of smell, and can be received into a watering-cart for horticultural purposes, or may pass away into the sewer for use in irrigation."

Passing on to the theory of the action, it is then said: "May not the unseen agents be those vibrions or anaerobes which, according to Pasteur, are destroyed by oxygen, and only manifest their activity in vessels from which the air is excluded?" Daily observations conducted with a glass model showed that "fæcal matters introduced on the 29th August were entirely dissolved on the 16th September." "Even kitchen refuse, onion peelings, &c., which at first floated on the surface, descended after a time to the bottom of the vessel and awaited decomposition. Everything capable of being dissolved acted in a similar way, and even paper wholly disappeared."

It is further said: "The principles on which M. Mouras bases the action of this machine is that the animal dejecta contain within themselves all the principles of fermentation or of dissolution necessary and sufficient to liquefy them, and to render them immediately useful in their return to the soil, and without appreciable loss."

In a later article of the Cosmos-les-Moudes (January, 1883, p. 110), entitled "Theory and Accurate Working of the Automatic Scavenger," and written by Abbé F. Moigno, certain additional information is given, by which the proper dimensions of such a tank may be ascertained. M. Mouras is reported to have made the following statements. For the complete solution of the floating matter a period of thirty days should be allowed. The superficial area of the tank should be $\frac{1}{10}$ metre per person. The thickness of the top layer of undissolved solid matter should not exceed 0·75 metre (say 3-in.). The depth of the deposit is assumed as 0·02 metre (say 1 in.). The depth of the submerged portion of the outflow pipe below the surface should be 0·18 metre (say 7 in.).

If we assume:—

v = daily volume of excreta per person,
n = number of persons,
a = area of tank,
d = depth of tank, which be at least 1 metre, if only excreta entered it,
s = thickness of floating layer of undecomposed solids,
c = thickness of layer of deposited detritus,

then the size of the necessary tank may be ascertained from the following formula:—

$$ a = \frac{30\,vn}{s} $$

$$ d = 1 \text{ metre} + ac $$

From the description of this interesting contrivance, continues the article, it will be seen that the process of anaerobic decomposition was practically applied many years ago. It does not seem to have been suggested, however, as a method to be adopted on a large scale until it was introduced at Exeter, England, in 1896, by Mr. Donald Cameron, city engineer.

## ALTERATIONS AT THE GUILDHALL, NEWCASTLE-ON-TYNE.

The interior of the old Guildhall at Newcastle-on-Tyne has been completely transformed by the alterations recently effected within it, and, according to a contemporary, the "New Exchange" was opened for the transaction of business on the 30th ult.

In the work of alteration the ten heavy stone piers carrying the arches which supported the north wall and floor of the Guildhall have been removed, the superstructure now being carried on steel girders resting on four steel stanchions. The work of demolishing the old interior and substituting the new, was one in which the greatest care was necessary, the more so as the Exchange business had all the time to be carried on on the floor above. Under the new scheme the Exchange proper covers an area of 3,800 square feet, with a cubical space of 77,000 ft., and it has entrances, on the north from the Sandhill and on the south from the Quayside. On the left of the Sandhill entrance are the porter's, reading and manager's rooms, with retiring accommodation. Adjoining the entrance from the Quayside are the writing-room, accommodation for the Chamber of Commerce, telegraph and telephone rooms and smoking-room. These apartments, all well lighted, are separated from the exchange proper by glazed screens. The reading-room occupies the eastern end of the building.

In the Exchange increased height has been effected by lowering the old floor 2 ft. 4 in., giving a height to the Exchange of 20 ft. 6 in. The windows have been increased in size, and now have a lighting area of 648 square feet, as against 370 square feet formerly. The floors are covered with wood-block flooring, supplied and fixed by Messrs. Greasy & Walker, of London. The heating is by hot water on the low-pressure system. The ventilation is effected by the introduction of fresh air on the Tobins tube principle, the foul air being extracted by a large Blackman's fan, worked by an electric motor, and supplied by Messrs. Henry Walker & Son, of Newcastle. The decorative fibrous plaster work has been modelled and carried out by Mr. W. R. Dodds, of Jarrow, the general contractor being Mr. Thomas Lumsden, of Jarrow. The supporting steel stanchions are encased in fibrous plaster columns, and finished in Ionic caps below the girders, which are also encased in plaster, moulded, the cross beams resting at the walls on pilasters treated in a similar way to the columns. Messrs. Armstrong & Knowles, of 38 Grainger-street West, Newcastle, are the architects.

Norwich.—On the 6th inst., at a meeting of the council, the City Committee asked for a further sum of £115, making £423 to be expended on the renovation of the sessions court, lobby and entrance to the guildhall; and also recommended that the tender of Messrs. Downing & Sons to undertake the work for £423, be accepted. The recommendation was agreed to.

# London Local Authorities and the Water Companies.

## THE QUESTION OF MAINS AND PIPES AND THE LOWERING OF ROADS AND FOOTPATHS.

The recent lawsuit between the Southwark and Vauxhall Water Company and the Board of Works for the Wandsworth district has more than a local interest, so far as the metropolis is concerned, and therefore an accurate report of the main points of the proceedings will be of interest. When the case was first heard a decision was given against the local authority, but, as will be seen, this was subsequently upset on appeal. We may mention that the surveyor for the Wandsworth district, in which the difficulty arose, is Mr. P. Dodd. The preliminary facts of the case may be briefly stated, after which the judgment on appeal will be quoted in full.

The Board of Works for the Wandsworth district having resolved, in June, 1898, to pave West Hill-road, Wandsworth, as a new street, under sec. 105 of 18 and 19 Vict., cap. 120, it was found necessary, in order to form the road and footpaths to a proper level and inclination, to lower the footpath at one place 10¼ in. The footpath in question was laid out over thirty years ago, and at the place in question it was apparently made up to a higher level, in order to facilitate entrance to the forecourt of a house erected there. A water main was laid under the footpath, about thirty years ago, to supply such house. This main was laid so as to follow generally the contour of the footpath, which was made up to a very irregular inclination. The depth of the main below the footpath averaged about 1 ft. 7 in. At the place where the footpath was proposed to be lowered the minimum depth of the main was 14¼ in. The lowering of the footpath 10¼ in. would therefore leave a thickness of only 4 in. of soil above the top of the main. The old footpath was made up with gravel. The new footpath was to be of tar paving 3 in. thick.

At the place in question the water main was frozen in the severe winter of 1894-95. The water company then took up one length of pipe (which had burst), and laid a new pipe in lieu thereof at the same depth.

Upon the water company observing the paving works which were being executed by the board in June, 1898, the engineer of the company requested the board, before lowering the footpath, to agree to the company lowering the water main at the cost of the board, the company stating that the lowering of the footpath would render the main more likely to be frozen. This the board declined to do, being of opinion that if the main required lowering the cost should fall upon the company. The company thereupon applied for an injunction. Upon the hearing of the application, on July 8, 1898, Mr. Justice Kekewich granted an injunction restraining the board from "lowering the surface of the streets and footways in their district whereunder the pipes and mains of the plaintiffs are laid in any manner which will leave such pipes or mains without a sufficient covering of soil or other material to protect them from injury from frost, or otherwise without first altering the position of the said pipes and mains, by placing them at such depth below the proposed new surface of such streets or footways as will not expose them to greater danger from frost or otherwise than they are at present."

The board appealed. The appeal was heard on the 27th and 28th July, 1898, and the following judgment was delivered on the 8th of August, 1898 :—

## JUDGMENT.

THE MASTER OF THE ROLLS: This is an appeal from an order of Mr. Justice Kekewich, by which he restrained the defendants, the Wandsworth District Board of Works, until after judgment or further order from lowering the surface of the streets and footways in their district whereunder the pipes and mains of the plaintiffs are laid in any manner which will leave such pipes or mains without a sufficient covering of soil or other material to protect them from injury by frost or otherwise, without first altering the position of the said pipes and mains, by placing them at such depths below the proposed new surface of such streets or footways as will not expose them to greater danger from frost or otherwise than they are at present.

The injunction was granted under these circumstances. It appears that the Wandsworth District Board of Works have, pursuant and in the exercise of powers conferred upon them, which I will refer to presently, by the Metropolis Management Act, 1855, lowered the surface of a certain public footpath under which there are some pipes of the plaintiffs, the Southwark and Vauxhall Water Company. The defendants have not touched the pipes, but the water company say by lowering the path the defendants have exposed these pipes to the action of frost, and that is their complaint.

Now, the section under which the defendants have lowered the surface of this street is sec. 98 of the Metropolis Local Management Act, 18 and 19 Vict., chap. 120. It runs as follows: "It shall be lawful for every vestry and district board from time to time" (and the defendants are exercising these statutory powers) "to cause all or any of the streets within their parish or district, or any part thereof respectively, to be paved or repaired when, and as often, and in such form and manner, and with such materials, as such vestry or board think fit, and to cause the ground or soil

thereof to be raised or lowered, and the course of the channels running in, into or through the same to be turned or altered, in such manner as they think proper, and to alter the position of any mains or pipes in or under such street, such alteration to be made subject to the approval of the engineer of the company to which such mains or pipes belong."

Now, the defendants do not want to move those pipes, but there is a controversy between them and the water company. The water company say, "You must move and drop the pipes down, so as to protect them from frost, and not have them exposed or nearly exposed as it is proposed to do." That is the controversy.

Now, sec. 98 of the Act which I have just read simply in its terms confers a power: its language imposes no duty. The words are "it shall be lawful, &c." These words may, no doubt, under certain circumstances impose a duty as well as confer a power, but it is for those who contend that they do both to make good their contention.

Nothing can be clearer on this point than the judgment of Lord Cairns in Julius v. The Bishop of Oxford, which will be found in 5 Appeal Cases, p. 214, and see pp. 223 and 224.

The defendants have not touched or disturbed the plaintiffs' pipes. They have in no way injured them, and this circumstance distinguishes the case from the Gas Light and Coke Company v. The Vestry of St. Mary Abbotts, Law Reports, 15, Queen's Bench Division, p. 1, in which the steam rollers used by the defendants broke the plaintiffs' gas pipes.

The same circumstances—namely, the non-interference with the plaintiffs' property—distinguishes this case from Geddis v. The Proprietors of the Bann Reservoir, which is reported in 3 Appeal Cases, p. 430, where the defendants flooded the plaintiffs' land and said, in effect, that they could not help it. The answer was that they could help it if they kept a stream into which they poured water free from obstruction by mud, which they could do if they chose. Lord Blackburn's remarks on p. 456, on which the plaintiffs mainly relied, had reference to that state of things, and do not show what the plaintiffs must show—namely, that sec. 98 imposes a duty on the defendants to lower the plaintiffs' pipes, although the defendants do not want to do so for their own purposes. Underlying the plaintiffs' contention is the assumption that they are entitled to have a certain amount of soil over their pipes. I can find no warrant for this assumption; and as the defendants are clearly empowered by sec. 98 to remove the soil above the pipes, I see no ground for saying that the additional power conferred upon them of lowering the plaintiffs' pipes imposes the duty of lowering them in order to protect them from injury. The plaintiffs pay nothing for the privilege of laying their pipes down in a public path or road, and they run the risk of having it made higher or lower by the road authorities under their statutory powers.

This conclusion is strengthened by sec. 61 of the Towns Improvement Act, 1847, 10 and 11 Vict., ch. 34, which is in pari materia, and which empowers the Improvement Commissioners to raise or lower pipes "if they deem it necessary" so to do. No duty to do so is cast upon them. Sec. 98 of the Metropolis Local Management Act, although not quite so clearly worded, has, in my opinion, the same meaning.

The appeal motion having by consent been treated as an appeal from a final judgment in the action, the order appealed from must be discharged and judgment be entered for the defendants with costs here and below, and the costs below must be taxed as between solicitor and client, pursuant to the Act of 56 and 57 Vict., ch. 61, sec. 1, which we have just dealt with in the previous judgment.

Lord Justice CHITTY: I am of the same opinion. The case is one of some importance; the decision will effect not only water companies, but gas and other like companies who have the like statutory privilege of laying pipes under the public streets in the metropolis. For these privileges they make no payment. The case turns on sec. 98 of the Metropolis Local Management Act of 1855. That section confers powers on the road authority to pave and repair the streets when and so often as, and in such manner as, that authority think fit, and to raise or lower the ground or soil in such manner as they think proper. This is the principal power; it is discretionary. Then they have power to alter the position of mains and pipes in or under the street. This is a supplemental or subsidiary power; if it is exercised the alteration of the position of the mains or pipes is subject to the approval of the engineer of the company to which the mains or pipes belong. In this case the road authority have not altered the position of the pipes, nor have they in any way disturbed or interfered with them. The effect of their works, which have been lawfully executed under their principle power, is to bring the surface of the street nearer to the pipes, which remain in situ. The consequence is that the water in the pipes, being but a few inches from the surface, is more exposed to frost. In executing the power the road authority has not been guilty of any negligence. I am unable to find in the section any express or implied duty cast upon the road authority when they exer-

## WATER DIVINATION.

### A FURTHER SURCHARGE.

Last year the Porthcawl Urban District Council were surcharged by the Government auditor the amount of fees paid to wielders of hazel sticks in efforts to reach a supply of water by "divining." At this year's audit, held on Saturday, Mr. Dolby further surcharged the council £248, spent in sinking a well on a "diviner's" advice, thus differentiating Porthcawl from other places, where the fees have been disallowed but subsequently the expenditure has been passed. The council appealed against last year's surcharge to the Local Government Board, but the matter is not yet decided.

## COST DESTRUCTION AT LEYTON.

### THE WORKING OF THE DESTRUCTOR.

In his annual summary of the reports of the district medical officers of health, Dr. Thresh, county medical officer of health, quotes from the Leyton report some interesting remarks on the subject of refuse destruction and its combined drainage. These remarks will be sufficiently interesting to our readers to bear reproduction. We are told that the destructor has now been working the whole of the year, and that the results have been most satisfactory. The conclusions of experts by whom the destructor was thoroughly tested are given as follows:—(1) The destructor is capable of consuming wet sewage cake and house refuse of poor character in a complete and satisfactory manner; (2) the combustion of the combustible matter in the material fed into the destructor is complete, and the gaseous products of combustion are inoffensive; (3) the gaseous products of combustion are sensibly free from any suspended matter by the time they pass into the flue in the chimney; (4) the clinker is well burnt and free from offensive half-charred carbonaceous matter. Even when working with a wet sewage cake and poor house refuse the destructor generates more heat than can be used with the present plant at Leyton. We examined one of the cells in its cold condition, and were unable to discover any signs of wear or abrasion. We therefore consider that your destructor provides an efficient and economical method of destroying the refuse of towns without injury to the neighbourhood. So far as we are aware, it is the only form of furnace yet adopted capable of burning a considerable proportion of sewage sludge, even when containing, as in this case, a high percentage of moisture.

## MUNICIPAL WORK IN SOUTHAMPTON.

### A NEW LODGING-HOUSE.

In our supplement this week we publish the plans of the new lodging-house which is being erected by the Southampton Corporation, and the foundation-stone of which was laid by the mayor some little time ago.

The new building will be four storeys high, with a basement at the lower end. It is simple in design, and will be built of red bricks with stone facings, and the roofs covered with red tiles, which have been taken from the old buildings demolished on the first of the areas now cleared. The building will have a frontage of 65 ft. 2 in. to Pepper-alley, and a depth of 129 ft. 6 in., extending to within a few feet of the ancient town wall, which has been thrown open to view by the removal of many old buildings formerly abutting upon it. It will be rectangular on plan, covering a superficial area of 940 yards, 40 ft. high to the eaves in front and 53 ft. at the back. The narrow roadway of Pepper-alley has been widened to 40 ft., and the building will be put back some 10 ft. further. The main entrance is from Pepper-alley and will open into a vestibule, beyond which, on the left side, is an office, situated to give the attendants control of a central corridor, which extends from the entrance to the rear of the building. The foundation-stone, laid by the mayor, is on the left side of the entrance. The manager's quarters are situated in the south-east corner, and comprise two bed-rooms, sitting-room, kitchen, bath-room and coal store. All these rooms are well lighted from the front and side of the building and from the yard, which also furnishes a supplementary light to the corridor at this end. On the right-hand side, and entered from the corridor, is the recreation and reading room, 51 ft. 6 in. long by 25 ft. wide. This will be excellently lighted from the front and the open space on the north side. Part of this space is reserved for the artisans' dwellings about to be erected facing Simnel-street, which is also to be widened. An open yard will be left over 50 ft. wide between the two blocks of buildings.

Near the recreation-room and adjoining the dining-room is a provision shop, 25 ft. 6 in. long by 7 ft. 3 in. wide, lighted from the yard and Blue Anchor-lane. It is provided with serving windows to the dining-room and the corridor, and communicates with a store of similar dimensions in the basement. Beyond the shop is a central hall, 14 ft. by 14 ft., in which are situated the stairs to the dormitories above and also to the basement. On the left of the hall is the dining-room, 51 ft. 6 in. long by 25 ft. 6 in. wide. It is well lighted by windows on the north side. At the end of the dining-room, and in communication with the same, is the lodgers' kitchen, which is well lighted on the south and west sides and provided with cooking stoves and washing troughs for the use of lodgers. A lift communicates with this kitchen, the dining-room and the administrative kitchen in the basement. The lavatory, which is entered from the central hall, is provided with twenty-three enamelled fire-clay basins. Leading from the lavatory, the urinals. eight in number, and seven water-closets are situated. beyond which is the feet washing-room and three bath-rooms. These offices are well lighted and ventilated from the sides, also to an open area. Hot and cold water supply is provided for this and all offices of the building. A work-room is provided, 11 ft. 6 in. by 10 ft. 6 in., at the end of the corridor, from which it is entered on the right side. The situation of this room enables an attendant to have full observation over the lavatory, water-closets, baths and urinals, as a door communicates with the central passage of the same. Leading out of this on the opposite side is a porter's store.

The lodgers' changing and locker room is approached by a separate passage in continuation of the corridor. It is 20 ft. by 12 ft., and provision is made for nearly 200 lockers. At the end of this passage is an external staircase giving access to the administrative portion of the basement below, and this is continued up to each floor above as an emergency exit. In the basement there is an administrative kitchen, 20 ft. by 15 ft., with a scullery and wash-house, 25 ft. 6 in. by 18 ft. 6 in., and drying chambers, ironing-room, stores, staff mess-room, sleeping-room, lodgers' box-room and a laundry. The whole of these apartments are lighted and approached by passages 5 ft. wide. Independent lavatory and water-closets are provided for the staff. The dormitories are designed in three separate pavilions, 30 ft. apart, approached from the central staircase by open corridors. The partitions of the cubicles will be composed of coke-breeze concrete on iron framing. Each cubicle has a separate window and also a ventilator under the bed. Each floor contains sixty-three cubicles, giving accommodation for 189 lodgers. It is proposed that the charge per head per night shall be 6d., and it is calculated that this will be sufficient to bring in a revenue to the corporation.

Messrs. Dyer & Sons are the contractors. The amount of their tender was £10,795. to which must be added £1,000 for the laundry and kitchen fittings, hot and cold water supply, boilers, furniture, &c., and £9 6d for cost of sundries. making the total cost £12,295.

The scheme has been worked out by the borough engineer, Mr. W. B. G. Bennett, and the medical officer of health, Dr. A. Wellesley Harris, both of whom have inspected nearly all similar buildings erected by other authorities. The drawings have been prepared by Mr. C. J. Hair, the architectural assistant appointed by the corporation for the purpose.

## MUNICIPALITIES AND CONTRACTORS.

As another instance of the terms that are being imposed on persons tendering for municipal work, a firm of contractors have addressed a letter to *The Times*, enclosing the following verbatim copy of the general conditions attaching to a certain undertaking for one of the largest corporations in the country. The stipulations, in the opinion of the writers, are such as no firm of free individuals should agree to :—

"*General Conditions.*—The contractor shall to the *(sic)* at all times during the continuance of this contract abide by, perform, observe, fulfil and keep all and singular the stipulations following—that is to say :

"*Wages of Workmen.*—The contractor shall pay every workman employed by him, whether in or about the execution of this contract, or otherwise, wages and wages for overtime respectively and at the rate not less than that recognised in the district where the work or any part of it is being done as the standard rate of wages in such workmen's trade.

"*Hours of Labour.*—The contractor shall observe the, and cause to be observed by each workman, hours of labour not greater than the hours of labour (other than that union men only be employed) usually observed in the trade of such workmen in such district.

"*Lock-Out.*—The foregoing conditions shall not apply to any trade, or trades, during the existence of a general lock-out in such trade or trades. The corporation shall be sole judges as to whether such a lock-out exists.

"*Underletting of Contract.*—The contractor shall not transfer, assign or underlet, directly or indirectly, this contract, or any part of it, share or interest therein, without the written consent of the corporation under the hand of the town clerk, which consent may either be withheld or given, subject to the terms such as the corporation may determine, and particularly that the person to whom such contract may, or any part of it, share or interest therein may be transferred, assigned, or underlet, shall abide by, perform, observe, fulfil and keep the stipulations on the part of the contractor herein contained.

"*Book-keeping.*—The contractor shall, to the satisfaction of the council, provide and keep proper books, in which shall be entered from time to time the names of, the wages paid to, and the hours of labour observed by, all workmen employed by him, whether *in or about the execution of this contract or otherwise*, and shall from time to time, when required by notice under the hand of the town clerk, produce the same, or any of them, to him or the deputy town clerk, who shall be at liberty to inspect and take copies or extracts therefrom.

"*Breach of Contract.*—In case of any breach of the contractor or by any person to whom this contract, or any part of it, may be transferred, assigned, or underlet, of any one or more of the stipulations in this clause contained, it shall be lawful for the council to determine this contract in the same manner and to the same extent as they have power so to do under clause 5 in the events therein specified, and if the contract shall be determined under the present power, then all the provisions of that clause shall apply as if the contract had been determined under that clause.

"Tenders to be suitably endorsed, and addressed to the Chairman of the Gas Committee, Municipal Buildings."

## AMERICAN COMPETITION.

A meeting of the Glasgow Corporation Waterworks Committee has just been held to consider offers for 1,000 tons of pipes required by the department. Four tenders had been received. The lowest of these was from Messrs. R. D. Wood & Co., Philadelphia, who offered to supply the pipes in 12-ft. lengths, the total amount of the contract being £4,592 1s The second lowest offer was made by Messrs. Robert Maclaren & Co., Glasgow, who offered to supply the pipes in 9-ft. lengths for £4,959 8s. 4d. The average price of the pipes was thus £4 15s. 4d. per ton in the case of the Philadelphia firm and £4 19s. 8d. in the case of the Glasgow firm, a difference of 1s. 4d. per ton. After the matter had been discussed a motion was made to accept the offer of the Philadelphia firm. An amendment was proposed to divide the contract, giving £2 079 of it to the Philadelphia firm and the balance to the Glasgow firm. Six members voted on each side, and the chairman gave his casting vote in favour of the motion, so that the recommendation to the town council is that the offer of the Philadelphia firm be accepted.

**Scarborough.**—In consequence of the slow progress being made with the construction of the new road round the Castle Hill, the subcommittee have passed a resolution requesting any unnecessary delay on the part of the contractors and expediting the work, and calling upon them to make the necessary arrangements for commencing operations at the south, or east pier, end without delay.

cise their power of altering the level of the road, whether by raising or lowering it, to exercise at their own expense their power of altering the position of the pipes for the benefit of the company owning the pipes, much less any duty to place the pipes at a depth below the new surface corresponding with the depth at which they stood below the old surface. I think that no such duty is imposed upon the appellants.

The real question is on whom the expense of altering the position of the pipes is to fall. It appears to me that it falls on the company. They are under no statutory obligation as to the particular depth at which their pipes are to be placed from the surface of the road; it is for them to place them at such a depth as will protect the water from freezing. As between the road authority and the company, I think that the road authority are paramount. They are entrusted with the powers over the street, not for their own profit as a statutory body, but for the benefit of the public using the streets as a highway. The statutory undertaking of the water company is vested in them with a view to their own profit as a company and for the purpose of affording a supply of water to the consumers of water within their district. When the road authority alter the level of the street, sec. 98 does not afford any means of ascertaining the point at which the supposed duty of the road authority begins in reference to the distance from the surface at which the pipes are to be left—subject only to this qualification, that where the position of the pipes themselves is altered the approval of the company's engineer is required in relation to the position where the pipes are to be re-laid.

In regard to the authorities cited, I think they are distinguishable, as stated by the Master of the Rolls, and I agree with Lord Justice Collins (whose judgment I have had an opportunity of reading) in his statement of the general principles of law derived from the authorities in reference to the exercise of statutory powers.

Lord Justice COLLINS: I am of the same opinion, but I will add a few words on the point, based on the dictum of Lord Blackburn in *Geddis v. The Proprietors of the Bann Reservoir* :—

The point urged is that the plaintiffs have suffered damage by the exercise by the defendants of their statutory powers ; that the defendants were armed by the same statute with other powers, which, if used, would have mitigated the damage, and that therefore they were bound to use them. I think it is quite clear, as pointed out by the Master of the Rolls, that the power to move the pipes is merely ancillary to the powers of levelling the highway, and that there is no statutory duty on the defendants to exercise it, unless they require it for the performance of their primary obligation. But it is not on the assertion of such a statutory duty that the argument for the defendants' liability is or must be based, but on the broader proposition—that being possessed of a power of mitigating damage arising from their proceedings under the statute they are bound to exercise it. So stated, it is merely an assertion of the proposition so frequently affirmed that where statutory rights impinge upon what, but for the statute, would be the rights of other persons, they must be exercised reasonably, so as to do as little mischief as possible. The public are not compelled to suffer inconvenience which is not reasonably incident to the exercise of statutory powers. The railway spark cases are instances of this principle. See *Vaughan v. The Taff Vale Railway Company,* 5 Thurlstone and Norman, p. 679 ; *Brand v. The Hammersmith Railway Company,* Law Reports, 4 House of Lords, p. 171, and see *Coates v. The Clarence Railway Company,* 1 Russell and Mylne. Lord Blackburn was dealing with a case in which the rights of adjoining owners had been in fact invaded, the statute under which the defendants acted not enabling them to flood the plaintiffs' lands when such flooding might have been avoided by dredging, as the defendants had power to do, the channel by which they sought to pass their compensation water back to the river. They were under a duty to pass the water down to the river, and they were given powers to make and maintain channels for this purpose, and where they had not exercised these powers they could not say that the damage to the adjoining proprietors was a necessary incident of the exercise of their statutory right. The statutory power which Lord Blackburn thought them bound to exercise was one without which their duty of passing the water on could not be properly carried out. Here the levelling of the road could be, and was, effectively carried out without in any way disturbing the plaintiffs' pipes or infringing any of their rights. I think the dictum of Lord Blackburn must be read with reference to the case he was dealing with, and cannot be pressed to cover this one. But it must be admitted that the defendants are bound to exercise their statutory powers with reasonable regard for the rights of other persons. I think, when it is once clear that the main purpose of the defendants could be completely carried out without recourse to the power of moving the pipes, the obligation of the statutory body must be tried by the same standard of duty as is applicable to private persons. Of course, being merely a creature of statute, they cannot exercise powers if the statute has not conferred them, but it does not follow that they are bound to use them because they possess them, any more than a private person would be. They merely fall under the general principle *sic utere tuo ut alienum non lœdas.* Here the plaintiffs have no right to any particular thickness

of soil above their pipes. They are subordinate in this respect to the duties of the road authority, see *Gas Light and Coke Company v. St. Mary Abbotts,* 15 Queen's Bench Division, p. 4. But they are not trespassers. Their pipes are lawfully in the road, and the defendants' acts have undoubtedly damaged if they have not injured them. I think they can have no higher claim to consideration at the hands of the defendants than the owner of a house for which no right of support from the adjoining house had been acquired would be entitled to claim against the adjoining owner, who, in pulling his own house down, withdrew support to which his neighbour is not entitled. I think it is clear in such case that, though the pulling-down owner must be careful to interfere as little as possible with the adjoining house, he is certainly not called upon to take active steps for its protection, as for instance by shoring it up. There is a broad distinction between exercising a right with reasonable care so as not to do avoidable damage and taking active measures to ensure the continuance of something that is not a right in the adjoining owner.

*Shadwick v. Trower,* 3 Bingham new cases, pp. 354 and 6 Bingham new cases, p. 1 (which goes perhaps further than any other case in the plaintiffs' favour) merely decides that supposing there is a duty upon a person pulling down his own house to take care not to injure his neighbour's vault in so doing, where he knows of its existence, though it has acquired no right to support, there can be no such duty where he does not know of it. And it cannot be the law that the pulling-down owner is bound to find a substitute or equivalent for the support which he has a right to remove. That he has such right is clear, see *Angus v. Dalton,* 6 Appeal Cases, p. 740.

I think the result is that, though the person pulling down is bound to do no unnecessary damage, he is not fixed with any obligation to take active steps to mitigate a mischief which follows inevitably upon the reasonable exercise of his own rights.

I think, therefore, the only obligation on the defendants was to use reasonable care to do no unnecessary damage to the plaintiffs, and I think the existence of the power to move the pipes, and the fact that it was unused, would afford no evidence of want of such reasonable care, and that therefore the judgment ought to be for the defendants.

Mr. Renshaw, Q.C., and Mr. Lyttleton Chubb were for the appellants; Mr. Warrington, Q.C., and Mr. Gore Brown were for the respondents. Solicitors, W. W. Young and Lanfear, Tanner & Lanfear.

## DUST DESTRUCTION AT LEYTON.

### THE WORKING OF THE DESTRUCTOR.

In his annual summary of the reports of the district medical officers of health, Dr. Thresh, county medical officer of health, quotes from the Leyton report some interesting remarks on the subjects of (1) the dust destructor and (2) combined drainage. These remarks will be sufficiently interesting to our readers to bear reproduction. We are told that the destructor has now been working the whole of the year, and that the results have been most satisfactory. The conclusions of experts by whom the destructor was thoroughly tested are given as follows :—

(1) The destructor is capable of consuming wet sewage cake and house refuse of poor character in a complete and satisfactory manner; (2) the oxidation of the combustible matter in the material fed into the destructor is complete, and the gaseous products of combustion are inoffensive; (3) the gaseous products of combustion are sensibly free from any suspended matter by the time they pass into the flue in the chimney; (4) the clinker is well burnt and free from offensive half-charred carbonaceous matter. Even when working with a wet sewage cake and poor house refuse the destructor generates more heat than can be used with the present plant at Leyton. We examined one of the cells in its cold condition, and were unable to discover any signs of wear or abrasion. We therefore consider that your destructor provides an efficient and economical method of destroying the refuse of towns without injury to the neighbourhood. So far as we are aware, it is the only form of furnace yet adopted capable of burning a considerable proportion of sewage sludge, even when containing, as in this case, a high percentage of moisture.

## WATER DIVINATION.

### A FURTHER SURCHARGE.

Last year the Porthcawl Urban District Council were surcharged by the Government auditor the amount of fees paid to wielders of hazel sticks in efforts to reach a supply of water by " divining." At this year's audit, held on Saturday, Mr. Dolby further surcharged the council £248, spent in sinking a well on a " diviner's " advice, thus differentiating Porthcawl from other places, where the fees have been disallowed but subsequently the expenditure has been passed. The council appealed against last year's surcharge to the Local Government Board, but the matter is not yet decided.

## MUNICIPAL WORK IN SOUTHAMPTON.

### A NEW LODGING-HOUSE.

In our supplement this week we publish the plans of the new lodging-house which is being erected by the South-ampton Corporation, and the foundation-stone of which was laid by the mayor some little time ago.

The new building will be four storeys high, with a base-ment at the lower end. It is simple in design, and will be built of red bricks with stone facings, and the roofs covered with red tiles, which have been taken from the old buildings demolished on the first of the areas now cleared. The build-ing will have a frontage of 65 ft. 2 in. to Pepper-alley, and a depth of 129 ft. 6 in., extending to within a few feet of the ancient town walls, which has been thrown open to view by the removal of many old buildings formerly abutting upon it. It will be rectangular on plan, covering a superficial area of 940 yards, 40 ft. high to the eaves in front and 53 ft. at the back. The narrow roadway of Pepper-alley has been widened to 40 ft., and the building will be put back some 10 ft. further. The main entrance is from Pepper-alley and will open into a vestibule, beyond which, on the left side, is an office, situated to give the attendants control of a central corridor, which extends from the entrance to the rear of the building. The foundation-stone, laid by the mayor, is on the left side of the entrance. The manager's quarters are situated in the south-east corner, and comprise two bed-rooms, sitting-room, kitchen, bath-room and coal store. All these rooms are well lighted from the front and side of the building and from the yard, which also furnishes a supplementary light to the corridor at this end. On the right-hand side, and entered from the corridor, is the recreation and reading room, 51 ft. 6 in. long by 25 ft. wide. This will be excellently lighted from the front and the open space on the north side. Part of this space is reserved for the artisans' dwellings about to be erected facing Simnel-street, which is also to be widened. An open yard will be left over 50 ft. wide between the two blocks of buildings.

Near the recreation-room and adjoining the dining-room is a provision shop, 25 ft. 6 in. long by 7 ft. 3 in. wide. It is supplied from the yard and Blue Anchor-lane. It is provided with serving windows to the dining-room and the corridor, and communicates with a store of similar dimensions in the base-ment. Beyond the shop is a central hall, 14 ft. by 14 ft., in which are situated the stairs to the dormitories above and also to the basement. On the left of the hall is the dining-room, 51 ft. 6 in. long by 25 ft. 6 in. wide. It is well lighted by windows on the north side. At the end of the dining-room, and in communication with the same, is the lodgers' kitchen, which is well lighted on the south and west sides and provided with cooking stoves and washing troughs for the use of lodgers. A lift communicates with this kitchen, the dining-room and the administrative kitchen in the basement. The lavatory, which is entered from the central hall, is pro-vided with twenty-three enamelled fire-clay basins. Leading from the lavatory, the urinals, eight in number, and seven water-closets are situated, beyond which is the feet washing-room and three bath-rooms. These offices are well lighted and ventilated from the sides, also to an open area. Hot and cold water supply is provided for this and all offices of the building. A work-room is provided, 11 ft. 6 in. by 10 ft. 6 in., at the end of the corridor, from which it is entered on the right side. The situation of this room enables an attendant to have full observation over the lavatory, water-closets, baths and urinals, as a door communicates with the central passage of the same. Leading out of this on the opposite side is a porter's store.

The lodgers' changing and locker room is approached by a separate passage in continuation of the corridor. It is 20 ft. by 12 ft., and provision is made for nearly 200 lockers. At the end of this passage is an external staircase giving access to the administrative portion of the basement below, and this is continued up to each floor above as an emergency exit. In the basement there is an administrative kitchen, 20 ft. by 15 ft., with a scullery and wash-house, 25 ft. 6 in. by 18 ft. 6 in., and drying chambers, ironing-room, stores, staff mess-room, sleeping-room, lodgers' box-room and a laundry. The whole of these apartments are lighted and approached by passages 5 ft. wide. Independent lavatory and water-closets are pro-vided for the staff. The dormitories are designed in three separate pavilions, 30 ft. apart, approached from the central staircase by open corridors. The partitions of the cubicles will be composed of coke-breeze concrete on iron framing. Each cubicle has a separate window and also a ventilator under the bed. Each floor contains sixty-three cubicles, giving accommodation for 189 lodgers. It is proposed that the charge per head per night shall be 6d., and it is calculated that this will be sufficient to bring in a revenue to the cor-poration.

Messrs. Dyer & Sons are the contractors. The amount of their tender was £10,798, to which must be added £1,000 for the laundry and kitchen fittings, hot and cold water supply, boilers, furniture, &c., and £500 for contingencies, making the total cost £12,298.

The scheme has been worked out by the borough engineer, Mr. W. B. G. Bennett, and the medical officer of health, Dr. A. Wellesley Harris, both of whom have inspected nearly all similar buildings erected by other authorities. The drawings have been prepared by Mr. C. J. Hair, the architectural assistant appointed by the corporation for the purpose.

## MUNICIPALITIES AND CONTRACTORS.

As another instance of the terms that are being imposed on persons tendering for municipal work, a firm of contractors have addressed a letter to The Times, enclosing the following verbatim copy of the general conditions attaching to a certain undertaking for one of the largest corporations in the country. The stipulations, in the opinion of the writers, are such as no firm of free individuals should agree to:—

"General Conditions.—The contractor shall to the (sic) at all times during the continuance of this contract abide by, perform, observe, fulfil and keep all and singular the stipu-lations following—that is to say:

"Wages of Workmen.—The contractor shall pay every workman employed by him, whether in or about the overtime respectively and at the rate not less than that recognised in the district where the work or any part of it is being done as the standard rate of wages in such workmen's trade.

"Hours of Labour.—The contractor shall observe the, and cause to be observed by each workman, hours of labour not greater than the hours of labour (other than that union men only be employed) usually observed in the trade of such workmen in such district.

"Lock-Out.—The foregoing conditions shall not apply to any trade, or trades, during the existence of a general lock-out in such trade or trades. The corporation shall be sole judges as to whether such a lock-out exists.

"Underletting of Contract.—The contractor shall not trans-fer, assign or underlet, directly or indirectly, this contract, or any part of it, share or interest therein, without the written consent of the corporation under the hand of the town clerk, which consent may either be withheld or given, subject to the terms such as the corporation may determine, and particularly that the person to whom such contract may, or any part of it, share or interest therein may be trans-ferred, assigned, or underlet, shall abide by, perform, observe, fulfil and keep the stipulations on the part of the contractor herein contained.

"Book-keeping.—The contractor shall, to the satisfaction of the council, provide and keep proper books, in which shall be entered from time to time the names of, the wages paid to, and the hours of labour observed by, all workmen em-ployed by him, whether in or about the execution of this con-tract or otherwise, and shall from time to time, when required by notice under the hand of the town clerk, produce the same, or any of them, to him or the deputy town clerk, who shall be at liberty to inspect and take copies or extracts therefrom.

"Breach of Contract.—In case of any breach of the con-tractor or by any person to whom this contract, or any part of it, may be transferred, assigned, or underlet, of any one or more of the stipulations in this clause contained, it shall be lawful for the council to determine this contract in the same manner and to the same extent as they have power so to do under clause 5 in the events therein specified, and if the contract shall be determined under the present power, then all the provisions of that clause shall apply as if the contract had been determined under that clause.

"Tenders to be suitably endorsed, and addressed to the Chairman of the Gas Committee, Municipal Buildings."

## AMERICAN COMPETITION.

A meeting of the Glasgow Corporation Waterworks Com-mittee has just been held to consider offers for 1,000 tons of pipes required by the department. Four tenders had been received. The lowest of these was from Messrs. R. D. Wood & Co., Philadelphia, who offered to supply the pipes in 12-ft. lengths, the total amount of the contract being £4,892 1s. The second lowest offer was made by Messrs. Robert Maclaren & Co., Glasgow, who offered to supply the pipes in 9-ft. lengths for £4,958 8s. 4d. The average price of the pipes was thus £4 18s. 4d. per ton in the case of the Phila-delphia firm and £4 19s. 8d. in the case of the Glasgow firm, a difference of 1s. 4d. per ton. After the matter had been discussed a motion was made to accept the offer of the Philadelphia firm. An amendment was proposed, to divide the contract, giving £2,078 of it to the Philadelphia firm and the balance to the Glasgow firm. Six members voted on each side, and the chairman gave his casting vote in favour of the motion, so that the recommendation to the town council is that the offer of the Philadelphia firm be accepted.

**Scarborough.**—In consequence of the slow progress being made with the construction of the new road round the Castle Hill, the sub-committee have passed a resolution regretting any unnecessary delay on the part of the contractors in not expediting the work, and calling upon them to make the necessary arrangements for commencing operations at the south, or east pier, end without delay.

# Comparative Reports of General Practice.

## XXVIII.—TRAMWAY TRACTION : BLACKPOOL REPORT.—III.

### CONCLUSIONS.

As the result of their inquiry, the deputation found, as has been set forth at length, that Continental tramway practice, like English and American, tended mainly towards the adoption of the overhead system of electric traction. In those cases where conduit and accumulator systems were at work the fact was distinctly stated that those systems were costly, and were only maintained to meet the æsthetic wishes of the various municipalities. Where the overhead system was installed the records show that the system was efficient and reliable, that it gave popular satisfaction, and that it was decidedly remunerative. But the main object of the deputation's visit was to inquire into the advantages, disadvantages and cost of the accumulator system, so as to be able to form a definite opinion upon the Board of Trade's recommendation to adopt this system.

They have found, as a consequence, that the accumulator system has undoubted advantages peculiar to itself. Each car is to all intents and purposes an independent installation. If one car fails the traffic arrangements are not deranged to the same extent as with the failure of an overhead or conduit system, inasmuch as the whole of the cars on service on the latter systems depend upon the maintenance of the supply of electricity from generators to motor; while in the case of accumulators, one car failing simply puts that car out of service without interfering with the others. The disadvantages, too, which have been urged against accumulators carried on cars on account of the smell of the acid, the injury to the car body and the clothing of passengers arising from spilt acid, were found by the deputation to be almost negligible. With modern equipped cars, such as are to be seen on the Continent, these disadvantages with old type car-carried accumulators have been overcome; the deputation having discovered only the faintest odour of acid, and no trace whatever of the effect of acid upon the car body. The opinion was formed that the accumulator system was an ideal one, if the question of cost were left entirely out of consideration. Accumulator traction is free from all possible objections on the score of unsightliness of overhead wire or of the existence of a slot in the roadway, and is certainly satisfactory from a public point of View.

But the Blackpool tramways, unlike the tramways the deputation inspected, are owned and operated by the municipality, and the public rightly demand that they shall not only be satisfactory as regards punctuality and reliability of service, but successful financially. Unfortunately for the adoption of this system, the cost of installing accumulators is, at the present time at all events, excessive; the life of the cells is short and their upkeep heavy; and the fact that no type of cell has been sufficiently long in use to demonstrate its efficiency and economy, and that one type of cell is being constantly displaced by a newer type, which in turn is again displaced, taken in conjunction with the fact that—with short-lived cells—extra ears are required to run a given service on account of the time occupied in charging the cells, effectually places the system out of consideration if a remunerative return is to be expected from the corporation's tramway undertaking.

As bearing upon the capital and maintenance cost of accumulators, the correspondence with the Tudor Accumulator Company, Limited (the English manufacturers of the Tudor cell, known on the Continent as the Hagen cell, and used at Berlin, Paris, Dresden, Hanover and elsewhere), already referred to, is given below. The questions and the answers were as follows:—

(1) What weight of accumulators would be required to drive a double-bogie tramcar weighing 11 tons, together with its load of eighty-six passengers, a distance of 5 miles with one charge? 5 tons 4 cwt. complete with acid.

(2) The same running 75 miles with one charge? A discharge of this duration is not practicable with our system of rapid charging. The battery would be of such weight that it would scarcely be able to propel itself.

(3) What space would be occupied—see No. 1? 68 cubic feet.

(4) What space would be occupied—see No. 2? See answer No. 2.

(5) At what maximum speed? About 12 miles.

(6) What is the ampere hour efficiency you would guarantee? 75 per cent.

(7) At what price per car mile would you be prepared to maintain the cells for a period of ten years? 1·6d. per car mile.

(8) At what price would you be prepared to fit up each car with accumulators? £370, including erection and delivery; but not the case in which the cells are contained. The case would form part of the car body.

(9) How long will the batteries require charging at the maximum rate at the end of the 5 miles journey? Ten to fifteen minutes.

(10) Are you prepared to enter into a contract on the above terms? Yes.

To a subsequent question as to the weights upon which these figures were based the following answer was received: "We have based our reply upon the following weights: Weight of car and equipment, 11 tons; weight of passengers, 6 tons; weight of battery, 5¼ tons; total, 22¼ tons."

From these particulars it will be seen that the weight of cells is given for one of our largest cars, carrying eighty-six passengers. But we have ten small cars carrying an average of fifty passengers each, so that the weights given will have to be reduced *pro rata*. These small cars weigh with equipment 7½ tons, the passengers approximately 3¾ tons, and the batteries, taken as above, 3½ tons, making a total car weight of 14¾ tons. Still proceeding on the same scale as for the larger cars, the cost of batteries for each of these smaller cars would be £247. Summarised, the estimated capital cost works out as follows:—

| | |
|---|---|
| Batteries for six large cars at £370 ... ... ... | £2,220 |
| " " ten small cars at £247 ... ... ... | 2,470 |
| | £4,690 |
| Plus, containing cases for sixteen cars at, say, £15 | 240 |
| | £4,930 |

Considering, for the sake of comparison, the cost of installing the overhead system, it would be well to turn to the tenders received. These amounted to £3,377, and were for overhead line and insulators, posts and brackets, trolleys, and that portion of feeding mains which would not be required with an accumulator system. It will be remembered in this connection that the posts were intended to be used both for electrically lighting the promenade and streets and suspending the tramway trolley wire, and that a portion of their cost should therefore be chargeable to the public lighting fund, which would reduce the gross cost accordingly. Taken as a capital item, consequently the accumulator system compares unfavourably with the overhead.

Another point requiring emphasis is the fact that a loan on capital account would probably not be sanctioned for a longer period than ten years, nor would it be advisable to ask for an extension of this period in view of the short life of the cells; whereas for an overhead system the general practice is to sanction a loan for repayment in twenty-five years, thus relieving the annual charges on the capital account.

Passing on now to the consideration as to the effect the adoption of accumulators would have upon the annual balance sheet of the tramway undertaking, it is necessary to find the annual cost of maintaining the accumulators, carrying them, and supplying electrical energy to them. The Tudor Accumulator Company, Limited, gave the cost of maintaining the cells at 1·6d. per car mile for the large cars; and the cost for the small cars, taken *pro rata*, may be estimated at 1·07d. per car mile. The mileage of the corporation tram cars at the present time is about 200,000, or, with the addition of the two large cars now being built, say 228,640 per year, being an average of 14,290 per car. Every car, for the present purpose, may be assumed to run the same number of miles. Thus the cost of maintaining the whole of the cells contained in the cars would be:—

| | |
|---|---|
| Ten small cars, 142,900 miles at 1·07d. ... ... | say £637 |
| Six large cars, 85,740 miles at 1·6d. ... ... | " 572 |
| | £1,209 |

To this, however, should be added an extra sum for increased supply of electricity, due in the first place to the additional weight carried, and in the second place to the inefficiency of the cells. As regards the increased weight, every ton of dead weight carried a mile on a given tramway track requires the same expenditure of energy to carry it, whether it be in the shape of car, passengers or battery; and it has been seen that the large cars would have to be increased in weight from 17 tons loaded to 22¼ tons, or 31 per cent., and with the small cars the increase would be from 11¼ to 14¾ tons, or 32 per cent. The energy taken per car mile at present is an average of ·9 of a unit, and the large cars running approximately 85,740 miles would take 77,166 units. But with 5¼ tons added by way of batteries to each car the total energy required to run the cars the same number of miles would be 101,087 units, or an increase of 23,921 units. For the small cars, taken on the same basis, the energy would be, without cells, 128,610; with weight of cells, 169,765 units, or an increse of 41,154 units.

As regards the inefficiency of the cells, it will be seen from the reply No. 6 of the Tudor Accumulator Company, Limited, that the guaranteed ampere hour efficiency is 75 per cent.; but it should not be forgotten that the cells have to be charged at a higher pressure than they discharge at, and that this difference of pressure amounts to some 20 per cent., making the real efficiency of the cells about 55 per cent. In the present calculations, however, it has been assumed that 60 per cent. is returned. Now, the units given above as requisite to drive the cars refer entirely to the energy given to the motors. Seeing, therefore, that only 60 per cent. of the energy put into the cells is given to the motors, there is a further increase of energy on this account, and the gross increase would be equal to some 245,600 units per annum. Bringing the units together, the following result is arrived at :

|  | Units. |
|---|---|
| Current used per annum for six large cars, without cells... ... ... ... ... ... | 77,166 |
| Current used per annum for ten small cars, without cells... ... ... ... ... ... | 128,610 |
|  | 205,776 |
| Plus extra energy required through loss in cells and additional weight... ... ... ... ... | 245,600 |
| Total ... ... ... ... | 451,376 |

If we assume the cost of current to the corporation themselves to be at the low figure of 1d. per unit, the cost of the additional current per annum would be about £1,023 if cells were used. Put in another way, the estimated annual maintenance account would be :—

WITH ACCUMULATORS.

| | £ |
|---|---|
| Interest and sinking fund on a capital of £4,930 at 11½ per cent. (repayable in ten years)... ... ... | 567 |
| Cost of upkeep of cells ... ... ... ... ... | 1,209 |
| Additional cost of current to supply cells, due to inefficiency and extra weight carried ... ... | 1,023 |
| | £2,799 |

Compared with this, the cost of the upkeep of the present conduit amounted last year to £2,238, though probably it will be rather less this year, and the estimated annual cost of the upkeep of that portion of the overhead system comparable with the accumulator system would be a sum not exceeding £600, including interest and sinking fund charges on a twenty-five years loan. Hence the relative costs of maintaining the similar portions—exclusive of repairs to roadway, rails, motors, gearing, cars, &c.—of the three systems are :—

| | £ |
|---|---|
| Overhead system (line, &c.) ... ... ... ... | 600 |
| Conduit system (conduit, &c.), cost, 1897 ... ... | 2,238 |
| Accumulator system (accumulators, &c., as per statement) ... ... ... ... ... ... | 2,799 |

But even were there no increase in the cost brought about by the installation of accumulators, the deputation are advised that it is the very definite opinion of the borough electrical and tramway engineer (Mr. Quin) and the general manager of the tramways (Mr. Lancaster) that in the event of the accumulator system being adopted it would be necessary to practically relay the present permanent way, owing to the additional load carried, and that the wear and tear of the road would be excessive, due to the accumulators, the extent and cost of which increased wear and tear would be difficult to estimate.

From the evidence brought before them, and from the result of their investigations, the deputation have unanimously come to the conclusion that the overhead trolley wire system is the only system of traction which can be made both successful and remunerative in Blackpool. If the council are prepared to incur what may probably be an annual loss for years to come on the tramway undertaking, then the deputation are not indisposed to the adoption of the accumulator system. But they believe that such an opportunity of relieving the rates by means of the profits which can be derived from their tramways by the adoption of an efficient and economical system should not be lost, and this fact alone leads them to strongly advise the adoption of the overhead trolley wire system. They are also of the opinion that the alleged danger of the overhead system, when properly installed and in conformity with latest electrical practice, is not justifiable; and that the overhead wires, if properly suspended, would not appreciably detract from the appearance of the promenade and streets of Blackpool.

One point, however, the deputation wish to emphasise is, that no system, whether overhead or accumulator, can be reasonably expected to work to its highest success until the promenade widening is accomplished and a double track laid, and they respectfully urge the Promenade Widening Sub-Committee to expedite matters in this direction. At the same time the deputation are fully of opinion that a change of system must take place immediately.

Finally, the deputation had the utmost confidence in recommending the council to ask the Board of Trade to receive a deputation from the corporation, to put before the board the evidence which has been obtained and the experience gained, and to press for the board's permission to replace the conduit system, at present in use in Blackpool, by the overhead trolley wire system, in accordance with the resolution of the Electric Lighting and Tramways Committee of August 26, 1897, confirmed by the council on September 7, 1897.

The report is signed by Councillor Joseph Brodie, chairman of the committee; Alderman James Cardwell; Councillors James Ward, Thos. Bickerstaffe, Jno. Grime and T. H. Smith; by Mr. Robert C. Quin, borough electrical and tramway engineer, and by Mr. John Lancaster, general manager of tramways.

## COMBINED DRAINAGE.

The medical officer to the Leyton Urban District Council, in a recent report, has expressed the opinion that the system of combined drainage so often used in the houses being erected in the district is open to considerable doubt. In discussing the problem the following points appear to him to be of great importance :—

(1) The difficulty of investigating and abating of nuisances. In some cases many owners are implicated, one being willing to rectify the defects, and a neighbour refusing to assist in the matter. This necessitates stringent measures, which, unfortunately, cannot legally be carried out without considerable delay, the nuisance in the meanwhile being a source of danger to the health of the inmates of the house. Moreover, this investigation by the sanitary staff does not only apply to the nuisance, but also is directed to determine the ownership of the various houses whose drains are combined; a matter of considerable delay, and really a necessary proceeding to be gone through before any legal process can be taken.

(2) As the law now stands it is distinctly advisable to have a separate drain to each house. This throws the responsibility upon the proper party, and makes the rectification of sanitary defects a much quicker process. I am certainly of opinion that these single drains, laid in accordance with your by-laws and those of the Local Government Board, being properly supervised by your officers, being intercepted from the sewer, and having proper air inlets and outlets, make it absolutely impossible for any danger to arise to the health of the inmates.

(3) In instances of combined drainage, when the drains have not been properly laid, cases of infectious diseases may occur (and I allude especially to typhoid fever), and prove a great danger to the health of the inmates in adjoining houses. The following remarks by the Walthamstow medical officer may also be quoted as supplementary to those made above :—

The question of combined drainage has been before your Sanitary Committee several times during the year. I would therefore like to draw attention to the decision in the case of Seal v. Merthyr Tydfil District Council, heard on July 10, 1897, before Mr. Justice Cave and Mr. Justice Ridley. The decision is a common-sense one, and to my mind fairly represents the meaning of the Public Health Acts relating to this subject.

Mr. Justice Cave said, by the Public Health Act, 1875, all sewers were vested in the local authorities, and sewers were defined as drains draining more than one house. This was found to create some difficulty, for when one man built two houses on his own land and drained them the drain became vested in the local authority and had to be paid for by them. That was one difficulty, but it was got over by holding that the Act did not apply to the houses in the same curtilage, and that the drain, until it came out of the private property into public property, could not be said to be a sewer. When houses belonging to different owners drained into a sewer, whereby they connected with a public sewer, in that case it was hard that the public should have to pay for what was in fact a private drain. Sec. 19 of the Act of 1890 was therefore passed.

The definition of " private drain " included a drain used for the drainage of more than one house. What, then, was a " private drain ?" In the opinion of the judge the term applied to a drain constructed in private grounds to which the public had no access. The intention was to relieve the public from paying for that which they were not allowed to use.

## LIVERPOOL ART GALLERY.

### PROPOSED EXTENSIONS.

A proposal to extend the Walker Art Gallery buildings, the plans in connection with which, prepared by Mr. Dyall, provide for a considerable addition at the rear of the existing buildings, was considered at the last meeting of the Library Committee of the Liverpool Corporation. The city surveyor reported that the scheme was an admirable one, but the addition would be equal to 57 per cent. of the old buildings, and would cost £29,000. The area of the present buildings was 16,000 square feet, and the addition proposed would occupy 14,000 ft. It was agreed that the city surveyor should submit plans within a month for an extension which would involve an expenditure of about £8,000, it being understood that the addition should be designed on such lines that a further extension could be made at some future date.

**A Valuable Find in a Dust-Cart.**—A purse containing four diamond rings has been taken away among some rubbish in a dust-cart from Roslyn House, New Cross Gate. Only a short time ago, says London, a fine necklace worth, it is said, over £400, was found by a South London dustman, who honestly restored the valuable ornament to its owner. He was offered 5s. for his trouble, and upon remonstrating was threatened with police proceedings. Several very similar cases are reported; but Mr. Layman, the owner of the missing diamond rings, has offered a reward of £3 for the recovery of his property.

# Some Annual Municipal Engineering Records.

## NUNEATON AND CHILVERS COTON : ST. PANCRAS : NEWARK.

In his last annual report to the Nuneaton and Chilvers Coton Urban District Council, Mr. J. S. Pickering, the engineer and surveyor, first refers to the number of newly-erected buildings. These have totalled 272, and have been much in excess of previous years. The removal of night-soil is a matter which has resolved itself into a most important question, and during the year 5,324 cart-loads of this particular refuse were collected from wet ash-pits and privies. From dry ash-pits there were taken 1,524 loads. In the maintenance of roads the quantity of macadam used from the council's quarry has been 3,172 tons and 508 tons of chippings, against 2,730 tons and 360 tons respectively during the previous year. In addition to this, 248 tons of macadam and 782 tons of chippings have been purchased from local quarries, against 650 tons and 1,360 tons respectively during the year 1896. A further loan has been obtained for general footpath paving, making a total of £4,000. More than half this amount has been expended during the year, and the work is proceeding as rapidly as the delivery of bricks will allow. The new pavements which have been laid in various parts of the district are much appreciated, and add considerably to the appearance of the streets and to the comfort and convenience of pedestrians.

New streets of a total length of about 750 yards (against 850 yards in the previous year) have been completed or are in course of construction by the owners of building land, while a sum of £1,150 has been expended out of current rates on the construction of sewers at Stockingford, the Local Government Board having refused to sanction a loan for that purpose. It has also been decided to spend about £750 yearly out of the current rates on the extension of sewers so long as the Local Government Board refuse their sanction to a loan. The Local Government Board have sanctioned a loan of £1,300 for additional pumping machinery, which will be erected during the present year. The pumping plant will then be capable of raising 120,000 gallons of sewage per hour, and will meet the requirements of the town for many years to come. The quantity of sewage received at the outfall works during the year has been 192,884,000 gallons, against 180,000,000 gallons in the previous year, showing an increase of 12,884,000 gallons.

In five years the sewage has increased by nearly 39 per cent. The quantity turned back into the sewers for retreatment has been gradually diminishing, and last year none was so dealt with. Mr. Pickering thinks that this is undoubtedly due to the increasing care exercised by manufacturers in the treatment of their waste liquors before discharging them into the sewers and to the better clarification of the sewage since the conversion of the tanks to the Cosham system. But, continues Mr. Pickering, while recognising the general improvement in the waste liquors from factories, it must still be pointed out that frequently they are discharged into the sewers with apparently little or no treatment. During the year 17,435 tons of sewage sludge have been received and pressed into 3,487 tons of solid manure, against 16,060 tons and 3,212 tons respectively during the previous year, showing an increase of about 8 per cent. This gives an average of 48 tons of sewage sludge received daily including Sundays, and 56 tons excluding Sundays, or 9¼ tons and 11 tons respectively of pressed cake. There has been no difficulty in disposing of the whole of the manure to farmers. The chemical account is still a heavy item, amounting in 1897 to over £440. The lime purchased for sludge-pressing cost nearly £60.

Upon the council acquiring the undertaking, Mr. Pickering presented a detailed report of the works to the Waterworks Committee, pointing out the insecurity and unsatisfactory nature of the present supplies, and urging the necessity of a new and increased supply from one source. A new reservoir, of a capacity of 500,000 gallons, was, at the time of the preparation of the report, in course of construction, at a cost of about £3,100. New pumping machinery, commenced by the water company to replace the temporary sinking pumps, has recently been fixed in the deeper well at the pumping station. This has enabled the cost of pumping to be reduced to a minimum, only two men being now permanently employed at these works.

\* \* \*

Some interesting details of matters which have lately occupied the attention of the department of works of St. Pancras Vestry are contained in the last report prepared by the chairman of the Highways, Sewers and Public Works Committee. In the introductory paragraphs following a reference to the rates levied during the year the opinion is expressed that if the general rate could be kept nearly at an equable figure without increase it was about as favourable a result of careful management as could reasonably be expected in the face of the constant demands for the extension of the wood paving system. Although it does not strictly appertain to the subject of the report, yet it was thought that it would be interesting to reprint a statement showing the "indebtedness" of the metropolis. This was as follows: London

County Council, £19,105,942; School Board for London, £9,271,131; Metropolitan Asylums Board, £1,918,225; Metropolitan Police (proportion), £298,337; vestries, City Commissioners of Sewers and district board of works, £4,469,479; board of guardians, £2,699,597; other local authorities, £921,518. Of the total—£38,684,229—the "indebtedness" of St. Pancras for local purposes is £644,893, divided thus: Vestry, £414,153 (including electricity, £149,887); guardians, £230,740.

The vestry apparently have long held an objection to overhead wires, and therefore they have hailed with satisfaction an application from the National Telephone Company for leave to lay several hundred miles of wires underground. The company proposed to commence by a line extending from Pentonville-road to Portland-road, and permission has been unanimously granted on condition that the work of making good the ground shall be executed by the vestry's workmen at the cost of the company. Consideration has also been given to a further application for permission to lay three pipes down the south side of Tottenham Court-road, along Grafton-street and Huntley-street, to connect with pipes already laid in St. Giles; but having regard to the course adopted by the vestry in dealing with a previous application, the committee had felt constrained to advise that the further consideration of the matter should be deferred until after the decision of the conference of vestries on the subject of telephone communication of the metropolis.

After a year's anxious work in connection with the refuse destructor, the vestry have thought it better to constitute a separate department to supervise it in connection with the removal of dust. When the vestry placed the control in the hands of the Works Committee they were not consulted in the matter, and it came as an addition to an already everworked department without any increase in the staff beyond a managing foreman six months after. As the committee did not seek the change, they have nothing to regret at being relieved of an unpleasant function, but while it remained in their hands they did what they could to improve the working; and the new committee have continued on those lines rather than enter on the responsibility of advising reconstruction, as was suggested (in part), after observing the effects of another mode of construction at Leyton. Mr. W. N. Blair, M.I.C.E., as is well known, is engineer and surveyor at St. Pancras, and his services are duly acknowledged in the report.

\* \* \*

Mr. Tom Vickers, the surveyor to the Newark Rural District Council, has furnished his second annual report to that body. The district comprises about 109 miles of highways and twenty-five parishes. Of first-class roads there are 55¼ miles, of second-class 39½ miles, third-class roads 11½ miles, and grass lanes 3 miles. The majority have a very poor subsoil and entail a heavy expenditure for manual labour. Of a total sum of £1,713 spent during the twelve months ended March last, £773 was devoted to manual labour, £685 to manual labour for ordinary repairs, £209 to team labour, and £45 to smaller repairs. Each mile of road in the district therefore costs about £15 14s. 5d. to maintain. In 1897 the expenditure per mile was £18 6s., and in 1896 £15 18s. The total cost of maintenance for the years 1896 and 1897 was £1,725 and £1,994 respectively. Roads of the first class, it may be stated, lie adjacent to the borough of Newark and receive an ever-increasing amount of the heavy traffic of that town. The quantity of stone actually used upon the roads was 2,296 tons, against 3,121 tons in the preceding year, being a decrease of 825 tons. There are 25 miles of footpaths in the district, and £60 was spent upon their maintenance, against £75 in the preceding year. The total expenditure of all works was £1,927.

**Eastbourne.**—At the last meeting of the council a letter was read from the Local Government Board stating that they were unable to supply any sketch plans of common lodging-houses. It was resolved that the council be recommended to sanction a scheme for the erection of a model common lodging-house, at a cost not to exceed £3,500. This does not include the cost of the site and furniture, the total cost including which would not exceed £5,000.

**Dewsbury.**—We understand from a contemporary that the town council, on Tuesday of last week, discussed the question of so altering the by-laws as to allow of the erection of back-to-back houses in blocks of four, a committee, after considering the cost in comparison with single through cottages, having reported against such alteration. The report gave rise to a spirited discussion. Mr. Denton moved an amendment referring the minute back to the committee, his object being to get official sanction to the erection of back-to-back houses in blocks of four, with side light and ventilation. His amendment was, however, rejected by a small majority, and the committee's report was adopted.

# Municipal Work in Progress and Projected.

Nothing unusual is contemplated in the metropolis at present, although the majority of the local authorities have resumed their deliberations. In the provinces, however, several extensive schemes are projected or in progress, notably at Bradford, Harrogate, Ipswich, Retford, Selby, Wallsend and other places.

## METROPOLITAN AUTHORITIES.

### METROPOLITAN ASYLUMS BOARD.

Sir E. H. Galsworthy presided on Saturday at the first meeting of this authority since the recess. A letter was read from the Local Government Board, enclosing an order authorising the expenditure of an additional sum of £149 in the erection of workshops and store-rooms at the Eastern Hospital. The communication also contained the board's sanction to the erection of an isolation pavilion, at a cost not exceeding £2,316, and the borrowing of the necessary money. In another letter to the managers the Local Government Board stated that they had directed their chief general inspector, Mr. W. E. Knollys, C.B., to hold, after the vacation, an inquiry into the causes of the excess of cost over the tenders received for the erection of the Brook Hospital, the architect's responsibility, and the supervision exercised by the committee and the managers as regarded expenditure. The letter was referred to the General Purposes Committee, with power to take such action as they might think necessary.

### VESTRIES AND DISTRICT BOARDS.

**Battersea.**—The vestry, on Wednesday, resolved to be represented at the conference to be held next month, at the instance of the Lee District Board of Works, to consider the question of the Workmen's Compensation Act in relation to the employees of the local authorities throughout the metropolis.—The Finance and Law Committee reported, in reference to the injunction granted against the County of London and Brush Electric Lighting Company, that the company had applied to the Court for a further suspension of the injunction in regard to the laying of electric light mains in Trinity-road until the hearing of the company's appeal. The case came recently before Mr. Justice Stirling, when, although opposed by the vestry, the application was granted, but the company was ordered to pay all costs in the matter.—The Health Committee announced that they had considered a letter from the Clerkenwell Vestry drawing attention to the fact that new buildings were erected to plans approved by the district surveyor or the London County Council without the plans being submitted to the vestry, many persons being under the impression that when the plans had passed the district surveyor the sanitary arrangements had received the sanction of the local authority, and resenting the subsequent action of the local authority. In this connection the Clerkenwell Vestry suggested that the county council should instruct the district surveyors to draw the attention of builders to the necessity for making application to the local authority before commencing to build and submitting details as to the proposed drainage arrangements. The Clerkenwell Vestry asked for co-operation in the matter, and, on the motion of the Health Committee, the vestry resolved to concur with the action of the former authority.—With reference to the views sought by the county council on the proposal to establish a bacteriological laboratory for the whole of the metropolis, the Health Committee recommended that no action should be taken. The recommendation was adopted.—The Works Committee reported the receipt of a letter from the county council, stating that the council had refused to consent to the application and plan submitted by Mr. W. D. Goodwin for the erection of blocks of residential flats, with projecting bays on the west side of Albert Bridge-road.—A letter was read from the Local Government Board stating that the board would direct an inquiry into the application made by the vestry for sanction to borrow £36,878 for the purchase of land and the erection of public baths and wash-houses in Battersea Park-road. On the motion of the Health Committee, it was decided to procure vans and receptacles for the collection and removal of fish offal throughout the district.

**Limehouse.**—Attention was last week called to the congested condition of Narrow-street, Broad-street and Three Colt-street, and it was said that it was a notorious fact that there was a very great congestion of traffic in these streets, and it was of importance that something should be done to improve the present state of affairs. It was moved that, in view of the injury to business and trade, not only to this district but to the port of London, owing to the insufficient width of the streets referred to, a special committee be appointed to consider the advisability of taking action thereon. The motion was carried.

**Marylebone.**—The vestry are at present seeking a site on which to erect a new town hall in lieu of the present inadequate court house, which was rebuilt in 1825.

**Rotherhithe.**—The public gallery in the town hall, which has been the subject of numerous complaints, has now been re-ventilated and otherwise improved. The vestry have

further decided to construct an open balustrade instead of the present plain front, and a tender, amounting to £50 10s., has been accepted for this purpose. Other improvements are in contemplation.—At last week's meeting a letter was received from the Local Government Board asking to be furnished with the observations of the vestry upon a letter received by the board from the London County Council relative to the Fulford-street and Braddon-street, Rotherhithe, improvement scheme.—It was decided to support certain resolutions passed by the Wandsworth Board of Works in favour of the telephone service being exclusively exercised by the Government, and not undertaken by the London County Council and the other local authorities; and of the undertaking and property of the National Telephone Company being taken over by the Post Office.

**Shoreditch.**—At the last meeting of the vestry it was decided to apply to the Public Works Loan Commissioners for a loan of £10,653 for works at the baths and wash-houses. —The Town Hall Committee reported having considered plans for the proposed alterations to the town hall and the adaptation for office purposes of adjoining premises recently acquired by the vestry. The committee recommended that tenders should be invited for the carrying out of the work, at a cost of £4,450.—It was resolved to authorise the Housing Committee to obtain tenders for the erection of a shelter and tool-shed at the Charles-square recreation ground.—The following tenders were considered for the supply of new boilers for the electric light station: R. Taylor & Sons (accepted), £3,410; E. Danks & Co., £3,900; J. Fraser & Son, £4,236; Fleming & Ferguson, Limited, £4,400; Tinkers, Limited, £4,750; S. Hodge & Sons, Limited, £5,150; Davey, Paxman & Co., Limited, £5,173; J. Jones & Sons, £5,300.—Tenders as under were dealt with for the supply of transformers: The General Electric Company, Limited, £2,010; The Electric Construction Company, Limited (accepted), £2,747; Thomas Parker, Limited, £2,800; Fuller Westrom Electric Manufacturing Company, Limited, £2,895.—For the extension of the buildings at the electric light station the following firms tendered: Merredew & Wort, £2,855; C. Gray Hill (accepted), £3,069; J. Dolman & Co., £3,330; H. G. Evans, £4,040.—It was decided to accept the tender of J. Bellamy for the supply of Alexander patent cisterns of 900 gallons capacity at the price of £21 10s. each, of 750 gallons at £20 10s., and of 500 gallons capacity at £16 10s. each. The other firms who tendered, and at higher prices, were: W. B. Bawn & Co., and F. Braby & Co., Limited.—The following tenders were opened and referred to committee for consideration: For the construction of an underground convenience in Hoxton-street—Dolman & Co, Poplar, £2,066; George Jennings, £2,025; and Doulton & Co., Lambeth, £2,150; for the construction of a sewer in Britannia-street—W. Manders, £414; T. Adams, £557; Robert Jackson, £409; J. Jackson, £512; Williamson & Son, £502; and Killingback & Co., £416.

**St. Pancras.**—At their last meeting the vestry decided to have lithographed the plan approved by the county council showing the line of buildings of the proposed new baths in the Prince of Wales-road.—It was also decided to attach the seal of the vestry to the Chapel-grove and Eastnor-place improvement schemes, and to forthwith take all necessary steps to carry them into effect, under Part II. of the Housing of the Working Classes Act.—The Electricity and Public Lighting Committee reported that, as the extensions in progress at the Regent's Park central station were not sufficiently advanced to enable the additional plant to be fixed and in working order to meet the demand for the electric light during the coming winter, they had had to consider the question of hiring temporary plant to tide over the difficulty. As the matter was of urgency the committee asked for and obtained permission to make arrangements to cope with the demand.—On the recommendation of the same committee the vestry resolved to charge all consumers in future requiring a combined day and night supply on the maximum demand indicator system.—The Health Committee reported that they had considered a letter from the Clerkenwell Vestry drawing attention to the fact that new buildings are erected to plans approved by the district surveyor or the county council, and that after the building is in position application is frequently made to the vestry to modify the by-laws relating to water-closets, soil pipes, &c., owing to the difficulty of complying with them. The Clerkenwell Vestry suggested that it might be advantageous for the county council to instruct the district surveyors to draw the attention of builders to the necessity for making application to the local authority before commencing to build and to submit details of the drains and sanitary conveniences. The Clerkenwell Vestry had resolved to forward suggestions to that effect to the county council, and on the recommendation of the Health Committee the vestry decided to support the former's action in this respect. It was further resolved to inform the county council that the vestry were in favour of the establishment of a central bacteriological laboratory, and that such an institution could be provided by the Metropolitan Asylums Board in the new premises now being built for the latter on the Victoria-embankment.

# PROVINCIAL AND GREATER LONDON AUTHORITIES.

## COUNTY COUNCILS.

**Westmoreland.**—The Light Railways Committee reported, at the last meeting of the county council, that the advisability of constructing a light railway from Kendal to Arkholme had been considered by them and the Kendal Corporation, and they recommended the council to vote £100 towards the cost of a survey of the district, Kendal Corporation contributing a like sum. The recommendation was agreed to.

## MUNICIPAL CORPORATIONS.

**Banbury.**—A Local Government Board inquiry was held on the 1st inst. respecting an application of the town council to borrow £1,000 for the improvement of the baths. There was no opposition to the application.

**Bournemouth.**—The town council have adopted a resolution, with one dissentient, to make application to the Board of Trade for a provisional order to authorise the council to supply electricity for any public or private purposes within the borough.

**Bradford.**—A new fire station is about to be erected by the corporation opposite St. James's church, Nelson-street, at a cost of £10,000, exclusive of the outlay on the purchase of the site, which is £11,000.

**Brighton.**—A revised scheme was recently submitted to the council by the Works Committee relative to the provision of conveniences in the northern part of the town. It was recommended that one at the north end of the level should be rebuilt near Union-road, at an estimated cost of £221; that the one in Lewes-road should be enlarged and improved, at a cost of £55; that a new one should be constructed in Oxford-street, at a cost of £150, in lieu of the proposed underground convenience; and that another should be erected in the public road at the north end of Queen's Park, at a cost of £140. The committee added that they hoped to report, at an early date, with a plan and an estimate for the erection of an underground convenience in the neighbourhood of the Clock Tower at the south end of Queen's-road. —The Waterworks Committee have decided to accept an offer from Mr. A. E. Nunn, of Tenterden, Kent, to drive headings in the wells at Mile Oak, Portslade, at a depth of 140 ft., for the sum of 37s. per lineal foot.

**Bristol.**—At last week's meeting of the Sanitary Committee, the report of Messrs. John Taylor, Sons & Santo Crimp on the Bristol main drainage scheme was presented. The scheme provides for an outfall at the north-east of Dunball Island, Avonmouth, the estimated cost of which is £379,700. The report states that in the opinion of the engineers such a scheme if properly designed would be sanctioned by Parliament. No decision was arrived at by the committee.

**Devonport.**—On the recommendation of the Water Committee, the town council, at a special meeting on Tuesday of last week, decided to apply for Parliamentary powers to acquire the undertaking of the Devonport Waterworks Company.

**Dorchester.**—Negotiations are to be opened with the Dorchester Gas Company by the town council with a view to the purchase of the undertaking. It was pointed out that the present was a desirable opportunity for moving in the matter, in view of the extension of the borough and the greatly-increased lighting area.

**Dover.**—At the town council meeting, on Tuesday afternoon, it was officially reported that the first year's working of the corporation's electric tramways, after allowing for payment of interest and instalments of the loans, had resulted in a profit of £1,300 being earned. A total of 1,794,903 persons have been carried, at the universal fare of 1d.

**Gateshead.**—The Parliamentary Committee of the town council have decided to take steps to obtain expert evidence as to the cost of laying down plant for the overhead electric traction system on the tramways, the probable cost of buying out the present company at the end of the term, and the advantage to be gained by working the trams and supplying electric light from one generating station.

**Glossop.**—A petition is being signed at Glossop against a proposal, carried by a narrow majority of the council, to introduce electric light into the borough. The opposition is based on the belief that the installation will prove unremunerative; and in this connection the petition points out that the fact that the price of gas has been reduced by the Glossop Gas Company will have a considerable effect in the way of diminishing the number of probable consumers of the electric light.

**Halifax.**—The municipality is about to begin the work of extending its tramways system, being now assured that it will prove a paying concern. The two sections now working are the railway station to King's Cross and to High-road Well. During eight weeks' running the weather has been fine, the result being that they averaged £300 per week during the last four weeks, but this can hardly be expected to continue.

**Harrogate.**—Mr. F. H. Tulloch, M.I.C.E., on Tuesday of last week, held an inquiry, on behalf of the Local Government Board, respecting an application of the town council for sanction to borrow £8,500 for surface-water drainage works, £580 for sewerage works, £500 for the purchase of a steam roller and a road scarifier, and £450 for the construction of a public convenience in High Harrogate.

**Ipswich.**—A Local Government Board inquiry was held on Friday by Mr. E. A. Sandford Fawcett respecting an application of the corporation for sanction to borrow £4,400 for the erection of a fire station, £4,000 for works of sewerage, £3,070 for works of street improvement, £600 for market purposes, and £450 for purposes of public walks and pleasure grounds.

**Liverpool.**—At the last monthly meeting of the council the Estate Committee recommended that the town clerk be authorised to give notice to the Mersey Docks and Harbour Board, in pursuance of the provisions of the Corporation Act, 1898, that the council intended to purchase a certain indicated portion of the land now occupied by the George's dock. The recommendation was passed.—The tender of Messrs. Waring & Sons, of West Kirby, has been accepted, at £2,635, for the erection of an electric sub-station in Lodge-lane.— The Tramway Committee having asked if the Lighting Committee could utilise for lighting purposes the poles being erected in connection with the electric tram lines, the matter has been referred to Mr. A. B. Holmes, city electrical engineer, and Mr. Charles R. Bellamy, superintendent of street lighting, for a report. It is understood that they will make experiments as to the most suitable lamp that can be used. An extension of mains in several thoroughfares has been resolved upon.

**Manchester.**—The lord mayor recently opened a new park in Bellott-street, Cheetham, which has just been presented to the city. It has an area of 7,500 superficial yards. Part of it is laid out for games of bowls and tennis, a second part is covered with grass and will form a children's playground, while the remainder is planted with one or more specimens, all labelled, of almost every indigenous tree or shrub, besides some that are not natives of Britain, the variety being greater than in any other of the thirty-eight parks and open spaces in Manchester.—A report has been drawn up, at the instance of the Rivers Committee, with reference to certain allegations of "errors and omissions connected with the erection of catch-pits at Davyhulme sewage works." The report is now in the hands of the Town Hall Committee.

**Oldham.**—In the minutes of the Gas Committee submitted to the meeting of the town council on Wednesday week it was stated that the gas manager, acting on instructions given to him, had made inquiries at a number of towns using carburetted water-gas, and that they all expressed themselves satisfied with that gas as an auxiliary to coal-gas. The Gas Committee had, however, decided to defer action in the matter until the Home Office Committee had made its report.

**Retford.**—The formal sanction of the Local Government Board to the borrowing of £40,000 for carrying out a scheme of sewerage has been received by the town council.

**Richmond, Surrey.**—A special meeting of the town council, on Tuesday, unanimously decided not to accept the option of purchasing Glover's island for £4,000. A special committee, who had considered the whole subject of its acquisition as a means of preserving from undesirable encroachment the view from Richmond Hill, and also the price, decided adversely, and this report the council adopted. The island had been entrusted by the owner to the mayor for sale by public auction on September 23rd, and the mayor meantime secured the refusal of the purchase at the reserve price of £4,000 for the public. A fund which was opened in the town to raise the £4,000 had only scanty support, and now the committee denounced the whole project. Although the mayor desired to join in the discussion on the committee's report, the council declined to hear him, and, in adopting the report, passed another resolution calling on the Thames Conservancy to introduce a Bill to prevent abuses of advertising on the river banks and islands.

**Salford.**—The town council last week decided to accept tenders as follows: De Bergue & Co. for the erection of purifying and oxide floors at the Liverpool-street gasworks; Bale & Co. for the supply of 100 tons of natural oxide of iron on the basis of 40 per cent. of moisture; Muller & Co. for the supply of 500 tons of natural oxide of iron, on the basis of 25 per cent. of moisture; and J. & J. Braddock for the supply of wet and dry pre-payment meters.

**Stockport.**—An effort is about to be made by the corporation to acquire the property of the waterworks company which supplies Stockport and the surrounding district, in which the total population is over 200,000.

**Stockton.**—At a meeting of the Stockton Town Council, on the 6th inst., the town clerk reported that he had received the sanction of the Local Government Board to the borrowing of £28,482 for the electric lighting of the town and also the approval of the board to the use of certain lands for the erection of the plant.

**Wells.**—Tenders for the erection of a new town hall and post office were opened at last week's meeting of the city council. There were six tenders, the highest being £10,698 and the lowest £9,192. The architect's estimate was £4,850, so that the prices read out caused very great surprise. None of the tenders were accepted, and the whole question was referred to a special meeting of the General Purposes Committee.

**Wolverhampton.**—A letter was on Monday received from the Local Government Board, stating that, with reference to the application of the council for sanction to borrow £1,855, for the formation of an open space and for paving over the vaults of the Exchange Hall, they had deferred their consideration of the matter until they were informed that the town council had definitely decided to adopt the scheme which formed the subject of the inspector's inquiry.—The following resolution was adopted without discussion: "That in pursuance of the provisions of the Tramways Act, 1870, and the Tramways Orders Confirmation Act, 1877, the mayor, aldermen and burgesses of the borough of Wolverhampton, acting by the council as the local authority under the said Tramways Act, 1870, do hereby resolve that, subject to the approval of the Board of Trade, notice in writing, under the corporate common seal of the said local authority, be given to the Wolverhampton Tramways Company, Limited, requiring them to sell to the council of this borough, as such local authority as aforesaid, so much of the undertaking of the said company as is within the borough of Wolverhampton, and as was authorised by the Wolverhampton Tramways Order, 1877, as confirmed by the Tramways Orders Confirmation Act, 1877."

## URBAN DISTRICT COUNCILS.

**Brandon and Byshottles, Durham.**—The contract for the pumping machinery required by the council for pumping water to Brandon village has been placed with Messrs. Robert Stephenson & Co., Limited, engineers, Newcastle, who are to supply a "Rocket" oil engine and a treble-ram pump for the duty.

**Buckley.**—On the 7th inst., at a meeting of this authority, it was reported that the council's offer to purchase the local gasworks for £3,500 had not been accepted, the gas company offering to sell for £4,750. A resolution to obtain a provisional order for lighting the district by electricity was unanimously carried, and it was resolved to engage the services of an electrical engineer. Tenders for electric lighting had been received from the Sandycroft Engineering Company and Messrs. Mather & Platt, Manchester.

**Chertsey.**—At the meeting of a committee of the council, held on the 5th inst., consideration was given to a draft prepared by the surveyor of particulars to be furnished to the competing engineers in connection with the proposed main drainage scheme. These were gone through seriatim, and were approved, as was also a plan drawn, by the surveyor on a large scale, showing the areas which it is suggested shall be sewered.

**Haworth.**—The Water and Fire Brigade Committee last week brought forward a recommendation that the council should take into consideration the desirability of concreting the bottom of the Hough reservoir, and also inquire into the condition of the water supply generally in the district. It was decided to discuss the question in committee.

**Ilkley.**—On Thursday, at the offices of the council, Mr. F. H. Tulloch, one of the Local Government Board inspectors, inquired into an application by the local authority for sanction to borrow £175, being half the estimated cost of forming new streets on the south and east sides of the proposed public offices, and to be known as Chantry-drive and Back-road. Details of the proposed works were then given, and the inquiry closed, the inspector subsequently visiting the locus in quo, and afterwards the sewage disposal works.

**Morecambe.**—At a meeting of the council, on Monday afternoon, the question was considered of constructing a marine lake on the foreshore fronting the Victoria Esplanade at the east end. This has recently been completed, and the council are now engaged in fixing arc lamps to complete the electric lighting of the whole of the sea frontage. It was resolved unanimously that the council considered it advisable to construct a marine lake, and that a special council meeting be called at an early date to consider the matter fully and in detail. From inquiry it has been estimated that the probable cost will be £40,000. This, in conjunction with the electric light undertaking, the proposed new sewage scheme and refuse destructor and street improvement works now in hand, is expected to place Morecambe in the forefront of pleasure resorts.

**Northwich.**—At last week's meeting of the council it was unanimously resolved to invite all local architects to prepare competitive plans for the erection of an isolation hospital on land at Shurlach, at a cost of £3,000.

**Selby.**—Lieut.-Colonel A. C. Smith, an inspector of the Local Government Board, held an inquiry on Friday in respect to an application of the council for sanction to borrow £8,400 for gasworks extensions, &c. The gas manager (Mr. W. J. Scott) stated that at nightfall there was a great draw, and they were sometimes unable to keep up with the demand. Last winter, on one or two occasions, the manager had to

reserve the pressure and otherwise restrict the supply. Then the council were under a very great obligation to the North-Eastern Railway Company, inasmuch as all their signals at the station, which is a very important junction, were lit by gas, and any interruption in the supply to them might be disastrous.

**Swinton and Pendlebury.**—It was on Monday stated that the Local Government Board had, after a long delay, given their sanction to the council contracting a loan of £1,100 for works of street surface-water drainage and to the borrowing of two sums of £875 for works of sewage disposal. In a further communication from the board it was stated that no recommendation was necessary in reference to the loan of £5,910 for works of street improvement.

**Teignmouth.**—The district council have adopted plans, prepared by Mr. Jones, their surveyor, for an enlargement of the isolation hospital, by which the number of beds will be increased from three to twelve, and the building will be doubled in size. The estimated outlay is £5,000.

**Wallsend.**—A Local Government Board inquiry was held on the 2nd inst. respecting an application of the district council for sanction to borrow about £5,000 for the formation of a new road and quay on the east side of the township, £3,885 for works of public and private street improvements, and £5,000 for the purpose of public walks and pleasure grounds. The clerk to the council said that the reason the council had resolved to take steps to put the improvements named into effect was due exclusively to the extraordinary development of the town consequent upon the shipbuilding and engineering industries and the recent re-opening of the coalfields in the immediate neighbourhood. No less than 48,000 tons of shipping had been set afloat in 1897 by the firm of Messrs. C. S. Swan & Hunter, or about one-fourth of the shipping launched on the Tyne that year. The population in 1861 was 2,371; in 1871, 4,159; in 1881, 6,150; and in 1891, 11,620. The present population was 18,192. No fewer than 425 houses were at the moment in course of erection, 375 of which were on the "flat" principle. The immense rush of working men to the district necessitated enlarged household accommodation, the buildings at present in course of erection being sufficient to house some 2,000 workmen and their families.

**Withington.**—On the 7th inst. Colonel J. G. Marsh, on behalf of the Local Government Board, heard an application, at the Withington Town Hall, for permission on the part of the district council to borrow a sum of £4,407 for sewage works, and a further sum of £608 to be spent upon private street improvements.

## RURAL DISTRICT COUNCILS.

**Bingham.**—The clerk has been directed, in replying to a recent communication from the Local Government Board inquiring what had been done in connection with the scheme of sewerage, to state that the council had instructed Messrs. Sands & Walker, civil and sanitary engineers, Nottingham, to prepare plans and an estimate for submission to the board, and that the plans were now ready, but the engineers were unable to complete their estimate until they heard from the clerk with respect to the land required for disposal purposes.

**Chesterton.**—An inquiry has been held by Mr. E. A. Sandford Fawcett, on behalf of the Local Government Board, concerning an application of the rural district council for sanction to borrow £5,000 for works of sewerage and sewage disposal.

**Flaxton.**—In response to an application by the rural district council to the Local Government Board for sanction to borrow £250 for the improvement of a main road in the township of Strensall, an inquiry was held by Lieut.-Colonel Albert C. Smith, R.E., Local Government Board inspector, in the St. Mary's Hall, Strensall, on Thursday. Mr. L. Dennis-Smith addressed the inspector on the need of the improvement and on the proposed scheme, and the road and new route were afterwards inspected. Lieut.-Colonel Smith remarked that the improvement was absolutely necessary, and if his report should be favourable work will be commenced soon after its receipt. There was no opposition.

**Goole.**—Lieut.-Colonel A. C. Smith, R.E., an inspector of the Local Government Board, held an inquiry at Swinefleet last week into the subject matter of an application from the Goole Rural District Council to borrow £1,000 for purposes of sewerage for the parish of Swinefleet. Mr. G. England, clerk to the district council, appeared on their behalf, and said it was their intention to re-lay the drains from Reedness to Swinefleet with pipes, and erect a flushing tank capable of holding 900 gallons of water. He said some of them were without pipes and sewage was deposited into manholes and afterwards taken away by scavengers.

**Sleaford.**—The rural district council having applied for power to borrow £900 for a water supply for Great Hale, the usual inquiry was held on Tuesday by Mr. H. Percy Boulnois at Hale. The council were represented by Mr. Clare, district surveyor, and Mr. C. Clements, clerk. Mr. Clare reported that the present supply was obtained from shallow wells, and was declared by Dr. Ashby's analysis to be wholly unfit for domestic purposes. The council had therefore decided to bore, the necessary site having been purchased. There was no opposition.

# Personal.

The salary of Mr. J. Smith, gas manager to the Corporation of Bangor, was last week increased by £20 per annum.

Mr. Edward Hall, borough surveyor of Pwllheli, was on Tuesday of last week appointed borough surveyor of Carnarvon.

Messrs. Samson & Cottam have been awarded the first premium of £100 for their designs for the proposed new town hall at Taunton.

Mr. M. Tutin, buildings inspector to the Stockton-on-Tees Corporation, has been appointed to a similar position under the Southend-on-Sea Corporation.

Messrs. Walker & Sons have been appointed architects of the new free public library which the Gloucester Corporation propose to erect, at a cost of £6,000.

Mr. Leonard Harvey Combe has been selected by the Eccles Town Council to fill the position of borough electrical engineer, at a commencing salary of £150 per annum.

Mr. John Henry Teague, of Lincoln, son of the late engineer (Mr. Henry Teague, deceased), was appointed waterworks engineer to the Lincoln Corporation on Tuesday of last week.

Mr. W. A. Boothroyd, of Barry, has been appointed engineering assistant in charge on the sewage scheme now being carried out by the Coventry Corporation, at a salary of £3 3s. per week.

Mr. Alfred H. Dunkin, of Colne, was on Monday appointed by the General Works Committee of the Bacup Town Council to the position of assistant in the office of Mr. Francis Wood, borough engineer.

Mr. J. Freebairn Stow, surveyor to the Bridlington Urban District Council, was on Tuesday selected to fill the position of surveyor to the Chertsey Urban District Council. Five other gentlemen came up for interview.

The Electric Lighting Committee of the Derby Corporation have reduced the applications for the post of borough electrical engineer and manager to three—namely, Messrs. J. T. Baron, London; E. A. Lancaster, Birmingham; and T. P. Wilmshurst, Halifax.

Mr. H. L. Taylor, of Blackburn, has been unanimously appointed assistant engineer and surveyor to the Sudbury Corporation. Mr. Taylor has had considerable experience as a mechanical engineer, which will be of great service in his present appointment as assistant water engineer.

With some dissentients the Manchester City Council last week adopted a resolution asking Mr. Callison, the superintendent of the Cleansing Department, to resign. On Monday Mr. Callison handed in his resignation, and Mr. George Plant, outdoor superintendent, was appointed to take charge of the duties.

Mr. Corbett Woodall, an expert in gas manufacture, has been appointed by the Corporation of Southport to make an examination of the gas estate and report as to the best methods by which an improvement can be effected in the profits accruing from the same. The results have for some years past been unsatisfactory.

An interesting ceremony took place at Darwen, on Thursday, the occasion being the marriage of Mr. H. B. Longley, chief assistant in the city engineer's department, Coventry, to Miss Ada Beet, eldest daughter of Mr. J. Beet, of Darwen. Mr. J. Ainsworth Settle, borough engineer of Heywood, officiated as best man. The happy couple spend the honeymoon at Llandudno and Barmouth.

The result of the competition in connection with the proposed new town hall of Singapore, India, has been announced. The first prize of £200 has been awarded to Messrs. Francis Sills & Francken, of Norfolk-street, Strand, London, and the second prize of £100 to Mr. William A. Tunstall, of Colombo, Ceylon. Plans submitted by Messrs. Swan & Maclaren, of Singapore, and Messrs. Sevenoaks & Lavelle, of Bangalore, have been commended.

At the first meeting of the St. George's (Southwark) Vestry after the recess, on Tuesday of last week, a member spoke in highly eulogistic terms of Mr. Winter, the late surveyor, and moved that an honorarium of 25 guineas be granted to Mr. Winter in consideration of the extra work performed by him and the able manner in which that work had been carried out. Other members endorsed the praise of Mr. Winter's services, and the motion was unanimously carried.

A special meeting of the Llandudno District Council was held on the 6th inst. for the purpose of presenting the surveyor, Mr. Paley Stevenson, with a handsome marble timepiece, on the occasion of his marriage, which took place on the day following at Ashbourne, in Derbyshire. The chairman (Mr. T. T. Marks), who presided, remarked upon the unanimity and cordiality which had characterised the movement for making this testimonial to the surveyor. Other members spoke, and the surveyor acknowledged in suitable terms the kind feeling which had prompted the presentation.

We regret to announce the death, which took place suddenly on Friday morning, of Mr. John Tate, the surveyor to the Pickering (Yorks) Rural District Council. The deceased was well known and much respected, and a very large company attended the funeral, which took place on Sunday. At a meeting of the council, on Monday, the chairman moved, and the vice-chairman seconded, a resolution of sympathy and condolence with the widow and family of the deceased, both speaking in high terms of the good services rendered by him in the management of the highways for a period extending over nearly thirty years. Other members added to the tribute of respect. A meeting of the council will be held on the 26th inst. to consider the question of the appointment of a surveyor in succession to the late Mr. John Tate. Mr. T. Tate, the deceased's son, has agreed to carry out the duties in the meantime.

On the 5th inst. the Oswestry Town Council were recommended to adopt a resolution of the General Purposes Committee accepting the resignation of Mr. R. O. Wynne Roberts, the borough surveyor, who would, it was stated, shortly take up the post of city engineer of Cape Town. The motion also proposed the granting of a testimonial and a sum of £75 as remuneration for past services. The mayor, in seconding the motion, said he did so with pleasure, not unmixed with feelings of regret. Mr. Wynne Roberts had earned for himself their respect and good feeling, and they wished him every possible success in his new sphere of labour. He was sure that what would be a great loss to them would prove a great acquisition to Cape Town. A councillor, in the course of a highly complimentary speech, expressed his appreciation of the manner in which Mr. Wynne Roberts had discharged his duties as borough surveyor, and said that although it was their privilege to differ frequently with each other, as well as with their officials, as to the methods and manner of doing their work, no one would deny that he (Mr. Wynne Roberts) had worked like a slave on their behalf. The motion was eventually adopted, and the mayor, in a brief address to Mr. Wynne Roberts, remarked that the council had parted with no officer with greater feelings of regret than they would part with him. Mr. Wynne Roberts then replied, saying that words failed to express his gratitude for the kind way in which he had been treated during the past four years. He had always endeavoured to do his duty, and he was glad that his efforts on their behalf had been appreciated.

## A FOUNTAIN POLLUTED BY SEWAGE.

### REMARKABLE CASE AT HALSTEAD.

In his summary of the reports of the district medical officers of health for 1897, Dr. Thresh, medical officer of health for the county of Essex, refers to a somewhat remarkable case of the pollution of a public fountain at Halstead by sewage from the isolation hospital. A subsequent outbreak of typhoid fever in the district was attributed to the drinking of water from the fountain in question. The chief features of the case were summed up in the following way by the medical officer of health to the Halstead Urban District Council: We have therefore this remarkable chain of evidence, from which no link is wanting, to prove that the isolation hospital was the origo mali.

(i.) Initial case of typhoid being treated in isolation hospital.

(ii.) Untreated excreta from which were being frequently put down drain.

(iii.) Although the hospital drains are perfect, the main sewer pipes are only pugged at points, with defective flanges, and one cracked pipe.

(iv.) Spring water led across the road and sewers in tops and bottoms minus joints or any means to prevent pollution.

(v.) Twenty yards lower down, catch-pit, badly constructed, from which drinking fountain is supplied.

This evidence appears overwhelming, the only thing against the theory being that there were no signs of sewage pollution round the defective sewer, the light, sandy soil being, when opened, dry and nowhere discoloured; but, be it remembered, water may be teeming with typhoid bacilli and yet quite clear, and yet a few drops of such a solution would be ample to pollute the well and cause the mischief. It is most probable that the pollution occurred after the heavy falls of rain, which data from the Halstead climatological station prove to have fallen during the first ten days of the year, when the sewer was full of surface water from higher up the hill, the pressure of which would force the water through joints which at ordinary times would be nearly watertight. At such a time, also, the sewage would be dilute, and unlikely to discolour the surrounding soil.

**Tunbridge Wells.**—It has been decided to open the new baths, which have been erected by the corporation, on September 5th next.

## ASSOCIATION OF MUNICIPAL AND COUNTY ENGINEERS.

### MIDLAND DISTRICT MEETING AT BILSTON.

A meeting of the members of the midland district will be held to-morrow at Bilston. The following are the arrangements:—

**11 a.m.**— The members will be received in the council chamber, Town Hall, by the chairman (Councillor R. A. Harper, J.P.) and other members of the council. Minutes of Stafford and Rhyader meetings. Election of hon. district secretary.

**11.30 a.m.**—Leave in brakes, kindly provided by Councillor J. W. Sankey, chairman of the Water and Baths Committee, for a visit to the Spring Vale furnaces, arriving about 11.40 a.m., where, by the kind permission of Sir Alfred Hickman, the process of steel manufacture will be witnessed. A short descriptive paper will be given.

**12.30 p.m.**—Leave in brakes for a visit to the waterworks covered service reservoir (which will be specially emptied for the inspection of the members), arriving about 12.45.

**1.15 p.m.**—Leave in brakes for the Hinley Arms Hotel, arriving about 2 p.m., where a light luncheon will be provided by Councillor R. A. Harper, J.P., chairman of the council.

**3 p.m.**—Leave in brakes for a visit to the Bilston waterworks pumping station, arriving about 3.30 p.m.

**4.15 p.m.**—Leave in brakes for the Technical School, Bilston, arriving about 5 p.m.

**6 p.m.**—Dinner at the Technical School. Tickets, 3s. 6d. each (exclusive of wine).

Arrangements will be made for any members desirous of doing so to inspect the public baths and the public market.

Mr. C. L. N. Wilson, the water engineer and surveyor to the Bilston Council, will give a descriptive paper of the works. As the paper will be in the hands of members intimating their intention to attend some days before the meeting, it will be taken as read.

Among the hotels at Bilston may be mentioned the Pipe Hall, Globe and Great Western.

Wolverhampton is within 2½ miles and Birmingham 10½ miles, and there is a good service of trains from these towns. The Great Western station at Bilston is the nearest to the Town Hall.

J. S. PICKERING, A.M.I.C.E.,        THOS. COLE, A.M.I.C.E.,
*Hon. District Secretary,*                *Secretary,*
Council Offices, Nuneaton.    11 Victoria-street, S.W.

## WISHAW WATER SCHEME.

A special meeting of the Wishaw Town Commissioners was held recently to consider a report of Mr. James Tait, the engineer, as to the probable cost of a new water supply for the burgh. The report contained the cost of constructing a compensation reservoir, and bringing in a supply of water to the present burgh reservoirs in the parish of Carluke from the streams of Potrail, Potrinick and Redin, in the parish of Crawford, in terms of the Wishaw Water Act, 1898. The probable estimates were made with piping in four different diameters. The cost of carrying out the works, including land, wayleaves and surface damages, was as follows : Reservoir, with 18-in. pipe line (delivering 2,200,000 gallons of water per day), £93,000; 16-in. pipe line (1,640,000 gallons), £81,000; 15-in. pipe line (1,400,000 gallons), £78,000; 12-in. pipe line (780,000 gallons), £67,000. Attached to the report was a certificate, signed by Mr. R. Copland, C.E., Glasgow, saying he had examined the estimates on which the report was based, and he considered the sums sufficient. After discussion it was unanimously agreed to adopt the 18-in. size of pipe, at a cost of £93,000, and the engineer was instructed to prepare specifications and schedules.

## APPOINTMENTS VACANT.

*Advertisements which are received too late for classification cannot be included in these summaries until the following week.*

BOROUGH SURVEYOR AND SANITARY INSPECTOR.—September 17th.—Borough of Oswestry. £200.—Mr. J. Parry Jones, town clerk.

ENGINEERING ASSISTANT.—September 17th.—Ilfracombe Urban District Council.—Mr. O. M. Prouse, engineer and surveyor to the council.

ELECTRICAL ENGINEER. — September 20th. — Willesden Urban District Council. £400.—Mr. O. Claude Robson, M.I.C.E., engineer and surveyor to the council.

TEMPORARY ASSISTANT.—September 20th.—Llantrisant and Llantwit Fadre Rural District Council.—Mr. Gomer S. Morgan, surveyor to the council, Pontyclun.

SECRETARY AND CITY MANAGER.—September 21st.—York Waterworks Company. £300 with house.—The Directors of the Company, Lendal Hill, York.

BURGH AND ROAD SURVEYOR, SANITARY INSPECTOR, &c.—September 23rd.—Commissioners of the Burgh of Carnoustie. £100.—Mr. William Cæsar, town clerk.

SANITARY INSPECTORS (Two).—September 29th.—Chelsea Vestry. £120.—Mr. Thomas Holland, clerk to the vestry.

GENERAL ASSISTANT FOR BOROUGH ENGINEER'S DEPARTMENT.—October 1st.—Corporation of Plymouth. £100.—Mr. James Paton, borough engineer and surveyor.

## COMPETITIONS.

*Advertisements which are received too late for classification cannot be included in these summaries until the following week.*

PLYMOUTH.—September 24th.—Erection of shops and dwelling-houses fronting Tavistock-road. £250.—Mr. J. H. Ellis, town clerk.

WIVENHOE.—September 20th.—Works of drainage and water supply, for the urban district council.—Mr. C. W. Denton, clerk.

REIGATE.—October 6th.—Erection of municipal buildings, fire station, public offices, &c.—Mr. Clair J. Grece, town clerk.

ABERAVON.—December 1st.—Extension of the covered market, at a cost not to exceed £5,000. £21.—The Borough Surveyor.

CURRNEY.—December 23rd.—Sewerage and sewage disposal scheme for the No. 1 and 2 wards of the district. £50, £30 and £20.—Mr. T. E. Harland Obaldecott, clerk to the council.

## MUNICIPAL CONTRACTS OPEN.

*Advertisements which are received too late for classification cannot be included in these summaries until the following week.*

ROTHBURY.—September 17th.—Supply of a ½-ton steam roller, one sleeping-van and one water-cart, for the rural district council.—Mr. James Wood, surveyor to the council.

EVESHAM.—September 17th.—Building of a new bridge, altering course of brook, and other works connected therewith, at the boundary of Bengeworth and Badsey parishes, for the urban district council.—Mr. Edward Wadams, clerk to the council.

NOTTINGHAM.—September 17th.—Construction of new sewer.—Mr. Arthur Brown, city engineer.

ABERDEEN.—September 17th.—Supply for one year of electricity meters, house fuse-boxes and house service cables.—Mr. J. Alex. Bell, city electrical engineer.

STAINES.—September 17th.—Making-up of Sidney-road, Bremer-road, Farnell-road and Billet-road, for the urban district council.—Mr. E. J. Barrett, A.M.I.C.E., surveyor to the council.

STAINES.—September 17th.—Supply and delivery of about 200 tons of 1½-in. hand-broken Guernsey granite, for the urban district council.—Mr. E. J. Barrett, A.M.I.C.E., surveyor to the council.

DOWNPATRICK.—September 17th.—Improvement of the storage reservoir at Tannaghmore.—The County Surveyor, Downpatrick.

CAMBERWELL.—September 19th.—Painting of the exterior of Camberwell and Dulwich baths, for the vestry.—The Clerk to the Vestry.

WEST RIDING.—September 19th.—Erection of a farm residence at the asylum at Menston.—Mr. J. Vickers Edwards, county surveyor, County Hall, Wakefield.

GLOUCESTER.—September 19th.—Erection of new electricity works.—Mr. George Sheffield Blakeway, town clerk.

HORNSEY.—September 19th.—Sewering, levelling, paving, metalling, channelling and making good certain roads, for the urban district council.—Mr. F. D. Askey, clerk.

HULL.—September 19th.—Construction of engine foundations and setting of economiser and four boilers at the Springhead pumping station.—Mr. F. J. Bancroft. water and gas engineer, Town Hall, Hull.

SWANSEA.—September 19th.—Completion of the main sewerage of the district, for the urban district council.—Messrs. Francis Newman & Cocks, 8 St. Thomas-street, Ryde.

LYTHAM.—September 19th.—Construction of about 900 yards of 3-ft. diameter brick sewer, about 1,500 yards of 24-in. and 18-in. pipe sewer, and concrete and storage tanks, together with sea embankment, roadway and other contingent works, for the urban district council.—Messrs. Newton, 17 Cooper-street, Manchester.

WAKEFIELD.—September 19th.—Construction of a cast-iron water-tank, to hold 18,000 gallons, at Woolley-edge in the township of Criggleston, for the rural district council.—Mr. Frank Massie, A.M.I.C.E., engineer and surveyor to the council.

PADDINGTON.—September 19th.—Supply of about 600 cubic yards of fine crushed Thames shingle, for the vestry.—Mr. Frank Dethridge, surveyor to the vestry.

AYRTH.—September 19th.—Supply of 100 tons of broken whinstone, for the urban district council.—Mr. W. Gibson, surveyor to the council.

TORQUAY.—September 19th.—Supply of meters and are lamp carbons for twelve months from 1st October.—Mr. P. Storey, borough electrical engineer.

LIVERPOOL.—September 19th.—Alterations at the Stable-street public wash-house, for the corporation.—Mr. R. Court, engineer and chief superintendent, Cornwallis-street baths, Liverpool.

LONDON. — September 20th. — Construction of underground conveniences at Queenhitho.—The City Engineer, Guildhall, E.C.

LEEDS.—September 20th.—Supply of (a) poles and (b) trolley wire and attachments in connection with the extension of the electric tramway systems.—The City Engineer.

ANDLE.—September 20th.—Excavating, levelling and paving works in Alley-street Back-lane and Middleton-street Back-lane, for the urban district council.—Mr. W. Gibson, surveyor to the council.

BUCKLOW.—September 20th.—Repaving of certain boulder pavements and channels in Carrington, Partington and Warburton, for the rural district council.—Mr. Joseph Burgess, highway surveyor, Tabley, Knutsford.

BARNWOOD.—September 20th.—Supply of 1,000 cubic yards of blue Guernsey granite, for the urban district council.—Mr. Nowell Parr, surveyor to the council.

GOSPORT AND ALVERSTOKE.—September 20th.—Supply of various materials during the year ending 30th September, 1899, for the urban district council.—Mr. H. Frost, surveyor to the council.

TOTTENHAM.—September 20th.—Supply of forage for the half-year ending Lady Day, 1899, for the urban district council.—Mr. Edward Crowne, clerk to the council.

NELSON.—September 20th.—Construction of two filter-beds at the sewage works.—Mr. B. Ball, A.M.I.C.E., borough engineer and surveyor.

BARKING TOWN.—September 20th.—Supply of a 6 or 10-ton steam road-roller adaptable for traction, for the urban district council.—Mr. E. H. Lister, clerk to the council.

South Hornsey.—September 21st.—Supply of road materials for one year from the 29th September, 1898, also dusting, and masons' and paviors' work, for the urban district council.—Mr. Edward B. Bennett, clerk to the council.

Hollingbourn.—September 21st.—Supply of steam rollers for use on the district roads during a period of about fifty days, for the rural district council.—Mr. J. Stanley Roper, surveyor to the council.

Bradford.—September 21st.—Supply of about 150,000 jarrah or karri wood paving blocks.—Mr. J. H. Cox, borough engineer.

Mile End.—September 21st.—Supply of gulley grates and frames, manhole covers and ventilating gratings, for the vestry.—Mr. J. M. Knight, surveyor to the vestry.

Easington.—September 21st.—Water supply works for Wingate Mill, Wingate-lane and High Wheatley Hill, for the rural district council.—Messrs. D. Balfour & Son, 3 St. Nicholas-buildings, Newcastle-on-Tyne.

Leek.—September 21st.—Erection of a science and art school and county silk school, for the urban district council.—Mr. Chas. Henshaw, clerk to the council.

Hull.—September 21st.—Supply of steel roofs and sundry iron and steel work for the tramway power station.—Mr. A. E. White, city engineer.

Hoyland.—September 22nd.—Construction of about 73 yards of 15-in., 1,690 yards of 12-in. and 1,086 yards of 9-in. pipe sewers, in connection with the King-street and Platts Common sewerage, for the urban district council.—Mr. William Farrington, A.M.I.C.E., engineer and surveyor to the council.

Portsmouth.—September 22nd.—Laying of compressed and asphalte paving in Palmerston-road, Russell-street, and part of Hyde Park-road and Charlotte-street.—Mr. Alexander Hellard, town clerk.

Dewsbury.—September 22nd.—Macadamising, kerbing, flagging, &c., works in Oxford-street and James-street.—Mr. G. Trevelyan Lee, town clerk.

Tamworth.—September 22nd.—Supply of about 8¼ miles of 4-in. and 3-in. cast-iron water mains, for the rural district council.—Mr. Henry J. Clarson, surveyor to the council.

Blaydon-on-Tyne.—September 22nd.—Erection of new public offices and a technical school, for the urban district council.—Mr. H. Dalton, clerk to the council.

Glasgow.—September 23rd.—Erection of a fence at the new park at Rutherglen-road.—Mr. A. B. M'Donald, city engineer.

Kingsbridge.—September 23rd.—Hire of a steam roller, for the rural district council.—Mr. William Beer, highway clerk to the council.

Glasgow.—September 23rd.—Erection of a retaining wall at the bowling green in Rutherglen-road over Polmadie burn.—Mr. A. B. M'Donald, city engineer.

Gloucester.—September 23rd.—Erection of cattle lairs, horse sheds, &c., in the cattle market.—Mr. R. Read, A.M.I.C.E., city surveyor.

East Sussex.—September 23rd.—Erection of two temporary buildings for 100 patients at the county lunatic asylum.—Mr. Henry Card, county surveyor, County Hall, Lewes.

Nelson.—September 24th.—Construction of about 110 lineal yards of culverting over the river Walverden, alongside the wall of the gasworks in Bradley.—Mr. B. Ball, A.M.I.C.E., borough engineer and surveyor.

Malvern.—September 24th.—Supply of a 10-ton steam road-roller, scarifier, stone-breaker and sleeping-van, for the urban district council.—Mr. H. P. Maybury, surveyor to the council.

Bath.—September 24th.—Construction of a steam disinfector house at the refuse destructor works, Upper Bristol-road.—Mr. Chas. R. Fortune, city surveyor.

Exmouth.—September 24th.—Erection of a cart-shed at the town yard, for the urban district council.—Mr. Walter D. Harding, surveyor to the council.

Dorchester.—September 24th.—Supply of coal for the year ending September 30, 1899.—Mr. H. Symonds, town clerk.

Willenhall.—September 24th.—Supply of various stores and materials during the six months ending March 31, 1899, for the urban district council.—Mr. Chas. J. Jenkin, town surveyor.

Beckenham.—September 26th.—Widening of Croydon-road and East End-road, for the urban district council.—Mr. John A. Angell, surveyer to the council.

Beckenham.—September 26th.—Erection of about 200 cast-iron ventilating columns, 13 ft. 6 in. high, on concrete beds, together with the laying of 9-in. stoneware pipe connections to the main sewers, &c., for he urban district council.—Mr. John A. Angell, surveyor to the council.

London.—September 26th.—Erection of a cleft pale oak boundary fence at Brockwell Park, for the county council.—Mr. C. J. Stewart, clerk to the council, County Hall, Spring-gardens, London, S.W.

Darwen.—September 26th.—Supply and fixing of a 10-ton overhead travelling crane in the generating-room of the new electricity works.—Mr. Chas. Costeker, town clerk.

St. Marylebone.—September 26th.—Supply of 500,000 Australian jarrah wood paving blocks, for the vestry.—Mr. W. H. Garbutt, clerk to the vestry.

Buxton.—September 26th.—Rebuilding of the Otterhole bridge, St. John's-road, and the erection of stabling, &c., in the cattle market, for the urban district council.—The Town Surveyor.

Witney.—September 26th.—Main drainage of Eynsham, for the rural district council.—Mr. Nicholas Lailey, A.M.I.C.E., 16 Great George-street, London, S.W.

Willesden.—September 27th.—Paving works in Baker-passage, Harlesden, and Newton-mews, Kilburn, for the urban district council.—Mr. O. Claude Robson, M.I.C.E., engineer to the council.

Sheerness.—September 27th.—Supply of about 360 tons of quartzite or granite, 300 tons of clean pit flints, and 200 tons of hoggin or Aylesford gravel, for the urban district council.—Mr. C. A. Copland, surveyor to the council.

London.—September 27th.—Erection of a new bothy and alterations to the conveniences at Parliament Hill, and the erection of a new cart-shed, bothy, office, &c., at Southwark Park, for the county council.—Mr. C. J. Stewart, clerk to the council, County Hall, Spring-gardens, London, S.W.

Hastings.—September 27th.—Excavating and steining two wells, about 270 ft. deep, at Brede.—Mr. D. H. Palmer, M.I.C.E., borough engineer.

Hastings.—September 27th.—Construction of two covered service reservoirs (each 1,500,000 gallons capacity) at Ore.—Mr. P. H. Palmer, M.I.C.E., borough engineer.

Bexhill.—September 28th.—Supply of various electric light plant, for the urban district council.—Mr. A. H. Preece, A.M.I.C.E., 39 Victoria-street, London, S.W.

Lee.—September 28th.—Supply of horse fodder for the parishes of Eltham, Lee and Kidbrook, for the district board of works.—Mr. George Whale, clerk to the board.

Basingstoke.—September 29th.—Paving of the Market-square with wood blocks.—Mr. George Fitton, borough surveyor.

Hartlepool.—September 29th.—Erection of a destructor-house, engine and mill house, cottage, boundary walls and chimney at the proposed new sanitary depot in Clifton-street.—Mr. H. C. Crummack, A.M.I.C.E., borough engineer.

Wood Green.—September 30th.—Making-up of King's-road and Western-road, for the urban district council.—Mr. C. J. Gunyon, surveyor to the council.

Calstock.—September 30th.—Laying of about 2,803 yards of 3-in. cast-iron socket pipes, from Buddles adit to Harrowbarrow, and 1,487 yards from Figgie Dowdie adit to Todsworthy and Albaston, in the parish of Calstock, for the rural district council.—Mr. John P. Blight, clerk to the council, Callington.

Hull.—September 30th.—Supply of forty-five electric motor cars, twenty trail cars, two sprinkler cars and two traversing platforms.—Mr. A. E. White, city engineer.

Birmingham.—October 1st.—Reconstruction of the sewer in Needless-alley, New-street, also the construction of new pipe sewers in a portion of Wentworth-road, Harborne.—Mr. John Price, city engineer and surveyor.

Pembroke.—October 1st.—Construction of a pumping station and night storage tank and other works at Milton in connection with the water supply of Pembroke Dock.—Mr. W. O. Hulm, town clerk.

Wolverhampton.—October 1st.—Making-up of Hilton-street.—Mr. J. W. Bradley, borough engineer and surveyor.

Leeds.—October 1st.—Extension of Kirkgate market.—Mr. Thomas Hewson, M.I.C.E., city engineer.

Northam.—October 3rd.—Construction of an impounding reservoir at Melburg Moor to hold 30,000,000 gallons of water, with the necessary outlet works, filters, pure water reservoir, diversion of a public road, fencing, the construction of a covered service reservoir at Northam, the supply and laying of cast-iron socket pipes, and the supply and fixing of hydrants, sluice valves, &c., in connection with the water supply of the towu, for the urban district council.—Mr. Charles Wm. Hole, clerk to the cenncil.

London.—October 4th.—Erection of two blocks of dwellings, to be known as Benson and Abingdon dwellings respectively, on the Boundary-street area, Bethnal Green, and also the erection of cottage dwellings at Brook-street, Limehouse, for the county council.—Mr. C. J. Stewart, clerk to the council, County Hall, Spring-gardens, London, S.W.

Rathmines (Ireland).—October 5th.—Supply of various electric light plant, for the township commissioners.—Mr. Robert Hammond, consulting engineer, 64 Victoria-street, London, S.W.

Ramsgate.—October 5th.—Erection of a refuse destructor.—Mr. T. G. Taylor, borough surveyor.

Hastings.—October 7th.—Laying of about 9,000 yards run of 16-in. water main and about 2,850 yards of 10-in. main in connection with the Brede Valley water scheme.—Mr. P. H. Palmer, M.I.C.E., water engineer, Town Hall, Hastings.

Southampton.—October 11th.—Supply and fixing of three high-pressure Lancashire boilers, economisers, calorifiers, radiators, steam and hot-water mains, and all necessary pumps, valves, &c., required for the extension of the heat and power generating plant at the county lunatic asylum at Knowle, Fareham.—Mr. W. J. Taylor, county surveyor, The Castle, Winchester.

Edinburgh.—October 17th.—Various works in connection with gasholder tank at Granton.—Mr. James M'G. Jack, clerk to the commissioners.

Birkenhead.—October 17th.—Erection of public baths on a site adjoining Livingstone-street and Price-street.—Mr. Charles Brownridge, A.M.I.C.E., borough engineer and surveyor.

# TENDERS.

*Accepted.

ALDERSHOT.—Accepted for the supply of 2,000 tons of granite (more or less), for the urban district council.—Mr. W. E. Foster, clerk to the council:—

C. M. Manuelle, 12 Lime-street, E.C.—1¼in., 14s.; (750, more or less) 2in., 13s. 6d.

ALDERSHOT.—Accepted for metalling Albert-street, West End, for the urban district council.—Mr. W. E. Foster, clerk to the council:—

| | |
|---|---|
| W. Norris, Heath End, Farnham | £81 |

BEXHILL.—Accepted for the erection of boundary walls, the railing, kerbing, paving and channelling of footpaths, and other works opposite the town hall, for the urban district council.—Mr. George Bail, A.M.I.C.E., surveyor to the council:—

| | |
|---|---|
| E. Gutsell, Silverhill, St. Leonards-on-Sea | £614 |

BIRKENHEAD.—For the flagging, paving, channelling and sewering of various passages in the borough.—Mr. Charles Brownridge, A.M.I.C.E., borough engineer and surveyor:—

T. Horrocks, Walton, Liverpool; C. J. Shaw & Co., Birkenhead; Executers W. F. Chadwick, Liverpool.

DEVONPORT.—For the erection of convenience at Northcorner quay.—Mr. John F. Burns, borough surveyor:—

| | |
|---|---|
| J. Healy, Devonport | £264 |
| T. Jenkin & Son, Devonport | 229 |
| S. Rinper, Plymouth | 219 |
| S. Perkins, Devonport* | 198 |

DEVONPORT.—For the construction of drainage culvert.—Mr. John F. Burns, borough surveyor:—

| | |
|---|---|
| R. T. Horton, Plymouth | £3,623 |
| W. C. Shaddock, Plymouth | 3,606 |
| T. Shaddock, Plymouth | 3,563 |
| J. Shaddock, Plymouth | 3,434 |
| J. Fisher Plymouth | 3,413 |
| C. T. Duke, Plymouth | 3,228 |

HALIFAX.—For the supply and erection of retort-house fittings.—Mr. Thomas Holgate, gas engineer:—

West's Gas Improvement Company, Limited, Manchester; W. J. Jenkins & Co., Limited, Retford; J. Drake & Son, Halifax; Clayton, Son & Co., Limited, Leeds; W. C. Holmes & Co., Huddersfield; J. Abbot & Co., Limited, Gateshead; Newton, Chambers & Company, Limited, Sheffield; R. Dempster & Sons, Limited, Elland.*

LEEDS.—Accepted for the extension of Kirkgate market roof and the building of new fish shops and a boundary wall.—The City Engineer:

| | |
|---|---|
| H. Braithwaite & Co., Leeds | £11,690 |

NEWMARKET.—Accepted for the supply of best broken Leicestershire granite metalling, for the urban district council.—Mr. S. J. Eunion, clerk to the council:—

Enderby and Stoney Stanton Granite Company, Narborough, near Leicester.—At Newmarket station, Great Eastern Railway, 11s. 1d. per ton; at Burwell station, Great Eastern Railway, 10s. 9d. per ton.

Ellis & Everard, Bardon Hill Granite Quarries, near Leicester.—At Newmarket station, 12s. 3d. per ton; at Burwell station, 12s. per ton.

PORTISHEAD.—For widening the lower portion of West Hill-road, for the urban district council.—Mr. T. J. Moss-Flower, Carlton Chambers, Bristol :—

| | | | | | | | |
|---|---|---|---|---|---|---|---|
| J. & T. Binns, Portishead | ... | ... | ... | ... | ... | ... | £108 |
| E. Monks, Fishponds, Bristol | ... | ... | ... | ... | ... | 249 |
| J. Woolford, Portishead | ... | ... | ... | ... | ... | 215 |
| G. Biss & Son, Portishead* | ... | ... | ... | ... | ... | 173 |

ST. GEORGE-THE-MARTYR.—For the construction of a ladies' lavatory at the rear of the Public Library buildings in the Borough-road.—Mr. Oliver E. Winter, vestry surveyor :—

| | | | | | | | |
|---|---|---|---|---|---|---|---|
| B. Finch & Co., Lambeth | ... | ... | ... | ... | ... | £378 |
| J. Smith & Son, Junction Works, South Norwood* | ... | ... | 363 |

TENBURY.—For the building of a retaining wall, about 200 ft. long by 12 ft. high, at the side of Kyre brook, for the rural district council.—Mr. R. W. Jarvis, surveyor to the council :—

| | | | | | | | |
|---|---|---|---|---|---|---|---|
| Vale, Stourport | ... | ... | ... | ... | ... | ... | £240 |
| H. Hewitt & Sons, Cross-street, Tenbury | ... | ... | 189 |
| W. Howells, Worcester-road, Tenbury* | ... | ... | 167 |

THORNHILL (Yorks).—Accepted for the supply of flushing vales, manhole and lamphole covers, &c., for the urban district council.—Mr. S. W. Parker, surveyor to the council :—

Newsome & Askham, Batley Carr, near Dewsbury... ... £193

WALSALL.—Accepted for the painting and other works at the Science and Art Institute, Bradford-place.—The Borough Surveyor :—

E. Howens, 53 Vicarage-street, Walsall.

WETHERBY.—For the construction of about 7,000 lineal yards of earthenware pipe sewers, varying from 8 in. to 16 in. in diameter, with the necessary valves, manholes, lampholes, &c.; also for the construction of filtration area, works and new road to same, with all necessary valves, manholes, &c., at Boston Spa, for the rural district council.—Mr. J. Waugh, Tunbridge Chambers, Bradford :—

| | | | | | | | |
|---|---|---|---|---|---|---|---|
| H. Wilson, Great Horton, Bradford | ... | ... | ... | ... | £6,173 |
| W. Brigg, Frizinghall | ... | ... | ... | ... | ... | 5,935 |
| M. E. Arundel, Ardsley | ... | ... | ... | ... | ... | 5,822 |
| Graham & Son, Huddersfield | ... | ... | ... | ... | 5,700 |
| A. Braithwaite & Co., Leeds | ... | ... | ... | ... | 5,344 |
| M. Hall & Sons, Bradford | ... | ... | ... | ... | ... | 5,189 |
| H. M. Nowell, Leeds | ... | ... | ... | ... | ... | 5,000 |
| W. Binns, Swan Arcade, Bradford* | ... | ... | ... | ... | 4,931 |

## MEETINGS.

SEPTEMBER.

10.—Plumbers' Company : Public meeting at Manchester, for the distribution of prizes awarded in connection with the recent exhibition of plumbers' work at Manchester.

27, 28, 29 and 30.—The Sanitary Institute: Annual Autumn Congress at Birmingham.

OCTOBER.

1.—The Sanitary Institute: Annual Autumn Congress at Birmingham.

## NOTICES.

THE SURVEYOR AND MUNICIPAL AND COUNTY ENGINEER may be ordered direct, through any of Messrs. Smith & Son's book-stalls, or of any newsagent in the United Kingdom. Applications to the Offices for single copies by post must in all cases be accompanied by stamps.

The Prepaid Subscription (including postage) is as follows :

| | Twelve Months. | Six Months. | Three Months. |
|---|---|---|---|
| United Kingdom | 15s. | 7s. 6d. | 3s. 9d. |
| Continent, the Colonies, India, &c. | | | |
| United States, &c. | 19s. | 9s. 6d. | 4s. 9d. |

The International News Company, 83 and 85 Duane-street New York City; The Toronto News Company, Toronto; and The Montreal News Company, Montreal, have been appointed agents in the United States and Canada for the sale of THE SURVEYOR AND MUNICIPAL AND COUNTY ENGINEER. A thin paper edition is printed for circulation abroad.

EDITORIAL OFFICES :—
24 BRIDE-LANE, FLEET-STREET, LONDON, E.C.

ADVERTISEMENT AND PUBLISHING OFFICES :—
13 NEW STREET-HILL, FLEET-STREET, LONDON, E.C.

## THE SURVEYORS' INSTITUTION.
(Incorporated by Royal Charter.)
TEMPORARY ADDRESS—
SAVOY-STREET, VICTORIA-EMBANKMENT, W.C.

### EXAMINATIONS, 1899.

PRELIMINARY EXAMINATION.

Notice is given that the Preliminary Examination for the admission of Students will be held on the 18th and 19th of January next.

It is proposed to examine candidates from the counties of Lancashire, Cheshire, Yorkshire, Durham, Cumberland, Westmoreland and Northumberland at Manchester. Candidates from other counties in England and Wales will be examined in London.

PROFESSIONAL EXAMINATIONS.

Notice is also given that the Annual Professional Examinations for Land Agents, Valuers and Building Surveyors (held under the provisions of the Charter), qualifying for the Fellowship and Associateship of the Institution, will commence on the 20th of March next.

English candidates for the Professional Examinations will be examined in London.

Irish candidates will be examined in Dublin.

Particulars as to subjects, course of examination, prizes and scholarships can be obtained of the Secretary.

All applications for the Professional Examinations, Divs. II., III., IV. and V., must be sent in before the 31st of October, and applications for the Students' Preliminary Examination before the 30th of November. The necessary entry forms for the various Examinations can be obtained of the Secretary.

## APPOINTMENTS OPEN.

BOROUGH OF PLYMOUTH.
The Corporation is prepared to receive applications for the position of General Assistant in the Borough Engineer's department.

Candidates must be neat and expeditious draughtsmen, competent to survey and level accurately, prepare plans, sections and detail drawings for works of sewerage, road-making and other works incidental to a borough engineer's department; also competent to take out quantities and measure-up works.

Preference will be given to applicants having had previous experience in a borough engineer's department.

Salary, £100 per annum, increasing by annual increments of £10 to £130. The engagement to be terminable by a month's notice from either side.

Applicant's age must be between twenty-two and thirty.

Applications, in candidate's own handwriting, accompanied by copies of not more than three recent testimonials only, which will not be returned, to be forwarded to me not later than Saturday, October 1st, endorsed "General Assistant."

Canvassing members of the Council, either directly or indirectly, will be deemed a disqualification.

JAMES PATON,
Borough Engineer and Surveyor.
Municipal Offices.
September 13, 1898.

YORK WATERWORKS COMPANY.
Wanted, a Secretary and City Manager. One having had previous experience in a waterworks office preferred. Salary, £300 a year with house.

Application, with not more than three testimonials, to be forwarded by the 21st September instant, addressed to the Directors of the York Waterworks Company, Lendal Hill, York.

## TENDERS WANTED.

BUXTON URBAN DISTRICT COUNCIL.
TO CONTRACTORS.
The above Council invite tenders for (1) the Rebuilding of the Otterhole Bridge, St. John's-road ; (2) the Building of Stabling, &c., in the cattle market.

Plans may be seen at the office of Mr. W. H. Grieves, Town Surveyor, Town Hall, Buxton, where specifications and forms of tender may be obtained for a deposit of £1 1s., which will be returned on receipt of a bonâ-fide tender.

Tenders, endorsed "Otterhole Bridge" or "Stabling," as the case may be, to be sent in not later than Monday, the 26th inst.

The Council do not bind themselves to accept the lowest or any tender.

(By order of the Council)
JOSIAH TAYLOR,
Clerk.
Town Hall, Buxton.
September 8, 1898.

CITY OF BIRMINGHAM.
The Public Works Committee invite tenders for the Reconstruction of the Sewer in Needless-alley, New-street; also the Construction of New Pipe Sewers in a portion of Wentworth-road, &c., Harborne.

Drawings and specifications may be seen, and bills of quantities, schedules of prices and forms of tender obtained, on application to this office on and after Wednesday next, the 21st instant, upon deposit of a cheque, value 2 guineas, for each set of quantities. The cheque will be returned in each case upon receipt by the Public Works Committee of a bonâ fide tender with prices filled in as required.

The contractor whose tender is accepted (in each case) will be required to pay not less than the minimum standard rate of wages current in the district.

Tenders, sealed and endorsed "Tender for Sewer, Needless-alley," and "Tender for Sewers, Wentworth-road, &c.", to be delivered here not later than 10 a.m. on Saturday, the 1st of October.

The Committee do not pledge themselves to accept the lowest or any tender.

(By order)
JOHN PRICE,
City Engineer and Surveyor.
The Council House, Birmingham.
September 15, 1898.

COUNTY BOROUGH OF WOLVERHAMPTON
NEW STREET WORKS.

The Public Works Committee invite tenders for Forming, Levelling, Sewering, &c., of Hilton-street.

Plans can be seen, and specifications, with bill of quantities and form of tender obtained, on application at the office of the undersigned. Sealed tenders, addressed to the Chairman of the Public Works Committee, and endorsed "Tender for New Street Works," to be delivered at the Town Clerk's office not later than Saturday, October 1, 1898.

The Contractor will be required to enter into an undertaking to pay not less than the minimum standard rate of wages of the district, and to observe certain hours of labour in accordance with the resolution of the Town Council.

The Committee do not bind themselves to accept the lowest or any tender.

J. W. BRADLEY, C.E.,
Borough Engineer and Surveyor.
Town Hall, Wolverhampton.
September 13, 1898.

BOROUGH OF DARWEN.
TO ENGINEERS AND ELECTRICIANS.

The Corporation are prepared to receive tenders for a 10-ton Overhead Travelling Crane, to be fixed in the generating-room of the new Electric Works, and for a Lightning Conductor to the chimney of their refuse destructor, to be erected adjoining the said works, at Robin Bank, Darwen.

General conditions and specification, with forms of tender, can be obtained from the Borough Engineers, Darwen.

Tenders, properly endorsed, to be delivered to me before 10 a.m. on Monday, the 26th September.

No tender necessarily accepted.
(By order)
CHAS. COSTEKER,
Town Clerk.
Town Clerk's Office, Darwen.

MALVERN URBAN DISTRICT COUNCIL.
The Council is prepared to receive tenders for the following :—

Steam Road-Roller.—Weight, 10 tons, Compound High and Low Pressure Cylinders, Steam Jacketted. Tenders must set out a full description of roller tendered for.

Scarifier.—With all necessary fittings and set of tynes complete. To be attached to steam roller. Tenders must set out a full description of scarifier tendered for.

Stone-Breaker.—"Patent Improved Blake." To be a fixed machine, fitted with hammered-steel eccentric shaft, drawback motion, steel toggle grooves, reversible cubing jaws, with faced backs. Tenders must set out a full description of stone-breaker tendered for.

Sleeping-Van.—To accommodate three men, to be fitted with boxes, lockers, bunks, bedding, vice bench, vice, stove and piping, &c. Tenders must set out a full description of van tendered for.

Further particulars may be obtained at the office of Mr. H. P. Maybury, Town Surveyor, Council Offices, Malvern.

Sealed tenders, endorsed "Tender for Steam Roller, &c.," to be sent to me not later than 5 o'clock in the afternoon of Saturday, the 24th day of September, 1898.

The lowest or any tender will not necessarily be accepted.

H. P. MAYBURY,
Surveyor.
Council Offices, Malvern.
September 12, 1898.

SHEERNESS URBAN DISTRICT COUNCIL.
ROAD MATERIALS.

The above Council invite tenders for the supply of Road Materials, as specified hereunder :—

About 300 tons of Quartzite or Granite ;
" 300 " Clean Pit Flints ; and
" 200 " Hogging or Aylesford Gravel.

The above quantities are not guaranteed.

The Quartzite or Granite and Flints must be broken to pass through a 2-in. ring, and the whole must be delivered into store (free of all dues) either at Mile Town or at West Minster, as directed, within a month, dating from the receipt of the order from the Surveyor to the Council (Mr. C. A. Copland), and to his entire satisfaction. The quantities will be ascertained by means of the weighbridge at the council's yard in Trinity-road, and be paid for accordingly.

Tenders, endorsed outside "Road Material," which must state price per ton, should be delivered or sent to the undersigned, and samples of the respective materials to the surveyor, before noon on the 27th day of September, 1898.

(By order)
VINCENT H. STALLON,
Clerk to the Council.
Council Offices, Trinity-road, Sheerness.
September 12, 1898.

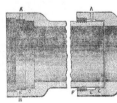

## COUNTY BOROUGH OF SOUTH SHIELDS.

### UNDERGROUND SANITARY CONVENIENCE.

#### TO SANITARY ENGINEERS.

The Town Council invite tenders for the whole of the works required in the Construction and Completion of an Underground Public Convenience at the Market-place, South Shields.

Specifications and forms of tender, with a blue print of contract plan, may be obtained from Mr. S. E. Burgess, A.M.I.C.E., Borough Engineer, Chapter-row, upon payment of a deposit of £2, which will be returned on receipt of a *bonâ-fide* tender. Remittances to be made payable to Mr. W. Anderson, Borough Accountant.

Tenders, sealed and endorsed "Tender for Underground Convenience," must be sent in to the undersigned by 12 noon on Wednesday, the 28th September next.

The Corporation do not bind themselves to accept the lowest or any tender.

(By order)
J. MOORE HAYTON,
Town Clerk.

Court Buildings, South Shields.
September 12, 1898.

## TAMWORTH RURAL DISTRICT COUNCIL.

### CONTRACT No. 1.

The Rural District Council of Tamworth are prepared to receive tenders for about 8¼ miles of Cast-Iron Pipes from 4 in. to 3 in. in diameter, and other castings to be made in accordance with the specification of their engineer.

Persons desirous of tendering may obtain a copy of the specification by application to me, at my offices, in Tamworth, on and after the 14th inst., and on payment of 1 guinea, to be returned in the event of a *bonâ-fide* tender being received.

Tenders, addressed to me, endorsed "Tenders for Cast-Iron Pipes," to be sent in on or before Friday, the 23rd day of September, 1898.

The Council do not bind themselves to accept the lowest or any tender.

HENRY J. CLARSON, C.E.

Tamworth.
September 12, 1898.

## CITY OF GLOUCESTER.

### NEW BUILDINGS FOR ELECTRICITY WORKS.

#### TO BUILDERS AND CONTRACTORS.

The Corporation of Gloucester invite tenders for the Erection of the New Buildings in connection with the above.

Plans and specification may be seen at the office of Mr. Harry A. Dancey, 26 Clarence-street, Gloucester, between 10 a.m. and 5 p.m., after Monday, 5th September next.

The quantities are being prepared by Mr. Dancey, and may be obtained from him on payment of a charge of £2 2s., which will be returned on receipt of a *bonâ-fide* tender.

The Committee do not pledge themselves to accept the lowest or any tender.

Tenders, endorsed "Tender for Electricity Works," to be delivered at the Town Clerk's office, Guildhall, Gloucester, before 11 o'clock on Monday, the 19th September, 1898.

(By order)
GEO. SHEFFIELD BLAKEWAY,
Town Clerk.

Guildhall, Gloucester.
August 30, 1898.

## WILLESDEN DISTRICT COUNCIL.

### TO CONTRACTORS.

The Willesden District Council are prepared to receive tenders for the execution of certain Paving Works in Baker-passage, Harlesden, and Newton-mews, Kilburn.

Plans and specification may be seen, and all further particulars obtained, on and after Monday, September 19, 1898, upon application to Mr. O. Claude Robson, M.INST.C.E., Engineer to the Council, Public Offices, Dyne-road, Kilburn, N.W.

The tenders, upon printed forms and endorsed "Private Streets," to be delivered at the offices of the Council not later than 4 p.m. on Tuesday, September 27, 1898.

The Council do not bind themselves to accept the lowest or any tender.

(By order)
STANLEY W. BALL,
Clerk to the Council.

Public Offices, Dyne-road, Kilburn, N.W.
September 14, 1898.

BECKENHAM URBAN DISTRICT COUNCIL.
TO CONTRACTORS.

The Beckenham Urban District Council invite tenders for Erecting about 200 Cast-Iron Ventilating Columns, 13 ft. 6 in. high, on concrete beds, together with the laying of 9-in. Stoneware Pipe Connections to the main sewers, &c.

Plans and sections may be seen, and bills of quantities, specifications and forms of tenders obtained, on application to Mr. John A. Angell, Surveyor, on or after September 7th, on deposit of £1, which will be returned on the receipt of a *bonâ-fide* tender.

A clause will be inserted in the contract providing that the contractor shall pay to the workmen employed in the execution of the work the wages generally accepted as current for workmen engaged on similar work in the district.

Tenders, duly sealed and endorsed "Tender for Erection of Ventilating Columns," to reach undersigned not later than 4 p.m. Monday, September 26, 1898.

The Council do not bind themselves to accept the lowest or any tender.

(By order)
F. STEVENS,
Clerk to the Council.

August 30, 1898.

BECKENHAM URBAN DISTRICT COUNCIL.
TO CONTRACTORS.

The Beckenham Urban District Council invite tenders for Widening Croydon-road and Elmers End-road. The works comprise the widening of Croydon-road for about 800 lineal feet and of Elmers End-road for 150 lineal feet, together with the formation of new footways. In connection therewith the following works are necessary—viz., about 800 lineal feet 9-in. pipe sewer, 700 lineal feet 9-in. pipe surface-water drain, with manholes, gullies, &c., 110 lineal feet concrete retaining wall about 4 ft. high, 1,000 lineal feet curb and channelling, making-up roadways, &c.

Plans and sections may be seen, and bills of quantities, specifications and forms of tender obtained, on application to Mr. John A. Angell, Surveyor, on or after September 7th, on deposit of £1, which will be returned on receipt of a *bonâ-fide* tender.

A clause will be inserted in the contract providing that the contractor shall pay to the workmen employed in the execution of the work the wages generally accepted as current for workmen engaged on similar work in the district.

Tenders, duly sealed and endorsed "Tender for Widening Croydon and Elmers End Roads," to reach undersigned not later than 4 p.m., Monday, September 26, 1898.

The Council do not bind themselves to accept the lowest or any tender.

(By order)
F. STEVENS,
Clerk to the Council.

August 30, 1898.

WITNEY RURAL DISTRICT COUNCIL.
EYNSHAM MAIN DRAINAGE.

The Rural District Council are prepared to receive tenders, under the advice of their Engineer, from contractors for the execution of this work.

The plans and specifications can be seen, and information obtained, upon application to Mr. Nicholson Lailey, F.G.S., ASSOC.M.INST.C.E., the Council's Engineer, at his chambers, 16 Great George-street, Westminster, between the hours of 10 and 4 o'clock on and after September 12th next.

Sealed tenders, endorsed "Eynsham Main Drainage," are to be delivered at my offices at Witney not later than 6 o'clock p.m. on Monday, September 26th.

The Council do not pledge themselves to accept the lowest or any tender.

A copy of the plans and specification are also deposited at the offices of Mr. W. George Eaton, Surveyor to the Council, Witney, and information can be obtained upon the dates and times before named.

The Engineer will give due notice to persons proposing to tender of the date and time that he or his chief assistant will attend at Eynsham in order to explain the nature of the proposed undertaking.

(By order)
Mr. JOHN G. RAVENOR, Solicitor,
Clerk to the Rural District Council.

Witney.
August 15, 1898.

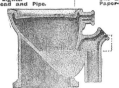

## BECKENHAM URBAN DISTRICT COUNCIL.
### TO CONTRACTORS.

The Beckenham Urban District Council invite tenders for Erecting about 200 Cast-Iron Ventilating Columns, 13 ft. 6 in. high, on concrete beds, together with the laying of 9-in. Stoneware Pipe Connections to the main sewers, &c.

Plans and sections may be seen, and bills of quantities, specifications and forms of tender obtained, on application to Mr. John A. Angell, Surveyor, on or after September 7th, on deposit of £1, which will be returned on the receipt of a *bonâ-fide* tender.

A clause will be inserted in the contract providing that the contractor shall pay to the workmen employed in the execution of the work the wages generally accepted as current for workmen engaged on similar work in the district.

Tenders, duly sealed and endorsed "Tender for Erection of Ventilating Columns," to reach undersigned not later than 4 p.m. Monday, September 26, 1898.

The Council do not bind themselves to accept the lowest or any tender.

(By order)
F. STEVENS,
Clerk to the Council.

August 30, 1898.

## BECKENHAM URBAN DISTRICT COUNCIL.
### TO CONTRACTORS.

The Beckenham Urban District Council invite tenders for Widening Croydon-road and Elmers End-road. The works comprise the widening of Croydon-road for about 800 lineal feet and of Elmers End-road for 150 lineal feet, together with the formation of new footways. In connection therewith the following works are necessary—*viz.*, about 800 lineal feet 9-in. pipe sewer, 700 lineal feet 9-in. pipe surface-water drain, with manholes, gullies, &c., 110 lineal feet concrete retaining wall about 4 ft. high, 1,000 lineal feet curb and channelling, making-up roadways, &c.

Plans and sections may be seen, and bills of quantities, specifications and forms of tender obtained, on application to Mr. John A. Angell, Surveyor, on or after September 7th, on deposit of £1, which will be returned on receipt of a *bonâ-fide* tender.

A clause will be inserted in the contract providing that the contractor shall pay to the workmen employed in the execution of the work the wages generally accepted as current for workmen engaged on similar work in the district.

Tenders, duly sealed and endorsed "Tender for Widening Croydon and Elmers End Roads," to reach undersigned not later than 4 p.m., Monday, September 26, 1898.

The Council do not bind themselves to accept the lowest or any tender.

(By order)
F. STEVENS,
Clerk to the Council.

August 30, 1898.

## WITNEY RURAL DISTRICT COUNCIL.
### EYNSHAM MAIN DRAINAGE.

The Rural District Council are prepared to receive tenders, under the advice of their Engineer, from contractors for the execution of this work.

The plans and specifications can be seen, and information obtained, upon application to Mr. Nicholson Lailey, F.G.S., ASSOC.M.INST.C.E., the Council's Engineer, at his chambers, 16 Great George-street, Westminster, between the hours of 10 and 4 o'clock on and after September 12th next.

Sealed tenders, endorsed "Eynsham Main Drainage," are to be delivered at my offices at Witney not later than 6 o'clock p.m. on Monday, September 26th.

The Council do not pledge themselves to accept the lowest or any tender.

A copy of the plans and specification are also deposited at the offices of Mr. W. George Eaton, Surveyor to the Council, Witney, and information can be obtained upon the dates and times before named.

The Engineer will give due notice to persons proposing to tender of the date and time that he or his chief assistant will attend at Eynsham in order to explain the nature of the proposed undertaking.

(By order)
Mr. JOHN G. RAVENOR, Solicitor,
Clerk to the Rural District Council.

Witney.
August 15, 1898.

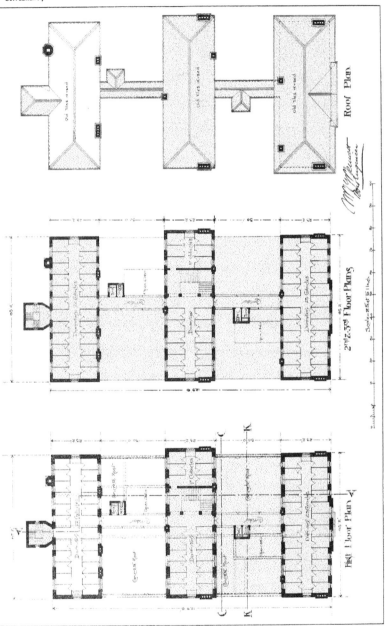

Roof Plan.

2nd & 3rd Floor Plans.

First Floor Plan.

[September 16, 1898.

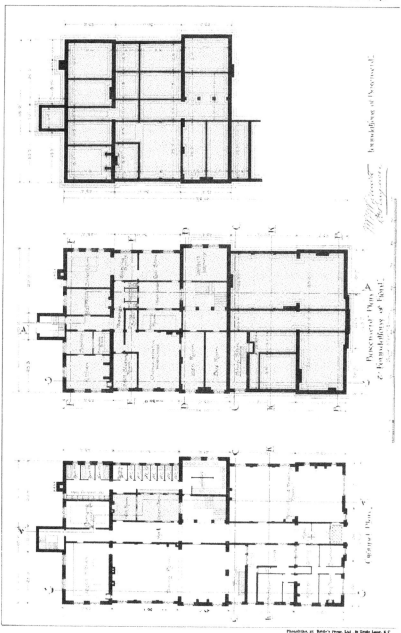

Photolitho, St. Bride's Press, Ltd. St. Bride Lane, E.C.

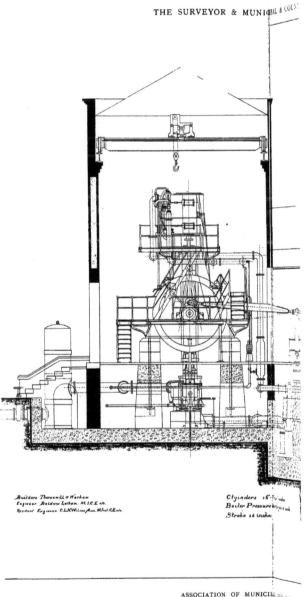

Builders Thornewill + Warham
Engineer Baldwin Latham. M.I.C.E. etc.
Resident Engineer. C.L.N.Wilson Assoc. M.Inst. C.E. etc.

Cylinders 16" Diameter
Boiler Pressure 80 lbs per inch
Stroke 36 inches.

# —BILSTON WATER WORKS—

## —PUMPING ENGINES—

SCALE.

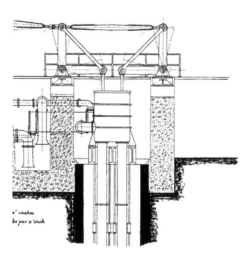

o´ inches
bs per o inch

C.L.N. Wilson. Anne M Inst C E ete
Water Engineer & Surveyor.
Bilston. Aug 1ᵗᴴ 9t

Photolitho, 81, Bride's Press, Ltd., 24 Bride Lane, E.C.

# The Surveyor

## And Municipal and County Engineer.

Vol. XIV., No. 349.    LONDON, SEPTEMBER 23, 1898.    Weekly, Price 3d.

## Minutes of Proceedings.

**Sanitary Condition of Alnwick.** In December, 1897, the Local Government Board received representations from the Northumberland County Council concerning the sanitary condition of Alnwick, an urban district with an estimated population of 6,700. The alleged defects had reference chiefly to the faulty arrangement and construction of certain dwellings of the poorer classes. Attention had been drawn to the matter last year by the county medical officer, whereupon the district council instructed their own medical officer to report, possibly in the expectation that the statements of the county medical officer would be contradicted. If so, disappointment was the result, for in material particulars the second report only served to confirm the first. For many years past medical officers have been drawing attention to the unhealthy condition of some of the poorer-class habitations, but there is nothing to show that any effective action has ever been taken by the sanitary authority. Hence came Dr. Buchanan's inquiry, the report of which is to hand. As far back as 1849 Sir Robert Rawlinson reported to the General Board of Health that a variety of unwholesome conditions existed in the district. These conditions comprised unhealthy, damp and overcrowded dwellings, packed away in narrow courts and alleys behind the main thoroughfares, abundance of privy and midden nuisances, unpaved or badly-paved yards, no public water supply, and no system of sewerage. Between 1852 and 1854 a large improvement scheme was carried out by the newly-appointed Alnwick and Canongate Local Board. The town was sewered, under Rawlinson's direction, privies were abolished and water-closets provided, and a public water supply was obtained. Unfortunately, these improvements were not followed by a diminution in the general mortality, and the late Sir George Buchanan, father of the inspector who now reports, and then at the head of the Medical Department of the Privy Council, pointed out that that the construction of the courts and dwellings occupied by the poorer classes in Alnwick remained as unwholesome as before, and that the provision of sewers had effected no drying of the subsoil. The subsequent action of the sanitary authority is not altogether satisfactory; in fact, the inspector describes it as conspicuously lax, though certain useful public works, such as the erection of public slaughter-houses and the laying of additional sewers, had been carried out, and in scavenging and a few other matters the administration was considered efficient. No attempt, however, had been made to remedy a multiplicity of serious sanitary defects, especially in connection with the courts and dwellings of the poorer classes, where overcrowding was actually on the increase.

In dealing with the present sanitary condition of the town Dr. Buchanan points out that the dwellings occupied by the poorer classes are to be found huddled on small areas, behind the main thoroughfares, and that this close aggregation of dwellings, which has long been a characteristic feature of Alnwick, must in part be attributed to the enclosure of the town in former centuries by walls, but to a greater extent is the outcome of later conditions. Dr. Buchanan gives an interesting account of the form which this overcrowding of buildings takes. Open spaces at the backs of buildings are conspicuous by their absence, for the simple reason that they have invariably been built upon. The following passage may be quoted :—

The commonest example is where a property first consisted of a single dwelling in a row abutting on the main street, having at the back a long strip of garden or yard, the width of which is no greater than the breadth of the house to which it belongs. Buildings have subsequently been packed on this strip of back yard, and access to the "court" so formed is had by a narrow "entry," driven through the ground floor of the house in the main street. Going through an entry into a court of this kind, one finds a passage, some 4 ft. to 6 ft. wide, extending the length of the property, sometimes terminating blindly, sometimes leading, by a second "entry" at its far end, into a neighbouring street or court. Along one side of the passage is a high wall, which forms the back of structures in the adjoining "property;" along the other side is a row of buildings, most of them two-storey dwelling-houses, out-houses, stables or cow-sheds. Here and there an irregularly-shaped common yard is met with, surrounded by buildings of a similar sort. Dwellings in these courts have thick walls, rudely constructed out of the local stone. Some habitations appear to have originally been stables or out-houses. As a rule, the only windows and doors are those facing the passage or common yard. These dwellings are thus without through ventilation, and commonly they receive insufficient light. Windows are frequently small, and often can be opened only to a trifling extent. Standing on a wet soil, constructed of porous stone, and unprovided with damp-proof course, these houses are conspicuously damp. In places the wall of the dwelling has been built against the hill-side, and here dampness is increased. In a few cases an additional source of wetness arises where eaves-gutters and down-spouting are wanting or are deficient.

Needless to say, these dwellings are generally more or less dilapidated and dirty. The courts are unlighted, and either unpaved or irregularly paved. Each is drained to a sewer in the main street by means of a gulley or gulleys placed in the yard or passage. Open gulleys, designed to convey to these gulleys rain water and slop water from the dwellings, have often been constructed in rudimentary fashion. Liquid refuse thrown into the gutters or on to the surface of the yard is thus apt to accumulate in pools in front of the houses. To the unhealthiness produced by the crowding together of insanitary dwellings upon area has to be added the evils attending overcrowding of persons, and the state of affairs can then be readily realised.

The sanitary circumstances of the town in other respects may be briefly summarised. Natural drainage and surface water from the principal roadways finds its way to the Aln, partly by open gutters and partly by rude, covered channels laid just beneath the surface. The greater part of the town was sewered by 1854, and until recently a main outfall sewer discharged unpurified contents into the river about a mile below Alnwick Castle, the chief seat of the Duke of Northumberland. A new main outfall sewer, however, has been laid at a higher level, the contents being delivered to disposal works, where the sewage is treated by "aluminoferric," and then passes to 5 acres of land laid out in irrigation plots, the effluent finally passing into the river. Some sewers through low ground to the west of the Castle are connected to a separate outfall sewer. A precipitant (sulphate of iron) is added in the sewer, and the sewage is then received in small covered catch-pits, the overflow from which passes, without further treatment, into the river. The council have undertaken to give this matter their attention. A separate plot of land will be secured, as levels do not permit of the sewage being taken by gravitation to the new works. The gradients of the sewers render artificial flushing for the most past unnecessary, but their ventilation apparently leaves something to be desired. That part of the water supply which is derived from springs is fairly satisfactory, but the same cannot be said of the supply from the natural drainage of the high ground in the neighbourhood, as the land is mostly agricultural. Formerly, even the water from the springs was much exposed to pollution, owing to offensive matter of various kinds finding its way into the small open streams contributing to the supply. Improvements, however, have been effected in recent years, chiefly with a view to the exclusion of surface water. The water is conveyed by gravitation to a service reservoir on high ground above Alnwick, but the storage capacity represents little more than twenty-four hours' supply. Mr. Wilson, the surveyor, is preparing a scheme to utilise the water from certain additional springs. Of this official the inspector remarks that he "appears to perform with thoroughness a multiplicity of duties attaching to the office." But it is not to such matters as water supply and sewerage that the heavy mortality to which Dr. Buchanan draws attention is to be ascribed. Improvements have been made in many directions in recent years, and the district council has a somewhat better record than the local board had. "But," says the inspector, "in the matter of dealing . . . . with some of the gravest insanitary conditions of Alnwick, and, above all, with its notoriously unhealthy courts and dwellings and with the overcrowding of persons therein, local board and district council alike must be held to have seriously neglected their duty." They have been reluctant to make demands upon property owners—or increase the rate. "Wherever individual interests have to be opposed," said a previous report, "or seemingly opposed, sanitary administration has been paralysed." In many cases the only possible remedy is wholesale demolition, and it is some satisfaction to learn that, as a result of the publicity which has been given to the matter, the urban district council show a disposition to grapple more seriously with the evil.

\* \* \*

**Sewer Ventilation.** In the report of the surveyor to the Kensington Vestry for the year ended March 25th reference is made to the subject of sewer ventilation. In Kensington the number of pipe ventilators for sewers has been increased during the year, in accordance with the instructions of the vestry. In consequence of complaints made in the end of 1897, Mr. Weaver presented a lengthy report, which led to the passing of the following resolutions by the vestry:—

(1) That offensive street gullies be efficiently trapped.
(2) That all new gullies constructed in the parish be pan gullies with syphon-trapped outlets.
(3) That the London County Council be requested to trap with syphon traps all offensive gullies on the main line sewers.

Mr. Weaver then goes on to refer to the conference on the subject of sewer ventilation which the surveyors to the various metropolitan sanitary authorities held with Sir Alexander Binnie in his capacity of chief engineer to the London County Council. The idea of the conference, it is worth noting, originated with Mr. Weaver, who in the report referred to above suggested that the London County Council should be requested to convene such a conference. Our readers will no doubt remember that the metropolitan officers of health also participated in the proceedings; but whether this was part of Mr. Weaver's original suggestion does not appear. As the meeting was private, we were unable to report it beyond giving the mere text of the resolutions that were ultimately adopted. Mr. Weaver, however, informs us that the fixing of interceptors on the main house drains was generally condemned by the conference as being bad from an engineering point of view, antagonistic to sanitation, and responsible for the offensive smells complained of in connection with the surface sewerventilators. This condemnation was not specifically recorded in the resolutions adopted, but it will be remembered that the second resolution recommended that in all cases where an intercepting trap is fixed on the main house drain a ventilating pipe should be carried up the premises on the outlet or sewer side of the interceptor. Mr. Weaver recalls that in 1885, when intercepted house drains were coming into vogue, he obtained little support in his opposition to syphon interceptors, and he naturally feels some gratification in finding that there has been a considerable change of opinion in the interval among those best able to arrive at a sound practical judgment on the subject. Mr. Weaver further remarks that the surveyors who attended the conference are not abstract theorists, but practical men responsible for the supervision of all the drainage work of the metropolis. Whatever the value of the resolutions may have been, the fact remains that nothing further has been heard of them or of any steps being taken to give effect to them. In this respect they are in the same interesting position as the proposed bylaws by means of which the London County Council intended to secure uniformity among the metropolitan sanitary authorities. Like legislation on the subject of combined drainage, these questions seem to hang fire indefinitely. We observe that, in concluding his report, Mr. Weaver almost apologises for any occasional deviation into subjects of a controversial nature, his rule being to confine himself in his annual reports as much as possible to statements of work. Such a view of the function of an annual report is not one that we can bring ourselves to support. A report confined to mere statements of work must of necessity be dry, bald and unhelpful. The discussion of some of the more difficult problems and recent developments of municipal engineering must obviously add greatly to the interest and value of these periodical statements. Of course it should be remembered that the larger questions confronting a local authority are dealt with from time to time in special reports.

\* \* \*

**The Bilston Meeting.** As we ventured to predict in our last issue, the Bilston meeting proved thoroughly successful in regard alike to attendance, weather, and the general interest of the proceedings. Generally speaking, the meeting was a profitable one, as providing an excellent object-lesson in municipal work as found in a comparatively small town in the Black Country; and, so far as that is concerned, Bilston has no reason to fear comparison with districts more favoured in other respects. There is no lack of civic spirit and intelligence, either in the inhabitants generally or in those to whom they entrust the local administration. So long as the town can command the services of public-spirited men like Councillor Harper, chairman of the council, Councillor Sankey, chairman of the Water and Baths Committee, Councillor Jordan, chairman of the Technical Education Committee, and others, the municipal prospects of the district must always be hopeful. From the engineering point of view the great work of the council has been that of water supply, in regard to which there is plenty of information in Mr. Wilson's able and comprehensive paper, with the accompanying illustrations. It is an axiom of municipal and sanitary engineering that the provision of an abundant supply of pure water is more important than, and should take precedence of, a system of sewerage; and that should be sufficient to justify the Bilston Urban District Council in replying to critics who find fault with them for delay in carrying out a thorough scheme of sewerage and sewage disposal. In a town with the population and rateable value of Bilston the carrying out of two such schemes simultaneously would have been out of the question. Municipal representatives are in the position of stewards, and must never lose sight of the question of ways and means. Hasten slowly is a good motto in their case, if they do not wish the ratepayers to call them to account. Undue delay in sanitary matters cannot be too strongly condemned, but the financial position and rate-paying capacity of a community must be carefully considered. No doubt when municipal engineers next visit Bilston they will find as much to commend in connection with sewerage and sewage disposal as on Saturday they found in connection with the water supply and the technical school. For a small town these problems have been attacked with remarkable pluck, enterprise and intelligence. In regard to the technical school, Mr. Wilson tells us that the total cost of the building and fittings is equal to about one-seventh of the total rateable value of the township; and yet it was built by public subscriptions and grants from the Staffordshire County Council and the South Kensington authorities, without putting a penny on the town rates. When we consider the great progress in technical education of our German commercial rivals, Mr. Wilson might well say, "In this respect Bilston can show the whole of Great Britain a noble example." He also reminds us of the prominent part taken in this work by Councillor Saukey, who has done so much for the town, not only by his labours as a municipal representative, but by the important industrial undertaking he has established in Bilston. The work of Mr. Wilson is evidently appreciated in the town, and it was pleasant to note the unstinted acknowledgment of it which fell from the chairman of the council and from Councillor Sankey. In conclusion, a word should be said in praise of the hearty hospitality extended to the visitors. Mr. Wilson evidently co-operated vigorously with Mr. Pickering in arranging all the details of the meeting, and especially in taking time by the forelock. General satisfaction was expressed with the issue of the paper several days in advance to those intending to be present. Mr. Wilson's paper contained sufficient to justify a visit to Bilston, without the members of the association in any way humbling themselves, as the chairman of the council seemed to fear they were doing.

\* \* \*

**The Applications of Small Electric Motors.** That municipal electricity works may do much for the community besides supplying it with a healthy light is shown in the case of Bradford, where the use of electricity for small power purposes has been developed to a remarkable extent It is hardly necessary to enumerate the trades which have been beneficially affected in the town by the use of the electric motor, but that they are numerous is instanced in the paper which Mr. Gibbings, the city electrical engineer of Bradford, recently brought before the Mechanical section of the British Association. There is not much doubt that the use of electric motors on public supply circuits is extending very rapidly, and the extension is not confined to large industrial centres, such as Manchester and Bradford, for a comparatively non-industrial town, such as Edinburgh, can claim to have 167 motors, aggregating 343 horse-power. The chief drawback against the adoption of

electric motors, especially among small power-users, is that of initial expense in purchasing the necessary electrical plant, especially when it may mean the discarding of other plant which is in fair condition. To meet that objection the Bradford Corporation have adopted a bold course, which is nothing less than the hiring-out of electric motors. It is an interesting experiment, because it was felt in many quarters that municipalities could not legally undertake such work. No doubt the success achieved at Bradford will influence local authorities to insert the necessary clauses in future Parliamentary Bills. The scheme of hiring-out motors was adopted by the Corporation of Bradford at the end of 1896, and, while it was taken up somewhat slowly at first, it was not long before consumers began to appreciate the idea. There have been forty-eight new motors added to the mains during this year, and of these forty-two are let on hire by the corporation. Indications are not wanting, however, that the supply of electricity for motor purposes will not be restricted to small power-users, for it is becoming generally accepted that a municipal supply can give economies over large private installations.

\* \* \*

**The Bristol Electricity Works.** The paper recently read before the British Association by Mr. Proctor, the city electrical engineer of Bristol, though mainly relating to auxiliary plant, was nevertheless of great importance, because it clearly demonstrated the chief direction in which losses are likely to arise in electricity works. It may interest those concerned in the growth of municipal electrical systems to note the extent of the plant which is now in use at Bristol. There are twelve Lancashire boilers, which are all fitted with such labour-saving devices as coaling, stoking, coal elevators and conveyors. The aggregate horse-power of the engines and dynamos is 3,700 horse-power, while there are 130 miles of cable laid underground. It affords an indication of the wide area which is fed by the Bristol Electricity Works when it is mentioned that there are no fewer than thirty-eight sub-stations, at which points the high-pressure current is transformed down to a pressure suitable for distribution. Returning for a moment, however, to the question of auxiliary plant, with which Mr. Proctor mainly dealt in his paper, it is to be regretted that such useful adjuncts to central station equipment as feed-pumps should be so extremely inefficient. Pump makers have, as a rule, exhibited marked indifference to the efficiency of their machines, but it is hardly likely, when so much publicity is brought to bear upon them, that they will not endeavour to improve them. That electric motors when applied to driving pumps will show considerable saving over steam-driven pumps is evidenced by the fact that at Bristol a steam-driven centrifugal pump takes 90·65 lb. of steam per brake horse-power while an electric motor pump took 48·26 lb. per brake horse-power. It was almost generally accepted at the recent annual meeting of the Municipal Electrical Engineers that it was distinct economy to drive as much as possible of the auxiliary machinery by electric motors.

\* \* \*

**Two Colonial Appointments.** Within a short period two important colonial vacancies have been filled up. It was a coincidence that the vacancies should have occurred about the same time and in the same colony, that the salary should be the same in each case, and that the appointments will remove from England two well-known members of the Association of Municipal and County Engineers. The appointment of Mr. Wynne Roberts, Oswestry, as municipal engineer of Cape Town has now been followed by the appointment of Mr. G. B. Laffan, Twickenham, to a similar office at Pietermaritzburg. Both will depart with best wishes for a successful career in South Africa.

# Association of Municipal and County Engineers.

## MIDLAND DISTRICT MEETING AT BILSTON.—I.

BILSTON: THE TOWN HALL.

The district meeting, which had been so carefully arranged at Bilston, took place on Saturday, and proved both highly interesting and thoroughly successful. The attendance was satisfactory, the weather was good, and there was much of a profitable character both to be seen and heard. Those who have never visited the Black Country, and who have gathered some vague ideas from word pictures of the lurid and gloomy order, such as those of Dickens in "The Old Curiosity Shop," are no doubt often tempted to think that it is a very undesirable land indeed. The reality, however, is very far from being as dreadful as the pre-conceived notions. This so-called Black Country is in many respects the heart of industrial England, and it was inevitable that it could have become so within the compass of a single century without the face of the country being affected for the worse and acquiring a somewhat grimy complexion. Like some dust-stained and perspiring toiler, the Black Country, appropriately enough, shows signs of the strenuous and incessant labour, extending over so many years, which have given it such industrial pre-eminence. Vast development industrially must involve loss of advantages in other directions. In this part of England the loss from the æsthetic point of view cannot be ignored, but it is a price that must be paid for the great material progress achieved. Apart from the industrial question, however, there are qualities of the best kind which find expression here in as marked a form as anywhere in England. Here are to be found intelligence, civic spirit, and a strong desire for improvement. As one of the speakers remarked at the banquet on Saturday, there are brains in the the Black Country. In municipal matters the visitors found that Bilston was no exception. From the engineering point of view the great work is the water supply scheme, of which a full account will be found in Mr. Wilson's paper, in connection with which we have reproduced some extremely interesting plans. Works of less magnitude, but no less significant when their social effect is remembered, are the technical school and the baths. By the former the intelligence of the younger members of the community will be cultivated and industry fostered; by the latter something is done to alleviate the discomfort of the conditions under which the inhabitants labour. For a town of the size and population of Bilston the enterprise shown in connection with the technical school is probably unique, and it is gratifying to learn that there is every promise of complete success, and that the benefits to be conferred by such an institution are appreciated by those for whom they were intended.

Bilston is an interesting example of a town which owes its prosperity to the iron and allied trades; but of the history and development of the town itself it is unnecessary to say anything here, owing to the fulness with which Mr. Wilson has dealt with the subject in his paper. We therefore proceed with our account of the meeting

## AT THE TOWN HALL.

At 11 o'clock the members assembled at the Town Hall, and were received by the chairman of the urban district council, Councillor R. A. Harper, J.P., and other members of the council. Among those present were the following :—

PAST-PRESIDENT: Mr. J. T. Eayrs, Birmingham.

MEMBERS OF COUNCIL: Messrs. J. S. Pickering, Nuneaton, and J. Price, Birmingham.

MEMBERS: Messrs. J. Baker, Slough; H. J. Clarson, Tamworth; A. T. Davis, Shrewsbury; N. H. Dawson, Banbury; E. J. Elford, Portland; J. Gammage, Dudley; A. D. Greatorex, West Bromwich; A. Greenwood, Todmorden; J. Haigh, Abergavenny; W. T. House, Hinckley; C. F. Marston, Sutton Coldfield; J. Mortimer, Tettenhall; J. Myatt, Leek; B. Perrins, Halesowen; R. Richardson, Aston Manor; C. W. Shackleton, Coseley; T. R. Smith, Kettering; C. D. M. Trinder, Claypole; G. M. Whitehead, Cannock; C. L. N. Wilson, Bilston; and J. Wilson, Bacup.

GRADUATES: Messrs. W. S. Bissell, Wolverhampton; S. S. Gettings, West Bromwich; A. J. Price, Worcester; D. S. Sutherland, Walsall; and J. J. Topping, West Bromwich.

VISITORS: Messrs. A. E. N. Aldridge, Bilston; E. H. Bailey, Leamington; T. R. Bailey, M.D., Bilston; J. P. Baker, Willenhall; C. H. W. Biggs, London; A. Bulyer, M.R.C.S., Ettingshall; J. Bundley, Wolverhampton; C. A. H. Clarry, Sutton Coldfield; T. W. Eayrs, Birmingham; S. Haddock, Ettingshall; J. Harper, J.P., Bilston; J. Howarths, Sedgley; E. J. Jansen, Birmingham; W. Jordan, Bilston; G. J. Ketteringham, Handsworth; J. E. Mawdesley, Bacup; J. T. Parker, Bilston; W. Paton, London; T. R. Phipps, Worcester; F. W. Plant, Bilston; W. Preston, Bilston; W. H. Reynolds, Birmingham; J. W. Sankey, Bilston; F. W. Shepheard, Wolverhampton; W. Small, Birmingham; G. H. Smith, Birmingham; J. E. Wilkes, Nuneaton; and V. Wilson, Bilston.

The CHAIRMAN, in opening the proceedings, said he had great pleasure in welcoming the members of that Association to Bilston, and added that he hoped their visit would not only enhance the importance of Bilston but would be a source of instruction to the visitors. The town had a population of 24,000, and he was inclined to think that the members of the Association would not go away dissatisfied.

Councillor SANKEY, in endorsing the chairman's welcome, said he was very pleased indeed to be associated with the chairman in extending a hearty welcome to the members of the Incorporated Association of Municipal and County Engineers. He regarded it as a great honour that the association should have decided to come to Bilston. Ten years ago they could not have expected that such a body would have made Bilston the scene of one of their visits. But during the last seven years they had obtained claims to consideration, and to-day there were in the district one or two matters of considerable interest to such an association. Nothing was more important than water supply, and at Bilston they had an installation that was unique in its way. They had a satisfactory plant and a supply that was practically inexhaustible. They

Mr. R. A. HARPER, J.P.,
Chairman of the Council.

had to congratulate themselves on the arrangement they had been able to make with Wolverhampton a few years ago, for if the old arrangement had continued both Wolverhampton and Bilston might now be in a very uncomfortable position owing to scarcity of water. Bilston was only a Black Country town, but he thought that what would be seen that day would leave upon their minds the impression that Bilston was well supplied with water, though the town had a rateable value of only £64,000. There was another matter in regard to which they were entitled to credit, and that was the technical school, which was superior to anything in the country in proportion to population and rateable value, and was abundantly

Mr. J. W. SANKEY,
Chairman of the Water and Baths Committee.

appreciated in the town. Last year, which was the first session, there were 22,000 attendances, or 835 per week, at the classes, and the report of the examiners was most satisfactory. The school had started under the happiest auspices in the work of technical education in the district. He had read with great interest the excellent paper prepared by Mr. Wilson, their engineer and surveyor. In his paper he told them many things they did not know, among others that the name Bilston meant the "village of the sun." The sun would continue to shine upon Bilston if the inhabitants showed the same interest in the affairs of the town and if the work of the council was done as heartily and cordially as during the last few years. He was glad that Bilston had a claim upon the consideration of their visitors and that they had honoured the town with their presence.

Mr. J. T. EAYRS (Past-President) now took the chair in the absence of the president, Mr. O. Claude Robson, who found it impossible to attend. They knew, the chairman remarked, that engineers and surveyors to large districts had many claims upon their time, and were often obliged to put away any personal matters of their own in order to carry out their public duties, and he was sure the members of the Bilston Council appreciated their self-denying efforts in that respect. He wished to point out that municipal engineers and surveyors derived great benefit from attending these meetings,

and he hoped the various councils would give them facilities for so doing. Bilston was different from a great many towns, being a purely industrial town and situated in the heart of the Black Country. It was a town in which great energy had been shown in sanitary matters, and in such towns that was much needed. Where the population of a town was entirely industrial, greater attention to sanitary matters was required than in more-favourably situated places, such as Cheltenham and Leamington. They were glad to be able to inspect the unique undertaking of the Bilston waterworks. He had resided in the district for a quarter of a century, and remembered the difficulties with the Wolverhampton Corporation and the troubles in regard to the old connection. He was glad that they had surmounted those difficulties and had obtained a water supply sufficient for all future needs.

Mr. PICKERING then read the minutes of the Stafford and Rhyader meetings, and these were unanimously adopted. Letters of apology for absence were read from Mr. Pritchard, who is recovering from illness, from Messrs. Parker (Hereford), Bradley (Wolverhampton), Lobley (Hanley), Cartwright (Bury), and others.

Mr. GREATOREX (West Bromwich) proposed the re-election of Mr. Pickering as honorary district secretary for the Midlands, referring in eulogistic terms to the excellence of the arrangements in connection with the Stafford and Rhyader meetings, and also the meeting that day. Special reference was made to the fact of the paper being printed and circulated well in advance of the meeting and to the manner in which it was illustrated.

Mr. MARSTON (Sutton Coldfield) said that Mr. Pickering had fulfilled all the promises made on his behalf, and they could not do better than leave the work in his hands.

The CHAIRMAN expressed his personal gratification at the way in which Mr. Pickering had carried out his duties as honorary district secretary.

The motion having been unanimously adopted,

Mr. PICKERING, who was received with cheers, thanked the members for the honour they had conferred upon him by re-electing him to the office, an honour that he greatly appreciated. It was at all times a pleasure to work on behalf of the Association. As in the past, so in the future; he would endeavour to make the meetings of the Association thoroughly successful.

This concluded the purely business part of the meeting, and, as arranged in the programme, the members at once entered the brakes that were in waiting at the Town Hall in order to proceed on the round of visits to various works, beginning with the Spring Vale furnaces. Of course. Mr. C. L. N. Wilson, water engineer and surveyor to the urban district council, had prepared a long and valuable paper on the municipal works of the district. As the paper had been sent several days before the meeting to those who had intimated their intention to be present, it was arranged that it should be taken as read. The paper, however, may appropriately be given at this point, before proceeding with our account of the visits and other functions. It was as follows :—

## SEVEN YEARS IN A BLACK COUNTRY TOWN.

By C. L. N. WILSON, ASSOC.M.INST.C.E.,
Bilston.

[Mr. C. L. N. Wilson, A.M.I.C.E., &c., the water engineer and surveyor of Bilston, was born in Blackburn, and was educated at the Mount Pleasant Wesleyan schools, at the Collegiate Grammar School, Blackup, and at Owen's College, Manchester, where he came out third in the first class in civil engineering. In April, 1888, he passed the examination of the Association of Municipal and County Engineers and Surveyors. He served his articles under his father (Mr. John Wilson, then borough engineer of Bacup) and was assistant borough engineer there for over five years. In March, 1890, he won the first prize in an open competition under scaled motto for the Bacup public baths, and he also prepared the surveys, plans, sections and details for the Stacksteads sewerage scheme and outfall works. In March, 1891, he was appointed town surveyor of Bilston. He was also one of the three men selected to go to Jamaica, but elected to stay at Bilston. In 1891 he was appointed town surveyor of George Town, but, being appointed resident engineer on the water scheme for Bilston, he again declined removal therefrom. While he has been at Bilston he has prepared plans for and carried out several street improvements, the erection of shops, stalls and offices in the new market-house, and the electric lighting of that building, the alterations, additions, and electric lighting of the public baths, the Bradley new road and bridges, the Ettingshall new road, and the technical schools. Besides acting as resident engineer under Mr.

Baldwin Latham, m.i.c.e., &c. on the Bilston water scheme from 1893 to its completion at the end of 1897. He has at present in hand the extension of the cemetery, the division of the water area into districts for the detection of waste water, extension of the water mains, water-works manager's house, new stables, and numerous other works. Mr. Wilson is a captain of the 3rd V.B.S. Staffordshire Regiment, and a lieutenant in the Army Reserve of officers, a Freemason, and a member of the Oddfellows, Free Gardeners and Buffaloes Friendly Societies. Needless to say, his services are thoroughly appreciated by the council, who would probably be very loth to part with him.]

Bilston, Bilson, Bylston, Bylstone, Bileston and Bilsone, as it has been spelt at various times, but from whence it was derived has not been clearly ascertained. It has been supposed that it took its name from its stone quarries, so famous for grind-

BILSTON: INTERIOR OF THE MARKET.

stones for edge tools, &c.; but this is certainly wrong, because it had its name years before its quarries were known. Dr. Oliver, a learned writer, tells us in his "History of Wolverhampton Collegiate Church" that Bilston is derived from "Beli," the principal male divinity of Ancient Britain, who was none other than Hu, or the sun; the Apollo, in fact, of classical mythology, who was worshipped by the Druids, and in whose honour the midsummer-eve festival of "Bel-tein" was celebrated. Dr. Oliver does not give any evidence in support of his supposition, yet a little examination serves to confirm his opinion. In the first place, we have the name written by Sigeric "Belstona," in which form the name of the god appears distinctly; in the second place, there are evidences extant of the existence of a Saxon temple founded by Oswy, King of Mercia, on the occasion of his victory over the army of Penda, King of Northumberland, at Bilston, dedicated to the "Sun," and afterwards given to the see of Lichfield. Bilston was situated in the very heart of the Druidical retreats, only 6 miles from Great Barr and Aldridge, the summer residence of the Arch Druid; and within 1¼ miles of Beacon Hill, anciently called "Druid's Hill," on whose summit the Druids are traditionally believed to have offered up their sacrifices. There therefore seems no better etymology of Bilston than the Gaelic "Beal-turin," the fire of Bel, Bael, or Bil, the great Gaelic god, the termination of the word "tona," or "ton," being an abbreviation of the Saxon word "tynan," a town or dwelling-place. Bilston, therefore, becomes a name full of strange significance, calling up pictures of antiquity of absorbing interest, for it literally means the "Village of the Sun."

During the time of Alfred the Great a measure was passed for the dividing of the kingdom into counties, hundreds and tithings, and Bilston was one of these tithings. It is first mentioned in Lady Wulfruna's charter, which she granted to the church at Wolverhampton in the year A.D. 994 or 996. Bilston is also mentioned in Doomsday-Book, and also the manor of Stowheath and the manor of Bradley. A curious coincidence is that at one time the manor of Bradley was held by the Lord of Wombourn, who derived his name and title from Wombourn, the district to which the council went to obtain a water supply for Bilston, and the site selected being a portion of a farm left to the living of St. Leonard's, Bilston. It is mentioned in Edward III.'s charter, and in those of Henry III. and IV., Henry VI., and so on.

Sir Richard Pype, who built a mansion near the present Pipe Hall Hotel, and who was born in Bilston and spent the greater part of his time here, was elected a councillor for the ward of Bishopsgate, and in 1570 he was elected an alderman. In the year 1572 he became sheriff, and had the honour of representing the City before Elizabeth, when business or policy induced the city council to appeal to the Queen. In 1578 he became lord mayor of London, and it was during his term of office that a dispute arose respecting the boundaries of Aldgate and Bishopsgate wards, Sir Richard Pype being for his own ward of Bishopsgate and Sir Richard Rowland for Aldgate, the result being that Sir Richard Pype secured the houses for his own ward. And in recent times the late Bishop Fraser, if not born here, spent the greater portion of his youth here. Bilston is situated upon the Holyhead to London main road, and the area is just over 1,845 acres.

This slight history of Bilston would not be complete unless reference was made to the cholera visitation of 1832, which was the most terrible and fateful event connected with the town. So near was this visitation to the town, that on March 8, 1832, a meeting of the inhabitants was held at the school-house, pursuant to public notice thereof given in the chapel on the Sunday previous by W. Salter, parish clerk, and by notices fixed to the gates of the chapels of St. Leonard's and St. Mary's on the same day, in the following words: "I hereby give notice that a meeting of the inhabitants will be held at the school-house on Thursday next, at 10 o'clock in the forenoon, to take into consideration the necessity of forming a board of health in this township, in consequence of the grievous disease with which it has pleased Almighty God to visit various parts of the kingdom."

At this meeting it was unanimously resolved:—

"That it appears to this meeting that the general health of the township is so good that there is no necessity for establishing a board of health, at least under the present circumstances.

"That the medical gentlemen of the township be requested to give the earliest information to the chairman of this meeting should the cholera unhappily present itself in this place or neighbourhood, and that he is hereby authorised and empowered to call a public meeting of the inhabitants by handbill immediately after the receipt of such information.

"That a copy of the above resolution be forwarded by the vestry clerk to each of the medical practitioners within the township.

"That the surveyors of the turnpike roads and highways, and all other public officers of the township, be earnestly requested to use their utmost endeavours to remove filth and all other nuisances which may come under their notice.

(Signed)　Rev. W. Leigh, Chairman."

"How history does repeat itself!"

On July 23rd the cholera attacked Tipton, and on August 3rd

BILSTON: THE PUBLIC BATHS.

reached Bilston, the first victim being a woman in Temple-street. On the 5th a meeting was held and a board of health appointed, subject to the approval of His Majesty's Privy Council, and on August 7th a letter confirming it was received; on the same day the board held its first meeting. To give all the particulars of cholera various meetings, &c., would be too long, and would also be outside the scope of this paper, but I purpose giving a few statistics in connection with the visitation.

Weekly State of New Cases of Disease.

| Weeks. | Date. | Cases of Disease. | Deaths. | Ratio of Deaths to Cases. |
|---|---|---|---|---|
| 1 | Aug. 4 to 10, 1832 | 150 | 36 | 1 in 4 |
| 2 | „ 11 to 17, „ | 616 | 133 | 1 in 4½ |
| 3 | „ 18 to 24, „ | 924 | 298 | 1 in 3 |
| 4 | „ 25 to 31, „ | 832 | 184 | 1 in 4½ |
| 5 | Sept. 1 to 7, „ | 694 | 62 | 1 in 11 |
| 6 | „ 8 to 14, „ | 250 | 23 | 1 in 11 |
| 7 | „ 15 to 21, „ | 102 | 6 | 1 in 17 |
| | Totals | 3,568 | 742 | 1 in 5 |

BILSTON: INTERIOR OF PUBLIC BATHS.

Weekly State of the Mortality in Bilston, August and September, 1832.

| Weeks. | Date. | Children under Ten Years. | Above Ten Years. Males. | Females. | Totals. |
|---|---|---|---|---|---|
| 1 | To Aug. 10th | 5 | 15 | 16 | 36 |
| 2 | „ „ 17th | 23 | 54 | 56 | 133 |
| 3 | „ „ 24th | 58 | 135 | 105 | 298 |
| 4 | „ „ 31st | 34 | 77 | 73 | 184 |
| 5 | „ Sept. 7th | 18 | 23 | 21 | 62 |
| 6 | „ „ 14th | 6 | 6 | 11 | 23 |
| 7 | „ „ 21th | 4 | 2 | 0 | 6 |
| | Totals | 148 | 312 | 282 | 742 |

Summary.

| | Children to Ten Years. | Above Ten Years. Males. | Females. | Total. |
|---|---|---|---|---|
| Estimated population of Bilston, Aug. 4, 1832 ... | 3,675 | 5,703 | 5,322 | 14,700 |
| Reported cases of disease, Aug. 4 to Sept. 21 ... | — | — | — | 3,568 |
| Ascertained deaths from cholera | 148 | 312 | 282 | 742 |
| Ratio of cases to population, say as 1 in 4 ... | — | — | — | — |
| Ratio of deaths to cases, say as 1 in 5 ... | — | — | — | — |
| Ratio of deaths to population, say as 1 in 20 or 1 in 23½ ... | 1 in 18 | 1 in 18½ | 1 in 20 | |

Deaths for August and September in the Years 1828 to 1832.

| August and September. | | Children to Ten Years. | Above Ten Years. Males. | Females. | Totals. |
|---|---|---|---|---|---|
| No cholera, | 1828 | 47 | 15 | 14 | 76 |
| „ | 1829 | 28 | 8 | 7 | 43 |
| „ | 1830 | 25 | 9 | 11 | 45 |
| „ | 1831 | 66 | 17 | 13 | 96 |
| Cholera only, | 1832 | 148 | 312 | 282 | 742 |
| Of other diseases, | 1832 | 18 | 9 | 12 | 39 |
| | Totals for 1832 | 166 | 321 | 294 | 781 |

| Orphans by cholera, without father or mother, under twelve years of age. | Orphans who lost their fathers by cholera, under twelve years of age. | Orphans who lost their mothers by cholera, under twelve years of age. | Widowers who lost their wives by cholera. | Widows who lost their hus- bands by cholera. |
|---|---|---|---|---|
| 28 males. | 94 males. | 105 males. | | |
| 34 females. | 105 females. | 93 females. | 103 | 131 |
| 62 total. | 199 total. | 198 total. | | |

Amount subscribed for relief of sufferers, £8,536 8s. 7d.

Comparisons with Neighbouring Towns.

| Town. | Population. | Deaths. |
|---|---|---|
| Sedgley ... | 20,577 ... | 289 |
| Darlaston ... | 6,667 ... | 68 |
| Wolverhampton ... | 30,600 ... | 193 |
| Willenhall ... | 6,900 ... | 8 |
| Wednesfield ... | 7,000 ... | 0 |
| Bilston ... | 14,492 ... | 742 |

In 1847 the cholera again visited Bilston, which retained its title of the "epidemic centre of the Midland coalfields," and in about the same time as in 1832 there were 730 deaths, but this time the lessons learnt at such a cost failed not in the object, and steps were immediately taken to improve the township.

The author offers no apology for giving these statistics, but hopes they may help some of his professional brethren to hurry up their councils to improve their respective districts by carrying out all those things needful to make them sanitary, healthy and clean, and also to point out to any lagging authority the awful responsibility they incur, and the vast amount of suffering they entail upon innocent children, and adults also, by neglecting to carry out these necessary sanitary schemes.

IMPROVEMENT BILL.

In 1850 a Bill was presented to Parliament "for paving, lighting, cleansing and improving the township of Bilston; for improving the market for supplying the town with water; and for providing a cemetery." This Public Improvement Bill was one of the first, if not the first, Bill obtained in England, and, as is usual on these occasions, met with a great opposition, and at a town's meeting a poll was demanded. This was granted, and the poll opened on June 3rd, but on the same day the opposition was withdrawn, and the Bill in due time became law. Under this Act the improvement commissioners had a system of sewerage and sewage disposal scheme designed, but only for a portion of the district, at a cost of about £13,000. The outfall was into the river Tame, the system adopted being very rough precipitation— and it is very rough indeed; in fact, almost useless. So bad was the effluent that it had to be taken out of the river Tame, and, by permission of the Birmingham Canal Naviga- tion Company, it was turned into their canal, the commis- sioners having to pay for the dredging of the canal from time to time. But so bad has this effluent become that in the early part of this year notice was served upon the present council to discontinue putting the effluent into the canal, and the council have in hand a scheme for a main sewer and out- fall works, at an estimated cost of about £26,000. The sew- age here is a very peculiar one, containing a large percentage of iron salts, which varies greatly in quantity. A number of experiments have been and are being carried out, and the

BILSTON: THE BRIDGE OVER THE RIVER TAME.

author hopes to publish them in due course. Besides the £13,000 spent by the commissioners under their Act of 1850, about £7,000 has also been spent on sewers by their successors up to the present time.

MARKET.

On May 17, 1825, it was represented to Parliament that Bilston was one of the largest villages in England, having a population of nearly 14,000 souls, and yet it had no market in which they might sell their wares; and the petitioners humbly prayed that they might be permitted to hold a weekly market in a place appointed for that purpose, believing that it would conduce to the prosperity of the town. The Royal assent was accordingly given. This Act also empowered the

BILSTON: THE FOUNTAIN IN THE CEMETERY.

trustees to erect a town hall and other public offices, as soon as the receipts were sufficiently large to enable them to do so. Before the granting of this Act the market was held in Church-street, near to the old church. When the Improvement Act of 1850 was obtained power was taken to purchase the property of the market for £7,000. In 1890 this market was not considered suitable for its purpose, and the commissioners had designs got out for a new covered market, and in 1891 a contract was entered into for the walls and roof. After this was finished, for reasons which need not be stated here, the author was called upon to put in the floor, design the shops, stalls and fittings, and also to superintend the putting in of the electric light. This market was among the first, and the author is of opinion that it was the first, public market in England to be so lighted; it was opened on Tuesday, August 9, 1892. In 1893 the lighting, about which there had been great complaints, had to be reconsidered, and the author was then instructed to get out a scheme for improving the lighting, but to use the then existing plant as far as it would go. He therefore decided to use the Brush dynamo for the arc lamps alone, and to put down a new compound wound dynamo for the incandescent lighting, and this was accordingly done. Since then complaints have ceased. The cost of lighting the market-house in this manner works out at per unit 2⅞d. It was also decided not to use accumulators on account of cost, but to drive direct; the light has not failed once for over three years. The plant consists of two locomotive type boilers, to work at 90 lb. pressure; two Robey 37 indicated horse-power engines, working at 250 and 350 revolutions; and one 12 and one 15 unit dynamo at 110 volts, the dynamos being by the Brush Company and Paterson & Cooper respectively. There are 120 32 nominal candle-power, ten 16 nominal candle-power and two 100 nominal candle-power incandescent lamps and sixteen 10 ampere arc lamps 2,000 nominal candle-power, twelve Brush, two Brockie Pell and two Royce. The dynamos were originally belt-driven, but it was found necessary to alter them, and they have for over three years been rope-driven, without any trouble whatever.

The site of the present market was purchased in the first place from the then lords of the manor, the Duke of Sutherland and the ancestors of W. G. Giffard, of Codsall. The old market was opened on July 26, 1825, and the last instalment of the £7,000 was paid off in 1884.

The new market is 300 ft. long and 65 ft. wide, the front being of best red bricks, with terra-cotta ornaments. The architects were Horton & Co., of Wednesbury, and the contractors Dorse & Co. After the completion of this work it was handed over to the author, who designed and carried out the work before mentioned, at a total cost of about £3,500. The floor is of granolithic, the vestibule floors being of marble mosaic; the stalls are 140 in number, comprising eleven butchers, eight fishmongers, twenty-six general shops and ninety-five general stalls; the woodwork is pitch and yellow pine, the butchers' stalls are fitted with iron bars and sliding hooks; the fish stalls are constructed with white enamel brick fronts, marble slab tops, enamelled channel in centre, and fresh water is also laid on to each. Messrs. Morrell Brothers, of Bilston, were the contractors, and it may be mentioned that the extras on the author's portion of the work, £3,500, came to 4s. 6d.; the total cost of the market up to the present being close upon £10,000.

PUBLIC BATHS.

In 1853 public baths and wash-houses were erected at a cost of £2,700, but turned out a failure, and in 1870 they were offered to the commissioners, who bought them and put them into order at a total cost of £1,100. They continued to be used until 1890, when a new boiler was required, but the building was in a very bad state, and it was thought best to go in for a complete new building, and designs were got in for new baths at a cost of £7,000. This was more than the commissioners were prepared to spend. In the early part of 1892 the roof fell in, after which the author was instructed to prepare plans for enlarging the swimming bath, providing extra dressing-boxes, new boiler, engine and laundry plant. This was done, and in 1893 an inquiry was held by the Local Government Board for their sanction to a loan of £2,500 for this purpose. The loan was sanctioned, but nothing was done until 1895, when the costs of the alterations, instead of being £2,500, were £3,500. The alterations consisted of taking down the south wall and setting it back 6 ft., providing ten new pitch pine dressing-boxes, providing a new roof, relining swimming bath, providing twelve new slipper baths, a soap bath, new floors and new boiler, engines and dynamo, and laundry and electric light fittings complete. The roof over swimming bath is elliptical in shape, with wrought-iron principals, and so constructed that the bath can be used as a gymnasium if required; the glazing is Heywood's patent. The whole building consists of one soap bath, one swimming bath, two ladies' and five gentlemen's first-class slipper baths; and four ladies' and thirteen gentlemen's second-class slipper baths, office, caretaker's-house, boiler-house, engine-room and laundry. The water is heated and circulated by means of a Bradford's patent calorifer; the boiler is a Cornish boiler, 18 ft. long and 5 ft. 6 in. diameter, flue 2 ft. 6 in. diameter, working pressure 60 lb. on the square inch; the laundry engine is a 4 nominal horse-power vertical engine, 7-in. cylinder and 9-in. stroke. The laundry also contains a Bradford's A 7 vowel washing and wringing machine, one of Bradford's No. 22 wringing and mangling machines, and a drying closet, containing six drying horses, 5 ft. 6 in. by 1 ft. 3 in. The electric lighting plant consists of a Robey 50 indicated horse-power inverted cylinder engine, running at 300 revolutions, one 18-unit dynamo at 110 volts, by the Electric Construction Company, to the author's specification, and is, like the dynamos at the market, rope-driven; there are sixty 32 nominal candle-power, eighty-seven 16 nominal candle-power and two 100

BILSTON: THE TECHNICAL SCHOOL.

nominal candle-power lamps; this plant also drives the sixty-five 16 nominal candle-power lamps in the town hall; no accumulators are used, the plant being driven direct. The cost per unit for this installation is 1⅓d, and there has not been the slightest trouble with it from the day it started. The whole of the oil from the engines and dynamos is collected and passed through Turner's patent oil filters, and re-used time after time. These filters do their work very well indeed, and without any trouble; valvoline oil is used, and it does not seem to suffer from being filtered in this way.

Messrs. Morrell Brothers were the contractors for the whole of the work, the engineering being done by Messrs Bradford & Co., of Salford, and the electric light installation by the Universal Electric Light Co., of Liverpool. The total cost of the alterations was £3,500, of which the engineering cost £1,000 and the electric lighting £600.

CEMETERY.

The cemetery was opened in 1855, the area being 9 acres 2 roods and 23 poles. The chapels are built with best blue bricks, with Bath stone dressings, the style being Gothic; the total cost was £5,000. It is about to be extended. It contains a rustic fountain and a Bath stone monument to the

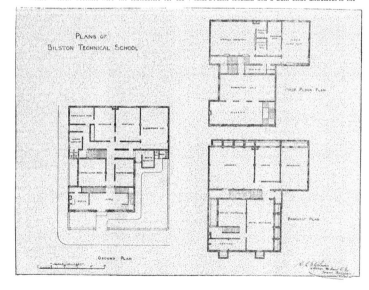

PLANS OF
BILSTON TECHNICAL SCHOOL

GROUND PLAN

BILSTON: THE MUSEUM AT THE TECHNICAL SCHOOL.

memory of the late John Etheridge, who gave away with his own hands 10,000 Bibles, 41,000 prayer books, 15,000 Testaments and 100,000 religious tracts, and was followed to the grave by 15,000 people of all grades ; but I am sorry to say that the monument is in a very bad state of repair.

TOWN HALL.

The town hall is a stone building in the Italian style of architecture, and was erected in 1871 and enlarged in 1880. It contains the usual public offices, council chamber and committee-rooms, a large assembly hall, a news-room, a free library and a reference library, both of which are well stocked with books. The architect was the late Mr. Bidlaker, and the total cost was £7,500.

NEW ROADS.

During the past seven years the council have, under the author's supervision and with their own workmen, cut two new roads and erected two bridges, at a cost of about £5,000. The main road (a portion of the Great Holyhead to London main road) is beautifully planted with trees, and there are very few towns with a better approach than the one coming into Bilston from Wolverhampton ; there is a straight length of over half a mile, planted with trees on each side. Last year the Willenhall-road and one or two smaller streets were also planted, and I think it is the intention to plant more this year.

The tramways are owned by the Wolverhampton Tramways Company, and run from Moxley through Wolverhampton to Tettenhall, with a junction from Wolverhampton to Willenhall.

TECHNICAL SCHOOLS.

The technical school is a large building situated on the Willenhall-road. It is built of bricks, the front being Doulton's best red bricks, with Doulton's terra-cotta quoins, plinths, jambs, heads, &c., the rest of the building being common red bricks. The building is Italian in style. It contains engineering and metal-working room, 54 ft. by 20 ft., fitted with gas engine, lathe, drilling machine, four smiths' hearths, &c.; a wood-working-room, 30 ft. by 20 ft.; a cooking-room, 20 ft. by 24 ft., fitted with a good range, a cottager's range and a gas stove, sink, &c.; a large modelling and casting-room, 30 ft. by 20 ft.; elementary art-room, 30 ft. by 20 ft.; antique-room, 24 ft. by 20 ft.; advanced drawing-room, 24 ft. by 20 ft., and a masters'-room, 12 ft. by 16 ft.; three class-rooms, each 20 ft. by 20 ft.; ladies' and gentlemen's cloak-rooms ; a large examination hall, 40 ft. by 20 ft., with a stained-glass window ; a chemical laboratory, 30 ft. by 24 ft., fitted with three double benches for thirty-six students, gas and water being laid on for each student, and also a down-draught chamber, five fume chambers, two chemical cup-boards and stands, sinks, &c.; a chemical balance-room, 8 ft. by 24 ft.; master's preparation-room, 10 ft. by 24 ft., fitted with desk, working table, waggon, sink and fume chambers ; and a chemical lecture-room, with a master's working table, with gas and water laid on to each end, two mercury trays, down-draught extractors, and a large water tank with plate-glass front for experimental purposes, sliding black-boards,

fume chambers, diagram frames and lantern sheet, the room being 20 ft. by 30 ft.

A museum, 45 ft. by 15 ft., is also provided ; and a large entrance hall, containing a piece of sculpture from the Shrewsbury collection, of Raphaelle (gazing at a picture of the Transfiguration), by Ceccarini, and a secretary's office. The museum is filled with a large number of curios, &c., collected by Mr. James Dangerfield during his travels round the world ; and in the entrance hall and examination hall are a number of valuable oil paintings, given or loaned by Messrs. Phœnix, Kelly, Sankey & Kirkland. The building is heated on the low-pressure system, by means of radiators, and is lighted by gas. The building was erected from the author's designs and under his supervision, the contractors being, for the building, Mr. Thomas Tildesley, amount £5,087, the extras being £10 0s. 8d.; the heating by C. D. Harris, at a cost of £363 15s.; the chemical laboratory fittings, by the Midland Educational Company, at a cost of £418 5s. 4d. The whole of the fittings in the chemical department were designed by the author. In this respect Bilston can show the whole of Great Britain a noble example. The total cost of the buildings and fittings is equal to about one-seventh of the total rateable value of the township, and yet it was built by public subscriptions, and grants from the Staffordshire County Council and the South Kensington authorities, without putting a penny on the town rates. It was not too much to say that Mr. J. W. Sankey, the chairman of the Water and Baths Committee, is entitled to all the credit of this undertaking ; and, to show how much the people value it, it is only necessary to state that during the last session, out of a population of about 25,000, there was an average weekly attendance of over 800 students.

FOUNTAINS.

There are three drinking fountains in the town, given by the late John Mason, and last year another one was erected by public subscription, in memory of the late Walter Hughes, who for a great number of years was nuisance inspector, and died August, 1896. This latter also forms a horse drinking-trough, with small basins for dogs, &c. In this respect the author thinks Bilston stands alone—i.e., that a town official received a public memorial.

LIGHTING.

There are 400 lamps in the district, and the total cost of street lighting for the year 1897 was £1,041 17s. 1d.

|  | £ | s. | d. |
|---|---|---|---|
| Amount paid for gas ... ... ... ... | 682 | 6 | 9 |
| „ „ „ lighting and cleaning, &c. ... | 218 | 15 | 8 |
| „ „ „ repairing and painting ... | 65 | 0 | 0 |
| Miscellaneous repairs ... ... ... ... | 75 | 14 | 8 |
| Cost per lamp per annum for gas ... ... | 1 | 8 | 5¼ |
| Cost per lamp per annum for lighting and cleaning ... ... ... ... ... | 0 | 10 | 11 |
| Cost per lamp per annum for repairing and painting ... ... ... ... ... | 0 | 3 | 0 |
| Total cost per annum per lamp ... ... | 2 | 7 | 1 |

Price of gas 2s. 7¼d. per 1,000 cubic feet.*

* This has since been reduced to 2s. 6d. per 1,000 cubic feet.

The gasworks belong to the Bilston Gas Light and Coke Company.

MAIN AND TOWN ROADS.

There are about 8½ miles of main roads, and the traffic is very heavy. They cost in 1897 £1,670 2s. 8d. for repairs, including about £200 for footpaths, or the sum of £230 18s. 8d. per mile per annum. The town roads repairable by the council are about 22 miles in length, and cost for the year ended March 31, 1897, £2,537 17s. 1d., or £115 7s. 2d. per mile per annum. The price of materials used in the repair of the roads is :—

10-in. by 5-in. by 2½-in. plain blue paving bricks, being 59s. per 1,000 delivered.

Rowley rag,* 3½-in., hand broken, 7s. 6d. per ton.

Hopton wood edging, 10 in. by 5 in., 2s. 1d. per lineal yard, dressed.

Lancashire (Lee quarries) edging, 10 in. by 6 in., 2s. 7d. per lineal yard, dressed.

Lancashire (Lee quarries), channels, 10 in. by 6 in, 2s. 8d. per lineal yard, dressed and machine faced.

Lancashire (Lee quarries), 12 in. by 8 in., bull-nosed, machined faced and dressed, 4s. 1d. per lineal yard.

Lancashire (Lee quarries), ditto circular, 6s. 8d. per lineal yard.

Lancashire (Lee quarries), 12 in. by 6 in., channels, 3s. per lineal yard.

Sand, 3s. 6d. per ton delivered.

Hopton wood setts, 6 in. by 4 in., 18s. 6d. per ton.

Rowley rag setts, 6 in. by 4 in., 17s. 6d. per ton.

BILSTON : THE KEY USED AT THE OPENING OF THE TECHNICAL SCHOOL.

The bulk of the town roads are coated and repaired with broken slag, which costs from 1s. 6d. to 2s. 6d. per yard cube.

OFFICE STAFF, &c.

The whole of the work in the water engineer and surveyor's department is carried out by the author, with the aid of a pupil.

The rateable value of Bilston for 1897 was £64,778, the

* The author has found it better to buy Rowley rag in the lump and have it broken in the council's yard by their own workmen. Lancashire flagging, 3 in. thick, costs 6s. 6d. per square yard, including foundation and dressing, and Nelson & Co.'s patent granolithic flagging, about the same.

poor rate for 1897 was 3s. in the £1, and the improvement rate for the same was 3s. 9d. in the £1. Below is a summary

BILSTON: ENTRANCE HALL OF THE TECHNICAL SCHOOL.

showing the position of the Council Mortgage Debt, to the end of March, 1897 :—

| Purpose for which applied. | Amount borrowed. | Principal paid off to March 31, 1897. | Outstanding Debt, March 31, 1897. |
|---|---|---|---|
| | £ | £ s. d. | £ s. d. |
| Market ... ... | 15,000 | 8,220 13 4 | 6,779 6 8 |
| Sewers ... ... | 13,800 | 12,166 19 1 | 1,633 0 11 |
| Cemetery ... | 5,000 | 5,000 0 0 | — |
| Water ... ... | 70,350 | 13,326 17 1 | 57,023 2 11 |
| Cost of Bilston Improvement Act, 1850 ... | 5,000 | 4,833 6 8 | 166 13 4 |
| Public Baths ... | 5,050 | 1,519 14 11 | 3,530 5 1 |
| Town Hall ... | 7,500 | 5,491 19 8 | 2,008 0 4 |
| Paving footpaths | 2,500 | 2,500 0 0 | — |
| Public library ... | 1,200 | 446 17 1 | 753 2 11 |
| Steam roller, &c. | 580 | 290 0 0 | 290 0 0 |
| Making new streets | 4,000 | 451 2 3 | 3,548 17 9 |
| Totals | 129,980 | 54,217 10 1 | 75,732 9 11 |

We regret that, owing to the pressure of other matter on our space this week, we are compelled to hold over the balance of our report, including the continuation of Mr. Wilson's paper. This portion of the paper deals exclusively with the waterworks and will be given next week, together with the rest of our report and additional plans and other illustrations.

## HOUSING OF THE WORKING CLASSES AT NOTTINGHAM.

In connection with a scheme for making a new thoroughfare at Nottingham, involving in its course the utilisation of the site of an old gaol, an important point has arisen as to the conditions under which the corporation should be required to erect dwelling-houses for the accommodation of those who might be dispossessed of their previously existing tenements. The matter has on several occasions engaged the attention of the corporation, it being suggested that the municipal authorities should be allowed to put up the vacant land by auction, with a view to it being leased for a period of ninety-nine years, under conditions as to the erection of buildings which would be in accordance with the requirements of the Local Government Board. The latter authority declined to allow the arrangement, directing that the corporation should themselves undertake the work of erecting the dwellings. Recently a deputation waited, by appointment, upon Mr. Adrian, one of the assistant secretaries of the Local Government Board, and urged reasons in favour of the course originally suggested by the corporation. They pointed out that in the interests of the municipality the best purpose would be served by the land being leased, as proposed. The interview was of a prolonged character, and Mr. Adrian promised that the whole matter should be carefully reviewed, and an answer given in due course.

# The British Association.

## SOME PAPERS ON ELECTRICAL WORK.

Last week we pointed out that, of the papers read at the recent meeting of the British Association at Bristol, those which came within our scope were practically, though not exclusively, confined to the Mechanical Science section, and the Economic Science and Statistics section. With the proceedings of the latter section we have already dealt. In the former section some interesting papers on electrical subjects were given, and abstracts of these will, no doubt, be welcome to our readers.

### TRANSMISSION OF POWER BY ELECTRICITY.

Mr. ALEXANDER SIEMENS read an extremely valuable paper on "The Transmission of Power by Electricity." The greatest achievement, he remarked, of the century which now approached its close was the intimate connection which had been established between science and practice, the effects of which were noticeable in every feature of modern civilisation, and in none more so than in electrical engineering. Among the solution of problems the transmission of power promised to become one of the most important. He reviewed the developments of science in this direction. In the case of the transmission of power there were three factors common to all systems which determined the cost of the motive power at the place where it was utilised, and thereby indicated what was the proper system to use. The first factor was the source of the energy to be used. The second was the means of transmitting; and the third the apparatus for utilising the energy. With their present experience there was no need to dwell on the advantages of electric traction in the streets of towns and suburbs, and there was little doubt that in the near future horse and steam tramways would disappear everywhere. The great success on tramways had naturally led to attempts to move trains on the railways by means of electric locomotives on all existing railways by electric motors, as the feasibility of such changes depended ultimately only on economical considerations. The changes might be technically possible, but an alteration could only be produced if a saving of expense was thereby effected. In spite of one or two drawbacks, electric transmission of power was applicable in a great many cases on account of the unquestionable superiority of the means of distributing electricity over the means of dealing with any other form of energy. The ease with which the current could be carried over a long distance, the certainty with which the losses could be determined beforehand, and the flexibility of the conductors, constituted advantages which no other system presented, while the inevitable loss of the double conversion, added to the losses in the conductor, militated against the application of electricity in cases where the source of power and the apparatus for utilising the same could be brought close together. He described the installation of electric plant at the works of Siemens Brothers & Co., at Charlton, and entered into figures, with a view to indicating the total cost of motive power during the year 1897—viz., £9,900, or 2d. per Board of Trade unit, and 1·71d. per brake horse-power per hour exerted by the motors. It was not pretended that these results were the best obtainable. They might, however, be utilised for drawing some general conclusions which applied to transmission of power by electricity generally. An obvious solution of the problem how to obtain cheap fuel was evidently to erect the plant for generating electricity close to a coal mine, and to distribute power to the various works which were usually found in the neighbourhood. Such an installation had been erected at Brakpan, in the Transvaal, and he gave a description of the plant. In the month of July, 1895, the works at Brakpan were commenced, and on January 27, 1897, the first dynamo commenced working. Since then the works had been steadily added to, but the data as to cost could obviously not be taken as a guide for other cases, as the regular working of the full plant had not yet settled down properly. A somewhat similar system of distributing power over a district had been in operation near Waldenburg, in Silesia, for the last two years. It was characteristic for this country that these examples of transmission of power by electricity over a large district had to be taken from foreign practice. However enterprising and progressive the individual Englishman was, when a novelty could be introduced only by the co-operation of a municipality, or a county council, or, worst of all, of Parliament, everybody appeared to consider it a patriotic duty to throw obstacles in its way, and in most cases it was quite impossible to find out who benefitted by such action. After awhile the public discovered that the introduction of the novelty would be a great convenience, and an agitation was set on foot to remove the obstacles, which were, in many cases, introduced only to satisfy prejudices.

### ELECTRIC MOTORS AND SMALL INDUSTRIES.

Mr. ALFRED H. GIBBINGS, M.I.E.E., president of the Municipal Electrical Association, city electrical engineer, Bradford, read an important paper on "The Application of the Electric Motor to Small Industrial Purposes and its Effects on Trade and on the Community generally." He remarked that the electric motor was rapidly becoming the most favoured medium for the transmission of energy for all industrial operations, whether on a large or small scale. This was due to the paramount advantages it possessed over any other method of utilising potential energy. These advantages were well known to electrical engineers, but indifferently appreciated by a large number of mechanical engineers, and almost unknown by the general manufacturer and tradesman. The paper went on to consider the reason why the application of the electric motor up to the present time had been confined to a few special trades and manufactures. The

PRINCIPAL OBSTACLES

to its adoption were: (1) The extreme aversion to innovations which characterised the industrial world, in this country especially. (2) The existence of other motors in good working condition. (3) The unsuitability of alternating currents of electricity for motors where the power required exceeded 2 horse-power or 3 horse-power. (4) The want of capital to lay out in new machinery. And (5) the want of confidence in the electric motor by the non-technical manufacturer. The chief obstacle to the more rapid adoption of electric motive power, especially in the case of small tradesmen, throughout the country was undoubtedly the want of capital to purchase the necessary motor; but where the power to purchase existed the buyer would probably have little or no experience or knowledge of electrical matters to guide him in his purchase; if his means were at all limited he would be tempted to venture on a cheap line and become the dupe of those who simply made to sell. The solution of these difficulties was that the owners of electricity supply undertakings, whether a public company, municipality or other local authority, should themselves purchase good, reliable motors and let them out on hire. Antecedently this scheme might appear a sort of parental régime, but it was suited to present circumstances, at any rate, and experience proved it to work well. Unfortunately, all local authorities had not got powers to borrow money for this purpose, although it appeared from the Electric Lighting and Public Health Acts that borrowing powers might be granted by the Local Government Board for works of a permanent nature. Electric motors did not yet come within that category, although gas stoves did, a legal decision having been given in their case. All future municipal Parliamentary Bills should therefore contain clauses which would confer such powers and secure freedom of action in this respect. He did not propose to run into elaborate details, but he might say that in Bradford they had found a rental charge of 10 per cent. upon the initial cost of each motor to be amply sufficient. That was made up of 3 per cent. for interest, 3 per cent. for sinking fund, and 4 per cent. for depreciation and contingent expenses. After giving some further details of the Bradford scheme, Mr. Gibbings gave the accompanying interesting table, which had been compiled from replies to an inquiry which he had recently made of each municipal electrical engineer where the continuous current system had been adopted. From it might be gathered

THE EXTENT

to which electric motors driven from electric lighting mains had been employed. The figures given are up to the end of 1897. The table was as follows:—

| Town. | Population. | Number of Motors Supplied. | Total Horse-Power of Motors. |
|---|---|---|---|
| Aberdeen ... | 140,000 | 14 | 65 |
| Bradford ... | 231,260 | 119 | 470 |
| Brighton ... | 122,310 | 100 | Not given |
| Belfast ... | 320,000 | Not given | 165 |
| Birkenhead... | 110,030 | 4 | 15 |
| Bury ... | 63,000 | 5 | 12 |
| Blackpool ... | 40,000 | 7 | 7 |
| Burnley ... | 90,000 | 8 | 32 |
| Chester ... | 37,100 | 20 | 70 |
| Dewsbury ... | 29,847 | 4 | 16½ |
| Dundee ... | 169,000 | 15 | 20 |
| Edinburgh ... | 295,000 | 167 | 343 |
| Glasgow ... | 750,000 | 37 | 131 |
| Hull ... | 213,000 | 14 | 46 |
| Lancaster ... | 38,224 | 28 | 80 |
| Liverpool ... | 641,063 | 57 | 152 |
| Manchester... | 505,368 | 257 | 696 |
| Norwich ... | 101,000 | 61 | 120 |
| Nottingham ... | 213,877 | 18 | 50 |
| Oldham ... | 148,000 | 11 | 60 |
| Southampton ... | 90,000 | 18 | 23 |
| Shoreditch ... | 124,000 | 31 | 43½ |
| Sunderland... | 147,000 | 23 | 240 |
| Wolverhampton ... | 92,000 | 2 | 8 |
| Whitehaven ... | 20,000 | | |
| Walsall ... | 72,000 | 7 | 13½ |

In closing his paper the author referred to the beneficial effects of the motor upon the trade and productions of the country, and the hygienic and social effect on the community generally. The effect of hiring-out was mutually advantageous, and its natural tendency was to create fresh demands; in fact, the municipality which included this scheme in its electric light undertakings offered a great inducement to the influx and establishment of new industries within its area. With a more complete return to a municipality of industrial operations there might also revive some neglected trades—such as those which had passed from us to other countries, and which now form our imports. From an hygienic point of view the electric motor was far and away the best; it was cleanly in its working, gave off no deleterious gases, and displaced the boiler and smoky chimney. One of the ultimate results must also be the raising of the status of the working part of the community. By becoming his own master the artisan gained self-respect, became more resourceful, and therefore a more important member of society; and the more intelligent interest which he would display in his business must appreciably affect the general welfare of the country.

## ELECTRIC POWER ON THE THREE-PHASE SYSTEM.

Mr. W. GIEPEL read an interesting paper on "Electric Power and its Application on the Three-Phase System to the Bristol Waggon and Carriage Works." The author remarked that while there had been several papers read in this country before engineering societies on the application of electric power in works, yet this subject did not appear to have been brought prominently before the members of the British Association. The author's main object was to localise the causes of the present enormous waste of coal in the case of our important workshops and factories, and to discuss how this might best be obviated by the use of electricity. Other objects which he had in view, however, were the attainment of the maximum output of machine tools, which could only be obtained by driving the tools at a steady maximum speed and the greatest economy in labour, and otherwise in producing the driving power. The advantages and economy obtained by substituting electric power in works using scattered engines were probably more distinct than in the case of works using a single large motor. One of these works alone would use as much energy as was demanded by an average provincial town for its electric lighting. The Bristol Waggon and Carriage Works, for example, used 710,000 horse-power hours per annum, that was the equivalent of over 400,000 Board of Trade units of electric energy, and was considerably more than last year's electricity supply in such towns as Aberdeen, Belfast, Cardiff or Dover. The directions in which improvement might be looked for were chiefly the following: Saving of coal, saving of water and stores, saving of labour and attention, reduction of loss in shafting and gearing, increased output owing to steady speed of machinery, and facility of extending by adding extra motors. The author gave details under these heads, and proceeded to a consideration of the application of electricity to the Bristol Waggon and Carriage Works, and various tests which had been made at the works. Full consideration was given to the merits and demerits of the direct-current and three-phase systems, and the directors of the Bristol Waggon Works took the opportunity of seeing both systems in practical work under conditions analogous to those in their own works. The first cost of the two systems was approximately the same, but several advantages of the three-phase system appealed to the Bristol Waggon Works—namely, (1) The absence of commutators on both the generator and motors, and the fact that the current passed direct through clamped terminals from the generator to the motors. (2) The more mechanical design and construction of the generator and motors, the windings of the latter being entirely enclosed by the iron frame of the machine, protecting them from accidental damage. (3) The fact that the three-phase motors could be left running for long periods without any attention, even when considerably overloaded, which was not advisable in the case of the direct-current motors. (4) The freedom from possibility of breakdown as compared with the direct-current system.

## DISCUSSION.

The three papers summarised above were discussed together.

Prof. SILVANUS THOMPSON observed that he must seriously differ from Mr. Siemens in his statement that in most cases the distributions of continuous currents were perfect. Prof. Thompson also complained of the one-sided set of figures submitted by Mr. Gibbings, who had actually suppressed all the data on the other side. It astonished him, after what he had seen in other countries, and particularly in Switzerland, which was ten years ahead of England in this matter, that electrical engineers should stick to the old idea of the continuous-current instead of adopting more freely the modern alternate-current system. There was one fact of special interest to Leicester and Bristol, where the boot and shoe industry still flourished. A Swiss boot factory four years ago struggled for existence, but having got rid of its steam machinery and adopted the alternate-current system it could now compete successfully with Bristol and Leicester.

Mr. PARKER, with many years of experience at Wolverhampton, spoke in favour of the continuous method, and claimed for it superiority over the alternate system.

Mr. BAILEY joined with Prof. Thompson in his condemna-

tion of British firms in refusing to favour the three-force and alternate system.

Mr. W. H. PREECE said the General Post Office was a great user of motive power, and all its new buildings in the provincial centres were fully equipped with motors, which were used for almost all kinds of work. These were found not only economical as regarded cost, &c., but as regarded human labour. With regard to the adoption of electric traction on the inner circle of the Metropolitan Railway, he might say that the directors had decided to go most thoroughly into this matter. They would not be prejudiced by any single system or manufacture, but would give to each every possible opportunity to lay their individual schemes before them, and, whether the three-phased or continued current, the best in their consideration would be adopted. In Bristol there had been a great question as to whether the current should be supplied to the tramways company from the city mains, or whether the tramways company should supply from their own works their own current. Unfortunately, the tramways company and their interests were too powerful, and they succeeded in inducing the local authority to agree that they should erect their own works. If the company could have come to terms with the Bristol authorities to supply the energy at the same price which the company could have done it for themselves, then the corporation would have been enabled to reduce the price of the power 1d. per unit, which was one of the most economical questions which local authorities could take into consideration, because it meant that the ratepayers and the users of the electric light would benefit by the introduction of motive power.

## BRISTOL ELECTRIC LIGHTING.

Mr. H. FARADAY PROCTOR, A.M.I.C.E., M.I.E.E., city electrical engineer, Bristol, submitted a practical paper, giving an outline of the electric lighting undertaking at Bristol, and the results of the working of some of the auxiliary plant. The author described the generating station, boilers, engines and dynamos, switch-houses, cables, and he also gave the results of trials made with sundry of the auxiliary plant. The conclusions arrived at were: (1) The motor feed-pump would work with from 27 per cent. of the steam consumption of the steam pump; (2) the output of a motor pump should be controlled by regulating the speed of the pump, the employment of by-pass cocks resulting in the loss of much energy; (3) with a motor driver feed-pump, where the motor runs at 580 revolutions per minute and the pump at 45, an efficiency of 67 per cent. could be obtained.

Mr. PARKER, in the course of some discussion, said that, seeing the enormous loss by steam, he looked forward to the time when they would see electrically-driven pumps more in use. The information given by Mr. Proctor was the first data which had been supplied to the section on the subject, and would be very valuable.

Mr. W. H. PREECE mentioned that the electric light station at Bristol was five years old, and there were now 54,700 lamps affixed to the system. In addition to that, the price, which was originally 6d., had been reduced to 5d., and at the same time the price of gas had been forced down by the introduction of the electric light from 2s. 10d. to 2s. 2d. During the five years of the existence of the station there had never been one breakdown. There had been occasional breakdowns at dinner parties, when fuses went, but as regarded the central station not a single mishap had occurred, which was a great credit to Mr. Proctor.

## OVERHEAD ELECTRIC WIRES.

Prof. SILVANUS THOMPSON submitted and discussed the details of his method, in association with Mr. Miles Walker, of electric traction by surface contact, with the object of getting rid of overhead wires. Prof. Thompson also detailed other systems to effect the same purpose. The subject was illustrated by diagrams thrown on the screen. At the close of the paper a brief discussion ensued, and the author was thanked.

## STANDARDS OF PURITY FOR SEWAGE EFFLUENTS.

In one or two isolated cases papers of some interest to our readers were read in other sections. In the Chemistry section, for example, Dr. S. RIDEAL made a communication on "Standards of Purity for Sewage Effluents." For some time it had occurred to him and others that they had been in difficulty as to recording or interpreting the results of examining sewage and water. Various figures had been put forward by different authorities as standards, and he thought there was a consensus of opinion that these standards should be done away with and others substituted. All existing standards were liable to give erroneous conclusions, inasmuch as the purity of an effluent depended upon the ratio of the amount of organic matter which had been oxidised and the amount left. Thus it was found that in most cases a considerable quantity of the organic matter disappeared in the form of nitrogen gas; and this loss could be expressed in the form of a ratio to the amount of chlorine or salt which remained in such a liquid and was not so dissipated. Secondly, with regard to the organic matter left, that similarly could be expressed in the form of a ratio showing the amount of matter which had undergone oxidation, and the amount which had not. Lastly, he drew attention to the fact that when standards have been put forward no attention has been paid to the volume of the river into which the effluents were

## SANITATION NEAR MARGATE.

### THE CONDITIONS OF VILLAGE LIFE.

## ROTHERHAM GASWORKS EXTENSIONS.

### OPENING CEREMONY.

## STRATFORD'S POLLUTED RIVER.

# Conditions Necessary for the Successful Purification of Sewage by Bacteria.

By W. J. DIBDIN, F.I.C., F.C.S., &c., and GEORGE THUDICHUM, F.C.S., &c.*

## INTRODUCTION.

### HISTORY OF BACTERIAL PROCESSES.

The recognition of the fact that the natural destruction of waste organic material is effected solely through the agency of living organisms is quite modern. Although casually observed or referred to by various authors, the first and practical attempt to apply such knowledge was in 1884, when the late Metropolitan Board of Works, on the initiative of its scientific advisers, resolved to adopt a system of sewage purification which would produce an effluent readily assailable by oxidising microbes; and also recognised and acted upon the principle that sterilising or destruction of the germs was wrong, and that on the contrary they should be encouraged. This led to the chloride of lime *versus* manganate controversy, which lasted until 1887, when a return to attempted sterilising proved finally disastrous and the upholders of the microbe theory were vindicated. The contention of the latter, which was actually the first step taken towards solving the problems indicated in the title of this paper, was that for the purposes of deodorising sewage an agent should be employed which would oxidise and destroy the putrescent matters which gave rise to nuisance, but should itself be destroyed in so doing, in order that no antiseptic element should be introduced which could interfere with the action of the oxidising bacteria. In a report made by one of the authors to the Metropolitan Board of Works in January, 1887, and in a paper read before the Institution of Civil Engineers in the same month, this proposition was clearly laid down, and remains now the basis of all bacterial treatment.

The next great step in advance was made by the authorities of the State of Massachusetts, under whose directions elaborate experiments were carried out at Lawrence. This result was to demonstrate absolutely that, given certain specified conditions, practically the whole of the organic matters of sewage could be removed by microbial action in artificial filters. The conclusion arrived at has been quoted, but is of such importance historically that it may well be mentioned here. The mechanical separation of any part of the sewage by straining through sand is but an accident, which under some conditions favourably modifies the result; but the essential conditions are very slow motions of very thin films of liquid over the surface of particles having spaces between them sufficient to allow air to be continually in contact with the films of liquid. With these conditions it is essential that certain bacteria should be present to aid in the process of nitrification. These, we have found, come in the sewage at all times of the year, and the conditions just mentioned appear to be most favourable for their efficient action, and at the same time most destructive to them and to all kinds of bacteria that are in the sewage. The work done at the Lawrence station, however, although of the greatest possible importance from a theoretical point of view, failed to indicate the conditions necessary for the practical application of the knowledge which had been gained, the quantity of sewage (60,000 gallons per diem) which could be treated on an acre of filter-bed being so small that the cost of an installation was quite prohibitive. Acting on the advice of one of the authors, the Main Drainage Committee of the London County Council instituted a series of experiments at the outfall works at Barking creek; and the result, which is now too well known to be gone into in detail, was to demonstrate the practicability of purifying large quantities of sewage effluent on an area of filter, which would make the adoption of the method possible from the economic point of view. The consideration of various data in connection with these experiments led to the belief that the crude sewage itself might be similarly treated, and experiments in this direction soon showed that such a belief was well founded.

In the meantime others had not been idle. Mr. Cameron, the city surveyor of Exeter, had been elaborating his ideas with regard to the preliminary treatment of crude sewage by means of anaerobic organisms, and had successfully demonstrated the possibility of such use being applied practically. Lowcock, also in this country, had been trying to purify sewage effluents by means of air forced by artificial means into a filter through which the effluent was constantly running; and Waring, in America, was perfecting a method whereby the solid residue retained in a filter, after the passage of a quantity of crude sewage, was oxidised by bacterial agency, aëration being obtained by a blast of air. Colonel Ducat also devised a filter in which the constant aëration was supposed to be kept up by natural means consequent on the method of construction. Others have also experimented, chiefly in the direction of ascertaining the most suitable material for filling the filter-beds, the general method followed being that laid down as a result of the work at Barking creek.

* A paper read in Section G (Mechanical Science) of the British Association.

## GENERAL CONDITIONS.

Speaking generally, the following are the points which the authors have found to be most noteworthy of the conditions which must be observed to ensure success—*viz.*,—

(1) Air supply, or its absence in the case of the septic tank.
(2) Temperature.
(3) Admission or exclusion of light.
(4) Reaction to test paper of the sewage to be purified.
(5) Time of contact.
(6) Nature of bed material.
(7) Depth of bed.

### (1) AIR SUPPLY.

This question must be considered from two distinct points of view, according to the method of preliminary purification to be adopted. In either case the final treatment is the same. Acting in the presence of a free supply of atmosperic oxygen, the aerobic organisms present in a bacterial filter-bed are able to liquefy, break down and oxidise the solid organic matters suspended in sewage, without such decomposition being accompanied by any of the ordinary phenomena of putrefaction. To such an extent is this action carried under favourable circumstances, that within two hours an effluent is produced which contains considerable quantities of nitric acid, 0·5 grains of nitric nitrogen, and in which nitrification is afterwards continued at an extremely rapid rate. In order to attain these results the bed which receives the crude sewage must be kept very open, the interstices being large. In practice the bed material, whether burnt ballast, coke or stone, has been found most efficacious when of a size varying from ½ in. diameter at the smallest to 4 in. or 5 in. at the largest. Smaller material than that which is rejected by a sieve having a mesh of ¼ in. square does not leave the bed sufficiently open, not only because the air has not free admission, but also because the solid particles held in suspension in the sewage are unable to work their way into the body of the bed.

This necessity for full aëration has been recognised by all who have attempted to utilise the aerobic organisms. In Colonel Ducat's filter it is intended to gain the object sought for by building the containing walls of drain pipes, in order that air shall have free access from all sides. Lowcock proposes to arrive at the same condition by pumping air into the body of the filter-bed, allowing the same effluent, which in his case is alone employed, to pass continuously. Waring, in America, runs crude sewage through the filter until the latter is fully charged with sludge, which is then oxidised and destroyed by forcing a current of air through it. In the method adopted at Sutton the object is attained by emptying the bed completely after each charge, when, as the water leaves the air necessarily enters.

In all these cases it is clear that a free air supply enters largely into the success of the operations; in the case of the anaerobic processes the conditions are not so plain. The septic tank, as worked at Belleisle, Exeter, is covered in with brickwork and cement; yet, on the authority of Dr. Sims Woodhead, the aerobic organisms increase during the passage of the sewage through the tank in a greater proportion than the anaerobic, a fact which would tend to show that air is not absolutely excluded. The same anaerobic action may also be effected in tanks which are open to the air, or even in a flowing river, as was the case with the Thames in 1884-87, when the foul condition of the water was undoubtedly due to the action or organisms working with an insufficient air supply. It is therefore a question whether sewage, if left to itself, without artificial aids or protection of any kind, will not always effect the first stage of its purication with the aid of anaerobic, or, at all events, of mixed organisms; whilst if the aerobic action is to preponderate some artificial assistance must be given. Regarding the greater desirability of the one method as compared with the other, the authors are not prepared at present to express an opinion; experience alone can solve this question. The fact remains that both systems effect the result aimed at.

### (2) TEMPERATURE.

The greater number of micro-organisms can only flourish within a very small thermometric range—namely, from about 50 deg. Fahr. to 100 deg. Fahr. Some there are which can exercise their life functions at the temperature at which water freezes, whilst others can exist when the thermometer registers as high as 150 deg. Fahr., and are killed at relatively high temperatures. The bulk, however, flourish at the degree of warmth first indicated. It will be seen at once how important this factor is, in view of the fact that artificial warming of a sewage purification plant is practically impossible, owing to the great expense involved. The effect of the seasons upon the process going on in a bacteria-bed or a septic tank forms a most interesting study. The experiments made by the Massachusetts authorities first showed to be discharged. This was a most important factor. He therefore suggested a formula which gave the relation between the quality of an effluent and the volume of the river.

Mr. Douglas Archibald, in the course of the discussion that followed, expressed the hope that the Royal Commission which had been appointed would adopt some such formula as those suggested for effluents discharged into rivers. If anything like a definite way of measuring the standard could be adopted it would be of great use.

Mr. F. W. Stoddart remarked that what was wanted in ideal sewage treatment was an effluent of constant quality, to which no possible objection could be taken. He was interested in a system, of which he was not at liberty to give a full description, which did produce an effluent of this character; and he hoped to see it very generally adopted. The effluent contained practically no saline ammonia, the quantity being ·025 per gallon, the oxygen absorbed in four hours being ·3·

Mr. Archibald admitted that this was a very high standard of purity, much higher than any of the river boards required.

Mr. Stoddart : But we have proved it to be attainable.

### CORROSION OF GAS AND WATER PIPES.

In the course of the proceedings in the Mathematical and Physical Science section

Prof. Fleming called attention to the electrolytic corrosion of gas and water pipes by the earth currents from electric railways and tramways. He stated that in the case of street railways with an uninsulated return circuit no amount of bonding of the rails would entirely prevent earth currents, which might be gathered by gas or water pipes. The danger of corrosion of such pipes would generally be greatest when they extended for some distance parallel with the rails, and the current must pass from the pipe into the surrounding soil. In rapidity of destruction a new clean pipe might possibly succumb even sooner than an old one protected by a dense coating of oxide, but when actual perforation of the pipe did not occur there might be an ageing action that shortened its life.

Prof. S. P. Thompson pointed out that by the use of alternating currents all disturbances could be entirely obliterated, whether magnetic or electrolytic. Even with continuous currents, if the third rail were on or below ground and between the other two, the trouble from both magnetic and chemical effect was very slight. He contended that they were fighting a phantom.

Prof. Rucker objected to the statement of Prof. Thompson. Whatever be the future arrangements of electric tramway systems, they had in the past to fight against actual proposals of electrical engineers and to legislate against threatened dangers.

This concludes our notes of the papers and discussions at the recent meeting, with the exception of the paper contributed by Messrs. Dibdin and Thudichum, which, as will be seen, we are dealing with separately. Sir John Wolfe Barry's address as president of the Mechanical Science section was excellent in many ways, but as we are pressed for space, and as the paper had very little reference to municipal work, we have not reproduced it either in whole or in part.

## ROTHERHAM GASWORKS EXTENSIONS.

### OPENING CEREMONY.

On the 12th inst. an interesting opening ceremony took place in connection with the extensions of the gasworks of the Rotherham Corporation. The works have been erected on an old fair ground, and the road leading thereto has been enclosed for the purpose. The new inclined retort-house is fitted with all the latest improvements for the automatic handling of coal and for the economical consumption of coke in the furnaces where the coal is handled for carbonising processes. Upon the coal being tipped up by the carters in the shed it is passed through a crusher, which crushes the coal into suitable size for passing through other apparatus. After crushing the coal is lifted by buckets upon an endless chain worked by a gas engine. From the elevator, which is 60 ft. high, the coal is conveyed to the bunkers, each of which is capable of holding about 40 tons, and from thence dropped through shoots into the retorts. The coke used for heating the retorts is about 10 per cent. of what is made, whereas in the old system the quantity ranged from 25 to 30 per cent., thus throwing the remainder upon the market for sale, and becoming a means of considerable saving to the corporation. The labour on the inclined retorts is unskilled, any man being able to work the system without previous training, and for the same quantity of coal carbonised one man will be able to do the work of nine under the old system, and the whole charging of the retorts is done in about a quarter of the time. The cost of the retort-house as at present completed ranges up to £14,000, but the retort-house is only half-filled. There are six benches of nine retorts each bench, and the contracts have been let for the setting of six more benches of nine retorts each bench, which will double the present capacity of

the works. The production of gas in the new retort-house will then be 1,800,000 cubic feet, and with the old retorts the total capacity of the works will be 3,000,000 of cubic feet of gas per day. The contractors for the work have been Messrs. Chadwick & Co., Rotherham, and for the ironwork and retort settings, Messrs. R. & J. Dempster, Manchester. Mr. G. Winstanley, of Coventry, is the consulting engineer, and Mr. F. A. Winstanley the resident engineer of the corporation gasworks.

## SANITATION NEAR MARGATE.

### THE CONDITIONS OF VILLAGE LIFE.

A Press representative, who has been inquiring into a serious outbreak of typhoid which has broken out in Garlinge, a village contiguous to Margate and Westgate-on-Sea, and only 3 miles from Ramsgate, has obtained some rather startling information. The enteric fever, he learns, has extended into some neighbouring villages, where investigation has revealed a condition of things which, at the close of the nineteenth century, is simply astounding. Garlinge is stated to contain some 300 inhabitants, who for the greater part are composed of the labouring classes, and mainly work in Ramsgate and Margate.

A gentleman living near the infected village described to the Press representative the sanitary, or rather insanitary, arrangements of the place. The village, he said, was absolutely undrained. All the slop water, &c., was thrown down a sink, which drained into a cesspool. These cesspools were emptied every ten or twelve years, when they got full. He estimated that it would cost £8,000 or £10,000 to drain the place ; and the people were too poor to pay it. An addition of 1d. in the £1, he said, would not produce more than £5 per annum. In conclusion, he said : " Do not mention my name, or they would set fire to my house." Subsequently the pressman visited several of the fever-stricken cottages in Crow Hill. In one of these lay a patient who could not be moved because the hospital was full. There was only one small room downstairs, 6 ft. 6 in. in height, and a pantry and two bedrooms. There were no means of ventilation except through the door, and although the place was very clean and tidy, the odour was not agreeable. The slops and foul water had to go down a " sink " close to the door in the back-yard, which flows into a cesspool common to three cottages.

The gravity of the situation has become more acute in consequence of the hospital being full, as there are no other means of isolation. Up to the 9th inst. there had been fifteen cases of typhoid fever and three deaths, and two fresh cases were reported on Sunday. The district council are adopting active measures to check the progress of the disease. Under the advice of the medical officer disinfectants are being liberally distributed, and an extra staff of men has been engaged to remove the dry ash-pails with regularity every morning. The council have decided to build a new infectious diseases hospital, at a cost of £30,000, on a site near the present hospital, which is insufficient to meet the requirements of the times.

The question of sewering Westgate-on-Sea has been the subject of discussion for several years, and now the council have bowed to the pressure brought to bear by the ratepayers, and a scheme of drainage will be carried out at a cost of £15,000. The work will be commenced early next month, and will be completed by the end of March. The council are also going to drain Birchington. There seems no fault to be found with the water supply. Dr. Robinson has prepared a report on the outbreak, which will be submitted to an early meeting of the district council, and then forwarded to the Local Government Board, who will, no doubt, send down one of the medical inspectors to confer with the local authorities as to the best means of checking the epidemic.

## STRATFORD'S POLLUTED RIVER.

An inquiry, on behalf of the Local Government Board, was held on Wednesday into complaints lodged by the inhabitants of Stratford regarding the polluted state of the Channelsea river, which communicates with the Lea. It was alleged that an outbreak of diphtheria had resulted in Stratford from this pollution, which was caused by the system of sewage disposal. A week ago the Channelsea was almost dried up.

Mr. Corble, for the Lea River Conservators, said they were anxious to establish a system of drainage which would run from Hertford to the outfall, a distance of 27 miles, and a conference with the local authorities would be held next month.

Mr. Gray, M.P. for West Ham, said the local authorities were squabbling, and the Local Government Board ought to decide which is responsible for the purity of the Channelsea, as that river is of the greatest importance to Stratford.

Mr. Angell, borough engineer, West Ham, stated that his corporation were spending £80,000 to open up connection between West Ham sewage works and the metropolitan sewers.

The inspector, before closing his inquiry, stated that he would inspect the area complained of.

# Conditions Necessary for the Successful Purification of Sewage by Bacteria.

By W. J. DIBDIN, F.I.C., F.C.S., &c., and GEORGE THUDICHUM, F.C.S., &c.*

## INTRODUCTION.

### HISTORY OF BACTERIAL PROCESSES.

The recognition of the fact that the natural destruction of waste organic material is effected solely through the agency of living organisms is quite modern. Although casually observed or referred to by various authors, the first and practical attempt to apply such knowledge was in 1884, when the late Metropolitan Board of Works, on the initiative of its scientific advisers, resolved to adopt a system of sewage purification which would produce an effluent readily assailable by oxidising microbes; and also recognised and acted upon the principle that sterilising or destruction of the germs was wrong, and that on the contrary they should be encouraged. This led to the chloride of lime versus manganate controversy, which lasted until 1887, when a return to attempted sterilising proved finally disastrous and the upholders of the microbe theory were vindicated. The contention of the latter, which was actually the first step taken towards solving the problems indicated in the title of this paper, was that for the purposes of deodorising sewage an agent should be employed which would oxidise and destroy the putrescent matters which gave rise to nuisance, but should itself be destroyed in so doing, in order that no antiseptic element should be introduced which could interfere with the action of the oxidising bacteria. In a report made by one of the authors to the Metropolitan Board of Works in January, 1887, and in a paper read before the Institution of Civil Engineers in the same month, this proposition was clearly laid down, and remains now the basis of all bacterial treatment.

The next great step in advance was made by the authorities of the State of Massachusetts, under whose directions elaborate experiments were carried out at Lawrence. This result was to demonstrate absolutely that, given certain specified conditions, practically the whole of the organic matters of sewage could be removed by microbial action in artificial filters. The conclusion arrived at has been quoted, but is of such importance historically that it may well be mentioned here. The mechanical separation of any part of the sewage by straining through sand is but an accident, which under some conditions favourably modifies the result; but the essential conditions are very slow motions of very thin films of liquid over the surface of particles having spaces between them sufficient to allow air to be continually in contact with the films of liquid. With these conditions it is essential that certain bacteria should be present to aid in the process of nitrification. These, we have found, come in the sewage at all times of the year, and the conditions just mentioned appear to be most favourable for their efficient action, and at the same time most destructive to them and to all kinds of bacteria that are in the sewage. The work done at the Lawrence station, however, although of the greatest possible importance from a theoretical point of view, failed to indicate the conditions necessary for the practical application of the knowledge which had been gained, the quantity of sewage (60,000 gallons per diem) which could be treated on an acre of filter-bed being so small that the cost of an installation was quite prohibitive. Acting on the advice of one of the authors, the Main Drainage Committee of the London County Council instituted a series of experiments at the outfall works at Barking creek; and the result, which is now too well known to be gone into in detail, was to demonstrate the practicability of purifying large quantities of sewage effluent on an area of filter, which would make the adoption of the method possible from the economic point of view. The consideration of various data in connection with these experiments led to the belief that the crude sewage itself might be similarly treated, and experiments in this direction soon showed that such a belief was well founded.

In the meantime others had not been idle. Mr. Cameron, the city surveyor of Exeter, had been elaborating his ideas with regard to the preliminary treatment of crude sewage by means of anaerobic organisms, and had successfully demonstrated the possibility of such use being applied practically. Lowcock, also in this country, had been trying to purify sewage effluents by means of air forced by artificial means into a filter through which the effluent was constantly running; and Waring, in America, was perfecting a filter whereby the solid residue retained in a filter, after the passage of a quantity of crude sewage, was oxidised by bacterial agency, aëration being obtained by a blast of air. Colonel Ducat also devised a filter in which the constant aëration was supposed to be kept up by natural means consequent on the method of construction. Others have also experimented, chiefly in the direction of ascertaining the most suitable material for filling the filler-beds, the general method followed being that laid down as a result of the work at Barking creek.

* A paper read in Section G (Mechanical Science) of the British Association.

## GENERAL CONDITIONS.

Speaking generally, the following are the points which the authors have found to be most noteworthy of the conditions which must be observed to ensure success—viz.,—

(1) Air supply, or its absence in the case of the septic tank.
(2) Temperature.
(3) Admission or exclusion of light.
(4) Reaction to test paper of the sewage to be purified.
(5) Time of contact.
(6) Nature of bed material.
(7) Depth of bed.

### (1) AIR SUPPLY.

This question must be considered from two distinct points of view, according to the method of preliminary purification to be adopted. In either case the final treatment is the same. Acting in the presence of a free supply of atmospheric oxygen, the aerobic organisms present in a bacterial filter-bed are able to liquefy, break down and oxidise the solid organic matters suspended in sewage, without such decomposition being accompanied by any of the ordinary phenomena of putrefaction. To such an extent is this action carried under favourable circumstances, that within two hours an effluent is produced which contains considerable quantities of nitric acid, 0·5 grains of nitric nitrogen, and in which nitrification is afterwards continued at an extremely rapid rate. In order to attain these results the bed which receives the crude sewage must be kept very open, the interstices being large. In practice the bed material, whether burnt ballast, coke or stone, has been found most efficacious when of a size varying from ½ in. diameter at the smallest to ½ in. or 5 in. at the largest. Smaller material than that which is rejected by a sieve having a mesh of ¼ in. square does not leave the bed sufficiently open, not only because the air has not free admission, but also because the solid particles held in suspension in the sewage are unable to work their way into the body of the bed.

This necessity for full aëration has been recognised by all who have attempted to utilise the aerobic organisms. In Colonel Ducat's filter it is intended to gain the object sought for by building the containing walls of drain pipes, in order that air shall have free access from all sides. Lowcock proposes to arrive at the same condition by pumping air into the body of the filter-bed, allowing the same effluent, which in his case is alone employed, to pass continuously. Waring, in America, runs crude sewage through the filter until the latter is fully charged with sludge, which is then oxidised and destroyed by forcing a current of air through it. In the method adopted at Sutton the object is attained by emptying the bed completely after each charge, whereby, as the water leaves the bed, air necessarily enters.

In all these cases it is clear that a free air supply enters largely into the success of the operations; in the case of the anaerobic processes the conditions are not so plain. The septic tank, as worked at Belleisle, Exeter, is covered in with brickwork and cement; yet, on the authority of Dr. Sims Woodhead, the aerobic organisms increase during the passage of the sewage through the tank in a greater proportion than the anaerobic, a fact which would tend to show that air is not absolutely excluded. The same anaerobic action may also be effected in tanks which are open to the air, or even in a flowing river, as was the case with the Thames in 1884-87, when the foul condition of the water was undoubtedly due to the action or organisms working with an insufficient air supply. It is therefore a question whether sewage, if left to itself, without artificial aids or protection of any kind, will not always effect the first stage of its purification with the aid of anaerobic, or, at all events, of mixed organisms; whilst if the aerobic action is to preponderate some artificial assistance must be given. Regarding the greater desirability of the one method as compared with the other, the authors are not prepared at present to express an opinion; experience alone can solve this question. The fact remains that both systems effect the result aimed at.

### (2) TEMPERATURE.

The greater number of micro-organisms can only flourish within a very small intermediate range—namely, from about 50 deg. Fahr. to 100 deg. Fahr. Some there are which can exercise their life functions at the temperature at which water freezes, whilst others can exist when the thermometer registers as high as 150 deg. Fahr., and are killed at relatively high temperatures. The bulk, however, flourish at the degree of warmth first indicated. It will be seen at once how important this factor is, in view of the fact that artificial warming of a sewage purification plant is practically impossible, owing to the great expense involved. The effect of the seasons upon the process going on in a bacteria-bed or a septic tank forms a most interesting study. The experiments made by the Massachusetts authorities first showed that organic matter was stored in the filter-bed in the winter months and destroyed by nitrification, as the atmospheric temperature increased with the coming spring. The authors have shown how, in the case of the septic tank, the amount of free ammonia is increased in cold weather, owing to the inability of the organisms to carry the process further; whilst in summer, in spite of the destruction of the suspended organic impurities, the free ammonia is reduced in quantity.

The problem of keeping the temperature of the beds well above the freezing point is partly solved by the sewage itself being in the winter time considerably warmer than the external air. The action taking place in the body of the bacteria-bed will also tend in the right direction. A further point, at all events so far as the Sutton system is concerned, is the short time during which the sewage must be submitted to bacterial influences. Since the whole process occupies only some three or four hours in each bed, there is no time for such a bulk of sewage to cool down appreciably. Effluent from the septic tank at Exeter, entering the bacteria-beds at a temperature of 47·3 deg. Fahr. on an average, escaped at 48 deg. Fahr. This was in the earlier part of April, 1897, the weather being very cold, with frequent snowstorms. Judging from the experience gained in the Massachussetts trials, and at Barking, Sutton and Exeter, it does not appear that there is danger of the temperature of bacteria-beds in this country falling to a point sufficiently low to destroy the vitality of the organisms. Thus in the case of Massachussetts, although there was ice over the surface of the filters during a considerable period, yet a good effluent was constantly produced. The chief effect observed was the non-production of nitric acid, which, however, was again formed when the warm weather returned, the nitrogenous matters having remained in great part stored in the filter. At Barking, during the severe frost of February, 1895, similar results were obtained, the filter continuing its work, although for six weeks it was covered with a sheet of ice.

In this connection it may be well to point out a danger that may arise from too careful distribution of the sewage over the surface of a bed. In such a case the incoming sewage itself may be frozen and fail to penetrate the bed at all, as was actually the case with an experimental filter on another plan at Sutton, even during the extremely mild winter of 1897-98.

### (3) LIGHT.

The following series of experiments will prove interesting, as showing that the organisms chiefly concerned in the aerobic purification of sewage seem to be unaffected by conditions of light or darkness. Two vessels were taken, of similar shape and size, and fitted with broken glass as a bed material; the one was left bare and fully exposed to the light, whilst the other was covered all over with black light-proof paper and fitted with a cap of similar material. Both being used as bacteria-beds, all the conditions except the exclusion of light being precisely the same, the following were the results:—

| | Light. | | | Dark. | | |
|---|---|---|---|---|---|---|
| No. of Filling. | Free. | Ammonia Albuminoid. | Oxygen absorbed in Four Hours. | Free. | Ammonia Albuminoid. | Oxygen absorbed in Four Hours. |
| 25 | — | — | 0·82 | — | — | 0·76 |
| 29 | — | — | 0·71 | — | — | 0·90 |
| 33 | — | — | 1·08 | — | — | 1·08 |
| 37 | 1·64 | 0·06 | 0·65 | 1·47 | 0·05 | 0·55 |
| 41 | 1·23 | 0·056 | — | 1·23 | 0·056 | — |
| 58 | 1·47 | 0·056 | 0·91 | 1·47 | 0·056 | 0·91 |
| 62 | 1·68 | 0·07 | 1·24 | 1·89 | 0·08 | 1·24 |
| 66 | 1·68 | 0·07 | 0·75 | 1·68 | 0·06 | 0·75 |
| 70 | 1·47 | 0·06 | 0·76 | 1·39 | 0·06 | 0·76 |
| Average | 1·53 | 0·062 | 0·86 | 1·52 | 0·06 | 0·83 |

It will be seen that equally good results were obtained by either method.

### (4) REACTION.

The most favourable condition of the sewage for bacterial activity is that of very slight alkalinity, a condition which occurs naturally in ordinary domestic sewage. Occasional variations, even though relatively large, appear to exert but little prejudicial influence, but a continuance of excess of either acid or alkali will put a bacteria bed out of action for a time. Sewage containing the highly acid liquor obtained from the preliminary treatment of iron for galvanising will yield to a very considerable extent to bacterial influences; but if its use be continuous the purification effected becomes gradually less, and the bed requires a prolonged period of rest. Very alkaline effluents, such as those produced by the use of lime in excessive quantities, are very liable to putrefy instead of becoming purified by oxidising organisms. The oxidation of iron is, of course, effected by direct combination with the oxygen of the atmosphere, the bacteria playing but a small part, if any, in this process. In the case of the dilution of either acid or alkaline sewage a considerable number of reactions are brought into play, with the result of more or less neutralising the deleterious action of the original crude liquor, and thus rendering it more susceptible to bacterial influences.

### (5) TIME OF CONTACT.

This point constitutes the main difference between the

system now known as the "Sutton" and the former method of intermittent downward filtration. It was found necessary for the sewage to be subjected to the action of microbes under proper conditions for a certain period of time. If this were not allowed the purification was incomplete; when it was greatly exceeded the aeration and consequent recuperation of the bed was affected disadvantageously. For this reason the bacteria-beds are locked, and the sewage kept in them for a period of about two hours; the effluent being then allowed to escape, the organic matter held in the bed is vigorously attacked by the organisms under the most favourable circumstances of combined dampness and air supply, and the bed is thus prepared for a further charge. The necessity for the locking has been proved by numerous experiments, from which also the most suitable time limit has been arrived at.

The work done during the empty period can be well demonstrated by taking the drainings at intervals, and estimating the amount of oxygen absorbed from permanganate and the quantity of nitric acid present. It will be found that the former steadily diminishes whilst the latter increases. For example, five minutes after opening the valve the following results were obtained:—

| | |
|---|---|
| Albuminoid ammonia ... ... ... ... ... | 0·100 |
| Oxygen absorbed in four hours ... ... ... | 0·280 |
| Nitrogen as nitrites ... ... ... ... | 0·224 |
| Nitrogen as nitrates ... ... ... ... | 0·290 |

One hour after practically empty :—

| | |
|---|---|
| Albuminoid ammonia ... ... ... ... ... | 0·070 |
| Oxygen absorbed in four hours ... ... ... | 0·112 |
| Nitrogen as nitrites ... ... ... ... | 0·326 |
| Nitrogen as nitrates ... ... ... ... | 0·499 |

The falling of the oxygen absorbed figure is well shown in the following table:—

*Oxygen absorbed from Permanganate in four hours by Samples taken at various periods during Filter Discharge at Belleisle, Exeter.*

| | Oct. 14, 1897. Filter No. 2. | Oct. 15, 1897. Filter No. 1. |
|---|---|---|
| 2 minutes after discharge ... | 0·400 | 0·372 |
| 5 " ... | 0·395 | — |
| 15 " ... | 0·360 | 0·305 |
| 25 " ... | 0·251 | — |
| 30 " ... | — | 0·214 |
| 35 " ... | 0·214 | — |
| 45 " ... | 0·210 | 0·203 |
| 55 " ... | 0·167 | — |
| 60 " ... | — | 0·136 |
| 65 " ... | 0·140 | — |
| 75 " ... | 0·134 | 0·125. |
| 85 " ... | 0·130 | — |
| 90 " ... | — | 0·210 |
| 95 " ... | 0·130 | — |
| 105 " ... | 0·126 | 0·125 |
| 115 " ... | 0·120 | — |
| 125 " ... | 0·120 | — |

Figures represent grains per gallon.

### (6) NATURE OF BED MATERIAL.

Many experiments have been made with a view to ascertaining the best material with which to construct bacteria-beds. It is clear that in many cases the local conditions would render the use of one or other special substances very advantageous from the point of view of original cost of installation; burnt ballast when the land is clay, broken slate in some districts, gravel in others, and so forth. The general experience of the authors is that coarsely-broken coke or burnt ballast indifferently may be used for the first treatment by "coarse grain beds;" whilst for "fine grain beds" the best material is undoubtedly coke, or pan breeze or cinder. This was first indicated at Barking Creek in 1892, where the degree of purification effected by various substances was as follows — :

| | | | | | |
|---|---|---|---|---|---|
| Burnt ballast ... | ... | ... | ... | ... | 43·3 per cent. |
| Sand ... | ... | ... | ... | ... | 46·6 " |
| Pea ballast ... | ... | ... | ... | ... | 52·3 " |
| Coke (pan) breeze ... | ... | ... | ... | ... | 62·2 " |

At Sutton in 1894 the following degrees of purification were indicated: —

| | | | | | |
|---|---|---|---|---|---|
| Sand ... | ... | ... | ... | ... | 36·5 per cent. |
| Coke breeze ... | ... | ... | ... | ... | 41·5 " |

and in April, 1895:—

| | | | | | |
|---|---|---|---|---|---|
| Sand ... | ... | ... | ... | ... | 62·1 per cent. |
| Coke breeze ... | ... | ... | ... | ... | 74·1 " |

The average purification effected by the 1-acre bed at Barking Creek was 75 per cent. to 80 per cent.

The authors have recently made a special series of experiments with coke, coal and glass, with a view to ascertaining not only the purification effected by each, but also the water capacity of the beds, this being a matter of great importance as determining the area of bed required to deal with a given volume of sewage. The three beds were similar in shape and size, and the materials were riddled through the same mesh, the sewage effluent placed on them being also the same for all three at each charging. From the following table it will be seen that the results obtained from the use of coke breeze were greatly superior to those produced by coal or glass :—

# BILSTON W

CREGEEN'S AIR INLET

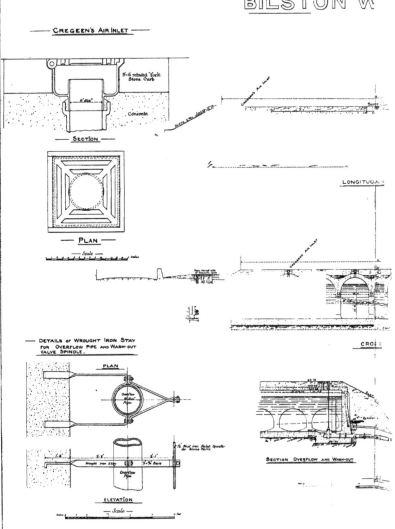

SECTION

PLAN

Scale

DETAILS OF WROUGHT IRON STAY
FOR OVERFLOW PIPE AND WASH-OUT
VALVE SPINDLE.

PLAN

ELEVATION

Scale

LONGITUDINAL

CROSS

SECTION OVERFLOW AND WASH-OUT

# ATER SUPPLY.

## RESERVOIR

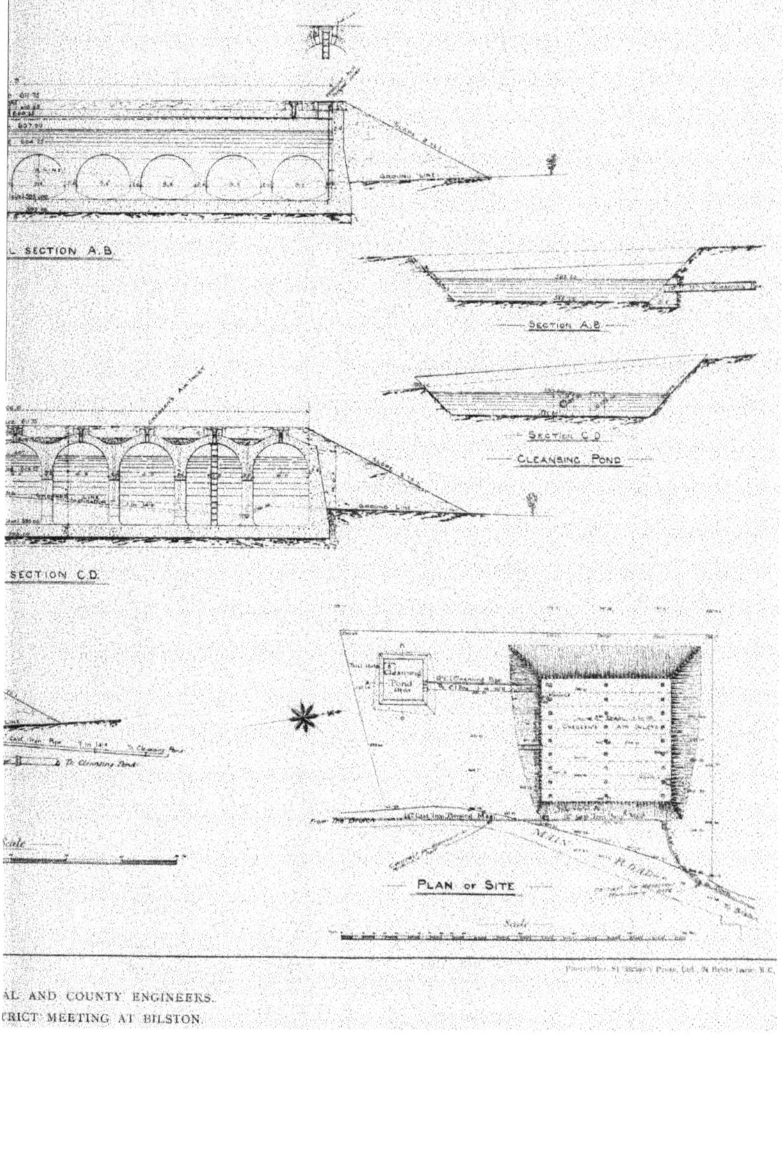

L SECTION A.B
Ground Line
Ground Line
SECTION C.D.
Section A.B
Section C.D
Cleansing Pond
To Cleansing Pond
Scale
Plan of Site
Main Road
Scale

Photolitho. St Bride's Press, Ltd., 24 Bride Lane, E.C.

AL AND COUNTY ENGINEERS.
RICT MEETING AT BILSTON.

*Free Ammonia.*

| No. of Filling. | Coke. | Coal. | Glass. |
|---|---|---|---|
| 4 | 1·05 | 2·65 | — |
| 6 | 0·88 | 1·89 | 2·27 |
| 10 | 1·23 | 2·73 | 3·06 |
| 13 | 1·57 | 2·52 | 2·53 |
| 17 | 6·30 | 8·45 | 7·40 |
| 21 | — | — | — |
| 25 | — | — | — |
| 29 | — | — | — |
| 33 | — | — | — |
| 37 | 0·76 | 0·97 | 1·60 |
| 41 | 0·18 | 0·77 | 1·23 |
| 58 | 0·63 | 1·26 | 1·47 |
| 62 | 1·26 | 1·47 | 1·89 |
| 66 | 1·34 | 0·67 | 1·68 |
| 70 | 0·36 | 0·63 | 1·43 |
| Mean | 1·41 | 2·18 | 2·47 |

*Albuminoid Ammonia.*

| No. of Filling. | Coke. | Coal. | Glass. |
|---|---|---|---|
| 4 | 0·060 | 0·005 | — |
| 6 | 0·040 | 0·060 | 0·110 |
| 10 | 0·050 | 0·140 | 0·160 |
| 13 | 0·070 | 0·200 | 0·270 |
| 17 | 0·060 | 0·120 | 0·130 |
| 21 | — | — | — |
| 25 | — | — | — |
| 29 | — | — | — |
| 33 | — | — | — |
| 37 | 0·050 | 0·060 | 0·050 |
| 41 | 0·035 | 0·056 | 0·056 |
| 58 | 0·031 | 0·042 | 0·056 |
| 62 | 0·060 | 0·070 | 0·080 |
| 66 | 0·050 | 0·060 | 0·080 |
| 70 | 0·040 | 0·040 | 0·060 |
| Mean | 0·050 | 0·086 | 0·103 |

*Oxygen Absorbed in Four Hours.*

| No. of Filling. | Coke. | Coal. | Glass. |
|---|---|---|---|
| 4 | 0·890 | 1·300 | 1·780 |
| 6 | 0·650 | 0·950 | 1·360 |
| 10 | 0·710 | 1·390 | 1·470 |
| 13 | 0·820 | 1·640 | 2·020 |
| 17 | 0·540 | 0·980 | 1·030 |
| 21 | 0·540 | 1·050 | 0·820 |
| 25 | 0·710 | 1·090 | 0·790 |
| 29 | 0·600 | 0·820 | 0·660 |
| 33 | 0·680 | 1·130 | 1·050 |
| 37 | 0·440 | 0·760 | 0·600 |
| 41 | — | — | — |
| 58 | 0·560 | 0·760 | 0·910 |
| 62 | 0·810 | 1·130 | 1·240 |
| 66 | 0·700 | 0·920 | 0·750 |
| 70 | 0·650 | 0·970 | 0·760 |
| Mean | 0·660 | 1·060 | 1·090 |

Figures represent grains per gallon.

Taking the impurity in the coke breeze effluent as unity, the following ratios are arrived at :—

| | Coke. | Coal. | Glass. |
|---|---|---|---|
| Free ammonia | 1·00 | 1·55 | 1·75 |
| Albuminoid ammonia | 1·00 | 1·72 | 2·06 |
| Oxygen absorbed | 1·00 | 1·60 | 1·65 |

In this series the superiority of the coke breeze is plainly demonstrated, every possible care having been taken to ensure exactly similar conditions for all three beds.

The experiments regarding water capacity also placed coke first, the positions of glass and coal, however, being reversed from those shown in the table of quality. After many measurements, extending over seventy-two fillings of each bed, the water capacities were found to be as follows :—

Coke ... ... ... 40·4 per cent. of total cubic contents.
Glass ... ... ... 39·0 „ „
Coal ... ... ... 29·9 „ „

In these experiments, therefore, the coke did not only produce a better result, but with the same total volume of bed purified more sewage, as follows :—

Sewage purified by coke being taken at 100; then sewage purified by glass equals 96·4; and sewage purified by coal equals 74·1

Put into other words, 4 acres of coal filter of a given depth would be required to treat the sewage which could be dealt with by 3 acres of coke breeze of the same depth.

Experiments on a larger scale have been tried, using as materials for coarse grain beds broken granite, chalk and slate. In each case considerable purification was effected, but the results did not compare favourably with those obtained from burnt ballast. The main object, however, the removal and destruction of the sludge, was accomplished, and the purification could be satisfactorily completed by the fine bed.

Having regard to these various results, it is evident that the question of efficiency of a material resolves itself into the character of its surface ; thus coal, &c., presents a minimum surface per unit acre, whilst coke may be taken as affording a maximum surface for the same area.

(7) DEPTH OF BED.

With regard to this point it is difficult to speak with any certainty. Experience of working on a large scale has led the authors to believe that the maximum limit of depth for the best results to be obtained is about 3 ft. to 3 ft. 6 in. Beds have worked well at a depth of 4 ft. to 5 ft., but the alteration of a bed from 3 ft. 6 in. to 5 ft. was accompanied by some reduction in the quality of the effluent produced. On the other hand, a laboratory experiment with a bed 8 ft. in depth appears to show that such increase is an advantage, samples drawn at each foot down exhibit a steadily-increasing degree of purification.

*Oxygen Absorbed in Four Hours.*

| No. of Filling. | 1 ft. | 2 ft. | 3 ft. | 4 ft. | 5 ft. | 6 ft. | 7 ft. | 8 ft. |
|---|---|---|---|---|---|---|---|---|
| 32 | 1·01 | 1·01 | 0·86 | 0·71 | 0·71 | 0·56 | 0·06 | 0·61 |
| 45 | 0·68 | 0·69 | 0·52 | 0·46 | 0·52 | 0·46 | 0·46 | 0·34 |
| 62 | 1·09 | 0·98 | 0·86 | 0·74 | 0·69 | 0·52 | 0·40 | 0·34 |
| 99 | 0·89 | 0·78 | 0·39 | 0·39 | 0·33 | 0·33 | 0·22 | 0·22 |
| 130 | 1·28 | 1·22 | 1·15 | 1·10 | 1·10 | 0·99 | 0·82 | 0·82 |
| 146 | 0·88 | 0·82 | 0·88 | 1·00 | 1·00 | 0·88 | 0·82 | 0·76 |
| 163 | 2·22 | 1·79 | 1·57 | 1·47 | 1·47 | 1·31 | 0·98 | 0·87 |
| 192 | 1·89 | 1·70 | 1·64 | 1·38 | 1·22 | 0·96 | 0·74 | 0·74 |
| 228 | 3·48 | 3·05 | 2·57 | 2·19 | 1·98 | 1·71 | 1·44 | 0·86 |

*Nitrogen as Nitrites and Nitrates.*

| No. of Filling. | 1 ft. | 2 ft. | 3 ft. | 4 ft. | 5 ft. | 6 ft. | 7 ft. | 8 ft. |
|---|---|---|---|---|---|---|---|---|
| 32 | 0·00 | 0·00 | 0·00 | T | T | 0·08 | 0·10 | 0·30 |
| 45 | 0·00 | 0·00 | 0·00 | T | T | 0·12 | 0·14 | 0·22 |
| 62 | 0·00 | 0·00 | 0·00 | 0·00 | 0·00 | T | T | HT |
| 99 | 0·00 | 0·00 | 0·00 | ST | T | T | HT | T |
| 130 | 0·00 | 0·00 | 0·00 | 0·09 | 0·23 | 0·31 | 0·46 | 0·64 |
| 146 | 0·02 | 0·03 | 0·06 | 0·32 | 0·21 | 0·25 | 0·35 | 0·25 |
| 163 | 0·24 | 0·08 | T | 0·03 | 0·11 | 0·34 | 2·00 | 2·94 |
| 192 | 0·00 | 0·00 | 0·00 | 0·00 | 0·00 | 0·12 | 1·02 | 1·70 |
| 228 | 0·00 | 0·00 | 0·00 | 0·00 | T | T | 0·13 | 1·28 |

Figures are grains per gallon. Abbreviations : T, Trace ; HT, heavy trace ; ST, slight trace.

In this special matter of depth, however, it is difficult to produce in a laboratory conditions comparable with those obtaining outside, owing to the necessarily small diameter of the bed, and the therefore abnormally large proportion of side to body of filter. It may be, therefore, that the experiment, if repeated on working lines, would yield a very different result. The above table is put forward to show what was obtained, but must not at present be taken as expressing the authors' views on the matter.

# THE NATIONAL REGISTRATION OF PLUMBERS.

## MEETING IN MANCHESTER.

Mr. Lees Knowles, M.P., who has charge of the Plumbers' Registration Bill in the House of Commons, speaking on Monday, at Manchester, on the occasion of the distribution of prizes by the Lord Mayor of Manchester, in connection with the competition and exhibition of plumbers' work in April last, held under the auspices of the council for Manchester and district for the National Registration of Plumbers, said that all parties in the House were committed to the principle of the Bill, the main object of which was to afford additional safeguards to the public health by enabling persons employing plumbers to select, when they desired to do so, those who had given evidence of their qualification for plumbers' work. There were some opponents to the Bill, but when it was explained that it was not in any way intended to create a monopoly they withdrew their opposition. The Bill conferred, as it were, a degree upon plumbers, and what they wanted was that this degree of registered plumbers should be recognised by the law. They had numerous illustrations of registration. Solicitors were registered in 1843, chemists in 1852, the general medical council in 1858, dentists in 1878, and veterinary surgeons in 1881, and he could not help but think that this subject was worthy of consideration. He was speaking without experience. He had steered five Bills through the House, and he advised them to get representative meetings such as that. What they should do was to submit a representation to the Government, and say that a Bill for the registration of plumbers was not merely an advantage for them but for the country. He was asked to take up the Bill in 1891, and in 1892 a select committee was appointed. A blue-book was published, and valuable information could be got from it.

**Glasgow.**—At a meeting of the Telephone Committee of the corporation, held on Thursday, a letter was presented from the Postmaster-General, in reply to the city's renewed application for a corporation telephone licence, stating that the Government had under their serious consideration the report of the Select Committee on Municipal Telephones, and that it was unnecessary meantime to receive any deputation from the corporation. The committee instructed a reply to this communication to the effect that, as the time was very limited and much would require to be given for powers for the corporation to work the telephone system, it was highly desirable that the Postmaster-General should at once give Glasgow a licence or assurance that a licence will be given.— Recent minutes of the Parks Committee contained a reference to the anonymous offer of a gift of £12,000 towards the erection of new public halls for the Springburn and Cowlairs district and a winter garden in the Springburn Park.

### Free Ammonia.

| No. of Filling. | Coke. | Coal. | Glass. |
|---|---|---|---|
| 4 | 1·05 | 2·65 | — |
| 6 | 0·88 | 1·80 | 2·27 |
| 10 | 1·23 | 2·73 | 3·06 |
| 13 | 1·57 | 2·52 | 2·83 |
| 17 | 6·30 | 8·45 | 7·40 |
| 21 | — | — | — |
| 25 | — | — | — |
| 29 | — | — | — |
| 33 | — | — | — |
| 37 | 0·76 | 0·97 | 1·69 |
| 41 | 0·18 | 0·77 | 1·23 |
| 58 | 0·63 | 1·26 | 1·47 |
| 62 | 1·26 | 1·47 | 1·89 |
| 66 | 1·34 | 0·67 | 1·68 |
| 70 | 0·36 | 0·63 | 1·43 |
| Mean | 1·41 | 2·18 | 2·47 |

### Albuminoid Ammonia.

| No. of Filling. | Coke. | Coal. | Glass. |
|---|---|---|---|
| 4 | 0·060 | 0·095 | — |
| 6 | 0·040 | 0·060 | 0·110 |
| 10 | 0·050 | 0·140 | 0·160 |
| 13 | 0·070 | 0·200 | 0·270 |
| 17 | 0·060 | 0·120 | 0·130 |
| 21 | — | — | — |
| 25 | — | — | — |
| 29 | — | — | — |
| 33 | — | — | — |
| 37 | 0·050 | 0·060 | 0·050 |
| 41 | 0·035 | 0·056 | 0·056 |
| 58 | 0·031 | 0·042 | 0·056 |
| 62 | 0·060 | 0·070 | 0·080 |
| 66 | 0·050 | 0·060 | 0·060 |
| 70 | 0·040 | 0·040 | 0·060 |
| Mean | 0·050 | 0·086 | 0·103 |

### Oxygen Absorbed in Four Hours.

| No. of Filling. | Coke. | Coal. | Glass. |
|---|---|---|---|
| 4 | 0·890 | 1·300 | 1·780 |
| 6 | 0·650 | 0·950 | 1·360 |
| 10 | 0·710 | 1·290 | 1·470 |
| 13 | 0·820 | 0·980 | 2·020 |
| 17 | 0·540 | 0·980 | 1·030 |
| 21 | 0·540 | 1·050 | 0·820 |
| 25 | 0·710 | 1·090 | 0·790 |
| 29 | 0·600 | 0·920 | 0·600 |
| 33 | 0·680 | 1·130 | 1·050 |
| 37 | 0·440 | 0·760 | 0·600 |
| 41 | — | — | — |
| 58 | 0·560 | 0·700 | 0·910 |
| 62 | 0·810 | 1·130 | 1·240 |
| 66 | 0·700 | 0·920 | 0·750 |
| 70 | 0·650 | 0·970 | 0·760 |
| Mean | 0·660 | 1·060 | 1·090 |

Figures represent grains per gallon.

Taking the impurity in the coke breeze effluent as unity, the following ratios are arrived at:—

| | Coke. | Coal. | Glass. |
|---|---|---|---|
| Free ammonia ... ... ... | 1·00 | 1·55 | 1·75 |
| Albuminoid ammonia ... ... | 1·00 | 1·72 | 2·06 |
| Oxygen absorbed... ... ... | 1·00 | 1·60 | 1·65 |

In this series the superiority of the coke breeze is plainly demonstrated, every possible care having been taken to ensure exactly similar conditions for all three beds.

The experiments regarding water capacity also placed coke first, the positions of glass and coal, however, being reversed from those shown in the table of quality. After many measurements, extending over seventy-two fillings of each bed, the water capacities were found to be as follows:—

| | | | |
|---|---|---|---|
| Coke ... | ... | ... | 40·4 per cent. of total cubic contents. |
| Glass ... | ... | ... | 39·0 " " |
| Coal ... | ... | ... | 29·9 " " |

In these experiments, therefore, the coke did not only produce a better result, but also with the same total volume of bed purified more sewage, as follows:—

Sewage purified by coke equals 100; then sewage purified by glass equals 96·4; and sewage purified by coal equals 74·1

Put into other words, 4 acres of coal filter of a given depth would be required to treat the sewage which could be dealt with by 3 acres of coke breeze of the same depth.

Experiments on a larger scale have been tried, using as materials for coase grain beds broken granite, chalk and slate.

In each case considerable purification was effected, but the results did not compare favourably with those obtained from burnt ballast. The main object, however, the removal and destruction of the sludge, was accomplished, and the purification could be satisfactorily completed by the fine bed.

Having regard to these various results, it is evident that the question of efficiency of a material resolves itself into the character of its surface; thus coal, &c., presents a minimum surface per unit area, whilst coke may be taken as affording a maximum surface for the same area.

#### (7) DEPTH OF BED.

With regard to this point it is difficult to speak with any certainty. Experience of working on a large scale has led the authors to believe that the maximum limit of depth for the best results to be obtained is about 3 ft. to 3 ft. 6 in. Beds have worked well at a depth of 4 ft. to 5 ft., but the alteration of a bed from 3 ft. 6 in. to 5 ft. was accompanied by some reduction in the quality of the effluent produced. On the other hand, a laboratory experiment with a bed 8 ft. in depth appears to show that such increase is an advantage, samples drawn at each foot down exhibit a steadily-increasing degree of purification.

### Oxygen Absorbed in Four Hours.

| No. of Filling. | 1 ft. | 2 ft. | 3 ft. | 4 ft. | 5 ft. | 6 ft. | 7 ft. | 8 ft. |
|---|---|---|---|---|---|---|---|---|
| 32 | 1·01 | 1·01 | 0·86 | 0·71 | 0·71 | 0·56 | 0·66 | 0·61 |
| 45 | 0·68 | 0·69 | 0·52 | 0·46 | 0·52 | 0·16 | 0·46 | 0·3 t |
| 62 | 1·09 | 0·98 | 0·86 | 0·74 | 0·69 | 0·52 | 0·40 | 0·34 |
| 99 | 0·89 | 0·78 | 0·39 | 0·39 | 0·33 | 0·33 | 0·22 | 0·22 |
| 130 | 1·28 | 1·22 | 1·15 | 1·10 | 0·99 | 0·82 | 0·82 | |
| 146 | 0·88 | 0·82 | 0·88 | 1·00 | 1·00 | 0·88 | 0·82 | 0·76 |
| 163 | 2·22 | 1·79 | 1·57 | 1·47 | 1·47 | 1·31 | 0·98 | 0·87 |
| 192 | 1·89 | 1·70 | 1·64 | 1·38 | 1·22 | 0·96 | 0·74 | 0·74 |
| 228 | 3·48 | 3·05 | 2·57 | 2·19 | 1·98 | 1·71 | 1·44 | 0·86 |

### Nitrogen as Nitrites and Nitrates.

| No. of Filling. | 1 ft. | 2 ft. | 3 ft. | 4 ft. | 5 ft. | 6 ft. | 7 ft. | 8 ft. |
|---|---|---|---|---|---|---|---|---|
| 32 | 0·00 | 0·00 | 0·00 | T | T | 0·08 | 0·10 | 0·30 |
| 45 | 0·00 | 0·00 | 0·00 | T | T | 0·12 | 0·14 | 0·22 |
| 62 | 0·00 | 0·00 | 0·00 | 0·00 | 0·00 | T | T | HT |
| 99 | 0·00 | 0·00 | 0·00 | ST | T | T | HT | T |
| 130 | 0·00 | 0·00 | 0·00 | 0·00 | 0·23 | 0·31 | 0·46 | 0·64 |
| 146 | 0·02 | 0·03 | 0·06 | 0 32 | 0·21 | 0·25 | 0·35 | 0·25 |
| 163 | 0·24 | 0·08 | T | 0·03 | 0·11 | 0·34 | 2·00 | 2·94 |
| 192 | 0·00 | 0·00 | 0·00 | 0·00 | 0·0 | 0·12 | 1·02 | 1·70 |
| 228 | 0·00 | 0·00 | 0·00 | 0·00 | T | T | 0·13 | 1·28 |

Figures are grains per gallon. Abbreviations: HT, heavy trace; ST, slight trace.

In this special matter of depth, however, it is difficult to produce in a laboratory conditions comparable with those obtaining outside, owing to the necessarily small diameter of the bed, and the therefore abnormally large proportion of side to body of filter. It may be, therefore, that the experiment, if repeated on working lines, would yield a very different result. The above table is put forward to show what was obtained, but must not at present be taken as expressing the authors' views on the matter.

## THE NATIONAL REGISTRATION OF PLUMBERS.

### MEETING IN MANCHESTER.

Mr. Lees Knowles, M.P., who has charge of the Plumbers' Registration Bill in the House of Commons, speaking on Monday, at Manchester, on the occasion of the distribution of prizes by the Lord Mayor of Manchester, in connection with the competition and exhibition of plumbers' work in April last, held under the auspices of the council for Manchester and district for the National Registration of Plumbers, said that all parties in the House were committed to the principle of the Bill, the main object of which was to afford additional safeguards to the public health by enabling persons employing plumbers to select, when they desired to do so, those who had given evidence of their qualification for plumbers' work. There were some opponents to the Bill, but when it was explained that it was not in any way intended to create a monopoly they withdrew their opposition. The Bill conferred, as it were, a degree upon plumbers, and what they wanted was that this degree of registered plumbers should be recognised by the law. They had numerous illustrations of registration. Solicitors were registered in 1843, chemists in 1852, the general medical council in 1858, dentists in 1878, and veterinary surgeons in 1881, and he could not help but think that this subject was worthy of consideration. He was speaking without experience. He had steered five Bills through the House, and he advised them to get representative meetings such as that. What they should do was to submit a representation to the Government, and say that a Bill for the registration of plumbers was not merely an advantage for them but for the country. He was asked to pilot the Bill in 1891, and in 1892 a select committee was appointed. A blue-book was published, and valuable information could be got from it.

**Glasgow.**—At a meeting of the Telephone Committee of the corporation, held on Thursday, a letter was presented from the Postmaster-General, in reply to the city's renewed application for a corporation telephone licence, stating that the Government had under their serious consideration the report of the Select Committee on Municipal Telephones, and that it was unnecessary meantime to receive any deputation from the corporation. The committee instructed a reply to this communication to the effect that, as the time was very near when notice would require to be given for powers for the corporation to work the telephone system, it was highly desirable that the Postmaster-General should at once give Glasgow a license or assurance that a license will be given.— Recent minutes of the Parks Committee contained a reference to the anonymous offer of a gift of £12 000 towards the erection of new public halls for the Springburn and Cowlairs district and a winter garden in the Springburn Park.

# Some Annual Municipal Engineering Records.

## STOCKPORT : KENSINGTON : GLOUCESTER.

Judging from the report of the borough surveyor (Mr. John Atkinson), the past municipal year at Stockport has again been an extremely busy one. The report, which covers some eighty pages, contains much information of an interesting character. It is, as usual, exceedingly well arranged. At present the population of Southport stands at 81,000, the number of inhabited houses being about 18,006 ; the rateable value is £284,159. The borough has an area of 2,200 acres, the number of people to the acre being estimated at 36·8 ; in 1897 the death rate was 21·6 per 1,000. The average rateable value per head of the population is £3 10s. 1d. Parks and other open spaces extend over 62 acres. There are now 1,907 lamps erected and kept lighted within the borough, thirty-six having been added this year. As 54 miles of public highways and about 12 miles of streets and roads are provided for, the average distance apart throughout the entire borough is about 62 yards. Within recent years, however, the lamps have been placed at an average distance of 40 yards. The cost per lamp fixed averages about £4 10s. The Gas Committee charge £2 15s. 3d. per lamp per annum for lighting, cleaning and maintenance. An inquiry, it may be mentioned, was held on April 1, 1897, and another on May 4th of the same year, by an inspector of the Local Government Board into an application for sanction to borrow £124,882 for sewage, street, gas and public building purposes.

The highways account for the year exceeded £24,215, the work of this department, including an expenditure of £13,394 on private works, totalling over £37,609. Public highways—that is to say, those repairable by the inhabitants at large—had at the time of the publishing of the report a length of over 56½ miles. As private streets have an extent of nearly 21 miles, the length of roads in the borough is thus about 77½ miles.

Under the heading of "private street works" we find that forty streets have been completed, have been declared highways and transferred to the Sanitary Committee for cleansing and scavenging. Their length is 2½ miles. Thirty-six streets and passages, having a length of about 2 miles, have also been completed, measured off, and the cost (less asphalting pavement) apportioned upon the property owners. The average cost per lineal yard of frontage to owners amounts to about 42s., but as the value of grouting paving with boiling pitch is defrayed by the corporation, the total per yard of frontage equals 45s. 6d., and the full value of the works executed amounts to £10,827, after adding £946, the cost of asphalting pavements. The average cost per lineal yard of frontage for paving, &c., passages 9 ft. wide amounts to about 11s. 3d.

The materials generally used on the footpaths are fine machine-faced Haslingden flags and 5-in. edgings, and on the carriageways best Haslingden setts racked with limestone chippings and grouted with boiling pitch. At the end of the year under review there were nineteen streets and passages in progress, their total length being slightly over 5 furlongs. On carriageways the pavements are principally composed of Lancashire and Derbyshire grit setts, while Welsh and Dalbeattie granite are laid in places on the important thoroughfares and main roads. The macadamised roads of the borough are of comparatively small extent ; they, however, measure over 6 miles. There are only some small sections of boulder paving on public highways, altogether amounting to about 6,926 yards in length and 8,651 superficial yards in area.

The principle of assisting the ventilation of the sewage system of the town (originally designed to be supplied with fresh air through surface gratings only) by the erection of tall shaft ventilators at the upper extremities of the various sewers has been continued, and the absence of complaint as to sewer gas rising into the atmosphere at the surface of the streets, or other places in the districts already provided with shafts, is quoted as evidence that the provision of the latter is of considerable benefit. The shafts, when the report was issued, numbered eighty-one, while the total number of flushing tanks was eight. The tanks are not used in rainy seasons. A scheme of subsidiary sewerage has, according to the report, been occupying the attention of the borough surveyor, and plans and sections have been prepared for the reversion of the drainage from the river of the properties lying between the new intercepting sewers and the river. These subsidiary sewers have become necessary owing to the great depths at which the new intercepting sewer has had to be laid.

\* \* \*

From the last annual report of Mr. William Weaver, the surveyor to the Vestry of Kensington, we find that the total length of sewers cleansed during the year by manual labour was 3½ miles 550 yards. In addition to the brick sewers cleansed as aforesaid, 1⅞ miles of pipe sewers were flushed with water. The cost of water used for this purpose amounted to £124. The contract for jobbing drain work was retained by Messrs. G. Nowell & Co. on similar terms as in the preceding year—viz., 5 per cent. above a schedule of prices. During the year 143 drains under public roads were laid by this firm, at a cost of £2626.

The vestry made the following rule as regards the testing of soil pipes and ventilating pipes : "Builders and others when constructing house drains shall test the soil pipes and ventilating pipes with smoke, in the presence of the vestry's surveyor or other authorised representative, before such drains are passed as sound." In carrying out this rule considerable difficulty was in many cases encountered in getting builders to supply the required smoke-testing rockets. Upon this difficulty being reported to the Works Committee it was ordered that the matter should be left in Mr. Weaver's hands to deal with. Mr. Weaver subsequently gave instructions for smoke-rockets to be supplied at the vestry's expense where required, and this instruction has been acted on for the past five months.

Five new streets, of a total length of 430 yards, were made up during the year, while masons' and paviors' jobbing work, costing £1,597, was also executed. Further work of the latter description, costing £5,835, was carried out under contract. The roads in the charge of the vestry now total 85·11 miles, and the following materials were used on their maintenance during the year : Granite, 8,661 yards ; flint, 3,021 yards ; and gravel, 673 yards. The granite was supplied by Messrs. A. & F. Manuelle, 101 Leadenhall-street ; Mr. C. M. Manuelle, 12 Lime-street, E.C. ; and the Kensington Board of Guardians ; the flints by Messrs. Eastwood & Co., Belvedere-road, Lambeth, and the gravel by Messrs. W. & J. Studds, Iver, Bucks. Some 4,215 trenches, representing 11,571 superficial yards of surface, were opened by the gas and water companies and the postal authorities. These were afterwards made good, and the expenses (£1,639) charged to the various bodies.

\* \* \*

During the past municipal year the expenditure of the General Purposes Committee of the Gloucester County Council on manual and team labour, bridges, footpaths, stocks and stores, the central offices, steam rollers and other matters, has, according to the ninth annual report of the chairman of the committee, amounted to over £68,320. This, however, was considerably under the sum allowed for in the report of Mr. Robert Phillips, the county surveyor. Superintendence has cost the following percentage on the total outlay : Central offices, ·90 per cent. ; salaries of clerks and surveyors 2·61 per cent., and county surveyor's salary (including buildings and bridges) ·87 per cent. The council have now fourteen steam rollers, but have had to hire four others for short periods. For the urban road maintenance during the year (including contributions) the sum of £10,205 has been paid, together with a sum of £732 towards improvements and interest on loans.

Owing to the extension of the Bristol City boundaries, the Urban Districts of St. George and Stapleton, and part of the Urban District of Horfield, have been transferred from the county to the city. The committee have to report that there are now four authorities that do not contract. Failing agreement with these, arbitration must ensue, as provided by the Local Government Act. In the urban districts there is a marked tendency to increased expenditure ; in some cases, it is considered, this is justified by an increasing population and increasing rateable value, in others this justification cannot be pleaded, and in such districts the expenditure requires to be very carefully scrutinised.

Two bridges have been rebuilt during the year—one at Preston, near Ledbury, and the other at Ampney Crucis, near Cirencester. On rural main roads £4,504 has been expended, while a sum of £732 has been contributed towards improvements and footways on urban roads.

Accompanying the committee's report, we may mention, is the county surveyor's estimate of the main roads expenditure for the forthcoming year. Last year's estimates and actual expenditure are also shown.

═══

**St. Andrews.**—At a recent special meeting of the burgh commissioners consideration was given to the report of Messrs. Belfrage & Carfrae, Edinburgh, with reference to the proposed additions to the water supply. They state that the dry-weather flow of the present sources is 180,000 gallons daily over and above the storage capacity of the reservoir, which is 33,250,000 gallons. They recommend that an additional reservoir, in connection with the present supply in the glen to the west of North Lambiethham, be constructed to hold 10,000,000 gallons. The engineers further recommend that the water from the catchment area of Kinaldy burn should be utilised. The dry-weather flow of this stream is 100,000 gallons daily, and they suggest the construction of a reservoir capable of holding 36,000,000 gallons. The estimated cost of the extension of the present scheme is £3,000, and of the new scheme £15,000, exclusive of compensation, way-leave, &c. The meeting called to consider the question met in committee, and after a long discussion resolved to appoint a committee to confer with Mr. Parvis, Kinaldy.

## CREMATION OF SEWAGE.

In view of its highly interesting nature, we are reprinting a second communication, signed "Non-Pollution," received by *The Times* as a result of the Archdeacon of Gloucester's letter, published in our issue of the 9th inst. on this subject. "Non-Pollution" writes:—

Your correspondent, Archdeacon T. W. Sheringham, Canon of Gloucester, calls attention to the failure of our present methods of sewage disposal in England and the scandalous pollution of our rivers and sea coast, and pleads for "the erection of huge furnaces at the outfalls of our drains" and the cremation of sewage. No one who travels in England can fail to agree with Archdeacon Sheringham as to the disgraceful state of things at present, or withhold sympathy with him in his desire to render the rivers and sewage farms more pure and less offensive. But the improvement of these matters is not a simple problem, but one calling for much study and special knowledge, as will at once be apparent from a consideration of the circumstances under which the existing conditions of our rivers and sewage farms have grown up. So far back as 1875, when the Public Health Act of that year was passed, the disposal of the sewage of our towns was sufficiently important to call for legislative action, and in the following year the Rivers Pollution Prevention Act of 1876 was passed, under which Act no one, neither a sanitary authority dealing with the sewage of a district nor a private manufacturer dealing with the trade waste of his business, was allowed to discharge any polluting matter into a stream unless he could show that he was using the "best-known and available means of rendering such polluting matter harmless." Here we find an authoritative admission of the difficulty to be overcome, and a loophole of escape for an offender which has naturally been made the most of during the past twenty odd years. But the Government of that day, recognising how real were the difficulties to be overcome, appointed a special committee to investigate the subject and assist with advice, which they did in a report issued in 1881. In that report, the commission having ascertained the very great intricacy of the problem and the insufficiency of our scientific knowledge at that time to deal satisfactorily with it, declined to fix any definite standard of purity which should be legally considered unpolluting, and uncertainty and considerable variability on that point exists to this day. The only practical result arrived at by that commission was that no treatment of sewage by chemical precipitation and filtration was good enough to give an effluent sufficiently pure to be discharged into a stream, but that the safest method of purifying sewage was to irrigate land with it, trusting to the nitrifying action of the micro-organisms in the soil to dispose of the nitrogenous organic putrescible matter in the sewage. This rather vague and uncertain finding of that commission has formed the basis of what may now be considered as the law in England—*viz.*, that all sewage shall be treated on land before it can be allowed to flow into a stream; hence the universality of the sewage farm. At the time this ruling of the special commission was published the action of the bacteria in different soils had not been carefully or sufficiently studied. It had not been considered how slow this action is under natural conditions at different seasons of the year, even in suitable soils, and how practically useless such treatment is on many soils.

The elements of failure by land treatment are too numerous and too important ever to make this method a safe and satisfactory process of sewage disposal. The unsuitability of the soil, the great difficulty of proper and even distribution of the sewage, the fall of the temperature below 37 deg. Fahr., when bacterial action is practically suspended, all these are elements of failure which are more than sufficient to account for the state of our sewage farms, which, as Archdeacon Sheringham points out, are in most cases "miserable subterfuges." Though the sewage farm, in ninety-nine cases out of 100, may be admitted to be a failure, we see there was some good reason for its adoption, and in principle it is sound. Can as much be said for Archdeacon Sheringham's suggestion of huge furnaces in which to cremate liquid sewage, and is such treatment likely to effect the object sought for—*viz.*, the purification of our rivers? Anyone who has had experience of the evaporation of sewage, or even the burning of dry-pressed sewage sludge, knows what fearful offence is caused. Such works can be felt for half a mile at least. The nuisance could, no doubt, be minimised by the construction of lofty chimneys and the use of chemical ingredients as suggested, and the introduction of scientific and costly destructors, but will not the great cost of such treatment prevent its being used or enforced.

To hang a man for sheep-stealing is not the readiest way to put an end to the stealing of sheep, but would in these days only make it impossible to get a conviction; and, in the same way, to make the cost of sewage purification practically prohibitive would make it impossible to put pressure on an offender.

The difficulty of enforcing the law would seem to be great enough now, when our large cities, like Manchester, Salford, Leeds, Bradford and others, are allowed to continue to pollute because the sums of money involved in purification are so great and the influence brought to bear to avoid such heavy outlay is so powerful. I fear the only effect of Archdeacon Sheringham's suggestion would be that, while the water of our rivers and the land of our sewage farms remained polluted much as at present, we should in addition foul our air as well.

To put a stop to the scandalous pollution of our rivers is perfectly feasible, and to do this at such a trifling cost as shall afford no excuse for non-performance of their duty on the part of any sanitary authority, or the non-enforcement of the law on the part of any county council or river authority, is also within easy reach, and it is to be hoped that the Royal Commission now sitting to consider this very important subject will, in the light of the knowledge of to-day, give a more certain sound than could be obtained in 1881. The principle laid down by the commission in 1881 was correct. Sewage can practically only be purified by means of micro-organisms as proved and designed by Nature; but to suppose that man may convert millions of gallons of pure water, stored and collected for the use of crowded communities, into foul sewage, and then, on whatever land may be within reach, reconvert this into pure water again, is to expect too much. The requirements of civilised man have created certain artificial conditions which can only be met by corresponding artificial treatment, but the law of nature need not be transgressed or departed from. In the working of Nature it will be found that the purification of sewage on land is effected only in the upper few inches of the soil, where air in the necessary quantities can penetrate, and that the land itself must be open and porous, and under such conditions the area of land required must be large and the distribution of the sewage on it must be regular and even.

Now, if an artificial filter be prepared in which the interstices in the filtering medium be sufficiently open to allow a free passage of air, and the sides of the filter be made porous, so that air can enter throughout the entire depth of the filter, we have the same condition as Nature works with, only the operation, instead of being confined to the upper few inches, can be continued through a depth of many feet, thus enabling the area of treatment to be greatly curtailed, whereby accurate distribution of the sewage can be effected at little expense, artificially warmed air can be supplied in winter and all the conditions of nature can be complied with.

The operation of such an aërated bacterial filter as above described has been tested for a considerable time at the sewage farm at Hendon on the Brent, within an hour's drive of London, and should be seen by all those interested in the non-pollution of our rivers.[*]

---

## EAST-END WATER SUPPLY.

There has as yet been no rain to speak of, so that the East London Company's reservoirs are still in a state of depletion. The cooler weather, however, has brought sensible relief to the inhabitants of the waterless district, and connection has at last been made with the Southwark and Vauxhall system. Not a few people maintain that it might have been made long ago, while others maintain the contrary.

Full flow of water through the 20-in. pipes in the Tower Subway is now giving at least an additional 6,000,000 gallons per day to the thirsty East-Enders. Connection with the Southwark and Vauxhall system is made in Bermondsey-street, and with the East London mains in Leman-street, Whitechapel, Deck-street and Hooper-square. These receiving pipes are 12 in. and 9 in., but Leman-street is partially "up," and the new main is being laid on to Osborne-street, where it will join another 20-in. pipe. Distribution is at present going on through Whitechapel, Bethnal Green, Shoreditch, Limehouse, and low-lying districts where the pressure from the other side should be sufficient to send water up to the highest storeys. The East London Company, thus relieved, should be able to give somewhat improved service to the higher localities.

---

## AN UNSAFE BUILDING IN WESTMINSTER.

The London County Council, acting on the advice of their building surveyor, on Wednesday condemned the Abbey Mansions, which have frontages to Victoria-street and Orchard-street, Westminster, as unsafe and dangerous to the public. Five months ago, it will be remembered, the concrete roof of the building fell and brought all the flooring with it. Seven workmen were killed and about twenty were more or less seriously injured. Since then workmen have been engaged putting on a new roof and shoring up the cracked tires of bay windows and walls. On Wednesday it was found that the foundations were giving way, hence the condemnation. All vehicular traffic from Victoria station to Westminster was immediately diverted, as the authorities feared that the vibration might cause the collapse of the building. A cordon of policemen was placed round it, and later in the evening pedestrians were not allowed to approach the building. The structure cost £80,000.

---

[*] The reference here is cheaply to the Local Inventor(?) singular that no reference could be made ... purification which have at least a much ... THE SURVEYOR.

## Municipal Work in Progress and Projected.

The most important news received this week respecting extensive municipal works in progress or projected in the provinces will be found in the paragraphs relating to Truro, Bradford, Burnley, Colchester, Heywood, King's Lynn, Scarborough, Stockport, Walthamstow and Bath. Among the metropolitan authorities, Camberwell, St. Pancras, Newington and Shoreditch are all contemplating more or less extensive undertakings.

### METROPOLITAN AUTHORITIES.
### VESTRIES AND DISTRICT BOARDS.

**Bermondsey.**—The vestry, on Monday, considered a lengthy report of the Electric Lighting Committee in regard to the vestry's electric lighting provisional order, the Bill to confirm which was read a third time in the House of Commons last session, and was read once in the House of Lords. Owing to a sessional order of the latter House the Bill could not be read a second time. All attempts made by the Board of Trade to induce Lord Morley, chairman of committees, to move for the suspension of the order were unsuccessful. It was also sought to get the Bill suspended, so that it might be allowed to proceed next session at the same stage as it stood in the last, as in the case of the General Power Distributing Company's Bill, but Lord Morley said that that course was impossible, and had only been done in that case because the Bill had been referred to a joint committee of both Houses. As a result, should the vestry desire to obtain a provisional order, the Electric Lighting Committee stated that it would again be necessary to apply to the Board of Trade for electric lighting powers. The committee accordingly recommended that a provisional order should be applied for, and that a special meeting should be held to pass a resolution to that effect, in conformity with the Electric Lighting Acts. Mr. Cox, chairman of the committee, formally moved the adoption of the recommendations, which were unanimously carried. In connection with this matter the Electric Lighting Committee reported the receipt of notice from the London Electric Supply Corporation of intention to lay high and low pressure mains in Bermondsey New-road and join other thoroughfares. The committee recommended that the proposed works should be disapproved, as so far as they related to the low-tension distributing mains and to the laying of mains on both sides of the streets, and that the company should be informed of the vestry's decision to apply to the Board of Trade for a provisional order. The recommendations were adopted.—It was resolved, on the suggestion of the Works Committee, to increase the rate of pay to masons and paviors from 9d. to 9½d. per hour, in accordance with the request of the Footway Masons' and Carriage Paviors' Trade Protection Society.—The vestry decided to take similar action to the Clerkenwell Vestry in requesting the county council to instruct the district surveyors to draw the attention of builders to the necessity for making application to the local authorities before commencing building operations, in order that the drains and sanitary conveniences may be made to comply with the local by-laws without unnecessary trouble to the builders after the structures are up.—It was also resolved to suggest to the county council, in support of the action of the Battersea Vestry, (1) that all district surveyors should devote the whole of their time to the duties of district surveying; (2) that they should be paid a salary by the London County Council, and that all building fees (if continued) should be paid by the council direct; and (3) that an office be provided for the district surveyor at the local vestry hall or offices, so that he may be brought into closer touch with the local authorities.—The Baths Committee reported on the following tenders, received for various works at the laundry : E. Mills, £64; W. Mills, £72; G. F. Morgan (accepted), £44; R. Athey, £65; Leaf & Co., £70; Stewart & Co., £87. The tender of E. Mills was stated to have been accepted, at £193, for sanitary work at the laundry, the only other offer received being from W. Mills, for the sum of £196.

**Camberwell.**—The vestry on Wednesday decided to inform the Lee District Board of Works that they were willing to take part in the conference to be convened by the latter authority to consider the question as to the desirability of establishing a system of mutual insurance against liabilities under the Workmen's Compensation Act.—It was resolved, on the recommendation of the Finance Committee, to apply to the London County Council for a loan of £11,800 for wood paving works in Hill-street and Peckham Park-road.—The General Purposes Committee recommended that tenders should be invited for the supply of wood blocks for the paving of Church-street and other thoroughfares, and that a clerk of works should be engaged by the surveyor to supervise the work.—The Sanitary Committee recommended that the London County Council should be approached with a view to the erection of a public convenience on Peckham Rye.—It was suggested by the Libraries Committee that tenders should be invited for painting the outside of the central library.—The following tenders were received for furnishing rooms at the vestry hall : R. Pearson, £39 5s.; Airey & Co. (accepted), £42 3s.; Tarn & Co., £48 7s. 4d.; Silk & Son, £53 8s.; and Scale & Sons, £54 14s. 6d.

**Greenwich.**—On Wednesday of last week, at a meeting of the district board of works, the tender of Messrs. Mowlem & Co., £998, for paving as a new street Fergus-street, Greenwich, was accepted.—Tenders for paving Dentford-street were referred to the Greenwich Committee.—The Board had again before them a letter from the London County Council, stating that their Bridges Committee, in consequence of the summer recess, were unable to fix an earlier day than Wednesday, the 28th inst., at 3 o'clock p.m., when they would be prepared to receive a deputation from the board on the subject of the construction of a tunnel between Rotherhithe and Shadwell. A reply was ordered to be sent, stating that having received no answer from the Rotherhithe Vestry, the board were not prepared to take action in the matter.—A suggestion of the London County Council, that in cases where a street lamp was within a few feet of a fire alarm the lamp-post should be painted a bright red, was referred to the District Committee.

**Lambeth.**—A circular-letter was last week received from the Battersea Vestry asking Lambeth to join in seeking powers for local authorities to erect dwellings for the working classes under Part III. of the Working Classes Act. It was decided, after a short discussion, to join in the movement.

**Newington.**—On Wednesday of last week, at a special meeting of the vestry, a resolution suggesting an application to the London County Council for sanction to borrow £50,000 for electric lighting purposes was adopted by a large majority of the members. The Electric Lighting Committee reported that under the power vested in them they had during the recess accepted the tender of the British Insulated Wire Company for the insulated electric mains, conduits, junction boxes, &c., at £9,081 19s. 6d; the tender of the General Electric Company, Limited, at £1,457, for the main switchboard and instruments; and the tender of Messrs. Pritchetts & Gold, for £900, for the battery of accumulators and accessories, which now covered the whole of the work to be let under contract. The following was a summary of the contracts—namely : The station, £12,928; supply and fixing engines, generators and public lighting plant, £8,975; supply and erection of boilers, £9,348; electric mains, conduits, &c., £9,082; main switchboard and instruments, £1,457; accumulators and accessories, £900.

**Shoreditch.**—The vestry, on Tuesday, received a report from the Law and Parliamentary Committee stating that they had acknowledged a communication from the St. James (Westminster) Vestry relating to the interruption in the telephone service attributed to the recent fire in Heddon-street.—Mr. Chant presented a report of the Parliamentary Committee referring to the letter received from the Battersea Vestry asking for assistance in opposing the General Power Distribution Company's Bill, and Bills of a similar nature which sought to empower companies to supply electrical energy in bulk over large areas in districts where provisional orders had already been granted to local authorities. The committee stated that if these Bills were passed an absolute monopoly would be established, as the companies would not be constituted under the Electric Lighting Acts. On the recommendation of the committee it was unanimously decided to ask the local members of Parliament to strenuously oppose the Bills.—It was reported that Mr. Newton Russell, the chief electrical engineer, had written to the Lighting Committee asking for a reconsideration of the question of his salary. The committee had, however, resolved to refer the subject to the vestry. After some discussion the consideration of the question was referred to the Officers' Committee.—The Works Committee reported that they had considered the estimates prepared by Mr. Rush Dixon, the surveyor, for repaving Old-street and Great Eastern-street with setts and hard wood, at a cost of about £9,000 and £8,500 respectively. The committee recommended that the repaving of the portion of Old-street from Great Eastern-street to Hoxton-street should for the present be deferred, that the rest of the paving should be proceeded with in hard wood, and that advertisements should be issued inviting tenders for carrying out the work. After some discussion an amendment was carried, by thirty-nine votes to eight, postponing the consideration of the question for twelve months.—The Works Committee reported that they had considered the following tenders for the construction of an underground convenience in Hoxton-street : George Jennings (accepted), £2,025; Doulton & Co., £2,150; J. Dolman & Co., £2,666. The committee had also had under consideration the following tenders for the construction of a new pipe sewer in Britannia-street : W. Manders, £414 18s. 6d.; C. W. Killingback & Co., £416; Robert Jackson, £494 8s. 3d.; John Jackson, £512; Thomas Adams, £557 16s. 3d.; Williamson & Son, £562 13s. 2d. As the surveyor's estimate was only £404, and as the vestry had means for carrying out the work by direct labour, the committee recommended that the work should be executed without the intervention of a contractor. After considerable discussion the recommendation was adopted.

**St. Luke.**—The Wharf Committee of the vestry have deferred the question of buying three of the three-wheeled type of barrows, though these are urgently needed. The present contract for horse-hire expires at the end of this month, but the committee have decided to allow the existing arrangement to continue for a peripd of three months. Additional orderly street-bins are to be fixed throughout the parish. A Barnard Smith's rotary machine, taken by the vendor as a bad debt, is to be acquired at a cost of £25.—The Public Health Committee have approved of various applications for house drains, &c.—The vestry are informing the London County Council that they are not in favour of the proposal to establish a bacteriological laboratory.—The Works Committee are to construct some ten sewer manholes. Tenders were opened for the execution of paving works in the parish. The amounts were: Limmer Asphalte Company, £3,236 17s. 6d. (amount allowed for old material, £55 17s. 6d.); French Asphalte Paving Company, £3,332 7s. 6d. (£103 2s. 6d.); and Val de Travers Asphalte Paving Company, £3,166 16s. 9d. (£66 5d.). The tender of the Val de Travers Company has been accepted. For wood paving the following tenders were received ; Acme Wood Flooring Company, £3,998 ; Improved Wood Pavement Company, £3,640 ; William Griffiths, £3,380 ; and Mowlem & Co., £3,864. The tender of Mr. Griffiths has been accepted. For the construction of an underground convenience in Old-street, by City-road, the followin tenders were received : George Jennings, £2,505 ; B. Finch & Co., £2,895 ; George B. Davis, £2,375 ; and William Shurmur, £2,772. The tender of Mr. Jennings has been accepted. It has also been decided to construct an underground convenience in Golden-lane, by Old-street, at an estimated cost of £2,700.

**St. Pancras.**—At a meeting of the vestry on Wednesday the Finance Committee recommended and it was decided to apply to the Local Government Board for permission to borrow £6,557 for the construction of underground conveniences in Mansfield-road, Fortess-road and Camden-broadway. —It was also resolved to apply to the London County Council for a loan of £10,836 for wood and asphalte paving purposes. —The Highways Committee recommended the expenditure of £1,450 on further work of wood paving in Euston-road, and this was agreed to.—Tenders as under were submitted by the Highways Committee for the supply of 140,000 jarrah or karri wood blocks, 5 in. by 3 in. by 9 in., required for the repaving of a portion of Guilford-street and Midland-road : For jarrah—W. Griffiths, £11 2s. 6d. per 1,000 ; Acme Wood Flooring Company, £11 15s.; Jarrahdale Jarrah Forests, Limited, £11 6s. 3d.; Miller's Karri and Jarrah Forests, Limited, £11 5s.; Palfreman, Foster & Co., £10 19s. 6d.; and B. G. Elliott, £12 6s. 8d. For the supply of karri—W. Griffiths, £11 per 1,000 ; Acme Wood Flooring Company, £10 17s. 6d.; and Miller's Karri and Jarrah Forests, Limited, £11 2s. 6d. The tender of Messrs. Palfreman, Foster & Co. to supply jarrah at £10 19s. 6d. per 1,000 was accepted. The following tenders were considered for the erection of a boundary fence at Finchley cemetery : N. C. Torring, junr., High-road, £55 ; Joyce & Co., High-road, £61 2s.; and W. Luck & Sons, High-road (accepted), £57.

## PROVINCIAL AND GREATER LONDON AUTHORITIES.

### COUNTY COUNCILS.

**Cumberland.**—The county council are at present finishing a skew bridge in the. Penrith district at Sickergill, between Kirkoswald and Renwick. The structure has a span of 25 ft. Another bridge will also shortly be completed in the Brampton district, at Walton Mill. It is being erected across the Camp beck, with a 35-ft. square span. In the spring a bridge, having a span of 25 ft. square, will be erected across the Ellen at Ireby, in the Wigton district.

**Worcestershire.**—The county council last week resolved to purchase, for £10,534, Bundy's farm, near Malvern, as a site for the proposed isolation hospital.

### MUNICIPAL CORPORATIONS.

**Bath.**—Mr. Robert H. Bicknell, inspector of the Local Government Board, conducted an inquiry on the 15th inst. into an application of the corporation for sanction to borrow a sum of £18,000 for the purposes of street improvements.

**Birmingham.**—The corporation water department have found it necessary to issue a notice warning consumers of the necessity of exercising economy in the use of water. The danger of a water famine in the district is by no means unreal, and very shortly an intermittent and restricted supply must be resorted to unless the drought should break or a very material reduction in the consumption be effected. At a conference between the city surveyor and the secretary of the department it has been deemed necessary to discontinue entirely for the present the watering of all roads in suburban districts except main roads on which the traffic is very heavy.

**Blackburn.**—The designs of Messrs. Lockerbie & Wilkinson, Limited, of Birmingham, have, together with their tender of £1,495, been accepted by the corporation for the erection of a new palm-house and conservatories in the public park.

**Bradford.**—The Gas and Electricity Supply Committee of the corporation propose to borrow £10,000 for the extension of the electricity cables in the city.—Owing, it is thought, to the slippery state of the lines, one of the cars on the corpo-

ration system of electric tramways, in descending a steep hill on Monday with a large number of passengers, went beyond the control of the driver and dashed with tremendous force into the boundary wall of a church at the foot of the slope. Fifteen persons sustained serious injuries and one died an hour after the accident. The Board of Trade have appointed Major Cardew, R.E., to open an inquiry on Monday.

**Burnley.**—Application is to be made to the Local Government Board by the Gas and Electric Lighting Committee of the corporation for sanction to the borrowing of £5,000 for mains, £3,000 for stoves, and £1,500 for lamps.

**Caine.**—An inquiry was held at the Town Hall, Caine, last week, relative to an application by the town council to the Local Government Board for permission to borrow £695 for the improvement of certain main road footpaths, and £775 for the construction of works for the purpose of obtaining water for sewer-flushing and street-watering.

**Canterbury.**—One of the inspectors of the Local Government Board recently conducted an inquiry with reference to an application of the town council for sanction to borrow an additional £3,000 for the infectious diseases hospital.

**Carlisle.**—Local Government Board sanction will shortly be sought in connection with a proposal to borrow £2,850 for the erection of artisans' dwellings in Willow Holme.

**Colchester.**—The sanction of the Local Government Board to the proposed loan of £36,000 for the erection of the new town hall has been granted, with the exception of £1,424, the estimated cost of the portion of the new structure to be used as a police station. The mayor, Alderman J. N. Paxman, will lay the stone of the new building on the day of the annual oyster feast in October. The architect is Mr. John Belcher, of London, whose design was selected in competition.

**Coventry.**—At the fortnightly meeting of the city council on Thursday it was decided, on the recommendation of the Works Committee, to pave Cross Cheaping and Burgess-street with granite setts, at an estimated cost of £1,000.

**Dewsbury.**—Consideration was last week given to a resolution of the Gas and Electricity Committee suggesting that, for the purpose of relieving the present overloaded condition of the existing feeding mains and distributors, the principle of increasing the voltage from 220 volts to 440 volts should be adopted in preference to that of duplicating the mains, the estimated cost of such increase being £2,232.

**Durham.**—The city council have resolved to take initial steps towards improving the banks of the river Wear. They have agreed to invite tenders for carrying out a small portion of the work between Framwellgate bridge and the site of the proposed shire school in accordance with plans prepared by Mr. Jones.

**Exeter.**—The Local Government Board have sanctioned the application of the town council for leave to borrow £7,000 for electric lighting purposes.

**Falmouth.**—The corporation on Thursday adopted a resolution recommending the purchase of certain land, known as the Gyllyngdune estate, for £13,000.

**Godalming.**—As a result of negotiations between the corporation and the directors of the Frith Hill, Godalming and Farncombe Water Company, an extraordinary meeting of shareholders was held recently, at which a resolution was proposed agreeing to the acquisition of the waterworks by the council for the sum of £51,000. Although there was a majority in favour of the municipalisation of the undertaking, there was not a three-fourths majority, as legally required, and the resolution was rendered abortive. Mr. J. C. Collier, chairman of the meeting, resigned his position as director in consequence.

**Haslingden.**—The town council recently decided to apply for an electric light provisional order.

**Herne Bay.**—The serious landslip which has just occurred has again brought prominently to the fore the question of commencing the permanent sea-wall to take the place of that which was destroyed in the heavy gales last year, and was temporarily repaired for this season. The plans, &c., for the new wall have been prepared, and it is felt in the town that the building of a solid wall should not longer be delayed, as anything like a heavy gale might produce serious effects.

**Heywood.**—The manager of the sewage works has been instructed by the town council to obtain an estimate for the electric lighting of the works and also for the infectious diseases hospital.—Local Government Board sanction has been received by the corporation to the borrowing of £8,000 for gasworks purposes. Of this amount £1,500 is required for land, £2,000 for prospective new mains, £3,000 for stoves and prepayment meters, £500 for a coke-breaking machine, and £900 for new buildings for stores, &c.

**Horsham.**—The council's engineer, in accordance with a request of the Local Government Board, is now preparing a detailed estimate of the cost of the proposed sewerage works, plans of the land involved in the scheme, and detailed drawings of the outfall works, &c. Sanction to borrow £3,000 to carry out the improvement has already been applied for.

**Hyde.**—At Monday's meeting of the town council the Highways Committee reported that they had considered a communication from the Oldham, Ashton and Hyde Electric Tramways Company, Limited, asking why they had been prevented from laying cables under the footpaths. The committee had resolved that consent should be given to the execution of the work on condition that the company contributed a further sum of £500, in addition to a similar amount already promised, towards the cost of widening the roads at various points along the tramway route.

**King's Lynn.**—Mr. Sandford Fawcett, A.M.I.C.E., on the 7th inst. held an inquiry, on behalf of the Local Government Board, with reference to an application of the town council for sanction to borrow £30,100 for electric lighting purposes. Particulars relative to the provisional order, &c., were given by the town clerk, and Prof. Robinson, who is acting as consulting engineer, explained that he had been authorised to obtain tenders and make plans, &c., for the various works. The mayor and other members of the council attended to support the scheme, but Alderman Pridgeon opposed, on the ground that the ratepayers did not want the installation. He thought it curious to advertise for tenders, &c., before the Local Government Board had given their sanction.

**Lincoln.**—The price of gas in Lincoln will in future be 2s. 1d. per 1,000 feet.

**Lowestoft.**—The Sanitary Committee last week reported that the surveyor had submitted the revised plans and estimate of the Horsfall Company for erecting a refuse destructor and mortar mill on Smith's Marsh, their tender for the whole work being £4,700. The committee recommended that the tender be accepted, and that application be made to the Local Government Board for their sanction to the borrowing of the necessary money. This was carried.

**Maidstone.**—The town council on Wednesday decided to promote a Bill in the next session of Parliament for the compulsory acquisition of the waterworks company and the extension of the present sources of supply. The undertaking, it is stated, will cost the town about £120,000.

**Middlesbrough.**—The corporation's electric lighting order has received the Royal assent, and the committee, in consultation with Mr. Hammond, electrical engineer to the corporation, have decided that the station be erected on the land belonging to the Gas Committee at the corner of Snowdon-road and Washington-street, on condition that the Gas Committee agree thereto and subject to the sanction of the Local Government Board. Mr. Hammond has been instructed to prepare specifications and estimates for lighting the compulsory area. These will be submitted to a future meeting of the corporation.

**Newcastle.**—A meeting of the joint committee of the Newcastle and Gateshead Corporations was held on Friday afternoon, in the Town Hall, Newcastle, to consider the reports of the engineers on the proposed new bridge across the Tyne. In pursuance of a resolution adopted by the two committees, it was agreed that the bridge should cross from Pilgrim-street to High-street, but there was found to be a little difference of opinion between the engineers as to the exact point of landing in High-street. It was therefore resolved that the two borough engineers, along with Messrs. Moncrieff and Sandiman, should further consider and determine the most satisfactory point on the Gateshead side; and also that they should present a report at the next meeting of the committee, a month hence.

**Ramsgate.**—At last week's meeting of the town council the General Purposes Committee and Parliamentary Committee recommended that an agreement be entered into with Messrs. Tomson & Wotton, Limited, to purchase the Queen's Head Inn, with vacant possession, for the sum of £4,000, the corporation taking the tenant's fixtures and trade effects at a valuation. The report was adopted without opposition. The last item on the agenda was: "To consider the subject of widening the road between the Elms and Grove-road, and to take the necessary steps to purchase for the purpose a piece of land on the north side of that road for the sum of £200 and a piece of land on the south side for the sum of £50. The whole cost of the improvement is estimated at £450." This also was adopted.

**Richmond, Surrey.**—The highest bid made at Wednesday's attempt to sell Glover's Island was £200—£3,000 short of the sum at which it had been offered to the corporation. The auction, which was held at Tokenhouse-yard, was very largely attended.

**Rotherham.**—An important enlargement of the corporation gasworks was inaugurated last week, when a new retort-house was opened. The extension scheme practically means the doubling of the facilities for the manufacture of gas, and an expenditure of £30,000. The new retort-house represents an addition of 650,000 cubic feet per day, and the whole plant will be capable of yielding 2,000,000 ft. In the system the newest methods for the automatic handling of the coal and for the economical consumption of coke in the furnaces have been adopted. Mr. C. Winstanley, of Coventry, has been the engineer.

**Scarborough.**—A Local Government Board inquiry is to be held on Monday relative to an application of the corporation for permission to borrow £33,575 for the purchase of the St. Nicholas House estate, which it is proposed to lay out as a park, the house at present being used as a town hall.

**Southampton.**—A letter was, last week, read from the Local Government Board adverting to an application of the council to borrow £10,076 for the purposes of a new road, quay and wharf, and stating that the board had been informed that the Board of Trade would be prepared to approve, so far as the interests of navigation were concerned. The board went on to state that they approved generally of the scheme, but that, as it was proposed to use corporate land for the purposes of the scheme, the town council should make formal application by memorial under seal for approval of the appropriation of the land for such purposes.

**Stockport.**—The borrowing of £28,482 by the town council for electric lighting purposes has been sanctioned by the Local Government Board.

**Sunderland.**—Powers to work the local tramways will shortly be applied for by the corporation. It was on Wednesday decided to establish the overhead trolley wire system in the place of horse haulage.

**Taunton.**—At a meeting of the town council on the 13th inst. the Main Drainage Committee presented the surveyor's report containing a scheme for the alleviation of the floods in North Town. The scheme provided for the laying of a separate sewer along Station-road, to carry off the storm water, and the committee recommended the council to have it carried out at once, at a cost of £275.—Alderman Spiller, chairman of the committee, said that the scheme would not effectively do away with the flooding in that part of the town, but would greatly lessen it, and that was all they could hope to do until they had received the sanction of the Local Government Board to proceed with the high-level scheme, which they hoped would permanently stop the flooding. In the discussion it was urged that, as there was a possibility of receiving the sanction of the Local Government Board very shortly to the high-level scheme, it would do no harm to postpone this scheme for a time. This course was adopted, and the mayor and town clerk were authorised to proceed to London to have an interview with the secretary of the Local Government Board with regard to various loans that had been applied for by the council for works which were urgently needed.

**Walsall.**—At the last monthly meeting of the council the Electric Lighting Committee recommended that with a view to encourage the use of electric motors, and so endeavour to secure a day load for the generating plant, a special charge of 2½d. per unit be made for current supplied for motor purposes only. The committee had also instructed the engineer to reply that they did not see their way clear at present to recommend the extension of the cable to Lichfield-road, as they had been requested to do. The committee's report was adopted.

**Widnes.**—The corporation have decided to apply to the Local Government Board for permission to borrow £2,000 for alterations and extensions at the gasworks.

**Wolverhampton.**—The town council have given notice to the tramways company to purchase their undertaking.

**Yarmouth.**—It is intended to purchase a 10-ton steam roller and a scarifier, at a cost of £450.

## URBAN DISTRICT COUNCILS.

**Aylesbury.**—On Saturday week the district council were fined £5 and costs for polluting a tributary of the river Thames by sending into it sewage matter which had not been properly treated.

**Barnoldswick.**—An inquiry was held last week, on behalf of the Local Government Board, respecting an application of the district council for power to borrow £2,000 for the purpose of erecting an infectious diseases hospital upon a site at Banks-hill.

**Burnley-in-Wharfedale.**—Mr. F. H. Tulloch, M.I.C.E., held an inquiry on the 5th inst., on behalf of the Local Government Board, relative to an application of the district council for sanction to a loan of £200 for water supply works and £150 for gasworks.

**Chadderton.**—The new sewage purification works at Chadderton, constructed from the designs of Mr. James Diggle, of Heywood, were formally opened on Saturday by the chairman of the Sewage Committee. The site, situated at Slacks Valley, contains 15 statute acres, and the total cost of the disposal works and the sewage scheme has been £80,000, of which £50,000 has been expended on sewerage.

**Clacton.**—The council have decided to make an application to the Local Government Board for sanction to borrow a sum of £1,660 for making a path on the cliffs, providing a mortuary, and erecting a town yard and fire station.

**Cleethorpes.**—The surveyor, Mr. E. Rushton, last week submitted his estimate of the cost of widening a portion of Grimsby-road. This amounted to £2,715. It was decided to consider the matter at a future meeting.

**Hucknall Huthwaite.**—At the last monthly meeting of the district council, Mr. H. Silcock, surveyor to the Blackwell Rural District Council, presented plans of the tanks and filters in connection with the sewerage farm in Pit-lane, and estimated the cost to carry out the work at £180. The scheme, he said, was on the same lines as at Tibshelf, where the works were going on very satisfactorily. It was decided to proceed with the works at once.

**Ilford.**—The medical officer of health reported, at a recent meeting of the district council, that he was afraid the elements of a wide-spread epidemic of typhoid were present at a watercress bed on the banks of the Roding, as the river water, which was now dreadfully polluted with sewage, flowed over some of the watercress, and made it dangerous to eat. He suggested that if the council had no power to prohibit the sale of the 'cress, they might buy up the crop, so as to prevent the public having it. The surveyor was instructed to inspect and report. The council also decided to give notice of intention to the gas company to purchase their undertaking.

**Llandudno.**—An important meeting of the Electric Lighting Committee was held last week, at which Mr. Preece reported that current would be definitely available from this date. The erection of the chimney at the generating station had now been completed, and consequently the chief cause of delay removed. Some discussion ensued as to getting a demonstration to celebrate the switching on of the light. The arrangements were deputed to a sub-committee.

**Moss Side.**—At the last monthly meeting of the council a communication was read from the town clerk of Salford referring to and enclosing copies of the resolutions passed at the late conference of authorities in the watershed of the Irwell on the treatment of sewage. The letter called special attention to the second resolution, which proposed the formation of an association of local authorities in the Mersey and Irwell watershed, on which each authority should have two representatives, for the purpose of reporting on the treatment of sewage problems by the Local Government Board and the Mersey and Irwell Joint Committee. The election of two representative, as suggested, was eventually decided upon by the council.

**Newmarket.**—The council have adopted the following resolutions: "In the event of no feasible agreement with the Burwell Fen Commissioners being arrived at, that the main drainage alternative scheme be divided into two parts, to be called (a) the Newmarket scheme, and (b) the Exning scheme. (2) That the Newmarket scheme, as explained by Mr. Beesley and Mr. Metcalf, shall be carried out on the present sewage farm, the area of which the surveyor considers sufficient to effectually treat by bacteria-beds the sewage of the old urban area and added parts, with the exception of Exning proper, which shall be dealt with by the Exning scheme; and that permission be sought to raise a loan to carry out the sewerage of Cheveley-road immediately. (3) That the Local Government Board be requested to hold a public inquiry for the purpose of sanctioning the urban district council raising loans to carry out the Newmarket scheme of drainage, and to fix an early date for that purpose, as it is urgent. (4) That, if possible, the Exning scheme be considered at the same time."

**Redditch.**—On the 13th inst., at a special meeting of this authority, it was stated that at a meeting of the Public Works Committee, held earlier in the evening, the question of the best means of adapting the present police station in Evesham-street, which was recently purchased by the council for council meetings and other purposes, had been considered. The surveyor had presented a plan for the adaptation of the buildings. It appeared that the cost of a swimming bath would be £2,500, and the committee were of opinion that that portion of the scheme should stand over for the present. It was resolved, after considerable discussion, to recommend the council to accept the proposed plans, with the exception of that dealing with the swimming bath. The report of the committee was adopted. A sub-committee were subsequently appointed to confer with the surveyor as as to the preparation of modified plans for the required alteration, to be submitted at the next meeting of the Public Works Committee.

**Rhyl.**—It was reported, at last week's meeting of the district council, that a committee had had under consideration draft schemes for supplying certain parts of the town with electric light, and also for laying down a tramway from near the entrance to the Grand Pavilion to Prestatyn. Plans had been submitted by the engineers, Messrs. Alfred Dickinson & Co., and, without pledging the council to them, the committee who inspected them expressed approval of them, and requested Messrs. Dickinson to submit a detailed scheme for consideration. It was resolved that the members should in a body visit some of the Lancashire seaside towns, including Southport, Blackpool, Morecambe and Fleetwood, to inspect similar works carried out there.

**Ruskington.**—A largely-attended public inquiry was held at Ruskington, near Sleaford, last week by Mr. H. Percy Boulnois, Local Government Board inspector, respecting the borrowing of £1,900 by the council for waterworks, ordered to be constructed by the Local Government Board, in answer to a petition signed by the late Earl of Winchilsea and forty other leading parishioners. Mr. J. Clare, the engineer, stated that he expected to find water at a depth of 130 ft.—probably 40,000 gallons daily.

**Skipton.**—The council on Thursday unanimously resolved to promote a Bill in the next session of Parliament empowering them to acquire the works of the Skipton Gas Company

upon such terms as may be agreed upon or determined by arbitration. The council recently made an offer to the Gas Company to purchase the undertaking for £300 00. In refusing to accept this sum the company intimated that if they sold the works their price would be £250 00, but that they were not at all desirous of relinquishing the undertaking at any price. The feeling of the ratepayers on the question of compulsory powers will be gauged at a forthcoming public meeting, which is being called at the request of twenty-eight property owners and ratepayers.

**Walthamstow.**—Local Government Board sanction will shortly be applied for by the council in connection with a proposed loan of £16,000 for the provision of public baths.

**Waterloo.**—It has been reported that at a meeting of the Tramway Committee the surveyor presented a detailed estimate of the cost of constructing the tramway track and maintaining and working the tramways. After being duly considered it was resolved that before coming to any decision as to the desirability of maintaining and working the tramways further inquiries be made with inference to the cost and other matters relating thereto, for the guidance of the council, and the council authorised the committee to make such inquiries.

**Wombwell.**—A committee has been appointed by the district council to consider the question of providing a recreation ground for the town.

## RURAL DISTRICT COUNCILS.

**Chapel-en-le-Frith.**—It has been decided by the council to purchase a steam roller and a water-cart, at a cost of £300.

**Kiveton Park.**—On Thursday Mr. H. Percy Boulnois held an inquiry, on behalf of the Local Government Board, respecting a scheme of sewerage and sewage outfall works for the districts of North and South Anston, prepared by the surveyor, Mr. William Atkinson.

**Newbury.**—The Thames Conservancy on Thursday prosecuted the district council for polluting a tributary stream of the Thames in the parish of Doddington. Mr. Bunting, for the conservancy, explained that the proceedings had become absolutely necessary in consequence of the great delay on the part of the local authority in carrying out a proper system of drainage for the village of Doddington. In defence, Mr. Pinniger said the district council had been doing their best to remedy the evil, but had been met with a number of obstacles. They had been unable to obtain a site for a pumping station, and it seemed likely they would be driven to put compulsory powers into force. The justices said they were of opinion that the complainants had made out their case, and therefore the district council must pay a penalty of £3 and £5 costs.

**Soulcoates.**—At last week's meeting of this council a letter was read from Messrs. A. M. Jackson & Co., solicitors, stating that certain gentlemen had in contemplation a scheme for the construction of an electric tramway from Hessle to connect with the new system at Hull. All they wanted was the consent of the authorities concerned, and if the scheme was to go through it would be necessary to apply for a provisional order early next session. On the motion of the chairman it was resolved to appoint a committee from the council to meet the promoters and discuss the scheme.

**Sleaford.**—Mr. H. Percy Boulnois conducted an inquiry on the 13th inst., on behalf of the Local Government Board, with reference to an application of the district council for permission to borrow £900 for the water supply of Great Halo. Mr. Clare, the surveyor to the council, said that the present supply was obtained from shallow wells, and was declared by Dr. Ashby's analysis to be wholly unfit for domestic purposes. The council had therefore decided to bore, the necessary site having been purchased. There was no opposition to the application.

**Tamworth.**—At a recent meeting of the district council a letter was read from the Local Government Board sanctioning the proposed scheme of water supply for the parish of Kingsbury. The council instructed their surveyor, Mr. H. J. Clarson, to proceed with the work at once. This scheme, which will involve the expenditure of about £1,000, is greatly needed to supply the wants of the mining districts in that parish.

**Truro.**—The district council have resolved to apply to the Local Government Board for sanction to borrow £550 for carrying out a water supply scheme for St. Agnes, from plans prepared by Mr. Worth.

**Yardley.**—Local Government Board sanction has been received to the borrowing by the council of a sum of £140 for the purchase of land for the purpose of a depot, and for the erection of a fire station and a mortuary. The board, however, have refused to sanction a loan of £100 for the purchase of a site for proposed public offices at Sparkhill.

## SCOTLAND AND IRELAND.

**Aberdeen.**—The town council have authorised the Finance Committee to consult Mr. H. G. Wilson, architect, and to obtain from him plans for extending the fish market along Market-street, and, alternately, along Commercial-street.

**Inverness.**—A reduction in the price of gas from 3s. 9d. to 3s. 4d. per 1,000 cubic feet has been resolved on by the town council. This resolution was the outcome of a recommendation made by the engineer, Mr. J. Thomson, who pointed out that there was a surplus of £1,586 on last year's working. Since Mr. Thomson took charge of the works, over twenty-two years ago, the price has been reduced 5s. per 1,000 cubic feet.

## A CLOSET DEODORISER.

We illustrate a little apparatus for use in water-closet cisterns. The object of the apparatus is to leave a portion of the deodoriser in the pan every time it is flushed, and thus decompose and render innocuous any sewer-gas which may

rise up the waste pipe. The *modus operandi* is to place a quarter or half an ounce of permanganate of potash in the vessel, which is then placed in any unoccupied corner of the closet cistern, so as to be under water when the cistern is full. The theory is that every time the closet cistern is emptied a portion of the deodoriser comes down with the final rush of water ; that it is therefore not immediately washed away down the drain, but remains in the pan performing its sanitary duties until flushed away with the next emptying of the cistern. It is considered that one charge of the permanganate of soda will last a month or more, according to the frequency of use of the closet, and that thus a few pence will cover the cost for a whole year. Assuming that the arrangement works all right, a good deal might by its means be effected in keeping water-closets in good condition. The apparatus is sold at the moderate price of 2s. 6d., Messrs. Underwood, 13 Granville-street, Birmingham, being the sole patentees and manufacturers.

## THE SANITARY INSTITUTE CONGRESS AT BIRMINGHAM.

THE MUNICIPAL ENGINEERS' CONFERENCE.

In connection with the conference of municipal and county engineers, on Wednesday, at the annual autumn congress of the Sanitary Institute, the following arrangements have been made :—

10 a.m.—The President will deliver his address, and the following papers will then be read and discussed : (1) "Precautions to be Observed in the Ventilation of Sewers and Drains," by Mr. T. J. Moss-Flower, A.M.I.C.E.; (2) "By-Laws Relating to New Streets and Buildings," by Mr. J. S. Pickering, A.M.I.C.E., surveyor to the Nuneaton Urban District Council; (3) "Some Sanitary and Allied Advantages Attending the Introduction and Use of Motor Vehicles," by Mr. Shrapnell Smith.

1 p.m.—Adjournment for lunch.

2.15 p.m.—Visit Public Convenience in course of construction in the Bull Ring.

3.40 p.m.—Visit Salkey, to inspect the diversion of the Rea main sewer (7 ft. diameter), now in progress.

3.30 p.m.—Visit Edward-street depot, which is now approaching completion.

4.15 p.m.—Visit the river Rea improvement works, recently commenced.

5.0 p.m.—Visit the Queen's Ride.

6.0 p.m.—Return to Birmingham.

Tickets for the brakes (price 2s. 6d.) and for lunch (price 3s.) should be secured from the secretaries of the confer-

ence (Messrs. H. Ashton Hill, A.M.I.C.E., Birmingham, and A. D. Greatorex, A.M.I.C.E., West Bromwich) between 9.30 a.m. and 10 a.m., who will attend at the conference meeting for this purpose.

On Thursday afternoon, at 2.15 p.m., a party will leave Birmingham on a visit to the Croft Granite, Brick and Concrete Works, near Leicester, by kind permission of the directors of the company. The company will provide saloon carriages free of charge, and also invite the party to tea at the works at 4.30 p.m. The party will return to Birmingham about 6.50 p.m.

The following, we may mention, are the officers of the conference :—

PRESIDENT: Mr. T. de Courcy Meade, M.I.C.E., city surveyor, Manchester.

VICE-PRESIDENTS : Messrs. W. B. G. Bennett, A.M.I.C.E., borough engineer, Southampton; R. E. W. Berringer, A.M.I.C.E., Wolverhampton ; W. Blackshaw, A.M.I.C.E., borough engineer, Stafford ; A. T. Davis, A.M.I.C.E., county surveyor, Salop; J. T. Eayrs, M.I.C.E., F.S.I., Birmingham ; E. Purnell Hooley, A.M.I.C.E., county surveyor, Nottingham ; F. J. C. May, M.I.C.E., F.S.I., borough engineer, Brighton ; J. Price, M.I.C.E., city surveyor, Birmingham ; J. Willmot, county surveyor, Warwick ; J. E. Worth, M.I.C.E., district engineer, London County Council; T. H. Yabbicom, A.M.I.C.E., city engineer, Bristol.

BOROUGH OF SOUTHEND-ON-SEA.
    TO ROAD CONTRACTORS AND OTHERS.
The Corporation invite tenders for the Kerbing, Channelling and Paving of High-street.

Plans, sections and specifications may be seen, and bills of quantities and forms of tender obtained, on and after Monday, the 26th September (on payment of £1 1s., which will be returned on receipt of a *bond-fide* tender), upon application to Mr. Alfred Fidler, ASSOC.M.INST.C.E., Borough Surveyor, Clarence-road, Southend.

No tender will be considered unless made on the prescribed form.

Sealed tenders, marked "Tender for Paving High-street," to be delivered at my office before 10 o'clock in the morning of Thursday, the 6th October.

The Corporation will not be bound to accept the lowest or any tender.

(By order)
            WILLIAM H. SNOW,
                Town Clerk.

Southend-on-Sea.
    September 21, 1898.

BOROUGH OF SOUTHEND-ON-SEA.
    TO ROAD CONTRACTORS AND OTHERS.
The Corporation invite tenders for the Laying-out of Darlow's Green, and for the Making-up of the Esplanade and Roads adjacent thereto, also for the Construction of a short length of Sea-Wall.

Plans, sections and specifications may be seen, and bills of quantities and forms of tender obtained, on and after Monday, the 26th September (on payment of £1 1s., which will be returned on receipt of a *bond-fide* tender), upon application to Mr. Alfred Fidler, ASSOC.M.INST.C.E., Borough Surveyor, Clarence-road, Southend.

No tender will be considered unless made on the prescribed form.

Sealed tenders, marked "Darlow's Green," to be delivered at my office before 10 o'clock in the morning of Thursday, the 6th October.

The Corporation will not be bound to accept the lowest or any tender.

(By order)
            WILLIAM H. SNOW,
                Town Clerk.

Southend-on-Sea.
    September 21, 1898.

BOROUGH OF RICHMOND (SURREY).

*SURVEYOR'S DEPARTMENT.*

JUNIOR CLERK WANTED,
In the Borough Surveyor's office, Richmond (Surrey); good writing and thorough knowledge of shorthand indispensable ; speed to be not less than 100 words per minute.

Salary, 24s. per week, rising, by annual increments of 2s., to a maximum salary of 30s. per week.

Personal application to members of the Council is strictly prohibited, and will disqualify the candidate.

Applications, accompanied by copies of not more than three testimonials of recent date, stating age and present occupation, are to be sent to me not later than noon on Monday, the 3rd of October, 1898, marked " Junior Clerk, Borough Surveyor's Department.

                J. H. BRIERLEY,
                    Borough Surveyor.

Town Hall, Richmond, Surrey.
    September 22, 1898.

# Personal.

Mr. H. Mence, of St. Albans, has been appointed surveyor to the St. Albans Rural District Council.

Mr. J. Walker Smith, chief assistant on the sewerage works of the Burton Corporation, has had his salary advanced to £130 per annum.

We hear that Mr. William Cumming, burgh surveyor of Carnoustie, has received an appointment as manager for a large contracting firm in Hull.

The chief assistant in the electricity department of the Stafford Corporation has had his salary increased from £120 per annum to £150 per annum.

The Bournemouth Town Council have appointed Mr. F. Dawkins, at present engaged by the Thames Conservancy Board, to the post of assistant buildings inspector.

Mr. G. B. Laffan, of Twickenham, has been selected to fill the post of borough engineer of Pietermaritzburg, South Africa. Mr. Laffan's salary will commence at £800 per annum.

The salary of Mr. F. Latham, assistant surveyor to the Margate Town Council, has, on the recommendation of the General Purposes Committee of that body, been increased to £150 per annum.

Mr. H. T. Chapman, district council offices, Chapel-en-le-Frith, and Mr. L. D. Thompson, district council offices, Haydock, Lancs., have been elected district surveyors under the Lancashire County Council.

Much sympathy is felt in Lambeth with Mr. W. Macintosh, the former surveyor of the parish, who has recently lost his wife. The vestry feelingly expressed their condolences in a resolution passed on Thursday evening.

We are glad to hear that Mr. Edward Pritchard, M.I.C.E., of London and Birmingham, the well-known past-president of the Association of Municipal and County Engineers, who has been seriously ill during the last four weeks, is now recovering.

On Tuesday of last week the employees of the Hammersmith Vestry's electricity department presented Mr. F. C. Pay, one of the engineers in charge, with a handsome marble timepiece, on the occasion of his marriage, and as a mark of their respect and esteem.

The names of the following firms of engineers have been placed before the Hackney Vestry, who are considering a combined scheme of electric lighting and dust destruction : Messrs. Burstall & Monkhouse, Mr. Robert Hammond, and Messrs. Kincaid, Waller & Manville.

Mr. Henry Masterton, surveyor to the Devonshire County Council, died at Barnstaple on Sunday, from cancer of the liver. He was very highly regarded in North Devon. At Plymouth he was connected with some of the recent large engineering work, and it was his skill which supplied Saltash with water from the Plymouth source carried on the bed of the Tamar. The interment will be in London.

A presentation was, on Thursday, made at the town hall, Grimsby, to Mr. R. S. F. Dring, of the borough surveyor's office, by the staff, on the occasion of his leaving the town for a Government appointment as assistant surveyor at Accra, Gold Coast, Africa. A supper was provided in honour of the occasion, the surveyor, Mr. M. Petree, presiding. The presentation took the form of a solid silver cigarette case. Mr. Dring suitably responded.

The Harrogate Corporation, at their meeting on Monday of last week, passed without comment the following recommendation of the Wells and Baths Committee : "That advertisements be inserted inviting competitive designs for a new Royal pump-room, and that £50, £30 and £20 be offered for first, second and third prizes; also that competitive designs be invited for alterations to the present building to increase the accommodation, and £30, £20 and £10 be offered as prizes."

Mr. Walter Percival, of the borough surveyor's office, Wolverhampton, has been appointed assistant architect for outposts under her Majesty's Lords of the Admiralty. The borough surveyor of Wolverhampton, Mr. J. W. Bradley, in presenting to him numerous tokens of the esteem in which he is held, spoke highly of his work and expressed the general regret which was felt at his approaching departure. Mr. Percival is a Gassell prizeman and a gold medallist of the Royal Institution of British Architects.

At the last monthly meeting of the Chesterfield Town Council the Finance Committee of that body reported that they had considered the qualifications of the applicants for the post of surveyor to the northern district and had selected six for interview. There were originally forty-three. Mr. C. Thorpe, who has represented the district of Calow on the council for many years, was eventually elected by a large majority, and in returning thanks said he hoped he would be able to so carry out the duties of the office as to merit a continuance of the members' confidence in him.

At last week's meeting of the Blackrock Commissioners consideration was given to the appointment of a surveyor. For this position there were originally twenty candidates. The names were afterwards submitted to a committee of the whole board, by which only three were sent forward. These were Messrs. Price, Grey and Going. After the first ballot Mr. Going fell out, and a long discussion followed on various matters connected with the appointment. Eventually a division was taken, when Mr. Price and Mr. Grey received eight votes each. The chairman gave his casting vote in favour of Mr. Price, who was thereupon declared elected.

An interesting gathering of officials of the Vestry of St. George-the-Martyr, Southwark, is reported to have taken place on Friday, at the Tower Tavern, Westminster Bridge-road, where, during the course of a smoking concert held in his honour, Mr. Oliver Winter, the late surveyor, was presented with a handsome American writing-desk bearing a suitable inscription. Mr. A. Johnson, the Vestry clerk, made the presentation, and paid a warm tribute of praise to Mr. Winter, both as a surveyor and a man. Mr. Winter, in the course of returning thanks, introduced his successor, Mr. Harrison, who met with a hearty welcome. The testimonial, it is understood, was subscribed to by 126 subscribers, representing every department of the vestry's work.

As we last week mentioned, the number of candidates for the post of borough electrical engineer of Derby were reduced to three. There were originally sixty-two applicants. The names of those selected were, on Wednesday of last week, submitted to the town council, and Mr. T. P. Wilmshurst, chief of the Halifax Corporation's electric lighting works, was then appointed to the vacant post. The appointment is worth £350 a year, with the privilege of taking two pupils. The principal points in Mr. Wilmshurst's favour were that the same system of electric lighting is in vogue in Derby as in Halifax, and that he had laid down the electric tramway there. This work is contemplated in Derby. Mr. Wilmshurst secured fifty-two votes out of fifty-five, the number of members present.

The announcement, says a contemporary, of the impending retirement of Mr. Stewart from the position of electrical engineer-in-chief of the corporation electricity supply works, Derby, with which he has been connected from their inception, was received with much regret by the whole of the staff employed under him ; and it was felt by all that this was a fitting opportunity of showing their esteem for him and their appreciation of the many kindnesses received from him during his tenure of the office of engineer and manager of the works. An appeal for subscriptions was generously responded to, and as a result a walnut cabinet of dessert knives and forks was, in the name of the whole staff, presented to him on Friday afternoon, September 9th. Mr. Stewart, in returning thanks on behalf of Mrs. Stewart and himself, said that both of them, whilst highly valuing the gift, would especially value the kindly thought which prompted it.

On Wednesday, at a meeting of the St. Pancras Vestry, the Baths Committee reported that thirty-six applications had been received from architects willing to submit designs for the erection of the proposed new baths and wash-houses in the Prince of Wales-road. The following six gentlemen were chosen by the committee as possessing the best qualifications for this class of work : T. W. Aldwinckle, 1 Victoria-street, S.W.; R. Stephen Ayling, Parliament Mansions, Victoria-street, S.W.; Harnor & Pinches, 5 John-street, W.C.; I'Anson & Co., 7 Laurence Pountney-hill, E.C.; F. T. Smith, Parliament Mansions, Victoria-street, S.W.; and Spalding & Cross, 15 Queen-street, E.C. The committee recommended that the foregoing architects should be invited to compete for the new baths and wash-houses, and that the president of the Royal Institute of British Architects should be invited to communicate the names of three gentlemen competent to advise the vestry on baths architecture, for the selection of one as assessor, to advise and report on the designs sent in. The recommendations were adopted.

## BACTERIOLOGICAL EXAMINATION.

The London County Council a short time ago addressed a communication to each of the vestries and district boards throughout the metropolis, asking them whether they would be in favour of the council applying for Parliamentary powers to establish a bacteriological laboratory. The idea is to appoint an expert or experts in connection with the projected institution, or otherwise to make arrangements whereby medical officers of health and medical practitioners in London could obtain, at the expense of the county, the examination by a competent bacteriologist of material from suspected cases of infectious disease, with a view to aiding in the diagnosis. Among those authorities which have already pronounced in favour of the project are the vestries of Shoreditch and St. Pancras.

## PREPAYMENT ELECTRICITY METERS.

As various corporations in the country have evinced considerable interest in the system of prepayment meters, and as one or two have practically decided to adopt such an arrangement, it will be interesting to describe a practical form of it at present on the market. It is known as the Bastian prepayment meter, and is the result of numerous experiments from various forms. This prepayment arrangement does not imply a special form of meter, for the device

FIG. 1.

can be attached to any of the well-known types of meter. The illustrations by which we shall endeavour to explain the working of the instrument show the prepayment mechanism applied to a Thomson watt-meter. The operation of the instrument, by means of a coin, is an interesting and ingenious one. Until a coin is inserted the handle, which projects from the cover, is free to move; a coin, when pressed through the slot, falls into a groove, and forms a rigid connection between the handle and the interior mechanism, and a turn of the handle switches on the current. The arrangement of the meter will be better appreciated by referring to the detailed parts. Fig. 1 shows the meter and prepayment attachment entirely enclosed, the form in which the

FIG. 2.

mechanism will be usually sold. Fig. 2 is the front view of the meter, the only features to be noticed here being the coin receiver or shoot shown at O and the pointers N, N, the exact function of which will be referred to subsequently. Fig. 3 gives a detailed view of the prepayment mechanism seen from the back of the meter.

We will now follow the action of the apparatus. Upon the insertion of the coin at B, which makes a mechanical connection, the handle, H, is turned. One result of this is to operate on the pivoted end of the switch, T, which is depressed into the mercury cups, M, thus completing the circuit through the meter. The switch is held in the mercury cups, against the tension of a spring, by means of a clutch, D. The turning of the handle does more than merely put the switch on. In fact, the operation that we are about to describe is probably the most important in the complete action of the mechanism. Above the dials of the meter (Fig. 2) will be observed two pointers, and the relation of these to one another is very important. The handle, H, being in connection with a rod, G, its movement will cause a partial revolution of the pulleys, $L_1$ and $L_2$. These pulleys are connected together by means of a miniature raw-hide belt. Pulley $L_1$ is mounted on an axle which carries one of the pointers already alluded to. It will be seen therefore that when the handle is turned one of the needles, through the medium of the pulleys, is moved away from the other pointer, the exact distance of its movement being predetermined. The second pointer is geared to the train wheels of the meter, and when the switch has been put on by the agency of a coin the meter commences to run and the second pointer travels slowly after the first one. The exact distance it has to traverse before it overtakes the first pointer is a measure of the current consumed; in fact, the first pointer is caught up by the second pointer in a time inversely proportionate to the amount of current flowing through the meter. The distance that the first is separated from the second is determined by the gear wheels, which are proportioned according to the price per unit and the value of the coin with which the mechanism is intended to be operated.

The more coins that are dropped in up to a certain limit the further the first pointer will be separated from the

FIG. 3.

second, and they will be a proportionately longer time in coming together. One side of the first pointer is insulated, so that it can come in contact with one side of the second pointer with impunity. The other side, however, carries a platinum contact, and when the second overtakes it and comes into actual contact a current of electricity at once flows round the electro-magnet, E, whose armature is immediately raised and pulls the clutch, D, away from the switch, F, which immediately flies into the off position. From observations we have made the action of the meter seems to be certain, and the instrument ought to meet with considerable success. It is manufactured and sold by the Penny-in-the-Slot Electric Supply Syndicate, Limited, 41 and 42 Parliament-street, S.W.

## ARBITRATIONS AND AWARDS.

Mr. W. Ambrose, Q.C., who acted as arbitrator in the hearing of the claim of the executors of the late T. Danby against the Leigh District Council (see p. 302 ante), has issued his award. The claim was for £13,000 for the acquisition, by the council of the shop and premises, 24 Market-street, Leigh, for the purposes of street improvement. It included the value of the land, buildings, stock-in-trade, goodwill and damages for injury to trade by compulsory removal, &c. Witnesses on behalf of the claimants gave the value of the freehold, interest and fixtures as £7,975, and estimated that the premises would let on lease at £250. On behalf of the council, however, witnesses valued the property at £4,574. The arbitrator's award is £7,142.

## ASSOCIATION OF MUNICIPAL AND COUNTY ENGINEERS.

Vᴏʟᴜɴᴛᴀʀʏ Pᴀss Exᴀᴍɪɴᴀᴛɪᴏɴ.

Candidates whose names have been entered for the above examination must attend at the Technical School, Princess-street, Manchester, on Friday, the 30th September, at a quarter before 10 a.m., and the following day at 8.45 a.m.

Candidates will only require to take with them a small pocket set of drawing instruments.

Intending candidates for these examinations will greatly facilitate the work of the secretary by enclosing an addressed postal wrapper when asking for a copy of the syllabus.

11 Victoria-street,  Tʜᴏᴍᴀs Cᴏʟᴇ,
London, S.W.  Secretary.

## THE WEST RIDING RIVERS BOARD AND TRADE REFUSE.

Major-General Crozier, R.E., on the 14th inst. conducted two inquiries at Diggle, on behalf of the Local Government Board, with reference to applications made by the West Riding Rivers Board for power to take proceedings against Messrs. A. W. Lawton & Sons, of Court Mill, Diggle, and Messrs. Jonathan Chambley, Sons & Co., of Stone Bottom Mills, Dobcross, respectively, for having turned their trade effluent, without any purifying treatment whatever, into the Brun clough and the Diggle brook respectively, both tributaries of the Thame.

Mr. A. Lawton, on behalf of Messrs. Lawton & Sons, admitted the pollution, but stated that his firm were merely yearly tenants of the mill, and contended that it was the duty of the landlord to provide works of purification. The inspector pointed out that the Act did not give the rivers board any power over the landlord. He added that he supposed there were other mills to be got.

Mr. E. Rowbotham, of Oldham, appeared for Messrs. Chambley, and urged that it was for the local sanitary authority, to whom they paid a considerable amount each year in rates, to receive the trade effluents into their sewers. The authority had been asked to do so, but had refused.

## APPOINTMENTS VACANT.

*Advertisements which are sieed too late for classification cannot be included in these summaries until the following week.*

Bᴜʀɢʜ ᴀɴᴅ Rᴏᴀᴅ Sᴜʀᴠᴇʏᴏʀ, Sᴀɴɪᴛᴀʀʏ Iɴsᴘᴇᴄᴛᴏʀ, &c.—September 23rd.—Commissioners of the Burgh of Carnoustie. £100.—Mr. William Cæsar, town clerk.

Sᴜʀᴠᴇʏᴏʀ.—September 29th.—Stone (Staffs.) Rural District Council. £200.—Mr. J. Buckley Norris, clerk to the council.

Iɴsᴘᴇᴄᴛᴏʀ ᴏғ Nᴜɪsᴀɴᴄᴇs.—September 26th.—Highworth and Swindon Rural District Council. £120.—Mr. John P. Kirby, clerk to the council.

Sᴀɴɪᴛᴀʀʏ Iɴsᴘᴇᴄᴛᴏʀ.—September 26th.—Vestry of St. George-the-Martyr, Southwark. £120.—Mr. J. A. Johnson, clerk to the vestry.

Sᴜʀᴠᴇʏᴏʀ.—September 27th.—Bridlington Urban District Council. £160.—Mr. Chas. Gray, clerk to the council.

Cʟᴇʀᴋ ᴏғ Wᴏʀᴋs.—September 27th.—Corporation of Guildford. £2.—Mr. Ferdinand Smallpiece, town clerk.

Hɪɢʜᴡᴀʏ Sᴜʀᴠᴇʏᴏʀ.—September 27th.—Tendring (Essex) Rural District Council. £175.—Mr. A. J. H. Ward, clerk to the council, 42 Church-street, Harwich.

Assɪsᴛᴀɴᴛ Iɴsᴘᴇᴄᴛᴏʀ ᴏғ Nᴜɪsᴀɴᴄᴇs.—September 29th.—Corporation of Leicester. 30s.—Mr. James Bell, town clerk.

Sᴀɴɪᴛᴀʀʏ Iɴsᴘᴇᴄᴛᴏʀs (Tᴡᴏ).—September 29th.—Chelsea Vestry. £120.—Mr. Thomas Holland, clerk to the vestry.

Fᴏʀᴇᴍᴀɴ ᴏғ Sᴛʀᴇᴇᴛ Gᴀs Lɪɢʜᴛɪɴɢ.—October 1st.—Corporation of Plymouth. £2 5s.—Mr. James Paton, borough engineer and surveyor.

Gᴇɴᴇʀᴀʟ Assɪsᴛᴀɴᴛ ғᴏʀ Bᴏʀᴏᴜɢʜ Eɴɢɪɴᴇᴇʀ's Dᴇᴘᴀʀᴛᴍᴇɴᴛ.—October 1st.—Corporation of Plymouth. £100.—Mr. James Paton, borough engineer and surveyor.

Sᴜʀᴠᴇʏᴏʀ ᴀɴᴅ Iɴsᴘᴇᴄᴛᴏʀ ᴏғ Nᴜɪsᴀɴᴄᴇs.—October 3rd.—Arlecdon and Frizington Urban District Council. £120.—Mr. John Bowly, clerk to the council, Council Offices, Frizington.

Eɴɢɪɴᴇᴇʀ ᴀɴᴅ Mᴀɴᴀɢᴇʀ ᴏғ Sᴇᴡᴀɢᴇ Wᴏʀᴋs.—October 5th.—Hampton Urban District Council. £3.—Mr. John Kemp, engineer and surveyor to the council.

## COMPETITIONS.

*Advertisements which are received too late for classification cannot be included in these summaries until the following week.*

Wɪᴠᴇɴʜᴏᴇ.—September 29th.—Works of drainage and water supply, for the urban district council.—Mr. C. W. Denton, clerk.

Rᴇɪɢᴀᴛᴇ.—October 6th.—Erection of municipal buildings, fire station, public offices, &c.—Mr. Clair J. Grece, town clerk.

Aʙʙᴇᴀʟᴏɴ.—December 1st.—Extension of the covered market, at a cost not to exceed £5,000. £21.—The Borough Surveyor.

Cʜᴇʀᴛsᴇʏ.—December 23rd.—Sewerage and sewage disposal scheme for the No. 1 and 2 wards of the district. £50, £30 and £20.—Mr. T. E. Harland Chaldecott, clerk to the council.

## MUNICIPAL CONTRACTS OPEN.

*Advertisements which are received too late for classification cannot be included in these summaries until the following week.*

Eᴀsᴛ Sᴜssᴇx.—September 23rd.—Erection of two temporary buildings for 100 patients at the county lunatic asylum.—Mr. Henry Card, county surveyor, County Hall, Lewes.

Nᴇʟsᴏɴ.—September 24th.—Construction of about 110 lineal yards of culverting over the river Walverden, alongside the wall of the gasworks in Bradley.—Mr. B. Bell, A.M.I.C.E., borough engineer and surveyor.

Mᴀʟᴠᴇʀɴ.—September 24th.—Supply of a 10-ton steam road-roller, scarifier, stone-breaker and sleeping-van, for the urban district council. —Mr. H. P. Maybury, surveyor to the council.

Bᴀᴛʜ.—September 24th.—Construction of a steam disinfector house at the refuse destructor works, Upper Bristol-road.—Mr. Chas. R. Fortune, city surveyor.

Exᴍᴏᴜᴛʜ.—September 24th.—Erection of a cart-shed at the town yard, for the urban district council.—Mr. Walter D. Harding, surveyor to the council.

Dᴏʀᴄʜᴇsᴛᴇʀ.—September 24th.—Supply of coal for the year ending September 30, 1899.—Mr. H. Symonds, town clerk.

Wɪʟʟᴇɴʜᴀʟʟ.—September 24th.—Supply of various stores and materials during the six months ending March 31, 1899, for the urban district council.—Mr. Chas. J. Jenkin, town surveyor.

Bᴇᴄᴋᴇɴʜᴀᴍ.—September 26th.—Widening of Croydon-road and East End-road, for the urban district council.—Mr. John A. Angell, surveyor to the council.

Bᴇᴄᴋᴇɴʜᴀᴍ.—September 26th.—Erection of about 200 cast-iron ventilating columns, 13 ft. 6 in. high, on concrete beds, together with the laying of 6-in. stoneware pipe connections to the main sewers, &c., for the urban district council.—Mr. John A. Angell, surveyor to the council.

Lᴏɴᴅᴏɴ.—September 26th.—Erection of a cleft pale oak boundary fence at Brockwell Park, for the county council.—Mr. C. J. Stewart, clerk to the council, County Hall, Spring-gardens, London, S.W.

Dᴀʀᴡᴇɴ.—September 26th.—Supply and fixing of a 10-ton overhead travelling crane in the generating-room of the new electricity works. —Mr. Chas. Costeker, town clerk.

Sᴛ. Mᴀʀʏʟᴇʙᴏɴᴇ.—September 26th.—Supply of 500,000 Australian jarrah wood paving blocks, for the vestry.—Mr. W. H. Garbutt, clerk to the vestry.

Bᴜxᴛᴏɴ.—September 26th.—Rebuilding of the Osterhole bridge, St. John's-road, and the erection of stabling, &c., in the cattle market, for the urban district council.—The Town Surveyor.

Bɪʟʟᴇʀɪᴄᴀʏ.—September 26th.—Sinking of a well at Little Wakey, for the rural district council.—Mr. C. Edgar Lewis, clerk to the council, Brentwood.

Wɪᴛɴᴇʏ.—September 26th.—Main drainage of Eynsham, for the rural district council.—Mr. Nicholas Lailey, A.M.I.C.E., 16 Great George-street, London, S.W.

Rᴏᴡʀᴏᴛʜ.—September 27th.—Supply of 1,500 tons of blue Guernsey granite, 400 yards of gravel and 300 yards of hoggin, for the urban district council.—Mr. George Bailey, clerk to the council.

Lᴇᴀᴍɪɴɢᴛᴏɴ.—September 27th.—Construction of a concrete wall in the river walk.—Mr. W. de Normanville, borough surveyor.

Wɪʟʟᴇsᴅᴇɴ.—September 27th.—Paving works in Baker-passage, Harlesden, and Newton-mews, Kilburn, for the urban district council. —Mr. O. Claude Robson, M.I.C.E., engineer to the council.

Sʜᴇᴇʀɴᴇss.—September 27th.—Supply of about 300 tons of quartzite or granite, 300 tons of clean pit flints, and 200 tons of hoggin or Aylesford gravel, for the urban district council.—Mr. C. A. Copland, surveyor to the council.

Lᴇᴀᴍɪɴɢᴛᴏɴ.—September 27th.—Erection of a refreshment arbour in Jephson-gardens.—Mr. H. Consett Passman, town clerk.

Lᴏɴᴅᴏɴ.—September 27th.—Erection of a new bothy and alterations to the conveniences at Parliament Hill, and the erection of a new cart-shed, bothy, office, &c., at Southwark Park, for the county council.—Mr. C. J. Stewart, clerk to the council, County Hall, Spring-gardens, London, S.W.

Lᴇᴀᴍɪɴɢᴛᴏɴ.—September 27th.—Providing and fixing of various wrought-iron fencing.—Mr. W. de Normanville, borough engineer.

Hᴀsᴛɪɴɢs.—September 27th.—Excavating and steining two wells, about 270 ft. deep, at Brede.—Mr. D. H. Palmer, M.I.C.E., borough engineer.

Eᴅᴍᴏɴᴛᴏɴ.—September 27th.—Supply of Portland cement from September 30, 1898, to September 30, 1899, for the urban district council. —Mr. G. Eedes Kachus, engineer to the council.

Pᴏɴᴛʏᴘᴏᴏʟ.—September 27th.—Supply of various materials, &c., for the six months ending March 31, 1899, for the urban district council.— Mr. H. H. Baden, clerk to the council.

Cᴏᴠᴇɴᴛʀʏ.—September 27th.—Supply of about 300 tons of 3-in. by 5-in. by 6-in. setts, and 4-in. granite cube setts.—Mr. J. E. Swindlehurst, city engineer and surveyor.

Aᴍᴇsʙᴜʀʏ (Wilts.).—September 27th.—Supply of flints from the 1st October, 1898, to the 30th September, 1899, for the rural district council.—Mr. John T. Hoskins, surveyor to the council.

Hᴀsᴛɪɴɢs.—September 27th.—Construction of two covered service reservoirs (each 1,500,000 gall. capacity) at Ore.—Mr. D. H. Palmer, M.I.C.E., borough engineer.

Bᴇxʜɪʟʟ.—September 28th.—Supply of various electric light plant, for the urban district council.—Mr. A. H. Preece, A.M.I.C.E., 39 Victoria-street, London, S.W.

Bᴀɴʙᴜʀʏ.—September 28th.—Reconstruction of the public swimming bath adjoining the public recreation ground.—Mr. N. H. Dawson, borough surveyor.

Sᴀʟᴇ.—September 28th.—Making-up Goodier-street, Brogden-terrace, Brogden-grove, Eliza-street, Mason-street, Eden-place, Joynson-street, Clarendon-road, Beech-road and St. Ann-street, for the urban district council.—Mr. A. G. M'Beath, A.M.I.C.E., surveyor to the council.

Dᴜʀʜᴀᴍ.—September 28th.—Erection of a retaining wall and footpath along the bank of the river near South-street, for the urban district council.—Mr. F. Marshall, town clerk.

Iʀᴇ.—September 28th.—Supply of horse fodder for the parishes of Kilham, Leo and Rudbrook, for the district board of works.—Mr. George Whale, clerk to the board.

Hᴜʟʟ.—September 29th.—Extension of the electric light station in Sculcoates-lane.—Mr. A. E. White, city engineer.

LLANDOVERY.—September 29th.—Construction of abutments, wing walls, piers, &c., for a highway bridge to be erected over the river Towy at Glanrhyd, for the rural district council.—Mr. Rees James, surveyor to the council.

EAST BARNET.—September 29th.—Supply of broken granite, gravel, hoggin, water-vans, &c., for the year ending September 29, 1899, for the urban district council.—Mr. Henry York, surveyor to the council.

EAST BARNET.—September 29th.—Making-up of Jackson-road and Warwick-avenue, for the urban district council.—Mr. Henry York, surveyor to the council.

BASINGSTOKE.—September 29th.—Paving of the Market-square with wood blocks.—Mr. George Fitton, borough surveyor.

MIDDLESBROUGH.—September 29th.—Reconstruction of Pearson, Derby, Welford, Croft and Stanley streets.—Mr. Frank Baker, borough engineer.

SALFORD.—September 29th.—Alterations to the water-closets, lavatories, &c., at the model lodging-house in Bloom-street.—Mr. Samuel Brown, town clerk.

HARTLEPOOL.—September 29th.—Erection of a destructor-house, engine and mill house, cottage, boundary walls and chimney at the proposed new sanitary depot in Clifton-street.—Mr. H. C. Crummack, A.M.I.C.E., borough surveyor.

WEDNESBURY.—September 30th.—Erection of isolation hospital buildings, boundary walling, &c., on a site in Dangerfield-lane.—Mr. E. Martin Scott, borough engineer and surveyor.

EDINBURGH.—September 30th.—Reconstruction of part of the tenement at the north-west corner of Bank-street.—The Burgh Engineer.

RAWSGATE.—September 30th.—Supply of 250 12-ft. lengths of 12-in. gas pipes, and 10 tons of ordinary specials.—Mr. William A. Valon, engineer of the corporation gasworks.

WOOD GREEN.—September 30th.—Making-up of King's-road and Western-road, for the urban district council.—Mr. C. J. Gunyon, surveyor to the council.

AUCHINLECK (Scotland).—September 30th.—Construction of a pier or boat-landing stage.—Mr. James Brims, county clerk, Thurso, N.B.

CALSTOCK.—September 30th.—Laying of about 2,803 yards of 3-in. cast-iron socket pipes, from Duddles adit to Harrowbarrow, and 1,487 yards from Fuggle Dowdie adit to Tossworthy and Albaston, in the parish of Calstock, for the rural district council.—Mr. John P. Blight, clerk to the council, Callington.

EAST RIDING.—September 30th.—Erection of registrar's offices and extension of the county offices at Beverley, for the county council.—Mr. J. J. Bickersteth, clerk to the county council, Beverley.

HULL.—September 30th.—Supply of forty-five electric motor cars, twenty trail cars, two sprinkler cars and two traversing platforms.—Mr. A. E. White, city engineer.

LEEDS.—October 1st.—Construction and erection of a wrought-iron roof for the new coal store at the New Wordy gasworks.—Mr. R. H. Townsley, general manager, Municipal Buildings, Leeds.

BIRMINGHAM.—October 1st.—Reconstruction of the sewer in Needless-alley, New-street, also the construction of new pipe sewers in a portion of Wentworth-road, Harborne.—Mr. John Price, city engineer and surveyor.

PEMBROKE.—October 1st.—Construction of a pumping station and night storage tank and other works at Milton in connection with the water supply of Pembroke Dock.—Mr. W. O. Hulm, town clerk.

LEICESTER.—October 1st.—Alterations and additions to the Museum buildings in Hastings-street.—Mr. E. G. Mawbey, M.I.C.E., borough engineer.

WOLVERHAMPTON.—October 1st.—Making-up of Hilton-street.—Mr. J. W. Bradley, borough engineer and surveyor.

LEEDS.—October 1st.—Extension of Kirkgate market.—Mr. Thomas Hewson, M.I.C.E., city engineer.

BURTON-ON-TRENT.—October 3rd.—Making-up of Eldon-street and Nelson-street.—Mr. George T. Lynam, borough engineer and surveyor.

HANWELL.—October 3rd.—Supply of broken Guernsey or Channel Islands granite during the year ending the 31st March, 1899, for the urban district council.—Mr. Warren S. James, clerk to the council.

ASHTON-UNDER-LYNE.—October 3rd.—Installation of the necessary wires, fittings, &c., for the electric lighting of the public market.—Mr. John Neal, borough comptroller.

WEMBLEY.—October 3rd.—Supply of broken granite, granite chippings, slag and fine gravel, for the urban district council.—Mr. John Smith, clerk to the council.

FAIRFIELD (Derbyshire).—October 3rd.—Supply of 1,035 yards of 6-in. cast-iron socket and spigot pipes, for the urban district council.—Mr. Charles Slater, clerk to the council.

NORTHAM.—October 3rd.—Construction of an impounding reservoir at Melbury Moor to hold 30,000,000 gallons of water, with the necessary outlet works, filters, pure water reservoir, diversion of a public road, fencing, the construction of a covered service-reservoir at Northam, the supply and laying of cast-iron socket pipes, and the supply and fixing of hydrants, sluice valves, &c., in connection with the water supply of the town, for the urban district council.—Mr. Charles Wm. Role, clerk to the council.

WATFORD.—October 4th.—Levelling, paving, kerbing, metalling, flagging, channelling, lighting, &c., works in Liverpool-road, Parker-street, Milton-street and Shakespeare-street, for the urban district council.—Mr. H. Morten Turner, clerk to the council.

CROYDON.—October 4th.—Various repairs at the Abbey Mills and Isle of Dogs pumping stations, for the county council.—The Engineer to the Council, County Hall, Spring-gardens, S.W.

CROYDON.—October 4th.—Repair of portions of Crowther, Holland and Dale Park roads.—Mr. E. Mawdesley, town clerk.

CROYDON.—October 4th.—Supply of 10,000 ft. of 12-in. by 8-in. Norway granite kerb and 10,000 ft. of 12-in. by 6-in. Norway granite channel.—Mr. E. Mawdesley, town clerk.

CLACTON.—October 4th.—Provision and laying of a 11-in. cast-iron main, about 9½ miles in length, from Great Bentley to the present waterworks, for the urban district council.—Messrs. John Taylor, Sons & Santo Crisp, engineers, 27 Great George-street, London, S.W.

LONDON.—October 4th.—Erection of two blocks of dwellings, to be known as Benson and Abingdon dwellings respectively, on the Boundary-street area, Bethnal Green, and also the erection of cottage dwellings at Brook-street, Limehouse, for the county council.—Mr. C. J. Stewart, clerk to the council, County Hall, Spring-gardens, London, S.W.

IPSWICH.—October 5th.—Supply of about 500 tons of best Welsh or other unscreened or hand-picked hard steam coal.—Mr. Hamlet Roberts, engineer and manager of the corporation waterworks.

HALIFAX.—October 5th.—Erection of a tramway car-shed at the junction of Free School-lane and Skircoat-road.—Mr. Edward R. S. Escott, borough engineer.

LITTLEHAMPTON.—October 5th.—Various improvement works in Gloucester-road and Purbeck-place, for the urban district council.—Mr. H. Howard, surveyor to the council.

RATHMINES (Ireland).—October 5th.—Supply of various electric light plant, for the township commissioners.—Mr. Robert Hammond, consulting engineer, 64 Victoria-street, London, S.W.

RAMSGATE.—October 5th.—Erection of a refuse destructor.—Mr. T. G. Taylor, borough surveyor.

DARTFORD.—October 6th.—Laying of a surface-water drain and the paving of the footways, crossing and channelling in Fulwich-road, for the urban district council.—Mr. W. Harston, A.M.I.C.E., surveyor to the council.

PLYMOUTH.—October 6th.—Supply of an enclosed (iron-clad) continuous-current motor.—Mr. John H. Rider, borough electrical engineer.

QUARRY BANK.—October 6th.—Supply of about 500 tons of Rowley granite as required during the ensuing twelve months, for the urban district council.—Mr. Alfred Homfray, clerk to the council, Cradley Heath, Staffs.

HULL.—October 7th.—Supply and erection of a 7-ton overhead traveller (hand-power) for a span of 42 ft. 9 in.—Mr. A. E. White, city engineer.

HASTINGS.—October 7th.—Laying of about 9,000 yards run of 16-in. water main and about 3,340 yards of 10-in. main in connection with the Brede Valley water scheme.—Mr. F. H. Palmer, M.I.C.E., water engineer, Town Hall, Hastings.

BISHOP STORTFORD.—October 8th.—Supply of from 1,200 to 1,500 tons of 1½-in. broken granite and from 100 to 150 tons of 1-in. granite chips, for the urban district council.—Mr. William Gee, clerk to the council.

PRESTON.—October 5th.—Various sewerage and sewage disposal works for the township of Farington, for the rural district council.—Mr. James Clarke, clerk to the council.

SOUTHAMPTON.—October 11th.—Supply and fixing of three high-pressure Lancashire boilers, economisers, calorifiers, radiators, steam and hot-water mains, and all necessary pumps, valves, &c., required for the extension of the heat and power generating plant at the county lunatic asylum at Knowle, Fareham.—Mr. W. J. Taylor, county surveyor, The Castle, Winchester.

TUNBRIDGE WELLS.—October 15th.—Sewering and making-up of new roads on the site of the proposed workmen's dwellings.—Mr. W. C. Cripps, town clerk.

EDINBURGH.— October 17th.— Various works in connection with gasholder tank at Granton.—Mr. James M'G. Jack, clerk to the commissioners.

BIRKENHEAD.—October 17th.—Erection of public baths on a site adjoining Livingstone-street and Price-street.—Mr. Charles Brownridge, A.M.I.C.E., borough engineer and surveyor.

TUNBRIDGE WELLS.—Erection of fifty-three four-roomed cottages and five blocks of tenements.—Mr. W. C. Cripps, town clerk.

## TENDERS.

*ACCEPTED.

CARSHALTON.—For the supply of about 345 ft. of 18-in. cast-iron socket and spigot pipes in 12 ft. lengths, for the urban district council. — Mr. S. Willis Galo, A.M.I.C.E., surveyor to the council :—
J. & S. Roberts, West Bromwich.—Straight, £5 15s. per ton ; specials, £9 5s. per ton.
Pontifex & Co., Coleman-street, E.C.—Straight, £5 8s. per ton.
Gibbs & Co., Fenchurch-street, E.C.—Straight £5 7s. 6d. per ton ; specials, £7 per ton.
J. Ritchie, Middlesbrough.—Straight, £5 6s. 6d. per ton ; specials, £9 5s. per ton.
Stanton Iron Company, Nottingham.*—Straight, £5 3s. 6d. per ton ; specials, £9 per ton.

CHAPEL-EN-LE-FRITH.—For the construction of a concrete service reservoir and the providing and laying of about 1½ miles of cast-iron mains for the water supply of the township of Bamford, for the rural district council.—Mr. J. Burton Boycott, clerk to the council :—
W. Bull & Son, Glossop-road, Sheffield* ... ... ... £1,384

DISS.—For the supply of about 260 tons of Belgian granite, for the urban district council.—Mr. Henry O. Lyus, clerk to the council :—
Per ton.
Whitwick Granite Company, Whitwick ... ... ... 13s. 3d.
W. Grimley & Co., Sutton Bridge ... ... ... 13s. 2d.
Enderby and Stoney Stanton Company, Narborough ... ... 13s. 1d.
L. Sommerfeld, King's Lynn ... ... ... 12s. 1d.

GRAYS.—Accepted for the supply of 1,000 tons of granite and quartzite, for the urban district council.—Mr. Arthur C. James, surveyor to the council :—
The Cherbourg Quartzite Company, Mark-lane, E.C.—Quartzite from Imperial Quarries—1½-in., 9s. per ton ; 1½-in., 9s. 3d. per ton.

HALIFAX.—For the laying of about 800 yards super. of setting at King's Cross, for the rural district council.—Mr. F. Gordon, C.E., Brighouse :—
A. Beverley, Skircoat, Halifax ... ... ... ... £220
S. Bedford, Halifax* ... ... ... ... 171
G. Kenyon, Halifax ... ... ... ... 170

NORWICH.—For alterations, &c., at the cattle market offices.—Mr. Arthur E. Collins, city engineer :—
J. Evans, Nelson-street, Norwich ... ... ... £550
A. Hipperson, Adelaide-street, Norwich ... ... 505
R. Hayes, Kimberley-street, Norwich ... ... 490
Barton & Son, Spencer-street, Norwich ... ... 468
R. Daws & Son, Dereham-road, Norwich ... ... 447
Tyrell Brothers, Whitefriars-street, Norwich* ... ... 535
† Recommended for acceptance.

PANTEG.—For the erection of offices, &c., at Pontymoile, Pontypool, for the urban district council.—Mr. Thomas Williams, clerk to the council, Albion-road, Pontypool :—
F. C. Parfitt, Newport ... ... ... ... £1,365
Morgan & Evans, Pontnewynydd ... ... ... 1,347
G. H. Hambleton, Pontnewynydd ... ... ... 1,295
W. Arthur, Aberystwyn ... ... ... ... 1,015
Bailey Brothers, Pontnewynydd* ... ... ... 922

SLOUGH.—Accepted for the supply of 300 tons of 2-in. broken clean field flints and about 500 tons of 1½-in. machine-broken and hand-broken granite, for the urban district council.—Mr. W. W. Cooper, surveyor to the council :—
Per Ton.
s. d.
Clee Hill Dhu Granite Company, Ludlow ... ... ... 11 1
Mendip Stone Company, Shepton Mallett ... ... ... 9 0

TAMWORTH.—Accepted for the supply of about 300 tons of broken granite, for the rural district council.—Mr. Henry J. Clarson, surveyor to the council :—
M. A. Barlow (agent for Hartshill Granite Quarries), Glascote, Tamworth.—Average price, 6s. per ton.
Messrs. Nugent & Sons (agents for the Cliffe Hill Granite Company), Tamworth.—Average price, 9s. 2d. per ton.

WALTHAMSTOW.—Accepted for the erection of public baths, for the urban district council.—Mr. E. J. Gowen, clerk to the council :—
Killby & Gayford, Worship-street, E.C. ... ... ... £14,838

TEDDINGTON.—For the making-up of Clarence-road, for the urban district council.—Mr. M. Hainsworth, surveyor to the council :—
Tar-paving. Road-making.
Lawrence & Thacker, Clapham Common ... £211 £1,123
W. Adamson, Kingston-on-Thames ... ... — 1,050
T. Adams, Wood Green ... ... ... 202 1,145
R. Ballard, Limited, Kilburn ... ... 196 1,328
F. G. Sheppard, Southend-on-Sea ... ... 195 —
R. Newell & Co., Kensington, S.W. ... ... 192 1,203
North England Asphaltic Co., Manchester ... 186 —
T. Free & Son, Maidenhead ... ... ... 172 1,150
J. J. Inghams, Bradford ... ... ... 165 —
Asphaltic Limestone Concrete Co., Birmingham 160 —
J. Wainwright & Co., Shepton Mallett ... 160 —

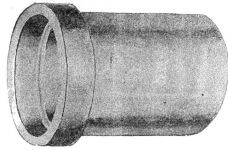

## MEETINGS.

SEPTEMBER.

27, 28, 29 and 30.—The Sanitary Institute: Annual Autumn Congress at Birmingham.

OCTOBER.

1.—The Sanitary Institute: Annual Autumn Congress at Birmingham.

## NOTICES.

THE SURVEYOR AND MUNICIPAL AND COUNTY ENGINEER *may be ordered direct, through any of Messrs. Smith & Son's book-stalls, or of any newsagent in the United Kingdom. Applications to the Offices for single copies by post must in all cases be accompanied by stamps.*

*The Prepaid Subscription (including postage) is as follows :*

|  | Twelve Months. | Six Months. | Three Months. |
|---|---|---|---|
| United Kingdom | 15s. | 7s. 6d. | 3s. 9d. |
| Continent, the Colonies, India. | | | |
| United States, &c. | 19s. | 9s. 6d. | 4s. 9d. |

*The International News Company, 83 and 85 Duane-street New York City; The Toronto News Company, Toronto; and The Montreal News Company, Montreal, have been appointed agents in the United States and Canada for the sale of* THE SURVEYOR AND MUNICIPAL AND COUNTY ENGINEER. *A thin paper edition is printed for circulation abroad.*

EDITORIAL OFFICES :—
24 BRIDE-LANE, FLEET-STREET, LONDON, E.C.

ADVERTISEMENT AND PUBLISHING OFFICES :—
13 NEW STREET-HILL, FLEET-STREET, LONDON, E.C.

## THE SURVEYORS' INSTITUTION.

*(Incorporated by Royal Charter.)*

TEMPORARY ADDRESS—
SAVOY-STREET, VICTORIA-EMBANKMENT, W.C.

EXAMINATIONS, 1899.

PRELIMINARY EXAMINATION.

Notice is given that the Preliminary Examination for the admission of Students will be held on the 18th and 19th of January next.

It is proposed to examine candidates from the counties of Lancashire, Cheshire, Yorkshire, Durham, Cumberland, Westmoreland and Northumberland at Manchester. Candidates from other counties in England and Wales will be examined in London.

Irish candidates will be examined in Dublin.

PROFESSIONAL EXAMINATIONS.

Notice is also given that the Annual Professional Examinations for Land Agents, Valuers and Building Surveyors (held under the provisions of the Charter), qualifying for the Fellowship and Associateship of the Institution, will commence on the 20th of March next.

English candidates for the Professional Examinations will be examined in London.

Irish candidates will be examined in Dublin.

Particulars as to subjects, course of examination, prizes and scholarships can be obtained of the Secretary.

All applications for the Professional Examinations, Divs. II., III., IV. and V., must be sent in before the 31st of October, and applications for the Students' Preliminary Examination before the 30th of November. The necessary entry forms for the various Examinations can be obtained of the Secretary.

## APPOINTMENTS OPEN.

BRIDLINGTON URBAN DISTRICT COUNCIL.

APPOINTMENT OF SURVEYOR.

Applications are invited for the appointment of Surveyor to this Council, at a salary of £160 per annum. The person appointed will be required to devote the whole of his time to the duties of the office, and must be able to prepare plans and superintend works of sewerage, repairs of highways, &c.

The applications, marked "Surveyor," with copies of not more than three recent testimonials, to be forwarded to me not later than Tuesday, the 27th instant.

Canvassing the members of the Council will be held a disqualification.

CHAS. GRAY,
Clerk to the Council.

Clerk's Office, 39 High-street, Bridlington.
September 19, 1898.

BOROUGH OF PLYMOUTH.

The Corporation is prepared to receive applications from suitable persons for the position of Foreman, who will be required to take charge of the street gas lighting of the borough under the direction of the Borough Engineer.

The person appointed must be competent to test all burners and governors and the illuminating power of the gas by means of the photometer.

Applicants in applying must state their age and full particulars of past experience and present employment.

Applications, accompanied by copies of not more than three recent testimonials, to be forwarded to me not later than the 1st October, endorsed "Foreman."

Canvassing members of the Council, either directly or indirectly, will be deemed a disqualification.

The salary will be £2 6s. per week.

JAMES PATON,
Borough Engineer and Surveyor.

Municipal Offices.
September 20, 1898.

BOROUGH OF PLYMOUTH.

The Corporation is prepared to receive applications for the position of General Assistant in the Borough Engineer's department.

Candidates must be neat and expeditious draughtsmen, competent to survey and level accurately, prepare plans, sections and detail drawings for works of sewerage, road-making and other works incidental to a Borough Engineer's department; also competent to take out quantities and measure-up works.

Preference will be given to applicants having had previous experience in a Borough Engineer's department.

Salary, £100 per annum, increasing by annual increments of £10 to £130. The engagement to be terminable by a month's notice from either side.

Applicant's age must be between twenty-two and thirty.

Applications, in candidate's own handwriting, accompanied by copies of not more than three recent testimonials only, which will not be returned, to be forwarded to me not later than Saturday, October 1st, endorsed "General Assistant."

Canvassing members of the Council, either directly or indirectly, will be deemed a disqualification.

JAMES PATON,
Borough Engineer and Surveyor.

Municipal Offices.
September 13, 1898.

## TENDERS WANTED.

THE BRIDGEWATER TRUSTEES invite tenders for the Wiring, Supply of Fittings, Lamps, &c. for the electric lighting of Bridgewater House Picture Gallery, St. James's Park, S.W.

Copies of the specification may be obtained and plans seen at the offices of Messrs. O'Gorman & Cozens-Hardy, Consulting Engineers, 66 Victoria-street, S.W., on and after September 27th, on deposit of 1 guinea.

URBAN DISTRICT COUNCIL OF DARTFORD.

TO CONTRACTORS AND OTHERS.

The Council invite tenders for laying a Surface-Water Drain and for Paving the Footways, Crossing and Channelling in Fulwich-road, within their district, in accordance with plans, sections and specification prepared by their Surveyor, Mr. W. Harston, A.M.I.C.E., and which may be inspected at his office, High-street, Dartford.

Tenders, in envelopes endorsed "Tender for Works in Fulwich-road," and addressed "The Chairman, General Purposes Committee, Session's House, Dartford, Kent," must be sent in not later than 5 o'clock, p.m., on Thursday, 6th October prox.

Forms of tender may be obtained of the Council's Surveyor on payment of £10, which will be returned to the person whose tender is accepted on execution of a contract and bond for ensuring the due carrying out of the works and to the persons whose tenders are not accepted upon acceptance of the successful tender.

The person whose tender is accepted will also be required to provide two sureties to the bond, to be approved by the Council.

The contract will contain a clause providing that the wages paid to the workmen employed in the execution of the works shall be those generally accepted as current for competent workmen for similar work in the district.

The Council do not bind themselves to accept the lowest or any tender.

(By order)
T. G. HAYWARD,
Clerk to the Council.

Sessions House, Dartford.
September 18, 1898.

## BOROUGH OF TUNBRIDGE WELLS.
### NEW ROADS.

The Corporation are prepared to receive tenders for Sewering and Making-up New Roads on site of proposed workmen's dwellings, Tunbridge Wells.

Plans and specification can be seen at the Borough Surveyor's office, and quantities and form of tender obtained from me on payment of 2 guineas, which will be returned on receipt of a *bona-fide* tender.

Tenders to be sent to me on or before the 15th October, 1898.

The Corporation do not bind themselves to accept the lowest or any tender.

(By order)
W. C. CRIPPS,
Town Clerk.

Town Hall, Tunbridge Wells.

## COUNTY BOROUGH OF SOUTH SHIELDS.

*UNDERGROUND SANITARY CONVENIENCE.*

#### TO SANITARY ENGINEERS.

The Town Council invite tenders for the whole of the works required in the Construction and Completion of an Underground Public Convenience at the Market-place, South Shields.

Specifications and forms of tender, with a blue print of contract plan, may be obtained from Mr. S. E. Burgess, A.M.I.C.E., Borough Engineer, Chapter-row, upon payment of a deposit of £2, which will be returned on receipt of a *bona-fide* tender. Remittances to be made payable to Mr. W. Anderson, Borough Accountant.

Tenders, sealed and endorsed "Tender for Underground Convenience," must be sent in to the undersigned by 12 noon on Wednesday, the 28th September next.

The Corporation do not bind themselves to accept the lowest or any tender.

(By order)
J. MOORE HAYTON,
Town Clerk.

Court Buildings, South Shields.
September 12, 1898.

## BOROUGH OF TUNBRIDGE WELLS.
### WORKMEN'S DWELLINGS.

The Corporation are prepared to receive tenders for the Erection of fifty-three Four-roomed Cottages and five blocks of Tenements.

Plans and specification may be seen at the Borough Surveyor's office, and quantities and forms of tender obtained from me on payment of 2 guineas, which will be returned on receipt of a *bona-fide* tender.

The Corporation do not bind themselves to accept the lowest or any tender.

(By order)
W. C. CRIPPS,
Town Clerk.

Town Hall, Tunbridge Wells.

## CITY OF BIRMINGHAM.

The Public Works Committee invite tenders for the Reconstruction of the Sewer in Needless-alley, New-street; also the Construction of New Pipe Sewers in a portion of Wentworth-road, &c., Harborne.

Drawings and specifications may be seen, and bills of quantities, schedules of prices and forms of tender obtained, on application to this office on and after Wednesday next, the 21st instant, upon deposit of a cheque, value 2 guineas, for each set of quantities. The cheque will be returned in each case upon receipt by the Public Works Committee of a *bona-fide* tender with prices filled in as required.

The contractor whose tender is accepted (in each case) will be required to pay not less than the minimum standard rate of wages current in the district.

Tenders, sealed and endorsed "Tender for Sewer, Needless-alley," and "Tender for Sewers, Wentworth-road, &c.", to be delivered here not later than 10 a.m. on Saturday, the 1st of October.

The Committee do not pledge themselves to accept the lowest or any tender.

(By order)
JOHN PRICE,
City Engineer and Surveyor.

The Council House, Birmingham.
September 15, 1898.

## BOROUGH OF TUNBRIDGE WELLS.
### NEW ROADS.

The Corporation are prepared to receive tenders for Sewering and Making-up New Roads on site of proposed workmen's dwellings, Tunbridge Wells.

Plans and specification can be seen at the Borough Surveyor's office, and quantities and form of tender obtained from me on payment of 2 guineas, which will be returned on receipt of a bonâ-fide tender.

Tenders to be sent to me on or before the 15th October, 1898.

The Corporation do not bind themselves to accept the lowest or any tender.

(By order)
W. C. CRIPPS,
Town Clerk.

Town Hall, Tunbridge Wells.

## COUNTY BOROUGH OF SOUTH SHIELDS.

*UNDERGROUND SANITARY CONVENIENCE.*

### TO SANITARY ENGINEERS.

The Town Council invite tenders for the whole of the works required in the Construction and Completion of an Underground Public Convenience at the Market-place, South Shields.

Specifications and forms of tender, with a blue print of contract plan, may be obtained from Mr. S. E. Burgess, A.M.I.C.E., Borough Engineer, Chapter-row, upon payment of a deposit of £2, which will be returned on receipt of a bonâ-fide tender. Remittances to be made payable to Mr. W. Anderson, Borough Accountant.

Tenders, sealed and endorsed "Tender for Underground Convenience," must be sent in to the undersigned by 12 noon on Wednesday, the 28th September next.

The Corporation do not bind themselves to accept the lowest or any tender.

(By order)
J. MOORE HAYTON,
Town Clerk.

Court Buildings, South Shields.
September 12, 1898.

## BOROUGH OF TUNBRIDGE WELLS.
### WORKMEN'S DWELLINGS.

The Corporation are prepared to receive tenders for the Erection of fifty-three Four-roomed Cottages and five blocks of Tenements.

Plans and specification may be seen at the Borough Surveyor's office, and quantities and forms of tender obtained from me on payment of 2 guineas, which will be returned on receipt of a bonâ-fide tender.

The Corporation do not bind themselves to accept the lowest or any tender.

(By order)
W. C. CRIPPS,
Town Clerk.

Town Hall, Tunbridge Wells.

## CITY OF BIRMINGHAM.

The Public Works Committee invite tenders for the Reconstruction of the Sewer in Needless-alley, New-street; also the Construction of New Pipe Sewers in a portion of Wentworth-road, &c., Harborne.

Drawings and specifications may be seen, and bills of quantities, schedules of prices and forms of tender obtained, on application to this office on and after Wednesday next, the 21st instant, upon deposit of a cheque, value 2 guineas, for each set of quantities. The cheque will be returned in each case upon receipt by the Public Works Committee of a bonâ-fide tender with prices filled in as required.

The contractor whose tender is accepted (in each case) will be required to pay not less than the minimum standard rate of wages current in the district.

Tenders, sealed and endorsed "Tender for Sewer, Needless-alley," and "Tender for Sewers, Wentworth-road, &c.", to be delivered here not later than 10 a.m. on Saturday, the 1st of October.

The Committee do not pledge themselves to accept the lowest or any tender.

(By order)
JOHN PRICE,
City Engineer and Surveyor.

The Council House, Birmingham.
September 15, 1898.

Both St:

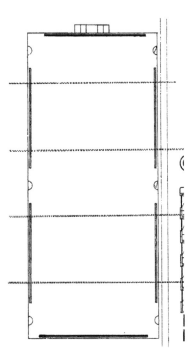

Ground Plan

10    5    0

ASSOCIATION OF MUNICII
MIDLAND COUNTIES DIS

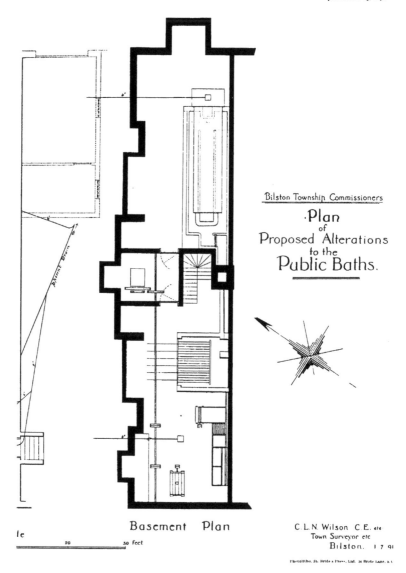

Bilston Township Commissioners

·Plan
of
Proposed Alterations
to the
Public Baths.

Basement Plan

C. L. N. Wilson C.E. etc
Town Surveyor etc
Bilston. 1 7 91

Photolitho. St. Bride s Press. Ltd. 24 Bride Lane. E.C.

le
20        50 feet

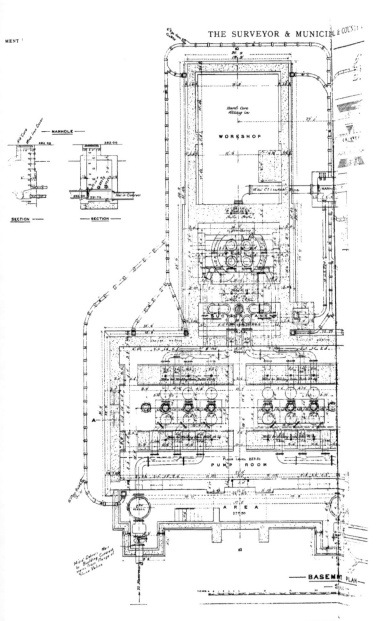

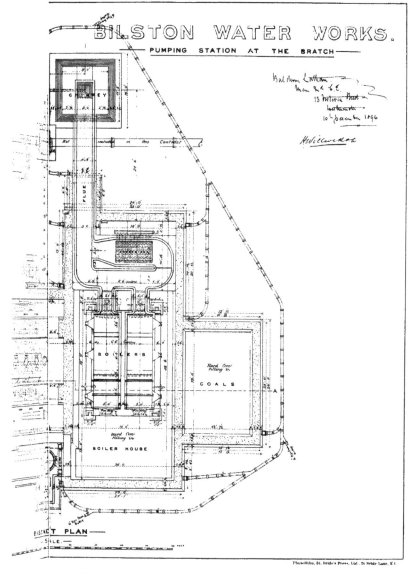

# BILSTON WATER WORKS.
## — PUMPING STATION AT THE BRATCH —

# The Surveyor

## And Municipal and County Engineer.

Vol. XIV., No. 350.   LONDON, SEPTEMBER 30, 1898.   Weekly, Price 3d.

## Minutes of Proceedings.

**Sanitarians in Congress.** From our point of view it must be confessed t1at the president's address to the Sanitary Institute Congress was disappointing. Coming, as it did, from Sir Josep1 Fayrer, it could not 1ave been ot1er t1an able, but one looked in vain to it for pregnant suggestions for the future, or even for new presentations of facts w1ic1 1ave become familiar to us in the past. Wit1 the 1istory of the Sanitary Institute most people who take any sort of interest in matters of public 1ealt1 are now familiar, wit1 the familiarity t1at breeds respect. In its twenty-second year of existence, and on the occasion of its seventeent1 annual congress, one may be permitted again to congratulate it on its magnificent work, and it is satisfactory to find t1at it has reaped its reward in a well-deserved increase of prosperity, w1ic1 means increased powers of influence for good in the years to come. W1en its first congress was 1eld, in 1877, it had 150 members and an income of £240. In 1897 its members were 2,028, and its income £6,000. In the former year five candidates were examined for its now coveted certificates; in 1896 t1at number had risen to 521. All its great work, Sir Josep1 Fayrer tellingly pointed out, has been effected entirely by private enterprise, unaided by any subsidy eit1er from Government or other public aut1ority; and he would have been justified in adding t1at no little of its influence and prosperity has been due to the marked ability of its secretary, Mr. E. W1ite Wallis. It was not news to the president's audience to 1ear how, within the past quarter of a century, public opinion has been educated up to bringing pressure to bear upon legislators, in tangible witness w1ereof has come a crop of sanitary statutes. Unfortunately, 1owever, we can feelingly agree wit1 Sir Josep1 that, as some of t1ese are permissive and ot1ers utterly neglected, muc1 of the benefit t1ey mig1t confer is lost. In spite of the popular belief t1at public aut1orities have neit1er souls to be saved nor bodies to be kicked, Parliament has been too prone to credit municipal boards wit1 consciences. And the result? The association of ideas is not exactly the president's, but his is the allegation t1at tainted water is still drunk, as was illustrated by the condition of Maidstone and King's Lynn last year; t1at c1imneys still vomit fort1 t1eir smoke and c1emical fumes; that rivers are still polluted; t1at cesspools and imperfect drains, badly-constructed and ill-ventilated 1ouses still defy alike sanitary law and common sense. One could turn back to records of past congresses and point to the same complaints in similar definite words. Year after year t1ese, and a dozen ot1er sources of deat1 and disease, claim t1eir scores and hundreds of victims; year after year sanitarians clamour for the stern, systematic and scientific enforcement of remedies. We may point wit1 satisfaction, as does Sir Josep1 Fayrer, to our great advances since Elizabet1an days; but, God knows, our latter-day progress, in proportion to our increased knowledge and resources, has been criminally slow. "It will, per1aps, not be," says Sir Joseph, "until the more complete organisation of the public 1ealt1 administration under a Minister of Public Healt1 be effected, t1at the full benefits of sanitary legislation will be realised and the people attain to t1at standard of 1ealt1 and duration of life for w1ic1 t1ey 1ave a rig1t to 1ope." We can only re-ec1o "Per1aps!"

To his reference to tainted water, smoky chimneys and ot1er c1eris1ed ills Sir Josep1 later adds the careful preservation in t1eir streets by the metropolitan vestries of the fermenting filt1 t1at is allowed to accumulate over the day t1at comes between the Saturday and Monday, and to the practice of t1ose bodies in collecting refuse at all 1ours of the day. Here, again, is an evil 1oary wit1 age and gloriously victorious over opprobrium. T1ey nouris1 it wit1 antiquarian zest in the 1eart of London. As in the insanitary days of our forefat1ers. the citizens of our capital daily place t1eir matutinal muck out on the public ways in all sorts of improvised receptacles; the prowlers of the streets rake it over and distribute muc1 of it to the four winds of 1eaven, and at t1eir leisure the refuse carts of the first city of the world, foul and uncovered, wind in and out of the 1eavy traffic "collecting." It is t1ese, and even more petty, anachronisms t1at we must watc1 and eradicate. Many forms of deat1-dealing disease we 1ave eit1er secured immunity from, or at least 1ave reduced from epidemic proportions. But Sir Josep1 warns us t1at our vigilance must never be relaxed. Small-pox must "gang its gait," at least for the five years during w1ic1 "conscience" is to 1ave full play; enteric fever, the president 1opes, is to become less prevalent wit1 improved drainage, the removal of excretal filt1 and the supply of pure water; c1olera is to be similarly influenced; scarlet fever is satisfactorily decreasing, but wit1 regard to dip1t1eria it would seem t1at sanitary arrangements as suc1 1ave had little or no effect upon the sustained prevalence of the disease. We must wait, so far as Sir Joseph carries us, for more knowledge of the be1aviour of the micro-organism of the scourge. As to malarial diseases, we may include t1em, says the president, among t1ose t1at 1ave become all but extinct in England, thoug1 they are still the prominent cause of deat1 in our Eastern empire; but w1en he turns to tuberculous disease the record is not so satisfactory. It is true that sanitation has in t1is connection done good by attending to ill-ventilated and crowded dwellings, damp and waterlogged soil, impure water and noxious trades. "We 1ave witnessed," says Dr. James Pollock, "an enormous decrease of deat1s from p1t1isis, and a decided lengt1ening of its duration. Fewer die of it, and are slower to die w1en affected." As yet no agents are known w1ic1 can be applied locally to the interior of the body for the destruction of bacilli or septic material. In this direction we may look wit1 with eager hope to the furt1er researc1es of bacteriologists; in the meantime one misses from the inaugural address the suggestion for compulsory isolation, which we hope some day may be made and acted upon.

From the fulness of his intimate knowledge of India Sir Joseph drew a hopeful picture of the beneficial results of sanitary work there during the last half-century. From 1800 to 1830 the ordinary death rate of the British soldier stood at 84·6; in 1895 it was 15·26, and it has been even as low as 10 per 1,000. The death rate of the native army does not show so great a diminution, but here, too, there is an improvement. So, also, is there with the jail population, though 27·61 per 1,000 was the mortality in 1895. As regards the vast civil population, the president points out that not only have there to be dealt with epidemics, famine and long-established modes of living, which obstruct improvement, but also ignorance, prejudice and religious scruples, which tend to make the people doggedly resist all measures taken for the amelioration of their condition. Yet the published mortality returns during the period between 1882 and 1895 have oscillated between 23 and 33 per 1,000—not, after all, says Sir Joseph, a very high death rate considering the circumstances, but one which is susceptible of diminution. The interest of sanitarians the world over has of late been centred upon the plague which has appeared in India within the last two years, and one notes with relief the optimistic opinion of so high an authority as the president, that already it has been shown to be amenable to sanitary laws, like other epidemics, and that there is a hope that it may be ultimately controlled and got rid of altogether, though there is reason to fear that this will not take place for some time to come.

Returning, finally, to the more general observations in the inaugural address, there are some sentences which come early in the paper but which may fitly close these passing comments. "In some parts of England, where health is the main object considered, it (the death rate) has been as low as 9 per 1,000; in others, where the chief objects are manufacture, trade or money-making, it has been 30 per 1,000. The death rate is susceptible of considerable modification, and we know how it may be increased or diminished; it behoves the nation to exert its power and stand credited with the lowest figure. In fact, it is, within certain limits, at our own control, and whether the people shall die at the rate of 13 or 23 per 1,000 depends on how we recognise our responsibility and put in force sanitary regulations. It is mainly a question of finance. Our sanitarians can say how it is to be done, and are perpetually saying it; but more money, more faith, more energy are needed to deal with this question satisfactorily." One of the first and most practical steps, we venture to add, should be a simple codification of existing sanitary statutes; a second, their more complete, universal and impartial enforcement.

\* \* \*

**The Opening of Streets.**    In his annual report submitted to the Teddington Urban District Council for the year ended June 30th the surveyor, Mr. Marshall Hainsworth, refers to one or two interesting points of practice. About a year ago the Grand Junction Waterworks Company decided to cast upon all persons seeking a supply of water the statutory duty of making good and maintaining the surface of roadways over trenches cut for that purpose, and in consequence of this decision the council undertook the responsibility of repairing this damage on certain terms. The disturbance of the surface of a public highway is only allowed after a license or permit for the purpose has been obtained from the council, and thus a record of and supervision over these operations is obtained, the work being facili-

tated by the courtesy of the water company in submitting regular notifications of the applications made to them for a supply of water. Very few of the parish roads escaped damage from opening during the past year, and Mr. Hainsworth takes particular exception to the clumsy method of opening down to the water mains for the purpose of cutting off the services in cases of non-payment of water rates, a process that is obviated by other companies in various ways. The opinion of the borough engineer of Birkenhead is quoted, to the effect that *replacement* is not *reinstatement*, trenches being often closed without any serious attempt to consolidate the loose excavations, that are often indiscriminately composed of road materials and soil obtained in the cutting of the trench. The consequence of these operations is that the road surface is never made good until the road is re-coated or re-formed. Further difficulties have been experienced, owing to the failure of the water company to submit prior to the execution of the work plans showing the position of the new mains to be laid, the result being that they are often laid in very undesirable positions in the roadways. Inferior foundation for plug boxes has also been a cause of unevenness in the road surfaces, but it is expected that the introduction of concrete as a foundation will remove this factor of dis-repair. The experience of the year confirms Mr. Hainsworth in the opinion previously formed that the responsibilities of the maintenance of all public highways should vest solely in one authority—the urban district council acting as the highway authority. He therefore concludes by recommending that the excavation of trenches in public highways for the laying of house drain connections, or gas or water services, be undertaken by the council for the various companies and owners of property upon a schedule of prices based upon the nett cost of similar work, as he is convinced that any loss that might accrue from such an arrangement would be more than compensated by the proper reinstatement of the roadways and footways.

\* \* \*

**Manchester Corporation Electricity Regulations.**    The city electrical engineer of Manchester has recently issued a revised set of regulations in connection with the supply of electrical energy which will repay some consideration. Comprising, as they do, some thirty-three pages, the rules may appear to be a little alarming from the consumer's point of view, but, seeing that they are really intended to safeguard the interests of the consumer, few objections ought to be raised. The special feature of the Manchester system of supply —viz., the five-wire arrangement—enables the corporation in many streets to give a supply of electrical energy at a different voltage, ranging from 100 to 400 volts, which is a matter of some importance to many consumers. The majority of the regulations do not differ from those usually adopted by municipalities and companies. The most striking alterations are those relating to wiring and fittings, and the innovation proposed by the city electrical engineer is somewhat startling. Practically all wiring, electrical fittings and appliances of every description situated on any premises intended to be used for the supply of electrical energy from the corporation mains must be approved by the city electrical engineer before the installation is connected. In other words, every detail of an installation has to be submitted to the city engineer before they will be permitted to be erected. Hitherto it has usually been felt that if the consumer's wiring and fittings were reasonably safe, that is if the electrical test applied was moderately satisfactory, current was then supplied without demur. It was generally felt that the test applied was of a somewhat perfunctory nature, and certainly could not reveal much of the inferior work that might exist. It was merely a test of the insulation which might alter from day to day. Mr. Wordingham, the Manchester engineer, proposes to sweep all this away, and the changes coming upon what have been undoubtedly lax methods may cause some perturbation. From a consumer's point of view it does appear to be somewhat parental to insist that all fittings should be submitted to the city engineer before they can be used. It is putting an obstacle in the way of pushing the electric light, and might have the effect of deterring some householders or shopkeepers from having their premises wired if they are compelled to go through the formula prescribed by the city electrical engineer. If the articles were to be submitted only by a contractor, we think there is a good deal to be said for the regulation, but it will never do to make it difficult for the consumer to obtain electric light.

\* \* \*

**An Appointment at Axminster.**

Our readers will find in our issue of September 2nd a reference to the circumstances of an appointment by a rural district council in Devonshire. The details were so extraordinary that but for the fact that we knew our correspondent to be thoroughly reliable we should have hesitated to credit them. We have been at pains, however, to make some inquiries, and find that the story is only too true. We did not previously mention the name of the place, but we shall do so now. It is Axminster. The facts of the case may be briefly given. Last month a special adjourned meeting was held to consider applications for the appointment of a highway surveyor, and select three candidates to attend the next meeting of the council. There were a large number of applicants, and it was stipulated that each candidate should state the salary he would require. One of the selected three was the assistant, or "partner," as he is sometimes called, of the late surveyor, and this candidate, who, we understand, is only twenty-three years of age, was ultimately appointed in preference to more experienced men, at a salary of £150 a year, a higher figure, we believe, than was asked by the other selected candidates. Before the election was made it was thought that the local candidate stood very little chance. One of our correspondents relates a peculiar story in connection with the proceedings. Prior to the final selection the question arose as to whether certain plans of roads under the jurisdiction of the council were the property of that body or not. These plans were then in the possession of, and claimed by, the outgoing surveyor. The council decided that, though the plans were prepared by their surveyor during his term of office, they could not or would not claim them, and the retiring surveyor having given the council to understand that the plans would be at the disposal of his successor if he were elected, elected he accordingly was. Another correspondent informs us that, while the appointment has caused some dissatisfaction in the district on account of the youth and inexperience of the new surveyor, the majority of the members excuse themselves on the ground that he is a near relative of the chairman, and that a year or two ago he paid a large sum of money to the retiring surveyor to become his partner and ultimate successor. These seem to us to be two very good reasons why he should not have been elected.

\* \* \*

**An Appointment at Bridlington.**

In another column we give some details of the resignation of Mr. Stow, the surveyor to the Bridlington Urban District Council, in consequence of his appointment to Chertsey. At the meeting of the council there was unanimity in praising the work of Mr. Stow, but a disposition to complain because he had not applied for an increase of salary instead of a new situation, the implication evidently being that he might have had the former for the asking. It does not

seem to have occurred to the members that if they thought their surveyor's services were worth more than they were paying it would have been more graceful on their part to have raised his salary spontaneously without waiting for an application. It would also have been more in accordance with the moral fitness of things, for it is the sheerest sophistry to say that anything can justify employers in accepting underpaid work, which is simply a case of taking something for which nothing is given in return. It must be rather annoying to the retiring surveyor to know that, after the admitted excellence of his work, a successor is to be appointed at an increased salary, but he undoubtedly did the right thing in finding another situation in preference to throwing himself on the tender mercies of the Bridlington Urban District Council, however much they may now profess to value his services. We observe that during the discussion at the council meeting a member objected to the salary proposed to be given to the new surveyor, the objection being based on the ground that many tradesmen at the present time were not earning as much. We shall not attempt to analyse the peculiar beauty and subtlety of this argument. There was some compensation, however, in coming across a remark on the part of another member to the effect that a surveyor should be remunerated so that he would be above influence in the discharge of his duties.

\* \* \*

**The Bradford Tramway Accident.**

Without in any way desiring to anticipate the result of the inquiry that is being held into the lamentable disaster on the recently-opened tramway system at Bradford, the accident ought to have very little bearing upon the subject of electrical working, because it was evident from the very outset that whatever the motive power may have been a similar catastrophe might have occurred. Many of our readers will remember the terrible calamity that occurred on the Huddersfield municipal steam lines some years ago, when one of the steam cars got beyond the driver's control and was capsized at the bottom of a steep gradient in a manner very similar to what happened at Bradford. It may be shown at Bradford that slightly different handling of the controlling apparatus might have averted the danger, but the same may be said of practically every railway accident that occurs. Although the matter seems to be clearly explainable, it will be regrettable if the accident influences any corporation when deciding upon the merits of electrical and other tramway methods, as appears to be the case in Newcastle, where, to judge from the local agitation that is rife, the occurrence at Bradford is likely to have considerable weight. In order to show that the question of gradients is not wholly responsible for the Bradford accident, it may be pointed out that at Bristol and Halifax much more severe gradients are being constantly traversed by electric cars.

\* \* \*

**Stratford's Polluted River.**

In our last issue we gave a brief report of a Local Government Board inquiry which was held last week respecting complaints lodged by the inhabitants of Stratford as to the polluted state of the Channelsea river, which communicates with the Lea. Among other things it was alleged that an outbreak of diphtheria in Stratford had resulted from the pollution. As the brevity of the report may create an incorrect impression, we print in another column a report on the subject recently presented by the borough engineer of West Ham, Mr. Lewis Angell. There seems to be no evidence that the cases of diphtheria are attributable to the state of the river, and the general health of the district is continuously very good. Cases of diphtheria occur in other parts of the district.

# Association of Municipal and County Engineers.

## MIDLAND DISTRICT MEETING AT BILSTON.—II.

Bilston: View of Wellington-road.

We now conclude our report of this meeting. It will be remembered that before giving an account of the visits and other functions we reproduced Mr. Wilson's long and valuable paper, but were compelled to hold over the latter part, which dealt exclusively with the waterworks. This concluding part of the paper is as follows :—

### SEVEN YEARS IN A BLACK COUNTRY TOWN
*(continued),*
By C. L. N. WILSON, ASSOC.M.INST.C.E.

#### WATERWORKS.

Under the 1850 Act the commissioners obtained powers to construct waterworks and to supply the town with water, and they commenced to pump water from the mines by the Sandy gay engine direct into the water mains, but, as might have been expected, this did not prove satisfactory. About the same time that our Act was obtained the Wolverhampton Waterworks Company was established, and took power to supply Bilston, and then, in a few years after, the South Staffordshire Waterworks Company also took power to supply Bilston, and the Wolverhamptom Waterworks Company actually commenced to supply water in the town. The then commissioners made a bargain with the Wolverhampton Waterworks Company for them to supply the town with water in bulk, and the company to withdraw from supplying the township in detail, the charge to the commissioners being 6d. per 1,000 gallons, and the commissioners to do the distribution themselves. At the end of this term the commissioners negotiated with the South Staffordshire Waterworks Company for their price to supply Bilston, but whilst these negotiations were going on the South Staffordshire Waterworks Company, without the knowledge of the Bilston commissioners, entered into an agreement with the Wolverhampton Waterworks Company by which the South Staffordshire Waterworks Company were prohibited from supplying Bilston with water under a penalty of £5,000. Therefore the commissioners entered into a second agreement for a further term of twenty-one years, the water to be taken in bulk, and the price to be 5d. per 1,000 gallons, the commissioners to pay for not less than 220,000 gallons per day, and any excess over the 220,000 gallons per day to be paid for at the same rate. In 1868 the Wolverhampton Corporation proposed to purchase the undertaking of the Wolverhampton Waterworks Company, and promoted a Bill in Parliament to which was scheduled for confirmation by Parliament the before-mentioned agreement between the South Staffordshire Waterworks Company and the Wolverhampton Waterworks Company. The Bilston Township Commissioners opposed this Bill, on the ground that it would place them in the hands of the Wolverhampton Waterworks Company, and would prohibit them obtaining water from the South Staffordshire Waterworks Company. The result of this opposition was that the agreement between the commissioners and the Wolverhampton Waterworks Company was made perpetual as between the Wolverhampton Corporation and the Bilston Commissioners, subject to a revision in price every twenty-one years. The first term of twenty-one years expired in 1889, and the Wolverhampton Corporation gave notice for an advance from 5d. to 6d. per 1,000 gallons; the Bilston Township Commissioners gave notice for a reduction from 5d. to 4d. per 1,000 gallons. An arbitration followed, Mr. Baldwin Latham being the engineering adviser for the Township Commissioners, and he advised that 3d. per 1,000 gallons was the outside price the Wolverhampton Corporation ought to charge, and that it would be better and cheaper for the Bilston Township Commissioners to construct their own waterworks and become independent of Wolverhampton. He further advised that within 6 or 7 miles of Bilston it would be possible to obtain a good and plentiful supply of water, and, acting upon his advice, the Township Commissioners determined to construct their own waterworks. To do this Parliamentary powers were required, to get rid of the agreement with the Wolverhampton Corporation, which had been made perpetual. The commissioners, however, first of all sought the advice of the Local Government Board, who advised that it appeared to them that the Township Commissioners were only bound to the Wolverhampton Corporation for 220,000 gallons per day, and that the Township Commissioners might construct works for the supply required beyond that. They then applied for a loan for this purpose, where-upon the Wolverhampton Corporation gave them notice that unless they abandoned their purpose they (the corporation) would move for an injunction in the Supreme Court to restrain them. The commissioners refused to abandon their proposal, and the application of the Wolverhampton Corporation for an interlocutory injunction was refused. The Township Commissioners were then advised to promote a Bill in Parliament, so that there was a Chancery suit and Parliamentary proceedings running at the same time. The Bill came before a committee of the House of Commons, who took evidence, but ultimately decided not to pass the Bill, having regard to the Chancery proceedings. The action commenced by the Wolverhampton Corporation for an injunction came on soon after, when the First Court held that the agreement held the Bilston Township Commissioners to the Wolverhampton Corporation for all the water they required.

From this decision the Bilston Township Commissioners appealed, and on this occasion the Court was divided: two judges held that the Bilston Township Commissioners were bound to take all the water they required from the Wolverhampton Corporation, and the other judge held that they were only bound to 220,000 gallons per day. The Township Commissioners were strongly advised to appeal to the House of Lords against this decision, and the appeal was in the list for hearing. At this stage in the proceedings negotiations were entered into by the two authorities, which ended in the Bilston Commissioners agreeing to pay the Wolverhampton Corporation the sum of £9,000 to be released from the terms of the agreement, and also to promote a Bill in Parliament for powers to supply the township of Bilston with water, and to construct their own waterworks; the Wolverhampton Corporation agreeing to help the commissioners to obtain their Bill. The commissioners, in accordance with this agreement, promoted a Bill which became law in 1893 after some slight opposition. In 1895 another agreement was entered into between the two authorities, under which Bilston agreed to pay Wolverhampton the sum of £7,750 for the right to supply such portion of the Coseley District Council as is in the Wolverhampton area of supply; and also for certain mains, valves, hydrants, &c., in this district, and along the Parkfield - road and other roads from the corporation's pumping station at Goldthorn Hill, to the boundary of the Bilston Urban District Council on the Willenhall-road and this was incorporated in the Bilston Improvement Act of 1896; and, after some slight opposition from the Seisdon Rural District Council, was approved, subject to certain concessions to this council. The water area for supply consists now of the township of Bilston, such portion of the Coseley area as was in the Wolverhampton area of supply, and the parishes of Himley, Wombourn, Swindon, Trysull and Woodford in the Seisdon rural district.

The average daily amount of water pumped is about 840,000 gallons, or about 30 gallons per head per day for all purposes; of this about 5 gallons per head per day is for trade purposes. The water rate is practically 7 per cent. per annum upon the rateable value; nothing is charged for the first water-closet, but a charge of 10s. is made for every water-closet beyond the first per annum, and the sum of 8s. for every bath.

### DESCRIPTION OF THE WORKS.

The whole of the works were designed by Mr. Baldwin Latham, M.I.C.E., &c., of Westminster, and the author acted as resident engineer. In June, 1892, a test bore-hole was put down, 4-in. in diameter and 66 ft. deep; and the first come of water was met with at a depth of 30 ft. below the surface. After this bore-hole had been put in a 3-in. pump with 7-in. stroke was lowered into the well, and a steam engine and boiler obtained to drive it : this pump lifted 16 gallons per minute. Below is a table showing the effect of two and a quarter hours' pumping—viz.:—

|  |  |  | ft. | in. |  |  |  |
|---|---|---|---|---|---|---|---|
| After 30 minutes pumping water | 7 | 0 | below top of bore-holes. |
| „ 45 | „ | „ | 9 | 0 | „ | „ | „ |
| „ 60 | „ | „ | 10 | 0 | „ | „ | „ |
| „ 75 | „ | „ | 10 | 0 | „ | „ | „ |
| „ 90 | „ | „ | 10 | 0 | „ | „ | „ |
| „ 105 | „ | „ | 10 | 4 | „ | „ | „ |
| „ 120 | „ | „ | 10 | 4 | „ | „ | „ |
| „ 135 | „ | „ | 10 | 0 | „ | „ | „ |

After the pump was stopped it took forty-seven minutes for the water to rise in the bore-hole until it just overflowed; on no occasion afterwards were we able to lower the water in the bore-hole to a greater depth than 10 ft. from the surface. In October, 1893, a contract was entered into with Messrs. H. Hughes & Sons to sink the well and drive the adits, and they commenced work on Monday, January 15, 1894. On February 6th the well was down 34 ft., and the hand-pumps and pulsometer were beaten, and a 10-in. steam pump was then put to work. On March 22nd the shaft was down 65 ft., and the come of water was 7,363 gallons per hour. On April 11th the shaft was down 91 ft. 8 in., and the come of water was 13,748 gallons per hour. On April 18th the large steam pump was beaten; the water then rose to within 1 ft. 10½ in. from the surface when the bore-hole was plugged, but when the water was overflowing from the bore-hole, in fifteen minutes it fell to 2 ft. 2 in. below the surface and remained constant at that level. The sandstone in the well was tested, when dry, and broken up into sand; 1,061 grains taken; of this, 1,054 grains went through a 2,500-mesh sieve, and 1,047 grains of this passed through a 4,900-mesh sieve. A second 10-in. steam pump was then obtained, and on June 13th the well was down 134 ft., and the come of water was 801,700 gallons in twenty-four hours. From then up to August 8th the water could not be got out, and Messrs. H. Hughes & Sons threw up the contract; from that time Mr. John Hughes, their surety, carried on the sinking of the shaft, and on September 3rd a third pump was got to work, and the men commenced sinking again on September 10th, and went on until September 17th, when the pit was down 142 ft.; at this point the pumps were beaten again. The men got to work again on October 9th, but failed again on October 15th, with the well only 149 ft. deep. It was then decided to sink a second shaft and connect the two by means of headings, and after this was done we still could not go on with the sinking, and it was found necessary to put down our permanent pumps

and allow the contractor to use them in addition to his own; by this means the wells were got down to their full depth and the headings driven for a short distance, and the brickwork finished in December, 1897, as it at present stands. It was decided not to put down the bore-hole in No. 1 well or to drive the headings any further. For the last sixty-seven days, upon which it was necessary to pump from the bottom of the shaft whilst the cast-iron tubbing, the oak curbs, and the lower portion of the brickwork were got into position, 101,440,942 gallons of water was raised, or an average of 1,514,044 gallons per day, or 251 gallons per minute. The shafts are both sunk in a trough in what are known as the hunter beds, the particular bed being the upper soft red sandstone, which at this point is about 160 ft. thick, and overlies the pebble beds, which are probably 350 ft. thick. This rock is well known as a good water-bearing strata. The shafts are two in number, one 150 ft. deep and 8 ft. 6 in. in diameter, the other 140 ft. deep only. They are connected by a heading, 6 ft. by 4 ft. and 45 ft. long. The steining in each case consists of the best Staffordshire blue bricks, built in cement mortar, the upper 15 ft. being 14-in. work and the remaining portion 9-in.; the water is carried down behind the walls by means of perforated cast-iron pipes packed round with gravel. The adits are driven the following distances only—viz., north adit, 43 ft. instead of 132 ft.; south adit, 32 ft. instead of 258 ft.; east adit, 79 ft. instead of 343 ft.; and the west adit, 84 ft. instead of 99 ft. The whole of the cement, bricks, &c., were tested on the ground before using.

|  | £ | s. | d. |
|---|---|---|---|
| The original contract was ... ... ... | £3,351 | 10 | 5 |
| The cost of work, including pumping, was ... | 6,822 | 0 | 1 |

Of this latter sum no less than £2,208 9s. 10d. represents money paid for extra pumping alone. In connection with this contract a wharf, 90 ft. long, was constructed on the side of the canal, and a small brick bridge overflow drain, measuring chamber and a length of roadway, at a cost of £376 12s. 3d.

During the whole of the time the works were in progress the whole of the wells in the district were carefully measured

BILSTON: THE METER-HOUSE.

every week, the water passing down the stream gauged daily, and the amount of rainfall was also taken daily, and a register of the whole kept for reference. The level of the ground round well is 235·5 ft. above ordnance datum, the bottom of the tank is 252·5 ft. above ordnance datum, the surface of the stream 252·5 ft. above ordnance datum, and the surface of the water in canal 255 ft. above ordnance datum. The reservoir is situated at Goldthorn Hill, a distance of 6,617 yards from the pumping station at the Bratch; the bottom of the reservoir is 595 ft. above ordnance datum; the inlet from the rising main being 597 ft. above ordnance datum, the outlet to Bilston 505·33 ft. above ordnance datum, the top water level 607 ft. above ordnance datum, and the surface of the ground on the top is 611·75 ft. above ordnance datum. It is a covered service reservoir only, constructed entirely of cement concrete with a floated face; it is 116 ft. 9 in. by 100 ft., divided into nine compartments by eight cross walls, 2 ft. thick, and covered with semicular arches,

BILSTON WATERWORKS: VIEW OF THE SERVICE RESERVOIR.

the cross walls themselves being each pierced with ten suitable openings; the drains run in the cross walls, and are all collected and connecting to the cleansing pond; twenty-seven Cregeens air-inlets are provided, and a by-pass, so that the water can be pumped direct into the mains whilst the reservoir is being cleaned out, &c. The bottom is 2 ft. thick, and the sides and ends taper from 3 ft. 6 in. at the bottom to 2 ft. at the top; an overflow and draw-off pipe is also fixed and connected to the cleansing pond, and the necessary manholes, ladders and valve chambers are also fixed. The concrete used consisted of six parts by measure of mixed stone and sand to one of cement, the cement being fresh burnt finely ground Portland, weighing 116 lb. per striked bushel when filled from a hopper with a fall of not more than 1 ft., and to stand 350 lb. to the square inch when tested on a section of 2¼ square inches after seven days' immersion in water, and not more than 10 per cent. residuum left in a 2,500-mesh sieve; the stone dressings for gates, &c., are "Pennant." Before the contract was advertised two trial holes were sunk, and it was found that the site was sand and gravel; in fact, the contractor found all the sand and gravel he required on the job. The sand required washing, however, before being used, and the concrete was carefully placed in position; strips of iron, No. 16 B.W.G. and 1¼ in. wide, were also put in the concrete work, and after the shutters had been drawn the whole of the inside of the work and the top of the arches outside were floated at two different times with coats of mortar ¾ in. in thickness, and composed of one of cement and one of sand. The work is very well done, and is perfectly watertight, the contractor being Henry Hill, of Maidenhead, and the amount of contract £3,601 17s., the actual cost being £3,574 12s. 9d.

The rising main is 6,617 yards in length, of 14-in. cast-iron pipes, properly tested at the foundry and on the ground to the following tests—*viz.*,—

| Diameter of Pipes. | Description and Mark. | Thickness of Metal. | Length of Pipe in Work. | Depth of Socket. | Thickness of Joint. | Weight of Pipe. | Deviation allowed. | Head of Water in ft. |
|---|---|---|---|---|---|---|---|---|
| in. | | in. | ft. | in. | in. | lb. | lb. | ft. |
| 3 | For hydrants | ½ | 9 | — | — | 172 | 8 | 1,000 |
| 12 | Straight | 9/16 | 9 | 3 | 5/16 | 715 | 35 | 500 |
| 12 | Radial | ⅝ | 4 | 3 | ¼ | 382 | 17 | — |
| 14 | Straight, A | 1 | 12 | 3½ | 5/16 | 1,953 | 97 | 1,000 |
| 14 | " B | ⅞ | 12 | 3½ | 5/16 | 1,717 | 85 | 800 |
| 14 | " C | ¾ | 12 | 3½ | 5/16 | 1,484 | 74 | 600 |
| 14 | " D | ⅝ | 12 | 3½ | 5/16 | 1,262 | 63 | 500 |
| 14 | Radial A | 1 1/16 | 4 | 3½ | ¼ | 844 | 42 | — |
| 14 | " C | 13/16 | 4 | 3½ | ¼ | 680 | 34 | — |
| 14 | Branch, A | 1 | 3 | 3½ | 5/16 | 667 | 33 | 1,000 |
| 14 | " B | ⅞ | 3 | 3½ | 5/16 | 604 | 30 | 800 |
| 14 | " C | ¾ | 3 | 3½ | 5/16 | 524 | 26 | 600 |
| 14 | " D | ⅝ | 3 | 3½ | 5/16 | 466 | 23 | 500 |

The joints are made entirely of lead, cold rings of drawn lead being driven into the socket first until they were half full, and then filled with molten lead and well caulked. Every length of pipe was tested by a force pump to a pressure of 200 ft. above the working head at its upper end, the force pump being fixed at the lower end for all the tests. The hydrants are extra strong, of the loose valve screw-down type for bayonet-joint connection, 2½ in. in diameter; the air valves are of the single self-acting type, 3⅜ in. in diameter, with floating ball and leather diaphragm; the stop-cocks are also on the screw-down principle, with loose valves and stuffing boxes, and tested for 300 lb. pressure, of the following weights: ½ in., 10 oz., ¾ in., 20 oz., ⅞ in., 26 oz, 1 in. 31 oz. metal, 14 lb. copper, 1¾ lb. lead and 1 lb. block tin. Morris & Penny's ferrules are used for house connections with cone joints, and their patent apparatus for tapping mains under pressure are used for fixing them. The rising main is laid at a uniform depth to bottom of sockets of 4 ft. 7 in. below the surface of the roadway. This work was also well carried out by the contractor, Mr. Herbert Holloway, of Wolverhampton; not one single joint had to be re-run, and very few wanted setting up a second time. The contract price was £7,154 2s. 4d., and the actual cost £7,115 3s. 7d.

The pumping station is very prettily situated at the Bratch, Wombourn, and consists of a noble castle-like red (Ruabon) pressed-brick building, with Hollington stone dressing, window heads, &c. The building has a Gothic feeling, and the principal portion has four turrents, one at each corner, and embattled parapets. The building consists of area and pump-room, engine-house, well-house, and a small fitting shop, boiler-house and coal store. The pump-house is in the basement, and the walls are constructed of concrete; the remaining walls, both inside and out, are built with red Ruabon pressed bricks. The stack is also built of red Ruabon bricks, and it is 90 ft. in height, surmounted with a cast-iron ornamental railing 3 ft. high, a weathercock and vane; and, to prevent a pollution, Moule's patent earth-closet, with galvanised iron pails, is provided. The contractors for this portion of the work were Messrs. H. Willcock & Co., of Wolverhampton. The contract price was £5,718 6s. 6d., and the actual cost £6,133 6s. 9d.

### ENGINES, PUMPS AND BOILERS.

This contract was let in the first place to Messrs. Jas. Watt & Co., of Soho Works, Birmingham, under conditions to be hereinafter stated; but, unfortunately, this old-established firm came to grief before they had half completed their contract, but what work they had finished was very well done indeed, and the author is very glad that the old name of Watt in connection with steam engine works in Birmingham is not to die out, Messrs. Averys, who purchased the works, having given notice of their intention to trade under the old name of James Watt & Co., Limited. I have also given the same particulars with regard to the tenders of Messrs. Thornewill &

BILSTON: GENERAL VIEW OF THE PUMPING STATION.

Warham, of Burton-on-Trent, who have successfully completed this portion of the work.

On these figures James Watt & Co.'s tender for the engines and pumps, with Hornsby's boilers and Green's economiser, was accepted. The engines are of the vertical triple-expansion type, and surface condensing, with the three force pumps placed directly underneath the crank shaft, and two well pumps driven from a pin in a disc at the end of the crank shaft, connected by a pitman of pitch pine to a pair of rocking bobs placed over the well, the pumps being about 140 ft. from the surface of the well.

Each engine has a high-pressure, intermediate-pressure and low-pressure cylinder, the internal diameters of which are 16 in., 26 in. and 40 in. respectively. These cylinders were all tested hydraulically to a pressure of 320 lb. on the square inch before leaving the maker's works, have a 3-ft. stroke, and are fitted with valve chests, indicator cocks, escape valves, auxiliary starting valves, cylinder drain cocks, jacket drain cocks, and the necessary gear for working them. The cylinders are lagged and covered, with planished steel and brass bands and screws; each cylinder is fitted with main and expansion valves, the latter ranging from nine to three. The whole of the valve gear is of the Corliss trip type.

The pistons are fitted with Bickle's improved metallic packing. The piston rods are 5-in. diameter, of forged scrap steel. The crank shaft is set at angles of 120 deg. with each other, the sequence of the cranks being H.P., L.P., I.P. The disc on fly-wheel is set to give a stroke of 3 ft.; the fly-wheels are six-armed, 13 ft. diameter, and weigh 7¼ tons; square holes are cut on the face, for barring round. Boiler feed pumps and auxiliary feed pumps are provided; a single air pump, 13½ in. diameter with a 3-ft. stroke, is driven from a disc on the outside fly-wheel.

The condensers contain 600 square feet of cooling surface each; the tubes are solid-drawn brass, 1¼ in. inside diameter

and 22 B.W.G. in thickness, fastened to tube plates with screwed ferrules and packed with asbestos. The force pumps are 11 in. in diameter; the poles are connected to cross-heads under the crank shaft, and worked by side rods; the suction and delivery valves are double-beat and made of gun metal. The air vessels are 3 ft. 9 in. diameter, and from the centre of discharge from force pumps to the top of the dome is 12 ft. 6 in.; these air vessels were tested to 800 ft. A Westinghouse air compressor is fixed on the west side of engine-house, for charging the air vessels.

The well pumps are 14 in. diameter, with a 3-ft. stroke, and are suspended by means of two wrought-iron suspension rods 2½-in. diameter, and a 15-in. rising main from specially strong cast-iron girders over the top of the well, the landers being fixed on the top of these girders; each pump has a Babbitt's metal double-beat valve. The quadrants are of wrought-iron; and the spear rods are pitch pine, 7 in. by 5 in., fitted with strapping plates and bolts.

The materials used had to stand the following tests:—

| Iron. | Tensional Strains per square inch. Tons. | Percentage of Contraction of Fractured Area. |
|---|---|---|
| Bars and rods under ½ in. in sectional area | 24 | 40 |
| Bars and rods over ½ in. in sectional area | 24 | 30 |
| Plates | 21 | 10 |
| Channel, angle and tee iron | 22 | 20 |
| Steel. | | |
| Plates, bars, rods, angles and tees... | 27 to 30 | 40 |

Overhead travelling cranes are provided both in engine and well houses and fitting-shop. The fitting-shop contains one of Thornewill & Warham's horizontal steam engines; one 10-in. by 12-ft. box gap bed, self-acting, sliding, surfacing and screw-cutting lathe; one 6-in. by 6-ft. gap bed, self-

| | JAS. WATT & Co., Birmingham. | | | THORNEWILL & WARHAM, Burton-on-Trent. | | |
|---|---|---|---|---|---|---|
| | 1. Babcock's Boilers and Economiser, or Green's Economiser. | 2. Hornsby's Boilers and Green's Economiser. | 3. Sterling's Boilers and Economiser. | 1. Babcock's Boilers and Economiser. | 2. Hornsby's Boilers and Green's Economiser. | 3. Sterling's Boilers and Economiser. |
| | | | | Corliss Gear and Automatic Out-off Gear. | | |
| 1. Amount of tender | £8,550 | £8,470 | £8,300 | £13,100 | £12,800 | £12,500 |
| 2. Equivalent for engines off 100 mills at 1 per cent. reduction | £8,464 | £8,004 | £7,843 | £11,790 | £11,520 | £11,250 |
| 3. Equivalent for engines off 100 mills at 2s. penalty | £8,379 | £7,453 | £7,304 | £10,480 | £10,240 | £10,000 |
| 4. Extra, two fly-wheels | — | — | — | £50 | £50 | £50 |
| 5. Extra for four tye rods | £125 | £125 | £125 | £50 | £50 | £50 |
| 6. Six months' coals when pumping 400,000 gallons per day of eight hours, coals at 10s. per ton | 97 | 93 | 93 | 90 | 90 | 90 |
| 7. Wages, one driver and one stoker for six months, as above | £123 | £123 | £123 | £91 | £91 | £91 |
| 8. Guaranteed weight in tons | 352 | 352 | 352 | 404 | 404 | 404 |
| 9. Duty, in million foot-lb. | 101 | 105½ | 105½ | 110 | 110 | 110 |
| 10. Lb. coal per P.H.P. per hour | 2·195 | 2·1 | 2·1 | 2·016 | 2·016 | 2·016 |
| 11. Lb. feed water per 1,000,000 gallons pumped | 47,800 | 57,120 | 57,120 | 54,000 | 54,000 | 54,000 |
| 12. Lb. feed water per P.H.P. per hour | 19 | 21 | 21 | 18 | 18 | 18 |
| 13. Lb. water evaporated per lb. of coal at and from 212 deg. Fahr. | 9 | 10· | 10 | 9 | 9 | 9 |
| 14. Time for completion, in months | 9 | 9 | 9 | 9 | 9 | 9 |
| 15. Price per ton | £24 5s. 9d. | £24 1s. 3d. | £23 11s. 7d. | £32 8s. 6d. | £31 13s. 8d. | £30 18s. 9 |

BILSTON: THE PUMPING STATION.

acting, sliding, surfacing and screw-cutting lathe; one 6-in. stroke shaping machine; one planing machine, and one 30-in. double-geared drilling machine; one 2-ft. grindstone, and a bench with vice. There is also a portable smith's hearth outside.

The boilers are Hornsby's water-tube boilers, with about 1,426 square feet of heating space and about 26 square feet of grate space. The tubes are 4 in. internal diameter and about 18 ft. long; the steam and water drum is 3 ft. 6 in. diameter and 23 ft. 7 in. long. They are tested to 200 lb. pressure, and the working pressure is 145 lb. on the square inch. They are fitted with safety valves to blow off at 150 lb. pressure. At first considerable difficulty was experienced with these boilers, said to be caused from the large amount of oil passing from the cylinders through the condensers into the boilers; for the past twelve months, however, they have worked very well, and now that a double feed-water filter (Reeves') has been fixed, there does not appear to be any reason why they should not continue to do so. The econo-miser is one of Green's, of Wakefield, the heating surface being about 784 square feet; it was tested hydraulically to 300 lb. pressure, and is provided with a safety valve to blow off at 150 lb. pressure.

A number of tests were made by the author on January 26, 1897, when, with an average piston speed of 141 ft. per minute, the average indicated horse-power was 139·2725, and the coal consumption 1·7232 lb. of coal per indicated horse-power per hour. On February 10, 1897, another test for coal consumption alone was made, and came out at 1·79 lb of coal per indicated horse-power per hour; the contractor's speed was 150 ft. per minute. Thornewill & Warham's contract to complete the work was £8,622 10s. 6d.

The water mains in Wombourn, Trysull and Seisdon, containing several miles of 2-in., 3-in. and 4-in. pipes, with hydrants, sluice valves and air valves, were laid by Mr. Hy. Roberts, of West Bromwich. These water mains have to carry an average pressure of, say, 160 lb. on the square inch, and the pipes had to be made extra strong on that account. The joint used was the same as the one on the pumping mains—i.e., it was all of lead. The pipes had to undergo the following tests at the works and on the ground—viz.,—

| Diameter of Pipe. | Thickness of Metal. | Length of Pipe. | Depth of Socket. | Thickness of Joint. | Weight of Pipes. | Deviation Allowed. | Head of Water. |
|---|---|---|---|---|---|---|---|
| in. | in. | ft. | in. | in. | | | ft. |
| 2 | ⅜ | 6 | 2¼ | 5/16 | 67 | 2 | 900 |
| 3 | ½ | 9 | 2½ | 3/8 | 168 | 4 | 900 |
| 4 | ½ | 9 | 2¾ | 7/16 | 213 | 6 | 900 |

For testing the joints the full working pressure from the reservoir was used, the pipes being laid from the rising main outwards, so that this could be done before the lengths were filled in; the hydrants and air valves were the same as those on the rising main. Where the pipes are less than 3 ft. from the surface of the ground they are surrounded with slag wool and wood covers screwed together; where the pipes

cross canal or other bridges they are covered with slag wool and then cased in wrought-iron casing bolted together, the internal diameter of the wrought-iron covering being 9 in. The cost of this portion of the work was £3,533 12s. 11d.

For the prevention and detection of waste of water the author has divided the whole water area into eight separate districts, each district being controlled either by a Deacon's, or Siemen's, or a Kennedy water meter fitted with a clock and clockwork arrangements for taking diagrams. The districts themselves are divided into streets and sections by means of sluice valves, and by this means it is possible to find the street or sub-section in which the waste is going on, and by means of the stop taps on each service to find the house, and by means of inspection from service to service to exactly locate the leak, either on the service pipe or the main itself. In addition to this, before any water can pass to the town from the reservoir it can be passed through three Kennedy's water meters, two 8-in. and one 6-in.; these meters are also fitted with clockwork arrangements for taking diagrams. When the whole of these meters are fixed and in working order the author hopes to get down the water consumption to about 750,000 gallons per day. The cost of this work is about £900.

To complete the scheme the commissioners in the Bilston Improvement Act, 1896, took power to lay down a telephone from the author's office to the pumping station, and a water-level indicator to indicate the depth of water in the reservoir; this indicator to be connected to instruments at either end—i.e., one in the author's office at Bilston, and the other at the Bratch. This telephone line, &c., is also part of Mr. Latham's scheme. The sanction of the Local Government Board has just been given to a loan for the erection of a manager's house, and the question of enlarging and extending the water mains in the township is now under consideration.

*Total Cost of Water Undertaking to Date.*

| | | £ | s. | d. | £ | s. | d. |
|---|---|---|---|---|---|---|---|
| Paid Wolverhampton for Bilston | | 9,000 | 0 | 0 | | | |
| „ „ Coseley | | 7,750 | 0 | 0 | | | |
| „ John Hughes, for well ... | { | 6,657 | 0 | 0 | } 6,822 | 0 | 1 |
| | { | 165 | 0 | 1 | | | |
| „ H. Hughes & Sons, for wharf and bridge ... | | 367 | 12 | 3 | | | |
| „ Henry Hill, for reservoir ... | | 3,574 | 12 | 9 | | | |
| „ R. Holloway, for rising main | | 7,115 | 3 | 7 | | | |
| „ H. Willcocks & Co., for pumping station ... ... | | 6,133 | 6 | 9 | | | |
| „ H. Roberts, for Wombourn, &c., mains ... ... ... | | 3,533 | 12 | 11 | | | |
| „ Thornewill & Warham's en- gines, &c. ... ... | { | 8,472 | 10 | 6 | } 8,622 | 10 | 6 |
| | { | 150 | 0 | 0 | | | |
| „ for obtaining bills, meters and pumping, &c.... ... | | 6,121 | 0 | 0 | | | |
| „ Rev. C. Lee, for land, &c. ... | | 1,525 | 0 | 0 | | | |
| | | | | | | | |
| Total ... | | £60,564 | 18 | 10 | | | |

With the engineer's charges, the manager's house and

several other items, the total cost will not be much under £70,000. Last year supplied by Wolverhampton Corporation, April 1, 1895, to March 31, 1896. Paid Wolverhampton £3,353 0s. 8d. for 160,945,300 gallons, at 5d. per 1,000 gallons. The cost of distribution was £650 6s. 6d., or say, 1d. per 1,000 gallons. Making a total cost of 6d. per 1,000 gallons. Gallons per day 440,672, or gallons per head per day 19·16, cost first twelve months in our own hands. Total cost, including nothing for loan charges, £3,403 16s. 9d.; water pumped, 307,370,000, or 2½d. per 1,000 gallons; loan charges, 1d. per 1,000 gallons; and distribution, 1d. per 1,000 gallons: this equals 4½d. per 1,000 gallons. Gallons per day, 842,657; gallons per head per day, 27·18. The second year's working will be much less than this, but the returns are not complete yet, but I hope to send them in for insertion in the "Proceedings." In the year 1896 about 4 gallons per head per day trade purposes. In 1897 about 5 gallons per head per day trade purposes.

*Summary for Rising Main.*

| | £ | s. | d. |
|---|---|---|---|
| Conditions of contract ... ... ... ... ... | 272 | 0 | 0 |
| The rising main ... ... ... ... ... | 6,058 | 6 | 4 |
| The delivery main ... ... ... ... | 365 | 7 | 9 |
| The air valves, hydrants, &c. ... ... ... | 162 | 19 | 0 |
| Spares ... ... ... ... ... | 166 | 0 | 4 |
| Quantities and printing ... ... ... ... | 120 | 8 | 11 |
| Total ... ... ... ... | £7,154 | 2 | 4 |

*Cost of a few Items.*

| | £ | s. | d. | |
|---|---|---|---|---|
| Screw metropolitan hydrants ... ... | 2 | 0 | 0 | each |
| Air valves ... ... ... ... ... | 1 | 10 | 0 | ,, |
| 14-in. cast-iron pipes ... ... ... | 3 | 15 | 0 | per ton |
| 14-in. ,, specials ... ... ... | 8 | 0 | 0 | ,, |
| 12-in. ,, pipes ... ... ... | 3 | 16 | 6 | ,, |
| 12-in. ,, specials ... ... ... | 8 | 0 | 0 | ,, |
| Cost per yard run ... ... ... ... | 1 | 0 | 3 | |

*Summary for Boiler-House, Engine-House, Well-House, Pump-House, Coal Store and Chimney, &c.*

| | £ | s. | d. |
|---|---|---|---|
| Conditions... ... ... ... ... ... | 222 | 10 | 0 |
| Engine and boiler house, &c. ... ... ... | 4,283 | 3 | 9 |
| The chimney shaft ... ... ... ... | 337 | 17 | 11 |
| Drains ... ... ... ... ... ... | 145 | 16 | 8 |
| 14-in. main... ... ... ... ... ... | 154 | 15 | 10 |
| Fences and roads ... ... ... ... ... | 431 | 14 | 4 |
| Quantities and printing ... ... ... ... | 142 | 8 | 0 |
| Total ... ... ... ... | £5,718 | 6 | 6 |

*Particulars of a few Items.*

| | £ | s. | d. |
|---|---|---|---|
| Ruabon bricks, per 1,000 ... ... ... ... | 4 | 10 | 0 |
| Common bricks, per 1,000 ... ... ... ... | 1 | 12 | 0 |
| Blue bricks, per 1,000... ... ... ... ... | 4 | 0 | 0 |
| Portland cement, per bushel... ... ... ... | 0 | 6 | 0 |
| Common brickwork in cement, per cube yard ... | 1 | 4 | 0 |
| Sand, per cube yard ... ... ... ... ... | 0 | 6 | 0 |
| Gravel, per cube yard... ... ... ... ... | 0 | 6 | 6 |
| Timber, per cube foot... ... ... ... ... | 0 | 3 | 0 |
| Cast-iron work, per cwt. ... ... ... ... | 0 | 10 | 6 |
| Wrought-iron work, per cwt. ... ... ... | 1 | 2 | 0 |

*Principal Levels.*

| | Above Ordnance Datum. | |
|---|---|---|
| Level of top of water in reservoir ... ... | 607·00 | feet |
| ,, floor of reservoir... ... ... ... | 595·00 | ,, |
| ,, ground at the Brateb ... ... ... | 258·50 | ,, |
| ,, basement of engine-house ... ... | 257·50 | ,, |
| ,, water in tank between engine and well house ... ... ... ... ... | 257·00 | ,, |
| ,, bottom of above tank ... ... ... | 253·50 | ,, |
| ,, surface of stream ... ... ... | 250·51 | ,, |
| ,, formation ground ... ... ... | 262·00 | ,, |
| ,, engine-house door ... ... ... | 267·00 | ,, |
| ,, bottom of well ... ... ... ... | 108·50 | ,, |
| ,, surface of water in canal ... ... | 255·00 | ,, |

*Particulars of a few Items in Reservoir Contract.*

| | £ | s. | d. |
|---|---|---|---|
| Washed sand, per cube yard ... ... ... | 0 | 6 | 0 |
| Excavating average 8 ft. 4 in., per cube yard ... | 0 | 1 | 0 |
| Forming slopes, per yard super. ... ... ... | 0 | 0 | 4 |
| Cement concrete, 6 to 1, per cube yard ... ... | 0 | 12 | 0 |
| Boarding for concrete and struts, per super. square | 0 | 5 | 0 |
| Cement rendering, per super. yard... ... ... | 0 | 1 | 6 |
| Gregeen's air-inlets, each ... ... ... ... | 1 | 5 | 0 |
| Wrought-iron work, per cwt. ... ... ... | 1 | 5 | 0 |
| Cast-iron pipes, 6-in., per ton ... ... ... | 6 | 0 | 0 |
| ,, ,, 6-in., specials, per ton ... ... | 10 | 0 | 0 |
| ,, ,, 12-in., per ton ... ... ... | 6 | 0 | 0 |
| ,, ,, 12-in. specials, per ton ... ... | 12 | 0 | 0 |

*Particulars of a few Items in Wombourn and Seisdon Water Mains Contract.*

| | £ | s. | d. |
|---|---|---|---|
| Wrought-iron casing, per cwt. ... ... ... | 1 | 8 | 0 |
| 3-in. slag wool filling, per foot lineal ... ... | 0 | 1 | 4 |
| Common brickwork in cement, per cube yard ... | 1 | 5 | 0 |
| Cast iron generally, per cwt.... ... ... ... | 0 | 8 | 0 |
| Wrought iron generally, per cwt. ... ... ... | 1 | 8 | 0 |
| Cement concrete, per cube yard ... ... ... | 1 | 0 | 0 |
| Hydrant, cover, index-plate and chamber, each ... | 5 | 10 | 8 |
| Air-valve ,, ,, ... | 6 | 4 | 11 |
| 4-in. sluice ,, ,, ... | 4 | 10 | 6 |
| 3-in. ,, ,, ... | 4 | 0 | 6 |
| 2-in. ,, ,, ... | 3 | 13 | 6 |
| 4-in. pipes, iron, each ... ... ... ... ... | 0 | 9 | 3 |
| 3-in. ,, ,, ... ... ... ... ... | 0 | 7 | 6 |
| 2-in. ,, ,, ... ... ... ... ... | 0 | 3 | 0 |
| 4-in. bend iron and junctions, each ... ... ... | 0 | 9 | 3 |
| 3-in. ,, ,, ... ... ... | 0 | 7 | 6 |
| 2-in. ,, ,, ... ... ... | 0 | 3 | 0 |
| Hydrant, with cover and plate, each ... ... | 2 | 2 | 6 |
| Air valve ,, ,, ... ... ... | 3 | 7 | 6 |
| One 4-in. sluice valve, with cover and plate, each | 3 | 2 | 6 |
| One 3-in. ,, ,, ... | 2 | 12 | 6 |
| One 2-in. . | 2 | 5 | 6 |
| 4-in. pipes, per ton ... ... ... ... ... | 4 | 15 | 0 |
| 3-in. ,, ,, ... ... ... ... ... | 4 | 17 | 6 |
| 2-in. ,, ,, ... ... ... ... ... | 5 | 2 | 6 |
| Specials... ... ... ... ... ... ... | 10 | 0 | 0 |

*Summary of Technical School.*

| | £ | s. | d. |
|---|---|---|---|
| Excavator and drains ... ... ... ... | 406 | 0 | 0 |
| Bricklayer ... ... ... ... ... ... | 1,595 | 0 | 0 |
| Terra-cotta ... ... ... ... ... ... | 556 | 0 | 0 |
| Stonemason ... ... ... ... ... | 189 | 0 | 0 |
| Slater ... ... ... ... ... ... | 124 | 0 | 0 |
| Carpenter and joiner ... ... ... ... | 935 | 0 | 0 |
| Smith and founder ... ... ... ... | 279 | 0 | 0 |
| Plumber, glazier and painter ... ... ... | 515 | 0 | 0 |
| Contingencies ... ... ... ... ... | 150 | 0 | 0 |
| Quantities and printing ... ... ... ... | 122 | 10 | 0 |
| Walls and fences ... ... ... ... ... | 295 | 3 | 6 |
| Total ... ... ... | £5,166 | 13 | 6 |
| Reduced to ... ... ... | £5,087 | 0 | 0 |

*Particulars of a few Items in above Contract.*

| | £ | s. | d. |
|---|---|---|---|
| Excavating to 15 ft. deep, per cube yard... ... | 0 | 1 | 6 |
| ,, 17 ,, ,, ... ... | 0 | 2 | 0 |
| Cement concrete (6 to 1) ,, ... ... | 0 | 11 | 0 |
| ,, 4 in. thick, per sup. yard ... | 0 | 1 | 4 |
| 9-in. common brickwork ... ... ... ... ... | 0 | 4 | 0 |
| Facing with Doulton's pressed bricks, per sup. yard | 0 | 0 | 6 |
| Red deal floors, double ¼-in., per sup. square ... | 1 | 10 | 0 |
| Steel joists, per cwt. ... ... ... ... ... | 0 | 7 | 0 |
| Cast iron ,, ... ... ... ... ... | 0 | 8 | 0 |
| 2-in. iron windows, per super. foot ... ... | 0 | 0 | 9¼ |
| Slating, 20 in. by 10 in. Bangor slates, 3-in. lap and torched with hair mortar, per sup. square ... | 1 | 14 | 0 |

*Bilston Waterworks. Analysis of Water.*

| | |
|---|---|
| | Parts per Million. |
| Ammonia free ... ... ... ... ... ... ... | 0·082 |
| Ammonia albuminoid ... ... ... ... ... ... | 0·104 |
| | Grains per Gallon. |
| Chlorine ... ... ... ... ... ... ... | 5·18 |
| Nitric acid... ... ... ... ... ... ... | Trace |
| Sulphuric acid ... ... ... ... ... ... | 37·99 |
| Carbonate of lime ... ... ... ... ... | 34·91 |
| Lime otherwise combined ... ... ... ... | 2·24 |
| Magnesia ... ... ... ... ... ... ... | 10·74 |
| Total solid residue ... ... ... ... ... | 116·14 |
| Organic and volatile matter ... ... ... ... | 15·12 |
| Saline residue at 212 deg. Fahr. ... ... ... | 101·02 |
| Soda (calculated) ... ... ... ... ... ... | 15·97 |

The following represents the most probable composition of the saline residue:—

| | Grains per Gallon. |
|---|---|
| Calcic carbonate ... ... ... ... ... ... | 34·91 |
| ,, sulphate ... ... ... ... ... ... | 5·43 |
| Magnesia sulphate ... ... ... ... ... | 30·42 |
| ,, carbonate ... ... ... ... ... | 1·22 |
| Sodium sulphate ... ... ... ... ... | 25·77 |
| ,, chloride ... ... ... ... ... | 8·55 |
| | 106·30 |

The author begs to thank Mr. Wassell, the town clerk of Bilston, for the assistance given to him in preparing this paper, Mr. Baldwin Latham for allowing him the use of the drawings in connection with the water scheme, and Mr. George T. Lawley, the author of the "History of Bilston."

## THE ROUND OF VISITS.

When the formal business was concluded at the Town Hall the company left in brakes, which had been kindly provided by Councillor Sankey, in order to visit the Spring Vale furnaces, where, by the courtesy of Sir Alfred Hickman, the process of steel manufacture was watched. Mr. W. Moore, manager of the works, conducted the members over the works and explained the various processes, including the heating, rolling and shaping of ingots, and the sawing and shearing of bars and plates, all of which was followed with the closest interest and attention. As Mr. Greatorex subsequently remarked at luncheon, the heat was rather greater than most of them were generally accustomed to, and on account of the thick white dust they could have wished that the dust-cart had preceded them, but it was an undeniable boon to have an opportunity of visiting works of the kind, which are among the largest in the country, and in which over 1,000 men are employed.

Having re-entered the brakes, the company proceeded on their way, the next stoppage being made for the purpose of a brief inspection of the covered service reservoir, which has been so fully dealt with by Mr. Wilson in his paper that no further reference need be made to it. One of the special supplements in our last issue consisted of a reproduction of the plans of the reservoir, and in this issue we give a view of the interior.

The drive was then resumed through a most attractive district just outside the Black Country, the destination being the Himley Arms Hotel, where a very pleasing function took place in the shape of a luncheon, provided by Councillor Harper, chairman of the council. A number of toasts were proposed, and the various sentiments expressed deserve some record.

Mr. A. T. Davis (Shropshire) proposed the health of the "founder of the feast," to whom a hearty vote of thanks should be accorded for his hospitable treatment, thanks being also due to the council for their kind reception, for the use of the council chamber and the technical school for the purposes of the meeting and for arranging the visits to the various places of interest. Under such favourable circumstances they would be very pleased to come into the Black Country again.

Mr. Gammage (Dudley), in seconding the vote of thanks, testified to the instruction to be derived from the visit.

Councillor Harper, in replying, expressed pleasure in receiving a visit from such a body of men. He hoped they would have no cause to be disappointed with their visit. They were about to see one of the finest waterworks in the country, overhead a magnificent building, underneath the best water procurable. Bilston had a history of which few towns could boast. Not only did it possess its iron works and its various manufactories, but they had here a stone quarry which brought to light some of the finest grindstones obtainable. The town was notable for its Japan work, and was some time back extremely rich in its minerals. This industry, however, was dying away, owing to the first layer of coal having been got and it being impossible to get at it lower down because of the enormous floods of water. He thought that the works of Councillor Sankey might have been included among the places to be visited, as the visit would certainly have been profitable.

Mr. Price (Birmingham) moved a vote of thanks to Councillor Sankey for providing the conveyances. The cordial reception they had met with proved the kindly feelings that existed in the Black Country. Staffordshire, as he had himself experienced, was noted for hospitality and other good qualities, and Bilston was evidently no exception. The people of Staffordshire had a large share of local patriotism.

Mr. A. T. Davis, having seconded, and the vote having been carried with acclamation,

Councillor Sankey, in reply, said that such a meeting being held at Bilston gave a fresh status to the town, and he regarded it as an interesting epoch in the town's history. He was pleased that they had works in the town worthy of being visited, and he hoped the Bilston meeting would be remembered by them and that many of them would gain instruction by the visit. He also felt very strongly that when he had the power to make their engineer and surveyor, Mr. Wilson, better known it was his duty to do so, for he knew that he had devoted himself almost night and day for the past seven years to the good work of the town. Bilston, he continued, had been very fortunate in receiving the services it had from Mr. Wilson during these years.

Mr. A. D. Greatorex (West Bromwich) moved a vote of thanks to Sir Alfred Hickman for granting them permission to visit the Spring Vale works, and to Mr. Moore, the manager of the works, for so kindly and courteously showing them round and explaining the processes.

Mr. Moore having briefly acknowledged the vote of thanks,

Mr. Clarson (Tamworth) proposed that a hearty vote of thanks be accorded to the author of the paper which had been submitted. Mr. Wilson had evidently devoted a great deal of time, thought and trouble in producing so able and comprehensive a paper, from which the members could gather information of great interest and profit. It was a great advantage to secure the paper prior to the meeting, and thus acquaint themselves with its contents and prepare themselves better for discussing it. He hoped it would not be their last visit to Bilston.

Mr. Price said he had pleasure in seconding the vote of thanks, which was carried unanimously.

Mr. Wilson in acknowledging the vote of thanks said he would be sufficiently repaid if any members were able to gather from his paper information which would be useful to them.

When this interchange of courtesies had been concluded, the party resumed their drive, the destination now being the Bilston waterworks pumping station at the Bratch, Wombourne. As our readers will observe, the station has been fully described and illustrated in connection with Mr. Wilson's paper. After going through the ordeal of being photographed, the visitors were conducted through the building, in four sections, by Messrs. Sankey, Wilson, Sutherland and Carne (works manager). They then assembled in front of the building, and a brief discussion ensued.

## DISCUSSION OF MR. WILSON'S PAPER.

The Chairman having invited remarks on the paper,

Mr. Mortimer (Tettenhall) pointed out that under the Rivers Pollution Act a canal was defined as a river or stream, and he was curious to know why they were allowed to run the effluent into this canal for so long.

Mr. Pickering (Nuneaton) wished to refer to one matter. As the work was carried out by so able an engineer as Mr. Baldwin Latham, he would like to know whether the idea as to the size of the reservoir was Mr. Latham's. In most waterworks schemes the storage capacity was for three days, and certainly not less than two. Here there was only storage capacity for one day.

Mr. Price (Birmingham) pointed out that the nett total cost of pumping worked out at 2½d. per 1,000 gallons. The water seemed pretty hard, and if that was a permanent condition he was surprised that the authorities did not go in for a softening process. They had not yet seen the technical school, but judging from the plans and photographs, Mr. Wilson was to be congratulated on a very simple and effective elevation. The district council had been successful in obtaining a fairly good building at a reasonable cost.

Mr. Clarson also referred to the cost of pumping, and cited a case in his own experience in which the cost was only a little over 1d. per 1,000 gallons. There was the same depth, 150 ft., and the same rising main. Coal was delivered at 6s. 6d. per ton. Mr. Wilson was to be congratulated on his elaborate figures. They were glad to have the papers in advance, so that they could come prepared for discussion.

Mr. Dawson (Banbury) said that in constructing a concrete floor for the swimming bath Mr. Wilson had put iron bars the whole length, 12 in. apart. As he was about to construct a swimming bath, he would like to know whether that was desirable. He proposed to put down 10 in. of Portland cement concrete, and cover with 2 in. thick of cement rendering.

Mr. Smith (Kettering) referred to the amounts which had been expended on the baths, and wished to know if there was any likelihood of the baths being a paying concern. His council would go in for baths if they did not require to sacrifice more than £300 a year. He would like some particulars as to the number of persons and the revenue.

Mr. Price (Worcester) referred to the height to which the water was pumped, which ought to be taken into consideration in connection with the cost per 1,000 gallons. The great pressure must prove a drawback after a time, and must lead to a great waste unless reducing valves were used. He did not think that mains less than 3 in. in diameter were advisable, and in towns of any size they should not be less than 4 in. At Bilston there was a very great pressure and a good supply of water. Generally speaking, 3-in. mains had to be taken out after a time. The district council should congratulate themselves on the cheap rate at which the concrete had been obtained.

Mr. Greatorex (West Bromwich) congratulated Mr. Wilson on his excellent paper, for which a great deal of credit was due. The council had had their work done in a very cheap manner, especially as Mr. Wilson had only had the assistance of one pupil. Considering the amount of work that had been carried out in a very short space of time, he thought the surveyor should have been provided with a better staff.

Mr. Myatt (Leek) inquired as to whether steam fire-engines would not be of service.

Councillor Sankey said it was not fair to judge of the capacity of the plant by the work of the first twelve months, and from the initial cost. They aimed at reaching 1d. per 1,000 gallons, and they would probably reach it. They had started with only one engine, and, in addition to delays and other difficulties, they had also to pay schedule prices for engineers and others.

Mr. Eayrs, after a reference to the difficulties under which Bilston had started in connection with the water supply, said that Mr. Wilson was to be congratulated on the way in which his contracts were carried out. On page 8 it was mentioned that in connection with a contract of £3,500 the extras amounted to only 4s. 6d. As a rule, extras formed a large item in contracts, and in the majority of cases were unavoidable. The cost of the electric lighting in the baths and the markets was exceedingly low, and if it could be produced at this rate in a small installation the substitution for the dearer gas was worth consideration. In connection with the technical schools he noted that the extras were only £10 in a £5,000 contract, and he would like to know if Mr. Wilson could give the cost of management and say whether the grants covered expenses, or had to be supplemented by a rate or contribution. The attendance was certainly exceedingly good. A point that was new to him was the jointing of water pipes entirely with lead and without using yarn. He thought it was a good idea to get rid of the yarn difficulty in the way Mr. Wilson had done. They were also told that where the pipes were less than 3 ft. from the surface of the ground they were covered with slag wool. That, as they were aware, was probably to counteract the effects of frost, and it seemed to him quite a new departure. The particulars of cost given in the latter part of the paper were exceedingly valuable and interesting, as showing the details of each item. They could then form a good opinion as to the economy effected. The total cost told them nothing, but when they had the prices of bricks and other materials they could judge better than when figures were lumped together. He would like to know if Mr. Wilson could supplement the details given by a few figures as to the cost of laying and jointing the mains.

Mr. WILSON, in replying, referred first to the question of Mr. Mortimer in regard to the canal. As pointed out in the paper, only the effluent was discharged into the canal. The canals in the Black Country were not so pure as elsewhere. The canal company wanted water, and were glad to take the effluent. A scheme was now being considered to deal with the difficulty, but it was not completed. If desired he could give all the particulars. He had tried all experiments, including the new bacteriological craze. Mr. Pickering had referred to the size of the reservoir. Originally the scheme was for Bilston alone, and they had a supply for two days. They had subsequently taken in a large outlying district, and thus it came that they had only one day's supply. He agreed with Mr. Pickering in regard to the question of capacity. Mr. Price had referred to the cost of 2½d. per 1,000 gallons, but, as Councillor Sankey had pointed out, it was not fair to assume that the price would be always 2½d. After referring to some of the causes which had led to the heavy cost at first, Mr. Wilson said that Mr. Price had recommended a softening process, but that gentleman was evidently not in the brewing trade, or he would have known the advantage of having the water hard. The employment of the bars of iron to which Mr. Dawson had referred had given good results, and he had no cause to regret it. Dealing with the remarks of Mr. Smith (Kettering), Mr. Wilson pointed out that the baths had originally been built only as wash-houses and slipper baths, at a cost of £2,700, and had been bought for £1,100. Since then the town had spent £3,500, including the laundry and the electric lighting, part being borrowed for thirty years and part for ten years. He could, if necessary, give the number of bathers from the time the baths were started. Baths would neither pay working expenses nor interest on capital, and he did not think this should be taken into account in providing baths in such a district, in which they were a great boon to the labouring class. In reply to Mr. Price (Worcester), Mr. Wilson said he did not believe in reducing values. So far they had found very little loss. He quite agreed with what had been said as to the size of mains, but, when they found that at a distance of about a mile they had only one house to supply, they found with the pressure available that a 2-in. pipe was sufficient. In low-lying parts the mains were not less than 3 in. in diameter. In connection with the price of concrete they should note that the material excavated—sand and gravel—was afterwards used for the composition of the concrete. In reply to Mr. Myatt, Mr. Wilson said that steam fire-engines were not thought necessary. Referring finally to the points raised by Mr. Eayrs, Mr. Wilson reminded them that in connection with the electric light the same plant was used for the heating and for supplying power to the laundry. The technical schools did not pay for themselves, the town being rated to the extent of 1d., while the county council made a similar grant. This year the schools would be even more successful than last year. In regard to the jointing of the pipes with lead, he pointed out that the water found its way through when yarn was used, while with lead there was no such risk. He would, if desired, supply the cost of jointing and other particulars desired by Mr. Eayrs.

As soon as the discussion had closed the members of the party proceeded to drive back to Bilston, the destination being the technical school. After an examination of this interesting building, which reflects so much credit on a town of the population and rateable value of Bilston, a goodly number assembled there later to do justice to an excellent dinner provided by Mr. J. S. Iliffe, of the Pipe Hall Hotel, Bilston. Various toasts formed the text of excellent speeches, and thus ended an interesting and instructive visit to a Black Country town.

## THE EAST LONDON WATER FAMINE.

### DEPUTATION TO MR. CHAPLIN.

On Saturday afternoon Mr. Chaplin, the President of the Local Government Board, received a deputation from members of the East-End local authorities, organised by the Social Democratic Federation, with reference to the water famine and the London water question generally.

Mr. HYNDMAN having formally introduced the deputation, Mr. GEORGE LANSBURY said the deputation had been got together by the people of the East-End at various public meetings, and they wanted to assure the Government that there was a feeling of indignation at a water famine occurring again in two years. He submitted the following resolution, which was passed at a mass meeting held at Victoria Park,

West Ham and Trafalgar-square: "That this mass meeting of London citizens protests against the infamous conduct of the East London Water Company in cutting off the water supply of East London twenty hours each day, and calls upon the Government to use such pressure as is necessary to compel the companies responsible for the water supply of the metropolis to connect their mains, and so allow all classes to be treated alike; further, to call upon the Government to summon an autumn session, to place the whole water supply under public ownership and control; and, further, to urge the people not to pay for what they did not get."

Miss KERRISON, a member of the West Ham Board of Guardians, described the sanitary condition of the East-End district. The drains, she said, had not been flushed for a long time, and the smell was indescribable. The deaths from diarrhœa had increased very much in the past two weeks. In fact, there was great danger of an epidemic if the supply of water was not increased.

Mr. R. R. TAYLOR having also spoken,

Mr. CHAPLIN, in the course of his reply, admitted the force of many of the representations that had been made, was quite sensible of the serious nature of the calamity, and was not surprised at the demand that this state of things should be permanently remedied. Before discussing the question of the permanent remedy, he would consider what had been, was being and could be done to relieve the strain of the immediate emergency. After citing the testimony of a medical inspector that the scarcity of water had not yet had an appreciable effect in increasing disease in East London, he proceeded to enumerate the various connections already effected and in process of being carried out by the water company, which would increase their available supply by 12,000,000 gallons a day. He had proposals from the company which, if carried out, would add 16,500,000 gallons a day to their normal supply before the next dry season. The cause of the scarcity in East London was primarily the exceptional dryness of the past sixteen months, and secondly, the circumstance that the East London Company depended mainly for their supply on the river Lea, after the requirements of the New River Company had first been met. An obvious remedy for that state of things was that a connection should be made between the mains of all the water companies in London. He had always entertained that opinion himself, and when the Royal Commission was appointed last year that was one of the matters on which it was instructed to inquire and report. The chairman of the commission had written to him expressing a hope that they might be able to make an early interim report on the subject. In reference to the policy of transferring the whole water supply, it was one on which his mind was perfectly open; but there would be great difficulty in carrying out such a policy, because there was a large area now supplied by the London water companies which was outside the jurisdiction of the London County Council, and the ratepayers of which strongly objected to their water supply being under the control of the council. After reviewing the action of his department, to show that there was no foundation for the charges of neglect and incapacity brought against it, and explaining his attitude on the subject of waste water, Mr. Chaplin doubted whether, even if Parliament were summoned for an autumn session, the object of the deputation would be forwarded in the least. He closed by promising that the representations made to him should be submitted to his colleagues in the Government.

Mr. HYNDMAN thanked the right hon. gentleman for his courtesy, and the deputation then withdrew.

## INVERNESS AND ELECTRIC LIGHTING.

At a meeting of the Electric Light Committee of Inverness Town Council, on Thursday, a report was submitted by a southern expert on the question of introducing electric light into Inverness under municipal auspices. It was favourable to a scheme whereby the water of the Caledonian canal could be utilised, it being calculated that a fall of 30 ft. can be obtained within a short distance of the town. He recommends the provision of 500 horse-power to begin with, which he thinks could maintain 5,000 lamps of 16 candle-power each. There is little doubt, he adds, that the Caledonian Canal Commissioners would sanction the use of a much larger water-power at any future time if it was desired to extend the light, and that without producing an undue velocity of water in the canal, the latter point being one which has given rise to considerable discussion among local experts. It is estimated that for an annual payment of £600 water to produce 500 horse-power can be obtained from the canal. The committee considered the latter estimate rather high, but agreed to defer consideration of the whole scheme until a future meeting.

**The New Penny Magazine** is the title of Messrs. Cassell & Co.'s new weekly periodical, of which the first number is to appear on October 19th. The publishers inform us that it will provide a greater amount of reading matter and illustrations than has been hitherto given for a penny in any magazine. Each issue is to contain sixty-four large pages, fully illustrated.

# The Sanitary Institute.

## THE SEVENTEENTH ANNUAL CONGRESS.—I.

It is not necessary to detail here the aims and objects of the Sanitary Institute. They are already widely known and upheld. Summarised, they are the promotion of the advancement of sanitary science in all or any of its branches, and to diffuse knowledge relating thereto. That they have attained a very full measure of success is evidenced by the fact that the Institute has been in existence for twenty-two years, and that its seventeenth annual congress this year finds it numerically stronger than ever in membership, with an increasing income, more influential as an educational body and yet full of the vigour of youth.

Its congress of this year was opened on Tuesday, in Birmingham, and in its earliest stages everything pointed to a success which will undoubtedly compare favourably with any of the previous gatherings in its history. Something of this is due to the admirable arrangements made by the Institute's executive; much of it is due to the splendid facilities offered for such a meeting by a city with a central position and such fine public buildings as Birmingham possesses. Nor is the enterprising city to be outdone in the hospitality it extends to its officially-recognised visitors, albeit we have it on the authority of the Lord Mayor that the visits of learned societies have of late assumed the proportions of an epidemic. Social functions, general and sectional meetings, and the early days of the Health Exhibition, which is a feature of the congress, all passed off with those satisfactory signs of success which are marked by full attendances and sustained interest.

### OFFICIAL RECEPTION OF MEMBERS.

Altogether the number of the visitors totalled up to some 1,800, of whom 800 are delegates sent by about 400 authorities scattered throughout the country. The majority of them met on Tuesday in the Council House, where they were formally received by the Lord Mayor (Councillor C. G. Beale), who was accompanied by the Lady Mayoress.

The Lord Mayor cordially welcomed the members and delegates. Whether the present gathering was destined to be a success or not, he said, no one could doubt that the Sanitary Institute's congress was entitled to rank with the highest of the important gatherings of the kind which had been held in Birmingham. There they stood practically upon the backbone of England, within a few miles of the ridge which divided the watershed of the Severn from that of the Trent. As a consequence, the corporation was called upon to deliver a large amount of water for domestic supply, at an altitude approaching something like 700 ft., a physical difficulty with which few cities had to contend. It followed, also, that they had no great river running through their midst. If they had possibly their forefathers would, in all innocence, have turned it into a common sewer. Apart from these physical conditions, every community had artificial ones of its own creation. There was one in Birmingham which, to his mind, played no unimportant part in its difficulties. Probably no large city was so considerably built upon the leasehold system—a system under which the landlord laid down conditions of building, under which it was assumed that the conditions were to be permanently suitable. They knew with what result. Probably no city had a finer residential suburb. That was due to the fact that the whole parish was in the hands of one landowner, who could dictate the type of residence. The fine street of which the Council House formed one end, and the Great Western Railway station the other, was a remarkable instance of the beneficial co-operation between the landowner and the municipality. The landowner gave up his frontage, and the municipality spent the money in laying it out, and the buildings had a character and uniformity which could not exist if a large number of small owners had to be consulted. The corporation had developed that great Corporation-street without incurring the expenses of buildings, and ultimately would become the owner of the whole property down that street. That was the beneficial view of the leasehold system, but within a stone's throw there were blocks of small properties laid out on plans which eighty years ago seemed all sufficient, and upon which at the present time no one interested spent a farthing, and the Health Committee were face to face with insanitary property. This matter seemed to have a direct local bearing on the great question of the housing of the working classes. In conclusion, his lordship said that upon these and all kindred questions the congress would find no lack of interest in Birmingham.

Sir Douglas Galton (chairman of the council of the Institute) cordially acknowledged the Lord Mayor's welcome to the members. They hailed, he said, the opportunity of coming to Birmingham, for the municipality of Birmingham stood pre-eminent in the efforts which it had made to advance both education and sanitation. It had spent thousands in endeavouring to solve the problem of dealing with the sewage of inland towns. It was now seeking to bring pure water from the Welsh mountains. Birmingham had solved some of those problems in municipal life which the larger metropolis of London was still in the throes of debating. The

Institute, therefore, thanked the corporation for giving them an opportunity of closely studying their work.

Major Lamorock Flower and Sir Joseph Ewart also tendered their thanks on behalf of the members and delegates.

### THE PUBLIC LUNCHEON.

Subsequently the members and delegates lunched together at the Grand Hotel, under the presidency of the Lord Mayor. Among others present were Earl Beauchamp, Sir William Pink and Sir Arthur Hodgson. After the customary loyal toast, the Lord Mayor proposed "The Sanitary Institute," expressing admiration of the great national work it was accomplishing. The public relied on the Institute to guarantee the efficiency of the men to whom they looked to carry out the Sanitary Acts, and the value attached to that guarantee was evidenced by the fact that that week there were present at the congress some 800 representatives of authorities who were sufficiently interested to meet together and compare notes on subjects of sanitation.

Sir Douglas Galton, whose name was coupled with the toast, responded. The Institute watched over, as far as it could, the legislation of Parliament; but he was sorry that in last year's legislation they had to lament that Government took the view that vaccination might be relaxed. He was not one of those who would say that vaccination could not be relaxed, but he said it could not possibly be relaxed under the conditions which the Government had sanctioned (Loud applause). It could be relaxed if the Leicester system of isolation were introduced everywhere, but without that safeguard it was absolutely wrong to have made any change.

Sir Joseph Fayrer gave the toast of "The Lord Mayor and Corporation of the City of Birmingham," referring to the many suggestive object lessons which Birmingham presented to sanitarians; and Alderman Cook, whose name was associated with the toast, mentioned that, after a good deal of experience in Birmingham, he knew that very much remained to be done there in sanitary matters, and he hoped the visit of the Institute would prove mutually stimulating.

### THE PRESIDENT'S INAUGURAL ADDRESS.

The inaugural address was delivered in the large lecture theatre of the Midland Institute, before an imposing audience. Having been introduced by Sir Douglas Galton, who said that Sir Joseph Fayrer's experience in Indian and general sanitation distinguished him as the most worthy representative whom they could select to preside over the congress, the president then read an address, in which he did not deal with any special branch of preventive medicine or hygiene, but took a general survey of progress during recent times. By way of preface he detailed the steps which led to the formation in 1876 of the Sanitary Institute, and the good work by which it has since steadily developed its purpose of diffusing practical sanitary knowledge throughout the country and has attained its present influential position. The story is now a familiar one to our readers. What the scope of the Institute's work is may be gathered from such facts as these—that in 1897 it organised in London forty sessional meetings and lectures, thirty-six practical demonstrations, four examinations, and 138 classes at the Parkes Museum. This last, by the way, was visited by some 17,500 persons. In the provinces eight examinations were held; while at the Leeds congress there were seventeen sectional and other meetings, and a health exhibition which was visited by 75,790 persons. All this is effected entirely by private enterprise, unaided by any subsidy either from Government or other public authority.

But in addition to the Sanitary Institute there are now, Sir Joseph Fayrer pointed out, many other sources of instruction in matters relating to hygiene and preventive or State medicine. Half a century ago the great mass of the population lived and died under conditions which violated all the now well-known principles on which health depends; now, were all the existing official provisions enforced, little would remain to be desired on the part of the executive Government. Still, the death rate is susceptible of further diminution, expectancy of life may be enhanced, and the general conditions of living and exemption from certain forms of disease are by no means as perfect as they might be. It will, perhaps, not be until the more complete organisation of the public health administration under a Minister of Public Health be effected that the full benefits of sanitary legislation will be realised and the people attain to that standard of health and duration of life for which they have a right to hope.

Although Birmingham could not be ranked by the president of the congress with the great cities which have reduced their death rates, it was hopefully shown that such a process had been going on elsewhere. When the last quinquennium was compared with the preceding decennium it was found that Blackburn and Huddersfield had reduced their death rate by 4, Halifax and Cardiff by 3·8, Oldham by 3·7, Preston by 3·4 and Manchester by 3·3 per 1,000, while Birmingham had been practically at a standstill. If its death rate is to be reduced, thinks its eminent health officer, it is essential that there should be a continuation of the improvements which had such a good effect some years ago. *A propos* of London, Sir Joseph pointed to, as blots, the action of a certain vestry in leaving dead cats, dirty papers and various kinds of offal unswept from the streets from Saturdays to Mondays, and "the abominable and insanitary practice" of sending out the vestry dust-carts to remove house refuse at all times of the day. The question of pure water supply should also be settled.

A contrast between the present sanitary state of our country and that of the Elizabethan era brought Sir Thomas to congratulations that many of the forms of disease of those days had disappeared, and others had been mitigated. But he was afraid we could not feel confident this immunity would continue, though he showed that some well-known diseases have become less severe in their incidence, if not less frequent in their recurrence.

About a third of the president's address was devoted to the beneficial results of sanitary work in India during the last half-century, a subject upon which no one is better qualified to speak than Sir Thomas Fayrer.

Earl BEAUCHAMP, in moving a vote of thanks to the president, said the reference which it contained to the question of vaccination appealed to them all. It was difficult to find words sufficiently strong in which to condemn the action of the Government (Loud applause). His only fear was that such a state of things afforded little hope for the future, even if there were a Ministry of Health. He also wished that from that Institute they might get a wave of feeling as to the criminal action of the water companies which refused to supply water to the East-End of London (Applause). That such monopolies should exist in their present form was something more than a local question, for it must ultimately affect the health of the whole nation, and, unless they were prepared to approach the question in the future, they might find that there would be a fiasco such as had occurred in connection with the vaccination question.

Councillor MARTINEAU having seconded the vote of thanks, it was carried by acclamation.

### THE HEALTH EXHIBITION.

In the evening the Health Exhibition, which has been promoted by the Sanitary Institute, was formally opened by the Right Hon. the Lord Mayor. Mr. HENRY LAW, M.I.C.E., chairman of the Judges' Committee, contrasted the exhibition with the first held, seventeen years ago, observing that it clearly indicated the immense strides that had been made in sanitary knowledge and appliances. The congress all through its history had done its best to encourage improvements in sanitary appliances, and each year it offered awards in competition. Their main object was, however, the education of the general public. He bore testimony to the zeal displayed by the local committee, and to the excellent manner in which they had carried out the whole of the arrangements. Mr. Law, on concluding his speech, presented a handsome bouquet to the Lady Mayoress, who was wearing her right arm in a sling.

The LORD MAYOR said various kinds of exhibitions had been held in Bingley Hall, but the present exhibition, he thought, appealed to every class. But even if it did nothing more than instruct builders and architects, upon whose advice they so much depended in arranging sanitary matters, then it conferred a great benefit upon the community.

His lordship then declared the exhibition open.

A vote of thanks was passed to him on the motion of Prof. LANE NOTTER, seconded by Prof. BAILING, and, in acknowledging it, the LORD MAYOR said he had attended exhibitions and exhibitions, but he had never before seen one which was so complete and ready for opening.

In later issues of THE SURVEYOR we shall, as usual, devote considerable attention to the exhibits, many of which mark important advances in sanitary appliances. In the meantime it may be explained that these exhibits are classified in four divisions: (1) Science in relation to hygiene; (2) hygiene of special classes, trades and professions; (3) construction and sanitary appliances, which include building materials, construction and machinery, water supply and sewerage, and heating, lighting and ventilating; and (4) personal and domestic hygiene. Bingley Hall is most admirably adapted to the purposes of such an exhibition, and the exhibits are more numerous than on previous occasions. As usual, Mr. A. T. Thompson is indefatigable in attending to the comfort of exhibitors and others who have to spend considerable time at the hall.

The judges of the exhibition are: Messrs. A. Wynter Blyth, H. Percy Boulnois, T. W. Cutler, Rogers Field, E. T. Hall, H. Law, A. Newsholme, J. Lane Notter, Louis C. Parkes, G. Reid, J. Osborne Smith and W. C. Tyndale. Their first award is as follows:—

We append the first List of Awards:—

*Silver Medals.*

Jaeger Woollen Underclothing.—Allport's, 21 and 23 Celmore. row, Birmingham.

Case for Water Analysis, and Chemicals in Solcids for Water Analysis.—Burroughs, Wellcome & Co., Snow-hill Buildings, London, E.C.

Compressed Chemical Substances.—Burroughs, Wellcome & Co., Snow-hill Buildings, London, E.C.

Products of Coal Tar and Ammoniacal Liquid.—Burt, Boulton & Hayward, Limited, 64 Cannon-street, London, E.C.

Cocoa.—Cadbury Brothers, Bournville, near Birmingham.

Pure Carbolic Acid.—F. C. Calvert & Co., Bradford, Manchester.

Enamelled Cast Iron.—The Cannon Hollow Ware Company, Bilston, Staffs.

Pasteur Chamberland Filter.—J. Defries & Sons, Limited, 147 Houndsditch, London, E.C.

Pure Cocoa.—J. S. Fry & Sons, Limited, Union-street, Bristol.

Brougham Ambulance.—Wilson & Stockall, County Ambulance Works, Bury, Lancashire.

Accident Ambulance.—Wilson & Stockall, County Ambulance Works, Bury, Lancashire.

*Bronze Medals.*

Method of Aërating Water by Means of Compressed Carbondioxide.—Aërators, Limited, Broad-street-avenue, London, E.C.

Simplex Cinder-sifter. — Arkinstall Brothers, Milk-street, Birmingham.

Liquid Sulphur Dioxide for Disinfection.—A. Boake, Roberts & Co., Limited, Stratford, London, E.

Petanello Fabrics.—Brion, Pate, Burke & Co., 15 Walbrook, London, E.C.

Whitehead's Automatic Taps, for Drawing Off Liquids.—Clark's "Optimus" Coffee Company, Limited, Queen's-road, South Lambeth, S.W.

Jackson's Self-feeding Water Boiler.—Eclipse Brass and Copper Company, Limited, Harrison-road Works, Halifax.

The "Helliwell" System of Glazing.—Farrer, Barber & Co., 36 Cannon-street, Birmingham.

Combined Sink and Lavatory.—Farrer, Barber & Co., 36 Cannon-street, Birmingham.

Hutching's Food-steamers.—G. J. Hutchings, 94 Clerkenwell-road, London, E.C.

Jeyes' Fluid.—Jeyes' Sanitary Compounds Company, Limited, 64 Cannon-street, London, E.C.

Chinosol.—Bernard Kuhn, 38 St. Mary-at-Hill, London, E.C.

Mellin's Food for Invalids.—Mellin's Food Company, Limited, Peckham, London, S.E.

Salt-glazed Wash-Tub and Rubber Combined.—Oates & Green, Limited, Halifax.

Dr. Quine's Ash-Bin.—Pendleton Sanitary Engineering Company, Leaf-square, Pendleton, Manchester.

Thermometer for Hospital Wards.—W. W. Rolston, 120 Pope-street, Albion-street, Birmingham.

Aërated Waters prepared from Distilled Water.—Southall Brothers & Barclay, Lower Priory, Birmingham.

Triple Vegetable Sink.—Twyfords, Limited, Hanley.

"Ideal" Sink in Two Compartments.—Twyfords, Limited, Hanley.

Chloros.—United Alkali Company, Limited, Gaskell and Deacon Works, Widnes.

Concentrated Vimbos.— Vimbos, Limited, 130 Queen Victoria-street, E.C.

### CONFERENCES.

On Wednesday conferences were held at the Mason University College.

Of the municipal representatives, Alderman J. Cook, J.P., chairman of the Health Committee of the Birmingham City Council, was president; and there was a strong list of vice-presidents, which included Earl Beauchamp (chairman of the Health Committee of Worcester), the Lord Mayors of Liverpool and Leeds, the Mayor of Brighton, Sir William Pink (chairman of the Sanitary Committee, Portsmouth), and other mayors and chairmen of sanitary committees. The secretaries were Councillor J. H. Lloyd and Mr. E. V. Hiley, of Birmingham; the recording secretary, Dr. W. Collingridge.

Dr. J. C. McVail presided over the medical officers of health, who included among their vice-presidents a number of names famous in medical and sanitary science. Drs. S. Barwise (Derby) and A. S. Underhill (West Bromwich) were the secretaries; and Mr. Henry Kenwood (London), recording secretary.

Mr. T. de Courcy Meade, city surveyor of Manchester, presided over the conference of municipal and county engineers, whose vice-presidents were: Messrs. W. B. G. Bennett, Southampton; R. E. W. Berrington; W. Blackshaw, Stafford; A. T. Davis, Salop; J. T. Eayrs; E. Parnell Hooley, Nottingham; F. J. C. May, Brighton; J. Price, Birmingham; O. Claude Robson, Willesden; J. Willmot, Warwick; J. E. Worth, district engineer, London County Council; and T. H. Yabbicom, Bristol. The secretaries were Messrs. H. Ashton Hill (Birmingham) and A. D. Greatorex (West Bromwich); and the recording secretary, E. G. Mawbey (Leicester).

Over the Sanitary Inspectors' Conference Mr. W. W. West (Walthamstow) presided; and Messrs. X. Deeks, J. Parker and A. Taylor were the secretaries. There were twelve vice-presidents.

The conference on Domestic Hygiene was "run" by ladies, under the presidency of the Lady Mayoress. The vice-presidents included the Countess of Warwick, Lady Holder, Lady Martineau and others.

In all these divisions of the congress a number of most interesting papers were read, many of them of considerable value from the point of view of the municipal and county engineer. We shall deal with these in due course as amply as space permits. Some special resolutions were also passed. The municipal and county engineers devoted their afternoon to the practical work of inspecting, under the guidance of Mr. Price, the city surveyor, some of the municipal works of the city, including a public convenience in course of construction, the diversion of the Rea main sewer now in progress, the nearly-finished Edward-street depot, the river Rea improvement works, and the "Queen's Ride." To these, also, we hope to refer more specifically in a later issue.

In the evening a conversazione was given in the Council House by the Lord Mayor.

Yesterday was devoted to sectional meetings at Mason University College. Over the first of the three sections—that on Sanitary Science and Preventive Medicine—Dr. Alfred Hill, medical officer of Birmingham, presided. The Engineering and Architecture section met under the presidency of Mr. W. Henman, F.R.I.B.A., the vice-presidents including the following: L. Angell, W. G. Bagnall, C. E. Bateman, Sir A. R. Binnie, E. H. Collins, J. A. Cossins, E. Day, W. Hale, C. Hunt, H. Lea, J. Lemon, W. Martin, E. Pritchard and H. A. Roechling. Messrs. H. T. Buckland, S. R. Lowcock and Major Lamorock Flower were the secretaries. The remaining section—Physics, Chemistry and Biology—was presided over by Dr. G. Sims Woodhead. The Institute has been unusually fortunate this year in securing papers on interesting topics by men who are entitled to be heard, and among the work of the sections many of these contributions were found.

In the evening Dr. Christopher Childs delivered the usual "lecture to the congress," his subject being "The Prevention of Pollution of our Streams and Rivers." His paper was received with every mark of appreciation and interest.

To-day the work of the sections will be resumed, various excursions have been organised, there is to be a garden party at Egbaston Botanical Gardens in the afternoon, and there will be a formal closing general meeting of the congress. This will not imply, however, that its proceedings are over, for at night the "popular lecture" will be delivered, on "Unnatural Death," by Dr. A. Hill. Further excursions, moreover, will carry the congress on to to-morrow, when some of the members will visit Stratford and Malvern.

In our next issue we shall proceed with our report on the proceedings of the various sections and conferences so far as they are likely to concern our readers, particular attention being given to the conference of Municipal and County Engineers.

## THE PRESIDENT OF THE SANITARY INSTITUTE.

Sir Joseph Fayrer, the president of the Sanitary Institute, is the second son of the late Commander Fayrer, of Haverbrack, Westmoreland, and was born in 1824. He was educated privately, at Charing Cross Hospital, London, and at Edinburgh University. He served at the sieges of Palermo and Rome in 1847-48, and in 1850 he entered the Bengal Medical Service, retiring in 1874, becoming surgeon-general in the following year. Sir Joseph took part in the Burmese war of 1852 and in the suppression of the Indian Mutiny, being present at the siege of Lucknow. He was for some time civil surgeon at Rangoon, and Residency surgeon and Assistant Resident, Lucknow, was professor of surgery in the Medical College of Bengal from 1859 until 1874, acted as a magistrate for Calcutta from 1868 to 1874, and was president of the Asiatic Society of Bengal. Sir Joseph, in 1870, accompanied the Duke of Edinburgh in his tour through India, and when the Prince of Wales paid his visit Sir Joseph accompanied him in the capacity of physician to his Royal Highness and chief medical officer to the expedition. He is hon. physician to her Majesty and to the Prince of Wales, Physician in Ordinary to the Duke of Edinburgh, is a F.R.S. of London and Edinburgh, a member of the Academy of Medicine of Paris, and of many other learned societies. Sir Joseph has the third-class Medjidie and Redeemer of Greece, and the second-class of the Order of Conception of Portugal. He has held the position of president of the Medical Board at the India Office, was a member of the Army Sanitary Committee, and is a member of the Senate of the Army Medical School at Netley. He was created C.S.I. in 1868, K.C.S.I. in 1876, and was made a baronet in 1896. In 1855 he married Bethia Mary, the eldest daughter of the late Major-General Andrew Spens, of the Bengal army.

**Royal Commission on Sewage Disposal.**—The Royal Commission on Sewage Disposal are this week inspecting the works erected at Exeter for the purification of sewage by the "septic" system. Next week they will inspect the sewage disposal works of the town councils of Manchester, Oldham, Chorley and Rochdale. The offices of the Commission have been removed from 16 Victoria-street to 23 Great George-street, Westminster.

**Typhoid Fever and Flies.**—The commission, consisting of Drs. Lee, Vaughan and Shakespeare, and other medical men appointed to inquire into the cause of the severe epidemics of typhoid which carried off so many men in the American camps during the war, report that the disease was undoubtedly spread by flies, and had it not been for these little pests there would only have been a few isolated cases. They are willing to stake their reputations on these conclusions.

## THE BRADFORD CAR ACCIDENT.

### BOARD OF TRADE INQUIRY.

Last week, at Bradford Town Hall, an inquiry was opened by Major Cardew, on behalf of the Board of Trade, into the circumstances attending the tramcar accident which we reported in our last issue. At the outset Major Cardew referred to the comments which had been made upon his appointment, inasmuch as he had also made the inspection of the line originally. He pointed out that the construction of the line was determined by Act of Parliament, and if any one believed that the line was not safe and desired to give evidence on the point, he should not be afraid to say so.

Witnesses were first called to prove that when the cars went out that morning they were in perfect order, and were fitted with electric brakes and sand. There was heavy traffic that morning, and two extra cars had been put on. It was in connection with one of those cars that the accident occurred.

Mr. Spencer, the manager of the electric tramways, admitted that he did not regard the brake power as sufficient, and had recommended the committee to attach other brakes, which they agreed to do. He saw danger when the lines were greasy, and accordingly he recommended slipper brakes.

Mr. Cox, city surveyor, expressed the opinion that the cause of the accident was that the hand brake had been applied with such pressure as to stop the wheels, and so put the electric brake out of use.

After hearing other evidence to the effect that the speed of the cars was often excessive, and that the drivers were in some cases incompetent to perform their duties, the inspector adjourned the inquiry.

## WATER SUPPLY AT CHARD.

Mr. Frederick H. Tulloch, M.I.C.E., an inspector of the Local Government Board, held an inquiry at Chard, last week, relative to an application of the corporation to borrow the sum of £2,500 for works of water supply. It was pointed out that the council contemplated laying a new service of water mains in place of the existing mains, which are old and defective. The present water supply is derived from springs just above the centre of the town, and the parts situate above the level of the springs are without any town supply. Opposition was offered to the scheme by residents outside the area of the town supply, on the ground that it would be unfair to charge them a share of the cost of laying pipes from which they would derive no benefit, and it was urged that the town council should carry out a proper scheme of water supply for the whole borough. On the other hand, it was stated that the town council had had various schemes before them, but for one reason and another they had been abandoned. Mr. G. Hodson, C.E., of Loughborough, attended the inquiry, and in very strong terms condemned the present springs from which the town water supply was derived. He declared that he would refuse to be associated with any scheme which contemplated the continued use of water from this source, which he found was liable to contamination at any time. The inspector said one thing was obvious—that there was need for a proper water supply for the whole town, and this would have to be carried out. He strongly commented on the delay and inaction of the town council.

## PAVING CHARGES.

### WHAT IS A "NEW STREET?"

At the South-Western Court, on Thursday, Mr. John Brett, A.R.A., of Daisyfield, West-hill, Wandsworth, appeared to answer the complaint of the Wandsworth District Board of Works, who sought to obtain the payment of £145 17s. 11d., being the share of expense for paving Putney Heath-lane. Mr. Michael Brett, barrister, and a son of the defendant, appeared for the defence. He raised the point that the lane was not a new street within the meaning of the Act, and therefore repairable at the expense of the general body of ratepayers. He cited cases showing that the judges had held that in deciding whether a certain thoroughfare was a new street or not attention should be paid to the general character of the houses in the neighbourhood. Mr. Rose concurred. Mr. W. W. Young, who supported the summons, urged that it was a most serious matter for the board. If the contention of counsel were accepted it would amount to this—that a road lined with small houses could be called a street, while a road sparsely lined with large houses of rental of over £100 a year could not be termed a street. Surely his worship could not say that the board would have to wait till the gaps between the large houses were filled before calling on the owners to pay for the paving. Mr. Rose: They can call on the ratepayers to pay. Mr. Young: Well, if you are of that opinion, may I be allowed to withdraw the summons. Mr. Brett objected, and asked his worship to dismiss the summons. Mr. Rose: Yes; it is a question of fact, and I decide, wrongly it may be, but I do not think so, against the board, and I dismiss the summons.

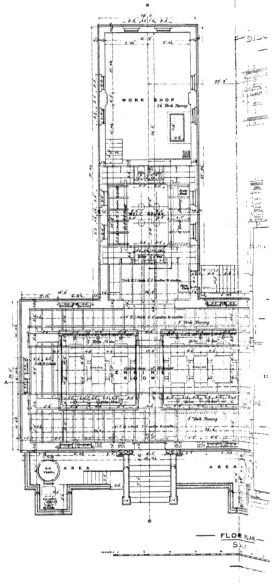

FLOOR PLAN

# —BILSTON WATER WORKS—
## —PUMPING STATION AT THE BRATCH—

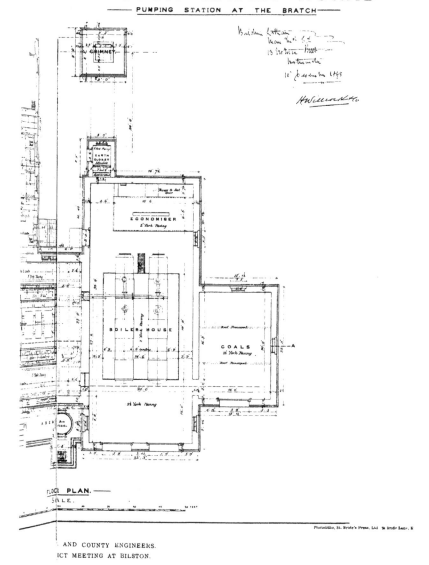

FLOOR PLAN.

SCALE.

Photolitho, St. Bride's Press, Ltd. 24 Bride Lane, E.

AND COUNTY ENGINEERS.
ICT MEETING AT BILSTON.

# Some Annual Municipal Engineering Records.

## ASTON MANOR : TONBRIDGE : MIDDLETON.

The last report of the work done in the department of ᵭr. Harry Richardson, engineer and surveyor to the Urban District Council of Aston ᵭanor, opens with some information concerning the maintenance of the town highways. ᵭain roads have a length of over 2 miles, while the remaining highways measure 40 miles, the exact total length being 42 miles 1 furlong 119 yards. ᵭost of the old roads were constructed without having proper paved crossings at the junction of the carriageways; and it would, in ᵭr. Richardson's opinion, greatly improve the roads and add considerably to the comfort of pedestrians if all important street crossings were paved. Stone used upon the roads amounted to 6,287 tons and cost £3,052. The carriageways now present a marked improvement on what they were last year, when the expenditure on macadam was very much below the average. Consequently later repairs have been of a rather extensive character.

ᵭr. Richardson is firmly of the opinion that it is impossible (except at great expense) to maintain busy roads, the centres of which are paved and the sides macadamised, in good condition. The relative hardness of the two materials is so widely different, that unless the macadamised portion is continually under repair a most irregular contour is the result, and until the carriageway is paved from kerb to kerb such roads will always be a source of unduly heavy annual expense. Plans and estimates for the paving of the carriageways of the main roads in the district have been submitted to the county council. In the period covered by the report 7,617 loads of mud were carted from the streets to the various tips, as against 9,487 loads last year. It will be noticed from this that the result of not expending the usual quantity of stone upon the roads during 1896 was an increase of 1,870 loads of mud to be removed. As regards the tramways, ᵭr. Richardson has noticed that the condition of the permanent way of the City of Birmingham Company is in a better condition than that of the Birmingham and Aston Company, this difference being, he thinks, attributable to the fact that, in compliance with his suggestion, the latter company use pitch for running in the joints of their paving, while the other still persist in using cement grouting composed of two parts of sand to one of cement, which material ᵭr. Richardson considers unfit for the purpose. ᵭr. Richardson has had cause to complain of the worn-out setts which are from time to time re-laid by both companies. Plans were submitted for the council's approval by ᵭr. W. H. Robins, of Birmingham, of three new streets, proposed to be constructed on the Aston Park estate, in the vicinity of Prestbury and Witton roads. When this work is put into effect nearly all the land available for building in the district will have been opened up. There are, it may be stated, only two urban districts with a larger population than Aston ᵭanor, whose rateable value now stands at £175,929.

For the purpose of street-watering 3,304,546 gallons of water were used. The sum paid to the water department up to December last was £145, which includes rent of hydrants. The price charged per 1,000 gallons is 6d. The total number of hydrants in use for the purpose of street watering and fire extinguishing is 479, for which a rental of 3s. 9d. for each hydrant is paid to the Birmingham water department. When sewers are required to be laid for the drainage of two or more houses the *modus operandi* is as follows : The owner or builder first makes application for an approximate estimate of the cost of the work, and at the same time requests the council, in writing, to execute the work. The cost is then estimated, and a copy of the estimate forwarded to the owner or builder, who on the receipt of it deposits the estimated amount with the accountant clerk. An order, accompanied by a tracing showing position of houses, sewers and drains, together with sizes, gradients and depths, is sent to the council's contractor. The work is then proceeded with and superintended by the staff. All measurements are taken on the works, and afterwards booked and priced-out, a duplicate copy of the measurements being sent to the contractor. Should the actual cost of the work be greater than that estimated, the owner or builder pays to the council the amount of such deficiency. In case the deposit exceeds the cost of the work, the council repay to the owner or builder any excess. ᵭr. Richardson finds that under this system the work is carried out in a much more uniform manner, and the dangers arising from badly-constructed sewers brought to a minimum, the construction throughout being of a much higher class.

In accordance with instructions received from the Health Committee, plans and estimates were prepared for extensions to the administrative building of the infectious diseases hospital at Upper Witton. These extensions comprised a dining hall, lobby, office, four bed-rooms, linen store, coal store, pantry, verandah, two water-closets, and also one bed-room over the stores for the accommodation of a coachman. The total estimated cost of the works was £1,450.

\* \* \*

According to the report of ᵭr. William Laurence Bradley, the engineer and surveyor to the Tonbridge Urban District

Council, the great activity in the building trade of the town, which commenced in 1895, still continues to increase. Buildings in course of erection have been inspected from time to time, and only seven notices have been served for breaches of the by-laws. It is satisfactory, says ᵭr. Bradley, that there has been no occasion to take legal proceedings. There is, it seems, a general willingness on the part of local builders to adopt any reasonable suggestions. The total number of plans approved by the council has been 111, the number of houses certified for occupation being 113, as against fifty in 1895 and 125 in 1896.

Flushing has been carried on in all the main sewers of the town during the year, both by means of the valve chambers and the flushing van. Important new sewerage works have been executed during the year, a Local Government Board inquiry having previously been held concerning an application for sanction to borrow money for the purpose. The surveyor was instructed to carry out the work departmentally without a contractor, tenders being obtained for the supply of materials. In the report it is stated that considerable progress has been made with the work, which is considered to have been executed in a thoroughly substantial manner. In addition to the above work, 3,200 ft. of sewers have been laid in private streets, together with the necessary manholes and flushing chambers. Several new manholes have been built, while six new ventilating shafts have been erected in various parts of the town.

The work of the department dealing with the sewage works and farm has, in the opinion of the surveyor, been carried on in a fairly satisfactory manner. About 800 ft. of new brick effluent carriers have been constructed, these being a very great improvement on the old system. A considerable portion of land has been levelled and underdrained, and an experimental bacteriological filter will be constructed early in the year.

Satisfactory results have been obtained in connection with the scavenging which has been undertaken. Over 3,000 loads of refuse have been deposited at the farm. In this part of the engineer's report, we may remark, the attention of the council is called to the very rapid growth of their district and to the increasing amount of work done in the scavenging department. The report next states that no new work of a constructional nature has been required at the isolation hospital during the year. But new roads, of a total length of about 4,000 ft., have been made up; several also have been taken over by the council. ᵭr. Bradley is pleased to be able to state that Local Government Board sanction has been granted in respect of an application for sanction to borrow a sum of £9,000 for the purchase of Tonbridge Castle and grounds for the purposes of pleasure grounds, public offices, depot, an electric light station and fire-brigade station.

Several other properties have been acquired by the council, including the site of a proposed free library and technical institute, which will, it is expected, in a short time be seen nearing its completion.

\* \* \*

In the report of ᵭr. W. Wellburn, the borough surveyor of ᵭiddleton, on the work carried out under his supervision during the year ended March last, it is stated that the area of the district is 4,741 statute acres, the population about 25,000, and the rateable value £71,200. Of main roads there are about 8½ miles, of secondary roads 2 miles 5 furlongs, and of highways over 10 miles. The county council allow towards the maintenance of the main roads £2,350, and for secondary roads £100. During the year 257 visits have been made to new buildings in course of erection, and 136 new dwelling-houses have been certified fit for habitation. The number of times the surfaces of the streets have been opened for drains, gas and water mains has been 258. The number of fresh water-closets in the borough is 257 ; of slop water-closets there are 651, making a total of 908. This shows that the water-carriage system is making a steady progress and saving a large amount of expense in carting the offensive matter through the streets. This the surveyor has no doubt adds greatly to the comfort of the burgesses. There have been several slop water-closets stopped up during the year, caused by tins, bricks, pots, shoes, lanterns and many other articles being thrown down. There is a great improvement in this respect, as the users of the slop-closets are given to understand that they must not throw these articles into them.

The cost of cleansing and scavenging the highways in the borough has been £417, while £915 has been spent upon drainage and other works. There are now 176 manholes, 152 ventilators, and 1,872 street gullies.

Plans, &c., for a light railway in the borough have been submitted, and a committee of the Light Railways Commissioners have held an inquiry, but their decision has not yet been given. Should the promoters agree to the council's requirements, ᵭr. Wellburn is satisfied that it would be a benefit to the town at large.

## PLYMOUTH WATER SUPPLY.

THE NEW RESERVOIR.

The Mayor of Plymouth on Wednesday week laid the last stone of the dam which has been constructed in connection with the new Plymouth waterworks. Large crowds of people witnessed the proceedings, which were followed in the evening by a banquet, presided over by the mayor.

The history of the water undertaking of the town dates from the reign of Queen Elizabeth, when Sir Francis Drake, under the powers of an Act of Parliament obtained by the corporation, made a leat some 17 miles in length which brought into Plymouth the waters of the river Meavy. In the years 1881 and 1891 serious difficulty was experienced owing to the blocking of the leat by snow and frost, and more recently trouble has arisen from a diminution of the supply by drought. In consequence of this the corporation in 1892 obtained powers to make a storage reservoir in the neighbourhood of the head weir which is the intake of the leat, and also to substitute a pipe line for the open watercourse which has served the town for so many generations. The pipe line was completed in 1894, and the reservoir has now been finished.

The reservoir has been made by constructing a dam of masonry across the bed of the Meavy at a point about 1 mile below the head weir, where the river ran through a narrow channel known as Burrator Gorge. This dam rises to a height of 145 ft. from its foundation and 77 ft. above the bed of the river. Its length is 410 ft. along the parapet, or 361 ft. at the water line, and its greatest thickness is 80 ft. The face and top of the dam have been constructed of uncoursed ashlar, consisting of square blocks of granite, and the core of the structure is composed of cyclopean rubble, consisting of large masses of granite embedded in concrete. On the side of the dam which has to resist the water pressure the granite blocks have been rebated to a depth of 6 in., leaving a space ¾ in. wide to that depth between each of the blocks. These spaces have been filled in with cement slightly damped and driven in by an iron chisel. By this process an exceedingly hard and watertight joint has been obtained, so as to prevent water percolating into the core of the structure. A secondary dam has been made near the village of Sheepstor, where there was a depression in the ground which had to be filled up. When full the reservoir will contain 650,000,000 gallons of water. Its length will be 1¾ miles, its greatest width ½ mile, and its greatest depth 77 ft. The work was designed by Mr. Edward Sandeman, the corporation's engineer, and Mr. James Mansergh, consulting engineer, and it has been carried out by the corporation under the supervision of these engineers. The estimated cost was £150,000.

## ELECTRIC LIGHT AT HANLEY.

A FURTHER LOAN REQUIRED.

Colonel W. R. Slacke, R.E., on the 14th inst. held an inquiry, on behalf of the Local Government Board, with reference to an application of the Hanley Town Council for sanction to borrow a further sum of £4,000 for electric lighting purposes. Among those present were Messrs. A. Challiner, the town clerk; J. Lobley, the borough surveyor; and C. Sutherland and W. Cowell, the electrical engineers.

The Town Clerk explained that the annual rateable value of the borough was £197,912, and the balance of outstanding loans was £216,557. On February 6, 1893, the corporation obtained sanction to borrow £21,000 for electric lighting, repayable in twenty-five years. On June 14, 1894, they borrowed a further sum of £1,100, repayable in ten years; on May 29, 1895, £5,000, on November 28, £19,000, and on July 27, 1897, £14,880, repayable in twenty-five years. The present loan being part of the general scheme, it was desirable that its repayment should be extended over twenty-five years also. They had at present 363 private customers, and these were rapidly increasing. Mr. Cowell produced diagrams, and stated that the private lamps were equal to 25,750 lamps of 8 candle-power. They were supplied from four feeders, and they wanted now to put down a new high-tension feeder to supplement these. Owing to the great demand in the evening the tension dropped to 94 volts, whereas the minimum allowed was 97 volts. It was also explained that the council wished to take advantage of the ground being opened for telephone purposes to lay down some new low-pressure distributing mains. The present application was to meet the estimated requirements during the next twelve months. With regard to a proposal to purchase 100 additional meters to enable the corporation to carry out what was termed the Brighton system, by which they charged 5d. per unit for the first one and a half hours and 2½d. an hour afterwards, a member of the town council remarked that it was the most absurd system that was ever invented.

At the close of the inquiry, which was of a formal character, a vote of thanks was accorded to the inspector; and, in replying, Colonel Slacke said it must be very gratifying that the introduction of the electric light in Hanley had been such a success, and that they could supply electricity at such a rate as to induce so many customers to take it.

## SANITATION UP TO DATE.

The accompanying illustration is reproduced from a photo received from Mr. J. Owen-Jones, engineer and surveyor to the Biggleswade Urban District Council.

Our correspondent remarks: The pan is earthenware, and the trap outlet is made of lead. How long it had been in use I cannot say, the pan in some parts was worn into small holes. Excreta was well adhered inside the trap and

pipe (of course I need not mention what the stench was like). At point A another closet of the same pattern was connected, and both emptied into a small brick channel in the outer wall, the pipe B being the ventilation pipe from the brick channel. This channel was connected to a 6-in. socket pipe, and carried into the main sewer without an intercepting trap of any form.

## SEWER VENTILATION.

DECISION OF THE CAMBERWELL VESTRY.

The Sewers and Sanitary Committee of the Camberwell Vestry reported, at a meeting of that body on Wednesday week that they had again considered the report of the delegates to the recent conference on the subject of sewer ventilation.

The resolutions passed were as follows: (1) That the closing of surface sewer ventilators in response to complaints increases the general evil, the diminution of which is to be attained by the multiplication of the ventilators, both surface and up-cast shafts, at regular frequent intervals. (2) That in connection with any interceptor hereafter fixed on a main house drain it is advisable to carry a ventilating pipe from the sewer side of the interceptor, up the front side or back of the house, to the satisfaction of the local sanitary authority, and that the outlet drain from the interceptor shall not be flap-trapped in sewer unless required by the local sanitary authority. (3) That pipe ventilators up buildings, or otherwise, where possible should always be adopted, in addition to surface ventilation. (4) That copies of these resolutions be forwarded to the London County Council and the various vestries and district boards, and their co-operation asked for in giving effect to same.

The committee expressed themselves as being entirely in accord with these resolutions, subject to the following words being added to the second recommendation: "And that such ventilating pipes be 3 ft. above and 6 ft. away from the highest window or chimney where possible."

## SUPERANNUATION OF MUNICIPAL OFFICERS.

The conference convened by the Municipal Officers' Association, at a meeting held on Thursday, at 117 Holborn, E.C., had under consideration the question of again promoting legislation in the next session of Parliament, and decided to invite all associations and societies representing municipal officers to again send delegates to the conference. The chairman and secretary presented a joint report, together with balance-sheet, showing what had been done last session in promoting the Local Authorities Officers' Superannuation Bill. In order to further the movement, a conference will be held in London at the end of October, to which municipal officers throughout the country will be invited to attend, and a very large gathering is anticipated. Particulars of the place and time of meeting will be announced in due course, and any further information can be obtained by letter from the hon. secretary, Mr. C. J. F. Carnell, 117 Holborn, E.C.

**Bloemfontein.**—We understand that the town council have adopted a scheme for lighting the town with electricity, and have accepted the tender of Messrs. Reumert & Sons, at £16,500, for carrying out the work.

# Law Notes.

### Edited by J. B. REIGNIER CONDER, 11 Old Jewry Chambers, E.C.

#### Solicitor of the Supreme Court.

*The Editor will be pleased to answer any questions affecting the practice of engineers and surveyors to local authorities. Queries (which should be written legibly on foolscap paper, one side only) should be addressed to "The Law Editor," at the Offices of* THE SURVEYOR. *Where possible, copies of local Acts or documents referred to should be enclosed. All explanatory diagrams must be drawn and lettered in black ink only. Correspondents who do not wish their names published should furnish a nom de plume*

## QUERIES AND REPLIES.

STRIPS OF LAND ADJOINING ROADWAY.—" J. S. C." writes : There is a strip of land on the road side that has not been macadamised up to the present time, about 6 ft. wide, next to the fence. The surveyor of the district is cutting away the ground and macadamising it to the fence, behind which is a clean-water drain that supplies some property. Is the surveyor justified in doing so? The property abuts on the Rochdale and Halifax turnpike road.

*Primâ facie*, strips of land adjoining the highway form part of the highway (per Mr. Justice Crompton in *The Queen* v. *United Kingdom Telegraph Company*, 31 L.J., M.C., 166). Unless, therefore, there is something to rebut this presumption in the present instance it would appear that there is nothing illegal in the action of the surveyor, assuming that he is acting under the instructions of the highway authority. See *Locke-king* v. *Woking Urban District Council* (THE SURVEYOR, vol. xii., p. 096).

COMBINED DRAIN : ALTERATION.—" R. M. F." writes : In a combined system of drainage a number of houses are each connected with the "sewer" in the rear by means of a pipe, which enters the sewer through a hole in side of same and cemented round as in Fig. (1). The "sewer" is a fire-clay pipe, and the sanitary authorities have called upon the owners of the houses to re-form the connections (which were made a

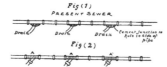

Fig. (1)
PRESENT SEWER

Fig (2)

few years since under their own supervision) by putting in new junction lengths in the sewer, as in Fig. (2). (1) Is the owner obliged to put in these new lengths in the "sewer" and reconnect with same? (2) As the new lengths, with the junction pieces on same, will form part of the "sewer," are the sanitary authorities bound to put in such lengths themselves?

Assuming the combined system to be a " sewer " and the drains to have been connected therewith in accordance with the regulations of the authority, any alterations in the sewer would have to be made at the expense of the authority.

BY-LAWS.—" X. Y. Z." writes : In 1882 B erected under our old b_-laws a suite of offices two storeys high. The old by-laws, made in 1863 under sec. 34 of the Local Government Act, 1858, prescribed a minimum thickness of 9 in. for all external and party walls, and the offices referred to were erected with walls thicker than those prescribed by such by-laws. The old by-laws also required that " where buildings are proposed to be raised the outer walls and the party walls, or separate side or end walls, shall be of sufficient strength, and so far sound and in good repair, as to be fit to bear the proposed additional walls." In 1894 the old by-laws were repealed and new by-laws adopted, under sec. 157 of the Public Health Act, 1875, based on the Model By-Laws of the Local Government Board. B has now deposited plans showing an additional storey to be erected on the top of the existing two-storey office building. This additional storey includes a new suite of offices, which will be connected with the existing offices. Taking such additional storey by itself, the walls comply with the requirements of the new by-laws as to thickness, but if the old and new portions are taken as a whole, then the walls of the existing two storeys are not found to be of the proper thickness to carry the additional storey, but would require thickening in order to comply with the new by-laws. We have Part III. of the Public Health Acts Amendment Act, 1890, in force in the borough, sec. 23 of which enables local authorities to make by-laws to prevent buildings which have been erected in accordance with by-laws made under the Public Health Acts from being altered in such a way that if at first so constructed they would have contravened the by-laws. We have, however, not yet made any by-laws under this section. Having regard to the fact that no such by-law is in existence, can the corporation insist that the walls of the existing two-storey building shall be thickened so as to comply with the new by-laws? And would they be justified in disapproving the plans unless the same show such walls to be thickened, and the old and the intended new part of the building (regarded as a whole) to be made so that the walls thereof comply with such now by-

laws? If your reply is in the affirmative, will you kindly quote cases in support of the same?

The question is whether the proposed addition amounts to the erection of a new building, or merely to an addition to the old building. This would be a question of fact for the decision of the magistrate. I think it is hardly likely that it would be held to be a new building, and, in my opinion, the corporation would not be justified in disapproving the plans.

PUBLIC HEALTH ACT, 1875, SEC. 23.—Mr. Percy Johns, A.M.I.C.E., borough surveyor of Maidenhead, writes : The whole question of the construction to be put on sec. 23 so frequently arises in my district that I should be glad to have your opinion thereon. At present my council is being urged by the waterworks company to compel three large properties, whose otherwise satisfactory system of drainage are connected to cesspools, quite efficient for the purpose, and so constructed and situated in the grounds of each as to be no nuisance to the inhabitants or the public at large. The properties, however, in these particular instances are located on what forms probably a portion of the area which is drained by the water company's wells, and therefore a possible danger by contamination. The company have called the attention of the council to this fact, and have asked that steps may be taken by the council to insist on the drainage of each house being connected to the public sewers, which are available and within the prescribed distance. Will you be good enough to state what power, in your opinion, the council have, if any, to compel the connections being made : (1) In these particular instances, and (2) supposing the question of danger to the public water supply were not a feature in the case.

This section does not justify a local authority in requiring an owner to alter his system of drainage, though it may be sufficient in itself (*Attorney-General* v. *Clerkenwell Vestry* [1891], 3 ch., 527.). If a nuisance arises the authority can proceed under sec. 41.

NEW STREETS.—" Nemo" writes : Eighteen months ago the owners submitted plans of a new street from A to B, ending in a *cul de sac* at B, which are approved by the urban authority. Street C to D is also laid out to the authority's approval. Sewers are put in the centre of street as shown, not being in the *cul de sac*. Buildings are erected in the portions etched. The owner, before proceeding with further buildings, proposes to do away with the *cul de sac* at B, and, instead of

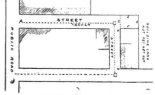

STREET

PUBLIC

PRIVATE

his buildings fronting E and F, to make them front H, and submits plans to alter the street accordingly. Can the urban authority refuse to sanction the amended plan and compel the owner to carry out his original plan, which will thus assist another owner in developing his estate?

In my opinion the authority are not bound to sanction the amended plan.

APPOINTMENT OF DISTRICT COUNCILLOR AS SURVEYOR : DISQUALIFICATION.—Mr. W. Hollingsworth, Eckington, Sheffield, writes : Will you please inform me if it is legal for a man who is a member of the district council to be appointed surveyor before his retirement from the council or not : also say when he should retire?

Under sec. 46, sub-sec. (d) of the Local Government Act, 1894, the member would become disqualified as a councillor by being appointed surveyor. He should retire before being appointed.

If " A Young Surveyor " will forward his name and address his query will receive attention. All queries must be accompanied by these particulars, though not necessarily for publication.

**Oban.**— New municipal buildings, which have been erected at a cost of about £5,000, were recently formally opened by Lord Strathcona, the High Commissioner for Canada.

## PLYMOUTH WATER SUPPLY.

### THE NEW RESERVOIR.

The Mayor of Plymouth last Wednesday week laid the last stone of the dam which has been constructed in connection with the new Plymouth waterworks. Large crowds of people witnessed the proceedings, which were followed in the evening by a banquet, presided over by the mayor.

The history of the water undertaking of the town dates from the reign of Queen Elizabeth, when Sir Francis Drake, under the powers of an Act of Parliament obtained by the corporation, made a leat some 17 miles in length which brought into Plymouth the waters of the river Meavy. In the years 1881 and 1891 serious difficulty was experienced owing to the blocking of the leat by snow and frost, and more recently trouble has arisen from a diminution of the supply by drought. In consequence of this the corporation in 1892 obtained powers to make a storage reservoir in the neighbourhood of the head weir which is the intake of the leat, and also to substitute a pipe line for the open water-course which has served the town for so many generations. The pipe line was completed in 1894, and the reservoir has now been finished.

The reservoir has been made by constructing a dam of masonry across the bed of the Meavy at a point about 1 mile below the head weir, where the river ran through a narrow channel known as Burrator Gorge. This dam rises to a height of 145 ft. from its foundation and 77 ft. above the bed of the river. Its length is 410 ft. along the parapet, or 361 ft. at the water line, and its greatest thickness is 80 ft. The face and top of the dam have been constructed of uncoursed ashlar, consisting of square blocks of granite, and the core of the structure is composed of cyclopean rubble, consisting of large masses of granite embedded in concrete. On the side of the dam which has to resist the water pressure the granite blocks have been rebated to a depth of 6 in., leaving a space ¾ in. wide to that depth between each of the blocks. These spaces have been filled in with cement slightly damped and driven in by an iron chisel. By this process an exceedingly hard and watertight joint has been obtained, so as to prevent water percolating into the core of the structure. A secondary dam has been made near the village of Sheepstor, where there was a depression in the ground which had to be filled up. When full the reservoir will contain 650,000,000 gallons of water. Its length will be 1¾ miles, its greatest width ¼ mile, and its greatest depth 77 ft. The work was designed by Mr. Edward Sandeman, the corporation's engineer, and Mr. James Mansergh, consulting engineer, and it has been carried out by the corporation under the supervision of these engineers. The estimated cost was £150,000.

## ELECTRIC LIGHT AT HANLEY.

### A FURTHER LOAN REQUIRED.

Colonel W. R. Slacke, R.E., on the 14th inst. held an inquiry, on behalf of the Local Government Board, with reference to an application of the Hanley Town Council for sanction to borrow a further sum of £4,000 for electric lighting purposes. Among those present were Messrs. A. Challinor, the town clerk; J. Lobley, the borough surveyor; and C. Sutherland and W. Cowell, the electrical engineers.

The Town Clerk explained that the annual rateable value of the borough was £197,912, and the balance of outstanding loans was £216,557. On February 6, 1893, the corporation obtained sanction to borrow £21,000 for electric lighting, repayable in twenty-five years. On June 14, 1894, they borrowed a further sum of £1,100, repayable in ten years; on May 29, 1895, £5,000, on November 28, £19,000, and on July 27, 1897, £14,880, repayable in twenty-five years. The present loan being part of the general scheme, it was desirable that its repayment should be extended over twenty-five years also. They had at present 363 private customers, and these were rapidly increasing. Mr. Cowell produced diagrams, and stated that the private lamps were equal to 25,750 lamps of 8 candle-power. They were supplied from four feeders, and they wanted now to put down a new high-tension feeder to supplement these. Owing to the great demand in the evening the tension dropped to 94 volts, whereas the minimum allowed was 97 volts. It was also explained that the council wished to take advantage of the ground being opened for telephone purposes to lay down some new low-pressure distributing mains. The present application was to meet the estimated requirements during the next twelve months. With regard to a proposal to purchase 100 additional meters to enable the corporation to carry out what was termed the Brighton system, by which they charged 5d. per unit for the first one and a half hours and 2½d. an hour afterwards, a member of the town council remarked that it was the most absurd system that was ever invented.

At the close of the inquiry, which was of a formal character, a vote of thanks was accorded to the inspector; and, in replying, Colonel Slacke said it must be very gratifying that the introduction of the electric light in Hanley had been such a success, and that they could supply electricity at such a rate as to induce so many customers to take it.

## SANITATION UP TO DATE.

The accompanying illustration is reproduced from a photo received from Mr. J. Owen-Jones, engineer and surveyor to the Biggleswade Urban District Council.

Our correspondent remarks: The pan is earthenware, and the trap outlet is made of lead. How long it had been in use I cannot say, the pan in some parts was worn into small holes. Excreta was well adhered inside the trap and

pipe (of course I need not mention what the stench was like). At point A another closet of the same pattern was connected, and both emptied into a small brick channel in the outer wall, the pipe B being the ventilation pipe from the brick channel. This channel was connected to a 6-in. socket pipe, and carried into the main sewer without an intercepting trap of any form.

## SEWER VENTILATION.

### DECISION OF THE CAMBERWELL VESTRY.

The Sewers and Sanitary Committee of the Camberwell Vestry reported, at a meeting of that body on Wednesday week that they had again considered the report of the delegates to the recent conference on the subject of sewer ventilation.

The resolutions passed were as follows: (1) That the closing of surface sewer ventilators in response to complaints increases the general evil, the diminution of which is to be attained by the multiplication of the ventilators, both surface and up-cast shafts, at regular frequent intervals. (2) That in connection with any interceptor hereafter fixed on a main house drain it is advisable to carry a ventilating pipe from the sewer side of the interceptor, up the front, side or back of the house, to the satisfaction of the local sanitary authority, and that the outlet drain from the interceptor shall not be flap-trapped unless required by the local sanitary authority. (3) That pipe ventilators up buildings, or otherwise, where possible should always be adopted, in addition to surface ventilation. (4) That copies of these resolutions be forwarded to the London County Council and the various vestries and district boards, and their co-operation asked for in giving effect to same.

The committee expressed themselves as being entirely in accord with these resolutions, subject to the following words being added to the second recommendation: " And that such ventilating pipes be 3 ft. above and 6 ft. away from the highest window or chimney where possible."

## SUPERANNUATION OF MUNICIPAL OFFICERS.

The conference convened by the Municipal Officers' Association, at a meeting held on Thursday, at 117 Holborn, E.C., had under consideration the question of again promoting legislation in the next session of Parliament, and decided to invite all associations and societies representing municipal officers to again send delegates to the conference. The chairman and secretary presented a joint report, together with balance-sheet, showing what had been done last session in promoting the Local Authorities Officers' Superannuation Bill. In order to further the movement, a conference will be held in London at the end of October, to which municipal officers throughout the country will be invited to attend, and a very large gathering is anticipated. Particulars of the place and time of meeting will be announced in due course, and any further information can be obtained by letter from the hon. secretary, Mr. C. J. F. Carnell, 117 Holborn, E.C.

**Bloemfontein.**—We understand that the town council have adopted a scheme for lighting the town with electricity, and have accepted the tender of Messrs. Reunert & Sons, at £16,500, for carrying out the work.

# Law Notes.

EDITED BY J. B. REIGNIER CONDER, 11 Old Jewry Chambers, E.C.

Solicitor of the Supreme Court.

*The Editor will be pleased to answer any questions affecting the practice of engineers and surveyors to local authorities. Queries (which should be written legibly on foolscap paper, one side only) should be addressed to "The Law Editor," at the Offices of THE*　　|　*SURVEYOR. Where possible, copies of local Acts or documents referred to should be enclosed. All explanatory diagrams must be drawn and lettered in black ink only. Correspondents who do not wish their names published should furnish a nom de plume*

## QUERIES AND REPLIES.

STRIPS OF LAND ADJOINING ROADWAY.—"J. S. C." writes: There is a strip of land on the road side that has not been macadamised up to the present time, about 6 ft. wide, next to the fence. The surveyor of the district is cutting away the ground and macadaming it to the fence, behind which is a clean-water drain that supplies some property. Is the surveyor justified in doing so? The property abuts on the Rochdale and Halifax turnpike road.

*Primâ facie, strips of land adjoining the highway form part of the highway (per Mr. Justice Crompton in The Queen v. United Kingdom Telegraph Company, 31 L.J., M.C., 166). Unless, therefore, there is something to rebut this presumption in the present instance it would appear that there is nothing illegal in the action of the surveyor, assuming that he is acting under the instructions of the highway authority. See Locke-King v. Woking Urban District Council (THE SURVEYOR, vol. xii., p. 696).*

COMBINED DRAIN: ALTERATION.—"H. M. F." writes: In a combined system of drainage a number of houses are each connected with the "sewer" in the rear by means of a pipe, which enters the sewer through a hole in side of same and cemented round as in Fig. (1). The "sewer" is a fire-clay pipe, and the sanitary authorities have called upon the owners of the houses to re-form the connections (which were made a

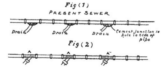

*Fig (1)*

PRESENT SEWER

Drain　　Drain　　Drain　　Cement Junction in hole in side of pipe

*Fig (2)*

few years since under their own supervision) by putting in new junction lengths in the sewer, as in Fig. (2). (1) Is the owner obliged to put in these new lengths in the "sewer" and reconnect with same? (2) As the new lengths, with the junction pieces on same, will form part of the "sewer," are the sanitary authorities bound to put in such lengths themselves?

*Assuming the combined system to be a "sewer" and the drains to have been connected therewith in accordance with the regulations of the authority, any alterations in the sewer would have to be made at the expense of the authority.*

BY-LAWS.—"X. Y. Z." writes: In 1882 B erected under our old by-laws a suite of offices two storeys high. The old by-laws, made in 1865 under sec. 34 of the Local Government Act, 1858, prescribed a minimum thickness of 9 in. for all external and party walls, and the offices referred to were erected with walls thicker than those prescribed by such by-laws. The old by-laws also required that "where buildings are proposed to be raised the outer walls and the party walls, or separate side or end walls, shall be of sufficient strength, and so far sound and in good repair, as to be fit to bear the proposed additional walls." In 1894 the old by-laws were repealed and new by-laws adopted, under sec. 157 of the Public Health Act, 1875, based on the Model By-Laws of the Local Government Board. B has now deposited plans showing an additional storey to be erected on the top of the existing two-storey office building. This additional storey includes a new suite of offices, which will be connected with the existing offices. Taking such additional storey by itself, the walls comply with the requirements of the new by-laws as to thickness, but if the old and new portions are taken as a whole, then the walls of the existing two storeys are not found to be of the proper thickness to carry the additional storey, but would require thickening in order to comply with the new by-laws. We have Part III. of the Public Health Acts Amendment Act, 1890, in force in the borough, sec. 23 of which enables local authorities to make by-laws to prevent buildings which have been erected in accordance with by-laws made under the Public Health Acts from being altered in such a way that if at first so constructed they would have contravened the by-laws. We have, however, not yet made any by-laws under this section. Having regard to the fact that no such by-law is in existence, can the corporation insist that the walls of the existing two-storey building shall be thickened so as to comply with the new by-laws? And would they be justified in disapproving the plans unless the same show such walls to be thickened, and the old and the intended now part of the building (regarded as a whole) to be made so that the walls thereof comply with such new by-

laws? If your reply is in the affirmative, will you kindly quote cases in support of the same?

*The question is whether the proposed addition amounts to the erection of a new building, or merely to an addition to the old building. This would be a question of fact for the decision of the magistrate. I think it is hardly likely that it would be held to be a new building, and, in my opinion, the corporation would not be justified in disapproving the plans.*

PUBLIC HEALTH ACT, 1875, SEC. 23.—Mr. Percy Johns, A.M.I.C.E., borough surveyor of Maidenhead, writes: The whole question of the construction to be put on sec. 23 so frequently arises in my district that I should be glad to have your opinion thereon. At present my council is being urged by the waterworks company to compel these large properties, whose otherwise satisfactory system of drainage are connected to cesspools, quite efficient for the purpose, and so constructed and situated in the grounds of each as to be no nuisance to the inhabitants or the public at large. The properties, however, in these particular instances are located on what forms probably a portion of the area which is drained by the water company's wells, and therefore a possible danger by contamination. The company have called the attention of the council to this fact, and have asked that steps may be taken by the council to insist on the drainage of each house being connected to the public sewers, which are available and within the prescribed distance. Will you be good enough to state what power, in your opinion, the council have, it any, to compel the connections being made: (1) In these particular instances, and (2) supposing the question of danger to the public water supply were not a feature in the case.

*This section does not justify a local authority in requiring an owner to alter his system of drainage, though it may be sufficient in itself (Attorney-General v. Clerkenwell Vestry [1891], 3 Ch., 527.). If a nuisance arises the authority can proceed under sec. 41.*

NEW STREETS.—"Nemo" writes: Eighteen months ago the owners submitted plans of a new street from A to B, ending in a cul de sac at B, which are approved by the urban authority. Street C to D is also laid out to the authority's approval. Sewers are put in these new lengths in the "sewer" not being in the cul de sac. Buildings are erected in the portions etched. The owner, before proceeding with further buildings, proposes to do away with the cul de sac at B, and, instead of

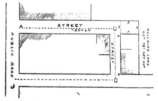

STREET

PUBLIC ROAD

his buildings fronting E and F, to make them front H, and submits plans to alter the street accordingly. Can the urban authority refuse to sanction the amended plan and compel the owner to carry out his original plan, which will thus assist another owner in developing his estate?

*In my opinion the authority are not bound to sanction the amended plan.*

APPOINTMENT OF DISTRICT COUNCILLOR AS SURVEYOR: DISQUALIFICATION.—Mr. W. Hollingsworth, Eckington, Sheffield, writes: Will you please inform me if it is legal for a man who is a member of the district council to be appointed surveyor before his retirement from the council or not; also say when he should retire?

*Under sec. 46, sub-sec. (d) of the Local Government Act, 1894, the member would become disqualified as a councillor upon being appointed surveyor. He should retire before being appointed.*

If "A Young Surveyor" will forward his name and address his query will receive attention. All queries must be accompanied by these particulars, though not necessarily for publication.

Oban.—New municipal buildings, which have been erected at a cost of about £6,000, were recently formally opened by Lord Strathcona, the High Commissioner for Canada.

# Municipal Work in Progress and Projected.

Hampstead Vestry is the only metropolitan authority from whom we have information this week of contemplated works of any magnitude. From the provinces, however, comes information of large and important undertakings projected at Halifax, St. Helens, Liverpool, Newcastle-on-Tyne, Scarborough, Leigh, Stretford, Chesterfield and elsewhere.

## METROPOLITAN AUTHORITIES.

### COURT OF COMMON COUNCIL.

The members of the above body held their first meeting after the summer vacation on Thursday, under the presidency of the Lord Mayor. The Streets Committee presented a report relative to the suggested erection, near the City hydrants, of receptacles or cupboards for fire-hose, with key of hydrant, so that the same might be avilable for use on the first outbreak of fire. A letter from the London County Council was included in the report, and from this document it appeared that the chief officer of the fire brigade was opposed to the suggestion. The committee consequently recommended the discharge of the reference. The recommendation was adopted.—The same committee presented a report on the dispute between the corporation and the Post Office authorities relative to the laying of telephone tubes without the permission of the former body. The committee submitted a letter from the secretary of the Post Office intimating that the provision of wires between exchanges of the National Telephone Company and the houses of their subscribers was not contemplated. The letter further contained an assurance from the Postmaster-General that if his present policy should be departed from he would not construct any telegraphs under consent of the corporation within the City between the exchanges of the National Telephone Company and the houses of their subscribers without conveying to the corporation an intimation that the policy had been changed. The committee stated that, subject to this understanding and to the usual condition that the contractors to the corporation would be employed to make good the pavements disturbed, they had consented to the various applications of the Post Office authorities for permission to open the public ways. The report was adopted.—In reply to a question, Mr. Turner said that water to the amount of about 11,000 gallons daily was being supplied from the artesian well to the Whitechapel district. The water would be supplied as long as it was required.—The Court agreed to an arrangement for acquiring the leasehold interest in 82 Fleet-street for £4,000.—On the motion of Mr. Deputy Johnson, it was referred to the Sanitary Committee to take into consideration the present position of Montague-court, Bishopsgate, and to report forthwith to this Court thereon. Mr. Deputy Johnson pointed out that the present was an excellent opportunity for sweeping away a highly insanitary area, and added that the inhabitants of Bishopsgate-street felt very strongly that the corporation should avail itself of it.

### VESTRIES AND DISTRICT BOARDS.

**Hampstead.—** The Works Committee of this body last week reported that they had given instructions for the London County Council to be informed that they agreed with the suggestion of the council that, where a street lamp was within a few feet of a fire alarm, the lamp-post should be painted a bright-red colour. This was approved.—The Baths and Wash-Houses Committee reported that they had considered the question of the advisability of the vestry applying to the Local Government Board for sanction to raise a loan in respect of expenditure on works carried out or authorised by the vestry to be executed at the Finchley-road baths. The matter was referred to the Finance Committee, with instructions to apply to the Local Government Board for permission to raise a loan of £5,800.

**Kensington.—** The Works and Sanitary Committee last week reported the consideration of several resolutions, passed at a conference of local authorities, relative to the housing of the working classes. They were of opinion that it was desirable that the vestry should have power to put the particular provisions of the Housing of the Working Classes Act into operation, and they accordingly recommended " that the London County Council be requested to include in their next General Powers Bill a clause giving the sanitary authorities concurrent power with the council to put in force Part III. of the Housing of the Working Classes Act." After some discussion the committee's recommendation was agreed to.—The Vestry of St. Margaret and St. John, Westminster, wrote, stating that they had decided to contribute £5,000 towards the cost of the High-street improvements. It was decided that the clerk should be instructed to write accepting that sum.

**St. George's, Southwark.—** At last week's meeting of the vestry the Open Spaces Committee reported that the vestry clerk had completed the purchase of the Paragon open space, and had received the following contributions towards the purchase money : London County Council, £1,700 ; Lord Llangattock, £1,000 ; Newington Vestry, £100. It was agreed that the open space should be laid with Hobman's tar paving.

## PROVINCIAL AND GREATER LONDON AUTHORITIES.

### COUNTY COUNCILS.

**Cumberland.—** The completion of the new stone bridge over the Irthing at Gilsland was celebrated last week by the members of the county council. The bridge is built on the skew principle, and has cost £1,400, including road diversions. The erection is in substitution of a narrow bridge with a square span and a very awkward approach on the left bank of the river. The bridge has been designed by Mr. G. J. Bell, the county surveyor, and built by Mr. Thos. Telfer, Langholm.

### MUNICIPAL CORPORATIONS.

**Birmingham.—** At a meeting of the Gas Committee of the corporation, on Monday, the progress of the various new works now in course of construction at Saltley was reported upon. The works have now reached a stage at which some idea can be formed of their extent and nature. The committee intend some time next month to invite the members of the council to view the tank which is now ready for the reception of the new four-lift gasholder at Nechells. This will hold 8,000,000 cubic feet of gas. A smaller gasholder has had its capacity doubled by telescoping, and will now hold 4,000,000 ft. The council will have pointed out to it the site of the new retort-house, also the improvements in the sewerage works and the bed of the river Rea, which have been undertaken by the Gas Committee. These and other works form part of the scheme sanctioned by the council in February, last, and the total expenditure on which was estimated at £366,000.

**Bristol.—** The scheme for providing docks at Portishead, at an estimated cost of £360,000, was, after a long discussion, rejected at the last meeting of the city council. The result of this decision is that Bristol is, officially speaking, once more without a policy of docks extension, and that a further period of twelve months must elapse before steps can be taken for depositing a Bill in Parliament.

**Cardiff.—** The town council have under consideration a report by the borough surveyor, Mr. W. Harpur, as to the space required for the town hall, law courts, technical college, Welsh University buildings, museum and other institutions which are to be provided for on the site of Cathays Park. They have instructed Mr. Harpur to define the several sites provisionally with flags, and all the members are then to meet the architect, Mr. Lanchester, of London, on the site.

**Croydon.—** We understand that the Local Government Board have refused, on sanitary grounds, to sanction the town council's scheme of new waterworks at Whaddon. Strong evidence against the proposal was submitted on behalf of the riparian and mill owners on the river Wandle at the inquiry, which was recently held by an inspector of the Local Government Board.

**Devonport.—** A largely-attended statutory meeting of ratepayers decided on Tuesday, by a considerable majority, to apply to Parliament for compulsory powers to acquire the rights of the Devonport Waterworks Company. The company were recently approached by the Water Committee of the corporation, but refused to treat at the price named by the committee—£350,000.

**Gloucester.—** The mayor recently laid the foundation-stone of the public free library, which is to be built on a site adjoining the municipal technical schools. The building, with additions to the schools, will cost £9,000. Messrs. Waller & Son, of Gloucester, are the architects.

**Halifax.—** The town council, at a special meeting on Wednesday of last week, decided to proceed forthwith with the construction of the three new reservoirs comprising the Walshaw Dean scheme; at a cost of £157,000.

**Harrogate.—** The sanction of the Local Government Board has been received by the corporation to the purchase of Harlow Moor, an open space some 52 acres in extent, which has hitherto been rented at a nominal rent from the Earl of Harewood. A loan of £30,500 has been sanctioned for the purchase and laying-out of the moor.

**Horsham.—** The information which, under this heading, was given in our last issue should, we find, has been included with the proceedings of rural district councils instead of municipal corporations. We regret the error.

**Hull.—** At a meeting of the Gas Committee, held on the 20th inst., the chairman reported that he and the deputy-chairman had made numerous inquiries with a view to securing a suitable site for the required station meter, and had arranged for the purchase of two houses and shops, with a plot of ground behind, situated on the east side of Dock Office-row, immediately adjoining the north quay of the Queen's Dock basin, and containing an area of 278 square yards, for £2,000. The main to the meter would be carried underneath one of the shops, and as there was sufficient land behind to erect a meter-house, it would not be necessary to interfere with the shops, which produced an annual rental of £80. They did not think they had done badly, as they would practically get their site for nothing. The report was adopted.

**Keighley.**—The Health Committee have secured provisionally 9,080 square yards of ground in Lawkholme-lane as a site for a proposed public slaughter-house.

**Liverpool.**—Plans have been approved by the city council for the extension of the City Fever Hospital, East Mill-lane, Old Swan, and an application is to be made to the Local Government Board for sanction to the borrowing of £40,000 to carry out the work.

**Maidstone.**—A letter has been received by the town council from the Local Government Board stating that a loan to cover the expenses incurred by the town council in connection with the typhoid epidemic which devastated the borough last autumn can only be granted for three years. The council had applied for sanction to borrow £18,000 and to spread repayments over twenty years. The Local Government Board intimate that they are disposed to grant a loan of £15,000 only. This decision, both as to the amount and period of the loan, has caused great surprise in the borough, to which it means an annual rate of 1s. in the £1 for the three years.

**Manchester.**—The special committee of the corporation appointed to consider and report with reference to the city telephone service on Thursday resolved to recommend to the city council that authority should be given them " to communicate with the Postmaster-General, the adjoining local authorities and the representatives of any telephone company who may desire an interview; also to make such further inquiries as they may think desirable, and to present a further report to the council." The matter will be submitted to the council at their meeting in October.

**Nelson.**—At a recent joint meeting of the Health and Gas Committees it was resolved to use the waste heat from the proposed new refuse destructor for the generation of electric energy, and the borough surveyor was instructed to at once proceed with the preparation of the necessary plans, &c.

**Newcastle-on-Tyne.**—At the last meeting of the Town Improvement Committee of the corporation it was reported that a communication had been received from the Local Government Board sanctioning the loan of £6,500 for the extension of the Ouseburn sewerage scheme. It was agreed that the city engineer, Mr. Law, should take steps to have the scheme carried into practical effect as soon as possible. About five years ago the scheme was first initiated, and the proposal was that the sewage discharged at the bridge, Byker Bank, from Byker, Heaton, Benton and Jesmond, and also that from Gosforth, should be discharged into the river at low-water mark. The carrying out of the scheme will remove a grievance complained of by the residents in the neighbourhood of Byker.—The new branch library at Heaton, erected at the cost of Alderman W. H. Stephenson, and presented by him to Newcastle-on-Tyne, is to be opened by Earl Grey on Thursday. The library will be called the Victoria Library, and it is a building almost identical with the Stephenson Library in Elswick-road, also given to the town by the same donor, and opened by Sir M. W. Ridley.

**Plymouth.**—At the Municipal Buildings, on Friday, Mr. E. A. Sandford Fawcett, A.M.I.C.E., one of the Local Government Board inspectors, sat to inquire into an application for sanction to borrow £1,325 for police station and fire brigade purposes, £300 for the reconstruction of the urinal at the west of the Promenade pier, and £227 for works of street improvements.

**Saffron Walden.**—A Local Government Board inquiry was held here on Friday last by Mr. G. W. Willcocks, M.I.C.E., with reference to the application of the town council for sanction to borrow £400 for works of street improvements. The town clerk opened the inquiry, and the borough surveyor, Mr. G. William Lacey, produced the plans and gave information as to the work proposed. Some opposition was raised on the ground that the sewerage of the borough should be improved and extended before the work proposed. The inspector inquired closely, therefore, into the question of the sewerage of the streets, as to when the new paving was intended to be done, and also as to the general system of sewers and sewage disposal.

**Scarborough.**—Plans for the erection of a new isolation hospital, at a cost of £15,000, have been passed by the town council. Thirty-two beds will be provided, sixteen in the scarlet fever block (four private), ten in the typhoid block (two private), two for measles and diphtheria, and two for observation.—A proposal is at present before the town council for the establishment of a system of 14 miles of electric tramways. There is not unanimity of feeling on the subject, and it is expected that the question will give rise to much controversy both in and out of municipal circles. A part of the scheme is to make a circular route of some 6 miles in extent. There is no doubt whatever that the departure would be eminently popular.

**Sheffield.**—A proposal of the Leicester and Nottingham Corporations to acquire the water of the famous Derbyshire rivers, the Derwent and the Ashop, has created some alarm to the Sheffield Corporation, and the Water Committee of that body have recommended the council to take steps in

defence of their own rights to the water. The scheme of the Midland towns is to construct four reservoirs at Ashopton, one of the most beautiful spots in Derbyshire, and a favourite resort of Sheffield people. Not only is the place within 10 miles of Sheffield, but some of the water to be acquired drains from hillsides which are in Yorkshire. A conference between the various local authorities interested in the subject is to be held, and, failing a satisfactory agreement, Sheffield Corporation is advised to promote a Bill to secure a portion of the threatened supply.

**Southend-on-Sea.**—The Local Government Board have sanctioned the borrowing by the corporation of £3,845 for the construction of the tramway passing-place and new buildings on the pier.

**St. Helens.**—It was last week reported that the Local Government Board had sanctioned the borrowing of £20,000 for street works, £15,000 of this amount being for street paving. For the paving of Corporation-street £900 was sanctioned and £5,000 for the construction of the subway in Church-street. With respect to the subway, the borough surveyor read a letter he had received from the Local Government Board requesting the council to construct the brick arch of 9 in. instead of 4½ in. The surveyor said that on receipt of this letter he wrote stating that, as the Local Government Board had delayed giving their consent so long, the work had been commenced, and a considerable part had been completed. He pointed out that a large quantity of concrete was being put above the 4½-in. arch. The Local Government Board had subsequently given consent to the work.

**Sunderland.**—Last week the corporation resolved to take steps to obtain powers to work the tramways in the town, which are at present worked by a company. They also resolved to establish the electric overhead trolley wire system of traction in lieu of horse-power.

**Swansea.**—At a recent meeting of the Sanitary Committee it was decided, upon the recommendation of the medical officer, to add a new wing to the borough fever hospital.

**Taunton.**—As a result of a visit of the mayor of Taunton to the secretary of the Local Government Board, that body have, it is stated, sanctioned a high-level drainage scheme for the prevention of floods at the north end of the town. The work is to be proceeded with at once.

## URBAN DISTRICT COUNCILS.

**Audenshaw.**—The council have decided to apply for provisional orders for the construction of tramways between Fairfield and Guide Bridge within their district, and also for electric lighting. Mr. J. P. Wilkinson, A.M.I.C.E., of St. Mary's Gate, Manchester, is the engineer.

**Bognor.**—The district council have decided to erect a new fire brigade station in the High-street, and also a new depot, workshop, stables and cottages for the foreman and head horseman upon land recently acquired in Circus-street. The plans for the buildings have been prepared by Mr. Oswald A. Bridges, the surveyor to the council, and he will supervise the erection of the buildings.

**Chingford.**—A public inquiry has been held by Colonel Hepper, on behalf of the Local Government Board, with reference to an application of the district council for sanction to borrow £1,350 for sewerage works at Chingford Hatch. No opposition was offered to the application.

**Cowes.**—It was reported, at the last meeting of the district council, by the manager of the gasworks that, owing to the increasing consumption of gas, it would be necessary to appropriate the present coal store as a retort-house and to erect two benches of sixes there, at an estimated cost of £789. Another coal store would also be necessary, estimated to cost £440.

**Crediton.**—The council having applied to the Local Government Board for leave to borrow £500 for the purpose of sewerage works at Fordton and the improvement of the drainage in the town, Colonel A. J. Hepper, D.S.O., R.E., has been directed to hold an inquiry into the circumstances. Colonel Hepper has fixed the inquiry to-day, at 11.30 a.m., at the council offices.

**Ilford.**—At their last meeting the district council resolved to take steps to acquire the undertaking of the Ilford Gas Company, and also the right of supply in that portion of the district at present supplied by the Barking Gas Company.

**Ilfracombe.**—The Local Government Board have declined to sanction the council's application to borrow £5,000 for an improvement of the vegetable market, on the ground that the approach road on the west side would be but 24 ft. wide, and that on the south side 15 ft. 6 in. This decision has placed the council in a fix, as now they will have to come to terms with the owners on the opposite side, who two years ago offered to give the council the necessary 12 ft. of land throughout, which they declined.

**Leigh.**—A special meeting of the council was held on Thursday, when it was agreed to apply to the Local Government Board for sanction to borrow £15,000 for works of sewerage.

**Llandudno.**—The loan required by the district council for the purpose of erecting the proposed municipal buildings has been sanctioned by the Local Government Board, and the contract has been given to Mr. Samuel Warburton, of Manchester, who is carrying out the extension of the Denbigh Asylum. The work will be commenced without delay.

**Machynlleth.** — The Local Government Board have declined to sanction a loan of £3,000 to the council for works of sewerage, being of opinion that the proposed scheme was incomplete and unsatisfactory in many important respects.

**Matlock.** — Local Government Board sanction to the borrowing of £5,500 for a further extensive improvement scheme is to be applied for by the district council. The scheme comprises the provision of open spaces, promenades and other works.

**Morpeth.** — Works of water supply have just been completed for the district council, and will be opened shortly. The works, which are situated at Tranwell, have been carried out from plans by, and under the direction of, Mr. A. S. Dinning, of Newcastle-on-Tyne.

**New Swindon.** — At the last fortnightly meeting of this council it was decided not to entertain the idea of purchasing the New Swindon Gas Company's undertaking. There was a great deal of discussion on the subject, and it was stated that the market value of the gas undertaking was between £90,000 and £100,000. The council have obtained a provisional order to provide electric light for the town, and the members felt they could not go to the extent of purchasing the gas undertaking just now.

**Romford.** — At last week's meeting of the district council a letter was read from the Local Government Board sanctioning the borrowing of an additional £1,000 for bath purposes.

**Ruskington.** — A Local Government Board inquiry was held on the 15th inst. by Mr. H. Percy Boulnois, with reference to an application of the district council for sanction to borrow £1,900 to construct waterworks ordered by the Local Government Board.

**Saxmundham.** — A scheme for the drainage of the town, prepared by Mr. H. J. Wright, of Ipswich, has been adopted by the district council.

**Southgate.** — The Local Government Board have sanctioned the borrowing of £1,280 for improvement works in the Green-lanes main road.

**Stretford.** — Colonel W. Langton Coke has held an inquiry, on behalf of the Local Government Board, with reference to an application of the district council for permission to borrow £6,000 to provide a technical institute and free library, and £4,000 for the purchase of a plot of 18½ acres of land, at Pennington-lane, for the purpose of a public recreation ground.

## RURAL DISTRICT COUNCILS.

**Bridgwater.** — At a meeting of this authority, last week, the question of providing a supply of water for the parish of Nether Stowey was again considered, and it was reported that the ratepayers of Stowey had almost unanimously decided to recommend the council to adopt the scheme for obtaining a supply from the Brucombe spring, the cost of which was estimated at £1,000. The council decided to adopt this scheme, and to arrange satisfactory terms, if possible, with Sir Alexander Hood for obtaining a supply from the source named.

**Chesterfield.** — A Local Government Board inquiry was held at Chesterfield, on the 16th inst., into an application by the council for sanction to borrow a large sum of money for the purpose of extending the northern water supply system. The authority proposed to apportion the cost as follows: Barlow, £955; Beighton, £11,092; Coal Aston, £850; Dronfield Woodhouse, £950; Eckington, £14,346; Holmsfield, £561; Killamarsh, £4,217; Staveley, £14,551; and Unstone, £1,352. The inquiry was also relative to an application by the Dronfield Urban District Council for sanction to borrow £5,189. After a lengthy discussion, the inspector, Mr. H. Percy Boulnois, said that he would report on the matter in due course.

**St. Germans.** — Mr. Sandford Fawcett held an inquiry last week, on behalf of the Local Government Board, respecting an application of the district council for permission to borrow £933 for sewerage works for the village of Downderry. Mr. S. Jenkin, engineer of the works, explained the plans.

**Stratford-on-Avon.** — At a meeting on Friday afternoon, Mr. J. E. Willcox, of Birmingham, attended to report upon the water supply of Alveston. An artesian well had been sunk, and the works now contemplated, including service mains, &c., were estimated to cost £3,693, which, Mr. Willcox submitted, was too costly for the parish. He suggested modifications of the plans for a high-level supply to the neighbouring farmhouses by reducing the size of the reservoir and pipes, which would save about £600. After a long discussion Mr. Willcox's modifications were agreed to. The contract was signed. It was decided to commence the work forthwith. Several members complained that the water from the well had been running to waste for three or four months.

**Wem, Salop.** — At a recent meeting of this authority a letter was read from the Grinshill Parish Council stating that many of the inhabitants of Grinshill were suffering from

what might be termed a water famine, and requesting the district council to render what assistance they could in the matter. It was stated that they were in a most deplorable state for want of water. The supply from the parish pump had given in, and there was no water at all. They would be glad to obtain the water supply for the neighbourhood from the council, and Mr. Stooke, the engineer, had stated that there was quite sufficient for the purpose, there being almost an unlimited supply at Oreston.

## SCOTLAND AND IRELAND.

**Aberdeen.** — Acting on the instructions of the town council, Mr. Rust, the city architect, has completed the valuation of the different slaughter-houses in the city, in view of the proposal to erect a public abattoir, and the estimate will be submitted to the committee. As it is felt desirable to have the Bill empowering the council to proceed in the matter ready for the ensuing session of Parliament, it is likely that several points in the draft scheme may be left over in the meantime. — An agreement has been entered into by the corporation with the Rubislaw Granite Company to widen Queen's-road, at an estimated cost to the ratepayers of £1,640.

**Annan.** — The Finance Committee have been instructed by the town council to report on the question of the purchase of the gasworks.

**Ayr.** — An important decision with reference to the domestic water supply of the burgh was come to by the town council at a recent meeting. The pipe conveying the water from Loch Finlas to the filters at Knockjarder, a distance of 15 miles, is proving too small to convey sufficient water to keep up with the consumption. A number of schemes to increase the supply have been considered; but it has been decided to lay down a pumping plant, at a cost of £4,400, which involves the eventual construction of a storage reservoir, at a cost of £2,650, to pump the water from the old water supply in the Careline reservoir to the filters about a mile distant and at a considerably higher level.

**Buckie.** — At a special meeting of the commissioners, held recently, plans of the new bridge to be erected across the Buckie burn were submitted to Mr. Barron, C.E., Aberdeen. Three plans were submitted, the estimated cost being £1,800, £1,650 and £1,750 respectively. It was agreed to adopt the plan costing £1,650.

**Coleraine.** — Mr. Charles P. Cotton, chief engineering inspector of the Local Government Board of Ireland, recently held an inquiry respecting an application of the rural sanitary authority for sanction to a supplemental loan of £1,600 for sewerage works for Portstewart. Mr. W. J. Given, engineer of the works, explained the plans.

**Dublin.** — A Local Government Board inquiry was recently held by Mr. O'Brien Smyth into an application of the town council for sanction to borrow a sum of £9,000 for the erection of additional class-rooms at the Kevin-street technical schools. — On Thursday last, as a drove of bullocks were passing through Beresford-place, Dublin, four of them fell through a large manhole leading to the main drainage excavation. Two men and a boy who were working below received severe, though not dangerous, injuries from the fall of the bullocks, and were rescued with difficulty.

**Dunoon.** — The commissioners have at present under consideration a scheme for the electric lighting of the principal thoroughfare of the town. It is also proposed that an application for power to erect a pavilion be inserted in the Bill to be promoted. — It was decided, at the last meeting of the commissioners, to borrow £17,800 for the purposes of water extension, hospital, special sewers, roads and pier.

**Helensburgh.** — The Burghs Gas Supply (Scotland) Act has been adopted by the town council, and it has been unanimously agreed to apply its provisions to the town. Further consideration of the matter has been deferred until after the forthcoming municipal elections.

**Kilsyth.** — The commissioners have a new water scheme under consideration, and have appointed Mr. Frew, of Messrs. Kyle, Denison & Frew, Glasgow, to report on the most suitable place on the Gandihill for a reservoir. Sir Archibald Edminstone has agreed to give the ground free of charge under certain reservations, the chief of which is that his tenants along the wayleave must be supplied with water.

**Paisley.** — The corporation, it is stated, have successfully objected to an application of the British Electric Traction Company for an order to run electric cars in their district. The corporation have arranged with Glasgow for that city to purchase the tramways, control them for twenty-one years, and then hand them over to Paisley for nothing.

# Personal.

Mr. Pettitt, of Stanway, has been appointed assistant surveyor to the Braintree Rural District Council, at a commencing salary of £75 per annum.

At a meeting of the Portmadoc Urban District Council, on Wednesday of last we k, Mr. Thomas Harris, of Bootle, was appointed surveyor and sanitary inspector.

We are informed that Mr. R. W. Hartley, of Eccles, has been appointed to the position of third assistant in the office of Mr. T. Hunter, the engineer and surveyor to the Leigh (Lancs.) Urban District Council.

Mr. Gilbert Dickinson, son of Mr. John Dickinson, of Greenbank, Ulverston, Lancashire, has qualified as a graduate of the Institution of Mechanical Engineers. He is articled to Mr. J. W. Bradley, borough engineer of Wolverhampton.

A letter was last week received by the Newton Rural District Council from Mr. S. Sugar, the chief inspector, resigning his position under that body. He has, it is understood, obtained an appointment as architect to a building estate.

Mr. Henry Hewitt Bridgman, a Fellow of the Royal Institute of British Architects and at one time a member of the London Court of Common Council and the City Commission of Sewers, has, we regret to learn, succumbed to a serious illness.

At a meeting of the Court of Common Council on Thursday a letter was submitted from Mr. Walter Swale, announcing the death of his father, Mr. William Swale, late superintendent of cleansing, who in 1892 was granted a retiring allowance of £500 a year.

Mr. Bertie Wake, son of Mr. H. H. Wake, engineer to the River Wear Commissioners, while having a trip in a steam launch on Saturday week, on the river Wear at Southwick, with a party of young men, fell overboard and was drowned. His body was recovered shortly afterwards.

A few days ago, according to a contemporary, the Milton-next-Sittingbourne Urban District Council received a letter from Mr. Amos B. Acworth, their surveyor, intimating that he had resigned his post, owing to private reasons. Mr. Acworth was in the service of the council for twelve years.

Mr. William Heston, who for four years has held the post of divisional inspector of highways on the staff of the borough engineer of Wolverhampton, has resigned, in order to commence business with his brother, under the style of Heaton Brothers, contractors for public works, St. Helens, Lancashire.

In our reference of last week to the election of district surveyors to the Lancashire County Council, Mr. H. T. Chapman, who is at present a district surveyor of main roads under the Derbyshire County Council, was inadvertently mentioned as being with the Rural District Council of Chapel-en-le-Frith.

The Sandgate Urban District Council, at their meeting on Friday last, presented their surveyor, Mr. A. R. Bowles, with a handsome spirit tantalus on the occasion of his marriage. They wished him every happiness, and expressed a hope that he might long remain among them. Mr. Bowles thanked the council for the confidence reposed in him and for their kindness.

At the last meeting of the Haltwhistle Rural District Council, Mr. Harry W. Taylor, A.M.I.C.E., of Newcastle-on-Tyne and Birmingham, presented his scheme for the sewering of West End. The council considered the scheme very satisfactory, and instructed Mr. Taylor to also prepare a scheme of sewerage for Town Foot and report upon the disposal of the whole of the sewage of Haltwhistle.

A special meeting of the Wareham Town Council in committee was held on Tuesday of last week, for the purpose of electing a surveyor in the place of Mr. George Hobbs, who has resigned the office. The salary is £20 per annum. There were four candidates—namely, Messrs. William Laws, W. Feekes, J. Laws and J. Bridle. The voting was as follows: W. Laws, seven; W. Feekes, four; J. Laws, one. Mr. W. Laws was therefore elected.

Ventnor Urban District Council last week recommended that a draft agreement with the surveyor, Mr. E. J. Harvey, be approved, the arrangement being that, in consideration of salaries of £120 as surveyor and £80 as inspector of nuisances, Mr. Harvey would carry out the duties and devote the whole of his time during office hours to the work of the council; he also stipulated to undertake no private practice that would clash with the interests of the council. The report was adopted.

The Finance Committee of the Mile End Vestry on Wednesday of last week recommended that the resignation of Mr. W. F. Loveday, assistant surveyor, who has been appointed surveyor to the South Hornsey District Council, be accepted, and that advertisements be issued inviting candidates for the vacant post, and that the salary to commence with be at the rate of £104 per annum. The resignation was

accepted, but the subsequent portions of the report were referred back to committee.

A special committee dealing with the borough surveyorship of Preston have recommended to the council that Mr. Thomas Cookson, heretofore deputy surveyor, be appointed the borough engineer and borough surveyor during the pleasure of the council, at a salary of £500 per annum. The title of steward is to be transferred to the borough treasurer. It is also recommended that, "to ensure efficiency in the engineer's and surveyor's department, there be appointed an assistant surveyor, at a salary after the rate of £200 per annum, and a draughtsman, at wages of 35s. per week.

The remains of Mr. H. Masterton, district surveyor under the Devonshire County Council, whose death, we regret to state, occurred recently at Barnstaple, were on the 22nd inst. removed to London for burial. The deceased gentleman was resident engineer in connection with the construction of the first section of the North Cornwall Railway and the line from Lydford to Devonport, while he was engineer for several important works at Plymouth. He succeeded ten years ago to the business of Mr. J. C. Ingliss, engineer, Plymouth, Mr. Ingliss being now chief engineer of the Great Western Railway.

The question of appointing a surveyor to the northern, or Finchingfield, division of the rural district of Braintree led, at last week's meeting of the council, to a discussion as to the advisability of continuing the old arrangement of having two divisions, with a surveyor to each, or the appointment of one surveyor to do the whole of the work, with an assistant. The chairman favoured the latter arrangement, and moved the appointment of Mr. G. H. Bright, the surveyor of the southern district, as surveyor and sanitary inspector for the whole district, at an inclusive salary of £200 a year, with an assistant at £75. This was seconded, and eventually agreed to by a majority of thirteen votes to four.

At a meeting of St. George's (Southwark) Vestry, on the 20th inst., the Public Health Committee reported that they had considered a report from the surveyor, drawing attention to the large amount of work in his department, and asking that a permanent professional assistant should be appointed. The committee, taking into consideration that much work had to be done in connection with new public conveniences, new sewers, &c., recommended that an assistant surveyor be appointed, at a salary commencing at £130 per annum, rising by annual increments of £10 per annum to a maximum of £180 per annum, the Public Health and Sewers and Works Committees to make the appointment. The recommendation was adopted.

An interesting ceremony took place at the Shire Hall, on Saturday, when Mr. H. T. Wakelam was presented with an illuminated address and a gold watch by the district surveyors of the county on the occasion of his resigning the surveyorship of Herefordshire to take up the position as county surveyor of Middlesex. Mr. John Parker, city surveyor of Hereford, in making the presentation said it had been subscribed to by the district surveyors and the surveyors of the boroughs and urban authorities in the county. It was with great regret that they looked upon the departure of Mr. Wakelam from their midst. During the time Mr. Wakelam had been associated with them in their work he had found a warm place in their hearts, and they all wished him every success and prosperity in his new sphere of labour. Mr. Wakelam suitably acknowledged the presentation.

Last week, at a meeting of the Bridlington Urban District Council, a letter was received from Mr. J. Freeburn Stow intimating his desire to be relieved of his duties as town surveyor at the end of October. Mr. Stow, as will be remembered, was recently appointed, out of a large number of applicants, to the position of surveyor to the Chertsey Urban District Council. The chairman of the Highway Committee, in moving the acceptance of the resignation, said he had had, officially, a great deal to do with Mr. Stow, who had been at all times both able and willing to perform his duties. He regretted very much his leaving, and he only hoped and trusted that the change he had decided upon would be so beneficial to him, and that the appointment might prove all he desired. The motion, which also proposed the granting of a testimonial in recognition of Mr. Stow's past services, was subsequently adopted, the chairman of the council remarking that they all regretted losing such a valuable official. Following upon this business the council proceeded to discuss the appointment of a new official, and decided to issue the usual advertisements inviting applications for the vacant post, the salary being fixed at £160 per annum.

**Society of Engineers.**—The next ordinary meeting of the above society will be held at the Royal United Service Institution, Whitehall, S.W., on Monday, when a paper will be read by Mr. Sherard Cowper-Coles, A.M.I.C.E., M.I.M.E., M.I.E.E., on "Protective Metallic Coatings for Iron and Steel." The chair will be taken at 7.30 p.m. precisely.

## POLLUTION AT STRATFORD.

### THE CHANNELSEA RIVER.

Mr. Lewis Angell, borough engineer of West Ham, has submitted the following interesting report with regard to the state of the Channelsea river. He says: The recurring and continuously-increasing complaints of the condition of the Channelsea has been the subject of many reports by the borough engineer over a long period. The great increase of the populations north of the borough, abutting on watercourses which flow into the north-western parts of West Ham, intersecting the Stratford district, has resulted in an amount of sewage pollution of the most offensive character. Abundant evidence of such pollution was given before the House of Commons Select Committee on Police and Sanitary Regulations, June 15th and 16th, when the chairman, Sir Stafford Northcote, made the remark, page 50: "I must say that the committee accept the fact of the foulness of the brook. The only question is, who is to have jurisdiction?" Further evidence was submitted to the same committee, June 29th, by the borough engineer, pages 116–128, explaining the conditions affecting the offensiveness of the Channelsea, which, omitting details, may be generally stated as follows: The tidal flow from the Thames, which is not in itself pure, is intercepted on the river Lee by gates at the Bromley lock, the Three Mills and the Abbey Mills, above which gates the waters are penned up.

Various "backwaters" connect with the main river Lee— viz., Waterworks river, City Mill river, Pudding Mill river, Three Mills Wall river, Channelsea river, and other streams.

The West Ham sewage is discharged about 1¾ miles below the Channelsea tidal gates, and for the last ten years upon the ebb tide only, the discharge being discontinued for about 1½ hours, more or less, before the turn of the incoming tide, the sewage being stored during the interval in extensive tanks. Some time ago the borough engineer made experiments with floats discharged with the sewage, which showed that such floats did not return so high as the Channelsea gates at Abbey Mills. The greatest offensiveness of the Channelsea occurs during neap tides, when tidal waters do not enter the pen above the gates. The penned-up water containing the sewage discharged from the districts above is held up without change for several days, and during warm weather increases in offensiveness. In consequence of the abstraction of water very little, in the absence of rain, flows down the Channelsea; in fact for long periods of dry weather the only flow is the sewage "effluent" discharged from Walthamstow and Leyton. As neap tides do not reach the Abbey Mill gates by about ¼ mile, even if the West Ham sewage did return upwards from Canning Town, it could not reach the Channelsea. The black sewage "effluent" penned up by the Abbey Mill gates deposits mud or "sludge" along the beds of the Channelsea, producing foul scum and vegetation, which decomposes and emits large volumes of sewage gas, rising in bubbles to the surface.

The flow and accumulation of sewage is a daily-increasing quantity. Neither the water nor the flood-gates are under the control of the corporation. Arrangements are made, by consent of the West Ham Gas Company, to open the gates for the escape of the sewage as frequently as possible, corporation men remove offensive mud deposits and apply disinfectants to the river bed, but no amount of cleansing within West Ham effects any practical good, nothing short of an arrest of the pollution from above will be effectual.

West Ham has been accused of contributing to the pollution, but, as previously stated, in no case can West Ham sewage flow through the Abbey Mill gates during neap tides; during spring tides, when, if at all, it may be thought possible for sewage to flow up the Channelsea, no complaints arise by reason of the volume of water. There is a West Ham storm overflow immediately below the Abbey Mill gates, which acts only at times of storms, and cannot act when the tide flows up the Channelsea, nor do complaints arise at storm times. Rainfall entering the Channelsea, either in Stratford or from up river, reduces its offensiveness.

In less than a year the West Ham sewage will be diverted from the river Lee, but it will take a long period to divert the sewage of Walthamstow from the Channelsea. The evidence before the Police and Sanitary Committee last month shows that injunctions have been issued, also an order of sequestration (against Walthamstow) without result. So long as sewage is discharged from the districts above West Ham, Stratford must continue to suffer increasingly.

## ELECTRIC TRACTION IN DUDLEY.

### DETAILS OF THE SCHEME.

Although the Dudley portion of the proposed electric tramway remains in abeyance pending the corporation and the British Electric Traction Company coming to terms, that portion of the Dudley and Stourbridge line from Hart's Hill to Stourbridge will be in full working order before the end of the year. The generating station at Hart's Hill is being rapidly pushed forward by Messrs. Whittaker & Co. It comprises a car-shed, 102 ft. by 54 ft.; a workshop, 102 ft. by 27 ft.; a boiler-house, 40 ft. by 48 ft.; and an engine-room,

57 ft. by 30 ft. The contract is for £7,000, and over 1,000,000 bricks will be used up. The site has been acquired from the Earl of Dudley, and sufficient space has been obtained to double the operations, if such expansion should be needed. Two large Lancashire boilers will be placed in the boiler-room, capable of working up to 140 lb. pressure on the square inch, whilst two non-condensing compound engines will work the cable of the two electrical generators. There will be nine cars, capable of carrying twenty-eight passengers in each, the cars being worked by two motors rated up to 25 horse-power geared to the axles.

The span-wire system will be utilised. A cable runs from the generating station to the end of the line, and is tapped at every half-mile, and connected to a feeder-box. From the latter cables convey the current to the trolley wires. From the trolley wires the current goes to the controller at each end of the car, and from the controllers to the motors, then to the wheels, and back through the track to the power-house. Enough power could be generated at the station to work the whole of the original system—viz., from Dudley to Kinver vid Kingswinford, from Dudley to Stourbridge vid Brierley Hill, and from Dudley to Cradley Heath, as well as providing for lighting if required. At present the line will be 3¼ miles in length, and has been entirely reconstructed. It is proposed to run a ten minutes' service.

## AMERICAN COMPETITION.

### A GLASGOW MUNICIPAL CONTRACT.

The last, it seems, has not been heard of the water pipes contract, and it is said that the muddle is now worse than ever. It will be remembered that the Water Committee recommended the acceptance of the offer of Messrs. Robert Maclaren & Co., Glasgow, to supply 1,000 tons of cast-iron piping, at a cost of £4,958, while Messrs. Wood & Co., Philadelphia, had offered to take the contract for £4,892. This proposal the corporation upset, and divided the contract, giving about two-thirds to the Glasgow firm and one-third to Messrs. Wood. Messrs. Maclaren & Co. have since written stating that they decline to accept the contract on those conditions, having made an overhead price for the whole quantity, or that they will require to be paid an additional 13s. per ton. The matter is in the hands of the town clerk and Mr. Osborne, convener of the committee; and apparently all that can be done is to re-advertise the contract or give it in its entirety to the American firm.

## APPOINTMENTS VACANT.

*Advertisements which are received too late for classification cannot be included in these summaries until the following week.*

FOREMAN OF STREET GAS LIGHTING.—October 1st.—Corporation of Plymouth. £2 5s.—Mr. James Paton, borough engineer and surveyor.

GENERAL ASSISTANT FOR BOROUGH ENGINEER'S DEPARTMENT.—October 1st.—Corporation of Plymouth. £100.—Mr. James Paton, borough engineer and surveyor.

SURVEYOR AND INSPECTOR OF NUISANCES.—October 3rd.—Arlecdon and Frizington Urban District Council. £120.—Mr. John Bowly, clerk to the council, Council Offices, Frizington.

ENGINEER AND MANAGER OF SEWAGE WORKS.—October 5th.—Hampton Urban District Council. £3.—Mr. John Kemp, engineer and surveyor to the council.

MEASURING CLERK FOR ARCHITECT'S DEPARTMENT.—October 5th.—London County Council. £100.—The Clerk to the Council, Spring-gardens, S.W.

CLERK OF WORKS.—October 6th.—High Wycombe Corporation. £3.—Mr. T. J. Rushbrooke, borough surveyor.

INSPECTOR OF NEW BUILDINGS AND DRAINAGE WORK.—October 8th.—Hornsey Urban District Council. £160.—Mr. E. J. Lovegrove, engineer and surveyor to the council.

HARBOUR ENGINEER.—October 10th.—Waterford Harbour Commissioners. £150.—Mr. J. Allingham, jun., secretary to the commissioners, Harbour Office, Waterford.

BOROUGH AND HIGHWAY SURVEYOR, WATER ENGINEER INSPECTOR OF NUISANCES, &c.—October 10th.—Pwllheli Corporation. £140.—Mr. Evan R. Davies, town clerk.

DISTRICT ROAD SURVEYOR. — October 11th. — Derbyshire County Council. £160.—Mr. N. J. Hughes-Hallet, county clerk, County Offices, Derby.

## COMPETITIONS.

*Advertisements which are received too late for classification cannot be included in these summaries until the following week.*

REDRATH.—October 6th.—Erection of municipal buildings, fire station, public offices, &c.—Mr. Clair J. Grece, town clerk.

ABERAVON.—December 1st.—Extension of the covered market, at a cost not to exceed £5,000. £21.—The Borough Surveyor.

CHERTSEY.—December 23rd.—Sewerage and sewage disposal scheme for the No. 1 and 2 wards of the district. £60, £30 and £20.—Mr. T. R. Harland Claddecott, clerk to the council.

# MUNICIPAL CONTRACTS OPEN.

*Advertisements which are received too late for classification cannot be included in these summaries until the following week.*

Hartlepool.—September 29th.—Erection of a destructor-house, engine and mill house, cottage, boundary walls and chimney at the proposed new sanitary depot in Clifton-street.—Mr. H. C. Crummack, A.M.I.C.E., borough engineer.

Wednesbury.—September 30th.—Erection of isolation hospital buildings, boundary walling, &c., on a site in Dangerfield-lane.—Mr. E. Martin Scott, borough engineer and surveyor.

Edinburgh.—September 30th.—Reconstruction of part of the tenement at the north-west corner of Bank-street.—The Burgh Engineer.

Ramsgate.—September 30th.—Supply of 250 12-ft. lengths of 12-in. gas pipes, and 10 tons of ordinary specials.—Mr. William A. Valon, engineer of the corporation gasworks.

Wood Green.—September 30th.—Making-up of King's-road and Western-road, for the urban district council.—Mr. C. J. Gunyon, surveyor to the council.

Auckingill (Scotland).—September 30th.—Construction of a pier or boat-landing stage.—Mr. James Brims, county clerk, Thurso, N. B.

Calstock.—September 30th.—Laying of about 2,803 yards of 3-in. cast-iron socket pipes, from Buddles adit to Harrowbarrow, and 1,487 yards from Figgie Dowdie adit to Todsworthy and Albaston, in the parish of Calstock, for the rural district council.—Mr. John P. Blight, clerk to the council, Callington.

East Riding.—September 30th.—Erection of registrar's offices and extension of the county offices at Beverley, for the county council.—Mr. J. J. Bickersteth, clerk to the county council, Beverley.

Hull.—September 30th.—Supply of forty-five electric motor cars, twenty trail cars, two sprinkler cars and two traversing platforms.—Mr. A. E. White, city engineer.

Leeds.—October 1st.—Construction and erection of a wrought-iron roof for the new coal store at the New Wortly gasworks.—Mr. R. H. Townsley, general manager, Municipal Buildings, Leeds.

Birmingham.—October 1st.—Reconstruction of the sewer in Needless-alley, New-street, also the construction of new pipe sewers in a portion of Wentworth-road, Harborne.—Mr. John Price, city engineer and surveyor.

Pembroke.—October 1st.—Construction of a pumping station and night storage tank and other works at Milton in connection with the water supply of Pembroke Dock.—Mr. W. O. Hulm, town clerk.

Leicester.—October 1st.—Alterations and additions to the Museum buildings in Hastings-street.—Mr. E. G. Mawbey, M.I.C.E., borough engineer.

Wolverhampton.—October 1st.—Making-up of Hilton-street.—Mr. J. W. Bradley, borough engineer and surveyor.

Leeds.—October 1st.—Extension of Kirkgate market.—Mr. Thomas Hewson, M.I.C.E., city engineer.

Burton-on-Trent.—October 3rd.—Making-up of Eldon-street and Nelson-street.—Mr. George T. Lynam, borough engineer and surveyor.

Hanwell.—October 3rd.—Supply of broken Guernsey or Channel Islands granite during the year ending the 31st March, 1899, for the urban district council.—Mr. Warren S. James, clerk to the council.

Ashton-under-Lyne.—October 3rd.—Installation of the necessary wires, fittings, &c., for the electric lighting of the public market.—Mr. John Neal, borough comptroller.

Wembley.—October 3rd.—Supply of broken granite, granite chippings, slag and fine gravel, for the urban district council.—Mr. John Smith, clerk to the council.

Fairfield (Derbyshire).—October 3rd.—Supply of 1,035 yards of 6-in. cast-iron socket and spigot pipes, for the urban district council.—Mr. Charles Slater, clerk to the council.

Northam.—October 3rd.—Construction of an impounding reservoir at Melburg Moor to hold 30,000,000 gallons of water, with the necessary outlet works, filters, pure water reservoir, diversion of a public road, fencing, the construction of a covered service reservoir at Northam, the supply and laying of cast-iron socket pipes, and the supply and fixing of hydrants, sluice valves, &c., in connection with the water supply of the town, for the urban district council.—Mr. Charles Wm. Hole, clerk to the council.

Watford.—October 4th.—Levelling, paving, kerbing, metalling, flagging, channelling, lighting, &c., works in Liverpool-road, Parker-street, Milton-street and Shakespeare-street, for the urban district council.—Mr. H. Morten Turner, clerk to the council.

London.—October 4th.—Various repairs at the Abbey Mills and Isle of Dogs pumping stations, for the county council.—The Engineer to the Council, County Hall, Spring-gardens, S.W.

Barnes.—October 4th.—Removal by barge of the refuse collected in the district from Small Profit Wharf, for the urban district conneil.—Mr. G. Bruce Tomes, A.M.I.C.E., surveyor to the council.

Aberdeen.—October 4th.—Construction of about 195 lineal yards of a brick circular sewer, 3 ft. diameter, in St. Swithin-street, and the supplying and laying of 9-in., 12-in. and 18-in. fireclay pipe sewers in Bedford-place, Bon-Accord-terrace, Wallfield-crescent, Albert-street and Walker-road.—Mr. William Dyack, burgh surveyor.

Croydon.—October 4th.—Repair of portions of Crowther, Holland and Dale Park roads.—Mr. E. Mawdesley, town clerk.

Croydon.—October 4th.—Supply of 10,000 ft. of 12-in. by 8-in. Norway granite kerb and 10,000 ft. of 12-in. by 6-in. Norway granite channel.—Mr. E. Mawdesley, town clerk.

Clacton.—October 4th.—Provision and laying of a 11-in. cast-iron main, about 9¼ miles in length, from Great Bentley to the present waterworks, for the urban district conneil.—Messrs. John Taylor, Sons & Santo Crimp, engineers, 27 Great George-street, London, S.W.

Dundee.—October 4th.—Supply of lead-covered cables and underground conduits for the extension of feeder mains, for the gas commissioners.—Sir Thos. Thornton, clerk to the commissioners.

Lewisham.—October 4th.—Kerbing and tar paving of the footpaths, and channelling and metalling of the roadway of Colfe-road, Forest Hill, for the district board of works.—The Surveyor to the Board.

Urmston.—October 4th.—The flagging and kerbing of various public footpaths, for the urban district council.—Mr. C. C. Hooley, surveyor to the council.

Keighley.—October 4th.—Paving, flagging, &c., of Moses, Aaron, Barn, Bee and Fly streets, and a yard off Park-lane.—Mr. W. H. Hopkinson, A.M.I.C.E., borough engineer.

London.—October 4th.—Erection of two blocks of dwellings, to be known as Benson and Abingdon dwellings respectively, on the Boundary-street area, Bethnal Green, and also the erection of cottage dwellings at Brook-street, Limehouse, for the county council.—Mr. C. J. Stewart, clerk to the council, County Hall, Spring-gardens, London, S.W.

Ipswich.—October 5th.—Supply of about 500 tons of best Welsh or other unscreened or hand-picked hard steam coal.—Mr. Hamlet Roberts, engineer and manager of the corporation waterworks.

Halifax.—October 5th.—Erection of a tramway car-shed at the junction of Free School-lane and Skircoat-road.—Mr. Edward R. S. Escott, borough engineer.

Littlehampton.—October 5th.—Various improvement works in Gloucester-road and Purbeck-place, for the urban district council.—Mr. H. Howard, surveyor to the council.

Rathmines (Ireland).—October 5th.—Supply of various electric light plant, for the township commissioners.—Mr. Robert Hammond, consulting engineer, 64 Victoria-street, London, S.W.

Ramsgate.—October 5th.—Erection of a refuse destructor.—Mr. T. G. Taylor, borough surveyor.

Blaydon-on-Tyne.—October 6th.—Supply of broken whinstone, limestone and slag as required up to March 31, 1899, for the urban district conneil.—Mr. W. H. Stephenson, surveyor to the council.

Halifax.—October 6th.—Private improvement works in Beecher-street, Brewery-street, Brier-street, Rothery's-court and Back Glen View-terrace.—Mr. Edward R. S. Escott, borough engineer.

Dartford.—October 6th.—Laying of a surface-water drain and the paving of the footways, crossing and channelling in Fulwich-road, for the urban district conneil.—Mr. W. Harston, A.M.I.C.E., surveyor to the council.

Plymouth—October 6th.—Supply of an enclosed (iron-clad) continuens-current motor.—Mr. John H. Rider, borough electrical engineer.

Manchester.—October 6th.—Erection of two blocks of conveniences in the Helmet-street recreation ground, also the construction of a new entrance gateway to Philips Park.—The City Surveyor.

Quarry Bank.—October 6th.—Supply of about 500 tons of Rowley granite as required during the ensuing twelve months, for the urban district conneil.—Mr. Alfred Homfray, clerk to the council, Cradley Heath, Staffs.

Islington.—October 7th.—Supply and fixing of pipes, valves, &c., in connection with the provision of a supply of water to the public gardens and recreation grounds in Market-road, Holloway.—Mr. J. Patten Barber, vestry surveyor.

Hull.—October 7th.—Supply and erection of a 7-ton overhead traveller (hand-power) for a span of 42 ft. 9 in.—Mr. A. E. White, city engineer.

Totnes.—October 7th.—Erection of post and rail fencing at Lower Longcombe, Berry Pomeroy, for the rural district conneil.—Mr. Thos. W. Windeatt, clerk to the council.

Hastings.—October 7th.—Laying of about 9,000 yards run of 16-in. water main and about 2,850 yards of 10-in. main in connection with the Brede Valley water scheme.—Mr. P. H. Palmer, M.I.C.E., water engiacer, Town Hall, Hastings.

Swinton and Pendlebury.—October 8th.—Repaving of Swinton Hall-road, Station-road and Partington-lane, for the urban district conneil.—Mr. Henry Entwistle, surveyor to the council.

Hull.—October 8th.—Sinking and construction of cast-iron shafts and subway at the Queen's dock basin, for the corporation.—Mr. F. J. Bancroft, water and gas engineer.

Swinton and Pendlebury.—October 8th.—Construction of a surface-water drain, for the urban district conneil.—Mr. Henry Entwistle, surveyor to the council.

Swinton and Pendlebury.—October 8th.—Supply of 175 tons of granite setts, for the urban district couneil.—Mr. Henry Entwistle, surveyor to the council.

Bishop Stortford.—October 8th.—Supply of from 1,200 to 1,500 tons of 1½-in. broken granite and from 100 to 150 tons of ½-in. granite chips, for the urban district council.—Mr. William Gee, clerk to the council.

Staines.—October 8th.—Supply of mackintoshes and waterproof everalls for the use of the out-door staff, for the rural district conncil.—Mr. G. W. Manning, surveyor to the council.

Preston.—October 8th.—Various sewerage and sewage disposal works for the township of Farington, for the rural district couneil.—Mr. James Clarke, clerk to the council.

Featherstone.—October 10th.—Laying of about 2½ miles of 5-in. cast-iron water main, for the urban district conncil.—Mr. W. A. Palliser, engineer and surveyor to the council.

Sittingbourne.—October loth.—Supply of about 400 yards of Guernsey or Alderney granite, for the urban district conneil.—Mr. W. J. Harris, clerk to the council.

Ossett.—October 10th.—Levelling, making-up and surface draining of a portion of the new road between Grays and Tilbury dock, and also the construction of a bridge culvert on the road, for the rural district council.—Mr. R. T. Stewart, surveyor to the council.

Ossett.—October loth.—Levelling, making-up, kerbing and surface-draining works in certain streets in the parish of Chadwell St. Mary, for the rural district council.—Mr. R. T. Stewart, surveyor to the council.

Southampton.—October 11th.—Supply and fixing of three high-pressure Lancashire boilers, economisers, calorifiers, radiators, steam and hot-water mains, and all necessary pumps, valves, &c., required for the extension of the heat and power generating plant at the county lunatic asylum at Knowle, Fareham.—Mr. W. J. Taylor, county surveyer, The Castle, Winchester.

Eccles.—October 12th.—Construction of a urinal in Barton-lane.—Mr. G. W. Bailey, town clerk.

Hertford.—October 12th.—Erection of a new bridge at Totteridge for the county council.—Mr. Urban A. Smith, county surveyor, 41 Parliament-street, London, S.W.

Cheltenham.—October 12th.—Erection of a new boiler-house at the waterworks at Tewkesbury.—Mr. E. T. Brydges, town clerk.

Cheltenham.—October 12th.—Supply of a new boiler at the waterworks at Tewkesbury.—Mr. E. T. Brydges, town clerk.

Croydon.—October 13th.—Supply of earthenware drain pipes, stores, &c., for the year from the 9th November.—Mr. E. Mawdesley, town clerk.

Leigh.—October 14th.—Supply and erection of various electric lighting plant, for the urban district conneil.—Mr. Peregrine Thomas, clerk to the council.

Leigh.—October 14th.—Alteration of a bench of inclined retorts, for the urban district conncil.—Mr. Peregrine Thomas, clerk to the council.

Romford.—October 14th.—Erection of public baths, for the urban district council.—Mr. George Bailey, clerk to the council.

Bangor.—October 16th.—Erection of buildings, chimney shaft, &c., for the electric light station.—Mr. John Gill, A.M.I.C.E., borough surveyor.

Southborough.—October 15th.—Erection and completion of the proposed Victoria Hall and buildings in London-road, for the urban district council.—Mr. William Harmer, surveyor to the council.

Tunbridge Wells.—October 15th.—Sewering and making-up of new roads on the site of the prop sed workmen's dwellings.—Mr. W. C. Cripps, town clerk.

Edinburgh.—October 17th.—Various works in connection with gasholder tank at Granton.—Mr. James M'G. Jack, clerk to the commissioners.

Birkenhead.—October 17th.—Erection of public baths on a site adjoining Livingstone-street and Price-street.—Mr. Charles Brownridge, A.M.I.C.E., borough engineer and surveyor.

Wilmslow.—October 21st.—Construction of certain sewers, for the urban district conneil.—Mr. William Cobbett, clerk to the council.

Hull.—October 27th.—Supply and erection of various electric lighting plant.—Mr. A. S. Barnard, city electrical engineer.

## TENDERS.

*ACCEPTED.

AMBLE.—For the execution of excavating, levelling and paving works in Albert-street Back-lane and Middleton-street Back-lane, for the urban district council.—Mr. W. Gibson, surveyor to the council:—

| | |
|---|---|
| J. Scott, Hope House, Alnwick | £313 |
| A. Douglas, Amble | 263 |
| G. Brown, Amble* | 225 |
| E. Cotisoe, Amble | 219 |
| Surveyor's provisional estimate (including 3 per cent. for plans, &c.), £232. | |

BRIDGWATER.—For the construction of about 587 lineal yards of sanitary pipe sewer in Washington-terrace and Washington-gardens.—The Borough Surveyor:—

| | |
|---|---|
| H. Meredith, Gloucester | £646 |
| T. Stockham, Bridgwater | 524 |
| Thomas & Webb, Bristol | 483 |
| C. Bryer, junr., Friarn-street, Bridgwater* | 427 |
| W. Hollard, Bridgwater | 400 |

HASTINGS.—Accepted for the supply of about 1,797 tons of 16-in., 169 tons of 10-in. and 84 tons of 6-in. cast-iron water pipes, and about 33 tons of irregulars.—Mr. R. H. Palmer, M.I.C.E., borough engineer :—

H. R. Merton & Co. (on behalf of Messrs. R. D. Wood & Co., of Philadelphia).—About 910 tons of 16-in., delivered at Rye station, £4 19s. per ton; about 15 tons of irregulars, delivered at Rye station, £9 6s. 3d. per ton; about 1,050 tons of 16-in. and 10-in., delivered at Hastings station, £4 17s. 9d. and £4 18s. 9d. per ton respectively; about 84 tons of 6-in., delivered at Hastings station, £5 0s. 9d. per ton; about 20 tons of irregulars, delivered at Hastings station, £9 6s. per ton.

HOLLINGBOURN.—For the supply of steam rollers for use on the district roads during a period of about fifty days, for the rural district council.—Mr. J. Stanley Roper, surveyor to the council:—

Jesse Ellis & Co. Limited, Maidstone ... ... 3s. 3d. per hour.

HORNSEY.—For the making-up of Barrington-road (3rd section), Hare-field-road and Hampden-road (2nd section), for the urban district council.—Mr. E. J. Lovegrove, engineer and surveyor to the council ;

| | Barrington-road (3rd section). | Harefield-road. | Hampden-road (2nd section). |
|---|---|---|---|
| Pedretto & Co., Finsbury Park | £1,078 | £928 | £1,803 |
| J. A. Dinmore, Crouch End | 981 | 929 | 1,637 |
| H. Clarke, Andover-road | 979 | 937 | 1,642 |
| Killingback & Co., Camden Town | 962 | 911 | 1,617 |
| W. Griffiths, Bishopsgate-street Without... | 948 | 804 | 1,610 |
| Williamson & Sons, Green-lanes | 930 | 889 | 1,609 |
| G. Bell, Tottenham | 917 | 803 | 1,547 |
| T. Adams, Wood Green* | 905 | 706 | 1,534 |

HUNSLET.—For the laying and jointing of about 6,150 yards of 3-in. cast-iron pipes, also fixing and walling-in of about twenty valves and hydrants, for the Templenewsam and Thorpe Stapleton water supply, for the rural district council.—Mr. W. B. Pinder, clerk to the council :

| | |
|---|---|
| J. Bentley, Leeds | £674 |
| J. Keighley, Hunslet | 567 |
| C. Rhodes & Sons, Huddersfield | 501 |
| T. Rowland, Northwich | 455 |
| T. Young & Co., Cullingworth | 450 |
| Batchelor & Snowden, Cardiff | 420 |
| H. Wilson, Bradford | 381 |
| W. Barrick, Garstang | 369 |
| W. Jowett, Hemsworth | 360 |
| J. Gott, Preston | 321 |
| A. Henson, Leeds | 313 |
| W. Gould, Preston* | 311 |

NORTH RIDING.—For the rebuilding, &c., of Tanton bridge, near Stokesley.—Mr. Walter Stead, M.I.C.E., county surveyor, Northallerton :—

| | |
|---|---|
| P. O. Hetherington, Garnford, Darlington | £1,045 |
| R. P. Brotton, Rilsdale, Middlesbrough | 688 |
| W. Blackburn, Broughton, Malton | 666 |
| A. Atkinson & Co., Grove-terrace, Stockton* | 655 |

RUSHDEN.—For painting, &c., work at the waterworks pumping station at Wymington and at the isolation hospital, for the urban district council.—Mr. W. S. Madin, town surveyor :—

| | Waterworks Pumping Station and Residence. | | | Isolation Hospital. | | |
|---|---|---|---|---|---|---|
| | £ | s. | d. | £ | s. | d. |
| W. Spencer, Rushden | 23 | 0 | 0 | 24 | 0 | 0 |
| G. L. Shelton, Higham Ferrers... | 23 | 0 | 0 | 13 | 0 | 0 |
| A. T. Nichols, Rushden | 13 | 10 | 0 | 13 | 0 | 0 |
| Wheeler & Son, Church-lane, Rushden* | 7 | 10 | 0 | 13 | 0 | 0 |

SHOREDITCH.—For the construction of an underground convenience in Hoxton-street.—Mr. J. Rush Dixon, A.M.I.C.E., engineer and surveyor to the vestry :—

| | |
|---|---|
| J. Dolman & Co., Poplar | £2,565 |
| Doulton & Co., Lambeth | 2,150 |
| G. Jennings, Lambeth* | 2,035 |

STEVENAGE.—For the supply of 500 tons of 1½-in. broken Guernsey, Leicester or other granite, for the urban district council.—Mr. William Onslow Times, clerk to the council :—

| | Per ton. |
|---|---|
| W. Griffiths, Hamilton House, E.C. | 16s. 7d. |
| Ellis & Everard, Hitchen* | 11s. 9d. |
| Mountsorrell Granite Company, Mountsorrell | 11s. 9d. |
| Whitwick Granite Company, Whitwick | 11s. 3d. and 9s. 9d. |
| Van Praagh & Co., East India-avenue, E.C. | 11s. 0d. |
| W. Pearson, Stevenage | 11s. 0d. |
| A. & F. Manuelli, Gracechurch-street, E.C. | 10s. 9d. |
| Forest Rock Granite Company, Whitwick | 10s. 9d. |
| Enderby Stony Stanton Company, Narborough | 10s. 7d. |
| W. B. Murray & Co., King William-street, E.C. | 10s. 6d. |
| Narborough and Enderby Granite Company | 10s. 3d. |

## MEETINGS.

### SEPTEMBER.

30.—The Sanitary Institute: Annual Autumn Congress at Birmingham.

### OCTOBER.

1.—The Sanitary Institute: Annual Autumn Congress at Birmingham.
3.—Society of Engineers: Ordinary meeting; Mr. Shepard Cowper-Coles, A.M.I.C.E., &c., on "Protective Metallic Coatings for Iron and Steel. 7.30 p.m.
17.—Sanitary Institute: Sir Douglas Galton's introductory lecture to the 26th course of lectures and demonstrations for sanitary officers.
19.—Sanitary Institute: Visit of sanitary officers to the disinfecting apparatus and model steam laundry at St. John's Wharf, Fulham. 3.30 p.m.
19.—Sanitary Institute: Lecture for sanitary officers; Dr. Louis Parkes, M.D., D.P.H., medical officer of health, Chelsea, on "Sanitary Laws and Regulations governing the Metropolis." 8 p.m.
21.—Sanitary Institute: Lecture for sanitary officers; Mr. H. Manley, medical officer of health, West Bromwich, on "Sanitary Law—English, Scotch and Irish; General Enactments Public Health Act, 1875; Model By-Laws, &c." 8 p.m.
22.—Sanitary Institute: Visit of sanitary officers to the Wimbledon sewage works, under the guidance of Mr. C. H. Cooper, A.M.I.C.E., engineer and surveyor to the Wimbledon Urban District Council. 3 p.m.
24.—Sanitary Institute: Lectures for sanitary officers; Mr. W. A. Bond, medical officer of health, Holborn and St. Olave, Southwark, on "The Law Relating to the Supervision of Food Supply," 8 p.m.
26.—Sanitary Institute: Visit of sanitary officers to the parish of St. George, Hanover-square, under the guidance of Mr. A. Taylor, chief sanitary inspector. 2 p.m.
26.—Sanitary Institute: Lecture to sanitary officers; Prof. A. Bostock Hill, medical officer of health, Sutton Coldfield, on "Trade Nuisances." 8 p.m.
28.—Sanitary Institute: Lecture to sanitary officers; Dr. J. F. J. Sykes, medical officer of health, St. Pancras, on "Objects and Methods of Inspection, Nuisances, &c." 8 p.m.

## NOTICES.

THE SURVEYOR AND MUNICIPAL AND COUNTY ENGINEER may be ordered direct, through any of Messrs. Smith & Son's book-stalls, or of any newsagent in the United Kingdom. Applications to the Offices for single copies by post must in all cases be accompanied by stamps.

The Prepaid Subscription (including postage) is as follows :—

|  | Twelve Months. | Six Months. | Three Months. |
|---|---|---|---|
| United Kingdom | 13s. | 7s. 6d. | 4s. 9d. |
| Continent, the Colonies, India, United States, &c. | 19s. | 9s. 6d. | 4s. 9d. |

The International News Company, 83 and 85 Duane-street New York City; The Toronto News Company, Toronto; and The Montreal News Company, Montreal, have been appointed agents in the United States and Canada for the sale of THE SURVEYOR AND MUNICIPAL AND COUNTY ENGINEER. A thin paper edition is printed for circulation abroad.

EDITORIAL OFFICES :—
24 BRIDE-LANE, FLEET-STREET, LONDON, E.C.

ADVERTISEMENT AND PUBLISHING OFFICES :—
13 NEW STREET-HILL, FLEET-STREET, LONDON, E.C.

## APPOINTMENTS OPEN.

### HORNSEY URBAN DISTRICT COUNCIL.
#### APPOINTMENT OF INSPECTOR OF NEW BUILDINGS AND DRAINAGE WORK.

The Urban District Council of Hornsey require the services of an Inspector of New Buildings and Drainage Work, at a salary of £160 per annum, which will be paid monthly.

Candidates must be between twenty-five and forty years of age and have had some previous similar experience.

Preference will be given to candidates holding certificates of competency from some recognised examining body, such as the Sanitary Institute.

Written applications only, with particulars of past and present employment, and copies of two recent testimonials as to character and competency, with copy of certificates (if any), marked outside "Building and Drainage Inspector," must be received not later than 4 p.m. on Saturday, the 8th day of October, 1898, and be addressed to Mr. E. J. Lovegrove, Engineer and Surveyor, Council's offices, Southwood-lane, Highgate, from whom particulars of the duties to be performed can be obtained.

Original testimonials will not be returned.

Canvassing members of the Council will disqualify.

(By order)
F. D. ASKEY,
Clerk to the Council.

District Council Offices,
99 Southwood-lane, Highgate, N.
September 28, 1898.

CLERK OF WORKS.
The Corporation require the services of a Clerk of Works, to superintend construction of Sewage Precipitation Tanks. Salary not to exceed £3 per week.
Applications, in candidate's own handwriting, stating age, qualifications, experience and salary required, together with not more than four recent testimonials, and endorsed "Clerk of Works," should be sent to Mr. T. Rushbrooke, Borough Surveyor, High Wycombe, by noon on 6th October.
Canvassing will be considered a disqualification.

High Wycombe.
October 6th.

## TENDERS WANTED.

FEATHERSTONE URBAN DISTRICT COUNCIL.
WATERWORKS COMMITTEE.
Tenders are invited for the labour, laying and jointing, about 2¼ miles 5-in. Cast-Iron Water Main.
Specification and particulars may be obtained at the office of the undersigned.
Tenders, endorsed "Water Main," to be delivered at the Council offices not later than noon, 10th October next.
W. A. PALLISER,
Engineer and Surveyor.

Council Offices, Featherstone.
September 26, 1898.

VESTRY OF ST. MARY, ISLINGTON.
TO PLUMBERS AND WATERWORKS FITTERS.
The Vestry is prepared to receive tenders for Supplying and Fixing Pipes, Valves, &c., in connection with the provision of a supply of water to the Public Gardens and Recreation Ground in Market-road, Holloway.
Copies of the specification, bills of quantities and forms of tender can be obtained on application to the Chief Surveyor, Mr. J. Patten Barber, M.INST.C.E., at the Vestry Hall, Upper-street, Islington, N., upon the payment of 1 guinea, which will be returned upon the receipt of a bonâ-fide tender and the return of the whole of the documents issued.
Sealed tenders, endorsed "Tender for Water Supply," must be delivered to the undersigned not later than 4 p.m. on Friday, 7th October, 1898.
The Vestry does not bind itself to accept the lowest or any tender.
WM. F. DEWEY,
Vestry Clerk.

Vestry Hall, Upper-street, Islington, N.
September 27, 1898.

BOROUGH OF TUNBRIDGE WELLS.
NEW ROADS.
The Corporation are prepared to receive tenders for Sewering and Making-up New Roads on site of proposed workmen's dwellings, Tunbridge Wells.
Plans and specification can be seen at the Borough Surveyor's office, and quantities and form of tender obtained from me on payment of 2 guineas, which will be returned on receipt of a bonâ-fide tender.
Tenders to be sent to me on or before the 15th October, 1898.
The Corporation do not bind themselves to accept the lowest or any tender.
(By order)
W. C. CRIPPS,
Town Clerk.

Town Hall, Tunbridge Wells.

## CLERK OF WORKS.

The Corporation require the services of a Clerk of Works, to superintend construction of Sewage Precipitation Tanks. Salary not to exceed £3 per week.

Applications, in candidate's own handwriting, stating age, qualifications, experience and salary required, together with not more than four recent testimonials, and endorsed "Clerk of Works," should be sent to Mr. T. Rushbrooke, Borough Surveyor, High Wycombe, by noon on 6th October.

Canvassing will be considered a disqualification.

High Wycombe.
       October 6th.

## TENDERS WANTED.

### FEATHERSTONE URBAN DISTRICT COUNCIL.
#### WATERWORKS COMMITTEE.

Tenders are invited for the labour, laying and jointing, about 2½ miles 5-in. Cast-Iron Water Main.

Specification and particulars may be obtained at the office of the undersigned.

Tenders, endorsed "Water Main," to be delivered at the Council offices not later than noon, 10th October next.

W. A. PALLISER,
       Engineer and Surveyor.

Council Offices, Featherstone.
    September 26, 1898.

### VESTRY OF ST. MARY, ISLINGTON.
TO PLUMBERS AND WATERWORKS FITTERS.

The Vestry is prepared to receive tenders for Supplying and Fixing Pipes, Valves, &c., in connection with the provision of a supply of water to the Public Gardens and Recreation Ground in Market-road, Holloway.

Copies of the specification, bills of quantities and forms of tender can be obtained on application to the Chief Surveyor, Mr. J. Patten Barber, M.INST.C.E., at the Vestry Hall, Upper-street, Islington, N., upon the payment of 1 guinea, which will be returned upon the receipt of a bond-fide tender and the return of the whole of the documents issued.

Sealed tenders, endorsed "Tender for Water Supply," must be delivered to the undersigned not later than 4 p.m. on Friday, 7th October, 1898.

The Vestry does not bind itself to accept the lowest or any tender.

WM. F. DEWEY,
       Vestry Clerk.

Vestry Hall, Upper-street, Islington, N.
    September 27, 1898.

### BOROUGH OF TUNBRIDGE WELLS.
#### NEW ROADS.

The Corporation are prepared to receive tenders for Sewering and Making-up New Roads on site of proposed workmen's dwellings, Tunbridge Wells.

Plans and specification can be seen at the Borough Surveyor's office, and quantities and form of tender obtained from me on payment of 2 guineas, which will be returned on receipt of a bond-fide tender.

Tenders to be sent to me on or before the 15th October, 1898.

The Corporation do not bind themselves to accept the lowest or any tender.

(By order)
       W. C. CRIPPS,
       Town Clerk.

Town Hall, Tunbridge Wells.

## STAINES RURAL DISTRICT COUNCIL.

Tenders are invited for the supply of Mackintoshes and Waterproof Overalls for the use of the outdoor staff.

Tenders to reach the Surveyor, Mr. G. W. Manning, from whom all particulars may be obtained, not later than October 8th next.

(Signed) G. W. MANNING.

Surveyor's Office, Ashford, Staines.

## ORSETT RURAL DISTRICT COUNCIL.

*PRIVATE STREET WORKS.*

### CHADWELL ST. MARY PARISH (TILBURY).

Tenders are invited for the Levelling, Making-up, Kerbing and Surface Draining the following streets or parts of streets in the parish of Chadwell St. Mary—viz., Montreal-road, for a distance of 1,880 ft. from its junction with Dock-road; Quebec-road, Toronto-road, for a distance of 1,501 ft. from its junction with Dock-road; Calcutta-road, for a distance of 692 ft. from its junction with Montreal-road; Sydney-road, for a distance of 785 ft. from Toronto-road; and Dock-road, from the boundary of the London, Tilbury and Southend Railway Company's property to the boundary between the parishes of Chadwell St. Mary and Little Thurrock.

Plans and specifications can be seen, and bills of quantities obtained, at the office of the Council's Surveyor, Mr. R. T. Stewart, Orsett, Essex, by making an appointment with him.

Sealed tenders, to be endorsed "Tilbury Streets," to be delivered to the undersigned not later than Monday, October 10, 1898.

The Council do not bind themselves to accept the lowest or any tender.

(By order) JAMES BECK,
Clerk to the Orsett Rural District Council.

South Ockenden.

## ORSETT RURAL DISTRICT COUNCIL.

*PRIVATE STREET WORKS.*

### LITTLE THURROCK.

Tenders are invited for the Levelling, Making-up and Surface Draining of a portion of the new road between Grays and Tilbury Dock, being about 550 yards in length from the commencement of the highway formerly known as Curtis-road, to the boundary of Little Thurrock parish near the Shepherds' Arms; also the Construction of a Bridge Culvert on the said road.

A plan and specification can be seen, and bills of quantities obtained, at the office of the Surveyor of the Council, Mr. R. T. Stewart, Orsett, Essex, by making an appointment with him.

Sealed tenders, to be endorsed "Little Thurrock Road," to be delivered to the undersigned not later than Monday, October 10, 1898.

The Council do not bind themselves to accept the lowest or any tender.

(By order) JAMES BECK,
Clerk to the Orsett Rural District Council.

South Ockenden.

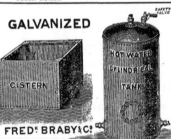

STAINES RURAL DISTRICT COUNCIL.
Tenders are invited for the supply of Mackintoshes and Waterproof Overalls for the use of the outdoor staff.
Tenders to reach the Surveyor, Mr. G. W. Manning, from whom all particulars may be obtained, not later than October 8th next.

(Signed)    G. W. MANNING.
Surveyor's Office, Ashford, Staines.

ORSETT RURAL DISTRICT COUNCIL.

*PRIVATE STREET WORKS.*

CHADWELL ST. MARY PARISH (TILBURY).
Tenders are invited for the Levelling, Making-up, Kerbing and Surface Draining the following streets or parts of streets in the parish of Chadwell St. Mary—viz., Montreal-road, for a distance of 1,880 ft. from its junction with Dock-road; Quebec-road, Toronto-road, for a distance of 1,501 ft. from its junction with Dock-road; Calcutta-road, for a distance of 692 ft. from its junction with Montreal-road; Sydney-road, for a distance of 785 ft. from Toronto-road; and Dock-road, from the boundary of the London, Tilbury and Southend Railway Company's property to the boundary between the parishes of Chadwell St. Mary and Little Thurrock.
Plans and specifications can be seen, and bills of quantities obtained, at the office of the Council's Surveyor, Mr. R. T. Stewart, Orsett, Essex, by making an appointment with him.
Sealed tenders, to be endorsed "Tilbury Streets," to be delivered to the undersigned not later than Monday, October 10, 1898.

The Council do not bind themselves to accept the lowest or any tender.

(By order)
JAMES BECK,
Clerk to the Orsett Rural District Council.
South Ockenden.

ORSETT RURAL DISTRICT COUNCIL.

*PRIVATE STREET WORKS.*

LITTLE THURROCK.
Tenders are invited for the Levelling, Making-up and Surface Draining of a portion of the new road between Grays and Tilbury Dock, being about 550 yards in length from the commencement of the highway formerly known as Curtis-road, to the boundary of Little Thurrock parish near the Shepherds' Arms; also the Construction of a Bridge Culvert on the said road.
A plan and specification can be seen, and bills of quantities obtained, at the office of the Surveyor of the Council, Mr. R. T. Stewart, Orsett, Essex, by making an appointment with him.
Sealed tenders, to be endorsed "Little Thurrock Road," to be delivered to the undersigned not later than Monday, October 10, 1898.
The Council do not bind themselves to accept the lowest or any tender.

(By order)
JAMES BECK,
Clerk to the Orsett Rural District Council.
South Ockenden.

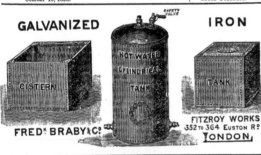

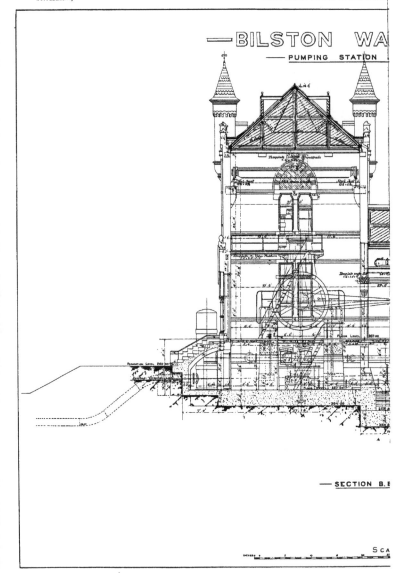

BILSTON WA
PUMPING STATION

SECTION B.

SCA

ASSOCIATION OF MUNICIPAL
MIDLAND COUNTIES DISTRI

# TER WORKS—
## T THE BRATCH—

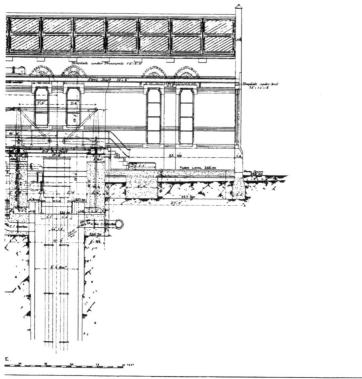

E.

# The Surveyor

## And Municipal and County Engineer.

Vol. XIV., No. 351.    LONDON, OCTOBER 7, 1898.    Weekly, Price 3d.

## Minutes of Proceedings.

**Municipal Engineers at Birmingham.** The conference of municipal and county engineers in connection with the congress of the Sanitary Institute at Birmingham, like most of the conferences of municipal engineers, was in every way a complete success. Much of this was, no doubt, due to the excellent arrangements which had been made by the local secretaries, who earned a well-deserved meed of praise for their successful exertions to provide subjects for discussion, and also objects of especial interest to municipal engineers to be viewed. In the latter respect the city surveyor of Birmingham, Mr. Price, with characteristic geniality assisted most materially to arrange at short notice for the inspection of numerous municipal works in progress in Birmingham, so that there was not an idle half-hour spent the whole day. The attendance of municipal engineers was large, and, it appears to us, increases at each successive conference. It is not, we believe, generally understood that the conference is unconnected and quite independent of the Incorporated Association of Municipal Engineers, but such is the case. In view, however, of the undoubted success of these foregatherings, it might, we venture to think, be a matter for the consideration of the council whether the conference should not be officially recognised and arranged by them, to the advantage of the Association. There are, we observe, a considerable number of engineers who attend these conferences who are not members of the Association, and who would be brought into touch with the body, to the benefit of themselves and the Incorporated Association of Municipal and County Engineers. It would further result, we believe, in eliciting papers on a wider variety of subjects interesting to municipal engineers than appears to be now practicable, and it would also appeal to the attention of municipal representatives and others who would at such times attend its meetings and who in many cases would not under ordinary circumstances have the opportunity of doing so. Another point, and one which it will be seen from our report was strongly emphasised at Birmingham. The council of the Sanitary Institute held that it is not practicable to print congress papers beforehand and to place them, if applied for, in the hands of intending speakers at the debates. A congress is an unwieldly function, but, so far as concerns the special section of it with which we are particularly interested, experience has shown that the course suggested is practicable; and, moreover, the local secretaries, given a free hand, could secure its enforcement. The council of the Institute have not seen fit to act upon the resolution passed at the Newcastle congress; it may be hoped they will earnestly consider the similar resolution adopted at Birmingham, as assuredly it is calculated, if put in practice, to increase vastly both the interest in the papers to be read and the value of the discussions upon them. One may, perhaps, be permitted to instance, as a timely illustration, the case of Mr. Moss Flower's paper. It was not even printed before being read, with the result that it was listened to with less interest than it deserved, and comment upon it was conspicuous by its complete absence. And while in the vein of suggestion, it may perhaps be permitted to submit to the council of the Institute that they should in future years mete out more consideration to the Press. The daily struggle for sets of papers, too incomplete to be of use when obtained, is an unnecessary waste of time; the "reporters' room" at the Mason University College was of such a character that not a journalist used it; at the Health Exhibition there was no Press accommodation of any sort; nor was it possible for reporters to work at the conferences or sectional meetings with any degree of convenience. These are but few instances of minor matters which might be remedied with advantage at the next congress, at Southampton.

It will be observed that, in continuing our report of the work of the congress, we give special attention to the proceedings of the conference of municipal and county engineers, as that in which our readers are specially interested, though not a few papers bearing more or less directly on municipal engineering problems were read in other sections. The municipal engineers were presided over by Mr. T. de Courcy Meade, the city surveyor of Manchester, whose able address was evidently kept within rather brief limits owing to a consciousness of the amount of work to be subsequently done. It was generally regretted that the plans which were to have accompanied the address were not forthcoming, but it should be understood the fault was neither with the president nor the local secretaries. After a brief reference to the multifarious duties of the municipal engineer and the necessity thus imposed upon him of an unceasing search after knowledge, the president devoted the remainder of his address to a general but interesting commentary on one or two matters to which he is at present giving special consideration. Practically he confined himself to two topics—the housing of the working classes and the treatment of sewage. With great clearness, brevity and precision he indicated the methods by which the Manchester Corporation have met the difficulties of providing sufficient suitable accommodation at reasonable cost for persons of the working class displaced from insanitary areas, or from areas cleared for street improvements and railway works. The Manchester Corporation are to be equally congratulated on the steady progress which is being made in the substitution of water-closets for pail-closets and privies. The completion of such a work must, as Mr. Meade remarked, be a question of time. In his observations on sewage treatment the president gave some interesting figures as to the cost of treatment and the amount of work done at the Manchester outfall works, and these details are certainly of interest and value for the purposes of comparison. The solution of the sewage disposal problem is now generally looked for in connection with artificial filtration. Towards the close of his address Mr. Meade referred to the experiments which have been continued at Manchester since 1895 with coke and cinder filters, and gave details of their respective capacities, together with the capacity of a coal filter. Those who are following the experiments in various parts of the country in connection with bacterial treatment will, no doubt, duly note the conclusions and results so pithily expressed by the president in regard to the working of the filters.

Three papers were read and discussed at the conference. Mr. Pickering, engineer and surveyor to the Nuneaton Urban District Council, took for his subject by-laws relating to new streets and buildings; Mr. Moss Flower, engineer and surveyor to the Portishead Urban District Council, dealt with the precautions to be observed in the ventilation of sewers and drains; and, finally, Mr. E. Shrapnell Smith, honorary secretary of the Liverpool Self-propelled Traffic Association, pointed out some of the sanitary and allied advantages attending the introduction of motor vehicles. A paper from Mr. Pickering may safely be anticipated as a thoughtful contribution, and the present occasion was no exception. He was undeniably successful in pointing out some weak joints in the sanitary armour of which we are so proud. He insisted strongly on the initial error involved in the Model By-Laws of the Local Government Board—the error of assuming that there could be drawn up one set of by-laws which would apply to all districts alike, rural and urban. This is probably the only objection that Mr. Pickering sees to making the adoption of by-laws compulsory and not permissive on the part of local authorities. He is strongly in favour of sanitary authorities being obliged to adopt by-laws, but holds with equal firmness that the adoption of a rigidly uniform code throughout the country would be impracticable, if not actually impossible. Certainly it would be difficult to dispute that, as local needs and conditions vary in different districts, the by-laws adopted should be modified in accordance with the needs and conditions of each district. Mr. Pickering's position, then, is that the adoption of by-laws should be compulsory, but that at the same time greater latitude should be given to sanitary authorities to frame by-laws adapted to the circumstances of their own particular districts. Probably the great majority of municipal engineers support the view enunciated by Mr. Pickering. Of course the granting of such discretionary power to sanitary authorities would be on the understanding that it was to be exercised within reasonable limits. Mr. Pickering chose a very effective illustration to enforce his argument when he referred to the risk of checking building operations in, and the growth of, a small district if the by-laws are found oppressive. Among other important points referred to in a suggestive and helpful paper was the necessity of proper facilities being given for the enforcement of by-laws. There is very little to choose between no by-laws at all and by-laws which cannot be enforced. Mr. Moss Flower, who read the next paper, had, like Mr. Pickering, the credit of introducing, in an able and closely-reasoned paper, a problem which provides municipal engineers with many anxious moments. He has long given close attention to the question, and the result was seen in his contribution to the proceedings of the congress. Though the last word has by no means been said, the subject of sewer and drain ventilation, as Mr. Moss Flower admitted, has been exhaustively discussed ; but there was room for his paper at such a gathering as that at Birmingham, and also for the discussion upon it which did not take place. Apparently it was considered necessary that the discussion of this paper should be taken together with that on the not

very cognate subject treated by Mr. Shrapnell Smith, and, judging from the results, the topic of motor vehicles seemed to be the more fascinating of the two. Mr. Moss Flower's paper certainly deserved discussion, if only for the reason that it was essentially practical, the object being not to advocate any cut-and-dried method but to suggest certain desirable precautions. Municipal engineers, however, may think that they have discussed the subject sufficiently for the present. So far as London is concerned, the question remains where it was left at the conference last year between Sir Alexander Binnie and the metropolitan officials. It is not necessary in the course of these remarks to examine Mr. Moss Flower's suggestions in detail, but the majority of them will no doubt commend themselves to municipal engineers. Turning to the last of the three papers, it is obvious, from our report of the discussion elicited, that the subject excited no small interest. It cannot be said, however, that the speakers were quite so enthusiastic as Mr. Shrapnell Smith There was some diversity of opinion, as will be seen from a comparison of the remarks of Mr. Mawbey with those of Mr. Hooley, who thought the paper was "too previous" by about ten years. Mr. Hooley, as becomes a county surveyor, spoke with reference to the adaptability of motors to the highways; Mr. Mawbey and others with reference to the possibility of effecting a saving by the employment of motors in municipal work. The purely sanitary aspect of the question, so much emphasised by the reader of the paper, was largely ignored in the discussion in favour of the other aspects referred to. Taking the proceedings of the conference as a whole, it can safely be said that they reached a high standard of excellence and interest.

\* \* \*

**The Dover Municipal Tramways.** The results of the first year's working of the Dover electrical tramways are as successful as the most ardent advocate of municipalisation could desire. The report recently presented by the surveyor demonstrates beyond all doubt, as far as Dover is concerned, the success of municipal electrical tramways and the economy of electrical working. The total receipts for the year have been £7,487 15s. 3d.; the receipts averaging per car mile 12·39d. The operating expenses per car mile, including all wages for staff, electrical energy, &c., was 6·41d. To sum up the result, the Dover Corporation, after payment of interest and instalment on loans, and all expenses of repairs, &c., are £1,300 to the good, which is sufficient evidence of the popularity of the venture. The cost of operating the line, 6·41d., is of interest not only to municipal officials, but is of importance so far as electrical engineers are concerned, because it was generally urged, when presenting the claims of electrical traction, that the cost per car mile w. uld not exceed 6d. As a matter of fact, under most arrangements it would have been considerably lower at Dover than really obtained last year, for the undertaking is handicapped by the corporation having to purchase electricity to operate the tramway system. We are not saying that they are not justified in adopting this course with so short a length of line—viz., 3 miles ; we merely contend that if electricity had been generated by the corporation themselves, or if they had obtained their supply of electrical energy from a municipal lighting station, it is extremely likely that the cost would not have exceeded 4½d. per car mile. As it is, on account of a maximum and minimum arrangement with regard to the consumption of energy, the cost per car mile would have been 5·9d., had it not been that the corporation had to pay £302 for current they did not use. The result of operating this short length of line ought to encourage municipal authorities who are contemplating the adoption of electrically operated tramways.

**Theory of Local Government.** We have again pleasure in drawing the attention of our younger readers, and especially those of them who reside in London or within easy reach of it, to the opening of another session of the London School of Economics. We have on a previous occasion referred to the admirable work this institution is doing, though it is entirely the result of private enterprise. A syllabus embodying the arrangements for 1898-99 has recently been issued, and should be obtained and consulted by all who are interested in a good work which, perhaps, does not get all the appreciation it deserves. There is a special course for municipal officials, which includes general instruction in economics and political science, attention being subsequently given to statistics, public finance, constitutional law and the government of London. Mr. F. W. Hirst, B.A., will conduct a class for the study of the structure and working of modern local government, Mr. J. Kemp, M.A., one for the study of the government of London, and the subject of local government will also form part of the course of instruction to be given in the class to be conducted by Mr. G. Lowes Dickinson, M.A., for the study of the structure of the modern State. In addition to the classes, supplementary courses of lectures are given, and among them we observe courses on the problems of local government, foreign municipal government, the principles of local taxation, the theory of local taxation, and the incidence of taxation. Among the lecturers are Mr. Hobhouse, M.P., Mr. R. Cunningham Glen, Mr. G. Laurence Gomme (statistical officer to the London County Council), Prof. Edgeworth, and others. We may mention that the sesssion opens this evening, when the principal, Prof. Hewins, will give the inaugural lecture at the school, 10 Adelphi-terrace, W.C., where all information can be obtained. We may say, in conclusion, that a glance at the syllabus is enough to show that the courses are arranged with marked ability and knowledge.

\* \* \*

**Another Colonial Appointment.** We have recently had the pleasure of announcing the appointment of two English municipal engineers to important and lucrative posts in South Africa. We refer, of course, to the appointment of Mr. Wynne Roberts, borough engineer and surveyor of Oswestry, to be city engineer of Cape Town, and the appointment, a few weeks later, of Mr. G. B. Laffan, engineer and surveyor to the Twickenham Urban District Council, to be municipal engineer of Pietermaritzburg in the neighbouring colony of Natal. To these a third appointment has now to be added, for we have pleasure in announcing that Mr. R. S. Rounthwaite, borough engineer of Sunderland, has been appointed city engineer of Wellington, the capital of New Zealand, and is expected to leave Sunderland for his new sphere of labour in December. The salary is the same as in the case of Cape Town and Pietermaritzburg—£800 a year. In Mr. Laffan the Incorporated Association of Municipal and County Engineers lose an energetic district secretary, and in Mr. Rounthwaite an enthusiastic supporter. The district meeting held at Sunderland last year enabled some idea to be gleaned of the ability and application Mr. Rounthwaite has brought to bear upon his work, and of the manner in which he is appreciated in the town he has served so long and so faithfully. His work in Sunderland is a good augury for a successful career in New Zealand, and the best wishes of his many friends will accompany him.

\* \* \*

**An Application as She is Wrote.** As our readers are well aware, singular notions prevail in many quarters as to the qualifications requisite for municipal engineers. The following is a copy of an application received in connection with a recent vacancy in the office of surveyor, &c.:—

DEAR SIR,

Replying to the advisement in . . . . . . . respecting the vacancy Sanitary Inspector.

I beg to offer myself as one of the applicants for the vacant appointment as Sanitary Inpector of this Borough age 29 years.

I am grandson to late Mr. —— this town who was well known to the gentlemen of the Counsell.

In the of you knowing me personlly I should feel greatly indebted you if you would kindly intercede your influeuce on my behalft.

I am native of the town there are severall named gentlemen who speak of my respectiabliaty is Ald —— whom I am personlly from a boy.

My occupation is Railway Cooch Trimmer I am sorry I cant send you my referances respecting my abliuty and experance.

I have written my employers and there are rules is not to grant any workmen there referances to carry about with them untill written for.

My present employer who has to engaged or appoint to refer to last employers bring letter.

For reference I have enclosed the Pass and Present employers.

Your Influence much esteemed.

Yours obediently.

\* \* \*

**Qualified Candidates!** A reference to a recent meeting of the Saltburn Urban District Council has just come under our notice, but we sincerely hope the statements are just a little bit exaggerated. The meeting was a special one, held to consider applications for the position of surveyor to the council, and we are told that the applicants were ninety-nine in number and "comprised representatives of nearly every trade, including tinkers, tailors, butchers, plumbers, farmers, lawyers, tobacconists, joiners, commercial travellers, engine drivers, secretaries, foremen, overseers, schoolmasters, and a grocer and a draper." The list is a formidable one, and, though we have expressed a hope that it may be somewhat exaggerated, there is no doubt that in connection with appointments by district councils applications are often received from singular quarters. The mental condition of some of those applicants, and their conception of a district council surveyor's duties, responsibilities and qualifications are easy neither to imagine nor describe. In the preceding paragraph we reproduce an actual bonâ-fide application which was received in connection with a vacancy, not in an urban or rural district, but in a borough. Considering the source from which we have received it, we can vouch for the fact that it is genuine.

\* \* \*

**Loughborough Water Supply.** At a meeting of the Loughborough Town Council, on Monday, an important decision was arrived at with regard to the water supply of the borough. It was decided unanimously to proceed at once with the construction of the proposed storage reservoir at Blackbrook, Parliamentary powers having been obtained last year to complete the Blackbrook scheme by impounding the whole of the water flowing off the watershed. The time fixed for the completion of the work was eight years from the passing of the Act. It has been pointed out by the Water Committee that the works must necessarily take several years to complete, even if proceeded with continuously; but, owing to the necessity of depending upon the Blackbrook stream, it may be necessary to suspend the works during the summer months each year, so that a much longer time might be occupied than would otherwise be the case. In moving, at the council meeting on Monday, that the Water Committee be empowered to begin the work at once, Councillor Cartwright, chairman of the committee, explained clearly the necessity for the scheme and also dealt with its financial bearings. In our next issue we shall give an abstract of the elaborate and highly-interesting report which has been prepared by the engineers, Messrs. G. & F. W. Hodson.

# The Sanitary Institute.

## THE SEVENTEENTH ANNUAL CONGRESS.—II.

In our last issue we gave a report of the opening proceedings of the congress last week, together with a brief outline of the sectional proceedings and conferences. We now proceed to deal in greater detail with the papers read and discussed, beginning with the

### CONFERENCE OF MUNICIPAL AND COUNTY ENGINEERS.

There were five special conferences—municipal representatives, medical officers of health, municipal engineers, sanitary inspectors, and a conference of ladies on the subject of domestic hygiene. The work of all five conferences began on Wednesday. The municipal and county engineers assembled in the Physics Lecture Theatre, where a large and representative attendance was presided over by Mr. T. de Conroy Meade, M.I.C.E, city surveyor of Manchester.

Among members of the Incorporated Association of Municipal and County Engineers who were present were the following:—

Messrs. Lewis Angell, West Ham; T. W. A. Hayward, Sudbury, Suffolk; T. H. Yabbicom, Bristol; H. Hatch Gammell, Perry Barr; W. L. Sugden, Stoke; T. Caink, Worcester; E. Rushton, Cleethorpes; J. Saville, Heckmondwike; E. Purnell Hooley, Nottingham; W. J. Press, Burnham, Somerset; R. Read, Gloucester; R. M. Gloyne, Eastbourne; H. G. Keywood, Maldon, Essex; W. K. L. Armytage, Yeovil; R. C. Ivy, Ormskirk; J. Chadwick, Bletchley, Bucks; T. Biker, Barnoldswick; R. Dickinson, Berwick-on-Tweed; A. A. Tarriff, Elgin, N.B.; A. Waddington, Oldham; J. A. Barton, Ryde, I.W.; H. T. Sidwell, Herne, Canterbury; J. Gammage, Dudley; C. W. Shackleton, Coseley, Shropshire; J. E. Willcox, Birmingham; T. Gregory, Newburn-on-Tyne; R. Dixon, Stratford-on-Avon; T. Young, Sunderland; G. H. Wild, Littleborough; G. J. Hunt, Dorchester; J. Spencer, Keighley; J. Rushworth, Haworth; A. J. Price, Worcester; F. C. Cook, Nuneaton; G. S. Fraser, Eccleston Park, Prescot; T. Hibbert, Cirencester; C. T. Jenkin, Willenhall; W. F. Y. Molineux, Winchester; A. L. Rodwell, Skipton; W. B. Morgan, Weymouth; F. Massie, Wakefield; J. Munce, Belfast; W. P. Pattison, Benwell and Fenham; G. F. Moody, Grimsby; J. Smith, Ballinasloe; R. O. Wynne Roberts, Oswestry; W. E. A. Williams, Festiniog; J. S. Pickering, Nuneaton; T. de Courcy Meade, Manchester; J. T. Eayrs, Birmingham; J. Price, Birmingham; E. G. Mawbey, Leicester; J. E. Worth, district engineer, London County Council; A. D. Greatorex, West Bromwich; R. Collins, Enfield; W. L. Bradley, Tonbridge; W. R. Prescott, Reigate; B. Boulton, Burslem; F. Mager, Aldridge, Walsall; G. P. Milnes, Stroud; W. G. Fletcher, Wimbourne, Dorset; W. F. Bird, Midsomer Norton; T. J. Moss Flower, Portishead; S. Churchward, St. Thomas, Exeter; J. E. Swindlehurst, Coventry.

Of non-members of the Incorporated Association of Municipal and County Engineers the following were among those present:—

Messrs. S. G. Driver, J. Foulds and W. Sugden, Bradford; W. Gane and B. Greaves, Cleethorpes; T. E. Coleman, Gosport; J. Clark, Broughton-in-Furness; J. Wrigley, Lenscale; C. Harper, Bath; F. Bettany, Burslem; S. R. Lowcock, Birmingham; A. Smith, Lowestoft; P. Kitt, Lowestoft; J. G. Mills, West Kirby; W. T. Mills, Liscard, Cheshire; J. D. May, Dublin; J. Robinson, Durham; W. Boulton, Burslem; O. C. Apted, Reigate; J. J. Galloway, Royal Engineers, Birmingham; T. Hutchinson, Warrington; J. Chew, Stroud; H. C. Broome, Failsworth Urban District Council; S. S. Gettings, West Bromwich; H. Vickery, Kingsbridge Rural District Council; G. Price, Harborne; H. Silcock, Wakefield; J. Eastwood, Warley Urban District Council; W. Dawson, Birkenhead; A. Oddy, Pontefract; G. Owen Dunn, Bombay; D. Turson, Warrington; J. Evans, Warrington; J. Dean, Warrington; W. E. Coles, Stratford-on-Avon; J. Actnmley, Skipton; R. Pitzbills, Oxenhope; E. Thomas, Beaumaris; H. Vickery, Kingsbridge; F. W. Mason, Enfield; H. Swire, Skipton; F. Wicks, Walsall; G. F. Moody, Grimsby.

The proceedings of the conference were opened by

### THE PRESIDENT'S ADDRESS.

BY T. DE COURCY MEADE, M.I.C.E.

With feelings of much pleasure I accepted the invitati n of the council of the Sanitary Institute to occupy the chair at this conference, which enables me again to take some part in the excellent work the Institute is annually performing. This is the fifth occasion on which municipal and county engineers have assembled at congresses of the Sanitary Institute. The former meetings took place at Portsmouth in 1892, at Liverpool in 1894, at Newcastle-upon-Tyne in 1896, and at Leeds last year. Upon all these occasions the Incorporated Association of Municipal and County Engineers were well represented by individual members—although not collectively—showing that municipal engineers are ever ready to embrace all opportunities afforded to them of meeting for the discussion of matters appertaining to their profession, for exchange of ideas, and for mutual advancement.

The interest taken in these meetings proves also that the council of the Sanitary Institute were well advised in making this new departure in the programme, which has been, I believe, fully justified by the results. At the first of these meetings the chairman, Mr. H. Percy Boulnois, M.I.C.E., submitted his excellent diagram indicating the duties of the municipal engineer under six heads, which embrace no less than ninety-eight distinct subjects. Is it therefore surprising that the municipal engineer should always be a student, anxious to learn all that is new, and desirous to benefit by the experience of other engineers, and by the discussion of papers and criticisms of the views expressed by the authors? It should not, however, be forgotten that the communities whose representatives we have the honour to serve reap the benefits of the knowledge thus gained; and when this fact becomes better known and generally recognised the attendance of officials at meetings of this character will doubtless be still more numerous. For the information of visitors who may be present, I would add that the Incorporated Association of Municipal and County Engineers was founded upwards of a quarter of a century ago, and numbers among its members the surveyors and engineers of all the principal towns in Great Britain and Ireland, and that meetings of that Association are held annually in one or more large centres of population, when papers are read and discussed and works in progress are viewed.

#### THE HOUSING OF THE WORKING CLASSES.

It is not the custom to discuss the points raised in the chairman's opening address. I shall therefore refer in very general terms to a few matters that are likely to be of interest to which I am at present giving special consideration, commenoing with that well-worn topic—the housing of the working classes. The difficulties of providing sufficient suitable accommodation at reasonable cost for persons of the working class displaced from insanitary areas, or from areas cleared for street improvements and railway works, are in most instances very great, and are generally enhanced by the tendency to overcrowd, which in many cases unduly increases the number of persons to be provided for upon areas already too limited. These difficulties have been met in Manchester by the erection on the cleared sites of (a) blocks of five-storeyed tenements, approached by a common stairs and balconies; (b) blocks of tenements of two and three storeys, with separate entrance and stairs to each set of tenements; (c) terrace cottages of five rooms each; (d) a model lodging-house. By the kindness of the chairman of the Sanitary Committee of the Manchester Corporation, Alderman Walton Smith, J.P., drawings of all these buildings have been lent for the inspection of visitors to the congress. The Manchester Corporation are also erecting (e) cottage dwellings in the outskirts of the city, about 2½ miles from the cleared areas, where land is less costly. These cottages vary somewhat in character, and contain from five to seven rooms each. The buildings class (a) have been occupied about three years, and are let at rents which yield a moderate return upon the cost of erection. The two blocks (a) of five-storeyed buildings cost about £87,000 exclusive of the cost of sites. The latter, with old buildings thereon, cost about £54,000. Single-room tenements are let at 2s. 6d. per week, the rent of two or three roomed tenements varies from 3s. to 5s. per week.

In addition to the above-mentioned new buildings, much has been done in the improvement of existing dwellings and the conversion of "back-to-back" houses into "through" houses. This work, though excellent where it is effected, has a tendency to cause overcrowding elsewhere, as the number of persons that can be accommodated in the converted and improved dwellings is much less than was crowded into the "back-to-back" houses before alteration. Full details of the procedure of the Manchester Corporation regarding the treatment of insanitary "back-to-back" houses will be found in Dr. Niven's interesting paper on the subject (see "The Journal of the Sanitary Institute," vol. xvi., page 254). That paper is accompanied by plans showing the methods generally adopted in the alteration of "back-to-back" houses. From these it will be seen that in all cases the groups of pail-closets used by the occupiers of one or more blocks of houses are removed, and that each "through" house is provided with a proper water-closet. The substitution of private water-closets for common pail-closets and privies is thus gradually proceeding, but will doubtless be a work of time.

There are at present in the city of Manchester 76,913 pail-closets, 22,990 privies and 13,014 middens, but these numbers are annually becoming less, as water-closets are being provided wherever alterations to property are effected by the corporation. About 900 tons of fæcal matter is collected from the pail-closets per week, and about half this quantity is dried and converted into concentrated manure and sold; the remainder is mixed with ashes and rubbish and disposed of among farmers on the corporation estates at Carrington and Chat Moss. These estates have an area of about 3,750 acres, and it is estimated that about 93,000 tons of mixed night-soil can be thus annually disposed of.

THE TREATMENT OF SEWAGE

is a subject of general interest to most of those present, therefore a few particulars of the cost, &c., of treatment at the Manchester outfall works may not be out of place. The population contributing to the sewage system increased from 400,360 on the 1st of January, 1897, to 512,500 on the 31st of December, 1897. The average daily flow during 1897 was 20,426,363 gallons. The flow per head of the population ranged from 39·3 gallons per day in May to 50 gallons per head in December last. The quantity of water supplied by the corporation is about 28 gallons per head per day. It is estimated that about 17 gallons are supplied for domestic use, and the remaining 11 gallons for trading and public purposes. The difference between the total quantity of water supplied and the average quantity of sewage reaching the works is largely due to the admission of underground water, which passes into the old sewers and drains through defective joints. The nett cost of treatment for 1897 was £19,089 9s. 7d. exclusive of interest and repayment of capital, or £2 11s. 9d. per 1,000,000 gallons treated, apportioned as follows :—

|  | 1896. Per 1,000,000 gallons. £ s. d. | 1897. Per 1,000,000 gallons. £ s. d. |
|---|---|---|
| Precipitation (labour and chemicals only) | 1 2 11 | 1 0 7·1 |
| Sludge disposal (labour and materials only) | 0 14 3·6 | 0 13 9·7 |
| Filtration (a small proportion only of the sewage was filtered) | 0 1 1 | 0 0 5·9 |
| Coal (this includes all steam-power used on the works, but does not include coal for the steamer) | 0 3 11·5 | 0 2 10·1 |
| Sundries | 0 0 6·5 | 0 0 7·7 |
| Incidental expenses (less credits and receipts) | 0 11 5·3 | 0 13 4·6 |
| Total | £2 14 2·0 | £2 11 9·1 |

The above summary of the cost of treating the sewage for the year 1897 shows a reduction of 2s. 5·8d. per 1,000,000 gallons on the cost of treatment for the year 1896. The proportion of chemicals used during the year 1897 was lime, 5·32 grains per gallon ; sulphate of iron, 5·29 grains per gallon—total, 10·61. The quantities of lime and copperas used are adjusted by frequently testing the sewage after admixture with chemicals. The effluent is kept as far as possible faintly alkaline. For this purpose the addition of a slight excess of lime is necessary, owing to subsidence and precipitation of carbonate of lime in the tanks. The amount of copperas added varies with the sewage, and is estimated by the character of the precipitation observed. The composition of the sewage varies within wide limits. The sewage begins to attain its maximum strength about noon on each day, and continues strong until midnight or a little after. The composition of the effluent does not vary so abruptly as that of the sewage, owing to the mixture of the sewage in the precipitation tanks. The effluent begins to attain its maximum strength about 2 o'clock in the afternoon.

The average amount of wet sludge precipitated in 1897 was equal to 21·16 tons per 1,000,000 gallons, as against 21·84 tons for the previous year, yielding 7 tons 12 cwt. of pressed cake per 1,000,000 gallons, as compared with 7 tons 18·4 cwt. for the year 1896. One ton of wet sludge equals 33·7 cubic feet, and 1 ton of pressed cake equals 32·12 cubic feet. The average proportion of wet to pressed sludge was at the rate of 2·73 to 1. The amount of lime used in pressing has averaged 1·40 per cent. by weight of wet sludge, and 3·83 per cent. by weight of pressed cake. The amount of sludge cake removed by farmers during 1897 was 14,233 tons, equal to an average of about 39 tons per day. The balance of 41,875 tons was deposited in a tip adjoining the works. The cost of pressing sludge during the year 1897 was 7·7d. per ton of wet sludge for labour, lime, cloths and sundries, but exclusive of cost of tip, repairs to presses, rolling stock and insurance. The cost of conveying the sludge to the sea for the first three months of this year amounts to 6·2d. per ton of wet sludge, and includes wages, insurance of steamer, coal, repairs and incidental expenses and ship canal charges. Experiments have been continued since 1895 with coke and cinder filters. The capacities of these filters and of a coal filter as measured on several occasions are :—

| Date of Measurement. | Capacity in Gallons. Coke. | Cinder. | Coal. | Time of resting before Measurement. |
|---|---|---|---|---|
| At commencement of use, in 1895 | 1,750 | 1,750 | — | — |
| April 26, 1897 | 1,296 | 1,260 | 756 | 1 hour. |
| April 28, ,, | 1,332 | 1,404 | 828 | 8 hours. |
| May 27, ,, | 1,380 | 1,477 | — | 17 hours. |
| July 2, ,, | 1,446 | 1,548 | — | 15 hours. |
| July 2, ,, | 1,425 | 1,476 | — | 2 hours. |
| July 2, ,, | 1,404 | 1,476 | — | 2 hours. |
| October 6, ,, | — | — | *1,260 | |
| January 5, 1898 | 1,260 | 1,350 | — | 2 hours. |
| January 6, ,, ,, | 1,278 | 1,308 | — | 2 hours. |
| January 7, ,, ,, | — | — | 1,026 | |
| January 24, ,, ,, | 1,368 | — | — | { After a fortnight's rest. |

* The filters had been refilled with washed and screened material.

The results of these measurements show that a considerable amount of moisture is retained in the filtering medium, and that this is slowly drained off or evaporated when the filter is allowed sufficient rest before refilling. The cinder filter has throughout given better results than the coke, both as regards the percentage reduction of impurity effected and in non-putrescibility.

To-day we shall have the opportunity of hearing several interesting papers read and discussed. I therefore feel that I must not unduly occupy the limited time at our disposal, and will content myself with directing your attention to the drawings before referred to, and to the photograph and models which have been placed here for your inspection.

BY-LAWS RELATING TO NEW STREETS AND BUILDINGS.

Mr. J. S. PICKERING, surveyor to the Nuneaton Urban District Council, read a paper entitled "By-Laws Relating to New Streets and Buildings." He said it was scarcely possible within the limits of a short paper to make any detailed reference to by-laws affecting new streets and buildings. It was more with a view to elicit an expression of opinion on the subject generally that it was introduced. He proposed to refer more particularly to by-laws made in England, under the provisions of the Public Health Acts, rather than to by-laws made under local Acts, but his remarks would, however, apply in some measure to by-laws relating to sanitary matters in general.

THE PUBLIC HEALTH ACT, 1875,

empowered sanitary authorities to make by-laws with respect to new streets and buildings, and repealed previous Acts under which such by-laws were made. It also provided that by-laws made under those repealed Acts were to be deemed by-laws under the Act of 1875, if not inconsistent with the provisions of such Act.

In 1877 the Local Government Board drew up a " Model" series of by-laws for the guidance of local authorities. These had been somewhat amended from time to time, and had been framed with great care and under the best legal advice. What was also of the utmost importance, their provisions were considered to be in accordance with the statutory enactments by which they were authorised. But, notwithstanding these [conditions, the Model By-Laws had not been received with general approval. It was true that by-laws made since the passing of the 1875 Act generally adhered closely—and in the greater number of cases almost word for word—to the "Model" series, but this was not so much on account of their general suitability to the districts for which they were adopted, as to the fact that the Local Government Board would not sanction any important departure from their "Model" code. The result was that many authorities did not possess any by-laws at all, others depended upon by-laws of doubtful validity made under former sanitary Acts, while the great majority did not enforce the particular by-laws they had been compelled to include in adopting the "Model" series.

"It is somewhat astonishing," said Mr. Pickering, "that this state of affairs should be allowed to continue with the extension of local government which has taken place in the country, and when there is a general desire on the part of local authorities to carry out the provisions of the Sanitary Acts. The varying circumstances of different districts make it impossible to frame a series of by-laws applicable to all. By-laws, for instance, affecting new streets and buildings in large towns would be altogether unsuited to the requirements of, say, the villages of rural districts. But obvious as this is, it is a matter which is overlooked and accounts for the absence of by-laws in many rural sanitary districts. Sec. 157 of the Public Health Act, 1875, provides that every urban authority may make by-laws with respect to the following matters: The level, width and construction of new streets, and the provision for the sewerage thereof ; the structure of walls, foundations, roofs and chimneys of new buildings for securing stability and the prevention of fires, and for the purposes of health ; the sufficiency of the space about buildings to secure a free circulation of air, the ventilation and drainage of buildings, and the closing of buildings unfit for habitation. Surely these provisions are of sufficient importance to make their adoption imperative. Possibly twenty-three years ago, when the Act came into force, it would not have been desirable to make the adoption of by-laws compulsory, but, considering the advance of sanitary science since 1875, and the general determination of the community to live in greater comfort, and consequently under healthier conditions, there now appears to be no valid reason against the adoption of proper by-laws in every sanitary area. It is evident that the legislature do not accept this view, or they would not continue to make the adoption of important sanitary measures permissive on the part of local authorities." Speaking of

THE PUBLIC HEALTH ACTS AMENDMENT ACT, 1890,

Mr. Pickering said this Act contained many important provisions affecting the health of the community, but they could not be put into force without months of delay in complying with the wearisome details provided for in the adoption of the Act. Sec. 23 of this Act gave to sanitary authorities increased powers as to making by-laws affecting new streets and buildings. Under this section a by-law might be made with reference to the height of bed-rooms, and other rooms used for human habitation. It seemed almost incredible that until the passing of the 1890 Act sanitary authorities had no control over the height of such rooms, although many authorities possessed a by-law fixing their minimum height. This was one of many by-laws inconsistent with the provisions of the Public Health Act, 1875, and therefore ultra vires, but it had been carried out as though it possessed full legal force. In many of the larger towns by-laws made under the Public Health Act, 1848, the Local Government Act, 1858, and other Acts repealed by the Public Health Act, 1875, had not been amended, though repugnant to the laws of the country, and the authorities possessing them preferred to retain these, trusting to their legality not being questioned, rather than adopt the more modern by-laws as sanctioned by the Local Government Board. This position on the part of local authorities should scarcely be possible; in any case, it should not be a necessary position to take up in order to secure by-laws adapted for the health and convenience of a district, for it must not be overlooked that many of these ancient by-laws, as in the case of the one referred to, were eminently desirable, whatever might be said of their validity from a legal point of view. By-laws made under Acts previous to the Public Health Act, 1875, were, as a rule, so conveniently elastic that this was another reason given for their retention in preference to the rigid by-laws of the present day. The following were specimens of the by-laws in force in a town with a population of upwards of 130,000 :—

"The walls of every new building shall be constructed of such thickness as shall be approved by the said council."

"The owner or occupier of every house shall provide proper ventilation in the drainage thereof by means of the rain-water pipe from the roof of the house, or by such other method as the said council shall direct."

These were, Mr. Pickering said, a striking contrast to the detailed by-laws referring to the thickness of walls and the ventilation of drains in the "Model" series, and yet they were only examples of similar by-laws in force in numerous large towns.

Another convenient old by-law was one giving the authority discretionary power with respect to the enforcement of air space at the rear of buildings. The Local Government Board would not now sanction a new by-law which provided for this discretionary power. But most sanitary authorities, nevertheless, did not hesitate to exercise their discretion when an occasion arose, such, for instance, as in the pulling down and re-erection of a building where the provision of the by-law could not be adhered to without considerable sacrifice of property. It might, of course, be contended that the air space was necessary for the health of the occupants of a dwelling wherever the building was situated, and more especially in a populous district, where property as a rule is the most valuable. But an authority had often either to allow a building to be re-erected (and possibly improved from a sanitary point of view) without the requisite air space, or submit to is being altered in such a way that it would not come within the scope of the by-laws as a new building. Discretion in a case of this description seemed desirable, but it must be admitted that any general admission of discretionary power in the by-laws would probably result in frequent acts of indiscretion on the part of some authorities. By-laws of the "Model" series relating to the thickness of walls were seldom carried out in their entirety, especially where they had been adopted in the smaller towns and rural districts, where there was often a feeling that their enforcement might prejudicially affect the desirable growth of the district. So far as by-laws could be prepared to meet the varying conditions affecting the thickness of the walls of a building, the "Model" by-laws did not appear to leave much to be desired. Possibly the thickness prescribed for the walls of small houses up to three storeys might be somewhat modified to meet the objections usually raised against them in the smaller districts; but there would always be a difference of opinion as to what should be regarded as the reasonable and necessary strength of a building, and much would, of course, depend upon the quality of the material and workmanship. As the powers and privileges to make (and necessarily to enforce) by-laws under the Sanitary Acts have not been so fully appreciated as the framers of the Acts must have anticipated, it is a question as to the proper course to be adopted to bring about a better state of things. That it was desirable for all sanitary authorities to have proper by-laws affecting new streets and buildings there could be no doubt. However seldom it may be necessary to bring such by-laws into operation, they would be of service at some time or other, even in the most sparsely-populated districts. If, then, suitable by-laws were essential in rural districts, how much more important that populous towns should possess by-laws framed with the highest possible considerations for health and convenience. This, in the author's opinion, would only be brought about by the adoption of by-laws being made compulsory, and a greater latitude being given to sanitary authorities to frame by-laws adapted to their own particular districts. But the possession and value of by-laws would, however, be of little effect if the necessary means were not adopted for enforcing them. Even in districts where there was an apparent desire to see the by-laws strictly carried out the surveyor's staff was generally so inadequate that the necessary amount of supervision could not be given. In the author's opinion no new house should

be occupied without a certificate from the surveyor that it had been erected in accordance with the by-laws, and that it was fit for human habitation. It would be manifestly unfair, however, to expect a surveyor to give such a certificate unless he had satisfied himself by systematic and regular supervision on the part of a competent staff during building operations that such certificate was justified. Then, again, such a certificate could not be given where the by-laws were not enforced. In some of the older by-laws this certificate was required to be given, but it was not probable that a by-law would now be sanctioned to this effect. Indeed, it would scarcely be desirable until the necessity for a better supervision of new buildings was recognised by sanitary authorities.

BY-LAWS versus ACTS.

It appeared to the author that many provisions contained in by-laws might with advantage be incorporated in the Sanitary Acts, making them statutory enactments rather than measures to be adopted at the option of local authorities. It also seemed desirable that by-laws should be made less comprehensive, many matters of detail now included being made the subject of regulations varying according to the requirements of each particular district. Under these conditions a general series of by-laws more acceptable than the present "Model" series could probably be framed, and sanitary authorities would be able to include in their regulations many important matters, which would make by-laws cumbersome and unnecessarily lengthy. In the case of new streets, for instance, the by-laws might very properly lay down the requirements as to widths under various conditions, but the actual method of construction would be better dealt with in detailed regulations, forming a practical specification of the requirements. Then, again, matters connected with the drainage of a building could be more conveniently and in greater detail be referred to in regulations. It would add to the value of such regulations to accompany them with a complete set of descriptive drawings. Many authorities supplemented their by-laws with regulations as to drainage and other matters, but as these were not confirmed by the Local Government Board, and very frequently contained conditions which could not be legally enforced, they could not be said to be wholly satisfactory.

In concluding, Mr. Pickering said that in any revision of the "Model" by-laws, and the Acts under which they were framed, the Incorporated Association of Municipal and County Engineers might afford most valuable assistance. Throughout the Sanitary Acts and the "Model" series of by-laws there were many technical defects which the municipal surveyor could very readily rectify, and thus put an end to much much unnecessary litigation. The Local Government Board in 1877 acknowledged the assistance rendered by the Royal Institute of British Architects, in framing the by-laws dealing with new streets and buildings, and they would no doubt equally value the help of a professional body whose members must, by their every-day experience, possess a most intimate knowledge of the subject. It was to be hoped that the time was not far distant when every sanitary authority in the country would be in possession of by-laws which it would be deemed a duty to carry out in the interests of the health of the community.

THE DISCUSSION.

Mr. J. Price (Birmingham) proposed a vote of thanks to Mr. Pickering for his paper on by-laws; always, he said, a delicate subject. One would like to know how far the Public Health Acts Amendment Act of 1890 was in force. In very few cases, in his experience, had full advantage been taken of the various clauses, more especially in regard to details in respect of the height of rooms. By-laws might be divided into two classes—one in which they would be general and applicable to every authority, and another in which they were simply applicable to particular districts. Birmingham had one or two of the discretionary by-laws, and he thought they had been carried out with great advantage to the city. After referring to various points of detail concerned with the thickness of walls, Mr. Price expressed his opinion that new by-laws would have to be made for Birmingham, as those in existence were in some respects not sufficiently stringent and in others were oppressive to builders.

Mr. T. Longdin (Warrington) said he knew that for the last fifteen or sixteen years the question of adequate by-laws had been before them, but they had not yet been able to get a model set of regulations. He thought something like that might be effected if they could get a consensus of the opinions of municipal engineers.

Mr. J. T. Eayrs (Birmingham) said Mr. Pickering had given them a valuable and interesting paper on an important subject. By-laws had been a burning question for many years. He knew that in many districts they were afraid to adopt new by-laws, because the Local Government Board insisted on the Model By-Laws being carried out with very little modification. Local authorities felt that some discretionary power should be left to them, so that they could deal with incidents in their own districts which the Local Government Board would not recognise. He agreed with the author that a series of revised by-laws might be drawn up with advantage. There ought to be powers in them to deal with the strength of timber, as well as the thickness of walls; such powers as Salford had, and, he thought, Manchester also. In 75 per cent. of the cases where the Model By-Laws existed they were not enforced. It was no use having these restrictions if they were not acted upon ; but he wanted to know what power local authorities had to enforce by-laws. It is true they could be compelled by mandamus to exercise them, but who would take this action ? A surveyor had not the power, and if he tried to exercise it he would at the next meeting get the —— (laughter). "Well, gentlemen, you know what I mean," was Mr. Eayrs' conclusion.

Mr. T. CAINK (Worcester) referred to certain concessions which had been obtained from the Local Government Board as to the thickness of walls for three-storey buildings, and expressed his opinion that others could get similar concessions.

Mr. G. J. HUNT (Dorchester) said that if local authorities had no discretionary power they must either stop building progress or allow building to proceed without taking action. He also dealt with the by-laws as to air space in the rear of buildings and as to the thickness of walls.

Mr. R. READ (Gloucester) said that when his authority had adopted by-laws every regulation they had made was struck out by the Local Government Board, but they had discretionary by-laws which applied to the older parts of the city. When any building there had to be rebuilt they could adopt the same air space as the old building had. The Model By-Laws appeared to have been drawn up on the assumption that all materials were bad, builders unscrupulous, and architects fools. They were altogether out of date, and wanted revising, with the assistance of the Association of Municipal and County Engineers. When this was done he hoped they would be written in English. At present they could only be understood by a Philadelphia lawyer.

Mr. A. J. PRICE (Worcester), as a building inspector, referred to the necessity of providing in by-laws for a proper damp course in basements. He would like to know what was "a new building," as the difficulties of defining " ground floor" left it in doubt. In Liverpool and Brighton they provided in their by-laws a definition of "ground floor" and "ground storey." In close conjunction with this question of new building was that of new drains. In Brighton they insisted upon proper plans being deposited, a course which he thought was followed in a few other places, but not generally. One could sometimes get a plan, but there was nothing in the by-laws which empowered them to insist upon it. Nor was there any power to enable them to deal with high factories in narrow streets as they could with private houses.

The PRESIDENT expressed their obligations to Mr. Pickering for putting before them a subject of so difficult a character that even those who had spoken upon it disagreed in their views for amendment. Some would have discretionary powers given to local authorities, others would not. If they sought the other point of view they would find that architects had difficulties which did not occur to local surveyors.

Mr. PICKERING, in acknowledging the vote of thanks which had been cordially given to him, was sorry his paper had not been distributed before the meeting (hear, hear!). He could not agree with the approval by the Local Government Board, as referred to by Mr. Read, of the same air space in a new building as in the old one taken down (Mr. Read : Within the discretion of the local authority). The very idea of by-laws was to enable new buildings to be improvements upon the old. Mr. Price (of Worcester) had referred to the alteration of drains. It seemed that builders could alter without consulting the authority, and he thought there should be by-laws to prevent that.

AN OFT-REPEATED COMPLAINT.

Mr. T. DE COURCY MEADE, referring to general complaints as to the papers of the conference not being printed before the meeting and as to the mislaying of the drawings referred to in his (the speaker's) presidential address, said that he wished it to be understood that these shortcomings were not due to the local secretaries.

Mr. E. G. MAWBRY (Leicester), as recording secretary to the conference, said he had written to the secretary of the Sanitary Institute pointing out that at the Newcastle congress a request was specially made that their papers should be printed in time to enable them to be properly discussed. If the Association of Municipal and County Engineers could work with the Sanitary Institute in some way, he thought this might be effected.

Mr. J. T. EAYRS pointed out that the early distribution of many of the papers was most important with regard to the Municipal and County Engineers' Association ; it was always their practice, as far as possible, to get the papers out and in the hands of members, especially of those who had announced their intention of taking part in the discussion. Mr. Eayrs then intimated that he also had written to Mr. White Wallis, the secretary of the Sanitary Institute, in these terms, and he read a reply in which the secretary said in effect that in the case of the Sanitary Institute congress such a course was " impracticable." Mr. Eayrs, continuing, said he was still of opinion that if a strong view were expressed by the conference the Sanitary Institute might do something.

Mr. C. MASON (Nottingham) cordially supported Mr. Eayrs, and moved that such a resolution should be passed and forwarded to the council of the Sanitary Institute.

After having been seconded by Mr. A. T. DAVIES (Shropshire), the resolution was carried unanimously.

## THE VENTILATION OF SEWERS AND DRAINS.

Mr. T. J. MOSS FLOWER, A.M.I.C.E., F.G.S., engineer and surveyor to the Portishead Urban District Council, then read a paper, entitled "Precautions to be Observed in the Ventilation of Sewers and Drains." The author at the commencement of his paper apologised for attempting to deal with a subject already well worn and upon which there exists an abundance of literature, but he believed the very great importance of the subject was in itself a sufficient excuse for his dealing with it. He then continued :—

The ventilation of sewers and drains is a matter which during recent years has been discussed controversially by eminent chemists, doctors, engineers and others. It has been dealt with at meetings of the Institution of Civil Engineers, the Association of Municipal and County Engineers, and nearly all of the other professional institutions and associations the members of which are, more or less, brought into contact with sewers and drains. At conferences of the Royal Institute of Public Health, and at former meetings of the Sanitary Institute, the matter has been brought forward, and at the present time it is considered to be a very important question from a ratepayer's point of view, and is being dealt with at ratepayers' meetings in various places in the country. Well may it reasonably be said, then, that this subject has been well nigh exhausted. It would be mere presumption on the part of the author to attempt to introduce anything new in connection with the subject, as he is fully aware that among his hearers there are a considerable number of eminent gentlemen who have devoted much time and attention to the ventilation of sewers and drains, and who are past-masters of the art of the application of the principles underlying the successful ventilation of these necessary evils —sewers and drains. It is, therefore, primarily not the author's intention to discuss controversially the various systems in vogue at the present date for ventilating sewers and drains so much as to refer to a few precautions which, in his opinion, should be observed in carrying out this work, so as not only to reduce to a minimum the chances of the gases from the sewers causing injury to health, but also to prevent nuisances arising therefrom. A nuisance is understood to mean something the law does not require to be proved to be injurious to health, but which is disgusting and unpleasant to the olfactory nerve. The author does not quite see where the line of demarcation comes in between something that is "injurious to health" and that which is legally only a "nuisance," for, in his opinion, that which is a nuisance must have more or less a bad influence upon health, and is therefore injurious to health in the true sense of the word.

### THE OBJECTS AIMED AT.

In indicating the objects to be aimed at the author said : Shortly, the object aimed at in ventilating sewers is to prevent as far as possible the evolution of gases ; to carry harmlessly from the sewers the gases that cannot, owing to the physical conditions that exist in sewers under the very best of circumstances attainable, be prevented ; to prevent such an abnormal increase in the pressure of the sewer air or gas within the sewer as would make the possibility of the water-seal of the traps fixed in connection with drains discharging into the sewers, becoming broken, within reasonable bounds, or cause the sewer air to be forced out at defective or inconvenient points in the sewers and drains where it could be inhaled, and to purify the air of sewers sufficiently to enable men to work in them. Probably it will be said that this latter object can be attained by opening the manholes at each end of that part of the sewer in which the men are to work. No doubt something can be said in support of this argument, yet it is unreasonable, to say nothing of its being most dangerous, to allow men to enter unventilated sewers. By unventilated sewers I mean, of course, sewers where no attempt has been made to ventilate them in the ordinary sense of the word. It is necessary, perhaps, to mention this distinction, as, whether we appreciate it or not, sewers will ventilate themselves, and where no general system of ventilation has been adopted the sewer gas makes its way out of the sewers through weak spots in the system, either at the side of the pavement through untrapped or defective street-gulley traps, or into the house through defective drains, or into the subsoil, polluting the subsoil, air and water. There are other objects aimed at in ventilating sewers, but probably those mentioned are among the most important.

It may appear too grotesquely ridiculous and unnecessary, in the light of past experience and having regard to the weighty arguments that have been supported over and over again in favour of sewers being ventilated, for the author to have referred to the necessity for ventilating sewers ; but the fact is he comes from one of the greatest cities in the United Kingdom, where no special means are provided for ventilating the sewers. By special means it is to be understood that no attempt is made to ventilate the sewers in his town, and if the air does get in and out the sewers—and get in and out it must do—it must be through unprovided openings and in ways calculated to cause injury to the public health. The objects aimed at in the ventilation of house drains to a very large extent are the same as in the case of sewers. By properly ventilating the drains the traps connected with the various sanitary fittings are relieved from undue pressure caused by the discharge of water-closets and other fittings, and are thus assisted in maintaining their water-seal ; and should any gases from the public sewer by any means pass to the house drain beyond the disconnecting trap, they would be carried harmlessly away, instead of remaining stagnant in the house drain, to pour perhaps into the house through some defect which might at any time occur.

### SEWER GAS AND HEALTH.

It is perhaps unnecessary, the author continued, to say anything upon the question of what effect the sewer gases may have upon health. One may say, What has this to do with engineers, since this can only be dealt with by medical men? Certainly engineers are not, properly speaking, entitled to express an opinion, but it is generally admitted by medical men that at least the inhalation of sewer gases by human beings is conducive to ill-health, and that although no specific forms of disease may result from this, that it must produce a low condition of health, and thus more or less predispose persons to an attack of any form of bodily disease. And whilst there is, probably, no doubt in the mind of any person as to the danger and ill-effects of taking into the human system sewer or drain air, the degree of danger in so doing, and as to the possibility of drains and sewers spreading certain forms of disease, are much more debateable points. It is unnecessary in this paper for the author to refer to the many published reports of the investigations of men of eminence, which go to prove that there is, one may say, overwhelming evidence to show that sewer and drain air is injurious to health.

As far as the author's experience goes, he has made a very large number of inspections in almost all classes of houses in which there have been cases of infectious disease and illnesses attributed by the medical attendant to defective sanitation, and without exception he has always been able to prove that drain or sewer air has had a comparatively free ingress into the house, and in most of these cases the medical attendants have deemed the defects brought to light to have in some way or another assisted in producing or aiding the illness, and on several occasions he has found to his own cost the ill-effects of inhaling foul air from bottled-up drains and sewers, in one case causing him blood poisoning which affected his system for months. In one instance, in which there were several cases of very bad blood poisoning, in the house, it was found that the air from an unventilated sewer in an elevated district was discharged directly through an untrapped trumpet-mouth waste pipe in a water tank fixed under the window on the landing of the bed-room floor. In this case it was found that the current of air passing up this pipe about mid-day was something extraordinary and sufficient to blow a large piece of paper a considerable distance. In another case a fracture was found in the drain at a spot where a person who had had diphtheria very badly was accustomed to stand many times during the day. This defect was believed by the doctor in attendance to have been the cause of the disease, or, at any rate, to have predisposed the patient to the disease from which he suffered. The house was in an elevated position in the town, and was connected to an unventilated system of sewers. Many other cases could be cited, and this is probably the experience of most men who have to make investigations of this character.

In considering the question of the probability of sewers and drains spreading disease, the elaborate experiments and investigations into sewer air made by Mr. J. Parry Laws, at first by himself and subsequently in conjunction with Dr. F. W. Andrews, and which have been from time to time referred to in several professional papers, will throw some light upon the subject. In one report Mr. Parry Laws says: "The whole of my results point unmistakably to the conclusion that the principal, if not the only, source of micro-organisms in sewer air is the air without the sewer, and not the sewage, and they also tend to prove that there is very little ground for supposing that the micro-organisms of the sewage, in the absence of violent splashing, become disseminated in the sewer air." Mr. Laws in the body of his report also says: "It has been shown by previous experimenters that if the splashing is sufficiently violent to produce a very fine state of division of the sewage, organisms will be carried some distance, even 50 or 60 yards." In his second report Mr. Laws states: "The results of these investigations strengthen very considerably the conclusion I arrived at from previous experiments—viz., that micro-organisms in the sewer air are related to the micro-organisms in the air outside, and not to the micro-organisms of the sewage." Mr. Laws further says: "Although one is led irresistibly to the conclusion that organisms found in sewer air probably do not constitute any source of danger, it is impossible to ignore the evidence, though it be only circumstantial, that sewer air in some instances has had some casual relation to zymotic disease." In the conjoint report of Mr. Parry Laws and Dr. Andrews it is shown that the investigators found by experiment that in ordinary sewage typhoid organisms do not tend to survive, and their death is probably only a matter of a few days, or at most seven to fourteen days. But this degree of resistance may, nevertheless, be sufficient to allow of their being able to produce disastrous results should they gain access to the water supply. It was found that in a drain from a typhoid fever block of a fever hospital, when the stools have not been disinfected for two days, a bacillus can be found which, so far as demonstration can go, is identical with that believed to be the actual cause of typhoid fever :—

Prof. J. F. J. Sykes, M.D., medical officer of health for St. Pancras, in a paper read at a sessional meeting of the Sanitary Institute in April, 1895, in referring to these reports, says that they "show that typhoid organisms do appear in the sewage of specifically-infected drains, and that splashing will cause organisms to be carried considerable distances." Dr. Sykes further says: "What the effect of hot vapour, together with violent splashing—invariable conditions in house drains—may be in the presence of the typhoid bacillus it is not difficult to surmise, and tends to support the opinion of large numbers of medical officers of health and medical practitioners that typhoid may be spread aerially by defective drainage," and further, "if specific organisms do gain access there is a possibility of specific disease being conveyed." It may be reasonably inferred that if specific organisms gain access to drains they will pass on to the sewer, and under certain conditions may travel along the sewer a little way and up the next house drain, connected to which there may be a pipe ventilating the sewer discharging near an opening into the house to which it is fixed, or near the point of connection between the drain and sewer there may be a manhole with an open grating at the top thereof, and if at the time of the discharge of the undisinfected excreta from a typhoid patient into the drain the air is passing out of the grating, owing perhaps to its being in an elevated part of the district, a person passing over the grating might inhale the typhoid bacillus and perhaps become infected with the specific form of disease due to this organism.

### LEGAL BEARING OF THE SUBJECT.

Having briefly discussed the objects aimed at in ventilating sewers and drains, and referred to the dangers attributed to inhaling the gases from them, the author thought it would be interesting, before briefly referring to the plan most generally adopted in ventilating sewers and drains, and some of the precautions to be observed in connection therewith, to see how the law bears upon the subject. In regard to this he said :—

The Public Health Act, 1875, sec. 19, enacts that "Every local authority shall cause the sewers belonging to them to be constructed, covered, ventilated and kept so as not to be a nuisance or injurious to health, and to be properly cleansed and emptied," and by sec. 15 "Every local authority shall keep in repair all sewers belonging to them." In sec. 13 the following sewers are not vested in the local authorities—viz.,

(1) Sewers made by any person for his own profit, or by any company for the profit of the shareholders.

(2) Sewers made and used for the purpose of draining, preserving or improving land under any local or private Act of Parliament, or for the purpose of irrigating land.

(3) Sewers under the authority of any commissioners of sewers appointed by the Crown.

Consequently, secs. 15 and 19 do not apply to this class of sewer as regards repairing, cleansing and ventilation, and where any such sewers exist and they are unventilated it would be difficult to insist upon their being ventilated. Why there is the omission one is at a loss to know. It may be said that where a nuisance arises in consequence of the non-ventilation of any sewers excepted in sec. 13 they can be dealt with under other sections in the Public Health Act, 1875, or under Acts amending same, but it is difficult to say how far success would attend the efforts of any local authority attempting to make the proprietors of the excepted sewers above referred to ventilate their sewers.

Under sec. 150, Public Health Act, any local authority with urban powers can compel owners to sewer private streets to their satisfaction, and of course can insist upon the said sewers being properly ventilated. The same may be done under the Private Street Works Act, where such has been adopted.

In cases where local authorities do not carry out their duties in providing their district with sufficient sewers, or in the maintenance of existing sewers, or have made default in enforcing any provision of the Public Health Act, 1875, which it is their duty to enforce, appeal can be made to the Local Government Board, which body has the power to enforce performance by the defaulting authority. Considering the frequency with which local authorities make default, the Local Government Board are remiss in not bringing such authorities to task. Probably in matters which are very debateable there is some reluctance on the part of the central authority to insist upon local authorities observing certain duties imposed upon them by the Public Health Acts, yet there does not seem to be any reason why the Local Government Board should not insist upon all sewers and drains being efficiently ventilated.

The Public Health Acts Amendment Act, 1890, sec. 17, enacts that "Every person who turns or permits to enter into any sewer of a local authority, or any drain connecting therewith, (a) any chemical refuse, or (b) any waste steam, condensing water, heated water or other liquid (such water or other liquid being of a higher temperature than 110 deg. F.), which either alone or in combination with the sewage causes a nuisance or is dangerous or injurious to health, shall be liable to a penalty not exceeding £10 and to a daily penalty not exceeding £5." This is a most important provision. Unfortunately, the Act is an adoptive one, and has not therefore been in operation in all districts, and it is doubtful if these provisions are properly enforced at all times. The exclusion of the above-mentioned matters is an important factor to be considered in providing for the ventilation of any sewer.

The ventilation of drains does not appear to be specially mentioned in any of the Acts of Parliament applying generally to the whole of England. Provision is made for the effectual draining of houses, and under secs. 23 and 25, Public Health Act, 1875 (sec. 23 applies to rural and urban authorities, but sec. 25 to urban authorities only), the surveyor can specify the materials, size, level and fall, but no mention is made of ventilation, and it does not appear that these clauses give power to insist upon special arrangements for ventilating the drains or the materials to be used for such purpose. Sec. 157 of the last-named Act enables urban and rural authorities invested with urban powers to make by-laws with regard to the ventilation of drains. The Model By-Laws of the Local Government Board, which were drawn up upwards of twenty years ago, have been adopted in most places where by-laws are in force, but in a very large number of parts of this country no by-laws have been adopted, and where such have been adopted -they are by no means properly carried out. The author is of opinion, notwithstanding the useful purpose these by-laws have served, that in the light of past experience, a modification of them in so far as the ventilation of drains is concerned is most desirable, and this matter will be again referred to in dealing with the precautions to be observed in connection with the ventilation of drains.

It may be well said that the law upon this matter is very vague and somewhat difficult of application, and, like most of the law connected with sanitation, requires much modification, and after the Model By-Laws have been revised it should be made compulsory for every local authority throughout the country to adopt them; and not only to adopt them, but to insist upon their being enforced. In this connection one may say that it may not be wise to create additional public officers, but the author considers it desirable that there should be a Government staff of officers whose duty it should be to pay periodical visits to every district in the country; to see that local authorities are doing their duty, and I believe much good in this way could be done. In cases of epidemics special officers are sent from the Local Government Board to make inspections and reports, and every now and then a frightful condition of things is revealed. What is wanted is that these inspections should be made prior to the outbreak of epidemics, so that the root of the evil can be struck at before much harm can be done.

### SUGGESTED PRECAUTIONS.

In the time given it is impossible to enumerate all the precautions to be observed in providing for the ventilation of sewers and drains, but having seen the necessity of carrying out this work, so that the chances of the sewer or drain air making its exit at points where it is likely to be inhaled shall be reduced to a minimum, we are guided to some extent in arriving at the ventilating methods. The plan to be adopted cannot be the same under all sets of circumstances, and it is probably the endeavour to apply the same plan in all cases that leads to non-success. If success is to be attained, it is useless to consider the question of the ventilation of sewers or drains apart from the question of the construction and maintenance of those sewers and drains and the size of the sewer compared with the work it has or may have to do; the gradients, flushing arrangements, materials of which they are constructed, width of streets and distance across from houses on one side of street to the other, and as to whether there are any manufacturers sending injurious liquids into the sewers, for it is pretty certain that no system of ventilation yet devised will give satisfactory results where the sewers are sewers of deposit, or the materials of which the sewers are made are of an absorbent nature, or there are not proper flushing arrangements; and it is practically certain that to attempt to ventilate such sewer by open gratings at the road level or shafts up the side of houses, by both these methods, or even by special columns fixed at suitable spots away from houses (such spots in crowded districts cannot be found) must end in failure. It appears, to the author in such cases that, in the absence of total reconstruction of the sewers, nothing can be done unless means are provided for destroying the gas by burning it or by rendering it innocuous by bringing it in contact with some chemical agent that will rob it of its smell and destroy its dangerous properties. Either of these plans is bound to be costly; yet, on the other hand, if at a moderate expense such plan can be devised the cost would no doubt be justified. The author has seen public sewers opened which have been nothing more nor less than elongated cesspools, and to have ventilated such sewers with open gratings would have been simply ridiculous, even though the most perfect flushing arrangements had been devised. The only remedy in such cases is to reconstruct the sewer. It is an accepted rule that flushing arrangements must be provided in all cases if the ventilating arrangements are to be successful, and even in cases where the materials used in the construction, and the full and volume of flow are all that could be desired, regular and systematic flushing, although not required to the extent as where adverse conditions exist, is indispensable.

The author recently inspected the sewers of a seaside town much frequented in the summer by persons seeking rest and health, and found the ventilating openings for the most part at the ground level. The district is a hilly one,

the falls for the most part very good, but objectionable smells come from the gratings. Open gratings are fixed in comparatively narrow passages, with large boarding-houses on either side, and on several occasions in this district most offensive odours were perceived coming from the gratings. It appears to the author to be a very bad practice to allow open gratings at the road level in such places, and certainly not in streets of a less width than 40 ft. to 50 ft.

The sewers should be capable of removing all the foul matter sent into them to its ultimate place of deposit before decomposition sets in, and with good falls, plenty of flushing and proper attention this object can be obtained, and unless this can be done, the air coming from the sewers, no matter how many openings there may be, even if the sewer is one open channel, a nuisance must arise from the sewage. It is desirable to see that the following conditions are observed:—

(1) Sewers of deposit should be reconstructed if it is desired to remove complaints.

(2) Surface gratings should not be fixed in narrow streets.

(3) In fixing shafts up the sides of houses they should be fixed to the tallest buildings, high factories, and churches and chapels might well be used for fixing the shafts to, and the gases delivering at a high altitude could do no harm. The law should allow of local authorities fixing sewer vents to the houses.

(4) The shafts to be carried well above the ridge of the roof, and in no case should a pipe be fixed to a house unless at its highest point it can be fixed clear of all doors and windows. This applies to drains.

(5) The shafts to be not less than 5 in. or 6 in. diameter, and to be surmounted with a cowl to prevent down blows.

(6) The pipe at foot to be provided with a duck's-foot bend, with well at bottom, for the reception of the rust, a cleaning-out hole being provided, so that any obstruction could be removed.

(7) The dead end of all sewers to be ventilated by a 6-in. to 9-in. shaft fixed clear of all windows and door openings to houses.

(8) The sewers cut up in sections, so as to prevent the gases from the lower districts getting to the sewers in the higher part of the town.

(9) To see that, in the event of open gratings being used they shall not be placed near the pavement or near the entrance to dwellings.

(10) To pay constant attention to the ventilating appliances, to see that they are kept in working order.

With regard to drains, it is desirable—

(1) That the drain from end to end be properly ventilated, and not, as in the majority of cases in detached and semi-detached villas, by ventilating the soil pipe, which is usually connected about the centre of the drain longitudinally, by fixing a 4-in. pipe on the inlet side of the disconnecting chamber in front of the house, and fixing in front of the 4-in. pipe a piece of freestone with four or five small holes in it, leaving that part of the drain from the foot of the soil pipe to the back of the house unventilated.

(2) To dispense with the use of mica flap-valves, and, if a site for a low-level inlet pipe clear from all doors and windows or places much frequented can be found, to run the inlet shaft from the drain side of the trap to the ridge of the roof, as it seems simply ridiculous to carefully make all the pipes sound and leave a free opening for the discharge of the drain air in front of the larder or drawing-room window, as is so often found.

(3) To arrange the vent pipes so that the outlets shall not only be clear of the windows, doors and other openings in the house to which the pipe belongs, but also clear of all openings to other houses. This object is seldom kept in view, and much inconvenience and ill-health is believed to be caused by the foul air from neighbour's vent-shafts.

### CONCLUSION.

Mr. Moss Flower concluded his paper as follows: The Local Government by-laws bearing upon this subject are very vague and permit inlets at as near the ground level and outlets as low as 10 ft.; and where builders and owners are determined to defy local authorities there is very considerable difficulty in getting them to carry out the ventilating arrangements in a proper manner. They use for the most part the very cheapest kind of material for ventilating pipes, and simply make their joints with a little red lead or something of the sort; the pipes generally are barely carried above the eaves, and every precaution should be taken to prevent this class of work being done. All this could be prevented by the adoption of by-laws specifying in greater detail how the house drains should be ventilated, giving particulars as to the kind of pipe, the joints, &c.

(4) To see that in exposed positions at least a cowl to prevent down blows should be fixed at the top of the soil pipe ventilators. This the author has found to be absolutely necessary after taking observations over a period of four years in exposed positions. He has found that the water seals in the traps of water-closets become destroyed by the wind blowing down the soil pipe ventilators with wire globes at their top.

As in the case of sewers, the construction of the drainage plays a most important part in the successful ventilation of drains. The drains must have good falls, be constructed of proper materials and be well flushed. The disconnecting trap should be of a self-cleansing nature, although, in the absence of special flushing arrangements, it cannot be expected that the trap can be properly cleaned with the appliances generally in use.

## SOME SANITARY AND ALLIED ADVANTAGES ATTENDING THE INTRODUCTION AND USE OF MOTOR VEHICLES.

Mr. E. SHRAPNELL SMITH, honorary secretary, Liverpool Self-propelled Traffic Association, then read a paper with the above title. In the course of it he said :—

The present age is essentially utilitarian in its tendencies, upon which fact we may reasonably congratulate ourselves ; yet few of us desire to see custom and sentiment ruthlessly swept aside by or sacrificed to a belief which in some instances amounts to nothing less than a fetish. Utility is, no doubt, a good plea for many of the changes which we see being wrought around us, but unless strengthened by the argument of expediency is by no means a sufficient one.

Years of admirable service rendered by that artist in haulage, the horse, have taught us beyond question that it is a useful and usually a reliable animal ; but to-day there are evidences of the revival of a perhaps equally useful and reliable means of locomotion—_viz._, mechanical self-propelled self-contained vehicles for use on common roads. That these motor vehicles are in their development is, I think, sufficiently attested by their behaviour during the recent competitive trials in France, America and this country, when loads up to 5 tons nett were successfully carried over average roads and up and down more than average gradients, and by the expericnce gained in quarters where they have been in use for many months under trying conditions. Granting, then, that the motor vehicle is no longer in the experimental stage, we have alternate methods of transport at our command, each of which has proved its practicability and utility, and are led to inquire whether we shall support the old order or the new. If considerations of expediency, under which head ? I think matters affecting the public health, convenience and expenditure, are to determine the question. It appears to me to be almost a foregone conclusion that this conference will support the resolution which it is my good fortune to be afforded the opportunity of moving to-day.

The object of this short paper is to lay before the members of the Institute and delegates to the conference, with a view to discussion, some of the advantages which are claimed for motor vehicles by those who have possibly welcomed the automobile movement with too great enthusiasm, a quality commendable in itself but sometimes dangerous. It is not proposed to attempt to discuss the merits or demerits of the several systems now upon the market, but by a brief contribution in somewhat general terms to lead up to a discussion which will probably be the most interesting part of the proceedings. The subject will be considered under two heads, although it is somewhat difficult at times to prevent their merging one into the other, and an endeavour will be made to render apparent some of the advantages which may be expected to accompany the progressive adoption of motor vehicles. The two divisions are—(1) improvements in sanitary conditions ; (2) reduction in public expenditure.

IMPROVEMENTS IN SANITARY CONDITIONS.

The first and most obvious advantages as affecting the public health and convenience will be the almost entire elimination of the trouble of dealing with horse manure and the general improvement in the condition of our streets. Manure heaps, with their attendant emanations, will in every case where a service displaces horse-drawn conveyances disappear, and the avoidance of these accumulations is a matter of no small moment. Too frequently are these heaps allowed to grow to large dimensions in centres of dense population, and at least to assault our olfactory nerves, if not to constitute a real danger to those who are obliged to inhale the noxious reducing gases of putrefaction which arise therefrom, especially in hot weather. The problem of dealing with horse manure is not, unfortunately, confined to the vicinity of the stables, in which event the nuisance could be a more localised and treated accordingly in a simple manner, but extends over the whole area covered by the traffic of our towns and cities. Thus we have the droppings exposed to the disintegrating and pounding action of hoofs and wheels, dried under the sun's rays and impartially distributed on the wind, to cause various unpleasant personal consequences and to contaminate articles of food exposed for sale uncovered. In the open, in addition, the nuisance is aggravated by the incorporation of the dust (also largely produced by the horse) with the manure, whereby the total bulk of sweepings is largely augmented, to produce the elusive particles of summer or the troublesome pasty slime of winter. In short, the horse—firstly by reason of its excrements, and secondly by reason of its pedium extremitates—is the veritable _bête noir_ of those who are responsible for the scavenging and cleaning of our streets, and the great cause of all the difficulties which beset them. This matter of street cleansing is undoubtedly recognised as one of the most serious which public health officers have to face, the degree of its importance being proportionate to the traffic, and most intense in the streets of London, the main thoroughfares of our large provincial cities, the neighbourhood of railway or shipping depots, and station approaches or other cab and cart ranks.

How many devices exist to combat the nuisance, and how far successful are they ? By means of mechanical sweeping, manual scraping and brushing and street-orderly bins, perhaps 90 per cent. of the matter is intercepted, but a considerable quantity is already under the traffic and in a state of transition to the insidious dust before it can be coped with. To this residuum of fæcal matter, which is inevitably flattened out upon the road, must be added the whole of the urine, and the characteristics of the resultant compound are too well known to require further words from me. The ordinary methods have in some instances been supplemented by a system of thorough washing of the streets at night, this treatment being practised by certain of the London district boards of works in particular. The mere fact that so much thought and labour are extended in street scavenging and cleansing proves that sanitarians accord this work a high place in the scale of operations which conduce to the improvement of the public health ; but, however efficiently the work is carried out, a nuisance must exist during an appreciable part of the twenty-four hours, and even the washing of the foul matter down the gulleys is not always a solution of the difficulty ; further, it will probably be admitted that it would be better to avoid as far as possible the necessity for all the elaborate steps named above by materially reducing the source of the nuisance. The introduction of motor vehicles and the gradual extension of their uses in place of horse-drawn vehicles must reduce the filth and dust of our streets to an ultimate minimum, and, quite apart from financial considerations, I submit that any change which contributes to such sanitary betterment is, on the principle that prevention is better than cure, both desirable and expedient as affecting the health and convenience of the community at large.

REDUCTION IN PUBLIC EXPENDITURE.

Economy is always a good reason to put forward in support of any new proposal if it can be put forward and substantiated, and it is perhaps one of the strongest arguments that can be adduced in favour of the change from horse-drawn to self-propelled vehicles, in the conducting of sanitary work more especially. The connection between sanitation and economy is a close one—too close sometimes. Committees have a way of fixing round sums which must not be exceeded, and earnest hard-working officers have a penchant for wanting more and more in order to do what they feel to be necessary, so that my intention to deal at some length with the financial side of the question may be, and I trust is, acceptable to all. I hope to show that a saving can be effected in more than one direction, and think it best to subdivide this section of my subject as follows : (a) Working expenses ; (b) road maintenance ; (c) congested thoroughfares ; (d) means of communication ; (e) incidental advantages.

(a) _Working Expenses._—It is of vital importance in making estimates, before coming to a decision as to the expediency of the change, to know the exact conditions of the work to be done, particularly the light-load contingency, the amount of time idly spent in waiting for loads, and the gradients to be encountered. The necessity for taking these features into account cannot be too strongly emphasised, for the economy to be effected is, owing to the relatively high prime cost of the motor vehicle, chiefly determined by the factors of regular work and steep gradients. The more regular the work and the higher the gradients the more economical does the motor vehicle become. Most corporations will be ready to guarantee regular work, and many of our towns possess irregular contours ; hence the advantages of the motor vehicle can be turned to account in refuse and rubbish removal more readily than in many other directions. Speaking, as I do, to those who are directly interested in the efficient conducting of sanitary work, it will suffice to endeavour to establish a comparison between the costs of refuse removal by the two means at our disposal. Assumptions must in any case be made, and the figures given are intended to indicate what might be realised in a town where the gradients are nominal both in number and degree. If any of those present have occasion to know that their dust-carts carry weights differing from those which I have taken as cases of calculation, it will be found a simple matter to make the necessary corrections.

COMPARISON OF COSTS OF WORKING.

| Type of Vehicle. | Capacity. Cub. Yds. | Maximum Load. Tons. Cwt. | Daily Mileage. | Work per Annum. Days. |
|---|---|---|---|---|
| Two-wheeled cart ... | 2·5 | 1　5 | 16 | 310 |
| Four-wheeled cart (London) ... | 3·5 | 1　15 | 12 | 310 |
| Motor vehicle ... ... | 7·5 | 3　15 | 24 | 300 |

TWO-WHEELED DUST-CARTS.

| | | | | |
|---|---|---|---|---|
| _Prime cost_— | | | | |
| Four dust carts at £20 | ... | ... | ... | £80 |
| Four horses at £60 | ... | ... | ... | 240 |
| Four sets harness, rugs, &c. ... | | | ... | 27 |
| | | Capital outlay | ... | £347 |
| _Annual expenditure_— | | | | |
| Interest, at 5 per cent. per annum ... | | ... | £17　7　0 |
| Depreciation, at 15　,,　　,, | | ... | 52　1　0 |
| | | | | £69　8　0 |

|  | £ | s | d |
|---|---|---|---|
|  | £09 | 8 | 0 |
| Fodder and litter, at 11s. per horse per week ... | 114 | 8 | 0 |
| Horsekeeper's wages ... ... ... ... | 12 | 0 | 0 |
| Shoeing, at 5s. per horse per month ... ... | 12 | 0 | 0 |
| Veterinary surgeon, at 20s. per horse per annum | 4 | 0 | 0 |
| Rent, rates and taxes ... ... ... ... | 14 | 0 | 0 |
| Repairs to carts and harness ... ... ... | 8 | 0 | 0 |
| Four drivers, at 25s. each per week ... ... | 260 | 0 | 0 |

Total per annum ... ... £493 16 0

Say, 80 per cent. of the maximum load is carried,
50 per cent. of the total distance traversed :
Work done = (1·25 × 0·8) × (16 × 310 × 0·5) × 4 nett ton-miles
per annum = 9920.
Cost = (£493 16s.) ÷ 9920 = 11·95d. *per nett ton-mile.*

FOUR-WHEELED DUST-CARTS (LONDON).

*Prime cost—*

| Four dust-carts at £50 ... ... | £200 |
|---|---|
| Four horses at £70 ... ... ... | 280 |
| Four sets harness and rugs... ... ... | 27 |

Capital outlay ... ... ... £507

*Annual expenditure—*

| Interest, at 5 per cent. per annum ... | 25 | 7 | 0 |
|---|---|---|---|
| Depreciation, at 15 „ „ ... | 76 | 1 | 0 |

£101 8 0

| Fodder and litter, at 15s. per horse per week ... | 156 | 0 | 0 |
|---|---|---|---|
| Horsekeeper's wages ... ... ... | 16 | 0 | 0 |
| Shoeing, at 5s. per horse per month ... ... | 12 | 0 | 0 |
| Veterinary surgeon, at 20s. per horse per annum | 4 | 0 | 0 |
| Rent, rates and taxes ... ... ... | 24 | 0 | 0 |
| Repairs to carts and harness ... ... | 16 | 0 | 0 |
| Four drivers, at 28s. each per week ... | 291 | 4 | 0 |

Total per annum ... ... £620 12 0

Say, 80 per cent. of the maximum load is carried,
50 per cent. of the total distance traversed :
Work done = (1·75 × 0·8) × (12 × 310 × 0·5) × 4 nett ton-miles
per annum = 10,416.
Cost = (£620 12s.) ÷ 10,416 = 14·30d. *per nett ton-mile.*

MOTOR VEHICLE.

*Prime cost* ... ... ... ... ... £420

*Annual expenditure—*

| Interest, at 5 per cent. per annum ... | £21 | 0 | 0 |
|---|---|---|---|
| Depreciation, at 15 „ „ ... ... | 63 | 0 | 0 |

£84 0 0

Fuel.—0·5 gallon kerosine per vehicle-mile :
0·5 × 24 × 300 = 3,600 gallons at 5d. per

| gallons ... ... ... ... | £75 | 0 | 0 |
|---|---|---|---|
| 1·0 gallon per diem for raising steam ... | 6 | 5 | 0 |
| Methylated spirit ... ... ... ... | 2 | 0 | 0 |

Water.—3·5 gallons per vehicle-mile :
3·5 × 24 × 300 = 25,200 gallons at 1s. per

| 1,000 gallons ... ... ... ... | 1 | 5 | 0 |
|---|---|---|---|
| Lubricating oil and waste ... ... ... | 10 | 0 | 0 |
| Rent, rates and taxes ... ... ... | 5 | 5 | 0 |
| License ... ... ... ... ... | 5 | 0 | 0 |
| Repairs ... ... ... ... ... | 60 | 0 | 0 |
| Driver, at 35s. per week ... ... ... | 91 | 0 | 0 |

Total per annum ... ... £340 0 0

Say, 80 per cent. of the maximum load is carried,
50 per cent. of the total distance traversed ;
Work done = (3·75 × 0·75) × (24 × 300 × 0·5) nett ton-miles per
annum = 10,125.
Cost = 8·06d. *per nett ton-mile.*

*Summary.*—A motor dust-cart ought, by reason of its
greater capacity and speed, to replace four horse-drawn carts.
The economies to be effected by the change are approximately
as follows :—

| | London. | Provincial Cities. |
|---|---|---|
| Cost per horse per annum | ...£155 | £123 |
| Cost of same work by motor | ... 85 | 85 |
| Saving per annum | ... 45 per cent. | 31 per cent. |

(b) *Road Maintenance.*—The vagaries of our old friend the
traction engine have caused so bad an impression to be formed
regarding the effects of mechanical haulage on road surfaces
that in many quarters the opinion is held that motor vehicles
of all types must do more damage than horse-drawn vehicles,
and opponents of the revived locomotion may even now be
contemplating an attempt to apply the clause of "extra wear
and tear " thereto. Whatever have been the just objections
to traction engines, it must be remembered that these ponder-
ous machines possess few, if any, points in common with the
motor vehicle and weigh very much more. Again, whilst the
traction engine does most harm by reason of its great weight,
it is the boots of the horse that do most of the damage at the
present day. Both these faults are absent in the modern
motor vehicle. It is interesting in this connection to recall
the treatment meted out to the pro-Victorian steam coach
pioneers—James, Gurney, Hancock, Church, Macerone and
others—in the form of prohibitive tolls, which were ostensibly
levied to cover the expense of extra road repairs. A Select

Committee of the House of Commons, which sat in the year
1831 with reference to the heavy steam coaches of that
period, and before which a great deal of valuable information
was given in evidence by Farey, McNeill, Telford and
M'Adam, gave the following as their eighth conclusion, "That,
as the roads are not acted on so injuriously as by the feet of
horses in common draught, such carriages will cause less
wear of roads than coaches drawn by horses." I do not think
that it is wide of the mark, or incompatible with the experience of engineers and road surveyors to-day, to accept the
proportion of the wear and tear caused by the action of the
horses' hoofs as two-thirds of the whole to which our roads
are subjected. Personal observation of and reflection upon
the differences between the effects of the combined anchoring
and levering action of the horse and of the mere rolling contact of the wheel tyres must lead one to concur in these findings. The further question arises, however, as to whether
the driving contact in the case of a self-propelled vehicle will
affect the surface of the road prejudicially as compared with
the rolling contact of the wheels of a vehicle which is hauled
by an external tractive force. In venturing the opinion that
at most an important difference here exists, I desire to point
out that the motor vehicle of to-day is not constructed with
cross-bars, studs, or other forms of " gripping " contrivances
upon the tyres, and, consequently, the adhesion is obtained
solely by what may be termed simple contact between the
road and the tyres. The difficulty of ensuring sufficient adhesion on greasy surfaces is best met by fitting a sanding-box
in front of each driving-wheel. The horse distorts the crown
of our macadam roads, causes unequal wear of our sett pavements, and disintegrates in a greater or lesser degree any
substance that the ingenuity of man can devise, and only so
soon as the motor vehicle shall come into more general use in
our streets will these troubles begin to grow less. To this
end municipal and other authorities, directly as large users
and indirectly by encouraging their adoption for hackney
purposes, can give the movement a healthy stimulus.

(c) *Congested Thoroughfares.*—The enormous increase of
vehicular traffic in our cities has caused another problem to
loom large in the minds of those who watch over our local
interests in these closing years of the nineteeth century, and
there seems to be no small apprehension that the motor
vehicle will serve only to increase the worries of the constable
on point duty and to add to the terrors of the crossings where
omnibuses, hansoms, four-wheelers, drays, cyclists and other
products of civilisation already jostle one another and pede-
trians with a considerable degree of confusion. Although
the value of wider streets is clearly seen, the value of the
frontages is apparently even more clearly seen by the fortunate parties who own the title deeds to these appreciated
spots. In the fact that the motor vehicle reduces the longitudinal distance monopolised by each unit of traffic to about
50 per cent. of what we are accustomed to to-day, there is,
I think, a possible solution to this pressing question. The
available street area will be used to better advantage, more
room and less risk will be secured to the harassed pedestrian,
less valuable time will be wasted in tantalising blockages and
stoppages, and the loans for street-widening purposes will be
less numerous.

(d) *Means of Communication.*—A Select Committee of the
House of Commons, which reported in the year 1808, said :
"Next to the general influence of the seasons, upon which
the regular supply of our wants and a great proportion of
our comforts so much depend, there is, perhaps, no circumstances more interesting to men in a civilised state than the
perfection of the means of interior communication." Since
that period the introduction and extension of railways and
tramways has done much to improve our means of transport
and communication, but the completion of the network of
lines of internal communication and of traffic in our outlying and rural districts will, I think, be accomplished by the
adoption of motor vehicles. Their absolute independence of
route, of prepared way, of central generating station, and of
one another, renders it possible for us to use them where
the railway, the tramway and the horse fail to meet our requirements. In rural districts, owing to insufficient or
fluctuating traffic, it frequently does not pay to lay down
either a rail or a tram way in, in consequence of which considerable inconvenience, and even hardship, is inflicted upon
a long-suffering portion of the population. Motor vehicles,
which require neither metallic path nor ballasted track and
can change their routes according to demand, offer a solution
of the difficulty and a means of assisting the depressed
agriculturalist. I venture to commend the motor vehicle to
representatives of county councils and rural district councils
as a possible means of reaching markets from which their
constituents are now shut out by excessive railway rates or
absolute lack of connection, and of putting their districts
into closer touch with latter-day progress by affording the
inhabitants increased facilities for travel.

(e) *Incidental Advantages.*—There are not a few minor
advantages attached to the use of motor vehicles. In towns,
for circulation within a prescribed area, it is highly probable
that accumulator propulsion of cabs and similar light vehicles
will provide a moderate day-load for electric generating
stations. Motor vehicles will not bolt, take fright, shy, or
cause damage to persons or property, so long as they are in
charge of a man of ordinary intelligence, for their control is
simple and certain. Another matter, one also which affects

the public health, is the prospective diminution of the diurnal roar of street traffic which distracts our attention and tries our nerves. This will be achieved by removing the horse in a number of instances and, in order to protect the mechanical parts of the motor vehicle, fitting rubber tyres to the wheels. Again, as affecting the public health and the prosperity of the country wayside, a means of supplementing the bicycle for touring purposes is presented which could scarcely be improved upon.

#### CONCLUDING REMARKS.

In concluding his paper the author said :—

Before concluding, I wish to direct attention to the fact that in the few years that have elapsed since the revival of interest in the value and scope of motor traffic the most striking feature in this country has been the marked lack of public interest as compared with that evinced by our near neighbours, the French. This apparent apathy does not of necessity, indicate anything beyond that peculiar conservatism which is so characteristic of a Briton, even when his personal welfare and convenience are affected ; but I submit that the movement deserves and demands recognition and encouragement. There is no reason to call for the extinction of the horse, which has a higher calling than a life of drudgery in hauling conveyances laden with goods and human beings through the streets and up the steep hills of our towns. It will ease our consciences to let this work devolve upon the motor. The present contention is that as the inconvenience, trouble, expense and general sanitary difficulties of street cleansing are almost entirely due to the excretions of the horse and to the hammering and distorting action of its hoofs, and as the same can be diminished by the use of motor vehicles, which also possess advantages as affecting the expense of refuse removal, the relief of congested thoroughfares, and the perfection of internal communication, sanitarians, as a body, should encourage the introduction and use of the more novel means of locomotion. In conclusion, I desire to acknowledge the fact that the subject of motor vehicles has already attracted the attention of some sanitarians, the engineers of Chelsea, Leicester, Wolverhampton and Liverpool having to my knowledge already taken steps to adopt them. I am also indebted to the cleansing superintendents of Glasgow, Derby, Huddersfield, Hull, Leeds and Sheffield for information bearing on part of my paper.

Mr. Shrapnell Smith, on concluding the reading of his paper, proposed that the conference should pass the following motion : " That this conference of municipal engineers, assembled in connection with the congress of the Sanitary Institute, this 28th day of September, 1898, is of opinion that the introduction and use of efficient motor vehicles should be encouraged by county, municipal, urban and other authorities, in view of the fact that the extended use of such vehicles would contribute to the general improvement of the sanitary condition of our streets and towns; and this meeting recommends that the council of the Sanitary Institute make known this opinion as widely as possible."

#### DISCUSSION.

It having been agreed to discuss both Mr. Moss Flower's and Mr. Shrapnell Smith's papers together,

Mr. PRICE (Birmingham) opened the debate by seconding the resolution proposed by the reader of the latter paper, especially as Mr. Smith had added the word "efficient." If all vehicles used in Birmingham were motor cars, Mr. Price said, the corporation could afford to have all the streets paved with wood.

Mr. EAYRS said that, so far as his own experience went, he had seen motor cars which worked well and were free from excessive noise, but he had seen others which were abominations. He was sure that if there was a demand manufacturers would be able to put something on the road which was "efficient."

Mr. J. WILLIAMS (Mountain Ash, South Wales) referred to the tests of road metal published in The Western Mail, and made by Prof. Elliott, tests which were called those for " percussivo-attrition," and which it was alleged had never been made before. He had had the pleasure of correcting this impression, as he had many years ago devised a machine similar to that used by Prof. Elliott. Cardiff was using a material which might not stand the test of " percussive-attrition " but was good for all the purposes of road-making. One of the great advantages of motor cars would be their enabling them to use local material which, though not necessarily the best, would make a road that would be good and easy for locomotion.

Mr. E. P. HOOLEY (Notts) thought Mr. Shrapnell Smith might possibly have read his paper with advantage in ten years' time. Mr. Smith had spoken of a motor car to carry 5 tons. Well, there had been started at Mansfield a company which was going to run motors to take the place of tram cars, but their vehicles could not even carry five persons, much less 5 tons. He thought the figures in the paper were mostly "jumped at." The Mansfield company had said they must have special roads for their motor cars, as granite were out the rubber. It struck him that motor cars wanted not only special roads, but the whole of a road, if not for their steering for room for the horses they caused to shy. Roads for them would either have to be wood or tar paved. He would like to hear whether there was any chance of county authorities getting the benefit of the 5-guinea license for

meter cars. Referring to locomotives on highways, he thought municipal engineers who had not yet seen the new Locomotives on Highways Act, which would come into force on January 1st, should certainly do so, as it contained clauses which should be carefully studied.

Mr. PHILLIPS (Gloucester), as a county surveyor thought all county authorities would welcome "efficient" motor cars —that is, those that would not frighten horses, would travel without undue noise, and would carry freight at reasonable rates. It seemed to him, however, that motor cars improved as slowly as had traction engines. It was only the poverty of his county that caused him to employ these latter.

Councillor GLOVER (Mayor of Warwick), as a manufacturer said his firm were giving every attention to the subject. He thought it unwise to "rush" the matter, and to put on the roads motor cars of any sort which were not effective. He had been giving prolonged thought and experiments to a motor car he was making for dusting and watering, but he did not think it wise to put it on the market until he felt it was as perfect as it could be made.

Mr. MAWBEY (Leicester) had advertised for tenders for motor cars. The difficulty seemed to be in the fuel for power. He had only had four proposals—two for Welsh coal and two for oils—and none were satisfactory. He had worked the matter out, and had come to the conclusion that if in Leicester they could use motor cars in their scavenging department they would effect a saving, and he would have no hesitation in adopting them if they could get a good one. He had been to Chiswick and seen a car working on a flat gradient. He then saw it, loaded with 3½ tons, go splendidly up a gradient of 1 in 12. He found also the driver could easily stop on an incline and start again, and that the car could be turned in a radius of 15 ft. He came away very highly satisfied on these points. He agreed with the author that as soon as they could get good meter cars they could be used with advantage in many ways.

Mr. SHRAPNELL SMITH, in reply, said the horse-power of motor vehicles on gradients was one of the most vital questions. They must be able to stop and start. In Liverpool they had been put to the severest test with satisfactory results. They had been run, carrying 5 tons, over the most horrible cobble roads, up gradients of 1 in 17, 35 miles for four days in succession, and had come through with the consumption of oil he had mentioned. They started from the river side and ran through traffic, and the delay was only nine minutes for the four days for the four vehicles under test. The use of kerosene or the best coal avoided the smoke nuisance. As to whether it was wheels or horses' hoofs that did all the damage to the roads, he would ask them, if they were cyclists, which part of the road they chose for riding. Was it where the horses' hoofs went ? He had not said motors were ready for adoption; he had asked them to encourage their introduction and use. The Mansfield car Mr. Hooley had referred to was only made to carry 2 tons.

The resolution proposed by Mr. Shrapnell Smith was then put and carried, and on the motion of the president of the conference votes of thanks were unanimously awarded to Mr. Moss Flower and Mr. Shrapnell Smith for their papers.

The members of the conference then lunched together at the Grand Hotel, and in the afternoon visits were made to various works in Birmingham, in accordance with the programme given in our issue of September 23rd. We hope to be able to give some account of these works in a subsequent issue.

#### THE HEALTH EXHIBITION.

#### FIRST NOTICE.

Space will not permit us to give anything like an exhaustive notice of the numerous stands at the Health Exhibition, which, as noted in our last issue, was opened at Birmingham by the Lord Mayor on the 27th ult., and will remain open until the 22nd of the current month. Generally speaking, it may be said that, while there is little that is absolutely novel, the exhibition as a whole shows that great strides have been made, even in the past twelve months, in the artistic finish and practical development of the details of sanitary appliances. We give hereafter a few particulars of the more notable of the exhibits, taking them in the numerical order of the catalogue.

Mr. WILLIAM EGGINTON, of 176 Waterloo-road, Birmingham, occupies Stand No. 1 with a portable sewer-gas extractor and destroyer. A fan, driven by any convenient motive power, is intended to extract the gas and to force it through a fire. In conjunction with the extractor and destroyer there is an arrangement for vapourising chemicals under the action of another fire, so that with the assistance of drop-plates and airproof mats a section of sewer can be disinfected. The idea is to treat specially-infected areas.

Messrs. SHANKS & Co., of the Tubal Works, Barrhead, have a show which is perhaps the most conspicuous of its kind at Bingley Hall. Its chief feature is the collection of beautifully-decorated baths and really exquisitely designed and finished bath-room accessories. Here are to be seen applications of the well-known firm's vitreous enamel for baths and lavatories, which gives a surface equal to white porcelain enamel but at considerably less cost; spray baths, for public baths and other institutions, fixed in ranges and intended to replace plunge baths; hospital baths, lavatories, sinks and closets; and trough-closets and latrines for schools. Especially noticeable is the new 1808 pattern of the "Fin de Siècle" bath, with splayed end, dispensing with soap dish, and sponge rack and soap tray attached to the end of the bath; while among their closets conspicuous is the "Barrhead" syphonic closet, with a new vulcanite seat which is quite non-absorbent and is claimed to be more sanitary than wood. It is being used in several hospitals and infirmaries now being erected. A feature of another closet, the "Silent Combination," is indicated in its title. A strong objection to syphonic closets has been their noisiness. Messrs. Shanks really seem to have overcome this, and at last to have produced a closet which is practically silent in working without sacrifice of efficiency in flushing.

Mr. GEORGE JENNINGS, of Lambeth Palace-road, London, has also a stand which will compare favourably with any in the exhibition. We hope to have an opportunity of referring to it in more detail in a later issue, but it may be noted here that he includes a splendid array of baths, lavatories, closets, urinals, sinks and the like, many of them incorporating recent improvements.

Messrs. DOULTON & Co., of Lambeth, have also an exhibit worthy of their world-wide reputation. Baths of all kinds—shower, douche, spray and plunge—are again conspicuous. One is struck with the attractive qualities of their vitreous enamelling, an effective process which is cheaper than porcelain and the older enamels, is really artistic, and is impervious to the acids of soap. Some sinks shown are also remarkable for the beauty of the white-glazed fireclay and for the "truth" of their lines. A ceramic ware fireplace, erected in terra-cotta and suitably glazed and decorated, will also be noticed; and of course one sees, too, some beautiful examples of Doulton ware panels. The artistic and the practical combine harmoniously on Messrs. Doulton's two stalls.

Messrs. THOMAS WRAGG & SONS, of Swadlincote, Burton-on-Trent, have a goodly show of Hassall's well-known pipes, channels in white enamel and salt-glazed, gulleys, intercepting traps, sinks, lavatories, closets and other appliances.

THE SEPTIC TANK SYNDICATE, Limited, of 7 and 8 Bedford-circus, Exeter, show a model of a complete installation of the Cameron septic tank and five filters, and another working model of an installation for small isolated residences and explanatory diagrams. Mr. Cameron's system of sewage treatment is so well known to our readers that we need not further refer to it here. Adjoining is the stand of Messrs. FARRER, BARBER & Co., of Cannon-street, Birmingham, who, as agents, show automatic tanks, baths, lavatories, the Helliwell patent system of glazing, and other appliances; next we come to the five earth-closets shown by the BRITISH SANITARY COMPANY, of Bothwell-street, Glasgow; and beyond that to the large and attractive exhibit of Messrs. W. HARRIMAN & Co., Limited, of Newcastle-on-Tyne, in which the prominent features are yard sinks, gulleys, channels and intercepting traps for inspection chambers, closets, lavatories, and the well-known specialities associated with the name of "Barron."

Messrs. S. DIBBLE & SON, of Ledsam-street, Birmingham, show a sink and automatic waste-water closet, in which the pan is flushed by the water from the sink without the aid of a separate flushing apparatus; Messrs. JOSEPH SANKEY & SONS, of Bilston, show three steel-clad and copper-lined baths; Messrs. F. C. CALVERT & Co., of Bradford, are represented by a show-case of their well-known disinfectants and other preparations; Mr. W. T. ALLEN, of Whitehouse-street, Aston-road, Birmingham, shows automatic latrines and water-closets; Messrs. CALLENDER & MONTGOMERY, of 11 Victoria-street, London, show samples of those excellent inventions—Callender's bitumen damp course and "Jhilmil" lathing; Messrs. L. HUGH BRISTOWE & Co., Limited, of Victoria-street, London, show a portable plant of Riddell's patent filter; and Messrs. C. ISLER & Co., of Bear-lane, Southwark-street, London, exhibit their invaluable tube-well driving apparatus.

TWYFORDS, Limited, of Cliffe Vale Potteries, Hanley, have an exhibit of considerable importance and interest. One notices the beautiful design of their "Bidet" closet, which in compact form comprises all the arrangements for spray, douche and thorough flushing; their "Deluge" closet, too, well known to need description; the "Orion," a new feature in wash-down closets, made of a special kind of ware ("Vitrina"), for which they claim non-absorption, even should the surface glaze be in any way accidentally removed; the "Twyford," a syphonic closet for which it is claimed that it has the advantages of a large surface area of water, depth of seal, almost noiselessness in action, and particularly simplicity of construction and ease of fitting. A new bath shown is one of fireclay, with all the appearance of a first-class marble bath, but with the advantage over marble of being non-porous and practically undestructible. It is fitted for spray, douche or hand-douche, and its arrangements for hot and cold water are in most compact form. One notices particularly its handsome hand-douche appliance, the india-rubber tube being encased in a patent bright spiral metal covering, its large extended tray at the back, its mahogany inserted rim, and a ribbed bottom to do away with the possibility of accidents from slipping. The "Athena" dual lavatory is a neat arrangement of two basins on one slab of earthenware; and near it is the "Adamant" urinal, made in various styles and designs and in a great variety of marbled fireclay, with inlaid tile treads and concealed channel. A noticeable feature of the stand is a three-division sink, 6 ft. long by 2½ in., a

size very seldom attempted, owing to difficulties of manufacture. Here also are a hospital sink, consisting of slop-hopper and drains, with treadle action for hot and cold flushing purposes—a sink which has been adopted at the hospital in connection with the Birmingham Workhouse; combination hospital sinks, consisting of ordinary washing sink, with "Neros" standing waste fitting, spray for bed-pans and enlarged outlet; the "Beresford" butler's sink, consisting of double compartment sink for washing purposes, soap drawer, and receptacle for garbage to be retained and collected for burning, and with the firm's patent "Inserta"—an inserted wooden rim to prevent chipping; a surgical instrument sink, a most useful appliance for washing surgical implements; the "C.V." lavatory range, marbled with the new design of marbling; and the "Athena Neros" range of three lavatory basins. Space will permit us to notice only one more of the many exhibits—the "Inserta" combination closet, an ingenious adaptation of wood to the rim so as to avoid risk of fouling or of destruction of the usual seat arrangement. This is the closet which has been adopted by the Manchester Corporation for their municipal lodging-houses.

The PENDLETON SANITARY ENGINEERING COMPANY, of Pendleton, Manchester, have erected an elaborate red-brick wall to show the working of Dr. Quine's sanitary ash-bin; Messrs. ROWE BROTHERS & Co., of the City Lead Works, Manchester, have on view specimens of lead manufactures; and Messrs. EVERED & Co., of London, Birmingham and Smethwick, show closets, flushing-tanks and plumber's brass work of considerable merit.

Messrs. ADAMS & Co., of York, Leeds, London, Birmingham and other places, are the occupants of the next stall. The new ware, "Titanite," manufactured by this firm, has a beautiful appearance and should find favour. It is composed of a new mixture of clays, which are claimed to give the strength of fire-clay with the finish of queen's ware. Lavatories, slep-sinks and closets are all shown in this ware. The hospital closet is especially designed for this work, and, combined with enamelled iron-casing for flush pipe on a special cistern, is particularly useful for asylum work, where it is desirable that no projection or ledges should be visible. The Adams insular multiple closets are for school and factory use, a great improvement on the old latrine and trough closet. Other fittings are surgeon's lavatory and a slop-sink, with drainer and water jet for cleansing bed-pans for hospitals and infirmaries; and two special types of urinals. One special feature is the Adams new improved disconnecting syphoned trap, which has the eye for inspection in a direct line with the drain, and thus gives greater facility for rodding and enables it to be used as a lamp-eye as well. Besides these advantages, the trap itself has its outlet much nearer the inlet than in the ordinary type, and it is thus easily reached, by hand from the inspection chamber. The Adams patent sewage lift is shown in operation. This apparatus is now widely known in this country and abroad for its ingenious adaptation to the raising of low-lying sewage to any desired level. Where available the high-level sewage in the same district can be used by means of this apparatus to raise the low-level sewage. In other cases clean water may be used to do the work in such a way that this water may be afterwards applied to other purposes, so that whether sewage or water is used to give the power required, the first cost of the apparatus is, in nearly all cases, the only cost, there being no outlay whatever for maintenance and repairs. These sewage lifts already installed in actual works (some for four and five years now) are giving every satisfaction, and can be inspected on application to Adams' Patent Sewage Lift Company at York.

Passing on to the exhibit of Messrs. GEORGE SKEY & Co., Limited, of Tamworth, there will be found an array of closets, drain pipes, damp-proof courses, chimney tops, sinks and other useful appliances, most of them well tried and appreciated; while adjoining are the shows of Messrs. SUTTON & Co., of Overseal, near Ashby-de-la-Zouch, who exhibit their selected salt-glazed stoneware pipes, bends, junctions, channels and other connections, their street and other gulleys, and a well-chosen variety of their other appliances; and of DAY'S AUTOMATIC WASTE-WATER CLOSET Co., Limited, whose chief feature is the well-known "Stafford" automatic waste-water closet.

The following is the full list of awards:—

*Silver Medals.*

Adams' Automatic Sewage Lift.—Adams & Co., Birmingham.
Jaeger Woollen Underclothing.—Allports, 21 and 23 Colmore-row, Birmingham.
Case for Water Analysis and Chemicals in Soloids for Water Analysis.—Burroughs, Welcome & Co., Snow-hill Buildings, London, E.C.
Compressed Chemical Substances.—Burroughs, Welcome & Co., Snow-hill Buildings, London, E.C.
Products of Coal Tar and Ammoniacal Liquor.—Burt, Boulton & Haywood, Limited, 64 Cannon-street, London, E.C.
Coeum.—Cadbury Brothers, Bournville, near Birmingham.
Pure Carbolic Acid. F. C. Culvert & Co., Bradford, Manchester.
Enamelled Cast Iron. The Cannon Hollow-Ware Company, Bilston, Staffs.
Pastour Chamberland Filter.—J. Defries & Sons, Limited, 147 Houndsditch, London, E.C.

Equifex Pressure Disinfecting Apparatus.—J. Defries & Sons, Limited, 147 Houndsditch, London, E.C.

"Fryston" Range.—Ferrybridge Foundry Company, Ferrybridge, Yorks.

Pure Cocoa.—J. S. Fry & Sons, Limited, Union-street, Bristol.

Shone's Hydro-Pneumatic Ejector.—Hughes & Lancaster, 47 Victoria-street, London, S.W.

Automatic Water Steriliser.—Maiche, Limited, 4 St. Mary-axe, London, E.C.,

Mercury Gas Governor.—J. Stott & Co., Vernon Works, Oldham.

Vaillard Desmaroux Water Steriliser.—Jas. E. Webb, 52 Queen Victoria-street, London, E.C.

Brougham Ambulance.—Wilson & Stockhall, County Ambulance Works, Bury, Lancashire.

Accident Ambulance.—Wilson & Stockall, County Ambulance Works, Bury, Lancashire.

*Bronze Medals.*

Adamant Plaster for Walls and Ceilings.—The Adamant Company, Limited, 6 Commercial-street, Birmingham.

Wedge Disc Valve.—Adams & Co., Birmingham.

Method of Aërating Water by Means of Compressed Carbon Dioxide.—Aërators, Limited, Broad Street-avenue, London, E.C.

Simplex Cinder-sifter. — Arkinstall Brothers, Milk-street, Birmingham.

Liquid Sulphur Dioxide for Disinfection.—A. Boake Roberts & Co., Limited, Stratford, London, E.

Petanelle Fabrics.—Brion, Pate, Burke & Co., 15 Walbrook, London, E.C.

Expanding Drain Stopper.—Burn Brothers, 23 Charing-cross, London, S.W.

Rapid Mixer for Liquids.—Burt, Boulton & Haywood, Limited, 64 Cannon-street, London, E.C.

Callender Pure Bitumen for Linings.—Callender & Montgomery, 11 Victoria-street, London, S.W.

"Perfect" Straining Cover for Cooking Utensils. — The Cannon Hollow-Ware Company, Limited, Bilston, Staffs.

The "Chef" Gas-cooker.— The Cannon Hollow-Ware Company, Limited, Bilston, Staffs.

Aërated Waters.— Chemists' Aërated and Mineral Water Associations, Limited, The Rock Spring Works, Cheston-road, Aston, Birmingham.

Whitehead's Automatic Taps for Drawing off Liquids.—Clark's "Optimus" Coffee Company, Queens-road, South Lambeth, London, S.W.

Automatic Gas-Stove.—Davis Gas-Stove Company, Limited, Camberwell, London, S.E.

Low-pressure Ventilating Radiator.—A. R. Dean, Limited, Corporation-street, Birmingham.

Fibrous Plaster.—A. R. Dean, Limited, Corporation-street, Birmingham.

Louvre Air Bricks.—J. Duckett & Sons, Limited, Burnley, Lancashire.

Enamelled Glazed Urinals.—J. Duckett & Son, Limited, Burnley, Lancashire.

Jackson's Self-feeding Water-boiler. — Eclipse Brass and Copper Company, Limited, Harrison-road Works, Halifax.

The "Helliwell" System of Glazing.—Farrer, Barber & Co., 36 Cannon-street, Birmingham.

Combined Sink and Lavatory.—Farrer, Barber & Co., 36 Cannon-street, Birmingham.

Formalin.—Formalin Hygienic Company, 9 St. Mary-at-Hill, London, E.C.

Adaptation of the Braille System to Phonetic Reporting for the Blind.—General Institution for the Blind, Birmingham, Edgbaston, Birmingham.

New Rotary Watering-Van.—W. Glover & Sons, Limited, Eagle Works, Warwick.

Floor Channels, with Sockets for Waste Pipes.—W. Harriman & Co., Limited, Fenkle-street, Newcastle-on-Tyne.

Barron's Channel Bends made to pass a Drain Plug.—W. Harriman & Co., Limited, Fenkle-street, Newcastle-on-Tyne.

Biscuits.—A. Hughes, 88 Moor-street, Birmingham.

Hutching's Food-steamers.—G. J. Hutchings, 94 Clerkenwell-road, London, E.C.

Tube Wells.—C. Isler & Co., Bear-lane, Southwark, London, S.E.

Jeyes' Fluid.—Jeyes' Sanitary Compounds Company, Limited, 64 Cannon-street, London, E.C.

Reversible Window with Lines and Weights.— Jones James, 317 Albert-road, Aston, Birmingham.

Paragon Washer, Wringer and Mangle.— E. N. Kenworthy & Co., Alpha Works, Oldham.

"Equipoise" Wringer and Mangle.—E. N. Kenworthy & Co., Alpha Works, Oldham.

Chinosol.—Bernard Kuhn, 36 St. Mary-at-Hill, London, E.C.

Wall Decorations in Leeds Faience.—Leeds Art Pottery and Tile Company, Leathley-road, Leeds.

Willesden Paper.—C. A. Line, Burlington Chambers, New-street, Birmingham.

Tynecastle Canvas.—C. A. Line, Burlington Chambers, New-street Birmingham.

Mellin's Food for Invalids.—Mellin's Food Company, Limited, Peckham, London, S.E.

Boiler Bath.—Mould's Patent Boiler Bath Company, 3 Union-passage, Birmingham.

Izal.—Newton Chambers & Co., Thorncliffe, Sheffield.

Glazed Stoneware Manger.—Oates & Green, Limited, Halifax.

Salt-glazed Wash-Tub and Rubber Combined. — Oates & Green, Limited, Halifax.

Jones' Combination Bath.—Parker, Winder & Achurch, Limited, Broad-street, Birmingham.

Ventilated Hot Closet for Eagle Stove.—Parker, Winder & Achurch, Limited, Broad-street, Birmingham.

Penny-in-the-Slot Prepayment Gas-meter.—W. Parkinson & Co., Bell Barn-road, Birmingham.

Dr. Quine's Ash-Bin.—Pendleton Sanitary Engineering Company, Leaf-square, Pendleton, Manchester.

Thermometer for Hospital Wards.—W. W. Rolston, 120 Pope-street, Albion-street, Birmingham.

Lead Pipe made in any Length.—Rowe, Brothers & Co., City Lead Works, Clement-street, Birmingham.

Water-Closet Ventilating Fan Worked by High-pressure Supply to Flushing Cistern.—Sanitary Ventilating Syndicate, 40 Lower Ormond-quay, Dublin.

Aërated Waters.—Schweppes, Limited, Colwall, Malvern.

Perfecto Lavatory.—Shanks & Co., Barrhead, N.B.

Perfecto Bath.—Shanks & Co., Barrhead, N.B.

"Duresco."— Silicate Paint Company, Limited, Charlton, London, S.E.

Aërated Waters Prepared from Distilled Water.—Southall Brothers & Barclay, Lower Priory, Birmingham.

Steam Tip-Waggon.—Steam Carriage and Waggon Company, Homefield, Chiswick.

Hydraulic Ram with Valve.—Stocks, Sons & Taylor, Berkeley-street, Birmingham.

Improved "Challenge" Ironing Machine.—Summerscales & Co., Phœnix Foundry, Keighley, Yorks.

Washing Machine for Disinfecting under Steam-pressure.— Summerscales & Co., Phœnix Foundry, Keighley, Yorks.

Green's Wyvurst Channels and Inlets for Manholes.—Sutton & Co., Union Pottery, Overseal, near Ashby-de-la-Zouch.

"Axis" Water-Closet, with screw brass joint.—Twyfords, Limited, Hanley.

Triple Vegetable-Sink.—Twyfords, Limited, Hanley.

"Ideal" Sink in two compartments.—Twyfords, Limited, Hanley.

Chloros.—United Alkali Company, Limited, Gaskell and Deacon Works, Widnes.

Concentrated Vimbos.—Vimbos, Limited, 130 Queen Victoria-street, London, E.C.

"Whitely" Exerciser.—Whitely Health Exerciser, Limited, 29 Maltby-street, Bermondsey, London, S.E.

*Deferred for Practical Trial.*

Automatic Flushing-Tank.—Wm. Thomas Allen, Whitehouse-street, Aston-road, Birmingham.

"Acme" Ventilator.—T. Ash & Co., 37 Cannon-street, Birmingham.

Eureka Lead Waterpipe.—A. Barraclough & Co., Limited, Eureka Lead Works, Heckmondwike.

Steam Heater for Hot-Water Warming and Supply.—Burn Brothers, 23 Charing Cross, London, S.W.

A Court and Binny's System of Hot-Water Warming and Supply.—Burn Brothers, 23 Charing Cross, London, S.W.

Automatic Grease-flusher.—J. Duckett & Son, Limited, Burnley, Lancs.

Automatic Syphon-Cistern. — J Duckett & Son, Limited, Burnley, Lancs.

Automatic Flushing-Tank.—Evered & Co., Limited, 27 Drury-lane, London, W.C.

Automatic Flushing-Tank.—Farrer, Barber & Co., 36 Cannon-street, Birmingham.

Fischer System of Water Filtration.—Hughes & Lancaster, 47 Victoria-street, London, S.W.

Duplex Supply and Sanitary Waste-Valve.—George Jennings Palace-road, Lambeth, London, S.E.

"Viking" Condensed Milk.—Fred Lomax, 27 Freeman-street, Birmingham.

Chimney Pot.—Mansfield Patents Company, Queen-street Chambers, Mansfield, Notts.

Mansfield Ventilator.—Mansfield Patents Company, Queen-street Chambers, Mansfield, Notts.

Pullen's "Scorcher" Paint-Lamp.—Martineau, Beames & Madeley, Holloway Head, Birmingham.

"Victoria" Ventilator.—Parker, Winder & Achurch, Limited, Broad-street, Birmingham.

"Empress" Ventilator.—Parker, Winder & Achurch, Limited, Broad-street, Birmingham.

"Standard" Ventilator.—Parker, Winder & Achurch, Limited, Broad-street, Birmingham.

Zinc Roofing.—Plant & Co., 66 Dale-end, Birmingham.

"Proteus" Food.—Protene Company, Limited, 36 Welbeck-street, London, W.

"Septic" Tank.—"Septic" Tank Syndicate, 7 Bedford-circus, Exeter.

Non-concussion Taps.—Shanks & Co., Barrhead, N.B.

Spiralvent Chimney Top.—G. Skey & Co., Wilnecote Works, Tamworth.

Sterilite Filters.—Sterilite Filter Company, 15 Haymarket-street, Bury.

Quarries for Heating Drying-Sheds.—Sutton & Co., Union Pottery, Overseal, near Ashby-de-la-Zouch.

"Twycliff" Syphon Closet.—Twyfords, Limited, Hanley.

"Excel" Silver.—J. E. Webb, 52 Queen Victoria-street, London, E.C.

In our next issue we shall continue our report of the general proceedings of the congress, selecting, in accordance with our usual custom, the papers and discussions in which our readers are likely to be interested. We shall also conclude our notice of the exhibits.

## MUNICIPAL OFFICERS' ASSOCIATION.

### THE QUESTION OF SUPERANNUATION.

In our last issue we made a brief reference to the joint report of the chairman and secretary of the Municipal Officers' Association in regard to the superannuation conference convened by that body. The following is the text of the report:

In continuation of the report presented last year we regret being unable to place on record the passing of the Local Authorities Officers' Superannuation Bill. The conference, at its meeting, held at 117 Holborn, on the 4th November, 1897, decided to re-introduce the Bill again in Parliament in the session of 1898, and to ask the delegates to approach members of Parliament with the view of getting promises for the ballot. A number of members balloted, but, unfortunately, none were successful in obtaining a good place.

Sir H. Seymour King, K.C.I.E., very kindly undertook the charge of the measure, which was read a first time on February 22, 1898, and was put down for second reading on April 5th, 13th, 19th, May, 17th, 18th, and finally on June 17th; but, finding that it was hopeless to proceed further, the measure was then dropped. At the same meeting Mr. C. William Tagg was appointed to take charge of the Bill on behalf of the conference, and Mr. C. J. F. Carnell, hon. secretary, and the associations and societies represented on the conference, were asked to subscribe £10 each towards the expenses. The question of the introduction of other Bills was very fully gone into, and a committee of four—viz., Messrs. C. W. Tagg, Dr. Dudfield, Geo. Chaloner, and C. J. F. Carnell—was appointed to confer with other associations and societies (who might be contemplating such action) as to the best method of bringing the passing of the Bill to a successful issue.

The Metropolitan Local Government (Officers') Association, on being informed of the appointment of this committee, wrote a letter stating that a special meeting would be held on January 17, 1898, to confer with it. Messrs. Dudfield, Geo. Chaloner and C. J. F. Carnell attended. As a result of this interview a letter was received from the Metropolitan Local Government Officers' Association expressing the hope that in the interest of the two Bills all reference to the officers to whom the Superannuation Act, 1866, applies should be omitted from the Conference Bill. This letter was submitted to the conference on January 24th, and the following resolution was passed:—

"That this conference, representing every section of municipal officers throughout the country, cannot see its way to omit from the Conference Bill all reference to the officers to whom the Superannuation Act, 1866, applies, and that it sees no reason why the two Bills should not be introduced side by side; moreover, the Bill promoted by the Metropolitan Local Government Officers' Association is deemed to be unsatisfactory, inasmuch as officers are unable to count their years of service from one local authority to another."

They were also informed that the conference would be prepared to give all possible support to the measure, feeling sure that their association would reciprocate the kindly feeling, and if both Bills passed a second reading and were referred to the same committee, arrangements would doubtless be made to meet the necessities of the case and to prevent clashing of interests.

## THE DRAINAGE OF NEWHAVEN.

The following extract is taken from *The East Sussex News.* We understand that the sewer in question is about a mile long, and was laid twelve years ago by a contractor without proper supervision. The extract is as follows: The Newhaven Urban District Council have received a report from their surveyor (Mr. F. J. Rayner) which caused them great anxiety. It is in reference to the main sewer from Elphick-road to the culvert, and the information contained in the document will be found to be of a very startling character. This particularly refers to the portions from Haggett's Barn to Essex-place, from Bishopstone-terrace to Sea View House, and from Messrs. Colgate & Gray's office near the cricket ground to the pond, as in each instance the fall is the wrong way, while two other lengths are reported as being dead level—viz., from the Bridge Hotel to the Ship Hotel and from 74 to 73 Chapel-street. There is an insufficient fall in four cases, the incline varying from 1 in 375 from the river bank to the Bridge Hotel, to 1 in 1,372 from the coastguard station

to Messrs. Coalgate's offices, while the portions from 73 Chapel-street to Bishopstone-terrace and from Sussex-place to 74 Chapel-street are even worse, the fall in one case being 1 in 6,500 and in the other 1 in 8,450. The only satisfactory feature of the report is the last item, in regard to the sewer from the ventilator to the culvert, which is spoken of as good, the inclination being 1 in 56. To summarise the results arrived at it may be mentioned that three portions fall the wrong way, three are spoken of as having an insufficient fall, two as being dead level, four as being fair, one as being bad, four as being very bad, and one as being good. The obvious inference is that nearly the whole of the main sewer from Elphick-road to the culvert will have to be taken up and relaid, and the ratepayers may therefore rest assured that their contributions towards the cost of local government will not decrease at present. However, they will be able to console themselves with the fact that even a high rate is preferable to periodical outbreaks of infectious disease, and that there will be such outbreaks no doubt as long as sewage is expected to run uphill.

## NEW PUBLIC BUILDINGS AT WEST HAM.

Mr. J. Passmore Edwards yesterday opened a new technical institute and central free public library erected by the West Ham Corporation. He also laid the foundation-stone of a natural history museum, which will be built close by. The new buildings, which stand at the corner of Romford-road and Water-lane, Stratford, are in the form of a large quadrangle. The technical institute has its main front and entrance in the Romford-road, its upper floor extending over the library premises in Water-lane. It is in what may be called a free Renaissance style, the exterior being of Portland stone and red brick. The design of the interior is throughout utilitarian. In the large hall lectures will be given and examinations held. The hall may be let for purposes which will not interfere with the work of the institute. Every department is well equipped, special attention being paid to the chemical laboratories and the engineering workshops. The institute will be wholly under the control of the municipality, and will be financed from municipal sources. The buildings have cost £45,000, and a further £15,000 has been spent on equipment and fittings. The new central library is wholly on the ground floor, and is fitted with all the modern appliances of such institutions. The reading-room is 110 ft. long by 30 ft. wide. It is surrounded with a tiled dado embellished with literary maxims in an ornamental border. The cost of the building has been between £8,000 and £9,000, and about £4,000 has been spent on the furniture and fittings. Messrs. Gibson & Russell were the architects of the buildings. The whole of the buildings will be lighted by electricity supplied from the corporation mains.

## QUERIES AND REPLIES.

*Sketches accompanying Queries should be made separate on white paper, in plain black-ink lines. Lettering or figures should be bold and plain.*

**213. Sewage Disposal : Triplicate Treatment.**—"A.C." writes : Can you or any of your readers inform me of cases in this country where town sewage is subjected to the combined treatment of chemical precipitation, artificial filtration and land filtration ?

We are not aware of any instance where sewage is treated on the triplicate system, such as that referred to by our correspondent. We believe that at Sutton (Surrey), Wimbledon, Friern Barnet and one or two other places in the south the several systems may be seen at work side by side, portions of the sewage being precipitated in settling tanks, and the topwater drawn off and treated on fine grain artificial filters or on land, according as one or the other may be ready to receive it, while another portion is treated on coarse-grain bacteria filters, the filtrate being further treated on fine-grain bacteria filters or on land. But we do not know of any town which in practice treats its sewage on the lines named by the querist. Perhaps some of our correspondents will be able to assist us with information which may be useful to our correspondent.

**Street-watering in London.**—Mr. Henry C. Jones, clerk to the Board of Works for the St. Giles district, has addressed the following letter to *The Times* : "In your issue of the 29th ult., "C. F. M." suggests that the practice of watering the gutters of the carriageway pavements should be discontinued, on the ground that very serious inconvenience ensues to the riders in cabs and drivers of vehicles in consequence of this partial watering. May I claim a brief space in your issue to say that this course was suggested by Sir E. R. C. Bradford, Chief Commissioner of Police of the metropolis, in a circular which he issued to local authorities so recently as August 24th last, as he attached great importance to this work being carried out in the way now complained of, as it was found that the practice which had largely hitherto obtained of watering led to accidents ?"

# Comparative Reports of General Practice.

## XXIX.—ELECTRIC LIGHTING : BECKENHAM REPORT.—I.

Mr. John A. Angell, engineer and surveyor to the Beckenham Urban District Council, not long ago submitted to that body a preliminary report on the proposed electric lighting of the district. After pointing out that a provisional order was obtained in 1890, and that in 1893 a report on the subject was presented by Mr. Gisbert Kapp, the report proceeds as follows:—

THE MUNICIPALISATION OF ELECTRIC LIGHTING.

Until within recent years it was the usual practice of local authorities to favour the undertaking of electric lighting by private companies. Latterly, however, public opinion has changed, so that, whilst formerly the majority of undertakings were private companies, in the year 1896 only fifty-nine companies existed, as compared with seventy-four municipal undertakings. Again, in 1890, out of fifty-seven provisional orders applied for one-fourth only were granted to local authorities, whilst in 1896 twenty-seven out of a total of thirty provisional orders were taken up by local authorities. During the present year over thirty local authorities have applied to the Board of Trade for provisional orders.

The loans raised by local authorities, on the sanction of the Local Government Board, for electric lighting have also steadily increased during recent years, thus: In 1890-91 the loans sanctioned amounted to £10,000; in 1891-92, £101,000; 1892-93, £115,000; 1893-94, £572,000; 1894-05, £560,000; and in 1895-96, £796,500. During 1896 loans were raised by forty local authorities, the maximum period allowed by the Local Government Board for repayment being (with one exception) twenty-five years.

Among other more or less cogent reasons in favour of municipalisation are: That (1) the creation of a monopoly (certain to be profitable in the *future*, though not in the immediate present) is prevented. (2) Greater confidence is felt and greater public support obtained. (3) A heavy cost is involved in buying out a private company prior to the termination of the statutory period.* (4) Public street lighting should be in the hands of local authority. (5) The capital cost is raised on easier terms by a local authority.

There is, perhaps, but little force in the latter contention (No. 5), inasmuch as a local authority must from the outset pay annual instalments of sinking fund and interest (equivalent approximately to 6 per cent.† on the total amount of the loan) out of revenue, or, in default, out of public rates. Whilst admitting that in the earlier years deficits are almost inherent to the undertaking,‡ yet the prevention of a monopoly would in itself seem to be all-important, and, in the light of present experience (especially in relation to water and telephones), an imperative duty on the present generation. Indeed, as to the wisdom of municipalisation, there appears to be no *doubt*, inasmuch as, whilst the deficits of early years will probably represent a less burden on the rates than the subsequent cost of buying out a private company, ultimately, under proper management, all such undertakings cannot be otherwise than profitable. The policy, therefore, of leasing to a private company for a term of years the rights of supply does not appear to me to recommend itself.

As to whether a local authority shall of its own initiative enter upon an undertaking purely on its own merits, and in advance of suggested competition by a private company, is, of course, a matter for consideration, the determining factors

being public feeling, character and needs of the districts, and probability or otherwise of early success.

In the matter of electric lighting, as in most other things, Beckenham presents features special to itself. Its large area, unusually scattered houses, distance apart, great depth of front gardens, prevalent leasehold system, migratory habits of its residents and consequent diminished interest in local affairs, long summer and winter vacations, absence of any convenient central site for the generating station, represent disadvantages. On the other hand, the wide roads, bordered with trees, lend themselves effectively to street lighting from the centre of the road; laying of cables, &c., is facilitated by gravel paths or margins; and high-class residences are precisely those from which demand is likely to be active. Absence of many shops is no grave disadvantage, for, although a fair proportion of shops to houses is preferable, shop supply in itself is brief and heavy and to that extent unremunerative.

Whilst the growth of incandescent gas lighting during the past four or five years has checked and probably will continue to check the development of electric lighting generally, Beckenham has neither more nor less to fear in this respect than other districts. In my opinion the time is approaching when gas companies will of their own initiative substitute incandescent gas for ordinary street lighting.

Speaking generally, metropolitan suburbs, such as Beckenham, do not present such favourable conditions of success as provincial towns, partly owing to the less migratory habits of their inhabitants, and partly to the fact that local energy, enterprise and initiative is more concentrated on local concerns in such self-contained centres.

The sanitary and economic advantages of electric light do not require emphasising. The non-consumption of air and absence of impure waste products of combustion are important recommendations. A very considerable saving (not sufficiently appreciated by the public generally) is also effected in whitewashing and cleansing walls, ceilings, re-papering, re-decoration, renewing delicate fabrics, &c. The comparative immunity from fire afforded by electric light is also a point in its favour.

The street lighting also, if effectively done, presents a very attractive feature, serving not only to advertise the light, but tending to attract residents to the district, and when here to induce them to stay, inasmuch as but few persons will by choice quit a brilliantly-lighted, and consequently cheerful, district for one in which comparatively depressing feeble yellow gaslight prevails.

In considering the financial, as distinct from the technical, aspect of municipalising electric light three considerations present themselves—*viz.*:—

(1) Capital cost.
(2) Working expenses (including repayment of loan).
(3) Revenue.

Capital cost can be determined with a fair degree of accuracy; even if somewhat under-estimated, the comparatively small increased repayments do not materially affect the prosperity of the scheme. Estimates of both working expenses and revenue are merely conjectural, especially so in respect to revenue, based as it is on a supposititious rate. Nevertheless, says Mr. Angell in concluding this part of his report, as on revenue depends the success of the undertaking, some effort should be made to determine possibilities.

MR. GISBERT KAPP'S REPORT.

In referring to Mr. Kapp's report Mr. Angell tells us that, for the purposes of estimates, he divided the scheme into two stages, the first stage comprising compulsory streets and streets down which the mains must necessarily pass to reach these latter, and the second stage, streets in which a supply will *eventually* be required. Mr. Angell, however, has submitted new proposals, under which the scheme may be divided into three stages, each stage working progressively outwards from the generating station in Arthur-road, and including on its way (where deemed advisable) all minor streets. It is not considered that the operations in any one stage need necessarily await the completion of the previous stage or stages. On the contrary, it is held that the principal cables once laid in stage No. 1, as indicated in the schedule which forms Appendix II. of the report, subsequent stages and minor streets could be dealt with wholly or partially as riper experience might determine. Stages Nos. 1 and 3, it is thought, might be carried out, in whole or in part, at one and the same time.

Having thus created two stages of lighting, Mr. Kapp estimated that in each stage respectively one-fourth and one-half of the total number of houses would take current, and he further assumed that the first stage (one house in four) would take supply *shortly*, and the second stage (one house in two) be reached in from *three to five years*. Mr. Angell, however, is of opinion that two or three years of deficit must elapse before one house in four is supplied, and that it is doubtful whether any electric lighting scheme in this country has arrived at the second stage (one house in two) even after

---

* Under the Electric Lighting Act, 1888, sec. 2, the council may, by compulsory purchase, acquire an electric light undertaking after the expiration of forty-two years, or thereafter at subsequent intervals of ten years, at the then fair market value, without addition for compulsory sale, goodwill or profits.

At Bromley the provisional order has been transferred to a private company for the statutory period of forty-two years, under agreement for re-transfer to, and at the option of, the council on the following terms—*viz.*, Purchase price after seven years from date of transfer 20 per cent. above capital expended (less depreciation), after fourteen years 16 per cent. twenty-one years, 12 per cent., twenty-eight years 8 per cent., thirty-five years 4 per cent. Assuming Beckenham to adopt the same course, purchasing, say, after fourteen years, the comparative financial results of the two modes of working, by (*a*) company, (*b*) local authority, would be approximately as follows:—

I. COMPANY.

| | | £ | £ |
|---|---|---|---|
| For compulsory purchase of Stage I. by local authority after, say, fourteen years, 16 per cent. on capital cost (£20,000) ... ... ... ... | | | 3,200 |

II. LOCAL AUTHORITY.

| | | £ | £ |
|---|---|---|---|
| Aggregate deficits (Appendix I.) of first three years of working ... ... ... ... | | 2,000 | |
| Balance in favour of council as undertakers ... ... | | 300 | |
| Annual profits for eleven years, at £500 per annum ... | | 5,500 | |
| Balance in favour of council on fourteen years' working | | | £5,800 |

This amount, £5,800, would therefore represent the estimated loss to the council during the fourteen years if the provisional order were transferred to a private company.

(In connection with this footnote Mr. Angell points out that computation of annual profits for eleven years at £500 a year is a low estimate, being the probable profit of the fourth year, which amount would increase year by year.)

† As the Local Government Board would probably not extend the repayments of loan beyond twenty-five years.

‡ Brighton and Tunbridge Wells are exceptions, no call whatever having been made on the rates.

several years of existence. He points out that, in the case of the Crystal Palace District Electric Supply Company, out of 140 houses in the Beckenham district only nineteen, or one in seven, have taken current, although available for ever five years. It is admitted, however, that better results may be obtained where the local authorities are undertakers.

AMENDED ESTIMATES, CHARGE PER UNIT, AND REVENUE PER LAMP.

Mr. Angell has accordingly prepared the following amended estimates of the capital cost of the combined installation, indicating what to him appears to be the reasonable probabilities of the case. These estimates do not include supply to secondary streets, which, says Mr. Angell, must be dealt with gradually, as the success of the scheme warrants.

| | No. of Houses. | Length of Mains. Miles. | Estimated Cost. |
|---|---|---|---|
| District No. 1 | 796 | $6\frac{1}{2}$ | £21,000* |
| " " 2 | 232 | $5\frac{1}{2}$ | 9,000 |
| " " 3 | 376 | $2\frac{3}{4}$ | 6,000 |
| | 1,404 | $14\frac{3}{4}$ | £36,000* |

The estimated cost of stage I. is higher than that of Mr. Kapp, as it includes (1) the cost of a dust destructor and (2) the cost of a generating station large enough to preclude the necessity of extension for the second stage of development. In an appendix Mr. Angell has endeavoured to indicate the approximate financial development of stage I., the cost of each scheme being dealt with separately. As the dust destructor alone involves an average annual cost of £600, this is not placed to the debit account of the electric lighting installation. Mr. Kapp's estimates were based on an assumed revenue of 8s. 4d. per 10 candle-power lamp. The following table indicates the average charge per unit and revenue per lamp in seventy-nine towns :—

| | Average Charge per Unit. | Average Revenue per Lamp. |
|---|---|---|
| Local Authorities— | | |
| 3 Metropolitan | $6\frac{1}{3}$d. | 11s. 4d. |
| 42 Provincial... | $5\frac{3}{4}$ | 6 $5\frac{3}{4}$ |
| Private Companies— | | |
| 24 Metropolitan | $6\frac{1}{2}$ | 8 6 |
| 10 Provincial... | $6\frac{3}{4}$ | 7 7 |

The highest revenue per 8 candle-power lamp is 17s. 3d. (Islington), and the lowest 3s. 7d. (Kelvinside). In Mr. Angell's amended estimate the revenue per 8 candle-power lamp has been taken at 7s. 6d. The report then proceeds as follows :—

CHARGE TO CONSUMERS.

Returns from the whole of the provincial installations (local authorities and companies) indicate that the maximum charge per unit is 9d., the minimum $4\frac{1}{2}$d., and the average 6d., the maximum charge (9d.) occurring once only (*viz.*, at Hastings). The Crystal Palace District Electric Supply Company charge from $6\frac{1}{2}$d. to 7d. per unit. Usually, also, a material reduction in price is made after a given number of hours' consumption per term (determined by Wright's indicator, recording the maximum number of lamps lighted simultaneously during the said period). Mr. Kapp's proposed charge of 8d. per unit is therefore considerably above the average price throughout the country.

The equivalent cost of current at 8d. per unit is from 4s. 8d. to 5s. 4d. per 1,000 cubic feet of gas—(*viz.*, from seven to eight times the cost per unit). Electric light, therefore, presents no *pecuniary* advantages (except as previously indicated), nor can it be said that fewer 16 candle-power electric glow lights are usually used than 5 cubic feet gas-burners. On the other hand, the greater facility for turning off current affords opportunity (more especially in the lighting of bedrooms and cellars) for a *considerable* reduction in consumption.

The supply of current at day time for heating, lighting, &c., purposes, at a low charge (2d. or 3d. per unit), would probably be appreciated by householders and would prove a source of profit to the council. As such a high charge as 8d. per unit would seriously discourage possible consumers, and so prolong the years of loss, Mr. Angell considers that the lowest possible price should be fixed, say, at the outset not exceeding 7d. per unit. In this connection, he says, the economic effect of a combined scheme of electric lighting and dust destruction has a bearing. Mr. Angell then proceeds to deal as follows with the subject of

DUST DESTRUCTION.

Whilst it is, of course, possible to determine experimentally the exact thermal equivalent of any given *sample* of refuse, the determination of its calorific value on a large scale is a much more difficult matter, and, as yet, but little practical knowledge or experience exists on the subject. Although in the case of Shoreditch† no accounts have yet been published nor exact results obtained, it would appear from the six months' practical working that 7 tons of refuse approximate in value 1 ton of coal. It is, however, stated that the refuse at Shoreditch is of an exceptionally favourable character due to the presence of large quantities of wood and shavings, the refuse of the staple industry (cabinet making). One very favourable feature certainly exists—*viz.*, that, owing to the *daily* house-to-house collection, the refuse is received at the works in a dry condition, not wet or damp as in districts where weekly collections prevail. Taking a less favourable view, therefore, of the value of the Beckenham refuse (although also supposed to be of a more than usually valuable character), and accepting 14 tons refuse (in lieu of 7) as the equivalent of 1 ton coal, the economic effect (provided, of course, that thermal storage be effected during day) would be approximately as follows :—

In the earlier period of the first stage coal, practically, could be entirely dispensed with. As this stage progressed, however, and the second stage became operative, the refuse would prove insufficient in quantity (its increase in bulk not keeping pace with demand for current), and coal or coke would be requisite, the coal account then being reduced to the extent of about 500 tons per annum (*viz.*, the assumed equivalent of 7,000 tons of refuse). The cost of current in the earlier stages of the combined scheme may therefore be reduced by $\frac{3}{4}$d. per unit (*viz.*, the average cost of coal per unit of current generated in the case of forty-two electric light stations), the reduction in later stages being somewhat less. This economy, together with that due to the combined scheme in respect to (*a*) the provision of a common chimney shaft and boiler-house, and (*b*) the reduced working expenses of either scheme in respect to stokers' wages, &c., should enable the council to supply consumers at 7d.* per unit, without decrease of revenue, in lieu of 8d. as proposed by Mr. Kapp.

Of course the saving thus effected might be carried towards reducing the annual deficits of the earlier years rather than to lower the charge to consumers. In my opinion, however, such a course is not desirable. The aim of the council should be directed rather towards lowering price as far as possible, bearing in mind that, whilst high charges deter, a reasonable scale encourages consumers to *immediate* demands for supply, and that popularisation of the light is the surest means of decreasing the number of lean and hastening the advent of fat years.

It may be suggested that the value of house refuse as a fuel, and the economic effects of a combined scheme generally, have been underestimated. So little reliable data exists, however, as to the financial results of such schemes, that I have felt it desirable to err, if at all, in the direction of under- rather than over-stating possibilities.

Objection may be taken to a combined scheme on the grounds that refuse is an uncertain fuel and may lead to fluctuating light; also that dust and dirt must impair the efficiency of the electric plant. Whilst there is some force in both contentions, careful design and good management will no doubt obviate substantial evil. At any rate no difficultice are complained of at Shoreditch. If fuel is to be *purchased*, admittedly the best is cheapest. Where, however, fuel in the shape of house refuse *is* available, unless more potent objections than those already forthcoming are discovered its use as an economical factor in the generation of electric light is, in my opinion, more than justifiable.

In the few cases where dust destructors, not originally intended as a means of generating electricity (and not therefore specially designed for the purpose) have been so utilised, the results have not been very satisfactory, St. Pancras being a case in point. Much of this ineffectiveness can doubtless, however, be avoided if due consideration be given in the original design to the ultimate *subsidiary* purpose of the destructor. Even thus, however, much of the constructional economy of a combined scheme would be lost. Combination, therefore, at the outset would be distinctly advantageous, if not opposed to more important considerations of policy.

* Inclusive of capital cost of dust destructor.

† As far as I can learn, says Mr. Angell in a footnote, Shoreditch, St. Pancras, and Oldham are the only places in which dust is at present actually being used as fuel. According to THE SURVEYOR, however, several other districts—*viz.*, Gloucester, Hackney, Fulham, Swansea, Ashton-under-Lyne, Pembroke, Weston-super-Mare and Llandudno are about to enter upon combined schemes.

* With sliding scale reduction of price after a certain consumption.

## REFRESHMENT KIOSKS IN CEMETERIES.

"These English are so practical." The French press is, says *The Pall Mall Gazette*, paying this compliment to the "parish council" of Battersea for having voted the erection of a refreshment kiosk in Battersea cemetery. "The conceptions of this council may," says *The Débats*, "be wanting in picturesqueness, but then they are so solid"—as solid as the refreshments which the contractors will supply, and fancifully called light. The dead must be remembered, and the living must not be forgotten; what, then, can be more natural than that the *placens uxor*, the bereaved heir, the son-in-law who mourns a mother-in-law, should comfort themselves after fulfilling the duties of piety? Sorrow in the cemetery must not be a hollow sorrow, and therefore the need of the kiosk. Near the great Paris cemeteries the funeral restaurants discharge the same office. They line the roads near the cemetery gates, sandwiched in between the monument men and the sellers of funeral flowers. They style themselves "A la Consolation," "A la Terre Promise," "A la Vue du Cimetière," with other cheering titles. But they have not yet found their way into consecrated ground. "Imagine," says *The Figaro*, "a brasserie in the middle of Père-Lachaise."

# Law Notes.

EDITED BY J. B. REIGNIER CONDER, 11 Old Jewry Chambers, E.C.,
Solicitor of the Supreme Court.

*The Editor will be pleased to answer any questions affecting the practice of engineers and surveyors to local authorities. Queries (which should be written legibly on foolscap paper, one side only) should be addressed to "The Law Editor," at the Offices of THE*

*SURVEYOR. Where possible, copies of local Acts or documents referred to should be enclosed. All explanatory diagrams must be drawn and lettered in black ink only. Correspondents who do not wish their names published should furnish a nom de plume.*

SEWER "MADE FOR PROFIT": PUBLIC HEALTH ACT, 1875, SECS. 13 AND 144: HIGHWAY ACT, 1835, SECS. 67 AND 68.—An interesting contribution to the cases relating to the definition of a "sewer" is afforded by the decision in *Croydale v. Sunbury-on-Thames Urban District Council* (Chancery Division, Mr. Justice Stirling). The plaintiff was the owner of a field on the west side of a road known as Green-street. The field slopes downward from the street, and then rises again. In the dip are two ponds. On the same side of Green-street was at one time an open ditch, from which there ran down a line of pipes, which discharged into one of the ponds. The end of this line of pipes next to the ditch was protected by a grating at a level of more than 2 ft. below the surface of the road, while the end next the pond projected to the extent of 6 in. or thereabouts. In December, 1896, the plaintiff, with a view to filling up the pond, removed the line of pipes so far as it existed on his land. Subsequently the council entered on the plaintiff's lands, and cut a trench between the ditch and the field, for the purpose of running off the surface water from Green-street. The present action was thereupon brought, claiming (1) a declaration that the defendants are not entitled without the leave or license of the plaintiff to draw the surface water from Green-street, or from any of the roads or streets in the parish of Sunbury-on-Thames, into the plaintiff's pond or land, or to lay down or make on the plaintiff's land or use any drain pipe or trench for any such purpose, and (2) an injunction. Mr. Justice Stirling, in giving judgment, said that the defendants justified their acts under (1) the powers conferred on them as the urban authority by the Public Health Act, 1875; (2) their powers as the highway authority under sec. 144 of that Act and the Highway Act, 1835. His lordship then referred to the evidence, and came to the conclusion that the line of pipes was laid down in 1858 or 1859 by the then tenant of the field for the purpose of getting a better supply of water for the use of cattle, and that subsequently the surveyors of highways from time to time caused the rubbish deposited on the grating at the ditch end of the pipes to be removed, but that it was not established that such surveyors repaired or even cleansed the pipes themselves. The first question was whether the defendants could justify what they had done under the powers conferred by the Public Health Act, 1875, secs. 13 to 17. It was established by *Durrant v. Branksome Urban District Council* (L.R., 1897, 2 ch., 291) that the sewers to which the Act applied include sewers for the removal of surface water. That being so, the pipes constituted a sewer within the definition contained in sec. 4. It was, however, contended by the plaintiff that they fell within the definition contained in sec. 13—viz., "sewers made by any person for his own profit." In *Minehead Local Board v. Luttrell* (L.R., 1894, 2 ch., 178) it was held that sewers constructed by a landowner for the use of persons by whom he was to be remunerated by a direct money payment for the use of them fell within the exception. The word "profit," however, was not, in his opinion, to be restricted to a direct money payment, *Ferrand v. Hallas Land and Building Company* (L.R., 1893, 2 Q.B., 135). When the object of making the sewer was neither for sanitary or ordinary drainage purposes, but to enable the land to be occupied more profitably, or to avoid an expenditure which would otherwise have to be incurred in order that the occupation might be equally beneficial, it seemed to him that the sewer was made for the profit of the occupier. Sec. 16 was referred to, but, whatever might be done hereafter, the defendants had not as yet brought themselves within its terms. So far as the evidence went no report was obtained from a surveyor, nor any notice given to the owners and occupiers. It was, then, to be considered whether the defendants derived any sanction for their acts from the Highway Act, 1835. The clauses relied on were secs. 67 and 68. The former authorised the highway authorities to "make, skour, cleanse and keep open all ditches, gutters, drains or watercourses, and also to make and lay .... trunks, tunnels, plats or bridges .... in and through any lands or grounds adjoining or lying near to any highway." That section, however widely it was construed, only authorised the making and keeping open of ditches and drains in and through lands adjoining a highway, and did not authorise the discharge of the contents of any ditch or drain on such lands. Unless, then, the pond could be treated as part of the drainage system under the control of the authorities, those sections did not empower the defendants to discharge the surface water into the plaintiff's pond, and the case of *Croft v. Rickmansworth Highway Board* ([1888] L.R. 39 ch., D. 272) shows that the pond could not be so regarded. In his judgment, therefore, this defence also failed the defendants. It was, lastly, contended that an injunction ought not to be granted, because the defendants

might thereafter put in force the powers conferred by sec. 16 of the Public Health Act, 1875. At present, however, they did not show that they were in a position to do so. Down to the present time they had been in the wrong. His lordship therefore made the declaration and granted the injunction asked for by the plaintiff.

PUBLIC HEALTH ACT, 1875, SEC. 16: CARRYING SEWER THROUGH PRIVATE LANDS: "REASONABLE NOTICE."—The above section, it will be remembered, empowers a local authority, "after giving reasonable notice in writing to the owner or occupier (if, on the report of the surveyor, it appears necessary)," to carry any sewer into, through or under any lands whatsoever in their district. In *Hutchings v. Seaford Urban District Council* (Chancery Division, 21st September), the plaintiff was the owner of an estate near Eastbourne, adjoining a high road, in which a sewer had recently been laid. Parallel with the high road there ran another road, known as Sutton-road, and a road called Hindover-road ran into it at an angle. All the land between the high road and Sutton-road was the plaintiff's property. A drainage scheme being in progress, it was desired to drain certain houses on the Hindover-road which were at present drained by a cesspool arrangement. On August 23, 1898, the defendants served the plaintiff with the following notice: "Take notice that the urban district council for the urban district of Seaford, in the county of Sussex, intend, under and by virtue of the powers in that behalf conferred upon them by the Public Health Act, 1875, to carry a sewer into, through or under certain lands in the district of which you are the owner—that is to say, across the lands situated between Sutton-road and Eastbourne-road, in the parish of Seaford, from points A and B as shown on the enclosed plan." On August 29th the defendants acted upon the notice by entering upon the plaintiff's land and commencing the works. The report made by the defendants' surveyor as to the necessity for carrying the sewer through the plaintiff's land was in the following terms: "The cesspool into which the houses in Hindover-road drain has again filled and requires emptying. I have had great difficulty in finding a place for the disposal of its contents, and have had to cart it nearly half a mile. I consider it very necessary that the property should be drained into the main system, which is now laid sufficiently far to connect in Sutton-road. The course should be across the fields into Sutton-road at right angles." It was submitted, on behalf of the plaintiff, that the notice, being only a five-day notice, was not a reasonable notice as required by the section; and, further, that the report made by the surveyor did not show that it appeared to be necessary that the sewer should be carried through the plaintiff's land. The report merely said that the course "should" be across the fields, not that it was necessary. *Lewis v. Weston-super-Mare Local Board* (40 Ch. Div., 55) was referred to. The plaintiff therefore asked for an interim injunction to restrain the defendants until the trial of the action or further order from trespassing on his land and from opening up the soil or laying pipes thereunder. Mr. Justice Channell, however, without calling upon the defendants' counsel, refused the application. He said: I have no doubt that in this case the real question is merely one as to the amount of compensation to be paid by the defendants. There is no ground for granting an injunction. Personally, I think that the action is misconceived. I see no necessity for an interim injunction. The defects in the notice and report (if they exist) could be remedied in a very short time, and the injunction must be refused. As to costs, they will be costs in the action.

## QUERIES AND REPLIES.

BUILDING PLANS.—"Plans" writes: Will you be so good as to inform me through the medium of your paper whether I have power to refuse to accept any plans unless they are drawn upon tracing linen? Our local by-laws say nothing whatever about the matter, and I do not care to do anything unless I have the power to enforce what I ask.

In the absence of any by-laws requiring plans to be drawn upon tracing linen, I do not think this can be insisted upon.

LONDON UNITED TRAMWAYS.—The directors of the London United Tramways, Limited, have addressed a letter to the London County Council requesting that sanction may be given to the early introduction of overhead electric traction upon the few miles of the system inside the county of London, in order that the system may be simultaneously applied to all the company's lines.

## Some Recent Publications.

### REMOVAL AND DISPOSAL OF TOWN REFUSE.

A comprehensive, accurate and thoroughly adequate text-book on this subject has long been wanted, and we have no hesitation in saying that the want has been at last supplied by Mr. Wm. H. Maxwell, assistant engineer and surveyor to the Leyton Urban District Council, in his book, THE RE-MOVAL AND DISPOSAL OF TOWN REFUSE (London : The Sani-tary Publishing Company, 5 Fetter-lane, Fleet-street, E.C. Price 15s.). The author correctly remarks that a good deal has been written on the subject from time to time, either in the form of detached "papers," reports or pamphlets, but that no attempt had been made to deal with the subject practically in the compass of a single volume and with any-thing like completeness. To accomplish this was the object Mr. Maxwell set before himself, and the better to carry out his task he tells us that he divided his subject into four primary divisions—a resumé of the law bearing on the subject ; a consideration of the nature of town refuse ; a dis-cussion of the various systems of collection ; and, finally, an investigation of the methods of its sanitary and economical disposal, or in some cases utilisation.

It will thus be seen that Mr. Maxwell started with a very adequate conception of this problem, and there can be no ques-tion of the thorough, intelligent and conscientious manner in which the work has been accomplished. The book is the out-come of extensive knowledge, wide reading and a firm com-prehension of the whole problem in all its bearings. In his excellently-worded preface the author gives a lucid statement of the general question, and also clearly indicates the scope of his book and the limits of the task he set himself. His chief aim has been to give, in a clear and impartial form, such a statement of facts and results as would enable any intelligent student to put himself abreast of our present knowledge of the subject, to understand what has been done in the past, and thus be in a position to keep pace with future develop-ments. The book is not put forward as a medium for the exposition of new and original views with regard to the collec-tion, disposal or utilisation of town's refuse. This can no doubt be largely explained by the fact that progress in municipal work depends to a very great extent on accumulated experi-ence, and of no problem is this more true than of that now dealt with by Mr. Maxwell. With this reservation, however, we cannot but consider that the author might have allowed himself a little more latitude in the expression of purely personal opinions. From what we know of his work we have no hesitation in saying that such a course would certainly not have detracted from either the interest or the value of the book. As a compilation and work of reference it has very distinct value, but to many who will consult its pages it would have been of much greater utility had it been more critical in character. In closing his preface the author trusts that the book may be found of service, not only to municipal engineers and surveyors, but also to members of sanitary authorities in carrying out their investigations into a subject which must ever constitute one of the most arduous and important duties which a local authority has to perform. Experienced municipal engineers and surveyors will, no doubt, be able to discriminate for themselves amid the mass of information that Mr. Maxwell provides, but the novice and the amateur generally stand in need of some critical assistance, which Mr. Maxwell would have been justified in attempting to supply. This is shown by the temperate and impartial way in which the author in his preface discusses the much-debated question of combined undertakings—that is to say, the utilisation of refuse as fuel for steam produc-tion in connection with electric lighting. In a subsequent edition the author would do well to develop criticism and comment in the body of this book. We observe that in con-nection with the typical combined undertaking—that of Shoreditch—there is little that is new forthcoming, though the promoters of the experiment have promised much and long.

We can only refer briefly to the contents of the various chapters, which have been very carefully and methodically arranged. The first chapter is general, and, in addition to a sketch of the legal aspect of the question, there are remarks on the scavenging and cleansing of streets, the disposal of street refuse and on street-watering. The second chapter is devoted to the collection and ultimate disposal of house refuse. The term "refuse" is defined, its composition, quality and temporary storage are discussed, and an account given of the different methods of collection. The third and fourth chapters discuss respectively the removal of excreta and the disposal of town refuse by the various methods in vogue. The importance of these opening chapters from the point of view of the municipal engineer is obvious. Naturally, much of a book devoted to the subject of town refuse will be taken up with the discussion of dust destructors, and Mr. Maxwell has done a real service in bringing together all the information available to date on so important a subject, though the service would have been greater still had the author's plan permitted of an attempt to discriminate between the relative values of the various types of destructors instead of merely describing them from information obtained. A special

word of commendation is due for the carefully-compiled in-formation contained in Chapter X., in which a most interest-ing and valuable mass of details are brought together with reference to refuse disposal and destructor installations at various towns. This body of information will retain its value for a long time to come, and Mr. Maxwell duly expresses his obligations to the borough engineers and surveyors who sup-plied him liberally with plans and details. The volume con-cludes with a chapter on the interesting subject of thermal storage, from which the author expects a good deal ultimately. The book is well illustrated, both in regard to the quantity and the quality of the illustrations. The printing is good, and the general get-up tasteful and pleasing.

### LIGHT AND AIR.

THE LAW OF LIGHT AND AIR (London : Estate Gazette Office. Price 6s.) is the subject and the title of a work by Mr. Alfred A. Hudson, author of the well-known work on building contracts, and Mr. Arnold Inman, both, as is cus-tomary in connection with such compilations, being barristers-at-law. The object of the authors has been to produce, in a compact form, a digest of the law of light and air, for the use of lawyers, surveyors and students, and they have been tolerably successful in achieving their object. The principle adopted for the arrangement of the work can also be com-mended. An endeavour has been made, as far as possible, to explain the rules of the law and then to set out in chrono-logical order the cases from which such rules have been de-duced, thus placing before the reader a short but complete history of the law under each branch of the subject. Naturally the greater part of the volume is devoted to the subject of light, the last chapter only being devoted ex-clusively to the cognate subject of air. The first chapter consists of introduction and definitions, and among the vari-ous aspects of the question to which subsequent chapters are devoted are : The creation of the easement of light by pre-scription (apart from statute) or by lost grant, creation of the easement of light by express grant, creation of the easement of light by statute (Prescription Act), extent of light con-ferred by prescription, creation of the easement of light by implied grant, right to light acquired by acquiescence, extinc-tion of the easement of light, tenant and reversioner, inter-ference with the easement of light by obstruction, remedies by action, and proceedings generally. There are some use-ful illustrative diagrams given ; an appendix contains the full text of the Prescription Act, and one or two forms of agree-ment which have come before the Courts ; a table of cases in which reference has been made to all the recognised reports ; and an index, which is fairly complete.

### TWO WORKS OF REFERENCE.

The eighth edition of KELLY'S DIRECTORY OF THE BUILD-ING TRADES (Kelly's Directories, Limited, High Holborn, W.C. Price 30s.) has recently been issued, and the result is that a work of reference indispensable to all engaged in any branch of the building trade has been brought thoroughly up to date. The arrangement and classification are excellent, but the many merits of the compilation are too-well known at this time of day to require pointing out. The great volume and importance of the building trade in its various ramifications is illustrated by some exceptionally significant figures in the preface, from which we take the following concluding remarks : "It may not be out of place to add that the amount of labour involved in the production of this work has been very great. As on former occasions, the whole of the names therein have been personally visited by a large staff of canvassers, and the returns made by them have afterwards been arranged by a staff of clerks specially trained to the work. Every care has been taken to render the work as accurate and as complete as possible, and the proprietors believe that this edition will be found equal in every respect to the previous editions of the work." Those who have occasion to use the volume will have no difficulty in endorsing any of these statements.

THE LONDON MANUAL (London : Edward Lloyd, Limited, Salisbury-square, E.C. Price 1s., cloth 1s. 6d.) for 1898-99 has an introduction by Sir Walter Besant on the survey of London, and has a number of illustrations by Alfred Parsons, Joseph Pennell, Herbert Railton and Fred. Pegram. It is a companion volume to the MUNICIPAL YEAR-BOOK published by the same firm, and also edited by Mr. Robert Donald, editor of London. The compilation when first issued created a highly-favourable impression which cannot fail to be con-firmed by this re-issue. It seems a model of what such a work of reference should be, and is not likely to be supplanted by any similar work. The got-up is tasteful and pleasing, the arrangement is good, the matter is well-condensed and presented, exactly what is required being given, and finally there is the crowning merit of extreme accuracy.

Simla.—The Government of the Punjab have sanctioned the application of the municipality for permission to borrow 3 lakhs of rupees to complete the extension of the water-works.

# Municipal Work in Progress and Projected.

The paragraphs referring to Croydon, Lancaster, Middlesbrough, Lowestoft, Reigate, Ripon, Scarborough, Coalville, Leatherhead and Herne Bay contain all the important news that has come to hand this week with respect to the progress of extensive municipal undertakings in the provinces. In the metropolis it will be noticed that the London County Council have resumed business, while St. George-in-the-East Vestry and the Strand District Board of Works are engaged in carrying out fairly extensive works.

## METROPOLITAN AUTHORITIES.

### LONDON COUNTY COUNCIL.

The members of the County Council on Tuesday met for the first time since the summer vacation, and obviously they had to face an unusually full agenda. Before the sitting closed the old subject of the London water supply was introduced by a motion which had been placed on the paper by Mr. W. Crooks, one of the labour members for Poplar. This subject has been receiving an unusually large amount of attention in the Press during the vacation, owing to the failure of the East London Water Company's supply, and, naturally, some public interest was felt as to the attitude the council would take up in the matter. No decision was, however, arrived at, the debate being adjourned until the next sitting. An important report of the Highways Committee, dealing with the purchase of the undertakings of the London Tramways Company, was also postponed for consideration until next week. Full particulars of this report will be found in another column.

*Loans for Public Works.*—Upon the recommendation of the Finance Committee, it was agreed to lend the Battersea Vestry £1,545 for the erection of public conveniences; the Islington Vestry £21,010 for street improvements, laying-out open space by Cattle Market, &c.; St. George's (East) Vestry £3,000 for paving works; and the Westminster Vestry £15,000 for similar purposes.

*Proposed Transfer of Powers.*—Consideration was resumed of the report of the Local Government and Taxation Committee dealing with proposals for the transfer to local authorities of certain powers now possessed and exercised by the council. The recommendations of the committee, it will be remembered, were based upon resolutions passed by a conference held some time ago between members of the council and representatives of the local authorities of the metropolis. Several of the recommendations were adopted when the matter was first before the council. The council now adopted, without comment, the two recommendations referring to powers for the removal of unauthorised signs and the storing of wood and timber. After some discussion they also adopted the following recommendation: "That the maintenance of the Victoria-embankment and portions of streets adjoining in the precincts of the Savoy and the footways of the Albert and Chelsea embankments be transferred to the local authorities, and that the lighting, watering and cleansing of the Victoria-embankment and the footways of the Albert and Chelsea-embankments be transferred to the local authorities, subject to the maintenance and lighting of the walls of the embankments being retained by the council." The council further agreed: "(1) That the maintenance of main roads be transferred to the local authorities. (2) That the power of sanctioning the closing of streets for repairs be transferred to the local authorities. (3) That the words 'with the sanction of the council' be omitted from the provision enabling vestries and district boards to close or stop up streets during paving or sewerage works. (4) That the power of the council to require main roads when maintained by a vestry or district board to be repaired to the council's satisfaction be repealed on transfer of such roads to the vestry or district board. (5) That the local authorities be given concurrent power with the council to apply to Parliament for powers to make improvements of public utility wholly within their districts and intended to be paid for wholly out of their funds." Several other minor recommendations were adopted; and the whole of the various recommendations were referred to the Parliamentary Committee, in order that a report might be presented on the proper steps to be taken to give effect to them.

*Greenwich Tunnel.*—The Bridges Committee recommended the council to invite tenders for the construction of the proposed tunnel under the river Thames at Greenwich. This was agreed to.

*Purchase of the London Tramways.*—A report of the Highways Committee recommending the council to purchase the undertakings of the London Tramways Company for £860,000 was postponed for consideration till next week.

*London Water Supply.*—Mr. Crooks obtained urgency for the following motion: "That, in view of the existing difficulty in obtaining an adequate supply of water in a large portion of the county of London, it be an instruction to the Water Committee to forthwith submit its proposals with regard to legislation affecting the water supply in the ensuing session of Parliament." In moving the resolution he said that the council knew the urgency of the case. They had been told over and over again that the water companies

were quite capable of minding their own business, and of giving the people of London a full, adequate, and above all, pure supply of water. He was sick and tired of the promises of the water companies and the platitudes of the Government, and hoped the council would go for a full, efficient and pure supply from Wales or from any other source that was capable of giving it. Mr. Stuart, M.P., in seconding the motion said the present distress in the East-End was due to the culpable negligence of the East London Company in putting into effect the legislation which they themselves promoted for the very purpose of avoiding a scarcity of water. Mr. Beachcroft supported the motion, but moved the addition of words directing the committee to obtain the opinion of an engineer as to the works required for connecting the mains and works of the several companies, for use in cases of urgency. After discussion, in which Mr. McDougall, the Rev. F. Williams and Sir A. Arnold took part, the debate was adjourned.

*Tenders.*—It was announced that no tenders had been received in reply to the council's invitation in respect to the erection of two blocks of working-class buildings on the Boundary-street area and some cottage dwellings at Brook-street, Limehouse.—The following tenders were opened by the chairman for painting works at the Abbey Mills pumping station, &c.: Messrs. A. J. Wick, £2,092; A. H. Inns, £2,154; B. Proctor, £2,172; F. W. Harris, £2,251; D. Gibb & Co., £2,558; E. F. Folley, £2,774; Vigor & Co., £2,812; and J. Kybett, £4,872.

### VESTRIES AND DISTRICT BOARDS.

**Bermondsey.**—On Monday the vestry considered a long report from the Sanitary and Public Health Committee in reference to the conference held some time ago on the subject of overcrowding and housing of the working classes, when twenty-three vestries and district boards were represented. The committee recommended that the county council should be asked to exercise its powers under Part III. of the Housing of the Working Classes Act, so as to provide accommodation within the county of London. This was agreed to.—It was also resolved to approach the county council with a view to the insertion of a clause in their General Powers Bill for 1899 to enable vestries and boards of works to erect municipal buildings under Part III. of the same Act.—The Sanitary Committee further reported on the result of negotiations with the Rotherhithe Vestry on the subject of the construction at joint expense of two underground conveniences at the end of Southwark Park-road by Jamaica-road and at the junction of Galleywall-road with Southwark Park-road. The committee stated that the Rotherhithe authority had referred the question to committee for consideration, and this, in the opinion of the committee, showed that there was every prospect of some arrangement being arrived at.—On the recommendation of the General Purposes Committee it was decided to invite tenders from six firms for a steam crane to be fixed at the wharf.—The following tenders were considered for the purchase of old iron at the depot: Isaacs & Son (accepted), £1 14s. per ton; B. Hyams, £1 12s.; and C. H. Lloyd, £1 10s.

**Hackney.**—At last week's meeting of the vestry the public analyst reported that the sample of water taken from Tumbling Bay, Hackney Marshes (river Lea), possessed a foul sewage odour and was undistinguishable from sewage.

**Hammersmith.**—The vestry, at their meeting last week, decided not to support the proposal of the London County Council for establishing a laboratory for the examination of pathological matter by a bacteriologist.—The clerk was instructed to inform the Battersea Vestry, in reply to their circular-letter, that the vestry were in favour of district surveyors being under the direct control of the vestries or district boards.—A letter was read from Mr. J. C. Robinson, managing director of the London United Tramways, to the effect that the directors felt the time was opportune to re-open negotiations with the London County Council asking its assent to the introduction of the overhead trolley system of electric traction on the lines in Hammersmith. The matter was referred to a committee of the whole vestry.

**Holborn.**—At Monday's meeting of the district board of works tenders were received for asphalte paving works in the carriageway in Farringdon-road, footways in Farringdon-road, and asphalte paving works in Emerald-street.—The surveyor was instructed to prepare plans and obtain estimates for a new urinal in Cross-street, Leather-lane; also for an underground convenience at Rosebery-avenue and Clerkenwell-road.—It was decided to repave a portion of Theobald's-road with wood.

**Lambeth.**—A meeting of this vestry was held on Thursday, when the Sewers Committee recommended the vestry to join with Battersea in urging the London County Council to adopt regulations with regard to district surveyors, with the view to minimising the dangers of accidents from buildings in course of erection and alteration.—The vestry agreed to support Battersea on recommended. In May of last year the vestry accepted an offer, made by the late Sir Henry Doulton, of a statue of her Majesty, which (at the close of the Victorian Exhibition at Earl's Court, where it was to be exhibited) Sir Henry desired should be erected in the enclosure on the east side of Lambeth Bridge. Messrs. Doulton have now written informing the vestry that they were prepared to proceed with the erection of the statue, but the General Purposes Committee found that the enclosure referred to was under the charge of the London County Council. They therefore directed that the matter should be placed before the London County Council, with the view to the erection of the statue on the site in question.—The Baths Committee reported that, in the absence of Mr. Tiltman on the Continent, they were unable to take any action in relation to the latter's letter on the subject of the cost of the Kennington-road baths, which was published in The Surveyor on August 12th.—In connection with the heavy expenditure anticipated for the repairs of Brixton Hill, the General Purposes Committee pointed out that, as the tramways in the district would shortly pass into the possession of the county council, they had given instructions for only those repairs that were absolutely necessary to be carried out. In the meantime Mr. J. P. Norrington, the surveyor, had been requested to place himself in communication with the county council, with a view to arrangements being made for the complete repair of Brixton Hill.

**Lewisham.**—At a special meeting of the district board of works, last week, it was resolved to apply to the Board of Trade for a provisional order for supplying the district with electricity.

**Newington.**—The vestry, on Wednesday of last week, concurred in the following suggested regulations with regard to district surveyors—namely, that all district surveyors should devote the whole of their time to the duties of district surveying; that they should be paid a salary by the London County Council, and that all building fees (if continued) should be paid to the council direct; that an office be provided for the district surveyor at the local vestry hall or offices, so that he may be brought into closer touch with the local authorities.—Resolutions were adopted in favour of by-laws being made for the regulation generally of search and flash light advertisements, and in favour of street lamp-posts that are within a few feet of a fire alarm being painted a bright red colour, in order to indicate the positions of the fire alarms.—The vestry also resolved to construct an underground convenience for both sexes in South-place, by the side of the Kennington Theatre.

**Paddington.**—The vestry, at their meeting on Tuesday, decided to object to the theory of certain other vestries, that vestries and local authorities should have the power of erecting dwellings for the working classes. Their opinion is that the only effective way to stop overcrowding and improve the housing of the working classes is to enforce by-laws with respect to houses let in lodgings.—The tender of Messrs. Boyer & Son was accepted for the supply of about 800 cubic yards of river Colne coarse shingle, for frosty roads, at the rate of 4s. 8d. per ton.—The carriageway paving in Westbourne Street-mews was ordered to be relaid with old redressed pitching stones as far as possible, at an estimated cost of £325.—The roadway in Warwick-place in front of the Warwick Castle public-house was also ordered to be relaid with granite pitching.—The surveyor was instructed to embody in his report on the cost of the wood paving works for the year a statement as to the condition of the Baltic deal pavings which have been removed from the streets recently repaved with wood.—A deputation was appointed to wait upon the Improvement Committee of the London County Council and explain the necessity of carrying out the proposed Westbourne-terrace road bridge improvements forthwith.

**Poplar.**—The board have adopted a report of the Electric Lighting Committee recommending that the offer of the trustees of the German estate to sell to the board, for the purpose of an electric station, the piece of vacant ground now in the occupation of the board, and situated between Violet-road and Glaucus-street, and adjoining the Board School site, for the sum of £3,000, the board to forego a claim for paving, amounting to £104 12s. 5d. in respect of the land, and to pay all costs, including negotiation, &c., be accepted.

**Shoreditch.**—The vestry, at a meeting on Tuesday, resolved to renew the fire insurance of the electric lighting station and refuse destructor with the Fine Art and General Insurance Company, at the annual premiums of £65 12s. 6d. and £32 3s. 9d. respectively for the sum of £62,000.—On the recommendation of the Lighting Committee it was decided to order a 100-kilowatt transformer from the Electric Construction Company for the sum of £881, and to advertise for tenders for two smaller transformers of 66-kilowatt capacity each.—The Scavenging Committee asked for authority to dispose of an old gas engine and to substitute an electric motor, at a cost not exceeding £100. This was agreed to.—The undermentioned tenders were submitted for the erection of a shelter in the Charles-square recreation ground : Messrs. Schooley & Son (accepted), £68 10s.; Messrs. J. Ivory, £68 10s.; and Messrs. Jarvis & Son, £73.

**Strand.**—A meeting of the district board of works was held on Wednesday of last week. On the recommendation of the Works Committee it was decided to construct an underground latrine in Leicester-square, at an estimated cost

of £4,500.—The board declined to accede to the application of the Charing Cross Hospital authorities and others for the closing of Bedford-court, Chandos-street.—A long discussion took place on the application of the National Telephone Company for permission to erect a wood and iron hut at Holles-street, Clare Market, but the recommendation of the Works Committee to give the requisite permission to the company was, however, agreed to.—The Improvements and Parliamentary Committee reported that they had been asked to take common action with other metropolitan authorities in favour of vesting the water supply in the people of London, but, while of opinion that the control of the supply should be placed in the hands of a central authority, they were not prepared to express any further opinion until the report of the Royal Commission now considering the subject was published. The report was adopted.—It was decided to erect a dust destructor, on the Horsfall system, on the Shot Tower Wharf.—A letter was read from Mr. Sydney Smith, late hon. secretary of the Sir Augustus Harris Memorial Fund, asking the board to take over the repair and control of the drinking fountain erected to the memory of Sir Augustus at Drury-lane Theatre. The subject was remitted to the Works Committee for consideration and report.

**St. George-in-the-East.**—The vestry have decided to invite tenders for the enlargement of the vestry hall. The cost of the work is estimated at £7,000, and it is thought that the seating accommodation will be increased from 300 to 500.

**St. Marylebone.**—At the last meeting of the vestry, Mr. Waddington, the surveyor, drew attention to the lack of accommodation for his staff, which was shortly to be increased. During the discussion reference was made to the projected new vestry hall, but eventually the representations of the surveyor were referred to the Works Committee for consideration and report.—It was resolved, on the recommendation of the Works Committee, to give permission to Messrs. Peter Robinson, Limited, to erect six electric arc lamps in Oxford-street and to Messrs. Gardiner to put up seven lamps of a similar type in Edgware-road.

**St. Pancras.**—On Wednesday the vestry received a report from the Electricity and Public Lighting Committee giving details of the position of the municipal electric light undertaking. The accounts, which related to the six months ended the 30th June last, showed that during that period the total revenue amounted to £17,408, being an increase of £3,088 over the corresponding half of last year. The expenditure on trading account reached £11,556, leaving a surplus of £5,852 to meet interest charges and instalments on loans amounting to £4,686. The nett result of the six months was a profit of £1,166, which, together with the sum of £1,717 brought forward from last year, made a total of £2,883. The introduction of the maximum demand indicator system and other reductions had resulted in an actual decrease of £800 in the income, whilst the coal bill had been increased by £500, largely owing to the troubles in the coal trade.—The Health Committee reported that they had considered a representation from the medical officer of health directing attention to the fact that when the vestry takes over a sewer that has hitherto been regarded as a drain there is a transfer of responsibilities and liabilities which makes matters extremely complicated. The medical officer had suggested that it should be made perfectly clear to the tenant, leaseholder and freeholder what the transfer meant in each case, and obtain the consent and undertaking in writing from each of the parties interested. Having considered the matter in connection with an opinion obtained on the subject from the solicitors, the Health Committee recommended that no action should be taken in the matter. This was agreed to.—The Dusting and Refuse Destructor Committee announced that they had considered the question of erecting in the destructor yard the three boilers removed from the Regent's Park central electric light station, and had conferred with Mr. S. Baynes, the chief electrical engineer, on the subject. The engineer explained that it would be necessary to place the boilers over the cells, and expressed the opinion that it would require at least three cells to heat each boiler. He proposed that two of the boilers should be fixed above the six south cells, and be provided with a by-pass for the escape of the heat when the boilers were not in use. He also informed the committee that it would be advisable for an arrangement to be made whereby the furnaces might be stoked with fuel, if found necessary, during the hours of full load. On the recommendation of the committee the vestry authorised the arrangement suggested to be carried into effect.

# PROVINCIAL AND GREATER LONDON AUTHORITIES.
## COUNTY COUNCILS.

**Norfolk.**—The county council have decided not to pay the claim of the Walsoken Urban District Council for highway repairs because English granite was used instead of Belgian, which is cheaper. The district council thereupon appealed to the Local Government Board, but that department have declined to interfere. As the result of negotiations, the county council have offered to pay if the claim is reduced to the amount that foreign granite would have cost. The district council have decided to invoke an arbitration.

## MUNICIPAL CORPORATIONS.

**Birmingham.**—Contract No. 12 on the Elan aqueduct, being the section from Cleobury Mortimer to Hagley, has been let to Messrs. Morrison & Mason, Limited, of Glasgow, at £412,445 19s. 5d. This firm are already the contractors for three sections of the aqueduct, and the new contract places the continuous length from Dolaa to Hagley, a total of 51¼ miles, in their hands. The aqueduct over contract No. 12 is all in pipes or syphon, and includes the bridges over the Severn and Stour.

**Canterbury.**—Plans for the erection of the proposed new Guildhall, which have been prepared by the city surveyor are under the consideration of the city council. They show a frontage of 118 ft. in Guildhall-street and 56 ft. in High-street. On the ground floor will be a magistrates' court and the county and bankruptcy court. The upper floor will be taken up with the council chamber, committee-room and mayor's parlour, together with the offices of the town clerk. The chief entrance will be in Guildhall-street. The style is described as "a free Gothic treatment of secular character."

**Croydon.**—The Local Government Board have sanctioned the corporation's application for a loan of £23,262 for the purposes of electric lighting extensions at Norwood.

**Doncaster.**—Last week the town council, in committee, resolved to carry out a scheme for lighting the town by electricity. Mr. Schulebred, of London, is to be engaged to carry out the work.

**Dudley.**—A recent report of the Public Works Committee stated that several members of the council had purchased a building estate between the Buffery-road and the recreation ground, containing 17 acres, or thereabouts, upon which it was contemplated to erect houses, mostly for the artisan classes, and that they were prepared to sell to the corporation a piece of land adjoining the recreation ground, containing 7,000 square yards or thereabouts. The committee, having considered the offer, are of opinion that the enlargement of the recreation ground as proposed would be advantageous and a great improvement, and recommended that it be accepted on the following terms: "That the corporation purchase the land to be thrown into the recreation ground at the amount of the accepted estimate for making the roads; that the purchase money shall be paid when the roads are made to the satisfaction of the borough surveyor and when not less than fifty houses, yielding an annual gross rental of £600, are erected and finished; possession of the land to be added to the recreation ground to be given on the adoption by the council of these recommendations and a conveyance executed to the corporation; and that the amount of the purchase be included in a future loan."

**Eccles.**—It has been decided by the town council to apply to the Local Government Board for sanction to a loan of £275 for the construction of a sewer in Liverpool-road, Peel Green.

**Hythe.**—The town council recently considered the advisability of applying for a provisional electric lighting order. The question arose in consequence of an application from the Folkestone Electric Supply Company. It was decided to take preliminary steps, but before expense is incurred the matter will be confirmed by the council.

**Keighley.**—The town council have resolved to purchase 9,650 square yards of land as a site for the proposed public slaughter-house. They have also resolved to apply to the Board of Trade for a provisional order to enable them to supply electricity within the borough.

**Kidderminster.**—Last week a deputation from the Thornhill, Liversedge and Heckmondwike councils visited Kidderminster and inspected the Kidderminster and Stourport electric tramway, in view of electric developments in the district they came from. They were met by Mr. Lycett, district manager of the British Electric Traction Company, and the information they desired was given to them.

**Lancaster.**—At a meeting of the town council, held last week, it was resolved to apply for sanction to borrow £20,250 for extending the electric lighting, constructing a new river wall and railing on the rampart at Skerton, carrying out improvements in Church-street and Horse Shoe Corner, &c.

**Leicester.**—Representatives of the corporation and of the tramways company have agreed to an arrangement for the sale of the tramways undertaking to the town council for the sum of £155,000, or £11 15s. per £10 share. The undertaking has paid 5 per cent. since 1891, and the gross annual receipts are £40,000.

**Lincoln.**—It has been decided by the council to abandon a scheme for providing workmen's dwellings, in consequence of the Local Government Board requiring amendments in the plans, estimated to cost an additional £200.

**Lowestoft.**—Mr. W. C. C. Hawtayne has been instructed by the town council to prepare a scheme for lighting the borough by electricity, and to include the provision of power for traction purposes in consequence of an application by Messrs. Seaton & Beer as the East Anglian Electric Light Railway. This railway is intended to extend from Caistor to Southwold, running through Lowestoft and Yarmouth, Hop-

ton, Corton, Kessingland and Wrentham. In and near the towns and villages the rails are to be laid along the public roads flush with the surface, whilst the remaining length of the line will follow the roadside. Except at the termini, there are to be no stations. The cost is estimated at £300,000.

**Manchester.**—A meeting of the special committee of the Manchester Corporation appointed to consider the question of the telephone service in Manchester was held at the Manchester town hall last week. The subject was fully debated, and it was resolved that the chairman should prepare a report and submit it to a subsequent meeting.

**Middlesbrough.**—At a special meeting of the Sanitary Committee of the corporation, on Thursday, a report by Mr. J. Mansergh, with regard to the drainage of the town, and, more particularly, the preventing of the flooding in the marsh district, was considered. The recommendations of Mr. Mansergh embodied a scheme which would cost £40,000. The surveyor was requested to prepare specifications for the new iron sewer in Marsh-road, this being a very small portion of the entire scheme.

**Newport, Mon.**—On the 28th ult. a Local Government Board inquiry was held into a proposal of the corporation to borrow £6,150 for electric light extension, and £760 for providing a steam roller, road scarifier, &c. There was no opposition. The electric light has been in use for some years in Newport.

**Reigate.**—Dr. R. D. R. Sweeting, Local Government Board inspector, held an inquiry at the town hall, Reigate, on the 21st ult., relative to the council's application for sanction to borrow £11,000 for the purchase of a site and the erection thereon of a new hospital for infectious diseases. The town clerk, in opening the inquiry, explained that the present building was erected to meet an emergency, but the corporation proceeded to devote their attention to the acquisition of a site for a hospital of a more permanent character, whereupon the old small-pox hospital might be remitted to its old purpose, or used as an auxiliary temporary establishment to the permanent structure it was now proposed to erect. He also stated that negotiations had been entered into with the rural sanitary authority with a view to having a joint hospital, but these had failed, owing to the exorbitant terms imposed by the rural authority. The total area of the proposed site was about 3½ acres; it was situated about half a mile beyond the boundary of the borough, in a very salubrious situation, and was far removed from any source of infection or any objection on the part of any person whatsoever.

**Ripon.**—Colonel C. E. Luard, R.E., Local Government Board inspector, held an inquiry last week with reference to an application of the corporation for sanction to borrow £10,000 for purposes of gas improvements and £500 for the construction of public underground conveniences in the Market-place.

**Saffron Walden.**—A Local Government Board inquiry has been held by Mr. George Willcocks with respect to an application of the town council for sanction to borrow £1,400 for works of street improvement.

**Scarborough.**—Colonel Luard, R.E., Local Government Board inspector, held an inquiry at the Scarborough town hall last week with respect to the application of the corporation for their approval to the disposal by the council of certain corporate land situated in Seamer-read, and of the borrowing of £33,575 for the purchase of the St. Nicholas House estate for municipal purposes and for purposes of public walks and pleasure grounds. In referring to the proposed purchase of the St. Nicholas estate the town clerk said that the accommodation in his department was most unsuitable and inadequate. The reason the corporation were purchasing the grounds was that they would make most attractive and beautiful public pleasure grounds in the centre of the town. There was also a danger of the property getting into the hands of speculative builders.

**Worcester.**—At the meeting of the city council on Tuesday the Water and Sewerage Committee reported that the Local Government Board objected that the area of irrigation land for the new sewage works, in connection with which the council had resolved to apply for sanction to a loan of £52,000 to carry out, was not sufficient. The board had since expressed themselves satisfied with the increased area provided by alteration in the site of tanks and filters. The board also raised the point of the method of crossing the river, which Messrs. Beesley intended to carry out by pipes laid in the bed of the river by means of a coffer dam. Messrs. Beesley had since recommended the crossing of the river by a double line of pipes in an iron tunnel, stating that the plans, with the alterations proposed, could be carried out for the original estimate of £48,165.

**York.**—A Local Government Board inquiry has been held with respect to an application of the city council for sanction to borrow £2,500 for the purchase of certain land for hospital purposes.

## URBAN DISTRICT COUNCILS.

**Coalville.**—The sanction of the Local Government Board has been received by the district council to the borrowing of £22,902 for sewerage and water schemes.

**Herne Bay.**—The reconstruction of the sea wall and promenade at Herne Bay, which were so extensively damaged in the destructive gales of last November, is to be proceeded with at once, the estimated cost being placed by Mr. Baldwin Latham at £40,000.

**Holyhead.**—Colonel Durnford recently held an inquiry, on behalf of the Local Government Board, with reference to an application of the district council for sanction to borrow £1,000 for the purchase of land as a site for the proposed public abattoir.

**Leatherhead.**—The urban district council have resolved to apply to the Local Government Board for sanction to a loan of £30,000 to carry out Mr. Frederick Beesley's scheme for the drainage of the town. The amount includes the council's proportion of the joint outfall works with Ashtead.

**Newton Abbot.**—A loan for the purchase of Courtenay Park and the improvement of the sewage outfall works has been sanctioned by the Local Government Board.

**Rainford.**—An important meeting of the council was held recently, the details of a new water scheme being made public. At a special meeting, held a month ago, the council decided to adopt a scheme by which the St. Helens Corporation should supply the water, and that the council should apply to the Local Government Board for power to borrow £6,000 for the purpose. The necessary information has been forwarded to the Local Government Board by the clerk to council, Mr. B. Smith, and by the water engineer of the St. Helens Corporation, Mr. J. J. Lackland, by which it appears that the estimated cost of the whole scheme will be £6,000. The water will be supplied from the Eccleston Hill pumping station of the corporation to a concrete covered reservoir to be constructed at an elevated point in the township on ground near the quarry alongside the Occupation-road. A Local Government Board inquiry will be held at an early date with respect to the proposal.

**Tottenham.**—At a meeting of the district council on Wednesday it was decided to apply to the Board of Trade for a provisional order to supply electricity within the district and to oppose the applications which have been made for the purpose by several companies. The working of the electric light in connection with a dust destructor is also contemplated.

**Wadebridge.**—The urban district council having applied to the Local Government Board for sanction to borrow an additional sum of £1,000 for purposes of water supply, Colonel A. G. Hepper, R.E., held the usual inquiry on the 28th ult. There was no opposition.

**Wellingborough.**—Sir Philip Magnus on Thursday last opened a new technical school at Wellingborough. The building has been erected by the council at a cost of £3,000 exclusive of the site.

**Woking.**—At the last meeting of the district council it was decided, on the recommendation of the engineer, to accept the tender of Messrs. S. H. Johnson & Co., at £2,496, for the supply of sludge-pressing machinery, and the tender of the Hydraulic Engineering Company, of London and Chester, at £958, for the supply of generators, and £3,150 for the supply of out-station motors and pumps in duplicate. It was also decided to erect two cottages at the outfall site for workmen, and to purchase a piece of land in Walton-road for the erection of a tank and pumping machinery in connection with water-storage and flushing. The drainage scheme is being carried out under the supervision of Mr. W. Santo Crimp, of the firm of Messrs. Taylor, Sons & Santo Crimp, and another few months will see the completion of the main sewer by the contractor, Mr. H. Weldon, of Birmingham.

## RURAL DISTRICT COUNCILS.

**Axbridge.**—An inquiry was held on Friday by Mr. H. Percy Boulnois, an inspector of the Local Government Board, touching an application by the council for sanction to borrow £3,200 for works of water supply for the parish of Winscombe. Mr. A. Powell explained his scheme. He had taken several gaugings at the spring head; that in April last showed 95,000 gallons per twenty-four hours, that in May 90,000, and on the 23rd ult. 85,000. The population to be supplied was 700, and they would require 30,000 gallons per day. The scheme involved no engineering difficulties.

**Congleton.**—On Tuesday of last week Colonel A. G. Durnford, R.E., conducted an inquiry respecting an application which the rural district council had made to the Local Government Board for sanction to borrow £250 for works of sewerage for the township of Holmes Chapel. Mr. H. Ferrand, clerk to the rural district council, appeared in support of the application.

**Eaton Bray.**—At a meeting of this council, held on Friday, a letter was read from the Local Government Board notifying their consent to the borrowing of £1,750 for the proposed water scheme prepared by Mr. McKenzie, the engineer to the council. At the same meeting Mr. McKenzie received instructions to prepare plans, &c., for a sewerage scheme which is now being urged forward by the Upper Board.

**Epsom.**—The council have applied to the Local Government Board for sanction to borrow £13,000 for the drainage of Ashtead, including a proportion of the joint outfall with Leatherhead. The engineers are Messrs. Fredk. Beesley & Son, of Westminster.

**Luton.**—At a recent meeting of the rural district council it was reported by the surveyor that the water supply at Leagrave, near Luton, had totally failed, and boring operations had been commenced near to the bed of the Lea to secure water. The council decided to give a guarantee to the Luton Water Company to insure a return of 10 per cent. on the cost of the company laying water mains to Stopsley.

**Ruthin.**—Mr. E. Evans, surveyor for the Llandyrnog district, at the last monthly meeting of the district council submitted a further report upon the proposal to construct waterworks to supply a number of parishes on the eastward slope and floor of the Vale of Clwyd, in view of the fact that Llandyrnog now asked to be included. The total estimate for a supply sufficient to meet the requirements of many times the present population was £3,287, and the interest and sinking fund was to be borne by the consumers. After some discussion it was agreed to engage Mr. Thomas, Wrexham, to report on the scheme, and to prepare working plans, estimates, &c.

**Shepton Mallet.**—A Local Government Board inquiry has been held by Mr. H. Percy Boulnois relative to an application of the council for sanction to borrow the sum of £1,400 for the carrying out of a scheme of water supply for portions of the parish of Doulting. Mr. William Phelps, surveyor to the council, explained the scheme, which includes the erection of a wind engine for pumping. Mr. J. Wallis Titt, of Warminster, Wilts, a specialist on wind engines, also gave evidence.

**Sunderland.**—A mysterious and extensive underground fire was reported at the meeting of the district council on Wednesday. The sewers at Grangetown are in a very heated condition, and water pipes are also affected, the drinking water coming warm from the taps. The surveyor has been instructed to examine and report upon the outbreak, which it is feared will be extinguished only with much difficulty. Since the great conflagration in July last there has been quite an epidemic of fires occurring almost daily in Sunderland, and the corporation are making public trials of fire engines from leading firms in the country.

**Wing.**—A new brick bridge has recently been constructed for this council, situate at Northall, from the plans and under the superintendence of Mr. McKenzie, the council's surveyor. This bridge takes the places of a single arched ring of brickwork of a very flat curvature, which was much too light for the increased traffic of the district. Another improved feature at Slapton bridge (now in course of construction) is the alteration of the approaches, whereby the gradients will be 1 in 30 and 1 in 18, in lieu of 1 in 9·6 and 1 in 11·2 ; the side walls are constructed of brick in cement to a batter, with 5-in. square oak posts and diagonal side-rails. The road formation is made up with good hard materials, the contract having been let to Mr. Hammerton, of Wing, at £351.

# Personal.

Mr. T. H. Nogus, surveyor to the Glemsford Urban District Council, has received an increase of salary.

Mr. E. Davies, of Shrewsbury, has been appointed second engineering assistant to the Edmonton Urban District Council.

Carmarthen Town Council have acceded to the request of Mr. Finglah, the borough surveyor, for leave of absence on the occasion of his forthcoming marriage.

Mr. Kiddy has been appointed municipal electric light inspector at Buluwayo, at a salary of £150 per annum. This is in addition to his present position as Government electrician.

Twenty-nine applications have been received for the position of resident electrical engineer at Greenock. Three of the applicants have been selected to appear before the Finance Committee.

Mr. D. M'Leod, assistant at the Aberdeen Corporation electricity works, was recently the recipient of a smoker's cabinet and two engineering books, on the occasion of his leaving the station to become manager of some Dublin manufacturing works.

A letter was last week received by the Chelmsford Town Council from Mr. G. H. Sasse, stating that he was feeling very much out of health, and asking to be relieved of his duties for a period of three weeks. The application was at once acceded to.

The paper on "Gasworks Machinery," which was read by Mr. Edward A. Harman, engineer and manager of the Huddersfield Corporation gasworks, before the Society of Engineers, some few months back, has been published by the society in pamphlet form.

The town council of Norwich last week adopted a resolution of the General Purposes Committee recommending the appointment of Mr. T. O. Cudbird, a temporary assistant in the city engineer's department, as an assistant, at an annual salary of £110 per annum.

We regret to announce the death, which occurred on Sunday, of Mr. Jeremiah Jowett, the surveyor to the Rural District Council of Lancaster. Mr. Jowett, who was sixty-nine years of age, had served the council for some twenty years. He had to supervise a wide area.

The borough surveyor of Retford, Mr. J. D. Kennedy, was last week made the recipient of a handsome set of fish carvers, in return for his valuable services as honorary secretary to the Ground Committee of the Retford Bowling Club and as a mark of the general esteem of the members.

The town council of Sutton Coldfield have adopted a resolution of the Highways Committee recommending the increasing of the salary of Mr. A. Riley (who for the past four years has filled the position of superintendent of the Highways Department) to £156 per annum.

The following are the selected candidates for the appointment of surveyor to the Bridlington Urban District Council: Messrs. W. Pym Jones, surveyor, Lymington; P. Mawbey, assistant surveyor, Rugby; G. Goddard, surveyor, Ware; and F. Matthews, assistant surveyor, Hastings. There were, we learn, sixty-nine candidates, and some remarkably good applications. The above-named gentlemen will appear before the council to-day.

The remains of Mr. Davidson Hainsworth, building inspector to the Leeds Corporation, who died on Thursday, at Blackpool, after a brief illness, were interred in Woodhouse Cemetery on Saturday. A preliminary service took place in Woodhouse Moor Wesleyan Chapel, and the gathering there and at the graveside indicated that the deceased had many friends. The whole of the staff of the late gentleman's department was present.

Prior to a recent meeting of the Sanitary Committee of the Broadstairs Urban District Council an interesting ceremony took place, Mr. H. Hurd, the surveyor, being presented with an elegant polished walnut-wood secretaire, upon which had been fixed a silver plate with the following inscription: "Presented by the members and officers of the Broadstairs and St. Peter's Urban District Council to Howard Hurd, district surveyor, on the occasion of his marriage, September, 1898. H. S. D. Byron, Chairman."

A special meeting of the High Furness Highway Board was held last week, when consideration was given to the question of appointing a successor to the late surveyor, Mr. R. P. Nelson. There were thirteen applications for the post. The number was, however, reduced to three—namely, Messrs. R. T. Johnston and Ellwood (members of the board) and Mr. William Newby, architect, Kirkby-in-Furness. The latter gentleman (Mr. Newby) was appointed by a substantial majority. The appointment of Mr. Newby has caused a feeling of general satisfaction.

The names of the following three gentlemen have been submitted to the St. Pancras Vestry by Mr. E. A. Grouning, vice-chairman of the Royal Institute of British Architects, as being competent to act as assessors in respect of competitive designs to be submitted to the vestry for the erection of new public baths and wash-houses in Prince of Wales-road: Mr. Aston Webb, 19 Queen Anne's Gate, S.W.; Mr. John Slater, 46 Berners-street, W.; and Prof. T. Roger Smith, 130 Temple Chambers, E.C. The nomination of these gentlemen by the vice-president is due to the absence abroad of the president of the Institute.

At a meeting of the Shoreditch Vestry, on Tuesday, the Town Hall Committee reported that they had under consideration the question of the proposed alterations to the old fire-station buildings, and had deemed it advisable to vary the vestry's reference to the name of only one architect. The committee accordingly recommended that the three following architects should be asked to submit plans for the carrying out of the work, at a fee of £10 10s. each, such fee to be merged into the commission in the case of the successful architect: Mr. R. S. Ayling, Parliamentary Mansions, Westminster, S.W.; Mr. R. P. Day, Bloomsbury-square, W.C.; and Messrs. Spalding & Cross, Queen-street, Cheapside, E.C. The recommendation was, however, not adopted, it being eventually decided to advertise for competitive designs.

A spirit of unrest has lately been in evidence within the area governed by the Wakefield Rural District Council, and several of the townships are applying to the West Riding County Council for powers to become urban authorities. The Wakefield City Council are at the same time endeavouring to make terms with some of these townships which more immediately adjoin its boundaries to enter the city area on special rating terms. As a result of these changes Mr. Frank Massie, who for the last nine years has been the engineer to the rural authority, has commenced private practice in Wakefield as a civil engineer and surveyor, whilst still retaining his position as engineer to the rural council until the necessary arrangements for the transfer are made. Mr. Massie has quite recently been unanimously appointed to the position of consulting surveyor to the Sandal Magna Urban District Council.

The roadmen of the western district of Perthshire met recently at Dunblane and presented Mr. George A. Calder, road surveyor, with a handsome marble timepiece, on the occasion of his marriage. His intended wife was also made the recipient of a gold bangle. There was a full representation of the road staff, and also a few of Mr. Calder's personal friends, present at the meeting. The chairman, in making the presentation, said that Mr. Calder's quiet and affable manners had won him the esteem of his superiors as well as the respect and love of those who had the good fortune to work under him, the former knowing that in him they had a servant who would do his duty under any circumstances whatsoever, and the latter being convinced that under him they would always get justice and that kind and considerate treatment which bound master and servants together and created harmony and confidence between them.

The death took place on Tuesday, in his sixty-third year, of Mr. Christopher Oakley, past-president of the Surveyors' Institution, and senior partner in the firm of Messrs. Daniel Smith, Son & Oakley, auctioneers and surveyors, of Waterlooplace, Pall Mall. He was one of the original members of the Surveyors' Institution, and last year occupied the position of president. He was a Fellow of the Geological Society, a director of the Auction Mart Company, a member of the Committee of the Estate Exchange, and one of the trustees of the Auctioneers and Surveyors Clerks' Provident Institution. Mr. Oakley was engaged in innumerable compensation cases, and was for many years one of the surveyors to the Board of Trade and one of the consulting surveyors to the Charity Commissioners. For many years, too, he had resided at Chislehurst, he had served on the Kent County Council, and was a member of the Kent Antiquarian Society. The funeral will take place at the parish church, Chislehurst, to-morrow, at 2 o'clock.

Mr. William Welch, superintendent of the waterworks pumping station at Aston, Birmingham, on Friday completed his term of service with the corporation. He retires on superannuation. Mr. Welch entered the service of the late waterworks company on July 1, 1863, as superintendent at Aston, and has held that position continuously since that date, first under the company, and then under the corporation. Mr. Welch's term expired on June 30th last, but by resolution of the council his services were continued to September 30th, so as to enable him to complete the erection of certain new plant which was being carried out under his personal supervision. During the term of his long service many important extensions and alterations at Aston have taken place, and Mr. Welch's experience and thorough acquaintance with the station have been of great advantage to the corporation. On Friday he was presented with a gold watch as a parting token of respect from the members of the staff and the workpeople of the station. The presentation was made by the secretary in the presence of the contributors, and Mr. Welch feelingly and appropriately acknowledged the gift and bade farewell to his old associates.

## THE SOUTH LONDON TRAMWAYS.

PROPOSED PURCHASE BY THE COUNTY COUNCIL.

The Highways Committee of the London County Council have prepared another report on the negotiations for the purchase by the council of the London Tramways Company's system. Early in July last the committee reported that they were in negotiation for the purchase by the council of the whole of the London Tramways Company's system, including not only that portion with regard to which the council on the 21st of June preceding decided to give notice to purchase under the purchase sections of several of the company's Acts, but also certain tramways at Streatham and Tooting not immediately purchasable by the council, but exclusive of the 2½ miles of tramways and one depot which the council had already arranged to purchase for the sum of £22,872. They then stated that they had authorised the valuer to negotiate with the company's representative up to £800,000, which included a sum in consideration of the prospective profits of the Streatham and Tooting lines referred to. This offer the company was not prepared to accept, but suggested that the value of certain of the assets of the company, property and buildings, rolling stock, leases, harness, and plant and machinery, should for the purposes of the purchase be taken at the total amount shown in respect of them in the company's books on the 31st December, 1897—namely, £509,570—and as there was little difference between this amount and the valuer's estimate in respect of these items, the committee provisionally agreed to the suggestion. At that time they anticipated that the question of the value of the lines and the amount to be allowed in respect of prospective profits on lines not immediately purchasable would have to be referred to arbitration.

The committee now report that, as the result of further consideration and negotiations, they authorised the valuer to increase the offer on behalf of the council to £850,000, and the directors of the company stated they were prepared to advise the shareholders to accept that sum for the whole of the company's undertaking, exclusive, of course, of the 2½ miles of tramway and one depot the purchase of which had already been provided for. This offer the committee considered both fair to the council and the company, having regard to all the circumstances, and especially to the fact that by its acceptance all the expense and trouble of arbitration would be avoided, and they then intimated that they would recommend the council to purchase on those terms. At an extraordinary general meeting of the shareholders of the company, held on the 5th of August last, the directors were authorised by a special resolution to take the necessary steps for completing and carrying out the sale of the undertaking to the council upon the terms above stated, and that resolution was confirmed at a subsequent meeting. So far, therefore, as the company were concerned the matter was settled, and it only remained for the committee to obtain the sanction of the council to the arrangement provisionally made by them on their behalf with the company. After communication with the company's representatives as to the date for the transfer of the undertaking, they had come to the conclusion that, in order to give time for the purchase to be completed and the other necessary preliminary arrangements to be made, January 1st next would be the most convenient date, and the company had given an assurance in writing that the whole of the property would be thoroughly maintained until the day of transfer. The company had also undertaken to continue until December 31, 1898, the arrangement sanctioned by the council in May last, by which the company works and accounts to the council for the profits on the 2½ miles already purchased by the council. The agreed purchase price of £850,000 was for the company's undertaking only, and did not cover the provender and other consumable stores which would be in hand at the date of the transfer, nor the value of unexpired terms of licenses, Excise duties, insurance policies, and other outgoings at that date. The amount to be paid by the council under those heads would have to be settled by agreement, or, failing that, by arbitration after the purchase of the undertaking should have been completed. No provision had been made in the annual maintenance estimates for those items of expenditure, the necessity for which could not be foreseen when the estimates were prepared, and they proposed at a later date to ask the Finance Committee to submit to the council the necessary estimate on maintenance account to cover that and other expenditure in connection with the working of the tramways up to March 31, 1899, the end of the council's financial year. With reference to the working and the management of the tramways should the council agree to the purchase, the committee point out that in July last the council decided to establish a tramways department, and referred it to the Highways and General Purposes Committees to confer and report upon the organisation of the department. They were in communication with the General Purposes Committee upon the subject, and there was little doubt that they would be in a position, before the time for the transfer of the undertaking should arrive, to report jointly with that committee upon the subject of the reference.

At the conclusion of their report the committee submit a definite recommendation, asking the council to sanction the purchase on the terms agreed and to pass a vote of £860,000 for that purpose, £850,000 being for the purchase money and £10,000 provision for payment of stamp duty and other expenses of the transfer. The committee also seek to be authorised to settle the precise terms of the agreement to give effect to the purchase.

## THE WATER SUPPLY OF PAISLEY.

GRAVE ACCUSATIONS.

On Friday, at a meeting of the Public Health Committee of the Paisley Town Council, the medical officer, Dr. Donald, submitted a report on an epidemic of enteric fever, which at present exists in the town. From substantial evidence which had been brought before them he had no hesitation in affirming that the water had become locally polluted. Possibly the majority of the committee were not aware of the fact that terminal end pipes were retroverted into the sewer, to be used for flushing purposes, separated from any direct communication by a valve—the whole system being underground, with no means by which this dangerous arrangement could be submitted to frequent examination. He had consulted prominent engineers with regard to these valves, and they informed him that they readily went wrong, particularly if used for a long period.

Was it right that the water should be separated from poison by a valve which was down under the ground for years and years and was never seen, and, further, might become imperfect in its workings? Should it by any chance become obstructed, regurgitation up the connecting pipe must take place, and if the valve were in the slightest degree defective, with the additions in the water pipe favourable, what was the unfortunate result? Pollution of the water. He submitted a sample of water pipe taken from East Buchanan-street, which was occluded almost entirely with incrustations irregularly distributed to form cavities, which in the admittance of fluid matter or gas from the drain became nothing more nor less than little cesspools within the pipes. He felt convinced he had laid sufficient evidence before them in support of this very feasible theory, and that the majority would agree that the risk they ran was too appalling. He was not without hope that this contention would have the support of some, and that the public health would not be permitted to suffer from arrangements in the water system which were undoubtedly wrong, and demanded most urgent reform, by having certain structural alterations made and a systematic examination of the water from time to time, so that the element might be rendered above suspicion. Meantime he suggested extra flushing of the water and pipes and thorough disinfection of the sewers. A long discussion took place on the report, and it is understood that the committee agreed to the suggestions made by the medical officer.

**Peebles.**—At the last annual meeting of the Peebles Gas Light Company the annual report, which was submitted, showed the sum of £1,012 to be at the credit of the profit and loss account, and the directors recommended payment of the usual dividend of 10 per cent., which would absorb £580, leaving £432 to be carried forward. The chairman intimated that the craft of the agreement between the company and the town council for the acquisition of the company's undertaking had now been adjusted by the agents of the parties, and that in all probability that would be the last annual meeting of the company.

## APPOINTMENTS VACANT.

*Advertisements which are re eived too late for classification cannot be included in these summaries until the following week.*

INSPECTOR OF NEW BUILDINGS AND DRAINAGE WORK.—October 8th.—Hornsey Urban District Council. £160.—Mr. E. J. Lovegrove, engineer and surveyor to the council.

HARBOUR ENGINEER.—October 10th.—Waterford Harbour Commissioners. £150.—Mr. J. Allingham, jun., secretary to the commissioners, Harbour Office, Waterford.

SURVEYOR OF HIGHWAYS.—October 10th.—Pickering Rural District Council.—Mr. Robert Kitching, clerk to the council.

BOROUGH AND HIGHWAY SURVEYOR, WATER ENGINEER, INSPECTOR OF NUISANCES, &c.—October 10th.—Pwllheli Corporation. £140.—Mr. Evan R. Davies, town clerk.

SEWER FOREMAN.—October 11th.—Borough of Maidstone. £1 15s.—Mr. Herbert Monckton, town clerk.

DISTRICT ROAD SURVEYOR.—October 11th.—Derbyshire County Council. £160.—Mr. N. J. Hughes-Hallet, county clerk, County Offices, Derby.

SURVEYOR OF HIGHWAYS.—October 11th.—Spalding Urban District Council. £100.—Mr. H. H. Harvey, clerk to the council.

STEAM ROLLER DRIVER.—October 12th.—Maidstone Rural District Council. 28s.—Mr. Sidney Stallard, surveyor to the council.

MANAGER FOR SEWAGE PURIFICATION OUTFALL WORKS.—October 13th.—County Borough of Stockport.—Mr. Walter Hyde, town clerk.

FOREMAN.—October 14th.—Staines Rural District Council. 27s. 6d.—Mr. George W. Manning, engineer and surveyor to the council.

ASSISTANT SURVEYOR.—October 17th.—Garston Urban District Council. £110.—Mr. F. W. Bowden, A.M.I.C.E., surveyor to the council.

SURVEYOR.—October 17th.—Twickenham Urban District Council. £260.—Mr. H. Jason Saunders, clerk to the council.

ENGINEER, SURVEYOR AND SANITARY INSPECTOR.—October 19th.—Wembley (Middlesex) Urban District Council. £220. —Mr. John Smith, clerk to the council.

GENERAL ENGINEERING ASSISTANT.—October 20th.—Corporation of Birkenhead. £110. — Mr. Charles Brownridge, A.M.I.C.E., borough engineer and surveyor.

ELECTRICAL ENGINEER.—October 24th.—East Ham Urban District Council. £300.—Mr. W. H. Savage, A.M.I.C.E., engineer and surveyor to the council.

## COMPETITIONS.

*Advertisements which are received too late for classification cannot be included in these summaries until the following week.*

ABBAVON.—December 1st.—Extension of the covered market, at a cost not to exceed £5,000. £21.—The Borough Surveyor.

CUERTSEY.—December 23rd.—Sewerage and sewage disposal scheme for the No. 1 and 2 wards of the district. £50, £30 and £20.—Mr. T. E. Harland Chaldecott, clerk to the council.

## MUNICIPAL CONTRACTS OPEN.

*Advertisements which are received too late for classification cannot be included in these summaries until the following week.*

ISLINGTON.—October 7th.—Supply and fixing of pipes, valves, &c., in connection with the provision of a supply of water to the public gardens and recreation grounds in Market-road, Holloway.—Mr. J. Patten Barber, vestry surveyor.

HULL.—October 7th.—Supply and erection of a 7-ton overhead traveller (hand-power) for a span of 42 ft. 9 in.—Mr. A. R. White, city engineer.

TOTNES.—October 7th.—Erection of post and rail fencing at Lower Longcombe, Berry Pomeroy, for the rural district council.—Mr. Thos. W. Windeatt, clerk to the council.

HASTINGS.—October 7th.—Laying of about 9,000 yards run of 16-in. water main and about 2,850 yards of 10-in. main in connection with the Brede Valley water scheme.—Mr. P. H. Palmer, M.I.C.E., water engineer, Town Hall, Hastings.

SWINTON AND PENDLEBURY.—October 8th.—Repaving of Swinton Hall-road, Station-road and Partington-lane, for the urban district council.—Mr. Henry Entwistle, surveyor to the council.

HULL.—October 8th.—Sinking and construction of cast-iron shafts and subway at the Queen's dock basin, for the corporation.—Mr. F. J. Bancroft, water and gas engineer.

SWINTON AND PENDLEBURY.—October 8th.—Construction of a surface-water drain, for the urban district council.—Mr. Henry Entwistle, surveyor to the council.

SWINTON AND PENDLEBURY.—October 8th.—Supply of 175 tons of granite setts, for the urban district council.—Mr. Henry Entwistle, surveyor to the council.

BISHOP STORTFORD.—October 8th.—Supply of from 1,200 to 1,500 tons of 1½-in. broken granite and from 100 to 150 tons of ¾-in. granite chips, for the urban district council.—Mr. William Gee, clerk to the council.

STAINES.—October 8th.—Supply of mackintoshes and waterproof overalls for the use of the out-door staff, for the rural district council.—Mr. G. W. Manning, surveyor to the council.

PRESTON.—October 8th.—Various sewerage and sewage disposal works for the township of Farington, for the rural district council.— Mr. James Clarke, clerk to the council.

FEATHERSTONE.—October 10th.—Laying of about 2½ miles of 5-in. cast-iron water main, for the urban district council.—Mr. W. A. Palliser, engineer and surveyor to the council.

SITTINGBOURNE.—October 10th.—Supply of about 600 yards of Guernsey or Alderney granite, for the urban district council.—Mr. W. J. Harris, clerk to the council.

OBSETT.—October 10th.—Levelling, making-up and surface draining of a portion of the new road between Grays and Tilbury dock, and also the construction of a bridge culvert on the road, for the rural district council.—Mr. R. T. Stewart, surveyor to the council.

OBSETT.—October 10th.—Levelling, making-up, kerbing and surface draining works in certain streets in the parish of Chadwell St. Mary, for the rural district council.—Mr. R. T. Stewart, surveyor to the council.

ROTHWELL.—October 11th.—Levelling, paving, flagging and making-up of Smithson-street, Melbourne-street, Melbourne-grove, Melbourne-place and Sidney-street, for the urban district council.—Mr. J. T. Pears, surveyor to the council.

BRIDGWATER.—October 11th.—Making-up, channelling, metalling, kerbing and tar paving of Washington-terrace and Washington-gardens.—Mr. W. T. Baker, town clerk.

BRIDGWATER.—October 11th.—Repairing of the roof at the Market House, Cornhill.—Mr. W. T. Baker, town clerk.

SALFORD.—October 11th.—Erection of new lodges in the Albert and Ordsal parks.—Mr. Samuel Brown, town clerk.

LEES.—October 11th.—Erection of a brick wall, about 90 yards long, 7 ft. high and 14 in. thick, with a buttress every 10 ft., for the urban district council.—The Surveyor to the council.

SOUTHAMPTON.—October 11th.—Supply and fixing of three high-pressure Lancashire boilers, economisers, calorifiers, radiators, steam and hot-water mains, and all necessary pumps, valves, &c., required for the extension of the heat and power generating plant at the county lunatic asylum at Knowle, Fareham.—Mr. W. J. Taylor, county surveyor, The Castle, Winchester.

ROTHERHAM.—October 12th.—Heating with hot water of the Mechanics' Hall and buildings in Howard-street.—Mr. Geo. Jennings, borough surveyor.

HALIFAX.—October 12th.—Supply of fireclay goods for inclined retorts during the period ending 31st December, 1899, for the corporation. —Mr. Thomas Holgate, gas engineer.

HOOTON.—October 12th.—Construction of a urinal in Barton-lane.— Mr. G. W. Bailey, town clerk.

HERTFORD.—October 12th.—Erection of a new bridge at Totteridge for the county council.—Mr. Urban A. Smith, county surveyor, 41 Parliament-street, London, S.W.

HERDEN BRIDGE.—October 12th.—Erection of various machinery, consisting of boiler, engine, pumps, presses, &c., at the sewage works, for the urban district council.—Mr. R. Crabtree, clerk to the council.

CHELTENHAM.—October 12th.—Erection of a new boiler-house at the waterworks at Tewkesbury.—Mr. E. T. Brydges, town clerk.

BARNET.—October 12th.—Construction of roads and footways at Bell Hill and Mays Lane roads, for the urban district council.—Mr. H. Mansbridge, surveyor to the council.

CHELTENHAM.—October 12th.—Supply of a new boiler at the waterworks at Tewkesbury.—Mr. E. T. Brydges, town clerk.

BENFIELDSIDE.—October 12th.—Construction of a new street at Blackfine, for the urban district council.—Mr. John Dixon, surveyor to the council.

CHESTER-LE-STREET.—October 12th.—Laying of about 2,000 yards of asphalte footpath, near Washington, for the rural district council.— Mr. G. W. Ayton, surveyor to the council.

REIGATE.—October 13th.—Construction of a bacteriological filter at the precipitation works at Earlswood.—Mr. W. H. Prescott, borough surveyor.

NANTWICH.—October 13th.—Supply of cast-iron water pipes, hydrants, sluice valves, &c., and the laying of cast-iron water mains to the water supply of Alpraham and Calveley, for the rural district council.—Mr. C. E. Speakman, clerk to the council.

---

St. Pancras.—October 13th.—Supply, for eight months, of Welsh and other steam coal for use at the Regent's Park and King's-road electricity stations, for the vestry.—Mr. C. H. F. Barrett, clerk to the vestry.

Croydon.—October 13th.—Supply of earthenware drain pipes, stores, &c., for the year from the 9th November.—Mr. E. Mawdesley, town clerk.

Leigh.—October 14th.—Supply and erection of various electric lighting plant, for the urban district council.—Mr. Peregrine Thomas, clerk to the council.

Leigh.—October 14th.—Alteration of a bench of inclined retorts, for the urban district council.—Mr. Peregrine Thomas, clerk to the council.

Preston.—October 14th.—Levelling, paving, channelling, &c., works in the back roads between St. Christopher's-road and St. Andrew's-road, and the back roads between St. Andrew's-road and St. David's-road.—The Borough Engineer.

Norfolk.—October 14th.—Erection of a steel and iron bridge at East Harling, for the county council.—Mr. T. H. B. Heslop, M.I.C.E., county surveyor, Norwich.

Romford.—October 14th.—Erection of public baths, for the urban district council.—Mr. George Bailey, clerk to the council.

Hull.—October 14th.—Supply of sixty standards of creosoted red-wood stringers, 4 in. by 7 in., and 700,000 creosoted redwood paving blocks.—Mr. A. E. White, city engineer.

Bangor.—October 15th.—Erection of buildings, chimney shaft, &c., for the electric light station.—Mr. John Gill, A.M.I.C.E., borough surveyor.

Westmorland.—October 15th.—Widening of that portion of the Kendal to Ockenthwaite-road near the back gateway of Levens Park, for the county council.—Mr. Joseph Bintley, county surveyor, Kendal.

Southborough.—October 15th.—Erection and completion of the proposed Victoria Hall and buildings in London-road, for the urban district council.—Mr. William Harmer, surveyor to the council.

Betchouse.—October 15th.—Providing and fixing at the sewage outfall works, Cooper Bridge, various boilers, engines, economiser, &c.—Mr. James Parkinson, town clerk.

Glasgow.—October 15th.—Supply of about 150 tons of 27-in. tubes, 1,273 tons of 24-in. spigot and socket turned and bored pipes and special castings.—Mr. James M. Gale, engineer of the corporation water department, City Chambers, Glasgow.

Tunbridge Wells.—October 15th.—Sewering and making-up of new roads on the site of the proposed workmen's dwellings.—Mr. W. C. Cripps, town clerk.

Twickenham.—October 16th.—Supply of 2,000 cubic yards of 2-in. broken blue Guernsey granite or Cherbourg quartzite, for the urban district council.—Mr. M. Jason Saunders, clerk to the council.

Southampton.—November 10th.—Supply of two engines and dynamos at the county lunatic asylum at Knowle, Fareham.—Mr. W. J. Taylor, county surveyor, The Castle, Winchester.

Pontypool.—October 17th.—Alteration, repair, &c., of the town hall, for the urban district council.—Mr. R. H. Haden, clerk to the council.

Kingstown.—October 17th.—Supply during the ensuing twelve months of various stores, &c.—Mr. John Donnelly, town clerk.

Edinburgh.—October 17th.—Various works in connection with gasholder tank at Granton.—Mr. James M'G. Jack, clerk to the commissioners.

Wishaw.—October 17th.—Supply of 12,000 tons of cast-iron pipes of 16-in., 18-in. and 19-in. diameter.—Mr. James Logan, town clerk.

Lancaster.—October 19th.—Erection of a new stone bridge over Newhouse burn, near Moor-side, for the rural district council.—Mr. W. H. Ritson, clerk to the council.

St. George-in-the-East.—October 20th.—Erection of an addition to the vestry hall, in Cable-street, for the vestry.—Mr. G. A. Wilson, surveyor to the vestry.

Blackpool.—October 21st.—Construction of two main outfall sewers to the sea (2,400 ft. and 1,400 ft. in length respectively), with all necessary manholes, &c.—Mr. J. Wolstenholme, borough surveyor.

Wilmslow.—October 21st.—Construction of certain sewers, for the urban district council.—Mr. William Cobbett, clerk to the council.

Cowes.—October 22nd.—Supply of about 1,500 yards of 6-in. and 500 yards of 4-in. cast-iron socket pipes, for the urban district council.—Mr. J. W. Webster, engineer and surveyor to the council.

Cowes.—October 22nd.—Construction of a cast-iron water tank to hold 70,000 gallons, for the urban district council.—Mr. J. W. Webster, engineer and surveyor to the council.

Wiltshire.—October 23rd.—Erection of the new county offices at the back of Arlington House, Trowbridge, for the county council.—Mr. Charles S. Adye, county surveyor, Stallard-street, Trowbridge.

Regny.—October 24th.—Laying of about 500 yards of cast-iron pumping main from the Avon waterworks to Railway-terrace, for the urban district council.—Mr. D. G. Macdonald, A.M.I.C.E., engineer and surveyor.

Hoddesdon.—October 24th.—Making-up of three streets in the district and the construction of various surface-water sewers, &c., for the urban district council.—Mr. J. Salkield, surveyor to the council.

Hull.—October 27th.—Supply and erection of various electric lighting plant.—Mr. A. S. Barnard, city electrical engineer.

---

## TENDERS.

*ACCEPTED.

DARWEN.—For the supply and fixing of a 10-ton overhead travelling crane in the generating-room of the new electricity works.—Mr. C. Costoker, town clerk —
　The Chatteris Engineering Works Company, Chatteris, Cambs.*

DOVER.—For the erection of a workshop, &c., adjoining the car sheds at Maxton.—Mr. Henry E. Stilgoe, A.M.I.C.E., borough engineer —

| | | | | | |
|---|---|---|---|---|---|
| J. Parsons, Beaconsfield-road, Dover | ... | ... | ... | ... | £409 |
| G. Munro, Heathfield-avenue, Dover | ... | ... | ... | ... | 423 |
| Austen & Lewis, Randolph-gardens, Dover | ... | ... | ... | 389 |
| H. B. Ellis, Priory-hill, Dover | ... | ... | ... | ... | 382 |
| | Surveyor's estimate, £375. | | | | |

EAST SUSSEX.—For the erection of two temporary buildings for 100 patients at the county lunatic asylum.—Mr. Henry Card, A.M.I.C.E., county surveyor, County Hall, Lewis :—

| | | | | |
|---|---|---|---|---|
| E. C. & J. Keay, Limited, Birmingham | ... | ... | ... | £5,768 |
| Longley & Co., Crawley | ... | ... | ... | 5,565 |
| Humphreys, Limited, London | ... | ... | ... | 5,180 |
| Clark & Co., Croydon | ... | ... | ... | 5,117 |
| Milton & Co., London | ... | ... | ... | 5,265 |
| W. Harlow, London | ... | ... | ... | 5,200 |
| T. White, Hampstead Heath | ... | ... | ... | 4,990 |
| Hawkins & Co., Ashford, Middlesex | ... | ... | ... | 4,959 |

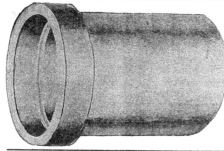

HOYLAND.—For the construction of about 73 yards of 15-in., 1,690 yards of 15-in., and 1,086 yards of 9-in. pipe sewers in connection with the King-street and Platts Common sewerage, for the urban district council.—Mr. William Farrington, A.M.I.C.E., engineer and surveyor to the council :—

A. Brunton & Son, Hull*　...　...　...　...　...　£1,203

Engineer's estimate, £1,337.

ILFORD.—For the construction of an underground latrine in The Broadway, for the urban district council.—Mr. Herbert Shaw, A.M.I.C.E., surveyor to the council :—

| | | | | | | | |
|---|---|---|---|---|---|---|---|
| Cross & Co. | ... | ... | ... | ... | ... | ... | £947 |
| F. Willmott | ... | ... | ... | ... | ... | ... | 717 |
| A. E. Symes | ... | ... | ... | ... | ... | ... | 675 |
| Merrydew & Wort, Stevenage, Herts* | ... | ... | ... | 506 |

Surveyor's estimate, £630.

ILFORD.—For various works at Valentine's, the site of the public park, for the urban district council.—Mr. H. Shaw, A.M.I.C.E., surveyor to the council :—

| | | | | | | | |
|---|---|---|---|---|---|---|---|
| C. Ford, Harlesden, N.W. | ... | ... | ... | ... | £2,290 |
| J. Jackson, Forest Gate | ... | ... | ... | ... | 2,275 |
| G. Bell, Tottenham | ... | ... | ... | ... | 2,363 |
| D. T. Jackson, Barking* | ... | ... | ... | ... | 2,200 |

MILE END.—For the supply of gulley grates and frames, manhole covers and ventilating gratings, for the vestry.—Mr. J. M. Knight, surveyor to the vestry :—

| | | | | | | s. | d. |
|---|---|---|---|---|---|---|---|
| Edie, Hewey & Co., Bow | ... | ... | ... | ... | 5 | 0 | per cwt. |
| Woodgate Engineering Company | ... | ... | ... | 5 | 0 | " |
| W. F. Butler & Co., Mile End Old Town | ... | ... | 4 | 5 | " |
| Durham Brothers, Bow | ... | ... | ... | ... | 4 | 3 | " |
| E. & F. Wright, Hanbury-street, Mile End New Town* | 4 | 3 | " |

NELSON.—For the construction of two filter-beds at the sewage works.—Mr. B. Ball, A.M.I.C.E., borough engineer and surveyor :—

W. Chew, Barkerhouse-road, Nelson*

SHEERNESS.—For the supply of about 900 tons of clean pit flints and 200 tons of hoggin or Aylesford gravel, for the urban district council.—Mr. C. A. Copland, surveyor to the council :—

Knight & Hodgkin, Sittingbourne.*—Flints, 5s. 5d. per ton ; hoggin, 5s. 1d. per ton.

ST. PANCRAS.—For the supply of about 140,000 jarrah or karri wood paving blocks for repaving Guildford-street and Midland-road, for the vestry.—Mr. Wm. N. Blair, engineer and surveyor to the vestry :—

| | | | Jarrah, per 1,000. | | | Karri, per 1,000. |
|---|---|---|---|---|---|---|
| | | | £ | s. | d. | £ s. d. |
| B. G. Elliott | ... | ... | 12 | 6 | 6 | |
| W. Griffiths | ... | ... | 11 | 2 | 6 | 11 0 0 |
| Acme Wood Flooring Company | 11 | 15 | 0 | 10 17 6 |
| Jarrahdale Jarrah Forests, Limited... | 11 | 6 | 3 | |
| Miller's Karri and Jarrah Company... | 11 | 5 | 0 | 11 2 6 |
| Palfreman, Foster & Co.* | ... | 10 | 19 | 6 | — |

WIMBLEDON.—For the supply of pipework, for the urban district council.—Mr. A. R. Preece, 30 Victoria-street, S.W. :—

| | | | | | | | |
|---|---|---|---|---|---|---|---|
| Mannesman Tube Company | ... | ... | ... | ... | £2,421 |
| Hopkins & Sons | ... | ... | ... | ... | ... | 1,568 |
| H. Ingle & Co. | ... | ... | ... | ... | ... | 1,471 |
| Babcocks & Wilcox* | ... | ... | ... | ... | 1,341 |
| J. Spencer & Co. | ... | ... | ... | ... | ... | 1,260 |

WILMSLOW.—For the construction of about 1,300 yards of 16-in. and 15-in. earthenware pipe sewers, &c., for the urban district council.—Mr. John Bowden, 14 Ridgefield, Manchester :—

| | | | | | | | |
|---|---|---|---|---|---|---|---|
| J. Dale, Northwich | ... | ... | ... | ... | ... | £4,036 |
| E. Cheetham, Pendleton, Manchester | ... | ... | 2,650 |
| G. Bosson, Church-road, Ashton-on-Mersey | ... | 2,600 |
| W. Briggs, Cheetham, Manchester | ... | ... | 2,450 |
| J. J. Blackborn, Cross-street, Urmston | ... | ... | 2,327 |
| J. & J. Lee, Wellington-road South, Stockport | ... | 2,098 |
| G. G. Rayner, Aintree, Liverpool | ... | ... | 1,880 |
| J. C. Shaw, David-street, Rochdale* | ... | ... | 1,877 |

## MEETINGS.

OCTOBER.

17.—Sanitary Institute : Sir Douglas Galton's introductory lecture to the 36th course of lectures and demonstrations for sanitary officers.

19.—Sanitary Institute : Visit of sanitary officers to the disinfecting apparatus and model steam laundry at St. John's Wharf, Fulham. 3.30 p.m.

19.—Sanitary Institute : Lecture for sanitary officers ; Dr. Louis Parkes, M.D., D.P.H., medical officer of health, Chelsea, on "Sanitary Laws and Regulations governing the Metropolis." 8 p.m.

21.—Sanitary Institute : Lecture for sanitary officers ; Mr. H. Manley, medical officer of health, West Bromwich, on "Sanitary Law—English, Scotch and Irish ; General Enactments Public Health Act, 1875 ; Model By-Laws, &c." 8 p.m.

22.—Sanitary Institute : Visit of sanitary officers to the Wimbledon sewage works, under the guidance of Mr. C. H. Cooper, A.M.I.C.E., engineer and surveyor to the Wimbledon Urban District Council. 3 p.m.

24.—Sanitary Institute : Lectures for sanitary officers ; Mr. W. A. Bond, medical officer of health, Holborn and St. Olave, Southwark, on "The Law Relating to the Supervision of Food Supply." 8 p.m.

26.—Sanitary Institute : Visit of sanitary officers to the parish of St. George, Hanover-square, under the guidance of Mr. A. Taylor, chief sanitary inspector. 3 p.m.

26.—Sanitary Institute : Lecture to sanitary officers ; Prof. A. Bostock Hill, medical officer of health, Sutton Coldfield, on "Trade Nuisances." 8 p.m.

28.—Sanitary Institute : Lecture to sanitary officers ; Dr. J. F. J. Sykes, medical officer of health, St. Pancras, on "Objects and Methods of Inspection, Nuisances, &c." 8 p.m.

29.—Sanitary Institute : Visit of sanitary officers to the Express Dairy Company's farm at Finchley. 3 p.m.

31.—Sanitary Institute : Lecture to sanitary officers ; Prof. W. H. Corfield, medical officer of health, St. George, Hanover-square, on "Water Supply, Drinking Water, Pollution of Water." 8 p.m.

## NOTICES.

*The Prepaid Subscription (including postage) is as follows:*

|  | Twelve Months. | Six Months. | Three Months. |
|---|---|---|---|
| United Kingdom ... ... | 15s. | 7s. 6d. | 3s. 9d. |
| Continent, the Colonies, India, | | | |
| United States, &c. ... ... | 19s. | 9s. 6d. | 4s. 9d. |

*The International News Company, 83 and 85 Duane-street New York City; The Toronto News Company, Toronto; and The Montreal News Company, Montreal, have been appointed agents in the United States and Canada for the sale of* THE SURVEYOR AND MUNICIPAL AND COUNTY ENGINEER. *A thin paper edition is printed for circulation abroad.*

EDITORIAL OFFICES :—

24 BRIDE-LANE, FLEET-STREET, LONDON, E.C.

ADVERTISEMENT AND PUBLISHING OFFICES :—

13 NEW STREET-HILL, FLEET-STREET, LONDON, E.C.

## APPOINTMENTS OPEN.

WEMBLEY (MIDDLESEX) URBAN DISTRICT COUNCIL.

APPOINTMENT OF ENGINEER, SURVEYOR AND SANITARY INSPECTOR.

The Wembley Urban District Council is prepared to receive applications from gentlemen desirous of filling the above posts, at the combined and inclusive salaries of £220, rising by annual increments of £15 to a maximum of £280 per annum.

Forms of application, and full particulars as to the duties, can be obtained by sending a stamped directed envelope (foolscap) to my office.

Application forms, duly filled up and accompanied by copies of not more than three recent testimonials, should be sent to me, in sealed envelopes, marked "Engineer, &c.," by not later than 6 o'clock on Wednesday, the 19th October, 1898.

Selected candidates will be written to, and third-class railway fare only will be allowed.

Canvassing the members, directly or indirectly, is strictly prohibited and will be deemed a disqualification.

(By order)
JNO. SMITH,
Clerk to the Council.

Public Offices, Wembley, Middlesex.
September 22, 1898.

BOROUGH OF BIRKENHEAD.

The Corporation of Birkenhead are prepared to receive applications for the position of General Engineering Assistant in the Borough Engineer and Surveyor's office, at a salary of £110 per annum, rising by annual increments of £10 to £150 per annum.

Candidates must have had experience in a municipal engineer's office, and be not less than twenty-three years of age nor more than twenty-eight years of age.

Applications, in candidate's own handwriting, stating age and experience, and accompanied by copies of not more than three recent testimonials, sealed and endorsed "Engineering Assistant," must be delivered at the office of Mr. Charles Brownridge, A.M.I.C.E., Borough Engineer and Surveyor, Town Hall, Birkenhead, by 12 o'clock noon, on Thursday, the 20th October, 1898.

Canvassing will be deemed a disqualification.
Borough Engineer's Office, Town Hall, Birkenhead.
September 29, 1898.

BOROUGH OF MAIDSTONE.

SEWER FOREMAN.

The Drainage Committee of the Corporation are prepared to receive applications from qualified persons for the post of Sewer Foreman.

Applicants must have had experience in the construction of brick and pipe sewers and the maintenance of the same, and will be required to take charge of the staff engaged in construction and maintenance of the sewerage system, and assist in the work when necessary.

The person appointed will act under the immediate direction of the Borough Surveyor, and his hours will be the same as the working staff, and he will be required to keep all the necessary books.

Wages will be at the rate of £1 15s. per week.

Applications, in candidate's own handwriting, stating age (which must not exceed forty-five years), experience, past and present employment, accompanied by copies of not more than three recent testimonials, and endorsed "Sewer Foreman," to be sent to the undersigned on or before Tuesday, 11th October, 1898.

Canvassing, directly or indirectly, will be considered a disqualification.

HUBERT MONCKTON,
Town Clerk.

Maidstone.
September 29, 1898.

MAIDSTONE RURAL DISTRICT COUNCIL.
The above Council require the services of a competent
Steam Roller Driver.

Applicants must have had previous experience in the driving
and management of steam roller, and must be competent to
execute any slight repairs thereto.

The appointment in the first instance will be for about
four months, but, if the selected driver gives satisfaction, the
appointment will in all probability be made a permanency.

Wages, 28s. per week.

Applications, stating age and previous experience, accompanied by two testimonials of recent date as to character and
suitability, must be sent, in own handwriting, to the undersigned not later than Wednesday, October 12, 1898.

SIDNEY STALLARD,
Surveyor.

October 1, 1898.

TWICKENHAM URBAN DISTRICT
COUNCIL.
APPOINTMENT OF SURVEYOR.

The Council invite applications for the appointment of
Surveyor for their district, which has a population of about
18,000 and a rateable value of £121,000, and approaching
40 miles of roads.

The salary will be £260 for the first year, with annual
increments thereafter of £20 until a maximum salary of £400
per annum is obtained.

The person appointed must reside within the district and
devote his whole time to the duties of his office (no private
work being allowed).

He must be thoroughly competent to carry out the duties
prescribed by the Public Health Acts, and to undertake and
superintend works usually performed by sanitary authorities.

The appointment will be subject to one month's notice on
either side.

Sealed applications, endorsed "Surveyor," stating age,
qualifications and experience, accompanied by copies of not
more than four testimonials, must reach me on or before
Monday, the 17th October, 1898.

Personal canvassing will be a disqualification.

(By order)
H. JASON SAUNDERS,
Clerk to the Council.

Town Hall, Twickenham.
September 30, 1898.

COUNTY BOROUGH OF STOCKPORT.
SEWAGE PURIFICATION WORKS.

Wanted, a Manager, to take charge of Sewage Outfall Works,
situate at Heathside Farm, Cheadle Heath, about 1½ miles
from Stockport. The estate is 95 acres in extent, 60 acres
being prepared for sewage treatment. The sewage is pumped
into the tanks; dry weather flow about, 2,500,000 gallons per
day. The buildings contain chemical tanks, boilers, duplicate
centrifugal pumps, duplicate engine-power grinding mills,
mixers, three mud presses, and other machinery.

Applicants must be experienced in the treatment of sewage
by precipitation, the pressing of mud, and the farming of land
by sewage effluent.

Applications, stating age, salary required, extent of experi-
ence, accompanied by copies of testimonials, and endorsed
"Sewage Farm Manager," to be addressed "The Town
Clerk, Stockport," and sent in not later than October 13, 1898.

WALTER HYDE,
Town Clerk.

EAST HAM URBAN DISTRICT COUNCIL.
ELECTRICAL ENGINEER.

The above-named Council require the services of an Electrical Engineer for the preparation of a scheme of electric
lighting combined with tramways, and the ultimate management and maintenance of the same after completion.

The person appointed must be prepared to reside in the
district and devote the whole of his time to the duties of the
office. The salary will be £300 per annum, with necessary
offices and assistance, and, as the district is a rapidly increasing one, the position is likely to improve.

All further particulars, together with a Form of application,
may be obtained upon application to Mr. W. H. Savage,
A.M.I.C.E., the Engineer and Surveyor to the Council, at the
Public Offices, East Ham.

Applications to be sent, in the printed envelope provided for the purpose, and enclosing copies of three recent
testimonials, or on or before Monday, October 24th next.

Canvassing members of the Council, either directly or indirectly, is strictly prohibited and will disqualify any candidate.

C. E. WILSON,
Clerk to the Council.

Public Offices, East Ham, London, E.
September 27, 1898.

## GARSTON URBAN DISTRICT COUNCIL.

The above Council require a qualified Assistant in the Surveyor's office; must be an accurate surveyor and leveller and neat draughtsman, having a thorough knowledge of building construction and competent to prepare working drawings and specifications. Applicants must be well acquainted with the Model By-Laws of the Local Government Board, and be competent to undertake the inspection of new buildings and the construction of drains, and have had at least five years' experience in a borough or district surveyor's office.

Salary to commence at £110 per annum.

Written applications only, in the candidate's handwriting, stating age, qualifications, present and past experience, together with copies of not more than four recent testimonials (which will not be returned), may be sent to the undersigned on or before the 17th day of October.

Canvassing will disqualify.

F. W. BOWDEN, Assoc.M.Inst.C.E.

Public Offices, Grassendale, West Liverpool.
October 5, 1898.

## DRAUGHTSMAN (Junior) required. — Permanency; London. One used to railway or tramway construction preferred. State age, experience and salary required.—Box 81, office of THE SURVEYOR, 24 Bride-lane, Fleet-street, E.C.

## STAINES RURAL DISTRICT COUNCIL.—
Wanted, Road Foreman, used to steam roller, tar paving, kerbing, and general work. Wages, 27s. weekly.— Apply, stating age and experience, to Mr. G. W. Manning, Surveyor to the Council, not later than the 12th proximo.

# TENDERS WANTED.

## BOROUGH OF REIGATE.
TO CONTRACTORS.

The Council of the Borough of Reigate, acting as an urban district council, invite tenders for the construction of a Bacteriological Filter and other incidental works at the Precipitation Works, Earlswood, within the said borough.

The whole of the work is to be executed in accordance with a plan, section and specification prepared by Mr. W. H. Prescott, C.E., the Borough Surveyor, and which may be seen at his office at the Market Hall, Redhill, Surrey, where also forms of tender may be obtained.

Sealed tenders, endorsed "Tender for Filter," are to be delivered at my office, No. 84 Station-road, Redhill, not later than 12 o'clock at noon on Thursday, the 13th day of October next.

The Council does not bind itself to accept the lowest or any tender.

Given under my hand this 26th day of September, 1898.

(By order of the Council)

CLAIR J. GRECE,
Town Clerk.

## RUGBY URBAN DISTRICT COUNCIL.

### PUMPING MAIN.

### TO CONTRACTORS AND OTHERS.

The Urban District Council of Rugby invite tenders for supplying, laying and jointing about 960 yards of Cast-Iron Pumping Main from the Avon Waterworks to Railway-terrace, Rugby.

The drawings can be seen at my office, where a copy of the specification, bill of quantities and form of tender can be obtained on payment of 1 guinea, which will be returned on receipt of a bond-fide tender.

Sealed tenders, endorsed "Pumping Main," to be sent to Mr. T. M. Wratislaw, Clerk to the Council, Rugby, on or before the 24th instant.

The Council do not bind themselves to accept the lowest or any tender.

(By order)

D. G. MACDONALD, Assoc.M.Inst.C.E.,
Engineer and Surveyor.

Rugby.
October 4, 1898.

HODDESDON URBAN DISTRICT COUNCIL.
TO ROAD AND SEWER CONTRACTORS.

The above Council invite tenders for the Making-up of three Streets in their district, comprising a total length of 3,400 ft.

The works include Carriageways, Footways and Kerbs.

Tenders are also invited for the construction of Surface-Water Sewers, comprising 44 yards of 15-in. Cast-Iron Pipe, 32 yards of 15-in. Stoneware Pipe, 383 yards of 12-in. Stoneware Pipe, 953 yards of 9-in. Stoneware Pipe and 131 yards of 6-in. Stoneware Pipe, with the necessary Junctions, Manholes, Tumbling Bays, Ventilators, Catchpits, &c.

Plans and sections may be seen at the office of the undersigned, from whom the specifications, quantities, forms of tender and contract may be obtained on payment of 3 guineas, which sum will be returned to non-successful contractors on the receipt of a *bonâ-fide* tender and the return of the specifications, quantities, forms of tender and contract, and to the successful contractor on his executing his contract and bond.

Tenders must be on the forms supplied by the council and accompanied by the schedule of prices, and must be delivered at the office of the Council, addressed to the Chairman, Highways Committee, Council Offices, High-street, Hoddesdon, sealed and endorsed "Tender for Works," by not later than noon on Monday, the 24th day of October inst.

The Council do not bind themselves to accept the lowest or any tender, and reserve the right of letting both contracts to one contractor or otherwise.

T. SALKIELD,
Surveyor.

Briscoe-road, Hoddesdon.
October 1, 1898.

TWICKENHAM URBAN DISTRICT COUNCIL.
BROKEN GRANITE.

The Twickenham Urban District Council invite tenders for the supply of about 2,000 cubic yards of 2-in. Broken Blue Guernsey Granite or Cherbourg Quartzite, suitable for road-metalling, to be delivered alongside Richmond Bridge or Church Draw Docks, within the parish of Twickenham, as required.

Tenders, with samples, to be sent in to me, endorsed "Tender for Granite," on or before noon on Thursday, 13th October, 1898.

Forms, on which the tenders only will be received, and full particulars may be obtained at the office of Mr. G. B. Laffan, Surveyor to the Council, Town Hall, Twickenham.

The party whose tender is accepted will be required to enter into a contract and deliver 100 cubic yards of the granite within fourteen days from the date of the Surveyor's order, and the remainder of the granite to be delivered within three months from the date of the signing of the contract.

The Council does not bind itself to accept the lowest or any tender.

(By order)
H. JASON SAUNDERS,
Clerk to the Council.

Town Hall, Twickenham.
October 1, 1898.

ORSETT RURAL DISTRICT COUNCIL.

*PRIVATE STREET WORKS.*

CHADWELL ST. MARY PARISH (TILBURY).

Tenders are invited for the Levelling, Making-up, Kerbing and Surface Draining the following streets or parts of streets in the parish of Chadwell St. Mary—viz., Montreal-road, for a distance of 1,880 ft. from its junction with Dock-road; Quebec-road, Toronto-road, for a distance of 1,501 ft. from its junction with Dock-road; Calcutta-road, for a distance of 602 ft. from its junction with Montreal-road; Sydney-road, for a distance of 785 ft. from Toronto-road; and Dock-road, from the boundary of the London, Tilbury and Southend Railway Company's property to the boundary between the parishes of Chadwell St. Mary and Little Thurrock.

Plans and specifications can be seen, and bills of quantities obtained, at the office of the Council's Surveyor, Mr. R. T. Stewart, Orsett, Essex, by making an appointment with him.

Sealed tenders, to be endorsed "Tilbury Streets," to be delivered to the undersigned not later than Monday, October 10, 1898.

The Council do not bind themselves to accept the lowest or any tender.

(By order)
JAMES BECK,
Clerk to the Orsett Rural District Council.

South Ockenden.

# The Surveyor

## And Municipal and County Engineer.

Vol. XIV., No. 352.     LONDON, OCTOBER 14, 1898.     Weekly, Price 3d.

## Minutes of Proceedings.

**Value of Municipal Trading.**

The question of the appropriate limits of municipal enterprise—or "municipal trading," to use the phrase that has been coming into fashion—has of late received a good deal of attention from economists. This was especially noticeable at the recent meeting of the British Association, when the section devoted to economics spent considerable time in debating the subject in various aspects. In connection with the special undertakings with which municipalities have for some time been closely identified, several erroneous statements have been made; and these, in the interests of all concerned, but particularly in the interests of municipal trading, invite some criticism. There can, of course, be no question as to the great development of municipal undertakings at the present day. In the valuable paper published in our issue of September 16th Mr. Pearson clearly demonstrated the vitality with which municipalities have been animated in their various enterprises. The total indebtedness of £93,000,000 sterling, which figure represents municipal loans at the present moment, is a measure of the activity of corporations in undertaking work for the benefit of the community. It is true that nearly half of that sum is invested in waterworks, but the capital account of those departments that are more distinctly trading in their character, such as electric lighting, gasworks and so on, stands at a very considerable figure. Nor can it be said that the results of such work suggest any immediate limit to the indebtedness that is being cheerfully undertaken by almost every municipality in the kingdom. It is hardly necessary to repeat some of the stock arguments that can be always deduced in favour of municipal trading, but these arguments are considerably strengthened by what we may term the extraordinary success that has followed the operations of corporations in the direction of tramways and electric lighting. Examples in connection with electric tramways are few, but we have already shown that in the completed systems success has been pronounced from the commencement. In speaking of the indebtedness of local authorities it must not be forgotten that these gigantic sums have been raised at exceedingly low rates of interest, probably a half, and in some cases a third, of what it would cost any joint-stock company. Dealing, however, with some of the misconceptions that have been promulgated, we must raise a strong protest against the remark, frequently repeated, that "there is no special reason why the credit of the ratepayers should be pledged to enable a capitalist to procure power for his mills at a cheaper rate." This especially relates to those cases in which a municipality undertakes to supply energy, no matter in what form, for power purposes throughout its district, but it is the very essence of municipal activity that it should supply a ratepayer with lighting, even when pledging the credit of the majority, more cheaply than he can supply it himself or be supplied by any other person. It is obvious that when a municipality undertakes a supply of power and lighting some one or more consumers are bound to derive relatively more advantage than many others. In particular, take the case of electric lighting. Its introduction by a corporation in many towns has permitted the owners of textile industries to work longer hours during the winter months, because by the aid of electric lighting they are enabled to match colours, which they could not possibly do previously by any other artificial light. If the owners of such a factory obtain their light from the public mains they pay in a correspondingly greater degree for the greater relative advantage than does the man who merely uses two or three lights for household purposes. The same truism will hold in the case of any other municipal supply; it is obvious that it will be cheaper to make power on a large scale and distribute to users than it will be for consumers to make it themselves. Iron workers, for example, may, in the exercise of their special work, employ large lengths of steam pipes for the operation of scattered steam engines. This is an uneconomical, though in some circumstances a necessary, method, but if a municipality will offer in such a case to supply electrical energy at a fairly low rate, the iron worker may abandon his steam engines and use electric motors. Nor could it be seriously urged that a municipality was exceeding its duties to the ratepayers if it sought to supply power in such a case. Moreover, a consumer is usually a ratepayer, and according to his value as a consumer so is his value as a ratepayer. If he is a large user of power or lighting, it may be taken for granted that he is a large ratepayer. It would not be difficult to produce other instances in which a municipality may be ostensibly benefitting one man more than another. The householder whose premises abut on main streets may be said to obtain a greater relative advantage from a good system of street sweeping and scavenging than the man who lives a considerable distance away from the main thoroughfare. One of the most unfair statements, however, made against municipalities is that "in those cases where they own the gasworks they show considerable reluctance to admit electric lighting into the district, because it might depreciate the value of the gasworks." Such a suggestion is absolutely erroneous, and it can be shown conclusively that electric lighting has been most successful in those towns where the corporations have for years owned the gasworks. The Manchester gasworks are among the largest municipally-owned undertakings in the world, but it would be difficult for anybody to say that the electric lighting system had suffered in the slightest degree; indeed, the very contrary can be shown, for the Manchester Corporation electric lighting works may be held to be pre-eminent among provincial works.

On the vexed question of what shall be done with the profits derived from municipal activity we have previously made some remarks, and we see no reason to alter the opinion formerly expressed to the effect that until the majority of ratepayers are obtaining some direct benefit from a corporation undertaking there should be some distribution of profit, when obtained, in the shape of a reduction of rates. Electric lighting is especially an instance where profits, at any rate for the first few years, should be devoted to some extent towards alleviating rates, because, in spite of the success that has attended the introduction of electricity, some years must elapse before it can be in any sense a universal illuminant. The whole matter is put into a nutshell in the case of Bristol, where at the present moment there are 1,000 consumers and 60,000 ratepayers. The credit of those ratepayers was pledged when the work was first undertaken, and it would be grossly unfair if the 1,000 consumers were, in their capacity of ratepayers, to receive the whole of the advantages that might arise from the successful operation of the system. Turning to another aspect of the question, it is surprising to find such an antiquated statement being repeated as that "municipalities cannot command the same ability as companies"; such a suggestion argues a lack of knowledge and experience of what really obtains. The engineers and surveyors, the lawyers, the agents, and officials generally, who are directly connected with municipal interests stand, it is needless to say, very high in their respective professions; nor is there any neglect of work merely because there is likely to be a change of employers from time to time. Members of committee may come and go, but the body corporate as directly representing the interests of the ratepayers is always in existence, and there is too much light thrown upon the doings of municipal departments for there to be much likelihood of waste occurring in time or money. In a sense there is probably more responsibility felt in the conduct of municipal work than in the undertakings carried out by companies. The record of joint-stock enterprise in this country on the grounds of probity and excellence of work does not stand on the same level as that of municipalities. We are often referred to America as furnishing an example of the disastrous effects of municipalities undertaking public supplies, but the life and institutions of the two countries are totally at variance. In comparison with this country America is new to municipal life, and has not yet freed itself from the tyranny of cliques, Tammany Halls and caucuses generally. But if municipal work has not been a success in America, can it be urged that the operations of companies in the United States have done very much for the consumer? It is the country above all others in which monopolist rings and trusts have exercised the most potent influence for evil. Leaving that phase of the subject, we come to another, equally important from the municipal point of view, What should be the limits of municipal trading? It is obviously difficult to lay down any hard and fast rules. We should not, however, like to see corporations or other local authorities embark upon the sale of provisions or become universal milk sellers, and we must confess even to some apprehension regarding the "Gothenburg" system of running beershops. But in such essentially public work as lighting, water supply, the distribution of power and the operation of tramway systems there is surely little to be said against it. The limit of municipal enterprise should be found in restricting it to those operations that are confined for the most part within the locality. Tramways occasionally, in order to make a complete system, might with advantage be extended beyond the municipal boundary, with the concurrence of the outlying local authorities, just in the same way as water is supplied to some outside authorities by large towns. We admit that the very fact of going beyond a municipal boundary tells against the telephone system, because, as we have pointed out, the utility of the telephone service depends upon the distance and area over which

conversations can be held, and this will become more marked with the greater development of trunk line services.

*          *          *

**Superannuation.** We note with satisfaction that the agitation over the question of superannuation for municipal officers is once more being resumed, and that those who are exerting themselves in the matter are in no way discouraged by the want of success which has hitherto attended their efforts. Given the necessary amount of energy and intelligent adaptation of means to the end in view, success must come sooner or later, though the sooner it comes the better. The conference convened by the Municipal Officers' Association, as we have already announced, have been considering the question of again promoting legislation in the next session of Parliament, and it has been decided to invite all associations and societies representing municipal officers to again send delegates to the conference. In this connection we would draw the attention of our readers to the letter from Mr. C. J. F. Carnell, honorary secretary of the Municipal Officers' Association, which appears in another column. We expect to be able to report a good attendance of municipal officers at the forthcoming meeting, and that a satisfactory course of action will be unanimously decided upon. Above all, we hope that municipal engineers will be adequately represented at the gathering. The Incorporated Association of Municipal and County Engineers will no doubt give the Bill the same hearty support as last year, though it will be remembered that it was considered desirable to extend support also to the Bill promoted by the Metropolitan Local Government Officers' Association, so long as the two Bills did not clash. The object of the smaller Bill, of course, is to make compulsory the provisions in the Superannuation Act, 1866, by which metropolitan local authorities are given discretion to grant superannuation to their officers. Last week we published a report from the chairman and secretary of the Municipal Officers' Association dealing with the present position of affairs, and from that report it will be seen that some slight friction has arisen in connection with the two Bills. The promoters of the smaller Bill apparently wish that all reference to metropolitan officers be omitted from the larger, a request to which the conference, as representing municipal officers all over the country, cannot very well agree, especially as the smaller Bill makes no provision for counting years of service from one local authority to another. A Bill of only partial application is not likely to stand as good a chance as a complete measure representing a unanimous demand on the part of municipal officers, both metropolitan and provincial. If the larger Bill were sure of acceptance by Parliament there would, of course, be no necessity for the smaller and sectional one; but, as things are, metropolitan officials naturally argue that they should not be expected to surrender their chance of making the Bill of 1865 compulsory. On the other hand, in spite of the discretionary powers vested in metropolitan authorities by that measure, it may reasonably be doubted if Parliament would make superannuation compulsory without extending the privilege to municipal officers throughout the country generally. At the same time there is no saying what Parliament in its wisdom may or may not do. There is the analogous case of the poor law officers as a precedent. In their case superannuation had long been permissible, and Parliament made it compulsory, though why they have a greater claim than other classes of local government officers would be very difficult to say. In regard to the two Bills under discussion, it should not be difficult to come to a harmonious understanding. The right policy, as in other things, will be that which tends to the greatest good of the greatest number, and a sectional measure is certainly to be deprecated if it can possibly be avoided without injustice. We hope to find that the forthcoming meeting will result in a satisfactory arrangement.

\* \* \*

**The Ventilation of House Drains and Sewers.**

Notwithstanding the difficulties which beset the question of the ventilation of house drains and of sewers, —for the two are interdependent— and notwithstanding that the subject is being repeatedly considered and discussed at all sanitary congresses, it is apparent that we get no nearer a solution of the difficulty. It is, we must admit, somewhat of a reflection on municipal engineers and medical officers that progress is so slow, and that practically we are no further advanced in our knowledge as to how to compass the evil than we were twenty years ago. There is, it cannot, we think, be gainsaid, no approach to any consensus of opinion among health officers on any phase of the question. In some districts it is found that the free ventilation of sewers by road-surface ventilators and shafts carried up the sides of houses is carried out, and that house drains are also ventilated in themselves, but disconnected, so far as sewer air is concerned, from the sewerage system. In a closely adjacent district road-surface ventilators are entirely abolished, as being an unmitigated nuisance, and tall expensive columns are erected in the footways of every street, while the house drains are constructed without disconnecting traps, the private drains being utilised to ventilate the sewer; or, where disconnecting traps are provided, each house is "adorned" with two ventilating shafts, one for the "ventilation" of the sewer and the other for the "ventilation" of the house drain—an incongruity which the poor householder is unable to fathom, and which experts are generally unable to explain away. In another district may be found a system of sewers in which no ventilation whatever is provided for, and in still another artificial means of disinfection of sewer air is provided for.

Each of the systems has its advocates, who claim that their particular method is, and only can be, right, and medical men are for ever proclaiming that almost all the ills that flesh is heir to are due to the influence of sewer gas. We venture to state that all this diversity of practice is due to an ignorance of the subject, which ought not to be permitted to continue. Medical officers of health, we notice, claim that the subject is one in regard to which surveyors should not have a monopoly of opinion as to a solution of the question, but, from a perusal of papers and opinions given by them at the recent Sanitary Institute congress, they are as widely chaotic in their views as municipal engineers, and though unable, as it appears to us, to suggest a remedy, they are enabled to work mischief, for in one case we noticed that a medical officer of health announced that a corporation acting on his advice had removed all ventilators of sewers up private houses, and no alternative means of ventilation appears to have been substituted for the ventilators displaced. Unless the medical officer can show, as he appears to have been unable to show at the recent congress, that his abilities are limited to criticism only, he must of necessity not be seriously counted upon as being able to assist in a solution of the problem. We think, however, that this is not the case; but we hope that the engineer and the chemist will jointly be able to do much, and we would suggest that the matter be taken up in a proper spirit and that experiments be carried out on strictly scientific lines to investigate and determine the remedy for what is at present a very unsatisfactory and chaotic muddle.

\* \* \*

**Progress in Sanitary Engineering.**

In matters of detail there are many points of difference in engineering practice in England and in America, but the essentials must, of course, be the same in both countries, and, indeed, in all civilised countries. This was illustrated at the recent convention of the American Society of Civil Engineers, when the president, Mr. Alphonse Fteley, gave, as the annual address, a comprehensive review of engineering progress during the preceding year. In connection with water supply he drew attention to some pressing aspects. He pointed out that extravagant consumption, or rather waste, appears to increase as increased provision is made to meet it, and that unless some more rational method than that now in use be employed to regulate consumption it will be impossible to make reasonable provision to meet it. With the increased demand for water come also more exacting requirements as to its purity. Filtration processes have been installed, their action studied, and much valuable information gathered. Radical chemical and biological changes have been found to take place in the operation of filtering, and bacterial life has been recognised as the most potent instrument for the conversion of organic matters into mineral compounds. Mr. Fteley also proceeded to sum up the equally vital question of sewage disposal and the pollution of rivers. The necessity for the final discharge of sewage into streams that may subsequently be used as sources of water supply makes equally necessary the application of means for rendering the sewage innocuous. The worst pollution of streams, of course, has arisen, not from domestic sewage, but from trade refuse, and at the present moment the solution of the problem seems much nearer realisation in the former respect than in the latter, even without Archdeacon Sheringham's wonderful suggestions of "huge furnaces," "lofty chimneys" and "chemical ingredients."

\* \* \*

**Remuneration for Special Work.**

When a municipal engineer carries out successfully some extensive scheme outside the ordinary routine of his duties, and thereby probably saves the town a large sum of money, surely no wrong is done to the ratepayers, but rather the reverse, by making due recognition in the shape of some special remuneration over and above the official's salary. A little encouragement judiciously given is generally a profitable investment, but if some people had their way there would be none. One or two members of the Waterford Corporation are of this type, but we are glad to say that on a recent occasion they did not have their own way. At the last meeting of the council a proposal was under consideration to increase the salary of the borough engineer, and the recommendation of the committee also contained a reference to the granting of some special remuneration for the designing and carrying out of the sewage works when these works were completed. This proposal gave offence to one or two members, and it was even described as a "dangerous precedent." The recommendation, however, was passed, and it is not likely that the corporation or ratepayers will have any reason to regret their generosity.

\* \* \*

**A Chairman Infringing By-Laws.**

It is never a very easy task for the surveyors to local authorities to enforce by-laws, but the difficulty is much greater when an infringement is committed by a member of the local authority and the chairman to boot. This was the case the other day at Bray, where the chairman of the commissioners, who might have been expected to know better and to set an example, appears not only to have ignored the by-laws, but to have made a complaint against the surveyor, because the latter insisted on the by-laws being complied with. This the offended chairman called "red-tapeism." He had applied for water to be turned on where he was carrying out certain building operations. That was not done, for the reason, as afterwards transpired, that no plans had been deposited. Much was said about the unwisdom of hampering and checking building operations, and thus injuring the town; but by-laws are made with a necessary object in view, and if even the chairman does not respect them, who will?

# Principal Features of Electric Lighting Systems.—VI.*

## TWO MODERN LOW-PRESSURE SYSTEMS.

In the last article on this subject it was suggested that perhaps the best way of bringing out the principal features of modern municipal works employing low-pressure current would be to describe systems of the latest type. With this object in view it is proposed to set forth the principal features of the Bradford system and the one owned by the Chester Corporation.

### THE BRADFORD WORKS

provide an instance of the best practice that obtains to-day. Both in size and arrangement the works rank among the best in the kingdom, the plant having been arranged and carried out by the present city electrical engineer, Mr. H. Gibbings. The dynamo and engine-room is 85 ft. long, 61 ft. wide and 28 ft. high, with steel roof, which is in one span and boarded with pitch pine. Accommodation is provided for twelve engines and dynamos. The boiler-house is 105 ft. long, 48 ft. wide, and 28 ft. high to the steel lattice girders which carry the roof. The latter is provided with large louvred ventilators for carrying away escaping steam and skylights for giving light. In order that the coaling arrangements may be expeditiously carried out, and with as little labour as possible, the coal carts enter by special entrance gates, and, after being weighed in the weigh-house, pass up a slight

running in a bath of oil lubricating all the working parts by splash. The range of speed capable of being regulated by hand is from 270 to 300 revolutions per minute. Four of the dynamos are of Siemens' multipolar type and coupled direct to the engine. They give an output of 750 amperes and 500 volts at a speed of 300 revolutions per minute. The armature is of the usual Siemens' drum pattern, with stranded bar conductors, but the diameter in this case is nearly twice the length of the pole pieces.

### THE BOILER-HOUSE.

Considerable interest attaches to the boiler-house, for the type of boiler used is radically different from what one usually meets in electricity works. There are two of the marine type, made by Messrs. John Brown & Co., Limited, providing steam for 600 horse-power when working on a consumption of 20 lb. of water per indicated horse-power, and capable when forced of providing 800 indicated horse-power. They are 9 ft. 9 in. mean diameter by 10 ft. 6 in. long, and fitted with two Purves' flues each, the diameter of flues being 2 ft. 10 in. inside. There are in each boiler 110 Servé tubes, which are 3¼ in. outside diameter; the shell plates are 1⅛ in. thick, front and back end plates ⅞ in., furnaces ½ in., the

Chester Corporation Electricity Works: Engine and Dynamo Room.

incline to a roadway running alongside the boiler-house, from which the coals can be easily tipped through the large doorways direct into the extensive bunkers below. For condensing purposes a cooling reservoir has been constructed near a brook, some 90 yards distant from the works. The water, controlled by a sluice, can be drawn from the brook through a settling tank into the reservoir. The latter is constructed of brickwork in cement, concrete and masonry. Efficient cooling of the condensing water is attained by the architect's system of guide-walls, by which the water is given time to part with its heat by travelling a maximum distance before returning to the condenser. From the reservoir the water travels in large cast-iron pipes to a well—built of brickwork in cement and concrete—near the engine-house, whence it is drawn by the circulating pumps to the surface condenser, from which it returns in open cast-iron troughs to the reservoir.

The engines are Willans' patent central-valve triple-expansion type, having three cranks at 120° apart, two of the engines being each of 600 indicated horse-power when running at 300 revolutions per minute with a steam pressure of 180 lb. per square inch at the stop-valve; the cranks

working pressure 200 lb. per square inch, and grate area 34 square feet. It is stated that at the six and a half-hours' evaporative test 626 horse-power was obtained easily, burning 40 lb. of coal per square foot of grate per hour. By reference to the illustrations† of the boilers some idea of the draught system may be gained. The cold air for the combustion of the fuel enters from the back end of the boiler, passing along the outer space, A A¹ to the valves, B and B¹, in furnace fronts; on its way this cold air is guided round the outside of the "inner" space C, in a "helical" direction by partitions set up as shown. After combustion the waste hot gases leaving the boiler pass through the smoke-box into inner space C, and are made by similar partitions to pass round and in close contact with the boiler in a "helical" direction on their way to the suction fan. The boiler by these means is thoroughly enveloped in the escaping heat, effectually preventing either "radiation," "condensation" or straining of the boiler under forced conditions, such as rapid

* Through a printer's error in the last article in this series was numbered VI. instead of V. The remaining contributions will be published in quick succession.—Ed. The Surveyor.

† See special Supplement sheet.

generation of steam from cold water or sudden and greatly-increased evaporation. The cold air on its way to the valves also absorbs a large amount of heat from the escaping gases, and so enters the furnaces at a greatly-increased temperature, with resultant economy. No blocking up of the bottom boiler tubes through any deposit in the smoke-box can take place, as such a deposit, if any, drops to the bottom of the inner casing C, from whence it is easily removed by doors at front. The doors D are placed so as to allow of a brush being passed through to sweep away any sooty deposit from the boiler shell, should any such deposit take place.

The surface-condenser which is employed has been manufactured by Messrs. Cole, Marchent & Morley, of Bradford, and is large enough to deal with 30,000 lb. of steam per hour at 200 deg. Fahr.; it consists of about 2,500 square feet of solid-drawn brass tubing, secured into brass tube plates with screwed ferrules; on each end of the condenser doors are provided, to give access to the tubes for cleaning out, &c. To the side of the condenser two single-acting air-pumps are bolted, each being 12 in. diameter and 9 in. stroke. These pumps draw the condensed water from the condenser, and deliver it into a storage cistern some distance above their own level; they are driven by a Reuling & Appleby electric motor and spur gearing, the former being coupled direct to the main switchboard close by; the pump resistances are arranged with seven notches, so that the speed and power of the motor can be varied to suit the requirements of the load on the station. The centrifugal circulating-pumps for the same plant deliver together 2,500 gallons per minute through the condenser; the pumps draw their water from a well close to the engine-house, which well is connected by means of a large pipe to the cooling reservoirs, the delivery from the pumps is taken through the condenser and delivered by 12-in. pipes outside the engine-house, from which place the water runs in open troughs back into the cooling reservoirs. The main steam pipes consist of one horizontal ring of 10-in. bore lap-welded steel tubes, having cast-iron tee-pieces for derivation of boiler and engine branch pipes. The branch pipes are of solid-drawn copper. The main exhaust pipes consist of 20-in. bore cast-iron pipes, made in sections, with inlets formed for connecting the branch pipes, which are from 14-in. to 18-in. bore.

The distribution of electrical energy from this station is on the most modern lines and entails distributing electricity to consumers at 200 volts, and from the consumer's point of view the system has worked extremely well. The cables, which are of the British Insulated Wire Company's manufacture, consist of five lines, each 1,030 yards in length, of 1·5 square inch sectional area, high-conductivity copper. The insulation material used consists of high-class hemp paper, specially manufactured and impregnated with resin oil. The insulation is protected with a solid lead tube of a radial thickness of ⅛ in. A further protection consists of two ribbons of mild sheet steel, wound one over the other so that the convolutions of the upper layer overlap those portions of the cable left unprotected by the lower layer. One thousand and fifty yards of three-core pilot wire is also laid with the above cable, to which the registering instruments on the switchboard are connected.

### THE CHESTER WORKS.

The chief points of interest in the Chester Corporation electric lighting system arise from the employment of a three-wire system with 420 volts across the two outers and the use of 210 volts in the houses. It clearly shows the unmistakable extension of area which is permitted to the low-pressure system by the use of 200 volts in the houses, and that the objections from the consumer's point of view are immaterial compared with those that might arise in a system which is changed over from 110 to 220 volts. The distance of the extreme feeding point from the generating station is 1,622 yards, and the greatest distance of a consumer's terminals from the generating plant is 1,900 yards; but we believe it is the intention to go considerably beyond these points, and there seems to be no reason against a further extension. In the use of 200 volts in the houses no trouble of a serious nature seems to have been experienced, nor has it been necessary to materially alter the methods of wiring that are usual with the lower pressure.

Commencing with the steam-raising plant, the boilers consist of three Babcock-Wilcox boilers, the working pressure of which is 160 lb., each evaporating 5,000 lb. of water. An interesting feature in connection with the steam-raising plant is the Green's economiser, consisting of 144 tubes, the scrapers of which are driven by an electric motor. The economiser is intended to raise 1,000 gallons of water per hour from 60 deg. to 200 deg. Fahr. There is a feed-water tank, which is kept supplied with water from the town mains; it is also connected with the discharge pipe from the condenser. The engine-room plant consists of Belliss two-crank compound engines combined with Parker dynamos. The dynamos, which are of the shunt-wound type, are mounted upon an extension of engine bed-plate, and coupled direct to the crank shafts. The machines shown in the foreground of the illustration are of great interest and play a very important part in the operation of the system. It will be observed that the four machines are connected together, the two middle machines forming in themselves a motor dynamo, or, as it is more commonly termed, a balancing transformer, which serves,

as a matter of fact, to balance the system. In other words, it helps to steady the voltage on the two sides of the three-wire mains. One of these two machines is the motor, and not only drives its companion, but also the two end dynamos, whose function is to assist in charging the battery of accumulators. The accumulators, of which there are two sets, furnish current for the demand during the day and also at night. There is nothing very unusual in the arrangement of mains; main feeders are run to one central point, from which five branch sub-feeders are run and connected at different points to the distributing mains.

## TYPHOID NEAR PLYMOUTH.

According to a morning contemporary, a serious outbreak of typhoid fever has taken place at Honicknowle, a village containing about 600 inhabitants, 4 miles north of Plymouth. At present there are twenty-three cases under treatment, while in another village close by there are fourteen more patients, and signs of the disease are now showing themselves at a third village, called Egg Buckland. All these places are within the area of the Plympton Rural District Council, and one of the most serious features of the outbreak is that from this area comes a great deal of the dairy produce with which Plymouth is supplied daily.

The epidemic is ascribed to the defective drainage, or rather to the absence of any proper system, and the consequent pollution of the streams and wells from which the people draw their water. The district council are now being openly accused of procrastination, and all the blame for the present disastrous outbreak is being laid at their door. As far back as 1893 strong representations were made to this body as to the insanitary condition of the area affected.

"Grossly polluted" is the description applied to the water supply by the council's own medical officer of health. It is alleged that from all points of the compass the people of Honicknowle are confronted by obnoxious odours, and samples of the water taken by visitors to the fever-stricken districts have a most disgusting smell. The village is surrounded on almost every side by accumulations of offensive matter.

Six children from one family are now in Plymouth borough isolation hospital, and one case has proved fatal. The usual precautions are being taken to prevent the spread of the disease.

## LOCAL AUTHORITIES AND ELECTRIC LIGHTING.

Lord George Hamilton, M.P., has forwarded the following letter to the Acton Urban District Council, who had asked him to oppose the Bill promoted in the last session of Parliament by the General Power Distributing Company. The Bill excited much opposition among local authorities which had taken up electric lighting orders or were proposing to do so. "India Office, Whitehall, S.W. Sir,—I have to acknowledge the receipt of your letter of July 22nd. I am in favour of local authorities having control over the lighting in their districts, and, where practicable, applying the profits of such enterprise to the reduction of the rates of the locality. On the other hand, private enterprise will often develop experiments and initiate improved methods of lighting which the local authority may not be able to conduct themselves, and it is by the combination of the two methods that the community at large may be most benefitted. The Bill to which you call my attention is postponed till next session, and I shall be glad, when it comes up in a new shape, to hear what the views of the Acton District Council are."

**Trade Publications.**—Mr. John Jones, the well-known sanitary specialist, of 16 Church-street, Chelsea, S.W., has sent us a copy of a recent catalogue of sanitary goods. He draws special attention to the many new improvements, patent and otherwise, that have been submitted to and tested by sanitary experts, and these he especially recommends for use. Among these goods may be mentioned his automatic-seal airtight manhole covers, which were awarded the medal of the Sanitary Institute at the Liverpool Health Exhibition in 1894, his patent drain ventilation system, improved deep-seal gullies, air-inlet ventilators, drain and pipe stoppers, and drain-testing appliances. The catalogue is well printed and contains numerous illustrations. It should certainly be referred to by architects, builders and others, who require information relative to all kinds of sanitary specialities.—From Mr. W. Duncan Tucker, Phœnix Saw Mills, Lawrence-road, South Tottenham, we have also received an illustrated catalogue and price list of doors, mouldings, sashes, cornices, &c. A new feature of the catalogue is the horticultural sections, which have been prepared to meet the growing demands for horticultural buildings; and a special page at the end of the catalogue is devoted to illustrations of various horticultural buildings which have been manufactured by the firm. This gives a good idea of the class of work they are prepared to undertake. Among the various goods manufactured, electric light wire casings may also be mentioned.

# The Sanitary Institute.

## THE SEVENTEENTH ANNUAL CONGRESS.—III.

In our last issue it will be remembered that we gave a full report of the papers and discussions in connection with the conference of municipal and county engineers at the recent congress at Birmingham. This week it will be seen that, instead of adhering to the formal and arbitrary divisions into sections and conferences, we have made a variation in our method of dealing with the proceedings, and trust that it will be acceptable to our readers.

### HOUSING THE LABOURING CLASSES.

In resuming our report we have grouped together some of the references to the difficult and pressing problem of dealing with insanitary areas in the larger towns and providing dwelling accommodation therein for the poorer classes. At the conference of municipal representatives interesting papers were read by Dr. J. F. J. Sykes, medical officer of health to the St. Pancras Vestry, and by Mr. Peter Addie, F.S.I., lately the manager of the Birmingham improvement scheme.

### DWELLING ACCOMMODATION IN LARGE CITIES.

Dr. SYKES in his paper said it was profitable to review the subject from a social as well as a structural aspect, since usage and sanitary precautions must form the basis of structural accommodation. He proceeded to point out that the functions and requirements to be provided for the individual in the modern dwelling were in approximate order of greatest necessity: (1) sleeping, (2) food storage, (3) cooking, (4) warming, (5) excretion, (6) ablution, (7) clothes washing, (8) deposit of refuse, (9) open space for refuse, drying clothes, &c., (10) bathing, not partial but total ablution of the body, and (11) living, including reading, writing, work, recreation, &c., for brevity called "living." In the next place it was advisable to picture the possibilities, whether desirable or not, of the case of a single individual living in one room, and the provision that would be necessary if separate rooms or places were required for the purposes mentioned. These points were thrown by Dr. Sykes very neatly into tabular form. In the first column the various purposes to be provided for were enumerated as follows: Living, sleeping, food storage, cooking and warming, ablution, clothes washing, bathing, deposit of refuse, and an open space (for drying clothes and storing refuse). The provision in a single room for these purposes would be: Table and chairs, bed, cupboard (ventilated into open air), range, draw-tap and sink, wash-tub, bath or tub, pail, and window-cill. The corresponding provision in separate places would be: Parlour, bed-room, larder, kitchen, scullery, wash-house with copper, bath-room, bin, and yard or balcony. The water-closet, it was pointed out, must in any case be provided for separately. As not only individuals, but whole families, in our cities and large towns existed in single rooms under such conditions, it was necessary to form some idea of the

#### PROVISION REQUIRED

to be made for those who had neither the means nor the knowledge to provide for themselves. In providing dwelling accommodation healthy family life should, above all things, be most encouraged and bettered, and no amount of collective accommodation for men only or women only would touch that great question. The two-roomed dwelling was the very minimum family accommodation possible; but it must be recognised that family life entirely carried on in two rooms could not be regarded as the standard of "home" in which the bulk of the young population of the nation should be reared and trained as future citizens, however humble their walk in life. As both of these rooms might, sooner or later, require to be used as bed-rooms, they must further consider how the second room may have removed from it such provision as might be made elsewhere. Food storage, cooking and warming, ablution and clothes washing might be so removed to a combined kitchen, larder, scullery and wash-house, and so they reached a three-roomed self-contained dwelling. The possibility of installing a food cupboard, a cooking range, a draw-tap and sink and a washing copper in the same room must be admitted. The combination of kitchen, larder, scullery and wash-house had this great disadvantage—that the room being applied to so many purposes it could not well be used for any other. The separation of this into two rooms, a scullery and a kitchen, enabled the kitchen to be freed from the other purposes and to be usable as a living-room, this in turn dispensing with a bed-room being so used, as must of necessity otherwise be the case. Here, then, they reached the four-roomed self-contained family dwelling. In proof of the fact that progress is being made in this direction, Dr. Sykes quoted some extremely interesting figures drawn up by Dr. J. B. Russell, the well-known medical officer of health of Glasgow, showing that during the last quarter of a century there had in that city been a steady increase in the percentage of the population living in two, three and four rooms, and a corresponding decrease in the percentage of those in one room and also in the case of those living in five rooms and upwards. The

number of people living in four-room dwellings, as well as those in three-room dwellings, showed a continuous and increasing proportion, the greatest gain of all being ultimately in the three-room dwellings. But the remarkable point was that, whereas in the decennium 1871-81 the proportion of persons living in two-room dwellings increased 3·2 per cent., and the proportion in three-room 2·8, in the decennium 1881-91 the proportion in two-room dwellings only increased 2·8, whereas the proportion in three rooms rose 3·7 per cent. Above all towered the notable fact that the proportion of persons living in one-room dwellings fell between 1871 and 1891 from 30·4 to 18·0 per cent. of the total number of the population, and it was significant that the increase of proportion appeared to be converging towards the three and four roomed dwelling. Unfortunately, no such valuable comparative figures were available for England and Wales, or any English towns, Dr. J. B. Russell's method having only been adopted at the last census in 1891, but he presented a table showing the percentage of population in one, two, three and four rooms in the whole of England and Wales, in the rural districts, in the urban districts, in St. Luke's, one of the most crowded, and in Lewisham, one of the least crowded districts in London. Comparing the St. Luke's figures with those of Glasgow, Dr. Sykes pointed out that the former had about the same proportion of population housed in three rooms, and a slightly larger proportion in four rooms, a very much larger proportion in five rooms and over, and a much smaller proportion in two rooms, but a somewhat larger proportion in one room. Comparing Lewisham with St. Luke's, the great difference was that in Lewisham 53·8 per cent. less of the population lived in one and two rooms and 55·3 per cent. more in five or more rooms than in St. Luke's. That, no doubt, was due to the difference between the classes inhabiting a semi-rural and choice residential suburban area as compared with a crowded central area in a large city. After a reference to the difficulty of accurately estimating the normal proportion of urban population living in several-roomed houses, Dr. Sykes proceeded to consider whether it was possible to reduce

#### THE NUMBER OF ROOMS

in the ideal self-contained large family dwelling of four rooms—namely, two bed-rooms, a kitchen and a living-room, a scullery, wash-house and larder, and a water-closet, with yard or balcony. If the family were very small one bed-room might suffice, and the number of rooms be reduced to three, constituting what might be regarded as the ideal self-contained small family dwelling. Could any further reduction be made, and how? At some sacrifice of family life and independence in the construction of buildings containing numerous dwellings, another room might be lopped off by setting the larder in the kitchen wall, opening to the air, and constructing a scullery and wash-house for the common use of several families, and where that form of construction was adopted the water-closets were treated in a similar manner. In some cases the scullery was also separated from the wash-house, the scullery being placed close to the dwellings and the wash-houses collected together at a distance. That class of dwellings might be better known as associated dwellings, in contra-distinction to self-contained dwellings. It was important that the water-tap and the water-closet should be as nearly accessible to the dwellings they served as possible, in every case on the same floor of the building, and that such provision should be made for every twelve occupants or less. The water supply and drainage should strictly conform with official regulations, for in buildings in which the number of occupants was multiplied the danger incident to defects was proportionately increased. Proceeding to refer to

#### VENTILATION,

Dr. Sykes said that some years ago Dr. Arthur Newsholme, in a paper read before the Royal Statistical Society, showed that in London houses constructed in separate dwellings or common-stair dwelling-houses appeared statistically not to have any particular influence upon health except in this respect—that they produced a greater prevalence of those forms of infectious diseases for which there was no hospital provision, such as measles, whooping-cough, &c. The lesson to be learnt from these statistical researches was that the staircases and passages of such houses must be so constructed as to be fully and permanently open to the outer air. That necessity was the more obvious when it was pictured that the separate dwelling all open on to the common stair and passages, and that the dwelling-rooms of each dwelling were also all in direct aërial communication with each other and were not separated by a ventilated staircase-well as in the older type of house. The statistical researches of Dr. Tatham, superintendent of statistics at Somerset House, when medical officer of health for Manchester, into the mortality and morbidity of back-to-back houses furthermore pointed to the necessity for having through ventilation to each dwelling —that is, that a back-to-back type must not be adopted, but that one or more of the rooms must be situated on the opposite front of the building to the other room or rooms, so as to allow of thorough perflation when windows and doors were opened. In this connection it need scarcely be added no water-closet should have direct aërial communication with any room of a dwelling, and especially where the rooms were in direct aërial communication with each other, and, furthermore, that every dwelling should have close access to a modicum of open space, in the form of a yard or balcony, wherein to place refuse or any objectionable matters and for other purposes. In planning, this open space might be made the means of cutting off the water-closet from aërial communication with the dwelling. As to open spaces at the front and rear of the building, it was now accepted that these should be as wide, and might be as wide again, as the height of the house. The erection of baths in corridors and spare corners had not met with successful application, and the only provision that appeared to succeed in large blocks of separate dwellings was the erection of a separate building, fitted with baths and furnished with hot and cold water under the care of an attendant. To that building also might be conveniently added another containing the wash-houses of associated dwellings. The concluding part of the paper was devoted to the question of

CUBIC SPACE,

which divided itself into (1) the cubic capacity or size of dwelling-rooms, and (2) the cubic space per head. Although it had been necessary for the purpose of lucid description to regard a scullery and wash-house as a room, it was not a fit place for living or sleeping in, and could not be included in the term dwelling-room. One of the principal points governing the size of dwelling-rooms was the means of ventilation, and the smaller a room the greater the difficulty of ventilating it, so that restriction must be placed upon the resolution of size in new buildings. The standard height now generally adopted was 9 ft. and the minimum area 90 square feet, say 12 ft. by 8 ft., or 11 ft. by 9 ft. or 10 ft. by 10 ft., a cubic capacity of something under 900 cubic feet. The cubic space per head was the most difficult point of all to deal with in practice, and must be regarded sanitarily as the most important. In 1851 the Common Lodging-Houses Act was passed, which placed the control of common lodging-houses in the hands of the police, with power to make by-laws. At that period there was no doubt some difficulty in fixing the minimum amount of cubic space per head to be enforced, and it appeared to have been fixed successively at 240, 260, 280 and 300 cubic feet, at which point it stood at present. It would be interesting to know how this amount was reached, and it was a curious coincidence that if they measured a bedstead 6 ft. long with a 2 ft. gangway at the bottom and 2½ ft. wide with a 1½ ft. gangway at the side, they arrived at an area of 8 ft. by 4 ft., the minimum amount of floor space in which it was possible to put an approachable bedstead, and if that be multiplied by 7½ ft., the minimum height probably adopted at that period, since cellar dwellings of a less height than 7 ft. were illegal, they arrived at a cubic space of 240 cubic feet, and it required but the addition of a few inches to each dimension to raise that space to 260, 280 and 300 cubic feet. It was highly probable, therefore, that that minimum was a purely mechanical calculation in packing, the requirement of the human subject being overlooked; 300 cubic feet still remained the minimum standard of cubic space for sleeping-rooms. It was true that a recent Factory and Workshop Act only provided for 250 cubic feet per head, but a person awake had more control over the condition of the air breathed than a person asleep for perhaps eight hours at a stretch. The Local Government Board's Model By-Laws provided for 400 cubic feet in tenement-rooms, used both for living and sleeping, and the 300 was recommended to be increased in the dormitories of common lodging-houses that might require it. Many years ago the late Dr. Edmund Parkes showed that, calculated on a physiological basis, the human adult required 10,008 cubic feet of space, because in order to maintain the air in a sufficient state of average purity in a dwelling-room it was necessary to supply 3,000 cubic feet of air per hour, and the air in this climate could not be changed more often than three times per hour. The medical profession were now strongly advocating the cure and mitigation of consumption, or tubercular phthisis—essentially a disease spread by crowding—by fresh air treatment. Was it into of place to advocate even more strenuously the prevention of the disease by fresh air, by the provision of more cubic space, and especially by raising the present inadequate minimum standard. The adoption of the maximum as a working standard was scarcely practicable, but it was practicable to advance the minimum standard to 400 cubic feet at the very least in all cases, and if the lauded fresh air treatment meant anything it meant, firstly, a decided step in that direction. A standard of two persons per room was adopted in schemes for re-housing and in census returns for measuring overcrowding. With regard to the latter, it gave no idea of the amount of cubic space per head, inasmuch as the sizes of the rooms were not known. In reference to the former, to design dwellings allowing 500, 600 or 700 cubic feet per head, without providing any means of preventing that allowance to be reduced, was practically futile. Dr. Sykes concluded his paper with a further plea in favour of increasing the minimum limit.

INSANITARY AREAS AND IMPROVEMENT SCHEMES.

Mr. Addie, whose paper was entitled "The Removal of Insanitary Areas and the Management of Improvement Schemes under the Housing of the Working Classes Act," said that most of the improvement schemes were carried out under the Artisans' and Labourers' Dwellings Improvement Act, 38 and 39 Vic., and the Housing of the Working Classes Act, 53 and 54 Vic., and then proceeded to give details of schemes carried out at Swansea and Birmingham, both of which towns had adopted the 1875 Act immediately after its passing. In the case of the Swansea scheme a very heavy charge remained, but an undesirable colony had been removed from the centre of the town, a marked improvement made upon the death rate of that particular area (40 per 1,000), the rateable value had been increased, and a continual source of complaint, both as to health and crime, absolutely abolished. What was known as Alexandra-road was evolved and cut through a very squalid and dilapidated area. It included 14 acres, 3 acres of which were devoted to streets. The usual stipulation was made for the housing of the disturbed population, but it was shown that local enterprise was sufficient in the undeveloped portions of the borough to provide for the people displaced, and the scheme was accordingly modified and the salvages were relieved from the embargo of being used only for the purpose of the re-erection of artisans' dwellings. The cost of the scheme was estimated to be—for the property required, £79,166, and the estimated value of salvages and houses not taken down was £67,078. Deducted from this was the corporation interest in property to be taken in the Greenhill district—viz., £11,044—leaving an estimated permanent charge to the borough of £11,044. That amount, however, was very much exceeded, the actual amount borrowed for the purposes being £120,000. In

THE BIRMINGHAM SCHEME

the area dealt with was 45 acres, of which 9 acres were used for new streets. In St. Mary's ward the death rate was 26·82 per 1,000, as compared with 13·11 in Edgbaston ward. Corporation-street, the principal thoroughfare, was begun in August, 1878, and completed for traffic early in 1882. The width of the street was ultimately fixed at 66 ft., of which each footway absorbed 14 ft. The length of the portion now opened was 851 yards. The length of the section still to be made was 633 yards, making a total length of 1,484 yards. Several other new streets had been constructed and others materially widened. During the progress of the scheme it was found necessary to obtain modification orders, varying the powers originally given, but no unnecessary difficulties were raised by the confirming authority. For the accommodation of persons of the labouring classes displaced by the scheme an outlying area lying between Newtown-row and Summer-lane was acquired, and upon the site sixty-two workmen's houses and twenty retail shops had been erected by lessees of the corporation. Upon the land in the area set apart for the erection of similar dwellings 103 houses had been erected by the corporation. The total quantity of land purchased was 218,099 square yards, or about 45 acres. This had been disposed of as follows, the figures, of course, denoting square yards: Let on building lease, 57,872; sold or exchanged, 17,393; site of Victoria-courts, 5,600; site of artisans' dwellings in Ryder-street, 9,706; required for new streets and widening old ones, 40,526; still occupied by rent-producing property, 76,375; cleared for letting, 10,567. About 1,867 houses and 814 other buildings had been acquired, and of these 1,002 houses and 427 other buildings had been taken down. Fifty-seven licensed premises were included in the above, and up to the present time twenty-three had been abandoned, the remainder being still in existence or transferred to new buildings erected upon the area. The town clerk of Birmingham, in a paper read to the Royal Statistical Society on the

FINANCIAL ASPECT

of the scheme, said: "The dwelling-house improvement fund, created under the Artisans' and Labourers' Dwellings Act and order, has been a great cost to the corporation, but the results have amply justified the expenditure." The Dwelling-House Improvement Account at March 31, 1898, was as follows: Nett expenditure on general capital account, £1,551,137; nett expenditure on artisans' dwellings, £18,000; deficiency on revenue account accumulated during the years 1880-92, now capitalised, £117,011; the total nett expenditure on capital account being thus £1,686,148. The money required for the scheme was borrowed for a term of sixty years, with the exception of the £18,000 expended on the erection of the artisans' dwellings, which was borrowed partly for forty and partly for fifty years. An amount was provided from income each year for the repayment of these loans sufficient to repay the whole within the periods for which they had been borrowed. The amount set aside for the purpose last year was £15,539, and the total amount so provided since the commencement of the scheme was £221,977, and the sum deducted from the nett capital expenditure as above, left the present liability in respect of the undertaking at £1,464,171. In return for the large expenditure the corporation were now in possession of an income from well-secured ground rents amounting to about £11,000 per annum, which would be further increased during the next four years (without any new lettings) to about £15,000

# The Sanitary Institute.

## THE SEVENTEENTH ANNUAL CONGRESS.—III.

In our last issue it will be remembered that we gave a full report of the papers and discussions in connection with the conference of municipal and county engineers at the recent congress at Birmingham. This week it will be seen that, instead of adhering to the formal and arbitrary divisions into sections and conferences, we have made a variation in our method of dealing with the proceedings, and trust that it will be acceptable to our readers.

### HOUSING THE LABOURING CLASSES.

In resuming our report we have grouped together some of the references to the difficult and pressing problem of dealing with insanitary areas in the larger towns and providing dwelling accommodation therein for the poorer classes. At the conference of municipal representatives interesting papers were read by Dr. J. F. J. Sykes, medical officer of health to the St. Pancras Vestry, and by Mr. Peter Addie, F.S.I., lately the manager of the Birmingham improvement scheme.

DWELLING ACCOMMODATION IN LARGE CITIES.

Dr. SYKES in his paper said it was profitable to review the subject from a social as well as a structural aspect, since usage and sanitary precautions must form the basis of structural accommodation. He proceeded to point out that the functions and requirements to be provided for the individual in the modern dwelling were in approximate order of greatest necessity: (1) sleeping, (2) food storage, (3) cooking, (4) warming, (5) excretion, (6) ablution, (7) clothes washing, (8) deposit of refuse, (9) open space for refuse, drying clothes, &c., (10) bathing, not partial but total ablution of the body, and (11) living, including reading, writing, work, recreation, &c., for brevity called "living." In the next place it was advisable to picture the possibilities, whether desirable or not, of the case of a single individual living in one room, and the provision that would be necessary if separate rooms or places were required for the purposes mentioned. These points were thrown by Dr. Sykes very neatly into tabular form. In the first column the various purposes to be provided for were enumerated as follows: Living, sleeping, food storage, cooking and warming, ablution, clothes washing, bathing, deposit of refuse, and an open space (for drying clothes and storing refuse). The provision in a single room for these purposes would be: Table and chairs, bed, cupboard (ventilated into open air), range, draw-tap and sink, wash-tub, bath or tub, pail, and window-cill. The corresponding provision in separate places would be: Parlour, bed-room, larder, kitchen, scullery, wash-house with copper, bath-room, bin, and yard or balcony. The water-closet, it was pointed out, must in any case be provided for separately. As not only individuals, but whole families, in our cities and large towns existed in single rooms under such conditions, it was necessary to form some idea of the

PROVISION REQUIRED

to be made for those who had neither the means nor the knowledge to provide for themselves. In providing dwelling accommodation healthy family life should, above all things, be most encouraged and bettered, and no amount of collective accommodation for men only or women only would touch that great question. The two-roomed dwelling was the very minimum family accommodation possible; but it must be recognised that family life entirely carried on in two rooms could not be regarded as the standard of "home" in which the bulk of the young population of the nation should be reared and trained as future citizens, however humble their walk in life. As both of these rooms might, sooner or later, require to be used as bed-rooms, they must further consider how the second room may have removed from it such provision as might be made elsewhere. Food storage, cooking and warming, ablution and clothes washing might be so removed to a combined kitchen, larder, scullery and wash-house, and so they reached a three-roomed self-contained dwelling. The possibility of installing a food cupboard, a cooking range, a draw-tap and sink and a washing copper in the same room must be admitted. The combination of kitchen, larder, scullery and wash-house had this great disadvantage—that the room being applied to so many purposes it could not well be used for any other. The separation of this into two rooms, a scullery and a kitchen, enabled the kitchen to be freed from the other purposes and to be usable as a living-room, the scullery in turn dispensing with a bed-room being so used, as must of necessity otherwise be the case. Here, then, they reached the four-roomed self-contained family dwelling. In proof of the fact that progress is being made in this direction, Dr. Sykes quoted some extremely interesting figures drawn up by Dr. J. B. Russell, the well-known medical officer of health of Glasgow, showing that during the last quarter of a century there had in that city been a steady increase in the percentage of the population living in two, three and four rooms, and a corresponding decrease in the percentage of those in one room and also in the case of those living in five rooms and upwards. The

number of people living in four-room dwellings, as well as those in three-room dwellings, showed a continuous and increasing proportion, the greatest gain of all being ultimately in the three-room dwellings. But the remarkable point was that, whereas in the decennium 1871-81 the proportion of persons living in two-room dwellings increased 3·2 per cent., and the preportion in three-room 2·8, in the decennium 1881-91 the proportion in two-room dwellings only increased 2·6, whereas the proportion in three rooms rose 3·7 per cent. Above all towered the notable fact that the proportion of persons living in one-room dwellings fell between 1871 and 1891 from 30·4 to 18·0 per cent. of the total number of the population, and it was significant that the increase of proportion appeared to be converging towards the three and four roomed dwelling. Unfortunately, no such valuable comparative figures were available for England and Wales, or any English towns, Dr. J. B. Russell's method having only been adopted at the last census in 1891, but he presented a table showing the percentage of population in one, two, three and four rooms in the whole of England and Wales, in the rural districts, in the urban districts, in St. Luke's, one of the most crowded, and in Lewisham, one of the least crowded districts in London. Comparing the St. Luke's figures with those of Glasgow, Dr. Sykes pointed out that the former had about the same proportion of population housed in three rooms, and a slightly larger proportion in four rooms, a very much larger proportion in five rooms and over, and a much smaller proportion in two rooms, but a somewhat larger proportion in one room. Comparing Lewisham with St. Luke's, the great difference was that in Lewisham 53·8 per cent. less of the population lived in one and two rooms and 55·8 per cent. more in five or more rooms than in St. Luke's. That, no doubt, was due to the difference between the classes inhabiting a semi-rural and choice residential suburban area as compared with a crowded central area in a large city. After a reference to the difficulty of accurately estimating the normal preportion of urban population living in several-roomed houses, Dr. Sykes proceeded to consider whether it was possible to reduce

THE NUMBER OF ROOMS

in the ideal self-contained large family dwelling of four rooms—namely, two bed-rooms, a kitchen and a living-room, a scullery, wash-house and larder, and a water-closet, with yard or balcony. If the family were very small one bed-room might suffice, and the number of rooms be reduced to three, constituting what might be regarded as the ideal self-contained small family dwelling. Could any further reduction be made, and how? At some sacrifice of family life and independence in the construction of buildings containing numerous dwellings, another room might be lopped off by setting the larder in the kitchen wall, opening to the air, and constructing a scullery and wash-house for the common use of several families, and where that form of construction was adopted the water-closets were treated in a similar manner. In some cases the scullery was also separated from the wash-house, the scullery being placed close to the dwellings and the wash-houses collected together at a distance. That class of dwellings might be better known as associated dwellings, in contra-distinction to self-contained dwellings. It was important that the water-tap and the water-closet should be as nearly accessible to the dwellings they served as possible, in every case on the same floor of the building, and that such provision should be made for every twelve occupants or less. The water supply and drainage should strictly conform with official regulations, for in buildings in which the number of occupants was multiplied the danger incident to defects was proportionately increased. Proceeding to refer to

VENTILATION,

Dr. Sykes said that some years ago Dr. Arthur Newsholme, in a paper read before the Royal Statistical Society, showed that in London houses constructed in separate dwellings or common-stair dwelling-houses appeared statistically not to have any particular influence upon health except in this respect—that they produced a greater prevalence of those forms of infectious diseases for which there was no hospital provision, such as measles, whooping-cough, &c. The lesson to be learnt from these statistical researches was that the staircases and passages of such houses must be so constructed as to be fully and separately open to the outer air. That necessity was the more obvious when it was pictured that the separate dwelling all open on to the common stair and passages, and that the dwelling-rooms of each dwelling were also all in direct aerial communication with each other and were not separated by a ventilated staircase-well as in the older type of house. The statistical researches of Dr. Tatham, superintendent of statistics at Somerset House, when medical officer of health for Manchester, into the mortality and morbidity of back-to-back houses furthermore pointed to the necessity for having through ventilation to each dwelling—that is, that a back-to-back type must not be adopted, but that one or more of the rooms must be situated on the opposite front of the building to the other room or rooms, so as to allow of thorough perflation when windows and doors were opened. In this connection it need scarcely be added no water-closet should have direct aërial communication with any room of a dwelling, and especially where the rooms were in direct aërial communication with each other, and, furthermore, that every dwelling should have close access to a modicum of open space, in the form of a yard or balcony, wherein to place refuse or any objectionable matters and for other purposes. In planning, this open space might be made the means of cutting off the water-closet from aërial communication with the dwelling. As to open spaces at the front and rear of the building, it was now accepted that these should be as wide, and might be as wide again, as the height of the house. The erection of baths in corridors and spare corners had not met with successful application, and the only provision that appeared to succeed in large blocks of separate dwellings was the erection of a separate building, fitted with baths and furnished with hot and cold water under the care of an attendant. To that building also might be conveniently added another containing the wash-houses of associated dwellings. The concluding part of the paper was devoted to the question of

CUBIC SPACE,

which divided itself into (1) the cubic capacity or size of dwelling-rooms, and (2) the cubic space per head. Although it had been necessary for the purpose of lucid description to regard a scullery and wash-house as a room, it was not a fit place for living or sleeping in, and could not be included in the term dwelling-room. One of the principal points governing the size of dwelling-rooms was the means of ventilation, and the smaller a room the greater the difficulty of ventilating it, so that restriction must be placed upon the reduction of size in new buildings. The standard height now generally adopted was 9 ft. and the minimum area 96 square feet, say 12 ft. by 8 ft., or 11 ft. by 9 ft. or 10 ft. by 10 ft., a cubic capacity of something under 900 cubic feet. The cubic space per head was the most difficult point of all to deal with in practice, and must be regarded sanitarily as the most important. In 1851 the Common Lodging-Houses Act was passed, which placed the control of common lodging-houses in the hands of the police, with power to make by-laws. At that period there was no doubt some difficulty in fixing the minimum amount of cubic space per head to be enforced, and it appeared to have been fixed successively at 240, 260, 280 and 300 cubic feet, at which point it stood at present. It would be interesting to know how this amount was reached, and it was a curious coincidence that if they measured a bedstead 6 ft. long with a 2 ft. gangway at the bottom and 2½ ft. wide with a 1½ ft. gangway at the side, they arrived at an area of 8 ft. by 4 ft., the minimum amount of floor space in which it was possible to put an approachable bedstead, and if that be multiplied by 7½ ft., the minimum height probably adopted at that period, since cellar dwellings of a less height than 7 ft. were illegal, they arrived at a cubic space of 240 cubic feet, and it required but the addition of a few inches to each dimension to raise that space to 260, 280 and 300 cubic feet. It was highly probable, therefore, that that minimum was a purely mechanical calculation in packing, the requirement of the human subject being overlooked; 300 cubic feet still remained the minimum standard of cubic space for sleeping-rooms. It was true that a recent Factory and Workshop Act only provided for 250 cubic feet per head, but a person awake had more control over the condition of the air breathed than a person asleep for perhaps eight hours at a stretch. The Local Government Board's Model By-Laws provided for 400 cubic feet in tenement-rooms, used both for living and sleeping, and the 300 was recommended to be increased in the dormitories of common lodging-houses that might require it. Many years ago the late Dr. Edmund Parkes showed that, calculated on a physiological basis, the human adult required 10,008 cubic feet of space, because in order to maintain the air in a sufficient state of average purity in a dwelling-room it was necessary to supply 3,000 cubic feet of air per hour, and the air in this climate could not be changed more often than three times per hour. The medical profession were now strongly advocating the *cure* and *mitigation* of consumption, or tubercular phthisis—essentially a disease spread by crowding—by fresh air treatment. Was it out of place to advocate even more strenuously the *prevention* of the disease by fresh air, by the provision of more cubic space, and especially by raising the present inadequate minimum standard. The adoption of the maximum as a working standard was scarcely practicable, but it was practicable to advance the minimum standard to 400 cubic feet at the very least in all cases, and if the lauded fresh air treatment meant anything, it meant, firstly, a decided step in that direction. A standard of two persons per room was adopted in schemes for re-housing and in census returns for measuring overcrowding. With regard to the latter, it gave no idea of the amount of cubic space per head, inasmuch as the sizes of the rooms were not known. In reference to the former, to design dwellings allowing 500, 600 or 700 cubic feet per head, without providing any means of preventing that allowance to be reduced, was practically futile. Dr. Sykes concluded his paper with a further plea in favour of increasing the minimum limit.

## INSANITARY AREAS AND IMPROVEMENT SCHEMES.

Mr. AURIE, whose paper was entitled "The Removal of Insanitary Areas and the Management of Improvement Schemes under the Housing of the Working Classes Act," said that most of the improvement schemes were carried out under the Artisans' and Labourers' Dwellings Improvement Act, 38 and 39 Vic., and the Housing of the Working Classes Act, 53 and 54 Vic., and then proceeded to give details of schemes carried out at Swansea and Birmingham, both of which towns had adopted the 1875 Act immediately after its passing. In the case of the Swansea scheme a very heavy charge remained, but an undesirable colony had been removed from the centre of the town, a marked improvement made upon the death rate of that particular area (40 per 1,000), the rateable value had been increased, and a continual source of complaint, both as to health and crime, absolutely abolished. What was known as Alexandra-road was evolved and cut through a very squalid and dilapidated area. It included 14 acres, 3 acres of which were devoted to streets. The usual stipulation was made for the housing of the disturbed population, but it was shown that local enterprise was sufficient in the undeveloped portions of the borough to provide for the people displaced, and the scheme was accordingly modified and the salvages were relieved from the embargo of being used both for the purpose of the re-erection of artisans' dwellings. The cost of the scheme was estimated to be—for the property required, £79,166, and the estimated value of salvages and houses not taken down was £67,078. Deducted from this was the corporation interest in property to be taken in the Greenhill district—viz., £1,044—leaving an estimated permanent charge to the borough of £11,044. That amount, however, was very much exceeded, the actual amount borrowed for the purposes being £120,000. In

### THE BIRMINGHAM SCHEME

the area dealt with was 45 acres, of which 9 acres were used for new streets. In St. Mary's ward the death rate was 26·92 per 1,000, as compared with 13·11 in Edgbaston ward. Corporation-street, the principal thoroughfare, was begun in August, 1878, and completed for traffic early in 1882. The width of the street was ultimately fixed at 66 ft., of which each footway absorbed 14 ft. The length of the portion now opened was 851 yards. The length of the section still to be made was 633 yards, making a total length of 1,484 yards. Several other new streets had been constructed and others materially widened. During the progress of the scheme it was found necessary to obtain demolition orders, varying the powers originally given, but no unnecessary difficulties were raised by the confirming authority. For the accommodation of persons of the labouring classes displaced by the scheme an outlying area lying between Newtown-row and Summer-lane was acquired, and upon the site sixty-two workmen's houses and twenty retail shops had been erected by lessees of the corporation. Upon the land in the area set apart for the erection of similar dwellings 103 houses had been erected by the corporation. The total quantity of land purchased was 218,099 square yards, or about 45 acres. This had been disposed of as follows, the figures, of course, denoting square yards: Let on building lease, 57,872; sold or exchanged, 17,393; site of Victoria-courts, 5,600; site of artisans' dwellings in Ryder-street, 9,700; required for new streets and widening old ones, 40,526; still occupied by rent-producing property, 76,375; cleared for letting, 10,567; About 1,867 houses and 814 other buildings had been acquired, and of these 1,002 houses and 427 other buildings had been taken down. Fifty-seven licensed premises were included in the above, and up to the present time twenty-three had been abandoned, the remainder being still in existence or transferred to new buildings erected upon the area. The town clerk of Birmingham, in a paper read to the Royal Statistical Society on the

### FINANCIAL ASPECT

of the scheme, said: "The dwelling-house improvement fund, created under the Artisans' and Labourers' Dwellings Act and order, has been a great cost to the corporation, but the results have amply justified the expenditure." The Dwelling-House Improvement Account at March 31, 1898, was as follows: Nett expenditure on general capital account, £1,551,137; nett expenditure on artisans' dwellings, £18,000; deficiency on revenue account accumulated during the years 1880-92, now capitalised, £117,011; the total nett expenditure on capital account being thus £1,686,148. The money required for the scheme was borrowed for a term of sixty years, with the exception of the £18,000 expended on the erection of the artisans' dwellings, which was borrowed partly for forty and partly for fifty years. An amount was provided from income each year for the repayment of these loans sufficient to repay the whole within the periods for which they had been borrowed. The amount set aside for the purpose last year was £15,323, and the total amount so provided since the commencement of the scheme was £221,977, and the sum deducted from the nett capital expenditure as above, left the present liability in respect of the undertaking at £1,464,171. In return for the large expenditure the corporation were now in possession of an income from well-secured ground rents amounting to about £41,000 per annum, which would be further increased during the next four years (without any new lettings) to about £43,000 per annum, but from that figure must be deducted a rent charge of £3,000 payable in respect of property acquired from the trustees of King Edward VI. Grammar School, leaving the nett income from ground rents at £40,000 per annum. A rental of about £18,500 per annum was also being derived from the shops, houses and other buildings still standing on the improvement area, and after deducting £4,000 from that item in respect of rates, repairs and other outgoings, a nett income was available from that source of about £14,500 per annum. There was still some uncleared land unlet near Corporation-street which was at present producing no rental, but it was estimated that that would bring in, sooner or later, a further income of about £1,000 per annum. On the other hand, interest on loans, sinking fund charges and management expenses entailed a total outgoing of about £69,000 per annum, which was £16,500 in excess of the present income. That deficiency had to be provided from the rates, and since the scheme was initiated in 1876 sums varying from £460 in 1876 to £25,000 in 1891, and £17,000 in 1898-99, and making a total up to the present time of £234,607, had been provided by the ratepayers. The annual contributions from the rates would continue to be reduced every year until the loans were paid off—about forty-four years hence. The undertaking would then be free of charge, and the whole of the nett rental income of, say, £53,000 per annum, could be carried to the credit of the funds of the city. The town clerk had pointed out that the income would be further increased some fifteen years later by the expiration of the leases which were for seventy-five years, and the consequent reversion to the corporation of the valuable land with the costly buildings that had been erected thereon in Corporation-street and the adjoining thoroughfares; and that if no great change took place in the value of property in the city during the interval it might be safely assumed that the corporation will then be in possession of a clear income of over £100,000 per annum from the scheme. From calculations made by the town clerk it appeared that if the £100,000 income was the ultimate estimated rental, were capitalised at 3 per cent., and the necessary deduction made for the difference in date at which the full benefit accrued, the result would be about £3,000,000, or about the same sum as the contributions from the rates would realise at 3 per cent. compound interest. The town clerk had further said that the scheme would, in fact, have formed a kind of savings bank for the benefit of posterity, while the sacrifice made by the present ratepayers had had its reward in the street improvements, increased rateable value, vastly improved sanitary condition of the area, involving a greatly decreased death rate, and the impetus that had been given by the construction of the new streets to the trade of the city and the general circulation of money occasioned by the improvements. The corporation had themselves erected workmen's dwellings for the working class on the area acquired. They would gladly have allowed private persons to provide suitable dwellings for the working class on the cleared ground, but, with the exception of the land on which the sixty-two houses mentioned were erected, none was let for the purpose. It was consequently proposed by the Improvement Committee that the corporation should sanction the expenditure of £5,250 on the erection of a block of model dwellings on the flat system, but that proposal was not accepted. Some time afterwards the council sanctioned the erection of twenty-two through cottages before mentioned, at an estimated cost of £4,000. These dwellings were at once let to respectable tenants at 5s. 6d. per week. The applications were largely in excess of the number of houses. Encouraged by the first experiment, the corporation afterwards embarked in the erection of eighty-one additional artisans' dwellings, at a cost of about £14,000. These houses were similar to those previously built, their accommodation consisting of a front living-room, 13 ft. by 12 ft. 6 in.; front bed-room, first floor, 13 ft. by 12 ft. 6 in.; kitchen, 12 ft. by 9 ft.; back bed-room, 12 ft. by 9 ft.; and attic, 13 ft. by 13 ft.; a separate water-closet being provided for each family. There was an asphalted or concreted yard common to each block, and wash-houses in proportion to the number of dwellings. These houses were let at rents of 5s., 5s. 6d. and 6s. per week, and produced a nett income of £790 per annum, which, after providing for the interest and sinking fund, was sufficient to pay an average ground rent, spread over seventy-five years, of 10d. per square yard per annum. The Local Government Board always insisted on the erection of dwellings for the working classes on the area acquired. Mr. Addie then proceeded to give a few particulars of the

DIFFERENT KINDS OF DWELLINGS

that had come under his notice. The dwellings erected by the Birmingham Corporation in Ryder-street he had already described. In Dublin the corporation erected five-storey flats, dual houses and one-storey cottages. In Liverpool five and six-storey flats, and in Manchester the same course was followed; but in each of these cities huge flats had been abandoned, and the dual houses were now in favour. In London the flat system, by reason of the scarcity of land, seemed imperative. Under the Act of 1890 the Birmingham Corporation had formulated a small scheme for the removal of an insanitary area in Milk-street, the site being very near to the centre of the town. The acquisition of the land and of the buildings necessitated an expenditure of about £5,000. Under the provisional order the corporation were required

to house 170 persons of the working classes, and for that purpose the city council had recently adopted plans, prepared by his successor, Mr. Tart, on the dual house principle. The plans now awaited the sanction of the Local Government Board. The tenements were arranged in four terraces, and comprised twenty-four houses, each containing one living-room and one bed-room, and thirty-seven containing more than one bed-room. The rooms averaged: Living-room, 13 ft. 4 in. by 14 ft.; bed-room, 8 ft. 2 in. by 14 ft.; and bed-room, 9 ft. by 9 ft., the smaller bed-room being designed for children only. The rents had been fixed at 1s. 6d. per week per living-rooms, that is 3s., and 4s. 6d. per dwelling. Each tenement would be provided with a separate water-closet, scullery accommodation and ash receptacle. It would be noticed that the upper storey was approached by a balcony, and that design permitted each door and window to have the maximum sunlight and air. The financial aspect of the Milk-street scheme was: Estimated cost of building, including paving, &c., £8,975; road-making, £146; contingencies, £897; and land at 5s. per yard (4,030 yards), £1,007; giving a total of £11,025. The estimated annual statement would be: Estimated rental, £659 2s.; outgoings, £219 14s.; giving a balance of £439 8s., against which had to be put interest and sinking fund on £11,025, amounting to £441. The Improvement Committee, in reporting to the council, had said: "The cost of the Milk-street site was £6,000. Deducting from this sum the £1,007 charged to the houses, leaves £4,993 to be provided for. The interest and sinking fund will amount to £199, and this annual payment from the rates must be considered as the city's payment for the sanitary improvement thus made." Mr. Addie devoted the latter part of his paper to some interesting general observations. As municipal representatives were aware, the housing of the working classes was

A MOST DIFFICULT PROBLEM,

and any scheme which was formulated received considerable opposition. It was difficult to provide for a population of so diverse a character as the working classes. What he might term the respectable element was hampered and weighed down by a number of thriftless and unclean people who abused any provision which was made for them. Possibly that difficulty might be removed in the future by universal education, but he was afraid that many years would elapse before the dwellings which municipalities so liberally provided would be appreciated and used to the best advantage. He would add a word or two with reference to the second and third parts of the Act. Part II. was utilised at present by local authorities for the purpose of closing isolated houses, or groups of houses, which were unfit for habitation because their condition was dangerous or injurious to health. He was afraid that the operations of authorities were frequently hindered by the reluctance which magistrates sometimes exhibited in making the necessary orders. In many instances the justices appeared to disregard the evidence of medical men and surveyors skilled in the subject; and as the authorities had no power to appeal against the magistrate's decision, a great many insanitary dwellings continued to exist. There could be no doubt that that was one of the greatest blots on the Act, and until it was removed no lasting and permanent benefit could ensue. The subject of appeal had, he believed, been discussed by the Municipal Corporations Association at the instance of the Nottingham Corporation, and he sincerely trusted that some result might follow their deliberations. This part of the Act also provided machinery to enable local authorities to purchase houses, in order to open up alleys and courts. If a medical officer found that any building, although not in itself unfit for habitation, was so situate that by reason of its proximity to, or contact with, any other buildings it stopped ventilation, or conduced to other buildings being unfit for habitation, or if it prevented proper measures being carried out to remedy a nuisance which was injurious to health, he might represent such first-mentioned building as an obstructive building, whereupon the local authority might take steps to secure its removal. It was worthy of note that the local authority would only have to pay compensation for the actual space taken, and would not be obliged to buy the whole of the owner's land, but would only bear the cost of the severance. Under the third part of the Act the local authority was empowered to provide lodging-houses or cottages for the working classes. Several municipalities have acted under this part of the Act—viz., Manchester, Southampton, Glasgow, &c. It was, however, beyond the scope of his paper to discuss the character of the buildings provided. Mr. Addie's

CONCLUDING REMARKS

were as follows: "I can only add that it is a matter of deep regret that many of the houses inhabited by the working class are not in the state of repair they should be, and that infectious diseases claim the majority of their victims from these houses. A wide field is offered in most towns for the application of both part one and part two of the Act; for there is no doubt that, as the landlords execute as few repairs as possible, the decay of the property increases year by year, and the classes of tenants thereby degenerate. If the local authority do not stop in area after area become insanitary. In many of our large towns there exist courts and alleys without number where perpetrators of crime and vice congregate. It is to be earnestly hoped that municipal representatives will study closely the provision of the Housing of the Working Classes Act, so that these plague spots may be abolished, light and air admitted, and the lives of the working men rendered brighter and happier.

## DISCUSSION.

The two foregoing papers were discussed together, and in opening the debate Alderman Coek, the president of the conference, said the great trouble was in clearing the sites. All manner of difficulties had to be encountered in clearing the land. The only way of getting rid of these plague spots, however, was for the municipal authorities to take the land over.

The papers were further discussed at some length, most of the speakers agreeing that the great thing needed was provision for the very poor, and that those who could pay 4s. 6d. a week could obtain proper accommodation, as a rule, without the intervention of the local authorities. The need of a legal definition of overcrowding and of legal provision for the prevention of the evil was also generally emphasised.

The PRESIDENT said that in the latest scheme the Birmingham Corporation altogether ignored the term "artisan" and "working classes" and went in boldly for a scheme for the labouring classes. The committee estimated the loss at £200 a year, and the council adopted the scheme unanimously.

In the course of the replies of the readers of the papers Mr. ADDIE met with sympathy in his remark that the Local Government Board had been a great stumbling-block, and had put the drag on the wheel of all enterprise and public spirit in the housing of the poor.

Alderman SUTTON (chairman of the Health Committee of Warrington) felt so strongly on the subject that he suggested a resolution asking the legislature to consider the necessity of passing a law to enable corporations to provide suitable dwellings for the very poor, and to compel them to reside in such dwellings when so provided. The latter clause provoked considerable laughter, and the chairman ruled the proposition out of order.

In the conference of medical officers of health Dr. H. Scurfield, medical officer for Sunderland, read a paper on the

## NECESSITY FOR AMENDMENT OF PART I. OF THE HOUSING OF THE WORKING CLASSES ACT, 1890.

Dr. SCURFIELD, in the opening paragraph of his paper, ventured to express the opinion that the beneficial effect of Part I. of this Act would be much greater if the proceedings preliminary to the execution of an improvement scheme were simplified and more liberty given to the local authority in determining the type of buildings to be erected on the "unhealthy area." In most towns the proposal to spend the ratepayers' money over such schemes would arouse great opposition, and would only be carried by the strenuous efforts of a few ardent sanitary reformers. Before the long-drawn-out proceedings in connection with the execution of the scheme were carried to a conclusion the enthusiasm of even a very ardent sanitary reformer would probably have been considerably cooled, and he would think twice before he advocated a second improvement scheme. In Sunderland there was a large district occupied by property in a very insanitary condition which could only be dealt with by improvement schemes. So far

### ONE SCHEME,

dealing with a small portion of this district known as the "Hat Case" area, had been attempted. The area was about half an acre in extent, and there were about 480 persons living on it when the official representation was made to the council by the medical officer of health on August 31, 1893. The improvement scheme was completed in September and advertised in October, 1893. The petition to the Local Government Board for the confirmation of the scheme was forwarded on November 27, 1893. The Local Government Board inquiry was held on January 18, 1894, and the provisional order was made on May 8, 1894. On September 26, 1894, a second Local Government Board inquiry was held, on an application to modify the scheme. On September, 1896, the purchase of properties was so far completed as to enable a competition for designs for workmen's dwellings to be advertised. The prizes in the competition were awarded in January, 1897. The first prize plans were then somewhat amended, and provisionally approved by the council in March, 1897. The architect who drew up the plans and the borough surveyor were then deputed to interview the architect to the Local Government Board, with a view to making such modifications, if any, in the plans as might be necessary for securing the approval of the Local Government Board. After this interview the plans were again amended. The amended plans were approved by the council in June, 1897, and formally submitted to the Local Government Board on July 12, 1898. In submitting the plans the town clerk represented that there was practically no one living on the area, and that the buildings were mostly in ruins, and that the council therefore wished to build on the whole area at once, instead of only on one-half. On November 30th a reply was received from the Local Government Board desiring to know the exact proposals of the council as to the relaxation of the regulations requiring only one-half of the area to be cleared and built upon at a time, and at the same time stating that the plans were not satisfactory for the following reasons: (1) The plans provided insufficient open space; (2) the plans pro-

vided accommodation for too few persons; (3) the plans provided one-room tenements. As regards objection (2), the plans provided accommodation for 454 persons, instead of accommodation for the 480 persons displaced. On December 18th a deputation waited on the Local Government Board with regard to their objections to the plans. As a result of the interview the plans were again amended, by providing more open space and accommodation for fewer persons, and by doing away with the one-roomed tenements. The amended plans were approved by the Health Committee, and provisionally submitted to the Board on February 4, 1898. On March 11th the plans were returned by the Board, with an intimation that if the plans were now formally submitted to the Board by the council the Board would be prepared to direct a local inquiry to be held. On May 25th the plans were approved by the council, and on June 6th they were submitted to the Local Government Board. On June 13th an inquiry was held by the Local Government Board. Four years and eight months had thus elapsed since the petition was made to the Local Government Board for the confirmation of the scheme. Of this period two years were spent in the purchase of properties, and about four months in the competition for the plans of workmen's dwellings, the remainder of the time having been spent in correspondence and negotiatiations with the Local Government Board. Already more than eighteen months had elapsed since the architects were awarded the prize in the competition, but there was no prospect of an early start in the erection of the buildings. All

### THIS DELAY

was very disheartening to citizens who were really anxious to see the sanitary condition of their town improved. It appeared to Mr. Scurfield that the local authority might safely be entrusted with the erection of workmen's dwellings under this Act without having to submit every detail of the plans for the approval of the Local Government Board. Surely a local authority had a more valuable opinion than the Local Government Board on such a question as whether it was desirable to provide one-roomed tenements or not. In Newcastle-upon-Tyne an improvement scheme was given up because the Local Government Board would not sanction one-roomed tenements, and this part of the Act had become a dead letter. "In other towns," remarked Mr. Scurfield in conclusion, "I expect the same result will ensue unless the Act is amended so as to simplify the proceedings and give more liberty to the local authority in the execution of improvement schemes."

### DISCUSSION.

Dr. R. S. MARSDEN (Birkenhead) strongly condemned one-roomed tenements, as likely to create pig-like conditions of living; but Dr. EUSTACE HILL urged that tenements of three or four rooms were often let off to lodgers and greatly overcrowded. He favoured a great limitation of the Local Government Board's powers of supervision. Dr. H. MANLEY (West Bromwich), Dr. F. VACHER (Birkenhead), Dr. ROBERTSON (Sheffield) and Dr. S. BARWISE (Derby) all thought one-roomed tenements would be an advantage in dealing with a certain class of people.

On the conclusion of the discussion a motion was carried recommending the council of the Institute to take steps to secure an amendment of the Act, to simplify the execution of improvement schemes, and to give more liberty to local authorities in the erection of buildings on unhealthy areas.

At the conference of sanitary inspectors Mr. T. C. Barralet read a paper on

### OVERCROWDING AND ITS REMEDIES.

Mr. BARRALET in the course of his paper, said that the tendency of populations to concentrate into towns was one of the characteristics of the human race, and became accentuated by civilisation. All attempts to stop that tendency by legislation had failed, as evidenced by the growth of London. Civilised commercial life tied the labourer to the towns as completely as the serfs of the middle ages were tied to the soil. The price we paid for being the leading manufacturers of the world was the divorce of half our population from the fields and the decay of rural life. Railways and manufactures had proved potent forces in concentrating populations on small areas, and the spread of education in rural districts had swelled the immigration to the towns. On the other hand, there was a growing tendency among richer townsmen to live in the country, but the number was so infinitesimal as to have practically no effect on overcrowding in the cities, while it positively aggravated it in the villages. An abnormal growth of population was not necessarily a good thing in itself, but might imply that the conditions of life were unfavourable. A high standard of comfort generally implied a low birth rate. The mere aggregation of dwellings, however, would not appear to be so inimical to health, inasmuch as the mortality returns from densely-populated urban districts did not much differ from those of less density, and the urban rates generally were yearly approximating to the rural. It was the overcrowding in dwellings that was fraught with such physical and moral degradation, and the various Public Health Acts had failed to cope with the difficulty. Indeed, there was reason to believe that such overcrowding was more prevalent than ever, pere the revelations of the 1891 census, the evidence of the late Lord Shaftesbury before the Parliamentary Commission of 1885, and published results of investigations into the housing of the working classes in the villages. The Public Health Acts were punitive and coercive, not remedial; they gave no definition of overcrowding, and were powerless to deal with the type of overcrowding which might be described as intermittent; they failed also in giving a sanitary officer no right to initiate proceedings. The writer gave several instances occurring in his own district. At seaside lodgings and boarding-houses it was notorious that overcrowding was rampant, but one seldom heard of proceedings. Overcrowding would continue to exist while it paid the owner, and while such owners dominated local authorities. Rents, especially of cottages, had risen universally, and in rural districts within easy reach of London were 50 per cent. higher than twenty-five years ago. The Model By-Laws, though good in essence, had intensified overcrowding by increasing the cost of building; the writer urged that timber-framed cottages should be permitted in the country under restrictions, and that provision should be made to ensure a minimum air space in bed-rooms. Public authorities had not availed themselves to a great extent of the powers to provide dwellings conferred by the

HOUSING OF THE WORKING CLASSES ACT OF 1890

and cognate Acts. Many of the large towns, however, had attempted to grapple with the overcrowding problem by the erection of dwellings, either in blocks, detached cottages or lodging-houses, generally with favourable financial results. In rural districts the Act had proved practically abortive through its clumsy and unworkable procedure and the composition of rural governing bodies. Ireland was far ahead of Great Britain in the public provision of labourers' cottages. Municipal ownership had obvious advantages, and in the writer's opinion economic objections were overborne by the crying evils of overcrowding and the urgent need for the erection of decent dwellings. All measures aiming at making a working man the nominal owner of the house he lived in by advances from the public funds were to be deprecated as inimical to good sanitation in general and strongly provocative of overcrowding. Much might be done in mitigation by the encouragement and extension of cheap travel, but it must not be sectional or it would aggravate the evil it was intended to remedy; the zone system, as in Austria-Hungary, if adopted by our railways would cause our cities to grow symmetrically, instead of at the least desirable extremities. Emigration might be a palliative for overcrowding, but it was not to be recommended, for our country is not overcrowded, no matter how our dwellings may be. Though we could not attain the late Sir B. W. Richardson's ideal in our cities of twenty-five persons to the acre, and the late Prof. Nuxling's minimum of 800 cubic feet in a room for each individual, we could keep them steadily before us, and by using all the means in our power remove to some extent one of the greatest blots on our civilisation.

## THE HEALTH EXHIBITION.
### SECOND NOTICE.

In continuing our notice of the prominent exhibits, a brief reference may be made to the list of awards published in our last issue. Of the firms whose exhibits we noticed a silver medal has been awarded to Messrs. Adams & Co., Leeds and York, for their automatic sewage lift. Bronze medals have been awarded to the following firms mentioned in last week's notice : Shanks & Co., Barrhead, for their " Perfecto " lavatory and " Perfecto " bath; Callender & Montgomery, 11 Victoria-street, S.W., for Callender's pure bitumen for linings; C. Isler & Co., Bear-lane, Southwark, S.E., for their well-known tube wells; Twyfords, Limited, Hanley, for their axis water-closet, with screw brass joint, their triple vegetable sink, and for their " Ideal " sink in two compartments; Pendleton Sanitary Engineering Company, Pendleton, Manchester, for Dr. Quine's ash-bin; Rowe Brothers & Co., City Head Works, Clement-street, Birmingham, for lead pipe made in any length; Farrer, Barber & Co., 36 Cannon-street, Birmingham, for the " Helliwell " system of glazing and a combined sink and lavatory; Adams & Co., for a wedge disc valve; Sutton & Co., Union Pottery, Overseal, near Ashby-de-la-Zouch, for Green's " Wyvurst " channels and inlets for manholes; and W. Harriman & Co., Limited, Newcastle-on-Tyne, for floor channels, with sockets for wash pipes, and Barron's channel bends made to pass a drain plug.

At Stall No. 27, Messrs. WM. BOYDELL & SONS, Brown-street Ironworks, Leigh, Lancs., had two interesting gully exhibits—a self-flushing gully for house drains and a street gully, with appliance for flushing for town mains, testing with smoke test and ventilation.—A new boiler bath for small villas and workmen's dwellings was the chief exhibit of MOUN'S PATENT BOILER BATH COMPANY, 3 Union-passage, Birmingham. This bath, for which a bronze medal has been awarded, is 4 ft. 6 in. by about 2 ft. inside measure. It is heated underneath by a small coal or slack fire, having a fire-box at one end for that purpose. It has a double flue, so that when the water is sufficiently hot the heat is cut off by closing a damper, which closes one flue and opens the other.—Mr. JOHN JONES, the well-known sanitary expert, of Carlyle Works, Church-street, Chelsea, S.W., had quite a formidable array of sanitary appliances on view, comprising drain-testing apparatus, manhole covers, cisterns, gullies and other goods, the mere mention of which would occupy considerable space. Mr. Jones recently issued and revised a

very comprehensive illustrated catalogue, from which those interested in sanitary manufactures can obtain full details of his manufactures.

Some cisterns, closets and general sanitary fittings shown by Messrs. MARTINEAU, BEAMES & MADELEY, Limited, Holloway Head, Birmingham, were deserving of notice. The " Vortex " valveless syphon cistern (Madeley's patent) is constructed both in enamelled iron and in fireclay. Other cisterns are the " Appleford " and the " Whirlpool," and among the closets may be mentioned the " Clyde," the " Isis " and the " Dart."—A general but very attractive display of baths, lavatories, urinals, flushing cisterns, closets, &c., was given by Messrs. PLANT & Co., 66 Dale-end, Birmingham.—A noticeable exhibit was that of Messrs. BURN BROTHERS, of Charing Cross, S.W. We have had occasion from time to time to draw attention to some of the more noteworthy of this well-knew firm's specialities in the manufacture of sanitary appliances. To mention only a few of the exhibits, there were on view drain pipes, inspection chambers, branches, bends, traps, gullies, lavatories, sinks, manhole covers, drain stoppers, &c. The firm have been awarded a bronze medal for their expanding drain-stopper.

Mr. H. PULLEN CANDY, Ashley-road, Altrincham, near Manchester, was in evidence with a working model of his automatic self-propelled distributor. The object of this invention is to enable sewage to be delivered in an even manner, irrespective of the size of the filtering material, upon bacteria filter-beds, and for continually aërating them. This arrangement, we are told, enables sewage to be filtered at the rate of 1,000 gallons per square yard per twenty-four hours, and produce as good a result as can otherwise be obtained while filtering at about 200 gallons per square yard per twenty-four hours. Mr. Candy had also on view automatic changers for alternately delivering sewage to and discharging effluent from bacteria filter-beds, and these appliances will, no doubt, receive attention from municipal and other engineers interested in sewage disposal.—The stall of the MANSFIELD's PATENT COMPANY, Queen-street Chambers, Mansfield, Notts, was conspicuous with a display of the various patents with which the name of the company is associated, these comprising sanitary connections for lead and earthenware, and for lead and iron pipes respectively ; wash-down pedestal closet basins; ventilators for soil, drain and sewer pipes; and the company's patent chimney pots.—Six pedestal closets with Edwards' patent connection between lead and earthenware were shown by the inventor, Mr. CHARLES HOWARD EDWARDS.

The number and variety of the appliances exhibited by Messrs. GASKELL, CHAMBERS & FOULKES, Dale End Works, Birmingham, made their display one of the most noticeable in the exhibition, but we can mention only a few of the prominent articles, such as the " Municipal " closet, the " Chantry " cistern, the " Sampson " closet, the " Vesta " closet, the " Spedon " closet, and a remarkable variety of fittings, among which the " Warrior " brackets were conspicuous. Some well-finished urinals, lavatories, baths and sinks were also on view.—Mr. A. T. COOPER, 92 Moray-road, N., exhibited his suction and vacuum pump, to which we have drawn attention on previous occasions; and Messrs. S. & T. UNDERWOOD, 130 Granville-street, Birmingham, had on view their automatic deodoriser, which was recently described and illustrated in our columns.

At stall No. 41 models of the Horsfall refuse destructor, with recent patented improvements of grate bars and parts of furnaces, were to be seen, together with diagrams and photographs of destructors and smoke-consuming boiler furnaces. Our readers are too familiar with the work of the Horsfall Furnace Syndicate, Limited, Leeds, of which Mr. F. L. Watson is manager, to render any further details necessary here. It will be remembered that the installations at Norwich and Edinburgh have recently been described in our columns.—Another firm with whose work our readers are familiar is HUGHES & LANCASTER, 47 Victoria-street, S.W., so well-known as the manufacturers of Shone's hydro-pneumatic ejector, a model of which was on view. This system of dealing with the sewage of low-lying and flat areas by gravitation alone is familiar to the great majority of our readers. Additional interest attached to the model from the fact that the compressed air for its working was supplied by a hydraulic or gravity air-compressor and a small electrically-driven air compressor. An equally interesting display by the same firm was the model of the celebrated Fischer system of water filtration, of which some details have appeared in our columns. A silver medal has been awarded in connection with Shone's ejector.

Messrs. J. DUCKETT & SON, Limited, the well-known sanitary ware manufacturers, of Burnley, exhibited an interesting variety of articles made in their highly-glazed amber ware. Among their exhibits our attention was particularly attracted by a row of isolated syphonic latrines, flushed from a cistern of similar material. A set of urinals for three persons showed this glazed amber ware to great effect. For the latter exhibit Messrs. Duckett have been awarded a bronze medal, and a similar recognition has been awarded for a louvre air-brick in salt-glazed ware. Slop-water closets, which are well-known to be one of this firm's specialities, were to be seen in two varieties. Their familiar B arrangement has an improved access to the tipper, and the alteration seems to be a very good device. The other form has a top flush, and is provided with a combined pedestal and trap above the floor level. In the isolated latrines, which embody a clever idea, syphonic force is employed in the flushing-cistern and also in the latrines, the latter being cut off before the cistern has ceased working, when a sufficient quantity of water is kept back to re-fill the basins after each flush. By simply turning a tap the closet basins and horizontal pipe can be entirely emptied if required. Among other prominent features of an interesting display we may mention the "Clincher" clean-water closet, for which a medal was awarded last year, grease traps, street gulleys and automatic flushing tanks. Some of these appliances were to be seen at work. Bronze medals have been awarded to Messrs. Duckett for louvre air-bricks and enamelled-glazed urinals.

Another firm whose exhibits were too numerous to admit of mention in detail were Messrs. OATES & GREEN, Limited, well known for the excellence of their salt-glazed ware. In addition to a variety of gullies and traps, there were several specialities worthy of notice on the part of the visitor interested in sanitation. Among those which caught our attention were some lavatory basins in cream and salt-glaze, for use in schools, public offices, &c., and a new form of urinal, in the construction of which the object has been to ensure that the water in flowing down would not fail to cover the whole surface, and thus keep the face of the urinal absolutely clean—a very essential condition our readers will admit. The "Wilby" patent tipper for waste-water closets, for which the firm claim an almost perfect flush, was shown at work side by side with the ordinary forward flush, and a test, we understand, showed that the backward flush possessed an undoubtedly greater power. With the water-tipper the tipper box is cleared with every flush, which is not the case with the ordinary forward flushing arrangement. The firm are introducing a new method for fixing their mangers in stalls and boxes, and other minor improvements. Altogether their exhibit was one of undeniable merit. We may mention that Messrs. Oates & Green have just issued a new catalogue, to which we shall have occasion to refer in a future issue. As would be observed from our report last week, they have been awarded bronze medals in connection with the Birmingham Exhibition for their salt-glazed wash-tub and rubber combined, and their glazed stoneware manger.

The manufactures of JOHNSON'S SANITARY APPLIANCES, Limited, Cobden Chambers, Corporation-street, Birmingham, have come into considerable prominence and favour. The exhibits on the firm's stall comprised Johnson's street gully, Johnson's circular gully, Johnson's yard and sink gully, and Price & Johnson's patent lifting and locking apparatus. We may mention some of the advantages claimed by the makers for their appliances, and no doubt our readers, as opportunity offers, will test for themselves the merits of the inventions. In regard to the gullies, a number of claims are made: (1) They have water seals of sufficient depth to prevent sewer gas escaping, but allowing the water to pass down the drain as fast as the drain pipe can take it away. (2) The seals are so arranged that frosty or dry summer weather does not affect them. (3) Nothing can pass through likely to obstruct the drain. (4) No sticks, straws, cloth, stones, &c., can pass beyond the mud receiver. (5) They effectually stop rats or vermin entering from the sewer. (6) They can be cleansed in one minute without breaking the seals and without any tools. (7) They have mud receivers, which retain the more solid particles. (8) No brick or stone work is required, nor skill in fixing. (9) They are adapted for use for all domestic purposes, and in urinals, stables, cowsheds, slaughter-houses, street gullies, manholes, and any place where there is likely to be sediment or refuse which obstructs other gullies or traps, these seals being self-cleansing. (10) The street gullies and manholes are so constructed that a steam roller, or any heavy weight, does not affect them or the earthenware connection and other settings. (11) They can be obtained in cast or malleable iron, or other metals, galvanised if necessary, or earthenware, made any size or strength, to suit all positions and purposes. In the twelfth and last place the makers claim that the cost of the gulleys and their advantages will compare favourably with any others in the market. The advantages claimed for the lifting and locking apparatus are not quite so formidable in point of number. We are told, however, that (1) the cover when dropped is automatically locked; (2) by means of a hook the lock can be released, and at the same time a leverage of ten to one is obtained in freeing the cover; (3) it obviates the great trouble and expense hitherto entailed in taking up a cover and frame rusted or fixed by mud together; (4) the cover is retained in a vertical position when in use, thus preventing accidents which might occur consequent on the cover dropping; and (5) that the apparatus, while considerably enhancing the practical usefulness of covers, can be attached to them at very small cost.

In continuing our report next week reference will be made to two remaining papers on the subject of the housing of the labouring classes, after which we shall deal with the interesting papers that were read in the various sections and conferences on the subject of sewage treatment and disposal. The third and concluding notice of the exhibits at the Health Exhibition will also be given. Owing to the pressure of other matter we were compelled to hold over a portion of this.

## ARBITRATIONS AND AWARDS.

Mr. J. Mansergh sat at the Hotel Victoria, London, on Thursday and Friday in last week, as umpire in an arbitration to fix the price to be paid by the Morley Corporation for the acquisition of the undertaking of the local gas company. Mr. Corbet Woolfall and Mr. T. Newbigging were engaged as arbitrators, the former for the corporation and the latter for the company. The valuers for the company assessed the value of the undertaking at about £133,000 and the corporation valuers at about £80,000. The umpire reserved his award.

Mr. S. H. Crowther, of Huddersfield, the umpire in the Gomersal waterworks arbitration, has awarded the sum of £8,410 as the price to be paid by the district council for the undertaking and interest of the water company. The costs of the arbitration are, by agreement, to be also paid by the council. The undertaking was valued by Mr. Fenwick, one of the expert witnesses for the company, at thirty years' purchase of the nett annual profit (£660), and by Mr. Charles Gott at twenty-five years' purchase. For the council it was contended that not more than five years' purchase should be allowed as compensation for disturbance, the company having no statutory powers. The company had, however, an agreement with the Bradford Corporation, which had yet fifteen and a half years to run, and it would appear that the award had been made on the basis of this agreement.

## INSTITUTION OF CIVIL ENGINEERS.

### ASSOCIATION OF BIRMINGHAM STUDENTS.

We have received a copy of the syllabus of this association for the session 1898-99, which in a neat form gives a list of the meetings arranged, names of members, and all other information as to the association and its objects. This association appears to be forging its way steadily ahead, each session showing an improvement on the last. Several successful visits have been carried out during the summer, and now an excellent list of papers is issued. Among others, Dr. Bostock Hill will read a paper on "Some Observations on Sewage and Modern Methods of Treatment," and Prof. H. F. Burstall, of Mason College, will give a paper on "The Experimental Study of Heat Engines." The session opens on Thursday, October 27th, when the president, Mr. J. C. Vaudrey, M.I.C.E., will deliver his inaugural address.

As a rule the members dine together before the meetings, and at the close light refreshments are served. The annual dinner has been fixed to take place at the Grand Hotel on February 2, 1899, when Mr. Preece, president of the Institution of Civil Engineers, has promised to be present. We note that Mr. Henry C. Adams, of the city surveyor's office, Birmingham, still retains the honorary secretaryship, this being the fifth year in succession that he has been called upon to fulfil the arduous duties of that post.

## CROYDON MUNICIPAL OFFICERS' ASSOCIATION.

At a recent meeting of public officials of the Corporation of Croydon, the Croydon Rural District Council and the local school board, it was resolved to adopt a resolution suggesting the formation of an association to be known under the above title. The objects of the body are, briefly, to promote a knowledge of the principles of local government and provide means of social intercourse and recreation among the members. In the course of the proceedings it was announced by the hon. secretary (Mr. John Earwicker, borough engineer's department) that the town clerk, Mr. E. Mawdesley, would read a paper at the first meeting of the association, which will be held in the town hall on Friday, the 28th inst., at 8 p.m.

**Fire Insurance.**—We have received the "special risks" supplement to the electrical installation rules of the Liverpool and London and Globe Insurance Company. These supplements are to be issued from time to time, dealing especially with the particular precautions which are shown by experience to be desirable. Various classes of buildings are dealt with, including, of course, central stations. The hints as to the arrangement of details tending to diminish the risks of fire form a useful addition to the general rules and assist in achieving one of the objects of the company—viz., the elimination of all unnecessary restrictions.

**The Sewage Commission.**—A visit was paid, on Tuesday of last week, to the sewage works of the Manchester Corporation at Davyhulme by several members of the Royal Commission on Sewage Treatment. The visitors made a complete inspection of the works, and the processes of treatment and purification of the sewage carried on there. On Friday the commission also paid a visit to the Rochdale Corporation sewage works on the Roach Mills estate. The works were thoroughly inspected, Mr. S. S. Platt, the borough engineer, supplying all the necessary information. Special attention was paid to the nature and action of the filter-beds.

# Loughborough and its Water Supply.

## THE NEW BLACKBROOK SCHEME : ENGINEERS' REPORT.

In our last issue we mentioned that the Loughborough Corporation had decided to proceed at once with the important scheme for the extension of the water supply, for which Parliamentary powers were obtained last year. The engineers, Messrs. G. & F. W. Hodson, have prepared an exhaustive report, from which we take some details which will be of interest to many of our readers.

### HISTORY OF THE LOUGHBOROUGH SUPPLY.

Beginning with a historical sketch of the Loughborough water supply, the engineers state that in 1866 a proposal was made to incorporate a private company to obtain water from the Blackbrook valley, and make a reservoir of 75,000,000 gallons capacity on the site of the old canal reservoirs, bringing the water to filter-beds at Nanpantan, and thence to the town. The old canal reservoir at Blackbrook was made in 1797, before the forest was enclosed, to feed the Charnwood Forest canal, which was constructed for the conveyance of coal from the collieries at Coleorton to Loughborough and Leicester, and thence to London. The canal terminated at Nanpantan, where the coal was to be loaded into waggons, and brought along a tramway to the coal wharf on the Derby road. The embankment of the reservoir was of earthwork, but its construction showed that works of that kind were very

proved to be quite wrong, and the population of 12,000, for which the works were designed, was reached in 1871, and further increased to 14,611 at the census of 1881, when one-sixth of the total supply was being taken by three customers for trade purposes. In 1878 the board were made aware that the occurrence of a summer drought would jeopardise the supply to the town, but no steps were taken till 1880, when negotiations were opened for the acquisition of the Blackbrook water rights; but as the rainfall of intervening years had sufficed to maintain the supply, the negotiations were dropped.

Nothing further was done until 1882, when Mr. Eaton, of Sheffield, was called in to advise. He considered that if provision were made for 18,000, or a prospective increase for forty years on the population then supplied (14,000), the board would have made all needful provision for the future, and he reported strongly against a reservoir at Blackbrook, and in favour of one above that at Nanpantan, at a cost of £26,125. As the estimate of population was obviously much too low, and the extra supply would only be 150,000 gallons a day, nothing was done on this report. In 1883 Prof. Henry Robinson was consulted in reference to the Woodbrook only, and he advised a reservoir on that source of supply immediately above Buck Hill Bridge, for a population of 25,000. No

LOUGHBOROUGH WATERWORKS: SITE OF THE PROPOSED BLACKBROOK DAM.

little understood in those days, and the materials used were quite unsuitable. The tradition among the old residents in the forest was that the reservoir was never brought into use. As soon as it commenced to fill, leaks appeared, and at the first flood the embankment was carried away. It was probable that the proposed water company intended to restore the old embankment, but the scheme was vigorously opposed by the local board, and an agreement was eventually come to by which it was withdrawn.

The local board having undertaken to make waterworks themselves, a scheme was drawn up in 1866 for the construction of the Nanpantan reservoir as it now exists, and an Act of Parliament obtained for carrying it out. The money was borrowed for a period of forty years, and the greater part had now been repaid, so that in the course of a few years these works would become the absolute property of the town. The engineer, Mr. James Simpson, stated that the population having remained stationary at 11,000 for some years past, and there being " no probability of a large increase at any time," it was therefore assumed that " a quantity of 25 gallons for a population of 12,000 persons, or 300,000 gallons per day, will be an ample supply for all purposes for some time to come." This estimate of the increase in population

action was taken on these suggestions, because it was apparent that the Woodbrook valley could not possibly yield the quantity estimated. During this period of indecision the population continued to increase, and with it the water consumption, and on the occurrence of the drought of 1884, which lasted into December, notwithstanding all precautions, the reservoir at Nanpantan was completely emptied, and remained so for many weeks, the town being dependent upon the small flow of the brook, and a temporary waterworks constructed on the Derby-road, for which all the water yielded by the Burleigh brook was pumped into the mains after filtration. This latter measure considerably mitigated the inconvenience arising from the want of an ample water supply, and very fortunately the town remained free from epidemic disease.

After this experience the necessity for an augmented supply was plainly apparent, and as the conviction had gained ground that the Blackbrook scheme was the only one which could be safely relied upon to meet the increasing demands of the growing population, Mr. de Lisle was again approached, to ascertain his terms for the water rights. In the meantime the Leicester Corporation prepared a scheme for the construction of a reservoir to hold 475,000,000 gallons, from which water was to be pumped over the Forest into their district. This was approved by a majority of one only on the Leicester Council, and was therefore not carried further. The Loughborough authority had meanwhile purchased lands lower down the Blackbrook, and prepared Parliamentary plans for a scheme to intercept and pump the water through Shepshed to the Nanpantan reservoir, and on the intimation that the Leicester Corporation did not intend to proceed negotiations were again resumed with Mr. de Lisle, and an agreement entered into for the purchase of his rights. When Leicester found Loughborough had effected this agreement and were proceeding to Parliament to secure the watershed, they deposited a Bill in opposition, and the result of the fight in the committee-rooms was the defeat of the Leicester Bill and the passing of the Loughborough Bill, which secured the Blackbrook watershed for ever for the use of the inhabitants of Loughborough. The works contemplated in the 1886 Act were immediately carried out, consisting of the laying of a 15-in. pipe from Blackbrook along the bed of the old canal to Nanpantan, and the execution of simple works for diverting the water out of the Blackbrook into the Nanpantan reservoir, forming the first instalment of the work necessary for utilising all the water the Blackbrook is capable of yielding. The existing supply, therefore, consists of the Woodbrook watershed, averaged by the small reservoir at Nanpantan, and in addition the dry-weather flow of the Blackbrook brought down to Nanpantan reservoir by the 15-in. main.

### THE NEW DAM AND RESERVOIR.

After referring to the general principles of water supplies from surface streams, the engineers explain that the general purpose of an impounding reservoir is to store up the winter rains, which yield the larger proportion of the annual flow to the streams, so as to make them available in the summer months, when the yield of the stream is below the needs of the population; but a reservoir only of sufficient size to do this would necessarily fail in its intended object, because of the variation in amount of rainfall from year to year. It is therefore necessary that the reservoir should be capable of averaging the yield over an extremely dry year, when the rainfall may amount to only two-thirds of the average, and also over a succession of dry years, such as are known to be of common occurrence, when the continued rainfall of three consecutive years may fall as much as one-fifth below the average. The yield of the Woodbrook is some extent averaged by the reservoir at Nanpantan, but it is not sufficiently large to equalise the winter and summer water, and into this reservoir is conducted during the summer months, as soon as there is any room, the whole of the dry weather flow of the Blackbrook, the winter water from which is absolutely lost for want of storage.

For some years past it has been apparent that the existing arrangements are insufficient for the increasing population and consumption of the borough, and the future increase will in all probability be at a still greater rate, considering the extension of existing industries and the introduction of new ones, and the favourable conditions for the growth of the borough. Under these circumstances it must be obvious that the time has come when the augmentation of the water supply can no longer be safely delayed. The Act of Parliament obtained last year to enable the Water Committee to complete the scheme of water supply from Blackbrook empowered the corporation to impound the whole of the water flowing off the watershed. It authorises the construction of a reservoir by forming a dam across the narrowest part of the gorge in the Blackbrook valley at or about the site of the old canal embankment. This dam will be 61 ft. 6 in. high above the level of the brook, and will form a lake nearly 1 mile in length and 2½ miles round. The dam is intended to be a solid construction, with concrete and masonry, extending across the valley, and excavated below the bed of the brook right down to the solid rock. The total height of the dam from the foundation to the summit will be 85 ft. or thereabouts, and the length across the valley will be 475 ft. A calculation as to the capacity of the reservoir shows that when filled to the height of 365 ft. above mean sea-level it will contain 506,000,000 gallons, or 253 days' supply of 2,000,000 gallons a day, which is sufficient to balance the yield of the brook over three dry years. The Act permits a slight variation of this level, and careful gaugings of the rainfall flowing off the watershed are now being taken to give further data for finally settling the exact height of the dam, a matter of great importance, in view of the fact that an additional foot in height will increase the capacity by 20,000,000 gallons, and a further foot by 42,000,000 gallons, thus making ample provision for the evaporation which will take place from the surface of the reservoir.

The report next discusses the construction of an earthen embankment and a masonry dam, and states that the natural conditions of the Blackbrook valley are more favourable to the latter. Details as to the materials are also considered, and the engineers continue their statement with the information that the profile of the Blackbrook valley happens to be such that no large storage of water can be obtained until the dam is carried up to a considerable height. At 10 ft. above brook level the storage capacity is only the insignificant quantity of 10,000,000 gallons, at 20 ft., which is the level of the highest of the present intakes, it only reaches 36,000,000,

when for practical purposes the reservoir may be considered empty. Beyond this point the increase becomes more rapid, and at 36 ft. the storage capacity is 135,000,000, at 41 ft. 250,000,000, at 60 ft. 506,000,000, so that one-half the total quantity is held in the top 14 ft. In the discussions which have taken place from time to time with the Water Committee it has been suggested that, as the town may not require the whole of the Blackbrook water in the immediate future, part of the work authorised by the Act should be omitted, but the committee have come to the conclusion that it is not advisable to do this for the following reasons. If the capacity of the reservoir was reduced by one-half, then only the 14 ft. of concrete and masonry at the top of the dam would be saved, because the foundations and lower part would have to be built of the full strength if it was ever intended to carry it to its proper height at a later period. The top portion of the dam is comparatively thin in proportion to the sub-structure, and the reduction of the reservoir to half its size would only save the comparatively small sum of £4,605. The effect of this would be that the Blackbrook could then only be made to yield 1,330,000 gallons instead of 2,000,000 per day, and 660,000 would overflow from the reservoir to the sea, and be for ever lost, whereas if the reservoir is constructed to retain it, it will be available for profitable sale. A further objection, and by far the most serious one, is that the powers of the council to make this reservoir entirely lapse in June, 1905, and all work not completed on that date must necessarily be abandoned.

The height to which the water will be held will cause a submersion of a portion of the road leading from Botany Bay to One Barrow Lodge, rendering a diversion of the road necessary. It will therefore be carried along the hillside at a higher level, and the reservoir itself crossed by a viaduct of three spans. The Charnwood Forest railway affords great facilities for bringing the materials necessary for the construction of the works, and a siding connection can be cheaply made direct to the site of the dam. A matter of vital importance, both from the point of security and economy, will be the washing thoroughly clean of all materials to be built into the dam. In the winter there will be an ample quantity of water for this, but the works will often have to be altogether suspended at that time of the year owing to the weather, and during the dry months of the year it is necessary to take the whole yield of the Blackbrook to maintain the supply of the town. The engineers point out that every year the works are delayed will accentuate this trouble and will necessarily add materially to the ultimate cost. It is desirable, therefore, both on grounds of prudence and economy, that a commencement should be made. Works of this nature, if they are to be securely built, cannot be unduly hurried, whatever the urgency may be, and they will take possibly from three to four years for their construction after a commencement has been fairly made, and as it will occupy some months to work out all the drawings and prepare the specifications, it will not be possible to get the contract let much before next spring. In conclusion the engineers say : "We are, therefore, clearly of opinion that the council ought now to pass the resolutions necessary to authorise the commencement of the works."

As already stated, the decision to proceed with the works was adopted unanimously, on the motion of Councillor Cartwright, chairman of the Water Committee, who ably expounded the necessity of the scheme and its financial bearings. We give an illustration of the spot at which the dam is to be constructed.

---

**Tenders Wanted.**—The Secretary of State for Foreign Affairs has received a despatch from her Majesty's Consul-General at Warsaw stating that the municipal council of that city invite tenders for the working of the tramways of Warsaw under municipal control. Horse traction is at present in use, but it is intended to introduce electricity as soon as possible. Information as to the conditions can be obtained from the Magistrat de la Ville de Varsovie, Varsovie, Russie.

**New Artificial Stone.**—A Scotch firm is manufacturing an artificial stone which is said to stand every test and to be impervious to all vagaries of the weather. The process, says a contemporary, is a simple one, and the ingredients of the stone, chiefly lime and sand, are not expensive commodities, so that it is believed that the artificial product will be able to compete with the real. The lime and sand having been thoroughly incorporated, are passed into moulding boxes, which may be of any convenient size or shape, and these are placed within the converter. Water at high pressure and having a high temperature is then pumped into the converter, to cause the necessary chemical union between the lime and sand, and the moulding boxes are also submitted to a temperature of about 400 deg. Fahr. by the action of superheated steam. In about thirty hours the surplus water is run off, but the heat is continued, in order to remove moisture from the moulding boxes, for another fifteen hours. The boxes are then removed from the converter, and the stone within them is practically ready for use. Experiments are now in progress from which it is hoped that other products of Nature's laboratory, such as slate and marble, will presently be successfully imitated.

# Comparative Reports of General Practice.

## XXIX.—ELECTRIC LIGHTING : BECKENHAM REPORT.—II.

CHOICE OF SYSTEM AND BOARD OF TRADE REGULATIONS.*

As regards the system to be adopted, the report continues, in view of the large area and straggling character of the district a high-pressure system alone (with underground cables) is suitable, but whether high-pressure alternating† or high-pressure continuous (Oxford system) is a matter for future consideration. The latter system possesses several advantages, more especially in relation to street lighting, motive power for machinery, cars, cabs, &c. A low-pressure system is out of question, as even its adoption in conjunction with high pressure would involve complications and prevent that simplicity of working so essential to economical administration.

Apart from the utilisation of house refuse for fuel, thermal storage, and some minor improvements in plant, no important modifications have occurred since Mr. Kapp's report, such as would materially reduce the capital cost of the undertaking.

WIRING OF HOUSES.

On this subject Mr. Angell says:—

As regards the cost to householders of wiring houses, inclusive of plain 8 candle-power lamps, switches, wiring, &c., on house side of meter, a charge of £1 per point or lamp should suffice.—(Appendix IV.) Elaborate fittings, brackets, &c., would considerably enhance the cost, according to the taste of each individual consumer. The approximate cost of wiring a six-roomed house of, say, £30 rental, would be £11, of a twelve-roomed house of, say, £60 rental, £27, of a sixteen-roomed house of, say, £100 rental, £55, and so on.

In most towns consumers are left to make their own arrangements for the wiring of their houses, with the result that progress is slow and demand for current inactive. In a few towns some system of free wiring prevails, *and to this system I wish to direct the council's special attention.* By this system householders are enabled to get their houses wired by a free wiring syndicate or by the local authority free of initial cost, the wiring agency recouping themselves by a slightly increased charge per unit of current or by quarterly repayments of their outlay.

To many persons the initial cost is a fatal objection ; to others, short leases, agreements and tenancies are equally fatal objections. Apart from mere inertia also, in view of their inexperience of electrical matters generally, a tendency exists on the part of private householders to shirk the responsibility, trouble, risk and enterprise involved in arranging with contractors for the execution of the work.

For the local authority to lay down costly plant and miles of cables, &c., and to then await private customers, without recognition of their (the customers') difficulties and without endeavour to meet them, is, in my opinion, a suicidal policy, and, doubtless, accounts largely for the non-success of local undertakings. In some localities, under specially favouring circumstances, success comes early, despite lack of originality and lack on the part of the local authority in the absence, however, of natural inducements, and where, especially, leasehold system and migratory habits prevail. Early success is entirely dependent on the extent to which the local authority foster the demand for current by assisting private householders over the initial difficulties of house wiring.

There are five methods in vogue by which wiring may be effected—*viz.*, by private householders employing—

(1) A local or other contractor and paying the actual cost of the work.

(2)‡ Free wiring company, who bear the capital cost, but recoup themselves by charging the householder an extra amount (¾d. to 1d.) per unit of current consumed.

(3) The local authority, the consumer paying the actual cost of work, plus 10 per cent. for supervision.

(4) The local authority, the consumer paying a percentage on the cost of the works for a term of years.

(5)‡ The local authority an increased quarterly charge per unit being made to the consumer, to cover interest and sinking fund, with option of purchasing the wiring by consumer at any period after five years.

As I consider, Mr. Angell continues, the question of free wiring to be of the *utmost importance*, I have given a synopsis of the various methods of dealing with this most complicated question, adopted in the few towns in which the difficulty has been recognised and met.

It will be seen therefrom that free wiring does not necessarily entail a loss to the local authority. The risk that, where a house has been free-wired, succeeding tenants may

---

refuse to take current, is obviously nominal. Who that has electric light for the same, or even a somewhat higher charge (with its hygienic advantages, cleanliness, convenience and comfort), will revert to gas *in preference?* In respect to landlord's fixtures, protection is obtained in the same manner as by a gas company who supply gas fittings on the "penny-in-the-slot" principle. Additional protection is also afforded in this matter by the Shoreditch agreement (Appendix III). Sec. 25, Electric Lighting Act, 1882, further protects the council against distress on wires, fittings, &c., or on bankruptcy of tenant.

PUBLIC LIGHTING.

Under this head Mr. Angell has the following remarks :—

Mr. Kapp does not refer to public street lighting or include the cost in his estimates. In my opinion the substitution of electricity for gas in public lighting should evidence a distinct improvement. Residents are apt to judge of the probable brilliancy of the light in their own dwellings by that of the street lighting, and disappointment with the latter may considerably modify private demand.

In other words, street lighting should be sufficiently brilliant and impressive to act as an advertisement.

If no greater illuminating power be provided than that of the present gas burners the cost would be much the same— *viz.*, about £3 per 16 candle-power lamp. If, however, a greater illuminating power is required, say, equal to that of the present incandescent gas lighting (40 to 60 candle-power), the cost would be increased considerably. Arc lights† (from 1,500 to 2,000 candle-power) in main thoroughfares (each costing about £20 annually) would entail still further expense, but when spaced at not greater intervals than 80 yards would give a most brilliant and inspiriting effect.

I would suggest, therefore, says Mr. Angell, that at the outset arc lamps of from 1,500 to 2,000 candle-power* should be placed at intervals of 80 yards in the High-street and Southend-road (from Croydon-road to Copers Cope-road), in Rectory-road and Bromley-road to its junction with Manor-road ; these lights to be automatically changed at, say, 11 p.m. to 16 candle-power glow lamps, one or two to each column. Ultimately, as cables are laid down the principal roads, No. 2 glow lights of 16 candle-power† each, and in secondary streets No. 2 glow lights 3 candle-power each, with double lens, should be fixed to each existing lamp column. The estimates include a sum of £300 (to be increased subsequently when the profit-earning stage arrives or as may be found desirable) for improved street lighting.

FINANCIAL STATISTICS *re* MUNICIPAL UNDERTAKINGS.‡

In an appendix to the report are statistics respecting the electric lighting installations of various towns, specially obtained for the information of the council. Whilst statistics from other towns may or may not be of great value generally, the districts dealt with are, mostly, somewhat akin to Beckenham in respect to population and general conditions. It will be seen, the surveyor continues, that generally years of profit are as yet but in anticipation (mostly in the immediate future), and that much valuable information awaits districts in which local enterprise is restrained for the next few years.

Electric light is now supplied in 132 provincial towns in the United Kingdom ; in seventy-four cases by the respective local authorities and in fifty-nine by private companies. Excluding towns containing populations of over 100,000,§ and those from which no information is to hand, it appears that in the remaining twenty-six towns in which the local authority are the undertakers the following averages obtain :—

| | | | |
|---|---|---|---|
| Average expenses | ... | ... | £3,780 |
| Average revenue | ... | ... | 3,665 |
| | | | |
| Average annual loss | ... | ... | £115 |

Of twenty-four provincial private companies, the average percentage paid for the year 1896 was 3 per cent.

In only four cases in the metropolis are the local authorities the undertakers—*viz.*, St. Pancras, Shoreditch, Islington and Hammersmith. In eleven cases the lighting is effected by private companies, the approximate average dividend being 5 per cent., of which the most adjacent—*viz.*, the Crystal Palace District Electric Supply Company—*is the only company showing a loss.*‖

---

In the case of the few localities *most closely akin to Becken-ham* the following results obtain for the past year (1896):—

| Name of District. | Population. | Supply commenced. | Profit. £ | Loss. £ |
|---|---|---|---|---|
| Ealing ... ... | 30,000 | 1894 | — | 300 |
| Hampstead ... ... | 75,449 | 1894 | 1,832 | — |
| Kingston-on-Thames | 27,000 | 1893 | — | 1,326 |
| Lancaster ... ... | 31,000 | 1894 | 68 | — |
| Taunton ... ... | 20,000 | 1890 | — | 215 |
| Tunbridge Wells ... | 30,000 | 1895 | 890 | — |

Of these Ealing, Tunbridge Wells and Hampstead give favourable results; concerning the two former (the one a London suburb and the other a provincial centre) a few words may not be out of place.

### EALING.

Ealing bears the reputation of being an enterprising and up-to-date suburb, with swimming baths, dust and sewage-sludge destructor works, wood-paved streets, electric lighting, &c. Not only is it, of course, a metropolitan suburb and high-class residential district, such as Beckenham, but it is in other respects more comparable with it than are provincial towns and districts. Electric supply, &c. (high-pressure alternating system with sub-transformer stations), has now been available for three years, the annual losses being first year, £1,500; second year, £1,100; third year, £300. A certain profit is, however, anticipated this year, application for supply being now more than can readily be dealt with. The street lighting is by seventy-eight arc lamps, at intervals of 75 yards, also by 300 incandescent lights (16 candle-power) fixed to existing lamp-posts. The charge to consumers is 6d. per unit, or for over 1,000 units per quarter 5d., with a 10 per cent. discount for prompt payments.

The comparative success of this installation is, doubtless, partly owing to the provision of "free services," the services being laid by the council to the meter inside the house; a great concession, inasmuch as under the Board of Trade regulations it otherwise devolves on occupiers to lay the entire services, whether situate on private ground or in the road. way, distant more than 60 ft. from the distributing main. The cost of wiring churches and board schools is also advanced by the council, repayable by annual instalments covering a period of seven years; a wise policy, not on account of the profit on the supply, but in regard to its advertising value.

### TUNBRIDGE WELLS.*

At Tunbridge Wells the last financial year realised a profit of £890, than which (having regard to capital sunk) no more favourable results have been obtained elsewhere. The in-stallation appears to have been popular from the outset, since in its third year the number of lamps average fifty-three per 100 persons, as against an average of twenty-nine per 100 in the twenty-eight towns (with populations under 100,000) given in Appendix V., a not inconsiderable demand being made by occupiers of comparatively small property. Having regard to the present profit, realised with only 300 customers out of a possible 4,000 (who can be supplied without further extension of mains, 32½ miles having already been laid), the profit of future years will be is doubtless a matter of pleasant speculation in the district.

The engineer states that "the light is a thorough success and greatly appreciated," that the demands for light are con-tinuously increasing, and that new machinery is being laid down as a consequence. He further states that "the council have cause to congratulate themselves on being the *only* town working on the high-pressure system that has not made a call on the rates in their first completed year's working."

As a favourite pleasure resort Tunbridge Wells is perhaps more comparable with a seaside watering place than with ordinary suburban residential districts—for purpose of com. parison, therefore, perhaps Ealing or Hampstead provide more useful data.

Mr. Angell concludes his preliminary remarks as follows:—

As the council will doubtless, in the event of proceeding with the scheme, decide to take expert advice, the following, among other engineers, may be mentioned: Lord Kelvin, Profs. Hopkinson, Kennedy, Robinson and Ayrton, Messrs. Kapp, Preece, R. Hammond, Manville, Shoolbred, R. P. Wilson and Dobson. The usual fee is 5 per cent. on the cost of the installation.

After interviews with many leading borough electrical engineers, and after endeavour to diagnose, so to speak, the causes of comparative success or failure in various districts, both in respect to general local conditions and to means adopted for creating a demand, I am of opinion that condi. tions of success are not absent in the case of Beckenham, and that, whilst partial and insufficient measures may prove stale and unprofitable for many years, a well-conceived scheme, pushed forward with the energy and intelligence generally associated with large *commercial and industrial* undertakings, must within a few years become not only a self-supporting but a profit-earning institution, tending to lessen local rates, and to give to the district during winter time an attractive. ness similar in degree, though different in kind, to that which so abundantly characterises it during the summer season.

* High-pressure alternating system with sub-transformer stations.

## THE SURVEYORS' INSTITUTION.

### ORDINARY GENERAL MEETING.

The first ordinary general meeting of the session 1898-99 will be held at the temporary premises of the institution on Monday, November 14th, when the president, Mr. Robert Vigers, will deliver an opening address. The chair will be taken at 8 o'clock.

### STUDENTS' PRELIMINARY EXAMINATION, 1899.

Those proposing to enter their names for the students' pre-liminary examination, to be held on the 18th and 19th of January next, must intimate their intention to the secretary before the last day of November. It is proposed to examine candidates from the counties of Lancashire, Cheshire, York-shire, Durham, Cumberland, Westmoreland and Northumber-land at Manchester. Candidates from other counties in Eng-land and Wales will be examined in London. Irish candi-dates will be examined in Dublin.

### PROFESSIONAL EXAMINATIONS, 1899.

Students eligible for the proficiency examinations (which will commence on the 20th of March next) must give notice of the sub-division (Table A of Rules) in which they elect to be examined, not later than the 31st inst. Examinations qualifying for the classes of "Professional Associates" and "Fellows" will also commence on the 20th of March next. Names of applicants for these latter examinations to be sent in before the 31st inst. All particulars as to days, subjects and course of examination will be forwarded on application to the secretary. English candidates for the professional examinations will be examined in London. Irish candidates will be examined in Dublin.

### PROPOSED SPECIAL-CERTIFICATE EXAMINATIONS (FOR MEMBERS), 1899.

Notice is also given that the next special-certificate ex-aminations in forestry, sanitary science and land surveying and levelling are proposed to be held on Tuesday, Wednes-day and Thursday, the 13th, 14th and 15th of June. Par-ticulars of these examinations can be obtained from the secre-tary.

### JUNIOR MEETINGS.

The first of four meetings of examinees and students au-thorised (subject to certain conditions) by the council to be held during the present session will take place at the tem-porary premises of the institution on Monday, the 21st November, 1898, the chair to be taken at 7 o'clock. All in-quiries with reference to the junior meetings should be ad-dressed to Mr. A. Norman Garrard, 8 Frederick's-place, Old Jewry, E.C.

## NEW PUBLIC LIBRARY AND MUSEUM AT KILMARNOCK.

The memorial-stone of a new public library and museum which is in the course of erection at Elmbank, Kilmarnock, was laid on the 17th inst. by Mrs. Robert Dick, of Glasgow, the wife of the donor. The building is of the Italian style of architecture. The leading feature of the design is the portico at the front entrance, its pediment terminating with the figure of Britannia, and on tympanum, the Kilmarnock arms, with supporters. The building is partly two storeys and partly one storey in height, the frontage being about 135 ft. in length, with a total depth of 114 ft. At the main entrance there is a spacious entrance hall, to the right of which is the reading-room and to the left the library-rooms. In the rear is a lecture hall, 60 ft. by 36 ft., with a platform and gallery. On the second floor the main staircase leads to a large vestibule, with a dome of coloured glass, to the right and left of which are the two wings of the museum, each having a floor area of 1,750 square feet. Here ample accommodation is provided for the magnificent Thomson and Braidwood collections presented to the town. All the ap-pointments are on the most modern and liberal scale. The estimates for the work amount to about £11,000. The architect is Mr. R. S. Ingram and the builder Mr. Andrew Calderwood.

After the foundation stone was laid Mrs. Dick was pre-sented with a silver trowel from the contractor, ex-Bailie Calderwood, and with a handsome mallet and spirit-level from Mr. W. S. Ingram, the architect. The proceedings were favoured with very fine weather.

**Surveyors' Institution Proceedings.**—The Surveyors' Institution have issued a revised index to the "Professional Notes," vols. i.-viii. (1886-9b), together with two appendices. This index has been designed to save members of the institution the trouble and inconvenience of searching for information through the contents of the eight completed volumes of the "Professional Notes." Moreover, the opportunity of its pre-paration has been taken to combine and simplify many of the entries and to add numerous cross references. The appendices, we may mention, contain an alphabetical list of names of the contributors to the eight volumes, and a similar list of law cases reported in the "Professional Notes" during the same period.

## CORRESPONDENCE.

**Superannuation of Municipal Officers.**—Mr. C. J. F. Cartnell, hon. sec. of the Municipal Officers' Association, 117 Holborn, London, E.C., writes: May I be permitted to call attention, through your columns, to the conference of municipal officers, to be held at Sion College, Victoria-embankment, London, E.C., on Monday, the 31st inst., at 8 o'clock p.m., in furtherance of the superannuation movement. The Local Authorities Officers' Superannuation Bill has already been twice introduced into Parliament, but has not yet been passed into law, and every effort will have to be made by municipal officers throughout the country during the next session to bring the measure to a successful issue. The present Government have recognised the poor law officers' and the teachers' just claims by giving them superannuation Acts, and we are only asking that similar benefits may be conferred upon the officers of the municipal service. I trust every municipal officer will endeavour to be present and make this meeting known as much as possible. Further particulars will be announced in due course.

**Royal Commission on Sewage Treatment.**—"Egawes" writes: During the past few days the above commission have been visiting some sewage works in different parts of the country. Now it is well know that Lancashire contains a very large number of towns; in most of them sewage works (more or less successful) are in operation. I have received certain information which makes me somewhat anxious as to the soundness of the conclusions the commission may eventually arrive at, and I should like to ask, through you, two questions, which someone with more knowledge than I possess may be able to answer: (1) Is it a fact that the commission have spent only two or three days in Lancashire inspections? (2) Is it a fact that the commission made most of their visits (few as they are) to towns where very little useful information could be gained, and have kept away from towns where artificial filters (not bacteria ones) have worked most successfully for years without any land treatment? If the answer to these questions is in the affirmative, I say the commission will not have all the evidence before them why land treatment is in a very many cases quite unnecessary; and I also fear the bacteria system is unduly pressed upon them to the exclusion of the oxidising system of filtration, which has done and is doing such good work when intelligently managed. In conclusion I may instance the commission's visits to Manchester sewage works. What did the members learn there? Chiefly, I imagine, how sewage works ought not to be constructed. There is nothing reliable there to help them as to the land question, nor as to the relative merits of the two systems of "filtration" I have named. In this connection I just want to point out what is often overlooked in comparing the two systems. However efficient the bacteria system may be, the cost of an installation is four or five times as great as one with oxidising filters. Moreover, the recent trials at Davyhulme are merely experimental and quite unreliable as yet.

**Sanitary Institute Congress: The Question of Papers.**—Dr. Charles Porter, M.D.IRE., D.PH.CAMB., medical officer of health, Stockport, writes: With reference to your well-timed remarks as to the inefficiency of the arrangements in regard to papers read at the recent congress, may I be permitted to state that on 21st September I sent to the secretary of the institute a paper upon "The Flushing of Sanitary Conveniences, &c., and the Effect of Disconnecting Traps thereupon," embodying the results of a careful inquiry conducted by direction of the Sanitary Committee of this county borough. On the 23rd September I received from him an intimation of its receipt and submission to the committee appointed to consider and group the papers. In the meantime I had an elaborate model made of the apparatus used in the large number of experiments which the paper recorded, and took the same to Birmingham with me. On Wednesday, 28th, the first working day of the congress, on looking through the programme I saw no mention of my paper, and naturally concluded that on account of the comparative lateness of its receipt, or for some other reason, it was not proposed that the paper should be read. At the closing meeting of the congress, however, Major Lamorock Flower, the recording secretary of your section, stated in his report, to my great surprise and annoyance, "that a paper by Dr. Porter on 'The Flushing of Sanitary Conveniences, &c.,' had not been read." I think I have much reason for complaint, that, though my paper was received on 22nd September, I received no intimation whatever from the secretary of the Institute either of its acceptance or of the section to which it had been assigned. I quite admit that the lateness of its receipt (six days before the congress) may account for its non-appearance on the programme, but it certainly does not account for the secretary's very discourteous failure to send any intimation as to its fate either to my official address or to the congress post office. The secretary in a subsequent communication appears to imply that I was to some extent in fault for not having attended the Engineering section on Thursday, 29th ult., but as he had omitted to inform me in what section my paper was to be read, or whether it was to be read at all, I am unable to understand why I should be supposed to have attended the Engineering section. I feel that this explana-

tion is due to the section, and if your suggestions result in more efficient and courteous methods of organisation at Southampton you will undoubtedly have done a public service.

## ELECTRIC TRACTION IN LONDON.

ATTITUDE OF THE LONDON COUNTY COUNCIL.

The Highways Committee of the London County Council have prepared a report relative to the application of the London United Tramways Company, Limited, for permission to apply to the Board of Trade for authority to use the overhead trolley system of electrical traction on those parts of the company's lines which are situated in the county of London—viz., (a) from the Askew Arms to the Uxbridge-road railway station, (b) from the Uxbridge-road station by Goldhawk-road to Young's-corner, and (c) from Young's-corner to Hammersmith-broadway, the total distance being rather more than 4½ miles. Mr. J. C. Robinson, engineer and manager of the company, states, that with a view to facilitating an arrangement being come to, the directors of the company would be prepared to hand over, free of charge, to the council, should they decide to purchase the undertaking at the expiration of the statutory period (which in this case will, in accordance with the provisions of sec. 13 of the London United Tramways Order, 1896, be after July 6, 1909) the whole property in the feeder cables or main laid down in the streets, together with the standards and overhead wires there, thus leaving the question of the purchase of the tramways, &c., under the purchase clause of the Tramways Act, 1870, absolutely unprejudiced. The directors would, further, it is stated, be willing to enter into agreement to remove the standards and other electrical apparatus at any time during the currency of the term on receiving a year's notice from the council to do so; and the company would adopt, subject to the approval of the Board of Trade, any other mode of traction which the council may at any future time find in practical operation, and acknowledged to be superior to, and more efficient than, the overhead trolley system. It is stated, moreover, that, should the council hereafter construct tramways to connect with the company's system, the company will, if required by the Board of Trade, adopt on their lines such method of mechanical haulage as the council may have adopted for their connecting lines.

In the report the committee state that they are still of the opinion, which they have previously expressed, that the overhead trolley system of electrical traction is unsuitable for the more crowded of the London thoroughfares; but they think that, as the company are desirous of making an experiment, and have offered to make concessions which will probably be of considerable benefit to the council should the experiment ultimately prove successful, and have, further, expressed their willingness to adopt any other system which may be proved superior after further experience shall have been gained, the council might in the circumstances give consent to the application being made by the company for authority to use the overhead trolley system of electrical traction, but so far only as regards that part of the company's tramways as is between the Askew Arms and the Uxbridge-road railway station. This consent, if given, will enable the company to apply to the Board of Trade to be allowed an opportunity for a full and satisfactory trial of the experiment upon a road quite at the outskirts of the county; and the committee consider that the council should, for the present at any rate, not go further than this, and that before giving consent to the use of the overhead system on the two routes (b) and (c), above indicated, the council should ascertain whether the system proves successful in the Uxbridge-road and is not a source of inconvenience.

The committee therefore decided to recommend the council: "That Mr. J. C. Robinson, managing director and engineer of the London United Tramways, Limited, be informed, in reply to his letter, dated September 27, 1898, that the council will consent, on the terms stated in that letter, to an application being made to the Board of Trade by the company for authority to use the overhead trolley system of electrical traction on the portion of the company's tramways between the Askew Arms and the Uxbridge-road railway station, a distance of 1 mile 3 furlongs and 3 chains; but that this consent will only be given on the company giving a written undertaking that the underground conduit system of electrical traction, or failing that horse traction, shall be used on the other tramways referred to in the letter—namely, (1) from the Uxbridge-road railway station by Goldhawk-road to Young's-corner, and (2) from Young's-corner to Hammersmith-broadway."

**Devonport.**—Terms have been arranged between the corporation and the Great Western Railway Company for the erection of a high-level bridge over Western Mill lake, and an application is to be made to the Local Government Board for sanction to borrow the money for the purpose.—On Thursday, at a meeting of the council, the Sanitary Committee submitted a report from the Burial Sub-Committee recommending the purchase of about 52 acres of land at Weston Mill for a new cemetery, at a price of £25,000. The report was unanimously adopted.

# Law Notes.

EDITED BY J. B. REIGNIER CONDER, 11 Old Jewry Chambers, E.C.,

Solicitor of the Supreme Court.

*The Editor will be pleased to answer any questions affecting the practice of engineers and surveyors to local authorities. Queries (which should be written legibly on foolscap paper, one side only) should be addressed to "The Law Editor," at the Offices of THE* | *SURVEYOR. Where possible, copies of local Acts or documents referred to should be enclosed. All explanatory diagrams must be drawn and lettered in black ink only. Correspondents who do not wish their names published should furnish a nom de plume.*

HIGHWAY: STEAM ROLLER: DANGEROUS NUISANCE.—In the recent case of *Moon v. The Wharfdale Rural District Council and the Otley Urban District Council* (Otley County Court) the plaintiff sought to recover damages for injuries to his horse and waggonette sustained in consequence of the horse being frightened by a steam roller belonging to the Otley Council, and hired from them by the Wharfedale Council. The plaintiff's contention was that the roller was not properly attended, and that the men in charge, or some of them, were drinking in a public-house at the time of the accident. From the evidence of his witnesses it appeared that the roller was standing in the middle of the road, and emitting black smoke and steam; that there was no one near it except a young man, believed to be the son of the driver; and that the driver himself was in the tap-room of an adjacent public-house. According to the evidence for the defence, on the other hand, there was no smoke or steam, the men in charge were at their posts, and the accident was due to the driver of the waggonette whipping up the horse. The learned judge, however, was dissatisfied with the defendants' witnesses, and came to the conclusion that their evidence could not be relied on. He was of opinion that the roller was left in such a position that it was likely to frighten horses, that it had been left in that position while the driver went into the inn to have something to drink, and without any of those protections which under the circumstances should have been made by those responsible. He therefore gave judgment in favour of the plaintiff for £40 as against the Wharfedale Council, the question of the liability of the Otley Council being left over for further consideration.

## QUERIES AND REPLIES.

STREETS IN URBAN DISTRICTS.—"A Builder" writes: Has an urban district council power to take action for offences under sec. 149, Public Health Act, 1875, when the streets are under the jurisdiction of the county council but within the urban district? Also under the same circumstances regarding the non-erection of hoardings, &c., when altering buildings?

As to offences under sec. 149, in my opinion the district council could proceed for penalties, notwithstanding the fact of the streets being under the jurisdiction of the county council. Sec. 253 provides that proceedings for the recovery of any penalty under this Act shall not be had or taken by any person other than by (*inter alia*) the local authority of the district in which the offence is committed. As to the hoardings required by sec. 34 of the Public Health Acts Amendment Act, 1890, the case is similar, it being provided by sec. 6 of that Act that offences and penalties thereunder may be prosecuted and recovered in like manner and subject to the same provisions as offences, &c., under the Public Health Acts.

BY-LAWS: "WALL" OF WATER-CLOSET: IS A DOOR A WALL? "Perplexed" writes: On inspecting a building in my district I find the water-closet on the ground floor so constructed that only the entrance door is external, and no window is constructed in accordance with By-Law 68. The builder contends the doorway is an external wall, in which he intends to construct a window, to comply with By-Law 68. We have adopted the Model By-Laws, and I enclose a sketch of same. I have refused to pass the building, in consequence of "one of its sides not being an external wall," and "the window of water-closet not being constructed in an external wall." Would you kindly state whether I am correct?

In my opinion "Perplexed" is justified in refusing to pass this building. I am not aware of any decision to the effect that a door is a wall, and should be surprised to learn that the builder can give any authority for his contention, which appears to me absurd upon the face of it.

ENGINEER AND SURVEYOR TO RURAL DISTRICT COUNCIL. —"Surveyor" writes: I shall feel obliged if you will let me know through your valuable paper whether an engineer and surveyor to a rural district council has a right to sign orders for materials required in his department, or is it necessary that all such orders be signed by the clerk to the council? I am told that under the old administration, when rural sanitary authorities consisted of members of the board of guardians, it was a rule, or rather an order of the Local Government Board, that all orders required by the surveyor should be signed by the clerk, and probably that order still applies to officials under board of guardians. Since the formation of district councils district councillors are, by virtue of their office, members of the board of guardians, and not, as hitherto, when rural sanitary authorities consisted of the rural members of the board of guardians. Does this rule therefore still apply to rural district councils, the same clerk acting for both authorities?

I can find no reference to this point either in Lumley's "Public Health Acts" or Glen's "Law of Public Health." Lumley refers to

certain orders of the Local Government Board, dated 23rd March, 1891, but on referring to these I find they apply only to sanitary inspectors and medical officers of health. I should advise "Surveyor" to apply for information to the Local Government Board.

BUILDING ESTATE: NEW STREET.—"Saltonstall" writes: I shall be greatly obliged if you will kindly favour me with your opinion in regard to the following: The plan enclosed represents an estate proposed to be laid out for building purposes, and plans have been submitted to the local authority for nine new streets and 360 houses, somewhat on the lines shown on plan. A B is a highway repairable by the council, and varies in width from 16 ft. to 32 ft. A D and B C are "occupation roads" and have never been repaired by the public. A D varies in width from 8 ft. to 14 ft., and B C from 9 ft. to 14 ft. There are no other buildings adjoining the estate except those shown. Our by-laws (copy enclosed) require a 36 ft. new street. (1) Will the laying-out of the

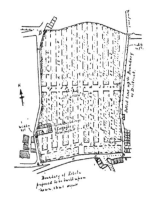

estate as shown constitute A B, B C and A D, or any of them, new streets within the meaning of By-Law No. 4? (I am aware that this is a question of fact for decision by the magistrates, but should like your opinion.) (2) What width (*i.e.*, width as interpreted in By-Law No. 1) can the council compel these streets to be laid-out? (3) Supposing answer to Question 2 to be "18 ft. from centre of present road," will this apply to opposite buildings as at southern end of "street" B C, in which case the entire width would only be 22 ft. 6 in. (4) If answer to Question 1 is in the affirmative, can the person laying-out streets be compelled (a) to flag, pave, sewer and make good streets A D and B C; (b) to lay footpath or sewer in street A B?

(1) In my opinion the erection of the proposed buildings would constitute the laying-out of A B, A D and B C as new streets. (2) If intended as carriage roads, the required width would be 36 ft. under By-Law No. 4. (3) In a case under the Metropolis Management Act, inst. sec. 98 (which requires a new street to be widened to the width of 40 ft.), it was held that the enactment would be satisfied by the owner of land on one side of the street setting back his fence 20 ft. from the crown of the road, although the result would be to leave the road less than 40ft. wide (*Taylor v. Metropolitan Board of Works, L.R., 2 Q.B., 213*). This case would probably be followed in interpreting local by-laws requiring a specified width of street. (4) Under By-Law 6, clause (e) he could be compelled to construct footways. In my opinion he could not be compelled to kerb, as, although clause (e) of the same by-law refers to the kerb, it does not in express terms require a kerb to be provided, but merely prescribes the height of the "kerb or outer edge of such footway." There appears to be no by-law under which he could be compelled to flag, pave or sewer. As to roads A D and B C, however, the council could of course proceed under sec. 150 of the Public Health Act, 1875, or (if adopted) under the Private Street Works Act, 1892.

DORKING.—The end now seems near in connection with the much-vexed water question, the shareholders of the water company having decided to sell their undertaking to the urban district council. This decision was arrived at by a small majority only.

# Municipal Work in Progress and Projected.

The most important news which has this week come to hand with reference to the progress and inception of municipal works in the provinces will be found in the paragraphs relating to Bournemouth, Brighton, Middlesbrough, Erdington and Southend. In regard to the metropolis similar information is given in connection with Battersea, Hampstead and Lewisham.

## METROPOLITAN AUTHORITIES.

### LONDON COUNTY COUNCIL.

The discussion on Mr. Crook's motion instructing the Water Committee to submit forthwith proposals with regard to legislation affecting the London water supply in the ensuing session of Parliament was the chief feature of the meeting at Spring-gardens on Tuesday. Several of the members took part in the discussion, and nearly all seemed to be of opinion that the only solution of the present state of affairs in the East-End was the municipalisation of London's water supply. This, as Mr. Shaw-Lefevre pointed out, would have prevented the famine in that district, as the various companies would have been connected. Two other important matters also occupied the attention of the council—viz., the telephone service and the proposed introduction of public slaughter-houses. Further particulars are given below.

*The Purchase of the Tramways.*—The Highways Committee presented a report recommending the council to enter into an agreement with the London Tramways Company for the purchase of the whole of the company's undertaking, with the exception of the 2½ miles and the Lawson-street depot already purchased, for the sum of £850,000, and an additional amount, to be settled by agreement or arbitration, in respect of the provender and other consumable stores in hand at the date of transfer. The details of this report appeared in the last issue of THE SURVEYOR. The recommendation of the committee was adopted, and the committee were authorised to settle the precise terms of the agreement, to give effect to the resolution and to report to the council.

*The East London Water Supply.*—The debate was resumed on the following resolution, moved last week by Mr. Crooks: " That, in view of the existing difficulty in obtaining an adequate supply of water in a large portion of the county of London, it be an instruction to the Water Committee to forthwith submit their proposals with regard to legislation affecting the water supply in the ensuing session of Parliament." To this Mr. Beachcroft had moved an amendment to add to the resolution the words: " And also to obtain the opinion of the engineer as to what works are required or provide for connecting the mains and works of the several companies for use in cases of emergency." Mr. Dickinson opened the debate, and said the proposal of going to Wales for a water supply was not a visionary one at all, but the only solution of the difficulty that would meet the necessities of the case. Dr. White, Mr. Shaw-Lefevre, Mr. Westacott and others also took part in the discussion, nearly all supporting Mr. Dickinson's opinion of the present state of affairs. Ultimately, on a division, the amendment was carried by eighty-eight votes to fifteen. Colonel Ford then moved a further amendment, but it was rejected by a large majority, and the resolution as previously amended was adopted.

*Public Slaughter-Houses.*—The Public Health Committee presented a report with reference to the provision of public slaughter-houses, and recommended that, as a first step towards ensuring the proper inspection of meat, private slaughter-houses should cease to exist, and that butchers should, in substitution, be afforded such facilities as are necessary for the killing of animals in public slaughter-houses to be erected by the council. They further recommended that a copy of the committee's report, and of the council's resolution upon it, should be sent to the Local Government Board, with an intimation that the council were prepared to accept such responsibilities as might be necessary to give effect in London to the recommendations of the Royal Commission on Tuberculosis, and that the board be asked whether they will include in any legislation introduced in connection with the Royal Commission's report the provisions which would be necessary for this purpose. Some discussion followed, in the course of which a desire was expressed by several members for the production of the medical officer's report on the question. The discussion was therefore adjourned.

*The Telephone Service.*—The Highways Committee reported that since the report of the Select Committee on Telephones was issued it had been stated in the newspapers that the Postmaster-General had informed the Corporation of Glasgow that he would grant a license, terminable in 1911, subject to the corporation obtaining next session the necessary powers to establish and work a telephone system. The committee thought the council were clearly of opinion that a competing service was necessary, and it appeared to them that, having regard to the evidence given before the select committee and to the terms of a certain portion of the report, the best course for the council to take at the present juncture would be to ask the Postmaster-General whether he intended to take the necessary measures for establishing an

efficient telephone service for London, independent of the National Telephone Company's system. Should he state that he was not in a position, or was not disposed to do so, it would be open for the council to renew their application for a license, and if such license were obtained to apply to Parliament for powers to establish and work a municipal telephone service for London. They recommended : " That the attention of the Postmaster-General be called to the expression of opinion in the report of the Select Committee on Telephones that general, immediate and effective competition by either the Post Office or the local authority is necessary, and that a really efficient Post Office service affords the best means for securing such competition ; and that he be asked whether, in view of that expression of opinion, it is his intention to take the necessary measures for establishing an efficient telephone system for the county of London." This was agreed to without discussion.

*The Smoke Nuisance.*—On the motion of Mr. Fletcher it was agreed to refer to the Public Control Committee to report the steps they are taking to enforce the Public Health (London) Act so far as it relates to the smoke nuisance, and whether they need any additional powers for that purpose.

*Supervision of Buildings.*—It was agreed, on the motion of Mr. Beachcroft, " That as the present system which obtains in London with regard to the supervision of buildings and the responsibility for their proper construction, both from a structural and sanitary point of view, is unsatisfactory, it be an instruction to the Building Act Committee to report fully on the subject."

### COURT OF COMMON COUNCIL.

At last Thursday's meeting of this body a member asked whether the court could be informed if any steps had been taken by the Streets Committee with regard to the lighting of the side streets of the City by electricity or the purchase of the City of London Electric Lighting Company's undertaking. It was stated that endeavours would be made to prepare a report on the subject.—A report was received from the Officers' Committee asking for authority to obtain the necessary fittings for the installation of the electric light in the court-room of the late Commissioners of Sewers and the offices of the engineer, at an additional cost of £15 beyond the £120 provided for the installation. The new offices, it was mentioned, were practically completed, and it was hoped that it would be possible before the end of the year to present a report setting out the entire cost of the buildings.

### METROPOLITAN ASYLUMS BOARD.

Sir E. H. Galsworthy occupied the chair at a meeting of this authority on Saturday. A letter was received from the Local Government Board proposing that the inquiry into the cost of the erection of the Brook Hospital should commence on Monday, the 17th inst., at 12 noon. They asked if the manager's offices would be available for the purpose. It was resolved to reply in the affirmative. The chairman, in reply to a question, said that no official information had been received in regard to the mode of procedure which it was intended to follow.—Upon the recommendation of the Finance Committee it was resolved to submit an application to the Local Government Board for an order sanctioning a further expenditure of £2,413 in connection with the contract of Messrs. W. Johnson & Co., Limited, for alterations and additions to the South-Western Hospital.—The following resolution was also adopted : " That it be referred to the General Purposes Committee to consider the desirability or otherwise of the board establishing a bacteriological laboratory for London, or of making other arrangements for providing bacteriological assistance in the diagnosis of infectious diseases, with power to obtain the opinion of the several metropolitan sanitary authorities upon the subject."

### VESTRIES AND DISTRICT BOARDS.

*Battersea.*—At the vestry meeting on Wednesday the Finance and Law Committee stated that they had considered the Workmen's Compensation Act, in conjunction with a report from the solicitor, and that it was not intended to specially deal with the question, but to treat each case as occasion might arise.—It was resolved to approve an estimate of £10,000 for the channelling and kerbing of various streets throughout the parish, and one of £11,935 for paving Bridge-road, Park-road and a portion of Albert Bridge-road with creosoted deal blocks.—In connection with the change in the incidence of diphtheria, it was decided to draw the attention of the London County Council to the matter, and to urge that steps should be taken to ventilate the main sewers in the district, and in the meantime it was resolved to take action in order to ventilate the local sewers.—The Health Committee announced the receipt of a letter from the Hon. Stephen Coleridge, hon. secretary of the Anti-Vivisection Society, with reference to the proposal of the London County Council to apply to Parliament for powers to establish a bacteriological laboratory, stating that the society hoped that the vestry would pause before giving adhesion to a scheme for endowing the torture of animals out of the rates, and would refuse to support the proposals of the council in the matter.—In was announced that a Local Government Board inquiry had been held the previous day in reference to the vestry's application for permission to borrow £42,178 for the erection of new baths and wash-houses in Battersea Park-road.—It was decided to refer to the Finance and Law Committee a letter received from Mr. H. S. Samuel, M.P., on the subject of a Bill which the hon. member proposes to introduce in the next Parliamentary session in order to compel the water companies to connect their mains so as to provide for cases of emergency.

**Clerkenwell.**—The vestry have been informed by the London County Council that they will accept the latter's offer of £100 for the small triangular plot of land at the Farringdon-road corner of Rosebery-avenue on condition that the vestry will pave it, plant it with trees and maintain it as an open space, a condition with which, it is understood, they are ready to comply.

**Fulham.**—On the recommendation of the Lighting and Dust Destructor Committee the vestry resolved, at their meeting last week, to accept the tender of the Horsfall Furnace Syndicate for the erection of a dust destructor.

**Hampstead.**—After a long discussion, it was on Thursday resolved "That no action be taken at present with reference to the circular letter, received 21st July from the vestry of Battersea, stating that they had requested the London County Council to insert a clause in their next General Powers Bill empowering local authorities to erect dwellings for the working classes under the Housing of the Working Classes Act, 1890."—The Finance Committee reported that, pursuant to the authority delegated to them, they had instructed the vestry clerk to make the necessary application to the Local Government Board for sanction to raise a loan of £5,920 in respect of the expenditure on the new baths buildings. This was approved.

**Kensington.**—Last week the vestry adopted a resolution, which was ordered to be sent to the London County Council, in favour of the duties of district surveyor and parish surveyor being discharged by one official appointed by the local authority, corresponding to the borough and town surveyors and engineers outside London, a change which has received the approval of three conferences of delegates from the metropolitan vestries and district boards, and will do away with the defects in the present system resulting from overlapping of jurisdiction and want of regular, systematic supervision.

**Lewisham.**—At a recent meeting of the district board of works the Works Committee reported that they had considered the notice of the Blackheath and Greenwich District Electric Lighting Company, Limited, of their intention to lay main and electric wires from the boundary of their parish next Greenwich, along Lewisham-road, Lewisham-hill, and Aberdeen-terrace, Haddo-villas, Eliot-vale, and Eliot-place, Blackheath. The surveyor recommended that from the bottom of Lewisham-hill to Walerand-road the mains should be laid in the footpath, and in the other streets in the roadways, and on those and the usual conditions as to reinstatement of roads, &c., the committee recommended the approval of the works, subject to the consent of the London County Council. This was agreed to.—It was decided to request the Works Committee to give their consideration to a recommendation of the local committee to construct an underground convenience, at an estimated cost of £1,800 or £2,000.

**Rotherhithe.**—It was last week reported that the Local Government Board had addressed to the London County Council a letter stating that they were not satisfied that proper accommodation could be prepared for 550 persons by the erection of block tenements on the Fulford-street and Braddon-street area, as proposed in the scheme submitted. They were prepared, however, to consider any further observations which the London County Council and the vestry might offer with respect to the scheme. The clerk was directed to reply that the matter was being dealt with by Mr. Scorgie, the surveyor, and the county council officials.

**St. George-the-Martyr.**—On Tuesday week, at a meeting of the vestry, a letter was received from the clerk to the London County Council stating that he had laid before the Improvements Committee the vestry's letter inquiring whether it was true that considerable delay was likely to ensue in carrying out a certain improvement in Long-lane, and urging the desirability of proceeding with the work without delay. In reply he had to inform the vestry that the committee regretted that delay had certainly occurred, owing to the Home Office not having yet approved the scheme for rehousing the persons of the labouring classes who would be displaced. Under the Act of Parliament authorising the improvement the council were prevented from acquiring the necessary property until they had received the approval of the Home Secretary to the rehousing scheme. It was hoped, however, that the approval would not be longer withheld, so that the council might commence and press forward the work to completion with all expedition.

**St. Pancras.**—The ratepayers of St. Pancras have, by a majority of 3,420 votes, negatived the proposal, made for the second time, to adopt the Public Libraries Act, 1892. On the last occasion that a poll on this subject was taken (in 1894) the proposal was negatived by a majority of 1,674 votes.

# PROVINCIAL AND GREATER LONDON AUTHORITIES.

## COUNTY COUNCILS.

**Essex.**—At last week's meeting of the county council the Highways Committee recommended that footpath improvements at Ilford, involving an outlay estimated at £9,232, should be authorised to be carried out. Some discussion followed, and eventually the council referred the matter back, declining to agree to so large an expenditure.

**Norfolk.**—At the last quarterly meeting of the county council the special committee entrusted with the consideration of the strengthening of those county bridges not sufficiently strong to carry traction engines reported that they had received a report, with estimates, from the county surveyor regarding eleven bridges, to do the necessary work to which would cost £2,625. The committee recommended the repair of Spong Bridge, £190, on the Holt and Dereham-road; East Harling Bridge, £460, near the station; and Claxton Bridge, £20, between Langley and Bramerton, subject in the latter case to the Loddon and Clavering Rural District Council paying half the cost. Denton Wash Bridge, £140, between Harleston and Bungay, was recommended to stand over for the present; and with regard to Shadwell Bridge, £240, on a district road between Shadwell and Brettenham, it was reported that the clerk was investigating as to the liability of the county council to repair the bridge. The committee suggested that they should be reappointed and authorised to accept tenders for the work they recommended to be done. This the council agreed to.

## MUNICIPAL CORPORATIONS.

**Bournemouth.**—The Local Government Board have sanctioned a loan of £8,926 to reconstruct the sewer in the valley of the Bourne.—A technical and secondary school is to be built, at a cost of £6,000.—A scheme for municipal tramways is to be discussed by the council at an early date.

**Brighton.**—The town council on Thursday adopted a scheme for clearing a condemned area in the eastern part of the borough. Over 700 persons will be displaced, but accommodation for 400 will be provided on the site, where a better class of houses have been erected. Making allowance for the value of the land, it is estimated that this improvement will cost nearly £25,000.—According to a statement by the mayor, a committee of the corporation are being inundated with proposals of companies to construct tramways in Brighton. Hitherto such means of locomotion have been vetoed, but a feeling is growing in favour of the introduction of tramways, at any rate in the hilly districts of the borough.

**Chester.**—It was announced at the last meeting of the city corporation that the Duke of Westminster had presented to the city 3 acres of ornamental ground near Curzon Park, known as the Dingle, for recreation ground purposes.

**Derby.**—At a monthly meeting of the town council, on Wednesday of last week, the Baths Committee reported that after a careful consideration of the whole question they had decided to recommend the council to provide both swimming and slipper baths for the southern end of the town, instead of any extension being made at Full-street. The reception of the report was moved by Mr. A. Ottewell, who, after it had been carried, moved "That the Baths Committee be instructed to look out for a site for a new baths at the southern end of the town." In doing so Councillor Ottewell said there was no doubt about it, baths were greatly needed in the southern end of the town. In the matter of baths Derby was far behind Sheffield and other Midland towns, where there were central baths and branch baths established all over the town. After some discussion the resolution was adopted.— At the same meeting Alderman Sowter moved that the sum of £149 15s. be granted for the purchase of portions of land in Old Chester-road, the Morledge, Devonshire-street and Osborne-road for street widening, and that application be made to the Local Government Board for sanction to borrow the sum of £149 15s. for this purpose. The resolution was also adopted.

**Durham.**—The city council last week resolved, on the recommendation of the Electric Lighting Committee, to apply for an electric light provisional order and to hold a special meeting to further consider the matter. At that special meeting a report will be submitted by Mr. W. C. C. Hawtayne on a scheme for the city.

**Falmouth.**—The question of promoting a Bill for the purchase of the gas and water undertakings was considered at a statutory meeting of the corporation on Monday of last week. In moving a resolution in favour of the purchase the mayor said that it was only by such a resolution that they could bring the matter before the ratepayers. The gas company's Act gave the town the option of taking over the works within ten years, and that would be the last opportunity the ratepayers would have of saying yea or nay within that period. There was a good deal of increase, and complaint was made that not sufficient data was put forward to allow of an opinion being formed as to the advisability or otherwise of the purchase. It was promised, however, that the data would be forthcoming, and that Mr. A. Silverthorne's report would be submitted to the council and to the ratepayers. The resolution was then carried by ten votes to four.

**Gateshead.**—At the monthly meeting of the town council, held last week, the Town Hall Committee recommended the confirmation of a provisional agreement for the purchase of the office of the Permanent Building Society for £2,800, it being proposed to utilise the late post office for the offices of the medical officer, inspector of nuisances and inspector of weights and measures, and to use the large room at the back as part of the public library. The report was, after considerable discussion, adopted.—The Watch Committee recommended that a new police station should be erected on the site belonging to the corporation at the junction of Old and New Durham roads, in accordance with the plan prepared by the town surveyor, and that the cost be paid out of the revenue. After discussion the report was referred back to the committee for further consideration.

**Hartlepool.**—At a meeting of the town council on the 5th inst. it was resolved to apply to the Board of Trade for a provisional order to empower the corporation to adopt electricity for public and private use within the borough. The town clerk is to be instructed to take the necessary steps to carry out the resolution.

**Hastings.**—The corporation are promoting a new town's Bill, by which they seek to obtain powers to enable them to carry out various schemes for the improvement of the borough. An innovation completed this year—the construction of green enclosures on the front line, to give a relief from the monotony of asphalte—has been warmly applauded by the numerous summer visitors.

**Hull.**—The Electric Lighting Committee, at a recent meeting, accepted the tender of Messrs. Newton & Chambers, Sheffield, at £473, for the erection of an iron roof in connection with the extended portion of the electricity works in Sculcoates-lane. Mr. Good's tender, at £2,532, for the extension of the station buildings, was also accepted. The opening of the station in Sculcoates-lane is to take place on Thursday.

**Macclesfield.**—On Monday of last week a museum, presented to the town by Mr. Pownall Brocklehurst, of Macclesfield, and Miss Brocklehurst, was formally handed over to the corporation with public ceremonial. The building and endowment will cost the donors £10,000.

**Middlesbrough.**—A special meeting of the Electric Lighting Committee was held on the 5th inst. for the purpose of considering plans and specifications for a proposed scheme of electric lighting for the borough. It was originally intended to lay down plant estimated to cost £25,000, but a larger scheme was suggested, and it was unanimously thought that this would prove more advantageous to the town. This scheme was adopted, and it was decided to apply to the Local Government Board for sanction to borrow £36,000.

**Oswestry.**—The Sanitary Committee last week recommended that an infectious diseases hospital be provided for the borough, and reported that they had appointed a sub-committee to visit suggested sites. The recommendation was adopted.

**Penzance.**—The town council have resolved not to accept the offer of the Edmundson's Electricity Corporation, Limited, to undertake the supply of electricity for the town.

**Reigate.**—The question of purchasing the undertakings of the Redhill and Reigate gas companies was the subject of a special meeting of the town council recently. The mayor reminded the meeting that upon the House of Lords refusing to pass the Bills promoted by the gas companies last session the council were authorised to give the companies notice that they would promote a Bill for the purchase of both undertakings. It was with that object in view that the special meeting of the council was called. He moved that the council be authorised to promote the necessary Bill. A somewhat lengthy discussion followed, but in the end the motion was rejected.

**Southend.**—A special meeting of the town council is to be held on the 26th inst., to decide whether to apply for a light railway order for laying down a system of electric trams for the principal streets of the borough, including Prittlewell, Leigh, Southchurch, Westcliff, &c. The council already have an electric lighting order, and it is proposed to put down a combined lighting and tram plant. The tram scheme would include 10 miles of system, and the total cost, including buildings, would be about £80,000.

**Wells.**—The General Purposes Committee reported at last week's meeting of the corporation that inasmuch as the successful architect's estimate of a proposed new hall and post office, built according to his own designs, would only cost £4,850, and the lowest tender was £9,192, they had written asking the architect to return the £25 premium paid him.

**West Bromwich.**—The Electric Lighting Committee have decided to ask the town council to authorise them to engage an expert to advise them as to the best means of carrying out the electric lighting order.

## URBAN DISTRICT COUNCILS.

**Dorking.**—At the district council meeting on Thursday a report, by Mr. James Lemon, M.I.C.E., on the suggested treatment of Westcott drainage at Dorking outfall, was read. The report stated it was desirable, in the interest of all parties, that Dorking should accept the responsibility of the sewage disposal of Westcott. It was resolved to refer the financial question to the Finance and General Purposes Committee for consideration and report.

**Erdington.**—The sanction of the Local Government Board has been received by the council to the following loans—viz., £1,321 for sewage works, £3,000 for surface-water drainage works, and £420 for the purchase of a tip, wharf, &c.—The board will hold an inquiry on Wednesday next in connection with an application of the council for sanction to a loan of £2,300 for public street improvement works. Colonel W. M. Ducat, R.E., will conduct the proceedings.

**Eton.**—The five following tenders were received at the last monthly meeting of the district council for the erection of an engineer's cottage at the pumping station: Messrs. Goddard & Sons, £999; Mr. H. Burfoot, £978; Mr. Willett, £865; Messrs. H. Cooper & Sons, £857 10s.; and Messrs. Butcher & Henry, £984 9s. 6d. The tenders were referred to the Pumping Station Committee for consideration.

**Coole.**—At their last meeting the district council decided to erect a public swimming bath on a site in Pasture-road. The building will comprise two swimming baths, one 75 ft. long by 25 ft. wide and the other 50 ft. long by 25 ft. wide; ten slipper baths, gallery to the large bath, waiting-rooms, laundry and boiler-house, and caretaker's residence.

**Levenshulme.**—Local Government Board sanction to the borrowing of £2,624 for private street improvements has been received by the district council.

**Llanelly.**—The following motion was last week considered by the council: "That the council make inquiry of the Llanelly Gas Light Company as to their being prepared to negotiate the sale of their works and undertaking, and as to the possible cost of acquiring the same." In support of the motion it was contended that under good management the gasworks should prove a profitable undertaking. The tendency throughout the country was the municipalisation of such works, and there was no reason why municipalisation should not be adopted in Llanelly. The motion was eventually rejected.

**Maidstone.**—The council had under consideration last week a letter recently received from the Local Government Board intimating to the corporation that they could be granted a loan of only £15,000 for three years to cover the cost of the typhoid epidemic of last autumn. The borough authorities had applied for sanction to borrow £18,000, the actual cost of the epidemic to the ratepayers, the repayments to be spread over a period of twenty years, and the decision of the Local Government Board had come as a great surprise to them. Last week the council resolved that Mr. Chaplin should be asked to receive a deputation on the subject, to be introduced by Mr. Cornwallis, M.P. It was pointed out that Worthing was granted a loan for ten years in similar circumstances, and it was urged that Maidstone, having regard to the greater severity of the epidemic from which it had suffered, had a right to expect equally generous treatment.

**Matlock.**—Through the Duke of Rutland the devisees of the late Sir Joseph Whitworth on Thursday presented to the public of Matlock for ever the Whitworth Institute and Park and the Whitworth Hospital at Darley Dale. The gifts cost considerably over £100,000, and they are endowed in perpetuity with a considerable income.

**Portishead.**—Dealing with the question of the water supply, the clerk recently read a letter which had been received from the Portishead Water Company in reply to a communication from the council with regard to the deficient supply. The letter stated that a previous letter of the company had reference solely to the resumption of the supply as it existed before the drought. If, however, the letter was with reference to obtaining a new supply, the company informed the council that the borings referred to had been most satisfactory. Instructions had been given for estimates to be obtained, and for the work to be proceeded with at once. The company were determined to do all in their power to give the district a continuous and good supply. The reply was considered to be satisfactory.

**Slough.**—The district council on Monday unanimously resolved to instruct a committee to prepare a scheme for supplying the town with electric light. It was intimated that the light might be generated by the superfluous steam-power at the sewage pumping station, and that it would pay to do this for the supply of public lamps alone.

**Stourbridge.**—Colonel A. G. Durnford, an inspector of the Local Government Board, held an inquiry on Thursday relative to the application of the district council for sanction to borrow £600 for the erection of stables and for the provision of asphalte manufacturing plant. There was no opposition to the proposal, and the necessary information was submitted to the inspector by Mr. Goddard, the town clerk, and Mr. Fiddian, the surveyor.

**Uttoxeter.**—A special meeting of the council was recently held to consider the question of a more abundant water supply. In some parts of the town, it was stated by the chairman, water was only obtainable for about an hour in the morning. As they all knew, the negotiations for additional water had been going on for some time, but they must push the business forward as much as possible. They had also to consider the question of sewage disposal. Things in this respect have been bad enough for some time, but if they had a larger water supply there would be still more need for adequate sewage disposal. The district was reported free from infectious disease, but this could not be expected to continue if sanitation were neglected. He suggested that the two schemes should be taken at the same time. The report of the Sanitary Committee was read, in which it was advised that the water scheme be carried out as soon as possible, and that Mr. Wilcox, of Birmingham, be asked to come over at an early date and advise the council as to which scheme would be most advisable, as good springs were available at Cresswell and at Quickshill. The council went into committee on the sewage question.

**Waterloo.**—A Local Government Board inquiry was held recently respecting an application of the district council for sanction to borrow £750 for public lighting purposes. It was explained that the application was divided into two heads. The first was for £550 for the lighting of Great George's-road and South-road. In these roads gas is to make way for electricity. The Liverpool and District Lighting Company, Limited, had obtained an order in 1896 for supplying the district with power of lighting. They had erected a generation station, and the works were now in operation. The lamps to be used were similar to those used in Liverpool. Half the cost of the service loss was to be defrayed by the lighting company and half by the council. The Electric Lighting Company would lay the mains, the council provide the standards and carriers, and the lighting company would fix and maintain them. The remaining £200 was in respect of an electric light installation in the town hall.

## RURAL DISTRICT COUNCILS.

**Hollingbourne.**—The attention of the district council was on Thursday called to the insufficient water supply at Sandway. Lenham, where there was only one well to supply sixteen houses. The owners are to be called upon to obtain an increased supply.

**Maldon.**—An inquiry into the application of the district council for permission to borrow £10,775 for the carrying out of the Purleigh water supply scheme, which includes the parishes of Althorne, Cold Norton, Hazeleigh, Latchington, North Farnbridge, Purleigh, Stow Maries and Woodham Mortimer, has been held by Major-General H. D. Crozier, R.E., an inspector of the Local Government Board.

**Shepton Mallet.**—A Local Government Board inquiry has been held by Mr. H. Percy Boulnois relative to an application of the council for sanction to borrow the sum of £1,400 for the carrying out of a scheme of water supply for portions of the parish of Doulting. Mr. William Phelps, surveyor to the council, explained the scheme, which includes the erection of a wind engine for pumping. Mr. J. Wallis Titt, of Warminster, Wilts., a specialist on wind engines, also gave evidence.

## SCOTLAND AND IRELAND.

**Aberdeen.**—In accordance with the provisions of the Housing of the Working Classes Act, the town council recently made an application to the Secretary for Scotland for an arbitrator to decide as to the disputed properties in Exchequer-row area. Lieutenant-Colonel Frederick Bailey, Edinburgh, has been appointed to adjudicate the claims affected by the scheme.

**Belfast.**—The following resolution has been adopted by the Electric Committee of the corporation: "That the corporation be recommended to promote a Bill in Parliament for the laying and working of electric tramways in the city of Belfast, especially in those streets not already provided with a tram service, with power to acquire rights over any existing tramways within the city, and for all other purposes necessary for the establishment of an electric tram service in the city."

**Cupar, Fife.**—A long report was submitted to the town council at a recent meeting by the committee appointed to consider the question of purchasing the gasworks. The report, after dealing with the company's accounts, expressed the opinion that it was not in the public interest to purchase the works unless a decided eventual profit could be shown or some immediate advantage to consumers secured; but the purchase price suggested (£16,000 or £14,000) would not admit of this. Turning to the question of electricity, the report stated that it compared favourably in price with gas. A London company had offered to pay the expenses of obtaining a provisional order, to work the order, and to sell the undertaking, if necessary, to the council at the end of twenty years for capital and 15 per cent. premium. This company would light the streets at 4d. per unit, a price described as equal to gas at 2s. 6d. per 1,000 cubic feet. There was some opposition to the report being adopted, one member declaring that it was "entirely unsound in its premises, misleading in its conclusions, and not worth the printer's ink." It was, however, adopted.

**Glasgow.**—The memorial-stone of a new bridge spanning the tributary river Cart, between Langside and the rapidly-growing suburb of Newlands, was recently duly laid. The old Millbrae bridge was only 12 ft. wide. The new structure, which is in the course of erection alongside of it, is 50 ft. wide. The total cost of £4,523 is borne to the extent of £1,300 by the Renfrewshire County Council, which shares the responsibility for the bridge along with the Glasgow Corporation. The bridge is of Locharbriggs red sandstone, with ring heads, springers and parapet of grey granite, and the inside of the arch of white rock. The abutments will be surmounted by iron railings in extension of the parapet, and the foundations are of concrete, 12 ft. below the scour of the river. Messrs. John White and James Lang are the joint engineers, and Messrs. Morrison & Mason, Limited, of Glasgow, are the contractors.—The Statute Labour Committee of Glasgow Corporation had again under consideration, at a meeting last week, the proposal to widen Buchanan-street at its junction with Argyle-street, by acquiring a strip of ground from Messrs. Stewart & M'Donald, who are about to reconstruct their premises. A proposal to offer the firm £8,000 was defeated by three votes, and it was then agreed to leave the matter in the hands of the whole corporation.—The new service of electric cars on the Springburn route of the corporation tramways was inaugurated yesterday.

**Kirkcaldy.**—Considerable interest was manifested at the last meeting of the town council owing to the proposal, to which we have previously made reference, to municipalise the electric lighting and tramways. Letters were read from a local company offering to take up the scheme and allow the council to take them over at the end of thirty-five years, at a price fixed by arbitration. The Edmundson Electric Lighting Company offered to introduce electric lighting to the burgh, allowing the town to purchase the scheme at the end of ten years at 15 per cent. on the cost. A long and amusing discussion took place, a strong feeling being prevalent against the town taking up the scheme. It was ultimately agreed that the town council should apply for a provisional order to introduce the electric light themselves; while a subsequent motion was made to apply further for an Act of Parliament or provisional order to empower the council to introduce electric tramways. The idea is that the town, having got Parliamentary sanction for these schemes, could then hand them over to any company offering the best terms. A committee was appointed to arrange for procuring these orders.

**Stirling.**—At a recent meeting of the Eastern District Committee of the county council, a sub-committee appointed to consider the question of supplying the Polmont district with water reported on the matter. The committee said they had had under consideration three sources of supply. The first of these was from the Lochcote reservoir, belonging to the Bo'ness Commissioners, and the second the Forestburn reservoir, belonging to the Linlithgow County Council. To both of these schemes there was the objection that they could not be carried out except at very considerable cost, whilst with regard to a supply from the Lochcote reservoir there was the further disadvantage that the Bo'ness Commissioners could not guarantee a full supply of water. The committee afterwards considered the Lily Loch scheme, which was reported upon in 1895, and they were of opinion that that source of supply, if obtainable, would, on account of its altitude and purity, solve many of the difficulties in the way of supplying the higher-lying villages, and would in the long run prove the most satisfactory source. The report was, after discussion, adopted.

---

**University College.**—Prof. Osbert Chadwick, chairman of the Chadwick Trust, delivered his inaugural address at this institution on Wednesday afternoon, to open the course of municipal engineering, and lectures and demonstrations on municipal hygiene, instituted by the trustees. In our next issue we expect to refer in greater detail to the address, which was listened to with close attention by a large number of students.

**Institution of Heating and Ventilating Engineers.**—At the inaugual meeting of this body, held on Wednesday evening, at the Albion Hotel, Ludgate-circus, E.C., Mr. Walter Jones (vice-president), of Stourbridge, read an interesting paper, entitled "Heating and Ventilation." Mr. John Grundy, of Tyldesley and London, presided, and the proceedings, to which we hope to make further reference, terminated with a vote of thanks to the author.

**The Sanitary Inspectors' Association.**—The annual general meeting of the members of the above association will be held at Carpenters' Hall, London-wall, E.C., to-morrow, at 6 p.m., when the fifteenth annual report of the council will be considered, together with the annual financial statement and the report and certificate of the scrutineers on the election of chairman and members of the council for the 1898-99 session. An election of members and associates will also take place.

# Personal.

Mr. R. O. Wynne Roberts, the newly-appointed city engineer of Cape Town, leaves England on the 29th inst.

Mr. James Pursey has been selected by the Street Urban District Council to fill the post of town surveyor and inspector.

Mr. Richard Fleming, of Dundee, has been selected to fill the post of burgh and road surveyor of Carnoustie, at a salary of £100.

Mr. J. G. Griffin has been appointed assistant engineer at the electricity works of the Llandudno Urban District Council, at a salary of £100 per annum.

Mr. Richard Simmons, surveyor to the Porthcawl Urban District Council, has been appointed surveyor to the Little Woolton Urban District Council.

Erdington Urban District Council at their last meeting increased the salary of their engineer and surveyor, Mr. Herbert H. Humphries, by the sum of £100 per annum.

At the last monthly meeting of the Rathmines Township Commissioners it was decided to increase the salary of Mr. Dixon, the township engineer, from £400 to £500 a year.

Mr. D. W. Slocombe, late assistant surveyor to the Nantyglo and Blaina Urban District Council, has been appointed surveyor and inspector of nuisances to the Thame Urban District Council, Oxfordshire.

At a meeting of the Littlehampton Urban District Council, on the 6th inst., it was resolved to award the surveyor, Mr. H. Howard, 50 guineas for services as engineer in connection with the auxiliary water supply from Arundel.

The Herefordshire County Council on Saturday appointed Mr. Alfred Dryland, assistant surveyor to the Kent County Council, to the county surveyorship of Herefordshire, at a salary of £400 per annum. There were seventy-four applications for the position.

At a special meeting of the Bridlington Urban District Council, on Friday, Mr. Ernest R. Matthews, of Hastings, was appointed surveyor to the council, in succession to Mr. J. Freebairn Stow, who was recently appointed surveyor to the Chertsey Urban District Council.

Mr. A. B. Powell, assistant in the office of Mr. Herbert H. Humphries, engineer and surveyor to the Erdington Urban District Council, has recently received the appointment of assistant surveyor in the office of the engineer to the Birmingham, Tame and Rea Drainage Board.

At the last fortnightly meeting of the Merthyr Urban District Council applications for the post of temporary assistant surveyor to the council, at a salary of £150 a year, were considered, and it was decided to request three of the candidates to appear before the council at their next meeting.

Mr. E. Cross, of the Bradford Corporation electricity department, has been presented with a handsome writing desk, which had been subscribed for by the whole of the staff, on the occasion of his leaving to take up the appointment of assistant to Mr. J. A. Bell, city electrical engineer of Aberdeen.

We regret to announce the death of Mr. Cundall, senr., of the firm of Messrs. E. Cundall & Sons, Limited, of the Airedale Ironworks, Shipley, and 20 and 22 St. Bride-street, London, E.C., which took place at his London residence, 28 Ballater-road, Acre-lane, Brixton, S.W., on Saturday, the 24th ult., in his sixty-ninth year.

A wedding gift, in the form of a handsome dining-room clock and bronze ornaments en suite, has been presented to Mr. Frederick A. Price, deputy superintendent of the Manchester Corporation Gas Department, with a salver for Mrs. Price. The presentation was made, in the name of the subscribers, by Mr. C. Nickson, superintendent of the department.

The Highways Committee of the Salford Corporation have decided to submit the following recommendation to the town council in regard to the appointment of adviser on the proposed electric tramways for the borough : " That Mr. Charles Hopkinson be appointed to advise this committee upon the same terms as those upon which the late Dr. Hopkinson was appointed."

On Friday, at a meeting of the Annan District Committee, it was decided to amalgamate with the Dumfries District Committee in the supervision of the roads, and Mr. A. V. Hart, surveyor of the Dumfries district, was appointed to work also the Annan district, at a salary of £250, to be contributed equally by each district. There were 116 applicants for the post.

At the annual general meeting of the Architectural Association, held on Friday evening, the president, Mr. G. H. Fellowes Prynne, delivered an address and congratulated the association on its prosperous position. The body was popular in every branch of the profession, its financial position was sound, and their able instructors offered students advantages in architectural education superior to those supplied by any other institution of the kind.

On Wednesday of last week, at a meeting of the Bridg-

water Rural District Council, a letter was read from Mr. S Ingram tendering his resignation as surveyor to the council, in consequence of his having been appointed surveyor to the Devon County Council. The resignation was accepted, and several members were in favour of advertising for a successor at once, at a salary of £250 a year, whilst others favoured the adjournment of the consideration of the appointment to a special meeting, in order that the question might be considered with any alterations in the duties or the salary. The latter course was adopted.

Ninety-four applications for the office of borough surveyor were received by the Oswestry Town Council. Six of these candidates were subsequently selected, and Mr. G. W. Lacey, borough surveyor and waterworks manager, Saffron Walden, has since been unanimously appointed. The new official received his early training in the borough surveyor's office at Luton, and was chief assistant there for over three years, after which he was elected assistant surveyor and engineer of Kettering, which appointment he vacated, after three years' service, in favour of his present post.

Dr. James Burn Russell, who has been appointed medical member of the Local Government Board, is the author of a number of important works dealing with the subject of public health, and has held a number of public appointments. He succeeded Prof. Gairdner in 1872 as medical officer of health for Glasgow, and has held that post for twenty-two years. After graduating B.A. in 1858 he assisted Lord Kelvin, then Prof. Thomson, in his preparations for the Atlantic cable expedition, and was present at the splicing of the cable. In 1862 he graduated M.D., and some twenty-three years later the University of Glasgow conferred upon him the honorary degree of LL.D. Dr. Russell is a member of the Royal Commission on Sewage Disposal at present sitting.

At a recent meeting of the Reigate Town Council a member, in moving the adoption of a resolution recommending the increasing of the salary of the borough surveyor, Mr. W. H. Prescott, commented very favourably upon the satisfactory nature of the latter's work, and expressed the opinion that he (Mr. Prescott) had shown very great activity in personally superintending the various improvements that had been carried out. A local paper, in referring to the decision of the council to advance the salary to £300 per annum, remarks that it is worth while offering some inducement to Mr. Prescott to remain in the services of the borough. It would have been easy for him to have improved his position financially by getting an appointment elsewhere, and they all felt proud to be able to retain his services.

The following gentlemen, among others, were present on Tuesday at an inspection of the Central London Railway works, at the Post Office station, by a party of the Society of Engineers: Mr. W. Worby Beaumont, president; Mr. Henry Adams, past-president; Messrs. J. C. Fell and Charles Mason, vice-presidents; Messrs. J. Patten Barber, Joseph Bernays, George Burt, Percy Griffith, and R. St. George Moore, members of council; Mr. Perry F. Nursey, hon. secretary and treasurer; Messrs. H. W. Andrews, R. L. Andrews, J. C. Belton, A. R. Burch, W. G. Bower, H. O. Carr, S. O. Cowper-Coles, G. B. Cutler, F. E. Duckham, P. M. Faraday, N. Harker, W. H. Hill, A. E. Hubert, E. Hulburd, A. J. Lenton, W. R. Phillips, H. Pupleit, J. J. Rawlings, G. M. Robins, F. A. Robinson, J. Waddington, Captain Walter Wood; and Mr. G. A. Pryce Cuxson, secretary.

A proposal of the Electricity Committee of the Bolton Town Council to advance the salary of Mr. Arthur Ellis, the electrical engineer, from £300 to £450 per annum from the 1st October and during the equipment of the tramways for electric traction, was the subject of a lengthy discussion at last week's meeting of the council. Some feeling was imparted into the matter by two so-called labour representatives, because the council on a division, just taken previously, had refused to give an advance in wages to the street sweepers. Councillor James Holt opened the discussion by moving an amendment to the effect that the advance to Mr. Ellis be £100, and not £150, per annum. On a division only six voted for the amendment, forty-three being against. The recommendation was therefore confirmed by an overwhelming majority.

Eighteen competitive designs were sent in from various parts of the country for the erection of the new constabulary offices, police and coroners' court, proposed to be erected by the Warrington Corporation on the site of the old barracks in Arpley-street. Mr. Bennett, president of the Manchester Society of Architects, who was appointed assessor on the nomination of the Royal Institute of British Architects, has awarded £100 for the first premiated design to Mr. R. Burns Dick, Northumberland-street, Newcastle-on-Tyne. The corporation have also decided to appoint him as the architect, and he will therefore superintend the carrying out of his own plans. The second premiated design is that of Messrs. Tapper & Crouch, 12 Gray's Inn Buildings, London, W.C., who receive £50; and the third design is that of Mr. J. Lane Fox, Bond-street, Dewsbury, who receives £25.

## MUNICIPAL TRAMWAY ENTERPRISE.

While there is considerable disparity between the number of tramway systems owned by private companies and those operated by municipalities, the advocate of municipalisation need scarcely despair when he contemplates the following list of lines already in operation and those under construction and projected. When one remembers that it is only within the past few years that the legal restrictions which somewhat cramped municipal enterprise in the direction of tramways have been modified, the progress that has been made is somewhat remarkable. Electric working is the basis of most tramway developments at the present moment, and all municipal schemes have that method in view; indeed, it is no exaggeration to say that electricity has been the means of showing what a useful undertaking a local tramway service can be made. As we have pointed out in these columns, a local authority by combining lighting with tramway working is enabled not only to provide an efficient means of illumination at low rates, but can also furnish a quick tramway service at popular fares.

As we have mentioned before in the working of tramways, companies predominate at the present moment, but it would appear that the early conditions of electric lighting will be reproduced. For the first few years the chief work in public lighting was done by private enterprise, but how much that has been altered is shown by the fact that of the fifty-seven electricity works opened in this country since 1893 forty-four are owned by municipalities and the remainder—thirteen—by companies.

Municipal electric tramways have been projected in the following towns: Aberdeen, Birkenhead, Birmingham, Cardiff, Cheltenham, Chesterfield, Derby, Dundee, Edinburgh, Gates-

| MUNICIPAL ELECTRIC TRAMWAYS IN THE UNITED KINGDOM. | | | | | |
|---|---|---|---|---|---|
| Town. | System. | Number of Cars. | Length of System. | The Source of the Electricity Supply. | Max. Gradient. |
| Blackpool | Open conduit | 10 | 3 miles | Separate plant | 1 in 50 |
| Bradford | Overhead | 18 | 7 miles | Corporation lighting works | 1 in 14 |
| Dover | Overhead | 13 | 4 miles | Local electric lighting company | 1 in 25 |
| Halifax | Overhead | 10 | 6 miles | Corporation lighting works | 1 in 12 |
| Leeds | Overhead | 40* | 12 miles | Separate plant | 1 in 20 |
| Southend | ... | This line traverses the pier | | ... | ... |

| LINES IN COURSE OF CONSTRUCTION. | | | | | |
|---|---|---|---|---|---|
| Blackburn | Overhead | 8 | 3 miles | Corporation lighting works | 1 in 13 |
| Glasgow | Overhead | — | 3 miles | Corporation lighting works | — |
| Hull | Overhead | — | 18 miles | Corporation lighting works | 1 in 20 |
| Liverpool | Overhead | — | 6 miles | Corporation lighting works | 1 in 20 |
| Plymouth | Overhead | 6 | 3 miles | Corporation lighting works | 1 in 15 |
| Sheffield | Overhead | 25 | 0 miles | Corporation lighting works | 1 in 10 |

head, Huddersfield, Kirkcaldy, Leicester, Manchester, Newport, Nottingham, Oldham, Portsmouth, Salford, Southampton, St. Helens, Sunderland, Southport, Tynemouth, Wallasey, Wigan, Tunbridge Wells, Reading and York. Out of this list the undertakings in the following towns include the purchase of the existing tram lines from the local companies : Birmingham, Cardiff, Derby, Edinburgh, Leicester, Manchester, Nottingham, Oldham, Portsmouth, Salford, Southampton, St. Helens, Reading and York.

## TRAMWAYS MUNICIPALISATION AT SUNDERLAND.

### OVERHEAD SYSTEM ADOPTED.

As we briefly announced in a recent issue, the Corporation of Sunderland have decided to take over the control of the borough tramways. This decision was arrived at as the result of a special meeting, which was held to consider the report of a committee dealing with the question. The committee's report recommended that steps should be taken to acquire the service and work it by means of the overhead trolley system. The extension of the lines was also recommended. The total cost of the carrying out of the scheme will be about £250,000. The tramways company's lease will expire on August 16, 1899.

A letter was read from the British Electrical Traction Company, offering to purchase the whole system and to extend it as desired, and suggesting that the decision of the council should be deferred until a conference with the company took place.

The chairman of the special committee presented his report, in the course of which he pointed out the advantages that would accrue to the town by the acquisition by the municipal authorities of the tramway service. A long discussion took place on the question of the working of the trams by the corporation, several members expressing the opinion that it would be well to retain in their own hands the power of leasing the trams. Ultimately, however, it was decided, by forty-two votes to three, to adopt clauses which bind the council to go to Parliament for powers for the purchase and the working of the tramways by the corporation.

\* Including new cars on order.

After a lengthly discussion as to the proposed routes, the report, with a few slight amendments, was adopted.

## PROPOSED PUBLIC LIBRARY FOR GLOUCESTER.

A proposal is on foot at Gloucester to erect new public library buildings in Brunswick-road as an addition to the existing technical school buildings.

The library, says a contemporary, will comprise a hall, lending library, reference library, librarian's-room and news-room. It is proposed to appropriate the large room, formerly used as a museum but latterly as a technical drawing-room, for the reference library, and to utilise a small section of it at the west end, together with the waste space beneath the principal stairs to the art school for a librarian's private-room, and also to erect on the south of the reference library a lending library, with entrance hall. The lending library will be two storeys in height, with a large glass dome light over, the upper storey having galleries round and an open centre, and with wall space for a large number of stock and extra books. The galleries will be reached by a staircase direct from the lending library—a book-lift being also provided. Adjoining the lending library, and occupying the whole length of the land on the south side, will be the reading and news room, and in the basement accommodation will be provided for extra papers and stores, cloak-room, lavatories, &c. To compensate for the loss to the school of art of the technical drawing-room taken by this scheme for the reference library, additional accommodation for the school of art is to be provided above the free library- viz., a lecture-room and technical drawing-room over the reading and news rooms, two class-rooms over the new hall, the space over the reference library to be rearranged to suit the new conditions, but affording, as at present, a class-room, art master's-room, with lavatory and cloak-room. The buildings are estimated to cost about £5,000. The architects are Messrs. Waller & Son, of Gloucester.

## VILLAGE WATER SUPPLIES.

### A YORKSHIRE SCHEME.

The popular health resorts of Spaunton, Lastingham, Appleton-le-Moors and Cropton, villages situated in a particularly beautiful part of Yorkshire, have for some time past, it seems, been dependent for their water supply upon a number of more or less inadequate wells, giving water of a rather doubtful purity. To remedy this state of affairs a joint committee, formed by the Pickering and Kirby-Moorside District Councils, in the autumn of last year advertised for an engineer to advise them with respect to a joint scheme of supply, and Mr. J. E. Parker, A.M.I.C.E., of Durham and Newcastle, was eventually instructed, as a result of that advertisement, to prepare the necessary plans.

A week or two ago the joint committee met at Pickering for the purposes of discussing the report, which was submitted by Mr. Parker, and which recommended that, owing to the varying volume of the springs from which he proposed to take the supply, it would be advantageous to divide the scheme into two parts—one part for Spaunton, Lastingham and Appleton-le-Moors, and the other for Cropton alone. The first portion would comprise impounding tanks, together with a closed aqueduct leading to a covered service reservoir in Spaunton village, and from thence to Lastingham and Appleton. The second part of the scheme would deal with the impounding of the water from the Rigg End spring, Hartoft, conveying it by means of iron pipes to Cropton village, where a service reservoir would be provided.

The joint committee unanimously decided to give their approval to the scheme, and recommended that the work should be proceeded with as soon as possible.

**Geneva.**— The switching apparatus of the great electricity works of the city of Geneva, situated on the Rhone, near Chevres, gave fire recently, and in a short time the entire works were destroyed. In consequence of the transmission of the electric current for motive power and illumination ceased throughout the canton of Geneva,

## SPRING VALE FURNACES AND STEEL WORKS.

The visit of municipal engineers to these works, on the occasion of the recent district meeting at Bilston, was inevitably a hot and somewhat dusty experience, but one that was undeniably interesting and instructive. A brief account of the works will therefore be acceptable to our readers. We are indebted to Mr. C. L. N. Wilson, engineer and surveyor to the Bilston Urban District Council, for the following description :—

The works are situated in Bilston, adjoining the Grand Junction Canal, and are connected to the London and North-Western and Great Western Railway systems. They are the property of Alfred Hickman, Limited, and are very extensive. Nine locomotives are kept at work in the yards and in taking the slag to the spoil banks. There are upwards of 10 miles of rails, and employment is found for over 1,000 men. There are six large blast furnaces, but only four of them are in blast at present, with eleven regenerative hot blast stoves of the Cowper, Ford & Moncur type, heating the air supplied to the furnaces to a temperature of 1,400 deg. Fahr. The whole of the furnaces are blown by five massive blowing engines developing about 1,500 indicated horse-power. The furnaces turn out about 2,000 tons of pig iron per week, most of which is used in the adjoining steel works, where it is converted into Thomas Gilchrist steel by the now well-known process bearing that name. The minerals from which the pig iron is made are obtained in the neighbourhood, the North Staffordshire district and from Northamptonshire, and the fuel from Yorkshire and Wales.

The process of making steel by the Basic method is being largely carried on here, about 1,600 tons of ingot steel being produced per week. The pig iron from the furnaces is remelted in cupolas and then poured into the Bessemer converters in about 10-ton lots. It is then blown for about twenty minutes, so as to oxidise all the phosphorous, silicon, &c., in the iron, which now comes off as basic slag. The steel is next poured into ingot moulds, and after standing a few minutes the moulds are "stripped" from the ingot of steel. The ingot is then put into a Siemens' gas furnace, to be heated for rolling. This occupies but a few minutes, and the ingot of steel appears once more coming out of the gas furnace, and is tipped down in front of a powerful cogging mill, which rolls the ingot into greater length with less width and depth. In connection with this mill there is a tilting machine, to turn over and otherwise manipulate the rolled ingot, which saves a great deal of manual labour. The "bloom," as the steel is then called, is cropped off at each end by very strong shears, and is next passed on to be rolled either into plates, bars, angles, tees, flats, channels, or any other section necessary for constructional works, such as bridges, piers, roofs and waggons. The finished bars are sawn into lengths by a steam saw, and then are straightened ready for shipment.

There is a bar mill near the steel works rolling smaller sections of steel, provided with all the accessories required for that purpose.

The basic slag contains a large percentage of phosphate of lime, and about 600 tons of it is ground into powder each week and sold to farmers and root-growers for manurial purposes; it is specially valuable for grass and root growing, and is in great request.

There is a large colliery and a clay pit and brickworks in connection with the works and adjoining them, and altogether the works constitute a very good illustration of a Staffordshire iron and steel enterprise, and I think they are the largest in the county. There is in connection with the works a large and well fitted-up laboratory, where a number of expert chemists are engaged in making chemical analyses of the various ores and samples of the iron and steel produced, and also in making microscopic examination of these ores and samples.

## APPOINTMENTS VACANT.

*Advertisements which are re ceived too late for classification cannot be included in these summaries until the ollowing week.*

Foreman.—October 14th.—Staines Rural District Council. 27s. 6d.—Mr. George W. Manning, engineer and surveyor to the council.

Assistant Surveyor.—October 17th.—Garston Urban District Council. £110.—Mr. F. W. Bowden, A.M.I.C.E., surveyor to the council.

Slaughter-House Superintendent.—October 17th.—Corporation of Doncaster. 30s.—The Town Clerk.

Time and Store Keeper.—October 17th.—Vestry of Rotherhithe. 30s.—Mr. James J. Stokes, clerk to the vestry.

Building Inspector.—October 17th.—Edmonton Urban District Council. £130.—Mr. Wm. Francis Payne, clerk to the council.

Temporary Assistant.—October 17th.—Hampton Urban District Council. £3.—Mr. John Kemp, A.M.I.C.E., surveyor to the council.

Surveyor.—October 17th.—Twickenham Urban District Council. £260.—Mr. H. Jason Saunders, clerk to the council.

Stores Clerk for Surveyor's Department.—October 17th.—Ealing Urban District Council. 25s.—Mr. W. Ruston, clerk to the council.

Engineer, Surveyor and Sanitary Inspector.—October 19th.—Wembley (Middlesex) Urban District Council. £220.—Mr. John Smith, clerk to the council.

Assistant Surveyor.—October 20th.—Vestry of St. George-the-Martyr, Southwark. £130.—Mr. J. A. Johnson, clerk to the vestry.

General Engineering Assistant.—October 20th.—Corporation of Birkenhead. £110.—Mr. Charles Brownridge, A.M.I.C.E., borough engineer and surveyor.

Sewage Farm Manager.—October 21st.—Willenhall Urban District Council. 21s.—Mr. Chas. J. Jenkin, A.M.I.C.E., engineer and surveyor to the council.

Surveyor.—October 21st.—Andenshaw Urban District Council. £140.—The Chairman of the Council.

Inspector of House Drains.—October 21st.—Vestry of St. John, Hampstead. £110.—Mr. Arthur P. Johnson, clerk to the vestry.

Temporary Engineering Draughtsman.—October 22nd.—Corporation of Tiverton. £2.—Mr. J. Siddalls, borough surveyor.

Building and Drainage Inspector.—October 24th.—Corporation of Stockton-on-Tees. £100.—Mr. M. H. Sykes, borough engineer.

Temporary Assistant Engineer.—October 24th.—Drumcondra, Clonliffe and Glasnevin Township Commissioners. £80.—Mr. Michael Petit, town clerk, Drumcondra, co. Dublin.

Electrical Engineer.—October 24th.—East Ham Urban District Council. £300.—Mr. W. H. Savage, A.M.I.C.E., engineer and surveyor to the council.

Highway Surveyor.—October 28th.—Warwick Rural District Council. £120.—Mr. H. Consett Passman, clerk to the council.

Building Inspector.—October 28th.—Walthamstow Urban District Council. £3.—Mr. E. J. Gowen, clerk to the council.

Assistant Inspector of Nuisances.—October 29th.—Stretford District Council. £80.—Mr. George H. Abrahams, clerk to the council.

Municipal Engineer and Surveyor.—October 29th.—Municipality of Woodstock, Cape Colony. £500.—Messrs. J. C. Mackinlay & Co., 27 Walbrook, London, E.C.

Inspector of Nuisances.—October 29th.—Windsor Rural District Council. £130.—Mr. J. E. Gale, clerk to the council.

Deputy Surveyor.—November 3rd.—Brierley Hill Urban District Council. £100.—Mr. William Waldron, clerk to the council.

## COMPETITIONS.

*Advertisements which are received too late for classification cannot be included in these summaries until the following week.*

Fylde.—October 24th.—Sewerage scheme or schemes for the townships of Bispham-with-Norbreck, Carleton and Thornton, for the rural district council.—Mr. Fred. H. Brown, clerk to the council.

Abrayon.—December 1st.—Extension of the covered market, at a cost not to exceed £5,000. £31.—The Borough Surveyor.

Chertsey.—December 23rd.—Sewerage and sewage disposal scheme for the No. 1 and 2 wards of the district. £50, £30 and £20.—Mr. T. E. Harland Chaldecott, clerk to the council.

## MUNICIPAL CONTRACTS OPEN.

*Advertisements which are received too late for classification cannot be included in these summaries until the following week.*

Leigh.—October 14th.—Supply and erection of various electric lighting plant, for the urban district council.—Mr. Peregrine Thomas, clerk to the council.

Leigh.—October 14th.—Alteration of a bench of inclined retorts, for the urban district council.—Mr. Peregrine Thomas, clerk to the council.

Preston.—October 14th.—Levelling, paving, channelling, &c., works in the back roads between St. Christopher's-road and St. Andrew's-road, and the back roads between St. Andrew's-road and St. David's-road.—The Borough Engineer.

Norfolk.—October 14th.—Erection of a steel and iron bridge at East Harling, for the county council.—Mr. T. H. B. Heslop, M.I.C.E., county surveyor, Norwich.

Romford.—October 14th.—Erection of public baths, for the urban district council.—Mr. George Bailey, clerk to the council.

Hull.—October 14th.—Supply of sixty standards of creosoted redwood stringers, 4 in. by 7 in., and 700,000 creosoted redwood paving blocks.—Mr. A. E. White, city engineer.

Bangor.—October 15th.—Erection of buildings, chimney shaft, &c., for the electric light station.—Mr. John Gill, A.M.I.C.E., borough surveyor.

Westmoreland.—October 15th.—Widening of that portion of the Kendal to Ockenthwaite-road near the back gateway of Levens Park, for the county council.—Mr. Joseph Bintley, county surveyor, Kendal.

Scarborough.—October 15th.—Erection and completion of the proposed Victoria Hall and buildings in London-road, for the urban district council.—Mr. William Harmer, surveyor to the council.

Reighouse.—October 15th.—Providing and fixing at the sewage outfall works, Cooper Bridge, various boilers, engines, economiser, &c.—Mr. James Parkinson, town clerk.

Glasgow.—October 15th.—Supply of about 156 tons of 27-in. tubes, 1,273 tons of 24-in. spigot and socket turned and bored pipes and special castings.—Mr. James M. Gale, engineer of the corporation water department, City Chambers, Glasgow.

TUNBRIDGE WELLS.—October 15th.—Sewering and making-up of new roads on the site of the proposed workmen's dwellings.—Mr. W. C. Cripps, town clerk.

TWICKENHAM.—October 16th.—Supply of 2,000 cubic yards of 2-in. broken blue Guernsey granite or Cherbourg quartzite, for the urban district council.—Mr. H. Jason Saunders, clerk to the council.

PONTYPOOL.—October 17th.—Alteration, repair, &c., of the town hall, for the urban district council.—Mr. H. H. Haden, clerk to the council.

BIRKENHEAD.—October 17th.—Erection of public baths on a site adjoining Livingstone-street and Price-street.—Mr. Charles Brownridge, A.M.I.C.E., borough engineer and surveyor.

KINGSTOWN.—October 17th.—Supply during the ensuing twelve months of various stores, &c.—Mr. John Donnelly, town clerk.

EDINBURGH.—October 17th.—Various works in connection with gasholder tank at Granton.—Mr. James M'G. Jack, clerk to the commissioners.

WISHAW.—October 17th.—Supply of 12,000 tons of cast-iron pipes of 16-in., 18-in. and 19-in. diameter.—Mr. James Logan, town clerk.

MOUNTAIN ASH.—October 17th.—Supply and planting of trees and shrubs at the pleasure grounds, for the urban district council.—Mr. John Williams, surveyor to the council.

WARRINGTON.—October 18th.—Erection of a public convenience.—Mr. John Deas, Bank House, Sankey-road, Warrington.

LANCHESTER.—October 18th.—Erection of a new stone bridge over Newhouse burn, near Moorside, for the rural district council.—Mr. W. H. Ritson, clerk to the council.

LEWISHAM.—October 18th.—Concreting the bed of the river Quaggy from the Plough building to the river Ravensbourne (about 240 ft. in length), for the district board of works.—The Surveyor to the Board.

AMBLE.—October 18th.—Levelling, channelling, paving, &c., of Byron-street, for the urban district council.—Mr. W. Gibson, surveyor to the council.

KEIGHLEY.—October 18th.—Sewering, paving, flagging and making-good of Salisbury-road and Clifton-road.—Mr. W. H. Hopkinson, A.M.I.C.E., borough engineer.

LEYTON.—October 18th.—Widening of a portion of Grove Green-road, for the urban district council.—Mr. William Dawson, M.I.C.E., engineer and surveyor to the council.

FULHAM.—October 19th.—Making-up and paving of Felden-stree (section 1) and Friston-street, for the vestry.—Mr. Charles Botterill surveyor to the vestry.

DROGHEDA.—October 19th.—Construction of filter-beds and other works in connection with the waterworks.—The Borough Engineer.

SOUTH SHIELDS.—October 19th.—Supply and erection of various electric lighting plant.—The Borough Electrical Engineer.

GLAMORGANSHIRE.—October 19th.—Improvement of the main road at Whitchurch, near Cardiff, for the county council.—Mr. T. Mansel Franklen, clerk to the council.

WATFORD.—October 19th.—Supply of 900 tons of broken granite, for the urban district council.—Mr. H. Morten Turner, clerk to the council.

BETHNAL GREEN.—October 20th.—Supply of 100 gulley gratings, for the vestry.—Mr. F. W. Barratt, surveyor to the vestry.

ST. GEORGE-IN-THE-EAST.—October 20th.—Paving of certain footways in the parish with compressed asphalte, for the vestry.—Mr. G. A. Wilson, surveyor to the vestry.

KEIGHLEY.—October 20th.—Supply of 1,700 tons of 6-in. by 3-in. granite setts.—Mr. W. H. Hopkinson, A.M.I.C.E., borough engineer.

ST. GEORGE-IN-THE-EAST.—October 20th.—Erection of an addition to the vestry hall, in Cable-street, for the vestry.—Mr. G. A. Wilson, surveyer to the vestry.

CARLISLE.—October 21st.—Erection of a caretaker's lodge on the Sauceries.—Mr. Henry C. Marks, A.M.I.C.E., city engineer and surveyor.

RHONDDA.—October 21st.—Laying of about 1,000 yards of 10-in. gas mains at Tonypandy, for the urban district council.—Mr. Walter H. Morgan, clerk to the council.

BLACKPOOL.—October 21st.—Construction of two main outfall sewers to the sea (2,400 ft. and 1,400 ft. in length respectively), with all necessary manholes, &c.—Mr. J. Wolstenholme, borough surveyor.

WILMSLOW.—October 21st.—Construction of certain sewers, for the urban district council.—Mr. William Cobbett, clerk to the council.

NEWTON-IN-MAKERFIELD.—October 22nd.—Construction of a 2-in. storm overflow sewer, for the urban district council.—Mr. W. W. Shirley, clerk to the council.

COWES.—October 22nd.—Supply of about 1,500 yards of 6-in. and 400 yards of 4-in. cast-iron socket pipes, for the urban district council.—Mr. J. W. Webster, engineer and surveyor to the council.

COWES.—October 22nd.—Construction of a cast-iron water tank to hold 70,000 gallons, for the urban district council.—Mr. J. W. Webster, engineer and surveyor to the council.

LEDBURY.—October 22nd.—Construction of certain sewers, for the urban district council.—Mr. R. E. W. Berrington, engineer, Bank Buildings, Wolverhampton.

WILTSHIRE.—October 23rd.—Erection of the new county offices at the back of Arlington House, Trowbridge, for the county council.—Mr. Charles S. Adye, county surveyor, Stallard-street, Trowbridge.

MANCHESTER.—October 24th.—Supply and erection of a new shafting, brackets, pulleys, &c., at the sewage works at Davyhulme, near Urmston.—The City Surveyor.

NEW SHOREHAM.—October 24th.—Supply of 400 cubic yards of clean hand-picked land flints, for the urban district council.—The Town Surveyor.

RUGBY.—October 24th.—Laying of about 900 yards of cast-iron pumping main from the Avon waterworks to Railway-terrace, for the urban district council.—Mr. D. G. Macdonald, A.M.I.C.E., engineer and surveyor.

HODDESDON.—October 24th.—Making-up of three streets in the district and the construction of various surface-water sewers, &c., for the urban district council.—Mr. J. Salkield, surveyor to the council.

ST. LUKE.—October 25th.—Construction of an underground sanitary convenience in Golden-lane at its junction with Old-street, for the vestry.—The Surveyor to the Vestry.

BIRMINGHAM.—October 25th.—Erection of stabling and offices at Saltley Wharf at the corner of Crawford-street and Saltley Viaduct.—Mr. John Price, city engineer and surveyor.

HARROW.—October 25th.—Making-up of Byron, Kingsfield and Valentine roads, for the urban district council.—Mr. T. Charles, surveyor to the council.

LONDON.—October 25th.—Supply and erection of eight large gas engines, with starting engines and four small gas engines at the proposed Lots-road pumping station, Chelsea, for the county council.—Mr. C. J. Stewart, clerk to the council, Spring-gardens, London, S.W.

ERDINGTON.—October 25th.—Levelling, metalling, channelling, paving and making-up of South-road, Leamington-road, Woodland-road and Bridge-road, under the Private Street Works Act, 1892, for the urban district council.—Mr. H. H. Humphries, engineer and surveyor to the council.

ERDINGTON.—October 25th.—Sewering of Minstead-road and the surface-water draining of Oakfield-road, for the urban district council.—Mr. Herbert H. Humphries, engineer and surveyor to the council.

ERDINGTON.—October 25th.—Supply of about 7,500 yards of 24-in., 21-in., 18-in., 15-in., 12-in., 9-in. and 6-in. earthenware socketted pipes, for the urban district council.—Mr. Herbert H. Humphries, engineer and surveyor to the council.

ERDINGTON.—October 25th.—Supply of broken and unbroken stone for a period of twelve months, for the urban district council.—Mr. Herbert H. Humphries, engineer and surveyor to the council.

DOVER.—October 25th.—Laying of a new 12-in. cast-iron supply pipe from the sea to the baths.—Mr. Henry E. Stilgoe, A.M.I.C.E., borough engineer.

HACKNEY.—October 26th.—Construction of a public underground convenience at the north-east corner of the town hall grounds, for the vestry.—Mr. James Lovegrove, surveyor to the vestry.

BURY.—October 26th.—Electric wiring of public baths in St. Marie's-place.—Mr. John Hasham, town clerk.

HULL.—October 27th.—Supply and erection of various electric lighting plant.—Mr. A. S. Barnard, city electrical engineer.

BRECON.—October 28th.—Erection of a concrete wall and the execution of drainage and other works to support the landslip between the main road and the river Usk, near the village of Llangrwyne, for the county council.—Mr. H. Edgar Thomas, clerk to the council, County Hall, Brecon.

WILMSLOW.—October 28th.—Sewering, kerbing, channelling and making-up of a private street about 200 yards in length, for the urban district council.—Mr. William Cobbett, clerk to the council.

KIRKBY-IN-ASHFIELD.—October 29th.—Laying of about 9,500 lineal yards of 15-in., 12-in., 9-in. and 6-in. stoneware and cast-iron pipe sewers; construction of precipitation tanks, filter-beds, &c.; and the erection of a cottage at the sewage outfall works in Park-lane, for the urban district council.—Mr. Herbert Walker, A.M.I.C.E., Newcastle Chambers, Angel-row, Nottingham.

KIRKBY-IN-ASHFIELD.—October 29th.—Sinking of a well to yield 15,000 gallons hourly, for the urban district council.—Mr. W. H. Radford, Angel-row, Nottingham.

MIDDLESEX.—November 1st.—Widening of Turkey-street bridge, in the parish of Enfield, and the rebuilding of Kendal bridge, in the parish of Isleworth, for the county council.—Mr. Henry T. Wakelam, county surveyor, Guildhall, Westminster, London, S.W.

CUCKFIELD.—November 3rd.—Supply and erection of various pumping machinery at the waterworks at Balcombe, for the rural district council.—Mr. James Mansergh, 5 Victoria-street, London, S.W.

DEAL.—November 4th.—Construction of about 10 miles of brick and pipe sewers, the erection of a pumping station, the provision of pumping machinery, the construction of a tidal storage tank, penstock chambers and sea outfall, and all works incidental thereto.—Mr. Alfred C. Brown, town clerk.

ROYTON.—November 10th.—Supply and erection of pumping machinery to lift about 60,000 gallons of water per hour to a height of 60 ft., at the sewage works, Streetbridge, for the urban district council.—Mr. Theo. S. McCallum, A.M.I.C.E., 4 Chapel-walks, Manchester.

COVENTRY.—November 12th.—Erection of buildings at the proposed two new sewage pumping stations on the side of the main road from Coventry to Daventry.—Mr. Lewis Beard, town clerk.

SOUTHAMPTON.—November 16th.—Supply of two engines and dynamos at the county lunatic asylum at Knowle, Fareham.—Mr. W. J. Taylor, county surveyor, The Castle, Winchester.

CARMARTHENSHIRE.—November 18th.—Erection of a stone building of three arches over the river Towry at Dryslwyn, for the county council.—Mr. Thomas Jones, clerk to the council, Llandovery.

JOHANNESBURG, S.A.—January 6th.—Supply of a complete carburetted water-gas plant, for the corporation.—Messrs. Robert Whyte & Co., 22 Bury-street, St. Mary Axe, London, E.C.

## TENDERS.

*ACCEPTED.

BARKING TOWN.—For the supply of a 6 or 10 ton steam road-roller adaptable for traction, for the urban district council.—Mr. E. H. Lister, clerk to the council:—

| | 10 ton. | 6 ton. |
|---|---|---|
| J. Fowler & Co., Limited, Leeds | £340 | £320 |
| T. Green & Son, Limited, Blackfriars-road, S.E. | 337 | — |
| Wallis & Stevens, Rochester | 330 | — |
| Aveling & Porter, Limited, Rochester | 329 | 302 |

BECKENHAM.—For the widening of Croydon-road and Elmers End-road, for the urban district council.—Mr. John A. Angell, surveyor to the council:—

| | |
|---|---|
| W. G. Cloke & Co., Queen Victoria-street, London | £2,342 |
| E. Iles, Mitcham, Surrey | 1,591 |
| G. Wilson, Westbury-road, Walthamstow | 1,566 |
| W. Wadey, Carysfort-road, Stoke Newington | 1,500 |
| J. Mowlem & Co., Westminster† | 1,493 |

† Recommended for acceptance.

BLAYDON-ON-TYNE.—For the erection of new public offices and a technical school, for the urban district council.—Mr. H. Dalton, clerk to the council:—

| | |
|---|---|
| H. Dishman, Blaydon-on-Tyne | £3,737 |
| R. J. Harbottle & Co., Gateshead-on-Tyne | 3,045 |
| J. Bewley, Dunston-on-Tyne | 2,950 |
| H. Atkinson, Blaydon-on-Tyne | 2,880 |
| J. Dockey, Blaydon-on-Tyne | 2,806 |
| M. A. Armstrong, Blaydon-on-Tyne | 2,708 |
| R. Thompson & Co., Blaydon-on-Tyne | 2,693 |
| Davison & Belam, Blaydon-on-Tyne* | 2,626 |

DURHAM.—For the execution of private street works in the parish of Neville's Cross, for the rural district council.—Mr. George Gregson, surveyor to the council, Eastwood, Western-hill, Durham:—

| | |
|---|---|
| **Section 1.** | |
| J. G. Bradley, Durham | £666 |
| G. T. Manners, Durham | 652 |
| J. Carrick, Durham* | 628 |
| **Section 2.** | |
| G. T. Manners, Durham | 156 |
| J. G. Bradley, Durham | 155 |
| J. Carrick, Durham* | 154 |
| **Section 3.** | |
| G. T. Manners, Durham | 886 |
| J. Carrick, Durham | 871 |
| J. G. Bradley, Durham* | 817 |
| **Section I.** | |
| G. T. Manners, Durham | 186 |
| J. Carrick, Durham | 180 |
| J. G. Bradley, Durham* | 171 |

NELSON.—For the construction of about 110 lineal yards of culverting over the river Walverden, alongside the wall of the gasworks in Bradley.—Mr. B. Hall, A.M.I.C.E., borough engineer and surveyor:—

T. Dent & Sons, Ripon-street, Nelson.*

BECKENHAM.—For the erection of about 200 cast-iron ventilating columns, 13 ft. 6 in. high, on concrete bels, together with the laying of 9-in. stoneware pipe connections to the main sewers, &c., for the urban district council.—Mr. John A. Angell, surveyor to the council :—

| | | | | | | |
|---|---|---|---|---|---|---|
| E. Iles, Mitcham, Surrey | ... | ... | ... | ... | ... | £1,366 |
| J. Mowlem & Co., Westminster | ... | ... | ... | ... | 1,327 |
| G. Wilson, Westbury-road, Walthamstow† | ... | ... | 1,152 |

† Recommended for acceptance.

EAST RIDING.—For the erection of registrar's offices and extension of the county offices at Beverley, for the county council.—Mr. J. J. Bickersteth, clerk to the county, Beverley :—

| | | | | | | |
|---|---|---|---|---|---|---|
| T. Hodgson, Malton | ... | ... | ... | ... | ... | £4,829 |
| J. Constable, Beverley | ... | ... | ... | ... | 4,548 |
| G. Pope, Beverley | ... | ... | ... | ... | 4,239 |
| J. R. Foley, Beverley | ... | ... | ... | ... | 4,163 |
| R. Potts, Beverley* | ... | ... | ... | ... | 4,161 |

LAMBETH.—For the supply of 2,000 loads of Australian hard-wood, during the months of May to August, 1899, for the purpose of wood paving works, for the vestry.—Mr. J. P. Norrington, surveyor to the vestry :—
Millar's Karri and Jarrah Forests Company, Limited.—Karri, 2,000 loads, £5 5s. per load ; jarrah, 2,000 loads, £5 6s. 6d. per load.
Foymorgan & Co.—Blackbutt and tallow wood, 1,000 loads, £5 7s. 6d. per load.
Churchill & Sim.—Jarrah, 2,000 loads, £5 9s. 3d. per load.
A. & F. Manuelle.—Jarrah or karri, 2,000 loads, £5 9s. 11d. per load.
Foymorgan & Co.—Jarrah, 2,000 loads, £5 10s. per load.
W. Griffiths.—Jarrah, 2,000 loads, £5 13s. 9d. per load ; karri, 2,000 loads, £5 12s. 6d. per load.
McLean Brothers & Rigg.—Jarrah, 2,000 loads, £5 16s. 6d. per load.
Davies Karri and Jarrah Company, Limited.—Jarrah or karri, 2,000 loads, £5 16s. 11d. per load.
Paltreman & Foster.—Jarrah, 2,000 loads, £5 10s. per load.
The vestry accepted the tender of Millar's Karri and Jarrah Forests, Limited, for the supply of 2,000 loads of hard wood, the deliveries to consist of 1,000 loads of karri and 1,000 loads of jarrah.

LEEDS.—For the supply of (a) poles and (b) trolley wire and attachments in connection with the extension of the electric tramway systems.—The City Engineer :—

| | | | | | |
|---|---|---|---|---|---|
| (a) J. Russell & Son, Wellington-street, Leeds* | ... | ... | £5,058 |
| (b) Thomson, Houston & Co., London* | ... | ... | 4,248 |

POPLAR.—For the construction of an underground convenience in Bow-road, for the district board of works.—Mr. Leonard Potts, clerk to the board :—

| | | | | | |
|---|---|---|---|---|---|
| J. Dolman & Co., Ellesthorpe-street, Poplar | ... | ... | £2,100 |
| Thomas & Edge, Anglesea-avenue, Woolwich | ... | ... | 1,927 |
| A. E. Synes, Albert Works, Stratford | ... | ... | 1,915 |
| W. Johnson, Limehouse | ... | ... | ... | ... | 1,700 |

POPLAR.—For the erection of a footbridge over the North London Railway between Carmen-street and Railway-street, for the district board of works.—Mr. Leonard Potts, clerk to the board :—

| | | | | | |
|---|---|---|---|---|---|
| J. Dolman & Co., Ellesthorpe-street, Poplar | ... | ... | £2,400 |
| M. T. Shaw & Co., Limited, Millwall | ... | ... | 2,491 |
| Somervail & Co., Dalmuir, near Glasgow | ... | ... | 2,455 |
| Stephens, Smith & Co., Millwall | ... | ... | 1,945 |
| Power, Power & Co., Philpot-lane, E.C. | ... | ... | 1,950 |

TAMWORTH.—For the supply of about 8½ miles of 4-in. and 3-in. cast-iron water mains, for the rural district council.—Mr. Henry J. Clar. son, surveyor to the council :—

| | | | | | |
|---|---|---|---|---|---|
| Staveley Coal and Iron Works, near Chesterfield | ... | ... | £1,852 |
| Acklam Foundry, Middlesbrough | ... | ... | 1,671 |
| Stanton Ironworks Company, Nottingham | ... | ... | 1,516 |
| Merton & Co., London (for R. D. Wood & Co., Philadelphia, U.S.A.) | ... | ... | 1,440 |
| J. Blakeborough & Sons, Brighouse, Yorkshire* | ... | ... | 1,423 |
| D. J. Russell-Duncan, London (for the McNeal Pipe and Iron Foundry, Philadelphia, U.S.A.) | ... | ... | 1,409 |

WHITLEY.—For the widening of the road from Marine-avenue to St. Paul's church and the road from Park-road, Front-street, to the south end of Whitley-road, for the urban district council.—Mr. J. P. Spencer, Newcastle-on-Tyne :—
G. Maughan, Jarrow-on-Tyne.*

## MEETINGS.

### OCTOBER.

15.—Sanitary Inspectors' Association : Annual general meeting at Carpenters' Hall, London-wall, E.C. 6 p.m.
17.—Sanitary Institute : Sir Douglas Galton's introductory lecture to the 26th course of lectures and demonstrations for sanitary officers. 8 p.m.
18.—The Lord-Lieutenant of Ireland lays the foundation-stone of the new town hall at Belfast.
19.—Sanitary Institute : Visit of sanitary officers to the disinfecting apparatus and model steam laundry at St. John's Wharf, Fulham. 3.30 p.m.
19.—Sanitary Institute : Lecture for sanitary officers ; Dr. Louis Parkes, M.D., D.P.H., medical officer of health, Chelsea, on "Sanitary Laws and Regulations governing the Metropolis." 8 p.m.
21.—Sanitary Institute : Lecture for sanitary officers ; Mr. H. Manley, medical officer of health, West Bromwich, on "Sanitary Law—English, Scotch and Irish ; General Enactments Public Health Act, 1875 ; Model By-Laws, &c." 8 p.m.
21.—The Mayoress of Shrewsbury lays the foundation-stone of the Coleham pumping station. 12 noon.
22.—Sanitary Institute : Visit of sanitary officers to the Wimbledon sewage works, under the guidance of Mr. C. B. Cooper, A.M.I.C.E., engineer and surveyor to the Wimbledon Urban District Council. 3 p.m.
24.—Sanitary Institute ; Lectures for sanitary officers ; Mr. W. A. Bond, medical officer of health, Holborn and St. Olave, Southwark, on "The Law Relating to the Supervision of Food Supply." 8 p.m.
25.—Lord Rosebery opens the Sanderson public library at Perth.
26.—Sanitary Institute : Visit of sanitary officers to the parish of St. George, Hanover-square, under the guidance of Mr. A. Taylor, chief sanitary inspector. 2 p.m.
26.—Sanitary Institute ; Lecture to sanitary officers ; Prof. A. Bostock Hill, medical officer of health, Sutton Coldfield, on "Trade Nuisances." 8 p.m.
27.—Association of Birmingham Students of the Institution of Civil Engineers : Presidential address by Mr. J. C. Vaudrey, M.I.C.E.
28.—Croydon Municipal Officers' Association : First General Meeting. 8 p.m.
28.—Sanitary Institute : Lecture to sanitary officers ; Dr. J. F. J. Sykes, medical officer of health, St. Pancras, on "Objects and Methods of Inspection, Nuisances, &c." 8 p.m.

31.—The Duke of Cambridge lays the foundation-stone of the new town hall at Colchester.
31.—Sanitary Institute : Lecture to sanitary officers ; Prof. W. H. Corfield, medical officer of health, St. George, Hanover-square, on "Water Supply, Drinking Water, Pollution of Water." 8 p.m.

### NOVEMBER.

1.—Institution of Civil Engineers : Inaugural address by the president, Mr. W. H. Preece ; presentation of the council's awards and reception in the library. 8 p.m.

## NOTICES.

THE SURVEYOR AND MUNICIPAL AND COUNTY ENGINEER may be ordered direct, through any of Messrs. Smith & Son's book-stalls, or of any newsagent in the United Kingdom. Applications to the Offices for single copies by post must in all cases be accompanied by stamps.

The Prepaid Subscription (including postage) is as follows :

| | Twelve Months. | Six Months. | Three Months. |
|---|---|---|---|
| United Kingdom | 16s. | 7s. 6d. | 3s. 9d. |
| Continent, the Colonies, India, United States, &c. | 19s. | 9s. 6d. | 4s. 9d. |

The International News Company, 83 and 85 Duane-street New York City ; The Toronto News Company, Toronto ; and The Montreal News Company, Montreal, have been appointed agents in the United States and Canada for the sale of THE SURVEYOR AND MUNICIPAL AND COUNTY ENGINEER. A thin paper edition is printed for circulation abroad.

EDITORIAL OFFICES :—
24 BRIDE-LANE, FLEET-STREET, LONDON, E.C.
ADVERTISEMENT AND PUBLISHING OFFICES :—
13 NEW STREET-HILL, FLEET-STREET, LONDON, E.C.

## APPOINTMENTS OPEN.

WEMBLEY (MIDDLESEX) URBAN DISTRICT COUNCIL.
APPOINTMENT OF ENGINEER, SURVEYOR AND SANITARY INSPECTOR.

The Wembley Urban District Council is prepared to receive applications from gentlemen desirous of filling the above posts, at the combined and inclusive salaries of £220, rising by annual increments of £15 to a maximum of £280 per annum.

Forms of application, and full particulars as to the duties, can be obtained by sending a stamped directed envelope (foolscap) to my office.

Application forms, duly filled up and accompanied by copies of not more than three recent testimonials, should be sent to me, in sealed envelopes, marked "Engineer, &c.," by not later than 6 o'clock on Wednesday, the 19th October, 1898. Selected candidates will be written to, and third-class railway fare only will be allowed.

Canvassing the members, directly or indirectly, is strictly prohibited and will be deemed a disqualification.

(By order)
JNO. SMITH,
Clerk to the Council.
Public Offices, Wembley, Middlesex.
September 22, 1898.

BOROUGH OF BIRKENHEAD.
The Corporation of Birkenhead are prepared to receive applications for the position of General Engineering Assistant in the Borough Engineer and Surveyor's office, at a salary of £110 per annum, rising by annual increments of £10 to £150 per annum.

Candidates must have had experience in a municipal engineer's office, and be not less than twenty-three years of age nor more than twenty-eight years of age.

Applications, in candidate's own handwriting, stating age and experience, and accompanied by copies of not more than three recent testimonials, sealed and endorsed "Engineering Assistant," must be delivered at the office of Mr. Charles Brownridge, A.M.I.C.E., Borough Engineer and Surveyor, Town Hall, Birkenhead, by 12 o'clock noon, on Thursday, the 20th October, 1898.

Canvassing will be deemed a disqualification.

Borough Engineer's Office, Town Hall, Birkenhead.
September 29, 1898.

EALING DISTRICT COUNCIL.
SURVEYOR'S DEPARTMENT.

A Stores Clerk required ; age not to exceed twenty-five ; must be a neat writer, quick at figures and have a good knowledge of accounts ; will be required to fill up his time in the Surveyor's office. Salary, 25s. weekly.

Applications, stating age, previous experience, and enclosing copies of three testimonials, to be sent to the undersigned, marked "Stores Clerk," on or before the 17th instant.

W. RUSTON,
Clerk.
Public Buildings, Ealing.
October 5, 1898.

## VESTRY OF ST. GEORGE-THE-MARTYR, SOUTHWARK.

The Vestry are prepared to receive applications for the position of Assistant Surveyor, at a salary of £130 per annum, rising by £10 per year to £180.

Candidates must be between twenty-five and thirty-five years of age, and have had experience in a municipal engineer's office.

Application, in candidate's handwriting, stating age and experience and accompanied by copies of not more than three testimonials, sealed and endorsed " Assistant Surveyor," must be sent to the Vestry Clerk in the form provided, not later than 12 noon on Thursday, the 20th October, 1898.

Canvassing will be deemed a disqualification.

Forms of application and conditions of appointment may be obtained at the Vestry Clerk's office.

J. A. JOHNSON, Vestry Clerk.

Vestry Hall, Borough-road, S.E.
October 10, 1898.

## DRUMCONDRA, CLONLIFFE AND GLAS-NEVIN TOWNSHIP COMMISSIONERS, DUBLIN.
### TEMPORARY ASSISTANT ENGINEER.

The Township Commissioners require the service of a Temporary Assistant in the Engineer's office.

The person who shall be appointed must have experience in levelling and making surveys and other duties connected with a municipal engineer's office.

The salary will commence at £80 per annum, paid monthly.

Applications, endorsed " Assistant Engineer," accompanied by not more than three testimonials, with statement of experience and age, are to be received by the undersigned on or before Monday, the 24th instant, 1898.

MICHAEL PETIT, Town Clerk.

Town Hall, Drumcondra, co. Dublin.
October 7, 1898.

## AUDENSHAW URBAN DISTRICT COUNCIL.
### SURVEYOR.

Wanted, an experienced Surveyor, fully acquainted with the laying-out and execution of sewers, paving, flagging, drainage, sewage, and other works under the Public Health Acts, and the examination of building, street, and other plans and erections.

Commencing salary, £140 per annum.

Required to devote whole time to Council's work without liberty to practise on own account. Offices and fixtures provided.

Apply, not later than the 21st October next, with copy testimonials and stating where last employed, to Chairman, District Council Offices, Audenshaw, near Manchester, from whom printed copy list of duties can be had.

## WALTHAMSTOW URBAN DISTRICT COUNCIL.
### BUILDING INSPECTOR.

The Walthamstow Urban District Council invite applications for the post of Building Inspector.

Applicants must be fully qualified and competent by knowledge and experience to carry out the duties.

The salary offered is £3 weekly.

Candidates must apply in their own handwriting, stating their age and qualifications, particulars of past and present employment, and enclosing copies of three testimonials of recent date. Applications, marked " Building Inspector," to reach the undersigned before 5 o'clock p.m. on Friday, October 28, 1898.

Canvassing will disqualify.

E. J. GOWEN, Clerk to the Council.

Town Hall, Walthamstow.
October 4, 1898.

## WARWICK RURAL DISTRICT COUNCIL.
### APPOINTMENT OF HIGHWAY SURVEYOR.

Applications are invited for the office of Highway Surveyor for the above district.

The district comprises thirty parishes, with a population of 11,363, an area of 55,178 acres, and about 150 miles of district roads to be superintended and maintained.

The salary is £120 per annum, and the Surveyor will be required to devote the whole of his time to the duties of his office, to provide himself with means of locomotion, and to reside in the district.

The person appointed must be fully competent to perform his duties, to keep the accounts prescribed by the Local Government Board's order, and generally to comply with the instructions of the Council.

Applications (marked " Highway Surveyor"), in the candidate's own handwriting, with age, present and previous occupation, and accompanied by not more than three recent testimonials, to be forwarded to me not later than Friday, the 28th instant.

(By order of the Council)
H. CONSETT PASSMAN, Clerk.

48 Bedford-street, Leamington Spa.
October 10, 1898.

## VESTRY OF ST. JOHN, HAMPSTEAD.
### INSPECTOR OF HOUSE DRAINS WANTED.

The Vestry invite applications for the above office from competent men not under thirty nor over forty-five years of age.

The person appointed will be required to superintend the drainage of houses, including internal fittings, &c., and to see that the regulations and orders of the Vestry in respect of such work are carried out.

Further particulars may be obtained at the Surveyor's office, at the Vestry Hall.

Commencing salary, £110 per annum.

Applications, in candidate's own handwriting, stating age, previous experience and present employment, and accompanied by not more than three testimonials of recent date, to be sent in to me not later than 10 a.m. on Friday, 21st October.

(By order)
ARTHUR P. JOHNSON, Vestry Clerk.

Vestry Hall, Hampstead, N.W.
October 5, 1898.

## HAMPTON URBAN DISTRICT COUNCIL.
### TEMPORARY ASSISTANT.

Wanted, at once, for a few months, a Temporary Assistant, to undertake the preparation of surveys, plans, sections, &c., for private street works, and to supervise the construction of private street works now in progress.

Applicants must be good and accurate surveyors, levellers and draughtsmen, and have had experience in the superintendence of the construction of similar works. Salary, £3 per week. Age not to exceed thirty-five years.

Applications, in writing, accompanied by copies only of recent testimonials, to be sent to me not later than the 17th October inst.

JOHN KEMP, Assoc.M.Inst.C.E., Surveyor to the Council.

District Council Offices, Hampton, Middlesex.
October 6, 1898.

## GARSTON URBAN DISTRICT COUNCIL.

The above Council require a qualified Assistant in the Surveyor's office; must be an accurate surveyor and leveller and neat draughtsman, having a thorough knowledge of building construction and competent to prepare working drawings and specifications. Applicants must be well acquainted with the Model By-Laws of the Local Government Board, and be competent to undertake the inspection of new buildings and the construction of drains, and have had at least five years' experience in a borough or district surveyor's office.

Salary to commence at £110 per annum.

Written applications only, in the candidate's handwriting, stating age, qualifications, present and past experience, together with copies of not more than four recent testimonials (which will not be returned), may be sent to the undersigned on or before the 17th day of October.

Canvassing will disqualify.

F. W. BOWDEN, Assoc.M.Inst.C.E.

Public Offices, Grassendale, West Liverpool.
October 5, 1898.

## EAST HAM URBAN DISTRICT COUNCIL.
### ELECTRICAL ENGINEER.

The above-named Council require the services of an Electrical Engineer for the preparation of a scheme of electric lighting combined with tramways, and the ultimate management and maintenance of the same after completion.

The person appointed must be prepared to reside in the district and devote the whole of his time to the duties of the office. The salary will be £300 per annum, with necessary offices and assistance, and, as the district is a rapidly increasing one, the position is likely to improve.

All further particulars, together with a form of application, may be obtained upon application to Mr. W. H. Savage, A.M.I.C.E., the Engineer and Surveyor to the Council, at the Public Offices, East Ham.

Applications to be sent, in the printed envelope provided for the purpose, and enclosing copies of three recent testimonials, or or before Monday, October 24th next.

Canvassing members of the Council, either directly or indirectly, is strictly prohibited and will disqualify any candidate.

C. E. WILSON, Clerk to the Council.

Public Offices, East Ham, London, E.
September 27, 1898.

## BOROUGH OF STOCKTON-ON-TEES.

The Corporation require the services of a Building and Drainage Inspector, at a salary of £100 per year.

For particulars of the duties apply to the Borough Engineer.

Applications, endorsed " Building Inspector," with copies of not more than three recent testimonials, which will not be returned, to be sent to the undersigned not later than Monday, the 24th October, 1898.

M. H. SYKES, Borough Engineer.

Stockton-on-Tees.

## COUNTY BOROUGH OF HANLEY.

Tenders and schemes are invited for the Erection of a Refuse Destructor.

The building in which the destructor is to be placed, or the brick chimney shaft, is not included in this contract.

Further particulars, together with copies of the plan of two suggested sites, may be obtained on application to the undersigned.

Contracts will only be given to firms paying the standard rate of wages.

The lowest or any tender not necessarily accepted.

Sealed and endorsed tenders to be sent to me before Tuesday, November 15, 1898.

JOSEPH LOBLEY,
Borough Engineer and Surveyor.

Town Hall, Hanley.
October 4, 1898.

## WILMSLOW URBAN DISTRICT COUNCIL.
### TO CONTRACTORS.

Tenders are invited for the Sewering, Kerbing, Channelling and Road-making of a Private Street about 200 yards in length.

Drawings and specifications may be seen, and bills of quantities and form of tender obtained, at the Council's offices, from 10 to 11 a.m., on payment of 1 guinea, returnable if a *bonâ-fide* tender be furnished.

Sealed tenders, to be addressed to the Clerk of the Council and endorsed "Private Street Works," to be delivered not later than Friday, the 28th October, 1898.

WILLIAM COBBETT,
Clerk to the Council.

Council Offices, Swan-street, Wilmslow.

## URBAN SANITARY DISTRICT OF ROYTON.
### TO PUMP MAKERS.

The Royton Urban District Council solicit tenders for the Supply and Erection of Pumping Machinery to lift about 60,000 gallons of water per hour to a height of 60 ft., at the Council's sewage works, Streetbridge, Royton.

Specifications and other particulars may be obtained on application to Mr. Theo. S. McCallum, A.M.I.C.E., 4 Chapelwalks, Manchester, on sending a deposit of £1, which sum will be returned after receipt of a *bonâ-fide* tender.

The Council does not bind itself to accept the lowest or any tender.

Tenders (endorsed "Contract No. 17") must be delivered to the undersigned on or before the 10th day of November, 1898.

(Signed)　　THOS. BLEASDALE,
Clerk to the Council.

Town Hall, Royton.
October 5, 1898.

## ERDINGTON URBAN DISTRICT COUNCIL.
### SUPPLY OF STONE FOR ROAD REPAIRING.

The Highways and Buildings Committee of the above Council are prepared to receive tenders for the supply of Broken and Unbroken Stone to various points in their district for a period of twelve months.

Specifications, forms of tender and all information may be obtained upon application at my office, Public Hall, Erdington.

Tenders accompanied by samples and endorsed "Tender for Stone," to be delivered to me not later than Tuesday, October 25, 1898.

The Council do not bind themselves to accept the lowest or any tender, and the tender of any firm paying less than the standard rate of wages current in their district will not be considered.

HERBERT H. HUMPHRIES,
District Engineer and Surveyor.

Public Hall, Erdington, Birmingham.
October 10, 1898.

## HODDESDON URBAN DISTRICT COUNCIL.
### TO ROAD AND SEWER CONTRACTORS.

The above Council invite tenders for the Making-up of three Streets in their district, comprising a total length of 3,400 ft.

The works include Carriageways, Footways and Kerbs.

Tenders are also invited for the construction of Surface-Water Sewers, comprising 44 yards of 15-in. Cast-Iron Pipe, 32 yards of 15-in. Stoneware Pipe, 383 yards of 12-in. Stoneware Pipe, 953 yards of 9-in. Stoneware Pipe and 131 yards of 6-in. Stoneware Pipe, with the necessary Junctions, Manholes, Tumbling Bays, Ventilators, Catchpits, &c.

Plans and sections may be seen at the office of the undersigned, from whom the specifications, quantities, forms of tender and contract may be obtained on payment of 3 guineas.

# PLACE'S PATENT LOCK JOINT

The composition being cast on the lower half of the pipe in the form of a ball and socket joint, it necessarily follows that immediately the pipes are put together and fastened with a wedge at the top the lower half of the pipe is absolutely watertight and perfect alignment of invert is secured.

### POINTS:—

Easily and quickly laid by unskilled workmen.
Perfect alignment of invert secured.
Joint readily made absolutely watertight.
Cheapest Patent Joint in the market.

Prices and further particulars on application to J. PLACE & SONS, Ltd., Darwen.

which sum will be returned to non-successful contractors on the receipt of a *bonâ-fide* tender and the return of the specifications, quantities, forms of tender and contract, and to the successful contractor on his executing his contract and bond.

Tenders must be on the forms supplied by the council and accompanied by the schedule of prices, and must be delivered at the office of the Council, addressed to the Chairman, Highways Committee, Council Offices, High-street, Hoddesdon, sealed and endorsed "Tender for Works," by not later than noon on Monday, the 24th day of October inst.

The Council do not bind themselves to accept the lowest or any tender, and reserve the right of letting both contracts to one contractor or otherwise.

T. SALKIELD,
Surveyor.

Briscoe-road, Hoddesdon.
October 1, 1898.

# ERDINGTON URBAN DISTRICT COUNCIL.

### PRIVATE STREET WORKS ACT, 1892.

#### TO CONTRACTORS.

The Highways and Buildings Committee of the above Council are prepared to receive tenders for Levelling, Metalling, Channelling, Paving and Making Good South-road, Leamington-road, Woodland-road and Bridge-road, within their district.

Drawings may be seen and specifications, bills of quantities, forms of tender and all information obtained upon application at my office, Public Hall, Erdington, from Thursday, the 13th inst., to Tuesday, the 25th inst., upon which latter day tenders, endorsed "Tender for making-up ——— road," must be delivered at my office not later than 12 o'clock at noon.

The Council do not bind themselves to accept the lowest or any tender, and the tender of any firm paying less than the standard rate of wages will not be considered.

HERBERT H. HUMPHRIES,
District Engineer and Surveyor.

Public Hall, Erdington, Birmingham.
October 10, 1898.

# CITY OF BIRMINGHAM.

### TO BUILDING CONTRACTORS AND OTHERS.

The Public Works Committee are prepared to receive tenders for proposed Stabling and Offices at Saltly Wharf (corner of Crawford-street and Saltly Viaduct).

The drawings and specification for the proposed works may be inspected, and quantities and forms of tender obtained, on and after Saturday, the 15th instant, on deposit of 1 guinea (which will be returned on receipt of a *bonâ-fide* tender) at the undermentioned office.

Tenders are to be sent in not later than 10 a.m. on the 25th instant, endorsed "Stabling." The tender of any firm or person paying less than the minimum standard rate of wages current in the district will not be accepted.

The lowest or any tender not necessarily accepted.

JOHN PRICE,
City Engineer and Surveyor.

City Surveyor's Office,
The Council House, Birmingham.
October 10, 1898.

# ERDINGTON URBAN DISTRICT COUNCIL.

### EARTHENWARE PIPES FOR SEWERAGE AND STORM-WATER DRAINAGE WORKS.

The Highways and Buildings Committee of the above Council are prepared to receive tenders for the supply and delivery to various parts of their district of about 7,500 yards of 24-in., 21-in., 18-in., 15-in., 12-in., 9-in. and 6-in. Earthenware Socketted Pipes.

Specifications, forms of tender and all information may be obtained upon application at my office, Public Hall, Erdington.

Tenders, endorsed "Earthenware Pipes," must be delivered at my office not later than Tuesday, the 25th October, 1898. The Council do not bind themselves to accept the lowest or any tender, and the tender of any firm paying less than the standard rate of wages current in their district will not be considered.

HERBERT H. HUMPHRIES,
District Engineer and Surveyor.

Public Hall, Erdington, Birmingham.
October 10, 1898.

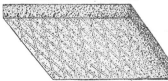

ERDINGTON URBAN DISTRICT COUNCIL.

*PRIVATE STREET WORKS ACT, 1892.*

TO CONTRACTORS.

The Highways and Buildings Committee of the above Council are prepared to receive tenders for the Sewering of Minstead-road and the Surface-Water Draining of Oakfield-road within their district.

Drawings may be seen and specifications, bills of quantities, forms of tender and all information obtained, upon application at my office, Public Hall, Erdington, from Thursday, the 13th inst., to Tuesday, the 25th inst., upon which latter day tenders, endorsed "Tender for ——— in ——— road," must be delivered at my office not later than 12 o'clock at noon.

The Council do not bind themselves to accept the lowest or any tender, and the tender of any firm paying less than the standard rate of wages will not be considered.

HERBERT H. HUMPHRIES,
District Engineer and Surveyor.

Public Hall, Erdington, Birmingham.
October 10, 1898.

LEDBURY URBAN DISTRICT COUNCIL.
SEWERAGE WORKS.

The Urban District Council of Ledbury is prepared to receive tenders from competent persons for the construction of certain Sewers and other work connected therewith.

The drawings may be seen, and copies of the specification, bill of quantities and form of tender, may be obtained from the Engineer, Mr. R. E. W. Berrington, Bank Buildings, Wolverhampton, on and after Saturday, October 8th next, on payment of 2 guineas, which will be returned on receipt of a *bond-fide* tender.

The contractor must not pay less than the standard rate of wages paid in the district and must observe the proper conditions of labour, and no sub-letting will be allowed except by permission of the Council.

Sealed tenders, addressed to me and endorsed "Tender for Sewerage Works," are to be delivered at my office, Ledbury, at or before noon on Saturday, October 22nd next.

The Council does not bind itself to accept the lowest or any tender.

JESSE GARROOD,
Clerk to the Council.

Clerk's Offices, Ledbury.
October 3, 1898.

ST. LUKE (MIDDLESEX) VESTRY.
CONSTRUCTION OF UNDERGROUND SANITARY CONVENIENCE.

The above Vestry invite tenders for the construction of an Underground Sanitary Convenience in Golden-lane, at its junction with Old-street, in accordance with the plans, specifications, &c., and bill of quantities prepared by the Surveyor to the Vestry and Mr. H. Williams Mellor, Quantity Surveyor, respectively.

These may be seen, and forms of tender and bill of quantities had, any day except Saturday, after 13th instant, from 11 to 5 o'clock, and on Saturdays from 11 to 1 o'clock, on application to the Surveyor's department and upon depositing the sum of 2 guineas, which will be returned upon receipt of a *bond-fide* tender.

Tenders must be upon the official form only, properly filled up, and signed by the contractor and the proposed sureties, and marked outside "Sanitary Convenience," must be delivered before noon on 25th October instant.

(By order)
GEORGE WHITEHEAD PRESTON,
Vestry Clerk.

Vestry Clerk's Office,
St. Luke Vestry Hall, City-road, E.C.
October 1, 1898.

---

## ADVERTISEMENTS.

QUANTITIES, &c., LITHOGRAPHED accurately and with despatch. METCHIM & SON, Abbey-buildings, Princes-street, Westminster, S.W. "Surveyor's Diary and Tables for 1898," price 6d, post 7d.; in leather 1s., post 1s. 1d.

---

THE ENGINE AND DYNAMO ROOM.

THE BOILER HOUSE.

PRINCIPAL FEATURES OF MUNICIPAL ELECTRIC LIGHTING SYSTEMS.
BRADFORD NEW WORKS.

# The Surveyor

## And Municipal and County Engineer.

Vol. XIV., No. 354.    LONDON, OCTOBER 28, 1898.    Weekly, Price 3d.

## Minutes of Proceedings.

**The Local Government Board and the Housing Problem.** There have recently been one or two vigorous deliverances in regard to the policy of the Local Government Board in connection with schemes for the housing of the poor. In the paper read at the recent Sanitary Institute congress at Birmingham, and reported in our issue of October 14th, Dr. Scurfield, medical officer of health for Sunderland, gave an account of the experience of that town. The first steps were taken in August, 1893, and in October of the same year the petition for the confirmation of the scheme was forwarded to the Local Government Board. The inquiry was held early in January, 1894, and the provisional order issued in the following May. In September of the same year a second inquiry was held to modify the scheme, and two years later the purchase of properties was so far advanced as to permit of advertising a competition. The premiums were duly awarded, and the first premiated designs provisionally approved by the council after some amendment. Then it was thought advisable that the architect and the borough surveyor should interview the architect to the Local Government Board, in order to ensure the ultimate approval of the plans by making any required modifications. The amended plans were quickly approved by the council, and then formally submitted to the Local Government Board, with a request that, as there was no one living on the area and the buildings were mostly in ruins, the council wished to build on the whole area at once instead of only on one-half. More than four months afterwards the Local Government Board wanted further information as to the latter proposal, and suddenly discovered that the plans provided (1) insufficient open space, (2) accommodation for too few persons, and (3) one-room tenements. In regard to objection (2) it is worth noting that while 480 persons were displaced the plans provided for the accommodation of 454 persons. The close of last year saw another deputation, and as a consequence thereof further amendments in regard to open space, the number to be provided for, and abolishing one-roomed tenements. The amended plans were submitted to the Local Government Board early in 1898, but the council were informed that another inquiry must be held. This duly took place in June, but there is not as yet a prospect of any early start in the erection of the buildings. Four years and eight months have elapsed since the Local Government Board were asked to confirm the scheme. Of this period about two years were spent in the purchase of the properties, about four months in the competition for the plans of the dwelling, and the balance in correspondence and negotiations with the Local Government Board.

So much for Dr. Scurfield, but he is by no means alone in his protest. Mr. MacBrair, the city surveyor of Lincoln, recently found an opportunity of entering the arena in connection with the diocesan conference in that city, and he delivered himself vigorously in speaking to a motion " that overcrowded and unsuitable dwelling-houses are detrimental to the spiritual, as well as to the sanitary welfare of the people." He first referred to the difficulty of finding a suitable term to define those for whom accommodation should be provided. " The labouring classes " was rather a vague term, and in Dublin they had coined a new expression—" the very poor." He himself confined his remarks to those who were earning 20s. a week and under. Flats, he said, were not wanted at Lincoln, for they were not cared for. The rents should be 3s. and under per week. In Hull lately they had been building a large number of houses at 3s. 9d. per week. At the present time in Dublin there was a scheme to provide dwellings at rents varying from 1s. to 1s. 3d. per week; but to do that a free site was asked for and no rates or taxes were paid, which meant a reduction of at least 30 to 35 per cent. off the cost. Mr. MacBrair finds that the provision required could only come from three possible sources: —(1) Ordinary commercial enterprise, (2) local authorities, and (3) sympathetic private enterprise —a phrase of his own coinage. The first source, he thought, might be dismissed, as the prospect was not sufficiently attractive. He then proceeded to ask why municipal enterprise should be behind benevolent private enterprise in this matter. We have always contended that municipal enterprise in this direction should be confined as much as possible to providing decent accommodation for those who could not provide for themselves and whose condition might otherwise be a danger to the community. In such a case the work must impose some burden on the rates, though it can scarcely fail to prove indirectly remunerative through its beneficial effects on the health of the community generally. But Mr. MacBrair's point is that, even assuming that there would be no burden upon the rates, the local authorities have a difficulty in providing the accommodation required. Why? Because as a loan is required the central authorities intervene, and their policy has been to insist on requirements which render it impossible to provide the accommodation necessary. Mr. MacBrair did not advocate the lowering of the ideal standard, but he contended—and he will have plenty of support in his contention— that the ideal cannot always be attained, and in that case they should be allowed to do the best possible under the circumstances. He also denied the contention of the Local Government Board that the modification of their demands necessarily meant insanitary dwellings, and bluntly asserted that these requirements practically vetoed the building of self-supporting houses. He argued, further, that as the Local Government Board insisted upon the repayment of the principal as well as the interest, an additional shilling a week, if not more, was thus placed upon the rent, and that it became a question whether the houses did not appear at the end of the thirty years to be the property of the working men themselves, who were paying both principal and interest in their rent, and might naturally be expected to reap some ultimate benefit from so doing. In short, Mr. MacBrair charges the central authorities with obstructing a beneficent movement, and calls upon them to consider the special circumstances of localities, to demand the minimum and not the maximum of requirements, to make their rules less cast-iron, and not to insist in season and out of season with absolute compliance irrespective of local conditions. Mr. MacBrair's arguments on the economic side of the question are strongly enforced by the concrete illustration in the case of Sunderland of the vexatious delays arising partly from procrastination and partly from rigid and unvarying requirements. Dr. Scurfield maintains that the local authority might safely be entrusted with the erection of workmen's dwellings under the Housing of the Working Classes Act, 1896, without having to submit every detail of the plans for the approval of the Local Government Board. The dissatisfaction is sufficiently great to make it desirable that the central authorities should seriously consider whether their requirements are not so great and so inflexibly insisted upon as to do more harm than good. Surely local considerations may be such as to justify, upon the report of a competent inspector after due inquiry, or after consideration of all the facts submitted by a local authority, an occasional modification of " model " requirements.

\* \* \*

**Municipal Work in Shoreditch.** The municipal reports and accounts of the borough of Shoreditch forms a portly and handsome volume of over 400 pages. It contains special reports from all the chief officials, including the surveyor, the lighting engineer and the chief electrical engineer. In municipal circles Shoreditch has for some time past been attracting no small share of attention on account of the combined scheme of electric lighting and dust destruction that is being carried out in the district, and the controversy that has arisen on the subject. At present, however, we have no intention of entering into the pros and cons of the matter, or of commenting on such figures or other details as are given in this volume. Mr. T. W. Baker has already criticised the figures, and we may have an early opportunity of dealing with the subject separately. In the meantime we may note one or two other points from the volume before us. The electricity station and the dust destructor are really part of a still larger combined scheme which consists in placing a remarkable collection of municipal institutions upon one site. During the year three of the main sections were completed, the electricity station, the dust destructor and the public library, leaving the baths and wash-houses and the technical institute, which will be completed in the ensuing year. The great event of importance last year was the opening of the combined works, which were duly blessed by Lord Kelvin. A scheme is also being carried out for the utilisation of the heat from the exhaust steam of the engines in the electricity station in heating the baths and wash-houses adjoining, and a contract for the necessary condensers, steam pipes and plant has been entered into, at a cost of £4,695. It is expected, according to the report of the town clerk, Dr. Mansfield Robinson, that this outlay will not only complete the economy of the electricity and dust destructor undertaking, but will save the Baths Committee a capital expenditure of £4,500 for boilers, which they would otherwise require, and an annual maintenance charge of £1,575 for fuel and the upkeep of boilers, while the condensation of the steam of the electricity engines is expected to be an advantage to their working, the scheme adopted costing nothing beyond the provision and upkeep of the condensers and the plant. From the resolution passed by the vestry

in March last it will be seen that superannuation for local government officials meets with scant favour in Shoreditch. That vestry is one of the few local authorities in the metropolis which have declared against the principle or petitioned against the Bill. In view of the conference on Monday next, and the fresh steps that are being taken to obtain the passing of the Bill, the resolution may be quoted here. It is to the following effect:—

That this vestry considers that the passing of the Poor Law Officers' Superannuation Act Amendment Act, 1896, was a gross injustice to the overburdened ratepayers, the great majority of whom are unprovided for in their old age, and hereby most emphatically condemns the Bill to amend the same so as to extend its provisions to the officers of vestries and other parochial bodies.

A petition against the Bill was duly presented to Parliament. It has been shown, however, that since the passing of the Act above referred to the amount obtained through the deduction of a percentage of salaries has far exceeded the amount which had to be paid away in allowances. So far, therefore, it has involved no " gross injustice to the overburdened ratepayers," and this argument, at all events, falls to the ground. The question, however, may be left in the meantime. In regard to the report of the surveyor, Mr. Rush Dixon, some of the more interesting facts and figures will appear among our abstracts of annual engineering records.

\* \* \*

**Municipalities and Rival Electric Companies.** The discussion which took place last week at the autumn general meeting of the Association of Municipal Corporations showed the unanimity that exists among corporations and their legal advisers as to the attitude that should be adopted in regard to the encroachments of private enterprise into districts which have been already exploited, as far as electric lighting is concerned, by the representatives and at the expense of the ratepayers. It is obvious that if Parliament were to grant power to the General Power Distributing Company or any similar enterprise it would not only seriously injure those undertakings, in which vasts sums of money have been already embarked, but it would seriously cripple municipalities in their future operations. It is generally recognised that a municipality is well within its legitimate sphere of operations in undertaking to distribute electricity for lighting and power purposes. It is clear, therefore, that some protection ought to be given against the intrusion of a private enterprise, which first and foremost carries out its work for the purpose of obtaining profits for shareholders. If it could be pointed out that in any single instance a municipality had failed to do its duty to a consumer or to the ratepayers, then something might be urged in favour of an undertaking having joint powers in such a district, but it is beyond all dispute that corporations have in distributing electricity been able to supply at lower rates than those usually charged by private enterprise. To permit a great organisation, such as the General Power Distributing Company gives evidence of becoming, to enter a town and undersell a municipality would be to strike a vital blow at the security of capital, and in the interests of the community and, one may say, of the well-being of the nation indirectly, the protection that has hitherto been given to the investment of capital, whether in municipal undertakings or in private enterprise, should not be departed from at the present moment. Moreover, if such a policy were ever brought to a practical issue, it would be reversing the effect of previous legislation, which has granted large facilities to municipalities for carrying out works for the good of the ratepayers. It was evident in the discussion which took place last week that the association recognised the fact that the generation of electricity on a large scale, such as is proposed by the distributing companies, would enable them to sell electricity in towns at probably lower rates that is at present being done. But the association was willing to admit that in those towns where electrical works have not yet been erected by municipalities that some arrangement might be arrived at between the corporation and the company. This is exactly the line on which we suggested that companies and municipalities should be able to carry on work together. A power distributing company might undertake to sell electricity in bulk to the municipality, and the whole of the distribution to consumers should be done by the local authority. It is probable that some such guarantee will be given when the Bill of the Power Distributing Company comes before Parliament next session for discussion.

*    *    *

**Local Government Board Inquiries in 1897.** In our review of the annual report of the Local Government Board, last week, we referred in passing to the local inquiries that had been held by the engineering inspectors of the department named with regard to applications made to that department under the Local Government Acts of 1888 and 1894, and the Municipal Corporations Act, 1882. In view of the increased staff at the Local Government Board, it is interesting to note that, in addition to the inquiries mentioned, no fewer than 949 others were held. The majority of them had reference to applications from sanitary authorities for the sanction of the Board or the borrowing of money for the carrying out of works of a permanent character under the provisions of the Public Health Act, 1875, the Public Health (Interments) Act, 1879, the Public Libraries Acts, the Baths and Wash-Houses Act, the Allotments Act, 1887, the Electric Lighting Act, 1882, the Technical Instruction Act, 1889, the Housing of the Working Classes Act, 1890, the Public Health (London) Act, 1891, the Museums and Gymnasiums Act, 1891, the Highways and Bridges Act, 1891, the Private Streets Works Act, 1892, and local Acts. Fifty-five inquiries related to petitions for the issue of provisional orders under the Public Health Act, 1875, the Gas and Water Works Facilities Act, 1870, and the Housing of the Working Classes Act, 1890; ten to proposals to fix general scales for the compulsory supply of water under sec. 62 of the Public Health Act, 1875, and sec. 8 of the Public Health (Water) Act, 1878; nine to objections made to the construction by local authorities of works of sewerage, sewage disposal and water supply beyond the limits of their districts; and eight to applications for approval of schemes for providing accommodation for persons of the working class in lieu of houses demolished under the powers of local Acts. Among the subjects of other inquiries may be mentioned complaints under sec. 299 of the Public Health Act, 1875, of the default of sanitary authorities in the performance of their duty in the matter of sewerage and water supply, applications for urban powers, for the powers of the Public Health (Water) Act, 1878, for consent to take proceedings against manufacturers under the Rivers Pollution Prevention Act, 1876, and the Mersey and Irwell Joint Committee Act, 1892, for polluting streams by trade refuse, applications for approval of the constitution of special drainage districts, and for orders under Part II. of the Housing of the Working Classes Act, 1890, approving schemes for the reconstruction of insanitary areas.

*    *    *

**Street Cleansing: Its Cost and Efficiency.** Another neat and well got-up volume is the report of the Hampstead Vestry for the year ended March 25, 1898. An abstract of the report of the surveyor, Mr. C. H. Lowe, will

appear in the usual course among our annual engineering records. In the meantime we may draw attention to some general remarks by Mr. Lowe on the subject of the cost and efficiency of street cleansing. He has something to say in regard to those fussy and irritable members of the public who are upset by every slight inconvenience, and who apparently think that the streets might be kept something like the deck of a liner. Mr. Lowe maintains that the work is now done regularly and systematically, and that the efficiency arrived at is as great as can be looked for while the existing means—men, money and appliances—remain as at present. Mr. Lowe points out that many of the suggestions made by those who write letters to the papers cannot be taken seriously; because, except at enormous cost, they are generally thoroughly impracticable. " All streets cannot be swept during the night, presenting a spic-and-span appearance to the parishioner as he leaves his house the first thing in the morning, nor can arrangements be made for a sprinkling machine to precede the men in dry weather to keep down the dust when the operation of sweeping goes on." Mr. Lowe also points out that comparisons with other parishes, boroughs or districts, are generally more or less worthless, as they do not take into account different sizes, situations, conditions and surroundings, and that municipal engineers are generally well-informed as to the many different plans followed throughout the country for the removal of objectionable matter from the streets. The point of the following remarks will at once be recognised by municipal engineers: " Surveyors exchange views freely, and seek and obtain information from each other on all points of importance, and it is certain that if there were an ideal in road-cleansing anywhere to be found which could readily be converted into the real and practical, it would soon become the common property of all concerned." But Mr. Lowe puts the whole thing in a nutshell when he says that it is chiefly a question of money, a fact which is generally lost sight of by ratepayers when they write to the papers, but is keenly remembered when they are invited to pay their rates.

*    *    *

**Engineers and their Rewards.** Last week we had occasion to draw attention, in connection with the case of a certain urban district council, to the absurdly low terms that local authorities frequently offer as premiums in competitions. In the case in question the work required would probably have cost a competitor, on a moderate estimate, about three times as much as the amount of the first premium. That is bad enough, but the cutting process is being extended to the fees for work to be carried out. From a report of a district council to consider a scheme for the sewerage and sewage disposal of Bletchley, we observe that an engineer, who had been invited to submit proposals, had suggested a scheme estimated to cost £1,200. Questioned as to the fee expected, he is reported to have given the following somewhat remarkable reply: " I should be prepared, if engaged to get out the plans, to accept a fee approaching, say, 3 per cent. on the cost." The chairman generously ignored any distinction between a fee of 3 per cent. and one " approaching " 3 per cent., and by a strenuous mental effort arrived at the conclusion that the total fee would be £36. That sum the engineer agreed to accept, and, not to be outdone by the chairman in magnanimity, he " preferred it to be a lump sum, as then, should the cost be more than his present estimate, it could not be said that he ran it up to draw the percentage." At all events he is to be congratulated on his professional scruple in regard to the district council, though scarcely in regard to his brother engineers. As we remarked in regard to premiums last week, the remedy lies practically with engineers themselves.

# Principal Features of Electric Lighting Systems.—VII.*

## THE OXFORD SYSTEM.

The principal features of the generation of electricity, both in the low-pressure continuous and the high-pressure alternating systems, have now been referred to. There is, however, another system to which reference may be made before discussing methods of distribution. It is that known as the Oxford system and involves the generation of direct currents at high potential and their transmission to sub-stations where motor transformers are employed. The motor transformer is a machine which practically reduces a high-voltage current to one of low voltage suitable for distribution to consumers. The machine is provided with an armature which has a double winding. It may be observed that an ordinary continuous-current machine has a single winding, and current is collected at the commutator bars and led off in the ordinary way. In the motor transformer, however, the armature carries a commutator at each end, to which the two distinctive windings are connected. A high-voltage current is brought to one set of brushes, which rub over the surface of the commutator, and at the other commutator a low-voltage current of 120 volts or 240 volts is obtained, in accordance with the requirements of the district. The advantages of this system are that it is possible to distribute electricity over a very wide area with a minimum expenditure of copper in the mains. The objections generally raised against the system are that it necessitates using high-voltage current at commutators, and this in the opinion of most electrical engineers, is a feature of some weakness. Certainly the distribution from the main power-house to the sub-stations, in which the motor transformers are placed, is by no means as simple as the distribution from power-houses to sub-stations, which is effected by high-pressure alternating current.

The most notable system on these lines is that at Oxford, which, though laid down some years ago, has continued to work until the present day without giving any trouble whatever. Moreover, considerable extensions have been carried out on a similar plan. There are three other towns in this country which employ a similar system, and in each case considerable success has been obtained with them. One of the last towns to adopt this system is Walsall, and it may be interesting to refer to the chief features of it. Walsall is a widely-scattered district, and it was considered that with the possibility of developing the use of electricity for motive power purposes, a high-pressure continuous with a sub-station distribution at low pressure, was the best system to adopt. The generating station is situated on the site of the old gasworks of the corporation, which some years ago were abandoned for the manufacture of gas, but subsequently proved an admirable site for a generating station. The building which contains the plant was really re-modelled from an old retort-house, and this building had a further advantage in being situated on the banks of a canal, from whence coal is easily shipped and ashes carried away. There is nothing unusual in the steam-raising plant which has been erected here. Lancashire boilers are employed. There are various mechanical details in connection with the steam pipes which are worthy of some note: the ring system of steam mains is employed, by which it is possible to completely isolate any steam plant that is necessary. The pipes in the engine-room are carried on pillars, but where they pass through the walls, and, indeed, on the pillars, iron rollers are employed, which permit of considerable movement at the time of expansion. The exhaust steam pipes are laid in underground pipes, and are led to the exhaust feeder, and afterwards they exhaust to the atmosphere.

The generating plant consists of compound engines, which work at a steam pressure of 125 lb. per square inch, directly coupled to generators, capable of giving an output of 40 amperes at 2,000 volts when running at a speed of 350 revolutions per minute. These are excited by means of small shunt-wound machines, which are driven by similar engines to those driving the large generators, and give a current of 60 amperes at 100 volts. The most interesting feature in the generating station, however, is the method of switching and operating the generators. In the system laid down some time previously at Oxford the sub-stations which contained the motor transformers were usually in charge of an attendant, who switched on the direct-station machines as required. In the case of Walsall, however, an attempt has been made to dispense with the services of an attendant at each sub. station, and automatic means were adopted by which it was possible for the switchboard attendant at the main power. house to start any of the machines in the various sub-stations. This has probably involved some complication in the switch. ing devices and in the mains, but, as far as we know, the system has been worked with very little trouble. The main switchboard is divided, as is customary, into various sections or panels. There is a panel for each generator, which is fitted with the usual ammeter and an automatic cut-out, main switch, regulating devices, and sundry other apparatus. Other panels are devoted exclusively to the feeders, which are the mains connecting the main generating station with the sub-stations. These are provided with the usual measuring instruments, cut-outs and main switches, and other apparatus, to which we will now refer.

It will be seen from the reference we have made to the exciting plant that it is necessary to excite the large generators, that is, pass a current of electricity through the windings when starting them up. This excitation current is obtained from the small generators, or, if necessary, a storage battery can be utilised. The generators are run in parallel, and feed on to what is known as the main omnibus bar of the switchboard; to this bar all the feeders are connected, and through these the main supply of the station passes out to the sub-stations placed in different parts of the town. In order, however, to provide a supply of electricity to the consumers it is necessary to start up the transformers at the sub-stations, because it must be understood that the main station itself does not supply direct to the houses. To start the transformer, therefore, at one of the distant points the main switch on the feeder board is put on. The operation of this switch is a gradual one. First of all a resistance is placed in series with the high-tension side of the armature at the distant station and the series winding on the magnets of the transformer; by the aid of this resistance a small current will pass through the feeders which starts up the transformer. As it is brought up to the requisite speed the secondary winding of the armature becomes energised, and this current circulates through a special automatic switch, which has the effect of cutting out the series winding already referred to, leaving the shunt only to energise the magnets. The process of this operation can be watched very closely by the switchboard attendant at the main station. Then there comes into operation at the sub-station a long-range switch, which has the effect of connecting the secondary winding of the transformers to the distributing network, which is directly connected to the consumers' premises. A motor transformer is taken out of action by a process which is the reverse of that already referred to.

Perhaps, however, the matter will be a little clearer if we describe the contents of one of the sub-stations. In each sub-station there is a main transformer giving an output at the secondary terminals, or that portion of the machine which feeds direct in the low-pressure main, of 400 amperes at 105 volts. This, however, only occurs when a primary current of 1,950 volts is supplied through the primary terminals. The field magnets have two windings, one being in series with a primary high-tension armature or winding, and the other has a shunt across the low-tension armature. A long range switch is provided with each of the transformers, its purpose being to close the secondary circuit from the transformer to the network, it being operated from the central station. Combined with this switch is what is known as an automatic magnetic cut-out, which breaks the circuit in the event of too great a current being demanded, or in the event of a transformer for any reason failing to give its proper voltage, preventing current coming back from the network. That is not the only plant, however, which is provided at the main sub-stations, for here are arranged batteries of accumulators; and for the purpose of charging these there is provided what is known as a battery-charging transformer, which takes its primary current at 105 volts from the distributing network, giving an output at the secondary of 300 amperes at 35 volts. The network of distributing mains is very much on the usual lines, it is entirely fed from the transformers and sub-stations as well as from the main battery. The concentric type of mains are employed, and these are drawn into cast-iron pipes. The distribution is carried out on the two-wire system, the mains being single conductor lead sheathed and steel armoured. The system has now been in operation for over two years, and although the cost of production has not been very low, the system has done moderately well.

It cannot be denied, however, that this method of generation and distribution apparently possesses more complications than commend themselves to the electrical engineer as a rule, and, although it is possible by the aid of unremitting care and skill on the part of the engineer in charge to keep such a system in a perfect state, it is questionable whether there will be much extension on this plan. Moreover, it must be pointed out that the Oxford system was adopted at a time when direct-current stations were not permitted to supply electricity to houses at a greater voltage than 120. Since the introduction of 220 volts to houses the applications of the Oxford system have naturally become limited.

The next two or three articles will deal especially with combined stations for lighting and tramways, the distributing portion of electric lighting; and remarks will be made on the commercial aspects of electricity supply, with special reference to the methods adopted for charging consumers.

---

**Dundee.**—A central fire brigade station is about to be built in Ward-road and Courthouse-square, from plans by Mr. Mackison, the brigade engineer. The building will be five storeys in height, with a tower, capped with a domical roof, at the angle of the streets. The estimated cost is £6,150.

* The last article of this series appeared in our issue of October 14th.

# The Sanitary Institute.

## THE SEVENTEENTH ANNUAL CONGRESS.—V.

In continuing our report of the proceedings at the recent congress we give another instalment of the important papers read on the subject of the treatment and disposal of sewage. The following is the conclusion of the paper by Drs. Kenwood and Butler, read in the Physics, Chemistry and Biology section :—

### THE NATURAL PURIFICATION OF SEWAGE
#### (concluded).
##### THE VALUE OF SECONDARY FILTERS.

It must be remembered, in speaking of the work of a filter, that it is not always manifest in the terms of a chemical analysis. Changes which can only be expressed in terms of stability and resistance are repeatedly made manifest. Thus, to take an illustration, the albuminoid ammonia figure of the effluent of No. 2 filter on June 23rd was 0·40. After an hour's rest in No. 3 it was reduced to 0·16, or 60 per cent. No. 3 in this instance had been charged with the effluent from No. 1 after the sewage had rested twenty-four hours in the anaerobic filter. Neither the twenty-four hours' rest in No. 1 nor the hour's rest in No. 2 had effected a satisfactory reduction in the albuminoid ammonia, but their combined action had doubtless so shaken the stability of the organic matter, which was expressed in terms of albuminoid ammonia, that in its passage through No. 3 filter it was reduced by 60 per cent. The example is one of many that were noted, and is taken as first to hand to illustrate the importance of multiple filters in completing a purifying process, the initial stages of which may not be disclosed in the ordinary form of an analysis. We satisfied ourselves by many experiments that by the use of secondary filters a much greater degree of purification can be obtained in a shorter time than by means of single filters.

A filter, like a living organism, not only ingests but excretes, and we have found it a useful working hypothesis to look upon each filter as possessing a state of equilibrium which affects its powers of absorption and excretion. The important point about this equilibrium of a filter worked regularly is that it tends to adjust itself to an average of the pollution of the intake. Thus the equilibrium of No. 1 differs from that of No. 2, and that of No. 3 from that of No. 3, the affluent of each, of course, having a pollution figure higher or lower than that of the other. It is for this reason that the necessity for multiple filters appear so great where strong sewages have to be dealt with. A filter will effect only a given percentage reduction on the pollution of its affluent when it has reached its maximum biological efficiency. If the pollution is high, and if we represent the purification which can be effected by the filter as 50 per cent., the effluent will still be a filthy liquid, and another 50 per cent. of reduction in another filter will leave 25 per cent. of the original pollution still to be disposed of.

The fact that the effluent which is first drawn off from an aerobic filter is relatively so much worse than that which comes away at a later stage, and that the filter may suddenly and unaccountably become overtaxed are further arguments for always making arrangements for passing the effluent through more than one aerobic filter. If a filter has rested the state of equilibrium should have been approached, and therefore its capacity for absorption should be greater—i.e., the percentage reduction should exceed the mean. On the other hand, if the effluent exceeds the mean two things occur : Firstly, to adjust to its habitual equilibrium the filter should absorb less per cent., and thus give a smaller percentage reduction ; secondly, its state of equilibrium being determined by this as by other effluents, the equilibrium figure is raised and the percentage reduction increased in obedience to this new demand. These facts are supported by a study of the figures of our experiments.

The facts which we ascertained with reference to ammonia elimination into the atmosphere appear to show—first that where no material nitrification goes on in a filter the nitrogen equilibrium is established by elimination of free ammonia. It was while the filters were rested that the most striking differences were observed. The nitrifying filter gave off no free ammonia at rest ; the non-nitrifying filter, on the other hand, gave off during the first twenty-four hours of rest ammonia at a mean of 0·39 milligram per square foot per hour. During the next twenty-four hours the ammonia eliminated was 1·8 milligram per square foot per hour, the mean for the succeeding forty-eight hours being only 0·06. The most active period of elimination is probably coincident with that of the most active reduction of the stored albuminoid ammonia to the free state, and the later stage of very low elimination with the attainment of the condition of nitrogen equilibrium. If this be so, we have a convenient means of discovering the period of rest required by a filter which has been overtaxed. It is only necessary to make daily estimations of the ammonia eliminated, and when the active elimination has ceased we should know that the filter had attained its equilibrium and was again ready for work.

The same tendency to equilibrium has been noted in the estimation of the total and volatile solids, and to favour this equilibrium solids may be sometimes taken up from the filter and at others deposited in it ; that something more than a mere straining of suspended mineral matter occurs, and that often an actual precipitation of dissolved solids takes place has been shown by the fact that often the reduction of non-volatile solids by rest in a comparatively coarse filter has been far in excess of anything we have been able to effect by filtering through a double thickness of fine filtering paper.

It has been repeatedly observed that the first rush of filtrate after opening the exit valve of a filter is associated with the escape of a large amount of suspended matter, some of which is of an organic character. Before the coke-breeze was placed in the model at University College it was very carefully washed in small quantities, yet when we removed it it was found to be charged, even in No. 3 filter, with large quantities of fine particles of organic matter. This fact is suggestive, and points to the conclusion that, however the filter may be constructed as to material and size of the filtering medium, organic matter tends to collect in the filter, and is liable to be washed out from its lower zones when the rate of outflow is rapid. We found that by constructing our filters with a stratum of sharp sand at the bottom we were able to obviate this difficulty.

Our lowest albuminoid ammonia figures were got with the longest rest in our secondary filters. The point always to be borne in mind is that what has to take place is not merely the reduction of unstable matter to the ultimate stable condition, but the reduction of the more stable organic matter to the unstable. The reduction of the unstable to the stable or ultimate appears to be best effected by change of filters, that of stable to unstable by rest in a filter. High albuminoid ammonia, then, is an index for rest in a filter, high oxygen absorbed an index for passing to another filter under conditions permitting of good oxygenation.

##### GAS ABSORPTION BY SEWAGE.

A stoppered flask, containing about 200 c.c. of sewage, was placed under anaerobic conditions by replacing its superincumbent atmospheric air with hydrogen gas. Anticipating from what we had observed in our No. 1 tank, and from what is known to occur in Cameron's tank—a large evolution of gas from the sewage—provision was made for the escape of such gases. The flask was hermetically sealed by an india-rubber stopper, perforated so as to admit a piece of glass tubing, which, opening at one end into the superincumbent gas in the flask, was sealed at the other by dipping into a cylinder of mercury. On examining the flask next day the mercury had risen in the tube and stood over an inch above that in the cylinder.

This could not be accounted for by any change in the atmospheric temperature and pressure, and was manifestly due to diminished pressure in the flask from absorption of the hydrogen gas. Flasks containing atmospheric air, coal gas and nitrogen were placed under similar conditions, with the invariable result that the mercury rose in the tube, until in some cases it was sucked right over into the flasks. These gases are used by the micro-organisms in their life processes, and doubtless we have here one of Nature's provisions for maintaining the earth's supply of fixed nitrogen, although perhaps not so active a process as that suggested by Sir William Crookes for the salvation of the wheat consumers of the twentieth century. The absorption was most rapid in respect of atmospheric air, and fresh sewage seemed greedy for air ; and if it could not get atmospheric air it took whatever came to hand.

After some weeks the mercury sinks in the tube, with the formation of black sulphide on the surface exposed to the flask atmosphere ; but never in the flasks kept in the light, even for a period of many weeks, does it sink to its original level. Gas absorption was found to go on in fresh sewage in the dark and in the light, but more slowly in the dark. It was observed to occur in sewage kept at rest and in sewage kept in motion by slow continuous flow through a flask where a limited quantity of air or gas was exposed to it. Under such conditions it was found to absorb every particle of the available gas imprisoned in the flask, and that in the case of fresh sewage in a very short time. As the sewage got older less gas was absorbed, and there came a time, in the case of sewage kept in the dark, when gas was given off in considerable quantities. A quantity of this gas was allowed to collect in a flask, through which the sewage slowly flowed, and this gas was exposed to the action of fresh sewage, which very quickly absorbed it. Light, temperature and the age and amount of sludge in the sewage appeared to be the determining factors of gas production and absorption. To what extent each of these factors played a part was not determined, but it may safely be said that light and freshness seemed to favour gas absorption ; darkness and age, gas production.

##### THE SEPTIC TANK.

Sewage kept out of contact with atmospheric air in the dark and at rest, so as to deposit its sludge—these are the

conditions under which the microbes work in the septic tank, and by reproducing these conditions on a small scale one is able to make sure that the same sewage is being dealt with. In comparing sewage kept under such conditions in bulk, as in the septic tank with sewage kept in the dark under similar conditions in a filter constantly sewage-logged, our investigations point decidely in favour of the filter. As stated, the effect of the sewage resting in our No. 1 filter-bed was distinctly and progressively to reduce the colour, opacity and odour; sewage kept in the dark in a closed receptacle, on the other hand, showed a marked and for a time progressive increase in colour and less reduction of opacity. As we have seen, the albuminoid ammonia is reduced very considerably both for the hour and the twenty-four hours' period of rest in No. 1, but in fresh sewage kept in the dark in a closed vessel the albuminoid ammonia remains the same or is very little reduced after twenty-four hours' rest under these conditions, although the free ammonia goes up. Thus a fresh sewage was found to have free ammonia 11·0, albuminoid 0·92, ammonia and oxygen absorbed in two hours 6·8. After twenty-four hours' rest in the dark the free ammonia was 13·05, albuminoid ammonia, 0·9, and oxygen absorbed 7·08. It would appear from this that the same changes which appear to occur in our No. 1 bed take place under these circumstances much more slowly and with less tendency to continuously progressive purification.

In order to satisfy ourselves upon this point, two separate quantities of fresh sewage were hermetically sealed and kept in the dark for several days. The following are the mean of the analytical results in parts per 100,000 :—

| | | | | Free and Saline N H₃ | | Albuminoid N H₃ |
|---|---|---|---|---|---|---|
| Fresh sewage after sedimentation | | ... | | 6·0 | ... | 0·69 |
| Same sewage after 24 hours | | ... | | 7·0 | ... | 0·64 |
| 48 ,, | ... | ... | ... | 8·5 | ... | 0·68 |
| 72 ,, | ... | ... | ... | 8·2 | ... | 0·61 |
| 96 ,, | ... | ... | ... | 9·5 | ... | 0·44 |
| 144 ,, | ... | ... | ... | 10·4 | ... | 0·47 |
| 168 ,, | ... | ... | ... | 9·8 | ... | 0·46 |
| 192 ,, | ... | ... | ... | 10·0 | ... | 0·45 |
| 216 ,, | ... | ... | ... | 10·5 | ... | 0·46 |
| 240 ,, | ... | ... | ... | 10·5 | ... | 0·51 |

It appears to us, then, that upward filtration offers a better prospect of effecting the separation and solution of the suspended matters of sewage, and at the same time of reducing the pollution of the effluent, than does any system which aims at their removal by digestion in a hollow chamber such as the septic tank. The particles of filtering material seem to form a large area, from which organisms can more effectively work. A filter more completely reproduces the conditions under which the purification of polluted water is effected in Nature where anything analogous to a septic tank is unknown.

What are the results claimed for the septic tank? According to Dibdin, the oxidisable organic matter was reduced 30·8 per cent., the albuminoid ammonia 17·5 per cent., whereas in his coarse bacterial filter at Sutton the oxidisable organic matter in four hours was reduced 66 per cent. and the albuminoid ammonia 58·4 per cent. According to Moor, the albuminoid ammonia is reduced 36·4 per cent. and the oxidisable organic matter 67·4 per cent. Our No. 1 filter, however, effects a reduction in the oxygen absorbed amounting to 40 per cent., and in the albuminoid ammonia amounting to 37 per cent., if the sewage rests in it but one hour. There is not much reason to doubt, therefore, that a bacterial filter is better than a tank, and doubtless analytical results would show a greater difference between the two processes if the sewage experimented with conformed more to the standard of the sewage employed in our experiments. The Exeter sewage experimented with is very exceptionally weak. The total solids of all those analyses which we have seen furnish a mean of under 60, and the volatile solids of under 30 parts per 100,000; nitrates are sometimes present in it, the chlorine is about 6, and the free and albuminoid ammonia 1·4 and 0·17 respectively.

METHODS OF ANALYSIS AND STANDARDS.

Our experiments show that the value of the figures of the oxygen absorbed in four hours is not as great as many maintain; it is only an expression of that which is in a condition to be immediately oxidised, and takes no account of the pollution which has not reached that stage, and which may be far in excess of that which has. We found that both in sewage samples and in sewage effluents permanganate is reduced by them at a temperature of 80 deg. Fahr, even when stopped bottles scarcely larger than the bulk of the fluid placed within them are employed, in such variable and irregular quantities hour by hour up to and beyond twenty-four hours that it was impossible to fix upon a period of time when it might be held that the oxygen absorbed formed a fairly approximate proportion to the entire amount of oxidisable organic matter in the liquid. Much time was spent in trying to work out this subject, but our results do not warrant more than this statement.

The presence of putrescible matter as indicated by a high figure of oxygen absorbed in two hours may denote merely that a large proportion of the dissolved impurity has been reduced to that transitional phase which immediately precedes purification of an ultimate character. In other words,

the oxygen absorbed figure is often more a measure of purification or of a stage of purification than it is a term of pollution. Nitrates are a measure not of that pollution which may be oxidised, but of that which has been oxidised, and their presence gives no indication of what remains to be purified. Nor is their presence inconsistent with profound pollution, even of a sewage effluent. If high nitrates are a good sign, then free ammonia cannot be considered a bad one, for the only value of the nitrates depends upon their power of yielding nascent oxygen for the oxidation of residual pollution in the effluent, and this very action necessitates an increase of free ammonia by the reduction of the nitrates.

The presence of nitrates in an effluent must not therefore be regarded as in any sense an index of purification. With breeze and clinker we invariably got nitrates, with fine filtering material, such as coal dust or granite chips, they soon disappeared completely, and yet these effluents repeatedly showed higher standards of purification than many in which nitrates were present in abundance; the explanation being that there was a further burning up of residual organic matter at the expense of the oxygen of a nitrate. Abundant nitrates were found in stinking effluents which looked and acted like fermenting sewage, where the free ammonia exceeded 5 parts, and the organic ammonia 1·4, where the oxygen absorbed in two hours exceeded 4 and the volatile solids amounted to 75 parts per 100,000. On the other hand, we have had effluents where the albuminoid ammonia was 0·1 and the oxygen absorbed was 0·23, where no nitrates were present; and we have found nitrates in the effluent from one filter to disappear when the same effluent was collected and passed through another filter in which it had undergone a further stage of purification. The presence of nitrates appears to be very much a question of the calibre of the filtering material as affecting the aeration of the filter. If the material is coarse, nitrates will be found even in offensive effluents, if it is fine they may be absent from an exceedingly pure effluent. The presence of nitrates is no more an indication of active bacteriolysis than is the presence of free ammonia, since both are the products of biological action, and can be produced at will by modifying the conditions of filtration. It is interesting to note in this connection that in a filter constructed of granite chips, where practically no nitrification occurred, the filter gave off free ammonia far in excess of a filter constructed of coarse breeze, where nitrification was very active.

The evidence of purification, as afforded by good physical characters, is added to by oxidised nitrogen only if the organic nitrogen is low; and standards should not be based upon estimations of the amount of oxygen required to partially purify and the amount available in combination with nitrogen for the reduction of residual pollution, but rather on an estimation which finds expression in neither of these figures—viz., that of the total organic nitrogen in the effluent. The albuminoid ammonia figure is a fair indication of the organic pollution, but the organic nitrogen as estimated on Kjeldahl's principle is a much more inclusive estimation than the albuminoid ammonia, and it is almost as easily arrived at. Although it will be found that the organic nitrogen of Kjeldahl's process averages a little over twice the nitrogen of the albuminoid ammonia, though sometimes showing marked differences from the average, the fact that the two analytical figures do not bear a constant ratio to one another is significant and points to the adoption of the more inclusive estimation. The process as we employed it was as follows : 25 c.c. of effluent was made up to 500 c.c. with ammonia free distilled water, a little pure sodium carbonate was added, and then by means of a condenser the free and saline ammonia was distilled over and rejected. What remained behind in the boiling flask, generally 250 c.c., was allowed to cool and then 10 c.c. of pure concentrated sulphuric acid was added. All the water was next boiled off in the fume cupboard, the flask being supported on the slant. When nothing but a very pale yellow coloured acid remained this was allowed to cool, 200 c.c. of ammonia free water were added, and the acid was neutralised by sodic hydrate solution. The flask was then connected with the condenser, and the organic nitrogen was calculated from the total ammonia which came over in the distillate.

Experiments have convinced us that a standard for effluents having a low limit of organic nitrogen is to be preferred to any standard of oxygen absorbed, or of oxidised nitrogen, or to any figure of percentage purification on the original sewage, or to any ratio between the oxidised nitrogen and the oxygen taken from permanganate in a limited period of a few hours. It has been suggested that a standard of loss on ignition of the total solids should be established; but will any two chemists precisely agree upon the exact extent of such loss? It would, besides, be unfair to compare on such a basis the effluent with the original sewage. Such a comparison would indicate too small a degree of purification on account of the greater quantity of oxidised nitrogen and carbon in the effluent.

Again, the practice of calculating to a uniform standard of chlorine is misleading. Thus a raw sewage with 0·74 albuminoid ammonia and 6 of chlorine is treated on Cameron's method, and a sample of effluent yielded by the process gave albuminoid ammonia 0·11, chlorine 4·5. The percentage reduction of the albuminoid ammonia is 85 per cent., and this reduced to a common chlorine standard shows a purification of 80 per cent. It is thus admitted that the effluent is not the effluent of the sample of sewage analysed, as judged by the chlorine, but that if the sewage which produced this effluent had been as strong as the sewage analysed the purification would have been 5 per cent. less. It is difficult to see on what grounds such an assumption can be based.

The fact is that no general standard applicable to all cases is possible or desirable. The best possible results must always be arrived at, and should be insisted upon with due regard to the nature of the sewage and to the conditions, volume and uses of the stream which is ultimately to receive it. The maximum impurity permissible will in certain cases be very slight indeed, in others a greater latitude may be conceded. It appears to us that what is most wanted is an uniform method of procedure in the taking of samples and *in the performance of the analysis;* as matters stand at present it is difficult to know what interpretation to place upon the results of different analysts when for any reason an attempt is made to compare their figures.

In the same section the following paper was read by Dr. Samuel Rideal, D.SC., F.I.C.:—

QUALITY OF SEWAGE AS INFLUENCING ITS MODE OF DISPOSAL.

Sewage may contain varying quantities of :—

(a) *Excretory substances.*

(1) Solid Fæces.—These consist of nitrogenous partially-digested matter, together with vegetable non-nitrogenous residues of the food. The former are easily liquefied, but the latter are slow in dissolving, being gradually attacked, chiefly by anaerobic bacteria, and broken down into soluble compounds of fetid odour and into black amorphous flocculi, which slowly deposit as black sludge.

(2) Urine.—The main source of ammonia, from fermentation of the urea, the proportion of urine being approximately indicated by the content of chlorine in excess of the content of chlorine in the water supply of the town.

(b) *Household waste :*—The larger solid substances pass to the ash-pits, but the drainage of these and their washings by

storm overflows in a sewage farm scheme the ground is liable to become waterlogged, and in a filtration process the excess of water by its volume and velocity tends to derange the purification plant, hence it is usually allowed to escape from the sewers by special outlets when above a certain amount, carrying with it a mixture of the unpurified sewage. The combined system also involves the construction and maintenance of sewers very much larger than the volume of the regular flow, in order to provide for occasional contingencies. This greater capacity presents inducements to the disposal of grosser refuse which would not be tolerated in a smaller sewer, and often it is impossible, except at rare intervals, to properly flush the entire surface of these large channels.

The "separate system," in which the sewage proper is kept apart from rainfall and storm water, has conduits of such size only as to preclude the possibility of the sewage becoming stagnant therein, the size being governed by the bore of the water main, since if a given diameter of pipe supplies all the water needed, a little above the same diameter is sufficient as an exit. Storm water passing rapidly off the land carries with it disease germs, as is shown by the repeated occurrence of epidemics when a sudden storm succeeds a period of drought. But the liquid is ordinarily supplied with abundance of the liquefying and oxidising bacteria, which if it be allowed to subside in auxiliary reservoirs will effect its purification rapidly, aided by the oxygen derived from the air, and by the nitrites and nitrates that rain water always contains. The sand, chalk, or especially the clay, may be a long time in subsiding, but when deposited will leave the water comparatively pure, and fit for flushing sewers, watering roads or for supplying the deficiency in rivers during dry seasons. Whatever system be adopted, the raw storm water of populous districts should never be allowed to pass in large volumes directly into a stream.

I may give, from my own analyses, an example of the influence both of the time of day and the rainfall on a strong sewage from one source.

Table showing Influence of Rain on Quality of Sewage. Parts per 100,000.

| Time and Circumstances. | | | Flow in gallons per twenty-four hours. | Solids in Solution. | Cl. | O consumed. | Free NH₃. | Albd. NH₃. | Nitric N. | Nitrous N. |
|---|---|---|---|---|---|---|---|---|---|---|
| *Dry Weather, no Rain* | | | | | | | | | | |
| 10 a.m. to 5 p.m. | ... | ... | — | 77·5 | 12·25 | 7·23 | 8·0 | 1·5 | None | None |
| 6 p.m. to 1 a.m. | ... | ... | 54,000 | 45·0 | 6·25 | 6·91 | 2·90 | 0·6 | ,, | ,, |
| 2 a.m. to 9 a.m. | ... | ... | — | 34·0 | 4·25 | 5·57 | 0·90 | 0·35 | ,, | ,, |
| | | | | | | Total chlorine—41 lb. per day. | | | | |
| *Heavy Storm.* | | | | | | | | | | |
| 10 a.m. to 5 p.m. | ... | ... | — | 54·4 | 7·75 | 3·58 | 11·5 | +1·2 | ·056 | None |
| 6 p.m. to 1 a.m. | ... | ... | — | 45·6 | 5·25 | 2·66 | 3·5 | 1·75 | ·014 | Trace |
| 2 a.m. to 9 a.m. | ... | ... | 79,000 | 34·4 | 3·75 | 0·74 | 4·5 | 5·5 | Trace | Very heavy |
| | | | | | | Total chlorine—44 lb. per day. | | | | |

Physical Characters.—Dry weather: Thick and fetid, fragments of paper and lumps of fæcal matter abundant.
,,          ,,     Heavy storm : Turbid, yellow-brown, earthy odour.

rain, if they are uncovered, are received into the sewers, together with liquid food residues discharged down sinks. Vegetable refuse yields a liquid which is very foul and fermenting, developing butyric odours and sulphuretted hydrogen. Fragments of animal food putrefy and furnish a product allied to that from fæces. Diluting these is a fluctuating amount of soap water, varying at different days and times. Its advent is often conspicuous in sewages of small volume, through the white opalescence of the effluent, the alkalinity and odour—the latter occasionally indicating scents or disinfectants. Household discharges other than urine may also temporarily raise the amount of chlorine.

(c) *Rain and storm water.*
(d) *Grit and detritus.*
(e) *Manufacturing waste products.*

*Rainfall and Storm Water.*—Although, according to Baldwin Latham, a rainfall of 0·1 in. to 0·2 in. in an hour increases the outflow of a sewer to five or more times its volume, there is, as Santo Crimp found in gaugings at Wimbledon, no exact relation between the rainfall as ordinarily recorded and the increment of flow at the outlet. The size, length and inclination of the sewer also clearly influence the result. At Exeter five-eighths of the ordinary rainfall is estimated to find its way into the sewers.

Both the quality of sewage and its quantity as affected by local circumstances therefore determine the choice of a system of sewerage. Under the "combined system" the effect of rain must not be considered as simple dilution, since the rain water carries the washings of the surfaces over which it has travelled. Where the rock or a clay bed is near the surface the showers will run off almost unchanged. From manured or peaty land there will be an addition of brown humous liquids, which are particularly difficult to decolorise. In towns the street drainage, even after prolonged rain, is mixed with complex dust, abraded clothing and wood, castings and emanations of man and animals, and particles of soot, iron, earth and stone, and is usually worse in character, especially from wood pavements, than an average sewage. Samples taken during rain have contained 18 to 38 parts per 100,000 of chlorine, 2 to 3 of albuminoid ammonia in solution, and as much as 80 to 120 of organic solids, suspended and dissolved.

For the safety of the sewers and the avoidance of flooding of basements, it is necessary under the combined system to construct special arrangements for storm overflow. Without

In the morning urine is prominent, as shown by the chlorine and by other signs ; later on soapy water makes its appearance, with a white scum of fatty lime salts that tends to clog filters and leave a greasy deposit on channels ; fixed alkalinity also appears, with an increase in the sodium salts ; subsequently the sulphuretted odour of vegetable washings is evident, and the liquid may even become temporarily acid. The road detritus and heavier matters are usually caught in a grit chamber, while paper, string, and animal and vegetable fragments are commonly carried forward with the mixture, which rapidly becomes black, alkaline and putrescent.

FILTRATION OF CRUDE SEWAGE.

Crude sewage passed direct on to a filter-bed will usually cause fouling of the upper layers and an obstruction to the entrance of oxygen, so that the surface requires scraping and renewal with a frequency proportional to the amount and character of the solids. The following analyses show the alteration occasioned by mere mechanical straining or filtration. They are averages of thirteen hourly samples, from 6 a.m. to 6 p.m., taken from different sewers of a large town on the water-closet system in 1897.

Table showing Variation in Quality of Sewage in different Sewers of the same town.

| Parts per 100,000. | Organic N. | Solids. | Cl. | Free NH₃. | Albd. NH₃. | O consumed. | Nitric N. | Nitrous N. |
|---|---|---|---|---|---|---|---|---|
| A.—Dissolved ... | 7·21 | 94·0 | 20·8 | 6·5 | 3·1 | 5·34 | ·096 | None |
| Suspended, | 6·18 | 35 | ... | ... | ... | 5·86 | ... | ... |
| Total ... | ...13·39 | 129 | | | | 11·2 | | |
| B.—Dissolved ... | 5·56 | 57 | 11·1 | 5·0 | 1·6 | 5·86 | ·12 | None |
| Suspended, | 3·71 | 51 | ... | ... | ... | 9·38 | ... | ... |
| Total ... | ...9·27 | 108 | | | | 15·24 | | |
| C.—Dissolved ... | 7·2 | 72 | 12·7 | 7·0 | 3·65 | 6·59 | ·08 | None |
| Suspended, | 1·55 | 60 | ... | ... | ... | 7·68 | ... | ... |
| Total ... | ... 8·75 | 132 | | | | 14·27 | | |

*Table showing Variation in Quality of Sewage in different Sewers of the same town.*

| Parts per 100,000. | Organic N. | Solids. | Cl. | Free NH₃ | Alb. NH₃ | O consumed. | Nitric N. | Nitrous N. |
|---|---|---|---|---|---|---|---|---|
| D.—Dissolved ...11·33 | 90 | 12·0 | 7·0 | 2·05 | 8·67 | ·12 | None |  |
| Suspended, 1·85 | 45 | ... | ... | ... | 5·28 | ... | ... |  |
| Total ... ...13·18 | 135 |  |  |  | 13·95 |  |  |  |
| E.—Dissolved ... — | 66 | 10·4 | 5·5 | 1 53 | 5·41 | ·14 | None |  |
| Suspended, — | 33 | ... | ... | ... | 3·39 | ... | ... |  |
| Total... ...11·12 | 99 |  |  |  | 8·80 |  |  |  |
| Average— |  |  |  |  |  |  |  |  |
| Dissolved ... 7·82 | 76 | 13·4 | 6·2 | 2·39 | 6·37 | ·11 | ... |  |
| Suspended, 3·32 | 45 | ... | ... | ... | 6·32 | ... |  |  |
| Total .. ...11·14 | 121 |  |  |  | 12·69 |  |  |  |

These examples show that the suspended solids contain about one-third of the organic nitrogen and half the carbonaceous matter of the sewage. It is easily seen that in systems where they are removed by sedimentation or by filter-presses a "sludge" will be produced which is highly putrescent and difficult of disposal, and of less manurial value than the matter left in solution. If sent on to land, the surface will be matted and clogged with an unhealthy deposit unless the soil is sandy or otherwise porous, as in the neighbourhood of Berlin, and, in addition, possesses other characters favourable to nitrification, such as the presence of lime, &c., as I pointed out in my paper at the Sanitary Institute in December, 1896 ("Journ. San. Inst.," Vol. 18, Part I.). Such land is frequently impossible of attainment near large towns, as is notably the case in the lower Mersey valley, where difficulties are still at an acute stage; moreover, it would be expensive, on account of its value for ordinary agriculture.

Septic systems like those of Cameron and Scott-Moncrieff submit the entire sewage, with only the deposition of grit, to the liquefying action of anaerobic bacteria, in an air-free dark space, with the result that the solids are dissolved to simpler organic compounds, with the final production of carbonic acid, ammonia and volatile gases, which are easily dealt with. Notwithstanding the fact that the experimental tank at Exeter has never been cleaned out, many people still cannot believe that paper, string, rag, feathers, &c., are dissolved. But it is undoubted that these substances do disappear, since only an amorphous peat-like residue is found. Brown and Morris have isolated a ferment, called "cytase," produced by fungi, which quickly dissolves celluloses ("Trans. Chem. Soc.," 1890, 497-503).

Van Tieghem describes several bacteria, especially *B. amylobacter*, which possess this hydrolysing power. ("Zeit phys. Chem." VI., 287, and De Bary's lectures; also J. G. Green, "Phil. Trans." 1887, clxxviii., 57, Marshall Ward, "Annals of Botany," II., 319, 1888, and Reinitzer, "Zeit. phys. Chem." xxiii., 175-208, 1897). *B. amylobacter* is always found in putrefying infusions; it hydrolises sugars, starches and cellulose, giving butyric acid and hydrogen, and is strongly anaerobic. In my own experiments I have found that the deposit from the effluent of a septic tank is capable of dissolving paper and cotton wool with evolution of gas. The putrefactive germs, as Sims Woodhead observes in a report on the Scott-Moncrieff septic process at Towcester, "have nothing to do with the production of disease under natural conditions; in fact, the addition of large quantities of putrefactive germs interferes with the action of or destroys entirely many disease-producing germs."

In both of these septic systems the tank effluent contains dissolved in simpler forms all the solids and liquids which were present in the raw sewage, minus the considerable proportion that has disappeared by being converted into carbonic acid, marsh gas, hydrogen and nitrogen. I estimated that in the Exeter septic tank of 50,000 gallons about 12 lb. to 15 lb. of organic carbon (corresponding to 2 parts to 3 parts per 100,000) are completely oxidised each day to carbonic acid and removed in solution as the tank effluent, in addition to the gases evolved in the tank, which are considerable.

In the Dibdin or Sutton process, the sewage is pumped on to beds of coarse burnt ballast 4 ft. in depth, allowed to stand for two hours, and then discharged, and the bed allowed to remain "full of air" for five to seven hours, the object aimed at is aerobic, but the primary process is still a septic one. I have shown that in the Exeter filters a large volume of CO₂ and N was given off in the filters, and as a number of the liquefying bacteria are facultatively aerobic, I am of the opinion, as expressed in my Sanitary Institute paper, that since the breaking down of solids is mainly a process of hydrolysis without the necessary presence of oxygen, it is better to carry out the *preliminary* liquefaction in a closed space than in an open bed. I believe, further, that the "resting full" period necessary in the Exeter filter and the Sutton beds is only necessary because the anaerobic change is not completed before. Nitrification is simply the conversion of ammonia into nitric acid in presence of air, and it should therefore be the object of all systems to get the organic matter of sewage *entirely* resolved into ammonia before the final oxidation upon the filter-bed.

Where, then, a concentrated sewage with a large proportion of coarse organic solids is to be dealt with, a septic system is indicated for the initial treatment, as requiring no previous screening nor settling basins, no large acreage of land, and as effectually settling the difficulty of sludge. Although fæces contain considerably less organic soluble matter than urine, yet, owing to the fact that they are composed to a large extent of cellulose and other materials not readily broken down in the alimentary canal during the short period they remain there, they will always, in common with vegetable matters, peelings, stalks, rags, &c., occasion great difficulties in any system of treatment except a septic tank or roughing filter, in which, as we have seen, they are easily broken down by the bacteria. One strong reason for dissolving the solids is the deposit they form on the banks and in the slower parts of the streams. The Exeter tank has shown that ballast or stones are not necessary in the first part of the process, whilst upward roughing filters still commend themselves to others. This will be the case whether the sewage proceeds from midden or from water-closet towns. The average figures for these, as given by the Rivers Pollution Commissioners, show no very conspicuous difference in composition, while in earth-closet localities a similar uniformity was observed (Frankland).

It seems as if the inclusion of solid excreta was balanced by the water used for their carriage, and that in midden towns much of the chlorine of urine soaks into the earth.

*Parts per 100,000.*

| | Solids. | Cl. | Org. C. | Org. N. | NH₃ | Total Combined N. | Suspended Matter. | | |
|---|---|---|---|---|---|---|---|---|---|
| | | | | | | | Mineral | Org. | Total. |
| Midden towns } | 82·4 | 11·54 | 4·18 | 2·97 | 5·43 | 6·45 | 17·8 | 21·3 | 39·1 |
| Water-closet towns } | 72·2 | 10·66 | 4·70 | 2·20 | 6·70 | 7·73 | 24·2 | 20·5 | 44·7 |

Back-to-back houses, where such an arrangement is still tolerated, by decreasing the influx of flush water give increased concentration to the sewage. Although the temperature of large sewers does not vary much, a hot and dry season usually causes a greater foulness and a more rapid putrefaction. Other circumstances that modify the quality or volume of the sewage are the size of the flush in water-closets and the number of public urinals. The behaviour of urine alone is somewhat different from that of mixed sewage, and will be further considered.

### MANUFACTURING WASTE PRODUCTS.

In the case of manufacturing towns it was at first thought that the large amount of effluent which reaches the sewers dark from dyes, impregnated with special foul odours, or unduly acid or alkaline from chemicals, would be inimical to bacterial purification. The Local Government Board has, however, of late declined to sanction schemes for the drainage and sewage disposal of districts unless the manufacturers submitted their effluents to a preliminary treatment before passing them into the sewers.

Since the operation of the various Public Health Acts it has been found possible, and even remunerative, for manufacturers to utilise such waste products; and yet, especially in the North of England, there is frequently very great difficulty through this cause. On the whole, however, the effect of trade refuse has been greatly exaggerated. In the case of small settlements collected round factories the domestic products may be only in small proportions, and the effluent must be treated periodically by chemical methods and not as a sewage proper. In large towns these discharges are usually so largely diluted that they cannot interfere with a bacterial process when rightly carried out.

It has been said that the antiseptic action of some chemicals would arrest the bacterial changes. But by actual cultures it has been shown that the amount of disinfectant required to kill, or even inhibit, the organisms is far in excess of what can be present in the mixed sewage. For example, at Yeovil, where arsenic as sulpharsenite of calcium is derived from the refuse of glove-making, I found that the maximum quantity of orpiment, $As_2S_3$, that could enter the sewers per week, if the whole amount escaped, was 2 cwt., equal in 120,000 gallons of sewage daily to 3·9 parts of $As_2O_3$ per 100,000, or ·003 per cent., whereas Miquel observed that 0·6 per cent. of $As_2O_3$ was required to prevent bacterial growth, and Frankland and Ward assert that it has little effect on lower forms of life ("Journ. Soc. Chem. Ind.," 1893, p. 1,053).

As an instance of an acid effluent, I found that a soap works at Exeter was discharging ¼ ton of acid liquor daily. Even if this contained 1 per cent. of sulphuric acid, it would amount on 1,000,000 gallons of sewage to 0·1 parts per 100,000. But crude sewage has sufficient alkalinity to neutralise more than this amount of acid, provided the latter be not supplied in spurts, as when poured direct on a filter. I have already remarked on the beneficial mixing and "smoothing" effect of the septic tank on the great fluctuations that occur at different times in all varieties of sewage. I believe that the same natural neutralisation and precipitation would dispose of most metallic admixtures, such as iron salts, galvanizing pickle, &c.

With regard to tanning refuse, the antiseptic power of tannin itself is very small, and, moreover, it does not pay to let much of it escape. At Exeter I estimated the daily quantity from the large tannery in that town as equivalent to that in 6 fluid ounces of brewed tea per head of population, and it certainly could have no influence. Effluents containing animal or vegetable matters, either suspended or in solution, as those from breweries, starch factories, &c., however foul and unfit to be discharged into rivers, present no difficulty to bacterial treatment, as the large numbers of the liquefying bacteria which they contain contribute to the efficiency of the process.

Popp and Becker ("Chem. Hyg. Inst., Frankfort," 1896) found that "liquefying bacteria" were killed by 0·5 por cent. of sulphuric acid, or by 1 per cent. of sodium carbonate, an acidity or alkalinity that would be higher than the ordinary factory runnings, and would be brought down when mixed with the whole of the sewage to an unimportant factor. As an example I ascertained that at a certain paper mill 35 lb. of soda ash were used daily: the maximum addition to the alkalinity of the whole daily sewage was 0·3 parts per 100,000 or ·000003 per cent.

Gas liquor and the effluents from timber works often contain a large quantity of suspended tar, which clogs up filter-beds and presses, and fouls the catch-pits and sewers. Therefore they must usually be excluded. The floating tarry film may possibly somewhat hinder the activity of the upper bacterial layer of a septic tank, but the aqueous liquid itself in its dilution would not be likely to interfere either by its sulphides, cyanides, ammonia or tar acids, inasmuch as many bacteria generate and live in a medium impregnated with ammonium sulphide, while cyanogen compounds are far less poisonous to lower organisms than to higher animals, and the strongest of the tar derivatives are not bactericidal, under 0·5 per cent., or 500 parts per 100,000, an impossible amount to be present. In exceptional cases, however, where intense acidity or other strong admixture cannot be avoided, the use of lime and a settling tank would become necessary; in this case a sludge would be created which would not be that of sewage.

The time of sojourn for an aerobic decomposition must vary with the age of the sewage. Many sewages require very little such change, so that the preliminary process is resolved into one of settling and of ensuring a liquid of more uniform composition for the filter-beds. Where the sewers are steep and not more than half to one mile in length the house discharges come very quickly down with little appreciable alteration, whereas an old sewage which has undergone considerable fermentation and hydrolysis by meandering through a long old sewer of somewhat sluggish flow will scarcely require much stay in a tank except for purposes of mixing, and may almost be trusted to a well-aërated filter-bed alone, especially if a large amount of free ammonia be present and the nitrification be carefully maintained. Where, on the other hand, "albuminoid ammonia" is predominant, a longer stay in the tank and an encouragement of further septic change is desirable, as although there are many aerobic or facultative bacteria which will change "albuminoid" into "free" (and gases) in a filter designed to have a "resting full period," it is better that this change should precede nitrication in a separate plant.

Laundry effluents and excessive quantities of slop water such as emanate from large institutions are often troublesome, on account of their greasy deposit of lime soaps, which soon became fetid. If passed on to filters, the scum has a great tendency to produce clogging and to hinder oxidation. But under alkaline anaerobic conditions such grease becomes emulsified by admixture with other solids, and will be attacked and dissolved as ammonia salts. They should, however, proceed to the works as far as possible without dilution with other water, and with a rapid flow to avoid deposition outside.

EFFLUENTS AND POLLUTION.

A question frequently raised is the possibility of an effluent conveying disease germs. By this time it is well known that, fortunately, pathogenic bacteria as a rule do not thrive much below blood heat, and that they are rapidly crowded out and destroyed by the ordinary bacteria existing in common waters, and still more by the immense numbers present in sewage. I need hardly refer to the fact that the typhoid bacillus has only in rare cases been found even in waters and sewages to which it must obviously have penetrated. This disappearance is clearly explained by some experiments of Dr. Sims Woodhead at Exeter, when he found that crude sewages containing about 500,000 organisms per cubic centimetre, when inoculated into the filtered effluent of a septic tank, developed more than 1,000,000,000 in five days, thus overwhelming any pathogenic bacteria that might be present. In the same Local Government Board inquiry Dr. Pickard specially investigated the typhoid microbe, with reference to the action of crude sewage on it, and to the effect of a filter-bed on those germs which had survived a short exposure. He concluded that the sewage itself, even when sterilised, "was not only a bad food, but an actual poison" to these bacteria, that in the septic tank they suffered a rapid destruction, and that the filter-beds effect a further biological elimination, "so that there is no chance whatever of the filtered effluent causing typhoid fever if passed into the river."

Strong Sewages, smaller in volume but more concentrated in

organic matter, require special consideration and sometimes a separate treatment. If admitted untreated into minor water courses, the local pollution is evident and will give rise to legal troubles. Among natural effluents that are exceptional in concentration, those from moors and bogs are frequently strongly brown in colour and devoid of dissolved oxygen; the humous matters, being singularly stable, have occasioned, especially in America, serious difficulties in all systems of sewage filtration by rendering the effluent coloured, and increasing the "oxygen consumed" figure, and possibly the "albuminoid ammonia," which are relied on in judging from arbitrary standards. A chemical treatment with lime, or lime with aluminium or ferric salts, is found to furnish a clean, colourless and particulary pure effluent, which in this case would actually have its value as a drinking water.

On the other hand, an effluent from works or large institutions, the flow from a collection of houses on the midden or earth-closet system, or the runnings from farmyards, piggeries and ditches of highly-manured land, will often by the odour and yellow colouration show that the main constituent is recent urine. Such a liquid is eminently unsuitable for either precipitation or passing through a porous filter of any kind, or even for placing on land until the first change, the hydrolysis of urea into ammonium carbonate, has been effected by organisms. The liquid will even then be so loaded with ammonia that it will not readily undergo nitrification; its tendency, in fact, will be to reduce any nitrate already formed into nitrite and nitrogen or its lower oxides, and to derange all systems of filtration through porous materials. For a strong or urinous sewage of this description, a preliminary detention until fermentation is completed is obviously essential before being diluted with naturally oxygenated water, as when discharged into a river, or before being admitted to a nitrifying filter, and in this latter case without special precautions the nitrification may be slow and incomplete.

NITROSIFICATION AND NITRIFICATION.

It is also important to remember, as pointed out in a former paper ("Journ. Soc. Arts," December 10, 1897), that the changes in the natural purification of sewage lead more to the production of nitrites than of nitrates. For the group of transformations working to this end, I use the term nitrosification, implying the production of nitrites and of nitrogen and its lower oxides by partial oxidation, as distinguished from the special reduction of nitrates called "denitrification," which was proved by Gayon and Dupetit to be "a fermentation involving direct burning up of the organic carbon at the expense of the oxygen of a nitrate." Nitrosification is not nearly so delicate a process or so difficult to initiate or control as nitrification, which it seems to invariably precede. It occurs best in the presence of diffused light and of a moderate amount of air, and is quite consistent with the growth of large numbers of green or brown algae which are at the same time engaged in reducing any nitrates present. The following experiments show some of the conditions of the changes.

*Experiment 1.*—Nine volumes of a tank effluent free from nitrate or nitrite were mixed with one volume of a coke-breeze filtrate containing 4·34 parts per 100,000 of nitric nitrogen (no nitrite), sealed in a flask without air, and kept for five days in a dark chamber at 150 deg. C. By this time the whole of the nitric nitrogen, amounting to 0·434 parts in the mixture, had disappeared, *without formation of either nitrite or free nitrogen.* The same liquid afterwards in a vessel partially full and exposed to light yielded nitrites in abundance.

*Experiment 2.*—A strongly urinous effluent to which potassium nitrate had been added in the proportion of 10 parts per 100,000 was seeded with the organisms (collected by a Pasteur filter) from a coke-breeze filter, and kept *in the dark* at room temperature in bottles nearly full. After fourteen days the liquid was turbid and had a sweetish urinous odour: a partial vacuum had been produced, as air entered freely on opening the stopper. The composition before and after was in parts per 100,000:—

| | Nitric N. | Nitrous N. | Free NH₃. | Org. N. other Forms. | Loss of N in N. |
|---|---|---|---|---|---|
| At commencement ... | 10 | 0 | 8·0 | 2·89 | — |
| After fourteen days... | 7·06 | 1·77 | 7·5 | 2·38 | 1·17 |

*Physical Characters.*—At commencement : Yellow, turbid.
　　　　"　　　" After fourteen days: As above, odourless.

In one day the formation of nitrite from nitrate in the dark was found to be equal to 0·21 parts of nitrous N. per 100,000.

*Experiment 3.*—A urinous effluent similar to the above preserved in a closed bottle containing air in *diffused daylight.* Analyses :—

| | Cl. | Nitric N. | Nitrous N. | Free NH₃. | Org. N. | Loss of N |
|---|---|---|---|---|---|---|
| Original ... | 23·5 | None. | Trace. | 35·0 | 6·17 | — |
| After sixty-seven days } | 23·5 | Trace. | 1·87 | 34·5 | 3·30 | 1·0 |

*Physical Characters.*—Original : Yellow-brown, turbid, odour very foul, urinous.
　　"　　　　" After sixty-seven days : Much less colour, deep brown flaky sediment, slight musty odour.

At first a white bacterial scum had formed, but had sunk with the sediment. No algæ were visible.

*Experiment 4.*—The result of the last experiment was diluted with four times its volume of tap water, containing 7 c.c. of free oxygen per litre and 0·2 parts per 100,000 of nitric nitrogen, and preserved in the light in a half-full bottle. In five days it was clear, inodorous and nearly colourless, and had only a very slight deposit in which green algæ had made their appearance. But the nitrifying change was still prominent: the nitrous N had increased to 3·375 parts, calculated on the original, while the nitric N in the mixture was ·091; so that the nitrate had actually been reduced. After this the nitrifying organism seems to have become predominant, as in fourteen days the liquid contained 3·06 parts per 100,000 of nitrogen as nitrate, and only traces of nitrite and of free ammonia, the green algæ (apparently *protococcus viridis*) being luxuriant, and the water clear, nearly colourless and almost devoid of dissolved organic matter. These experiments explain the causes of failure noticed when attempts have been made to deal with raw sewage by bacterial action without due provision for allowing the changes to take place in natural sequence.

The amount of oxygen required for the processes of nitrification and nitrosification is shown in the following table :—

One Gramme of Nitrogen requires:—

| For production of | Grammes of Oxygen. | Litres of Oxygen. | Litres of Air. | Litres of Oxygen saturated water at 7 c.c. per litre. |
|---|---|---|---|---|
| $N_2O_5$ | 2·85 | 2·0 | 10·0 | 286 |
| $N_2O_3$ | 1·7 | 1·2 | 6·0 | 170 |
| $N_2O_2$ | 1·13 | 0·8 | 4·0 | 114 |
| $N_2O$ | 0·57 | 0·4 | 2·0 | 57 |
| N | 0· | — | — | — |

So that to nitrify in an effluent five parts of nitrogen per 100,000 (1 gramme in 20 litres) will demand about half its volume of air, or about fifteen volumes of fully aërated water. This explains the comparative failure and frequent collapse of filter-beds in large masses, especially if the fluid is a raw sewage or a newly screened or precipitated effluent without preliminary hydrolytic change, as with every 100,000 gallons of sewage about 50,000 gallons of air must be continuously supplied. Contrivances like fountains, cascades and weirs, can only raise the dissolved oxygen to the saturation point of about 7 c.c. per litre, or 700 gallons per 100,000; although useful, if simple, like the aërator at Exeter, they are quite inadequate.

The most rapid nitrification that I have seen occurs in the nitrifying trays of Scott-Moncrieff, using the effluent flowing from his special form of upward roughing filter in which the anaerobic change takes place. The plant in use at Ashtead for a house sewage of strong character consists of nine perforated shallow trays of cast iron containing coke, supported vertically one above another at about 3 in. apart. It requires only about eight minutes for the liquid to pass through all the trays. In the early part of this year I collected samples from the different trays and obtained the results indicated in the annexed curves, on which I may offer the following remarks: (1) The nitrate has developed with extraordinary rapidity and to an extent that exceeds any other known process. (2) The nitrosification is much less marked—it rapidly reaches a maximum and then declines. (3) The free ammonia has been almost completely oxidised; at the same time the original yellowish colour, black suspended matter and sewage odour had disappeared.

In the table below I give the other figures for the first and last stages.

| | Chlorine. | Dissolved Oxygen. c.c. per litre. | Oxygen consumed by organic matter. | Available oxygen. |
|---|---|---|---|---|
| January 25th—Original ... | 9·0 | ... | 9·84 | minus 9·57 |
| Last tray, „ | ... | ... | 0·39 | plus 20·1 |
| February 8th—Original ... | 6·3 | 0 | 9·05 | minus 9·05 |
| Last tray, „ | 6·84 | 0·44 | | plus 12·99 |

Thus the organic matter has been very greatly reduced for so brief a time of contact. The effluent is now in a state of rapid natural purification by means of its "available oxygen," a term I some time ago proposed for effluents rich in nitrates. We know by the researches of Warrington, Munro, Adeney, Gayon and Dupetit, and others, that the oxygen of a nitrate is available for the burning up of organic matter, *provided it has been properly fermented*, as this has been. In my own experiments I have found that the large loss of nitrogen so often noticed was not accounted for by nitrous acid, ammonia, nor by nitrogen gas. Gayon and others have observed the production of nitrous oxide, which being soluble is not evolved, and has no doubt been overlooked by many observers. Therefore, to be on the safe side, I have allowed 4 atoms of "useful oxygen" to every 2 $RNO_3$—i.e., $N_2O_5$ to $N_2O$. Deducting from this the "oxygen consumed" figure, as representing the organic matters which are fairly easy of destruction, I call the surplus "available oxygen," ready to be drawn on to complete the purification. In the above case the quantity is obviously far greater than would be supplied by any process of mere aëration, hence such an effluent could be easily "finished" by a mechanical filter without fouling the latter, or could be beneficially applied to a small area of land, or mixed with a river of moderate volume not only without pollution, but possibly with an actual benefit to the stream.

I have hardly alluded to *chemical purification*, as I have frequently concurred in the opinion which is rapidly gaining ground that the use of chemicals is commonly a mistake.

In the recent Manchester report on sewage treatment it is stated that sewages at Oldham and Swinton after treatment by ferrous sulphate and lime, failed to nitrify in large cinder filters. The result could have been foreseen, as not only does chemical precipitation remove a very large percentage of the useful bacteria present in sewage, and therefore hinders the hydrolytic change which must precede nitrification in the filters, but in this particular case the ferrous hydrate formed removed the whole of the dissolved oxygen from the sewage immediately before it reached the filters, where the maximum amount of free oxygen is obviously desired.

Still in the same section of the congress, Mr. W. E. Adeney, D.SC., F.I.C., of the Royal University of Ireland, read a paper on

## THE BACTERIO-CHEMICAL ANALYSIS OF SEWAGE AND SEWAGE EFFLUENTS.

In the opening of his paper Mr. Adeney remarked that as it had been generally accepted that the purification of polluted waters, under natural conditions, was the work of bacteria, and that all processes for the purification of sewage must, to be satisfactory, recognise this fact as a central principle, the question arose, Should not the methods employed for the analysis of the same water be based upon the fact that they are fermentative liquids, and that the information we ought to seek from analysing them was the amount of fermentative matter they contained apart from their other possible constituents. Mr. Adeney then proceeded :—

METHODS OF ANALYSIS.

The methods in use at the present time for the analysis of polluted waters were originally worked out for the examination of potable waters, and although experience has shown them to be trustworthy for that particular purpose, they are, as it is now generally admitted, wholly unsuitable for the analysis of polluted waters. In making this statement I should like to guard myself against any idea that I wish to cast any discredit upon the classical work of Sir Edward Frankland on potable waters, or upon the work of the authors, Messrs. Wanklyn and Chapman, of that most valuable method of potable water analysis known as the albuminoid ammonia process. It is only necessary, to dispel any such idea, to point out the fact that the influence of bacteria in Nature, so far as their being the true agents concerned in the restoration of polluted waters to a condition of purity under natural conditions, was quite unknown and unsuspected at the time the researches of these chemists were being carried out.

It has been shown by bacterio-chemical researches[*] that the organic constituents of a potable water suffer practically no change by bacteria, and that the system of classification of potable waters into good, suspicious and bad, mainly according as the organic matters they contain come within certain well-defined and understood limits, is scientifically sound so long as the classification is confined to potable waters. Bacterio-chemical research has demonstrated, however, with even more force that the presence of organic matters in a water which can undergo change by bacteria gives rise to an entirely different set of considerations. We then require to know, not that the quantity of organic matter is represented by a certain figure or comes within certain limits, but what chemical changes they will undergo in the water, and what attendant influences such changes will exert in the water and everything that comes in contact with it—*e.g.*, fish and vegetable life, and also the atmosphere and public health of the neighbourhood—and how these changes may be ascertained and put into concrete form for analytical purposes.

I propose to describe in this paper a simple process for the chemical analysis of polluted waters, based upon the considerations which I have above stated. I much regret it is not in my power to also deal with the bacteriology of the problem. I can only hope that bacteriologists will themselves take up the problem and work out systematically the part of it which belongs to their subject, as I feel confident that results of great interest and practical importance will follow such study. In order to gain a clear conception of the kind of information we require to know concerning foul waters, let us consider the nature of the changes which the polluting matters in them may undergo during the restoration of the water to a condition of purity by natural agencies.

THE CHANGES INVOLVED.

These changes have been fairly well worked out, at least in broad outline. It is known, for instance: (1) That the agents which bring about the purifying changes are bacteria. (2) That the germs of these organisms exist practically everywhere in Nature. (3) That the ordinary bacteria of Nature can attack, and completely oxidise, probably most, if not all, known organic substances with the exception of antiseptics. (4) That the chief condition necessary for the continued healthy life processes of these organisms is an adequate supply of oxygen in the free state or in certain forms of combination. This holds good for the *solid* matters *in suspension*, as well as for those *in solution*. (5) That the chemical changes set up by these organisms under the condition of a sufficient oxygen supply result in the complete break down of the organic matters in a foul water, and in their conversion to carbonic acid, ammonia, water, and nitric

* See "Chem. Soc. Journal," vol. xlix., p. 577; also "Transactions, Royal Dublin Society," vol. v., Part II., 1895.

acid, together with the formation of small quantities of colouring matters, which although organic in composition are not to be regarded as polluting matters, since they are to be found present in more or less small quantities in all natural waters, including first class potable waters.

The process, then, of purification of foul waters by natural agencies is a true bacterial fermentation—a process presenting per se no danger to health if an adequate supply of oxygen be maintained during its continuation, but capable, in the absence of such adequate supply, of engendering conditions in the highest degree dangerous to public health. It is evident, therefore, that a method of analysis for drainage waters, to be satisfactory, must be capable of indicating the true polluting power of such a water—that is to say, it must indicate the quantity of fermentable organic matters the water may contain, the volume of oxygen which the bacteria will require to bring about their complete oxidation or fermentation, and the rate at which they will undergo fermentation. This information is necessary, it will be observed, before we can calculate what damage any drainage water will do if discharged into a given river, before we can state in fact whether the discharge of a foul water into a river will give rise to the evils of over-pollution in the river water or not.

We may take it, from what has already been said, that a river becomes over-polluted when the bacteria fermentation in its waters becomes so rapid that the atmospheric oxygen dissolved in them is consumed by the bacteria more quickly than it can be replenished in the ordinary way, that is by ordinary solution and diffusion through the water of fresh quantities of oxygen from the atmosphere. When this state of things arises anaerobic fermentation sets in, attended with all the offensiveness and dangers of putrifaction. The rapidity of the consumption of the dissolved oxygen depends upon the activity of the bacteria, and their activity depends upon the quantity and kind of polluting organic matters present in the water, the greater the quantity and the more favourable to growth of bacteria of the polluting matters the greater their activity and the more rapidly the chemical changes which they can bring about are completed,

SOME FUNDAMENTAL CONSIDERATIONS.

It will not, of course, escape the attention of the members of this section that a method of examination such as here indicated raises a number of fundamental considerations. All these fundamental points have been fully investigated. A description of the methods employed, and records of the experimental results obtained in the investigation, have already been published in the "Scientific Transactions of the Royal Dublin Society," Parts I., II. and III. in Vol. 5 (Series 2), Part 11, 1895; and Part IV. in Vol. 6, Part 11, 1897, under the title, "The Course and Nature of Fermentative Changes in Natural and Polluted Waters and in Artificial Solutions, as indicated by the Composition of the Dissolved Gases." An abridgment of these papers has been published in "The Transactions of the Institution of Civil Engineers of Ireland," 1896* and 1898. It is unnecessary for me to take up the time of the section by making a detailed reference to the results of this investigation, as those especially interested in them can refer to them at their leisure. I need only draw attention to some conclusions which bear directly upon the particular points I wish to deal with in this paper. They are as follows : (1) That the mixed organisms natural to foul waters practically behave as constant chemical factors during the complete fermentation or purification of the same under aerobic conditions; that is to say, they have been found to consume similar volumes of atmospheric oxygen during their complete fermentative action upon similar volumes of the same polluted water; (2) That the volumes of atmospheric oxygen consumed by the bacteria during their complete fermentation, under aerobic conditions, of a polluted water are directly proportional to the quantity of polluting matters in the waters; (3) That the mixed organisms of foul waters effect the complete fermentation of the polluting matters in the same in two separate and perfectly distinct stages.

During the first stage the organic matters are alone attacked, and they are completely changed into carbonic acid, ammonia water, and the colouring matters already referred to. After the completion of this stage a period of apparent rest ensues; then the second stage sets in, and during it the ammoniacal nitrogen is the central object of attack, and it is oxidised to nitric acid. The colouring matters formed during the first stage are also more or less completely converted into carbonic acid, water, and nitric acid. I have proposed to term these two stages of fermentation the carbon-oxidation and the nitrogen-oxidation stages respectively. The second stage may also be appropriately called the nitrification stage. Time will not permit me to dwell upon the interesting considerations suggested by the above conclusions. I will only remark here that the chemical changes effected by bacteria have been found, so far as they have been studied, to come under, without exception, the principles of thermochemistry, and that it is not suprising, therefore, to find that bacteria function as constant chemical factors under the condition of a constant supply of oxygen. It is also, for the same reason, not surprising to find that the carbon-oxidation or first stage of fermentation is always found to be complete before the commencement of the nitrogen-oxidation stage.

---

* Reprinted in Engineering, vol. lxi., pp. 728-730 and 762-764, 1896.

We should have anticipated this from thermo-chemical principles.

BACTERIO-CHEMICAL ANALYSIS: A NEW METHOD.

Turning now to the question of formulating a method of analysis for foul waters based upon bacterio-chemical principles, it is scarcely necessary to observe that the main object of such a method must be the determination of the volume of atmospheric oxygen consumed during the carbon-oxidation stage of a known volume of a foul water. It should also be an object of the method to approximately indicate the rate of consumption of oxygen if necessary. I may remark here that in the rational analysis of polluted waters, for river pollution purposes, it is really only necessary to examine the first stage of fermentation, since we may take it from what has been stated that it is only during this stage that putrefaction could be set up in a river. The methods employed in the investigations already referred to can, of course, be used for the analysis of foul waters, but they are unnecessarily elaborate and slow for general analytical purposes. I have accordingly recently worked out a simple method suitable for general use. This method is carried out as follows :—

A bottle, generally an ordinary Winchester quart, is fitted with an india-rubber cork, in the centre of which a hole has been bored, and in which a short glass tube is fixed. The outer end of this tube is fitted with a short length of capillary india-rubber tubing, which can be closed, when necessary, by a piece of glass rod. The capacity of the bottle, with the cork in position, is first found. A known volume of the water to be analysed is then transferred to the bottle, and the cork securely fitted in, the free end of the rubber tube being left open. The bottle is then put aside for about an hour, to allow its contents to assume the temperature of the surrounding air, and to allow also the air in the bottle to become saturated with aqueous vapour. The temperature of the laboratory and the barometer are then noted, and the rubber tube is immediately closed by means of the glass rod. Finally, all the rubber parts are coated with shellac varnish, to prevent gaseous diffusion, and the bottle is put aside in the dark for fermentation for about four to six days.

Knowing the capacity of the bottle, the volume of the water introduced, and the temperature and pressure of the air at the time of corking, and remembering the fact that the air left in the bottle is saturated with aqueous vapour, we can calculate, from the known composition of the atmosphere, the exact volumes of nitrogen and of oxygen left in the bottle at the time of corking. Then if after the completion of the first stage of fermentation a small quantity of the air in the bottle be withdrawn by means of a suitable gas apparatus, measured and analysed, we shall have all the data necessary for determining the exact volume of oxygen consumed during the first stage of fermentation of the organic matters in the volume of the water taken for analysis.

The analysis is extremely simple; it only involves the determination of the volume of carbon dioxide, and of oxygen, by absorption, and of the nitrogen by difference. The calculation is also very simple. The experiments recorded in the researches already referred to show that it may be taken, with close approximation to the truth, that the nitrogen does not alter in volume to any appreciable extent during the fermentation, if the contents of the bottle be preserved at a fairly constant temperature, and if the volume of air in the bottle be not too small in proportion to that of the water. With this assumption as to the nitrogen, we can calculate the consumption of oxygen by deducting the volume of it, at N.T.P., found by analysis to be associated with the nitrogen in the bottle, at the end of the experiment, from the volume found to be present at the commencement of the experiment. The method, it will be observed, presents no difficulties either in manipulation or in calculation, and possesses the very great advantage of securing the examination of a water under conditions very similar to those which obtain in nature. The gas apparatus required is also extremely simple. Lunge's nitrometer, or Hempel's gas burette and absorption pipettes, may be employed for the purpose. After a little experience no difficulty will be found in making an air-free connection between the gas apparatus and the experimental bottle.

SOME EXAMPLES.

A few examples of analyses by this method and by the albuminoid ammonia method will perhaps be the best means of demonstrating its value. The first four of the analyses quoted afford a very interesting study of river pollution, besides indicating the great practical value of the method as a means of investigating the nature of the polluting matters of a foul water. The fifth example demonstrates the impossibility of the old methods to even indicate the presence of a non-nitrogenous substance in a foul water, while, on the other hand, it proves the capability of the new method of indicating, not only the presence, but also the quantity, of such a substance in a foul water, in terms of the volume of atmospheric oxygen required for its complete bacterial fermentation. It must be noted that the matters in suspension in the samples were separated by subsidence and decantation before analysis.

*Analyses of Polluted Waters showing the volumes of Atmospheric Oxygen required for the oxidation of the organic matters they contain by bacterial fermentation.*

Results expressed as parts per 100,000, except the oxygen determinations, which are expressed as volumes, at N.T.P., per 100,000.

*Results obtained before fermentation.*

| | 1 | 2 | 3 | 4 | 5 |
|---|---|---|---|---|---|
| N. as albuminoid ammonia ... | ·052 | ·048 | ·09 | ·052 | ·012 |
| N. as nitrites ... ... ... | 0 | 0 | 0 | 0 | 0 |
| N. as nitrates ... ... ... | trace | ·059 | ·1 | ·03 | 0 |
| N. as ammonia... ... ... | ·022 | ·19 | ·64 | ·052 | ·012 |

*Results obtained after first stage of fermentation.*

| | | | | | |
|---|---|---|---|---|---|
| N. as ammonia... ... ... | ·02 | ·3 | ·9 | ·16 | 0 |
| Oxygen consumed ... ... | 229 | 845 | 2724 | 609 | 3324 |

*Note.*— In calculating the above volumes of oxygen the composition of the atmosphere was taken to be—nitrogen 79·1 and oxygen 20·9 per cent. by volume.

The first four samples were collected from a somewhat sluggish but fairly large river at points selected, to ascertain the effect of a number of discharges of sewage, more or less considerable in volume, along a flow of some 3 miles. The fifth sample was a solution of common soap. Sample 1 was collected at a point on the river above which, for at least a considerable distance, no discharge of sewage was discernible. Sample 2 was collected at a short distance lower down the river, and just below the outfall of a moderate-sized sewer. Sample 3 was also collected lower down than point 1, but immediately after the discharge of a large volume of sewage into it. Sample 4 was collected some distance below points 2 and 3. A glance at the results recorded in the above table shows that the albuminoid ammonia determinations afford no information either as to the kind or as to the degree of pollution of the waters, but that the volumes of oxygen consumed, when considered together with the free ammonia determinations made before and after fermentation, indicate at once the state of the waters, both as to kind and degree of pollution. For example, the results from sample 1 prove that a slight fermentation took place, but, inasmuch as the free ammonia shows no change after fermentation, it is evident from what I have stated above that the river water was slightly, but only very slightly, polluted with carbon-oxidisable substances at point 1.

The like determinations for the samples 2 and 4 show at once a decided pollution by carbon-oxidisable substances; but if we take into account the fact that 100,000 volumes of good river water will hold in solution 700 to 800 volumes of oxygen at N.T.P., according to the season of the year, it becomes evident that the river was at neither point over-polluted in the sense above explained. It is not surprising, therefore, to find that these samples did not develop any odours when kept in a corked bottle and out of all contact with air. The oxygen and ammonia determinations for sample 3 indicate an amount of pollution by carbon-oxidisable bodies which must be regarded as over-pollution, from the definition of that state which I have given above. That this was the case is proved by the fact that a portion of it, which was kept in a closed air-free bottle, became extremely offensive.

If we now refer to the albuminoid ammonia determinations, it will be seen they exhibit no such indications of great variation in the degree of pollution. The determinations for samples 1, 2 and 4 show practically no variation from one another, and but very little even from sample 3. The results obtained from sample 5 clearly demonstrate the impossibility of the albuminoid ammonia process of even indicating the presence of a large class of organic substances —viz., non-nitrogenous substances—which commonly occur in sewage and in other drainage waters, and which give rise to a very active bacterial fermentation, as the results above quoted prove.

SOME POINTS OF DETAIL.

Before concluding this paper there are one or two points of detail to which it may be well for me to make some reference. The first is as to the relative volume of a foul water, and of air-space to allow for in the bottles in which the fermentation tests are to be made. They must, of course, be varied according to the water to be examined—the greater the foulness the less will be the volume of the water required, or the greater will be the air-space which must be allowed for. I have found a convenient and suitable proportion to take is one of air to four, six or eight volumes of the water. I hope to shortly publish the record of a number of experiments dealing with this and some cognate points.

Another important detail is to decide how long the experiment be allowed to go on; a good working indication of this may be gained from the appearance of the water itself; after it has been fermenting for a day or two the turbidity, which from the first is more or less marked, decidedly increases and continues to increase for two or three days more, according to the foulness of the water; the turbidity then begins to lessen, and in a day or two more the water becomes almost clear, and a deposit of bacterial *débris* settles down to the bottom of the bottle. When this appearance has decidedly set in the first stage of the fermentation may be considered as finished.

It is advisable to dilute a very foul sewage with four to five times its volume of distilled water, otherwise the fermentation will be unduly prolonged. It is unnecessary, for reasons I have already given, to allow the fermentation to proceed to the second stage. As a general rule live or seven days ought to be a sufficient time to allow a water to ferment, when the analysis is required for river pollution purposes. When the water to be examined is a sewage effluent or a trade waste liquor care must be taken to separate before analysis traces of sulphate of alumina or other like bodies, which exert an unfavourable influence on bacterial fermentation, and which may be present in such waters. This may be effected by the careful addition of a few drops of sodium carbonate solution; after the precipitate, which is then formed, has settled down, the water may be decanted and subjected to fermentation.

One or two papers dealing with the question of sewage disposal still remain to be noticed, one of them being the extremely interesting contribution by Mr. Scott Moncrieff. We shall then give abstracts of some of the remaining papers of interest to our readers.

## ARBITRATIONS AND AWARDS.

The resumed inquiry as to the value of the properties affected by the Tottenham Court-road improvement scheme of the London County Council, which scheme will be subject to "betterment," was held on Tuesday, before Mr. James Green, the arbitrator appointed by the Local Government Board. The cases dealt with comprised the Oxford Music Hall and the freehold and leasehold interests therein, and in Nos. 4, 14 and 16 Oxford-street, 1 and 1a Tottenham Court-road, and part of 11, 12 and 13 Beziers-court. Professional evidence on both sides was given before the arbitrator, whose award will be published simultaneously with that in the Strand improvement scheme. The Hon. Alfred Lyttleton, M.P., appeared for the London County Council; and Mr. Glen, Mr. Greene, Mr. Moresby, Mr. Brown and Mr. Courthope Munroe for the various owners.

At the Grand Hotel, Manchester, on Friday, the 7th inst., an arbitration was opened before Messrs. William Spinks, Leeds, and William Eagle, Manchester, with Mr. Jos. Brierly, Blackburn, as umpire, to determine the amount to be paid by the Middleton Corporation to Messrs. Langton & Gilmour, the owners of an estate in Middleton, for compensation for damage sustained by reason of the defendants laying a sewer through the claimants' land. Mr. Sutton, Rochdale, appeared for the claimants and Mr. Bradbury for the defendants. Evidence was given by Mr. F. W. Stott, surveyor, Rochdale, and Mr. Breweton, Manchester, to the effect that a line of 15-in. pipes, 569 yards in length, with three manholes and three lampholes, having been laid through claimants' land, the property has sustained great damage as regards its value as building land, for which purpose it was intended, the defendants' action making it impossible to build on those plots under which the sewer is laid. A question was raised by the defendants as to the difficulty of draining the property there would be when built over. The claimants contended that there would be no difficulty in this matter, as two open ditches on the property, which they contended are sewers— as they have been partially piped—might be utilised. Claimants' valuation was as follows: 6,484 square yards of land not available for building on at 1½d. per yard and twenty years' purchase, £810 10s., deferred twenty years at 5 per cent., £305 9s. 5d.; 7,991 square yards of land depreciated in value at 1s., deferred twenty years at 5 per cent., £150 11s. 11d.; three manholes at £10, £30; three lampholes at £5, £15; total, £501 1s. 5d.

The further hearing of the case was then adjourned till Wednesday, the 12th inst., when the defendants' witnesses— viz., Messrs. H. Batey, Manchester, W. Evans, and W. Welburn, borough surveyor, Middleton, gave evidence. It was explained by those witnesses that the land in question was most unsuitable for building on, as it would have to be filled up to a great depth, and it would be a long time before it would be ready for building operations to commence. They contended that when built upon the property could not be drained except into the defendants' sewer, as the open ditches referred to were not sewers; also that the land could be laid out so that the line of the sewer would not interfere so much with the building plots, and therefore so much land ought not to be claimed for or so high a price asked. Their valuation for the full value of the land was: 480 square yards at 1d. per yard and twenty years' purchase, deferred twenty years at 4 per cent., £15 5s. 5d.; 2,785 square yards at 1d. per yard and twenty years' purchase, deferred thirty-five years at 4 per cent., £58 14s. 4d.; total, £73 19s. 9d. Estimating the damage sustained by the claimants to be two-thirds of the full value of the land, the following figures would be obtained: Two-thirds of full value (£73 19s. 9d.), £49 6s. 6d.; 550 lineal yards by 3 yards wide, land occupied by sewer, at 1d. per yard and twenty years' purchase, deferred thirty-five years at 4 per cent., £42 18s. 4d.; allowance for manholes, &c., £20; total, £112 4s. 10d. The arbitrators failing to agree, the case was referred to the umpire, who will make his award in due course.

**County Councils' Association.**—The executive council of this body met on Wednesday, under the presidency of Sir John Hibbert, and, among other things, it was resolved to make a representation to the Earl of Morley, urging him to propose that the standing order of the House of Commons which gives a *locus standi* to county councils in Water Bills should be adopted for the House of Lords.

# "The Genesis of Street Mud."

## CARDIFF AND THE TESTING OF ROAD METAL.—II.

At the conclusion of our comments on the above subject in last week's issue of THE SURVEYOR we mentioned that just as we were going to press we had received a copy of *The Western Mail* of the previous Wednesday, in which appeared a further article on "The Genesis of Street Mud," consisting chiefly of a letter written by Prof. Elliott (in answer to a pamphlet which had been prepared and circulated by the owner of the Penlee quarries) correcting an error of transcription which appeared in the tests of Prof. Elliott as first published in *The Mail*. These corrected figures so materially affect the question at issue, that it is necessary to call further attention to them.

For the purpose of showing the effect of the error of transcription in Prof. Elliott's first report, together with the correction now made, we refer our readers to the following table, which places Prof. Elliott's first and second figures in reference to the two competitive stones in question in parallel columns, and we also give the results of the tests of the same two kinds of stones by Mr. Lovegrove, as published in our issue of November 5, 1897 :—

mittee, the latter in correcting Prof. Elliott made two errors in calculation.

The following is the borough engineer's statement to which *The Mail* refers :—

Mr. Harpur, referring to articles which had appeared in *The Western Mail*, said that certain statements had been made which he considered reflected upon him in respect of the advice he had given to the committee. He wished to explain that the whole foundation upon which the articles referred to had been built up had been absolutely and completely upset by Prof. Elliott's report, which appeared in Wednesday's *Western Mail*. In giving the quantity of mud produced by basalt in the first instance, he put it down at 3·2 per cent. from sample C. On Wednesday he corrected an error in transcription, which appeared in the original report, and stated that the figures "3·2 per cent." should have been 5·8. It was contended in *The Western Mail* that Penlee stone produced twice as much mud as basalt sample C, and 50 per cent. more mud than the average of samples A, B and C, but according to

| Stones. | PROF. ELLIOTT'S ATTRITION TESTS. | | | MR. LOVEGROVE'S ATTRITION TESTS, | | |
|---|---|---|---|---|---|---|
| | As published in *The Western Mail* of September 23, 1898. | As corrected in *The Western Mail* of October 19, 1898. | | As published in THE SURVEYOR of November 5, 1897. | | |
| | Dry Test. | Dry Test. | | Dry Test. | Wet Test. | Mean of Dry and Wet Tests. |
| | Mud produced. | Mud produced. | | Mud produced. | Mud produced. | Mud produced. |
| German Basalt A | 5·9 per cent. | 5·9 per cent. | | | | |
| " " B | 6·5 per cent. | 6·5 per cent. | | 8·25 per cent. | 11·47 per cent. | 9·86 per cent. |
| " " C | 3·2 per cent. | 5·8 per cent. | | | | |
| Penlee | 7·2 per cent. | 7·2 per cent. | | 6·54 per cent. | 7·81 per cent. | 7·17 per cent. |

It was upon the figures given in the first of the above columns that the whole case of *The Western Mail* was founded, and upon the strength of these figures our contemporary, in its issue of September 23rd, held that Prof. Elliott's tests proved that Penlee stone produced twice as much mud as the German basalt sample C, and 50 per cent. more mud than the average of the three tests of the German stone A, B and C.

The argument deduced from these figures was, it will be remembered, that there was no economy in using Penlee stone as compared with German basalt ; in fact, that the Cardiff surveyor was absolutely in the wrong in his recommendations to the corporation. Now, by applying the same method of calculation to the figures in the second column (which are Prof. Elliott's corrected figures) the results reduce the cent. per cent. to 24·14 per cent. upon sample C and the 50 per cent. to 18·69 per cent. upon the average of the three samples of basalt, while if we apply the same method of calculation to the tests of Mr. Lovegrove we find that the German stone produces 26·15 per cent. in the dry test, 46·86 per cent. in the wet test, and 36·5 per cent. in the mean of the dry and wet tests—more mud than is produced by the Penlee stone. Again, if we take the mean of Prof. Elliott's and Mr. Lovegrove's tests, it shows slightly in favour of Penlee stone, and we venture to think this would prove to be a very fair result if the tests were in all respects equal.

Even supposing that the two stones are practically of equal merit, the question of price has then to be taken into consideration, as we previously pointed out ; and on this count again it would appear to be obvious that Mr. Harpur justifiably adopted the ordinary common-sense view of the matter. On the day on which our last issue was published *The Western Mail* contained an account of a meeting of the Public Works Committee of the Cardiff Corporation, at which the borough engineer drew attention to the correction made by Prof. Elliott in his figures, and to the effect of this error upon the deductions *The Mail* had published in its first report.

The Cardiff borough engineer (says *The Mail*, in the remarks introductory to its account of the above meeting) is once more exhibiting his "backbone" over the mud question. Would it not be more conducive to the public interest if he showed greater readiness to calmly discuss matters, avoiding excitement on the one hand, and *ad misericordiam* appeals on the other ? Surely the Cardiff borough engineer is capable of grasping the fact that the public have a right to call in question the action of the corporation, and even of its officials, while the latter have no right to attempt to reduce every controversy to a personal level. The borough engineer is certainly very badly advised in the course he has pursued—a public official should not allow himself to become a partisan. The borough engineer or the Public Works Committee yesterday laid great stress upon a single error in transcription which had occurred in Prof. Elliott's report on the attrition tests. Singularly enough, as shown by a note received from the borough engineer subsequently to the meeting of the com-

Prof. Elliott's amended figures Penlee stone only produced 24·14 per cent. more mud than basalt sample C, and 18·69 per cent. than the average of the three tests A, B and C. He was very sorry himself, and expected Prof. Elliott was sorry, that the mistake had occurred. The papers containing the articles had been distributed widely. They had reached members of his profession, and were calculated to do him a considerable amount of damage. He did not like the soundness of his advice to the corporation being called into question by irresponsible journalism. Mr. Lovegrove's test, the result of which was given at the last meeting, showed that basalt stone produced a very much larger percentage of mud than the Penlee stone. He did not wish to call into question anything Mr. Elliott had done, but, as the committee would see, he had corrected an error which crept into his first report, and he (Mr. Harpur) thought it was only right the committee should have their attention called to it, otherwise, he thought, it would not be noticed. If the committee thought there was anything in those tests, he would be glad to pay the expenses of two members of the committee to London, to see the tests which Mr. Lovegrove had taken.

We note, in passing, that *The Mail* now seeks to throw upon Mr. Harpur the responsibility for importing personality into the discussion. This is no concern of ours, and we imagine that those who have read *The Mail* articles, which carry upon the face of them the desire to effect an end with but little regard for the professional reputation of an engineer of the highest standing among those best qualified to judge, will need no comment of ours to enable them to form a fair judgment upon the point. They will not forget that Mr. Harpur has been forced, as a public official, into defending himself against a series of attacks which might conceivably have lost him the confidence of his corporation, and under the circumstances, it appears to us, his justification has been urged by him with dignity, consistency and complete success. That this view is shared by those whom Mr. Harpur so loyally serves is evidenced by the following concluding lines of the report of the meeting already referred to :—

The mayor said the committee had no reason to underrate Mr. Harpur's ability, and he was certain the committee had absolute confidence in his recommendations and advice.

This, we take it, is a final answer to *The Western Mail*, and we imagine both Mr. Harpur and the Cardiff Corporation will in future treat with absolute disregard any further "technical lucubrations"—to quote from the *Mail's* own graceful reference to our first article—from the same quarter.

**Wallasey.**—Mr. W. O. E. Meade-King recently held an inquiry, on behalf of the Local Government Board, with reference to an application of the district council for sanction to borrow £40,000 for gasworks purposes, £1,790 for street improvement purposes, and £1,198 for fire brigade purposes,

## PUBLIC WORK IN MANCHESTER.

### LOCAL GOVERNMENT BOARD INQUIRY.

Mr. George W. Willcocks recently held an inquiry at Manchester, on behalf of the Local Government Board, with reference to an application of the city council for sanction to borrow the sum of £20,000 for purposes of public works and pleasure grounds. The inquiry was attended, among others, by Mr. T. Hudson, deputy town clerk, and Mr. T. de Courcy Meade, city surveyor.

Mr. HUDSON, in opening the inquiry, explained that the application had reference to three grounds—the first at Oakroad, Crumpsall Park, the second at Boggart Hole Clough, and the third a new recreation ground to be formed in Higher Openshaw. The Openshaw scheme was an entirely new one, but both at Crumpsall Park and Boggart Hole Clough the land was already in the possession of the corporation, who, however, were desirous of erecting certain necessary buildings thereon. At Crumpsall it was proposed to erect a toolshed, two blocks of conveniences, two flights of terrace steps, entrance lodge, band-stand, and propagating-house, at a cost of £2,350; to expend on laying-out and planting £1,500; and on forming a draining passage on the Crumpsall Hall side, £250; a total of £4,100. At Boggart Hole Clough they desired to spend £2,000 on road-making and banking, £250 on footbridges, £2,000 on soiling, turfing and planting the banks, £1,000 on boundary hurdling, £500 on two blocks of conveniences, and £1,200 on six shelters; a total of £7,900. With regard to the Higher Openshaw ground, a provisional contract had been entered into by correspondence with Colonel Legh, lord of the manor of Openshaw, for the purchase of between 7 and 8 acres of freehold land, at a cost of £1,000 per acre. The nett purchase money was estimated at £7,500, expenses incidental to the purchase £120, and necessary works in adjacent streets £380; giving a total of £8,000.

Alderman EVANS said the works at Crumpsall Park would complete the estate in a satisfactory manner. Unless the land at Openshaw was acquired at the present time it would very soon be built upon. Crumpsall Park adjoined the Manchester workhouse, and was in the midst of a large, mixed population. It was acquired by the Crumpsall Local Board before the amalgamation of the district with Manchester, and he believed the ground would be of considerable benefit to the inhabitants. The Boggart Hole Clough would really accommodate the whole side of North Manchester, and hundreds of houses had recently been erected within a short distance of it. About 80 acres of the Clough were bought about five years ago for the purposes of a cemetery, and the recreation ground was rather more than 60 acres in extent. The Openshaw ground was also in the midst of a large working-class population.

Mr. T. DE COURCY MEADE, the city surveyor, presented plans of the proposed grounds and buildings, and fully explained them.

Mr. R. LAMB, general superintendent of the parks, open spaces and nurseries connected with the corporation, also gave evidence, and said some of the work had been proceeded with. That work consisted of repairing unsafe roads and excavating, and was executed in order that the corporation's workmen should not be dismissed.

Further evidence was also given, and the inquiry closed.

## SEWAGE DISPOSAL AT CHELTENHAM.

The Local Government Board have, says *The Birmingham Daily Post*, practically refused to sanction an application of the Cheltenham Corporation for permission to raise £13,410 for the purposes of sewerage and sewage disposal. The corporation are the owners of sewage farms in villages to the west of the borough, and these farms have hitherto been let to farmers. The manner in which the sewage has been treated on the land has been the subject of loud and frequent complaint from the villagers of Staverton and Boddington, and it was with the object of meeting and remedying these complaints that much of the work was proposed to be done with the £13,410 in question. At the inquiry, held a few weeks ago by Colonel Marsh, on behalf of the Local Government Board, further expression was given to these complaints, with the result that, as appears from a letter now received by the town clerk of Cheltenham, the Local Government Board are "satisfied that the present arrangements for the treatment and disposal of the sewage are unsatisfactory." In particular the letter goes on to state: "It is observed by the inspector that there appears to be no proper supervision of the farms by the town council, that the system of irrigation adopted by the farmers is inefficient, and that there were indications of a great deal of the liquid sewage finding its way untreated into the ditches and watercourses. The board's experience shows that as a general rule the results which ensue upon a local authority divesting themselves of the direct control of sewage lands by letting the lands for agricultural purposes are unsatisfactory, as it not infrequently happens that the farmers are more concerned to make a profit for themselves than to properly purify the sewage. The board therefore consider it most desirable that the management of sewage farms should be entirely in the hands of the local authority, whose primary object would be to avoid creating a nuisance or infringing the provisions of the Rivers Pollution Prevention Acts." Accordingly, the Local Government Board request that the town council will take this question into their immediate consideration, with the view of determining the present arrangements and taking the entire management of the sewage farms into their own hands. In any case, the town council are advised to consider the expediency of applying some such remedy for the complaints referred to as the use of aluminoferric or lime at the sewage works before the sewage is taken to the farms.

## SHREWSBURY MAIN DRAINAGE SCHEME.

The laying of the foundation-stone of the Coleham pumping station, which was performed by the mayoress of Shrewsbury on Friday, marks the approaching completion of the Shrewsbury main drainage scheme, which has been in progress during the past eighteen months. All the main intercepting sewers surrounding the town have been laid, together with a high-level gravitation outfall, discharging at the outfall works at Monknoor. The work has been one of unusual difficulty, on account of the physical characteristics of the town, the subsoil on arriving at water level consisting of extremely fine silt, a circumstance which led to the failure and abandonment of a scheme having the desired object in view which was commenced about twenty-five years ago.

The experience gained in that scheme, however, was not without its influence upon the design of the works now completed, since the engineers (Messrs. J. Taylor, Sons & Santo Crimp, of Westminster) determined to adopt a central position for the pumping station, in order to construct all the works above the level of the running silt. After its collection and delivery at the pumping station the sewage will be pumped by means of a pair of compound beam pumping engines, with a capacity of 6,000,000 gallons per day, into the gravitation outfall above mentioned. The outfall works consist of a set of tanks for the precipitation of the suspended matters, sludge-pressing plant and other works of the modern type. After clarification the effluent will be applied for its final purification to land, of which the town council have acquired 180 acres.

## A VILLAGE WATER SUPPLY.

Mr. F. Drake Brockman, of Beechborough, we learn, is providing the inhabitants of Newington, a village near Folkestone, with a supply of water for drinking and domestic purposes, and for some time past the work has been in progress under the supervision of Mr. A. R. Bowles, engineer to the Sandgate Urban District Council, who himself was responsible for the preparation of the scheme. The source of supply, locally known as the Spring Head, is situated up in the hills, at a distance of about 1½ miles from Newington. A storage reservoir of adequate capacity has been constructed there, and a 3-in. service main has been laid to the village. The works, when completed, will have cost about £600.

## INSTITUTION OF CIVIL ENGINEERS.

### ORDINARY GENERAL MEETING.

The first ordinary general meeting of the 1898-99 session of the above Institution will be held on Tuesday, at 8 p.m., when Mr. W. H. Preece, C.B., F.R.S., the president, will deliver an address, which will be followed by the presentation of medals and prizes awarded by the council. At the close of this meeting the president will hold a reception in the library.

**Maidstone Water Supply.**—A meeting of the ratepayers convened by the mayor, was held at Maidstone on Wednesday, for the purpose of passing a resolution authorising the corporation to promote a Bill in Parliament to empower them to purchase the undertaking of the local water company. The resolution was carried by an overwhelming majority, but a poll was demanded. The result, it is expected, will be favourable to the purchase scheme, the epidemic of last year having converted many who were opposed to the proposal two years ago, when it was vetoed by the ratepayers.

**"House Drainage: Its Inspection and Testing,"** by Richard J. Jenkins. (London: St. Bride's Press, Limited. Price 1s. nett).—On the whole, says *The Engineer*, this is a useful little book; but every sanitary engineer has his own notions, and there is no scheme of house drainage that will not be criticised. Mr. Jenkins' views on the subject of water-closets, for example, will not be accepted generally as final. All valve closets are bad, in our opinion. A 2-gallon flush is not sufficient. Mr. Jenkins seems to be unaware of the agitation against the intercepting chamber and the ventilating shaft now in progress. In the London clay a cement pipe joint may be the worst possible. But we cannot have everything in a little book like this, and it is so good that we feel somewhat ashamed of calling attention to its defects, which are, after all, more matters of opinion than reality.

## CORRESPONDENCE.

**Surveyor Baiting.**—" An Interested Looker On " writes :
It is refreshing to see that you have raised your powerful
voice in defence of Mr. Harpur, the borough surveyor, &c., of
Cardiff. There are a considerable number of the non-think-
ing public who consider that surveyors are appointed and
hold office simply to be kicked whenever the fit comes upon
them for that sort of amusement. But I think a deal too
much is being made of a very simple practical question. Of
experts and professors I have a wholesome dread, and do not
see the utility of erecting (figuratively) two steam-hammers
to crack so small a nut as this at Cardiff. Here are two
samples of road metal, about the wearing quality of which
there is a dispute ; why not lay down a coat of each sort of
metal on a certain road where equal traffic would pass over
each section or sample, and let the public judge at the end of
a year which has stood the wear and tear best. This would
be a practical test, not an expert's or professor's fad under
conditions which do not come into the practical solution of
this simple problem, and the nut would be cracked minus the
aid of the two steam-hammers, so needlessly introduced.

**Shoreditch Combined Electric Light and Dust De-
structor Works.**—Mr. H. E. Kershaw, chairman of the Electric Light Committee of the Shoreditch Vestry, writes : I am
at a loss to understand Mr. T. W. Baker's attack on the above
scheme, especially when viewed in the light of the fact that
Mr. Baker submitted a scheme to our vestry for dust destruction, in conjunction with the electric light, in 1893, but
that scheme was so ridiculous in its proposals that the vestry,
with but few dissentients, refused to have anything to do
with it. Is it a bid for cheap notoriety ? Or is Mr. Baker's
criticism the justification of his own scheme, for he states,
" I do not infer or wish to be understood that all dust destructors are or will be financial failures." Or is it the outcome of his chagrin that a more successful engineer should
be in the happy position of being the first to successfully
instal an electric light and dust destruction combined scheme?
Your contemporary, London, having facts at its disposal,
cleverly answers this attack in the last issue, for it must be
known to you, sir, that Mr. Baker's letter appears simul-
taneouly in THE SURVEYOR, London, The Contract Journal,
The Electrical Engineer, Lightning, The Electrician and The
Hackney Express of this week—and, no doubt, there are more
to follow—and I am put to the trouble, for the benefit of the
many who are desirous of knowing the truth of our scheme,
to reply to this unwarrantable attack. As London points
out, the basis of Mr. Baker's calculations of financial results
fall to the ground in the face of the fact that he has taken
our vestry's financial reports, which only give accounts up to
March this year and is based upon a twelve months' expenditure with a nine months' income, the first quarter of which
is invariably a heavy loss to any undertaking. Mr. Baker
very ably connects the two schemes—the sale of electricity
and the destruction of dust—and asks which is correct. The
vestry clerk's stated profit of £1,268 17s. 9d., or Mr. Baker's
supposed total loss of £1,525 16s. 7d. ? Well, I emphatically
state, not Mr. Baker; and the vestry clerk is correct, so far
as he goes, but from my point of view he does not go far
enough. I will state here—and within the course of a few
weeks justify my statement, as my committee's report on
this matter will shortly be before the vestry; and when it
has passed that board it can be made public—on our combined scheme we made a profit in the first year's working,
after making all allowances, of £2,000 nett. This is as emphatic
as I can put it, although probably Mr. Baker will again say,
" I note no amount for depreciation is allowed." I sincerely
hope there never will be, because it must be remembered that
we are paying back something like £5,000 per annum interest
and capital on these undertakings, which means that in thirty
years the dust destructor and electric lighting station will
become a valuable freehold asset. That being so, where is
the need of depreciation with the maintenance charges included in our estimates year by year? Further, I might
add, as London reminds me, that the London County Council
have practically verified the figures I have given you. Their
valuer, in valuing us for assessment, went fully into these
figures, and based our assessment upon a profit of £1,800. I
cannot, without violating my position as chairman of this
committee, give you details of the Scavenging Committee's
figures, but they will all be included in the report I have
mentioned, which I know is being anxiously awaited throughout the whole country, and which, I venture again to say, will
give the satisfaction that this phenomenal scheme deserves.

Mr. H. Mansfield Robinson, vestry clerk, Shoreditch, writes:
Mr. Baker, in his lengthy criticism of the above accounts in
your last issue, makes such palpable blunders that, whilst I
have no intention of entering into a controversy as to the
success or otherwise of this scheme, it is necessary that I
should correct Mr. Baker's misreading of plain English, as it
is to similar perversion of facts that some of the " conflicting
statements " he refers to are due. Mr. Baker's case consists
of showing that the figures in my report (p. 2) do not
harmonise with the surveyor's report and the electricity and
destructor accounts. My statement, that the " destructor has
also succeeded in destroying the whole of the dust in this
parish and more besides up to a total of 18,842 tons in nine
months " (P. 2) is not inconsistent, as Mr. Baker suggests,

with the surveyor's statement at p. 188, that " during the
year " 18,378 tons were collected by the scavenging department, as the latter figures refer only to the refuse of Shoreditch, whereas my figures expressly include " more besides,"
such as parish refuse from St. Luke's and trade refuse from
the City sent to the destructor, and not collected by the
scavenging department at all. Again, my figures as to coal
burned were expressly stated to be for nine months, and were
taken from the revenue account (p. 361), whereas the conflicting figures at pp. 350 and 323 of the accounts are headed
in large type as accounts from March 25, 1897, to March 25,
1898 ; and Mr. Baker, as an engineer, ought to know that it
takes many weeks' slow firing to prepare a destructor and
make tests, &c., before steam-raising can be attempted. He
makes the same mistake in the dust destructor maintenance
cost, by comparing my figures for nine months with those
for a year in the accounts, and when he asks dramatically,
" Which are correct ?" the obvious answer is that both figures
are correct, as they are for different periods, and are so expressly stated. On the one item of repayment of debt and
interest one quarter's charge exceeds £288 alone. Now,
either Mr. Baker knew he was comparing figures for dissimilar
periods, and so tried to wilfully mislead your readers, or he
had not read the paragraphs or figures which he criticises,
and criticism displaying such gross carelessness is unworthy
of a schoolboy. Moreover, if Mr. Baker were to follow up
the methods of his critique by suggesting to any trading company that they must pay back a large proportion of their
capital (including cost of freehold land) to their shareholders
out of income before they could declare a " profit," they
would, I think, invite Mr. Baker to communicate his opinion
to the marines. It may interest him to know that the valuer
of the London County Council, from the nine months' figures
out of which Mr. Baker distorts a loss of £1,522, values the
first year's profits of this joint undertaking at £1,800, after
allowing £800 for depreciation and £300 for establishment
charges. As to the other " curious feature " Mr. Baker discovers in the increase of the Scavenging Committee's accounts, it hardly needs to be pointed out that the destructor
undertaking has no more to do with the cost of collecting
refuse and sweeping roads than it has to do with flushing
gullies or mending the streets. The increase in the stokers'
wages over the contractor's estimate is due to the vestry
adopting three shifts of eight hours each in place of the two
shifts of twelve hours each, which were reckoned by the contractors on the lines of those destructors where the cost is
" sweated " down out of labour. Possibly Mr. Baker has
some cheaper and better scheme up his sleeve (as he darkly
hints), but I would remind him that when he placed his
scheme for this joint undertaking before the Shoreditch
Vestry in 1893 (which found some curious support), he admitted he had not then built either an electricity station or
dust destructor (his patent for the latter being then only on
paper). Shoreditch has, at least, been wise enough not to
trust the spending of what amounts to date to nearly
£100,000 to amateur adventurers, and the results of the
first full year's working (which should be published in about
a fortnight) will, I think, bring quietness, if not conviction,
to the most unreasoning opponents of this pioneer undertaking.

## YARMOUTH SEA WATERWORKS.

### A PROFITABLE UNDERTAKING.

For thirteen years the sea waterworks of the corporation
have been at work without any serious breakdown. During
the first five years 40,000,000 gallons were raised per annum ;
the last eight years over 100,000,000 gallons have been taken
from the sea every year and used for flushing sewers,
lavatories, urinals, baths and street-watering. So great has
been the demand, that the engine has been at work 120 hours
per week. The water costs less than 1¼d. per 1,000 gallons,
and when the water company supplied it the corporation
used to pay 1s. per 1,000 gallons. Not only has the 1¼d. per
1,000 gallons paid all charges for capital repayment and interest, the use of salt water has effected considerable saving
in repairs to gravel-made roads. The total expenditure on
the existing works has been £5,600, and the gas engine raises
25,000 gallons per hour. The annual cost at first was £450,
latterly it has reached £600. Now a larger supply is required,
which necessitates an extension of the plant. The borough
surveyor therefore recommended the town council, at their
last week's meeting, to place electrically-driven triple pumps
to raise 25,000 gallons per hour in a building at the north end
of the South Beach gardens, with a service of 4-in. 5-in. and
8-in. pipes about the town, at a cost of £3,000, for which the
annual interest and sinking fund charges would amount to
£150. The recommendations of the surveyor were adopted
without comment.

**Llandudno.**—A Local Government Board inquiry was recently held at Llandudno into an application of the district
council for permission to borrow £4,701 for the provision of
public slaughter-houses and £032 for a market and fire
station. It was stated that the public slaughter-house is intended to take the place of seven private slaughter-houses, as
to the positions and insanitary state of which complaints have
frequently been made by residents and visitors.

## QUERIES AND REPLIES.

*Sketches accompanying Queries should be made separate on white paper in plain black-ink lines. Lettering or figures should be bold and plain.*

**215. Municipal Engineering Appointments in Canada, Qualifications Required for.**—" B. B " writes : How are the engineering appointments made in the Canadian municipalities ? Are the men trained at college, or are vacancies open to competition ? Have English municipal engineers any chance of obtaining such berths in like manner to the appointments at Cape Town (South Africa) and Wellington (New Zealand) ? I have a great desire to go to Canada, and I should like to know if it is possible to get a berth from here.

The reply to this query has been delayed, in order that we might obtain absolutely reliable information for the querist and others who may be similarly desirous of obtaining appointments in Canada. To this end we have been directing inquiries to engineers in Canada, and are now enabled to announce the following: (1) No qualifications are prescribed by law for a person to possess before he can become a municipal engineer in Canada ; but in the majority of cities and towns the municipal engineers are members of the Association of Ontario Land Surveyors, which is what is known as a close corporation, admission to which is gained only by passing two examinations, classed as preliminary and final, in addition to which the candidate must have served his articles for a not less period than three years. The exceptions to this rule are in the case of surveyors duly authorised in other portions of her Majesty's dominions, or in the case of graduates in civil engineering from some recognised university. The secretary of the Association of Ontario Land Surveyors is Mr. A. J. Van Nostrand, Room D, Yonge-street Arcade, Toronto, who will, we understand, send a copy of the Surveyors' Act upon application. (2) When a city or town are about to engage an engineer, the vacancy is generally advertised in the leading provincial newpapers ; but in many cases we are informed the local surveyor is also made the engineer. (3) Municipal engineers from England would at the present time, it is stated, stand a very poor chance of securing employment in Canada, although several English engineers have attained good positions in a few years. Such engineers would have, however, there is no doubt, it is said, made their mark if they had remained in England. (4) No special training is required of municipal engineers by law, but cities and towns are beginning to realise that an engineer should have a university training.

**216. Highway Surveyorship : Certificate Recommended.** —" Assistant Surveyor " writes : I wish to become a rural district surveyor. I am at present an assistant surveyor to a highway board. Would you kindly tell me what certificate would be of most help to me in seeking to obtain the above ?

We are of opinion that the querist should obtain by examination the certificate of the Incorporated Association of Municipal and County Engineers, this being the best recognised and most valuable certificate an intending municipal or highway surveyor can obtain, which certificate will be of service to him in securing an appointment and in his future career. The secretary of the association is Mr. Thomas Cole, A.M.I.C.E., 11 Victoria-street, Westminster, S.W., from whom particulars and syllabus of the examinations may be obtained on application.

## MUNICIPAL WORK IN BIRMINGHAM.

### NEW SEWERAGE WORKS.

Important works of sewerage, which are roughly estimated to involve an expenditure of £60,000, formed the subject of a Local Government Board inquiry recently, Colonel A. G. Durnford, R.E., attending to receive evidence in support of the application of the council for sanction to borrow a sum of £35,760. The application was unopposed. By far the larger proportion of the money, the town clerk explained, was in respect of the reconstruction of the Rea main sewer, between Lawley-street and Nechells, the estimate for which was £33,500. The old sewer was egg-shaped, and 5 ft. 9 in. in height and 3 ft. 6 in. in width. From gaugings recently taken it had been found that the sewer conveyed about half of the sewage delivered at the outfall at Saltley, and its maintenance in proper working order was a matter of great consideration. When the sewer was examined it was found that the arch was cracked, the inverts were much worn, and in the opinion of the late experienced surveyor (Mr. Till) and the present surveyor (Mr. Price) immediate reconstruction was necessary. Owing to the large volume of sewage to be dealt with, any attempt to repair the sewer would be excessively costly, and for this and other reasons it was proposed to entirely do away with the old sewer. As the result of a conference between the city surveyor and the engineer of the Midland Railway Company, it was arranged that a new sewer, 6 in. circular, should be constructed upon a line almost parallel and close to the river Rea. The cost of constructing this new sewer, putting in the foundation and wall, was estimated by the surveyor at £28,000, and towards that amount the Midland Railway Company were willing to contribute £8,333, a third of the estimated cost. The company also requested the

Public Works Committee to divert and reconstruct that portion of the sewer between Lawley-street and Viaduct-street, and of the estimated cost of £2,800 they agreed to contribute £2,300. From the boundary of the Midland Railway Company's property the existing sewer ran through land of the corporation gas department, and in connection with extensions going on there the Gas Committee thought that it would be very advantageous if the new retort-house could be built over the site of the existing sewer. The diversion and reconstruction of the sewer was suggested to the Public Works Committee, and the total cost of that portion of the works, providing for a 7-in. circular sewer, was estimated at £21,000, towards which the Gas Committee agreed to contribute £13,000. Smaller items brought the total expenditure involved up to £57,000 odd, and the contributions thereto amounted to £23,633, leaving £33,000 odd to be borrowed. The application for sanction to borrow in respect of sewers included a further item of £2,260. The town clerk also called evidence before the inspector in support of the applications to borrow £7,000 for extensions at the Saltley depot wharf, and £4,730 for purposes of paving and other street improvements. In the latter connection £2,800 was required in respect of the purchase of property and other matters necessary for the rounding-off of an awkward bend in Longmore-street and Gooch-street, an improvement greatly to be desired in the public interest and safety. The inspector took careful notes of the evidence and promised to make an early report to the Local Government Board.

## SUPERANNUATION OF MUNICIPAL OFFICERS.

### LOCAL AUTHORITIES' OFFICERS' SUPERANNUATION BILL.

In connection with the conference, which has been convened for 8 o'clock on Monday, at Sion College, Victoria-embankment, E.C., the Municipal Officers' Association have, through their hon. secretary, Mr. C. J. F. Carnell, issued a circular, in the course of which he states :—

The object of the conference is to bring before the officers of the municipal service the absolute necessity of doing their utmost in the next session of Parliament to induce the local authorities under which they serve to view with favour the above Bill, and to secure promises of support from the member of Parliament representing their division. The conference, composed of three delegates sent by associations and societies representing municipal officers, is anxious to reintroduce the Bill next session, and with the assistance of every individual officer throughout the country is satisfied that the measure will eventually be passed into law.

I may say that in some quarters it has been urged that the fund would be a charge upon the rates, but this is not borne out by the working of the Poor Law Officers' Superannuation Act, 1896, and you will see from the following extract that for the six months ended Lady Day, 1897, there is a surplus in favour of the rates of £15,424.

Extract from the twenty-seventh annual report of the Local Government Board, 1897-98, p. 369 :—

"Amount of percentage deducted from salaries, &c., under the Poor Law Officers' Superannuation Act, 1896... ... ... ... £17,683.

"Amount paid as superannuation allowances under the provisions of the above Act ... £1,259."

The following resolutions will be submitted : (1) "That this meeting, representing municipal officers throughout the country, pledges itself to do all in its power to secure the passing of the Local Authorities' Officers' Superannuation Bill in the next session of Parliament." (2) "That a copy of the above resolution be sent to the members of Parliament, asking them to support the measure."

Notice of motion by Mr. F. Cliffe (Incorporated Society of Inspectors of Weights and Measures) : "In view of the passing of the Elementary Teachers' (Superannuation) Act, 1898, and the extension of that Act to Scotland, together with the statement in the House of Commons by Mr. Balfour when introducing the Bill, that 'he saw no reason why Scotch teachers should be placed in a different position in regard to superannuation to those in England,' this conference decides that the Local Authorities' Officers' Superannuation Bill, when next introduced into Parliament, shall also be extended so as to apply to Scotland."

The chair will be taken by Mr. C. William Tagg, chairman of the conference, supported by Sir John Blundell Maple, M.P., Major P. H. Dalbiac, M.P., John Lowles, Esq., M.P., and other influential gentlemen. No tickets will be required.

**Johannesburg Sewerage Scheme.**—The following special cable has been received at the London office of *The Johannesburg Standard and Diggers' News* : "The Government has arranged to inaugurate an adequate sewerage scheme for Johannesburg and the mines of the Witwatersrand. The water will be drawn from the surplus supplies of Zuurbekom, where there is more than ample for all requirements. The sewerage contract has been granted to Mr. E. Mendelssohn, who was largely responsible for the discovery of the Zuurbokom source and its addition to Johannesburg water supply."

# Law Notes.

EDITED BY J. B. REIGNIER CONDER, 11 Old Jewry Chambers, E.C.,

Solicitor of the Supreme Court.

*The Editor will be pleased to answer any questions affecting the practice of engineers and surveyors to local authorities. Queries (which should be written legibly on foolscap paper, one side only) should be addressed to "The Law Editor," at the Offices of* THE

SURVEYOR. *Where possible, copies of local Acts or documents referred to should be enclosed. All explanatory diagrams must be drawn and lettered in black ink only. Correspondents who do not wish their names published should furnish a nom de plume.*

PUBLIC HEALTH (LONDON) ACT, 1891, SEC. 120, SUB-SEC. (3).—This sub-section provides that where only some of the persons responsible for a nuisance have been proceeded against they may recover summarily from the others a proportionate part of the costs of and incidental to such proceedings and abating the nuisance, and of any fine or costs inflicted. In *Precost* v. *Jolly* (Worship-street Police Court, 3rd October) the point in dispute was : What are costs of and incidental to the proceedings within the meaning of the section ? The complainant had been summoned by the Poplar Board of Works in respect of a nuisance arising from a choked combined drain used for the drainage of several houses, some of which belonged to the complainant and some to the defendant. The complainant engaged a solicitor to appear in the proceedings by the board and called witnesses. An order was, however, made against him, in compliance with which he abated the nuisance. He now sought to recover from the defendant under this section a proportion of his solicitor's bill of costs and fees paid to witnesses, &c., as well as of the expense of putting the drain right. On behalf of the defendant it was contended that he had from the first been ready and willing to contribute to the expenses of abating the nuisance, that the complainant in allowing himself to be proceeded against and engaging a solicitor and defending the case had unnecessarily increased the expenses, and that these additional items were not costs of and incidental to the proceedings within the meaning of the section. The magistrate (Mr. Corser) decided in favour of the complainant and made an order for the payment of the proportion claimed, amounting to £17 3s. 9d.

## QUERIES AND REPLIES.

PUBLIC HEALTH LAW RELATING TO SCOTLAND.—"Public Health Student" writes; Will you kindly inform me what Acts of Parliament to study that affect the public health of Scotland—*e.g.*, the Act or Acts corresponding to Public Health Act, 1875, which does not apply to Scotland.

The law of public health relating to Scotland was consolidated in the Public Health (Scotland) Act, 1897 (60 and 61 Vic., c. 38), repealing wholly, or in part, several previous Acts. The unrepealed portions of the Local Government (Scotland) Act, 1889 (52 and 53 Vic., c. 50), and of the Local Government (Scotland) Act, 1894 (57 and 58 Vic., c. 58), should also be referred to, as well as 39 and 40 Vic., c. 31, sec. 0 (Public Works Loans), 30 and 40 Vic., c. 75, and 56 and 57 Vic., c. 31 (Rivers Pollution), 44 and 45 Vic., c. 37, secs. 5, 19 and 27 (Alkali, &c., Works).

BORROWING POWERS OF LOCAL AUTHORITY : PUBLIC HEALTH ACT, 1875, SEC. 235.—"Nemo" writes : Sec. 235 of the Public Health Act, 1875, gives power to raise a mortgage on land or works possessed by an authority for works of sewage disposal. My council have land, buildings and pumping plant at their sewage farm on a lease, the unexpired term of lease being thirty-eight years. Will the council be able to borrow on such lands, buildings, &c.? In other words, does the term "possessed," used in the section, mean that the authority must possess the freehold in order to borrow on such works?

In my opinion the borrowing powers conferred by this section are applicable to the land and buildings referred to. The Interpretation Act, 1889, sec. 3, provides that in every Act passed after the year 1850 the expression "land" shall include messuages, tenements and hereditaments, houses and buildings *of any tenure.*

SURVEYOR TO DISTRICT COUNCIL : SECURITY PREMIUM.—"Surveyor" writes : I have just been requested by my council to obtain a guarantee (according to the Public Health Act) for £100 from a guarantee society. This I have done, and have to pay an annual premium of 12s. 6d. Is there anything to prevent the council (if willing) paying the annual premium ?

There appears to be nothing absolutely prohibiting this, but it might give rise to a question on the audit of the accounts. The better plan would be to make a trifling increase of salary to cover it.

TEMPORARY IRON MISSION HALL.—"Surveyor" also writes: Plans have been deposited for approval which is to be of a wood and iron structure (Humphries, Limited). The urban district council will not pass the plans, as they say they are not in accordance with the by-laws; they maintain that the walls should be of bricks. I enclose copy of by-laws for your reference. Will you kindly give me your opinion on the matter.

Assuming that the mission hall does not fall within the category of "exempted buildings" enumerated in By-law 2, the question is whether it is a "new building." This is a "question of fact" for the magistrates to decide (*James* v. *Wyell*, 61 L.T. [N.S.], 237). The High Court has, however, in some cases considered the question, and it may be useful to note one or two of these. In *Richardson* v. *Brown* (60 J.P., 644) a wooden structure, 30 ft. by 13 ft., standing on wheels, with spouts, a down corner and a supply of gas, and used as a butcher's shop, was held to be a new building. In *Stevens* v. *Gourley* (23 L.J.,

C.P. 1) a wooden shop resting on joists, but having no fastenings or foundations in masonry, and capable of being lifted from the ground, was held to be a building. In *Watson* v. *Cotton* (17 L.J., C.P. 64) a shed standing against a wooden paling, but not fastened thereto, and consisting of six posts fixed in the ground and supporting a tarpaulin which formed the roof, one side being boarded up with boards nailed to the posts, was held to be a building. Perhaps the case most in point, however, is *Budley* v. *Cuckfield Union Rural District Council* (! THE SURVEYOR, 450), where the Queen's Bench Division held that a corrugated-iron sanatorium was a building, and overruled the owner's contention that it was exempt from by-laws requiring brick walls. In my opinion, having regard to these cases, the council are justified in refusing to pass the plans.

PARTNERSHIP.—"A Young Surveyor" writes: (1) I shall be glad if your Law Editor will inform me, through the columns of your valuable paper, if it is possible and legal for a young surveyor (B) to join another in partnership (A finding all capital and B being a working partner), to receive a share of the profits of the business, and have all the usual powers as may be necessary or proper for the enjoyment of his rights and discharge of his duties as partner encumber, and yet not to have any financial liability in respect of the business if this is expressly stipulated in the deed ? (2) Can you kindly refer me to any book in which I shall find a really good form of a partnership deed with the usual mutual covenants ?

(1) If B becomes a partner he cannot avoid financial liability, and any agreement (whether verbal or in writing) between two or more persons to share profits is *prima facie* evidence of partnership. He could, however, become manager to A at a salary equal to a proportionate share of profits, but in that case he would not have the rights of a partner, and a very carefully drawn agreement would be required. (2) I advise it to have a proper agreement prepared by a solicitor. It will be the cheapest in the end.

BY-LAWS : WALL OF WATER-CLOSET: IS A DOOR A WALL ? —"R. O." writes : I cannot but express my surprise at the opinion given by you in your answer to "Perplexed," in your issue of the 14th inst. Although it may at first sight appear absurd to contend that a door is a wall, you must remember that the side of a room may contain a doorway, and that one speaks of the whole as a "wall," not a "wall and doorway," although the doorway may take up the greater portion of the wall. In the case of a water-closet the side is usually so small that a doorway takes up the whole of the wall ; but it is, nevertheless, I maintain, a wall. Looking at the matter from a sanitary point of view, what earthly objection is there to the arrangement ? The objects of the by-law are, I take it, that the light and air from outside may have direct access to the water-closet, and that any drain from the water-closet may pass direct to the outside. Are not these advantages fully secured by this arrangement ? I should feel sincerely sorry for the builder whose house is condemned on, what appears to me, a paltry quibble.

I am quite ready to admit that a window in the door might answer every purpose, though as to this I am hardly qualified to express an opinion. This, however, is not the point. The query propounded by "Perplexed" was not whether "the objects of the by-law" would be "fully secured" by a window in the door, but whether he was "correct" (*i.e.*, as I understand it legally justified) in refusing to pass a water-closet with this arrangement. Upon this point I adhere to the opinion already expressed. "R. O." argues that where "a doorway takes up the whole of the wall," "*it* is, nevertheless, a wall." This is rather a puzzling proposition. In the first place the phrase "a doorway takes up the whole of the wall," if it has any meaning at all, must mean that the doorway occupies the place of, and is substituted for, a wall, and therefore that there is no wall. Notwithstanding which "R. O." contends that "*it*" is a wall. What is a wall? Surely not the *doorway* ? And yet there is nothing else left. To what then does "*it*" refer? Perhaps, however, "R. O." will consider this a "paltry quibble," and say that of course he means the *door*, and obviously a window cannot be inserted in an empty doorway. But if a door may be a wall, what becomes of all the by-laws as to the construction and thickness of walls? With regard to the argument that where there is a doorway in the side of a room the whole is, nevertheless, called a "wall," not a wall and doorway," I do not see that this affects the question. Surely "R. O." would not contend that if in such a case a by-law required a window in the "wall," it would be a compliance with that by-law to put a window in the door? And if not in that case, why in the case of a water-closet? It may or may not be that the by-law operates harshly, but as it stands it seems to me that it would be contrary to plain language to adopt the construction for which "R. O." contends.

**A Presentation Portrait.**—We have to acknowledge the receipt from the New York Insurance Company of a beautiful photogravure of Mr. V. McKinley, president of the United States, with his signature attached.

**Bravery Rewarded.**—In a recently issued list of awards the Royal Humane Society state that they have awarded a bronze medal to William Travis, employed by Messrs. Underwood Brothers, contractors, Dukinfield, for having at great risk rescued a fellow-workman from a sewage pipe, in which he had got jammed.

# Municipal Work in Progress and Projected.

We are able this week to publish particulars of several important municipal works—namely, those being carried out by the local authorities at Hastings, Abercorn, Barry, Bexhill, Batley, Dorchester, Leeds, Manchester, Nelson and other places.

## METROPOLITAN AUTHORITIES.

### LONDON COUNTY COUNCIL.

The county council on Tuesday managed to dispose of their agenda—a comparatively small one—without much discussion. The only matter which elicited a discussion at all was the General Purposes Committee's report in reference to the proposed appointment of a "chief officer of tramways." Some members considered that the salary proposed to be offered—viz., £1,500—was excessive, but eventually the committee's recommendation was adopted, after two amendments that the salary should be £1,000, and £1,250 rising by £50 per annum to £1,500 were rejected. The important joint report of the Housing of the Working Classes and the Improvement Committees, the recommendations of which involve an expenditure of £118,740, was again brought up and adopted without discussion.

*Loans for Public Works.*—Upon the recommendation of the Finance Committee it was agreed to lend the Chelsea Vestry £8,000 for paving works, the Islington Vestry £22,500 for electric lighting purposes, the St. Martin's Vestry £2,860 for paving works, the Shoreditch Vestry £8,200 for electric lighting purposes, and the Westminster Vestry £15,000 for paving works.

*The Tramways Department.*—The General Purposes Committee presented a report recommending that a head of the new Tramways Department, to be styled "Chief Officer of Tramways," should be appointed at a salary of £1,500 a year, and that advertisements should be issued inviting applications for the appointment. This was agreed to, after the rejection of amendments that the salary should be £1,000 and £1,250 per annum.

*Retirement of the Superintending Architect.*—The General Purposes Committee reported that Mr. Blashill, the superintending architect, had attained the age of sixty-eight years, and was entitled to retire on a pension. The normal age for retirement is sixty-five, but under special resolutions of the council Mr. Blashill's services had been retained during the past three years. The committee expressed the opinion that Mr. Blashill's services had been most devoted and valuable, and recommended that his pension should be £525 a year, being at the rate of 21-60ths of his salary of £1,500 a year, ten years being added to his eleven years of actual service, as authorised by the Superannuation Act, 1866. They also recommended that an advertisement should be inserted inviting applications for the appointment of a superintending architect, at a salary of £1,500 per annum. After considerable discussion, in the course of which several members paid high tributes to the value of Mr. Blashill's services to the council, the recommendation of the committee was adopted.

*The Clare Market Rehousing Scheme.*—The Housing of the Working Classes and the Improvements Committee presented a joint report, in which they recommended the council to purchase from the Duke of Bedford, for £118,740, two plots of land in Drury-lane and one in Herbrand-street, near Woburn-place, Russell-square, in order to erect thereon dwellings to rehouse persons to be displaced by the Clare Market improvement scheme and the proposed new street from Holborn to the Strand. Full particulars of the report are published in another column. The recommendations of the committees were adopted without discussion.

*Water Connections.*—On the motion of Mr. Purchese, the Water Connections were instructed to consider and report as to the best means of compelling the London water companies to bear the cost of conveying the water from their mains to the houses, buildings, &c., of the consumers.

*Proposed New Embankment.*—Mr. Gilbert moved : "That it be referred to the Improvements Committee to report as to the cost of making an embankment on the south side of the Thames from Westminster Bridge to Blackfriars Bridge, and that they specially report on the following points—(a) on the desirability of retaining the whole of the property benefited by the improvement as the property of the council ; (b) on the desirability of reserving a part of the site for a large housing scheme ; and (c), after consultation with the Establishment Committee, on the advisability of reserving a site at the western end of the proposed embankment for a new council chamber and offices." As, however, the resolution found no seconder, the matter was dropped.

*Tenders.*—The following tenders were opened for the supply of gas engines for the Lots-road pumping station : Premier Gas Engine Company, Limited, £9,500 ; Campbell Gas Engine Company, Limited, £10,000 ; J. E. H. Andrews & Co., Limited, £10,300 ; Fielding & Platt, Limited, £10,450 ; J. Taylor & Sons, Limited, £10,520 ; and Crossley Brothers, Limited, £10,744.

### COURT OF COMMON COUNCIL.

The Lord Mayor presided on Thursday at the usual meeting of the whole body at the Guildhall. The City Lands Com-

mittee presented a report with reference to the throwing open to the public of the garden in the centre of Finsbury-circus. The committee recommended that the reference should be discharged, and in their report stated that the corporation had not exercised any right over the garden for many years past, and that the leaseholders objected to the garden being turned into an open space. One person having the "right of user" objecting to the opening of the garden could prevent the corporation from carrying out the proposal. Even if it were done, it would probably involve the compensation of various interests, while nothing could be done without an Act of Parliament. The members of the London Institution strongly objected to the proposition, believing that it would be highly detrimental to the institution and the objects for which it was established. Some discussion followed, in the course of which Mr. Morton moved, as an amendment, that the question should be referred to the Streets Committee to consider and report. Further discussion followed, Alderman Smallman suggesting that the court should take the present report as an answer to the reference to the committee, and that Mr. Morton should give notice of motion that the Streets Committee should consider the way in which the garden could be thrown open. This suggestion was accepted, and the amendment as altered adopted.—The court agreed to the expenditure of £530 in fitting improved dust-shoots to the dwellings in Corporation Buildings, Farringdon-road, to replace those condemned by the sanitary authorities. The court next proceeded to deal with the business of the Public Health Department, but no officers of the department being present (with the exception of Mr. H. M. Bates), the Lord Mayor adjourned the court, leaving the whole of the work of the department untouched.

### METROPOLITAN ASYLUMS BOARD.

The Metropolitan Asylums Board met on Saturday, at the County Hall, Spring-gardens, Sir E. H. Galsworthy, the chairman of the board, presiding. It was mentioned that the inquiry ordered by the Local Government Board with regard to the cost of the Brook Hospital had been held, and proposed that a sum of £101,830, which remained unsanctioned by the board, should be applied for. This was agreed to.—After some discussion the managers decided to adopt a resolution of the General Purposes Committee to the effect that a reference to the committee from the board on the the 5th inst. respecting the proposed establishment of a bacteriological laboratory for London should be discharged. It was pointed out that the reference had only been made after the London County Council had taken up the matter. It would be time enough for the board to take up the question if the county council decided to do nothing.

### VESTRIES AND DISTRICT BOARDS.

**Battersea.**—At a meeting of the vestry on Wednesday, the Finance Committee reported that the London County Council had offered to lend £1,546 at 3½ per cent. for the construction of public conveniences in the shrubberies in Battersea Park. As the rate of interest was in excess of that charged in the past, the committee had applied to the Public Works Loan Commissioners, who were prepared to advance the amount required at 2½ per cent. On the recommendation of the committee it was resolved to borrow the money from the commissioners.—The vestry appointed two delegates to represent them at the forthcoming conference to be held at the Islington Vestry Hall to consider the question of the reform of the local government of London.—The Cemetery Committee announced that they had considered the drawings and specification prepared by the surveyor, Mr. J. T. Pilditch, together with the bills of quantities by the quantity surveyor, for the erection of six cottages at the Morden cemetery. As it appeared that the cost, as estimated by the quantity surveyor, would amount to £2,025, or £585 in excess of the surveyor's approximate estimate, the committee recommended that the proposal to build the cottages should be abandoned. The recommendation was, however, referred back to the committee for further consideration.—The Works Committee submitted a statement showing the actual cost of carrying on by direct labour the extension of the central library, Lavender Hill, as compared with the estimate. According to this statement the total cost, including 7½ per cent. for establishment expenses, amounted to £2,159, being £94 in excess of the original estimate. The vestry decided to receive the report.—A letter was read from the London County Council stating, in reply to the vestry's communication relative to the erection of workmen's dwellings, that the council had adopted a recommendation in favour of vestries and district boards of works being empowered to adopt Part III. of the Housing of the Working Classes Act, 1890. The council added that the subject had been referred to the Parliamentary Committee to report upon the steps to be taken in the matter.—In reply to a question as to the position of the electric lighting scheme, the chairman of the Lighting Committee stated that the project was "on the move."—The vestry sealed contracts with Messrs. Adams & Co. for the supply of sanitary fittings for the new chalets in Victoria-circus, and with the Tees Scoriæ Brick Company for the supply of Tees scoriæ channelling setts.

**Greenwich.**—A meeting of this board was held recently with reference to a suggestion from the chief officer of the fire brigade that where a street lamp was within a few feet of a fire alarm it should be painted a bright red. The District Committee recommended that the county council be informed that the board were prepared to adopt the suggestion, and that such lamps be painted that colour accordingly. This was agreed to.

**Hampstead.**—At last week's meeting of the vestry the Free and Open Spaces Committee reported that they had viewed the Golder's Hill estate, towards the purchase of which as an extension of Hampstead Heath the vestry recently voted £10,000 ; that they had taken part in a joint conference with the Acquisition Committee ; and that, as a result of the conference, they recommended the vestry to forward the following recommendations to the London County Council : (1) That the estate should be dedicated absolutely to the use of the public for ever. (2) That the council should have power to enclose, or keep enclosed, the whole or any part of the estate, and to restrict by by-laws the use of such enclosed space by the public to the hours of daylight only. (3) That the council should take power to use the mansion, or any part thereof, for a museum, library, refreshment-rooms or any other purpose conducive to the instruction, amusement, health or convenience of the public. (4) That the Parks Committee of the council be asked to receive a deputation, consisting of the Tree and Open Spaces Committee of the vestry and of the Golder's Hill Estate Acquisition Committee, when these recommendations are considered. The recommendations were adopted.

**Lewisham.**—Last week, at a meeting of the district board of works, the Blackheath and Lewisham Local Committee reported that their attention had been called to the condition of the concrete wall forming the bank of the mill pond at Southend, next the roadway. It had been suggested that the roadway should be widened and improved by throwing into it the strip of land along the pond. The committee recommended that the plan submitted be approved and forwarded to the freeholder for his approval, and that he be asked to give up the ground necessary for widening the road in the manner proposed. The committee were of opinion that this improvement, if carried out, would be one to the cost of which the board would be able to ask the London County Council to contribute. The recommendation was adopted.—The Works Committee reported that they had considered the memorandum from the Chief Commissioner of Police referring to the difficulty in dealing with the congested traffic of public thoroughfares occasioned by the watering of the sides of the streets. The surveyor had reported on the memorandum, and the committee concurred in the opinion expressed by him that it did not apply to streets such as these in the Lewisham district, but rather to paved and asphalted streets in the more crowded parts of London. They recommended, and the board approved, therefore, that no action be taken in the matter.

**Limehouse.**—A letter has been received from the London County Council stating that the Improvements Committee could not see their way to recommend the council to incur so large an expenditure as £1,030 for the purpose of providing hydraulic machinery to work the Wapping swing bridge. The letter has been referred to the Works Committee for consideration.

**Paddington.**—The vestry resolved last week, on the recommendation of the Finance Committee, to contribute the sum of £500 towards the purchase of the Golder's Hill estate for the extension of Hampstead Heath.

**Westminster.**—Last week, at a special meeting of the vestry, it was resolved " that, in view of the very large increase in the price to be paid to the contractor for slopping and dusting, a small committee be formed to consider and report to the vestry as to the practicability and advisability of the vestry doing their own slopping and dusting."

# PROVINCIAL AND GREATER LONDON AUTHORITIES.
## COUNTY COUNCILS.

**Hertfordshire.**—The county council, at a meeting on Monday, decided to memorialise the Local Government Board complaining that serious injury had been done to the water supply of the county by the enormous quantity daily abstracted from it by the London water companies. Sir John Evans stated that the Chadwell spring had failed, and the great spring at Woolmers Park, which formerly discharged over 1,000,000 gallons a day, had gone dry, in addition to which other springs had totally failed or were greatly reduced in volume. The heads of rivers were lower down the valleys than they had ever been known before. Numerous wells on the highlands were completely dry, and the bore pipes in watercress-beds had ceased to discharge. The council also gave instructions for evidence to be collected as to the condition of the springs, rivers, and water supply generally, to enable them to secure protection.

**Middlesex.**—The General Purposes Committee of the county council, who have been considering the request of the syndicate which purchased Golder's Hill to give £1,000 towards the purchase price, have recommended that a grant of £500 be made. It was understood by the committee that

that would be sufficient, as the remaining £500 would be forthcoming from another source. These two sums will complete the £41,000 required.

**Somersetshire.**—At a meeting of the county council on the 18th inst. the Sanitary Committee reported that they had considered a further report from the Long Ashton Rural District Council with regard to the alleged pollution of the Long Ashton stream, and, in view of the unsatisfactory nature of such report, again recommended the council to direct that an independent report upon the state of the stream be made. The recommendation was adopted.

# MUNICIPAL CORPORATIONS.

**Bacup.**—On the recommendation of the General Works Committee the town council have decided to transfer their electric lighting order to a company.

**Batley.**—Local Government Board sanction has been received by the corporation to a loan of £15,500 for works of surface-water drainage.

**Birmingham.**—Sir Francis Marindin, Board of Trade inspector, recently visited the city for the purpose of making the septennial examination of the tramway lines. Among those who gave their assistance were Mr. T. Arnall (of the city surveyor's department) and Mr. H. Richardson (surveyor to the Aston Urban District Council), who met the party at the borough boundaries.

**Bournemouth.**—At the last meeting of the town council it was proposed to apply for powers, under the Light Railway Act, to lay down and work tramways in the borough. The proposal was, however, defeated.

**Brighton.**—The town, it is stated, was plunged into darkness on Thursday night owing to the temporary failure of the electric light. Just after 9 o'clock the current failed, and caused considerable inconvenience in the central thoroughfares, in business establishments, and in the main streets generally. Darkness reigned for twenty minutes, and there was much excitement in the theatres and music halls.

**Bristol.**—The city council have declined to proceed with the dock extension at Avonmouth. They, however, have instructed the Docks Committee to report within three months on the cost of docksising the river Avon and making provision for the largest class of steamers afloat. The cost of the extension at Avonmouth hitherto has been reckoned at £1,500,000 and of docksisation at £2,000,000.

**Bury.**—At a recent meeting of the town council the Health Committee reported that the abattoirs Sub-Committee had inspected the Birmingham abattoirs, and as a result had instructed Mr. Neill to draw up sketch plans ; these plans had been submitted to a subsequent meeting of the sub-committee, the estimate for abattoirs, refrigerators and all necessary plant amounting to £14,000. The Health Committee recommended the council to adopt the principle of such plans and to instruct Mr. Neill to prepare the necessary working drawings and specifications. The recommendation was adopted.

**Eccles.**—On Saturday Major-General H. D. Crozier, R.E., inspector to the Local Government Board, opened an inquiry into an application of the town council for sanction to borrow £1,031 for works of private street improvements in Eccles and Patricroft. There was no opposition.

**Hastings.**—A Local Government Board inquiry was held on the 18th inst. into an application of the corporation to borrow a sum of £58,000 for the purpose of acquiring the undertaking of the Hastings Electric Light Company. The proceedings occupied a considerable time.

**Ipswich.**—The sanction of the Local Government Board has been received to the borrowing by the corporation of £4,000 for the construction of an overflow sewer from Hyde Park-corner to Constantine-road, and for the construction of the exteriors of sewers in Belstead-road and Branford-road. The plans for the works have been prepared by Mr. E. Buckham, the borough surveyor.

**Kidderminster.**—The seal of the council has been fixed to the agreement with the British Electric Traction Company for the sale of the Electric Lighting Order, 1891, to that company.

**Leamington.**—It was resolved, at a recent special meeting of the town council, to apply to the Board of Trade for a provisional order under the Electric Lighting Acts, 1882 and 1888, to authorise the council to supply electricity for public and private purposes within the borough.

**Liverpool.**—Since the Liverpool tramways were taken over by the corporation the question of electric traction has occupied the attention of the Tramways Committee. Already a new line on the overhead electric trolley system has been constructed, connecting the city with one of the southern suburbs, and at their next meeting the city council will be asked to authorise a scheme recommended by the city engineer, by which it is proposed to apply the system of electric traction to several of the existing routes, as well as to some short new lines about to be constructed.

**Loughborough.**—At a special meeting, held last week, the town council decided to promote a Bill in the next session of Parliament to authorise the corporation to purchase and acquire, either by agreement or compulsorily, the undertaking of the Loughborough Gas Company; to authorise the corporation to generate and supply electricity for public and private lighting purposes and for motive power, and to establish the necessary undertaking aud works for that purpose ; to enable the corporation to acquire land, either by agreement or compulsorily, and to borrow moneys for the purposes of their proposed gas and electric undertakings; to confer upon the corporation further powers with reference to streets, buildings, sewers, common lodging-houses, infectious diseases and other sanitary matters. They also decided to oppose any Bill promoted by the gas company for increased borrowing powers.

**Lymington.**—A special committee has been appointed by the town council to consider the question of the purchase of the gasworks.

**Manchester.**—A letter has been received from the Local Government Board granting authority for the borrowing of £110,570 for the purpose of sewerage and sewage disposal. This is a part of £170,000 spent by the old Rivers Committee, for which borrowing powers had not previously been obtained.

**Middleton.**—It has been intimated to the corporation that the Light Railway Commissioners have reported to the Board of Trade in favour of a proposal to construct tramways from Cheetham Hill through Rodes, Middleton and Castleton to Rochdale and through Chadderton to Oldham. The corporation intend to oppose the scheme.

**Monmouth.**—A special meeting of the town council was held recently to meet Mr. Graham Harris, the engineer for the sewage disposal and electric lighting works. After a discussion on the sewage disposal scheme notice was given by the chairman of the Drainage and Electric Lighting Committee to rescind the resolution in favour of the septic tank system, so as to leave the council open to adopt any other system.

**Nelson.**—On Friday an inquiry was conducted by Mr. H. H. Law, representing the Local Government Board, in reference to an application of the town council for sanction to a loan of £6,500 for the laying-out of an extension to Victoria Park.

**Southampton.**—The question of substituting electric traction for the horse-power now employed on the tramway undertaking is being considered by the corporation.—The borough engineer has prepared a report recommending the ventilation of certain sewers, at an estimated cost of £9,800.

**Warrington.**—The Water Committee on Tuesday stated that they had received the report of Mr. James Mansergh on proposals of the corporation to obtain an increased supply of water for both domestic and manufacturing purposes, aud Mr. Mansergh having advised the construction of a new reservoir in the southern part of the district of supply, and an extension of the works at Winwick, it was resolved that the town clerk be instructed to obtain the necessary powers for the construction of the proposed works.

**Wolverhampton.**—During the past week a deputation of the Tramways Committee of the corporation have been visiting Glasgow, Leeds, Halifax and other towns in order to obtain the latest information respecting municipal tramways worked on the electric overhead system.

## URBAN DISTRICT COUNCILS.

**Abercarn.**—A communication has been received from the Local Government Board sanctioning the borrowing by the district council of £7,833 for water improvements.

**Barry.**—On Friday Mr. E. A. Sandford Fawcett, an inspector of the Local Government Board, conducted an inquiry into an application of the urban district council for sanction to borrow two sums of £4,210 and £6,235 respectively for carrying out public improvement works in the district. No objection was raised to the applications.

**Bexhill.**—On the 19th inst., at the town hall, a Local Government Board inquiry was held by Mr. Frederick H. Tulloch, with reference to a proposed loan of £14,719 for works of private street improvement and £910 for works of public street improvement by the council. Mr. Ball, the surveyor, was present.

**Bexley Heath.**—The urban district council have instructed their surveyor to prepare a scheme to deal with the sewage of the low-lying portion of the district.

**Bonsall.**—Colonel A. T. Hopper, R.E., on Friday held an inquiry, on behalf of the Local Government Board, respecting an application of the district council for power to borrow £700 for the purposes of extending and improving the water supply of the district.

**Burnham.** — At a meeting of the council on Friday evening it was unanimously resolved to extend the proposal of the new sea front from the pier further northwards. This scheme involving a further outlay of £2,000, making in all £9,000, it was decided to petition the Local Government Board to grant the extended loan without further public inquiry. An offer of the Somerset Drainage Commissioners, confirming their committee's proposal of £60 per annum for thirty years and £30 afterwards towards maintaining the new sea front, was received and unanimously adopted.

**Cowes, I.W.**—The district council having applied to the Local Government Board for sanction to borrow £47,471 for the purpose of the gas undertaking, an inquiry was recently

held at the town hall, before Mr. F. H. Tulloch, M.I.C.E., an inspector of the board.

**Fleetwood.**—The urban district council have decided to apply to the Local Government Board for sanction to borrow over £3,000 for the purpose of erecting a pavilion on the mount facing the sea. The main purpose of the structure is to find amusement for the visitors who come on the electric tramway from Blackpool, 500,000 having come in two months this year, while it is expected when the full service of cars is completed that over 1,500,000 will come next summer. The pavilion will provide shelter for over 1,000 persons.

**Friern Barnet.**—Mr. J. Reynolds, the surveyor, at a recent meeting of the district council submitted plans and estimates for sewering Wetherill-road, which were approved, and the clerk was instructed to apply to the Local Government Board for sanction to borrow the necessary amount to carry out the work. The surveyor was also directed to prepare plans and estimates for re-sewering Holly Park-road.

**Hornsey.**—On Thursday Mr. Robert H. Bicknell, a local Government Board inspector, held an inquiry into an application of the council for sanction to borrow £1,876 for works of sewerage and surface-water drainage, £1,464 for street improvements, and £580 for works of paving. The inspector promised to review the evidence given and report to the Local Government Board as speedily as possible. The inquiry then terminated, there having been no opposition whatever, nor, indeed, were any of the ratepayers other than officials present.

**Idle.**—Mr. R. H. Bicknell recently held an inquiry, on behalf of the Local Government Board, with respect to an application of the district council for permission to borrow £700 for the purpose of sewerage and sewage disposal, and for consent to certain deviations from the scheme sanctioned by the Local Government Board in 1894. Among those present was Mr. J. Woodhead, of Messrs. W. B. Woodhead & Sons, engineers for the scheme. The grounds of the application, as stated by the clerk, were that in 1894 the Local Government Board sanctioned a loan of £1,800 for the purposes of sewage disposal for the Thackley portion of the district. The site, which had been taken under compulsory powers conferred on the council by a provisional order, formed the subject of an arbitration, and the arbitrator fixed the price which the council should pay for the land at £1,906. To this would have to be added legal charges on both sides, and it was estimated that the total cost of the land when conveyed to the council would be £2,500, or some £700 more than the amount previously sanctioned. The suggested deviations were considered by the inspector from the plan submitted, and one or two minor alterations were made. There was no opposition to the application, and at the conclusion of the inquiry the inspector viewed the district concerned.

**Mexborough.**—The council have been much troubled with the system of air injectors put down some ten years ago, and have since, under pressure from the West Riding Rivers Board, had to find a reply for the large quantity of sewage running into the Don. The Local Government Board have now sanctioned the scheme of the surveyor, Mr. G. Fenwick Carter, and the work will soon be in hand. The present plant of 350-gallon ejectors and compressors will be removed and a gravitation main of 5-ft. 6-in. egg-shaped sewer laid down to the pumping station (about 350 yards in length). This will also hold the night flow, and the sewage will then be lifted by direct-action pumping engines, treated by aluminoferric, and filtered by tanks on the biological system. The township has an estimated population of 10,000, the farm consists of 3 acres, and the area of the new filter-beds will be about one-quarter of an acre. The estimated cost of the alterations will be about £3,000.

**Rawmarsh.**—On Saturday, the 15th inst., a new public market which has been constructed by the district council was formally opened. The market is situated on a plot of land adjacent to the council offices, plenty of room being allowed for any future extensions. The laying-out, &c., of the market cost about £185.

**Romford.**—The district council have accepted a tender for the erection of public baths, at a cost of £5,682.

**South Hornsey.**—At last week's meeting of the district council the chairman gave notice that at the next meeting he would move that a committee be appointed to consider the advisability of the adoption of the Baths and Wash-Houses Act.

**Thornton.**—Mr. H. L. Law, one of the Local Government Board inspectors, held an inquiry at the council offices on Thursday in regard to a proposal of the council to borrow a sum of £2,500, required for the carrying out of sewerage and street improvement works. The proceedings were of a formal character. Evidence as to the details of the work was given, and the inspector afterwards visited the sites of the proposed improvements.

**Stowmarket.**—The work of laying the sewerage for the town has commenced in earnest. The contractor, under the supervision of Mr. Henry Richards, the resident engineer, began at the recently-built pumping station, near the gasworks. The main sewer has to cross the river Gipping, and possibly this will be the most difficult portion of the work. The fixing of the large cast-iron tubes, each being over 2 ft.

in diameter, measuring about 14 ft., and weighing upwards of 1 ton each, under the bed of the river has been accomplished, notwithstanding the large quantity of water and the looseness of the soil.

**Swadlincote.**—The district council propose to obtain sanction to a loan of £42,900 for the purchase of the gasworks and the carrying out of necessary improvements. The improvements include the connection of the gasworks with the Midland Railway by means of a siding, at a cost not exceeding £190, and the extension of the gas mains to Stanton and Castle Gresley.

**Wallasey.**—At a special meeting of the district council, held last week, it was decided to promote a Bill for taking over the tramways and working them by electricity, extending the promenade and widening roadways.—A public meeting of ratepayers to sanction the promotion of the Bill was afterwards held, and an animated discussion took place, dwellers in Wallasey township objecting that their district was neglected while other parts were disproportionately improved. On a vote being taken, the chairman declared that the result was close, but that the resolution approving the Bill was carried. Mr. R. W. Preston then demanded a poll of the district, which will be taken.

**Yeovil.**—The town council have appointed their surveyor, Mr. W. K. L. Armytage, engineer for the sewage disposal scheme about to be undertaken by them. The principle to be adopted is the septic tank system, the corporation having satisfied themselves of its efficiency after two years' working of the trial installation put down in September, 1896, under the surveyor's supervision, in conjunction with the Septic Tank Syndicate.

## RURAL DISTRICT COUNCILS.

**Eastry.**—At a recent meeting of the council it was stated that the Local Government Board had sanctioned a loan of £1,900 for the purpose of providing a water supply.

**Hayfield.**—Local Government Board sanction has been received to a loan of £1,200 for the completion of the sewerage works.

**Penistone.**—At a meeting of the district council on Thursday a letter was read from the Local Government Board declining to modify their requirements in regard to the proposed scheme of sewage for Langsett. The clerk reported that the Sheffield Corporation would in all probability devise a less expensive scheme, which would meet the requirements until the waterworks were completed.

**St. Thomas.**—Members of public bodies, surveyors to councils and others have been anticipating with some degree of interest a case which it was announced would have been tried at the Devonshire Quarter Sessions at Exeter on Tuesday of last week. It would appear that the council, acting upon the reports of their surveyor from time to time, called the attention of Mr. Wm. Gibson, of Exeter, to the excessive wear and tear of their roads caused by his traction engines, particularly in the conveyance of large quantities of stone hewn from quarries west of Exeter. A good deal of correspondence ensued between the clerk to the council (Mr. Arthur Ward) and the solicitors to Mr. Gibson (Messrs. Ford, Harris & Ford, Exeter), which culminated in an offer by the latter of a large quantity of stone, free and delivered without charge to any part of the council's district, in satisfaction of all claims against him up to the date of delivery. The offer was made without prejudice. It came before a meeting of the council on September 2nd. As the value of the stone offered was considerably below the claim preferred by the council against Mr. Gibson, this proposed compromise was rejected, and the council authorised their clerk to commence proceedings against the owner of the engines for the recovery of the amount of their bill. The tribunal for such suit is the court of quarter sessions, where it was stated the action would be heard. As the result of further negotiations between the parties, however, the matter is understood to have been arranged.

**Tarvin, Cheshire.**—An inquiry was on Thursday held by Colonel A. G. Durnford, R.E., on behalf of the Local Government Board, concerning an application of the council for sanction to borrow a sum of £4,500 for the purpose of providing a water supply for the townships of Tiverton, Tilston, Fearnall and Beeston. The wells in these villages are few and far between and yield a most scanty supply, many cottagers being dependent upon dip wells, which, of course, are exceedingly liable to pollution. Mr. Birch Killon, of Manchester, in explaining the scheme he had prepared, said that 20,000 gallons per day could be raised by the proposed works going three days a week. This would mean approximately about 20 gallons daily per inhabitant. If one well (already bored) proved insufficient, the scheme provided for the sinking of another near the present one.

## SCOTLAND AND IRELAND.

**Alloa.**—On the 13th inst. the provost, magistrates and commissioners made their annual inspection of Gartmorn waterworks. The party, beginning with the old service supply works, inspected in succession the settling ponds, filters, hydraulic pumps, store-houses and reservoirs in connection with both systems, afterwards proceeding by way of the upper aqueduct as far as Forestmill, where lunch was served. The visitors found everything in good working order, and were gratified to find that an abundant supply of water was passing from the upper lade into the old dam.

**Clydebank.**—The proposed new municipal buildings, as shown by the amended plans prepared by Mr. Miller, the architect of the 1901 Exhibition buildings, are a palatial pile, and will cost, it is estimated, £27,000, which is £9,000 more than that of the previous plans drawn up by him. The public hall, especially, is remodelled on larger lines, and will now accommodate from 1,500 to 2,000 persons.

**Edinburgh.**—Some time ago the town council resolved to erect a new bridge over the Water of Leith at Bonnington. Negotiations were afterwards opened with the Leith Corporation, a portion of the bridge being in that burgh, and a deputation from Edinburgh had an interview with the Leith Town Council on the subject. The Leith representatives acquiesced in the Edinburgh proposals. The only point which now remains to be adjusted is the proportion of cost which each municipality should be asked to bear. The proposals, which involve an expenditure of over £5,000, include the widening and levelling of the roadway up to the railway station.

**Glasgow.**—The Gas Committee of the corporation have at present under consideration the question of extending the gasworks of the city. Mr. W. Foulis, the engineer, recommends the purchase of ground, extending to about 110 acres, Monkland canal and the Caledonian railway branch line, for the erection of works capable of manufacturing 40,000,000 cubic feet per day, thus enabling the corporation to close the Dalmarnock works, which at present produce only 6,000,000 cubic feet per day.—The Telephone Committee have agreed, in view of the proposed municipal installation, to erect as an experiment an automatic switchboard in the municipal buildings for trial. The system is in use in one or two cities in America. Its object is to dispense with the services of the telephone girls, the subscribers, by aid of this device, making their own connections.

**Limerick.**—The Board of Works have intimated to the corporation that the Treasury are now prepared to grant the application of the corporation for sanction to a loan of £6,000, with which it is proposed to carry out improvements in Irishtown and Englishtown. A provisional order authorising the scheme under the Housing of the Working Classes Act, 1890, has already been obtained.

**Perth.**—The Lord Provost recently inaugurated the new manure depot at Friarton, new stables and a culvert, by means of which a lade and the sewage of the general prison and the Craigie district are conveyed direct to the river, leaving a valuable piece of ground to be used for other purposes. The works have been carried out at a cost of upwards of £8,400.—At the last quarterly meeting of the Central District Committee of this authority it was remitted to the Special Water Committee of Comrie to instruct Mr. Copeland, C.E., Glasgow, to prepare working plans and specifications and to obtain estimates for the proposed works. Mr. Copeland estimated the total expenditure at £1,500, when it was resolved to borrow the sum of £1,600.

**Port Glasgow.**—At last week's meeting of the town council it was agreed to carry out improvements at the baths, at a cost of £150. It is proposed to extend the dressing-room accommodation and to erect a gymnasium.

## Personal.

Birstall Urban District Council have increased the salary of their surveyor, Mr. John I. Longden.

Portsmouth Town Council have decided to insure the whole of their electrical staff against accidents.

The Erdington Urban District Council have increased the salary of their surveyor by £100 per annum.

Mr. R. E. Hughes, surveyor to the Prestatyn Urban District Council, has submitted his resignation to that authority.

The salary of Mr. A. Wyllie, borough electrical engineer of Walsall, has been raised from £200 to £300 per annum.

The Urban District Council of Mold, Flintshire, have accepted the resignation of Mr. John Rowlands, engineer at their sewage farm.

Mr. C. H. Robinson, of Oldham, has been appointed an assistant at the central electric lighting station of the Dewsbury Town Council.

Mr. Sidney R. Smith, of Manchester, has been appointed to the position of engineering assistant under the Ilfracombe Urban District Council.

Mr. H. T. Hughes, Tilston, Malpas, has been appointed district road surveyor to the Chapel-en-le-Frith district of the Derbyshire County Council.

Mr. David Rosser, Newbiggin, has been appointed, from a number of applications, to the post of surveyor to the Newbiggin Urban District Council.

The death has occurred, at the early age of thirty-eight, of Mr. James Young, of the well-known firm of James Young & Son, railway and public works contractors.

Messrs. Lomax & Lomax, of Westminster and Manchester, have received instructions to report upon the best means of disposing of the sewage of Mödling, Vienna.

Mr. Peers, Deansgate, Manchester, has been appointed electrical engineer to the Buckley Urban District Council. There were thirty-four applications for the position.

Mr. Streether, of Desborough, Derbyshire, has been appointed surveyor and inspector of nuisances to the Winton Urban District Council, at a salary of £140 per annum.

Mr. A. Colson, gas and electrical engineer to the Leicester Corporation, recently opened the winter session of the Leicester Literary and Philosophical Society with a lecture on "Electricity."

Mr. William Farnham, of the surveyor's department of the Vestry of St. Margaret and St. John, Westminster, has been appointed to the post of surveyor to the Milton-next-Sittingbourne Urban District Council.

The value of the estate of Dr. John Hopkinson, F.R.S., of "Holmwood," Wimbledon, and 26 Victoria-street, S.W., electrical engineer, who was killed on the Alps on the 27th August, has been sworn at £74,672.

On Friday, at a special meeting of the Pickering Rural District Council, Mr. J. W. Plews, who holds the position of surveyor to the Sherburn Rural District Council, was elected to a similar post under the first-named body.

The death has taken place of Mr. Philip Bracegirdle, the oldest servant of the Wilmslow Urban District Council. The deceased gentleman had been surveyor to the council for some twenty years, and was well known in all parts of the country.

Last week's business of the Merthyr Urban District Council included the appointment of an assistant surveyor. Three gentlemen, selected at a previous meeting, appeared, and the voting resulted in the election of Mr. Richard Abraham, of Cefn. The salary is £150 per annum.

The Building Clauses Committee of the Leeds Corporation have recommended the appointment of Mr. William Towers for the position of chief inspector of buildings, a post rendered vacant by the death of Mr. David Hainsworth. Mr. Towers has for twenty-two years acted as Mr. Hainworth's assistant.

Mr. W. J. Dibdin was on Wednesday examined before the Royal Commission on Sewage Disposal sitting in Great George-street, Westminster. The commissioners were expected to visit the Sutton works this week, with a view to seeing the operations of the bacterial system in use at the sewage farm.

Major-General Phipps Carey, chief engineering inspector to the Local Government Board, and Mr. Rienzi Walton, deputy chief engineering inspector of the Local Government Board, visited Sutton recently to inspect the sewage works and examine the system of sewage purification adopted there. They were shown over the works by Mr. W. J. Dibdin, chairman of the council, and the surveyor, Mr. Chambers Smith, and both inspectors seemed highly pleased with the system and the result obtained. A full report of an interesting Local Government Board inquiry at Sutton is unavoidably held over, but will appear in our next issue.

At the last meeting of the Tendring Rural District Council the clerk reported that three of the six candidates selected by the Highways Committee for the appointment of highway surveyor were in attendance—namely, Mr. W. Coles, surveyor to the Stratford-on-Aven Rural District Council; Mr. G. F. Taylor, assistant surveyor in the Leeds Corporation Highway Department; and Mr. J. Garratt, Fakenham, surveyor of main roads under the Norfolk County Council. Two other candidates had written declining the invitation to attend on finding that the salary was inclusive of the keep of a horse. The candidates present having each been before the council, Mr. Coles was elected to the position.

The Baths Committee reported, at the meeting of the St. Pancras Vestry on Wednesday, that they had considered a letter from Mr. E. A. Gruning, vice-president of the Royal Institute of British Architects, nominating, on behalf of the president, three gentlemen for the vestry to select one for the appointment of assessor in respect of designs for the new baths. The committee pointed out that the assessor to be appointed should have practical experience in the planning and carrying out of public baths and wash-houses, and the names of the gentlemen submitted, although architects of eminence, did not appear to them to possess this qualification. The president was asked to nominate three gentlemen *competent to advise on the subject of baths architecture*, and the committee thought it was possible that the vice-president may have misconstrued the meaning which was intended to be conveyed by these words. In these circumstances the committee had instructed that a further communication should be addressed, thanking him for his letter and asking, in view of the probable misconception of the meaning of the words used, whether he would desire to reconsider his reply.

The council of the Institution of Civil Engineers have made the following awards out of the trust funds at their disposal for the purpose for original papers dealt with during the year 1897-98. The formal presentation will take place at the institution on Tuesday, November 1st, at 8 p.m.: Telford medals and premiums—A. H. Preece (London) and H. C. Stanley (Brisbane, Queensland); Watt medals and premiums—H. L. Callendar, M.A., F.R.S. (London), and J. T. Nicolson (Montreal, Canada); George Stephenson medals and premiums—Whiteley Eliot (Plymouth), W. O. E. Meade-King (London), and W. P. Marshall (Birmingham); the Crampton prize—E. W. Anderson (Erith); Telford premiums—L. B. Atkinson (Cardiff), Henry Fowler (Horwich), W. L. Strange (Bombay), F. J. Waring, C.M.G. (London), D. W. Brunton (Denver, U.S.A.), Wilfred Airy, M.A. (London), E. M. Bryant, B.SC. (Newcastle-on-Tyne), D. B. Butler (London), and H. V. Champion (Victoria); the James Forrest medal—W. L. Brown, M.SC. (London); Miller prizes—C. E. Wolff, B.SC. (Derby), A. D. Keighwin (Ashford), Harrold Williams (Kingston), J. T. Morris (London), E. O. Adams (Birmingham), H. O. Enrich (Bradford), B. K. Adams (Colombo), A. B. E. Blackburn (Wednesbury), Thomas Carter (Newcastle), P. F. Storey (Manchester), D. E. Lloyd-Davies (Bewdley) and Wilfred Hall, B.A. (Corbridge-on-Tyne).

As intimated in last week's issue of THE SURVEYOR, several of Mr. G. B. Laffan's professional friends and neighbours entertained him to dinner at the Trocadero Restaurant on Saturday, in order to offer their congratulations and wish him success previous to his departure to take up the duties of his new appointment as engineer to the Pietermaritzburg Corporation. Mr. O. Claude Robson, president of the Association of Municipal and County Engineers, occupied the chair, and Mr. W. Weaver, the vice-chair. In addition to the guest of the evening, there were also present Messrs. C. Jones and A. M. Fowler (past-presidents), C. Botterill (Fulham), J. H. Brierley (Richmond), C. H. Cooper (Wimbledon), W. Fairley (Mortlake), S. G. Gamble (Metropolitan Fire Brigade), M. Hainsworth (Teddington), J. Kemp (Hampton), E. J. Lovegrove (Hornsey), G. B. Tomes (Barnes) and F. Summer (Bermondsey). Between thirty and forty telegrams and letters were received from brother surveyors, the editor of THE SURVEYOR and other friends expressing regret at their inability to be present, and conveying their best wishes to Mr. Laffan. In a particularly happy speech the chairman proposed the principal toast of the evening, in the course of which he referred in eulogistic terms to Mr. Laffan's past services as hon. district secretary for the Home Counties. In so doing he paid a high tribute to Mr. Laffan's professional abilities, which had at all times been freely placed at the disposal of the association and his professional brethren, and of behalf of those present offered Mr. Laffan hearty congratulations, and wished him God-speed, health and happiness in his new home. Mr. Laffan, in replying, desired to assure not only those present, but also many other friends who had written him in such kind terms, of his sincere appreciation of their good wishes and the kindly feeling evinced towards him that evening, and which he should never forget, and stated that he would endeavour to further the interests of the association and try to bring his brother engineers in South Africa into closer touch with those in the old country. The usual votes of thanks, &c., terminated a most successful and enjoyable function.

## CLARE MARKET RE-HOUSING AND IMPROVEMENT SCHEME.

### REPORT TO THE LONDON COUNTY COUNCIL.

In connection with the Clare Market re-housing scheme, now in progress, and with the proposed construction of a new street from Holborn to the Strand, in respect of which application is to be made to Parliament in the next session, the Housing of the Working Classes and Improvements Committees of the London County Council have drafted a joint report relative to the question of obtaining sites for re-housing purposes in the immediate vicinity of the two schemes.

The report states that in carrying into effect the first-named scheme about 3,038 persons will be displaced. Of this number it is proposed to make provision on the area for 750 persons, and for 1,500 on the Millbank site, leaving 788 unprovided for. By the formation of the new street about 3,030 persons, including women and children, will also be displaced, and the proposal to be made to Parliament is that all the persons who are dependent on fixed employment in the neighbourhood should be re-housed within about a mile of their residences, and that adequate provision should be made for the remainder of the persons to be displaced. This would mean that 1,815 persons would have to be accommodated within about a mile of the improvement.

Learning that land in the neighbourhood of Drury-lane was vacant, the report states, the committees entered into negotiations with the owner, the Duke of Bedford, with the result that he expressed his willingness to sell two sites in Drury-lane, and also a larger site fronting Herbrand-street, near Woburn-place. The duke, however, stipulated, as one of the conditions of the sale, that the council should undertake, in the event of their obtaining and exercising powers to construct the new street, to convey to him a strip of land which will front a portion of the western born of the crescent which it is proposed to form at the southern end of the main street. This is to enable the duke to develop the adjoining land, of which he is the owner. With regard to this stipulation of the duke, the committees consider that it may well be accepted. They therefore strongly advise the acquisition of the three sites, such acquisition to be effected under Part III. of the Housing of the Working Classes Act, 1890. If this be done accommodation can be provided for 180 persons on the site in Drury-lane, adjoining Drury-lane Theatre, for 360 persons upon the other site in Drury-lane, and for 460 persons upon the site in Herbrand-street, making a total of 1,000 persons on the three sites. This will enable the council to accommodate on the Clare Market area a large number of the persons displaced by the formation of the new street from Holborn to the Strand. In the event of the council failing to obtain Parliamentary powers for the new street (a contingency which the committees think it is hardly necessary to contemplate) the cost of the three sites may be recouped, as an amendment of the Clare Market scheme may be sought to enable the council to sell land on the Clare Market area, which but for the acquisition of the three sites would have been used for housing purposes. Failing this, the additional accommodation for re-housing can, with much advantage, be utilised in connection with other clearance schemes where the council are required to make provision within a certain distance from the scheme. The price asked for the three sites (£118,740) is, in the opinion of the committees, perfectly reasonable.

In concluding the report, the committees state: "It will be observed that one of the conditions of sale is that the three sites shall be purchased by the council by November 1, 1898, or as soon as practicable thereafter, whilst the other proposals are made subject to the council obtaining and exercising powers to form the new street from Holborn to the Strand. We have thought it right, before reporting to the council, to take the opinion of the solicitor on the question whether the council have full statutory powers to enter into the complete arrangement with the duke. The solicitor advises that the council at present possess full statutory powers, and we have ascertained that there is sufficient financial provision under the vote made in connection with re-housing persons of the working classes to enable the purchase of the three sites to be at once effected. Having regard to the favourable character of the proposals and to the expressed desire of the council to do all within their power to assist the poor persons of the labouring class now housed under such unhealthy conditions in the district in question, we have no hesitation in strongly advising the council to complete the arrangement with the duke."

At the end of the report are the formal resolutions embodying the above suggestions of the committees.

---

**Dorchester.**—The town council last week adopted a new scheme of sewerage and sewage disposal for the town. The council have decided not to adopt the Exeter septic system, but the sewage will be chemically treated at the outfall. A loan of £16,000 to cover the entire cost will be at once applied for. The council also decided to promote a Bill in Parliament for the compulsory purchase of the undertaking of the Dorchester Gas Company.

## THE BROOK HOSPITAL.

### CONCLUSION OF THE INQUIRY.

The Local Government Board inquiry into the circumstances under which the cost of the **Brook** Hospital largely exceeded the estimates has been concluded. A report of the previous sittings appeared in our last issue.

Mr. Aldwinckle, who was further examined, produced a further list of "extras," including one of £363 for fire insurance. This, he said, was an item in excess, because the work was stopped on account of the severity of the weather, and two instalments of insurance had to be paid instead of one. The inspector said he could not understand how it was that the sum was paid to the contractors without the board knowing what it was for.

Mr. T. D. Mann, clerk to the board, said the managers were bound to pay the amounts certified for by the architect. The inspector replied that it was the duty of the board to inquire of the architect what the sums were for. No one could justify a public body placing the expenditure of public money in the hands of one individual. There was a duty resting with the board to see what the certificates were granted for. Mr. Mann said that would imply suspicion of the architect. The inspector replied that all public bodies should have suspicion; they should not accept anybody's statement without proof.

Mr. Monson, one of the managers, said the inspector had raised one of the most important questions in connection with the proceedings of the board. Neither on the Finance nor on the Works Committee could he get any details of the accounts.

Mr. Brown, who was the chairman of the Brook Hospital Committee at the time of the construction of the building, stated that certain small items were authorised by himself, in company with other members of the committee, when going over the building, and he was ready to accept full responsibility for everything he did.

Mr. E. White, chairman of the special committee of investigation, said the whole of the extras, with trifling exceptions, would have been included in the specification if the board had not built the hospital so hurriedly. The board should be protected by a clause in the contracts to the effect that no extras would be paid for unless countersigned by the clerk. The architect should not have the power of spending the money of the ratepayers without the sanction of those who represented them. In this case the architect very nearly had *carte blanche*. With regard to the £19,000 expenditure upon the foundations, it had to be remembered that enormous quantities of concrete were used, and some of the blocks were 30 ft. by 20 ft. The hospital as completed was, however, a first-class one.

Mr. Brown also addressed the inspector, alluding especially to the difficulties of the site, and to the fact that the whole scheme for the hospital was prepared in three weeks. He added that the ultimate amount paid was in excess of the various contracts by about £50,000. He thought it fair to the architect to say that very few things which he ordered could be called unnecessary.

The inquiry was concluded, and the inspector said he would make his report to the Local Government Board.

## ROYAL COMMISSION ON SEWAGE DISPOSAL.

The Earl of Iddesleigh, in a circular letter to the Press, states that it has been brought to the notice of the Royal Commission on Sewage Disposal that there is a tendency on the part of some manufacturers and local authorities to postpone the carrying out of works for the purification of trade refuse and sewage until the commission have issued their report, his lordship thinks it desirable to state that a considerable time, perhaps even some years, must elapse before the commission can arrive at any final conclusions on a subject which necessarily involves detailed and prolonged scientific investigation. Any such postponement, he adds, would be viewed by the commission with the gravest concern.

## PROPOSED PIER FOR LYNMOUTH.

We understand that a provisional order is to be sought in the next session of Parliament for the construction of a pier at Lynmouth, from plans prepared by Mr. T. Milward. The scheme provides that a pier (a screw-pile one) shall run out from the eastward—at Blacklands, near the Manor house—upwards of 1,000 ft., and the end will be of double-face construction, for the convenience of steamer traffic up and down the channel. At the end of the pier will be a band-stand and pavilion, and it is also intended to erect a few shops as well. Communication with the pier will be by a 16-ft. wide roadway, which will come out at the Countisbury-road, a short distance from the Torrs hotel. The cost will be about £25,000.

**Swindon.**—On the 18th inst. Mr. G. W. Willcocks held an inquiry, on behalf of the Local Government Board, into an application of the Swindon Water Board for power to borrow £2,500 for an extension of mains at Wroughton and for other works.

## THE SURVEYORS' INSTITUTION.

### Ordinary General Meeting.

The first ordinary general meeting of the session 1898-99 will be held at the temporary premises of the institution on Monday, November 14th, when the president, Mr. Robert Vigers, will deliver an opening address. The chair will be taken at 8 o'clock.

### Students' Preliminary Examination, 1899.

Those proposing to enter their names for the students' preliminary examination, to be held on the 18th and 19th of January next, must intimate their intention to the secretary before the last day of November. It is proposed to examine candidates from the counties of Lancashire, Cheshire, Yorkshire, Durham, Cumberland, Westmoreland and Northumberland at Manchester. Candidates from other counties in England and Wales will be examined in London. Irish candidates will be examined in Dublin.

### Professional Examinations, 1899.

Students eligible for the proficiency examinations (which will commence on the 20th of March next) must give notice of the sub-division (Table A of Rules) in which they elect to be examined, not later than the 31st inst. Examinations qualifying for the classes of "Professional Associates" and "Fellows" will also commence on the 20th of March next. Names of applicants for these latter examinations to be sent in before the 31st inst. All particulars as to days, subjects and course of examination will be forwarded on application to the secretary. English candidates for the professional examinations will be examined in London. Irish candidates will be examined in Dublin.

### Proposed Special-Certificate Examinations (For Members), 1899.

Notice is also given that the next special-certificate examinations in forestry, sanitary science and land surveying and levelling are proposed to be held on Tuesday, Wednesday and Thursday, the 13th, 14th and 15th of June. Particulars of these examinations can be obtained from the secretary.

### Junior Meetings.

The first of four meetings of examinees and students authorised (subject to certain conditions) by the council to be held during the present session will take place at the temporary premises of the institution on Monday, the 21st November, 1898, the chair to be taken at 7 o'clock. All inquiries with reference to the junior meetings should be addressed to Mr. A. Norman Garrard, 8 Frederick's-place, Old Jewry, E.C.

## ASSOCIATION OF MUNICIPAL CORPORATIONS.

Sir A. K. Rollit, M.P., presided, on Wednesday of last week, at the autumn general meeting of the Association of Municipal Corporations, hold at the Westminster Palace Hotel. There was a large attendance, and among those present were the Lord Mayors of Manchester and Sheffield, and the Mayor of Nottingham.

Following an address by the president,

The Mayor of Nottingham moved : " That this association affirms the principle that where local authorities have, with the sanction of Parliament, established, or are in the course of establishing, undertakings for public benefit, and have not failed in the performance of their duties, it is not right or expedient that powers should be granted to companies to compete with such local authorities." He severely criticised the action of the House of Lords in passing the General Electrical Power Distributing Company's Bill, which contained most revolutionary proposals. The motion was adopted unanimously, while a further resolution requesting the council of the association to organise an opposition to the Bill was also agreed to.

The deputy town clerk of Huddersfield moved : " That the association represent to the Local Government Board, the Postmaster-General and the Treasury the expediency of legislation being so framed that the Postmaster-General be empowered to grant licenses which shall be self-contained, and confer all necessary and incidental powers for the supply of telephony by local authorities, including borrowing powers." He pointed out that under the present system there must be delay in the spread of telephony, as before local authorities could be fully invested with the powers to undertake the installation of telephones two Parliamentary sessions must elapse. The motion was seconded, but was eventually rejected, it being remarked that the principle involved in the proposition was absolutely contrary to the line adopted throughout by the association in regard to telephones.

Mr. S. Compston, of Rawtenstall, moved : " That, in the opinion of this association, such advance in the means of sewage disposal has been made that the continued demand of the Local Government Board for not less than 1 acre of filtering land per 2,000 of population is not necessary in all cases, but is often a hardship on sanitary authorities ; that the time has come when some option of method should be allowed to authorities, according to quality of sewage and local circumstances ; and that the Law Committee be and is hereby requested forthwith to use its utmost influence with

the Royal Commission now sitting and the Local Government Board in such manner as it deems best to secure such option." No support being given to the resolution, it was allowed to drop.

APPOINTMENTS VACANT.

*Advertisements which are received too late for classification cannot be included in these summaries until the following week.*

## APPOINTMENTS VACANT.

Assistant Inspector of Nuisances.—October 29th.— Stretford District Council. £80.—Mr. George H. Abrahams, clerk to the council.

Municipal Engineer and Surveyor.—October 29th.— Municipality of Woodstock, Cape Colony. £500.—Messrs. J. C. Mackinlay & Co., 27 Walbrook, London, E.C.

Inspector of Nuisances.—October 29th.—Windsor Rural District Council. £130.—Mr. J. E. Gale, clerk to the council.

Sewer Foreman.—November 1st.—Tottenham Urban District Council. £150.—Mr. P. E. Murphy, engineer to the council.

Working Engineer and Superintendent of Waterworks and Mains.—November 1st.—Leighton Buzzard Urban District Council. £150.—Mr. G. L. B. Calcott, clerk to the council.

Borough Surveyor.—November 1st.—Corporation of Saffron Walden. £175.—Mr. W. Adams, town clerk.

Clerk of Works.—November 2nd.—Shoreditch Vestry. £3 3s.—Mr. H. Mansfield Robinson, clerk to the vestry.

District Surveyor.—November 2nd.—Bridgwater Rural District Council.—£225.—Mr. T. M. Reed, clerk to the council.

Deputy Surveyor.—November 3rd.—Brierley Hill Urban District Council. £100.—Mr. William Waldron, clerk to the council.

District Building Inspector.—November 4th.—Corporation of Wolverhampton. £2 5s.—Mr. J. W. Bradley, borough engineer and surveyor.

Surveyor.—November 4th.—Lancaster Rural District Council. £150.—Mr. Joseph Ennion, clerk to the council.

Temporary Assistant.—November 7th.—St. Helens Corporation. £2 15s.—Mr. Geo. J. C. Broom, M.I.C.E., borough engineer.

General Foreman.—November 7th.—Morecambe Urban District Council. 33s.—Mr. Jno. Bond, surveyor to the council.

Second Assistant.—November 12th.—County Borough of Hanley. £80.—Mr. Joseph Lobley, borough engineer and surveyor.

Superintendent at the Corporation Wharf.—November 12th.—County Borough of Southampton. £200.—Mr. George B. Nalder, town clerk.

Assistant for Abstracting and Billing.—" A. B.," office of The Surveyor, 24 Bride-lane, Fleet-street, E.C.

Assistant for Taking-out and Measuring-up.—" A. B.," office of The Surveyor, 24 Bride-lane, Fleet-street, E.C.

## COMPETITIONS.

*Advertisements which are received too late for classification cannot be included in these summaries until the following week.*

Abergavon.—December 1st.—Extension of the covered market, at a cost not to exceed £3,000. £21.—The Borough Surveyor.

Chertsey.—December 23rd.—Sewerage and sewage disposal scheme for the No. 1 and 3 wards of the district. £60, £30 and £20.—Mr. T. E. Harland Chaldecott, clerk to the council.

Bradford.—January 2nd.—Erection of a central fire brigade station. £100, £50 and £30.—Mr. George McGuire, town clerk.

## MUNICIPAL CONTRACTS OPEN.

*Advertisements which are received too late for classification cannot be included in these summaries until the following week.*

Brecon.—October 28th.—Erection of a concrete wall and the execution of drainage and other works to support the landslip between the main road and the river Usk, near the village of Llangrwyne, for the county council.—Mr. H. Edgar Thomas, clerk to the council, County Hall, Brecon.

Brecon.—October 28th.—Laying of about 9,500 lineal yards of 15-in., 12-in., 9-in. and 6-in. stoneware and cast-iron pipe sewers; construction of precipitation tanks, filter-beds, &c.; and the erection of a cottage at the sewage outfall works in Park-lane, for the urban district council.—Mr. Herbert Walker, A.M.I.C.E., Newcastle Chambers, Angel-row, Nottingham.

Kirkby-in-Ashfield.—October 29th.—Sinking of a well to yield 15,000 gallons hourly, for the urban district council.—Mr. W. H. Radford, Angel-row, Nottingham.

Walton-le-Dale.—October 29th.—Construction of a filter at the sewage disposal works at Carr Wood, for the urban district council.— The clerk to the Council.

Newquay.—October 29th.—Erection of new council buildings and sanitary conveniences, for the urban district council.—Mr. Thurstan Collins, clerk to the council.

Islington.—October 29th.—Supply of about 300 lamps for the water vans, and dust and slop vans, for the vestry.—Mr. J. Patten Barber, surveyor to the vestry.

Bilston.—October 29th.—Construction of telephonic and electric communication between the waterworks pumping station at the Bratch, in the parish of Wombourne, and the town hall, with electric communication between the pumping station and the covered service reservoir at Goldthorn Hill, and also between the reservoir and the town hall, for the urban district council.—Mr. John D. Wassell, clerk to the council.

CONSETT.—October 29th.—Erection and completion of foreman's house, store-houses, cart-sheds, &c., and fence walls to stone yard in Hartington-street, for the urban district council.—Mr. William S. Shell, surveyor to the council.

NORTH RIDING.—October 29th.—Alterations to Malton and Scarborough-road at Brompton, near Scarborough, for the county council.—Mr. Walker Stead, M.I.C.E., county surveyor.

MOUNTAIN ASH.—October 31st.—Sewering, levelling, paving, metalling, flagging and channelling works in Augustus-street, Paget-street, Archer-street and Other-street at Ynysybwl, for the urban district council.—Mr. H. P. Linton, clerk to the council.

MORLEY.—October 31st.—Various works at the stables, town hall and public conveniences.—Mr. W. E. Putman, A.M.I.C.E., borough engineer and surveyor.

HULL.—October 31st.—Erection of a crematorium at the Hedon-road cemetery.—Mr. A. E. White, city engineer.

GAINSBOROUGH.—October 31st.—Supply of about 900 tons of granite and about 400 tons of slag, for the urban district council.—Mr. Henry Riley, engineer and surveyor to the council.

BURTON-UPON-TRENT.—October 31st.—Provision of a supply of water to the farm buildings, houses and cottages upon the sewage farm at Egginton.—Mr. George T. Lynam, borough engineer and surveyor.

WATERLOO-WITH-SEAFORTH.—October 31st.—Flagging on the north side of Church-road, Seaford, for the urban district council.—Mr. F. Spencer Yates, A.M.I.C.E., surveyor to the council.

FLEETWOOD.—November 1st.—Construction of an underground convenience, for the urban district council.—Mr. Robert T. Hayes, A.M.I.C.E., surveyor to the council.

MIDDLESEX.—November 1st.—Widening of Turkey-street bridge, in the parish of Enfield, and the rebuilding of Kendal bridge, in the parish of Isleworth, for the county council.—Mr. Henry T. Wakelam, county surveyor, Guildhall, Westminster, London, S.W.

WALTHAM.—November 1st.—Making-up, sewering and paving of Lee-road, for the urban district council.—Mr. C. W. Wiggs, surveyor to the council.

BROMLEY.—November 1st.—Sewerage and surface-water drainage works in Southborough-road, for the urban district council.—Mr. Fred. H. Norman, clerk to the council.

ACTON.—November 1st.—Erection of a new public library, for the urban district council.—The Surveyor to the Council.

PLYMPTON ST. MARY.—November 3rd.—Supply of 1,000 5-in., 650 4-in. and 3,250 3-in. cast-iron socket pipes and special castings in connection with the Plymstock waterworks, for the rural district council.—Mr. Fred. Wm. Cleverton, clerk to the council, 4 Buckland-terrace, Plymouth.

PLYMPTON ST. MARY.—November 3rd.—Supply of sluice valves, pressure-reducing valves, air valves, hydrants, surface boxes, &c., in connection with the Plymstock waterworks, for the rural district council.—Mr. Fred. Wm. Cleverton, clerk to the council, 4 Buckland-terrace, Plymouth.

PLYMPTON ST. MARY.—November 3rd.—Construction of a covered service reservoir near Elburton, the excavation of pipe trenches, and the laying of about 5,550 yards of 5-in., 1,030 yards of 4-in. and 9,730 yards of 3-in. cast-iron mains, in connection with Plymstock waterwork, for the rural district council.—Mr. Fred. Wm. Cleverton, clerk to the council, 4 Buckland-terrace, Plymouth.

CROMER.—November 3rd.—Construction of an underground convenience, comprising accommodation for both sexes, on the sea front, for the urban district council.—Mr. A. F. Scott, surveyor to the council.

NEW HUNSTANTON.—November 3rd.—Erection of one of Messrs. Meldrum Brothers' patent refuse destructors and a Cornish boiler, for the urban district council.—Mr. J. S. B. Glasier, clerk to the council.

CUCKFIELD.—November 3rd.—Supply and erection of various pumping machinery at the waterworks at Balcombe, for the rural district council.—Mr. James Mansergh, 5 Victoria-street, London, S.W.

KEIGHLEY.—November 3rd.—Supply of 1,700 tons of 6-in. granite setts.—Mr. W. H. Hopkinson, A.M.I.C.E., borough engineer.

BRADFORD.—November 3rd.—Extension of Rawson-place market in Godwin-street and James-street.—Mr. J. H. Cox, city surveyor.

BARRY.—November 4th.—Erection of a fire-engine station, tower and mortuary, for the urban district council.—Mr. J. C. Pardoe, A.M.I.C.E., surveyor to the council.

WIDNES.—November 4th.—Erection of new administrative and other blocks at the infectious diseases hospital.—Mr. H. S. Oppenheim, town clerk.

DEAL.—November 4th.—Construction of about 10 miles of brick and pipe sewers, the erection of a pumping station, the provision of pumping machinery, the construction of a tidal storage tank, penstock chambers and sea outfall, and all works incidental thereto.—Mr. Alfred C. Brown, town clerk.

NOTTINGHAM.—November 4th.—Erection of a new electricity station in Talbot-street, Hanley-street and Wollaton-street.—Mr. Arthur Brown, M.I.C.E., city engineer.

MACCLESFIELD.—November 5th.—Erection of a new police station at Church-side.—Mr. Edward E. Adshead, borough engineer.

DUBLIN.—November 5th.—Erection of a public library in North William-street.—Mr. Henry Campbell, town clerk.

ST. OLAVE'S (Southwark).—November 7th.—Supply of 50,000 black-butt wood blocks and 5,000 yellow deal blocks dipped in oil, for the district board of works.—Mr. G. L. Hawker, clerk to the board.

ST. ANNE'S-ON-THE-SEA.—November 7th.—Laying of about 124 yards of 15-in., 287 yards of 12-in. and 203 yards of 9-in. Hassall's patent pipe sewers in Glen Eldon-road and St. David's-road North, for the urban district council.—Mr. Thomas Bradley, clerk to the council.

HORNSEY.—November 7th.—Supply of 100 cast-iron lamp columns, 1,500 cast-iron telephone pipes, 30 cast-iron telephone pit covers and 100 wrought-iron tree guards, for the urban district council.—Mr. E. J. Lovegrove, engineer to the council.

HORNSEY.—November 7th.—Construction of a new road, 40 ft. wide, through Queen's Wood, Highgate, for the urban district council.—Mr. E. J. Lovegrove, engineer to the council.

BECKENHAM.—November 7th.—Paving works in Beckenham and Elmers End roads, for the urban district council.—Mr. J. A. Angell, surveyor to the council.

HORNSEY.—November 7th.—Supply and fixing of library fittings at the central public library in Tottenham-lane, for the urban district council.—Mr. E. J. Lovegrove, engineer and surveyor to the vestry.

WIMBLEDON.—November 7th.—Supply and erection of transformers and accessories, for the urban district council.—Mr. A. H. Preece, A.M.I.C.E., 30 Victoria-street, London, S.W.

BERMONDSEY.—November 7th.—Supply of two slop vans, for the vestry.—Mr. Frederick Ryall, clerk to the vestry.

FLEETWOOD.—November 8th.—Excavating, pile-driving, concreting, paving and other works in connection with the raising of the concrete landing at Knots End, for the urban district council.—Mr. Robert T. Hayes, A.M.I.C.E., surveyor to the council.

WILLESDEN.—November 8th.—The extension of Glynfield-road, Willesden, the widening of Rockhall-passage, Cricklewood, and the re-laying of a sewer in Church-road, Willesden, for the urban district council.—Mr. O. Claude Robson, M.I.C.E., engineer and surveyor to the council.

WILLESDEN.—November 8th.—Road-making and paving works in Preston-mews, for the urban district council.—Mr. O. Claude Robson, M.I.C.E., engineer and surveyor to the council.

HITCHIN.—November 8th.—Erection and completion of a new town hall and offices on a site at the corner of Brand-street and Grammar School-walk, for the urban district council.—Mr. Wm. Onslow Times, clerk to the council.

CHURCH.—November 9th.—Supply of about 550 tons of non-slipping granite setts, for the urban district council.—Mr. John R. Reddish, clerk to the council.

CARDIFF.—November 9th.—Supply and erection of iron sheep and cattle troughs and pens in Roath market.—Mr. W. Harpur, M.I.C.E., borough engineer.

HEYTEN.—November 10th.—Supply and erection of pumping machinery to lift about 60,000 gallons of water per hour to a height of 60 ft., at the sewage works, Streetbridge, for the urban district council.—Mr. Theo. S. McCallum, A.M.I.C.E., 4 Chapel-walks, Manchester.

SOUTHEND-ON-SEA.—November 10th.—Supply of 1,200 cubic yards of Kentish flints.—Mr. Alfred Fidler, A.M.I.C.E., borough surveyor.

BATLEY.—November 10th.—Levelling, paving, flagging, channelling and completing of Grafton-street and Brown's-street.—Mr. O. J. Kirby, borough surveyor.

SOUTHEND-ON-SEA.—November 10th.—Excavation of a lake, supply and erection of a wrought-iron unclimbable fence, and the construction of a cast-iron conduit and a concrete groyne.—Mr. Alfred Fidler, A.M.I.C.E., borough surveyor.

BIRMINGHAM.—November 11th.—Supply of certain goods for use in the general and Elan Valley supply departments for one year from January 1, 1899, for the corporation.—Mr. E. Antony Lees, secretary, Water Department, 44 Broad-street, Birmingham.

TAUNTON.—November 12th.—Supply of about 67 tons of 8-in. and 6-in. cast-iron spigot and socket bituminised water pipes.—Mr. George H. Kite, town clerk.

LAUNCESTON.—November 12th.—Construction of a new cattle, sheep and pig market.—The Town Clerk.

COVENTRY.—November 12th.—Erection of buildings at the proposed two new sewage pumping stations on the side of the main road from Coventry to Daventry.—Mr. Lewis Beard, town clerk.

BIRKENHEAD.—November 14th.—Erection of public baths on land adjoining Livingstone-street and Prince-street.—Mr. Charles Brownridge, A.M.I.C.E., borough engineer and surveyor.

LONDON.—November 15th.—Erection of new public conveniences at Blackwall Tunnel (north side), for the county council.—The Clerk to the Council, County Hall, Spring-gardens, S.W.

LONDON.—November 15th.—Erection of a new coroner's court building at Manor-place, Paddington, for the county council.—The Clerk to the Council, County Hall, Spring-gardens, S.W.

HANLEY.—November 15th.—Erection of a refuse destructor.—Mr. J. Lobley, borough engineer.

AYLESBURY.—November 16th.—Construction of sewage disposal and other works, for the urban district council.—Mr. J. H. Radford, surveyor to the council.

WORTHING.—November 16th.—Supply of 2,500 ft. of 12-in. by 6-in granite curbs and a quantity of broken granite.—Mr. Frank Roberts, A.M.I.C.E., borough engineer and surveyor.

SOUTHAMPTON.—November 16th.—Supply of two engines and dynamos at the county lunatic asylum at Knowle, Fareham.—Mr. W. J. Taylor, county surveyor, The Castle, Winchester.

CARMARTHENSHIRE.—November 18th.—Erection of a stone building of three arches over the river Towry at Dryslwyn, for the county council.—Mr. Thomas Jones, clerk to the council, Llandovery.

ASHTON-UNDER-LYNE.—November 21st.—Construction of precipitation tanks, artificial filters, land filters, subways, culverts, roads and other appurtenant works.—Mr. J. T. Earnshaw, A.M.I.C.E., borough surveyor.

JOHANNESBURG, S.A.—January 6th.—Supply of a complete carburetted water-gas plant, for the corporation.—Messrs. Robert Whyte & Co., 22 Bury-street, St. Mary Axe, London, E.C.

## TENDERS.

*ACCEPTED.

BURTON-ON-TRENT.—Accepted for the making-up of Eldon-street and Nelson-street.—Mr. George T. Lynam, borough engineer and surveyor:—

| | |
|---|---|
| Nelson-street.—Holloway & Son, Bilston-road, Wolverhampton | £121 |
| Eldon-street.—G. F. Tomlinson, City-road, Derby ... ... ... | 291 |

DARTFORD.—For the laying of a surface-water drain and the paving of the footways, crossing and channelling in Fulwich-road, for the urban district council.—Mr. W. Harston, A.M.I.C.E., surveyor to the council:—

SURFACE-WATER DRAIN.

| | |
|---|---|
| J. Mowlem & Co., Westminster... | £1,160 |
| T. Adams, Wood Green | 1,145 |
| Kent Road Company, Gravesend* | 1,041 |

PAVING OF FOOTWAYS.

| | Per super. yard. s. d. | | s. d. |
|---|---|---|---|
| T. Adams, Wood Green | 5 9 | and | 6 3 |
| Kent Road Company, Gravesend | 4 9 | and | 5 6 |
| J. Mowlem & Co., Westminster | 4 6 | and | 5 0 |
| Jones' Annealed Concrete Company, Middlesbrough,* | 3 7 | and | 3 10 |

FEATHERSTONE.—For the laying of about 2¼ miles of 5-in. cast-iron water main, for the urban district council.—Mr. W. A. Palliser, engineer and surveyor to the council:—

| | Price per yard Laying. s. d. | Price per Valve Fixing. s. d. | Price per Chamber. s. d. |
|---|---|---|---|
| Jenkins & Son, Leamington Spa... | 3 0 | 7 6 | 7 6 |
| H. W. Jowitt, Brighouse | 2 0 | 3 0 | 10 0 |
| T. Rowland, Northwich | 1 5½ | 2 6 | 6 0 |
| W. Barrick, Garstang | 1 0 | — | — |
| | | £ s. d. | |
| E. Cheetham, Pendleton | 3 0 | 2 10 0 | |
| N. Doleman, Dewsbury | 1 [illegible] | 0 15 0 | |
| M. Arundel, East Ardsley | 1 6 | 0 10 0 | |
| A. Henson, Leeds* | 1 3½ | 0 10 0 | |

DROGHEDA.—For the construction of filter-beds and other works in connection with the waterworks.—The Borough Engineer:—

| | |
|---|---|
| Barnes, Navan | £3,857 |
| Smullen, Drogheda | 2,673 |
| McLaren, Belfast | 2,648 |
| Henley, Drogheda | 2,588 |
| Small & Geoghegan, Newry* | 2,186 |

Borough engineer's estimate, £2,530.

ECCLES.—For the construction of a urinal in Barton-lane.—Mr. C. W. Bailey, town clerk:—

| | |
|---|---|
| J. F. Moore, Chadwick-road, Eccles* | £85 |

FULHAM.—For the making-up and paving of Felden-street (Section 1) and Friston-street, for the vestry.—Mr. Charles Botterill, surveyor to the vestry :—

FELDEN-STREET (Section 1).

Roadway.—J. Mears, Crabtree Wharf, Fulham, £212 ; H. Greenham, Hammersmith, £219 ; E. Parry, Chesilton-road, Fulham, £203 ; Nowell & Co., Warwick-road, Kensington, £200 ; Wimpey & Co., Hammersmith, £225.

York Stone.—Nowell & Co., Warwick-road, Kensington, £100.

Victoria Stone.—Victoria Stone Company, Bishopsgate-street Without, £106.

Imperial Stone.—Imperial Stone Company, East Greenwich, £119.

FRISTON-STREET.

Roadway.—J. Mears, Crabtree Wharf, Fulham, £225 ; H. Greenham, Hammersmith, £235 ; E. Parry, Chesilton-road, Fulham, £236 ; Nowell & Co., Warwick-road, Kensington, £234 ; Wimpey & Co., Hammersmith, £258.

York Stone.—Nowell & Co., Warwick-road, Kensington, £151.

Victoria Stone.—Victoria Stone Company, Bishopsgate-street Without, £90.

Imperial Stone.—Imperial Stone Company, East Greenwich, £97.

WYFOLD-ROAD (Section 1).

Roadway.—J. Mears, Crabtree Wharf, Fulham, £80 ; H. Greenham, Hammersmith, £140 ; Nowell & Co., Warwick-street, Kensington, £122.

York Stone.—J. Mears, Crabtree Wharf, Fulham, £40 ; Nowell & Co., Warwick-road, Kensington, £73.

Victoria Stone.—J. Mears, Crabtree Wharf, Fulham, £30 ; Victoria Stone Company, Bishopsgate-street Without, £45.

Imperial Stone.—J. Mears, Crabtree Wharf, Fulham, £30 ; Imperial Stone Company, East Greenwich, £51.

GOSPORT AND ALVERSTOKE.—Accepted for the supply of various materials during the year ending September 30, 1899, for the urban district council.—Mr. H. Frost, surveyor to the council :—

Jersey Granite.—Winter & Son, Southsea.

Guernsey Granite, York Stone and Broken Stone.—A. & F. Manuelle, London.

Keinton Paving, Kerbing and Channelling.—Hard Stone Firms, Limited, Bath.

Purbeck Paving, Kerbing and Channelling.—Chinchen & White, Swanage.

Artificial Paving.—E. Bradshaw, Southsea.

Stoneware Drain Pipes.—J. Jennings, Parkstone.

Cement and Lime.—T. Bailey & Son, Portsmouth.

HEXHAM.—For providing and laying cast-iron water pipes, for the rural district council.—Mr. John Marriner, Hedley-on-the-Hill, by Stokesfield-on-Tyne :—

PIPES AND RESERVOIR (Contract No. 1).

| | | | | | | | |
|---|---|---|---|---|---|---|---|
| J. Thompson, Gosforth | ... | ... | ... | ... | ... | ... | £948 |
| J. C. Archibald, Gateshead | ... | ... | ... | ... | ... | ... | 650 |
| J. Symm, Newton | ... | ... | ... | ... | ... | ... | 501 |
| G. Bailey, Newcastle | ... | ... | ... | ... | ... | ... | 562 |
| T. Heddeley, Wallsend | ... | ... | ... | ... | ... | ... | 483 |
| W. Carr, Hexham | ... | ... | ... | ... | ... | ... | 479 |
| J. Carrick, Durham | ... | ... | ... | ... | ... | ... | 476 |

WINDMILL AND PUMP (Contract No. 2).

| | | | | | | | |
|---|---|---|---|---|---|---|---|
| R. D. Bachelor, London | ... | ... | ... | ... | ... | ... | 246 |
| J. Carrick, Durham | ... | ... | ... | ... | ... | ... | 245 |
| Dinning & Cooke, Newcastle | ... | ... | ... | ... | ... | ... | 182 |
| H. Sykes, London | ... | ... | ... | ... | ... | ... | 165 |
| A. Williams & Co., London | ... | ... | ... | ... | ... | ... | 154 |
| Swinney Stewart & Co., Newcastle | ... | ... | ... | ... | ... | 150 |
| J. Symm, Newton | ... | ... | ... | ... | ... | ... | 140 |
| W. J. Richardson, Newcastle* | ... | ... | ... | ... | ... | ... | 135 |

LEYTON.—For the widening of a portion of Grove Green-road, for the urban district council.—Mr. William Dawson, M.I.C.E., engineer and surveyor to the council :—

| | | | | | | | |
|---|---|---|---|---|---|---|---|
| G. J. Anderson, Poplar | ... | ... | ... | ... | ... | ... | £874 |
| G. Wilson, Walthamstow | ... | ... | ... | ... | ... | ... | 791 |
| W. Griffiths, Bishopsgate-street | ... | ... | ... | ... | ... | 769 |
| W. & C. French, Buckhurst Hill* | ... | ... | ... | ... | ... | 734 |

Surveyor's estimate, £830.

ROTHWELL.—For levelling, paving, flagging and making-up of Smithson-street, Melbourne-street, Melbourne-grove, Melbourne-place and Sidney-street, for the urban district council.—Mr. J. T. Pears, surveyor to the council :—

Keighley & Riddiough, Globe-road, Leeds.*

WILLENHALL.—Accepted for the supply of various stores and materials during the six months ending March 31, 1899, for the urban district council.—Mr. Charles J. Jenkin, town surveyor :—

Cement.—Lee Brothers, Bilston.

Lime.—J. Brawn, Walsall.

Macadam.—W. Davis, Walsall.

Disinfecting Powders.—P. Spence & Sons, Manchester.

Aluminoferric.—P. Spence & Sons, Manchester.

Disinfecting Fluids.—A. Andovie & Co., Battersea.

Machine Oil.—E. Walker, Willenhall.

Cylinder Oil.—E. Walker, Willenhall.

Lamp Oil.—E. Walker, Willenhall.

Petroleum Jelly.—E. Walker, Willenhall.

Stoneware Pipes, &c.—Doulton & Co., Smethwick.

Coal.—T. Walker, Willenhall.

Cotton Waste.—Henley & Co., Willenhall.

Shovels.—Henley & Co., Willenhall.

Brooms.—B. Dawes, Wolverhampton.

Picks.—J. Baker, Willenhall.

TWICKENHAM.—For the supply of 2,000 cubic yards of 2-in. broken blue Guernsey granite or Cherbourg quartzite, for the urban district council.—Mr. H. Jason Saunders, clerk to the council :—

Cherbourg (per cubic yard).—L. Somerfeld, 12s. 11d.; H. L. Cooper, 12s.; A. & F. Manuelle, 12s. 6d.

Guernsey (per cubic yard).—L. Somerfeld, 14s. 7d.; G. le Maitre, 15s.; Fry Brothers, 15s.; A. & F. Manuelle, 15s. 2d.; J. Mowlem & Co., 14s. 7d.; R. & L. Fennings, London Bridge,* 13s. 9d.

## MEETINGS.

*Secretaries and others will oblige by sending early notice of dates of forthcoming meetings.*

OCTOBER.

28.—Croydon Municipal Officers' Association : First General Meeting. 8 p.m.

28.—Sanitary Institute : Lecture to sanitary officers ; Dr. J. F. J. Sykes, medical officer of health, St. Pancras, on "Objects and Methods of Inspection, Nuisances, &c." 8 p.m.

29.—Sanitary Institute : Visit of sanitary officers to the Express Dairy Company's farm at Finchley. 3 p.m.

29.—Opening of the St. George-in-the-East new public library by the Lord Chief Justice of England.

31.—The Duke of Cambridge lays the foundation-stone of the new town hall at Colchester.

31.—Sanitary Institute : Lecture to sanitary officers ; Prof. W. H. Corfield, medical officer of health, St. George, Hanover-square, on "Water Supply, Drinking Water, Pollution of Water." 8 p.m.

31.—Superannuation Conference at Sion College, Victoria Embankment. 8 p.m.

NOVEMBER.

1.—Institution of Civil Engineers : Inaugural address by the president, Mr. W. H. Preece ; presentation of the council's awards and reception in the library. 8 p.m.

2.—Sanitary Institute : Visit of sanitary officers to the disinfecting station, Chelsea. 3 p.m.

2.—Sanitary Institute : Lecture to sanitary officers ; Dr. A. Hill, medical officer of health, Birmingham, on "Diseases of Animals in Relation to Meat Supply ; Characteristics of Vegetables and Methods of Disinfection." 8 p.m.

4.—Sanitary Institute : Lecture to sanitary officers ; Dr. H. R. Kenwood, medical officer of health, Stoke Newington, on "Infectious Diseases and Methods of Disinfection." 8 p.m.

8.—Institution of Civil Engineers : Ordinary general meeting ; Prof. W. C. Roberts-Austen, C.B., F.R.S., on "The Extraction of Nickel." 8 p.m.

## NOTICES.

*THE SURVEYOR AND MUNICIPAL AND COUNTY ENGINEER may be ordered direct, through any of Messrs. Smith & Son's book-stalls, or of any newsagent in the United Kingdom. Applications to the Offices for single copies by post must in all cases be accompanied by stamps.*

*The Prepaid Subscription (including postage) is as follows :*

| | Twelve Months. | Six Months. | Three Months. |
|---|---|---|---|
| United Kingdom ... ... | 15s. | 7s. 6d. | 4s. |
| Continent, the Colonies, India, | | | |
| United States, &c. ... ... | 19s. | 9s. 6d. | 4s. 9d. |

*The International News Company, 83 and 85 Duane-street, New York City ; The Toronto News Company, Toronto ; and The Montreal News Company, Montreal, have been appointed agents in the United States and Canada for the sale of THE SURVEYOR AND MUNICIPAL AND COUNTY ENGINEER. A thin paper edition is printed for circulation abroad.*

EDITORIAL OFFICES :—

24 BRIDE-LANE, FLEET-STREET, LONDON, E.C.

ADVERTISEMENT AND PUBLISHING OFFICES :—

13 NEW STREET-HILL, FLEET-STREET, LONDON, E.C.

## APPOINTMENTS OPEN.

MORECAMBE DISTRICT COUNCIL.

The above Council require the services of a General Foreman over the outside men in their employ. He must be fully qualified and competent by knowledge and experience to carry out his duties.

The wages offered are 33s. weekly.

Also the services of a Time and Store Keeper, one accustomed to such duties preferred.

The wages offered are 22s. weekly.

Lists of duties can be seen by applying at the offices of the Council.

Applicants must apply in their own handwriting, stating their age and qualifications, particulars of their past and present employment, enclosing not more than three testimonials of recent date. All applications to be sent under cover, and endorsed "General Foreman" or "Time and Store Keeper," to the undersigned not later than noon on Monday, the 7th day of November next.

(By order)

JNO. BOND,

Surveyor to the Council.

Council Offices, Morecambe.

October 25, 1898.

BOROUGH OF SAFFRON WALDEN.

BOROUGH SURVEYOR.

The Council of the Borough of Saffron Walden invite applications for the appointment of a Borough Surveyor, at a salary of £175 a year.

The person appointed must devote the whole of his time to the service of the Corporation.

He must be thoroughly competent to carry out the duties prescribed by the Public Health Acts, to act as waterworks manager, and to undertake and superintend works usually performed by sanitary authorities.

Further particulars of the duties and the conditions of employment may be obtained at my office.

Applications, endorsed "Borough Surveyor," stating age, qualifications and experience, accompanied by copies of three testimonials, which will not be returned, must reach me on or before Tuesday, the 1st November next.

Personal canvassing will be a disqualification.

(By order of the Council)

W. ADAMS,

Town Clerk.

Saffron Walden.

October 17, 1898.

## COUNTY BOROUGH OF SOUTHAMPTON.
### APPOINTMENT OF SUPERINTENDENT AT THE CORPORATION WHARF.

The Corporation of Southampton invite applications for the appointment of Superintendent at the Wharf.

The person appointed to have the entire charge of the wharf and the employees, and be responsible for all materials coming in and going out. To superintend the precipitation of the sewage, and have the entire charge of the works under the Borough Engineer as Chief officer. To be responsible for the safe keeping of the horses, carts, fodder, materials and everything on the wharf.

Applicants having a knowledge of machinery preferred.

Salary, £200 per annum.

The person appointed will be required to devote the whole of his time to the duties of the office.

Applications, endorsed "Superintendent," and copies of three recent testimonials, with full particulars as to previous experience, age, &c., to be sent to my office on or before the 12th November next.

Canvassing will disqualify.

(By order)
GEORGE B. NALDER,
Town Clerk.

Municipal Offices, Southampton.
October 20, 1898.

## COUNTY BOROUGH OF WOLVERHAMPTON.

The Public Works Committee is prepared to receive applications for the post of District Building Inspector.

Applicants must have had experience in the working of the Model By-Laws and be well versed in sanitary building construction and the interpretation of plans. Wages, 40s. per week. A bicycle provided; staff hours.

Applications, in own handwriting, with not more than three recent testimonials (copies), to be sent to the undersigned on or before the 4th prox.

J. W. BRADLEY,
Borough Engineer and Surveyor.
Town Hall, Wolverhampton.

## LEIGHTON BUZZARD URBAN DISTRICT COUNCIL.
### APPOINTMENT OF WORKING ENGINEER AND SUPERINTENDENT OF WATERWORKS AND MAINS.

The above Council invite applications for the post of Working Engineer and Superintendent of Waterworks and Mains. Applicants will be required to devote their whole time and attention to the Council's work at the pumping station and ejector stations, and to superintend the connections to the sewers and water mains, and to assist generally in matters appertaining to the work and management of the sewers and waterworks. Preference will be given to one having a knowledge of Shone's system. The salary offered is £120 a year, rising £5 a year to £130, with use of house adjoining the waterworks (except a committee-room) rent free, rates and taxes to be paid by the Council. The engagement will be monthly, to be terminated by one month's notice on either side.

Applications, in the handwriting of the candidates, stating age and qualifications, with three recent testimonials, to be sent to me not later than the 1st day of November, 1898.

Canvassing is prohibited and will be considered a disqualification.

G. L. B. CALCOTT,
Clerk to the Council.
Leighton Buzzard.
October 17, 1898.

## COUNTY BOROUGH OF HANLEY.

A Second Assistant is required in the Borough Surveyor's office, Hanley, at a salary of £80 per annum, rising £10 a year to £100.

Applicants should have had practical experience in surveying, levelling, and general work of a town surveyor's office.

Applications, in candidate's own handwriting, stating age and experience, together with copies of not more than three recent testimonials, sealed and endorsed "Assistant Surveyor," must be delivered at the office of the undersigned not later than 12 o'clock noon on November 12, 1898.

JOSEPH LOBLEY,
Borough Engineer and Surveyor.
Town Hall, Hanley.
October 25, 1898.

## LANCASTER RURAL DISTRICT COUNCIL.
### APPOINTMENT OF SURVEYOR.

The above-named Council invite applications for the appointment of Surveyor for their district, which has an area of 55,174 acres, a population of about 11,830, an assessable value of £110,970, and about 190 miles of highways.

The appointment will be for one year, at a salary of £150, with reasonable and necessary travelling expenses allowed.

The person appointed must reside in or near Lancaster and devote the whole of his time to the duties of his office.

He will be required and must be thoroughly competent to carry out the duties devolving on a surveyor under the Public Health Acts; superintend the making, repairing and improving of all parish highways and bridges within the district

of the Council; and also must be well acquainted with the Model By-Laws of the Local Government Board.

The appointment will be determinable by one month's notice on either side.

Personal canvassing will be deemed a disqualification.

Applications, in candidate's handwriting, stating age, qualifications, when at liberty, and experience, accompanied by copies of not more than four testimonials, must reach me not later than Friday, the 4th day of November, 1898.

JOSEPH ENXION,
Clerk to the Council.
5 Dalton-square, Lancaster.
October 24, 1898.

## COUNTY BOROUGH OF ST. HELENS.

Wanted, for six or eight months, a fully-qualified Assistant, to prepare plans for the completion of sewage system in outlying districts. Salary, £2 15s. per week.— Apply, not later than the 7th November, to Mr. Geo. J. C. Brown, M.INST.C.E., Borough Engineer, St. Helens.

WANTED, a thoroughly competent Assistant, for abstracting and billing. State salary to "A. B.," office of THE SURVEYOR, 24 Bride-lane, Fleet-street, E.C.

WANTED, a thoroughly competent Assistant, for taking-out and measuring-up. State salary to "A. B.," office of THE SURVEYOR, 24 Bride-lane, Fleet-street, E.C.

# COMPETITION.

## CITY OF BRADFORD.
### INTENDED CENTRAL FIRE BRIGADE STATION.

#### TO ARCHITECTS.

The Corporation of the City of Bradford are prepared to receive Competitive Designs for the Erection of a Central Fire Brigade Station. Three premiums are offered to competing architects—viz., £100, £50 and £30. Plan of the site, with printed instructions, may be had on application at the City Surveyor's office on and after Monday, the 31st inst., on payment of 1 guinea, to be returned after receipt of design.

The designs must be sent in not later than Monday, the 2nd of January, 1899.

(By order)
GEORGE McGUIRE,
Town Clerk.
Town Clerk's Office, Bradford.
October 25, 1898.

# TENDERS WANTED.

## WILLESDEN DISTRICT COUNCIL.
### TO ROAD CONTRACTORS.

The Willesden District Council are prepared to receive tenders for the execution of the following works:—

*Road-making Works.*—Extension of Glynfield-road, Willesden (150 ft. lineal); widening Rockhall-passage, Cricklewood (115 ft. lineal).

*Sewer Work.*—Relaying sewer, Church-road, Willesden (891 ft. lineal).

Plans and specifications may be seen, and all further particulars obtained, on and after Monday, October 31, 1898, upon application to Mr. O. Claude Robson, M.INST.C.E., Engineer to the Council, Public Offices, Dyne-road, Kilburn, N.W.

The tenders, upon printed forms and endorsed "Improvements," to be delivered at the offices of the Council not later than 4 p.m. on Tuesday, November 8, 1898.

The Council do not bind themselves to accept the lowest or any tender.

(By order)
STANLEY W. BALL,
Clerk to the Council.
Public Offices, Dyne-road, Kilburn, N.W.
October 26, 1898.

## BOROUGH OF WORTHING.
### TO GRANITE MERCHANTS.

The Corporation are prepared to receive tenders for 2,500 ft. of 12-in. by 6-in. Granite Kerbs and a quantity of Broken Granite, delivered at Worthing station.

Forms of tender and further particulars may be obtained from the undersigned.

Sealed tenders, endorsed "Tender for Kerbs" or "Tender for Broken Granite," as the case may be, to be sent in to me on or before Wednesday, November 16, 1898.

The Corporation do not bind themselves to accept the lowest or any tender.

FRANK ROBERTS, A.M.INST.C.E.,
Borough Engineer and Surveyor.
Municipal Offices, Worthing.
October 24, 1898.

## WILLESDEN DISTRICT COUNCIL.
### TO ROAD CONTRACTORS.

The Willesden District Council are prepared to receive tenders for the execution of certain Road-making and Paving Works in Preston-mews, Willesden.

Plan and specification may be seen, and all further particulars obtained, on and after Monday, October 31, 1898, upon application to Mr. O. Claude Robson, M.INST.C.E., Engineer to the Council, Public Offices, Dyne-road, Kilburn, N.W.

The tenders, upon printed forms and endorsed "Private Streets," to be delivered at the offices of the Council not later than 4 p.m. on Tuesday, November 8, 1898.

The Council do not bind themselves to accept the lowest or any tender.

(By order)
STANLEY W. BALL,
Clerk to the Council.

Public Offices, Dyne-road, Kilburn, N.W.
October 26, 1898.

NEW HUNSTANTON URBAN DISTRICT COUNCIL.
CONTRACT FOR REFUSE DESTRUCTOR AND BOILER.

The Urban District Council of New Hunstanton is prepared to receive tenders for the Erection of one of Messrs. Meldrum Brothers' Patent Refuse Destructors and a Cornish Boiler.

Copies of the specification and tender can be obtained, on and after Friday, the 21st of October next, at the offices of the Council, Hunstanton, or at the office of the Engineers, Messrs. Stevenson & Burstall, 38 Parliament-street, Westminster, S.W., on payment of 1 guinea.

Sealed tenders, endorsed "Tender for Refuse Destructor, &c.. are to be forwarded to the undersigned not later than Thursday, November 3, 1898.

J. S. B. GLASIER,
Clerk.

BOROUGH OF SOUTHEND-ON-SEA.
TO CONTRACTORS AND OTHERS.

The Corporation invite tenders for the Excavation of a Lake, the supply and erection of a Wrought-Iron Unclimbable Fence, the construction of a Cast-Iron Conduit, and the construction of a Concrete Groyne.

Plans, sections and specifications may be seen, and bills of quantities and forms of tender obtained, on and after Monday, the 31st day of October (on payment of £1 1s., which will be returned on receipt of a *bonâ-fide* tender), upon application to Mr. Alfred Fidler, ASSOC.M.INST.C.E., Borough Surveyor, Clarence-road, Southend.

No tender will be considered unless made on the prescribed form.

Sealed tenders (marked "Tender for Lake, &c.") to be delivered at my office before 10 o'clock on the morning of Thursday, the 10th day of November.

The Corporation will not be bound to accept the lowest or any tender.

(By order)
WILLIAM H. SNOW,
Town Clerk.

Southend-on-Sea.
October 24, 1898.

BOROUGH OF SOUTHEND-ON-SEA.
TO STONE MERCHANTS.

The Corporation invite tenders for supplying 1,200 cubic yards of Kentish Flints, to be delivered alongside at Southend or at the railway station.

Specification and form of tender may be obtained, on and after Monday, the 31st instant, on application to Mr. Alfred Fidler, ASSOC.M.INST.C.E., Borough Surveyor, Clarence-road, Southend.

Each person tendering must send to the office of the Borough Surveyor a half-bushel sample of the flints offered.

Sealed tenders, endorsed "Tenders for Flints," to be delivered at my office before 10 o'clock a.m. on Thursday, the 10th November.

The Corporation will not be bound to accept the lowest or any tender.

(By order)
WILLIAM H. SNOW,
Town Clerk.

Southend-on-Sea.
October 24, 1898.

FLEETWOOD URBAN DISTRICT COUNCIL.

*FERRY WORKS.*

RAISING THE CONCRETE LANDING AT KNOT END
(CONTRACT No. 3).

The Urban District Council of Fleetwood invite tenders for the Excavation, Pile-driving, Concreting, Paving and other works in connection therewith.

Plans may be seen, and copy of the specification, general conditions, bill of quantities, with form of tender, obtained on

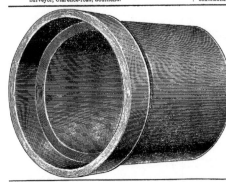

application to Mr. Robert T. Hayes, A.M.I.C.E., Surveyor's Office, Town Hall, Fleetwood, on payment of the sum of £2, which will be returned on receipt of a bond-fide tender.

Sealed tenders, accompanied by the priced bill of quantities, endorsed "Tender for Ferry Works," to be addressed to me and sent in not later than Tuesday, the 8th day of November, 1898, at 12 o'clock noon.

The Council do not bind themselves to accept the lowest or any tender.

(By order)
JOSEPH TILDSLEY,
Clerk and Accountant.

Town Hall, Fleetwood.
October 20, 1898.

## BOROUGH OF BATLEY.

The Town Council of the borough are prepared to receive tenders for the Levelling, Paving, Flagging, Channelling and completing of each of the following streets—viz., Grafton-street and Brown's-street—in the said borough.

Plans, sections and specifications of the said works respectively may be seen on application to the Borough Surveyor (Mr. O. J. Kirby), whose offices are situated in the Market-place, Batley.

Sealed tenders, on forms which may be obtained from the Borough Surveyor, properly endorsed, to be delivered at my office not later than Thursday, the 10th day of November prox.

The Council do not bind themselves to accept the lowest or any tender.

(By order)
JOSEPH HANSON CRAIK,
Town Clerk.

Town Clerk's Office, Batley.
October 20, 1898.

## BECKENHAM URBAN DISTRICT COUNCIL.
### TO CONTRACTORS.

The Beckenham Urban District Council invite tenders for Paving Works in Beckenham and Elmers End roads. The works comprise about 1,200 super. yards of red brick paving, 330 lineal feet of 6-in. by 12-in. Norwegian kerb, 800 lineal feet of Aberdeen or Guernsey granite channelling, together with other works in connection with the formation of the footpaths.

Plans and sections may be seen and bills of quantities, specifications and forms of tenders obtained on application to Mr. John A. Angell, Surveyor, on or after October 27th, on

deposit of £1, which will be returned on receipt of a bond-fide tender.

A clause will be inserted in the contract providing that the contractor shall pay to the workmen employed in the execution of the work the wages generally accepted as current for workmen engaged on similar work in the district.

Tenders, duly sealed and endorsed "Tender for Paving Works," to reach the undersigned not later than 4 p.m. on Monday, November 7, 1898.

The Council do not bind themselves to accept the lowest or any tender.

(By order)
F. STEVENS,
Clerk to the Council.

## BOROUGH OF TAUNTON.

The Corporation of the Borough of Taunton invite tenders for the supply of about 67 tons of 8-in. and 6-in. Cast-Iron Spigot and Socket Bituminised Water Pipes.

Full particulars may be obtained on application to the Waterworks Manager, Municipal Buildings.

Tenders to be sent into me, the undersigned, endorsed "Tender for Cast-iron Pipes," on or before 12th November, 1898.

The Corporation do not bind themselves to accept the lowest or any tender.

GEORGE H. KITE,
Town Clerk.

Municipal Buildings, Taunton.
October 21, 1898.

## HORNSEY URBAN DISTRICT COUNCIL.
### TO ROAD AND SEWER CONTRACTORS.

The Hornsey Urban District Council are prepared to receive tenders for the construction of a new road, 40 ft. wide, through Queen's Wood, Highgate, in the urban district of Hornsey.

Plans and specifications may be seen, and forms of tender and all information obtained, on application to Mr. E. J. Lovegrove, Engineer to the Council, at the offices mentioned below, or any morning between the hours of 10 and 12 o'clock, on a sum of £2 being deposited with the Clerk to the Council, which sum will be retained by the Council and deemed to be forfeited if a bond-fide tender is not made by the depositor.

If a tender is made which is not accepted the sum deposited will be returned, and if a tender is accepted such sum will be retained by the Council until the contract has been

executed by the depositor, and will be forfeited in the event of his or his sureties failing or neglecting to execute such contract or the bond accompanying same within seven days after he or they respectively shall have been requested to execute the same.

No tender will be considered except on the prescribed form.

Sealed and endorsed tenders are to be deposited in the tender-box in my department not later than 4 o'clock p.m. on Monday, the 7th proximo.

The Council reserve to themselves the right to decline all, or any, or any portion of, the tenders so sent in.

(By order)

F. D. ASKEY,

Clerk to the District Council.

Offices: Southwood-lane, Highgate, N.

October 18, 1898.

## HORNSEY URBAN DISTRICT COUNCIL.
### TO ENGINEERS AND IRONFOUNDERS.

The Hornsey Urban District Council are prepared to receive tenders for the supply of the following:—

    100 Cast-Iron Lamp Columns.

    1,500 Cast-Iron Telephone Pipes.

    30 Cast-Iron Telephone Pit Covers.

    100 Wrought-Iron Tree Guards.

Tender forms, specifications and particulars, may be obtained on application to Mr. E. J. Lovegrove, C.E., Engineer to the Council, and samples may be inspected at the Council's Offices.

No tender will be considered unless on the prescribed form.

Sealed and endorsed tenders are to be deposited in the tender box in my department not later than 4 p.m. on Monday, the 7th proximo.

The Council reserve to themselves the right to decline all, or any, or any portion of, the tenders so sent in.

(By order)

F. D. ASKEY,

Clerk to the District Council.

Offices: Southwood-lane, Highgate, N.

October 18, 1898.

## HORNSEY URBAN DISTRICT COUNCIL.
### TO LIBRARY FURNISHERS AND OTHERS.

The Hornsey Urban District Council are prepared to receive tenders for the Supply of Library Fittings and Fixing at the Council's Central Public Library, situate in Tottenham-lane, Hornsey.

Specifications and forms of tender and all information can be obtained on application to Mr. E. J. Lovegrove, Engineer to the Council, at the offices mentioned below, on any morning between the hours of 10 and 12 o'clock, on a sum of £2 being deposited with the Clerk to the Council, which sum will be retained by the Council and deemed to be forfeited if a bond-fide tender is not made by the depositor.

If a tender is made which is not accepted the sum deposited will be returned, and if a tender is accepted such sum will be retained by the Council until the contract has been executed by the depositor, and will be forfeited in the event of his or his sureties failing or neglecting to execute such contract, or the bond accompanying same, within seven days after he or they respectively shall have been requested to execute the same.

No tender will be considered except on the prescribed form.

Sealed and endorsed tenders are to be deposited in the tender-box in my department not later than 4 o'clock p.m. on Monday, the 7th day of November proximo.

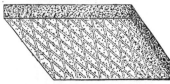

The Council reserve to themselves the right to decline all, or any, or any portion of, the tenders so sent in.

(By order)
F. D. ASKEY,
Clerk to the District Council.

Offices: Southwood-lane, Highgate, N.
October 25, 1898.

## AYLESBURY URBAN DISTRICT COUNCIL.

*WORKS OF SEWAGE DISPOSAL FOR THE TOWN OF AYLESBURY.*

CONTRACTS Nos. 1 TO 7, INCLUSIVE.

Tenders are invited for the Construction of Sewage Disposal and other Works for the Aylesbury Urban District Council, according to the plans and specification prepared by Mr. J. H. Bradford, Surveyor to the said Council.

Plans and specification of the works may be seen at the office of the Urban District Council, in Aylesbury, and the form of tender obtained on application to the undersigned, at his office, 1 Rickford's-hill, Aylesbury, on and after the 26th day of October instant.

The quantities of the several works have been taken out by Messrs. W. F. Taylor & Son, of Aylesbury, and may be had on application to them, or the undersigned, on deposit of £5, which will be returned only upon receipt of a *bona fide* tender, together with all documents entrusted to the contractors.

Sealed tenders, upon the form supplied, endorsed "Tender for Sewage Works," are to be delivered at the office of the undersigned on or before the 16th day of November, at noon.

The Council will not be bound to accept the lowest or any tender.

Dated this 17th day of October, 1898.

GEORGE FELL,
Clerk to the Council.

## URBAN SANITARY DISTRICT OF ROYTON.
TO PUMP MAKERS.

The Royton Urban District Council solicit tenders for the Supply and Erection of Pumping Machinery to lift about 60,000 gallons of water per hour to a height of 60 ft., at the Council's sewage works, Streetbridge, Royton.

Specifications and other particulars may be obtained on application to Mr. Thos. S. McCallum, A.M.I.C.E., 4 Chapel-walks, Manchester, on sending a deposit of £1, which sum will be returned after receipt of a *bona-fide* tender.

The Council does not bind itself to accept the lowest or any tender.

Tenders (endorsed "Contract No. 17") must be delivered to the undersigned on or before the 10th day of November, 1898.

(Signed)     THOS. BLEASDALE,
Clerk to the Council.

Town Hall, Royton.
October 5, 1898.

# The Surveyor

## And Municipal and County Engineer.

Vol. XIV., No. 355.  LONDON, NOVEMBER 4, 1898.  Weekly, Price 3d.

## Minutes of Proceedings.

**Limits of Municipal Enterprise.** As our readers are aware, we have frequently referred to the question of the just limits of municipal enterprise and municipal trading, and we observe with interest that the topic, which may be said to belong to the philosophy of local government, was discussed very effectively by Sir Henry Fowler in a speech delivered on Monday at a mayoral banquet at Wolverhampton. On the whole, we find very little cause to find fault with the views of Sir Henry, who as a former president of the Local Government Board and the author of the Local Government Act, 1894, must command attention when he deals with such a subject. There is undoubtedly a tendency to increase municipal powers and responsibilities, and, as Sir Henry Fowler says, the basis of the argument in favour of municipalisation is a tendency towards combination, so that the public may secure greater advantages in various departments more easily and more cheaply than could be secured by private enterprise. But the question is, Where is the line to be drawn? Broadly speaking, we have always maintained that those great public services which are necessarily in the nature of monopolies—water supply, sewerage, sewage disposal, lighting, and tramway services are the most prominent—can be most advantageously undertaken by the local authorities; but it is as well that we should be reminded occasionally, as we were by Sir Henry Fowler, that private enterprise, controlled by practical men and carried on under the supervision of those whose pecuniary interest is bound up in the success and development of such enterprise, is the basis of our commercial life. While disclaiming any attempt to draw a rigid frontier line between municipal and private enterprise, Sir Henry Fowler endeavoured to point out some of the conditions which seemed to him necessary for the successful carrying on of municipal enterprises. His first endeavour was to define—broadly, it is true, but on the whole judiciously—the limits of municipal enterprises. These, he thinks, should be confined to undertakings which require Parliamentary sanction and legislative powers for their establishment and control, or, in other words, they should deal only with those enterprises which no private company or proprietors could establish or conduct themselves—enterprises requiring compulsory powers. Companies can, of course, obtain the necessary powers in certain cases, as we see in connection with water supply, lighting and tramways. Sir Henry's meaning can be this, though, but the wording of his sentence was rather defective. The question really is to decide whether enterprises such as those mentioned can, from the point of view of the public good, be more advantageously undertaken by the local authorities or by companies. There is no doubt as to the general trend of public opinion on the subject. As a better illustration of his meaning, Sir Henry Fowler referred to the question of the streets and roads of a borough, which cannot be

disturbed by any private company or individual unless legislative powers are first obtained, and he maintained that the municipality alone should have full control over enterprises requiring the breaking up of the thoroughfares—an opinion with which only a small minority, we imagine, would disagree.

The second condition formulated by Sir Henry Fowler is that enterprises undertaken by local authorities should be for the common good and for the general use of the community. The cycle industry was cited as not a suitable object of municipal solicitude, while water supply, lighting and tramways were cited on the other side. Public control, of course, necessarily implies monopoly, unless in certain exceptional cases. In some matters it is impossible there can be any competition; in others it is undesirable. In regard to tramways, for example, it is impossible to have two sets of tram lines running through a street. They must be under one control. In other words, there must be a monopoly, and if there is to be a monopoly in matters directly affecting the health and well-being of the whole community, the balance of argument is in favour of entrusting it to the local authority as directly representing the interests of the ratepayers. Another condition suggested—and one with which there is not much cause to quarrel—is that a municipal enterprise should be one which can be carried on not only more efficiently, but more cheaply, than it can be carried on by a private company. Before concluding Sir Henry Fowler referred to the much-debated question which we have frequently discussed in our columns, especially in connection with electric lighting—whether undertakings acquired by the community should be carried on by the local authority at a profit; in other words, whether profits should be devoted to a general reduction of rates, or whether advantage should be taken of the opportunity to reduce the price of the particular service. Sir Henry Fowler cited the case of the controversy which had taken place in the North of England in connection with the manufacture of gas. One municipality, he said, had carried on the manufacture and supply at a profit, and transferred the profit for various public improvements, whilst another municipality had acted on the principle of supplying gas to the community at a little more than its bare cost. As we have pointed out on previous occasions, much depends on whether the thing supplied is of general consumption or is restricted to a minority. So long as the latter is the case, to reduce the price unduly is to favour this minority at the expense of the general ratepayers, who are entitled to demand that a share of the profits should be devoted to the relief of the general burden of rates. Sir Henry Fowler himself forcibly emphasised the point, when, according to the report, he said :—

> The community must pay for certain services by taxation, such, for instance, as the police, the necessary works for the protection of the public health, the lighting and repairs of

the streets, and many other matters which he need not detail; but they must always remember that the general use did not justify universal taxation. Many of them, for instance, were votaries of tobacco. He (Sir Henry) did not smoke, and they had no right to tax him so that they might buy their tobacco (laughter). The same with regard to tea-drinking. If they charged a higher price for any article than the cost of its production the consumer was taxed, but if, on the other hand, they charged a lower price then they put the tax on the general taxpayer.

But whatever difference of opinion there may be on this question in regard to matters of detail, there should be general agreement with the sentiment with which Sir Henry Fowler concluded his remarks—that the true secret of strength and success in any municipal enterprise in which we may embark is having at our back the full force of a favourable public opinion.

\*     \*     \*

**The Position of "Superannuation."** The conference of municipal officers held at Sion College on Monday fully bore out the opinion we previously held, and do not hesitate to express, as to the supineness of municipal officials on the question of superannuation. In the special issue of THE SURVEYOR published at the beginning of this year we dealt with the matter from several points of view and endeavoured to elicit signs of interest in the subject. They were not forthcoming. The statements of several speakers at the conference convince us that general, active and united interest does not exist. Never was there a measure of more vital importance to municipal officials than the Local Officers' Superannuation Bill. To us it is simply incredible and inexplicable that its chances of becoming a statute should have been damned by faint, half-hearted and disunited support. Municipal engineers cannot be exempted from this reproach, yet of all sections of local officers they have perhaps the greatest stake in the securing of compulsory superannuation. Among chief officials they alone, almost without exception, give their whole time—the best of their years, their abilities, their experience—to their employers. Medical officers and clerks to authorities have in many cases private practices to which they devote a portion of their time. Yet we are inclined almost to say that among officials it is the municipal engineers of the country who have been least energetic and effective in supporting those who have laboured to secure for them the certainty of at least a living income in the day of permanent infirmity or old age. Why? Is it indolence? Is it want of unity? Is it failure to realise the indisputable boon the Bill seeks to confer upon them? Is it that abject sort of pessimism which cannot fight against odds? If we can sting the inactive into such mental activity as is involved in subjecting themselves to this sort of catechism, we venture to think they will find that there is not one of these attitudes which is excusable or tenable. In 1896 poor law officials secured compulsory superannuation by dint of fine generalship and persistent pegging away. Next year board school teachers, thanks to a precedent of such obvious application, were equally successful. This is the year of grace, 1898, but the sequence has not been sustained. The bringing into line of other local officers cannot yet be recorded, nor can we honestly say that their case has made much progress. When the poor law officials urged their claims they were able to quote the resolutions "in favour" of 400 boards of guardians, while there was not one of such authorities "against." In the Local Officers' Superannuation Bill there are 1,932 authorities interested, and up to the present actually only 400 of these have even got to the length of expressing any sort of opinion at all about the measure. And we conjecture—the able chairman of the conference is no doubt in possession of the exact figures—that it would have been better if the 400 had been still fewer, for their resolutions were in the majority of instances "against." In a few words, the position of the Bill is this. There are sufficient members of Parliament in its favour

to secure its being adopted as a Government measure if the Local Government Board commend it. But the Local Government Board will not support it unless—and this is the crux of the whole unless matter—a majority of the municipal authorities who will have to administer the Bill petition in its favour. One is irresistibly reminded of the stick that would not beat the dog, and the dog that would not bite the pig, and the pig that would not get over the stile, and the old lady who was thereby troubled. Some one has got to move the municipal authorities, and then there will be progress all along the line. Until this is accomplished there will be a deadlock. We incline to the opinion, though we whisper it with bated breath, that authorities may occasionally be guided aright by united, persistent and tactful efforts of officials. Moreover, it is worth remembering that the Press is usually credited, especially by journalists, with some power in the land. Let it be somebody's business in every district to secure the interest of local journals to at least such an extent as, one may reasonably expect, a conscientious and fair-minded editor would be willing to go; and such an extent need involve no more than educating ratepayers and their representatives up to a knowledge of the fact that superannuation, as proposed by the Bill we have referred to, is not going to be another tax upon the rates. This, in the words of the chairman of the conference, is a "trump card," and it should be played for all it is worth.

\*     \*     \*

**Provisional Orders in 1897.** An appendix to the recently-issued report of the Local Government Board for 1897 contains tables with respect to the Provisional Orders issued during last year, showing the areas affected, the purposes of the orders, and the titles of the confirming Acts. In addition to seventeen Provisional Orders under the Local Government Act, 1888, sixty-seven Orders were also issued under the Public Health Act, 1875, and one under the Gas and Water Works Facilities Act, 1870. Of these sixty-eight Orders all but one were included in confirming Bills in the session of 1897. Twenty-six of the Orders issued in pursuance of the Local Government Board's powers under the Public Health Act, 1875, put in force with reference to the lands described in the schedules to the orders, the powers of the Lands Clauses Acts with respect to the purchasing and taking of lands otherwise than by agreement by twenty urban and six rural district councils. The purposes for which the lands were authorised to be acquired included the widening and improvement of streets, the formation of new streets, the disposal of sewage, the construction of waterworks, and the provision of sites for pleasure grounds. Of the remaining Provisional Orders thirty-seven were issued in pursuance of the Local Government Board's powers under the Public Health Act, 1875, for the repeal, alteration and amendment of Local Acts and Provisional Orders Confirmation Acts. The Provisional Orders altering and amending local Acts dealt with a variety of matters. For example, the corporations of Bootle, Chorley and Scarborough were authorised to require the provision of water-closets in the cases of new buildings and in lieu of other accommodation in existing buildings; the Birmingham Corporation to make superannuation allowances to their officers and servants; and the St. Helens Corporation, with the consent of the Duchy of Lancaster, to alienate certain specified portions of Thalto Heath, which had been granted to them as a recreation ground. Other local authorities were authorised to carry out gas and water works, and in the case of Harrogate mineral waterworks, and to purchase and use lands, make and carry out agreements, and borrow moneys for the purposes specified. Not a few Provisional Orders had reference to by-laws. A number of local authorities were authorised to make by-laws with respect to water and waste-water closets, the regulation of parks, and the width and construction of new streets and passages. Three of the Provisional Orders were issued with the object of combining urban and rural areas for the execution of schemes of main sewerage. Under sec. 276 of the Public Health Act, 1875, sec. 5 of the Public Health Acts Amendment Act, 1890, and sec. 4 of the Private Street Works Act, 1892, no fewer than 117 orders were issued investing rural district councils with the powers conferred on urban district councils by certain sections of those Acts. In a large number of cases the urban powers given were those contained in secs. 42, 44, 157 and 158 of the Public Health Act, 1875, and sec. 23 of the Public Health Acts Amendment Act, 1890, relating to the cleansing and watering of streets and the making of by-laws for the prevention of nuisances and with respect to new buildings. In a number of cases the Board conferred the powers contained in secs. 39 and 66 of the Act of 1875 as to the provision of sanitary conveniences and fire-plugs, those of sec. 154 for the widening of streets or the construction of new streets, of the first and second paragraphs of sec. 160 with regard to the naming of streets and the numbering of houses and to ruinous or dangerous buildings, and the powers given by the first paragraph of sec. 161 to enter into contracts for lighting purposes and to provide lighting apparatus; also the powers of secs. 169 (paragraphs 2 and 3) and 170 for the sanitary regulation of slaughter-houses, of sec. 171 with regard to obstructions and nuisances in streets, and of the Private Street Works Act, 1892, as to the making-up of specified private streets.

\* \* \*

**Local Authorities and the Royal Commission on Sewage Disposal.** The letter of Lord Iddesleigh to *The Times*, which we reproduced in our last issue, has attracted a good deal of attention and some adverse criticisms, including two rejoinders in the columns of our Printing House square contemporary. These we give in another column. It will be remembered that the members of the commission, through their noble chairman, expressed the " gravest concern " on account of the statements that many local authorities and manufacturers proposed to delay the execution of schemes of sewage disposal and for the purification of trade effluents until the report of the commission has been published. It would be more correct to say that the grave concern arises from the fact that, according to his lordship, " a considerable time, perhaps even some years, must elapse before the commission can arrive at any final conclusions on a subject which necessarily involves detailed and prolonged scientific investigation." The noble chairman has been answered, more or less bluntly, that there is an alternative to the terrifying prospect that causes him and his fellow-commissioners so much concern, and that is for the commission to bestir themselves and issue their report within a reasonable time, say a year, for it is averred that there is nothing in the nature of the investigations to justify a longer period being required. As for the delay of which local authorities and manufacturers are suspected, a possible alternative for them is the carrying out of schemes which, on the strength of the forthcoming report, may ultimately be described as inadequate. One of the correspondents of our contemporary, in the course of an incisive letter, points out that the proper function of the commission is not to evolve an ideal system by means of exhaustive experiments in bacteriology and chemistry, but " to collate, digest and report upon the enormous mass of practical experience and knowledge obtained from the actual working of numerous sewage disposal systems, but never yet brought to a focus or treated as a whole. Only a very small minority of the commission are really experts in this particular question, and even if they formulated a system satisfactory to themselves it would be just as likely to become obsolete as any of its predecessors, and any attempt to give it finality

by dint of official authority would be disastrous in the extreme. Finally, the correspondent above referred to draws attention to the serious difficulty arising from the private financial interests involved in the sewage disposal question. Another correspondent, signing himself " District Councillor," makes the somewhat startling statement that a certain rural district council which proposed to treat the sewage by means of bacteria beds on the Dibdin lines has been informed that no loan for the purpose will be sanctioned by the Local Government Board unless the process is recommended in the report of the Royal Commission now sitting. We should be much surprised to hear that this deliverance came from the Local Government Board, at all events without the usual qualification that no loan would be sanctioned without subsequent treatment of the effluent on land. The whole correspondence, however, points to the existence of a highly unsatisfactory state of affairs. In another column we give a full report of the recent inquiry at Sutton, where it is proposed to extend the treatment by Dibdin bacteria beds. The inquiry should provide a good test of the present attitude of the Local Government Board, and the decision of the department will be awaited with no small interest. To say nothing of the inquiry, it is significant, as we stated last week, that the chief engineering inspector and the deputy chief engineering inspector of the Local Government Board—Major-General Carey and Colonel J. Ord Hasted—have both recently visited the works at Sutton.

\* \* \*

**London Water Supply.** As will be seen from our report of the London County Council meeting on Tuesday, that body have decided to resume their water supply campaign without waiting for the report of Lord Llandaff's Commission, now sitting. A lengthy report, which we give in another column, has been drawn up by the Water Committee, and has been before the council for a fortnight. On Tuesday the whole of the recommendations with which the report concludes were adopted. The proposals of the council divide themselves into two great schemes, which will be formulated in the shape of Bills—the acquisition of the present undertakings of the companies and the provision of a long-distance supply from Wales. The former scheme would naturally weld the present undertakings into one, and would have the advantage of facilitating that inter-connection between the mains the necessity of which was so plainly demonstrated during the recent scarcity in the East-End. In connection with a long-distance supply from Wales, there is something to be said both for and against the attempt to obtain Parliamentary powers without waiting for the report of Lord Llandaff's Commission. It must be admitted that Royal Commissions rarely result in any definite action being taken, however much the air may be cleared in certain directions, and the opinion has been strengthened during the past two years of scarcity that the commission appointed in 1891 and presided over by Lord Balfour of Burleigh, quite under-estimated the gravity of the situation when their report was published two years later. On the other hand, it may reasonably be doubted if either the Government or the legislature will countenance schemes the verdict on which might be materially influenced if postponed till after the publication of the report of the Royal Commission now sitting. The weight of argument has always seemed to us to be in favour, not only of the acquisition of the present undertakings on reasonable terms by a representative body, but of the ultimate provision of a long-distance supply. It is to be feared, however, that until the publication of the report referred to the prospects of success for the council's proposals are none too rosy. Even should the report of the commission be of an adverse nature, the question is one which must ultimately be decided by public opinion.

# The Sanitary Institute.

## THE SEVENTEENTH ANNUAL CONGRESS.—VI.

We continue our abstracts of the papers and discussions at the recent Birmingham congress. In the section devoted to Physics, Chemistry and Biology, one of the most interesting papers in connection with sewage disposal was that read by Mr. W. D. Scott-Moncrieff on

### THE BIOLYSIS OF SEWAGE.

In the course of his paper Mr. Scott-Moncrieff said that he had been engaged in the solution of the sewage problem, upon purely biological lines, since 1891, but he had refrained from reading a paper on the subject because until quite recently there had been a lack of facts necessary to the formation of definite conclusions. But within the last twelve months he had not only been able to reach finality in the results obtained, but the method of obtaining them threw the whole process open to examination in detail at any required number of stages. The state of knowledge at the time he commenced to make experiments, in 1891, might be judged from the fact that the apparatus now spoken of as the first in England to have proved the capacity of micro-organisms to throw the organic matter of sewage into solution and produce nitrates in the effluent was referred to at that time by a high authority as dependent wholly upon mechanical causes for the results obtained. He referred to the roughing filter at the high-level outfall at Wimbledon. He mentioned this to show that definite information was of very recent date, and it was hardly necessary to add that a nebulous condition often gave rise to inaccurate statements, not to speak of still more nebulous claims to originality. Mr. Scott-Moncrieff then proceeded as follows :—

#### THE WORKING HYPOTHESIS.

The working hypothesis of the advocates for the purification of sewage by biolysis is based upon a belief that the effete substances contained in sewage are within the capacity of Nature to deal with unaided by the use of chemicals. Seeing that Nature does carry out the work of purification, sooner or later, without any assistance from man, and that, as a matter of fact, no great accumulations of inert effete substances exist at all, the hypothesis may be regarded as a truism, and the problem really resolves itself into the discovery of methods by which Nature can be so aided in the case of sewage that it can be purified on the largest scale at a reasonable cost without creating a nuisance and without the use of chemicals. This is which has to be proved, not as a laboratory experiment, but as an available and practical process.

I have made use of the term " biolysis " because the decomposition which occurs in the conversion of food into its original elements are not due to bacterial processes only, but to changes which take place in the digestive organs as well. In dealing with sewage the advocates of purely natural methods contend that after the changes which have taken place in the digestive organs, or even without them, bacteria are capable of completing the work of purification. Now, supposing there were no apparatus in existence to show that this is true, there are, nevertheless, certain facts available for forming a judgment as to the conditions which such an apparatus would have to comply with in order to obtain the best results. These facts may be arranged in the following sequence : (1) The process of purification by biolysis is not instantaneous, but gradual. (2) Dividing it into any convenient number of stages or periods, each of these must represent a different character of food supply. (3) No one kind of organism is capable of flourishing in all the different media or stages equally well. It follows that each stage should occur regularly if each differentiated group of organisms is to work to the best advantage.

Working upon these data, the conditions theoretically most favourable would be first to sterilise the sewage, then subject it to a special cultivation of organisms best suited to throw the organic matter into solution, then, when these had performed the maximum amount of work, sterilise again, subject it to another special cultivation of organisms, and so on. If this were done we know that the organisms employed in the last stage would be incapable of flourishing in the conditions favourable to the first stage, and vice versâ. This I have been able to prove by the very simple experiment of disarranging the various stages of nitrification—placing the seventh in the place of the second, the second in the place of the seventh, and so on. Now, although the process of repeated sterilisations with different cultivations between each is not practicable, it was very important to keep those theoretical conditions clearly in one's mind, because it was obvious that the principle would have to be realised in practice if the best results were to be obtained.

#### PRECIPITATION versus SOLUTION.

It had long been observed in the chemical treatment of sewage that there were greater difficulties in carrying out the process of purification after suspended matters had been disposed of than occurred in their removal. Sir Edward Frankland in a summary of the work done in the laboratory of the Royal Commission on Rivers Pollution says : "All classes of processes are to a great extent successful in removing polluting organic matter in suspension . . . but the getting rid of suspended matters is a simple problem compared with the removal of organic matters in solution." This was written years before the employment of micro-organisms had taken a tangible form. It was a strong argument for the removal of as much suspended matter as possible, so that the organic matters in solution might be reduced in quantity and more easily disposed of.

This opinion becoming widely embraced by those responsible for the carrying out of sewage works, led to the general adoption of precipitation of the suspended matters by chemicals as a cardinal preliminary to all further treatment. Whatever views may be held by Sir Edward Frankland in the light of recent developments, there is little doubt that he would have looked upon the bacterial treatment of sewage, at the time of the Rivers Pollution Commission, with anything but favour if he had understood that the first step in the process was to throw the whole of the organic matters into solution. This would appear, on the face of it, to be opposed to all the prevailing beliefs, because it seemed to add to the difficulty of dealing with what was generally admitted to be the most difficult part of the process. We now know that the question altogether hinges not upon the amount of the organic matter in solution but upon its instability and susceptibility to further and rapid changes in the direction of complete mineralisation, and we also know that this condition of instability can be much more easily produced by biolysis than by any artificial chemical means. As to the relative difficulty between the first and second stages of the process indicated by Dr. Frankland and very generally accepted, it is evident that if the process of throwing the matters into solution by a bacterial fermentation produced the necessary amount of instability required for a further natural process of mineralisation, the problem would be solved if this process could be completed, and it would follow that there would be no sludge, and that the effluent would be a theoretically perfect fertilising medium with all the original organic matter decomposed into the form most readily assimilated by plants. All the experience obtained from my earlier experiments went to show that the process of throwing the organic matter into solution was even more easily carried out than that of getting rid of the suspended matters referred to by Sir Edward Frankland, and the apparatus I have used is shown on Diagram I., Fig. 1 being a plan, Fig. 2 a longitudinal, and Fig. 3 a transverse, section of what has been generally called a "cultivation" tank. The following is a description of the first apparatus of this kind, which was constructed in 1891 and is still in use. It is about 2½ ft. wide, 10 ft. in length, and about 3 ft. deep at the deepest part. The entire sewage discharges and waste waters from a household of ten to twelve persons, with the exception of the grease, which is held back as far as possible by a grease trap, finds its way into one end of this tank at the point CC. The liquid portion rises through a perforated grating E, and then through a layer of flints till it reaches the level of the outflow pipe JJ, which is about 2 in. below the level of the invert of the drain AA. The depth of the filtering material is only about 14 in.

#### THE RESULTS OBTAINED.

The invariable results obtained from several installations of this apparatus proved that practically complete liquefaction of the organic matter could be obtained without trouble of any kind, and that the amount of organic sludge was a negligable quantity. Where there was inorganic detritus it had, of course, to be provided for by deposition in the ordinary way in a sump or catch-pit. It remained to be found out whether or not the breaking up of the organic matter which occurred in the "cultivation" tank was carried sufficiently far to insure its complete mineralisation under natural conditions by some convenient and inexpensive apparatus, and this part of the problem I found to be the most difficult. Several proofs of the sufficiency of the breaking up process were soon available. When discharging the effluent from a "cultivation" tank into a stream of relative greater volume I found that no perceptible pollution occurred, but that there was a fall in the quantity of free and albuminoid ammonia out of all proportion to the amount of dilution.

It will be noticed, from the following analysis that the ratio of dilution could be closely estimated by the chlorine content of the effluent and that of the stream, and while the dilution was about as 3 to 1, the fall in the quantity of albuminoid ammonia was from '25 to '035, or about as 7 to 1 and the free ammonia as about 20 to 1. This proved beyond doubt that the organic matter contained in the effluent from the "cultivation" tank was capable of being rapidly oxidised in the stream, and from this I argued that if channels could be provided with the same amount of dilution they would be all that was necessary to give similar results.* The chemists, however, insisted upon judging the process from the analysis of the effluent as it escaped from the "cultivation" tanks. The argument about the instability of the organic matter was never entertained at all, and although in the case above referred to there could be no reasonable objection made to the water that was passed into the river, they said that the process must be judged from the results obtained from the apparatus itself.

embodies the third part of the process, which, again, is subdivided into any required number of stages, according to the standard of purification which it is wished to maintain. This analysis is shown on the first line of the table, which gives analyses of the changes which occur during the process of nitrification.

### THE APPARATUS DESCRIBED.

The original apparatus was as follows: I constructed nine wooden boxes with perforated bottoms, each of them 2 ft.

*Scott-Moncrieff System of Purification. Date when Sample taken, September 12, 1893.*

| Description. | Smell. | Reaction. | Clearness—Inches through which type could be read | Chlorine. | | Total Solids. | | Ammonia (Wanklyn). | | | |
|---|---|---|---|---|---|---|---|---|---|---|---|
| | | | | | | | | Free. | | Albuminoid. | |
| | | | | Grains per gallon. | Parts per 100,000 | Grains per gallon | Parts per 100,000 | Grains per gallon. | Parts per 100,000 | Grains per gallon. | Parts per 100,000 |
| Effluent ... ... | Slightly unpleasant | ...Practically neutral... | 6·8 | 3·3 | 4·71 | 43 | 61·4 | 1·72 | 2·46 | ·17 | ·25 |
| Brook water taken 5 yards from effluent outlet | Slightly musty | ... Neutral | ... | — | 2·0 | 2·86 | 38 | 54 | ·52 | ·74 | ·04 | ·06 |
| Brook water at bottom corner, about 30 yards | More musty than above... | Neutral | ... | — | 1·3 | 1·86 | 27 | 39 | ·09 | ·13 | ·024 | ·035 |

This impressed me more than ever with the necessity for providing more highly oxidising conditions, and also for separating, if possible, the various stages of the process into differentiated colonies of nitrifying organisms, as already referred to. Accepting the analysis of the diluted effluent as a proof that the first stage of anaerobic fermentation was sufficient to produce the required amount of instability in the organic content of the effluent, it was evident that in sewage containing a certain amount of free oxygen the first changes that occurred would be aerobic in character, and even when all available oxygen was absent it only showed that it had been used up and that some organic change had occurred as a consequence. The process as a whole must then consist of several stages, in the first of which the available oxygen will be used up by aerobic organisms, and the second would depend upon the action of anaerobic organisms with liquefactions of the organic matter, and a conversion of its nitrogenous constituents into nitrogen as free ammonia with other changes due to the fermentative conditions.

The case could therefore be stated in another way, and the necessary sequence would be—first, that favourable conditions should be provided by well-ventilated and self-cleansing sewers for the work of a mixed group of aerobic organisms; that the conditions should then be reversed, becoming unfavourable to the aerobic and favourable to the anaerobic organisms, and that the conditions should again be reversed, being unfavourable to the anaerobic organisms and highly favourable to differentiated colonies of nitrifying organisms, which are best suited to carry on and complete the final mineralisation of the organic matter by converting the free ammonia into nitrogen as nitric acid.

Presuming that the "cultivation" tank as above described

long by 7 in. wide by 7 in. deep, an allowance of ¼ in. on each side being made, so that each box had an effective area of 1 square foot through which the effluent passed. These boxes I placed one above the other upon a framework, and filled them to a depth of 6 in. in each box with coke, broken so as to pass through a ring 1 in. diameter. Over the uppermost box I fixed two small tilting V-shaped trays, which automatically discharged their contents when the liquid reached a level that upset their equilibrium, as they were hung upon small trunnions fixed at the proper point to effect this movement, working upon supports fixed to the ends of the highest box. Over this column of boxes a large tank was fixed, into which the effluent was pumped after it came through the "cultivation" tank. The flow of the effluent was so regulated and measured that an estimate could at any moment be made of the rate in terms of gallons per acre per twenty-four hours. Between each of the boxes there was an air space of about 2 in., and a receptacle was provided at the bottom which held about twelve hours' flow. By placing shallow dishes between the boxes samples could be taken simultaneously and a complete set of analyses of the whole series of changes could be made consecutively. The arrangement of the trays is shown on Diagram 1., Figs. 4, 5 and 6, also Diagrams II., III. and IV. The apparatus was set to work on October 25th last, and kept constantly going both night and day for about three months, this lengthy trial being made with the object of discovering if there was any tendency to clogging of the material in the boxes, everything being perfectly free from accumulations and the effluent running at the rate of a little over 1,000,000 gallons per acre during the whole period. Dr. Rideal made a series of analyses which are shown in the table.

*Table showing successive stages of Mineralisation by Nitrifying Organisms. Ashstead Experiments, February, 1898.*

| Description of Samples. | A Chlorine. | B Free NH₃ | C ≥ N | D Albuminoid NH₃ | E = N | F Oxygen consumed. | G O. consumed being O. required by Nitrous Nitrogen. | H Nitrous Nitrogen. | I —Oxygen Nitrogen. | J Nitric required. | K Nitric Nitrogen. | L = Useful Oxygen N₂A₂ to N₂A. | M Total Oxidised Nitrogen. | N Available Oxygen used ᵗⁿ₄, consumed. | O Total Unoxidised N. (Kjeldahl). | P Total Inorganic Nitrogen. | Q Total Nitrogen of all kinds. |
|---|---|---|---|---|---|---|---|---|---|---|---|---|---|---|---|---|---|
| Effluent from cultivation tank, taken 3 and 5 p.m. | 9·0 | 12·5 | 10·30 | 1·50 | 1·23 | 0·843 | 9·843 | Nil. | — | 0·12 | 0·274 | 0·12 | — | 9·57 | 12·35 | 2·05 | 10·42 | 12·47 |
| (1) Effluent from first tray ... | 9·0 | 10·5 | 8·65 | 1·25 | 1·03 | 0·694 | 5·56 | 0·99 | 1·13 | 0·006 | 6·219 | 1·036 | — 6·47 | 11·5 | 2·8 | 9·74 | 12·59 |
| (2) Effluent from second tray | 8·5 | 9·0 | 7·42 | 1·00 | 0·82 | 5·773 | 4·74 | 0·90 | 1·03 | 0·48 | 1·00 | 1·33 | — 4·66 | 11·10 | 3·08 | 8·80 | 12·48 |
| (3) Effluent from third tray ... | 8·5 | 5·0 | 4·12 | 0·60 | 0·49 | 4·493 | 3·60 | 0·78 | 0·59 | 1·87 | 4·27 | 2·65 | — 0·22 | 6·60 | 2·48 | 0·77 | 9·25 |
| (4) Effluent from fourth tray | 8·0 | 4·0 | 3·3 | 0·3 | 0·29 | 1·728 | 0·98 | 0·66 | 0·75 | 2·76 | 6·30 | 3·42 | + 4·58 | 5·15 | 1·85 | 6·72 | 8·57 |
| (5) Effluent from fifth tray ... | 7·75 | 1·5 | 1·24 | 0·15 | 0·12 | 1·28 | 0·73 | 0·48 | 0·55 | 4·08 | 10·70 | 5·16 | + 9·42 | 1·75 | 0·51 | 6·40 | 6·91 |
| (6) Effluent from sixth tray ... | 8·0 | 1·75 | 1·44 | 0·35 | 0·29 | 1·497 | 0·92 | 0·31 | 0·55 | 4·416 | 10·10 | 4·926 | + 8·61 | 2·25 | 0·81 | 6·37 | 7·18 |
| (7) Effluent from seventh tray | 7·5 | 0·35 | 0·29 | 0·30 | 0·25 | 0·755 | 0·755 | Nil. | — | 6·6 | 15·08 | 6·6 | + 14·33 | 0·85 | 0·56 | 6·80 | 7·45 |
| (8) Effluent from eighth tray | 7·5 | 0·20 | 0·165 | 0·65 | 0·53 | 0·397 | 0·397 | Nil. | — | 7·32 | 16·73 | 7·32 | + 16·34 | 1·03 | 0·865 | 7·48 | 8·35 |
| (9) Effluent from ninth tray... | 7·5 | 0·25 | 0·206 | 0·60 | 0·49 | 0·580 | 0·580 | Slight trace. | — | 9·0 | 20·0 | 9·0 | + 25·1 | 0·10 | 1·394 | 9·21 | 9·60 |

was a satisfactory method of carrying out the first two stages, I give a typical analysis of the effluent obtained from it, and will then go on to describe the very simple apparatus which

---

* The method of treating sewage by dilution only has been seriously considered both in Germany and the United States, and it is now being used for dealing with the sewage of Chicago, but no notice seems to have been taken of the important element of instability of the organic matter produced by previous bacterial fermentation.

### THE MOST INTERESTING RESULT

of the experiments is the rapid conversion of the nitrogen compounds into nitrogen as nitric acid, and a high figure has been maintained throughout, varying from 7 to about 9 parts per 100,000. The conversion from the first line of results to the bottom line, which gives an analysis of the effluent from the ninth tray, occurs in something under ten minutes, showing the extraordinary rapidity with which mineralisation

# The Sanitary Institute.

## THE SEVENTEENTH ANNUAL CONGRESS.—VI.

We continue our abstracts of the papers and discussions at the recent Birmingham congress. In the section devoted to Physics, Chemistry and Biology, one of the most interesting papers in connection with sewage disposal was that read by Mr. W. D. Scott-Moncrieff on

### THE BIOLYSIS OF SEWAGE.

In the course of his paper Mr. Scott-Moncrieff said that he had been engaged in the solution of the sewage problem, upon purely biological lines, since 1891, but he had refrained from reading a paper on the subject because until quite recently there had been a lack of facts necessary to the formation of definite conclusions. But within the last twelve months he had not only been able to reach finality in the results obtained, but the method of obtaining them threw the whole process open to examination in detail at any required number of stages. The state of knowledge at the time he commenced to make experiments, in 1891, might be judged from the fact that the apparatus now spoken of as the first in England to have proved the capacity of micro-organisms to throw the organic matter of sewage into solution and produce nitrates in the effluent was referred to at that time by a high authority as dependent wholly upon mechanical causes for the results obtained. He referred to the roughing filter at the high-level outfall at Wimbledon. He mentioned this to show that definite information was of very recent date, and it was hardly necessary to add that a nebulous condition often gave rise to inaccurate statements, not to speak of still more nebulous claims to originality. Mr. Scott-Moncrieff then proceeded as follows :—

#### THE WORKING HYPOTHESIS.

The working hypothesis of the advocates for the purification of sewage by biolysis is based upon a belief that the effete substances contained in sewage are within the capacity of Nature to deal with unaided by the use of chemicals. Seeing that Nature does carry out the work of purification, sooner or later, without any assistance from man, and that, as a matter of fact, no great accumulations of inert effete substances exist at all, the hypothesis may be regarded as a truism, and the problem really resolves itself into the discovery of methods by which Nature can be aided in the case of sewage that it can be purified on the largest scale at a reasonable cost without creating a nuisance and without the use of chemicals. This is which has to be proved, not as a laboratory experiment, but as an available and practical process.

I have made use of the term "biolysis" because the decomposition which occurs in the conversion of food into its original elements are not due to bacterial processes only, but to changes which take place in the digestive organs as well. In dealing with sewage the advocates of purely natural methods contend that after the changes which have taken place in the digestive organs, or even without them, bacteria are capable of completing the work of purification. Now, supposing there were no apparatus in existence to show that this is true, there are, nevertheless, certain facts available for forming a judgment as to the conditions which such an apparatus would have to comply with in order to obtain the best results. These facts may be arranged in the following sequence : (1) The process of purification by biolysis is not instantaneous, but gradual. (2) Dividing it into any convenient number of stages or periods, each of these must represent a different character of food supply. (3) No one kind of organism is capable of flourishing in all the different media or stages equally well. It follows that each stage should occur regularly if each differentiated group of organisms is to work to the best advantage.

Working upon these data, the conditions theoretically most favourable would be first to sterilise the sewage, then subject it to a special cultivation of organisms best suited to throw the organic matter into solution, then, when these had performed the maximum amount of work, sterilise again, subject it to another special cultivation of organisms, and so on. If this were done we know that the organisms employed in the last stage would be incapable of flourishing in the conditions favourable to the first stage, and vice versâ. This I have been able to prove by the very simple experiment of disarranging the various stages of nitrification—placing the seventh in the place of the second, the second in the place of the seventh, and so on. Now, although the process of repeated sterilisations with different cultivations between each is not practicable, it was very important to keep these theoretical conditions clearly in one's mind, because it was obvious that the principle would have to be realised in practice if the best results were to be obtained.

#### PRECIPITATION versus SOLUTION.

It had long been observed in the chemical treatment of sewage that there were greater difficulties in carrying out the process of purification after suspended matters had been disposed of than occurred in their removal. Sir Edward Frankland in a summary of the work done in the laboratory of the Royal Commission on Rivers Pollution says ; "All classes of processes are to a great extent successful in re. moving polluting organic matter in suspension , , , but the getting rid of suspended matters is a simple problem com. pared with the removal of organic matters in solution." This was written years before the employment of micro-organisms had taken a tangible form. It was a strong argument for the removal of as much suspended matter as possible, so that the organic matters in solution might be reduced in quantity and more easily disposed of.

This opinion becoming widely embraced by those responsible for the carrying out of sewage works, led to the general adop. tion of precipitation of the suspended matters by chemicals as a cardinal preliminary to all further treatment. Whatever views may be held by Sir Edward Frankland in the light of recent developments, there is little doubt that he would have looked upon the bacterial treatment of sewage, at the time of the Rivers Pollution Commission, with anything but favour if he had understood that the first step in the process was to throw the whole of the organic matters into solution. This would appear, on the face of it, to be opposed to all the pre. vailing beliefs, because it seemed to add to the difficulty of dealing with what was generally admitted to be the most difficult part of the process. We now know that the question altogether hinges not upon the amount of the organic matter in solution but upon its instability and susceptibility to further and rapid changes in the direction of complete mineralisation, and we also know that this condition of instability can be much more easily produced by biolysis than by any artificial chemical means. As to the relative difficulty between the first and second stages of the process indicated by Dr. Frank. land and very generally accepted, it is evident that if the process of throwing the matters into solution by a bacterial fermentation produced the necessary amount of instability re. quired for a further natural process of mineralisation, the problem would be solved if this process could be completed, and it would follow that there would be no sludge, and that the effluent would be a theoretically perfect fertilising medium with all the original organic matter decomposed into the form most readily assimilated by plants. All the experi. ence obtained from my earlier experiments went to show that the process of throwing the matters into solution was even more easily carried out than that of getting rid of the suspended matters referred to by Sir Edward Frankland, and the apparatus I have used is shown on Diagram I., Fig. 1 being a plan, Fig. 2 a longitudinal, and Fig. 3 a transverse, section of what has been generally called a "cultivation" tank. The following is a description of the first apparatus of this kind, which was constructed in 1891 and is still in use. It is about 2½ ft. wide, 10 ft. in length, and about 3 ft. deep at the deepest part. The entire sewage discharges and waste waters from a household of ten to twelve persons, with the exception of the grease, which is held back as far as possible by a grease trap, finds its way into one end of this tank at the point CC. The liquid portion rises through a perforated grating E, and then through a layer of flints till it reaches the level of the outflow pipe JJ, which is about 2 in. below the level of the invert of the drain AA. The depth of the filtering material is only about 14 in.

#### THE RESULTS OBTAINED.

The invariable results obtained from several installations of this apparatus proved that practically complete liquefac. tion of the organic matter could be obtained without trouble of any kind, and that the amount of organic sludge was a negligable quantity. Where there was inorganic detritus it had, of course, to be provided for by deposition in the ordi. nary way in a sump or catch-pit. It remained to be found out whether or not the breaking up of the organic matter which occurred in the "cultivation" tank was carried suffi. ciently far to insure its complete mineralisation under natural conditions by some convenient and inexpensive apparatus, and this part of the problem I found to be the most difficult. Several proofs of the sufficiency of the breaking up process were soon available. When discharging the effluent from a "cultivation" tank into a stream of relative greater volume I found that no perceptible pollution occurred, but that there was a fall in the quantity of free and albuminoid ammonia out of all proportion to the amount of dilution.

It will be noticed, from the following analysis, that the ratio of dilution could be closely estimated by the chlorine content of the effluent and that of the stream, and while the dilution was about as 3 to 1, the fall in the quantity of albu. minoid ammonia was from ·25 to ·035, or about as 7 to 1 and the free ammonia as about 20 to 1. This proved beyond doubt that the organic matter contained in the effluent from the "cultivation" tank was capable of being rapidly oxidised in the stream, and from this I argued that if channels could be provided with the same amount of dilution they would be all that was necessary to give similar results.* The chemists, however, insisted upon judging the process from the analysis of the effluent as it escaped from the "cultivation" tanks. The argument about the instability of the organic matter was never entertained at all, and although in the case above referred to there could be no reasonable objection made to the water that was passed into the river, they said that the process must be judged from the results obtained from the apparatus itself.

embodies the third part of the process, which, again, is subdivided into any required number of stages, according to the standard of purification which it is wished to maintain. This analysis is shown on the first line of the table, which gives analyses of the changes which occur during the process of nitrification.

### THE APPARATUS DESCRIBED.

The original apparatus was as follows: I constructed nine wooden boxes with perforated bottoms, each of them 2 ft.

*Scott-Moncrieff System of Purification. Date when Sample taken, September 12, 1893.*

| Description. | Smell. | Reaction. | Clearness.—Inches through which pearl type could be read. | Chlorine. | | Total Solids. | | Ammonia (Wanklyn). | | | | | |
|---|---|---|---|---|---|---|---|---|---|---|---|---|---|
| | | | | | | | | Free. | | Albuminoid. | | | |
| | | | | Grains per gallon. | Parts per 100,000. | Grains per gallon. | Parts per 100,000. | Grains per gallon. | Parts per 100,000. | Grains per gallon. | Parts per 100,000. | | |
| Effluent ... ... | Slightly unpleasant | ...Practically neutral... | 6·8 | 3·3 | 4·71 | 43 | 61·4 | 1·72 | 2·46 | ·17 | ·25 | | |
| Brook water taken 5 yards from effluent outlet | Slightly musty | ... Neutral | — | 2·0 | 2·86 | 38 | 54 | ·52 | ·74 | ·04 | ·06 | | |
| Brook water at bottom corner, about 30 yards | More musty than above... | Neutral | — | 1·3 | 1·86 | 27 | 39 | ·09 | ·13 | ·024 | ·035 | | |

This impressed me more than ever with the necessity for providing more highly oxidising conditions, and also for separating, if possible, the various stages of the process into differentiated colonies of nitrifying organisms, as already referred to. Accepting the analysis of the diluted effluent as a proof that the first stage of anaerobic fermentation was sufficient to produce the required amount of instability in the organic content of the effluent, it was evident that in sewage containing a certain amount of free oxygen the first changes that occurred would be aerobic in character, and even when all available oxygen was absent it only showed that it had been used up and that some organic change had occurred as a consequence. The process as a whole must then consist of several stages, in the first of which the available oxygen will be used up by aerobic organisms, and the second would depend upon the action of anaerobic organisms with liquefactions of the organic matter, and a conversion of its nitrogenous constituents into nitrogen as free ammonia with other changes due to the fermentative conditions.

The case could therefore be stated in another way, and the necessary sequence would be—first, that favourable conditions should be provided by well-ventilated and self-cleansing sewers for the work of a mixed group of aerobic organisms; that the conditions should then be reversed, becoming unfavourable to the aerobic and favourable to the anaerobic organisms, and that the conditions should again be reversed, being unfavourable to the anaerobic organisms and highly favourable to differentiated colonies of nitrifying organisms, which are best suited to carry on and complete the final mineralisation of the organic matter by converting the free ammonia into nitrogen as nitric acid.

Presuming that the "cultivation" tank as above described

long by 7 in. wide by 7 in. deep, an allowance of ¼ in. on each side being made, so that each box had an effective area of 1 square foot through which the effluent passed. These boxes I placed one above the other upon a framework, and filled them to a depth of 6 in. in each box with coke, broken so as to pass through a ring 1 in. diameter. Over the uppermost box I fixed two small tilting V-shaped trays, which automatically discharged their contents when the liquid reached a level that upset their equilibrium, as they were hung upon small trunnions fixed at the proper point to effect this movement, working upon supports fixed to the ends of the highest box. Over this column of boxes a large tank was fixed, into which the effluent was pumped after it came through the "cultivation" tank. The flow of the effluent was so regulated and measured that an estimate could at any moment be made of the rate in terms of gallons per acre per twenty-four hours. Between each of the boxes there was an air space of about 2 in., and a receptacle was provided at the bottom which held about twelve hours' flow. By placing shallow dishes between the boxes samples could be taken simultaneously and a complete set of analyses of the whole series of changes could be made consecutively. The arrangement of the trays is shown on Diagram I., Figs. 4, 5 and 6, also Diagrams II., III. and IV. The apparatus was set to work on October 25th last, and kept constantly going both night and day for about three months, this lengthy trial being made with the object of discovering if there was any tendency to clogging of the material in the boxes, everything being perfectly free from accumulations and the effluent running at the rate of a little over 1,000,000 gallons per acre during the whole period. Dr. Rideal made a series of analyses which are shown in the table.

*Table showing successive stages of Mineralisation by Nitrifying Organisms. Ashstead Experiments, February, 1898.*

| | Description of Samples. | A Chlorine. | B Free NH₃. | C = N | D Albuminoid NH₃ = N | E Oxygen consumed | F O, required by combined amines (O₂ required by combined amines) | G | H Nitrous Nitrogen. | I = Oxygen required. | J Nitric Nitrogen. | K Useful Oxygen N₂O₃ to N₂O₅. | L Total Oxidised Nitrogen. | M Available Oxygen per useful O, estimated. | N Total Dissolved N. (Kjeldahl). | O Total Organic Nitrogen. | P Total Inorganic Nitrogen. | Q Total Nitrogen of all kinds. |
|---|---|---|---|---|---|---|---|---|---|---|---|---|---|---|---|---|---|---|
| Colonies of Aerobic Nitrifying Organisms. | Effluent from cultivation tank, taken 3 and 5 p.m. | 9·0 | 12·5 | 10·30 | 1·50 | 1·23 | 9·843 | 9·843 | Nil. | — | 0·12 | 0·274 | 0·12 | — | 9·57 | 12·35 | 2·05 | 10·42 | 12·47 |
| | (1) Effluent from first tray ... | 9·0 | 10·5 | 8·65 | 1·25 | 1·03 | 6·694 | 5·56 | 0·99 | 1·13 | 0·096 | 0·219 | 1·086 | — | 6·47 | 11·5 | 2·85 | 9·74 | 12·59 |
| | (2) Effluent from second tray | 8·5 | 9·0 | 7·42 | 1·00 | 0·82 | 5·773 | 4·74 | 0·90 | 1·03 | 0·48 | 1·09 | 1·38 | — | 4·68 | 11·16 | 3·68 | 8·80 | 12·48 |
| | (3) Effluent from third tray... | 8·5 | 5·0 | 4·12 | 0·60 | 0·49 | 4·493 | 3·60 | 0·78 | 0·59 | 1·87 | 4·27 | 2·65 | − 0·22 | 6·60 | 2·48 | 6·77 | 9·25 |
| | (4) Effluent from fourth tray | 8·0 | 4·0 | 3·3 | 0·3 | 0·29 | 1·728 | 0·98 | 0·66 | 0·75 | 2·76 | 6·30 | 3·42 | ÷ 4·68 | 5·15 | 1·85 | 6·72 | 8·57 |
| | (5) Effluent from fifth tray ... | 7·75 | 1·5 | 1·24 | 0·15 | 0·12 | 1·28 | 0·73 | 0·48 | 0·55 | 4·68 | 10·70 | 5·16 | ÷ 9·42 | 1·75 | 0·51 | 6·40 | 6·91 |
| | (6) Effluent from sixth tray... | 8·0 | 1·75 | 1·44 | 0·35 | 0·29 | 1·497 | 0·92 | 0·61 | 0·58 | 4·416 | 10·10 | 4·926 | ÷ 8·61 | 2·25 | 0·81 | 6·37 | 7·18 |
| | (7) Effluent from seventh tray | 7·5 | 0·35 | 0·29 | 0·30 | 0·25 | 0·755 | 0·755 | Nil. | — | 6·6 | 15·08 | 6·6 | ÷11·33 | 0·85 | 0·56 | 6·89 | 7·45 |
| | (8) Effluent from eighth tray | 7·5 | 0·20 | 0·165 | 0·65 | 0·53 | 0·307 | 0·397 | Nil. | — | 7·32 | 16·73 | 7·32 | ÷16·34 | 1·03 | 0·865 | 7·18 | 8·35 |
| | (9) Effluent from ninth tray... | 7·5 | 0·25 | 0·206 | 0·60 | 0·49 | 0·589 | 0·589 | Slight traco. | — | 9·0 | 20·0 | 9·0 | ÷20·1 | 0·6 | 0·394 | 9·21 | 9·60 |

was a satisfactory method of carrying out the first two stages, I give a typical analysis of the effluent obtained from it, and will then go on to describe the very simple apparatus which

### THE MOST INTERESTING RESULT

of the experiments is the rapid conversion of the nitrogen compounds into nitrogen as nitric acid, and a high figure has been maintained throughout, varying from 7 to about 9 parts per 100,000. The conversion from the first line of results to the bottom line, which gives an analysis of the effluent from the ninth tray, occurs in something under ten minutes, showing the extraordinary rapidity with which mineralisation

---

* The method of treating sewage by dilution only has been seriously considered both in Germany and the United States, and it is now being used for dealing with the sewage of Chicago, but no notice seems to have been taken of the important element of instability of the organic matter produced by previous bacterial fermentation.

occurs when the conditions are favourable. By transposing the trays so as to upset the natural survival of organisms in the sequence the whole process was arrested, a high-coloured and inferior effluent being the immediate result, and one or two days were required to re-establish the conditions which had been disturbed.

It occurred to me that the arrangement as described could be used to obtain graphic illustrations of the changes as they took place, and the nitrogen lines are shown upon Chart I. All the other changes can be graphically shown in a similar manner, and when these are superimposed one upon the other a complete view is obtained of how they are related to each other. The lines of increase crossing the lines of decrease afford a practically perfect method of obtaining information as to what is going on, and a curious setting back of the lines of increase with a corresponding change in the line of oxygen consumed in the case of the 5th Colony pointed to a critical state of the biological conditions at that part of the process; that is shown upon Chart No. 2. It is a subject of great regret to me that a large installation at Caterham, dealing with the entire discharge from the barracks, has not been completed in time to allow of the results being brought into this paper. These I hope will soon be made public.

What appears to be certain is that full information can now be obtained, both chemically and bacteriologically, as to what actually goes on during the whole process of nitrification. I should add that I have made provision for discovering, if possible, the point to which the anaerobic changes should be carried and beyond which they ought to be arrested. Estimation by error appeared to me to be the only way of arriving at any certainty with regard to this important element in the process. With this end in view, I have constructed a closed chamber, in which the anaerobic conditions are greatly intensified by means of inverted glazed earthenware vessels piled up inside the chamber. As each of these forms a separate cell, in which the gases of decomposition accumulate, and as these, numbering over 500, are placed in the body of the liquid, and as arrangements are also made for discharging the effluent at various stages of the anaerobic decomposition over the nitrifying trays, it is hoped that some definite knowledge may be gained as to the proper point to which these first stages should be carried. As I have already said, my apology for reading this paper is that there is now a prospect of light being thrown upon the process of biolysis at all its stages, and that we shall be no longer working in the dark. Two analyses are given in addition to those made by Dr. Rideal, one by Sir Edward Frankland and the other by Mr. Raymond Ross.

*Analysis by Sir E. Frankland, F.R.S. Ashstead Experiments.*

| February 10, 1898. | Total Solid Matters. | Organic Carbon. | Organic Nitrogen. | Ammonia. | Nitrogen as Nitrates and Nitrites. | Total Com. binel Nitro. gen. | Chlorine. |
|---|---|---|---|---|---|---|---|
| Sample of Crude Sewage. | 85·6 | 5·538 | 1·054 | 11·25 | 0 | 10·31 | 7·1 |
| Sample of Sewage Effluent. | 79·3 | ·713 | ·111 | ·42 | 5·940 | 6·40 | 5·9 |

*Remarks.*—Sample of crude sewage: Foul odour.
" Sample of sewage effluent: No odour.

*Analysis by Raymond Ross, F.I.C., F.C.S., Member of the Society of Public Analysts. Ashstead Experiments.*

Samples taken by Dr. Fosbroke, M.O.H. for Worcestershire.

| | Parts per 100,000. | |
|---|---|---|
| | Sewage. | Effluent. |
| Total Nitrogen (Kjeldahl) | 38·42 | ·17 |
| Free Ammonia | 11·72 | ·013 |
| Albuminoid Ammonia | 4·5 | ·075 |

The concluding paper in this section was one entitled "The Flora of Sewage," by Prof. Rubert Boyce, M.B. As this paper does not seem to be procurable, we regret that we are unable to give an abstract. If opportunity offers, however, we shall make good the deficiency in an early issue.

## DISCUSSION.

The papers of Messrs. Kenwood, Rideal, Scott-Moncrieff, Adeney and Boyce, were discussed together.

Prof. FRANKLAND said the rapid disposal of sewage was first gone into by chemists, and under them obtained greatest perfection. He did not think there was anything which could surpass the results obtained by intermittent downward filtration and irrigation. In many manufacturing parts of the country the streams were in a shockingly polluted state, so that there was no chance of them ever being able to be used for drinking purposes. What they desired to ascertain was whether the effluent was capable of entering into putrefaction or not, and whether similar action took place when the sewage was mixed with the stream. He should like to see more generally introduced the incubator test for sewage effluent, which should also be extended to sewage mixtures. Manufacturers were frequently guilty of wholesale pollution, and it seemed to him that the only remedy open to public authorities was to obtain powers to coerce the manufacturers to distribute as much as possible the escape of waste liquors over twenty-four hours, and in the case of really dangerous liquids to make them first undergo a process of purification. Powers had been obtained at Bilston that nothing should be admitted into a sewer that would damage the sewer or living crops. They also had the additional power to exclude anything which damaged purification processes.

Lieutenant-Colonel JONES, V.C. (London), argued that until they had filters on a large scale and they were tried with all matters that came down a sewer for a considerable time they must proceed with great caution.

Dr. PORTER (Stockport) said in the Mersey and Irwell district of Lancashire there were streams which could never be used for purposes of water supply. He therefore submitted that no unnecessary harassing of manufacturing interests should be insisted upon merely for sentimental and æsthetic reasons.

Dr. KAYE PERRY (Dublin) urged that until the question of the cost of filters and working was put aside with other systems of sewage purification engineers were not in a position to get off the fence on which they had sat so long.

Mr. W. J. DIBDIN (Sutton, Surrey), said if they treated sewage by excessive doses of lime, by carbolic acid, or any material which would act as a disinfectant, they arrested that systematic process of destruction of the organic matters and simply held up for a time the natural purifying action.

Dr. HEWITT (Cheshire) gave the results of some experiments at Manchester, which showed, he said, that the effluent in the tanks could be so dealt with under Mr. Dibdin's process that it was good enough to turn into a slow-moving large body like the Ship Canal. He considered that the incubator test was a safe addition to the oxygen absorbed test.

Mr. A. J. MARTIN (Exeter) said the use of a sewage tank was preferable at Exeter. Unless they were dealing solely with domestic sewage on a separate system they would have a large amount of mineral matter and mud in suspension coming down the sewage. The effect of this in cultivation filters must be very disastrous. It had also been proved that the destruction of organisms in a tank was considerable, owing to the time of exposure to action.

Dr. G. SIMS WOODHEAD, who presided over the section (Physics, Chemistry and Biology) in which the papers were read, spoke with satisfaction of the great advance made since last year's congress. Then they could only deal with generalities, but now they had definite data to go upon, and the authors of the various papers had provided data to keep them going for at least another twelve months. (Laughter.)

Other gentlemen taking part in the discussion were Messrs. R. Burford (Taunton) and A. S. Ackermann (Westminster), and the authors of the papers replied.

The papers already given may be supplemented by one read at the conference of municipal representatives by the Rev. Dr. Cox, F.S.A., chairman of the Brixworth Rural District Council. The paper, which dealt with both the sewerage and sewage disposal of rural districts, was entitled

## VILLAGE SEWERAGE SCHEMES: EXPERIMENTS IN THE RURAL DISTRICT OF BRIXWORTH.

In the opening of his paper the author remarked that there was no rural district of England, of at all similar area and population, that could compare for a moment with the Brixworth district in the large number of its sanitary experiments. It might be of profit to others to know of their attempts and their failures. He then proceeded as follows:—

The Brixworth district consists of thirty-six distinct villages or hamlets, with an aggregate population of 12,000, and an area of 62,648 acres. Out of the total seventeen are sewered. The seventeen sewered villages have an approximate population of 3,000, and the nineteen unsewered of 4,000. About 1873 the question of water-carried sewage was before the sanitary authority. In that year the experiment of water-flushed sewers discharging into a small filtration bed was begun at Moulton, the largest village in the district. The second to be sewered was Brixworth, the next largest in population; this experiment was carried out in 1877, together with that of Walgrave. The two last villages to be sewered were Pitsford and Boughton; the works for both these villages were finished in 1895, but they were ordered by the old authority. Since the Local Government Act of 1894, which provided for a popularly elected district council, attempts to extend sewerage schemes to other small villages have been successfully resisted. The resistance of the very large majority of the council has not been based upon economical considerations, but rather upon the belief that most of the previous experiments in this direction have been distinct failures.

The removal of refuse and excreta by water carriage, which is the ordinary sewage method of towns, pre-supposes (if the method is to be successful), five conditions:—(1) a copious water supply; (2) properly-laid sewers, with adequate fall; (3) a sufficiency of suitable land for irrigation or filtration purposes; (4) a large outlay; and (5) good and continuous management. It is my contention that the many experiments of the Brixworth district, several of a quarter of a century duration, prove that it is practically impossible to find these conditions co-existent in rural districts or amid small village populations, and that the health of the village will not be permanently improved by a water-carried system, but will rather in the long run materially suffer. Evidence was laid before the Public Health Amendment Bill Committee in 1877 as to the sewering of several Brixworth union villages, and the local nuisance inspector, when examined by Mr. Pell, stated that the system thoroughly answered. But at that time it was far too soon to draw any satisfactory conclusions. How have the five conditions mentioned above as essential to success worked out in our rural district? Let us take them *seriatim* after a brief fashion.

### (1) A COPIOUS WATER SUPPLY.

Surely in village sanitation this provision should stand absolutely first. At the same time, it is possible to have two copious a water supply running in your sewers, if the village is in a district abounding in surface springs. This has been and still is the case with the village Brixworth (sewered in 1877), where the amount of water that constantly gets into the sewers is sufficient (according to the estimate of our inspector) to cover the whole area of the filtration-bed 2 in. deep once in every twenty-four hours. The result is disastrous; the effluent into the adjoining brook is never good and occasionally singularly foul.

Throughout our seventeen sewered villages there is only one in which the question of the water supply was thought out and engineered before the sewerage scheme was begun, and it is the only one in which each closet is supplied with a cistern. Chapel Brampton is the solitary instance, with which I am acquainted, where a water-carried sewerage system, as applied to a rural village, can be said to be a success. This village, with a population of 217, is on Earl Spencer's estate. The water supply and sewerage works were executed by Mr. Griffiths at his lordship's charges, and were for the date (1880) admirable of their kind, and even now produce fairly satisfactory results.[*] It is difficult, however, to imagine that any rural sanitary authority would have undertaken such a scheme, and it would have been almost more than any rates could possibly have borne. Here, and here only in our district, was the right principle followed—*viz.*, the construction of a reservoir, fed by a wheel and pumped from a clear spring supply at some distance, before ever the sewers and the connected closets were constructed.

Nowhere, save at Chapel Brampton, out of our seventeen schemes are the connected closets technically water-closets. They are simply pan-closets, and to keep them sweet water has to be hand-carried and thrown down each day. The water in several of our sewered villages is at a considerable distance from many of the cottages. It is unreasonable to expect that the average cottage housewife, when she has fetched the water for varied domestic purposes, will care to regularly hand-flush the closet. The consequence is that many of the pans get coated with filth and choked up from time to time. To sewer a village without at first providing for the flushing of each pan, even if the flushing tanks of the main sewer are kept well supplied, is a curse instead of a blessing. The connections, often of considerable length, thus remain practically unflushed from year's end to year's end and occasionally get fouled and choked. I have seen several such connections opened which were in a very nasty condition.

### (2) PROPERLY LAID SEWERS WITH ADEQUATE FALL.

To secure a good fall to the filtration-beds, in an undulating district like ours, the risk is incurred of selecting a bed close to the brook or stream in that valley. This has been done by us at Walgrave, where the bed almost touches the brook, and is in consequence subject to an overflow during heavy rains, with disastrous results. A like mistake was made at Moulton and Harleston. The very last scheme at Boughton (1895) is also on the verge of the stream. At Brixworth the fall of the sewers was not sufficient, and there and elsewhere they were not laid straight. Outward angles sometimes occurred, whilst manholes and ventilation shafts were unknown in the earlier examples which were held up to admiration in 1878. In the earlier examples, and in some of later date, the sewer drain pipes were unsocketted and the joints were merely made of clay. In two cases— namely, at Guilsborough (a large village at Cold Ashby)— the main sewers are simply uncemented culverts. Into these closer connections have been made, and is it to be wondered at that Guilsborough has at the present time failed to purge itself of diphtheria. Into these have been constantly recurring during the past twelvemonth?

The grievous thing about a badly-laid system in a country village is the great difficulty in persuading the local authority to incur the necessary expenses of altering or improving the scheme. The inital expense is brought up against the reformer, and often nothing but a serious epidemic will rouse the parish and the authority to enter upon remedial measures.

### (3) A SUFFICIENCY OF SUITABLE LAND FOR IRRIGATION OR FILTRATION PURPOSES.

When the Local Government Board sanctioned the earlier of the Brixworth district schemes, their ideas as to the quantity of land required for effective natural filtration were very meagre, and remained so for some time. Moulton, with a population of 1,400, had 1½ acres; Brixworth with 1,700, 1 acre; and Walgrave with 600, half an acre. Even Pitsford, so late as 1894, with a population of 500, was only required to have half an acre. The consequence of this is that, although working fairly smoothly for two or three years, the land becomes sewage sick (or clogged with more or less solid organic matter), and a variety of expedients have to be tried

---

[*] This Chapel Brampton scheme was fully illustrated and described in Sir Henry Acland's treatise, " Health in the Village," published in 1884.

---

to freshen it. At last another small bit of land has to be added; but this is, after all, only a temporary expedient, for the old evils will be reproduced after the lapse of another year or two.

Our beds are for the most part planted with mangelwurzels, but one or two grow osiers, and another ash poles. In several cases the beds are of stiff clay—here the question of natural filtration (whatever the size) is altogether hopeless. Spratton is one of the worst of our examples of this kind. A satisfactory effluent has never been obtained there, save for very brief periods, and at times the discharge into the small adjacent stream has been very bad. The foulness of the effluent led some few years ago to legal proceedings against the old authority, when an injunction was obtained. It will be rembered that at last year's congress at Leeds, Dr. Barwise said that for drainage on to clay an acre of land would only suffice for twenty-five people. At this rate the Spratton bed ought to have an area of 37 acres, instead of consisting, as at present, of a single acre. In short, where there is a clay subsoil, any proposal to entrust to it sewage, without the use of tanks, is rank folly and doomed ere long to certain failure.

### (4) A LARGE OUTLAY.

Sir Henry Acland laid this down as an axiom of successful water-carried sewering some fifteen years ago, and year after year yields proof of its absolute truth. This is one of the chief reasons against such a system for small rural populations. The large populations and the successful commercial undertakings of our towns, together with the obviously stern necessity of having a reservoired water supply and some kind of sewage scheme, make such matters comparatively easy to carry out on a satisfactory scale in boroughs. But agricultural depression, dwindling population and common-sense opposition make it exceedingly difficult to carry out a thorough and therefore an expensive scheme in the country. One inspector tells me that several of our more recent instances of village sewering were rendered far less effective by the cutting down of the original estimates.

### (5) GOOD AND CONTINUOUS MANAGEMENT.

This was laid down by Mr. Roechling, at the Newcastle congress, as one of the two absolute necessities for successful sewage farming, whether big or small, the other being a good soil. Without considerable annual outlay, this good management cannot be attained in villages; and yet the rates seem scarcely able to bear it, and the proper control of a sewage system and its disposal bed is almost unknown. At all events continuous management does not exist in the Brixworth district. I cannot at this point do better than quote the words of our inspector in a recent communication to me: "To get a good effluent even from the best made bed on the best soil there must be good management. When a man is not constantly employed he should at least attend to the turning of the sewage twice a day. Many parishes pay a man to turn the sewage only 2s. 6d. a week, and the man has to walk a mile or more to and from the bed. Neglect of management is one of the main causes of beds going wrong." So late as May 9, 1880, it was resolved by the authority, on the motion of Mr. Albert Pell, to employ a man one *day each week* on the Brixworth and Spratton filtration grounds!

With regard to river pollution, our filtration-beds are serious and continuous offenders, as will be seen in detail from the appended table. They have recently been severely condemned by the surveyor of the county council. Comparatively small attention has hitherto been given to river pollution from beds so small as ours; the gravity of dealing with town effluents has been sufficient, but now that the county council has appointed so distinguished a medical officer of health as Mr. C. E. Paget further steps will probably be taken. The results to rivers from the foul effluents of small villages should not be disregarded, for it would be easy to work out a calculation which would prove that—if only the other rural districts of Northamptonshire had followed the lead of Brixworth in 1873, after a like ration and with like methods— the river Nene would long ago have become one continuous stinking open sewer.

With regard to the equally grave question of the effect on the health of the district itself from these numerous village sewer schemes, it is impossible to give full or accurate statistics. For the old authority was so enamoured of these schemes that other sanitary precautions were absolutely eschewed. Brixworth was the only rural sanitary authority in England that persistently defied the Local Government Board and the Public Health Act of 1875, by having no medical officer of health to make periodical visits and reports. This reproach was only removed last year. Brixworth, too, under the old *régime*, refused to adopt the Notification of Diseases Act; this reproach, after four defeats, was only removed last month. Still there is no doubt whatever that, broadly speaking, the health of our unsewered villages are better than those that are sewered; and this I have deliberately stated before a Local Government Board inspector at a public inquiry.

Under all the circumstances detailed in this paper, it is grievous to think that the Local Government Board refuse us leave, when wanting to improve the foul effluent at Brixworth and Walgrave, to try precipitating tanks, unless we add to the acreage of beds that have already failed. Whereas, if the tanks succeeded as well as elsewhere, no land would be required. The central authorities seem blindly wedded to natural as opposed to artificial filtration, though the former has proved a dismal failure in villages and a constant vexation in many towns.

It is even more astounding to have to state that, on the complaint of a single non-resident individual, the Local Government Board have recently declared the Brixworth Council in default as to the "sufficient sewering" of one of the healthiest of their villages, Holcot, with a dwindling population of only some 300. The inspector, who conducted the inquiry, refused to allow the question of the disposal of the sewage (if a scheme was adopted) to be even named, but as the subsoil is the stiffest clay in the district, and as the sewers would have to be laid in the used water-bearing bed, the council unanimously refused thus to jeopardise the health of the inhabitants.

Failure is written large right across the Brixworth district in their well-meant but disastrous attempts to deal with village sewerage by natural filtration. The moral of it all seems to be that rural authorities dealing with small populations should try every expedient rather than water-carried sewerage. But that if that system has to be adopted, water must be conveyed to every closet, and the outfall should enter precipitating tanks, or be treated in settling tanks before it reaches the filter-bed.

Some diagrams illustrative of Mr. Scott-Moncrieff's interesting paper reached us too late for this week's issue. We expect, however, to give them in our next issue, as they have an important bearing on certain passages of the paper. After a reference to Dr. Child's able lecture on the pollution of rivers, we shall proceed to deal with some remaining papers on various subjects of interest to our readers.

## MUNICIPAL PROGRESS IN LEICESTER.

### OPENING OF NEWARKE BRIDGE.

On the 24th ult the Mayor of Leicester, as the head of a progressive municipality, opened for public traffic the Newarke bridge, which has been erected to connect a large outlying industrial district with the centre of the town. The ceremony was attended by a large number of members of the corporation and others who take a deep interest in the public life and prosperity of the town. The bridge, which is a very imposing structure, built in the Gothic style of the Perpendicular period, so as to be in keeping with the ancient buildings and gateways in the neighbourhood, was designed by the borough surveyor, Mr. G. E. Mawbey, who is to be congratulated on the satisfactory character of the work, the cost of which, together with works of sewerage, paving, purchase of land and repairing the demolished buildings of Trinity Hospital, will compare very favourably with the £15,500 estimated and loaned for the purpose. It might be mentioned that the bridge will considerably reduce the distances from several points of the central part of the town to the Hickley and Narborough-road districts, and the gradients will be much easier than by the present Applegate-street route, no part of the carriageway being steeper than an inclination of 1 in 33. The land for the carrying out of this improvement was acquired from the Trinity Hospital trustees by an agreement on advantageous terms to both parties, which practically amounted to an exchange of that land for certain lands in Mill-lane and Jarrom-street, representing a cost of about £1,700, the corporation, in addition, paying to the hospital trustees the sum of £1,800, being the estimated cost of replacing that portion of the hospital building which has been demolished.

The bridge consists of two concrete elliptical arches, each 38 ft. span by 52 ft. 6 in. along the soffit. The arches are supported by massive concrete abutments, with a centre pier in the flood course. The work of construction, which has been carried out by Messrs. Bently, Son & Partington, was by no means an easy task, great difficulty having been experienced in getting in the foundations, owing to the large volume of water which found its way into the excavations from the flood course through the gravel overlying the marl, under a pressure varying from 10 ft. to 14 ft. The foundations are carried down to the solid red marl, a depth of about 9 ft. below the bed of the flood course. As proof of the solidarity of the work, it might be mentioned that among the material used in the bridge are about 5,580 tons of Portland cement concrete—the weight of the concrete in the arches being 1,400 tons—and about 524 tons of stone masonry. The concrete above the water and ground levels is faced with stone from Boden's Matlock quarries, and in the centre pier below the water-line with blue brickwork in cement. The concrete in the foundations of the abutments and pier is composed of one part of Portland cement to eight parts of broken granite and granite gravel, and in the abutments it was laid in layers at right angles to the thrust of the arches.

THE ARCHES

were built upon massive wood centres, carried on piles driven into the bed of the river. Those on the western side had to be specially constructed, so as to not only safely support the great weight of concrete and masonry of the arches, but to allow an opening through them 20 ft. wide and 9 ft. high, to provide for the boat traffic without interruption. The laggings or coverings of the centres were 2 in. thick, and covered

with very thick brown paper, which was coated with soft soap in order to give a smooth surface to the intrados of the *in situ* concrete of the arches. On this brown paper covering wrought V-shaped strips were nailed, to give the soffit the appearance of stone-worked Voussoirs; in fact, these concrete arches were actually constructed in separate courses, just as a stone arch would be, excepting that the concrete was laid in its plastic condition in radiated layers between wood frames instead of being set in solid blocks, as would have been the case with stonework. Nevertheless, the concrete, instead of being one homogeneous mass, has really bed joints between each layer similar to masonry construction, as each course of concrete was allowed sufficient time to set before another course was put in. The arches are 3 ft. thick at the crown and about 4 ft. 6 in. at the haunches, and the rise of them from the springing of the semi-ellipse is 8 ft. About five weeks after the arches were keyed in the centres were lowered from the weight they had supported by the gradual withdrawal of the numerous large pairs of folding wedges upon which they had been supported, and it is satisfactory to know that there is no sign of settlement or crack in any part of this somewhat unusual method of construction. Great care had to be taken throughout the winter months to protect the concrete from being damaged by frost ; in fact, this part of the work had to be stopped for several weeks on this account. The upper surfaces of the arches, abutments and counterforts are covered with a layer of asphalte 1 in. thick, and provided with " weep " drains to carry off any water which may percolate through the roadway.

The stone parapets have sunk traceried panels and mullions. Over the abutments and centre pier six ornamental towers or piers will be constructed; those over the abutments will be 10 ft. 3 in. and those over the centre pier 4 ft. 3 in. above the top of the parapets. They will be octagonal, with traceried panels and crenellated tops. Besides the ordinary storm, foul and clean trade-water sewers, which have been laid under the new road, a storm overflow culvert has been laid from the Newarke to the river, to give relief to the western main sewer in time of heavy rains. During the excavation for these sewers two underground passages were discovered and a few coins were found. The largest passage was about 2 yards wide by 3 yards high, with walls of granite rubble masonry, and with a Gothic-shaped roof very solidly constructed with Swithland slate built in lime mortar.

The bridge and new approach from the Newarke have a total width of 50 ft., consisting of a 30-ft. carriageway and two 10-ft. causeways. The Newarke has also been widened, mostly to 50 ft., all along the front of the almshouses from the Technical Schools to the corner of Asylum-street. The carriageway, excepting for a short length, is paved with 3-in. by 5-in. granite setts upon 9-in. of cement concrete, and grouted with pitch and tar. A piece, however, immediately opposite St. Mary's vicarage is paved with jarrah wood. The footways are also paved with concrete slabs, which were laid by the corporation staff as an additional attraction to the structure. Trees have been planted on each side of the new approaches, and the bridge and the approaches will be lighted by an ample number of ornamental lamp columns with the Victorian incandescent lamps, which are being provided. Messrs. Bentley, Son & Partington were the contractors for the bridge, the amount of their tender being £8,732; while Mr. H. C. Leadbeater has acted as the borough surveyor's chief assistant in the work and Mr. W. Thrall as clerk of the works.

## COMBINED DRAINAGE IN LAMBETH.

A short time ago the Sewers Committee of the Lambeth Vestry were instructed to submit replies to certain questions raised by Alderman Hubbard in relation to combined drainage. One of the points upon which information was sought was as to whether there is an order of the vestry regulating the width of a passageway along which combined drainage is sanctioned, and the size of the pipe in connection therewith.

In reply to this question the Sewers Committee reported, at the last meeting of the vestry, that there is at present no order regulating the width of a passageway along which a combined drain is sanctioned, nor the size of the combined drain. It has, however, for some time past been the custom of the committee to stipulate that the passageway down which the combined drain passes shall, if possible, be at least 5 ft. in width, in order that the footings of the walls of the houses may not be interfered with in excavating for laying the drain or for future repair of it. As regards the size of the drain, the committee consider that this is a matter for the exercise of their discretion.

The committee also stated that the whole question of combined drainage is at present under the joint consideration of themselves and the Sanitary Committee, and that a report on the matter will shortly be presented to the vestry.

A further question asked was as to whether an order has been issued requiring builders to put in improved gullies with back and side inlets. In reply to this the committee stated that according to their knowledge no such order has been issued ; so that a builder may, if he so chooses, terminate the sink, bath, or other wastes or rain-water pipes over gully gratings. The present drainage regulations mention back and side inlet gullies only, but this regulation does not appear to have been approved or adopted by the vestry.

# Comparative Reports of General Practice.

## XXIX.—ELECTRIC LIGHTING : BECKENHAM REPORT.—III.

The first and second instalments of Mr. Angell's report appeared in our issues of October 7th and 14th. Included in the report were a number of interesting appendices, with which we now proceed to deal.

### ESTIMATED PROFIT AND LOSS.

In his first appendix Mr. Angell presented a table showing the estimated profit and loss in district No. 1 at various stages of supply. For one house in eight, and with 2,953 8 candle-power lamps, the working expenses, including repayments, are estimated as follows : Private lighting, £1,887 ; street lighting, £300 ; and dust destruction, £600 ; a total of £2,787. The estimated revenue is £1,107, which gives a loss of £1,680. With one house in six, and with 3,937 lamps, the estimated working expenses are : Private lighting, £2,044 ; street lighting, £300 ; and dust destruction, £600 ; a total of £2,944. The revenue being estimated at £1,476, there is thus a deficit of £1,468. With one house in four, and 5,906 lamps, the estimated working expenses are : Private lighting, £2,357 ; street lighting, £300 ; and dust destruction, £600 ; a total of £3,257. Deducting an estimated revenue of £2,215, there is a loss of £1,042. With one house in three, and 7,874 lamps, the estimated working expenses are £3,570, of which £2,670 is for private lighting, the two remaining items being the same throughout. With an estimated revenue of £2,952 there is thus a loss of £618. Finally, with one house in two, and 11,812 lamps, the working expenses are estimated at £4,196, private lighting being put down at £3,296, and the other items as before. The revenue being estimated at £4,430, there is thus a profit of £234. Mr. Angell remarks in connection with this tabular statement, that as soon as an annual profit is realised a reserve fund should be created, to cover the cost of renewing cables, &c. In regard to street lighting, the cost of arc lighting is estimated at £400. Deducting £100, the saving on gas, the nett extra cost is thus £300. To ascertain the financial result of the electric lighting scheme alone, the cost of dust destruction (£600) must be deducted from the annual deficits and added to annual profits. The time interval between any of the stages is a matter of speculation, and may be one or more years, according to public demand for supply.

Appendix II. contains the schedule of streets, and Appendix III. matter relative to forms and agreements in connection with the

### FREE WIRING OF HOUSES.

A few notes abstracted from this appendix will no doubt be of interest. The Shoreditch Vestry in their circular to customers state that, as they will have to maintain a staff of electric wiremen and jointers, they have resolved to estimate for, and undertake the execution of, private work for installations. The vestry will charge for such work the actual cost to them of labour and material, plus 10 per cent. for supervision. A reasonable deposit will be required before the work is put in hand. The borough engineer of Hanley writes as follows : " The proposal is that an agreement for free wiring should be entered into and signed by both occupier and owner agreeing to pay, say, 10 per cent. on the cost of the work for a period of, say, ten years." The wiring will, of course, be executed and paid for by the council, and a loan for the purpose has been sanctioned by the Local Government Board.

At Shoreditch there is an alternative method. By an agreement between the vestry of the first part, the National Electric Free Wiring Company, Limited, of the second part, and the occupier (or owner or lessee for an unexpired term of years) of the premises on the third part, it is agreed, among other things, (1) That the wiring company should wire and fit up the premises in accordance with the fire insurance company's regulations free of cost to the consumer. (2) That the installation should be the property of the supply company unless paid for as provided in the agreement. (3) The consumer may, after the expiration of five years, purchase the installation at cost price, plus 20 per cent., and less 1½ per cent. per annum for depreciation. (6) Neither the supply company nor the wiring company are to be liable for repairs or maintenance, but the wiring company, without charge, to make good all defects of workmanship within six months after installation. (7) The consumer shall, until purchase, pay the supply company for the use of the installation ⅜d. per unit supplied, the minimum payment in any year to be 1s. per 8 candle-power lamp. (8) If a consumer ceases to take supply, or makes default in payment, the supply company may remove the installation, making good any damage. (9) The supply may be cut off if payments are in arrear and not paid on demand. When the consumer is only the occupier, the following memorandum is signed by the landlord : " I, the undersigned, being landlord of the above-named consumer, and being owner (or lessee for an unexpired term of . . . . years) of the said premises, hereby consent to the installation of wires and fittings in the said premises upon the terms and conditions of the above agreement."

At Wallasey, the consumer, having applied to be supplied with electric current, and for their premises to be wired and fitted up on the free wiring system, undertakes to conform in every respect to the conditions specified in the form of agreement. Among these conditions are the following : (1) The council, at their cost, undertake to wire and fit up the premises ready for electric supply, the consumer to be responsible for any damage to cables and fittings fixed on such premises and to pay for current at the rate of . . . . per Board of Trade unit. (The wiring is not actually executed by the Wallasey Council, but by the National Electric Free Wiring Company, Limited, as their agents and contractors.) (2) The consumer has the option of purchasing wires and fittings outright at any time after the expiration of five years at cost price, plus 20 per cent., but minus 1½ per cent. per annum for depreciation. (4) The council are to keep a stock of fittings at the show-room for customers' selection. (5) Renewals are to be made at the consumers' cost.

A fourth appendix contained a synopsis of Mr. Kapp's report of November, 1893. One of the suggestions was that, in order to arrive at the approximate demand, a circular letter be sent to each householder in the streets in which mains will be laid giving estimate of cost of fittings and inquiring what number of lamps, if any, such householders would be likely to require. In regard to this Mr. Angell remarks, " Such a preliminary canvass might serve as an advertisement, but otherwise at so early a stage it has little to recommend it, and is, indeed, misleading. As a rule, it would appear that but few advance premises are obtained, and that many of these are unfulfilled. On the other hand, many from whom no replies are received take the light notwithstanding. It is preferable to lay mains down streets where *in the judgment of the local authority a demand is likely to exist or to be created,* after which a canvass may be made, probably with some degree of profit."

### PARTICULARS OF INSTALLATIONS.

Appendix V. embodied in tabular form some interesting particulars in regard to various installations in reply to queries addressed to various towns. These details we reproduce as follows :—

#### AYR.

(Population, 26,000 ; rateable value, £151,149.)

Ayr, it might be stated, is the only Scotch town of which particulars are given in the report. A high-tension installation has been in operation in the burgh since May, 1896. Its original cost was £26,000, and it supplies the equivalent of 9,000 8 candle-power lamps. No demands have yet been received for power for motors. The revenue of the last financial year was £1,865, and the working expenses amounted to £3,192, so that a loss of £1,327 was experienced. The price per unit is 6d. and 4d., Wright's system being followed ; but a reduction, which is confidently expected to improve the affairs of the works, is contemplated. Gas is charged for at the rate of 3s. 9d. per 1,000 cubic feet.

#### BLACKPOOL.

(Population, 35,000 ; rateable value, £250,000.)

A sum of £80,000 was spent upon the works in this town, which are of the high-tension alternating type, with low tension distribution. They were opened in August, 1893, and supply the equivalent of 30,000 8 candle-power lamps. Last year's working resulted in a profit of £828, the revenue being £10,633 and the working expenses £9,805. Wright's system of charging has been adopted, the price for the first hour being ½d. per unit ; for subsequent hours the charge is 2d. per unit. Profits are expected to increase. Gas costs 2s. 4d. per 1,000 cubic feet.

#### BLACKBURN.

(Population, 126,000 ; rateable value, £441,111.)

The three-wire low-tension system is in operation in the centre of the town, while the outer districts have a high-tension alternating supply. The works, which have run since February, 1895, cost £35,000 to erect. They drive the equivalent of 12,700 8 candle-power lamps, and also supply current for motors. Last year's working showed a loss of only £5, the revenue being £3,642 and the working expenses £3,647. During the first hour a charge of 6d. per unit is imposed, and for subsequent hours 3d. per unit. A discount of 5 per cent. is also allowed. Profits are expected to increase. Gas cost 3s. 7d. and 2s. 9d. per 1,000 ft.

#### BOLTON.

(Population, 115,000 ; rateable value, £428,520.)

At Bolton the high-tension alternating system of lighting has been adopted. The works were erected at a cost of £65,615, and have supplied current since October, 1894. Power equivalent to 27,000 8 candle-power lamps is supplied, but none is used in connection with motors. The revenue and working expenses of last year were respectively £4,486 and £4,756—a loss of £270. Charges are made as follows : For the first hour 6d., afterwards 3d. per unit. A reduction of price is anticipated, as is a profit on the working of the installation. Gas costs 3s. per 1,000 cubic feet.

#### BRIGHTON.

(Population, 115,402 ; rateable value, £732,760.)

The low-tension continuous system is combined with the

high-tension alternating system at Brighton. Current was first supplied in September, 1891, and the output is now equivalent to 75,427 8 candle-power lamps. Motor power is supplied. Last year the revenue amounted to £26,527, and, as the working expenses only amounted to £20,644, a profit of £5,883 resulted. As regards the price, for the first hour a charge of 7d. per unit is made, this afterwards being reduced to 1½d. per unit. At present no reduction in the charges is contemplated, and the profits are not expected to increase. In Brighton gas costs 2s. 9d. per 1,000 cubic feet.

### BRISTOL.
(Population, 226,576; rateable value, £1,061,143.)

With a high-tension alternating plant, which was erected at a cost of £110,000, the Bristol authorities supply the equivalent of 43,615 8 candle-power lamps. Current was first supplied in October, 1893. The result of last year's working was a profit of £487, the revenue and expenses being respectively £14,388 and £13,901. The price per unit is 6d., and it is not expected that any reduction will be made; larger profits, however, are expected. A charge of 2s. 6d. per 1,000 cubic feet is made for gas.

### BURNLEY.
(Population, 95,000; rateable value, £320,000.)

A low-tension three-wire installation is at work here. The original cost of the works was £26,000, and the first supply dates from August, 1893. Power sufficient for 15,000 8 candle-power lamps is supplied, but none is used in connection with motors. A profit of £712 resulted from last year's working, the revenue being £3,579 and the expenses £2,867. The price per unit is 5d., less 5 per cent. No reduction is expected to be made. Gas costs 2s. 3d. per 1,000 cubic feet.

### BURTON-ON-TRENT.
(Population, 49,000; rateable value, £244,785.)

At Burton-on Trent an installation on the high-tension alternating system, which cost £30,000 to erect, is in use, and current has been supplied since February, 1894. The amount at present supplied is sufficient for 7,600 8 candle-power lamps. There is no demand for power for motors. A less of £1,579 is shown on last year's working. The revenue was £1,521 and the expenses £3,100. A charge of 6d. per unit is made, but a reduction is anticipated. Gas costs 2s. 6d. per 1,000 ft.

### BURY.
(Population, 57,000; rateable value, £244,785.)

The low-tension continuous system is in use at Bury, where current has been available since November, 1896. A sum of £22,000 was expended upon the erection of the works, which supply an equivalent of 3,185 8 candle-power lamps. No electricity is supplied for motors. The charge for the first hour is 6d. per unit, and for the second 3d. A reduction is not anticipated, nor is it expected that profits will increase. The price of gas in Bury is 2s. 2d. Nothing, it may be mentioned, is given in this return regarding revenue or expenditure.

### CHELTENHAM.
(Population, 47,500; rateable value, £272,610.)

At this town, where £36,416 was spent upon a high-tension alternating system, with sub-stations, the date of the first supply was May, 1895. Electric motors are not used. In the last financial year the revenue totalled only £1,945, as against £3,100 working expenses. This leaves a deficit of £1,155. No immediate change is expected in connection with the electric light charges, which are stated to be from 3½d. to 6d. Considerable profits are expected to result shortly, and the year dealt with in the report is itself likely to result favourably, as the revenue has increased. Gas in the district is charged for at the rate of 2s. 4d. per 1,000 cubic feet.

### COVENTRY.
(Population, 53,000; rateable value, £183,674.)

A high-tension alternating system is at work here. It cost £20,000 to erect, and was started in January, 1896; the equivalent of 8,000 8 candle-power lamps are supplied, but no power is distributed for the use of motors. With a fixed charge of 6d. per unit, last year's accounts resulted in the revenue and expenses balancing equally at £1,300. The authorities hope to be able to make both a reduction in price and earn a profit in the future working. The price of gas is 2s. 5d.

### DERBY.
(Population, 94,146; rateable value, £357,233.)

Here a high-tension system with transformer stations is in use. The original cost of the works was £258,650; they were started in October, 1893, and now supply power equal to dealing with 17,580 8 candle-power lamps. There is a small demand for power with which to drive meters. The last financial year's accounts showed a loss of £1,453, the income and expenditure being respectively £6,866 and £8,319. This deficit is, however, explained by large extensions which at present are earning no revenue, but future working will, it is confidently expected, result profitably. During the first one and a half hours the charge per unit is 6d.; afterwards it is 3d. per unit. Gas in the town costs 2s. 8d. per 1,000 cubic feet.

### DEWSBURY.
Population, 31,000; rateable value, £114,000.)

Current has been available in Dewsbury since December,

1894, the date when the electric lighting plant, which is on the high-tension system with transformer stations—and which cost £24,260—first started work. The equivalent of 7,155 8 candle-power lamps are supplied, and there is a slight demand in connection with motors. Here also a loss has been experienced on the working of the undertaking, the revenue for the last financial year having been £3,733, and working expenses £3,879, leaving a deficit of £146. A profit is shortly expected to be made. For the first one and a half hours 6d. per unit is charged, and afterwards 3½d. The price of gas per 1,000 cubic feet is 3s.

### EALING.
(Population, 30,000; rateable value, £200,000.)

A sum of £59,000 was spent upon the installation at Ealing, which is on the high-pressure alternating system with sub-stations. It has been working since October, 1894, and at present supplies power sufficient to deal with 12,684 8 candle-power lamps. No energy is used for motor purposes. Revenue and working expenses amounted to respectively £4,975 and £5,292, thus leaving a deficit of £317. Sixpence per unit is charged for current, but a reduction is anticipated. Profits, also, are expected. The price of gas is 2s. 11d.

### FAREHAM.
(Population, 7,034; rateable value, £24,000.)

A high-pressure alternating system with transformers is working in this town, where current has been available since September, 1891. The works cost £4,500 to build and supply power sufficient for 1,152 8 candle-power lamps. In this case a loss of £819 was experienced during the last financial year, the revenue being £543 and the expenses of working £1,362. The cost of maintaining the public lamps was not however, included in the accounts. The current costs 8d. per unit, while gas can be obtained at the rate of 1,000 cubic feet for 3s. 9d.

## NEW PUBLIC BATHS AT TUNBRIDGE WELLS.

The new public baths erected by the Tunbridge Wells Town Council in Monson-road, at a cost of £10,000, were recently recently opened. The interior walls of the swimming tank are of brick, with glazed tiles for the lower portion, and a gallery surrounds the bath, under which the dressing-boxes abut on to the platform which encloses the water surface, and which has a mosaic pavement. The dressing-boxes are of pitch pine, on the half-door system, and warmed with steam radiators. The sides of the bath are of white glazed tiles, and the bottom of mosaic pavement, in which the borough arms may be traced. The roof has a 55 ft. span, and is 70 ft. from the water surface to the apex of the glass lantern; the bath is 105 ft. long, and 55 ft. wide, the actual water surface is 90 ft. by 30 ft., with a depth varying from 6 ft. 6 in. to 3 ft. 6 in., which can be increased 6 in. for polo matches, while a spray is introduced for cleaning the surface of the water. The gallery will hold 400 spectators, and the walls are for a height of 8 ft. lined with glazed bricks, and the remaining portion with red bricks. At one end of the bath an alcove contains a shower-bath, and there is the usual lavatory accommodation. Behind the bath is the boiler-house, with a couple of Cornish boilers, a steam laundry for bath linen, and a drying oven for towels. A subway encircles the bath, in which the various pipes can be easily reached in case of need. Over the boiler-house is a tall chimney shaft. The building was designed and its erection superintended by Mr. W. Mallor, the borough surveyor. Messrs. Longley & Co. were the contractors for the building; Messrs. T. Bradford & Co., of Salford, for the engineering; and Messrs. Diespeker, for the mosaic paving. The electric light is utilised all over the building.

## THE WATER SUPPLY OF BROOMFLEET.

The water question, which has been a source of perplexity to the members of the Howden Rural District Council for some time, again came up for consideration at a recent meeting. A letter was received from the Local Government Board forwarding copies of letters from several residents of Broomfleet complaining of the condition of the water, which was described as sewage matter. They forwarded a sample of the water, which they said was "unfit for human nature to use," and complained that the matter had been in the hands of the council for three years without result. The Local Government Board concluded by asking for the council's observations on the matter. The council also received a report from Mr. Bohn, engineer, of Hull, on the subject. The purport of the report was that Rowdale, Weeddale and Wooddale springs on the wolds would furnish supplies equal to the demands. He recommended a 3-in. pipe to Broomfleet and a 2-in. pipe to the adjoining farms and lock cottages, and calculated that when the work was completed a discharge of 55,000 gallons per day would be given. The cost of the work to Broomfleet would be £1,287, and if the pipes were taken on to the farmhouses alluded to the extra outlay would be £778. After some discussion it was decided to refer the matter to a committee.

# London Water Supply.

## PROPOSALS OF THE WATER COMMITTEE OF THE COUNTY COUNCIL.

On the 11th ult. the London County Council passed the following resolution : "That in view of the existing difficulty of obtaining an adequate supply of water in a large portion of the county of London, an instruction to the Water Committee be forthwith submit its proposals with regard to legislation affecting the water supply in the ensuing session of Parliament." This resolution the Water Committee have now fully considered, and on Tuesday their report was considered by the members of the council.

The committee state that it will be remembered that in May last they submitted a report to the council stating that, owing to the continuance of the sitting of the Royal Commission on London Water Supply, they did not deem it advisable at that moment to make any proposals for legislation on the subject of water, but that in their opinion it would be well for the council to suspend their standing orders so as to leave them free after the summer recess to make any recommendations that might appear to be necessary. The council, therefore, have now to consider whether they will continue to wait for the report of the Royal Commission before taking any action in the direction of legislation, or whether they will at once formulate their proposals and lay them before Parliament in the coming session. In view of the very serious state of affairs that has been shown to exist during the last few months, the committee themselves believe that it is the duty of the council to take every possible step to enable the legislature to have before them in the coming session specific proposals for solving the problem of the London water supply upon the lines of the council's policy. There were two main facts appearing from the experience of the last twelve months. First, that one-quarter of the population of London had recently been subjected to a series of water famines by reason of the default of the East London Water Company ; and, secondly, that the drought of the present year had reduced the flow of the rivers Thames and Lea to so low a state as to make it certain that these rivers could not in a dry year yield the supply which the Royal Commission, presided over by Lord Balfour of Burleigh, relied upon in making their report. Those two matters, although closely connected, might for the purposes of discussion be kept distinct, because it was possible by temporary measures to satisfy the needs of East London immediately, whereas it would take ten or fifteen years to carry out the necessary works for providing for the permanent requirements of London generally.

Dealing with the question of

### IMMEDIATE REMEDIES,

the committee state that in their opinion the only satisfactory means of remedying the state of affairs in East London rests in pressing forward the old policy of the council—namely, the

ACQUISITION OF THE EIGHT METROPOLITAN WATER COMPANIES.

They point out that if the council's Bills of 1895 had become law there would have been no famine in East London in the present year. The council would have come into possession of all the undertakings in 1896, and would have been able with little difficulty to utilise for East London the water generally available for the metropolis, of which there had been sufficient even during the present drought. Any scheme which contemplated the continuance of the individual companies was open to the objection that each company possessing a margin of available water would naturally desire to retain such margin for the possible needs of its own consumers. It was only by uniform management that the whole of the water available for the metropolis could be efficiently made use of for all parts of the area. Although schemes of amalgamation, or of combination of the companies, had been put forward as capable of effecting this object, they were attended by so many difficulties and were open to so great objections that the committee were convinced that the only satisfactory system of uniform management lay in a public authority possessing the entire supply. They proposed, therefore, legislation upon the lines of the council's purchase Bills, subject to certain observations. The council's Bills had always provided for the

### IMMEDIATE TRANSFER

of the companies' undertakings, with subsequent arbitration as to price. That proposal had been the subject of some criticism, but they believed it to be indispensable in the pressing circumstances of the case, and quite capable of justification when accompanied, as it had been, by provisions assuring the shareholders against loss of income during the interval between the transfer and the payment of the purchase money. The actual vesting of the undertakings in the council could not prejudice the shareholders, nor did they wish it to prejudice the question of the future position of the outside areas, and they therefore proposed a resolution which made that clear.

The committee point out that the plan of proceeding by separate Bills was adopted formerly for reasons of Parliamentary expediency, but the consideration which the subject underwent in 1895 should operate so as to shorten the period of discussion in the coming session and make it possible to unite the proposals for purchase in one Bill. They accordingly propose that the council should proceed by one Bill for the purchase of all the companies, and, in order to make the council's proposals a complete and immediate protection against further famines in East London or elsewhere, they suggest that the Bill should contain clauses enabling the council to take in hand forthwith the work of consolidating the several systems, and connecting and laying mains, &c., so that the whole might be at the earliest possible moment adapted to meet the needs of the whole of the metropolis.

On the question of the

### ARBITRATION CLAUSE

the committee think that the precise form of the clause may be left to be considered by the Parliamentary Committee, and suggest that at present the council should only pass a general resolution on the subject. The views of the council throughout had been that, while prepared to pay the fair and reasonable value of the water undertakings, such value ought only to be decided with due regard to many important matters. One of those matters was the contention then put forward by the council, that the companies were rapidly nearing the end of their resources, and would shortly come face to face with a very large expenditure necessary for procuring an additional supply. The experience since gained had entirely borne out that view. In the last three years all the companies, except the Kent company, had been to Parliament for additional powers, and the default of the East London Company was a matter of notoriety. The present proposal was that the arbitration clause should be drafted in such a form that it should be certain that under it the arbitrator would, in the case of each company, have regard to all such circumstances as might be brought before him, such as, for instance, in the case of East London, its inability to provide for its population and the necessity of its obtaining other supplies.

As to the question of dealing with the

### OUTSIDE AREAS,

the committee state that the matter is naturally one of difficulty, but the council had already on other occasions agreed to the principle of according to the outside authorities the same freedom of administering their own supply as the council claimed for themselves. The further question, as regards the separation of sources, might be left over for negotiation with the outside authorities.

With reference to the council's agreement with

### THE CITY CORPORATION

to give one-eighth of the seats on the council's future Water Committee to nominees of the corporation, the committee state that they are not sure how far the corporation have abandoned their views in favour of purchase, the evidence put forward by them before the Royal Commission being somewhat uncertain. If, however, they still supported the principle of purchase, the committee thought the council were bound to adhere to their arrangement, and suggested that the corporation should be asked at once whether they would assist the council on the lines of the old agreement.

In the second portion of the report the committee deal with the

### FUTURE SUPPLY OF LONDON,

and in this connection they state :—

It will be remembered that the conclusion arrived at by Lord Balfour's Commission, that sufficient water to satisfy the requirements of London up to the year 1931 could be obtained from the valleys of the Thames and the Lea, were based upon the view that these valleys could be relied upon to yield at least an average daily supply of 300,000,000 gallons and 92,500,000 gallons respectively. Although from the outset entertaining grave doubts as to the correctness of this view, we have hitherto accepted it and devoted our attention specially to the question of the cost of a storage system necessary for giving such supply, as compared with the cost of bringing water from Wales, and, having become convinced that the storage scheme would prove in the end the most costly and least satisfactory of the two, we tendered evidence before the present Royal Commission, to show that reservoirs at Staines capable of supplying 300,000,000 gallons a day, without depletion of the Thames in dry years, must be very large and very costly. The present year has been dryer than any previous year in recent times, and it is evident now that a reservoir system capable of meeting the needs of a year such as 1898 must be of such magnitude as practically puts all storage schemes out of the question. But, beyond this, the experience gained in connection with the flow of the rivers Lea and Thames during the present season has entirely confirmed us in our belief that

LORD BALFOUR'S COMMISSION WERE MISLED

into erroneous views as to the quantity of water obtainable in dry years. The report of the commission with regard to the Lea was undoubtedly based to a great extent upon the evidence given on behalf of the East London and the New River Companies. This evidence was that between them they could supply over 110,000,000 gallons a day, and that this quantity could be largely increased by storage reservoirs in the Lea valley. Since then the New River Company have admitted that they can obtain from their wells only 24,000,000 gallons a day, instead of 34,000,000 gallons as stated to Lord Balfour's Commission, and the East London Company, although they have doubled the capacity of their storage reservoirs, have nevertheless made default. The fact is that during the whole of the present year the entire volume of the river Lea has been used, and yet there has been a famine. Moreover, the average flow in September last over Field's weir was only 8,250,000 gallons a day (of which it is believed a large proportion was water contributed by the New River Company), whereas the information before Lord Balfour's Commission was to the effect that the minimum known flow of the river for any month at that spot was 17,500,000 gallons. With regard to the Thames, the information before the commission showed that its minimum total flow in one month was 308,000,000 gallons a day. Last August the flow was only 272,000,000 gallons, and in September it dropped to about 200,000,000 gallons, out of which the Thames companies had the right to abstract 150,500,000 gallons, and did, in fact, in August draw 129,900,000 gallons. These facts have convinced us that it is impossible to depend in a very dry year upon the quantity of water which the commissioners reported as being obtainable; and if this is so their report affords no solution of the problem of metropolitan water supply. The evidence of the present year therefore seems to justify conclusively the views hitherto held by the council as to the necessity of immediately proceeding with some scheme for the future supply of the metropolis on lines other than those suggested by Lord Balfour's Commission. The council have already decided that in their opinion the solution lies in having

RESORT TO THE WELSH MOUNTAINS

to obtain the necessary supplementary supply, and the time has now arrived for giving effect to this resolution. Our report upon this subject, discussed at the council meetings on February 25 and April 21, 1896, gave a detailed statement of our entire proposals, and thereupon the council resolved that the requisite augmentation of the supplies of water should be derived from some other source than the Thames and Lea; that the valleys of the Usk, the Wye and the Towy would furnish a suitable area from which supplies might be derived, and that the Usk section should be undertaken in the first instance. After passing these resolutions, however, delay was incurred by reason of the council desiring further advice from Sir B. Baker and Mr. Deacon, and although in 1897 these engineers reported in favour of the Welsh scheme as compared with that of storage in the Thames valley, by that time the present Royal Commission had been appointed by the Government, and thus we again felt ourselves unable to recommend the council to take Parliamentary action. We proceeded, nevertheless, with the plans and sections, and these have all been completed for both portions of the Welsh scheme. The work that remains to be done in order to lay complete proposals before Parliament will take about three months to execute, but the referencing for the portion of land taken for the reservoirs, &c., can be completed in proper time, and it should not be impossible, if the referencing for the conduits is finished before Parliament meets, to obtain a suspension of standing orders so as to enable Parliament to have the scheme properly before it. We therefore propose that the council should deposit a Bill for obtaining water from Wales, but in doing so we advise the council to make an alteration in its former resolution. The Welsh scheme, as approved in 1896, was divided into two parts—namely, the Usk section and the Wye section. We then advised the council to take up the Usk section in the first instance, but since that date Sir Benjamin Baker and Mr. Deacon have expressed a preference in favour of the Wye section. The reasons which actuated us in recommending the former were purely reasons of policy, and as the engineer himself has throughout preferred to put forward the

WYE SECTION FIRST,

and recommends it now strongly as being the better and the cheaper of the two, we think the council would do well to rescind its former resolution and order a Bill to be promoted for obtaining water from the valleys of the Wye and Towy upon the lines set out in our former report with reference to that portion of the engineer's scheme. The estimate of cost in our former report has been slightly reduced, the total amount necessary for providing a daily supply of 200,000,000 gallons being £16,546,000, and this will probably be expended in three instalments.

In concluding the report the committee recommend the council to adopt the following resolutions: (1) That a Bill be promoted in the coming session of Parliament for the purchase by the council of the undertakings of the eight metropolitan water companies by agreement, or, failing agreement, by compulsion. (2) That, subject to such provision as may be made by Parliament as to the ultimate relationship between London and the outside authorities, provision be made for the undertakings of the companies vesting in the council at a date not later than six months after the passing of the Act. (3) That the Bill contain provisions authorising the council to proceed

forthwith with the connecting and laying of mains and other works necessary in order to enable it to protect any part of the metropolis from want of water. (4) That the arbitration clause be so framed as to render it certain that in the case of each company the arbitrator will have regard to all such circumstances as may be brought before him, and that no allowance shall be made in respect of compulsory sale except for cost of reinvestment (if any). (5) That, subject to further negotiation thereon with the local authorities, the clauses with respect to the supply of outside areas should follow the principle of the Bills promoted by the council in 1895. (6) That the understanding with the corporation of the City of London with regard to their representation on the Water Committee be adhered to, if they so desire. (7) That a Bill (or Bills) be promoted in the coming session of Parliament for the purpose of empowering the council to bring an additional supply of water to London from the watersheds of the Wye and Towy on the general lines of the report of the Water Committee approved by the council, April 21, 1896, in so far as it applies to the Wye section of the engineer's scheme. (8) That it be referred to the Parliamentary Committee to prepare and present to the council the necessary Bills for carrying out the above resolutions.

## QUERIES AND REPLIES.

*Sketches accompanying Queries should be made separate on white paper in plain black-ink lines. Lettering or figures should be bold and plain.*

**217. Passage of an Electric Current.**—Mr. Egbert Rushton, engineer and surveyor to the Cleethorpes District Council, writes: Would the presence of mud and dirt, &c., between sheet copper and rusty steel, though the two were bolted together, interfere with the efficient passing from one to the other of an electric current? Assuming that the answer to the above be "yes," is there anything cheap and efficient I could place between the two metals so as to prevent the entrance of mud and dirt, &c., and which would not interfere with the current.

Mud and dirt would certainly help to make the joint a bad one, but rust would, more than anything, tend to retard the passage of a current between the two metals. Under most conditions the best means of making the junction of the two metals an efficient one would be to remove the dirt and rust and solder them together.

**218. Motor Dust-Vans.**—Mr. D. J. Ebbets, engineer and surveyor to the Acton Urban District Council, writes: I am desirous of obtaining information concerning motor dust-vans. I should be greatly obliged if you can tell me of any authorities who are using them. I am aware that the Chiswick Urban District Council use them, but would be glad to know of any other authorities who so use them.

We are unable to discover that any local authority other than the Chiswick Urban District Council have adopted motor dust-vans. The Steam Carriage and Waggon Company, Limited, Chiswick, may be able to render some information on the point. Possibly Mr. E. Shrapnell Smith, honorary secretary of the Liverpool Self-propelled Traffic Association, Liverpool, the auther of a paper on "Motor Vehicles," read at the recent Sanitary Institute congress, may be able to assist the querist. We shall be glad if any of our subscribers can give any information.

**219. Curious Taste in Water after Filtration.**—"Puzzled" writes: Can you tell me the cause of a curious taste in water resembling cucumber? I have lately been troubled with this peculiarity in water supplied by some works of which I have the control. The works have been constructed for about forty years, and not until last autumn was this taste observed. The water is taken from a stream, filtered through sand and gravel, and is then pumped up to supply the inhabitants. The taste, which can be detected for some miles up the stream, can scarcely be distinguished as it leaves the filter-beds, but becomes very marked when it is in the mains and is under pressure. Analysis fails to give any information excepting that there is nothing deleterious in it?

The pollution referred to by the querist is most probably of organic origin, derived from vegetable matter over or through which the stream or some of the distributories passes. A careful examination of the banks should be made, and samples of water taken at different points, when the source of pollution should be by this means located. Having done this, the remedy will be comparatively easy.

**The Sanitary Inspectors' Association.**—An extraordinary meeting of the above association will be held at Carpenters' Hall, London-wall, E.C., to-morrow, at 6 p.m. At this meeting Mr. T. J. Moss Flower, chairman of the council, will deliver his inaugural address.

**Society of Engineers.**—The next ordinary meeting of this society will be held at the Royal United Service Institution, Whitehall, on Monday, when a paper will be read by Mr. Perry F. Nursey, past-president, on "The Preparation of Rhea Fibre for Textile Purposes." The chair will be taken at 7.30 p.m. precisely.

# Sewage Disposal at Sutton.

## LOCAL GOVERNMENT BOARD INQUIRY.

Mr. R. H. Bicknell, Local Government Board inspector, conducted an inquiry on the 18th ult. into an application of the Sutton (Surrey) Urban District Council for sanction to borrow £3,500 for works of street improvement, £1,600 for works of sewage disposal, and £199 for additions to the stables and the making of a cart-shed.

Mr. W. J. DUDDIN, J.P., who is the chairman of the council, was first examined in connection with the loan for purposes of sewage disposal. He stated that in 1887 both himself and Dr. Dupré expressed an opinion, from investigation, that the future treatment of sewage would be by bacteria. Experiments by the State Board of Massachusetts entirely confirmed that view, and in 1891 the London County Council decided to make experiments at Barking. Experiments were made, resulting in the construction of a coke-breeze bed of an acre in extent, and this was brought into use in 1892. The result was satisfactory, and the experiments had been continued under his supervision until he resigned his position as chemist to the London County Council, about eighteen months ago. He gave up his office in October last. In 1892 he was elected, being a resident of Sutton, as a member of the old local board, and he suggested to the board, they being about to institute their present sewage works, that they should try the system of treating the sewage by as economical a process as possible by relying upon

### COKE-BREEZE OR OTHER MATERIAL

for fine beds for the purification of the sewage, similar to those used at Barking, after preliminary treatment. These beds were made, the material being coke-breeze, sand, and sand and polarite. The Polarite Company offered the board polarite at £7 per ton, and he suggested other material costing shillings. The work was done by a paid servant of the public on the one hand (speaking of himself as chemist to the London County Council), and by ratepayers, speaking of the board and of himself as a representative of the ratepayers on the Sutton Local Board. He wanted the inspector to take particular notice that these coke-breeze beds were precisely similar to those beds used at Exeter by the Septic Tank Company, and which were found satisfactory, as would be seen by Mr. Cameron's statement submitted to the Local Government Board inspector at the inquiry at Exeter. As a result of the work done by these fine beds, it was shown that the tank effluent could be purified by this simple treatment over prepared land, because they showed that it did not matter what they used for preparing the beds. It really was a process of downward filtration worked intermittently. It was really prepared land, these beds. The result having been established, he submitted to the members of the council about two years ago that they should further experiment, by filling one of their precipitating tanks with coarse burnt ballast or coke-breeze for treating the crude sewage directly upon it, letting the effluent from this pass into the fine beds, and allowing the bacteria to eat up the sludge; and this was done. It was the outcome of public work, and not of work of a speculative character. It was a ratepayers' scheme entirely. The suggestion was carried out, and the first coarse bed was brought into use in November, 1896. As a result of the first six months' work he presented a report to the council, in his capacity as a townsman, to the chairman of the urban district council, and it came to this, that they found that the sludge was completely removed. Their

### NEW COARSE BACTERIA-BED

took the place of the precipitating tank, and the results showed that the sludge was done away with, and that the oxidisable matter was reduced by the coarse beds to the extent of 63 per cent. and by the combined beds to 85 per cent. If they measured by the albuminoid of ammonia process it was reduced in the coarse beds 58 per cent. and in the combined beds 78 per cent. The final effluent was free from all objectionable odour, and remained perfectly sweet on being kept either in open or closed vessels. Three other coarse beds were made from time to time by filling up the precipitating tanks, and were still working. They hoped, by the Local Government Board granting this loan, that they would be able to make a sufficient number of beds to deal with the whole of their sewage in accordance with the surveyor's report of February, 1898, which would effect an economy of nearly £500 per annum when this system was complete. Dr. Jacob, the medical officer to the council, would tell the inspector his opinion of the character of

### THE EFFLUENTS

he had examined from time to time, and they should also submit to the inspector that during the whole of this time they had completely satisfied the requirements of the Thames Conservancy, whose inspector informed him personally that they were quite satisfied with the effluent. The analysis would show a most important and interesting fact—that in March, 1897, when they were overworking the beds with a view to ascertaining their maximum power, their power fell off and the purification of the organic matter was reduced; but even then, under these abnormal conditions, taking the very worst time when they tried to put them out of order,

there was no nuisance whatever, and as soon as they gave them a few days' rest their recuperative power was so great that their full action was immediately restored. He pointed that out, because it had been used as an argument that the beds were not reliable; but it showed, on the contrary, that they were entirely under control and could be worked at all times. This was

### A RATEPAYERS' SYSTEM,

worked out at the cost of the ratepayers by the ratepayers' representatives, and given to the ratepayers by the united exertions of public men all along the line, because without the help and assistance received from the members of that council it could not have been done, and it went without saying that England had to thank the members of the Sutton Council for showing how this difficult problem might be solved without any question of royalties or patents. The cost was a minimum that any works could be made for, and a minimum of plant was required; and the results were such that they would be able to satisfy the inspector that they had only to extend the area of the beds, and sewage, as Sir Edward Frankland showed in his report to the Thames Conservators, could be brought back into the character of original drinking water. They had here a perfect system of land treatment, in which the action which generally took place on land properly worked was concentrated, accelerated and controlled. The treatment at sewage farms, as hitherto followed, had been a treatment prescribed from want of knowledge and the precise process through which sewage passed was haphazard and uncertain. In this case, knowing all the conditions, they submitted to the inspector that they had a system which was economical and efficacious in the highest degree, and they asked him to assist them in granting permission to adopt the system for the treatment of the whole of the sewage at Sutton, and thus assist the ratepayers in getting the work done most economically and as satisfactorily as possible.

Mr. C. CHAMBERS SMITH, surveyor to the council, said the estimated flow of sewage was 30 gallons per head of the population. The existing capacities of the coarse filters was 101,600 gallons, and it was proposed to increase this to 443,500 gallons. This was allowing for filling the tanks twice a day, but in practice they filled them three times per day, so that they had allowed one-third more, in order to be on the safe side always. The capacity of the present five beds was 233,586 gallons, and it was proposed to increase this to 462,786 gallons. They had 24 acres 17 perches of land at present available for the treatment of sewage. The land was stiff clay.

Mr. DIBDIN said one of the results of the increased purity of the effluent had been to enable them to grow mint, for which they had secured a net profit of £24 per acre, which, he ventured to think, was the highest profit ever obtained on a sewage farm. That was a natural advantage, and a very great one, but one that arose consequent upon their being better able to deal with the effluent. It was possible to fill the tanks six or seven times a day in case of storm.

Dr. JACOB, medical officer of health, supported the application from his observations of the results of the treatment of the sewage in the past.

On the termination of the inquiry the inspector paid a visit to the farm, and is understood to have been much gratified with the system and the condition of the works generally.

# ELECTRIC LIGHT IN BRUSSELS.

On the 22nd July last the first trial of the complete electric light installation in the Gare du Midi in Brussels was made, and, according to The Journal of the Society of Arts, pronounced thoroughly satisfactory. When the city authorities of Brussels a few years ago proposed lighting public places, such as railway stations, parks, &c., by electricity, and supplying electricity to subscribers at the same rate as gas, a great cry was raised and protestations made against the innovation, urging that it would ruin the gasworks and injuriously affect the communal exchequer. Recent statistics show that during the past year not only has the use of electricity increased, but that the profit from the sale of gas is considerably in excess of that of previous years. Deducting the amount expended for establishing plant, &c., the city derived a profit of £8,896. The most important installation recently made in Brussels is in the king's palace. When the work is finally completed there will be 7,500 lamps, of which a large number will be of 5 candle-power, employed in the chandeliers illuminating the ball and reception rooms. There are, according to the United States consul at Brussels, about 47,391 lamps, reduced in units of 16 candles, in the city system, averaging 117 lamps per 100 running motors of canalised streets. This number includes 770 arc lamps and twenty-eight electric motors, the latter varying from $\frac{1}{20}$th to 10 horse-power, with a total of 163 horse-power. In view of the increasing use of electricity in Belgium, the consul is of opinion that there is an excellent opportunity for the introduction of electric apparatus of all kinds.

## THE LOCAL OFFICERS' SUPERANNUATION BILL.

### MEETING OF THE MUNICIPAL OFFICERS' ASSOCIATION.

Mr. C. William Tagg, clerk to the Camberwell Vestry, on Monday evening occupied the chair at a conference, held at Sion College, Victoria-embankment, for the purpose of bringing before municipal officers the necessity of making efforts to induce their authorities to support the Local Officers' Superannuation Bill, and to take steps to secure assistance from the Parliamentary representatives of their districts.

The CHAIRMAN delivered a long address. He explained that the meeting had been convened for practical purposes, and that they desired to arrive at some practical decision as to how they were to get their Bill through the next session of Parliament. As yet there had been no really practical result, although a trump card had appeared in the annual report of the Local Government Board, which showed the result obtained in the working of the Poor Law Officers' Superannuation Act—namely, a profit in favour of the rate-payer of £15,000. It had been objected that the measure would place another burden on the back of the ratepayer, but they had always argued that that would not be the case, and that it would be a measure of justice to be equally fair to both the official and the ratepayer. The average salary of municipal officers in this country was £100 per annum, and it was impossible to make any provision for retirement out of that sum. They desired that the local authorities—who, he regretted to say, had not responded in the manner in which they had been expected to—should grant superannuation on a scheme under which the officers would contribute. As far as Parliament was concerned they were safe, but it was for themselves to obtain the consideration and support of their authorities, the majority of whom had up to the present refused to approve the movement. Several, however, had adopted resolutions in its favour. He thought that the allowance they asked for was a reasonable one. It was not a question of pension; it was one of deferred pay, and, in his opinion, it required settlement. Mr. Tagg, following a reference to the proposed inclusion of workmen in the Bill, then concluded his remarks by expressing a hope that the proceedings would be fruitful of good work, and, furthermore, that another step might be made in the right direction.

Mr. MATTHEW HALE, clerk to the Holborn District Board of Works, next submitted a motion pledging the meeting to do all in its power to secure the passing of the Local Authorities Officers' Superannuation Bill in the next session of Parliament, and, in the course of a brief address, said he considered the task of the association to be a gigantic one, and one which required much perseverance on the part of everyone engaged in municipal duties.

Dr. ORME DUDFIELD, medical officer of health to the Paddington Vestry—who has been connected with the association, as a member, since its formation—referred to the appointment of independent committees, which he agreed was satisfactory. Continuing, he mentioned that it had been contended that officers with good salaries should provide for their old age. The stipends, however, were generally so low that that was seldom possible. He felt sure he would have the approval of the meeting in seconding the motion.

Mr. JOHN LOWLES, M.P., in supporting the motion, remarked that it gave him great pleasure to be enabled to show his sympathy with the movement, which he promised he would do all in his power to support. Sympathy had been shown by Parliament, who really only required a little pressure from the various authorities. He spoke, he was sure, the opinion of a number of his fellow-members when he said that unless municipal officers were paid a higher salary in their earlier years they could not be expected to shift for themselves and provide for their old age. Local government in England, he went on, was of a very high standard compared with that of many foreign countries which he had visited, and it was because he wished to keep our municipal life pure and the officers free from corruption that he advocated their being treated in as handsome a manner as possible, and all their reasonable claims satisfied. He was always sorry, he added, to see good officers transferred because of a cheese-paring policy. In the present Government they had, he thought, a sympathetic body, and he was sure that their efforts would ultimately be crowned with success.

Mr. E. J. HALSEY, chairman of the Surrey County Council, also spoke in favour of the motion, and agreed that the arguments which had been used by Mr. Lowles were the right ones. There was a general reluctance on the part of local authorities to interest themselves in the superannuation question; but, speaking personally, he would do everything he possibly could to support the movement.

Mr. RUTHERGLEN (Kensington) expressed his thorough belief in the ultimate success of the scheme—which was perfectly reasonable in character—and strongly condemned the action of certain members of the House in endeavouring to prejudice Parliament as to the effects of the Bill if passed.

The CHAIRMAN made some further remarks, emphasising the importance of securing the support of the local authorities, and then formally moved the adoption of the motion, which was carried unanimously.

A discussion afterwards took place as to the best methods to be employed to ensure the success of the Bill, and the first speaker gave it as his opinion that that could be made all the more possible by influencing members of the House and persuading them to give their support to the measure in Parliament. Mr. W. J. FLETCHER, county surveyor of Dorset, however, differed from that view, and maintained that more good would result by furnishing the various authorities with statistics relating to the working of the scheme. He warned them not to rely upon their Parliamentary representatives. The CHAIRMAN remarked that it would be better to leave the members of Parliament to themselves, as Parliament would not stir in the matter until the members moved. Other speakers, including Messrs. COOK, READ (Dorset) and HUNTER, followed, and the proceedings terminated with the negativing of a motion proposing the extension of the association's Bill so as to apply to Scotland.

## CORRESPONDENCE.

"The Genesis of Street Mud."—Mr. Robert Phillips, county surveyor, Gloucester, writes: The crushing tests of stone are always interesting, and for the information of your readers I send you some I had taken in 1886. The 3-in. cubes were carefully selected, ground true, and bedded between pine. Your readers will notice that the Bristol limestone, a far inferior road stone, stood a greater test than the Clee Hill basalt, showing the fallacy of crushing tests. If you add to this, and the attrition tests heating to 120 deg. and immersion while hot, and a freezing test of three hours' duration, you have reached about the limit of tests, and must fall back on the test of user for a lengthened period.

[ENCLOSURE.]

Three specimens, carefully and impartially selected by an independent and experienced person from stone, actually supplied for use on the roads, of each of the kinds named below, have been sent up to Messrs. Kirkaldy & Son, of 99 Southwark-street, London, to be tested by them as to their comparative resistance to a thrusting stress.

The following are the results:—

| Supplied for Road use from | Three specimens of each kind sent up. | Cracked slightly at | | Crushed, dropped at | | Steelyard dropped at | |
|---|---|---|---|---|---|---|---|
| | | Pressure on 1 sq. inch. lb. | Pressure on 1 sq. foot. ton. | Pressure on 1 sq. inch. lb. | Pressure on 1 sq. foot. ton. | Pressure on 1 sq. inch. lb. | Pressure on 1 sq. foot. ton. |
| Clee Hill Granite Company, Salop | 1 | 13,214 | 849·7 | 15,847 | | 1,019·1 | |
| | 2 | 9,914 | 637·6 | 12,850 | | 826·4 | |
| | 3 | 8,495 | 546·3 | 12,559 | | 807·7 | |
| Mean | | 10,541 | 677·9 | 13,752 | | 884·4 | |
| Bristol Stone, Clifton, Bristol | 1 | 13,867 | 891·7 | 16,898 | | 1,086·7 | |
| | 2 | 13,073 | 840·7 | 14,932 | | 960·3 | |
| | 3 | 11,289 | 726·0 | 12,251 | | 787·2 | |
| Mean | | 12,743 | 819·5 | 14,694 | | 944·9 | |
| Tytherington Stone, Falfield, Gloucester | 1 | 12,888 | 828·8 | 14,662 | | 942·9 | |
| | 2 | 9,900 | 636·7 | 11,819 | | 760·1 | |
| | 3 | 10,080 | 648·2 | 11,810 | | 759·5 | |
| Mean | | 10,956 | 704·6 | 12,764 | | 820·8 | |
| Local White Limestone Oolite,* Gloucester | 1 | 4,082 | 262·5 | 4,749 | | 305·4 | |
| | 2 | 3,022 | 194·3 | 3,857 | | 248·0 | |
| | 3 | 2,170 | 139·5 | 3,197 | | 205·6 | |
| Mean | | 3,091 | 198·8 | 3,934 | | 253·0 | |

## LONDON'S STREETS.

In an address he gave the other day at King's College Prof. Simpson referred to the importance of cleanliness in the streets. The condition of public thoroughfares had, he declared, a very important influence upon the degrees of health of the people. It was impossible to say that London, except it was the City, was conspicuous for the cleanliness of its streets. London was magnificently paved, but the matter which was allowed to remain in the streets in a state of putrefaction was a serious menace to health. London was a healthy city, taken by the standard of its death rate, but if health consisted of being and feeling well it was possible that investigation in that direction might lead them to modify their views as to the healthiness of London.

London Water Supply.—Mr. H. S. Samuel has received promises from a number of members of Parliament to ballot next session for a place for his Metropolis Water Bill in the event of the Queen's speech not containing an assurance that legislation shall be introduced on the subject. Mr. Samuel's Bill, which has already been submitted to Mr. Chaplin, seeks to compel the various water companies in the metropolis to form junctions of mains, to enter into agreements with each other, and to give power to the Local Government Board to appoint an officer to report upon the quality, quantity and pressure of the water supplied by the companies.

* In common use in the county, the sample being above the average.

# Association of Municipal and County Engineers.

## MIDLAND DISTRICT MEETING AT BILSTON.

It will be remembered in connection with our report of the Midland Counties District Meeting of the Incorporated Association of Municipal and County Engineers at Bilston, on September 17th, that Mr. Wilson, the engineer and surveyor to the urban district council, in response to requests from Mr. J. T. Eayrs and others, readily consented to supplement his long and interesting paper entitled "Seven Years' Work in a Black Country Town," by additional particulars in regard to the public baths, the main roads, the technical school and the waterworks. These details have now been embodied in the following

### SUPPLEMENT TO SEVEN YEARS IN A BLACK COUNTRY TOWN.

By C. L. N. Wilson, A.M.I.C.E., &c.

#### PUBLIC BATHS.

It should be pointed out that, whilst the council would not object to making a profit out of the public baths, they never expected them to pay even working expenses, but considered that it would be conducive to the health and welfare of the town if they could induce the men employed in the ironworks and collieries to frequently use the baths and prevent youths from using the canal. With this object in view the charges for admission were fixed at so low a figure that it is possible, on three days per week, to obtain a slipper bath (hot and cold water), a cold-water shower bath and a swimming bath, with the use of one clean towel, for the sum of one penny.

The total number of bathers for the year ended March 31, 1897, was 23,088, or an average of 444 per week all the year round; the highest number using the baths in one week being 1,548 (week ended June 16, 1896), and the lowest fifty-six (week ended February 2, 1897); the average earnings from each bather being a fraction over 2¼d.

*Cost of Working for Year ended March 31, 1897.*

| | £ | s. | d. |
|---|---|---|---|
| Wages ... ... ... ... ... ... | 152 | 18 | 9 |
| Ironmongery, oil, &c. ... ... ... ... | 46 | 10 | 5 |
| Rates ... ... ... ... ... ... | 3 | 0 | 0 |
| Coal ... ... ... ... ... ... ... | 123 | 19 | 3 |
| Electric light plant ... ... ... ... | 24 | 9 | 3 |
| Soap and soda ... ... ... ... ... | 9 | 5 | 0 |
| Towels, drawers, brushes, &c. ... ... ... | 22 | 19 | 3 |
| Miscellaneous ... ... ... ... ... | 15 | 16 | 6 |
| | £398 | 18 | 5 |

*Receipts for Year ended March 31, 1897:* £218 16s. 9d.

| | £ | s. | d. |
|---|---|---|---|
| Cost of working ... ... ... ... ... | 398 | 18 | 5 |
| Receipts from bathers ... ... ... ... | 218 | 16 | 9 |
| Deficit ... ... ... ... | £180 | 1 | 8 |

| | £ | s. | d. |
|---|---|---|---|
| Cost of working ... ... ... ... ... | 398 | 18 | 5 |
| Interest on loans ... ... ... ... ... | 129 | 17 | 7 |
| Repayment of loans ... ... ... ... | 159 | 14 | 11 |
| Total cost ... ... .. | 688 | 10 | 11 |
| Receipts... ... ... ... | 218 | 16 | 9 |
| Total deficit ... ... ... | £469 | 14 | 2 |

#### MAIN ROADS.

The total cost for the year ended March 31, 1898, was £1,552 14s. 3d.; or, without making any deduction for cost of new footpaths and drains, £282 6s. 2¾d. per mile; or, after making these deductions, £1,316 9s. 2d., or £239 7s. 1½d. per mile.

#### TOWN ROADS.

| | £ | s. | d. |
|---|---|---|---|
| Total cost for year ended March 31, 1898 ... | 1,070 | 0 | 9 |
| Interest on loans ... ... ... ... ... | 11 | 12 | 0 |
| Repayment of loans ... ... ... ... | 72 | 10 | 0 |
| | £1,754 | 2 | 9 |

or £70 14s. 8¾d. per mile.

#### TECHNICAL SCHOOL.

*Working Expenses for Year ended March 31, 1898.*

| | £ | s. | d. |
|---|---|---|---|
| Teachers' salaries ... ... ... ... ... | 450 | 0 | 0 |
| Heating and light ... ... ... ... ... | 60 | 16 | 8 |
| Printing and stationery ... ... ... ... | 53 | 6 | 6 |
| Caretaker ... ... ... ... ... ... | 45 | 0 | 0 |
| Rates, taxes and insurance ... ... ... | 13 | 14 | 5 |
| Secretaries ... ... ... ... ... ... | 65 | 0 | 0 |
| Apparatus, wood, &c. ... ... ... ... | 30 | 0 | 0 |
| Miscellaneous ... ... ... ... ... | 15 | 0 | 0 |
| | £732 | 17 | 7 |

*Receipts.*

| | £ | s. | d. |
|---|---|---|---|
| General district rate ... ... ... ... | 204 | 3 | 8 |
| Grants—Staffordshire County Council ... | 102 | 0 | 0 |
| " Science and Art Department (app.)... | 99 | 0 | 0 |
| " Educational Department, Continuation School ... ... ... | 90 | 12 | 0 |
| " Cooking Kitchen ... ... ... | 15 | 0 | 0 |
| Students' fees ... ... ... ... ... | 105 | 0 | 0 |
| | £726 | 15 | 8 |

| | £ | s. | d. |
|---|---|---|---|
| Payments ... ... ... ... | 732 | 17 | 7 |
| Receipts ... ... ... ... | 726 | 15 | 8 |
| Deficit ... ... ... ... ... | £6 | 1 | 11 |

#### WATERWORKS.

*Year ended March 31, 1898.*

The quantity of water pumped was 355,258,365 gallons. The cost of pumping, distribution, repayments of loans and interest, and including £811 4s. paid to the contractors for extra wages and £457 9s. 5d. for new works, was £6,502 19s. 3d., and equals a total cost of just over 4⅝d. per 1,000 gallons. The receipts from water rents for the same period were £5,377 8s. 5½d.

*Weight of Lead Pipe Allowed by our By-Laws for Services, &c.*

| | Bilston Area. | Wombourn, &c. |
|---|---|---|
| ⅜ in. internal diameter | 5 lb. | 5 lb. per yard |
| ½ in. " " | 6 " | 7 " " |
| ⅝ in. " " | 7½ " | 9 " " |
| ¾ in. " " | 9 " | 11 " " |
| 1 in. " " | 12 " | 16 " " |
| 1¼ in. " " | 16 " | 22½ " " |

No wrought-iron tubing of any kind is allowed, above 1¼ in. diameter cast-iron pipes to be used, smallest size 2 in. diameter.

*Rising Main Contract.*

| | |
|---|---|
| Excavating to 4 ft. 7 in. deep and 3 ft. wide... ... ... ... ... | 10½d. per yard cube. |
| Excavating to 9 ft. deep and 3 ft. wide | 1s. 2d. per yard cube. |
| Excavating to 4 ft. 7 in. deep and 3 ft. wide radial ... ... ... ... | 1s. 3d. per yard cube. |
| Laying 14-in. pipes only ... ... | 7d. per yard run. |
| 14-in. joints, all lead, about 18 lb. each | 4s. each. |
| 12-in. joints, all lead, about 15 lb. each | 3s. 6d. each. |
| Laying 12-in. pipes only ... ... | 6d. per yard run. |

*Wombourn Mains.*

| | |
|---|---|
| Excavating to 3 ft. 6 in. deep and 2 ft. 6 in. wide ... ... ... | 8d. per lineal yard. |
| Filling in to 3 ft. 6in. deep and 2 ft. 6 in. wide... ... ... ... ... | 3d. per lineal yard. |
| 4 in. joints, all lead, 10d. each... ... | about 5 lb. each. |
| 3 in. " " 7d. each ... ... | " 3¾ lb. each. |
| 2 in. " " 5d. each ... ... | " 2¼ lb. each. |

Mr. Wilson concluded his supplementary paper with a short description of the Spring Vale Furnaces and Steel Works, which were visited on the occasion. This description has already appeared in our columns, and is therefore not reproduced.

## RIVER POLLUTION IN WALES.

### COUNTY COUNCILS' ACTION.

A joint committee, appointed by the county councils of Monmouth and Glamorgan, met at the county offices, Cardiff, on Saturday, to consider the question of the pollution of the river Rhymney. A letter was read from the Rhymney Urban District Council, in which they gave explanations as to why they had not proceeded with their sewerage scheme. The committee, having considered the letter at some length, gave instructions that notices should be issued to the Rhymney Urban District Council, the Bedwellty Urban District Council, and the Gelligaer Rural District Council, to the effect that unless effective sewerage schemes were formulated for the respective districts, and satisfaction afforded the committee that there was an intention to carry out efficient schemes, legal proceedings to prevent pollution of the river would be taken against the local authorities.

**Calcutta.**—After a hot discussion, lasting two sittings, the Calcutta Corporation have adopted, by a large majority, the terms of the agreement with the tramway company proposed by the special committee. The company are given a new lease of life for thirty years, and in order to continue the work of reform already begun a court of arbitration is formed to punish summarily any case of default. The company is now at liberty to introduce electric traction at any time.

## ASSOCIATION OF BIRMINGHAM STUDENTS OF THE INSTITUTION OF CIVIL ENGINEERS.

The opening meeting of the 1898-99 session of the above institution was held on Thursday, when the members paid a visit in the afternoon to the engine works of Messrs. G. E. Belliss,& Co., then dined together at the Grand Hotel, and assembled again at the Midland Institute at 7.30, to hear the inaugural address of the president, Mr. J. C. Vaudrey, M.I.C.E.

After transacting the usual formal business, the president announced that the council of the Institution of Civil Engineers had awarded four "Miller" prizes to the members of the association—viz., Messrs. A. B. E. Blackburn and D. E. Lloyd-Davis for papers read before the local association, and C. E. Wolff and Henry C. Adams (the hon. sec. of the association) for papers read before the students in London.

### THE PRESIDENT'S ADDRESS

brought forward some of the more prominent features that have marked the history and progress of electrical engineering. To be an electrical engineer, he said, a thorough engineering training is absolutely essential. Be an engineer first, and an electrician after if you will. Twenty years have hardly passed since Edison startled the scientific world by his discovery of the effect of passing an electric current through a carbon filament sealed in an air-exhausted globe. The old truism, that the road of pioneers was strewn with failures, was no exception in the case of electrical engineering.

THE EARLY SCHEMES OF PUBLIC LIGHTING

from an engineering point of view lacked system, uniformity and business prudence. The early dynamo was inefficient, and a machine producing 50 kilowatts was called " a jumbo." High-speed engines as a commercial factor were non-existent. Incandescent lamps were not made of a higher voltage than 60 volts, and cost about 5s. each. The first Electric Lighting Act was passed in 1882, and gave a limiting period of twenty-one years, the property passing to the local authority at the end of that time at the then value. This Act retarded progress, but effectually put a stop to many ill-natured and uncalled-for schemes. Since 1888 several systems have been adopted for underground distribution, but sufficient time has hardly elapsed to determine which will be the survivor. The conditions absolutely essential are that the copper should be permanently isolated and that the insulation should not be affected by damp or changes of temperature, and should be protected from mechanical injury. The Callendar system of laying insulated cables in iron troughs, the cable being surrounded by pure bitumen, was first adopted in Liverpool by Mr. Vaudrey and his colleague, Mr. Holmes, and the greater portion of the mains in Birmingham have been dealt with in a similar manner. With regard to

GENERATING MACHINERY,

the electrical engineer owes a deep debt of gratitude to Willans for the high-speed central-valve engine, which can be run safely at such a speed as to allow the dynamo to be coupled direct to the crank shafts. Messrs. Belliss & Co., of Birmingham, have established a well-earned reputation with their type of plant. Electric tramway engineering should not be lost sight of by the student, as it offers a new opening to those now entering the profession. Underground railways are being brought rapidly to the front. The railway engineer, the hydraulic engineer, and those in charge of our municipal work and gas supplies, will all have to know something of electrical work. A large railway contractor has recently spent some £10,000 in electrical plant for temporary motor work and other uses on a large railway contract he has on hand. There is a great tendency to specialise, and often the student is apt to think his own special subject is the one which will enable him to make his way in life; and I would advise him never to lose sight of the power a wide knowledge of engineering, added to that of a specialist, gives him. Buildings are all lighted now with a brilliancy that was inconceivable even ten years ago, and from a sanitary view the very air we live in must be purer.

THE NEW GENERAL HOSPITAL AT BIRMINGHAM

is perhaps the highest ideal of a pure condition of life, all owing to electricity. The world at large will be immeasurably richer for the advantages of electricity, and those taking part in such works, in whatever form they may assume, are engaged in a work with which they will hereafter be proud to have been associated.

## INSTITUTION OF CIVIL ENGINEERS.

### THE PRESIDENTIAL ADDRESS.

The above institution hold the first meeting of their eightieth session on Tuesday evening, when the president, Mr. W. H. Preece, C.B., F.R.S., engineer-in-chief and electrician to the Post Office, took the chair for the first time.

In delivering the customary inaugural address the PRESIDENT expressed his gratitude for the honour done him, and said he was very proud, not only for the sake of that branch of the profession to which he specially belonged, but also because he was a member of the great Civil Service of this country. After referring to the position occupied by the

institution as the representative of engineering science in this country, the president turned to the subject of

TECHNICAL EDUCATION.

He pointed out that a knowledge of matter and of energy was the foundation of all the engineer's actions, and this, combined with the power of thinking, was the root of technical training. There was a fashion for technical education just now in Great Britain, and enormous sums of money were being spent. It was well that the country had awakened from its conservatism and apathy. Our trade was suffering, even in our own colonies, from the competition of our Continental neighbours, who were said to be beating us by their technically superior hand labour. This was because we were suffering from the superior commercial skill of the principals at home and the accomplished polyglot traveller abroad, as well as from a financial system that was more moral and sound than that rampant in England through the gross abuses of the Limited Liability Act of 1862. In Germany financial support was readily subscribed for a new industry by the generous and enlightened policy of its banks. In England a syndicate, a pioneer company, and, finally, an appeal to the public for an enlarged limited company, were required. The industry was established, but with a capital overloaded by the harpies sprung from the operation of that Act. The same industry could be established in Germany with probably half the capital, the manufacture would be supervised with greater skill, and it would be developed as a business by better trained agents, for educational methods had begun at the wrong end. We ought to teach the masters first, and then the men ; moreover, we had to teach the teachers and those who had control of the purse-strings. Mr. Preece proceeded to refer to some of the practical applications of the science of electricity. Beginning with lightning conductors, he went on to speak of

TELEGRAPHY,

mentioning that he had used a portion of the first line ever constructed, made by Cooke & Wheatstone in 1837 to connect Camden Town and Euston-grove station, to complete a special circuit between Buckingham Palace and the General Post Office, used by the Queen on her Diamond Jubilee day. This pioneer line of 1837 was 1¼ mile long ; now the system of British telegraphs contained 1,111,366 miles of wire. Progress had never been checked. The introduction of the telephone was revolutionising the mode of transacting business. Its progress in Great Britain had been checked by financial complications. Telephony, like the post and telegraph, was an imperial business, and ought to be in the hands of the State. In the working of railways the employment of electricity had not only been highly beneficent in the security of human life, but it had vastly increased the capacity of a road to carry trains, while its introduction into our houses had added materially to the comfort and luxury of home. In supplying light without defiling the air of our dwellings electricity had proved a true benefactor of the human race, while on board ship the electric light had been pre-eminently successful. With regard to

ELECTRIC TRACTION,

everywhere our great cities were rising to the occasion. Indeed, to neglect to supply tramways where they would be useful, healthful and valuable was, to a certain extent, an abuse of the trust confided to the municipality by the legislature. Electrometallurgy was now a very large business, and destined to increase still more, for the generation of electrical energy was becoming better understood and more cheaply effected. It was remarkable that our coalfields had not been utilised in this direction, for on a coalfield where coal of good calorific value was raised at a cost of 3s. a ton electrical energy could be generated more cheaply than by a waterfall, even at Niagara. In conclusion, Mr. Preece hoped he had impressed on them the universality of electricity. Though its followers were now regarded as specialists, the period was not distant when it must cease to be a speciality. Every engineer must ultimately become an electrician, and electricity would be the most general, the most useful and the most interesting form in which he applied the fundamental principles of energy to the wants, the comforts and the happiness of mankind.

A vote of thanks was unanimously accorded Mr. Preece for his address. The distribution of the medals and prizes then followed.

---

"**Modern Opera Houses and Theatres.**"—The third volume of "Modern Opera Houses and Theatres," by Mr. Edwin O. Sachs, architect, is to be issued during this month, and this monumental work will thus see completion before the end of the year. As before, so with the impending volume, Mr. Sachs' programme will be materially extended, and there will, for instance, be no less than 900 illustrations, as compared with the 250 he originally promised his subscribers. The third volume will comprise a treatise on theatres generally, with various supplements ; and having special regard for the interest evinced in modern forms of construction, a particular chapter has been devoted to constructional ironwork as applied to the playhouse, both on cantilever principles and otherwise. The publisher is Mr. Batsford, of High Holborn, and with the completion of the work the subscription list will be closed, the price henceforward being 15 guineas.

# The Belfast Municipal Electricity Works.

Some years ago the Belfast Corporation instituted what proved to be a most interesting departure in electric lighting. They commenced a public supply of electricity, and relied upon gas engines as a source of power. The experiment, which it undoubtedly was, did not prove altogether successful, and although it cannot be said that the results of Belfast experience can be urged against the use of gas engines for electric lighting, it is clear that the faith of the Belfast Corporation is not sufficient to induce them to carry out extensions with similar plant. In dealing, then, with the demand that has arisen in Belfast and was growing rapidly, it was resolved to meet it by building a new station, which would be entirely equipped with steam plant. The works have now been completed, and were recently opened formally by the Viceroy of Ireland, on the same occasion as the laying of the foundation-stone of the city hall, of which proposed building we give some details in another column. They are in every respect among the most important in the country, not only on account of the size of the generating station, but by reason of the magnitude of the plant which has been erected. The works are situated within 150 yards of the river, from which an ample supply of water can be obtained. It also permits of the easy delivery of coal, and the site is in a central position with regard to distribution. It is computed that the ground will provide buildings sufficient to house 20,000 horse-power of plant. At the present moment four Lancashire boilers have been erected, which work at a pressure of 160 lb. per square inch. They are fitted with Hopkinson's mountings, and while one is to be fired by hand, the others are furnished with mechanical stokers; these, by the way, are driven through a countershaft by a motor. The inevitable Green's economiser is employed, which has 216 tubes, the scrapers for these being driven by an electric motor. Coal bunkers extend the whole length of the boilers, and are provided with doors which open on to an elevated road, from whence carts can be unloaded without much difficulty. We believe it is the intention to subsequently provide coal conveyors, and already provisions have been made for an overhead tramway from the riverside. The steam mains have been erected on the ring principle, the pipes are solid-drawn copper, and Hopkinson valves are employed. Tanks capable of storing 20,000 gallons have been erected below the boilers, and, in addition, there are two distinct supplies from the city mains.

THE ENGINE-HOUSE AND THE BATTERY-ROOM.

The engine-house is probably one of the finest in the country, and in it at the present moment are four Belliss steam dynamos, two having a capacity of 100 kilowatts and two of 200 kilowatts. The smaller sets consist of two crank compound engines, coupled direct to a 50 kilowatt dynamo. These are apparently intended for day supply, and in addition for charging the batteries. The larger sets—viz., the 200 kilowatt, develop current at from 400 to 500 volts. The engines which drive these machines are of the three crank compound type. With a view to dealing with the supply of current for traction purposes, which we trust will not be long before it is required, one of the sets has been furnished with a heavier type of fly-wheel. At the generating station there are also arranged a pair of boosters and a balancing motor generator. Adjoining this room is the battery-room, in which are arranged two batteries of accumulators, consisting of 130 cells of the "Faure-King" type, which have a capacity of 500 ampere hours at a discharge rate of 100 amperes. They are also capable of discharging at 300 amperes for one hour. The switchboard is placed on a platform some 13 ft. above the floor level, six being arranged for feeders, eight for dynamos, and others for the motor generators and battery generators. With a view to making it as fireproof as possible, the panels are carried on the steel framework, and there are the usual measuring and recording instruments; each machine has also in circuit with it an automatic cut-out. Feeders are provided on both poles, with ammeter, fuses and switches. From this board the regulation of the batteries can be carried on, the switches in the battery-room being actuated through shaft and level gearing. If necessary, the battery switch can also be operated in the battery-room. The system of distribution has been carried out on the three-wire system, with 440 volts between the outer wires and 220 between either outer and the middle wire.

The network of distributing mains is fed at several points by the feeders from the generating station. Meters are provided by which the engineer in charge can maintain a proper pressure in the network. The mains are of single-core cable, insulated with vulcanised bitumen, and drawn into Doulton earthenware conduits when laid under footways or into cast-iron pipes under roadways. In other portions of the town lead-covered and armoured three-core cable is used.

ESTIMATED CONSUMPTION.

It is interesting to mention that the demand indicator system of charging is now in operation, and it is considered that when the advantages of this become generally known there will be a considerable accession of consumers. At the present moment there are connected to the Belfast mains an equivalent to 29,000 8 candle-power lamps, and this includes 150 horse-power in motors. Just prior to the completion of the new station the total number of applications received

was up to an equivalent of 8,000 8 candle-power lamps, and it is estimated that in order to cope with the growing demands it will be necessary to order fresh plant at once. It may be interesting to observe that the whole of these extensions have been carried out by the city electrical engineer, Mr. Victor M'Cowen, and it was in consequence of his report, presented to the Electric Lighting Committee in 1896, that the scheme was adopted. In the report presented at that time Mr. M'Cowen observed that they had spent £33,000 in the gas engine station, that all the available room of the engines had been taken up, and that it was necessary to build another station. Although availing themselves as far as possible of the old system, it was necessary, in Mr. M'Cowen's opinion, to put the plant in a position more contiguous to the area where a large demand was likely to arise, and, in order to meet the demand that was likely to arise at a considerable distance from the old station, the engineer recommended the adoption of a 440-volt system, on the three-wire method, which gives 220 volts in the houses. This would enable the corporation to distribute current economically at a distance of about 2 miles from the station. It was suggested in the report that consumers beyond such area could be best supplied on the high-tension transformer system or from battery-sub-stations, these sub-stations being placed at the end of the feeders and the batteries being charged from the central station, in this manner obtaining longer running hours from the plant.

The conclusion of Mr. M'Cowen's report was to the effect that by the combination of a steam-driven and a gas-driven station supplying the same mains they would be able to get economical results. The steam station would take the bulk of the winter load, and the gas station would take the peak of the load, being, as well, always ready to take up a fog or dark-day load; the gas driven station would be able to do the summer load when the steam station might be shut down for a few months, with the exception of a run off and on to charge the batteries, or arrangements could be made to charge these batteries in summer from the gas-driven station.

## ARBITRATIONS AND AWARDS.

The award in an arbitration case of Coode, Shilston & Co. v. St. Austell Urban District Council, in respect of compensation for land acquired by the council for street improvements around a fine block of buildings just erected by the firm, has been received. The council offered £111. The claim before the arbitrators amounted to about £1,300, being based upon the actual rental, and doubled in consequence of the whole of the land (about £303) being frontage. The award to the company amounts to £303, the council to pay all costs. In a similar claim by R. W. Rogers, grocer, Fore-street, an award of £12 was made, and costs to be paid by the council. Coode, Shilston & Co. (who also represented Mr. Rogers) appointed Mr. H. Drew, of Exeter, their arbitrator, and Mr. A. Body, of Plymouth, acted for the council, the umpire being Mr. G. C. Smyth Richards, of Barnstaple.

At the Sheriff's Court, Red Lion-square, on Thursday, before Mr. Under-Sheriff Burchell and a special jury, a claim against the London County Council by the Clothworkers' Company was heard in respect of freehold wharf property on the Surrey side of Vauxhall bridge, let on lease to Messrs. Francis & Co. Limited, for a term, of which fifty-two years were unexpired, at a ground rent of £515 a year. Sir Edward Clarke, q.c., and Mr. Edward Boyle, q.c., were counsel for the claimants, and they called Sir J. W. Ellis, Mr. Bousfield and Mr. James Green, who all agreed that the value of the property, including the customary 10 per cent., was £22,660. For the London County Council Mr. Littler, q.c., and Mr. Morton were retained, and called Mr. Alderman Green, Mr. Farmer, Mr. Horsey and Mr. Field, whose valuations were £14,182, including the 10 per cent. The jury returned a verdict for the claimants for £22,660.

Mr. James Mansergh, of Westminster, the umpire appointed in the arbitration between the Morley Corporation and the Morley Gas Company to fix the price to be paid for the undertaking of the Morley Gas Company, has now made his award. The arbitration was held last month, at the Hotel Victoria, London. The amount of the claim for the gas company was about £133,650, and the witnesses for the corporation put the value at about £80,000, which latter amount, however, did not include any allowance for compulsory purchase or cost of re-investment, these matters being left by the corporation witnesses to be dealt with by the umpire. The amount of the award is £108,806 2s. In addition to the gas undertaking, the corporation will be entitled to the balance of various insurance and contingent funds, which amount to about £10,000 after the payment thereon of certain costs of the Morley Gas Company. The corporation will be able to acquire some freehold property in the centre of the town which belongs to the gas company, and some other land purchased by the company but not at present used for the purpose of the gasworks.

## ROYAL COMMISSION ON SEWAGE DISPOSAL.

### REPLIES TO THE CHAIRMAN'S LETTER.

The following letters have appeared in *The Times* in answer to the letter of Lord Iddesleigh, to which we made reference in our last issue. A correspondent, signing himself "A. B.," writes:—

"Lord Iddesleigh's letter in *The Times* of the 21st opens up a question the importance of which neither the public nor the legislature appears as yet to have realised.

"He says that the Commission on Sewage Disposal would view with the gravest concern any postponement on the part of local authorities of the carrying out of works for the purification of trade refuse and sewage until the commission have issued their report. He also says that a considerable time, perhaps even some years, must elapse before that report appears. Which does Lord Iddesleigh suppose will weigh most in the minds of local authorities—the grave concern of a little group of gentlemen at Westminster, or the serious risk that whatever plan they may adopt for the disposal of sewage and trade refuse will be condemned as inadequate by the Local Government Board, armed with the report of this commission? Lord Iddesleigh has struck the heaviest blow that has been dealt to sanitary progress for many years.

"The question for the public, and a very grave question it is from the ratepayers' point of view, is this—What is the proper scope and aim of a commission of this kind? Is its proper business to collate, digest and report upon the enormous mass of practical experience and knowledge obtained from the actual working of numerous sewage disposal systems, but never yet brought to a focus or treated as a whole? Or is it the proper business of the commission to neglect all that practical work and to embark upon a prolonged search for an ideal system of its own—a search carried out by means of laboratory experiments in bacteriology and chemistry, and therefore having at least but a dubious relation to practical needs? Common sense would choose the first alternative without hesitation, first because it alone offers the smallest practical help within a reasonable time, and secondly because it is the only kind of investigation which the composition of this commission fits it to undertake. The commission itself has chosen the second alternative, which commits it to an investigation of a highly speculative and theoretical character and of wholly indefinite duration. For such an investigation the commission is absolutely unfit. Were such a thing desired, it ought obviously to be entrusted to two or three experts. But nothing of the kind is desired or called for. Were such an investigation completed and published, the report would either be so much waste paper, or it would stereotype a method of sewage disposal which, on the one hand would be used to condemn existing and practically efficient systems, and on the other would be an absolute bar to advance. There is no finality in science. Whatever the commission may discover, at whatever point it may stop, there will be more to discover just beyond. The commission is repeating the blunder made some years ago in another department, when this country was allowed to drop fifteen years behind other nations in armaments, because some sapient persons at the War Office were waiting for the appearance of the ultimate and unimprovable type of gun. Sewage disposal is practically brought to a stand for an indefinite period, because this commission is looking for an ideal system of its own, which, when found, is as likely as not to be rendered obsolete in twelve months.

"But there is more than this. The commission, working on its present lines, is in great danger of becoming a gigantic job. There is money, a great deal of money, in this sewage question. It is one of the biggest social questions with which the people of this country have to deal. The fishing inquiry, on which the commission is embarked, means in itself a large expenditure, and it may be indefinitely protracted. It further opens the door to the creation of patent rights, controlling indispensable details of the machinery to be subsequently forced upon all local authorities by the action of the Local Government Board. Has the Government so much as made the stipulation, loudly called for in the interests of the public, that no such private rights shall be, directly or indirectly, founded upon any results arrived at in the progress of this inquiry?"

The second letter, which appeared over the *nom de plume* of "District Councillor," was as follows:—

"The letter of Lord Iddesleigh, pointing out the probable delay in issuing the report of the Royal Commission on Sewage Disposal, is of great importance to rural district councils which are anxious at once to make a sanitary disposal of their sewage, but cannot do so without obtaining from the Local Government Board the sanction of a loan. The rural district council to which I belong have determined to treat the sewage of a town of 1,000 inhabitants, which at present pollutes an important stream, by what is known as 'Dibdin's Biological Process,' which has been at work for the town of Winsford for many years, and has also been successfully adopted at Oswestry. The district council, however, is informed that no loan for the purpose will be sanctioned by the Local Government Board unless the process is recommended in the report of the Royal Commission now sitting."

## DOUGLAS SEWERAGE SCHEME.

Mr. S. H. Adams, of Adams' Patent Sewage Lift Company, York, writing under the date of 31st October, has addressed the following communication with reference to the above subject to the editor of *The Isle of Man Times* : I have read to-day, for the first time, the discussion upon Mr. Mausergh's report. One or two points are raised to which, with your permission, I would refer. (1) We were providing two distinct air pipes, so that each lift is independent of the other. (2) The screen is really a continuation of the sewer, perforated where it passes through the flush tank that liquid may enter the latter whilst solids pass on to the sewer. It is desirable, although not ordinarily essential, that the lift should be looked at once a week. An ordinary sewerman can do this, no special attendant being required. (3) I give a list of a few towns in which our lifts have been in constant work for varying periods: London, Glasgow, Grimsby, Bridlington, Ilkley, Hoylake, Barmouth, Bucknall, Maldon, Ebchester, Johnstone (N.B.), Newmarket, Portsmouth, Godalming, Beamish (county Durham), and on the Continent and abroad. In four of these the supply is crude sewage. Plans have passed and are still before the Local Government Board for other schemes. Malvern, the well-known health resort, has adopted our system, the work being now in progress—here the sewage is used for supply. In no sense is the sewage lift experimental. It has one moving part—a plain flap valve—against the many of engines and pumps. Every installation is absolutely guaranteed to do the work required of it. The adoption of the lift then becomes in a sense a question of cost. As sewage is the motive power this is costless, and as the lifts require no special attendant no provision under the head of maintenance is necessary, the first is then the only cost. The lifts will thus pay for themselves in a given number of years. Mr. Marshall Petree, borough engineer of Grimsby, writing on October 14th last, says: "In reply to your inquiry, the sewage lift you fixed for this corporation over four years ago continues working to my entire satisfaction, and I am pleased to say has cost us nothing whatever throughout the time in the way of repairs and maintenance. Several deputations have inspected the lift and have expressed themselves highly satisfied with it."

## SYPHONIC CLOSET TRAPS AND CLOSETS.

We give an illustration of a syphonic trap and closet which attracted some attention at the recent sanitary congress at Birmingham, as satisfying the chief requirements of a modern water-closet. This appliance is known as the "Kensington" syphonic closet trap and closet, and is manufactured by the Anchor Sanitary Potteries, Swadlincote. It has a water surface of 10 in. by 8 in., or more if required, and a water seal of 5 in., which, it is claimed, cannot under any circumstances be syphoned out. Among other advantages claimed for this closet are that it is fixed exactly as a

common hopper and trap, with earthenware or lead outlets; that it is self-cleansing, and without any puff pipes or other complicated parts that are liable to get out of order; that only 2 gallons of water are required to flush it properly, thus getting over the difficulty of the 3-gallon flush, a quantity which is not always forthcoming; and that its moderate cost enables it to be used in all classes of buildings. We may also mention that the trap can be fitted separately to other closets. The appliance is certainly worth the attention of sanitarians, architects, builders, property owners, and others.

**Road Locomotives.**—Under the Locomotives Act, 1898, county councils are empowered to make by-laws for the regulation of road locomotive traffic, and to fix the fees for licences granted to locomotives. In several instances scales of fees have already been adopted. In respect to the making of by-laws, however, the County Councils' Association have resolved to move the Local Government Board to issue model by-laws, and a committee, consisting of Lord Thring, Mr. D. Hobhouse, M.P., Mr. R. D. Littler, Q.C., and Mr. F. C. Hulton, have been appointed to draw up suggestions for submission to the board.

# Law Notes.

EDITED BY J. B. REIGNIER CONDER, 11 Old Jewry Chambers, E.C.,
Solicitor of the Supreme Court.

*The Editor will be pleased to answer any questions affecting the practice of engineers and surveyors to local authorities. Queries (which should be written legibly on foolscap paper, one side only) should be addressed to "The Law Editor," at the Offices of THE* SURVEYOR. *Where possible, copies of local Acts or documents referred to should be enclosed. All explanatory diagrams must be drawn and lettered in black ink only. Correspondents who do not wish their names published should furnish a nom de plume.*

HIGHWAY: STEAM ROLLER: DANGEROUS NUISANCE.—It will be remembered that in the case of *Moon v. The Wharfedale Rural District Council and The Otley Urban District Council* (noted at p. 489 *ante*), judgment was given in favour of the plaintiff as against the Wharfedale Council, the question of the liability of the Otley Council being reserved. The learned judge of the Otley County Court has now decided that question, holding that the latter council are also liable. In the course of his judgment his honour said : This was an action against the two councils to recover damages for injuries to the plaintiff's carriage through the horse taking fright at a steam roller belonging to the Otley Council, but, which was at the time being used by the Wharfedale Council. The Otley Council agreed with the Wharfedale Council to let them the roller, and a man to take charge of it, for a fixed sum per day. The Otley Council selected and paid the man whom they sent with the roller, whose name was Jennings. On the day in question the Wharfedale Council employed four other men, whose duty it was to go two before and two behind the roller, and to help persons desiring to drive past it needing assistance. The surveyor to the Wharfedale Council pointed out to Jennings what roads were to be rolled, and left him in charge. Jennings left the roller, and went to refresh himself at a public-house, the roller being at the time stationary. He left his son, who was one of the four men employed by the Wharfedale Council, on the engine. The other man, who would have been in front of the engine when in motion, went away also. Jennings' son, whilst his father was away, proceeded to get up steam, and in doing so caused the engine to emit a quantity of black smoke and create a considerable noise. Whilst it was doing so the plaintiff's carriage was driven past it. There was no one to give assistance, and the horses took fright, and, notwithstanding the efforts of the coachman, the carriage was upset and seriously injured. I am of opinion that the steam roller in the condition in which it was—giving off quantities of smoke, causing considerable noise, and not protected by men waiting to render assistance to vehicles—was a nuisance, and that as the Wharfedale Council were responsible for its being in the high road, they were answerable for the damages. I must therefore give judgment against them. The Otley Council were not, I think, responsible for the nuisance, as they had no control over the place to which the roller was sent, but it is agreed that the accident happened through the negligence of Jennings, and that the Otley Council were his masters and liable for his negligence. I am of opinion that Jennings was negligent in leaving the roller, and that, whether he ordered his son to get up steam or not, he was responsible for the way in which the engine was dealt with in his absence. It remains for me to consider which of the defendants was his master within the rule of law which makes a master responsible for the negligent act of his servant. This, I am of opinion, depends whether his negligence was in relation to an act which he was doing under the instructions of one defendant or the other. It appears to me that in all that he did in the management of the engine he was acting under the direction and for the benefit of the Otley Council. I am of opinion that the negligence of which Jennings in fact was guilty related to the management of the engine and the mode of getting up steam, and therefore that the Otley Council were for this purpose his masters and were liable for the damage that was caused. I give judgment, therefore, against them also.

## QUERIES AND REPLIES.

WATER RIGHTS.—"Kosmos" writes: A rural district council acquires the right to sink a well and take water from a piece of land for a village supply. The well is sunk 26 ft. deep and about 30 ft. from a spring issuing from the side of a hill. It is found that when the water is pumped from the well at a certain rate the spring ceases to flow. There is no channel connecting the spring with the well, except several natural crevices in the rock, through which the water flows when it rises above a certain level in the well. The owner of a mill into whose mill stream the spring used to flow threatens action. Has he any grounds? Would the grounds of action be any stronger if a trench were cut from the well to convey the water by gravitation, provided the site of the spring were not interfered with? The water would not again reach the stream.

The general rule is that a riparian proprietor's right extends only to the defined stream, and not to that portion of the water which, though eventually by percolation or otherwise it may reach and supply the defined stream, does not as yet run in a defined stream (*Broadbent v. Ramsbotham*, 11 Exch., 608). In that case the plaintiff's mill for more than fifty years had been worked by the stream of a brook, which was supplied by subterranean waters, a swamp and a well formed by a

stream flowing outside of a hill, the waters of all of which occasionally overflowed and ran down the defendant's land, in no defined channel into the brook. It was held that the plaintiff had no right, as against the defendant, to the natural flow of any of the waters. In the case given in the query it is not stated whether or not the water from the spring flows into the brook into a defined channel. Assuming that it does not flow in a defined channel, I do not think the millowner would succeed in an action, unless he has acquired a right by express grant (see also *Rawstron v. Taylor*, 11 Exch., 369). If, however, the water flows from the spring to the stream in a defined channel, the millowner may have acquired a right to its uninterrupted flow by prescription—*i.e.*, twenty years' uninterrupted enjoyment.

OFFICER TO LOCAL AUTHORITY: TERMINATION OF APPOINTMENT.—"Lex" writes: On the 10th day of July, 1895, I was elected surveyor and sanitary inspector to the —— Rural District Council (northern division), and received the following letter from the clerk—"I have to inform you that you were, at the meeting of the rural district council, elected to the post of surveyor and inspector for the Northern or —— sub-district. Your appointment is to be until December 31st next." The letter was dated July 12, 1895. I was reappointed in December for six months, and reappointed again in August for twelve months. My appointment terminates next Monday, and I understand that the surveyor for the Southern district is to take over the duties of both divisions on Monday next. My salary is paid quarterly. The question is, Am I entitled to any notice, as I have had none; and, if so, how much, as I presume that if I wished to leave next Monday I could not do so without giving the council notice, and I do not see why it should not cut both ways.

The appointment having been for a term certain, which has expired, "Lex" is not legally entitled to any notice nor required to give any. It would undoubtedly, however, have been no more than common courtesy dictates for the authority to have given him an earlier intimation of their intention not to renew his engagement.

HOUSE DRAINAGE: PUBLIC HEALTH ACT, 1875, SEC. 23.—(1) "X.Y.Z." has just completed an extensive sewerage scheme, which is to drain old property as a rule. The sewer in one case goes close past the end gable of a row of nine or ten houses which are not drained, the end house of which is close to the sewer. Would "X.Y.Z." be right in compelling owner to construct a branch sewer behind these houses and connect drains therewith, as per par 3, sec. 23, Public Health Act, 1875. If sewer can be charged on owner would a notice under sec. 23 be sufficient? (2) Could you call a house *effectually* drained where the drains are not laid straight to line or gradient and the joints are made of clay, but still are working fairly well and create no perceptible nuisance? (3) In several cases the old sewers are running through the back yards, about 6 ft. from the houses. Would "X.Y.Z." be justified in making owner connect drain into new sewer in back street, assuming he could prove the old drains were not as they should be?

(1) The effect of this section is briefly as follows: Where a house is without "a drain sufficient for effectual drainage" the authority *shall* require the owner or occupier to drain into a sewer not more than 100 ft. distant, or (failing such a sewer) into a cesspool, &c. If the owner, &c., fails to comply the authority may do the work and recover the cost from the owner. Then comes the proviso (referred to by "X.Y.Z." as par. 3) that where, in the opinion of the authority, greater expense would be incurred in causing the drains of two or more houses to empty into an existing sewer "*pursuant to this section*" than in providing and connecting with a new sewer they may construct a new sewer and require the owners to drain into it, and may apportion the cost of such sewer amongst the various owners. In my opinion the power conferred by this proviso is only exercisable where there is an existing sewer within 100 ft. of the property, as it is only in that case that the owner could be compelled to drain into it. The words "pursuant to this section" seem to me to show that this is the intention. It is not stated in the query whether or not there was, prior to the construction of the new sewer, any existing sewer within 100 ft. of these houses. If there was such a sewer, and if in the opinion of the authority the cost of draining into it would have exceeded the cost of providing and connecting with the new sewer, then I think the owners could be charged with the latter, pursuant to the proviso. If, however, there was no existing sewer into which the owners could have been compelled to drain, then, in my opinion, they cannot be charged with the cost of constructing the new sewer. They can, of course, be compelled (assuming they have no effectual drains) to drain into the new sewer, under the first part of the section. (2) I do not think a house would be held to be "without a drain sufficient for effectual drainage" in such a case. (See the notes to this section in Lumley's "Public Health Acts," fifth edition, p. 51.) (3) Yes, if the drains are not "sufficient for effectual drainage."

AUCTIONEERS' INSTITUTE.—The session of the Auctioneers' Institute will commence on Tuesday next, the 8th inst., when Mr. Alexander Macmorran, Q.C., will read a paper in the Lecture Hall, 57 Chancery-lane, W.C., upon "The Effect of Recent Decisions on the Liabilities and Rights of Owners in Respect of the Drainage of Buildings." The chair will be taken by the president, Mr. Edward Dobson, at 7.45 p.m.

# Municipal Work in Progress and Projected.

The paragraphs relating to Newmarket, Wimbledon, Barry, Llandudno, Croydon, Barnsley, Batley, Douglas (Isle of Man), Leamington, Salford and Southampton contain the most important news which has this week come to hand in reference to municipal works in the provinces. In connection with the metropolis similar news is given under the headings of Shoreditch and Lambeth.

## METROPOLITAN AUTHORITIES.

### LONDON COUNTY COUNCIL.

Practically the whole of the meeting of the county council on Tuesday was occupied in the consideration of the long and important report of the Water Committee dealing with the question of the water supply of London, both as regards the present supply and future requirements. Particulars of the report are given in full in another column. It is not therefore necessary to refer to them at any length here. The report elicited a lengthy discussion, but the recommendations of the committee were eventually adopted almost unanimously. The majority of the members of both parties in the council seemed to be of opinion that no time should be lost in remedying the present state of affairs, this opinion being evidently arrived at in view of the recent failure in the East-End supply. Some also thought that the Government would not be likely to sanction such a gigantic scheme until the report of the Royal Commission had been submitted, and that, consequently, the promotion of a Bill in the next session would only lead to a waste of money. These latter therefore proposed that the report should be postponed until the report of the Royal Commission had been submitted. The amendment was, however, lost by a majority of eighty-six votes.

*Loans for Public Works.*—Upon the recommendation of the Finance Committee, it was agreed to lend the Newington Vestry £10,000 for electric lighting purposes, the Shoreditch Vestry £10,470 for similar purposes, and the Wandsworth District Board of Works £3,000 for the extension of Wandsworth cemetery.

*London Water Supply.*—The Water Committee presented their report on the subject of the purchase of the undertakings of the London water companies and the provision of a supplementary water supply from Wales, a full summary of which will be found in another column. Mr. Dickinson, chairman of the committee, in moving the reception of the report, urged that the experience of the past summer had proved that any further delay would be a serious matter for London. The report was received. On the first recommendation—that a Bill be promoted in the next session of Parliament for the purchase of the undertakings of the water companies by agreement, or, failing agreement, by compulsion—Lord Onslow moved an amendment in favour of delay pending the report of the Royal Commission who are inquiring into the subject. After a long discussion the amendment was rejected by 101 votes to fifteen. The recommendation was then agreed to, as well as a series of subsequent recommendations, including one for the promotion of a Bill empowering the council to bring an additional supply of water to London from the watersheds of the Wye and Towy in Wales.

## VESTRIES AND DISTRICT BOARDS.

**Hackney.**—The Hackney baths are proving too small to meet the demands made by the ratepayers, and the Baths Committee have under consideration a scheme for enlarging their premises by pulling down an old building adjoining, and erecting new premises in harmony with the existing premises. This would provide accommodation for twenty additional men's private baths and six women's baths. It is estimated that the cost of the necessary alterations would be about £3,000.

**Lambeth.**—The Baths Committee, at the last meeting of the vestry, reported that they had again considered the question of the well at the Kennington-road baths. Messrs. Baker, the engineers for the work, recommended that the boring into the chalk below the bottom of the guide pipe should be continued for not less than 150 ft. to 200 ft. Acting upon this suggestion, the committee asked the vestry to sanction the boring being carried down to a depth not exceeding 200 ft., at the prices mentioned in THE SURVEYOR of the 21st ult. An attempt was made to get the report referred back for further consideration, but on a division this was defeated by thirty-nine votes to twenty-five. The recommendation of the committee was then put to the meeting and adopted.—The General Purposes Committee announced the receipt from Messrs. A. & F. Manuelle of a letter notifying the completion of all the vestry's orders for York paving, and asking that they might continue delivery in anticipation of future orders, so as to prevent the rubbing mills being shut down. At the suggestion of the surveyor, who reported that there was little stone in stock, the vestry adopted a recommendation of the committee to order a further 10,000 ft. from the firm under the existing contract.—It was reported by the Wharf Committee that a deputation waited upon the Lower River Committee of the Thames Conservancy with regard to the

scheme for a proposed embankment at Pedlar's Acre. The members of the deputation were informed that the Conservancy Commissioners would again give consideration to the subject.—The consideration of the recommendations of the Vestry Hall Committee, which were referred to in THE SURVEYOR a fortnight ago under the heading of "Lambeth's Proposed Town Hall," were postponed.—It had been intended to elect a committee of eight members to inquire into the statements and charges made on the subject of the transfer of the vestry's electric lighting provisional order, but in the absence of Mr. Cooper, on whose motion the original resolution was adopted, the matter was deferred until the next meeting. In connection with this subject Mr. Price proposes to move "that all members who voted against the vestry exercising the electric lighting order be invited to sign a document pledging themselves to take no action, either legal or otherwise, if Messrs. Hubbard, Lock & Wightman will attend and state to the special committee the full particulars of the information which they have stated in the vestry is within their knowledge."

**Marylebone.**—About two hours were last week again devoted by the vestry to the consideration of the question of the electric lighting of the parish. A fortnight ago the vestry resolved to give statutory notice of intention to apply again to the Board of Trade for an electric light provisional order, and last week Mr. Brooke-Hitching, chairman of the Electric Lighting Committee, brought forward a recommendation that the committee should be empowered to enter into preliminary negotiations with the Metropolitan Electric Supply Company for the purchase of that part of the company's undertaking situated in Marylebone, and to report to the vestry on the matter. The discussion was of a very animated nature, and at times assumed a personal character. Two amendments were moved, one seeking to vary the terms of the recommendation and the other proposing the postponement of the matter with a view to the reconstitution of the Electric Lighting Committee. These amendments were, however, rejected, and eventually the recommendation of the committee was adopted without any dissentient.—A letter was read from the London County Council drawing the attention of the vestry to the Canals Protection Act, which empowered the vestry to enforce the provision of proper fencing alongside canals. The letter was referred to the Works Committee.—The Works Committee recommended the vestry not to entertain a proposal to place a rest at the lower end of Mortimer-street, but this was allowed to stand over.—It was decided to refer to the Works Committee, with power to act, a petition referring to the wood paving of the north entrance to Devonshire-mews South.

**Poplar.**—Last week a deputation of members of the Bow Vestry waited on the district board with reference to the proposed erection of a footbridge over the canal between Wansbeck-road and Bonier-road. It was stated that a bridge at the place suggested would prove a great boon to the public. Since the closing of the canal gate there had been a great loss to the trade of Bow, and if the board would give the matter their favourable consideration their action would receive the approbation of the ratepayers generally. The matter was referred to the Works Committee for consideration.

**Shoreditch.**—The vestry, at their meeting on Tuesday, were recommended by the Finance Committee to apply to the Local Government Board for sanction to borrow £10,500 for additional works at the Hoxton baths and wash-houses, and, on permission being obtained, to ask the London County Council to advance the amount. After some discussion the recommendation was adopted, excluding that part referring to the proposed application to the county council on the ground that the loan might possibly be advanced at a lower rate of interest by the Public Works Loan Commissioners.—The Lighting Committee announced that they had considered a report from the chief engineer stating that many of the inhabitants of the Haggerston district had promised to take a supply of current to such an extent as to warrant the construction of a new sub-station. Pending that work being carried out, the committee recommended that a new main should be laid, at a cost of £2,200, the current to be supplied temporarily from two existing sub-stations. This was agreed to.—The Lighting Committee obtained sanction to an expenditure of £520 on the purchase of a further supply of electricity meters.—The surveyor, Mr. J. Rush Dixon, recently submitted to the Works Committee an estimate of the cost of paving the footways in Marlborough-road and other thoroughfares, the amount being £1,902. The committee recommended that the Finance Committee should be authorised to raise a loan for the carrying out of the work. By the consent of the vestry the report was, however, withdrawn.—The Baths Committee reported that they had considered an estimate from the architects for providing temporary flooring over the swimming baths, at a cost of £862. In view of the proposal to use these baths in the "off season" for places of entertainment, the committee recommended that the work should be proceeded with, and that they should be authorised to advertise for tenders for the carrying out of the work. After considerable discussion the recommendation was agreed to.—Having fully considered the question of sinking an artesian well, and bearing in mind the present cost of water, the joint Electric Lighting and Baths Sub-Committee expressed the opinion that it would be a distinct economy to sink a well at the Coronet-street premises, where there was every prospect of an ample supply of water being obtained. The committee accordingly recommended that the work should be undertaken, and that the Lighting Committee should be empowered to advertise for tenders for the work. The recommendation was adopted.

## PROVINCIAL AND GREATER LONDON AUTHORITIES.
### COUNTY COUNCILS.

**East Riding.**—With respect to a letter read from the Sculcoates Rural District Council suggesting that a hospital for the reception of patients suffering from infectious diseases should be provided by the county council for the whole of their district, the county council decided to inform the clerk be instructed to inform the Sculcoates Rural District Council that if they would make application under the Isolation Hospitals Act, 1893, in the manner provided by the Act, the committee would be prepared to carefully consider the matter.

**Middlesex.**—The county council decided, at the monthly meeting on the 27th ult., to acquire the lease of the chapel in Clarence-road, Teddington, for the purpose of a court-house, and to expend £250 in carrying out the necessary alterations and repairs.—On the recommendation of the Finance Committee it was resolved to approve an estimate of £2,500, being the council's contribution towards the cost of the wood paving of High-street and Kew Bridge-road, to be carried out on behalf of the Brentford Urban District Council. The wood paving is to consist of creosoted fir blocks.—It was decided to inform the Chiswick Urban District Council that the county council were willing to contribute a sum not exceeding £394 towards the cost of paving with Victoria stone a portion of the footpath of the High-road, Chiswick.—Reporting on the proposed new lines of the London United Tramways Company, the Highways Committee stated that the company had submitted drawings showing the projected construction of the tramways and plans indicating the position of the poles for carrying the overhead wires in the Acton district. The committee mentioned that they had given their approval to the drawings and plans, subject to the tram line in Kew Bridge-road and High-street being paved with creosoted fir blocks, to that in Halfacre and Boston-lane being paved partly with the same kind of wood and partly with granite setts, and to that in the main road in Heston and Isleworth and in Lower Boston-lane being laid with granite setts. On the recommendation of the committee the council endorsed their action, and authorised the committee to approve any further plans and take any other steps necessary in connection with the construction of the tramways in the five districts concerned.— Last July the council intimated to the Bucks. County Council their readiness to contribute £1,000 in respect of a bridge costing £3,500 to be built over the Colne between West Drayton and Iver. Since then the Bucks County Council found it unable to provide a similar amount towards the bridge. In this connection the Highways Committee announced the receipt of representations from the Uxbridge Rural District Council and the Iver Parish Council asking that the scheme should not be allowed to fall through by declining to furnish the requisite funds to meet the Bucks. County Council. On the recommendation of the committee, however, it was decided not to alter the previous decision to contribute £1,000.—The Finchley Urban District Council, according to a further report of the Highways Committee, had given notice of intention to proceed to arbitration with the Local Government Board in respect of the maintenance of the footways on the main roads in their district during the past two years. The committee recommended, and it was decided, that the county solicitor should be instructed to require that the arbitration shall extend to the question of the annual payment, not only as regards footways, but also as concerns carriageways, and that the solicitor should be empowered to employ counsel and obtain such engineering evidence as might be necessary in addition to that of Mr. Wakelam, the county surveyor.—The joint committee of the county councils of Middlesex and Surrey presented a report, which is referred to in another column, in regard to the proposed new bridge at Kew.—The following tenders were received for adapting part of the reporters'-room at the Guildhall as a reference-room for the surveyor's department: Phillips & Son, Baker-street (accepted), £35; A. Porter, Tottenham, £41 9s.; and Higgs & Hill, Limited, £57 10s.

## MUNICIPAL CORPORATIONS.

**Barnsley.**—Colonel W. Langton Coke, R.I.C.K., an inspector of the Local Government Board, held an inquiry on Friday, at the town hall, Barnsley, into an application of the town council to borrow £25,000 for an installation of the electric light. The works are proposed to be erected on a site adjoining the premises of the highways and waterworks departments, and will consist in the first instance of a plant for 6,000 8 candle-power lamps, so arranged that its capacity can be doubled by the expenditure of £2,000 in machinery and £500 in plant.

**Barrow-in-Furness.** — The Barrow-in-Furness Tramway Company, Limited, have agreed to sell their undertaking to the British Electric Traction Company, Limited, for the sum of £22,750, but before they can complete the transfer the corporation have the right of refusal to buy at the same price. The question has been considered by the General Purposes Committee of the council, and the feeling is in favour of allowing the tramways to be absorbed by the British Electric Traction Company, Limited. The corporation hope to supply the company with electricity from their new works. The tramways, which are between 6 and 7 miles in length, originally cost over £60,000.

**Batley.**—Local Government Board sanction has been received by the corporation to the borrowing of £15,500 for works of surface-water drainage.

**Chester.**—The city council have adopted plans by Messrs. Douglas & Minshall for the erection of public baths in Union-street, at an estimated cost of £11,000. The plans provide for one swimming bath, 60 ft. long by 30 ft., a second swimming bath, 80 ft. by 30 ft., with slipper baths, vapour baths, &c. In connection with the scheme a new road will be made from Foregate-street to the site of the baths, near Grosvenor Park.

**Cheltenham.**—It is stated that the Local Government Board have practically refused to authorise the borrowing by the corporation of £13,410 for sewerage and sewage disposal purposes.

**Darlington.**—The electric lighting scheme for the town is reported to be still making satisfactory progress. Prof. Kennedy, to whom the matter was referred, has just submitted the ground plans of the proposed works to the Gasworks Committee, and the borough surveyor has been instructed to draw up specifications for the buildings, &c. The next step will be to obtain the sanction of the Local Government Board to the borrowing of the necessary money.

**Devonport.**—Mr. Charles Chadwell, Mr. James Diggle and the borough surveyor have inspected Vauxhall Bridge, London (now being demolished by Messrs. Puthick Brothers, of Plymouth), with a view to acquiring a portion of it for use in reconstructing the Camel's Head Bridge. They advise the corporation not to purchase either of the spans, and recommend a steel bridge for the purpose required.

**Douglas, Isle of Man.**—On Thursday a committee of the Tynwald Court sat in the matter of the application of the corporation for authority to borrow £20,000 for the purpose of improving the drainage of Douglas, in addition to the sum of £35,000 already authorised to be borrowed for the purpose. The Clerk of the Rolls presided and there was a full attendance of the committee. There were fifty-eight basements in the town below the high-tide mark. Mr. E. H. Stevenson, of London, the author of the high and low level scheme adopted by the corporation, gave evidence as to the liability of the basements in the town to be flooded, and said that he had seen black sewage matter in some of the basements at high water. Several householders and owners of property in the low-lying part of Douglas gave evidence in support of the opposition. They declared that any flooding was not due to sea water, but heavy rains, and had been obviated since storm outlets had been provided. It was, they also declared, a simple matter to put in a contrivance to keep the water out.

**Huddersfield.**—On the 22nd ult. Sir W. H. Broadbent opened the new municipal sanatorium which has been erected at Mill Hill, Dalton, one of the outlying portions of the borough. The site of the hospital is about 2 miles from the centre of the town, and the buildings are erected on the pavilion principle. From the administration block there is a covered way leading to the three ward pavilions, each of which will provide accommodation for thirty patients. There is also an isolation block in course of erection. Further, there are the receiving and discharge blocks, laundry, disinfecting blocks, and other buildings. There are ninety beds, which, with seventy at the Birkby establishment, twenty in the small-pox department at Mill Hill, and ten in the additional isolation block, gives a total accommodation of 190 beds. The total cost of the sanatorium up to September last was £24,667 4s. exclusive of the land, and the total contracts amounted to about £30,000.

**Leamington.**—The town council propose to build a free library and technical institute on the Perkins'-gardens site, at a cost of £12,000, exclusive of land.

**Leeds.**—In connection with the York-street insanitary area improvement scheme, the Sanitary Committee of the corporation have provisionally arranged for the purchase of properties there involving an expenditure of, in the aggregate, over £12,000. Continuing, also, the improvements in North-street, it is proposed to buy a shop and premises on the east side of that thoroughfare, on the basis of an exchange of land in addition to a payment of £2,000.—An interesting report was recently presented to a committee of this authority in reference to the result of an experiment with the Diblin system at Knostrop, which was recently adopted by the council. The treatment of the sewage had, it was stated, given every indication of the possible solution of the difficulty of dealing with so large an accumulation as 20,000,000 gallons per day, including sewage created by the city and its trade effluents.

**Middlesbrough.**— On Saturday Colonel Hepper, Local Government Board inspector, held an inquiry at Middlesbrough into an application of the Middlesbrough Corporation to borrow £1,200 for the purpose of erecting public conveniences at the corner of Albert-road and Corporation-road. After an examination of the plans and estimates submitted by the borough engineer, Mr. Baker, the inspector visited the sites. It is anticipated that the income derived from the contemplated conveniences will be sufficient to pay interest and redemption on the money borrowed and also for their maintenance.

**Retford.**— At a special meeting of this authority, on Monday, it was unanimously decided that application be made to the Board of Trade to license the council to supply electricity under the Electric Lighting Act, 1882, for public or private purposes within the district of the borough of Retford, and that the town clerk take the necessary steps for carrying out the resolution.

**Salford.**— Major-General H. D. Crozier, R.E., Local Government Board inspector, held an inquiry on the 21st ult. concerning the application of the town council for approval of a modification of the scheme relating to the borough which was confirmed by the Local Government Board's Provisional Orders Confirmation (Housing of the Working Classes) Act, 1891. The town council asks for sanction to the borrowing of £45,000 for the purpose of the Housing of the Working Classes Act, 1890, £10,765 for purposes of street improvements, £8,000 for purposes of public walks and pleasure grounds, and £3,200 for the purpose of defraying half the cost of widening Regent-road bridge. There was a considerable attendance of members of the council and of the general public.—The borough engineer was recently instructed to submit a report as to the best method of laying and constructing the sewer in back passages so that the burden of their repair should be as small as possible. He recommended that all drains should be constructed with a good fall, be properly jointed, provided with a flushing eye and vent shaft at the upper end, and an inspection chamber at the outlet end; and that when thus laid the corporation should flush adequately, regularly and periodically. Sewers thus laid and flushed will throw practically no burden upon the ratepayers beyond the cost of flushing. This report was adopted by the committee, and approved by the council at its meeting last Friday.

**Sheffield.**— On Tuesday of last week, at a private meeting of the city council, the lord mayor brought up a proposal to purchase from the Duke of Norfolk the whole of his markets and market rights in Sheffield. A letter was read from his lordship agreeing to sell for £530,000. Twenty years ago, it was stated, the corporation endeavoured to acquire the markets, but disagreements arose and the negotiations came to nothing. The gross income of the markets is £18,866.

**Southampton.**— Mr. W. A. Ducat, Local Government Board inspector, held a public inquiry at Southampton on Thursday, in respect of an application by the town council for sanction to the borrowing of £7,000 for the erection of artisans' dwellings, £246 for a new manual fire engine and two fire escapes, and £72 for water vans.

**Worthing.**— Mr. F. H. Tulloch has held an inquiry, on behalf of the Local Government Board, respecting an application of the town council for sanction to borrow £345 for works of sewage disposal. Mr. F. Roberts, the borough surveyor, attended the proceedings, which were of a purely formal character.

**Wrexham.**— The Local Government Board recently held an inquiry in reference to an application of the town council for permission to borrow the sum of £3,125 for market purposes and £400 for certain footpath improvements.

## URBAN DISTRICT COUNCILS.

**Barry.**— Mr. E. Sandford Fawcett, an inspector of the Local Government Board, held an inquiry recently with respect to applications made by the council for power to borrow about £11,500 for street improvements in the town—namely, £6,340 for public and private street works, including £105 for the widening of St. Nicholas-road, Barry, together with £4,820 for the formation of a new road round the Victoria Park, late Cadoxton Common, the acquirement of which was empowered under the Council's Act of 1896. The necessary formal evidence was given, and, there being no objection whatever on the part of the ratepayers, the commissioner proposed to inspect the sites of the proposed new works.

**Bridlington.**— It has been decided by the Sanitary and Foreshore Committee to recommend the council to sanction the erection of an infectious diseases hospital for the town, at a cost of about £4,000. It has also been resolved to recommend the erection of a destructor, at an estimated cost of £1,000.

**Caerphilly.**— Local Government Board sanction has been received to an application of the council to borrow a sum of £36,000 for purposes of sewerage and sewage disposal. The district proposed to be drained by this scheme is about 17,000 acres. The scheme is in two sections—viz., Rhymney Valley and the Aber Valley. Future requirements are looked to in the arrangement of the scheme. Both mains will fall into a sewage farm called Gwainybara, in the hamlet of Vaes. This

farm has been purchased under a provisional order, and the sewage disposal scheme proposed to be adopted is the intermittent and broad irrigation system. The council had anxiously waited the result of the recent inquiry, as the state of sanitation in the district is such as demands immediate attention. It is considered to reflect very great credit on the officers of the council, especially Mr. Harpur, the surveyor, that the scheme has been approved in its entirety.

**Chiswick.**— At a recent meeting of the district council the Works Committee presented a report with reference to correspondence which had passed between the clerk and the London United Tramways Company upon the question of electric trolleys. The committee approved of the wires being fixed at a height of 21 ft. from the surface of the highway, the trolley poles to be so constructed that they may be used as lamp columns. The report was adopted.

**Fenny Stratford.**— At the last fortnightly meeting of this body the surveyor produced and explained amended plans for the treatment of the sewage of the district by the septic tank system, which would result in the annual saving of £100 in the working expenses. It was resolved to forward the plans to the Local Government Board.

**Felixtowe and Walton.**— The district council have decided to seek Parliamentary powers next session to carry out extensive works of sea defence, including the reconstruction of the sea wall and promenade in accordance with plans prepared by Mr. Henry Millar, of Ipswich, the county surveyor of East Suffolk.

**Ilford.**— In addition to the public park, the district council last week made arrangements for the purchase of 32 acres of land in the southern ward for the purpose of a recreation ground, at a cost of £350 per acre.

**Ledbury.**— At a special meeting of the council, held last week, the following tenders for sewerage works were received : Messrs. Johnson Brothers, Hereford, £2,528 ; J. Bentley, Southport, £2,516 ; H. Holloway, Wolverhampton, £2,733 ; Owen James, Wolverhampton, £2,849 10s. 2d. ; John Mackay, Hereford, £2,876 13s. ; George Law, Kidderminster, £2,878 ; T. Vale, Stourport, £3,063 ; W. L. Meredith, Gloucester, £3,374 16s. ; D. Smith, Ledbury, £3,397 ; and W. Braithwaite & Co., Leeds, £4,000. Messrs. Johnson's tender, being the lowest, was accepted.

**Llandudno.**— The council have decided upon a expenditure of £14,000 for the erection of municipal buildings, which are to be completed by May 1, 1900.

**Newmarket.**— The district council have under consideration a report and scheme by Mr. F. Beasley for the main drainage of the district. The estimated cost, including a refuse destructor and workmen's cottages, is about £37,500.

**Shipley.**— Last week, at a meeting of the council, the adoption of the minutes of the Electric Lighting Committee, which showed that the proposed compulsory area of supply of electricity had been determined upon, and steps had been taken in relation to the application for a provisional order empowering the council to supply electricity.

**Walker.**— A special meeting of the council, held last week, passed the following resolution, with one dissentient : " That application be made to the Board of Trade for a provisional order, under the Electric Lighting Acts, 1882 and 1888, to authorise the urban district council to supply electricity for the public and private purposes as defined by the Electric Lighting Acts within the urban district of Walker."

**Watford.**— The Local Government Board have informed the district council that they are willing to comply with their application for sanction to borrow £1,650 for water supply on the understanding that the mains are laid at a depth of 3 ft. —An inspector of the Local Government Board has held an inquiry respecting an application of the district council for sanction to borrow £4,800 for the purposes of public walks and pleasure grounds.

**Wimbledon.**— The works which the district council have at present in hand include the completion of the depot buildings, the contract for which was let at £9,444. The main block facing Queen's-road has a frontage of over 500 ft., and includes stabling for thirty-nine horses, with sheds which can be converted into stables and give room for an additional forty-seven horses. In the centre of the block are dwellings for the storekeeper and foreman. A rear block contains storekeeper's office, stores, workshops and six isolation boxes. The flood-prevention works, the contract for which was let to Messrs. B. Cooke & Co. in June last, at £3,302, is almost completed. There are also in hand at the present moment private street improvement works which have been let at a total of £10,187. During the year a Johnson's twin tandem air-compressor, 20-in. stroke with 10-in. diameter steam cylinders, has been erected. A new bridge, carrying Gap-road over the London and South-Western Railway Company's and the District Railway Company's property, is being fixed. Considerable progress has been made in the construction of the station and the laying of mains for supplying the district with electricity. Quantities for the isolation hospital, in accordance with plans prepared by the surveyor, are being taken out by Messrs. Arding, Bond & Buzzard. The council are, with their own men, also constructing 2 acres of nitrification filters at the sewage works.

## RURAL DISTRICT COUNCILS.

**Belper.**—At a meeting on the 22nd ult. the district council resolved to lease 2 acres of land for dealing with the sewage disposal of South Wingfield, and also that application be made to the Local Government Board for their sanction to a loan of £750 for constructing works of water supply for the township of Holbrook.

**Chesterton.**—The council have purchased a 10-ton steam roller from Messrs. Aveling & Porter.

**Croydon.**—A Local Government Board inquiry was held at Beddington, on the 25th ult., into an application of the council to borrow £16,000 for the purpose of providing a joint cemetery for the parishes of Beddington, Wallington and Coulsdon. The application was opposed by several landowners in the neighbourhood on the ground of a possible contamination of the water supply. The plans for laying-out the cemetery and for the chapel were prepared by the council's surveyor, Mr. R. M. Chart, F.S.I., of Croydon, who gave evidence in support of the scheme. The inquiry will be reopened to-day (Friday).

**Ruthin.**—The district council have adopted the plans and a scheme, prepared by Mr. John E. Thomas, of Wrexham, for the proposed new water supply for the parishes of Llangwyfan, Llandyrnog, Llanychan, Llanynys and Llangynhafal, in the Vale of Clwyd. The source of supply will be Nant y Ne, on the western slopes of Moel Famman, the gathering ground being 307 acres on the open mountain, formed of Upper Silurian rocks.

**St. Germain's, Cornwall.**—The district council have decided to instruct Messrs. Jenkin & Son, engineers, of Liskeard, to prepare plans and specifications for taking water from their mains for the supply of the village of St. Stephen-by-Saltash.

**Wortley.**—On Thursday Colonel Coke, C.E., Local Government Board inspector, held an inquiry in reference to an application by the district council to borrow £3,700 for the purpose of supplying with water from Hall Broom—the source of the present Stannington supply—the villages of Worrall Stubbin, Holdworth, Loxley and Stacey Bank. Mr. G. E. Beaumont, the council's engineer, explained the plans and proposals. The water is stated to be exceptionally soft and pure, this being proved by analysis. About 6½ miles of pipes will be required, and a deep valley will have to be crossed. The altitude of the source of supply is 1,065 ft. above ordnance datum.

## SCOTLAND AND IRELAND.

**Arbroath.**—In forwarding to the town council a report of Sir Henry Littlejohn on the water supply of Arbroath the secretary of the Local Government Board at Edinburgh has stated that it is obvious that that gentleman, while anxious to give due credit to the local authority for their efforts to improve the water supply and fully disposed to await the issue of those efforts, still regards with apprehension the unflushed condition of the sewers and the absence of a margin of supply applicable to the extinction of fire.

**Belfast.**—It is stated that the Finance Committee, after considerable discussion, last week agreed to the construction of 6 miles of new tramway, it being understood that the corporation would lay the lines in such a manner that if any system of electric traction was afterwards decided upon they would not require to be relaid. The new lines are to be all double lines, and the tramway company, it is also understood, agree on their part to pay 5½ per cent. on the outlay to the corporation, the lines, of course, to be the property of the corporation and to be kept in repair by that body.

**Johnstone.**—The burgh commissioners and a number of local gentlemen recently met at the gasworks to witness the ceremony of turning on the gas at the new telescope gasholder. The holder has a capacity of 240,000 cubic feet. On the motion of Mr. M'Gilchrist (the engineer of the work), Provost Thomson was called upon to perform the ceremony. He said the storage capacity of the holder previous to the present enlargement was 120,000 cubic feet, and now it was doubled. The gasworks were acquired by the burgh in 1879. In 1880 the price was 5s. 1d. per 1,000 cubic feet, while at the present time the price is 3s. 4d. per 1,000 cubic feet, or a reduction of 2s. 1d. per 1,000 cubic feet. They had also reduced the debt of the purchase price by £11,000. The provost passed a high eulogium on the contractors who had done the excavation for the original holder, which was put down seven years ago. He also spoke highly of the contractors for the work of this holder, Messrs. Laidlaw & Co., Limited.

**Kirkcaldy.**—The town council have decided to apply for a special Act of Parliament for powers to construct the proposed tramways, and to have a clause inserted giving the council the option of handing over the construction and working of the tramways to a company.

**Motherwell.**—The Police Commissioners have had under consideration a scheme of electric lighting. The estimated cost of the scheme is between £23,000 and £24,000, which will give private lighting and also street lighting with thirty arc lamps and 400 32 candle-power incandescent lamps, and also for motive power. The report was approved and the convener of the Lighting Committee instructed to push forward the work as rapidly as possible.

## INSTITUTION OF CIVIL ENGINEERS.

### ORDINARY MEETING.

The second ordinary meeting of the 1898-99 session of the above Institution will be held on Tuesday, at 8 p.m., when a paper will be read by Prof. W. E. Roberts-Austen, C.B., F.R.S., on "The Extraction of Nickel." A discussion will follow the reading of the paper.

### STUDENTS' MEETING.

A meeting for students of the Institution will be held on Friday, the 18th inst., when a paper will be read by Mr. Cecil Lightfoot on "Liquid Air: A short description of its production and summary of its application to the chemical or other industries." The chair will be taken. at 8 p.m. by Mr. W. H. Preece, C.B., F.R.S., the president.

**Shoreditch Combined Scheme.**—A communication from Mr. T. W. Baker on this subject reached us just as we were going to press, having evidently been delayed in delivery owing to the envelope being insufficiently addressed. It will, however, appear in our next issue.

**Laundry Machinery.**—In these days of municipal baths and wash-houses the improvement of laundry machinery is of increasing importance. Mr. J. Appleyard, Harris-street, Bradford, said our contemporary, The Laundry Record, on a recent occasion, is placing on the market a new collar-ironing machine, which is likely to be very successful and a credit to the British laundry engineering interest. It is a six-roller machine, that is to say, the collar or other article that is to be ironed passes under five rollers and over a drum, and the machine has a capacity of fully 1,000 collars an hour. This we have tested, watch in hand. One or two minor details are being perfected, but the machine will very shortly be ready. The collars are delivered into a basket arranged conveniently to the hands of the operator.

**Santiago (Cuba).**—A remarkable change has come over the spirit of the dream of Santiago, which with an unenviable reputation as one of the dirtiest and most unhealthy cities in Cuba is, under the judicious system introduced by General Wood, who happens to possess the additional qualification of being a physician, becoming, it is said, almost a model of cleanliness. The city has been divided into five sections, each under the general supervision of a medical man, with inspectors of sewers, streets, &c., under whom are a number of street-cleaners. The refuse is burnt daily, disinfectants are used wherever necessary, and the people are fined, not only for uncleanliness against the public good, but for failure to report deaths and unhealthy conditions. The result on the death rate has been remarkable, for after only a month of this treatment the death rate was declared to have fallen from an average of 70 to 20 a day.

## Personal.

Mr. E. R. Matthews has succeeded Mr. J. F. Stow as surveyor to the Bridlington Urban District Council.

The Newington Vestry have decided to advertise for a resident engineer at their electrical works, at a salary of £250 per annum.

Mr. G. F. Deacon has been retained in connection with certain works of water supply which are being undertaken by the Todmorden Town Council.

Mr. G. H. Hamby, borough surveyor of Lowestoft, was among those present on Friday evening at the annual dinner of the corporation, held in the public hall.

The death took place last week of Mr. William John Mott. He was thirty-six years of age, and has been gas manager at Selby for six months. He was formerly in Halifax.

The town commissioners of New Ross, co. Wexford, have instructed Mr. W. Kaye Parry, of Dublin, to report upon the best source for the proposed water supply for the town.

Mr. D. Crampton, who has held the office of surveyor to the Spalding Urban District Council, has resigned that position, although he still retains the post of market inspector.

Port Glasgow Town Council have granted an honorarium of £20 to Mr. Wm. Mackie, the gas manager, in recognition of extra services rendered in connection with improvements at the gasworks.

The Preston Town Council have adopted a minute of the Streets and Buildings Committee recommending that Mr. J. H. Smethurst be appointed deputy surveyor, at a salary of £200 per annum.

On Friday, at a special meeting of the Selby Urban District Council, Mr. T. H. Alderson, assistant gas manager at Halifax, was appointed gas manager to the council, in the room of the late Mr. W. J. Mott, at a salary of £200 per annum.

We learn that Mr. Walter Percival, of Longton, has been appointed to the post of assistant surveyor to the Longton Town Council, rendered vacant by the resignation of Mr. C. A. Benbow. Mr. Percival's salary will commence at £120 per annum.

A very interesting lecture on the "Welsh Water Scheme" was delivered on Friday by Mr. E. Antony Lees, of the Water Department of the Birmingham Corporation, to a large and appreciative audience. A vote of thanks to Mr. Lees brought the proceedings to a close.

Whitechapel District Board have decided to grant a sum of £60 to Mr. Wilson for duties performed by him as acting surveyor between the time that Mr. Waddington resigned his appointment as surveyor and the time when such duties were undertaken by Mr. Jameson.

Mr. J. A. McPherson, A.M.I.C.E., contributed a paper, entitled "Notes upon Regulating and Recording Apparatus for Reservoirs, Gauge Weirs and the Flow of Water," at a meeting of the Bristol Association of Engineers, held on Saturday evening, under the presidency of Mr. T. H. Yabbicom.

Mr. A. J. Dickenson, of the building department of the Sheffield city surveyor's office, has been appointed borough surveyor and water engineer of Fwllheli, North Wales. Mr. Dickenson is one of the lecturers in building construction at the evening technical department of the Sheffield University College.

Mr. George J. Bouchier, assistant surveyor to the Ashton-in-Makerfield Urban District Council, has been appointed, by a unanimous vote of the Haydock Urban District Council, to the post of clerk and surveyor to that authority. Mr. L. Davenport Thompson, Mr. Bouchier's predecessor, has, we understand, secured a position under the Lancashire County Council.

Last week, at a meeting of the Lancaster Town Council, the Water Committee reported that the Lancaster Rural District Council had written to Mr. J. Cook, the borough engineer, asking him, on account of the death of Mr. Jowett, the surveyor to the district council, to undertake the preparation of the preliminary plans and estimates in connection with a certain application to the Local Government Board.

Prior to Tuesday's meeting of the London County Council, Mr. McKinnon Wood, the chairman of the council, presented Sir Arthur Arnold, who was the chairman of the council in 1895-96 and 1896-97, with his portrait, which has been painted by Mr. Leonard Watts. Sir Arthur was also presented with a silver casket containing the autographs of the subscribers, whilst Lady Arnold was presented with a replica of her husband's picture.

The death has taken place, after a brief illness, of Mr. John White, borough surveyor of Folkestone. The cause is stated to have been enteric fever and acute peritonitis. Mr. White, who was only thirty-one years of age, was the pupil of the late Mr. Conquest, whom he succeeded. He was a man of most amiable disposition, and all who came in contact with him speak of him in the most affectionate terms. The

funeral took place on Thursday afternoon amid every manifestation of sympathy and regret.

A letter was recently read from Mr. C. A. Benbow tendering his resignation as assistant borough surveyor of Longton. The following motion, which has been adopted by the Improvement Committee, has since been approved by the council: "That the resignation of Mr. C. A. Benbow, assistant borough surveyor, be accepted with regret, and that the members of this committee desire to express their sense of the valuable services rendered by Mr. Benbow for the past seventeen years, and their congratulations on his appointment as surveyor of highways for the parish of Stone, and their best wishes for his future success and prosperity."

After a lingering illness, Mr. Joseph Potts, burgh architect and surveyor of Partick, died at his residence late on Friday. Mr. Potts had been ill since February last, and the commissieners granted leave of absence in the hope that he might be benefited by change of air and scenery. Mr. Potts spent the summer months in Wigtownshire, but on returning home he was still unfit for his duties, and his illness for the past two months was serious. He entered the service of the burgh twenty-one years ago, and was fifty-six years of age. During that time he discharged his duties to the satisfaction of all, and he was held in high esteem by the burgh officials and the general public.

Mr. Fred. W. Pearce, the newly-appointed surveyor to the Twickenham Urban District Council, is thirty-two years of age, and has for the last twelve years been employed in the engineer's and surveyor's department of the Wimbledon Urban District Council, four years assistant under Mr. W. Santo Crimp, and eight years as assistant surveyor. He has assisted in the design and construction of many important works in Wimbledon, and has had a considerably varied experience in this capacity. His testimonials are excellent, and include one from Mr. W. Santo Crimp, who describes him as being particularly well-informed in matters relating to road and sewer maintenance and construction.

Sutton (Surrey) Urban District Council last week decided to increase the salary of their surveyor, Mr. C. Chambers Smith, by £50. A like advance, it is understood, will also be made next year, so as to bring the amount up to £350. A councillor, in endorsing certain remarks which had been made in reference to Mr. Smith's duties, said that there was no doubt that the latter had shown himself to be a superlatively good man. He was a man much above the average intelligence, and had carried out his duties in a manner which had evoked many favourable expressions of opinion from the ratepayers. Men in his position were looked upon as somewhat migratory. They went to the place where they could get the most money, and he thought it would be a graceful act on the part of the council, having regard to the fact that he started at £250—it would be a graceful way of showing their appreciation of the diligence and attention he had shown in important matters in the town, if they offered him some increment of salary, which would induce him to stay for at least another couple of years. Other members expressed themselves in similar terms. But the highest compliment to the surveyor is, in the opinion of a local journal, the fact that the ratepayers, in consequence of the general improvement of their roads and paths, and their appreciation of Mr. Smith's efforts, are generally agreed that he is worthy of the increase.

The death is reported of Mr. Latimer Clark, who was intimately associated with the developments of our present system of electric telegraphs and submarine cables. Born in 1822, at Great Marlow, he gained his first practical experience in railway engineering, being appointed in 1847 resident assistant engineer under Robert Stephenson at the building of the Britannia and Conway tubular bridges. A joint paper by Sir Charles Bright and Mr. Clark was contributed to the British Association in 1861, and was the means of putting electrical measurement on a firm basis. After it had been read, Sir William Thomson, now Lord Kelvin, obtained the appointment of a committee to decide a national system of electrical units, and the result of its labours was the absolute system now in universal use, the terms volt, ampere, ohm, &c., being adopted according to suggestions made in Bright and Clark's paper. The "Elementary Treatise on Electrical Measurement," which has become a standard work, appeared in 1868, and a few years later Mr. Clarke, in conjunction with Mr. R. Sabine, published "Electrical Tables and Formulæ." In 1873 he described the Clark standard voltaic cell, which has proved of great value in promoting accurate measurements of electrical potentials. Mr. Clark was deputy chairman of the St. James's and Pall Mall Electric Light Company, and as a partner in the firm of Clark, Ford & Taylor had to do with the manufacture and laying of thousands of miles of cable in various parts of the world. One of the founders of the Society of Telegraph Engineers (now the Institution of Electrical Engineers), he became the fourth president of that body in 1875, delivering an inaugural address that contained an interesting account of the early history of the electric telegraph. He was elected a member of the Institution of Civil Engineers in 1858 and of the Royal Society in 1889.

## BELFAST NEW CITY HALL.

### DESCRIPTION OF THE BUILDING.

In connection with the recent visit of Earl Cadogan, Lord Lieutenant of Ireland, to Belfast, for the purpose of laying the foundation-stone of the proposed new city hall and opening the corporation's new electric light station, the following particulars of the city hall will, no doubt, be of considerable interest to many of our readers.

The new hall is to be erected on the site of the old White Linen Hall, which some years ago ceased to be used for the purpose for which it was originally built. An Act of Parliament was obtained by the corporation in 1890 to enable them to utilise this site, and as soon as the old buildings of the hall were demolished competitive designs were invited for the erection of the proposed new buildings. Mr. Alfred Waterhouse, R.A., having been appointed to examine and report upon the designs, selected the designs of Mr. A. B. Thomas, of Westminster. This selection was approved by the corporation, and a contract was then entered into with Messrs. H. & J. Martin, Limited, of Belfast, to carry out the erection of the buildings, the contract price amounting to about £150,000.

The proposed buildings are in rectangular form, the external dimensions being 300 ft. in length and 250 ft. in depth, the internal quadrangle being 180 ft. by 130 ft. A large portion of the site remains outside the city hall, and will, we understand, be planted, but a great many of the trees will, of course, be preserved. The lower storey of the building is in the simple form of a heavily-rusticated basement. This will give effect to the upper or principal storey, which is divided regularly by an order of Ionic design, surmounted by a richly-carved cornice and balustrade. The principal feature will be the dome surmounting the entrance hall. It is upwards of 150 ft. high to the lantern, 56 ft. diameter at the peristyle—the circular range of columns—and 40 ft. diameter at the drum of the dome. At each corner of the building is an angle tower, and these are almost 100 ft. high by 25 ft. diameter. At the principal entrance is a small stone-domed carriageway, designed to give size and scale to the edifice. The portion devoted to a public hall includes a hall measuring 120 ft. by 60 ft., together with a refreshment-room and a stage and dressing-rooms. In the planning of the building the first special point which may be mentioned is that the suite of reception-rooms and the large public hall with its adjuncts are designed on the first floor and intercommunicate, thus forming a continuous set of apartments well adapted for the requirements of civic receptions and large functions of various kinds. With the spacious entrance hall and marble staircase under the dome, these may be considered the great feature of the design internally. The next point to be specially mentioned in that the large public hall and its adjuncts are so arranged that they can be shut off entirely from the rest of the building, and being provided with separate entrances and exits, can be employed quite apart from and with out in the least degree interfering with what may be described as the municipal portion of the building. Separate and distinct entrances and exits from the street have also been supplied to the offices in which the payment of rates and gas are made, and thus the inconvenience of so many people passing in and out of the main building is obviated. The various committees will in future each have a room adjoining the private offices of the principal of the respective departments, the object being to facilitate as much as possible the work of all the committees. In the internal arrangements accommodation has been provided for the city officials and the following departments : Town clerk, city surveyor, health department, accountant, city cashier, gas department, electric light department, rate offices, school attendance department, market department, weights and measures department, &c. The reception-rooms embrace, first, an apartment measuring 50 ft. by 30 ft., which will be specially set apart for receptions; next the council-chamber, the dimensions of which are 70 ft. by 38 ft., together with the following : Ante-room, robing-room, writing-room, banquet hall (70 ft. by 38 ft.), and three apartments for the Lord Mayor exclusively—viz., his reception-room, parlour and retiring-room.

## LITTLEHAMPTON WATER SUPPLY.

In accordance with instructions, Mr. H. Howard, surveyor to the Littlehampton Urban District Council, has prepared a report in reference to a proposal of his council to construct new permanent water supply works for their district.

The council, we understand from the report, propose to obtain the supply from Warningcamp by means of a bore, 12 in. diameter, sunk in the chalk to a depth of from 160 ft. to 200 ft. This bore-hole it is proposed to construct of steel tubing, which will be perforated from the bottom upwards for about 50 ft. The suction and delivery pipes, in duplicate, are also to be 12 in. in diameter, and will be connected directly to the bore. The engines and pumps (condensing triple expansion) will be duplicated and of the most modern and efficient type, each being capable of raising and delivering to the reservoir not less than 500 gallons per minute. The boilers, also in duplicate, will be of the Lancashire type, and will develop an ordinary working pressure of 100 lb. per square inch. The rising main, which is to be con-

structed from the pump to the reservoir, a distance of about 685 yards, will be 12 in. in diameter.

### THE SERVICE RESERVOIR

will be sunk for about half its depth on the side near road close to Batworth Park House, and the surplus soil will be used for forming the embankment. It will be constructed of selected hard-stock bricks in cement mortar, with asphalte watertight coursing in the wall on a concrete bottom, while the internal faces of the walls and bottoms will be finished in Portland cement or other suitable facing material. The reservoir will be rectangular in form, and its total capacity 500,000 gallons, equivalent to rather more than three days' supply, reckoned on the average amount used per day during the past summer. If required, extra space can be provided for the construction of an additional reservoir in the case of any increase in the present demands.

The buildings, which will be erected at the source of the supply at Warningcamp, will include engine and boiler houses, with chimney from 50 ft. to 60 ft. in height, store and coal sheds and engineer's cottage. They will be constructed of hard-stock bricks, red kiln bricks and stone. A cart road, 12 ft. wide and about 235 yards long, will also be constructed leading to the works. About 420 yards of 10-in. delivery main will also be laid from the reservoir through the grounds of Batworth Park to Crossbush, and will be connected with a 10-in. main recently laid by the council. This latter main will unite with the council's 6-in. main at Water-lane (Lyminster and Littlehampton boundary), where provision has been made for a 10-in. extension to that of the present main at Littlehampton waterworks, so as to complete the circuit. It is probable that the 6-in. off the 10-in. main at Arundel-road will be competent to serve the requirements of the town for a few years to come with the increased pressure from a higher reservoir, and as the laying down of about 1,700 yards of 10-in. pipe from Water-lane to the main at the present works, with valves, would represent a cost of £1,280, from which no material gain for some time would result in the general distribution, it does not appear to be absolutely necessary for this section of the scheme to be carried out in connection with the new works, though it is one which can be easily done at any time when the necessity arises. The council's present waterworks will, on the completion of this new undertaking, form a useful stand-by, and as the whole of the plant, buildings, &c., are in a fairly good condition, the annual cost of maintenance will be comparatively very small.

The above report was adopted by the district council at their last meeting, and Mr. Howard was instructed to proceed with the preparation of the necessary specifications, &c.

## PROPOSED NEW BRIDGE AT KEW.

At the last monthly meeting of the Middlesex County Council the Finance Committee, on behalf of the joint committee of Surrey and Middlesex, presented supplementary estimates to the extent of £35,000 for the rebuilding of Kew Bridge. The report of the joint committee showed that while the estimate of the total cost of the widening, given by their engineer, Sir J. Wolfe Barry, was £118,000, the lowest of seven tenders received for the work, that of Mr. Easton Gibb, of Skipton, Yorkshire, was £169,288. In reply to a request for an explanation, Sir J. Wolfe Barry reported that his estimate was based on the prices paid for similar work at the Tower Bridge, with a considerable addition. He suggested that the cost of all work in the neighbourhood of London had been steadily increasing during the past two years, owing to the obligations imposed by the Employers' Liability Act, the action of the London County Council with regard to the terms of labour, and the great demand for materials at the present time. He estimated that £20,000 to £25,000 might be saved by the substitution of internal brickwork or concrete for stonework. The committee further reported that they had ascertained that a reduction of about £20,000 might be made on Mr. Gibb's contract in the way suggested, and they recommended that the tender should be accepted for a sum not exceeding £150,000, and that a Bill be promoted to authorise the additional borrowing. It was moved as an amendment to the report of the joint committee that the council should not entertain the proposed additional expenditure, but should refer the matter back to the joint committee, with a view to bringing the total cost of the bridge approximately within the amount authorised by Parliament, and this was carried by thirty-two votes to eight.

**Huddersfield.**—At the last monthly meeting of the town council a letter was read from the Post Office authorities in London stating that when the necessary powers to enable the corporation to work an exchange system had been obtained, the Postmaster-General will be prepared to give the corporation a license for a telephone exchange. The matter was discussed at considerable length, and eventually the following resolution was passed : "That this council memorialise the proper authorities that the Postmaster-General should be authorised to grant self-contained licenses to corporations to work telephone exchanges, and that such licenses should confer all necessary and incidental powers, including borrowing powers."

## THE SURVEYORS' INSTITUTION.

### Ordinary General Meeting.

The first ordinary general meeting of the session 1898-99 will be held at the temporary premises of the institution on Monday, the 14th inst., when the president, Mr. Robert Vigers, will deliver an opening address. The chair will be taken at 8 o'clock.

### Students' Preliminary Examination, 1899.

Those proposing to enter their names for the students' preliminary examination, to be held on the 18th and 19th of January next, must intimate their intention to the secretary before the last day of November. It is proposed to examine candidates from the counties of Lancashire, Cheshire, Yorkshire, Durham, Cumberland, Westmoreland and Northumberland at Manchester. Candidates from other counties in England and Wales will be examined in London. Irish candidates will be examined in Dublin.

### Professional Examinations, 1899.

Students eligible for the proficiency examinations (which will commence on the 20th of March next) must give notice of the sub-division (Table A of Rules) in which they elect to be examined, not later than the 31st inst. Examinations qualifying for the classes of "Professional Associates" and "Fellows" will also commence on the 20th of March next. Names of applicants for these latter examinations to be sent in before the 31st inst. All particulars as to days, subjects and course of examination will be forwarded on application to the secretary. English candidates for the professional examinations will be examined in London. Irish candidates will be examined in Dublin.

### Proposed Special-Certificate Examinations (For Members), 1899.

Notice is also given that the next special-certificate examinations in forestry, sanitary science and land surveying and levelling are proposed to be held on Tuesday, Wednesday and Thursday, the 13th, 14th and 15th of June. Particulars of these examinations can be obtained from the secretary.

### Junior Meetings.

The first of four meetings of examinees and students authorised (subject to certain conditions) by the council to be held during the present session will take place at the temporary premises of the institution on Monday, the 21st inst., 1898, the chair to be taken at 7 o'clock. All inquiries with reference to the junior meetings should be addressed to Mr. A. Norman Garrard, 8 Frederick's-place, Old Jewry, E.C.

## APPOINTMENTS VACANT.

*Official and all similar advertisements received later than Thursday morning are too late for classification and cannot therefore be included in these summaries. No advertisements received after 3 p.m. can be inserted until the following week.*

District Building Inspector.—November 4th.—Corporation of Wolverhampton. £2 5s.—Mr. J. W. Bradley, borough engineer and surveyor.

Surveyor.—November 4th.—Lancaster Rural District Council. £150.—Mr. Joseph Ennion, clerk to the council.

Temporary Assistant.—November 7th.—St. Helens Corporation. £2 15s.—Mr. Geo. J. C. Broom, M.I.C.E., borough engineer.

General Foreman.—November 7th.—Morecambe Urban District Council. 33s.—Mr. Jno. Bond, surveyor to the council.

Clerk of Works.—November 7th.—Limehouse District Board of Works. £2 10s.—Mr. S. G. Ratcliffe, clerk to the board.

Surveyor, &c.—November 8th.—Fulwood (near Preston, Lancs.) Urban District Council. £130.—Mr. Arnold Brierley, clerk to the council.

Inspector of Nuisances.—November 9th.—Richmond Corporation. £175.—Mr. Fredk. B. Senior, town clerk.

Highway Surveyor.—November 11th.—Isle of Wight Rural District Council. £150.—Mr. H. Eldridge Stratton, clerk to the council, Pyle-street, Newport, I.W.

Second Assistant.—November 12th.—County Borough of Hanley. £80.—Mr. Joseph Lobley, borough engineer and surveyor.

Superintendent at the Corporation Wharf.—November 12th.—County Borough of Southampton. £200.—Mr. George B. Nalder, town clerk.

Superintending Architect.—November 14th.—London County Council. £1,500.—Mr. C. J. Stewart, clerk to the council, County Hall, Spring-gardens, S.W.

Assistant Surveyor. — November 14th. — Wimbledon Urban District Council. £200.—Mr. W. H. Whitfield, clerk to the council.

Chief Officer of Tramways.—November 14th.—London County Council. £1,500.—Mr. C. J. Stewart, clerk to the council, County Hall, Spring-gardens, S.W.

Road Foreman.—November 14th.—Corporation of Bacup.—Mr. Francis Wood, A.M.I.C.E., borough engineer and surveyor.

Road Foreman.—November 15th.—Heston and Isleworth Urban District Council. £2 10s.—Mr. W. A. Davies, A.M.I.C.E., engineer and surveyor to the council.

Surveyor of Highways and Inspector of Nuisances.—November 17th.—Tarvin Rural District Council. £130.—Mr. Edward Evans Lloyd, clerk to the council.

Building Inspector.—November 19th.—Corporation of Bury. £120.—Mr. J. Cartwright, borough engineer.

Sewage Farm Manager.—November 19th.—Longton Corporation. £150.—Mr. J. W. Wardle, borough surveyor.

Fire Brigade Engineer.—November 26th.—Corporation of Coventry. £1 15s.—The City Engineer.

Pupil.—Box 90, office of The Surveyor, 24 Bride-lane, Fleet-street, E.C.

Junior Draughtsman and Analyst. £65.—Box 91, office of The Surveyor, 24 Bride-lane, Fleet-street, E.C.

## COMPETITIONS.

*Official and all similar advertisements received later than Thursday morning are too late for classification and cannot therefore be included in these summaries. No advertisements received after 3 p.m. can be inserted until the following week.*

Abergavon.—December 1st.—Extension of the covered market, at a cost not to exceed £5,000. £21.—The Borough Surveyor.

Chertsey.—December 23rd.—Sewerage and sewage disposal scheme for the No. 1 and 2 wards of the district. £50, £30 and £20.—Mr. T. E. Harland Chaldecott, clerk to the council.

Bradford.—January 2nd.—Erection of a central fire brigade station. £100, £50 and £30.—Mr. George McGuire, town clerk.

## MUNICIPAL CONTRACTS OPEN.

*Official and all similar advertisements received later than Thursday morning are too late for classification and cannot therefore be included in these summaries. No advertisements received after 3 p.m. can be inserted until the following week.*

Deal.—November 4th.—Construction of about 10 miles of brick and pipe sewers, the erection of a pumping station, the provision of pumping machinery, the construction of a tidal storage tank, penstock chambers and sea outfall, and all works incidental thereto.—Mr. Alfred C. Brown, town clerk.

Macclesfield.—November 5th.—Erection of a new police station at Church-side.—Mr. Edward E. Adshead, borough engineer.

Dublin.—November 5th.—Erection of a public library in North William-street.—Mr. Henry Campbell, town clerk.

St. Olave's (Southwark).—November 7th.—Supply of 50,000 blackbutt wood blocks and 5,000 yellow deal blocks dipped in oil, for the district board of works.—Mr. G. L. Hawker, clerk to the board.

St. Anne's-on-the-Sea.—November 7th.—Laying of about 124 yards of 16-in., 287 yards of 12-in. and 203 yards of 9-in. Hassall's patent pipe sewers in Glen Eldon-road and St. David's-road. £15.—for the urban district council.—Mr. Thomas Bradley, clerk to the council.

Hornsey.—November 7th.—Supply of 100 cast-iron lamp columns, 1,500 cast-iron telephone pipes, 30 cast-iron telephone pit covers and 100 wrought-iron tree guards, for the urban district council.—Mr. E. J. Lovegrove, engineer to the council.

Hornsey.—November 7th.—Construction of a new road, 40 ft. wide, through Queen's Wood, Highgate, for the urban district council.—Mr. E. J. Lovegrove, engineer to the council.

Beckenham.—November 7th.—Paving works in Beckenham and Elmers End roads, for the urban district council.—Mr. J. A. Angell, surveyor to the council.

Hornsey.—November 7th.—Supply and fixing of library fittings at the central public library in Tottenham-lane, for the urban district council.—Mr. E. J. Lovegrove, engineer and surveyor to the council.

Wimbledon.—November 7th.—Supply and erection of transformers and accessories, for the urban district council.—Mr. A. H. Preece, A.M.I.C.E., 39 Victoria-street, London, S.W.

Bermondsey.—November 7th.—Supply of two slop vans, for the vestry.—Mr. Frederick Ryall, clerk to the vestry.

Fleetwood.—November 8th.—Excavating, pile-driving, concreting, paving and other works in connection with the raising of the concrete landing at Knots End, for the urban district council.—Mr. Robert T. Hayes, A.M.I.C.E., surveyor to the council.

Willesden.—November 8th.—The extension of Glynfield-road, Willesden, the widening of Rockhall-passage, Cricklewood, and the re-laying of a sewer in Church-road, Willesden, for the urban district council.—Mr. O. Claude Robson, M.I.C.E., engineer and surveyor to the council.

Willesden.—November 8th.—Road-making and paving works in Preston-mews, for the urban district council.—Mr. O. Claude Robson, M.I.C.E., engineer and surveyor to the council.

Brighton.—November 8th.—Erection and completion of a new town hall and offices on a site at the corner of Bristol-street and Grammar School-walk, for the urban district council.—Mr. Wm. Obadiah Times, clerk to the council.

Dudley.—November 8th.—Sewering works in the proposed new streets at Scott's Green and in a portion of Stourbridge-road.—Mr. John Gammage, borough surveyor.

Barrow-on-Soar.—November 8th.—Construction of brick carriers and cast-iron and stoneware pipe sewers in the parish of Syston, for the rural district council.—The Chairman of the Council.

Hackney.—November 9th.—Supply of Portland cement, for the vestry.—Mr. James Lovegrove, chief surveyor to the vestry.

Winchester.—November 9th.—Erection of a new public urinal at the Corn Exchange.—The City Surveyor.

Church.—November 9th.—Supply of about 550 tons of non-slipping granite setts, for the urban district council.—Mr. John R. Reddish, clerk to the council.

Cardiff.—November 9th.—Supply and erection of iron sheep and cattle troughs and pens in South market.—Mr. W. Harpur, M.I.C.E., borough engineer.

Royton.—November 10th.—Supply and erection of pumping machinery to lift about 60,000 gallons of water per hour to a height of 60 ft., at the sewage works, Streetbridge, for the urban district council.—Mr. Theo. S. McCallum, A.M.I.C.E., 4 Chapel-walks, Manchester.

SOUTHEND-ON-SEA.—November 10th.—Supply of 1,200 cubic yards of Kentish flints.—Mr. Alfred Fidler, A.M.I.C.E., borough surveyor.

BATLEY.—November 10th.—Levelling, paving, flagging, channelling and completing of Grafton-street and Brown's-street.—Mr. O. J. Kirby, borough surveyor.

SOUTHEND-ON-SEA.—November 10th.—Excavation of a lake, supply and erection of a wrought-iron unclimbable fence, and the construction of a cast-iron conduit and a concrete gulley.—Mr. Alfred Fidler, A.M.I.C.E., borough surveyor.

BRIDLINGTON.—November 10th.—Construction of sea defence works on the north beach, for the urban district council.—Mr. Chas. Gray, clerk to the council.

BLACKBURN.—November 10th.—Execution of the masonry work in connection with the erection of a conservatory in the corporation park.—Mr. Wm. Stubbs, A.M.I.C.E., borough and water engineer.

PADIHAM.—November 10th.—Supply and delivery of 530 yards of unclimbable iron hurdle fencing and 760 yards of wire fencing, for the urban district council.—Mr. J. Gregson, engineer to the council.

NORFOLK.—November 11th.—Erection of steel and iron bridges at East Harling and Beetley, near Dereham, for the county council.—Mr. T. H. B. Heslop, M.I.C.E., county surveyor, Norwich.

ALTRINCHAM.—November 11th.—Erection of new offices, council chamber, fire station, caretaker's house, &c., for the urban district council.—Mr. John Stokoe, clerk to the council.

BIRMINGHAM.—November 11th.—Supply of certain goods for use in the general and Elan Valley supply departments for one year from January 1, 1899, for the corporation.—Mr. E. Antony Lees, secretary, Water Department, 44 Broad-street, Birmingham.

TAUNTON.—November 12th.—Supply of about 67 tons of 8-in. and 6-in. cast-iron spigot and socket bituminised water pipes.—Mr. George H. Sile, town clerk.

LAUNCESTON.—November 12th.—Construction of a new cattle, sheep and pig market.—The Town Clerk.

COVENTRY.—November 12th.—Erection of buildings at the proposed two new sewage pumping stations on the side of the main road from Coventry to Daventry.—Mr. Lewis Beard, town clerk.

DEWSBURY.—November 12th.—Paving, flagging, kerbing, channelling, &c., works in Thornton-street.—Mr. Henry Dearden, borough surveyor.

LLANGYFELACH.—November 12th.—Construction of about 456 yards of 12-in. stoneware pipe sewer in Sterry-road and Mount-street, Gowerton, for the rural district council.—Mr. J. Thomas, A.M.I.C.E., engineer and surveyor to the council, 32 Fisher-street, Swansea.

BARROW-IN-FURNESS.—November 14th.—Supply and erection of cast-iron lamp columns, arc and incandescent lamps, and automatic switches and fittings.—Mr. O. F. Preston, town clerk.

ANNFIELD PLAIN.—November 14th.—Formation of the road and footpath in Victoria-terrace and other streets, for the urban district council.—Mr. T. J. Trowsdale, surveyor to the council.

BIRKENHEAD.—November 14th.—Erection of public baths on land adjoining Livingstone-street and 1 Prince-street.—Mr. Charles Brownridge, A.M.I.C.E., borough engineer and surveyor.

LONDON.—November 15th.—Erection of new public conveniences at Blackwall Tunnel (north side), for the county council.—The Clerk to the Council, County Hall, Spring-gardens, S.W.

LONDON.—November 15th.—Erection of a new coroner's court building at Manor-place, Paddington, for the county council.—The Clerk to the Council, County Hall, Spring-gardens, S.W.

HANLEY.—November 15th.—Erection of a refuse destructor.—Mr. J. Lobley, borough engineer.

ACTON.—November 15th.—Supply of a steam fire-engine, a 50-ft. fire-escape, and electric street alarms, fire calls, &c., for the urban district council.—Mr. D. J. Ebbetts, clerk to the council.

CARDIFF.—November 15th.—Erection of fish market and offices at The Hayes.—Mr. W. Harpur, A.M.I.C.E., borough engineer.

TOTTENHAM.—November 15th.—Making-up of Cunningham-road and The Avenue, for the urban district council.—Mr. P. E. Murphy, engineer to the council.

DOVER.—November 15th.—Supply of about 1,500 tons of broken Guernsey granite, 500 tons of Guernsey granite settings, and about 2,000 lineal feet of Guernsey granite kerbing, channelling and quadrant corners.—Mr. E. Wollaston Knocker, town clerk.

TOTTENHAM.—November 15th.—Providing and laying of about 3,000 yards super. of 2½-in. hard York paving on the east side of Green-lanes, for the urban district council.—Mr. P. E. Murphy, engineer to the council.

HERTFORD.—November 15th.—Laying of about 100 yards of 9-in. and 60 yards of 12-in. glazed stoneware pipe sewers.—Mr. John H. Jevons, A.M.I.C.E., borough engineer and surveyor.

LINEHAM.—November 16th.—Supply of hard wood blocks for street paving.—Mr. R. A. Macbriar, city surveyor.

PLUMSTEAD.—November 16th.—Paving and making-up of part of Formount-road and part of Old Mill-road, for the vestry.—Mr. W. C. Gow, surveyor to the vestry.

AYLESBURY.—November 16th.—Construction of sewage disposal and other works, for the urban district council.—Mr. J. H. Radford, surveyor to the council.

WORTHING.—November 16th.—Supply of 2,500 ft. of 12-in. by 6-in. granite curbs and a quantity of broken granite.—Mr. Frank Roberts, A.M.I.C.E., borough engineer and surveyor.

SOUTHAMPTON.—November 16th.—Supply of two engines and dynamos at the county lunatic asylum at Knowle, Fareham.—Mr. W. J. Taylor, county surveyor, The Castle, Winchester.

CARMARTHENSHIRE.—November 18th.—Erection of a stone bridge of three arches, over the river Towry at Dryslwyn, for the county council.—Mr. Thomas Jones, clerk to the council, Llandovery.

ABERTILLERY.—November 19th.—Construction of a new road from Abertillery to Aberbeeg, a distance of about 2 miles, for the urban district council.—Mr. James McBean, engineer and surveyor to the council.

STAFFORD.—November 21st.—Supply of a stone-breaking machine.—Mr. W. Blackshaw, borough engineer.

ASHTON-UNDER-LYNE.—November 21st.—Construction of precipitation tanks, artificial filters, land filters, subways, culverts, roads and other appurtenant works.—Mr. J. T. Earnshaw, A.M.I.C.E., borough surveyor.

SOUTHAMPTON.—November 22nd.—Supply and delivery of sluice valves, fire hydrants, air valves and surface covers required by the waterworks department during the ensuing three years, for the corporation.—Mr. W. Matthews, waterworks engineer.

BURTON-UPON-TRENT.—November 24th.—Supply of fireclay retorts, bricks and clay required at the gasworks during the year 1899.—Mr. F. L. Ramsden, manager and engineer, Corporation Gas and Electric Light Works, Burton-upon-Trent.

TAME.—November 25th.—Construction of stoneware and other sewers for the interception of the sewage of the town, together with the necessary manholes, inspection shafts, flushing tanks, outfall works and engine-house, for the urban district council.—Mr. Wm. Parker, clerk to the council.

EAST RETFORD.—November 25th.—Construction of about 20,000 lineal yards of stoneware and iron pipe sewers, with manholes, storm overflow, ventilators, ejector chamber and ejectors, cast-iron rising main and other works; also precipitation tanks, engine and boiler houses, chimney shaft, press-house, stores and offices, carriers, underdrains; and levelling land, roads, fencing and other works.—Mr. Samuel Jones, town clerk.

STOURBRIDGE.—November 28th.—Construction of 990 yards of 9-in. earthenware pipe sewer, for the main drainage board.—Mr. W. Fiddian, surveyor to the board, Town Hall, Stourbridge.

MIDDLESBROUGH.—November 29th.—Supply and erection of various electric lighting plant, for the corporation.—Mr. Robert Hammond, consulting engineer, 64 Victoria-street, London, S.W.

SALFORD.—December 1st.—Supply and erection of certain electric plant.—Mr. Sanl. Brown, town clerk.

JOHANNESBURG, S.A.—January 6th.—Supply of a complete carburetted water-gas plant, for the corporation.—Messrs. Robert Whyte & Co., 22 Bury-street, St. Mary Axe, London, E.C.

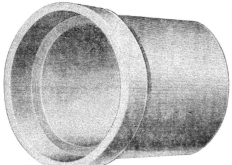

LONDON.—January 24th.—Construction of a tunnel for pedestrian traffic under the river Thames from Greenwich to Poplar, for the county council.—Mr. C. J. Stewart, clerk to the council, County Hall, Spring-gardens, S.W.

## TENDERS.

*ACCEPTED.

AMBLE.—For the levelling, channelling, paving, &c., of Byron-street, for the urban district council.—Mr. W. Gibson, surveyor to the council :—

E. Coulson, Amble ... ... ... ... ... ... £122
A. Douglas, Amble ... ... ... ... ... ... 88
R. & G. Brown, Amble* ... ... ... ... ... 73

BENFIELDSIDE.—For the construction of a new street at Blackfine, for the urban district council.—Mr. John Dixon, surveyor to the council :—

G. Christopher, Queen-street, Blackhill* ... £101 19s. 8d.

BETHNAL GREEN.—For the supply of 100 gully gratings, for the vestry.—Mr. F. W. Barratt, surveyor to the vestry :—

| | Per ton. |
| --- | --- |
| | £ s. d. |
| R. G. Phipps, Art Ironworks, Chippenham ... ... | 10 5 0 |
| Tingle Brothers, Cinderford, Gloucestershire ... ... | 7 10 0 |
| G. R. Hall, Newgate-street, Worksop ... ... | 7 2 6 |
| Viaduct Engineering Company, Crimlin, Monmouth | 6 12 0 |
| W. A. Oakley, Addington-road, Bow ... ... | 6 5 0 |
| Brockfield Foundry Company, St. Helens, Lancs. ... | 5 15 0 |
| J. Needham, Mulgate Foundry, Stockport ... ... | 5 5 0 |
| H. & G. Measures, East Surrey Ironworks, Croydon ... | 5 0 0 |
| Mackintosh & Sons, Cam Foundry, Cambridge ... | 4 10 0 |
| T. Morris, Potter-street, Worksop ... ... | 4 15 0 |
| Jukes, Coulson & Stokes, St. Leonards Works, Bromley, E.... | 4 15 0 |
| J. Gibb & Son, Fenchurch-street, E.C. ... ... | 4 10 0 |
| Beldam Foundry Company, Windmill-road, Brentford ... | 4 10 0 |
| E. & F. Wright, Whitechapel, E. ... ... | 4 5 0 |
| Moorgate Engineering Company, Featherstone-street, E.C.... | 4 2 6 |
| W. Harris, Stratford, E.* ... ... ... | 3 19 6 |

BEXHILL.—Accepted for the supply of various electric light plant, for the urban district council.—Mr. A. H. Preece, A.M.I.C.E., 39 Victoria-street, London, S.W. :—

Water Tube Boilers (Section A).—R. Hornsby & Sons, £1,746 10s.
Steam Dynamos and Balancer (Section B).—W. H. Allen, Son & Co., £2,570.
Storage Battery (Section D).—The Chloride Electrical Storage Syndicate, £1,020.
Underground Cables and Pipes, Arc Lamps and Posts (Section E).— The British Insulated Wire Company, Limited, £6,624 7s.

CONSETT.—For various kerbing, channelling, cementing and macadamising works.—Mr. William S. Shell, surveyor to the urban district council :—

T. W. Dobson, Consett ... ... ... ... ... £437
T. Hogg, Black Bill ... ... ... ... ... 409
G. J. Christopher, Black Bill ... ... ... ... 404
D. Omerod, Black Bill ... ... ... ... ... 381
W. J. & R. Walker, Consett and Black Bill* ... ... 381

LEDBURY.—For the construction of certain sewers, for the urban district council.—Mr. R. E. W. Berrington, engineer, Bank Buildings, Wolverhampton :—

J. Braithwaite & Co., Leeds ... ... ... ... £4,000
J. Smith, Ledbury ... ... ... ... ... 3,397
J. Meredith, Gloucester ... ... ... ... 3,374
H. Vale, Stourport ... ... ... ... ... 3,063
G. Law, Kidderminster ... ... ... ... 2,878
J. McKay, Hereford ... ... ... ... ... 2,876
J. Owens, Wolverhampton ... ... ... ... 2,849
H. Holloway, Wolverhampton ... ... ... ... 2,733
J. Bentley, Southport ... ... ... ... 2,616
Johnson Brothers, Hereford ... ... ... ... 2,528
Engineer's estimate, £2,700.

LEICESTER.—For alterations and additions to the Museum buildings in Hastings-street.—Mr. E. G. Mawbey, M.I.C.E., borough engineer :—

T. F. Scott, Leicester ... ... ... ... £1,912
W. G. Harrison, Leicester ... ... ... ... 1,872
F. Neal, Leicester ... ... ... ... ... 1,860
J. E. Tyers, Leicester ... ... ... ... 1,832
J. E. Johnson & Son, Leicester ... ... ... ... 1,830
G. Brown & Son, Leicester ... ... ... ... 1,787
H. Herbert & Sons, Leicester ... ... ... ... 1,746
J. Riddett & Son, Leicester ... ... ... ... 1,728
W. Hoddon, Leicester ... ... ... ... 1,701
Clark & Garrett, Leicester ... ... ... ... 1,696
H. T. & W. Chambers, Leicester ... ... ... ... 1,635
T. Herbert, Welford-road, Leicester* ... ... ... 1,608

SOUTHBOROUGH.—For the erection and completion of the proposed Victoria Hall and buildings in London-road, for the urban district council.—Mr. William Harmer, surveyor to the council :—

K. Jarvis, Tonbridge ... ... ... ... £4,620
Alliance Building Society, East Grinstead ... ... 4,217
Crates & Son, Tunbridge Wells ... ... ... 4,190
J. Jarvis, Tunbridge Wells ... ... ... ... 4,190
Punnett & Son, Tonbridge ... ... ... ... 4,097
Strange & Sons, Tunbridge Wells* ... ... ... 3,904
Logan, Maidstone ... ... ... ... ... 3,837
Avard, Maidstone ... ... ... ... ... 3,821

SOUTHEND-ON-SEA.—For the making-up of Claremont-road.—Mr. Alfred Fidler, A.M.I.C.E., borough surveyor :—

W. Iles, South-avenue, Southend-on-Sea* ... ... £288

TOTNES.—For the erection of post and rail fencing at Lower Long-combe, Berry Pomeroy, for the rural district council.—Mr. Thos. W. Windeatt, clerk to the council :—

R. Brimicombe, Stoke Gabriel ... ... ... ... £26
J. Collings, The Hayes, Stoke Gabriel* ... ... ... 15

WARRINGTON.—For the erection of a public convenience.—Mr. John Deas, Bank House, Sankey-road, Warrington :—

T. Davies, Warrington ... ... ... ... £124
Wood & Co., Liverpool ... ... ... ... 112
R. W. Collins, Warrington ... ... ... ... 100

WOLVERHAMPTON.—For the making-up of Hilton-street.—Mr. J. W. Bradley, borough engineer and surveyor :—

J. Owens, Skinner-street, Wolverhampton.*

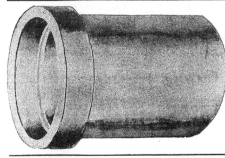

## MEETINGS.

*Secretaries and others will oblige by sending early notice of dates of forthcoming meetings.*

NOVEMBER.

4.—Sanitary Institute: Lecture to sanitary officers; Dr. H. R. Kenwood, medical officer of health, Stoke Newington, on "Infectious Diseases and Methods of Disinfection." 8 p.m.

7.—Society of Engineers: Ordinary meeting; Mr. Perry F. Nursey on "The Preparation of Rhea Fibre for Textile Purposes." 7.30 p.m.

8.—Institution of Civil Engineers: Ordinary general meeting; Prof. W. C. Roberts-Austen, C.B., F.R.S., on "The Extraction of Nickel." 8 p.m.

8.—Auctioneers' Institute: Opening meeting of the session; Mr. Alexander Macmorran, Q.C., on "The Effects of Recent Decisions on the Liabilities and Rights of Owners in respect of the Drainage of Buildings." 7.45 p.m.

8.—Royal Colonial Institute: The Hon. E. H. Wittenoom on "Western Australia in 1898." 8 p.m.

9.—Royal Institute of Public Health: Sir Richard Thorne Thorne, K.C.B., M.D., F.R.S., medical officer to the Local Government Board, on "The Administrative Control of Tuberculosis" (second Harben Lecture for 1898). 8 p.m.

## NOTICES.

THE SURVEYOR AND MUNICIPAL AND COUNTY ENGINEER *may be ordered direct, through any of Messrs. Smith & Son's book-stalls, or of any newsagent in the United Kingdom. Applications to the Offices for single copies by post must in all cases be accompanied by stamps.*

*The Prepaid Subscription (including postage) is as follows :*

|  | Twelve Months. | Six Months. | Three Months. |
|---|---|---|---|
| United Kingdom | 15s. | 7s. 6d. | 3s. 9d. |
| Continent, the Colonies, India, | | | |
| United States, &c. | 19s. | 9s. 6d. | 4s. 9d. |

ADVERTISEMENT AND PUBLISHING OFFICES :—
13 NEW STREET-HILL, FLEET-STREET, LONDON, E.C.

## ADVERTISEMENT.

## THE SANITARY INSTITUTE.

EXAMINATIONS IN SANITARY KNOWLEDGE.

The next Examinations in Practical Sanitary Science for Sanitary Inspectors will be held in London on December 2nd and 3rd.

The last day for receiving applications for Examination is November 19th.

Forms of application and full particulars can be obtained at the offices of the Institute, Margaret-street, London, W.

E. WHITE WALLIS, Secretary.

Newry.—At a recent meeting of the commissioners, a letter was read from the Local Government Board stating that they had been requested to withhold a loan of £5,000, asked for by the town commissioners some time since, for the purpose of erecting artisans' dwellings in Newry, until after the new board was elected under the new Local Government Act.

## APPOINTMENTS OPEN.

MORECAMBE DISTRICT COUNCIL.
The above Council require the services of a General Foreman over the outside men in their employ. He must be fully qualified and competent by knowledge and experience to carry out his duties.

The wages offered are 33s. weekly.

Also the services of a Time and Store Keeper, one accustomed to such duties preferred.

The wages offered are 22s. weekly.

Lists of duties can be seen by applying at the offices of the Council.

Applicants must apply in their own handwriting, stating their age and qualifications, particulars of their past and present employment, enclosing not more than three testimonials of recent date. All applications to be sent under cover, and endorsed "General Foreman" or "Time and Store Keeper," to the undersigned not later than noon on Monday, the 7th day of November next.

(By order)
JNO. BOND,
Surveyor to the Council.

Council Offices, Morecambe.
October 25, 1898.

COUNTY BOROUGH OF BURY.
BUILDING INSPECTOR.
The Sewering, Paving and Streets Committee invite applications for the appointment of Building Inspector in the Borough Engineer's department.

Candidates must be thoroughly qualified persons, and will be required to undertake the inspection of new buildings and drains, to fix levels, and make surveys of all new houses, buildings and drains, and to keep the necessary records in connection therewith. The commencing salary will be £120 per annum, increasing by yearly increments of £10 to £160 as a maximum. A list of duties may be obtained on application.

Applications, in candidate's own handwriting, stating age

(which must be between twenty-eight and thirty-five), accompanied by not more than three copies of recent testimonials, and endorsed "Building Inspector," to be sent to Mr. J. Cartwright, Borough Engineer, on or before Saturday, the 19th instant.

Canvassing will be considered a disqualification.

JOHN HASLAM,
Town Clerk.

TARVIN RURAL DISTRICT COUNCIL.
APPOINTMENT OF A SURVEYOR OF HIGHWAYS AND INSPECTOR OF NUISANCES.

The Tarvin Rural District Council invite applications for the appointment of Surveyor and Inspector for the Southern Division of their district, at a salary of £130 per annum.

Candidates must not be less than twenty-five nor more than forty years of age, and preference will be given to those who are able to prepare plans and drawings of sewerage works, &c.

The appointment will be made subject to the approval of the Local Government Board.

Applications, in candidate's own handwriting, accompanied with copies of not more than three recent testimonials, must reach the undersigned not later than the 17th November inst.

Canvassing will disqualify.

EDWARD EVANS LLOYD,
Clerk.

Crypt Chambers, Chester.
November 2, 1898.

CORPORATION OF THE CITY OF BIRMINGHAM.

The Public Works Committee are prepared to receive applications for the appointment of a District Road Surveyor in the City Surveyor's department, at a commencing salary of £130 per annum.

Candidates, whose age is not to exceed forty years, must be thoroughly qualified persons, having had active, practical experience in the construction, scavengering and maintenance of roads and streets; and on the various classes of pavement used therefor; and also in the management of large bodies of workmen; and should be able to set out works accurately, take all necessary measurements and prepare estimates of cost.

The candidate elected will have charge of one of the five districts into which the city is divided for road purposes.

He will be required to reside in his own district, and will be employed the same number of hours as the working staff. He will also be required to subscribe to the superannuation scheme, and to devote the whole of his time to the service of the Corporation.

Applications, in candidate's own handwriting, stating age, experience, past and present employment, and accompanied with copies of not more than three recent testimonials, endorsed "District Road Surveyor," to be sent to the undersigned not later than November 11th next.

Canvassing, either directly or indirectly, will be considered a disqualification.

JOHN PRICE,
City Engineer and Surveyor.

The Council House, Birmingham.
October 27, 1898.

WIMBLEDON URBAN DISTRICT COUNCIL.
ASSISTANT SURVEYOR.

The Wimbledon Urban District Council require an Assistant Surveyor. The salary is £200 a year, rising to £250 by annual increments of £10. Applicants must be under thirty years of age, must be conversant with all details of building construction, and must have had experience in the office of a surveyor to a municipal or local authority.

The area of the district is 3,220 acres, and the estimated population 38,500.

Applications, stating age and qualifications, and endorsed "Assistant Surveyorship," to be sent to me, accompanied by copies of three testimonials of recent date (which will be returned so as to be received not later than noon on the 14th instant.

Canvassing is prohibited.

W. H. WHITFIELD,
Clerk to the Council.

November 1, 1898.

WANTED, in a Provincial Gas Works, a young man as Junior Draughtsman and Analyst. Commencing salary, £65 per annum.—Apply, stating age and experience, to Box 91, office of THE SURVEYOR, 24 Bride-lane, Fleet-street, London, E.C.

PUPIL.—Engineer on a large modern gasworks, in a healthy Northern town, has a vacancy for a Pupil. Premium required.—Apply to Box 90, office of THE SURVEYOR, 24 Bride-lane, Fleet-street, London, E.C.

## COMPETITION.

### CITY OF BRADFORD.

*INTENDED CENTRAL FIRE BRIGADE STATION.*

#### TO ARCHITECTS.

The Corporation of the City of Bradford are prepared to receive Competitive Designs for the Erection of a Central Fire Brigade Station. Three premiums are offered to competing architects—*viz.*, £100, £50 and £30. Plan of the site, with printed instructions, may be had on application at the City Surveyor's office on and after Monday, the 31st inst., on payment of 1 guinea, to be returned after receipt of design.

The designs must be sent in not later than Monday, the 2nd of January, 1899.

(By order)
CEORGE McGUIRE,
Town Clerk.

Town Clerk's Office, Bradford.
October 25, 1898.

## TENDERS WANTED.

### WILLESDEN DISTRICT COUNCIL.

#### TO ROAD CONTRACTORS.

The Willesden District Council are prepared to receive tenders for the execution of certain Road-making and Paving Works in Preston-cnews, Willesden.

Plan and specification may be seen, and all further particulars obtained, on and after Monday, October 31, 1898, upon application to Mr. O. Claude Robson, M.INST.C.E., Engineer to the Council, Public Offices, Dyne-road, Kilburn, N.W.

The tenders, upon printed forms and endorsed "Private Streets," to be delivered at the offices of the Council not later than 4 p.m. on Tuesday, November 8, 1898.

The Council do not bind themselves to accept the lowest or any tender.

(By order)
STANLEY W. BALL,
Clerk to the Council.

Public Offices, Dyne-road, Kilburn, N.W.
October 26, 1898.

### BOROUGH OF STAFFORD.

The Corporation invite tenders for a Stone-breaking Machine, with jaws about 12 in. by 9 in., to have revolving screens, one to take out the dus', one to a ⅜ in. and one to 1¼ in. gauge, to be complete in every respect, and delivered at the corporation depot ready for fixing. Further particulars may be obtained on application to Mr. W. Blackshaw, Borough Engineer, Stafford.

Sealed tenders, endorsed "Tender for Stone Breaker," addressed to the Chairman of the Works Committee, to be left at the Town Clerk's office, Martin-street, not later than 10 a.m. on Monday, the 21st of November, 1898.

MATT. F. BLAKISTON,
Town Clerk.

Martin-street, Stafford.
October 31, 1898.

### URBAN DISTRICT OF ABERTILLERY.

#### TO CONTRACTORS.

The above Council are prepared to receive tenders for the making of a New Road from Abertillery to Aberbeeg, a distance of about 2 miles.

They are also prepared to receive tenders for the Widening of an existing Highway between Aberbeeg and Crumlin, a distance of about 2¼ miles.

Plans may be seen and specification, bill of quantities and form of tender obtained on application to Mr. James McBean, Engineer and Surveyor to the Council, at his office, No. 1 King-street, Abertillery.

A charge of £2 2s. will be made for each copy of the specification and bill of quantities, which will be returned on receipt of a *bonâ-fide* tender.

Sealed tenders, endorsed separately " New Road " or " Road Widening," as the case may be, to be sent to the undersigned on or before Saturday, the 19th day of November, 1898.

No tender will be entertained unless sent in on the prescribed form.

The Council do not bind themselves to accept the lowest or any tender.

(By order)
(Signed)   JNO. ALEX. SHEPARD,
Clerk to the Council.

District Council Office, Abertillery, Mon.
October 24, 1898.

## EAST RETFORD DRAINAGE.

The Corporation of East Retford, acting as the Urban District Council, invite tenders for the construction in the Borough of East Retford of about 20,000 lineal yards of Stoneware and Iron Pipe Sewers, with manholes, lampholes, storm overflow, ventilators, ejector chamber and ejectors, cast-iron rising main, and other works connected therewith; also precipitation tanks, engine and boiler houses, chimney shaft, press-house, stores and office, carriers, underdraining and levelling land, roads, fencing, and other works connected therewith; also the maintenance thereof for a period of twelve calendar months after completion.

Specification, with bill of quantities and schedule of prices, may be obtained from the Engineer, Mr. J. C. Melliss, M.I.C.E., 264 Gresham House, Old Broad-street, London, E.C., or from the Borough Surveyor, Retford, and the plans may be seen at their offices on and after November the 8th on payment of £10, which will be returned on receipt of a bonâ-fide tender.

Sealed tenders, properly filled in and addressed on the out-side, are to be sent to me before noon on Friday, the 25th day of November, 1898.

The Council does not bind itself to accept the lowest or any tender.

SAMUEL JONES,
Town Clerk.

Town Hall, East Retford.
October 31, 1898.

## PLUMSTEAD VESTRY.

### PAVING NEW STREETS.

### NOTICE TO CONTRACTORS.

The Plumstead Vestry invite tenders for Paving and Making-up part of Formount-road and part of Old Mill-road (as New Streets), comprising kerbing, channelling, roadway and tar paving.

The person or firm whose tender is accepted will, in the case of all workmen to be employed by him or them, be required to pay wages at rates not less, and to observe hours of labour not greater, than the rates an hours set out in the Vestry's list (such rates of wages and hours of labour will be inserted in a schedule, and form part of the contract), and will also be required to enter into a formal contract and bond, with two approved sureties, for the due performance of the contract.

Plans may be seen, and form of tender, specification and approximate quantities, also lists of wages and hours of labour, may be obtained on application to Mr. W. C. Gow, C.E., Surveyor to the Vestry, on and after Monday, the 7th November, on deposit of £2, which sum will be returned on receipt of a bonâ-fide tender, provided such tender is not sub-sequently withdrawn.

The Vestry does not bind itself to accept the lowest or any tender, and reserves the right to let the tar paving separately.

Sealed tenders, properly filled in, must be sent to me at the Vestry Hall, on or before Wednesday, the 16th November, 1898, not later than 4 p.m., in envelope marked "Tender for Paving."

(By order)
EDWIN HUGHES,
Vestry Clerk.

Vestry Hall, Maxey-road, Plumstead.
October 31, 1898.

## BOROUGH OF SOUTHEND-ON-SEA.

### TO STONE MERCHANTS.

The Corporation invite tenders for supplying 1,200 cubic yards of Kentish Flints, to be delivered alongside at Southend or at the railway station.

Specification and form of tender may be obtained, on and after Monday, the 31st instant, on application to Mr. Alfred Fidler, ASSOC.M.INST.C.E., Borough Surveyor, Clarence-road, Southend.

Each person tendering must send to the office of the Borough Surveyor a half-bushel sample of the flints offered.

Sealed tenders, endorsed "Tenders for Flints," to be de-livered at my office before 10 o'clock a.m. on Thursday, the 10th November.

The Corporation will not be bound to accept the lowest or any tender.

(By order)
WILLIAM H. SNOW,
Town Clerk.

Southend-on-Sea.
October 24, 1898.

# The Surveyor

## And Municipal and County Engineer.

Vol. XIV., No. 356.   LONDON, NOVEMBER 11, 1898.   Weekly, Price 3d.

## Minutes of Proceedings.

**Municipalities and Electric Tramways.**
Probably one of the most important papers published by the London County Council during recent years is Mr. J. Allen Baker's report on some forms of mechanical tramway traction.* Although the paper has special reference to the best form of traction for London, there is little doubt that the information collected and the conclusions arrived at will be of great use to all municipalities in considering the question of applying electricity to tramway work. One cannot but think that electricity for tramway purposes reaches its highest degree of utility when its growth coincides with that of the development of districts. It is this factor, no doubt, which accounts for the immense progress that has taken place in the United States and Canada during the past few years. The influence that a well-equipped tramway service has upon a town is demonstrated in the report under discussion. Mr. Allen Baker states:—

Cities that were hitherto confined to limited areas have had their congested inhabitants scattered to large suburban districts by the introduction of tramways, and property in suburban and outlying districts has in consequence immensely increased in value. In many districts numbers of towns and villages are connected by a perfect network of tramlines, and it is freely admitted that one of the greatest features in the improved social conditions of the people is the development of their mechanical tramways.

How great an influence electricity is exerting upon social life has been shown before in these columns, and it is of the utmost consequence that such an important body as the London County Council, the premier municipal organisation in the country, should recognise this fact. Apart from carrying passengers swiftly and efficiently, electric tramways in many towns are fulfilling functions of equal importance. In many cities they are utilised for municipal services of various sorts, such as street sweeping, sprinkling, postal delivery and collection. Although such functions could only be discharged properly when a tramway ran down every street, it is obvious that they can be relied upon to carry out some important work. It must be pointed out, however, that in considering American achievements in electric traction there is not likely to be the speedy development in this country that has characterised the States.

The very fact that municipalities are considering closely the question of tramways will in many cases delay the introduction of electricity; and that arises not so much from any want of conviction on the part of local authorities that electricity is not a suitable agent, but because most of the tramways of the country are still owned by companies, and it is not until their license has run its legal course that we may expect any startling development in the equipment of tramways for electrical working. At the same time there are many municipalities who have arrived at the point when they must either take over the local tramway service or grant an extension of leases to companies, with fuller powers as to the method of operating them. There is scarcely any local authority that has considered the subject of tramway traction and has not arrived at the conclusion that horses are quite unsuitable for such work, and that some form of mechanical traction must be adopted in order to provide an efficient and economical service. The tramways in London at the present moment are, judged by American conditions, not considered to have reached any magnitude, yet on the lines in existence no fewer than 25,000 horses are employed. If these were immediately removed the saving of wear to streets and the greater cleanliness effected would not be unimportant. The one great difficulty to be grappled with in London is that of dealing with the great congestion that forms so characteristic a feature of our present streets. Underground railways will do much to relieve the tension, but there is little doubt that if a well organised and equipped service of surface railways or tramways, offering rapid and cheap transit, were to be adopted it would aid very materially in enabling the masses of population to live outside the town. The question that has exercised the minds of town councillors, of county councillors and members of municipal bodies is, What is the system to adopt? A good deal of information has been collected by municipalities when considering the question, and it is perhaps a pity that the ideas and experiences of the various municipal bodies are not collected, or at any rate put in such a form that they would form a guide to the various municipalities that will, if not immediately considering the question, be shortly called upon to do so. It is an expensive matter to send deputations abroad and to different parts of the country where tramway systems are in operation, and although one might expect any given municipality to argue that the opinions of other towns would probably be useless to them, still one cannot help thinking that some joint action in a matter affecting the ratepayers all over the country should be arrived at.

It will now be of some interest to consider the various conclusions that Mr. Baker has arrived at with regard to different systems, and at the same time to offer some criticism where, in our opinion, it is needed. It will be difficult for anyone, even when not imbued with much enthusiasm for electrical methods, to disagree with the conclusions of the report that steam, so far as tramways are concerned, is not likely to be extended in any direction; and, moreover, if one may judge by the experience in Leeds, Huddersfield, Burnley and other towns, where tramways have been operated on such a system, we are likely to see the method almost immediately supplanted. In the most notable instance of steam tramways operated by a municipality, in fact, with the exception of Leeds, perhaps

* The report, which is well and profusely illustrated, can be obtained from Messrs. P. S. King & Sons, 9 Bridge-street, Westminster, S.W., price 1s., or 1s. 2d. post free.

the only instance in the country—we refer to that in Huddersfield—the experience has by no means been satisfactory. For some years the system has been practically run at a loss; yet the ratepayers were so dependent upon it as a means of conveyance from one part of the district to another that they preferred the levying of a small rate to meet the losses arising from the operation of the system rather than that the system should be abandoned. The expenses of operating the Huddersfield steam lines have been exceedingly heavy; at one time they were as much as 1s. 3d. per car mile, and even of later years have not been lower than 1s. per car mile. If electricity can show in the case of Huddersfield a reduction of 3d. or 4d. per car mile it will mean that a handsome profit would be derived from the operation of such a system. Electrical engineers claim that electricity should be able to operate almost any system in this country at 6d. or 7d. per car mile. Certainly the limited experience on tramway lines in this country bears out the fact. Whether, however, in the exceedingly difficult district of Huddersfield a similar experience will be obtained it is difficult to say. The Huddersfield Corporation, however, are convinced that electricity in some form or other is the most suitable means of operating their tramways, and we may shortly expect some developments in this direction. It was thought for some time that oil motors, which were tested in London, Croydon and Greenwich, were likely to be adopted to some considerable extent in the operation of tramways, but absolutely no progress has been made on this system since the first experiments, and if the extensive experiments in Chicago during 1893 go for anything this system may be considered completely out of court.

Gas motors, however, have proved to be by no means an inefficient and uneconomical system, and gas motor tramcars have been tried and are now in use on short lines in Dresden and Dessau; but what is of more interest to English municipalities is that a line of 7 miles has been very recently installed at Blackpool, running between Blackpool, St. Anne's and Lytham. Certainly the system has been shown to be capable of improvement; moreover, if we can accept the figures advanced by the Gas Motor Company, it appears to be a most economical one, but it is doubtful when any municipality considers the disadvantages arising from such a system whether this consideration is likely to help very much in its extension. It is interesting to mention, apart from the report under discussion, that in spite of elaborate estimates which were prepared for the Dover Corporation at the time when they were contemplating adopting electricity for tramway purposes, and in which it was shown that under certain conditions gas cars could in point of economy compare most favourably with electricity, yet, after a most careful investigation into the merits of the system, the Dover Corporation rejected the method in favour of electrical working. How successful this system has proved we have recently shown in these columns, the results being that at the conclusion of the first year's working a considerable profit was handed over to the alleviation of rates. Returning, however, to the question of gas-driven systems of tramcars, the following passage may be quoted :—

The cars are generally worked by means of a double-cylinder gas-engine placed under the seat, the fly-wheel being enclosed in a recess in the side of the car. Ordinary coal gas, at a pressure of 150 lb. to the square inch, is stored in the cylinders, which are carried under the seat. These require to be recharged at the compressing station every 9 miles. Thirty-five cubic feet of gas is used per car mile. The process of recharging occupies about one minute.

It is not difficult to place one's finger upon the drawbacks in such a system. In the first place, whether the car is running or at a standstill, it is necessary that the gas motor shall be continually rotating, on account of the difficulties in starting, and therefore the car, whether at a standstill or running, is subject to almost the same vibration. Moreover, it need hardly be urged how inconvenient and uncomfortable such a method will be to passengers, and, curiously enough, the Blackpool system, which has a somewhat steep gradient, has demonstrated another serious drawback, and that is that the laden cars have sometimes a difficulty in surmounting the gradient, and if stopped require to go back and recommence the ascent. There is also considerable smell given off from the motors, and though the practice may not be considered a dangerous one, still it is not a point in favour of any system of tramcars that reservoirs containing high-pressure gas have to be carried. The system, moreover, has not even the advantage of the self-contained electrical car, because the gas on the motors must necessarily be fired by a flame, and there may be always the danger of a fire occurring.

Compressed air has been long projected for cars, and Mr. Baker quotes instances where such systems have been working. In Paris, Berne, St. Quentin, Angouleme and Lyons systems have been at work for a considerable time. Cars have been used on the New York lines for some time, and the conclusion arrived at by Mr. Baker is that "they appeared to work well and to be under perfect control." Here, again, one could soon raise objection—it is necessary to carry cylinders in which compressed air is stored. Although it is claimed that properly-made cylinders can be ruptured without flying to pieces, still, some latent defects in the metal may at any time develop, with the consequent scattering of fragments. There appears to have been considerable improvements effected in this system, and certainly it is not open to the same objection as the gas-driven car, for there is, of course, an entire absence of smell, and the mechanism seems to admit of a considerable amount of flexibility. It is admitted by the engineers of the compressed air companies that the cars are heavier than those employed in the overhead wire system. Moreover, Mr. Pearson, in the report of the Liverpool Corporation Tramways Committee, stated that it would cost 1d. per car mile more than the electric conduit which had been installed in New York. We cannot, however, do better than quote Mr. Baker's final conclusion on the compressed air system. He states :—

Since I visited New York the Knight-Hoadley and Hardie Company, under the title of the American Air-Power Company, have been amalgamated, and I have been informed that the Metropolitan Traction Company of New York, upon whose lines I saw the trial air car, have decided to lay down a further compressing plant and extend the use of the system to some of the cross lines, in place of their present horse cars; but on the main avenues this company have shown their preference for electric traction, and have just completed a further 55 miles of electric conduit.

The further points raised by Mr. Baker in his report as to the merits and demerits of other systems we will leave for another article.

*          *          *

**The Making of By-Laws.**   The annual report of the Local Government Board for 1897 gives some interesting statistics respecting the making of by-laws during the year under the Public Health Act, 1875, the Public Health (Interments) Act, 1879, the Housing of the Working Classes Act, 1885, the Public Health Acts (Amendment) Act, 1890, the Public Health (London) Act, 1891, and the Acts incorporated with the first-mentioned Act. We are told that there is marked evidence of continued activity on the part of local authorities in making by-laws on the more important sanitary matters, such as scavenging, the prevention of nuisances, the regulation of common lodging-houses, the construction of buildings and the regulation of offensive trades. The majority of these by-laws were based on the model series prepared by the Local Government Board, and they comprised forty-two series relating to the cleansing of footways and pavements, the removal of house refuse and the cleansing of ash-pits, &c., and for regulating the times for the removal or carriage of noxious matter; fifty series relating to the prevention of nuisance arising from filth and of the keeping of animals so as to be injurious to health; thirty series dealing with the regulation of common lodging-houses ; 122 series with respect to the construction of new streets and buildings ; two series for the management, &c., of public slaughter-houses; six series with respect to houses let in lodgings or occupied by members of more than one family ; two series as to cemeteries ; four series with respect to mortuaries ; thirteen series for the regulation of offensive trades so as to prevent or diminish their noxious or injurious effects ; one series for securing the decent lodging and accommodation of persons engaged in picking hops, fruit and vegetables ; and eight series for securing the decent conduct of persons using public sanitary conveniences. Several series of by-laws, proposed to be made under sec. 9 of the Housing of the Working Classes Act, 1885, and sec. 95 of the Public Health (London) Act, 1891, with respect to tents, vans, sheds and similar structures used for human habitation, with a view to securing their habitable condition and for preventing the spread of infectious disease, &c., have been under the consideration of the Local Government Board during the year, and eight series were confirmed. A " model " series of these has been framed for the assistance of local authorities. The by-laws confirmed under the Public Health Acts also included twenty-four series with regard to public walks and pleasure grounds ; two series with respect to the regulation of horses and asses for hire ; six series as to pleasure boats and vessels ; and seven series with respect to whirligigs, swings and shooting galleries. Under the powers of the Acts incorporated with the Public Health Act, 1875, eight series of by-laws confirmed during the year were made with respect to markets, forty-two series with respect to private slaughter-houses, twelve series with reference to hackney carriages, twelve relating to omnibuses, and one series relating to public bathing. The Board approved eight series of by-laws made under the Baths and Wash-Houses Acts, and confirmed two series of rules and regulations under the Tramways Act, 1870. Twenty-four sets of by-laws or regulations submitted by local authorities and public companies in pursuance of provisions in various local Acts were also confirmed or approved by the Local Government Board in the course of the year. In an appendix to the report are given the names of the various local authorities and other particulars. Reference is again made to the practice of the Board in requesting that by-laws and regulations may be, in the first instance, submitted in draft, so that before they are actually made their details may be examined from legal, sanitary and technical points of view. It is also satisfactory to hear that advantage has been experienced from holding conferences between officers of the Board and representatives of the local authority proposing the by-laws. Many such conferences, we are told, took place during the year, and in several cases it was found desirable to hold local inquiries for the purpose of ascertaining the special circumstances in which certain exceptional clauses were deemed necessary. The discussion on by-laws initiated by Mr. Pickering at the recent congress of the Sanitary Institute at Birmingham indicated the existence of considerable dissatisfaction among local authorities and their officials with the too rigid attitude of the Local Government Board in practically demanding, irrespective of special local conditions and needs, one uniform code of by-laws throughout the country, based on their own " model " series. The Local Government Board, however, seem quite satisfied of the wisdom and correctness of their policy, but we doubt if it would obtain much support outside of Whitehall.

\*     \*     \*

**The Municipal Telephone.** Subject to the sanction of Parliament, which is by no means a foregone conclusion, we may be said to have reached the era of municipal telephones. The granting by the Postmaster-General of a license to the Glasgow Corporation to equip and carry on a system of telephones has naturally led other bodies to consider the question more closely than they have hitherto done. It would only be fair to grant powers to other municipalities that might apply for them, although the reasons that induced the Glasgow Corporation to apply for permission to erect their own system might not obtain in other towns. There is no doubt that Glasgow has been suffering for a good many years from a bad telephone system, and we can speak from personal experience on this point. Supposing, however, that the Postmaster-General grants various licenses in different parts of the kingdom, and such licenses receive the direct sanction of Parliament, it must be obvious that for some years much confusion would obtain. In a large town four, or even five, years would probably elapse before the system could be at the service of telephone users ; and it must not be forgotten that all licenses granted by the Postmaster-General will expire in 1911. It does not follow that these licenses may not be renewed, but it is clear that the Postmaster-General is reserving to himself the right of operating the entire telephone system of the country if conditions are favourable for such a course. Therefore a telephone system may be laid down by a municipality at considerable expense and in a few years be entirely superseded, because it is clear that the Post Office would not take over any system which did not commend itself to its engineering department. Hence it might follow that a large sum of money would have been invested in plant which had become practically useless. As we have before pointed out, the telephone service is not comparable with electric lighting, because the telephone subscriber wants more than the mere local service. Although the success of the agitation so persistently urged by the Glasgow Corporation may doubtless impress many municipalities, it is probable that those seeking relief from the present system will follow the lead of the London County Council in urging as strongly as possible the taking over of the telephone system by the Post Office. Unless some such course be adopted we are afraid municipalities will in many cases attempt to supply a telephone service and much public money may be wasted.

\*     \*     \*

**The Typhoid Bacillus in the Soil.** In the Shoreditch Vestry annual report, to which we have already referred, Dr. Fraser Bryett, medical officer of health, refers to the recent investigations of Dr. Sidney Martin, F.R.S., on behalf of the Local Government Board, respecting the behaviour of the bacillus of enteric fever in the soil. These investigations, so far as they have been pursued, tend, he thinks, to show that in earth which is originally polluted, as is likely to be the case in the vicinity of defective drains, leaky cesspits, or in the neighbourhood of dwellings in crowded and poor localities, the micro-organisms which give rise to enteric fever are capable not only of retaining their vitality for months, but of increasing and multiplying in numbers. On the other hand, in soils which are not exposed to pollution the micro-organisms are unable to flourish and rapidly become extinct. Dr. Bryett points out that similar results have been arrived at by at least one other investigator in the same field of research, and he is justified in saying that they go to emphasise the great importance of sanitary work executed under the supervision of the officials of local authorities in respect to such matters as the proper paving and drainage of yards and areas in connection with dwellings, and the construction of drains and other sanitary arrangements, in such a way as to prevent the pollution of the soil. A timely appeal is made for the paving with impervious material of courts, cul-de-sacs and narrow streets in localities occupied by poor people. When so paved every shower of water helps to wash them clean, and thus by facilitating, cleansing, and preventing the pollution of the soil the comfort of the people is promoted and the standard of health raised.

# Principal Features of Electric Lighting Systems.—VIII.

## COMBINED LIGHTING AND TRAMWAY SYSTEMS.

It is hardly necessary to say that one of the chief developments in a municipal supply is that of combining plant for furnishing electricity both for lighting and tramway purposes. This arises mainly from the desire of municipalities to cheapen the cost of electricity, and it is obvious that when a local authority is operating a tramway by electrical means considerable economy will be effected if the plant can be housed in the one building. It is held that such an arrangement would provide the electrical machinery with a day load, and by thus giving a good load factor during the greater part of the twenty-four hours a very considerable saving would be effected, with the result that the production of electricity would be materially cheapened. There is a good deal of experience to guide municipalities in this direction, for combined systems have been in operation for a considerable time in different parts of the Continent and in America. It has been held in this country that by combining plant in such a way electric current ought to be produced for all purposes at from 1½d. to 3d. per unit, according to the demand. Even when a company operates an electrical tramway system it is under some circumstances much better for it to obtain its electricity from the local supply, be it municipal or other-

wise, than to put down plant for the sole purpose of supplying electrical energy for tramway purposes. To quote from a paper communicated some time ago to the Association of Municipal Electrical Engineers:—

"This has been realised on the Continent, where in several large towns the tramway companies are buying current from municipal electric light works. The lowest price paid is at Geneva, where the tramway company guarantees a minimum consumption of 500,000 units per annum, and pays 1·15d. per Board of Trade unit. Hamburg is another example of a tramway company buying current from a lighting station. In this case the tramway company guarantees a minimum annual consumption of 2,500,000 units. The lighting company has to pay a fine of 9·6d. for every car mile which the tramway company may not be able to run, owing to any failure in the power plant. The total expenses of the tramway company, including depreciation, maintenance, interest on bonds, sinking fund, &c., are only 3·95d. per car mile. Hamburg is, so far, the largest electric tramway system in Europe, and its success is an accomplished fact. The management state in the last year's annual report that the introduction of electric traction has, without the slightest doubt, very much improved the earning capacity and diminished the working expenses of the system ; further, that on the lines where electricity has superseded horses the number of passengers carried has increased more than 32 per cent., and the receipts have increased nearly 35 per cent."

Although it is generally accepted that striking economies

can be effected by combining the interests in some such way, the most conspicuous departure from this rule is in the case of Glasgow, where the recently opened municipal tramways are not supplied with current from the existing lighting station, but separate plant has been erected. This, however, arises not so much from the belief on the part of the Glasgow Corporation that no economy can be effected by combined works, but it had its origin in a dispute between the Tramway Committee and the Lighting Committee, with the almost deplorable result that the former committee refused to obtain its supply from the already existing system. In all other systems, however, where tramways are being introduced, the prevalent desire on the part of municipalities is to obtain the advantages derived from a combined system of tramway and lighting plant. One of the most notable instances is that of Halifax, where a large system of municipal electric tramways is being operated in conjunction with the lighting of the town.

## THE HALIFAX WORKS.

This is a very interesting example, because the current supplied for lighting purposes in this town is wholly unsuited for propelling electric tramcars, and it has been necessary to

HALIFAX MUNICIPAL ELECTRICITY WORKS.

put down special plant to give a direct current supply ; but such an arrangement gives all the advantages arising from having the whole of the plant under the supervision of one staff. The illustration gives a general idea of the works as they exist to-day. The plant which is being used for the purpose of generating electricity for tramway purposes is the third machine visible in the illustration. It will be interesting to give some details of this particular plant, because no doubt it will have some bearing on future systems where combined plant is to be used. The generator is of the continuous-current type, and driven by ropes from an engine which was originally put down for driving an alternator. It is of the four-pole type, having an output of 220 amperes at 500 to 550 volts. But one of the most interesting machines in the present station is a motor alternator, which acts as a sort of buffer state between the tramway and the lighting systems. It consists of a continuous-current dynamo, which is driven, through ropes, by means of an alternating-current motor. This machine possesses two valuable functions. If an alternating current is sent into the motor it drives the continuous-current dynamo, which is thereby enabled to deliver current into the tramway circuit, but it is possible for the continuous-current machine to be turned into a motor, and thus reverse the operation and drive the alternating-current machine, thereby enabling it to give an alternating current which can be delivered into the lighting circuit. In order, however, that this should be done a battery of accumulators is provided, and thus it is possible to call upon this store of electrical energy to drive the continuous-current machine as a motor and the alternating machine as a generator. This combination will effect two purposes then. Through the medium of the alternating machine driving the continuous the whole of the tramway service will be operated during the early morning, and then by reversing the motor alternator the whole of the lights in the town will be kept going during the hours of light load. The arrangement provides what is undoubtedly a novel feature in alternating-current systems; previously all alternating works had been compelled to keep a staff all night to keep the few lamps supplied that may be burning, but by means of the combination adopted at Halifax it will be actually possible to shut down the station at night and thus rely on the battery to drive the continuous-current machines, which will in turn drive the alternator, and thus give off an alternating-current suitable for distribution into the lighting mains, without the necessity of having anybody in attendance. In the case of Halifax the whole of the switching devices are arranged on different boards, there is a board specifically used for controlling the whole of the lighting and a second board placed in a separate part of the building is used entirely for tramway purposes.

It will be interesting to quote the opinion of Mr. Stewart, who has until recently acted as municipal electrical engineer of Derby, on the subject of combined plants for lighting and tramway purposes. The conclusions are those shared by most municipal engineers, and were recently brought before the convention of municipal electrical men held some time ago:—

"The first consideration is, Shall the current be supplied from the existing works? This, I believe, should be answered in the affirmative, for the sufficient reasons that the same buildings, boiler, power and plant will answer the purpose, and the necessary spare plant will not be augmented, but, on the contrary, considerably reduced in proportion to the output, as accumulators would be introduced to, as far as possible, reduce the necessity of adding plant to take the load over the lines when the maximum load for the ordinary supply occurs at the same time as the traction load.

"Secondly, the cost of keeping accounts will be very much reduced, as the work that is necessary to keep the electricity works accounts will not be added to, as would be the case when a separate power-house is laid down. The power used would be metered as for an ordinary consumer and charged for as such. The interest and sinking fund on the capital outlay on buildings will not be increased, or only slightly so, which would not be the case if a separate power-house were decided upon. The same staff of men practically would do, or in any case with a small increase only necessary. The same engineer would in consequence control the whole supply. Having decided so far, that the one works should do all the work necessary to supply electrical energy for whatever purpose it may be required, it cannot too carefully be considered as to what arrangements should be made to save confusion and friction between committees or the various departments into which the work of corporations is divided. The committee, I think, should be composed of a definite number of gentlemen, which should be divided into two sub-committees —one to be responsible for the supply of electricity, arranging of prices and managing the supply works; the second to be responsible for the tramways' equipment and management; and each should report its recommendation to the ordinary committee meetings."

## MR. PREECE'S ADDRESS.

### THE PROGRESS OF ELECTRICITY.

In our last issue we gave a brief abstract of Mr. Preece's address as president of the Institution of Civil Engineers. The following communication, which we have received from a correspondent, embraces some interesting points not included in our abstract:—

It was only natural that Mr. W. H. Preece, C.B., the president of the Institution of Civil Engineers, should have chosen the subject of electricity for his presidential address on the 1st inst. There is no man living who has had so much practical experience in the application of this force to the uses of mankind, and his address was consequently listened to with wrapt attention by an appreciative audience. After an admirable defence of the Government "official," he gave some statistics of the present strength of the Institution of Civil Engineers, amounting to 7,008 members, of whom 71 per cent. are home members, 21 per cent. are colonial members, and 8 per cent. are foreign members. These he divided into the railway engineer, the mechanical engineer, the naval architect, the mining engineer, the sanitary engineer, the gas engineer, the hydraulic engineer, the electrical engineer, the chemical engineer and the marine engineer. He spoke of the advantage of examinations, but pointed out the difficulty of obtaining really competent practical teachers. "The ideal professor of pure abstract science is a very charming person, age, but he is a very arrogant and dogmatic individual, and, being a sort of little monarch in his own laboratory and lecture room, surrounded by devoted subjects, his word is law, and he regards the world at large, especially the practical world, as outside his domain and beneath his notice." Speaking later

on of "Energy," Mr. Preece thought that the title of "Engineer" should be rather that of "Energeer."

### THE TELEGRAPH AND THE TELEPHONE.

The president, turning to his familiar subject of electricity, said that he had studied under Michael Faraday fifty years ago, and he pointed out the practical advances of this form of energy since that time. With regard to telegraphy, he said that, whereas in 1837 the pioneer line was only 1¼ miles in length, there were at the present time no less than 1,111,366 miles of British telegraph wires and cables. Speaking of the insulation of underground cables, he strongly advocated paper covering, protected by lead. He spoke of the future advances which were almost perfected in connection with "Telangraphy," or writing telegraphs, and of wireless telegraphy, and in connection with the telephone he gave a history of its development, and pointed out that there were at present 152,019 telephones in use in this country. He gave some interesting details of the use of telegraphy in connection with the working of railways, whereby travelling had been rendered so safe, and he gave tables to show how accidents, in consequence, had decreased. For instance, in 1874 one person in 5,500,000 journeys was killed, in 1884 one person in 22,500,000 journeys, in 1894 one in 57,000,000 journeys, and in 1896 one in 196,000,000 journeys. In 1897, he said, twenty-four persons only were killed in railway accidents when travelling. A first-class compartment on one of our great railways is the safest place in the world. "It is safer than bed, for in 1896 1,800 persons were suffocated in bed. It is safer than a dining-room, for in the same year 148 persons were choked by food." And this with more than 20,000 miles of railway line open for passenger traffic.

### ELECTRIC LIGHTING.

After touching on the domestic electrical appliances, such as the bell, the fire and burglar alarms, lifts, ventilators, heating by radiators, cooking in ovens, boiling water, heating flat irons, and even curling tongs! Mr. Preece proceeded to give particulars with regard to the electric light, showing that, whereas there were only 135 electric light stations in this country, there were 2,580 in the United States. The capital invested in this country in such undertakings was nearly £8,000,000 and in the States £52,000,000. On the cost of production Mr. Preece said electricity could be generated continuously during the twenty-four hours at a fraction of 1d. per unit, but if used solely for light it may cost 3d. per unit. "The cheaper the supply of energy per unit the more certain and speedy the advent of the electric light as the poor man's lamp, and the more beneficial its introduction into the confined, ill-ventilated and overcrowded houses of the working classes. By improving the locomotion to the suburbs and enabling them to live in pure air, and by cleansing the air they breathe of the impurities due to the combustion of tallow, oil and gas, the more readily should the public fall down and worship the golden image which Parliament and science have set up."

On the question of traction Mr. Preece said that the first experimental line was constructed by Dr. Siemens, in Berlin, in 1879. In 1884 there was only one short experimental line in America—viz., in Cleveland, Ohio; now there are more miles of line so worked in Cleveland alone than in the whole of the United Kingdom, the reason being the climatic influences of the States, the habits of the people, the cost of horseflesh and the necessity for more rapid transit.

### ELECTRIC TRACTION.

He considered that the slow advance of electric traction in this country was due to the restrictive clauses of the Act of 1870; but as these are now removed there ought to be a rapid development of this form of traction. Speaking of the storage battery, Mr. Preece said it fulfils a very important function in the economical working of an electric railway. It equalises the pressure on the circuits, it meets the fluctuations of the load, it takes in current when the load is light, and it lets out current when the load is heavy. "Electric traction is invading even our streets. The number of unstable and weak-kneed cart horses seems destined to be reduced by their electric competitor, while the pride of London, the fleet hansom, will be freed from an obstructive and not always sweet-smelling avant courier. When the real storage battery is produced the auto-mobile problem will be solved."

Mr. Preece then referred to electro-chemistry, and also to the transmission of power. With regard to the latter he said "the energy wasted in waterfalls is enough to maintain in operation the industries of the world." At Tivoli, 15 miles from Rome, the energy of the falls lights Rome and drives the tramcars, and he gave other instances of similar transmission. Such transmission was effecting a great economy in coal consumption in workshops and factories. The efficiency of steam-driven shafting is poor, scattered steam engines and long steam piping run away with money; the motor is used only when and where wanted, and costs nothing when idle. In conclusion, Mr. Preece said that "every engineer must ultimately become an electrician, and electricity will be the most general, the most useful and the most interesting form in which he applies the fundamental principles of energy to the wants, the comforts and the happiness of mankind." After all there is nothing like leather, and President Preece may be right in his prophecy.

# Comparative Reports of General Practice.

## XXIX.—ELECTRIC LIGHTING : BECKENHAM REPORT.—IV.

We now give the remaining

### PARTICULARS OF INSTALLATIONS.

#### GREAT YARMOUTH.

(Population, 50,000; rateable value, £178,500.)

This town possesses a high - tension alternating installation, which cost £32,000 to erect. The works have been running since January, 1895, and supply power equal to dealing with 9,500 8 candle-power lamps; but there is no demand for motors. Here also there is shown a loss on last year's working, the revenue being £2,942 and the working expenses £3,558—a deficiency of £616. Profits, however, are anticipated. Current is charged for at the rate of 6d. per unit, and gas costs 3s. per 1,000 cubic feet.

#### HAMPSTEAD.

(Population, 75,449 ; rateable value, £805,443.)

A high-tension alternating system is at work here. It was started in October, 1894, and produces power sufficient to deal with the equivalent of 50,000 8 candle-power lamps. The original cost of the works was £83,330. Motor-power is not used. Last year's revenue and working expenses were respectively £12,810 and £10,987, leaving a substantial profit of £1,832. Current is charged for at the rate of 6d. per unit, but it is expected to be able to reduce this charge and at the same time to earn considerably larger profits. The cost of gas at Hampstead is 2s. 10d. per 1,000 cubic feet.

#### HUDDERSFIELD.

(Population, 96,000; rateable value, £435,000.)

The installation at Huddersfield is, like that of Hampstead, on the high-tension alternating principle, but the cost of erection was only £65,000. Current (which is now capable of supplying 40,000 8 candle-power lamps) has been available since July, 1893. There is no demand for power purposes. The profit on the last financial year's working totalled £445, the revenue being £6,864 and the expenditure £6,419. A charge of 6d. per unit, less discount, is imposed, but a reduction is anticipated, as is an increase of profits. Gas costs 2s. 9d. per 1,000 cubic feet.

#### KINGSTON-ON-THAMES.

(Population, 27,057 ; rateable value, £120,218.)

A high-tension alternating system is also in operation at Kingston, the date of the first supply being October, 1893. A sum of £29,497 was spent upon the works, which have a capacity of 10,050 8 candle-power lamps. No applications for motor-power have as yet been made. In this case a loss was experienced, as the working expenses—£4,339—exceeded the revenue by £1,326. Charging is made at the rate of 6d. for the first two hours and 4d. for subsequent hours, and no reduction is expected. A profit is expected on future working, and the corporation are so satisfied with the past results that large extensions are being carried out. The price of gas is 2s. 11d. per 1,000 cubic feet.

#### LANCASTER.

(Population, 31,034; rateable value, £131,978.)

The system adopted at Lancaster is a three-wire low-tension one, which cost £22,984 to erect. Current was first supplied in April, 1894, and the present output is capable of dealing with the equivalent of 10,500 8 candle-power lamps ; a small demand for motor-power is also met. The last financial year's revenue was £2,475 and the expenditure £2,387—a surplus of £88 ; 5d. per unit is charged, and this not likely to be reduced. A large profit, however, is expected. In Lancaster gas costs 2s. 6d. per 1,000 cubic feet.

#### LEYTON.

(Population, 80,000; rateable value, £217,750.)

At Leyton, where a low-tension system is at work, a sum of £26,000 was spent upon the works, and current, which is now capable of supplying 4,000 8 candle-power lamps, has been available since September, 1896. As a result of seven months' working the revenue and expenditure were respectively £600 and £1,000, thus showing a loss of £400. The charge for current is the same as at Lancaster—namely, 5d. per unit—and no reduction in this direction is expected to be made. It should be mentioned that the station is rapidly attaining a profit-earning state. Gas costs between 3s. and 4s. per 1,000 cubic feet.

#### NELSON.

(Population, 35,000; rateable value, £91,000.)

With a two-wire low-tension system, which was completed in 1892 and cost £10,600 to lay down, the equivalent of 5,620 8 candle-power lamps are supplied in Nelson. No demand for motor-power is made. Charging 5d. per unit, less 5 per cent., the authorities have earned a profit of £304, but are expecting to shortly be able to make a reduction in price together with an accompanying increase in profits. At present the installation is not being carried on to its full capacity. Gas in the district cost 2s. 6d. per 1,000 cubic feet.

#### NEWPORT, MON.

(Population, 54,695 ; rateable value, £249,422.)

At Newport, where a high-tension alternating system is carried on, current has been supplied since October, 1895. The original cost of the installation was £43,000, and the equivalent of 15,000 8 candle-power lamps is supplied. There is no demand for motors. The last financial year's working resulted in a loss of £962, the revenue being £3,386 and the working expenses £4,348, but a profit is expected to be made in the course of two years. A charge of 6d. per unit is made for current. Gas costs 3s. 2d. per 1,000 cubic feet.

#### NOTTINGHAM.

(Population, 213,877 ; rateable value, £857,479.)

The three-wire low-tension continuous-current system has been adopted here, and current has been supplied since September, 1894. The works, which can deal with the equivalent of 25,476 8 candle-power lamps, cost £67,387 to build. There is no demand for power for purposes of motors. Profits on last year's working amounted to £2,284, the charges for current being 6d. for the first hour and 4d. for subsequent hours. Larger profits are, however, expected. Gas costs 2s. 2d. per 1,000 cubic feet.

#### OLDHAM.

(Population, 131,463 ; rateable value, £634,496.)

At Oldham a low-pressure three-wire installation has been working since March, 1894, and is now supplying current capable of dealing with 15,766 8 candle-power lamps. The costs of the works was £39,600. Motor-power is supplied. Revenue and expenditure totalled £5,564 and £4,521 respectively, thus showing a profit of £1,043. Wright's system of charging has been adopted by the authorities, and the prices are 4½d. and 3½d. per unit. Considerably larger profits are expected. Gas costs 2s. 3d. per 1,000 cubic feet.

#### OSWESTRY.

(Population, 8,496 ; rateable value, £35,810.)

The installation here, which cost £6,000, is on the two-wire continuous direct-current system, and was first started in August, 1895. It supplies power sufficient to deal with 7,000 8 candle-power lamps, and meets a small demand for motors. A profit of £123 resulted from the last financial year's working, the working expenses being £348 and the revenue £471. The cost of the current is 6d. per unit, and no reduction in this price is anticipated. But considerably larger profits are expected, as experience has proved that once the light is used it is never discontinued and is appreciated far beyond any other.

#### PORTSMOUTH.

(Population, 180,000; rateable value, £624,495.)

Portsmouth, with a high-tension alternating system, which has been working since June, 1894, and cost £97,000, is supplied with power sufficient for some 32,000 8 candle-power lamps. The works last year produced the large profit of £2,324, the working expenses and revenue being respectively £11,950 and £14,274. The charge for current is 4½d. per unit, while gas costs 2s. 4d. per 1,000 cubic feet.

#### SOUTHPORT.

(Population, 47,243 ; rateable value, £299,831.)

An installation similar to that at Portsmouth is in working here. Its erection cost £47,000, and current has been available since November, 1894. Power equal to supplying 19,810 8 candle-power lamps is distributed, but none is used for motor purposes. Last year's results were as follows : Revenue, £4,426 ; working expenses, £4,827. This means a loss of £410, but a profit of at least £600 is anticipated during the present year, as the demand for electricity is increasing at a great rate. A reduction in charges, which are at present 7d. for the first hour, 4d. for the second, and 2d. for the third, is also expected. The cost of gas is 3s. per 1,000 cubic feet.

(Population, 21,000 ; rateable value, £61,356.)

In this town a three-wire continuous-current system has been adopted, and power equal to dealing with 7,000 8 candle-power lamps is supplied. The installation was completed in October, 1895, and cost £20,000. Motor-power is not used. The last financial year's working cost £1,516, while the revenue was £1,215—a loss of £301. Charges are made at the rate of 7d. for the first hour and 3d. for subsequent hours. The cost of gas in the town is 2s. 6d. per 1,000 cubic feet. It may be mentioned that the works were expected to pay their way this year.

#### TAUNTON.

(Population, 20,000; rateable value, £85,000.)

The system here is a high-tension one, with sub-stations. It cost £23,200, and has been working since October, 1890. The equivalent of 16,000 8 candle-power lamps is supplied, but no current is used in connection with motors. Revenue and expenditure last year totalled respectively £2,705 and

£2,980, but a profit is expected to accrue from the present year's working. The charge for gas in Taunton is 3s. 6d., while current during the first two hours costs 6d., and in subsequent hours 3½d. per unit. No reduction is considered to be yet possible.

### TUNBRIDGE WELLS.

(Population, 30,000; rateable value, £300,000.)

Power has been supplied in Tunbridge Wells since August, 1895. The cost of the installation, which is on the high-tension alternating system, was £35,000, and current equal to dealing with 16,000 8 candle-power lamps is now distributed. Motor-power is not used. The last financial year's revenue left a profit of £890, the charges being 6d. for the first one and a half hours and 4d. for the succeeding hours. It is both expected to be able to reduce these charges and to earn large profits in connection with the lighting, which is said to be a thorough success and much appreciated. Gas is sold at 3s. por 1,000 cubic feet.

### WALLASEY.

(Population, 41,000; rateable value, £215,000.)

The installation here is also on the high-tension alternating system, and is capable of dealing with 2,000 8 candle-power lamps. Its cost was £11,000, and the date of the first supply, February, 1897. Last year's revenue and working expenses were respectively £2,250 and £2,200 (a profit of £50), these figures resulting from a charge of 7d. and 5d., with an extra 1d. per unit for free wiring. The cost of gas in the town is 3s. per 1,000 cubic feet.

### WALSALL.

(Population, 71,791; rateable value, £202,876.)

At Walsall a high-tension continuous-current system, with motor-generator transformers, has been in use since December, 1895, supplying the equivalent of 5,720 8 candle-power lamps. A sum of £19,000 was spent in its construction, but last year's working resulted in a loss of £445, the revenue being £1,568 and the expenditure £2,013. Current (none of which is used for motors) during the first one and a half hours costs 6d. per unit; subsequent hours are charged for at the rate of 2d. per unit. No reduction is anticipated, although profits are expected to result from future working. In this town gas costs 3s. 6d. per 1,000 cubic feet.

### WHITEHAVEN.

(Population, 19,236; rateable value, £54,170.)

A three-wire continuous-current installation is working at Whitehaven, where the equivalent of 5,000 8 candle-power lamps is supplied. A sum of £18,500 was spent upon the works, which cost £18,500 to erect. Revenue and expenditure in the last financial year balanced equally at £2,791, this result being obtained from a charge of 5d. per unit. Gas in Whitehaven costs 3s. 6d. per 1,000 cubic feet. It might be stated that the above accounts were made to balance by including the cost of public lighting.

### WORCESTER.

(Population, 44,000; rateable value, £174,000.)

In Worcester the electric lighting installation, which cost £62,000 to erect, is on the high-tension system, with sub-stations, and has a capacity of 23,000 8 candle-power lamps. It has supplied current at a charge of 6d. per unit for the first hour and 2½d. for succeeding hours since October, 1894. Power for motors is used. The works, however, sustained a loss of £1,617 on last year's working, the revenue and expenditure being respectively £4,757 and £6,374; but profits are expected. The price of gas per 1,000 cubic feet is 2s. 7d.

## LAUNCESTON NEW SEWAGE DISPOSAL WORKS.

The mayor of Launceston on the 25th ult. formally opened the new sewage disposal works, which have been constructed by the Launceston Corporation from the designs, and under the superintendence of, Mr. A. P. I. Cotterell, M.I.C.E., of Bristol.

The system of purification adopted is said to embody some unique features. After passing the screens and mixing race (ferozone being the precipitant used), the sewage enters a vertical precipitation tank, passes by an iron pipe to the bottom, rises slowly to the surface, and then escapes through copper screens into the effluent channel. While thus rising the sewage is broken up by anaerobic micro-organisms, much of the solids in solution and suspension being liquefied, whilst the remainder falls to the bottom of the tank and gradually collects inside a conical base. The clarified liquid next passes on to biological filters, which contain layers of polarite. A novel feature in connection with the filters is that the liquid is discharged on to perforated corrugated galvanized-iron plates, and passing along them drips through the perforations on to the filtering material beneath. The effluent, it is stated, issues from the filters as clean water and in a high state of purity.

**Business Announcement.**—Mr. John Parker, proprietor of Hassall's patent safety joint for sanitary pipes, and director of Hamblet's, Limited, has removed his offices from Brougham Chambers, Nottingham, to 16 Long-row, Nottingham.

## ABERGAVENNY WATER SUPPLY.

On the 27th ult. the members of the Abergavenny Urban District Council paid a visit of inspection to their waterworks at Llwyndu, where extensions and improvements have been recently carried out from the plans of Mr. J. Haigh, engineer and surveyor to the council.

On arriving at the waterworks the members were received by Major Williams, the chairman of the Water Committee, who congratulated them upon the possession of such a supply. We append the following brief description of the works:—

The supply is derived from mountain springs and received in small chambers of masonry. Up to the year 1886 no provision for storage had been made, consequently the night overflow went directly to waste in the open stream, and was of course unavailable for the town mains. Acting upon the advice of their engineer, the then Improvement Commissioners determined to construct an underground reservoir of 60,000 gallons capacity to receive the night overflow. This work was carried out in the year 1887, and proved to be a decided advantage, affording a constant supply under high pressure; but with the continued increase of population it was soon found that, even with the addition referred to, the arrangements were inadequate. The engineer therefore recommended the construction of a second underground reservoir of the same capacity as the first, to be fed from an adjoining stream. Drawings were prepared in 1896 and approved by the council. The works were executed in 1897, and have afforded an ample and constant supply to every house in the town during the whole of the dry summer of the present year.

The two reservoirs may be worked alternately, one filling while the other is feeding the main supply pipes. The work is in hard brick, Portland cement and White's Hygian rock composition giving a perfectly watertight result and security against contamination. In connection with the works there have been constructed some well-arranged filters and intercepting tanks, with the necessary by-passes, sluice valves, overflow pipes, wash-out valves and ventilators. In connection with the distribution the town has been divided into nine districts, for the purpose of waste detection by nine of Deacon's meters and outside stop-cocks on all services; and to make the system still more perfect, the council have recently adopted their engineer's scheme for constructing a high-level main which will connect with the extreme end of the existing main, making a complete circuit of the town, and by an arrangement of reducing valves the pressure over the whole distributing area will be made nearly equal. The ordinary working pressure will be maintained at about 90 lb. per square inch, but by means of sluices and by-passes the pressure for fire-extinguishing purposes can be increased to 175 lb. if required. The supply is by natural gravitation. The whole of the works mentioned have been designed by Mr. J. Haigh, the council's engineer, and executed in a substantial manner under his personal supervision, the cost being £2,500.

The council expressed great satisfaction upon what they had seen, both with regard to the design and manner of execution of the works and the ample and pure supply of water secured.

## "THE IMMOVABLE LOCAL GOVERNMENT BOARD."

Under the above heading, The Manchester City News, on the 29th ult., published the following editorial note:—

A fortnight ago we drew attention to the stupidity and red-tapeism of the Local Government Board in refusing its sanction to the expenditure of £16 for the drainage of the park-keepers' lodges which the Salford Corporation propose to erect in Ordsall and Albert Parks. The ground of refusal was that the corporation had not carried out the requirements of the board in the matter of acquiring land for the purpose of sewage filtration. The council thereupon requested the three members for the borough to see Mr. Chaplin, president of the board, and bring before him the "unreasonable position taken up by the board" in this trumpery affair. One would have thought that the bluff commonsense of Mr. Chaplin would have settled the business in three seconds, but officialdom has been too strong for him. He has signed a long letter to Mr. Lees Knowles, M.P., in reply to the representations made to him. It is an historical survey of the position from the beginning, the inquiries and recommendations of the board, and the reports from the joint committee in regard to the character of the effluent, and ends by saying that the board cannot retreat from its position, and must refuse its sanction to the expenditure of £16. The lodges will not go without drains, of course, but the obstinacy of the Local Government Board is surely without parallel in the annals of official red-tapery. The first cost to Salford for interest and sinking fund for land filtration, even if suitable land was procurable in a convenient situation, would not be less than an increase on the rates of 3d. in the £1, and working expenses would probably be another 3d. But if the Local Government Board can block a small expenditure for drains of two houses, what is to be done for the 600 or 800 houses which are yearly being erected in Salford? The controversy between the Salford Corporation and the untenable Local Government Board is a suggestive one as it stands, and its solution will be interesting. The honours should remain with the corporation.

# The Sanitary Institute.

## THE SEVENTEENTH ANNUAL CONGRESS.—VII.

As mentioned in our last issue, we are now in a position to illustrate Mr. Scott-Moncrieff's interesting and valuable paper (see p. 572) on "The Biolysis of Sewage" by some very useful diagrams, to which he referred in the course of his remarks, and which are of material assistance in following the paper. The first diagram shown by Mr. Scott-Moncrieff included Figs. 1, 2, 3, 4, 5 and 6, illustrative of the apparatus used in his experiments, Fig. 1 being a plan, Fig. 2 a longitudinal and Fig. 3 a transverse section of what has been generally called a "cultivation tank." In describing the first apparatus of this kind, which was constructed in 1891 and is still in use, Mr. Scott-Moncrieff said: "It is about 2½ ft. wide, 10 ft. in length, and about 3 ft. deep at the deepest part. The entire sewage discharges and waste waters from a household of ten to twelve persons, with the exception of the grease—which is held back as far as possible by a grease trap—find their way into one end of this tank, at the point CC. The liquid portion rises through a perforated grating, E, and

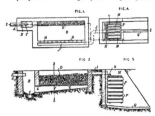

FIG. 1.    FIG. 4.

FIG 2    FIG 5

then through a layer of flints till it reaches the level of the outflow pipe, JJ, which is about 2 in. below the level of the invert of the drain, AA. The depth of the filtering material is only about 14 in."

The arrangement of the trap is shown in Figs. 4, 5 and 6, as well as in Figs. 7, 8, 9 and 10. This apparatus was described as follows: "I constructed nine wooden boxes with perforated bottoms, each of them 2 ft. long by 7 in. wide by 7 in. deep, an allowance of ⅛ in. on each side being made so that each box had an effective area of 1 square foot, through which the effluent passed. These boxes I placed one above the other upon a framework, and filled them to a depth of 6 in. in each box with coke, broken so as to pass through a ring 1 in. diameter. Over the uppermost box I fixed two small tilting V-shaped trays, which automatically discharged their contents when the liquid reached a level that upset their equilibrium, as they were hung upon small trunnions

fixed at the proper point to effect this movement, working upon supports fixed to the ends of the highest box. Over this column of boxes a large tank was fixed, into which the effluent was pumped after it came through the cultivation tank. The flow of the effluent was so regulated and measured that an estimate could at any moment be made of the rate

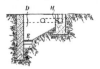

FIG. 3.

in terms of gallons per acre per twenty-four hours. Between each of the boxes there was an air space of about 2 in., and a receptacle was provided at the bottom which held about twelve hours' flow. By placing shallow dishes between the boxes samples could be taken simultaneously, and a complete set of analyses of the whole series of changes could be made consecutively."

Fig. 11 is a chart showing the changes which occur in successive stages of purification, the nitrogen lines being

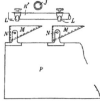

FIG. 6.

specially indicated. Fig. 12 is also a chart showing changes in successive stages of purification. In regard to these Mr. Scott-Moncrieff said: "It occurred to me that the arrangement as described could be used to obtain graphic illustrations of the changes as they took place, and the nitrogen lines are shown upon Chart 1. All the other changes can be graphically

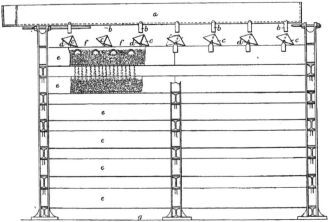

FIG. 7.

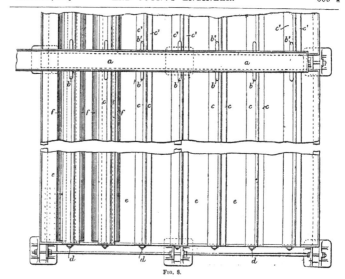

FIG. 8.

shown in a similar manner, and when these are superimposed one upon the other a complete view is obtained of how they are related to each other. The lines of increase crossing the lines of decrease afford a practically perfect method of obtaining information as to what is going on, and a curious setting back of the lines of increase with a corresponding change in the line of oxygen consumed in the case of the 5th colony pointed to a critical state of the biological conditions at that part of the process; that is shown upon Chart No. 2."

We may appropriately supplement the papers dealing with sewage disposal, which we have given at more or less length, by an abstract of the long and interesting lecture, given before the congress by Dr. Christopher Childs, M.A., M.D.OXON., D.P.H., lecturer on bacteriology in relation to hygiene, University College, London, who took for his subject the important question of river pollution.

### LECTURE TO THE CONGRESS.
### THE PREVENTION OF POLLUTION OF OUR STREAMS AND RIVERS.

After some introductory remarks of a general character and a reference to recent contributions on the subject, Dr. Childs said that it was commonly admitted that the Rivers Pollution Act of 1876 had generally and persistently failed in the purpose for which it was intended, and that pollution had very generally continued and progressed unchecked in defiance of the law and of the many efforts made to reduce it. He then proceeded to refer to difficulties in the way of reform. The chief difficulties in the way of the much-desired reforms were the ignorance and indifference of the people; the great cost of sewage purification and the uncertainty with regard to the best means to be employed; and last, but not least, the defects in the law itself and the impotence of the measures provided for its administration. The ignorance was of different kinds and degrees, was common to all classes, and could only be dispelled by systematic, persistent and widespread education in such matters as the laws of nature, the laws of health, the nature and causes of diseases which are conveyed through water, and of the ways in which such diseases are spread from man to his neighbour or to a large community. As to the cost and uncertainty of sewage purification methods, they might congratulate themselves that there was a definite prospect that these two difficulties would be reduced to a minimum. The researches and practical results obtained by the Massachusetts State Board of Health, Scott-Moncrieff, Dibdin, Dupré, Cameron and others, plainly demonstrated that the great difficulty, uncertainty and cost of purification which had blocked the way for so many years had been in a large measure due to our misconception of the true principles by which we should be guided in dealing with domestic sewage. We had persistently endeavoured to thwart and destroy these natural agents for the purification of foul matters, the liquefying and nitrifying bacteria, as if they were our greatest foes, instead of our best

and most indispensable allies. The discovery and practical application of the so-called biological methods of purification formed one of the greatest triumphs of modern sanitary science. Those methods had been on trial for sufficient time and on a sufficiently large scale to prove that they had to a great extent solved the clue to this most difficult and complicated problem. If they finally and completely succeeded they would remove the chief practical difficulties which blocked the way, and would save the country the annual expenditure of many millions.

OBJECTS AND MEANS OF PURIFICATION.

Dr. Childs then proceeded to consider the exact objects to be aimed at in the process of sewage purification and the means by which such purification might be obtained and secured. The chief object in the purification of sewage was to secure that the effluent from any sewage, manufacturing process, or filth accumulation to any "stream" (as defined in Clause 20 of the Rivers Pollution Prevention Act, of 1876), shall be purified in such a way that it shall not cause the water of the stream to be poisonous or dangerous to the health of those who drink it, nor be detrimental to the manufactures for which it may be used, nor offensive to the sight or smell, nor destructive to fish, nor obstructive to the flow of the stream. Of these conditions, that which made the water poisonous or dangerous to the health of those who drank it was the most important for our consideration and the most difficult to define. Proceeding to define the term " poisonous " or " dangerous to health," Dr. Childs said that from the time when serious attention was given to the pollution of our streams by foul matters, culminating in the work of the Rivers Pollution Commission of 1868, great stress had rightly been laid upon the amount of effete organic matter in the effluents and in the water used for drinking purposes. The limits of the amount of organic matter to be allowed in any effluent, as gauged with the help of Frankland's method by the amount of organic carbon and organic nitrogen in a given quantity of the fluid effluent, were laid down in the well-known suggestions of the Rivers Pollution Commission. At that time, however, the germ theory of disease was hardly known, bacteria were not recognised as the active agents, the vera causa of infectious diseases, and consequently the amount of organic matter in an effluent or in water became the recognised chief test of the danger or safety of those fluids. Now, although the amount of organic matter (and of certain inorganic compounds, such as chlorides) in a natural water was the most delicate test and indication of contamination with animal or vegetable matter, whilst in an effluent it was a measure of the putrescible matter which still remained to be oxidised, it could not be too much insisted upon that the amount of organic matter in an effluent or in water, as gauged by any of the recognised chemical methods (Frankland's, Wanklyn's, Tidy's and others), was not a test of the actual poisonous character of those fluids. Proceeding to further elaborate the subject, Dr. Childs said :—

" It is generally accepted that water polluted by sewage

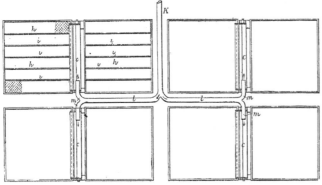

Fig. 9.

is always dangerous to health, and frequently the actual cause of outbreaks of cholera and typhoid fever. But it does not follow that the quantity or quality of organic matter which is dissolved in the water determines these outbreaks. In fact, water strongly contaminated with sewage may be drunk for an indefinite time without causing cholera or typhoid fever. It is necessary to lay stress upon these statements, because there is a tendency to regard a sewage effluent as "purified" when the putrescible matter contained in it is reduced down to a certain standard, whilst the idea, even in these days, seems to be prevalent that the actual poisonous or wholesome character of water for drinking may be decided simply by chemical analysis. It is only under certain conditions that water so polluted causes these diseases, those conditions being the introduction of the specific poisons of cholera or of typhoid fever under circumstances favourable for their development and convection. The poisons of cholera and typhoid fever, it has long been known, are contained in the excreta of patients suffering from those diseases, and according to the accepted teachings of bacteriology, those poisons consist of living bacteria, the *spirillum choleræ Asiaticæ* of Koch, and the *bacillus typhosus* of Eberth and Gaffky. Water strongly contaminated with sewage, unless it contains the bacterium of cholera or typhoid, cannot cause cholera or typhoid fever, any more than grapes may be gathered from thorns or figs from thistles. Though the quantity and quality of organic matter in any water are of great importance as an index of the degree, kind and source of pollution, they are not a measure of danger or safety. The real factor which determines the danger or safety of water for drinking purposes is the presence or absence of living germs of disease, the 'pathogenic bacteria.'"

Continuing, Dr. Childs said it must be admitted that but few diseases had definitely been proved to be due to drinking water contaminated with human excreta, for most authorities agreed that cholera and typhoid fever were the only diseases conveyed in this country by drinking water. It was probable, however, that diarrhœa and various ill-defined low states of health might be conveyed in the same way. As cholera was now practically banished from our shores, it followed that, having regard to the public health, the most important object in sewage purification was the destruction of those micro-organisms which were recognised as the cause of typhoid fever, the *bacilli typhosi* of Eberth and Gaffky. But the first step for the prevention of infection in our water supplies by the fever poison was not the purification of the sewage, but the destruction of the fever germs before they had escaped from the sick-room of the patient into the soil, the sewers or the drinking water. When the typhoid bacillus had been allowed to escape alive into the drain or cesspit, or other receptacle, it became most difficult to trace or detect it, or to destroy it effectively with germicidal agents. The first step for the prevention of the pollution of our water supplies began at the bedside of the typhoid fever patient, and thus a great responsibility lay with the nurse for the protection both of herself and of others. Disinfection in cases of typhoid fever was probably most imperfectly performed throughout the country. If complete disinfection were carried out in all cases of typhoid fever that disease would rapidly disappear, and the dangers resulting from sewage pollution of our water supplies would be greatly reduced. Dr. Childs then proceeded to consider the means available for the destruction of the typhoid bacilli and other pathogenic bacteria when they had once gained an entrance into sewage. He said :—

"There are no direct experimental proofs that the bacilli of typhoid fever are destroyed in sewage by any of the pro-

cesses of purification at present in use. Nor is there much prospect of obtaining such proof at present, owing to the great and special difficulty of detecting and verifying the presence of these bacilli in such fluids as sewage. This difficulty can only be fully realised by those who have had large experience in such investigations, and is due partly to the absence of any specific active properties peculiar to these bacilli (except, perhaps, in the "serum test"), partly to the strong resemblance between these bacilli and many others which almost invariably accompany them—notably those known as 'the bacilli of the coli group.' It is generally admitted that many of our best bacteriologists have been deceived by this resemblance, and that, though the presence of *bacilli typhosi* have frequently been reported in suspected waters, it is very doubtful whether the bacilli have actually been isolated and verified, even where the water has been contaminated by excreta of typhoid fever patients.

"The experiments of Laws and Andrewes, it is true, indicate that sewage does not form a medium in which much, if any, growth is possible for the *bacilli typhosi* under natural conditions, and that their death is only the matter of a few days, or at most a few weeks (Report to London County Council, 1894). Until the results obtained by these observers have been corroborated by repeated experiments under similar and under varied conditions it would be inadvisable to form a final conclusion or to base any practical system upon them. An exhaustive investigation of the quality and quantity of micro-organisms to be found in the sewage effluents obtained by different processes at present in use is much to be desired. But such investigations are very difficult, can only be conducted by skilled bacteriologists of great

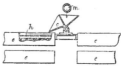

Fig. 10.

experience, and will require a long time for their completion. Similar information is needed with regard to the vitality of typhoid bacilli in various kinds of water."

Such experiments were also carried on in this country as well as on the Continent, and Dr. Childs made special reference to the work of Dr. Houston in making bacteriological analysis of the crude London sewage.

NATURAL AGENCIES.

Dr. Childs then went on to discuss the question, How far might we trust to natural agencies for the destruction of the *bacilli typhosi* when they have been conveyed by a sewage effluent into a large river, such as the Severn or the Thames? There, again, there was no experimental proof, owing to the difficulties already mentioned. It had been shown that those bacilli can live from one to three weeks in ordinary drinking water, but it was possible that they might live longer. From our general knowledge of them and by analogy we might infer that the chances were against their living very long in river water. They did not form spores, and were therefore not very resistant to adverse conditions. It had been shown that sunlight had a weakening and inhibitory effect upon them, and probably diminished their virulence. It was conceivable that before long some practical and economical method might be devised for completely sterilising sewage effluents, so that no living organisms—pathogenic or nou-pathogenic—might escape in them into the stream. Medical statistics and epidemiological facts supplied abundant evidence that the typhoid mortality in towns and cities supplied with water from upland surfaces did not seem to be less than that of towns and cities deriving their water supplies from rivers, provided that the river water is efficiently filtered. Such appeared to be the case on the Continent, in America, and in our own country. The evidence, however, was fragmentary and incomplete, and required most careful investigation before any final judgment could be formed from it. He was at present engaged in an inquiry with regard to the typhoid mortality of the chief towns and cities of the world in relation to their water supply, soil, drainage and other conditions, but it would be long before he would have sufficient evidence for the formation of a definite conclusion. If they could obtain sufficient evidence, extended over many years, with regard to the mortality from typhoid fever among several millions of people drinking water from a river which had been contaminated by sewage, and compared that mortality with the mortality of several millions supplied with water never so contaminated, other conditions being equal, we should have the conditions of an experiment on a vast scale, from which we might hope to form reliable conclusions.

Such conditions we had in the history of our great metropolis. According to the evidence brought before the Royal Commission on the Metropolitan Water Supply (1893), the typhoid mortality in London was exceptionally low. When compared with that of fourteen other great English towns " that have public water supplies which are not excrementally polluted," during the period 1881-90 it was found to be a very little higher than that of four of these large towns, and lower than that of the remaining ten. Moreover, all the medical, chemical and bacteriological experts examined by the commission stated unhesitatingly that they knew of no single instance in which the consumption of London water had caused disease. People were differently impressed by the significance of these facts. Some were convinced that water supplied under such conditions as obtained in London must be regarded as reasonably safe. Such was the opinion of the majority of the Royal Commission for the Prevention of the Pollution of Rivers of 1868 and the unanimous conviction of the Royal Commission previously referred to. Others, again, did not consider the water derived from the Thames and Lee could ever be used for drinking purposes with reasonable safety, even though the sewage effluents which entered those rivers be " purified to the highest extent known to science." Referring to the case of Altona, Dr. Child said that in the great cholera epidemic at Hamburg in the autumn of 1892 the contiguous town of Altona was comparatively free from the disease, although the source of the supply from the Elbe was far more polluted than that of Hamburg. The escape of Altona was generally attributed to the fact that the water supply was submitted to careful sand filtration, " whilst in Hamburg the Elbe water was distributed in its raw condition as taken from the river." Nevertheless a gross flaw in the Altona filters was suffered to pass unnoticed in the following December, and was detected only when too late by a sharp outbreak of disease among those supplied with water from the defective filter. " One of the filters which had been cleaned during the frost had become frozen over, and was in consequence not able to retain the bacteria," a fact which was subsequently proved by bacteriological examination of the water derived from this special filter. It was imperative that water supplied from any river or other source which had been polluted in the least degree by sewage or organic matter, after adequate storage and sedimentation, should be subjected to complete and carefully-managed sand filtration before being distributed into the water mains. Dr. Childs disclaimed any desire to plead on one side or the other, but felt compelled to adopt and uphold the following principles:—

" (1) That where a community is able to obtain a water supply free from the possibility of any contamination, instead of one liable to such contamination, that community is bound, for the sake of the safety and the welfare of its citizens, to procure the supply which is above suspicion. (2) That in cases where there is no alternative but to use the water of some adjoining river, or other source liable to pollution, no measures should be neglected whereby poisonous and noxious elements may be prevented from finding entrance into the water, and whereby the last traces of such poisonous elements, if they have found entrance, may with certainty be removed through the best means available."

Birmingham was to be congratulated on having acquired an unrivalled and magnificent watershed among the mountains of Wales, through which an ample and pure supply was secured for its growing population, the whole gathering

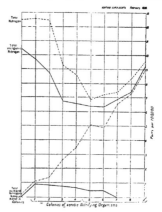

FIG. 11.

ground and every tributary and spring being the property and under the protection of the corporation. After a visit to the works he could bear evidence to the grandeur and completeness of this colossal triumph of engineering skill and human enterprise. To many towns and cities such irreproachable watersheds were impossible, and they had to rely upon neighbouring streams or rivers for their supply. Serious and complicated difficulties were felt owing to the competition for upland water supplies.

It would be seen that bacteriological and epidemiological evidence gave little or no help in deciding on " the best practicable and reasonably available means " for destroying the pathogenic bacteria in sewage. In the meantime they must be content with those means which are best for purifying an effluent to the extent that it will not cause putrefactive or other offensive processes in a stream. The difficulty of exactly defining this expression, " the best practical and available means," had proved one of the many obstacles to progress. The treatment by irrigation on land which had so generally been insisted upon (subsequent to filtration and

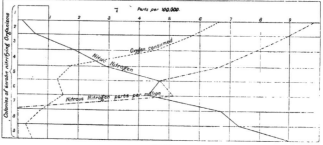

FIG. 12.

precipitation, or to both) had proved a heavy tax to many communities and a frequent obstacle to the adoption of any process of purification at all. In many cases either the high cost of land or its utter unsuitability for the purpose, or its position, had prevented it from being anything like available or practicable. But there was every reason for hoping that by the new biological methods recently established a way would be found by which the difficulties might be overcome; and though these methods might not altogether supplant that of irrigation, they would no doubt simplify the process in some cases, diminish the amount of land required, and in others do away with the necessity for land altogether. Whichever biological system proved the best, it had undoubtedly been shown that by withholding chemicals altogether, and by placing the countless hosts of bacteria which thronged every drop of domestic sewage under conditions favourable for their development and activity, the solid materials of sewage might be broken down and liquefied, and subsequently oxidised so as to form a clear and non-putrescible effluent. How far these methods would succeed in dealing with the manifold and complicated materials which were presented in sewage mixed with trade effluents remained to be seen. Almost every noxious and offensive trade effluent that existed was probably represented in Lancashire and West Riding, and as experiments had been for some time carried on at Leeds, Bradford and Sheffield, besides many other places, we should probably learn before long to what extent the biological processes were interfered with by these effluents, and also the means by which this interference might be checked or altogether counteracted.

In regard to standard effluents, Dr. Childs said that the conditions under which those standards had to be determined were so various, and there was so much difference of opinion with regard to them among authorities, that it seemed impossible to define them, although they would greatly facilitate the labours of all those who were concerned with the prevention of pollution. With regard to sewage, however, the principle on which a standard of purity should be formed might be defined—viz., that the effluent shall be purified in such a way that it would not undergo offensive putrefaction either by itself or when mixed with the stream into which it flows. With regard to trade effluents it was to be hoped that the present Royal Commission would lay down some definite lines. Meanwhile the settlement of standards might be made in friendly conference between manufacturers and river committees, as had been done in some instances with satisfactory results.

Proceeding to consider the law for the prevention of pollution, Dr. Childs said the Rivers Pollution Act of 1876 was universally condemned as a dead letter, the failure having been due chiefly to the faulty and imperfect arrangements for the administration of the law and to certain defects and difficulties in the Act itself. "The powers for taking action against pollution were entrusted to the sanitary authorities, and were enabling, not compulsory. Now, considering that the sanitary authorities were too often the greatest polluters, and were constantly subjected to the influence of local and vested interests, and the incessant cry for the reduction of the rates, it was not to be wondered at that the administration of these Acts has not been attended with success."[*]

COUNTY COUNCILS.

Great hopes were entertained that with the establishment of county councils by the Act of 1888 the indifference and opposition of interested or ignorant individuals and of the smaller local authorities would be overwhelmed and carried along by the larger and more powerful organisation. Unfortunately, the administration of the law for the prevention of pollution, which was still purely optional, was from its very nature unpopular and likely to be avoided. It could only be carried out thoroughly by men who would systematically devote much time and care to this duty, and would not be unduly influenced by local and vested interests, or by the clamour of short-sighted and parsimonious ratepayers. Several of the county councils no doubt had done and were doing much for the prevention of pollution. But all efforts for improvement must be hampered and curtailed by the defects and difficulties at present existing in the Act of 1876. These defects and difficulties were: (1) The vagueness and incompleteness of many of the terms, such as the definitions of polluting matters, liquid sewage, &c. (clauses 2 and 3); (2) The expense, delay and uncertainty involved in the restrictions imposed when any authority proposes to enforce the enactment for preventing pollution; (3) The absence of deterrent penalties ; (4) The absence of power of entry.

These defects were a serious impediment to action, as the joint committees of the Mersey and Irwell and of the West Riding of Yorkshire soon discovered when they began seriously and systematically to deal with the overwhelming sources of pollution which prevailed in their respective districts. No time was lost by these committees in appealing to Parliament for special Acts "to make more effectual provision for prevention of pollution," on the ground that "the restrictions contained in the Act (of 1876) were such as to preclude effective action." Parliament acknowledged the justice and the reasonableness of the appeal by giving assent, and the necessary Acts were passed. And yet a private Bill

* "Waterborne Typhoid Fever." *Journal of the Sanitary Institute,* vol. xix., p. 248.

which embodied all these reforms had been before the House of Commons for years. This Bill, modelled on the Acts of the Mersey and Irwell Joint Committee and the West Riding Rivers Board, remedied the defects which he had mentioned. It defined and catalogued the various possible kinds of polluting effluents, granted powers of entry to authorities for the taking of samples, and, whilst it amply protected the manufacturer from undue embarrassment and expenditure, it provided for the proper administration of the law, and the infliction of appropriate penalties upon actual offenders with as little cost, delay and uncertainty as possible. It had been pointed out, however, that the Bill as it at present stood was weaker in several respects than either of the Acts upon which it was based. The following were some of the points left undecided by the present Bill : The settlement of the question of the right of a manufacturer to discharge his trade refuse into a public sewer, or of the right of a sanitary authority to refuse to allow him so to discharge it ; the prohibition of the sludging of mill dams; the power to cause obstruction to the flow of stream to be removed ; the absolute prohibition of any new pollutions; and the proper supervision of the discharge of compensation water. Dr. Childs, however, strongly urged his hearers to support the passing of the Bill, even in its present form, either as a private Bill or as a Bill taken up by the Government. The amendment of the intrinsic defects in the Rivers Pollution Prevention Act would, without doubt, greatly facilitate and promote the abolition of much of the lawless and disreputable pollution which prevailed throughout the United Kingdom. On this subject Dr. Childs further remarked :—

"There still remains, however, the great difficulty of getting councils, boroughs and county boroughs to combine and insist that the law shall be duly observed throughout the whole watersheds in which they are situated. A borough or a county council may do its best to set its own house in order to prevent and abolish all pollution within its borders, but it is almost powerless to remove pollution—except when of the grossest and most intolerable kind—in parts of the stream and rivers which are higher up. The sources and tributaries of a river, for instance, which are above a given town or county may each contribute its share of pollution until the sum total of impurity in the main stream becomes intolerably offensive. Yet it will be very difficult to bring conviction home to the individual offenders.

"The solution of the difficulty lies in the formation of joint committees, who shall have the supervision and control over whole watersheds, or groups of streams and rivers; committees which shall be fairly representative of all the local interests concerned—of councils and water companies, manufacturers and industries—strong and extensive enough to resist the undue influence of local interests and local jealousies, and to overcome the *vis inertiæ* of ignorance and indifference ; and whose sole business it shall be to administer the law promptly and without fear or favour for the protection of the waters within their district. This is no paper scheme based on theoretical considerations. The Act of 1888 provides for such an organisation in clause 81, whereby the formation of such joint committees is sanctioned and regulated.

"The idea of the watershed as a proper area for administration is not at all new, but has been advocated by many competent authorities. In April of this year Mr. Middleton read a very interesting paper to the Institute on the desirability of making watershed areas and sanitary district coterminous. This proposition, however commendable, involves such a revolution and such an intricate shifting and resetting of our whole social organisation that it is not likely to find much favour. But for the constitution of joint committees for the prevention of pollution no new authorities are required. The existing authorities, who have not sufficient time, and who for reasons previously mentioned are not well qualified to carry out the work thoroughly, will merely depute their office to an authority provided for and sanctioned by the existing statute."

The principal watershed areas in England and Wales differed greatly in size. In some cases a conjoint committee was evidently undesirable, and in various cases the county council would be the more suitable central authority, but in that case it would be desirable to depute the work to a special representative board. Fortunately there were a few joint committees in existence which in their constitution, methods of work and results produced presented excellent models for the whole kingdom. Those were the Thames and Lee Conservancy Boards, the Mersey and Irwell Conjoint Committee.

Dr. Childs then proceeded to give some details of the constitution of these bodies, the methods employed, and the results obtained, after which reference was made to the responsibilities of waterworks companies and their relations to sanitary authorities, the conclusion arrived at being that under the existing state of the law the obligations laid on the companies are so insufficient that we have no ground for confidence in the power or desire of the companies to secure us against the introduction of poisonous material into the water with which they supply us. But after the disastrous epidemics of recent times the necessary reforms should be insisted upon at the earliest opportunity. The lecturer concluded as follows :—

"Parliament also appears to be ready for action, for although the clauses proposed by Mr. Chaplin last June, to be added—with a view to protecting the consumers—to twenty-one private Water Bills were withdrawn, the withdrawal was urged upon technical grounds, and all who spoke on the subject appeared to be ready to support those clauses if introduced in a public Bill. On looking at these clauses of Mr. Chaplin's I am astounded to find that the provision which, in my mind, is by far the most important one has been entirely omitted—viz., the regular and constant inspection and supervision of all parts of the water supply—from source to distribution. Instead of that, the taking and examination of samples is entirely relied upon for the detection and prevention of pollution. Combined with thorough and regular inspection of the water supply, it is true, chemical and bacteriological analyses can be of great service, for they can give indication of pollution which could not be detected merely by inspection. If relied upon alone, they give a false sense of security. Even if the analyses were made daily, they would not enable us to prevent pollution; they can only detect the pollution after it has taken place.

"As a rule, water-borne outbreaks of typhoid fever occur with explosive violence; so that most of the victims have imbibed the poison before the alarm conveyed by the means of analysis can possibly save them from infection. It is to be hoped that these reforms will be carried out as seen as possible, and that the serious omission with regard to inspection will be remedied. I trust, however, that amidst the agitation which springs out of recent calamity and alarm the old-standing evil will not be forgotten; that the nation will awake to a sense of the disgrace, loss and danger which must always exist as long as this foul and illegal pollution of our streams is suffered to continue. If the idea of constituting joint committees to control whole watersheds or groups of streams, according to circumstances and convenience, be approved of, I appeal to the Institute, to this congress, to all concerned in the health and welfare of the nation, to do all that is possible to urge the Local Government Board that they shall give every facility and encouragement for the formation of such joint committees. But, above all, I hope and trust that you and all who are so concerned will give cordial support to the Rivers Pollution Prevention Bill, by which the defective Act of 1876 will be amended, and through which we may hope eventually for the total abolition of the pollution of our streams and rivers throughout the United Kingdom."

The closing meeting in connection with the congress took place on Thursday, in Birmingham, the lord mayor presiding. The report of the local officers stated that the congress had been successful in all respects. The number of tickets issued exceeded those of any previous year, and the attendances were in like proportion. The total number of tickets issued was 1,979, as compared with 1,531 at Leeds last year, 1,225 at Newcastle in 1896, and 1,214 in Liverpool in 1895. The number of visitors to the Health Exhibition this year was 85,212, and was 10,000 greater than had been previously attained. Councillor Martineau submitted the financial statement, which showed that the general expenses of the congress amounted to £1,463. The amount of the guarantee fund to be called up was £1,460 14s. 7d., which would necessitate a call of 14s. 9d. in the £1 being made upon the guarantors. The report was adopted, and a vote of thanks was passed to the hon. treasurer (Councillor Martineau) and to the hon. secretaries (Messrs. A. Bostock Hill, W. B. Marshall and J. S. Wilcox). The chairman, in replying to a vote of thanks, expressed satisfaction at the success which had attended the meetings. There was a feeling of reality about the congress which impressed him very much, and he felt that the city had benefitted by his visit.

**Burnham, Somerset.**—It has been unanimously resolved by the district council to extend the new sea front from the pier further northwards to a point near Catherine-terrace, instead of to the church. This will involve a further outlay of £2,000, making in all £9,000. It has therefore been decided to petition the Local Government Board to grant the extended loan without holding a further public inquiry.

**Tenders Wanted.**—The Secretary of State for Foreign Affairs has received a despatch from her Majesty's Consul at Genoa stating that tenders are invited by the municipality of Spezzia for the supply of 2,500 tons of gas-coal for the municipal gasworks. Sealed tenders must be received at the municipality of Spezzia by 10 a.m. on the 10th inst. A copy and translation of the conditions of contract may be examined at the Commercial Department of the Foreign Office any day between the hours of 11 a.m. and 5 p.m. The Secretary of State has also received a despatch from her Majesty's Consul-General at Christiania, stating that tenders are invited by the town engineer of the port of Stavanger for the delivery of 4,800 water and drain pipes of different sizes. Tenders in sealed envelopes, marked "Anbud paa Rör," should be addressed to "Stavanger-Stadsingeniörkontor, Stavanger," where they should be received by the 15th inst. In view of the short time given to the tenderers, persons desirous of obtaining further information with respect to the above tender are recommended to apply direct by telegraph to Mr. Vice-Consul Berentsen, at Stavanger.

## THE TESTING OF CEMENT.

There is the promise of a useful enterprise in the Cement Users' Testing Association which has just been established and which should satisfy a manifest want. As the promoters of the enterprise truly enough remark, upon the testing of no class of structural materials do opinions differ so widely as upon cement. "A perusal of half-a-dozen different specifications (for the same class of work) reveals at once the absence of any agreed opinion among engineers, architects and surveyors as to the tensile and other standards which it is desirable to adopt. A few hours spent in watching various manipulators working at the mixing table shows a yet greater divergence in the practice of briquette-making. It is safe to say that at the present time there is not even an approximation to a standard specification of requirements, and, further, there is no standard method of mixing, so that a series of tests made by one experimenter will often not compare with the results obtained from the same cement by another. Most diverse and anomalous results are continually obtained, and, so far from affording a true gauge of the character of cement, many of the tests now made are entirely useless. There are two absolute ideas which must be banished by users of cement in constructional works:—

"(1) The fact of brickwork being 'in cement' or of concrete being made with 'Portland cement' is not any evidence *per se* of special excellence or durability in either material.

"(2) The fact of a cement standing a 350-lb. tensile strain per square inch seven days after mixing is not sufficient to prove that the work upon which it is used will prove a success; other tests are required, and *by itself the tensile test is of little guidance.*

"There is at present no material more important to the engineer or architect than is cement, and no material in use on public works is so completely at the mercy of the individual idiosyncrasies of the experimenter. This must to some extent remain the case until the users of Portland cement are brought into line in drafting their specification, and adopt some definite method of mixing which will eliminate individuality in the manufacture of briquettes.

"The advantage of submitting cement to an expert is obvious. The ordinary individual who is in charge of construction has no plant or time for anything but the most simple tensile test, which has been shown to be unsatisfactory. For a comprehensive report it is needful to have before one—(1) Specific gravity; (2) tensile test on a large section; (3) transverse breaking weight; (4) fineness to which ground; (5) condition as to heating; (6) analysis. It is not, of course, essential to carry out the whole of the above tests every time a sample is taken; but to secure a thoroughly sound material the manufacturer should be made aware that his cement may at any moment be subjected to examination on all the above points."

The object of the Cement Users' Testing Association is to undertake the testing of Portland cement under standard conditions and on the most moderate terms. Users of cement are therefore saved from the necessity of setting up expensive plant and the expenditure of the time and trouble necessary to obtain a correct estimate of the value of the material. Full particulars as to the manner of making the tests, the analysis of samples, specifications, fees, &c., can be obtained on application to the general secretary of the association, Mr. Edmund S. Spencer, B.SC., 136 Shaftesbury-avenue, W.C.

## ARTESIAN WELL SUPPLIES.

On the 4th inst., at a meeting of the Rhondda Urban District Council, Mr. W. D. Wright, agent of the Pentre, Gelli and Tynybedw Collieries, submitted a scheme which he maintained would enable the council, by boring to the limestone strata at Treherbert, to obtain a supply of 50,000 gallons of water per hour. The depth of the boring would be about 1,500 ft. He had had much experience in the matter in a district where 300,000 population were supplied by water pumped out of five wells sunk to the limestone strata. The risk of speculating to obtain water from the limestone strata was insignificant, because they were thoroughly saturated. The cost would be small compared with the enormous expense which would have to be incurred in tunnelling at Llyn Fawr from Blaenrhondda and constructing a huge reservoir there. The water would rise to sea level, and the depth to that part was about 600 ft. where he proposed sinking at Treherbert. He estimated the cost of the whole of the plant, the pumping machinery included, at £10,000.

**Indian Survey Report.**—We have to acknowledge the receipt from Major-General C. Strahan, R.E., Surveyor-General of India, of a copy of the general report of the Survey of India Department of 1896-97.

**Jarrahdale Jarrah.**—The *Rallo* has arrived at Hull with 792 leads and the *Dag* at Lendon with 512 leads of Jarrahdale jarrah on board, to the order of the agent of the Jarrahdale Jarrah Forests and Railways, Limited, Francis Chapman, 1 Fenchurch-avenue, London, E.C.

# Auctioneers' Institute.

## THE DRAINAGE OF BUILDINGS : THE RIGHTS AND LIABILITIES OF OWNERS.

On Tuesday evening Mr. Alexander Macmorran, Q.C., read a paper before the Auctioneers' Institute on "The Effect of Recent Decisions on the Liabilities and Rights of Owners in Respect of the Drainage of Buildings." As the paper will no doubt interest a large majority of our readers we publish it in full.

Mr. MACMORRAN, in opening his remarks, said he did not propose in the course of the paper to lay before them an exhaustive summary of the law relating to sewers and drains, but rather to direct their attention to certain important points which had been the subject of recent decisions. But he hoped to do this in a connected way, indicating what the general law was as he went along. He also did not propose to deal with the law in so far as it related to the metropolis only. He had found that it would be impossible to do so in the course of a single paper, and, although he should have to refer to decisions in cases arising in London, he should do so only so far as they bore upon points which were common both to the country at large and to the metropolis.

Continuing, he said : The first point which it is necessary to emphasise is the distinction between a drain and a sewer. Under the Public Health Act, 1875, which applies to the whole country outside of the metropolis, a drain may be said to consist of a channel for the conveyance of drainage or sewage from one building, or from buildings within the same curtilage. I have made use of the expression

"CURTILAGE."

On the meaning of this word there have been two recent decisions. In the first of these (*Vestry of St. Martin-in-the-Fields* v. *Bird*, 1895, 1 Q.B., 428) it was held that the houses in the Lowther-arcade were not buildings in the same curtilage, although they all opened into a common passage, the ends of which were closed by gates at night and on Sundays. In the other (*Pilbrow* v. *Vestry of St. Leonard's, Shoreditch*, 1895, 1 Q.B., 433) two blocks of industrial buildings within the same enclosure, but separated by a causeway from which only one of them was entered, were held to be within the same curtilage. Both of these decisions relate to exceptional cases, which are not likely to recur. The Shoreditch case (in which, by the way, Lord Justice Rigby delivered a dissenting judgment) is not likely to be extended or followed except with reference to facts precisely similar. It may be said that a curtilage is the enclosure in which a house stands, or perhaps the space of ground which would pass by a simple conveyance of a house and its appurtenances. The drain, therefore, from a dwelling-house and the stables adjoining it, and contained within the same enclosure, would be a drain. A similar channel for drainage from the same house would be a sewer if the drains from the stables and adjoining premises were led into it. It would become a sewer, however, only from the point at which it received the drainage of the second building. So much for the distinction itself as contained in the interpretation clause of the statute. The importance of the distinction is obvious. The duty of repairing a drain and keeping it in good order, so as not to be a nuisance, is upon the owner or occupier of the premises drained. A sewer, on the other hand, belongs to, and is vested in, the local authority. The duty of repairing it, cleansing it, ventilating it, and keeping it so as not to be a nuisance, is imposed upon the local authority. Every owner of premises who can reach it without committing a trespass upon private land may lawfully connect the drains of his premises with it on the sole condition of giving notice to the local authority and complying with their regulations as to the manner in which the connection is to be made. He has this right even if the sewer discharges itself into a stream so as to be in contravention of the Rivers' Pollution Prevention Act, or otherwise causes a nuisance, for it is for the local authority to provide an outfall for the sewer which belongs to them. These are some of the more important points of distinction between a drain and a sewer, and they will be illustrated later in this paper.

WHAT IS A SEWER ?

I proceed now to point out that a channel for receiving drainage—I use this expression because I know of no other which is quite neutral—if it receives such drainage from more than one building is none the less a sewer vested in the local authority because it is laid in private ground. On this subject a case, decided in 1894, may be regarded as having opened the eyes at once of local authorities and of the public to the importance of the distinction already pointed out. The case is *Travis* v. *Utley*, 1894, 1 Q.B., 233. In that case there was a number of houses in a street belonging to one owner. Those houses had been drained in groups of three. The drain began, say, at No. 1, passed through No. 1 into the collar of No. 2, where it received the soil and other pipes of the house, thence passed into No. 3, where it received similar pipes, and then was carried out through the front of No. 3 into the street, in which a main sewer was laid. The local authority had found defects in this common drain, and they had required the owner to abate the nuisance consequent upon such defects. The owner refused. The case came before the magistrates,

and through them to the High Court, and it was held that the common drain was a sewer vested in the local authority, which they were bound to repair, and consequently that the nuisance complained of was one which they were bound to abate. This decision is important and involves serious consequences alike to the local authority and the owner of the property. In the first place the local authority must accept their liability to repair a common drain of this kind, although it is laid in private ground or even under private houses. On the other hand the owner must give them free access to his premises at all times when it may be necessary for them to inspect, alter or otherwise deal with the common drain, and he may not himself interfere with or in any way deal with it except with the consent of the local authority. In an urban district he cannot lawfully build over it without such consent. In the course of his judgment upon the case Mr. Justice Wills made use of some expressions which seemed to imply that, in his opinion, the entire drain, in *Travis* v. *Utley*, from the first house to its termination in the street was a sewer. But the same learned judge had afterwards reason to reconsider this in the case of the *Beckenham Urban District Council* v. *Wood* (CO J. P. 490), decided in 1896, which now establishes that a common drain such as this is only a sewer from the point at which it receives the drainage of the second house. This leads me naturally to bring to your notice a curious fact —namely, that in general, while a local authority have ample authority over private persons with reference to the making of drains from private houses, they have little or none in respect of the making of sewers except under private streets. In a rural district there is nothing to prevent a private person from making a drain to receive the drainage of two or more houses and making it as he may think fit ; yet, however badly it may be made, it will vest in the local authority and be repairable by them. There is no means by which such a person can be prevented from making it, or required to make it properly. This is undoubtedly the law in a rural district. It is also the law in an urban district, but with this important qualification—that with regard at least to a new house a district council may prescribe the manner in which that house is to be drained under sec. 25, and in this way may defeat the intention of an owner to make a combined system of drainage, with the result that the common drain would be a sewer of which they would have the burden of repair ; but however it may be made, if it is ever drained by two houses, it vests in the local authority. There was at one time some doubt whether a secret or a wrongful connection made with what would otherwise be a drain would have the effect of converting the drain into a sewer. In such a case the owner of the original drain would probably have a remedy against the trespasser ; but so far as the local authority were concerned, it is now well established that they must accept the *status quo*, and that, as between them and the private owners, the drain to which a secret or wrongful connection has been made is a sewer. The cases which establish this are, taking them in order of time : *Kershaw* v. *Taylor*, 1895 (2 Q.B. 208) ; *Holland* v. *Lazarus*, 1897 (66 L.J.Q. B. 285) ; and *Geen* v. *Newington Vestry*, 1898 (2 Q.B., 1). One other point while dealing with the subject of what is a sewer, may be mentioned. It is that there may be a sewer which is not covered, and that the common expression, "open sewer," is one which is recognised in law as well as in common talk. Thus, where the sewage of a number of houses drained into a pipe, and thence into an open watercourse, which in its turn ran into a brook, it was held that under the circumstances the open watercourse was a sewer within the meaning of the definition, that the local authority were charged with the duty of keeping it in proper condition, and might therefore enter upon the land where it was for the purpose of piping it in and cleansing it. This was the case of *Wheatcroft* v. *Matlock Local Board* (52 L.T. [N. S.], p. 356). It has since been decided that even a natural stream may have its character so altered by the sending of drainage into it from a large number of houses that it becomes a sewer. Such was the decision in *Falconer* v. *South Shields* (11 T. L. R., 223). It is obvious, however, that with regard to a natural watercourse the question must always be one of degree. It would be absurd to say that a considerable river or stream became a sewer merely because several houses drained directly into it. The true rule would appear to be that the stream must have lost its character of a natural stream and become substantially, if not exclusively, a conduit for the drainage of buildings in a district. I may here point out, however, that a conduit or channel may be a sewer, although it does not convey sewage in the ordinary sense of the term. The definition says that the expression "sewer" includes sewers and drains of every description, with the single exception of drains as already defined, that is to say, drains receiving the drainage of one building or premises within one curtilage. It is manifest, therefore, that a pipe or channel may be a sewer within the meaning in this definition though it receives surface water only, and accordingly this was so decided. In a recent case, *Ferrand* v. *Hallas Land and Building Company*, 1893, (2 Q.B., 135), Lord Justice Smith made use of the following language : "It will be noticed that a sewer need not necessarily convey sewage matter in order to constitute it a sewer. It would be none the less a sewer within the Act if it conveyed only rain or surface water. The draining off of rain or surface water collected from different premises or different feeders into one main drain would constitute that main drain a sewer within the meaning of the Act."

#### A SEWER MADE FOR PROFIT.

I have said that a sewer vests in the district council. Such is the general rule; but to this rule there are three statutory exceptions : (1) Sewers made by a person or company for his or their own profit; (2) sewers made for the purposes of land drainage or irrigation under a local Act; and (3) sewers under the authority of Commissioners of Sewers.

It is only to the first of these exceptions that attention need be drawn here. It was at one time thought that where a person made a sewer for the benefit of his own estate, with the intention of draining into it only such houses as he or his lessees or licensees might erect, the sewers so made were private property and came within the first exception. This notion has long been exploded. The first case was *Acton Local Board v. Batten* (28 Ch.D., 283), decided by Mr. Justice Kay. It has since been followed in a number of cases, among which I may mention *Ferrand v. Hallas Land and Building Company*, to which I have already referred, and *Fowles v. Colmer*, 1898 (W.N., 42). In the last case the owners of a building estate, on one side of which was a roadway, constructed a sewer in the soil of that moiety of the roadway adjoining the boundary of their own estate, that is to say, in that part of the road of which presumably they were the owners. They made this sewer for the purpose of draining the houses which it was proposed to erect upon the building plots upon their estates, and as the plots were sold the purchasers in every case entered into agreement to pay a sum of money in respect of the right to connect with the sewer. The defendant was the owner of a house on the other side of the road, and he claimed the right to connect the drains of his house with the sewer without payment. It was held that he was so entitled; that the sewer could not be said to have been made by the plaintiffs for their own profit within the meaning of the section; and the true meaning of the exception seems, therefore, narrowed down to this : that a sewer made for profit is one which is made not merely for the purposes of disposing of drainage, but for the purpose of realising some profit beyond and independent of any sanitary purpose. The most recent illustration of what is meant by a sewer made for profit is to be found in the case of *Croysdale v. Sunbury District Council* (W.N., 1898, p. 70), decided by Mr. Justice Stirling in the present year. In that case the owner of a field adjoining a highway had laid a drain from a ditch by the side of the highway to a pond in his field, for the purpose of supplying water to his cattle. It was held that this drain was a sewer, but that it was made for profit, and therefore did not vest in the district council. The most important decision, however, on the subject of a sewer made for profit was that of Mr. Justice Romer in *Minehead Local Board v. Luttrill* (2 Ch., 179). In that case a landowner, for the purpose of draining a town, the greater part of which stood on his own land, made sewers, and for the use of those sewers he levied and was paid a sewer rate by all persons whose houses were connected with his sewers. It was held that the sewers were made for profit and were not vested in the local authority. It is, however, difficult to now distinguish this case from the latter one, which I have already mentioned, and many doubts have been expressed as to whether it was correctly decided. This much may be said—the decision will probably be limited to facts exactly similar, and these are not likely again to recur.

#### SEWERS MADE FOR LAND DRAINAGE UNDER LOCAL ACT.

A recent case of some importance has been decided with reference to the second exception—*The London and North-Western Railway v. Runcorn Rural District Council*, 1898 (1 ch., 34, 561). In that case the railway company had made sewers for the purpose of draining the land adjoining their line. These were made under powers contained in their local Acts. After they were made the rural district council had, without the knowledge of the company, connected houses with them. It was held that although they were sewers, yet they were made and used for the purpose of draining land under a local Act, and did not vest in the local authority. I have mentioned this decision in passing, but to the general public it is one of little importance. Up to this point I have dealt only with the question, "What is a drain, and what is a sewer?" I have now to point out what are

#### THE RIGHTS AND LIABILITIES OF LOCAL AUTHORITIES IN CONNECTION WITH SEWERS

admitted or determined to be such. Now, the first is that they are bound to keep them in repair, to keep them cleansed, ventilated, and in such a condition as not to be a nuisance or injurious to health. That duty is imposed in express terms. It becomes important to the owner of property in this way : he may have a notice served upon him to abate a nuisance consisting of an alleged defective drain, but if he can show that that drain is in fact a sewer he is clearly under no liability to comply with the notice, for the nuisance exists by reason of the act or default of the local authority in failing to perform their statutory duty. But this liability of the local authority may not be an unmixed benefit to the owner,

for, as I have already pointed out, the local authority have the right of access, and the existence of a sewer upon his land, with which he cannot interfere and over which he cannot build, may be a serious drawback from the owner's point of view.

#### THE LIABILITY TO REPAIR,

however, brings me to the consideration of an attempt which has been made to amend the law in the Public Health Amendment Act, 1890, sec. 19. The consideration of this section is important, and I propose, therefore, to read the exact terms of it. It provides that "where two or more houses belonging to different owners are connected with a public sewer by a single private drain an application may be made under sec. 41 of the Public Health Act, 1875, relating to complaints as to nuisances from drains, and the local authority may recover any expenses incurred by them in executing any works under the powers conferred on them by that section from the owners of houses, in such shares and proportions as shall be settled by their surveyor, or, in case of dispute, by a court of summary jurisdiction. For the purposes of this section the expression 'drain' includes a drain used for the drainage of more than one building."

There can be little doubt what the intention of the legislature was in enacting this section. It was intended to provide for cases where sewers had been laid by private persons in private land for their own purposes, to prevent an unnecessary and probably improper burden being cast upon the public purse ; for, as I have already pointed out, once you can establish that a channel for drainage is a sewer the local authority must repair it. Such being the intention of the legislature, it is a little unfortunate that they did not employ some person in the drafting of the section who had some elementary acquaintance with the law of the subject. To begin with, the section applies only where there are two or more houses belonging to *different* owners. Why the section should not have applied to the case where two or more houses belong to the same owner I am unable to conceive. But the fact remains, for what it is worth, that the section with which I am now dealing may be put in force against the owners, say, of three houses draining into one common drain, while, if all three houses belonged to the same person, but the other circumstances were identically the same, the section would not apply. In the next place, the section makes use of two expressions which up to that time were quite unknown to the law. It deals with the case of "two or more houses connected with a public sewer by a single private drain." Now a sewer which is vested in the local authority is a public sewer, and all sewers are so vested, with the trifling exceptions to which I have already referred. But there is no such thing known to the law, or rather there was no such thing known to the law up to 1890, as a single private drain receiving the drainage of two or more houses, for such a drain was a sewer. But there the section is, and the Courts had to give some interpretation to it. After two somewhat unsatisfactory and, indeed, contradictory decisions—*viz.*, *Sell v. the Hove Commissioners*, 1895 (1 Q.B., 655), and *Hill v. Hair*, 1895 (1 Q.B., 906)—a Divisional Court, consisting of the Lord Chief Justice and Mr. Justice Wills, have arrived at an interpretation of the section which is at least intelligible. They have decided in effect that the section is intended to apply to what would otherwise be a sewer draining two or more houses belonging to different owners but laid in private land, so that the public could not have access to it. This decision was in *Bradford v. the Mayor, &c., of Eastbourne*, 1896 (2 Q.B., 205), and it has since been followed in *Scott v. Merthyr Tydvil*, 1897 (2 Q.B., 548). It must not, however, be imagined that the new enactment has transferred from the local authority to the owners of houses all liability in connection with what is referred to as the "single private drain." If I may again refer to the words of the section which I have already quoted, they merely enable the local authority to have recourse, in the case of such a drain, to the powers which they possess under sec. 41 of the Public Health Act, 1875, relating to nuisances in ordinary drains. Translated into intelligible language, their power is limited, as follows : There must be a written complaint from some person that the drain is a nuisance. The local authority must then authorise their officer to enter and examine the drain. If he reports it to be in bad condition the local authority may then give notice to the owners concerned to do the necessary work, and upon their default the local authority may do the work and recover the expenses. The amendment of the law effected by the Act of 1890 is therefore of a very limited character. In the restricted class of cases to which it applies it enables the local authority to compel the owners to bear the cost of repairs which, but for the Act, they would themselves have to bear. But unless they follow the procedure which I have mentioned, their duty in respect of the "single private drain" is exactly the same as if the Act had never passed. In other words, it is a sewer which they are bound to repair, and which, if necessary, they can be compelled to repair. This was pointed out by the Court in the case of *Reg. v. The Mayor of Hastings*, 1897 (1 Q.B., 46), where the local authority were ordered to do repairs to a common drain, although had the appropriate procedure been adopted it is possible that the owners might have been compelled to do them. There is one important subject connected with sewers which time will only now permit me to mention.

#### LIABILITY OF LOCAL AUTHORITY TO MAKE SEWERS FOR THE EFFECTUAL DRAINAGE OF DISTRICT.

One of the duties of a local authority imposed by the Public Health Act of 1875, sec. 15, is that of making such sewers as may be necessary for effectually draining their district for the purposes of the Act. A number of recent decisions relate to the liability of a local authority to carry out this obligation. They are cases of this character: Sewers are or have become insufficient to carry away the volume of drainage sent into them, particularly in cases of storm. The sewers become overcharged and flood the basements of premises which they ought to drain, occasioning in many cases much damage as well as discomfort to the occupiers. Claims have thereupon been made against local authorities for damages, and in some instances an attempt has been made to obtain a writ of mandamus to compel the local authority to enlarge their sewers, or to construct such additional sewers as are necessary to give the desired relief. Up to the present time the Court has dealt with such cases by applying to them a technical rule of law. The rule may be thus stated : Where a statute creates an obligation, and also provides a means of enforcing that obligation, no other remedy is open to a person aggrieved by the failure to perform that obligation. Now the Public Health Act, 1875, contains, in sec. 299, a provision enforcing the obligation of providing a district with sufficient sewers and of maintaining existing sewers. The procedure is by complaint to the Local Government Board, who, upon inquiry, make an order limiting the time for the performance of the duty, and such order may be enforced by mandamus. Acting upon this rule, the Courts, including the House of Lords, have held that where persons are damaged by floods caused by the insufficiency of sewers to take away the drainage from a district they have no remedy in damages or by mandamus, and can only complain to the Local Government Board. I need only refer to the last of these cases, that, namely, in the House of Lords, which affirms the principle in all the others. It is *Passmore v. Oswaldtwistle Urban District Council*, 1898 (Appeal Case, 387). This is a very important limitation of the rights of private persons. But it is worthy of note that it cannot apply in the metropolis, where there is no section in force corresponding to sec. 299 of the Public Health Act, 1875. Closely connected with the point which I have just mentioned is another, which I shall mention in conclusion. It is this : Suppose an owner wishes to lay-out a building estate, what are the rights and liabilities of the owner on the one hand, the local authorities on the other, in respect of the provision of means of drainage, without which, of course, no estate can be successfully developed ? That has been, I think, settled by the decision of the Court of Appeal in *Reg. v. Tynemouth Rural District Council*, 1896 (2 Q.B., 219). I may summarise what has been there decided. The local authority are under no obligation to bring their sewers up to the new estate for the purpose of enabling the owner to develop it for building. On the other hand, they cannot refuse to pass his plans because these do not disclose how the drainage of the streets and buildings he proposes to construct and erect will eventually be disposed of. They cannot, in other words, insist upon his showing on his plans a means of sewage disposal for the estate, once the buildings have been erected. What will happen is this : When the new streets are laid out the local authority will be in a position to require sewers to be laid in them, under sec. 150. These sewers, however, will only be sewers in the streets. As soon as connections are made with these sewers an outfall will have to be provided, but that duty will fall upon the local authority.

It is obvious that many difficult questions are likely to arise in connection with this branch of the law. Can an owner, in anticipation of his liability, lay sewers under his new streets, which end nowhere, and then, by connecting one or two of the houses with them force the local authority to find an outfall for him ? Such a result might be very unreasonable in many cases. On the other hand, at what point of time can the duty of the local authority to provide an outfall be said to arise ? Can they compel the owner for an indefinite time to drain house after house into cesspools, regardless of the fact that at some period or another these will have to be abolished and a system of sewers provided ? I do not trust myself to speculate as to the liabilities on either side of these matters. In many cases, no doubt, such difficulties will disappear by mutual arrangement. Until they are fought and decided by the Courts I can hardly care to venture an opinion on the points to which I have referred. There are one or two important points connected with the subject of this paper which regard for your time and patience compels me at present to leave unnoticed. I can only trust that you have not, by reason of the disconnected character of my observations, found them tedious or uninteresting.

**The Widening of Parliament-street.**—At the Surveyors' Institution, on Thursday, an arbitration was held to determine the sum to be paid to the Government in respect of premises Nos. 11 and 13 King-street, Westminster, which are required in connection with the scheme of widening Parliament-street. The amount claimed was £4,643, while witness for the plaintiffs (Messrs. Lewin, Gregory & Anderson, the occupants of the premises) submitted detailed estimates varying from £1,175 to £1,480. The award was reserved.

## QUERIES AND REPLIES.

*Sketches accompanying Queries should be made separate on white paper in plain black-ink lines. Lettering or figures should be bold and plain.*

**220. Underground Water Supplies and Well Sinking.**—" L. L. B." writes : I should be much obliged if you would inform me what books you recommend on underground water supplies and on wells and borings.

The best book on the subject of underground water supplies is " The Water Supply of England and Wales " (Price 24s. Stanford), by Chas. E. de Rance, C.E., F.G.S., secretary of the British Association Underground Water Committee. " The Modern Practice of Sinking and Boring Wells, with Geological Considerations and Examples of Wells," by Ernest Spon, C.E. (Price 10s. 6d. E. & F. N. Spon), is, we believe, the best work on the subject of which it treats.

**221. Designing Water Mains, Formula for.**—" Assistant " writes : A town with a population of 4,000 is about to have a public water supply. The amount fixed per head is 20 gallons per day. By what formula or principles could the diameter of the supply main be ascertained, and what should be the maximum allowable velocity in the pipes ?

In designing a scheme for water supply the mains should be of such a diameter as to allow for the total estimated daily supply being delivered in four hours. Thus in the case given the mains should be capable of delivering

$$\frac{4,000 \text{ population} \times 20 \text{ gallons}}{4} = 20,000 \text{ gallons per hour.}$$

Some engineers, however, prefer to allow for two-thirds of the estimated daily supply being delivered in eight hours, and if this were the basis then we should have

$$\frac{4,000 \times 20}{8} = 6,666 \text{ gallons per hour as the capacity for}$$

which the mains must be designed. In order to calculate the diameter of the main to supply this, or any other required quantity, the following formula should be used :—

$$D = \frac{1}{TA} \sqrt{\frac{G \cdot L}{H}} \text{ where}$$

G = Number of gallons delivered per hour.
L = Length of pipe in yards.
H = Head of water in feet.
D = Diameter of pipe in inches.

But in order to work this formula it is necessary to know the length of main and its fall, as to which the querist has omitted to furnish us. The maximum velocity of water in the main should not exceed 3 ft. per second. Burton's " Water Supply of Towns " (Crosby Lockwood & Son. 25s.), Crimp & Bruges' " Tables for Designing Sewers and Water Mains " (Biggs & Co. 10s. 6d.), Molesworth's " Civil Engineer's Pocket-Book " (E. & F. Spon. 6s.), and Box's " Hydraulics " (5s.), will be found highly useful to the querist.

## MARKET EXTENSIONS AT DEPTFORD.

We understood that, the City Corporation having obtained an Act of Parliament authorising them to considerably extend the foreign cattle market at Deptford, and connect it by means of a railway with the London, Brighton and South Coast Railway, the work, which will involve an expenditure of £100,000, will be carried out without delay. The services of Sir J. Wolfe Barry have been secured as engineer, and from a report he has made it would appear that the railway and tramway outside the market will cost £32,250. For the purpose of extending the market property in the near vicinity will be bought up, at a cost of £22,000. Increased accommodation will be also provided, in the shape of additional slaughter-houses, cooling-rooms, increased lairage and an extended river frontage. The estimated outlay on these works are as follows : Slaughter-houses (a first instalment), £5,000 ; lairage, £21,000 ; a junction of three jetties (providing a continuous river frontage of 880 ft.), £16,000 ; and property required, £22,000. The extension of the market has been rendered necessary owing to the great pressure which has been put upon the existing accommodation. The business increases every month, no fewer than 510,618 animals being slaughtered there during the last year. The financial position of the market is satisfactory, as, although the loan account at one time reached a total sum of £424,000, the amount outstanding at the close of last year was only £21,000.

**Heckmondwike.**—At a meeting of the district council on Monday week the chairman reported in reference to a visit last week to the sewage farm by Mr. Dibdin, the author of the bacterial system of sewage disposal. He stated that Mr. Dibdin had suggested a means by which the Heckmondwike scheme, which is one of land filtration, could be absolutely perfected by the outlay of an extra £2,000. The Drainage Committee would, no doubt, consider the suggestion in due course. The members of the committee were very much interested in the scientific explanations which had been made by Mr. Dibdin.

# Municipal Work at Nottingham.

## THE NEW BASFORD CEMETERY.

Park and cemetery competitions are, as a rule, conducted in such an unsatisfactory manner that it is a pleasant task to refer to a case in which the promoters showed laudable anxiety to place the awards beyond dispute, and in order to secure this result not only drew up conditions which were models in their way, but engaged experts of unquestionable authority in Messrs. Aston Webb and Ernest Milner to decide upon the respective merits of the schemes submitted. For this state of affairs the competitors were much indebted to the Nottingham Corporation and their city engineer, Mr. Arthur Brown. The designing of the cemetery was divided into sections—A, the laying-out of the ground, planting, &c.; and B, the chapels, crematorium, lodges, gates, &c. In section A, as we have already announced, the first premium was awarded to Mr. T. H. Mawson, the well-known park and garden architect, Windermere, the first premium in Section B going to Messrs. McKwan & Norton, architects, Birmingham.

In a special supplement plate we reproduce the general plan and the plan of the grave spaces as designed by Mr. Mawson. Some descriptive details will, no doubt, be of interest to our readers. The site chosen for the cemetery, which is about 30 acres in extent, is bounded on the north by Arnold-road and on the south by the Great Northern Railway. As will be seen by the levels, the ground is very undulating, that adjoining the railway embankment being, unfortunately, the lowest, thus making it very difficult to screen passing trains. Both soil and atmosphere are favourable to plant growth. The curves of the walks are for the most part suggested by the contour of the land, but the long straight avenue is raised for a part of its length considerably above the surrounding levels. This feature, however, will, it is expected, add considerably to the convenience and beauty of the cemetery when the limes have grown into character. This and other important details, however, are more particularly referred to in the following report, submitted by Mr. Mawson, together with his plans:—

### MR. MAWSON'S REPORT.

In preparing the accompanying design the author has adhered, so far as possible, to the suggested positions for chapels, crematorium, entrances and lodges, arranging the levels and positions of each in such a way as would be most likely to fall in with the schemes of architects competing under Section B. Some modification and readjustment is sure to be required, as it is quite impossible for the designers to plan their positions exactly alike. This scheme—i.e., so far as it refers to position of chapels—can be altered to suit any plan of chapels without in any way destroying the other portions of the scheme.

#### ENTRANCE AND DRIVE TO CHAPELS AND CREMATORIUM.

When mortuary chapels are grouped together, as in this scheme, it becomes necessary to prepare a wide drive, with entrance gates set well back from the road. The entrance from the centre of Arnold-road to the gates is shown as set back 50 ft., thus allowing of convenient turn in. The width of drive to chapels is 30 ft. and the stance or turning circle is 120 ft. A circular shrubbery is arranged in the centre of the stance. This would prove a useful screen between the chapels.

#### RETAINING WALL.

It will be noticed that to obtain this large circular carriage turn a retaining wall would be required. This might be treated architecturally, and so add very considerably to the effect of the cemetery. The advantages gained by having this large gravelled space would far more than compensate for the cost of the wall and building.

#### CREMATORIUM.

The crematorium is arranged to the south side of the circle, so as to obtain a lower level for the various chambers required for furnaces, &c.

#### LANDSCAPE TREATMENT.

The author of the accompanying scheme is, wherever practicable, in favour of a more formal treatment which allows of economical division of grave spaces, but in this instance the contour of the ground would not allow of such a treatment without incurring the expenditure of a sum quite out of keeping with any advantages which could be gained.

The landscape or gardenesque style adopted recognises the contour of the land, and, so far as possible, adapts itself to it. This being so, the effect would be much more pleasing than the more expensive formal style. The only portion of the scheme to which the foregoing does not apply is the avenue, which is straight and of easy gradient. A straight road would, however, be very valuable, both in respect to convenience division of the ground for church and dissent. It would also help the architectural features, which finish each end—i.e., shelters and chapels. It would also give the most direct route for pedestrians entering from Arnold-road from the west corner. The avenue would at all times form a delightful promenade.

A glance at the plan will show that the portion of land lying between the chapels and the nursery could easily be laid out without disturbing the land to the west of the chapels

(excepting the portion adjoining the Arnold-road, the excavation from which would be required for filling up the lower ground, as per sections A B. It would, however, add very considerably to the reposeful aspect of the cemetery if the southern boundary could be planted at once, so as to screen the railway and reduce the noise of passing trains.

#### ARRANGEMENT OF WALKS AND DRIVES.

In designing the walks and roads provision has been made for the hearse taking the corpse to any part of the ground. This has proved a most convenient arrangement in other cemeteries. The roads over which the hearse may be allowed are all connected with the main avenue or other return roads. This allows of roads being much narrower than if the hearse had to turn round and return on same road.

A road is shown from an entrance west of the registrar's house to the crematorium, passing under the avenue. This is for the convenience of the crematorium. The whole of the walks would, so far as possible, follow the natural contour of the ground.

Owing to the dryness of the subsoil very little surface drainage would be required, but where the gradients were less than 1 in 14 the sides should be formed into cobble-paved channels, with grates and catchpits every 20 yards apart. This would prevent severe washing of roads in times of storm.

#### FORMATION.

Much depends upon the way in which the work of formation is carried out, and a foreman who has worked under the direction of some recognised professional landscape gardener should be engaged to carry out the work, otherwise an appreciative rendering of the designer's intention would not be obtained.

In executing the work three points would require careful consideration : (1) Good soil beds for the various plantations; (2) careful merging of levels into the natural contour of the land, &c.; and (3) good pure grass seeds, carefully selected, and sown on well-prepared ground. The prescription for grass seeds which the author of this scheme recommends is as follows. The quantities are for an acre : Perennial Rye Grass, 20 lb.; Cynosurus Cristata, 4 lb.; Festuca diuriscula 3 lb.; Festuca tenuifolia, 3 lb.; Poa Nemoralis Sempervirens 2 lb.; Poa Trivalis, 2 lb.; Trisetum flavescens, 3 lb.; Trefolium repens, 7 lb.; Trefolium minus, 3 lb.; total, 47 lb.

In arranging the plantations in a cemetery it is advisable to introduce as many flowering shrubs and trees as possible, especially those varieties which are sweet scented. A glance at the enlarged detail of a plantation will show that the authors of this scheme propose to make the fullest use of the large number of varieties which would succeed on this ground. These varieties would be largely composed of the following : Almond, double-flowered and single ; Berberis, Darwinii and Vars ; Genista, Praecox, Andreana, &c.; Cerasus, of sorts ; Deutzia Crenata and Scabra ; Guelder Rose ; Hypericum, Moscriana, &c.; Hydrangea Paniculata and Grandiflora ; Mexicreum of sorts ; Prunus Sinensis flora plena ; Prunus Pissardii ; Philadelphicus Coronaria, &c.; Pyrus Maus floribunda ; Ribes, Flowering Currants ; Spiræa, shrubby varieties ; Symphoricarpus Racemosus ; Syringas, of sorts ; Weigelias Rosea and Amabilos, &c., Rhododendron Caucasicum Alba and Wilsonia ; Pernettya Mucronata and Hybreda ; Erica Cinera and Fragrans ; Azalea Pontica ; Diplapappus Chrysophylla ; Gorse, Spanish.

Among the evergreen trees and shrubs which would succeed are the following : Aucuba Vera ; Box Handsworth and golden ; Cotoneaster, Simmondsii and Microphylla ; Euonymus Japonica ; Hollies of all sorts ; Laurels, Portugal Rotundifolia ; Laurestinus floribunda ; Ligustrum Ovalifolia and Japonica ; Grislina, littorialis ; Mahonia Aquifolia ; Quercus Sinpervirens ; Olearia Haastic ; Osmanthus Illisifolia ; Yews, common, Adpressa and Washington ; Gaultheria Shalloon ; Tree, iries.

Among the conifers the following would succeed : Pinus, Cembra and Austriaca ; Retinosphora Plumosa, Aurea and Squarosa ; Retinospora Obtusa and Filifera ; Cedrus Atlantica, Deodora and Libanii ; Cupressus Macrocarpa ; Cupressus Lawsoniana, Aurea and Argentea ; Abies, Canadensis and Albertiana ; Picea, Nobilis and Nordmanniana ; Picea, Kosterii Glauca ; Thuja Lobbii ; Juniperus chinensis : American Arborvitæ ; Taxodium Sempervirens.

The deciduous trees of larger growth would chiefly consist of the following : Ash, Mountain and also Golden-Leaved ; Beech, Common, Purple and Fern-Leaved ; Chesnut, Scarlet, Common and Spanish ; Birch, Silver ; Cherry, Common : Crab, Liberian and John Downie ; Elms, Huntingdon and Wych ; Limes, Red-Twigged ; Maples, Norway and Schwedleriana ; Oak, Turkeys and Scarlet ; Poplar, New Golden and Lombardy ; Sycamore, common and Corstophine ; Thorns, Double Scarlet and Single Pink ; Willows, Silver and Apple-Leaved.

The foregoing lists might be considerably extended, but the author of this scheme strongly advises the planting of such sorts as are sure to grow. Far better do this than experiment with the whole list of a nurseryman's catalogue. Where single trees are shown, as in avenue, the best trees procurable should be planted, and each tree should be planted in a properly prepared pit, with selected soil, so as to give it a good start.

ESTIMATE OF COST.

The following estimate is based upon an average of the actual cost of laying-out public parks and cemeteries designed by the author of this scheme. There works are situated in various parts of the country, and have cost nearly £100,000.

| | £ | s. | d. |
|---|---|---|---|
| Cost of landscape formation, including walks and drives to ballast level ... ... | 3,868 | 0 | 0 |
| Cost of roads and walks... ... ... ... | 1,511 | 5 | 0 |
| Cost of preparing soil beds for plantations ... | 634 | 0 | 0 |
| Trees and shrubs ... ... ... ... ... | 792 | 0 | 0 |
| Specimen trees for avenues, &c. ... ... | 61 | 5 | 0 |
| Yews, &c., for hedges ... ... ... ... | 41 | 16 | 0 |
| Propagating houses and cemetery nursery ... | 320 | 0 | 0 |
| Total... ... ... ... £7,228 | | 6 | 0 |

## ELECTRIC LIGHTING AT LLANDUDNO.

### INAUGURATION CEREMONY.

An informal inauguration of the electric light, which has been installed at Llandudno under the superintendence of Mr. A. H. Preece, took place on Saturday evening, the official ceremony being postponed until the spring, when the district council hope to secure the attendance of the president of the Local Government Board.

THE GENERATING STATION.

This has been erected contiguous to the gasworks, which are also the property of the town and yield a remunerative return. It will be combined with a refuse destructor, which was greatly needed in a seaside resort such as Llandudno. The plant consists of three Babcock-Wilcox boilers, two of which will be fired from Beaman & Deas' destructors, while the third will be hand-fed with coal or coke; the whole of the boilers may be fired with coal or coke if necessary. Apart from the "eternal fitness of things," the proximity of the electric light and gas departments, each a municipalised undertaking, combines convenience with economy in the matter of fuel. The refuse destructor is one of most modern approved construction. The same may be said of the engine-room, which is at present equipped with two 100-kilowatt steam dynamos and one 50-kilowatt steam dynamo, together with a motor generator for regulation and charging the batteries. The two principal generating setts are each capable of giving an output of 100 kilowatt at 440 to 500 volts. There is also a third generating sett, capable of giving an output of 50 kilowatt at 600 volts. A balancer is provided, each armature capable of carrying a current of 100 amperes, and working at a voltage varying between 200 and 256 volts, so that it can transfer 25 kilowatt from one side of the three-wire system to the other.

STREET LIGHTING.

For street lighting there are altogether forty-eight arc lamps, erected on cast-iron pillars. The lamps along the front of the promenade, thirty in number, as well as those of important crossings, are fixed in carriers, protected from the weather by a canopy—an ornamental as well as useful appendage. The remaining eighteen lamps are all fixed along the kerb at the side of the road, suspended from overhanging brackets. The lamps are run in groups of eight in series, and are of the well-known Crompton-Pochin type. Fitted with opalescent globes, they are for single carbons, burning for eighteen hours without re-trimming. Each lamp is provided with an automatic "cut-out," which, in the event of the lamp "hanging-up" from any cause, immediately "short-circuits" it so that the other lamps in that particular circuit are not extinguished. The lamps on the sea front are fixed about 50 yards apart, those in the town at a slightly greater distance. The installation, the cost of which approximates £20,000, has been admirably carried out by Mr. Preece and his assistants, there not being a single hitch in the whole of the details.

Mr. T. T. MARKS, chairman of the district council, after switching on the current, touched upon the great progress Llandudno had made within late years. The utilisation of the light of the age afforded a further proof that Llandudno was determined upon keeping progress with the needs of the times. He was glad to see among those present Mr. Preece, c.b., the chief electrician of the General Post Office, whose sons had carried out the works so successfully. Mr. Preece, he need hardly remind the audience, had reached the highest profession and reputation, and, being a Carnarvonshire man and a resident in the county, had reflected lustre upon North Wales.

Mr. PREECE, in response, said there was no doubt that the electric light would prove a success at Llandudno. He strongly urged that the local authorities should turn their attention to the provision of electrical tramways.

Mr. W. A. Darbishire and other speakers followed, Mr. Marks remarking that Llandudno was much indebted to Mr. Darbishire for his liberal donation towards the building fund of the intermediate school.

## LONDON WATER SUPPLY COMMISSION.

The sittings of the Royal Commission on the question of the London water supply were resumed on Monday, at the Westminster Guildhall, under the presidency of Lord Llandaff.

The CHAIRMAN said he proposed to deal first with the separate question of inter-connection between the undertakings of the different companies.

Mr. POPE, Q.C., on behalf of the companies, said they were prepared to promote a Bill next session enabling them to consider what works were necessary to carry out inter-communication, and to submit proposals to the Local Government Board, who were to be empowered to approve, with or without modification, to authorise and order other works, and also to authorise any of the companies, in cases of emergency and for temporary purposes, to get more water from the Thames than they were now empowered to take. The expenditure under the Bill was to be deemed capital expenditure, and the issue of additional debenture stock authorised by the Local Government Board.

Mr. E. COLLINS, engineer to the New River Company, was, after some further discussion, examined. He said the connection of the systems of all the companies was practicable from an engineering point of view, but at the times of greatest pressure scarcely any of the companies had water to spare. At present the East London Company were receiving from other companies about 14,500,000 gallons per day. A scheme of inter-connection had been drawn up by the engineers of the different companies in October, 1897, but it would only meet the case of a temporary emergency, not of such a failure of supply as had occurred this summer. The witness explained a larger scheme that would facilitate interchange, resting on the assumption that more water might be taken from the Thames.

Mr. W. BRYAN, engineer to the East London Company, examined, said he was not at present prepared to say on what connections his company relied to ensure a proper supply next year in the event of another scarcity.

The commission met again on Tuesday, when

Mr. J. HOLLAMS, legal adviser to the associated water companies, gave further evidence on the scheme for connecting the systems of the different companies.

Sir H. KNIGHT, chairman of the Southwark and Vauxhall Company, who was next examined, gave a general approval of the scheme as practicable and as necessary to satisfy the public outcry, but was quite certain that if the works were carried out they would never or seldom be used. The present supply was quite sufficient to meet another drought. The connections already made between the different companies had not yet enabled the East London to resume a constant supply, because assistance was not available so early this year as it would be next year. He estimated that the companies, with their present powers and without any trouble whatever, had a surplus of 24,000,000 gallons per day which they might place at the disposal of the East London Company. It was not the East London Company which had broken down; the trouble was due to the ridiculous system of building houses without cisterns. He complained strongly of the opposition which the water companies met with from the London County Council.

Monday is the day fixed for the next sitting.

## IMPROVEMENTS AT MIDDLETON.

Having procured powers for the monopoly of electric light supply, the Middleton Corporation are now considering a scheme of some magnitude, which has been presented to them by their advisers. Great extensions have been going on at the gasworks, and it is proposed that here the electric supply works should be erected. It is estimated that the necessary plant and buildings would cost £19,300. It is further proposed to erect a refuse destructor, at a cost of £3,500, and also to so construct the plant as to make it suitable for the supply of power to the new tramways company if terms could be agreed upon. Altogether it is proposed to borrow £33,500 for the works.

Tramway Waiting-Rooms.—It has been suggested that waiting-rooms, similar to those erected at Bristol, should be provided near several of the recognised stopping-places on the routes taken by the tramways and omnibuses of the metropolis.

New Free Library for East Ham.—Mr. McKinnon Wood, the chairman of the London County Council, on Saturday afternoon laid the foundation-stone of the Passmore Edwards Free Library at Plashet. The new building, the cost of which will be defrayed by Mr. Passmore Edwards, is to be erected on a plot of the land set aside by the East Ham District Council as a recreation ground, at the western end of the parish. The architect is Mr. S. Trevail, F.R.I.B.A., who has designed a building to cost £4,000, without internal fittings, while the district council propose to put in the tower which is to be erected a clock, which will be bought by public subscriptions. All the departments for a good library will be provided on the ground floor, the upper floor being reserved for committee-rooms and apartments for the custodian.

# For Assistants and Pupils.

## THE CONSTRUCTION OF ROADS AND STREETS.—XIX.

By WILLIAM H. MAXWELL, Assistant Engineer and Surveyor, Leyton Urban District Council.

### ROAD MATERIALS AND CONSTRUCTION

*(continued).*

*Construction of French Roads.*—Large boulders, 8 in. or 9 in. deep, are placed at the sides, as in Fig. 28, and a stone bottoming about 6 in. in depth is formed of rubble stone, upon which comes about 3 in. of small stone packing filling the interstices of the pitched foundation, making together a depth of about 7½ in. This is covered with a coating of hard metalling, broken to pass, 1½-in. ring, and well rolled in with sand as a "*binding*," aided by watering.

CONCRETE MACADAM.—This was introduced by Mr. Joseph Mitchell as an improvement upon ordinary macadamised surfaces. He laid down a concrete macadamised road in Edinburgh of the following proportions: Portland cement, one; broken stones, four; sand, one and a quarter.

"The stones were well screened and watered, and the whole turned over, thoroughly mixed, and spread to a thickness of 3 in. to 5 in., and allowed to harden, after which a second layer was spread, and so on, until the required thickness was obtained. A road thus formed need only be about one-half to two-thirds as thick as ordinary broken-stone roads. The great objection to roads thus formed is, that when the surface becomes worn the cost for repairing them will be considerably more than that of an ordinary road."* Also, where streets are liable to be frequently opened for sewer, gas, water or other pipe tracks, the trenching will be expensive and repairs difficult.

Mr. H. U. McKie, A.M.I.C.E., as a result of his inspection of the concrete macadam streets of Edinburgh in 1883, stated† that "the streets paved with concrete macadam were in fair order. The pavement is non-absorbent and could be readily washed quite clean, and the scavenging of such streets is brought to the minimum. The cement concrete macadam varied from 9 in. to 12 in. deep. Two modes of forming the streets have been adopted, namely:—

"(*a*) After the street has been excavated to the proper depth and properly formed, and the ground thoroughly beat down, the first coat is laid down with 2-in. macadam, and blinded and made compact to form required.

"The top coat is laid down with clean-riddled 2-in. macadam, which is grouted with carefully-prepared cement grout, varying in strength from one of cement to three of sharp sand, to one of cement and one of sand, carefully formed to the proper contour of the street.

"(*b*) The second method is to make a concrete of the broken stone and cement, sand and gravel, and lay it on the road in sections in such lengths that each section can be completed before the cement sets. All the broken stones used are of hard metal, whinstone, granite or porphyry, all hand-broken.

"This class of pavement requires great care in construction to make it a success and to prevent unequal settlement in the street after it is completed. It makes a good street, and the cost varies from 6s. to 9s. per square yard."

TAR MACADAM.—Tar macadamised or bituminous concrete roadways are adopted in many towns, and for light traffic are found to be a good substitute for ordinary macadam roads, being impervious to moisture, noiseless,‡ more sanitary, and less muddy and dusty than macadam. Also, the cost of watering and scavenging is less, as well as the annual cost of maintenance.

This class of road is well adapted for use in the quiet quarters of large towns, in residential areas and the less busy thoroughfares of suburban districts. Mr. Deacon considered tar macadam roadways only suitable for roads having less traffic than 40,000 tons per yard of width per annum and macadam for roads with less than 30,000 tons per yard of width per annum.

The work should always be constructed in the spring or winter months, as if done in the summer the heat of the sun draws the tar out of the pavement. *Dry* weather is essential, and considerable care and experience will be necessary for successful construction.

The precise methods of laying tar paving for footways and tar macadam for roadways necessarily vary somewhat in different districts, according to local circumstances, but the general method is as follows*:—

The material used (in Leicester) is the blast-furnace cinder and limestone. For *footways* it is sorted by screening and sifting into four different sizes of 1½-in., ¾-in., ½-in. and ¼-in. gauges, and for roadways to 2½-in., 1½-in. and ¾-in. gauges. The cinder and limestone are both heated on an iron floor under which the flues from a fire run. The material is then mixed in its heated state with a sufficient quantity of a mixture (also in a heated state) of pitch, tar and creosote, boiled until they form a tough and thick consistency,† when it is, after lying for a few days in heaps, ready for use. The quantity of tar, pitch, &c., depends on the qualities of these articles, and particularly of the tar, which varies very frequently. The quantities are also regulated to the character of the traffic expected on the roadway or footway on which the material is to be used, but the average quantities may be taken to be as follows: 12 gallons of tar, ½ cwt. of pitch, 2 gallons of creosote, 1 ton of stone.

The work is laid down in either two or three layers. For *two-coat footway work* 1-in. material is used for the bottom layer, 1 in. thick, and ½-in. material for the top, 1 in. thick, making 2½-in. total thickness.

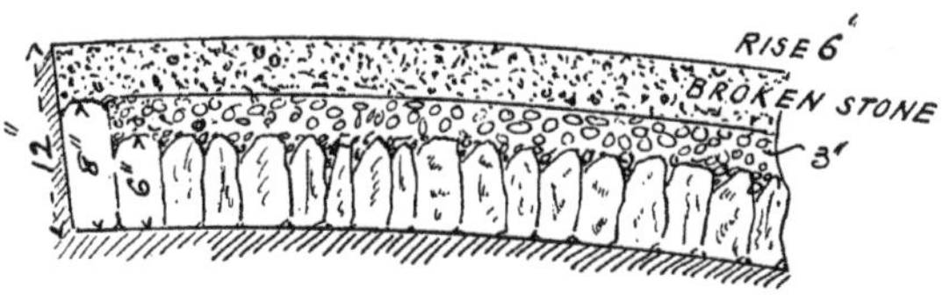


FIG. 28.—CROSS-SECTION OF FRENCH ROAD.

In *three-coat footway work* 1¼-in. material is used, 1½ in. thick, for the first or bottom layer, ¾ in. for the second, 1 in. thick, and ¼ in. for the top covering, ½ in. thick, with the addition of Derbyshire spar sprinkled on the top covering in both cases, to give it a white or variegated appearance, making 3 in. in all. Each layer of material is separately well rolled with hand rollers weighing 13 cwt. each.

The *tar macadam for roadways* is laid down in three layers, the preparation of the material being the same as in the case of footways. The road bed and foundations are prepared similarly as for an ordinary macadamised roadway, and the tarred macadam is laid as follows: The first layer is 3 in. thick and of 2½-in. gauge, the second layer is of 1½-in. gauge and 2 in. thick, and the top coat is 1 in. thick of ¾-in. gauge, and covered with cinder dust, sharp sand or grit, each layer being well rolled with a 15-ton steam roller.

As to the durability of this class of work, Mr. Gordon considered that the life of the roads may be fairly taken at about three years, at the end of which period they will in all probability require *topping*—that is, tracking over and recovering with the material used for the top coat—at a cost of from 9d. to 1s. per square yard.

The cost *of the tar paving*, laid as above described, exclusive of preparing the ground, for three-coat work averaged 1s. 6½d. per square yard and for two-coat work 11d. per square yard.

The cost *of tar macadam* for roadways was from 2s. 6d. to 3s. per square yard, exclusive of preparation of the ground on special formation.

In old paved streets it only involves the removal of the stones and some few inches of ground, if the foundation be already good, or possibly the carting of a few loads of dry material to make up any apparent soft places in the foundation.

* "Proceedings of the Association of Municipal and County Engineers," vol. vii. p. 30.

† "Proceedings of the Association of Municipal and County Engineers," vol. x.

‡ Tar pavement has been called the "silent macadam" in *Leicester*.

* As adopted by Mr. John Gordon, M.INST.C.E., at *Leicester—vide* "Proceedings of the Association of Municipal and County Engineers," vol. x., from which the following particulars are taken.

† The ingredients are boiled together until bubbles rise to the surface and in bursting emit puffs of brown smoke.

In other cases, where a street is being formed on maiden ground, the formation of a foundation with from 9 in. to 12 in. of what is locally called "rammel"* is necessary, and the covering of the same with furnace ashes, gravel or other suitable material to receive the tar macadam. This, with the necessary excavation, adds from one-third to one-sixth per square yard to the cost, but is requisite even for ordinary macadam roads. The cost of preparing the ground, where no such foundation is required, ranges from 3d. to 6d., the breaking up of the old macadam roads being the most costly, but to set against this there is the value of the old materials.

One important feature, Mr. Gordon further stated, is the *rolling* of the foundations before laying down the first layer of the tar macadam, and he considered a steam roller, of about 10 tons weight, to be necessary for success with such roadways.

Tar macadam is also sometimes laid by merely spreading a coating of broken stone, and, after consolidating it by means of a roller, a mixture of coal tar, pitch and creosote oil is poured over it, and upon this a layer of small stone is put down and well rolled in, the surface being finished as before with stone chippings and rolling.

The system of forming tar macadam roadways in Croydon is described† as follows by Mr. J. Walker, the borough engineer and surveyor:—

"The surface of the road was taken off to allow of an 8-in. coat of tar macadam. The bottom 5 in. consisted of the best of the old road material taken off, after it had been sifted, baked, and, while hot, well tarred. With the gas tar a little pitch was mixed, well boiled and used hot. The stones were turned over until all were well blacked. The material was then taken back to the road, laid on and well rolled. The top 3 in. were Kentish rag, baked and tarred similarly to the bottom coat, and well rolled with a heavy hand-roller; a day or two afterwards it was well rolled with the 10-ton steam roller. A little fine Kentish rag was used to bind it, having been previously baked and tarred as the other. The full cost was about 3s. 6d. per square yard. The old foundation was not disturbed, but if the foundation of a new road and new materials were required the cost would not be under 4s. per yard super."

The stones which have been used for tar macadam are granite, basalt, mountain limestone, Kentish rag and blast furnace slag. Hard limestone has been found to be preferable to the siliceous or igneous rocks, as it wears more evenly.

## CORRESPONDENCE.

### Shoreditch Combined Electric Light and Dust Destruction Scheme.

—Mr. T. W. Baker, 7 Broad-street House, E.C., writes: No one wishes for the success of the utilisation of towns' refuse for the generation of electricity more than myself, but let us not be led away by random generalisations and data unsupported by facts as to works' costs; and, inasmuch as the published accounts of the Shoreditch Vestry must be assumed to be correct, I await the promised figures for the year's working, although if the "initial expenditure that would not recur" were credited against the loss, as stated, the true working results would be apparent, and Mr. Kershaw and Dr. Mansfield Robinson evidently missed this salient fact in their respective replies to my previous communication. But the aforesaid gentlemen having imported into the controversy deliberate personalities — such as "virgin experimentalist," "amateur adventurer," and guilty of "schoolboy carelessness"—these epithets call for some contradiction by me. I now give the facts that did occur. In June, 1893, I was requested by the vestry clerk, being a ratepayer, to give him some idea of how and at what cost I would propose to light the Shoreditch area. I did so, and handed him a report as a ratepayer, which I understood was of some value at this initial stage. In November, 1893, I was employed, and received payment for a design and scheme to bring in the then idle large property in Ivy-street for the purposes of a similar scheme, with baths and wash-houses, as now erected. In 1894 a representative of the contractors and designers of the present destructor called on me, and asked if I would grant my patent rights to them for the Shoreditch schemes and row in their boat," which on the terms mentioned I refused. In 1895, upon the request for competing schemes by the Shoreditch Vestry, I designed that special scheme, according to my patents, that was submitted by the eminent firm of Messrs. Daniel Adamson & Co., who were lowest in price, and whose guaranteed cost for labour for 20,000 tons of refuse per annum was £1,100, and I beg to subjoin Messrs. Kincaid, Waller & Manville's report thereon to the Shoreditch Vestry:—

*Messrs. Daniel Adamson & Company, of Dukinfield.*

"This firm is one of the highest reputation in the manufacture of steam-raising apparatus, and they have submitted a scheme which in many respects is different from the majority of those placed before you, and for which, if erected in accordance with the specification issued by you, the cost

will amount to £14,400. They propose to supply only ten cells in place of twelve, but these cells will be of larger area than the twelve stipulated for, and will therefore burn the requisite amount of refuse daily. The refuse furnaces, in place of being ranged alongside the boilers, are placed, as in Messrs. Fraser & Sons' scheme, under the boilers. This likewise involves the clinkering floor being somewhat enclosed, since a second floor, in addition to the tipping floor, is provided opposite each row of furnaces, from which the boilers will be fired by coal, so far as that is required, and on which also the refuse may be screened to separate some of the cinder from it, should you adopt that portion of their scheme. The destructor furnaces are of a type that would enable the perfect combustion of the refuse and its gases to be relied upon, and the furnaces provided by them are arranged to both feed and clinker automatically. The amount of coal this firm considers necessary to obtain the necessary evaporation is extremely high—namely, 3 tons per day. We think, however, that this is probably only due to the fact that, as they have not heretofore erected a dust destructor, they have probably not attached sufficient importance to the calorific value of the refuse to be dealt with, and, in any case, the arrangement of their boilers and furnaces is such that the same evaporation could be relied upon as that suggested by other tenderers. They also estimate the cost of labour in working the plant at £1,100 per annum, but they do not make any statement as to the amount required to maintain the apparatus, merely stating that this would be very low. The scheme put forward is an extremely well worked-out one, and, considering the extra amount of work in the erection of the two extra floors which are included in their tender, is not by any means a dear one. They make an alternative tender at £13,150 if double-flued tubular boilers are provided by them in place of the water-tube boilers, and we have no objections to offer to this alternative, should you be prepared to consider their tender for recommendation. They also quote as extras for a screen and apparatus in connection therewith, and for other sundries, which you would probably not be prepared to consider at the present moment."

The Society of Engineers in 1894 awarded me their gold medal for my paper on "Utilisation of Towns' Refuse for Generating Steam." Further comment is needless.

## "GENESIS OF STREET MUD."

In reference to the articles which we published in our issues of October 21st and 28th, under the above title, *The Quarry* says:—

In our last issue we gave the results of experiments made by Prof. Elliott upon various samples of stone submitted to him by *The Western Mail*. We then stated that "physical tests are frequently extremely delusive," and an examination of the tests in question tends to confirm our opinion. We have carefully considered the numerous articles which have appeared in *The Western Mail*, based upon Prof. Elliott's report, and compared it with evidence in our possession, and, as a result, we were in no way surprised to hear that Prof. Elliott had found it necessary to make an important correction in his figures. This correction brings the whole of *The Western Mail's* castle to the ground and renders further argument quite unnecessary. Even taking Prof. Elliott's original figures, we cannot admit that *The Western Mail* has made out its case. The whole question has been most ably dealt with in an article in THE SURVEYOR of October 21st, and we have much pleasure in congratulating our contemporary upon the calm, painstaking and logical manner in which it has combatted the double attack upon the Penlee Elvan stone and the Cardiff borough engineer. We should imagine that after this experiment *The Western Mail*, which is not a technical paper, will appreciate the maxim *No sutor ultra crepidam*.

## INSTITUTION OF CIVIL ENGINEERS.

ORDINARY MEETING.

An ordinary meeting of the above Institution will be held on Tuesday, at 8 p.m., when a paper will be read by Mr. Wm. Beedie Esson, M.I.C.E., on "Electrical Transmission for Power in Mining." A discussion will follow the conclusion of the reading of the paper.

* The refuse of the granite quarries.
† *Vide* "Proceedings of the Association of Municipal and County Engineers," vol. x.

# Law Notes.

EDITED BY J. B. REIGNIER CONDER, 11 Old Jewry Chambers, E.C.,

Solicitor of the Supreme Court.

*The Editor will be pleased to answer any questions affecting the practice of engineers and surveyors to local authorities. Queries (which should be written legibly on foolscap paper, one side only) should be addressed to "The Law Editor," at the Offices of* THE SURVEYOR. *Where possible, copies of local Acts or documents referred to should be enclosed. All explanatory diagrams must be drawn and lettered in black ink only. Correspondents who do not wish their names published should furnish a nom de plume.*

## QUERIES AND REPLIES.

ENGINEER AND SURVEYOR TO RURAL DISTRICT COUNCIL.—"Assistant" writes: I shall be much obliged if you can tell me, through your valuable paper, whether a surveyor to a rural district council has a right to sign orders for materials required in his departments, or is it necessary that all such orders should be signed by the clerk? Are there any reliable books published setting forth the duties of a surveyor under a rural district council?

This depends upon the regulations of the council with regard to the point. "The Municipal and Sanitary Engineers' Hand-Book," by H. Percy Boulnois, M.I.C.E. (third edition), is an excellent work on the subject of the duties of municipal and sanitary engineers.

BY-LAWS: ALTERATIONS TO BUILDING.—"Surveyor" writes: Plans have been submitted to the local authority for the erection of a new billiard-room over two living-rooms, which were 7 ft. 6 in. in height, and the conversion of the two living-rooms into a large dining-room, 42 ft. by 15 ft., to be used in connection with a café. It is proposed to make the dining-room 8 ft. 9 in. in height, but the local authority refuse to approve the plans unless such room is made 10 ft., as, in their opinion, a room used as a public dining-room should be not less than 10 ft. in height. The by-laws in force in the district (a copy of which I enclose), page 34, clause 64, states that a room used for human habitation shall not be less than 8 ft. in height. (1) Taking into consideration the use to which the large room is to be put, and may at times be full of people, can the local authority insist upon the room being made 10 ft.? (2) Would you consider the erection of the billiard-room and the alterations to the dining-room (the walls on the two sides of which have been pulled down to the ground floor) constituted a new building?

(1) I do not see how the authority can require a greater height than 8 ft. under By-Law 64. (2) This would be a question of fact for the magistrates to decide (*James* v. *Wyeill*, 51 L.T. [N.S.], 237).

PUBLIC HEALTH ACT, 1875, SEC. 150: INTERSECTIONS OF STREETS.—"F. H. G." writes: I enclose a sketch of two private streets ordered to be made and completed by the corporation. Can you inform me the legal way of apportioning

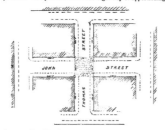

the costs of making the square piece at the junction of the two streets under the 1875 Act (1) when the work of making the two streets is carried out together, and (2) when only one street is completed and the other one left for, say, a year or two?

Under sec. 150 of the Public Health Act, 1875, the owners of premises fronting, adjoining or abutting on such parts of a street as may require to be paved, &c., are liable for the expense of making-up the street "according to the frontage of their respective premises." In any opinion the frontagers are not liable for the cost of paving, &c., the intersections. This view is strengthened by the fact that the corresponding section of the Metropolis Management Act, 1862 (sec. 77), expressly makes the owners of houses and land in the street liable for the paving, &c., of intersections; and it is to be presumed that the omission of a similar provision from the 1875 Act was intentional. The question remains whether where the soil of an intersecting street is vested in a private owner he is liable as a frontager. In *Lord North-brook* v. *Plumstead Board of Works (L.R.* 7, Q.B., 183) the owner of an intersecting private street was held liable; but in that case the intersecting streets had not been dedicated to the public. In a subsequent case where intersecting streets had been dedicated to the public it was held that the owners of the soil thereof were not liable as frontagers to contribute to the cost of paving, &c., the intersected street (*Plumstead Board of Works* v. *British Land Company, L.R.* 10, Q.B., 203). These cases were, however, under the metropolitan Act, under which (as already stated) frontagers are liable for the intersections, "and it remains to be decided whether in an urban district the owners of the soil of a public street abutting on a street within this section" (sec. 150, Public Health Act, 1875) "can be charged with a proportion of the expense of paving, &c., the latter." (Lumley's "Public Health Acts," fifth edition, p. 187.)

BY-LAWS: OPEN SPACE AT REAR OF BUILDING.—"W. D. H." writes: As questions are continually arising upon the interpretation of clause 53 in our local by-laws with regard to air space, I should esteem it a favour if you would kindly give me your opinion upon the following case. The house shown upon the plan has been newly erected, and the occupier

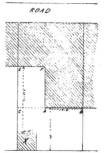

wished to erect a shed X in the position shown. Would this, in your opinion, contravene By-Law No. 53? or, in other words, would line A B be produced to C and the 15 ft. measured from this line, or should the 15 ft. be measured from E F?

In my opinion the shed would contravene By-Law 53. That by-law provides (*a*) that the open space shall extend laterally throughout the entire width of the building, and (*b*) that the distance across the open space from every part of the building to the boundary of premises opposite or adjoining shall be as prescribed (varying according to the height of the building). It seems to me that the effect of these two requirements is to preclude the erection of anything (except a water-closet, &c.) upon the open space. If a building were erected upon it, it would no longer be "an open space," and even if the distance to the boundary was measured from E F it could not be said to be "the distance across such open space."

HIGHWAY SURVEYOR: CLAIM FOR SALARY.—"Surveyor" writes: My late council in March last drew up a form of accounts to show in detail the expenditure on each road in the district, and it was passed that I, as their highway surveyor, should keep them from April 1st last. (I may say that these accounts did not have to be placed before the auditor, but were only for their private information.) Two years ago the clerk to the council wrote me saying that I was to do no new work of any kind without his written instruction, even if it had been passed by the rural district council. In the case of these books I received no instructions to commence them, so did nothing to them. Now, having left the council to take up duties here, they refuse to pay me a fortnight's salary, which is still owing to me, as they say in not doing these books I have not fulfilled my contract. I may say that I signed no contract or agreement as to my duties or the fulfilment of same, therefore I ask you can they legally keep back any money that is due to me?

Was the resolution of March last communicated to "Surveyor," and, if so, by whom? And did he thereupon, or at any time, communicate with the clerk and ask for instructions? How was the salary payable—quarterly, monthly or weekly? And when and under what circumstances did he leave the employ of the council? The law is that if a servant engage to render any particular service and refuse or neglect to render it he may be discharged without notice, and if he is guilty of such misconduct as to justify discharge he is not entitled to any salary from the time of the last period of payment. The facts are not stated with sufficient fulness to enable me to express an opinion as to whether the omission to keep the accounts was such neglect as would have justified dismissal, but it seems rather strange that "Surveyor" knew of the resolution he should not have taken some steps to arrive at a clear understanding as to whether he was to do the work or not.

Pontefract.—The purchase of Headlands House from Messrs. Lee & Shaw for £2,540, for market purposes, was discussed at a special meeting of the corporation last week. The chairman of the Market Committee proposed that the purchase be effected, but ultimately, after a long discussion, it was decided to leave the matter in the hands of the new council.

# Municipal Work in Progress and Projected.

The paragraphs under the headings of Aston Manor, Haworth, Lower Bebington, Otley, Romford, Sutton-in-Ashfield, Withington, Chorley, Lincoln and Yarmouth contain the most important news of municipal works which have come to hand this week from the provinces. In the metropolis, however, no specially extensive works seem to have been mooted during the week.

## METROPOLITAN AUTHORITIES.

### LONDON COUNTY COUNCIL.

The report presented by the Housing of the Working Classes Committee in reference to the future housing policy of the county council was unquestionably the chief matter which came up for consideration at Spring-gardens on Tuesday. The presentation of the report was followed by a long discussion, in the course of which several of the principal speakers opposed the erection of dwellings by the council except under legal obligations or exceptional circumstances. Sir Arthur Arnold thought the better policy was for the council to develope the tramway system so that people could get into the suburbs. This was the opinion expressed by most of the speakers, and the report was therefore referred back with an instruction to report again in three weeks. Several other less important matters were also considered, particulars of which are given below.

*Loans for Public Works.*—Upon the recommendation of the Finance Committee, it was agreed to lend the Hampstead Vestry £10,490 for electric lighting purposes, the Islington Vestry, £6,780 for similar purposes, the St. Martin's Vestry £5,000 for sewerage works, and the St. Pancras Vestry £10,110 for paving works.

*Maintenance of Small Open Spaces.*—The Parks Committee recommended the council to call a conference of local authorities to determine the future policy to be adopted in the management of the 105 small open spaces in London. This was agreed to.

*The Council's Housing Policy.*—The Housing of the Working Classes Committee presented a report dealing with the question of an extension in the near future of the housing policy of the council, and recommended: " (*a*) That it be the policy of the council to proceed from time to time, as opportunity shall offer, with the acquisition, under Part III. of the Housing of the Working Classes Act, 1890, of sites available for the erection of working-class dwellings within the county of London ; (*b*) that all clearances which involve rehousing be done at the sole cost of the council; (*c*) that housing accommodation should be provided for a number of persons equal to that of the working classes displaced by any scheme under the Housing of the Working Classes Act, 1890, or under the provisions of any Improvement Act ; (*d*) that housing accommodation for persons displaced be provided within the county of London, but not necessarily in the immediate neighbourhood of the displacement, due consideration being given to the needs of those living on any particular area." After a long discussion, during which several members protested against the idea that it was the duty of the council to house the people of London, the recommendation was referred back to the committee with an instruction to report further in three weeks.

*Proposed Purchase of Spitalfields Market.*—On the 12th July the Parliamentary Committee were instructed by the council to consider the advisability of including in one of the Bills to be promoted by the council in the next session of Parliament a clause empowering them to acquire by agreement or compulsorily the freehold and other interests in Spitalfields Market. They now reported that they had carefully considered the matter, and had come to the conclusion that the best course to adopt was to insert a clause in the council's General Powers Bill enabling the council to acquire by agreement the freehold interests in the market. They had instructed the agent accordingly, and recommended the council to approve their action. The recommendation was adopted.

*The Telephone Question.*—The Highways Committee submitted a letter from the Postmaster-General in reply to the council's letter of the 14th ult., which has already been published in THE SURVEYOR, stating that the Government were considering the proposals of the Select Committee on Telephones, and that if the proposals were adopted Parliament would be asked to legislate on the subject. The committee stated that in their opinion there was urgent necessity for the establishment of a telephone service for the London district, in competition with the service provided by the National Telephone Company, and they thought that every endeavour should be made to expedite the matter. They accordingly recommended that the clerk should be instructed to address a letter to the Postmaster-General pointing out the extreme urgency of the matter and the desirability of a decision being promptly arrived at by the Government upon the question whether the Post Office should establish a competing service. The recommendation was adopted.

### COURT OF COMMON COUNCIL.

At the usual meeting of the Court of Common Council on Thursday a petition was presented, on behalf of the Vestry of St. Botolph Without, Bishopsgate, asking for inquiries to be made into the condition of Montague-court, Bishopsgate, with a view to it being declared an insanitary area, so that it might be dealt with accordingly. The petition was referred to the Sanitary Committee with power to confer with the Finance and Improvement Committees.—The court unanimously adopted a resolution that the Streets Committee should be instructed to consider the desirability of the corporation applying for a license to establish a telephone service, either solely or in conjunction with the county council or any other local authorities within the London telephone area.—The Streets Committee presented a report from the City solicitor on the recent findings of the Select Committee of the House of Commons on the telephone service. The officer in question advised that the necessary steps should be taken to urge upon her Majesty's Government the extreme desirability of action being forthwith taken to give due effect to the recommendations of the Select Committee. The report was adopted.—The Streets Committee, reporting on a recent petition from the Metropolitan Drinking Fountain and Cattle Trough Association, recommended that the association should be relieved of all further expenses in connection with the drinking fountains and troughs in the City, and that the structures should be taken over, maintained and provided with water by the corporation. The recommendation was adopted.—The town clerk read an application from the Metropolitan Electric Supply Company, Limited, asking for the formal consent of the corporation to their intended application to the Board of Trade for a provisional order for the supply of electricity within the City.—The Cattle Markets Committee submitted a report with reference to the extension of the foreign cattle market at Deptford and the construction of a short line from the market to the railway station of the London, Brighton and South Coast Railway. The report set forth the fact that Sir J. Wolfe Barry, K.C.B., had been appointed the engineer to the new works. Notices had been served for the acquisition of a considerable amount of property, the amount involved being estimated at £22,000. The extended accommodation meant additional slaughter-houses, cooling-rooms, lairage and river frontage. The estimate for the slaughter-houses (a first instalment) was £5,000 ; lairage, £21,000 ; a junction of the three jetties, £16,000 ; and railway and tramway works, £32,250, making, with other expenditure, a total outlay of £105,000. The report of the committee was adopted without discussion.

### METROPOLITAN ASYLUMS BOARD.

A meeting of the managers was held on Saturday, under the presidency of Sir Edwin Galsworthy. Upon the recommendation of the *Exmouth* Committee it was decided to accept the tender of Messrs. Clark & Stanfield for the provision of new water-storage tanks. The tender of Messrs. Taylor & Sons, of Marsden, Yorks., was also accepted for the supply of auto-stokers, with hoppers, counter-shafting and engine, at the sum of £195. The following clause regarding the rates of wages to be paid to workmen by contractors was recommended to be inserted in all future contracts entered into: " The contractor shall on all work executed for the managers pay the rates of wages and observe the hours of labour agreed upon by the association of employers and the representatives of the workmen ; but in the case of any trade where no such agreement exists, then the rate of wages and the hours of labour must be those current in the district where the work is executed."

### VESTRIES AND DISTRICT BOARDS.

**Battersea.**—The Finance Committee, at a meeting of the vestry on Wednesday, reported that they had considered the draft Bill prepared by Mr. H. S. Samuel, M.P., which provided that the Local Government Board may in cases of emergency require the water companies to supply water to each other by agreement or as the Local Government Board may prescribe. The committee recommended that Mr. Samuel should be informed that the vestry were in favour of the draft provisions of the Bill. After some discussion an amendment was adopted approving of the Bill, with the name of the London County Council being substituted for the Local Government Board.—The Highways Committee announced that they had received a report from Mr. J. T. Pilditch, the surveyor, on the condition of the whole of the gullies in the parish. The committee recommended that the work of reconstructing and repairing the gullies in some of the streets should be carried out as a matter of urgency, and this was agreed to. The total cost of the scheme was estimated at over £1,300, although, as the surveyor pointed out, other work might be discovered which would cause the amount to vary.—A report from the Health Committee was submitted recommending the erection of a new urinal in Nine Elms-lane. The report was, however, referred back to the committee, with a view to the erection of a chalet in the neighbourhood.—At the suggestion of the Works Committee it was decided to postpone until March the work of wood paving in Battersea Park-road, owing to the inadvisability of carrying out the work in the winter months.—With reference to the additional land recently acquired for the extension of the site of the proposed electric light station, the Lighting Committee recommended that the land should be enveloped by a boundary wall with the necessary piers and gates. The recommendation was adopted.—The Lighting Committee also reported that notice had been given by Mr. Morse of the intention of the County of London and Brush Provincial Electric Lighting Company to apply for an electric lighting provisional order for Battersea in the ensuing session of Parliament.— It was decided to refer to the Health Committee a report by the surveyor of the flooding of many houses through the recent heavy storm.—A letter was read from the Lee District Board of Works on the subject of the Workmen's Compensation Act. The letter stated that in consequence of the expressions of opinion by other authorities that the risk was small, and the action of those authorities in the matter, it had been decided to postpone the proposed conference to consider the question.

**Bermondsey.**—At a meeting of the vestry, on Monday, the Sanitary Committee reported that they had again considered the question of providing underground conveniences. Though the Rotherhithe Vestry had declined to co-operate in the matter, the committee, in view of the urgent need of such accommodation, recommended that a convenience should be built near the junction of Galley Wall-road and Southwark Park-road. This was agreed to, and the question was referred to the committee for the selection of a site and the getting out of plans and estimates.—A letter was received from the Kensington Vestry in favour of the telephone service being in the hands of the Government, and stating that they had resolved to urge upon the Government the necessity of the Post Office establishing a more efficient telephone service in the metropolis. On the recommendation of the General Purposes Committee it was resolved to support the action of the Kensington Vestry.—The following tenders, which were opened, for the supply of slop vans were referred to committee for consideration and report : Austen Rendle, £43 10s. each ; Alfred Parker, £42 ; Horn, Limited, £45 ; Stone & Son (informal), £45 ; Glover & Son (alternative tenders), £43 and £44 ; McDonald, £46 ; and Baker & Son, £38 6s.

**Camberwell.**—At a meeting of the vestry, on Wednesday of last week, the Baths Committee reported that for some time past they had had under consideration the provision of public baths and wash-houses in the Old Kent-road. They had viewed numerous sites, and had selected one which contained an area of 18,000 square feet, and which consisted of the five freehold houses, Nos. 525, 527, 529, 531 and 533 Old Kent-road and Nos. 2, 4, 6 and 8 Marlborough-road. This site the committee estimated would be sufficiently large to enable the vestry to erect first and second class swimming baths, public wash-houses and slipper baths. The agents of the freeholders had agreed to give the vestry a short option of purchase and to accept the sum of £6,500 for their entire freehold interest. The leases of all the property would expire within the next five years. The committee unanimously recommended that the vestry purchase the freehold interest in the property ; that a cheque for £650 be drawn as a deposit, and that it be referred to the Finance Committee to negotiate and arrange a loan. After some discussion the recommendation of the committee was adopted.—The General Purposes Committee reported that the county council had not yet decided whether they would contribute towards the acquisition of the ground at the rear of 113A Sumner-road as a recreation ground. The owner of the land, which was a third of an acre in extent, now stated that he had received an offer to let it for stables, at a ground rent of £50 per annum. It was therefore necessary that the vestry should decide at once. The committee were of opinion that it was most desirable that it should be acquired as a public garden, and they therefore recommended that the land be purchased by the vestry for the sum of £1,000. The recommendation was adopted.—On the recommendation of the Sewers and Sanitary Committee it was resolved that the surveyor be empowered to carry out the work of laying a pipe sewer on the west side of Peckham Rye, which was estimated to cost £1,200, with the vestry's own workmen, and also to engage a clerk of the works.—The Plant and Scavenging Committee reported that they had considered a letter from the London County Council giving the result of the council's inquiry, extending over nearly three weeks, as to dust collection in the parish. The council stated that there were accumulations of two weeks or over in 162 cases, and that many householders said they were still compelled to give the dustmen money in order to obtain a clean removal. The committee had referred the matter to the surveyor. The committee's action was approved.—On the motion of Mr. Rogers the clerk was instructed to reply, informing the Islington Vestry that the Camberwell Vestry did not think it advisable to appoint delegates to attend another conference on London local government.

**Islington.**—At a meeting of the vestry, on Friday, a letter was read from the Limehouse District Board of Works drawing attention to the proposal of the London County Council to transfer the maintenance of the main roads to the local authorities, and suggesting that if this was done it would deprive the latter of the grant now made in regard to the maintenance of those thoroughfares. The board asked the vestry to appoint delegates to attend a conference of other local authorities to consider the question. It was decided to refer the matter to the Parliamentary Committee for report. —The vestry clerk submitted a communication from the

London County Council in regard to the by-laws made under the London Overhead Wires Act. The council asked the vestry whether they had appointed any inspectors under the Act, whether any steps had been taken to enforce the by-laws, and, in the event of this having been done, whether particulars would be furnished for the information of the Highways Committee. The letter was referred to the Works Committee, with power to act.—The vestry postponed the consideration of recommendations of the Works Committee in favour of the reconstruction of a 12-in. pipe sewer in Cambridge-terrace, at an estimated cost of £340, and the erection of greenhouses at the Finchley Cemetery, at a cost of £313. —The Public Health Committee submitted a report on the advisability of public abattoirs being established in London, and recommended that a copy of the report should be forwarded to the London County Council.—A report was presented by the Parliamentary Committee in respect to the draft Bill prepared by Mr. H. S. Samuel, M.P., dealing with the question of London water supply. As the vestry have previously passed a resolution declaring that the water supply should be vested in the county council, the committee recommended that no action should be taken in connection with the Bill, and that Mr. Samuel should be informed as to the vestry's views on the subject. The consideration of the question was postponed.—At the next meeting a resolution will be proposed by Mr. Stonelake to instruct the Electric Lighting Committee to report as to the cost of installing the electric light from Highbury-corner along Canonbury-road and the New North-road, in order that the installation may meet the electric lighting system now being carried out by the Shoreditch Vestry as far as the boundary of that parish.

**Lee.**—At the last meeting of the district board of works the General Purposes Committee reported that they had considered a recommendation from the London County Council in reference to the establishment of bacteriological laboratories in the board's district, and recommended that the clerk should be instructed to reply to the council stating that they considered the question to be one for the Government. This was agreed to.

**Lewisham.**—On Wednesday of last week, at a meeting of the district board of works, Mr. Carman moved that it be referred to the Works Committee to consider and report as to the desirability of substituting artificial stone or other paving for tar paving, at present generally used in the district. He said that at Sydenham and Forest Hill artificial stone had been found to be a great improvement. The proposal was unanimously agreed to.—The surveyor submitted a plan and estimate (£1,270) of the expenses of forming and paving part of the road at Honor Oak Park from Leasing-street to the railway station, together with an apportionment of such expenses on the several persons chargeable. It was resolved that such apportionment be made.

**Mile End.**—Last week the vestry resolved to request the London County Council to lower Victory Bridge (near Commercial gasworks), and the clerk was instructed to forward copies of the resolution to the councillors for Limehouse, Stepney and Mile End, and also to the Limehouse District Board of Works, asking for their active support.—On the recommendation of the Highways Committee, it was resolved to appoint four delegates to attend a conference on the subject of the recent action of the London County Council with regard to applying to Parliament for the transfer to the local authorities of the duty of maintaining main and disturnpiked roads.

**Newington.**—The Electric Lighting Committee, at a meeting of the vestry on Wednesday, recommended that the first instalment of £10,000 of the electric lighting loan of £50,000 should be taken up from the London County Council and be repaid by thirty-nine annual instalments (the first in 1902) within the period of forty-two years, over which the loan is to be granted. This was agreed to. It was also decided to give an undertaking to the county council to set apart a sinking fund to meet the necessary maintenance charges on the electric light installation during the period of the loan, and not to include in any future loan any sum for the renewal of the machinery and plant to be provided by the present loan.—The General Purposes Committee asked the vestry to approve the Bill, to be introduced by Mr. Sam Woods, M.P., in favour of cheap trains being instituted for the working classes.

**Rotherhithe.**—At the last meeting of this vestry the General Purposes Committee recommended that the vestry agree with the whole of the resolutions passed at the Bermondsey conference on the subject of overcrowding and the housing of the working classes, with the exception of the one expressing the opinion that local authorities should not be compelled to repay the cost of the land out of the income from the dwellings. The committee's recommendations were adopted without discussion. The vestry approved Mr. H. Samuel's Bill to amend the Metropolis Water Act, 1871. The Bill provides, inter alia, for the connection of the mains of the various water companies in cases of emergency.

**St. Luke.**—A letter from the clerk to the London County Council was read at last week's meeting of the vestry informing them that the council had agreed to contribute one-half of the nett cost of carrying out the proposed improvement at the corner of Old-street and City-road.

**St. Olave's.**—At last week's meeting of the district board of works the clerk was instructed to inform Bermondsey Vestry that the board, while sympathising with all efforts for improving the housing of the working classes, were not, in the absence of any practical scheme, able to take any action in the matter.—On the motion of the chairman it was resolved that a deputation wait upon the Highways Committee of the London County Council to ask them to contribute towards the cost of widening Queen Elizabeth-street as a public improvement.

**St. Pancras.**—The Highways Committee, at the last meeting of the vestry, reported that they had received a letter from Messrs. Jackson & Son asking for the transfer of their contracts in relation to scavenging works and the supply of stone to Messrs. Snowdon, Hubbard & Co. On the recommendation of the committee it was resolved to accede to the request and to enter into fresh contracts with the latter company.—The vestry decided to grant the application of the East London Waterworks Company to lay a new 36-in. main in Camden-road, passing Little Randolph-street and St. Paul's-road, to York-road. The application was made because the company possessed no statutory powers outside the line of their existing mains passing through the parish, and in order to enable the company to obtain more water from their Thames works.—The Highways Committee announced that they had further considered the application of the National Telephone Company for permission to lay a branch line to establish communication between the exchange at King's Cross and the company's exchange in the West-End. The committee again recommended that the scheme should be sanctioned, but this was withdrawn in view of action being probably taken to establish a competitive system in the metropolis.—On the recommendation of the Electricity Committee it was resolved to sanction an expenditure of £2,225 on the lighting (by means of arc lamps) of Albany-street and four other thoroughfares.

# PROVINCIAL AND GREATER LONDON AUTHORITIES.

## COUNTY COUNCILS.

**Middlesex.**—A special meeting of the county council was held on Monday to consider a further report presented by the Kew Bridge Joint Committee of Surrey and Middlesex. The further report renewed the former recommendation that a Bill should be introduced to give fresh spending powers, as the cost of rebuilding would be more than £50,000 over Sir John Wolfe Barry's estimate, and it was impossible to reduce the price within the authorised limits. Mr. Littler, Q.C., the chairman of the council, who is also chairman of the joint committee, in moving the adoption of the report said he had asked the council to meet that day out of courtesy to the Surrey Council, who were meeting on the following day. The county surveyors of the two counties had told the committee that the tendered price was very moderate, and in some cases decidedly low. Sir John Wolfe Barry had assured them that had the work been done at the time his estimate was given that estimate would probably have been nearly accurate; but the price of granite had gone up 100 per cent. since then. Mr. Peter Watson said that this matter was almost a scandal to the county council. He did not think they should have been called together again until after the meeting of the Surrey Council. He therefore moved that they adjourn until the 14th inst. This was seconded, and carried by twenty-one votes to thirteen. Mr. Littler said that he must ask the council to appoint another chairman of the joint committee, as in future he would have nothing to do with it in any shape or kind. The meeting then closed.

**Surrey.**—At their quarterly meeting, on Tuesday, the county council considered a report from the joint committee of Surrey and Middlesex similar in terms to that presented to the Middlesex Council on the previous day, stating that, after careful reconsideration, the committee were unable to recommend any further reduction in the revised estimate of £149,000 as the contract price for the rebuilding of Kew Bridge, and they repeated their recommendation that an Act should be obtained for fresh borrowing powers. Mr. Halsey, chairman of the council, in moving the adoption of the report, read a letter from Mr. Littler, chairman of the Middlesex Council, pointing out that, despite the action of his own council on the previous night postponing the matter, it was still open for the Surrey Council to go for an Act, leaving the Middlesex Council to confirm it at the adjourned meeting. Mr. J. Lawrence moved an amendment to refer the matter back to the committee; but this proposal was rejected by a large majority, and the recommendations to seal the contract and proceed with the Bill were adopted.

## MUNICIPAL CORPORATIONS.

**Brighton.**—The General Purposes Committee of the corporation have approved plans by which a great improvement will be effected at the Brighton Aquarium. The property has been for a long time in the market, and at length it has been acquired by a syndicate, who propose to form a winter garden on the site. Negotiations have been in progress, and an agreement has been arrived at under which 6,000 superficial yards will pass into the possession of the town, enabling the Marine Parade to be widened by 20 ft. from the new pier to the site of the toll-houses of the old Chain Pier.

**Cheltenham.**—The town council have decided to apply to the Board of Trade for an amendment of the Cheltenham Electric Light Order, 1890, by extending the area of supply to the whole of the borough as may be determined.

**Chorley.**—At the last monthly meeting of the town council it was resolved that a refuse destructor should be provided on land adjoining Stump-lane, and that tenders for the erection of the destructor be advertised for.—It was also resolved that on the 9th November an Electric Lighting Committee should be formed to take over the duties appertaining to the laying down of an electric lighting plant.—A letter was read from the Local Government Board sanctioning the borrowing of £6,500 for purposes of sewage disposal, but insisting on the necessity for passing the effluent of the sewage over land after being chemically treated.

**Colchester.**—The Duke of Cambridge last week laid the foundation-stone of the new town hall, which is being erected by the corporation at a cost, excluding private gifts, of about £35,000, from designs by Mr. John Belcher, F.R.I.B.A., of Hanover-square, W. A conspicuous feature of the building will be the Victoria Tower, with clock and chimes, costing £2,000, the gift of the mayor, Alderman James Paxman, J.P. After the conclusion of the ceremony the mayor entertained about 500 guests at the annual Oyster Feast in the adjoining Corn Exchange.

**Derby.**—The Parliamentary Committee of the corporation at a recent meeting entered into an agreement for the purchase of the tramways. The actual price to be paid will be made known shortly, and the tramways will probably come into the possession of the town at the beginning of the new year.

**Gloucester.**—The corporation recently accepted the tender of Messrs. John Gurney & Sons, Gloucester, at £7,676, for the construction of the electric light works. The tender was not the lowest, but it was accepted because the contractors were the only ones who guaranteed to complete the works in nine months. Mr. H. Forse's (Bristol) contract was £9,278, and that of Messrs. Stephens, Barstow & Co., Limited, £10,774.

**Lincoln.**—The city council have decided to apply to the Local Government Board for sanction to borrow the sum of £19,000 for the purpose of defraying the expenses of the extension of the electricity works, cables, &c., and other works.

**Liverpool.**—Major Cardew, on behalf of the Board of Trade, recently paid a special visit to Liverpool, for the purpose of inspecting the experimental line of electrical tramways which extends from South Castle-street to the Dingle. He was met by Mr. Holmes, corporation electrical engineer, and Mr. J. O'Neill, manager of tramways.

**Manchester.**—The committee of the corporation who have in their charge the municipalisation of the tramway system in Manchester are conducting negotiations with the various urban authorities into whose districts the lines extend. Arrangements have been come to with the Heaton Norris, Levenshulme, Gorton, Denton, Audenshaw, Droylsden and Failsworth urban district councils; but the councils which govern the affairs of Withington, Moss Side and Stretford are still in negotiation with the committee. In the case of the two former there seems to be nothing to prevent an adjustment of the difficulties which have presented themselves. With Stretford, however, the case is different. It is understood that this authority—no doubt for reasons which, in their opinion, are perfectly good—are holding out for terms which the committee cannot see their way to concede.

**Rotherham.**—The following resolution was adopted at a recent special meeting of the town council : That this corporation do join with the Sheffield Corporation in the promotion of a Bill in the ensuing session of Parliament for acquiring the waters, or a portion thereof, of the rivers Derwent and Aslop, subject to the detailed terms as between Sheffield and Rotherham being incorporated in an agreement and approved of by the present sub-committee.

**Tynemouth.**—The town council, at a special meeting on Monday, resolved : That the proposals made by the counsel for the North Shields Water Company, as contained in the terms of arrangement, dated October 19th, as to the price to be paid by the corporation to the company and Earl Percy for the purchase of the undertaking and the settlement of other matters, set forth in the terms of arrangement, for the sum of £75,000 be adopted and confirmed.

**Yarmouth.**—At a special meeting of the corporation, on Monday of last week, the question of establishing electric trams in the borough was considered. The borough surveyor had framed a scheme on the overhead principle, the total cost of which would be £100,000, but the Lands Committee had struck out some of the routes and reduced the scheme so that the total cost would be £40,000, including construction, rolling stock and equipment. The scheme was adopted by nineteen votes to one vote.

## URBAN DISTRICT COUNCILS.

**Haworth.**—On Tuesday of last week Mr. E. A. Sandford Fawcett, A.M.I.C.E., conducted an inquiry, on behalf of the Local Government Board, into an application of the district council for power to borrow £12,000 for sewerage works.

**Kingsbridge, Devonshire.**—At the last meeting of the council it was decided to apply for a provisional order to carry ont certain works of water supply. Messrs. Fredk. Beesley & Son, of Westminster, were appointed engineers for the work.

**Lower Bebington.**—Last week Colonel W. R. Slacke, R.E., held an inquiry, on behalf of the Local Government Board, regarding an application of the district council for power to borrow £10,000 for a sewerage scheme, £5,000 for new public offices, and £3,000 for a recreation ground.

**Middlewich, Cheshire.**—Magnificent technical schools and a free library, which were projected to commemorate the Queen's diamond jubilee, were opened on Saturday. The cost was £2,400, of which Sir John Brunner contributed £1,263. Lord Crewe, who performed the opening ceremony and made a speech, expressed his view that the popular vote for free libraries should be abolished, and local authorities be allowed to establish such institutions.

**Otley.**—A special meeting of the council was held on the 1st inst. to consider a report on the water supply. At present the supply is drawn from a bore-hole at Menston and other small sources, which yield a total of 240,000 gallons daily. This is sufficient for present requirements, but it is proposed to extend the supply so as to provide for the expected increase during the next twenty or thirty years. To do this it is proposed to construct a reservoir at a place called Bow Beck, on the north side of the river Wharfe, near Ilkley. It was mentioned that the cost of the scheme would be £35,000, and it would yield a supply sufficient for at least thirty years. Otley would also be able to supply other townships with water.

**Romford.**—On Friday Mr. Meade-King, a Local Government Board inspector, held an inquiry at Romford into an application of the council for permission to borrow £6,000 for the erection of public baths and £1,486 for the purchase of the lairs and stock-yards at Moore's yard and the erection of buildings thereon.

**Southgate.**—At a recent meeting of the district council a letter was read from the Local Government Board with reference to the council's application for power to borrow the sums of £4,500, £1,700 and £1,700 for purposes of sewerage, stating that before such application be acceded to a local inquiry would be held on the subject. With reference to the borrowing of an additional sum of £1,700 in respect of the sewer in the Green-lanes and Hoppers-road, for the construction of which a loan of £3,800 was sanctioned in October, the Local Government Board wished to be furnished with a revised estimate of the total cost on their own forms, and a detailed section of the proposed crossing under the New River in connection with the proposed construction of a new sewer from Tile Kiln-lane to Barrowell Green-corner, for which the sum of £4,500 was to be applied for. The clerk and the surveyor were instructed to supply the required information.

**Sowerby Bridge.**—An inspector of the Local Government Board held an inquiry last week with respect to an application of the district council for permission to borrow £800 for the purchase of land for storage purposes.

**Sutton-in-Ashfield.**—Mr. Frederick H. Tulloch, M.I.C.E., on Tuesday week held an inquiry, on behalf of the Local Government Board, in reference to an application of the district council for sanction to borrow £8,000 for water supply works. Messrs. F. W. & G. Hodson, the engineers of the proposed scheme, attended and submitted the plans for the works.

**Swinton and Pendlebury.**—In consequence of representations made to them, the Local Government Board recently sent Major Carey, one of their inspectors, to inspect the sewage works of the council, with a view to reporting as to their capacity for the treatment of the sewage of the district. The board recommended the council to take 125 acres of land for the treatment of their sewage; but the council pointed out that they were already producing an effluent which satisfied the Mersey and Irwell Joint Committee, and when other improvements now being carried out at the works have been completed the works will be "second to none for efficiency in Lancashire." The council's farm consists of 37 acres.

**Whitefield.**—The district council have resolved to apply to the Local Government Board for power to borrow money for important street improvements.

**Winsford.**—Last week, at a meeting of the council, the question of lighting the district by means of electricity was discussed. It was reported that the first installation to light the whole of the main streets would cost £7,700. Notice was given by a member of his intention to move that application be made to the Board of Trade for an electric lighting provisional order.

**Withington.**—A Local Government Board inquiry has been held into an application of the council for sanction to borrow £4,720 for the improvement of various thoroughfares and £1,560 for sewerage purposes. The surveyor, Mr. Mountain, showed the necessity for the improvements, and there was no opposition.

## RURAL DISTRICT COUNCILS.

**Halifax.**—The council are about to construct water tanks in Norland and Upper Greetland, for the purpose of improving their supply of water to these loftily-situated districts. The districts are within the area of supply of the Halifax Corporation.

**Hemsworth**—Colonel W. Langton Coke and Dr. H. T.

Bulstrode recently held an inquiry, on behalf of the Local Government Board, in reference to the application of the district council for sanction to a loan of £4,300 for the carrying out of the South Emrall and Moorthorpe sewerage scheme. The clerk to the council said that for some time the council had had great difficulty in obtaining a suitable site for the disposal works. Now all arrangements had been made with Major Allatt, who was going to sell 4½ acres of land at £140 per acre. A committee had inspected the septic tank system at work in Exeter, and recommended that system for adoption. In formulating the scheme the council had had regard to the wishes of the inhabitants, and all proposals had been approved by the parish councils of the two townships. Mr. T. H. Richardson, the surveyor, explained the plans, and said the surface water and drainage water would be dealt with separately. The only trade effluents which would enter the sewers were from two malt kilns at South Elmsall. The sewers would lie on the average about 3 ft. below the surface. The area for irrigation purposes was 3 acres 1 rood, and the tanks were to be on the septic principle. Other evidence was given, and the inquiry closed.

**Maldon.**—Mr. F. St. George Mivart, an inspector of the Local Government Board, has held an inquiry into an application of the council for permission to borrow £1,800 for the purchase of a site and the erection thereon of an isolation hospital at Southminster.

**Newton Abbot.**—Plans and estimates have been adopted by the district council for the construction of a reservoir, to hold 60,000 gallons, and the laying of the necessary pipes to supply Kingskerswell with water. The estimated cost is £1,900.

**Reigate.**—It has been announced that the Local Government Board, having had under consideration a report of their inspector on a recent inquiry with reference to an application of the council for sanction to borrow £1,000 for works of sewerage and sewage disposal, were advised that the site acquired on lease for the treatment and disposal of sewage was not suitable for such purpose, owing to its position and character, its liability to floods, and its close proximity to a public road and occupied houses. The board understood that the owner of the site was willing to lease and grant to the council another site. Under these circumstances the board must request the council to consider the matter, with a view to the adoption of a more suitable site. The council went into committee on the question at the conclusion of the highway business, and it was understood that it had been decided to take steps to acquire compulsorily a certain other site which was suggested.

## SCOTLAND AND IRELAND.

**Larne.**—A specially-convened meeting of the town commissioners was held on the 28th ult., to take into consideration, along with other matters, "the report received from Mr. J. Finlay Peddie in reference to the sewerage of Larne," which this gentleman had been deputed and employed by the members to undertake. Mr. Peddie was present and produced his plans. After discussion it was resolved that the report be printed and circulated among the principal ratepayers, as well as copies sent to the members of the board, and that a special meeting of the commissioners be summoned, at a time to be appointed at next monthly meeting, to consider the question.

**Linlithgow.**—The police commissioners, who are at present considering the best method for disposal of the town's sewage, have received a report from Messrs. Warren & Stuart, Glasgow, with reference to the bacteriological method of sewage disposal in preference to the system of chemical treatment by precipitation and filtration which had been recommended by them some years ago.

**Motherwell.**—At a recent special meeting the town council had under consideration the question of introducing an electric light installation in the burgh. A committee submitted a report by Prof. Alexander B. W. Kennedy, who has been retained by the burgh. The total capital expenditure is calculated to be over £23,000, this scheme providing for private lighting thirty arc lamps and 400 32 candle-power incandescent lamps for street purposes, and for power for mechanical purposes. After some discussion the report was adopted.

**Port Glasgow.**—The formal completion of additional waterworks, designed by Mr. James Wilson, Edinburgh, took place recently at Parkhill, near Port Glasgow. The works consist of a pure water tank capable of holding 500,000 gallons, and two new filters of about 800 square yards, the cost being £4,000. The contractors were Messrs. D. Cunningham & Sons, Kilbarchan. The ceremony of formally laying the last copestone was performed by Provost Rodger. It is calculated that in this department the requirements of the burgh have been met for the next twenty years.

**Ross and Cromarty.**—The county council of Ross and Cromarty have agreed to construct a new road from Kyle to Balmacara, in the vicinity of the terminus of the Dingwall and Skye railway, the length of which will be 5 miles, and the estimated cost £5,000. The existing road is of a circular nature, over 7 miles in length, besides being most dangerous. It was also decided to construct a few iron bridges at different points in the island of Lewis, at a cost of £1,214.

# Personal.

Llandudno Urban District Council have decided upon the appointment of an electrical engineer.

Mr. Percy G. Beckley, of Brierley Hill, has been appointed deputy surveyor to the Brierley Hill Urban District Council, at a salary of £100 per annum.

Mr. Morgan Thomas, of Pentre, was on Thursday appointed surveyor to the Porthcawl Urban District Council. There were twelve applicants for the post.

Mr. Thomas Jenkins, who has been a district superintendent under the Lambeth Vestry for several years, has been appointed to a similar position at Marylebone.

At the last monthly meeting of the Leeds Association of Engineers a paper was read by Mr. F. Leslie Watson, A.M.I.C E., on " The Designing and Construction of Refuse Destructors."

Warmley Rural District Council have adopted a motion recommending the appointment of Mr. H. W. Bennett as surveyor for the parishes of Bitton, Siston Oidland and Hanham Abbots.

Carlisle Town Council have approved the appointment of Mr. C. D. Burnet as resident electrical engineer, at a commencing salary of £250 per annum, with liberty to take not more than two pupils.

The successful candidate for the post of engineering assistant in the department of Mr. S. A. Pickering, borough surveyor of Oldham, is Mr. William Shackleton, of the borough surveyor's office, Nelson.

At last week's meeting of the St. George's (Southwark) Vestry Mr. R. H. Jeffes, at present engaged in the surveyor's department at Thames Ditton, was elected to the vacant position of assistant surveyor.

Mr. J. Willcocks, surveyor to the Buckfastleigh Urban District Council, recently gave notice of his intention to resign his post. At the request of the council, however, he agreed to continue in office until Christmas.

Mr. Sydney Baynes, chief electrical engineer to the St. Pancras Vestry, has been voted an immediate increase in his remuneration of from £600 to £700 per annum, with two further increases of £50 each up to a maximum of £800 per annum.

Last week the Spalding Urban District Council appointed Mr. J. H. Helé, of Stoke-on-Trent, as assistant borough surveyor. This office, which was rendered vacant by the resignation of Mr. D. Crampton, carries with it a salary of £100 per annum. There were forty-three applicants.

A new surveyor to the Audenshaw Urban District Council has just been appointed, the previous official, Mr. J. H. Burton, having resigned after holding the position for over twenty years. There were forty-eight applicants, from whom Mr. J. S. Green, of Haslingden, was selected. His salary will commence at £180 yearly.

Upon the recommendation of the Sewage Committee, the Yeovil Town Council recently decided to appoint Mr. W. K. L. Armytage, the borough surveyor, as engineer for the corporation's sewage scheme, which was on the septic tank system. Mr. Armytage's remuneration will be as follows: £100 at the conclusion of the Local Government Board inquiry; £50 if and when the scheme is accepted and the loan granted; and £100 at the completion of the works.

On the 4th inst., at a meeting of the Ayr Town Council, a letter was read from Mr. John Eaglesham, burgh surveyor, resigning the appointments held by him under the town council and police commissioners. He stated that he had for some time been considering the advisability of resuming private practice. He desired to be relieved of the duties as soon as possible. Eventually a committee was appointed to approach Mr. Eaglesham with a view to get him to reconsider his decision.

At a smoking concert, held at the Midland Hotel, Birmingham, on Friday evening last, under the presidency of the city surveyor, Mr. A. W. Lee (deputy building surveyor) was presented with a cellarette and cabinet by the members of the Public Works Department on the occasion of his marriage. On the same evening Mr. Charles Grubb, who is retiring after forty-six years of active service as superintendent of sewermen, and whose career was recently made the subject of an article in a London daily paper, was also presented with a handsome marble clock, suitably inscribed, and a purse of gold.

An interesting presentation has been made in Chester to Mr. William Holland, late surveyor to the Cheshire County Council. The presentation, which came from the foremen and workmen of Mr. Holland's district, consisted of a very handsome black marble clock, striking the hours and half-hours on a richly-toned cathedral gong. On a gilt plate on the clock was engraved the following inscription : " Presented to Mr. William Holland, district surveyor of the No. 1 district (Cheshire County Council) on his promotion, by the foremen and workmen of his district, as a mark of respect and esteem, 26th October, 1898."

The death occurred on Sunday night of Mr. Daniel Roberts, district surveyor to the Derbyshire County Council. The deceased, who had been ailing for some time, was sixty-six years of age. He was one of the first surveyors appointed when the county council took control of the main roads, having previously been employed in a similar capacity for the Bakewell Union. He leaves three sons and three daughters. Up to the last he was most active in the discharge of his duties, and enjoyed the respect, not only of the workmen whom he employed, but also of a wide circle of friends in Bakewell and the neighbourhood.

Last week, at the usual monthly meeting of the Folkestone Town Council, the mayor, speaking with deep feeling, moved a resolution of condolence, on behalf of his colleagues in the council, upon the sad occasion of the death of Mr. John White, the borough surveyor. It was a very painful duty to him, as he had known Mr. White for many years. His loss would be greatly felt, and he most sincerely offered the family his deepest sympathy. The chairman of the Highways Committee endorsed the remarks of the mayor and expressed the opinion that the council had lost a most estimable and valuable servant, who has carried out his duties in a most admirable manner. Other members spoke, and the resolution was passed in silence.

Saltburn Urban District Council have appointed Mr. G. S. Baynes, of Jarrow, as surveyor, at a commencing salary of £125 per annum. Two months ago Mr. R. A. Jackson resigned the office, but intimated that he was willing to continue to serve until the council appointed his successor. The council regretted to lose Mr. Jackson's services, but they had no alternative but to advertise the vacancy. This invitation attracted ninety-nine applications, coming from all sorts and conditions of people; and the sifting process brought the number down to three, who were asked to interview the council. Mr. Baynes has had a good deal of experience, having had charge of contracts in London, besides having been for some time the chief assistant to the borough engineer of Jarrow.

A limited competition was recently held for the erection of new municipal buildings at Godalming, on the site of the present town hall, which is to be incorporated in the new construction of London. It was a great triumph for architects that they were converting a rather dull city, mostly composed the new municipal buildings will include a court-house, with rooms for the magistrate and officials, as well as parochial offices. The council chamber will be on the first floor, with committee-room and offices for the town clerk. The scheme also includes a fire-engine station and men's quarters. The limit of the outlay was £27,000. The choice has been made of the premiated designs from eight sets of plans submitted ; but Mr. A. H. Tiltman, who was among the invited architects, did not prepare a plan. Messrs. Lanchester, Stewart & Rickards were awarded the first place, Mr. E. R. Robson, F.S.A., was awarded the second premium, and Messrs. Ardron & Dawson the third. Mr. E. W. Mountford acted as assessor.

On Monday evening Prof. Aitchison, R.A., delivered the opening address of the session to the members of the Royal Institute of British Architects. He congratulated his audience on the improvement that was taking place in the appearance of London. It was a great triumph for architects that they were converting a rather dull city, mostly composed of brick walls with holes in them, into a town almost as picturesque and varied as the old towns of France or Flanders. Architecture was the poetry of construction, and the noblest poetry was naturally found in buildings that were applied to the highest transcendental uses. A certain amount of comeliness was necessary to every building, except such buildings as were required to create fear, horror or a sense of ignominy, such as castles, gaols and pillories. Having dealt with the principal things which want teaching when construction and the art of planning had been mastered, the professor said, as regarded the practice of some of the younger members, there was too much straining after effect, too much recourse to easy means of arresting attention, too much partiality for curious and incongruous forms; the sewer arch or water opening was too much adopted for entrance doorways and attic windows—anything for a novelty. In his opinion there was nothing like straight lines for dignity, and the rounded corners and bellied door and window heads mostly produced meanness. The simplicity, grace and restraint of Greek work could not be too much studied, and that profusion of ornament that was now so common was not only opposed to Greek practice, but to good taste. They wanted badly a well-designed large window. They might increase one incentive by insisting on being paid for their work, for they were not paid now, and the powers that be might make another incentive more common by bestowing honours on the profession, which was now hardly recognised. In conclusion, he urged that they should devote themselves to architecture, and the art of planning their work, so that it might vie with the best Greek work in grace and with the Medieval in impressiveness. On the motion of Colonel Lenox Prendergast, seconded by Prof. Roger Smith, a vote of thanks was passed to the president for his address.

## BRADFORD WATER SUPPLY.

### PROGRESS OF THE NIDD VALLEY WORKS.

The report of the Waterworks Committee of the Bradford Corporation for the municipal year just ended contains the following particulars in reference to the progress of the new water supply works in the Nidd valley :—

GOUTHWAITE RESERVOIR.

The building of the masonry wall, the gauge basin, river retaining walls and river channel works are all completed. The whole of the arches, fourteen in number, over the dam, for carrying the roadway, as well as the parapet walls on each side, are completed. The narrow trench on the west side of the masonry dam, for about 180 yards in length, has been excavated, and 9,700 cubic yards of concrete have been put into place. The new road diversion along the western side of the reservoir, to replace the existing public road, has been pushed forward during the year, and the two bridges carrying the road over Colthouse Beck and Burn Gill are practically completed.

THE NIDD AQUEDUCT.

The work on this contract has progressed fairly well during the past year, and but for the flooding by water of the middle section of the Greenhow tunnel on December 11, 1897, which prevented two of the faces being worked for a period of some months, the work would have been further advanced. The masonry dam on the Nidd, which is being constructed to intercept the water of the Nidd for the supply of the city, is about one-third completed. The pipes, valves, &c., therefrom, which join up to the Rain Stang tunnel, are laid ; the Rain Stang tunnel, 2,486 yards in length, has been driven for a length of 2,360 yards, and the main aqueduct, consisting of 36-in. pipes and cut and cover work, together with the branch aqueducts connected therewith, arecompleted to Burn tunnel. The Burn tunnel, 1,844 yards in length, is finished. The pipes, aqueduct, bridges, &c., from Burn tunnel to Greenhow tunnel are all completed. The Greenhow tunnel, which has been kept back, as notified above, has been driven to a length of 4,850 yards, out of a total length of 6,200 yards. From thence to Chellow Heights reservoir and filter-beds the main line aqueduct, pipes, valves, manways, bridges, &c., are practically completed. The 30-in. pipe line from the main aqueduct to Barden reservoir is two-thirds finished, and the intercepting dam on the Barden Beck is in progress. The whole of the pipes for the Nidd aqueduct have, with the exception of a few special pipes, been supplied.

CHELLOW HEIGHTS SERVICE RESERVOIR AND FILTER-BEDS.

This work has been pushed steadily forward during the past year. The walling encircling the reservoir is nearly finished and coped, the bottom of the reservoir for about one-third of its area has been puddled with 14 in. deep of clay puddle, and on the top of this a layer of concrete has been laid 14 in. thick. The masonry of the upstand outlet and superstructure is complete. Seventy-six per cent. of the walling, concreting and puddling of the reservoir is complete. Twenty-eight per cent. of the work in formation of the filter-beds, including walling, concreting and puddling, is completed. Fifty-two per cent. of the outlet valve wells of the filters is completed. Of the distributing canal 9 per cent. is done. Of the sand-trap 79 per cent. is completed. Of the pipe trenches and laying 73 per cent. is completed. In all 57·6 per cent. of this work is complete.

## SEWER-FLUSHING APPARATUS.

The drought from which we have suffered during this year, and also the preceding years, has caused considerable anxiety to sanitary authorities on account of the want of water for sewer-flushing. During the long periods of drought the smaller street sewers gradually silt up and become almost choked with solid matter, which soon decomposes, liberating myriads of fever germs, which are soon carried into the atmosphere we breathe. Thus, at the very time when water is most scarce, sewer-flushing is most required. The ordinary mode of flushing, by pouring water down the sewers, is of little use, as it runs over the deposit and leaves things almost as bad as before, although requiring large quantities of water. A better system, however, was recently tested at Eccles, Lancs. where the local authority were in difficulty with the pipe sewers. A 12-in. pipe was opened and found to contain over 6 in. of solid matter, the flow of water over this being very small. In fact, there was every probability, in the event of a few weeks' longer drought, that the system would become entirely choked. Messrs. Merryweather, the hydraulic engineers, were consulted, and sent down their patent hydraulic sewer-flusher. Mr. A. C. Turley, the borough surveyor, and a number of the members of the town council were present at a test of this apparatus, and the work done was very satisfactory. In one case a length of 12-in. pipe, 120 ft. long and 12 in. in diameter, more than half choked with solid filth, was thoroughly cleansed in forty-five minutes. Further experiments, we understand, are to be carried out, and it is hoped that reliable data will be obtained in reference to the advantages or otherwise of the apparatus and in reference to its

economy compared with ordinary flushing. This data we hope to publish in due course. We are informed that the sewer in which the above-mentioned test was carried out could not have been cleansed by any ordinary process of flushing, as the filth it contained was very much consolidated and could only have been removed by opening out the whole sewer trench, taking up the pipes and cleansing them by hand labour. It will be seen, therefore, that immense advantage is obtained by using the apparatus in cases where the sewers are in a similar condition to the one mentioned above.

## HULL NEW PUBLIC BATHS.

The new public baths which have been erected by the Hull Corporation in the eastern division of the city were recently formally opened. The building is a brick structure, situated in Holderness-road. The front elevation is of red brick and terra-cotta, harmonising with the adjoining Reckitt Library. There is a swimming bath, 96 ft. by 30 ft., with 3 ft. 9 in. to 6 ft. 6 in. of water ; a boys' bath, 60 ft. by 30 ft., with 3 ft. 6 in. to 4 ft. 6 in. of water ; nine ladies' slipper baths, and ten men's first-class baths and twelve men's second-class baths. The large swimming bath occupies a position at the back, and has a semi-circular roof of iron and glass. A gallery for spectators runs over the dressing-boxes, and provision has been made for turning the room into a meeting hall in the winter. The boys' bath, behind the library, is built on the same plan, only the dressing-rooms are open recesses. The boiler-house and laundry stand between the swimming baths, whilst the waiting-rooms face the slipper baths in the central corridor. The slipper baths are arranged in short corridors, and are all fitted up with hot and cold showers. The manager's house is over the front part of the building. The plans were prepared by the city engineer, Mr. A. White, and the assistant engineer, Mr. Bricknell, and under their supervision the work has been carried out, at a cost of about £15,000.

## TYPHOID FEVER AT LEIGH.

Recently, at a meeting of the Leigh (Lancs.) Urban District Council, a member submitted a request for particulars in regard to the typhoid of typhoid fever in the town. It was, he thought, absolutely necessary that everything should be done to trace the source of the outbreak. Leigh obtained its water supply from Rivington, and he had noticed from the newspapers that there were one or two cases of pollution in that district in the neighbourhood of reservoirs.

The chairman of the Health Committee said the medical officer of health had found it impossible to trace the cause of the outbreak directly. There were many causes, one of the chief of which was the system of closets and ash-pits which the council permitted. It was a system which was fruitful of any kind of infectious diseases, and so long as the council allowed property owners to make ash-pits in the way they did at present the medical officer of health was strongly of opinion that they would always have intermittent epidemics of typhoid fever. In fact, they could not possibly be avoided.

## APPOINTMENTS VACANT.

*Official and all similar advertisements received later than Thursday morning are too late for classification and cannot therefore be included in these summaries. No advertisements received after 3 p.m. can be inserted until the following week.*

HIGHWAY SURVEYOR.—November 11th.—Isle of Wight Rural District Council. £150.—Mr. H. Eldridge Stratton, clerk to the council, Pyle-street, Newport, I.W.

SECOND ASSISTANT.—November 12th.—County Borough of Hanley. £80.—Mr. Joseph Lobley, borough engineer and surveyor.

SUPERINTENDENT AT THE CORPORATION WHARF.—November 12th.—County Borough of Southampton. £200.—Mr. George B. Naldor, town clerk.

SUPERINTENDING ARCHITECT.—November 14th.—London County Council. £1,500.—Mr. C. J. Stewart, clerk to the council, County Hall, Spring-gardens, S.W.

ASSISTANT SURVEYOR. — November 14th. - Wimbledon Urban District Council. £200.—Mr. W. H. Whitfield, clerk to the council.

CHIEF OFFICER OF TRAMWAYS.—November 14th. London County Council. £1,500.—Mr. C. J. Stewart, clerk to the council, County Hall, Spring-gardens, S.W.

ROAD FOREMAN.—November 14th.—Corporation of Morley. £2 2s.—Mr. W. E. Putman, A.M.I.C.E., borough engineer and surveyor.

ROAD FOREMAN.—November 14th.—Corporation of Bacup. —Mr. Francis Wood, A.M.I.C.E., borough engineer and surveyor.

ROAD FOREMAN.—November 15th.—Heston and Isleworth Urban District Council. £2 10s.—Mr. W. A. Davies, A.M.I.C.E., engineer and surveyor to the council.

SURVEYOR OF HIGHWAYS AND INSPECTOR OF NUISANCES.—November 17th.—Tarvin Rural District Council. £130. - Mr. Edward Evans Lloyd, clerk to the council.

BUILDING INSPECTOR.—November 19th.—Corporation of Bury. £120.—Mr. J. Cartwright, borough engineer.

SEWAGE FARM MANAGER.—November 19th.—Longton Corporation. £150.—Mr. J. W. Wardle, borough surveyor.

ENGINEER.—November 19th.—The Cork, Blackrock and Passage Railway Company. £500.—Mr. R. J. Copinger, secretary to the company, Cork.

GENERAL SURVEYOR'S ASSISTANT.—November 19th.—Bexhill Urban District Council. £75.—Mr. Fred. A. Langham, clerk to the council.

GENERAL SURVEYOR'S ASSISTANT.—November 21st.—Corporation of Maidenhead. £80.—Mr. Percy Johns, borough surveyor.

CLERK OF WORKS.—November 21st.—Corporation of Sunderland. £3 10s.—Mr. Fras. M. Bowey, town clerk.

FIRE BRIGADE ENGINEER.—November 26th.—Corporation of Coventry. £1 15s.—The City Engineer.

## COMPETITIONS.

*Official and all similar advertisements received later than Thursday morning are too late for classification and cannot therefore be included in these summaries. No advertisements received after 3 p.m. can be inserted until the following week.*

ABERAVON.—December 1st.—Extension of the covered market, at a cost not to exceed £5,000. £21.—The Borough Surveyor.

CHERTSEY.—December 23rd.—Sewerage and sewage disposal scheme for the No. 1 and 2 wards of the district. £50, £30 and £20.—Mr. T. E. Harland Chaldecott, clerk to the council.

BRADFORD.—January 2nd.—Erection of a central fire brigade station. £100, £50 and £30.—Mr. George McGuire, town clerk.

## MUNICIPAL CONTRACTS OPEN.

*Official and all similar advertisements received later than Thursday morning are too late for classification and cannot therefore be included in these summaries. No advertisements received after 3 p.m. can be inserted until the following week.*

NORFOLK.—November 11th.—Erection of steel and iron bridges at East Harling and Beetley, near Dereham, for the county council.—Mr. T. H. B. Heslop, M.I.C.E., county surveyor, Norwich.

ALTRINCHAM.—November 11th.—Erection of new offices, council chamber, fire station, caretaker's house, &c., for the urban district council.—Mr. John Stokoe, clerk to the council.

BIRMINGHAM.—November 11th.—Supply of certain goods for use in the general and Elan Valley supply departments for one year from January 1, 1899, for the corporation.—Mr. E. Antony Lees, secretary, Water Department, 44 Broad-street, Birmingham.

TAUNTON.—November 12th.—Supply of about 67 tons of 8-in. and 6-in. cast-iron spigot and socket bituminised water pipes.—Mr. George H. Kite, town clerk.

LAUNCESTON.—November 12th.—Construction of a new cattle, sheep and pig market.—The Town Clerk.

COVENTRY.—November 12th.—Erection of buildings at the proposed two new sewage pumping stations on the side of the main road from Coventry to Daventry.—Mr. Lewis Beard, town clerk.

DEWSBURY.—November 12th.—Paving, flagging, kerbing, channelling, &c., works in Thornton-street.—Mr. Henry Dearden, borough surveyor.

LLANGYFELACH.—November 12th.—Construction of about 456 yards of 12-in. stoneware pipe sewer in Sterry-road and Mount-street, Gowerton, for the rural district council.—Mr. J. Thomas, A.M.I.C.E., engineer and surveyor to the council, 32 Fisher-street, Swansea.

BARROW-IN-FURNESS.—November 14th.—Supply and erection of cast-iron lamp columns, arc and incandescent lamps, and automatic switches and fittings.—Mr. C. F. Preston, town clerk.

ANNFIELD PLAIN.—November 14th.—Formation of the road and foot-path in Victoria-terrace and other streets, for the urban district council.—Mr. T. J. Trowsdale, surveyor to the council.

BIRKENHEAD.—November 14th.—Erection of public baths on land adjoining Livingstone-street and Prince-street.—Mr. Charles Brownridge, A.M.I.C.E., borough engineer and surveyor.

STOCKTON-ON-TEES.—November 14th.—Execution of various private street improvement works.—Mr. M. H. Sykes, borough engineer.

LEWISHAM.—November 15th.—Kerbing, tar-paving, channelling and metalling works in Vancouver-road, for the district board of works.—The Surveyor to the Board.

BROMLEY.—November 15th.—Works of surface-water drainage in Plaistow-lane, for the urban district council.—Mr. Fred. H. Norman, clerk to the council.

LONDON.—November 15th.—Erection of new public conveniences at Blackwall Tunnel (north side), for the county council.—The Clerk to the Council, County Hall, Spring-gardens, S.W.

LONDON.—November 15th.—Erection of a new coroner's court building at Manor-place, Paddington, for the county council.—The Clerk to the Council, County Hall, Spring-gardens, S.W.

HANLEY.—November 15th.—Erection of a refuse destructor.—Mr. J. Lobley, borough engineer.

ACTON.—November 15th.—Supply of a steam fire-engine, a 50-ft. fire-escape, and electric street alarms, fire calls, &c., for the urban district council.—Mr. D. J. Ebbetts, clerk to the council.

CARDIFF.—November 15th.—Erection of fish market and offices at The Hayes.—Mr. W. Harpur, A.M.I.C.E., borough engineer.

TOTTENHAM.—November 15th.—Making-up of Cunningham-road and The Avenue, for the urban district council.—Mr. P. E. Murphy, engineer to the council.

DOVER.—November 15th.—Supply of about 1,500 tons of broken Guernsey granite, 500 tons of Guernsey granite siftings, and about 2,000 lineal feet of Guernsey granite kerbing, channelling and quadrant corners.—Mr. E. Wollaston Knocker, town clerk.

TOTTENHAM.—November 15th.—Providing and laying of about 3,098 yards super. of 2½-in. hard York paving on the east side of Green-lanes, for the urban district council.—Mr. P. E. Murphy, engineer to the council.

HERTFORD.—November 15th.—Laying of about 100 yards of 9-in. and 60 yards of 12-in. glazed stoneware pipe sewers.—Mr. John H. Jevons, A.M.I.C.E., borough engineer and surveyor.

LINCOLN.—November 16th.—Supply of hard wood blocks for street paving.—Mr. R. A. Macbriar, city surveyor.

PLUMSTEAD.—November 16th.—Paving and making-up of part of Formount-road and part of Old Mill-road, for the vestry.—Mr. W. C. Gow, surveyor to the vestry.

AYLESBURY.—November 16th.—Construction of sewage disposal and other works, for the urban district council.—Mr. J. H. Radford, surveyer to the council.

WORTHING.—November 16th.—Supply of 2,500 ft. of 12-in. by 6-in granite curbs and a quantity of broken granite.—Mr. Frank Roberts, A.M.I.C.E., borough engineer and surveyor.

SOUTHAMPTON.—November 16th.—Supply of two engines and dynamos at the county lunatic asylum at Knowle, Fareham.—Mr. W. J. Taylor, county surveyor, The Castle, Winchester.

RADCLIFFE.—November 16th.—Sewering of Market, Seed and Roscow streets, for the district council.—Mr. J. Sharples, clerk to the council.

BARNSLEY.—November 16th.—Draining, paving, flagging and metalling of Beckett-street and Vernon-street.—Mr. J. Henry Taylor, borough engineer.

EASTLEIGH.—November 17th.—Providing and fixing of a chain pump at the sewage pumping station at Chickenhall, for the urban district council.—Mr. Henry White, clerk to the council.

CARMARTHENSHIRE.—November 18th.—Erection of a stone bridges of three arches over the river Towry at Dryslwyn, for the county council.—Mr. Thomas Jones, clerk to the council, Llandovery.

BIRMINGHAM.—November 18th.—Supply of engine slack, cast-iron pipes, special castings, &c., at the various pumping stations and wharves during the year 1899.—Mr. E. Antony Lees, secretary to the Corporation Water Committee, 44 Broad-street, Birmingham.

ABERTILLERY.—November 19th.—Construction of a new road from Abertillery to Aberbeeg, a distance of about 2 miles, for the urban district council.—Mr. James McBean, engineer and surveyor to the council.

LEICESTER.—November 19th.—Supply and delivery of retorts and firebricks.—Mr. Alfred Colson, M.I.C.E., engineer and manager, Corporation Gasworks, Millstone-lane, Leicester.

ERPINGHAM.—November 19th.—Execution of protection works in the parishes of Sheringham and Beeston-Regis, for the rural district council.—Mr. Thos. Ling, clerk to the council, Northrepp, Norwich.

BOGNOR.—November 21st.—Construction of a new sea wall and esplanade, 487 ft. in length, for the urban district council.—Mr. O. A. Bridges, town surveyor.

DROYLSDEN.—November 21st.—Construction of 607 lineal yards of 24-in. pipe sewer, 615 lineal yards of 18-in. pipe sewer and 345 lineal yards of 15-in. pipe sewer, for the urban district council.—Mr. W. Curry, engineer to the council.

STAFFORDSHIRE.—November 21st.—Laying of about 5,000 yards of 12-in., 9-in., 6-in. and 4-in. cast-iron and stoneware pipe sewers and surface-water drains at the County Lunatic Asylum, for the county council.—Mr. Walter H. Cheadle, county surveyor, Stafford.

ULVERSTON.—November 21st.—Various sewerage and drainage works, for the rural district council.—Mr. Chas. W. Dean, clerk to the council.

WEDNESBURY.—November 21st.—Widening of the bridge over the Birmingham Canal on the Holyhead-road, near Moxley.—Mr. E. Martin Scott, borough engineer and surveyor.

CAMBERWELL.—November 21st.—Supply of 2,050,000 Australian hardwood blocks, 3 in. by 9 in. by 5 in.; 2,050,000 creosoted deal blocks, 3 in. by 9 in. by 5 in.; and 3,260 loads of Australian hardwood in 9 in. by 3 in. planks, for the vestry.—Mr. W. Oxtoby, engineer and surveyor to the vestry.

LANCASTER.—November 21st.—Supply of about 1,850 lineal yards of 7-in. cast-iron pipes.—Mr. John Cook, A.M.I.C.E., water engineer, Town Hall, Lancaster.

STAFFORD.—November 21st.—Supply of a stone-breaking machine.—Mr. W. Blackshaw, borough engineer.

ASHTON-UNDER-LYNE.—November 21st.—Construction of precipitation tanks, artificial filters, land filters, subways, culverts, roads and other appurtenant works.—Mr. J. T. Earnshaw, A.M.I.C.E., borough surveyor.

SOUTHAMPTON.—November 22nd.—Supply and delivery of sluice valves, fire hydrants, air valves and surface covers required by the waterworks department during the ensuing three years, for the corporation.—Mr. W. Matthews, waterworks engineer.

GLASGOW.—November 22nd.—Supply of about 800 lineal feet of cast-iron pipes, 21 in. in diameter, and certain cast-iron pipes, 22 in. and 29 in. in diameter, with special castings, for the new electricity works at Port Dundas.—Mr. J. D. Marwick, town clerk.

NEWCASTLE-ON-TYNE.—November 22nd.—Supply during the twelve months ending December 31, 1899, of various materials, &c.—The City Engineer.

EDMONTON.—November 22nd.—Execution of about 5,252 ft. of 1-in. kerbing, about 4,086 ft. of 1-in. channelling, and about 3,048 ft. of crossings in Queen's-road, Station-road, Hyde-lane, Eldon-road, Hertford-road, Silver-street and Fore-street; about 3,111 yards super. of indurated concrete slab paving in Queen's-road, Claremont-street, Station-road, Hyde-lane and Eldon-road; and about 1,057 yards super. of patent Victoria stone paving in Hertford-road and Fore-street; for the urban district council.—Mr. G. Eedes Eachus, M.I.C.E., surveyor to the council.

CASTLE DONNINGTON.—November 23rd.—Execution of various sewerage works for the rural district council.—Mr. Herbert Walker, A.M.I.C.E., Newcastle Chambers, Angel-row, Nottingham.

WITHAM (Essex).—November 24th.—Supply of 300 tons of granite, for the urban district council.—Mr. Wm. Bindon Blood, clerk to the council.

BIRMINGHAM.—November 24th.—Construction of brick and pipe sewers in Church-street.—Mr. John Price, city engineer and surveyor.

BURTON-UPON-TRENT.—November 24th.—Supply of fireclay retorts, bricks and clay required at the gasworks during the year 1899.—Mr. F. L. Ramsden, manager and engineer, Corporation Gas and Electric Light Works, Burton-upon-Trent.

TAME.—November 25th.—Construction of stoneware and other sewers for the interception of the sewage of the town, together with the necessary manholes, inspection shafts, flushing tanks, outfall works and engine-house, for the urban district council.—Mr. Wm. Parker, clerk to the council.

EAST RETFORD.—November 25th.—Construction of about 20,000 lineal yards of stoneware and iron pipe sewers, with manholes, storm overflow, ventilators, ejector chamber and ejectors, cast-iron rising main and other works; also precipitation tanks, engine and boiler houses, chimney shaft, press-house, stores and offices, carriers, underdraining and levelling land, roads, fencing and other works.—Mr. Samuel Jones, town clerk.

STOURBRIDGE.—November 28th.—Construction of 900 yards of 9-in. earthenware pipe sewer, for the main drainage board.—Mr. W. Fiddian, surveyor to the board, Town Hall, Stourbridge.

BROMSGROVE.—November 28th.—Construction of stoneware pipe sewers comprised in the scheme of sewerage for the parish of Pedmore, for the rural district council.—Mr. H. D. Holloway, clerk to the council.

ERDINGTON.—November 29th.—Supply of about 6,500 lineal yards of kerb and about 820 tons of 4-in. cube setts, for the urban district council.—Mr. Herbert H. Humphries, engineer and surveyor to the council.

BUCKLOW.—November 29th.—Reconstruction of the main sewers of the township of Hall, for the urban district council.—Mr. J. M'D. M'Kenzie, surveyor to the council, 7 Market-street, Altrincham.

WEST HARTLEPOOL.—November 29th.—supply of various materials and goods required during the year ending December 31, 1899.—Mr. J. W. Brown, borough engineer.

MIDDLESBROUGH.—November 29th.—Supply and erection of various electric lighting plant, for the corporation.—Mr. Robert Hammond, consulting engineer, 64 Victoria-street, London, S.W.

SALFORD.—December 1st.—supply and erection of certain electric plant.—Mr. Saml. Brown, town clerk.

JOHANNESBURG, S.A.—January 9th.—supply of a complete carburetted water-gas plant, for the corporation.—Messrs. Robert Whyte & Co., 22 Bury-street, St. Mary Axe, London, E.C.

LONDON.—January 24th.—Construction of a tunnel for pedestrian traffic under the river Thames from Greenwich to Poplar, for the county council.—Mr. C. J. Stewart, clerk to the council, County Hall, Spring-gardens, S.W.

HORNSEY.—Sale of manual fire engine, for the urban district council. —Mr. E. J. Lovegrove, engineer and surveyor to the council.

## TENDERS.

*ACCEPTED.

CARDIFF.—For forming, metalling, paving, kerbing, channelling and sewering works in Teilo-street, Gardens-lane North, Portmanmoor-road and splott-lane.—Mr. W. Harpur, M.I.C.E., borough engineer :—

| | Portmanmoor-road. | Splott-lane. | Teilo-street. | Gardens-lane North. |
|---|---|---|---|---|
| J. Rich, Cardiff ... | £1,026 | £45 | £372* | £24* |
| T. Rees, Cardiff ... | 1,077 | 50 | 398 | 25 |
| R. Osmond, Cardiff | 1,270 | 43 | 380 | 23 |
| C. Davies, Cardiff | 911* | 44* | 376 | 23 |
| W. Ellis, Cardiff... | 1,176 | 46 | 303 | 24 |
| J. Vevers, Barry | 973 | 51 | 440 | 29 |

CARLISLE.—For the erection of a caretaker's lodge on the Sauceries. —Mr. Henry C. Marks, A.M.I.C.E., city engineer and surveyor :—

| | |
|---|---|
| Beaty Brothers, Lampleigh-street, Carlisle ... | £741 |
| R. Little, Norfolk-road, Carlisle ... | 721 |
| J. H. Reed, Edward-street, Carlisle ... | 699 |
| W. Lattimer, Sheffield-street, Carlisle ... | 684 |
| E. J. Hill, Crown-street, Carlisle... | 679 |
| G. Hill & sons, south Henry-street, Carlisle... | 667 |
| J. Laing, Denton-street, Carlisle* | 654 |
| surveyor's estimate, £616. | |

EAST BARNET.—For the making-up of Jackson-road and Warwick-avenue, for the urban district council.—Mr. Henry York, surveyor to the council :—

JACKSON-ROAD.

| | |
|---|---|
| Swaker, Chiswick ... | £1,060 |
| Griffiths, Bishopsgate-street, E.C. | 1,089 |
| Nowell & Co., Kensington, W.... | 1,087 |
| Clark, Finsbury Park, N. | 1,078 |
| Kitteringham, Enfield | 1,072 |
| Adams, Wood Green* | 1,011 |

WARWICK-AVENUE.

| | |
|---|---|
| Griffiths, Bishopsgate-street, E.C. | £342 |
| Swaker, Chiswick ... | 330 |
| Nowell & Co., Kensington, W.... | 320 |
| Kitteringham, Enfield | 320 |
| Clark, Finsbury Park, N. | 319 |
| Adams, Wood Green* | 303 |

EAST BARNET.—For the supply of broken granite, gravel, hoggin, water-vans, &c., for the year ending September 29, 1899, for the urban district council.—Mr. Henry York, surveyor to the council :—

Broken Granite.—W. Muir, Coleman-street, E.C., 11s. per ton at New Barnet.
Gravel.—J. smart, Finsbury Park, 4s. 9d. per ton at New Barnet.
Hoggin.—F. Pre, New Barnet, 5s. 3d. per cubic yard on to road.
Cartage.—F. Pye, New Barnet, 8s. 6d. per day.

EDINBURGH.—For various works in connection with gasholder tank at Granton.—Mr. James M'G. Jack, clerk to the commissioners :—
C. Macandrew, Lauriston-gardens, Edinburgh* ... ... £17,804

GLOUCESTER.—For the erection of the new electricity works.—Mr. George Sheffield Blakeway, town clerk :—

| | |
|---|---|
| Stephens, Bastow & Co., Limited, Bristol ... | £10,774 |
| H. A. Forse, Bristol ... | 9,278 |
| W. Bowers & Co., Hereford ... | 8,691 |
| A. King, junr., and A. E. King, Gloucester ... | 8,378 |
| Collins & Godfrey, Tewkesbury ... | 8,146 |
| P. Ford, Stroud ... | 8,026 |
| W. Jones, Gloucester ... | 7,711 |
| J. Gurney & sons, Gloucester* | 7,676 |
| Freeman & Jones, Gloucester* | 7,300 |

HARROW.—For the making-up of Byron, Kingsfield and Valentine roads, for the urban district council.—Mr. T. Charles, surveyor to the council :—
G. Wimpey & Co., Hammersmith, W.* ... ... £1,214

HEBDEN BRIDGE.—For the erection of various machinery, composed of boiler, engine, pumps, presses, &c., at the sewage works, for the urban district council.—Mr. R. Crabtree, clerk to the council :—
Goddard, Massey & Warner, Nottingham* ... ... £1,170

NEWHAVEN (Sussex).—For levelling, paving, kerbing, channelling, metalling, lighting, &c., Lawes-avenue, for the urban district council. —Mr. F. J. Rayner, town surveyor and engineer :—

| | |
|---|---|
| H. A. Chambers, Seaforth ... | £925 |
| Grounds & Newton, Bournemouth | 814 |

NEWHAVEN (Sussex).—For the drainage and sewerage of nineteen houses in Lewes-road, for the urban district council.—Mr. F. J. Rayner, surveyor and engineer to the council :—

| | |
|---|---|
| M. Woolger, Newhaven ... | £135 |
| C. Cook, Newhaven ... | 127 |

NEWHAVEN (Sussex).—For the erection of a brick and iron building, for the urban district council.—Mr. F. J. Rayner, surveyor and engineer to the council :—
Redman Brothers, Newhaven* ... ... £100

NEWHAVEN (Sussex).—For the alteration of coach-house, &c., for the urban district council.—Mr. F. J. Rayner, surveyor and engineer to the council :—
Redman Brothers, Newhaven* ... ... £60

NEWHAVEN (Sussex).—For the drainage and sewerage of seventeen houses in Chapel-street, for the urban district council.—Mr. F. J. Rayner, surveyor and engineer to the council :—
M. Woolger, Newhaven* ... ... £135

---

NEW SHOREHAM.—For the supply of 400 cubic yards of clean hand-picked land flints, for the urban district council.—The Town Surveyor :—

| | Per Cubic Yard. |
|---|---|
| W. Hillman, Portslade ... | 6s. 9d. |
| H. Bridger, Shoreham* ... | 6s. 4½. |

RAMSGATE.—For the erection of a refuse destructor.—Mr. T. G. Taylor, borough surveyor :—
Horsfall Furnace syndicate, Leeds* ... ... £7,245

WELLS.—For the erection of public hall and post office building.—Mr. R. L. Foster, town clerk :—

| | |
|---|---|
| Stevens, Bastow & Co., Limited, Bristol ... | £10,780 |
| General Builders, Limited, London ... | 10,000 |
| W. Gibson, Exeter | 10,118 |
| F. W. Bray, Wells, Somerset . . | 9,855 |
| H. W. Pollard, Bridgwater | 9,800 |
| R. E. Cock, Wells, Somerset | 9,592 |

## MEETINGS.

*Secretaries and others will oblige by sending early notice of dates of forthcoming meetings.*

NOVEMBER.

11.—Sanitary Institute : Lecture to sanitary officers ; Prof. T. Roger Smith, F.R.I.B.A., on " Sanitary Building Construction." 8 p.m.

12.—Sanitary Institute : Visit of sanitary officers to the Richmond main drainage works, Mortlake, under the guidance of Mr. W. Fairley, A.M.I.C.E. 3 p.m.

14.—Sanitary Institute : Lecture to sanitary officers ; Dr. Geo. Reid, M.D., D.P.H., medical officer of health to the Staffordshire County Council, on " Sanitary Appliances." 8 p.m.

15.—Institution of Civil Engineers : Ordinary meeting ; Mr. William Beedie Esson, M.I.C.E., on " Electrical Transmission of Power in Mining." 8 p.m.

16.—Sanitary Institute : Visit in the parish of St. George's (Hanover-square), under the guidance of Mr. Albert Taylor, chief sanitary inspector. 2 p.m.

16.—Sanitary Institute : Lecture to sanitary officers ; Mr. J. Wright Clarke on " Details of Plumbers' Work." 8 p.m.

16.—Royal Institute of Public Health : Sir Richard Thorne Thorne, F.C.B., M.D., F.R.S., medical officer to the Local Government Board, on " The Administrative Control of Tuberculosis " (third Harben Lecture for 1898). 5 p.m.

17.—Association of Birmingham Students of the Institution of Civil Engineers : Ordinary meeting ; Mr. J. G. Marshall, A.M.I.C.E., on " Light Railways and Rolling Stock." 7.30 p.m.

18.—Sanitary Institute : Lecture to sanitary officers ; Mr. W. C. Tyndale, M.I.C.E., on " House Drainage." 8 p.m.

## NOTICES.

THE SURVEYOR AND MUNICIPAL AND COUNTY ENGINEER may be ordered direct, through any of Messrs. Smith & Son's book-stalls, or of any newsagent in the United Kingdom. Applications to the Offices for single copies by post must in all cases be accompanied by stamps.

The Prepaid Subscription (including postage) is as follows :

| | Twelve Months. | Six Months. | Three Months. |
|---|---|---|---|
| United Kingdom | 18s. | 9s. | 4s. 6d. |
| Continent, the Colonies, India, | | | |
| United states, &c. | 19s. | 9s. 6d. | 4s. 9d. |

The International News Company, 83 and 85 Duane-street, New York City; The Toronto News Company, Toronto ; and The Montreal News Company, Montreal, have been appointed agents in the United States and Canada for the sale of THE SURVEYOR AND MUNICIPAL AND COUNTY ENGINEER. A thin paper edition is printed for circulation abroad.

EDITORIAL OFFICES :
24 BRIDE-LANE, FLEET-STREET, LONDON, E.C.

ADVERTISEMENT AND PUBLISHING OFFICES :
13 NEW STREET-HILL, FLEET-STREET, LONDON, E.C.

## APPOINTMENTS OPEN.

### BEXHILL URBAN DISTRICT COUNCIL.
ASSISTANT SURVEYOR.

The Bexhill Urban District Council require a General Assistant in the Surveyor's Department.

Candidates must be neat draughtsmen, competent to take levels, prepare plans and detail drawings for works of sewerage, road-making, private street works and apportionments, and the general routine of a surveyor's office. Preference will be given to applicants having had previous experience in a municipal engineer's office. Salary, £75 per annum, payable monthly. Duties to commence on December 1, 1898.

Applications, stating age, with copies of not more than three recent testimonials (which will not be returned), to be forwarded to the undersigned not later than the 19th inst.

Personal canvassing will disqualify.

FRED. A. LANGHAM,
Clerk.
Municipal Buildings, Bexhill.
November 8, 1898.

### BOROUGH OF MAIDENHEAD.
SURVEYOR'S ASSISTANT.

The Town Council of the Borough of Maidenhead require the services of a General Assistant in the office of the Borough Surveyor, at a salary of £80 per annum.

Candidates must not be less than twenty-eight years of age and have received a thorough training in a municipal office. They should be competent to survey and level accurately, prepare plans and detail drawings for private street improvements and other works, have a knowledge of building construction, and generally be able to assist in the duties of a borough surveyor's department.

Applications, in the handwriting of the candidate, stating age and qualifications, accompanied by copies of not more than three testimonials, and endorsed "Surveyor's Assistant," must be sent in to me not later than Monday, the 21st day of November, 1898.

PERCY JOHNS,
Borough Surveyor.

Guildhall, Maidenhead.
November 7, 1898.

COUNTY BOROUGH OF BURY.
BUILDING INSPECTOR.

The Sewering, Paving and Streets Committee invite applications for the appointment of Building Inspector in the Borough Engineer's department.

Candidates must be thoroughly qualified persons, and will be required to undertake the inspection of new buildings and drains, to fix levels, and make surveys of all new houses, buildings and drains, and to keep the necessary records in connection therewith. The commencing salary will be £120 per annum, increasing by yearly increments of £10 to £160 as a maximum. A list of duties may be obtained on application.

Applications, in candidate's own handwriting, stating age (which must be between twenty-eight and thirty-five), accompanied by not more than three copies of recent testimonials, and endorsed "Building Inspector," to be sent to Mr. J. Cartwright, Borough Engineer, on or before Saturday, the 19th instant.

Canvassing will be considered a disqualification.
JOHN HASLAM,
Town Clerk.

COMPETITION.

CITY OF BRADFORD.

*INTENDED CENTRAL FIRE BRIGADE STATION.*

TO ARCHITECTS.

The Corporation of the City of Bradford are prepared to receive Competitive Designs for the Erection of a Central Fire Brigade Station. Three premiums are offered to competing architects—viz., £100, £50 and £30. Plan of the site, with printed instructions, may be had on application at the City Surveyor's office on and after Monday, the 31st inst., on payment of 1 guinea, to be returned after receipt of design. The designs must be sent in not later than Monday, the 2nd of January, 1899.

(By order)
GEORGE McGUIRE,
Town Clerk.

Town Clerk's Office, Bradford.
October 25, 1898.

TENDERS WANTED.

TAUNTON RURAL DISTRICT COUNCIL.
ROAD-ROLLERS WANTED.

Wanted immediately, on Hire, at least two Road-rollers for 200 days' work in total.

The owner of such machines to provide a water-cart, with pump for each; also driver and boy, and all necessary oil, &c. Time of working only to be paid for, the council providing coal.

Tenders, stating price per day of at least eight hours, to be sent to me, the undersigned, on or before the 18th November instant.

(By order)
W. F. B. DAWE,
Clerk.

Taunton Rural District Council.
November 9, 1898.

HORNSEY URBAN DISTRICT COUNCIL.
FIRE ENGINE FOR SALE.

The Hornsey Urban District Council invite offers for their Manual Fire Engine (London Brigade pattern), 6-in. pumps, in thorough condition, with spare set of wheels, improved pole crab and double-lever brake.

For permission to view and further particulars apply to Mr. E. J. Lovegrove, Engineer and Surveyor to the Council, at the Council's offices as below.

(By order)
F. D. ASKEY,
Clerk to the Council.

Offices, Southwood-lane, Highgate, London, N.
November 9, 1898.

## ERDINGTON URBAN DISTRICT COUNCIL.
### TO QUARRY OWNERS.

The Highways and Buildings Committee of the above Council are prepared to receive tenders for the supply and delivery of about 6,500 lineal yards of Kerb.

They are also prepared to receive tenders for the supply and delivery of about 820 tons of 4-in Cube Setts.

Specifications, forms of tender and all information may be obtained upon application at my office, Public Hall, Erdington, from Monday, the 14th inst., to Tuesday, the 29th inst., upon which latter day tenders, endorsed "Kerbing" or "Setts," must be delivered to me not later than 12 o'clock at noon.

The Council do not bind themselves to accept the lowest or any tender, and the tender of any firm paying less than the standard rate of wages current in their district will not be considered.

The work may be let in two or more contracts.

HERBERT H. HUMPHRIES,
District Engineer and Surveyor.

Public Hall, Erdington, Birmingham.
November 9, 1898.

## THAME DRAINAGE.
### TO CONTRACTORS.

The Urban District Council of Thame are prepared to receive tenders for the construction of Stoneware and other Sewers for the interception of the sewage of Thame, together with the necessary manholes, inspection shafts, flushing tanks, outfall works and engine-house.

The works are to be in accordance with plans and specification prepared by Messrs. John Taylor, Sons & Santo Crimp, civil engineers, 27 Great George-street, Westminster, at whose office the plans may be inspected, and copies of the specification and bill of quantities obtained, upon depositing £5 (cheque only), which will be returned on receipt of a *bond-fide* tender.

Sealed tenders, endorsed "Thame Drainage," are to be delivered at my office before noon on the 28th day of November, 1898.

The Council do not bind themselves to accept the lowest or any tender.

WILLIAM PARKER,
Clerk to the Council.

2 High-street, Thame.
October 28, 1898.

## CITY OF BIRMINGHAM.

The Public Works Committee invite tenders for the Reconstruction of the Brick and Pipe Sewers in Church-street, in the city of Birmingham.

Drawings and specification may be seen, and sets of quantities and forms of tender obtained, by applying at this office on and after Tuesday, the 8th inst., upon depositing a cheque for 1 guinea, which will be returned on receipt of a *bond-fide* tender.

The contractor whose tender is accepted will be required to pay not less than the standard rate of wages current in the district.

Tenders, sealed and endorsed "Tender for Sewers in Church-street," to be delivered here not later than 10 a.m. on Thursday, November 24th.

The Committee do not pledge themselves to accept the lowest or any tender.

(By order)
JOHN PRICE,
City Engineer and Surveyor.

Council House, Birmingham.
November 4, 1898.

## VESTRY OF CAMBERWELL.
### TO TIMBER MERCHANTS.

The General Purposes Committee of this Vestry will meet at the Vestry Hall, Peckham-road, on Monday, November 21 1898, at 7 p.m., to receive alternative tenders for the supply of :—

2,050,000 Australian Hardwood Blocks, 3 in. by 9 in. by 5 in.;
2,050,000 Creosoted Deal Blocks, 3 in. by 9 in. by 5 in.;
3,200 loads Australian Hardwood, in 9-in. by 3-in. planks.

Specification and all particulars can be obtained on application to Mr. W. Oxtoby, Engineer and Surveyor, Vestry Hall, as above, on and after Thursday, 10th November, 1898.

The Vestry does not bind itself to accept the lowest or any tender.

Contractors or their agents must be in attendance at the time first above mentioned.

Persons tendering must comply with the conditions with regard to rates of wages and hours of labour as contained in the form of contract.

(By order)
C. WILLIAM TAGG,
Vestry Clerk.

November 8, 1898.

## BASFORD CEMETERY COMPETITION : FIRST PREMIATED DESIGN.
### Mr. T. H. Mawson, Park and Garden Architect, Windermere.

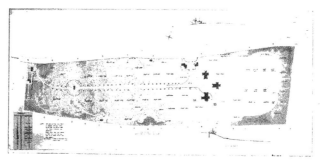

PLAN OF GRAVE SPACES.

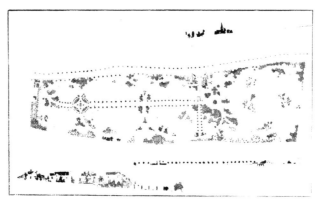

GENERAL PLAN WITH SECTION OF MAIN AVENUE, &c.

## MUNICIPAL WORK IN NOTTINGHAM.

# The Surveyor

## And Municipal and County Engineer.

Vol. XIV., No. 357.   LONDON, NOVEMBER 18, 1898.   Weekly, Price 3d.

## Minutes of Proceedings.

**Municipalities and Electric Tramways.—II.** Whatever may be the merits of systems other than electrical, and we have pointed out that there are certain distinct ones, it is extremely improbable that, for some time at least, they will be extended. Having regard to all things, it is impossible to avoid coming to the same conclusion as that arrived at by Mr. Baker—in the report to which we referred in our last issue—that in solving the problem of our tramways we must look to some form of electric traction. As the report points out, "with the great improvements that have been made during recent years in electrical appliances, the comparatively low cost at which electric energy can to-day be produced, the more perfect means of insulation and consequent greater safety and economy in transmitting the electric current to considerable distances by means of cables, there can be no doubt that the best and cheapest mode of tramway traction to-day is the electric." From the public point of view an electrical system bases its chief claim to favour on various grounds. That which affects the public most is the greater comfort provided by electric cars and the greater smoothness with which an electrically-propelled car runs; but what is of special importance, and this applies particularly to large towns having connections with suburban districts, is that a much greater average speed will be obtained on an electrical system as compared with any other form of mechanical traction or with horse traction. A special feature of an electric tramcar obtaining its energy from an external source, such as an overhead wire or a conduit, is that it will take the steepest gradient without diminution of speed. It must be remembered that such a vehicle is rendered more flexible in meeting varying conditions, either of track, gradients or of passengers, by the fact that it has almost unlimited power to draw upon from the main power-house, subject, of course, to what its electric motors can safely take. A general practice nowadays in equipping an electric tramcar is to provide electric motors which can, on emergency, develop 80 horse-power, and it will be seen at once how great an improvement that is upon other methods. Then the control and regulation of a tramcar is one of its greatest features; the modern car is so equipped that by means either of a band or electric brake it is possible to stop it, when travelling at full speed, in almost its own length. There is little doubt that these points account in a great measure for the extraordinary rapidity with which electric traction has been adopted in the United States. The most important portions of Mr. Baker's report are those relating to figures of costs which he has collected. He deduced a general statement from these that the cost of operating horse traction is from 50 to 100 per cent. greater than by electricity. As an instance of the increased popularity of tramways, it is interesting to point out the experience in some of the North American

towns. We find that in Bridgport the adoption of electricity on the existing tramlines resulted in an increase in traffic of 150 per cent., and exactly similar results were obtained in the case of New Orleans and Carleton. Washington increased its traffic by 80 per cent.; Pittsburg by 95 per cent.; Columbia and Brooklyn by some 100 per cent. No doubt the question of fares has a very great bearing on the popularity of a line, and perhaps one of the chief points of difference between the existing tramway systems in this country and those in America is the distance that can be travelled for a certain fare. Generally speaking, New York City charges a fare of 5 cents. Although this may be a comparatively heavy one for a short journey, it is possible in Brooklyn to travel for the same fare a total distance of 18 miles; in Chicago 15 miles : St. Louis, 15; and in no town is the distance less than 10 miles for a 5-cent. fare. It will be seen at once how different the conditions are in this country. We find from Mr. Baker's report that Glasgow, with its municipal tramways, charges 3d. for a little over 5 miles, while in Liverpool 5d. is charged for 6 miles; in Dublin 5d. for 8 miles, in Edinburgh 7d. for 8 miles; and in Manchester the fare is, generally speaking, 1d. per mile. It is true that in London a much better state of things prevails, for it is possible to travel from Wood Green to Moorgate-street and back again, a total distance of 7 miles, for 3d. Moreover, on the South London lines a 3d. fare will carry a passenger from Blackfriars Bridge to Lower Tooting, a total distance of 6¼ miles. It is probable that some modification of the American system will be generally applied in this country, and, as a matter of fact, it has been introduced in a modified form on the recently - opened electric lines of Middlesbrough and Stockton. The question, however, that mostly concerns municipalities at the present moment is, Which is the best system to adopt? Even if they have decided that electrical methods are to be adopted, they are immediately confronted with four systems—the accumulator, the surface contact, the overhead wire with the trolley or side connections, and the underground conduit with connection by plough, shoe or trolley. Many engineers consider that the accumulator is the ideal system; but probably, because we never achieve ideals, it is quite unlikely that the accumulator system will receive much extension. It is quite true that continued improvements in accumulators may to some extent enable engineers to apply them on moving vehicles, but up to the present time experience has been entirely against them, and the most successful instances of the employment of accumulators have been when used in conjunction with the overhead trolley system in running cars over short sections of city lines where the overhead system would not be permitted. For practical purposes the accumulator may be dismissed. The surface contact may be considered to be the modern development of the underground conduit. It claims, to some extent on good grounds, to obviate the disadvantages of the conduit system, and it also dispenses with the overhead wires and posts that are necessary in the trolley system. It overcomes those disadvantages, but at once introduces some of its own. All surface contact systems rely upon contact plates fixed to the surface of the road, making occasional contact with the cables conveying the current from the power-house. Contact with these studs is usually made by a skate or collector carried underneath the car, and the principle of operating the stud is that current can only pass out of the contact plate at the time when the car is passing over it, and that it is completely put out of action as soon as the car passes. It is obvious that such an operation calls for certain delicate mechanism, and, whether it be magnetic or mechanical, it is easy to see that troubles may constantly arise. Beyond a system that has existed in Paris for some time and one laid down at Monaco, there are practically no such systems in operation on a commercial scale. In other words, whatever position the surface contact system may occupy in the future it can be definitely said that there are no instances of sufficient importance to justify municipalities undertaking the responsibility of laying down such a system. It is perfectly true that many inventors are working on the subject, and recently two or three systems have been brought to prominent notice which may possess the advantages without the disadvantages previously noted in surface contact systems.

When we come to consider the trolley, there is probably no question of its practical utility. As Mr. Baker points out, there can be no doubt that the trolley has many advantages, that where in use it soon becomes very popular, and that the great rapidity with which it has been adopted in leading cities, not only in America but also on the Continent of Europe, and more recently in this country, is ample proof that the advantages are in the majority of cases considered to outweigh the disadvantages. There are, however, some cities, such as New York, Paris and Edinburgh, which, permitting and encouraging other forms of mechanical traction on their tramways, entirely refuse to permit the overhead trolley wires, while others, such as Brussels, Berlin, Dresden and Buda-Pesth, though permitting the overhead wires in the suburbs and less important streets, prohibit them in the public and more important thoroughfares, insisting that for such streets the electric accumulator or conduit system must be used. If, therefore, this or any other system can be made to compare favourably in price of construction and economy of working with the trolley, without its corresponding disadvantages and objections, it would be welcomed by all municipalities interested in street locomotion. It is hardly necessary to trace out in detail the operation of the overhead trolley system. Briefly, it embraces the erection of overhead wires, which are fed with electric energy from a central power-house, and the electric cars obtain their energy through the medium of a long trolley pole which keeps in permanent contact with the overhead wire. The chief objection urged by Mr. Baker is that of the disfigurement of streets. We need hardly combat that, because it is only necessary to point to Bristol, Glasgow, Liverpool, Coventry and other towns to show that there is probably less disfigurement than is generally supposed, When, however, Mr. Baker brings forward as an objection against this system that, there is a certain loss of electric energy by utilising the rails for the return current, and a danger of electrolysis destroying gas and water pipes by stray currents, we think that he has overestimated both the danger and the defects. There is bound to be some slight loss of energy in all systems. No mechanical form of motor is free from a certain loss of efficiency. It is exactly the same with the overhead tramway system ; but the only serious point is whether the loss of electrical energy in a tramway system is likely to cause trouble to anything else. The slight

loss will make absolutely no difference to the system, the only fear is whether it should cause electrolysis or interfere to any extent with the telephone service. But the Board of Trade have been alive to the dangers that may arise from stray currents of electricity, and they have not only formulated a somewhat rigid set of rules which limit the leakage from any tramway system, but insist that if leakage continues they may exercise their powers of stopping the working of the system. As a matter of fact, with the efficient methods of. bonding at present used in this county it is extremely unlikely that electrolysis would be set up. The third objection raised is that of a certain danger arising from telegraph and telephone wires falling on the overhead wire. This is exaggerated on two grounds. The first is that most telephone lines are being gradually put underground, and telegraph wires cross electric lines at very rare intervals ; as a matter of fact, telegraph lines and electric lines usually run parallel with each other. But wherever there has been a system of overhead wires erected in this county they have been completely protected from one end to the other of the system by guard wires. It is a little unfortunate for the trolley system that it has been necessary to guard against falling telephone and telegraph wires. The fourth reason given against the system relates to the sparking of the car wheels and the fact that this may frighten horses in the streets. As far as our experience goes, we know of no instance of a horse shying from sparking caused between the wheels and the tram ; the sparking, as a matter of fact, is no more serious as far as horses are concerned than a person striking a match in the street. We venture to think that Mr. Baker is labouring under a misapprehension when he says that the Board of Trade rules relating to the operation of tramways "seem to some extent permissive in their application, and, even if complied with in the first instance, there is no certainty that compliance will not become more difficult or impossible as time goes on and deterioration sets in in the underground and inaccessible parts of the return current." So far from these rules being permissive, a Board of Trade inspector carefully tests the line before a system is permitted to run, and, moreover, every tramway system is compelled to employ a special switchboard, the sole purpose of which is to make tests in order to see that the Board of Trade rules are complied with. These are not casual tests —tests have to be made definitely every day, every week, every month, and every quarter. Records of these have to be sent to the Board of Trade, and the slightest departure from them will be immediately followed by vigorous action. It is apparent, however, that Mr. Baker, in unintentionally exaggerating the objections to the overhead trolley, is merely preparing the way for a favourable consideration of the conduit system, but it will be necessary to postpone our remarks and criticisms on this section of the subject, as well as on the article which has appeared in an American contemporary, and to which Mr. Baker, who kindly favours us with a copy of the article in question, refers in the communication published in another column.

* * *

**Combined Drainage.** If an apology were needed for returning once more to this perennial topic, it would be found in the fact that it formed the subject of a valuable and interesting paper read by Mr. Priestley at the recent Birmingham congress of the Sanitary Institute. After pointing out the tendency of the present state of the law to cause local authorities to look askance at all plans for combined drainage, and deprecating such an extreme view on sanitary grounds, Mr. Priestley proceeded to show the advantages, in the case of a row or terrace of houses, of a combined system of drainage, as against a separate drain and connection for each house, provided the number of houses to each combined drain were restricted to six, or less. Turning to the legal aspect of the matter, the author of the paper referred to the case of *Appleyard v. Lambeth Vestry.* The effect of that case, it may be remembered, was to relegate to the category of sewers all combined drains in the metropolis constructed prior to 1848 (at which date the Metropolitan Commissioners of Sewers were constituted), whether with or without the approval of the authorities having jurisdiction at the time of their construction. Mr. Priestley characterised this decision as laying down the law very simply, and so, no doubt, it does so far as combined systems constructed before 1848 are concerned ; but it, of course, leaves unaffected systems constructed after that date, which, as is well known, are drains if made with the approval of the sanitary authority, but otherwise are sewers. As to districts under the Public Health Act, 1875, reference was made to the definition of a sewer contained in that Act, and to the modification of that definition effected by sec. 19 of the Public Health Acts (Amendment) Act, 1890 ; although, if Mr. Priestley is correctly reported, he omitted any reference to the limitation of the latter section to cases of houses belonging to different owners, which is an important point. In the course of the discussion on the paper Mr. Lewis Angell (West Ham) referred to the efforts which had been made by his corporation to bring about an alteration in the law on this subject, and, although these efforts have not been successful so far as the general law of the land is concerned, he was able to point to a conspicuous success achieved as regards West Ham itself. The corporation in their Omnibus Bill of the present year inserted the following clause :—

In and for the purpose of sec. 41 of the Act of 1893 the word "drain" shall be deemed to include any sewer or drain, whether constructed before or after the passing of this Act, with which two or more houses or premises (whether belonging to the same or different owners) are at the date of the passing of this Act, or may at any time thereafter be, connected, or which is used or capable of being or intended to be used for the conveyance of the drainage of such houses or buildings directly, or by means of any other sewer or drain, to any public sewer situate under a street repairable by the inhabitants at large, but shall not include any sewer which has been constructed to the satisfaction of the corporation under sec. 152 of the Public Health Act, 1875, or any sewer which has been constructed by the corporation for the effectual drainage of the borough.

This comprehensive clause was passed ("whether Parliament was asleep or the Local Government Board was nodding," Mr. Angell could not say), and is now the law in the West Ham district, forming sec. 42 of the West Ham Corporation Act, 1898. We congratulate this "fighting corporation" (to again quote Mr. Angell) on having achieved this result, and we trust that the day is not far distant when a similar clause may be embodied in a public statute applicable to the entire country.

* * *

**Surveyors'
Institution:
President's
Address.**
The surveyor's profession is a many-sided one. We are speaking at present of the surveyor in private practice as represented by the great majority of the members of that flourishing body, the Surveyors' Institution. Naturally the different aspects of the profession are reflected from year to year in the addresses of the president for the time being. On Monday Mr. Vigers dealt at more or less length with some topics of municipal interest, such as the growth of London, and the housing and street traffic problems which confront us in the metropolis. In referring to the housing question, he was evidently more impressed with the achievements of private enterprise as exemplified by the Peabody Trust than with those of municipalities. Certainly the latter sometimes go beyond their legitimate province, but they occasionally do the right thing. The appalling congestion of traffic in the central parts of the metropolis has long been a grievous and almost intolerable affliction to Londoners, and it would be well if the authorities could accelerate their present snail's pace in carrying

out those street-widening improvements which constitute the most obvious remedy. We are glad that Mr. Vigers hammered away at the subject. This question calls more urgently for the attention of the London County Council than does even that of electric traction for tramways. Until means of relieving the congestion of traffic have been found electric traction of any kind will be quite impossible in certain parts of the metropolis. In the latter part of his paper Mr. Vigers referred to the question of sewage disposal, a subject which does not often come up at the Surveyors' Institution. Here we have an indication of the attention which the new methods are attracting, for the president practically confined his remarks to the bacteriological developments, especially as exemplified by the septic tank. He did not, however, commit himself to much in the way of opinion. We observe with gratification that Sir John Wolfe Barry, in his address on Wednesday, as President of the Society of Arts, also attacked the great transit problem of the metropolis, but space compels us to hold over any further reference till next week.

* * *

**The late Colonel
George
E. Waring.**
Many municipal engineers and others connected with local Government in this country will hear with deep regret of the death of Colonel George E. Waring, who achieved so signal a success as commissioner of street cleaning in New York during the reign of Mayor Strong, under whom also General Collis did so much good as commissioner of works, especially in connection with paving and other street operations. Details in regard to Colonel Waring's system and the peculiar efficiency with which it was carried out have appeared from time to time in our columns. It is not too much to say that he completely reformed and reorganised the street-cleaning department, of which he was placed in charge in 1895, and his compulsory retirement after Tammany's municipal victory was a notable illustration of the evils resulting from the municipal system prevailing in America, and especially the subordination of that system to politics and the changing of officials after a party victory at the polls. Colonel Waring was sent by President McKinley to examine into the sanitary condition of Havana and devise means for stamping out yellow fever. He returned to New York at the end of last month and a few days later he was dead.

* * *

**Royal
Commission on
Sewage
Disposal.**
It may be remembered that in a recent issue we reprinted some correspondence which appeared in *The Times,* the opening communication having come from the chairman of the Commission, Lord Iddesleigh, who warned local authorities and manufacturers of the unwisdom of delaying schemes for the treatment of sewage and effluents until the report of the Commission had appeared. One of the letters elicited by the noble chairman's communication was signed "District Councillor," and was to the effect that a district council, after having decided to adopt a certain biological means for treating sewage, was "informed that no loan for the purpose would be sanctioned by the Local Government Board unless the process is recommended in the report of the Royal Commission now sitting." We questioned at the time whether such a statement was likely to come direct from the Local Government Board, as the probability was that the aforesaid district council had simply been "advised" by some more or less weighty authority to the effect indicated. Our surmise has now been corroborated officially, as "A Member of the Royal Commission," has sent to *The Times* a letter in which the following passage occurs :

This statement has been assumed by a number of persons to imply that this was a pronouncement of the Local Government Board, and hence I have made inquiry of that Board in the matter. The result is, as I anticipated, that the Local Government Board have pronounced no such opinion nor given any such decision.

# Comparative Reports of General Practice.

## XXX.—TRAMWAY TRACTION : WEST BROMWICH REPORT.—I.

In March, the Highway Committee of the West Bromwich Corporation appointed a sub-committee, consisting of the chairman, deputy chairman, the mayor, councillors Wilson and Baggott, and the borough surveyor, to obtain all information necessary to enable the committee to come to a decision as to the system of traction most suitable to adopt. The sub-committee decided to inspect for themselves the systems of mechanical traction most recently adopted, and in doing so visited the following towns in which a system of electric traction is in operation: Leeds, Bristol, Dover, Coventry, Wednesbury and Kidderminster (in all of which the overhead trolley system is in operation), Blackpool (underground conduit system), and Birmingham (cable and electric accumulator systems). The borough engineer, Mr. A. D. Greatorex, who accompanied the sub-committee throughout, also visited Prescot, where a system of underground conduit has been put down as an experimental line, and is described in the report.

### THE EXISTING LINES.

Before describing the systems in the towns visited the report gives a brief history of the present South Staffordshire line. The company was formed in 1881, and, the Provisional Order being obtained in August of the same year, the twenty-one years' lease will expire in August, 1892. The lines were constructed in 1882-83 and duly certified by the Board of Trade. Steam-power was used as the form of traction. In 1886 complaints were made respecting the undue emission of steam, excessive speed, &c., and these formed the subject of a Board of Trade inquiry. In November, 1888, the Highway Committee reported that the paving of the tramway had not been kept in such good repair as they would like, and about the same time the corporation were successful in taking legal steps to stop goods traffic, which the company had refused to discontinue. A conference of surrounding authorities was also held in Birmingham to consider the general question of nuisances in connection with steam traffic. Repeated ex-

tensions of time were granted to the company for the use of steam traction, always, however, on the understanding that some better system would be adopted. Previous to sanctioning a twelve months' extension from March 25, 1896, the Board of Trade deputed Major Marindin to inspect the tramways and report, which he did to the following effect :—

"The lines were laid in 1882-83, and there has been no relaying except for a length of one-quarter mile.

"The rails are very much worn, the check rail nearly throughout being higher than the top of the running rail.

"The points are in many places low and cannot be considered satisfactory, and the paving setts require adjustment over a considerable portion of the tramway. As, however, the lines ought to be relaid within two years, the extension ought not to exceed a period of twelve months from March 25, 1896."

Ultimately it was arranged in the beginning of the present year to hold a conference between an inspector of the Board of Trade and representatives of the various local authorities concerned. The conference was duly held on May 3rd, and was presided over by Sir Francis Marindin, R.E., C.M.G., of the Board of Trade. Representatives, including officials, were present on behalf of the following local authorities interested : West Bromwich, Handsworth, Dudley, Darlaston, Tipton and Wednesbury. As a result of the conference, Mr. Sellons, on behalf of the British Electric Traction Company, Limited, undertook to forward to the local authorities within a month a copy of the proposals of his companies in connection with the undertaking of the South Staffordshire Tramways Company. It should be mentioned that a provisional agreement had been entered into by the tramway company with the Electric Construction Company for the installation of a system of electric traction, but the latter company subsequently assigned their entire interest in the agreement to the British Electric Traction Company, Limited. Various powers have been conferred upon the South

LEEDS CITY TRAMWAYS: CENTRE POLES IN BOAR-LANE,
(Trolley wires not in position.)

Staffordshire Company from time to time since 1882. In 1889 an order was obtained for incorporation and other purposes, and in 1894 an Act was obtained to empower the company to construct the tramways so as to use cable, electric or other mechanical traction. That Act, however, through lapse of time has become a dead letter, so the committee advised the insertion of many of the clauses in whatever Act should be promoted by the South Staffordshire

by horses, but lately by steam. In 1891 the concession of the company expired, when the council decided to purchase the entire undertaking. The transfer took place in February, 1894. The tramways, as they then stood, cost the corporation approximately as follows : Lines constructed by the corporation, £20,330 ; undertaking purchased from the company and cost of arbitration, £118,814 ; total, £139,144.

After completing the negotiations and obtaining possession

LEEDS CITY TRAMWAYS : BRIGGATE.

Tramways Company or any other company. The following are the lengths of the lines in the various towns and districts : Handsworth (double track), 4 furlongs, 73 yards ; West Bromwich (double), 5 miles, 179 yards ; Tipton (single), 4 miles, 2 furlongs, 183 yards ; Dudley (single), 5 furlongs, 73 yards ; Coseley (single), 6 furlongs ; Wednesbury (single), 2 miles, 1 furlong, 77 yards ; Wednesbury (single, but not

of the lines, the corporation invited bids for the lease of the tramways, but none of the offers received were considered sufficiently advantageous. Meanwhile the working of the system was continued under the direction of the town council, who had retained most of the old staff. This arrangement had proved quite successful, and the result gave encouragement to the popular desire to have the system remain under

LEEDS CITY TRAMWAYS : ROUNDHAY-ROAD.

worked), 2 furlongs, 37 yards ; Darlaston (single), 6 furlongs ; the total being thus 14 miles, 4 furlongs, 182 yards.

After this account of the existing lines the report is continued with description of systems in operation in towns visited by the sub-committee. These we may reproduce practically as given in the report.

## LEEDS.

The tramways in Leeds were originally constructed in 1872, and extended in 1877, and the lines were originally worked

the direct control of the corporation. In November, 1896, the corporation decided to at once equip the line from Kirkstall to Roundhay.

The electric tramway, opened July 28, 1897, extends from a point opposite the entrance to Kirkstall Abbey, on the northwest outskirts of the city of Leeds, to the north-easterly end of Princes-avenue at Roundhay Park, a suburban resort in the north-eastern district. The route is not direct, but forms the two arms of what may be roughly termed a right-angle, the centre of the city being at the apex, the total extent of the line being 7 miles and the length of track 14 miles. The gradients throughout the route are easy, and the steepest not exceeding 1 in 21. On most of the route the vehicular traffic is fairly heavy, while Boar-lane, Leeds, is one of the most crowded thoroughfares in the provinces. Altogether the conditions are such as will give a very thorough test of electric traction in city service.

*Permanent Way.*—The permanent way was designed and constructed under the supervision of Mr. Thomas Hewson, the city engineer. The rails weigh 100 lb. per yard, of the usual grooved section, the gauge being 4 ft. 8½ in. The paving is of granite setts, except in Boar-lane and a part of Briggate, where wood paving is used.

*Conducting System.*—From Kirkstall Abbey to the Midland station in Wellington-street, and from North-street to Roundhay Park, the trolley wire is carried by single brackets attached to tubular steel poles placed at the side of the roadway. These poles are placed at an average interval of 120 ft., they measure 31 ft. in length, and are in two parts. In Boarlane and Briggate centre poles with double brackets have been used, and they serve also to carry arc lamps for street lighting. All the poles have been manufactured by Messrs. James Russell & Sons, of Wednesbury.

There is a minimum width of roadway in Roundhay-road and Kirkstall-road of 32 ft., and in Briggate and Boar-lane the width is greater, and admits of a space of 5 ft. 6 in. for the centre poles between the tracks; there is thus plenty of space between the rails for the islands, and a clear way on either side of the road outside the tracks for vehicular traffic.

*Rolling Stock.*—The rolling stock consists of twenty-five four-wheel double-deck motor cars, six double-decked trailers and six single closed cars, and the committee were informed that the Tramway Committee contemplated purchasing an additional twelve trailer cars. This would make the total number of trailer cars twenty-five, one for each motor car. The bodies were built by Messrs. Milnes & Co., of Birkenhead, and are of the cantilever extension type, the trucks being from designs of the Peckham Motor and Wheel Company, New York. The bodies of the cars present a neat and attractive appearance. They are painted in blue, and decorated with gilt, the body panels bearing in the centre the coat of arms of the city of Leeds. Inside the motor cars there are seats for twenty-two passengers and outside for twenty-nine, making a total of fifty-one. The double-decked trailers carry twenty passengers in and twenty-four out, and the single cars twenty-two passengers. The cars are lighted by electricity, each being wired for ten lights of 16 candle-power each, connected five in series between the main conductor and the rails, and provided with switches, so that either or both groups of lights can be cut out. The trolley poles and supports are of the swivelling-arm type. The total weight of the car and truck complete is about 7 tons. The cars travel at a speed of 8 miles per hour, there is a seven and a half minutes' service, and they stop when required, the charge being 1d. per mile.

*Power Station.*—The building for the power station is of brick and iron, was designed by the city engineer, and is close to the line and midway between the termini. The building is glazed with white bricks, and has a clean and neat appearance. The engines are two pairs of horizontal compound condensing-engines, supplied by Messrs. John Fowler & Co., of Leeds, and the dynamos are driven from the fly-wheel of the engine by fifteen ropes. The station can be enlarged as required. To house the cars and to provide the necessary repair shops and other offices the corporation have erected very extensive buildings of brick and iron in Kirkstall-road. They are designed for future requirements, and will hold nearly 200 cars.

*General Notes.*—The sub-committee wish to express their admiration of the thoroughly substantial and durable manner in which the work has been carried out. At present all systems used the same tracks—namely, horse cars, steam and electric—but the sub-committee were informed that it was the intention of the corporation to convert the entire system into the overhead system in course of time.

The committee rode on the cars inside and out, and found them very superior to the cars at Wednesbury. Since the committee visited Leeds the corporation of the latter city have decided to equip the following lines on the overhead system : The Headingley, Chapeltown, Hunslet and Dewsbury routes.

**Locomotives, on Highways.**—The Local Government Board announce that, with respect to the wheels of locomotives on highways, they have issued an amending order further varying the provisions of sub-sec. (4) of sec. 28 of the Act of 1878, by the substitution for the condition numbered 6 in the order of November 26, 1807, of the following condition : " No such wheel shall be used any block of which is so worn that any metal rim surrounding the block protrudes beyond the surface of the block." Circulars have been issued by the Board to the councils of counties and county boroughs, to boroughs other than county boroughs, and to urban and rural districts, calling attention to the Locomotives Act, 1898 (61 and 62 Vic., c. 29), by which important changes have been made in the law with respect to the use of locomotives on highways and to extraordinary traffic.

## AN EXPERIMENT IN MUNICIPAL TRAMWAYS.

### CO-OPERATION OF COMPANY AND MUNICIPAL .AUTHORITY.

An interesting experiment in municipal enterprise is now being made in the Lancashire borough of St. Helens, whose extensive area and the contiguous district contain nearly 200,000 inhabitants. The experiment takes the form of an effort to place the workings of the tramway system under the joint proprietorship of the corporation and private enterprise. The corporation will generate and supply the electric power, the company will provide the vehicles and working staff, and it is hoped that this combination will prove advantageous to both parties, as well as to the public. The St. Helens Corporation, recognising that rapid and cheap locomotion is essential to their scattered industrial population, obtained Parliamentary powers to establish electric stations both for light and energy. They also obtained powers to lay down a complete network of rails through the whole district, to be worked by electricity. Instead of managing the tramways themselves, the council have preferred to delegate this duty to men with practical experience. They have therefore granted a lease for twenty-one years to a company, who will undertake to provide an efficient service of cars and to run at frequent intervals at cheap fares. On their side the corporation undertake to lay down rails of the most approved type, to equip the lines on the trolley system, and to supply electric energy at a fixed charge—namely, 2d. per unit for the first 400,000 units, and reducible to 1d. per unit when the full quantity of power is consumed. Some of the advantages claimed for the arrangement are that the corporation will be assured of a fair return on the capital they have invested and a profitable use of their electric plant, so that they will secure a good return to the ratepayers without incurring any responsibility for the actual working and conduct of the tramway business. The company, on their side, anticipate material advantage, because the charge for electric power under the lease will be far less than the cost of steam or horse haulage, which they now use. The future extension of the system, they also anticipate, will bring St. Helens into direct connection with Liverpool at lower fares than are now charged by the railway companies.

## HARBOUR IMPROVEMENTS AT ABERDEEN.

### AN EXTENSIVE SCHEME.

At a recent special meeting of the Aberdeen Harbour Board the Works Committee recommended that in the Bill for which the commissioners are to apply in the ensuing session power should be taken to borrow for the purposes of the harbour, including the reconstruction of the graving dock, the sum of £200,000. Among the works which Mr. Gordon Nicol, the engineer, considers it might be desirable to undertake during the next ten years are : Deepening the navigation channel to 30 ft. at high water of spring tides, including the removal of rock, £54,000 ; deepening the Albert Basin, tidal harbour, river Dee and dock, £9,000 ; improvement of Pocra Harbour, £9,500 ; improvement of Point Law, £17,000 ; improvement of river Dee, £13,000 ; reconstruction of part of Provost Blaikie's quay, £12,000 ; reconstruction of part of Provost Matthews' quay, £2,500 ; reconstruction of goods sheds, new houses for officials, and extension of workshops, £4,500 ; strengthening the quays for steam haulage, £1,800 ; extension and renewal of rails, £16,000 ; causewaying of roads and quays, £12,000 ; hydraulic machinery for lock gates, £2,800 ; new cranes and steelyards, £5,500 ; electric light fittings for buildings and sheds, £1,100 ; additions to plant, £14,000 ; contingent allowance for repairs to sea works, £6,000 ; engineering expenses, £7,000 ; new sea lock, £40,000 ; total amount, £227,700.

After a long discussion the report was adopted by twenty votes to two, and the Finance Committee were empowered to proceed with the Bill.

## SOUND PROOFING.

What is known as the lino-lattice system of sound proofing for floors, partitions, &c., is claimed to be produced by means of a non-conducting and wood-preserving material and an entirely new method of fixing. It is pointed out that an absolute sound-proof system is impossible except in vacuum, but that the aim of the inventor has been to come as near as possible to such a system. By this system the pugging is laid on lattice work between the joists, combined with the use of non-conducting sound strips laid on the top of the joists or on the face of partition studs, and it is claimed that this ensures the almost complete non-conduction of sound. The non-conducting strips may be used alone. The system is also claimed to be an effective preventive of dry-rot, to be non-inflammable, and vermin and insect proof, and, in addition to non-conducting and preservative qualities, various advantages over other materials are claimed with respect to cost and weight. The manufacturers are the Lino-Lattice Company, Marsh Bridge, St. Philip's Marsh, Bristol, from whom full information can be obtained.

# The Sanitary Institute.

## THE SEVENTEENTH ANNUAL CONGRESS.—VIII.

### HOUSE DRAINAGE AND SEWERAGE.

Several of the addresses contributed at the Birmingham congress of the Sanitary Institute dealt with questions connected with house drains and with sewers.

### TYPHOID AND CLOSETS.

In his paper on "Typhoid Fever," read before the Sanitary Science and Preventive Medicine section, Mr. PHILIP BOOS-DYER, M.B., the able medical officer of Nottingham, sought, by means of diagrams and statistics, to demonstrate the effects of privies and water-closets respectively in the spread of that disease. In Nottingham, during the last ten years, he said, the average rate of disease was one in every 120 houses fitted with pail-closets, one in thirty-seven houses fitted with privies, and one in every 555 houses fitted with water-closets.

Dr. COOPER PATTIN (Norwich) expressed similar views from his experience of that city, and Dr. EUSTACE HILL, medical officer of health for the county of Durham, a son of Birmingham's medical officer, emphasised the fact that nowadays it was becoming recognised more generally in the profession that typhoid was spread by other means than in a defective water or milk supply. He quite agreed that endemic typhoid was encouraged by the conditions to which Dr. Boobbyer had alluded, and, apart from soil pollution, thought that flies were frequently the means of carrying the germs of typhoid.

Dr. SCURFIELD (Sunderland) added his testimony to that of Dr. Hill, and thought the conditions under which colliers existed in the mining districts might be responsible for certain soil contamination.

Lieut.-General PHELPS, after agreeing with the observations of those who had preceded him, suggested that there was one more possible source which had not been considered, and which might possibly be the nidus from which the disease germ was diffused. He should "like to know whether it had been ascertained if the sources of vaccine lymph were free from contamination," an observation that was met with laughter. The general, however, insisted that vaccine lymph should be subjected to the same tests that Dr. Alfred Hill had proposed with regard to food preservatives.

Dr. A. WATERS (Southend) thought that after all they had heard about the causes of typhoid it would be well if someone would suggest a practical way of dealing with the matter.

Dr. CHARLES PORTER (Stockport) declared that General Phelps's suggestion that the typhoid germ might be carried in vaccine lymph was the most novel he had ever heard. It was, however, a remarkable fact, established by statistics he had compiled in Stockport, that the incidence of endemic typhoid was greater as the rateable value of the houses increased.

Mr. R. H. WILLIAMS (St. Austell) asked what means could be suggested to force local authorities, landlords and others to promote those sanitary measures beneficial to the preservation of health.

Dr. CLARE (Hanley) said his experience was that typhoid was more frequent where pail-closets existed.

Mr. BAKER (Maidstone) asked for information as to whether chemical analysis could be relied upon to protect a town from an epidemic of typhoid.

Dr. BOOBBYER, having replied to the points raised in the discussion, the chairman (Dr. Alfred Hill) pointed out that no analysis of water would reveal the presence of typhoid poison. Bacteriology and chemistry might be made use of as far as possible, but in conjunction with these two methods it was necessary to look to the surroundings of the source of the supply.

### INTERCEPTORS AND TRAPS.

In his opening address to the Engineering and Architectural section THE PRESIDENT (Mr. W. Henman, F.R.I.B.A.) sketched the evolution of domestic sanitation, and predicted that the day would come when all interceptors and traps would be abolished, and with them the sewer-gas which they retained about our dwellings. With good ventilation of house drains, air inlets to sewers, ample flushing, impervious and well-laid drains and sewers, all entrapped and free from obstruction, gas, he asserted, might become a thing of the past. Engineers had sinned deeply in the construction of sewers. Apart from their general design and the method of construction and gradients adopted, the work had too often been defective in execution, so that, instead of aiding the quick removal of solids by water carriage, they had acted as filters or separators, permitting the fluids to escape and soak into the ground, or to run off and leave the solids to fester and become offensive.

Major LAMOROCK FLOWER proposed, and Mr. LEWIS ANGELL (West Ham), seconded, a vote of thanks for the address, the latter joining in Mr. Henman's condemnation of "interceptors."

Prof. A. BOSTOCK HILL, M.D., D.P.H., contributed to the Engineering and Architectural section a paper on the subject of

### THE CONSTRUCTION AND VENTILATION OF HOUSE DRAINS.

In opening his paper Prof. BOSTOCK HILL remarked that it might at first sight be thought that a subject like this in the present stage of sanitary science had been definitely settled, but, as a matter of fact, we found that on some points authorities still held divergent views. The questions of amount of fall, materials of pipes, &c., no doubt were agreed upon; but certain other points gave rise to controversy on different forms of procedure in different districts. He had not the least intention to occupy their time by reiterating those parts of the subject upon which all were agreed, but he desired for a few moments to call attention to certain points, especially in connection with what were known as compound drains, more particularly as this subject had had of late a local interest. This question of the relation of house drains to so-called compound drains and sewers had been forced on public attention by certain well-known decisions of the High Court, decisions given mainly to settle the point, What is a drain and what is a sewer? The subject was of importance, because sewers, by sec. 13 of the Public Health Act, were vested in the local authority, while drains, of course, were the property of the private individual. Dr. Bostock Hill then proceeded as follows :—

In the past, at all events in the Midlands, it has been customary for the small contributory drains from a row of houses to join a larger one which connects with the public sewer. Most of the difficulties have arisen in cases of this kind. As regards the construction of these drains, the size and methods of disconnection and ventilation are the chief points to be considered. As to size of drains, the smallest which will convey the necessary quantity of liquid is certainly best for reasons of cleanliness. From a single house a 6 in. pipe is ample, yet I have been very surprised to find that in case of recently-erected cottages a 6-in. pipe has been insisted upon by some surveyors, and, as far as I can understand, the only reason urged for this is the less likelihood of the pipe becoming blocked. But even if this be true, which I take leave to doubt, there are many corresponding disadvantages. From small houses the soiled water chiefly comes down in gushes, the pipe itself, if it be as much as 6 in., is never nearly filled, but the sides get splashed, and they are in a very short time dirty and have on their surfaces matter in a state of putrefaction. Again, it is impossible to flush a pipe as large as 6 in. coming from a single small house; so that, although such a pipe may not become so frequently stopped up, still it is in a condition in which sanitary science has conclusively proved a house drain should not be.

#### DISCONNECTION AND VENTILATION.

It is, however, on the questions of disconnection and ventilation that the greatest differences occur. The by-laws in many towns state that every drain shall be cut off by an intercepting trap from the sewer. The judges have decided that a so-called compound drain on private property is a sewer. Therefore, say certain authorities, we must insist on the presence of an intercepting trap between each of the contributory drains and the common drain, which has become a sewer. Let us suppose, for the sake of argument, that legally a compound drain, though on private ground, is a sewer. As the by-laws were formulated some years previous to the legal decision, we may take it as at least doubtful whether the compound drain was intended by the sanitary advisers of those who framed the by-laws to be so considered; and we may also consider whether, though legally a sewer, it is desirable, from a sanitary point of view, to treat it as such as regards our methods of interception and ventilation. Let us consider this for a few moments. The object of a drain is to remove, as quickly as possible, from the neighbourhood of the dwelling foul water which has passed into it. The law steps in, and those who choose to consider it binding insist that at each junction of the sub-drain with the compound drain (legally a sewer) there shall be a disconnecting trap between the house drain and the compound drain, so that in a row of six houses we shall have six intercepting traps between the various sub-drains and the compound drain. Each of these traps holds a considerable quantity of liquid and solid matter, and as a trap is an obstruction to the regular flow of the liquid passing through the drain, each of these syphons becomes for the time being a small depositing tank where solids in suspension precipitate themselves. The compound drain is treated in one of two ways : Either it is made to discharge into the street sewer without an intercepting trap at all, and connected with a ventilating shaft running up to the roof of one or more houses, or else an intercepting trap is put just where it enters the road, an air inlet as in the case of the other traps being provided, and a ventilating shaft being taken from it at or near its highest point. In the latter case we ventilate only that part of the sewer which is on private property. In the former case we utilise private property for the ventilation to some extent at least of the public sewer.

Under this system, which I regret to say is becoming common in many instances in the Midlands in new property, the following must of necessity occur. Each of the syphons on the branch drain holds foul water ; in the case of the house having a water-closet, which is the rule at the present time, the trap holds fæcal matter as well. The inlet, which is on the drain just on the house side of the interception trap and which, when no water is coming down, may act as such, becomes an outlet every time a flush of water is sent down, and the fouled air, which the length of house drain contained, coupled with the gas which has been given off by the fouled matters in the trap, is discharged into the air in close proximity (in some instances not more than 6 ft. or 7 ft.) to the back-doors of the houses.

My experience, then, is that from these so-called inlets, acting frequently as outlets, constant smells from foul gases arise, and I have had ample evidence that the tenants complain loudly of the existing state of things. The diagram which I have here shows an actual occurrence observed by a sanitary official in Birmingham, where it will be seen that the so-called inlet is being used as an outlet, while the flushing of the closet is performing the function of a bellows, and thus enabling the children of the cottages to amuse themselves by utilising the soiled air from the house drain for the purpose of blowing up their miniature bonfire.

In a close and crowded neighbourhood such a condition of things is undoubtedly bad, even if there be no specifically contaminated matter in the drains; but in the case, say, of typhoid fever existing in property drained in this way, it seems to me that, even if disinfection of stools had been carried out in the best-known possible way, there would be considerable risk of further dissemination of the disease. It is certainly undesirable to store the sewage, even for a short time, near premises ; and I am strongly of opinion that the method which I have described, while no doubt complying with the letter of the law, induces a state of things, from the sanitary point of view, very much worse than the system which it superseded. I have known of instances where, to avoid the odours arising from these so-called inlets in front of the intercepting trap, tenants have on their own account stopped up the opening, and under the circumstances, in my opinion, they are quite justified in doing so.

VENTILATION OF DRAINS AND SEWERS.

Closely connected with this question is that of the ventilation of drains and sewers. I have been somewhat surprised to find that many surveyors at the present time are recommending the ventilation of sewers up houses on private ground. Such a proceeding is—and as, I believe, I have shown on other occasions—attended with considerable danger to health ; and I wish to enter a protest against a method which I believe to be utterly wrong in principle, and which tends to distract public attention from the real source of the nuisance, and which palliates an evil instead of removing it. It is common knowledge that nearly all newly-laid sewers on the separate system, if they be ventilated by ventilators at the crown of the road, are, when first put into operation, a nuisance to the public. It is equally well known, I believe, that the cause of this nuisance is the stagnation of sewage, the deposition of solids in some portion of the sewer, consequent putrefaction, and the production of offensive gases, so that when a sewer gives offence to the nose it is a sign that it is not doing what it was intended to do—viz., carry fresh sewage, which in itself is always inoffensive. When this state of things occurs the public demands that the nuisance be abated. Owing to the very large number of schemes which have been completed of late in the smaller towns and rural districts these complaints have become quite common, and there has been a tendency, which I consider to be unscientific, to endeavour to remove the nuisance from the nose, instead of removing the cause which produces it.

THE MUNICIPAL ENGINEER AND THE MEDICAL OFFICER.

It is no part of my subject to-day to deal with this question, as it refers to public sewers, but I do wish to take this opportunity of entering my protest against some of the systems which are officially being carried out, and notably that which, instead of preventing the formation of noxious gases, tends to bottle them up and discharge them some few feet above the roofs of private houses. I have on a previous occasion shown instances where, I believe, a system similar to this has been productive of suffering and death, and I may say that, acting on my advice in a neighbouring town, for which I act as medical officer of health, all ventilators of sewers up private houses have been removed by the corporation.

It is to be regretted that in considering a question of this kind the matter should be treated as one belonging only to the department of the surveyor. In matters sanitary, as in other professional matters, no doubt there is a tendency at the present time to specialise unduly, but while it is the duty of the sanitary engineer to formulate and carry out a system for the removal of sewage and waste waters, it is no reason why the medical side of the question should be forgotten, and I maintain that this can only be definitely and properly settled by the harmonious working of medical and engineering experts. In this matter of ventilation of sewers it is no doubt comparatively easy to abate the nuisance as far as the nose is concerned, but I think in the past we have been too ready to forget the real meaning of the proverb that the remedy may be worse than the disease.

In the same section Dr. Joseph Priestley, B.A., M.D., D.P.H., read a paper entitled

COMBINED DRAINAGE : ITS *PROS* AND *CONS.*

In the course of his paper Mr. Priestley said that there had recently been such difficulty in connection with combined drains, which were " sewers " in the present state of the law, and for which the sanitary authority were liable as to repairing or relaying, owing to the combinations not having received at the time of construction the formal approval, sanction, order or direction of the sanitary authority concerned, that there was a tendency to-day to look askance at and refuse all plans of drainage showing a combined system. Of recent years, too, sanitary authorities had had to expend thousands and thousands of pounds upon combined drains, so that they felt justified in insisting upon a separate drain to each house or building. Such an extreme view was unwarranted, as all sanitarians were agreed that a first principle in drainage was to keep the drains as far as possible outside, so that, in the event of defects in connection with the drains, no harm should result to the occupiers by the escape of sewer or drain gas—a condition of things which might and did arise even in these days of expert drain-laying, farm settlements, &c.

Detached and semi-detached houses could have a separate drain to each house, the drains being kept easily outside. In the case of a row or terrace of houses a back line of drainage could be provided, discharging into a branch sewer in a side roadway, or be turned into the sewer in the road-way in front, either through an open uncovered passageway between two adjacent houses (and not less than 5 ft. for the width of such passageway) or by the side of one house, or even, where necessary, through and under one of the houses. By branching each house separately into this back line of drainage all drains were kept outside, or, at the most, one house only had a drain running under and through it; whereas, if a separate drain and separate connection into the main sewer was insisted upon, each house had to have a drain underneath and through it. How many houses ought to be allowed in a combined drain ? In practice he would restrict the number to six (or less), and have the combined drain itself intercepted and ventilated *separately*; but with more than six houses the main drain might be regarded as a " sewer," and treated accordingly—each house drain being separately intercepted therefrom and ventilated. In the exceptional cases, where the combined drain had to pass under a house, great care must be taken in laying the same—*e.g.*, manhole back and front, joints absolutely air watertight, drain (if not iron) embedded in concrete, intercepted trap provided, &c.

THE LAW.

In the metropolis, with which he was concerned officially, the recent case of *Appleyard v. The Lambeth Vestry* had laid down the law very simply. Sec. 74 of the Metropolis Local Management Act, 1855, allowed a combined system which had, previous to laying, received the formal order of the vestry or district board concerned ; whilst sec. 17 of the Metropolis Local Management Amendment Act of 1862 extended the powers of the previous Act beyond vestries and district boards (which were created in 1855) to metropolitan commissioners of sewers, who came into existence in 1848. Prior to that date all combined drains constructed were in London " sewers," repairable by the sanitary authorities—a very large order. The new Public Health (London) Act, 1891, gave no definition of drain. In districts served by the Public Health Act, 1875, a combined drain receiving the drainage of two or more houses was a " sewer," repairable by the sanitary authority, but the Public Health Acts Amendment Act, 1890 (sec. 19 of Part I.), gave the sanitary authority power to deal with a combined drain, and to recover the expenses incurred in dealing with such combination under sec. 41 of the 1875 Act. The 1890 Act was permissive.

His conclusions were: (1) Where a scheme of drainage was simplified and the drains kept outside by means of a combined system (or even in the rare case when the combined drain had to be taken through and under one house), it ought to be allowed, instead of insisting upon a separate drain and passing through and under each house—such a combined system being best hygienically, financially or otherwise. (2) When six (or less) houses were combined, the combined drain was to be intercepted and ventilated separately as a whole, but where more than six houses joined the main drain had better be treated as a " sewer," and each house separately intercepted therefrom and ventilated—the main drain itself not being intercepted, except in the rare instance where such main drain passed through and under a house or building.

DISCUSSION.

Mr. W. HENMAN, the president of the section, opened the discussion on the two foregoing papers. Those who were studying the question, he said, were realising the danger of multiplying traps and interceptors. They were a result of the " Model " By-Laws of the Local Government Board. He himself was afraid of anything " model," and, above all, of the Model By-Laws of the Local Government Board. He hoped that a very strong feeling would be raised at that congress to show the Local Government Board that these by-laws ought to be thrown into the fire or the waste-paper basket, and sensible and reasonable ones adopted in their place.

Mr. T. J. PERRY, chairman of the Sewers and Sanitary

Committee of the Camberwell (London) Vestry, ventured to differ from Dr. Priestley concerning the combined drainage question. He had presided over a conference on the subject of London medical officers, surveyors and others, and as a result did not advocate combined drains under houses. Back drainage, if it could be adopted, was a different thing. In practice intercepting traps and inspection chambers were lamentably bad. He would have liked to see a gentleman come forward at that meeting with a perfect system of ventilation of sewers (Hear, hear, and laughter). The president would have them do away with traps, but he would like to hear of a satisfactory alternative.

Mr. E. M. CLOSE (chairman of the Health Committee, St. Pancras) said he rose in response to Mr. Perry's challenge. He believed that our present system of drainage was wrong so far as outside traps were concerned. These should be abolished, but inside traps were necessary. The system of sewerage in London was different to that of smaller villages, of which he had no experience. In a sewer 4 ft. or 5 ft. high there must be a deposit and they must have gas, so it was absolutely necessary that these should be ventilated. But he would entirely abolish fresh-air inlets, and would put in ventilating pipes of 4 in. diameter, carried up the side of the building on the sewer side of the inspection trap. He would take away all gully traps from the foot of rain-water pipes, and would have a system of free ventilation throughout. He regretted the London vestries did not take up this matter when the London County Council were considering the question of new by-laws. He complained that architects had in the past entirely lost sight of the question of drainage.

Mr. T. LONGDIN (Warrington) was glad to hear the Local Government Board by-laws condemned, and he hoped the Association of Municipal and County Engineers would consider them, and, as practical men, send up suggestions for their improvement. The great thing was to have sewers giving self-cleansing velocities.

Councillor A. C. CAMPKIN (Cambridge) said he had found, as chairman of the Sewage Disposal Committee of his town, that ventilation by manholes in the crown of the road was an unmitigated nuisance, and he had endeavoured, but without success, to have them removed. Shafts carried up houses were successful in removing the smells, but the parties concerned complained of them. If these were condemned, where was the remedy? He doubted whether any ventilation of well-constructed sewers was necessary if they had proper gravitation and sufficient velocity. In the metropolis, however, where they had such large sewers, he could understand the necessity of ventilation.

Mr. LEWIS ANGELL (West Ham) said his corporation had circularised the authorities of the country, asking them to endeavour to get the new law as to combined drainage altered, but they had not succeeded in getting Parliament to do so. West Ham was a fighting corporation, and in their Omnibus Bill of this year they sought to introduce the old interpretation. Whether Parliament was asleep or the Local Government Board was nodding he could not say, but the West Ham clause had been passed, and that district had now succeeded in making for themselves a law under which private owners were responsible for combined drains. Moreover, the West Ham powers were retrospective.

Mr. S. R. LOWCOCK said he preferred "combined drain " to Prof. Bostock Hill's term "compound drain," because combined drainage used to mean the combination of rain water and sewage, in contradistinction to the separate system. He agreed with the suggestion that the Association of Municipal and County Engineers should give the Local Government Board the benefit of their advice as to by-laws, but what was wanted should first be settled, as at present there was great divergence of opinion. He also agreed with Dr. Bostock Hill that the multiplication of traps should be avoided; but they should not all be done away with, because of the difficulty of ventilating a sewer on account of the outlets at times becoming inlets. In his view the number of traps should be kept down, and some six or ten houses, according to local conditions, should be connected to a section of drain cut off from the main sewer. The sewer should be treated by itself and the section of drain by itself.

Mr. E. DAY (Worcester) thought they were all agreed that some outlet should be provided for sewer gases. Personally he favoured exhaust shafts, with a destroyer at the top to draw vitiated air from the sewer and destroy any microbes that might exist. For these shafts some arrangement might be devised for using the waste heat from gasworks or refuse destructor works.

Mr. W. IKKNMAN (Birmingham) said the real point was to prevent altogether the formation of sewer-gas. He knew that a complicated system of house drainage could be kept free from sewer-gas, and therefore engineers should be able to find a remedy for it in the sewers. Fresh sewage did not give off sewer-gas. But if there were traps, one to every house, there must be gallons and gallons of putrefying sewage matter which at the next flushing was discharged into the sewers, and there was the material for making sewer-gas. It was true that there could not be found any perfectly model method for all towns. Each must have its own. All that had been said pointed to the fact that they were rather overridden by the law. He was not an advocate for uniting drains together where they had to go under houses. In Birmingham they did not know back passages, and, though they

were convenient for drainage purposes, he did not advocate them because of other evils connected with them. Mr. Lowcock advocated the ventilation of sewers as distinct from drains. Well, do away with traps and the distinction ended.

Dr. BOSTOCK HILL, in his reply, referred to the fact that there was at times a covert feeling of hostility between engineers and medical officers, but he was pleased to see it had not shown itself in that discussion. With what Dr. Priestley had said as to drainage under houses he absolutely disagreed. Under no conditions should a drain go under a house at all. He preferred to see the evils of, and he believed there were several that were creeping in through, compound drainage. The position as to ventilating shafts might be summed up in what the president of the section (Mr. Henman) had said as to fresh sewage having no smell. If sewers and drains could hold only fresh sewage, and not stale, then there would be no noxious gases which arose from putrefaction. The scientific method was not to close up gratings to hide smells, but to go to the root of the matter and see why there was a deposit in any particular drain, and remove the deposit. He was sorry Mr. Willcox, one of the best authorities in the Midlands, had not illumined the discussion. Mr. Day had suggested exhaust shafts and destructors for sewers. They had had many of these brought under their notice, but if they looked to the principle they would see such remedy was wrong. They could not in large towns, such as Birmingham, with hundreds of miles of sewers, possibly get such a draught as would consume all sewer gas and render it inoffensive. The expense would be prohibitive, nor would it be necessary. What was wanted was to so rearrange the sewers in large towns that offensive gases would not be generated. With reference to the question of "drain " and "sewer," he thought it was a mistake to quibble, because what everybody had thought to be a drain the judges had decided was a sewer. It had been suggested that it was unfair on ratepayers that they should be saddled with the cost of looking after drains that had become sewers. Well, in this age of socialism, he thought it was one of the best principles for all drains, whether private or not, to be looked after by the State, in the interests of the public health.

Dr. PRIESTLEY, in reply, said Dr. Bostock Hill had not made it clear that he (Dr. Priestley) did not advocate drains under houses. His contention was that they should only be so placed where necessary. With regard to Mr. Lewis Angell's remarks, he thought the West Ham Omnibus Bill would not override the general law of the land.

Dr. CHARLES PORTER, M.D., D.P.H., medical officer of health for the county borough of Stockport, also read an interesting paper in the Engineering and Architectural section, his subject being

THE QUANTITY OF WATER REQUIRED FOR DOMESTIC FLUSHING PURPOSES, AND THE INFLUENCE OF INTERCEPTING TRAPS THEREUPON.

In the course of his paper Dr. Porter said that the water-carriage system of refuse disposal, which was yearly becoming increasingly prevalent throughout the country, aimed at the cleanly and rapid removal, through drains, of excremental matter from the neighbourhood of dwellings. For its successful application and working adequate flushing of water-closets and house drains was absolutely essential, in order to prevent the latter from becoming " nothing better than elongated cesspools charged with foul, festering filth," as was shown to be the case at Maidstone. The recent Government report on the typhoid epidemic in that town told us that half its 6,000 odd houses had water-closets without any mechanical means of flushing, and that the sanitary authority's lamentable " failure of duty in this respect had led to the gravest consequences," a large number of the typhoid cases being officially ascribed to soil and air pollution from blocked and defective drains. In advocating conversion to water carriage we ought, therefore, to satisfy ourselves that the public health was protected from the results of such deficiencies; and with this object in view he was directed in April last by the Stockport Corporation to ascertain experimentally the quantity of water required to flush efficiently a water-closet with drain and intercepting trap. Dr. Porter then continued :—

Upwards of 120 experiments were shortly afterwards carried out on the lines adopted by the Sanitary Institute in 1893, the apparatus used being the following: (a) Duckett's wash-down closet, with 8 outgo, and afterwards a "Unitas" wash-out closet; (b) water waste-preventing cistern, graduated for 6, 4, 3½, 3, 2½, 2 and 1½ gallons, and connected to closet by 5 ft. of 1¼-in. vertical lead piping; (c) 47 ft. of glazed earthenware 6-in. and 4-in. pipe drain, with puddle joints, and having a right-angled curve onto pipe's length from closet outgo. In upper surface of each length of pipe was cut a slot 15 in. to 18 in. long and about 2 in. in width, for inspection purposes; (d) disconnecting traps (or " interceptors ") of a good type, attached to end of drain, discharging over a weighed pail, and having glass windows inserted in the lowest part or " throat." Fæcal matter and paper, from a " Rochdale Pail," filled by actual use at a mill, were used for charging the closets, 4 oz. to 6 oz. being employed in most cases, but 8 oz. and 12 oz. were used in a smaller number. In the Sanitary Institute experiments artificial material was used for this purpose.

The first series of trials (fifty in number) were made with

a *4-in. drain* (fall 1 in 40) and *4-in. disconnecting* trap. This trap was filled by *8 pints* of water and at the lowest part measured 3½ in. transversely and 4 in. vertically. Flushes of 3, 2½, 2 and 1½ gallons were employed, the result being that 3 gallons invariably sufficed to thoroughly flush closet, drain and 4-in. trap; a 2½-gallon flush generally failed to clear the 4-in. trap; with 2 gallons the interceptor was not once cleared, and most of the solids were left in the trap. By repeated 2-gallon flushes in rapid succession, causing a head of water in the drain, the trap was eventually cleared with a rush, but this did not happen if one flush were allowed to trickle away before the next followed it. A 1½-gallon flush was found to be of little use. The drain was never cleared and became rapidly blocked.

*The second series* included twenty-one experiments, and was made with a 6-in. drain (fall 1 in 60) and *6-in.* disconnecting trap, which, it is noteworthy, required *12 pints* of water to fill it, and at its lowest part measured 5½ in. transversely and 5½ in. vertically. Flushes of 6, 4, 3½, 3 and 2½ gallons were used, and it is a remarkable fact that, though 3 gallons and upwards sufficed to clear the closet and drain each time, the *6-in. trap was cleared by a 6-gallon flush in only two out of four cases*; 4 gallons cleared it in only one out of six cases, and anything less than 4 gallons altogether repeatedly failed to clear the trap.

*The third series* numbered twenty-two experiments with a 6-in. drain and a 4-in. intercepting trap. With a *3-gallon* flush the closet, drain and trap were efficiently cleansed every time, but a flush of less than 3 gallons failed each time to clear the drain and to reach the trap.

*The fourth series* (eighteen trials) with a "Unitas" *wash-out* closet, 4-in. drain and 4-in. interceptor, flushes of 3, 2½ and 2 gallons being used; 3 gallons sufficed to clear the trap in two out of six cases. With smaller flushes the trap retained a portion of the charge in every case; in five cases the drain was not cleared, whilst in eight the closet trap was not cleared, due evidently to the inherent faults of the *wash-out* closet. I shall be pleased to supply fuller details of these results to anyone interested in the matter, and I venture to submit the following

CONCLUSIONS.

(1) That *3 gallons is the minimum amount that can be relied upon for efficient flushing*—i.e., prompt carriage of dejecta through closet, drain and interceptor to sewer, even with a good form of *wash-down* closet well laid, 4-in. or 6-in. drain, and good 4-in. interceptor. (2) That *if an inferior type of closet* be used, or *if the intercepting trap exceed 4 in. in diameter, 3 gallons is clearly not sufficient* for effective flushing. The proper remedy then, however, is to correct such structural deficiencies rather than to increase the flush. (3) That *if no intercepting trap be employed a flush of 2½ gallons* is the minimum amount that can be relied upon to efficiently cleanse the closet trap and drain. (4) That *the invariable employment of a disconnecting trap, as recommended by the model by-laws, is far from being an unmixed benefit*, and, owing to the obstacle the disconnecting trap presents to the cleansing of house drains, *its use should be strictly limited to those dwellings inside which a drain opening exists* —e.g., in the cellar—and that if such drain openings inside houses were prohibited in new dwellings disconnecting traps might, with great advantage, be entirely dispensed with. There is much reason to believe that we have hitherto exaggerated the potency of sewer air; assuming, however, that it is noxious in its effects, the object of a disconnecting trap is wholly gone if we keep all drain openings outside our dwellings; and having done this, it is absurd to continue to insist on disconnecting traps, which only diminish the efficiency of the flush of water.

IS ECONOMY IN WATER EFFECTED BY THE USE OF WASTE-WATER-CLOSETS?

In order to elucidate this question two blocks of exactly similar houses were recently selected in Stockport. At the request and expense of the Sanitary Committee the water supplied to each block between 7 a.m. on October 28, 1896, and 7.30 a.m. on May 13, 1897, was metered by the water company, with the following results: Lot *A.*—Ten houses with waste-water-closets used 65,720 gallons, or 33·3 gallons per house per day. Lot *B.*—Fourteen houses with ordinary water-closets used 151,320 gallons, or 54·8 gallons per house per day, showing *a saving of exactly 21·5 gallons per house per day in slop-water houses.* In a similar and more recent experiment in Manchester the city surveyor, Mr. T. de Courcy Meade, M.I.C.E., has, curiously enough, obtained an exactly identical result.

**New Mersey Docks.**—The Mersey Docks and Harbour Board have accepted the tender—amounting to over £250,000 —of Mr. C. J. Wills, of Manchester, for the construction of a new dock, &c., in connection with the Queen's dock, and the work will be commenced immediately.

**Business Announcement.**—Messrs. J. H. Sankey & Son, Iron Bridge and Essex Wharves, Canning Town, London, E., inform us that they have purchased the business of Messrs. A. Gregory & Co., lime, cement, brick and sanitary goods merchants, carried on by them at Plumstead, Woolwich Arsenal (South-Eastern Railway) Bexley Heath and Erith. Messrs. Gregory & Co. still, however, retain their brickfields at Wickham-lane.

## QUERIES AND REPLIES.

*Sketches accompanying Queries should be made separate on white paper in plain black-ink lines. Lettering or figures should be bold and plain.*

**222. Building By-Laws: Wooden Bay Windows not Permissible.**—"M. S. A." writes: In submitting plans for some houses with bay windows on ground and first floors it is proposed to put brick mullions at angles to ground floor, only the upper bay having no angle mullions, but simply the wood frame, and finished with moulding and gutter above. These were submitted to two different local authorities. One authority passed the plans as in accordance and complying with the by-laws; the other refused to pass them, as they contend that the upper bay does not comply with the by-law. The by-laws of each authority are alike, and state that the woodwork shall be 4 in. from the face of the wall. I consider that the woodwork of the upper bay is 4 in. from the face of the wall. Which authority is right?

The construction of bay windows formed of wood is contrary to the provisions of clause 24 of the by-laws which are in force in the district, and the local authority are entitled to refuse approval of the plans. The clause referred to requires that "every person who shall erect a new building shall cause all woodwork in any external wall of such building (except any bressumer, or any storey post under a bressumer, and any frame of a door or window of a shop) to be set back in reveal *4 in.* at least from the outer face of such wall." The object of this clause, as pointed out in Knight's "Annotated Edition of the Model By-Laws," is to require window frames, &c., to be set back from the outer face of any external wall of a new building, in order that, in the event of fire, the burning of the woodwork referred to shall be less dangerous to adjacent property and less liable to interfere, by falling out or otherwise, with persons outside the building. For convenience of business, woodwork about any shop-front is exempted from the operation of the clause, and in the case of buildings of the warehouse class doors for the ingress or egress of merchandise are allowed by another part of clause 24 (not reproduced) to be nearly flush with the outer face of the wall. Bay windows formed of wood only cannot be erected to comply with the by-laws.

## THE LONDON WATER SUPPLY COMMISSION.

The Commission held their thirty-fourth meeting at the Westminster Guildhall, on Monday, Lord Llandaff presiding.

Mr. W. B. BRYAN, chief engineer to the Eäst London Water Company, was examined, and gave detailed statistics as to the supply of water in the company's district during the present scarcity. He asserted that there had been much waste from taps being kept continually running, and that the lack of storage in the district greatly aggravated the hardships of the drought, which really began about sixteen months ago, and had exceeded all previously recorded droughts. He estimated that in the event of the recurrence of a similar scarcity the company, with the assistance of 12,000,000 gallons daily from other companies, would be able to keep up a constant supply. They were taking measures for increasing their storage, and hoped to be independent of the other companies in two years.

In the course of cross-examination on Tuesday, Mr. BRYAN said the East London Water Company's supply of water from its own sources was in September last less by 17,343,000 gallons per day, and in October less by 18,040,000 gallons, than in the corresponding months of 1897.

Sir ALEXANDER BINNIE, engineer to the London County Council, recalled, gave it as his opinion that what had been done by the company this autumn was sufficient for present purposes. On the part of the county council he strongly objected to their being saddled, in the event of purchase, with an expenditure of £500,000, which the companies proposed to expend upon the intercommunication scheme. In the event of water having to be obtained from Wales hereafter, it was undesirable to have the scheme complicated by a system of intercommunication from the centre to the outside. In case of an amalgamation of the companies the intercommunication should be from the outside to the centre, and on this account he preferred what had been described as the No. 1 scheme. If it was an insurance, an intercommunication scheme, whilst increasing the debenture stock of the companies, might decrease their selling price. If the East London Water Company were bought now, they should buy them as a defaulting company, which they could not do if they were able to avail themselves of the intercommunication scheme.

**Tenders Wanted.**—The Secretary of State for Foreign Affairs, has received a despatch from her Majesty's representative at Rio de Janeiro, stating that tenders are invited by the Government of the State of Para for the purchase and working of the waterworks of the city of Belem (known as Para). Tenders must be received at the Treasury of Para by March 15, 1899. A copy of the conditions of the contract may be examined at the Commercial Department of the Foreign Office any day between the hours of 11 a.m. and 5 p.m.

# The Surveyors' Institution.

## PRESIDENT'S ADDRESS : GROWTH OF THE METROPOLIS : SEWAGE DISPOSAL.

On Monday evening Mr. Robert Vigers delivered his inaugural address as president of the Surveyors' Institution. In his opening remarks he said it was the wise policy of those who founded the institution to establish it on the broadest possible basis, so as to make it representative of every branch of their many-sided calling. The list of members now comprised nearly 3,000 names. He proposed to confine his observations very largely to matters connected with the great metropolis, which presented such an immense and unique field for professional activity. In dealing with this subject the president continued as follows :—

### THE GROWTH OF LONDON.

"To begin with, the material growth of London during the fifty years covered by my personal experience almost transcends belief. A comparison of a map of London in the forties with a map of our present London will show how rapid and complete has been the absorption of the open spaces which separated it at the earlier period from the surrounding hamlets and villages—spaces which have been taken possession of in the interval by the extra 2,000,000 persons for whom house accommodation has had to be provided.

"Take, by way of example, the parish of Kensington. The population of the parish was in 1856 54,000 persons, in 1896 it had risen to 170,000 persons—in other words, it had more than tripled. In 1856 the inhabited houses numbered 6,300, in 1896 22,580, or three and a half times as many as forty years previously. The roads under the control of the vestry measured 27 miles at the earlier date, in 1896 they measured 85 miles. The rateable value was £287,665 in 1856, and had risen to £2,300,000 in 1896. This amazing growth can no doubt be matched in other districts, but it may serve as a measure of the problem which awaits some of us, and certainly our successors, to conservation of the health of and the providing for the housing of a population expanding at this astonishing rate.

"I have given some statistics of the growth of a single London parish during the last forty years. Let me now take the wider area of what is known as the administrative county of London, which, subject to a slight correction, is co-extensive with the old Metropolitan Board of Works district as defined by the Act 18 and 19 Vic., cap. 120. The several areas on which the census for the years 1851, 1861, 1871, 1881 and 1891 were respectively based are difficult to reconcile, and I am indebted to the courtesy of the Registrar-General for a reduction of these areas to uniformity for the purposes of the following analysis. The population of the area now known as the administrative county of London, comprising 75,422 acres, was : In 1851, 2,363,274; 1861, 2,808,862; 1871, 3,266,987; 1881, 3,834,194; 1891, 4,232,118; or, putting it another way, about fifty-six persons to the acre. In the decade 1851-61 the population increased by 445,588 persons, or 18·85 per cent.; in the decade 1861-71 by 458,125 persons, or 16·31 per cent.; in the decade 1871-81 by 567,207 persons, or 17·36 per cent.; and in the decade 1881-91 by 397,924 persons, or 10·37 per cent. The number of inhabited houses was : In 1851, 306,064; 1861, 360,065; 1871, 419,642; 1881, 488,885; 1891, 548,315. But I should explain that an inhabited house is for census purposes a house or tenement in which one or more persons slept on the night of enumeration.

"I will not labour the point by setting out the figures in detail, but it is a fact worth observing that, while the ratio of the growth of the population showed in the first three decennial periods a tendency to exceed the ratio of increase in the number of houses in the last census decade, the growth of house accommodation exceeded the growth of population by about 2 per cent., and I think I am entitled to argue from this that the work done during the last twenty years in the demolition of overcrowded slum neighbourhoods is beginning to bear fruit and to reveal itself in our statistics. The number of persons per house has fallen 0·30 per cent. in the last two decennial periods (the figure is now about 7·64 persons per house, compared with 7·94 in 1871), and my point is : that not only has the number per house fallen appreciably in the last twenty years (despite an increase of nearly 2,000,000 in the population), but that in an enormous number of cases the 7·64 persons per house are now living in far larger and healthier dwellings than the 7·94 persons per house of twenty years ago, and that, with improved dwellings, 7·64 persons per house is not by any means excessive."

Mr. Vigers then proceeded to refer to

### THE HOUSING PROBLEM IN LONDON.

In regard to this he said :—

"I am not very conversant with the work done under the Housing of the Working Classes Acts, but it is stated that the value of sites for rehousing on the route of the Strand to Holborn improvement would involve a loss to the county council of £260 per person provided for, or for a family of seven persons an unremunerative expenditure of £1,820 for land only, if reinstated close to their former dwellings. This is in startling contrast to the experience of the Peabody Trustees; but then the philanthropy of the trustees is not of so exalted an order as to induce them to select sites in expensive situations for the mere purpose of saving the persons to be benefitted a quarter of an hour's journey to their work. There is the less necessity for this plan of rebuilding on the old sites, seeing the facilities in the way of cheap workmen's trains for rehousing the dispossessed persons in the far healthier atmosphere of the suburbs. Indeed, this system of workmen's trains is in some danger of abuse and of becoming a check to enterprise. There can be no doubt that the conditions in this respect imposed on the new railway beneath Oxford-street are oppressive in the highest degree, whatever may be their justification from the point of view of modern sociology.

"It will perhaps be remembered that Mr. Peabody's superb gift to the poor of London amounted in the aggregate to £500,000, to which had been added up to the end of last year over £720,000 in respect of rent and interest, bringing up the total fund to £1,220,446 on December 31, 1897. It will thus be seen that the trustees in their management of the fund have had due regard to the wishes of the donor that it should minister to the wants of 'future generations of the London poor' by making it reproductive, while at the same time rendering it a model for all future efforts to relieve the congestion of the poorer districts of this crowded city.

"I find that the capital expended on land and buildings to the end of the year 1897 was £1,250,390 10s. 8d.; that the artisan and labouring poor of London had been provided with 11,367 rooms, besides bath-rooms, laundries and lavatories, and that these rooms were comprised in 5,121 separate dwellings, of which eighty-six were of four rooms, 1,781 of three rooms, 2,426 of two rooms and 828 of one room. The average weekly earnings of the head of each family was £1 3s. 2½d., while the average rent of each dwelling was 4s. 9¼d. a week and of each room 2s. 2d. a week. The total number of persons in residence in December last was 19,741, giving a mean density of 725 per acre. I have already shown that the average density of the population of London is about 56 per acre, and it is therefore a significant circumstance that, notwithstanding that the number of persons in the Peabody Buildings represents a mean density nearly thirteen times as great as that of London as a whole, the death rate was 2·8 per 1,000 below the average of London, while the infant mortality (the most telling factor in the death rate) was actually 21·9 below that of London as a whole.

"To show this class of persons for whom accommodation has been provided I may set out the occupations principally represented : Carmen, 283 ; charwomen, 372 ; labourers, 673 ; letter carriers, 104 ; needlewomen, 267 ; packers, 136 ; police constables, 186 ; porters, 513 ; printers, 129 ; and warehouse labourers, 194. It will, I think, be agreed that no better example could be found of a charity administered in such a manner as to be entirely free from the familiar reproach of pauperising the beneficiaries, or of one in which the expenses of management bears such a small proportion to the total income as 2½ per cent."

### THE TRANSIT PROBLEM IN LONDON.

The next subject taken up by the president was the important one of transit, in regard to which he said :—

"But the serious problem still confronts us how to provide a population increasing at the rate of about 500,000 in ten years with those means of internal communication necessary for the free movement of the vast traffic traversing the restricted area comprising the principal centres of business activity. Speaking broadly, it may be said that the bulk of the heavy commercial traffic of London (taking the area lying between Westminster and the Tower) is between north and south—that is, between the termini of the great railways on each side of the river, the Port of London, and the warehouses and manufactories of Southwark and Bermondsey.

"The opening up of new routes for vehicular traffic has done a good deal to relieve the pressure, and the effect was strikingly displayed in the case of the Tower Bridge. Most of us have had bitter experience of former blocks on London Bridge. I have not the latest figures before me, but I find from the report of the City engineer that within a year of the opening of the Tower Bridge London Bridge had been relieved of about 5,200 vehicles per day, Eastcheap of 2,200, and Fenchurch-street of about 3,000, whereas the traffic in the streets to which it was deflected by the new bridge was increased in the following ratio : The Minories by 2,200 vehicles daily, Liverpool-street by 900, Houndsditch by 700, and Bishopsgate-street by 600.

"The lighter traffic and the ebb and flow of the pedestrian tide is, on the other hand, mainly from east to west. Every one must have been struck with the crowded condition of the footways along the main thoroughfares during the greater part of the day. A man who wishes to make his way rapidly between such points as Liverpool-street and St. Paul's, Moorgate-street and the Mansion House, or the bottom of Fleet-street and Charing Cross, finds his progress checked, and at times absolutely arrested, by the double stream of people on the narrow pavements he has to traverse, where the pace is set by the slowest walkers, who are frequently mere loiterers or sightseers. It must have occurred to him to wonder what the state of things will be in this respect in twenty or thirty years' time. Yet practically no attempt has been made to mitigate this great and growing inconvenience.

"There is no lack of schemes for widening the roadways, but, so far as I am aware, the equally serious consideration of facilitating the progress of the pedestrians by the provision of wider pavements has, except in a few instances, not been deemed worthy of attention. It is not sufficient to widen a street like the Strand from 53 ft. to 80 ft., as indicated by the setting-back at the corner of Wellington-street, unless the footways are also doubled in width, nor does it meet the case to provide parallel thoroughfares, for people will not quit the direct track from point to point, whatever the inconvenience may be of attempting to traverse it.

"The system of tube railways, now in its infancy, will probably absorb in time some of the foot traffic of the main thoroughfares, and may even result in a temporary diminution in the number of omnibuses, but the limits of the carrying capacity of these railways will soon be reached, and the provision of wider roads and pavements and new arteries for wheeled traffic will become imperative.

"One of my predecessors in this chair, the late Mr. C. J. Shoppee, put forward an ingenious suggestion for carrying the heavy north and south traffic *under* the Strand. This suggestion met with less attention than it deserved, and I should not be surprised if some enterprising engineer some day rediscovered the idea.

"No doubt there have been vast improvements in the means of external communication within the last few years. Without these increased facilities the more remote districts would have been inaccessible to those whose daily business lies in the great commercial centres; but these rather tend to increase than to diminish the congestion of the centres, by throwing a vast population into them within a limited period of the day.

"I am of opinion that the time is not far distant when the people of London will be called upon to incur an enormous expenditure in further widening streets like Oxford-street, Holborn, the Strand, Fleet-street and Ludgate-hill, originally laid out for a population one-tenth the present size; for what has hitherto been done in this direction is a mere tinkering with the problem of free locomotion."

After some remarks on the great rise in the value of land in the City, the president referred to the valuable report prepared by Mr. Percy J. Edwards, and published by Messrs. King, of Bridge-street, Westminster, dealing with metropolitan improvements. The report comprised a list of thirty new streets and street widenings effected between 1857 and 1885 inclusive, with gross and nett costs, and the approximate area of building land absorbed in their execution. From a table which gave the results in a condensed form it appeared that the area of building land lost to the market by these improvements was 1,606,650 square feet, or nearly 37 acres. The president next referred briefly to dealings with property in connection with the new Central London Railway, and then said that a few words would not be considered out of place on the perennial subject of

SEWAGE DISPOSAL.

On this subject he spoke as follows: "A few words will not be considered out of place on the perennial subject of sewage disposal. Some of us are old enough to remember papers read before this institution thirty years ago, to prove not only that a way had been found of ridding our towns of what had even then become an intolerable nuisance, but promising fortunes to those who had the sense to utilise this good gift of Nature on the land. We were all thrilled with tales about 10 tons of rye grass to the acre and of crops stimulated to the almost visible growth of ½ in. per hour. We were reproached with our folly in depending for manure on the legacy left to us by the 'provident penguins' of by-gone centuries, and were assured that each man's excreta, properly applied, was sufficient to grow crops for his maintenance. Alas for human enthusiasm! This noble dream of a self-supporting community faded in the light of realities. There was no money in it beyond that which was put there. Nitrogen tables were forthcoming to any amount, but no balance sheets, and in a few years all that could be definitely predicated was this, that, under favourable conditions, a dry-weather flow of sewage could be dealt with on a sufficient area of land in a suitable situation, and that such heavy crops of rye grass could be grown that there was no market for them. So we were not much the wiser for all that had been said and done in the matter.

"Gradually it came to be recognised that sewage, so far from being of commercial value, was a nuisance to be got rid of, in the least expensive way, but at any rate get rid of. This more reasonable gospel now meets with general acceptance, and processes innumerable have been devised for dealing with crude sewage in such a way as to secure an effluent sufficiently innocuous for discharge into rivers and watercourses without danger to the public health. It must be admitted that local authorities have been placed in a cruel predicament between the demands of legislation, the resulting pressure of public departments, the necessity of getting rid of their sewage and the immaturity of the methods for so doing. The solution seemed at first to be exclusively in the hands of the surveyor and the agriculturist. Later on the engineer became enlisted, then the chemist; and now the bacteriologist, assisted by a few bricklayers, appears intent on making the question his exclusive monopoly. For the moment it is that much-maligned creature, the micro-organism, that holds the field, and it is with its benignant aid that a way is to be found out of all our troubles. The annual report (1898) of the London County Council affords a measure of the immensity of the task of dealing with the sewage of a great city. The crude sewage treated at the two outfalls in the course of twelve months amounted to 77,103,364,000 gallons. The chemical precipitating agents employed were 15,500 tons of lime and 3,914 tons of proto-sulphate of iron, while the sludge produced weighed 2,136,683 tons. The disposal of this latter required the services of six sludge vessels (with a carrying capacity of 1,000 tons each), which made an aggregate of 2,124 passages for the purpose of depositing it at Barrow Deeps, some 15 miles beyond the Nore, at a cost for maintenance of nearly £30,000 per annum.

"There is no attempt here, so far as I can gather, at anything more than the removal of the solid matter, and vast as is the expense involved, it is small in comparison with the cost that would be incurred in endeavouring to obtain the innocuous effluent so necessary where the outfall is situated on a non-tidal river. However, the subject is too great for treatment in any detail in this address, and I will therefore confine myself to a brief reference to two modern methods of sewage treatment that are for the moment attracting some attention.

THE SEPTIC SYSTEM.

"First, I may refer, as the more hopeful of the two, to the ingenious system invented by Mr. Cameron, the city surveyor of Exeter, which has recently formed the subject of a Local Government Board inquiry. Mr. Cameron maintains that all other systems show but poor results, that they all bear a strong family likeness, and have been adopted as mere makeshifts; that they all aim at merely clarifying the sewage by chemical means previously to turning the effluent on the land or passing it through an artificial filter; that this effluent is frequently found to undergo subsequent fermentation; and that the nuisance which results is often greater than if the crude sewage were put at once upon the land without previously undergoing these costly processes. He argues that the soluble organic matter passes away in the effluent, while the more solid matter still remains to be dealt with in the highly inconvenient form of unmarketable sludge, which has very little, if any, manurial value.

"He is under the impression (a very reasonable one) that the production of sewage has been going on in these islands from prehistoric times, and he naively remarks that, notwithstanding this fact, no difficulty has ever arisen as to its disposal until artificial means were resorted to for getting rid of it in some other than the time-honoured manner of turning it into the nearest stream, to be dealt with by natural oxidation—a somewhat odd reflection for a sanitary reformer. He does not, of course, advocate a return to so unscientific a system, but he contends that crude sewage, minus manufacturing refuse, is, when poured into the rivers, in most cases completely destroyed in a few hours; that this is done by a purely natural process, and that the true key to the problem is to imitate these natural processes with such facilitating means as science may afford. It is at this point that the bacteriologist appears upon the scene, with battalions of friendly microbes, doing their work of chemical metamorphosis under conditions favourable to their development and beneficent activity. His plan is simplicity itself. He passes the crude sewage into what he calls septic tanks, from which light and air (those foes of the microbe) are as much as possible excluded. He claims that on entering the still waters of the tanks the solid matters are disengaged, the heavier falling to the bottom and the lighter rising to the surface; that the organisms present in the sewage under these circumstances increase enormously and rapidly attack all the organic matters, converting them into simple compounds in a descending scale of complexity, and that the ultimate remaining products are merely ammonia, carbonic acid and other gases, with an almost inappreciable residuum of black earthy matter representing the burnt-out ash of the solids of the sewage. The principal points on which Mr. Cameron insists are that no refractory residuum remain in the shape of sludge, and that the effluent leaves the tanks clear and inoffensive and (most important of all) free from all liability to subsequent fermentation and decomposition. If this be so—and scientific evidence is forthcoming in support of the claim—it represents a very distinct advance, and the days of the claimant with a sentimental grievance over the propinquity of a sewage farm should be numbered.

"As a matter of fact, Mr. Cameron's so-called septic tank is a species of glorified cesspool, with this difference, that in a cesspool the septic changes constantly going on are uncontrolled and liable at any moment to invade the houses with which it is connected, whereas in the case of the septic tank all deleterious gases are cut off from the drains, and can be conducted away and dealt with without damage to human health. It is as well, however, not to be too sanguine, or to forget that old fallacies under fresh names are apt sometimes to be hailed as new truths.

"Just a few words about another system. I will be very brief, as it has already been described in our 'Transactions.' I refer to what is called the 'Electrozone Sterilising Process,' carried on at Maidenhead. The liquid called electrozone is described by our member, Mr. Henry Robinson, as produced by the electrolytic decomposition of sea water, resulting in the evolution of chlorine. One-fifth of a grain of chlorine per gallon of effluent is found, it is said, to be quite sufficient for the purposes of complete sterilisation. I do not gather that the system is primarily intended for the treatment of crude sewage, which is best dealt with by bacteric action, but rather as a means of absolutely sterilising the effluent for a time long enough for the processes of natural oxidation in the streams and rivers to check any tendency in it to generate morbific organisms. This also sounds promising, but the system has yet to stand the test of time and of those varying conditions which are so liable to upset the most confident predictions."

The concluding part of an interesting address was devoted to a discussion of various points in connection, first, with the ethics of practice especially as affecting the younger members of the profession in their desire to obtain business, and, secondly, with certain strictures which had been made in regard to the giving of

EXPERT EVIDENCE ON OATH.

In the course of his remarks on the latter subject, Mr. Vigers pointed out that the difference between the extreme valuations on the same side was just as great as that between the extreme valuations on the two sides. So long as the value of property remained a matter of opinion and speculation divergencies must arise. The surveyor for the claimant was bound, in view of potential changes affecting the value of property, always liable to occur in a densely-peopled country, to see that no contingent element of value was overlooked, however remote it might be; while the surveyor for the purchaser was equally bound to secure his client, if possible, against paying ready money in respect of any future element of value which was not certain to accrue sooner or later. It was necessary to consider what was the position of the surveyor as a witness on oath. He has sworn to tell "the truth, the whole truth, and nothing but the truth." Now as this adjuration was much too precise and comprehensive for application to matters into which purely speculative opinion must, from the nature of things, largely enter, it followed that what in effect the witness swears was not that all he has to say is fact, but that what he had to say was his honest opinion. The critics were probably suffering from some confusion of mind, being apparently under the impression that because the witnesses on both sides were on their oath their valuations should practically agree, whereas it was not likely, in the nature of things, that they would even approximately agree in some cases, having regard to the different standpoints from which the respective parties approached the matter at issue. An opinion was one thing and a fact another thing altogether. The question, therefore, could not but suggest itself whether the examination of expert witnesses on oath was not a mistaken endeavour to apply to the region of opinion a procedure imported from the courts of law, and appertaining in principle to the region of pure fact. Might it not be contended, with some show of reason, that the position in which the surveyor should really be placed was that of a technical advocate for his side, a species of assessor to counsel, and that it should be left to a sworn umpire to settle, after hearing the witnesses on both sides, the degree to which the more speculative elements in the valuations should be allowed to prevail?"

THE INSTITUTION.

Mr. Vigers concluded an interesting address with the following remarks in regard to the institution:—

"The retrospect of the last thirty years should inspire us with a pardonable pride. No institution with which I am acquainted has ever achieved such a remarkable success in so brief a period of time, and, so far as it can be ascribed to any one circumstance, I think this has been due to the habits of caution, so characteristic of surveyors, which have governed our procedure. It has been the policy of your council, while availing themselves of every real opportunity of advancing the interests of the profession, to avoid that fussiness which some persons consider the first duty of a professional society. We have not sought to harry public departments on small pretexts or on none at all, and, as a consequence, when we have approached them on questions of moment we have received attention and consideration at their hands, and have been able to usefully influence in this way the course of legislation and the tendency of departmental procedure. In the result the society is stronger to-day than at any period of its history, and whether regard be had to numbers, to financial position, to internal organisation, to the freedom of its constitution, or to the beautiful new home which it has provided for itself, and which will be completed early next year, it may challenge comparison with any other professional body in the kingdom. But the future is with the rising generation, not with that which is passing from the scene. You younger men cannot say that you are not entering into a goodly heritage, and it rests with you to decide whether you will dissipate and destroy it by indifference or even by mistaken activity, or whether you will hand it on unimpaired, and even extended, to your successors."

**Ilford.**—The district council have decided to take steps to promote a Bill in Parliament with the object of acquiring the gasworks.

## THE LOCAL GOVERNMENT BOARD AND "WATER-FINDING."

Mr. Leicester Gataker, of Bath, has forwarded us an extract from *The Leighton Buzzard Reporter* of November 5th, with reference to his "water-finding" proceedings in Bedfordshire. It will be remembered that Mr. Gataker was employed last year to "find" water by a district council, and that the district auditor refused to pass the account. He disallowed the payment to Mr. Gataker on three grounds: (1) That Mr. Gataker's claim to be able to discover subterranean sources of water was such a pretence as constituted an indictable offence, and that therefore the consideration for his employment was illegal and the contract void. (2) That in disregarding a certain geological report and employing Mr. Gataker the district council incurred expenditure without any sufficient ground and recklessly wasted the public money under their control. (3) That Mr. Gataker's claim to be able to discover subterranean sources of water was practically an attempt at imposition; and that, therefore, he was not a proper person for the district council to employ. However, the Local Government Board have now, according to the journal quoted, reversed the auditor's decision, and have written a letter on the subject to the following effect: "As regards the auditor's first reason, the board do not consider that it has been proved that Mr. Gataker committed an indictable offence; or that, if he did so, the members of the district council were aware that his pretences were illegal. This being the case, the board are of opinion that it must be held that the first reason assigned by the auditor fails to support his decision. As regards his second reason, the board cannot but consider the action of the district council as unwise, but it does not appear to them, having regard to the recommendations the council received as to Mr. Gataker's capabilities, that the council can be considered as having acted with such recklessness that the disallowance and surcharge can be confirmed on this ground. In view of the above considerations respecting the auditor's first and second reasons, the objection taken by him in his third reason appears to this board to be insufficient to support his decision, and in the circumstances the board propose to reverse the disallowance and surcharge. An order will shortly be issued accordingly."

## FIRE PROTECTION IN LONDON.

NEW STATIONS AT WOOLWICH AND LEWISHAM.

On Saturday afternoon Mr. A. M. Torrance, the chairman of the Fire Brigade Committee of the London County Council, laid the foundation-stones of two new fire stations at North Woolwich and Lewisham.

The station at the former place is rather a small affair, affording accommodation for only three married men. The district abuts on the borough of West Ham, but further protection for fire has been rendered necessary owing to the growth of the neighbourhood, which contains many large factories. The cost of the building will be something over £4,000.

At Lewisham a much larger station is in course of erection. The existing fire station at Catford has been found to be altogether below the wants of the district. The building itself contains accommodation for one officer only, the coachmen and firemen having to live some distance away. It is away from that part of Lewisham where most of the business premises were placed. Five years ago the Fire Brigade Committee recommended that a new station should be built. A site had been selected, having a frontage of 77 ft. to the High-street of Lewisham, next to St. Mary's Church. It contains an area of 6,100 square feet, and the station will cost £13,600 to build. It is hoped that the buildings will be completed by next summer. Accommodation will be provided for fourteen married men, four horses, one steamer, one hose-tender and escape, and one hose and ladder truck.

A large number of people gathered to witness the ceremony of laying the respective stones, after which Mr. Torrance and the party accompanying him paid a visit, during the afternoon, to several stations on the south side of the river.

---

**Trade Catalogue.**—Mr. A. G. Thornton, manufacturer of drawing and surveying instruments, St. Mary's-street, Manchester, has just issued a new edition of his illustrated catalogue. The new edition has not only been entirely rewritten and revised, but has been considerably enlarged. It comprises, indeed, nearly 200 pages, is profusely illustrated, and contains full particulars of new articles and improvements introduced since the issue of the last edition.

**Bedworth Waterworks.**—On Saturday, the 5th inst., the foundation-stone of the water tower, in connection with the above works, was laid by Mr. William Johnson, the chairman of the parish council. At the ceremony a silver trowel, suitably engraved, was presented by the engineer, Mr. H. Bertram Nichols, A.M.I.C.E., of Birmingham. Afterwards a luncheon was held in the central schools by the invitation of the chairman. The works are being carried out by Mr. Amos Jenkins, of Southwell, Notts, whose contract amounts to £9,700.

## CORRESPONDENCE.

**Tramway Traction in London : Mr. Baker's Report.—**
Mr. J. Allen Baker writes: I note, from an issue of your
paper, that on the 11th inst. you noticed at some length my
report to the London County Council on some forms of
mechanical tramway traction, and that you purpose continuing same in a later issue. I have just received from
New York a very striking confirmation of my recommendation of the conduit system for London, in the form of an
article in *The Street Railway Journal*. I considered this of
so much importance that I immediately had it reprinted and
circulated to the London County Council, and have pleasure
in handing you herewith a copy of same. The experience
of the Metropolitan Street Railway Company of New York (who
have had the largest and best experience with the conduit
system, and have installed the latest improved type of same)
proves conclusively that the "conduit" is not only minus
the disadvantages of the "trolley," but works satisfactorily
in every way ; and, further, and most important, this report has
proved it to work with greater economy than any other
system or installation that has come under my notice.

THE BRITISH GAS TRACTION COMPANY, Ltd., 22 Chancery-
lane, E.C., write : We notice in your issue of the 11th inst.
some abstracts from Mr. J. Allen Baker's report to the
London County Council on mechanical traction and your
comments on the subject. The line at Blackpool, running to
St. Anne's and Lytham, to which allusion is made as having
been very recently installed, has been in regular work since
July, 1896, and the consumption of gas of 35 cubic feet per
car mile, which includes that used in driving the compressing engines, represents a cost of less than 1d. per car mile.
Comparison is made between this system and the overhead
electric system, and the Dover Corporation is cited as having
adopted the latter, after careful investigation of the merits
of the two methods. We have reason to believe that the
overhead electric system was adopted chiefly because of
larger apparent profit shown on their estimate ; and it should
be noticed in this connection that the experience of the Dover
Corporation has shown a consumption of electrical energy of
0·95 unit per car mile, for which they pay at the rate of 3d.
per unit. Wherever horse traction is replaced by a mechanical system the receipts increase and the conditions become
more favourable to economical working. There are, however,
some grave errors in the further statements made on the
subject of gas cars, which we beg your leave to correct. It
is stated that " it is necessary that the gas motor shall be
continually rotating . . . . and therefore the car, whether at
a standstill or running, is subject to almost the same vibration." The motors are most carefully balanced, and when
the car is standing the speed is reduced. The amount of
vibration then produced is less than 1/10 in. movement; less,
in fact, than that caused by a passenger when walking over
a car. When running the vibration is no greater than, if as
great as, that observable on an ordinary horse car. It is
further stated, in reference to Blackpool, that "the laden cars
have sometimes a difficulty in surmounting the gradients, and
if stopped require to go back and recommence the ascent."
This statement is probably founded on an observation
made during the first few weeks the line was opened, when
at a point where curve and gradient are combined the gauge
was laid too tight ; the cars are capable of starting from
rest on the gradients, and do so when required. Smell is
again raised as an objection to this system, but no mention
is made of the special means that have been so successfully
adopted to obviate this by ensuring more regular and efficient
lubrication. Further remarks are also made, including that the
storage of compressed gas on vehicles is a source of danger ;
the storage arrangements are identical with those employed
on the majority of railway carriages for lighting, and in this
connection no accident has occurred, with the exception of
one on the Metropolitan Railway, which was directly traceable
to outrage. The advantages of a self-contained system
which does not involve expensive alterations to the permanent
way has not been alluded to, nor is mention made of the
difficulty of laying the conduit in our streets, which in many
cases contain the loads of two or three electric lighting companies with their branches and feeders, gas, water and
hydraulic power mains, telegraph and other wires, besides
the sewers. The conduit system, with its very high first cost,
though liable to complete stoppage in case of breakdown,
would, however, probably pay better than the overhead electric with its disadvantages of greater losses of current and
of damage done by electrolysis, which must ultimately be
paid for.

**Shoreditch Combined Electric Light and Dust De-
struction Scheme.—**Messrs. Manlove, Alliott & Co., Limited,
Bloomsgrove Works, Nottingham, contractors and engineers
of the Shoreditch destructor, write : We notice in your issue
of the 11th inst. a letter signed " T. W. Baker," which makes
some statements with respect to ourselves which are absolutely contrary to fact. We observe that Mr. Baker appears
to attach great value to our judgment with respect to his
schemes, but, unfortunately, his memory in regard to this
particular matter is entirely untrustworthy. It is not the
fact that we ourselves, or any of our representatives, ever
asked Mr. Baker if he would grant his patent rights to us
either for the Shoreditch scheme or for any other. It is not

the fact that we ever asked Mr. Baker to "row in our boat."
It is not the fact that we ever proposed any terms at all to
Mr. Baker. And therefore, of course, it is not the fact that
we ever proposed any terms which he refused. Mr. Baker
appears to be very anxious to find fault with the arrangements at Shoreditch and with the figures—which are admittedly not complete—which have been put forward by the
Shoreditch authorities. What can his object be in this correspondence? If it were simply to elicit or elucidate facts,
that could be effected as thoroughly by a letter to a single
paper as by identical letters to half-a-dozen, and probably it
could be effected better still if, before he had entered into the
correspondence at all, he had sought to understand the things
which he states he cannot understand, while certainly correspondence would have been more likely to be valuable if
based upon complete figures—known to be very shortly forthcoming—than when based upon figures admitted by himself to
be incomplete. We have not cared to join in the correspondence upon figures, partly because the consulting engineers to
the scheme (Messrs. Kincaid, Waller & Manville) and the
authorities connected with it (that is, all those who have
complete information concerning it) most fully admit that
the results which we promised from the arrangement have
been attained and much more than attained—and therefore
we are not very much concerned with the discussion of the
matter by people less fully informed—and partly because we
have not wished to engage in correspondence, since to have
done so might have looked like a wish to obtain a gratuitous
advertisement. There is the further excellent reason that
complete figures have not been as yet before the public. Mr.
Baker's letter, however, attempts to give importance to his
own plans by suggesting that we consider them better than
ours, which of course is not the truth ; and in attempting to
give importance to himself and his arrangements he, by inference, depreciates our arrangements and our own capacity for
dealing with the destruction of refuse. As we feel that these
incorrect statements, which have been made not only in your
journal but in so many others, ought not to pass without contradiction, we request that you will be good enough to insert
this letter.

Mr. T. W. BAKER, 7 Broad-street House, E.C., writes : Referring to the recent controversy on this question, the items
for the year June 24, 1897, to June 24, 1898, showing the
income and expenditure, are now before me, and I find the
following to be the correct reading of them as a joint
scheme :—

*Revenue Accounts for the Financial Year from June 24, 1897,
to June 24, 1898.*

(1) ELECTRICITY WORKS.

| Dr. | Expenditure. | £ | s. | d. |
|---|---|---|---|---|
| To Coal (490 tons, £432 15s. 9d.), stores, water and insurance | ... ... | 1,328 | 19 | 9 |
| „ Wages (562,167 units) | ... ... | 1,472 | 13 | 10 |
| „ Engineers' salary (proportion) and expenses | | 459 | 10 | 9 |
| „ Parochial rates, £125 2s., and sub-station do., £33 10s. 3d. | ... ... | 158 | 12 | 3 |
| „ Interest and redemption | ... ... | 2,641 | 13 | 1 |
| „ Interest and redemption on temporary loan (overdraft from bank) | ... ... | 815 | 9 | 4 |
| „ Balance carried down | ... ... | 1,707 | 16 | 0 |
| | | £8,504 | 15 | 0 |

| Cr. | Income. | £ | s. | d. |
|---|---|---|---|---|
| By Sales of current to consumers, &c.... | ... | 3,254 | 2 | 1 |
| „ Miscellaneous income | ... | 120 | 4 | 7 |
| „ Sales of stores to other departments | ... | 130 | 8 | 4 |
| | | £8,504 | 15 | 0 |

(2) DUST DESTRUCTOR STATION.

| Dr. | | £ | s. | d. |
|---|---|---|---|---|
| To Wages (25,404 tons) ... | ... | 2,746 | 1 | 7 |
| „ Engineers' salary (proportion) | ... | 83 | 6 | 8 |
| „ Stores and charges ... | ... | 411 | 16 | 4 |
| „ Cost of removing clinkers ... | ... | 612 | 10 | 5 |
| „ Insurance ... ... | ... | 43 | 4 | 2 |
| „ Interest and redemption | ... | 1,435 | 13 | 4 |
| „ Interest and redemption on temporary loan (bank overdraft) | ... | 79 | 10 | 4 |
| „ Balance carried down | ... | 344 | 9 | 2 |
| | | £5,756 | 12 | 0 |

| Cr. | | £ | s. | d. |
|---|---|---|---|---|
| By Balance of income brought down ... | ... | 1,707 | 16 | 0 |
| „ Destroying trade refuse | ... ... | 238 | 1 | 9 |
| „ Amount of money saved by use of dust destructor instead of the old method of barging of the refuse (25,404 tons at 3s.) | | 3,810 | 14 | 3 |
| | | £5,756 | 12 | 0 |

Balance of income over expenditure, £344 9s. 2d., exclusive
of the following items and charges—viz., depreciation and
bad debts; also management charges, such as proportion of
salaries of vestry clerk, accountants' department collectors,
&c., estimated by the London County Council valuer to be at
least £600 per annum (see official minutes). I note that
these items do not emanate from the accountant of the
vestry, but from the Electric Lighting Committee, although

individually I have reason to believe them to be correct. I will leave the results to the judgment of your readers to find where the profit occurs, of £2,000 and upwards, that has been claimed for this joint undertaking, and enlighten some other public authorities. I have taken the bank overdrafts as they occur at March, and assume them to be the same in June.

**Municipal Officers' Association: Superannuation.**—Mr. C. J. F. Carnell, hon. secretary of the Municipal Officers' Association, writes: I have the pleasure to announce that the Right Hon. the Lord Mayor (Sir John Voce Moore) has accepted the presidency of this association, which, as most of your readers are aware, is actively engaged on the question of superannuation for municipal officers, and its increasing membership shows, as its aims and objects become known, that the officers are appreciating more and more the efforts being made by it on their behalf. A number of town clerks, clerks to urban and rural district councils, medical officers of health, and municipal engineers and surveyors, have recently enrolled themselves as members, and the continued support of officers will do much to strengthen the organisation, which is absolutely necessary to ensure the success of the Superannuation Bill. If officers would join from every local authority throughout the country and appoint a correspondent it would enable the association to place all the latest information in the hands of its members. For years the poor law officers had been working to this end, and when Mr. Rutherglen took over the charge of the Poor Law Officers' Superannuation Bill he had behind him an organisation which had been plodding away for years on the superannuation question, but at last they reaped their reward. Municipal officers have now the opportunity of doing the same thing, and if they do not see their way to co-operate with the association, they might at least, I venture to suggest, send a contribution to the special superannuation conference fund. If officers wish the Superannuation Bill to become law they must be prepared to make some little sacrifice, either of time or money, or both, and I do most earnestly appeal to every officer to give active support to the movement, which must prove successful if persevered in. No one should feel discouraged because the Bill introduced last session was not successful, and it must be borne in mind that the poor law officers previously had a permissive statutory right. It will therefore be much more difficult to convince the local authorities of the justice of the measure, as they have not been in the habit of granting superannuation allowances.

## SOME RECENT PUBLICATIONS.

SOME PERIODICALS.

In *The Architectural Review* for November there is an excellent coloured lithograph, the first of a series depicting the old inns of England. The chief articles, which are profusely illustrated, deal with the architecture of Michael Angelo, the work of G. F. Watts, romance in sculpture, and Greek bronzes. Both letterpress and illustrations maintain the high standard which the conductors have set themselves from the first.—In *Cassier's Magazine* this month there is an excellent portrait of Sir William Arrol, accompanying an interesting and readable biographical sketch of the great bridge-builder, written by Mr. A. S. Biggart, who was Sir William's engineer and manager during the construction of the Forth Bridge, and who has been his partner since its completion. The article is accompanied by some excellent illustrations of the three great bridges—Forth, Tay and Tower. In the discussion of current topics we note some interesting remarks in reference to the growth of open conduit electric street railways in America.—The Earl of Cottenham is the subject of the portrait and biographical sketch in *Baily's Magazine* this month. Among the subjects dealt with are jumping, sporting celebrities, spots on the cricket sun, Dianas of to-day, saddles, judging at horse shows, the hunting season, and the usual sporting intelligence, comments, and reviews of the month.—Our American contemporary *The Sanitarian*, reprints a paper recently read by Dr. A. Campbell Munro, president of the Scottish branch of the Incorporated Society of Medical Officers of Health, the burden of the paper being the points of contrast and contact in the public health administration of England and Scotland. There is also an interesting article by Mr. William R. Hill, Syracuse, on early methods of collecting, storing and distributing water, and abstracts of some interesting contributions on sewage disposal, read at the recent conference of the American Public Health Association.—The last quarterly issue of *The Journal of the Sanitary Institute* is chiefly devoted to the proceedings of the Sanitary Congress at Birmingham, but there is, in addition, the usual miscellaneous information of an interesting character with regard to sanitation. *The Journal of State Medicine* contains a further instalment of papers read at the Dublin Congress of the Royal Institute of Public Health. There is a useful article on the bacteriological examination of water, abstracts from foreign journals, reports, reviews, and other information.—*Work* (Cassell & Co., Limited), has articles on acetylene gas, drawing for metal-plate work, the calculation of magnetic losses in armatures, locomotives and railway waggons, and the construction of small-power water-motors.—The scientific articles in *Knowledge*

this month are remarkably varied and interesting.—In *The Quarry* there is the first instalment of a series of articles on the stone industry of the United Kingdom, and a continuation of the useful series on applied geology.—We have also to acknowledge the following monthlies: *The Italian Engineer*, *The Plumber and Decorator*, *The Sanitary Inspectors' Journal*, *The Digest of Physical Tests and Laboratory Practice*, *The Journal of the Society of Estate Clerks of Works*, *The Analyst*, *The Quiver* (Cassell & Co., Limited), and from A. W. Hall, Hutton-street, Whitefriars, *Great Thoughts*, *The Model Reciter* and *Helping Words*.

## SUPERANNUATION CONFERENCE.

Mr. C. William Tagg, vestry clerk of Camberwell, presided over a largely attended meeting, convened by the Municipal Officers' Association, and held at 117 Holborn, E.C., on Monday. The hon. secretary reported as to the replies received from the associations and societies which had been invited to send delegates, and as to premises of financial support, and pointed out that it would be useless for him to continue to act as the hon. secretary unless the officers were prepared to give the movement more financial support, as it was quite impracticable to carry on an active campaign with the small amount subscribed during the last twelve months.

The chairman in his remarks dwelt upon the absolute necessity of unity among officers, and said that they must be prepared to find the necessary funds if they wished the Bill to become law. It was ultimately decided, in addition to asking the associations and societies sending delegates to the conference to make an appeal to officers throughout the country to subscribe to a special superannuation conference fund.

At the request of the chairman, a special committee was appointed to consider important proposals with regard to the Bill to be submitted in the next session of Parliament. The conference unanimously expressed its continued and unabated confidence in the chairman and the hon. secretary for their conduct of the Local Authorities Officers' Superannuation Bill.

Subscriptions to the Special Fund should sent to the hon. secretary (Mr. C. J. F. Carnell), 117 Holborn, London, E.C.

## THE BRADFORD CAR ACCIDENT.

BOARD OF TRADE REPORT.

The report of Major Cardew to the Board of Trade on the fatal tramway accident which occurred at Bradford on September 19th last has just been issued. Major Cardew states that the accident was due to the car being run at an excessive speed, to the unfortunate combination of a driver with very little experience and a conductor with none at all, a slippery road, and extra pressure on traffic. The driver certainly used the brake-power in an injudicious manner, the conductor put on the hand brake, and thus deprived the driver of full control of the brake-power, and the conductor also caused the trolley to be disconnected, thus depriving the driver of the power of reversing, which might have prevented the accident. Although the accident was in great measure due to the inexperience and injudicious action of the driver and conductor, in his opinion they both did their duty to the full extent of their skill and ability. Major Cardew considers the brake-power ample, but says the fact is that, if a car be allowed to acquire such a speed as 20 miles an hour on such a steep gradient, no brake acting by friction on the running rails will stop it in a distance that can be considered safe. He insists that on this line the speed on the downward journey must not exceed 6 miles an hour. The tramways company considered the report on Wednesday, and decided to accept liability, and to see that a rate of 6 miles an hour was observed.

## INSTITUTION OF CIVIL ENGINEERS.

STUDENTS' MEETING.

A meeting for students of the Institution will be held tonight, when a paper will be read by Mr. Cecil Lightfoot on "Liquid Air: A short description of its production and summary of its application to the chemical or other industries." The chair will be taken at 8 p.m. by Mr. W. H. Preece, C.B., F.R.S., the president.

ORDINARY MEETING.

An ordinary meeting of the above Institution will be held on Tuesday, at 8 p.m., when the paper which was read at the last meeting by Mr. Wm. Beedie Esson, M.I.C.E., on "Electrical Transmission of Power in Mining," will be further discussed.

**Sewerage Work in Birmingham.**—The Public Works Committee of the Birmingham Corporation have prepared a long report on the redrainage of Edgbaston and Harborne, which will be considered by the city council at their meeting on Tuesday. A few of the more important details of the report will be given in our next issue.

# Municipal Work in Progress and Projected.

Owing to the annual municipal elections, very little news in reference to important engineering works has come to hand during the week. It will be seen, however, that the authorities at Accrington, Croydon, Birmingham, Bury St. Edmunds, Weston-super-Mare and Mountain Ash are not remaining idle.

## METROPOLITAN AUTHORITIES.

### LONDON COUNTY COUNCIL.

The large and expensive schemes which have lately occupied the attention of the county council so largely were on Tuesday conspicuous by their absence. The only matter which came up for consideration that seemed of any magnitude was the proposal of the Technical Education Board to spend £35,500 on the purchase of the lease of Oxford Mansions for the purpose of converting them into a Central School of Arts and Crafts. This proposal was, however, after considerable discussion, referred back, to enable the board to present a recommendation for acquiring the freehold of the premises. The most important matters which were disposed of are summarised below.

*Loans for Public Works.* — Upon the recommendation of the Finance Committee it was agreed to lend the Westminster Vestry £23,670 for street improvements, the Lambeth Vestry £3,920 for paving works, and the Islington Vestry £2,223 for street improvements.

*Proposed Central School of Arts and Crafts.*—The Technical Education Board presented a report recommending the council to authorise the expenditure of £35,750 for the purchase of the leasehold property known as Oxford Mansions, off Oxford-street, to provide permanent accommodation for the board's Central School of Arts and Crafts. The board, in their report, stated that the school was at present housed in temporary premises in Regent-street. The number of students had increased so that the capacity of these premises had been severely taxed, there having been 539 individual students on the books last session, of whom about 140 attended each night. Every room in the premises was now fully occupied, and there was no further room for the further extensions of the work which appeared desirable. After considerable discussion the report was referred back to the board, with the view to the purchase of the freehold of the property.

*Housing of the Working Classes at Poplar.*—A long discussion took place upon a proposal of the Housing of the Working Classes Committee to sell a piece of land, known as the Cotton-street site, Poplar, for the purpose of allowing the purchaser to rehouse 260 persons displaced by the Blackwall Tunnel scheme. The subject of the disposal of this land has already been before the council on several occasions, when it has been explained that it would be impossible for the council themselves to build on this land within the terms of the standing order, which requires that the erection of dwellings shall entail no charge upon the rates. Mr. Piggott moved that the recommendation should be referred back, arguing that if it was possible for a private builder, who certainly would require a profit, to erect buildings on this land, it should be competent for the council's architect to devise some plans for buildings which would entail no loss to the council. After discussion the amendment was carried, upon a division, and the further consideration of the matter was adjourned.

*Pensions for Employees.*—The General Purposes Committee, in the course of a long report, recommended the council to adopt their view—that it was inexpedient to obtain power to pension the employees on a higher scale than was now possible under the existing powers of the council. This was agreed to.

*Tramway By-Laws.*—The Highways Committee recommended, and it was resolved, " that in view of the fact that the undertaking of the London Tramways Company will be transferred by agreement to the council at the end of the year 1898, the Board of Trade should be requested, in the exercise of the powers conferred upon them by sec. 7 of the London County Tramways Act, 1896, to re-enact the existing by-laws and regulations applicable to the undertaking, and prescribe the manner in which the council shall give notice of the making of the by-laws referred to."

*Tenders.*—The following tenders were opened by the chairman : (a) for the erection of conveniences at Blackwall Tunnel —Messrs. Doulton & Co., £1,891 ; and (b) for the erection of a coroner's court at Paddington—Messrs. Marchand & Hirst, £3,869 ; Spencer, Santo & Co., Limited, £4,261 ; General Builders, Limited, £4,400 ; H. H. Sherwin, £4,698 ; J. Shillitoe & Son, £5,299 ; and H. C. Clifton, £5,527.

## VESTRIES AND DISTRICT BOARDS.

**Lambeth.**—The Sanitary Committee presented to the vestry, at their last meeting, a report by the medical officer of health (Dr. J. Priestley) in regard to the smoke nuisance at the works of Sir Joseph Causton, Messrs. Clowes and the Electricity Supply Company. The medical officer had visited these works and inspected the boilers, and in consequence of the improvements being made in order to abate the evil he stated that he was unable to advise the vestry to take action before the magistrate for the present. The committee endorsed the report of the medical officer in regard to taking

no action. In a further report by the same committee reference was made to the proceedings taken by the London County Council against two firms in Lambeth without advising the vestry of intention to apply for a summons for smoke nuisance. The committee intended to submit a further report on the subject, and the present report, after a long discussion, was passed.—On the recommendation of the Sewers Committee the vestry sanctioned the reconstruction of a sewer in Commercial-road, at a cost of £487.— The Baths Committee stated that they had received a full report from Mr. Hessel Tillman, architect, as to the extras in connection with the Kennington-road baths, but that further explanations were necessary before the matter could be properly placed before the vestry. It was hoped, however, to present a full report on the subject at the next meeting.— Messrs. Kellett, of Hammersmith, the contractors for the excavation on the extension of the City and South London Electric Railway, have applied to the Cemetery Committee for permission to tip earth from the railway tunnel on the land purchased for the Tooting cemetery. As the soil was suitable for the purpose and there was a considerable hollow in the land, the committee had arranged with Messrs. Kellett for the latter to pay a lump sum of £75 for the privilege.— The General Purposes Committee reported that the London Basalt Stone Company had submitted to them samples of basalt imported by the company. As the samples appeared to be good, and as the quotation was 12s. 6d. a yard alongside the wharf, as against 14s. 1d. for granite, the vestry decided to make a trial of the material, and to purchase three large loads, at a cost of about £150 per load of from 80 to 100 yards.—A letter was received from the Thames Conservancy Commissioners stating that, subject to certain conditions, the conservators would be prepared to grant permission to the vestry to construct an embankment, 105 ft. 6 in. long and extending 141 ft. into the river at the upper end and 136 ft. 6 in. at the lower end, at the wharf in Belvedere-road. The commissioners intimated that they would communicate further with the vestry on the subject.—Some discussion took place on the report of the Vestry Hall Committee in regard to the present office accommodation, to which reference has previously been made in The Surveyor. It was pointed out that the only real remedy was the erection of municipal buildings. It was eventually decided to ask the churchwardens and overseers to meet the vestry to confer on the subject.

**Marylebone.**—The vestry, at their last meeting, considered as a matter of urgency a motion by Mr. Brooke-Hitching, on behalf of the Electric Lighting Committee, in reference to the position of the authority in regard to electric lighting in the parish. Mr. Hitching stated that the committee had received information from the best of sources that the Board of Trade, under the circumstances of the Select Committee of the House of Commons having refused last session to confirm the provisional order granted by the board, would not grant another order to the vestry. After a full consideration of the question the committee decided to recommend that the solicitors should be instructed to take all preliminary steps with a view to obtaining a private Act to authorise the vestry to supply electricity in the parish. After a long discussion the recommendation was adopted by forty votes to seven, and an expenditure of £50 was sanctioned for the insertion of the necessary official advertisements.—It was resolved to refer to the Works Committee three communications received from ratepayers suggesting the substitution of wood paving for the existing form of carriageway in certain thoroughfares.—The Parliamentary Committee submitted a recommendation in favour of simply acknowledging the receipt from the Battersea Vestry of a communication asking the authority to support them in requesting the London County Council to seek powers to authorise metropolitan vestries and district boards to erect dwellings under Part III. of the Housing of the Working Classes Act, 1890. An amendment was eventually adopted deciding to concur with the action of the Battersea Vestry.—On the motion of Mr. Garrould it was resolved to refer to the Works Committee to consider and report as to the desirability, in cases of renewal of lanterns on the public lamp columns, of substituting lanterns of a modern pattern.

**Shoreditch.**—A long time was occupied at the meeting of the vestry on Tuesday in discussing a report of the Lighting Committee submitting the accounts relating to the electric light undertaking and dust destructor for the year ended the 24th June last. The figures submitted in the case of the former showed that the excess of income over expenditure amounted to £5,826, and that after providing for interest and redemption of capital there remained a surplus of £3,184, which the committee regarded as a highly satisfactory result. In the opinion of the committee the charge for interest and redemption of capital was more than sufficient to provide for the depreciation of the undertaking. With regard to the dust destructor, the accounts for this part of the joint scheme exhibited a debit balance of £1,758, which the committee stated was represented by steam used in the lighting station and library. If to the credit balance on the electricity undertaking was added the "saving on previous expenditure of barging refuse," amounting to £1,253, this made a total of £4,437, and deducting from this the debit balance on the destructor of £1,758, the nett profit and saving, in the opinion of the committee, amounted to £2,679 for the year. The committee recommended that the report should be received, and that it should be referred back to them to allocate the disposal of the profits. During the severe criticism to which the trading accounts were subjected it was shown that there was no saving over the previous cost of barging the refuse, but that the expenses were now even greater. Several speakers declared that the accounts were bogus, false, and a farce, but by thirty votes to eleven the recommendation of the committee was carried.—In connection with this subject the Lighting and Scavenging Committee reported that they had considered the question of the amount to be charged for destroying refuse in the destructor. Although the previous charge for barging was 3s. 1d. per ton, the committee thought the scavenging department should have the prior claim upon any profits from the combined scheme. On the recommendation of the joint committee it was resolved to make a fixed charge of 2s. per ton against the scavenging department for destroying refuse in the destructor. It was also decided to pay out of the general rate the charge for interest and repayment of capital, amounting to £1,435, in respect of the refuse destructor.—The Parliamentary Committee reported that they had considered the Bill prepared by Mr. H. S. Samuels, M.P., to amend the Metropolis Water Act, 1871, and to make provision for the due supply of water in London. The committee recommended, and the vestry decided, to disagree with the Bill, as being insufficient to deal with the question satisfactorily.—A report was submitted by the Town Hall Committee referring to the proposed extensions of the town hall. It was decided to empower the committee to advertise for designs from architects in general competition.

**St. Pancras.**—At a meeting of the vestry on Wednesday the Parliamentary committee presented a report in reference to the tramways in Kentish Town-road. On the recommendation of the committee it was decided to inform the London County Council that it was desirable for the carriageway of that road to be widened, so as to double the tramway along a portion of the thoroughfare, and that the improvement should be carried out by the county council.— The Health Committee announced that they had considered a communication from the Local Government Board with reference to the Brantome-place and Prospect-terrace areas. The board asked to be supplied with copies of the amended scheme and plans showing the additional lands proposed to be acquired for the purpose of rehousing displaced persons who would not be accommodated on the sites which were to be cleared and the number of persons who would thus be rehoused, and plans showing how it was proposed to lay out the areas, with a revised estimate of the cost of the schemes. In reference to this question the Health Committee stated that they had decided to view certain properties in the parish and to report further on the subject.—A special report was submitted by the Health Committee, covering reports by the medical officers of health of the London County Council, in reference to the sanitary condition and administration of St. Pancras. The council's assistant medical officer, Dr. Hamer, had inspected St. Pancras, and as a result he recommended the appointment of seven additional sanitary inspectors. This recommendation was supported by Dr. Shirley Murphy, the council's chief medical officer of health, and the county council asked for the vestry's observations on the subject. The chairman of the Health Committee in a lengthy speech moved the reception of the report. An amendment by Mr. Barnes was, however, adopted, appointing a special committee to inquire into and report upon the reorganisation of the Health Department, and deciding to inform the London County Council of the vestry's intention.—The Highways Committee recommended that a portion of Euston-road now paved with yellow deal blocks should be repaved with jarrah wood blocks, at an estimated cost of £2,500, to be defrayed by loan. On the recommendation of the committee it was decided to put the work in hand at once, although an amendment to adopt asphalte in place of wood was only rejected by a majority of five votes.—In reply to questions, Dr. Smith, chairman of the Electricity Committee, stated that the delay in the supply of electric light in the Brecknock-road was due to a peculiar state of affairs. The houses in the road were in St. Pancras, but the roadway was in Islington. The committee had approached the Islington Vestry to ascertain whether permission would be given for the main to be laid, but that authority contended that they had no power in the matter. The Electricity Committee had therefore decided to ask the Board of Trade for sanction to erect the conductors overhead.

## PROVINCIAL AND GREATER LONDON AUTHORITIES.

### COUNTY COUNCILS.

**Middlesex.**—The county council held a special meeting on Monday to consider further the question of rebuilding Kew Bridge. In view of the fact that Surrey agreed, on Tuesday of last week, to accept Mr. Gibbs' tender and seek a fresh Bill, the Middlesex Council now resolved to do the same. A member expressed the opinion that the plans did not show a bridge of

sufficient width to meet the increasing traffic. The chairman concurred, but said that under the terms of the tender it would be open to require the contractor within six months to increase the width. The member then gave notice to move at the next meeting that it should be an instruction to the joint committee to increase the width to 50 ft.

**Staffordshire.**—At the last meeting of the county council the Sanitary Committee reported that they had considered a report of a sub-committee, and recommended that the council request them to require all local authorities within the administrative county to provide efficient isolation hospitals. The Earl of Lichfield said that the possession of isolation hospitals would contribute largely to the prolongation and saving of many lives, more especially among the poorer classes of the community. Hospitals could now be built at an estimated cost of £220 to £250 per bed, whereas three or four years ago the cost would have been £350 a bed. The recommendation was adopted.

**Surrey.**—It was recently recommended that, provided possession could be arranged for on reasonable terms, the Asylum Committee should be authorised to enter into a provisional contract for the purchase of Nethern House estate, at a cost of £10,000.

### MUNICIPAL CORPORATIONS.

**Accrington.**—Last week, at the Accrington town hall, Mr. W. A. Ducat conducted an inquiry, on behalf of the Local Government Board, into an application of the council for sanction to borrow £1,758, for the purpose of street improvements. There was no opposition.

**Birmingham.**—The preparation of the scheme mooted a considerable time back for what amounts to practically a resewering of the Edgbaston district of the city, including Harborne, is being pushed forward in the city surveyor's department. Complaints of the nuisance arising from the present sewers have been loud and prolonged, and the Health Committee and Public Works Committee, in considering the matter, found that nothing short of a complete reconstruction of the sewers would meet the case. It is anticipated that the outlay will not fall short of £100,000.

**Blackpool.**—On Friday last Mr. W. A. Ducat, Local Government Board inspector, held an inquiry into an application of the corporation for sanction to borrow £8,100 for the purchase of property for the extension of the town hall. There was no opposition to the scheme.

**Bridgwater.**—A specially-convened meeting of the town council was held recently for the further consideration of the Parrett navigation improvement scheme, as recommended by Mr. Wheeler, at an estimated cost of £110,000. A resolution was carried approving the scheme and authorising the town clerk to take the necessary steps to apply for Parliamentary authorisation.

**Bury St. Edmunds.**—After a somewhat lengthy discussion the town council last week passed a resolution to adopt a modified scheme of electric lighting, at a cost of £16,000.

**Chelmsford.**—The corporation have instructed the town clerk to apply for an injunction to restrain the rural district council from polluting the river Cann with sewage.

**Croydon.**—On Friday, at the town hall, Croydon, Mr. W. O. E. Meade-King, one of the inspectors of the Local Government Board, held a public inquiry into the application of the corporation to borrow £5,000 for the provision of fire stations, £2,250 for the purchase of that portion of the undertaking of the Crystal Palace Electric Lighting Company, which is situated within the borough of Croydon, and £850 for electric lighting purposes (the erection of a sub-station in Upper Norwood).

**Durham.**—Last week a special meeting of the city council was held to consider the advisability of applying to the Board of Trade for a provisional order under the Electric Lighting Acts, 1882 to 1890, authorising the authority to supply electricity for any public or private purpose within their district. After the engineer's report was read and discussed it was decided to make the necessary application.

**Hereford.**—It has been decided to construct a new filterbed at the waterworks, at a cost of £3,000.—An application will shortly be made by the council to borrow £8,400—part of the sum to be expended upon the city and county asylum.

**Heywood.**—Colonel A. G. Durnford, R.E., held an inquiry, on Tuesday, into an application of the town council for sanction to borrow £18,000 for street improvements and for the provision of a fire station, mortuary and depot in Hind Hill-street; £1,700 for the purchase of land as a site for a town hall, council house, justices'-room and police station; and £420 for the provision of a steam road-roller. It was stated that there had been great inconvenience because the town had not a complete town's yard. Mr. J. A. Settle, the borough surveyor, gave evidence in support of the application. He stated that the central yard would include firemen's dwellings, fire stations, stables for the health and surveyor's yard, and yards and other buildings for these departments. The application for £1,700 for the site of a town hall, &c., was to pay for a plot of land recently acquired by the corporation to complete their town hall site in the centre of the town. The site had been all acquired with this ex-

ception. There was no objection to the applications, and at the close of the inquiry the inspector went to view the different places.

**Hull.**—A Local Government Board inquiry has been held in reference to an application of the city council for sanction to borrow £120,150 for street improvement purposes and the formation of new streets, £26,000 for electric lighting, £6,774 for the purchase of a site for a public library, and £4,103 for the purchase of a site for a refuse destructor in West Dock-road.—The Burial Committee of the corporation have accepted the tender of Mr. T. Goates, to erect a crematorium for £2,153. The engineer's estimate was £1,784.—The corporation have decided to obtain Parliamentary power to carry out the scheme for the construction of a new street from White-friargate to Drypool Bridge, for extending Brook-street to Anlaby-road, and for completing the Great Passage-street improvement and the widening of Holderness-road. They have also decided to take active measures for the opening of South Bridge.

**Liverpool.**—On the 3rd inst. Mr. Frederick H. Tulloch, M.I.C.E., an inspector of the Local Government Board, held an inquiry respecting the application of the city council for sanction to borrow various sums of money for various purposes. It was explained that the town council had applied to the Local Government Board for sanction to borrow £30,688 for the provision of a refuse destructor in Fenistone-road, £9,756 for additional works at the Lumley-street refuse destructor, and £12,000 for the completion of the town hall. Evidence was given by Mr. C. F. Wike, city surveyor, who produced plans and estimates of the work to be dealt with. No opposition was offered.

**Madeley.**—At the last meeting of the town council a committee reported that the water supply works at Hanington had been completed, and that the boring and testing had proved successful. Ample water was found, enough, in fact, to supply other districts. The boring and testing operations had cost £882 2s. 6d., £400 more than estimated, therefore £400 was required to be raised by a loan, which was decided upon. , The engineer, Mr. Stroke, of Shrewsbury, said the water was described by Mr. Blunt, the analyst,  as excellent, and of moderate hardness. The mayor proposed that the report be adopted, and said they could raise 1,000,000 gallons every twenty-four hours. The motion was carried. A sub-committee was appointed to proceed with the work, and the engineer was instructed to make out an estimate and provide a plant that would supply 250,000 gallons every twelve hours.

**Manchester.**—The following resolution has been passed by the Telephone Committee : "That a report be prepared in due form for presentation to the city council setting forth the recent communications with the Postmaster-General and embodying the general conclusion that, in view of the proposed action of her Majesty's Government in this matter in the next Parliamentary session, it is desirable not to proceed further with respect to the insertion of clauses in the Manchester General Powers Bill for conferring powers upon the corporation to provide and work telephones under license from the Post Office."

**Margate.**—The new municipal offices, which take the place of an old market, and which have been presented to the town by Mrs. Kendall, the widow of a late alderman of the council, were formally opened last week. A stone recording the gift was unveiled by the mayoress (Mrs. G. F. Brown), and the building itself was opened, on behalf of Mrs. Kendall, by Miss Wootton, daughter of Alderman Wootton, J.P. The new offices, which have been erected at a cost of £23,000, make a handsome adjunct to the town hall, which they adjoin and are connected with. They comprise magistrates' retiring and mayor's robing-room, together with offices for the various officials ; the market stalls being under a glass-covered colonnade.

**Norwich.**—The town council having applied to the Local Government Board for sanction to borrow £1,316, for police station and fire brigade purposes, an inquiry was held on the 9th inst. by Mr. H. Percy Boulnois.

**Preston.**—On the recommendation of the Streets and Buildings Committee, the town council have decided to pave and flag Tulketh Brow from Fylde-road to the railway arches, at an estimated cost of £450.

**Wolverhampton.**—It is understood that the corporation purpose making a number of important improvements in regard to the sewerage of the borough in the near future. In some cases the sewers will be extended over an area which has not yet been brought in touch with the existing sewage scheme. The expenditure will represent several thousand pounds.

## URBAN DISTRICT COUNCILS.

**Aston Manor.**—At a meeting of the district council on the 1st inst. the Health Committee presented a detailed report and estimate in reference to the erection of the proposed new destructor cells and other works at the Chester-street wharf, and also for electrically lighting the works, yard and fire station, at an estimated cost of £11,500.—The Highways Committee announced that they had had under consideration the application of the Birmingham and Aston Tramways Company for the sanction of the council to the using of steam

for traction purposes on their lines running through the district. The surveyor having reported that he had recently inspected the lines in question and had found that his requirements had been seen to, it was decided, on the recommendation of the committee, to grant the application of the company.—The same committee laid upon the table the final apportionment of the cost of making-up Priory-road, amounting to £890, with a recommendation that it be approved and that notice thereof be served upon the respective owners and occupiers liable in respect of the works.—The same committee also laid upon the table an agreement between the Birmingham Canal Company and the council relative to the laying of a sewer under the canal at Thimble Mill-lane and under the Bloomsbury wharf, and the construction of manholes in connection therewith, and recommended that it be approved and that the clerk be authorised to affix the seal of the council thereto.—The Baths Committee stated that they had instructed the surveyor to make arrangements with the Auto-Electro Feed-Water Purifier Company to fix one of their purifiers to the boilers at the baths on trial, free of cost to the council.

**Bexhill.**—Major-General H. Darley-Crozier, R.E., held an inquiry, on behalf of the Local Government Board, on Thursday, with reference to the application of the council for sanction to borrow the sum of £9,000 for the purposes of sewerage at Little Common. Both the clerk (Mr. F. A. Langham) and the surveyor (Mr. Ball) gave evidence during the inquiry.

**Bredbury and Romiley.**—On the 9th inst. an inquiry was held by Mr. Walter A. Ducat, inspector from the Local Government Board, into the application of the council to borrow a sum of £2,200 for the purpose of widening a bridge over the Peak Forest Canal. Opposition was offered on behalf of a number of ratepayers, on the ground that the land proposed to be purchased was not required and that the price fixed was too much. The improvement itself was not opposed.

**Droylsden.**—An inquiry has been held at Droylsden, by Mr. Walter S. Ducat, one of the engineering inspectors of the Local Government Board, into an application of the council for sanction to borrow the sum of £6,200 for works of street improvement. In the course of evidence it was stated that there was only one main road in the district—namely, that from Manchester to Ashton. The Local Government Board inspector, having promised that the decision of the Local Government Board would be forwarded in due course, proceeded to make a tour of the district.

**Handsworth.**—Colonel W. Langton Coke conducted an inquiry on Friday into an application of the council for sanction to borrow £3,000 for works of sewerage and sewage disposal.

**Heage.**—Last week, at a meeting of this council, a letter from the Local Government Board was read respecting the sewerage scheme, and in relation to a Government inquiry to be held by Colonel W. Langton Coke, M.I.C.E. The council had applied to the Local Government Board for consent to the application of £50, being part of the unexpended balance of a loan of £1,260, for the execution of certain works of sewerage which were not included in the estimate on which the loan was sanctioned.

**Itchen.**—It was last week proposed and agreed that the Local Government Board be requested to give their sanction to the adoption of the septic tank system of sewage disposal in lieu of the system previously sanctioned. The council also accepted an offer of Messrs. Cameron, of Exeter, to provide a set of plans of the sewage disposal works for 10 guineas.

**Matlock Bath.**—A special meeting has been held to consider the question of applying next session for electric lighting powers. It was explained that as the site upon which electric supply works would in all probability be erected was that adjoining the gasworks, which were situated in the area of their neighbour, the Matlock District Council, it would be necessary to serve that body with notice before July 1st, as a preliminary to applying for a provisional order. Therefore, as the time for this had gone by, it would be impossible to obtain powers in the coming session. The meeting thereupon decided to leave the matter over until next year.

**Mountain Ash.**—Local Government Board sanction has been received to loans of £16,600 and £4,000 by the council for purposes of sewerage and sewage disposal. Negotiations had for some years been carried on between the Pontypridd and the Mountain Ash Councils with a view to some share of the latter district being carried away by the Pontypridd and the Joint Sewerage Board sewers, but the terms of the Pontypridd Council were considered exorbitant, and the Mountain Ash Council decided to provide a sewage farm outside the Pontypridd district.

**Wanstead.**—The district council have refused to accept a contribution of 80 per cent. of the cost of main road improvements from the Essex County Council, and the matter will now be referred to arbitration.

**Weston-Super-Mare.**—An inquiry will shortly be held by the Local Government Board concerning an application of the district council for sanction to borrow £14,300 for the erection of a pavilion at Knightstone.—It has been resolved by the council to apply for sanction to borrow £430, the amount expended in excess of a loan granted for the erection of new offices.

## THE TELEPHONE SERVICE.

### A FEW WORDS FOR THE COMPANY.

The following letter has been addressed to *The Times* by Mr. Wm. E. L. Gaine, general manager of the National Telephone Company, Limited, in reference to the debate which took place in regard to the telephone service at the London County Council meeting last week, a report of which was published in the last issue of THE SCRVEYOR :—

I have to ask you on behalf of the company to afford me the opportunity of placing a few facts before your readers. It is charged against the company that its service in London is inefficient and inadequate. My reply is that to whatever extent it may be so at this moment is entirely the fault of the London County Council.

In May, 1896, the company applied to the county council for the consent of that body, as required by the Telegraph Act, 1892, to enable the company to place its wires underground—the only solution of the serious difficulties which otherwise beset the company from the use of overhead wires.

Prolonged negotiations followed, and finally terms were agreed and embodied in a series of resolutions passed by the county council on June 1, 1897. Nothing further remained to be done but to prepare and execute a formal agreement to give effect to the bargain. These negotiations, it will be seen, occupied rather more than a year. It took the county council nearly seven months to prepare the draft of the formal agreement, and this document was submitted to the company for consideration on January 29, 1898. It was then found that two additional conditions not forming part of the bargain had been inserted. These conditions were: (1) That the company should make a wayleave payment to the county council which would impose a burden upon the company amounting to several thousand pounds per annum, and (2) that the company should reduce its tariffs to an arbitrary scale as fixed by the county council, which would involve the company in an immediate loss of revenue of upwards of £40,000 per annum.

The company considered that the importation of these conditions after more than twelve months had been spent in concluding the bargain was not in accord with good faith. The company replied that, as it had agreed to make wayleave payments to a large number of provincial cities and towns, it was willing to do so in the case of London, but pointed out that, differing from the provincial cities, the county council was not the road authority, and that it could only do so if the county council indemnified the company against any claims which might be made by the road authorities in the metropolis, and, as regards tariffs, it respectfully declined to discuss the impossible proposition submitted to it, but offered to agree to fix the company's present tariffs as the maximum charges to be made, and to come under an obligation to supply all intending users equally and without undue preference.

On May 19, 18?8, the county council broke off the negotiations. The position may therefore be summed up as follows: Twelve months occupied in negotiations finally resulting in a bargain being arrived at ; further twelve months occupied in preparing a formal document to give effect to the bargain ; finally resulting in the county council withdrawing from it.

On the 3rd inst. there were 992 people in London waiting to be joined up to the company's system. As regards the bulk of these they will have to wait an indefinite time, on account of the difficulties in the way of the company in physically connecting their premises with its exchanges, owing to the want of facilities which it is in the power of the county council to give.

Whether it is or is not desirable to import competition into such a service as that of the telephone appears to the company to afford no reason why the company should be denied facilities for doing its work. Even if competition is set up, it must, in the nature of the case, take years before it can meet fully public requirements, and in the meantime the public suffers and blames the company for not doing the impossible.

I see that it was stated in the course of the debate that the Highways Committee is prepared to recommend the requisite facilities being given to the company if the company will concede to London similar terms as to tariffs and wayleave payments as the company has given to Manchester, Liverpool and other towns.

The position of London is not comparable with that of any other town. It covers an area of 634 square miles. The working cost of a telephone system throughout this great area is nearly double what it is anywhere else, and the tariffs must therefore be proportionately higher. At the same time I may add that the company is considering whether it cannot meet the requirements of small users and those requiring a more limited service. It is the intention of the company to invite the county council to reopen negotiations, and it will not be the fault of the company if a proper arrangement is not come to.

Let me give one instance of the treatment to which the company is subjected. When the bargain was concluded with the county council on June 1, 1897, the company was allowed to go on with certain portions of underground work which were very urgently needed. Among the works authorised is a system of pipes for upwards of 6,000 miles of wires which the company has laid down in the districts governed by the Holborn Board of Works and the Vestry of St. Giles, all

centring upon a large exchange of the company situate at the corner of Holborn-viaduct and St. Andrew-street. These pipes are stopped close to the north-west corner of Holborn-viaduct, and for months they have been lying idle, and so far as can be seen are likely to remain so, because the company cannot obtain from the local authority the permission to carry them across one road and into the exchange.

In conclusion, I have only to say that it is not reasonable to blame the company for the deficiencies of its service if proper facilities are refused and every impediment and difficulty placed in its way.

## MUNICIPAL ENTERPRISE AT YARMOUTH.

### LOCAL GOVERNMENT BOARD INQUIRY.

At Yarmouth, on Tuesday of last week, Mr. H. Percy Boulnois, an inspector of the Local Government Board, conducted an inquiry with reference to an application of the corporation for sanction to loans of £6,000 for the erection of a shelter hall at Gorleston, of £3,000 for the extension of the sea waterworks, and of £850 for repairing a part of the market area.

In reference to the shelter hall at Gorleston, the borough surveyor stated that it would consist of a room 45 ft. by 90 ft. on the ground floor, with a gallery above at one end, providing seating accommodation for 750. A small stage would be provided, concerts would be given in the hall, and in wet weather the band would play therein. There would be a reading-room above and two refreshment-rooms, and a balcony round the outside of the building would afford fine sea views. It was stated that the hall was principally designed for visitors, of whom it was estimated there had been 200,000 during the past season. There was no opposition to this proposal, nor to the partial repayment of the market with granite setts, bedded in concrete, in substitution of the present cobbles. In reference to the sea waterworks extension, the borough surveyor explained that a new pumping station would be provided, and that fresh mains would be laid to meet the increased demand that had arisen for street watering, sewer flushing, &c. The pumps would be driven by electricity from the corporation's main.

## LEICESTER WATER SUPPLY.

The Water Committee of the Leicester Town Council, on Monday, unanimously decided to recommend the corporation to promote a Bill in Parliament to acquire the water of the upper Derwent and the Ashop, at a cost of £1,500,000. It is proposed either to assume the entire responsibility for the vast undertaking and supply the Derbyshire authorities, or to form a joint board with Derby and Derbyshire. The watersheds yield 50,000,000 gallons daily ; but at first three reservoirs would be constructed, to yield 10,000,000 to 12,000,000 gallons daily, or sufficient for Derbyshire, and then to convey the water a distance of 66 miles to Leicester. The scheme is strongly recommended by eminent engineers and experts.

## ELECTRIC TRACTION IN LIVERPOOL.

The first electric tramway cars commenced running on Monday on the Dingle line in Liverpool. The whole of the tramway system of the city has been acquired by the corporation, whose decision to adopt for electric tramways the overhead trolley system has been the topic of heated local discussion, mainly on the ground of the disfigurement of the streets by the posts and network of overhead wires. The new cars run in couples, one being reserved for smoking. They are ornamental in appearance, and appear to be well constructed. They have no outside seats. The Dingle line is nearly 3 miles long, and the fares are fixed at 2d. for the non-smoking and 1d. for the smoking cars. The cars run every four minutes. The inauguration attracted general attention. The working of the cars seemed to be satisfactory, both as regards speed and smoothness.

# Personal.

Mr. Sloan, surveyor to the Linsdale Urban District Council, has resigned his position, owing to bad health.

Mr. David Edwards, of the borough engineer's office, Neath, has been appointed engineering assistant in the city engineer's office, Hull.

Mr. Edward Dobson, J.P., president of the Auctioneers' Institute, was last week elected an alderman of the borough of Bradford.

A gratuity of £25 has been granted Mr. F. E. G. Bradshaw, surveyor to the Trowbridge Urban District Council, for extra work performed by him.

The Saltburn Urban District Council have appointed Mr. G. S. Baynes, of Jarrow, to the vacant position of surveyor. There were ninety-nine applications for the position.

Messrs. Belfage & Carfrae have been appointed engineers in connection with a new scheme of water supply which is being carried out by the burgh commissioners of St. Andrews.

Mr. Streather, the newly-elected surveyor to the Winton Urban District Council, has stated, in a letter to that body, that he will be able to enter upon his duties on the 26th inst.

Mr. F. H. Chaplin, of Portsmouth, has been appointed electrical engineer under the Southampton Corporation, at a salary of £350 per annum. There were sixty-six applicants for the post.

It is understood that Mr. John Eaglesham, burgh surveyor of Ayr, has, in spite of a request of the town council, declined to withdraw his resignation. Mr. Eaglesham is to resume private practice.

The death is announced of Mr. Joseph William Wilson, first principal of the Crystal Palace School of Practical Engineering. The funeral of the deceased, who was sixty-nine years of age, took place on the 9th inst.

Mr. A. D. Price has resigned his position as town surveyor of Bray, Ireland, having recently been selected to fill the surveyorship of Blackrock. The resignation was received with regret by the Bray Town Council at their meeting last week.

Southmolton Rural District Council have increased the salary of Mr. W. S. Gardiner, one of their surveyors, by £10 per annum. Mr. Gardiner, it was mentioned in the course of the discussion which ensued upon the matter, was a most efficient officer.

In a recent open competition for schemes of sewerage, sewage disposal and water supply for the district of Wivenhoe, Essex, the schemes submitted by Messrs. Sands & Walker, civil engineers, Nottingham, have been selected as the best and unanimously adopted.

Mr. T. Swaffham Brown delivered a lecture on "Ecclesiastical and Domestic Art Metalwork" at the ordinary monthly meeting of the Sheffield Society of Architects and Surveyors on Tuesday of last week. Mr. J. Smith, the vice-president of the association, occupied the chair.

In a limited competition for the erection of the proposed baths, &c., by the Leyton Urban District Council, the designs of Messrs. Harrop & Duffield, of Queen-street, Cheapside, have been accepted. The cost, it is estimated, will be about £15,000. Mr. Rowland Plumbe was the assessor.

Mr. J. H. Helé, who at present holds the position of assistant surveyor under the Stoke-on-Trent Corporation, has been appointed surveyor to the Spalding Urban District Council. By an inadvertence we last week stated that he had been appointed assistant surveyor to the latter authority.

A special meeting of the Diss Urban District Council was held last week for the purpose of appointing a surveyor. Originally there were twenty candidates, but at a recent meeting these were reduced to four. After an examination of these gentlemen it was decided to appoint Mr. Lait, of Diss, to the post, at a salary of £80 yearly.

Mr. A. Hessel Tiltman, of 6 John-street, Bedford-row, W.C., is to be invited by the St. Pancras Vestry to become the assessor to assist in the preparation of instructions and conditions for the guidance of architects competing for the new baths and wash-houses to be erected in the Prince of Wales-road, and to report on the designs submitted in the competition. The fee offered to the assessor is 100 guineas.

On the 12th inst. Mr. J. F. Thorrold, engineer and surveyor to the Redditch Urban District Council, having made application for extra remuneration, the council unanimously resolved to vote him a substantial increase of salary from the 14th inst., as well as commission on extra works. Mr. Thorrold has been seven years with this authority, and is now engaged in the preparation of plans, &c., for new municipal offices, baths and wash-houses, and workmen's dwellings.

Mr. Thomas Harris, the new surveyor to the Portmadoc Urban District Council, has commenced his duties under the latter authority, at the last meeting of which he was formally introduced to the members. Before leaving Bootle Mr.

Harris was presented by the officials of the corporation with a handsome American oak roll desk as a parting gift and as a small token of the esteem in which he was held. The ceremony was an interesting one, the town clerk of Bootle presiding over the proceedings, referring in most eulogistic terms to the work performed by Mr. Harris, who was described as a zealous and straightforward official.

On the 5th inst., Mr. William Cumming, the late burgh surveyor of Carnoustie, was the recipient of a public testimonial from the inhabitants. A member of the council, in making the presentation, dwelt on the many services Mr. Cumming had rendered the burgh, and asked him to accept a gold lever watch as an appreciation of his many good qualities. Mrs. Cumming was also made the recipient of a gold bracelet. Mr. Cumming replied in a very characteristic speech, assuring all that he had only tried to do his duty according to his knowledge. He has also, it might be mentioned, been presented by the corporation employees with a handsome umbrella, suitably inscribed, and a silver-mounted pipe.

Mr. Cecil R. W. Chapman, surveyor to the Swaffham (Norfolk) Urban District Council, was last week elected to the vacant position of engineer, surveyor and inspector of nuisances to the Wembley (Middlesex) Urban District Council, which carries with it a salary of £220 per annum. There were over 120 applicants for the post, six of whom were selected to appear before the council. Mr. Chapman was for three years in the sanitary department of the Norwich Corporation, seven years with Mr. T. H. B. Heslop, M.I.C.E., county surveyor of Norfolk, and subsequently an assistant under him. During his four years' service under the Swaffham Urban District Council Mr. Chapman has carried out a system of sewage precipitation and an extensive sewerage scheme. He is a member of the Incorporated Association of Municipal and County Engineers, and holds, among many others, the certificate of the Sanitary Institute.

The death has taken place, at his residence in Carrickfergus, of Mr. James M'Neill, assistant surveyor of co. Antrim, Ireland. Although comparatively fresh and vigorous in appearance till within a few months back, Mr. N'Neill had been in failing health for some time past, and latterly he succumbed rapidly to an affection of the liver. Mr. M'Neill was one of the oldest county officials in Ireland, his period of servitude extending over forty-one years. He was one of the most conscientious and painstaking of officials, and spared no trouble to have the many public works of which he had the supervision under the county surveyor carried out in the most satisfactory manner possible. His genial disposition, the unaffected simplicity of his character, and his unvarying kindliness of heart endeared him to all with whom he came in contact, both young and old, and his friends were many and spread over a very wide area. He leaves a widow and two sons.

At the Crown Hotel, Chertsey, recently, a hurriedly-convened gathering assembled for the purpose of bidding farewell to the late surveyor to the urban district council, Mr. A. W. Smith, who later that day departed to take up the duties of a new appointment. The real purpose of the meeting was to enable Captain F. B. Harrison to publicly present to Mr. Smith an extremely valuable theodolite. The instrument, which was enclosed in a handsome mahogany case, has quite unique historical associations, having been used by the world-famed firm of Brassey, Peto & Betts (in which Captain Harrison's father was a partner) in connection with their construction of the Mont Cenis tunnel. In responding to the toast of his health, proposed by Captain Harrison, Mr. Smith said he would value the present very highly, because of the giver, and also for its usefulness to him in his work, its intrinsic worth, and its historic associations. While he had been in Chertsey he had endeavoured to do his duty, although it had not always been a pleasant one. Public officials were often targets for mud-throwing, as he had occasionally experienced, but altogether his sojourn in Chertsey had been a happy one.

Mr. F. W. Richardson, city analyst of Bradford, on Monday of last week delivered a lecture on "Microbes, the Friend of Man," in the course of which he said, referring to the bacteriological treatment of sewage, in which experiments are being made at the Bradford sewage works at Frizinghall, that it had been found that if sewage, particularly domestic sewage, was allowed to run over beds of coke, engine ashes, gravel or sand, the filters soon got into working order, and countless quadrillions of microbes got to work on the impurities, converting them first into ammonia, then into nitrites, and afterwards into nitrates, and finally splitting up the nitrogen and sending it back into the great aerial reservoir. The Bradford sewage was one of the worst kinds. It was contaminated with trade effluents from different works, the worst of all being from wool-combing establishments. This effluent contained a large quantity of grease, which got on the outer surface of the filtering media and choked it up. Until they got the sewage separated into two classes—domestic, which could undoubtedly be treated on this principle, and trade—he did not think that the bacteriological treatment would be very successful.

## APPOINTMENTS VACANT.

*Official and all similar advertisements received later than Thursday morning are too late for classification and cannot therefore be included in these summaries until the following week. No advertisements received after 3 p.m. on Thursday can be inserted until the following week.*

GENERAL SURVEYOR'S ASSISTANT.—November 21st.—Corporation of Maidenhead. £80.—Mr. Percy Johns, borough surveyor.

SURVEYOR OF HIGHWAYS.—November 21st.—Fylde Rural District Council. £120.—Mr. F. H. Brown, clerk to the council, Kirkham.

BOROUGH SURVEYOR AND INSPECTOR OF NUISANCES.—November 21st.—Corporation of Penryn.—Mr. G. Appleby Jenkins, town clerk.

CLERK OF WEAKS.—November 21st.—Corporation of Sunderland. £3 10s.—Mr. Fras. M. Bowey, town clerk.

INSPECTOR OF NUISANCES.—November 22nd.—Carlisle Rural District Council. £130.—Mr. H. B. Lonsdale, clerk to the council.

ROAD FOREMAN.—November 25th.—Walthamstow Urban District Council. £2 10s.—Mr. E. J. Cowen, clerk to the council.

SURVEYOR AND SANITARY INSPECTOR.—November 26th.—Gnosall (Salop) District Council. £110.—Mr. H. G. N. Elliott, clerk to the council.

FIRE BRIGADE ENGINEER.—November 26th.—Corporation of Coventry. £1 15s.—The City Engineer.

GENERAL OUTDOOR FOREMAN.—November 28th.—Corporation of Stockton-on-Tees. £100.—Mr. M. H. Sykes, borough engineer.

ROAD SURVEYOR.—November 30th.—County Borough of Sunderland. £130.—Mr. Fras. M. Bowey, town clerk.

MANAGER OF GAS AND WATER WORKS.—November 30th.—Ambleside Urban District Council. £125.—Mr. George Gatey, clerk to the council.

MAIN ROAD INSPECTOR. — December 1st. — Bedfordshire County Council. £160.—Mr. W. W. Marks, clerk to the council, Shire Hall, Bedford.

MECHANICAL ENGINEER.—December 6th.—Tyne Improvement Commissioners. £250.—Mr. R. Unwin, secretary to the commissioners, Newcastle-on-Tyne.

PUPIL.—Cleethorpes-with-Thrunscoe Urban District Council.—Mr. Egbert Rushton, engineer and surveyor to the council.

## COMPETITIONS.

*Official and all similar advertisements received later than Thursday morning are too late for classification and cannot therefore be included in these summaries. No advertisements received after 3 p.m. can be inserted until the following week.*

HULL.—January 1st.—Erection of a central public library in Albion-street. £50, £30 and £20.—Mr. E. Laverack, town clerk.

HARROGATE.—January 2nd.—Erection of a pump-room, &c., at a cost not exceeding £8,000. £50, £30 and £20.—Mr. Samuel Stead, borough surveyor.

## MUNICIPAL CONTRACTS OPEN.

*Official and all similar advertisements received later than Thursday morning are too late for classification and cannot therefore be included in these summaries. No advertisements received after 3 p.m. can be inserted until the following week.*

CARMARTHENSHIRE.—November 18th.—Erection of a stone bridge of three arches over the river Towy at Dryslwyn, for the county council.—Mr. Thomas Jones, clerk to the council, Llandovery.

BIRMINGHAM.—November 18th.—Supply of engine slack, cast-iron pipes, special castings, &c. at the various pumping stations and wharves during the year 1899.—Mr. K. Antony Lee, secretary to the Corporation Water Committee, 44 Broad-street, Birmingham.

ABERTILLERY.—November 19th.—Construction of a new road from Abertillery to Aberbeeg, a distance of about 2 miles, for the urban district council.—Mr. James McBean, engineer and surveyor to the council.

LEICESTER.—November 19th.—Supply and delivery of retorts and firebricks.—Mr. Alfred Colson, M.I.C.E., engineer and manager, Corporation Gasworks, Millstone-lane, Leicester.

ERPINGHAM.—November 19th.—Execution of protection works in the parishes of Sheringham and Beeston-Regis, for the rural district council.—Mr. Thos. Ling, clerk to the council, Northrepp, Norwich.

BENSON.—November 21st.—Construction of a new sea wall and esplanade, 487 ft. in length, for the urban district council.—Mr. O. A. Bridges, town surveyor.

STAFFORDSHIRE.—November 21st.—Laying of about 5,000 yards of 12-in., 9-in., 6-in. and 4-in. cast-iron and stoneware pipe sewers and surface-water drains at the County Lunatic Asylum, for the county council.—Mr. Walter B. Cheadle, county surveyor, Stafford.

ULVERSTON.—November 21st.—Various sewerage and drainage works, for the rural district council.—Mr. Chas. W. Dean, clerk to the council.

WEDNESBURY.—November 21st.—Widening of the bridge over the Birmingham Canal on the Holyhead-road, near Moxley.—Mr. E. Martin Scott, borough engineer and surveyor.

CAMBERWELL.—November 21st.—Supply of 2,050,000 Australian hardwood blocks, 3 in. by 9 in. by 5 in.; 2,050,000 creosoted deal blocks, 3 in. by 9 in. by 5 in.; and 3,200 loads of Australian hardwood in 9 in. by 3 in. planks, for the vestry.—Mr. W. Oxtoby, engineer and surveyor to the vestry.

LANCASTER.—November 21st.—Supply of about 1,850 lineal yards of 7-in. cast-iron pipes.—Mr. John Cook, A.M.I.C.E., water engineer, Town Hall, Lancaster.

STAFFORD.—November 21st.—Supply of a stone-breaking machine.—Mr. W. Blackshaw, borough engineer.

ASHTON-UNDER-LYNE.—November 21st.—Construction of precipitation tanks, artificial filters, land filters, subways, culverts, roads and other appurtenant works.—Mr. J. T. Earnshaw, A.M.I.C.E., borough surveyor.

SOUTHAMPTON.—November 22nd.—Supply and delivery of sluice valves, fire hydrants, air valves and surface covers required by the waterworks department during the ensuing three years, for the corporation.—Mr. W. Matthews, waterworks engineer.

BRADFORD.—November 22nd.—Erection of a slab-making shed at the Hammerton-street destructor yard.—Mr. George McGuire, town clerk.

GLASGOW.—November 22nd.—Supply of about 800 lineal feet of cast-iron pipes, 21 in. in diameter, and certain cast-iron pipes, 22 in. and 20 in. in diameter, with special castings, for the new electricity works at Port Dundas.—Mr. J. D. Marwick, town clerk.

EDMONTON.—November 22nd.—Execution of about 5,253 ft. of 1-in. kerbing, about 4,085 ft. of 1-in. channelling, and about 3,948 ft. of crossings in Queen's-road, Station-road, Hyde-lane, Eldon-road, Hertford-road, Silver-street and Fore-street; about 3,111 yards super. of indurated concrete slab paving in Queen's-road, Claremont-street, Station-road, Hyde-lane and Eldon-road; and about 1,057 yards super. of patent Victoria stone paving in Hertford-road and Fore-street; for the urban district council.—Mr. G. Eedes Eachus, M.I.C.E., surveyor to the council.

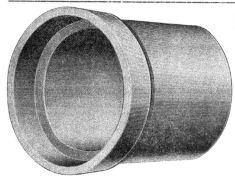

NEWCASTLE-ON-TYNE.—November 22nd.—Supply during the twelve months ending December 31, 1899, of various materials, &c.—The City Engineer.

WORCESTER.—November 23rd.—Laying of surface-water drains in the Stratford main road and other roads adjoining in the parish of Yardley, for the county council.—Mr. J. H. Garrett, county road surveyor, Shire Hall, Worcester.

HARTLEPOOL.—November 23rd.—Supply of various goods and materials required during the year ending December 31, 1899.—Mr. H. C. Crummack, A.M.I.C.E., borough engineer.

HACKNEY.—November 23rd.—About 600 superficial yards of yellow deal wood paving at Northwold-road and about 1,000 superficial yards of hardwood paving in Kingsland-road, for the vestry.—Mr. James Lovegrove, surveyor to the vestry.

ILKLEY.—November 23rd.—Supply of 1,000 tons of 2-in. machine-broken granite, for the urban district council.—Mr. Frank Hall, clerk to the council.

CASTLE DONINGTON.—November 23rd.—Execution of various sewerage works for the rural district council.—Mr. Herbert Walker, A.M.I.C.E., Newcastle Chambers, Angel-row, Nottingham.

WITHAM (Essex).—November 24th.—Supply of 300 tons of granite, for the urban district council.—Mr. Wm. Bindon Blood, clerk to the council.

BIRMINGHAM.— November 24th.—Construction of brick and pipe sewers in Church-street.—Mr. John Price, city engineer and surveyor.

GRAYS THURROCK.—November 24th.—Supply of about 475 yards of wrought-iron fencing and a pair of gates, for the urban district council.—Mr. A. C. James, surveyor to the council.

MIDDLESBROUGH.—November 24th.—Reconstruction and repair of Emily-street and the back street between Beaufort and Cook-street and the alterations of the old town hall police station.—Mr. Frank Baker, borough engineer.

BURTON-UPON-TRENT.—November 24th.—Supply of fireclay retorts, bricks and clay required at the gasworks during the year 1899.—Mr. F. L. Ramsden, manager and engineer, Corporation Gas and Electric Light Works, Burton-upon-Trent.

TAME.—November 25th.—Construction of stoneware and other sewers for the interception of the sewage of the town, together with the necessary manholes, inspection shafts, flushing tanks, outfall works and engine-house, for the urban district council.—Mr. Wm. Parker, clerk to the council.

BATLEY.—November 25th.—Supply of (a) flagstones, setts, paviors and kerbs; (b) sanitary tubes; (c) pitch and oil; (d) cement; and (e) broken granite.—Mr. O. J. Kirby, borough surveyor.

HULL.—November 25th.—Supply of about 316 ft. of railing for the corporation field, consisting of cast-iron posts, with two rails of steam tube.—Mr. A. E. White, city engineer.

SHOREDITCH.—November 25th.—Construction of temporary floorings to the first and second class swimming ponds at the baths buildings in Pitfield-street, for the vestry.—Mr. H. Mansfield Robinson, clerk to the vestry.

EAST RETFORD.—November 25th.—Construction of about 20,000 lineal yards of stoneware and iron pipe sewers, with manholes, storm overflow, ventilators, ejector chamber and ejectors, cast-iron rising main and other works; also precipitation tanks, engine and boiler houses, chimney shaft, press-house, stores and offices, carriers, underdraining and levelling land, roads, fencing and other works.—Mr. Samuel Jones, town clerk.

TONBRIDGE.—November 26th.—Supply of crude sulphate of iron and disinfectants, for the rural district council.—Mr. Frank Harris, surveyor to the council.

EASTRY.—November 26th.—Supply and laying of 1,460 yards of 6-in., 940 yards of 4-in. and 2,920 yards of 3-in. cast-iron socket pipes, for the rural district council.—Mr. F. S. Cloke, clerk to the council.

WATERLOO-WITH-SEAFORTH.—November 28th.—Supply of sixteen electric arc lamp columns and carriers, for the urban district council.—Mr. F. Spencer Yates, A.M.I.C.E., surveyor to the council.

HARTWOOD.—November 28th.—Supply and delivery of a steam road-roller and scarifier, for the urban district council.—Mr. Joseph Tildsley, clerk to the council.

HARROGATE.—November 28th.—Laying of about 2½ miles of surface-water drains and culverts in the borough and in the parish of Bilton.—Mr. Samuel Stead, borough surveyor.

STOURBRIDGE.—November 28th.—Construction of 990 yards of 9-in. earthenware pipe sewer, for the main drainage board.—Mr. W. Fiddian, surveyor to the board, Town Hall, Stourbridge.

BROMSGROVE.— November 28th.— Construction of stoneware pipe sewers comprised in the scheme of sewerage for the parish of Pedmore, for the rural district council.—Mr. H. D. Holloway, clerk to the council.

EDDINGTON.—November 28th.—Supply of about 6,500 lineal yards of kerb and about 820 tons of 4-in. cube setts, for the urban district council.—Mr. Herbert H. Humphries, engineer and surveyor to the council.

BUCKLOW.—November 29th.—Reconstruction of the main sewers of the township of Hall, for the urban district council.—Mr. J. M'D. M'Kenzie, surveyor to the council, 7 Market-street, Altrincham.

WEST HARTLEPOOL.—November 29th.—Supply of various materials and goods required during the year ending December 31, 1899.—Mr. J. W. Brown, borough engineer.

MIDDLESBROUGH.—November 29th.—Supply and erection of various electric lighting plant, for the corporation.—Mr. Robert Hammond, consulting engineer, 64 Victoria-street, London, S.W.

MIDDLESBROUGH.—November 29th.—Supply and erection of various electric lighting plant, for the corporation.—Mr. Robert Hammond, consulting engineer, 64 Victoria-street, London, S.W.

HYAWON.—November 29th.—Supply of 250 street gullies, 18 in. diameter by 2 ft. deep, for the urban district council.—Mr. John Holbrook, surveyor to the council.

DROYLSDEN.—November 30th.—Construction of 607 lineal yards of 24-in. pipe sewer, 615 lineal yards of 18-in. pipe sewer, and 345 lineal yards of 15-in. pipe sewer, for the urban district council.—Mr. W. Curry, engineer to the council.

BLACKPOOL.—November 30th.—Extension of the town hall buildings.—Mr. T. Loftus, town clerk.

SALFORD.—December 1st.—Supply and erection of certain electric plant.—Mr. Saml. Brown, town clerk.

LANCASTER.—December 2nd.—Supply and delivery of about 5,680 lineal yards of 7-in. cast-iron water pipes, for the rural district council.—Mr. Joseph Eunion, clerk to the council.

ST. JAMES, WESTMINSTER.— December 5th.—Construction of underground conveniences for both sexes in Broad-street, Golden-square, for the vestry.—Mr. T. Hensman Munsey, clerk to the vestry.

WEST HAM.—December 13th.—Erection of a quarter sessions court, police cells and mortuary in West Ham-lane, Stratford.—Mr. Lewis Angell, borough engineer.

MANSFIELD.—December 14th.—Construction of about 1,650 yards of brick sewer and storm overflows and 570 yards of pipe sewers.—Mr. R. Frank Vallance, borough surveyor.

JOHANNESBURG, S.A.—January 6th.—Supply of a complete carburetted water-gas plant, for the corporation.—Messrs. Robert Whyte & Co., 22 Bury-street, St. Mary Axe, London, E.C.

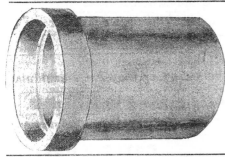

LENNON.—January 24th.—Construction of a tunnel for pedestrian traffic under the river Thames from Greenwich to Poplar, for the county council.—Mr. C. J. Stewart, clerk to the council, County Hall, Spring-gardens, S.W.

## TENDERS.

#### *ACCEPTED.

ABERDEEN.—For the supply for one year of electricity meters, house fuse boxes and house service cables.—Mr. J. Alex. Bell, city electrical engineer :—

House Service Cables.—British Insulated Wire Company, Limited, Prescot; Callender's Cable and Construction Company, Limited, Cannon-street, London*; Western Electric Company, North Woolwich; Siemens Brothers & Co., Limited, Westminster, London; Telegraph Manufacturing Company, Limited, Helsby; W. T. Henley's Telegraph Works Company, Limited, London.

House Fuse Boxes.—A. Stark, Aberdeen*; E. F. Moy, Limited, Camden Town, N.W.; Reason Manufacturing Company, Limited, Brighton; British Insulated Wire Company, Prescot; General Electric Company, Limited, Glasgow.

Electricity Supply Meters.—Penny-in-the-Slot Syndicate, London, S.W.; S. de Ferranti, Limited, Hollinwood*; Venner & Co., Westminster, S.W.; General Electric Company, Limited, Glasgow; British Insulated Wire Company, Limited, Prescot; Premier Electricity Meter Company, London, W.C.

ERDINGTON.—For making-up various roads, for the urban district council.—Mr. Herbert H. Humphries, surveyor to the council :—

##### SOUTH-ROAD.

| | |
|---|---|
| S. W. Harrison, Mitchley-lane, Harborne | £2,417 |
| Crawys & Hobrough, Gloucester | 1,661 |
| G. Law, Kidderminster | 1,390 |
| J. White, junr., Handsworth | 1,317 |
| W. H. Jones, Birmingham | 1,319 |
| J. C. Trueman, Swanley, Kent | 1,292 |
| J. Biggs, Farm-street, Birmingham | 1,281 |
| J. Mackay, Smethwick | 1,256 |
| Heap Brothers, Aston | 1,204 |
| Currall, Lewis & Martin, Birmingham | 1,202 |
| Fitzmaurice & Co., Birmingham | 1,174 |

##### LEAMINGTON-ROAD.

| | |
|---|---|
| S. W. Harrison, Mitchley-lane, Harborne | £757 |
| Crawys & Hobrough, Gloucester | 425 |
| G. Law, Kidderminster | 387 |
| J. C. Trueman, Swanley, Kent | 364 |
| W. H. Jones, Birmingham | 360 |
| J. White, junr., Handsworth | 341 |
| Currall, Lewis & Martin, Birmingham | 325 |
| Fitzmaurice & Co., Birmingham | 317 |
| J. Biggs, Farm-street, Birmingham | 313 |
| Heap Brothers, Aston | 310 |
| J. Mackay, Smethwick | 304 |

##### WOODLAND-ROAD.

| | |
|---|---|
| S. W. Harrison, Mitchley-lane, Harborne | £442 |
| Crawys & Hobrough, Gloucester | 254 |
| J. C. Trueman, Swanley, Kent | 254 |
| G. Law, Kidderminster | 229 |
| W. H. Jones, Birmingham | 223 |
| J. White, junr., Handsworth | 222 |
| Currall, Lewis & Martin, Birmingham | 199 |
| Fitzmaurice & Co., Birmingham | 196 |
| Heap Brothers, Aston | 195 |
| J. Biggs, Farm-street, Birmingham | 185 |
| J. Mackay, Smethwick | 178 |

##### BRIDER-ROAD.

| | |
|---|---|
| S. W. Harrison, Mitchley-lane, Harborne | £225 |
| Crawys & Hobrough, Gloucester | 126 |
| J. C. Trueman, Swanley, Kent | 112 |
| G. Law, Kidderminster | 109 |
| W. H. Jones, Birmingham | 104 |
| J. White, junr., Handsworth | 105 |
| Fitzmaurice & Co., Birmingham | 96 |
| Heap Brothers, Aston | 94 |
| J. Biggs, Farm-street, Birmingham | 90 |
| Currall, Lewis & Martin, Birmingham | 89 |
| J. Mackay, Smethwick | 85 |

##### MINSTEAD-ROAD SEWER.

| | |
|---|---|
| Crawys & Hobrough, Gloucester | £251 |
| J. White, junr., Handsworth | 247 |
| S. W. Harrison, Mitchley-lane, Harborne | 234 |
| J. Biggs, Farm-street, Birmingham | 213 |
| Currall, Lewis & Martin, Birmingham | 208 |
| J. C. Trueman, Swanley, Kent | 204 |
| Fitzmaurice & Co., Birmingham | 204 |
| G. Law, Kidderminster | 197 |
| Heap Brothers, Aston | 182 |
| J. Mackay, Smethwick | 151 |

##### CARFIELD-ROAD, S.W., DRAIN.

| | |
|---|---|
| Crawys & Hobrough, Gloucester | £104 |
| S. W. Harrison, Mitchley-lane, Harborne | 83 |
| J. C. Trueman, Swanley, Kent | 79 |
| Fitzmaurice & Co., Birmingham | 77 |
| G. Law, Kidderminster | 77 |
| Currall, Lewis & Martin, Birmingham | 75 |
| J. Biggs, Farm-street, Birmingham | 70 |
| J. White, junr., Handsworth | 69 |
| Heap Brothers, Aston | 65 |
| J. Mackay, Smethwick | 56 |

FLEETWOOD.—For the construction of an underground convenience, for the urban district council.—Mr. Robert T. Hayes, A.M.I.C.E., surveyor to the council :—

| | |
|---|---|
| O. Ashworth, Crawshawbooth* | £1,968 |
| Moore Brothers, Rawtenstall | 1,909 |
| J. Kirkbride, Fleetwood* | 1,909 |

Surveyor's estimate, £1,918 10s.

† Informal.

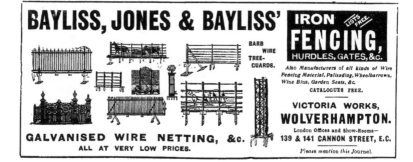

FLEETWOOD.—For excavating, pile-driving, concreting, paving and other works in connection with the raising of the concrete landing at Knots End, for the urban district council.—Mr. Robert T. Hayes, A.M.I.C.E., surveyor to the council :—

| | | | | | |
|---|---|---|---|---|---|
| J. Dale, Northwich | ... | ... | ... | ... | £4,588 |
| O. Ashworth, Crawshawborth | ... | ... | ... | ... | 4,122 |
| Gradwell & Co., Limited, Barrow-in-Furness | ... | | | | 3,624 |
| Ainsworth & Son, Oldham | ... | ... | ... | ... | 3,379 |
| Preston & Hirst, Wigan | ... | ... | ... | ... | 3,337 |
| E. Teppest, Blackpool | ... | ... | ... | ... | 2,999 |
| J. Kirkbride, Fleetwood* | ... | ... | ... | ... | 2,900 |

Surveyor's estimate, £3,202 13s.

HODDESDON.—For the making-up of three streets in the district and the construction of various surface-water sewers, &c., for the urban district council.—Mr. T. Salkield, surveyor to the council :—

FOR THE COMBINED WORKS.

| | | | | | |
|---|---|---|---|---|---|
| G. Wilson, Walthamstow | ... | ... | ... | ... | £2,903 |
| W. Lawrence, Waltham Abbey | ... | ... | ... | ... | 2,776 |
| Merndew & Wort, stevenage | ... | ... | ... | ... | 2,639 |
| T. Adams, Wood Green | ... | ... | ... | ... | 2,534 |
| G. Bell, Tottenham | ... | ... | ... | ... | 2,515 |
| Broomfield, Tottenham | ... | ... | ... | ... | 2,466 |
| Grounds & Newton, Tottenham | ... | ... | ... | | 2,427 |
| C. Ford, Harlesden | ... | ... | ... | ... | 2,392 |
| S. Kitteringham, Cheshunt* | ... | ... | ... | ... | 2,363 |

FOR ROAD WORKS ONLY.

| | | | | | |
|---|---|---|---|---|---|
| W. Griffiths, London | ... | ... | ... | ... | 1,381 |

ISLINGTON.—For paving with wood blocks the carriageways of Copenhagen-street and Tollington Park, for the vestry.—Mr. J. Patten Barber, M.I.C.E., chief surveyor to the vestry :—

| | Copenhagen-street. | Tollington Park. |
|---|---|---|
| A. Jackson & Son, Stroud Green, N. | £4,285 | £7,426 |
| J. Mowlem & Co., Westminster, S.W. | 4,154 | 7,444 |
| W. Griffiths, Bishopsgate-street Without, E.C. | 3,871 | 6,836* |
| Acme Wood Flooring Company, Hackney, N.E. | 3,727* | |

KIRKBY-IN-ASHFIELD.—For the laying of about 9,500 lineal yards of 18-in., 15-in., 9-in. and 6-in. stoneware and cast-iron pipe sewers, construction of precipitation tanks, filter-beds, &c., and the erection of a cottage at the sewage outfall works in Park-lane, for the urban district council.—Mr. Herbert Walker, A.M.I.C.E., Newcastle Chambers, Angel-row, Nottingham :—

CONTRACT No. 1.

| | | | | | |
|---|---|---|---|---|---|
| R. Lomax, Leigh | ... | ... | ... | ... | £13,270 |
| J. H. Vickers, Limited, Nottingham | ... | ... | ... | 9,797 |
| J. D. Nowell & Sons, Westminster | ... | ... | ... | 9,404 |
| R. Holmes, Chesterfield | ... | ... | ... | ... | 9,400 |
| W. & J. Foster, Shipley | ... | ... | ... | ... | 9,334 |
| H. Weldon, Birmingham | ... | ... | ... | ... | 8,944 |
| M. Hall & Sons, Bradford | ... | ... | ... | ... | 8,275 |
| H. H. Barry, Radcliffe-on-Trent | ... | ... | ... | 8,225 |
| J. F. Price, Nottingham | ... | ... | ... | ... | 8,199 |
| J. Hawley & Son, Ilkeston | ... | ... | ... | ... | 8,080 |
| Cope & Raynor, Lenton, Nottingham | ... | ... | ... | 7,860 |
| J. Lane & Son, Skegby* | ... | ... | ... | ... | 7,284 |

Engineer's Estimate, £7,656.

CONTRACT No. 2.

| | | | | | |
|---|---|---|---|---|---|
| R. Holmes, Chesterfield | ... | ... | ... | ... | £430 |
| M. Hall & Son, Bradford | ... | ... | ... | ... | 438 |
| H. Weldon, Birmingham | ... | ... | ... | ... | 423 |
| W. & J. Foster, Shipley | ... | ... | ... | ... | 380 |
| J. F. Price, Nottingham | ... | ... | ... | ... | 348 |
| J. Lane & Son, Skegby* | ... | ... | ... | ... | 342 |
| J. H. Vickers, Nottingham | ... | ... | ... | ... | 319 |
| Cope & Raynor, Nottingham | ... | ... | ... | ... | 260 |

Engineer's Estimate, £273.

NEW HUNSTANTON.—For the erection of one of Messrs. Meldrum Brothers' patent refuse destructors and a Cornish boiler, for the urban district council :—

| | | | |
|---|---|---|---|
| Meldrum Brothers, City-road, Manchester* | ... | ... | £760 |

WATERLOO-WITH-SEAFORTH.—For the flagging of the north side of Church-road, Seaford, for the urban district council.—Mr. F. Spencer Yates, A.M.I.C.E., surveyor to the council :—

| | | | |
|---|---|---|---|
| T. Horrocks, Greenwich-road, Walton, Liverpool* | ... | ... | £105 |

## MEETINGS.

*Secretaries and others will oblige by sending early notice of dates of forthcoming meetings.*

### NOVEMBER.

18.—Sanitary Institute : Lecture to sanitary officers by Prof. Henry Robinson, M.I.C.E., on "Sewerage and Sewage Disposal." 8 p.m.
18.—Institution of Civil Engineers : Students' meeting ; Mr. Cecil Lightfoot on "The Production of Liquid Air and its Application to Chemical and other Industries." 8 p.m.
19.—Sanitary Institute : Visit of sanitary officers to Messrs. Harrison & Barber's knacker yard, Winthrop-street, Whitechapel. 3 p.m.
21.—Inner Temple Hall : Discussion on "Treasure Trove." 8 p.m.
21.—Society of Arts : First Cantor Lecture by Prof. Vivian B. Lewes, on "Acetylene." 8 p.m.
21.—Sanitary Institute : Visit of sanitary officers to the Metropolitan Cattle Market, York-road, N.
22.—Surveyors' Institution : First junior meeting. 7 p.m.
22.—Institution of Civil Engineers : Ordinary meeting ; further discussion on Mr. Wm. Beedie Esson's paper on "Electrical Transmission of Power in Mining." 8 p.m.
23.—Sanitary Institute : Visit of sanitary officers to the London County Council municipal lodging-house, Parker-street, Drury-lane. 3 p.m.
23.—Sanitary Institute : Lecture to sanitary officers by Mr. Charles Jones, M.I.C.E., engineer and surveyor to the Ealing Urban District Council, on "Scavenging, Disposal of House Refuse." 8 p.m.
23.—Society of Arts : Prof. G. Forbes, on "Long-Distance Transmission of Electric Power." 8 p.m.
26.—Sanitary Institute : Lecture to sanitary officers by Mr. W. C. Tyndale, M.I.C.E., on "House Drainage." 8 p.m.

26.—Sanitary Institute: Visit of sanitary officers to the Ealing sewage and destructor works, under the guidance of Mr. Charles Jones, M.I.C.E., engineer and surveyor to the district council.   2.15 p.m.

DECEMBER.

1.—Association of the Birmingham Students of the Institution of Civil Engineers: Dr. A. Bostock Hill on "Some Observations on Sewage and Modern Methods of Treatment."   7.30 p.m.

5.—Royal Institute of British Architects: Mr. R. W. Gibson, New York, U.S.A., on "Fireproof Construction in America."   8 p.m.

## NOTICES.

THE SURVEYOR AND MUNICIPAL AND COUNTY ENGINEER *may be ordered direct, through any of Messrs. Smith & Son's book-stalls, or of any newsagent in the United Kingdom. Applications to the Offices for single copies by post must in all cases be accompanied by stamps.*

*The Prepaid Subscription (including postage) is as follows :*

|  | Twelve Months. | Six Months. | Three Months. |
|---|---|---|---|
| United Kingdom ... ... | 15s. | 7s. 6d. | 3s. 9d. |
| Continent, the Colonies, India, United States, &c. ... ... | 19s. | 9s. 6d. | 4s. 9d. |

*The International News Company, 83 and 85 Duane-street, New York City; The Toronto News Company, Toronto; and The Montreal News Company, Montreal, have been appointed agents in the United States and Canada for the sale of THE SURVEYOR AND MUNICIPAL AND COUNTY ENGINEER. A thin paper edition is printed for circulation abroad.*

EDITORIAL OFFICES :—
24 BRIDE-LANE, FLEET-STREET, LONDON, E.C.
ADVERTISEMENT AND PUBLISHING OFFICES :—
13 NEW STREET-HILL, FLEET-STREET, LONDON, E.C.

## APPOINTMENTS OPEN.

### COUNTY BOROUGH OF SUNDERLAND.
ROAD SURVEYOR.

Wanted, by the Corporation of Sunderland, a Road Surveyor, to discharge all the duties of a surveyor of highways, subject to the Borough Surveyor as the Surveyor of Highways for the Borough.   Salary, £130 per annum.

Candidates must have had a thoroughly practical experience in road making and maintenance, paving of all descriptions, flagging, &c., and the person appointed will be required to devote his whole time to the duties of the office.   Personal canvassing for the appointment will be a disqualification.

Applications, in the handwriting of the candidates, stating age, residence, and past and present occupation, accompanied by copies of not more than six testimonials of recent date, must be delivered to me, at the address undermentioned, not later than 4 p.m. on Wednesday, the 30th November instant, endorsed "Road Surveyor."

(By order)
FRAS. M. BOWEY,
Town Clerk.

Town Hall, Sunderland.
November 14, 1898.

### BOROUGH OF MAIDENHEAD.
SURVEYOR'S ASSISTANT.

The Town Council of the Borough of Maidenhead require the services of a General Assistant in the office of the Borough Surveyor, at a salary of £80 per annum.

Candidates must not be more than twenty-eight years of age and have received a thorough training in a municipal office.   They should be competent to survey and level accurately, prepare plans and detail drawings for private street improvements and other works, have a knowledge of building construction, and generally be able to assist in the duties of a borough surveyor's department.

Applications, in the handwriting of the candidate, stating age and qualifications, accompanied by copies of not more than three testimonials, and endorsed "Surveyor's Assistant," must be sent in to me not later than Monday, the 21st day of November, 1898.

PERCY JOHNS,
Borough Surveyor.

Guildhall, Maidenhead.
November 7, 1898.

### CORPORATION OF STOCKTON-ON-TEES.
The above-named Corporation invite applications for the appointment of a General Outdoor Foreman.

Candidates (whose age must be between thirty and forty-five years) must be thoroughly qualified persons, having had practical experience in the cleansing and maintenance of roads and streets and of the various materials used in their construction, and also in the management and control of workmen, horses and carts.

He must be able to set out work accurately and take all necessary measurements.   He must also have had experience in the measurement and construction of sewers and drains.

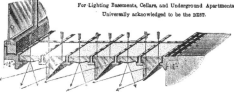

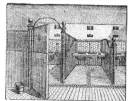

He must devote the whole of his time to the service of the Council and under the direction of the Borough Engineer. He will be required to keep all necessary books in connection with his work.

Salary, £100 per annum, with house, coals, gas, rates, &c.

List of duties and forms of application can be obtained from the Borough Engineer.

Applications, in candidate's own handwriting, stating age and qualifications, particulars of present and past employment, including copies of not more than three recent testimonials, must be sent to me before 10 a.m. on Monday, the 28th November, endorsed "General Foreman."

M. H. SYKES,
Borough Engineer.

Town Hall, Stockton-on-Tees.
November 14, 1898.

COUNTY OF BEDFORD.
APPOINTMENT OF A MAIN ROAD INSPECTOR.

The Highways and Bridges Committee of the Bedfordshire County Council are prepared to receive applications for the appointment of a Main Road Inspector, to act under the superintendence and directions of the County Surveyor.

Salary, £100 per annum, to include all travelling and other expenses, with the exception of stationery and postages.

The person appointed must have had experience in all branches of road-making and structural works connected therewith.

He will be required to devote the whole of his time to the service of the Council. A list of the duties of the office and all other information can be obtained from the undersigned.

Candidates must not be more than thirty-five years of age.

Applications, in candidate's own handwriting, accompanied by recent testimonials, not exceeding three, in number, must be sent to the undersigned, marked "Main Road Inspector," not later than 3 o'clock on Thursday, the 1st day of December, 1898.

The engagement will commence on the 1st day of February, 1899, and the person appointed will be required to enter upon his duties on that day.

Candidates canvassing, either directly or indirectly, will be disqualified.

It is desirable that the Inspector should be a good cyclist.

W. W. MARKS,
Clerk to the County Council.

Shire Hall, Bedford.
November 15, 1898.

CITY OF SHEFFIELD.
BUILDING INSPECTOR.

The Highway and Sewerage Committee are prepared to receive applications for the post of Building Inspector in the City Surveyor's department.

Candidates must be thoroughly qualified persons, and will be required to undertake the inspection of new buildings and drains and other duties.

The salary is £120 per annum.

A list of duties and form of application, which must be returned by the 24th inst., may be obtained on application to the undersigned on and after Monday next, the 14th inst.

CHARLES F. WIKE,
City Surveyor.

City Surveyor's Office, Sheffield.
November 11, 1898.

CLEETHORPES - WITH - THRUNSCOE
URBAN DISTRICT COUNCIL.
The undersigned has a vacancy for a Pupil. Premium required.
Splendid opening for a pushing youth at this popular watering-place. Population in 1891 was 4,306; population at present time over 13,000.
Further particulars on application from

EGBERT RUSHTON, C.E. (BY EXAM.),
Engineer, Surveyor and Inspector.
Cleethorpes.

WANTED.—Two responsible men, under forty and of slight build, one for Venezuela and one for South American Columbia. Must be fully qualified in one of the following subjects, with some knowledge of the others—namely, Gold and silver mining engineering, assaying, surveying. None need apply without first-class references, of which copies only must be sent. Good salaries for capable men.—Apply, by letter only, to "C. S.," 28 Bury-street, St. Mary Axe, London, E.C.

## COMPETITION.

CITY OF BRADFORD.

*INTENDED CENTRAL FIRE BRIGADE STATION.*

TO ARCHITECTS.

The Corporation of the City of Bradford are prepared to receive Competitive Designs for the Erection of a Central Fire Brigade Station. Three premiums are offered to competing architects—viz., £100, £50 and £30. Plan of the site, with printed instructions, may be had on application at the City Surveyor's office on and after Monday, the 31st inst., on payment of 1 guinea, to be returned after receipt of design.
The designs must be sent in not later than Monday, the 2nd of January, 1899.

(By order)

GEORGE McGUIRE,
Town Clerk.

Town Clerk's Office, Bradford.
October 25, 1898.

## TENDERS WANTED.

CORPORATION OF MANSFIELD.
The Town Council, acting as the urban sanitary authority for their district, are prepared to receive tenders from competent persons for the construction of about 1,650 yards of Brick Sewer and Storm Overflows, and 570 yards of Pipe Sewers, with all necessary lampholes, manholes, ventilators, flushing arrangements and works incidental thereto.
Plans and specifications of the works may be seen, and the form of tender and schedule of quantities obtained (on deposit of £10), at the office of Mr. R. Frank Vallance, C.E., F.S.I., Borough Surveyor, Mansfield, the Engineer for the works, on and after the 1st day of December next.
The deposit will be returned, after a contract has been entered into, to every person making a *bond-fide* tender and on the return of the documents entrusted to him.
In the event of a tender being withdrawn the deposit will be forfeited.
The successful contractor will be required to pay the standard rate of wages recognised in the district in the several trades.

Sealed tenders (on the form supplied) endorsed "Tender for Intercepting Sewer," are to be delivered at the office of the undersigned, in the envelope provided for the purpose, on or before the 14th day of December, 1898, at noon.

The Town Council will not be bound to accept the lowest or any tender.

Dated this 16th day of November, 1898.

J. HARROP WHITE,
Deputy Town Clerk.

## BROMSGROVE RURAL DISTRICT COUNCIL.

### PEDMORE SEWERAGE.

#### TO CONTRACTORS.

The above Council is prepared to receive tenders for the Construction of the Stoneware Pipe Sewers comprised in the scheme of sewerage for the parish of Pedmore, together with manholes, lampholes, flushing chambers and other works in connection therewith.

Plans, sections and detail drawings may be seen, and specifications and bills of quantities obtained, at the office of the Engineer, Mr. E. B. Marten, M.I.C.E., Church-street Chambers, Stourbridge, on and after Wednesday, November 2nd, on payment of £5 5s., which will be returned after the receipt of a bonâ-fide tender, with the schedules duly filled in, and the return of all documents.

Sealed tenders, addressed to me, and endorsed "Tender for Pedmore Sewerage," are to be delivered at my office on or before Monday, the 28th day of November next.

The Council do not bind themselves to accept the lowest or any tender.

(By order)
H. D. HOLLOWAY,
Clerk to the Council.

Union Offices, Bromsgrove.
October 27, 1898.

## COUNTY BOROUGH OF WEST HAM.

#### TO BUILDERS AND CONTRACTORS.

The Council hereby invite tenders for the Erection of Quarter Sessions Court, Police Cells and Mortuary, West Ham-lane, Stratford, E.

Plans may be seen, and specification, form of tender and further particulars obtained, on and after Monday, 28th November, 1898, at the office of Mr. Lewis Angell, Borough Engineer, Town Hall, Stratford, E., upon the deposit of a £5

Bank of England note, which will be returned upon receipt of a bonâ-fide tender.

Tenders, endorsed "Tender for Quarter Sessions Court, &c.," to be sent to my office not later than 4 o'clock on Tuesday, 13th December, 1898.

The Council do not bind themselves to accept the lowest or any tender. The contractor will be required to enter into a bond, with two sureties, for the due performance of the contract; and no work will be ordered under the contract until such bond has been duly executed.

As regards all work to be done at the site or elsewhere within a radius of 20 miles from Charing Cross, the contractors will be bound by the contract to pay to all workmen (except a reasonable number of legally-bound apprentices) employed by them wages at rates not less, and to observe hours of labour not greater, than the rates and hours set out in the Council's list, and such rates of wages and hours of labour will be inserted in and form part of the contract by way of schedule.

(By order of the Council)
FRED. E. HILLEARY,
Town Clerk.

Town Hall, West Ham, E.
November 15, 1898.

## DROYLSDEN URBAN DISTRICT.

### CONSTRUCTION OF SEWERS.

The above Council invite tenders for the construction of 607 lineal yards of 24-in. Pipe Sewer, 615 lineal yards of 18-in. Pipe Sewer, and 345 lineal yards of 15-in. Pipe Sewer, together with Manholes, Junctions, &c.—namely, from Manchester-road to Ashton Old-road, Fairfield, and from Copperas-lane to the "Barley Mow," Fairfield-road.

Particulars and specifications may be seen on application to Mr. W. Curry, F.I.S.E., the Engineer to the Council.

Quantities and forms of tender will be supplied to intending contractors on payment of 1 guinea, which will be returned on receipt of a bonâ-fide tender, together with all documents given to contractors.

Tenders, endorsed "Sewers," must be addressed Chairman, Sewage Committee, Council Offices, Droylsden, and sent in on or before the 30th inst.

The Council do not bind themselves to accept the lowest or any tender.

(By order)
JOHN RICHARDS,
Clerk of the Council.

Council Offices, Droylsden.

# The Surveyor

## And Municipal and County Engineer.

Vol. XIV., No. 358.    LONDON, NOVEMBER 25, 1898.    Weekly, Price 3d.

## Minutes of Proceedings.

**Municipalities and Electric Tramways.—III.** The report on tramway traction, which we have already discussed at considerable length in the two last issues, concludes with the firmly-expressed opinion that the solution of the traction problem in London lies in the electric conduit. This is a very important declaration, coming from one who has so closely studied the question as Mr. Baker. It is not only of importance, however, as far as London is concerned, but it equally affects all towns and cities suffering from congestion of traffic. It will be as well, therefore, to consider some of the reasons that have led to the report being in favour of this system. We have already indicated in our previous remarks that if any system will give the advantages that accrue from electrical methods for propelling vehicles, without the necessity of erecting overhead wires and their requisite supports, a good deal will have been achieved in making the way easy for the general adoption of electricity in crowded thoroughfares. Fortunately, as far as this country is concerned, there is on the subject of conduits a good deal of experience and knowledge which may serve as a guide to some extent. At the same time it must not be forgotten that the conditions obtaining in London, and for the matter of that in the chief English cities, are totally at variance with those found either on the Continent or in America. It is apparent from the report that the conclusions expressed in favour of this form of traction are based upon systems which have been in existence in America for some years. Indeed, Mr. Baker almost admits that the examples on the Continent may be regarded as only a qualified success. Many of our readers are no doubt familiar with the fact that one of the first public systems of tramways operated by electricity was that of Blackpool, where the conduit was laid down in the middle of the rails. That system demonstrated beyond all question the economy of electrical working. It obviously had many defects, and, although it has continued almost to the present day, it is now being superseded by an overhead trolley. We admit at once that the partial failure at Blackpool must not be taken as an argument against the conduit. The chief conduit systems on the Continent are in Brussels, Buda-Pesth and Berlin. In the case of Buda-Pesth the slot is formed by two rails, and below them in a sort of tube are the conductors. Brussels and Berlin do not differ very materially from this, and the same remark applies to the system which has been erected at Dresden. Probably the most noted system in Europe is the one at Buda-Pesth, to which we have just alluded. This system had been chosen because local authorities would not permit the overhead wires to be erected in the streets. It is stated in Mr. Baker's report that wet weather does not affect the working, but in the same paragraph it is admitted that it may cause more leakage of current at the insulators, which is a very important point. We have already pointed out that the conditions regarding the construction and working of electric tramways in this country are different to those which prevail either on the Continent or in America. Definite regulations have been laid down by the Board of Trade, and, in spite of the fact that these are considered in many quarters to be to some extent permissive, there is every reason to think that their transgression would be followed by some restriction. The question, therefore, that naturally arises is whether at any time there will be sufficient leakage from a conduit system to cause electrolytic troubles or inconvenience to telegraph and telephone services. It is interesting to quote at this point some remarks in the report, because they embody the arguments generally advanced to induce the London County Council to adopt the conduit system:—

The steady opposition of the city authorities, in both Washington and New York, to the overhead trolley wire has made it imperative upon the operating companies in those cities to find a substitute for this and the horse lines, which could be no longer tolerated. Accordingly, at much expense, the cable lines were laid down in Broadway, Lexington-avenue and other leading thoroughfares in New York, and similar lines were also installed in parts of Washington. These have worked with great success and economy, the operating expenses in New York being given at less than 50 per cent. of the gross earnings. Subsequently, in 1894, the first trial line on the electric conduit system was laid on Lenox-avenue, New York. This was a very expensive construction, having an unnecessarily deep conduit. It has worked, however, with great satisfaction and economy, and proved to the company that it possesses many advantages over the cable. In the succeeding year 26 track miles of conduit line were laid down in Washington, with shallower conduit and less expensive construction than that laid down at Lenox-avenue line. The success of this installation induced the Metropolitan Traction Company in New York to extend their conduit system and lay down a further 55 miles on Maddison, Fourth, Eighth, Second and Amsterdam avenues. These are now working with entire success and great satisfaction to the public and the company, as manifested by largely-increasing receipts and the "stealing of traffic" from parallel cable lines . . . . The latest development and the most striking proof of the perfect success and economical working of the conduit system is the fact that the Metropolitan Traction Company of New York have just applied to the New York State Railroad Commissioners for permission to convert their Broadway, Columbus-avenue and Lexington-avenue cable lines (their entire cable system) to the underground conduit electric, in spite of the fact that the Broadway cable had cost £200,000 per mile of double track to construct. This is all the more striking when it is considered that the tramway traffic on Broadway is heavier than that of any other city in the world, cars running every ten to fifteen seconds. It was thought previously that no system of the cable could economically cope with such a service.

These are undoubtedly important facts, and should no doubt be very carefully considered by any municipality that is contemplating the adoption of some form of mechanical traction. At the same time it must be pointed out that the conduit was not adopted by the companies because they considered it better than the overhead wire, for it is noted in the report that Congress decreed that all overhead wires in Washington should be removed and be replaced by other forms of traction. Any local authority is, of course, justified in taking up such a position, and we would not think of arguing that the conduit is at all impracticable ; in fact, if a local authority conscientiously considers that the overhead wires are in any sense a disfigurement, then we admit without hesitation that it is desirable to adopt a conduit system. It is perfectly feasible to work a conduit system, and there is no reason why, if properly constructed, it should not in every respect conform to the Board of Trade regulations. There is distinct evidence adduced by the report that the system is mechanical and economical. It would be almost impossible to find an electrical man at the present time who would suggest that there were any mechanical difficulties in the way of working the conduit, but there must be some reason why there are so few systems at the present moment. It is somewhat strange that the municipalities of Glasgow, Liverpool, Dover, Sheffield and Manchester should have declared in favour of the overhead trolley when the information that Mr. Baker has so admirably set forth was quite open to them. Without, therefore, desiring to prejudice the minds of our readers against the conduit system, it is necessary to point out why this system has not been more largely adopted. The most careful investigations into all systems have been undertaken by various municipalities, and we cannot do better than quote the objections raised against the conduit by the deputation of the city of Sheffield. They are as follows :—

(1) The great expense.
(2) Prolonged interference with the streets during construction and repairs.
(3) The difficulty in locating any defect of the underground part of the system.
(4) The difficulty and expense of carrying out any sewerage works in streets in which there are conduits.
(5) The danger to traffic through the presence of a slot in the street, varying in width from ⅜ in. to 2 in.
(6) The difficulty in keeping conduits clean and maintaining satisfactory insulation.
(7) The liability to stoppage through storms.

There can be no question about the first objection raised by the Sheffield Committee. It has been stated by Messrs. Siemens & Halske, of Berlin, who have equipped more conduit lines than any other firm in Europe, that the conduit costs £4,000 to £5,000 more per mile of double line than the overhead. The tramway company in Berlin state that the price per mile of overhead electric is £2,400, and for exactly similar equipment the conduit system costs £6,450. The municipal engineer of Brussels states that the overhead electric line in that city costs £5,410 per mile and a mile of conduit single track £9,800. Mr. Baker shows in his report that the cost of the conduit in Washington and the electric installation of it, and repaving mostly with asphalte, was £7,000 per mile of single track, and this is considered to be a moderate figure. The question is whether the advantages provided by such a system are worth the very heavy initial outlay that must be incurred. On the point of prolonged interference with streets during construction and repairs there is equally clear evidence in existence. In the case of Buda-Pesth it is stated by the engineer that 1 kilometre (equal to ·6 of a mile) of conduit tramway could be laid in about a month, or, working three gangs, in a fortnight. In regard to Berlin, where a more modern system of conduit is in operation, the Sheffield report states that the inconvenience arising from the time occupied in the construction of the lines was so great that, although the police authorities prohibit overhead apparatus in the streets of Berlin, it has been decided not to allow the construction of any more conduit lines on account of the inconvenience arising in this way. It might be said with reason that if such towns as Washington and New York can withstand the inconvenience arising from such prolonged construction, there ought to be no difficulty in the way of London following in their footsteps ; but we merely point out the objections, leaving the municipal authorities to consider them.

At this stage it is interesting to quote two or three opinions from a very eminent American engineer—Mr. Pearson—on the subject of the conduit, and these opinions are particularly interesting and instructive at the present moment, because this authority has been the consulting engineer for the very large conduit systems in New York to which Mr. Baker refers so fully. Mr. Pearson states that "it is useless to consider any cheap form of conduit, because it should be well built and capable of withstanding the excessive weights which pass over it." That, of course, is admitted. In considering the question of applying electric tramways to the streets of Liverpool, Mr. Pearson estimates that the cost of 1 mile of straight track for overhead trolley would be £5,822, but 1 mile of straight track slotted conduit would cost £9,648. But heavy charges do not cease when the system has been erected. It is in maintenance that the conduit is shown to be inferior to the overhead trolley. It was stated that under the street conditions prevailing in Liverpool the cost of cleaning the conduits per mile of track would probably amount to £40 per year, and as the cost of maintaining what is described as the special work would be very much greater in the case of the conduit than in the case of the overhead wire, the expense of maintenance would vary in the same ratio as the original cost, and would be at least three times as much for the underground system as for the overhead. According to Mr. Pearson, if there had been 70 miles of track in Liverpool used for electric tramways the special charges would amount to £60 per year per mile of track for the maintenance of the special work of the overhead trolley system, and £180 per year per mile of track for the maintenance of the special work for the underground conduit system. In other words, the total yearly cost of maintaining in efficient condition an underground conduit would amount to £12,500 per annum against £4,200 for the overhead. Put in another way, if 9,000,000 car miles were run annually the cost per car mile for the special work maintenance would be ·11d. for the overhead trolley and ·33d. for the underground conduit. These are some of the points that will have to be carefully considered by all authorities who are contemplating adopting a conduit system. It is argued by many authorities that the objection to the overhead is a sentimental one. The question is whether getting rid of this objection is worth the heavy cost in first construction, and the undoubtedly heavy charges for maintenance that would thus be entailed.

* * *

**A Benighted City.** A smoke-enveloped and traffic-congested metropolis is the description that might appropriately be applied to London after a perusal of the daily papers during the past week or so. Mr. Vigers, in his opening address as president of the Surveyors' Institution, commented at some length on the congested state of the London streets and insisted on the necessity of widening improvements being carried out a little more vigorously and promptly. Then Sir John Wolfe Barry, at the Society of Arts, made London's traffic problem the subject of an entire address which had plenty of interest, and is given by us this week as fully as space will permit. It is to be feared, however, that the somewhat heroic remedies proposed by the eminent engineer will not meet with a great deal of support. It is the old question of ways and means, and we fear that Londoners must reconcile themselves to piecemeal improvements from time to time, while patiently awaiting the construction of further underground railways, the development of the motor car, and other improvements in our transit facilities. After the traffic problem comes the smoke problem —an appropriate enough subject of discussion in November, the fogs of which are often due as much to smoke as to purely atmospheric causes. Sir B. W. Richmond led off with a vigorous impeachment of vestries and district boards for their neglect in putting into force the powers vested in them by sec. 23 of the Public Health Act, 1891. This artistic protest was followed next day by a letter which attracted more attention on account of the signature than by any exceptional originality or information. The initials were "C. T. R.," which easily reveal the identity of a member of the present Cabinet who had so much to do with the establishment of county councils, including the London one of that ilk. Mr. Ritchie simply pointed out that under sec. 100 of the Public Health (London) Act, 1891, the County Council, in the case of default by the sanitary authority in removing any nuisance, instituting proceedings, or enforcing any by-law, is empowered to take any action which the sanitary authority might have taken and recover the expenses from the defaulting body. Since Mr. Ritchie's contribution to the discussion there has been plenty of rather aimless talk in the columns of the daily papers, most of the writers being apparently under the impression that the clause in question has been lying buried and unknown since the passing of the Act in 1891. We have no intention of defending the vestries and district boards, for it is difficult to believe that many of them make any sincere effort to check the smoke nuisance, to say nothing of others, but it is not quite just to imply that the County Council do absolutely nothing, though there may be ground for contending that they do not act so vigorously as they might do. Those who have occasion to follow the proceedings of London local authorities know that the County Council do frequently intervene in regard to the smoke nuisance. At the meeting of the Council this week, as will be seen from our report, the Public Control Committee reported with regard to proceedings in default of the Vestry of Lambeth, penalties and costs being obtained in two cases. The committee admit, however, that this is the first time the intervention of the Council has gone the length of legal proceedings. Let us hope that they will not weary of well-doing, for a little persistence in this policy should have salutary results. The following paragraph from the report should be of interest to Sir B. W. Richmond, "C. T. R.," the editor and leader writers of *The Times*, and one or two others:—

We have from time to time reported the steps we have taken for enforcing the provisions of the Public Health (London) Act, 1891, as to smoke prevention. In almost every instance either the sanitary authority has carried out its duties under the Act, or, as a consequence of the direct intervention of the council, the parties creating the nuisance have found means for abating it. Out of 228 premises from which serious and persistent nuisance was observed about July last, either by the police or the Council's officers, in over 200 cases means were found for abating the nuisance, although in some cases this was only after legal proceedings had been instituted by the sanitary authority.

\* \* \*

**Waste Strips Adjoining Highways.** There is, we believe, some confusion of thought, to some extent even among those whose duties tend to familiarise them with matters appertaining to highways, and to a greater extent among landowners and others with regard to those strips of land which are so frequently found between the metalled portion of a country road and the boundaries of adjoining property. The idea so deeply ingrained in the English character, which finds expression in such sayings as "An Englishman's house is his castle" and "A man may do what he likes with his own," leads many to confuse the question of the "owner-ship" of the soil with the question of the rights of the public. If a landowner discovers, or thinks he discovers, that the plans on his title deeds include such strips, he is apt to jump to the conclusion that he can fence them in, utterly irrespective of the length of time that they may have been left unenclosed, or of any rule of law, or evidence of fact, which may curtail his rights. We have not to go far afield to find claims of this kind actually brought into court. In *Locke-King v. Woking Urban District Council* (noted at p. 696 of vol. xii.), the plaintiff produced a deed of conveyance upon which strips of this kind were

included as part of the land conveyed, and asked the Court to declare that he was entitled to enclose them. Mr. Justice Kekewich, before whom the case was tried, visited the spot, and found that the strips were remarkably irregular, being sometimes of considerable width and at other times running to a point, the boundary hedges themselves not being very regular in shape. He also found that there was nothing to render them impassable or to rebut the ordinary presumption of law in such cases—viz., that where there is a highway running between fences, unless there is something to show the contrary, the whole space between the fences, whether metalled or not, forms part of that highway and is subject to the right of the public to use it, be the soil vested in whom it may. The action therefore failed; not, be it observed, because the plaintiff was not the "owner" of the soil of the strips of land, but because, they having become part of the highway, his ownership was limited by and subject to the rights of the public. It must not, however, be assumed too hastily that such public rights exist in every case. There may be evidence to rebut the presumption referred to, and then it will be for the Court or the jury to decide whether the ground has been dedicated and become part of the highway. Through overlooking this aspect of the question, and taking the law into their own hands, highway authorities have sometimes got themselves into difficulties. In *Absalom v. Corporation of Norwich* (noted at p. 140 of vol. vi.), for example, the corporation were saddled with £20 damages and costs for pulling up some posts which the plaintiff had erected on a vacant piece of ground in front of his shop, they contending, unsuccessfully, that the ground formed part of the street. And, again, in *The Medway Lower Navigation Company v. the Hollingbourne Rural Sanitary Authority* (noted at same page of vol. vi.) damages and costs were obtained against the defendants for taking forcible possession of a triangular piece of ground, which was alleged by them to form part of the highway, but which was found upon the evidence not to have been dedicated to the public. It is true that these cases had reference not precisely to such grassy strips as we have been considering, but in one instance to land adjoining a street and in the other to a triangular or corner plot of ground. But the same principle applies to all. Other cases might be quoted, but enough has been said to show that a question of this kind is always one of considerable nicety, depending upon the application of the principle mentioned to facts which are not always easy of ascertainment, and the elucidation of which may necessitate the sifting of conflicting evidence.

\* \* \*

**Another Lucrative Appointment.** In the town of Penryn, the local authority must have very little work for officials, have very little money, or be remarkably parsimonious. They have recently advertised for a "person" to perform the duties of inspector of nuisances and surveyor, at a salary not less than £40 a year. On further perusal of the advertisement, however, one gathers that this magnificent sum represents only the remuneration on the sanitary inspector side, for candidates are further tempted by the announcement that "the person appointed will also be required to perform the duties of surveyor to the council, at a salary of £5 per annum." The discrepancy between the remuneration as inspector of nuisances and that given as surveyor is, we are all aware, due to the fact that when the appointment of an inspector of nuisances is made with the sanction of the Local Government Board half the salary is paid by that department. We trust, however, that before sanctioning this appointment the Local Government Board will carefully consider whether £45 a year is adequate remuneration for discharging the duties of inspector of nuisances and of surveyor, even in a place like Penryn.

# Comparative Reports of General Practice.

## XXX.—TRAMWAY TRACTION : WEST BROMWICH REPORT.—II.

BLACKPOOL (ELECTRIC CONDUIT SYSTEM).

The system in operation at Blackpool is known as the electric conduit system. In 1885 the corporation laid down the tramway and leased the running powers to a company for seven years. At the expiration of this period, in September, 1892, the corporation purchased the undertaking and plant for the sum of £15,587. In addition to this, they had expended £13,435 in the construction of the permanent way, making a total of £29,022. On the completion of the purchase it was found necessary to relay part of the conduit and to replace and repair part of the plant and machinery.

Permanent Way.—The electric tramways run through 5 miles of streets, 3 miles being single and 2 miles double. The gauge is 4 ft. 8½ in., and the rails are of the girder type, 92 lb. to 97 lb. per yard. The paving is generally of granite, but there is also some wood paving. The conduit is in the centre of the rails, the slot being ⅜ in. and ⅝ in. The conductors are of pure copper tubing, insulated from the channel, the insulators being 9 ft. apart.

Rolling Stock.—The electric cars are of two sizes. There are four large ones, each capable of carrying eighty-two passengers—forty-four inside and thirty-eight outside. They weigh 11 tons 14 cwt., and are of the double-decked four-wheeled bogie type. The small cars are ten in number and carry fifty-four persons. They weigh 4½ tons each. All the cars are lighted by electricity, as at Leeds. The speed of the electric cars is 8 miles per hour, they stop when required, and the charge is 1d. over the entire distance in the winter and 2d. in the summer.

Power Station.—The power for the electric tramways is supplied from the general electric lighting station, which is about midway, the engines being 25 horse-power compound engines, coupled to two four-poled generators. The current is direct, no accumulators being used either in the station or on the cars. The deputation were very much struck with the class of engines in use for driving the generators, which, they were informed, were in use for the first time for electric works.

General Notes.—The capital invested in the electric lines is £55,372. The circumstances in Blackpool are very different to those in any large commercial town. Not only is the population subject to enormous fluctuations, but in the case of the conduit line the effects of the sea water and sand have to be contended with. The Blackpool Corporation had during the winters of 1894-96 to relay the whole of the conduit along the promenade on a new principle, at a nett cost of £6,754. In spite of this large expenditure on the conduit, supplemented as it was by a further expenditure during the following years of £1,196 for repairs, &c., the trouble increased rather than decreased and the committee decided that a radical change in the system was necessary. They therefore, after consideration, recommended the corporation to abandon the conduit system and substitute for it the overhead trolley system. In a report of the sub-committee of the Blackpool Corporation the relative costs of maintaining the similar portions, exclusive of repairs to roadway, rails, motors, gearing, cars, &c., of the three systems—viz., overhead, conduit and accumulators—on the present Blackpool system is stated as follows: Overhead system (line, &c.) estimated, £600 ; conduit system (conduit, &c.) cost 1897 actual, £2,238; and accumulator system (accumulator, &c.) estimated, £2,799.

GAS TRAMS (BLACKPOOL TO LYTHAM).

Permanent Way.—The gas trams run between South Shore, Blackpool (where the line joins the electric conduit line) and St. Anne's and Lytham. The line is 7 miles long, and is single, with passing places, the gauge is also 4 ft. 8½ in. and the steepest gradient is 1 in 26. One mile of this line is within the borough boundary, and has been laid by the corporation and is leased to the company.

Rolling Stock.—The cars, of which there are sixteen, are smaller than those on the electric line. Four of the cars carry forty—sixteen inside and twenty-four out—and weigh about 7 tons. The remaining twelve cars carry fifty-two passengers —twenty-two in and thirty out—and weigh from 7½ to 8 tons. They are supplied with ordinary gas at the depot, one charge

BRISTOL ELECTRIC TRAMWAY: OLD MARKET-STREET TERMINUS.

being sufficient for 9 miles. The speed is 8 miles per hour, and the cars run at intervals of fifteen minutes in the borough and thirty to forty minutes outside. In the winter a twenty minutes' service to and from Lytham and Blackpool is maintained, and in the summer a ten minutes' service.

*General Notes.*—The advantages of this system are stated to be : (1) The low cost of traction ; (2) the absence of the overhead apparatus or conduit. The disadvantages are : (1) The unpleasant smell ; (2) the vibration ; (3) the difficulty of ascending gradients ; (4) the noise and rattle of machinery. This system has only been in operation about eighteen months, and is therefore still in the experimental stage, and as the track is quite local (with two exceptions) it is exceedingly doubtful whether the cars could mount the steep gradient at Holloway Bank. Your sub-committee are of opinion that, taking all the various conditions into consideration, this system would not be suitable for this district.

## BRISTOL.

There are two systems of tramways in Bristol—*viz.*, horse and overhead electric—both owned and worked by a company, the latter having been in use since 1895. The lease to the company was for twenty-one years, and it has still sixteen years to run.

*Permanent Way.*—The various lines, with the exception of one small length, were constructed by the company. The electric line commences at the western or city end of Old Market-street, where it joins two lines of horse cars. There is a double track for most of the route. The power station, which is in Beaconsfield-road, a turning south of main road close to St. George's Church, is about equi-distant from the extreme ends of the route. On leaving Old Market-street the line continues in an easterly direction, *vid* Lawrence-hill and Redfield-road to Kingswood ; there is also a branch line along Stapleton-road. The total distance of track is now about 8 miles, a total length measured in single track of 10 miles. The gradients vary from 1 in 15 (a length of 220 yards), and half a mile from Kingswood terminus it has an elevation of 300 ft. over the starting point in Old Market-street. The gauge is 4 ft. 8½ in., and the rails are of the girder pattern, 96 lb. per yard. The paving is generally granite, but wood paving is used in the centre of the city.

*Conducting System.*—The standards are of steel tubes in three lengths, which overlap, and are shrunk together whilst hot. The tube enters 6 ft. into the ground, and over it a cast-iron base is passed and bedded in concrete. They are placed at the edge of the footway on the south side of the road, except in Old Market-street and Lawrence-hill, where they are placed in the centre and have brackets on either side. The standards erected in the middle of Old Market-street are surmounted alternately by electric arc lamps, the wires being 22 ft. above the road.

*Rolling Stock.*—The rolling stock consists of twenty-one motor cars, each sufficiently powerful to draw an ordinary trailer car. The car bodies were built by Messrs. Milnes & Co., of Birkenhead, and are mounted on cantilever trucks made by the Peckham Motor Truck and Wheel Company of New York. The cars are all fitted with a bell arrangement on the top of the car, by which passengers on the top can easily and expeditiously communicate to the conductor their desire to get off. They will carry forty-four passengers—eighteen inside and twenty-six out—and weigh 5½ tons. Six new motor cars have lately been added, which are mounted on Peckham cantilever expansion trucks. They are larger than the earlier cars, and carry fifty-three passengers—twenty-four inside and twenty-nine out. Each car is provided with two motors of 15 horse-power ; the weight of each motor is 19 cwt. The colours of the cars are different on each route, and at night different coloured lamps are also used, the arrangement contributing very much to public convenience and utility. There are two separate systems of lighting the cars, which are employed simultaneously. In both incandescent lamps are used, but the one system is from the main circuit, whilst the other is supplied from accumulators. On the trolley wire circuit are five lamps of 16 candle-power each. One is placed on a standard 4 ft. 6 in. high on the roof and four are placed inside the cars over the seats. The lamps served by the accumulators consist of one lamp on a standard on the roof, a coloured bull's-eye at either end of the car, and a head lamp on the hood over the driver. The employment of accumulators ensures that the car will always be adequately lighted, even though the current from the power station should be cut off, either by the trolley being disconnected from the trolley wire or by

stoppage of the generators at the station. The accumulators supply sufficient current to light the lamps for eight hours. The speed is 8 miles per hour, and the service is at intervals of six and twelve minutes, except on Saturdays, when it is every four and a half and nine minutes. Convenient stopping places have been established on the line of route, these positions being indicated by rings conspicuously painted round the poles, and the system is said to answer remarkably well, having many advantages. The line is divided into three 1d. stages, and the charge from end to end is 3d. Workmen's cars are run at certain hours, the first car being at 4.50 a.m., and the fare on them is 1d. for any distance. They are greatly appreciated and extensively patronised.

*Power Station.*—The power station and tramway sheds are situated midway on the route at St. George's. The boilers are four Lancashire boilers of Siemens-Martin steel, manufactured by Messrs. D. Adamson & Co., and are fitted with Green's fuel economisers and mechanical stokers. The engines are four of MacIntosh & Seymour's horizontal compound engines, with high-pressure cylinders, direct coupled to 150-kilowatt generators of the six-pole type. The engines are 250 horse-power each, and the station is the largest tram-

BRISTOL ELECTRIC TRAMWAY : CENTRE POLES AND BRACKETS.

way station in England, and this is the first instance of the use of engines of this class in England. The engine and boiler house is at the rear of the car shed, and there are fitting and paint shops attached for repairs, also a superintendent's house and general stores.

*General Notes.*—The tram company supply eight public lamps with electricity, each lamp being equipped with five incandescent glow lamps of 16 candle-power each, and these lamps are supplied by the company free of charge. No accidents have happened from falling wires, and very few through frightening horses, and none of a serious character. The total cost of the present installation, including conversion of lines, overhead work, power station and cars, was about £50,000. It is stated that the cost per car mile run with a seven and a half minutes' service is 5½d. as against 9½d. with horses, and the receipts have largely increased since the conversion. The cost per electrical unit is 1·66d.

**Coole.**—Local Government Board sanction has been refused in connection with an application of the council for sanction to borrow £1,000 for works of sewage disposal at Swinefleet. A more expensive scheme will have to be provided.

## THE VALUE OF STREET SWEEPINGS.

### AN INTERESTING INVESTIGATION.

An investigation of much practical interest has been carried out by the United States Department of Agriculture concerning the fertilising or manurial value of street sweepings. Letters of inquiry were sent to the officials in charge of street-cleaning departments in the 354 cities and towns of the United States having 10,000 or more inhabitants. As the result, more or less complete data relating to the disposal of the street sweepings of 204 cities and towns were obtained. It appears, says *The Times*, that sixty of these succeed in disposing of some portion of their street sweepings for agricultural purposes, seventy-four make no attempt to turn to account the fertilising value of the material, though some part of the latter is used for filling in low land, for reclaiming marsh land, &c., and the remaining seventy dump the material in streams or other bodies of water, or on land, without any systematic attempt at utilisation. In general terms it may

BRISTOL ELECTRIC TRAMWAY: SIDE POLE AND BRACKET.

be said that cities representing one-fourth of the entire urban population of the country make an effort to utilise the fertilising value of some portion of their street sweepings. Reasons are assigned for estimating the total quantity of street sweepings annually collected throughout the country at not far short of 3,000,000 tons, this being based upon a calculated average of 160 tons per 1,000 inhabitants per annum.

The fertilising value of the sweepings varies greatly with the nature of the pavements, being practically nothing in the case of material off macadamised roads, and approaching that of good stable manure in the case of material collected on the band-swept and well paved streets of crowded cities. The regulations in different cities as to the nature of the substances which may be thrown into the alleys and streets, and thus find their way into the material collected by the sweepers, vary so widely that there is necessarily a corresponding difference in the cost of sorting and preparing the material for spreading on the land. It is believed that the rapidly increasing sentiment in favour of the careful separation and systematic utilisation of all kinds of city waste will tend to remove this difficulty, and thus increase the value of sweepings, particularly of such as are collected in alleys, where the percentage of miscellaneous rubbish is now often very great. In autumn the quantity, and in many cases the quality, of the street sweepings are much enhanced by the falling leaves. There appears to be a dearth of recent literature on the subject of the fertilising value of the material under notice.

In 1892 the *Landwirtschaftliche Presse* published an analysis of sweepings from the asphalt-paved streets of Berlin, which yielded the following percentages: Moisture, 38·69; ash, 37·67; organic matter, 22·44; total nitrogen, 0·479; ammoniacal nitrogen, 0·004; phosphorus pentoxide, 0·452; potash, 0·370; lime, 1·491; magnesia, 0·347. A sample representing the accumulations for four weeks of the sweepings from a street in Trenton, New Jersey, in 1895 yielded on analysis 0·18 per cent. of nitrogen, 0·3 per cent. of phosphorus pentoxide, and 0·19 per cent. of potash; this material was valued at 90 cents per ton. From the tabulated results of analysis of eighteen samples of sweepings obtained from the streets of Washington City we learn that the percentages of the substances named ranged between the following extremes: Organic matter, 35·5 and 10·2; nitrogen, 1·18 and 0·17; phosphorus pentoxide, 0·16 and 0·1; potash, 0·5 and 0·08.

An effort was made to supplement the analytical data with the results of practical tests made by farmers to determine the value of street sweepings as a source of plant food for field and garden crops, and as a source of the humus which is indispensable to the good mechanical condition of many soils. Evidence was forthcoming to show that well-selected and judiciously-used street sweepings possess considerable manurial value. Out of sixteen quoted letters, only four of which report unfavourable results, we may briefly notice two or three. A farmer who uses the sweepings from Atlanta, Georgia, finds 1 ton of them to be about equal to half a ton of mixed stable manure (two-thirds cow, one-third horse); he has used the sweepings for three years for maize, wheat, oats, rye and potatoes, broadcasting about 20 tons per acre, and his lands have greatly improved. At Norfolk, Virginia, a grower has been using street sweepings for several years, and with much profit, on spinach, cabbage, kale and potatoes; he finds that their effect on the land is much more lasting than that of stable manure. At Pittsburg, Pennsylvania, street sweepings are used very largely in the parks, with excellent results; the material is powerful and quick in its action, and gives a capital growth of grass, whilst its effect is more lasting than that of artificial manures. A Californian hop-grower puts the street sweepings of Sacramento direct on the hop hills.

The exact monetary value of street sweepings is, of course, not easy to determine. Using the very conservative estimate of 10 cents. per pound for the nitrogen, and disregarding the phosphoric acid and the potash, Mr. Ervin Ewell, the chemist who has prepared the bulletin, calculates that the samples analysed would range in value between $1·46 and 34 cents. per ton. The material, however, has its uses in addition to the fertilising value of the plant food it contains. Gardeners, for example, appreciate it on account of its improving the mechanical condition of stiff and badly-aërated soils. Sixteen cities reported the prices at which street sweepings are sold to farmers, and these prices vary from 15 cents. to $2 per ton. It is hoped that the publication of this bulletin will result in improved methods for the collection of street sweepings and in the extension of their use for maintaining the productiveness of land.

---

**Bakewell.**—A Local Government Board inquiry has been held by Colonel A. J. Hepper with respect to an application of the council for sanction to borrow £1,120 for the carrying out of sewerage and sewage disposal works in the village of Longstone.

**A Useful Russian Practice.**—Prompted by a letter that recently appeared in *The Times* with reference to the difficulties cyclists had to contend with owing to the absence of any notification in England enabling them to discover the names of railway stations or of villages through which they pass, Mr. Francis H. E. Palmer writes to a contemporary that at the entrance and exit of every Russian village a notice board is placed upon which is inscribed, not only the name of the village and of the administrative district, but also the number of adult male and female inhabitants, and of the *izbas* that it contains. To this other information is often added, such as the area of the land in the hands of the peasants and of small local proprietors respectively, as well as the names of and distance to the nearest village or town. The village signboard also generally indicates where the nearest licensed country doctor can be found in case of accident.

# The Traffic Problem in London.

## THE VIEWS OF SIR JOHN WOLFE BARRY.

Sir John Wolfe Barry, F.R.S., is the new chairman of the council of the Society of Arts, and at the opening meeting of that body for the session, last week, he delivered the customary address, selecting as his subject " The Internal Traffic of London." The particular question he proposed to consider was, he said, that of the means of communication of London's inhabitants with each other by means of its streets and thoroughfares. This he took to be one of the pressing matters of the present time, not only in respect of the existing state of things, but still more in view of the future requirements of our ever-growing population ; and if he could bring forward sufficient information and such a view of the questions involved as to induce some systematic consideration of that great subject he should feel his labour had not been thrown away. The first part of the paper was devoted to a discussion of the factors which have led to the enormous expansion of the traffic in London streets during the last thirty or forty years, and some interesting figures were produced showing the increase in the means of bringing traffic from the extremities to the central parts, and the movements of population to which, with other causes, their development is due. No one who had lived in London could, be said, doubt that the pressure on the streets was getting yearly heavier and heavier and becoming more and more unmanageable. Considering the new streets and widenings of streets effected in the last fifty years or so with the view of facilitating the constantly-growing streams of traffic, he remarked on the smallness of the mileage and capital expended as compared with the outlays of railway and tramway companies.

### LONDON STREET IMPROVEMENTS.

In the matter of street improvements in London one could not but notice an almost entire absence of grasp of a large subject, and in the history of the past forty years we looked in vain for any new arterial thoroughfares traversing inner London from end to end and proportioned in width to the demands upon them at different parts of their route. On the contrary, we found in the new streets, as in the old, that the nearer they were to the heaviest of the traffic the narrower they were in absolute dimensions. Cheapside, Fleet-street, Piccadilly, the Strand, Marylebone and Euston roads remained very much as they were fifty years ago, when the traffic was a mere fraction of what it is now. He desired to speak with all respect of those who executed the idea of Regent-street, for Nash's wide Waterloo-place and Regent-street, with its circuses at Piccadilly and Oxford-street, was a work conceived in a large-minded way. But most at least of modern street improvements seemed piecemeal and patchwork enterprises, narrowed to the smallest dimensions that would pass muster, and without any but the most meagre provision for the future, or, except in the case of Regent-street, the slightest attempt at systematic artistic treatment. In fact, there had been and was now a hitherto incurable petitesse in dealing with such matters in London which was in great contrast to what we saw in foreign cities of far less importance and wealth. It was to be carefully borne in mind that the want of accommodation for traffic in London streets was not merely a question of grumbling from those that suffered from it, but involved many other considerations, such as loss of money in the delays to men of business, loss of time to vehicles and horses, the practical impossibility of introducing cheaper and more expeditious means of transit, like electric trams, and the great want of free circulation of air. His plea was that to meet the traffic of London it was not so much additional railways, underground or overground, traversing the town and connected with the suburbs that were wanted as wide arterial improvements of the streets themselves. Strictly urban railways, or rather trains that only traversed the town itself, though carrying immense numbers of passengers, had not dealt with the question and would not produce the desired result of relieving the streets ; on the contrary, they tended to add to the congestion from the point of view of both urban movement and suburban influx.

### SIR JOHN WOLFE BARRY'S SCHEME.

In his judgment street improvements in London should be considered as a whole and in a large-minded way, unless we were to be doomed to perpetual disappointment. A scheme of new main thoroughfares of adequate width for present and future traffic should be laid down and realised as time and finance permitted. There should be continuity of effort towards radical amelioration by the construction of great main lines of through communication as distinguished from merely local improvements, and all local improvements, as was the case in Paris and other foreign cities, should be devised so as to form parts of a harmonious whole. Apart from wide streets, a matter which had been too much lost sight of was the provision of means for allowing the north and south traffic to cross the east and west traffic with the least possible confusion. If some means could be devised for the crossing of north and south traffic over or under that going east and west at places like Hyde Park-corner, Piccadilly-circus, Ludgate-hill and Wellington-street, the relief to the main thoroughfares at those points would be enormous. The results would be well worth the expenditure, heavy though it might be, and, having given some consideration to the subject at the points above mentioned, he could say there was nothing impracticable in the suggestion. After a few words on the thoroughfares of the south sides of the Thames, the speaker referred to what he recognised as of more importance and urgency—viz., the north bank and the three main lines of east and west communication. The Euston-road (with Praed-street and Chapel-street at the west and the Pentonville and City roads at the east), Oxford-street (including Uxbridge-road, Holborn and Cheapside), and the Strand (including Fleet-street, Ludgate-hill and Cannon-street) were all almost ludicrously inadequate. In the case of the Euston-road route, where shortcomings were the least glaring, the necessary widenings and improvements would involve less serious consequences than in the other thoroughfares. The Oxford-street route, with the exception of some narrow places near Notting Hill-gate station and the confused crossing at the Marble Arch, was fairly adequate as far east as Edgware-road, but from that point a radical improvement, either by means of important widenings or by a new street, was wanted, and should be carried through the City so as to connect at its eastern end with the Mile End-road. In the case of the Strand, Fleet-street and Piccadilly, it seemed to him that the only course was a systematic widening of all three thoroughfares, with a broad diagonal street from Piccadilly-circus, viâ Coventry-street, to join the widened Strand near Wellington-street. Another want that was beginning to be pressing was a route for bicycle traffic. One could not but recognise what an advantage it would be to the bulk of Londoners if they could travel safely at perhaps 8 miles or 10 miles an hour to and from their work. He did not suppose the present price of bicycles would last very long, and it did not seem too sanguine to expect that a few years hence they would be sold at about one-fourth their present price. When this took place were Londoners to be debarred from their use because the streets were so crowded with vehicular traffic as to be too dangerous for bicycles ? That would seem hereafter to be as absurd a proposition as that foot passengers ought not now to be accommodated in the streets because of the requirements of vehicular traffic. If these views of future requirements were correct, he thought they wanted one new and spacious thoroughfare east and west, about 120 ft. wide—as wide, that was, as Whitehall opposite the Horse Guards. It might leave the Bayswater-road near Westbourne-terrace, follow the line of Wigmore-street to Russell-square behind the British Museum, and thence run to near Bread-street station. In addition, there should be two or three thoroughfares north and south, slightly less in width, which should be carried over the east and west route by bridges at the points of intersection ; and all these new routes should have a raised or sunken road for bicycles, so that they should not mix either with vehicular or pedestrian traffic. The cost of such a work doubtless presented rather an alarming prospect, for a street 120 ft. wide and 4 or 5 miles long must mean many millions of money, though the recoupment from the new frontages would be very important. Such, however, was the kind of undertaking required for London of the future.

### WAYS AND MEANS.

In conclusion, he said he feared that in the street improvements he had sketched he would be thought to hold extravagant and Utopian views, but when he contemplated the vast sums spent by railway and public companies to bring traffic to London, and realised what had been done by Continental nations to improve their means of transit in their capitals and to embellish them, he could not see that Londoners should consider the cost of such measures in the metropolis of the kingdom (might he not say of the Greater Britain ?) as prohibitory. The heavy expenditure should not affright us, for it would be repaid by the increased facilities both for trade and pleasure. He could not but think that the relief of the present congestion of our streets by a well-considered enlargement of the arteries of London was a subject which must commend itself as of primary importance to the whole city—nay, more, to the whole nation. It was worthy of the fullest consideration by those who would devote themselves to no peddling treatment, but to such a large-minded plan of a remodelled town as was made by Wren in respect of the City of London after the great fire, and as had been so successfully carried out in Paris, where he supposed the cost of land and construction differed but little from similar values in London.

---

**Redditch.**—A Board of Trade inquiry was recently held by Lord Jersey and Colonel Boughey with respect to the proposed light railway for Redditch and district. Mr. Pritchett is the engineer of the scheme, which is estimated to cost £15,500. It is opposed by the district council on the ground that one of the streets through which the line would pass is but 16 ft. 10 in. wide at one point.

# The Sanitary Institute.

## THE SEVENTEENTH ANNUAL CONGRESS.—IX.

### WATER SUPPLY.

In addition to several incidental references to the important question of water supply, four valuable papers, which dealt exclusively with one phase or other of the subject were read at the recent Sanitary Institute congress at Birmingham. We refer first to the contribution of Dr. J. SPOTTISWOODE CAMERON, medical officer of health for Leeds, on

THE PURCHASE OF THE CATCH MENT AREA AS A
MEANS OF PROTECTING THE SOURCES OF
A PUBLIC WATER SUPPLY.

In the opening of his paper Dr. CAMERON remarked that the duty of cleansing wells, the honour given to well-borers, the many lawsuits on account of the diversion of springs, all testified to the importance the community had always, in all countries, attached to the sufficiency and, so far as their knowledge went, to the purity of common water supplies. The impounding of river and surface waters, their storage in reservoirs and tanks—interfering, as it so frequently did, with private rights—was in this country almost impossible on any large scale except by the exercise of special powers only to be obtained by Act of Parliament. While public health law had conferred upon sanitary authorities the right to provide their district, or part of it, with a proper water supply by constructing waterworks, digging wells, leasing or hiring waterworks, or by contracting with other persons for a supply, the rights of private owners so continually interfered with the carrying out of such powers that it was usually necessary to obtain the sanction of Parliament for the construction of any important works. The writer then continued :—

WATERWORKS CLAUSES ACT, 1847.

·All waterworks undertakers, whether sanitary authorities or others, are required by statute law to conform to certain conditions, and they have, on the other hand, certain powers of protecting the water supply given to them. The Waterworks Clauses Act of 1847 contains the more important of these powers. These clauses, it will be remembered, were the consolidation into an Act of provisions which it had been usual before that time to insert in private Acts. Certain of these clauses (18 to 27), restrictive in their nature and applicable to mines, are incorporated, with modifications, by the Public Health Act, 1875, Support of Sewers (Amendment Act), 1883, into the sanitary Acts incumbent upon all authorities. Other clauses of the 1847 Act require that the undertakers, whether a waterworks company or a sanitary authority, shall keep and provide in their pipes pure and wholesome water sufficient for the domestic use of all the inhabitants of the town or district within the limits of the special Act. But this section (35), while requiring them to keep this pure water in their pipes, does not confer any special powers for so doing. The sections of this 1847 Act, referring to protection of water, deal (54) with the providing of cisterns and cocks, enact penalties (55) on persons allowing such apparatus to get out of repair, give rights of repair and observation in regard to the structures, and protect the undertakers against waste.

More cognate, however, to the subject of this paper is sec. 61, which makes it penal for anyone (1) to bathe, or wash or throw an animal into a stream, reservoir, aqueduct or other works belonging to the undertakers; to (2) throw any rubbish into or do any kind of washing in such stream, &c. ; (3) cause the water of any sink, sewer or drain, steam engine, boiler or other filthy water belonging to him or under his control to run or be brought into any stream, &c. ; or do any other act whereby the water of the undertakers shall be fouled. The penalty for any offence against this section is limited to £5, but there is a recurring penalty of 20s. a day should the last-mentioned offence be continued. There are also other sections relating to protection against effluents from gasworks, which I need not remind you of.[*]

It is therefore principally sec. 61 of the 1847 Act that has to be relied upon by a waterworks authority as a means of protection against the fouling of the sources of supply. There are, it is true, certain powers in the Rivers Pollution Prevention Act, 1876, dealing specially with sewage pollutions and mining or manufacturing effluents. But this Act is hampered with such restrictions as to make it extremely difficult to administer against an old offender. With the exception of the ordinary public health powers for the abatement of nuisances, these are the essential powers possessed by water authorities for the protection of their supply, and the question naturally arises, Are they sufficient ?

While sec. 61 practically prohibits personal bathing or washing of an animal, the washing of clothes, or skins, &c., or the throwing of dirt into a " watercourse," it does not say exactly what a watercourse is. In many of our upland districts a fairly pure water is collected from large areas of moor

[* The further Act of 1863, dealing principally with the security of reservoirs, enabled the undertakers to cut off water supply where injury had been done and increased the strength of the law in regard to waste or the fouling through the pipes, but practically left the powers of protection much as in the Waterworks Clauses Act of 1847.]

and pasture land. The whole surface of the hills sloping to its river basin is really part of the water catchment, but only certain habitual courses of water could be called streams. These hills are often steep, and practically anything put upon the land is liable to be carried down by the rain to the watercourses. The average farmer cannot be made to understand that the heap of manure from his stable, midden or byre, the liquid from which is allowed to trickle over his land, can be in any way objected to by a water authority; and yet he generally selects for the site of his manure heap, if not the actual bank of the stream, some steeply sloping ground, which would in heavy rain contribute surface water to the neighbouring runnels.

WHAT CONSTITUTES INFRINGEMENT ?

The question then arises, Does he in any way infringe this section ? He does not throw this rubbish into the stream, or reservoir or aqueduct. The rain which passes over the ground, carrying with it some of the filth, is not, he would contend, exactly filthy water belonging to him or under his control which he can be said to cause to run or be brought into the stream. He does not intentionally make a channel from his manure heap to the watercourse. On the other hand, in a sort of half-hearted way he will dig grips across the course of this liquid to keep it longer upon the land ; and having done this he will consider that he has done all that can be required of him under the section.

The convenience attached to his house is generally placed in the garden, a little away from the dwelling, but not unfrequently it is on some high bank, the surface water from which gravitates towards the stream ; but this place, he will tell you, has been so situated within the memory of man and he does not see how anybody can reasonably object to it. A wayside inn receiving travellers and fishermen, who are not always necessarily exempt from infective disease, has a convenience of the kind mentioned at the back, and the night-soil has to be removed from the immediate neighbourhood of the trout stream. The person who removes it is not as careful of it as if it were refined gold, and if a little escapes from his wheelbarrow as he takes it away he will regard such an accident as of trifling consequence. But possibly, with the march of civilisation and increasing visits of fishermen, the landlord places a water-closet for the convenience of his customers in an upper storey, and conducts the pipes into the drain or the cesspool bordering upon the stream.

His cesspool has to have an overflow, and is supposed to be emptied on to the land at some distance from the stream; but I can assure you that such is really the case. Such conditions as I have described are not imaginary, but are drawn from fact. What power has the waterworks authority, say the corporation of a neighbouring town, under the section to get rid of this nuisance. If they catch the man emptying his filth into the river they can go to the rural magistrates and ask to have him fined £5. If they find that he has made a distinct channel from his house to convey the slops to the stream they can do the same. In one instance, in the house attached to an almost disused flour mill, after remonstrance from the authority, the drain from a slop-sink at the front had been cut off from the stream, but it was afterwards found that a small gutter at the back had evidently been utilised instead for the conveyance of slops into the mill-lead, and thence of course into the stream. But who is to watch the family in this house, to see that they send no foul liquids into the back ?

The authority have, I take it, no power to seal up these apertures and to say " Not only shall you not use them, but we shall take them away." A conviction could, of course, only be obtained against an offender by proving the actual commission of the offence. But the object of sanitary science surely is the prevention rather than the removal of nuisances ; and I suggest that a water authority ought to have powers of entering upon premises and making alterations of such premises, at their own expense, of such a character as shall make it easier for the occupiers to use them in a cleanly than in a dirty manner.

It is not to be expected that a farmer living on the side of a stream which has been impounded for waterworks purposes should himself go the expense of rearranging the position of his midden, or of his stable, or of making a small sewage farm for the slops from his house, and carrying such slops carefully over land, so that they may be purified before reaching the stream, and of doing this, moreover, in such a way that a heavy rainfall shall not carry any of the unpurified effluent directly into the water catchment.

The expenditure of money for such purposes is evidently one for the water consumer who comes into the valley and takes the water. I say advisedly that the farmer does not intentionally foul the water, and that in many cases it would be difficult to convict him of so doing. A fortiori, it would be impossible to make him provide such necessary works that the lines of least resistance should be on the side of purity.

CONTROL OF CATCHMENT AREAS.

Many towns have experienced these difficulties, and the

increasing stress laid by health officers and engineers upon the importance of having the supply of a large town not only pure, but above suspicion, has driven many towns to seek to obtain not merely the right of catching comparatively pure water as it flows, but by acquiring the rights of a landlord to be able to make such structural alterations as may be necessary on the various farmsteads within their catchment area. Manchester, I believe, claims to be one of the first towns to have acquired the freehold of the catchment area of a new waterworks. I am told that they have done this around Thirlmere. They have also, I believe, acquired a strip of land along their Longdendale areas. Birmingham, I understand, has acquired the absolute ownership of the basin feeding the Elan and Claerwen, and Liverpool has also acquired the ownership of such of the land as is not common land carrying the water to their reservoir at Vyrnwy.

Leeds, in the 1896-97 session of Parliament, applied for compulsory powers of purchase of a large portion of their catchment area in the Washburn Valley. The circumstances were a little unusual and may warrant a word or two about them. The Waterworks Committee had been aware for some time that there had been certain undesirable conditions in the farmsteads in the valley, and had made various endeavours, in the first instance through the local authorities and afterwards through the West Riding Rivers Board, to bring pressure to bear upon the various occupiers of these places to prevent possible pollution. In a great many cases by mutual consent a rearrangement of structure was made at the expense of the Leeds Corporation, but a few of the dangers were of such a nature that it was difficult to see how they could be averted without somewhat expensive alterations.

One of the worst of the cases was carefully gone into with a view of considering whether legal action should be taken under existing powers, and we were advised that it would be difficult to get a conviction before rural justices on such evidence as it was possible to furnish. About this time it was thought desirable to build some further reservoirs higher up the valley, and the waterworks engineer suggested that in going to Parliament for this purpose we should acquire the land necessary for the reservoirs and the ground feeding them, and at the same time that we should acquire compulsory powers of purchase of a wide margin along the side of all our streams tributary to the existing reservoirs.

The Act was prepared, but before it went through its final stages it was thought desirable to postpone the erection of these reservoirs and works, but the committee were unwilling to forego the occasion of seeking for powers of compulsory purchase of land; and I am told that the Leeds Act of 1897 has established a precedent, as it is the first Act in which compulsory powers of purchase of land for the protection of waterworks has been given apart from the construction of works. If this is so, it will probably make it easier in future for corporations having existing reservoirs to go to Parliament and ask for power to purchase the land around these reservoirs merely for the purpose of protecting the purity of their supply, and although they are not intending to erect upon them reservoirs or other structural works. It is, of course, evident that the owner of the land can insist upon his tenant conforming to such regulations for the protection of water as he may choose to make. If the tenant refuses he gets notice to quit. The advantages are so obvious that I need not detain the section by enlarging upon them.

## DISCUSSION.

Mr. WM. WHITAKER (Croydon) could only find one fault with the paper—it viewed the subject from a Northern aspect. What would be easy to do in the North might be difficult in the South. In the North they had large populations, great wealth, and cheap land in the moorland districts. In the South they found large towns with well supplies. The land was very often valued as agricultural land, and consequently more expensive. On the other hand, they could perhaps deal with sewage more advantageously than in the North. He was dealing with the supply of a large town, which was fairly wealthy, and had a catchment area of pasture land, more or less, with occasional habitations. It would be impossible to buy the land; how could they protect it? He agreed with Dr. Cameron's suggestion that a water authority should have powers of entering upon premises and altering them. In Croydon they had made arrangements to take into their own sewerage system the sewage of other places. Each county must take its own line, without reference to a central authority, which, as a general rule, he thought should only come in when the councils failed to do their duty. This, he considered, they were not inclined to do. It would be good if the Local Government Board could be made to prevent damage to water supplies rather than to prevent water supplies doing damage.

The Rev. Dr. COX (chairman of the Brixworth District Council) said Northampton, which had two-thirds of its catchment area in the Brixworth district, was anxious to get the latter authority to put their powers in action, and they found on farmer's premises defects which were not sufficiently grave to need taking into account if they had not been on a catchment area. The farmers felt that complaints would not have been made if the Northampton reservoir had not been there. He hoped Northampton would see their way to purchase the catchment area, and so to relieve the rural district council of their responsibility.

Mr. HENMAN having added a few remarks, Dr. CAMERON, in reply, said that he did not consider the question of the cost of land entered so much into account as Mr. Whitaker seemed to think. A corporation could borrow at some 2½ per cent., and, as the land purchased did not lose its value after purchase, no loss need be made.

## THE WATER SUPPLY OF RURAL DISTRICTS.

In his paper on some sanitary defects in rural districts Mr. G. H. SMITH, New Malden, Surrey, gave some space to the above subject, as follows :—

In the reports of the medical inspectors of the Local Government Board one of the most frequent matters complained of in rural districts is the water supply ; and yet how terribly slow are the local authorities in taking action. The usual sources of dietetic water in the country are three in number —viz., shallow wells, the rivers and the ponds. The shallow wells are perhaps the largest source of supply. They are usually sunk in the garden attached to the house, often without steining, seldom provided with protection from surface pollution, and rarely cleaned out. The cesspool is generally in the same plot of land, and not unfrequently geologically above the well and within 50 ft. of it, and, of course, not watertight ; in fact, the chief advantage of a cesspool in the eyes of a villager is that it seldom requires emptying. The dangers here are obvious to all of you, especially when dry seasons occur, when the action of the pump, where there is one, tends to draw in the soakage from the cesspool.

The rivers as they pass through the villages generally receive the drainage, directly or indirectly, from some houses, as well as the surface washings from the roads and cultivated lands ; where they run through pastures the cattle are often to be found standing in them, and in the case of small streams dipping ponds for sheep-washing are frequently constructed across them ; yet, polluted as they are, they provide the sole source of potable water for many houses. Ponds are open to the same polluting sources as the rivers, and with more serious effects, there being no self-purifying action taking place with them, as is the case with rivers; the water is stagnant and affords a good breeding place for frogs and other reptiles.

These defects admit of only one remedy—proper supply of pure water from waterworks wherever the houses are sufficiently close together to render it possible, and in other cases deep wells ought to be sunk and carefully guarded against pollution. The question of cost has here to be faced. The Public Health Act, 1875, sec. 62, will not allow the water rate to exceed 2d. per week, and this limit raises great difficulties; but it would appear that the limit might well be raised to 3d. without causing any hardship, as then much could be done, as Mr. R. E. Middleton has shown in a paper read before the Surveyors' Institution in 1895. What is really wanted is a water supply judiciously designed, simple and inexpensive in working, providing about 10 or 12 gallons per head per day. We do not want in country districts a water supply for fire-extinguishing purposes ; the present sources can do for that. Another difficulty, which is being increasingly felt, is the present arrangement of parishes and districts in curious interwoven boundaries. A rearrangement is needed on the lines of the natural watersheds. If such boundaries were adopted water supplies would be greatly facilitated and the pollution of rivers more easily prevented.

Rural authorities are proverbially slow in carrying out sanitary improvements, and it would appear desirable for the Local Government Board to have power to compel a district council to construct waterworks forthwith, after due public inquiry, on the complaint of their medical inspector.

## RECENT PROGRESS IN THE METHODS OF WATER ANALYSIS.

In the Physics, Chemistry and Biology section a paper on the above subject was read by Mr. CLARENCE A. SEYLER, B.SC., F.I.C., who classified the objects of hygienic water analysis under three heads: (1) To determine the general suitability of a new supply for drinking and domestic purposes ; (2) to control the purity of a supply by periodic examination ; (3) to determine the condition of a polluted water (effluent) and its suitability for discharge into a stream or river. A purely chemical side existed to the first of these problems in the action of water upon the metals used for storing it. The author, while admitting that apart from this the biological aspect was fundamentally the most important one in all these questions, drew attention to the failure of direct bacteriological methods to realise the exaggerated expectations formed of them. The enumeration of organisms he considered valueless in ground waters without a previous sterilisation of the well, which was usually impossible ; while in surface waters it rarely afforded any fresh information. The actual detection of pathogenic organisms in polluted waters he regarded as a practically unsolved problem, and the importance attributed to the so-called *bacillus coli communis*, much exaggerated. The true place of the method was in the control of artificial filtration, but all such methods were open to the objection that their results were only known after the mischief was irremediable. For the control of the condition of surface waters he recommended the determination of the colour by Tidy's or Lovibond's colorimeter, coupled with the use of Dibdin's microfilter. In the case of ground waters the author considered that chemical methods were alone available, and discussed the basis on which the interpretation of the chemical results was founded.

METHODS OF WATER ANALYSIS.

The standard methods of water analysis were mostly of long standing, and had undergone little real improvement in recent times. These methods, though not ideal, served their purpose well enough. But the imperfections and difficulties in the processes for the determination of the dissolved oxygen and carbonic acid had delayed the recognition of the importance of these determinations. It was in respect to these two substances that recent progress in the methods of water analysis has been most marked. The gasometric methods, though now very satisfactory, were too laborious, and had the disadvantage of giving only the total carbonic acid, and not its various forms. Pettenkofer's well-known method for carbonic acid was open to the same objection, and was deficient in accuracy. The volumetric methods for dissolved oxygen, such as Schutzenberger's, required very complicated apparatus, and as usually carried out were infected by an error due to diffusion which rendered the results nearly valueless. Recently, Thresh had proposed a method in which nitric oxide acted as an oxygen-carrier and liberated an equivalent of iodine, which could then be titrated. That method gave excellent results, but required an atmosphere of hydrogen or coal-gas, and was still somewhat complicated. The method which he strongly recommended was that of Ludwig Winkley (described by him in *The Chemical News* in 1894). In that method recently precipitated manganese hydrate acted as the carrier of oxygen, and the equivalent iodine was liberated and titrated as in Thresh's method. It was very accurate and of marvellous simplicity. No neutral atmosphere or special apparatus of any kind was necessary, and it could be carried out upon the spot if required. Among the results obtained by the use of this method was the fact that water can be supersaturated with oxygen and remain so. This fact had been proved by himself and Gill independently by saturating the water at a low temperature and raising its temperature, when the water remained supersaturated. He had also proved that if saturated under pressure the water remained largely supersaturated upon removal. He had found this condition of supersaturation not at all uncommon in surface waters. The oxygen available for bacteriological was not, therefore, limited to the solubility of the gas at the actual temperature of the water, and the degree of aëration must strictly be referred, not to the temperature, but to the ratio of oxygen to the dissolved nitrogen.

DETERMINATION OF CARBONIC ACID.

With regard to the carbonic acid, it had long been known that the fixed carbonates in water could be simply titrated with standard acids, and the use of methyl orange as an indicator had vastly simplified this process. Since Trillich, in 1890, showed that free carbonic acid could be accurately titrated by the use of standard sodium hydrate or carbonate with phenolphthalein as indicator a great advance had been possible. It had hitherto been doubted or disputed that natural waters contain calcium carbonate dissolved as bicarbonate. The use of Trillich's method, however, showed him that ground waters constantly contained an excess of carbonic acid over that required to form bicarbonates, and that the total carbonic acid in such cases was divisible into three parts : the free portion, which was acid to phenolphthalein, the fixed, which was combined with the lime, the remainder, which had no effect upon the indicator. By experiments upon artificial and natural water he showed, in 1894, that this remaining carbonic acid was equal to the fixed portion, and that the water therefore behaved analytically, exactly as though containing its lime and magnesia as bicarbonate. This assumption led to correct results for the total carbonic acid, and this was also proved simultaneously in Germany by Kippenberger. This was a very strong argument for the existence of calcium bicarbonate, a question which he was at present further investigating. In the case of potable waters, therefore, he might claim that the question of determining the carbonic acid in all its forms was now solved in a very simple and expeditious manner. He had found it of great value in characterising a ground water and showing the condition of surface waters, and also in investigating the action upon lead, iron and zinc. Recent experiments also enabled him to state that he had tested the methods upon waters deficient in carbonic acid, and therefore alkaline to phenolphthalein, such as sea and estuary waters, and found it gave accurate results. Dittmar, in the *Challenger* reports, strongly urged the search for such a method, which he predicted would have valuable results if systematically applied. He (the author) was at present engaged upon the applicability of the method to sewage and highly polluted effluents, in which case he feared that the presence of ammonia and organic acids, such as butyric acid, would interfere. He had succeeded in completely eliminating the effect of the butyrates, but in strong sewage the ammonia had, unfortunately, proved to interfere seriously. In dilutions such as are necessary to study the process of bacteriolysis in polluted waters he had, however, obtained very good results; and in any case, combined with Dittmar's so-called "vacuum process," he had found a method which he believed fully answered, in a simple way, the exigencies of the problem both as to accuracy and simplicity. The details of those inquiries he would leave for another occasion.

The PRESIDENT (Dr. G. Sims Woodhead), in the course of

the discussion that followed disagreed with the opinion expressed by Mr. Seyler, claiming that a bacteriological examination was very valuable.

WATER ANALYSIS.

In the same section Dr. SIDNEY BARWISE, M.D., D.P.H., read a paper, entitled "The Interpretation of Results of Water Analysis," in the course of which he said that he read it as a protest against the too-frequent practice of some analysts giving definite reports upon the suitability of samples of water for drinking water merely upon the results of single chemical analysis; and he wished to submit that it would be a much better practice for analysts to submit the results of their analyses, to be interpreted by some person who had a thorough knowledge of the pedigree of the water in question, derived from a careful inspection of its source. In the discussion which followed the importance of both biological and bacteriological analysis was laid down, and special stress was laid upon the importance of the samples being properly taken. Hearty votes of thanks were accorded to the readers of the papers.

One of the most interesting contributions to the proceedings of the congress was Mr. Mansergh's able paper on the Birmingham water scheme. This paper, which was illustrated by lantern views, will be given in our next issue, with illustrations.

## ARBITRATIONS AND AWARDS.

At the Midland Hotel, Bradford, on the 5th inst., Mr. R. B. Brosser, Keighley, sat as arbitrator in a case in which Mr. Elias Heaton, dentist, Manningham-lane, Bradford, sought damages against the Ilkley Urban District Council for the construction of a sewer through his land at Ben Rhydding. Mr. J. J. Wright appeared for the plaintiff and Mr. Compston for the council. Witnesses for the plaintiff put the damages at £760. Mr. Charles Gott, Mr. Armistead and Mr. Rhodes Calvert supported this view. For the council, Mr. John Waugh, Mr. W. B. Woodhead and Mr. Prest estimated the damage at £39.

The Southampton Corporation received, at their last meeting, the award of Mr. Gutteridge, architect of that borough, the arbitrator in reference to Tudor House, St. Michael's-square, which was compulsorily acquired in connection with a working classes housing scheme. The owners' claim was for over £300, and the sum awarded was £120.

A series of important arbitration cases was heard at Exeter last week. There were some nine cases dealt with under the recent Torquay Water Act, which gave the corporation power to acquire the whole of the watershed of their water supply, covering some 2,300 acres and seven farms. About one-fifth of this area has already been purchased by private agreement, but several owners have declined to treat in this manner. Hence arbitration became necessary. Mr. A. S. Rendell, of Newton Abbot, was the arbitrator on behalf of the Torquay Corporation in all the cases, and Messrs. A. C. Loveys, of Moreton and Ellis and Drew, of Exeter, were the arbitrators for the respective vendors. Mr. Squirey, land agent, was the agreed umpire, and Mr. Balfour Brown, Q.C., was retained on behalf of the corporation, whilst Mr. H. E. Duke represented the other side. About half the watershed was affected by these cases, and the total sum allowed under the Act for the purchase of the properties and laying-out the land was £40,000. Of this only about one-sixth has been so far expended. The witnesses included, for the claimants, Messrs. A. E. Ellis, F.S.I., Exeter ; J. Bowerman, timber merchant, Bridgewater ; Arthur C. Loveys, F.S.I., Moreton-hampstead ; J. Bellamy, consulting water engineer to the Plymouth Corporation ; E. Osmond, sen., land surveyor ; and for the Torquay Corporation, A. S. Rendell, F.S.I.; Arthur Body, A.R.I.B.A., Plymouth ; E. J. Sawdye, surveyor, Ashburton ; J. Ingham, water engineer to the Torquay Corporation ; and Mr. H. Hoskings.

## SEWAGE DEPOSIT AS MANURE.

The following letter has been addressed by Mr. J. Garrett, J.P., to *The Yorkshire Post* in reference to the above subject:—

I have read with much interest the able articles on agriculture which appear weekly in *The Yorkshire Post*. I have been carrying out an experiment, for the last two or three years, which, I think, is worth recording. I have a quantity of rich grass land adjoining the Otley sewage works, and have made use of the deposit from the sewage works on this land with remarkable results. This year I mowed about 10 acres in June, a very heavy crop. At the end of September I again mowed the fog, a very good crop; and I have now a third very nice crop of fog. The result of my experiments has been to give such a demand for the sewage deposit that what a few years ago appeared to be likely to be a difficulty as to its removal is now readily disposed of, and many applicants for it. I am quite satisfied if the sewage deposit from our town could be easily removed and used on much of the poor land on the north side of the Wharfe the produce would be vastly increased. I strongly recommend any parties who have access to sewage systems to try the experiment.

## CORRESPONDENCE.

**Gas Traction for Tramways: An Experiment at Neath.**
—Mr. D. M. Jenkins, A.M.I.C.E., borough surveyor, Neath, writes: With reference to your comments upon gas traction as applied to tramways, it may be of interest to some of your readers to know that the Neath Corporation have adopted this system on their tramways, and have, with the approval of the Board of Trade, leased the lines for a period of seven years to the British Gas Traction Company. The tramways have been recently reconstructed, and the necessary preparations are being made for commencing the working of the new system at an early date. The decision to discontinue horse traction and to adopt the gas system was arrived at after very careful consideration of the merits of the various mechanical systems and of horse traction in relation to the particular conditions involved. The length of route to be worked is about 4 miles; the gradients (excepting a short length of 1 in 22) and curves are easy, and the traffic variable during the day and week, not requiring a very frequent service of cars. These conditions suggested a self-contained in preference to a central power system, and the only form that has been successfully applied in this country being the gas system, this was adopted after an inspection of the installation at Blackpool and a comparison of first costs and working expenses. Further factors in the consideration of the matter were that the gasworks are owned by the corporation, that coal gas is certain to remain the illuminant for the town for many years to come, and that the supply required for traction purposes will be for the most part a day load, and will not involve a material increase of plant in manufacture. Many of the smaller towns in this country are, doubtless, very similarly situated, as to local conditions, to Neath; and for tramways in such towns I believe the compressed gas system to be the cheapest and best at present available. Under certain conditions, combining heavy gradients and a heavy and continuous traffic, no doubt the cable system is to be preferred to any other; but the present position of electric traction, it appears to me, is not such as to encourage its adoption except in special cases. The difficulties and objections that have been recently pointed out, the improvements suggested by Prof. Silvanus Thompson and others, the great diversity of expert opinion upon details, and the special works of construction involved, all these considerations suggest great caution in adopting electric traction at present. Having regard also to the heavy capital expenditure entailed upon plant and details of construction generally which may be out of date in a few years' time, some of the larger towns may do well to adopt a self-contained system which will not commit them for an unlimited time, which will not prevent their adopting electrical traction when a system or method with some measure of finality has been evolved, and which will not involve a heavy initial expenditure and cost of working. That electric traction is the system of the future for large towns, except in cases specially suitable for cable traction, I have no doubt, but that it has not yet realised expectations as to efficiency and cost of working is abundantly clear. Referring to the objections in detail to the gas system, stated in THE SURVEYOR of the 11th inst., I think that these have been fairly replied to by the British Gas Traction Company. I had an opportunity of inspecting the working of their system in September, 1896, and then formed the opinion that the odour (which was perceptible, though faint) and vibration, urged as objections to the system, wore matters of detail that were not difficult of remedy. I have since seen a model of the improved motor car made for the use to be placed on the Neath tramways, and having received independent information of the results I do not think the objections can now be sustained. As to the inability of a motor car to take a particular gradient, this surely, if there were no other explanation of the matter, is merely a matter of engine power and cannot be maintained as an objection to the system.

**Professional Etiquette.**—"An Expert Witness" writes: It is to be regretted that the old-world etiquette among professional men is slowly but surely dying out in these days of furious competition. The boundaries of the professions of architect, surveyor, and estate agent, nay, even the lawyer, are so packed upon in the race for self-advancement that the honourable rules and customs of many of the professional societies are perforce secretly ignored, with the result that confidence in professional men is often talked of as a thing of the past. That this canker is entering into municipal life is very evident, and is doubtless tending to the destruction of that *esprit de corps* so necessary for carrying into effect the local government legislation of the country. To quote cases, Mr. Editor, would be to invite lawsuits innumerable; yet, suffice it to say that salaried officials are daily selling their birthrights, the knowledge of the intricacies and difficulties of their calling, yes, and even the severest criticism of works other than their own that they are able to propound, and all for a very thin veneer of gold. Men of high standing consider it compatible with their duties to play into the hands of wealthy gas and water companies, to the detriment of near neighbouring authorities, whilst others have supported that enemy of sanitation, the jerry-builder, to the extent, in one instance that has come to my knowledge, of presenting a

written report, uninvited, to a local authority to the effect that their professional adviser's opinion was incorrect, doubtless with the sole object of staying a prosecution. Truly, money works wonders! Actions of this character do not add lustre to officialdom; whilst more than one authority, in consequence of this questionable form of neighbourliness, has found itself in a deadlock, and the health of the district under its charge seriously endangered. We are told there is a code of honour among thieves, and it is in the hope, Mr. Editor, with your kind assistance, of waking up one or other of the societies formed with the object of advancing the interests of local government to the unkind, not to say unfair, actions of their members that I have been induced to draw attention to acts that would appear to be unworthy the prestige of even the marauders above referred to.

## THE BROOK HOSPITAL.

### REPORT OF THE LOCAL GOVERNMENT BOARD INSPECTOR.

At a meeting of the Metropolitan Asylums Board on Saturday a letter was read from the Local Government Board enclosing a copy of the report of Mr. W. E. Knollys on the recent inquiry held by him, on behalf of the board, with reference to the Brook Hospital. In this it was stated that of the excess of £50,100 the managers, upon representations made to them, had assented to an expenditure of rather over £20,000, and it might be held that that expenditure, although not included in the original contracts, was practically necessary in connection with the erection of the hospital. There was a further expenditure in different items of somewhat £4,000 incurred with the consent, or, at any rate, with the knowledge of the Hospital Committee, but there remained an expenditure of at least £25,000, which was incurred on the architect's own responsibility without any consent or knowledge on the part of the managers or the Hospital Committee. This amount included the sum of £14,000 in connection with extra foundations, which were found to be necessary. He (the inspector) had been struck in the course of the inquiry by the view that seemed to be taken of the helplessness of public bodies to control expenditure. The continuing expenditure of public money, amounting, as in this case, to very large sums, must clearly not be left in the hands of a single individual. It was evident that the expediture of the ratepayers' money had been considerably in excess of what would have been requisite if further time could have been given to the choice of a site; and that further excess had been caused by the architect exercising his own discretion in his wish to provide a hospital in every respect the best obtainable, as he supposed, instead of one in accordance, as far as possible, with the contracts entered into by the managers.

The Local Government Board, commenting on this report in their letter, said it was admitted that Mr. Aldwinckle, the architect employed by the managers in connection with the hospital, under-estimated the cost of the building, &c., to a serious extent; that works which should have been included in the contracts were omitted; that as regarded foundations and the substitution of fireproof floors for others his reports were most misleading; and that he authorised deviations from and additions to the works specified in the contracts, involving a large expense, on his own responsibility and without any authority whatever from the Hospital Committee or the Board of Managers. The Board had not failed to consider the explanation offered by Mr. Aldwinckle, but they could not but regard his proceedings as deserving of grave reprobation, and, in the opinion of the Board, he altogether failed to realise what was due to the committee of the hospital, and also to the managers, as the architect appointed by them. In their opinion there was not such supervision of the works by the committee as was desirable, while, with respect to the managers, they considered that the practice of drawing cheques for the amounts included in the certificates of the architect without any information being furnished to them by the architect or the Hospital Committee as to the works, &c., for which the certificates were given was open to serious objection.

The CHAIRMAN moved a resolution referring the letter and accompanying report to the Brook Hospital Committee with instructions to consider and to report to the managers on the points dealt with in the letter—namely, the supervision of building works in progress and the payment of contractors upon architects' certificates.

After a long discussion the motion was adopted, it also being decided to forward a copy of the report and the Local Government Board's letter to Mr. Aldwinckle, the architect.

**Northwich.**—The new technical schools and free library, which were formally opened at the beginning of the month, were built from designs by Mr. E. T. Worth, A.M.I.C.E., until recently surveyor to the district council, who acted as honorary architect. The contractors were Messrs. Clarke & Son, of Middlewich. The style adopted is English Renaissance, and the facings are of red Ruabon bricks with terra-cotta dressings, supplied by Mr. J. C. Edwards, of Ruabon.

# Some Annual Municipal Engineering Records.

## BUCKINGHAMSHIRE : WEST HAM.

In submitting his last annual report of the works of the Highways and Bridges Committee, Mr. R. J. Thomas, county surveyor of Buckinghamshire, draws the attention of the county council to the continued increase in the expenditure upon the main roads maintained by the council, and also upon those maintained by urban district councils. The payments towards contributory roads or district highways, he adds, slightly exceeded those of the previous year. The actual mileage of roads maintained directly by the council is 435 miles, 4 furlongs, 47 yards.

The total expenditure by the council on rural main roads and those in the newly-formed urban districts for the year ended March 31, 1898, was £22,388, compared with £23,152 for the previous year, £22,394 for the year ended March, 1896, £23,356 for 1895, and £25,542 for 1894. It will thus be seen that a reduction of £764 has been effected in the expenditure as compared with that of the previous year, although the mileage has been increased by 5¼ miles. The cost per mile was £51 8s. 1d., compared with £53 17s. 7d. for the previous year, £52 8s. 7d. for 1895-96, £54 14s. for 1894-95 and £60 for 1893-94. The expenditure for the year ended March, 1893, was abnormally high, in consequence of the council deciding to increase the quantity of metalling above the ordinary requirements by 50 per cent., in order to improve the general character of roads and produce a more solid foundation for the effectual working of the steam rollers which were bought in the previous year.

Granite used on the rural main roads during the past year totalled 16,356 tons, the cost of this material, including cartage from stations and wharves, being £9,771. This gives an average of 11s. 11½d. per ton. In the year ended March, 1897, 16,631 tons of granite were used, the cost per ton averaging 12s. 0½d. For the present year 16,900 tons have been ordered. Of flint there was used some 11,730 cube yards, the cost, including measuring and breaking, being £3,006. The accepted local custom (remarks Mr. Thomas) of adding two bushels to every yard of flints when measured after breaking, in order to allow for "shrinkage," dies hard, and quite recently it was necessary, in order to convince an irate contractor that there was no such "shrinkage" (and that therefore it was immaterial whether flints were measured through the box unbroken or broken), to have a yard measured in his presence before and after breaking. It is difficult to imagine (continues the county surveyor) how this erroneous idea came to be accepted by purchasers of flints in the past; but certain it is that the belief has been an expensive one to the ratepayers. Where hand-picked flints have not been obtainable, and railway stations have been too far away, it has been found necessary to use clean pit gravel, and, as the roads so repaired have but a moderate amount of traffic, this material has answered fairly well.

Gravel to the amount of 2,238 cube yards, and costing £445, was also used during the year. The average per cube yard works out at 3s. 11½d. Last year's figures were 1,501 cube yards, at an average cost of 3s. 8½d. per cube yard. From the foregoing figures it will be seen that the quantity of materials used has again been reduced. This is accounted for by the absence of frosts and their accompanying thaws during the past year, and to the consequent sounder condition of roads. The total cost of manual labour for the year, including measuring and breaking flints, repairs to paths, steam rolling, &c., and surfaces over county bridges, was £5,864, which, compared with £5,818 for the previous year, shows an increase of £46. The three 10-ton rollers owned by the council have continued to work effectively during the year, at a cost of £673, compared with £619 for the previous year. These figures include drivers and attendants and hire of horses and men for water-carts, in additional to fuel, oil, waste, &c., for the three. The sum of £338 was expended on the hire of rollers.

It is evident (the report continues) that the outlay upon footpaths, especially where they pass through non-urban towns and larger villages, must gradually increase, as numerous lengths of old pavements are in a more or less worn-out condition, calling for considerable outlay in the near future. The expenditure on main road footpaths during the year was £891, compared with £1,765 for the previous year and £1,476 for 1895-96. This great reduction in cost is accounted for by the fact that during the previous two years exceptionally large paving and improvement works were effected, towards which local contributions approximating one-half cost were received; but such contributions having, by direction of the Local Government Board auditor, to be paid unto the county fund and not into the highways and bridges account, the latter has necessarily to show in its balance-sheets the gross total cost of such improvement works, and not the half. The cost of urban and rural main roads maintained by the council is now about £15 per mile less than it was when they were maintained by the various parishes; but Mr. Thomas thinks that to keep them up to their present standard, and to provide for reasonable alterations and improvements, it will be necessary to maintain the present expenditure of about £50 per mile; otherwise a fatal mistake would be made, calculated to undo the work of the past nine years.

* * *

The last annual report of Mr. Lewis Angell, borough engineer of West Ham, states that the length of dedicated roads maintained by his corporation is approximately 100 miles—an increase of about 2¾ miles on the previous year; new streets dedicated since the incorporation of the borough have a length of nearly 34½ miles. The area of the district is 7¼ square miles. In connection with private streets, of which a length of nearly 2¾ miles has been dedicated during the year, the report mentions that four contracts, amounting in all to about £12,830, have been let for works on twenty-four roads. Final apportionments have been made in twenty roads, in the sum of £8,351. Since the adoption, in 1895, of the Private Street Works Act, 1892, it may be mentioned, plans, specifications, estimates and provisional apportionments have been made for sixty-seven roads, at an aggregate cost of £47,101.

Public lamps have increased by forty-seven, and now number 2,704; their cost during the year has been £9,940. Some 1,242 plans have been deposited—an increase of 227, but 301 of these have been disapproved owing to non-compliance with the various Acts and by-laws. The building fees received have amounted to over £945, making a total of £13,625 since the introduction of the Local Board Act of 1882. Plans have been deposited for eight new estates, with roads of a length of 3¾ miles. Since the date of the incorporation of the borough plans have been deposited for 13,557 new houses, 1,600 other buildings, and 1,503 works of alteration and extension. According to the report, the reconstruction of defective private drainage has been very expensive to the council; but the new West Ham Corporation Act (sec. 42) has now placed upon owners the obligation of maintaining drains situate on private premises. Progress is being made with the new pumping station at Abbey Mills, the boilers of which will also supply steam for the electric lighting station connected therewith. When the pumping station is completed, next year, the sewage of the town will be intercepted from the river and discharged by a 40-ft. lift into the metropolitan system, but the sewage discharged from other districts beyond West Ham will continue to foul the rivers which flow through the borough, become increasingly offensive. At this point it may be mentioned that the matter of the pollution of the Channelsea has since been the subject of inquiry at the hands of the Local Government Board.

The fire brigade continues to maintain a high state of efficiency. Its cost for the past year has been £4,608. Six stations are at present in use, employing twenty-five men and eight horses. Mr. Angell again calls attention to the large number of fires caused by the dangerous oil lamps in common use, by which seven persons have been injured, two dying. Eleven persons have been injured by fire from other causes, one dying.

Among the more important works which have engaged the attention of the borough surveyor during the year have been a lunatic asylum (contract No. 1, £10,130; contract No. 2, £6,000; and contract No. 3, £209,531), a new sewage pumping and electric lighting station (buildings, £35,430; and engines, boilers, &c., for the sewage pumping, £20,751), the Dagenham Hospital (£20,475), a recreation ground (£497), and pitching works in North Woolwich-road, Victoria Dock-road, and Church-street and Portway (£13,995, £11,992 and £9,502 respectively); while various private street works (£12,830) have also been advanced. In addition to the above, plans have been prepared for artisans' dwellings (£11,976), a police court extension (£4,440), mortuaries in West Ham and Canning Town (£1,580), fire brigade barracks at Canning Town (£16,000), town hall extension (£42,500), water scheme (£28,560), northern and southern sewers (£19,991), pitching of The Grove, Leytonstone, Leyton, Chobham and Major roads (£18,759), and private street works (£9,413) in addition to those mentioned above. With the addition of the general expenditure connected with the engineer's department on account of highways and the cost of jobbing, &c., the above works, it is interesting to note, represent work (either in execution or preparation) to the value of over £500,000. In conclusion, it may be stated that the number of workmen of all classes (excluding the stable department) in the direct employ of the council on March 25th was 449. The total number pensioned has been sixty-eight, the amounts of the pensions varying from 5s. to 10s. weekly. There are forty on the list at the present time, and the annual disbursement amounts to over £600.

---

**Lasswade.**—The commissioners have decided to take action against the Loanhead Commissioners in order to put a stop to the nuisance caused by sewage matter from Loanhead discharging through Lasswade. The clerk has been instructed to communicate with the Loanhead Commissioners, and, as the sewage also affects the landward district, it was agreed to communicate with the Lasswade District Committee of the Mid-Lothian County Council.

# For Assistants and Pupils.

## THE CONSTRUCTION OF ROADS AND STREETS.—XX.

By WILLIAM H. MAXWELL, Assistant Engineer and Surveyor, Leyton Urban District Council.

THE CONSTRUCTION OF ROADS AND STREETS.

*Cost of Construction of Macadamised Roadways.*—The cost of constructing a macadamised roadway varies very widely, according to the locality, facility for obtaining road materials, the price of labour, and many other considerations.

For a first-class macadam roadway the following is a brief specification: Excavate to a depth of 16 in. below finished level of proposed road surface; level and properly consolidate surface formation to the required contour; lay in a bed of "hard core" of broken stone or brick, 12 in. in thickness, and consolidated to 9 in. by rolling with a 10-ton steam roller,

FIG. 29.—CROSS-SECTION OF A FIRST-CLASS MACADAM ROAD.

and make up all hollow places; spread a layer of Thames ballast or gravel, 5 in. thick, consolidated to 3 in. by rolling; lay down two 3 in. layers of 2-in. blue Guernsey granite, and roll in to a finished thickness of 4 in., sharp sand or fine gravel to be spread during the process and the surface well watered (see Fig. 29).

In London a road constructed after the above manner would cost about 6s. per square yard. A lighter section (Fig. 30) suitable for suburban roads, and consisting of 9 in.

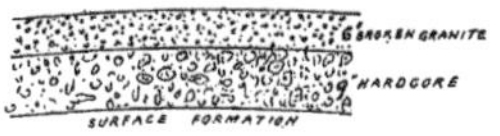


FIG. 30.—SUBURBAN MACADAM ROAD.

of hard core covered with a 6-in. layer of broken granite and well rolled, would cost about 3s. 6d. per square yard.

The following are the approximate prices of road materials in the vicinity of London:—

| | | Per ton. |
|---|---|---|
| Blue Guernsey granite, broken to pass a | 2-in. ring, | 13s. 10d. |
| " " " " " | 1½-in. " | 14s. 4d. |
| Alderney granite " " | 2-in. " | 14s. 0d. |
| " " " " | 1½-in. " | 14s. 6d. |
| Quenast* (limestone) " " | 2-in. " | 13s. 0d. |
| " " " " | 1½-in. " | 13s. 6d. |

Flints (best Kentish chalk), from 7s. 6d. to 9s. per cubic yard.
Double-screened ballast, from 5s. 6d. to 6s. 6d. per cubic yard.
Hard core (broken stone or brick), about 2s. 6d. per cubic yard.

The following are the particulars of the cost of materials used in road-making in Plymouth† (1895):—

Road metal, Elvan stone, unbroken, 3s. 5d. and 3s. 10d. per ton.
" " broken to pass through a 2-in. ring, 5s. and 5s. 5d. per ton.
Limestone, for tar paving, 3s. per ton.
First-class granite setts, 3 in. by 6 in. by 6 in. to 8 in. long, 22s. per ton.
" " 3 in. to 5 in. by 6 in. to 8 in. long, 23s. per ton.
Second-class " 3 in. to 4 in. by 6 in. by 9 in. long, 18s. 9d. per ton.
Granite flagging, 10s. per square yard.
Granite curb, bevelled, 12 in. by 8 in., 1s. 2d. per lineal foot.
" " 12 in. by 8 in., circular on plan, 1s. 5d. per lineal foot.
Granite channel blocks, 12 in. by 6 in., 1s. per lineal foot.
" " 12 in. by 6 in. (circular), 1s. 3d. per lineal foot.
" " 15 in. by 8 in., 1s. 5d. per lineal foot.
" " 15 in. by 8 in. (circular, 2½ in. to 2¾ in. thick), 1s. 9d. per lineal foot.
Caithness flagging, laid complete, 6s. per square yard.
Coverack concrete slabs, 2 in. thick, laid complete, 6s. 3d. per square yard.
Limestone flagging, laid complete, 9s. 6d. per square yard.

In Birmingham the average cost per square yard per annum of cleansing, watering and macadamising the carriage-ways for 1880 was 5d.; the maximum cost for any one street for that year was 4s. 3·35d., whilst the first cost of making was about 2s. 3d. per square yard. In streets of heavy and concentrated traffic, like Bull-street and High-street, the respective costs for macadam, wood and granite were*:—

| Material | First cost per square yard. | | Average annual maintenance, including first cost and repayment in sixteen years. | | | Cleansing. | | Watering. |
|---|---|---|---|---|---|---|---|---|
| | s. | d. | s. | d. | | s. | d. | |
| Macadam | 3 | 0 | 3 | 0 | per square yard | 1 | 3 | ·35 |
| Wood | 15 | 0 | 1 | 11¾ | " " " | 0 | 5 | ·25 |
| Granite | 14 | 0 | 1 | 4 | " " " | 0 | 5 | ·25 |

A macadamised street in Bristol, 718 yards long, 13 yards wide, cost per annum nearly £1,000 to repair and maintain, or 2s. 1½d. per square yard = £2,425 per mile. It is also on record that Regent-street, when macadamised, cost 3s. 7d. per square yard per annum to maintain.

In Norwich† the cost of constructing syenitic granite macadam, including gravel foundation, is 4s. 6d. per square yard; tarred macadam costs 6s. per square yard, including 2s. for gravel foundation. The tarred macadam requires refacing once in five years, and with this attention has a life of about twenty years in the class of streets where it is suitable.

ROAD-ROLLING.

Some particulars of the history of the evolution of the practice of steam road-rolling have already been given, and need not again be referred to. The use of steam rollers in the consolidation of road metal has become general, both in urban districts and also upon county main roads.

The undoubted advantages of steam road-rolling over the former method of allowing road surfaces to be consolidated by the traffic are briefly as follows:—

(1) Economy combined with efficiency; the roads are better made, and the necessity for such frequent sweeping and scraping is obviated. The saving effected is given as varying from 30 to 50 per cent. The road metal is economised, as a thinner coating can be used, the metal need not be broken so small, and there is less abrasion of the stones, there being only one surface exposed.
(2) The cruelty inflicted upon animals passing over a newly-metalled unrolled road is avoided.
(3) Road-making and repairs can be carried out at any time of the year, and the constant employment of men raking metal into the ruts is avoided.
(4) The steam roller soon shows which is good and which is bad metal for the roads.
(5) Steam-rolled streets are easier for the traffic, are harder, of a more even surface, and have also a better appearance.
(6) The roller is oftentimes found useful for other work.

When thrown open to traffic an unrolled road presents a surface of stones without any mutual cohesion, and every wheel in passing over the loose stones acts somewhat like a plough, pressing down the stones over which it passes and raising up those on each side. This requires the stones to be constantly raked smooth, whereby fresh corners are presented for the next wheels to chip off, and ultimately the surface of the road is uneven, consisting of minute hills and valleys, as it were, which make it far more vulnerable to traffic than when perfectly smooth.

The interspaces in a layer of newly-broken stones occupy, when the stones are first loosely spread upon the road, about one-half the area covered by them, but only one-fourth the area after they have settled into the compactness of an ordinary road surface. This compactness has to be attained by compression or by wear, by a heavy roller, or by the traffic. In the former case the stones are driven into a prepared compressible bed, with their sharp ends downwards and their flat sides uppermost, and form a level, regular and solid pavement of interlocked angular stones; in the latter case they are rolled and kicked about by the traffic until at least one-third of the metalling is destroyed—ground into dust or mud—and removed as refuse by the sweepers; and when, with their angles rounded off, the stones are worn into the worst possible shape for consolidation they are stamped into place to form a road surface, which no mending, filling-up of hollows or other expensive attention will make smooth and durable, and over which the first dry weather of summer will again set the loose stones rolling.

"The main difference between an unrolled and rolled road, at the outset, is that the first contains nearly three times more empty space than the latter. It is clear that a road cannot be hard and strong until these spaces are filled up.

* *Quenast* is a limestone from Belgium, of brownish grey colour. At first sight looks like granite, but is softer, and does not wear so well.
† "Proceedings of the Association of Municipal and County Engineers," vol. xxi.

* "Proceedings of the Association of Municipal and County Engineers," vol. vii., p. 81.
† "Proceedings of the Association of Municipal and County Engineers," vol. xxii.

Without the use of rolling this can only be done by the particles ground by the traffic off the edges of the stones, by dirt and foul excrementitious matter .... The main causes of the longer duration afforded by the roller are, therefore : (1) That it diminishes the actual wear by the traffic ; (2) the interlocking of the stones prevents the injurious action of mud, dirt and moisture ; (3) that it allows thinner coatings to be used.

"One of the main advantages attending the rolling of roads by steam-power consists in the diminished proportion of mud or soluble matter which in then incorporated in the structure of the road surface. If the surface of an ordinary road that has not been rolled is broken up and the material washed it is found that as much as half of it is soluble matter—mud, dirt and very fine sand ; the stones, having only been thrown loosely upon the road, have lain so long before becoming consolidated by the traffic, and have undergone in the meantime such extensive abrasion, that the proportion of mud, dirt and pulverised material in the metalling is increased to that extent, and the stones are really only stuck together by the mud. This accounts for the fact that although an unrolled macadamised road may, indeed, after long use have a surface that is pretty good and hard in dry weather, and may offer then a very slight resistance to traction, yet it will quickly become soft and muddy when there is any rain. By the employment, however, of a steam roller upon the newly-laid metalling of a macadamised road the stones are rolled in and well bedded at once, and the surface is thus consolidated into a sort of stone felt, capable of resisting most effectually the action of ordinary traffic and containing the smallest quantity of soluble matter to form mud in wet weather."[*]

The disadvantages attending the use of steam rollers include the following :—

(1) Risk of damage to gas and water mains and services.
(2) Interference to traffic and the risk of frightening horses whilst the roller is in use.
(3) Nuisance from noise and smoke, though the latter is reduced to a minimum by the use of wood and coke for fuel.
(4) The road metal may be crushed instead of bedded, or the road foundation may be injured, if the roller used is too heavy.
(5) The first cost is a difficulty in small districts which often delays the introduction of a steam roller.

A road-roller should not exceed about 12 tons in weight, or the road metal may be crushed and damage done to gas, water and other pipes, as well as to culverts or cellar arches under the roadway.

The following are the particulars of one of Messrs. Aveling & Porter's modern type 12-ton rollers, well suited to use on county roads :—

Weight, about 12 tons.
Bearing weight on road, 401·2 lb. per square inch.
Length over all, 18 ft. 6 in.
Width of roller surface, 6 ft. 5 in.
Height of top of funnel from ground, 9 ft. 10 in.
Six horse-power nominal.
Driving wheels, 5 ft. 6 in. diameter, 1 ft. 5 in. wide.
Front rollers, 4 ft. diameter, 2 ft. wide.
Boiler made of special brand milled steel.
Plates flanged by hydraulic flanging press.
Large grate area and heating surface.
Gearing made of fine crucible cast steel.
Crank and intermediate shafts carried by patent steel brackets.
Sides of fire-box being intended to form brackets.
Constructed with feed pump and injector for filling.

The fire-box, being intended to form the brackets, allows the gear to be brought closer together, thus reducing the width of the roller, so that whilst narrow streets can be rolled easily the shape of the road is retained.

**The Telephone Service.**—The National Telephone Company intend to apply next session for an Act to dissolve the company and reincorporate the shareholders into a new company, empowered to maintain and extend the undertaking, and to possess such other powers, rights and privileges as may be necessary for the purpose of effectively providing telephonic communication throughout the United Kingdom, the Channel Islands and the Isle of Man.

**Electric Traction on the Underground Railway.**—The directors of the Metropolitan and District Railway Companies have decided to undertake a series of experiments prior to the introduction of electric traction on the inner circle lines. An electric installation is to be laid down between Earl's Court and High-street, Kensington, by which a train fully as heavy as those running at the busiest times of the day on the Metropolitan line will be run for several months without any interruption of the present locomotive steam traffic. The work will be under the direction of Sir John Wolfe Barry, consulting engineer to the Metropolitan Railway Company, and Mr. W. H. Preece.

[*] "Report on the Economy of Road Maintenance and Horse Draught through Steam Road-rolling, with special reference to the Metropolis," by F. A. Paget, c.e. 1870,

## QUERIES AND REPLIES.

*Sketches accompanying Queries should be made separate on white paper in plain black-ink lines. Lettering or figures should be bold and plain.*

**223. Sewage Sludge, Weight of : How ascertained.**—
"Regular Reader" writes: Would you furnish me with a formula for estimating the weight of sewage sludge when containing various percentages of moisture ?

Sludge from any system of sewage disposal contains about ninety parts of water and ten parts of solid matter. As the sludge is dried its weight diminishes in a ratio which is defined by the following simple rule, devised by Prof. Henry Robinson, and given in his book, " Sewerage and Sewage Disposal " (E. & F. N. Spon. 12s. 6d.).

Let X = weight of sludge, to be ascertained.
S = weight of solids in the sludge (which is constant).
P = percentage of moisture in the sludge.

Then $X = \dfrac{S \times 100}{100 - P}$

Thus, to ascertain what weight 25 tons of sludge containing 90 per cent. of moisture would be reduced to when it is dried to 15 per cent. of moisture. Now, 25 tons of sludge with 90 per cent. of moisture contain 2·5 tons (i.e., 10 per cent. of 25 tons) of solids, and therefore applying the formula

$$X = \frac{2·5 \times 100}{100 - 15} = 2·94 \text{ tons.}$$

**224. Building By-Laws and Regulations.**—"J. W. M." writes: I send you herewith plans and particulars of a new building and drainage scheme, together with the by-laws, such plan having just been passed by the local authority. I shall esteem it a favour if you will give me your opinion upon the drainage system. My own opinion as a surveyor is that the drainage system is entirely wrong and not according to the aforementioned by-laws.

We are unable to advise properly with the information before us. The querist accompanies his letter with what appears to be a newspaper cutting showing a block plan of two houses and an outbuilding, whereon is shown the line of drainage, together with several extracts from the by-laws. Excepting that the disconnecting chamber appears to be a considerable distance from the sewer, and there appear to be no branch drains to take the waste from sinks and baths, the plan is not otherwise irregular. The querist has placed the information before us in a very imperfect manner. The newspaper cutting shows that his plan of drainage has been disapproved, yet he informs us it is approved. If the latter, why is he now taking exception to it ?

**225. Levelling, Book on, required.**—"D. W." writes: Could you recommend me a good book on levelling. I have had some experience in levelling, but require a good text-book by means of which I can thoroughly master the subject.

Usill's " Practical Surveying," price 7s. 6d. (Crosby Lockwood & Son), will be found an excellent book for the purpose required.

**226. Surveying, Cross-Section of River.**—"Semper Eadem" writes : How would you obtain a cross-section of a river when there is neither a boat nor a raft available ? The method must, I presume, be equally applicable to rivers whether 10 yards or 200 yards wide, as in this country a boat will be always available. I should be glad if you would give me a reasonable solution such as an engineer might adopt, as to my mind the question is a ridiculous one, for though I have thought out several methods I have not found one by means of which accurate results could be obtained. I may add that the question was set at a recent examination of the Municipal and County Engineers' Association.

If the querist has correctly copied the question we are bound to state that it is neither intelligibly nor fairly placed before the examinees. If the river is not more than 100 links in width the distance may be ascertained without difficulty, and by sending a man round by the nearest bridge to the point required with a staff the levels may also be ascertained so far as the banks and water-level are concerned. Where the river is a wide one the distance must be obtained by the formula for measuring inaccessible points, several formulæ for the purpose being given in Molesworth's " Pocket-Book of Engineering Formulæ " (E. & F. N. Spon. Price 7s. 6d.), and in Usill's " Practical Surveying " (Crosby Lockwood & Son. Price 6s.). The " Wells system of levelling " may often be adopted in such cases, and should be learnt. We gave a description of the system in reply to Query No. 60 in our issue of April 30, 1897. Further information may be obtained from the book " Hints on Levelling Operations as applied to the reading of distances by the law of perspective, and the saving thereby of chainmen in a level survey, &c.," by W. H. Wells (E. & F. N. Spon. Price 1s.).

**Ormskirk.**—Last week Colonel A. G. Durnford, R.E., one of the Local Government Board inspectors, held an inquiry respecting an application of the council for sanction to borrow £1,600 for the erection of a fire engine station, £250 for water supply, £220 for public offices, £80 for public walks and pleasure grounds, and £65 for a fire escape.

## EXETER WATER SUPPLY.

### APPLICATION TO BORROW £30,000.

Mr. G. W. Willcocks, M.I.C.E., last week conducted an inquiry, on behalf of the Local Government Board, at Exeter, in reference to an application of the city council for permission to borrow £30,000 for water supply purposes. Among those who attended the inquiry were Mr. G. R. Shorto, town clerk, Dr. Woodman, medical officer of health, and Mr. D. Cameron, the city surveyor.

In the course of the evidence it was explained that under the Exeter Corporation Water Act of 1878 the parishes of St. Thomas, Heavitree, Alphington and Pinhoe, all outside the city, were included within the limits of supply, but St. Thomas also had a water supply of their own, although the Exeter supply was laid throughout the district. The St. Thomas supply provided for about 5,000, and Exeter had to make provision for about 55,000 in all. The present demand for water was about 1,750,000 gallons per day. The conduit from the intake would carry 2,250,000 gallons, and the rising main would carry all the water required for consumption, but only by an extravagant expenditure of power. The filtration was done by two filters only, with a combined area of 36,000 superficial feet. Their capacity was not sufficient, and the corporation would not have been satisfied with them during the last five years had there been any ground upon which they could have extended them. There was greater strain upon one filter when periodically the other had to be thrown out of work for cleansing. The water was taken from the Exe above the junction of the Culm, not by a direct flow but by filtration through a bed of gravel into a tank at the intake, which was 60 ft. long by 12 ft. wide. This provided for filtration at the intake. It was thence conveyed by a culvert of tiles of 2 ft. internal dimension to the city pumping station. This culvert had manholes at intervals, and it was found that roots of trees had penetrated these manholes, and through the gaps thus caused surface water obtained admission. The culvert, which was 7,652 ft. in length, was found to be very unsatisfactory from its insufficient size and on account of its construction, and was to be replaced. The water was conveyed in the conduit to the pumping wells at Pynes, where there were three turbines in use, and two more which were intended to be used. As an auxiliary power, when the water-power failed, there was a pumping engine of 48 horse-power, which would raise over 1,000,000 gallons a day, and there was also another temporary engine which would raise 270,000 gallons. The water was pumped through two mains, one of 10 in. and the other of 12 in. internal dimensions, and the velocity was at present a little over 3 ft. per second. They were obliged to keep up that rate to get enough water, and this was considered wasteful. The water was pumped from Pynes to Dane's Castle reservoir, a height of about 150 ft. above the pumping station at Pynes, where it was filtrated and gravitated to the lower district, while what was required for the higher part of the city was pumped to Marypole Head reservoir. The increase of population and consequent increase of demand for water was on the higher level. The capacity of the Dane's Castle reservoir was 4,500,000 gallons, and Marypole Head 1,000,000. This was the present state of affairs, and the council considered it necessary to have (1) increased means of filtration, and (2) an increased supply, which involved an increased size of the conduit, increased pumping power of water and steam, increased capacity of the rising mains, and a diminution of unnecessary waste of power in unnecessary friction in the rising main, owing to its small size, by the formation of an immediate level reservoir. The council now proposed to take the whole of the filter tanks out to Pynes, on land for the purchase of which a provisional agreement had been made with the Earl of Iddesleigh. It was intended to construct here two settling basins, each to contain 1,500,000 gallons. The water would then be lifted an average height of about 8 ft. from the settling tanks on to the filters to be constructed immediately alongside. These filters would be six in number, each of 12,000 ft. superficial area. Fixed filters would do all the work required for a largely-increased water supply, the five filtering 3,000,000 gallons daily, at the rate of 4 in. per hour under a head of 2 ft. The sixth filter would always be in reserve for cleansing or other purposes. The water would pass from the filters to the proposed suction wells. This was all the increased means of filtration. Another proposal was to improve in construction and increase the size of the present conduit by replacing the existing one by a 30-in. internal dimension cast-iron pipe without manholes. The power, both of water and steam, was to be increased, the council proposing to raise the depth of the water in the tost by 2 ft. The proposed works would increase the water-power by nearly one-fourth, so far as the existing machinery was concerned. Two new pumps would be provided to utilise the increased power. With the turbines and new works it would be possible to raise 3,000,000 gallons a day with the normal flow of the river. Coming to the steam, the existing machinery was to be increased by a new steam engine capable of raising to the level of Dane's Castle 96,000 gallons per hour, or 2,250,000 gallons per day. The Dane's Castle pumping station would be abandoned, and the steam engine at present there would be removed to Pynes, where it would be capable of raising 500,000 gallons a day to a proposed intermediate level reservoir. The new mains to be provided were also explained. The present rising main between Pynes and Dane's Castle would be replaced by a larger one, and that between Dane's Castle and Marypole Head would be tapped for a new main to the proposed intermediate level reservoir. With this new reservoir and the turning of a filter-bed at Dane's Castle into a reservoir the storage for city water would be increased from 5,500,000 to 7,500,000 gallons. There was at present a waste of power through water being pumped up to Marypole Head when a lesser height would do for a large part of the service now supplied by the Marypole Head reservoir. The new reservoir to supply this intermediate service was to be provided at Pennsylvania, on land in a line with the terrace, to be purchased from the Freehold Land Society. The council had to purchase 2½ acres —the society would not sell less—at £1,325. Only half an acre would be required, and the remaining 2 acres would be resold. An increase of the estimate would be necessary in regard to this matter. The new reservoir would be circular in form, constructed of concrete or brickwork, covered in, and with a capacity of 600,000 gallons.

The inspector subsequently visited the reservoirs and the waterworks, and will report in due course.

## LONDON WATER SUPPLY.

### COUNTY COUNCIL PROPOSALS.

The London County Council announce their intention of applying for leave to bring in a Bill empowering them to construct a storage and service reservoir at Borehamwood, Hertfordshire, "and aqueduct, conduit or line of pipes, to commence at the dam or embankment of a reservoir proposed to be made on the river Yrfon, in the county of Brecknock, and to terminate at the Borehamwood reservoir," and filter-beds near Edgware and Hendon, Middlesex. By other clauses the council will seek for powers to lay down, &c., conduits, &c.; to enter into and carry into effect contracts for the supply of water in bulk or otherwise within the counties mentioned in the notice; to enable them from time to time to raise money by stock or annuities, terminable or otherwise, to such amount as may be necessary for the purposes of the intended Act, or to use for those purposes, or any of them, money standing to the credit of the Consolidated Loans Fund; and to make such provisions as to the redemption of such stock or repayment of loans, and the payment of interest or dividend thereon, out of any water rates and charges and revenue derived by the council from the undertaking, or out of the Consolidated Loans Fund and county rate, and to include in their estimates and precepts for the purpose of the county rate such sums as may be requisite for those purposes. By other clauses provision will be made for defraying all costs and expenses of the council in the execution of the powers of the intended Act (except so far as they may be otherwise provided for) as payments for general county purposes within the meaning of the Local Government Act, 1888, and for the payment by the council in like manner of their costs, &c., "preliminary to, and of and incidental to, the preparing, applying for, obtaining and passing the intended Act." The Bill will also contain a clause providing for the keeping of separate accounts by the council in relation to expenditure and revenue in connection with the undertaking to be authorised under the intended Act.

## NORTHAMPTON COUNTY BUILDINGS.

### EXTENSIVE IMPROVEMENTS.

At a recent meeting of the Northamptonshire County Council the Building Committee recommended the adoption of plans, prepared by Mr. Aston Webb, for alterations and enlargements of the existing County Buildings at Northampton. By these plans such parts of the existing buildings as have any architectural or historical interest will not be altered, nor will the façade be touched except for the interchange of a doorway and window on the ground floor. The courts will remain as they are, and so will the walls of the main wing, which contain the grand jury-room, but the modern buildings at the back between the main buildings and the county council chamber will be pulled down. The main entrance will be removed to the western extremity of the wing. The alterations will provide more rooms and offices, all more conveniently placed, and better accommodation will be given to the police department. The roughly-estimated cost of the alterations will be £15,000, and the committee recommend that Messrs. Aston Webb and E. Ingress Bell be appointed architects for the erection of the buildings.

**Cannock.**—Letters were last week read from the Local Government Board and the county council with respect to the removal of house refuse, pointing out that it was essential that proper arrangements should be made for the removal of the refuse during the proper hours and in an efficient manner in the populous places. It was decided to write to the parish councils of Cheslyn Hay, Great Wyrley, Essington, Brewood and Penkridge, asking for their observations on the matter, and calling the attention of the parish councils to the clauses

# Law Notes.

EDITED BY J. B. REIGNIER CONDER, 11 Old Jewry Chambers, E.C.,

Solicitor of the Supreme Court.

*The Editor will be pleased to answer any questions affecting the practice of engineers and surveyors to local authorities. Queries (which should be written legibly on foolscap paper, one side only) should be addressed to "The Law Editor," at the Offices of* THE SURVEYOR. *Where possible, copies of local Acts or documents referred to should be enclosed. All explanatory diagrams must be drawn and lettered in black ink only. Correspondents who do not wish their names published should furnish a nom de plume.*

COMBINED DRAINAGE: NOTICE BY LOCAL AUTHORITY TO REPAIR: LIABILITY OF AUTHORITY.—The recent case of *North and Millhouse v. Walthamstow Urban District Council* (Queen's Bench Division, 27th October) is of interest as a further contribution to the precedents relating to the subject of combined drainage. It was an action by Miss Sarah Ellen North and Mr. Charles Millhouse to recover £35 for work done and materials supplied as a builder by the plaintiff Charles Millhouse to the plaintiff Sarah Ellen North, at the direction of the defendants. The facts were as follows: The plaintiff Miss North is the owner of seven houses, 22 to 34 (even numbers) Cambridge-road, Walthamstow. The plaintiff Mr. Millhouse, throughout the matters which led to the present action acted as Miss North's agent and builder. At the end of November, 1897, the sanitary inspector for the district complained of the state of the drain of No. 22 Cambridge-road, and served a notice in respect of that house in the form set out below. The ground was opened, when it was discovered that the drain drained more than one house. Subsequently the following notice was served on the plaintiffs in respect of all the houses 22 to 34 Cambridge-road. Both the above-mentioned notices were in the following form, the first being limited to No. 22: "Walthamstow Urban District Council. To Mr. Millhouse, of 13 Cassland-road. Notice is hereby given you to abate a nuisance at 22, 24, 26, 28, 30, 32 and 34 Cambridge-road, arising from defective drains, within seven days from the service of this notice, and for that purpose to take up and relay, properly trap, ventilate and provide means of access to drains. Dated this 27th day of November, 1897. Signature of officer of local authority, W. W. West, inspector of nuisances." The work was done in accordance with the notices and according to the instructions of the sanitary inspector as the work went on. The plaintiff Mr. Millhouse admitted that he believed that the pipe to which the repairs were done was a sewer, and that the plaintiffs were not liable to do the work, but he said that he believed he was obliged to do it after he received the notice. It was agreed by both sides that the pipe upon which the work was done was in fact a sewer. On behalf of the plaintiffs it was contended that the notice was not given by them, but by the sanitary officer on his own responsibility, and the case of *Selfe v. Hove Commissioners* (1895, 1 Q.B., 685, THE SURVEYOR, vol. vii., p. 203) was relied on. For the plaintiffs *Andrew v. St. Olave's Board of Works* (1898, 1 Q.B., 775, THE SURVEYOR, vol. xiv., p. 70) was cited, and it was argued that the notice constituted an implied request to the plaintiffs to do work which the council were legally bound to do. Mr. Justice Channell characterised (during the arguments) *Selfe v. Hove Commissioners* as "about as unsatisfactory a decision as ever came into court," and in the course of his judgment in favour of the plaintiffs said: In my opinion I ought to act upon the authority of the decision in *Andrew v. St. Olave's Board of Works*. I do not think it desirable to draw refined distinctions, and, further, I am inclined to think that *Andrew v. St. Olave's Board of Works* involves the same principles as the present case. Upon behalf of the defendants it was said that that case was distinguishable and inconsistent with *Selfe v. Hove Commissioners*. That case is, no doubt, not an entirely satisfactory decision, but it is not necessary to discuss it further, as the present case is not governed by it. Upon behalf of the defendants it was conceded that the sections in the Public Health (London) Act, 1891 (54 and 55 Vic., cap. 76), upon which *Andrew v. St. Olave's Board of Works* was decided, were similar to the corresponding provisions in the Public Health Act, 1875. In that case the work had to be done at once; in the present case that is not so. It is admitted that it was the duty of the plaintiffs to do the work. If any persons other than the plaintiffs had done the work it would have been a voluntary act, and they could not have recovered the cost of it from the defendants. The principle upon which the cost of doing the work is sought to be recovered by the plaintiffs in the present action is that if a person is compelled to do that which another person is legally liable to do a request is implied by the person who is so liable. The question is, What degree of compulsion is necessary to entitle the plaintiffs to recover? The compulsion need not be irresistible. It is not sufficient for the defendants to say that if the plaintiffs went before the magistrates they would have had a defence. If a public body comes to a person and either commences or threatens proceedings such person is no longer a volunteer. A person in such a position is under an obligation to do the work. It is immaterial whether the notice given to the plaintiffs was a statutory notice or not. The law implies practical compulsion. In the present case there was no legal compulsion, but a mere indirect compulsion is sufficient. It has been held in betting cases that a mere threat to turn a man out of a club is sufficient to enable him to recover money paid by him to avoid being turned out. Where a man repaired a sea wall as a matter of practical necessity, which it was the duty of the commissioners to repair, he recovered the costs of the repairs. The fact that in the present case there was no actual statutory notice is immaterial.

## QUERIES AND REPLIES.

SURVEYOR TO URBAN DISTRICT COUNCIL : PRIVATE PRACTICE. —"A. B." writes: Has an urban district council (having granted their surveyor permission to engage in private practice) power to revoke the same after a period of seventeen years without granting compensation, he (the surveyor) having during that time received a smaller salary in view of the accorded privilege?

In the absence of any agreement under seal binding the council to employ the surveyor for a fixed period, his engagement could be determined by the council "at their pleasure" (see sec. 189 of the Public Health Act, 1875 ; *Reg. v. Darlington School*, 6 Q.B., 682. In *re Teather*, 19 L.J., M.C., 70). It follows that they could revoke the permission to engage in private practice, since dismissal would doubtless follow any continuance of such practice subsequent to the revocation.

DUTIES OF BOROUGH SURVEYOR. —"Borough Surveyor" writes: I have filled my present position for three years, during which time a considerable amount of work has been carried out in the extension of water mains, sewers, new streets, &c. At the present a sewage scheme, estimated to cost about £2,000, is under consideration, for which I have prepared plans, estimate and report. A resolution was proposed that I be instructed to carry out the work without any extra remuneration. This I objected to, contending that I had fulfilled my obligations by the preparation of plans, &c. (see condition of appointment enclosed), at the same time I made application to be paid a commission on new works on contracts above £200 of 2½ per cent., I agreeing to provide at my own cost any extra assistance I may require. I shall be glad to know if, in your opinion, the conditions of appointment and salary include all work I may be requested to do.

Under clause 1 of the "Statement of Duties" the surveyor is to perform "all duties which may be imposed by the authority of the council," and under clause 2½ he is to "devote his whole time to the duties of the office," while clause 23 specifies the salary he is to receive. Having regard to these clauses, I do not think "Borough Surveyor" has any legal claim for extra remuneration for carrying out the sewage scheme.

BUILDING LINE : PUBLIC HEALTH ACT, 1875, SECS. 154 AND 155 : BUILDINGS IN STREETS ACT, 1888, SEC. 3.—"B. L." writes : Along the east side of a common within a rural district having urban powers there is a public footpath, bounded on the east by a ditch, and on the east of the ditch there is a field belonging to A, who purposes to fill up the ditch and build a row of six houses a few feet back from the ditch. At the southern extremity of A's field, and divided from it by an occupation road 8 yards wide, there is an old row of houses set back 18 ft. from the line of this ditch. The local authority require A to set back his new houses in a line with the old houses, and to give up sufficient land where added to the footpath to form a new street 36 ft. wide, under the authority of sec. 3 of the Buildings in Streets Act, 1888. (1) Can A be compelled to set back in this way? He is not, in my opinion, erecting his buildings in a street nor proposing to lay out a new street. (2) Can the local authority prescribe a building line and pay compensation for the land which A has to give up in order to conform to such building line?

(1) The word "street," as defined in sec. 4 of the Public Health Act, 1875, includes any highway (not being a turnpike road) and any lane, footway, &c., whether a thoroughfare or not. This definition is incorporated in the Public Health (Buildings in Streets) Act, 1888 ; consequently that Act would, in my opinion, apply to the public footpath in question if it were in an urban district. Whether the Act applies to this rural district depends upon the order conferring urban powers. Assuming the Act to be applicable, it would be a question of fact for the magistrates whether the new buildings were "in" the "street" ; and also whether the old houses were sufficiently near to be on one side of the new buildings within the meaning of the Act (*Warren v. Mustard*, 61 L.J., M.C. 18). Another question that arises is whether (apart from the Act) A would, by the erection of the proposed buildings, be laying out, or commencing to lay out, the public footpath as a new street, so as to render applicable any by-law that may be in force in the district requiring new streets to be of a certain width. This also would be a question of fact for the magistrates (see reply to "Unus"). (2) Assuming that they possess the requisite urban powers, the authority could, by agreement with A, purchase part of his land for the purpose of widening the highway under sec. 154 of the Public Health Act, 1875, or they could (after obtaining a provisional order under sec. 176 of that Act) purchase the required land compulsorily. But they could not proceed under sec. 155, which only applies where a building has been taken down to be rebuilt or altered.

# Municipal Work in Progress and Projected.

This week information of important undertakings will be found in connection with Canterbury, Douglas, Leicester, Loughborough, Marlborough and other towns. No doubt the recent heavy snowfalls and gales have taxed the energies of many a borough engineer's department.

## METROPOLITAN AUTHORITIES.

### LONDON COUNTY COUNCIL.

As many of our readers will be aware, complaints have recently been rife in regard to the smoke nuisance in London. It is therefore all the more satisfactory to learn that the county council have not been so idle, nor their efforts so unsuccessful, as many have supposed. But, as Mr. Crooks, the chairman of the Public Control Committee, remarked, the local sanitary authorities are difficult to move in the matter, and after their fashion read the special provisions of the Public Health (London) Act, 1891, in two or three different ways.

*The Slaughter-House Question.*—The adjourned report of the Public Health Committee, originally submitted on October 14th, was again brought up for consideration. The recommendations for discussion contained in the report were: (*a*) That, in the opinion of the council, it is desirable that, as a first step towards abolishing the proper inspection of meat, private slaughter-houses should cease to exist in London, and that butchers should, in substitution, be afforded such facilities as are necessary for the killing of animals in public slaughterhouses to be erected by the council; (*b*) that a copy of this report and of the council's resolutions thereon be sent to the Local Government Board, with an intimation that the council is prepared to accept such responsibilities as may be necessary to give effect in London to the recommendations of the Royal Commission on Tuberculosis, and that the board be asked whether they will include in any legislation introduced by them in connection with the Royal Commission's report the provisions which would be necessary for this purpose. Mr. Laughland, chairman of the committee, asked leave to withdraw the report until the architect and other officers had prepared plans and provided further information. This was agreed to.

*Rehousing in Poplar.*—The Housing of the Working Classes Committee submitted a report recommending the council to undertake the rehousing of 180 persons displaced by the Ann-street, Poplar, scheme. In 1896 the East-End Dwellings Company negotiated to purchase the cleared land, in order to provide the dwellings, but the plans deposited by the company were not approved by the Local Government Board, who intimated that single-room tenements could only be allowed if the council guaranteed that they would be occupied by childless married couples, two girls, or two elderly persons of the same sex. To these conditions the company objected. The committee reported that under these circumstances there was no likelihood of any agreement being arrived at with the company. The council had for three years been under a legal obligation to house these persons, and, as there was a great demand for accommodation in the neighbourhood, they thought there should be no further delay. They accordingly recommended that negotiations with the company should be terminated and the standing orders should be suspended, in order to enable the council themselves to erect forthwith dwellings on the cleared area. After a long discussion, the recommendation was agreed to, on a division, by sixty-nine votes to thirty.

*The Smoke Nuisance.*—The Public Control Committee presented a report in reference to the steps they had taken for enforcing the provisions of the Public Health (London) Act, 1891, as to smoke-prevention in London. The report stated that in almost every instance either the sanitary authority had carried out their duties under the Act, or, in consequence of the direct intervention of the council, the parties creating the nuisance had found means for abating it. The report concluded with a narrative of the events which led up to the council's taking proceedings in default of the Lambeth Vestry against two firms in the Lambeth district, which resulted in the maximum fine of £10 being imposed in each case. After some discussion the report was adopted.

*The Telephone Service.*—In reply to Mr. Beachcroft, who asked if it was the case that more than 900 persons were unable to take advantage of the telephone system in London because the council had declined to give their consent to the company carrying out certain works underground, Mr. Benn said that this was the case, and it was due to the fact that certain consents had been withheld by the council. That permission had not been granted because the National Telephone Company had not seen fit to concede terms to London similar to those conceded in other cities. Very shortly, however, a conference would be held between the company and the council, to see if these difficulties could not be overcome.

*Tenders.*—The following tenders were opened for the supply and erection of boilers and fittings at the western pumping station : Messrs. E. Danks & Co., Limited, £2,775 ; R. Taylor & Sons, £2,880 ; J. & J. Horsfield, £3,250 ; W. Arnott, £3,420 ; J. Thompson, £3,500 ; J. Musgrave & Sons, Limited, £3,717.

### COURT OF COMMON COUNCIL.

The lord mayor presided, for the first time, at a meeting of the Court of Common Council on Thursday. The town clerk read a letter from the vestry clerk of Hackney asking for the use of the Guildhall for a proposed conference on the subject of trade obstructions and costermongers' stalls on the highways. On the motion of Mr. Buddeley the necessary permission was granted.—Mr. Wallace was nominated to represent the corporation at a conference to be held by the London County Council with a view to formulating some general scheme for the maintenance of small open spaces in the county of London.—A letter was read from the clerk to the London County Council, enclosing copies of the report of the Water Committee and the resolutions passed by the council to promote in the ensuing session of Parliament a Bill for the purchase of the water companies' undertakings, and also a Bill for the introduction of a new water supply from Wales. The corporation were asked whether it was still their wish to assist the council under the agreement which was entered into between the two bodies some years ago. Mr. Cloudsley moved that the question should be referred to the County Purposes Committee for consideration. Mr. Wallace, however, moved an amendment, that the question should be referred to a committee of the whole court. Considerable discussion ensued, but on a show of hands the amendment was adopted by a sweeping majority.— Mr. Timbrell asked the chairman of the Streets Committee to make some inquiry into the condition of London Bridge. Its present muddy state was, he declared, disgraceful. The footpaths were kept clean, but so muddy and greasy was the roadway that a pedestrian could scarcely keep his foothold. Mr. Turner said he would make the necessary inquiries.— The Improvements and Finance Committee submitted a report relative to the petition of certain inhabitants of Crutched-friars and the neighbourhood directing attention to an opportunity for improving the means of communication between Crutched-friars and Fenchurch-street. The committee submitted for adoption an arrangement and plan for making a new street, 40 ft. wide, connecting the said thoroughfares, the corporation to construct the new thoroughfare with sewer, subways, vaults, &c., and the owners of the vacant site to contribute £6,000. The scheme was approved without discussion.—The same committee also submitted a plan for making Lothbury 50 ft. wide between Old Jewry and Prince's-street, at an estimated cost of £42,000, together with a letter from the London County Council agreeing to contribute one-third of the nett cost of the improvement, such contribution not to exceed £15,000. The committee recommended that the improvements should be carried out accordingly. The committee further recommended, relative to the proposed improvement at the western end of Cheapside, that the leasehold and trade interest of Messrs. Dunn's trustees in 4A Cheapside should be acquired for £3,750 ; and also that the ground needed to widen the public way in front of the premises, 39 and 40 Hutton-street, and 40 and 42 Primrose-hill, should be acquired for the sum of £240. The recommendations of the committee were approved.—The Streets Committee presented a report relative to a letter from the Metropolitan Electric Supply Company, Limited, asking for the formal consent of the corporation to their intended application to the Board of Trade for a provisional order for the supply of electricity within the City. The committee recommended that the company should be informed that the corporation regretted that they were unable to give their consent to the application. After some discussion the recommendation was agreed to.—On the recommendation of the Streets Committee the court agreed that an application should be made for a license to establish a telephone service, in conjunction with the London County Council and other local authorities within the London telephone area.—Sir Albert Altman moved : " That it be referred to the Streets Committee to consider and report on the dangerous condition of Ludgate-hill station and the necessity of more accommodation being provided for passengers, with power to communicate with the Board of Trade on the subject." Sir Albert said that, owing to the enormous increase in the passenger traffic, Ludgate-hill station had become absolutely dangerous. The staircases were only 6ft. wide, and in some places less than that. The entrance to the platforms was by means of a hole cut through them, and from it a passenger emerged like a Jack-in-the-box. To make matters even worse, there was a continual block on the staircase, owing to the passengers who had detrained meeting those who were eager to catch a train. The station was built of wood many years ago, and if the station caught fire it would result in a fearful catastrophe. The motion was adopted with unanimity.

### METROPOLITAN ASYLUMS BOARD.

The usual fortnightly meeting of the above body was held on Saturday, Sir E. H. Galsworthy, J.P., the chairman, presiding. A letter was received from the Local Government Board enclosing a copy of the report of Mr. W. E. Knollys on the recent inquiry held by him with reference to the Brook Hospital. Full particulars of the board's letter and Mr.

Knolly's report are given in another column.—In a second communication the Local Government Board, adverting to the managers' application for an order authorising the borrowing of a further sum of £101,830 14s. 4d. in connection with the erection, &c., of the Brook Hospital, stated that under the circumstances they deemed it right to omit from the order the amount due to the architect in consideration of the extra works. As that amount appeared to be £375, the order would authorise the borrowing of the sum of £101,456 instead of £101,830. The Local Government Board further wrote enclosing copies of an order authorising the reconstruction of the North-Eastern Hospital and the erection of a water tower thereat, at a cost not exceeding the sum of £126,850, and the borrowing of the amount.

## VESTRIES AND DISTRICT BOARDS.

**Battersea.**—The vestry on Wednesday received a deputation from the Butchers' Trade Society with reference to the proposals of the London County Council in connection with the abolition of private slaughter-houses and the establishment of public abattoirs. In the course of his arguments against the proposal Mr. Lindsay, the spokesman of the deputation, stated that the scheme, if carried into effect, would necessitate an expenditure of £1,500,000, and that someone would have to pay for it. In reply to questions, Mr. Lindsay stated that in consequence of representations made by his society and by agricultural societies the London County Council had the previous day postponed the consideration of the question until after Christmas, that making the fourth postponement of the matter. The vestry resolved to refer the subject to the Health Committee for consideration.—With reference to the proposal to erect a refreshment kiosk at the Morden cemetery, as sanctioned by the vestry in September last, the Cemetery Committee reported that they had deferred the consideration of the question until next March.—The Highways Committee announced that they had considered a report by the surveyor on the condition of the gullies throughout the parish, and that the total estimated cost of thoroughly carrying out the work amounted to £8,268. On the recommendation of the committee it was resolved to proceed with the work, the cost to be defrayed by loan.—A letter had been received by the Highways Committee from the manager of the South London Tramways Company concerning the lowering of the roadway under the West London Extension Railway bridge over Falcon-road. At the suggestion of the committee the vestry decided to give permission to the company to skim the present concrete and use a 5½-in. girder, instead of a 7-in. girder as at present laid, and to defer until the new year the paving works proposed to be carried out under all the bridges crossing Falcon-road.—The special committee appointed to consider the question of the steps to be taken to vest the water supply in the people of London reported that they had been in communication with the various vestries and district boards on the subject. It appeared from the replies received that twenty-two of the authorities were in favour of the water supply being vested in a public authority, six were in favour of the control of the water being placed in the hands of a public authority, and thirteen reserved their opinion until the issue of the report of the Royal Commission. With regard to the constitution of the authority, the Special Committee stated that only nine local authorities suggested the London County Council as that body. In a further report the committee stated that since instituting the above-mentioned inquiries the county council had adopted various resolutions on the water question. On the recommendation of the committee it was decided to approve generally of the conclusions arrived at by the county council.—A short time ago the Works Committee were instructed to consider the question of preparing a scheme for the unloading of barges, under which the barges would be discharged at the vestry's wharf and the material carted direct to where it was required, instead of being carted from the wharf to the various depots of the vestry. The committee found that in order to arrange a system for carrying out the bargework upon the above lines additional wharfage accommodation would be reqired. The conclusion arrived at was that the Falcon and granite wharves in Lombard-road were the most suitable premises, and the committee recommended that negotiations should be entered into for the purchase of the premises. After considerable discussion the proposal of the committee was adopted by a large majority.—A long report was submitted by the Baths Committee notifying the consent of the Local Government Board to the borrowing of £34,370 for the erection of baths and £1,380 for the boring of artesian wells, the latter sum to be repaid in five years.

**Bermondsey.**—The vestry on Monday discussed a report of the Sanitary Committee in reference to letters received in connection with the proposals of the London County Council relative to the abolition of private slaughter-houses and the erection of public abattoirs. The committee, while not feeling competent to express an opinion on the subject, reported that the medical officer of health was of opinion that the establishment of abattoirs would be of considerable advantage to the public health and would largely facilitate the detection of diseased meat. Eventually the report was referred back to the committee for further consideration and for the reception of a deputation representing the butchering interests.—The London County Council, in reference to the

visit of a deputation from the vestry in regard to the housing of the working classes in Bermondsey, had asked to be furnished with information as to any vacant site in the district which might be suitable for the erection of artisans' dwellings. In this connection the Sanitary Committee reported that they had investigated the subject, and submitted a list of sites likely to be suitable, a copy of which was directed to be forwarded to the council.—The Electric Lighting Committee stated that on attending the inquiry held by Major Cardew at the Board of Trade, consequent upon the appeal of the London Electric Supply Corporation against the vestry's disapproval of the laying of mains in certain streets, the company produced the written consent of the London County Council to the execution of the works objected to. This was the first intimation received of the approval of the council, and the committee expressed the opinion that before sanctioning works in the parish the council should first ask for the vestry's views thereon. On the recommendation of the committee it was resolved to inform the council to that effect.—A motion was proposed by Mr. Dumphreys in favour of the surveyor being requested to prepare an estimate for the cleaning and redecoration of the town hall, board-room and offices, and that the estimate should be submitted for the immediate consideration of the General Purposes Committee.—The General Purposes Committee reported that they had considered the following tenders for the supply of slop vans: Bristol Waggon Company, £46 each; Glover & Sons, £44; E. & H. Hora, £45; A. Parker, £42; A. Randell, £43 10s.; and T. Baker & Son, £38 5s. Mr. A. Parker's tender was accepted.

**Islington.**—The vestry clerk at the last meeting read a letter from the solicitors to the North Metropolitan Tramways Company, intimating the intention of the company to apply to the Light Railway Commissioners for powers to construct a light railway from the county boundary in Archway-road through Finchley to Whetstone. The letter asked the vestry to urge the necessity of constructing a light railway from the Archway Tavern to the Archway, the boundary of the metropolitan area. It was decided to refer the letter to the Works Committee for consideration.—Messrs. Mills & Simons were appointed to represent the vestry at the conference to be held at the Islington Vestry Hall to-day (Friday) to consider the question of the reform of London local government. It was mentioned that many of the vestries and district boards had agreed to send delegates to the conference.—The Public Health Committee reported that they had reconsidered the communication from the London County Council inviting an expression of opinion on the proposal of the council to establish a bacteriological laboratory for London. On the recommendation of the committee it was resolved to take no action in the matter until further information on the subject had been obtained.—The committee also announced that they had considered a report from the medical officer of health on the subject of establishing public abattoirs in London. The medical officer expressed the opinion that the London County Council, who were proposing to take steps in the direction of providing public slaughter-houses, should be supported by the vestry. It was decided to approve the report and forward a copy to the county council.—The Parliamentary Committee submitted a report on the subject of the draft Water Bill proposed to be introduced by Mr. H. S. Samuel, M.P., and recommended that the author should be informed that the vestry were of opinion that the remedy sought to be effected by the Bill would be more satisfactorily attained by the whole of the undertakings of the various water companies being placed under the control of the county council. The recommendation was adopted without any discussion.—It was decided, at the suggestion of the Works Committee, to reconstruct the pipe sewer in Cambridge-terrace, at an estimated cost of £340; to repair a portion of Essex-road, at a cost of £200; and to expend £313 on the erection of greenhouses to keep the plants in at the Finchley cemetery.—With regard to the question of the maintenance of main roads, the Parliamentary Committee stated that they had considered the letter on the subject from the Limehouse Board of Works, who drew attention to the proposal of the London County Council to transfer the maintenance to the local authorities. The board pointed out that the effect of such transfer would be to deprive the local authorities of the contributions now received from the council towards the cost of the upkeep of those thoroughfares, and that it was proposed to convene a conference to consider the question.—A long discussion took place on the presentation of a report by the Electric Lighting Committee recommending the suspension of one of the by-laws in order to enable the committee to invite tenders from a selection of firms for the projected large extension of the electric light station. The committee were of opinion that, in order to avoid a repetition of past delays, it was desirable to invite building firms of the highest standing to tender privately, as experience had shown that many first-class firms would " not reply to advertisements for tenders in the public Press." An amendment was moved in favour of advertising for open tenders, and on a division this was adopted by thirty-six votes to thirty-one. Owing, however, to the operation of the by-laws the amendment could not be put as a substantive motion, and its further consideration was postponed to the next meeting.—A report was submitted by the Baths Committee announcing that they had received and considered tenders for the extension of Hornsey-road baths. The committee recommended the acceptance, at £14,630, of the tender of Mr. H. L. Holloway, Union Works, Deptford. The report was deferred until the next meeting.

**Lewisham.**—Upon the receipt of a communication from the London Butchers' Trade Society, forwarding a copy of a petition presented to the London County Council in reference to the proposed closing of private slaughter-houses and the establishment in lieu thereof of public abattoirs, the board have decided that to do away with private slaughter-houses would not be in the interests of either producer or consumer, nor required in the interests of the public health. It was stated that the cost of establishing public abattoirs would be £1,000,000, and it might be £1,500,000.—The board have decided to take the necessary steps for the construction of an underground convenience in High-street, Lewisham, at an estimated cost of £1,800.

**St. James, Westminster.**—An important question, arising out of the proceedings of the Public Health Committee, was brought before the vestry at their last meeting by Mr. W. H. Watson. The speaker drew attention to the committee's recommendation in favour of the soil pipes at the new Carlton hotel being permitted to be placed inside the building. Quoting from the by-laws made by the London County Council under the Public Health (London) Act, 1891, Mr. Watson stated that under these regulations all soil pipes in the case of new buildings must be erected outside the structures, and that in existing buildings the pipes should, whenever practicable, also be placed outside. After a long discussion it was decided to refer the question to the Public Health and Works Committee for consideration and report.— The Public Health Committee reported that they had received a certificate from Mr. Monson, the surveyor, for the payment of £206 9s. to Messrs. Finch & Co. for fixing semi-circular back urinals at the Piccadilly conveniences, in lieu of those existing. Having been informed by the surveyor that the work had been completed in a satisfactory manner, the vestry decided to refer the matter to the Finance Committee for payment. —The Works Committee recommended the recision of a previous resolution declining to sanction the application of the London Hydraulic-Power Company to lay mains in three streets unless the Company agreed to pay an adequate rent for the privilege. The motion was, however, not carried, the voting being thirteen for and thirteen against recision.—It was decided to refer to the Works Committee complaints made as to the alleged forcing of steam into the sewers in Carnaby-street from the premises of electric light company. In connection with this question the surveyor stated that he had not been able to ascertain that steam was turned into the sewers, but that the evils probably arose from hot water being passed out, from which steam was given off.—The Works Committee reported that they had invited tenders from six firms and by public advertisement for the supply of horses, carts and men for snow cartage during the winter. The only tenders received were from Messrs. Mead & Co., of Paddington, and Mr. J. Bolton, 11 Little James-street, Bedford-row, these being at a schedule of prices. On the recommendation of the committee it was decided to accept both tenders.

**St. Marylebone.**—At the last meeting of the vestry the surveyor was asked whether any of the district superintendents had been appointed. In reply, Mr. Waddington stated that the cleansing superintendent had been selected and was on the point of taking up his duties. In this connection Mr. White asked whether the Sanitary Committee had considered the question of applying to the London County Council for a moiety of the salaries of the staff. Mr. W. H. Garbutt, vestry clerk, replied that the authority had always stood outside of any such arrangement, preferring to pay their own salaries. On the motion of Mr. White it was decided to refer the consideration of the question to the Sanitary Committee, the proposer stating that the vestry were paying £1,700 a year, of which one-half should be contributed by the county council.—The Works Committee presented a report in regard to a previous suggestion that the renewal of the trenches in Oxford-street should be carried on both day and night. On the recommendation of the committee it was resolved not to adopt this course.—A motion stood in the name of Mr. G. B. Crook, proposing that the Electric Lighting Committee should be instructed to inquire and report whether the Metropolitan Electric Supply Company have power to sell that portion of their undertaking situated in Marylebone, and whether the vestry can legally purchase it; and that the committee should be authorised to employ experts to advise them on the subject. The consideration of the motion was postponed.—The Works Committee recommended the acceptance, at £127 10s., of the estimate of Mr. George Jennings for erecting a four-stall urinal in Acacia-road, and that of the same firm, amounting to £158 10s., for a six-stall urinal in Market-place.

## PROVINCIAL AND GREATER LONDON AUTHORITIES.

### MUNICIPAL CORPORATIONS.

**Bristol.**—Colonel C. H. Luard, R.E., Local Government Board inspector, conducted an inquiry on Friday in respect of the proposed transfer by the corporation of certain consolidated stock and to the application of the proceeds of such transfer in purchasing certain land at Portishead for the improvement of the corporate estates, and certain lands at Bedminster-down and Ashton-gate as sites for pleasure-grounds. Further, respecting the corporation's application to borrow £11,050 for purposes of streets improvement and £1,420 for the provision of a steam roller and other plant.

**Burnley.**—A Local Government Board inquiry was held on Thursday into an application of the town council for sanction to borrow £10,000 for electric lighting. It was stated that the works had been profitable from the start, yielding a surplus of £500 a year. A sum of £25,000 is already being spent in extending the works and engine-power, and now £10,000 is needed for new mains to meet the rapidly-increasing demand.

**Canterbury.**—Colonel Durnford, R.E., an inspector of the Local Government Board, has conducted an inquiry into an application by the town council for sanction to loans of £6,050 and £1,150 respectively, for the provision of public baths and the erection of dwellings for the labourers employed on the sewage farm. The town clerk and city surveyor attended, on behalf of the council, in support of the application. This application is but a further item of the ambitious programme of the city council, who we are glad to record are now going thoroughly ahead, determined to speedily bring themselves quite abreast of the times. Having completed the sanatorium, there is now being installed a combined electricity and refuse destructor plant, at an initial cost of about £30,000. These works are rapidly approaching completion, so that it is hoped the current may be switched on for shop lighting by Christmas. The question, so much combatted at present, as to the real calorific value of town refuse will have excellent opportunity of being tested at these works. The refuse destructor plant is by Messrs. Beaman & Deas. The new public library and museum is also nearing completion. The chief works in immediate project include a lunatic asylum, new municipal buildings and extended main sewerage; also a central corporation depot and workmen's dwellings. During the last three years the city has been well nigh repaved throughout in all its principal streets, whilst now attention is being directed to the numerous by-lanes. The road surfacing is gradually undergoing a conversion from the old granite and flint macadam road into the more welcome surface, known as "tarred macadam." It is thus evident that Canterbury is by no means lagging in the forward movement.

**Dorchester.**—The town council have decided to apply to the Local Government Board for sanction to borrow £1,900 for purposes in connection with the extension of the municipal buildings.

**Douglas.**—The corporation are applying for powers to borrow £50,000 for the construction of a new reservoir in West Baldwin Valley. The present water supply, the source of which is at Onchan, is sufficient for all the probable demands that will be made upon it for some years, but, in view of the growth of Douglas and its position as a health resort, it is thought advisable to have two distinct watersheds and be able to meet almost any emergency. The two reservoirs now in use hold 73,000,000 gallons; the new reservoir is to have a capacity of 300,000,000. The cost will mean an increase in the rates of 3d. in the £1.

**Hartlepool.**—On Tuesday an inspector of the Local Government Board conducted an inquiry into an application of this authority for sanction to borrow £5,730 for the purchase of a refuse destructor. The mayor gave evidence bearing upon the sanitary aspect of the question, adding that the proposed site was, in his opinion, the best that could be selected. Its area consisted of 2,420 square yards, and its cost would be £700. The inquiry having closed, the inspector visited the locus in quo.

**Hull.**—The Electric Lighting Committee of the corporation on Tuesday accepted the tenders of Messrs. T. Parker & Co., Limited, for switchboards, transformers and motor generator at £3,630; Messrs. Siemens Brothers for cables, &c., at £10,655; and Messrs. Barker & Aspey (Hull) for pump condensers and steam-water pipes, at £915.

**Ilkeston.**—The town council are applying to the Board of Trade for two provisional orders authorising the provision of electric tramways and the supply of electricity in the borough. The estimated cost is £80,000.

**Ipswich.**—At the last meeting of the corporation it was announced that Mr. T. H. Tacon, the present high sheriff of Suffolk, had offered to give to the town a drinking fountain and cattle trough, to be erected near the cattle market at the junction of Princes-street and Portman-road. The design, prepared for the donor by Mr. F. Wheeler, F.R.I.B.A., of 6 Staple-inn, E.C., showed an erection of Portland stone, with granite base and basin. The gift was accepted with hearty thanks.

**Leicester.**—The town council, at a large and protracted special meeting, held on Tuesday, unanimously approved of a scheme for bringing the water of the Upper Derwent and Ashop, a distance of 66 miles, to Leicester, at a cost of £4,250,000. The scheme drains the watershed of 31,000 acres, yielding over 50,000,000 gallons daily.

**Lichfield.**—An inspector of the Local Government Board has held an inquiry into an application of the city council for sanction to borrow £1,083 for the extension of the sewerage system of the city. Mr. C. J. Corrie, the city surveyor, explained the plans.

**Loughborough.**—A Local Government Board inquiry was held on the 11th inst. respecting an application of the town council for approval to the borrowing of £7,750 for various public works. The items making up this amount are alterations and additions to the town hall, £4,500; works of sewerage, £2,500; public walks and pleasure grounds, £550; and a depot in Dead-lane, £200. The surveyor, Mr. A. H. Walker, was present at the inquiry, at the termination of which the inspector made the usual inspection of the various sites.

**Manchester.**—In the course of his remarks on election as lord mayor, Mr. W. H. Vawdrey said that the electric light had been in every way a success. It had only been in operation five years, and there were over 200,000 8 candle-power lamps connected with the electric light stations. The charge for the current was one of the lowest in the kingdom, averaging 3¾d. per unit. Everyone connected with the city deserved the greatest credit. He had no doubt their electric tramway system, when completed, would give every satisfaction to the citizens, and would also produce large annual profits in relief of the rates.

**Marlborough.**—At a special meeting of the town council, which was held last week, to consider matters affecting the main drainage scheme, a letter was read from the Local Government Board formally sanctioning the borrowing by the council of £7,400 for works of sewerage and sewage disposal.

**Nelson.**—The town council, having decided to apply for powers to construct a light railway from Nelson to Colne, have instructed the borough surveyor to prepare the necessary plans, sections, &c. The overhead electric system is proposed to be adopted.

**Norwich.**—The work of laying tramway lines through the central thoroughfares of the city has been in progress for some six months past. There will be termini on Earlham-road (near the cemetery), Dereham-road, Silver-road, Thorpe-road, Trowse railway bridge, Household Heath, Aylsham-road, Newmarket-road and City-road, and all the lines will converge near the General Post Office. Electric power will be used for traction.

**Okehampton.**—Mr. G. W. Willcocks held an inquiry recently in regard to an application of the town council for sanction to borrow £130 for works of sewerage. There was no opposition.

**Portsmouth.**—By thirty-nine votes to three the town council on Tuesday decided to give twelve months' notice to the Provincial Tramways Company of their intention to purchase the local tramways, the question of price to be settled by arbitration. It is proposed, on taking over the system, to substitute electricity for horse traction. The precise kind of electrical traction has yet to be settled, and a deputation is to be sent to various towns in England and on the Continent to obtain information on the subject. The estimated cost of the purchase of the tramways and their equipment is about £245,000.

**Sheffield.**—We regret to state that a paragraph relating to a Local Government Board inquiry at Sheffield appeared in our " Municipal Works in Progress and Projected " column of our last issue under the heading of " Liverpool."

**York.**—On the recommendation of the city engineer, the city council have sanctioned the expenditure of £1,000 on the provision of experimental plant for the purification of the city sewage. The lime and aluminoferric process is now in operation, the resulting sludge being pressed in the ordinary manner into cakes, which are disposed of to farmers in the district.

## URBAN DISTRICT COUNCILS.

**Abergavenny.**—On the 17th inst. Colonel C. H. Luard, R.E., held an inquiry, on behalf of the Local Government Board, respecting an application of the district council for sanction to borrow £1,640 for sewerage works, according to plans prepared by their engineer, Mr. J. Haigh. At the close of the inquiry the inspector visited the site of the proposed works, in company with Mr. E. Martin, the chairman of the council, and Major Williams, the chairman of the Sanitary Committee.

**Barking.**—An inquiry was held at the public offices on Thursday morning by Mr. Herbert H. Law, Local Government Board inspector, relative to an application made by the district council for sanction to borrow £6,500 for works of sewerage and sewage disposal and £3,150 for purposes of public walks and pleasure grounds.

**Bexley.**—The urban district council have instructed their surveyor, Mr. Tom Vickers, to prepare a scheme and submit the necessary plans for dealing with the sewage of the low-lying portion of the town. Mr. Vickers has already submitted a long detailed report dealing with a proposed scheme for the erection of electric lighting works in the district, and a resolution has been adopted by the council deciding upon an application for a provisional order. The surveyor was at the same time congratulated on his able report.

**Bognor.**—The district council recently advertised for tenders for the construction of a new sea wall and esplanade, 487 ft. in length. Only one tender was, however, received, the tenderers being Messrs. Grounds & Newton, Bournemouth, who offered to carry out the work for £2,667. This amount being considerably above the surveyor's estimate, the council have decided to do the work themselves.

**Brigg.**—At a special meeting of the council, held recently, the following resolution was adopted : " That a Bill be promoted in the next session of Parliament by this council, authorising them to purchase the undertaking of the Brigg Gas Company, Limited, to manufacture and supply gas, and for other purposes, and that the costs and expenses attending the same shall be paid out of the general district rate, or other public funds or rates under the control of this council."

**Gainsborough.**—The council are about to promote a Bill in Parliament to authorise and empower them to acquire the gasworks of the town on such terms as may be agreed on between the council and the company, or, failing an agreement, by arbitration under the provisions of the Lands Clauses Acts. The initial cost will be heavy, but as the company are at present paying a good dividend there is no reason why the works should not be a source of revenue.

**Comersal.**—A Local Government Board inquiry is to be held here on Tuesday next into certain applications of the council for sanction to borrow £10,000 for purchasing the undertaking of the Gomersall Waterworks Company and £8,000 for carrying out sewage works within the Birstall township.

**Leyton.**—On Friday last Mr. Robert H. Bicknell, an inspector of the Local Government Board, held an inquiry at the town hall, Leyton, with respect to applications made by the district council for sanction to borrow £3,230 for private street improvement and £4,965 for public street improvements. Mr. Dawson, the council's surveyor, explained the plans. There was no opposition.

**Newport Pagnell.**—Mr. E. A. Sandford Fawcett conducted an inquiry last week, on behalf of the Local Government Board, into an application of the urban district council for sanction to borrow £9,000 for works of sewerage and sewage disposal. Messrs. D. Balfour & Sons, of London and Newcastle, are the engineers for the works, to which, it may be mentioned, considerable opposition is being made.

**Uckfield.**—A Local Government Board inquiry was held last week with regard to an application of the urban district council for sanction to a loan of £600 for sewerage extensions at the north end of the town. Mr. C. Thompson, the surveyor, explained the working of the scheme, to which no opposition was offered.

**Walton-on-the-Naze.**—The district council have adopted the scheme prepared by Messrs. Frederick Beesley & Son for the improvement of the drainage of the town, whereby the sewage will be conveyed to a point locally known as the Twizzle. Application is to be made for sanction to a loan of £6,000 to carry out the work.

**Wath-upon-Dearne.**—On the 16th inst. an inquiry was held by Mr. R. J. Reece, M.D., Local Government Board inspector, into an application of the Wath, Swinton, Greasborough and North Rotherham Joint Hospital Board for sanction to borrow a sum of £9,000 for the purpose of purchasing land and building an infectious diseases hospital for the district. Evidence was given by Mr. W. T. Campsall, architect to the board, and Mr. H. C. Poole, surveyor to the urban district council. No opposition was offered to the scheme.

**Wilmslow.**—On Thursday last Colonel Smith, an inspector of the Local Government Board, held a public inquiry at Wilmslow respecting the district council's application for sanction to borrow £2,000 for the purchase of land required for new public offices and street improvements. The council propose to remove old buildings near Swan-street, erect offices, and widen the Manchester and Alderley main road.

**Withington.**—A meeting of the council was held on Thursday. The proceedings of the Parliamentary Committee, which were adopted, included a resolution instructing the clerk to arrange for an interview with the Tramways Committee of the Manchester Corporation, with the view of discussing the terms upon which the corporation will be prepared to take a lease of the trams in the district; and providing that, in the event of an arrangement not being made, a Bill be promoted in the next session of Parliament empowering the council to work the tramways themselves.

## RURAL DISTRICT COUNCILS.

**Alnwick.**—At a meeting of the council, held last week, it was resolved to apply to the Local Government Board for sanction to borrow £650 for additional works of water supply for Alnmouth.

**Brailes, Warwickshire.**—The district council have instructed Mr. J. E. Willcox, of Birmingham, to report upon a question of water supply for the district of Little Compton.

**Cwyrfal.**—At a meeting of this body on Saturday a committee were appointed for the purpose of taking the preliminary steps to obtain an Act of Parliament to enable them to secure the waters of the lake and tarns in their district which have not already been appropriated, for their own use, and to take over all the waterworks in their district. A letter was read from the Local Government Board sanctioning the borrowing of £2,000 for the construction of a waterworks at Portdinorwic, and it was resolved to proceed with the work forthwith.

## LONDON WATER SUPPLY COMMISSION.

The Royal Commission on the subject of the London water supply held their thirty-fifth meeting at the Guildhall, Westminster, on Monday. The proceedings, however, were conducted in private. Another sitting was held on Tuesday.

Mr. REGINALD E. MIDDLETON, asked for his view as to the effect upon the consumer of the purchase of the water companies' undertakings, said there would be a loss to the consumer, and still more to the ratepayer, if the conditions of revenue spoken of by the witness of the London County Council were carried out; that was to say if the rates were reduced to one level for all London. Several of the costs now borne by the companies would in future be borne by the ratepayers, such as frosts and droughts. Then he did not think the purchase would be remunerative, because the price would be such as to prevent it from being remunerative at once; but no doubt it would be remunerative in time. He thought it was more fair to have differential rates than one rate for London, because it cost more to supply higher than lower districts. He thought that a company worked by a board who had been in existence for a great many years, and who were paid to do their duty, were more likely to be economical than one of a fleeting character, who were unpaid and who were unlikely to effect economies. Moreover, he thought municipal management did not, as a rule, effect economies. He did not believe in the necessity of going to Wales for an additional supply. If there was such a necessity there would be a deduction on that account from the cost of purchase. In his opinion it would be practicable for the county of London to purchase the whole existing supply and give the outside districts their present supplies with a margin, but it would be inconvenient and expensive. He was opposed to severance between London and the outside counties, because he thought it undesirable that there should be division of authorities.

The commission will meet again on Monday, when the examination of Mr. Reginald Middleton will be resumed.

## LOCAL GOVERNMENT.

On Friday, at the London School of Economics and Political Science, London, Mr. H. Hobhouse, M.P., delivered a lecture upon " Devolution and the Limits of Local Government." He said that we had in this country a vast and complicated array of machinery for conducting our local government, but this machinery was somewhat imperfectly organised and lacked coherence amongst its various members. The existing local bodies were dependent on Parliament, either being the creatures of statute, or, if created by charter, being invested with statutory powers. Thus Parliament could at any time modify their constitution and their powers. But melancholy as was the abject subjection of all local authorities to Parliament, still more humiliating were their relations to the central executive. They were, as a rule, subject to a twofold control, administrative and financial. The relations of the local bodies to each other afforded still more room for reflection than their relations to the central executive; indeed, if Englishmen were not generally gifted with common sense and a prejudice in favour of low rates, it was appalling to think of the waste of money which might be caused by the present want of organisation. But the existing want of co-ordination would perhaps be tolerable, and might certainly be remedied if it were not for another element which greatly aggravated and complicated the situation—namely, the constant struggle of the minor local authorities for autonomy. He mentioned that local affairs were best administered locally, because local knowledge was essential to meet the varying circumstances of the district, and that decentralisation resulted in greater economy, more freedom from politics, and in the encouragement of local public spirit.

## THE SANITARY INSTITUTE.

### NEWCASTLE-UPON-TYNE EXAMINATIONS.

At an examination for inspectors of nuisances, held at Newcastle-upon-Tyne, by the Sanitary Institute, on the 11th and 12th inst., thirty-six candidates presented themselves, twenty-four of whom were certified as to their sanitary knowledge, competent to discharge the duties of inspectors of nuisances.

The following were the questions set for answer in writing: (1) What is the difference between a disinfectant, an antiseptic and a deodorant? Name the best means of disinfecting (a) dejecta, (b) bed linen, (c) mattresses and (d) rooms. (2) What statutory provisions exist for preventing the use of polluted well water for drinking purposes? (3) What is the

usual procedure adopted when an inspector finds unsound meat exposed for sale? (4) What nuisances are likely to arise in the following trades: (a) Manufacture of kid gloves, (b) the storage of carbide of calcium, (c) the manufacture of illuminating gas from crude petroleum, and (d) blood boiling. (5) A nuisance arises from a foul accumulation of manure on private premises. What power of entry is given by the Public Health Acts, and how would you deal with the nuisance? (6) How would you proceed to test (a) new drains and (b) old drains? (7) Describe the various forms of stoneware and lead traps in common use. Give sketches showing the diameters of the traps and the positions in which they should be placed. (8) How long will it take to fill a cistern 5 ft. by 4 ft. by 3 ft. 6 in. through a pipe 1 in. diameter, the rate of flow being 3 ft. per second.

## INSTITUTION OF CIVIL ENGINEERS.

### ORDINARY MEETING.

An ordinary meeting of the Institution of Civil Engineers will be held on Tuesday, at 8 p.m., when a paper will be read by Mr. Stanley Robert Kay, A.M.I.C.E., entitled "The Effect of Subsidence due to Coal Workings upon Bridges and other Structures." A discussion will follow the reading of the paper.

### STUDENTS' MEETING.

A meeting for the students of the Institution will be held on Friday, at 8 p.m., Mr. T. Forster Brown, member of the council, in the chair. Mr. Charles Benjamin Saner will read a paper on " The Sunlight Gold-bearing Reef, Lydenburg, Transvaal."

**Self-propelled Traffic.**—At the opening meeting of the Liverpool and district centre of the Self-propelled Traffic Association, held at Liverpool on Wednesday, Prof. Hele Shaw, one of the judges, gave a description of the different vehicles in the late competition. The report of the judges in the trials was also submitted and adopted. The report stated that the judges did not consider the motor vehicles could successfully compete for traffic with railways at reduced rates except under special circumstances, while greater maintenance and depreciation charges for common roads would be involved than were used in the judges' calculations. The limit of tare imposed by the Highway Act of 1896 tended to reduce seriously the strength of the working parts and prevented the construction of a really satisfactory motor vehicle. An increase in the limit from 3 tons to 4 tons would have no inconvenience, while a tare of 6 tons might be allowed in certain localities, but such increase should not be accompanied by new restrictions.

**Electrical Transmission of Power.**—On Wednesday, at the Society of Arts, Prof. George Forbes, F.R.S., read a paper on the " Long-Distance Transmission of Electric Power." In the course of the paper the lecturer remarked that, though long-distance transmission had been much talked about, little had been done, and there were few people who realised what a vast field there was in that way for investment of capital on a sound commercial basis. He proceeded to refer to some instances with which he had to deal in India, New Zealand and Egypt, in which long distances were concerned. Thus he found, when considering the utilisation of the Nile cataracts, that the electric lighting of Cairo could be done more cheaply by power generated at the first cataract—400 miles distant as the crow flies—than by steam engines at Cairo, and he believed that if the gold mines in Rhodesia were really good it would pay handsomely to transmit electric energy 500 miles from the Victoria Falls of the Zambesi, provided the surveys showed the falls to be as satisfactory as they appeared by the photographs, and provided that fever was not an insurmountable obstacle.

## THE PURIFICATION AND STERILISATION OF DRINKING WATER.

HOWATSON-BERGE SYSTEM.

The question of the purification and sterilisation of water has never attracted so much attention as at present. A few notes on the above-named system may therefore be of interest. It is a combination of the Howatson filter with a method of sterilisation devised by Profs. Henri and Albert Bergé, of Brussels. The germicide employed is chlorine peroxide ($ClO_2$), prepared by the action of sulphuric acid (specific gravity 1·711) on chlorate of potash, at a temperature of 15 deg. Centigrade, and used either in the gaseous condition or in the form of a standardised solution. It is claimed for the Bergé germicide that it possesses a greater oxidising energy than ozone, by virtue of which power it rapidly burns up (in the chemical sense) any organic matter with which it comes in contact; and, furthermore, that whilst fatal to bacteria and the germs of micro-organisms and microscopic plants generally, it is innocuous towards man, animals and the higher members of the vegetable kingdom, both fishes and ordinary plants thriving in water charged with an excess of the peroxide. The advantage of cheapness is also claimed for this reagent, the quantity required for ordinary natural waters in a relatively pure condition being 2 grammes per cubic metre of water, and the cost 1d. per 100 cubic metres (22,000 gallons). In the case of waters polluted by sewage the quantity has to be increased to about 5 grammes per cubic metre, in order to ensure the destruction of the micro-organisms present.

No inconvenience attends the employment of the peroxide—so far as risk of overloading the water with chlorine is concerned—since the amount of chlorine in 2 milligrammes is only 0·0004 grammes, whilst the town water of Brussels, which contains 0·011 grammes of chlorine per litre (*i.e.*, twenty-seven times as much), is considered as very low in that constituent. The water treated by the Bergé method has an agreeable flavour, and is not subjected to any great modification in chemical composition, the only changes produced—*viz.*, diminution of organic matter, increase of oxygen in solution, and complete destruction of micro-organisms—being quantitatively slight, though highly advantageous.

In the report issued by Messrs. E. André, chief inspector of waterworks to the Belgian Board of Works, and A. Verraert, municipal engineer of Ostend, are detailed the results obtained by the Howartson-Bergé system in the purification of the water supply of the above-named seaside resort. The water is passed through a Howartson purifier, where it is freed from calcareous salts and most of the suspended organic matter, and is afterwards conducted through sand filters and a polarite filter. For the sterilisation process a small pneumatic pump is employed to force air, under a pressure of about two atmospheres, into a reservoir, for the purpose of washing out the generating apparatus producing the peroxide and for driving the gas into the solution vessels. The solution is drawn off into a lead-lined tank, fitted with a graduated tap leading to the conduit containing the water to be sterilised, and the mixture of germicide and water is allowed to run through a coiled pipe, in order to ensure a thorough admixture of the two before reaching the open air. A slight excess of the peroxide is necessary for the destruction of the organic matter, a condition which may be regarded as attained when the purified water gives a decided blue colouration to potassium iodide and starch.

The bacteriological examination of the water, both before and after purification, was performed by Profs. Van Ermenghem, De Molinari and Petermann, who report that of the various micro-organisms — including *Bacillus liquefaciens*, *Bacillus ramosus*, *Bacillus coli commune*, *Bacillus subtilis*, &c. —practically none survived the treatment. The engineers' report concludes with an expression of opinion very favourable to the process, on account of its rapidity and reliability.

In connection with the use of chlorine peroxide, however, it should not be forgotten that it is a very unstable gas, which decomposes on exposure to light, and at a temperature of about 50 deg. centigrade explodes with violence. This explosion is also liable to occur at low temperatures if the chlorate of potash used contains any potassium chloride.

**The Parliament-street Improvement.**—The First Commissioner of Works has, through the Hon. R. B. Brett, written to the vestry of St. Margaret and St. John, Westminster, stating that the remaining blocks of buildings between Parliament-street and King-street will very shortly be demolished, and the site between those streets entirely cleared. In these circumstances it is desirable, he states, that the new line of street adopted by the Government should be formed without delay, and it is suggested that steps should be taken as soon as possible to carry out the requisite alterations. The Works and General Purposes Committee of the vestry recommended that body, at their meeting on Wednesday, to inform her Majesty's Office of Works that the vestry concur in the desirability of the new line of street being formed without delay, but that it does not appear that the Act of Parliament under which the improvement is being carried out imposes any obligation upon the vestry in the matter.

## SOME RECENT PUBLICATIONS.

*Any of the Books noted below will be sent post free if the published price be forwarded to the offices of* THE SURVEYOR.

SHROPSHIRE, by Augustus J. C. Hare, with illustrations by the author; 7¾ in. by 5¼ in., 340 pp. George Allen. Price 7s. 6d.

AN OLD ENGLISH HOME AND ITS DEPENDENCIES, by S. Baring Gould, with illustrations by F. Bligh Bond; 7¾ in. by 5½ in., 336 pp. Methuen & Co. Price 6s.

THE STORY OF THE FARM, Some Essays on Agricultural Economy by James Long; 7¼ in. by 5 in., 158 pp. The Rural World Publishing Company. Price 1s.

THE YOUNG ESTATE MANAGER'S GUIDE, by Richard Henderson, F.S.I., with an introduction by R. Patrick Wright, F.R.S.E.; 7½ in. by 5 in., 266 pp. William Blackwood & Sons. Price 5s.

GENERAL REPORT OF THE OPERATIONS OF THE SURVEY OF INDIA DEPARTMENT, 1896-97, prepared under the direction of Major-General C. Strahan, R.E., Surveyor-General of India, with photo. etchings and numerous maps; 13 in. by 8½ in., 166 pp., office of the Superintendent of Government Printing, Calcutta. Price 3 rupees (3s. 6d.).

LOWESTOFT IN OLDEN TIMES, by Francis D. Longe; 9 in. by 6 in., 103 pp. Simpkin, Marshall, Hamilton, Kent & Co., Limited. Price 1s. nett.

APPLIED GEOLOGY, Part I., by J. V. Elsden, B.SC.LOND., with numerous illustrations; 8¾ in. by 5¾ in., 96 pp. *The Quarry* Publishing Company, Limited. Price 5s.

BLACK'S GUIDE TO CANTERBURY AND THE WATERING-PLACES OF EAST KENT, edited by E. D Jordan, B.A., with six maps and plans; 6¾ in. by 4½ in., 128 pp. Adam & Charles Black. Price 1s.

GAS AND PETROLEUM ENGINES (The Electro-Mechanical Series), translated and adapted from the French of Henry de Graffigny, and edited by A. G. Elliott, B.SC., with illustrations; 7 in. by 5 in., 140 pp. Whittaker & Co. Price 2s. 6d.

PHOTOGRAMS OF 1898: A Pictorical and Literary Record of the Best Photographic Work of the Year, compiled by the editors and staff of *The Photogram*; 10 in. by 6¾ in., 112 pp. Dawbarn & Ward, Limited. Price 1s. nett, or in cloth 2s. nett.

DISINFECTION AND DISINFECTANTS, together with an Account of the Chemical Substances used as Antiseptics and Preservatives, by Samuel Rideal, D.SC.LOND. (second edition), with diagrams; 9½ in. by 6½ in., 372 pp. The Sanitary Publishing Company, Limited. Price 12s. 6d.

THE HOUSING OF THE WORKING CLASSES ACT, 1890, AND AMENDING ACTS, Annotated and Explained, together with Statutory Forms and Instructions, by Charles E. Allan, M.A., LL.B., assisted as to the Practice by Francis J. Allan, M.D., D.P.H.; 8½ in. by 5¾ in., 186 pp. and index. Butterworth & Co. Price 7s. 6d.

THE ARGUS GUIDE TO MUNICIPAL LONDON, for the Local Government Year, 1898-99, edited by Fredk. J. Higginbottom; 7¼ in. by 4¾ in., 263 pp. *The London Argus* Office. Price 1s.

THE PROPERTY PROTECTION SOCIETY, Eighth Annual Report of the Council, 1897-98; 8½ in. by 5½ in., 8 PP. Offices of the Society, 45 Parliament-street, S.W.

MODERN OPERA-HOUSES AND THEATRES: Examples selected from Play-Houses recently erected in Europe, with numerous plates and illustrations, by Edwin O. Sachs, architect; three vols., 1898, 21 in. by 16 in. Price £15 nett.

PROCEEDINGS OF THE ASSOCIATION OF ONTARIO LAND SURVEYORS, 1898.

"THE INDIAN AND EASTERN ENGINEER" DIARY, 1899.

Publications of the British Fire-prevention Committee, edited by E. O. Sachs, vol. i. Published by the Committee. Price 7s. 6d.

## FOUNTAINS AND TROUGHS.

Among bodies that have done good work in their time is the Metropolitan Drinking Fountain and Cattle Trough Association. It is therefore a matter for regret to hear that, owing to the necessity for retrenchment, the association have deemed it desirable to close their works department and place the care of the fountains and troughs under the various vestries. For upwards of thirty years the work of the association at Clapham has been under the management of Mr. R. D. Gibbs, who has thus had a long and perhaps unique experience in the design and manufacture of fountains and cattle troughs, seeing that the first granite trough erected in the metropolis was not only designed by him, but manufactured and erected under his supervision. Since then about 1,000 fountains and troughs have been erected by him in the metropolis and its suburbs on behalf of the association. It has been suggested to Mr. Gibbs that he should continue to carry on the work as a private enterprise of his own, and we understand that he has decided to do so, and has succeeded in making arrangements with a good firm of granite quarry owners, who will supply the raw material on favourable terms. Mr. Gibbs will be found at 265 Clapham-road, S.W., and will be glad to submit to those interested estimates for fountains, cattle troughs, public memorials, and for the repair, inspection and cleaning of existing structures.

# Personal.

Matlock Bath Urban District Council have granted their gas manager, Mr. W. Gaffrey, an increase of salary.

Mr. B. F. C. Costelloe, L.C.C., delivered a lecture on Saturday at Toynbee Hall on "The County Council of London."

Mr. Balfour, it is stated, will introduce and take charge of the London Municipalities Bill, which is to be brought forward in the next session of Parliament.

Mr. David Rayne Wright, 13 West-street, Stockton-on-Tees, has been appointed a drainage and building inspector under the Stockton-on-Tees Corporation.

Mr. Wm. Dixon, surveyor to the Lytham Urban District Council, has been appointed to the position of surveyor to the Lancaster Rural District Council.

The council of King's College, London, have appointed Mr. Ernest Wilson, M.I.E.E., professor of electrical engineering in succession to the late Dr. Hopkinson.

Mr. E. E. Hoadley, of the Worcester Corporation electricity works, has been appointed resident electrical engineer to the Barking Town Urban District Council.

At their usual meeting, on Thursday, the Court of Common Council decided, on the recommendation of the Streets Committee, to appoint four new inspectors of pavements, at salaries of £200 per annum.

A debate upon the question of "Municipal Control v. Companies Control" (with reference to the gas and water companies) was opened last night by Lord Monkswell, L.C.C., at the South-Western Polytechnic.

Messrs. Simpson & Havey, engineers and surveyors, Leicester, have been instructed by the Lutterworth District Council to prepare a report on the best available method of disposing of the sewage of the town.

The burgh surveyor and electrical engineer of Aberdeen will accompany a committee of the town council on a visit to Glasgow on December 6th, for the purpose of making an inspection of the electric system of tramways in that city.

Stretford Urban District Council have adopted the resolution of a sub-committee recommending the appointment of Mr. Reginald P. Wilson, of London, as engineer in connection with a scheme for the electric lighting of the town.

After considerable discussion the Gwyrfai Rural District Council on Saturday adopted the resolution of a committee recommending the appointment of a surveyor of highways at a salary of £150 per annum. At present each parish has its own official.

At their meeting on Wednesday the Battersea Vestry decided, on the recommendation of their Lighting Committee, to appoint Mr. H. Riley, of 28 Victoria-street, Westminster, S.W., to prepare the bills of quantities in connection with the projected electric light station to be erected by the vestry.

In connection with a recent public baths competition at Wimbledon the first prize, of £50, has been awarded to Mr. Robert J. Thomson, a resident of the town; the second, of £25, to Mr. Francis J. Smith, of Victoria-street, Westminster; and the third, of £10, to Messrs. George A. Lansdowne and A. R. Jennit, also of Wimbledon.

In the recent open competition for schemes of sewerage and sewage disposal for the districts of Baildon Wood, Baildon Green, Lower Holme and Low Mill, the Baildon Urban District Council have, on the advice of Mr. G. Chatterton, M.I.C.E., the assessor, adopted the scheme submitted by Mr. H. Bertram Nichols, of Birmingham.

The appointment is announced of Mr. A. C. Richmond, surveyor to the Keynsham Rural District Council, and formerly surveyor to the Dulverton Rural District Council, to the position of surveyor to the Bridgwater Rural District Council, in succession to Mr. S. W. Ingram. Mr. Richmond is the son of a former surveyor to the Taunton Highway Board.

The first annual dinner of civil engineers, architects and surveyors of Newport was held recently at the Westgate Hotel. The toast of the evening—viz., "The Professions of the Civil Engineers, Architects and Surveyors," was given by Mr. W. Lyndon Moore, and responded to by Mr. R. H. Haynes (the borough engineer of Newport), Mr. John Brain and Mr. John J. Swalwell.

At the first meeting of the Institution of Electrical Engineers after the recess the president, in alluding to the loss sustained by the death of Dr. John Hopkinson, spoke of the sincere sorrow and great regret which the council felt, and said he thought it would be the wish of the members to unite in giving expression to that regret. A motion to this effect was subsequently adopted.

A special meeting of the Saffron Walden Town Council was held on Friday morning for the purpose of electing a borough surveyor in succession to Mr. G. W. Lacey, resigned. There were sixty applicants for the post, and in the end Mr. A. H. Forbes, who is at present under the Chesham (Bucks.) Urban District Council, was unanimously elected. Mr. Forbes commences his duties in January next, at a salary of £175 per annum.

At a recent meeting of the Badgeworth Highway Board consideration was given to the appointment of a successor to the late Mr. G. Gorey in the surveyorship of the roads of the district. There were only eleven applicants, and Mr. E. H. Attwater was eventually appointed. The position, it might be stated, is of a temporary character, as the county council take over the duties of the highway board at the end of March next.

Mr. R. Moffatt Ford, manager of the Motor Car Company, 93 and 94 Long-acre, W.C., has addressed a letter to The Times on the London traffic problem. The congestion in the streets would be diminished by one-half, the writer says, if the horses which supply its muscular motive force, and take up half the space of the traffic, could be eliminated. It rests with engineers to effect this reduction by the adaptation of the motor system, and ten years is given in the letter as the period in which the reform should be effected.

We regret to announce the death, which occurred at his residence in Tranmere, after a brief illness, of Mr. Peter Blair, one of the oldest officials of the Birkenhead Corporation. Mr. Blair was employed in the engineer's department at Woodside Ferry for many years, having been there under the old commissioners prior to incorporation twenty years ago. He was superintendent engineer at the ferry for a long period, and a few years ago, upon retiring from active work, was appointed consulting engineer. He was seventy-three years of age.

News was received in Durham on Saturday of the death, on the previous day, of Mr. James McGregor, recently of Durham, and for over a quarter of a century the surveyor under the now extinct Durham and Chester-le-Street Highway Board. Mr. McGregor, who spent his early life in Perthshire and Sterlingshire, came to Durham, when comparatively a young man, as surveyor of the Great North Road between Durham and Gateshead. He became well known throughout the north of Durham, and retired in 1894, when, on the introduction of the Local Government Act, the Durham and Chester-le-Street Highway Board became absorbed in the Durham Rural District Council.

We recently mentioned that Mr. S. C. Eagles had entered upon private practice as a consulting sanitary engineer and surveyor at Clarendon Chambers, 1 and 2 Waterloo-street, Birmingham. Mr. Eagles began his professional career as a pupil under Mr. J. Edward Wilcox, and for ten years has had considerable experience in the various branches of sanitary engineering. For three years he was deputy surveyor to the Erdington Urban District Council, and in this capacity he had an opportunity of gaining experience in the different branches of municipal engineering work. Until recently Mr. Eagles was acting as engineering assistant to the city surveyor of Birmingham, being specially engaged in connection with the new sewerage scheme for Harborne and Edgbaston.

By the death of Sir John Fowler, Bart., at Bournemouth, on Sunday night, one of the most celebrated civil engineers is removed from our midst. Many of the railways in the kingdom bear the marks of his genius, and his association with the engineering history of our times is not confined to these islands. He had his share, for example, in the British assistance of Egypt, for he was consulting engineer for a time in the dominion of the Khedive. He was very early associated with railway engineering. His parents, Mr. and Mrs. John Fowler, of Wadsley Hall, Yorkshire, apprenticed him to Mr. J. T. Leather, a hydraulic engineer, and he was afterwards an assistant to Mr. Rastrick in the construction of the London and Brighton Railway. He was but twenty-seven years of age when he received, in 1844, the appointment of engineer for the construction of the Manchester, Sheffield and Lincolnshire Railway. He was engineer for the original underground railway of London, and he built the Severn Valley Railway, the Launceston and South Devon Railway, the Isle of Wight Railway, the Birmingham and Stourbridge Railway, and the Great Northern and Western of Ireland systems. With the docks and river improvements of the country, also, his name has been largely associated, but the engineering achievement with which Sir John Fowler's name is now mainly associated in the public mind is the Forth Bridge, which he and Sir Benjamin Baker designed for spanning the Firth of Forth at Queensferry. The Prince of Wales opened the bridge in 1890, and announced that the Queen had conferred a baronetcy upon the engineer. He had previously been made a K.C.M.G. for his work in Egypt, and the honorary degree of LL.D. was conferred upon him by Edinburgh University in the year the Forth Bridge was opened. Sir John Fowler married, in 1850, Elizabeth, daughter of Mr. James Broadbent, Manchester. His son, who succeeds to the baronetcy, is married to Alice, daughter of Sir Edward Clive Bayley, K.C.S.I. Sir John Fowler, who was eighty-one years of age, had been in delicate health for some time at Bournemouth, but his death came unexpectedly. The funeral took place at Brompton cemetery yesterday afternoon, the first part of the service being held at St. Mary Abbot's, Kensington.

## THE SHOREDITCH DUST DESTRUCTOR AND ELECTRIC LIGHT UNDERTAKING.

### THE FIRST YEAR'S WORKING.

In our last issue we referred to a report which had been presented to the Shoreditch Vestry by the Lighting Committee of that body, and which embodied the accounts for the year ended June 24, 1898, in connection with the combined electric light and dust destructor undertakings. In view of the attention and criticism which these schemes have attracted, our readers will no doubt be glad to have the full text of the report, which is as follows:—

#### I. — ELECTRIC LIGHT UNDERTAKING.

ACCOUNTS FOR YEAR ENDED JUNE 24, 1898.

*Cr.*

| 1897. | | £ | s. | d. |
|---|---|---|---|---|
| Sep. quarter—To sale of current to consumers | | 549 | 14 | 2 |
| Dec. quarter.— ,, ,, ,, ,, | | 2,141 | 16 | 0 |
| 1898. | | | | |
| March quarter.— ,, ,, ,, | | 3,410 | 18 | 9 |
| June quarter.— ,, ,, ,, | | 2,151 | 13 | 2 |
| | | £8,254 | 2 | 1 |
| To sale of current to dust destructor from June, 1897, to June, 1898 | | 536 | 5 | 8 |
| ,, miscellaneous receipts from June, 1897, to June, 1898 | | 120 | 4 | 7 |
| ,, sale of stores to other departments from June, 1897, to June, 1898 | | 130 | 8 | 4 |
| | | £9,041 | 0 | 8 |

*Dr.*

| | | £ | s. | d. |
|---|---|---|---|---|
| By coal | | 432 | 15 | 9 |
| ,, water | | 217 | 11 | 3 |
| ,, stores, &c. | | 362 | 12 | 6 |
| ,, insurance | | 226 | 0 | 3 |
| ,, wages | | 1,472 | 13 | 10 |
| ,, engineer's salary, proportioned | | 145 | 16 | 8 |
| ,, miscellaneous expenses | | 323 | 14 | 1 |
| ,, rent, rates and taxes—principally on sub-stations | | 33 | 10 | 3 |
| | | £3,214 | 14 | 7 |
| ,, interest and redemption | | 2,641 | 16 | 2 |
| ,, nett balance | | 3,184 | 9 | 11 |
| | | £9,041 | 0 | 8 |

Leaving a surplus for the year of £3,184 9s. 11d.

It will be seen from the above that the excess of income over expenditure of this part of the undertaking was £5,826 6s. 1d., and that, after providing for interest and redemption of capital on this account of £2,641 16s. 2d., it leaves a surplus balance (being profit) of £3,184 9s. 11d., which your committee cannot but regard as a very highly satisfactory result in view of the fact that in the first quarter a loss of about £500 was actually incurred, when the demand for electricity was small.

The charge for interest and redemption of capital is more than sufficient to provide for the depreciation on this undertaking, as it is really redeeming the cost of buildings and land, which will be a clear asset to the vestry in forty-two years; independent of which all charges for the up-keep and maintenance in full working order of the plant has been included in the expenditure items of the above accounts.

#### II.—DUST DESTRUCTOR UNDERTAKING.

ACCOUNTS FOR YEAR ENDED JUNE 24, 1898.

*Cr.*

| | | £ | s. | d. |
|---|---|---|---|---|
| By work done for electric lighting department | | 59 | 0 | 0 |
| ,, trade refuse receipts | | 238 | 1 | 9 |
| ,, charged to scavenging department, at 2s. per ton on 23,137 tons | | 2,313 | 14 | 0 |
| ,, debit balance | | 1,758 | 14 | 6 |
| | | £4,369 | 10 | 3 |

*Dr.*

| | | £ | s. | d. |
|---|---|---|---|---|
| To wages (including proportion of engineer's and clerical salaries) | | 2,829 | 8 | 3 |
| ,, stores, &c. | | 130 | 8 | 1 |
| ,, carting clinker | | 612 | 10 | 5 |
| ,, insurance | | 43 | 4 | 2 |
| ,, current for light and power used in destructor, 128,708 units at 1d. | | 536 | 5 | 8 |
| ,, sundry expenses, including water and rates, &c. | | 217 | 13 | 8 |
| | | £4,369 | 10 | 3 |

Leaving a debit balance of £1,758 14s. 6d., against which is to be set off the cost of steam supplied to the lighting station and library.

It will be observed in the above accounts that your committee have agreed with the Scavenging Committee that a fixed charge of 2s. per ton should be made against that department for the cost of disposing refuse, which will result in

a saving to the vestry (on its previous expenditure of 3s. 1d. per ton) of a sum of £1,253 5s. 1d.

With regard to the debit balance of £1,758 14s. 6d., this is represented by steam used in the lighting station and library, &c. Even if this debit balance be charged against the surplus of the electricity undertaking, the following would be the nett result to the vestry of the combined scheme:—

| | | £ | s. | d. |
|---|---|---|---|---|
| Credit balance on electricity undertaking | | 3,184 | 9 | 11 |
| *Add* saving on previous expenditure of barging refuse | | 1,253 | 5 | 1 |
| | | £4,437 | 15 | 0 |
| *Deduct* debit balance on destructor | | 1,758 | 14 | 6 |
| Nett profit and saving | | £2,679 | 0 | 6 |

In view of the high initial cost of disposal of clinker, and the sale of electricity being very small at the commencement of the year, your committee think the above result one upon which they can well congratulate themselves, and they are advised that no previous municipal electrical undertaking has ever yielded such a result in the first year of working. Moreover, it is manifest from the increased supply of electricity now being given and the reduced cost of disposal of clinker and the use of the exhaust steam for heating the baths, that the result for the second year's working should show an immense advance upon the above accounts, although it must be borne in mind that the prices have been reduced 25 per cent., which is the lowest charge in London, and compares favourably with any provincial station. In the above accounts all charges for repairing and maintaining the destructor, cells, building, &c., have been included.

Your committee therefore recommend that the above report be received, and it be referred back to your committee to allocate the disposal of the profits.

#### A JOINT REPORT.

The Lighting and Scavenging Committees also presented the following joint report:—

Your committees have carefully considered the question of the amount to be charged for destroying refuse in the destructor, and although the previous charge for barging refuse was 3s. 1d. per ton, exclusive of redemption of interest and capital for wharf shoots, buildings, &c., your committees think that the scavenging department should have the prior claim upon any profits made from the combined scheme, and therefore recommend: (1) That a fixed charge of 2s. per ton be made against the scavenging department by the lighting department for destroying refuse in the destructor.

In order to maintain the same basis with regard to the dust destructor as exists with regard to the barging system, and in view of the fact that an amount of £2,641 16s. 2d. (which corresponds to depreciation) has been charged in the above accounts for redemption of capital, &c., whereas the valuer of the London County Council in rating the property estimated £800 per annum as sufficient to replace plant and machinery when worn out: Your committees recommend: (2) That the charge for interest and repayment of capital of £1,435 13s. 4d., in respect of the dust destructor, land and buildings, &c., should be paid out of the general rate.

As we stated last week all the recommendations were agreed to, in spite of some very hostile criticism.

### ELECTRIC LIGHT AT RATHMINES.

#### £50,000 REQUIRED.

On Monday of last week Mr. Charles P. Cotton held an inquiry at Rathmines, on behalf of the Local Government Board, in reference to an application of the town commissioners, acting as the urban sanitary authority, for sanction to a loan of £50,000 for the purpose of lighting the district by electricity.

Mr. F. P. Fawcett, secretary to the commissioners, said the commissioners had had the matter under consideration for some time. A good deal of pressure was put on them by the inhabitants to introduce electric lighting in the township. In 1895 the commissioners consulted the eminent electrical engineer, Mr. Robert Hammond, who submitted a report to them. Finally, by resolution, the commissioners determined to apply to the Board of Trade for an electric lighting order. A provisional order was made, and the Act confirming it obtained the Royal assent on July 20, 1896. Mr. Hammond had laid a complete scheme before the commissioners, which they approved of. Land at the rear of the town hall had been obtained as the site for the power-house.

Mr. Robert Hammond, electrical engineer, gave evidence, explaining in detail the scheme which had been adopted by the commissioners. Under the provisional order, mains would have to be laid within two years of the commencement of the order. The total length of distributing mains proposed to be laid was 25,000 yards, or over 14 miles. He had advised the commissioners that they would be making an extremely good investment for the township by the erection of these electrical works. The total estimate was £35,000, and he estimated that the other small general expenses would total £50,000.

Mr. Dixon, township engineer, also gave evidence, and the inquiry closed.

## ASSOCIATION OF MUNICIPAL AND COUNTY ENGINEERS.

VOLUNTARY PASS EXAMINATION.

Notice is hereby given that the twenty-seventh examination for candidates for surveyorships under municipal corporations and district councils will be held at the Institution of Civil Engineers, Great George-street, Westminster, on Friday and Saturday, April 14 and 15, 1899.

*The council reserve to themselves the right to hold a second examination in case the entries received exceed the limits of accommodation. Such second examination will be held as soon after the first as circumstances permit. Applications will therefore be accepted strictly in the order of priority.*

Application forms, duly filled in by intending candidates, together with entrance fee of £2 2s., must be in my hands on or before the 5th of March, 1899.

THOMAS COLE, *Secretary.*

11 Victoria-street, Westminster, S.W.

## THE SURVEYORS' INSTITUTION.

STUDENTS' PRELIMINARY EXAMINATION, 1899.

Those proposing to enter their names for the students' preliminary examination, to be held on the 18th and 19th of January next, must intimate their intention to the secretary before the last day of November. It is proposed to examine candidates from the counties of Lancashire, Cheshire, Yorkshire, Durham, Cumberland, Westmoreland and Northumberland at Manchester. Candidates from other counties in England and Wales will be examined in London. Irish candidates will be examined in Dublin.

PROPOSED SPECIAL-CERTIFICATE EXAMINATIONS (FOR MEMBERS), 1899.

Notice is also given that the next special-certificate examinations in forestry, sanitary science and land surveying and levelling are proposed to be held on Tuesday, Wednesday and Thursday, the 13th, 14th and 15th of June. Particulars of these examinations can be obtained from the secretary.

## APPOINTMENTS VACANT.

*Official and all similar advertisements received later than Thursday morning are too late for classification and cannot therefore be included in these summaries until the following week. No advertisements received after 3 p.m. on Thursday can be inserted until the following week.*

ROAD FOREMAN.— November 25th.—Walthamstow Urban District Council. £2 10s.—Mr. E. J. Cowen, clerk to the council.

SURVEYOR AND SANITARY INSPECTOR.—November 26th.—Gnosall (Salop) District Council. £110. — Mr. H. G. N. Elliott, clerk to the council.

FIRE BRIGADE ENGINEER.—November 26th.—Corporation of Coventry. £1 15s.—The City Engineer.

ASSISTANT ENGINEER DRIVER.—November 28th.—Leigh-on-Sea Urban District Council.—Mr. G. Egerton Wright-Motion, clerk to the council.

GENERAL OUTDOOR FOREMAN.—November 28th.—Corporation of Stockton-on-Tees. £100.—Mr. M. H. Sykes, borough engineer.

JUNIOR ASSISTANT.—November 29th.— Wimbledon Urban District Council. £60.—Mr. W. H. Whitfield, clerk to the council.

ROAD SURVEYOR.—November 30th.—County Borough of Sunderland. £130.—Mr. Fras. M. Bowey, town clerk.

BOROUGH SURVEYOR.—November 30th.—Corporation of Folkestone. £350.—Mr. A. F. Kidson, town clerk.

MANAGER OF GAS AND WATER WORKS.—November 30th.—Ambleside Urban District Council. £125.—Mr. George Gatey, clerk to the council.

MAIN ROAD INSPECTOR. — December 1st. — Bedfordshire County Council. £100.— Mr. W. W. Marks, clerk to the council, Shire Hall, Bedford.

MECHANICAL ENGINEERING DRAUGHTSMAN.—December 1st.—London County Council.—Mr. C. J. Stewart, clerk to the council, County Hall, Spring-gardens, S.W.

SURVEYOR AND INSPECTOR OF NUISANCES.—December 1st.—Portishead Urban District Council.—Mr. J. Chaffrey Glyde, clerk to the council.

RESIDENT ELECTRICAL ENGINEER.—December 2nd.—Vestry of St. Mary, Islington. £250.—Mr. L. J. Dunham, clerk to the vestry.

GENERAL FOREMAN. — December 2nd.— Corporation of Bridgwater.—Mr. W. T. Baker, town clerk.

GAS MANAGER.—December 3rd.—Corporation of Newbury. £200.—Mr. F. Quekett Louch, town clerk.

MECHANICAL ENGINEER.—December 6th.—Tyne Improvement Commissioners. £250.—Mr. R. Unwin, secretary to the commissioners, Newcastle-on-Tyne.

SEWAGE FARM MANAGER.—December 14th.—Willenhall Urban District Council. 30s.—Mr. Chas. J. Jenkin, surveyor to the council.

IMPROVER OR ASSISTANT.—£60.—" J. E. S.," office of THE SURVEYOR, 24 Bride-lane, Fleet-street, E.C.

## MUNICIPAL COMPETITIONS OPEN.

*Official and all similar advertisements received later than Thursday morning are too late for classification and cannot therefore be included in these summaries until the following week. No advertisements received after 3 p.m. on Thursday can be inserted until the following week.*

ABERAVON.—December 1st.—Extension of the covered market, at a cost not to exceed £5,000. £21.—The Borough Surveyor.

CHERTSEY.—December 23rd.—Sewerage and sewage disposal scheme for the No. 1 and 2 wards of the district. £50, £30 and £20.—Mr. T. K. Harland Chaldecott, clerk to the council.

HULL.—January 1st.—Erection of a central public library in Albion-street. £50, £30 and £20.—Mr. E. Laverack, town clerk.

HARROGATE.—January 2nd.—Erection of a pump-room, &c., at a cost not exceeding £8,000. £50, £30 and £20.—Mr. Samuel Stead, borough surveyor.

BRADFORD.—January 2nd.—Erection of a central fire brigade station. £100, £50 and £30.—Mr. George McGuire, town clerk.

## MUNICIPAL CONTRACTS OPEN.

*Official and all similar advertisements received later than Thursday morning are too late for classification and cannot therefore be included in these summaries until the following week. No advertisements received after 3 p.m. on Thursday can be inserted until the following week.*

TAME.—November 25th.—Construction of stoneware and other sewers for the interception of the sewage of the town, together with the necessary manholes, inspection shafts, flushing tanks, outfall works and engine-house, for the urban district council.—Mr. Wm. Parker, clerk to the council.

BATLEY.—November 25th.—Supply of (*a*) flagstones, setts, paviors and kerbs; (*b*) sanitary tubes; (*c*) pitch and oil; (*d*) cement; and (*e*) broken granite.—Mr. O. J. Kirby, borough surveyor.

HULL.—November 25th.—Supply of about 316 ft. of railing for the corporation field, consisting of cast-iron posts, with two rails of steam tube.—Mr. A. E. White, city engineer.

SHOREDITCH.—November 25th.—Construction of temporary flooring to the first and second class swimming ponds at the baths, buildings in Pitfield-street, for the vestry.—Mr. H. Mansfield Robinson, clerk to the vestry.

EAST RETFORD.—November 25th.—Construction of about 20,000 lineal yards of stoneware and iron pipe sewers, with manholes, storm overflow, ventilators, ejector chamber and ejectors, cast-iron rising main and other works; also precipitation tanks, engine and boiler houses, chimney shaft, press-house, stores and offices, carriers, underdraining, and levelling land, roads, fencing and other works.—Mr. Samuel Jones, town clerk.

TOWNELEY.—November 30th.—Supply of crude sulphate of iron and disinfectants, for the rural district council.—Mr. Frank Harris, surveyor to the council.

EARBY.—November 26th.—Supply and laying of 1,460 yards of 9-in., 960 yards of 4-in. and 2,020 yards of 3-in. cast-iron socket pipes, for the rural district council.—Mr. F. S. Cloke, clerk to the council.

WATERLOO-WITH-SEAFORTH.—November 28th.—Supply of sixteen electric arc lamp columns and carriers, for the urban district council.—Mr. F. Spencer Yates, A.M.I.C.E., surveyor to the council.

FLEETWOOD.—November 28th.—Supply and delivery of a steam road roller and scarifier, for the urban district council.—Mr. Joseph Tibbsley, clerk to the council.

HARROGATE.—November 28th.—Laying of about 2¼ miles of surface-water drains and culverts in the borough and in the parish of Bilton.—Mr. Samuel Stead, borough surveyor.

STOURBRIDGE.—November 28th.—Construction of 900 yards of 9-in. earthenware pipe sewer, for the main drainage board.—Mr. W. Fiddian, surveyor to the board, Town Hall, Stourbridge.

BRIDGNORTH.—November 28th.—Construction of stoneware pipe sewers comprised in the scheme of sewerage for the parish of Pedmore, for the rural district council.—Mr. H. D. Holloway, clerk to the council.

RUNCORN.—November 28th.—Construction of sewerage works in the parish of Helsby.—Mr. John Ashton, clerk to the council.

RHONDDA.—November 29th.—Erection of laundry and disinfecting block, discharging and mortuary block and stables in connection with the new isolation hospital at Ystrad, for the urban district council.—Mr. W. D. Morgan, architect, 23 St. Mary-street, Cardiff.

ST. SAVIOUR'S, SOUTHWARK.—November 29th.—Supply of three stop-vans, for the district board of works.—Mr. G. R. Norrish, surveyor to the board.

MARGATE.—November 29th.—Construction of about 4,000 ft. of main sewer outfall to connect the Westgate-on-Sea drainage with the Margate sewerage system.—Mr. Albert Latham, M.I.C.E., borough engineer.

EDDINGTON.—November 29th.—Supply of about 6,500 lineal yards of kerb and about 320 tons of 4-in. cube setts, for the urban district council.—Mr. Herbert H. Humphries, engineer and surveyor to the council.

BUCKLOW.—November 29th.—Reconstruction of the main sewers of the townships of Hall, for the urban district council.—Mr. J. M'D. M'Kenzie, surveyor to the council, 7 Market-street, Altrincham.

WEST HARTLEPOOL.—November 29th.—Supply of various materials and goods required during the year ending December 31, 1899. Mr. J. W. Brown, borough engineer.

MIDDLESBROUGH.—November 30th.—Supply and erection of various electric lighting plant, for the corporation.—Mr. Robert Hammond, consulting engineer, 61 Victoria-street, London, S.W.

MIDDLESBROUGH.—November 30th.—Supply and erection of various electric lighting plant, for the corporation.—Mr. Robert Hammond, consulting engineer, 61 Victoria-street, London, S.W.

HORNSEA.—November 30th.—Supply of 250 street gullies, 9-in. diameter by 2 ft. deep, for the urban district council.—Mr. John Holbrook, surveyor to the council.

PONTYPOOL.—November 30th.—Construction of 602 lineal yards of 24-in. pipe sewer, 615 lineal yards of 18-in. pipe sewer, and 342 lineal yards of 15-in. pipe sewer, for the urban district council.—Mr. W. Cafts, engineer to the council.

BLACKPOOL.—November 30th.—Extension of the town hall buildings.—Mr. T. Loftus, town clerk.

CROSTON.—November 30th.—Erection of a bailiff's house at Warlinghams.—Mr. K. Mawdesley, town clerk.

RYDE.—December 1st.—Erection of a new gasholder and tank at the gasworks.—Mr. M. Kirkby, town clerk.

SALFORD.—December 1st.—Supply and erection of certain electric plant.—Mr. Saml. Brown, town clerk.

LANCASTER.—December 2nd.—Supply and delivery of about 5,680 lineal yards of 7-in. cast-iron water pipes, for the rural district council. —Mr. Joseph Ennion, clerk to the council.

CHERTSEY.—December 2nd.—Execution of various works in connection with the recreation ground in Guildford-road, for the urban district council.—Mr. J. Freebairn Stow, surveyor to the council.

HULL.—December 2nd.—Supply of about 5,000 super. yards of the best hard Yorkshire 3-in. tooled flags.—Mr. A. E. White, city engineer.

SLEAFORD (Lincs.).—December 2nd.—Laying of about 2,100 yards of 3-in. cast-iron pipes for the water supply of the village of Great Hale, for the rural district council.—Mr. Edmund Clements, clerk to the council.

SHEFFIELD.—December 3rd.—Construction and erection of urinals and wall at lower entrance to Western Park, opposite Clarkson-street. —Mr. Charles F. Wike, city surveyor.

CHORLEY.—December 3rd.—Laying of water mains, hydrants, &c., in the townships of Anderton, Heath, Charnock and Adlington, for the rural district council.—Mr. A. Jolly, surveyor to the council.

ST. JAMES, WESTMINSTER.—December 5th.—Construction of underground conveniences for both sexes in Broad-street, Golden-square, for the vestry.—Mr. T. Hensman Munsey, clerk to the vestry.

GLASGOW.—December 5th.—Supply and erection of switchboards and instruments at the new electricity works, Port Dundas.—Mr. J. D. Marwick, town clerk.

PADDINGTON.—December 5th.—Supply from Lady Day, 1899, to Lady Day, 1900, of York paving and granite kerbs, for the vestry.—Mr. Frank Dethridge, clerk to the vestry.

PADDINGTON.—December 5th.—Supply of about 6,000 cubic yards of broken granite for repairing roads, for the vestry.—Mr. Frank Dethridge, clerk to the vestry.

MARGATE.—December 5th.—Supply of various articles, for the water department during the year ending December 31, 1899.—Mr. G. Foord-Kelcey, town clerk.

FLEETWOOD.—December 5th.—Sewage diversion scheme, for the urban district council.—Mr. Joseph Tildsley, clerk to the council.

EDMONTON.—December 5th.—Supply of corrugated-iron roofing and stoneware pipes, for the urban district council.—Mr. G. Eedes Eachus, M.I.C.E., engineer to the council.

HULL.—December 5th.—Supply of buff, terra-cotta or artificial stone for the string courses, tracery, &c., of the crematorium.—Mr. A. E. White, city engineer.

AUCKLAND.—December 5th.—Supply and fixing of sewer ventilating shafts at Coundon, for the rural district council.—Mr. Sam Adams, clerk to the council.

RUGBY.—December 6th.—Erection of a fire brigade station and stabling in the council's yard, Chapel-street, for the urban district council.—Mr. D. G. Macdonald, A.M.I.C.E., surveyor to the council.

LIMERICK.—December 6th.—Supply and delivery of a steam road-roller.—Mr. Wm. M. Nolan, town clerk.

BRENTFORD.—December 6th.—Making-up of Stile Hall-gardens, for the urban district council.—Mr. Nowell Parr, surveyor to the council.

ACTON.—December 6th.—Erection of a refuse destructor, for the urban district council.—Mr. D. J. Ebbetts, surveyor to the council.

CROYDON.—December 7th.—Erection of new buildings and additions to the borough hospital at Waddon.—Mr. E. Mawdesley, town clerk.

FELIXTOWE AND WALTON.—December 7th.—Sewering and making-up of Leopold-road North and Victoria-street North and the forming of a path in High-road, High-street and Lower-street, Walton, for the urban district council.—Mr. F. B. Jennings, clerk to the council.

NOTTINGHAM.—December 8th.—Supply of various stores and materials during the year ending 31st December, 1899.—Mr. Arthur Brown, M.I.C.E., city engineer.

BARNSLEY.—December 12th.—Supply of various electricity supply plant and the erection of tall chimney and engine, dynamo and boiler-house, storage-rooms and offices in Becket-square.—Mr. J. Henry Taylor, A.M.I.C.E., borough surveyor.

SHOREDITCH.—December 12th.—Boring of an artesian well at the electric light station in Coronet-street, Old-street, for the vestry.—Mr. H. Mansfield Robinson, clerk to the vestry.

ECCLES (Lancs.).—December 12th.—Erection of a bowl-house and pavilion, and the construction of a bowling-green on land in Edison-road, Patricroft.—Mr. G. W. Bailey, town clerk.

COVENTRY.—December 13th.—Construction of five electric light sub-stations.—Mr. J. E. Swindlehurst, city engineer.

WEST HAM.—Dcember 13th.—Erection of a quarter sessions court, police cells and mortuary in West Ham-lane, Stratford.—Mr. Lewis Angell, borough engineer.

MANSFIELD.—December 14th.—Construction of about 1,630 yards of brick sewer and storm overflows and 670 yards of pipe sewers.—Mr. R. Frank Vallance, borough surveyor.

MANSFIELD.—December 14th.—Construction of about 500 yards of 9-in. pipe sewer.—Mr. R. Frank Vallance, borough surveyor.

BECKENHAM.—December 17th.—Supply and erection of various electric light plant, for the urban district council.—Mr. F. Stevens, clerk to the council.

JOHANNESBURG, S.A.—January 6th.—Supply of a complete carburetted water-gas plant, for the corporation.—Messrs. Robert Whyte & Co., 22 Bury-street, St. Mary Axe, London, E.C.

LONDON.—January 24th.—Construction of a tunnel for pedestrian traffic under the river Thames from Greenwich to Poplar, for the county council.—Mr. C. J. Stewart, clerk to the council, County Hall, Spring-gardens, S.W.

SHANGHAI.—March 15th.—Construction and working of about 23 miles of electric tramways on the trolley system, for the municipal council.—Messrs. J. Pook & Co., 8 Jeffery's-square, St. Mary Axe, London, E.C.

## TENDERS FOR MUNICIPAL WORKS OR SUPPLIES.

*ACCEPTED.

BURTON-UPON-TRENT.—For the provision of a supply of water to the farm buildings, houses and cottages upon the sewage farm at Egginton.—Mr. George T. Lynam, borough engineer and surveyor:—

| | |
|---|---|
| Timmins & Son, Bridgwater Foundry, Runcorn* | £1,701 |

DOVER.—For the laying of a new 12-in. cast-iron supply pipe from the sea to the baths.—Mr. Henry E. Stilgoe, A.M.I.C.E., borough engineer:—

| | |
|---|---|
| Auston & Lewis, Salisbury-road, Dover* | £700 |

Engineer's estimate, £698.

DUDLEY.—For sewering works in the proposed new streets at Scott's Green and in a portion of Stourbridge-road.—Mr. John Gammage, borough surveyor:—

| | |
|---|---|
| J. Mackay, 257 Bearwood-road, Smethwick | £440 |
| J. Davies, 55 Hall-street, Dudley | 419 |
| H. Hughes & Son, Lower Gornal, near Dudley | 350 |

Borough surveyor's estimate, £406.

GLASGOW.—For the alteration of the lighting department's offices, &c., in Tobago-street.—Mr. John Lindsay, interim clerk, City Chambers, Glasgow:—

| | |
|---|---|
| W. & J. Boyd, Emily-place, Glasgow* | £116 |

HACKNEY.—For the construction of a public underground convenience at the north-east corner of the town hall grounds, for the vestry.—Mr. James Lovegrove, surveyor to the vestry:—

| | |
|---|---|
| T. J. West, Chesnut-avenue, Wood-street, Walthamstow, E. | £1,420 |
| B. Finch & Co., Belvedere-road, Lambeth, S.E. | 893 |
| Thomas & Edge, Anglesea-avenue, Woolwich, S.E. | 842 |
| G. Jennings, Lambeth Palace-road, S.E. | 805 |
| J. Dolman & Co., Ellerthorpe-street, Poplar, E. | 798 |
| F. Bull, Oldhill-street, Upper Clapton, N. | 785 |
| General Builders, Limited, Wharf-road, Notting Hill, W. | 700 |
| W. Shurmur, Riverside Works, Upper Clapton, N.* | 686 |

LAUNCESTON.—For the construction of a new cattle, sheep and pig market.—The Town Clerk:—

| | |
|---|---|
| E. Sharland, Launceston | £3,380 |
| R. G. Burt, Launceston | 3,250 |
| R. Nevill, Launceston | 3,183 |
| J. F. Broad, Launceston | 3,153 |
| Nankwell & Sons, St. Breward, Bodmin | 3,026 |

LEICESTER.—For the construction of about 1,713 yards of brick sewers, 286 yards of pipe sewers, with junctions, manholes, lampholes, and other works in connection therewith.—Mr. E. G. Mawbey, M.I.C.E., borough engineer:—

| | |
|---|---|
| J. Ainscouth & Son, Oldham | £6,063 |
| W. & J. Foster, Shipley | 5,005 |
| J. Holme, Leicester | 4,568 |
| Johnson & Langley, Leicester | 4,337 |
| J. D. Nowell & Son, London | 4,316 |
| Bentley & Loch, Leicester | 4,157 |
| T. Philbrick, Leicester* | 4,106 |

LEWISHAM.—For kerbing, tar-paving, channelling and metalling works in Vancouver-road, for the district board of works.—The Surveyor to the Board:—

| | |
|---|---|
| C. Pearce, Havelock-street, Forest Hill, S.E.* | £576 |

LLANGYFELACH.—For the construction of about 456 yards of 12-in. stoneware pipe sewer in Sterry-road and Mount-street, Gowerton, for the rural district council.—Mr. J. Thomas, A.M.I.C.E., engineer and surveyor to the council, 32 Fisher-street, Swansea:—

| | |
|---|---|
| J. Harvey, Swansea | £445 |
| W. Lane, Swansea | 420 |
| J. & F. Weaver, Swansea | 415 |
| Bennett Brothers, Swansea | 390 |
| C. Hanney, Morriston* | 317 |

RATHMINES (Ireland).—Accepted for the supply of various plant for the equipment of the electric lighting works, for the township commissioners.—Mr. Robert Hammond, consulting electrical engineer, 64 Victoria-street, London, S.W.:—

Boiler-House Plant (three 30-ft. by 8-ft. Lancashire boilers and accessories, mechanical stokers, feed pumps, injector, economiser and electric motor).—R. Taylor & Sons, Marsdon, £2,924.

Engine-House Plant (one 300-kilowatt and one 150-kilowatt high-speed steam dynamos and accessories, motor transformer, spare parts, &c.)—Mather & Platt, Limited, Manchester, £6,386.

Ten-Ton Overhead Travelling Crane.—Higginbottom & Mannock, Manchester, £204.

Switchboard and Instruments.—James White, Glasgow, £1,181.

Accumulators.—Tudor Accumulator Company, Limited, £1,958.

Underground Work (trenching, cables, &c.).—British Insulated Wire Company, Limited, Prescott, £14,123.

Meters.—Ferrante & Co., Limited, Hollinwood, £500.

ST. OLAVE'S (Southwark).—For the supply of 50,000 blackbutt wood blocks and 5,000 yellow deal blocks dipped in oil, for the district board of works.—Mr. G. L. Hawker, clerk to the board:—

| BLACKBUTT. | Per 1,000 Blocks. £ | s. | d. |
|---|---|---|---|
| Nicholson & Co., Fish-street Hill, E.C. | 10 | 15 | 0 |
| Improved Wood Pavement Co., Queen Victoria-street, E.C.,* | 10 | 5 | 0 |
| YELLOW DEAL. | | | |
| J. B. Lee & Sons, Gracechurch-street, E.C. | 6 | 11 | 6 |
| Burt, Bolton & Haywood, Limited, Cannon-street, E.C. | 6 | 11 | 0 |
| Improved Wood Pavement Co., Queen Victoria-street, E.C., | 5 | 15 | 0 |
| Acme Wood Flooring Co., Gainsborough-rd., Victoria-Park, E.* | 4 | 10 | 0 |

TAUNTON.—For the supply of about 67 tons of 8-in. and 6-in. cast-iron spigot and socket bituminised water pipes.—Mr. George H. Kite, town clerk:—

| | |
|---|---|
| Thomas Spittle, Limited, Newport, Mon.* | £5 7s. 6d. per ton. |

WEDNESBURY.—For the erection of isolation hospital buildings, boundary walling, &c., on a site in Dangerfield-lane.—Mr. E. Martin Scott, borough engineer and surveyor:—

| | |
|---|---|
| G. Summerhill, Wednesbury | £1,550 |
| J. Mitson & Co., London, S.E. | 1,477 |
| W. Harbrow, London, S.E. | 1,410 |
| T. J. Hawkins & Co., Ashford, Middlesex | 1,275 |
| E. Hadley & Sons, Old Hill, Dudley* | 1,083 |

## MEETINGS.

*Secretaries and others will oblige by sending early notice of dates of forthcoming meetings.*

NOVEMBER.

25.—Sanitary Institute: Lecture to sanitary officers by Mr. W. C. Tyndale, M.I.C.E., on "House Drainage." 8 p.m.

26.—Sanitary Institute: Visit of sanitary officers to the Ealing sewage and destructor works, under the guidance of Mr. Charles Jones, M.I.C.E., engineer and surveyor to the district council. 2.15 p.m.

28.—The Surveyors' Institution: Ordinary general meeting. 8 p.m.

29.—Institution of Civil Engineers: Ordinary meeting; Mr. Stanley Robert Kay, A.M.I.C.E., on "The Effect of Subsidence due to Coal Working upon Bridges and other Structures." 8 p.m.

DECEMBER.

1.—Association of the Birmingham Students of the Institution of Civil Engineers: Dr. A. Bostock Hill on "Some Observations on Sewage and Modern Methods of Treatment." 7.30 p.m.

2.—Institution of Civil Engineers: Students' meeting; Mr. Charles Benjamin Saner on "The Sunlight Gold-bearing Reef, Lydenburg, Transvaal." 8 p.m.

5.—Royal Institute of British Architects: Mr. R. W. Gibson, New York, U.S.A., on "Fireproof Construction in America." 8 p.m.

12.—The Surveyors' Institution: Ordinary general meeting. 8 p.m.

### NOTICES.

THE SURVEYOR AND MUNICIPAL AND COUNTY ENGINEER *may be ordered direct, through any of Messrs. Smith & Son's book-stalls, or of any newsagent in the United Kingdom. Applications to the Offices for single copies by post must in all cases be accompanied by stamps.*

The Prepaid Subscription (including postage) is as follows :

|  | Twelve Months. | Six Months. | Three Months. |
|---|---|---|---|
| United Kingdom ... ... | 13s. | 7s. 6d. | 3s. 9d. |
| Continent, the Colonies, India, United States, &c. ... ... | 19s. | 9s. 6d. | 4s. 9d. |

*The International News Company, 83 and 85 Duane-street, New York City; The Toronto News Company, Toronto; and The Montreal News Company, Montreal, have been appointed agents in the United States and Canada for the sale of* THE SURVEYOR AND MUNICIPAL AND COUNTY ENGINEER. *A thin paper edition is printed for circulation abroad.*

EDITORIAL OFFICES :—
24 BRIDE-LANE, FLEET-STREET, LONDON, E.C.

ADVERTISEMENT AND PUBLISHING OFFICES :—
13 NEW STREET-HILL, FLEET-STREET, LONDON, E.C.

## APPOINTMENTS OPEN.

### WIMBLEDON URBAN DISTRICT COUNCIL.
JUNIOR ASSISTANT IN THE SURVEYOR'S OFFICE.

The Wimbledon Urban District Council require a Junior Assistant in the Surveyor's Department. Salary commencing at £60 per annum. Applicants must be good levellers and have a knowledge of surveying and drawing.

Applications, in candidate's own handwriting, stating age and experience, which may be accompanied by copies of not more than three testimonials, to be addressed to me not later than Tuesday, the 29th inst.

Canvassing members of the Council is prohibited.

W. H. WHITFIELD,
Clerk to the Council.

Council Offices, Wimbledon.
November 19, 1898.

### COUNTY BOROUGH OF SUNDERLAND.
ROAD SURVEYOR.

Wanted, by the Corporation of Sunderland, a Road Surveyor, to discharge all the duties of a surveyor of highways, subject to the Borough Surveyor as the Surveyor of Highways for the Borough. Salary, £130 per annum.

Candidates must have had a thoroughly practical experience in road making and maintenance, paving of all descriptions, flagging, &c., and the person appointed will be required to devote his whole time to the duties of the office.

Personal canvassing for the appointment will be a disqualification.

Applications, in the handwriting of the candidates, stating age, residence, and past and present occupation, accompanied by copies of not more than six testimonials of recent date, must be delivered to me, at the address undermentioned, not later than 4 p.m. on Wednesday, the 30th November instant, endorsed "Road Surveyor."

(By order)
FRAS. M. BOWEY,
Town Clerk.

Town Hall, Sunderland.
November 14, 1898.

### WILLENHALL URBAN DISTRICT COUNCIL.

*AMENDED ADVERTISEMENT.*

SEWAGE FARM MANAGER WANTED.

Applicants must have had previous experience in sewage disposal and treatment and cropping of land (area of farm about 15 acres pasture and 13 acres arable.) Salary, 30s. per week, with house provided, rent and taxes free.

List of duties on application.

Sealed applications, with copies of three recent testimonials, to be sent to me on or before December 14, 1898, endorsed "Manager."

Canvassing will disqualify.

(Signed)    CHAS. J. JENKIN, C.E.,
Town Surveyor.

Council Offices, Willenhall.
November 19, 1898.

PORTISHEAD URBAN DISTRICT COUNCIL.
Wanted, by the above Council (population of the district under 3,000), a Surveyor and Inspector of Nuisances.
For particulars of appointment apply to the undersigned on and after Monday, November 21st.
Applications, stating salary required, and not more than three recent testimonials, to be sent to me not later than the 1st December.

(By order)
JNO. CHAFFEY GLYDE,
Clerk.
Portishead, Somerset.
November 18, 1898.

BOROUGH OF FOLKESTONE.
APPOINTMENT OF BOROUGH SURVEYOR.
The Folkestone Corporation are prepared to receive applications for the appointment of Borough Surveyor.
Salary, £350 per annum, with an increment of £25 per annum until £500 be reached. Candidates to be between thirty and forty years of age.
List of duties, &c., can be obtained from the undersigned, to whom applications must be addressed, endorsed "Borough Surveyor," and delivered at the Town Clerk's office on or before the 30th November, 1898.
Canvassing members of the Council will be a disqualification.

A. F. KIDSON,
Town Clerk.
Town Clerk's Office, Folkestone.
November, 1898.

A SURVEYOR to an urban district council in a suburban district of London has a vacancy in his office for an Improver or Assistant, at a salary of £60 per annum. A youth who has been in a similar office preferred. A vacancy also exists for an Articled Pupil.—Please apply for further information to "J. E. S.," office of THE SURVEYOR, 24 Bride-lane, Fleet-street, E.C.

## TENDERS WANTED.

CITY OF NOTTINGHAM.
The Works and Ways Committee are prepared to receive tenders for the supply of the undermentioned Stores

and Materials, the contracts to commence on the 1st January next, and to terminate on the 31st December, 1899 :—
1. Cement.
2. Blue Lias Lime.
3. Red Bricks.
4. Blue Bricks.
5. Timber.
6. Earthenware Pipes and Gulleys.
7. Earthenware Pipes (Hassall's Patent).
8. Iron Castings.
9. Yorkshire Flags, Kerbs, &c.
10. Granite Setts, Kerbs, Randoms and Broken Granite.
11. Broken Ironstone Slag, Chippings, &c.
12. River Gravel.
13. Coal.
{ 14. Picks, Shovels and Scoops. }
{ 15. Ironmongery. }
16. Scavenging and other Brushes.
Forms of tender may be obtained by applying at my office, the Guildhall, on payment of 5s. each, which sum will be returned on receipt of a bonâ-fide tender, and providing such tender is not withdrawn.
Patterns and samples may be inspected at the Eastcroft Depot, London-road, Nottingham. The committee will not consider any tender except those on the authorised form of tender, which must be sent in to the Town Clerk on or before Thursday, 8th December, 1898. The lowest or any tender will not necessarily be accepted, and tenders will only be accepted from persons who conform to the conditions as regards paying the local standard rate of wages, &c.
(By order)
ARTHUR BROWN, M INST.C.E.,
City Engineer.
The Guildhall.
November 24, 1898.

CITY OF HULL.
TO QUARRY OWNERS AND OTHERS.
The Corporation are prepared to receive tenders for the supply of about 5,000 super. yards of the Best Hard Yorkshire 3 in. Tooled Flags, delivered at Hull during the ensuing four months.
Forms of tender may be obtained of the City Engineer, Hull.
Tenders, endorsed "Tender for Flags," are to be addressed to the Chairman of the Works Committee, and to be delivered at the Town Clerk's office, Hull, before noon on Friday, December 2nd.

Firms who have not recently supplied flags to the Corporation may send sample trucks, carriage paid, to Neptune-street station, H. and B. Railway, to arrive not later than November 30th. Such sample trucks will be paid for at the rate in the accepted tender.

The Corporation do not bind themselves to accept the lowest or any tender.

(By order)
A. E. WHITE,
City Engineer.

Town Hall, Hull.
November 19, 1898.

## URBAN DISTRICT OF FLEETWOOD, LANCASHIRE.

The Fleetwood Urban District Council are prepared to receive, on or before Monday, the 5th day of December next, at 12 o'clock noon, suggestions from engineers as to the best method of carrying out a Sewage Diversion Scheme or Schemes for the above-named district; the terms upon which a detailed report will be made, together with the charges for preparing all necessary plans, specifications, &c., and carrying out the scheme or schemes if adopted.

The area of the district is 2,848 acres, and the estimated population is 13,500.

(By order)
JOSEPH TILDSLEY,
Clerk and Accountant.

Town Hall, Fleetwood.
November 17, 1898.

## CORPORATION OF MANSFIELD.

The Town Council, acting as the urban sanitary authority for their district, are prepared to receive tenders from competent persons for the construction of about 500 yards of 9-in. Pipe Sewer, with all the necessary lampholes, manholes, ventilators, flushing arrangements, and works incidental thereto.

Plans and specifications of the works may be seen, and the form of tender and schedule of quantities obtained (on deposit of £2), at the office of Mr. R. Frank Vallance, C.E., F.S.I., Borough Surveyor, Mansfield, the Engineer for the works, on and after the 1st day of December rext.

The deposit will be returned, after a contract has been entered into, to every person making a *bonâ-fide* tender and on the return of the documents entrusted to him.

In the event of a tender being withdrawn, the deposit will be forfeited.

The successful contractor will be required to pay the standard rate of wages recognised in the district in the several trades.

Sealed tenders (on the form supplied), endorsed " Tender for Outfall Sewer, Littleworth," are to be delivered at the office of the undersigned, in the envelope provided for the purpose, on or before the 14th day of December, 1898, at noon.

The Town Council will not be bound to accept the lowest or any tender.

Dated this 17th day of November, 1898.
J. HARROP WHITE,
Deputy Town Clerk.

## SHANGHAI MUNICIPAL COUNCIL.
### TRAMWAY CONCESSION.

The following resolution in reference to proposed tramways in Shanghai was passed at the last annual meeting of the ratepayers of the Foreign Settlements at Shanghai, north of the Yang-king-pang.

" Resolution 10.—That the Council be and is hereby authorised to consider the expediency of the establishment of a system of tramways in the streets of the settlement, and in its discretion to formulate a scheme for ratification by the ratepayers by which the system be carried into effect."

In accordance with the above resolution, the Council hereby invite tenders for a concession for constructing and working about 23 miles of Electric Tramways on the " trolley system " in the streets of Shanghai.

The special attention of tenderers is drawn to the fact that the tender (if any) recommended by the Council will require ratification by the ratepayers.

Plans may be seen and particulars obtained on application to Messrs. John Pook & Co., 8 Jeffreys-square, St. Mary Axe, London, E.C., on a Bank of England note for £100 (one hundred pounds sterling) being deposited with Messrs. Pook & Co., which sum will be retained by the Council and deemed to be forfeited unless a *bonâ-fide* tender be made by the depositor.

Further information may be obtained on application to Mr. Charles Mayne, Municipal Engineer, Shanghai, China

(telegraphic address, "Dynamo, Shanghai," "A.B.C.," 4th edition, and "Engineering" codes used).

Sealed tenders, endorsed "Tender for Tramway Concession," must be sent in to the undersigned and received not later than 12 noon on Wednesday, the 15th March, 1899.

The Council reserves to itself the right to decline all or any of the tenders so sent in.

(By order)
J. O. P. BLAND,
Secretary.

Council-Room, Shanghai, China.
September 5, 1898.

FELIXSTOWE AND WALTON URBAN DISTRICT COUNCIL.
TO ROAD CONTRACTORS AND OTHERS.

Tenders are invited for the Sewering and Making-up of Leopold-road North with Blue Staffordshire Kerb and Channel and Tar Paths.

Also for the Sewering and Making-up of Victoria-street North with Blue Staffordshire Kerb and Channel and Tar Paths.

Also for the Forming of a Path in High-road, High-street and Lower-street, Walton, with Blue Staffordshire Kerb and Gravel Paths.

Plans and specifications can be seen at the Surveyor's office on and after Tuesday, November 22, 1898.

Tenders to be sent to the undersigned not later than 11 a.m., Wednesday, December 7, 1898, endorsed "Tender for ———."

The Council do not bind themselves to accept the lowest or any tender.

F. B. JENNINGS,
Clerk to the Council.
Town Hall, Felixstowe.
November 19, 1898.

CORPORATION OF MANSFIELD.

The Town Council, acting as the urban sanitary authority for their district, are prepared to receive tenders from competent persons for the construction of about 1,650 yards of Brick Sewer and Storm Overflows, and 570 yards of Pipe Sewers, with all necessary lampholes, manholes, ventilators, flushing arrangements and works incidental thereto.

Plans and specifications of the works may be seen, and the form of tender and schedule of quantities obtained (on deposit of £10), at the office of Mr. R. Frank Vallance, C.E., F.S.I., Borough Surveyor, Mansfield, the Engineer for the works, on and after the 1st day of December next.

The deposit will be returned, after a contract has been

entered into, to every person making a bona-fide tender and on the return of the documents entrusted to him.

In the event of a tender being withdrawn the deposit will be forfeited.

The successful contractor will be required to pay the standard rate of wages recognised in the district in the several trades.

Sealed tenders (on the form supplied) endorsed "Tender for Intercepting Sewer," are to be delivered at the office of the undersigned, in the envelope provided for the purpose, on or before the 14th day of December, 1898, at noon.

The Town Council will not be bound to accept the lowest or any tender.

Dated this 16th day of November, 1898.

J. HARROP WHITE,
Deputy Town Clerk.

ACTON DISTRICT COUNCIL.

The Acton District Council require plans and tenders for the erection of a Dust Destructor.

The specification may be seen here, and forms of tender obtained on and after Monday, November 28th, during the usual office hours.

The Council do not bind themselves to accept the lowest or any tender.

Tenders must be left here, in sealed envelopes, endorsed "Destructor," not later than 3 p.m. on Tuesday, December 6th next.

(By order)
D. J. EBBETTS,
Surveyor to the Acton District Council.
242 High-street, Acton.

BROMSGROVE RURAL DISTRICT COUNCIL.

PEDMORE SEWERAGE.

TO CONTRACTORS.

The above Council is prepared to receive tenders for the Construction of a new Stoneware Pipe Sewers comprised in the scheme of sewerage for the parish of Pedmore, together with manholes, lampholes, flushing chambers and other works in connection therewith.

Plans, sections and detail drawings may be seen, and specifications and bills of quantities obtained, at the office of the Engineer, Mr. E. B. Marten, M.I.C.E., Church-street Chambers, Stourbridge, on and after Wednesday, November 2nd, on payment of £5 5s., which will be returned after the receipt of a

*bonâ-fide* tender, with the schedules duly filled in, and the return of all documents.

Sealed tenders, addressed to me, and endorsed " Tender for Pedmore Sewerage," are to be delivered at my office on or before Monday, the 28th day of November next.

The Council do not bind themselves to accept the lowest or any tender.

(By order)
H. D. HOLLOWAY,
Clerk to the Council.

Union Offices, Bromsgrove.
October 27, 1898.

## BRENTFORD URBAN DISTRICT COUNCIL.
### CONTRACT FOR MAKING-UP STILE HALL GARDENS.

The Council are prepared to receive tenders for the above work.

Forms of tender (on which alone tenders will be received), together with specification and conditions, may be obtained on application personally to Mr. Nowell Parr, the Surveyor, at his office, Clifden House, Boston-road, Brentford, between the hours of 10 a.m. and 5 p.m.

Tenders to be delivered (sealed) at the Clerk's office, New Brentford, on or before Tuesday, the 6th December next, by 12 o'clock, marked " Tender for Making-up Stile Hall Gardens."

The Council do not bind themselves to accept the lowest or any tender.

(By order)
STEP. WOODBRIDGE,
Clerk.

Brentford.
November 17, 1898.

## COUNTY BOROUGH OF WEST HAM.
### TO BUILDERS AND CONTRACTORS.

The Council hereby invite tenders for the Erection of Quarter Sessions Court, Police Cells and Mortuary, West Ham-lane, Stratford, E.

Plans may be seen, and specification, form of tender and further particulars obtained, on and after Monday, 28th November, 1898, at the office of Mr. Lewis Angell, Borough Engineer, Town Hall, Stratford, E., upon the deposit of a £5 Bank of England note, which will be returned upon receipt of a *bonâ-fide* tender.

Tenders, endorsed " Tender for Quarter Sessions Court, &c.," to be sent to my office not later than 4 o'clock on Tuesday, 13th December, 1898.

The Council do not bind themselves to accept the lowest or any tender. The contractor will be required to enter into a bond, with two sureties, for the due performance of the contract, and no work will be ordered under the contract until such bond has been duly executed.

As regards all work to be done at the site or elsewhere within a radius of 20 miles from Charing Cross, the contractors will be bound by the contract to pay to all workmen (except a reasonable number of legally-bound apprentices) employed by them wages at rates not less, and to observe hours of labour not greater, than the rates and hours set out in the Council's list, and such rates of wages and hours of labour will be inserted in and form part of the contract by way of schedule.

(By order of the Council)
FRED. E. HILLEARY,
Town Clerk.

Town Hall, West Ham, E.
November 15, 1898.

## DROYLSDEN URBAN DISTRICT.
### CONSTRUCTION OF SEWERS.

The above Council invite tenders for the construction of 607 lineal yards of 24-in. Pipe Sewer, 615 lineal yards of 18-in. Pipe Sewer, and 345 lineal yards of 15-in. Pipe Sewer, together with Manholes, Junctions, &c.—namely, from Manchester-road to Ashton Old-road, Fairfield, and from Copperas-lane to the " Barley Mow," Fairfield-road.

Particulars and specifications may be seen on application to Mr. W. Curry, F.I.S.E., the Engineer to the Council.

Quantities and forms of tender will be supplied to intending contractors on payment of 1 guinea, which will be returned on receipt of a *bonâ-fide* tender, together with all documents given to contractors.

Tenders, endorsed " Sewers," must be addressed Chairman, Sewage Committee, Council Offices, Droylsden, and sent in on or before the 30th inst.

The Council do not bind themselves to accept the lowest or any tender.

(By order)
JOHN RICHARDS,
Clerk of the Council.

Council Offices, Droylsden.

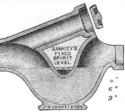

# The Surveyor

## And Municipal and County Engineer.

Vol. XIV., No. 359.     LONDON, DECEMBER 2, 1898.     Weekly, Price 3d.

## Minutes of Proceedings.

**Comparative [Costs and Profits of Cable, Electric and Horse Tramways.**

Probably one of the most important statements ever issued as to cost of operating the various systems of tramway traction is that which has been recently published by *The Street Railway Journal* of New York. The figures are especially important to municipalities at the present moment, because, as far as cost of operating is concerned, they bear out the statements of Mr. J. Allen Baker. It must be understood, however, that they demonstrate the superiority of electric over cable and horse tramways rather than the superiority of any particular system of electrical working over another. The figures are chiefly valuable from the fact that they are made up from the cost-sheets and records of one company (the Metropolitan Street Railway Company of New York) employing all three systems, and thus enable a true comparison to be made of the relative costs of operating these distinct systems in one city and under practically the same conditions. They demonstrate beyond all question the great superiority of electricity over both horse and cable traction, not only in traffic-handling capacity, but in economy of operation. It was generally supposed that the cable system under conditions of great traffic density was the cheapest and best motive power in existence, and it was thought that the rapid disappearance of the cable system in America was due rather to a desire for unification of motive power or to the general popularity and earning capacity of electric cars. It was not generally supposed that electric cars, replacing cable cars on heavy traffic roads, could be operated at a less cost per car mile, but such a supposition has been completely established by the New York figures. It is not necessary to refer to the various details of construction of either the cable or electric line, as it will suffice to confine one's attention entirely to the figures. During the twelve months under review, which, by the way, is down to the end of June this year, the company operated 34·2 per cent. of its car mileage by the cable system, 20·2 per cent. by the electric system, and 40·6 per cent. by horse haulage. The proportions had to a considerable extent altered in the quarter ended September 30th of this year, the cable mileage being then only 27·4 per cent. of the total, and the horse system only 33·7 per cent., while the mileage of the electric system had risen to 39·1 per cent. The relative earnings during the last quarter were as follows : Cable system, £7,800 per mile of track and 16d. per car mile ; electric system, £3,400 per mile of track and 13d. per car mile ; and horse haulage, £1,600 per mile of track and 14d. per car mile. It will be seen how important the results are from an electrical standpoint when it is mentioned that the cost of operating a single car mile was : Cable, 8·21d. ; horses, 8·93d. ; and electricity, 5·11d. For the three months period to which we have alluded the results are favourable to electric traction, probably on account of the greater popularity of the line. For the period in question the cable lines cost 8·77d. per car mile, the horse 8·94d., and the electric 5·03d. It is, however, when one considers the figures in detail that the great disparity is most clearly shown. For example, the maintenance of way in the cable system cost 1·72d. per car mile, in the electric ·11d. per car mile, and in the horse system ·80d. Even in regard to the maintenance of equipment, in which respect it would have been thought that the cable would have been able to show to great advantage, the respective costs are : ·47d. per car mile for cable, ·41d. for electricity, and ·33d. for horse traction. The cost of power, under which is included repairs, wages, &c., works out as follows : Cable, 1·01d. ; electricity, ·85d. ; and the horse, 1·97d. Perhaps the most remarkable feature is the production of power, for it has been found possible to operate heavy electric cars, which we understand vary from 22 ft. to 28 ft. in length, at a cost of 33 per cent. less than can be done in two cable-power stations which operate cables so heavily loaded as to make the proportion of live to dead weight greater probably than that of any cable railway system in the United States. It might be expected that the costs of repairs of the cable and electric conduit systems respectively would show a marked difference in favour of electric traction. Of course it must be admitted that the amount of moving mechanism in the cable system is very considerable, while in the electric there is none. It is probable, however, that as the electric lines are quite new certain charges which are exceedingly favourable at the present moment will be slightly enhanced, because in one respect electric traction is less favourable to track work than either cable or horse. Electric cars are heavier, and no doubt deliver a more severe hammer blow to the joints than is experienced with either horses or cable. At the same time, taking into consideration the various directions in which the electric portion of the system will show slightly increased expenditure, it is one of the most remarkable achievements on record that electricity should have been able to beat the cable on its own ground.

\* \* \*

**Combined Drains and Nuisances.**

The unsatisfactory state of the law with regard to the combined drainage question has again been forcibly illustrated by the recent case of *North and Millhouse v. Walthamstow Urban District Council* (noted on page 676 *ante*), in which the council have been adjudged liable to pay for the repair of what is to all intents and purposes a private drain (though legally a "sewer"), as well as the costs of the legal proceedings. As is frequently the case, the existence of this "sewer," situated on private ground, but "vested" by statute in the local authority, was unknown until discovered in the course of operations consequent upon a nuisance having arisen in a portion of the combined system. Seven houses were, in fact, drained by the conduit in question, and as they all belonged to the same owner no question arose under sec. 19 of the Public Health Acts Amendment Act, 1890. Prior to the discovery of the combined drain the sanitary inspector served the usual form of nuisance notice on the owner in respect of the house in which the nuisance had occurred. When, the ground having been opened, it was found that all the seven houses were served by the one drain, the inspector served a second notice, in the same form, but mentioning all the houses, instead of only the one. The work specified in the notices was done by the owner's agent, who was also a builder, he being aware (as he told the Court) that the pipe was a sewer, for the repair of which the owner was not liable, but being, nevertheless, under the impression that he was obliged to do the work after receiving the notices. There seems to be some confusion of thought here, but however this may be, the agent, in conjunction with the owner, presumably sought legal advice, which resulted in the bringing of the action we are considering. The council were bound to admit that the combined drain was a sewer, but they nevertheless denied the plaintiff's legal right to be recouped the amount expended in remedying the nuisance. They relied upon the case of *Selfe* v. *Hove Commissioners*, decided in 1895. In that case the local authority (who had adopted the Act of 1890) gave notice to the owner of one of two houses drained by a combined system to abate a nuisance by doing certain works, and threatening proceedings in case of default. The owner having complied with the notice, it was held that the latter was not such a request to do the work as would support the action, and that no such request could be implied, because the commissioners were not themselves liable for the repair of the drain. The action therefore failed. This was one of the earliest cases under the Act of 1890, and was decided before sec. 19 of that statute had been whittled away by the decision in *The Queen* v. *Mayor of Hastings*, which was not given until 1897. Apart from this, however, *Selfe* v. *Hove Commissioners* is obviously distinguishable from the present case, to which the Act of 1890 was not applicable, the houses all belonging to the same owner. On the other hand, precedents in support of the owner's claim to reimbursement are to be found in *Florence* v. *Paddington Vestry*, decided in 1895 by Mr. Justice Chitty, and *Andrew* v. *St. Olave's Board of Works*, decided in March of the present year by Lord Russell of Killowen and Mr. Justice Mathew. The first of these cases does not seem to have been brought to the attention of the Court in the present action, but the second was referred to, and evidently influenced Mr. Justice Channell in his decision. It is significant to note, too, that (although not necessary for the purpose of the decision) the learned judge took occasion to express strong disapproval of *Selfe* v. *Hove Commissioners*, and it may be doubted whether that decision can now be regarded as sound law. The present case does but emphasise the anomalous condition of affairs under which there must be hundreds of these secret "sewers" all over the country waiting for the touch of the enchanter's wand, in the shape of a "nuisance notice," to reveal their existence and claim the protection of their lawful but reluctant owners—the local authorities. An inspector of nuisances might well hesitate before serving one of these notices, lest he should thus involuntarily be the means of adding yet another hitherto unsuspected "sewer" to the local authority's possessions.

**The London Water Supply Controversy.** The wordy warfare which has been raging in *The Times* between Lord Balfour of Burleigh, Lord Farrer, Mr. Dickinson, L.C.C., and the anonymous writer who signs himself "Thames," and one or two others, seems now to have burned itself out, probably from sheer exhaustion. We cannot say that the controversy has cleared the air much or added to the knowledge and understanding of one of London's most serious problems. For one thing, the discussion partook a little too much of the "You're another" character to be particularly helpful. In other words, one of the combatants would make certain categorical assertions, and another would follow next day with equally categorical denials, little trouble being taken on either side to unfold reasons or adduce satisfactory proof. The broad question at issue between Lord Farrer and his anonymous antagonist, "Thames," was whether there is any real necessity for going to Wales for a source of water supply to the metropolis. Lord Farrer, of course, is an uncompromising advocate of the affirmative view, and "Thames" an equally uncompromising advocate of the negative one, the latter holding that storage in the Thames valley will supply all needs, at all events, until the time specified by the Balfour Commission, 1931. Lord Farrer's objection to this view is that it is based on the average, instead of the minimum, flow, and in this interesting position the controversialists still seem to remain. One beneficial result of the discussion has been that attention has been drawn to the capacity of the stream chiefly relied upon in Sir Alexander Binnie's great scheme. "Thames" has asserted that it has recently been dry for a month, a statement that Lord Farrer has denied, apparently on the strength of information received rather than from his own personal knowledge. Surely the capacity of the stream might easily be settled by reference to Sir Alexander Binnie, who would do well to publish some reliable data on the subject, if he has not already done so. The figures, if satisfactory, would be reassuring, and their publication would do no harm. Strangely enough, however, the controversialists seem to have quite overlooked the important fact pointed out by Mr. Dickinson at last week's meeting of the London County Council, that the success of Sir Alexander Binnie's scheme, like that of Mr. Mansergh's Birmingham scheme, depends not on the dry weather flow of the streams but on storage during winter and spring. This fact notwithstanding, the exact figures as to the flow of the chief stream might as well be published. Mr. Dickinson, by the way, is deserving of sympathy in having been fathered in some newspaper reports with the absurd remark that in the Welsh scheme reliance is placed not upon rivers but on springs. What he did say we have already indicated. Whether in the Thames valley or in Wales, the question is essentially one of storage. It is admitted by many by no means unfriendly critics of the Balfour Commission that the members were somewhat astray in their calculations; but accepting the 1931 hypothesis, what likelihood is there of any adequate watersheds being available in Wales for the needs of London thirty years hence ?

*          *          *

**Building By-Laws in Rural Districts.** Another question that has been attracting public attention in the columns of our Printing House-square contemporary is that of building by-laws, especially in rural districts. Opinions have been freely expressed that in such districts building by-laws generally cause unnecessary expense and inconvenience. The force and truth of much that has been written on the subject must be conceded, but there seems to be a general tendency to place the responsibility on the wrong shoulders. Rural district councils, of course, have no authority under any Act of Parliament to make by-laws, and before they can do anything in the matter application must be made for urban powers. If this system does not work, the most obvious explanation is that urban powers are granted by the Local Government Board to rural district councils on inadequate grounds. But this is not the only point in regard to which the policy of the Local Government Board is open to criticism. Urban powers having been obtained in the usual way, a rural district council has little or no latitude in the framing of its by-laws, which must follow the code which the Local Government Board are pleased to describe as "model," and with which, generally speaking, they require a rigid compliance, irrespective of the particular needs of a district. It is true that modifications are occasionally allowed, but they are of too slight and trivial a character to do away with the objectionable features of the system. It is desirable that there should be some sort of building by-laws, even in rural districts, but that they should be practically the same as those in force in urban districts is absurd. There may also be some force in the argument that rural district councils should not be trusted to frame or adopt their own by-laws, but should have this work done for them by some higher authority; but the answer is that at present by-laws have to be approved by the Local Government Board, and if their working is not satisfactory and they are not adapted to local needs the responsibility should lie with that department. But the chief point is that the Local Government Board rigidly insist on their "model" code being followed in all cases, but it requires no demonstration that village houses with plenty of ground behind them and detached houses in rural districts generally do not call for such exacting requirements as houses crowded together in a town. The application of similar regulations must simply tend to veto building operations in rural districts, and thus be disastrous to the interests of the rural population. The absurdity of insisting on one practically uniform code of regulations, irrespective of special local needs and conditions was forcibly pointed out by Mr. Pickering, surveyor to the Nuneaton Urban District Council, in his paper read at the recent Birmingham congress of the Sanitary Institute. In default of the initiation of a more enlightened policy at the Local Government Board, it is to be hoped that the question will receive some attention in Parliament.

* * *

**The Housing Problem.** As our readers are aware, the Standing Orders of Parliament require that in any case in which it is proposed by a Bill in Parliament to authorise the taking in any urban sanitary district, or in any parish or part of a parish in a rural sanitary district, of ten or more houses, occupied either wholly or partially by persons of the labouring classes as tenants or lodgers there shall be deposited with the Local Government Board, as the central authority for England and Wales exclusive of the metropolis, as well as with the Clerk of the Parliaments and at the Private Bill office, on or before December 31st, a statement of the number, description and situation of such houses, the number (so far as it can be ascertained) of the persons residing in them and a plan of the buildings involved. During 1897 forty-three such statements were deposited, and from these it appeared that it was contemplated during the season of 1898, by means of thirty-eight railway and other Bills and five provisional orders under the Public Health Act, 1875, to obtain powers to acquire in England and Wales, exclusive of the metropolis, 5,199 houses wholly or partially occupied by persons of the labouring class. The number of persons residing in such houses was 27,115. In connection with applications for the approval of schemes for providing new dwellings for persons of the labouring class proposed to be displaced by the acquisition of their dwellings under powers conferred by local Acts and provisional orders, it is the rule of the Board to arrange for the holding of the local inquiries in the evening, so that the occupants of the houses in question may have an opportunity of being present. Printed notices, setting forth the nature of the application, are served at each house involved. Nine local inquiries of this character were held during the year. In Manchester last year improvements involved the disturbance of no fewer than 2,000 persons of the labouring class, and the

corporation proposed to provide substantial accommodation, at a cost of £75,000. Carlisle Corporation also required a loan of £2,500 for the provision of dwellings for 134 persons. The scheme of the Cardiff Corporation for the rehousing of 234 persons had to be amended so as to provide for a larger number of dwellings. Only two applications were made during the year under Part I. of the Housing of the Working Classes Act, 1890, and these had reference to schemes framed by the Devonport and Sheffield Corporations.

* * *

**The Maintenance of Roads.** In his annual report to which we have already referred, being for the year ended March 25, 1898, Mr. C. H. Lowe, surveyor to the Hampstead Vestry, remarks that the practice of the vestry in employing its own labour in the repair of the roads and footways is generally, if not universally, recognised as that which, on the whole, produces the best results. At the same time he takes occasion to point out that the standard of excellence which the cyclist has set up is scarcely possible of attainment, considering the wear and tear caused by the incessant heavy traffic over the main roads, and that to make special provision for cyclists is impracticable. Mr. Lowe surmises that had the speedy cycle been known to our forefathers main roads might have consisted at present of a carriageway, two footways, and a cycle track. The nearest available approach to the cyclist's ideal is the wood-paved carriageway, and now that the experimental stage in the use of jarrah and similar hardwoods has been passed, Mr. Lowe is of opinion that the only thing standing in the way of their more general adoption for paving purposes is the initial cost. A reduction of cost may, however, be looked for through trade competition, and then Mr. Lowe anticipates that hardwood may be used on many important roads which are now coated with the best quality of broken granite. Mr. Lowe does not consider that the utility of the motor car is yet quite assured, but with so much attention devoted to it, with a view to perfecting the machine, the time for its common use in business may, he thinks, be nearer than is generally thought. The effect upon the roadways he sums up in the following words: "If ever the day does come when we shall see the highways taken possession of by the horseless carriage, that same day will witness the difficulty of maintaining a smooth surface surmounted, for every wheel will have a rubber tyre, and the decrease in the number of horses pounding the roads with their hoofs will be so marked that the destroying agents in the roadway will be reduced to a minimum."

* * *

**The Smoke Question.** The discussion of the London smoke question has continued during the week with unabated vigour, and though it has been pointed out that the trouble is probably due in far greater degree to the accumulated effect of smoke from dwelling-houses than to emissions from works, most of the correspondents seem determined to attribute everything to the failure of the authorities to enforce their powers on offending owners of works. Sir W. B. Richmond's ambition is to form vigilance committees, whose function will be to apply the spur to local authorities. In the meantime various remedies are suggested for the domestic evil. By one authority we are told that the trouble is due to the use of grates unscientific in construction. Others see remedies in the universal adoption of gas for heating and cooking purposes, in the structural alteration of chimneys to prevent the creation of smoke, or in the general use of anthracite coal. Here, no doubt, we have possible remedies, but it is to be feared that there are serious practical difficulties in the way which will seriously impede the general adoption of any one of them, in the immediate future at all events.

# The Birmingham Water Scheme.—I.

## By JAMES MANSERGH, m.inst.c.e.

Caban Dam, Brecon Culvert Outlet, in Course of Construction (December, 1896).

.These articles are practically a reproduction of the interesting and valuable address delivered by Mr. Mansergh before the Engineering and Architectural section of the recent congress of the Sanitary Institute at Birmingham. The interest of the paper was enhanced by a large number of lantern views. It has, of course, been necessary to eliminate the references to these, but through the courtesy of Mr. Mansergh and Mr. T. Barclay we reproduce a number of the illustrations. In the course of his address Mr. Mansergh said :—

The city of Birmingham has an area of 12,365 acres, and the Parliamentary limits within which the corporation are bound to supply water extend to 83,221 acres, or 130 square miles, an area 10 per cent. in excess of that of the county of London. This district varies considerably in elevation, being 270 ft. above sea level in the north-east corner, and rising to 800 ft. in the south-west. As compared with this, the highest part of Hampstead Heath, in the north-west of London, is 450 ft. The population within the limits at the time of census-taking in 1891 was 647,972, and is believed to be now over 700,000. The water is at present obtained from five local streams and from six wells sunk in the New Red Sandstone, which underlies the city and its neighbourhood.

MR. MANSERGH'S ADVICE.

In 1890 I was called in to investigate the whole question of the future of the water undertaking. My advice to the committee, put shortly, was :—

(1) That the water obtainable from the local streams, flowing as they do through populous districts, would go on constantly increasing in impurity, and that the greatest care would have to be exercised in order to ensure its safely for domestic use.

(2) That the addition to their resources by any impounding works which could be constructed on these streams, or by sinking more wells, would carry them on for only a comparatively few years, at the end of which time they would inevitably have to go much further afield, and the money they had spent would be practically lost.

(3) That the distant unpolluted sources, at sufficient elevation to supply Birmingham by gravitation, were comparatively few, and that if their acquisition were delayed for even a few years the chances were that they would have been secured by some other community, possibly London.

This advice was accepted, the result being that a Bill was promoted in Parliament in the session of 1892, by which the corporation sought powers to utilise the waters of the rivers Elan and Claerwen, flowing from an area of 71 square miles in the counties of Radnor, Brecon and Cardigan. These rivers are tributaries of the Wye, which, passing through Radnor, Brecon, Hereford, Monmouth and Gloucester, joins the Severn near Chepstow.

PARLIAMENTARY PROCEEDINGS.

In order to obtain complete control of the drainage area, and thus secure the water from pollution, the corporation asked Parliament to allow them to acquire the whole of it by purchase, a proposition which induced the opposition of the landowners, the commoners and the Commons Preservation Society. Further, there was what I may call a national opposition. Gallant little Wales, full of fight, protested that this was Welsh water and should be reserved for Welshmen. Before the committees of both Houses the principality was represented by two doughty champions—the late Lord Swansea, better known as Sir Hussey Vivian, and Mr. Tom Ellis, the Liberal whip. They came before the hybrid committee of the House of Commons near the close of the case and fired off long patriotic speeches, which were listened to respectfully and patiently by Sir Campbell Bannerman, the chairman, and his colleagues, but without effect.

In the Lords they brought some professional evidence, with the hope of showing that the Elan watershed was the only one competent to supply Glamorganshire, with its great coal mining interests. This they essayed by pointing out that the colliery villages in the Rhondda and other districts were necessarily built high up on the hillsides, so as to be near the pits, and they fixed on a spot near Merthyr which was the lowest at which water, they said, must be delivered to meet their requirements, and stated that it was only from the Elan that that point could be reached. This specific allegation was fatal to their contention, for it was only necessary to lay

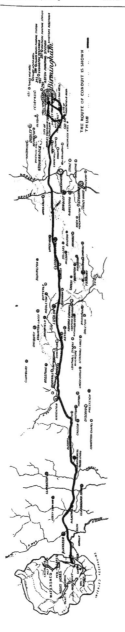

MAP SHOWING WATERSHED, RESERVOIRS AND AQUEDUCT.

out a line of aqueduct with a proper gradient from this point upwards to prove conclusively that it would cut the river Claerwen so high up that only about 8,000 acres out of our 46,000 could be utilised, and only one reservoir out of our six. For all practical purposes the Elan proper was too low. In the House of Lords I was able to show this to the committee by the model now on the table, and the Glamorganshire case was gone in ten minutes. I was also able to prove to the satisfaction of the committee that for the future needs of South Wales 250,000,000 gallons a day could be obtained from the river Usk and tributaries of the Wye, and, as these are the sources now proposed to be utilised for London in Sir Alexander Binnie's scheme, there will no doubt be "ructions"

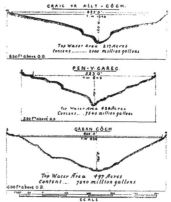

SECTIONS ON CENTRE LINES OF ELAN DAMS.

when the proposal comes before Parliament. In the second House, therefore, this opposition was also unavailing.

As a nation, therefore, the Welshmen failed, but the individual members of it, whose land we obtained powers to acquire for the works, have had their revenge. Radnorshire has "spoiled" Birmingham to the tune of scores of thousands, and during the last few years the ditty of my childhood has often recurred to my memory. It began "Taffy was a Welshman, Taffy was a thief;" but perhaps I had better not carry this any further. The Bill was also opposed by a number of property owners upon the line of aqueduct, by a small section of Birmingham ratepayers, by the Corporation of Hereford, and by the London County Council, the ground of the last-mentioned opposition being that the source of supply was an exceptionally good one, that therefore the council might some day like to get hold of it, and that Birmingham ought to wait until London had made up its mind. We were most effectively assisted in combating this opposition by Sir F. Bramwell. Sir Frederick had been engaged in

LONGITUDINAL SECTION OF ELAN RESERVOIRS.

the Liverpool fight twelve years previously, and was able to testify that a similar objection was made at the time by the Metropolitan Board of Works to the taking of the waters of the Vyrnwy to the great Lancashire seaport, and to show that the London question was no further advanced in 1892 than it was in 1880. This London contention was met by setting out in detail the many streams in the Welsh mountains which were available for the metropolis but too low for Birmingham, streams which when provided with proper storage reservoirs were competent to supply nearly 500,000,000 gallons a day without touching the Elan and Claerwen. This was one of the main features of the scheme before referred to as Sir Alexander Binnie's.

COMPENSATION WATER.

In addition to these oppositions, we had, of course, to fight, as happens in all Water Bills of this class, the question of the amount of compensation water to be paid to the river for the right to divert the water authorised to be taken for the supply of Birmingham. In the case of works established upon the rivers of Lancashire and Yorkshire, whose waters are utilised for manufacturing purposes nearly up to their sources, this is a serious question, but fortunately, in the whole course of the Wye and the Elan below the point of abstraction there is not a single case of such utilisation, even for driving the wheel of a corn mill. This did not, however, prevent most exorbitant claims being set up by

CABAN DAM, UP-STREAM FACE, BRECON END (February, 1898).

riparian owners on account of their fishing rights, not, however, by the net fishers in the lower reaches, who make their livelihood out of the fishing, but by sportsmen who handle a rod for diversion. In the Bill as deposited, we had proposed that the quantity of compensation water should be 22,500,000 gallons per day. The rod fishers demanded 40,000,000 gallons. They were assisted by the Wye Fishery Board, and in the background by the officials of the Board of Trade who administer the Salmon Fisheries Act, and ultimately a compromise was come to by which the quantity was fixed at 27,000,000 gallons per day. Since the works have been in course of construction we have had the opportunity of measuring the flow of the river at the spot where the 27,000,000 gallons will have to be discharged, and have found that in very dry weather it falls to something under 4,500,000 gallons, so that the quantity passing down will, so soon as any water is taken to Birmingham, be increased at such point six-fold. Of course the capability of so benefiting

CABAN DAM, BRECON CULVERT OUTLET (February, 1898).

the river is due to the storage of flood waters in the reservoirs to be constructed. Another incidental benefit arising out of this impounding will be the reduction in the volume and violence of destructive floods in the river below. The amount of compensation water in these cases is a fairly-well recognised proportion of the water collectable from the watershed area; that is to say, where the water is used for trade or manufacturing purposes the proportion is one-third, and where there are only ordinary riparian, including fishing, rights it is about one-fourth.

RAINFALL.

The quantity of water collectable is ascertained from the area of the gathering ground and the rainfall upon it, less the evaporation and the volume of water inevitably overflowing from the reservoirs in times of flood. Thus the area we are here dealing with was determined by accurately marking upon the plans the parting lines or watershed boundaries after careful examination, and in some cases instrumental levelling, upon the ground. By measurement from the plans the area was found to be 45,562 acres, the first factor in the calculation.

The rainfall might have been a much more difficult thing to determine than the area, but that, very fortunately, the lord of the manor, Mr. Robert Lewis Lloyd, and his father before him, had kept a rain gauge regularly from the year 1871 onwards at the family mansion of Nantgwilt, in the lower part of the Elan Valley, and at a spot on the watershed

area to be appropriated. So soon as it seemed probable that the matter would be proceeded with, several other rain gauges were erected at various points upon the shed with the assistance of Mr. Symons, the highest authority on British rainfall and the last and a most worthy recipient from the hands of H.R.H. the Prince of Wales of the gold medal of the Society of Arts. Then, by a comparison of these with the long term gauge at Nantgwilt and others in the surrounding country, it was decided that the mean annual fall of a long series of years upon the watershed might be taken at about 68 in., and the average of three consecutive dry years at 5 in. —this latter being the figure always used in these estimations—as first suggested by the veteran waterworks engineer and hydrologist, the late Mr. Hawksley. The greatest rainfall was in 1872—viz., 93·86 in., and the least was in 1892— viz., 43.44 in.

It is very usual to take 14 in. or 15 in. as the amount of evaporation, but, in order to be on the safe side and to allow amply for loss by overflow, 19 in. were deducted from the 55 in., leaving 36 in. as collectable by means of the reservoirs intended to be constructed. Taking the mean of three consecutive dry years, the rainfall in one year upon the watershed area would be equivalent to 252,495,491 tons of water, of which 63,950,823 would be lost by absorption or evaporation and 23,154,608 tons by overflow, leaving 165,390,060 tons as collectable in the reservoirs. In a year of maximum rain like 1872 the total quantity falling upon the watershed would be 431,116,756 tons, and the volume overflowing from the reser-

CABAN DAM, BRECON END, LOOKING NORTH (February, 1898).
(Showing Cyclopean Rubble.)

voirs into the river would be correspondingly increased Further observations since the Bill was in Parliament have satisfied me that we may calculate on obtaining from the works 75,000,000 gallons a day for supply in addition to the 27,000,000 gallons for compensation.

THE DAMS AND RESERVOIRS.

Considered geologically, the whole of the watershed area consists of rocks of Lower Silurian age, principally inferior slates, but in parts of very hard grits and conglomerates. It is the presence of thick bands of the latter stretching across the Elan at a place called Caban Coch and resisting disintegration which has determined the position of the contraction in the sides of the valley and rendered it so eminently suitable for the location of a barrier dam. At this spot the bed of the river is 700 ft. above ordnance datum, the bottom of the valley being about 200 ft. wide, and at 120 ft. higher only 600 ft. Immediately above this contraction the valley widens

CAREG-DDU CULVERT EXCAVATION, LOOKING UP-STREAM (July, 1896).

out into a broad "flat," and 1,540 yards higher up the river Claerwen joins the Elan on its right bank. These conditions pointed unmistakably to the Caban gorge as the site of the lowest dam, and consequently determined the area of gathering ground to be utilised.

The height of the wall to be built was, after much consideration, fixed at 122 ft. above the bed of the river, and the contents of the reservoir behind it will be nearly 8,000,000,000 gallons. As compared with the height of the wall above the river, the Vyrnwy (Liverpool works) is 85 ft. and the Thirlmere (Manchester works) 50 ft. The river Elan has in the point affected by this dam a rise of 30 ft. in a mile, so that the 122-ft. barrier backs the water up that valley 4 miles, and up the Claerwen, which is somewhat steeper, about 2½ miles.

The length of drought which it was deemed advisable to guard against was fixed at 180 days, and consequently the total storage to be provided was nearly 18,000,000,000 gallons, or 10,000,000,000 more than the Caban Coch reservoir would contain. For the purpose of selecting the positions of other reservoirs than the Caban higher up, the two valleys were levelled and closely contoured to above the highest possible site on each, and by this means the exact positions of five others were determined, *giving the greatest impounding capacity with the least amount of structural work.* There is to be a dam at Pen-y-Gareg, and another at Craig-yr-Allt Goch, and on the Claerwen at Dol-y-Mynach, Cil-Oerwynt and Pant-y-Ceddan.

### THE SUBMERGED DAM.

A unique feature in the scheme is the provision of what has been called a *submerged dam*, to be built across the Caban

CAREG-DDU DAM, LOOKING UP STREAM, FROM ROAD
(September, 1897).

Coch reservoir at a point nearly 1½ miles above the main wall, and called Careg-Ddu, its precise function being to hold the water up behind it high enough to charge the aqueduct conveying the water to Birmingham. It is described as submerged because until the water has been lowered 40 ft. it will be drowned and out of sight. The necessity for this device comes about in the following way—viz.,—

At the Birmingham end of the acqueduct the water is to be delivered into a large service reservoir at Frankley, about 6 miles from the centre of the city, whose top water will be 603 ft. above ordnance datum. From the commencement of the acqueduct inside the Caban reservoir to Frankley is a distance of nearly 74 miles, and in this length the fall required to convey the water is in round figures 170 ft., so that the invert of the acqueduct at its inlet will be 770 ft. above ordnance datum, or 70 ft. higher than the bed of the river at Caban Coch. Now the water must of necessity never fall

CAREG-DDU DAM FROM SOUTH-WEST ABUTMENT
(September, 1897).

below this inlet or the acqueduct could not be charged, and therefore the submerged dam is to have its crest at 782 ft. above ordnance datum, being high enough to fill the aqueduct, the cross-section of which will be described later on.

When the reservoir is full the layer of water between 822 and 782, 40 ft. thick, and having a surface area of 500 acres, contains 4,300,000,000 gallons. Now suppose no water were

coming down the rivers at all in a time of great drought, 27,000,000 gallons have still to be sent out for compensation every day, and dealing with the first instalment, another 27,000,000 have to go down the aqueduct to Birmingham, then this combined draught of 54,000,000 would draw down the water from 822 to 782 in eighty days. The quantity of water below 782, between Caban Coch dam and Careg-Ddu dam, is 2,700,000,000 gallons, and would therefore suffice to pay

PEN-Y-GAREG DAM CULVERT OUTLET AND CHANNEL WALL
(February, 1898).

the compensation water for another 100 days. In this way a drought of 180 days is provided for, the water for supply during the 100 days coming from the Pen-y-Gareg and Craig-Goch reservoirs higher up the Elan. They hold together 3,330,000,000 gallons, and are fully competent to ensure this. The water above the submerged dam and below 782 cannot, of course, be counted as effective storage, as it cannot be drawn down without leaving the aqueduct inlet high and dry, but it will, of course, be in no sense stagnant, because the quantity going to Birmingham must always be running through it.

When the second and following instalments are required for supply from the reservoirs on the Claerwen will have to be made in succession as required, and the addition of the water obtainable from them will enable the 40-ft. slice between 822

CRAIG GOCH PIT, LOOKING UP STREAM (February, 1898).

and 782—which they will always be repleting—to maintain the increased delivery by way of the aqueduct and the compensation as before, leaving the 2,700,000,000 below 782 for the last 100 days of the drought. In order to delay as long as possible the making of the Claerwen reservoirs, a tunnel 1½ miles long is to be driven from the Dol-y-Mynach reservoir on that river to above the submerged dam, so that its natural unstored waters can be used for supply, the respective levels at each end admitting of this being done comfortably.

**Tenders Wanted.**—The Under-Secretary of State for Foreign Affairs has received a despatch from her Majesty's consul at Genoa stating that tenders are invited by the municipality of Spezzia for the supply of 7,300 tons of gas coal. Sealed tenders must be received at the municipality of Spezzia on the 28th inst. A copy of the conditions of contract may be examined at the Commercial Department of the Foreign Office any day between the hours of 11 a.m. and 5 p.m.

**Private Bill Legislation.**—Official notice has already been given of several electric lighting schemes for the ensuing session of Parliament. Among other authorities seeking powers in this direction are the Erith Urban District Council, the Lewisham District Board of Works, the Glossop Corporation, the Keighley Corporation, the Electric Works Company, Limited (for Walton-on-Thames and Weybridge), the Castleford Urban District Council, the Ilkeston Corporation, and the Mirfield (Yorkshire) and Mexborough Urban District Councils.

# Comparative Reports of General Practice.

## XXX.—TRAMWAY TRACTION : WEST BROMWICH REPORT.—III.

### DOVER.

The rapid development of building operations and the advance of commercial enterprise made the construction of tramways in the town almost a necessity, particularly from the point of view of conveying the working population to and from their work and for the convenience of the general public. The corporation recognised the importance of these considerations and determined to avail themselves of a project which cannot fail to be a valuable property. A provisional order was obtained in 1896 and the lines constructed.

*Permanent Way.*—The tramways are single lines with passing places, the total length being 3·5 miles. The centre line of the tramway corresponds with the centre line of the road, except for a short length, where it was necessary to go to one side to pass round a sharp corner. The gauge is 3 ft. 6 in., and was decided by the narrowness of one or two streets through which the line passes. At the passing places, which are 3 chains in length, the distance between the centre of each pair of metals is 7 ft. 6 in. These are designed that

Dover Corporation Electric Tramways.

two or three cars may stand on one pair of metals while the same number of cars pass on the other. The reverse curves from the single to the double lines are 300 ft. radius, and allow the car to travel with great ease and with consequent comfort of the passengers and saving of wear and tear to the rolling stock. The steepest gradient on the lines is 1 in 25·69, and the sharpest curve is 45 ft. radius. The rails are of the girder type, weighing 87 lb. per yard, and the spaces between the rails and on each side are paved with granite.

*Conducting System.*—The overhead wires are carried on poles similar to those in Leeds and Bristol. Side poles are used throughout, except in King-street, Market-place and Biggin-street, where there is a double track. The poles are steel, 31 ft. long, the base has an ornamental cast-iron sleeve, and the top is fitted with a cast-iron terminal or lamp, as required. They are sunk into the ground and set in concrete, and are placed 40 yards apart where the line is straight. Side brackets are fixed to the poles when placed on the kerb, the lengths of the arms being adapted to the varying widths of the roads, and double brackets when the line is placed between double lines. Steel guard-wires, with insulated supports, are fixed where necessary for the protection of telegraph and telephone wires. The wires are 21 ft. 6 in. above the road. Acting on the advice of their electrical adviser, Mr. Stephen Sellon, A.M.I.C.E., the corporation entered

into an agreement with the Dover Electricity Supply Company to provide all the power required for working the tramways at a price of 3d. per Board of Trade unit, subject to reductions on a sliding scale as the consumption of energy increases.

*Power Station.*—The power station is situated about the centre of the system. The generating plant which the company installed consists of two 200 horse-power Babcock & Wilcox water-tube boilers, and two horizontal tandem compound engines, running at a speed of 235 revolutions per minute, and coupled direct to four-pole compound-wound railway generators, giving an output of 100 kilowatts at 500 volts. The tramways are divided into three sections, radiating from a central feeder pillar, and are further divided into half-mile sections at suitable switch pillars.

*Rolling Stock.*—The cars, which are capable of carrying forty-four passengers—twenty inside and twenty-four out—are carried on Peckham spring cantilever trucks, provided with two 25 horse-power motors. There are eight motors and two trailer cars; they are lighted by means of electric lamps. There are hand-bells in the cars for the use of passengers wishing to alight, and also covers for the outside seats in case of rain. Swivelling trolley poles are used, and the swing arms are fixed so as to be quite clear of the passengers. An important feature in the equipment of motor cars employed for the first time on the Dover cars is a recording meter, to check the consumption of energy used in driving the car. The meter is placed in a box on one of the platforms, and access to it is obtained by means of a door, opened from the outside of the platform, so that inspection can be quickly made. Two car-sheds have been erected, from the design of the borough engineer—one at Buckland and one at Maxton; one holds twelve cars and the other nine cars. The speed of the trams is 8 miles per hour, and there is a seven minutes' service, the charge being 1d. for the entire distance, and the cars stop whenever required. Both the drivers and conductors are provided with uniforms. No accidents of a serious nature have been recorded.

*General Notes.*—The cost of the undertaking has been £30,000, including laying lines, equipment, car-sheds, &c. Every attempt has been made to introduce an ornamental as well as thoroughly efficient system of tramway traction.

### WEDNESBURY AND WALSALL.

The electric system in Wednesbury and Walsall forms part of the South Staffordshire system, and is about 9 miles long. The line starts from "The White Horse," Wednesbury, and proceeds to Walsall, Darlaston and Bloxwich.

*Permanent Way.*—Generally the line is single, with passing places, the gauge being 3 ft. 6 in., and the rails are 76 lb. to the yard; most of the route is along macadam roads, but in all cases the track is paved across and for 18 in. on each side of the rails.

*Rolling Stock.*—The cars, of which there are sixteen, are double decked, 22 ft. long, and built to carry forty passengers—twenty-two inside and eighteen out—and they weigh 8½ tons

South Staffordshire Electric Tramways, Wednesbury.

The speed of the cars is 8 miles per hour, and they stop when required, but the end of each 1d. stage is a regular stopping place. The fare is generally a little less than a 1d. per mile, and the track is divided into 1d. stages.

*Conducting System.*—The trolley wire is suspended at a height of 21 ft. from the ground by insulators of usual design for electric street railways and attached to the end of tubular arms that screw into tees upon the street poles, a light guy rod, screwed at both ends, serving to keep the whole in proper tension. The poles are placed on the sides of the roads.

*Power Station.*—The generating plant at the central station, which is situated between Walsall and Bloxwich, consists of three Lancashire boilers and three compound horizontal surface-condensing engines of 350 horse-power, and these serve to drive three Elwell-Parker dynamos. No accumulators are used either at the station or on the cars. The station presents a very neat and tidy appearance.

*General Notes.*—There have been no serious accidents on this line, and there has never been any stoppage through breakdown of machinery. Once or twice the trolley wires have broken in frosty weather. The sub-committee have ridden on the cars, and consider that there is too much oscillation, owing, they were informed, chiefly to the old rails being used, the lines not having been reconstructed; but the committee are of opinion it is partly due to the make of the cars not being up to date.

## MANCHESTER MAIN DRAINAGE.

### MR. OLIVE AND THE CORPORATION.

We have pleasure in publishing the correspondence given below. It will be remembered that in connection with what was freely described as the Manchester sewerage scandals there naturally appeared in the Press a good deal of criticism which might have been construed as reflecting upon the manner in which various corporation officials had discharged their duties. Rightly or wrongly, Mr. W. T. Olive, then resident engineer, has chosen to regard much of the criticism as directed at himself personally. In his evidence, given on commission during the hearing of the arbitration case in the beginning of the year before Sir Benjamin Baker, Mr. Olive showed that the pressure of work compelled him to leave the supervision of the contractor's work almost entirely to subordinates, and both the evidence at the arbitration and the arbitrator's award pointed to employees of the contractors as directly responsible for the defective work, the contractors also being censured for neglecting to exercise proper supervision over their servants. Not satisfied with this, however, Mr. Olive has come specially to England for the purpose of courting the fullest inquiry, but, as will be seen below, no one has seen fit to take up his challenge. The matter therefore can only be regarded as settled definitely in Mr. Olive's favour. The correspondence to which we have referred is as follows:—

TO THE EDITOR OF "THE MANCHESTER CITY NEWS."

SIR,—Having spent fifteen years of my life in the active and honourable service of the Manchester Corporation, I claim I am entitled to some consideration at the hands of *The City News* and the public. The former has, unconsciously, been the means of publishing a slander upon me in its issue of October 31, 1896, in a report of the council proceedings, and I desire that the enclosed correspondence may be made public, in order that the true state of matters may become known. I feel confident that *The City News'* sense of justice and fairplay will allow of its publication.

WILLIAM THOMAS OLIVE, M.I.C.E.,
Cape Town C.C.
Thackeray Hotel, London.

[COPY.]
Manchester, July 13, 1898.
To William H. Talbot, Esq.

DEAR SIR,—In reference to my call on Friday, I received your message. All I wish to intimate is that it was simply a call of courtesy, and I desire now to state that I shall be in Manchester for another week or ten days from this date, and will willingly meet any member of the Manchester Council, should they desire it, in regard to any matters in connection with the sewerage scheme of the city as designed by me, and about which so much ignorance prevails in certain quarters. —I remain, dear sir, yours faithfully,

(Signed)　WM. THOMAS OLIVE, M.I.C.E.,
Cape Town.

Manchester, July 19, 1898.
To Sir Readin T. Leech, chairman of the Rivers Committee.

*Manchester Drainage Scheme.*

DEAR SIR BOSDIN,—Reflections have been made during my absence in Cape Town on the manner in which I have conducted these works; and not being able to answer these in person until now, although on hearing of the proceedings I wrote the town clerk offering to come to England, I am prepared and desire to attend any properly-constituted committee with a view to completely vindicate my conduct throughout or to attend a public inquiry should it be desired. Had I remained in England these statements dared not have been made. I have come here expressly with the above object at the earliest possible moment, and if prior to the middle of August be inconvenient to the committee or court of inquiry, I am prepared to come over from Cape Colony at any time on the payment of my bare expenses. My address in Cape Town is National Bank Chambers, St. George-street. I reserve the right to give publicity to this correspondence. Awaiting an early reply, I remain, yours faithfully,

WM. THOMAS OLIVE.

[COPY.]
Manchester, July 21, 1898.
Mr. Alderman Joseph Thompson, J.P., late chairman of the Rivers Committee.

*Alleged Defective Sewers.*

SIR,—In reference to the remarks you made in the council, as reported in *The City News* of October 31, 1896, page 6, column five: "A ratepayer had asked Mr. Mainwaring whether the defaulting officials were still in the employ of the corporation, and his reply was yes. That was not so. One of the officials left the employ of the corporation two years ago and the other seven months afterwards." I now formally ask you for an immediate answer as to whether you do or do not intend these remarks to apply to me.—I am, sir, yours truly,　WM. THOMAS OLIVE.

Booth-street, Manchester, August 2, 1898.
DEAR SIR,—Mr. W. T. Olive, of Cape Town, has consulted us as to the statements made to his detriment in the city council and elsewhere in connection with the recent investigation and litigation as to the defective sewers. Our client has returned from Cape Town expressly in order to have such statements investigated, and he has remained here for some time for that purpose. His communication to Mr. Alderman Thompson has not been replied to, although the alderman referred to Mr. Olive specifically in the council under the designation of a "defaulting official." No notice has been taken of our client's advertisement challenging an inquiry or investigation.

We desire to place upon record the fact that our client has returned to Manchester for the purpose of meeting any accusation made against him, and that, in spite of his challenge, none has been made. He has journeyed here at his own cost, and will return to this country at any time to attend any inquiry upon his bare travelling expenses being paid; but if any member of the council prove repeat in writing the statement of Mr. Alderman Thompson, our client will at once issue a writ against him for libel, so as to have the matter investigated, and will return to England at his own cost to pursue such action.—Yours truly,

BOOTE, EDGAR & Co.
W. H. Talbot, Esq.

[COPY.]
Town Hall, Manchester, August 3, 1898.
DEAR SIRS,—I beg to acknowledge the receipt of your letter of the 2nd instant, written on behalf of Mr. W. T. Olive.— Yours truly,　(Signed)
W. HENRY TALBOT, Town Clerk.
Messrs. Boote, Edgar & Co.

## A SEWER EXPLOSION.

Some particulars have just been published by the Main Drainage Committee of the London County Council with regard to the explosion which took place a fortnight ago in the filth-hoist over the northern low-level sewer at the council's Abbey Mills pumping station. The filth-hoist was practically wrecked, the roof was blown off entirely, and the force of the concussion also broke a large number of plate-glass windows in the main engine-house. A strong smell of paraffin had been noticed during the early morning, and the explosion was, no doubt, due to the ignition of a mixture of petroleum vapour and atmospheric air. It is thought that the petroleum vapour proceeded from refuse from stills used in the process of redistilling petroleum spirit, and the committee find that several other explosions of varying intensity have taken place in the past in the neighbouring districts. Some difficulty is experienced in definitely ascertaining where these inflammable substances are discharged into the sewers, but, in view of the grave danger to life and property arising from such discharges, the committee consider that notices should be served at once upon all persons carrying on the process of distilling or redistilling petroleum calling upon them to cease discharging such refuse into the sewers. They also think that intercepting chambers should be constructed on their premises in such a manner as to render the discharges more difficult, and that this matter might with advantage be taken into consideration in connection with the granting of licenses under the Petroleum Acts. They accordingly recommend the council to make an order under their General Powers Act, 1894, prohibiting the discharge into sewers of dangerous substances where the process of distilling or redistilling petroleum is carried on, and that copies of the order should be served on any persons carrying on the process.

**Dublin.**—On Wednesday of last week, while three men were endeavouring, by the aid of lighted candles, to locate a leakage in a sewer pipe in Dublin, an explosion of gas occurred, inflicting upon them serious injuries. They were hurled a considerable distance, and had to be taken for treatment to hospital.

# Principal Features of Electric Lighting Systems.—IX.*

## SYSTEMS OF DISTRIBUTION.

The various systems of electric lighting, which so far as the mere generation of electricity is concerned have already been described, depend for their economical working upon transmitting in an efficient manner the energy necessary to light the lamps. All conductors oppose a certain resistance to the passage of electric current, and it is the reducing of the losses that may arise from such resistance which constitutes one of the essential features of a well-designed distributing system. Resistance practically results in absorption of energy, and that obviously affects materially the running costs at the central station. The reduction of waste arising from the resistance opposed by conductors may be got rid of in two ways—(1) by increasing the size of the conductors, or (2) by increasing the pressure. It will be remembered that in the earlier articles in this series it was laid down that the question of electrical pressure did not affect the size of the conductors. It is clear that there must be some limit to the increase in the size of conductors, which constitutes a very material item in the capital expenditure. In proportioning the proper size of mains there are other considerations present in the mind of the electrical engineer besides the question of length. The further the main is from the power-house the greater will be the drop in pressure, and it is this that determines the brightness or otherwise of an incandescent lamp. It may therefore follow that lamps connected to the mains near the generating station are of considerable brightness while those at the most distant point are dim. It is the maintaining of the lamps throughout the distributing area at their maximum brightness which determines both the degree of pressure and the size of the mains. The three systems of generation which have been alluded to —the low-pressure continuous, the high-pressure continuous, and the high-pressure alternating—call in a sense for different methods of distribution. The first of these systems does not, in a sense necessitate great changes of pressure between the power station and the consumers' lamps, but both the other systems need some form of transforming device which will reduce the initial pressure from that in the mains connected to the power-house to the pressures in the mains connected to the consumers' houses.

### THE TWO-WIRE SYSTEM.

Dealing first of all with the low-pressure system, the simplest example would be that of a two-wire distribution. Electrical energy would leave the generators at something a little higher than 100 or 200 volts, and by means of feeders would be carried to certain points of the district, from whence it would be distributed to the consumers' houses at practically the same voltage. The feeders are ordinary conductors which are of sufficient section or size to carry the whole supply of the district, from which branch mains are taken. Such a system of distribution, however, has decided limitations, and it is only in small areas and in some of the older systems that the method is employed. It is obvious that the house connections and lamps on any system oppose considerable resistance to the passage of electricity, and therefore in order to maintain a lamp which is nominally rated for 100 volts it is necessary for electricity to leave the station at a higher pressure than that. The general practice with regard to variation of pressure in a consumer's lamps is that it should not fall below 96 volts or exceed 104 volts. Therefore in order to maintain the proper voltage throughout a district it is necessary to employ a certain size of conductor; and if the district were enlarged it would be necessary, in order to keep up the proper pressure in the lamps, to increase the size of the mains, and it is this one question which prevents any great extensions on the simple two-wire method.

### THE THREE-WIRE SYSTEM.

The next step, however, in the low-pressure system is that known as the three-wire method of distribution, which implies the use of a dynamo running at something over 200 volts or two dynamos coupled together in such a manner that they will transmit to the lighting circuits an electrical pressure equivalent to that of the 200-volt machine. In other words, if two dynamos of 100 volts each are connected together in series and are connected to mains they will give an effective pressure of 200 volts. The important feature, however, in the three-wire system is that a middle wire is employed, and such a method gives practically two circuits having a common return. The practical result of such a system is that the current required to supply a certain number of lamps would be only half that required to supply the same number of lamps on the two-wire system. Therefore, in order to pass the same amount of current through the mains, a conductor half the size of that employed in the two-wire system would be necessary. Let us take a typical case which illustrates the merits of the two system. It may be said that the electricity produced in a three-wire system is not increased in quantity, but is raised to twice the pressure of the two-wire system. A little thought enables one to see the difference between the two, and if we take, say, two 100-ampere 100-volt dynamos, the difference may be illustrated by saying

that in parallel they will give 200 amperes of current and with 100-volt pressure, whereas arranged in series the combined outputs of the machines will be 200 volts pressure and 100 amperes of current. It must be assumed that the number of lamps which could be lit would in each case be the same, but their arrangement on the wires would be different. It is the current flowing along the mains that causes a loss of head or pressure. If the current is reduced to half and the pressure doubled the lamp-lighting power remains the same but the actual loss of pressure is halved, and since the pressure is double its former value, the percentage of loss of pressure is only a quarter of what it was previously. At the same time the cables may be reduced in size considerably if the loss be kept the same; and as it is this that forms the basis of all systems, it is as well to make it clear, and to bear in mind the *rationale* of the higher-tension supplies. In other words, the three-wire system makes use of this fact and practically doubles the distance to which electricity can be supplied with reasonable financial success. We obtain all the advantages of the two-wire system, and can, if desired, make use of the same dynamos still. The consumers are in no way affected, the economy is marked, and the three wires are smaller than would be two for a similar supply in quantity upon a two-wire method, while not only is less power wasted in the mains themselves, but the first cost of the underground network is less. Where a low-pressure system is to be adopted the three-wire method is practically the only one to adopt if a fairly good demand can be obtained in a dense area. At the present moment most low-pressure continuous-current systems are laid down on the three-wire method. The adoption of the 200 volt supply in houses has increased very markedly the area to which a system can be supplied, and it is now possible for the low-pressure continuous system to be adopted in districts where previously it would have been uneconomical to supply with any other system than the high-pressure alternating or the high-pressure continuous.

#### PROF. FORBES ON THE LOW-TENSION SYSTEM.

Some interesting remarks which were made some time ago by Prof. Forbes, in one of his Cantor lectures, on the low-tension system might with advantage be quoted here :—

"My own experience is that mains ought to cost on the low-tension system about half the capital of the company, about equally divided in distributing mains and feeders. I think that far more copper would be put down in mains if people realised the low rate of interest at which money could be raised in debentures on them. Experience is the best guide as to the proportion between feeders and network mains. The smaller the latter the more numerous must the former be. The distance that can be covered by a feeder depends on many things, but, firstly, on the variation in pressure allowed at the house connections. The Board of Trade, where I think, has given great latitude—4 volts either above or below the normal 100 volts (i.e., no 3 per cent. variation), but it is to be hoped that supply companies will find it to their interest to attain a higher standard. If the feeder point is kept at a constant pressure of 100 volts the 4 volts will be lost in 80 yards if the section of copper is based upon a current density of 1,000 amperes per square inch, or that 330 amperes per square inch is chosen; and I am glad to say that in this country a large section like this is recognised as the best design. If now we use a three-wire system we can go to twice the distance, or 480 yards, with a current density of 330 amperes, still with a maximum drop of 4 volts. If the pilot wires which indicate pressure be not at each feeding point, but half-way to the most distant lamps supplied by a feeder, the length of main which can be fed is again twice as great, or 960 yards, the lamps at the feeding points varying from 100 volts at times of small demand to 104 volts at the maximum, the lamps at the distant end varying from 100 volts at times of small demand to 96 volts at the maximum. If now the lamps at the feeding points be 104-volt lamps and those at the distant end 96-volt lamps, with graduated voltages at intermediate points, we can increase the length of main supplied by a feeder to 1,920 yards, and no lamp will have a greater variation than 4 volts above or below its normal value. Of course this result has never been attained in practice, because in most cases it is difficult to accomplish. I do not generally approve of using lamps of different voltage on a circuit. The only time I ever sanctioned it was when I settled what was to be done by the St. James's and Pall Mall Company. Here the district was so compact that I could so easily that we would not be bothered by the future extensions. There is also some trouble in putting the pilot wires in the place indicated. There is also some difficulty in arranging the feeders so that they all feed into the network at the lowest pressure. Some engineers are also afraid of the three-wire system, having had no experience of its use. And, again, in a badly-fitted station it is difficult to ensure that the engines are working

* The eighth article of this series appeared in our issue of November 11th.

quite uniformly, so that a 2 per cent. variation, up and down, may be all that can be calculated for in order to conform with the Board of Trade requirements. All these reasons may reduce the workable distance, even when the low-current density here assumed is taken, from the above 1,920 yards down to 240 yards. I wish to impress strongly on you the fact that there are four distinct methods of improving the distribution : (1) Increasing the regularity of the engines, (2) using the three-wire system, (3) putting the pilot-wire connections half-way between feeder points, and (4) varying the voltage of lamps according to the distance from a feeder point. The last is the only one which cannot be safely done in all cases, and each of these four remedies enables us to go to double the distance, the introduction of the three wires being the only one which increases the weight of copper a little; or, we may say, especially with relation to the position of the pilot wires and the voltage of lamps, that these remedies each halve the weight and cost of copper in the mains, and, combined, reduce it to one quarter. The practical objection to using lamps of different voltage is that generally the network is first laid down and the feeders added in greater number as the demand increases, hence the voltage of lamps in any house will be changed. But the improvement on existing methods which I have advocated, of putting the pilot wire attachment half-way between feeder points, saves half the copper and can always be applied."

### INSULATION OF MAINS: THE BARE-WIRE SYSTEM.

In all systems of electric light mains it is necessary that they should be insulated from the earth. Insulation may take the form of india-rubber or gutta-percha, mechanically protected by special means. But there are instances in which the mains themselves are bare, but are insulated in such a way that they cannot possibly come into contact with the earth or set up any leakage between themselves and the ground. The system is known as the bare wire, and has been very extensively adopted in various low-pressure systems; and this particularly applies to the earlier installations laid down in this country. Generally speaking, bare wires are laid upon glass or porcelain insulators in a form of culvert. The chief advantage arising from such a method is that it is possible to a certain extent to increase the size of the conductor without increasing very materially the cost of insulation. Moreover, it is held, with some reason, that the depreciation on such materials must be very low, and, in addition, it is possible to make connections between the distributing mains and the houses at very little cost. At the same time it must be admitted that the construction of a culvert which will enable bare conductors to be laid with perfect safety must be considerable and occupies much more space than is usually given to electrical mains.

As this system, however, is still extensively employed in London, though it is in many cases being gradually superseded by ordinary insulated conductors, it may be as well to mention some of the features connected with it. The original form of bare-wire system was due to Mr. Crompton, who employed a concrete trench, usually built under the footway, and in this the conductors were laid upon glass insulators placed about 20 yards apart. The insulators themselves were attached to oak cross-bars, which were built into the concrete in such a way that they cleared the bottom of the culvert. Usually the conductor consisted of a copper strip about 1 in. wide and ¼ in. thick, the size depending, of course, upon the amount of current to be transmitted; and these were laid in the recess on the top of the insulator. In order to counteract any sag that might occur between the insulators, special straining boxes were used at intervals, on each set screws were arranged and connected to the strip, so that it was possible by tightening these to strain the bars up to the necessary requirements. Other forms of bare copper strip are employed, but they do not differ in principle from that already named. In the St. l'ancras system, where bare conductors were for a long time employed, in order to prevent the deposit of moisture upon the insulators, and also to keep the conductors dry, means of forcing dry air through the culverts or channels were provided. The most notable instance at the present time in which bare copper mains are employed is at Manchester; but as this is used in connection with a system that has some very special features, it will be necessary to consider it more in detail.

**Proposed Electric Tramways.**—The London United Tramways Company will make an application almost immediately, under the Light Railways Act, for permission to extend their system of electric tramways through Twickenham, Hampton, Hampton Court, Hampton Wick and Teddington. Last year the company obtained an Act authorising them to construct electric tramways from the London boundary at Hammersmith, through Chiswick, Brentford and Isleworth, to Hounslow. Arrangements are also in progress with the London County Council, under powers conferred by the same Act, by which the electric tramways will be continued within the London border to the terminal station of the Central London Electric Railway at Shepherd's Bush. Should the proposed extension southward be granted, electric tramcars will run direct from Shepherd's Bush to Bushey Park and Hampton Court, and to the nearer end of Kingston Bridge.

## ARBITRATIONS AND AWARDS.

Mr. Alexander R. Stenning, a member of the council of the Surveyors' Institution, recently sat at the Medical Examination Hall, Victoria-embankment, as arbitrator in the case of Gregory v. London Reservoirs Joint Committee—a claim for compensation in respect of the compulsory acquisition of land for the purposes of an easement through the estate known as Riverscourt, which adjoins the Thames at Staines. The joint committee are engaged in the construction of an aqueduct for conveying water from the Thames and the Colne brook to their extensive new reservoirs at Stauwell, belonging to the New River Company, the Grand Junction Company, and the West Middlesex Water Company. Mr. Freeman, Q.C., appeared for the claimant; while Mr. Baggallay, Q.C., and Mr. Lewis Coward represented the joint committee. Mr. R. Vigers said he valued the land, which was 3 acres 3 roods 7 perches in extent, at £300 per acre, which, with 10 per cent. for compulsory sale, would amount to £1,251. The general damage to the estate, including the severance, he estimated at £3,000, and with £100 deducted from his valuation for the proposed bridge this left £4,151. He understood the joint committee had refused to restrict their right to take water from the Colne brook, and if they exercised their full rights they would injure the property as well as ruin the fishing. For this injury he claimed £500, making his total valuation £4,651. Mr. Daniel Watney gave evidence of a total valuation of £4,575, and Mr. Howard Martin estimated the value of the property proposed to be taken at £4,365. On behalf of the defendants, Mr. R. E. Middleton, the joint engineer of the scheme, gave details as to the sites and construction of the aqueduct through the claimant's estate. In his view the works would do no appreciable damage to the property. The width of land taken was 100 ft., but this had been done in case it should be necessary in the future to increase the number of aqueducts to four. They had power to take 100,000,000 gallons a day from the Thames, the Colne, the Wraysbury, and the other streams, so long as there was a flow of 265,000,000 gallons over Bell Weir. They had statutory powers to take the whole waters of the Colne, but there was no intention of doing so, and, indeed, he did not consider this feasible. Sir J. Whittaker Ellis, Mr. Edward Tewson and Mr. E. H. Bousfield gave evidence as to the value of the estate. They agreed that the value of the easement should be £100, one-half the full value of the acre taken; the compensation for disturbance during the construction of the works they fixed at £100, £453 for the 2¾ acres of meadow taken for the open aqueduct, and £500 for the general depreciation in the value of the estate. That total of £1,153 they considered a fair and equitable, and even a generous and liberal, compensation for the works. The umpire reserved his award.

## BRITISH ASSOCIATION OF WATERWORKS ENGINEERS.

### SPECIAL GENERAL MEETING.

A special general meeting, of the above Association will be held at the Westminster Palace Hotel, Victoria-street, London, S.W., on Saturday, the 10th inst., for the purposes mentioned below. The chair will be taken by the president, Mr. W. Matthews, M.I.C.E., at 10 o'clock precisely.

PROPOSED ALTERATION OF RULES.

In substitution of Rules 30 and 31 :—

*Subsequent Councils and Term of Office.*

The council shall, after the above date, consist of the president, past-presidents (who are eligible for election as hereinafter provided), two vice-presidents, hon. secretary and treasurer, and ten ordinary members. The president, vice-presidents, hon. secretary and treasurer, and ten ordinary members shall go out of office each year, on the date fixed by the council for the annual general meeting, but shall be eligible for re-election. Voting papers, in a form to be determined by the council, shall be sent to each member by the secretary fourteen days before the half-yearly or winter general meeting, to be returned to the secretary at or before such meeting. Nominations for the two vacant offices shall be sent to the secretary thirty-one days before the winter general meeting. Two scrutineers shall be appointed at the said winter meeting to examine and report upon the voting lists. The result of the voting shall, upon the report of the scrutineers, be declared by the chairman. Every past-president shall, at the expiration of five years from the termination of his presidency, go out of office, but shall be eligible for election to the council in the ordinary way.

GENERAL MEETING.

A general meeting will afterwards be held, at 11 o'clock precisely, when the chair will be taken by the president, Mr. W. Matthews, M.I.C.E. Mr. H. Bertram Nichols, A.M.I.C.E., will read a paper, entitled : "Water Supply from the Lower Greensand and Constructional Works connected therewith at Leighton Buzzard." A discussion will follow the reading of the paper. At this meeting there will be a ballot for election of members and associates whose proposals have been received and approved by the council.

# Sewerage Work in Birmingham.

## RECONSTRUCTION OF EDGBASTON AND HARBORNE SEWERS.

At a special meeting of the Birmingham Corporation, last week, the Public Works Committee presented a report on the proposed reconstruction of sewers in the Edgbaston and Harborne districts. For several years past the council have received complaints of the offensive smells arising from the sewers in different parts of the city, but particularly in the districts of Edgbaston and Harborne. Efforts were made to lessen the evil by the erection of ventilation shafts at certain points and by more frequent and thorough flushing, but in October, 1896, it was found desirable to instruct the city surveyor to make a thorough examination of the sewers in the district mentioned. Where the dimensions would permit the interior of the sewer was traversed, in other cases the condition of the sewer was ascertained from the various manholes, and where manholes did not exist or were not sufficiently numerous trial holes were sunk for the purpose. The details of this examination formed the subject of a report by the city surveyor, Mr. Price, in November, 1897.

### THE CITY SURVEYOR'S REPORT.

In the city surveyor's report are given the results of the inspection in tabular form, the sewer in each street being briefly described, with its salient points and the condition in which it was found. The area reported upon comprised some 3,625 acres, with a population of 21,000. This area, with the exception of one portion, containing some 225 acres, with an estimated population of about 9,000, drains into the Rea main intercepting sewer above Balsall Heath-road, the small portion alluded to draining into the same sewer below this point. Into this branch of the Rea main intercepting sewer various areas of the King's Norton District Council's district are drained. These areas amount to an additional 2,715 acres, with an estimated population of over 20,000. The Rea main intercepting sewer receives the discharge from four principal branch intercepting sewers from Edgbaston and Harborne, which naturally divide the whole area into five drainage areas. It was also reported that an area of some 289 acres was then undrained, and would eventually have to be dealt with as a separate drainage area draining to the Rea main intercepting sewer. There are also five branch intercepting sewers conveying sewage from the King's Norton district into the Rea main intercepting sewer. On the subject of the drainage system generally the city surveyor said :—

"Generally speaking, the bulk of the sewers would seem to have been constructed between the years 1863 and 1879, and are therefore on principles which do not now obtain in sewer construction. At one time it was thought to be an advantage to have open joints in the soffit of the arch, with a view to admitting subsoil water, but now it is recognised that all foul-water sewers should be perfectly watertight, and that surface waters should be admitted only by properly trapped gullies or dealt with by separate surface-water drains.

"Very little advantage seems to have been taken of the natural facilities to deal with the surface waters by a separate system, although the area under consideration is one peculiarly adapted for such a system, being traversed by several brooks and watercourses, whilst the suburban character of the district is such that the surface waters should be of such a character as to be admitted into running streams without any danger of unduly fouling them.

"Certain of the branch sewers are giving trouble, owing to the fact that they have to carry both foul and surface waters, where the amount of surface waters is large in proportion to the foul waters, the result being that in dry weather the flow is insufficient to give the necessary velocity to keep them self-cleansing. Again, it must be remembered that until the storm overflows begin to act such surface waters pass down to the outfall at Saltley, causing difficulties there, of which the committee are no doubt quite aware."

The city surveyor strongly recommended that in this area the surface-waters generally should be dealt with by a separate system wherever possible, as that would do away with the necessity of reconstructing certain of the main sewers, which otherwise would have to be considerably enlarged. Mr. Price further remarked that, as might be expected, sewers which were constructed from twenty to forty years ago are not such as would be accepted nowadays, leaving out the fact of the ordinary wear and tear of that period. Thus they found miles of small brick sewers, 1 ft. 9 in. by 1 ft. 3 in. internal diameter, constructed half-brick in thickness, which would in more recent times consist of 12 in. and 15 in. stoneware pipes ; and it was pointed out that such sewers, when the joints give way or the bricks perish, cannot be repaired, and that a new sewer has to be substituted in such cases. Mr. Price further remarked that it is almost impossible to construct sewers with a single brick ring of a durable character, a fact which would be strongly impressed on the Public Works Committee when they heard the detailed report on such of the larger brick sewers as could be inspected internally, and he felt that no sewer constructed in such a manner could be considered safe. In the case of a sewer which was cited as an illustration the joints in the brickwork were found open and an accumulation of black filth at the back of the brickwork ; the pipes in the upper

length were badly jointed, open in places with the same result as before, the jointing material, if any, that had been used having generally disappeared. The sewer in question, it may be mentioned, has been entirely reconstructed. The report of the city surveyor continued as follows :—

"The manner in which connections for house drainage have been made in former years could scarcely be worse ; in the brick sewers a hole has been broken through and a pipe pushed in, nothing more being done, the hole thus made being left to take care of itself. Where the sewer has consisted of pipes, precisely the same method has been pursued in some of the cases which have come under notice in this examination.

"Generally the gradients are fair, although it is evident on certain lines of sewers that, for the sake of economy, the gradient has been sacrificed, with the result that what might have been a self-cleansing sewer has thus been made a sewer of deposit.

"In some portions of the general system the sewers have been divided into lengths, for the purposes of ventilation ; but in the case of reconstruction this system might be pursued to a much greater extent with advantage. Although many schemes of ventilation have been brought before the public from time to time by inventors, none have, so far, superseded the old system of open-air gratings, aided with ventilating shafts acting without any mechanical assistance.

"In some parts of the system, chiefly in Harborne, flushing chambers have been provided to assist sewers which evidently gave trouble through being badly constructed or not having self-cleansing gradients. Some of these chambers were found out of order, but instructions have been already given to have them put into order and regularly used.

"Some of the sewers, which are in fair condition, and for which reconstruction is not recommended, would be materially benefited by the addition of automatic flushing chambers. On all sewers reconstructed flushing manholes at regular distances apart should be provided."

Mr. Price also advised a considerable increase in the number of gullies, especially where it is not intended to provide a separate surface-water drain, as such a course, if proper attention were given to the cleansing out of such gullies, would prevent large quantities of detritus from getting into the sewers, from which it is very difficult to remove, and would also, in his opinion, relieve the outfall works at Saltley of a very large amount of the mud, which is now one of the great difficulties the Tame and Rea Drainage Board have to deal with.

### MR. EDWARD PRITCHARD'S REPORT.

As the result of Mr. Price's investigation was practically to condemn nearly the whole of the sewers in the district, the committee deemed it advisable before proceeding further to have an independent examination made, and they therefore instructed Mr. Edward Pritchard, M.I.C.E., who combines with an extensive practice in the designing and construction of sewerage works a long and intimate acquaintance with Birmingham, to make an independent personal examination of the sewers. To enable Mr. Pritchard to make his investigations, excavations were made in thirty different places. The report was presented in February of the present year, and in it Mr. Pritchard stated that the result of his inspection proved the sewers inspected to be in an unsatisfactory condition. With one exception he found the brick sewers to be only 4½ in. in thickness. Mr. Pritchard added :—

"In places along the intercepting sewers the arches are 'crowning in,' and the shapes of the sewers in their cross-sections are distorted. In places the bricks in the arches have dropped considerably, and in others have fallen right through, showing danger of collapse. The inverts in places are also in bad condition, having been much worn by erosion. In many places there have been deposits formed on the inverts of the intercepting and subsidiary sewers to an enormous extent, probably due to the gradients not having been carried out as intended and as shown upon the original drawings ; but my instructions not extending to a report upon the gradients or discharging capacity of the culverts, I did not check them by levelling. In fact, this would not be ascertained without baring the culverts to a much greater extent than has been done.

"The remarks generally as to the condition of the brick culverts of the intercepting sewers apply equally to the brick sewers comprising a portion of the subsidiary sewers. The jointing of the earthenware pipe sewers is faulty, and in many instances the spigot end of the pipe is not 'home,' thus permitting leakage to the subsoil. Where curved pipes should have been used straight ones have been substituted, with a result that it was impossible to make proper joints. In some instances the flow of the sewage is very sluggish ; in fact, at such places the flow is so slight that it is imperceptible, with a result that there is a great deal of excrementitious deposit in the pipes, from which emanate exceedingly offensive sewer gases. These facts indicate that the gradients are not self-cleansing for the volume of sewage passing down."

After indicating certain points at which the sewers (ignoring the imperfect private connections) appeared to be in a fairly good condition, Mr. Pritchard concluded his report by saying that the connections of the subsidiary sewers with the intercepting sewers, as well as the connections of the house drains with the sewers, generally were most imperfect, junction blocks and bends appearing to have been considered as quite unnecessary.

THE CITY SURVEYOR'S RECOMMENDATIONS.

The committee were convinced that nothing less than a scheme for the reconstruction of the whole of the sewerage system in the district would meet the requirements of the case, and they instructed the city surveyor to obtain the necessary levels, and to submit his recommendations for such a scheme. Accordingly, in July, Mr. Price presented a report embodying a scheme for dealing with both the foul and storm water sewers within the Edgbaston and Harborne district. The total area dealt with is 3,767 acres, with a population of about 26,500. Into the Rea main sewer is also drained an area of 2,535 acres, being a portion of King's Norton, which has an estimated population of 31,000. These figures give a total drainage area of 6,302 acres, and an estimated present population of 57,500. As a basis of calculation it was assumed that the period for which the sewers would have to be designed should be thirty years, having in view that such would be the period for which the Local Government Board would sanction a loan.

With regard to the area of King's Norton draining into the Rea main sewer, it has been assumed that in thirty years the present population of 31,000 would be doubled, and an allowance of 50 gallons per head per diem has been made, being 10 gallons per head in excess of the quantity which the corporation, under the terms of their agreement, are bound to provide for, the extra 10 gallons being allowed as a margin for special contingencies. The city surveyor finds, from inquiries which he has made, that a very rapid growth of population is taking place in certain parts of the King's Norton district, especially at Selly Oak, where the increase for the last seven years has been at the rate of 5 per cent. per annum.

For the sewers to be constructed within the city boundaries, each sub-drainage area has been dealt with separately, and a proportionate expansion has been allowed for. Thirty gallons per head per diem has been allowed for, and an addition for the surface and storm waters falling upon back roofs and yards of all houses, and also for the drainage of many of the larger houses, where the rainfall could not be economically separated from the foul waters, depending upon the character of the special area under consideration. The remainder of the rainfall will be carried off by a separate scheme of surface-water sewers having outfalls into the nearest watercourse. Two storm overflows are already provided in the Rea main sewer into the Rea river, and these will be so arranged that 150 gallons per head per diem will pass down the Rea main sewer before any dilute sewage will pass into the river. Under the river Rea improvement scheme a new storm overflow will be provided in Edgbaston-road for the one which has to be abandoned. The heaviest rainfall recorded during the past five years amounted to ¾ in. in half an hour. The sewers would be constructed on lines that would make them practically self-cleansing. The following part of the report may be quoted in full:—

"At dead ends, where the only trouble is likely to arise owing to the small flow which must necessarily occur, automatic flushing chambers will be provided, to be supplied with town's water. On all sewers reconstructed flushing manholes at regular distances apart are provided for.

"The estimate allows for the doubling of the number of gullies at present provided in this area, with a view to keeping as much road detritus as possible from getting into the sewers or surface-water drains, where the cost of removal is greatly increased.

"Wherever the gradients are good—and, fortunately, that obtains in many places all over the drainage area—valves will be provided for breaking up any tendency for a current to form and convey gases along the system of sewers, and with a view to limiting the area of ventilation at any one particular point. The city surveyor believes that if this is carried into effect it may enable him to entirely remove the ventilating columns which are at present erected at certain points in the Edgbaston district. The most practical authorities on the question of ventilation are of opinion that ventilation by means of open gratings placed in the centre of the roads is the best, and that where the roads are extremely narrow or where there are some peculiar circumstances which necessitate some other method of treatment, then ventilating shafts may be substituted, but not otherwise.

"In the new scheme it is intended that wherever possible the line of the existing sewer shall be followed, so that in excavating for the new sewer the existing one would be entirely removed; but in the larger trunk sewers this method is, unfortunately, impossible, owing to the large flow of water making the cost of construction in that way uneconomical. In such cases the new sewers will be laid as near to the line of the old sewer as possible, and the existing sewer, if not absolutely removed, will be cut off, cleansed and filled up where possible with gravel or some other clean substance.

"The whole system has been designed with a view to provide for the proper sewerage of the whole area, and consequently certain lengths of sewer may not require to be constructed for some years to come. The Rea main intercepting sewer will be reconstructed for part of its length as a brick sewer, 3 ft. 4 in. by 2 ft. 6 in., the least gradient being 1 in 260; for another length the sewer will be diminished to 3 ft. by 2 ft. 3 in., and for a third length it will be a pipe sewer 21 in. by 18 in. The estimated cost of relaying this main sewer and the branch sewers connected therewith is estimated at £48,439."

Mr. Price then proceeded to deal with the various sub-drainage areas in detail. In one area, comprising 357 acres, the intercepting sewer is a 3-ft. 6-in. by 2-ft. 6-in. brick sewer, which requires repair and partial reconstruction, and it is estimated that the cost of this work, together with the construction of the branch sewers draining into the intercepting sewer, will be £21,293. In another area, comprising 405 acres, it is estimated that branch sewers will require to be reconstructed, at a cost of £3,600. Dealing with two other areas, Mr. Price states that the reconstructed Chad Valley main sewer would consist of (1) a 3-ft. by 2-ft. 3-in. brick sewer, with a least gradient of 1 in 330 (the least gradient in the existing sewer for a considerable length is 1 in 920); (2) 24-in. and 21-in. pipes; 18-in. pipes at a gradient of 1 in 82, and, finally, 15-in. and 12-in. pipes instead of the existing 3-ft. 6-in. by 2-ft. 6-in. brick sewer. The cost of this work is estimated at £17,730. Various alterations are suggested in connection with the branch sewers discharging into the Chad Valley main, the cost of reconstruction being estimated at £20,812. There is also the area previously referred to as undrained. The cost of the proposed sewer and branches in this area is estimated at £5,237, and is included in the sum of £48,909 provided for the Rea main intercepting sewer. Mr. Price adds:—

"The total cost of the foul-water sewerage scheme, as set forth in this report, is estimated at £122,074, including a sum of £1,200 for flushing chambers; but, as already pointed out, it will probably not be necessary to construct for a few years sewers estimated to cost £9,000, the necessity for these depending upon the extension of building operations. After making this deduction the total amounts to £113,074.

"In estimating for the whole of the work I have allowed for the best workmanship and materials, and in all pipe sewers laid in valley lines, where bad ground is likely to be met with, Hassall's patent double-lined pipes have been estimated for, as these make the best watertight joint to be obtained at the present day."

In devising the surface-water system the city surveyor states that every opportunity has been taken of utilising the various streams and watercourses, these having no less than twenty-three outfalls, which enables the system to be economically carried out. At the outfalls detritus chambers will be constructed, with a view to arresting any matter which may pass through the gullies, and which otherwise would pass into the watercourses, some of which have a very small flow. In the central and more populous portions, where the flow for the first few minutes would be to a certain extent fouled, it is intended to divert such flow into the foul-water sewer by means of a leap weir arrangement. The total cost, including the additional gullies previously referred to, is estimated at £30,000. It is estimated that the surface-water system will deal with about five-eighths of the rainfall which would otherwise reach the sewers. This, says the city surveyor, means that if the sewers of the foul-water system had to be constructed large enough to deal with the surface-water system it would entail a probable increased cost of about £15,000; so that the actual saving of a combined system of sewers, as against a separate system, would only be £15,000 on the question of actual cost. Mr. Price concluded by pointing out the difficulty of estimating accurately what the saving would be at the outfall works, but gave some figures which would be of assistance in determining the value of the application of the separate system. He said :—

"Supposing that on the average 750,000 gallons per diem are diverted into the watercourses instead of passing into the sewage farm, then allowing that a proper sewage dressing day by day is 8,000 gallons per acre, it is clear that this quantity of sewage would represent a saving of 93¾ acres at the farm. Again, every acre at the farm, including tanks, roads, buildings, conduits, underdrainage, &c., represents an outlay of about £400; therefore 93¾ acres represents a sum of £37,500. The city surveyor is of opinion that the saving effected by the partially separate system proposed would not save less than 750,000 gallons; but it is probable that even a larger quantity than this may be diverted from the sewers, especially when the population increases in the area under consideration."

MR. MANSERGH'S REPORT.

The scheme thus projected by the city surveyor was duly approved by the corporation, but, having regard to the cost and importance of the work, it was considered desirable to obtain the opinion of an independent engineer of eminence. Mr. James Mansergh, who had in connection with the great water scheme obtained all details as to levels, &c., in the district, was therefore requested to consider the city surveyor's scheme and advise whether, in his opinion, it was the best for the purpose, and whether he would recommend any and what alterations in it, and also to consider whether the estimate of the cost of reconstruction was reasonable.

In the end of October Mr. Mansergh reported that the trial holes sunk on the present sewers have revealed a series of defects which justified the conclusion that sound, watertight sewers should be substituted for the present ones, and he pointed out that the levels of the districts are such that the engineering is of the simplest character. The main sewers are laid in the valleys, and the subsidiary branches are connected to the main sewers by the most direct lines, along the roads, and in some cases through private lands. Mr. Mansergh suggested a slight modification of the estimated increase of population in thirty years, and an increase in the estimated provision per head in regard to quantity. With these amendments he described the scheme as being based on the following lines:—

"The Chad Valley main sewer will drain 1,374 acres, on which a population of 31,030 is estimated to reside in thirty years time. The Hants Green and Rea main sewer will drain an area of 1,535 acres within the city, with a future population of 25,565, and 534 acres of the King's Norton district with a future population of 26,700. I regard these estimates as being reasonable and proper. The scheme is designed to admit into the sewers only that portion of the rainfall which comes off the back roofs and yards of the houses. This is a sound principle to work on in this case. By allowing for 500 gallons per head per day a provision will be made for carrying off nearly ¼ in. per hour from the back roofs and yards. In the case of the calculations for the Chad Valley I find that a total provision is made for 491 gallons per head per day, which is near enough for practical purposes."

Mr. Mansergh then went on to suggest some slight enlargements in the sizes of sewers, and concluded as follows:—

"The proposed surface-water drains call for little comment. For the present streets and roads, and also for some extension of them, the new drains will be sufficient, but as the district develops and additional streets are formed the system will require new outlets. These can very easily be obtained into the streams which intersect the areas.

"The estimated cost of the new sewers and drains will be increased slightly when the enlargements I have suggested are made, but substantially I approve of the city surveyor's estimate. The prices at which they are worked out are such as my experience confirms. It must be borne in mind, however, that in work of reconstruction like this the tendency is for the quantity of work to increase and for unexpected difficulties to reveal themselves. I do not think, therefore, that it would be a matter of surprise if the total cost, when finished, were 10, or even 20, per cent. in excess of that now estimated.

"In my view the committee may, with confidence, recommend the council to approve of the schemes with the small amendments I have named, for I regard them as well suited to the conditions of the areas they are designed to serve as well as to the sewerage system of the city as a whole."

FINAL REPORT FROM MR. PRICE.

Having perused Mr. Mansergh's report, the city surveyor submitted the following remarks:—

"The basis of 500 gallons per head per diem is equal to ¼ in. of rainfall from the back roofs and back yards, the front roofs and roads being dealt with by the separate surface-water system recommended. As a matter of fact the sewers will be able to discharge a heavier rainfall than ¼ in. in an hour, as it may be assumed that at the commencement of such a heavy fall the sewers will be discharging sewage, the maximum flow of which represents only one-tenth of the capacity of the sewers, thus leaving nine-tenths for the accommodation of the rainfall.

"The differences in sizes of the sewers recommended by Mr. Mansergh in his report, as against the sizes which were first proposed, are probably due to the fact that the calculations have been worked from different tables. The question is to what extent will their increases in size affect the estimates, and the city surveyor finds that the additional sum of £690 will be sufficient. This amount is small in proportion to the total estimated cost, especially bearing in mind that by using the larger sizes proposed the corporation will have in any case a greater safeguard against flooding; and the increase may, therefore, be accepted. The estimated cost of the sewers would therefore amount to £122,764, of which amount the sum of £9,000 is put down for sewers which may not be required for a few years, depending very much on the development which may take place in the area under consideration. The cost of the surface-water system is £30,000.

"This deals with the whole of the roads which are at present in existence; and, as development may take place, it may be necessary to provide for additional outfalls, although it may be presumed that the bulk of the surface-water drainage would be provided by the owners laying out the various estates.

"The city surveyor would suggest that a sum of £2,236 should be provided for the preparation of plans and other engineering expenses, bringing up the total cost of sewers and surface-water drainage to £155,000."

At the special meeting of the Birmingham Corporation held last week it was unanimously decided, on the motion of Alderman Sir James Smith, chairman of the Public Works Committee, seconded by Councillor Balden, to carry out the proposed scheme of reconstruction, at the estimated cost of £155,000.

## QUERIES AND REPLIES.

*Sketches accompanying Queries should be made separate on white paper in plain black-ink lines. Lettering or figures should be bold and plain.*

**227. The Construction and Working of Tramways, Book on.**—"Candidate" writes: Will you or any of your readers kindly inform me where I can obtain sufficient reliable information on the construction and working of tramways for the questions frequently set at the Municipal and County Engineers' examinations, as there does not appear to be any work on the subject published?

The only book containing a reasonably comprehensive amount of information on this subject is "Tramways: Their Construction and Working," by D. Kinnear Clark, M.I.C.E. (Crosby Lockwood & Son. Price 28s.). This work embraces a comprehensive history of the system, with an exhaustive analysis of the various modes of traction, including horse-power, steam, cable traction, electric traction, &c.; a description of the varieties of rolling stock, and ample details of cost and working expenses, with 400 illustrations, 8vo., 780 pp. The following books on electric tramways are recommended: Reckenyaun's "Electric Traction on Railways and Tramways," with 200 illustrations, 8vo., and 400 pp. text (Biggs & Co. Price 10s. 6d.), and Dawson's "Electric Tramway Construction, Equipment, &c.," 4to. (Batsford, 94 High Holborn, London, W.C. Price 42s. nett).

**228. Osiers, Damage to, by Sewage Effluent.**—"Surveyor" writes: Do you know of any case where the growing of osiers has been damaged by the effluent from sewage works passing through or over the ground? If so, can you give me particulars where compensation or damages has been awarded; also, if there is anyone who is an authority on the cultivation of osiers?

Correspondents should endeavour to give as many facts bearing on each query submitted to us as they possibly can consistent with due regard to conciseness. In the case now put before us it would have been helpful to know whether the osiers *had been damaged*, and if so how, by a sewage effluent, and what system, if any, of chemical precipitation was in use, and whether the osiers are being sewaged by the effluent on land other than that of the local authority. These and other material facts should not have been withheld. If the sewage is precipitated with proto-sulphate of iron, in combination or otherwise with lime or other chemicals, an excess of the proto-sulphate of iron will have an injurious effect upon vegetation. We are unable to give an instance where osiers have been injured by the application of sewage, nor do we know of any case where damages have been obtained against a local authority under circumstances similar to those suggested by the querist. We do not know of anyone who is an authority on osier cultivation.

**229. Reservoir Embankments, Pressure of Water on.**—"A Student" writes: Would you furnish me with a reliable formula for estimating the pressure on reservoir embankments when full and, say, when two-thirds full?

.. The rule for calculating the total pressure of quiet water against and perpendicular to any surface is: Multiply together the area in square feet of the surface pressed, the vertical depth in feet of the centre of gravity below the surface of the water (which is equal to half the depth), and the constant number 62·5. The product will be the required pressure in pounds. *Example.*—What will be the total pressure on a wall 50 ft. long when the depth of water pressing against its vertical back is uniformly 20 ft.? $50 \times 10 \times 62\cdot5 = 31,250$ lb., the total pressure. The same rule will apply to reservoirs when either full or two-thirds full, as the pressure is calculated from the actual height of water behind the wall.

**Building By-Laws and Regulations.**—We have received an interesting letter from Mr. A. R. Robinson, surveyor to the Clacton Urban District Council, with reference to Query 224, which appeared in our last issue, and shall have pleasure in publishing it next week.—[Ed. The Surveyor].

## LONDON LOCAL GOVERNMENT.

The Rev. Prebendary Barlow, chairman of the Islington Vestry, presided on Friday over a conference of local authorities, held at the Islington Vestry Hall, for the purpose of discussing the question of reform in the local government of the metropolis.

Following a short address by Mr. Lough, M.P., who was present, by invitation, to explain his Bill, the following resolution was, after some discussion, carried almost unanimously: "That in the opinion of this conference, representing the vestries and district boards of the metropolis, no reform in London government will be satisfactory unless it deals simultaneously with the constitution of the local authorities in all parts of the county of London and secures a uniform system throughout London."

A motion was also adopted agreeing that it is desirable that the local authorities of the metropolis should possess the power to purchase property compulsorily for all purposes for which they had, or might obtain, powers to acquire property. The meeting shortly afterwards terminated with a vote of thanks to the chairman.

# For Assistants and Pupils.

## THE CONSTRUCTION OF ROADS AND STREETS.—XXI.

By WILLIAM H. MAXWELL, Assistant Engineer and Surveyor, Leyton Urban District Council.

### ROAD-ROLLING (*continued*).

Messrs. Aveling & Porter, in their pamphlet on "Steam Road-rolling,"† give the following general description of the manner in which the roller should be used:—

"In the best practice the roadway is excavated, graded and properly formed to a depth of 14 in. from the level of the gutters, with a cross-section conforming to the cross-section of the road when finished, it is then thoroughly and repeatedly rolled with the steam roller, all depressions being carefully filled and rolled before the stone is put on.

"On the bed thus formed and consolidated a layer of stones, 8 in. thick, is set by hand, and rammed or settled to place by sledge hammers, all irregularities of surface being broken off and the interstices wedged with pieces of stone. The intermediate layer of broken stone, of a size not exceeding 3 in. in diameter, is then evenly spread to a depth of 4 in. and thoroughly rolled, and this is followed by rolling in ½ in. of sand. The surface layer of stone, broken to a size not larger than 2 in. diameter and to a form as nearly cubical as possible, is then put on to a depth of 3 in., thoroughly rolled, and

FIG. 31.

followed as before by sand, also rolled. Finally a binding, composed of clean, sharp sand, is then applied, well watered, and most thoroughly rolled with the steam roller, until the surface becomes firm, compact and smooth, the superfluous binding material being swept off and removed."

In "patching" a road by the aid of the steam roller the usual process is, as described by the county surveyor of Notts in a paper on "Steam Rolling,"* to thoroughly water the road surface before applying the new material, and then "opening the edge of the hole before covering with a patch, removing the fine detritus, applying the material of the gauge required, and covering the edges up with the removed detritus, blending, well watering, and finally well consolidating the whole with a roller."

As to the use of the roller in the repair of roads "when a road becomes so full of holes or so worn as to require coating throughout its entire length and width, it should be hacked completely over and raked into a segmental form in its transverse section to remove irregularities, and so that the road may have a fall from the crown to the channel of not less than 1 in. to 1 yard. It should then be coated with stone broken as nearly cubical as possible and to an uniform gauge. When spread it should be slightly coated with gravel screenings, or the grit sweepings from the roads, which are equally suitable for the purpose when in proper condition. The road should then be watered and rolled, beginning with the road at the channels and ending at the crown of the road, until a smooth surface is obtained, more stones being added to fill up any inequalities that may exist until the whole is consolidated. By constantly sweeping the grit from the sides to the crown of the road as the roller passes over every stone is thoroughly grouted into its bed.†

On the repair of roads the city surveyor of Gloucester observes‡: "The road should be thoroughly well lifted and the metalling spread in 3-in. layers evenly, and rolled once or twice before the gravel or other binding material is spread; then spread gravel or sand evenly and well watered with fine distribution until the stone is entirely covered and the sand does not adhere to the roller. Dam up the road channels to prevent water and sand running off into the sewers, and let men scoop up the water and throw it back on the road as it collects in the gutters."

The haunches of the road should always be rolled before the centre, so that when the roller passes over the crown of the road the weight, which will tend to spread the road metal toward the channels, will be resisted by the previously consolidated sides.

"Binding material," consisting of fine gravel, sand, chippings or road drift is essential in road-making with a roller, but should not be placed on the road until the roller has been at work for a short time, as its use is simply to bind the crust or surface of the road. Should too much binding material be used, it will be removed from the joints of the stones by heavy rains and the surface of the road will quickly go to pieces. Where the traffic is allowed to consolidate the newly-laid metal the stones are abraded against each other so as to form sufficient binding material for themselves.

An experiment was tried at New York* in consolidating by rolling of road metal by adhering strictly to the method practised by Macadam of excluding all binding material, but, although the bottom layer of stone could be compacted in this way, it was found impracticable to consolidate the top layer to a sufficiently firm surface to prevent the stones being displaced by the traffic. Increasing the weight of the roller produced the opposite effect to that intended, and the stones became rounded by excessive abrasion. It was thus shown that "broken stones of the ordinary sizes and of the very best quality for wear and durability, with the greatest care and attention to all the necessary conditions of rolling and compression, would not consolidate in the effectual manner required for the surface of a road while entirely isolated from and independent of other substances. The utmost efforts to compress and solidify them while in this condition after a certain limit had been reached were unavailing."

In regard to the rolling of country roads in America, the "Provincial Instructor in Road-making," Ontario, in his report for the year 1896, observes: "When the benefit to be derived from the use of rollers is better understood they will be more generally adopted." The advantages derived from their use are:—

(*a*) "A good track is immediately obtained, and vehicles at once take the centre of the road.

(*b*) "A dirt track is not made near the ditch, and by this means the side of the road is not cut up and made so uneven as to interfere with surface drainage.

(*c*) "Traffic is not inconvenienced in fall by having to drive through loose gravel or crushed stone.

(*d*) "The gravel or stone is not forced down into the subsoil by the wheels and feet of the horses, is not churned and mixed with the earth, and there is in this way a great saving in the amount of metal.

(*e*) "There is a great saving in manual labour, and repairs are more easily and effectually made."

*Cost of Steam Road-rolling.*—The cost of steam rolling per square yard, including all charges, may be taken as being between ½d. and 1d.; but this and the amount of work done in a given time necessarily varies with the system of working and the principle of calculating chargeable expenses. Some surveyors take the daily cost as consisting of wages, coal and oil for the roller alone; others add a percentage on the cost of the machine to cover depreciation and interest; others, again, include the collateral expenses of watching, watering, and sweeping in the sand, &c., sometimes even adding the cost of the hoggin to the account.

Also, the statements of work done in a given time show equal disparity, as so much depends upon the thickness of metal to be rolled, the proportion of sand or hoggin rolled in with it, the quantity of water used in rolling, the gradients of the roads, the degree of consolidation required for the traffic, and the number and gravity of the interruptions met with.

Under efficient management, where the roller is kept continuously at work by having stretches of road always prepared in advance of it, the number of square yards rolled in a day by Messrs. Aveling & Porter's rollers is given at from 1,000 to 2,000, according to the weight of the machine and to the influence of the other conditions on the work. If the items constituting the cost of rolling be restricted to the wages of the driver, the bills for coke and oil, and a sum of 10s. to 15s. to cover interest, wear and tear, the cost of rolling the above number of yards will average 22s. to 25s.—*i.e.*, from 3 to 8 square yards can be rolled and thoroughly consolidated for 1d.

In Edinburgh 10,000 tons of metal, covering an area of 100,000 super. yards of roadway, were consolidated at a cost, including all expenses, of ¼d. per square yard. Two thousand five hundred super. yards of 3-in. or 4-in. metal have been consolidated in a day, but the mean surface rolled has been stated as 1,000 yards for town roads and 2,000 yards for country roads where there is no interruption to the working of the roller.

In Bournemouth 9,666 super. yards were rolled in 116 days, at a cost varying from ¼d. to ½d. per yard super.; 4,800 super. yards were also picked up at a cost of from 1d. to 2d. per yard super.

The cost per day of steam roller in Bristol was reported as follows: Driver, 5s. 6d.; man with flag, 3s.; coke and coal, 2s.; oil and sundries, 2s.; interest, depreciation and repairs 6s. 1d.; hire of water-cart, 8s.; total, £1 6s. 7d. An area of 2,043 yards super. of roadway was consolidated at a cost of

*"Proceedings of the Association of Municipal and County Engineer," vol. xxii.

†"Steam Road-rolling" (Aveling & Porter).

‡"The Use of Steam Rollers," by A. W. Parry, Reading.

* "Roads, Streets and Pavements," by Q. A. Gillmore.

rather more than ½d. per yard super. Another example of 4,145 yards super. cost ·56d.

On the question of cost the following details, given by Mr. A. Greenwell, A.M.I.C.E. (Frome), in a paper on "Steam Road-rolling,"* will be of interest: "From careful experiments with blue limestone it has been found that to obtain consolidation with the usual coating of two stones in thickness (each cubic yard broken to 2½ in. gauge, and made to cover about 1·7 super. yard of road) the steam roller must traverse a patch equal to its own width about thirty-five times. From this it appears that a cubic yard of broken stone requires 1½ ton-miles of rolling to produce consolidation.

"With regard to the use of binding material, the blue limestone in this district (Frome) cannot be consolidated without it. The best results appear to be obtained by the use of well-weathered road scrapings, spread over the surface, when consolidation has been nearly effected, in the proportion of one of road scrapings to twenty of broken stone. Careful observation has shown that at least 25 per cent. of the material is saved by steam road-rolling.

"The cost of steam road-rolling a patch of mountain limestone about two stones in thickness (1 cubic yard broken to 2½ in. gauge, to cover 17½ superficial yards), 1 mile in length and 21 ft. wide, is found to be £31 1s. 7d.

"The cost of this coating is £189 11s. 8d., and under ordinary circumstances, when consolidated by the traffic alone, will last seven years; making the cost per mile per annum £27 1s. 8d. Taking the saving in materials resulting from the use of the steam road-roller at 25 per cent., the additional cost (for steam road-rolling) per mile per annum would be £3 6s. 7d., but the saving in material would be £6 15s. 5d.; and, allowing 16s. 8d. for after-raking, the nett profit resulting from the use of the steam road-roller is £4 5s. 6d., or 15 per cent."

## LONDON WATER SUPPLY COMMISSION.

On Monday, at the Westminster Guildhall, Lord Llandaff presided over the Royal Commission inquiring into the water supply of the metropolis.

Mr. REGINALD E. MIDDLETON was again examined on behalf of the water companies. In answer to the chairman, he said his general opinion was that to get the supply from Wales would be more costly than to get an equal supply from the Thames. He did not think it would be necessary to go to Wales within the next fifty years, but if it was necessary he would go there now. Supposing 400,000,000 gallons were taken from the Thames, there would still be sufficient water for sanitary purposes. It would be cheaper to take it from the Thames, as the Welsh water could not be distributed without first undergoing the process of filtration. In the Thames the watershed was obtained without being paid for. The London County Council's estimate of a supply from Wales of 12¾,500,000 gallons per day would be about £21,000,000, while the cost from the Thames storage reservoirs scheme to supply a like amount would be little more than £6,600,000, including £1,155,000 for additional mains. He suggested that the water drawn from the sources of supply should be managed by an amalgamated or joint board. Future Parliamentary powers should be granted, not to any one company, but to the whole of the companies in such proportions as the board should determine.

Mr. MIDDLETON, recalled at Tuesday's meeting, said the rainfall in Wales was 54 in. to 60 in., and in the Thames about 28 in. With regard to the Thames scheme, he thought there would be a great deal of revenue over the ordinary expansion. The Welsh scheme would be unprofitable for a very long period. The great difficulty about the Welsh scheme was the large expenditure that would have to be made before there was any return whatever. It was not inevitable to go to Wales. There was enough water from the Thames watershed to supply a population of 18,000,000 people, and if we got beyond that we should have to go to Scotland and Cumberland. He had considered the cost of the Thirlmere scheme for Manchester, the Vyrnwy scheme for Liverpool, and the proposed cost of the Elan Valley scheme for Birmingham. The cost per 1,000,000 gallons of supply from Thirlmere was £88,000, the Vyrnwy £97,500, and the Elan Valley £289,333, and the average cost of these supplies was £91,611. The lengths of the several aqueducts were: Thirlmere, 96 miles; Vyrnwy, 67 miles; and Elan Valley, 50 miles; or an average length of aqueducts of 81 miles. The Welsh scheme for London was 81 miles longer than the average length of the other three aqueducts. The estimated cost of the Welsh scheme to supply 123,500,000 gallons, when judged by the Manchester, Liverpool and Birmingham standards, would be £21,190,537; and at 215,000,000 gallons (the end of the first instalment from Wales) it was £33,297,251. He made the Welsh scheme five times that of Staines. The water from Wales required a great deal of filtration, because it contained so much peat. He thought the carrying out of the Welsh scheme would mean a financial deficit up to 1948, but could not say what the amount of it would be. Asked for his opinion as to the right of counties to the supply of water in their own district, he said he could not see how any county could claim that, because the water was merely passing

* "Proceedings of the Association of Municipal and County Engineers." Vol. xx.

through and did not belong to them. London had exactly the same right to go into Kent as into Wales. The argument of the counties was that Parliament ought not to give the right, and he expected Wales would say the same thing.

## NEW SOUTH LONDON INSTITUTE.

### OPENING CEREMONY.

The Duke of Cambridge on Monday performed the opening ceremony in connection with a new public institute which has been erected in Tooley-street, Southwalk, by the trustees of the United Charities of St. Olave and St. John, at a cost of £12,000. Besides adding to the beauty and importance of the neighbourhood, it is thought that the institute cannot fail to be of very great use, not only to the parishioners but to the public generally.

The buildings, which have been designed by Mr. Henry Stock, F.R.I.B.A., F.S.I., of London Bridge, occupy a very convenient position, and comprise a hall—to be used for meetings and entertainments—and a reading-room, together with a lending library, gymnasium, and rooms suitable for a small club, including a billiard-room. The gymnasium, with dressing-room, lockers and lavatory attached, a book store, club smoking-room and lavatory, and a boiler-room for the heating apparatus, are all in the basement. On the ground floor there is the principal entrance hall, which gives access to the billiard and private club-rooms. In addition to the staircase ascending to the hall, there is a separate one leading from Fair-street to the lending library, while from the open way on the south-east side the caretaker's apartments, the stairs down to the gymnasium and the exit stairs from the hall are approached. Iron spiral stairs give access to the smoking-room and book store in the basement. Ascending the stairs from the entrance, the large hall is reached on the first floor—wholly occupied by this chamber. The latter, owing to the peculiarity of the site, has of necessity had to assume a wedge-shaped form on the plan, without, however, in any way impairing its utility, the platform or small stage being placed at the narrow end, from which, it is expected, sound will emanate with good effect. A small staircase at the north-west angle gives access to a gallery for musicians on the main staircase, while in connection with the platform are retiring-rooms for ladies and gentlemen.

The hall itself, which has been constructed in accordance with the requirements of the county council, is about 78 ft. long on its central axis, with a width at the north-west end of about 55 ft., and at the south-east end of about 17 ft. It is about 25 ft. high to the ceiling, and will seat about 350 persons. The floor is laid with wood blocks on a fireproof foundation, composed of Stuart & Co.'s patent granolithic flooring; and the principal and exit staircases are also formed of this material. The lending library is of irregular shape, and contains bookcases and wallshelves capable of containing between 8,000 and 9,000 books. The bookcases and fittings have been supplied by Messrs. Wake & Dean. The several portions of the building to be used by the public are lighted by electric light, the installation and fittings having been executed by Mr. W. Mackie, of Turnmill-street, S.E. The contractor for the erection of the institute was Mr. William Shepherd, of Bermondsey New-road, S.E.

## THE HOUSING OF THE WORKING CLASSES.

Mr. H. M. Beachcroft, a member of the Housing of the Working Classes Committee of the London County Council, has forwarded to the members of the council some observations on the report and recommendations of that committee. He points out that the effect of the recommendations is to commit the council to three definite conclusions—namely, that in all clearance schemes accommodation shall be provided for as many persons as are displaced; that, independently of that, the council should proceed to buy land and build to meet the general wants of London; and that the council continue the policy of itself erecting dwellings. After pointing out the statutory obligations which bind the council when effecting clearances and the obstacles the council have had to meet in this work, Mr. Beachcroft suggests that the first duty of the council is to devise means by which, in the case of a clearance scheme, the neighbourhood can be secured from the curse of overcrowding. This, he believes, can be done by a judicious exercise of the powers which enable the council to buy land or hire houses for the accommodation of the people displaced. He thinks, however, that there should be a definition of the class of person to be included in the term "working classes." With regard to the proposal that the council shall build for the working classes generally, Mr. Beachcroft says that it is so startling that he is tempted to wonder whether it is meant seriously. The practical line for the council to take, as it seems to him, is to devote themselves to opening out communications between the suburbs and the most crowded districts. The most serious feature in the recommendation, he adds, is its deterrent effect on private enterprise. He contends that the time has come when the council should review its building policy and consider whether it is justified in continuing to build on existing lines.

# Law Notes.

ÉDITED BY J. B. REIGNIER CONDER, 11 Old Jewry Chambers, E.C.

Solicitor of the Supreme Court.

*The Editor will be pleased to answer any questions affecting the practice of engineers and surveyors to local authorities. Queries (which should be written legibly on foolscap paper, one side only) should be addressed to "The Law Editor," at the Offices of* THE

SURVEYOR. *Where possible, copies of local Acts or documents referred to should be enclosed. All explanatory diagrams must be drawn and lettered in black ink only. Correspondents who do not wish their names published should furnish a nom de plume.*

PUBLIC HEALTH ACT, 1875, SEC. 16: CARRYING SEWER THROUGH PRIVATE LANDS: "REASONABLE NOTICE."—In *Hutchings* v. *Seaford Urban District Council* (noted at p. 458 *ante*) Mr. Justice Channell, sitting as vacation judge, refused to grant an interim injunction against the council under circumstances set out in our note of the case. The Court of Appeal (the Master of the Rolls and Lords Justices Chitty and Vaughan Williams) have confirmed the decision of the Court below. It will be remembered that the council had, in exercise of their statutory powers, taken steps with a view to carrying a sewer through land belonging to the plaintiff, and that the latter sought to restrain them on two grounds—*viz.*, (1) That the report of the surveyor to the council did not state that it was "necessary" that the sewer should be carried through the land, and (2) that the five-day notice given by the council was not a "reasonable notice." The Master of the Rolls said that this could not be a case for a mandatory injunction, especially as the sewage was running; and their lordships made no order except that the costs should be costs in the action. It is, of course, open to the plaintiff to bring the action to trial in due course, in which event the case will be heard of again. It must not therefore be assumed that this decision is a final one on the points raised. All that the Court have actually decided at present is that this is not a case for an interim injunction. Mr. Justice Channell, however, expressed the opinion, when the matter was before him, that the action was misconceived.

HIGHWAY: RIDGE LEFT IN REPAIRING ROAD: PERSONAL INJURY: LIABILITY OF LOCAL AUTHORITY.—The recent case of *Hill* v. *Tottenham Urban District Council* (Queen's Bench Division, Mr. Justice Bruce and a common jury, November 21st) is one of that rather extensive class of cases which turn upon the somewhat nice distinction between "misfeasance" and "non-feasance." The facts were briefly as follows: In the defendants' district, and under their control and management, there was a road, known as Pembury-road, which at a certain point was spanned by a railway bridge. The road had been repaired by the council, and it was alleged by the plaintiff that in carrying out such repairs a ridge had been left in that part of the road which was underneath the bridge. The plaintiff (a furniture porter and blacksmith) was being driven in a van along the Pembury-road on September 14, 1897, when, on passing under the bridge, the van was jolted upwards by the ridge referred to, and the plaintiff was thrown against one of the girders of the bridge. In support of the plaintiff's case evidence was given by Mr. Lawson, architect and surveyor, who stated that he had examined the roadway under the bridge. There was a ridge extending across the road 3 in. high. The road had the appearance of being a newly made road. It appeared to the witness that the ridge had been formed in consequence of the rollers having left off rolling on either side of it. The height of the bridge at the crown of the road was 10 ft. 9 in. The road rose slightly westward with a gradient of 1 in 55. The plaintiff said that the van he was driving in was a pantechnicon van. Its height was 9 ft. 3 in. The height to the driver's seat was 9 ft. 1 in. The witness sat on the near side of the driver's seat. When he was three parts through the bridge he was jolted back, and the bottom of the girder squeezed him against the top of the van. His collar bone was broken and three of his ribs. The side boards at the top of the van were smashed. In cross-examination he said that he bobbed down as he passed under the bridge. He thought there was as much room at one end of the bridge as at the other. The driver bobbed too, and was not hurt. They were driving up the hill. Norman, a late police constable, who was on duty near the place where the accident took place and was summoned to the spot, stated that he saw no ridge. Mr. Philip Murphy, the defendants' surveyor, called on their behalf, said that the road was made up by contractors. It was finished on March 22, 1897, and was taken over by the defendants on September 22nd. The witness examined the road before it was taken over, and he saw no ridge under the railway bridge. Mr. Thomas Adams, the contractor who made up the road, said that when he gave up the road it was in a proper condition. It had been open to traffic since March 22nd. Other witnesses were called, all of whom denied the existence of the ridge. Mr. Murphy, recalled, said that prior to the taking over of the road on September 22, 1897, it was a private road, and the defendants employed their contractor to make up the road, under sec. 150 of the Public Health Act, 1875, having first served notices on the adjoining owners to do the work. Cross-examined, he said that under the terms of the con-

tract he had control over the work done by the contractors. During the six months before the road was taken over no repairs would be done to it by the defendants. The learned judge directed the jury to say whether or not there was a ridge on the road, and they returned a verdict for the plaintiff with £150 damages, but his lordship reserved the question of the defendants' liability for further consideration. The case therefore, it will be observed, cannot yet be regarded as decided, the verdict of the jury merely establishing the fact that there was a ridge in the road, and assessing the damages in the event of the council being held liable. We reserve further comment pending the decision of the Court on this point.

## QUERIES AND REPLIES.

MAIN ROADS.—"F. R." writes: Under the Local Government Act, 1888, my urban district council elected to hand over the main roads entirely to the county council. Would you please inform me if my council can obtain the management of the main roads again, and by what means; and if so, by what Act and section.

I assume that in stating that the district council elected to hand over the roads to the county council? F. R." means that the option reserved by sub-sec. (2), sec. 11 of the Local Government Act, 1888, was not exercised by the district council, so that sub-sec. (1) took effect. I do not think that the district council can now obtain the management of the main roads without the consent of the county council. But under sub-sec. (4) of the above section it would appear that this could be done by agreement between the two councils. See also the Highways and Bridges Act, 1891.

PRIVATE STREET WORKS ACT, 1892.—"Hazeldon" writes: Some four years since the council, in carrying out their main drainage scheme here, proceeded inadvertently to sewer a certain private street without previously serving the usual notices upon the owners concerned, and the works, being far advanced, were consequently completed, and paid for by the corporation themselves. The council are now about to take the usual steps for kerbing, channelling, road-making, and generally putting in order the same street at the expense of the private owners; but the question has been raised as to whether the action of the council, in sewering the road under the circumstances I have mentioned, has in any way constituted it a highway repairable by the inhabitants at large. It has also, I should mention, been a general custom in the borough to light all private streets when built upon to any extent at the public expense, and the road under consideration is one that has been so dealt with. Reading the provisions of sec. 6, sub-sec. (1) and sec. 15 of the Act of 1892, where, although the council did not formally resolve without any other evidence of the adoption of the road by the local authority, are you of opinion that it has ceased to exist as a "private street" within the meaning of the Act, and that therefore the owners are relieved from any further liability in regard to the road whatsoever?

In my opinion the sewering and lighting by the council are not sufficient to render the street repairable by the inhabitants at large, assuming that no such notice has been given as provided for by sec. 19 of this Act. If this view be correct, it follows that the cost of making up the road can be recovered from the frontagers under secs. 6 to 14.

BUILDING BY-LAWS: SCHOOL BUILDING: WATER TOWER.—"J. T. U." writes: I shall be greatly obliged if you will inform me in your next issue of THE SURVEYOR of the law (and also the usual practice observed) in the following cases. We have in this district by-laws with respect to new streets and buildings, of which I enclose a copy. (1) Are school buildings, plans of which have been approved by the Education Department, "exempted buildings" under by-law 2 (g)? (2) A water company proposes to erect a water tower in connection with their works (for which they have a private Act of Parliament); this tower does not come within the term "exempted building" in either by-law 2 (i) or (j). Is this building, or any building belonging to such a company, which does not come within the meaning of secs. (i) or (j), an exempted building? or are they beyond the jurisdiction of the district council under the by-laws? (3) Would the before-mentioned tower, which will exceed in height 30 ft., but will not exceed the cubic extent mentioned, be an exempted building if it stood 30 ft. from the boundary of adjoining lands or premises, or would it have to comply with the terms of by-law 2 (j)—*i.e.*, be 30 ft. from the boundary?

(1) So far as I can find, the plans of school buildings do not require the approval of a Secretary of State, and unless so approved I do not think they would be "exempted buildings" under by-law 2 (g). Notwithstanding the approval of the Education Department. (2) Probably there is some provision in the Private Act of Parliament exempting such buildings from the by-laws. In the absence of any such provision

it would be a question whether they are exempt under by-law 2 (i) or (j), which would depend upon the facts. (3) It would have to comply with the terms of by-law 2 (j). In order to be within clause (i) it would have not to exceed in height 30 ft., and not to exceed in extent 125,000 cubic feet.

House Drains: Public Health Act, 1875, secs. 18 and 23.—"Rural" writes: The rural district council have intimated to the owner of the four houses shown on Fig. 1 that the drains, which are not at present in a proper sanitary condition, must be taken up and relaid. The houses are provided with closets which are not connected to the drains and

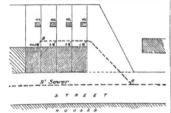

Fig. 1.

with slop-water gullies which are connected to the drains, but both gullies and connections are defective. The owner contends that the main line of pipes between A and B (Fig. 1) is a sewer, and as such is repairable by the district council. Is this line of pipes a drain or a sewer? If the line of pipes between A and B is a sewer and the property of the district council, have not the council power, under sec. 18 of the

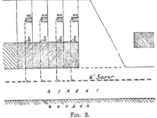

Fig. 2.

Public Health Act, 1875, to close such sewer and compel the owner to drain the houses into the 9-in. sewer in the street by means of separate drains laid under the houses, as shown in Fig. 2? The sewer in the street is within 100 ft. of the houses, as required by sec. 23 of the Public Health Act, and the line of pipes between A and B was laid by the owner.

The line of pipes is, in my opinion, a "sewer." It is not stated whether the Public Health Acts Amendment Act, 1890, has been adopted in the district, but as the houses belong to one owner this is not material. The council are empowered under sec. 18 of the Public Health Act, 1875, to close this sewer, if it has, in their opinion, become unnecessary, on condition of providing a sewer as effectual for the drainage of these houses, provided the closing is so done as not to create a nuisance. Whether the owner can be compelled to bear the expense of draining into the 9-in. sewer in the street by separate drains is rather a difficult question. If the actual "drains" of the houses (as distinguished from the combined drain or sewer, B A) are at the present time not "sufficient for effectual drainage" of the houses, then sec. 23 would appear to be applicable; in which case the authority could first compel the owner to drain into the street sewer, and then proceed to close the sewer B A, under sec. 18. But if it is the sewer B A only that is defective, I do not think the owner can be compelled to alter his system of drainage at his own expense (see Morylebone Vestry v. Vleet, 39 L.J., M.C., 214). This was a case under the Metropolis Management Act, 1855, sec. 75, whereof is somewhat similar in terms to sec. 23 of the Public Health Act, 1875. The vestry resolved that the drainage of several houses into an old sewer was insufficient, and that such sewer should be discontinued, and gave notice to the owners to drain into a new sewer. The magistrate refused to order the owners to bear the expense of new drains, and upon appeal the High Court held that there was nothing to show that the drains were insufficient, that the vestry could not, by their finding, conclusively bring the case within sec. 75, that it was competent for the magistrate to refuse the order on the ground that the case fell within sec. 69 (which is much to the effect of secs. 16 and 18 of the Public Health Act, 1875), and that his decision on the matter (which was a question partly of law and partly of fact) was right, as the facts showed that the new drains were rendered necessary by the draining into the new sewers, and not by the insufficiency of the old drains.

Dundee.—Mr. Baxter, the water engineer, at a meeting of the Water and Gas Committee, held recently, submitted a report suggesting the laying of new water mains along the proposed new tramway route to the east end of the town before the streets were prepared for the tramways. The cost of the work, which the committee eventually decided to recommend for execution, was estimated at £1,240.

## SUBSIDENCE FROM COAL WORKINGS.

EFFECT UPON BRIDGES AND OTHER STRUCTURES.

At an ordinary meeting of the Institution of Civil Engineers, on Tuesday, Mr. S. R. Kay, A.M.I.C.E., read a paper on "The Effect of Subsidence due to Coal Workings upon Bridges and other Structures," in the course of which the author expressed the opinion that a period of two or three years at least after coal was extracted should elapse before commencing works, and more if possible in the case of deep mines. In building ordinary road or railway bridges, or viaducts, the form of the arch should be avoided and steel superstructure employed having the requisite elasticity to adapt itself to any slight movement subsequent to erection. Waterworks and reservoirs, where certain heights above sea level were to be maintained, should not be constructed in mining districts unless the suitability of the site outweighed the cost of protection. Where coal was worked underneath canals the banks must be puddled and raised to the extent of about two-thirds of the thickness of the excavation. Locks should, as a rule, be protected by pillars. In the case of bridges, where a succession of seams would probably be worked, it was necessary to consider whether the subsidence of level, and possible rebuilding of the bridge, or the purchase of the mines for support in an increasing descending ratio, was the more economical or preferable.

Bridges with strong well-bonded abutments and wings and steel superstructure were frequently worked under, and sustained little or no damage, especially in the case of deep mines. Where, therefore, they must be built over an area to be subsequently mined, the intention being not to purchase support, they should be built in the manner described and the girders should have a good bearing upon the beds. The subsidence to be expected, amounting to about two-thirds of the thickness excavated, should, if necessary, be provided for in the first height of the bridge; otherwise provision should be made for the eventual raising of the superstructure to its former level if required. Lofty viaducts should be protected by pillars, and lower structures should be built as indicated; the piers should be solid and should not be pierced by an arch. In all cases, if possible, the goaf under the above should, at the time of working, be tightly packed.

## GAS SUPPLY IN MANCHESTER.

LOCAL GOVERNMENT BOARD INQUIRY.

At the Manchester Town Hall, on Tuesday, Mr. G. W. Willcocks held an inquiry, on behalf of the Local Government Board, relative to an application of the corporation for sanction to borrow £500,000 for the purposes of their gas undertaking. Among those present were Mr. Charles Nickson (superintendent of the gas department), Mr. F. L. Price (deputy superintendent), and Mr. G. E. Stevenson (gas engineer to the corporation). The latter, in the course of his evidence, said the works at present were just sufficient to meet the demand. That demand, however, was growing. There was a great increase during the year ended March, 1897, not so large an increase during the following year, owing to the mildness of last winter, and so far this year the increase was considerable. Mr. Stevenson explained the additions it was proposed to make to the works. In addition, he said that they wanted £140,000 for new mains and £100,000 for new meters and stoves. They had already spent £70,000 on meters and stoves, the demand for which had been above their expectation.

## CORRESPONDENCE.

Purification and Sterilisation of Drinking Water: The Howatson-Burge System.—Mr. Andrew Howatson, 88 Avenue de Neuilly, Neuilly-sur-Seine, writes: I see in your last issue, p. 682, an article on the "Howatson-Bergé System for the Purification and Sterilisation of Drinking Water." I am sure you will allow me to offer an explanation concerning the last paragraph. Immediately the gas ($ClO_3$) is produced it is forced through a column of water, and it enters at once in solution. It is this solution which is used for the sterilisation of the water, and if placed in properly stoppered and coloured bottles it can be preserved for a long time. I am now making arrangements for an experimental plant to be put up in England. As soon as it is ready and at work the scientific world will have an opportunity of examining it and making such experiments as may be necessary to satisfy even the most sceptical.

## THE SANITARY INSTITUTE.

Sessional Meeting.

A sessional meeting of the above Institute will be held at the Parkes Museum, Margaret-street, W., on Wednesday, the 14th inst., at 8 p.m., when a discussion will be opened on "Some Prevalent Fallacies in Vital Statistics," by Edward F. Willoughby, M.D.,LOND., D.P.H.,LOND. AND CAMB. The chair will be taken by Prof. W. H. Corfield, M.A., M.D.,OXON., F.R.C.P.,LOND., vice-president of the Institute.

# Municipal Work in Progress and Projected.

News of important municipal engineering works have this week reached us from Lambeth, Southport, Newcastle, Bury St. Edmunds, Sheffield, Wallasey, Truro, and several other places.

## METROPOLITAN AUTHORITIES.

### LONDON COUNTY COUNCIL.

The long and important report of the Housing of the Working Classes Committee, which was presented some weeks ago, came up for consideration at the council meeting on Tuesday. The recommendations of the committee, three in number, elicited considerable discussion, and consequently only two of them were disposed of, the consideration of the remaining one being adjourned. Particulars of the important appointment which was made by the council—namely, that of the new chief officer of tramways—will be found in our " Personal " columns.

*Loans for Public Works.*—Upon the recommendation of the Finance Committee, it was agreed to lend the St. George's, Hanover-square, Vestry £5,250 for the purchase of land and erection of depot, and the St. George-the-Martyr Vestry £1,235 for the erection of buildings, and for paving and sewerage works.

*The Council's Tramways.*—In reply to Mr. Beachcroft, Mr. Benn said he was unable to make any statement respecting the method of working the council's tramways until the Highways Committee had consulted with the newly-appointed chief officer of tramways. Replying to further questions, he said the draft agreement between the council and the London Tramways Company was now in the hands of the company, and would be considered by his committee the following day. He hoped to be able to present a report next week.

*The Telephone Question.*—Mr. Benn, replying to Colonel Ford and Mr. Phillimore, said he believed that the Postmaster-General had granted power to the Huddersfield Corporation to establish a municipal telephone system, but had refused to give similar powers to Bedford. His grace had not yet replied to this communication.

*Housing of the Working Classes.*—A long report was presented by the Housing of the Working Classes Committee as to the course they desired the council to pursue in connection with the housing of the working classes. The report pointed out that hitherto the council, when acting under Part I. or Part II. of the Housing of the Working Classes Act, 1890, had in many cases felt themselves justified in securing the provision of dwellings for a number slightly in excess of half of those displaced. Having regard, however, to the need of dwellings so acutely felt at the present time, they thought the council should no longer be satisfied with this minimum, and recommended : " That housing accommodation should be provided for a number of persons equal to that of the working classes displaced by any scheme under the Housing of the Working Classes Act, 1890, or under the provisions of any Improvement Act, but not necessarily in the immediate neighbourhood of the displacement, due consideration being given to the needs of those living on any particular area." Mr. Bruce, in moving the adoption of the report, said the great difficulty which faced the council was the enormous cost of the buildings. The requirements of their medical officer of health reduced the number of rooms available, and the council could not compete with a private builder. Sir Arthur Arnold moved, as an amendment, to refer the recommendation back. Considerable discussion followed, but eventually the council divided and the amendment was rejected by ninety-two votes to sixteen. Lord Onslow then moved a further amendment, to defer the report until the committee had agreed upon a definition of the term " working classes." Further discussion followed, in the course of which Mr. Bruce pointed out that the definition of " working classes " had been framed by Parliament, and the council were, of course, bound by that. The amendment was rejected by seventy-one votes to thirty-one. Two other amendments having also been rejected, Mr. Crooks moved to add words to the effect that a register should be kept of all persons displaced, and, if possible, such persons should have the first offer of tenancy in the council's buildings. Another long discussion followed, but in the end the amendment was carried, and the recommendation as amended adopted. It was also agreed that all clearances under the Housing of the Working Classes Act, 1890, which involved rehousing be done at the sole cost of the council; and the debate on the remaining recommendation of the committee—namely, " that, apart from the rehousing required in connection with clearance or improvement schemes, the council do approve of action being taken, under Part III. of the Housing of the Working Classes Act, 1890, with a view to the purchase of land and the erection of dwellings thereon for the purpose of supplying housing accommodation," was then adjourned.

*" Abbey Mansions."*—The Building Act Committee reported in reference to the above premises, which, it will be remembered, some time ago collapsed and caused the death of seven workmen, that the council summoned the persons responsible for the construction of the building, and sought to obtain a

conviction for an infringement of the London Building Act. The magistrate, however, refused to convict, on the ground that as the buildings were constructed for the Government they were exempted from the operation of the London Building Act. The Government have, however, repudiated the conditional agreements made with Mr. Paxley, and, as the magistrate had expressed his willingness to state a case, the committee recommended that proceedings should be taken in the High Court. This was agreed to.

## VESTRIES AND DISTRICT BOARDS.

**Camberwell.**—The usual fortnightly meeting of this authority was held on Wednesday evening. The Baths Committee reported that they had had under consideration the question of providing artesian wells at the Camberwell and Dulwich baths—adapting the present machinery—and had received a report from the surveyor on the subject. The latter, after acknowledging the advantages of the system, especially from the financial point of view, proposed that a number of the best-known practical well engineers should be invited to submit estimates and specifications for the sinking of the wells. This was agreed to.—On the recommendation of the same committee it was decided to carry out certain works of wood paving and tar paving at the Dulwich baths, at an estimated cost of £185.—The Finance Committee reported that they had given their consideration to a reference from the vestry of a report of a conference held in July with regard to the housing of the working classes, but it was decided to adjourn the further consideration of the matter until some proposals are introduced by Parliament dealing with London government.—The General Purposes Committee reported that they had considered a circular letter from the Hammersmith Vestry dealing with the report of both Houses of Parliament on the subject of electrical energy. The Hammersmith Vestry, it was stated, were of opinion that the local authority within an area of supply should have the power of deciding the route on which mains should be laid, as well as the power of breaking up and reinstating streets; that the veto of local authorities as to the erection of overhead wires should be maintained; and that the provisions of the Electric Lighting Act, 1888, requiring the consent of the local authority as a condition precedent to the granting of a provisional order, should be preserved. The committee recommended and it was decided that the support of the vestry should be given in the matter.—A report from the committee in regard to alterations in the vestry hall, which are estimated to cost £500, was ordered to stand over until the next meeting.—Approval was given to the action of the Plant and Scavenging (Public Health) Committee in empowering the surveyor to hire two motor cars from Messrs. Thornycroft for a period of one month. The results obtained were stated to be in every way satisfactory.—Among the communications received was one from the Clinical Research Association, Limited, with reference to the proposal of the London County Council to establish a bacteriological laboratory, pointing out that the association afforded equal facilities for bacteriological examination, and that it appeared probable that it would be more economical for local authorities to join the association than to pay a yearly subsidy to the support of a municipal laboratory.

**Holborn.**—At a meeting of the board of works, on Monday, a letter was read from the London County Council requesting the board to take over the maintenance of the Brook's Market open space. It was decided to comply with the request of the council.—The Works Committee reported that, in their opinion, the work of cleansing the streets could be done most effectively by a staff employed by the board, but having regard to the statistics obtained by them, they did not recommend the taking of any action at present. They, however, recommended that an additional inspector should be appointed to supervise the work of the contractor. The report was adopted.

**Lambeth.**—The Sanitary Committee presented a long report at the last meeting of the vestry relating to the summonses taken out by the London County Council over the head of the vestry in respect of smoke nuisances in Lambeth. As a result of the convictions obtained by the council the committee stated that the decision of Mr. Slade, the magistrate, now renders the vestry's course in connection with black smoke an easy and straightforward one, " as no regard apparently need be had to the appliances in use for the prevention of smoke or the expenses incurred in fitting up such appliances, the existence or non-existence of a coal strike, or other like considerations. The law is that a smoky chimney, as such, is a nuisance, no expert evidence being required." After considerable discussion the report was adopted, as was also a further report recommending the institution of legal proceedings against a company for alleged nuisance from smoke.—A letter and petition has been received by the Sanitary Committee from the London Butchers' Trade Society concerning the public abattoir question. The committee recommended that the letter should be acknowledged and that no action should be taken at present or any opinion be expressed on the question of private versus public slaughter-houses. An amendment was, however, carried referring the report back to the committee for further consideration.—The Baths Committee announced that the clerk has received another offer for the purchase of the Ferndale-road baths. In connection with this matter the committee recommended that the property should be put up for auction if the local committee formed to purchase the buildings for the purpose of a polytechnic institute could not satisfy the vestry by the 1st January that the £4,000 required would be obtained. The recommendation was adopted in an amended form by the substitution of the 30th June as the date.—The General Purposes Committee reported that at their last meeting a plan was submitted showing the position of two refuges proposed to be erected at Kennington Cross. The committee had directed wooden models to be laid down, so as to give members an opportunity of making any suggestions before proceeding with the work.—In accordance with the directions of the committee, the surveyor, Mr. J. P. Norrington, had prepared estimates for paving Commercial-road and Effra-road with hard wood. The estimated cost was about £8,400, and, on the recommendation of the General Purposes Committee, the vestry resolved to carry out the work.—It was decided, at the suggestion of the committee, to purchase from the Municipal Appliances Company, of Bamber Bridge, Lancs., a pitch boiler, at a cost of £16, conveniently portable, for small wood paving repairs.—A letter was received notifying the intention of the County of London and Brush Provincial Electric Lighting Company to apply for a provisional order to supply electrical energy in that part of Lambeth lying to the north of Westminster Bridge-road, including so much of Westminster Bridge-road as is within the parish.—At a future meeting Mr. Candler proposes to move the appointment of a special committee to consider the provisions of the Workmen's Compensation Act in relation to the vestry's employees.

**Poplar.**—At last week's meeting of the board of works the medical officer of health was instructed to make an official representation to the London County Council, as provided by the Housing of the Working Classes Act, with regard to Burford's-court, Tucker's-court, Dingle-court and Dingle-lane, so that they may be dealt with by the council under the Act as insanitary areas.—The Works Committee recommended, and it was agreed, that consideration of the application of the National Telephone Company for permission to lay a number of underground telephone cables and wires in the district be deferred for six months.—It was decided to accept the tender of Mr. W. Johnson for the construction of the proposed underground convenience in Bow-road, by the Gladstone statue, at the sum of £1,700, and the meeting then adjourned.—At the adjourned meeting of the board, on Tuesday, it was resolved, on the recommendation of the General Purposes Committee, to appoint a deputation to wait upon the Bridges Committee of the London County Council in support of the suggested provision of some direct means of communication across the Thames between Rotherhithe and Wapping.—The General Purposes Committee recommended that the Islington Vestry be informed that the board approves the provision contained in the Metropolis Management Amendment (By-Laws) Bill of last session proposing to authorise the London County Council to make by-laws "requiring persons about to construct, reconstruct or alter drains in connection with buildings, to deposit with the sanitary authorities of the district such plans, sections and particulars as may be necessary for the purpose of ascertaining whether such construction, reconstruction or alteration is in accordance with the statutory provisions relative thereto and with any by-laws under the said section." The recommendation was agreed to.—The Works Committee recommended that the roadway in front of the board schools in Glengall-road (western end) be pave with jarrah wood blocks, at an estimated cost of £373, and that the following streets be rolled and metalled : Albert-street, at an estimated cost of £74; Benledi-street, at £142; and Blair-street, at £413. The recommendations of the committee were adopted.—A report was presented by the Dust Destructor Committee with reference to the application of the forced draught apparatus at the refuse destructor, recommending that the offer received from Messrs. Goddard, Massey & Warner—viz., the contractors to provide and fit shafting, with roof, and all things necessary to make the driving gear complete, at the dust destructor to show they can deal with 100 tons of refuse per day of twenty-four hours, they being willing to take the shafting down again if required to do so, but if it is decided to retain it the board to pay for the same according to the price tendered for the work—viz, £229—be accepted without prejudice and an order be given to the contractors to proceed with the work. The report was, however, adjourned.

**St. George-the-Martyr, Southwark.**—A letter was, at a meeting of the vestry on Tuesday, read from the Union of Women's Liberal and Radical Associations, enclosing a copy of a resolution calling upon local authorities to provide free compartments in public conveniences for women.—The Clinical Research Association also wrote suggesting that it would be more economical for the vestry to join the association than to subscribe to the municipal laboratory which the London County Council propose establishing.—The Works Committee presented a report calling attention to the condition of the footway in Newington Butts, which is in a very

bad and worn state. A trench has recently been opened by the London Electric Supply Corporation, Limited, the cost of the reinstatement of which it is estimated would amount to £23 15s., and the committee think that it is an opportune time to thoroughly repair the whole footway. They therefore recommended that the footway be relaid with York paving, at a nett cost to the vestry, as estimated by the surveyor, of £132. The recommendation was approved.—The General Purposes, Trees and Open Spaces Committee reported that they had had under consideration a letter from the Bermondsey Vestry with regard to the housing of the working classes, asking for the vestry's support to the following resolutions : (a) That the London County Council be asked to exercise their power under Part III. of the Housing of the Working Classes Act to provide accommodation within the county of London where required ; (b) that the London County Council be approached with a view to the insertion of a clause in their General Powers Bill for 1899 to enable metropolitan vestries and district boards to erect municipal dwellings under Part III. of the Housing of the Working Classes Act, 1890 ; (c) that the London County Council should contribute towards the cost of building dwellings for the working classes by local authorities in London, such contributions to be determined, in cases of dispute, by the Local Government Board ; (d) that local authorities should be allowed to permanently retain and manage any dwellings for the working classes erected by them, and that the provision of sec. 12 (5) of the Housing of the Working Classes Act, 1890, requiring them to sell or dispose of such dwellings within ten years from the completion thereof unless the Local Government Board otherwise determine, should be repealed ; and (e), that in view of the heavy cost of land in London and the fact that the value of such land is more likely to increase than decrease, that local authorities should not be compelled to repay the cost of such land out of the income from the dwellings, and that the period for borrowing for buildings should be extended to 100 years. They recommended the vestry to concur with resolutions (a), (d) and (e), but disagree with clauses (b) and (c). The recommendations of the committee were adopted.

**St. Marylebone.**—The vestry clerk, at the last meeting of the vestry, read a letter from the Metropolitan Electric Supply Company in reply to the vestry's inquiry as to whether the company would be prepared to sell that part of their undertaking situated in Marylebone. The letter stated that the vestry's communication had been placed before the directors, whose attention had at the same time been drawn to the advertisement of a Bill intended to be promoted by the local authority in the next session of Parliament. The company further said that the Bill would not only authorise the compulsory purchase of their undertaking, but, as an alternative, would sanction that power of competition which was refused in the last session. In these circumstances the company, though anxious to meet the wishes of the Marylebone ratepayers, thought they might fairly ask the vestry for further information as to the basis upon which it was proposed to proceed with the negotiations suggested in the above-mentioned letter of the vestry. It was decided, after some discussion, to refer the consideration of the question to the Electric Lighting Committee.—The London County Council wrote announcing that Dr. Young, one of the assistant medical officers of health, had been appointed to inquire into the question of cemetery accommodation in Marylebone, and asking for the assistance of the vestry in the matter. The letter was referred to the Burials Committee for attention.—As the vestry have decided to promote a private Bill to authorise the supply of electricity, the chairman of the Electric Lighting Committee withdrew a proposal, of which notice had been given a month previously, to apply for a provisional order for the same purpose.—On the recommendation of the Sanitary Committee it was resolved to inform the Butchers' Trade Society that the vestry were not in favour of the abolition of private slaughter-houses and the establishment of public abattoirs.—The tenders of Mr. G. Jennings, to which reference was made in the last issue of The Surveyor, were accepted for the erection of two urinals, in Acacia-road and Market-place respectively.

**St. Pancras.**—On the motion for the adoption of the report of the Finance Committee, at a meeting of the vestry on Wednesday, Mr. Thornley asked whether all the money for which application had been made to the London County Council had been obtained for the electric light department. He stated that the vestry owed £40,000, upon which they were paying 4 per cent. Mr. Barrett, the vestry clerk, in reply, expressed the opinion that they ought to raise another loan.—The General Purposes Committee recommended that the attention of the London County Council should be called to the danger to life and inconvenience to traffic caused by the narrowness of Hampstead-road by Euston-road, and that the council should be requested to take into consideration the urgent necessity for steps being taken for widening that portion of the road. After some discussion the recommendation was adopted, and it was decided to ask the county council to receive a deputation on the subject.—With regard to the proposed new baths in Willes-road, the Baths Committee reported that it had been contemplated to clear the site on obtaining vacant possession at Christmas. As, however, the instructions for the guidance of competing architects had not yet been prepared, and as at least three months would have to be allowed for them to prepare the designs for the new baths, the committee did not deem it necessary to disturb the site before Lady Day next.—The Health Committee presented a report in reference to the unsatisfactory procedure of placing dust receptacles, drain manholes, gullies, and other sanitary conveniencies, inside houses in public mews, contrary to the methods adopted in private mews. The committee recommended that the attention of the Highways Committee should be directed to the matter, with a view to assisting in the modification of the procedure in the direction of improved sanitary arrangements. The recommendation was adopted.—A long discussion ensued on a motion of Mr. Hillyard that the Highways and Works Committee should be instructed not to order any more broken granite until the whole of the setts now lying at the various depôts were disposed of. An amendment was moved, and eventually carried, referring the consideration of the question to the Works and Dust Committees. A second proposal by the same member, that clinker from the refuse destructor should be used for all concrete, was lost by twenty-seven to twenty-two votes. During the discussion of the latter proposal it was mentioned that the surveyor already used the clinker on all possible occasions, but that there were cases where it could not be utilised.—A deputation appeared from the London Butchers' Trade Society to protest against the action of the London County Council regarding private and public slaughter-houses. After the deputation had withdrawn the Health Committee submitted a report recommending that the London Butchers' Trade Society should be informed, in reply to their communications, that the vestry were in favour of the establishment of public abattoirs. The motion was eventually adopted with the addition of the words "but that the vestry did not wish to suppress properly-kept private slaughter-houses."—In a further report the Health Committee recommended the vestry to inform the London County Council that they were in favour of the council including peat litter within the provisions of its by-laws, under sec. 16 of the Public Health (London) Act, 1891, prescribing the hours of removal of offensive matter and the construction of carts for its transport. The proposal was under discussion when, owing to the by-laws, the debate had to be adjourned.

## PROVINCIAL AND GREATER LONDON AUTHORITIES.
### MUNICIPAL CORPORATIONS.

**Bedford.**—In reply to an application of the corporation for a license to transact telephone exchange business, the Postmaster-General has written to state that he is unable to accede to their request, as he is advised that municipalities are not empowered to work such businesses.

**Birmingham.**—The city council last week approved a draft Bill for acquiring the electric lighting undertaking of the Birmingham Electric Supply Company, Limited. The council have to pay the company £420,000, and they propose to borrow £500,000 to carry out the bargain made and provide a reasonable working capital. It is intended to extend the area of present supply. The Bill empowers the corporation to make a profit up to 5 per cent. and to apply it in reduction of rates.

**Bradford.**—At a recent special meeting the city council adopted a proposal to promote a Bill in Parliament to authorise them to extend the tramways, to transfer the technical college, and to purchase the property of various gas companies in the outside districts and of the manorial rights over Baildon Moor.

**Bury St. Edmunds.**—As the Local Government Board will not sanction a loan for an electric lighting scheme as originally drawn up, the council have now resolved to adopt a modified scheme, at a reduced cost of £10,000.

**Devonport.**—The corporation have had a demand made on them by the Admiralty for the prevention of the discharge of sewage into the Hamoaze. The Admiralty consider the present state of things is inimical to the health of the crews on the various ships in the harbour. The effluvia which arises from the mud when the tide recedes from some portions is a pretty good indication of the unsanitary conditions, and the change indicated by the Admiralty will be hailed with delight by those on the ships. The corporation, however, will have to face an enormous outlay. The sewage of the town now practically empties itself into the Hamoaze, and hence the corporation will be called upon to provide a new system of sewerage, which will cost many thousands of pounds.

**Exeter.**—Messrs. Frederick Burt & Co., 80 Cornhill, London, E.C., have given notice of their intention to apply to the Board of Trade for a provisional order, under the Tramways Act, 1870, to empower them to construct, so as to be worked, and to work and use, the tramways authorised by the Exeter Tramways Act, 1881, by means of electrical power, on the overhead trolley system, or otherwise, or other mechanical power, and either in addition to or in substitution for animal power.—Two important matters came up before the city council at their meeting on Wednesday. The council having complied with the requirements of the Local Government Board's letter of June last, and the three months' notice to the adjoining authorities for works outside the city boundaries having expired without there being any opposition, the Local Government Board now wrote giving their formal sanction to the loan for works of sewerage and sewage disposal on the septic tank system. The sum to be borrowed is £40,000, which is to include cost of land (about £6,000) and the expenditure on the main intercepting sewer from Dur.yard, on the Cowley-road, to Belle Isle, together with a large outlay on subsidiary sewers through the city. This, we believe, is the first scheme of sewage disposal by the septic tank system of any magnitude for which the Local Government Board have given permission to borrow. The second matter which occupied the attention of the council was the question of the tramways. The Finance Committee reported adversely on the proposal for the introduction of electrical traction for trams by a syndicate or company, and recommended the council to carry out the scheme at the earliest possible date. A good deal of discussion arose on this recommendation, but it was eventually adopted. The council thus stand committed to the project of laying new tram rails and the introduction of some method of electric traction; and they are pledged to proceed with this project as soon as it is practicable to do so. The present owners of the tramways can block the council until the summer of 1902, but if the council then elect to become the purchasers the old company or syndicate is ousted, and the sale will be based upon and limited to the worth of the rails, &c., then laid in the streets through their system. If the present owners are, however, willing to entertain the question of selling now or at an intermediate date between 1899 and 1902, the council are prepared to treat with them. It has been referred to the committee to see if any arrangement on these lines can be carried out.

**Falmouth.**—The corporation's scheme for the municipalisation of the gas and water works, estimated to cost £120,000, has been rejected by the ratepayers by 1,238 votes against 773.

**Maidstone.**—The result of the poll which was demanded at the recent ratepayers' meeting on the proposal of the corporation to purchase the local waterworks was declared on Tuesday, as follows: For the purchase, 1,975; against, 2,536—majority against, 561. The result was very different from what was expected a few weeks ago, and the defeat of the corporation's proposal is attributed to a fear entertained by property owners that the purchase price would be so high as to necessitate an addition to the rates of the borough for some years. In 1896, when the previous poll was taken on the question, the ratepayers decided against purchase by a majority of nearly three to one.

**Manchester.**—An important decision was come to at a recent meeting of the Telephone Committee of the city council. The committee considered the Postmaster-General's reply to a deputation that had waited upon him, and eventually resolved that a report be prepared in due form for presentation to the city council, setting forth the recent communications with the Postmaster-General, and embodying the general conclusion that, in view of the proposed action of her Majesty's Government in this matter in the next Parliamentary session, it was desirable not to proceed further with respect to the insertion of clauses in the Manchester General Powers Bill for conferring powers upon the corporation to provide and work telephones under license from the Post Office.

**Newcastle.**—A Local Government Board inquiry has been held by Mr. W. O. E. Meade-King with respect to an application of the corporation for sanction to borrow £750 for the purchase of three freehold houses at the south end of Derby-street and east end of Douglas-terrace, Westgate-hill, for the purposes of improvement, and £7,000 for the improvement of the meat and provision market in Grainger-street. Of the last-named amount £3,500 was stated to be for the removal of the roof, which was constructed over fifty years ago.

**Salford.** — A special meeting of the town council was held recently, to consider and determine the expediency of promoting in the ensuing session of Parliament a Bill for the following (among other) purposes: To empower the corporation to make and maintain additional tramways in the borough, to be worked by animal or mechanical (including electrical) powers; to purchase, take leases of, work or run over the tramways in districts outside, but adjoining the borough; to widen and improve streets where requisite for tramway purposes; and to purchase the necessary fixed and movable plant for working the tramways. The present tramways, we may mention, are leased to a private company and have a total length of 20¾ miles. The proposed new system will extend to over 35 miles.

**Southport.**—Once again a scheme for bridging the estuary of the Ribble between Southport and Lytham is engaging attention. The latest proposal laid before the corporation is the erection of a structure, 90 ft. above high water, upon which tramway cars could run. The estimated cost is £300,000. Of the utility of the bridge and the important bearing it would have upon the fortunes of highly-popular places on the Lancashire coast, there is no question. Hitherto the magnitude of the plan has prevented anything being done. The bridge which is now projected would be a rival to the famous Tay Bridge at Dundee, which is about 2 miles long.

**Sheffield.**—It is understood that, in consequence of an emphatic protest forwarded by Mr. H. Sayer, the town clerk, on behalf of the City Hospital Committee, the Local Government Board have reconsidered their decision with regard to the loan for the extension of Lodge Moor hospital, and have now consented to sanction the borrowing by the corporation of £24,600, the sum voted by the city council for the provision of additional accommodation. The question of the hospital drainage is not yet settled, however. It is also understood that the sub-committee in charge of the sewage disposal works at Blackburn Meadows are recommending the Highway Committee to retain Mr. James Mansergh to advise them as to the suitability of the land in the neighbourhood of the sewage works which the Local Government Board have suggested that the corporation should acquire for the purpose of treating the effluent by land filtration, and also as to the advisability of extending the present works in order to deal with the increased quantity of the sewage.

**Sunderland.**—On the 25th ult. a Local Government Board inquiry was held by Mr. W. O. E. Meade King into an application of the corporation for sanction to borrow £10,000 for the erection of a technical college. There was no opposition to the application.

## URBAN DISTRICT COUNCILS.

**Bridlington.**—As the result of an arbitration, the company at present supplying the town with water have been awarded a sum of £66,260 as compensation for the acquirement of their works by the council, but the Water Committee of the latter body have since resolved to recommend that counsel's opinion should be taken before paying over the money. It is contended that in some way the arbitration award has been invalidated.

**Leigh.**—On Tuesday, at a meeting of the council, a letter was read from the Local Government Board sanctioning the borrowing of £18,860 for gasworks extensions and of £10,216 for the erection of electricity works.—It was decided to appoint a committee to report fully on the provision of a refuse destructor and to visit such towns as they might deem fit for the purpose of inspecting refuse destructors.

**New Mills.**—A poll of the ratepayers on the question of sanctioning or otherwise the council obtaining Parliamentary powers to purchase the present waterworks and construct new works, estimated to cost nearly £40,000, has been declared to be favourable to the scheme.

**Paignton.**—At a recent meeting of this authority it was reported that it had been decided to engage Mr. Baldwin Latham to visit Paignton, with a view to reporting on a couple of schemes for providing the town with a more adequate water supply. One of the schemes is a Dartmoor scheme, and the other refers to a source within 2 miles of Paignton.

**Sheerness-on-Sea.**—A Local Government Board inquiry has been held in regard to an application of the district council for sanction to a loan for the following works: The construction of a dwarf wall on the Esplanade, new wharves, a tunnel between two wells, at a depth of 275 ft., the raising of the level of Halfway House-road, the fixing of a 10-in. centrifugal pump at the sewage pumping station, the construction of new sewers in the Broadway and Jumea-street, and the paving of twenty-three passages. Plans, &c., for the various works were submitted by Mr. Chas. A. Copland, surveyor to the council. There was no opposition to the application.

**Surbiton.**—Mr. Robert H. Bicknell, an inspector of the Local Government Board, recently held an inquiry respecting an application of the town council for sanction to borrow £1,050 for works of private street improvement.

**Wallasey.**—On Wednesday next Major-General H. D. Crozier, R.E., will hold an inquiry at the public offices, Egremont, into an application of the council to the Local Government Board to borrow £12,000 for gasworks purposes and £42,000 for the purchase of a ferry undertaking.

**Whitchurch.**—A meeting, convened by the district council, was held recently to ascertain the opinion of the ratepayers with regard to the scheme recommended by the council for the purchase of the gasworks at a cost of £37,000. Several members of the council recommended the purchase upon commercial grounds. The scheme was, however, warmly opposed by a number of ratepayers, who pointed out that electric lighting works could be erected at less cost. The meeting, upon a vote, rejected the scheme by an overwhelming majority.

## RURAL DISTRICT COUNCILS.

**Blackwell.**—Mr. H. Walker, engineer of Nottingham, has written stating that he has gone through the estimates, which had been made twelve months ago, for the Pixton water scheme, and found that the price of small pipes had abnormally increased. Upon that ground he advised the council to make an application to the Local Government Board for a further loan of £200, which would make the cost of the scheme £1,000.

**Llandaff and Dinas Powis.**—Colonel C. H. Luard, R.E., held an inquiry, on Wednesday week, into an application by the rural district council for sanction to borrow £1,050 for

sewerage works in the parish of Whitchurch. Mr. William Fraser, the engineer to the council, explained the scheme.

**Lye.**—A special meeting of the council was held recently to discuss the desirability of applying for a provisional order to enable the council to supply electrical energy and electric light in their own district. After some discussion it was resolved that the council apply to the Local Government Board for the order. It was reported that the British Electric Traction Company had abandoned their intention to apply for an order.

**Nantwich.**—At a recent meeting of this council, a letter was received from the Cheshire County Council asking what progress had been made by the council towards providing general isolation hospital accommodation. It was moved that the council reply that they were of opinion that the suggested accommodation was not required. Several members, including the chairman, counselled moderation, and eventually the motion was withdrawn in favour of a suggestion that the clerk write to the Crewe Cottage Hospital authorities as to the terms upon which they would accept patients from the council's district, and then inform the county council of the arrangement come to.

**Tamworth.**—It has been reported that the Local Government Board have sanctioned an expenditure of £80 towards the widening of a canal bridge at Glascote.

**Truro.**—Mr. H. Percy Boulnois, on Thursday, conducted an inquiry into an application of the Local Government Board for sanction to borrow £5,000 for works of water supply in the parish of St. Agnes. It was stated that the place comprised scattered hamlets to a large extent and there were levels of supply in the scheme. The highest was Higher Bal, and to provide for this a water tower was proposed to be erected. The St. Agnes high level had a population of about 1,200, and these two levels would be supplied from a reservoir and water tower at the seventh milestone on the Truro road. Mount Hawke would be supplied from the same sources, but needed a special service reservoir. For the low level from the shore to Peterville the supply would be by gravitation. Gooninnis adit would supply the low level, and the rest of the water would be derived from Penhallow and Gover adits.

**Tutbury, Staffs.**—The council have instructed Mr. J. E. Willcox, of Birmingham, to prepare a scheme for the sewerage and sewage disposal for the township.

## SCOTLAND AND IRELAND.

**Edinburgh.**—At the meeting of the Electric Lighting Committee of the town council, last week, it was intimated that there has been 7,252 applications for electric light since the 17th October. The committee agreed to recommend the acceptance of estimates for machinery at the M'Donald-road station amounting to £45,000.

**Glasgow.**—At a recent meeting of the Buildings Regulation Committee of Glasgow Corporation the draft clauses of a proposed new Bill to regulate the height of buildings in Glasgow, which were adopted by the committee on the previous day, were again under consideration, and several modifications were made with the object of encouraging the formation of broad streets. It was agreed that, while 80 ft. to the top of the wall-head should be the absolute height limit for buildings in streets under 40 ft. in width, buildings should not be erected to a greater height than the width of the street, whilst in streets over 40 ft. and under 60 ft. in width the height of the buildings might be the height of the street plus 20 per cent. In streets over 60 ft. in width buildings might rise to any height up to 80 ft. The committee sat for nearly two hours.

---

**Bucks. County Council Report.**—We regret that in our summary last week of the annual report of Mr. R. J. Thomas, county surveyor of Buckingham, the word "increase" should have been printed in the fourth line. As the succeeding paragraph clearly shows, the word should have been "decrease."

**Society of Engineers.**—An ordinary meeting of the above society will be held on Monday, at the Royal United Service Institution, Whitehall, S.W., when a paper will be read by Mr. George Thudichum on "The Bacterial Treatment of Sewage." The chair will be taken at 7.30 p.m. precisely.

**Ancient Lights.**—A deputation from the Society of Architects waited on the Lord Chancellor, last week, and presented a petition praying that a Parliamentary Committee might be appointed to inquire into the present law regarding "ancient lights," with a view to saving the large amount of money expended in determining the rights of owners in respect of such lights. The society desires the appointment of a Building Act tribunal of the London County Council to deal, before the commencement of building operations, with applications made by building owners to define the limits within which they are entitled to build, having regard to the adjacent properties, and of a similar tribunal for other parts of the country. His lordship, after discussing the subject, informed the deputation that he would give the matter his careful consideration.

# Some Recent Publications.

### DISINFECTION AND DISINFECTANTS.

Among the books awaiting notice in our columns a prominent place must be assigned to the second edition of Disinfection and Disinfectants, by Samuel Rideal, D.SC.LOND., (The Sanitary Publishing Company, Limited, Fetter-lane, E.C., 12s. 6d.). As notified on the title page, the book also includes a full account of the chemical substances used as antiseptics and preservatives. The author states that "no recent attempt has been made to summarise and review the very voluminous literature on the subject of disinfection which is scattered through our own and foreign scientific and medical publications; and, notwithstanding the rapid development of sanitary science in this country, there does not exist at the present time in the English language any book which deals exclusively with the composition of disinfectants." An examination of the present volume readily shows that the information it contains is not only well adapted to the requirements of the chemist and bacteriologist, but will also be found useful to medical officers of health, municipal engineers, sanitary inspectors, and all others who are concerned with the practical work of disinfection. The progress of bacteriological science during the last few years permits of the methods of disinfection described in this work being reviewed under more exact conditions than was formerly the case. Dr. Rideal considers that "the time is not far distant when the importance of the thorough disinfection of all suspected areas will be fully realised by local authorities and when all such work will be entrusted to specially qualified men." In the meantime the author has rendered a service in providing an exhaustive review of the facts and an excellent summary of the practical knowledge at present available. At present the proper carrying out of the work of disinfection forms part of the duties of the sanitary inspector; and this being the case, the Sanitary Institute of Great Britain has for some years insisted, as a condition of granting certificates, that he should posses a considerable amount of practical experience and scientific knowledge. As a means of obtaining the latter requirement we may recommend Dr. Rideal's "Disinfection and Disinfectants." An intelligent study of its contents should enable responsible officials to discriminate between useful disinfection and the futile remedies which give a false sense of security in many localities during times of danger. The chapter following the introductionary one treats of mechanical disinfection, in the next disinfection by heat is described, and in the fourth chapter chemical disinfectants are dealt with. In succeeding chapters the various non-metallic elements and their derivations, metallic salts, and organic substances are summarised and reviewed in detail, practical methods of sanitation are reviewed in chapter xii., and personal and internal disinfection and food preservation are dealt with in that which follows. A chapter is then devoted to the consideration of legal statutes and regulations, and the final one is descriptive of the various methods of analysis. This new edition, embodying corrections and improvements, has been brought well up to date by incorporating the advances made in knowledge and practice during the last two years, and useful appendices and an excellent index enhance its value considerably. Reference to any section is also facilitated by the admirable systematic arrangement observed throughout, and we may add that the book is well printed on good paper.

### THE HOUSING PROBLEM.

A work, entitled The Housing of the Working Classes Act, 1890, and Amending Acts, Annotated and Explained, together with the Statutory Forms and Instructions, has been compiled by Charles E. Allan, M.A., LL.B., barrister-at-law (Butterworth & Co. Price 7s. 6d.). The author states that in preparing this work he has endeavoured, by full notes and explanations, to produce a practical manual for the use of lawyers and of members and officials of local authorities who may have occasion to study or put in force this somewhat involved and complicated, but highly useful, piece of legislation. In so doing he has afforded an excellent example of the manner in which a technical subject may be rendered not only intelligible, but also to a certain degree interesting, to non-professional readers. The introductory portion of the treatise gives a general view of the scope and purposes of the Act of 1890, and is preceded by a table of statutes and a list of the leading cases involved. Then follows a recital of the several sections of the Act, comprised under the principal headings of "Unhealthy Areas," "Unhealthy Dwelling-Houses" and "Working Class Lodging-Houses," which are copiously interspersed with explanatory notes and references. The forms prescribed by the Home Secretary and by the Local Government Board, together with the instructions of the latter authority as to the applications for provisional orders under the first part of the Act, are inserted in an appendix. Although intended primarily for English practice, the book includes an account of the various modifications in the working of the Act when applied to Scotland and Ireland. The different schedules in connection with the main provisions of the enactments are duly enumerated and satisfactorily explained in the later pages of the volume, and a carefully digested index is amply sufficient for all ordinary purposes of reference. In style of production and general appearance the book should give satisfaction.

### A CENTRAL STATION DIRECTORY.

The first edition of the Electrical Engineers' Central Station Directory (London: Biggs & Co., 139 and 140 Salisbury-court, Fleet street, E.C.) was found to contain a great amount of information and to constitute a valuable work of reference. Such a compilation undoubtedly serves the useful purpose of rendering easily accessible to electrical engineers, municipal authorities and others, details which might otherwise have to form the subject of special inquiry and report, involving the expenditure of time, money and labour. In the second edition some new features have been added. The scope of the work will be understood when we mention that, in addition to the information given of stations open, some details are given of stations contemplated; financial returns are tabulated; lists are given of municipal stations at work, provisional orders existing, provisional orders applied for in session 1898, electric tramways and railways, members of the Municipal Electrical Association, and of electrical engineers; the Board of Trade regulations, details of some electric tramways, and biographical notices with portraits, are also given; and, finally, there is a comprehensive list of reasons why electric lighting should be municipalised. The book has been prepared with care, and may be relied upon by those who have occasion to consult it.

### THE ARCHITECTURAL SURVEYORS' HANDBOOK.

Hurst's Architectural Surveyor's Hand-Book (E. & F. N. Spon)—or "Hurst," as this hand-book is familiarly called—is before us in its fifteenth edition, revised and enlarged, as the title page tells us. Since 1864, when the first edition appeared, it has been the office companion, friend and guide of many architects and surveyors, and with the careful revision it has received will in all probability, notwithstanding its competitors, still be the lending reference-book for all the little petty detail and formulæ so difficult to remember and yet so desirable to know. Next to a good memory a good reference-book is the most useful stock in trade of the average professional man; and "Hurst" supplies the memory in a very readable and systematic form. The index is the weak spot in the book, and in the next edition a thoroughly good cross-reference index should be included, by which its popularity will be much increased and its usefulness established, for there is little one wants to know that is not in the book, but the difficulty is where to find it.

*Any of the Books noted below will be sent post free if the published price be forwarded to the offices of* The Surveyor.

Sanitary Engineering: A Practical Treatise on the Collection, Removal and Final Disposal of Sewage, and the Design and Construction of Works of Drainage and Sewerage, by Colonel E. C. S. Moore, R.E., with 534 illustrations and 70 large folding plates; 622 pp., 9½ in. by 6½ in., 1898. Price 30s.

Notes on Water Supply, by J. T. Rodda; 142 pp., 11 in. by 8¾ in. Price 5s.

Petroleum Motor Cars, by Louis Lockhart; 218 pp., 7½ in. by 5 in.

Alphabets, Old and New, containing over 150 complete examples, by Lewis F. Day; 7¾ in. by 5¼ in. Price 3s. 6d.

The Conduct of Building Work, and the Duties of Clerks of the Works, by J. Leaning, F.S.I.; 6¾ in. by 4½ in., 140 pp. Price 2s. 6d.

The Elements of Sanitary Law, by Alice Ravenhill, with introduction by Sir Richard T. Thorne, K.C.B., &c.; 8½ in. by 5½ in., 44 pp. Price 6d.

The Eighth Annual Report of the Council of the Property Protection Society, 1897-1898.

A Forgotten Past, being Notes on the families of Tyssen, Baker, Hougham and Miller of five centuries, by F. H. Luckling; 134 pp., 9½ in. by 6¼ in. Price 10s. 6d.

Shropshire, by Augustus J. C. Hare; 340 pp., 7¾ in. by 5¼ in. Price 7s. 6d.

## INSTITUTION OF CIVIL ENGINEERS.

### Ordinary Meeting.

An ordinary meeting of the above Institution will be held on Tuesday, when the paper entitled "The Effect of Subsidence due to Coal Workings upon Bridges and other Structures," read by Mr. Stanley Robert Kay, A.M.I.C.E., at the last ordinary meeting, will be further discussed. Time permitting, a paper will also be read, with a view to discussion, on "The Ventilation of Tunnels and Buildings," by Mr. Francis Fox, M.I.C.E. At this meeting a ballot for members will be taken.

### Students' Meeting.

A meeting for the students of the Institution will be held to-night, at 8 p.m., Mr. T. Forster Brown, member of the council, in the chair. Mr. Charles Benjamin Sauer will read a paper on "The Sunlight Gold-bearing Reef, Lydenburg, Transvaal."

## Personal.

Mr. S. Edgar Fedden, Municipal Buildings, Greenock, has been appointed electrical engineer to the Greenock Board of Police.

A lecture on "The Engineering Triumphs of our Age" was delivered last night, at the Cripplegate Institute, by Prof. W. H. Goulding.

Mr. F. J. French, one of the inspectors of paving for Toronto, has recently invented an interlocking paving brick, for which he has applied for a patent.

By the will of the late Mr. Christopher Oakley, who left property to the value of £86,707, a sum of £250 is bequeathed to the Incorporated Auctioneers' Benevolent Fund.

Mr. William W. Carter, Eastham, has been appointed surveyor and inspector of nuisances for the southern division of the district, under the jurisdiction of the Tarvin Rural District Council.

Under the presidency of Mr. McKinnon Wood, chairman of the London County Council, a meeting was held last night, at the Hackney Town Hall, to celebrate the completion and adoption of the technical institute scheme.

Mr. Edward John Gammage, son of the borough surveyor of Dudley, has been appointed to the post of assistant in his father's department, at a salary of £120 per annum. He will be engaged in the work of sewering the Netherton and Woodside districts of the borough.

Mr. J. Finlay Peddie, 9 Donegall-square West, Belfast, has prepared a report for the the Kilkeel Board of Guardians on the sanitary condition of Newcastle, co. Down. Mr. Peddie has also, we may mention, been instructed to proceed with a sewerage and sewage disposal scheme next spring for the city of Armagh.

Mr. G. Chatterton, the assessor nominated by the president of the Institution of Civil Engineers for the competition schemes submitted for the water supply of Bricklade, Wilts., has awarded the first premium to Mr. F. Redman, of Swindon, and the second premium to Mr. T. George Caink, of Worcester. The number of schemes submitted was eighteen.

Mr. D. J. Diver, surveyor and inspector of nuisances to the Wirksworth Urban District Council, has resigned his appointment in order to take up a similar position under the Desborough Urban District Council, in the room of Mr. W. T. Streather, who has obtained the appointment of surveyor to the Winton District Council. Mr. Diver has been in the service of the Wirksworth Urban District Council for about three years.

Mr. Edwards, assistant surveyor to the Lambeth Vestry, is recommended by the special committee of the vestry on staff vacancies for the position of surveyor, due to the resignation of Mr. J. P. Norrington. The committee at the next meeting of the vestry will suggest that the appointment should be on probation for twelve months, at a salary of £500, and that Mr. Edwards should have such assistance as may be necessary during that period.

The London Municipal Society, at a meeting on Monday evening, passed a resolution welcoming the announcement that the Government intended to introduce next session a comprehensive measure dealing with the local government of London. Another resolution was also carried, urging that steps should be immediately taken to relieve the congestion of both vehicular and pedestrian traffic in the principal thoroughfares of London.

Mr. J. H. Vensey, who was at one time in the office of Mr. J. H. Pickering, surveyor to the Nuneaton Urban District Council, has succeeded in obtaining the appointment of assistant town engineer of Buluwayo. Since leaving the Midlands for South Africa Mr. Vensey, it is understood, has met with every success, his training at Nuneaton having made him thoroughly familiar with the work of public bodies. His new post is worth £350 per annum.

The town council of Southampton have confirmed a report of the Electric Lighting Committee appointing Mr. S. L. Smith, of London, as third assistant electrical engineer. They have also agreed to the appointment of Mr. F. H. Chaplin, chief assistant to the borough electrical engineer of Portsmouth, as electrical engineer, at a salary of £250 per annum. There were sixty-six applicants for the vacancy, and four of these were interviewed by the committee.

On Monday, before the Royal Scottish Society of Arts, at Edinburgh, Mr. Gilbert Thomson, of Glasgow, contributed a paper on "Drain Testing." He remarked that, although it was very common to find it reported that drains had been smoke-tested and found all right, all that could really be said was that nothing was found to be wrong. This was not the same thing, and might be very different. Mr. Thomson advocated the general use of the air test, which might be made a standard to which all drains and pipes put in under building by-laws might be made to conform.

Fifty-nine applications were last week reported to have been received for the position of surveyor for West Medina, under the Isle of Wight Rural District Council, and a committee, who had been entrusted with the work of selection, recommended the appointment of Mr. J. A. Harcourt Powell, of Little Bentley, near Colchester, Essex. The recommendation was unanimously adopted, and Mr. Powell, on being informed of the council's choice, briefly returned thanks and promised to do his best to give satisfaction. He will commence his duties on the 1st prox.

No fewer than seventy-five applications for the post of surveyor, rendered vacant by the resignation of Mr. Smethurst (who has obtained another appointment), were received by the Fulwood Urban District Council. This number was reduced to twenty-one, and several of the candidates subsequently attended a special meeting of the council, when it was decided to appoint Mr. W. Dickson, of Lytham, at the salary hitherto appertaining to the office—viz., £130 per annum, with house, coal, gas, &c. Mr. Dickson, however, has since intimated that he has been appointed surveyor to the Lancaster Rural District Council, and therefore desired to resign the position. He thanked the council for their kindness, and expressed the hope that he would not put them to any undue inconvenience. The resignation was accepted.

On Thursday, at Belfast, Mr. J. G. Zachary was presented with an address, to mark the occasion of his promotion to the position of chief of the Public Works Department under the Improvement Committee of the Belfast Corporation. The presentation took the form of a solid silver tea and coffee service. Mr. J. C. Bretland, city surveyor, took the chair during the proceedings, and, in the course of a short address, said he heartily joined in the congratulations which they all desired to offer Mr. Zachary, who had been at his hand for consultation for a great number of years, during which time he had seldom, if ever, found his judgment at fault. Mr. Munce, assistant city surveyor, spoke of the invaluable assistance which Mr. Zachary had always rendered him, and said he could endorse every word that had been said by the chairman.

The General Purposes Committee of the London County Council announced, at the meeting of the council on Tuesday, that in response to their advertisement inviting applications for the appointment of a chief officer of the council's tramways, at a salary of £1,500 a year, seventy applications were received. These applications were in the first instance considered by a joint sub-committee of the General Purposes Committee and the Highways Committee, who, after seeing nine of the candidates, submitted the names of five. These candidates had been seen by the committee, who, having carefully considered their qualifications, submitted to the council the names of three—Mr. John Young, Mr. A. Baker and Mr. J. Aldworth. The committee were strongly of opinion that Mr. Young was the best-qualified for the appointment, and they accordingly submitted a recommendation that he should be appointed to the position. The recommendation was adopted without discussion. Mr. Young at present holds the position of tramways manager to the Corporation of Glasgow.

A very successful smoking concert was held on Friday evening, under the presidency of the chief road surveyor, at the Great Western Hotel, Birmingham, in order to make a presentation from the officials of the Public Works Department of the corporation to Mr. Fred. T. Rundall, road surveyor for the Edgbaston and Harborne district, who has been appointed superintendent of the Streets Department of the St. Marylebone Vestry. The presentation took the form of a handsome timepiece with a suitable inscription. Before the presentation was made the vice-chairman, Mr. T. Arnall, said that Mr. Rundall took with him into his new sphere the best wishes of all, without exception, and that his future prospects ought only to be limited by his own desires and his friends' expectations. It had given widespread satisfaction that the committee had not gone outside the department for his successor. The chairman, Mr. T. J. Orme, apologised for the absence of the city surveyor, Mr. John Price, who would have been present but for a previous engagement. In making the presentation he wished Mr. Rundall success in his new undertaking. The previous night he had had the pleasure of presenting him, on behalf of the working men of Mr. Rundall's district, with an illuminated address, as a mark of their appreciation, and he was sure he had the good wishes of every man who had signed it. Mr. Rundall suitably acknowledged the presentation and thanked all very warmly for the kind things they had said of him. He re-echoed the sentiments expressed that the Public Works Committee had taken a step in the right direction in promoting one of their fellow-officials, without going to foreign parts; and that when it became known that deserving officials might look forward to promotion a better spirit would animate their servants. As far as their new chief road surveyor was concerned, he was sure he had the welfare of the officials under him at heart. The musical programme was contributed by Messrs. A. M. Rose, Rundall, W. H. Worthington, J. A. Dale, Farr, Pearce, James, Savage, Smith, Ballard, Cherrett, Bowes, Borg, and Richards, while Mr. A. J. Farr discharged the duties of accompanist in his usual efficient manner.

# THE EDUCATION AND REGISTRATION OF PLUMBERS

A conference on the subject of the education and registration of plumbers was held on Friday at the Carpenter's Hall, London-wall, E.C. The conference was called by the National Association for the Promotion of Technical and Secondary Education, in response to a suggestion made by Mr. T. W. Russell, M.P., the Parliamentary Secretary of the Local Government Board, to a deputation of educationalists and administrators, who submitted to him certain objections to the Plumbers' Registration Bill introduced into Parliament last session.

After considerable discussion the following resolutions were adopted : " Without prejudice to the question of whether any Bill for the national registration of plumbers should be introduced into Parliament or not, it is resolved that if a Bill be introduced it should provide : (a) That there shall be placed upon the registration council (1) directly-appointed representatives of local municipal authorities aiding plumbing classes at least equal in number to the representatives of the various branches and interests of the plumbing trade, and (2) an adequate number of directly-appointed representatives of teaching institutions and of such additional organisations as are specially interested in the education and registration of plumbers, including the following, among others : City companies connected with the various sections of the building trade, the Sanitary Institute, the Royal Institute of Public Health, the Royal Institute of British Architects, the City and Guilds of London Institute, the Institute of Builders, the London Polytechnic Council, the Association of Technical Institutions. (b) That the registration council be instructed to accept, as qualifying for registration, the certificate of such public examining body or bodies approved by a Government department, and that such acceptance be not withdrawn without due notice nor without the consent of the Government department concerned. (c) That only a small fee for registration be charged to operative plumbers, and that the registration council shall not remove from the register any operative plumber once entered thereon solely by reason of his failing to pay a subsequent fee. (d) That the examination for the purposes of registration should test the candidates' general knowledge of other sections of the building trade in addition to their special knowledge of plumbing. (e) That in any Bill the council created by the Bill should be the actual managing body and have direct charge of the registration, and, further, that the conduct of the Bill should not be left in the hands of any one body."

It was further resolved to transmit the foregoing resolutions to the Local Government Board and to the principal members of her Majesty's Government.

# DISSEMINATION OF TUBERCULOSIS BY MILK.

ACTION OF THE LONDONDERRY CORPORATION.

At the last meeting of the Public Health Committee of the Londonderry Corporation, Alderman O'Kane, M.D., the chairman, moved : " That, owing to the dissemination of tuberculosis by milk, all cows kept in city dairies be inspected periodically by a competent official." He said that the matter came up as a corollary from the report submitted by the deputation at the sanitary congress. Among the various subjects dealt with at the congress there was none that secured a greater share of attention than that dealing with the steps for the prevention of tuberculosis. The old opinion that this disease was beyond tracing to its source, and stamping out by systematic precaution, had been replaced by a more encouraging one. There was no reason why this disease should not be ranked among such as typhoid fever, typhus fever, scarlatina and small-pox, and combated successfully by employing proper precautions. Tuberculosis kills more, many more, than all the zymotic diseases put together. He asked the committee generally to join with him in what was but a first step towards stamping out a disease which was so terrible. He hoped the time would come when the county councils would take up the matter and adopt the precautions on like lines in the rural districts, for the corporation had only power to deal with the area within their own boundary. He considered that if the motion met with the approval of the committee they should appoint a competent official, such as a veterinary surgeon, to go round and make periodic inspections of the cows and ascertain whether any were suffering from tubercle.

The resolution, after further discussion, was carried unanimously, and the Hospital Committee were instructed to report upon the matter at some future meeting.

**Erosion of the Sea Coast.**—The council of the British Association recently appointed a committee to report on the following resolution, which was refered to them by the General Committee for consideration : That the council be requested to bring under the notice of the Admiralty the importance of securing observations upon the erosion of the sea coast of the United Kingdom, and that the co-operation of the coastguard might be profitably secured for this purpose.

# MUNICIPAL LONDON.

AN INTERESTING LECTURE.

Mr. G. A. Gomme, M.A., recently delivered a lecture at Toynbee Hall, Commercial-street, E., on "Municipal London." Premising that the government of the City was a subject that should be of great interest to all, he defined "the great place we call London" as the City (which included eighty parishes) added to "what is called the County of London." A parish took the place of the militant township, and in some cases the parish and township were one and had always been one. Previously to the Act of 1855 each parish grew up as it would. Then district boards were formed ; this was an attempt to get local government outside the parish. There were formerly fifty-two district boards in the London area ; then these increased to eighty-six different boards. The complexity of London government was one of the difficulties of 1855 which was not remedied till 1888. The variety of boards he likened to a kaleidoscope ; they interlaced and overlapped each other. Thirty additional local authorities, and no fewer than 116 different local boards, were formed after 1888. But this was far from being an accession of strength. Boundaries were quite anomalous. In Hyde Park there might be seen a stone on one side of which was St. Margaret, Westminster, and on the other side, Paddington. The boundary lines of Holborn were a puzzle ; they crossed Charterhouse-street several times. The lecturer called it a zigzag line, cutting in half the railway station and various warehouses and churches. When the Queen on one occasion paid a visit to the "Royal Borough of Kensington," an allusion was made to the "borough" as the place where her Majesty was born ; but the remarkable thing was that Kensington was not in Kensington at all, but in the parish of St. Margaret, Westminster. The lecturer, having referred to the central authority of the City Corporation and its administration, said the London County Council had done much good, but was handicapped by the existence of a multiplicity of official areas and local authorities. Speaking of the water authorities, the lecturer observed that as they had the "right" to tax us for the supply of water, the least they could do was to do their best to supply the water.

# MAIDSTONE SEWAGE WORKS.

THE NEW FILTER-BEDS.

The members of the Maidstone Corporation recently paid a visit to the sewage works of the town, situated at Allington, in order to inspect the filter-beds which have recently been constructed there for the purpose of experimentally dealing with the sewage of the town. The filters are on the lines of those adopted at Sutton, Surrey, and other places on the advice of Mr. W. J. Dibdin (late chemist to the London County Council), and they were decided upon by the Maidstone council after consultations with and reports from him. Maidstone being a low-level system of sewerage, the whole of the sewage will have to be pumped for the purpose of filling the filters.

The bacteria beds are two in number, constructed of concrete. They are filled with breeze or clinker, and consist of a coarse and fine bed, the material in the former having been rejected by a sieve having a mesh of ¾ in., while the latter has all passed through a ¼-in. mesh with the fine dust removed. The beds are 45 ft. long by 30 ft. wide, and 3 ft. 6 in. and 4 ft. 6 in. deep respectively, and hold from 12,000 to 15,000 gallons at one filling. The sewage which is treated upon these beds is conveyed to them in the same condition in which it arrives at the works, without any mixing with lime, in a perfectly crude state. A new sewer had to be constructed through the works from the southern end to the filters, a distance of over 800 ft. The sewage is raised by means of a 4-in. Gwynne's centrifugal pump, which fills the bed in one and a half hours. It is first pumped direct from the coarse bed and spread over its surface by distributing troughs. After filling it is allowed to remain for two hours, when it is gradually drawn off, by opening the penstock at the outlet, and run into the fine bed. The second bed having been filled, it is allowed to stand in the same way for two hours, after which the effluent is drawn off and runs into the main outfall sewer, which empties itself just below Allington locks into the river. The experimental beds deal with about nearly a twentieth part of the Maidstone sewage.

**The London Water Companies.**—The metropolitan water companies have given notice of their intention to introduce a Bill into Parliament next session for improving and facilitating intercommunication between the mains and works of the respective companies, so as to obviate the possibility of a deficiency in the quantity of water which any one or more of the companies may be able to supply within their districts. The East London Company have given notice of a Bill empowering them to construct new storage reservoirs, aqueducts, &c., and to require the owner of any dwelling-house supplied by them to provide a cistern of such size as they may prescribe.

## ASSOCIATION OF
## MUNICIPAL AND COUNTY ENGINEERS.

### VOLUNTARY PASS EXAMINATION.

Notice is hereby given that the twenty-seventh examination for candidates for surveyorships under municipal corporations and district councils will be held at the Institution of Civil Engineers, Great George-street, Westminster, on Friday and Saturday, April 14 and 15, 1899.

*The council reserve to themselves the right to hold a second examination in case the entries received exceed the limits of accommodation. Such second examination will be held as soon after the first as circumstances permit. Applications will therefore be accepted strictly in the order of priority.*

Application forms, duly filled in by intending candidates, together with entrance fee of £2 2s., must be in my hands on or before the 5th of March, 1899.

THOMAS COLE, *Secretary.*
11 Victoria-street, Westminster, S.W.

## A NEW IRON JOINT FOR STONEWARE PIPES.

There have been, as is well known, large numbers of patent joints for stoneware pipes for sewers and drains, some of which have been good, but many of them have been unable to maintain the tests of the sewerage engineer in every-day practice. These joints have been mostly formed by an adaptation of the collar and the addition of a patent composition, and with or without the use of cement. Mr. James Smith, of 82 Coldharbour-lane, London, S.E., has recently brought out a new joint, known as Ernest Smith's Patent Iron Joint for stoneware pipes, which differs entirely from anything we have yet seen in that the stoneware pipe is without the usual stoneware collar, but its place is supplied by a very light iron collar or socket, which is fitted on to the body of the

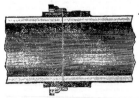

pipe with a cement composed of sulphur and precipitated gypsum, which is practically imperishable, as testified by the certificate of an eminent chemist, and an iron spigot is similarly fixed upon the opposite or spigot end of the stoneware pipe. The joint, as will be seen from the illustration, is practically the same joint that is used in cast-iron water mains, and is so simple and so easily made that any labourer could make it without any previous experience. The annular space between the spigot and the collar is fitted with a strip of blue lead cut for the purpose and of the proper thickness. The spigot is then pushed home, and a very slight amount of caulking makes the joint perfectly watertight.

We recently had the opportunity of seeing these pipes laid in a difficult piece of ground, for Mr. Capon, the surveyor to the Epsom Urban District Council, and were much interested to notice the expedition with which they were laid and the effective hydraulic test to which they were put, standing a pressure of 160 lb. to the square inch. It is also remarkable that the price at which the pipes can be supplied is not higher than that of most patent jointed pipes now in the market. The advantages claimed from the adoption of the joint are: (1) Excellence of work, strength, neatness and durability being especially pronounced. (2) Saving of time in laying pipes when water test is enforced. The pipes can be charged immediately the last joint is made, there being no necessity to wait for cement setting. Should a joint weep, it can be caulked up while the inspecting officer is present and the ground filled in. (3) Stoneware pipes of any length can be used. (4) The iron spigot and socket can be fixed by an unskilled labourer. (5) The joint can be used with the pipes of any manufacturer. (6) Special adaptability of joint for waterlogged ground, as it may be laid with the pipes partly or entirely under water.

We should not be surprised if the joint comes into considerable favour with sewerage engineers, as it has already been ordered for several important sewerage schemes.

**Otley.**—The district council are applying to Parliament for an Act to construct a reservoir at Bow beck, near Ilkley, at a cost of from £40,000 to £50,000. Mr. J. Waugh, of Bradford, is the engineer, and Mr. Mansergh has been called in as consulting engineer.

## BRYNMAWR WATER SUPPLY EXTENSIONS.

It is stated that the Brynmawr (Brecknock) Urban District Council propose to improve the water supply of the town by increasing the capacity of the present reservoir, near Crickhowell, from 8,500,000 gallons to 25,000,000 gallons, and to substitute 9-in. mains for the 5-in. pipes now in use. Great inconvenience and hardships are stated to have been experienced by the inhabitants of Brynmawr in the matter of water supply during the past summer, and it is considered gratifying to know that the council are taking such energetic action to prevent similar experiences. The work of raising the embankment of the reservoir will entail an expenditure of about £5,000, and the water supply area will be nearly doubled. Application, it is understood, has already been made to the Local Government Board for the necessary sanction to the execution of the works, which, it may be mentioned, include the provision of an additional filter-bed, at a cost of about £500.

## APPOINTMENTS VACANT.

*Official and all similar advertisements received later than Thursday morning are too late for classification and cannot therefore be included in these summaries until the following week. No advertisements received after 3 p.m. on Thursday can be inserted until the following week.*

RESIDENT ELECTRICAL ENGINEER.—December 2nd.—Vestry of St. Mary, Islington. £250.—Mr. L. J. Dunham, clerk to the vestry.

GENERAL FOREMAN.— December 2nd.— Corporation of Bridgwater.—Mr. W. T. Baker, town clerk.

GAS MANAGER.—December 3rd.—Corporation of Newbury. £200.—Mr. F. Quekett Louch, town clerk.

HIGHWAY SURVEYOR.—December 5th.—Keynsham Rural District Council. £150.—Mr. Fred. E. Whittuck, clerk to the council.

ROAD FOREMAN.—December 6th.—Winchester Corporation. —Mr. Walter Bailey, town clerk.

SURVEYOR AND SANITARY INSPECTOR.—December 6th.— Wirksworth Urban District Council. £80.—Mr. J. Gratton, clerk to the council.

MECHANICAL ENGINEER.—December 6th.—Tyne Improvement Commissioners. £250.—Mr. R. Unwin, secretary to the commissioners, Newcastle-on-Tyne.

CONSULTING ELECTRICAL ENGINEER.—December 6th.—Hoylake and West Kirby Urban District Council.—Mr. Roderick Williams, clerk to the council.

RESIDENT ELECTRICAL ENGINEER.—December 6th.—Wimbledon Urban District Council. £250.—Mr. W. H. Whitfield, clerk to the council.

ENGINEER, SURVEYOR, &c.—December 7th.—Chesham Urban District Council. £120.—Mr. Frederick How, clerk to the council.

ASSISTANT ELECTRICAL ENGINEER.—December 7th.—Ashton-under-Lyne Corporation. £130.—The Chairman, Electricity Committee, Town Hall, Ashton-under-Lyne.

CIVIL ENGINEERING ASSISTANT.—December 10th.—Corporation of Hull. £85.—Mr. A. E. White, city engineer.

ASSISTANT FOR THE INSPECTION OF BUILDINGS, &c.—December 12th.—Ilford Urban District Council. £120.—Mr. H. Shaw, A.M.I.C.E., surveyor to the council.

ASSISTANT SURVEYOR.—December 12th.—Corporation of Stockton-on-Tees. £91.—Mr. J. B. Ashwell, town clerk.

SEWAGE FARM MANAGER.—December 14th.—Willenhall Urban District Council. 30s.—Mr. Chas. J. Jenkin, surveyor to the council.

TEMPORARY ARCHITECTURAL DRAUGHTSMAN.—Aston Manor Urban District Council. £2 2s.—Mr. H. Richardson, surveyor to the council.

ENGINEER'S CLERK.—Box 90, office of THE SURVEYOR, 24 Bride-lane, Fleet-street, E.C.

## MUNICIPAL COMPETITIONS OPEN.

*Official and all similar advertisements received later than Thursday morning are too late for classification and cannot therefore be included in these summaries until the following week. No advertisements received after 3 p.m. on Thursday can be inserted until the following week.*

CHERTSEY.—December 23rd.—Sewerage and sewage disposal scheme for the Nos. 1 and 2 wards of the district. £50, £30 and £20.—Mr. T. E. Harland Chaldecott, clerk to the council.

HULL.—January 1st.—Erection of a central public library in Albion-street. £50, £30 and £20.—Mr. E. Laverack, town clerk.

HARROGATE.—January 2nd.—Erection of a pump-room, &c., at a cost not exceeding £8,000. £50, £30 and £20.—Mr. Samuel Stead, borough surveyor.

BRADFORD. — February 1st. — Erection of a central fire brigade station. £100, £50 and £30.—Mr. George McGuire, town clerk.

## MUNICIPAL CONTRACTS OPEN.

*Official and all similar advertisements received later than Thursday morning are too late for classification and cannot therefore be included in these summaries until the following week. No advertisements received after 3 p.m. on Thursday can be inserted until the following week.*

LANCASTER.—December 2nd.—Supply and delivery of about 5,680 lineal yards of 7-in. cast-iron water pipes, for the rural district council.—Mr. Joseph Ronion, clerk to the council.

CHERTSEY.—December 2nd.—Execution of various works in connection with the recreation ground at Guildfort-road, for the urban district council.—Mr. J. Frodsham Stow, surveyor to the council.

HULL.—December 2nd.—Supply of about 5,000 super. yards of the best hard Yorkshire 3 in. tooled flags.—Mr. A. E. White, city engineer.

SLEAFORD (Lincs.).—December 2nd.—Laying of about 2,100 yards of 3-in. cast-iron pipes for the water supply of the Village of Great Hale, for the rural district council.—Mr. Edmund Clements, clerk to the council.

SHEFFIELD.—December 3rd.—Construction and erection of urinals and wall at lower entrance to Western Park, opposite Clarkson-street.—Mr. Charles F. Wike, city surveyor.

CHORLEY.—December 3rd.—Laying of water mains, hydrants, &c., in the townships of Anderton, Heath, Charnock and Adlington, for the rural district council.—Mr. A. Jolly, surveyor to the council.

ST. JAMES, WESTMINSTER.— December 5th.—Construction of underground conveniences for both sexes in Broad-street, Golden-square, for the vestry.—Mr. T. Hensman Munsey, clerk to the vestry.

GLASGOW.—December 5th.—Supply and erection of switchboards and instruments at the new electricity works, Port Dundas.—Mr. J. D. Marwick, town clerk.

PADDINGTON.—December 5th.—Supply from Lady Day, 1899, to Lady Day, 1900, of York paving and granite kerbs, for the vestry.—Mr. Frank Dethridge, clerk to the vestry.

PADDINGTON.—December 5th.—Supply of about 6,000 cubic yards of broken granite for repairing roads, for the vestry.—Mr. Frank Dethridge, clerk to the vestry.

MARGATE.—December 5th.—Supply of various articles, for the water department during the year ending December 31, 1899.—Mr. G. Foord-Kelcey, town clerk.

FLEETWOOD.—December 5th.—Sewage diversion scheme, for the urban district council.—Mr. Joseph Tildsley, clerk to the council.

EDMONTON.—December 5th.—Supply of corrugated-iron roofing and stoneware pipes, for the urban district council.—Mr. G. Eccles Kachus, M.I.C.E., engineer to the council.

HULL.—December 5th.—Supply of buff, terra-cotta or artificial stone for the string courses, tracery, &c., of the crematorium.—Mr. A. E. White, city engineer.

ACCRINGTON.—December 5th.—Supply and fixing of sewer ventilating shafts at Coonion, for the rural district council.—Mr. Sam Adams, clerk to the council.

CHORLEY.—December 5th.—Supply of 178 tons of cast-iron pipes for water mains, for the rural district council.—Mr. Alban Jolly, surveyor to the council.

SOUTHEND-ON-SEA.—December 6th.—Various private drainage works.—Mr. Alfred Fidler, A.M.I.C.E., borough surveyor.

WALSALL.—December 6th.—Construction of surface-water sewers in Field-street, Bloxwich, and in Sandwell-street.—Mr. John R. Cooper, town clerk.

RUGBY.—December 6th.—Erection of a fire brigade station and stabling in the council's yard, Chapel-street, for the urban district council.—Mr. D. G. Macdonald, A.M.I.C.E., surveyor to the council.

LIMERICK.—December 6th.—Supply and delivery of a steam road-roller.—Mr. Wm. M. Nolan, town clerk.

HERTFORD.—December 6th.—Making-up of Stile Hall-gardens, for the urban district council.—Mr. Newell Parr, surveyor to the council.

ACTON.—December 6th.—Erection of a refuse destructor, for the urban district council.—Mr. D. J. Ebbetts, surveyor to the council.

TOTTENHAM.—December 6th.—Supply of a high-lift plunger and bucket pump at the Hale pumping station, for the urban district council.—Mr. E. Crowne, clerk to the council.

CROYDON.—December 7th.—Erection of new buildings and additions to the borough hospital at Waddon.—Mr. E. Mawdesley, town clerk.

GREENWICH.—December 7th.—Supply of 3,000 ft. of 3-in. and 1,000 ft. 2½-in. best tooled Yorkshire stone, for the district board of works.—The Surveyor to the Board.

FELIXSTOWE AND WALTON.—December 7th.—Sewering and making-up of Leopold-road North and Victoria-street North and the forming of a path in High-road, High-street and Lower-street, Walton, for the urban district council.—Mr. F. B. Jennings, clerk to the council.

FULHAM.—December 7th.—Laying of the sewer portions of combined drainage in private premises in various parts of the parish, for the vestry.—Mr. Charles Botterill, A.M.I.C.E., surveyor to the vestry.

TANDRIDGE.—December 7th.—Construction of about 156 yards of 9-in. pipe sewer in Romsey, for the rural district council.—Mr. T. W. Gold, surveyor to the council.

LEICESTER.—December 8th.—Supply of various stores and materials required during the year 1899.—Mr. E. Geo. Mawbey, M.I.C.E., borough engineer and surveyor.

CHATHAM.—December 8th.—Supply of various materials for the year ending December 31, 1899.—Mr. Charles Day, borough surveyor.

COLCHESTER.—December 8th.—Purchase and removal of four round cast-iron tanks.—Mr. Herbert Goodyear, A.M.I.C.E., borough engineer.

LEICESTER.—December 8th.—Supply of granite kerb, setts, ringwall, &c., required during the year 1899.—The Borough Surveyor.

NOTTINGHAM.—December 8th.—Supply of various stores and materials during the year ending 31st December, 1899.—Mr. Arthur Brown, M.I.C.E., city engineer.

CHESTERLE-STREET.—December 8th.—Levelling, paving, draining, &c., of the road past Clarence-terrace, for the rural district council.—Mr. G. W. Ayton, surveyor to the council.

WORCESTER.—December 10th.—Supply of lead water pipes (¾ in. to ¼ in. in diameter), pig lead and block tin during the year 1899.—Mr. T. Caink, A.M.I.C.E., city engineer.

KING'S LYNN.—December 10th.—Supply during the twelve months ending December 31, 1899, of various stores, &c.—Mr. H. J. Weaver, borough engineer and surveyor.

SOUTHAMPTON.—December 12th.—Supply of 1,000 tons of granite for macadamising.—Mr. W. B. G. Bennett, borough engineer.

CARMARTHEN.—December 12th.—Supply of about 270 yards of 21-in. socketed stoneware pipes, for the urban district council.—Mr. William Willis Gale, A.M.I.C.E., surveyor to the council.

CHURCH.—December 12th.—Excavating, flagging and paving of Water-street, for the urban district council.—Mr. John R. Roidisch, clerk to the council.

BARNSLEY.—December 12th.—Supply of various electricity supply plant and the erection of tail chimney and engine, dynamo and boiler-house, storage-rooms and offices in Racket-square.—Mr. J. Henry Taylor, A.M.I.C.E., borough surveyor.

SHOREDITCH.—December 12th.—Boring of an artesian well at the electric light station in Coronet-street, Old-street, for the vestry.—Mr. H. Mansfield Robinson, clerk to the vestry.

ECCLES (Lancs.).—December 12th.—Erection of a bowl-house and pavilion, and the construction of a bowling-green on land in Edison-road, Patricroft.—Mr. G. W. Bailey, town clerk.

WILLESDEN.—December 13th.—Execution of certain road-making and other works at Willesden Green, between Strode-road and Hawthorn-road, for the urban district council.—Mr. O. Claude Robson, M.I.C.E., engineer to the council.

COVENTRY.—December 13th.—Construction of five electric light substations.—Mr. J. E. Swindlehurst, city engineer.

WEST HAM.—December 13th.—Erection of a quarter sessions court, police cells and mortuary in West Ham-lane, Stratford.—Mr. Lewis Angell, borough engineer.

TURRIFF.—December 13th.—Various works in connection with the main drainage scheme, for the urban district council.—Mr. A. R. Wood, borough surveyor.

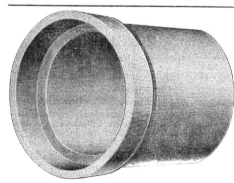

MANSFIELD.—December 14th.—Construction of about 500 yards of 9-in. pipe sewer.—Mr. R. Frank Vallance, borough surveyor.

MANSFIELD.—December 14th.—Construction of about 1,650 yards of brick sewer and storm overflows and 670 yards of pipe sewers.—Mr. R. Frank Vallance, borough surveyor.

TWICKENHAM.—December 14th.—Supply of 500 tons of Guernsey granite spalls, for the urban district council.—Mr. F. W. Pearce, surveyor to the council.

MACCLESFIELD.—December 14th.—Supply of drain pipes, castings, ironmongery, cement, bricks, &c., during the year ending 31st December, 1899.—Mr. W. Fredk. Taylor, town clerk.

HAMPSTEAD.—December 15th.—Removal of slop from the roads and gullies in the parish for one or three years from March 26th next, for the vestry.—Mr. Arthur P. Johnson, clerk to the vestry.

PRESTON.—December 15th.—Levelling, paving, channelling, &c., of the roads between St. David's-road and St. Michael's-road.—The Borough Surveyor.

BECKENHAM.—December 17th.—Supply and erection of various electric light plant, for the urban district council.—Mr. F. Stevens, clerk to the council.

BLACKPOOL.—December 21st.—Various sewering, levelling, paving, metalling, channelling, &c., works.—Mr. J. Wolstenholme, borough surveyor.

TAUNTON.—January 1st.—Construction of a sewer, about 1,300 yards long, from Railway-street to the site of the sewage outfall works in the Target Field.—Mr. James H. Smith, borough surveyor.

JOHANNESBURG, S.A.—January 6th.—Supply of a complete carburetted water-gas plant, for the corporation.—Messrs. Robert Whyte & Co., 22 Bury-street, St. Mary Axe, London, E.C.

LONDON.—January 24th.—Construction of a tunnel for pedestrian traffic under the river Thames from Greenwich to Poplar, for the county council.—Mr. C. J. Stewart, clerk to the council, County Hall, Spring-gardens, S.W.

SHANGHAI.—March 15th.—Construction and working of about 23 miles of electric tramways on the trolley system, for the municipal council.—Messrs. J. Pook & Co., 6 Jeffery's-square, St. Mary Axe, London, E.C.

## TENDERS FOR MUNICIPAL WORKS OR SUPPLIES.

*ACCEPTED.

ABERTILLERY.—For the construction of a new road from Abertillery to Aberbeeg, a distance of about 2 miles, and the widening of the main road from Aberbeeg to Crumlin, about 2½ miles, for the urban district council.—Mr. James McBean, engineer and surveyor to the council:—

| | |
|---|---|
| Preece, Hereford | £18,340 |
| W. Brown, Merthyr | 17,407 |
| Meredith, Gloucester | 16,166 |
| Mainwaring & Davies | 15,687 |
| Willis, Ystrad | 15,438 |
| N. Bayley, Abertillery | 14,347 |
| Howells, Caerphilly | 14,275 |
| Lewis, Llanhilleth | 13,713 |
| Monks & Parfit, Newport* | 12,313 |

ANNFIELD PLAIN.—For the formation of the road and footpath in Victoria-terrace and other streets, for the urban district council.—Mr. T. J. Trowsdale, surveyor to the council :—

| | |
|---|---|
| D. Champney, Lanchester | £738 |
| G. H. Bell, Bishop Auckland | 666 |
| R. Goldsborough, Chester-le-Street | 588 |
| T. Collinson, Annfield Plain | 584 |
| C. Smith, Annfield Plain | 580 |
| T. Gates, Annfield Plain | 546 |
| A. Stephenson, Blackhill | 526 |
| J. Dunn, Annfield Plain* | 464 |

BECKENHAM.—For paving works in Beckenham and Elmers End roads, for the urban district council.—Mr. J. A. Angell, surveyor to the council :—

| | |
|---|---|
| G. Wilson, Walthamstow, E. | £643 |
| J. Mowlem & Co., Westminster, S.W. | 479 |
| E. Iles, Mitcham Common* | 472 |

BIRMINGHAM.—For plumbing work and sanitary fittings at the Birmingham Eye Hospital.—Mr. J. E. Willcox, engineer, Birmingham :—

| | |
|---|---|
| T. Sneath, Stafford | £1,501 |
| T. Rowbotham, Birmingham | 947 |
| G. Robinson, Birmingham | 795 |
| Scull Brothers, Shrewsbury | 784 |
| H. Lea, Burton-on-Trent* | 711 |

BRIGHOUSE.—Accepted for providing and fixing at the sewage outfall works, Cooper Bridge, various boilers, engines, economiser, &c.—Mr. James Parkinson, town clerk :—

Boilers (Contract No. 8).—J. & J. Umpleby, Cleckheaton, £398.

Fuel Economiser (Contract No. 80).—The Clay Cross Company, Chesterfield, £68.

CARDIFF.—For the supply and erection of iron sheep and cattle troughs and pens in Roath market.—Mr. W. Harpur, M.I.C.E., borough engineer :—

| | |
|---|---|
| J. Allen, Woodville-road, Cardiff | £233 |
| H. Gibbon, Richmond-road, Cardiff | 223 |
| W. H. Ingleson, Tudor-street, Cardiff | 220 |
| Rees & Thomas, Clare-road, Cardiff | 210 |
| G. Griffiths, Working-street, Cardiff | 195 |
| Knox & Wells, Bangor-street, Cardiff | 179 |

CROMER.—For the erection of a public convenience, with accommodation for both sexes, on the sea front, for the urban district council.—Mr. A. F. Scott, surveyor to the council :—

BUILDINGS.

| | |
|---|---|
| R. Daws & Son, Norwich | £1,950 |
| J. Youngs & Son, Norwich | 1,592 |
| G. E. Hawes, Norwich | 1,565 |
| J. S. Smith, Norwich | 1,533 |
| T. Gill, Norwich | 1,495 |
| G. A. Lines, East Runton | 1,432 |

SANITARY FITTINGS.

| | |
|---|---|
| G. Jennings, Lambeth, S.E. | £312 |
| Shanks & Co., Barrhead | 234 |
| G. B. Davies, Westminster, S.W. | 233 |
| B. Finch & Co., Lambeth, S.E. | 223 |
| F. Barber & Co., Birmingham | 220 |
| Doulton & Co., Lambeth, S.E. | 210 |
| Adams & Co., London | 212 |
| Twyfords & Co., Hanley and London* | 175 |

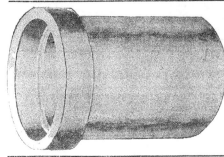

CARDIFF.—For the erection of a fish market, &c., at The Hayes.—Mr. W. Harpur, M.I.C.E., borough engineer :—

| | |
|---|---|
| G. Griffiths, Cardiff | £15,029 |
| R. Gibbon, Cardiff | 14,907 |
| Chubb & Co., Cardiff | 14,708 |
| J. Thomas, Cardiff | 14,363 |
| Powell & Mansfield, Cardiff | 14,325 |
| Latty & Co., Cardiff | 14,190 |
| Shepton & Sons, Cardiff | 13,941 |
| W. Thomas & Co., Cardiff | 13,766 |
| Evans Brothers, Cardiff | 13,739 |
| J. Allan, Cardiff | 13,608 |
| W. T. Symonds, Cardiff | 13,454 |
| Rees & Thomas, Cardiff | 13,285 |
| Turner & Sons, Cardiff | 12,988 |

GRAYS THURROCK.—For the supply of about 475 yards of wrought-iron fencing and a pair of gates, for the urban district council.—Mr. A. C. James, surveyor to the council :—

E. J. Raybould & Co., Workington.*—Fencing for level ground, 5s. 7½d. per yard; fencing for sloping ground, 5s. 9d. per yard; gates, £5 5s. per pair.

GRAYS THURROCK.—For the erection of stables, cart-sheds, stores, &c., in Stanley-road, and two blocks of latrines in the proposed park, for the urban district council.—Mr. A. C. James, A.M.I.C.E., surveyor to the council :—

| | Stables. | Latrines. |
|---|---|---|
| | £ s. d. | £ s. d. |
| W. White, Tilbury | 1,380 0 0 | 262 0 0 |
| J. J. Laurence, Grays | 985 15 0 | 185 10 0* |
| H. J. Carter, Grays | 980 0 0 | 305 0 0 |
| G. B. Rous, Grays | 875 17 0† | 242 5 0 |
| J. Brown, Grays | 843 0 0* | 203 0 0 |

† Informal.

HORNSEY.—For the supply of wrought-iron tree guards, for the urban district council.—Mr. E. J. Lovegrove, engineer and surveyor to the council :—

| | Each. |
|---|---|
| TREE GUARDS. | £ s. d. |
| Caversham Studio, Caversham-road, N.W. | 1 3 0 |
| Newton, Chambers & Co., Great George-street, Westminster | 0 15 0 |
| Beck & Co., Limited, Southwark, S.E. | 0 11 0 |
| Jukes, Coulson, Stokes & Co., Clements-lane, E.C. | 0 9 6 |
| Hayward & Sons, Wolverhampton... | 0 8 9 |
| Bayliss, Jones & Bayliss, Cannon-street, E.C. | 0 8 9 |
| Gibb & Co., Fenchurch-street, E.C. | 0 8 8 |
| Hill & Smith, Queen Victoria-street, E.C. | 0 8 6 |
| Pontifex & Co., Coleman-street, E.C. | 0 8 3 |
| Hollom & Co., Gracechurch-street, E.C. | 0 8 2 |
| Raybould & Co., Marsh Side, Workington | 0 8 0 |
| Priest & Sons, Limited, Castle Ironworks, Bristol | 0 8 0 |
| Neville & Co., Llanelly | 0 7 9 |
| M. McVay, Kennington Park-road, S.E. | 0 7 9 |

| | Per 100. |
|---|---|
| | £ s. d. |
| Miller & Sons, Wolverhampton | 175 0 0 |
| Henry Lebwitz, Ucres-road, Kingston-on-Thames | 70 0 0 |
| J. Kiwell, Sheepcote-street, Birmingham* | 36 5 0 |

HORNSEY.—For the supply of cast-iron telephone pipes and jut covers, for the urban district council.—Mr. E. J. Lovegrove, engineer and surveyor to the council :—

| PIPES. | Per ton. |
|---|---|
| H. & G. Measures, Pitlake, Croydon | 7 0 0 |
| Pontifex & Co., Coleman-street, E.C. | 7 0 0 |
| Stanton Ironworks Company, near Nottingham | 6 17 0 |
| Hollom & Co., Gracechurch-street, E.C. | 6 15 0 |
| Bird & Co., Great Castle-street, W. | |
| Jukes, Coulson, Stokes & Co., Clement-lane, E.C.* | 6 13 0 |
| Gibb & Co., Fenchurch-street, E.C. | 6 12 6 |

| COVERS. | Per ton. |
|---|---|
| Stanton Ironworks Company, near Nottingham | 1 17 6 |
| Newton, Chambers & Co., Great George-street, Westminster | 1 17 0 |
| Pontifex & Co., Coleman-street, E.C. | 1 10 0 |
| Hollom & Co., Gracechurch-street, E.C. | 1 7 6 |
| Gibb & Co., Fenchurch-street, E.C. | 1 7 0 |
| Bird & Co., Great Castle-street, W. | 1 6 4 |
| Jukes, Coulson, Stokes & Co., Clements-lane, E.C.* | 1 4 0 |
| H. & G. Measures, Pitlake, Croydon | 1 3 0 |

HORNSEY.—For the construction of a new road through Queen's Wood, Highgate, for the urban district council.—Mr. E. J. Lovegrove, engineer and surveyor to the council :—

| | |
|---|---|
| W. Langridge, Croydon | £4,875 |
| H. Clark, Andover-road, N. | 3,995 |
| E. T. Bloomfield, Tottenham, N. | 3,761 |
| W. T. Williamson & Sons, Limited, Green-lanes, N. | 3,570 |
| C. Ford, Harlesden, N.W. | |
| Killingback & Co., Camden Town, N.W. | 3,540 |
| Pedretti & Co., Finsbury Park, N. | 3,400 |
| R. Ballard, Limited, Childs Hill, N.W. | 3,316 |
| W. Walker, Holloway, N. | 3,204 |
| T. Adams, Wood Green, N. | 3,067 |
| J. A. Dunmore, Crouch End, N.* | 3,035 |

HORNSEY.—For the supply of cast-iron lamp columns, for the urban district council.—Mr. E. J. Lovegrove, engineer and surveyor to the council :—

| CAST-IRON LAMP COLUMNS. | Per ton. |
|---|---|
| | £ s. d. |
| E. Stevenson, Nottingham | 10 0 0 |
| Moorgate Engineering Company, Fetherstone-street, E.C. | 10 0 0 |
| T. Howden & Sons, Wakefield | 9 9 0 |
| Stanton Ironworks Company, Nottingham | 9 0 0 |
| J. Shaw & Co., Glasgow | 9 0 0 |
| F. Bird & Co., Great Castle-street, W.C. | 8 10 0 |
| Rowland, Carr & Co., Lime Street-square, E.C. | 8 10 0 |
| J. R. Hollom & Co., Gracechurch-street, E.C. | 8 5 0 |
| Newton, Chambers & Co., Westminster, S.W. | 8 1 5 |
| H. & G. Measures, Croydon | |
| Jukes, Coulson, Stokes & Co., Clements-lane, E.C. | 7 17 6 |
| J. Needham, Stockport | 7 15 0 |
| Gibb & Co., Fenchurch-street, E.C. | 7 5 0 |
| Pontifex & Co., Coleman-street, E.C.* | |

| | |
|---|---|
| G. Smith & Co., Upper Thames-street, E.C. | 1 3 0 |
| T. R. Kershaw, Nuneaton | 1 0 0 |

DOVER.—Accepted for the supply of about 1,500 tons of broken Guernsey granite, 500 tons of Guernsey granite siftings, and about 2,000 lineal feet of Guernsey granite kerbing, channelling and quadrant corners.—Mr. E. Wollaston Knocker, town clerk :—
Broken Granite Siftings.—Fry Brothers, Lion Wharf, Greenwich, 11s. 9d., 8s. 9d., and 8s. 9d. per ton.
Fry Brothers, Lion Wharf, Greenwich.—Kerb, 2s. per lineal foot; radiated kerb, 2s. 3d. per lineal foot; channelling, 2s. 6d. per lineal foot; radiated channelling, 2s. 10d. per lineal foot.

LINCOLN.—For the supply of hard wood blocks for street paving.—Mr. R. A. Macbriar, city surveyor :—

| | | | | Per 1,000. |
| | | | | £ s. d. |
| JARRAH. | | | | |
| Nightingale & Co., Grimsby | ... | ... | ... | 11 12 6 |
| W. Griffiths, London, E.C. | ... | ... | ... | 11 0 0 |
| Millar's Karri and Jarrah Forests, London, E.C. | ... | 10 19 6 |
| Acme Wood Flooring Company, London, N.E. | ... | 10 17 6 |
| H. Newsum, Sons & Co., Lincoln | ... | ... | ... | 10 10 0 |
| Falfreyman, Foster & Co., London | ... | ... | ... | 10 9 6 |
| W. E. Gandy, Shipley | ... | ... | ... | 9 10 0 |
| Jarrahdale Jarrah Forests and Railways, Ltd., London, E.C. | 9 3 4 |
| KARRI. | | | | |
| W. Griffiths | ... | ... | ... | ... | 10 18 0 |
| Millar's Karri and Jarrah Forests | ... | ... | 10 17 9 |
| Acme Wood Flooring Company | ... | ... | 10 17 6 |
| H. Newsum, Sons & Co. | ... | ... | ... | 10 10 0 |
| BLACKBUTT. | | | | |
| McEuen & Co., Cannon-street, E.C. | ... | ... | 10 0 0 |
| H. Newsum, Sons & Co. | ... | ... | ... | 9 5 0 |

† Subject to Council's approval.

STAFFORDSHIRE.—For reorganising the system of soil and surface-water drains at the county lunatic asylum.—Mr. J. E. Wilcox, engineer, Birmingham :—

| T. Vale, Stourport | ... | ... | ... | £4,790 |
| H. Law, Erdington | ... | ... | ... | 4,650 |
| F. Barke, Stoke-on-Trent | ... | ... | ... | 4,073 |
| C. J. Nevitt, Stafford | ... | ... | ... | 3,739 |
| J. Biggs, Birmingham | ... | ... | ... | 3,145 |
| J. Mackay, Smethwick | ... | ... | ... | 3,116 |
| G. Law, Kidderminster | ... | ... | ... | 3,099 |
| J. Jameson, Birmingham | ... | ... | ... | 3,070 |
| H. Holloway, Wolverhampton | ... | ... | ... | 2,926 |

WEYBRIDGE.—Accepted for the supply of stoneware pipes, gullies, Bristol blue pennant kerbing, prepared limestone or granite for tar paving, Thames ballast, Portland cement and gas tar, for the urban district council.—Mr. John S. Crawshaw, surveyor to the council :—
Stoneware Pipes and Gullies.—Albion Clay Company, Burton-on-Trent, 6in., 1s. 2¾d. per yard; 9in., 1s. 8½d. per yard; 12in., 3s. 2d. per yard; 15in., 5s. 0½d. per yard; 18in., 7s. 7¾d. per yard. Gullies (Sykes'), 18in. and 15in. by 3ft. 6in., 55s.; 18in. diameter by 3ft. 6in., 50s.
12-in. by 4-in. Bristol Blue Pennant Kerbing.—West Gloster Pennant Stone Quarries Company, Bristol, 9½d. per foot.
Prepared Limestone for Tar Paving.—Buxton Lime Firms Company, Limited, Buxton, ¾-in. topping, 2s. per ton; ¼-in. bottoms, 19s. 6d. per ton.
Portland Cement.—Eastwood & Co., Lambeth, S.E., 36s. per ton.

WEYBRIDGE.—Accepted for the supply and delivery of various materials, for the urban district council.—Mr. G. Wheeler, clerk to the council :—
About 3,000 Tons of Farnham Hungry Hill Flints.—Farnham Flint, Gravel and Stone Company, Farnham, 6s. 7d. per ton.
About 5,000 Tons of Fine Gravel Screenings.—Farnham Flint, Gravel and Stone Company, Farnham, 4s. 7d. per ton.
About 1,500 Yards of Local Gravel.—W. F. Egerton, Weybridge, 3s. per yard.
Hire of Steam Roller.—Oxfordshire Steam Ploughing Company, Oxon., 26s. per day.
Scarifying.—Oxfordshire Steam Ploughing Company, Oxon., flint 3s. 4d. per yard; granite, 1d. per yard.

## MEETINGS.

*Secretaries and others will oblige by sending early notice of dates of forthcoming meetings.*

### DECEMBER.

2.—Institution of Civil Engineers: Students' meeting; Mr. Charles Benjamin Saner, on "The Sunlight Gold-bearing Reef, Lydenburg, Transvaal." 8 p.m.
5.—Royal Institute of British Architects: Mr. R. W. Gibson, New York, U.S.A., on "Fireproof Construction in America." 8 p.m.
5.—Society of Engineers: Mr. George Thudichum, F.C.S., on "The Bacterial Treatment of Sewage." 7.30 p.m.
6.—Institution of Civil Engineers: Ordinary meeting; Mr. Francis Fox, M.I.C.E., on "The Ventilation of Tunnels and Buildings." 8 p.m.
10.—British Association of Waterworks Engineers: Special general meeting. 10 a.m.
10.—British Association of Waterworks Engineers: General meeting; Mr. H. Bertram Nichols, A.M.I.C.E., on "Water Supply from the Lower Greensand and Constructional Works connected therewith at Leighton Buzzard." 11 a.m.
12.—The Surveyors' Institution: Ordinary general meeting. 8 p.m.
13.—Liverpool Self-propelled Traffic Association: Discussion on "The Judges' Report on the 1898 Trials, and the Conditions for the 1899 Trials." 8 p.m.
14.—Sanitary Institute: Sessional meeting; Dr. E. F. Willoughby on "Some Prevalent Fallacies in Vital Statistics." 8 p.m.

## NOTICES.

THE SURVEYOR AND MUNICIPAL AND COUNTY ENGINEER may be ordered direct, through any of Messrs. Smith & Son's book-stalls, or of any newsagent in the United Kingdom. Applications to the Offices for single copies by post must in all cases be accompanied by stamps.
The Prepaid Subscription (including postage) is as follows :

| | Twelve Months. | Six Months. | Three Months. |
| United Kingdom | ... 15s. | ... 7s. 6d. | ... 3s. 9d. |
| Continent, the Colonies, India, United States, &c. | ... 19s. | ... 9s. 6d. | ... 4s. 9d. |

The *International News Company, 83 and 85 Duane-street, New York City; The Toronto News Company, Toronto; and The Montreal News Company, Montreal, have been appointed agents in the United States and Canada for the sale of* THE SURVEYOR AND MUNICIPAL AND COUNTY ENGINEER. *A thin paper edition is printed for circulation abroad.*

EDITORIAL OFFICES :—
24 BRIDE-LANE, FLEET-STREET, LONDON, E.C.

ADVERTISEMENT AND PUBLISHING OFFICES :—
13 NEW STREET-HILL, FLEET-STREET, LONDON, E.C.

## APPOINTMENTS OPEN.

### BOROUGH OF STOKE-UPON-TRENT.
ASSISTANT SURVEYOR.

The Town Council require the services of an Assistant to the Borough Surveyor.

Salary, £91 per annum.

Candidates must have a thorough knowledge of the duties appertaining to the appointment.

Personal canvassing will be a disqualification.

Applications, in own handwriting, accompanied by not more than three recent testimonials, and endorsed "Assistant Surveyor," to be received by me not later than December 12th.

JNO. B. ASHWELL,
Town Clerk.
Stoke-upon-Trent.
November 24, 1898.

### URBAN DISTRICT COUNCIL OF HOYLAKE AND WEST KIRBY.

The Urban District Council of Hoylake and West Kirby invite applications from Electrical Engineers desirous of acting as Consulting Electrical Engineer in connection with the works to be carried out by the Council under their electric lighting order.

Applications to be sent on or before 6th December next, addressed to the undersigned at the Council's offices, Hoylake, Cheshire.

RODERICK WILLIAMS,
Clerk.
November 25, 1898.

### ILFORD URBAN DISTRICT COUNCIL.

The Ilford Urban District Council require in the Surveyor's department an Assistant for the inspection of buildings and other work, at a salary of £130 per annum.

The person appointed will be required to devote his whole time to the discharge of his duties, a list of which can be obtained from Mr. H. Shaw, A.M.I.C.E., the Council's Surveyor, at his offices, 7 Cranbrook-road, Ilford.

Applications, in candidate's own handwriting, accompanied by copies of three recent testimonials, stating age (which must not be under twenty-five or over forty-five), qualifications and experience, endorsed "Application for Surveyor's Assistant," under seal, and addressed to the Chairman, must be sent to me on or before noon on Monday, the 12th December next.

Canvassing, directly or indirectly, is strictly prohibited and will be deemed a disqualification.

(By order)
JOHN W. BENTON,
Clerk to the Council.
Council Offices, Ilford, Essex.
November 25, 1898.

### KEYNSHAM RURAL DISTRICT COUNCIL.
APPOINTMENT OF HIGHWAY SURVEYOR.

The Council will, at their meeting on Tuesday, the 6th December, 1898, select Candidates for the office of, and will at their meeting on the 20th December, 1898, appoint a Surveyor for the Keynsham highway district (about 10 miles by 7, embracing fourteen parishes), at a salary of £150 per annum. Duties to commence 1st January next. Previous knowledge of road management essential.

The Surveyor will be required to devote his whole time to the duties of his office, must be able to draw specifications for laying stone pavement and gutters, stone, brick and pipe drains, and gratings; to keep a horse or other suitable means of locomotion. Preference will be given to candidates under the age of thirty-five years, with experience as aforesaid.

Candidates must send testimonials as to character and ability (not more than three) by Monday, the 5th December, to

FRED. E. WHITTUCK,
Solicitor.
Keynsham.
November 18, 1898.

CITY OF HULL.
The Corporation require a Civil Engineering Assistant in the City Engineer's office, at £85 per annum.
It is essential that candidates should be quick and neat draughtsmen.
Applications, stating age, experience and qualifications, are to be addressed to the undersigned, and delivered on or before Saturday, 10th December.
Testimonials need not be sent in the first instance.
(By order)
A. E. WHITE,
City Engineer.
Town Hall, Hull.
November 28, 1898.

BOROUGH OF GUILDFORD.
SUPERINTENDENT OF OUTFALL SEWAGE WORKS.
The Corporation of Guildford invite applications from persons competent to undertake the duties of Superintendent of the Outfall Sewage Works at Bellfields, Stoke-next-Guildford.
The person appointed will be required to devote the whole of his time to the work and to reside in the house provided at the works, and he will act under the directions of the Borough Surveyor.
Candidates must have a thorough knowledge of steam-engines, air compressor, and sludge-pressing plant, and to be able to work this machinery.
A schedule of the duties, and particulars of the salary to be paid, can be obtained, after the 30th inst., on application at the Town Clerk's office.
Applications, with copies of not more than three testimonials of recent date, must be sent to me on or before the 10th December next.
FERDINAND SMALLPEICE,
Town Clerk.
138 High-street, Guildford.
November 24, 1898.

ENGINEER'S CLERK wanted; must be rapid shorthand and type writer, competent book-keeper, and able to read drawings and trace neatly.—Apply, stating age, salary required, and full particulars of experience, to Box 90, office of THE SURVEYOR, 24 Bride-lane, Fleet-street, E.C.

## COMPETITION.

BRADFORD NEW FIRE BRIGADE STATION.
REVISED CONDITIONS OF COMPETITION.
The Corporation of the City of Bradford are prepared to receive competitive designs for the erection of a Central Fire Brigade Station. Three premiums are offered to competing architects—viz., £100, £50 and £30.
Plan of the site, with revised instructions, may be had on application at the City Surveyor's office on payment of 1 guinea, to be refunded after receipt of design, or on return of papers within three weeks.
The designs must be sent in not later than the 1st February, 1899.
(By order)
GEORGE McGUIRE,
Town Clerk.
Town Clerk's Office, Bradford.
November, 1898.

## TENDERS WANTED.

WILLESDEN DISTRICT COUNCIL.
TO ROAD CONTRACTORS.
The Willesden District Council are prepared to receive tenders for the execution of certain Road-making Work, together with Sewer, Surface-Water Drain, Fencing, and other work incidental thereto, at Willesden Green, between Steele-road and Hawthorn-road, and comprising a length of 325 ft. lineal or thereabouts.
Plan and specification may be seen, and all further particulars obtained, on and after Monday, December 5, 1898, upon application to Mr. O. Claude Robson, M.I.C.E., Engineer to the Council, Public Offices, Dyne-road, Kilburn, N.W.
The tenders, upon printed forms and endorsed "New Road," to be delivered at the offices of the Council not later than 4 p.m. on Tuesday, December 13, 1898.
The Council do not bind themselves to accept the lowest or any tender.
(By order)
STANLEY W. BALL,
Clerk to the Council.
Public Offices, Dyne-road, Kilburn, N.W.
November 28, 1898.

# The Surveyor

### And Municipal and County Engineer.

Vol. XIV., No. 360.    LONDON, DECEMBER 9, 1898.    Weekly, Price 3d.

## Minutes of Proceedings.

**Sewers made for Profit.** "Sewers made by any person for his own profit" are, as is well-known, excepted by sec. 13 of the Public Health Act, 1875, from the category of sewers which vest in local authorities. The phrase seems simple enough, but this is only one of the numerous instances in which the simplicity disappears when the attempt is made to apply the terms of the statute to the complexities of actual facts; and the cases are numerous in which the Courts have been called upon to decide whether or not a given sewer fell within the exception. Such a case was recently noted in our columns (*Croysdale* v. *Sunbury - on - Thames Urban District Council*, p. 458 ante); but before commenting upon this it may be of interest to make a brief reference to a few earlier decisions. In one of the earliest of the reported cases a builder had constructed a number of houses fronting on a street which had not at that time become a public highway, and made the following arrangements for their drainage: He made a drain and a cesspool, and connected them with the first house, and as he completed successive houses he continued the drain from one house to the other, carrying the cesspool forward, and finally, when all the houses had been completed, there was a line of pipes or sewer connecting them with the cesspool. It was held that this sewer was not made by the builder "for his own profit" within the meaning of the Act (*Acton Local Board* v. *Batten*). In another case the owners of a building estate laid out a street and made a sewer to drain the houses. This sewer was sufficient as long as sewage was allowed to be sent into the Thames, but upon this being prohibited it became necessary to construct a new sewer to carry the sewage in a different direction. It was held that the original sewer was not made by any person "for his own profit," but vested in the local board, who were bound to keep it in repair. Mr. Baron Huddleston in the course of his judgment suggested as an illustration of the mode in which the exception might apply the case of a sewer made for conveying sewage to works, to be utilised for manure, &c. (*Bonella* v. *Twickenham Local Board*). This decision was affirmed by the Court of Appeal. A similar view was expressed by Lord Justice Lopes in *Farrand* v. *Hallas Land and Building Company*—namely, that a sewer made for profit means not a sewer made merely for getting rid of sewage for sanitary purposes without utilising it in any way, but one made for the purpose of realising a profit above and beyond and independent of any sanitary purpose. And in further illustration of the kind of sewers falling within the exception, Lord Justice A. L. Smith called attention to the undoubted fact (which is apt sometimes to be overlooked) that the carrying of sewage is not necessary to constitute a sewer. There may be sewers for carrying off rain or surface water collected from different premises and its distribution, on payment among different receivers. Such sewers would be sewers "made for profit."

The sewer in question in that case was held not to fall within the exception, being an intercepting sewer constructed by the defendants and connected with the drains of a row of cottages, the sewage from which was thereby conveyed to a stream. In *Fowles* v. *Colmer* the plaintiffs constructed a sewer in a road adjoining their building estate, and on sale of the building plots charged the purchasers for connecting the drainage systems of their premises with the sewer. The defendant was the owner of a house on the other side of the road, and claimed the right to connect his drains with the sewer without payment. The plaintiffs asked for an injunction, but Mr. Justice Romer dismissed the action, holding that the sewer was not "made for profit," and therefore vested in the local authority, the case not being distinguishable from *Farrand* v. *Hallas Land and Building Company*. A very different set of circumstances existed in *Minehead Local Board* v. *Luttrell*, where it was held that the sewers did fall within the exception, and had been made by the defendant for his own profit, although they were not in any way sewers of the class referred to in the judicial illustrations previously mentioned. The facts were probably within the recollection of our readers, but we may briefly remind them that the defendant (who was the lord of the manor and owner of a large part of the town of Minehead) constructed in 1878, at his own expense and with the sanction of the local authority (where necessary), a sewerage system for draining the town, subsequently extending the system from time to time to new streets as required. The greater number of the houses in the town were connected with this system, and a voluntary annual sewage rate of varying amount was paid by the occupiers of these houses to the defendant. The Minehead Local Board unsuccessfully claimed these sewers as being vested in them. We do not know whether the circumstances of this case are absolutely unique, but we should think they are, at all events, very unusual.

In the case to which we referred at the beginning of these remarks (*Croysdale* v. *Sunbury-on-Thames Urban District Council*) we get an altogether different, but probably equally unusual, state of things: and the case is very interesting, not only as being (we believe) the latest decision under this section, but because the council relied for their defence in a great measure upon certain provisions of the Public Health Act, 1875, and the Highway Act, 1835, which therefore necessarily received careful examination by Mr. Justice Stirling, before whom the trial took place. The plaintiff was the owner of a field sloping downward from a street and then rising again, and having two ponds in the "dip" or hollow thus formed. In 1858 or 1859 the then tenant of this field laid down a line of pipes connecting these ponds with a ditch between the field and the street, with the object of getting a better supply of water for his cattle. At the ditch end of the conduit was a grating, from which the highway surveyors from time to time cleared away accumulations of rubbish, but it was not proved that they ever cleaned the pipes themselves. The plaintiff having removed the pipes, with a view of filling up the ponds, the council entered the field and cut a trench from the ditch to run off the surface water from the street. The Court granted an injunction against the council on the ground that the line of pipes constituted a sewer made by the plaintiff's predecessor for his own profit. This decision, it will be seen, gives a somewhat more extended meaning to the term "profit" than that which it bears in colloquial usage; indeed, Mr. Justice Stirling expressly stated that in his opinion the term was not to be restricted to a direct money payment, but that when the purpose of a sewer was "neither for sanitary nor ordinary drainage purposes, but to enable the land to be occupied more profitably, or to avoid an expenditure which would otherwise have to be incurred in order that the occupation might be equally beneficial," the term would apply. The statutory provisions above referred to, under which the district council sought to justify their action, are secs. 13 to 17 of the Public Health Act, 1875, and sec. 67 of the Highway Act, 1835. Our readers are, of course, familiar with these clauses, but it will, we think, be interesting briefly to consider their bearing on the case in the light of the judgment. Taking first the Public Health Act, sec. 13, which vests all sewers in the authority, with certain specified exceptions, it of course became inapplicable as soon as the sewer in question was held to fall within one of those exceptions. Sec. 14 enables the authority to purchase "or otherwise acquire" from any person any sewer, or the right of making or using any sewer. It was obvious, however, that this was not a case of purchase, and upon the evidence there was no "other acquisition" in this instance. Sec. 15 merely imposes on local authorities the duty of repairing sewers belonging to them, and of making such sewers as may be necessary. Sec. 16 at first sight might have seemed helpful. It empowers a local authority to carry a sewer into, through or under any lands. Setting aside, however, the fact that what the council had done was not to carry a sewer but to cut a trench in the plaintiff's field, the statutory power is, by its terms, only exercisable "after giving reasonable notice to the owner or occupier," and "if on the report of the surveyor it appears necessary." Neither of these conditions had been fulfilled, and therefore, in the words of the learned judge, "whatever might be done hereafter, the defendants had not as yet brought themselves within its terms." As to the provisions of the Highway Act, the section relied on empowers the authority to make, scour, cleanse and keep open all ditches, gutters, drains or watercourses, and also to make and lay trunks, tunnels, plats or bridges in and through any lands or grounds adjoining or lying near to any highway. In the opinion of Mr. Justice Stirling this section, however widely construed, only authorises the making and keeping open of ditches and drains in and through lands adjoining a highway, and does not authorise the discharge of the contents of any ditch or drain on such lands, which was what had been done in the present case. These cases, and others that might be cited, will serve as useful guides in determining whether a sewer has been made for profit. It cannot be supposed, however, that every possible state of circumstances is covered by them, and doubtless in this, as in numerous other instances, there remain problems to be solved at the expense of future litigants.

\* \* \*

**The London County Council Housing Policy.** A good deal of unnecessary apprehension seems to have been excited of late in connection with the housing proposals of the London County Council, but the result of Tuesday's debate at Spring-gardens should have a more or less soothing effect. The debate was in continuation of that of last week, and centred round the interesting report which was some time ago presented to the council by the Housing of the Working Classes Committee. It may be as well to note clearly how the apprehensions of the council's various critics were aroused. Apparently they were due, not so much to the report in question, as to a matter which came before the council at the meeting on the 22nd ult., and which, though it had reference to the housing problem, had no direct connection with the report which has been under consideration at the last two meetings. The question was the erection of dwellings on a specific area in Poplar. To put the matter briefly, difficulties had arisen which prevented the erection of the dwellings in the way originally contemplated, and the committee brought forward a suggestion which excited the fears of a number of people. A company had undertaken to purchase the cleared land and provide the dwellings, but found themselves unable to satisfy the requirements of the Local Government Board. The council are under a legal obligation to provide accommodation for those displaced, and, considering the demands of the neighbourhood, it was inexpedient that there should be any further delay. As the only obvious and practicable way of putting an end to the deadlock, the committee proposed that the council should suspend the very salutary standing order which provides that their dwellings should be self-supporting. A number of people assumed, rather hastily, that this was to be the basis of the entire future policy of the council in connection with the housing problem. Hence the outcry and the denunciations of the infringement of the laws of political economy and of the injury to private enterprise which the council were supposed to be contemplating by drawing upon the rates to cheapen the rents of a favoured few who would be the council's tenants. Alderman Beachcroft is a member of the committee, and he has been at considerable pains to point out that the case of the Poplar area is an exceptional one, and that the council have really no option in the matter. We may now refer to the report which was considered at the last two meetings, and which may be regarded as formulating the council's general policy for the future. Into the details of the report our purpose does not render it necessary to go. The essence of the council's policy was given in the form of three recommendations:—

(1) That housing accommodation should be provided for a number of persons equal to that of the working classes displaced by any scheme under the Housing of the Working Classes Act, 1890, or under the provisions of any Improvement Act, but not necessarily in the immediate neighbourhood of the displacement, due consideration being given to the needs of those living on any particular area.

(2) That all clearances under the Housing of the Working Classes Act, 1890, which involved rehousing be done at the sole cost of the council.

(3) That, apart from the rehousing required in connection with clearance or improvement schemes, the council do approve of acquiring land, under Part III. of the Housing of the Working Classes Act, 1890, with a view to the purchase of land and the erection of dwellings thereon for the purpose of supplying housing accommodation.

There is nothing very appalling in the first two recommendations, which were adopted last week, the first with an amendment to the effect that a register be kept of all persons displaced, and that, if possible, such persons should have the first offer of tenancy in the council's buildings. The third recommendation, however, has been more disquieting to a good many people who read it in connection with the suspension of the standing order already alluded to. In the course of the discussion on Tuesday more than one speaker on the Progressive side energetically disclaimed any intention of erecting dwellings which would not be self-supporting and would involve a charge upon the rates, but it will be observed that there was nothing in the wording of the recommendation which would have prevented that being done if at any time a majority of the council thought fit to suspend the standing order. It is better to be on the safe side and above suspicion. So evidently thought Lord Monkswell, who accordingly persuaded the council to insert after the word "schemes" the words " providing that no charge be placed on the county rate thereby." There should, therefore, no longer be any cause for uneasiness on this particular score. But even as amended the clause will be a matter for misgiving to many people. Alderman Beachcroft, for example, though he felt compelled to support the suspension of the standing order in the specific case of the Poplar area, is by no means in favour of indiscriminate building, and the suggestion that the council should build for the working classes generally is to him so startling that he is tempted to wonder whether it is meant seriously. He suggests as an alternative policy that the council should endeavour to open out communications between the suburbs and the most crowded districts; but unfortunately the artisan and labouring classes have an obstinate preference for getting as near as possible to the scene of their labours, even at the expense of more or less insanitary surroundings. We have no doubt that the proposal of the council is meant quite seriously, and, like Alderman Beachcroft and others, we confess to some misgiving. We have consistently maintained that in this matter of building municipal authorities should avoid needless and undesirable competition with private enterprise, which such a policy must tend to discourage and ultimately drive out of the field. If only as a matter of self-interest, the community, as represented by municipal authorities, may be justified in doing something towards housing the very poorest, whose condition might otherwise become a social danger. It is notorious, however, that this is precisely the class which the London County Council have hitherto failed to reach, and there is nothing in the new recommendations which will remedy the deficiency. The remedy may be found in less expensive construction, but in any case some revision or modification of the lines on which the council carry out their building policy is evidently urgently called for.

\* \* \*

**Incandescent Gas Lighting in Streets.** In his report for the year ended March 25, 1898, Mr. George Weston, surveyor to the Paddington Vestry, gives the results of his experience with incandescent lamps for street lighting. As the outcome of a second year's experiment with twelve incandescent burners he finds that the success or failure of incandescent lighting from the financial point of view depends entirely on the state of efficiency in which the mantles are maintained. He points out that a mantle is at its best, and gives a maximum of light, when first put on, but that day by day this light is decreasing; and the question then is, When shall the mantle be removed ? Mr. Weston adds :—

It follows that the longer the mantles remain unchanged, even after the light is very sensibly diminished, the less will be the yearly maintenance charge; but it is not then fair to state that a light of three to four times that of the ordinary flat-flame burner is obtained at a less annual cost. I desire here to state that it would be easy to so leave the mantles on these lamps that an actual saving, or at least no additional expenditure, could be shown for a year's working, but I am afraid the lighting of the streets would then hardly meet with the approbation of the committee.

In comparing the relative annual cost of a single incandescent burner in place of an ordinary flat-flame burner as used by the vestry Mr. Weston found that a saving in gas amounting to 7s. 11d. in the first year and 9s. 10d. in the second year is effected, but that the additional cost for mantles and the upkeep of incandescent burners generally was respectively £1 9s. 1d. and £1 2s. 1d. for the first and second years. Deducting the amount saved in gas from these items of additional expenditure, Mr. Weston gets for the first year £1 1s. 2d., and for the second year 13s. 1d., as the total increased cost per lamp per annum by the adoption of these burners. Obviously, when the extra cost of mantles does not exceed the amount saved on gas the expenditure will be equal in both cases, and it is estimated that for this to take place the cost of mantles, rods,

chimneys, &c., and extra labour and attention, must not exceed 8s. 10½d. per annum—the average of 9s. 10d. and 7s. 11d., the amounts saved in the first and second years respectively. This, with mantles costing 1s. 2d. each, does not allow for many breakages in the year. It should be mentioned that the burners on trial are of the earliest pattern, and, as Mr. Weston remarks, many improved patterns have since been introduced which would, no doubt, reduce the number of breakages of mantles. It may be admitted that incandescent burners of any pattern are far behind the ordinary simple burner for withstanding the hard and rough usage of street lighting; but the question is, Does the improved light outweigh any objections which may be urged against the system ? To this question Mr. Weston does not seem to give a very definite answer. He points out that to get the best results from incandescent burners only specially-constructed lanterns should be used, those used in Paddington being ill-adapted to obtain the highest efficiency. In one respect the trial was favourable to the incandescent system, the thoroughfare in which the experiment was made having a small amount of light traffic only. Mr. Weston, in conclusion, expresses a decided opinion that the adoption of any of the latest pattern of burners in any quantity would not reduce the cost for mantles and labour to 8s. 10½d. per lamp per annum, assuming, that is. that the mantles are kept in a proper state of efficiency. This is equivalent to saying that the lamps fitted with incandescent burners would cost more per lamp per annum than those with ordinary burners, but would give additional light; or, in other words, if the vestry wish to increase the lighting of any street or district by substituting incandescent for ordinary burners they must pay more for it.

\* \* \*

**Sewage Disposal and Bacteriology.** About two years ago Mr. Thudichum read a paper before the Society of Engineers on "The Ultimate Purification of Sewage." The new methods were not so familiar then as now, and, not having been tested to the same extent, they were viewed with a good deal of scepticism. Wherever there is scepticism there is naturally a certain amount of hostility, and Mr. Thudichum had to face some adverse, and it may be rather harsh, criticism. On Monday he again read a paper before the same society and on the same subject, but dealing, of course, more particularly with recent developments in connection with the septic tank system and that associated with the name of Mr. Dibdin. Among the audience on Monday were some of those who had severely condemned two years ago, but who now found themselves able to view the new methods from a much more favourable point of view. The approval expressed may not have been of a specially enthusiastic order, and was at times accompanied by certain reservations; but, nevertheless, it was significant enough. In this connection the remarks of Mr. Baldwin Latham were specially interesting. The most adverse criticism came from Mr. C. H. Cooper, of Wimbledon, who still maintains an obstinate disbelief in the statement that the Barking filters dealt with sewage at the rate of 1,000,000 gallons per acre in twenty-four hours. But in view of the express, and naturally somewhat indignant, declaration made by Mr. Thudichum on Monday, we think the figures may safely be accepted and the matter allowed to rest. Now that bacteriological methods are meeting with approval from engineers generally, the time may possibly not be far distant when even the Local Government Board will relax somewhat. The verdict of the Royal Commission now sitting will be awaited with no small interest, but one of the speakers on Monday no doubt expressed a very general feeling when he remarked that it was not conceivable that the commission could fix upon one particular system as applicable alike to the needs of every district apart from special local conditions.

## The Birmingham Water Scheme.—II.

BY JAMES MANSERGH, M.INST.C.E.

SUBMERGED DAM CULVERT IN COURSE OF CONSTRUCTION (December, 1896).

### CONSTRUCTION OF THE DAMS.

In this country hundreds of impounding reservoirs have been constructed for the storage of water for canal purposes and for town supply, and a very large majority of these have banks of earth supporting an internal wall of puddled clay, which forms the watertight part of the barrier. Underground watertightness is secured by a tongue of concrete 6 ft. thick founded on impervious shale; above, a puddle wall resting in a concrete shoe is carried up to nearly top bank with supporting earth on each side. In this case we had to go down 70 ft., in the middle of the valley and over 150 ft. at the sides to obtain a watertight foundation. There are still only very few stone dams of any great size in England, although many are to be found on the continent of Europe. The Elan and Claerwen valleys were, however, practically adapted for such structures, the dam sites being all on rock, practically to the surface, and plenty of stone for building at no great distance, the material for earth banks being, on the other hand, deficient.

Mr. Mansergh then exhibited views of various dams. The Abbeystead dam is a small work of the class above referred to, and was built by him nearly twenty years ago to take the place of a much smaller structure erected by Sir Robert Rawlinson in 1852. It is the dam of the Lancaster Corporation's compensation reservoir on the river Wyre, the capacity of the reservoir being 180,000,000 gallons and its drainage area 12,000 acres. The water has gone more than 4 ft. deep over the crest of this overflow. The dam of Lake Thirlmere, in connection with the Manchester waterworks, was constructed by Mr. W. Hill, and the Vyrnwy dam of the Liverpool waterworks by Messrs. Hawksley & Deacon. In showing interesting cross-sections of the Caban dam, in the Elan Valley, and of the Bouzey dam, near Epinal, in France, which failed three years ago with such disastrous results, Mr. Mansergh drew attention to the relative thickness of the walls at the same depth below the water surface, which, of course, determines the pressure. In the Bouzey dam, continued Mr. Mansergh, the line of stress, instead of being within the middle third of the profile—as it should be—

was very much nearer the downstream face at the point of failure; the weight of the structure was under 130 lb. per cubic foot, and neither the stone nor the mortar of which it was built was of good quality. The failure was, no doubt, due to the fact that when the reservoir was full the water-face of the wall at the point of fracture, owing to the improper form of cross-section, was subjected to a tensile strain which the material was not competent to bear. This strain Prof. Unwin has calculated at 1¼ ton per square foot, which was sufficient to make a horizontal tear or rent along the back of the wall. Once this was made the water would enter it and, acting upwards as a wedge, widen the rent and ultimately overturn the part of the wall above, cutting it right across vertically at each end of the disturbed part—a length of about 190 yards.

The structure of all the walls in the Elan valley will be identical in character; they are being formed of blocks of stone ("plums" as the men call them) practically unhewn, varying from 5 yards or 6 yards to as many tons in weight, built so as to avoid horizontal bedding planes, but with good vertical bonding, and embedded in and surrounded by a matrix of high-class Portland cement concrete. Both the up and down stream faces are being finished with heavy broken coursed and rock-faced grit, or conglomerate blocks closely jointed. The stone weighs about 170 lb. per cubic foot, and the concrete about 146 lb., and we are aiming at getting a little more than half the mass of "plums," so that the finished weight of the dams shall be as nearly as possible 160 lb. per cube foot.

The design of the walls is such that no effective tensile strain can ever come upon their water faces; but if it did, the structures as put together will resist a tensile strain of at least 12 tons per square foot. When the Caban reservoir is full the total water pressure against the exposed face of the dam will be about 60,000 tons. The work is being so built that there shall be no interstices in it, and that each dam, when furnished, shall be to all intents and purposes a monolith, only movable by some great convulsion of nature. Without reckoning anything for the cohesibility of the structure, but only considering the weight the factor of safety against overturning (as did the Bourzey) is from three and a half to four.

The drainage area above Caban Coch in by far the largest that has been hitherto dealt with in this country in construct-

CRAIG GOCH CULVERT OUTLET (February, 1898).

ing works of this character. Deducting the reservoirs, the Manchester Thirlmere area is 11,000 acres, the Liverpool Vyrnwy 22,000, and this is 44,000. The provision to be made for passing flood waters during the execution of the works is consequently a very important matter.

FLOOD WATERS.

Proceeding to describe the way in which they dealt with a flooded condition of the river during construction, and how flood water would be disposed of when they came with all the reservoirs full, Mr. Mansergh said : First of all we cleared out of the bed of the river on and for some distance below the base of the wall a very great number of large boulders and some rocks *in situ*, in order to enable the water to run freely away. We then erected a concrete and timber stank on the Breconshire side of the river, to exclude the water and thus allow of the excavation for the foundation of that end of the wall being got out and the base of the wall and the Brecon culvert built. This has all been done, the wall having been carried up to 730 ordnance datum, or 30 ft. above the bed of the river, the water passing meanwhile along the left side of its old course. We have now completed a similar

stank on the Radnor side, and nearly finished getting out the foundation inside of it, and the building of the wall and the Radnor culvert is being proceeded with. When this is finished a stank of concrete will be erected up to the level of 730, abutting against the wall at the upper and inner end of each culvert.

This stank being finished, we shall be in a position to impound water behind it to the extent of 240,000,000 gallons and to charge the two culverts (which are 16 ft. in diameter) under a head over the centre of 22 ft., and this combined storage and power of discharge through the culverts will enable us to pass a maximum flood without interfering with the conduct of the works. The excavation for the foundation of the central part of the wall can then be got out and the wall be built between the two ends (which are being finished

NANTGWILLT.

with vertical joints, dovetailed in plan) up to 730, after which the remaining 92 ft. of the wall can be erected without further trouble. When the wall has been finished to its full height the inlet ends of the two culverts will be closed.

Whilst they are performing their function of passing the river in its normal state and during floods they are fitted with

CAETHON SYPHON STREAM CROSSING, LOOKING EAST (February, 1897).

cast-iron trumpet or bell-mouthed inlets to facilitate the entrance of the water. At the proper time these castings will be removed, and the face plate to which they are attached will then become the seating of a steel caisson, which will be lowered into its place by means of guides previously fixed and drawn home so as to form a watertight junction by bolts inside. These doors, or caissons, are competent to bear the

CAETHON SYPHON STREAM CROSSING, LOOKING WEST
(February, 1897).

pressure due to a full reservoir—viz., about 560 tons—and under their protection the pipes, with their valves, will be laid in the culverts for conveying the compensation water to the measuring chambers outside. Afterwards each of the caissons will be reinforced by a mass of concrete and brickwork inside the culvert, so that there may be no risk of the perfect and permanent soundness and watertightness of the stop.

In connection with the measuring apparatus there will be self-recording gauges and testing chambers, and turbines, driven by the compensation water, actuating accumulator pumps for working the hydraulic valves and dynamos for electric lighting. With a full reservoir the passing of the 27,000,000 gallons a day of compensation water will give about 650 horse-power gross. When the reservoir is full the water will overflow the whole 600 ft. length of the wall; unimpeded in any way, at the time of a high flood the depth will be about 3 ft. on the crest. This will be a magnificent sight, which I hope some of us may live to see. On each side of the valley a channel, lined with masonry and concrete, will be constructed in front of the ends of the main wall to conduct the water harmlessly down and train it into the main channel

FRYDD WOOD DINGLE CROSSING (July, 1896).

of the river, which will be enclosed within masonry side walls 150 ft. apart.

At the dams higher up the river similar means are being provided for the passing of flood waters, modified, of course, to meet the circumstances of each case. The Craig Gôch dam is to be built on a curve in plan—all the other main drains being straight—and will have a roadway carried over it on arches. The submerged dam will also have a road over it, and as upon it must be laid a railway for the conveyance of materials up the Claerwen valley, its left bank end must be built on a practicable railway curve.

Before closing this much-condensed description of the general scheme and the works in the valley I should like to say that out of the 45,562 acres of the collecting area probably 40,000 consist of open mountain pasture or moorland, carrying not more than one small sheep per acre. In the lower parts of the valleys there is some cultivated land, which will for the most part be occupied by the reservoirs, roads and railway, the small farmsteads being submerged, and all trees and fences being removed below top-water level of the reservoirs. Practically the whole area will be expropriated, only the cottages of the very few shepherds needed being left. The old manor house of Nantgwillt will be submerged, and also Cwm Elan House, for a while the residence of Shelley, and the very small Nantgwillt church and a Baptist chapel, from the graveyard of which the remains of between

sixty and seventy bodies have been removed and reinterred near a new chapel erected below Caban Côch. The chapel, after having its roof riddled with holes by the blasting operations in the Careg-Ddu trench adjoining, has been repaired and converted into the Cwm Elan Literary Club, supported by the assistant engineers and the book-keeping staff.

### THE AQUEDUCT.

I will now shortly describe the course and mode of construction of the aqueduct. As has already been stated, it commences in the side of the Caban Coch reservoir, above the submerged or Careg-Ddu dam, and terminates in the Frankley service reservoir, nearly 74 miles distant. At its inlet there will be a tower containing the controlling valves and simple screens to keep out floating matters. The aqueduct goes immediately into tunnel, 1¼ miles in length, through the Feel, and emerges on the side of the hill about 800 yards below the Caban dam. At about 4½ miles is crosses over the Mid-Wales Railway, where that line is in tunnel, and at 5 miles under the river Wye, a little south of the small town of Rhaydder. At 10 miles it passes the village of Nantmil, and at 17 goes under the Central Wales Railway at Dolau, where it enters a tunnel 4¼ miles long.

At 26 miles it is just south of Knighton, that point being at the east end of another tunnel, 2½ miles long. At 35 miles it crosses over the river Teme, south of Leintwardine; then runs along Bringwood Chase to just south of Ludlow, where it again crosses the Teme. At 52½ miles it is half a mile north of Cleobury Mortimer, and at 58 miles it crosses over the river Severn 3 miles north of Bewdley, where the pressure

FRYDD WOOD DINGLE CROSSING (July, 1896).

in the pipes will be about 240 lb. on the square inch. At 62½ miles it is just north of Wolverley, and at 68 close to Hagley, reaching the intended Frankley reservoir at 73 miles 54 chains. In addition to the two railways above mentioned, the aqueduct crosses the Shrewsbury and Hereford Railway at 42 miles 10 chains, the Severn Valley Railway at 58 miles 54 chains, the Stafford and Worcester Canal at 62 miles 70 chains, and the Halesowen and Bromsgrove Railway at 72 miles 2 chains. In its course it also crosses the rivers Ren and Stour, and the Teme a third time.

There are altogether 13½ miles of tunnel, 23 miles of cut and cover, and 37¼ miles of iron and steel pipes crossing valleys under pressure; a total of 73¾ miles.

The meaning of "cut and cover" is that the aqueduct is laid in ground approximately parallel to and slightly higher than the hydraulic gradient line, so that an open trench may be cut, the aqueduct built in it, and the ground filled in and restored over it to its original condition. In tunnel and cut

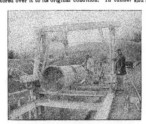

WYE SYPHON, PREPARING TO LOWER A PIPE
(February, 1897).

and cover the structure consists of blue brick lining on a concrete backing so far as the invert and side walls are concerned, the arch being of concrete only. This conduit is laid almost throughout with a fall of 1 in 4,000, or about 16 in. in a mile, the exception being in the long tunnels, which have slightly better gradients. It will carry, running something under full, 75,000,000 gallons a day, and the first instalment of 27,000,000 gallons a day will flow about 3 ft. deep and with a speed of 150 ft. a minute, taking about forty-four hours in its passage from the Elan to Birmingham. In crossing valleys below the hydraulic gradient line the aqueduct will consist at first of two 42-in. cast-iron or steel pipes, with a fall of 3 ft. in a mile, or 1 in 1,760. As the demand for water increases a third, fourth, fifth and sixth pipe of similar size will be laid.

### FRANKLEY RESERVOIR.

The service reservoir at Frankley is to be divided into two equal parts, each holding 100,000,000 gallons. The surface-water area will be 25 acres, and the depth 30 ft. The side walls will be of concrete faced with blue brickwork, a skin of asphalte coning between them and being laid also on the concrete floor.

Below this reservoir will be built a series of filter-beds sufficient in area at all times to efficiently filter all the water that is required. From a pure-water tank below the filters the gravitation mains will start into the district, and from it will be pumped such water as is wanted for a high fringe of sparsely-populated country too high to be commanded by gravitation.

## THE MAINTENANCE OF MAIN ROADS.

### AN ARBITRATION CASE AT BOURNEMOUTH.

A long-standing dispute between the Hampshire County Council and the Bournemouth Corporation, as to the amount to be paid by the former in respect of the maintenance of main roads in the borough, was recently submitted to the arbitration of Colonel Slacke, R.E., one of the Local Government Board inspectors. Mr. T. W. Wheeler, Q.C., instructed by the town clerk (Mr. J. Druitt, junr.), appeared on behalf of the town council; and Mr. Balfour Browne, Q.C., instructed by the county clerk (Mr. H. Barber), represented the county council.

### THE CASE FOR THE CORPORATION.

Mr. WHEELER, in opening the case for the corporation, said the original dispute went back to 1889, when, on April 4th of that year, the corporation, under sub-sec. 2 of sec. 11 of the Local Government Act, 1888, claimed the right to construct and maintain the roads, and to look to the county council to reimburse them for the outlay. The dispute arose almost immediately after the transfer of the roads had been taken over by the corporation. In 1890 the total amount expended on account of main roads, inclusive of footways, was £3,887 6s. 5d. The county council offered the sum of £1,415 in settlement of the claim, but when the case came on for arbitration the town council were awarded £2,608. In the succeeding four years the claims were settled amicably and without arbitration. In 1891 the amount claimed was £6,178 8s. 4d., and the amount received from the county council £4,395; in 1892 the amounts were respectively £4,736 10s. 11d. and £3,650; in 1893 £7,303 7s. 8d. and £4,000; and in 1894 £4,094 8s. 4d. and £3,230. Roughly, in those four years the cost of maintenance came to £22,311, and the amount received from the county council was £15,275, so that the corporation had borne an outlay on their own shoulders of something like £7,000. The first amount now in dispute was as concerned the year 1895, when the sum expended in the maintenance of the road was £2,963 19s. 0d.; in 1896 the total cost was £3,918 11s. 5d., and in 1897 £2,831 12s. 4d., whilst the estimate for 1898 was £4,479 6s. 0d. It would be seen that in the three years there had been expended by the town council a total sum of £9,359 18s. 9d., including a sum of £3,000 for metalling. Payments had from time to time been made on account (without prejudice) and the amount now in dispute was £3,359 18s. 0d. The cost of the repairs to footways, which was not in dispute, but which would have to be included in the award, was, for the three years, £312 12s. 11d. Mr. Wheeler proceeded to describe the character of the main road between Pokesdown and the county gates, and also pointed out that with increasing traffic came the necessity to spend more money on the maintenance of the road. He then called evidence, the first witness being

Mr. F. W. LACEY, borough surveyor of Bournemouth, who said that when he came to the town (in March, 1889) the annual expense of maintenance of main roads was estimated at about £1,300. He soon came to the conclusion that that was too little, and he put the estimated cost for the year ended March, 1890, at £1,800. As a matter of fact the actual expenditure, including establishment charges and the cost of the footways, was £3,887 6s. 5d. Up to that time the road, in his judgment, had been starved. In reference to 1895 (the first year in dispute), he said that his estimate for the repair of main roads in that year was £3,834 5s., and footways £105. The actual outlay was £2,765 7s. 11d. for carriageways, and footways brought the total to £2,922. The difference between the estimate and the actual expenditure was largely due to the weather.

On the conclusion of Mr. Lacey's evidence the proceedings were adjourned until the following day, when the whole of the morning was occupied by the inspector in visiting the locus in quo, the hearing of evidence being resumed after luncheon.

A question by the inspector at the outset of the second day's proceedings elicited from Mr. Barber, who represented the county council in the absence of his learned chief, the main grounds of objection taken by the county council to the claim made by the corporation. The materials, said Mr. Barber, were admitted, but the cost of spreading was deemed excessive; the steam rolling was agreed to; the cost of cleansing was deemed excessive; the quantity of water used was accepted, but the cost of distribution was objected to.

Mr. LACEY was recalled and examined as to details in the accounts, after which

Mr. E. PURNELL HOOLEY, county surveyor of Nottingham, was called. He said he had had frequent opportunity of noticing the roads of Bournemouth, and he had looked with a professional eye at the main road. In his judgment it was a well-kept roadway, and he did not think the cost of maintenance at all extravagant. At first £800 per mile per annum appeared a big sum to him, but on going through the items he found that the expenses were cut down to the minimum, and he did not think the road could be maintained as it should be maintained in a town like Bournemouth for less money.

Mr. SANTO CRISP, who said he had been professional adviser to the local authority at Wimbledon in the matter of the maintenance of main roads and had had experience with the London County Council, said the main road of Bournemouth was as well kept as he thought it should be kept, having regard to the nature of the locality. He had been through the items charged by the local authority for the maintenance of the road, and could find no evidence of extravagance in any particular.

At this stage the case was again adjourned until the following day, when Mr. Wheeler concluded his case for the corporation by calling Mr. Weaver, M.I.C.E., vestry surveyor of Kensington, and Mr. T. de Courcy Meade, M.I.C.E., city surveyor of Manchester, both of whom considered the expenditure on the main road very reasonable, nothing being extravagant or unnecessary, considering the continual heavy traffic.

### THE CASE FOR THE COUNTY COUNCIL.

Mr. BALFOUR BROWNE, before producing evidence on behalf of the county council, briefly addressed the inspector. His learned friend, he said, in opening the case for the corporation claimed the actual cost, but who was to say what the actual cost was? It was almost entirely a matter of estimate, and he should bring forward witnesses whose estimates would differ materially from the estimates put forward by the other side. Where the actual cost was definitely known the amount was not in dispute. Proceeding to deal with the points at issue, Mr. Browne said that the only criticism he had to offer with regard to the spreading of material on the road was as to the cost of the foreman's (or the walking gangers') wages. He contended, should be eliminated from this account and put under the establishment charges. If this item was struck out the only items in dispute were the cost of "siding and scraping, including team labour," and the cost of spreading the water. This, he urged, was extravagant. Moreover, the scavenging, cleansing, watering, &c., was largely carried out for sanitary purposes and for the comfort of the inhabitants, and this should be differentiated from watering and scavenging for purely maintenance purposes. The money was no doubt properly expended, but it should not come out of the pockets of the county council.

Evidence on behalf of the county council was offered by Mr. T. Codrington, who was the arbitrator in the dispute between the parties in 1891; Mr. J. E. Swindlehurst, city engineer of Coventry; Mr. J. Fletcher, county surveyor of Dorset; Mr. W. J. Taylor, county surveyor of Hants; and Mr. E. Bicker, of Messrs. Bicker Brothers & Pettit, accountants, Bournemouth.

## A REMARKABLE POISONING CASE.

An extraordinary occurrence was reported at a recent meeting of the Works Committee of the Birmingham City Council. The men who had been employed to clear the streets of snow were supplied with overcoats, which on becoming soaked by the sleet and rain apparently gave off a poisonous gas. As a result, a large number of the men have since suffered from poisoned hands and arms, and have been treated at the hospital. Sir James Smith, chairman of the committee, stated that about sixty of the corporation employees had complained of the effects of the chemical dressings of the coats and overalls. An examination of the coats has been made by Dr. Hill, medical officer of health, who reports that the cloth contains chloride of zinc.

**Blackfriars Bridge.**—A correspondent of The Times writes: "Owing to there being no catch-pits at the end of the northern slope of Blackfriars Bridge, the whole of the dirty water and mud draining from this portion of the bridge in wet weather is allowed to flow across the footpaths leading to New Bridge-street, on to the Embankment on the one side and towards Queen Victoria-street on the other, with a result that (to the annoyance and detriment of) hundreds of foot passengers, well and badly shod, have to wade through a stream of water or a quagmire of mud, and the footpaths adjoining become in a like state. Surely this state of things might be altered."

# Comparative Reports of General Practice.

## XXX.—TRAMWAY TRACTION : WEST BROMWICH REPORT.—IV.

### KIDDERMINSTER AND STOURPORT.

The new tramway which has just been opened between Kidderminster and Stourport forms what is known in America as an "inter-urban line." It commences at Somerleyton-avenue, about half a mile in an easterly direction from the Great Western station at Kidderminster. The line passes by the station and traverses the principal streets of the town, and proceeds in a southerly direction along the Stourport-road. The line enters Stourport from the north, and crosses the town ends in Bridge-street close to the bridge over the river Severn.

*Permanent Way.*—The line is a single track, with numerous passing places, and has a length of 4½ miles, the gauge being 3 ft. 6 in., and the rails are of the girder type, 75 lb. to the yard. In the borough of Kidderminster the line has been laid as an ordinary tramway, upon a bed of concrete 6 in. in thickness. Between the rails and for 18 in. on either side it is paved with 3-in. by 5-in. Clee Hill granite setts. Along the Stourport-road the line, with the exception of one short length, is laid on the north side of the road ; and here the rails are laid on transverse creosoted sleepers, and the space between the rails and on each side is made up with macadam. Considerable road improvements have had to be made by the company in order to leave a clear carriageway for the ordinary traffic of the road. This has necessitated the widening of the road and also of three bridges.

*Conducting System.*—The two trolley wires are suspended at a height of 21 ft. from the ground, at the side of the road, from bracket arms attached to a single line of posts, which are placed at average intervals of 150 ft. These poles are in one length and stand 22 ft. above the ground, and are bedded in concrete to a depth of 6 ft. below the surface of the road. The lengths of the bracket arms vary considerably, the longest being 8 ft. 6 in. and the shortest 2 ft. 6 in. They are of plain but neat design, and were manufactured by Messrs. James Russell & Sons, of Wednesbury.

*Rolling Stock.*—The rolling stock consists of six closed motor cars with a carrying capacity of twenty-four passengers, and three open cars carrying forty passengers. The motor cars weigh 6½ tons and the trailer cars 4 tons. Each motor car is equipped with two 15 horse-power motors, and they are each lighted with ten 16 candle-power incandescent lamps, arranged in two circuits of five lamps in series. Inside the cars there are three clusters of lamps, one containing four lamps and one containing two lamps, and there is also a headlight projecting above the hood or roof of the car. The cars are mounted on brill trucks, and this is the first tramway in this country with rolling stock entirely equipped with this kind of truck. There are no top seats to the cars, and on each end of the motor car is an enclosed cab, which presents a very great improvement on the present class of tramway cars. The speed of the cars is 8 miles per hour in Kidderminster, and in certain streets in Stourport the rate is reduced to 5 miles per hour, but 15 miles when travelling between the two towns. They stop when required, but have regular stopping places, and the through fare, a distance of 4½ miles, is 3d., with 1d. sections. There is a half-hour service in the morning, and twenty minute service in the afternoon, but on market days and holidays there is a quicker service when necessary. The company carried in Whit-week, the first week it was opened, 47,000 passengers.

*Power Station.*—The power station and car-shed is about a mile from Kidderminster, and contains two Babcock & Wilcox boilers, two 200 indicated-horse-power engines of the Raworth type, and they are direct coupled to 6-pole compound dynamos manufactured by the Brush Electric Engineering Company. The station is simple in construction, but contains all that is required for the working of the line.

*General Notes.*—The sub-committee were extremely pleased with the ease, comfort and absence of oscillation when riding in the cars, and believe that ears of this class would be found very serviceable in West Bromwich. The saving of time by using the trailer instead of the old-fashioned type deckers will be no doubt considerable, both for passengers and conductors. The line has been constructed by the British Electric Traction Company, which is the same company at present working the Wednesbury line, and the one proposing to take over the South Staffordshire Company.

### COVENTRY.

*Permanent Way.*—The Coventry overhead electric line commences at the London and North-Western Railway station, and continues to Bedworth, a distance of about 6 miles. It is a single line with passing places, the gauge is 3 ft. 6 in., and the old lines are used, which were originally constructed for steam traction and have been down fourteen years. The rails weigh 85 lb. to the yard. The route is along macadam roads, but in all cases the track is paved across and for 18 in. on each side of the rails.

*Conducting System.*—The trolley wire is suspended at a height of 21 ft. from the ground by insulators attached to the ends of tubular poles, known as the span-wire system. Side poles are also used, and in some of the narrow streets the wires are fastened from house to house with rosettes, with the result that the overhead construction is scarcely observable and certainly not offensive. On the other hand, the span-wire system is much more objectionable than the single poles, in that extra poles are required and also more wires. The feeders are also carried above ground from pole to pole. The poles are placed 120 ft. apart, as in other towns, but none are used for street-lighting purposes, the tramway being in the hands of a company who have obtained a lease for another twenty-one years.

*Rolling Stock.*—The cars are of two sizes. There are six large ones, weighing about 7 tons, and capable of holding fifty-two passengers, and four small ones, to carry forty passengers, and weighing about 6½ tons. They are lighted by means of lamps, and have four lights on each end. They are mounted on Peckham trucks. The speed is 8 miles per hour, and they stop when required. There is a ten minutes' service, and the fare is about 1d. per mile, the conductor and guard being in uniform.

*Power Station.*—The generating plant is situated at Foleshill, and consists of two Babcock & Wilcox's boilers and two 125 horse-power Browett & Lindley's engines, coupled by belts to two Westinghouse dynamos. The machinery is rather too small for the work it has to do.

*General Notes.*—The line has been in operation for two years, and is very popular. No accidents of a serious character have happened, and there has never been a stoppage through breakdown of the machinery. An extension is in course of construction through another portion of Coventry, and this will be a single line of a length of 5·25 miles. In this case side poles are being used. A new power-station, which will be erected, with larger and more modern machinery, to work both lines, will be almost in the centre of the district, and the existing station will be made into a car-shed. The oscillation was very great, so much so as to be uncomfortable at a high speed, and the sub-committee were informed that this was largely owing to the old steam track being used.

### BIRMINGHAM (CABLE TRAMS).

The cable line belonging to the City of Birmingham Tramways Company (as is well known to the members of the committee) runs from Snow-hill to New Inns, Handsworth, a distance of 3 miles, and is a double track. The gauge is 3 ft. 6 in., and the rails weigh 92 lb. per yard. The line was constructed in 1888. The paving on each side of the rails is wood, but between the lines granite setts. The motion is obtained by attaching the cars, by means of a gripper worked by the driver, to an endless moving cable formed of steel wires with a rope centre, and running in a conduit laid in the centre of each pair of rails. In the top of the conduit is a slot, with opening ¾ in. wide, through which the gripper passes. The action of the gripper somewhat resembles that of the human hand clutching a rope. The cable is guided at curves and gradients, or changes of gradient, by pulley wheels fixed at the sides or in the bottom of the conduit. The depth of the conduit is 2 ft. 7 in. from the surface.

*Power Station.*—The cables pass, near the centre of the route at Hockley brook, into and out of the power-house, where they wind round large drums or pulley-wheels driven by steam engines. These are two single-cylinder horizontal high-pressure engines of 250 horse-power each, both geared on to one set of driving drums. One of the engines is being replaced with a 370 horse-power Galloway's compound condensing engine. Only one engine is used to run the full service of cars (about twenty-seven), except in very heavy snowy weather, when at times it has been found necessary to run both engines. There are two cables, with lengths of 4,666 yards and 6,340 yards, the weight of the two being 27 tons 5 cwt. The cable has to be renewed about every nine months on the city portion and every twelve months on the Handsworth portion, and they cost £300 and £400 respectively.

*Rolling Stock.*—There are thirty-two cars, each mounted on bogies, and carry forty-four passengers—twenty inside and twenty-four out. They weigh 6½ tons, and are lighted with compressed gas. Cars run every one and a half minutes ; the speed is 7 miles per hour in the city and nine miles in Handsworth. The cars stop when required, and the charge is 1d. per mile. Very few accidents have occurred.

*General Notes.*—The financial results of this mode of traction have been very satisfactory to the company. There is a constant and very observable humming noise in the streets while it is working, and the presence of the third rail is very objectionable ; but the objections to the cable system generally are fully set forth in the general conclusions. As the adoption of the cable system was largely experimental, the Birmingham Corporation (who constructed virtually all the lines in the city and leased them to the company at a yearly rental, and the cost of repairs is also paid by the company, the work being done by the corporation) were unwilling to incur any financial responsibility in connection therewith, and it was therefore arranged that the tramway company should enter into a contract in the usual way for the construction of an ordinary tramway along the route, having permission to adapt the tramway at their own cost to cable traction. The extra cost of so adapting the line—*i.e.*, construction of conduit, pulley pits, manholes, alteration of gas and water pipes, besides the erection of the power station and provision of machinery—being paid for by the company.

BIRMINGHAM (ELECTRIC ACCUMULATOR SYSTEM).

The Birmingham Central Tramway Company possesses the unique distinction of combining under one management tramways worked on four different systems. The Bristol-road electric accumulator system has been in operation since 1890. It extends from a point in Navigation-street, near its junction with John Bright-street, where the steam tramway terminates, and adjacent to the London and North-Western Railway station, through Bristol-street and Bristol-road to Bournbrook, a distance of 3 miles, and is a double track throughout. All the gradients and curves, except two or three, are comparatively easy. The rails are steel girder type, 92 lb. to the yard, and the space between and for a distance of 2 ft. on each side is paved with deal blocks.

*Power Station.*—The power station, which forms one of the most important features, is situated at Bournbrook. It is built of brick, and covers some three-quarters of an acre. There are three boilers—two of Davey & Paxman's and one of Babcock & Wilcox's. The two engines are compound engines made by Messrs. Davey & Paxman, and there are two Elwell & Parker dynamos.

*Rolling Stock.*—The cars, of which there are seven, have a capacity of fifty passengers—twenty-four inside and twenty-six out—and weigh, when loaded, 12 tons. The body is mounted on a pair of bogies, one of which is fixed a 15 horse-power motor. It can be driven from either end, and by means of suitable switching apparatus any required speed or power can be obtained without the use of the resistance, which would entail a loss of energy. The cars are lighted by electric lamps from the accumulators. The accumulators are carried under the seats, and are charged at the depot, the charge being sufficient for a journey of 21 miles. There is a regular ten minutes' service, and the fares range from 1d. to 3d. for the entire distance. The cars travel at a speed of 8 miles per hour, but slower up hills—about 6 miles per hour.

*General Notes.*—Many minor objections against this system may be named. The vibration rapidly destroys the batteries, and at times causes an objectionable smell. Complaints have been made that the acids have discoloured and destroyed the clothing of passengers, and claims have been made against the company on account of damage sustained from this cause. The acids have a very injurious effect on the cars themselves, and destroy the woodwork—the life of the bottom of the cars being only four years—the ironwork and the floors; and, in consequence of the fumes from the acid, which discolours the paint, it is very difficult to keep the cars from looking shabby. The accumulator system is very far from being a success commercially, the maintenance being very heavy, and the sub-committee do not recommend its adoption in West Bromwich.

## GIBRALTAR SANITATION.

Gibraltar is now in possession of a proper system of drainage. The new sewer has involved an immense amount of labour and skill during the two years or so of its construction. It is of solid concrete, and high enough for a man to walk erect through its entire length of 2 miles from the north end of the town to the southern outlet at Europa Point, where all the matter is carried away into the waters of the Mediterranean. The pumping engines and machinery are fine specimens of British handiwork, from the firms of Crossley (Manchester) and Schorm (London) respectively, and are situated at the north end of the garrison. By means of a tank of large capacity, fitted with flood-gates, some hundreds of tons of water are discharged with tremendous force through the sewer at each flushing, which is carried to the sea outlet in five minutes. It now remains for the Sanitary Commissioners to see that the catch-pits and connections from the houses to the sewer are kept clean, and then, doubtless, all the bad odours for which "Gib." has been noted in past years in her streets will be a thing of the past, together with the periodical outbreaks of fever that must have increased the death rate, which should be very low in such a mild climate.

**Light Railways.**—Applications for light railways are received by the Light Railway Commissioners twice a year—in the months of May and November. The applications received in November amounted to fifty-four, under which it is proposed to construct 492½ miles of line, at an estimated cost of £3,344,563. This estimate is for construction only, and does not include the cost of plant and rolling stock for their equipment. This is the largest number of applications that has yet been received by the commissioners in any one half-year. The total number of applications previously received in the four half-years since the appointment of the Light Railway Commission in 1896 amounted to 121 for 1,302¼ miles of line, at an estimated cost of £7,555,976 for construction.

## IDEAL LONDON.

At Toynbee Hall, on Saturday evening, a lecture was delivered by Mr. Frederic Harrison on the subject of ' Ideal London."

By " Ideal London " Mr. Harrison said he meant " London as it might be, as it should be, and as it shall be." The true ideal was no idle dream, but the justification of study and the motive of all useful endeavour. London was his birthplace, and for nearly sixty years had been his home. For two generations he had watched its growth and rebuilding; and as a member of the county council he had experience of the practical difficulties of making improvements. In suggesting the ideal London he should try to keep within the bounds of practical statesmanship; but he was not bound by limits of time or by the exigencies of existing prejudices and legislation. An ideal London should contain all that pertained to pure and perfect citizenship. Now modern civilisation had failed to carry on some of the best elements of city life as known to the ancient and mediæval worlds. London did not inspire in Englishmen the feelings which Athens, Rome, Florence and Venice excited in their citizens. It was now valued as a market, an exchange, an office, or a playground, though that had not always been the case. But a city that covered 120 square miles of buildings was not a city, but a wilderness of houses, and city life was impossible for a population of 4,000,000 or 5,000,000. People must be within walking distance of the country, or the town became a prison and not a city. Therefore ideal London would not exceed 2,000,000 inhabitants—and it would be better with only 1,000,000—and it would be but a third of its present size. He was no lover of the tenement or flat system, but it was absolutely necessary if a great city were not to grow to unmanageable bulk. London at present had no ideal tenements, and few satisfactory ones; but when spacious, airy, clean and lofty blocks, provided with common libraries, baths, play-rooms and sick-rooms, were available the economy of such wise co-operation would leave room for boulevards, parks, gardens and playgrounds. He repudiated the idea that London would go on increasing at its present rate, for he was sure that the causes which had led to that increase were only temporary. In ideal London the Thames would run as clear as at Henley, and again it would be the great highway of traffic. The bridges would be doubled in number, and the disfiguring railway bridges would have to be suitably treated. Steam engines would probably be prohibited within the City, and the air would cease to be polluted by the poisonous fumes of millions of chimneys. It was really strange how long we had allowed preventable nuisances to choke us. A pure and unlimited water supply would be carried through great aqueducts, as in Rome, from inexhaustible lakes and reservoirs. This would have been done long ago for London but for commercial self-interest, political intrigue and administrative jealousy. Water, no more than fresh air, would be bought from money-making speculators. It was a prime necessity of life, and as such it was the duty of the State to supply it, pure and in abundance. Science and organisation would annually save many thousands of lives now sacrificed by preventable diseases. Already the death-rate of London had been reduced by one-half in the present century, and there was no reason why it should not be reduced very much further. With regard to the question of burial grounds, he believed that London would return to the ancient and honoured practice of cremation. This practice would obviate the danger of infection to the living and the difficulty of visiting cemeteries which could only be reached by a long and fatiguing journey. It was too much forgotten that cremation was only the scientific process of preparing the remains of the dead for disposal. The problem of the reorganisation of London had taken a new phase since London had been broken up into so many Parliamentary boroughs. He did not advocate " tenification," but he looked forward to the different districts of London, while united under a strong central government, having each a separate civic life of its own, available for all citizens within a mile of their homes and within reach of their own influence. The buildings of London, which had now neither permanence nor self-respect, would be changed in character, and be made more worthy of the genius which built Westminster Hall and the Abbey. But through all reconstruction he hoped that the historic associations and landmarks of a city which had an unbroken record of 1,000 years would be preserved, even at the expense of some regularity. New lines of traffic would be created, and the heavy traffic would be diverted to deep electric railways. With easy and open avenues of communication London might become as bright and gay, as full of fountains and flowers and statues as Paris and Florence.

At the conclusion of the lecture Mr. Harrison invited questions from the audience, and being asked how he thought the population of London could be brought within the smaller limits which he had contemplated, he replied that the efficient cause would be economic. He did not suggest any legislative restrictions, but he could not believe that London would always continue to occupy its present unique position as the centre of the financial and commercial world.

A vote of thanks to Mr. Harrison for his lecture brought the proceedings to a close.

## QUERIES AND REPLIES.

*Sketches accompanying Queries should be made separate on white paper in plain black-ink lines. Lettering or figures should be bold and plain.*

**224. By-Laws as to House Drainage and their Interpretation.**—Mr. A. R. Robinson, surveyor to the Clacton-on-Sea Urban District Council, writes: In your "Queries and Replies" for November 25th I notice Query No. 224, by "J. W. M.", relating to building by-laws and regulations I have no doubt this refers to a case in my district which is now exciting a good deal of local interest, and I should be glad to have a full expression of opinion on the merits of the case. The facts of the case are as follows: A plan for a new building was deposited and recommended for approval by me, and was, in fact, approved at the next council meeting. At a subsequent meeting "J. W. M.", who is a member of my council, contended that the plan should not have been passed, and quoted the opinion of Mr. Winship to prove it; he based his contention on the following two points—viz., (1) That every building is required to have a separate drain, and (2) that the drains, if laid as shown on plan, would form a right-angle junction or worse. A and B on accompanying plan are existing buildings, while C is the proposed new building, all belonging to the same owner. The existing drain is shown by a firm black line and the new drains by dotted lines. The existing drain is furnished with a disconnecting chamber near the sewer, and the inspection chamber shown has proper curved channels. My reply to the first objection is : (a) The buildings are within the same curtilage; but even if they were not I should not recommend a separate

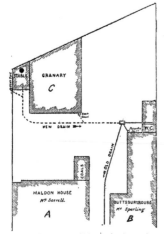

connection with the sewer, with its attendant inconveniences, such as breaking the road and tapping a pipe sewer, for the sake of taking the drainage from two gullies; and (b) the regulation quoted is intended to apply to houses, and not to outbuildings. My reply to the second objection is that branch drains running at right angles, or acute angles, may be joined by the introduction of proper bends, so as to avoid what is known as a right-angle junction. . . . Mr. Martin has not made public his case as sent to Mr. Winship, and on writing to the latter as a fellow-surveyor he declines to give his reasons for his published opinion.

We have pleasure in publishing our correspondent's communication, and in complimenting him upon the able and proper manner in which he has interpreted the by-laws in question. With regard to the opinions (1) and (2), expressed by another engineer, Mr. Winship, we may observe that neither the Public Health Acts nor the Model By-Laws anywhere prescribe "that every building is required to have a separate drain," and, moreover, such a by-law would, if made, be in our opinion, ultra vires. Local authorities frequently provide by their regulations that the drain from each house (not from each building) shall, except where the local authority otherwise approve, be connected to the sewer by a separate drain. But, even when such a regulation is in force, it frequently happens that it is impracticable and detrimental from a sanitary point of view to require separate sewer connections in every instance. If the contention of Mr. Winship were a sound one each building within the

area at the rear of every dwelling-house would require a separate connection to the sewer, which would be absurd. The mode of drainage approved on the recommendation of Mr. Robinson is correct, as the buildings are within the same curtilage. The second objection raised by Mr. Winship, that "the drains if laid as shown on plan would form a right-angle junction, or worse," is also, we are bound to observe, an incorrect one. The new drain from the stable and granary will join the existing drain in the chamber obliquely in the direction of the flow of such drain, and complies with the building by-laws. A reference to Knight's "Annotated Edition of the Model By-Laws" shows a similar mode of connection (illustrated) to that approved.

**229. Reservoir Embankments, Pressure of Water on.**—"O. D. B." writes: I have to draw your attention to a mistake in the reply to Query No. 229, in your issue of December 2nd. The vertical depth of the centre of gravity of the surface pressed is equal to two-thirds of the depth, and not to one-half of the depth as your reply stated.

We are pleased to have our correspondent's communication. The rule that is given by us is, however, quite correct, and he has evidently fallen into the somewhat common error of confusing "centre of gravity" with "centre of pressure." The centre of gravity of a right line of uniform density is the point which bisects its length; hence it follows that the centre of gravity of a reservoir wall, as stated by us, is situate at a point at half its depth. The centre of pressure, however, in a vertical wall is at a point below the centre of gravity. If the pressure exerted at different depths of a plane side were equal, the point of application of their resultant, the centre of pressure, would obviously coincide with the centre of gravity of the side. But since the pressures increase with the depth, the centre of pressure is necessarily below the centre of gravity. The vertical depth of the centre of gravity, therefore, as already pointed out by us, is at half the depth of the side; but the centre of pressure of the surface pressed is at a point two-thirds of the depth from the surface. Our correspondent has evidently omitted to notice a clerical error in our working of the example which has been kindly pointed out to us by another correspondent, "Index," and is a self-evident error from the rule given. The working should appear thus : Total pressure = 50 (length) x 20 (depth) x 10 (depth of centre of gravity) x 62·5 = 625,000 lb.

## THE SMOKE NUISANCE.

### AN ASSOCIATION FORMED.

On Monday night the Earl of Meath presided at a meeting held at 6, Onslow-gardens, South Kensington, when the question of the "Smoke Nuisance" was considered. The Chairman said that in the attempt to minimise the evil they were there for the purpose of forming an association to do what seemed best.

Sir W. B. RICHMOND, in supporting the suggestion for the formation of such a society, said the proposed body would not take over the duties already consigned to the local governing authorities, but they could assist those authorities to carry out the law at present dealing with the question. If they could strengthen and encourage the powers that be, in a very short space of time London would be rid of a considerable portion of a very serious and dangerous nuisance. It was not an æsthetic or artistic agitation, but one which was of great interest to every class and section of Society. Sir John Brunner, M.P., had written to him as follows: "My experience as a manufacturer proves to me that the evolution of black smoke could be stopped with profit, simply by taking care to burn coal scientifically. I congratulate you on having initiated this movement at a time when your efforts will be helped by the adoption, now becoming general, of gas-cooking appliances." He had received letters in favour of the movement from the Duke of Westminster, Lord Hobhouse, Mr. Ruskin, and others.

The association was formally inaugurated, after some discussion.

**Selkirk.**—The question of the water supply was discussed at a recent meeting of the police commission, when a copy of resolutions passed at a meeting of ratepayers favourable to improving and augmenting the present pumping scheme was considered. A deputation from this meeting were present and gave expression to their views, after which it was moved : "That with the view of introducing to the burgh a gravitation water supply from Lewinshope, and on the assumption that the estimated cost will be found to be approximately correct, the commissioners resolve to proceed with the scheme and to instruct Messrs. Leslie & Reid, Edinburgh, to forthwith prepare specifications and working plans and take in offers; also that all necessary steps be taken to complete the arrangement with Captain Johnstone, of The Hangingshaw (on whose ground the reservoir will be placed), and all others interested." It was pointed out that the commissioners had spent years on this question and had come to the conclusion that a gravitation supply was the best in all respects for the community. Eventually the motion was adopted. The estimated cost of the scheme is over £17,000.

# The Bacterial Treatment of Sewage.

## By GEORGE THUDICHUM, F.C.S.[*]

On the last occasion upon which the author had the honour of reading a paper before the society he dealt with the principles involved in the successful biological treatment of sewage effluents, more particularly as deduced from the results obtained from the 1-acre filter-bed at the northern outfall at Barking creek. At the same time he hinted at the advance then being made by the local authority at Sutton, Surrey—viz., the direct treatment of the actual sewage by the same agencies, but under conditions, as regards bed material chiefly, necessarily somewhat altered. The progress in this direction has since that time been remarkable, and very many authorities, all over the kingdom, have followed in the footsteps of the Sutton Council by adopting their method in its entirety.

It is not the intention of the author on the present occasion to deal with the question from its scientific or theoretical aspect; this has lately been fully discussed upon many occasions. It is rather sought to bring before the notice of the members of the society the practical outcome of a large amount of experimental work, and to show how the system can be adapted to meet local requirements in various cases, it being now evident that the general principle of biological treatment, in one form or another, is acknowledged by the majority of those practically concerned in the disposal of waste matters. The author has also no intention of entering into matters of history, claims as to priority of ideas, or even as to the relative merits of the various schemes suggested, except with regard to those two systems which are at present most prominently before the public.

During the last eighteen months the author, together with his partner, Mr. W. J. Dibdin, formerly chief of the chemical and gas department of the London County Council, has had numerous opportunities of applying in practice the principles learned during many years of experiment; and it is the general result of such practical experience, illustrated by certain concrete examples, that he now proposes to lay before the society. In addition to dealing with this matter as applied to larger communities, he also proposes to discuss the question of the treatment of the sewage of isolated country houses, workhouses, schools, asylums, or other public institutions, a question which, more especially latterly, has become of the greatest importance.

### THREE CONSIDERATIONS.

In attempting to apply the biological method to the treatment of the sewage of any given place three questions of paramount importance have to be considered; these are (1) the available fall, (2) the nature of the soil, and (3) the possibility of the sewage containing ingredients which are hostile to microbial life. The first two questions, those of fall and nature of soil, will in great measure determine, according to the author's views, the method to be adopted in the particular case. In gravitation schemes in which the sewage is delivered at less than 4 ft. above the point at which it must be finally discharged it would appear that the septic or Exeter method possesses some advantages, in that a fall is required into and out of one set of bacteria-beds only, no head being lost by passage through the septic tank, in which the preliminary solution of the solid matter is effected. It must be understood that in discussing arguments of this kind the author is not siding with the septic tank against the Sutton, nor with the Sutton against the septic tank system. He desires merely to point out what are the particular advantages of either according to the local conditions, and the final results produced by either process are in all respects comparable. If the sewage be naturally delivered at a point very near the level of the final outfall it must then be quite evident that a system requiring a fall through one bacteria-bed only has an advantage from an economic point of view over a scheme which necessitates a fall through two beds. If, however, the sewage must in any case be pumped, or is delivered by gravitation at a height above the outfall sufficient to allow of the interposition of two sets of bacteria-beds, it then becomes a matter for consideration as to which of the two should be adopted; and the decision, it appears likely, will usually be arrived at from economic reasons mainly, if not entirely.

The extent of fine-grain bed to be provided will be the same in either case; the difference, therefore, so far as first cost is concerned, will be the difference between the cost of a coarse-grain bacteria bed and of a septic tank. Where the soil is light and porous, so that all tanks and beds must be built of brickwork or concrete bottoms, it is possible that such difference may be extremely small, since the extra cost of covering the septic tank will be compensated by its being of smaller cubic contents than bacteria beds to do the same work, and by its requiring no bed material. Where, however, the nature of the soil is such as to permit of the construction of bacteria beds in the open ground, merely puddling the bottom and sides, the advantage from a pecuniary point of view is entirely with the system adopted at Sutton. On suitable land, such as the heavy clay at Sutton itself, bacteria beds can be made by merely excavating, burning the soil, laying drains on the bottom and returning the burnt ballast; and this has actually

been done at a cost, for a bed 3 ft. in depth, of 4d. per foot super, or £726 per acre. In places where the bacteria beds must be erected above the ground level, but where clay is readily obtainable, such beds can be prepared at a relatively small cost; and in these instances also the first installation will cost less on the Sutton than on the septic system.

With regard to the third point, that of the sewage possibly containing matters hostile to the growth of microbes, the author has found, as a matter of experience, that the majority of trade effluents, especially if diluted with a reasonable proportion of ordinary domestic sewage, will yield to the influence of either aerobic or anaerobic organisms. In a joint paper by Mr. Dibdin and the author, read before the Society of Chemical Industry in April, 1897, this question was specially discussed; and it was shown that bacterial treatment was applicable to sewage containing considerable quantities of refuse liquors from many trades, including, as in the case of Leeds, effluents from tanneries, galvanising works, copper works (wet process), and the solid matters from shoddy; in the case of Maidstone, from tanneries and breweries; at West Bromwich, pickle liquor from galvanising works; at Yeovil, from the yards of fellmongers and leather dressers; and in various instances in which the sewage to be treated was highly charged with refuse from gasworks, margarine factories, dairies and distilleries. Taken as a whole, the experience of the last two years goes to prove that in the large majority of cases the manufacturing refuse which may be present in the sewage does not prevent the application of the principles of biological treatment throughout; whilst in cases in which preliminary precipitation or other treatment is necessary the final purification can be best effected by means of the fine bacteria-bed, as described by the author in his paper read before the society in 1896.

### A CONCRETE EXAMPLE.

Turning to a concrete example of the advantages possessed by a bacterial process as compared with chemical precipitation and land treatment, the author would point to the Worcester Park outfall works of the Cheam and Cuddington Council, in the area administered by the Epsom Rural District Council. This is one of those cases, alluded to by the author in his previous communication, in which the successful working of the farm is rendered practically impossible by the very nature of the soil, which is a heavy clay, waterlogged in wet seasons, and in dry ones full of cracks which admit of the direct passage of the sewage effluent to the underdrains, whence it escapes, unpurified, into the brook. But it is just in such a soil that aerobic bacterial treatment can be adopted in the most economical manner possible.

The daily quantity of sewage delivered at the Worcester Park farm is about 80,000 gallons, the high-level sewage containing considerable quantities of brewery refuse, the low-level being ordinary domestic sewage. The high-level delivers by gravitation near the highest point of the farm, whilst the low-level, entering at the bottom, is pumped to precipitation tanks about the centre of the area. Two small artificial filters were also provided. The effluent produced was very bad and the general condition of the farm unsatisfactory. It was accordingly determined to establish coarse and fine bacteria-beds on the Sutton method, both sets, since the fall was sufficient, to be excavated, and the bed material to be burnt ballast obtained on the farm itself.

Pending the carrying out of these alterations it was necessary to deal by some temporary means with the high-level sewage, which was responsible for the larger proportion of the effluent complained of. The method adopted for effecting this purpose is highly instructive, as showing the identity of land treatment with so-called bacterial treatment, and at the same time demonstrating the reason for the superiority of the artificial over the natural method of rendering microbial life available for this purpose. A plot of land of about 1 acre in area having been selected, the main effluent drain was locked, and the sewage (which in order to reach the highest portion had to be backed up in the outfall sewer) was allowed to flow on to the land until no more could be received; in fact, the whole plot was considered and treated as a Sutton bacteria bed. This operation occupied about three days. At the expiration of this period the damming of the outfall sewer was stopped, and the sewage allowed to flow freely for a short time into the precipitation tanks, in order to remove any accumulation of sludge from the sewer; the backing up was repeated, and the sewage diverted on to a second plot treated in a similar manner to the first. The valve locking the latter was opened and the nature gradually discharged from the plot. The work was continued in this way, using the plots alternately, and the result was a remarkable improvement in the quality of the effluent. That which before was black and stinking was clear, and had only a slight sewage odour, analysis bearing out the conclusions arrived at from inspection by sight and smell.

Such an operation must, of course, not be looked upon as a typical bacterial treatment. The time occupied in filling the

[*] A paper read on Monday before the Society of Engineers.

bed, and consequently the period during which the organisms are submerged, is far too long, whilst the bed material is so fine that the re-entry of air is necessarily imperfect, and choking of the surface by the suspended matters in the raw sewage would take place probably at an early date. But as an object lesson it is worthy of the most careful consideration. By compelling the intimate contact of the sewage matters with the purifying bacteria, and by ensuring that such contact should be of some duration, work was effected which under the original conditions was impossible. The action of the organisms existing in the soil was controlled as in an artificial bed, and the desired result was arrived at with practically no expenditure whatever.

But, as just pointed out, such a method, however admirable as a temporary expedient, could not be looked upon as a radical cure, since the fineness of the bed material and its softness would infallibly cause a breakdown in the course of time. The bed material must be of a size sufficient to admit the passage, in the case of the coarse beds, of the suspended particles in the sewage; and in both sets of beds of the free admission of atmospheric air as the water is withdrawn. It must also be of a more or less hard and resistant nature, in order that it may retain its original size and shape and not break down into a mud. To provide, therefore, for the permanent treatment of the sewage, coarse-grain beds, having a united area of 4,500 superficial feet and a depth of 3 ft., were designed, the bed material to be burnt ballast, the whole of which had been rejected by a screen having a ¼-in. mesh; and a similar number of fine beds, with a united area of 4,950 superficial feet and a depth of 3 ft., the bed material being also burnt ballast, but in this case of a size which would pass a screen having a ¼-in. mesh, the fine dust only being rejected. The beds were constructed by excavating, puddling the bottoms and sides, and laying agricultural drains on the bottom, leading to an outlet controlled by a valve. The cost of the beds, to deal with the dry weather flow of 80,000 gallons daily, amounts to £325 only. The result of the work is what was anticipated—namely, the production of a perfectly satisfactory effluent.

A similar method will be found generally applicable on a large number of sewage farms which are at present yielding unsatisfactory results, and it is this facility that constitutes one great advantage of the Sutton system. Existing precipitation tanks can be utilised, in small part as sand traps, in the greater part as coarse beds, being converted into the latter by the simplest form of drainage being laid on the floors and by being then filled with burnt ballast, coke, or whatever material can be readily provided in the neighbourhood. Fine beds can then be constructed as indicated, and the effluent from these can then be passed on to the land when desired, or may be discharged directly into a watercourse when the condition of the crops or the soil renders irrigation useless or harmful. The immediate benefits derived from such a conversion of the method of treatment are well marked, the use of chemicals is abandoned, saving both cost of materials and labour. The collection and subsequent treatment of sludge is abolished, since there is no sludge, merely a small quantity of rags, paper, and similar matters collected by the screens, and amounting in ordinary cases to about thirty barrow loads per 1,000,000 gallons, the sludge item also making a marked difference in the working cost. There is at no time danger of nuisance arising from the works, such as is necessarily the case when sludge has to be dealt with and an effluent liable to secondary putrefactive decomposition is spread over the land; and, lastly, the crops can receive the full benefit of the manurial constituents of the sewage at such times as irrigation is wise or needful, without being drowned and compelled to grow in sodden soil by its being always necessary to pass the effluent through the land. The Sutton works themselves form a typical instance of the advantage of conversion. By the time the alterations are completed the whole cost will have been less than £2,000, whilst the annual saving in working expenses already or to be effected amounts to no less than £500, or about 8d. per head of population.

### SOME PRACTICAL POINTS.

Practical points requiring further investigation, and which can be elucidated only by the co-operation of engineers, and more especially of borough surveyors, are the questions relating to the trapping of sand, the duration of the working life of the coarse beds, and the degree of fineness necessary for the screens. In the case of the septic tank process the last named requires no consideration, as everything that is organic may be permitted to enter the tank. The sand question, however, remains, and the study of the life of a bed is passed on, though in lesser degree, to the fine beds, since the effluent from the septic tank, taking Exeter as an example, contains considerably more suspended organic matters than that from a coarse bacteria bed.

The duration of the active and useful life of a coarse-grain bed has not yet been determined; the original one at Sutton, which commenced working over two years ago, being still in excellent condition, and treating its proportion of crude sewage daily with results equally as good as those obtained after it had been in operation a couple of months. But certain important observations have been made which tend to show that the water capacity of a bed diminishes according to the time during which it is kept at work, increasing again when rest is allowed, but never equalling that of the bed in

its early stages. A considerable portion of this loss in capacity is no doubt due to organic growths in the interstices of the material, and until a certain amount of such has taken place the purifying powers of the bed are not fully developed. But there must also be a quantity of mineral matter from the sewage deposited in the bed, and much of this can never be brought into solution, and thus carried away with the effluent water. Intimately connected with this question is that of trapping the actual sand carried by the sewage, and so preventing it from getting into the bed. This is not of very great importance in the case of towns provided with a separate system of drainage; but where such does not exist, and the water from the roads is removed by the same channel as that which carries the sewage proper, it assumes proportions which on some occasions are startling. This can be well seen by anyone at the Barking outfall works, where there are thousands of tons of road sand which has been removed from the precipitation channels, having subsided almost as soon as the sewage had passed the penstocks into the channels, and had therefore ceased to flow at a high speed. The amount of such sand brought down and deposited after a single thunderstorm following a period of drought is some hundreds of tons.

It is, of course, obvious that this could not be permitted to pass on to a bacteria bed, as the choking up would only be a matter of a relatively short time; and the question to be solved is, to what rate must the flow be reduced, or how long must the sewage be quiescent in settling tanks, in order that the sand may be deposited and the organic matters in suspension left. Too short a period will allow sand to enter the bacteria bed; too long a one will permit of the subsidence of organic matter, which will result in the production of sludge, a product by all means to be avoided. The life of a fine-grain bed is, of course, not affected by similar considerations. The coarse-bed effluent which passes on to the fine contains only a small amount of suspended solids, principally organic, and silting up of the fine bed would not occur. A certain amount of loss of water capacity, due to growth, always takes place; but when the point of highest efficiency is arrived at the capacity remains practically constant.

An important point in connection with sewage treatment by any method is to minimise the attention required. In many recent cases where the Sutton system has been adopted attendance during the night hours has been dispensed with by providing a pair of beds, coarse and fine, each having a water capacity sufficient to take the whole of the night flow. Syphons are provided, so that if, owing to rain or other cause, the level of the water in the bed exceeds a certain height it is automatically discharged from the coarse bed into the fine, or from the fine on to the land.

### PUBLIC INSTITUTIONS AND SMALL COMMUNITIES.

For dealing with the sewage from a small community, such as a public school or an asylum or a small hamlet, one of two biological methods may be employed, according to the fall available. In the first method, which may be either on the lines of the Sutton or the septic system, or a combination of the two, the sewage is passed continuously through the tank, or for twenty-four hours on to a coarse bed, and then on to fine beds, where it remains for two hours and is then discharged. If bacteria beds only are employed, they should be four in number—viz., two coarse and two fine grain—each being of sufficient capacity to take a whole day's flow. The sewage, or the overflow from the cesspit where such exists, is allowed to pass into one of the coarse beds for twenty-four hours, and is then diverted to the second bed, the effluent from the first being discharged into the corresponding fine bed. Here it is allowed to remain during two hours, and is then finally removed. By this method there is no doubt far more anaerobic action in the coarse bed than is the case when the system is worked normally; but the rest, which is given every alternate day, gives an opportunity for the destruction by oxidation of the organic matters retained by the bed. The attendance required is very slight, and can be readily given by a gardener; it consists merely in turning a few valves, with an interval of three hours between the first and second operations, and in an occasional raking of the surface. If the fall be sufficient to admit of the employment of two sets of beds, the septic tank and the fine beds only can be employed; and in this case the alternating gear used with the latter is essential, as otherwise the attendance would prove a severe tax.

In the second method it is presupposed that the sewage cannot be delivered at or sufficiently near the surface to be passed on to a bed. In this case the best plan is to provide a storage tank, a coarse-grain and a fine-grain bacteria bed, each of the three being capable of containing the sewage of an entire day of twenty-four hours. At a fixed time on each day the sewage should be pumped from the storage tank into the coarse bed, should remain there two hours and then be passed into the fine bed, and after a similar period of rest in the latter be finally discharged.

The sewage from the Claybury Asylum of the London County Council has been treated by a single pair of coarse-grain bacteria beds with perfect success for over three years. At Radley College an installation has recently been completed, in which the overflow from a cesspit is treated by two pairs of beds—viz., two coarse and two fine grain. These beds are constructed by excavating, the sides being of brickwork and the bottoms of clay puddle. The coarse beds are 16 ft. by 10 ft. by 3 ft. deep each, and the fine 16 ft. by 12 ft. by 3 ft. deep each. The bed material is coke, that in the coarse beds being all rejected by a screen having a ½-in. mesh, and that in the fine having all passed a mesh of ⅜ in., with the fine dust removed. The water capacity of each bed is 160 cubic feet, that being the maximum quantity of sewage which they have to deal with daily.

It is a source of much gratification to the author that further experience has caused no alteration of the views expressed by him in the paper read before the society two years ago regarding general principles and methods of working. Much additional knowledge has been gained, and the applications of the bacterial method have been shown to be of wider scope than was at that time generally recognised; but the facts then related still form the basis on which such knowledge is founded, and the theories set forth have been only amplified and verified, without suffering any integral change. The method of working the beds, by alternately filling and emptying, allowing them to stand full for a limited time and empty for as long a period as possible, has been proved over and over again to be the correct one. Where the method of constant flow through a filter is employed the results have so far not been shown to be satisfactory. In many instances, as for example at Wimbledon, the effluent escapes from the burnt-ballast filter, surface-choked and, being cut off from air by its covering of earth, in a semi-putrid and stinking condition. This fact was noticed by many members of the Association of Municipal and County Engineers on the occasion of their visit to the farm. Whatever be the first treatment, the final purification must be aerobic; and, so far as the author has yet seen, this is best accomplished on the lines laid down as a result of the Barking experiments between 1892 and 1896.

## DISCUSSION.

Mr. BALDWIN LATHAM said that it almost appeared to be a settled matter that the sewage disposal problem would be solved in the manner suggested by Mr. Dibdin and Mr. Thudichum in the paper read by the latter before the society two years ago. There was no doubt that in this biological treatment of sewage they had an element of success which would provide a means of solving the sewage difficulty by purifying sewage before it was turned into the watercourses. He may have been rather hard on the process on former occasions, but there was no doubt that those gentlemen who were giving their attention to the matter were doing a great work. Both in regard to the septic process and that which relied on aerobic organisms, those engaged in the work were deserving of thanks. He himself had been carrying on experiments in a large manufacturing town in Central England. The result from these, he would not say filters but contact chambers, was that the effluent was equal to that obtained from the best irrigation process ever carried out in this country. The sewage in the town of Bilston was charged with salts of iron and was the colour of mahogany. When the sewage had been reduced to a liquid state by an arrangement corresponding to the septic tank, which need not be a closed vessel, it was passed on to one of those contact filters, and the effect was perfeotly marvellous. In the case of the Bilston sewage the amount of albuminoid ammonia has been reduced as much as ·03 and ·028 grains per gallon, and this from a sewage containing refuse from galvanising works and showing as much as 28 grains of chlorine per gallon. At Friern Barnet the results were not quite so good as those at Bilston. The sewage showed 1·16 grains of albuminoid ammonia per gallon and ·05 in the effluent. In the case of Manchester the sewage contained an enormous amount of trade effluents of all descriptions, especially from chemical and dye works, but after treatment by contact filters the amount of albuminoid ammonia was only ·07 grains per gallon, and the improvement was going on. Week by week the experiments showed that a process of purification had been going on throughout the whole period, and final results had not yet been reached. At Friern Barnet the amount of oxygen absorbed in twenty-four hours was reduced from 6·53 to ·30, and at Manchester from 5·15 to 1·24. The results showed that sewage could be satisfactorily treated by this method. In the districts he had mentioned there was no land to which sewage could be applied so as to produce such results. In future no chemicals would be required, and their rivers would be purified if the methods were pushed to their ultimate issue.

Mr. MAXWELL LAWFORD asked whether the condition of the Pill Brook was to be attributed to the condition of the Sutton sewage works. He believed it took the whole of the Sutton effluent. When the neighbouring golfers lost a ball in the stream they had to take it out of what could only be described as black sludge; he had, however, been told that many of the houses in Sutton were not connected with the sewers and discharged direct into the stream. That had, no doubt, something to do with the condition of the brook. In regard to the question of sludging up at Leeds, Mr. Dibdin and Mr. Thudichum had recommended, if he remembered aright, sedimentation-beds as a preliminary. A similar process had also been recommended at Choam as a preliminary treatment before the sewage went into the coarse and line beds respectively. He took exception to the statement that in the case of institutions only two biological methods were available. In addition to the septic tank system and Mr. Dibdin's system there was the system associated with the name of Mr. Scott-Moncrieff. The success of the new methods all went to show that the late Mr. Bailey Denton was quite right in saying that the final purification was effected by intermittent downward filtration. In the one case land was laid out to deal with the sewage by intermittent downward filtration. In the other case artificial filters were used for the same process. They often heard of the effects of discharging crude sewage into the sea, the sewage sometimes collecting as a seething mass. In a case in which his firm were at present engaged they had arranged, in consultation with Messrs. Dibdin & Thudichum, to put down filters and send a purified effluent into the sea. Some information was wanted as to how biological methods applied respectively to towns drained on the combined system and those drained on the separate system. In the late Mr. Bailey Denton's experience of fifty years no two towns had been treated in the same way, and he did not see that it was any more likely to be so in the future. Filters were of the greatest use to engineers generally, but he did not see that it was possible for any Royal Commission to say that one system should be adopted to the exclusion of others. He congratulated Mr. Dibdin and Mr. Thudichum on having decided to act in a professional and consultative capacity only and keep themselves free from circulars and syndicates.

Dr. RIDEAL said that a comparison of the size of filters and the number of gallons of sewage treated at Leeds and at Exeter respectively showed a slight superiority in favour of the latter place. It was desirable to understand clearly what was meant by a coarse and what was meant by a fine filter. In one case they found that a coarse bed was made up of material that had been ejected by a ½-in. mesh, and a fine bed of material which would pass a screen with a ⅛-in. mesh. In another case the material for the fine bed passed through a ⅜-in. mesh. At Exeter the material used passed through a screen with a ½-in. mesh, and was therefore coarser than that advocated by Mr. Thudichum for the fine bed. It was, in fact, intermediate between the material used by Mr. Dibdin and Mr. Thudichum for their coarse beds and that used for their fine beds. It was also necessary to consider what was meant by screening the sewage before passing it into the coarse and fine beds respectively. The figure given in connection with the Worcester farm was thirty barrow loads per 1,000,000 gallons. That quantity, therefore, would have to be dealt with in some other way. Then there was the question of sand and the utilisation of settling tanks to reduce the flow of the sewage and obtain the deposition of the sand.

Mr. E. G. MAWBEY said that it must be admitted that Mr. Dibdin and others were deserving of thanks for the progress made by them in connection with bacteriological treatment by means of artificial filters. Some of them were tempted to cling to land treatment, which had served them well. At all events they were inclined to support it as a supplement to bacteriological treatment. Great headway, however, had been made in clarifying sewage without chemicals. For about eight years they had treated the sewage of Leicester on clay land, but during the last four years there had been an enormous increase of population, to the extent of 6,000 a year, and they found themselves face to face with the necessity either of increasing the area of the land or of adopting some means of clarification. He himself was in favour of clarification, but wished to find out the best system. By the aid of an illustration on the blackboard Mr. Mawbey then went on to describe the system of preliminary purification adopted at Leicester, consisting of (1) a detritus tank, (2) a settling tank, and (3) coarse filter-beds. Since the adoption of the system they found themselves able to treat 1,000,000 gallons on 22 acres, as against 1,000,000 gallons on 52 acres when land alone was used. For final purification he was in favour of land, when there was plenty of it to be had, but otherwise they should fall back on bacteria beds.

Mr. C. H. COOPER (Wimbledon) said that the Worcester farm was drained to death, as clay grounds usually were, and such a farm must of necessity be a failure. To say that they could not treat sewage on clay grounds was wrong, as was shown by the example of Leicester and other places. He would like to know how the beds at Worcester would deal with extra rains—say five times the dry weather flow. He had had a sample of the effluent taken that day, which he would hand up to the chairman to have a sniff (Laughter). Mr. Cooper concluded by disputing the statement that the filters at Barking had treated 1,000,000 gallons a day per acre. He doubted if they had treated even 500,000, and expressed a regret that the figures given in connection with these matters could not be relied upon.

Dr. THUDICHUM agreed with those who did not think it was possible for the Royal Commission to lay down one system for all cases, but they could consider details and principles. He was glad to find that the system was meeting with so much approval, and spoke of the progress it was making in Germany, in which work he had taken a considerable part. It was one of the greatest advances in our times, but the details of one town would not apply to those of another.

Mr. PENFOLD referred to the remarks of Mr. Cooper, and corroborated the statements that the filters at Barking had treated 1,000,000 gallons per acre a day. The filters were charged twice a day, and had a depth of 6 ft. The sewage was treated chemically before it went into the filter-bed.

Mr. WM. BROWN expressed the opinion that this preliminary

treatment made all the difference. He took exception to the statement that there was an economy effected at Sutton of £500 per annum. If the original expenditure was £1,200, and there was a saving of £500, then the annual cost would be £700. But that would compare unfavourably with a system not mentioned in the paper. It was a weakness of the paper that it only recognised two systems. Before the present system had been adopted at Sutton an offer had been made to the local authority not only to treat the sewage but to keep the sewers free from sewer air for £700. The nett cost of treating the sewage would have been £600. He agreed that the circumstances of each case must determine the method of treatment. If the particulars of each treatment and cost were fully gone into, the economy would not prove to be so great.

Mr. DAWSON spoke of the efficiency of a septic tank installation he had seen at Barrhead, near Glasgow. The filters were not working, but the effluent from the septic tank only was better than what he had seen from any precipitating process. The installation at Barrhead was on the same lines as that at Exeter. Three things recommended the system. There was a small initial cost, the cost of maintenance was small, and there was no sludge. He hoped that at Leyton they would, in a very short time, follow the example of other places.

Mr. THUDICHUM in the course of his reply referred at length to the remarks of Mr. Cooper, which, he said, constituted the only adverse criticism he had received. He denied the accuracy of that gentleman's statements in regard to the Barking filters, and strongly insisted on the accuracy of the official figures of the London County Council, for which he had been himself responsible. He thanked Mr. Baldwin Latham and others for the more favourable way in which they were now inclined to express themselves in regard to bacterial methods.

## ELECTRIC LIGHTING IN SHOREDITCH.

### THE SIGNING OF THE BOARD OF TRADE ACCOUNTS.

We give below the reasons submitted by Dr. Mansfield Robinson, the vestry clerk, at a meeting of the Shoreditch Vestry on Tuesday, for his inability to sign the accounts of the electric light works for the past year. The reasons were stated in a report presented by the Finance Committee and adopted by the vestry:—

(1) The Board of Trade nett revenue account does not harmonise with the vestry's nett revenue account for the same period printed, together in the last annual report, pp. 363 and 352 (and annexed hereto), the balance of excess of income over expenditure in the account at p. 363 being £781 1s.; whilst in the account at p. 352 it is £2,063 0s. 4d. (which is carried forward to the appropriation account at p. 355 as a balance of £807 12s. 2d.). This appears to arise from treating the entry from "deficit account," at p. 352, of £1,255 8s. 2d. (being the advance by the vestry out of rates to refund the deficit on the years ended 25th March, 1896 and 1897) as income earned by the undertaking during March, 1897, to March, 1898, when no charge for the corresponding expenditure is made on the other side, whereas this is done in effect in the Board of Trade account, at p. 363, by debiting a balance from the last account of £1,281 19s. 4d. I am unable to follow how the above advance from the vestry out of rates to meet deficiencies in the years ended March, 1896 and 1897, can be called income for the year ended March, 1898, although, of course, it is properly entered under the heading of receipts during the latter period.

(2) The chief electrical engineer declined to take responsibility for the Board of Trade accounts before the Lighting Committee, on the ground that some of the items are classed under the wrong heading—e.g., there is no expenditure under the headings of public lamps, (a) to attending and repairs, and (b) to renewals of lamps, whereas it appears from his books that the first item should be £154 10s. 5d. and the second £83 14s. 1d., and, again, that the items relating to wiring and fitting work are inserted in the accounts, whereas the printed Board of Trade form make no provision for them.

(3) In view of the statements, made at the last vestry meeting, that the electric lighting accounts made up for the year ended June, 1898, were "cooked," on the ground (as I understand) that no charge for steam raised from burning refuse, or for payment of interest on and redemption of bankers' overdraft, was made, it is evident that the same allegation (if correct) is applicable to the Board of Trade accounts up to March, 1898, as there appears to be no charge made in them in respect of those items.

**Swansea.**—The Water and Sanitary Committee recently had before them the insanitary state of Morriston. It was reported that plans were prepared and approved, and that only the invitation of the tenders was necessary, for the laying down of the remaining main sewers in the locality. A resolution was adopted calling upon the Water and Sewers Committee to proceed with the work forthwith, so that the owners in the private streets might connect their property and the corporation take over the control in accordance with the terms of the Public Health Act.

## LONDON LOCAL GOVERNMENT.

### PROPOSED MUNICIPALITIES.

At the request of the executive committee of the Westminster conference—a committee on which the parishes of Marylebone, Clerkenwell, Hammersmith, Deptford, Mile End Old-town, Kensington, Westminster, Camberwell, St. Martin's-in-the-Fields, Bermondsey, and Paddington are represented.

Mr. T. W. Wheeler, Q.C., the chairman of the conference, has addressed to the Lord President of the Council a letter making certain representations with reference to the memorial recently adopted by another conference at Islington regarding the proposed municipalities for London. The letter points out that thirteen of the vestries of the larger parishes and two of the district boards designedly held aloof from the Islington conference, on the ground that it was unnecessary, and could only go again over the ground already covered by the earlier conference at Westminster. The fifteen authorities represent a population of 2,024,000, and a rateable value of £15,494,000 or 45 per cent. of the population and 42 per cent. of the rateable value of the entire metropolis. The memorial of the Islington conference stated that twenty-six of the forty-two vestries and district boards in London were represented thereat, but Mr. Wheeler's committee explain that seven of the twenty-six authorities were and are members of the Westminster conference, the majority of whom "attended at Islington, not for the purpose of reconsidering their position, but for the purpose of observation only." These seven parishes comprised 794,000 inhabitants and £6,337,000 rateable value, so that the nineteen authorities left could claim to represent at the utmost only 1,500,000 out of the 4,493,000 people in the metropolis, and £9,363,000 out of the £36,571,000 rateable value. The nineteen localities in question—Battersea, Bethnal Green, Hackney, St. George's-in-the-East, St. George-the-Martyr, St. Luke's, Old-street, Newington, Shoreditch, Stoke Newington, Holborn, Limehouse, Lee, Poplar, St. Giles's, St. Olave's, St. Saviour's, Strand, Wandsworth and Whitechapel—comprised the smaller areas with which the Royal Commission of 1894 did not deal. "It is gratifying to find, however," writes Mr. Wheeler, "that they assent to the principle of incorporation, notwithstanding that objections and difficulties might be experienced in treating them on a par with the larger areas." The letter proceeds to discuss details of the proposal for creating new municipalities, and expresses satisfaction that the differences between the two conferences on essential points are so few, the real measure of the differences between Islington and Westminster, it is said, being in truth, "the extent to which the powers of the London County Council are proposed to be interfered with, or even assailed, and this by the later conference."

## SEWERAGE AND SEWAGE DISPOSAL AT BUCKLOW.

The application of the Bucklow Rural District Council for sanction to borrow £5,524 for sewerage and sewage disposal works in the township of Dunham, was the subject of the Local Government Board inquiry which was held on Thursday by Mr. Robert H. Bicknell. Among those who attended the inquiry was Mr. J. Mackenzie, surveyor to the district council.

In the course of the evidence it was stated that the land proposed to be acquired was 10 acres 3 roods 9 perches in extent, the cost of which was £540 6s. 3d., which sum included all wayleaves for sewers, right of ways, etc. The existing filters at Oldfield have not been in operation for 20 years, and the lease of 21 years expired in March next. The north-easterly portion of the township was treated by the Altrincham Urban District Council's sewers. The Broadheath portion of the township had rapidly developed latterly, and sewers were urgently required. At the present time between 70 and 80 houses were being treated in a small temporary tank in a field, the effluent from the tank going into a ditch on the roadside, and eventually into Sinderland Brook. A memorial was presented to the Council on September 28th, requesting prompt attention to the existing state of things from residents along Sinderland-lane, Broadheath. It was proposed to abolish the existing outfall at Oldfield, and to continue the main sewer to the new outfall. The total cost of the works would be £4,984.

At the conclusion of the inquiry the inspector visited the site of the proposed outfall.

**Private Bills in Parliament.**—The time expired last week for depositing at the Private Bill Office, Westminster, and elsewhere, plans and other documents in connection with private Bills to be proceeded with during the ensuing session. The plans deposited number 363, made up as follows: Railways 58, tramways 14, miscellaneous 102, general provisional orders 75, and electric lighting provisional orders 114. The deposits on the corresponding day of last year for the session of 1898 were: Railways 61, tramways 15, miscellaneous 86, general provisional orders 85, electric lighting provisional orders 85; total, 332.

# Some Annual Municipal Engineering Records.

## WALSALL : FULHAM.

The borough of Walsall, according to the last annual report of Mr. R. H. Middleton, the surveyor, now has an area of 8,711 acres, with a population (1891 census) of 71,789. In September last the total length of sewers was over 60 miles 7 furlongs, and of surface-water drains 5 miles 3 furlongs 210 yards. The length of sewers and surface-water drains constructed and relaid during the year was nearly 3½ miles. Since September, 1892, forty-seven ventilating shafts have been erected, the adjoining manholes being closed in order to prevent the recurrence of complaints of offensive smells from the sewers. The shafts were distributed as follows: Against houses, twenty-four; into factory chimneys, twenty; and in other positions, three. The number of private drains laid and connected to sewers from 1897 to 1898 was 125. We may here remark that Mr. Middleton again suggests that all hand-flushed closets should be supplied with an efficient flushing cistern. As regards the sewage farm, the precipitation tanks and filter-beds worked in a very satisfactory manner during the year, and good results were obtained. From the monthly returns of the rainfall, as recorded by the gauge fixed at the Brockhurst farm, it appears that the heaviest falls were experienced in May, when the total reached 5·22 in. Rain fell on twenty-one days, the fall recorded on the 22nd day of the month being 1·25 in.

Streets repairable by the corporation in September measured over 64½ miles. The number of loads of materials used and refuse, &c., removed during the past municipal year were as follows: Broken stone, 5,301; gravel, 116; broken cinders, 2,526; fine gravel and binding, 1,466; rough ashes, 1,848; water, 25,966; refuse and street sweepings, 11,582; other materials, including pitching, 3,064. Materials used by contractors are not included in the foregoing. In connection with footpaths, the quantity of paving executed and materials used were: Blue brick paving, 3,817½ square yards; flagging, 781⅙ square yards; sett paving in crossings, 1,343¼ square yards; kerb, new and relaid, 2,128¾ lineal yards; gutter, 2,454⅜ lineal yards; ashes used on roads and footpaths, 1,769 loads; and ashes used during frosty weather, seventy-nine loads. In addition to the above the following work was carried out: Ashed footways, 465 square yards; blue brick paving, 5,331 square yards; new kerbing, 2,341¼ lineal yards; new gutters, 2,134 lineal yards; and new asphalte, 138 square yards. Some 4,614 super. yards of asphalte were retopped. At the end of the period under review the total number of gas lamps in the borough, exclusive of those supplied by meter, was 1,183; the cost of lighting and maintaining 1,120 of these being £2 7s. 6d. each; fifty-seven others cost £4 2s. each, and the remaining six £5 16s. each. A sum of £360 is annually spent on electric lighting. This year the number of plans of new buildings approved was 811, as against 677 in the preceding twelve months.

It is interesting to note that the Local Government Board have given their sanction to the first instalment of a scheme for the surface-water drainage of the town, and the preparation of the plans and contract is already in hand. Plans have also been prepared for the construction of three underground conveniences, and instruction given for the necessary application to be made to the Local Government Board for powers to borrow money in order to carry out the work. In addition to this estimates and plans have been prepared for the sewerage of the northern part of the borough, and they are now under the consideration of a committee. Additional stabling and a new depot are also proposed. The rubbish and night-soil department during the year dealt with 24,255 tons of rubbish and 4,756 tons of night-soil, at a cost, including the usual expenses of maintenance, of £3,281. This is equal to an average cost of removal per ton of 2s. 3·14d. It may be mentioned that the Streets Committee recently gave their consideration to several schemes for providing a refuse destructor; but efficient tips have since been found, and it has been decided not to erect one for the present. An inventory taken of the horses, carts, implements, stock and furniture in the borough surveyor's department states that there are twenty-seven horses, of a value of £879. The carts, street cleaning machines and harness are valued at £185; the steam engines and machinery at £599; tools, timber, stores, iron-work and loose stock at £499; sanitary pipes and kindred materials at £65; office furniture at £200; and the stock of market timber at £225.

* * *

Mr. Charles Botterill, surveyor to the Vestry of Fulham, has presented the twelfth annual report of works carried out in his department. The area of the parish is 1,700 acres, the area of foreshore 56 acres, and the area of tidal waters 99 acres. There is a population of 120,835, for which there are some 18,249 houses. The rateable value of the parish is £612,564. Carriageways measure about 55½ miles, and footways nearly 98 miles, there being only 7 miles of public footway without carriageway. Since the your 1886, it may be mentioned, the number of new streets made up and taken over has been 281, those having a tolul length of 25 miles 2 furlongs 131 yards. Drainage plans submitted to the vestry during the past year have numbered 813, and an increasing amount of "sewer" portions of combined drains have been laid by the latter. This heavy liability, amounting to an annual expenditure of about £3,000, is one (the surveyor thinks) which should never have fallen upon the authority. The work of maintenance, Mr. Botterill feels sure, will be considerable, as the works are nearly all within enclosed premises, over which very little purview can be exercised. Cast-iron ventilating shafts upon the walls of houses, 6 in. by 4 in. in section, have been erected by consent of the owners in various parts of the parish, making a total of 172 shafts erected since March, 1886. Good results, we are told, have been obtained, and wherever a shaft has been supplied complaints of sewer emanations in its immediate neighbourhood have ceased. The difficulty in obtaining consents is in many cases insuperable, and in most cases difficult, involving a good deal of correspondence.

Reference is made to a conference of delegates invited by the Hammersmith Vestry from the various parishes and riparian authorities from Richmond down to Wandsworth, with a view to considering the expediency of constructing a lock and weir across the Thames at a point somewhere between Putney and Wandsworth bridges. A meeting took place, at which Fulham was represented by four delegates, including the clerk and surveyor. Mr. E. Pritchard, of Westminster, was engaged to draw up a report, which he did, and presented it to the conference on October 8, 1897. According to his instructions the site reported on was by Broomhouse Dock, which did not appear to the Fulham representatives a suitable position, and on their initiative, after a view of the river at low water had taken place, a further report was submitted by Mr. Pritchard, showing the site to be below Wandsworth Bridge, at a point between the Vestry's Town Mead Wharf and the West London Extension Railway bridge. This was thought to be better, and reported upon as less expensive, and unanimously adopted by the conference at a meeting held in November, 1897. As to the final outcome of the scheme, remarks Mr. Botterill, prophecy would be futile, but the desirability of the ponding of the river between the points mentioned cannot be questioned. The conference is still at work, and hopeful of a satisfactory result.

The process of night scavenging continues to be a success (although it has been found desirable to slightly increase the number of sweepers to obtain this), and the parish has now established for itself quite an enviable reputation among the drivers of vehicles, who naturally appreciate the cleanliness of the roads in the early morning and the attention which is also given to the work of sanding in frosty weather. Wages paid to the vestry workmen amounted to £15,615 in the year covered by the report, an average of £300 6s. weekly. In connection with the removal of dust, some 27,356 loads have been dealt with, the average loads per horse being 3·887. The daily cost of horse and cart hire has been 6s., so that the cost of each horse and cart per load works out at 1s. 6¼d. The wages per load were 1s. 9d., and the cost of tip or barge per load 2s. 3d. For the work of street cleansing and slopping the following staff and plant are engaged: Seventy-four day and twelve night scavengers, thirty horses, eight horse brooms, eight horse scrapers, eighteen orderly hand-trucks, six sanding machines, thirty-five slop-carts, twenty shoot-carts, twenty-six water-vans, and two water-carts. There are about 2,500 gullies in the parish.

## ELECTRIC LIGHTING IN COLCHESTER.

On Thursday evening last a new system of electric lighting, which has been laid down by the Colchester Corporation, was formally inaugurated, and a number of shops in the town were supplied with current for the first time.

The electric light station is centrally situated, at the junction of Osborne and Stanwell-streets, near St. Botolph's station. It is a large red-brick building with white facings, divided, under one roof, into a boiler-house, a battery-house and an engine-house. Mr. Goodyear, the borough surveyor, is responsible for the very suitable design, and the work has been well carried out by Messrs. Grimwood & Sons, of Sudbury. All the appointments are of the most approved pattern, and ample room has been left for a developing business—for the enterprise on the corporation's part is essentially a business one, animated by no little public spirit. In the boiler-house are two Davey Paxman economic boilers of 200 horse-power nominal. They are lagged with asbestos and cased with enamel tiles. The arrangements for feeding the boilers are in duplicate, and there is a large condenser-pit in which the waste steam is returned to the boilers. In the engine-house, which immediately adjoins, are three 300 horse-power Pouche engines coupled direct to the dynamos of 250 amperes at 230 volts. The dynamos are each capable of supplying 2,000 8 candle-power lamps. It may be mentioned that the corporation intend to, as far as possible, utilise the works during the hours of daylight for supplying motive power, and already several orders have been received in this connection.

# For Assistants and Pupils.

## THE CONSTRUCTION OF ROADS AND STREETS.—XXII.

By WILLIAM H. MAXWELL, Assistant Engineer and Surveyor, Leyton Urban District Council.

### TOWN ROADS.

When it is found that the traffic in a road has so increased as to render it more economical and more advantageous to the public convenience, as well as to that of the residents in the road, to provide it with some harder and more durable surface than macadam, the roadway is then usually pitched with stone, paved with either wood, asphalte, brick or other suitable material.

As in the case of macadamised roads, a good and properly constructed *foundation* is absolutely essential in order to carry the weight of the traffic, the surface material of the roadway being regarded more in the light of a veneer to withstand the *wear* of the traffic and to preserve the foundation underneath.

The best foundation for paved roadways is that composed of cement concrete. This is prepared in various proportions upon "bankers," or boarded platforms, as follows: Four parts of broken stone or brick are mixed with two parts of clean sharp sand and one part of Portland cement. After being turned over twice in a dry state water is added from a watering-pot fitted with a rose, and the mixture again turned over twice in its wet state. Being thoroughly mixed, it is at once placed in the excavation prepared for the foundation, consolidated by ramming, brought to the proper level, and the surface finished with a shovel. Wood pegs are usually inserted in the roadway surface to guide the workmen in attaining the required contour and heights. The concrete should be in position within a quarter of an hour of the time of mixing.

In Liverpool another method is adopted for laying in this foundation; it is that of the *béton* horizontal wall or slightly cambered arch. Mr. H. Percy Boulnois, formerly city engineer, Liverpool, has described this method as follows*:—

"The ground having been prepared in the usual way, and the channel and kerb stones fixed in position, a stratum of stones (which should by preference be of a non-absorbent character), broken so as to pass all ways though a 3-in. ring, is spread evenly over the surface of the ground, and upon this is placed a layer of cement mortar, mixed, in the proportions of one of Portland cement to six of fine, sharp, clean gravel, in the method to be described hereafter. Upon this layer of mortar is placed another layer of broken stone—the whole of the stones in each layer to be thoroughly watered while the work is proceeding—and this stone is forced into the interstices of the first layer by the use of flat beaters of wrought iron weighing 16 lb. each, shaped like square shovels, with handles at an angle of 33°.

"This process is repeated until the proper level and contour is reached, and the surface is finished off parallel to the exact curvature of the carriageway. The foundation thus prepared is left until the concrete is sufficiently set or hardened to receive the pavement, which, if possible, should not be less than ten days, although this period may be shortened where the exigencies of the traffic render it imperative by strengthening the proportion of cement to the gravel, care to be taken in all cases to periodically water the surface of the concrete to assist the ultimate hardening, and in very hot weather it is advisable to cover the surface of the concrete with old cement bags thoroughly saturated with water.

"The proportions of broken stone, gravel and cement used in such a concrete are as follows:—

"*Before Mixing.*—Broken stone, eight parts; gravel, six parts; cement, one part.

"*After Mixing.*—Broken stones and gravel, mixed together, eleven parts; cement, one part; three parts of gravel having been expended in filling the interstices of the stones."

Another description of foundation is that known as "bituminous concrete"; it is made as follows:—

The ground is excavated to the required depth and contour, and broken stone as used for macadam is laid in for a depth of from 6 in. to 9 in., and levelled and rolled. A boiling mixture of pitch and tar, or creosote oil, is next poured over the surface to fill all interstices, and a thin layer of stone (broken small) is then spread and well consolidated by rolling. The cost per square yard of bituminous concrete foundation in Liverpool, 6 in. deep, including all charges, is about 3s. 6d.

#### STONE PAVEMENTS.

A pavement of granite setts, laid upon a good cement concrete foundation, makes the most durable carriageway that can be constructed, and is particularly suited to streets of heavy traffic. It can be used upon all ordinary gradients, is suited to all classes of traffic, and affords ease of traction and a very fair foothold to horses. Also, it is easily cleansed, and creates the minimum of dust and mud.

The objections to this class of pavement are that it becomes greasy and slippery under certain atmospheric conditions and that the incessant noise from the traffic in any busy thoroughfare so paved is a great inconvenience to tradesmen and others. It is also considered that the jar upon the legs and hoofs of horses is injurious to them.

Granite setts of large dimensions (6 in. to 8 in. wide by 10 in. to 20 in. long by 9 in. deep) were at first employed, but subsequent experience has shown that narrow setts, about 3 in. in width, are much to be preferred and afford a much better foothold to horses. The noise nuisance may also be lessened by running the joints with asphaltic composition instead of ordinary grouting.

The following useful table, given by Mr. H. Percy Boulnois,* gives the sizes of pitchers now in general use, and also shows the number of square yards that 1 ton in weight of the different sizes of setts, cubes and blocks will cover.†

| Stone. | Depth × Width × Length. | Area in square yards which 1 ton will pave. |
|---|---|---|
| Setts | 5 in. × 3 in. × 5 to 7 in. | 4·5 square yards. |
| " | 5¼ in. × 3¼ in. × " | 4·3 " |
| " | 6¼ in. × 3¼ in. × " | 3·6 " |
| " | 7¼ in. × 3¼ in. × " | 3·1 " |
| Cubes | 3¼ in. × 3¼ in. × 3¼ in. | 6·7 " |
| " | 3½ in. × 3½ in. × 3½ in. | 6·2 " |
| " | 3¾ in. × 3¾ in. × 3¾ in. | 5·8 " |
| " | 4 in. × 4 in. × 4 in. | 5·4 " |
| Blocks | 4 in. × 4 in. × 6 in. | 3·6 " |
| " | 4 in. × 3 in. × 3 in. | 5·4 " |
| " | 5 in. × 3 in. × 3 in. | 4·4 " |
| " | 6 in. × 3 in. × 3 in. | 3·7 " |
| " | 6¼ in. × 3¼ in. × 3¼ in. | 3·25 " |

The suitable *width* of a stone is to some extent regulated by the size of the horses' hoof, about 4 in. being the maximum. A *depth* of 7 in. is found sufficient for stability under any class of traffic, and the *length* should be such as to properly break joint with the adjoining stones. If too long the stones are apt to tilt and work loose. The stones should be well and uniformly dressed, so as to make as close a joint as possible, and should not be allowed to vary but very slightly from the specified sizes. The finer the joints the less will be the noise produced by traffic, and the wear will also be reduced to a minimum. In good work the setts are laid upon a cushion bed of fine sand ½ in. in thickness, so as to provide an elastic bed, and to convey the pressure equally to the foundation.

In regard to the cleaning of old setts for re-use, Mr. H. Percy Boulnois, when city engineer of Liverpool, found that the expense of cleaning off the grouting of bitumen, or cement, by hand with the sett-cleaner's hammer cost 10½d. per square yard, as compared with 4·07d. per square yard when the old setts were boiled in a pitch boiler with creosote oil heated to about 266 deg. Fahr.

Local circumstances often determine the class of stone to be used as paving material, but care should be taken that the stone selected should be hard and durable, and not apt to wear slippery, or brittle. The hard igneous and metamorphic rocks are the best for pavement setts where the traffic is heavy, but where comparatively light millstone grit and other hard sedimentary rocks are used. Carnarvonshire syenite is one of the most durable materials that can be used for heavy traffic, and most of the granites are also largely used. Of the latter, the Balbeattie granite is considered the best.

A pitched roadway, consisting of 7 in. by 3 in. Norway granite setts, laid on 6 in. of Portland cement concrete, costs about 17s. per superficial yard in the neighbourhood of London.

Penmaenmawr stone has been much used in the North, but was discontinued in London owing to its slipperiness. It is a hard and durable stone, but wears smooth and is noisy.

Aberdeen blue granite is preferred in London to either Guernsey or Mountsorrel, as it retains a rougher surface, but wears faster. Colonel Haywood's observations showed that in London the wear of Aberdeen granite pavements was from ·14 in. to ·23 in. per year, whilst the wear of Penmaenmawr and Carnarvonshire setts in the city of Liverpool, under heavy traffic, is said to seldom exceed ·02 in. per annum.

The cross-section of a paved street should have a rise to the crown of one-sixtieth the width of carriageway.

**Oldbury.**—An inquiry has been held, on behalf of the Local Government Board, respecting the council's application for sanction to borrow £3,500 for purpose of sewage disposal.

* "The Construction of Carriageways and Footways," by H. Percy Boulnois, C.E. (Biggs & Co.).

* "The Municipal and Sanitary Engineers' Hand-Book" (Spon).

† This, of course, will vary with the specific gravity of the stone.

# Law Notes.

EDITED BY J. B. REIGNIER CONDER, 11 Old Jewry Chambers, E.C.,

Solicitor of the Supreme Court.

*The Editor will be pleased to answer any questions affecting the practice of engineers and surveyors to local authorities. Queries (which should be written legibly on foolscap paper, one side only) should be addressed to "The Law Editor," at the Offices of* THE SURVEYOR. *Where possible, copies of local Acts or documents referred to should be enclosed. All explanatory diagrams must be drawn and lettered in black ink only. Correspondents who do not wish their names published should furnish a nom de plume.*

THE MAINTENANCE OF MAIN ROADS: SEA WALL. — The House of Lords, on the 25th November, confirmed the judgment of the Queen's Bench Divisional Court in the case of *Sandgate Urban District Council v. Kent County Council* (noted at p. 517 of vol. xi.), and overruled the decision of the Court of Appeal reversing that judgment. It will be remembered that this was a special case stated by the arbitrator appointed by the Local Government Board (Mr. Thomas Codrington, M.I.C.E.). The points in dispute had reference to the liability of the county council to contribute to the maintenance and repair of part of the main road between Folkestone and Hythe. In the year 1883, when it became a main road, the condition of things was as follows: Commencing at the east end or Folkestone boundary, there was private property lying between the road and the sea up to the coastguard station. Adjoining the coastguard station there was a piece of ground, formerly foreshore, which had been leased by the local board, and on which they had erected a platform paved with concrete, and faced on the sea or south side by a concrete wall, to protect it from the sea. This was sublet by the local board for the purposes of a bathing establishment. Westward of this, and between the carriage road and the sea, was what was then, and still is, known as the "Esplanade." It had been made at various times, and was of various widths. Beyond that there was a piece of land between the esplanade and the carriage road, which was laid out ornamentally and planted with shrubs. As early as 1867 the local board had repaired and improved it, for the purposes of a public promenade, by regulating the width, kerbing and paving the same throughout. Throughout the entire length it was faced by a sea wall, the outer edge of the esplanade being on the top of the sea wall. This sea wall had been erected at different times and under different circumstances, and besides protecting the esplanade and ornamental grounds from the inroads of the sea, it helped to protect parts of the carriage road also. By the award (some items of which were in favour of each party) the county council were ordered to pay £6,188 to the district council in respect of the costs incurred in repairing, maintaining and improving the road for four years, ended March, 1893. The Queen's Bench Division having confirmed the award, both parties appealed. The Court of Appeal reversed the confirmation and directed the arbitrator to find for the county council on all points. From that decision the district council appealed to the House of Lords, with the result already stated. In the Court of Appeal Lord Esher indulged in some extremely harsh criticisms of the arbitrator, criticism in which the majority in the House of Lords by no means concurred. The Lord Chancellor said that, in his opinion, scant justice had been done to the arbitrator, and those who had criticised him had not sufficiently considered the complex nature of the problem which he was called upon to determine. It was part of the arbitrator's task to deal with a part of the road which was close to the sea. He had found that this part was part of the main road. It was certainly within the arbitrator's jurisdiction to award a contribution in respect of the maintenance and repair of this portion of the road. Then there was another portion, which, though not actually part of the main road, was necessary for its maintenance, because, if not maintained, the main road itself would be continually in a state of disrepair. The arbitrator was of opinion that what was so necessary for the support of the main road was itself part thereof. These and other questions the arbitrator had treated with great minuteness, and had not contented himself with the determination simply of the total amount to be paid by the county council, and had solved the problem put before him with great care and perfect accuracy. The award had been so divided into its several items that it was possible for the Court to consider each head of contribution on its own merits. One question of law, and only one, had been raised, with which he would afterwards deal; and on that also the arbitrator had afforded materials to enable the Court to put matters right. It was a remarkable fact that the arbitrator was so dealt with every one of the facts of the case that neither party had been able to suggest any omission of which he had been guilty. The arbitrator had conclusively determined against the county council that the road was part of the main road. But it was gravely argued that there was a construction which ought not to be held part of the main road, although if it were not there the road itself would be washed away. To his mind such a contention was absurd. It was common sense that where the obligation was to maintain and keep in repair it was the duty of the persons subject to that obligation to take steps which would prevent the road being washed away. Whatever was necessary for the road the local authority charged with its maintenance and repair were bound to uphold. The arbitrator had also found that the esplanade was necessary to the road, and that there was a finding of fact with which their lordships were not entitled to interfere. The same observation was to be made in respect of the sea wall and of the groynes and as to the latter, he had been struck with the remarkable care with which the arbitrator had dealt with each groyne separately, so as to give the Court of Appeal the opportunity of discriminating between one item and another. The proposition had been advanced that nothing outside the road could be done, and that the road itself should be allowed to go out of repair every year. But that argument lost sight of the word maintain. The one solitary question of law was with respect to the annual contribution. But on that question also, in his opinion, the arbitrator had been perfectly right. There was no foundation for such an argument, and, in his opinion, the award was a perfectly good one, and the original judgment of the Queen's Bench was right.

## QUERIES & REPLIES

BUILDING BY-LAWS: OPEN SPACE: CORNER PLOTS.— "Corner Plot " writes: (1) Model By-Law No. 54 requires the space at the rear of a domestic building to contain 150 square feet, and such space to extend laterally the entire width of the building and to measure across at least 10 ft. &c. This by-law seems difficult to apply to corner plots of land which are not square. The enclosed plan marked A is a case in point. Please say in what way the plan fails to comply, and whether it seems possible to erect a building upon such a plot to fully comply with the by-law; and do you know how the by-law is applied in other towns under similar conditions?

Public Street.　　　　Public Street.
PLAN A.　　　　　　PLAN B.

(2) Suppose the premises were made into a lock-up shop, would the same requirements as to space be necessary? The building is proposed to be two storeys and 23 ft. high half way up to ... le. (3) I also enclose a plan, marked B, in which the , and floor is intended for business, and the domestic part provided on the first floor, with the bed-rooms on the second floor, the total height being over 35 ft. high. The open space at the rear contains 376 square feet. Does this plan comply with the By-Law No. 54; if not, why?

(1) *See* reply to "Urban," on p. 313 of vol. xiii. (April 1, 1898). The fact is that in framing this by-law irregularly-shaped plots seem to have been altogether left out of contemplation. I do not see how it is possible to literally comply with the by-law in the present case—that is, with any buildings as shown in the plan. And it must be remembered that unless by-laws themselves give the authority a dispensing power or discretion the authority are bound by the by-laws and cannot waive their requirements (Lumley's "Public Health Acts," 5th edition, p. 200). (2) Yes, in my opinion. See the definition of " domestic building" in by-law i. (3) I do not think this plan complies with the by-laws, for the following reasons: (a) The open space is not "free from any erection thereon above the level of the ground except a water-closet, earth-closet, or privy, and an ash pit," inasmuch as there is a coal receptacle shown. And although the area of the open space may be sufficient independently of the space occupied by the receptacle, the presence of the latter precludes compliance with the requirement that

the distance *across the open space* from the building to the boundary shall be 25 ft.  (b) The open space does not "extend laterally throughout the entire width of such building."

LOCK-UP SHOPS.—"Assistant" writes : Can you oblige me by answering the following queries : (1) Have any legal decisions been given on the point of whether the conversion of portions of existing dwelling-houses (not erected under any by-law) into lock-up shops amounts to erecting a "new building" under the Public Health Acts, the remaining portions of the building being still used as a dwelling-house ? If you know of any such decisions, please name them. (2) Would plans of a block of buildings, consisting of lock-up shops at front and dwelling-houses at rear (the houses being attached to the shops, but having no direct communication with them), be in accordance with the Model By-Laws as regards air space unless the amount of space required under these by-laws was provided at the rear of each lock-up shop, thus entailing an open space between back of shop and front of dwelling-house ?

(1). The question whether the conversion would amount to the erection of a new building is a question of fact for the decision of the magistrates.  I have not been able to find any reported cases in which this particular kind of building has been dealt with, Sec. 158 of The Public Health Act, 1875, provides that the conversion into a dwelling-house of any building not originally constructed for human habitation shall be considered the erection of a new building, but it does not provide for the converse case of the conversion of a dwelling-house (or part of a dwelling-house) into a building to be used as a shop, &c. (2) "Domestic building" is defined in the Model By-Laws as "a dwelling-house, or an office building, or other outbuildings appurtenant to a dwelling-house, whether attached thereto or not, or a shop, or any other building, not being a public building, or of the warehouse class." We think, therefore, that the by-laws as to air space applicable to new domestic buildings would apply to the lock-up shop, whether it be considered as a separate building or as an outbuilding appurtenant to the dwelling-house.

## THE SEPTIC TANK SYSTEM AT EXETER.

### A DEPUTATION FROM BEDFORD.

A deputation from the Bedford Town Council recently visited Exeter for the purpose of examining the working of the septic tank system, and the event has inspired a local scribe to perpetrate the following paragraphs :—

And it came to pass that certain elders of the city of Bedford journeyed unto Exeter, to look upon the cistern that digesteth that which the cloaca bringeth thereto. And they marvelled greatly, and said unto the prophet whose device it was, "O prophet! Is it true that the microbes rend asunder bass brooms and scrubbing brushes, bones, bottles, and date stones, so that they come to nought ?" The prophet spake and said unto them, "Behold this dead dog, to which I attach collar and chain."  And he placed it in the cloaca which passeth into the cistern that is called septic.  But the elders said, "We are sceptic."  Then did they tarry awhile, even for the space of five and twenty minutes.  When they came to the mouth of the cistern whence issues the beverage that is called effluent, and they saw two links of the chain and nought of the dog, then did the prophet fill a cruse and say : "Drink!  Let them all come!"  And they all came and had some.  Then they all with one consent said it was good, since which, in the words of that which is written, "they have used no other."

Just so, but, joking apart, it is well that councillors from this district have seen the system in operation. Theoretically, a committee of half a dozen ought to have been enough, but in a disputatious body the remainder would have probably wrangled and wasted money on useless experiments. Even this system, however successful it may seem to be, cannot be adopted without experiment. Some of the senators who have been to Exeter are still sceptical, and, since there is something to pay by way of royalty on the patents or its equivalent, let wholesome scepticism by all means be encouraged.  Some of the more enthusiastic believers in the system are talking about an expenditure which is much larger than the amount Exeter has seen fit to ask for in the shape of a loan, even though the Exeter scheme included land and a good deal of sewering as well.

## ASSOCIATION OF BIRMINGHAM STUDENTS OF THE INSTITUTION OF CIVIL ENGINEERS.

At the meeting of this association, held in the Midland Institute, Birmingham, on Thursday last, the first of the special lectures arranged for the present session was delivered by Dr. A. Bostock Hill, county medical officer of health for Warwickshire, on "Some Observations on Sewage and Modern Methods of Treatment," before a large audience. The president, Mr. J. C. Vaudrey, M.I.C.E., occupied the chair, and among others present were Messrs. J. E. Willcox and S. R. Lowcock, past presidents; T. S. Stooke, J. S. Pickering, J. Garfield, R. Angel, H. P. Raikes, A. B. E. Blackburn, and Henry C. Adams, honorary secretary.

Dr. Hill, at the outset, showed how sewage varied according to the construction of the sewers—whether they were old or modern, whether they received the storm water, whether they were constructed on the separate system, or whether they received much manufacturing waste.  The variations in quantity also depended largely on whether the sewers received the storm water.  Speaking of the Birmingham Tame

and Rea sewage farm at Saltley, he said it had for years been so overtaxed that it was no exaggeration to say that it might be taken as "an object lesson of how not to purify the sewage."  If they did, as had been done on certain portions of the farm, waterlog the land, and turn it into a filthy morass and swamp by letting sewage stand on it for days, and even weeks, it was absolutely certain that purification could not take place.  He submitted several analyses of sewage, and then proceeded to deal with his subject historically.  He pointed out how the question of the treatment of sewage became important from the time of the appointment of the Rivers Pollution Commission, and went on to show how the old views with reference to the chemical treatment of sewage were false, both in theory and practice, and were only maintained in places into which the more advanced views had not penetrated.  He dealt at some length with the disposal of sewage by the modern bacteriological methods, affirming that any system that was opposed to the principle on which the bacteria which produced resolution of the sewage depended was false and must fail.

A good discussion followed the lecture.

## LONDON WATER SUPPLY COMMISSION.

The Royal Commission held their thirty-ninth sitting on Monday, at the Westminster Guildhall, under the presidency of Lord Llandaff.

Mr. REGINALD E. MIDDLETON was recalled and further examined.  In cross-examination he said that he had not constructed any large reservoirs or a masonry dam such as that proposed to be constructed by the London County Council on the Upper Wye.  No doubt Sir Alexander Binnie's, Sir Benjamin Baker's and Mr. Deacon's experience was greater than his own.  He dared say that the whole of the line between Wales and London had been levelled and surveyed by a large staff of engineers.  The design of the Staines scheme of the Balfour Commission was that an average of 300,000,000 gallons per day should be taken from the Thames on condition of allowing a minimum of 200,000,000 gallons per day over Teddington weir.  He was aware that when the Balfour Commission reported in 1891 the average consumption in the metropolis was 29·73 gallons per head per day, and that their idea was that in 1931 the consumption would be 35 gallons.  It was quite possible that since that report of the commission the Chelsea company had increased their consumption per head per day by 9·6 gallons, the Kent by 1·51, the Lambeth by 3·18, the New River by 9·3, the Southwark and Vauxhall by 11·29, and the West Middlesex by 5·61.  He did not think it would be safer to assume that the consumption in 1931 would be 40 gallons per head.

## THE LATE MR. HENRY KNOWLES.

It is with regret that we announce the death of Mr. Henry Knowles, the head of the Albion Clay Company, Limited, the well-known firm of sanitary engineers, of Woodville, near Burton-on-Trent.  Some time ago Mr. Knowles was seized with a paralytic stroke, from the effects of which he never fully recovered.  Our readers scarcely require to be told of the success of the Albion Works, founded by the deceased gentleman, and of the many well-known sanitary manufactures associated with the name of the firm.  It should, however, be remembered that Mr. Knowles was the first to establish works in the provinces for the purpose of supplying the London market, so far as sanitary goods are concerned.  Previous to the establishment of the Albion Works the needs of the metropolis in this direction were supplied entirely from works established there.  The deceased gentleman, who leaves a widow but no children, was sixty-five years of age.  The interment took place at Matlock, where Mr. Knowles was a large property and land owner.

**Ottery St. Mary.**—At the last meeting of the district council attention was drawn to the bad state of the roads leading from Ottery station to Tipton, with the two branches leading to Metcombe.  On the suggestion of the surveyor it was decided to grant a sum of £50 to put the roads complained of in good condition.—Mr. Pope again brought forward the question of repaving the town, and moved that steps should be taken with a view to obtaining a loan in order to provide new pavements throughout the town. After some discussion, however, an amendment was adopted postponing the matter until a public meeting of ratepayers had been held to consider the matter.—A letter was read from the county council asking what steps had been taken with reference to the disposal of the town sewage.  The chairman said the septic tank system impressed those members of the council who visited the works in Exeter very favourably, but the Local Government Board would only sanction it under conditions which rendered it more expensive than they at first considered.  He suggested that the council should advertise for suitable schemes and plans, and offer a premium to the most acceptable.  A resolution to this effect was proposed and carried unanimously.

# Municipal Work in Progress and Projected.

Though news is at present rather scarce, we are able this week to publish details of several extensive municipal works, notably those at Gomersall, Runcorn, Wigan, Dudley, Manchester, Blackburn, Bolton and other places.

## METROPOLITAN AUTHORITIES.

### LONDON COUNTY COUNCIL.

The meeting of the county council on Tuesday was almost entirely occupied by the debate on the report of the Housing of the Working Classes Committee, which was left adjourned at the conclusion of the last meeting. It will be remembered that last week the council came to a decision with respect to the first two recommendations of the committee (in reference to rehousing), so they now had under consideration the third recommendation, which dealt with "housing" as distinguished from "rehousing." At the conclusion of the discussion this third recommendation was passed, but not before several amendments had been adopted, which made it read as follows: "That apart from the rehousing required in connection with clearance or improvement schemes, provided that no charge be placed on the county rate thereby, the council do approve of action being taken, under Part III. of the Housing of the Working Classes Act, 1890, with a view to the purchase of land and the erection of dwellings thereon, and also with a view to purchasing or leasing suitable houses, already or hereafter to be built or provided, for the purpose of supplying housing accommodation." The general question of the council's housing policy, it will be seen, is dealt with in our editorial columns.

*Proposed New Fire Station at Wapping.*—The Fire Brigade Committee recommended the council to agree to an estimated expenditure of £11,000 for providing a new fire station in Red Lion-street, Wapping. This was agreed to without discussion.

*The Works Department.*—On the reception of the report of the Finance Committee Mr. Westacott asked when the council might expect to have the statement of works executed by the works department for the half-year ended September 30th last, and whether it was true, as stated in a newspaper, that there had been a loss of £22,000 on the construction of the Lewisham sewer. Lord Welby, chairman of the Finance Committee, replied that the statement was ready, and would be presented next week, when the reports of the executive committees had been received. The statement would contain full information with regard to the Lewisham sewer.

*Golder's Hill Estate.*—The Parks and Open Spaces Committee recommended the council not to let for private use the house and gardens included in the 36 acres forming Golder's Hill estate, recently purchased with the object of adding it to Hampstead Heath. The committee suggested that the house should only be let as a refreshment house or for some other public purpose. After some discussion, in the course of which Mr. Shaw Lefevre pointed out that the loss to the council by making no use of the house or gardens would amount to about £1,000 a year, the recommendation of the committee was adopted.

*Housing of the Working Classes.*—The debate was resumed on the report of the Housing of the Working Classes Committee. When the council adjourned last week Sir Arthur Arnold had moved as an amendment to refer back to the committee their third recommendation, which was as follows: "That, apart from the rehousing required in connection with clearance and improvement schemes, the council do approve of action being taken under Part III. of the Housing of the Working Classes Act, 1890, with a view to the purchase of land and the erection of dwellings thereon for the purpose of supplying housing accommodation." Mr. Antrobus now seconded Sir A. Arnold's amendment, stating that he objected to the proposal of the committee on the ground that it committed the council to a general line of policy, instead of their being allowed to deal with each particular case as it came forward. A long discussion followed, in which Mr. Boulnois, M.P., Mr. Cohen, M.P., and Mr. Boachcroft supported the amendment, and Mr. Taylor, Lord Carrington, Mr. Dickinson, Mr. Phillimore, Mr. Lawson and Mr. Burns, M.P., spoke in favour of the recommendation. Eventually the council divided, with the result that thirty-six voted for the amendment and seventy-eight against. Sir J. Dickinson-Poynder, M.P., then moved a further amendment, that the words " in anticipation of " should be substituted for the words of the recommendation "apart from" the housing required. This amendment was also rejected, but, on the motion of Lord Monkswell, another amendment recommending the addition to the recommendation of the words " provided that no charge be placed on the county rate thereby " was adopted, as was a further one by Mr. Campbell giving power for the purpose of purchasing or leasing suitable houses already or hereafter to be built or provided. When the recommendation as amended was put from the chair a division was demanded, but as the " noes " failed to appoint tellers the amended recommendation was declared carried and became the finding of the council.

## COURT OF COMMON COUNCIL.

The lord mayor presided, on Thursday, at a meeting of the Court of Common Council. It was mentioned that the Streets Committee had made an application to the Board of Trade asking that department to institute a provisional inquiry into the condition of Ludgate-hill station.—The committee had also agreed that a conference on the subject of the granting of a telephone license to the corporation should be held at some convenient date at the Guildhall, and that the local authorities within the London telephone area should be invited to attend. Permission to hold the conference in the Guildhall was subsequently given, it being left to the lord mayor to fix the date.—A petition from a number of ratepayers in and near Salisbury-square, Fleet-street, asking that the existing stone carriageway pavement should be replaced by either wood or asphalte, was referred to a committee.—Authority was given for the expenditure of £200 upon a small building at Ilford for the storage of carts and fodder, and of £444 for repointing and repairing the boundary walls and fences at the City cemetery.—Relative to the improvement in Upper Thames-street, a letter was read from the London County Council intimating that they were prepared to pay their promised contribution of one-third of the nett cost, amounting to £11,413, if the corporation would undertake to complete the improvement by setting back the remainder of the property in front of No. 36 Upper Thames-street at the expiration of the lease. The court at once gave this undertaking.—They decided to accede to certain requests of electric lighting companies for sanction to their (the companies') intended applications for provisional orders for the supply of electricity within the City.

## METROPOLITAN ASYLUMS BOARD.

The managers met on Saturday, at the County Hall, under the presidency of Sir E. Galsworthy. A letter was read from the Local Government Board referring to the managers' application for an order authorising the borrowing of a further sum of £2,413 in respect of alterations and additions to the South-Western Hospital, stating that they observed that there had been similar irregularities on the part of Mr. Aldwinckle, the architect, as in the erection of the Brook Hospital, and that they would therefore omit from the order the amount which, under ordinary circumstances, would be due to him as commission on the cost of certain works—namely, £62. The chairman moved that a copy of the letter be forwarded to Mr. Aldwinckle, but it was moved as an amendment that the letter should be referred to the General Purposes Committee for consideration and report. It was, it was stated, a matter of considerable importance. The Local Government Board were taking very strong action in relation to the excessive expenditure, and whenever that department intervened it had always been in the interests of the public. Seeing that Mr. Aldwinckle was engaged in connection with the North-Western Hospital, it was thought that they ought to consider the question of his further employment by the board. The amendment was not seconded, and the chairman's motion was accordingly adopted. A long letter was read from Mr. Aldwinckle in reference to the Local Government Board's report. Although not agreeing with all the conclusions at which Mr. Knollys, the inspector, arrived, he (Mr. Aldwinckle) could not, he said, fail to recognise the inspector's manifest desire to be fair to him. He had carefully classified all the items which were authorised by or executed with the knowledge of the committee, leaving only £12,000 to be accounted for. Only two items, £655 for teak flooring and £663 for ward stoves, were mentioned as having been ordered by him without any justification whatever. There was no suggestion that there had been any waste of public money, and no complaint that the managers had not received full value for the expenditure. He was glad to have the inspector's opinion that in acting as he did he was actuated by the desire to produce a hospital of the best possible type and fitted with all the newest improvements. He did not find in the Local Government Board's letters any evidence of the fair spirit that was displayed by Mr. Knollys. The expression, " grave irregularities," should not be used in relation to an architect of his professional standing, especially as he had done so much important public work, chiefly under the control of the Local Government Board, simply because some items had been ordered by him without authority, while no suggestion was made that public money had been wasted thereby. It was admitted on all hands that the Brook Hospital was a good hospital, completely finished, and in all respects worthy of London. He was, and always should be, proud of being its architect. It was resolved to enter the communication on the minutes, to forward a copy to the Local Government Board, and to circulate it generally.

## VESTRIES AND DISTRICT BOARDS.

**Bermondsey.**—The vestry at the meeting on Monday were recommended by the Sanitary Committee to construct an underground convenience at the junction of Galley wall road and Southwark Park-road in accordance with plans prepared by Mr. F. Sumner, the surveyor, at a cost of £1,800. It was resolved to issue advertisements inviting tenders for the work.

—A further report was submitted by the committee in reference to the proposed abattoirs for the county of London. The committee stated that there were only four slaughter-houses in Bermondsey, that these received efficient supervision from the vestry's staff, and that they were not in any sense detrimental to public health.—The Sanitary Committee also announced that intimation had been given of three other sites available for the housing of the working classes, and that information to this effect had been conveyed to the London County Council.—On the recommendation of the Electric Lighting Committee it was resolved to inform the London Electric Supply Corporation that the vestry disapproved of works of laying low-pressure distributing mains on both sides of certain thoroughfares. It was also decided to oppose the application of the County of London and Brush Provincial Electric Lighting Company for a provisional order to supply the electric light in Bermondsey, and to co-operate with Hammersmith in opposing certain of the recommendations of the Parliamentary joint committee on the supply of electrical energy.

**Hampstead.**—At a meeting of the vestry, on Thursday, the General Purposes Committee reported that they had fully considered the memorial presented by the deputation consisting of the metropolitan superintendent of the National Telephone Company, Limited, and a number of residents of the parish requiring telephonic communication, in support of the company's application to the vestry for permission to lay underground wires in the parish, and, having in view the resolution recently passed by the vestry on the subject—*viz.*, " That no further action be taken at present in the matter of the agreement proposed to be entered into by the vestry with the National Telephone Company on the subject of underground mains "—they saw no reason for departing from the resolution. They therefore recommended that the National Telephone Company should be informed accordingly. The report was adopted.—The surveyor was instructed to prepare an estimate and apportionment of the cost of making-up a new street, known as The Grange, Parkhill-road, at the cost of the owners of the property abutting on the street.—The Works Committee recommended that the remaking of the roadway over the Metropolitan Railway bridge in West End-lane should be completed by the laying of extra wood paving northwards to Blackburn-road and southwards to Broadhurst-gardens, at an estimated cost of £150. The recommendation was agreed to.—The Tree and Open Spaces Committee presented a report recommending that, without in any way pledging themselves to the proposed scheme put forward by the London County Council on the subject of the maintenance of the small open spaces in the county, the vestry do appoint a representative to attend the conference with the council on the question. The recommendation was adopted.

**Islington.**—At the last meeting of the vestry Mr. W. F. Dewey, the vestry clerk, read a letter from the London County Council stating that the Building Act Committee had had under consideration the question of district surveyors employed in connection with the London Building Act, 1894. The committee had come to the following conclusions : That the suggestion that all district surveyors should devote the whole of their time to the duty of district surveying could not be carried out, but that Parliamentary powers would be required for the purpose. At the same time the committee pointed out that the practice was being gradually introduced as fresh appointments were made, and that thirteen district surveyors had already been appointed on that basis. With regard to the question of paying district surveyors by salary, the committee were not prepared to alter the existing system of payment by fees until further experience had been gained. As to the proposal that an office should be provided at the local vestry hall, the committee expressed the opinion that it had much to recommend it, but that they did not see their way to recommend the council to take any steps in the matter, as unfortunately the districts did not coincide with the local government areas, and Parliamentary powers might be required before the suggestion could be carried out. The committee added that notices would in due course be issued to the district surveyors, for posting up in their offices, intimating that they were not concerned with the question of drains, water-closets and other sanitary matters which are under the control of the local authorities. The vestry decided to enter the communication on the minutes.—A letter was read from the Hammersmith Vestry in reference to the recommendations made in the report of the Parliamentary Joint Committee on Electricity Generating Stations. In connection with these the Hammersmith Vestry expressed the opinion that the local authority within the area of supply should have the power to decide the route along which the mains are to be laid, as well as the power of themselves breaking up and reinstating the streets. The vestry strongly objected to the second and third recommendations of the joint committee, and had resolved in the event of any legislation being brought forward on the subject to take up a strong position in opposition, and to use every endeavour to retain its power of veto both in regard to wires for the purpose of traction and applications for provisional orders. In conclusion, the Hammersmith Vestry asked for the co-operation of Islington, with a view to combined action being taken in the matter. It was decided to refer the letter to the Parliamentary Committee for consideration and report.—The vestry clerk submitted a memorial

from the National Telephone Company in regard to the retention of overhead telephone wires in the parish, announcing at the same time that a number of letters had been received from local subscribers to the telephone system protesting against the proposed action of the vestry in regard to the overhead telephone wires. It was decided to refer the matter to the Works Committee. The intended action in question was referred to in a report of the Works Committee, who recommended the vestry to instruct the solicitor to at once institute proceedings against the National Telephone Company for failing to comply with the by-laws made by the London County Council in regard to the length of the spans of overhead wires. The report was, however, withdrawn for further consideration of the question.—The amended motion of the Electric Lighting Committee in reference to the proposed extensions of the electric light station, at a cost of £22,000, was again discussed for a considerable time. It was eventually decided, by forty votes to nine, to adopt an amendment by Mr. Varley referring the report back to the committee with instructions to advertise for builders willing to tender for the carrying out of the work.—The Works Committee reported that they had considered a letter from Mr. R. C. Godfray, 42 Finsbury-square, intimating his intention to apply for powers to construct a light railway from Archway-road, through Finchley to Whetstone, and asking the vestry to request the London County Council to construct a line between Highgate Archway and the metropolitan boundary, so as to afford a direct route of communication. The committee recommended the vestry to again approach the county council on the matter, but on the report being reached the chairman obtained permission to withdraw it without giving any reason for so doing.—The vestry postponed until the next meeting the consideration of various recommendations in respect of wood and stone paving works, involving an expenditure of several thousands of pounds.—The tender of Mr. H. L. Holloway, Union Works, Deptford, amounting to £14,630, was accepted for the enlargement of the Hornsey-road baths.—The Works Committee recommended the acceptance of the tender of Messrs. Steavenson & Co. for the supply of sixty-two shingle bins at £4 15s. each.

**Poplar.**—The Finance Committee recommended, at a meeting of the district board of works on Tuesday, that an application should be made to the Public Works Loans Commissioners for a loan of £5,000 for the carrying out of sundry sewer and paving works and the purchase of land for public improvements, already approved by the board. The recommendation was agreed to.—The Dust Destructor Committee again submitted their report, which was adjourned at last meeting, in reference to application of forced draught apparatus at the refuse destructor. They recommended that the offer of Goddard, Massey & Warner, which was given in full in the last issue of THE SURVEYOR, be accepted without prejudice, and an order be given to the contractors to proceed with the work. The recommendation was adopted. — On the recommendation of the Sanitary Committee, the board being of opinion that a proper system of inspection and the marking of meat would be sufficient, decided to disapprove the scheme of the Public Health Committee of the London County Council for the abolition of private slaughter-houses in London and the establishment of public abattoirs.—It was decided to refer the question of the provision of an underground convenience, near Gladstone statue in Bow-road, for women to the Works Committee for consideration.—On the motion of Mr. J. R. Smith the following resolution was adopted : " That the surveyor prepare statement of cost that would have been incurred for shooting dust at contractor's shoots, as compared with cost of shooting same at the destructor, from May 25 to November 25, 1898."

**Rotherhithe.**—A deputation from the London Butchers' Trade Society waited upon the vestry, at their meeting on Tuesday, to urge them to oppose the proposal of the Public Health Committee of the London County Council to establish public abattoirs in London and to abolish private slaughter-houses. The matter was referred to a committee for consideration and report.—A letter was read from the secretary of the Union of Women's Liberal and Radical Association of the Metropolitan Counties, enclosing a copy of a resolution passed by the executive committee of the association, to the effect that the union considers it should be made incumbent upon all vestries to provide at least one free compartment for women at each of their public conveniences.—The County of London and Brush Provincial Electric Lighting Company, Limited, also wrote stating, in reference to the formal notice served upon the vestry in July last, of their intention to apply during the ensuing session of Parliament for a provisional order covering the district of Rotherhithe, that they had duly made application to the Board of Trade, and would therefore be glad to receive the vestry's consent to the grant of an order, and enclosed a pamphlet setting forth the reduced rates adopted by the company for the supply of electric energy. They also stated that they were prepared to enter into a contract with the vestry for the supply of current for all-night public lighting, at an uniform rate of 3d. per unit ; and that they would agree that the vestry should have the right to purchase the undertaking, as applied to the district, at any time after the expiration of seven, fourteen or twenty-one years from the date of the order, on terms to be mutually agreed upon. The communication was referred to the General

Purposes and Works Committee for consideration.—A further communication was read from the secretary of the Clinical Research Association, Limited, suggesting that it would be more economical for vestries to join the association than to undertake to pay a yearly subsidy to the support of the municipal bacteriological laboratory which the London County Council propose to establish. The letter was referred to the Sanitary Committee.—On the motion of Mr. Vezey the vestry resolved "to express its satisfaction with the action taken by the London County Council, at its meeting on the 1st November, in relation to the question of a future reliable supply of water to London, and trusts its efforts will have the sanction of Parliament at an early date—as the matter is too urgent to admit of delay." They also decided to send a copy of the resolution to the London County Council; to Mr. Cumming Macdona, M.P., urging him to give the matter his support in Parliament; and to each London vestry and district board, urging them to take similar action.—On the recommendation of the General Purposes and Works Committee it was decided to accept the tender of Messrs. Boswall & Son, at £50 10s., for the purchase of the vestry's vans and gig.

**Shoreditch.**—The Vestry, on Tuesday, discussed a report by the Finance Committee covering a statement made by the vestry clerk as to his reasons for not having signed the electricity accounts and his inability to sign them at the present time. As a result of the report, which is given in another column, and after hearing an explanation of the accountant, the committee had resolved to strike out of the Board of Trade return the words "To balance from last account, £1,281 19s. 0d.," as printed in the annual report, and to also strike out "By deficiency of income, £1,255 8s. 2d.," as given in the same report, leaving the balance to be carried forward as £807 12s. 2d.; and to also omit the words "present available surplus." This report was adopted. In connection with this matter the accountant had asked for instructions as to the sale of copies of accounts in the amended form now resolved upon, and it was decided to sell the amended copies. It was also decided to include the accounts for wiring and fitting in the Board of Trade return. The Finance Committee further recommended that, in view of the statements made that the electricity and dust destructor accounts had b-en "cooked," a firm of chartered accountants should beſin-structed to audit and report on the accounts for the year as presented to the vestry. After a long discussion an amendment was adopted referring the recommendation back to the committee for further consideration and report.—The vestry clerk reported the receipt of a letter from the Hammersmith Vestry relating to the recommendations made by the Parliamentary Joint Committee on the supply of electrical energy in the last session of Parliament. That vestry opposed those recommendations, and it was resolved to refer the matter to the Lighting Committee for consideration and report.—A letter was read from the Clinical Research Association pointing out the work of the society in regard to the bacteriological examination of material from cases of infectious diseases.—It was announced by the Lighting Committee that they had considered a report by the chief engineer on the quotation of the British Insulated Wire Company for the supply and laying of conduits in the Haggerstone district, at a cost of 10s. 8d. per yard. On the recommendation of the committee it was decided to accept that company's tender. It was resolved, at the suggestion of the Works Committee, to inform the Hammersmith Vestry that a letter had already been forwarded to the London County Council protesting against the proposed by-laws for controlling the fixing of lamps overhanging the public footways.—The Works Committee recommended that the carriageways of Hoxton Market should be asphalted and the footways relaid with York stone, at a cost of £500. The recommendation was adopted.—With reference to the proposal to erect a public clock-tower in the High-street, the Works Committee reported having considered various designs submitted by Mr. J. Rush Dixon, the surveyor. The committee were of opinion that the design exhibited in the vestry hall for an iron clock-tower, 30 ft. high, with a dial 2 ft. in diameter, would he the most suitable, the cost being estimated at £270. The committee recommended the vestry to adopt the design and carry out the work.—A report had been submitted to the Works Committee by the surveyor on the cost of sewer works carried out by the vestry without a contractor. It appeared from the report that the sewer works in Angrave-street had resulted in a nett saving of £122 on the estimate of £841, and on those in Grange-street a saving of £150 had been gained upon an estimate of £613.—The following tenders were considered for providing temporary flooring for the first and second class baths, the figures in parenthesis being those for the second-class baths: Messrs. Thomason & Son, £614, (£200); Tupthorne & Co., £571 (£254); E. Houghton & Son, £542 (£240); J. Dolman & Co., £518 (£237); Walter Lawrence, £519 (£235); C. Gray Hill, £490 (£210); and the General Builders, Limited, £440 (£190). The tender of the latter firm was accepted.

**St. James, Westminster.**—At the last meeting of the vestry the Works Committee recommended, and it was decided to approve, the laying by the St. James and Pall Mall Company and the London Electric Supply Corporation of electric light mains and the construction of street boxes in various streets.—A report was submitted by the Public Health and Works Joint Committee in relation to the proposal of the Public Health Committee to consent to the construction of soil pipes inside the Carlton Hotel, instead of being arranged on the exterior of the building as required by the by-laws of the London County Council. The joint committee recommended that, subject to the approval of the county council, the arrangements for the additional soil pipes should be accepted by the vestry, and that a communication should accordingly be forwarded to the county council. After considerable discussion the recommendation was unanimously adopted. It was resolved, at the suggestion of the St. James Dwellings Committee, to assent to the extension of the trust in acquiring the Marshall-street site and the erection of dwellings for the poor, and to invite the guardians to appoint representatives to confer with the overseers and the committee with a view to the sale of the property to the vestry for the purpose in question.—The Clinical Research Association wrote in reference to the proposal to establish a central bacteriological laboratory. The association pointed out that it was undertaking, at very small cost, for many sanitary authorities throughout the kingdom the work for the performance of which it was proposed to erect the new laboratory, and suggested that it would be more economical for local authorities to join the association than to pay a yearly subsidy to support a county council laboratory. The communication was referred to the Public Health Committee.—Notices were read from the St. James and Pall Mall Electric Lighting Company of their intention to apply to Parliament for authority to compulsorily acquire certain property in the parish for the purpose of the company's undertaking, and from the Brompton and Piccadilly-circus Railway Company of intended application to Parliament to empower the company to extend the railway.

**St. Marylebone.**—The Sanitary Committee, at the last meeting of the vestry, drew attention to the buildings in the area comprised in Nightingale-street, Samford-street, and a portion of Salisbury-street. In the opinion of the committee the bad condition and sanitary defects were of such a nature as to render necessary the demolition of the buildings and the construction on the site of dwellings suitable for the working classes. The committee accordingly recommended the vestry to direct that a scheme should be prepared for the improvement of the area under Part II. of the Housing of the Working Classes Act. Dr. Snape, chairman of the committee, stated that the superficial area was 7,000 square yards and that the number of persons proposed to be displaced and re-housed amounted to 500. As an amendment, Mr. E. White moved that a statement of the facts should be forwarded to the London County Council, with a request that the council would prepare and carry out a scheme for the improvement of the area in question. On being put to the meeting the amendment was adopted by thirty-eight votes to twenty votes.—The Works Committee presented a report recommending that Harley-street, Old Cavendish-street and Upper Berkeley-street should be paved with wood next year, the estimated cost, if yellow deal were used, being £6,930. In connection with this matter the committee stated that Mr. Waddington, the surveyor, estimated the cost of hard wood pavement at 75 per cent. more than that of yellow deal. Being equally divided in opinion as to the relative merits of hard and soft wood paving, the committee left it to the vestry to decide which wood should be used for the thoroughfares, as also in the case of the renewal of a portion of Oxford-street from Hereford-gardens to Edgware-road, estimated to cost £1,575 in yellow deal. The discussion of the subject was adjourned till the next meeting.—It was decided, on the motion of Mr. E. J. Physick, to refer to the Burials Committee to consider and report on the following arrangements in connection with the Marylebone cemetery: (1) The expensive system of drainage of private earth graves (not brick graves), not known to be adopted in other cemeteries; (2) the placing of common interments both at head and foot of private graves; (3) the waste of ground involved by having a space of 4 ft. wide between the rows of private graves, instead of a space from 1 ft. 6 in. to 2 ft. as in other cemeteries.—The following tenders were accepted for the cartage of snow during the winter, the first prices being at per day and the second at per hour: Henry Boyer & Co., 11s. and 1s. 4d.; R. Ballard, 11s. and 1s. 6d.; Robert Bunce, 11s. and 1s. 6d.; A. Salamon & Co., 11s. and 1s. 5d.; and Joseph Latter, 11s. and 1s. 6d.

**Whitechapel.**—The board have given their approval to a recommendation of the Electric Lighting Committee to lay down an installation for lighting the district with current for lighting and power purposes, at an estimated cost of £60,500.

## PROVINCIAL AND GREATER LONDON AUTHORITIES.
### MUNICIPAL CORPORATIONS.

**Andover.**—The formal sanction of the Local Government Board has been received by the town council to the loan for the construction of sewage disposal works on the septic tank system.

**Bedford.**—A deputation of the members of the corporation recently visited Yeovil for the purpose of inspecting the septic tank system of sewage treatment at work there. The conditions, says a local paper, were very exacting, inasmuch as the sewage was black with refuse from the tanneries, breweries and factories. The work of purification seemed to be very effectually carried out, as the effluent was perfectly clear.

**Blackburn.**—On the recommendation of the Health Committee, the medical officer was on Thursday directed to prepare a full report on the question of providing further accommodation at the fever hospital. The gas engineer having recommended that the corporation should purchase their own railway waggons for the conveyance of coal and cannel, the council confirmed a resolution of the Gas Committee that the gas engineer should obtain specifications from various firms for the supply of fifty of these vehicles.—On the recommendation of the Finance Committee it was also resolved to borrow a sum of £4,400 for market purposes.

**Blackpool.**—On Wednesday, at a meeting of the town council, a discussion took place in regard to the overhead system of electrical traction, letters from the Blackpool Tradesmen's Association and from the Blackpool Municipal Reform Union protesting against it being read. Several councillors objected to the system, but any discussion on its merits or demerits was ruled out of order. Some speakers wanted to stop the work of instituting the overhead system on the Promenade until all the councillors had had an opportunity of discussing the whole subject again. However, it was stated that the work was already begun, and that the contractor was bound to finish the work by Easter, under a heavy penalty. One member stated that during his canvass he found his constituents entirely unanimous against the overhead system, and for that reason he rose to give his protest. An amendment referring the whole matter for discussion by the General Purposes Committee was carried by a large majority.

**Bolton.**—A Local Government Board inquiry has been held respecting an application of the town council for sanction to borrow £10,500 for the extension of the water supply. This had been necessitated by the rapid growth of the population in the Chorley-road district. There was no opposition.

**Brighton.**—On Tuesday, at the Royal Pavilion, Brighton, Mr. H. Percy Boulnois held an inquiry into an application of the town council to the Local Government Board for sanction to borrow £3,396 for slaughter-house purposes. The surveyor explained in detail the various items which the loan asked for embraced, and referring to the sanitary arrangements, said they were most satisfactory and that there had not been a single drain choked.

**Bury.**—It has been decided to promote a Bill in Parliament to authorise, among other things, the construction of new waterworks for the borough and other districts within the water limits of the corporation; the compulsory purchase of lands in order to protect the water from pollution, the alteration of charges, and the borrowing of additional moneys.

**Doncaster.**—The corporation of Doncaster having obtained a provisional order last session for electric lighting, are seeking powers for the construction, in the session of 1899, of 7½ miles of tramways on the overhead trolley system. The tramways will serve not only Doncaster, but the outlying suburbs of Balby, Hexthorpe, Bentley and Wheatley. The corporation, it may be mentioned, are just completing a new isolation hospital for the use of the borough and suburbs. —A new bridge over the river Don, which is being constructed at the joint cost of the West Riding County Council and the corporation, will be opened very shortly.

**Dudley.**—On Thursday, at a meeting of the town council, the Sanitary Committee reported that they had fully considered plans, produced by the borough surveyor, for the laying-out of certain land at Queen's Cross provisionally decided upon for acquirement as a cemetery, and recommended that the council should make an application to the Local Government Board for sanction to borrow £12,500 for the purchase of the ground. The Public Works Committee mentioned that plans had been produced of land at Netherton and Woodside which would be suitable for recreation grounds.

**Lancaster.**—The corporation have accepted the tender of Messrs. J. & S. Roberts, Limited, Swan Foundry, West Bromwich, for the supply of about 1,850 lineal yards of 7-in. cast-iron pipes.

**Leeds.**—New public baths, which have been erected by the corporation in Hunslet, are to be opened on the 17th inst. The premises have cost about £12,000.

**Leicester.**—The town council, by practically a unanimous vote, recently decided to promote a Bill in Parliament to obtain powers to utilise the extensive watersheds of the Upper Derwent and Ashop rivers, near Derbyshire, for the purpose of securing an additional water supply. The scheme provides for the construction of five immense reservoirs in the Derwent and Ashop valleys; but in the first instance only a portion of this huge undertaking will be proceeded with, the cost of the first instalment being £1,500,000. It is hoped that the Derbyshire authorities, who are promoting a scheme of their own in reference to the same watersheds, will be induced ultimately to co-operate with Leicester.

**Manchester.**—The Local Government Board have sanctioned the borrowing by the corporation, for public walks and pleasure grounds, of £12,000.

**Scarborough.**—Mr. H. H. Law, Local Government Board inspector, has held an inquiry into an application of the town council for sanction to borrow £2,879 for the purposes of pleasure grounds, £1,205 for the construction of a bridge, and £340 for the provision of an underground convenience.

**Sheffield.**—A special meeting of the city council has been summoned for the 14th inst., to consider the various Bills that are being promoted in Parliament for dealing with the waters of the Derwent. The council will be asked to approve the Bill of the Sheffield Corporation for taking the waters of the Derwent, Ashop and other rivers, and to consider the desirability of authorising opposition to the Bills of the Leicester and Derby Corporations. The council will also be asked to approve the Bill of the Sheffield Corporation for the purchase of the markets and the market and fair rights of the city from the Duke of Norfolk.

**Wigan.**—For some time past the Electric Lighting Committee of the Wigan Corporation have had under consideration the question of having the town lighted with electricity, and deputations have visited Leeds, Bradford and Wakefield. The committee have now decided that an installation be put down to supply Wigan with electric light. The council are at present waiting the report of the committee, who also have under consideration the running of the trams by electrical traction.

## URBAN DISTRICT COUNCILS.

**Camborne.**—Mr. H. Percy Boulnois, Local Government Board inspector, has held an inquiry respecting an application of the council for sanction to erect a grand stand in the town recreation ground, at a cost of £300. No opposition was offered.

**Levenshulme.**—At Monday's meeting of the council a letter was read from the Local Government Board sanctioning an application of the council to borrow £2,334 to complete the purchase of land for the purpose of a recreation ground, and a further sum of £1,382 to be expended in laying out the ground, which is about 4 acres in extent.—Notice was given by a member of his intention to move the adoption of the Artisans' Dwellings Act.

**Llanelly.**—A letter has been received from the Board of Trade pointing out that the time allowed for the carrying out of the electric lighting scheme had now expired, and they desired to know whether the council intended to proceed with the work.

**Maidstone.**—At the last fortnightly meeting of this authority the medical officer, in his capacity as public analyst, reported that the nitrates in the Boarley and Ewell waters were too high. The Cossington water also showed a marked increase in the free ammonia, which was now higher than it had been any time since October, 1897. By comparison with the other water the albuminoid ammonia and the oxygen absorbed were likewise somewhat high in this water. After some discussion it was resolved to request the water company to furnish a monthly analysis of their water.—The Sanitary Committee brought up a report, in which they stated that the result of a deputation to the Local Government Board as to the typhoid loan had been that the Local Government Board had expressed their willingness to sanction the borrowing of £17,500 (being practically the whole of the money expended), in lieu of the £15,000 originally granted.

**Northallerton.**—A letter has been received from the Local Government Board approving the borrowing of £376 for the purchase of property adjoining the fire station.

**Northwich.**—The district council, at a recent meeting, agreed to amalgamate with the Northwich Rural Council in the carrying out of a sewerage scheme for the Castle portion of the urban and the Winnington portion of the rural districts. The cost of the work is estimated to be about £30,000.

**Redditch.**—At a recent meeting of this body the surveyor presented plans and estimates for the alteration of the old police station, which has been purchased for council offices and other purposes. The cost of the work is estimated at £1,600. The plans and estimates were passed, and it was decided to apply to the Local Government Board for permission to borrow the money.

**Stretford.**—At a recent special meeting of the council a resolution was carried by an absolute majority of the council to promote a Bill in the next session of Parliament to enable the council to work the tramways in their own district, and any adjoining district by agreement with other district councils, by animal, mechanical or electrical power; to enable the council to agree with the Manchester and Salford Corporations, and the district councils adjoining, for the exercise by the council of running powers or the leasing to the council of the tramways in such adjoining districts; to empower the council to borrow money for the purposes of the Bill; and to confer upon the council all such other powers as might be deemed expedient for, or in relation to, the foregoing purposes.

**Walker.**—A special committee have reported that an electric lighting provisional order had been advertised, and plans prepared in accordance with the rules. A memorial has also been prepared, and will shortly come up for consideration.

**Warminster.**—On Friday a Local Government Board inquiry was held by Colonel Smith, R.E., relative to an application of the council for sanction to borrow £7,500 for the purposes of a sewerage and sewage disposal scheme.

## RURAL DISTRICT COUNCILS.

**Bucklow.** — Mr. Robert H. Bicknell on Thursday conducted an inquiry, on behalf of the Local Government Board, in reference to an application of the district council for sanction to borrow £2,100 for sewerage works in the township of Hale. Among those present at the inquiry was Mr. J. McKenzie, surveyor to the council. It was explained that the proposed works included the construction of a total length of 3,225 yards of new sewers, these being necessary to cope with the property erected and now in course of erection. It was sought to borrow the money for thirty years in respect of the works along Bank Hall-lane, Broad-lane and Handloy-lane as far as the Unitarian Chapel, but the laying of the sewers from Yollandlane to Aldcroft's cottage, at a cost of £600, would be proceeded with as soon as possible, while the remainder would be done as immediate necessity arose.

**Comersall.**—Mr. H. H. Law, one of the Local Government Board inspectors, conducted an inquiry last week with reference to an application of the district council for sanction to borrow £10,000 for the purchase of the Comersall waterworks undertaking and £8,000 for the purpose of works of sewerage and sewage disposal. There was no opposition to the application for sanction to the purchase of the waterworks, and this part of the inquiry was quite of a formal character. With regard to the proposed sewage outfall works, it was contended that the site chosen was building land and that if the owner was paid a proper price for it the scheme could not be carried out for £8,000. Apart from that, the scheme was described as an extravagant one, inasmuch as it was only intended to provide for less than 400 houses.

**Runcorn.**—At a recent meeting of the council a letter was read from the clerk to the Cheshire County Council intimating to the council that, in the opinion of the Rivers Pollution Committee of the county council, the sewage from their district polluted the rivers and streams therein, contrary to the provisions of the Rivers Pollution Act, 1876, and that whether such pollution created a nuisance injurious to health was immaterial. Unless the district council made arrangements for stopping this pollution the committee would feel bound to advise the county council to put the Act into operation. The clerk was instructed to reply to the communication and inquire what streams were referred to.—The district council are extending the sewers of Frodsham and Frodsham Lordship, at a cost of over £1,000, from plans prepared by Mr. William Diggle, their surveyor. They are also about to carry out a sewage scheme for the village of Helsby, at a cost of from £4,000 to £3,000.

**Sleaford.**—A tender of Mr. Skinner, of Heckington, for the construction of waterworks at Great Hale, for £635, has been accepted. It has also been resolved to apply to the Local Government Board for permission to borrow the necessary money.

**Wigan.**—On Friday a Local Government Board inquiry was held by Mr. G. W. Willcocks with regard to an application of the rural district council for sanction to borrow £6,700 for works of water supply for a portion of the township of Wrightington.

## SCOTLAND AND IRELAND.

**Aberdeen.**—It has been decided by the Finance Committee to recommend the extension of the fish market building along the Market-street wharf. The cost of the works is estimated at from £3,000 to £4,000.

**Coleraine.**—A Local Government Board inquiry has been held relative to an application of the town commissioners for sanction to carry out a sewerage scheme for the northern district of the town.

**Glasgow.**—At a meeting of the Corporation Statute Labour Committee, held on Friday, consideration was given to the question of erecting additional bridges over the Clyde east of Albert Bridge. It was stated that to utilise the materials of the present temporary wooden bridge across the Clyde at Jamaica-street for the erection of two bridges would cost £8,100, being £5,700 for an ordinary cart bridge at Govan-street and £2,400 for a bridge (16 ft. wide), also for carts, at Polmadie-street. To erect a suspension bridge at Polmadie-street would cost £8,600. The former proposal was favourably considered, but no decision was come to in the meantime.

## FOREIGN AND COLONIAL.

**Toronto, Ont.**—Mr. C. H. Rust, the city engineer, has prepared an exhaustive report on the sewage disposal of the city. In concluding the report he recommends the construction of intercepting sewers on the general plan proposed by Messrs. Hering & Gray in 1889, and the provision of purification works in addition. The cost of the intercepting sewers is estimated at £820,000. Final disposal works are estimated at £910,000 for intermittent filtration and £720,000 for chemical precipitation, with filtration of the effluent. The annual charges for filtration would be less than for precipitation. Before deciding on a purification system Mr. Rust advises the employment of a consulting engineer.

**Sanitary Inspectors' Association.**—A general meeting of the members of the above association will be held at Carpenters' Hall, London-wall, E.C., on Saturday, the 17th inst., at 6 p.m., when a paper will be read by Mr. W. H. Grigg, of Fulham, and an election of members and associates will take place. This meeting will be followed, at 8 p.m., by an extraordinary general meeting, at which the following resolution will be submitted on behalf of the council: That the number of members in the association shall be increased by the addition thereto of seven hundred (700) members beyond the present registered number.

# Some Recent Publications.

SOME SHORT NOTICES.

THE ELEMENTS OF SANITARY LAW, by Alice Ravenhill, lecturer to the Health Society (The Sanitary Publishing Company, Limited. Price 6d.), has a brief introduction by Sir Richard T. Thorne, K.C.B., F.R.S., LL.D., and will prove of much practical utility to many of our readers who are debarred by various causes from having recourse to the pages of Glen or Lumley. The design and compass of the pamphlet are appropriately set forth in the author's words: "This little book has been compiled with a view to meet a growing demand for some concise and inexpensive summary of the leading points of our existing system of public health law, some items of the most practical value having been selected and presented in a form as simple as is compatible with accuracy, and permitting of easy and rapid reference to any particular subject on which information is desired. For these reasons the alphabetical system of arrangement has been adopted, and great pains have been taken to preserve correctness of interpretation while condensing lengthy sections into simple sentences."

THE GENERAL REPORT OF THE OPERATIONS OF THE SURVEY OF INDIA DEPARTMENT, ADMINISTERED UNDER THE GOVERNMENT OF INDIA, DURING 1896 AND 1897 (Calcutta. Price 3 rupees), has been prepared under the direction of Major-General C. Strahan, R.E., Surveyor-General of India, and is issued from the office of the Superintendent of Government Printing, India. It contains much that is calculated to interest and instruct those persons who are intimately associated with our Eastern empire, as well as many others whose acquaintance with that great country is necessarily limited. Without entering into a minute analysis or detailed account of the valuable, statistical and descriptive information comprised in this folio volume, amply illustrated by maps and plates, we may mention that the first part is devoted to an account of the various surveys undertaken and of the progress hitherto made in each instance, the second to a recital of the operations of several field parties, the third division treats of the work performed at the headquarters offices, and sundry appendices embody reports made by executive officers.

SURVEYING, by T. Baker and F. E. Dixon (Crosby Lockwood & Co. Price 2s.), is a revised edition of a well-known book. Baker's "Surveying" has long been the favourite text-book of the student in land surveying, and we see no reason why the great measure of success it attained should not, under the new editor, be much increased. We are rather surprised to find no mention of the tacheometer, an instrument much used as an angle and distance measure, and in future editions we think it would be well, in the interests of students, especially in the colonies, to add some description of it. As in most of the books on surveying, we find the author clings somewhat to the antiquated chain, whereas those constantly at work in the field do not hesitate to decide in favour of the steel band as a more accurate and certainly more convenient instrument. A more lengthy description of the planimeter would be of great use, as, notwithstanding the faint praise accorded it, we have found it extremely accurate, and with reasonable care not easily injured.

"THE ARGUS" GUIDE TO MUNICIPAL LONDON, edited by Mr. Frank J. Higgingbottom ("London Argus" office. Price 1s.), will be found a handy medium of reference in all matters of interest connected with the local governing authorities of both the city and county of London. It contains a full list of members of the City corporation, the county council, school board, the administrative vestries, district boards and boards of guardians, with biographical notes and a variety of additional particulars. Special features of this little hand-book are the numerous portraits of prominent persons associated with the various bodies enumerated, and the personal notices concerning the principal members of the City corporation are certain to meet with due appreciation in many quarters. Statistical matters are fully entered into, and a systematic arrangement of details has been strictly adhered to in the several sections.

Mr. F. Latham, the author of THE SANITATION OF DOMESTIC BUILDINGS (The Sanitary Publishing Company, Limited. Price 2s. 6d.), has been fortunate in getting an introduction by so well known a sanitarian as Mr. Baldwin Latham. The book will thus probably ensure a greater meed of success than might otherwise have fallen to its lot as a work on the details of sanitation. It travels over well-worn ground, and nothing that is particularly new is described. The catalogue blocks which are used for illustrating do not add to its appearance, as the variety of scale is confusing; we are so used now to process work, even in small text-books, that these appear rough by comparison. What does "F. Inst. Architects and Surveyors" mean? Is it a new society?

APPLIED GEOLOGY, Part I., by J. V. Elsden, B.SC.LOND. (The Quarry Publishing Company, Limited. Price 5s.), is stated in the preface to be "an attempt to combine as much geology as the practical man should know with as much practical detail as should interest the geologist." Although the author advances no claim to originality, and admits that all available sources of information as to facts recorded have been freely utilised in the compilation of this little book, as the result of a careful examination of its contents we unhesitatingly recommend it to the notice of any of our readers who may be personally or professionally interested in the subject therein treated with marked ability and considerable success.

THE STORY OF THE FARM, by James Long (The Rural Publishing Company. Price 1s.), consists of a series of essays on agricultural economy, some of which have been reprinted from *The Nineteenth Century*, *The Fortnightly Review*, and *The Manchester Guardian*, and it contains an introductory article by the Countess of Warwick, entitled "Women and the Future of Agriculture." A lengthened experience in agricultural matters generally, and an intimate acquaintance with the many social problems discussed, has enabled Mr. Long to treat the wide range of subjects referred to in this little hand-book with clearness, efficiency, and a thoroughly practical insight into all details.

From the EIGHTH ANNUAL REPORT OF THE COUNCIL OF THE PROPERTY PROTECTION SOCIETY, 1897 to 1898, we learn that "during the past session the society was unremittingly engaged in watching what they consider to be confiscatory Bills in Parliament, and took what steps seemed necessary in each case." Among such Bills introduced in the House of Commons were the Agricultural Holdings Bill, the Occupying Tenants' Enfranchisement Bill, and the Workmen's Houses Tenure Bill.

"THE INDIAN AND EASTERN ENGINEER" DIARY AND REFERENCE-BOOK (presented to yearly subscribers of that periodical) contains a considerable amount of practical information specially interesting to those persons for whom it is primarily intended. The matter in the present issue appears to have been kept up to the standard of previous years, and in particular we note the very complete table of metrical equivalents and the singularly convenient manner in which the other varied particulars therein included are arranged.

*Any of the Books noted below will be sent post free if the published price be forwarded to the offices of* THE SURVEYOR.

"THE LIVE STOCK JOURNAL" ALMANAC, 1899; 268 pp., 9¾ in. by 6½ in. Price 1s.

CLASSICAL AND FOREIGN QUOTATIONS, LAW TERMS AND MAXIMS, PROVERBS, MOTTOES, PHRASES AND EXPRESSIONS, in French, German, Greek, Italian, Latin, Spanish and Portuguese, by W. F. H. King, M.A. (new edition); 624 pp., 7½ in. by 5¼ in. Price 5s.

UNDER THE SHADOW OF ST. PAUL'S: a page from the history of London, by Henry Johnson; 192 pp., 7½ in. by 5 in. Price 2s. 6d.

HAZELL'S ANNUAL FOR 1899; 676 pp., 7¼ in. by 5¼ in. Price 3s. 6d.

THE NEW GUIDE TO BRISTOL AND CLIFTON AND THE BRISTOL CHANNEL CIRCUIT, by James Baker, F.R.H.S., F.R.G.S.; 306 pp., 6¾ in. by 4½ in. Price 2s.

JUDGES' REPORT OF THE LIVERPOOL TRIALS ON MOTOR VEHICLES FOR HEAVY TRAFFIC, 1898; 126 pp., 9¾ in. by 6 in. Price 5s.

NOTES ON WATER SUPPLY, by J. F. Rodda; 140 pp., 11 in. by 8¾ in. Price 5s.

THE "COMPLEAT" AND UNIVERSAL GUIDE TO HOTELS, &c., 1898; 368 pp., 7½ in. by 4¾ in. Price 1s.

TRIGONOMETRY AT A GLANCE, by G. W. Usill, ASSOC.M.INST.C.E., and F. J. Browne, C.E.; 7½ in. by 10 in. Price 2s.

THE "GLOUCESTER" DIARY AND DIRECTORS' CALENDAR FOR 1899; 300 pp., 6¼ in. by 4 in.

AN INQUIRY INTO THE RELATIVE EFFICIENCY OF WATER FILTERS IN THE PREVENTION OF INFECTIVE DISEASE, by G. Sims Woodhead, M.D., F.R.S.E., and C. E. Cartwright Wood M.D., B.SC; 136 pp., 8½ in. by 5½ in. Price 2s. 6d.

## INSTITUTION OF CIVIL ENGINEERS.

ORDINARY MEETING.

An ordinary meeting of the above Institution will be held on Tuesday, at 8 p.m., when a discussion will be opened on the paper which was read at the last meeting by Mr. Francis Fox, M.I.C.E., on "The Ventilation of Tunnels and Buildings."

STUDENTS' MEETING.

A meeting for the students of the Institution will also be held on Friday, when a paper, entitled "The Kentish Town Widening, Midland Railway," will be read by Mr. Walter Daniel. The chair will be taken at 8 p.m. by Mr. Horace Bell, member of the council.

**Surveyors and Bicycles.**—At a recent meeting of the Berwick Town Council it was decided to provide Mr. R. Dickinson, the surveyor, with a bicycle.—At the Queen's Hotel, Macclesfield, Mr. Boyd, road surveyor to the Cheshire County Council, was recently presented by Mr. J. Naylor, on behalf of about 200 cyclists in Macclesfield and the neighbourhood, with a handsome bicycle, fully equipped, as a mark of the esteem in which he is held, and in recognition of the admirable condition in which the roads in the Macclesfield district under his charge are kept.

# Personal.

The death is announced of Mr. de Witt C. Cregier, ex-city engineer of Chicago.

Worcester City Council have appointed Mr. C. J. Sutherland, of Hanley, electrical engineer, at a salary of £350 per annum.

Mr. G. A. Calder, road surveyor, Dunblane, was recently presented with a handsome escritoire on the occasion of his marriage.

Penryn Town Council have selected Mr. J. Partridge Jenkins to fill the posts of borough surveyor and inspector of nuisances.

Mr. A. M. Cutler, the city engineer of Cork, last week delivered an interesting lecture on the subject of "Healthy Dwellings."

Mr. William J. Crawford, of Stirling, was on Thursday appointed assistant borough surveyor of Stirling, at a salary of £80 per annum.

The salary of Mr. E. J. Reynolds, surveyor to the Friern Barnet Urban District Council, has been increased from £225 to £275 per annum.

At a meeting of the Wigmore Rural District Council, held last week, it was proposed by the chairman and unanimously decided to grant the surveyor, Mr. H. W. Bowen, an increase in his salary of £30 per annum.

Mr. Lee, the late borough electrical engineer of Southampton, has been presented with a silver cigar, cigarette and vesta case by some of his friends on the council and the staff at the works, on the occasion of his leaving the works.

Mr. F. J. M. Whittaker, surveyor to the Peterborough Rural District Council, has been selected to carry out a water supply scheme for the parish of Werrington, Peterborough. The boring operations, we understand, have proved very successful.

Mr. Arthur Fuller, burgh electrical engineer, Ayr, has been granted an increase in his salary of £50 a year. The motion for granting the increase was opposed, but the opposition elicited such a volume of testimony in Mr. Fuller's favour that it was withdrawn, and the increase granted unanimously.

Maidstone Urban District Council have increased the salary of their surveyor, Mr. T. F. Bunting, from £250 to £300 per annum. The mayor, on the adoption of the report of the committee recommending the advance, said he was glad that the council had thus recognised that they had in Mr. Bunting a good honest servant.

The Lambeth Vestry have decided to grant Mr. Norrington, the surveyor, a testimonial so soon as he asks for one, it being left to a small committee to draw up the terms of the testimonial. They have also decided that Mr. Edwards, assistant surveyor, be appointed chief surveyor for twelve months on probation, at a salary of £500.

We are informed that Mr. W. Taylor, of Chipping Sodbury, Glos., has been appointed surveyor to the Swaffham Urban District Council, in the place of Mr. Cecil Chapman, who has received the appointment of engineer under the Wembley Urban District Council. There were thirty-seven applicants for the vacancy. The salary commences at £100 per annum.

At a meeting of the Fylde Rural District Council, held recently, the chief business was the appointment of a surveyor, in place of Mr. Henshaw. The salary was fixed at £120 per annum. Out of a large number of candidates six were selected to appear before the council, and ultimately the appointment was given to Mr. Henry Swire, assistant surveyor at Skipton.

The death has occurred, somewhat suddenly, of Mr. Thomas Claridge, for eight years surveyor to the Swinton Local Board, for twenty years surveyor to the Stockport and District Highway Board, and up to his decease surveyor to the Disley District Council. He was formerly engaged upon engineering works in Brussels and other Continental cities. He was fifty-eight years of age, and was well known throughout Cheshire and Lancashire.

We hear with regret of the death of Mr. John G. Livesay, which has taken place at Ventnor, Isle of Wight. The deceased gentleman was in 1864 appointed to the Ventnor Local Board as surveyor, and on his resigning that office, eleven years later, he took the position of consulting engineer to the authority. During his tenure of office he inaugurated and carried out an extensive sewerage scheme, extended the sea walls, and undertook several other important public works.

The Long Eaton Urban District Council have shown their appreciation of the services of their engineer and surveyor, Mr. Frank Worrall, by giving him an advance of salary. The vice-chairman of the council, in moving the resolution, remarked that no application had been made by Mr. Worrall for an increase in his salary, but he felt confident that the council would recognise the ability and energy he had displayed in his work during the past twelve months by granting him an increase, and so endeavour to retain his services.

Mr. William Hamilton Beattie, an eminent Scottish architect, whose death has occurred very suddenly at his residence in Edinburgh, was chief expert adviser to the Edinburgh Corporation, and performed important duties of a similar kind for the North British Railway Company. He was also well known as a skilled witness in Parliamentary inquiries, while he was responsible for the design of a large number of important buildings in Edinburgh and elsewhere. Mr. Beattie was highly esteemed, and his death in his prime—he had only reached the age of fifty-five—will be deeply regretted by a very wide circle.

At the last meeting of the St. George-the-Martyr (Southwark) Vestry the Joint Public Health and Sewers and Works Committee reported that they had considered the application received for the post of assistant surveyor and had selected five candidates to appear before the vestry. After these five candidates had been interviewed the vestry resolved to appoint Mr. R. T. Millar, 37 Hercules-road, Westminster Bridge-road, S.E., to the post. Mr. Millar, who is twenty-five years of age, is at present an assistant to Mr. W. H. Woodroffe, 214 Great Dover-street, S.E., previous to which he was an assistant to another firm.

An arrangement has been made by which the private practice established in Manchester in 1859 by the late Mr. William Radford, M.I.C.E., and carried on until recently by him in conjunction with his son, Mr. William Harold Radford, under the style of Messrs. William Radford & Son, civil engineers, surveyors and valuers, at 19 Brazennose-street, Manchester, has been transferred to Mr. Joseph Swarbrick, A.M.I.C.E., of Temple Chambers, 33 Brazennose-street, Manchester, consequent upon the appointment of Mr. W. H. Radford to the position of bridgemaster for the County of Lancaster, in succession to his father.

On Tuesday, at the meeting of the London County Council, the General Purposes Committee announced that twenty-seven applications had been received in response to the advertisement for an architect to fill the position of superintending architect to the council, rendered vacant by the retirement of Mr. T. Blashill. The committee had carefully considered the applications, and nine of the candidates were interviewed, but they regretted to have to report that they could not see their way to submit the names of any of the candidates as possessing, in their opinion, the qualifications necessary for so important a position. They were now considering what course should, in the circumstances, be taken with a view to filling the appointment, which carries with it a salary of £1,500 a year.

At the close of a meeting of the Leighton Town Council on Thursday, Mr. C. A. Benbow, the late assistant surveyor, was presented with a purse of £40 in recognition of his long and diligent services. The mayor, in making the presentation, alluded to the propriety with which Mr. Benbow had conducted himself during his seventeen years' stay with the corporation, and said he hoped that before long he would attain a high position under the county council. Mr. Benbow, it may be stated, has recently been appointed to the position of highway surveyor under the Stone District Council. Several members of the council also spoke of Mr. Benbow's high abilities as an engineer, while the town clerk, on behalf of the officials, bore testimony to his courtesy and expressed their gratification at his promotion.

At the Hotel Victoria, Northumberland-avenue, S.W., Mr. Baines Dudley, as president, recently delivered an opening address before the Civil and Mechanical Engineers' Society, in the course of which he referred to the various railway extensions in progress in London, especially the underground tubular system originally introduced by the late Mr. Greathead, which he described as a great step forward in the science of practical engineering. Dealing with the bridges over the Thames, he suggested that when a railway company was granted permission to construct a railway bridge over the river it should be on condition that a road bridge was combined with it. Such a regulation, he understood, already existed in some of our colonies. The steamboat traffic on the river had greatly fallen off, because the land service had improved to an extent which had not been imitated by the river service, but with covered landing stages, improved boats, running at greater speed, at more frequent intervals, there was no reason why an all-year-round service should not be resuscitated. The river was also badly lighted, and the public lost after dusk the advantage of this splendid highway through the centre of the metropolis. Were the bridges and banks lighted with diffusive electric arc lamps traffic could be carried on by night as well as by day. The proceedings closed with a vote of thanks.

Clontarf. Mr. C. P. Cotton, engineering inspector to the Local Government Board, held an inquiry recently in regard to an application of the town commissioners for sanction to borrow a sum of £300 for the defrayal of the cost of concreting and kerbing a number of footpaths.

## ASSOCIATION OF MUNICIPAL AND COUNTY ENGINEERS.

### VOLUNTARY PASS EXAMINATION.

Notice is hereby given that the twenty-seventh examination for candidates for surveyorships under municipal corporations and district councils will be held at the Institution of Civil Engineers, Great George-street, Westminster, on Friday and Saturday, April 14 and 15, 1899.

*The council reserve to themselves the right to hold a second examination in case the entries received exceed the limits of accommodation. Such second examination will be held as soon after the first as circumstances permit. Applications will therefore be accepted strictly in the order of priority.*

Application forms, duly filled in by intending candidates, together with entrance fee of £2 2s., must be in my hands on or before the 5th of March, 1899.

THOMAS COLE, *Secretary.*

11 Victoria-street, Westminster, S.W.

## BRITISH ASSOCIATION OF WATERWORKS ENGINEERS.

### SPECIAL GENERAL MEETING.

A special general meeting of the above Association will be held at the Westminster Palace Hotel, Victoria-street, London, S.W., to-morrow, for the purposes mentioned below. The chair will be taken by the president, Mr. W. Matthews, M.I.C.E., at 10 o'clock precisely.

PROPOSED ALTERATION OF RULES.

In substitution of Rules 30 and 31 :—

*Subsequent Councils and Term of Office.*

The council shall, after the above date, consist of the pre   dent, past-presidents (who are eligible for election as hereinafter provided), two vice-presidents, hon. secretary and treasurer, and ten ordinary members. The president, vice-presidents, hon. secretary and treasurer, and ten ordinary members shall go out of office each year, on the date fixed by the council for the annual general meeting, but shall be eligible for re-election. Voting papers, in a form to be determined by the council, shall be sent to each member by the secretary fourteen days before the half-yearly or winter general meeting, to be returned to the secretary at or before such meeting. Nominations for the vacant offices shall be sent to the secretary thirty-one days before the winter general meeting. Two scrutineers shall be appointed at the said winter meeting to examine and report upon the voting lists. The result of the voting shall, upon the report of the scrutineers, be declared by the chairman. Every past-president shall, at the expiration of five years from the termination of his presidency, go out of office, but shall be eligible for election to the council in the ordinary way.

GENERAL MEETING.

A general meeting will afterwards be held, at 11 o'clock precisely, when the chair will be taken by the president, Mr. W. Matthews, M I.C.E. Mr. H. Bertram Nichols, A.M.I.C.E., will read a paper, entitled : " Water Supply from the Lower Greensand and Constructional Works connected therewith at Leighton Buzzard." A discussion will follow the reading of the paper. At this meeting there will be a ballot for election of members and associates whose proposals have been received and approved by the council.

## COMBINED DRAINAGE IN LAMBETH.

REPORT OF THE JOINT COMMITTEE.

The Lambeth Vestry have received the following report from the joint committee of the Sewers and Sanitary Committees on combined drainage :—

The committee have taken this subject into their very careful consideration, and after considerable discussion it was resolved to make the following recommendations to the vestry :—

*Combined Drainage for New Buildings (excepting Flats).—* (1) That combined drainage, where advantageous, shall be approved ; (2) that combined drainage shall not be approved where the plan shows that separate drains can be laid outside each house ; (3) that combined drainage shall be limited to a maximum of six houses to drain into one drain, with one interceptor from the main sewer ; (4) that in no case where combined drainage is sanctioned shall any part of the combined drain pass under any house without the special consent of the vestry ; (5) that the passageway under which the main portion of the combined drain is laid shall be of the minimum width of 4 ft., such passageway being open to the sky ; (6) that where the passageway is more than 7 ft. wide, such passageway shall be considered as open to the air, if open at both ends to a minimum height of 10 ft. ; (7) that the owner shall sign an agreement, to the satisfaction of the clerk to the vestry, that the passageway shall never be built upon ; and (8) that when it is proposed to drain more than six houses by a combined system, for the maintenance and

repair of which the owner or owners are to be liable for all time, a main combined drain shall be placed at the rear of the houses and treated separately as to ventilation, means of access, &c., and into this back line of drainage each house shall be drained separately (with drains outside), and separately intercepted and ventilated.

*Combined Drainage of Flats.—*That each self-contained block of flats or tenement dwellings shall be drained separately.

*Records of Combined Drains.—*That the recommendation made by the clerk to the vestry as to a reference-book being kept, such book to contain particulars of each case of combined drainage sanctioned by the vestry (Minutes, p. 1,525), be adopted.

APPENDIX TO REPORT.

The committee resolved to submit the following information, prepared by the medical officer, as an appendix to their report : The medical officer reported to the committee that he had received communications from thirty-five metropolitan districts with reference to the subject of combined drainage, and had tabulated the information received as follows : Five—*i.e.*, 14·3 per cent.—do not allow or approve of combined drainage—two in connection with new, and three with new or old buildings ; thirty—*i.e.*, 85·7 per cent.— allow and approve of combined drainage. The only districts that disapprove of and do not allow combined drainage are : (1) In new or old buildings—Fulham, St. George's (Hanover-square) and St. Martin's-in-the-Fields ; (2) in new buildings only—Clerkenwell and Bermondsey. The districts that approve of and allow combined drainage are : (1) *Conditionally*—Camberwell, Whitechapel, St. Marylebone, Holborn, Newington, St. George-the-Martyr, Kensington, Clapham, Rotherhithe, Chelsea, St. Olave's, St. Pancras, Islington, Hammersmith, Strand, Westminster, Paddington, Hampstead, Strentham, St. James's, St. Luke's, St. Giles's and St. George's-in-the-East ; (2) *Unconditionally*—Hackney, Shoreditch, Bethnal Green, Wandsworth, Limehouse, Woolwich and Poplar.

## THE SEPTIC TANK SYSTEM OF SEWAGE TREATMENT AT EXETER.

A great deal of misunderstanding exists as to the terms upon which the Local Government Board have granted the loan applied for by the Exeter City Council for carrying out sewage disposal works by means of the septic tank system. It has been stated that the Local Government Board had allowed the scheme at Exeter, but had attached certain conditions which would involve a very much greater expenditure than the scheme itself—namely, that the effluent should be spread over a certain quantity of land.

It is hardly necessary to inform those who are at all conversant with the subject, says *The Devon and Exeter Daily Gazette*, that this condition is always enforced by the Local Government Board, no matter what system of dealing with sewage is adopted. It is a rule from which they never depart unless the outfall be into a tidal river or direct into the sea. Moreover, the quantity of land which the Local Government Board have required in connection with the Exeter scheme is the minimum quantity which they allow under any circumstances. Again, the requirement that the Exeter City Council shall accept the entire responsibility of the success or failure of the scheme is nothing exceptional, as it is well known that the Local Government Board never accept responsibility for the satisfactory working of any scheme which is laid before them. No matter what kind of a scheme is adopted, if unsatisfactory results followed its operation the Local Government Board would be the first to call upon the authority concerned to rectify it, even though the Board had a year or so before granted a loan for carrying out the works. It will thus be seen that no unusual conditions have been attached to the granting of the loan for carrying out sewage disposal works at Exeter by means of the septic tank system. As a matter of fact, too, it may be mentioned that the loan granted for land represents less than one-fifth of the amount sanctioned for the other portion of the scheme.

**Railway Companies and Road Locomotive Traffic.**—In view of the provision of clause 6 of the Act of Parliament recently passed at the instance of the Lancashire County Council, that a county council may, if they see fit, contribute, or join with other local authorities in contributing, to the rebuilding, widening or improvement of any bridge in the county belonging to any railway, canal or other company, corporation or person, and to the widening and improvement of the approaches thereto, and that any such contribution of the county council shall be paid out of the county fund and shall be deemed a special county purpose, the executive council of the County Councils Association addressed a circular to county councils requesting information as to whether railway companies have prohibited the passage of locomotives across over-line bridges ; and, if so, whether any inconvenience has arisen from such prohibition, and had the council taken any steps in the matter ; and also whether in the opinion of the council it would be desirable to promote a bill applying to counties generally the principles of the clause quoted. Replies to the circular have been received from twenty-eight councils.

## THE SURVEYORS' INSTITUTION.

### ORDINARY GENERAL MEETING.

The next ordinary general meeting will be held on Monday, when a paper will be read by Mr. Wm. Weaver, entitled "The London Building Act and the Official Supervision of Buildings." The chair will be taken at 8 o'clock.

### STUDENTS' PRELIMINARY EXAMINATION, 1899.

Those proposing to enter their names for the students' preliminary examination, to be held on the 18th and 19th of January next, must intimate their intention to the secretary before the last day of November. It is proposed to examine candidates from the counties of Lancashire, Cheshire, Yorkshire, Durham, Cumberland, Westmoreland and Northumberland at Manchester. Candidates from other counties in England and Wales will be examined in London. Irish candidates will be examined in Dublin.

### PROFESSIONAL EXAMINATIONS, 1899.

Students eligible for the proficiency examinations (which will commence on the 20th of March next) must give notice of the sub-division (Table A of Rules) in which they elect to be examined, not later than the 31st inst. Examinations qualifying for the classes of "Professional Associates" and "Fellows" will also commence on the 20th of March next. Names of applicants for these latter examinations to be sent in before the 31st inst. All particulars as to days, subjects and course of examination will be forwarded on application to the secretary. English candidates for the professional examinations will be examined in London. Irish candidates will be examined in Dublin.

## APPOINTMENTS VACANT.

*Official and all similar advertisements received later than Thursday morning are too late for classification and cannot therefore be included in these summaries until the following week. No advertisements received after 3 p.m. on Thursday can be inserted until the following week.*

CIVIL ENGINEERING ASSISTANT.—December 10th.—Corporation of Hull. £85.—Mr. A. E. White, city engineer.

ASSISTANT FOR THE INSPECTION OF BUILDINGS, &c.—December 12th.—Ilford Urban District Council. £120.—Mr. H. Shaw, A.M.I.C.E., surveyor to the council.

ASSISTANT SURVEYOR.—December 12th.—Corporation of Stoke-upon-Trent. £91.—Mr. J. B. Ashwell, town clerk.

DISTRICT ROAD SURVEYOR.—December 13th.—Gwyrfai Rural District Council. £150.—Mr. J. Henry Thomas, clerk to the council, Carnarvon.

SEWAGE FARM MANAGER.—December 14th.—Willenhall Urban District Council. 30s.—Mr. Chas. J. Jenkin, surveyor to the council.

INSPECTORS OF PAVEMENTS (FOUR).—December 15th.—Corporation of London. £200.—The Town Clerk, Public Health Department, Guildhall, E.C.

WATERWORKS PUMPING STATION ENGINEER, INSPECTOR OF WATER SERVICES, &c.—December 16th.—Newport Pagnell Urban District Council. 33s.—Mr. J. E. Hargreaves, surveyor to the council.

GENERAL ROAD FOREMAN.—December 17th.—Corporation of Cambridge. £2 14s.—Mr. J. E. L. Whitehead, town clerk.

ASSISTANT BOROUGH SURVEYOR AND INSPECTOR OF NUISANCES.—December 17th.—Corporation of Wenlock. £80.—Mr. Godfrey C. Cooper, town clerk.

DISTRICT MAIN ROAD SURVEYORS (Four).—December 19th.—Hertfordshire County Council. £130.—Mr. Urban A. Smith, county surveyor, 41 Parliament-street, London, S.W.

SURVEYOR.—December 20th. — Lytham Urban District Council.—Mr. Chas. A. Myers, clerk to the council.

HIGHWAY SURVEYOR.—December 21st.—Uxbridge Rural District Council. £200.—Mr. Charles Woodbridge, clerk to the council.

BUILDING INSPECTOR.—December 22nd.—Corporation of Stockport. £2 2s.—Mr. John Atkinson, borough surveyor.

## MUNICIPAL COMPETITIONS OPEN.

*Official and all similar advertisements received later than Thursday morning are too late for classification and cannot therefore be included in these summaries until the following week. No advertisements received after 3 p.m. on Thursday can be inserted until the following week.*

CHERTSEY.—December 23rd.—Sewerage and sewage disposal scheme for the Nos. 1 and 2 wards of the district. £50, £30 and £20.—Mr. T. E. Harland Chaldecott, clerk to the council.

HULL.—January 1st.—Erection of a central public library in Albion-street. £50, £30 and £20.—Mr. E. Laverack, town clerk.

HARROGATE.—January 2nd.—Erection of a pump-room, &c., at a cost not exceeding £8,000. £50, £30 and £20.—Mr. Samuel Stead, borough surveyor.

BRADFORD.—February 1st.—Erection of a central fire brigade station. £100, £50 and £30.—Mr. George McGuire, town clerk.

## MUNICIPAL CONTRACTS OPEN.

*Official and all similar advertisements received later than Thursday morning are too late for classification and cannot therefore be included in these summaries until the following week. No advertisements received after 3 p.m. on Thursday can be inserted until the following week.*

WORCESTER.—December 10th.—Supply of lead water pipes (2 in. to 1¼ in. in diameter), pig lead and block tin during the year 1899.—Mr. T. Caink, A.M.I.C.E., city engineer.

KING'S LYNN.—December 10th.—Supply during the twelve months ending December 31, 1899, of various stores, &c.—Mr. H. J. Weaver, borough engineer and surveyor.

SOUTHAMPTON.—December 10th.—Supply of 1,000 tons of granite for macadamising.—Mr. W. B. G. Bennett, borough engineer.

CARSHALTON.—December 12 h.—Supply of about 270 yards of 21-in. socketed stoneware pipes, for the urban district council.—Mr. William Willis Gale, A.M.I.C.E., surveyor to the council.

CHURCH.—December 12th.—Excavating, flagging and paving of water-street, for the urban district council.—Mr. John R. Redditch, clerk to the council.

BARNSLEY.—December 12th.—Supply of various electricity supply plant and the erection of tall chimney and engine, dynamos and boiler-house, storage-rooms and offices in Becket-square.—Mr. J. Henry Taylor, A.M.I.C.E., borough surveyor.

SOUTHPORT.—December 12th.—Boring of an artesian well at the electric light station in Coronet-street, Old-street, for the vestry.—Mr. H. Mansfield Robinson, clerk to the vestry.

ECCLES (Lancs.).—December 12th.—Erection of a bowl-house and pavilion, and the construction of a bowling-green on land in Eldon-road, Patricrofts.—Mr. G. W. Bailey, town clerk.

WILLESDEN.—December 13th.—Execution of certain road-making and other works at Willesden Green, between Strode-road and Hawthorn-road, for the urban district council.—Mr. O. Claude Robson, M.I.C.E., engineer to the council.

COVENTRY.—December 13th.—Construction of five electric light sub-stations.—Mr. J. E. Swindlehurst, city engineer.

WEST HAM.—December 13th.—Erection of a quarter sessions court, police cells and mortuary in West Ham-lane, Stratford.—Mr. Lewis Angell, borough engineer.

TURSTALL.—December 13th.—Various works in connection with the main drainage scheme, for the urban district council.—Mr. A. R. Wood, borough surveyor.

NEW HUNSTANTON.—December 13th.—Alterations to engine-house and engine foundations, for the urban district council.—Mr. J. S. B. Glasier, clerk to the council.

HORWICH.—December 13th.—Supply and delivery of one road-sweeping machine, for the urban district council.—Mr. G. J. Woolridge, surveyor to the council.

HORWICH—December 13th.—Laying of about 800 square yards of flagging, for the urban district council.—Mr. Peter Taberrer, clerk to the council.

BARKING (Essex).—December 13th.—Erection of eighty-three cottages for the working classes in Creekmouth-lane, for the urban district council.—Mr. C. J. Dawson, F.R.I.B.A., surveyor to the council.

FULHAM.—December 13th.—Alterations to the coroner's court, Munster-road for the vestry.—Mr. Charles Botterill, A.M.I.C.E., surveyor to the vestry.

BARNOLDSWICK.—December 14th.—Supply and fixing at the water-works of one non-condensing steam engine, for the urban district council.—Mr. D. E. Garlick, gas and water engineer to the council.

ATHERTON.—December 14th.—Erection of new council offices on the site of the present premises in Bolton New-road, for the urban district council.—Mr. Daniel Schofield, clerk to the council.

HACKNEY.—December 14th.—Supply of gulley grates, manhole covers and other sewer ironwork, for the vestry.—Mr. James Lovegrove, surveyor to the vestry.

MANSFIELD.—December 14th.—Construction of about 500 yards of 9-in. pipe sewer.—Mr. R. Frank Vallance, borough surveyor.

MANSFIELD.—December 14th.—Construction of about 1,050 yards of brick sewer and storm overflows and 870 yards of pipe sewers.—Mr. R. Frank Vallance, borough surveyor.

TWICKENHAM.—December 14th.—Supply of 500 tons of Guernsey granite spalls, for the urban district council.—Mr. F. W. Pearce, surveyor to the council.

MACCLESFIELD.—December 14th.—Supply of drain pipes, castings, ironmongery, cement, bricks, &c., during the year ending 31st December, 1899.—Mr. W. Frodk. Taylor, town clerk.

HAMPSTEAD.—December 16th.—Removal of slop from the roads and gullies in the parish for one or three years from March 26th next, for the vestry.—Mr. Arthur P. Johnson, clerk to the vestry.

PRESTON.—December 15th.—Levelling, paving, channelling, &c., of the roads between St. David's-road and St. Michael's-road.—The Borough Surveyor.

WALLASEY.—December 15th.—Supply of waste-water meter and fittings, for the urban district council.—Mr. H. W. Cook, clerk to the council, Public Offices, Egremont.

LEICESTER.—December 15th.—Supply of brushes, &c., as may be required during 1899.—Mr. E. Geo. Mawbey, M.I.C.E., borough surveyor.

RYDE.—December 16th.—Erection of a fire brigade station and stabling in the council yard, Chapel-street, for the urban district council.—Mr. D. G. Macdonald, A.M.I.C.E., surveyor to the council.

PRESTON.—December 16th.—Alteration of the cattle stage at the cattle market, Brook-street North.—The Borough Surveyor.

PRESTON.—December 16th.—Extension of the cellars at the "Regatta Inn" in Fishergate-hill.—The Borough Surveyor.

PRESTON.—December 16th.—Alteration of the grammar school in Cross-road.—Mr. Henry Hamer, town clerk.

HULL.—December 16th.—Draining, macadamising, flagging, &c., of Reed-street, Little Reed-street, Tynemouth-street, and Tulls-street.—Mr. A. E. White, city engineer.

BIRKENHEAD.—December 17th.—Supply and erection of various electric light plant, for the urban district council.—Mr. F. Stevens, clerk to the council.

GALWAY.—December 17th.—Supply of ironwork for bridges and the construction of a new road near Moon, for the county council.—Mr. James Perry, M.I.C.E., county surveyor, Galway.

NORTH RIDING (Yorkshire).—December 17th.—Widening of Thornaby and Stainborough main road from Stainsby Beck to Oswald terrace, for the county council.—Mr. Walker Stead, M.I.C.E., county surveyor, Northallerton.

LOSTOCK.—December 17th.—Supply, during the twelve months ending December, 1899, of broken granite, granite setts, kerbs, cast iron work, Portland cement, blue paving bricks, earth-ware pipes, &c.—Mr. J. W. Wardle, borough surveyor.

PADIHAM.—December 19th.—Supply of gravel at per ton, for the vestry.—Mr. Frank Rothridge, clerk to the vestry.

MORLEY (Yorkshire).—December 19th.—Supply and kerbing of Mitchell-street.—Mr. W. Putman, A.M.I.C.E., borough engineer and surveyor.

UXBRIDGE.—December 19th.—Supply of 265 tons of cast-iron pipes and special castings, for the rural district council.—Mr. John Anstie, engineer, 10 Marchwood-crescent, Ealing, W.

WEST RIDING (Yorkshire).—December 19th.—Erection of two new police stations, with cells and officers' residences. at Worsborough Dale and Ardsley, near Barnsley, for the county council.—Mr. J. Vickers Edwards, county surveyor, Wakefield.

HORNSEY.—December 19th.—Sewering, levelling, paving. metalling, channelling and making-good of Temple-road and Rathcoole-gardens (1st section), for the urban district council.—Mr. E. J. Lovegrove, engineer to the council.

ULVERSTONE.—December 21st.—Supply and laying of about 207 yards of 3½-in. turned and bore iron water pipes and the construction of a storage tank, for the rural district council.—Mr. Chas. W. Dean, clerk to the council.

BLACKPOOL.—December 21st.—Various sewering, levelling, paving, metalling, channelling, &c., works.—Mr. J. Wolstenholme, borough surveyor.

PORTSLADE-BY-SEA.—December 22nd.—Construction of stoneware and other sewers for the drainage of the district, for the urban district council.—Mr. Charles O. Blaber, M.I.C.E., 64 Ship-street, Brighton.

EDEYRNION (Wales).—December 22nd.—Excavation, masonry and other works in connection with the proposed new bridge over the river Dee at Corwen, for the rural district council.—Mr. Thomas Hughes, clerk to the council. Corwen.

HENGOE.—December 22nd.—Extension of the main sewer along the Edgware-road to Elstree, for the rural district council.—Mr. F. J. Seabrook, clerk to the council.

LEICESTER.—December 23rd.—Erection of working-class dwellings in Winifred-street.—Mr. James Bell, town clerk.

DARTMOUTH.—December 24th.—Ventilating, painting and other works at the Guildhall.—Mr. T. O. Veale, borough surveyor.

WILLENHALL (Staffs.).—December 30th.—Erection of a new span-roof greenhouse, 30 ft. by 12 ft., at the new cemetery at Bentley, for the urban district council.—Mr. Chas. J. Jenkin, engineer and surveyor to the council.

ROTHERHAM.—December 31st.—Supply and erection of sludge-pressing plant, boilers, sewage ejectors and sewage lifts, for the corporation.—Mr. R. E. W. Berrington, Bank-buildings, Wolverhampton.

RAMSGATE.—December 31st.—Supply of a compound condensing beam engine at the Whitehall pumping station.—Mr. William A. Valon, gas and water engineer to the corporation.

DUNDEE.—December 31st.—Supply of 500 2-in., 1,000 4-in., 500 6-in. and 500 9-in. turned and bored cast-iron pipes, for the water commissioners.—Mr. George Baxter, engineer and manager to the commissioners, 93 Commercial-street, Dundee.

TAUNTON.—January 1st.—Construction of a sewer, about 1,800 yards long, from Railway-street to the site of the sewage outfall works in the Target Field.—Mr. James H. Smith, borough surveyor.

JOHANNESBURG, S.A.—January 5th.—Supply of a complete carburetted water-gas plant, for the corporation.—Messrs. Robert Whyte & Co., 22 Bury-street, St. Mary Axe, London, E.C.

WEST HAM.—January 7th.—Enlargement of the hospital in Southern-road, Plaistow, E.—Mr. Fred. E. Hilleary, town clerk.

SOUTHAMPTON.—January 16th.—Construction of concrete foundations, erection of brick, steel and concrete superstructures of new infirmary wards, sanitary blocks, boiler-house, tail chimney shaft, and sundry other work at the county lunatic asylum at Knowle, near Fareham, for the county council.—Mr. W. J. Taylor, county surveyor, The Castle, Winchester.

LONDON.—January 24th.—Construction of a tunnel for pedestrian traffic under the river Thames from Greenwich to Poplar, for the county council.—Mr. C. J. Stewart, clerk to the council, County Hall, Spring-gardens, S.W.

SHANGHAI.—March 15th.—Construction and working of about 23 miles of electric tramways on the trolley system, for the municipal council.—Messrs. J. Pook & Co., 8 Jeffery's-square, St. Mary Axe, London, E.C.

## TENDERS FOR MUNICIPAL WORKS OR SUPPLIES.

*ACCEPTED.

BERMONDSEY.—For the supply of two slop-vans, for the vestry.—Mr. Frederick Ryall, clerk to the vestry :—

|  | Each. |
|---|---|
| British Waggon and Carriage Works, Limited | £46 |
| E. & H. Hora, Limited | 45 |
| Glover & Sons, Limited (with patent tipping gear) | 44 |
| Glover & Sons, Limited (with screw rear) | 43 |
| A. Randell | 43 |
| A. Parker* | 43 |
| T. Baker & Son | 38 |

COWES.—For the supply of about 1,500 yards of 6-in. and 400 yards of 4-in. cast-iron socket pipes, for the urban district council.—Mr. J. W. Webster, engineer and surveyor to the council :—

R. Laidlaw & Son, Alliance Foundry, Glasgow.*—4-in. pipes, £5 14s. per ton ; 6-in. pipes, £5 10s. 6d, per ton ; special castings, 10s. per ton ; hydrants, £1 13s. 6d. each ; 4-in. sluice valves, £1 16s. each ; 4-in. sluice valves, £2 5s. 6d. each ; 6-in. sluice valves, £2 7s. each ; 5-in. by 3-in. rolled steel joists, £9 10s. per ton ; standpipes and valves, £37 per ton.

COWES.—For the construction of a cast-iron water tank to hold 70,000 gallons, for the urban district council.—Mr. J. W. Webster, engineer and surveyor to the council :—

| T. Howden & Sons, Wakefield* | £1,034 |
|---|---|
| Engineer's estimate, £1,100. | |

EASTRY.—For the supply and laying of 1,460 yards of 5-in., 940 yards of 4-in. and 2,020 yards of 3-in. cast-iron socket pipes, for the rural district council.—Mr. F. S. Cloke, clerk to the council :—

| G. Green, Hatherley, Cheltenham | £1,840 |
|---|---|
| Hextel, Sons & Peattie, Ebury-street, London | 1,800 |
| Seamark & Hudson, Faversham | 1,620 |
| S. White & Son, Queen Victoria-street, E.C. | 1,599 |
| H. Shardlow, Nottingham | 1,530 |
| A. C. Oatley, Lloyd-square, S.W. | 1,486 |
| Jenkins & Son, Leamington Spa | 1,347 |
| S. V. Bond, Ramsgate* | 1,205 |

PORTSMOUTH.—For the laying of compressed and asphalte paving in Palmerston-road, Russell-street, south of Hyde Park-road and Charlotte-street.—Mr. Alexander Hellard, town clerk :—

|  | Per Yard. |
|---|---|
|  | s. d. |
| French Asphalte Company | 13 4 |
| Val de Travers Asphalte Company | 13 3 |
| Limmer Asphalte Paving Company* | 12 9 |
| Trinidad Lake Asphalte Company | 12 |

RADCLIFFE.—Sewering of Market-street.—Mr. J. Sharples, clerk to the council :—

| J. Cunningham, Manchester | £315 |
|---|---|
| T. Rowland, Northwich | 263 |
| J. Foster, Ramsbottom | 256 |
| S. Seadon, Bolton | 226 |
| E. Ellis, Bury | 219 |
| Etheonge & Clark, Crumpsall, Manchester* | 216 |

## MEETINGS.

*Secretaries and others will oblige by sending early notice of dates of forthcoming meetings.*

### DECEMBER.

10.—British Association of Waterworks Engineers : Special general meeting. 10 a.m.

10.—British Association of Waterworks Engineers : General meeting ; Mr. H. Bertram Nichols, A.M.I.C.E., on " Water Supply from the Lower Greensand and Constructional Works connected therewith at Leighton Buzzard." 11 a.m.

12.—Surveyors' Institution : Ordinary general meeting ; Mr. William Weaver on " The London Building Act and the Official Supervision of Buildings." 8 p.m.

13.—Liverpool Self-propelled Traffic Association : Discussion on " The ' Judges' Report on the 1898 Trials, and the Conditions for the 1899 Trials." 8 p.m.

14.—Sanitary Institute : Sessional meeting ; Dr. E. F. Willoughby on " Some Prevalent Fallacies in Vital Statistics." 8 p.m.

14.—Society of Arts : Mr. Albert Rollit, M.P., on " Commercial Education." 8 p.m.

17.—Sanitary Inspectors' Association : General meeting. 6 p.m.

17.—Sanitary Inspectors' Association : Extraordinary meeting. 8 p.m.

19.—Royal Institute of British Architects : Messrs. Burnell and Drake on " The Application of Electric Power to Practical Purposes in Buildings, and the Production and Use of Electricity for Lighting Country Houses." 8 p.m.

**Berlin.** — The municipal council recently determined to approve of a contract between the municipality and the various Berlin electrical works, according to which these firms and companies will supply electricity to the city of Berlin till the year 1915, while the municipality will participate to a considerable extent in their profits. A violent controversy has raged for some time around the question of the contract. The view ultimately prevailed, however, that the electric industry was still in an early stage of its development, and that new inventions might easily place the capital value of the existing works and machinery in a doubtful position. The contract was finally approved by sixty-six votes to fifty-one votes.

## NOTICES.

THE SURVEYOR AND MUNICIPAL AND COUNTY ENGINEER may be ordered direct, through any of Messrs. Smith & Son's book-stalls, or of any newsagent in the United Kingdom. Applications to the Offices for single copies by post must in all cases be accompanied by stamps.

The Prepaid Subscription (including postage) is as follows :

|  | Twelve Months. | Six Months. | Three Months. |
|---|---|---|---|
| United Kingdom | 15s. | 7s. 6d. | 3s. 9d. |
| Continent, the Colonies, India, | | | |
| United States, &c. | 19s. | 9s. 6d. | 4s. 9d. |

The International News Company, 83 and 85 Duane-street, New York City ; The Toronto News Company, Toronto ; and The Montreal News Company, Montreal, have been appointed agents in the United States and Canada for the sale of THE SURVEYOR AND MUNICIPAL AND COUNTY ENGINEER. A thin paper edition is printed for circulation abroad.

EDITORIAL OFFICES :—
24 BRIDE-LANE, FLEET-STREET, LONDON, E.C.

ADVERTISEMENT AND PUBLISHING OFFICES :—
13 NEW STREET-HILL, FLEET-STREET, LONDON, E.C.

## APPOINTMENTS OPEN.

WEALDSTONE URBAN DISTRICT COUNCIL.

TEMPORARY ASSISTANT SURVEYOR.

Applications are invited for the above appointment from persons between the ages of twenty-five and thirty-five, who have had good experience in a municipal surveyor's office, in surveying and levelling, are good draughtsmen, and able to prepare accurate working drawings, specifications, bills of quantities, and to assist generally.

Salary at the rate of £125 per annum ; at least six months' engagement for satisfactory services. The whole time must be devoted to the duties, which are to be commenced as soon as possible after the appointment is made.

Further particulars may be obtained from Mr. F. J. Hopwood, Engineer and Surveyor, Council Chambers, Wealdstone.

Applications, stating age, present and previous occupation, together with copies of three recent testimonials, to be sent to me and addressed to the Chairman of the Council, and endorsed " Assistant Surveyor," not later than Monday, the 26th day of December, 1898.

R. J. BRYANT,
Clerk to the Council.

Council Chambers, Peel-road,
Wealdstone, Middlesex.

# BOROUGH OF STOKE-UPON-TRENT.
## ASSISTANT SURVEYOR.

The Town Council require the services of an Assistant to the Borough Surveyor.

Salary, £91 per annum.

Candidates must have a thorough knowledge of the duties appertaining to the appointment.

Personal canvassing will be a disqualification.

Applications, in own handwriting, accompanied by not more than three recent testimonials, and endorsed "Assistant Surveyor," to be received by me not later than December 12th.

JNO. B. ASHWELL,
Town Clerk.

Stoke-upon-Trent.
November 24, 1898.

# ILFORD URBAN DISTRICT COUNCIL.

The Ilford Urban District Council require in the Surveyor's department an Assistant for the inspection of buildings and other work, at a salary of £120 per annum.

The person appointed will be required to devote his whole time to the discharge of his duties, a list of which can be obtained from Mr. H. Shaw, A.M.I.C.E., the Council's Surveyor, at his offices, 7 Cranbrook-road, Ilford.

Applications, in candidate's own handwriting, accompanied by copies of three recent testimonials, stating age (which must not be under twenty-five or over forty-five), qualifications and experience, endorsed "Application for Surveyor's Assistant," under seal, and addressed to the Chairman, must be sent to me on or before noon on Monday, the 12th December next.

Canvassing, directly or indirectly, is strictly prohibited and will be deemed a disqualification.

(By order)
JOHN W. BENTON,
Clerk to the Council.

Council Offices, Ilford, Essex.
November 25, 1898.

# HERTFORDSHIRE COUNTY COUNCIL.
## APPOINTMENT OF FOUR DISTRICT MAIN ROAD SURVEYORS.

Applications are invited for the post of District Main Road Surveyor from persons who have had thorough experience in all the duties pertaining to a road surveyor.

Salary, £130 per annum clear of all travelling and office expenses, rising to a maximum of £160 per annum.

Preference will be given to applicants who are cyclists and not more than thirty-five years of age.

The persons appointed will act under the instructions of the County Surveyor, and will have charge of a district comprising about 120 miles of rural main roads. They will be required to devote the whole of their time to the service of the County Council.

Particulars of duties, terms of appointment, and form of application, may be obtained by applying, by letter, to the County Surveyor.

Applications, in candidate's own handwriting, accompanied by copies of not more than three testimonials, must be sent to the undersigned not later than Monday, December 19, 1898.

URBAN A. SMITH, C.E.,
County Surveyor of Hertfordshire.

41 Parliament street, Westminster, S.W.
December 7, 1898.

# BOROUGH OF WENLOCK.
## APPOINTMENT OF ASSISTANT SURVEYOR AND INSPECTOR OF NUISANCES.

The Town Council of the Borough of Wenlock are prepared to receive applications for the appointment of an Assistant to the Borough Surveyor and Inspector of Nuisances for one year commencing from 1st February next, at a salary of £80.

The person appointed will be required to devote the whole of his time to the duties of the office and to reside in Much Wenlock. He must be fully competent to perform the duties of the office and to act under the direction of the Borough Surveyor and Inspector of Nuisances.

Applications, stating age and previous experience, with not more than three recent testimonials, to be forwarded to me, the undersigned, not later than Saturday, the 17th instant, endorsed "Application for Position of Assistant Surveyor and Inspector."

Canvassing any member of the Council is strictly prohibited.

GODFREY C. COOPER,
Town Clerk.

Much Wenlock.
December 6, 1898.

# CORPORATION OF LONDON.
## PUBLIC HEALTH DEPARTMENT.

The Corporation of London hereby give notice that they are about to appoint Four Inspectors of Pavements, at a salary of £200 per annum each, to be increased from time to time, according to merit and ability, to a maximum of £300 per annum.

The appointments will be subject to three months' notice on either side.

The officers appointed will be required to devote their whole time to the duties of their office, and must be prepared to undergo a medical examination.

Applicants must have been accustomed to the superintendence of paving, building and drainage works, and must understand the qualities of building materials.

Applications, in candidate's own handwriting, stating age (not under thirty or over forty-five years), height, whether married or single, with copies of not more than three recent testimonials, must be delivered on or before Thursday, the 15th day of December, 1898, addressed "Town Clerk, Public Health Department, Guildhall."

The Act of Parliament under which the appointments are made requires that the inspectors shall reside within the district to which they are appointed.

Copies of the list of duties may be seen on application at the Guildhall, as above.

MONCKTON.
Guildhall.
December, 1898.

# URBAN DISTRICT OF LYTHAM.
## SURVEYOR.

The Lytham Urban Council are prepared to receive applications for the appointment of Surveyor.

The population of the district is 7,200, and the nett rate-able value £36,608.

Candidates must have had experience of the duties under a local authority.

All applications must be on the prescribed form, which can be obtained at the offices of the Council by forwarding stamped addressed envelope.

Applications, stating salary required, and endorsed "Surveyor," and addressed "The Chairman of the Council," must be delivered at these offices not later than noon on the 20th instant.

Canvassing, directly or indirectly, will disqualify.

(By order)
CHAS. A. MYERS,
Clerk to the Council.

Urban Council Offices, Lytham.
December 5, 1898.

# NEWPORT PAGNELL URBAN DISTRICT COUNCIL.

The above Council invite applications for the position of Engineer at their Waterworks Pumping Station, Inspector of Water Services and General Waterworks Fitter.

Applicants must be competent to take full charge of the machinery and have a good knowledge of waterworks fittings, be able to execute ordinary waterworks repairs, and be prepared to undertake not to engage in any other business.

Wages to commence at 30s. per week, rising by increments of 1s. per week per annum to a maximum of 33s. per week, with free use of garden at the Water Tower. The engagement will be determinable by one month's notice on either side.

Age not to exceed forty years.

Particulars of duties may be obtained on application to Mr. J. E. Hargreaves, Surveyor to the Council, at his office, Newport Pagnell.

Application, in own handwriting, accompanied by three recent testimonials, endorsed "Waterworks Engineer," to be sent to me, the undersigned, not later than Friday, December 16, 1898.

(By order)
E. P. WARD,
Clerk.

# COUNTY BOROUGH OF STOCKPORT.
## APPOINTMENT OF BUILDING INSPECTOR.

The General Purposes Committee invite applications for the appointment of Building Inspector in the Borough Surveyor's department.

Candidates must be thoroughly qualified persons, to be accurate surveyors and levellers, and will be required to undertake the inspection of new buildings and drains, set out and fix levels for new streets, and make surveys of all new houses, buildings and drains, and to keep the necessary records in connection therewith, and to be well up in building construction and the Model Building By-Laws.

Salary, £2 2s. per week. Age to be between thirty and forty years. A list of duties may be obtained on application.

Applications, in candidate's own handwriting, stating age, and accompanied by not more than three copies of recent testimonials, and endorsed "Building Inspector," to be sent to Mr. John Atkinson, Borough Surveyor, on or before Thursday, December 22, 1898.

Canvassing will be considered a disqualification.

WALTER HYDE,
Town Clerk.

# UXBRIDGE RURAL DISTRICT COUNCIL.

The above Council are prepared to receive applications for the appointment of a Highway Surveyor for the Uxbridge Rural District.

The district comprises nine parishes and about 90 miles of parish highways.

The Surveyor will be required to devote the whole of his time to the duties, and to reside within the district or in Uxbridge, as may be approved by the Council.

Salary, £200 per annum, to include all travelling expenses, but an office will be provided by the Council.

Applications, in the candidate's own handwriting, stating age, previous experience in road maintenance, and keeping the accounts, &c., relating thereto, accompanied by three recent testimonials as to character and practical knowledge of road work, to be sent to me on or before Wednesday, the 21st December instant.

The person appointed must be prepared to enter into a bond in the sum of £200.

Notice will be sent to any candidate who may be required to attend before the Council.

Canvassing, directly or indirectly, is prohibited.

Any further particulars may be obtained on application to me.

CHARLES WOODBRIDGE,
Clerk.

Council Offices, 38 High-street, Uxbridge.
December 5, 1898.

## GWYRFAI RURAL DISTRICT COUNCIL.

*WANTED, A DULY-QUALIFIED SURVEYOR.*

### QUALIFICATIONS.

Competent to discharge the duties of a district road surveyor, and capable of preparing plans, specifications, estimates, &c., to accompany applications to the Local Government Board for sanction to loans for the construction of works as the Council may require.

### DUTIES.

To undertake the care of all the roads belonging to the Council.

To prepare plans, &c., superintend works of drainage and water supply that may be constructed by orders of the Council.

To see that the by-laws with respect to new streets and buildings are duly observed.

To attend all meetings of the Council, to submit reports with respect to the roads and sanitary works that he may be overlooking, and to submit the workmen's pay-sheets and accounts of all expenses connected with the roads and sanitary works.

To keep all accounts and to discharge all duties of road and sanitary surveyors, and to obey all directions of the Council.

### CONDITIONS.

Salary, £150 per annum.

To devote all his time to the duties of the office.

To provide security for the proper discharge of the duties in a bond given by a duly-approved guarantee society in the sum of £500.

The person appointed must be conversant with the Welsh and English languages, and must not be over forty years of age.

Canvassing the councillors, directly or indirectly, strictly prohibited, and will be deemed a disqualification.

### APPLICATIONS,

with not more than four testimonials of recent date, stating age, qualifications and experience, to be received by me not later than Tuesday, the 13th day of December.

The selected candidates will be asked to attend the meeting of the Council at which the final selection may be made, but no expenses will be allowed.

J. HENRY THOMAS,
Clerk to the Council.

Carnarvon.
November 26, 1898.

## BOROUGH OF CAMBRIDGE.
### GENERAL ROAD FOREMAN.

Wanted, by the Corporation, a Foreman, to take charge of the whole of the men, horses, plant, &c., in the Highway Department, under the Borough Engineer and Surveyor.

Applicants must have a thorough knowledge of paviors' and masons' work, the setting-out of new and the maintenance of old roads, and none but those who have been previously employed in a similar capacity need apply.

Wages, £2 10s. per week, with an additional 4s. per week for superintending the erection and removal of the market stalls.

Applications, accompanied by *copies* of not more than two recent testimonials, to be sent in to me not later than Saturday, the 17th instant.

Canvassing, either personally or by letter (except by circular enclosing testimonials), will be viewed with disfavour.

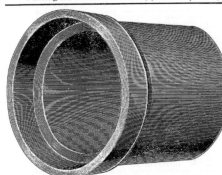

Candidates must state in their applications the earliest date they would be prepared to enter on their duties.

J. E. L. WHITEHEAD,
Town Clerk.

Guildhall.
December 5, 1898.

## TENDERS WANTED.

RUGBY URBAN DISTRICT COUNCIL.
TO BUILDERS.

The Urban District Council of Rugby invite tenders for the Erection and Completion of a Fire Brigade Station and Stabling in the Council Yard, Chapel-street, Rugby.

The drawings may be seen, and a copy of the specifications, bill of quantities and form of tender obtained, on application at the office of the undersigned on payment of 2 guineas, which will be returned on receipt of a *bonâ-fide* tender.

Sealed tenders, endorsed "Fire Brigade Station," to be sent to Mr. T. M. Wratislaw, on or before the 16th day of December next.

The Council do not bind themselves to accept the lowest or any tender.

(By order)
D. G. MACDONALD, ASSOC.M.INST.C.E.,
Surveyor to the Council.

Rugby.
November 17, 1898.

TWICKENHAM URBAN DISTRICT
COUNCIL.
GRANITE SPALLS.

The Twickenham Urban District Council invite tenders for about 500 tons of Guernsey Granite Spalls.

Persons tendering must quote prices for the granite delivered at the Brentford Union Workhouse, at Isleworth, Middlesex.

The granite must be delivered at such a time or times as the Surveyor to the Council may direct, in quantities to suit the convenience of the Council, but the whole of the granite to be delivered within one month from the date of the contract to supply.

Tenders, endorsed "Tenders for Granite," to be delivered to me on or before 1 o'clock on Wednesday, 14th December next.

Forms, on which tenders will only be received, and further information, if required, may be obtained of Mr. F. W. Pearce, Surveyor to the Council, Town Hall, Twickenham, to whom samples of the granite tendered are to be sent on or before the time named for sending in tenders.

The Council does not bind itself to accept the lowest or any tender.

(By order)
H. JASON SAUNDERS,
Clerk.

Town Hall, Twickenham.
November 28, 1898.

COUNTY OF SOUTHAMPTON.

*COUNTY LUNATIC ASYLUM, KNOWLE, NEAR
FAREHAM.—CONTRACT No. 1.*

TO BUILDING CONTRACTORS.

Persons desirous of tendering for the Construction of Concrete Foundations, the Erection of Brick, Steel and Concrete Superstructures of New Infirmary Wards, Sanitary Blocks, Boiler-House, Tall Chimney Shaft, and sundry other works connected therewith, at the County Lunatic Asylum, Knowle, Fareham, may see the plans and specification, and obtain bills of quantities and all other information, on application at the office of Mr. W. J. Taylor, County Surveyor, The Castle, Winchester, on and after Monday, December 12th next, between the hours of 9 a.m. and 5 p.m.; Saturdays between 9 a.m. and 1 p.m. A deposit of one £10 Bank of England note will be required for each bill of quantities, and will be refunded on receipt of a *bonâ-fide* tender.

The foundations are to be commenced in February, 1899, and the superstructures in March, as the weather may permit.

Tenders, strictly in accordance with forms supplied by the County Surveyor, to be delivered to me on or before Monday, January 16, 1899.

The Committee of Visitors do not bind themselves to accept the lowest or any tender.

JOHN R. WYATT,
Clerk to the Committee of Visitors.

Knowle.
November 30, 1898.

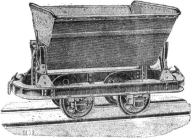

## UXBRIDGE RURAL DISTRICT COUNCIL.
### COWLEY, HILLINGDON EAST, WEST DRAYTON AND YIEWSLEY MAIN DRAINAGE WORKS.

The above Council are prepared to receive tenders for the Supply and Delivery at West Drayton station of about 265 tons of Cast-Iron Pipes and Special Castings.

Copy of specification and drawing can be obtained on application to Mr. John Anstie, the Engineer to the Works, 10 Marchwood-crescent, Ealing, W., on deposit of the sum of £2 with him, which will be repaid on the return of the said documents.

Copies of the schedule of pipes and specials, with form of tender, can also be obtained from the Engineer.

Sealed tenders, marked " Tender for Iron Pipes," to be delivered to me, at my office, 38 High-street, Uxbridge, before 12 noon Monday, the 19th December next.

The Council do not bind themselves to accept the lowest or any tender.

CHARLES WOODBRIDGE,
Clerk to the Council.
November 29, 1898.

## HORNSEY URBAN DISTRICT COUNCIL.
### TO ROAD AND SEWER CONTRACTORS.

The Hornsey Urban District Council are prepared to receive tenders for Sewering, Levelling, Paving, Metalling, Channelling and making good the following road and portion of road situate within the district of Hornsey—viz.,—

(1) Temple-road, and
(2) Rathcoole-gardens (first section).

Plans and specifications may be seen, and forms of tender and all information obtained, on application to Mr. E. J. Lovegrove, Engineer to the Council, at the offices mentioned below, on any morning between the hours of 10 and 12 o'clock, on a sum of £2 being deposited with the Clerk to the Council, which sum will be retained by the Council, and deemed to be forfeited if a bond-fide tender is not made by the depositor.

If a tender is made which is not accepted the sum deposited will be returned, and if a tender is accepted such sum will be retained by the Council until the contract has been executed by the depositor, and will be forfeited in the event of his or his sureties failing or neglecting to execute such contract, or the bond accompanying same, within seven days after he or they respectively shall have been requested to execute the same.

No tender will be considered except on the prescribed form.

Sealed and endorsed tenders are to be deposited in the tender-box in my department not later than 4 o'clock p.m. on Monday, the 19th day of December instant.

The Council reserve to themselves the right to decline all, or any, or any portion, of the tenders sent in.
(By order)
F. D. ASKEY,
Clerk to the District Council.
Offices, Southwood-lane, Highgate, N.
December 6, 1898.

## PORTSLADE-BY-SEA DRAINAGE.
### TO CONTRACTORS.

The Urban District Council of Portslade-by-Sea are prepared to receive tenders for the Construction of Stoneware and other Sewers, together with the necessary Manholes, Inspection Shafts, Flushing Tanks, &c., for the drainage of their district into the intercepting sewer of the joint parishes of Portslade by-Sea and Southwick, in the county of Sussex.

The works are to be in accordance with plans and specifications prepared by Mr. Charles O. Blaber, Civil Engineer, M.I.C.E., 64 Ship-street, Brighton, at whose office the plans may be inspected, and copies of the specification and bill of quantities obtained on payment of a deposit of 5 guineas, which will be returned on receipt of a bond-fide tender.

Sealed tenders, endorsed "Portslade-by-Sea Drainage," are to be delivered at my office before noon on the 22nd day of December, 1898.

The Council do not bind themselves to accept the lowest or any tender.
THOMAS AUSTEN,
Clerk to the Council.
Council Office, Portslade-by-Sea.
November 29, 1898.

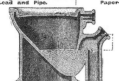

# The Surveyor

### And Municipal and County Engineer.

Vol. XIV., No. 361.    LONDON, DECEMBER 16, 1898.    Weekly, Price 3d.

## Minutes of Proceedings.

**The Repair of Main Roads.**

The provisions of the Local Government Act of 1888 with reference to main roads have been somewhat fruitful in litigation. Sec. 11 of that Act, it will be remembered, provides for the handing over to the county councils of all main roads, with all the powers and duties of highway boards in connection with them, subject, however, to this qualification, that an option is given to urban authorities to retain their own main roads, with a further provision that where this option is exercised the county council is to make an annual payment "towards the costs of the maintenance and repair and reasonable improvement connected with the maintenance and repair" of the roads retained. The amount of this payment is to be determined (unless agreed between the councils) by arbitration of the Local Government Board. There are further clauses in the section, including a provision enabling the county council to require the district council to undertake the maintenance of any main road in consideration of an annual payment "for the costs of the undertaking," to be determined in the same manner. With these latter clauses, however, we are not immediately concerned, our present purpose being to recall one or two decisions bearing upon those instances in which district councils have exercised the option of retaining the control of main roads. The provision that in such cases the county council is to contribute "towards" the cost of maintenance, &c., at first gave rise to considerable discussion. It was argued on the one hand that the use of the word "towards" showed that the legislature did not intend to make the county council liable for the whole of the cost; whilst, on the other hand, it was contended that the word was used merely to enable the council to dispute improper or unreasonable charges, there being apparently no reason why they should not bear the entire cost (properly incurred) in these instances, just as much as when they themselves managed the roads. This question, however, may now be regarded as practically set at rest in favour of the latter view. In *Wiltshire County Council* v. *Marlborough Borough Council*, which was a special case stated for the opinion of the Court on several points in difference between these two councils, one of the questions submitted for decision was "whether the obligation of the county council under sec. 11, sub-secs. 2 and 3, is to repay annually to the borough the actual cost (assuming it to be reasonably and properly incurred) of the maintenance, repair and reasonable improvement of the said footpaths during the preceding year, whether such cost be normal or increased by reasonable improvements connected with maintenance and repair, and whether it be defrayed by the borough out of current rates or by means of a loan." The Court (Lord Coleridge and Mr. Justice Day) expressed a very decided opinion that the county council were bound to reimburse the borough council the whole of the cost incurred, and that, in fact, the

term "towards" as used in the section did not necessarily imply something less than the whole. It is manifest that even had the Court felt compelled to construe the term *au pied de la lettre*, an award of the total cost *minus* the smallest coin of the realm would have sufficed to satisfy such a literal interpretation, whilst at the same time giving the borough council in substance all that they obtained by the contrary decision. Another important point which this case settles is as to the mode of reimbursement by the county council where the district council has borrowed the necessary funds for repairing the roads, the loan being repayable by instalments extending over a fixed period. The question, indeed, was raised, as we have seen, whether the liability of the county council arose at all where this method had been adopted. But the point was not contested very seriously, and the Court decided that, although undoubtedly liable, the county council could only be called upon to pay the amount so borrowed by the same instalments and at the same time as the district council themselves were bound to repay it.

Another question which arose in connection with this subject was as to the footpaths of main roads. In ordinary language the word "road" is, it must be admitted, an ambiguous term. When we talk about "the London Road" or "the Brighton Road," and so forth, we refer to the entire highway, comprising both the carriageway and the footpaths (if any). But, on the other hand, scores of instances will occur to the reader in which the term "road" is used of the carriageway only, in contradistinction to the footpath. It was in this latter sense, according to the contention raised on behalf of certain county councils, that the word was used in the Act. It will have been noticed that in the case last referred to the cost of maintaining and repairing footpaths was claimed and allowed, but the point does not appear to have been contested in that case, the dispute being, as we have seen, limited to other matters. One of the first cases in which the question was fully considered was *Warminster Local Board* v. *Wilts County Council*, in which Mr. Justice Charles decided against the narrow interpretation to which we have referred, holding that the footpaths were parts of the road within the meaning of the Act, and that the liability of the county council extended to the cost of their maintenance and repair and reasonable improvement, whether gravelled, paved, or asphalted, &c. This case was followed in *Matlock Urban District Council* v. *Derby County Council*, and also in *Burslem Corporation* v. *Staffordshire County Council*. Both these cases, which originally came before the Queen's Bench Division, were taken to the Court of Appeal, where the decision of the Court below was confirmed in each instance. Nevertheless, the county council in the former case had the hardihood to go to the House of Lords. But the result was a confirmation of the view of the Courts below; and this long-vexed question was thus, once for all, definitely set at rest beyond the risk of overruling, since even the House of Lords itself (as was recently seen in *London Tramways Company, Limited,* v. *London County Council*) cannot revoke its own decision upon a point of law. There were one or two other points decided in *Warminster Local Board* v. *Wilts County Council* which are worth noting, although they have not aroused the same amount of discussion as those previously referred to. It was held in that case that the liability of the county council extended to the cost of maintaining and repairing paved or pitched crossings, and to the cost of scavenging, cleansing and watering (so far as necessary for maintenance and repair), but not to lighting; and also to the cost of altering the paving of footways (as—*e.g.*, by substituting flagging, pavement, wood, or asphalte, for gravel, &c.) in so far as it is a reasonable improvement connected with maintenance and repair, how far it is so being a question for settlement (in case of dispute) by arbitration.

In *Sandgate Urban District Council* v. *Kent County Council,* which has just reached its final stage in the House of Lords, the principal bone of contention was whether the county council were liable for the cost of the maintenance and repair of a sea wall, which, though not actually part of the road, protected it from the sea, and was alleged by the district council to be on that account a necessary work of "maintenance." The arbitrator appointed by the Local Government Board made his award in the form of a special case, some items of which were in favour of the county council, others of the district council, the nett result being that the former were ordered to pay a sum of £6,188 towards the cost of the repair of the main road, which sum included costs applicable to some portions of the sea wall. The award was confirmed by Mr. Justice Cave and Mr. Justice Lawrance in the Queen's Bench Divisional Court; but their judgment was reversed by the Court of Appeal, who sent the case back to the arbitrator with the direction to reject the whole of the claim of the district council and to award entirely in favour of the county council. The Court of Appeal, however, have, in their turn, been reversed by the House of Lords, who have restored the judgment of the Queen's Bench Division and confirmed the award in every particular. The case is perhaps as remarkable for the different estimates of the award and of the arbitrator, prevailing in their Lordships' House and in the Court of Appeal, as for the conflicting judicial views of the points of law involved. Lord Esher appeared to feel particularly aggrieved at the length of the award "by this gentleman, who, unfortunately for himself, was called an arbitrator." "I pity the arbitrator," continued his lordship, "because I cannot help thinking that if he had counsel before him it was they who led him into such an abomination as this." The Lord Chancellor, however, took a diametrically opposite view. "In his opinion scant justice had been done to the arbitrator, and those who criticised him had not sufficiently considered the complex nature of the problem which he was called upon to determine." The questions submitted to him "the arbitrator had treated with great minuteness . . . . and had solved the problem put before him with great care and perfect accuracy . . . . It was a remarkable fact that the arbitrator had so dealt with every one of the facts of the case that neither party had been able to suggest any omission of which he had been guilty." The majority of the other learned lords expressed full concurrence with the Lord Chancellor on this point, and after reading their calm and judicial comments one cannot help feeling somewhat surprised at the very different tone adopted by Lord Esher in the Court of Appeal. This, however, is by the way. The Lord Chancellor was equally emphatic on the main question. "It was gravely argued," he said, "that there was a construction" (*i.e.*, the sea wall) "which ought not to be held part of the main road, although if it were not there the road itself would be washed away. To his mind

such a contention was absurd. It was commonsense that where the obligation was to maintain and keep in repair it was the duty of the persons subject to that obligation to take steps which would prevent the road being washed away . . . . The proposition had been advanced that nothing outside the road could be done, and that the road itself should be allowed to go out of repair every year. But that argument lost sight of the word 'maintain.'" The tendency of the Courts, it will be seen from these cases, is to interpret the provisions of the Act in no narrow spirit, but liberally and from a common-sense point of view.

\* \* \*

**Sanitation in West Bromwich.** In 1895 Dr. G. S. Buchanan, on behalf of the Local Government Board, made an inquiry into the sanitary condition of West Bromwich. In his report he recommended, among other things, (1) that thorough and systematic attention should be given to insanitary premises in the borough, especially with reference to houses unfit for habitation, premises with drains improperly constructed, unpaved or insufficiently paved yards, and nuisances arising from the accumulation of refuse and excrement; (2) that a satisfactory system for the removal of dry refuse and excrement should be substituted for the present objectionable privy middens and pit privies in the borough, water carriage being adopted where possible, and (3) that a fresh series of by-laws, based on the "model" series of the Local Government Board, should be adopted. In May last he was again instructed to visit the district, and in his report, recently issued, he is able to state that on the whole the corporation have, during the three years under review, shown greater activity than before in dealing with insanitary conditions, but that a variety of conditions will continue to demand careful consideration and sustained effort on the part of the sanitary authority of the borough. A few points may be referred to in greater detail. Some progress has been made in remedying dilapidations of houses, overcrowding of persons, faulty paving and drainage of yards, objectionable middens, want of eave spouting, and other unwholesome conditions. But owners called upon to make repairs are apt to do so in a makeshift fashion. Thus the demand for the proper drainage of common yards is still met by the provision of open channels, roughly constructed of brick, laid without regard to level, and having right-angled bends in their course. New paving in these common yards often turns out to be an insufficient patch of brickwork, which has not been carried as far as the midden, and in consequence pollution of the soil is apt to continue. Dr. Buchanan, on being told that the town council doubted their powers to compel more thorough action, pointed out that by-laws might be adopted under sec. 23 of the Public Health Acts Amendment Act, 1890. As to the substitution of water-closets, the report is that proposals to that effect meet with opposition from those who are interested in the numerous small properties in the borough, and that the opposition has been in a large measure successful. He cites the case of an owner who was called upon to demolish an ashpit and two privies situated about 10 ft. from dwellings, but who pleaded successfully to the stipendiary that the structures complained of had been erected twelve years before with the approval of the town council, and called tenants to express their satisfaction with the existing arrangements. The enlightened stipendiary was not satisfied that the structures in question did constitute a nuisance, and said that even if he had been he would have hesitated to order the provision of a water-closet. Under such circumstances it is not surprising to find a corporation rather discouraged. "Dry refuse" is tipped on waste ground within the borough, but the council have been urged, so far in vain, to provide a refuse destructor. The town clerk and the borough engineer have drafted new by-laws. Officials, however, may draft new by-laws, but only the council can adopt them. In his former report Dr. Buchanan said that sewage was discharged on a farm at Friar's Park, " of large area, but comprising much land covered by old pit mounds and little suited for sewage treatment." In his later report, however, he was able to say that the town council had recently applied to the Local Government Board for sanction to a loan for the purpose of providing tanks for the bacterial, or as an alternative the chemical, treatment of sewage, and of laying out 35 acres of land for irrigation. He was also able to report that during the interval between the two inspections the council had carried out some satisfactory street improvements, enlarged the public baths and wash-houses, paved a considerable number of footpaths, and had made desirable additions to the public parks and recreation grounds. We are glad to observe that Dr. Buchanan does not forget to point out that sanitary improvements in the Black Country are carried out in the face of exceptional difficulties, and demand " judicious and resolute action from those who undertake the duty of safeguarding the public health of their districts." Therefore such progress as has been made in West Bromwich is the more commendable.

\*     \*     \*

**District Surveyors under the London Building Act.** We agree with one of the speakers at the Surveyors' Institution, on Monday, who thought that Mr. Weaver, the well-known surveyor to the Kensington Vestry, was a bold man in bringing up before such an audience so contentious a question as the position and functions of the officials appointed by the London County Council under the London Building Act and known as district surveyors. Most, if not all, of these gentlemen are members of the Surveyors' Institution, and it was only to be expected that they would vigorously defend the maintenance of the *status quo* as superior in every way to anything that Mr. Weaver might suggest. It was a pity, however, that Mr. Weaver's proposals should have been misinterpreted, as they were by one or two speakers. He does not propose that the present district surveyors should simply be swept aside and their duties handed over to the surveyors to the local bodies. He simply puts forward the broad contention that the duties of the surveyor to the local authority and those now carried out by the district surveyors might and ought to be combined in and discharged by one official, as is the case in the large provincial cities and towns. There is nothing preposterous in the proposal that the present surveyors to the vestries and district boards should, where competent, discharge the duties in question, as borough engineers do in the provinces, with satisfactory results. The present position is certainly anomalous, and Mr. Weaver had no difficulty in demonstrating the inconvenience and delay that result from the divided jurisdiction which now prevails, one official acting under the London Building Act and another under the Public Health (London) Act. This evil of divided jurisdiction has been in no way diminished by the decision of the London County Council some years ago to debar district surveyors appointed after the passing of the order from engaging in private practice. It was asserted by more than one speaker on Monday that the surveyors to the local authorities are more engineers than architects, but, as a matter of fact, the majority of them have a very considerable architectural training and experience. Again, surely the engineer requires as intimate an acquaintance with materials and construction as the architect. In view of the intention of the Government to bring in a Bill to reorganise the municipal work of the metropolis, Mr. Weaver and the Surveyors' Institution have done well to bring this important matter to the front. As the discussion will be resumed at the next meeting of the Institution, we may be able to refer to the question in greater detail.

**Honorary Surveyors.** The Urban District Council of Phillack, in Cornwall, find themselves floundering in a position which is probably unique in its way. About six months ago their surveyor resigned, and ever since the duties of the office have been performed (?) by three members of the council. This noble triumvirate, we are given to understand, are carrying out their duties gratuitously, and, like the Gracchi of old, they no doubt expect that their public-spirited and self-sacrificing devotion will secure the approbation of their fellow-citizens. For do they not save the latter from the unpleasant necessity of paying the pampered official's salary, which, we believe, reached the colossal figure of £50 per annum? Whether each of these amateur, but self-confident, surveyors takes charge of some special district or branch of the duties, or whether they meet in solemn conclave to discuss important questions before taking action, we know not. At all events, the arrangement is a remarkable one and has certainly the merit of originality, and it remains to be seen whether the ratepayers do not suffer in proportion to the inexperience of their self-elected officials. It may be doubted, however, whether such an arrangement is in accordance with sec. 189 of the Public Health Act, 1875, which says: " Every urban authority shall, from time to time, appoint fit and proper persons to be medical officer of health, surveyor, inspector of nuisances, clerk and treasurer." Unfortunately, however, we are not aware of any legal machinery by which such an administrative scandal as this at Phillack can be prevented. Could not that august body, the Local Government Board, be persuaded to do something in the matter if it were brought to their notice? But who will undertake the task of moving the Local Government Board? The question is one that directly affects the interests of surveyors to local authorities, and, possibly the council of the Association of Municipal and County Engineers may see their way to take some action.

\*     \*     \*

**Councillor and Surveyor.** There has been an instructive but somewhat melancholy episode at Chertsey. A member of the urban district council has been convicted for infringing the building by-laws and mulcted in penalties. Among those who gave evidence for the council was the late surveyor, and naturally the convicted one and his friends on the council did their best to prevent the payment of the surveyor's bill, but, fortunately, without success, though a fair-minded member of the council felt compelled to make a spirited protest against blackguarding an official after he' had gone, at the same time pointing out that two guineas was a recognised fee for attendance, and that the remainder of the charge was not too much for expenses. Nor was the present surveyor to the council, Mr. J. Freebairn Stow, allowed to escape without some unpleasantness; but when the matter came up for discussion he did not hesitate to speak to the point. He stated that only since he had entered upon office had the work been done by the offending councillor, " who had threatened to take out a mandamus with respect to one of the chimney backs." Still no certificate could be granted, because there was reason to believe that some of the walls were built brick-on-edge, and that the bay windows were not in accordance with the plans. Mr. Stow took exception to the remarks of a councillor who had said that a surveyor was not a professional man, in the same sense as a lawyer for example, and reminded the council that if he had not been a duly-qualified civil engineer they would not have appointed him. Finally, he pointed out the mischievous results that must ensue if the council did not support him adequately in the discharge of his duties. We have ourselves been for years insisting on the necessity of proper relations between officials and authorities, but the need for agitating the matter seems as great as ever.

# The Birmingham Water Scheme.—III.

## By JAMES MANSERGH, M.INST.C.E.

CUT AND COVER WORK.

### THE ELAN VILLAGE.

I should like now to be allowed to say a few words about the arrangements which have been made by the Elan Supply Committee—with whom I am in constant touch—for the housing and general well-being of the bulk of the men engaged on the works in the Elan Valley and of their families. At my recommendation the committee determined to undertake the construction of the reservoirs and all collateral works in the valley under the direct administration of their own staff and without the intervention of contractors. This is not the time nor the place either to defend or apologise for this decision ; suffice it is to say that up to the present time the method is giving complete satisfaction.

Having thus decided, the question arose of how the people were to be kept together in close proximity to the works, and it was answered by the erection of a village below Caban Coch with sufficient accommodation for about 1,000 people. The houses are of wood, and are built of different types to suit varying grades ; thus, there are huts for officials such as the missioner and schoolmaster, for gangers, for married workmen and for navvy lodgers. In the latter there is a good kitchen and living-room, rooms and offices for the hut-keeper, his wife and family, and a larger room for lodgers. It has been not unusual on public works to put twenty-four men into such a hut, sleeping in pairs in twelve beds ; and where work was going on day and night I believe there have been occasions when these beds have not had time to get cold. This, to say the least of it, is not nice. The committee needed no pressing from me to sanction the erection of the huts above described. In the larger ones the eight men sleep in one large room, but each man has his own separate cubicle and single bed.

Water is laid on under pressure throughout the village ; the drainage is as good as can be, and there is a fire brigade. There is also a canteen, where good beer and aërated waters are to be had at certain hours and under strict regulations ; schools for infants and older children, with one male and two female teachers, these rooms being used on Sundays for religious services. There is also a large recreation hall, with gymnasium games, writing accommodation and a circulating library, and in the hall are given concerts, theatrical entertainments, and last winter a ball. Then there are baths and wash-houses and a general and accident hospital in the village, and another for infectious diseases far away up the hillside. The baths are, of course, patronised principally on Saturday afternoon and Sunday morning. When first opened there was only one charge—viz., 1d. It was soon found that this would not do. Account had to be taken of different grades. If a nipper or ordinary tramp labourer—who is not a proud man—paid 1d., the legitimate navvy demanded to pay

SPECIMEN OF CUT AND COVER WORK (February, 1898).

more, so as to be select. The foreman posed on a still higher platform. Now a warm bath, soap and one towel costs 1d. Ditto with two towels 1½d. Ditto, ditto, and high-class toilet soap, 2d. There are, of course, ladies' days, but into the particulars of their prejudices I have not ventured to inquire.

To keep out infectious diseases there is also a "doss-house" on the opposite side of the river to the village, in which men tramping in search of work are taken in. They are made to take a warm bath and their clothes are disinfected ; and for

brigade, some members of which are on duty every evening. The village is perambulated throughout the night by two watchmen. All of the huts are, moreover, inspected weekly by the village superintendent, with a view to the removal of all refuse and the prevention of the use of oil lamps of dangerous type, and other articles likely to occasion an outbreak of fire.

" The village day school is placed under the Education Department, the school manager being the chairman of the Water Committee with three officials, two of whom are resident at the works and one in Birmingham. The buildings are certified by the department as sufficient for the accommodation of 168 scholars. At first considerable difficulty was experienced in bringing the navvies' children under the discipline of regular instruction, but now good progress is being made, and at the last examination by the Government inspector the general school earned the highest possible grant."

THE CANTEEN AND ITS SOCIAL RESULTS.

I must now refer to the canteen. To this institution a special interest attaches, as we have here an experiment embodying some of the suggestions thrown out for the regulation of the liquor traffic. In point of fact, the canteen is a municipal public-house, and is, I think, the only instance of the kind in the United Kingdom. On the question of the drink traffic there were the three proverbial courses open to the Water Committee : (1) To do nothing, and allow any enterprising publicans who could obtain licenses to set up their establishments and conduct their trade in the usual manner. (2) To attempt to prohibit the traffic altogether. (3) To undertake the provision of beer for the use

ELAN VILLAGE (April, 1895).

a week they sleep here, and are under the supervision of the doctor before being allowed to take up their quarters in the village. These arrangements have hitherto proved successful, and whilst two years ago small-pox was epidemic in many parts of South Wales, and especially on some large public works, we escaped.

With the permission of Mr. Lees, the highly esteemed and most competent secretary of the Water Committee, I will now quote from a lecture he has delivered with great success on several occasions in the city :—

" The village is on the opposite side of the river to the road, and access is given to it by a suspension bridge constructed across the river by the corporation. The position of the village in that it has to be approached by this bridge, and that it is erected on private ground to which there is no public right of way is unfortunate, in that the corporation thereby have the means of exercising a beneficent supervision which would be impossible were it in the ordinary sense of the word a public place. Nor is the supervision of the corporation merely nominal. No strangers are allowed in the village without permission. Every tradesman who wishes to deliver goods is required to furnish himself with a pass, on which somewhat stringent regulations are laid down. For instance, the owner undertakes he will not deliver any intoxicating drinks within the village, and the Sunday quiet and rest of the inhabitants are protected by a regulation that, with the exception of milk, no goods shall be delivered or sold on that day ; and these regulations are not a dead letter, for at the end of the bridge on the village side a gate is situate at which the bridge-keeper is constantly in attendance and examines the contents of every cart before it is permitted to proceed.

" Fire hydrants are fixed on the water mains throughout, fire-extinguishing appliances are provided at convenient points, and in the middle of the village there is a small fire station surmounted by a fire bell. This is the rendezvous of the fire

of the community, but under such regulations as should render it least hurtful.

The objection to the first course is obvious. The navvies —in common, alas, with many others—readily yield to temptations when they have the means of gratifying the appetite, and during the summer months, when regularity in the gangs is of the utmost importance, and at the same time when earnings are highest, there would be the greatest likelihood of the demoralising and disastrous effects of drunkenness asserting themselves. To the second course the objection was none the less marked. The people, rightly or wrongly, will have their beer, and without facilities to obtain it in a legitimate manner they would decline the place altogether or resort to illicit means to supply themselves. It was held, therefore, to be impolitic to attempt prohibition ; and I think it would have been unwise to prohibit altogether the sale of beer.

The third alternative course, then, was that adopted—namely, to provide beer under stringent regulations. The canteen is placed in charge of a manager, in whose name the license stands. The manager has no interest whatever in the sale of the drink. His salary is fixed, and is sufficiently liberal to command the services of a thoroughly reliable and respectable man. The points against which he must guard himself is incivility towards customers on the part of himself or his assistants, lack of cleanliness in the house and drinking vessels, selling out of hours, and disorder and drunkenness on the part of his customers. If he is able to avoid offence in any of these respects he is thought no worse of if the takings fall off, and no better of if they increase.

To promote the objects in view stringent regula-

STREET IN ELAN VILLAGE.

THE DOSS-HOUSE JUNCTION (April, 1895).

tions have been enacted; and the regulations are not merely printed and hung on the walls, but are actually enforced. The sale of drink is refused to men who show signs of having had enough, or who have already been supplied up to the stipulated limit. No women or children are permitted in the bar. Even in the outdoor department no woman under twenty-one years of age is served and no boy under sixteen. The house is closed every night at 9 o'clock, and the inspection and co-operation of the police are courted in every way. Every effort is made to sell a thoroughly wholesome and pure beer. A regular system of sample taking and testing is carried out, samples being taken without notice from time to time and forwarded to Birmingham for analysis in cases marked with numbers only, so that the analyst cannot tell from what brewers the beers are purchased.

Now as to the social results. While we cannot say that by our attempt to regulate the drink traffic we have created a "Utopia," we may firstly say—and indeed we claim—that we have reduced the evil results of drinking to a minimum, taking into consideration the fact that on the opposite side of the river, within a mile of the village, another public-house exists, which is conducted on the usual lines. Persons qualified to judge speak in the highest terms of the results of the experiment.

One of the declared bases of the Elan village canteen is that the profits are devoted to the social well-being of the community. First, the whole of the cost of the day school beyond the Government grant, and including the cost of the building, is provided from the canteen profits; in other words, the profits take the place of what, in an ordinary community, would be the school board rate. Secondly, the cost of erecting and maintaining the public hall, with the library, gymnasium, reading-room, &c., is provided from the same source. Recreation grounds for the workmen and clerical staff, the deficit on the bath-house and occasional help to charitable institutions are all defrayed from the canteen profits.

The men are taken up the valley from the village early in the morning, and brought back after their work in railway carriages, so as to save time and their exposure in open trucks, and the children from the upper works huts are brought down to school and returned home in the same way. With this ride in view the parents have no trouble in getting them away to their lessons.

———

For the series of smaller half-tone illustrations used for the elucidation of Mr. Mansergh's lecture in this and the two previous issues we are indebted to the kindness of Mr. Thomas Barclay, formerly a member of the Water Committee of the Birmingham City Council, and the author of an admirable volume, entitled "The Future Water Supply of Birmingham," in which work the illustrations to which we have referred first appeared along with others. Those who wish for more details than Mr. Mansergh could compress into his lecture cannot do better than obtain Mr. Barclay's book, which is published by Cornish Brothers, 37 New-street, Birmingham, and Simpkins, Marshall & Co., Limited, London, at 3s. 6d. nett. The main features of water supply schemes for large towns can be more clearly indicated by following the details of some typical concrete example than by mere theoretical disquisition. The Birmingham scheme is not only typical but is in some respects unique, and is being carried out on a gigantic scale. From this point of view Mr. Barclay's volume, with its maps, plans and other illustrations, the lucid explanations and painstaking accuracy of the writer, is a distinctly valuable contribution to the literature of water supply. The first five chapters deal with the present supply, the conditions of a suitable supply, the cost of the necessary works, the action of moorland water on lead, and the answering of objections to the scheme. The subsequent chapters give particulars of the passing of the Act, the provision made for the interim supply of Birmingham, and a description of the works in the Elan valley, showing the progress made in the construction of the reservoirs on the watershed and at Frankley and what had been accomplished on the line of aqueduct at the time of writing. The last chapter is devoted to interesting and useful notes on the Liverpool, Manchester and London water supplies, embodying information which the reader can turn to account for purposes of comparison.

———

**Salford.**—In view of the doubt as to the liabilities thrown upon local authorities by the Workmen's Compensation Act, 1897, the corporation are attaching the following clause to all specifications, forms of tender, contracts, &c.: NOTE.—The contractor shall pay to the corporation any sum or sums of money, and all costs, claims and damages whatsoever, which the corporation may, in pursuance of proceedings brought against them under sec. 4 of the Workmen's Compensation Act, 1897, have to pay as compensation to any workman employed by the contractor in respect of any accident arising out of and in course of his employment, and in default the corporation may recover the amount thereof by action at law, or may deduct the same from any moneys due to the contractor for the execution of the works under this contract, any certificate of the amount payable to the contractor in respect of such works, or any clause of this agreement, or any submission or reference therein contained, or any other matter or thing notwithstanding.

## THE SANITARY INSTITUTE.

### EXAMINATIONS IN LONDON.

At an examination in practical sanitary science, which was held by the above Institution, at Parkes' Museum, Margaret-street, London, W., on the 2nd and 3rd insts., six candidates themselves, and Mr. William Ord, 17 Cambridge-gardens, Hanwell, was granted a certificate. The following were the questions set for answer in writing: (1) What is the law relating to the diffusion of gases? What bearing has this on the ventilation of living-rooms? (2) Describe the wet and dry bulb thermometers. State how the relative humidity of the atmosphere can be arrived at by means of this instrument. (3) What is meant by "ground air" and "ground water"? What circumstances affect the movements of each, and how may they get polluted? (4) Specify the construction and materials of a fireproof floor, 60 ft. long and 20 ft. wide, capable of bearing a distributed weight of 25 tons. (5) How can a school-room best be ventilated? What should be the size of inlets and outlets provided, and what should be the relative positions of these openings. (6) Describe briefly a refuse destructor and its uses. What temperature is usually maintained to destroy ordinary town refuse, and what percentage of clinker remains after cremation. (7) In what state of combination does the largest proportion of nitrogen exist in fresh town sewage? Shortly describe the treatment you would recommend for defecating the sewage and utilising the nitrogen compounds in solution. (8) A drain with a fall of 1 in 40 has a velocity of flow of 3 ft. per second; what velocity would be secured if the same drain is relaid with a fall of 1 in 30?

On the same days an examination was held for inspectors of nuisances, at which 128 candidates presented themselves, seventy-four of whom were certified, as regards their sanitary knowledge, competent to discharge the duties of inspectors of nuisances. The following were the questions set for answer in writing: (1) Describe briefly how to lay domestic drains from house to sewer. Give plan to scale of 8 ft. to 1 in., and state diameters and fall to sewer. (2) In a case of typhoid fever occurring in a crowded tenement dwelling, describe in detail what steps you would take to prevent the spread of the disease with respect to the following points: (a) The sick; (b) the healthy members of the family; (c) the bedding, clothing, and other articles exposed to infection; (d) the rooms; and (e) the drainage. (3) Give a list of the offensive cargoes most frequently carried by canal boats, and state the precautions that should be taken to prevent nuisance. What are the chief regulations as to cargoes made by the Local Government Board under the Canal Boats Acts. (4) Define "hard" and "soft" water. State the action of the latter on lead, and how such action may be prevented. (5) Describe the appearance of measly pork, and the effects when eaten by men. (6) What are the cubical contents of a circular rain-water tank, 11 ft. diameter and 12 ft. deep, with a flat bottom? State the weight of the water that it would contain. (7) What are the provisions of the Sale of Food and Drugs Acts with regard to the purchase of samples for analysis? (8) Sketch a good form of slop sink for domestic use, and show the method of connecting the waste from the slop sink, situated on the first floor, to the drain.

———

## ELECTRIC LIGHTING IN THE CITY.

A memorial, signed by over 5,000 ratepayers and others, has been addressed to the Lord Mayor and Corporation of the City of London in opposition to an application made to the Board of Trade for a provisional order enabling the Charing Cross and Strand Electricity Supply Corporation, Limited, to supply electric energy within the City of London. The grounds for the memorial are set forth as follows: (1) That monopoly of supply by any one company is adverse to the interests of the ratepayers and the public; (2) that the rate charged for supply of electric energy by the corporation is very considerably less than that charged within the city by the present supply company; (3) that the service of the corporation is a more economical, steady and efficient service; (4) that the low tension distributing system is a safer system for many reasons, among others the avoidance of fireproof transformer-rooms or apparatus on the premises supplied with energy; (5) that the low-tension direct-current system appears, inter alia, to be the best adapted for arc lighting and motive power purposes. The memorial is signed by twenty-nine banks, as well as by eighty-one insurance companies and eighty-two newspapers.

———

**Notice of Removal.**—Messrs. Sheath Brothers, india-rubber, gutta-percha, general manufacturers and patentees, have informed us that they have removed to 87 City-road, London, E.C. These new premises, we understand, have been built specially commodious to meet the requirements of their largely-increasing trade, and to enable them to keep a much larger stock of their regular and special manufactures for india-rubber and gutta-percha manufacturers and dealers, ironmongers, coach builders, saddlers, upholsterers and the building trades.

# Comparative Reports of General Practice.

## XXX.—TRAMWAY TRACTION : WEST BROMWICH REPORT.—V.

### PRESCOT.

The borough surveyor, being in the neighbourhood of Prescot on other corporation business, availed himself of the opportunity, by the courtesy of Mr. B. Cookson the secretary of the company (to whom acknowledgement is also due for the useful information on the subject), of closely inspecting the experimental line of the "simplex conduit electric tramway" and inserted trolley system laid down at Prescot, near St. Helens, and the following is a description of the short experimental line and the advantages claimed for this system :—

The line has been laid down in the grounds of the British Insulated Wire Company at Prescot, and is one-quarter of a

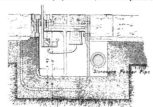

"SIMPLEX" TRAMWAYS.—CROSS-SECTION AT HATCHWAY, SHOWING CARRIER ARM AND COLLECTOR.

mile of single track, and includes some particularly difficult conditions, besides presenting continuous and varying gradients. For about half of the distance there is a gradient of 1 in 25. It includes a curve having a radius of about 45 ft.

The conduit is constructed of concrete, taking the form of the inner surface of cast-iron yokes, as in the case of conduits for cable tramways. These yokes are placed at intervals of 4 ft., except at the end of the rails, where a pair are placed only 18 in. apart. This arrangement is made to give greater support to the rails, which rest upon and are bolted to the yokes. The yokes are embedded in and are supported by the floor and walls of the conduit, which are 6 in. thick. The traction rail weighs 50 lb. per yard, and has the section shown in the illustration, while the inner rail of the conduit weighs 43 lb. per yard. At the surface the slot measures about 1 in., but as one of the rails projects slightly to form a groove, the actual width of the slot is reduced to ⅞ in., or even ⅝ in. Below the rails the conduit broadens out to 8 in. in width, so that, including the walls and concrete bottom, we have a total

removable. Bolted to this bar is a large insulator supporting a curved steel carrier bar, ⅜ in. in diameter, on which rests the cable. These bars are used only on straight sections of line and on slight curves. At all sharp curves modified appliances are necessary. Under tension at curves the cable would, of course, tend to assume a straight line. To prevent this and to secure the cable upon its insulated support when a collector is passing, a device of considerable ingenuity has been brought into play. The hatch boxes are placed at shorter intervals on sharp curves, the space between them decreasing on very sharp curves to 8 ft., and to the square iron bar let into the box are bolted two insulators, which support a carrier box swivelling vertically, to which is attached a carrier arm. The object of the device is to secure freedom for a vertical rise of the cable while allowing no lateral motion. As the cable is firmly secured in the carrier arm, it moves with this, and the swivel is so hung that it can rise or fall with perfect ease as the collector passes along underneath the cable, but it cannot move laterally, so that the alignment of the cable is maintained.

An even strain is kept on the cable throughout by a tension arrangement resembling somewhat the tension gear on a cable tramway. The conductor consists of a flexible wire cable, made by the British Insulated Wire Company. Owing to its great flexibility, it can be conveniently handled, and it can be removed and replaced, should this be necessary for any reason, with facility. For the return circuit the rails are employed, and they are bonded in the usual manner. Reference has been made to the collectors, by which current is conducted from the cable to the car. A hollow shank gives space for the passage of a conductor, properly insulated to a shoe of brass, which forms the rubbing surface. On this rests the cable, which is lifted from its support as the shoe passes beneath it, and again falls back on the insulating arms. The shoe has quite as smooth a passage along the conductor as has the trolley wheel or bar in the overhead system, and no difficulty is to be apprehended on this score. The shoe is attached to the truck of the car just in front of the wheels, and, while allowed free lateral motion in relation to the car, it is very firmly secured, so that it easily clears the slot of any stones or other matter that may be lodged there.

Any type of electric car can, of course, be used with this system. For the line at Prescot a small but neatly-designed car has been built, which weighs 5 tons 13 cwt., and has seating accommodation for twenty persons, the two motors being 15 horse-power each.

The advantages claimed by the promoters for this system are : (1) Freedom from street obstruction, such as poles and overhead wires ; (2) high permanent insulation ; (3) accessibility of electric fittings for repairs and renewals over ordinary electric conduit systems ; and (4) economy in construction and simplicity. As the system has not been as yet adopted

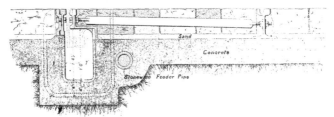

"SIMPLEX" TRAMWAYS.—CROSS-SECTION OF TRACK AND CONDUIT BETWEEN HATCHWAYS.

width of 1 ft. 8 in., with a total depth of 1 ft. 10½ in.; not a large excavation as tramway conduits go. In special cases, as, for instance, in crossing bridges, the total depth can be reduced to 12 in.

But the distinctive features of the system are the use of a flexible cable and the arrangements for supporting it in the conduit, and to these we now turn, taking first the ordinary insulator or carrying bar, on which the cable is loosely supported (see illustration). These occur on straight runs at intervals of 3 ft.—i.e., there is an insulator at the junction of every pair of rail ends. At these points hatchways are let into the conduit between the yokes, which are here 18 in. apart. A box or hand-hole is thus formed, with a framework and cover of cast iron. In the framework of each box, a little below the cover, there is a socket, into which a square bar of iron is dropped without any fastening, so that it is instantly

by any company or corporation, it is impossible to say what the cost of maintenance will be : and taking into consideration that the first cost in construction will of necessity be greater than for the overhead system, and whilst there will still remain the great objection—namely, the open conduit—the sub-committee are of opinion that it is too expensive and extensive an experiment to adopt in West Bromwich.

### SUMMARY.

Having briefly described the various electric and other tramway lines in the places visited, the sub-committee before drawing conclusions wish to draw your attention to the following summary, and it may be advisable to state that, in addition to the information obtained as to the various systems of mechanical traction, the deputation learned a great deal as to general arrangements, which cannot fail to be of use and which could not have been obtained without personal investigation. The sub-committee wish to emphasise the fact that they approach the consideration of the conclusions to be arrived at solely on the merits of the question, with but one aim and object in view—the general well-being, development and interest of the town.

THE CABLE SYSTEM.

*Advantages.*—The chief advantages of the cable system are: (1) The absence of overhead apparatus in the streets. (2) The regular speed and the freedom from accidents which might be caused by the driver losing control of the car. (3) The adaptability of a cable line to the demands of an increasing traffic. If extra cars are required at any time the extra cost and power required are comparatively small in proportion to the number of cars so required. (4) Economy of working. (5) Cleanliness.

*Disadvantages.*—The great objections to this system are: (1) Its great cost of construction and the prolonged interference with the streets during construction and repairs, when the traffic and business is greatly impeded. (2) The inflexibility of the traffic conveyed by it. If time is lost it cannot be regained, the speed of the cable limiting the speed of the car, and a car cannot be run back if required. (3) The objection to the slot, which, although much narrower than with the electric conduit, is still objectionable; and the noise from the cable running in the pulleys below the ground is found to be a constant annoyance to residents on the route. (4) The fact that any breakdown of the engines or cable stops the traffic entirely on that particular section.

*Sub-Committee's Recommendations.*—The sub-committee are not prepared to recommend the adoption of the cable system in West Bromwich, as on account of the very heavy cost in construction it is prohibitive for the entire line. If the entire route were laid on the cable system it would be an enormous expense, two power stations at least would be necessary, and the difficulty of getting over canal and railway bridges would have to be faced as in the conduit system, and if the portion from Carters Green to the New Inns, Handsworth, were laid down for the cable system it would, they are informed, cost at least £75,000. There would then remain the difficulty of changing at Carters Green for passengers to Great Bridge and Hill Top.

LIST OF TRAMWAY SYSTEMS WORKED BY CABLE IN THE UNITED KINGDOM.

| Name. | By whom worked. | Date opened | Length of route | Total length of track. | Gauge. |
|---|---|---|---|---|---|
| | | | miles. | miles. | ft. in. |
| Birmingham | Company | Mar., 1888 | 3 | 6 | 3 6 |
| Douglas | Company | Aug., 1896 | 1·5 | 3 | 3 0 |
| Edinburgh | Corporation | { Feb., 1888 } { Feb., 1890 } | 3 | 6 | 4 8½ |
| London | Company | { Jan., 1893 } { Jan., 1896 } | 3·5 | 7 | 4 8½ |
| „ (Highgate) | Company | May, 1884 | ·75 | 1·5 | 3 6 |
| Matlock* | { District } { Council } | Apr., 1893 | ·62 | ·8 | 3 6 |
| | | | 12·37 | 24·3 | |
| IN COURSE OF CONSTRUCTION. | | | | | |
| Edinburgh | Corporation | — | 16 | 32 | 4 8½ |

## A BUSINESS AMALGAMATION.

We are informed that the well-known business of the Patent Gully Company, Limited, Nottingham, has been amalgamated with that of Messrs. Ames, Crosta & Co., Limited, sanitary engineers, Nottingham. The business will henceforth be conducted under the title of the Ames-Crosta Sanitary Engineering Company, Limited, at City Chambers, South-parade, Nottingham. The Patent Gully Company was formed to place upon the market Crosta's patent surface-water gully, which is now well known to engineers and surveyors, and is being largely used in London and the principal towns and health resorts throughout the United Kingdom. This gully has on each occasion when it has been exhibited been awarded the medal of the Sanitary Institute of Great Britain.

The Ames and Crosta patent pipe joint is also now being largely adopted. This joint, which was placed upon the market by Messrs. Ames, Crosta & Co., is designed to dispense with composition rings, and to ensure a perfect water-tight joint, with a true invert, at a low cost. That company have also recently brought out an improved manhole cover, (patented by Mr. R. Ames), which appears to combine many excellent points, and has, we understand, already found great favour among engineers and surveyors. In addition to these specialities the new company propose to deal in all kinds of sewer ironwork and stoneware sanitary materials. With their present extensive connection and the assistance of an unusually strong board (among whom we notice the late surveyor to St. Martin's Vestry, Mr. Charles Mason, A.M.I.C.E.) the amalgamated firm should rank high among the first sanitary engineering firms in the country.

* Presented to town.

## IMPORTANT IMPROVEMENT AT SHEFFIELD.

### THE ERECTION OF BALL BRIDGE.

The erection of a new bridge over the river Don at Ball-street, Sheffield, which is to take the place of the old footbridge that for many years has afforded a scanty and, during the last period of its existence a rather risky, convenience to the people living in that locality, is progressing favourably, and it may safely be stated that in a comparatively short time an old and unsatisfactory state of things will have been replaced by a useful and much-needed means of communication between two busy parts of the city. That there is a necessity for a cartbridge over the river at this point is without a doubt. The two nearest places at which the Don is crossed are Corporation Bridge on the one hand and Rutland Bridge on the other. The bridge now in course of construction will stand almost midway between these, and will provide a means of communication between the two districts of Shalesmoor and Neepsend.

The dilapidated state of the old iron footbridge was frequently brought before the notice of the city council up to a short time ago, and the city surveyor, Mr. C. F. Wike, on being instructed to examine it, found the ironwork so corroded that he deemed the bridge unsafe, and advised the committee to close it. It was in three spans, and was only 10 ft. wide, and representations as to the desirability of having a wide bridge had been made for a considerable time. The council decided to build such a bridge, and, at the same time, to widen Ball-street on the Shalesmoor side. A quantity of old house property has been purchased on the side of the street opposite Messrs. Dixon's works, and the width of the street will be increased from 21 ft. to 40 ft. Unfortunately, the whole of the street cannot be so improved. For the last 100 ft. the approach to the bridge will remain at its present breadth, but, apart from this, there will be a good road, 40 ft. wide, both on the bridge and on each side of it.

ENGINEERING DETAILS.

The design submitted by Mr. Wike, and accepted by the council, is for an iron bridge of an ornamental and substantial character. The river here is about 200 ft. wide, and the bridge will rest on two central piers and an abutment on each bank. There will thus be three spans, each about 70 ft. long. They will be arched, and the segments of the arches fastened with buckle plates. From each pier will rise a heavy stone pilaster, the top of which will be nearly 15 ft. above the water line. From the crown of the arch to the waterway the space will be 6 ft. 6 in. The balustrades will be of handsome open ironwork running the whole length of the bridge except where interrupted by the stone pilasters. The bridge will be paved with wood, and there will be a footpath on each side, with a roadway 24 ft. wide between. Messrs. Braithwaite & Co., of Leeds, whose tender to do the work for £9,500 was accepted, have progressed very satisfactorily. The new bridge is being built at the same point as the old one, and a temporary footbridge has been erected a few yards away. This work occupied a month, and since August, when it was completed, the piers for the iron bridge have been put down, and built clear of the water line. On one pier the iron spring blocks are now ready to receive the ironwork, and all the work is so well assured that a flood in the river could scarcely affect it.

The method adopted of building the piers was that of constructing coffer dams. A number of piles are driven into the bed of the river, placed close together, and forming a circle. Outside these a second series of stakes are placed, and the space between the two circles is filled up with clay. The water thus enclosed is pumped away, and the men are able to work in the bed of the river. Some water, of course, finds its way into the enclosure, and pumping operations have to be carried on constantly. The river bed has been excavated for the concrete foundations, and these have been sunk to a depth of 3 ft. 6 in., resting on solid blue bind. On the top of the concrete is the stonework, which has now reached a height of about 7 ft. The stone is Ashlar, supplied from the Worrall and Horsforth quarries.

The work is not without one or two serious difficulties. One of these is caused by the fact that the pier nearest Mowbray-street has to be built on a weir. At the other end the abutment of the bridge adjoins the famous Cornish-place Works of Messrs. James Dixon & Sons. This building is very high, and in digging the foundations of the abutment great care has to be exercised lest anything should be done to imperil the stability of the works. Another obstacle to progress at this point is the great quantity of water that finds its way into the workings, notwithstanding the coffer dam. When the foundation at this end has been put in it will not be very long before the stonework of all the piers will be sufficiently high to receive some of the iron ribs for the bridge. The abutment at the Mowbray-street end, which is placed close to Messrs. John Bedford & Sons' works, does not give so much trouble.

**Jarradale Jarrah.**—The *Menelaus*, with 400 loads, and the *Ursus Minor*, with 600 loads, of Jarradale jarrah have arrived in London, and the *Bonâ Fide*, with 510 loads, at Hull, all to the order of the Jarrahdale Jarrah Forests and Railways, Limited.

# British Association of Waterworks Engineers.

## GENERAL MEETING IN LONDON.

Mr. William Matthews, president of the British Association of Waterworks Engineers, occupied the chair at a general meeting of that body, held on Saturday morning, at the Westminster Palace Hotel, Victoria-street, S.W.

The following other gentlemen were present:—

MEMBERS OF COUNCIL: Messrs. F. J. Bancroft, Hull; J. Cook, Lancaster; A. Davidson, Perth, N.B.; J. Deas, Warrington; J. B. Fenwick, East Retford; W. C. Finch, Luton, Kent; C. Gilby, Bath; W. W. Gray, Cambridge; G. Greenslade, Southampton; F. Griffith, Leicester; J. T. Harvey, Ryde, I.W.; T. W. A. Hayward, Sudbury; H. A. Hill, Birmingham; T. L. Hughes, Wigan; W. Ingham, Torquay; J. Johnstone, Brighton; C. E. Jones, Leyton; W. Jones, Pontypridd; J. Lees, Tonbridge; J. W. Lewis, Farnham; W. G. Peirce, Richmond; J. S. Pickering, Nuneaton; C. H. Priestley, Cardiff; H. Preston, Grantham; R. Roberts, Ipswich; J. T. Rodda, Eastbourne; C. Sainty, Windsor; E. Sandeman, Plymouth; J. Shaw, Boston, Lincs.; E. J. Silcock, King's Lynn; R. H. Swindlehurst, Bolton; H. Turner, Folkestone; W. Watts, Sheffield; J. W. Way, Newport, I.W.; A. Wells, Lewes; and E. A. B. Woodward, Wolverhampton.

ASSOCIATES: Messrs. C. J. Hobbs, London, W.; W. G. Kent, London, W.C.; R. Macintyre, London, S.E.; G. D. Robertson, London, W.C.; G. Watson, London, S.W.; and W. Whitaker, Croydon.

VISITORS: Messrs. D. Gore and C. A. Matthews were also among those present.

Previous to the commencement of the ordinary business of the meeting, it should be stated, the members held a special meeting, in order to discuss a proposal to substitute the following for the existing Rules 30 and 31:—

### *Subsequent Councils and Term of Office.*

"The council shall, after the above date, consist of the president, past-presidents (who are eligible for election as hereinafter provided), two vice-presidents, hon. secretary and treasurer, and ten ordinary members. The president, vice-presidents, hon. secretary and treasurer, and ten ordinary members, shall go out of office each year, on the date fixed by the council for the annual general meeting, but shall be eligible for re-election. Voting papers, in a form to be determined by the council, shall be sent to each member by the secretary fourteen days before the half-yearly or winter general meeting, to be returned to the secretary at or before such meeting. Nominations for the vacant offices shall be sent to the secretary thirty-one days before the winter general meetings. Two scrutineers shall be appointed at the said winter meeting to examine and report upon the voting lists. The result of the voting shall, upon the report of the scrutineers, be declared by the chairman. Every past-president shall, at the expiration of five years from the termination of his presidency, go out of office, but shall be eligible for election to the council in the ordinary way."

The proposal was eventually adopted, on the understanding that the new rule should not come into operation until after the next annual meeting.

On the opening of the ordinary meeting the minutes of the previous meeting of the association were read by Mr. W. H. Brothers, the secretary. Balloting was shortly afterwards proceeded with, and the whole of the names of the gentlemen shown for election were agreed to. They were as follows: MEMBERS—Messrs. J. R. Downes, Redhill; F. W. Talbot, Farnborough; W. A. Valon, Ramsgate; and C. L. N. Wilson, Bilston. ASSOCIATES—Messrs. J. H. Parkin, Fisher Tarn, Kendal; and H. C. Hawsthorne, Bolton. Mr. J. H. Teague, of Lincoln, was transferred from the Associates to the Member class.

On the invitation of the chairman, a paper was then read on the

### WATER SUPPLY FROM THE LOWER GREENSAND AND CONSTRUCTIONAL WORKS CONNECTED THEREWITH AT LEIGHTON BUZZARD

By Mr. H. BERTRAM NICHOLS, A.M.I.C.E.

[Mr. H. Bertram Nichols was articled to his father, Mr. George Benjamin Nichols, F.G.S., with whom he served until he was taken into a junior partnership in the year 1880 before which time he underwent a short course of study at Mason Science College. In 1890 he passed the sanitary Institute examination for surveyors, and was elected a member in 1886. He commenced to practice on his own account in the beginning of 1885, and during a varied and extensive practice he has been engaged on several water and sewerage works in different parts of the country; also arbitration, riparian cases and Parliamentary work. In the course of his professional career he has been successful in obtaining many water and sewerage schemes by competition, which he has successfully carried out. His scheme has been adopted for bringing the water from Dartmoor by gravitation for the supply of the town of Teignmouth. Among the works he has carried out are the Uckfield waterworks, Matlock Bath waterworks, the Leighton Buzzard water and sewerage works—completed at a cost of £21,230—and Redruth waterworks, completed at a cost of £10,500. The Redruth waterworks are now being carried out at his hands, at a cost of £9,700; also the Brownhills sewerage scheme and other works. Mr. Nichols' offices are in Corporation-street, Birmingham. During the present year he has been called in to prepare schemes for the improvement of the water supply]

to the towns of Mallow and Nenagh, Ireland, and he has been successful in winning in open competition the sewerage scheme of Montmorency, the

estimated cost of which is over £60,000. He is an Associate Member of the Institution of Civil Engineers. Our portrait of Mr. Nichols is taken from a photo. by Moull & Fox.]

The lower greensand is an important siliceous formation immediately underlying the gault, composed of soft yellowish sands with ferruginous seams, and invariably contains a large proportion of solid impurity in solution, nearly all of a saline nature, which, although imparting some hardness, is not injurious to health. Both the upper and lower greensands are of porous and oxidising strata, which rapidly destroy or remove the organic matter contained in the water percolating through them, leaving but mere traces behind; the proportion of organic elements in these waters is therefore almost invariably very small. Among their constituents they contain protoxide of iron, which probably exercises a reducing effect upon the nitrates and nitrites present in the water, thus removing their oxygen and transferring a portion of their nitrogen into ammonia, whilst the remaining nitrogen escapes as gas. Even the sulphates present in the water are in some cases attacked, and sulphuretted hydrogen generated. The evidence of previous animal contamination is thus diminished, or even obliterated altogether, whilst the water acquires a considerable proportion of ammonia.

The waters from the lower greensand are frequently slightly turbid, owing to the friable character of the water-bearing stratum; they are palatable, and generally of a moderate degree of hardness; occasionally they have a slight odour and flavour of sulphuretted hydrogen when first raised to the surface, these, however, soon disappear when the water is exposed to the atmosphere.

In connection with the water supply to the town of Leighton Buzzard a well and boring has been sunk into the lower greensand. The well is 8 ft. internal diameter, lined with cast-iron cylinders in segments carried down to a depth of 48 ft., and below this the well has been deepened a further 16 ft. with 7-ft. diameter cylinders. Beneath the well the bore pipes are carried down to a total depth of 200 ft. from the surface, the tubes varying from 10 in. to 8 in. in diameter. A great deal of difficulty was met with during the construction of the works, in consequence of the sand blowing below the depth of 48 ft. from the surface. Down to this depth stiff gault clay was met with, but below this level sand, some of a very loose nature, with bands of varying thickness of grey sandstone, congealed stone, pebbles and sand, and some very hard stone. Owing to the difficulties experienced, the well sinking and boring operations from beginning to finish took about two and a half years to complete, many stoppages having occurred and difficulties of an unforeseen nature having arisen.

The water above the depth of 175 ft. from the surface is entirely shut out from the well, as upon analysis by Prof. Attfield, PH.D., F.R.S., in November, 1892, although he reported the water as being most remarkably pure and among the slightly hard or comparatively soft class of well waters, he mentioned its slight but temporary fault of containing, when first pumped, a little iron in solution; and it was decided to take it to a lower depth, in the hope of finding the iron eliminated from the water. At the depth of 200 ft. the water was again tested by Prof. Attfield, who reported, in July, 1893, that the water was of good quality for all drinking purposes:—

"The sample contains a red ferruginous sediment. There was no trace of iron in solution. Poured off from the sediment—which is what everybody would do before drinking—the water, and which is what I did before analysing—the water is, as I have said, of good quality for all drinking purposes. I assume, however, that this ferruginous sediment was originally in solution; exposure to the air and the shaking in transit causing its deposition. If that be so, consideration must be given to the question of due exposure in reservoir or otherwise, and arrangements for periodical removal of the sediment if the water is to be used for supplying a town. Such depositing iron ensures purity in the drawn-off water."

Upon this report of the analyst the author of this paper suggested that an aërating spiral trough should be fixed

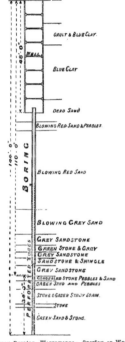

LEIGHTON BUZZARD WATERWORKS: SECTION OF WELL AND BORING, SHOWING GEOLOGICAL STRATA.

above the surface of the water in the circular tank in the tower, having level overflow lips each side the channel across the centre of the tank, to ensure spray action, and this was incorporated in the scheme of water supply.

In consequence of the severe frost in the winter of 1894 the then local board decided to protect the outside of the tank with felt, on account of its extent of surface and exposed situation. The material used for this purpose was the best hair felt, and it may be of interest at this point to give particulars as to the method of protection adopted. The hair felt was of a weight of 48 oz. to the foot, and was placed on in separate layers, each layer being glued to the tank in the first place, and the second layer glued to the back of the first, so that no twine or any other contrivance was necessary to keep it in position. Sixteen uprights were fixed from the concrete floor (which formed a passage round the tank), and on the outside of these uprights six oak hoops, 3 in. wide and ⅜ in. thick, were screwed, in order that the wood lagging to protect the felt could be securely fixed. These laggings were made of American redwood grooved and tongued boards, 5½ in. by 21 ft. deep, enclosed by four wrought-iron hoops, 2½ in. wide and ⅜ in. thick, each belt or hoop put on in four sections, wrought-iron joint ends having been made for ⅜-in. bolts, in order to tighten if the necessity arose. The result of this protection, which necessitated boarding over the top of the tank, was that the spiral trough arrangement did not answer so well as was previously anticipated under the former conditions.

After the works were completed, at the end of 1896, and the water had been regularly supplied to the consumers for some time, sentimental objections arose from a number of the townspeople with respect to the colour of the water, so Prof. Attfield was again resorted to in October, 1897, when he reported in a similar manner as before on the sample submitted to him: "It (the sample) contains a perfectly harmless trace

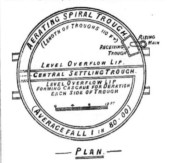

— PLAN. —

of iron, which soon settles, while settling the water is unsightly; on the other hand, the iron affords a guarantee against organic impurity. I should prize such water as a town supply, but more especially if the iron could be deposited by exposure in reservoirs or otherwise before delivery to consumers."

ANALYTICAL DATA.

One gallon contains the following number of grains and decimal parts of a grain of the respective substances:—

| | |
|---|---|
| Total suspended solid matter, dried at 250 deg. Fahr. | traces |
| Total dissolved solid matter, ,, ,, ,, | 20·5 |
| Ammoniacal matter, yielding 10 per cent. of nitrogen | 0·09 |
| (equal to ammonia per 1,000,000, 0·150.) | |
| Albuminoid organic matter, yielding 10 per cent. of nitrogen | 0·04 |
| (equal to ammonia per 1,000,000, 0·070.) | |
| Nitrites | none |
| Nitrates, containing 17 per cent. of nitrogen | 0·22 |
| (equal to grains of nitrogen per gallon, 0·04.) | |
| Chlorides, containing 60 per cent. of chlorine | 1·9 |
| (equal to grains of chlorine per gallon, 1·15.) | |
| Hardness, reckoned as chalk grains or degrees— | |
| Removed by ebullition | 11·0 |
| Unaffected by ebullition | 3·0 |
| Total hardness | 14·0 |
| Lead or copper | none |
| Physical examination, a faint brownish tinge (iron). | |
| Oxygen absorbed in three hours (by iron) | 0·16 |

The discolouration of the water still remaining a source of trouble to the urban district council, they consulted Mr. Holme, the manager of the waterworks at Hornsea, near Hull, at which place the water was stated to be of a similar nature and had been satisfactorily treated at his hands. He reported that the water when pumped from the well was clear and bright, but when delivered from the rising main emitted a sulphurous smell, and that this arose from the gas dissolving the oxide in the water, which, when exposed to the air, deposited in the pipes and domestic utensils. He recommended

SECTIONAL ELEVATION OF AERATING TROUGH.

a method of precipitation by breaking the water up and exposing it to the atmosphere, and then to pass it through filters of coarse gravel and sand which should retain the oxide, and then store it in a reservoir sufficient to hold one day's supply.

From the report of a deputation which visited Hornsea, accompanied by Mr. T. Hughes, the council's waterworks manager, they found there was a great difference between the water at Hornsea and that at Leighton. At Hornsea the water practically remained clear the whole time, and there seemed to be no difference in the colour of the water after exposure; at the same time there was a deposit of iron after standing only a short time, and this deposit was easily retained by the filters. It was considered, however, better to allow the Leighton water to stand in settling tanks and deposit before passing through the filters, as the Hornsen process would not take out the iron by working continuously. The deputation recommended that the council provide an aërator, settling tanks of sufficient capacity so as to allow ample time to deposit, afterwards passing the water through a sand filter into a reservoir, to allow a sufficient body of water for the pumps to draw on.

Mr. Hughes' opinion on the subject is that exposing the water to the atmosphere does not remove the iron; still, that it is necessary that it should be exposed before it can be

LEIGHTON BUZZARD WATER TOWER: GENERAL VIEW.

removed. When the water is pumped up from the well it is perfectly clear before its exposure to the atmosphere; but after being exposed it becomes very much discoloured, and this gives cause for numerous complaints. Mr. Hughes has fixed up an apparatus at the tower for the purpose of ascertaining whether aëration and filtration would remove the iron, and the experiment has proved successful, but in consequence of his leaving the town to take up a more lucrative appointment the experiments have been suspended. The water was first passed through an aërator, which consisted of a pipe carried up a height of about 25 ft., and on this pipe was fixed three perforated discs, placed one above the other and about 18 in. apart. The water, falling through these discs in the shape of rain, allowed the air to be thoroughly mixed with the water, which was afterwards conveyed into a tank through a trough, which again acted as an aërator. In this tank the water became much discoloured, owing to oxidation taking place as a result of the aëration. After this treatment the water was passed through a grave, and sand filter, when it became perfectly clear and bright, and did not show the least sign of discoloration after being exposed to the air for fourteen days. Mr. Hughes, from continued observation, considers it necessary that the water should remain some time in the settling tank, otherwise it would oxidise in the filter, with the result that the iron would be found near the invert of the filter, necessitating great expense in cleaning out. It would be found much better if it were allowed to stand twenty-four hours after aëration; the iron would be found at the top of the filter and could readily be removed; the water would then be freer from impurities.

The council are about adopting a scheme on the above method to remove the discoloration of the water, and this will probably form one of the first measures to be taken in hand by their new waterworks manager. The water from the well is raised into the wrought-iron tank, 30 ft. in diameter and 19 ft. 3 in. in depth, carried on the walls at a height of 62 ft. above the ground level. The tank is divided into two parts for a depth of 5 ft. from the bottom of the tank. This division was made in order to allow the whole of one side of the tank to be cleaned out; while there would remain on the

other side of the division a sufficient supply of water for the ordinary purposes of the town. The capacity of the tank is 80,350 gallons, the depth of water with this quantity being 18 ft. 3 in. The arrangement of the engines and pumps is in duplicate. Two 9 horse-power nominal Crossley gas engines work the two sets of three-throw pumps, and on the same floor there are fixed two other gas engines, with air compressors for working the ejectors in connection with the town's sewerage scheme.

The Leighton Buzzard water tower is an octagonal building, with buttresses and recesses of a Gothic character, the dimensions being 27 ft. 6 in. internally on the square. The average thickness of brickwork is about 2 ft. 8 in., but this is widened out in the bottom, immediately above the footings, to a width of 5 ft. 4 in., under which are the footings, spread out to 10 ft. The brickwork is carried on 5 ft. 6 in. of cement concrete, which extends some distance outside the footings all round the building. The detail work is of a solid character, enriched with terra-cotta mouldings, and special facing bricks from the Heather Brick and Terra-Cotta Company have been used throughout. The front and entrance of the tower faces towards the town, and the manager's residence is to the left looking from the town. There are two octagonal towers at the sides of the entrance, one carried up above the main tower, and having a spiral staircase for access to the various floors and to the top of the tank and balcony, the other being utilised as a meterhouse. The total height of the brickwork above the ground floor is 82 ft., and on the top of this a strong framed octagonal roof covered with red tiles is constructed with a balcony on the summit.

In connection with the discolouration of the water the "Fischer" system of water filtration is being considered by the council, and Mr. Hughes, the waterworks manager, has submitted proposals in conjunction with the experiments he has made, by which he estimates the required desiccation of the iron from the water could be arrived at by an expenditure of about £800.

For the water supply of small towns situated on the lower greensand, and where they are dependent upon a supply from this strata, it becomes a serious matter to abstract the iron from the water, necessitating, as it appears to do, additional machinery and pumping the water to an elevated tank after it has been raised from the well or bore-hole into the settling tanks or other apparatus requisite for its treatment. Where the water passes over or through the chalk or other calcareous stratum the hardness is sometimes excessive, as at the Barton boring, near Cambridge, where the total hardness reached 44 deg. 3. Generally speaking, however, the waters from the lower greensand are good and wholesome for drinking and cooking purposes, but in many instances are too hard for washing.

The above observations are brought under the notice of the British Association of Waterworks Engineers in the hope that the discussion following them will elicit some important information relative to treating the difficulty mentioned in the paper.

## DISCUSSION.

Mr. W. G. PEIRCE (Richmond) wished to draw attention to the question of cost. They always liked to know that, especially in well-sinking; and in the present case it was desirable that the author should state whether the work had been carried out by contract or under the supervision of the local authority. Also, as the pumping had been done by means of gas engines, he thought it would be interesting if Mr. Nichols could state the cost per 1,000 gallons, together with the quantity of water obtained daily.

Mr. W. COLES FISCH (Luton, Kent), following a question in regard to the ordnance datum of the water at the Leighton Buzzard works, asked whether in the opinion of Mr. Nichols it would not be possible for waterworks engineers to do their own boring. Personally he thought he could do it himself, and he would be glad to know if Mr. Nichols considered it necessary to engage professional men. The work was exceedingly profitable, the gain often amounting to 40 per cent. Tools, he remarked, could be bought at reasonable prices, or hired.

Mr. FRANCIS J. BANCROFT (Hull), referring to the question of yield, said he would like to know whether any test was made when the well spoken of by the author was put down. The difficulty of working in the lower greensand was, of course, due to the running in of the sand. The Hornsea water, to which reference had been made, should have been treated both chemically and mechanically. The work, in his opinion, was not tackled on a scientific basis, as the process of aëration had been carried out first. A sample should have been taken under water. The settling tank, he noticed, was boarded over at the top.'

The CHAIRMAN: What sort of filter is used?

Mr. BANCROFT: Sand. Continuing, he said he would like to ask the cost of the wrought-iron tank. It seemed to him that the raising of the water to a tank was useless, and if the money had been spent on aërating machinery instead it would have been better. At Hornsea they had now done away with cloth filters, and were devoting themselves entirely to sand filtration. The water, after analysis, only required to be treated in that way and he believed that success would follow.

Mr. W. W. GRAY (Cambridge) drew attention to the statement that at the Barton boring, near Cambridge, owing to the calcareous stratum over which the water passed, the hardness reached over forty degrees. He wished to know whether the author was sure that it was the Barton near Cambridge. The hardness of the water at Cambridge never reached such a surprising figure, and Barton was only 2 miles away. At his own works they experienced no difficulty, except with the buckets; and they found that the salt water acted on the gun-metal fittings of the machinery.

Mr. E. J. SILCOCK (Kings Lynn) said he would be glad if the author would give some further information in regard to the illustration showing the geological strata of the well and boring at the Leighton Buzzard works, as that contained in the diagram did not agree with the figures in the letter-press. Then the 7-ft. cylinders spoken of did not appear in the illustration. He agreed with the observation that some

details of cost might with advantage be introduced; and he suggested that the inclusion of figures in reference to the population supplied would also be of value to the members. No information of this character had been given. He quite agreed that where engineers were in the neighbourhood of their works boring should be done by administration. Personally, he had experience both ways. Prices asked for boring were generally excessive, but in the event of an engineer deciding to undertake the work himself he should purchase a plant outright, and not hire one, as it could be sold immediately on the completion of the work. The purchase of plant was not an expensive matter, even if a diamond rock drill were included. It did not follow, continued Mr. Silcock, that because water came from greensand it contained iron; neither did it follow that it contained iron simply because it was clouded. It would, he thought, be easy to arrange for the aëration of water by the adaptation of the air-compressing machinery of waterworks. That could be carried out at a very small cost indeed. Mr. Silcock then concluded with a request for some information respecting the manner in which Mr. Nichols had put down his bore tubes. He had, he mentioned, gathered that long lengths of blowing sand were passed through, and he would therefore be glad to know something of the methods employed.

Mr. T. W. A. HAYWARD (Sudbury) put a question in regard to the price of gas at Leighton Buzzard. The price varied a great deal, being in some towns 2s. 3d. per 1,000 cubic feet, and in others, notably his own, over 4s. He then went on to speak of the great uncertainty which always attended the work of well-boring, and related an instance in which the contractor, who was being paid at the rate of 12s. 6d. per foot, broke no less than three tools, his profit being of necessity swallowed by the purchase of new implements and the cost of the delay which resulted. That showed the extent of the loss to which the council would have been subjected had they themselves undertaken the boring.

Mr. W. WHITAKER (Croydon), in a reference to certain typographical errors which had crept into the paper, said he had to protest against the treatment of the names of the various geological formations. He asked how the author himself would like it if his name were spelt wrongly. But printers, he remarked, never would do these formations justice. He, however, hoped that Mr. Nichols would amend the statement that the upper and lower greensands consisted of porous and oxidising strata which rapidly destroyed or removed the organic matter contained in the water percolating through them; it was only in certain districts—for example, Kent. The same remarks applied to Mr. Nichols' description of the greensand itself. Mr. Silcock had anticipated some remarks of his concerning the illustration of the well and boring, which he also considered required something to make it agree with the text. The expression "congealed stone," which was included in the diagram, was not to his liking, and he thought the well sinkers' term should be adhered to; besides, there could not be such a thing as "congealed stone." Anything that would help to make the diagram perfect he would, he assured them, be glad to do; at present he considered it imperfect. The top sand was probably not a part of the lower greensand, but a part of the gault. He did not quite understand why there should be any difficulty in dealing with the analyses of Prof. Attfield. They had constantly before them expressions of people that it was only necessary to sink in the lower greensand to get good supplies of water, but the fact was a great deal more trouble was experienced with those waters than with the supplies from the limestone. As to the inrush of sand, that was the usual result when attempts were made to pump from a bore-hole in sand. In his analytical data Mr. Nichols had omitted to give the percentage of iron contained in the water, and it was important that that should have been included. He presumed that the oxide (shortly afterwards alluded to) was of iron, but failed to understand the phrase " breaking up of water"; it probably only meant the mechanical breaking up of water, but, nevertheless, might easily mislead. Then they were not told where the Hornsea water came

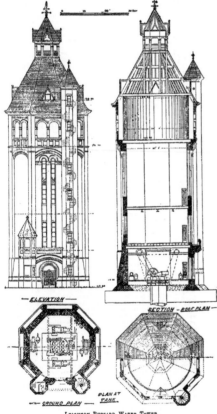

LEIGHTON BUZZARD WATER TOWER.

from — the chalk or the lower greensand — and that also required clearing up. He could not understand the statement that where water passed over or through the chalk or other calcareous stratum the hardness was sometimes excessive; neither was he able to understand the hardness of that particular water. A hardness of forty-four degrees was enormous, and there must be, he thought, some special reason for it; but it was interesting to get such a figure recorded. In his opinion the charges for boring were not excessive. But in America, in spite of the higher wages which were paid, this class of work was done very cheaply. Referring to the accidents spoken of by Mr. Hayward, he could only suggest that the contractor was not provided with a sufficient amount of tackle. But (continued the speaker amid laughter) it was not considered to be a finished work unless some tool was left in, though they had in the case recorded by Mr. Hayward started rather early.

Mr. CHRISTOPHER SAINTY (Windsor) asked for an explanation of the paragraph in the paper relating to the shutting out of the water from the well above the depth of 175 ft. He thought it must get in.

Mr. JONES (Leyton), speaking in regard to the samples of water submitted for analysis, considered that it would have been more scientific if the water had been followed in its various stages. The iron, he took it, could be precipitated. He would aërate the water by compressed air, atmospheric aëration being slow and expensive compared with that method, while it required time and space to carry it out. Then by charging the water with air more satisfactory results would be obtained. Regarding the analyses in the paper, he would, he said, be glad to know where the sulphuretted hydrogen came from, as he did not see how it could be accounted for. It would also be desirable to know the population supplied, the amount supplied to each person, and the birth and death rates of the town. He suggested that those points should be given in the paper before it was out of the printer's hands. He had also the idea that it would be much more satisfactory if the hardness of the water at Leighton Buzzard was reduced, and he would be glad to know if milk of lime was used in its treatment. People nowadays had a preference for clear waters, and disliked those discoloured with iron; but in many places the inhabitants habitually used brown water, and quickly became inured to it. Iron, if not present in excess, had a beneficial effect on the system, and people often went hundreds of miles to obtain sulphuretted water. It was very useful in some cases of medical treatment, but he did not like to imbibe it himself. They were all, he remarked in conclusion, glad to have information of the nature contained in Mr. Nichols' paper, the works of small towns being as interesting as those of the larger ones. He thought the exceptions which had been taken to the diagrams were certainly well founded.

Mr. J. S. PICKERING (Nuneaton) remarked that he had been interested in the paper, as he himself had to deal with works somewhat similar to those of Mr. Nichols. He would therefore watch with close attention the progress of the experiments in connection with the removal of the iron from the water. The method, however, was certainly an expensive one for small towns. The objections made to the discoloured water were of course only sentimental, but for all that people could hardly be expected to drink such waters. They would, he admitted, rather drink clear, and probably impure, waters from wells. The remedy was to aërate the discoloured waters and allow them to settle, after which they should be filtered. In his own case he had proposed to use sand in the filters, but it was subsequently suggested that gravel should be tried instead; sand, however, gave better results. Following filtration, the next thing was to discharge the water into a service reservoir, and from thence distribute it to the town. He would be very glad to communicate with Mr. Nichols if that gentleman desired any further information from him, but at present he was not quite prepared to say more. The water at his works, he mentioned in concluding his address, was perfectly clear and sparkling on being pumped.

Mr. S. H. NORMAN (Burgess Hill), in the course of a few remarks, stated that for many years past he had successfully treated the water at Burgess Hill by aëration and sand filtration, and not at any time had there been the slightest complaint. He also would be glad to supply any additional information to the author if the latter so desired.

Mr. J. SHAW (Boston, Lincs.) said he had listened to the paper with interest, but the analyses of the water had struck him as curious, and he had to say the hardness was very high. Paris went into the lower greensand for water, and the supply of that city, when unpolluted, never rose above 9 deg. of hardness. Another point in the analysis to which he wished to draw attention was the excessive amount of albuminoid organic matter. That, he would mention, when supplied to a town in any appreciable quantity, was looked upon with suspicion. But nowadays, he confessed, it was a fact that people drank with their eyes, and could not by any means be convinced that the consumption of a particular kind of water was likely to be beneficial to them.

Mr. W. WATTS (Sheffield), upon the invitation of the chairman, next contributed some remarks to the discussion. He had, he said, been hoping that he would be allowed to remain a quiet listener, as Mr. Nichols' paper dealt with matters in which he had had but little experience. The idea, he went on, had struck him that in clarifying water it would be best to

have as great a bulk as possible, in order to give it more exposure to atmospheric action. He quite agreed that corporations might themselves carry out works of boring; and he spoke from experience. Many years ago a boring company undertook to sink a certain well at the price of £3 per foot, on condition that the owner paid the actual expenses of the work. He (the speaker) thereupon offered to sink a shaft for £4 10s. per yard, the shaft to be 4 ft. in width, and the boring was subsequently carried out at that price. Referring to Mr. Nichols' statement in regard to the passing of water through a pipe, 25 ft. in height, for purposes of aeration, it seemed to him that when the water left the discs it would be blown away in spray. Then he failed to understand how the water rose to such a height.

Mr. H. ASHTON HILL (Birmingham) said that as so many remarks had been made respecting borings, he would have liked to have struck out in another direction. But he thought that engineers of waterworks should well consider the question before embarking upon those operations. Engineers with plenty of time on their hands might safely undertake the work, but he was speaking with his knowledge of boring companies when he said that they rarely paid a dividend exceeding 10 per cent. And that could scarcely be grudged them considering the risky character of their business. Therefore he was not of opinion that public officials should hamper themselves with such matters. It was easy to get low quotations for borings, the proper thing being to draw out plain specifications, with the end in view of getting tenders only from firms of the highest standing. He himself had just recently completed a boring, and now had others in hand, so that he was specially interested in the subject. But, he remarked in closing, he did not think that such large profits resulted from the work as was generally supposed; the real profit was as near as possible 10 per cent. Mr. Watts' prices for the sinking of shafts were extremely low.

Mr. J. JOHNSTONE (Brighton) said he desired to know, as it was specially interesting, whether Mr. Nichols had tried the yield of the Leighton Buzzard well—which was completed in 1896—during the present year, and, if so, what was the result. Although it might yet be impossible to discern any change, it was all the more important that steps should be taken to discover any because of the unusual dryness of the past few months. He was particularly anxious to know, because there had been a falling off in the supply of underground water; but his opinion was that the dryness would not yet be felt in the lower greensand. At Brighton they had easily overcome the difficulties in connection with oxide of iron.

Mr. PEIRCE, referring to the question of labour, said he must certainly say that for the benefit of the engineer in charge it was preferable that work should be placed in the hands of the contractor, although sometimes that course was impossible. In driving adits on one occasion he commenced with a contractor, but afterwards found it would be so expensive that it would be necessary to drive it himself, and he therefore bought the contractor's plant. If they had had to pay the contractor the cost would have been ruinous.

Mr. C. H. PRIESTLEY (Cardiff) at this stage added a few words in reference to the profits of contractors, and gave it as his opinion that a company might happen to lose money in the carrying out of one work, but would easily compensate themselves by the unfair profit which would accrue from some later contract.

The CHAIRMAN said that one thing that had struck him was the enormous time taken to sink the well described in the paper, and because of that he would have liked to have known more about the difficulties met with. Either the well was of an extraordinary character or the work was abandoned for a time. The most perplexing part of the paper, however, was that dealing with the analyses, as, for example, in the first item respecting the suspended matter. Only traces of suspended matter were said to have been found, and that appeared to answer the question as to whether sand was brought up in the boring. Regarding the figures in reference to the ammoniacal and albuminoid matters present in the water, he had, as many of those present also had, to deal with a medical officer of health who would make a long face if they had similar results. He felt convinced that the amounts were too high, and the excessive figure of 14 deg. of hardness suggested that there was a communication between the chalk and the greensand. It was a very simple matter to deal with this water. Continuing, he said he wished to know the reason for building a tank of the description mentioned by Mr. Nichols of wrought iron instead of steel, by which a considerable saving in weight would have been effected. The tank would also have been very much stronger. After commenting on the use of the term "nominal" in connection with the gas engines referred to by the author, the chairman then formally moved the accordance of a hearty vote of thanks to Mr. Nichols, and brought his address to a close.

The motion having been seconded, it was subsequently put to the meeting and adopted unanimously.

Mr. BERTRAM NICHOLS then proceeded to make his reply. He would, he said, endeavour to answer a number of the questions which had been put. He had not anticipated such a large discussion, and would, as he was unable to carry in his mind all that had been said, reply to the remaining questions at a future date. Mr. Hughes, the waterworks engineer to the Leighton Buzzard Council, he had hoped would have been present. He had said he would, and he (the speaker) was exceedingly sorry that he was not, as the information which might otherwise have been supplied was very valuable. Mr. Hughes would have dealt with the scheme from its start. Since the completion of the work his information had been derived partly from memory, from the local press, and from individual conversations with members of the council. If Mr. Hughes had been present it would have been easier to answer; but he would take the questions *seriatim*. The population of Leighton Buzzard had not been included in his paper, because the latter had been drawn up, not with the object of giving such points, but of getting some information which would help to overcome the difficulties which the townspeople had experienced. He would, however, mention that the population was about 7,000, and was not increasing very rapidly, or expected to. The total cost of the works was £22,500, the sinking of the well and boring absorbing about £1,350 of that sum; but the figures might not be quite accurate. The presence of the perforated tubes in the well he would explain. On reaching a certain depth the water was found to be impregnated with iron, in order to obliterate which a lining was put in, and the tubes were thereupon carried to a depth of 200 ft. When the first testing was made they pumped for a number of days. The quantity raised per day at the present time was 12,000 gallons. As to whether the supply had decreased since the time of the completion of the works, he would state that that pumping had been carried on constantly, but it had been found that the water had risen higher in the well, and at the present time stood higher than ever; the total rise was between 4 ft. and 5 ft. They did not pump directly from the borehole. The supply appeared to be quite sufficient for the present population as well as for a larger population in the future. Treatment by filters seemed to him a reasonable method if the water could be raised to high ground. That, however, had not been possible, there being no hill within reasonable distance to which the water might be pumped; and to his mind the only way out of the difficulty had been to build a water tower. There had, he ought perhaps to explain, been three analyses of the water, and he was sorry that he had not included them all, as they had differed from those given in his paper. The whole of the boring had been carried out by Messrs. Isler & Company. As to the delay in its execution, that had been due to the failure of water, which stopped the works for six or seven months and then went on with them again; that was the explanation. At the start a large amount of sand was encountered, but at the present there was little coming from the borehole. His information regarding the hardness of the water had been extracted from the Sixth Report of the Rivers Pollution Commissioners. Milk of lime had not been tried at Leighton Buzzard. The analyses, he would state, had not been taken only from samples of water drawn from the well, but also from samples from the mains. He would be glad, he said in conclusion, to avail himself of Mr. Pickering's kind offer, and also to amplify, to some extent, the matters contained in his paper.

## SCAVENGERS' POISONOUS OVERCOATS.

The effects of the poisoning upon the Birmingham scavengers are more serious than was at first anticipated. About seventy men were invalided in consequence of the poisonous effects of the overcoats and the overalls which they were wearing, and it was stated at the time that the skin eruption which the poisonous dye had caused was only such that in the majority of the cases the men would soon be at work again. Inquiries, however, show that quite half the number of men are still under treatment as out-patients at the hospitals, and that in many cases their injuries have been of a very painful character. The dye or solution of chloride of zinc which was discharged from the overcoats and overalls set up an acute irritation of the skin on certain parts of the body, principally about the arms, wrists, thighs and legs. It was hoped and believed at the time that the epidermis irritation would pass away in a few days, but it now appears that the acid had a cauterising effect upon those portions of the skin with which it came into contact, and either destroyed the epidermis or created nasty blisters and sores. It is likely to be some time yet before all the men are back at work again.

**Sewer Accident at Barcelona.**—The brickwork of a large sewer in course of construction fell-in this afternoon, says a *Reuter's* telegram, dated the 11th inst., having a number of men engaged on the work. Eighteen bodies have already been recovered from the *débris*. The accident is believed to have been caused by the infiltration of water.

**Sanitary Inspectors' Association.**—A general meeting of the members of the above association will be held at Carpenters' Hall, London-wall, E.C., to-morrow, at 6 p.m., when a paper will be read by Mr. W. R. Grigg, of Fulham, and an election of members and associates will take place. This meeting will be followed, at 8 p.m., by an extraordinary general meeting, at which the following resolution will be submitted on behalf of the council : That the number of members in the association shall be increased by the addition thereto of seven hundred (700) members beyond the present registered number.

## QUERIES AND REPLIES.

*We cannot undertake to reply to any queries which are not accompanied by the writer's name and address. These are required as a guarantee of good faith and not for publication. Sketches accompanying queries should be made separate on white paper, in plain black ink lines. Lettering or figures should be bold and plain.*

**224. By-Laws as to House Drainage, and their Interpretation.**—Mr. J. W. Martin, Station Chambers, Clacton-on-Sea, writes, enclosing plan of new building which was referred to in our last issue under this heading, and which we also reproduced. He points out (1) that fences to the two existing houses have been newly erected, diminishing the open space considerably from that which the premises enjoyed before; (2) the new granary has a basement 4 ft. 6 in. below the ground, but no provision is made for draining same, as required; (3) that the junction of the new drain with the old drain creates the latter into a public sewer; (4) copy of a letter from Mr. George Winship, borough surveyor, Abingdon, certifying that the proposed drainage of the new buildings is not in accordance with the regulations for drainage as set forth in Form A and in force within the district of the Clacton Urban Council; (5) an extract from another journal, that the plan submitted to them has a very ugly curve in it, and which appears to be unprovided by an inspection chamber; that it is connected with an old drain at right angles; and, according to the by-laws, each house must be connected with the sewer by a separate drain; (6) that Mr. Martin has no connection with the said plan, neither is he interested in any way with the matter, only to see his town properly drained and kept in a sanitary condition.

Several of the points urged by Mr. Martin have been already anticipated and answered by us in our last issue (December 9th). Taking them in the order given, we have to observe that (1) the erection of the fences named do not appear to have any bearing on the drainage of the building or the plan submitted and approved. (2) The drainage of the basement cannot be enforced under the by-laws, as is erroneously suggested. (3) We are of opinion that the drain has not been converted into a public sewer by the connection of the outbuilding to the existing drain. (4) See our reply of last week, which dealt with the points named. (5) These criticisms are scarcely worthy of serious notice, and we are of opinion that the writer has not read the by-laws. The by-laws do not prohibit (*a*) such a curve as that shown (*b*) nor require an inspection chamber (although such is provided); (*c*) the drain is not connected with the existing one at right angles, but obliquely in the direction of the flow, as required by the by-laws; and (*d*) the by-laws *do not* require that each house must be connected with the sewer by a separate drain. (6) We are obliged for Mr. Martin's avowal. Our experience and observation, however, teach us that municipal surveyors, with very few exceptions, may be depended upon, and are much more deeply concerned, in securing the proper drainage and sanitary condition of a town than individual members of a local authority, who, in the nature of things, have not the requisite experience and knowledge of the subject that a municipal surveyor possesses.

**228. Osiers, Damage to by Sewage Effluent.**—" W. H. D." writes : With reference to your reply to this query (December 2nd), and as to recommending the name of a person who is an authority on osier cultivation, I beg to say that Mr. J. Brown, 7 North-end, Wisbech, is an authority on the subject. Mr. Brown wrote a report for the Royal Commission on Agriculture upon osiers, and this report was printed in pamphlet form. He also reported to the Dublin Science and Art Committee and the Committee of the Herbarium at Dublin upon osiers—their kinds, cultivation, commercial value, &c., and he has been engaged in many similar respects throughout the kingdom.
We are much obliged to our correspondent for the information.

**230. Sewage Farms in the United Kingdom: Particulars Required.**—" Borough Surveyor " writes : Would you inform me of the name of any work or official publication giving the number of sewage farms in the kingdom worked by local authorities or let to farmers ?
The querist would, we think, most probably be able to obtain the necessary information from the Local Government Board. If we remember rightly; a return of the description named was compiled by the Board a few years ago. Possibly Messrs. Eyre & Spottiswoode, Queen's printers, East Harding-street, London, E.C., may have published the return, but we are unable to trace it.

**231. Appointments for Engineers and Surveyors : Advertisements as to Foreign Vacancies.**—" Alpha " writes : Will you kindly inform me whether there is any special paper which advertises foreign appointments, and could you give me any information respecting them and how to hear of them ?
There is not, so far as we are aware, any journal which is specially selected as a medium for the exclusive advertisement of foreign vacancies. The Surveyor and Municipal and County Engineer, having a circulation in all the colonies, will probably be found to contain advertisements or particulars of most of the vacancies.

## THE WIDENING OF PARLIAMENT-STREET.

### THE ACTION OF THE LONDON COUNTY COUNCIL.

The Improvements Committee · of the London County Council have prepared a report in reference to the application of Her Majesty's Office of Works for a contribution from the council towards the cost of the widening of Parliament-street. It appears that the council were asked to join in a conference at the Office of Works to determine the nature and extent of the contributions to be made by the council and the Westminster Vestry. To this request the Improvements Committee acceded, and deputed their chairman and their vice-chairman to wait upon the First Commissioner, having previously ascertained, however, that the vestry had resolved to take no part in the conference, as they had decided not to make any contribution towards the cost of the improvement. At the conference it was stated, on behalf of the Office of Works, that it was proposed to widen Parliament-street by setting back the line of frontage of the public buildings to be erected there so as to give a width of at least 135 ft., instead of about 60 ft. as at present. At the same time it was proposed to do away with King-street and to utilise its site in connection with the new public offices. The difference between the area of the land to be added to Parliament-street and that to be appropriated for buildings in King-street would amount to 17,858 square feet. It was contended that this widening of Parliament-street would be a great public improvement, relieving altogether the congestion of traffic there, and adding greatly to the dignity of the approach to the Houses of Parliament and Westminster Abbey. It was suggested, therefore, that the London County Council might properly contribute out of the county fund to this improvement, and that the proper measure of such contribution would be the value of the land thus added to Parliament-street, after accounting for that appropriated in King-street. If the value of this land to be given up were put at £10 per square foot the amount would be £178,580, but the First Commissioner freely admitted that as the Office of Works would not lose the frontage value of the lands, inasmuch as they would retain the frontage to the widened thoroughfare, the value should more properly be estimated at £6 per square foot. This would make the value of the land given up to the public way about £107,000, to which should be added the cost of the paving works of the widened street. It was further pointed out that it was proposed to double the width of Charles-street, which would also be a public improvement. Incidentally it was mentioned by the First Commissioner that the clearance of the block of buildings bounded by Parliament-street, Charles-street, King-street and Great George-street, had cost the Office of Works the sum of £405,000, which included £100,000, the value of land forming part of the Westminster Bridge estate, owned by the Office of Works.

After stating what has in the past been done in connection with the widening of Parliament-street, the committee mention that the clause authorising the council and the Westminster Vestry to contribute was not originally in the Public Offices (Westminster) Site Act, 1896, but was inserted during the progress of the Bill through Parliament without the council or the vestry being consulted in the matter. Neither was the council asked for a contribution until arrangements had been made for the acquisition of the land. These and other facts were stated by the chairman of the committee at the conference, and he suggested that the inference to be drawn from them was that the improvement about to be effected by the Government would not entail any cost when the commercial value of the land was taken into account. While admitting the very great public importance of the improvement in the widening of Parliament-street, he felt doubtful whether the council would be justified in making a contribution towards the acquisition of the land for the widening of the street, though he expressed the opinion that the cost of making up the roads would be a matter for consideration.

Since the conference the Improvements Committee have very carefully considered the whole subject, and now report : " It appears to us that the council would not be justified in making a contribution to a public improvement unless it were clearly shown that it was being carried out at a loss. As the Office of Works in 1882 so strongly represented to the Metropolitan Board of Works that in their opinion a scheme exactly similar to that now being undertaken by them could be carried out without loss, and as a body of private promoters were in 1896 also prepared to carry out this same scheme at their own cost and under the belief that they would make a profit thereby, it cannot be shown that the Government is incurring a loss by the transaction. Moreover, it must not be forgotten that the Office of Works are retaining for the purpose of the public offices the very valuable frontages to the widened thoroughfare of Parliament-street. We consider, therefore, that the council should not be asked to make a contribution towards the cost of the acquisition of the land needed for the scheme. We fully recognise the value of the scheme about to be carried out by the Government in the widening of Parliament-street and the improvement of the approaches to the Houses of Parliament and Westminster Abbey. We think that the council, as the central authority in London for carrying out large street improvements, may well desire to show their appreciation of the value of this work to the extent of taking upon themselves the cost of making the widened roads in Parliament-street and Charles-street. We think that a reasonable estimate for the two thoroughfares would be £12,000, and we consider that the council would do well to offer to contribute that amount." The committee accordingly submit a recommendation to this effect.

## LONDON WATER SUPPLY COMMISSION.

Another meeting of the commission was held on Monday, Lord Llandaff presiding, as before.

Mr. R. E. MIDDLETON was recalled and further cross-examined by Mr. Balfour Browne. Asked to give the calculation on which witness based the cost of the Staines scheme, he said that he had given the contract price, and he did not think it was fair to give the details. He did not think that flood-water brought down an enormous amount of manure from ditches and farms. The population of the Thames Valley watershed was about 1,000,000, and the population of the watershed of the proposed Welsh scheme was only 3,700. It was necessary to purchase in the latter case, because in the cases of Liverpool, Manchester and Birmingham they had purchased their watersheds ; and the water companies now paid rent to the Thames Conservancy, which was equivalent to purchase.

Mr. WALTER HUNTER, engineer and director to the Grand Junction Water Company, and joint engineer with Mr. Middleton to the Staines scheme, was the next witness examined. In reply to the chairman, the witness said the principle of the Staines scheme was to store the Thames water in large reservoirs as it came down the Thames. Whether the companies were purchased or not, either a Staines scheme for the added supply of the Thames must be adopted or the water must be got from Wales. The question for the commission to determine was what the cost of each of those two schemes was likely to turn out. In his judgment the Staines scheme would be much the less costly. He thought two days' rejection of flood water would leave sufficient time to cleanse the surface of the land and wash out the ditches. Although he thought that two days were sufficient, he had taken six days, so as to agree with Mr. Middleton's statement. In Sir William Crookes' and Prof. Dewar's report it was said that no advantage was gained by the rejection of the flood-water. The water contrasted favourably with that from mountain sources. If the Londoners had the brown water drawn from Wales and Thirlmere there would be an outcry.

Mr. BALFOUR BROWNE.—Sir William Crookes and Prof. Dewar said in their report of November, 1898 : " It has been said over and over again in these reports on the bacteriological quality of the London water supply that it does not depend upon the rejection or use of flood water, but upon the proper regulation of filtration. The direct use of water may result in a little additional vegetable matter, but in the last fifteen years none of the London water supply in that respect has equalled that of Thirlmere, Loch Katrine, or the Welsh lakes."

Witness said it was part of the Staines scheme that the companies should not draw any water at all to induce the flow to be less than 100,000,000 gallons at Teddington weir when their storage works were completed. He would not let the companies dry up the Thames.

At the sitting on Tuesday,

Mr. HUNTER, being asked whether he thought it desirable in the interests of London to take any steps to secure a fresh watershed in case of the need arising hereafter, expressed the opinion that it might be desirable if it could be shown that it was really wanted. That depended upon the growth of London. Some people believed that London would not increase in the future as it had increased in the past, and that therefore the Welsh water would never be wanted at all. The view which he took with reference to the utilisation of Thames water in preference to water taken from a distant watershed might be summed up somewhat in this way. Having a river at our feet with an average daily flow of something like 1,300,000,000 gallons, it was suggested that we should go to Wales and open up a supply from a watershed which at the outside would afford 415,000,000 gallons a day. If the county council, who were the promoters of that scheme, carried out what was at first their avowed intention of discarding the Thames altogether, what would happen would be that within a certain period these 415,000,000 gallons a day would be used up, and then, after having incurred all the expense of bringing water from Wales, the county council would have to come back to the Thames, which previously they had affected to despise, and make up the additional water which would then be wanted from the Thames. In these circumstances he felt that it was a question of expense as between the two schemes, and that, if the supply of good water from the Thames could be further developed at less expense, it would be absurd to go to a distant watershed until compelled to do so.

Sir FREDERICK BRAMWELL, F.R.S., who was the next witness, being asked by the CHAIRMAN whether he considered that purchase of the undertakings of the water companies by one or more authorities was financially desirable, gave it as his opinion that it was not expedient that the companies' undertakings should be acquired, in the interests either of the water consumers or of the ratepayers, because he felt convinced that the purchasing authority could not afford to make a less charge for water than at present.

## SHEFFIELD ELECTRIC TRAMWAYS.

**THE NEW POWER STATION AT KELHAM ISLAND.**

Of all the work of various kinds that is being carried on at Sheffield preparatory to the change in the system of tramway traction, the erection of the electric-power station on Kelham Island, from which all the power for driving the cars will be obtained, is considered to be the most important. As a centre for a power station Kelham Island is said to be admirable. It fulfils the essential conditions of being within a short distance of the lines, so that the current may be conveyed with as little waste as possible, and of providing space for any extensions of buildings that may be required in the future, as the tramway system is gradually enlarged, and lines cover all the principal streets of the city.

The buildings are so contrived that they can at any time be extended by additions to one end. The site of Crowley's Foundry premises, which the corporation have bought, is very large, and hardly half the land is at present being used for the provision of a station which is calculated to supply power to all the present lines and as many more as will be ready when it is completed. As a matter of fact, by no means the whole of the ground has been cleared, and the large portion of the old buildings left standing are being used as temporary stables and stores. The station consists of two large oblong buildings, the largest of which, the engine and dynamo house, occupies about 5,000 square feet, and the smaller, which is for the boilers, about 3,500 square feet. Thirty or forty men have been at work since the beginning of July, and very good progress has been made. The buildings are of brick, plain and neat, substantial, and in character with the kind of work for which they will be used. The most tasteful-looking elevation will be that on the south side, where the wall, 40 ft. high, will be pierced by two rows of windows, those in the lower storey placed together in pairs, and those higher in groups of three. This will be the wall of the engine-house, the inside measurement of which is 100 ft. by 50 ft.

The heavy foundations have been carried down to a depth of 10 ft. below the ground line, and afford space for six engines. At first only three engines are to be put in. These will be of 300 horse-power, supplied by Messrs. Allis, an American firm, and will be coupled to dynamos having a capacity of 225 kilowatts, and so arranged that they can be used independently or all worked together. A short time ago it was anticipated that one dynamo would probably prove sufficient to work the traffic, but the corporation seem now disposed to push on the extensions of the lines at a greater speed, and it is not unlikely that additional engines will be required before the house has been long in use. As already explained, however, it will not be necessary to extend the building for the first additions to the stock, as the beds of three more engines are already outlined. When extensions are needed the east end will have to be removed, and it will be possible to go on lengthening the building for a long time before all the land is covered. The same means will be adopted for enlarging the boiler-house, which adjoins the engine-house, standing nearer the river. This is at present 76 ft. long by 40 ft. 6 in. wide, and will hold three boilers, each of 800 horse-power, manufactured by Messrs. John Brown & Co., Limited, and fitted with patent induced draught supplied by fans working in the power-house. The boilers will be 10 ft. square at the base.

The brickwork of the engine-house is being filled into a skeleton of steel framework as large as any recently used in Sheffield. Ten upright steel stanchions are fixed, eight of which are 50 ft. high, and the others 10 ft. or 15 ft. lower. Across these are laid steel beams, which will support the roof trestles, and to which can also be fixed a travelling crane, by means of which any portions of the machinery can be removed without unnecessary delay. It was at first intended to have steel framework for the boiler-house as well, but there was a difficulty in obtaining the material, and this part of the design had to be abandoned. As it was, the work was considerably delayed by the slow arrival of the stanchions for the engine-house. The boiler-house will be lined with salt-glazed bricks, so that the sanitary measure of washing the sides can be taken from time to time, and glazed bricks of yellow will line the engine-house. The height of the two buildings from the floor to the eave of the roof will be about 40 ft. Along the roof of each will be a long lantern, which will admit sufficient light. The side of the boiler-house will be lined with coal bunkers some 12 ft. wide, and at one end there will be a tower for the tanks. Lavatories are provided in the building. Such good progress has been made with the work that if there is a continuance of fine weather the building will probably be completed by the end of March.

The work is being carried out under the supervision of Mr. C. F. Wike, the city surveyor. Mr. John Eshelby, of Sheffield, is the contractor for the buildings, his tender amounting to about £7,100; while the roofs will be supplied from the Phœnix Iron Foundry, Derby.

**Clayton-le-Moors.**—Application has been made by the district council for Local Government Board sanction to a loan of £5,075 for the purpose of paving, flagging, kerbing and channelling portions of the main roads in the district.

## THE VENTILATION OF BUILDINGS.

In the course of a paper on "The Ventilation of Tunnels and Buildings," which was read by Mr. Francis Fox, M.I.C.E., at an ordinary meeting of the Institution of Civil Engineers, last week, the author animadverted on the inconsistency of keeping houses clean, streets swept, and sewers flushed, with the object of preserving the air in a pure condition while allowing it to become absolutely foul and putrid for want of proper ventilation. Air that had passed through human lungs had, he said, been well designated "air-sewage." It was highly poisonous, and the breathing of it over and over again was fraught with the gravest consequences to health. It had been asserted by Dr. Ransome, F.R.S., that 70,000 deaths occurred annually in Great Britain from tuberculous disease, nearly all of which could be saved were the subject of fresh air both understood and acted upon by the community. Competent medical authority considered that the quantity of carbon dioxide in the air of rooms should not exceed 10 parts per 10,000, equivalent to about 16 cubic feet per head per minute. In French hospitals 50 cubic feet per patient per minute was allowed. Mr. Fox considered, however, that 20 cubic feet per minute would be sufficient for ordinary purposes. Tables were given of the impurity in the air of schools with different systems of ventilation, of that in dwelling-houses, and of that in sewers, from which it appeared that the latter was the least impure of the three.

Proceeding to consider the ventilation of particular public buildings, Mr. Fox illustrated his views by reference to special cases which had come within his experience. The fact should not be lost sight of, he said, that the air in a room might be quite cold and yet very foul; whilst, on the other hand, it might be warm and yet perfectly fresh. To avoid draught the air should enter through a large number of small orifices, so as to thoroughly diffuse the current. This was done by gratings, but unfortunately these seriously diminished the volume of air passing through, owing to the friction of the bars. The same remark applied to extracting flues. He was of opinion that no large building could be successfully ventilated without some mechanical force, furnished by steam, electricity, falling water, or other such agency. Then fans could be worked with certain results, whereas automatic extractors not infrequently became inlets, thus reversing the whole system. The inlets should be by Tobin or similar tubes, about 5 ft. above the floor. In one American State legislation building the warmed fresh air entered on the level and in front of the desks of each member. In conclusion, Mr. Fox urged the desirability of educating the public to the value and merits of fresh air.

## VENTILATION OF THE NEW NEWTON ABBOT HOSPITAL.

At the opening of the new hospital at Newton Abbott, on the 29th ult., the Right Hon. Charles Seale-Hayne, M.P., referring to the ventilation of the building, which is on the Boyle natural system, said : "I am a firm believer in what may be termed the philosophy of health. I believe also that it would be an excellent thing if in our primary schools greater attention was paid to instruction in hygiene. God has endowed us and blessed us with bodies that are wonderful machines, therefore it is our duty to keep these machines are kept in proper working order. This hospital seems to be admirably designed and well constructed, reflecting credit on both architect and builder. In presence of the crowded and distinguished company which I have the honour of addressing, I need not say, because the temperature attests it, that the ventilation of this hospital is upon the best and most scientific principles. I said just now how important was the subject of hygiene, and in no respects is it more valuable or necessary than in the subject of securing for our public buildings the necessary amount of fresh air. But if a pure atmosphere be necessary for us, who are in health by the blessing of Providence, how much more necessary is it that our afflicted fellow-creatures, stricken down by accidents or disease and denied for the time the blessings of outdoor exercise, should have secured to them the healthiest possible surroundings. I am glad, therefore, as I say, that in this new hospital the committee of management, or the architect acting on their behalf, have selected and adopted what I believe to be absolutely the best system of airing a public building that is known to sanitary science."

**London Local Government.**—The following letter has been received from the Lord President of the Privy Council in reply to the memorial addressed to him at the instance of the Islington conference on London Local Government: "Dear Sir, —I am directed by the Duke of Devonshire to acknowledge the receipt of the memorial which you left here on the 29th inst. The memorial has been laid by the Lord President before his colleagues. The Bill dealing with London government will be introduced in the House of Commons; and the Lord President will consider, with the member of the Government in charge of the Bill, whether there would be any advantage in receiving a deputation on the subject of your memorial before the meeting of Parliament.—I am, yours faithfully, Riversdale Walrond.—W. F. Dewey, Esq."

# Law Notes.

EDITED BY J. B. REIGNIER CONDER, 11 Old Jewry Chambers, E.C.,

Solicitor of the Supreme Court.

*The Editor will be pleased to answer any questions affecting the practice of engineers and surveyors to local authorities. Queries (which should be written legibly on foolscap paper, one side only) should be addressed to "The Law Editor," at the Offices of* THE

SURVEYOR. *Where possible, copies of local Acts or documents referred to should be enclosed. All explanatory diagrams must be drawn and lettered in black ink only. Correspondents who do not wish their names published should furnish a nom de plume.*

## QUERIES AND REPLIES.

ANCIENT LIGHTS.—"Lancastrian" writes : My council propose erecting the building coloured pink on the accompanying plan and section. The new building is sufficiently far away from the existing buildings to allow an angle of 45°

*Section on line A B*

from the sills of the ancient lights. At the rear of the private passage is a shop which has been erected within twenty years from this date. Would the owner have any chance in restraining the council or of being successful in an action for compensation in a court of justice ?

Under the Prescription Act (2 and 3 Will. IV., c. 71) the actual enjoyment of the access of light without interruption for twenty years gives an absolute right, unless the light is limited by agreement in writing. Nothing is to be deemed an interruption which has not been submitted to or acquiesced in for one year. If, therefore, the shop has been erected nineteen years and a day, the owner would have an inchoate right, which would become absolute when the period of twenty years is complete, interruption for a year not being possible. He may also have acquired a right by implied grant or implied reservation if both plots of land at any time belonged to one owner. Whether he has

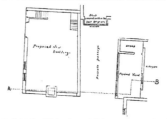

acquired such a right depends upon the facts. Assuming him to have acquired a right, either (a) under the Prescription Act or (b) by implied grant or reservation, the question would arise whether the obstruction of his light caused by the proposed building was sufficient for the Court to interfere, and whether it was a matter for an injunction or for damages, the general rule being that the Court will not interfere by way of injunction where damages will afford adequate compensation. If, however, the right is only an inchoate right under the Prescription Act, the Court would not grant an injunction (see *Lord Battersea* v. *Commissioners of Sewers*, vol. viii., THE SURVEYOR, p. 220). But the owner could probably recover damages if he brought an action the moment the twenty years' period expired and if he could prove substantial damage.

BY-LAWS : NEW STREET : HOUSE DRAINAGE.—"Unus" writes : A builder has deposited plans for a building estate of 20 acres (edged green on plan) which, physically speaking, lies low, being several feet below the main sewer in Sand Cross-lane, which is shown in blue. A portion of this estate has a frontage to Whitehall-lane of 1,060 ft., which is an old highway and averages 15 ft. wide (see A to B). Will the building of houses change the character of this old lane and transmute it into a new street, thereby enabling the corporation to ask for it to be made of the prescribed width in the by-laws—viz., 36 ft. wide ? The owner has offered to surrender the strip of land coloured blue to make Whitehall-lane 36 ft. wide, providing the corporation lay a new sewer from A to B, and so connect to the existing system in Sand Cross-lane ; as the land lies low, the laying of this sewer will entail a great outlay, the sewage having to be lifted by means of compressed air. Should the corporation decline the offer the owner declares he will leave Whitehall-lane at its present width and construct cesspools for the property. Sec. 23, Public Health Act, 1875, stipulates that property within

100 ft. of a public sewer should be drained into it. May I ask if this section does not apply in this case for the whole estate, as a portion thereof fronts on Sand Cross-lane, which is provided with a sewer. Can we compel the owner to make Whitehall-lane 36 ft. wide in the event of building operations being commenced ?

(1) It is a "question of fact" whether the carrying out of the building scheme would constitute the laying-out of Whitehall-lane as a new street, so as to entitle the authority to require it to be made 36 ft. wide. This question of fact would have to be decided by a magistrate in any proceedings to enforce the by-law (see *Taylor* v. *Metropolitan Board of Works, L.R.* 3, Q.B., 213 ; *Robinson* v. *Sutton Local Board*, 21 Ch. D., 436, and Lumley's "Public Health Acts, fifth edition, pp. 296, 297). This seems to me to be a case in which the authority might confidently anticipate the decision of the question of fact in their favour. (2) In my opinion the authority could, under the section referred to, compel the owners or occupiers of such houses on the estate as were within 100 ft. of the sewer in Sand Cross-lane to make drains emptying into that sewer, but this power would not extend to houses beyond that distance.

GAS EXPLOSION : LIABILITY.—"Gas Explosion" writes : I am the owner and occupier of a house abutting on a 36 ft. street. When the property was built, some three or four years ago, an old lane was filled up (about 10 ft.). The settlement of this filled-up stuff caused a sinkage in the footpath—under which the gas main is laid—exactly opposite my frontage, and resulted in the gas main being fractured, the gas escaping from the main under the house, and igniting at the lighted chandelier in back room caused an explosion, doing damage to the amount of £240, besides personal injuries and shock. The gas company deny liability, not being responsible for the state of the street, their pipes being stated to be of the usual and sufficient strength, &c. The street has not yet been declared a highway, and so has not been taken over by the corporation. The property was built by contract for a Building Company, Limited, who sold the houses and land freehold to the first purchasers. I am the third owner of this particular house. I may add that the water main in the centre of the street was broken some few weeks ago through the same cause—the settlement of street over the site of the old lane. It appears to me that the responsibility must rest with some party, and I shall be glad of your opinion in the matter.

I am afraid this is one of those cases in which it would be extremely difficult to fix liability anywhere. In order to render the gas company liable it would be necessary to prove negligence in the laying of the pipes, which would be difficult enough in any case, and especially so in this instance, seeing that the accident was really due to the subsidence of the road. The local authority would not be liable for merely not repairing the road ; it would have to be shown that they had been guilty of some active negligence—"misfeasance," as distinct from "nonfeasance." I presume, as the road has not been taken over, that the authority have not interfered with it in any way ; also, that the road was made and the old lane filled up by the building company, who, in that case, would seem to be the real culprits. But here, again, it is, in my opinion, very doubtful whether an action would lie against them, as the damage would be too remote. Although not declared a highway, the road probably has been informally dedicated, and thus actually becomes a highway ; and there is, so far as I am aware, no precedent for holding the landowner who lays out a road liable for accidents resulting from its subsidence.

NEW BUILDING.—"Surveyor" writes : About nine days ago, when visiting a part of my district, I found a new building was being erected—viz., a stable containing three or four loose boxes and a harness-room, and being built to join the gable end of the present block of stables, &c. I wrote to the builder asking him to submit plans for my committee, and to cease the works till the same were approved or otherwise ; he wrote back saying that the architect considered this was a simple addition and not a new building, and therefore the plans would not be submitted nor the works cease. The architect has written to our clerk to this effect, also saying he was prepared to defend the action. Our clerk has given the builder notice to cease the works, which was delivered on November 29th, and they have not done so. We are taking action, which will take place on the 5th or 6th of December. As all these cases are a matter of fact for the justices to decide, can you give me the most recent case that will help our case. I will send you full particulars of the decision in due course, as I feel sure it will be interesting to your readers. Our by-laws are the model ones, based on those of the Local Government Board, and of which you have a copy.

I am unable to refer to any recent cases which will assist. But in *James* v. *Wyeth* (51 J.P., N.S., 327) Lord Coleridge laid down the general principle on which the "question of fact"—viz., whether a building is a new building or not is to be decided, as follows :—" If a building were nearly all taken away and then rebuilt it clearly would be a new building ; on the other hand, it is quite clear that by a small addition, of say a door, the building would not therefore become a new building. Between these two extreme cases there may be thousands of cases, and it would be impossible to give a definition in each particular case as to what is or is not a new building, and it must be left to the discretion of each judge to decide for himself what is a new building.'

# Municipal Work in Progress and Projected.

The paragraphs under the headings of Morley, Manchester, Taunton, Worthing, Portslade-by-Sea and other places contain the chief information that has come to hand this week in regard to municipal works in the provinces. In the metropolis, St. Marylebone and Strand seem to be the only authorities that have any extensive works in hand.

## METROPOLITAN AUTHORITIES.

### LONDON COUNTY COUNCIL.

The county council evinced keen interest on Tuesday in the urgency report of the Highways Committee with regard to the refusal of Mr. John Young, manager of the Glasgow Corporation tramways, to accept the position of chief officer of the council's tramway department. The members tried to find out why he had refused the position, which carries with it a salary of £1,500 per annum, but they were unsuccessful. Mr. Benn, chairman of the Highways Committee, explained all he knew in connection with the matter, and also read the letter which his committee had received from Mr. Young. In the end the report of the committee, which recommended that Mr. Baker, manager of the Nottingham Corporation tramways, who was second on the list of three submitted by the General Purposes Committee a fortnight ago, should be appointed to the managership, at a salary of £1,000 per annum, was adopted. Full particulars are given in our "Personal" column.

*Loans for Public Works.*—Upon the recommendation of the Finance Committee it was agreed to lend the Hammersmith Vestry £11,020 for electric lighting purposes; the Newington Vestry £10,000 for the same purpose; and the St. Giles' District Board of Works £17,160 for the purchase of land as a site for a depot.

*The Council's Water Bills.*—The Parliamentary Committee brought up a report with reference to the draft Bills to be introduced in the ensuing session of Parliament. The first was the London Water (Purchase of Companies) Bill, the arbitration clause being known as the "Plunket" clause; the next was the London Water (Welsh Reservoirs and Works) Bill; and the next the London Water (Aqueducts and Works) Bill. Mr. Cornwall, in moving the reception of the report, said there was only one alteration in the estimates for the Welsh scheme. Sir Alexander Binnie had asked that the estimates should be raised from £16,500,000 to a round figure of £17,000,000. It had been found impossible to get the whole of the plans of the aqueducts finished in time to comply with the standing orders, but it was hoped that Parliament would see their way, after learning the circumstances, to suspend the standing orders and allow the Bills to proceed. The report was adopted.

*The Holborn to Strand Improvement.*—The Parliamentary Committee also presented the draft of the London Improvements (Holborn to Strand, Southampton-row widening, High-street, Kensington, and other works) Bill, and recommended that the seal of the council should be affixed to a petition for leave to bring in the Bill. Mr. Campbell moved as an amendment to insert in the recommendation words declaring that provision should be made for the interest on money raised to .pay for the purchase of property under the Bill, and generally for effecting the improvements, to be for the first few years before the completion of the improvements treated as part of the expenses payable out of the money borrowed. After a lengthy discussion, the amendment was rejected, on a division, by seventy-two votes to forty. The draft of the Bill was then approved, as well as the draft of the London County Council (General Powers) Bill.

*Housing of the Poor at Poplar.*—The Housing of the Working Classes Committee presented a report dealing with the provision of working-class dwellings on land known as the Cotton-street site, Poplar. This matter has already been the subject of several discussions in the council. A proposal to sell the land for the erection of dwellings was rejected. The committee found themselves unable to build on the land without incurring a charge on the rates, and now asked to be authorised to take no further action with regard to the erection of buildings on the site. After discussion an amendment was accepted to the effect that the recommendation should be referred back to the committee, with an instruction to see whether plans could not be prepared for erecting dwellings upon this site which should not involve any charge on the county rate.

*The Widening of Parliament-street.*—The Improvements Committee presented a report with reference to the proposed contribution to the widening of Parliament-street now being undertaken by Her Majesty's Office of Works. A summary of the report will be found in another column. The committee reported against any contribution being made to the cost of the acquisition of the land needed, but recommended the council to contribute £12,000 in respect of the making-up of the widened streets. A long discussion followed, during which two amendments were negatived, but eventually the recommendation of the committee was adopted, with a verbal amendment that the sum contributed should not exceed £12,000.

## COURT OF COMMON COUNCIL.

The Lord Mayor presided on Thursday at a meeting of the above body called specially to clear off the arrears of business left over at the last ordinary meeting. A letter was received from the London County Council relative to the application made by the court for a grant towards the cost of widening London-wall and Blomfield-street. The Improvements Committee of the council stated that, after full consideration, they did not see their way to recommend the council to entertain the suggestion for widening the thoroughfare to 60 ft. With regard to the proposal to widen it to 50 ft., they understood that the trustees of the Bridge House estates were the owners of the property in the vicinity, and had arranged to undertake the widening in connection with the sale of part of their property. Under those circumstances the committee did not feel prepared to recommend the council to accede to the request made by the corporation for the contribution. The letter was referred to the Finance and Improvement Committee.—Mr. Moojen asked whether a report had yet been received from the engineer with reference to the condition of the footways and parapets of London Bridge. Mr. B. Turter, chairman of the Streets Committee, replied that he hoped a report from the engineer would be presented at the next meeting of his committee.—In reply to another question by Mr. Moojen, Mr. Turner stated that he was unable to say when the conference between the local authorities of the metropolis on the subject of telephones would take place. It was not necessary that there should be a preliminary inquiry, and when they had satisfied themselves on certain points the Lord Mayor would be approached for the purpose of convening the meeting of the conference.

## VESTRIES AND DISTRICT BOARDS.

**Battersea.**—The Finance Committee reported to the vestry on Wednesday that the County of London and Brush Provincial Electric Lighting Company had deposited plans in reference to their proposal to apply for powers to produce and supply electricity in the parish. It was decided to refer this matter, together with other plans submitted in regard to Parliamentary schemes, to the special committee on Parliamentary subjects.—The same committee also announced the receipt from the Local Government Board of sanction to borrow £34,370 for the erection of baths and wash-houses in Battersea Park-road, and £1,380 for the sinking of artesian wells at the Latchmere-road baths.—It was further reported by the committee that application had been made to the London County Council for a loan of £1,200 for the reconstruction of the sewer in Stewart's-road.—A letter had been received from the London County Council on the subject of district surveyors, stating that the Building Act Committee could not recommend the council to take any steps at present in respect of the duties and payment of district surveyors, whom the vestry had suggested should devote the whole of their time to their duties and be in the salaried employment of the county council.—A long discussion took place on the presentation by the Health Committee of a report dealing with cases of diphtheria in No. 2 sanitary district, the cause of the disease in twenty cases being attributed to insufficient ventilation of sewers and defective gullies in the streets. The committee found that the low-level sewer was inadequately ventilated, and they recommended that the attention of the London County Council should be drawn to the matter, with a view to the more efficient ventilation of the sewer. The recommendation was adopted. With regard to the ventilation of the local sewers, the vestry decided to fit automatic flushing chambers to the stump ends of the sewers in various streets, to connect the local sewers at the stump ends with the sewers in the adjacent streets where practicable, to ventilate the sewers at their highest point by 9-in. upcast shafts, and to provide inlet and outlet ventilation to each sewer in the district.—It was decided to reconstruct the sewers in Alfred-street and five other thoroughfares.—The Works Committee reported that they had had under consideration a letter from Mr. J. Pilditch, the surveyor, relating to the responsibility for the carrying out of contracts by the Works Department. The committee stated that they had decided to relieve the superintendent of works of the supervision of all building works estimated to cost £700 or more, and to engage a general foreman for any building work estimated to cost £700 or more, such foreman to have all control of the men engaged on the work, with full power to engage and discharge men. The committee had settled the duties and responsibilities of such foreman, and they recommended that on large jobs, such as the erection of the new baths and wash-houses, the foreman be paid a salary of £5 per week, and be provided with a timekeeper to keep the men's time, check all material, and generally to assist him in carrying out the duties. On the motion of Mr. Musser it was resolved to refer the report back to the committee.—On the recommendation of the Works Committee it was decided to invite tenders for the supply, among others, of bricks, cement, lime, granite, stoneware pipes and street lamp columns.—It was resolved to approve plans prepared by the surveyor for the erection of dwellings for men employed at the Morden cemetery. The cost was estimated at £1,550.

**Camberwell.**—A meeting of this body was held, on Wednesday, when an adjourned report of the General Purposes Committee, recommending the approval of plans for the carrying out of various alterations at the vestry hall, at an estimated cost of £500, was received. The report was, however, subsequently withdrawn.— The Finance Committee stated that all necessary arrangements had been made for the purchase of ground in Grove-vale for the purpose of a depot, and now proposed the drawing of a cheque for the sum of £8,100, the balance of the purchase money for a similar site in Peckham Park-road. This was agreed to.—The committee also reported that they had given further consideration to a report of a conference, convened by the Bermondsey Vestry, on the housing of the working classes, and recommended that the approval of the vestry be given to the five resolutions adopted at the meeting which was subsequently held; they, however, took slight exception to the wording of the first resolution. It was decided to adopt the committee's recommendation, together with another suggesting that the surveyor should be instructed to at once cleanse and put in a sanitary condition a number of roads which had recently been taken over, until such time as they were made up.— On the recommendation of the General Purposes Committee, the vestry resolved to empower the surveyor to invite tenders for the carrying-out of work in connection with the heating and ventilating of the vestry hall and offices.—A number of other recommendations were presented by various committees, but were opposed after 10 o'clock. The vestry rose at a very late hour.

**Lambeth.**—At the last meeting of the vestry a lengthy report was submitted by the Baths Committee giving the explanations of Mr. Hessell Tiltman, architect, on the subject of the extra expenditure incurred over the estimates of the Kennington-road baths.—The General Purposes Committee presented a report recapitulating the objections raised by the Hammersmith Vestry to the recommendations of the Joint Parliamentary Committee on the Supply of Electrical Energy. On the recommendation of the committee it was resolved to agree with the Hammersmith Vestry in submitting that the local authority within the area of supply should have the power of deciding the route the mains are to be laid, and the power of opening and reinstating the streets. It was also decided to concur in the view that the local authority should use every endeavour to retain its power of veto, both in regard to overhead wires for the purposes of traction and applications for provisional orders.—A special report was received from the Lighting Committee relating to the desire of the South London Electric Supply Corporation to submit a scheme for the lighting of some of the principal streets in Lambeth. By clause 20 of the transfer deed from the vestry to the company the latter undertook to supply electrical energy free of charge for twenty-five arc lamps. The company suggested that in addition to the twenty-five free lamps the vestry should agree to the erection of 225 other lamps, at an annual cost of £22 10s. per lamp, or a total yearly expenditure of £506. This proposal was, however, not entertained, but the vestry clerk then suggested that in addition to the twenty-five free lamps the company should erect twenty-five others, to be charged at the rate of £20 per lamp per annum for a trial period of twelve months. The company, with the exception of the price, which was adhered to at £22 10s. per lamp, consented to this scheme, and the Lighting Committee accordingly recommended its adoption. The subject was discussed at some length, but eventually an amendment was carried, by forty-two votes to eleven, adhering to the vestry clerk's suggestion, and instructing the committee to report as to the cost of the lamp standards and the relative cost of lighting the parish by electricity charged by meter as compared with the price asked by the company, or any other company.— The following tenders were received for repairs to Arlington Lodge : Messrs. H. Boulter, £239 ; J. Parsons, £530 ; Edwards & Bedway, £543 ; J. F. Ford, £562 ; and T. Leeks, £580. Since sending in his tender Mr. Boulter had asked leave to amend it to £284, but the Sanitary Committee declined to accede to the request. Considering all the circumstances of the case, and as £300 had been settled as the price of the work, the committee recommended and the vestry decided not to entertain any of the tenders, but to have the contract carried out under the direction of the surveyor.—The undernoted tenders were also received for the supply of six new sand-bins, 3 ft. long, 2 ft. wide, 3 ft. high in front and 4 ft. 6 in. high at back, with sliding door and hinged lid. The prices are, for bins without bottom : Messrs. Gibb & Co., £4 14s.; Knox & Co., £6 10s.; Bosher & Co., £7 8s. 6d.; Pontifex & Co., £7 8s. 6d.; Hammond & Hussey, £8 ; and Pfeil & Co., £7 12s. 6d. The tender of Gibb & Co. was accepted.

**Strand.**—On the recommendation of the Wharf Committee it was decided, at a meeting of the board of works on Wednesday of last week, to affix the seal of the board to a contract with the Horsfall Furnace Syndicate, Limited, for the erection of one of their dust destructors at the board's wharf. The contract provides that each furnace shall consume not less than 12 tons of refuse per day, which shall be so reduced by fire that a residue of not more than 33 per cent. is left. The contract price is £10,241.—The Improvements and Parliamentary Committee presented a report with reference to the necessity of making Little Newport-street a uniform width of 40 ft., as a further improvement, consequent on the adoption of the scheme for the closing of Earl's Court. The report states that on the 12th October the committee announced that they were unable to present a conclusive report, as the negotiations, having for their object the reduction of the cost of the improvement, were incomplete. They now reported that they had still been unable to come to any definite agreement to effect the improvement. The only method left of effecting the widening of the street as suggested, therefore, appeared to the committee to be by serving the statutory notices under sec. 73 of the Metropolis Management Amendment Act, 1862. They accordingly recommended that, if the board were still of opinion that the improvement should be carried out, the matter should be referred back to them, so that the necessary statutory resolutions could be framed and submitted to the board. The consideration of the report was adjourned.—The same committee announced that they had received a letter from Mr. H. S. Samuel, M.P., enclosing the draft of a Bill which he proposes to introduce in the next session of Parliament dealing with the London water question. The Bill provides for the connection of the mains of the various water companies, and makes provision for inspection as to quality, quantity and pressure of water, with liability to penalties in case of default. The committee stated that they had adjourned the consideration of the Bill until such time as the whole of the Water Bills come up before them.

**St. George-the-Martyr, Southwark.**—On the recommendation of the Public Health and Sewers Committee, the vestry, at their meeting on Tuesday, resolved to construct five surface ventilators in connection with the sewer in Southwark Bridge-road, at a total cost of £35.

**St. Marylebone.**—At the last meeting of the vestry the official seal was affixed to the petition asking for permission to introduce a Bill to authorise the vestry to establish electric supply works for the parish.—A letter was read from the London County Council in reference to the representation made to the council on the subject of district surveyors. The letter pointed out that the Building Act Committee were not prepared to recommend the council to take any action in regard to the duties and payment of district surveyors, and that on some points it would perhaps be necessary to obtain Parliamentary powers to accomplish the objects aimed at in the representations. It was decided to enter the communication on the minutes.—An hour and a half were occupied in discussing a report by the Works Committee relating to proposals for the extension of wood paving next year in Harley-street, Old Cavendish-street, and Upper Berkeley-street, the estimated cost being £6,930 for yellow deal. The committee stated that they were equally divided as to the merits of hard and soft wood paving, and left it to the vestry to decide which kind of wood should be used for those streets. Mr. Dennis, chairman of the Works Committee, stated that they now had an inspector to examine the wood blocks delivered to the vestry, and that as a result the supply of inferior soft wood had and would in future be prevented. The use of soft wood would be much cheaper than hard, but if the latter was adopted it would mean that wood paving would be restricted to fewer streets, owing to the large expenditure. Mr. Garrould said that from a return submitted to the vestry it appeared that metropolitan surveyors stated that no complaints had been made of hard wood paving on the ground of being noisy and slippery. In reply to questions, Mr. Waddington, the surveyor, expressed the opinion that the cost of soft wood was approximately three-fourths of the total cost of paving, and that hard wood had not been laid down sufficiently long to determine its durability. The only way to test the two woods was to lay them down in the same thoroughfare, subject to the same traffic, and laid in the same manner. The vestry eventually agreed to adopt yellow deal in the thoroughfares in question. —On the recommendation of the Sanitary Committee it was resolved to instruct the surveyor to reconstruct a portion of the sewer in Little Welbeck-street, at a cost of £50.

# PROVINCIAL AND GREATER LONDON AUTHORITIES.

## MUNICIPAL CORPORATIONS.

**Brighton.**—Mr. H. Percy Boulnois, M.I.C.E., one of the Local Government Board inspectors, held an inquiry, on the 6th inst., with reference to an over-expenditure upon the public abattoir. The town clerk and Mr. F. J. C. May, the borough engineer, explained how the over-expenditure, amounting to £3,396, had been incurred, and the inspector afterwards viewed the locality.

**Coventry.**—The contract for the erection of certain buildings at the proposed two new sewage pumping stations, on the side of the main road from Coventry to Daventry, has been let to Messrs. Wingrove & Stanley, of Northampton, who have offered to carry out the work for £11,276.

**Darwen.**—A special meeting of the Darwen Town Council was held on Monday to consider the question of purchasing the undertaking of the tramways company running between Blackburn and Darwen, in conjunction with the Blackburn Corporation. The town clerk explained that the apportioned price for Darwen's share of the tramways was £26,400, in which was included £2,000 for the depot, which would be the property of Darwen. As the Darwen Corporation were only applying for powers to work the system, a lease would be granted to the Blackburn Corporation, who would work the line and pay Darwen £85 per quarter for the repairs of the rails, &c., and £916 10s. by way of rent. The mayor proposed a resolution authorising the purchase of the tramways, and this, after some discussion, was carried.

**Grimsby.**—The following questions have been placed in the hands of the Highways Committee for consideration : To widen and improve certain public thoroughfares, in order to remedy the serious inconvenience and loss to the public in passing from east to west of the town, owing to the level crossings. To purchase the gasworks and undertaking. To purchase the waterworks and undertaking. To acquire certain properties for the future improvements of the town. To acquire further powers for enforcing by-laws for promoting better sanitation. That a committee be appointed to consider the promotion of an Omnibus Bill in Parliament, or such other methods as they may be advised are necessary to further these objects, and complete their report to the council.

**Liverpool.**—The arbitration between the corporation and the docks board as to the amount which the former body are to pay for the portion of the site of George's Dock, taken for city improvements, will take place about the beginning of next month.

**Manchester.**—It was reported at a meeting of the corporation Rivers Committee, on Monday, that the chairman (Sir Besdin Leech) and the deputy chairman (Dr. Dreyfus) had had an interview in London with Mr. Adrian, of the Local Government Board, with reference to the sewage difficulty. The experts appointed by the corporation some months ago have presented an interim report, and in view of their recommendations the committee asked for an extension of the time laid down by the Local Government Board for fulfilling certain requirements. An inquiry was suggested, and it was stated that the evidence to be produced would probably justify the board in granting the borrowing powers required by the corporation to the extent of £160,000. Mr. Adrian gave the deputation to understand that an inquiry would be held early in January.—The Gas Committee report that during the past year there has been a large increase in the consumption of gas within the area of supply of the Manchester Corporation. This has been brought about by the increased demand for gas-cooking appliances, and to some extent also by the use of prepayment meters. During the last week of November the total consumption reached 129,467,000 cubic feet, as compared with 120,262,000 in the corresponding week last year.

**Morley.**—Recent minutes of the town council contained a report of Mr. W. E. Putman, the borough engineer, upon his inspection of a leakage in the Victoria service reservoir, and his suggestions as to the best method for making good the reservoir. He thought that the council would be unwise to abandon the site, and he suggested that the whole of the puddle should be taken out, and that other work should be done. He estimated the cost at £3,175. The committee recommended that they should be empowered to proceed with the repair of the reservoir, in accordance with Mr. Putman's report. A short discussion ensued upon the motion, which, however, was eventually approved.

**Newcastle-under-Lyme.**—The Executive Sanitary Committee of the corporation have decided to proceed at once with the scheme of replacing the present isolation hospital with a permanent structure for the treatment of infectious diseases on the same site. Messrs. J. Lewis, of Newcastle, and F. Emery, of Stoke-on-Trent, have been appointed joint architects and will prepare the plans.

**Plymouth.**—Alderman J. Pethick, the mayor, last week opened the first block of workmen's dwellings erected by the corporation in Vauxhall-street. The block comprises seven houses to be let at a weekly rental of 5s., seven at 4s. 6d., and seven at 4s. The total cost of erection has been £5,847, and the price of the land was £760 10s. They have been built from plans by Mr. J. Paton, the borough surveyor, the contractors being Messrs. Wakeham Brothers.

**Retford.**—At the last monthly meeting of the town council the corporate seal was affixed to a contract with Messrs. Jenkins & Co., Limited, of Retford, for erecting a new retort at the gasworks. This was the lowest tender received.

**Salford.**—Numerous inquiries having been made respecting the Agecroft cemetery competition, we are authorised to state that twenty-two sets of plans were sent in, but they have not been opened pending the receipt of sanction to use the land for cemetery purposes. This has been delayed owing to the opposition raised by the local authority in whose district the site is situated. The Home Office inspection of the land was made as long ago as July 15th.

**Taunton.**—Colonel A. G. Durnford, R.E., yesterday attended at the town hall to hold an inquiry, on behalf of the Local Government Board, with reference to an application of the corporation for power to borrow £18,520 for the conversion of the existing precipitation works into an installation on the septic tank system. The sum mentioned includes the cost of the land, pumping, and all contingent expenses.

**Wednesbury.**—The tender of Mr. John Mackay, Smethwick, at £537, has been accepted for the widening of the

bridge over the Birmingham canal on the Holyhead road near Moxley.

**Worthing.**—A Local Government Board inquiry was held on the 8th inst., by Mr. H. Percy Boulnois, M.I.C.E., into an application of the town council for permission to borrow £589 for laying tar paving on the Esplanade and for £850 for laying new mains. After hearing evidence from the town clerk and the borough surveyor, Mr. F. Roberts, the inspector visited the Esplanade and also the waterworks. The large service reservoir at these works has recently been covered, on the advice of Mr. Roberts, in order to prevent a weed growth which used to formerly take place at certain seasons of the year. The water is pumped from a deep well in the chalk, and since the reservoir has been covered there has been no recurrence of this growth.

# URBAN DISTRICT COUNCILS.

**Aston Manor.**—At the ordinary monthly meeting of the district council, on Tuesday of last week, it was reported that the surveyor had been instructed to engage additional temporary assistance for the purpose of pushing forward the preparation of the plans, &c., in regard to the erection of additional cells at the refuse destructor.—The Highways Committee recommended that the surveyor should be instructed to prepare plans and estimates for the laying of storm-water sewers in Aston and Lichfield roads, from the city boundary to Salford Bridge, and the roads abutting thereon, and also in Witton-road. The recommendation was agreed to.—It was decided to direct the surveyor to make such alterations and do such work as may be necessary for the widening of the road opposite the new premises of the National Provincial Bank of England at Six Ways.—The Baths Committee reported that, in order to provide additional first-class slipper bath accommodation at the baths, they had resolved to purchase the dwelling house and premises adjoining the baths, at a price of £425.—The tender of Messrs. Butcher & Son, of Aston-road, Aston Manor, was accepted for the supply of two mud carts, at a further cost of £15 10s. each.

**Dukinfield.**—At the last monthly meeting of the council a recommendation was received from the General Purposes Committee suggesting that an application should be made to the Local Government Board for sanction to borrow £11,361 for the erection of a new town hall and municipal buildings. It was decided to consider in committee a proposal to add a large hall, at a cost of £5,000.

**Herne Bay.**—A Local Government Board inquiry was held on Saturday in reference to an application of the district council for sanction to a loan of £40,000 required for the renewal of the sea wall and parade, which was so extensively damaged in the great gale in November of last year. The clerk to the council, in the course of his evidence, said the damage was at that time caused to the whole of the sea-front and the lower part of the town, some 200 houses being affected. The sea front was temporarily repaired, at a cost of £700. It was explained by Mr. Baldwin Latham that the new sea wall would be 1,924 yards long and 20 ft. to 25 ft. high, being so constructed that it would allow of the promenade being widened by 15 ft. Evidence in support of the scheme and in opposition having been heard, the inquiry was closed.

**Littlehampton.**—Mr. H. Percy Boulnois, M.I.C.E., an inspector of the Local Government Board, held an inquiry on the 9th inst. with reference to the application of the district council for sanction to borrow £1,000 for street works, consisting of various paving, channels, kerb, &c. The surveyor, Mr. Howard, gave evidence, after which the inspector closed the inquiry, and then proceeded to inspect all the streets proposed to be dealt with.

**Llanidloes.**—The Local Government Board have sanctioned a loan of £7,326 for carrying out the water supply scheme which has been prepared by Messrs. Fredk. Beesley & Son, of 11 Victoria-street, London, S.W.

**Oldbury.**—An inquiry has been held, on behalf of the Local Government Board, respecting the council's application for sanction to borrow £3,500 for the purpose of sewage disposal.

**Portslade-by-Sea.**—This small village, not far from Brighton, is going ahead. Quite recently a new sewerage scheme has received the sanction of the Local Government Board, and last week an inquiry was held as to an application of the district council for permission to borrow £4,500 for the purchase and the laying out of land for a recreation ground or public park. "Sanitation first and pleasure afterwards" appears to be the motto of this local authority, and it seems to be a very good motto too. The water supply comes from Brighton, and, of course, is excellent.

**Rawmarsh.**—A special meeting of the council was held recently, in order to adopt by-laws for the district, about which communications have been passing between this authority and the Local Government Board for some time. The question at issue has been in regard to the construction of dwelling-houses, the model by-laws of London authority insisting upon a better class of structure, with stronger division walls and more precautions against fire, &c., than was deemed necessary by the local authority. The negotiations have, however, been brought to a conclusion, and the wishes of the Local Government Board complied with. A resolution was passed adopting the by-laws, which will immediately come into operation.

**Waterloo-with-Seaforth.**—Messrs. Killick & Cochran, 51 and 53 Seel-street, Liverpool, have obtained the contract for the supply of sixteen electric arc lamp columns and carriers for the district council.

**Worksop.**—At a recent meeting of the district council a letter was read from Messrs. Hodding & Co., solicitors, Worksop, offering, on behalf of Mr. Thomas Turner, of Scofton House, Worksop, to sell to the council a portion of the land required for street improvements fronting Park-street and Westgate. The portion proposed to be sold was about 80 yards, and the price £500. It was resolved not to accept the offer.

## RURAL DISTRICT COUNCILS.

**Guildford.**—At the last meeting of the district council it was decided to take over from the contractors the works of sewerage and sewage disposal at Shere, which are now completed. The works have been carried out under the supervision of and from plans prepared by the council's surveyor, Mr. Jas. Dewhirst. It was also decided to extend the system of sewers to the village of Gomshall, according to the plans prepared by Mr. Dewhirst, and to apply to the Local Government Board for sanction to borrow £1,700 to carry out such extension.

**Hollingbourne.**—A Local Government Board inquiry was recently held by Colonel A. G. Durnford, R.E., in reference to an application of the district council for permission to borrow the sum of £3,755 for the provision of an efficient water supply for Headcorn and the adjoining hamlet of Grafton Green. The engineers of the scheme are Messrs. Stephenson & Barstal, of Westminster.

**Romford.**—The district council have obtained the sanction of the Local Government Board to adopt building by-laws for their district under the Public Health Act, 1875, and the Public Health Act Amendment Act, 1890. Formerly building by-laws were in force only in the parishes of Hornchurch and Dagenham. The council have further obtained urban powers for the purpose of making-up certain new streets under the Private Street Works Act, 1890.

**Tendring.**—The district council have accepted the tender of Mr. T. Canham, High-road, Weeley, amounting to £198, for the construction of about 450 yards of 9-in. pipe sewer at Romsey.

## DUNDEE TRAMWAYS.

### OVERHEAD SYSTEM ADOPTED.

At a recent meeting of the Dundee Town Council, attention was called to recommendations of the Tramways Committee suggesting that the overhead system of traction should be adopted. A member, in moving the adoption of the minute, said that no person denied the utility of the overhead system, and the danger of it was comparatively *nil*. Besides, the Glasgow Corporation were going in for further extensions of the system. So far as he knew, no corporation in Britain had resolved up to the present to adopt the conduit system. They could not afford to experiment with that system, because it was too costly. Even supposing the conduit system was a success, and the initial expense was not less than between £3,000 and £6,000 a mile more than the overhead system, was anyone prepared to recommend the adoption of that system ? Besides, after a few years, if the conduit system were proved a success, what would they lose by meantime adopting the overhead system and subsequently introducing the conduit in the centre of the city ? This would simply mean the removal of the posts and wires to some suburban portion of the lines, and the saving in the first year by the adoption of the overhead system would be sufficient to enable them to meet any loss they had made by having first erected the overhead system and then had to take it down. The minute was eventually adopted by a large majority.

## CORRESPONDENCE.

**The Late Mr. Henry Knowles.**—Messrs. John Knowles & Co., 38 King's-road, St. Pancras, N.W., write : In your obituary notice of the late Mr. Henry Knowles we observe you have made one slight mistake. You have credited his firm with being the first to supply the London market from the provinces, but when we inform you that the deceased gentleman was connected for some years with our works before he commenced business on his own account, and that before he thus commenced we had begun in London of many years' standing we hope you will allow this correction to be made.

**Surveyors' Institution Meetings.**—We regret that, owing to the amount of matter it has been necessary to deal with this week, we have been compelled to hold over the interesting paper, read at the Surveyors' Institution on Monday, by Mr. W. Weaver, on "The London Building Act and the Official Supervision of Buildings." It will be given in our next issue, together with some notes of the discussion.

## INSTITUTION OF CIVIL ENGINEERS.

### ORDINARY MEETING.

An ordinary meeting of the above Institution will be held on Tuesday, at 8 p.m., when the paper which was read by Mr. Fancies Fox, M.I.C.E., at the last meeting, on "The Ventilation of Tunnels and Buildings," will be further discussed. Time permitting, a paper will be read by Mr. John Hawksley Dales, A.M.I.C.E., on "High-speed Engines."

### SPECIAL GENERAL MEETING.

A special general meeting (of corporate members) will also be held on Tuesday, at 9.15 p.m., to consider, and if approved enact, a supplemental by-law.

### STUDENTS' MEETING.

A meeting for the students of the Institution will also be held to-night, when a paper, entitled "The Kentish Town Widening, Midland Railway," will be read by Mr. Walter Daniel. The chair will be taken at 8 p.m. by Mr. Horace Bell, member of the council.

# Some Recent Publications.

SANITARY ENGINEERING.

The phrase "sanitary engineering" is by no means synonymous with "municipal engineering." The latter expression may be said to include the former, but it is at the same time much wider in scope, inasmuch as it embraces many branches of work which are not, strictly speaking, regarded as coming under the description of sanitary engineering. The phrase "sanitary engineering" must also be clearly differentiated from the more vague and elastic term "sanitation." It is not too much to say that students of sanitary engineering have awaited with no small interest the appearance of the promised work, entitled SANITARY ENGINEERING, by Colonel E. C. S. Moore, R.E. (London: B. T. Batsford, 94 High Holborn. Price 30s. nett). The author was formerly instructor in estimating and construction at the School of Military Engineering, Chatham, and has already published a smaller book, entitled "Sanitary Engineering Notes." It may be said at once that his more recent work amply justifies the interest with which it has been anticipated. The sense in which Colonel Moore employs the expression "sanitary engineering," and what he intends his title to connote, can be seen in his sub-title, which runs thus: "A Practical Treatise on the Collection, Removal and Final Disposal of Sewage, and the Design and Construction of Works of Drainage and Sewerage." To this is added "a special chapter on the disposal of house refuse and sewage sludge, and numerous hydraulic tables, formulæ and memoranda, including an extensive series of tables of velocity and discharge of pipes specially computed by Ganguillet and Kutter's formula." It will therefore be seen that the title of the book is practically synonymous with sewerage and sewage disposal, with the addition of some closely related questions, such as dust destruction, for example.

We hope it will not be gathered from the preceding remarks that we are either finding fault with the meaning which Colonel Moore attaches to the title of his book or with its scope. A glance either at the contents or the appearance of the volume, is quite enough to convince the reader that the field is certainly wide enough for a single volume or a single writer when the subject is treated so comprehensively and so thoroughly as Colonel Moore has treated it. The volume is of the kind that is usually described as "portly," extends to over 600 pages, and is provided with no fewer than 534 illustrations and seventy large folding plates. Colonel Moore points out that no attempt had previously been made to deal comprehensively with the subject as a whole, that is to say, in the course of a single work, a fact which may be taken as additional evidence of the extent of ground to be covered. Of course many able works have been published from time to time dealing with special branches of the subject, but Colonel Moore's object has been, in his own words, "to bring together, in a concise and practical manner, such information as I believe is most needed for the guidance of those engaged in the important work of preparing and carrying out schemes for the efficient sanitation of our cities, towns and villages, whether as engineers, surveyors, medical officers of health, municipal authorities and sanitary inspectors." The result is a work of reference which is likely to find its way into every sanitary engineer's library. The subjects to which chapters are devoted comprise collection and removal, sewerage, the flow of liquid in pipes and open channels, hydraulic memoranda, the application of the formulæ of D'Arcy and Bazin and also of Ganguillet and Kutter, construction and materials, ventilation, traps, latrines and watercloset, urinals, lavatory fittings, &c., surface-water collection, subsoil drainage, sewage disposal, and the disposal of sludge and household refuse. The extensive improvements of recent years have led the author to devote special attention to two subjects—sanitary apparatus and appliances, and the methods of sewage purification and disposal. Colonel Moore, like the Local Government Board, has not ventured to discriminate between the various systems of sewage disposal, on the grounds that no one system has so far established a claim to universal acceptance, and that special cases will always demand special treatment. He adds, however, that the progress that has been made during the last few years in the system of biological treatment tends to show that in this direction the ultimate solution of this troublesome problem will be found.

In discussing the subject of sewerage, the "absolutely separate" system is recognised as undoubtedly the most perfect when carried out in its entirety, but the author's conclusion is that the "partially separate" system commends itself, if judiciously applied, and if the principles on which the absolutely separate system are based are carefully kept in view. The chief sewage lifting systems—those of Shone, Liernur, and Adams—are described, but, as in the case of sewage disposal system, and sanitary appliances, the author generally contents himself with a careful description of each system and appliance, leaving the reader to draw his own conclusions as to merits or defects. It is only natural that a considerable portion of the book should be occupied with the discussion of hydraulic formulæ and memoranda, and with tables giving the velocity and discharge of sewers, pipes and conduits (circular and egg-shaped); the tables, as we have mentioned, being based on the formula of Ganguillet

and Kutter. In connection with the size of sewers, we should have expected some reference to the formula of Knichling. The chapter on construction and materials is long and fairly exhaustive. Writing on sanitary appliances is at times a thankless task, in connection with which it is impossible to please everybody, as manufacturers and patentees are sure to have very different ideas from the writer of a sanitary text-book as to what ought and ought not to be mentioned, approved or censured. There is no doubt, however, that on the whole Colonel Moore has carried out his task thoroughly well. In the chapter on ventilation the sewer gas question is discussed, though we are not carried further than the general conclusion that it is undoubtedly a predisposing cause in the spread of disease, through the lowering of vitality. The chapter closes with a full account of the Reeves system, which has been attracting so much attention of late. The contents of the remaining chapters are equally interesting, but it is impossible to deal with them in detail. A remarkable amount of information has been crammed into the chapter on sewage disposal, with reference to the numerous systems that have been brought forward, and especially the rapid advance of bacterial methods. To the author's general conclusions we have already referred. The final chapter deals with the disposal of sludge and refuse. As the author is no doubt aware, some additional information has now been forthcoming in regard to the Shoreditch combined scheme, and the figures have been subjected to a good deal of adverse criticism. Owing to the wealth of materials contained in the book a review might easily run to great length, but we must bring our remarks to a close. We may say, in conclusion, that we know of no single volume on this subject which contains such a mass of well-arranged information. The personal note of the author is, of course, not conspicuous, as the work is intended to be rather in the nature of a text-book and work of reference. In this respect it is encyclopædic, and should take its place as a standard book on the wide and important subject with which it deals.

ESTATE MANAGEMENT.

THE YOUNG ESTATE MANAGERS' GUIDE, by Richard Henderson, contains an introduction by R. Patrick Wright, F.R.S.E. (W. Blackwood & Sons. Price 5s.). The contents of this practical little manual indicates the number and variety of the branches of work which fall to the lot of an estate manager. Whilst realising that a due knowledge of the majority of these is only to be acquired through "actual experience in field and forest, in the workshop or yard, on the road and at the homestead," we endorse the author's views that it must prove detrimental to the higher interests of agriculture to have no institution in this country where an initiatory training, sufficient to embrace all the subjects indicated in the useful volume before us, can be adequately imparted. The aim of the present work, we are told, is "to instruct the beginner in estate management in the principles which lie at the root of the various departments, so that he may thereafter come to understand for himself their due application in practice, the plan adopted being first to take each branch of building by itself, commencing with the work of the mason and bricklayer, and to bring upon the stage the other tradesmen as they follow each other in due course. After this the nature and the relation of the respective buildings with regard to one another are dealt with, and next follow chapters devoted to other branches of work connected with estate management." Prof. Wright informs us that "the number of new text-books and other works relating to agricultural science that have been issued from the British press in the past few years has been unusually great; yet, rapid as has been their increase, it cannot be said that there exists any superfluity. Till within quite a recent period," he adds, "the literature of agricultural science in Britain was amazingly inadequate, and numerous as have been the additions made to it within the past decade, they have not yet nearly sufficed to fill up the wide blank that existed." Mr. Henderson's book forms a desirable contribution to our stock of agricultural reading, and the practical method of treatment enhances the value of the work. That most interesting, but somewhat neglected, branch of estate management comprised under the term of forestry, receives adequate treatment; and although the estate agent cannot aspire to be a forester, or be supposed to master the arts of the builder or the crafts of the drainer and the fencer, still a practical knowledge of these and numerous other subjects is indispensable; and this book may be commended to those aspiring to estate management as a profession. We may conclude our notice by quoting the following remarks from Prof. Wright's introduction to the volume. "No work," he says, "that deals with details of which many are well known can be altogether original, but the special value of this book lies in the fact that it is a record of the results of prolonged experience, of observation, and of reflection by a man whose education, and whose familiarity, both with the science and the practice of agriculture, have given him exceptional qualifications, and who has had ample opportunities of submitting his conclusions to the test of actual trial. It is especially noticeable all through the work that the facts that come under Mr. Henderson's observation have been made the sub ject of careful consideration in their relation to all other facts bearing on the same subject. Whether his conclusions are in all cases sound or not, they have always been carefully formed, and are entitled to be received with respect and attention." The quality of the illustrations, type and paper render the general appearance of the volume attractive.

### SOME SHORT NOTICES.

GAS AND PETROLEUM ENGINES, by A. G. Elliott, B.SC. (Whittaker & Co. Price 2s. 6d.), is translated and adapted from a French work by M. Henry de Graffigny, and forms one of "Whittaker's Electro-Mechanical Series." Although internal combustion motors have for many years been steadily gaining favour, and at present hold an assured position in the industrial world, their great and increasing importance is perhaps as yet scarcely realised by the general public. Hence we can confidently recommend this carefully-compiled and well-illustrated little volume to the non-technical reader who may desire to keep abreast of the times in matters of universal concern and interest. One chapter is devoted exclusively to an elucidation of the theory of the gas engine, but, as mathematical reasoning is as far as practicable avoided, the lay reader need not hesitate to enter upon its perusal, as he will not, we feel assured, experience much difficulty in following the author's lucid expositions, and thus clearly understand the deductions drawn and conclusions arrived at. We entertain no doubt that Mr. Elliott will be afforded opportunities for realising his anticipations by embodying later results in a future edition.

LOWESTOFT IN OLDEN TIMES, by Francis D. Longe, barrister-at-law (Dostoolo & Todd, Lowestoft. Price 1s.), embodies a course of lectures delivered by the author at the St. Margaret's Institute, in that town, with such additions as were considered desirable so as to render the narrative of historical facts more complete and interesting. We are accustomed to associate with Lowestoft of the present day a good harbour, a line fishing fleet and pleasant marine terraces; but these nineteenth century features are linked with the past by the retention of its largely-developed modern extensions. Mr. Longe's compilation is founded on materials furnished by leading authorities of early and recent periods, and he imparts a vast amount of entertaining historical lore associated not only with the annals of Lowestoft, but also with those of Yarmouth, in a pleasant narrative style; and the publishers deserve much credit for the acceptable form in which they have issued a volume which must be considered a marvel of cheapness.

THE PROCEEDINGS OF THE ASSOCIATION OF ONTARIO LAND SURVEYORS embraces the annual reports of the council and several committees, with the minutes of the yearly meeting of that incorporated body, held at Toronto in 1898; and also includes a selection of papers of more than usual interest read by prominent members, accompanied by a record of the salient points of discussions that ensued.

*Any of the Books noted below will be sent post free if the published price be forwarded to the officer of* THE SURVEYOR.

A HAND-BOOK OF HYGIENE AND SANITARY SCIENCE, by George Wilson, M.A., M.D., LL.D.,EDIN., F.R.S.,EDIN., D.P.H.,CAMB. (eighth edition); 798 pp., 8½ in. by 5½ in. J. & A. Churchill. Price 12s. 6d.

THE PURIFICATION OF SEWAGE, by Sidney Barwise, M.D.,LOND., D.P.H.,CAMB.; 150 pp., 7½ in. by 5 in. Crosby Lockwood & Son. Price 5s.

THE XMAS NUMBER OF "THE PROCESS PHOTOGRAM"; 9½ in. by 6½ in. The Photogram, Limited. Price 6d.

## SUPERANNUATION.

### MEETING OF THE CONFERENCE.

Mr. C. William Tagg, presided at a meeting, held on Thursday, at 117 Holborn, E.C., when there was a good attendance. The sub-committee—consisting of Messrs. C. W. Tagg, Dr. Dudfield, G. Chaloner, W. P. Hunter, and the hon. secretary —appointed to confer with the Metropolitan Local Government (Officers') Association submitted the following report as the result of its deliberations with that body.

"That this conference, consisting of representatives of the Metropolitan Local Government (Officers') Association and the conference convened by the Municipal Officers' Association, agrees to recommend to the several associations as under:—viz., (1) That metropolitan officers to whom the provisions of the Superannuation Act of 1866 apply be omitted from the Local Authorities Officers' Superannuation Bill. (2) That the efforts of both associations be mutually directed to assisting each other in regard to the two Superannuation Bills to be brought before Parliament, it being understood that precedence shall be given to the Superannuation (Metropolis) Bill, inasmuch as the circumstances connected therewith are the same as those of the Poor Law Officers' Superannuation Act, of 1896."

The hon. secretary (Mr. Carnell) stated that he was unable to attend the meeting when these resolutions were agreed to, and protested against the omission of the officers to whom the provisions of the Superannuation Act of 1866 applies from the Local Authorities Officers' Superannuation Bill, and

pointed out that it (the Metropolis Bill) did not provide for counting service from one authority to another in the area to which it applied, and he knew of a number of cases where officers will lose years of service, and he could see no reason why this could not be provided for as in the case of the Poor Law Officers' Superannuation Act, 1896 (sec. 4) and a clause inserted to the following effect:—" all service by an officer or servant under any authority to whom this Act applies shall be credited and reckoned for the purpose of this Act, whether the service has been continuous or not, and whether his whole time has been devoted to the service or not," and also to add, "and any contribution he may have made under the provisions of this Act shall be transferred and paid over to the local authority in whose service he shall enter," and all service under any local authority or under any other body whose duties and powers shall have been transferred to any local authority to whom this schedule applies shall be aggregated and reckoned for the purposes of this schedule." The report was ultimately adopted without alteration.

The conference also had under consideration the Local Authorities Officers' Superannuation Bill, and inserted a clause to provide for nurses contracting out if they so desire, and with this exception and the omission of the metropolitan officers to whom the Act of 1866 applies, decided to introduce the measure as in the last session.

It was decided to send a copy of the Bill to all local authorities to whom the Bill applies, asking them to pass a resolution in its favour, and also to do its utmost to get the officers themselves to petition their own local authorities to assist in the passing of the measure.

The hon. secretary (Mr. Carnell) writes to say that delegates were present from the associations representing metropolitan officers, who agreed to the exclusion of the officers who come under the 1866 Act from the general Bill, and he points out that should such officers feel aggrieved later on, through losing service by reason of holding office in more than one local authority, he did his best to safeguard their interests.

The Bill, having now been finally settled, will be ready for publication very shortly, and it only remains for the officers to make a liberal response to the appeal for financial support in order than an active campaign may be promoted. Subscriptions to the "Special Superannuation Conference Fund " should be sent to the Hon. Secretary (Mr. C. J. F. Carnell), 117 Holborn, London, E.C.

### MEETING OF THE EXECUTIVE COUNCIL OF THE MUNICIPAL OFFICERS' ASSOCIATION.

At a meeting, on Tuesday, the executive council of the Municipal Officers' Association had under consideration the report of their delegates to the above-mentioned conference, who submitted the resolutions which were adopted by that body.

A long discussion took place on the report, and the following resolutions, moved by the hon. secretary (Mr. Carnell), were carried by a large majority : (1) That, having heard the report of the delegates appointed to represent this association at the superannuation conference, this executive council is of opinion that the clauses referring to metropolitan officers should be reinstated in the Local Authorities Officers' Superannuation Bill, and that the Metropolitan Local Government (Officers') Association should be asked to insert the following clause in the Superannuation (Metropolis) Bill: All service by an officer or servant under any local authority or authorities, or under any other body whose duties and powers shall have been transferred to any local authority to whom this schedule applies, shall be aggregated and reckoned for the purposes of this schedule, whether the service has been continuous or not, and whether his whole time has been devoted to the service or not, and any contribution he may have made under the provisions of this Act shall be transferred and paid over to the local authority in whose service he shall enter. (2) That a copy of the above resolution be sent to the superannuation conference, to the Metropolitan Rate Collectors' Association, to the Incorporated Society of Medical Officers of Health, and to the Sanitary Inspectors' Association, asking them to take similar and immediate action in the matter and instruct their delegates to act in accordance with the foregoing resolutions. (3) That the Metropolitan Local Government (Officers') Association be informed of the action taken.

**St. Marychurch, Devonshire.**—At a recent meeting of this authority it was reported that it had been decided to approve a scheme for the drainage of the borough, and to make an application to the Local Government Board for sanction to borrow £7,500 to carry out the necessary work. The scheme as proposed is to improve the present drainage in St. Marychurch and to provide a drainage system for Barton and other parts. Dr. Winter said the council adopted the report of Mr. Worth, of London, who had examined the drainage and reported upon it, the cost being £10,000. Consequent upon an interview with Mr. Worth, that amount had been reduced to £7,000. He said it was advisable that the scheme should be carried, as St. Marychurch depended upon its visitors, and it was necessary to have the place in a thoroughly sanitary condition. Eventually it was decided that the work be carried out.

## Personal.

Mr. Edward Charles Griffiths, of Gnosall, has been appointed surveyor to the Gnosall Rural District Council.

We understand that 126 applications have been received for the vacant borough surveyorship of Folkestone.

Harrogate Town Council have increased the salary of Mr. E. W. Dixon, their waterworks engineer, by £100, making it now £400 a year.

Mr. William Clough, of the borough surveyor's office, Haslingden, has been appointed surveyor to the Audenshaw Urban District Council.

The Town Council of Wokingham have adopted a resolution agreeing to a proposal to increase the salary of their borough surveyor, Mr. J. Manley.

Mr. Robert M. Evans, assistant in the borough surveyor's office, Stafford, has been appointed second assistant in the office of Mr. Joseph Lobley, borough surveyor, Hanley.

The Southborough Urban District Council have voted their surveyor, Mr. Hamer, £150 for extra work in connection with planning and superintending the erection of the Victoria Hall, which has just been opened, in the town.

A letter has been received by the South Darley Urban District Council from their inspector, Mr. E. F. Lowe, stating that, having been appointed surveyor to the North Darley authority, he wished to resign his present appointment. The resignation was accepted.

Mr. W. H. Preece, C.B., was the guest of the evening at a dinner of the Whitehall Club on Monday, when Sir Charles Scotter occupied the chair. Mr. Preece was thus entertained in recognition of his occupying this year the important position of president of the Institution of Civil Engineers.

Mr. F. Rodley, who has held the position of surveyor and inspector to the Whitworth (Lancs.) Urban District Council for the last sixteen years, recently tendered his resignation. The resignation was accepted at the last monthly meeting of the district council, and will take place in three months' time.

The Pontardawe Rural District Council, at their last meeting, decided to increase the salary of Mr. John Morris Thomas Williams, their assistant surveyor. Mr. Williams, we may mention, was appointed about eighteen months ago, and is the son of Mr. Dawkin Williams, engineer and surveyor to the Ogmore and Garw Urban District Council, with whom he served his articles.

Mr. Edwin O. Sachs, of 11 Waterloo-place, Pall Mall, S.W., on Tuesday completed the first section of the new electrical stage installation at Drury-lane Theatre in time for the impending pantomime. The present works principally refer to the stage floor and its movability in sections above and below the footlights. The total area now already movable by mechanical power exceeds 1,200 square feet, and arrangements have been made for every possible safeguard against accident.

Mr. Frederick J. Dixon, who has for the last three and a half years held the appointment of district highway surveyor to the Spilsby (Lincs.) Rural District Council, was on Thursday presented by a few friends with a handsome set of electrum drawing instruments in an oak case and a gun-metal parallel ruler, 2 ft. in length, in a mahogany case, on the occasion of his leaving Spilsby to take up his residence in Lincoln, he having recently been taken into partnership by Mr. James Thropp, county surveyor of Lincoln.

At a meeting of the Penzance Town Council recently a letter was received from Mr. J. H. Small, the borough surveyor, stating that he had accepted an appointment at Port Elizabeth and asking the council's acceptance of his resignation at the end of December. He expressed to the council his grateful thanks for the many acts of kindness and consideration shown him during his long connection with the borough. The mayor said during the twenty-four years Mr. Small had been with them he had been a trustworthy and respected officer of the council. They must all congratulate him on his abilities being recognised in a manner so entirely satisfactory to himself. Everyone who knew his true worth to the town would experience the liveliest regret that they were about to lose his services. Mr. J. Caldwell, chairman of the Highways Committee, in moving the acceptance of the resignation, said he was surprised at Mr. Small remaining with them for so many years, for a man of his ability who had carried out works so successfully was deserving of a better position than that at Penzance. The motion was eventually adopted, it being referred to the General Purposes Committee to appoint a successor.

At the last monthly meeting of the Darwen Town Council the Highways Committee recommended that the salary of Mr. R. W. Smith-Saville, the borough engineer and surveyor, should be increased from £300 to £400 per annum. Councillor Halliwell moved an amendment that the increase should be to £350, and not to £400. He said he had not a single word to say in complaint of Mr. Saville, but the question was whether the raising of Mr. Saville's salary from £300 to £400

was not going too fast. If the corporation were to go on at this rate they would soon be in a difficult position. With regard to the expenses of the borough surveyor's department, he found that in 1884 the surveyor was receiving £350 a year, and that a clerk was employed at £39 a year—those were the expenses of the whole department. Now, for the last half-year they had been £627, which meant that the expenses for the current year would be £1,250. A long discussion ensued, several members speaking in very high terms of Mr. Saville's services. Eventually the council divided, with the result that only three votes were recorded for the amendment. The recommendation of the committee was, therefore, adopted by a large majority.

The forty-fifth annual general meeting of the Society of Engineers was held on Monday, at the rooms of the society, 17 Victoria-street, Westminster, S.W. The chair was occupied by Mr. William Worby Beaumont, the president. The following gentlemen were duly elected by ballot as the council and officers for 1899 : As president, Mr. John Corry Fell; as vice-presidents, Messrs. Henry O'Connor, Charles Mason and Percy Griffith ; as ordinary members of council, Messrs. J. Patten Barber, Joseph Bernays, D. B. Butler, G. A. Pryce Cuxson, R. St. George Moore, Nicholas J. West, Joseph William Wilson and Maurice Wilson ; as hon. secretary and treasurer, Mr. George Burt ; as hon. auditors, Messrs. Alfred Lass, F.C.A., and Samuel Wood, F.C.A. It was announced that, owing to the increase in his private practice, Mr. Pryce Cuxson, F.S.I., had been compelled to resign his position as secretary to the society, and a very flattering tribute was paid to him for the services which he had rendered to the society. It was also announced that Mr. Perry F. Nursey had been appointed to fill the vacancy, and will take office on the 1st of January next. The following were elected honorary members of the society : Sir J. Wolfe Barry, K.C.B., LL.D., F.R.S., M.I.C.E.; Prof. A. B. W. Kennedy, LL.D., F.R.S., M.I.C.E., Mr. W. H. Preece, C.B., F.R.S., M.I.C.E., and Mr. Alexander Siemens, M.I.C.E. The proceedings were terminated by a vote of thanks to the president, council and officers for 1898, which was duly acknowledged by the president. On Tuesday evening the society held their annual dinner in the Victoria Hall of the Hotel Cecil. Mr. W. Worby Beaumont, the president, presided, and among the guests were Sir Benjamin Baker, Sir J. Durston, General Sir O. Tanner, Mr. W. H. Preece, Mr. W. H. M. Christie (Astronomer Royal), Mr. Alex. Siemens, Mr. J. W. Swan, the Hon. C. S. Rolls, Mr. John Aird, M.P., Mr. J. C. Fell, and the secretary, Mr. G. A. Pryce Cuxson. The last-named gentleman during the evening was presented, on his retirement from his office after ten years' zealous work, with an address on vellum and a tea and coffee service. Following the usual loyal toasts, "Prosperity to the Society of Engineers" was proposed by Mr. A. J. Walter and responded to by the president. Mr. Preece, president of the Institution of Civil Engineers, proposed "Engineering Enterprise," and Sir B. Baker responded.

At the London County Council meeting on Tuesday the Highways Committee brought up an urgency report with reference to the refusal of Mr. John Young to accept the position of chief officer of the tramways department. The committee stated that they had received a letter from Mr. Young declining, for reasons given, to accept the appointment conferred upon him by the resolution of the council. In view of all the circumstances, they were of opinion that it was advisable that for the present the appointment of the chief officer of tramways should remain vacant ; but having regard to the fact that the council would take over at the end of the year the undertaking of the London Tramways Company, it was important that provision should be made for the proper administration of that system after that date. They therefore recommended that Mr. A. Baker, the manager of the Nottingham Corporation tramways, who was second on the list of three submitted by the General Purposes Committee a fortnight ago, should be appointed the manager, at a salary of £1,000 a year. Mr. Benn, chairman of the committee, read Mr. Young's letter, which was to the effect that he had hoped that the appointment would be made so as to admit of the council having the advice of the chief officer of the new department from the beginning of the arrangements. During the past few days it had gradually, but irresistibly, been borne upon his mind that the position would be so different from what he anticipated, and what he had been so long accustomed to, that it would be a mistake for him to come to London. Commenting on this letter, Mr. Benn said that Mr. Young saw the clerk at the outset, and was fully acquainted with all the particulars before he sent in his application. Replying to questions, Mr. Benn further said that Mr. Young made no stipulation as to the appointment of a second officer. He did ask that he might be allowed to bring his chief assistant with him, but was informed that the matter would have to be considered by the committee in the first instance before it was submitted to the council. The committee, however, did not offer any opposition to the suggestion that this officer should also be appointed, at £850 a year. No inducement had been made to Mr. Young, so far as he knew, to apply for the position. The report of the committee was adopted.

## ELECTRIC LIGHT FOR ROCHDALE.

### LOCAL GOVERNMENT BOARD INQUIRY.

At Rochdale, Colonel A. J. Hepper, R.E., last week held an inquiry, on behalf of the Local Government Board, in reference to an application of the Rochdale Corporation for sanction to borrow £30,000 for electric light purposes. Among those present were Mr. S. S. Platt, the borough surveyor, Mr. T. B. Dall, the gas manager, and Mr. E. M. Lacey, of London, the consulting engineer.

From the evidence it appeared that it was proposed to erect electricity works to supply the whole area of the borough, as well as the motive-power for tramway traction in the event of that system of traction being adopted when the tramway came into the possession of the corporation, as they will do in 1901 and 1902. The site of the works, which comprises 2,838 square yards, is in close proximity to the gasworks, and is believed to be very well and centrally situated for the purpose of an electric light station. A plan was submitted showing the streets where the light is first to be introduced, and it was explained that the corporation do not think it necessary to have subsidiary feeding stations in different parts of the town. The one at the generating station was thought sufficient, at the start at any rate. The corporation would be bound by their provisional order to complete works enabling them to supply electric light within a certain limited area within two years from the date of the order. The estimate of £30,000 was made up as follows: £9,500 for buildings; £4,700 for engines and dynamos; £4,000 for boilers, economisers, condensers and pumps; £1,000 for switchboards; £1,000 for accumulators; £5,000 for cables and laying them; £1,000 for meters and service; £1,000 for superintendence and legal expenses; and £2,000 for contingencies. It was proposed to charge 5d. per unit for the light, and it was anticipated that a profit of £800 would be obtained when 1,200 8 candle-power lamps were connected.

There was no opposition to the application, and, on the conclusion of the inquiry, the inspector visited the site of the proposed station.

## APPOINTMENTS VACANT.

*Official and all similar advertisements received later than Wednesday evening are too late for classification and cannot therefore be included in these summaries until the following week. No advertisements received after 3 p.m. on Thursday can be inserted until the following week.*

GENERAL ROAD FOREMAN.—December 17th.—Corporation of Cambridge. £2 14s.—Mr. J. E. L. Whitehead, town clerk.

ASSISTANT BOROUGH SURVEYOR AND INSPECTOR OF NUISANCES.—December 17th.—Corporation of Wenlock. £80.—Mr. Godfrey C. Cooper, town clerk.

SEWAGE FARM OVERSEER.—December 19th.—Corporation of Cheltenham. £100.—Mr. E. T. Brydges, town clerk.

DISTRICT MAIN ROAD SURVEYORS (Four).—December 19th. —Hertfordshire County Council. £130.—Mr. Urban A. Smith, county surveyor, 41 Parliament-street, London, S.W.

SURVEYOR.—December 20th.—Atherton Urban District Council. £160.—Mr. Danl. Schofield, clerk to the council.

SURVEYOR.—December 20th.—Lytham Urban District Council.—Mr. Chas. A. Myers, clerk to the council.

HIGHWAY SURVEYOR.—December 21st.—Uxbridge Rural District Council. £200.—Mr. Charles Woodbridge, clerk to the council.

FOREMAN OF PUBLIC WORKS.—December 21st.—Corporation of Canterbury. £2 2s.—Mr. Henry Fielding, town clerk.

ELECTRIC LIGHT MAINS SUPERINTENDENT.—December 21st. —Corporation of Hull. £120.—Mr. A. S. Barnard, city electrical engineer.

ASSISTANT TO THE CITY ARCHITECT.—December 21st.— Corporation of Dublin. £150.—Mr. Henry Campbell, town clerk.

BUILDING INSPECTOR.—December 22nd.—Corporation of Stockport. £2 2s.—Mr. John Atkinson, borough surveyor.

CLERK OF WORKS.—December 22nd.—Corporation of Rotherham. £3.—Mr. H. H. Hickmott, town clerk.

ASSISTANT FOR WATERWORKS ENGINEER'S OFFICE.—December 22nd.—Corporation of Cardiff. £80.—Mr. C. H. Priestley, A.M.I.C.E., waterworks engineer to the corporation.

INSPECTOR OF WEIGHTS AND MEASURES.—December 24th. —Corporation of South Shields. £120.—Mr. J. Moore Huyton, town clerk.

BUILDING INSPECTOR.—December 27th.—Corporation of Sutton Coldfield. 30s.—Mr. W. A. H. Clarry, A M.I.C.E., borough surveyor.

TOWN ENGINEER AND SURVEYOR.—December 30th.—Town Council of Ayr, N.B. £300.—Mr. A. G. Young, town clerk.

MANAGER AND BAILIFF OF SEWAGE FARM.—January 1st.— Corporation of Banbury. £100.— Mr. Oliver J. Stockton, town clerk.

DISTRICT ROAD SURVEYOR.—January 5th.—Norfolk County Council. £2.—Mr. T. H. B. Heslop, county surveyor, Norwich.

TEMPORARY ASSISTANT.— Corporation of Birmingham. £2 5s.—Mr. John Price, city engineer and surveyor.

## MUNICIPAL COMPETITIONS OPEN.

*Official and all similar advertisements received later than Wednesday evening are too late for classification and cannot therefore be included in these summaries until the following week. No advertisements received after 3 p.m. on Thursday can be inserted until the following week.*

CURRTSKY.—December 23rd.—Sewerage and sewage disposal scheme for the Nos. 1 and 2 wards of the district. £50, £30 and £20.—Mr. T. E. Harland Chaldecott, clerk to the council.

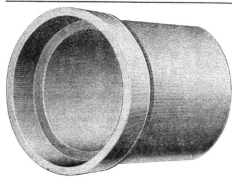

HULL.—January 1st.—Erection of a central public library in Albion-street. £50, £30 and £20.—Mr. E. Laverack, town clerk.

HARROGATE.—January 2nd.—Erection of a pump-room, &c., at a cost not exceeding £8,000. £50, £30 and £20.—Mr. Samuel Stead, borough surveyor.

BRADFORD.— February 1st.— Erection of a central fire brigade station. £100, £50 and £30.—Mr. George McGuire, town clerk.

## MUNICIPAL CONTRACTS OPEN.

*Official and; all similar advertisements received later than Wednesday evening are too late for classification and cannot therefore be included in these summaries until the following week. No advertisements received after 3 p.m. on Thursday can be inserted until the following week.*

PRESTON.—December 16th.—Alteration of the grammar school in Cross-road.—Mr. Henry Hamer, town clerk.

HULL.—December 16th.—Draining, macadamising, flagging, &c., of Reed-street, Little Reed-street, Tynemouth-street, and Talbot-street.—Mr. A. E. White, city engineer.

BECKENHAM.—December 17th.—Supply and erection of various electric light plant, for the urban district council.—Mr. F. Stevens, clerk to the council.

GALWAY.—December 17th.—Supply of ironwork for bridges and the construction of a new road near Moam, for the county council.—Mr. James Perry, M.I.C.E., county surveyor, Galway.

NORTH RIDING (Yorkshire).—December 17th.—Widening of Thornaby and Middlesbrough main road from Stainsby Beck to Oswald-street, for the county council.—Mr. Walker Stead, M.I.C.E., county surveyor, Northallerton.

LONGTON.—December 17th.—Supply, during the twelve months ending December, 1899, of broken granite, granite setts, kerbs, cast iron-work, Portland cement, blue paving bricks, earthenware pipes, &c.—Mr. J. W. Wardle, borough surveyor.

PADDINGTON.—December 19th.—Supply of gravel at per ton, for the vestry.—Mr. Frank Dethridge, clerk to the vestry.

MORLEY (Yorkshire).—December 19th.—Sewering and kerbing of Mitchell-street.—Mr. W. Putman, A.M.I.C.E., borough engineer and surveyor.

UXBRIDGE.—December 19th.—Supply of 265 tons of cast-iron pipes and special castings, for the rural district council.—Mr. John Anstie, engineer, 10 Marchwood-crescent, Ealing, W.

REDDITCH.—December 19th.—Supply and delivery of 2-in. broken stone, for the urban district council.—Mr. J. F. Thorrold, engineer and surveyor to the council.

WEST RIDING (Yorkshire).—December 19th.—Erection of two new police stations, with cells and officers' residences, at Worsborough Dale and Ardsley, near Barnsley, for the county council.—Mr. J. Vickers Edwards, county surveyor, Wakefield.

HORNSEY.—December 19th.—Sewering, kerbing, paving, metalling, channelling and making-good of Temple-road and Rathcoole-gardens (1st section), for the urban district council.—Mr. E. J. Lovegrove, engineer to the council.

TOTTENHAM.—December 20th.—Kerbing, paving and channelling part of the west side of High-road, and the paving and construction of crossings on part of the north side of Philip-lane, for the urban district council.—Mr. P. E. Murphy, engineer to the council.

BURY (Lancs.).—December 20th.—Forming, paving, kerbing, &c., of Back Ainsworth-road, Back Argyle-street and other streets.—Mr. John Haslam, town clerk.

LONDONDERRY.—December 20th.—Supply and delivery of all goods, tools, plant and materials required for the year from January 1, 1899.—The Town Clerk.

ABRAM (near Wigan).—December 21st.—Construction of permanent sewage outfall works, and the supply of oil engines and pumps, for the urban district council.—Mr. Wm. Aspinall, clerk to the council.

ROCHDALE.—December 21st.—Supply of retorts and other fireclay goods required during the year ending December 31, 1899, for the corporation.—Mr. T. Banbury Bail, gasworks manager.

GLASGOW.—December 21st.—Construction of public latrines at Camphill.—Mr. A. B. M'Donald, city engineer.

BIRMINGHAM.—December 21st.—Various forming, metalling, kerbing, channelling and flagging works in Harold-road and Noel-road.—Mr. John Price, city surveyor.

TWICKENHAM.—December 21st.—Supply of about 800 ft. of 6-in. by 12-in. Norway granite edge kerb, for the urban district council.—Mr. F. W. Pearce, surveyor to the council.

ULVERSTON.—December 21st.—Supply and laying of about 267 yards of 3¼-in. turned and bore iron water pipes and the construction of a storage tank, for the rural district council.—Mr. Chas. W. Dean, clerk to the council.

BLACKPOOL.—December 21st.—Various sewering, levelling, paving, metalling, channelling, &c., works.—Mr. J. Wolstenholme, borough surveyor.

PORTSLADE-BY-SEA.—December 22nd.—Construction of stoneware and other sewers for the drainage of the district, for the urban district council.—Mr. Charles O. Blaber, M.I.C.E., 64 Ship-street, Brighton.

ERTITHYON (Wales).—December 22nd.—Excavation, masonry and other works in connection with the proposed new bridge over the river Dee at Corwen, for the rural district council.—Mr. Thomas Hughes, clerk to the council, Corwen.

HENDON.—December 22nd.—Extension of the main sewer along the Edgware-road to Elstree, for the rural district council.—Mr. F. J. Seabrook, clerk to the council.

LEICESTER.—December 23rd.—Erection of working-class dwellings in Winifred-street.—Mr. James Bell, town clerk.

CARLISLE.—December 23rd.—Extension of the present water mains from Cumwhinton to Cocklakes, &c., for the rural district council.—Mr. George Armstrong, surveyor to the council.

SWINTON.—December 24th.—Repaving of Swinton Hall-road with 6-in. by 3¼-in. Welsh granite setts, for the urban district council.—Mr. Henry Entwistle, surveyor to the council.

DARTMOUTH.—December 24th.—Ventilating, painting and other works at the Guildhall.—Mr. T. O. Veale, borough surveyor.

BACUP (Lancs.).—December 26th.—Excavating and sewering of Baldwin-street, Hugh-street and Taylor-terrace.—Mr. Francis Wood, borough surveyor.

DUNDEE.—December 31st.—Supply of 500 2-in., 1,000 4-in., 500 6-in. and 500 8-in. turned and bored cast-iron pipes, for the water commissioners.—Mr. George Baxter, engineer and manager to the commissioners, 93 Commercial-street, Dundee.

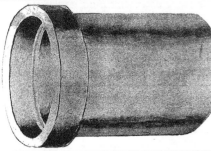

BOURNEMOUTH.—December 27th.—Making-up and extension of Bradlley-road.—Mr. F. W. Lacey, borough surveyor.

WEDNESBURY.—December 27th.—Erection of offices, for the urban district council.—Mr. J. T. Bownass, clerk to the council.

BROMLEY.—December 27th.—Widening of a portion of Homesdale-road, for the urban district council.—Mr. Fred. H. Norman, clerk to the council.

BROMLEY.—December 27th.—Diversion of the culvert in Homesdale-road, for the urban district council.—Mr. Fred. H. Norman, clerk to the council.

CARLISLE.—December 27th.—Extension of the water main from Wetheral Pasture to Shield Head, for the rural district council.—Mr. John Little, sanitary engineer, Viaduct-chambers, Carlisle.

PENZANCE.—December 28th.—Supply of cast and wrought iron work, granite, blue lias lime, &c., during the year ending December 31, 1899.—Mr. T. H. Cornish, town clerk.

EASINGTONE.—December 28th.—Widening of Victoria-street and the construction of a new street contiguous thereto, 36 ft. wide.—Mr. George Fitton, borough surveyor.

LEEDS.—December 29th.—Supply of (a) underground conductors, and (b) switchboards, &c., in connection with the extension of the electric tramway system, for the city council.—Messrs. Ronkinson & Talbot, 20 Victoria-street, London, S.W.

EMLEY (near Wakefield).—December 29th.—Laying of about 1,502 yards of 4-in. and 5,914 yards of 3-in. cast-iron water pipes, for the urban district council.—Mr. F. C. Heath, clerk to the council.

SUNDERLAND.—December 30th.—Supply of three 125-kilowatt direct-current high-speed steam dynamos, 400 volts.—Mr. J. F. C. Snell, A.M.I.C.E., borough electrical engineer.

HULL.—December 30th.—Supply of steel roof trusses, steel columns, &c., in connection with the erection of car sheds for the electric tramways.—Mr. A. E. White, city engineer.

HULL.—December 30th.—Erection of two car sheds and other buildings (area about 4,000 square yards) in connection with the electric tramways.—Mr. A. E. White, city engineer.

HULL.—December 30th.—Supply of pipes, fittings, &c., for the power station in connection with the electric tramways.—Mr. A. E. White, city engineer.

WILLENHALL (Staffs.).—December 30th.—Erection of a new span-roof greenhouse, 30 ft. by 12 ft., at the new cemetery at Bentley, for the urban district council.—Mr. Chas. J. Jenkin, engineer and surveyor to the council.

ROTHERHAM.—December 31st.—Supply and erection of sludge-pressing plant, boilers, sewage ejectors and sewage lifts, for the corporation.—Mr. R. R. W. Berrington, bank-buildings, Wolverhampton.

RAMSGATE.—December 31st.—Supply of a compound condensing beam engine at the Whitehall pumping station.—Mr. William A. Valon, gas and water engineer to the corporation.

ST. GEORGE, HANOVER SQUARE.—December 31st.—Supply of various materials for one year from March 25, 1899, for the vestry.—Mr. George Livingstone, surveyor to the vestry.

FOLKESTONE.—December 31st.—Supply of 1,000 to 2,000 yards super. of 24-in. York stone.—Mr. A. F. Kidson, town clerk.

DARTMOUTH.—December 31st.—Erection of stone boundary walls and public latrines on the reclaimed land, North-parade and Mayor's-avenue, for the urban district council.—Mr. T. O. Veale, surveyor to the council.

TAUNTON.—January 1st.—Construction of a sewer, about 1,300 yards long, from Railway-street to the site of the sewage outfall works in the Target Field.—Mr. James H. Smith, borough surveyor.

PADDINGTON.—January 2nd.—Supply of two dust-tipping vans, three slop-tipping vans and five pairs of wheels, for the vestry.—Mr. Frank Delbridge, clerk to the vestry.

STIRLING.—January 2nd.—Supply of various electric lighting plant, for the commissioners.—Prof. A. B. W. Kennedy, 17 Victoria-street, London, S.W.

LEAMINGTON.—January 2nd.—Erection of an entrance lodge to Victoria Park, for the corporation.—Mr. Fredk. G. Cundall, 41 Parade, Leamington.

RYDE (I.W.).—January 3rd.—Supply of two new pumping engines, overhead travelling crane and a Galloway boiler at the Knighton pumping station, near Newchurch.—Mr. C. G. Vincent, town clerk.

JOHANNESBURG, S.A.—January 6th.—Supply of a complete carburetted water-gas plant, for the corporation.—Messrs. Robert Whyte & Co., 22 Bury-street, St. Mary Axe, London, E.C.

WEST HAM.—January 7th.—Enlargement of the hospital in Southern-road, Plaistow, E.—Mr. Fred. E. Hilleary, town clerk.

TUNBRIDGE WELLS.—January 9th.—Construction of filter-beds at the waterworks at Pembury.—Mr. W. C. Cripps, town clerk.

WOLVERHAMPTON.—January 9th.—Levelling, paving, channelling, sewering, metalling, kerbing and completion of Raby-street extension (Melbourne-street to All Saints'-road) and Lever-street (Green-lane to Raby-street).—Mr. J. W. Bradley, borough engineer and surveyor.

SELBY.—January 10th.—Erection of public baths, for the urban district council.—Mr. Jno. Hy. Bansoft, clerk to the council.

SOUTHAMPTON.—January 10th.—Construction of concrete foundations, erection of brick, steel and concrete superstructures of new infirmary wards, sanitary blocks, boiler-house, tall chimney shaft, and sundry other work at the county lunatic asylum at Knowle, near Fareham, for the county council.—Mr. W. J. Taylor, county surveyor, The Castle, Winchester.

LONDON.—January 24th.—Construction of a tunnel for pedestrian traffic under the river Thames from Greenwich to Poplar, for the county council.—Mr. C. J. Stewart, clerk to the council, County Hall, Spring-gardens, S.W.

SHANGHAI.—March 15th.—Construction and working of about 23 miles of electric tramways on the trolley system, for the municipal council.—Messrs. J. Pook & Co., 8 Jeffery's-square, St. Mary Axe, London, E.C.

## MEETINGS.

*Secretaries and others will oblige by sending early notice of dates of forthcoming meetings.*

DECEMBER.

16.—Crystal Palace Company's School of Practical Engineering: Presentation of certificates, by Sir Charles Rivers Wilson, G.C.M.G., C.B. 12 noon.

16 and 17.—Sanitary Institute: Examinations in Practical Sanitary Science and for Inspectors of Nuisances at Manchester.

17.—Sanitary Inspectors' Association: General meeting. 6 p.m.

17.—Sanitary Inspectors' Association: Extraordinary meeting. 8 p.m.

19.—Royal Institute of British Architects: Messrs. Burstall and Drake on "The Application of Electric Power to Practical Purposes in Buildings, and the Production and Use of Electricity for Lighting Country Houses." 8 p.m.

JANUARY.

9.—Surveyors' Institution: Annual general meeting. 8 p.m.
17.—Liverpool Self-propelled Traffic Association: Mr. S. A. Sparkes on "Motor v. Horse Haulage; An Account of our Nine Months' Experiences." 8 p.m.
20.—Association of the Birmingham Students of the Institution of Civil Engineers: Mr. L. L. Baldwin, A.M.I.C.E., on "Coalville Water Supply; A few notes on the sinking of a trial bore-hole." 7.30 p.m.

## TENDERS FOR MUNICIPAL WORKS OR SUPPLIES.

*ACCEPTED.

CASTLE DONNINGTON.—For the execution of various sewerage works, for the rural district council.—Mr. Herbert Walker, A.M.I.C.E., Newcastle Chambers, Angel-row, Nottingham :—

| | £ s. d. |
|---|---|
| R. Lomax, Leigh, Lancashire | £9,377 |
| H. Weldon, Birmingham | 8,400 |
| W. Meredith, Gloucester | 6,905 |
| J. D. Nowell & Sons, Westminster | 6,780 |
| Walker & Slater, Derby | 6,750 |
| R. Holmes & Co., Chesterfield | 6,750 |
| Cope & Raynor, Lenton, Nottingham | 6,700 |
| C. E. Cox & Co., Ilkeston | 6,486 |
| H. H. Barry, Ratcliffe-on-Trent | 6,400 |
| A. B. Clarke, Nottingham | 6,350 |
| J. Hawley & Son, Ilkeston | 6,317 |
| J. F. Price, Nottingham | 6,300 |
| W. & J. Foster, Shipley | 6,035 |
| Main, Kendall & Main, Loughborough | 5,775 |
| J. H. Vickers, Limited, Nottingham* | 5,770 |
| M. Hall & Sons, Bradford | 5,621 |

CHERTSEY.—For the execution of various works in connection with the recreation ground in Guildford-road, for the urban district council.—Mr. J. Freeburn Stow, surveyor to the council :—

CONTRACT No. 1.

| | £ s. d. |
|---|---|
| W. Knight & Sons, Chertsey | £1,194 |
| Nesmyth & Co., Chertsey | 1,190 |
| R. Ballard, Limited, London | 1,187 |
| W. Greenfield, Weybridge | 910 |
| W. Norris, Farnham† | 820 |

CONTRACT No. 2.

| | £ s. d. |
|---|---|
| W. Greenfield, Weybridge | 446 |
| Nesmyth & Co., Chertsey | 375 |
| W. Knight & Sons, Chertsey | 356 |
| W. Norris, Farnham† | 203 |
| R. Ballard, Limited, London | 197 |

† Informal.

BRENTFORD.—For the making-up of Stile Hall-gardens, for the urban district council.—Mr. Nowell Parr, surveyor to the council :—

| | £ s. d. |
|---|---|
| B. Nowell & Co., Kensington, W. | £239 |
| J. Mowjem & Co., Westminster, S.W. | 199 |
| W. Parker, Brentford | 189 |
| W. Swaker, Chiswick | 188 |
| J. Ball, Chiswick* | 176 |

CHESTER-LE-STREET.—For the levelling, paving, draining, &c., of the road past Clarence-terrace, for the rural district council.—Mr. G. W. Ayton, surveyor to the council :—

| | £ s. d. |
|---|---|
| J. Carrick, Durham | £187 |
| C. Groves, Chester-le-Street* | 126 |

NORWICH.—For the widening of Fye Bridge (iron).—Mr. A. E. Collins, city engineer :—

| | £ s. d. |
|---|---|
| Cooke & Co., Westminster, S.W. | £1,235 |
| Downing, Norwich | 1,180 |
| T. H. Blyth, Foulsham, Norfolk* | 982 |

Engineer's estimate, £1,000.

NORWICH.—For the carrying out of private street works in Mousehold-street, Cavalry-street, Anchor-street, Wodehouse-street and Stracey-road.—Mr. A. E. Collins, city engineer :—

| | £ s. d. |
|---|---|
| Glenny, Colchester | £2,366 |
| Read, Norwich | 1,806 |
| Clarke, Norwich | 1,795 |
| G. Rackham, Norwich | 1,669 |
| H. Woodham, Blackheath Hill, London* | 1,471 |

PLUMSTEAD.—For the paving and making-up part of Tormount-road and part of Old Mill-road, for the vestry.—Mr. W. C. Gow, surveyor to the vestry :—

| FOR ALL WORKS. | Old Mill-road. | Tormount-road. |
|---|---|---|
| | £ s. d. | £ s. d. |
| Mowlem & Co., Westminster | 202 7 11 | 405 15 7 |
| Fry Brothers, Greenwich* | 198 19 0 | 482 17 6 |
| Bentham & Co., Plumstead | 183 10 0 | 467 8 5 |

TAR-PAVING WORKS ONLY.

| | £ s. d. | £ s. d. |
|---|---|---|
| D. Marchn, Bromley | 21 14 0 | 84 0 0 |
| Hobman & Co., Bermondsey | 21 0 0 | 80 10 0 |
| Chittenden & Lake, Malling | 19 6 6 | 74 16 3 |

SLEAFORD (Lincs.).—For the laying of about 3,100 yards of 3-in. cast-iron pipes for the water supply of the village of Great Hale, for rural district council.—Mr. Edmund Clements, clerk to the council :—

| | £ s. d. |
|---|---|
| Merridew & Worth, Stevenage | £1,417 |
| A. Jenkins, Southwell | 795 |
| W. Stone, Bolingbrooke | 739 |
| Jenkins & Co., Leamington | 722 |
| H. Shardlow, Hyson Green | 700 |
| L. Waterman, Honiton | 692 |
| J. Lee, Manchester | 673 |
| C. Stevenson, London | 668 |
| B. Roberts, Gainsborough | 642 |
| J. T. Barnes, Sleaford | 638 |
| S. C. Skinner, Berkington* | 635 |

## NOTICES.

THE SURVEYOR AND MUNICIPAL AND COUNTY ENGINEER *may be ordered direct, through any of* Messrs. Smith & Son's *book-stalls, or of any newsagent in the United Kingdom. Applications to the Offices for single copies by post must in all cases be accompanied by stamps.*

*The Prepaid Subscription (including postage) is as follows :*

|  | Twelve Months. | Six Months. | Three Months. |
|---|---|---|---|
| United Kingdom ... ... | 15s. | 7s. 6d. | 3s. 9d. |
| Continent, the Colonies, India, United States, &c. ... ... | 19s. | 9s. 6d. | 4s. 9d. |

*The International News Company, 83 and 85 Duane-street, New York City; The Toronto News Company, Toronto; and The Montreal News Company, Montreal, have been appointed agents in the United States and Canada for the sale of* THE SURVEYOR AND MUNICIPAL AND COUNTY ENGINEER. *A thin paper edition is printed for circulation abroad.*

EDITORIAL OFFICES :—
24 BRIDE-LANE, FLEET-STREET, LONDON, E.C.

ADVERTISEMENT AND PUBLISHING OFFICES :—
13 NEW STREET-HILL, FLEET-STREET, LONDON, E.C.

## APPOINTMENTS OPEN.

### COUNTY BOROUGH OF STOCKPORT.
APPOINTMENT OF BUILDING INSPECTOR.

The General Purposes Committee invite applications for the appointment of Building Inspector in the Borough Surveyor's department.

Candidates must be thoroughly qualified persons, to be accurate surveyors and levellers, and will be required to undertake the inspection of new buildings and drains, set out and fix levels for new streets, and make surveys of all new houses, buildings and drains, and to keep the necessary records in connection therewith, and to be well up in building construction and the Model Building By-Laws.

Salary, £2 2s. per week. Age to be between thirty and forty years. A list of duties may be obtained on application.

Applications, in candidate's own handwriting, stating age, and accompanied by not more than three copies of recent testimonials, and endorsed " Building Inspector," to be sent to Mr. John Atkinson, Borough Surveyor, on or before Thursday, December 22, 1898.

Canvassing will be considered a disqualification.

WALTER HYDE,
Town Clerk.

### ATHERTON URBAN DISTRICT COUNCIL.

The above-named Council invite applications from duly-qualified persons for the office of Surveyor to the Council.

Salary, £160 a year, increasing to £180 by two advances of £10 each on the completion of the first and second years' service.

Candidates may obtain forms of application and a statement of the terms of the appointment from the undersigned, to whom the applications (with copies of not more than three testimonials of recent date) are to be delivered not later than Tuesday, the 20th December inst.

Personal canvassing of members of the Council will be deemed a disqualification.

DANL. SCHOFIELD,
Clerk.

Atherton, near Manchester.
December 9, 1898.

### CORPORATION OF CANTERBURY.
FOREMAN OF WORKS.

Wanted, a qualified Foreman of Public Works, to work under the immediate direction of the City Surveyor. Must be experienced in the special department of municipal work consisting of road and paving formation and maintenance, also sewer and drain construction, and the management of Corporation workmen. Commencing wage at the rate of 42s. per week.

Applications, with copies of three testimonials of recent date, to be sent to me, the undersigned, not later than Wednesday, the 21st inst., at 10 a.m.

Canvassing members of the Council will disqualify.

HENRY FIELDING,
Town Clerk.

Town Clerk's Office,
15 Burgate-street, Canterbury.
December 7, 1898.

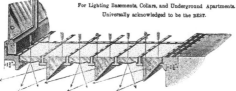
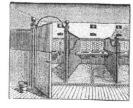

LAGOS, WEST COAST OF AFRICA.
INSTRUCTOR FOR TECHNICAL SCHOOL
required by the Government of Lagos, West Coast of Africa, for Technical School of the Public Works Department of the Colony. Engagement, one to three years. Salary, £300 per annum. Free quarters, or an allowance. Travelling expenses if sent on duty from station.

Free passage out, and home again on expiration of engagement. Leave of absence, if engagement extends beyond one year, six months on full salary, with free passage each way, after every twelve months' continuous residential service if exigencies of service permit.

Candidates must have had systematic training in building construction and surveying, with practical experience.

Candidates must be from twenty-six to forty years old. Character for steadiness and sobriety must bear the strictest investigation. Strict medical examination will be required. Single men preferred, and applicants must state whether they are single or married.

Applications, stating age and experience, and accompanied by copies (not originals) of testimonials as to personal character and qualifications, with the names and addresses of references of whom inquiry can be made, will be received by the Crown Agents for the Colonies, Downing-street, London, S.W., up to 29th December.

The Crown Agents possess no further particulars respecting the above appointment, and cannot therefore undertake to answer inquiries.

BOROUGH OF SUTTON COLDFIELD.
BUILDING INSPECTOR.
A Building Inspector is required, to inspect new buildings and drains and to assist in the office generally.

Salary, 30s. per week; engagement subject to a month's notice.

Written applications only, stating age and experience, and enclosing copies of not more than three recent testimonials, to be sent to the undersigned, endorsed "Assistant," before noon on December 27, 1898.

W. A. H. CLARRY, A.M.I.C.E.,
Borough Surveyor.

Town Hall, Sutton Coldfield.
December, 1898.

UXBRIDGE RURAL DISTRICT COUNCIL.
The above Council are prepared to receive applications for the appointment of a Highway Surveyor for the Uxbridge Rural District.

The district comprises nine parishes and about 90 miles of parish highways.

The Surveyor will be required to devote the whole of his time to the duties, and to reside within the district or in Uxbridge, as may be approved by the Council.

Salary, £200 per annum, to include all travelling expenses, but an office will be provided by the Council.

Applications, in the candidate's own handwriting, stating age, previous experience in road maintenance, and keeping the accounts, &c., relating thereto, accompanied by three recent testimonials as to character and practical knowledge of road work, to be sent to me on or before Wednesday, the 21st December instant.

The person appointed must be prepared to enter into a bond in the sum of £200.

Notice will be sent to any candidate who may be required to attend before the Council.

Canvassing, directly or indirectly, is prohibited.

Any further particulars may be obtained on application to me.

CHARLES WOODBRIDGE,
Clerk.

Council Offices, 38 High-street, Uxbridge.
December 5, 1898.

CITY OF BIRMINGHAM.
Required, immediately, in the Sewers Department of the Corporation of Birmingham, a Temporary Assistant, at a weekly salary of £2 5s. Age not to exceed twenty-six. Preference given to candidates holding certificates of the Association of Municipal and County Engineers.

Applications, stating age and full particulars of experience, with copies of recent testimonials, to be sent to the undersigned.

JOHN PRICE,
City Engineer and Surveyor.

Council House, Birmingham.
December 12, 1898.

CARDIFF CORPORATION WATERWORKS.
The Cardiff Corporation are prepared to receive applications for the appointment of an Assistant in the Waterworks Engineer's office. Salary to commence at £80 per annum, rising by annual increments of £10 to £110 per annum.

Preference will be given to candidates having a good knowledge of drawing, levelling and surveying; they should also be well acquainted with estimates and cost accounts usual in waterworks administration.

Further particulars as to duties may be obtained on application to Mr. C. H. Priestley, A.M.I.C.E., Waterworks Engineer, Town Hall, Cardiff.

Applications, in candidate's own handwriting, stating age, past and present employment, and accompanied by copies of not more than three recent testimonials, to be sent to me, endorsed "Assistant, Waterworks Engineer's Office," on or before Thursday, the 22nd inst.

Canvassing, directly or indirectly, will be a disqualification.
(By order)
J. L. WHEATLEY,
Town Clerk.
Town Hall, Cardiff.
December 12, 1898.

## TENDERS WANTED.

COUNTY OF SOUTHAMPTON.

*COUNTY LUNATIC ASYLUM, KNOWLE, NEAR FAREHAM.—CONTRACT No. 1.*

TO BUILDING CONTRACTORS.

Persons desirous of tendering for the Construction of Concrete Foundations, the Erection of Brick, Steel and Concrete Superstructures of New Infirmary Wards, Sanitary Blocks, Boiler-House, Tall Chimney Shaft, and sundry other works connected therewith, at the County Lunatic Asylum, Knowle, Fareham, may see the plans and specification, and obtain bills of quantities and all other information, on application at the office of Mr. V. J. Taylor, County Surveyor, The Castle, Winchester, on and after Monday, December 12th next, between the hours of 9 a.m. and 5 p.m.; Saturdays between 9 a.m. and 1 p.m. A deposit of one £10 Bank of England note will be required for each bill of quantities, and will be refunded on receipt of a bona-fide tender.

The foundations are to be commenced in February, 1899, and the superstructures in March, as the weather may permit.

Tenders, strictly in accordance with forms supplied by the County Surveyor, to be delivered to me on or before Monday, January 16, 1899.

The Committee of Visitors do not bind themselves to accept the lowest or any tender.
JOHN R. WYATT,
Clerk to the Committee of Visitors.
Knowle.
November 30, 1898.

BOROUGH OF SOUTHEND-ON-SEA.
TO GRANITE MERCHANTS AND OTHERS.
The Corporation invite tenders for the supply and delivery at the Railway Goods Station, or alongside, at Southend, of about 350 tons of Broken Granite.

Particulars and forms of tender may be obtained on and after Monday, the 12th instant, upon application to Mr. Alfred Fidler, ASSOC.M.INST.C.E., Borough Surveyor, Clarence-road, Southend.

Sealed tenders, marked "Granite," to be delivered at my office on or before Wednesday, the 21st December.

The Corporation will not be bound to accept the lowest or any tender.
(By order)
WILLIAM H. SNOW,
Town Clerk.
Southend-on-Sea.
December 7, 1898.

TWICKENHAM URBAN DISTRICT
COUNCIL.
TO GRANITE MERCHANTS.
The Council invite tenders for about 800 ft. of 6-in. by 12-in. Norway Granite Edge Kerb, to be delivered alongside Church Drawdock, within the parish of Twickenham.

Forms, on which tenders only will be received, and full particulars may be obtained from Mr. F. V. Pearce, Surveyor to the Council, Town Hall, Twickenham.

Tenders, endorsed "Granite Kerb," must be sent to me on or before Wednesday, the 21st inst. The person whose tender is accepted will be required to enter into a contract.

The Council do not bind themselves to accept the lowest or any tender.
(By order)
H. JASON SAUNDERS,
Clerk to the Council.
Town Hall, Twickenham.
December 10, 1898.

# URBAN DISTRICT COUNCIL OF BROMLEY.
### DIVERSION OF CULVERT, &c.

The Urban District Council of Bromley is prepared to receive tenders for certain works of Diversion of the Culvert in Homesdale-road, and other works connected therewith, within their district, in accordance with plans, sections, &c., which may be seen at the office of the Council's Surveyor.

The bill of quantities, specifications and form of tender may be obtained on payment of 1 guinea, which will be returned on receipt of a *bona-fide* tender.

Tenders, endorsed "Tender for Diversion of Culvert, Homesdale-road," must be delivered to me not later than 3 o'clock p.m. on Tuesday, the 27th day of December, 1898.

The Council do not bind themselves to accept the lowest or any tender.

(By order)
FRED. H. NORMAN,
Clerk to the Council.

District Council Offices, Bromley, Kent.
December 12, 1898.

# COUNTY BOROUGH OF WOLVER-
### HAMPTON.
### NEW STREET WORKS.

The Streets Committee invite tenders for the Forming, Levelling, Sewering, Draining, Metalling, Paving, Kerbing, Channelling and Completing Raby-street extension (Melbourne-street to All Saints'-road) and Lever-street (Green-lane to Raby-street).

Plans and sections can be seen, and specifications with bill of quantities and form of tender obtained, on application at the Borough Engineer's office, Town Hall.

Sealed tenders, addressed to the Chairman of the Streets Committee, and endorsed "Tender for New Street Works," to be delivered at the Town Clerk's office not later than January 9, 1899.

The contractor will be required to enter into an undertaking to pay not less than the minimum standard rate of wages of the district, and to observe certain hours of labour in accordance with the resolution of the Town Council.

The Committee do not bind themselves to accept the lowest or any tender.

J. W. BRADLEY, c.e.,
Borough Engineer and Surveyor.

Town Hall, Wolverhampton.
December 8, 1898.

# CITY OF BIRMINGHAM.

### HAROLD-ROAD EXTENSION.

### TO ROAD CONTRACTORS AND OTHERS.

The Public Works Committee of the Council of the said city are prepared to receive tenders for Forming and Metalling the Carriageway, and Kerbing, Channelling and Concrete Flagging, the Footpaths in Harold-road and Noel-road.

The drawings and specification may be seen, and forms of tender obtained, at the undermentioned office, where tenders, sealed and endorsed "Harold-road Extension," are to be delivered not later than the 21st instant.

The tender of any person or firm paying less than the minimum standard rate of wages current in the district will not be accepted.

The lowest or any tender not necessarily accepted.

The contractor whose tender may be accepted will be required to provide satisfactory security for the due performance of the contract.

JOHN PRICE,
City Surveyor.

City Surveyor's Office,
The Council House, Birmingham.
December 10, 1898.

# URBAN DISTRICT COUNCIL OF BROMLEY.
### WIDENING HOMESDALE-ROAD.

The Urban District Council of Bromley is prepared to receive tenders for certain works of Widening a Portion of Homesdale-road within their district, in accordance with plans, sections, &c., which may be seen at the office of the Council's Surveyor.

The bill of quantities, specification and form of tender may be obtained on payment of 1 guinea, which will be returned on receipt of a *bona-fide* tender.

Tenders, endorsed "Tender for Works of Widening Portion of Homesdale-road," must be delivered to me not later than 3 o'clock p.m. on Tuesday, the 27th day of December, 1898.

The Council do not bind themselves to accept the lowest or any tender.

(By order)
FRED. H. NORMAN,
Clerk to the Council.

District Council Offices, Bromley, Kent.
December 12, 1898.

# The Surveyor

### And Municipal and County Engineer.

Vol. XIV., No. 362.    LONDON, DECEMBER 23, 1898.    Weekly, Price 3d.

## Minutes of Proceedings.

**Building By-Laws and their Administration.** It may readily be admitted that the existing state of affairs in connection with building by-laws is in some respects not so satisfactory as it might be, and that those who suffer inconvenience thereby are justified in their endeavours to trace out the causes and indicate possible remedies. It will, however, be a matter for regret if this cannot be done without attempts being made to place the responsibility on the wrong shoulders, and without the publication of statements which have no apparent justification and which may cause undeserved annoyance and injury to a class of officials who are, as a rule, able and conscientious in the discharge of their duties. When such statements come from a source which may lead them to be accepted without question by the public it would certainly be a mistake to allow them to pass unchallenged. At a recent joint meeting in Birmingham of the Royal Institute of British Architects and the Birmingham Architectural Association the subject of discussion was "Building By-Laws and their Administration." It was explained that the subject had been selected by the local association because the Birmingham City Council are about to frame new building by-laws and had promised to submit the draft to the association, and that the members hope to have the assistance of the Royal Institute of British Architects in considering these by-laws and in obtaining greater uniformity in the by-laws of Birmingham and the surrounding districts. These objects are laudable enough, and it may well be that the absence of uniformity between the building by-laws of Birmingham and those of the surrounding districts causes a good deal of difficulty and annoyance. If within the range of possibility, it is certainly desirable in the interests of all concerned—builders, property owners, architects, and the community generally—that the by-laws of a large city should be uniform with those of the districts bordering on it, for it is not wise to perpetuate a system which may check industrial development and cause loss to the public. At the same time it should be remembered that a distance of a very few miles may mean an entire change of conditions, and that the by-laws of a district may require to be formulated in accordance with special needs. Such general considerations, however, affect only the system in operation. Like so much else in this world, that system is no doubt far from perfect, and criticism is in every way desirable; but to criticise a system is one thing, to attack the officials who administer that system, and to level at them a number of sweeping and general charges without any attempt to substantiate them by specific evidence, is quite another thing, and in every way reprehensible. This, in effect, is what has been done by an architect so well known as Mr. W. Henman, who opened the discussion to which we referred above. That gentleman has been president of the local association, and our readers will remember that he

acted as chairman of the Engineering and Architecture section at the recent Birmingham Congress of the Sanitary Institute. His professional eminence may therefore secure for his random, and by no means kindly, utterances a prominence they would not otherwise obtain, and it is therefore desirable that the unfairness of some of his statements should be pointed out.

Mr. Henman began by drawing a very dark picture indeed of the existing condition of things, and of what the future would hold if something is not quickly done. We note that he expressly excluded the metropolis from consideration, on the ground that the new Building Act "was administered by an experienced body of men, who, he believed, were generally architects or had had architectural training, while there was power of appeal to the London County Council." Mr. Henman apparently has not studied this subject closely enough to be aware that the "district surveyors," to whom he refers, carry out their duties under one Act, but that the sanitary equipment of new buildings in the metropolis is regulated by quite another Act—the Public Health (London) Act, 1890, and by another set of officials—the surveyors to the vestries and district boards. Mr. Henman, moreover, is apparently not aware that loss and inconvenience arise from this dual and often overlapping jurisdiction, and that many people, including not a few influential architects, would prefer to see the duties amalgamated in one official, provided he has the necessary qualifications; in other words, would prefer the system in operation in the large provincial towns and cities. It is with this system that Mr. Henman deals. In one sentence he admits that some latitude is required to meet local requirements, and then complains of the confusion that results from petty variations and of the annoyance and inconvenience caused to architects by having disapproved in one district plans which would be passed in another without question. There is, no doubt, a good deal of truth in this, but we fear that a certain amount of inconvenience is inevitable, and that architects can scarcely expect by-laws to be drafted and interpreted with an eye to their exclusive convenience. We are also convinced that the critic is anything but fair when he says that the trouble arises largely from the different interpretations surveyors put upon the same by-law or regulation. There is, no doubt, plenty of scope for variety of interpretation, but it is seldom that this scope is taken advantage of to an unreasonable extent. Then it is probably the fault of the by-laws rather than of the official who administers them, and who is probably only doing his duty. Mr. Henman asserts the desire of architects to comply with by-laws or regulations that are uniformly and reasonably enforced. He might therefore give some credence to what we know to be the general desire of borough and district surveyors—namely, to avoid causing unnecessary trouble or annoyance to others consistently with the conscientious discharge of their duties. He has, perhaps, some force on his side when he says that the so-called "model" by-laws of the Local Government Board are confused in their arrangement, go too much into detail on matters of minor importance or matters on which knowledge is as yet imperfect, omit reference to matters of structural importance, the neglect of which in some buildings might be a definite source of danger, and are wrapped up in unnecessary legal jargon and excessive verbiage. Hence the confusion and trouble, as by-laws sanctioned by the Local Government Board must be based on the "model" series. Obviously Mr. Henman's main grievance should be against the Local Government Board. As for regulations not so sanctioned, an architect should be aware that they cannot be legally enforced. The borough and district surveyor, however, is evidently Mr. Henman's *bête noir*, and in the course of his remarks he committed himself to statements which cannot be too severely reprobated, and should not have been made unless in connection with specific cases which the speaker was prepared to prove. But in the first place we must dispute the absurdly incorrect remark that, apart from the larger cities, surveyors to local authorities are usually selected from a class of men trained to road surveying and sewer laying and with little knowledge of building construction or architectural propriety, and the equally preposterous idea that they regard architects as their natural enemies, who should be hampered in every possible way. Even in smaller towns and districts the surveyor is probably a comparatively young man who has been trained in the office of a municipal engineer of a town of considerable importance; and given average intelligence, such an apprenticeship is impossible without obtaining a very considerable architectural knowledge and experience. In the more populous districts, according to Mr. Henman, the surveyors are assisted by building inspectors, who are endowed with still less knowledge and discretion. Now come the gravest of his various charges. In connection with them it is to be regretted that he has jumbled up surveyors and inspectors, but we take it that he means his remarks to apply indiscriminately. We may quote the following passage as reported :—

Dwellings for the working classes were still erected in the most flimsy fashion by the jerry builder, who generally went scot free, while architects who desired to build scientifically and well were continually harassed by unreasonable restrictions and requirements. Too many members of district councils were interested, directly or indirectly, in building operations, and the surveyor could serve such in many ways, and in turn obtained their support. Inspectors were but mortal, and were generally underpaid. It was therefore not surprising that some of them came under the influence of the speculative builder, and little credit accrued to them by drawing attention to his irregularites, but *éclat* was gained when an architect was reported as having contravened a by-law or regulation.

This can only mean one of two things. Either borough surveyors and building inspectors are accused of succumbing to bribery by speculative builders who are members of their councils, or they are accused of not carrying out their duties conscientiously and without fear or favour. The words are obviously those of a man who is speaking at random, and Mr. Henman can scarcely be congratulated on having achieved a courteous or considerate performance. In our columns cases have been reported of surveyors who have lost appointments through the conscientious discharge of their duties. As to remuneration and qualifications, we believe that no building inspector in Mr. Henman's own city has less than £150 a year, and probably all would bear favourable comparison with assistants in architects' offices and can boast of greater practical knowledge. We believe we are correct in saying that the building surveyor to the Birmingham Corporation is an Associate of the Royal Institute of British Architects and was trained in offices of the highest class.

Before concluding, Mr. Henman had something to say on the subject of borough surveyors carrying out buildings of an architectural character, such as isolation hospitals, baths, libraries, markets, town halls and council houses. Rarely, we are told, have they received suitable training for such work, and by their doing it architects are deprived of legitimate employment. The latter is, no doubt, the sore point, but we doubt if it can be regarded as otherwise than a matter of opinion and sentiment. There is really no reason why borough surveyors should not do such work if their other duties permit, and if they have the necessary training and capacity, as many of them undoubtedly have in spite of what Mr. Henman may say to the contrary. If otherwise, we should soon hear of it, and the practice would die a natural death. As it is, there is certainly a saving to the ratepayers. The buildings designed and carried out by borough surveyors are not, as a rule, of very great magnitude, and there should be plenty of other work for architects. The matter, we think, is one for compromise, say, on the lines suggested by a speaker from Leicester, where the corporation have decided that an outside architect should be engaged for all work over a certain amount. Mr. Henman's theory of the employment of architectural hacks by borough surveyors when some work has to be carried out is too ridiculous and offensive for serious consideration, and we should like him to advance some proof in support of another very sweeping and very general statement—that the actual outlay on buildings carried out under the control of borough surveyors is generally far in excess of what it would be under a "qualified architect," by which phrase we take it that Mr. Henman means an architect in private practice. Another matter that was exaggerated to absurd dimensions is the permission sometimes given to official surveyors to undertake private work, in which case it is at once assumed that the official abuses his position to obtain commissions. Mr. Henman has even "heard" of difficulties being thrown in the way of building proprietors and architects for the purpose of diverting work into the hands of the surveyor. "Heard" is good, but rumour has been described as a lying jade. We regret that anyone in Mr. Henman's position should assist in doing her work. How many borough or district council surveyors are now allowed to undertake private practice? He must know as well as anyone that the tendency, especially in populous districts, is to discountenance the system. If an official surveyor is allowed to take private work there is every probability that his plans are passed because he takes care to comply with the by-laws, and that if other plans are rejected the reason is that they do not so comply.

We may note some of the remarks made in the course of the discussion on Mr. Henman's paper, as that discontented gentleman occasionally suffered something like flat contradiction from members of his own camp. Mr. W. Woodward assured him that the same difficulties in regard to by-laws and their interpretation were equally applicable to London, to which Mr. Henman had pointed as an example. Thus, the architects who officiate as building surveyors in the metropolis are no more successful than other people, though they generally contrive to make out a very eloquent case in support of the present system. A second speaker said he had experienced no difficulty with surveyors, and in Birmingham, if the surveyor did not think a by-law was sufficiently elastic to justify him in taking the responsibility of meeting a special case, an appeal could be made to a committee of the council. Two other speakers testified that they had experienced little or no difficulty with official surveyors, either in Birmingham or elsewhere, the present city surveyor of Birmingham being specially mentioned. One of the speakers referred to expressed the very reasonable opinion that, while by-laws should vary to suit local conditions, uniformity is desirable in what is really one large town; but Mr. P. Gordon Smith, architect to the Local Government Board, pointed out that as Birmingham had special powers under the Consolidation Act the suburban districts could not exactly copy the Birmingham by-laws. He made the sensible suggestion that the neighbouring local authorities might appoint a joint committee to frame a common code of by-laws. He was sure that such a conference would receive every encouragement and assistance from the Local Government Board, who would probably point out to them what they could and what they could not do. Speaking in defence of the "model" by-laws, he said the Local Government Board could not enforce the adoption of any one of them; that they had stood the test of the courts very well, and that if their phraseology was obscure there was no objection to the local authority printing explanations or illustrations with them. The last remark provoked laughter. It cannot be denied, however, that the "model" by-laws might be still more "model," if we can employ degrees of comparison in such a case, and that they can best be improved by the Local Government Board listening to the advice of those who have the greatest experience. Needless to say, we include borough surveyors in that category, though Mr. Henman would no doubt deny their title. It is not possible that officials and architects should always see eye to eye. Borough surveyors, we have no doubt, appreciate the compliment with which Mr. Smith closed his remarks. He, at all events, has found them excellent officers and very amenable to reason, and he added that in many of the larger towns the surveyors are simply splendid men.

We certainly sympathise with Mr. Henman in the small amount of support he received in his somewhat distempered and misdirected crusade, which is likely to do more harm than good to what the resolution adopted at the meeting described as "the action that is being taken by the Birmingham Architectural Association as to the framing and administration of by-laws in Birmingham and the surrounding district." We have ourselves had occasion to point out some of the defects of the present system, and in some of the objects he aims at we have no doubt that Mr. Henman would command the support of most of those whom he regards as his natural enemies. He may count on a good deal of sympathy when he confines himself to principles and methods, and when he advocates changes which are not in themselves unreasonable. Revision of the "model" by-laws, the restriction of official control within reasonable limits, the sanctioning of only such regulations as are necessary to secure health and safety, a greater approach in adjoining urban districts towards uniformity in essential matters, and the establishment of easily-accessible courts of appeal —these are demands for which there is, no doubt, a good deal to be said. It may also be admitted that there is at times too much official control, and that now and again the surveyor to the local authority is apt to be over-zealous and fussy, but that is something very different from the exaggerated state of affairs which Mr. Henman depicts so gloomily, and which he would fain persuade us really exists. When he resorts to gratuitous and offensive charges against an estimable and deserving body of officials, and commits himself to reckless and inaccurate statements, marked equally by want of discretion and want of consideration for other people's feelings, he is more likely to injure his own cause than those whom he attacks. To make sweeping generalisations from conditions which only arise occasionally in individual cases is neither fair nor logical, and nothing is more significant than the fact that the members of Mr. Henman's own profession who were present on the occasion abstained from endorsing his charges. Architects who have listened to a discussion of by-laws on the part of municipal engineers are aware that these officials are by no means blind to existing defects, and that they are, as a rule, earnestly desirous, consistently with the proper discharge of their duties, to avoid anything detrimental to the interests either of the community in general or of any particular class. Some architects, however, speak as if they should be given an absolutely free hand. That experiment, we may safely say, would not be in the public interest.

* * *

**The Overhead versus the Conduit System of Electric Tramway Traction.** There is little doubt that the quasi-official report which was recently submitted to the London County Council on the various systems of electric tramways has caused quite a flutter among those corporations that were contemplating adopting an overhead wire system. The effect in some cases has been so great that work which was practically in progress has been actually stopped until further information was obtained on the working of the conduit systems. It is, however, satisfactory to find that the Manchester Corporation have had the courage to proceed in the course, which it adopted some time ago, of laying down electric tramways on the overhead wire system. The corporation committee who have charge of this matter are fortunate in possessing a mechanical engineer as its chairman, for Mr. Higginbottom has apparently considered almost every system of electric tramways in use at the present moment, and while we cannot altogether agree with all the arguments and estimates which he put forward in favour of the overhead wire system, it is interesting to quote them for the benefit of other municipalities. He stated that the reasons in favour of the overhead trolley systems were :—

(1) That the first capital cost per mile of track was £2,135, against £11,491 for the conduit system ; or, for the 67 miles required in Manchester, £144,000, against £773,897.

(2) The working cost per car mile was ½d. more for the conduit system, or £14,000 per year.

(3) Difficulties of construction of the conduit system in the narrow and congested Manchester streets.

These are arguments that will apply to a good many towns, and it is sincerely to be hoped that municipalities will recognise that the figures relating to such a special undertaking as that of the New York conduit system, on which most arguments are now based, will not apply to many places in this country. The Glasgow Corporation, after laying down its experimental overhead system, went very carefully into the system of the conduit, prompted, no doubt, by the report to which we have already alluded, but it was speedily discovered that the conduit system was quite impracticable in Glasgow, and the future extensions (some of which are already being undertaken) will be carried out on the overhead wire system. As we have previously pointed out, there is no difficulty in working the conduit system, but it needs some very special reasons to justify the extraordinary expense that such a system involves.

* * *

**Automatic Gas Meters and Cookers.** Our readers will, no doubt, peruse with interest the communication we publish this week from Mr. Edward A. Harman in reference to the success which has attended the adaptation of the penny-in-the-slot system for gas distribution. The Huddersfield Corporation are always to the fore in useful work of this kind, and it is gratifying to hear of the success which has attended their efforts in this particular direction. We have not now the space at our disposal to enter into the subject at length, in spite of its undeniable interest, but Mr. Harman's letter brings out clearly the essential points. He quotes figures to demonstrate that the system is practicable from a financial point of view, and enters at length into the future possibilities of the popular pennyworth, which certainly bids fair to simplify life a good deal, especially for those of straitened means. Nor must we lose sight of the fact that, by the extended use of gas for heating and cooking purposes, we may to a very large extent abolish the smoke nuisance, which so vexes the soul of Sir W. B. Richmond, R.A.

# Principal Features of Electric Lighting Systems.—X.*

## SYSTEMS OF DISTRIBUTION (continued).

THE FIVE-WIRE SYSTEM.

Some reference was made in the last article to what may be termed an extension of the three-wire system. It is, so far as its operation in this country is concerned, due entirely to the late Dr. John Hopkinson, who patented, simultaneously with Edison, applications of many wire systems, among which was included the five-wire method. In its first application, which was probably at Temesvar, in Hungary, a dynamo working at 400 volts was employed. It had five main wires in the distribution network, lamps being placed between the first and second wire, the second and third, the third and fourth, and the fourth and fifth. This practically gives four groups of lamps which would be in series with each other; but the important point about this arrangement is that each group of lamps would only receive current at a pressure of 100 volts, so that each group would be receiving a voltage the sum of which would be 400, in other words, the difference of pressure between the two outer mains would be 400 volts, while between one of the outer mains and the nearest inner one the difference of pressure would be only 100 volts, and there would be the same difference of potential between any two adjacent wires. The importance of this system was that it enabled the distance which could be operated economically from a low-tension station to be increased to four times the distance that could be accomplished with an ordinary two-wire system, or twice the distance that could be economically supplied by a three-wire system having 200 volts between the two outers. A still more notable five-wire system was that employed in Paris in connection with the central station, known as the "Secteur Clichy." In this case the armatures of the four separate dynamos were connected together on one common shaft and were coupled in series across the feeders. The two outer terminals of the combined set of machines and the three intermediate terminals were connected one to each of the five distributing wires. The important point was that all the dynamos were compelled to turn at the same speed, consequently any difference of pressure between any of the feeders would be equally divided between the four armatures so long as the resistance in each of the lamp circuits was ·qual. If it happened that one circuit was receiving too much pressure, because there were too few lamps, then the pressure on the dynamo corresponding to that group would be greater than the other four machines; and, consequently, that particular dynamo would be compelled to act as a motor and be driven at a higher speed than if it were out of the circuit. The consequence of this greater speed is to raise the pressure in all the other burning circuits, and thus in those circuits where there is least pressure the dynamos would act as machines generating electricity, and in those groups where there were fewer lamps they would act as motors, absorbing power and helping to drive the other machines. This system has been employed for a considerable period, but it was felt long ago that it was somewhere uneconomical, especially in the method of compensating for the difference in pressure on the different circuits. Consequently it is not surprising to find that the system has been almost completely abandoned.

The five-wire system adopted in Manchester was a very notable departure from the one adopted in Paris, and, moreover, it has successfully met extraordinary developments in the demand for electricity that has arisen in Manchester during the past few years. In this case the dynamos are of somewhat varying voltages. Thus one machine would be wound for 400 volts, and would feed on the two outer wires, while others on lower voltages would act as compensators. The flexibility of the Manchester arrangement has been very marked, and instead of the difficulties of regulation and compensating for varying pressures, which were held at one time to be insuperable, the system has gone steadily ahead, meeting the demand for electricity in the middle district of Manchester with unqualified success. It is true that during the past two or three years it has been necessary to supplement the original system with a battery sub-station, and to arrange also, at two or three different points of the city, two motor-dynamo sub-stations, which successfully meet any fall of pressure that might arise. It was felt that the difference of pressure between the two outer mains of 400 volts might be dangerous, but, so far from that being the case, it is interesting to mention that the whole five wires have been taken into some of the largest buildings, such as the town hall and other municipal buildings, without causing the slightest trouble whatever.

INSULATING MATERIAL.

The next point that one might satisfactorily consider is that of the material which is mostly employed for insulating electric light cables. In the opinion of many engineers the substance that is put before all others for its high insulating qualities is pure rubber, and it is not too much to say that for a long time, at any rate, the majority of distributing systems in this country depended upon rubber. Obviously high insulation is necessary in all systems of distribution. It is not everything, however, because a cable must be able to withstand a good deal of rough usage without showing very

marked signs of deterioration. Again, it must be sufficiently flexible that it can be bent and coiled readily, and, what is of equal importance, it should be able to withstand differences of temperature without showing any permanent injury. A matter of very great moment in those systems employing very high pressures is that the cable should be able to prevent to a very great extent what is known as disruptive discharge. Although later experience in some instances has tended to show that rubber cables have occasionally exhibited signs of weakness, it is not precisely clear at the moment whether this is due to any inherent fault in the insulator itself, or whether the troubles have been caused by carelessness in laying the cables. Speaking generally, it has been considered that rubber, when of good quality and applied properly, gives very high resistance and is probably incomparable in withstanding high pressures. Moreover, it is able without apparent signs of injury to withstand very great variation in temperature. The whole question, however, at the present moment is whether it is durable. It is quite true that while some engineers complain that rubber cables have given them considerable trouble, it is not difficult to find as many, or probably more, engineers to come forward and declare that rubber cables which have been in continuous use for some years have developed a minimum number of faults. It would be easy to quote instances which demonstrate that rubber cables have lasted for electric lighting purposes ten and eleven years without showing any signs of deterioration. The method of insulating a copper conductor would be to wrap round layers of pure rubber tape, and on this compound rubber would be applied, after which other strips of prepared rubber tape would be bound round and the whole vulcanised. A general practice nowadays is to place on the rubber cable a covering of lead, which affords very marked mechanical protection; but occasionally on the top of the lead covering a sheathing of galvanised-iron tapes may be laid on, and the complete cable could be then laid direct in the ground, or, if necessary, drawn into a pipe or conduit.

One of the best-known forms of cable employed for electric lighting purposes in this country is known as the bitumen type of cable, and in spite of the fact that it might be open to some objection from a mechanical point of view, many miles have been laid down in this country by the Callender Company, and the cables are giving extreme satisfaction. The insulating material in this system consists of a preparation of bitumen, and it is occasionally wrapped in some form of yarn or fibrous material served on tape. It is then covered with some insulating compound, again taped, and it is afterwards covered with hemp yarn. Very frequently this cable is laid in trenches, which are filled up solid with bitumen compound, or, as is very frequently the case, it may be drawn into what is known as Callender-Webber casing, which is practically a case containing a number of ducts, into which the cables are drawn. Previous to being drawn into position, however, the cases are jointed together by means of bitumen compound, and this gives almost all the advantages of a solid system, coupled with the advantage of being able to draw in the cables as required.

Another interesting type of cable which is very greatly used in this country at the present moment is what is known as the paper cable. In this class of cable the wire is insulated by means of paper, which is wrapped round in place of cotton or jute. Usually the paper is wound round the conductor in strips, and as each spiral of paper is laid on the wire is passed through a die, which presses it into a compact mass. After being exposed for some time the cable with its paper covering is passed through a special bath of compound, and it afterwards passes direct to a lead-covering press. This type of cable is the one which is made by the British Insulating Wire Company in this country, and, as we have already pointed out, it is very extensively used.

Of the many forms of conduit which are in use, one of the most durable is that known as Doulton ware casing, and, as this is used in very many systems, it may be interesting to mention the principal features of it. As a matter of fact, it consists practically of a conduit possessing a varying number of ducts. In the case of Belfast, the most recently completed system in which Doulton casings are employed, the conduits have two, three and six rectangular ducts, each 2½ in. by 2½ in.; and an interesting feature of this is that the joints between the lengths of conduit have been made by means of cast-iron clamp collars in two portions bolted together. The interior of the collars is recessed, and the upper piece is provided with an aperture, through which is poured rapidly-setting bituminous compound. This entirely surrounds the ends of the lengths, but it is prevented from entering the ducts by expanding joint mandrels, one of which is inserted in each duct while the joint is being made. Perfect continuity of the ducts is thus secured. Branch cable connections are provided for as follows: At suitable intervals in the line of conduits special lengths are laid,

* The ninth article of this series appeared in our issue of December 2nd.

which are grooved during manufacture in such a way that, while strength is preserved, a longitudinal division can be made by means of a chisel when desired. When a **T** connection is required the upper portion of the split length is detached, giving access to the cables. The cable joints having been completed, a junction cover, made for the purpose, is substituted for the piece which has been detached. This cover is fitted with a cast-iron socket piece to take the service pipe.

COST OF MAINS.

It may be interesting, before closing this article, to give a few figures relating to the cost of mains. It is not an easy thing, however, to obtain very reliable figures as to the exact cost per yard of many systems, but in the case of Kensington and Knightsbridge it was stated, when the system had been in operation for some time, that the cost was as follows:—

| | Per yard. £ | s. | d. |
|---|---|---|---|
| Five Pipes.—Four of 2 in. and one of 1½ in., with three cables 61/15 and two cables 37/16 ... ... | 3 | 2 | 2 |
| Three Pipes.—Two of 2 in. and one of 1½ in., and three 61/15 cables ... ... ... ... | 1 | 8 | 6½ |
| 15-in. culvert, including three strips 1 in. by ¼ in. | 1 | 3 | 9 |
| 20-in. culvert, including five strips 1 in. by ¼ in. ... | 1 | 9 | 0 |
| 24-in. culvert, including seven strips 1 in. by ¼ in. | 1 | 14 | 2 |

In another case the cost of supplying and laying Callender-Webber casing with three 2-in. ways, including all charges, with straightforward work was 6s. 6d. per yard; or, including the draw and service boxes, 8s. 9d. per yard. The usual cost of connecting a house varies from £10 to £15.

It is interesting to quote from a paper relating to the cost of underground mains by Major-General Webber, who stated, comparing the cost of insulated cable with bare copper strip, that he came to the conclusion as regards the economical aspect of the use of insulated conductors, "that practice shows in any position that where a small section of copper in each conductor in the same line only is required, other conditions alike, it is much cheaper to use insulation of the character of bituminous compound in ducts or ways of a small size and economical material than to look for insulation to non-conducting supporting surfaces, with a large surrounding of air space subsisting in a subway of which the minimum first cost must be represented by a substantial figure." Again, he says, "Generally speaking, if the section of copper in a pair of conductors is 1 in. and under, then a main constructed with insulated cables in separate ways is cheapest, increasingly so with small conductors between 1 in. and 1¼ in. The comparison varies, according to circumstances, over 1½ in. of section. Then insulated copper bears away the prize for economy."

Some figures contributed by Mr. Crompton to the discussion on Major-General Webber's paper are interesting, and although they are by no means new they are of some significance even at the present moment, and we have therefore reproduced them in the above table.

TABLE SHOWING COST PER YARD OF UNDERGROUND MAINS.

| — | Extract from Tables 1 and 2 of Mr. Crompton's Paper of 1888. I. Callender. | | II. Culvert. | | Webber. | | Crompton. Paper. | | Crompton. Culverts. | |
|---|---|---|---|---|---|---|---|---|---|---|
| Area of conductors ... ... | ½ in. s. d. | ¼ in. s. d. | ½ in. s. d. | ¼ in. s. d. | ½ in. s. d. | ¼ in. s. d. | ½ in. s. d. | ¼ in. s. d. | ½ in. s. d. | ¼ in. s. d. |
| Cost of Callender casing, wrought-iron pipes or culverts ... ... | 11 4 | 11 4 | 11 8 | 11 8 | 6 6 | 6 6 | 6 6 | 6 6 | 11 9 | 11 9 |
| Cost of surface boxes, 12 yards apart | 2 3 | 2 3 | — | — | 2 3 | 2 3 | 1 11½ | 1 11½ | 1 11½ | 1 11½ |
| Cost of insulators and straining gear | — | — | 3 0 | 3 0 | — | — | - | — | 0 7½ | 0 7½ |
| Cost of cables ... ... ... ... | 31 7 | 15 9 | — | — | 31 0 | 18 0 | 31 0 | 18 0 | — | — |
| Cost of copper (bare)... ... ... | — | — | 12 2 | 6 3 | — | — | — | — | 12 2 | 6 3 |
| Totals ... ... ... | 45 2 | 29 4 | 26 10 | 20 11 | 39 0 | 26 9 | 39 5½ | 26 5½ | 26 6 | 20 7 |
| If high-class rubber cable be used (extra) ... ... ... ... | — | — | — | — | — | — | 10 4 | 2 8 | — | — |
| Totals ... ... ... | | | | | | | 49 9½ | 29 1½ | | |

## ARBITRATIONS AND AWARDS.

The arbitration between the North Metropolitan Tramways Company and the London County Council to determine the price to be paid by the council to the company for the tramways recently acquired by the council was opened at the Surveyors' Institution, Savoy-street, recently. Lord James of Hereford was the sole arbitrator. Sir Edward Clarke, Q.C., M.P., Mr. Charles Mathews and Mr. F. Richardson appeared for the tramways company; while Mr. Dickens, Q.C., and Mr. Daldy appeared for the London County Council. At the outset of the proceedings Sir Edward Clarke, addressing the arbitrator, said he and his friend Mr. Dickens, representing the two parties, had agreed that, as the question to be decided was quite a private matter, it would be better if the proceedings were conducted in private. Lord James said the question was entirely in the hands of the two parties, and he must ask the representatives of the Press to withdraw. Sir Edward Clarke: And the witnesses also. The witnesses and the representatives of the Press then withdrew. The arbitration lasted some days.

## ELECTRIC LIGHTING AT ECCLES.

OPENING OF WORKS.

Alderman Kendall, chairman of the Electric Lighting Committee of the Eccles Town Council, last week performed the opening ceremony in connection with the new electric lighting works of the corporation.

The generating works occupy a modest block of brick buildings in Cawdon-street, Patricroft, and the whole scheme has been carried out under the direction of Mr. S. V. Clirehugh, of the firm of Messrs. Lacy, Clirehugh & Sellar, consulting engineers. The plant consists of two Lancashire boilers and two steam alternators, each of 200 horse-power, and capable of supplying together about 10,000 8 candle-power lamps. It is only intended to run one alternator at a time, the other being held in reserve in case of a breakdown. The engines are of the marine inverted type, running at 200 revolutions a minute, and direct coupled with the alternators. Accumulators are provided which will maintain 1,000 8 candle-power lamps for seven hours. These accumulators are charged off the alternators by means of motor generators, which in their turn are run by the accumulators and supply direct to the mains. The high-tension alternating-current system of distribution is adopted. The current is at a pressure of 2,000 volts, which is reduced at the consumer's premises to 200 volts. This system has been introduced in consequence of the scattered nature of the district to be supplied. It is intended to light the whole borough by electricity, which will involve a supply of some 1,700 lamp columns. Generally speaking, the existing gas-lamp columns will be utilised. At the present moment there are about 5 miles of mains laid in the district, and applications have already been received for over 4,000 8 candle-power lamps. The whole district contains about 30 miles of streets. The storage apparatus embraces separate accumulators capable of supplying 700 8 candle-power lamps for ten hours. In order to save expense these will be requisitioned during the day time and also after midnight. The apparatus for subdividing the currents and registering the quantity of energy distributed is of the newest kind.

## GAINSBOROUGH WATERWORKS EXTENSIONS.

A new reservoir and water tower, which form part of the Gainsborough water extension scheme, were opened on the 14th inst. by Mr. John Dixon, the chairman of the urban district council, who has, it may be mentioned, taken a great share in promoting the artesian borings and in the development of the scheme generally.

The total cost of the tower, reservoir and rising main will be approximately some £7,000. The length of the rising main from the artesian well to the tower is 2,000 ft., with a total rise of 103 ft. The pipes were made by the Stanton Iron Company. The reservoir is a fine piece of work, the walls and floor being of concrete, with salt-glazed bricks supplied by Messrs. Oates & Green, of Halifax. The depth is 16 ft., and the capacity if 1,004,350 gallons. The wall tower is a hexagonal structure 75 ft. in height. It is ornamental in design, and, taken in conjunction with the reservoir, forms a very pleasing feature in the landscape. The tank will hold about 7,200 gallons of water—sufficient to supply the town for three or four days. An automatic recorder constructed on scientific principles has been supplied by the Glenfield Iron Company. The whole of the works have been carried out under the supervision of Mr. H. Riley, engineer and surveyor to the council, and the contractor was Mr. Benjamin Roberts, of Gainsborough.

**Merthyr.**—Recently Colonel A. C. Smith, R.E., one of the inspectors of the Local Government Board, held an inquiry at the public offices, Merthyr, relative to an application made by the urban district council for sanction to borrow £1,115 for the construction of new sewer tanks at Troedyrhiw. Mr. Harvey, the surveyor, explained that it was proposed to close the existing tanks and to put the new ones lower down, nearer to the river.

# Municipal Authorities and Public Slaughter-Houses.*

The importance of the question to municipalities of the establishment of public slaughter-houses is not appreciated as it should be in this country, and it is only recently that we are giving that consideration to the subject which it deserves. Other countries, especially Germany, have gone a long way ahead of us, and it behoves those who have the health of the public largely in their hands to pay increased attention, not only to the sanitary question as to how a private slaughter-house affects the health of the inhabitants of the neighbourhood in which it is located, but to the securing of a large and wholesome food supply for the people, and to ensure that animals are prepared for food under sanitary conditions and with efficient supervision by meat inspectors. We are slow to move in this country, but, having once grasped the importance of the subject, I hope shall make up for lost time. It is a large question, and it is impossible for me to go into much detail with the time at my disposal.

There are four main divisions to consider : (1) The establishment of public slaughter-houses or halls, with all modern appliances, and with the sanitary arrangements as perfect as possible ; (2) the efficient inspection of meat by qualified persons ; (3) proper facilities for keeping dead meat ; and (4) mode of killing.

On the first point there is no doubt that the existence of so many private slaughter-houses, often in a very insanitary condition and placed in the midst of a dense population, is one of the greatest drawbacks we have in England in dealing with the whole subject. Our Parliamentary powers are insufficient to deal with them. In the case of new communities and new areas in this country no doubt it can be and is being dealt with, but in our large towns vested interests are so sacred, and the number of registered and licensed slaughter-houses so numerous, that it presents an almost impassable barrier to those who desire to see things altered for the better. In Germany, again, it is quite different. There the public powers are amply sufficient to deal with any nuisance arising from private slaughter-houses. It is no uncommon thing to find in the large towns that powers are exercised in abolishing the private slaughter-house, and, erected in their place in a suitable position outside the town, with good railway accommodation, fine new establishments, comprising market-halls for cattle, sheep and pigs, slaughter-halls, refrigerators, laboratories, destructors, refreshment-rooms, offices, and all appliances necessary for a complete market.

### THE LAW IN GERMANY.

In Germany the town council where the General Slaughtering Act has been applied by means of a local Act has power to erect and carry on public slaughter-houses. The town council may issue an order prohibiting the slaughtering of animals anywhere within the limits of their district, except at the public slaughter-houses. The prohibition may also be applied to the carrying on of all trades intimately connected with the slaughter of animals for food. The council may prohibit a further use of private or other slaughter-houses, except those erected or carried on by an association or guild of butchers.

The council may, after they have erected their slaughter-houses, make regulations for the examination by experts, both before and after slaughter, of all animals brought to the public slaughter-houses, in order that the condition of such animals may be ascertained ; and for the examination of all fresh meat not slaughtered in the public slaughter-houses, by duly appointed experts, before it is offered to the public for sale. A fee shall be payable by the owner of the meat to the council for such inspection. They may enact that fresh meat brought from outside the area of the town, and disposed of to restaurants, hotels, &c., shall not be prepared for food until it has been inspected. They may altogether prohibit the importation of prepared meats, and decide that in public markets, shops, &c., the flesh of animals which have not been slaughtered in the public slaughter-houses shall be kept and exposed for sale separate from that which has been so slaughtered. They may order that no meat shall be sold in any public market-hall which has not been slaughtered, &c., at the public slaughter-house ; and that butchers shall not offer meat for sale which has been slaughtered outside the area and within a prohibited district or radius.

The council may make and publish regulations as to the examination of meat, and fix the fees to be taken for such examination. Regulations as to the inspection of meat not slaughtered in the public slaughter-houses shall direct that all meat shall be submitted to the inspector—in the case of large animals in sides or quarters, and in the case of small animals in whole carcasses. The fees to be charged for the inspection of meat shall not in the aggregate exceed the cost of such inspection. Various lines and restrictions are laid down as to how and under what circumstances these regulations are to be carried into effect. The regulations of a local authority require the approval of the Provincial Government. The town council may close all private slaughter-houses after giving six months' notice of their intention so to do. It is within their discretion to allow a longer period to elapse. After the issue of such notice it is illegal to erect any new private slaughter-houses.

Compensation shall be paid by the council to the proprietors and tenants of the private slaughter-houses which are closed in pursuance of the council's orders, such compensation being for real damage or loss which can be proved by the aforementioned persons on account of the closing of their places, such places having been built for slaughtering purposes. In calculating the compensation to be paid the amount which may be realised from the properties and fixtures when used for other purposes shall be deducted. No compensation shall be paid for the extra trouble there may be involved by reason of a butcher having to slaughter away from his own place of business. Where the premises to be closed are held by the occupier on a lease, such lease shall terminate at the same time as the notice issued by the council. No claim shall stand as between landlord and tenant on account of such termination of a lease. It is necessary for the owners and tenants of premises to be closed to give notice to the Provincial Government of their intention to claim compensation within six months, or their claims will not be allowed. This Government appoints an arbitrator, who, with the assistance of two others—one to be appointed by the claimant and one by the town council—shall inquire into the claim that has been made. The above is a short description of German law on the question of inspection and private slaughter-houses.

The Royal Commission on Tuberculosis, in their report to our Parliament this year, recommend : (a) When the local authority in any town or urban district in England, Wales and Ireland have provided a public slaughter-house, powers be conferred on them to declare that no other place within the town or borough shall be used for slaughtering, except that a period of three years be allowed to owners of existing private slaughter-houses to apply their premises to other purposes. (b) That local authorities be empowered to refuse all meat slaughtered elsewhere than in a public slaughter-house and brought into the district for sale to be taken to a place where such meat may be inspected, and that the authorities be empowered to make a charge to cover the costs of such inspection. (c) Inspectors shall be engaged and shall stamp the joints of all carcasses passed as sound. (d) The commission further recommends that it shall not be lawful to offer for sale the meat of any animal which has not been killed in a duly-licensed slaughter-house.

These are drastic recommendations, but it is what other countries have had to do, and we shall be compelled to do likewise if we are to deal effectively with the question. It is worthy of the notice of other municipalities that the Public Health Committee of the London County Council are recommending the council to inform the Local Government Board that they are prepared to carry out the recommendations of the commission if the power be given to them by Parliament. In Germany, on the closing of private slaughter-houses compensation is paid to the owner and tenant, a definite procedure for ascertaining the amount being laid down by Act of Parliament. In Leipzig the prohibition of all private slaughter-houses and the provision that all slaughtering shall be done only in the public slaughter-houses is very stringent.

### EFFICIENT INSPECTION.

Equally important with having a suitable public slaughter-house is the question of efficient inspection of meat. This is conducted in a most scientific manner in Germany, and from all we learnt to most successful. So thorough especially is the microscopical examination of pork, that one of the members of our deputation which visited Germany was led to remark, " Well, after seeing the way they examine pork in Germany, I should have no hesitation in eating German sausages." In England there is no compulsion to have meat inspected at all. It is left to the conscience of the butcher, if he has any doubt about the quality, to call in the inspector, or to the perseverance and sharp eyes of that official to discover cases of inferior meat offered for public sale. In Germany it is compulsory that all meat should be inspected and stamped before it is used for the food of man. Our inspectors may be very vigilant, but in consequence of the large number of private slaughter-houses it is impossible for them to visit them all when the process of killing is going on.

The question of stamping meat has recently come up for discussion in this country, and there seems a great amount of prejudice against it, but in Germany it is exactly the reverse. Many stamps are placed on each carcase, and these stamps are a guarantee of soundness, and without them people there would hesitate to purchase. In Liepsig all cattle brought into the market are examined by experts. The staff consists of a director, who is the supreme officer, and acts, with the consent of the Minister of the Interior, as official veterinary inspector for contagious diseases in cattle for a given area and is responsible for all inspection. Besides the director there are the two veterinary surgeons, two assistant veterinary surgeons, the chief of the microscopical department, and microscopical assistants, and the officers engaged in taking the samples of meat. The chief officers are sworn in by taking the oath, and bind themselves to truly and con-

* A paper read at the Birmingham Congress of the Sanitary Institute, by Mr. E. Parkes, m.p., Chairman of the Markets and Fairs Committee of the Birmingham Corporation.

scientiously execute the work of meat inspection, to carefully watch the slaughtering of all animals by slaughtermen, and to observe the ordinary by-laws. Attached to all the large markets is a staff of veterinary and microscopical inspectors. In Berlin, for instance, we were told that there were 240 persons engaged in the microscopic examination of meat, ninety of whom were women.

There is no doubt that we are very much behindhand on the question of meat inspection in England, and without attempting to go into it as thoroughly as described above, there is a great deal that we might and ought to do to make inspection more thorough. A veterinary surgeon with a practical training is the ideal inspector, and the time is coming, no doubt, in this country when some such a law will be enacted. The opinion of such men will be taken generally without any question by the butchers, but an unqualified or inexperienced man is often the cause of a great deal of friction and unpleasantness in carrying out his work. In some districts in England, especially in country districts, the system of inspection is most lax, and the inspectors have often the flimsiest qualification to perform their duties. The whole question requires to be put on a different basis, and not left, as it often now is, to men with a mere smattering of knowledge and who have been able to answer a few questions at a sanitary science examination. There should be more uniformity of practice, the recommendation of the Royal Commission being very useful in this respect, and officers of different localities should work together, so that it would not be possible, as it sometimes is now, for dealers in bad meat to be driven out of a district or town where inspection is efficient and establish themselves over the border where inspection may be very lax. The whole question of meat inspection and public and private slaughter-houses requires the immediate attention of municipalities and of the legislature, with a due consideration, not only for the public health, but also for the interests of the traders concerned.

I think it is well that I should give some idea of the magnitude of the German establishments. In Berlin, with a population of 1,700,000, the general slaughtering law was applied in 1883, and that same year the markets in that city were opened for use, at a cost of £600,000; immediately after that date all private slaughter-houses in the city were closed. The cattle markets and slaughter-houses are in the outskirts of the city, and cover an area of 90 acres, 28 acres of which is reserved for railway sidings, including land for their extension. The cattle market-hall is a huge building, 240 yards by 80 yards wide, or about 4 acres in area. The population of Hanover is 126,000. The markets cost £140,000, and are situated about 1½ miles from the centre of the city, the area of site being about 17 acres. The population of Leipzig is 330,000. The cattle markets and slaughter-houses are nearly 2 miles from the centre of the city. The area, 29 acres. A main line of railway runs at the side of the markets, and tramways also into them. The total cost, including land and railway siding, was £235,000. These markets were erected in 1888, and are among the most complete of any in Germany. The population of Spandau is 35,000. The area of the markets was nearly 4 acres. The cost of building was £40,000.

The markets in Germany generally include market-halls for live cattle, sheep and pigs; slaughter-halls for the different animals, including one for horse-slaughtering; cold storage; bad meat destructors; ice-making plant; rooms for tripe-dressing; fat and tallow departments; and last, but not least, the inspection department. We generally noticed the scrupulous cleanliness and order which prevailed in these establishments, and everywhere they were laid out on a large scale, with plenty of room for each department. This is only possible where land is taken outside the city, and from what we saw it is certainly the best way of dealing with the problem; but in Germany they have Parliamentary powers to enable them to carry out their ideal, and they seem to have unlimited money to spend in the building of their markets. In Germany the whole question has been grasped boldly, thoroughly and successfully.

On the question of killing I do not know that it is necessary I should say much. We found that generally in Germany the pole-axe was used, as with us; in the case of beasts a mask was sometimes put over the face of the animal. In the slaughter of pigs a small cylinder, enclosing a pin and controlled by a spring, was used, a large wooden mallet being used to strike the pin when placed on the animal's head, which is really a spring pole-axe. We have tried several new methods of slaughtering animals, but generally there are drawbacks to the use of each of them, and in the hands of a duly-qualified slaughterman the pole-axe is as sure and expeditious as any other method.

THE BIRMINGHAM BUILDINGS.

In Birmingham a few years ago we were confronted with the problem of building new market-halls, slaughter-houses, &c., and after visiting many Continental and English markets, and giving the matter a great deal of thought, we decided upon the erection of the present buildings, which have now been opened about nine months. The plan shown and elevation will give some idea of the result of our labours. It is not exactly ideal, inasmuch as it is placed in the centre of the town, but we had no alternative, the land having been purchased some years ago.

We had about 12,000 yards of land to deal with, and our business was to make the best use of it. On the ground floor we have placed the large meat market, twenty separate slaughter-houses for wholesale butchers, the slaughter-hall, the offices, the fat stores, &c. On the upper floor we have placed the lairage for cattle and sheep, and the tripe-dressing, blood and gut-cleaning departments. In the basement we have the cold storage, the engines for electric lighting and for cold storage, &c., and steam boilers. The main hall is 305 ft. long, by 95 ft. wide by 63 ft. high to centre of roof. Over the stalls, in the centre of market, are thirty-four offices, approached by two staircases, for the use of the salesmen. We have two hydraulic lifts connecting the market-hall with the cold stores below; the meat market-hall is fitted to hang about 3,000 sides of beef. We have a complete system of overhead travelling-gear connecting the slaughter houses and halls with general market and cold stores.

We have a very complete electric lighting system, the motive power being supplied by four large gas engines of 85 break horse-power each, running 200 revolutions per minute. Hot water and steam is conveyed to the different departments all over the site, there being hot and cold water taps in all the slaughter-house departments. We have a tripery fitted with all necessary appliances, rooms for fat and hides, ropes, blood, &c. We have also, in addition to separate slaughter houses, a slaughter-hall for beasts, sheep and calves, 250 ft. long by 40 ft. broad. In Germany, as already explained, the system is to slaughter in open halls. They like it best for many reasons, and perhaps it is the best system on the whole. We could not very well adopt this system in its entirety—there was some feeling against it by the trade—but have adopted the two systems, but ere long I expect that the slaughter-halls will be extensively used. The pig slaughter-hall is 96 ft. by 40 ft., and is fitted with six scalding-tubs.

The cold stores and chill-rooms have been constructed by the Linde Refrigeration Company, who have leased a portion of basement from the corporation, and have constructed rooms which will store about 25,000 carcasses of mutton and 300 sides of beef. Accommodation is being provided for the slaughtermen in the shape of a mess-room, another room being allotted for the salesmen. The Birmingham Coffee House Company have a shop on the premises. A water tower is erected on the Bradford-street end of the site, in which is placed two large tanks, one of which contains a reserve of water (about 20,000 gallons) in case of a temporary shutting-off of the mains. The action of the corporation in erecting these premises has been fully justified, seeing that, although the area of the meat market-hall is six times that of the old market, nearly every stall is let. Nineteen out of the twenty separate slaughter-houses are let, and killing is now being carried on in the slaughter-halls. The total cost of the scheme, including the site, which was an expensive one, will be about £120,000.

Birmingham justly feels that in regard to its meat market and public slaughter-houses we have premises which are constructed on the most modern principles, due regard having been observed to a good hot and cold water supply, efficient lighting and ventilation, drainage arranged to prevent the escape of solids into the sewers, the manure, &c., being carted right out on to farms. The premises are capable of being properly cleansed, and it has been our endeavour to ensure that the surroundings of the fresh-killed meat shall be pure and clean, and that as little handling of the meat as possible shall take place. Although our new market-hall is six times the area of the old one, we find it none too large, nearly every stall at the present time being let. Since the premises have been erected many other municipalities who are moving in this matter have sent deputations to inspect the premises and arrangements here, and the Markets and Fairs Committee will be pleased at all times to arrange for such inspections and to give any useful information which they can on the matter.

The discussion on the paper brought several contrary opinions to light, though it appeared to be the general opinion that there should be more municipal control over the slaughtering of animals for food, albeit some of the speakers considered the German system unnecessarily costly. Dr. Marsden (Birkenhead) argued that the measures in Germany were carried to extremes, and that we could attain a result practically as good for our purposes without anything like the amount of paraphernalia and expense. Dr. W. Collingridge differed entirely from Mr. Parkes as to the ideal inspector, and contended that the medical officer of health ought to be responsible for the work of meat inspection. Mr. Edwards (superintendent of the Birmingham markets) thought a veterinary surgeon, with a staff of trained inspectors, would do the work best.

**The Royal Commission on Sewage Disposal.**—The Earl of Iddesleigh presided last week at two meetings of the above commission, when there were present General Carey, Prof. Ramsay, Prof. Foster, Mr. Killick, Colonel Harding, Dr. Russell and Mr. F. J. Willis (secretary). The witnesses examined were Sir E. Frankland, Mr. Scott-Moncrieff and Mr. Garfield.

# The Surveyors' Institution.

## THE LONDON BUILDING ACT AND THE OFFICIAL SUPERVISION OF BUILDINGS.*

In submitting the following short paper to the Surveyors' Institution I am desirous of drawing attention to the London Building Act and the manner in which it is carried out or enforced, with the view of considering the desirability of extending to London the system prevailing under the Public Health Act in the provincial towns throughout England. Included in the membership of the Institution are a majority of the surveyors connected with the development and management of estates, both in London and the country, and such members especially should, from their experience, be in a position to institute a comparison between London and provincial procedure in matters of the kind.

Recent unfortunate events in London have had the effect of directing public attention to the Building Act and its alleged shortcomings, and although the aid of the law has been invoked in several cases since January 1, 1895, when the new Act came into operation, I consider it would be a slur on the many professional associations (including the Surveyors' Institution) which gave so much time and consideration to the Act when in Bill form to admit that its provisions, if efficiently enforced, are not sufficient for the general attainment of the end for which they were devised. Members are aware of the many alterations made in the Bill, as the result of the consideration given to it, and the very different appearance which it presents in the form of an Act, and it may be fairly assumed that even if the same amount of consideration were given to the amendment of the present Act, the resulting measure would still fall short of perfection, and afford ample opportunity for the exercise of legal acumen and expert skill in the interpretation of its provisions.

I am of opinion that the remedy for the defects of the present official system of building supervision in the metropolis must be sought, not so much in the direction of amendments to the Act itself as in the system of supervision adopted in enforcing it; and it is to this view of the question that I would particularly call attention. During my thirty-nine years' official connection with the parish, Kensington has developed from fields and market gardens into one of the most important districts of the metropolis, and very exceptional opportunities have thus been afforded of acquiring practical acquaintance with the subject under consideration, not only in the particular district referred to, but in the metropolis generally.

THE DISTRICT SURVEYOR: HIS POSITION AND FUNCTIONS.

In the report of the London County Council for 1897 it is set forth that for the purposes of the Building Act the county of London is divided into sixty-four districts, each superintended by a district surveyor, whose duty it is (according to the said report) to see that all new buildings and all alterations and additions to buildings " are carried out in accordance with the law." This statement is not correct, for, as I shall point out, the district surveyors exercise no supervision outside the statutes governing their appointment.

The report of the council further states that a standing order of the council requires each district surveyor newly appointed or reappointed to devote the whole of his time to the duties of his office, and not to engage directly or indirectly in private practice. Of the existing district surveyors, forty-one can take private practice, twelve are precluded from private practice in their own districts, and the remaining eleven are, under the standing order above referred to, entirely precluded from private practice. The district surveyors are remunerated by fees in accordance with schedules attached to the Building Act, and during the year covered by the council's last report these fees amounted to the sum of £47,748 10s. 4d. The council has power, under sec. 158 of the Act, to substitute a fixed salary in lieu of fees, abolishing the latter and charging the salary to the county fund.

Prior to the passing of the order prohibiting private practice the office of district surveyor was sought, not so much for the direct income attaching to it, but for the opportunities afforded for enlarging the private practice of the official. A district surveyor acting as architect for a building in his own district is required to give notice of the fact to the London County Council, who appoint another district surveyor, generally from an adjoining district, to see that such building is erected in conformity with the provisions of the Building Act. After a short interval the positions are possibly reversed, and the first-mentioned district surveyor finds himself officially supervising the work of the *pro tem* district surveyor in *his* district. There can be no doubt that it is bad in principle for any public official to be allowed to engage in private practice in any way connected with his official work, and doubtless the London County Council acted wisely when they passed their resolution prohibiting district surveyors thereafter appointed from engaging in private practice. It is somewhat curious, however, to observe how this restriction actually works. When a new district surveyor is required candidates for the position are invited by advertisement, and in response applications and testimonials are sent in to the council. Each candidate must have passed the qualifying Royal Institute of British Architects' examination; but be-

yond that equal gauge the comparative merits of the candidates are assessed upon the skill and ability they have shown in the past exercise of their profession, and, in the result, an architect is appointed who has established some reputation for designing and planning buildings, and the situation does appear somewhat ironical when it is considered that the newly-appointed surveyor must no longer exercise the talents which have secured him the appointment, but must, as it were, wrap them in a napkin and relegate them to unprolific burial.

The man who has gained a name for designing a good elevation and getting but a clever plan is forthwith to stifle his own aspirations and inspirations, and be content with looking after the height and thickness of walls, &c., and other dry provisions of the Building Act. It is to be presumed that such self-sacrifice is loyally acquiesced in, but this castration of professional ability is for some reasons to be deplored. The training necessary for the production of a good architect is not required for and should be different from that of a building surveyor, in whose case the skill to plan and design, which is a necessity in the architect, is not so much required as a thorough acquaintance with building materials. A knowledge of strains and thrusts and of workmanship is much more desirable than expertness in the more artistic branches of the architect's profession.

A SUGGESTED TRANSFER OF POWERS.

In 1885, in response to an order of my board, I presented a report embodying suggestions for improving the local public work of the metropolis. Most of these suggestions have subsequently been carried into effect by legislative enactment, but among the recommendations awaiting adoption is one for the transfer to the local authorities of the metropolis of the duties now discharged by the district surveyors. I am of opinion that public benefit and administrative economy would result from the adoption of this recommendation, and I strongly urge that, in any scheme for the reform of the local government of the metropolis, the proposed district councils should be entrusted with the supervision of building operations in their several districts.

The policy of the proposed transfer has received the endorsement of the metropolitan vestries, as will be seen from the following statement of past action in the matter. As a result of two meetings, convened by thirty-four metropolitan vestries and district boards, and held at the Town Hall, Chelsea, a memorial was forwarded, on August 5, 1890, to the Prime Minister, stating (paragraph 4) : "That, in the opinion of this conference, the office and functions of the district surveyor under the Building Acts should be in the hands of the local boards and their officers, with an appeal to the London County Council."

On February 28, 1896, a conference took place between delegates from the London County Council and from the several vestries and district boards to consider, in view of contemplated changes in the government of London, what powers should be allocated respectively to the central and district authorities, and a resolution was carried similar in effect to that set forth above. The London County Council representatives did not vote on this resolution, and the committee of the council subsequently reported adversely to the view adopted by the conference, and that recommendation of the committee has since been confirmed by the full council. This line of action, however, was only to be expected, as the council has always been opposed to parting with power, whilst showing a ready disposition to undertake new functions—the more important the better. On March 16, 1894, in giving evidence before the Royal Commission on the Amalgamation of the City and County of London, I submitted (*inter alia*) the following statement :—

"Upon the occasion of the delegates from the conference on the Public Health (Amendment) Bill waiting upon the Local Government Board, on June 25, 1891, the Right Hon. C. T. Ritchie stated that it was his desire and intention in the District Councils Bill, which he hoped shortly to introduce, to enlarge the scope of usefulness and responsibilities of the local authorities. In connection with such statement it may be fitly asked, What duty more desirable and important can be cast upon the local authority than the responsibility of seeing that the buildings within its district are erected in a sound, substantial manner, suitable for human occupation, with due regard to fire risks and health risks of the general community? As urged in the memorial above referred to, all such work should be vested in the local authority, as is the case in provincial towns. Drawings for each new building should be deposited, the intended drainage, depth of foundation, line of frontage, open spaces, water supply and sanitary arrangements should be clearly shown. Upon the said drawings being approved the work should be executed under the supervision of the local authority, and on satisfactory completion a certificate given, which could be

* A paper read by Mr. William Weaver, M.I.C.E., F.S.I., before the members of the Surveyors' Institution on the 12th inst.

affixed inside the building. Such certificate would be of great advantage, both to the owner of and the individual contemplating residence in the house. Unauthorised alteration of the drains or sanitary arrangements, when completed as aforesaid, should be punishable at law. At the present time, after a drain has been completed, tested and passed by the vestry's officials, there is nothing to prevent the occupier or other person making, without notice, some alteration which may entirely destroy the perfection of the drain.

"In effecting any change on the lines hereinbefore advocated, Parliament would, of course, take care that no injustice should accrue to the present district surveyors, and the work of the future would have to be safeguarded by precautions being taken to ensure proper knowledge and experience on the part of the officials undertaking the transferred duties. One of the risks under this head is in the case of small districts where the work is not sufficiently extensive or responsible to justify the appointment of a properly-qualified man at a sufficient salary to give the whole of his time to his public duties. No public surveyor should be allowed to practise privately; the defects of such a dual system are well known and need not be dilated on here.

"The above difficulty (as to small districts) may be met by uniting two or more together, so as to create districts with a population of about 200,000 each. Such an enlarged district could afford to pay for the whole time of a properly-qualified surveyor or engineer, who would have no difficulty in finding ample scope for the useful employment of his skill. The work of a fairly large district can be better and more economically executed than that of a very small district, especially where the local authority performs it own work instead of executing it by the aid of contractors."

It will be seen from the preceding extract that my desire was to protect the present district surveyors from any unjust treatment; and I would take this opportunity of assuring those gentlemen—many of whom I am pleased to count as personal friends—that I have always been careful when advocating the transfer of their duties to emphasise the necessity of protecting their interests in the event of any change of the kind being effected.

It is possible, of course, that some individual cases of hardship may occur, but to anyone acquainted with the working work of London it must be apparent that the duties of district surveyor and parish surveyor should be discharged by one official corresponding to the borough engineer and surveyor in the towns throughout the rest of England. If the two offices were amalgamated, the district surveyor would in some parishes probably be the best man to discharge the duties of the combined office, and in other parishes the present engineers and surveyors would be fully equal to the task. At any rate, individual interest must not be allowed to stand in the way of public advantage, and if the latter demands a change there will be no more difficulty in getting qualified engineers and surveyors for the London district councils than is experienced in the large towns throughout the kingdom.

These points I strongly urged when reporting to my board on the London Streets and Buildings Bill, as the following extract will show:—

"It is a bad system to have two district surveyors, one responsible to the council and the other serving the local authority, and both going over the same ground and to a certain extent over the same work. The two officers should be rolled into one, responsible to the local authority, and discharging the same duties as now performed by the borough surveyors throughout the kingdom. The vestry will understand that the suggested amalgamation of offices is not proposed in the interests of the professional class of which I am a member, but is simply made in the interest of the government of the metropolis. Many of the district surveyors are better qualified to undertake the work of the local surveyors than the latter are to absorb the functions of the former, but, whenever such assimilation of officers does take place, properly-qualified men would be appointed to each locality, and that without injustice to any present surveyor, district or local."

SOME  ARGUMENTS.

In view of the general unanimity of the present local authorities on the question, the members of this Institution can hardly fail to be convinced that it is for the advantage of the public generally and for the convenience of the profession itself that the proposed change of administration should take place. In support of the policy of change I would submit the following considerations which have induced me to propose the suggested transfer of powers and amalgamation of duties under the Building Acts and Metropolis Management Acts.

I am distinctly of opinion that anyone desirous of developing an estate or erecting a building should be able to ascertain at the town hall of the district everything required by the public authorities relative to such building or estate. At the present time an applicant is informed, on attending at the town hall, that he must give the vestry seven days' notice before commencing the excavation of foundations, and must give concurrent notice to the district surveyor as to the commencement of building operations, and submit drawings of the proposed buildings for the approval of the district surveyor; but the local authority has no power to call for such drawings, the seven days' notice to them being only required in order to afford an opportunity of serving a counter

notice to keep the foundations up to a certain level, so as to insure proper drainage.

Should the applicant desire to develop some building land, he is referred to the London County Council, to whom he must first submit (in duplicate) plans of intended roads. The county council forward one of the copies to the vestry, and, guided more or less by their recommendation, approve or refuse them. Having received sanction to his plan for laying out the roads, the applicant becomes anxious to construct sewers, and is then told to send in duplicate plans to the vestry, who upon approving them forward one copy to the London County Council for their sanction. After this double reverse process, generally taking considerable time, the applicant, having succeeded in getting his plans of roads and sewers passed, proceeds to build, generally constructing the sewer first, this work being carried out under the supervision and to the satisfaction of the vestry. The foundations of the buildings are then proceeded with, the vestry surveyor attending to look after the level and frontage line. Simultaneously the district surveyor attends to look after the foundation site, with regard to the necessity for concrete and the thickness of walls and spread of footings.

The attendance of the vestry surveyor then ceases until the house drainage work is commenced, of which seven days' notice has to be given to the vestry, under whose supervision the whole of the work (in addition to water supply) has to be satisfactorily carried out. In alterations to buildings and in the erection of blocks of flats, building work and sanitary work will be found progressing simultaneously, and the district surveyor may be found looking after the proper construction of a wall, while the vestry surveyor is seeing to the soil pipe attached to it. Generally speaking, in the majority of buildings the drainage work is executed after the carcase of the building is completed, and it may be found, as in past cases, that the building, though erected in accordance with plans passed by the district surveyor under the Building Act, does not conform to the by-laws framed under the Public Health Act by the London County Council, and enforced and supervised by the vestry. Several such cases having occurred in Kensington, the London County Council were requested (March 16, 1894) to furnish the district surveyors with copies of the by-laws under the Public Health Act, with an instruction not to approve plans submitted to them under the Building Act when such plans showed intended violations of the council's by-laws. The council, in reply (April 14, 1894), considered it inexpedient to give such instructions to the district surveyors, whose duties were prescribed by the Building Acts. In consequence, at present it occasionally occurs that notice has to be served by the vestry requiring a newly-built structure to be altered and amended in order to meet the requirements of the council's by-laws.

Further overlapping supervision and occasional clashing arise with respect to lines of building frontage and the laying out of new streets, and also in relation to arches or vaults under public ways. With regard to the former, the district surveyor is entitled to special fees under sec. 155 of the Act, and as to the latter the fees are fixed under Schedule 3, Part I., of the Act.

Concurrently with the district surveyor's supervision of frontage lines and of the laying out of new streets, the vestry's surveyor is exercising similar supervision, with the additional work of setting out the levels of the new streets and their intersections. With regard to vaults under footways, the district surveyor's duty is limited to looking after the brickwork in relation to the span of the arch, and he has no power to disapprove any work provided it fulfils the conditions laid down in the Building Act; but the vestry's requirements, which their surveyor has to enforce, may demand 50 per cent. thicker head walls, set back 2 ft. from the kerb line, backed up with concrete, with 2 ft. of space for electric, gas and water mains, &c, left between the crown of the vaults and the paving.

Again, with regard to setting back buildings to be erected on open spaces within 20 ft. of the centre of the road, both the district surveyor and parish surveyor have corresponding duties, and it occasionally happens that the former, in approving building plans submitted to him, loses sight of the fact that the abutting highway is under the full width, and the parish surveyor has afterwards to stop the building work in progress.

If the work of the proposed new district councils for London followed the course of procedure adopted in all other towns throughout England these difficulties and cases of overlapping jurisdiction would not occur. In Leeds, Birmingham, Manchester, &c., by attending at the borough or town surveyor's office, anyone can obtain all information necessary for his guidance in carrying out any building operations, and the advantages of this simplicity of procedure should not be denied solely to the metropolitan districts, many of which at the present time exceed in population and rateable value most of the provincial towns possessing the advantage of self-government.

Another difficulty under the present system in London arises from the district surveyor having no knowledge of or responsibility as to the sewers. Plans for buildings at the rear of old houses are approved by him, notwithstanding the existence of sewers running under the site of the new building, which it is illegal to erect in such position, but which unless discovered by the vestry within six months from completion cannot be demolished. The connection of the district surveyor with any new building ceases on its completion and the payment of his fees; there is no subsequent periodical inspection to detect violations of the law after the completion of the building. If such inspections were made I suspect that many infringements of the Building Act would be discovered, notably the erection of sheds and buildings in back yards, with consequent increased fire risks and reduction of air space. If the Building Act was administered by the local authorities the drawings of each building would be lodged with them; such drawings would show the situation and construction of the building, its drainage, sanitary adjuncts, water supply, and open spaces attached to the premises, and the present officers to the local authorities, in making their regular inspections at short intervals, would be able to note any recent alterations to the premises.

As before stated, the district surveyors are remunerated by fees, out of which their assistants have to be paid, and it is unreasonable to expect the surveyor to provide and pay a body of perambulating assistants to the serious diminution of his nett income. I believe I am correct in stating that most of the cases of dangerous structures are notified to the district surveyor by the vestry surveyor, and it must be borne in mind that the district surveyor is not entitled to charge his fee for surveying any dangerous structure until directed by the council to make such survey, as under sec. 103 of the Act the existence of the dangerous structure must be notified to the council before an instruction for its survey is given by them. Under the present system, too, much is left to chance; it is nobody's duty to find out or discover dangerous structures, and the collapse of a building may be the first intimation of its dangerous condition.

I am of opinion that no fees should be charged in respect of new buildings or dangerous structures. At the present time the supervision of drainage and sanitary work, water supply, and regular sanitary inspection, are undertaken by the local authority and the expense thereof borne by the rates, and I fail to see any sound reason why one principle should not apply to the whole work of supervision.

### Metropolitan Local Authorities.

In amending the local government of the metropolis it is very desirable that the responsibilities and duties of the district councils should be enlarged beyond their present scope and limitations, in order to dignify the position of the members and raise the status of the chief officials. The latter should not, of course, become the masters of the councils, but at the same time they should be able men, fitted to discharge their duties fearlessly without any sacrifice of independence.

In support of my opinion as to the desirability of raising the tone of local administration, I would refer to the report of the Royal Commission on London Government (hereinbefore alluded to), and to the remarks made on June 25, 1891, by the Right Hon. C. T. Ritchie on receiving a deputation of delegates from a conference on the Public Health (Amendment) Bill. Mr. Ritchie (as I have mentioned) stated that it was his desire and intention in the District Councils Bill, which he hoped shortly to introduce, to enlarge the scope of usefulness and responsibilities of the local authorities. The report aforesaid of the Royal Commission states (page 17):—

" P. 47.—We have now to consider what the functions of the new corporation should be and its relations to the subordinate local authorities, especially to that of the Old City. As we have already intimated, we think the resettlement of the government of the Old City should be made on lines which are capable of being more or less rapidly adopted in the other component parts of London, so that the organisation may be regarded as an example to be followed."

" P. 48.—In developing this principle we think that everything possible should be done to maintain the strength, authority and dignity of the local bodies of London; and that in the partition of functions between the Corporation of London and local authorities the former should be relieved of all administrative details for which its intervention is not really necessary, and the latter should be entrusted with every duty they can conveniently discharge. In case of doubt our inclinations would lean to the allotment of functions to the local bodies, and we believe that in cases where uniformity of action is necessary this may often be best secured by giving to the corporation the authority to frame by-laws which should be locally administered, with provision, however, for the intervention of the corporation to secure their enforcement should they be neglected."

I therefore submit that the interests of the community would be served by casting upon any new district councils to be created for the future local government of London the duties now discharged by the district surveyors under the London Building Acts, and that the cost of carrying out such duties should be a charge upon the general rate of each district.

Finally, I beg to assure the members of the Institution that in recommending the foregoing alterations or reforms I have no personal object to gain—my official career is rapidly approaching its termination—and I simply place my views on record as honest convictions resulting from a life's working experience; and I am strongly of opinion if the District

Councils Bill for the improvement of the local government of the metropolis is shortly introduced (as promised) into Parliament, it should provide for the single, complete, systematic and regular supervision of all buildings on the lines I have advocated.

### DISCUSSION.

Mr. T. Blashill, superintending architect to the London County Council, said that in proposing a vote of thanks to Mr. Weaver he wished to recognise that gentleman's experience and the way in which he had brought it to bear upon that particular question. At the same time he was bound to disagree with much in the paper. The contention seemed to be that the Building Act was badly carried out by the district surveyors, and would be better administered by the surveyors to the vestries and district boards. He was disappointed with Mr. Weaver's evidence, for the points put forward were chiefly matters of opinion. Mr. Weaver might have enlarged more upon the available evidence, for no man had had a larger experience. He wished to refer to some points in the paper one by one. It was true that the district surveyors had the duty of supervising buildings, and he was quite convinced that anything that did not come under their cognisance in connection with building details was quite unimportant. The number of district surveyors now debarred from private practice was thirteen out of sixty-five. The change had been made by the London County Council about eight or nine years ago, after the most careful consideration. He was astonished to find the remark that " prior to the passing of the order prohibiting private practice the office of district surveyor was sought, not so much for the direct income attaching to it, but for the opportunities afforded for enlarging the private practice of the official." Mr. Weaver must have been misinformed. He (the speaker) had been a district surveyor for eleven years, and he had only once taken a job in his own district, and he had always regretted it. The advantage derived by district surveyors in this way was not worth considering. Mr. Weaver's remarks about one district surveyor supervising the private work of another in an adjoining district could only mean that they played into each other's hands. If the remarks did not mean that they meant nothing. The remark had also been made that district surveyors were appointed for their proficiency in design. His own experience was that the men who went in for the work were skilled not so much in design as in the more practical kinds of work. The idea that the training of an architect was not necessary for a district surveyor was really fallacious. There was really no ground for it. What had the district surveyor to do? He must have a good knowledge of architectural and building work, to begin with, and buildings had to be erected to his satisfaction. The recent Building Act had enlarged his responsibilities. To put such work into the hands of anyone not an architect would be wrong. How the parish surveyor would deal with the work he did not know, nor could he imagine how he would appear before the tribunal of appeal, which was composed, not of three engineers, but of three architects and surveyors, one of whom also combined the qualifications of a barrister. Mr. Weaver had also referred to the action of the London County Council in connection with the conference of delegates from that body and from the vestries and district boards in regard to transfer of powers. He (Mr. Blashill) ought to know as much of that as anyone, and he could assure those present that the officers of the London County Council had been distinctly instructed by the committee to examine the whole question carefully, to see if there was anything that could be handed over to the smaller authorities. The committee desired the help of the officers, not to retain the work in their own hands, but to hand it over to the vestries and district boards. He quite agreed with Mr. Weaver that the districts should be large, but he disputed the statement that there were two district surveyors. There was one only, for the surveyor to the vestry or the district board was not a district surveyor. He did not see much in the objection that the builder had to give notice in two different places. Nobody complained, so far as he knew. The duties of the two classes of officers were entirely distinct, and he did not see any sufficient reason why there should not be two. The same mistake was made in speaking of the frontage line. The district surveyor looked after the frontage of individual buildings, and the other surveyor looked after the frontage line of the street—two entirely different things. In the event of any infringement of the building line the surveyor to the local authority could complain. He would be sorry to say anything that would reflect upon parish surveyors, but only one out of forty-five belonged to the Royal Institute of British Architects, and only eight out of forty-five belonged to the Surveyors' Institution. Mr. Weaver had spoken slightingly of the examination of the Royal Institute of British Architects for district surveyors, but surely it was the most important of all examinations for them. What examinations did the parish surveyors pass to demonstrate their fitness to undertake the duties of district surveyors? One of the great advantages possessed by district surveyors was that they were independent—a qualification to which both Parliament and the Local Government Board attached great importance. The same could not be said of the parish surveyor. After giving the details of a case in illustration of this point, Mr. Blashill went on to say that it was not merely a case of the fitness of the surveyor to the local authorities, but of those bodies themselves. Vestries and district boards had before now tried to get rid of spaces in front of houses, merely for the sake of increasing the rates. As to dangerous structures, Mr. Weaver seemed to be afraid that a good many buildings fell down without notice, but he (Mr. Blashill) did not know of anything that had happened which could have been prevented by the district surveyor. Officials going about looking for dangerous structures would become an unbearable nuisance. He thought that the fees should certainly be paid by the builder, and this applied particularly to dangerous structures, for why should the owner of a block of slum buildings get off scot free? He did not know if the parish surveyor was prepared to do the work himself. There was no point that Parliament and the London County Council were more anxious about than that this work should not be done by a clerk or a low-paid official. How was the parish surveyor to survey these buildings himself? The London County Council had taken steps to ensure that the district surveyor would attend to the work personally. The parish surveyor would have a very disagreeable work to do without the consolation of the fees drawn by the district surveyor.

Mr. ALEXANDER PAYNE, district surveyor for South-East Hackney and North Bow, seconded the vote of thanks, but said that from the first word to the last he entirely disagreed with the paper. Mr. Weaver seemed to mix up two totally distinct offices. The parish surveyor was more of a civil engineer, whose duty was to look after sewerage, roads, and other matters, most important duties no doubt, but entirely different from the carrying out of the Building Act. Mr. Weaver was evidently of opinion that the duties of a surveyor did not require the systematic training of an architect; but in disproof of that statement it was only necessary to point to sec. 78, sec. 5 (27), and other sections. Was it possible for anyone without the training of an architect to be responsible for these matters? The duties could not be carried out by a sanitary engineer. They would have to be delegated to an assistant. How would the architects of public buildings care to have their work supervised by the parish surveyors? Was the parish surveyor qualified to carry out the legal part of the work, and could the supervision of dangerous structures be entrusted to those who had not a life-long experience? The author of a paper assumed that the present system of supervision was bad, though he was evidently of opinion that it was due, not to the law, but to the method of carrying it out. They should remember, however, that the system had been in operation for about fifty years, and had given every satisfaction. Dr. Longstaff had said that serious accidents were uncommon, owing to the skill of the men who had carried out the Act, and Sir John Hutton had expressed the opinion that the system had worked very well. He emphatically denied Mr. Weaver's statement that district surveyors took office with the object of increasing their private practice. There had scarcely been a single change of corruption on the part of district surveyors during the past fifty years. One peculiarity about the work of district surveyors was the great variation in the fees, and the author had proposed population as a basis. But in an outlying district which was being opened up there might be far more building going on than in a thickly-populated district, and thus population was no test. It was a great mistake to alter the status of a district surveyor from that a practising architect. He had never heard any objections to the present system. They rarely, if ever, heard of a district surveyor who was too busy with private work to carry out his duties under the Building Act, and in any case he could be asked to resign. It would be the fault of the individual rather than of the system. They were told that the object of the author's proposals was to raise the status of the parish officials and dignify the local bodies; but would these objects justify them in altering a system that had worked well for fifty years and attempting an experiment which could only end disastrously?

Mr. WM. WOODWARD said there was a general opinion in favour of the relaxation of rules if building operations were not to be hampered. He certainly thought Mr. Blashill and Mr. Payne had entirely and absolutely misapprehended the object of the paper. Mr. Weaver had not said that parish surveyors should take the place of district surveyors, and he did not condemn the latter. As a practical architect he (Mr. Woodward) could appreciate the advantage of going to one central authority. Why should not an architect be able to carry out the duties now carried out by the vestry surveyor? Mr. Weaver had not said that the district surveyor or the official proposed should not be an architect. There was no necessity for an art architect to supervise buildings. The ordinary practical architect was quite capable of doing that. He had had large experience of district surveyors, three of whom had continually hampered him, not for substantial reasons, but for trivialities. They simply pointed to the Act, and said " That is the Act we have to administer." If that was so they might just as well have a clerk of works, and he could not understand why Mr. Payne should have attacked Mr. Weaver so vigorously. Of course it was not to be expected that district surveyors would sit quietly and allow themselves to be wiped out. Mr. Weaver's proposal, as he understood it, was that the whole thing should be centralised. The reference to salaries might have been left

out, but with that exception he agreed with every word, and thanked Mr. Weaver for his paper.

Mr. H. H. COLLINS, district surveyor for the eastern division of the City, after an expression of personal regard for the writer of the paper, whom he had known for a great number of years, regretted that the paper should have been written at all, and that it should have contained so many misconceptions and innuendoes. The title of the paper might have been "The Desirability of Transferring District Surveyors to the Local Authorities," and it seemed to have originated in the Westminster accident. As he was engaged in that case he could give them the exact details, and he assured them that the district surveyor had nothing whatever to do with it. An erroneous view had been taken of the powers of the county council and the district surveyor under the Act. He regretted that the remarks in regard to the motives of district surveyors in taking office had ever been made, especially when he thought of the eminent men, such as Donaldson, Kerr, Aitchison, Wyatt and others, who had held office. He admired Mr. Weaver's courage in appearing there, for the council of their institution had expressed the strongest opinions in favour of maintaining the original status of the district surveyor. Similar views had been expressed by the Royal Institute of British Architects and the Institute of Builders. Surely those bodies represented the interests chiefly involved. He had heard no complaint except from Mr. Weaver. The present policy of the London County Council was most illegal, and he would like to see it tested. No complaints had been made as to the remuneration of district surveyors by fees. Then why should they change, simply for the sake of a change? Mr. G. M. Freeman, Q.C., had stated before the House of Commons' Committee on the London Building Act that the district surveyors were independent of the London County Council. That body made the appointments, but were not responsible for the actions of the surveyors. No one but a practical architect could know the difficulties that were constantly arising, and what was required was an architect and building surveyor rolled into one. Mr. Weaver's suggestions had been before the public for twenty years. It had been stated in the paper that the district surveyor had no chance of seeing the work again after approval, but within fourteen days after completion the district surveyor had the right of interfering with anything he thought wrong. Under sec. 163 the district surveyor was bound to give notice to the London County Council if he found anything done in contravention of the Act, and the council took action. The functions of the district surveyor were clearly laid down. Many recently-appointed district surveyors had applied for the position now held by Mr. Blashill, but were not considered fit to take his place. Thus it seemed that the district surveyors now appointed were scarcely equal to those appointed under former conditions. Mr. Collins concluded by proposing a motion condemning the views expressed in Mr. Weaver's paper, but the president said the motion was unnecessary, as the institution was in no way committed to the views in question.

On the motion of Mr. DOUGLAS MATTHEWS, district surveyor for Stoke Newington, seconded by Mr. H. LOVEGROVE, district surveyor for South Islington, Shoreditch and Norton Folgate, the discussion was adjourned until January 9, 1899.

## MEETING IN GLASGOW.

A meeting of the members practising in Scotland was held in the Masonic Halls, Glasgow, on Wednesday last, when there was a good attendance, over which Mr. Thomas Binnie, presided. It was reported that the membership had been largely increased since last meeting, and now included surveyors, estate factors and valuators practising in various districts of Scotland— from Orkney to Dumfries— and the number was expected to be further augmented before the 31st inst., after which it will be necessary to qualify for admission by examination. Records of legal decisions, statistics and other items of professional information are being published for the use of members.

Mr. Binnie afterwards delivered an interesting address, in which he referred particularly to the responsibility of surveyors and the large interest involved in advising clients as to matters connected with heritage. He referred, as an instance, to the case of Glasgow alone, where the annual rateable value is now above £4,300,000 and the probable capital value about £100,000,000. The rental of the city, increasing at the rate of £100,000 per annum represents a capital increase of probably more than £2,000,000. Besides the growth of the city, several other causes were referred to as leading to changes in the value of properties, such as the changes in mode of locomotion, improvements on the river Clyde, and the operations of the city improvement trustees and railway companies. Mr. Binnie gave many interesting reminiscences, and then drew particular attention to the concentration of traffic, owing to the principal railway stations being situated in such close proximity, and the tendency following thereon to increase the height of central buildings. He hailed with satisfaction the attempt now being made to set some limit to the height of business premises, and to secure that business shall be conducted under conditions consistent with health and safety. Mr. Binnie was cordially thanked for his instructive and valuable paper.

## CORRESPONDENCE.

**Automatic Gas Meters and Cookers.**—Mr. Edward A. Harman, Corporation Gasworks, Huddersfield, writes: As a side issue to the engineering world, the rapid development of the penny-in-the-slot system, which has astonished the millions, demands something more than a passing notice. Perhaps one of the most surprising adaptations is that for gas distribution. The enormous success of this system is possibly due mainly to the reasonable desire of the public for knowing what they are buying, the cash payment, and also to the immense popularity of the pennyworth. To such a state of perfection have automatic gas meters been brought, that it is impossible to foresee to what extent they will be ultimately extended. It is probable in the near future that different rooms, workshops, offices, &c., of the same institution will control the consumption of what is required for lighting and heating purposes by automatic interception meters, rather than allow an indefinite quantity of gas to be used without regard to cost, as in many cases existing at present. Such waste not only affects the cost of production of materials, but also the health of the workers, which is of the first importance. It may be found advantageous, where rooms are let as apartments in houses or hotels, to allow each tenant to be responsible for their own amount of gas, in preference to the unsatisfactory fixed charges so generally made. For internal arrangements in workshops slot meters might be employed by a mutual arrangement with the head of the department and the employees. Of course in such a case the meter would be the property of those directly concerned. The meters, being fixed in a passage or landing, can easily be available for examination and collection from time to time. In cases of illness the ready check afforded upon the consumption of a bed-room stove is a satisfactory element. Applications for automatic meters are so numerous that few gas undertakings can afford to be independent of the assistance afforded by them. It is not so much the financial side of the matter, as revenue earners, that has to be considered as the popularising of gas in every home, office or workshop. It has recently been pointed out that for city and town offices a gas fire is perhaps as useful a system of heating as can well be used, no attention being required from the time the stove is lit in the morning to when it is turned off at night, thus saving not only time in this, but avoiding annoyance of too large or too small a fire and other attendant inconveniences. For bed-rooms gas fires are becoming increasingly popular. Where properly fixed and connected by a flue direct into the chimney this method of heating is peculiarly suitable. The temperature of a room can be maintained most evenly night and day, which in severe cases of illness is of immense importance, while the necessity for making the fire up, and thereby disturbing a patient, are dispensed with. There is, moreover, the additional important consideration that the fire is always available. To those affected with asthmatical, bronchial or kindred complaints this cannot afford to be disregarded, especially considering the liability of a sudden attack, which often occurs in the middle of the night, when some hours must frequently necessarily elapse before a coal fire can be got ready. If this notice were from a medical point of view, instead of from an engineering one, much might be said upon this subject. The omission of reference to the convenience obtainable in cases of illness would, however, render any notice of gas fires incomplete. Many gas undertakings are now recognising the importance of giving every facility for supplying gas fires, and are fixing them free of cost, only making a nominal annual charge for the stove. The undertaking of which I have the honour to be the engineer is doing this with good results. In consequence of what has come to be known as the "fixed free" stove business, numerous stove and meter makers have been inundated with orders, the delays occasioned in consequence being vexing alike to the consumer and the gas officials. The method of calculating the desirability of adopting this penny-in-the-slot system is most simple. My experience is that for an ordinary automatic meter for lighting purposes only the annual gas consumption therefrom equals 10,000 cubic feet, and where a small cooker is supplied this consumption is doubled. This quantity of gas at the profit on cost of manufacture per 1,000 ft. will furnish the income available as interest on the small original outlay, depreciation, and the extra cost of collection. From 20 to 35 cubic feet of gas for 1d. is the general charge. An ordinary flat-flame burner, consuming 5 ft. per hour, will thus last from four to seven hours, or where an incandescent burner is used consuming from 3 to 4 cubic feet per hour the time the pennyworth will last is proportionately longer. Generally speaking, gas undertakings supply fittings, burners, meter and stove free of cost, so that the consumer's maximum liability is only 1d. The addition of a small cooking stove is as great a convenience comparatively in small-class property as in large, where gas cooking stoves are considered well nigh indispensable. Such a development in one of the branches of the great engineering profession is truly astounding.

**The Sewerage of Johannesburg.**—"Young Natalian" writes: I notice a footnote in your paper of October 28th, in which you say that "the Transvaal Government has arranged to inaugurate an adequate sewerage scheme for Johannesburg," and that "the sewerage contract has been granted, &c."

As your information has been culled from *The Standard and Diggers' News*, a Government organ, I am not by any means surprised at the ingenious manner in which this "latest vile bit of jobbery" has been published; but, lest you or any of your many readers should be deceived, I hasten to give you the facts of the case. At the outset it must be understood that nearly all public works in the Transvaal are carried out by those who have had concessions granted for this purpose; the usual method of securing a concession is by bribery. It is purely a matter of "the highest bidder gets the job." To tender for work on the approved system which obtains in Great Britain is useless in the Transvaal, for the whole system of Government is against this. Bribery is rife from the President to the postboy. Mr. Editor, I hardly need to point out to you that to secure a good road, for instance, one at least must employ independent supervision. What think you, then, of a contractor who secures a concession for carrying out a sewerage scheme and acts as his own engineer as well? If it were a less serious matter one might surely laugh to think of a contractor laying to "bone" and jointing (?) pipes in waterlogged ground and then "passing" these pipes himself! Moreover, not only has a contractor this power, but a right to compel every owner of property to connect with his sewers and pay his own price for the work, no person having authority to choose his own plumber or workman at a reasonable figure, but he must submit to this iniquitous system imposed upon him merely for the purpose of filling the pockets of Government officials! Here are a few clauses in the new agreement: (a) £5 per year for each water-closet containing not more than one collecting trough or pail, and £5 for every additional pail; (b) £5 per year for the removal of bath water or dirt; (c) the foregoing tariffs under (b) shall be applicable to private buildings containing not more than seven apartments—in the case of larger buildings and hotels, boarding-houses, theatres and other buildings the tariffs shall be increased *pro rata*; (d) all Government offices shall be served without payment. How truly noble and unselfish the Government are is revealed in this clause (d). Mr. Editor, you have in brief outline (for I fear to encroach further on your valuable space) an account of what has occurred between the Transvaal Government and its contractors. The concession is known throughout South Africa as the "latest bit of vile jobbery."

## DISTRICT SURVEYORS.

The Bermondsey Vestry were informed by the General Purposes Committee on Monday that the London County Council had forwarded a letter on the subject of district surveyors. The council stated that the Building Act Committee, who had had under consideration the representations made by different local authorities, had arrived at the following conclusions upon the points raised:—

(1) That the suggestion that all district surveyors should devote the whole of their time to the duties of district surveying could not be carried out without obtaining Parliamentary power; the committee would, however, point out that the principle advocated is being gradually adopted by the council as fresh appointments are made, thirteen district surveyors having already been appointed who give their whole time to the duties of their office.

(2) That the question of paying district surveyors by salary having been considered by the council on two occasions, the committee are not at present prepared to alter the existing system of payment by fees until they have had further experience of its working.

(3) That although the proposal that an office should be provided for the district surveyor at the local vestry hall has much to recommend it, the committee do not see their way to recommend the council to take any steps in the direction indicated, as, unfortunately, the districts do not coincide with the local government areas, and Parliamentary power might be required before the suggestion could be carried out.

(4) That a notice should be printed and posted up in the office of each district surveyor explaining that the authority of the district surveyor does not extend to drains, water-closets, or other sanitary matters, which in accordance with the Metropolis Management Acts, and the Public Health (London) Act, 1891, are under the control of local authorities. This notice will be prepared and issued by the council to the district surveyors in due course.

The General Purposes Committee expressed the opinion that the fourth clause would be of little use, as in the majority of cases builders do not personally attend at the office of the district surveyor, and that even if they did so, the notice would probably not be read. The committee had therefore suggested to the county council the desirability of having a short notice printed on the letter paper of the district surveyors, giving such an explanation.

**Goole.**—At a statutory meeting of the Goole Urban District Council, held lately, it was decided to promote a Bill in the next session of Parliament authorising the council to construct new waterworks and to borrow money for the same, also for the gas undertakings and other purposes.

# Comparative Reports of General Practice.

## XXX.—TRAMWAY TRACTION : WEST BROMWICH REPORT.—VI.

THE ELECTRIC CONDUIT SYSTEM.

The sole advantage of the electric conduit system seems to be that the overhead wires and poles are removed, while the principal objections to it are the great expense, more expense than the cable system, the prolonged interference with the streets during construction and repairs, when the traffic and business is greatly impeded, the difficulty in locating any defects in the underground part of the system, the difficulty and expense of carrying out any sewerage work in streets in which there are conduits, the danger to traffic through the presence of a slot in the street varying in width from ¾ in. (the slot is wider than with the cable system), the difficulty and expense in keeping the conduit clean and maintaining satisfactory insulation, and the liability to stoppage through storms.

If the apparatus in the conduit should require repairing the work is of necessity much more difficult and expensive than with the overhead wires. No matter what precautions may be taken to ensure efficient drainage of the conduit in ordinary rain, in times of heavy storms, when the drains become overcharged, the conduit would be filled with water and mud and the tram service stopped, and could not be restarted until the water and mud had been cleared away.

Should a conduit or cable system be decided upon, it would be objectionable as regards the gas and water pipes, which are very near the surface, the concrete foundation would also be disturbed, and there would be considerable difficulty in certain parts of the town in draining the conduits, owing to there being no surface-water drains, and the sinking caused through mining operations would very considerably interfere with the conduits. With regard to the chief objection against the cable and conduit systems, it is impossible to disguise the fact—a fact which must be patent to all—that the cable and conduit systems are most expensive in construction. It may be fairly and legitimately argued that the matter of construction and the cost necessarily entailed thereby is a matter for consideration by the directors of the tramway company, as being the parties most directly interested, and not for the corporation or the ratepayers, who are but indirectly affected, and that consequently the argument as to the cost is not applicable.

In the first instance, the question of cost is one which more particularly affects the company, seeing that the obligation to provide the necessary capital rests upon the company; but the sub-committee would point out that the fact is important, as the cost of construction may eventually be a serious and very important matter to the ratepayers, seeing that upon the termination of the concession the undertaking may be purchased at its "then value," and the capital to be provided to meet the "then value" of a cable or underground conduit system would surely be considerably in excess of that to be provided for the system of overhead wires.

On the other hand, should the corporation determine to municipalise the tramways, the extra cost in construction on either of these two systems would have to be borne by the ratepayers. With regard to the objection—namely, the expense involved in maintenance and keeping the system in a thorough state of efficiency and good working order—here, again, this objection appears to be equally fatal with the first as regards the two systems named. As regards the time taken to reconstruct the lines under these two systems, there is no doubt it would take considerably longer than the overhead system, and the inconvenience would therefore be greater.

With reference to the difficulty experienced in speedily locating any defect in the conduit system, this objection is very important and one which demands earnest consideration. If the apparatus in the conduit should need repairing—and repairs at times are imperative—the work is of necessity rendered much more difficult and more expensive than with the overhead wires, and the utility of the tramways system is frequently seriously imperilled, and in order to get access to the conduit the provision of a very large number of manholes, &c., is rendered absolutely necessary.

In connection with the conduit system the hitherto insurmountable difficulty in securing and maintaining efficiency in all weathers has also to be carefully considered. In this connection it may be stated that it is not necessary to flood a conduit to bring down the insulation of the electric cable, and so cause leakage. The insulators by which the electric cable is held in position are composed of either earthenware or porcelain. These in themselves when clean are perfect insulators, that is to say, there is practically no leakage over them, but whenever they become covered with even a slight coating of moisture the insulation immediately falls and leakage begins. Again, the traffic is likely to be interrupted through the lines being blocked by snow.

The conduit system has not as yet had an extensive trial in England, Blackpool being the only town where it has been laid down; and, unfortunately, the limited experience already acquired has not been very happy or assuring, either to corporations or companies, as to its ultimate success. Mr. W. G. Laws, city engineer of Newcastle-on-Tyne, in reporting to the corporation states that at Blackpool, where the conduit system was laid and promised well for a time, when taken over by the corporation it gave so much trouble, owing to excessive leakage and consequent deterioration of the apparatus generally, that for some time it has to be worked by horses. A moist climate is unfavourable to the rather delicate apparatus and promotes leakage of energy by keeping the conductors damp, and would presumably require very close attention to keep the tube clean.

Taking, therefore, all the circumstances into consideration, and weighing the same with strict impartiality, the sub-committee have to report that they cannot see their way to recommend the adoption of any conduit system for West Bromwich.

OVERHEAD ELECTRIC.

*Advantages.*—The special advantages of the overhead electric system, as compared with other forms of electric traction, are: (1) Cheapness and simplicity, the latter allowing any necessary repairs to be effected with a minimum of trouble, delay and expense). In case of an accident to a trolley wire on any part of the system, which is most unusual, only that section (a ½-mile length) is thrown out of use, and it is very quickly repaired. The units of power employed in the engine-house are all coupled together, sending current through feeders to all sections of the trolley wire. An accident to one engine does not affect the running of the cars, as another spare engine can immediately be run to take its place. (2) The rapidity with which the lines can be reconstructed and the comparatively small interference with the surface of the streets and traffic, as compared with the conduit system. (3) The overhead system is less liable to leakage than the underground system. (4) The overhead system is the most efficient, taken as a whole, of mechanical traction, which has hitherto been demonstrated by practical working.

*Disadvantages.*—The disadvantages and objections usually urged against this system are: (1) The unsightly and objectionable appearance of the poles and wires. (2) The danger of overhead telephone wires, &c., breaking and falling on the highly-charged trolley wires. (3) The danger of the highly-charged trolley wires breaking and coming into contact with persons passing near them; but the trolley wires are very strong and breakages are almost unknown. These dangers can, however, be completely guarded against by the exercise of due precautions and the use of proper appliances. The sub-committee only heard of one case of wires breaking in the places visited by them. (4) The danger of the electrolysis of gas and water mains, owing to the return current being taken by the rails. This would also refer to the conduit system.

*Remarks.*—With regard to the unsightly and objectionable appearance of the poles and wires, the deputation are of opinion that the advantages outweigh the disadvantages, and with neat and ornamental poles judiciously used for electric lighting they rather add to than detract from the appearance of the streets, and they can be erected so as not to offend the eye; and the sub-committee feel convinced that the public will soon become reconciled to the poles and wires, and will cease to notice them as soon as they become acquainted with the advantages afforded by this mode of traction. The overhead system of tramways has been carried through the principal streets of Rome, and particularly through the magnificent ruins of the Capitol, without causing any adverse comment. At Milan the overhead system has been admitted almost into the precincts of its magnificent cathedral. If this system has not destroyed the beauties of these places, residents in West Bromwich and surrounding districts need not fear that the appearance of any street in this district will be spoilt. We started our investigations more or less in sympathy with this objection, but where the system is carried out in the most approved manner we found that the wires gave only the very slightest offence to the eye, and that a few hours' familiarity removed the objections previously held. The simplicity which characterises the overhead system must be self-evident to anyone impartially studying the question. It is essentially clean, safe and comfortable in its application, as well as being under perfect control. It has distinctly passed the experimental stage in every particular and in every detail. The very simplicity of the system enables any necessary repairs to be effected with a minimum of trouble, inconvenience, delay or expense, being under all circumstances the most accessible for purposes of maintenance and repair. The rapidity with which the lines can be constructed or converted, and the comparatively small interference with the surface of the streets and general street traffic, is another argument which strongly demonstrates the superiority and efficiency of the system over the conduit system. Again, where standards of artistic design, with ornamental arms or brackets on either side of the centre pole, are placed in the centre of the roadway, arc lamps can be attached and the poles used with much advantage for the electric lighting of the streets from the same station as would supply the power for working and lighting the tramcars, thus removing the necessity for another set of poles on the causeways or in the roadway. This would certainly be an advantage in more senses than one. There is little or no leakage from this system, and it is very little affected by either rain or snow, except that the rails must be kept clean, as they must be in any system of tramways. The municipal authorities of the most important cities in England and Scotland have, we are informed, after exhaustive inquiries and consideration decided in favour of overhead electric traction—for instance, Liverpool, Manchester, Sheffield, Bradford, Hull, Leeds, Glasgow, Birkenhead, Nottingham and Bristol. The sub-committee are of opinion that this system is the best adapted for West Bromwich.

LIST OF TRAMWAY SYSTEMS WORKED BY OVERHEAD ELECTRIC TRACTION.

| Location of line. | By whom worked | Date of opening. | Length of route. miles. | Total length of track. miles. | Gauge. ft. in. |
|---|---|---|---|---|---|
| Bristol ... | Company | { Oct., 1895 }<br>{ Oct., 1897 } | 6 | 10 | 4 8½ |
| Coventry ... | Company | Dec., 1895 | 6 | 6 | 3 6 |
| Dover ... | Corporation | Sep., 1897 | 3·5 | 4·5 | 3 6 |
| Dublin ... | Company | { May, 1896 }<br>{ Nov.,1897 } | 8<br>3 | 15<br>6 | 5 3<br>5 3 |
| Hartlepool ... | Company | May, 1896 | 2·56 | 3·4 | 3 6 |
| Kidderminster | Company | May, 1897 | 4·48 | 4·72 | 3 6 |
| Leeds... ... | Corporation | Aug., 1897 | 7 | 14 | 4 8½ |
| Walsall ... | Company | Jan., 1893 | 8 | 8·5 | 3 6 |

48·54   72·12

LIST OF TOWNS IN WHICH TRAMWAYS ARE BEING LAID TO BE WORKED ON THE OVERHEAD ELECTRIC SYSTEM.

| Location of line. | By whom being constructed. | Length of proposed route. miles. | Length of proposed track. miles. | Gauge. ft. in. |
|---|---|---|---|---|
| Blackburn ... ... | Corporation | 3 | 3·4 | 4 0 |
| Bradford .. ... | Corporation | 6·31 | 9 | 4 0 |
| Cork ... ... | Company | 11 | 11 | 3 0 |
| Coventry ... ... | Company | 5·25 | 5·25 | 3 6 |
| Dublin ... ... | Company | 40 | 80 | 5 3 |
| Glasgow* ... ... | Corporation | 3 | 6 · | 4 8½ |
| Halifax ... ... | Corporation | 3·5 | 4·25 | 3 6 |
| Hull... ... ... | Corporation | 9 | 18·5 | 4 8½ |
| Liverpool* ... ... | Corporation | 3 | 6 | 4 8½ |
| Middlesbrough ... | Company | 11 | 22 | 3 6 |
| North Staffordshire | Company | 6·75 | 8 | 4 8½ |
| Norwich ... ... | Company | 19 | 19 | 3 6 |
| Oldham ... ... | Company | 8·11 | 10·35 | 3 6 |
| Plymouth ... ... | Corporation | 1·8 | 3·6 | 3 6 |
| Potteries ... ... | Company | 12·47 | 16·6 | 4 0 |
| Sheffield* ... ... | Corporation | 5·25 | 9 33 | 4 8½ |
| West Hartlepool ... | Company | 2·14 | 2·30 | 3 6 |

150·58   235·97

# THE PARLIAMENT-STREET IMPROVEMENT.

The demolition of the houses on the western side of Parliament-street, which has been proceeding for some months, is now nearly complete. So far have the operations for the purpose of widening the thoroughfare leading from the Local Government Board offices on the north side of Charles-street to the Houses of Parliament proceeded, that the formation of the site into a carriageway has been commenced. On Monday a large number of labourers were at work filling in the basements of the demolished houses, and before evening this work had so far advanced that several heavy four-horse rollers and a steam roller were engaged in smoothing the surface. The new roadway will be made and paved with wood before the meeting of Parliament. Already the effect of the improvement can be gauged. An uninterrupted view of Westminster Abbey can now be had from Whitehall, and Parliament-square, lying to the north of the abbey, is now seen to advantage.

# INSTITUTION OF CIVIL ENGINEERS.

### ORDINARY MEETING.

An ordinary meeting of the members of the above Institution will be held on Tuesday, the 10th January, 1899, at 8 p.m., when Mr. John Handsley Dales, A.M.I.C.E., will read a paper on "High-speed Engines." At this meeting a ballot for members will be taken.

### STUDENTS' MEETING.

At a meeting for the students of the Institution, on the 13th January, 1899, Dr. Archibald Barr, M.I.C.E. (Professor of Civil Engineering and Mechanics in the University of Glasgow), will deliver an address on "The Application of the Science of Mechanics to Engineering Practice." Dr. Alex. B. W. Kennedy, F.R.S. (member of council), will take the chair at 8 p.m.

* Experimental.

# ASSOCIATION OF MUNICIPAL AND COUNTY ENGINEERS.

### NEW MEMBERS.

At a meeting of the council, held on Saturday, the 17th inst., the following gentlemen were elected

*As Members—*

Frederick Ball, borough surveyor, Southwold, Suffolk.
Alfred S. Cartwright, surveyor to the urban district council, Wilmslow, Cheshire.
Thomas J. Guilbert, surveyor to the States of Guernsey.
Daniel Hinchcliffe, surveyor to the rural district council, Dorchester.
Ernest R. Matthews, surveyor to the urban district council, Bridlington.
Warden A. Moller, engineer and surveyor to Woosung, China.
Fred. W. Pearce, surveyor to the urban district council, Twickenham.
Robert M. Reid, road surveyor to Stirlingshire County Council.
Julius Spencer, surveyor to the Oakworth, Haworth and Oxenhope Urban District Councils.
George E. Vint, surveyor to the urban district council, Holmfirth.

*As Graduates—*

Bertram Bell, city engineer's office, Carlisle.
James P. Bennetts, council offices, Watford.
C. Arthur Clews, borough engineer's office, Derby.
David Ellison, Darwen.
Ernest H. Essex, engineer's office, Kettering.
Charles G. May, engineer's office, Ipswich.
George Mitchell, county engineer's office, Aberdeen.
J. Walker Smith, engineer's office, Burton-on-Trent.
John Taylor, borough surveyor's office, Colne.
W. Whitworth, Cradley Heath, Staffordshire.
Mr. Robert Henry Bicknell, A.M.I.C.E., engineering inspector to the Local Government Board, was elected an honorary member of the association.

# LONDON WATER SUPPLY COMMISSION

The forty-third sitting of the Royal Commission on the Metropolitan Water Supply was held on Monday, Lord Llandaff presiding.

Mr. CHARLES HAWKSLEY, a member of the council of the Institution of Civil Engineers, examined by the chairman, said that he was largely concerned in the designing and construction of waterworks both for local authorities and for water companies. He estimated that the population of the metropolis in 1941 might be 13,231,000, and the daily quantity of water required 463,085,000 gallons, and was decidedly of opinion that the Thames could supply all the additional water required, and considerably more. It would not be necessary to go to Wales, at any rate, for a 100 years; and it would, in his opinion, be an unnecessary precaution to secure ground without going to the expense of constructing works. In the course of further evidence he said he approved the project described to the commission by Mr. Hunter and Mr. Middleton (the engineers now engaged in carrying the authorised Staines reservoirs into execution) to enable a daily average of as much as 400,000,000 gallons to be taken from the Thames for the supply of Greater London and the outlying parts of Water London without reducing the flow at Teddington weir, so far as any increased supply of water was concerned, below 200,000,000 gallons a day, except during a drought of abnormal severity. There appeared to be a prevalent misconception in respect to the effect of the drought of this year on the findings of Lord Balfour's Commission in regard to the Thames storage scheme, but the only effect had been to necessitate a larger amount of storage than had been previously anticipated and to show that the minimum flow originally suggested of 200,000,000 gallons a day at Teddington weir was unnecessarily large. He expressed his strong preference for management by companies as compared with management by public bodies, and his belief that no advantage would result, either to the water consumer or the ratepayer, from the transfer of the water supply of London from the water companies to a public body, especially in view of the fact that control already existed to a greater extent in London than in any provincial town. He was convinced that if the precautions for the prevention of waste which were taken in provincial towns were adopted in London the consumption would be reduced to 30 gallons per head per day in a few years. He defended the existing method of levying the charges for water by a rate based on rental as compared with a supply by meter, and stated that the rates charged by the London companies compared favourably with those charged by provincial corporations.

The next meeting of the commission has been fixed for January 9th, when the examination of Mr. Hawksley will be continued.

**The Dwellings of the Poor.**—The monthly meeting of the Mansion House Council on the Dwellings of the Poor was held last week. The report showed that the number of houses inspected during the month was 557. Of these 191 were reported to the authorities.

# For Assistants and Pupils.

## THE CONSTRUCTION OF ROADS AND STREETS.—XXIII.

### By WILLIAM H. MAXWELL, Assistant Engineer and Surveyor, Leyton Urban District Council.

TOWN ROADS (continued).

I am indebted to the courtesy of Mr. John A. Brodie, M.I.C.E., city engineer, Liverpool, for the following particulars of standard specifications for paving of streets in that city, and which will serve as excellent examples of how this class of work should be carried out in districts of this character.

FIRST-CLASS SPECIFICATION.

Excavate or fill in the ground, as the case may be, to the requisite level, and remove all surplus material. Properly form and trim off the surface and thoroughly consolidate

The channel stones to be of granite or syenite, of a quality to be approved by the city engineer, and to be not less than 3 ft. in length. The upper surface, if not self-faced and perfectly true, must be accurately worked out of winding, the bed even and parallel to the face, the sides and ends truly square; the stones to be bedded on cement concrete, and the joints to be filled with clean shingle and grouted in a similar manner to the paving.

The curb stones to be granite or syenite, straight or circular as required, 6 in. thick at top, 7 in. thick at 5 in. below, and not less than that thickness for the remainder of the depth;

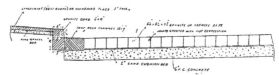

FIG. 34.—"FIRST-CLASS STREETS," LIVERPOOL.

same, and then lay a foundation of not less than 6 in. of Portland cement concrete, corporation standard. The paving shall consist of granite or syenite setts, 3½ in. wide by 6½ in. deep, from North Wales or other approved quarries, laid in regular, straight and properly-bonded courses, with close joints, and to be evenly bedded on a layer of fine gravel ½ in. in thickness. After the paving is laid the joints shall be filled with hard, clean, dry shingle; the setts shall then be thoroughly rammed, and additional shingle added until the joints are perfectly full. The joints shall then be carefully grouted until completely filled with a hot composition consisting of coal pitch and creosote oil, and finally the paving is to be covered with ½ in. of sharp gravel.

The crossings shall consist of three rows of 16 in. by 8 in.

to be not less than 12 in. deep, nor less than 3 ft. in length; to be carefully dressed on top, 9 in. down the face and 3 in. down the back; the remainder of each stone to be hammerdressed; the heading joints to be neatly and accurately squared throughout the entire depth.

SECOND-CLASS SPECIFICATION.

Excavate or fill in the ground, as the case may be, to the requisite level, and remove all surplus material. Properly form and trim off the surface and thoroughly consolidate the same, and then lay a foundation of (a) not less than 6 in. of Portland cement concrete, corporation standard, or (b) not less than 6 in. of bituminous concrete, consisting of clean and angular broken stone, grouted with a hot composition con

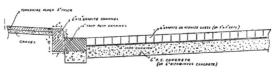

FIG. 35.—"SECOND-CLASS STREETS," LIVERPOOL.

granite crossing stones, and the remaining space shall be paved on each side of the crossing stones, to the full width of the footway, in a similar manner to the carriageway. The crossing stones shall be of granite of a quality to be approved by the city engineer, dressed perfectly true, and out of winding on the face; the sides and joints to be perfectly square and accurately dressed throughout their entire depth; the stones to be bedded on cement concrete, the joints to be filled with shingle and grouted in a similar manner to the paving. A triangular groove, 1 in. wide by ¼ in. deep, to be formed along the upper surface of each stone. No stone to be less than 3 ft. in length.

sisting of coal pitch and creosote oil, covered with chippings and thoroughly consolidated by rolling with a roller of sufficient weight. The paving shall consist of granite or syenite setts 3 in. wide by 5 in. deep, or of granite or syenite, 4 in. by 4 in. cubes, from North Wales or other approved quarries, laid in regular, straight and properly-bonded courses, with close joints, and to be evenly bedded on a layer of fine gravel, ½ in. in thickness. After the paving is laid the joints shall be filled with clean, hard, dry shingle; the setts shall then be thoroughly rammed, and additional shingle added until the joints are perfectly full. The joints shall then be carefully grouted until completely filled with a hot composition con-

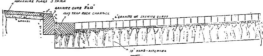

FIG. 36.—"THIRD-CLASS STREETS," LIVERPOOL.

The footways shall be paved with Lancashire ("Best Barns") or Yorkshire flags of the best quality, not less than 3 in. thick. No flag to measure less than 2 ft. in width nor to be of less area than 6 ft.; to be solid, free from laminations, the upper surface to be true and free from windings or hollows; the joints to be squared the whole thickness. The flags to be laid on a bed of fine gravel, with close, neat joints flushed in mortar, and in uniform courses breaking bond. The joints to be dressed after laying, where necessary.

sisting of coal pitch and creosote oil, and, finally, the paving shall be covered with ½ in. of sharp gravel.

The crossings, footways, channels and curbs shall be the same as specified for first-class streets.

THIRD-CLASS SPECIFICATION.

Excavate or fill in the ground, as the case may be, to the requisite level, and remove all surplus material. Properly form and trim off the surface, and thoroughly consolidate the same, and then lay a foundation of hand-pitched rock, 10 in. in depth, set on edge in the manner of a rough pavement. Over this a coating of gravel is to be laid of sufficient thickness to fill in the interstices and to form a smooth surface to the foundation, which must be thoroughly consolidated by rolling with a steam roller before the paving is laid. The paving shall consist of 4 in. by 4 in. granite or syenite cubes, from North Wales or other approved quarries, laid in regular, straight and properly-bonded courses, with close joints, and to be evenly bedded on a layer of fine gravel, ½ in. in thickness. After the paving is laid the joints shall be filled with clean, hard, dry shingle; the setts shall then be thoroughly rammed, and additional shingle added until the joints are perfectly full. The joints shall then be carefully grouted, until completely filled up, with a hot composition consisting of coal pitch and creosote oil, and, finally, the paving shall be covered with ½ in. of sharp gravel.

The crossings, footways, channels and curbs shall be the same as specified for first-class streets.

### FOURTH-CLASS SPECIFICATION.

After excavating the area of carriageway to a depth of 17 in. below the finished surface line, hand pitch the same with hard rock set on edge with the broadest sides downwards, 10 in. deep, break off the irregular corners of the

off after laying where necessary, but great care to be exercised in bedding the flags, so as to prevent the necessity for the after flogging. Natural asphalte upon concrete, granolithic or other artificial paving may be laid in substitution of flags at the discretion of the city engineer, and in accordance with his directions in each case.

Lay crossings, where required, consisting of three rows of 16-in. by 18-in. granite of a quality approved by the city engineer, and in lengths not less than 3 ft., dressed true and out of winding on the face, the sides and joints square, and accurately dressed throughout their entire depth; the joints to be filled with clean shingle, and grouted with pitch and creosote oil; a V grove, 1 in. wide and ½ in. deep, to be cut along the surface of each stone.

### FIFTH-CLASS SPECIFICATION.
(Specification for passages or back streets 9 ft. wide and upwards.)

After excavating the area of carriageway to a depth of 17 in. below the finished surface line, hand pitch the same with hard rock set on edge, with the broadest sides downwards, 10in. deep, break off the irregular corners of the stones, and fill in the interstices of the pitching with these fragments as well as with similar rock broken small. Consolidate the foundation thus formed by passing over it a steam roller until the whole is firm and compact.

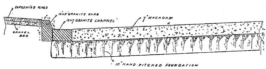

FIG. 37.—" FOURTH-CLASS STREETS," LIVERPOOL.

stones, and fill in the interstices of the pitching with these fragments as well as with similar rock broken small. Consolidate the foundation thus formed by passing over it a steam roller until the whole is firm and compact. When this is done spread over the surface evenly to a depth of 7 in. broken screened macadam free from slaty or flat fragments. This macadam to be durable granite or trap rock from the quarries of North Wales or from other approved quarries having similar class of rock. A layer of 2½-in. gauge stones to a depth of 3½ in. to be first spread and rolled until solid with a steam roller, then a layer of ·2-in. gauge stones to the finished level consolidated in a similar manner. Where binding is necessary, it should be sparingly used and must consist of granite chippings, preferably of the same rock as the macadam.

Lay channel stones over the hand pitching on each side of the carriageway of granite or syenite, of a quality approved by the city engineer, in lengths not less than 3 ft., in depth not less than 7 in., in width 12 in. The upper surface, if not

The paving shall consist of setts of Haslingden grit stone of the best quality, uniformly gauged to a depth of 6 in., laid in courses 6 in. wide, with a fall towards the centre of 1 in 48. Two courses to be laid longitudinally, to form a channel. After the paving is laid the joints shall be filled with hard, clean, dry shingle; the setts shall then be thoroughly rammed, and additional shingle added until the joints are perfectly full. The joints shall then be carefully grouted until completely filled with a hot composition consisting of coal pitch and creosote oil, and finally the paving is to be covered with ½ in. of sharp gravel.

The " Euston " Pavement was one of the first good granite pavements laid down in London. It derived its name from the fact of having been laid down (1843) at the departure side of the Euston station (London and North-Western Railway). It was laid in the following manner: The ground was excavated to a depth of 16 in. below the finished surface of the pavement and shaped to the proper road contour. Upon this bed a layer of coarse gravel, 4 in. thick, was spread and

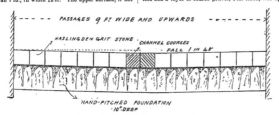

FIG. 38.—" FIFTH-CLASS STREETS," LIVERPOOL.
(Passages 9 ft. wide and upwards.)

natural faced and perfectly true, must be accurately worked out of winding, the bed as far as practicable parallel to the face, the sides and ends truly square, and the joints filled with clean shingle grouted with melted pitch and creosote oil.

Lay granite or syenite curb stones of a similar quality to that specified for channels, straight or circular as required, 5 in. thick at top, 6 in. thick at 5 in. below, and not less than that thickness for the remainder of the depth; to be not less than 12 in. deep, nor less than 3 ft. in length; to be carefully dressed on top, 8 in. down the face and 3 in. down the back; the remainder to be hammer dressed, the heading joints to be squared throughout the entire depth.

Pave the footways with " Best Barns " Lancashire flags, or Yorshire flags of the best quality, not less than 3 in. thick, 2 ft. in width, nor less than 6 ft. superficial area in each flag, which must be solid, free from laminations, windings, or hollows on the surface; the joints to be squared the full thickness; the flags to be truly laid on a bed of fine gravel, with close joints flushed with hydraulic lime mortar and in uniform courses, breaking bond; the surface to be flogged

well rammed. A second layer, 4 in. thick, consisting of gravel mixed with chalk or hoggin, to blind it, and again well rammed was next spread. A similar layer consisting of the same kind of materials but of finer quality was placed upon this, and again thoroughly well rammed to a solid surface for receiving the stones, which were bedded upon 1 in. of fine sand. The stone used was Mountsorrel granite, neatly dressed, and squared and well jointed, measuring 3 in. in width by 4 in. in length and about 4 in. deep. The whole surface of pavement was then thoroughly well rammed with a rammer, 55 lb. weight, and afterwards sprinkled with screened gravel, which entered the joints and so increased the rigidity of the pavement. The cost of the Euston pavement, including foundation, is given at 12s. per square yard.

**Kirkham.**—It has been decided by the council to make an application to the Local Government Board for sanction to borrow £500 to cover the cost of certain sewerage works and the erection of a new fire engine station and offices.

# Law Notes.

EDITED BY J. B. REIGNIER CONDER, 11 Old Jewry Chambers, E.C.,

Solicitor of the Supreme Court.

*The Editor will be pleased to answer any questions affecting the practice of engineers and surveyors to local authorities. Queries (which should be written legibly on foolscap paper, one side only) should be addressed to "The Law Editor," at the Offices of* THE SURVEYOR. *Where possible, copies of local Acts or documents referred to should be enclosed. All explanatory diagrams must be drawn and lettered in* black *ink only. Correspondents who do not wish their names published should furnish a* nom de plume.

BUILDING BY-LAWS: "NEW BUILDING."—Although a magisterial decision on a "question of fact" cannot be regarded in the light of a precedent, the recent case of *New Winchester Rural District Council* v. *Hutchings* (Winchester County Bench, December 17th) is of interest as an illustration of such an addition to an existing building as the magistrates considered to amount to a "new building" within the meaning of the by-laws in force in the district. The following evidence was given: Mr. W. F. Y. Molyneux, surveyor to the council, stated that on November 15th he visited the premises in question (which were known as Brambridge Lodge) and found that a new wing was in course of erection, consisting of a stable containing three or four loose-boxes and a harness-room, these additions being built to join the gable end of the existing block of stables, &c. In cross-examination he admitted that he saw nothing to object to in the additions, except that no plans had been submitted, as required by the by-laws. On being asked to define a "new building," he said "that is a matter of fact for the justices"; and in reply to the further question what led him to form the opinion that these additions amounted to a new building, explained that in his view any addition necessitating footways, walls, ventilation and drainage amounted to a new building, requiring the control of the sanitary authority and the supervision of their surveyor. For the defence Mr. W. J. Jennings, architect, of Canterbury, said he was instructed to make the additions in question to Colonel Little's stable. The existing building consisted of a coach-house, harness-room and three stalls, and, as this was not sufficient, the plan was for accommodation for four horses, with communication on the ground floor and above. When asked for plans by the district surveyor he pointed out to him that the work was only an addition, and not a new building, and offered to meet him on the works and explain to him what was being done. In witness's opinion it was an extension of an existing building. Mr. J. B. Colson, architect, of Winchester, said he had seen the building and the plan. In his opinion the work was clearly an addition to an old building. For the defence the case of *Shiel* v. *Sunderland Corporation* (30 L.J., M.C., 215) was cited, in which a building erected partly on the site of an old coach-house and stable attached to a house, and partly on adjoining ground, was held not to be the erection of a new building, but only an addition to an old building. The Bench, however, decided the "question of fact" in favour of the council, finding that the proposed additions constituted a "new building," and that plans ought to have been deposited, and the defendant was ordered to pay 15s. costs.

## QUERIES AND REPLIES.

PRIVATE STREET WORKS.—"Subscriber" wishes to know whether it is possible to carry out private street works under sec. 150 of the Public Health Act, 1875, for the urban district council, the said council having already adopted the Private Street Works Act, 1892, but have never yet put it in force?

No. Sec. 150 of the Public Health Act, 1875, does not apply to any district in which the Private Street Works Act, 1892, is in force. See sec. 25 of the latter Act.

PRIVATE STREET WORKS: VENDOR AND PURCHASER.—"E. A. S." wites: Purchaser agrees to buy a property fronting a private road, but before sale is completed the corporation serve a "private street works" notice on the vendor. Is the vendor liable for the amount of the apportionment of expenses, or will the purchaser be held responsible. The notices were issued after the purchaser agreed to buy, and the works will probably be commenced before the sale is completed. I think there has been a decision in a similar case within the last few months, and that it appeared in THE SURVEYOR, but I am unable to find reference of it.

There are two phases of this question to be considered—*viz.*, (1) As between the local authority on the one hand and the vendor or purchaser on the other hand, and (2) as between the vendor and purchaser. As to (1), I assume that the Private Street Works Act, 1892, has been adopted (since a "private street works notice" has been served). In that case "the owner for the time being" is liable under sec. 14, and under sec. 13 the apportioned sum is a charge on the property. So far as the local authority are concerned, therefore, the vendor is liable up to the time of the completion of the purchase, from which time the purchaser will be liable (see *East London Waterworks Company* v. *Kellerman* [1892], 2 Q.B., 72). (2) If the final apportionment is made before the date fixed for completion the vendor would, in my opinion, be bound, as between himself and the purchaser, to discharge it, because it is a charge on the premises, unless, of course, there is anything in the agreement to the contrary. If the final apportionment is not made until after the date fixed for completion the case is not quite so clear, and may depend upon the wording of the agreement for sale. In *Tubbs* v. *Wynn* (1897), 1 Q.B., 74, the vendor had agreed to clear all "outgoings" to May 8th. Before that date a "dangerous structures" notice was served by the local authority, which was not complied with. After May 8th the authority took down the building and demanded and received the expenses from the purchaser. It was held that the purchaser was entitled to recover the expenses he had so paid from the vendor. Having regard to this decision, I am inclined to think that in the present case, assuming the agreement to contain the usual undertaking by the vendor to clear outgoings up to the date fixed for completion, that he would be liable.

BY-LAWS: LAYING-OUT A NEW STREET.—Mr. G. Fenwick Carter, engineer and surveyor to the Mexborough Urban District Council, writes: A public road runs from our township to a village about 2 miles away, and there are a few houses dotted along its course, but in all probability it will soon be laid out as a building road. A plan is submitted for a villa, and the forecourt wall is shown to butt up to the stone fence wall, leaving the road about 19 ft. at this point. My council think that before any more buildings are erected a street plan should be submitted to the new street by-laws, and a frontage line shown to make a 36-ft. street. They have therefore rejected the plan. The owner intends to build in defiance, leaving the stone wall up and putting railings on top. Kindly let me have your advice in the matter, as it is a very important point to many authorities round here. If the owner on the other side was to claim 3 ft. from the centre of his hedge it would only make a 16-ft. street.

As a general rule the question whether a new street is being laid out is a question of fact for the magistrates, and if there is any evidence to justify the latter in finding that a street is a new street the Court will not inquire into its sufficiency. There are several reported cases, however, in which the Court have considered the question of what does and what does not amount to laying out a new street (see Lumley's "Public Health Acts, fifth edition, p. 206, *et seq.*). From these I think it may be gathered that if the proposed villa is the first of a series of buildings about to be erected (either by the same owner or by various owners, so that there is an intention to go on and make a street) its erection would amount to the commencement of the laying out of a new street (see the observations of Lord Esher in *Robinson* v. *Barton Local Board*, 21 Ch.D., p. 636). If, however, this is a solitary building and no such intention to make a street can be inferred, I think it is very doubtful whether there is evidence to justify a finding that a new street is being laid out. See *Williams* v. *Powning*, 47 J.P., 460, where the building of six cottages on one side of a lane, 250 ft. long and 6 ft. wide (there being no other houses in the lane), was held not to constitute the laying out of a new street.

GENERAL DISTRICT RATE: WATER RATE.—"J. H. M." writes: I own and live in a house which lets at 6s. per week clear, or £15 12s. per year. I pay—general district rate, £1 5s. 4d.; poor rate, £1 10s.; water rate, 18s. 9d.; fire insurance, 3s.; chief or ground rent, £2 5s.; total, £6 2s. 1d. per year. I have not made any allowance for repairs, painting, &c. I enclose poor and general district demand note for reference. Could you give me any information whether these demands are correct? I also enclose Private Waterworks Acts for reference, showing their scale of charges (*vide* page 3,192, sec. 31, of their 1861 Act). Am I, in your opinion, overcharged? Enclosed are also the Union Assessment Committee Acts, 1862 and 1864?

(1) As to the general district rate, the demand note shows that the premises are assessed at £11 5s. In sec. 1 of the statute 6 and 7 William IV., cap. 96, the "nett annual value" is defined as "the rent at which the property might reasonably be expected to let from year to year, free from all usual tenant's rates and taxes, and tithe rent charge (if any), and deducting therefrom the probable average annual cost of repairs, insurance and other expenses, if any, necessary to maintain it in a state to command such rent." The section has reference to rates for the relief of the poor, but the Union Assessment Committee Act, 1862, sec. 15, expressly preserves this definition of "nett annual value." It is not stated whether on the rental of 6s. per week the landlord or the tenant would pay the rates and taxes, and although he refers to the rent as "clear" (which would imply that the tenant pays them), yet he enumerates them as deductions which (apparently) he considers should be made from the rent for the purpose of the assessment. Assuming that the landlord would pay rates (amounting to £3 14s. 1d.), it would appear that the assessment is too high, as this only leaves a margin of 12s. 11d. per annum for repairs, insurance "and other expenses" referred to in the Act of William IV. If, on the other hand, the rates would be payable by the tenant, I do not think the assessment is too high, unless the state of the property is such as to require a proportionally large annual expenditure in repairs. The ground rent cannot be deducted in estimating the rateable value. (2) As to the water rate, sec. 31 of the Local Waterworks Act provides that where "the annual rack rent or value" of the premises shall not exceed £20 per annum the rate shall not exceed £7 10s. per cent. per annum. The annual charge in this case is 18s. 9d. = 7½ per cent. on £12 10s. But the company are also entitled to further charges for any water-closet beyond the first, and for any private bath, as to which no information is furnished. Probably, as the house is apparently a small one, there is not more than one water-closet and no bath. In that case the question is whether £12 10s. represents the "annual rack rent or value." In a case in which the special Act authorised charges calculated upon the "annual rack rent or value" (the identical words of the Act we are considering), and it was held that the rate must be calculated upon the "rateable value." (*Warrington Waterworks Company* v. *Longshaw*, 9 Q.B.D., 145). And in the well-known case of *Dobbs* v. *Grand Junction Waterworks Company*, 9 App. Cas., 49), the expression "annual value" in the special Act was held to mean "nett annual value," as defined by the statute of William IV., already referred to. I think, therefore, that the company in the present case are only entitled to charge upon the "nett annual value" as so defined. If, therefore, the assessment of £11 5s. is too high, *à fortiori*, the company's charges, based on a value of £12 10s., are excessive.

## QUERIES AND REPLIES.

*We cannot undertake to reply to any queries which are not accompanied by the writer's name and address. These are required as a guarantee of good faith and not for publication. Sketches accompanying queries should be made separate on white paper, in plain black ink lines. Lettering or figures should be bold and plain.*

**224. By-Laws as to House Drainage and their Interpretation.**—Mr. Geo. Winship, Borough Buildings, Abingdon, writes us on this subject, stating (1) that we have given his name somewhat unusual prominence, and more than is usually the case when any engineer differs from another in professional practice; (2) that the matter does not hinge upon the adaptability of the plan published; and (3) that the plan submitted to him was put with a question as to whether it was in accordance with the provisions and regulations as to drainage now in force within the district of the Clacton Urban District Council.

(1) We are sorry we are unable to sympathise with Mr. Winship in his disappointment that his name has been brought forward, but this is no fault of ours, but that of his client, who, we presume, paid for the use of it; and (2) and (3) we really cannot follow Mr. Winship's contention. He has advised that the plan is not in accordance with the by-laws and regulations as to house drainage, and to say that the matter does not hinge upon the adaptability of the plan published leaves us to infer that it was not upon the conformity or otherwise of the plan to the by-laws and regulations whereon he gave his opinion, which is a statement not reconcilable with his former written opinion. We feel it necessary also to add that considerations of professional etiquette do not appear to have been considered so fully as might have been expected, and it is most exceptional, and, for the advantage of surveyors generally, we trust it will remain so, for a municipal surveyor of one authority to advise an individual member of another local authority on cases such as this for purposes which are, to say the least of it, not conducive to satisfactory administration. Mr. Winship has had the opportunity to explain the reasons on which he based his opinion in this column in the same manner as Mr. Martin, but he has not done so, for reasons best known to himself. Further correspondence on the subject, so far as we are concerned, cannot be accepted for publication.

**230. Sewage Farms in the United Kingdom: Particulars Required.**—Mr. Robert Green, A.M.I.C.E., writes: Referring to the query in your last issue, Prof. Henry Robinson, in his book "Sewerage and Sewage Disposal," states on p. 153 that a return was obtained by the Local Government Board from towns in which sewage precipitation works were in operation to ascertain if the precipitant was soluble; 23½ places are given in the return, from which it will be seen that only at thirty places was anything obtained for the sludge, the amount varying from 1s. to 2s. 6d. per ton.

We are much obliged to Mr. Green for the information, which will, we are sure, be useful.

**232. Bridges: Wing Walls and Abutments.**—"F. A. D." writes: Will you kindly define which are the wing walls in

A is the wall carrying road on to bridge crown (composed of rubble); B is brickwork.

the sketch herewith, which roughly represents a canal bridge over which passes a highway?

Inasmuch as the querist appears to have an imperfect knowledge of the term "wing walls," &c., it may be useful if we give a few particulars relating thereto and to bridge abutments. In the construction of stone or brick built

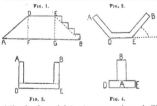

Fig. 1.          Fig. 2.

Fig. 3.          Fig. 4.

bridges four forms of abutments are more or less used: (1) A plain wall parallel to the current, as shown in Fig. 1, with or without the wings A D F and B E G. The slopes may be finished with an inclined coping, as A D, or by an offset at each course, as B E. This form is termed the straight abutment or wings. (2) The wings or abutment may be swung around into the bank at any angle, as shown in plan in Fig 2. The angle is usually about 30°. This form is known as the wing abutment. (3) When the angle of 30° becomes 90° we have Fig. 3, which is called the U abutment. (4) When the wings, as in Fig. 3, are moved to the centre of the head wall we get Fig. 4, which is known as the T abutment. The abutment of an ordinary bridge has two offices to perform—viz., (1) To support one end of the bridge, and (2) to keep the earth embankment from sliding into the water. In Figs. 2 and 3 the portion D E performs both offices, while the wings A D and B E are merely retaining walls. In Fig. 4 the "head," D E, supports the bridge, and the tail or stem, A B, carries the road; hence the whole structure acts as a retaining wall, and also supports the load. From the sketch which the querist has submitted it will be seen that the form of abutment is similar to that in No. 4 above. Strictly, the parts marked A A in his sketch are not wing walls, but merely retaining walls to carry the road. The querist will find Baker's "Treatise on Masonry Construction" (Wiley & Sons. Price 21s.), from which we have copied a portion of the lucid definitions given above, most useful.

## THE I. V. O. C.

"Invincible Veterans and Old Comrades," it has been suggested, are indicated by the above mystic letters. They stand, however, for the Islington Vestry Officers' Club, which held one of its social evenings on Wednesday, under the presidency of Mr. W. F. Dewey, the vestry clerk, at the Islington Vestry Hall. Comrades, indeed, are the members of the club, and we heartily commend their unity and good fellowship, and their methods of expressing these qualities in practice, to the staffs of local authorities the country over. Veterans some of them are, but length of service hath not dimmed their loyalty to their chiefs, their zest for work as public officials. Invincible they are not, for this year the representative team of the club failed, through the temporary indisposition of one of their most valiant swimmers, to bear off the national shield of the Life-saving Society. But they triumphantly bore away the Southern Counties Life-saving Championship shield, and on Wednesday Mr. Guy Campbell, chairman of the executive of the Life-saving Society, gracefully presented that trophy to the team which wrested it from the London and India Docks representatives, who had held it for the two preceding years. In addition, the four Islington champions were the recipients of the gold medals which accompany the shield, and for their prowess at Birmingham, where, as already mentioned, they were the runners-up for the national shield, they were awarded bronze medals. Moreover, Mr. J. B. Leggatt, who had trained the members of the team, was presented by them with a handsome silver cup in recognition of his services. Then came a scene of even greater enthusiasm. Mr. G. J. Eldridge, the most modest member of the Islington staff, was at Great Yarmouth in August last, no doubt studying the details of the sanitary administration there. He heard the despairing cries of a youth who had sunk for the third time at some distance from the shore. Mr. Eldridge swam out, dived, rescued the then insensible body, and not only brought it ashore but scientifically put into practice the theory of resuscitation which he had learnt at Islington's public baths. Pluckily, unostentatiously and effectively he performed the noblest deed it is given to man to achieve—he saved a fellow-creature's life. For this he deservedly received on Wednesday the honorary testimonial of the Royal Humane Society, which was presented to him, on the society's behalf, by Mr. Dewey, amidst the vociferous cheers of his colleagues. The setting of these inspiring incidents in a "pleasant evening all too-swiftly sped" was a varied programme to which many well-known entertainers contributed. The mere names of the veteran Clarance Holt, Prof. Lindsay, and Messrs. Charles Gardner, Willie Ronse, Frank Maitland and Harold G. Thompson are sufficient to suggest the quality of this programme.

**Leyton.**—The urban district council are favourably considering the adoption of the septic tank system of sewage treatment. It was stated, at a recent meeting of the council, that the new system would cost £3,000 a year less than the present method.

**Bridges in the Lake District.**—A correspondent of *The Times* writes: In consequence of the county council repudiating all responsibility for the bridges in the Keswick neighbourhood, the state of the roads is almost incredible in this nineteenth century. The inhabitants of the Portinscale district have now no safe access to church or market, nor to any railway station. Within 1½ miles from Keswick, on the main road to Cockermouth, there are four bridges. The Greta bridge has large gaps in the parapet mended with wooden fencing and an old door. The Crossing bridge has a large hole in it, where an accident took place lately. The Portinscale bridge has large gaps in the parapet, and the water in flood pours in torrents through the pier, and half of the Powe bridge is entirely swept away. Other bridges are in a most dilapidated state, some entirely destroyed. Is there no law in the land?

# Municipal Work in Progress and Projected.

We have this week received information in reference to several extensive municipal works which are being carried out at Accrington, Wolverhampton, Canterbury, Stafford, Ledbury, Glasgow and other places. The metropolitan authorities also seem to be more than usually busy, as a glance at the paragraphs relating to Islington, St. Marylebone and the Court of Common Council will prove.

## METROPOLITAN AUTHORITIES.
### LONDON COUNTY COUNCIL.

On Tuesday the London County Council sat for five and a half hours, after which they adjourned over the Christmas recess until January 24th. Among the large amount of business disposed of was the important report of the Housing of the Working Classes Committee in respect to the erection of working-class tenement houses in several districts of London. The total cost of the proposed works was estimated at £40,500. After some discussion the whole of the estimates were approved, except one, the approval of which would have involved a charge upon the rates. This one was rejected. Several other more or less important matters were also dealt with, the chief of which we give below.

*Housing of the Poor.*—The Housing of the Working Classes Committee submitted a report asking for the passing of supplemental estimates of £950 and £2,030 in respect of the erection of Benson and Abingdon buildings, on the Boundary-street area. In the case of these buildings the works manager declined to accept the original estimates, and accordingly tenders were advertised for, but none were received, and the committee now recommended that the work should be given to the Works Department at an increased estimate of £2,980. After some discussion the recommendation was adopted. The committee further asked the council to approve a supplemental estimate of £1,502 in respect of the erection of cottages in the Brock-street, Limehouse, scheme. The facts in this case were much the same as in the previous one, with the exception that in this instance the enhanced cost would entail a small charge on the rates. Mr. Boulnois, M.P., moved as an amendment that the recommendation should be referred back to the committee, with an instruction to offer the site to the Industrial Dwellings Company without any other condition than that the approval of the Home Secretary must be obtained to the plans of any buildings which might be placed on the site. A long discussion followed, but eventually a vote was taken, with the result that Mr. Boulnois' amendment was negatived by a large majority. The recommendation was then, on a division, rejected by fifty-six votes to forty-seven. Subsequently an estimate of £13,024 was approved in respect of the erection of Leighton and Millais buildings, Millbank estate, on condition that if the works manager found himself unable to undertake the work at that figure tenders should be invited for it.

*Sewer Ventilation in Chelsea.*—The Main Drainage Committee recommended the council to sanction an expenditure of £750 for the erection of nine ornamental ventilating columns on the northern low-level sewer in Cheyne-walk and Chelsea-embankment. The committee reported that their attention had from time to time been called to offensive emanations from the sewers in this neighbourhood, and their present suggestion was in order to obviate any further cause of complaint. Objection was taken by several members to the suggestion, on the ground that the columns would be detrimental to the neighbourhood from an æsthetic point of view. After the rejection of several amendments, the recommendation was adopted.

*A Munificent Gift to the Council.*—In reply to Mr. Phillimore, Mr. Bruce, chairman of the Housing Committee, stated that since the last meeting of the committee Sir Samuel Montagu, M.P., had called at the council offices and intimated his intention of making a gift of 25 acres of land at Edmonton for the purpose of the erection of working-class dwellings, subject to conditions which were now under consideration.

*Proposed Electrical Tramway Traction.*—On the recommendation of the Parliamentary Committee it was agreed to seek powers in the next session of Parliament, either by a separate Bill or by the insertion of provisions in the General Powers Bill, to enable the council to use electrical traction on all or any of their tramways.

*The Proposed Telephone Conference at the Guildhall.*—The Highways Committee reported that they had had before them a letter from the town clerk of the City forwarding a copy of a resolution, as follows, passed by the Court of Common Council on November 17th: "That application be made for a license to establish a telephone service in conjunction with the London County Council and other local authorities within the London telephone area," and asking the council to appoint six representatives to attend a conference at the Guildhall to consider the subject; and, if possible, to settle the necessary arrangements. They were of opinion that the council should give every assistance in their power in furtherance of the object which the corporation had in view in arranging for the conference, and they accordingly recommended that the invitation of the City corporation should be accepted. This was agreed to.

*Tenders.*—Reporting on the list of tenders sent in for the

separate items in respect to the construction of dwellings in Southwark, the Housing Committee recommende I that Standing Order No. 195 be suspended, so that advances to the extent of 80 per cent. of the value of the work done may be made to the contractors for general works and plastering in respect of the dwellings to be erected on the Borough-road site, Southwark; that the tender of Messrs. Brown, Son & Blomfield for the general works, amounting to £15,157, be accepted; that the offer of Mr. J. Bickley to carry out the plastering work for the sum of £1,686 be accepted; that the tender of Mr. N. Fortescue for the excavation of foundations, amounting to £1,923, be accepted; that the tender of Messrs. W. H. Lascelles & Co. for granolithic work, amounting to £770, be accepted; that the tender of Messrs. Yates, Heywood & Co. for chimney-pieces and iron railings, amounting to £498 10s. and £560 5s. respectively, be accepted; that the tender of Messrs. J. Wedgwood & Sons, Limited, for tiling work, amounting to £544 12s., be accepted; that the tender of Messrs. Shanks & Co. for water-closet apparatus and washtubs, amounting to £227 17s., be accepted; that the tender of Messrs. Homan & Rodgers for fireproof floors, amounting to £1,456, be accepted; that the tender of Messrs. Ewart & Son for dormers, amounting to £111 3s. 4 l., be accepted. The report was adopted.

## COURT OF COMMON COUNCIL.

A meeting of the Court of Common Council was held on Thursday, when the Lord Mayor presided.—Mr. Edward Lee presented a petition from the Charing Cross and Strand Electricity Supply Corporation, particulars of which we published in our last issue (p. 762), stating that they were desirous of supplying electrical energy within the city, and asking the court, notwithstanding their inability to consent to the application made to the Board of Trade, to permit the memorial to be put upon their records. Mr. Lee moved that the memorial should be referred to the Streets Committee for consideration and report, and after a prolonged discussion the motion was carried unanimously.—In reply to a question, Mr. Turner said the Streets Committee had received no further communication from the Board of Trade in reference to the proposed inquiry into the state of Ludgate-hill station.—The Improvement and Finance Committee submitted for adoption an arrangement for setting back the premises in Lothbury, between Old Jewry and Princes-street, at a cost of £36,586, to include all interests, the vaults being constructed at the expense of the corporation. This was agreed to.—The court also agreed to an arrangement for acquiring the ground needed to widen the public way in front of 82 to 86 Fenchurch-street and 1 Aldgate for the sum of £300.

## METROPOLITAN ASYLUMS BOARD.

A meeting of the managers was held at the County Hall, Spring-gardens, on Saturday, Sir E. H. Galsworthy presiding.—A claim for £34,445 was forwarded by Messrs. Mackrell, Maton, Godlee & Quincey, solicitors, on behalf of Messrs. Kirk & Randall, contractors, in respect of the increased cost entailed upon them owing to the delay that arose in connection with the erection of the Grove Hospital consequent on the non-supply of drawings and the supply of imperfect drawings by the board's architect. It was stated that further claims were in course of preparation and would be sent in due course. After some discussion the letter was referred to the Works Committee, with instructions to take the advice of the board's solicitors.—The General Purposes Committee reported that, acting under the authority accorded to them at the board meeting on July 2nd, they had instructed the Statistical Committee to assist the Social Science Sub-Committee of the Royal Commission of the Paris Exhibition of 1900, who were preparing a collection of exhibits illustrative of social science, by compiling for them a general report on the work of the Metropolitan Asylums Board from its commencement, and by showing at the exhibition certain models of the board's hospitals, asylums, ambulance stations, ambulances, &c. They had also instructed the Statistical Committee to submit estimates for giving effect to that decision. The architects of the North-Eastern Hospital, Messrs. A. & E. Harston, were instructed to prepare and submit to the Works Committee a plan and specification for the erection of a new laundry, together with the necessary additional boiler and engine-house, at the North-Eastern Hospital.

## VESTRIES AND DISTRICT BOARDS.

**Hampstead.**—The Lighting Committee, at a meeting of the vestry on Thursday, submitted a long report, in which they stated that they had had under consideration the question of the great increase in the number of consumers of electric current, and they were of opinion that the time had now arrived when it was necessary to make provision for the extension of the buildings at the central station, to enable them to cope with the probable increase in the demand for current in the future. They recommended that they should be authorised to prepare and lay before the vestry plans for the extension of the central station, with a view to the provision of additional plant of 4,000 horse-power for both engines and boilers. The report was adopted.—In a further report the same committee recommended the vestry to construct a transformer pit on Parliament Hill, at a total cost, including transformer, cable, &c., of £156, and also to support the action of the Hammersmith Vestry in reference to the report of the Joint Committee of both Houses of Parliament on the subject of electrical energy (generating stations and supply), and the question of breaking up of streets, route of mains, wires for traction, applications for provisional orders, &c. Both recommendations were adopted.—On the recommendation of the Works Committee it was decided to make-up the new street, known as Mackeson-road, at the cost of the owners of the property abutting on it.—The Public Libraries Committee recommended that the vestry clerk should be instructed to take the necessary steps for completing the purchase of the site for the branch library at West End. This was agreed to.—The Public Health Committee reported that they had carefully considered the question as to whether the present system of ventilating the sewers in the parish was the best that could be devised, and they had come to the conclusion that the system of ventilation by open grids, assisted by up-cast shafts at the ends of the sewers where necessary, was the best and the most practicable. They accordingly recommended: " (a) That up-cast shafts be used, only as heretofore, in some cases to assist the surface ventilators, especially at the ends of sewers; (b) that open grids be employed in the place of the wooden manhole covers in the centre of the roads; and (c) that the surveyor should gradually replace the smaller gratings in the lower parts of the parish with larger ones of 60-in. aperture." The report was adopted.

**Islington.**—At the last meeting of the vestry a letter was read from the Rotherhithe Vestry announcing that that authority had passed a resolution expressing their satisfaction with the recent action of the London County Council in deciding to seek powers to provide for the future water supply of the metropolis. The vestry hoped that the Bill would receive the sanction of Parliament at an early date, as the matter was too urgent to admit of delay. It was resolved to instruct the vestry clerk to communicate to the Rotherhithe Vestry the resolutions already passed by the vestry on the subject of the London water supply.—The Parliamentary Committee were instructed to report on the notice served upon the vestry by the East London Water Company of their intention to apply to Parliament for an Act to authorise them to construct additional storage reservoirs and other works.—In a letter received from Mr. C. B. Clay, district superintendent of the National Telephone Company, exception was taken to some statements made in a report by the Works Committee. The writer said that he had not stated to the committee that the company had no statutory powers to place their wires underground. He thought, however, the company had such powers subject to the approval of the necessary authorities, and that if he had failed to satisfy the vestry on the point he trusted the committee would look into the matter further. If that was done Mr. Clay opined that they would come to the conclusion of other authorities, and notably Kensington, and consent to the telephone wires being placed underground. The letter was referred to the Works Committee for report. In connection with this matter it was resolved, on the motion of Mr. Argyle, to tender the thanks of the vestry to Messrs. J. Howell Williams and Torrance for their action in inducing the London County Council to postpone until after the Christmas vacation a report by the Highways Committee dealing with the same question relating to overhead telephone wires in Islington.—The Works Committee reported that they had had under consideration the necessity for repaving the margins of the carriageway of Holloway-road between the Great Northern Railway bridge and the Seven Sisters-road. The committee recommended that the work should be carried out with hard wood, at an estimated cost of £6,500, and that the amount should be raised by loan. An amendment was moved by Mr. Tomkins in favour of the substitution of granite cubes for wood, but on a division this was rejected by thirty-seven votes to thirty-three. The committee's recommendation was then adopted.—On the motion of the Baths Committee it was decided to apply to the Local Government Board for sanction to borrow £4,000 to meet the deficiency arising from the extensions of the Caledonian-road baths.—The Public Health Committee presented a report on the question of dealing with nuisances occurring owing to the absence or insufficiency of urinal accommodation in connection with public-houses in the parish. Having regard to the great difficulty experienced in dealing with the subject, the vestry, at the suggestion of the committee, decided to ask the London County Council to promote legislation with a View to powers being conferred upon the council to act in the matter.—It was resolved to endorse the views of the Hammersmith Vestry in objecting to certain recommendations of the Parliamentary Joint Committee on the Supply of Electrical Energy, especially in regard to the breaking up of streets for the laying of mains, the use of overhead wires, and applications for provisional orders.—A long report was submitted by the Works Committee relating to the failure of the National Telephone Company to comply with the by-laws made by the London County Council under the London Overhead Wires Act, 1891. It was eventually decided, in consequence of the inconvenience which would otherwise be caused to the public, to allow the company to retain such existing overhead wires as do not conform to the by-laws for periods ranging from six to twelve months.

**St. James's, Westminster.**—The Health Committee reported, at the last meeting of the vestry, that they had considered a letter from the Clinical Research Association in reference to the work of the society in undertaking the bacteriological examination of material from cases of infectious diseases, the work being carried out, at small cost, for many sanitary authorities throughout the kingdom. The association suggested that it would be more economical for local authorities to join the society than to pay a yearly subsidy to support a laboratory as proposed by the London County Council. On the recommendation of the committee it was decided to acknowledge the receipt of the letter.—The Parliamentary Committee announced that they had considered the notice given by the St. James's and Pall Mall Electric Lighting Company of their intention to seek permission to introduce a Bill to authorise the company to acquire compulsorily property in the parish for the purposes of the undertaking. It was decided by the committee to defer the consideration of the subject until a copy of the Bill was obtainable.—In reply to an application made by the London Hydraulic Power Company for an extension of the hydraulic main from Bridle-lane to Marshall-street, it was resolved to inform the company that the vestry were prepared to assent to the proposal on the payment of an annual rental of £2 2s. Among the letters read was one from the London County Council stating the conclusions at which the Building Act Committee had arrived upon the points raised after consideration of the letters from local authorities on the subject of district surveyors employed in connection with the London Building Act, 1894.—A further letter from the county council was considered, announcing that application had been made to the council for approval of plans of proposed alterations adjoining St. James's Hall. The council asked the views of the vestry as to whether it would be desirable to use the opportunity to arrange for the widening of Piccadilly at the spot in question. It was decided to convene a special meeting of the vestry to consider the question.

**St. Marylebone.**—The vestry at their last meeting discussed a formal motion, proposed by Mr. T. H. Brooke-Hitching, chairman of the Electric Lighting Committee, to apply to Parliament for the grant of a special Act to empower the vestry to establish electric supply works. At the suggestion of Sir Edwin Galsworthy it was decided to adjourn the debate until after the recess, but in the meantime it was agreed to deposit the Bill.—It was decided to use hard wood in the case of the renewal of the carriageway of Oxford-street between Hereford-gardens and Edgware-road, and creosoted deal for the paving of Marylebone-road between York-place and Northumberland-street. The cost was estimated at between £3,000 and £4,000.—The Sanitary Committee reported that they had had under consideration a letter from the solicitors to Lord Portman on the subject of the proposed erection of an underground convenience in East-street by Marylebone-road. On the recommendation of the committee it was resolved to inform the solicitors that the vestry felt justified in adhering to the site in question.

# PROVINCIAL AND GREATER LONDON AUTHORITIES.

## COUNTY COUNCILS.

**Middlesex.**—A meeting of the county council was held on Thursday, when the Finance Committee recommended the council to approve a plan of the proposed court-house at Harlesden. This was agreed to, and the surveyor was directed to prepare detailed drawings and specification and the Finance Committee authorised to obtain tenders for the erection of the building.—It was decided to borrow £49,831 for the purchase of the Napsbury estate for the purposes of the proposed new county asylum, and to apply to the Local Government Board for permission to raise loans of £1,800 for road improvements at the Wandsworth asylum.—On the motion for the reception of the report of the Highways Committee a question was raised as to wood paving in Brentford. In reply, the chairman of the committee stated that the whole question of wood paving in relation to the different local authorities was about to be considered by the committee.—The Highways Committee further reported upon contributions received from various local authorities for contributions towards the carrying out of paving works. It was decided to grant £780 to Tottenham, £220 to Willesden, £517 to Hendon, £415 to Edmonton, and £625 to Teddington.—The Highways Committee recommended, and it was decided, that tenders should be obtained from not less than six firms for making good and restoring Hampton Court main road in accordance with a specification prepared by Mr. Codrington, and to engage a clerk of works at a salary not exceeding £3 10s. per week.—A report was submitted by the General Purposes Committee on the proposed new lock in the Thames below Wandsworth Bridge. On the recommendation of the committee it was resolved to take no action in the matter until it had been conclusively proved before an independent commission by the best hydrographic and engineering evidence that, while benefiting a particular district up stream, an extension of shoal ground and prolonged low water, with increasing difficulties to navigation, would not be brought about in the river below the intended new lock when erected. —It was resolved to formally oppose various electric lighting and light railway schemes in the county, in order to give the council a *locus standi* for the protection of their interests.— The Technical Education Committee recommended the council to contribute £1,800 towards the purchase of land and the building of a technical school at Harrow, provided that the remainder of the money required for the purpose be obtained from local sources. This was agreed to.—The following tenders were accepted : For the rebuilding of Kendal Bridge —George Bell, of Tottenham Hale, at £1,229 ; for the widening of Turkey-street bridge—George Bell, £927 ; and for works at Stratford Bridge—Fassnidge & Son, £85.

## MUNICIPAL CORPORATIONS.

**Accrington.**—At a recent meeting of the Health Committee it was unanimously decided to proceed with the erection of a destructor. It is estimated that the work will cost about £7,000.

**Batley.**—The town council have accepted the tender of Messrs. H. & W. Barraclough, Brighouse, for the execution of levelling, paving, flagging, channelling, &c., works in Brown's-street at a cost of £320 and Grafton-street at £563.

**Bradford.**—Recent minutes of the Waterworks Committee recommended that an agreement, dated June 12, 1871, between the corporation and Messrs. John & William Briggs as to supplying water to Crossflats be terminated, that an offer be made to them to purchase the service pipes according to their present value, and that the waterworks engineer be instructed to take the necessary steps to continue the supply direct to the consumers upon the termination of the notice. The minutes were passed.—On the recommendation of the Markets and Fairs Committee it has been decided to accept tenders, amounting to £5,722, for the extension of the Rawson-place markets.

**Burslem.**—The Local Government Board, it has been stated, have agreed to sanction the borrowing of a sum of £760 for the purposes of street improvements, and point out that in cases where it is proposed to defray expenditure by means of borrowed money the board's sanction should be obtained to the loan before the expense is incurred, and that any agreement which may be entered into for the purchase of land should be made conditional upon the board's sanction being obtained to the loan.

**Burton-on-Trent.**—At the last monthly meeting of the town council the tender of Messrs. Mobberley & Bailey, of Stourbridge, for the whole of the articles and goods required at the gasworks during the year was accepted, as was also that of Messrs John Fowler & Co., of Leeds, for a new engine, at £2,965.

**Canterbury.**—On the recommendation of the Lighting Committee it was recently decided to apply to the Local Government Board for sanction to a loan of £12,000 to cover an increase of expenditure and the cost of a proposed extension of plant.—At the same meeting the Guildhall Committee reported the receipt of a letter from the Local Government Board with reference to the proposed guildhall and municipal offices, to the effect that they were of opinion that the accommodation proposed was quite inadequate—no police station, offices for the medical officer of health, city surveyor and water engineer, sanitary inspector, rate collector, &c., being shown—while the offices intended for the town clerk's use appeared very inadequate. Under these circumstances the board could not consider the present proposals, and requested that a revised scheme should be submitted.

**Carmarthen.**—The council have agreed to the erection of a large market hall in the provision market, by putting the existing crockery and green-stuff sheds under one roof, instead of two as at present. The surveyor's plans showed that the building would be 125 ft. long and 67 ft. wide, the seating accommodation being for 1,500 to 1,800 people. On extra-ordinary occasions, such as the holding of eisteddfodau, they could find accommodation for considerably over 2,000. By using the available material such a structure would cost about £1,400.

**Dover.**—On Tuesday of last week, at a meeting of the town council, the surveyor brought up plans for the building of a waiting-room and public convenience adjoining the market place, with accommodation for ladies and gentlemen, the estimated cost being £850. The plan was referred to a small committee to confer with the surveyor as to the best mode of arranging the entrances, &c. Another report, on the lighting of the police station, the court hall and the council chamber by electricity, and the erection of two ventilating fans, was adopted.

**Harrogate.**—The tender (amounting to £5,620) of Mr. J. L. Hampton-Matthews, Kent-road, Harrogate, has been accepted by the corporation for the laying of about 2½ miles of surface-water drains and culverts in certain districts in the borough and in the parish of Bilton.

**Leeds.**—Recently, at a meeting of the Washburn Lands Purchasing Committee, it was decided to purchase certain farms in the Washburn valley, with the view of preventing the city's water supply from being polluted. So far the committee have purchased twenty-two farms, including two licensed houses and five blocks of cottage property, and com-

prising some 617 acres, for £32,474. This has been accomplished without having to go to arbitration.

**Plymouth.**—Reference was recently made to a proposal to purchase from Messrs. Pethick Brothers a hopper barge for £500, for conveying refuse to sea, and it was stated that when the destructor was erected and in working order, which might be within the next two years, the discharge of refuse into the sea would be discontinued. Since they had the disposing of the refuse they had been paying £5 a week for a hopper, and in that way about £400 has been spent. The recommendation was adopted.

**Retford.**—At a recent special meeting of the town council it was decided to affix the seal of the council to an application to the Board of Trade for a provisional order, under the Electric Lighting Acts, 1882 and 1888, to enable the council to supply electric energy for public and private purposes within the borough.

**Salford.**—An inquiry was held at the town hall, on Thursday, by Mr. H. H. Law, of the Local Government Board, with respect to an application of the corporation for sanction to borrow £2,500 for technical instruction purposes and £1,103 for street improvements. The proceedings were of a very formal character, there being no opposition to the proposals.

**Scarborough.**—The Local Government Board have written to the Scarborough Corporation with reference to the application of the town council for approval of the borrowing of £33,575 for the purchase of the St. Nicholas House estate, asking to be furnished with full information respecting the accommodation provided by the existing town hall and public offices, and also a statement showing in detail the loans sanctioned in respect of the town hall and offices. It is proposed to convert the house into municipal offices and the gardens into public grounds.

**Southampton.**—The contract for the supply during the next three years of sluice valves, fire hydrants, air valves, surface covers, &c., as may be required by the corporation's waterworks department, has been let to Messrs. J. Blakeborough & Sons, of Brighouse.

**South Shields.**—At the town hall, on Thursday, Mr. R. H. Bicknell held an inquiry, on behalf of the Local Government Board, into an application of the council for sanction to borrow £1,304 for the erection of an underground lavatory in the Market-place, £635 for improvement purposes, and £336 for additions to the manure straiths in Wapping-street.

**Stafford.**—A Local Government Board inquiry has been held by Colonel Langton Coke with respect to an application of the town council for sanction to borrow £5,000 for gasworks purposes. The loan, it was stated, was required for the extension of the works plant, which were necessary on account of the rapid increase of the department, and was made up as follows: Condensers, £1,250 ; sulphate of ammonia house and plant, &c., £1,750 ; river boundary wall, £300 ; amount already expended on purifying plant, £317 ; and extensions of mains during the past five years, £1,390 ; proposed further extensions of mains, £500 ; new meters, &c., £93 ; making a total of £5,600, from which the cost of sulphate house, &c., £600, had to be deducted. The town clerk added that at the time the corporation took over the works the price of gas was 4s. 2d. per 1,000 cubic feet, and customers were charged for meters, but the average price now charged was 2s. 6d., without meter rent.

**Taunton.**—Last week, at a meeting of the town council, the Electric Lighting Committee reported that on the evening of November 21st one of the improvers at the works happened to frame the alternator by contact with his hand, which was badly burnt, and the result was that the armature short circuited and put the lights out on No. 1 sub-station, the arc set fire to the internal casing of the armature wires. The staff at the works, with great promptitude, switched over the lights to the other machine in half a minute, so as to work on the alternator, and not only saved it from destruction, but had it running again by 1 o'clock in the morning.

**Wolverhampton.**—The corporation will make application during the ensuing session of Parliament for powers to construct and work 2½ miles of tramways. The system adopted is the electrical overhead, with side bracket poles. The borough surveyor's estimate, which has been approval by the council, amounts to £136,000 for track construction and electrical bonding and £90,000 for generating station, car depots and equipment.

## URBAN DISTRICT COUNCILS.

**Basingstoke.**—A committee have been appointed to report on the advisability of adopting the Housing of the Working Classes Act. It is proposed to build about 100 houses, at a cost of £20,000.

**Blackburn.**—The corporation, who recently acquired the tramway system of the borough and adopted electric traction on it, on Monday agreed to join with the Darwen Corporation in purchasing the steam tramways connecting the two towns and owned by the Blackburn and Over Darwen Tramways Company. The purchase money is £18,500, Blackburn's contribution being £23,000.

**Bournemouth.**—The council are applying to the Board of Trade for a provisional order for powers to supply electric light, and the surveyor has been empowered to consult an expert for assistance in preparing the necessary estimates.

**Christchurch.**—The town council are to have a special meeting shortly to consider the question of the drainage of the town, when the name of the engineer to be consulted will be decided on.

**Failsworth.**—Mr. Herbert H. Law, one of the inspectors of the Local Government Board, held an inquiry at the Failsworth town hall recently into the application of the Failsworth District Council to borrow the sum of £4,200 for purposes of sewerage and sewage disposal. It was explained that from the start of the works to the finish exceptionally bad ground had been met with. In consequence of this it had been found impossible to complete them at the estimated cost. With regard to the land which had been secured for intermittent filtration, it was not thought to be of any use, and the council had not therefore thought it advisable to go to the expense of underdraining. If, however, it was found necessary in the future, they would ask for a further loan. The loans previously sanctioned by the Local Government Board were £28,810 on October 26, 1893, and £2,132 on January 12, 1897. The inspector put a number of questions, with a view of clearing up certain discrepancies in the statements made at this and the previous inquiry, and subsequently visited the outfall works.

**Heston and Isleworth.**—At last week's meeting of the district council it was decided to oppose the application for an order for the construction of a light railway through the district, but at the same time it was decided to interview the engineer of the company with a view to settling clauses favourable to the council which are to be inserted in the order.—It was also agreed to oppose the Bill of the West Middlesex Waterworks Company which sought to confer powers to lay mains through roads in the district.—Mr. Button moved that the council should adopt sec. 3 of the Housing of the Working Classes Act, pointing out that there were many houses in the council's area which were unfit for habitation and should be demolished. The chairman said that owing to the financial condition of the council, with the prospective liability, it would be unwise to adopt an Act which would probably cause the spending of thousands of pounds. Colonel Clarke considered that the council should see if a profit could be derived from workmen's dwellings, and, on the motion of Mr. Loinaz, the question was deferred for six months.

**Heywood.**—Local Government Board sanction has been received by the town council to the borrowing of £1,700 for the purchase of land required by the town hall site. The corporation have also applied for borrowing powers for a new town's yard, fire station, firemen's dwellings, mortuary, &c., but nothing has yet been heard in regard to this application.

**Ledbury.**—Colonel W. Langton Coke, inspector of the Local Government Board, held an inquiry recently respecting an application of the council for sanction to borrow £5,500 for the execution of various works of water supply. The scheme, it was stated, provided for the pumping of the water from a well at Massington to a reservoir, capable of holding 37,000 gallons, to be erected at the Cross Hands, 1 mile from Ledbury, at a sufficient altitude to supply to the whole of the district by gravitation from the proposed new reservoir. The existing reservoir would be utilised, and either both or only one could be used, or one could be used whilst the other was cleaned out.

**Margam.**—Lieut.-Colonel Smith, R.E., held an inquiry at Taibach last week in reference to an application of the council for sanction to borrow £6,011 for a new market at Port Talbot.

**Portsmouth.**—The town council have adopted the following resolution: "That it be an instruction to the Tramway Committee to report at an early date the advisability of an extension of the system to other districts of the borough, with an estimate of the cost and probable income." They have also agreed to a recommendation of the Electric Lighting Committee that application be made to the Local Government Board for their sanction to borrow £18,000, being a further portion of £40,000 which was previously sanctioned by the council for the purchase of additional machinery and plant at the electric light station.

**Richmond.**—Upon the recommendation of the Highway Committee it has been decided to make an application to the Local Government Board for sanction to borrow £800 to cover the cost of laying a surface-water sewer.

**Rugby.**—The urban district council having applied to the Local Government Board for sanction to borrow a sum of £2,823 for works of private street improvement, Mr. G. W. Willcocks has recently held the usual inquiry. Mr. D. G. MacDonald, the surveyor, detailed the work it was proposed to carry out. There was no opposition.

**Sutton-in-Ashfield.**—The Local Government Board have given their sanction to a proposal of the council to borrow a sum of £8,000 for works of water supply.

**Tonbridge.**—On the 15th inst. Colonel A. J. Hepper, D.S.O., R.E., conducted an inquiry, on behalf of the Local Government Board, in reference to an application of the district council for sanction to borrow £1,500 for the purchase of the old town hall (and its subsequent removal for

street improvements), and a strip of land for the improvement of the Slade and the council's castle property; and £1,075 for the purchase of a Shone ejector, &c., for raising the sewage to the high-level tanks. The plans for the works were fully described by Mr. W. Lawrence Bradley, engineer to the council, and there was no opposition offered to the application.

## RURAL DISTRICT COUNCILS.

**Cwyrfai.**—On Saturday, at the usual monthly meeting of the council, it was mentioned that a report of Mr. E. Evans, the county surveyor, on a comprehensive scheme for supplying the villages within the area of the council with water, had been received. It was decided to refer the report to a special committee.—The Local Government Board, it was also stated, had given their sanction to an application to borrow £2,000 for works of water supply at Port Dinorwic.

**Gloucester.**—The rural district council, at a recent special meeting, agreed unanimously to the following resolution: "That this council is entirely opposed to any scheme which largely diminishes the mileage of roads to be under the control of the rural district council. The present mileages are only sufficient to keep up the necessary staff of clerks and surveyor and to keep the steam roller going, any diminution of which would practically leave to the district council the payment of establishment charges out of all proportion to the actual work to be done. This council considers also the supervision which could be given to the roads by a district council would be much more effective than any which could be given by the county council to the great mileage and work under their supervision."

## SCOTLAND AND IRELAND.

**Glasgow.**—The Statute Labour Committee have resolved to recommend that two bridges be erected across the Clyde east of the Albert Bridge, one for vehicular traffic at Govan-street, and another, for pedestrians only, at Polmadie-road. The estimated cost of the bridges is about £8,000, and they are to be constructed out of the materials of the temporary wooden bridge spanning the river at Jamaica-street.

**St. Andrews.**—At a recent meeting of this body a report in regard to the improvement of the water supply of this city was read from Messrs. Belfrage & Carfrae. The report recommended the formation of a reservoir in Langraw and Lambholetham Den to hold 13,000,000 gallons of water, and an additional clear-water well and filters upon a higher level than the present filters, &c., so as to give the requisite addition of pressure into the town. The estimated cost of reservoir, land and wayleave is £8,000. The provost explained that the proprietors were willing to give the commissioners every facility for the erection of the works, and some of them had promised wayleave at a nominal feu.

## FOREIGN AND COLONIAL.

**Nice.**—A most important step in the right direction has been taken by the Mayor of Nice, who has appointed a representative commission of all the local medical men to report on the sanitary condition of Nice, and the best means to take in order to effect satisfactory improvements. The English colony will be represented by Dr. Allen Sturge, and he says that the municipality are prepared to spend some millions, provided the commission agree that the expenditure is necessary. Some eight years ago £1,000,000 was spent on getting a supply of water on to the hill where the chateau stands wherewith to flush the old town, and five years ago nearly the same amount was granted for mending the drains. If a scheme proposed by Massou, of Paris, is adopted now the municipality will have to find 5,000,000 to 10,000,000 francs, which, it is understood, they are willing to do. Nice will then be a model town from a sanitary standpoint.

---

**Business Announcements.**—We have been informed that the business of Henry Hope, which has been established since 1818, has been converted into a private limited company, under the title of Henry Hope & Sons, Limited. The board of directors are composed of Messrs. Henry Hope (chairman), H. D. Hope, J. A. Hope and J. S. Nettlefold, and it will be the aim of the board to maintain, and if possible improve, the reputation of the firm for first-class work. The old-established conservatory and heating engineering business will be carried on, as before, under the personal superintendence of Mr. Henry Hope.—The Horsfall Furnace Syndicate have established a London office at 36 Great George-street, Westminster, S.W., where they will deal with inquiries for their well-known specialities—viz., refuse destructors and forced-draught boiler furnaces. It may be interesting to note that the firm is at present engaged upon a number of important contracts, among which are refuse destructors for the following: The Corporations of Ashton-under-Lyne, Huddersfield, Ramsgate, West Hartlepool and St. Helier's (Jersey); the County Councils of Lanarkshire and Cheshire; the Vestries of St. Luke and Fulham; the Strand Board of Works, and other authorities. Most of these works include complete steam-raising plant for use in connection with electric light and power stations.

# Some Recent Publications.

## MOTOR-CARS.

PETROLEUM MOTOR - CARS, by Louis Lockhart (Messrs. Sampson, Low, Marston & Co., Limited), forms the third section of a "Treatise on Auto-Cars on the Road" designed by the author to occupy four volumes, of which those treating of "Cycles" and "Steam Motor-Cars" have been already published, and that relating to "Motor-Cars worked by Electricity" has yet to appear. The book furnishes internal evidence of French sympathies and influence, the style of writing adopted is somewhat profuse, not to say inflated, and there is introduced much extraneous matter that must be deemed superfluous alike to the student and the general reader. Apart from these blemishes, a large amount of useful information on an interesting subject is afforded; and the letterpress is interspersed with an abundance of illustrations representing every variety of vehicle referred to in the text, as well as by diagrams of the different kinds of machinery, and the sundry appliances utilised in their construction or associated with their use. M. Ballif, president of the Touring Club of France, writes an introduction to the book, and in triumphant accents remarks: "People who two years ago would have been horrified at the very mention of travelling at a speed of 30 kilometres (18½ miles) an hour on a steam-car now look on calmly, if not with envy, as they see careering along omnibuses, brakes and victorias built by Serpollet, Lavassor or Peugeot." A perusal of this volume would, however, induce us to endorse the views expressed by M. Lockhart when discussing the future of auto-locomotion. "The application of motors worked by hydro carburets to the propulsion of auto-motor-cars, as well as the construction of these motors, more especially petroleum motors, is," he says, "at present, in an initial stage; it is therefore no easy task to write on a subject as yet undefined, and which is just in that state of indecision and uncertainty that when we have started we find that we have acquired just sufficient experience about direct-combustion motors to enable us to fully recognise their defects and to feel the necessity for introducing improvements. It is no exaggeration to say that, of all the motors now in use for propelling horse-less carriages, there is not one that gives complete satisfaction or is perfectly adapted to the purpose for which it is intended." The author at a later stage enters on more debateable ground when he contends that "auto-locomotion remains preeminently a French industry," and further declares that "it is French both by origin as well as by the relative perfection of the results obtained in our country (France), where it has certainly achieved the highest degree of development hitherto reached." These opinions are somewhat inconsistent with the information contained in a carefully-prepared and well-compiled volume that has reached us, and which describes in detail recent proceedings in this country. We refer to the JUDGES' REPORT OF THE LIVERPOOL TRIALS OF MOTOR VEHICLES FOR HEAVY TRAFFIC, 1898, edited by E. Shrapnell Smith (Wins'anley & Watkins, Liverpool. Price 5s.). The Self-propelling Traffic Association (Incorporated), under whose auspices these trials were conducted, has as its president Sir David Salomons, Bart., and numbers among its supporters many prominent persons whose names have been long identified with successful scientific experiments. The sections of the report preceding the general account of the trials give full particulars of the origin of the competition and the organisation of the preliminary arrangements, as well as a very complete description of the various vehicles that took part in the contests. A subsequent section deals with actual results relative to the cost of working these respectively, the calculations being determined to the nett ton-mile and the rate of speed per hour obtained. And here we may note that, apart altogether from the question of perfection or defect in construction and of success or failure in the practical working of self-propelling motor vehicles, the initial cost and the annual expenditure involved must for some years at least prove a serious obstacle to the general adoption of this convenient and desirable method of transit. From a series of estimates we learn that the prime cost of the vehicles engaged in these competitions ranged from £375 to £750, and that the annual working expenses, including interest on the purchase money and due allowance for depreciation, varied from £367 to £580. Diagrams on large folding sheets are introduced to illustrate in section the distances accomplished, with the various altitudes attained throughout each route. The clear letterpress and excellent reproductions of photographs are very attractively presented to us on fine art paper, and the report as a whole reflects credit on all who were concerned in its production.

## SOME PERIODICALS.

Cassier's Magazine (1s.) has always a good variety of interesting engineering matter. This month we observe such topics as luxury in American railway travelling, the Vesuvius cable railway, articles on aspects of military, naval and railway engineering, and an interesting speculation as to the transportation and lifting of heavy bodies by the ancients. There is a portrait and biography of Mr. John A. F. Aspinall, chief mechanical engineer to the Lancashire and Yorkshire Railway Company.—It is needless to repeat what we have said on previous occasions as to the general get-up of The Architectural Review (1s.). The contents, both literary and artistic, are always chosen with care and ability. Theatre-goers and readers of the elder Dumas will turn with interest to the first of a series of articles on the castles of "The Three Musketeers," a beginning being made with the Pierrefonds of the immortal Porthos. Restoration, the architecture of Michael Angelo, the arts of ancient Egypt, the work of G. F. Watts, and the architecture and antiquities of Cyprus, are also among the chief subjects dealt with. The special plates, including a photograve, need no praise.—The chief contents of our American contemporary, The Sanitarian, are an article on theatre sanitation and a report of the proceedings at the last meeting of the American Public Health Association.— Those of our readers who wish to read something lighter than matters of engineering and sanitary interest should find something to their taste in The Cornhill (1s.). The Rev. W. H. Fitchett continues his stirring "Fights for the Flag," the Bishop of London discourses on heroes, there is another instalment of the interesting Etchingham Letters; Mr. Garratt Fisher has a "Study in Imposture", Cavendish explains the game of "bridge," "Some Significant Acts of Parliament" are commented upon, and Mr. E. G. Henham gives an assortment of "Humours of Speech and Pen." These constitute not a bad programme for one number.—The North American Review (2s. 6d.) is of rather heavier calibre. "The Reorganisation of the Naval Personnel" is discussed by some well-known citizens of the United States, Max O'Rell gives us the first of a series of "Studies in Cheerfulness," and Lieut. Winston Churchill writes on "The Fashoda Incident." The prevention of yellow fever, the proposed Nicaragua canal, the Atlantic fisheries question, and ethics and etiquette, are among the other subjects which form the themes of articles.—The Christmas Bookseller (1s.) should be consulted by all who have any occasion to buy books at the festive season for presents or for their own use.—In Daily (1s.), "Borderer" deals with the etiquotte of field sports, "F. G." lifts "the curtain of the past," and Mr. G. H. Underhill has another sketch of a "sporting celebrity." There is the usual monthly record and comment, which, with other features, contribute to make this periodical so excellent an organ of field sports.—The American Review of Reviews provides an admirable monthly survey of the world's progress, with special reference, of course, to America and its problems, especially some recent ones of an Imperial character. There are some comments on the tasks that await American engineers in the new possessions. Many English municipal engineers and others will turn with sympathetic interest to Dr. Albert Shaw's appreciative notice of the life and work of the late Colonel Waring.—In Longman's (6d.) there are instalments of two serials, one by Mr. Rider Haggard. Mrs. Lecky describes the coming of age of the Queen of the Netherlands, and Mrs. Clement Parsons an etiquette-book of the seventeenth century, and Mr. Andrew Lang is still in evidence.—The Journal of State Medicine (2s.) is largely occupied with the subject of tuberculosis, the chief contribution being Sir Richard Thorne Thorne's "Harben" lecture. In an editorial article objection is taken to the combining of the duties of surveyor and sanitary inspector. — The chief articles in our instructive contemporary, Knowledge (6d.), deal with volcanoes and "The Christmas Customs of Shakespeare's Greenwood."—Among the subjects dealt with in Work (6d.) for December are photography, engine indicators, metal-plate work and railway waggons.—We observe that our enterprising monthly contemporaries, The Quarry and The Builders' Merchant, are to be amalgamated, and may soon be published as a fortnightly. We have no doubt the venture will meet with success.—We have also to acknowledge The Journal of the Royal Colonial Institute (6d.), The Sanitary Inspectors' Journal (6d.), The Journal of the Clerks of Works' Association (2d.), The Analyst (1s.), The Journal of the Society of Estate Clerks of Works, Great Thoughts, and Chums.

*Any of the Books noted below will be sent post free if the published price be forwarded to the offices of THE SURVEYOR.*

THE PROCEEDINGS OF THE INCORPORATED ASSOCIATION OF MUNICIPAL AND COUNTY ENGINEERS, vol. xxiv., 1897-98, edited by Thomas Cole, A.M.I.C.E.: 368 pp., 8, in. by 5½ in. E. & F. N. Spon.

THE TWENTY-SEVENTH ANNUAL REPORT OF THE LOCAL GOVERNMENT BOARD, 1897-98 (medical supplement); 344 pp., 9½ in. by 6 in. Her Majesty's Stationery Office. Price 4s. 11½d.

TILT EFFECT OF FIRE: A Report on the Horne Building Fire, Pittsburg, U.S.A., with fourteen plates and illustrations; 30 pp., 8½ in. by 5½ in. The British Fire-prevention Committee. Price 2s. 6d.

REPORT OF THE MORECAMBE BAY SEWERAGE SCHEME, by H. Bertram Nichols, A.M.I.C.E.: 12 pp., 8½ in. by 5½ in. Hodgetts, Limited. Price 6d.

# Personal.

On Saturday the Metropolitan Asylums Board decided to appoint an assistant engineer, at a commencing salary of £300 per annum.

We learn that Mr. J. T. Battersby, of Ambleside, has been appointed to the post of gas and water manager to the Ambleside Urban District Council.

Mr. T. H. Yabbicom, city engineer of Bristol, has been transferred from the class of "Associate Members" of the Institution of Civil Engineers to that of "Members."

At the last ordinary meeting of the Sheffield Society of Architects and Surveyors, Mr. Beresford Pite, of London, delivered a lecture on "Michael Angelo's Architecture."

Whitechapel District Board on Monday appointed Mr. Wright, electrical engineer to the Brighton Corporation, to carry out the electric lighting of the Whitechapel district, at a salary of £600 per annum.

Keynsham Rural District Council have selected Mr. James W. Hawkins, who is at present surveyor to the Weobley Rural District Council, to fill the post of highway surveyor, at a commencing salary of £150.

Mr. Harry Holmes, late assistant in the borough surveyor's department, Burton, has been successful in obtaining an appointment under the Works Department of the Birmingham Corporation, at a salary of £175 per annum.

Mr. Charles Henry Lawton, of Silverdale, North Staffs., has been appointed surveyor to the Wirksworth Urban District Council, and will commence his duties early in January. There were twenty-three applicants for the post.

Mr. G. McHarg, surveyor of highways under the Stoke Rural District Council, was, at a meeting of that authority, held last week, granted an increase of salary, several members bearing testimony to the satisfactory way in which he had discharged his duties.

Captain R. G. B. Crompton, who has been appointed major in command of the Electrical Engineer (Royal Engineers) Volunteers, in place of the late Dr. John Hopkinson, is not only a well-known electrical engineer, but served as an officer in the Rifle Brigade in the sixties.

Mr. R. E. W. Berrington, the late borough engineer of Wolverhampton, has been unanimously elected to the position of chairman of the Health Committee of the corporation. His experience as a specialist in sanitary engineering work should prove of great service to the borough.

Mr. W. A. Nicholson, who has for over two years acted as surveyor to the Brightlingsea Urban District Council, has submitted his resignation. Mr. Nicholson, it is understood, has been appointed to the position of chief assistant surveyor to the Tendring Hundred Rural District Council.

In consequence of inability to find a candidate to fill the position of superintending architect to the London County Council, the General Purposes Committee recommended, at a meeting of the council on Tuesday, that Mr. Blashill should be asked to retain the position until March next. This course was adopted.

At an adjourned meeting of the Court of Common Council, on Thursday week, the City Lands Committee asked for authority to retain the services of Prof. Aitchison, R.A., president of the Royal Institute of British Architects, in connection with the preparation of designs for the rebuilding of the Sessions House, Old Bailey, at an honorarium of 400 guineas. This was agreed to.

By a large majority the Penzance Town Council last week adopted a resolution of the General Purposes Committee, recommending that a testimonial should be presented to Mr. Small, the retiring surveyor, and that the corporation should head the list with a sum of £100. A committee is to be appointed to collect further subscriptions and to carry out the testimonial, the mayor acting as secretary.

Mr. J. R. Blackwall, a late pupil of Mr. E. Purnell Hooley, county surveyor of Nottinghamshire, was last month appointed to a district surveyorship under the Derbyshire County Council, and on Tuesday Mr. C. Hodges, an improver in Mr. Hooley's office, was appointed by the Highways Committee of the Bedfordshire County Council district surveyor, subject to the approval of the county council.

Mr. Rupert M. Evans, senior assistant in the office of Mr. W. Blackshaw, borough engineer and surveyor of Stafford, has been the recipient, on the occasion of his leaving Stafford, of a case of drawing instruments, as a slight mark of the esteem and respect in which he is held by the office staff. Mr. Evans is about to take up similar duties on the engineering staff of the County Borough of Hanley, under Mr. J. Lobley, the borough engineer.

At last week's meeting of the Plymouth Borough Council the chairman of the Works Committee raised the question of the appointment of a general assistant in the surveyor's department—a subject which provoked much discussion at a previous meeting—and emphasised the importance of the vacancy being filled. It was ultimately decided that one of the assistants to the water engineer should be appointed temporarily to the post.

There were forty candidates for the appointment of electrical engineer to the East Ham Urban District Council, and of these nine were selected to attend the final meeting of the council. Mr. W. C. Ullmann, who is at present engaged by the British Thomson-Houston Company, Limited, as resident engineer, superintending the construction of the city of Sheffield electric tramways, was subsequently appointed. He has had a varied practical experience, both in this country and abroad.

Consideration was, on Thursday, given by the Folkestone Town Council to the appointment of a surveyor in succession to the late Mr. J. White. Out of 126 applications seven were ultimately selected for interview, and after seeing these gentlemen and considering their applications and testimonials, the council, after further deliberation, reduced the number to three. All these ran one another close in qualification, but it was eventually decided to appoint Mr. A. C. Nichols, of Leeds, to the vacant post.

*The North China Daily News* states that on the 3rd November, at the Holy Trinity Cathedral, Shanghai, Mr. Charles Henry Godfrey, assistant municipal engineer of Shanghai, was married to Mary Elizabeth, daughter of Mr. James Reynolds Hewlett, of Chicago, U.S.A., and adopted neice of Mr. Daniel Hewlett, of Barnwood Court, Gloucester, England. The wedding presents, we understand, included a solid silver tea service from the members of the Shanghai Municipal Council in their private capacities.

An enjoyable evening was spent by the staff of the Willesden Urban District Council on Thursday, when the third annual dinner was given at the Frascati Restaurant. The chair was occupied by Mr. O. Claude Robson, and among those present were Messrs. Stanley Ball (clerk), H. H. Humphreys (deputy engineer), B. Hayior (assistant surveyor), H. Northcroft (quantity surveyor), and W. L. T. Brown and E. Willis (building surveyors). In responding to the toast of "The Chairman," Mr. Robson said they had been fortunate in possessing a local board and district council, not only willing to do justice to the public, but also to the officials; and it was due to this spirit of justice that the latter had ever a desire to do their work thoroughly and promote the prosperity of the district.

On the presentation of the report of the Highways Committee, at a meeting of the London County Council on Tuesday, Mr. Benn, chairman of the committee, stated, in reply to a number of questions, that it was the case, as reported, that Mr. A. Baker, who was last week appointed manager of the council's tramways, had written to say that the Nottingham Corporation had refused to relieve him from his duties in Nottingham for six months, or to give him facilities for attending to the work of the council. Mr. Baker added that great inducements had been offered to him to remain in Nottingham, but he had informed the corporation that he was pledged to the council, and he now left himself in their hands. Mr. Benn stated that the Highways Committee had felt it necessary to take this matter into immediate consideration. They felt they had to face some little difficulty, but he thought that after a few letters had passed between the council and the Nottingham Corporation the difficulty would be overcome. In the meantime, and for the protection of the council's interest, the committee had decided to appoint a special sub-committee, consisting of five members of the council, to undertake, on January 2nd, the management of the tramways.

Mr. Alfred Baker, the manager of the Nottingham Corporation tramways, who was last week appointed to a similar post under the London County Council, is a Lincoln man, but has spent nearly the whole of his life in Nottingham. During the last twenty years he has been on the staff of the tramway company there, and was appointed manager of the undertaking in 1891. In 1897, when the undertaking was municipalised, the corporation retained Mr. Baker's services, and he has since then had the absolute control of the system. Its owners have had under consideration the question of mechanical traction, and have visited all the principal towns in the United Kingdom for the purpose of inspecting the best systems and of finding out all that could be done to improve their possession. In these and other visits they have been accompanied by Mr. Baker. They have finally decided to make extensions of over 40 miles in length on the overhead electrical system. This scheme, as the town clerk, Sir Samuel Johnson, pointed out in recommending Mr. Baker for the London appointment, involved an outlay of over £500,000, and yet the corporation had not felt it at all necessary to call in expert advice. They were quite content to accept the recommendations of their manager. The people of Nottingham are sorry to lose Mr. Baker's services, and it is said that efforts have been made to induce him to stay, but at present the position of the tramways department there is not strong enough to justify its committee in increasing the salary of the post to such an extent as would offer him a strong inducement to reconsider his resolution.

## MAIN ROAD MAINTENANCE DISPUTE AT GAINSBOROUGH.

### LOCAL GOVERNMENT BOARD INQUIRY.

Colonel Slacke, R.E., recently held an inquiry at Gainsborough, on behalf of the Local Government Board, respecting the dispute between the urban district council and the Lindsey County Council as to the payment for main road improvements at Morton. In reference to the north section of the road leading from the vicarage to North Marsh-road, the county council argued that it was new work and was of purely urban benefit; and with respect to the southern section, from near Elm Cottage to Love-lane, that the widening was also on new ground, and that the work done was not in connection with reasonable repair and maintenance of the main road proper; that this also was of urban benefit solely, and, further, when the district council meditated undertaking the work they should have obtained the sanction of the county council if they wished them to pay for it as a main road charge. The contention of the district council was that the work was not new, but was in the nature of an improvement; that as the thoroughfare was one of the chief arteries for ingress and egress between the country and the town, the work was beneficial to the public at large.

#### THE CASE FOR THE DISTRICT COUNCIL.

Mr. D. M. Robbs, clerk to the district council, said the dispute between the two authorities was the question of the pavement of the two sections of the main road which was known as Morton-road. The expenses were incurred in the financial year ended on March 31, 1897. Dealing more particularly with the north section, he said the road was an awarded road under an Act of Parliament dated in the time of George III. He proceeded to argue that there could be no enlargement or widening of the Morton-road, because it was staked out in the award as 60 ft., and it was that distance to-day. The question in dispute, he said, was as to who should pay for the work which had been done to the road. The county council objected to pay any portion of the costs, on the grounds that being new works solely required in consequence of the erection of new houses within the urban district they were not liable for repayment. He maintained that it was not a new work. The district council had made a substitution or an improvement where a footway had existed. He then quoted written judgments and definitions by several well-known authorities in support of his contention that county councils were responsible for similar work to that done by the district council. As to the argument that the footway was of a purely local benefit, Mr. Robbs submitted statistics of the traffic on the road, and stated that it was the only artery leading into and out of the town by which persons coming from the northward could enter. Morton, Walkerith, Stockwith, Wildsworth, Laughton and Blyton were all within 6 miles, and the agricultural population on that side fed the town through that artery with all their country produce in the same way in which the town fed the country with town-made goods, &c. Therefore there was a constant journey backwards and forwards along the road. In reference to the south section, he held that old streets under certain circumstances, such as the erection of houses, &c., became new streets. When the new houses were built under their by-laws the road was bound to be made to the width of 40 ft. Prior to the widening it was only 30 ft. to 31 ft. from fence to fence, and was dangerous to traffic. It became congested, and people driving along it complained, while hundreds of cyclists now used it. It was dangerous to come from a road 60 ft. wide into a bottle-neck as it were.

Mr. CHARLES SCORER, clerk to the county council, here stated that it might shorten the proceedings if he admitted that the widening was a reasonable work for the district council to carry out.

Mr. ROBBS, continuing, impressed upon the Court that the improvement, if paid for or not, had been carried out on the most economical lines, because the landowner gave them the land required and also a contribution of £26 towards the cost of making the new footway. He then went on to show that the improvements had a distinct connection with the maintenance of the roads. In conclusion, he said that he had witnesses to prove the statements he had made, and he would also prove the statistics if necessary. He then called

Mr. HENRY RILEY, surveyor to the district council, who said that when he was appointed to his position (in 1894) the north section of the road in question had no proper footpath. It was formed of cinders and road scrapings, and was 2 yards wide. The condition of the path in winter weather was very bad, almost impassable after a heavy frost. The drainage was by means of pipes leading into a field ditch. He subsequently channelled, asphalted and kerbed the road, in fact, did the work, for which payment was now claimed from the county council, at a cost of £148 in the north section, while in the south section he did similar work at a cost of £118. The work was done by contract, was fair and reasonable, and would reduce the future cost of repair and maintenance. He therefore considered that it was a proper improvement to be carried out

Two ratepayers, who had resided in the road for a number of years, next gave evidence, after which

Mr. McBRAIN, city surveyor of Lincoln, was called. He said he thought the works very reasonable and necessary. They were of a permanent character, and, in his opinion, were properly included in the maintenance and repair of a main road. If the traffic increased to a certain degree he thought the county council ought to pay for the necessary widening.

#### THE CASE FOR THE COUNTY COUNCIL.

Mr. CHARLES SCORER, clerk to the county council, then stated his points in justification of the county council for the non-payment of the cost of the works. There was no question, he said, as to the reasonableness of the expenditure, but a very much larger question arose as to the liability of the county council for the payment of any portion of these works. If it were decided that the county council were liable, he submitted that the repayment should be extended over a considerable number of years. The Act did not say that the county council must pay for enlargement. The district council should keep their roads as originally mained, or come to the county council and ask them for a contribution. The proceedings of that day would not terminate the difficulty, for they had received an intimation that a similar application would shortly be made in respect of another section of the same road lying between the two sections in question. The district council had determined that they were masters of the situation, and seemed bent on making the county council pay.

Mr. THROPP, county surveyor, said the road was mained in 1883, and at that time it was in a fair condition. For traffic north of Morton-road the old footpath on the east side was sufficient. The improvements were more for the benefit of the town than of the adjoining district. He thought the work must be regarded as an enlargement rather than as an improvement. In cross-examination, witness said the county council had had slight differences with other urban authorities. They had had three arbitrations. It was not wise and necessary, from the county council standpoint, to have the road widened. He thought there was space sufficient for the traffic. Before the alterations on April 7, 1896, witness presented a report to the county council in which he said he did not think there was any course open to the Highways Committee but to recommend the consent of the county council to the expenditure in respect of the south section. He also reported that the increased width of the roadway would give more room for the heavy traffic, and cause that part of the road to be maintained at a comparatively less cost. Further, in his report he said that the north section was an entirely new work, and it might be open to question whether the county would have to pay the whole or any of the cost, but he feared the county council would have to pay the expense. If the district council had intended to widen their roadway without constructing a footway in the south section, the county council would not have allowed it.

Mr. CODRINGTON, formerly an inspector of the Local Government Board, took the view that no part of the works in the south section constituted an improvement connected with maintenance and repair, and no part was chargeable to the county council. The point had often arisen in disputes, and had been decided in favour of the county council whenever there had been any widening that had not been paid for by the county council.

Mr. ROBBS objected to the witness quoting his own decision in a number of cases of arbitration. It was not etiquette for Mr. Codrington to come there as a professional witness and to use the experience he had gained in the service of the Local Government Board. He asked the inspector to take note of his objection.

Mr. W. EMBLETON FOX, chairman of the Lindsey County Council, was the next witness, and the evidence closed.

Mr. SCORER informed the inspector that the Lindsey County Council were prepared to take a case to the High Court to test the question as to the liability of the county council for the cost of construction of works completed by the district council upon land added to the road. He knew it was contrary to the practice of the Local Government Board to give reasons for their decisions, but he hoped they would be able to gather from the award the grounds upon which the decision was made.

A vote of thanks to the inspector brought the proceedings to a close.

---

**Private Bill Legislation.**—Saturday night was the latest time for depositing in the office of the Clerk of the Parliaments copies of private or local Bills which it is proposed to introduce when the two Houses assemble in February. Plans in connection with those Bills requiring them were, it will be remembered, deposited at the Private Bill Office at the end of last month, and it was the measures themselves, some of which do not require plans, and were therefore not included in the former list, that were handed in on Saturday. The Bills of interest to London include the London County Council (General Powers), London Improvements (Holborn to Strand, Southampton-row Widening, High-street, Kensington, and other works), London Water (Welsh Reservoirs and Works), London Water (Aqueducts and Works), London Water (Purchase of Companies), and the London Water (Finance). The Scotch measures include the Glasgow Corporation Telephones Bill. The total number of Bills handed in was 207, as compared with 249 last year.

## EAST-END WATER SUPPLY.

### SOME EFFECTS OF THE DROUGHT.

In certain parts of the district which they cover the East London Water Company had already resumed the constant supply of water. The whole district did not, however, receive a constant service till Wednesday. It was on Monday, August 22nd, that the supply was first restricted to six hours a day, and on September 3rd the supply was still further reduced to two periods of two hours in each day. Assuming that all consumers obtained a full supply on Wednesday, it follows that the short service has been extended over about sixteen weeks. It was an immense effort to maintain even the restricted service.

The Grand Junction, Kent, New River, and Southwark and Vauxhall companies gave assistance by transferring water to the East London Company, the magnitude of this assistance being shown by the fact that during the month of October alone the quantity so transferred was no less than 359,160,000, an average of over 11,500,000 gallons a day. The supply of the East London Company, however, still fell short by 10,000,000 gallons a day, as compared with the supply they were able to furnish in the corresponding month of last year.

As to the effect of the drought upon the quality of the water, Sir William Crookes and Prof. Dewar make some interesting observations. They describe the drought as the most severe for forty years, but say that the average condition of the raw, unfiltered Thames and Lea waters continued exceptionally good. "The condition of the filtered water supplied to London was," they say, "excellent, and in the case of the East London supply the quality was substantially the same as during similar seasons, when the supply of water was ample." Again, they remark that the large rainfall in October had the effect of suddenly washing into the rivers organic matter accumulated in the watershed during the drought; and as the reservoirs of the East London Company were almost empty at the end of September, the company was forced in October to use the Lea, without the advantage of purification resulting from proper storage in the reservoirs. During that critical time Sir W. Crookes and Prof. Dewar took extra pains to ascertain the character of the East-End supply. They report with satisfaction that, "in spite of the severe strain thus thrown on their filtering appliances, the clear water supplied to East London has been bacteriologically better than it was during the months of August and September."

## STOCKPORT WATER SUPPLY.

### PROPOSED MUNICIPALISATION.

At an extraordinary meeting of the proprietors of the Stockport District Waterworks Company, last week, the chairman reported on the negotiations between the directors and the Corporation of Stockport, which had resulted in an agreement for the sale and transfer of the undertaking of the company to the corporation. The agreement having been read and explained, a resolution approving and adopting it was passed on the motion of the chairman. It is understood that the cost to the Corporation of Stockport will be nearly £800,000 for the transfer, to be followed by a large outlay on developments. Although the price is considered by many somewhat high, yet there is a general feeling of satisfaction in the town that the corporation, after various efforts extending over a long series of years, is likely to obtain control of the water supply. The area of supply extends also to Alderley, Wilmslow, Cheadle, Bredbury, Heaton Chapel, Reddish, Hazel Grove, Disley, &c.

**Electric Light in the City.**—*The City Press* state that they understand, on the very highest authority, that there is every possibility of a conference taking place in the near future between the Streets Committee of the corporation and the City of London Electric Lighting Company with reference to the purchase by the corporation of the company's undertaking. The directors, it is understood, are quite prepared to sell their property if the terms offered are sufficiently tempting. Naturally they are unable to give any indication of what the views of the board are as to the sum they will feel disposed to accept.

**A New Incandescent Electric Lamp.**—It is stated that a new form of incandescent electric lamp has been invented by Prof. Nernst, of Göttingen. Instead of a carbon filament in an exhausted bulb, it has a block of magnesia heated to an enormously high temperature. The principle relied upon is the fact that when magnesia is heated above 3,000 deg. C. it becomes a good conductor of electricity and will retain its brilliant incandescence without much expenditure of current. To start the lamp, however, it is necessary first to heat the magnesia up to a certain temperature, and this is effected by Prof. Nernst by placing it in the focus of a reflector, on the inner side of which is a spiral of platinum wire, which is readily brought to bright heat. As soon as a current starts in the magnesia the platinum wire is cut off. It is claimed that the new lamp is economical, and that it gives a purer light than the carbon filament; but this remains to be proved.

## THE SURVEYORS' INSTITUTION.

### ORDINARY GENERAL MEETING.

The next ordinary general meeting of the above Institution will be held on Monday, January 9, 1899, when the adjourned discussion on the paper read by Mr. Wm. Weaver at the last meeting, entitled "The London Building Act and the Official Supervision of Buildings," will be resumed. The chair will be taken at 8 o'clock.

### JUNIOR MEETING.

The second of four meetings of examinees and students of the Institution, authorised (subject to certain conditions) by the council to be held during the present session, will take place on Monday, January 30, 1899, when a paper will be read by Mr. H. M. Rogers on " Land and Land Tenure." The chair will be taken at 7 o'clock.

### STUDENTS' PRELIMINARY EXAMINATION, 1899.

Those proposing to enter their names for the students' preliminary examination, to be held on the 18th and 19th of January next, must intimate their intention to the secretary before the last day of November. It is proposed to examine candidates from the counties of Lancashire, Cheshire, Yorkshire, Durham, Cumberland, Westmoreland and Northumberland at Manchester. Candidates from other counties in England and Wales will be examined in London. Irish candidates will be examined in Dublin.

### PROFESSIONAL EXAMINATIONS, 1899.

Students eligible for the proficiency examinations (which will commence on the 20th of March next) must give notice of the sub-division (Table A of Rules) in which they elect to be examined, not later than the 31st inst. Examinations qualifying for the classes of "Professional Associates" and "Fellows" will also commence on the 20th of March next. Names of applicants for these latter examinations to be sent in before the 31st inst. All particulars as to days, subjects and course of examination will be forwarded on application to the secretary. English candidates for the professional examinations will be examined in London. Irish candidates will be examined in Dublin.

### PROPOSED SPECIAL-CERTIFICATE EXAMINATIONS (FOR MEMBERS), 1899.

Notice is also given that the next special-certificate examinations in forestry, sanitary science and land surveying and levelling are proposed to be held on Tuesday, Wednesday and Thursday, the 13th, 14th and 15th of June. Particulars of these examinations can be obtained from the secretary.

**Proposed Electric Ferry across the Thames.**—A novel scheme for a new ferry, by which passenger and vehicular traffic may be conveyed from Greenwich to Millwall, has, according to *The City Press*, just been completed. In the ensuing session of Parliament power will be sought to incorporate a company to construct and work the ferry by electricity or other power on submerged rails across the river. The line will run from a point near the site of Brewhouse-lane to the western boundary of the Island Gardens, Poplar. It is proposed to take power to sell or lease the undertaking to the corporation, the London County Council, or any corporate body.

## APPOINTMENTS VACANT.

*Official and all similar advertisements received later than Wednesday evening are too late for classification and cannot therefore be included in these summaries until the following week. No advertisements received after 3 p.m. on Thursday can be inserted until the following week.*

INSPECTOR OF WEIGHTS AND MEASURES.—December 24th.—Corporation of South Shields. £120.—Mr. J. Moore Hayton, town clerk.

BUILDING INSPECTOR.—December 27th.—Corporation of Sutton Coldfield. 30s.—Mr. W. A. H. Clarry, A.M.I.C.E., borough surveyor.

BUILDING INSPECTOR.—December 27th.—Corporation of Sutton Coldfield. 30s.—Mr. H. Clarry, A.M.I.C.E., borough surveyor.

TEMPORARY ENGINEERING ASSISTANTS (TWO) FOR UNDERGROUND TELEPHONE WORKS.—December 27th.—Manchester Corporation. £3 3s.—The City Surveyor.

TOWN ENGINEER AND SURVEYOR.—December 30th.—Town Council of Ayr, N.B. £300.—Mr. A. G. Young, town clerk.

ASSISTANT ENGINEER.—December 31st.—Carlisle Corporation. £130.—Mr. C. D. Burnet, city electrical engineer.

ASSISTANT ENGINEER FOR TRAMWAYS DEPARTMENT.—December 31st.—Manchester Corporation. £200.—Mr. Wm. Henry Talbot, town clerk.

TEMPORARY ENGINEERING ASSISTANT FOR TRAMWAYS DEPARTMENT. — December 31st. — Manchester Corporation. £2 10s.—Mr. Wm. Henry Talbot, town clerk.

MANAGER AND BAILIFF OF SEWAGE FARM.—January 1st.—Corporation of Banbury. £100.— Mr. Oliver J. Stockton, town clerk.

TEMPORARY ASSISTANT.—January 2nd.—Morley Corporation. £2 2s.—Mr. W. E. Putman, A.M.I.C.E., borough engineer and surveyor.

SUB-INSPECTORS OF NUISANCES (TWO).—January 2nd.—Bradford Corporation. £80.—The Town Clerk.

INSPECTOR OF ROADS.—January 2nd.—Vestry of St. Mary, Islington. £2 10s.—Mr. J. Patten Barber, chief surveyor to the vestry.

BOROUGH SURVEYOR.—January 4th.—Corporation of Penzance. £200.—Mr. T. H. Cornish, town clerk.

DISTRICT ROAD SURVEYOR.—January 5th.—Norfolk County Council. £2.—Mr. T. H. B. Heslop, county surveyor, Norwich.

ASSISTANT COUNTY ROAD SURVEYOR'S CLERK.—January 5th.—Worcestershire County Council. £52.—Mr. S. Thornely, county clerk, Shire Hall, Worcester.

ASSISTANT SANITARY INSPECTOR. — January 9th. — West Bromwich Corporation.—Mr. Alfred Caddick, town clerk.

INSPECTOR OF NUISANCES.—January 9th.—West Bromwich Corporation. £150.—Mr. Alfred Caddick, town clerk.

TEMPORARY CLERK OF WORKS.—£3 3s.—Box 95, office of THE SURVEYOR, 24 Bride-lane, Fleet-street, London, E.C.

TEMPORARY ASSISTANT. — Southend-on-Sea Corporation. £3 3s.—Mr. Alfred Fidler, A.M.I.C.E., borough engineer and surveyor.

PUPIL.—Mr. Alfred Fidler, A.M.I.C.E., borough engineer and surveyor, Southend-on-Sea.

## MUNICIPAL COMPETITIONS OPEN.

*Official and all similar advertisements received later than Wednesday evening are too late for classification and cannot therefore be included in these summaries until the following week. No advertisements received after 3 p.m. on Thursday can be inserted until the following week.*

CHERTSEY.—December 23rd.—Sewerage and sewage disposal scheme for the Nos. 1 and 2 wards of the district. £50, £30 and £20.—Mr. T. E. Harland Chaldecott, clerk to the council.

HULL.—January 1st.—Erection of a central public library in Albion-street. £50, £30 and £20.—Mr. E. Laverack, town clerk.

HARROGATE.—January 2nd.—Erection of a pump-room, &c., at a cost not exceeding £8,000. £50, £30 and £20.—Mr. Samuel Stead, borough surveyor.

BRADFORD.— February 1st. — Erection of a central fire brigade station. £100, £50 and £30.—Mr. George McGuire, town clerk.

KNUTSFORD.—February 28th.—Laying out of a plot of land at Tabley Hill for a cemetery, and also the erection of a chapel and caretaker's lodge for same, for the urban district council.—Mr. W. J. Downes, surveyor to the council.

## MUNICIPAL CONTRACTS OPEN.

*Official and all similar advertisements received later than Wednesday evening are too late for classification and cannot therefore be included in these summaries until the following week. No advertisements received after 3 p.m. on Thursday can be inserted until the following week.*

LEICESTER.—December 23rd.—Erection of working-class dwellings in Winifred-street.—Mr. James Bell, town clerk.

CARLISLE.—December 23rd.—Extension of the present water mains from Cumwhinton to Cocklakes, &c., for the rural district council.—Mr. George Armstrong, surveyor to the council.

SWINTON.—December 24th.—Repaving of Swinton Hall-road with 6-in. by 3½-in. Welsh granite setts, for the urban district council.—Mr. Henry Eniwistle, surveyor to the council.

DARTMOUTH.—December 24th.—Ventilating, painting and other works at the Guildhall.—Mr. T. O. Veale, borough surveyor.

BACUP (Lancs.).—December 26th.—Excavating and sewering of Baldwin-street, Hugh-street and Taylor-terrace.—Mr. Francis Wood, borough surveyor.

BOURNEMOUTH.—December 27th.—Making-up and extension of Braidley-road.—Mr. F. W. Lacey, borough surveyor.

WINDERMERE.—December 27th.—Erection of offices, for the urban district council.—Mr. J. T. Dowson, clerk to the council.

BROMLEY.—December 27th.—Widening of a portion of Homesdale-road, for the urban district council.—Mr. Fred. H. Norman, clerk to the council.

BROMLEY.—December 27th.—Diversion of the culvert in Homesdale-road, for the urban district council.—Mr. Fred. H. Norman, clerk to the council.

CARLISLE.—December 27th.—Extension of the water main from Wetheral Pasture to Shield Head, for the rural district council.—Mr. John Little, sanitary engineer, Viaduct-chambers, Carlisle.

PENZANCE.—December 27th.—Supply of cast and wrought iron work, granite, blue lias lime, &c., during the year ending December 31, 1899.—Mr. T. H. Cornish, town clerk.

WATERLOO-WITH-SEAFORTH. — December 27th. — Sewering, paving, flagging, kerbing, channelling, &c., works in Corinthian-street, Rownall-street, Ionic-street, Doric-street and various passages in the district, for the urban district council.—Mr. F. Spencer Yates, A.M.I.C.E., surveyor to the council.

PENRITH.—December 28th.—Supply of about 25 tons of 4-in. cast-iron water pipes, for the urban district council.—Mr. Wm. Speddy, surveyor to the council.

ISLINGTON.—December 28th.—Enlargement of the electric light station in Eden-grove, Holloway, for the vestry.—Mr. Wm. F. Dewey, clerk to the vestry.

DUBLIN.—December 28th.—Supply of a high-tension single-pole switchboard, for the corporation.—Prof. Alexander B. W. Kennedy, 17 Victoria-street, London, S.W.

STANLEY (Durham).—December 28th.—Various road improvements near South Moor, for the urban district council.—Mr. Joseph Routledge, surveyor to the council.

OSWALDTWISTLE (Lancs.).—December 28th.—Sewering, excavating, paving and flagging of Watson-street, and the sewering of Back Bank-meadow-street.—Mr. R. N. Hunter, borough surveyor.

WREXHAM.—December 28th.—Extension of the sewer at Grange, Ponkey, near Ruabon, for the rural district council.—Mr. J. Oswell Bung, clerk to the council.

TORQUAY.—December 28th.—Paving, &c., of Bank-street and a portion of Victoria-road.—Mr. C. R. Pease, borough engineer and surveyor.

BASINGSTOKE.—December 28th.—Widening of Victoria-street and the construction of a new street contiguous thereto, 36 ft. wide.—Mr. George Fixton, borough surveyor.

LEEDS.—December 29th.—Supply of (a) underground conductors and (b) switchboards, &c., in connection with the extension of the electric tramway system, for the city council.—Messrs. Hopkinson & Talbot, 26 Victoria-street, London, S.W.

EMLEY (near Wakefield).—December 29th.—Laying of about 1,942 yards of 4-in. and 5,911 yards of 3-in. cast-iron water pipes, for the urban district council.—Mr. F. G. Heath, clerk to the council.

LEAMINGTON.—December 29th.—Laying of about 141 yards of tar paving and about 1,300 yards of kerb and channelling.—Mr. W. de Normanville, borough engineer.

MIDDLESBROUGH.—December 29th.—Reconstruction of Bright-street and Abingdon-road, and the temporary repair of the carriageways in Lincoln and Innes streets.—Mr. Frank Baker, borough engineer.

SUNDERLAND.—December 30th.—Supply of three 125-kilowatt direct-current high-speed steam dynamos, 460 volts.—Mr. J. F. C. Snell, A.M.I.C.E., borough electrical engineer.

HULL.—December 30th.—Supply of steel roof trusses, steel columns, &c., in connection with the erection of car sheds for the electric tramways.—Mr. A. E. White, city engineer.

HULL.—December 30th.—Erection of two car sheds and other buildings (area about 4,000 square yards) in connection with the electric tramways.—Mr. A. E. White, city engineer.

HULL.—December 30th.—Supply of pipes, fittings, &c., for the power station in connection with the electric tramways.—Mr. A. E. White, city engineer.

WILLENHALL (Staffs.).—December 30th.—Erection of a new stand-roof greenhouse, 30 ft. by 12 ft., at the new cemetery at Bentley, for the urban district council.—Mr. Chas. J. Jenkin, engineer and surveyor to the council.

ELGIN.—December 30th.—Supply of road metal during the year ending May 15, 1900, for the various divisions of the county highways, for the county council.—Mr. Alexander Hogg, country road surveyor, 24 Academy-street, Elgin.

WEST SUSSEX.—December 31st.—Supply of picked surface flints, pit flints, local stone, and 2-in. broken granite or stone, from April 1, 1899, to March 31, 1900, for the county council.—Mr. W. R. Purser, county surveyor, 31 Bedford-road, Horsham.

DUNDEE.—December 31st.—Supply of 500 2-in., 1,000 4-in., 500 6-in. and 500 8-in. turned and bored cast-iron pipes, for the water commissioners.—Mr. George Baxter, engineer and manager to the commissioners, 93 Commercial-street, Dundee.

ROTHERHAM.—December 31st.—Supply and erection of sludge-pressing plant, boilers, sewage ejectors and sewage lifts, for the corporation.—Mr. R. B. W. Berrington, Bank-buildings, Wolverhampton.

RAMSATE.—December 31st.—Supply of a compound condensing-beam engine at the Whitehall pumping station.—Mr. William A. Valon, gas and water engineer to the corporation.

ST. GEORGE, HANOVER SQUARE.—December 31st.—Supply of various materials for one year from March 25, 1899, for the vestry.—Mr. George Livingstone, surveyor to the vestry.

FOLKESTONE.—December 31st.—Supply of 1,000 to 2,000 yards super. of 2¾-in. York stone.—Mr. A. F. Kidson, town clerk.

DARTMOUTH.—December 31st.—Erection of stone boundary walls and public latrines on the reclaimed land, North-parade and Mayor's-avenue, for the urban district council.—Mr. T. O. Veale, surveyor to the council.

TAUNTON.—January 1st.—Construction of a sewer, about 1,300 yards long, from Railway-gates to the site of the sewage outfall work in the Target Field.—Mr. James H. Smith, borough surveyor.

PADDINGTON.—January 2nd.—Supply of two dust-tipping vans, three slop-tipping vans and five pairs of wheels, for the vestry.—Mr. Frank Delbridge, clerk to the vestry.

STIRLING.—January 2nd.—Supply of various electric lighting plant, for the commissioners.—Prof. A. B. W. Kennedy, 17 Victoria-street, London, S.W.

LEAMINGTON.—January 2nd.—Erection of an entrance lodge to Victoria Park, for the corporation.—Mr. Fredk. G. Cundall, 41 Parade, Leamington.

EASTBOURNE.—January 2nd.—Relaying of the Tideswell-road district low-level sewer.—Mr. R. M. Cloyne, A.M.I.C.E., borough engineer.

WIMBLEDON.—January 2nd.—Making-up of Malcolm-road, for the urban district council.—Mr. W. H. Whitfield, clerk to the council.

LIMEHOUSE.—January 2nd.—Relaying the paving of Galt-street and parts of Rhodeswell-road and Belgrave-street, for the district board of works.—Mr. S. G. Ratcliff, clerk to the board.

EDINBURGH.—January 2nd.—Supply and delivery at the electric light works in Macdonald-road of a switch-board and boosters, for the corporation.—Prof. A. B. W. Kennedy, 17 Victoria-street, London, S.W.

BOOTLE (Lancs.).—January 2nd.—Certain private improvement works in College-view and various passages in the borough.—The Borough Engineer.

RYDE (I.W.).—January 3rd.—Supply of two new pumping engines, overhead travelling crane and a Galloway boiler at the Knighton pumping station, near Newchurch.—Mr. C. G. Vincent, town clerk.

GLASGOW.—January 3rd.—Supply and erection of generating plant at one of the new electricity works, for the corporation.—Mr. W. A. Chamen, 75 Waterloo-street, Glasgow.

HAMMERSMITH (Staffs.).—January 3rd.—Making-up of part of Putney-road, for the urban district council.—Mr. E. Kenworthy, engineer and surveyor to the council.

EPPING (Essex).—January 3rd.—Construction of about 1 mile of 12-in. and 9-in. iron and stoneware pipe sewers and the preparation of the outfall land, for the rural district council.—Mr. G. J. Child, clerk to the council.

HOVE.—January 4th.—Road-making and various works in Sackville-street and Molesworth-street.—Mr. H. H. Scott, borough surveyor.

MIDDLETON (Lancs.). — January 4th. — Sewering and drainage of Haworth and Wade streets.—Mr. W. Wilburn, borough surveyor.

JOHANNESBURG, S.A.—January 6th.—Supply of a complete air-buretted water-gas plant, for the corporation.—Messrs. Robert White & Co., 22 Bury-street, St. Mary Axe, London, E.C.

BIRMINGHAM.—January 6th.—Installation of inclined indents, together with coal and coke elevators and conveyors at the Millbank gasworks.—Mr. James Parkinson, town clerk.

WAKEFIELD.—January 6th.—Making-up of Mannington-road (southern portion) and Asylum-road (eastern portion), for the urban district council.—Mr. Wm. Blewitt, clerk to the council.

WEST HAM.—January 7th.—Enlargement of the hospital in Southern-road, Plaistow, E.—Mr. Fred. K. Hilleary, town clerk.

CARMARTHEN.—January 7th.—Supply of 11,400 yards of 9-in., 2,100 yards of 6-in., 1,500 yards of 4-in., and 4,500 yards of 3-in. cast-iron water pipes.—Mr. F. J. Finglah, borough surveyor.

SURBITON.—January 7th.—Making-up of St. James', Gladstone and Southborough roads, Southborough, and Orchard-road, Hook, for the urban district council.—Mr. Samuel Mather, A.M.I.C.E., surveyor to the council.

TUNBRIDGE WELLS.—January 9th.—Construction of filter-beds at the waterworks at Pembury.—Mr. W. C. Cripps, borough surveyor.

WOLVERHAMPTON.—January 9th.—Levelling, paving, channelling, sewering, metalling, kerbing and completion of Raby-street extension (Melbourne-street to All Saints'-road) and Lever-street (Green-lane to Raby-street).—Mr. J. W. Bradley, borough engineer and surveyor.

BECKENHAM.—January 9th.—Making-up of Border-crescent, for the urban district council.—Mr. F. Stevens, clerk to the council.

SOUTHAMPTON.—January 9th.—Construction of certain precipitating tanks, storm-water overflow and other works.—Mr. W. B. G. Bennett, borough engineer.

BECKENHAM.—January 9th.—Paving works in Trinity, Arthur and Croydon-roads, for the urban district council.—Mr. John A. Angell, surveyor to the council.

MALDON (ESSEX).—January 9th.—Supply of about 850 tons of 5-in., 4-in., 3-in. and 2-in. cast-iron water mains and special castings for the Purleigh district waterworks, for the rural district council.—Mr. Horace G. Keywood, engineer to the council.

SOUTHAMPTON.—January 9th.—Private street works in Brighton-road.—Mr. W. B. G. Bennett, borough engineer.

BARNES.—January 10th.—Erection of a new fire station in High-street, Mortlake, for the urban district council.—Mr. G. Bruce Tomes, M.I.C.E., engineer and surveyor to the council.

BURNLEY.—January 10th.—Supply and delivery at the electricity supply station of underground cables.—Mr. W. R. Wright, borough electrical engineer.

SELBY.—January 11th.—Erection of public baths, for the urban district council.—Mr. Jno. Hy. Bantoft, clerk to the council.

HORNSEY.—January 11th.—Alteration and extension of the heating system at the isolation hospital at Muswell Hill, for the urban district council.—Mr. E. J. Lovegrove, engineer to the council.

ISLINGTON.—January 11th.—Demolition of buildings abutting on the site of the electric light station in Eden-grove, Holloway, for the vestry.—Mr. William F. Dewey, clerk to the vestry.

KIDDERMINSTER.—January 11th.—Erection of a fire engine station.—Mr. Arthur Comber, borough surveyor.

SOUTHAMPTON.—January 16th.—Construction of concrete foundations, erection of brick, steel and concrete superstructures of new infirmary wards, sanitary blocks, boiler-house, tall chimney shaft, and sundry other work at the county lunatic asylum at Knowle, near Fareham, for the county council.—Mr. W. J. Taylor, county surveyor, The Castle, Winchester.

BERMONDSEY.—January 16th.—Supply of 60,000 bricks, for the vestry.—Mr. Frank Sumner, surveyor to the vestry.

LONDON.—January 24th.—Construction of a tunnel for pedestrian traffic under the river Thames from Greenwich to Poplar, for the county council.—Mr. C. J. Stewart, clerk to the council, County Hall, Spring-gardens, S.W.

SHANGHAI.—March 15th.—Construction and working of about 23 miles of electric tramways on the trolley system, for the municipal council.—Messrs. J. Pook & Co., 8 Jeffery's-square, St. Mary Axe, London, E.C.

## TENDERS FOR MUNICIPAL WORKS OR SUPPLIES.

*ACCEPTED.

BROMSGROVE.—For the construction of stoneware pipe sewers comprised in the scheme of sewerage for the parish of Pedmore, for the rural district council.—Mr. H. D. Holloway, clerk to the council:—

| | | | | | |
|---|---|---|---|---|---|
| J. Biggs, Birmingham | ... | ... | ... | ... | £4,310 |
| G. Trentham, Handsworth | ... | ... | ... | ... | 2,981 |
| G. Law, Kidderminster | ... | ... | ... | ... | 2,482 |
| T. Vale, Stourport | ... | ... | ... | ... | 2,474 |
| W. H. Meredith, Blackwood | ... | ... | ... | ... | 2,231 |
| J. Mackay, Smethwick* | ... | ... | ... | ... | 1,994 |

CARSHALTON.—For the supply of about 210 yards of 21-in. socketed stoneware pipes, for the urban district council.—Mr. William Willis Gale, A.M.I.C.E., surveyor to the council:—

| | | | s. | d. | |
|---|---|---|---|---|---|
| Duckett & Son, Burnley | ... | ... | 9 | 9 | per yard. |
| Doulton & Co., Lambeth (less 2½ per cent.) | ... | 8 | 0 | " |
| Oates & Green, Halifax | ... | ... | 7 | 9 | " |
| Albion Clay Company, New Bridge-street, E.C. (less 2½ per cent.)† | ... | ... | 7 | 6 | " |
| Wragg & Sons, Swadlincote (less 2½ per cent.)† | ... | 7 | 6 | " |

† Order divided between Albion Clay Company and Wragg & Sons.

CHATHAM.—Accepted for the supply of various materials for the year ending December 31, 1899.—Mr. Charles Day, borough surveyor :—
Trechmann, Weekes & Co., Rochdale.—Portland cement, £1 14s. 6d. per ton.
Chittenden & Co., West Malling.—Crushed ragstone, 10s. 9d. per yard.
E. D. Seagers, Chatham.—Gravel, 3s. 4d. per yard; sand, 3s. 6d. per yard; Thames ballast, 3s. 9d. per yard.
Thompson & Co., Chatham.—Coal, 12s. 3d. per ton; coke, 13s. per ton; coke, 13s. per chaldron.
Gibb & Co., Fenchurch-street, London.—Brooms with handles, £1 5s. per dozen; shovels, 16s. 6d. per dozen; picks, 4s. 4d. per dozen.
Farrars, Limited, Brighouse, Yorkshire.—York stone, 7s. 1d. per yard super.

FULHAM.—Accepted for the laying of the sewer portions of combined drainage in private premises in various parts of the parish, for the vestry.—Mr. Charles Botterill, A.M.I.C.E., surveyor to the vestry :—
No. 12 Bloompark-road.—C. Jones, £7 15s.
No. 36 Chesson-road.—J. Knight & Sons, £17.
No. 36 Coomer-road.—J. Meredith, £10.
No. 28 Chaldon-road.—E. Parry, £18 10s.
Nos. 25 to 27 Walham-avenue.—E. Parry, £9.
Nos. 25 to 27 Walham-avenue.—E. Parry, £13 10s.
Devon Laundry, Farm-lane.—E. Parry, £20 10s.
No. 41 Farm-lane.—J. Knight & Sons, £20.
No. 70 Lilyville-road.—J. Knight & Sons, £21.
No. 63 Claybrooke-road.—J. Knight & Sons, £22.
No. 11 Sherbrooke-road.—J. Meredith, £19.
No. 44 Parkville-road.—J. Meredith, £10.

FULHAM.—For alterations to the coroner's court, Munster-road, for the vestry.—Mr. Charles Botterill, A.M.I.C.E., surveyor to the vestry :—

| | | | | | |
|---|---|---|---|---|---|
| R. Goodman & Son | ... | ... | ... | ... | £539 |
| E. Swan & Son | ... | ... | ... | ... | 336 |

DEAL.—For the construction of about 10 miles of brick and pipe sewers, the erection of a pumping station, the provision of pumping machinery, the construction of a tidal storage tank, penstock chambers and sea outfall, and all works incidental thereto.—Mr. Alfred C. Brown, town clerk :—

| | | |
|---|---|---|
| H. Hill, Maidenhead* | ... | £39,000 |

STOURBRIDGE.—For the construction of 990 yards of 9-in. earthenware pipe sewer, for the main drainage board.—Mr. W. Fiddian, surveyor to the board, Town Hall, Stourbridge :—

| | | | | | | |
|---|---|---|---|---|---|---|
| J. Biggs, Birmingham | ... | ... | ... | ... | ... | £787 |
| G. Trentham, Handsworth | ... | ... | ... | ... | 650 |
| W. L. Meredith, Gloucester | ... | ... | ... | ... | 600 |
| T. Vale, Stourport | ... | ... | ... | ... | 545 |
| G. Law, Kidderminster | ... | ... | ... | ... | 528 |
| J. Mackay, Hereford | ... | ... | ... | ... | 471 |

ULVERSTON.—Accepted for various sewerage and drainage work for the rural district council.—Mr. Chas. W. Dean, clerk to the council :—
Wall End Drainage, Kirkby Irelett.—W. Simpson, Foxfield-in-Furness.
Urswick Main Sewer.—J. Pattison & Co., Urswick, near Ulverston.

## MEETINGS.

*Secretaries and others will oblige by sending early notice of dates of forthcoming meetings.*

### JANUARY.

9.—The Surveyors' Institution: Discussion on Mr. Weaver's paper on "The London Building Act and the Official Supervision of Buildings." 8 p.m.

10.—Institution of Civil Engineers: Ordinary meeting; Mr. J. H. Dales, A.M.I.C.E., on "High-speed Engines." 8 p.m.

13.—Institution of Civil Engineers : Students' meeting; Dr. Archibald Barr, M.I.C.E., on " The Application of the Science of Mechanics to Engineering Practice." 8 p.m.

17.—Liverpool Self-propelled Traffic Association : Mr. S. A. Sparkes on " Motor r. Horse Haulage; An Account of our Nine Months' Experiences." 8 p.m.

26.—Association of the Birmingham Students of the Institution of Civil Engineers : Mr. L. L. Baldwin, A.M.I.C.E., on " Coalville Water Supply : A few notes on the sinking of a trial bore-hole." 7.30 p.m.

## NOTICES.

THE SURVEYOR AND MUNICIPAL AND COUNTY ENGINEER may be ordered direct, through any of Messrs. Smith & Son's book-stalls, or of any newsagent in the United Kingdom. Applications to the Offices for single copies by post must in all cases be accompanied by stamps.

The Prepaid Subscription (including postage) is as follows :

| | Twelve Months. | Six Months. | Three Months. |
|---|---|---|---|
| United Kingdom ... ... ... | 15s. | 7s. 6d. | 3s. 9d. |
| Continent, the Colonies, India, United States, &c. ... ... | 19s. | 9s. 6d. | 4s. 9d. |

The International News Company, 83 and 85 Duane-street' New York City; The Toronto News Company, Toronto; and The Montreal News Company, Montreal, have been appointed agents in the United States and Canada for the sale of THE SURVEYOR AND MUNICIPAL AND COUNTY ENGINEER. A thin paper edition is printed for circulation abroad.

EDITORIAL OFFICES :—
24 BRIDE-LANE, FLEET-STREET, LONDON, E.C.

ADVERTISEMENT AND PUBLISHING OFFICES :—
13 NEW STREET-HILL, FLEET-STREET, LONDON, E.C.

## APPOINTMENTS OPEN.

BOROUGH OF PENZANCE.
APPOINTMENT OF BOROUGH SURVEYOR.
The Penzance Corporation are prepared to receive applications for the appointment of Borough Surveyor.
Salary, £200 per annum, with residence. List of duties, &c., can be obtained from the undersigned, to whom applications must be addressed, endorsed " Borough Surveyor," and delivered at the Town Clerk's office on or before the 4th January, 1899.
Canvassing members of the Council will be a disqualification.
T. H. CORNISH,
Town Clerk.
Town Clerk's Office, Penzance.
December 14, 1898.

COUNTY OF WORCESTER.
APPOINTMENT OF A CLERK TO AN ASSISTANT COUNTY ROAD SURVEYOR.
The Worcestershire County Council invite applications for the appointment of a Clerk to the Assistant County Road Surveyor for the No. 1, or Northfield, main road district of the county, at a commencing salary of £52 per annum, payable monthly, from persons between eighteen and twenty-five years of age.
Only persons need apply who possess a good knowledge of shorthand, and preference will be given to those candidates who have had experience in a surveyor's office.
The duties of the person appointed will comprise office correspondence, keeping of accounts, and the general office routine of a road surveyor's office.
The officer will be required to reside near the main road

depot at King's Norton, and to devote the whole of his time to the service of the Council.

Applications, stating the candidate's age, where educated, present occupation and previous experience, must be made in the applicant's own handwriting, on paper of foolscap size, accompanied by not more than three recent original testimonials, addressed to the undersigned, and marked "Clerkship to Assistant County Road Surveyor," to be received by 9 a.m. on Thursday, the 5th January. Any applications afterwards received will not be entertained.

The person elected will be appointed subject to the graduated scale of pay and advancement applicable to the junior clerks in the County Council's employ, particulars of which will be furnished on application to the undersigned.

The appointment will be held subject to three months' notice on either side, which may be given at any time.

Canvassing in any form will absolutely disqualify.

Selected candidates will be required to attend at the Shire Hall, Worcester, on a date to be fixed. The person appointed must be prepared to enter upon his duties forthwith, and to undergo a medical examination by an approved person.

S. THORNELY,
Clerk of the County Council.

Shire Hall, Worcester.
December 20, 1898.

## BOROUGH OF MORLEY.
### TEMPORARY ASSISTANT.

The Council of the Borough of Morley invite applications for the appointment of a Temporary Assistant from persons who have had good experience in a municipal engineer's office.

Candidates must be neat and expeditious draughtsmen, able to survey and level, prepare accurate working drawings and quantities.

Preference will be given to those having had experience in the construction of sewage works.

The whole time must be devoted to the duties, which are to be commenced as soon as possible after the appointment is made.

The engagement will be at least for three months for satisfactory service, and the salary will be at the rate of 2 guineas per week.

Applications, stating age, present and previous occupation,

together with copies of not more than three recent testimonials, to be delivered to Mr. W. E. Putman, ASSOC.M.INST.C.E., Borough Engineer and Surveyor, Town Hall, Morley, endorsed "Temporary Assistant," not later than noon on January 2, 1899.

## MANCHESTER CORPORATION TRAMWAYS DEPARTMENT.

The Tramways Committee of the Manchester Corporation require a competent Engineer to assist the City Surveyor in carrying out the engineering work required in connection with the permanent way. He must have a thorough knowledge of tramway construction, and be capable of preparing plans for and supervising the construction of all new lines, and the alteration and reconstruction of the existing track necessary in view of the introduction of electric traction. Salary, £200 per annum.

The Committee also require a Temporary Engineering Assistant. He must be a neat and expeditious draughtsman, and able to survey and level accurately. Wages, 50s. per week.

Applications, stating age, qualifications, and enclosing copies of recent testimonials, to be addressed to the Chairman of the Tramways Committee, Town Hall, Manchester, endorsed "Engineer" or "Engineering Assistant," and must be received on or before Saturday, December 31, 1898.

WM. HENRY TALBOT,
Town Clerk.

Town Hall, Manchester.
December 16, 1898.

## VESTRY OF ST. MARY, ISLINGTON.
### INSPECTOR OF ROADS.

The Works Committee of this Vestry are prepared to receive applications for the appointment of Inspector of Roads in one of the divisions of the district.

Candidates must have a practical knowledge of levelling, masons' and paviors' work, repairing roads, setting out and measuring up works, squaring dimensions, and making estimates, and none but those who have been engaged in a similar capacity need apply.

The person appointed will be required to devote the whole of his time to the duties of the situation, particulars of which can be obtained on application to the Chief Surveyor, Mr. J.

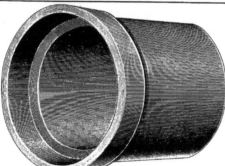

Patten Barber, at the Vestry Hall, and will be required to pass a medical examination as to his constitutional fitness for the appointment.

Salary to commence at 50s. per week, rising by two annual increments of 5s. per week to a maximum of £3 per week.

Applications, in the handwriting of the candidates, stating age and present employment, and accompanied by copies of not more than three testimonials of recent date, must be delivered to the undersigned not later than 4 p.m. on the 2nd January, 1899.

WM. F. DEWEY,
Vestry Clerk.

Vestry Hall, Upper-street, Islington, N.
December 20, 1898.

BOROUGH OF SOUTHEND-ON-SEA.
Wanted, a Temporary Assistant; must have had experience in preparing schemes for main sewerage and sewage disposal works. Salary, £3 3s. per week.

Apply to Mr. Alfred Fidler, ASSOC.M.INST.C.E., Borough Engineer and Surveyor, Clarence-road, Southend-on-Sea.

THE Borough Engineer of Southend-on-Sea has a vacancy in his office for a Pupil.—Apply, Mr. Alfred Fidler, ASSOC.M.INST.C.E., Clarence-road, Southend-on-Sea.

WANTED (Lancashire), for about nine months, Clerk of Works, to take charge of reconstruction of large brick main outfall sewer in deep cutting and headings. Must have had similar experience. Salary, £3 3s. per week. —Applications, with testimonials, to Box 95, office of THE SURVEYOR, 24 Bride-lane, Fleet-street, E.C.

WANTED, by a firm of waterworks contractors, one or two young men who have had experience in laying water mains, and who are capable of making their own drawings, getting out costs and controlling labour.— Address, stating experince, age and salary required, with copies of testimonials, to "S. 21," care of C. Birchall, Advertisement Contractor, Liverpool.

## TENDERS WANTED.

BOROUGH OF HOVE.
Tenders are invited for Executing Road-making and other works in Suffolk-street and Molesworth-street.

Further particulars may be obtained and plans and specification seen at the office of the Borough Surveyor (Mr. H. H. Scott), Town Hall, Hove.

The lowest or any tender not nessarily accepted.

Tenders, on forms supplied, addressed to the undersigned, and endorsed "Tender for Suffolk-street," or "Molesworth-street," as the case may be, will be received up to 6 o'clock on Wednesday, the 4th day of January next.

H. ENDACOTT,
Town Clerk.

Town Hall, Hove.
December 19, 1898.

HORNSEY URBAN DISTRICT COUNCIL.
TO ENGINEERS, CONTRACTORS, &c.

The Hornsey Urban District Council are prepared to receive tenders for Alteration and Extension of the Heating System, at the Council's Isolation Hospital, Muswell Hill.

Plans and specifications may be seen, and forms of tender and all information obtained, on application to Mr. E. J. Lovegrove, Engineer to the Council, at the offices mentioned below, on any morning between the hours of 10 and 12 o'clock, on a sum of £2 being deposited with the Clerk to the Council, which sum will be retained by the Council and deemed to be forfeited if a bonâ-fide tender is not made by the depositor.

If a tender is made which is not accepted the sum deposited will be returned, and if a tender is accepted such sum will be retained by the Council until the contract has been executed by the depositor, and will be forfeited in the event of his or his sureties failing or neglecting to execute such contract, or the bond accompanying same, within seven days after he or they respectively shall have been requested to execute the same.

No tender will be considered except on the prescribed form.

Sealed and endorsed tenders are to be deposited in the tender-box in my department not later than 4 o'clock p.m. on Wednesday, the 11th day of January, 1899.

The Council reserve to themselves the right to decline all, or any, or any portion, of the tenders so sent in.

(By order)
F. D. ASKEY,
Clerk to the District Council.

Offices: Southwood-lane, Highgate, N.
December 21, 1898.

## URBAN DISTRICT COUNCIL OF BROMLEY.
### DIVERSION OF CULVERT, &c.

The Urban District Council of Bromley is prepared to receive tenders for certain works of Diversion of the Culvert in Homesdale-road, and other works connected therewith, within their district, in accordance with plans, sections, &c., which may be seen at the office of the Council's Surveyor.

The bill of quantities, specifications and form of tender may be obtained on payment of 1 guinea, which will be returned on receipt of a *bona-fide* tender.

Tenders, endorsed "Tender for Diversion of Culvert, Homesdale-road," must be delivered to me not later than 3 o'clock p.m. on Tuesday, the 27th day of December, 1898.

The Council do not bind themselves to accept the lowest or any tender.

(By order)

FRED. H. NORMAN,
Clerk to the Council.

District Council Offices, Bromley, Kent.
December 12, 1898.

## CORPORATION OF CARMARTHEN.

### TO IRONFOUNDERS.

### NEW WATER MAINS.

The Corporation of Carmarthen are prepared to receive tenders for Supplying and Delivering, carriage free at Carmarthen, the following Pipes, &c.:—

| | | |
|---|---|---|
| 11,400 yards of 9-in. Cast-Iron Water Pipes. | | |
| 2,100 | " | 6-in. " " " |
| 1,500 | " | 4-in. " " " |
| 4,500 | " | 3-in. " " " |

Copy of specification and form of tender may be obtained upon application to Mr. F. J. Finglah, Borough Surveyor, Carmarthen, on and after Saturday next, the 24th inst.

Sealed tenders, on the proper forms supplied, must be sent in, addressed to the undersigned, not later than Saturday, the 7th January next, endorsed "Tender for Cast-Iron Pipes."

The Corporation do not bind themselves to accept the lowest or any tender.

R. M. THOMAS,
Town Clerk.

Carmarthen.
December 19, 1898.

## COUNTY BOROUGH OF SOUTHAMPTON.

### WESTERN DISTRICT SEWERAGE.
### PRECIPITATING TANKS.

### TO ENGINEERS, CONTRACTORS AND OTHERS.

The Corporation are prepared to receive tenders for the Construction of certain Precipitating Tanks, Storm-Water Overflow, and other works incidental thereto, in accordance with plans, specification and conditions, to be seen upon application to Mr. W. B. G. Bennett, C.E., Borough Engineer, from whom also bills of quantities may be obtained upon payment of £2 2s., which sum will be returned upon receipt of a *bona-fide* tender.

Sealed tenders upon the printed form, endorsed "Tender for Tanks," must be left at my office by Monday, the 9th prox.

Each person tendering will be required to pay not less than the minimum local standard rate of wages, as settled from time to time between the masters' associations and trade unions respectively, in each branch of the trade at the date of the contract.

No pledge is given to accept the lowest or any tender.

(By order)

GEORGE B. NALDER,
Town Clerk.

Municipal Offices, Southampton.
December 16, 1898.

## BECKENHAM URBAN DISTRICT COUNCIL.
### TO CONTRACTORS.

The Beckenham Urban District Council invite tenders for Paving Works in Trinity, Arthur and Croydon roads.

The work comprises about 500 super. yards of red brick paving, 220 lineal feet 6-in. by 12-in. Norwegian kerb, 500 lineal feet existing kerb reset, together with other works in connection with the foundation of the footpaths.

Plans and sections may be seen, and bills of quantities, specifications and form of tenders obtained, on application to Mr. John A. Angell, Surveyor, on or after December 20th, on deposit of £1, which will be returned on the receipt of a *bona-fide* tender.

A clause will be inserted in the contract providing that the contractor shall pay to the workmen employed in the execution of the work the wages generally accepted as current for workmen engaged on similar work in the district.

Tenders, duly sealed and endorsed "Tender for Paving Works," to reach undersigned not later than 4 p.m. Monday, January 9, 1899.

The Council do not bind themselves to accept the lowest or any tender.

(By order)
F. STEVENS,
Clerk to the Council.

December 20, 1898.

### BECKENHAM URBAN DISTRICT COUNCIL.
TO CONTRACTORS.

The Beckenham Urban District Council invite tenders for Making-Up Border-crescent, Beckenham. The works comprise about 1,600 lineal feet of Norwegian granite kerb and Guernsey or Aberdeen four-course channelling, 900 super. yards red brick paving, relaying existing surface-water sewers, building manholes, gullies, &c., together with the remodelling of 280 lineal yards of roadway, and other works incident thereto.

Plans and sections may be seen, and bills of quantities, specifications and forms of tenders obtained, on application to Mr. John A. Angell, Surveyor, on or after December 23rd, on deposit of £1, which will be returned on the receipt of a *bonâ-fide* tender.

A clause will be inserted in the contract providing that the contractor shall pay to the workmen employed in the execution of the work the wages generally accepted as current for workmen engaged on similar work in the district.

Payment under the contract will not be made until six months after the completion of the works.

Tenders, duly sealed and endorsed "Tender for Border-crescent," to reach the undersigned not later than 4 p.m. Monday, January 9, 1899.

The Council do not bind themselves to accept the lowest or any tender.

(By order)
F. STEVENS,
Clerk to the Council.

December 20, 1898.

### BOROUGH OF EASTBOURNE.
ENGINEER AND SURVEYOR'S DEPARTMENT.

The Highways and Drainage Committee are prepared to receive tenders for the Relaying of Tideswell-road District Low-Level Sewer—*viz.*,—

About 216 lineal yards of 18-in. Pipe Sewer,
About 469 lineal yards of 24-in. Pipe Sewer,

Together with the reconstruction of No. 8 Manholes, &c.

Plans and specifications may be seen and form of tender obtained at my office.

Tenders, endorsed "Tender for Relaying Low-Level Sewer," to be sent in to me not later than the 2nd day of January, 1899.

The Corporation do not bind themselves to accept the lowest or any tender.

(By order)
R. M. GLOYNE, ASSOC.M.INST.C.E.,
Borough Engineer.

Town Hall, Eastbourne.
December 16, 1898.

### URBAN DISTRICT COUNCIL OF BARNES.
TO BUILDERS AND CONTRACTORS.

The above Council are prepared to receive tenders for the Erection of a new Fire Station in the High-street, Mortlake.

The drawings and specification can be seen and forms of tender obtained on application to the Engineer and Surveyor to the Council, at the Council's offices, to whom tenders, sealed and endorsed "Tender for Fire Station," must be sent in not later than 12 o'clock noon on Tuesday, the 10th day of January, 1899.

The Council do not bind themselves to accept the lowest or any tender.

Dated this 20th day of December, 1898.

(By order)
G. BRUCE TOMES, ASSOC.M.INST.C.E.,
Engineer and Surveyor.

Council Offices, High-street, Mortlake.

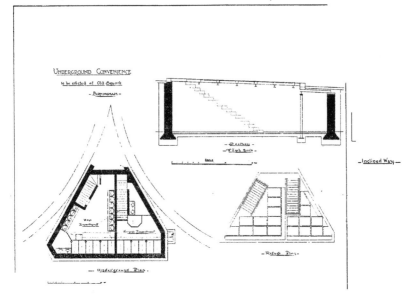

UNDERGROUND CONVENIENCE

to be erected at Old Square

— Birmingham —

— Inclined Way —

— Section —
— Flight Back —

— Underground Plan —

— Refuge Plan —

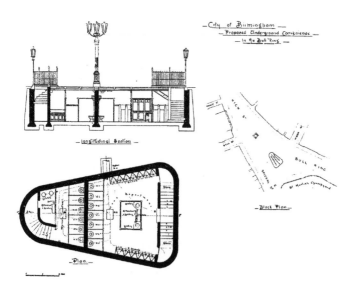

— City of Birmingham —
— Proposed Underground Convenience —
— In the Bull Ring —

— Longitudinal Section —

— Plan —

— Block Plan —

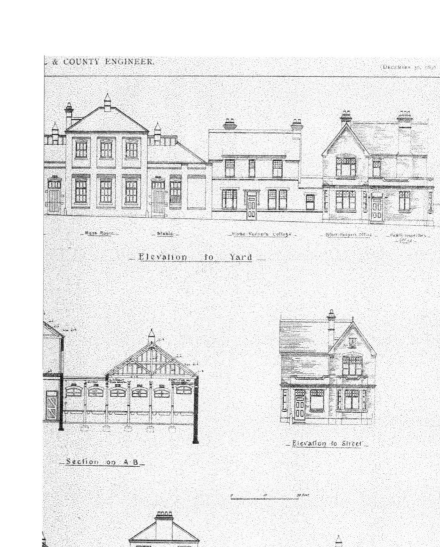

_Mess Room_     _Stable_     _Horse-Keeper's Cottage_     _Store-Keeper's Office_     _Health Inspector's Office_

_ Elevation to Yard _

_Section on A·B_

_ Elevation to Street _

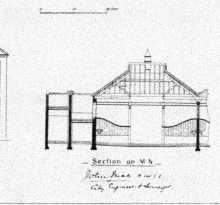

_Section on K·L_

_ Section on M·N _

# The Surveyor

## And Municipal and County Engineer.

Vol. XIV., No. 363.     LONDON, DECEMBER 30, 1898.     Weekly, Price 3d.

## Minutes of Proceedings.

**Municipal Water Supplies.** Those who are interested in the municipalisation of water supplies and wish to study the question in detail will find a great wealth of *data* in an elaborate return which has been prepared for the London County Council by their statistical offier, Mr. G. L. Gomme. The returns are presented in three groups —(1) county boroughs, (2) non-county boroughs, and (3) urban districts. The number of county boroughs is comparatively small, and for this, among other reasons, the information forthcoming in regard to them is more comprehensive than in the case of the other classes of authorities. Of the sixty-four county boroughs in England and Wales, forty-three have the water supply in their own control, and in practically every case a surplus revenue remains from the water rates and charges upon water consumers after paying for maintenance and other annual expenditure. The first table deals with income and expenditure, and the second gives much interesting information as to the various ways in which the surplus revenue is applied. In a number of cases there is a deficit after the payment of loan charges, but as a rule there are special circumstances to account for the fact. The third of the series of tables, constituting an analysis of county borough water accounts, deals with capital and capital expenditure, and subsequent tables set forth general statistics, the terms on which undertakings have been acquired, a comparison of charges made by county boroughs with those made by the London companies, and the system of charges for supplying water to outside areas. From his survey of the actual facts of municipal water supply Mr. Gomme concludes that not only do the majority of municipal water supplies yield a surplus revenue from the water rentals imposed, but that the corporations do more with the revenue derived from the consumers, in the interests of the consumers, than the water companies do. These extra services are stated as follows:—

(1) Repayment of debt, and hence a considerable cheapening of the water service as soon as the debt is paid off.

(2) Supply of water for municipal purposes, as at Liverpool, Birmingham, Glasgow, Edinburgh, Dundee, &c., and for charitable purposes as at Glasgow and Edinburgh.

(3) The security of a sufficient supply both as to quantity and quality.

(4) The economical expenditure of capital moneys on the keeping up of works in a high state of repair and efficiency to meet exceptional circumstances.

Even in cases of deficit revenue Mr. Gomme finds, wherever he has been able to make specific inquiries, that there is sufficient explanation afforded by the policy adopted by the corporation in the management of its water supply to show that the deficit, or apparent deficit, is not due to questions of management as between municipal and private supplies, but to different methods of administering the supplies in the interest of the public—methods which the public authority alone has the power to initiate. In any one case of deficit revenue shown by the figures in his return Mr. Gomme would hesitate to challenge it as an extra cost to the consumer. If it is extra, he points out that it is less cost in the municipal rate or there are more advantages to the consumers which the corporation has deliberately decided that it is necessary to provide.

Mr. Gomme then goes on to consider how far the financial results shown by the accounts have been attained by charges upon the water consumer which bear comparison with the charges imposed by water companies. That object, he thinks, can best be accomplished by ascertaining (1) whether the corporations have maintained the same charge as that levied by the companies whose undertakings they purchased, whether they have decreased or have increased the charge; (2) whether there are services included in the charge which were not included in the companies' charge. From the facts he presents Mr. Gomme deduces that generally water rates have been reduced as a consequence of municipal administration, and that the advantages, financial and administrative, which have accrued to the ratepayers have not been accomplished at the cost of increased charges upon consumers. His figures point to the fact that both general ratepayers and water consumers have gained by the transfer of water undertakings from private companies to public authorities, even though in the first instance the ratepayers have had to pay heavily for transfer. Mr. Gomme's comparison of the charges made by the London water companies with those made by the corporations of the large provincial towns is given under three forms: (1) A rough comparison of the scale of charges; (2) the result in respect of houses of particular values, assuming certain extras in each: and (3) a comparison of the charge per 1,000 gallons, arrived at by taking the income received and the total water supplied by the companies and the corporations respectively. The result of the comparison is to show that there are fewer charges for extras, and that in some cases no extras are charged at all; in many cases the charge is itself less than the London charges. It is pointed out, however, that the rental upon which the charges are levied is about one-half the rental of London.

The general effect of purchase is summed up by Mr. Gomme under two heads—(1) in respect of works executed by the companies, the creation of a perpetual annuity to the shareholders of the companies at a rate of interest generally higher than the dividends being paid at the date of purchase; and (2) in respect of works executed by the municipal authority after the date of purchase, the payment of a low rate of interest and the provision for redemption of capital. The general conclusion is that, according as the purchase was made, early or late, the effect is proportionately beneficial to the public, in spite of the high price paid for the purchase, but it is beneficial in every case. The particulars of the financial effect of purchase show, Mr. Gomme considers, that although recent cases of purchase are more beneficial to the companies, it has been beneficial to the consumers that the companies' control of water capital has been brought to a close. It has enabled the corporations to proceed with the necessary extension of works at a cost to the consumers very much less in amount of interest paid for capital, and Mr. Gomme is troubled with very little doubt that very much more care is exercised as to expenditure out of capital, both in amount and in application. Among the general advantages claimed for municipal waterworks is a smoother administration, that is to say, less friction and irritation between consumers and the administering authority. In illustration of this Mr. Gomme mentions that in the extremely poor borough of Middlesbrough there have been only three summonses for water rates since the company's undertaking was purchased in 1878. Consumers, remarks Mr. Gomme, pay attention to the rules of the corporation, because they are conscious of the fact that the water supply is their own. The special advantages of municipalisation, consisting of services not undertaken by companies but performed by municipalities for the benefit of the consumers, are thus stated :—

(1) The repair of supply pipes under the pavements and up to the joint inside the premises of the consumer, as at Manchester, Liverpool and other places.
(2) The registration of a body of plumbers who do their work to some extent under the eye of the corporation officials, as at Manchester, Birmingham, Nottingham and elsewhere.
(3) Facilities to traders and manufacturers using water in large quantities, as at Middlesbrough, for example.
(4) The settlement of the scale of charges in accordance with circumstances, such as residence, shop occupation, trade purposes, shipping purposes, &c., due regard always being paid to the particular interests of the town.
(5) Greater inspection and saving of waste water, to the advantage of the place generally and of the water administration.
(6) The keeping up of the works in a perfect state of repair, the repayment of capital, and the economical expenditure of capital moneys.
(7) The securing of the necessary pressure to force water up to the highest required point both for fire protection and for domestic use.
(8) The securing of the purest and most copious supply.

Part II. of this interesting and valuable return deals with the municipal waterworks controlled by the corporations of boroughs other than county boroughs. The financial statistics of these undertakings are given in tabular form, and these, taken in conjunction with the population at the last census, serve to indicate the size and importance of the water supply. As it was not possible to obtain information from each individual borough, Mr. Gomme availed himself of the official figures as published in the Local Taxation Accounts for the last available year (1895-96). He points out, however, that these are far from complete, as the charge on the water undertakings in respect of interest and repayment of capital is not stated, so that the financial results to each corporation cannot be more than approximately gauged. But in nearly all cases the amount of the loans outstanding is given, and from this it is possible to calculate roughly what the charge for interest and repayment is, and therefrom the financial result of the water undertaking on the year's working. In spite of any defects that may be urged, the information is undeniably useful as showing to what extent the supply of water is now a local government service and the relative importance of the water undertakings of the authorities throughout the country. The figures also give some indication of the financial result of the management of the undertakings, though Mr. Gomme admits that without further particulars as to the policy of the authority in respect of the system of charge a surplus or a deficit cannot be regarded as so much absolute profit or loss, as the authority may, and in the case of some county boroughs does, adopt a scale of charge purposely insufficient to meet all the expenses of the water undertaking, allowing the balance to fall on the borough rates. Of the 241 non-county boroughs in England and Wales, 139 appeared to have a regularly established system of

water supply under their control. For the purposes of his return Mr. Gomme has included only those towns which are known to have the management of their water supply, or which, owing to the fact that they have incurred indebtedness under the head of waterworks or show a material amount of receipts and expenditure, can be safely assumed as undertaking the provision of the water supply for their areas so far as such a supply is necessary. By a comparison of waterworks receipts with the receipts from other undertakings and from rates and all other sources of revenue Mr. Gomme illustrates the importance of this branch of local government work in the hands of these lesser municipalities. The receipts and expenditure from waterworks, though second to those from the gasworks, form a large proportion of the transactions of these corporations, while the indebtedness of the boroughs in respect of waterworks amounts to more than one-third of the total indebtedness for all purposes. By means of notes appended to the figures in each case Mr. Gomme indicates how these municipal waterworks came to be instituted; that is to say, whether by the corporation originally, or by the purchase of existing waterworks in the hands of companies. Where possible, the Parliamentary authority is given, and the terms of purchase when purchase has taken place. It can readily be understood, however, that without a very elaborate inquiry it is not possible to give full and reliable details of all these cases. But the information supplied is sufficient to show how the process of municipalisation of water undertakings goes on from year to year until the cases of water supply in the hands of companies are assuming comparatively small proportions throughout the country. Mr. Gomme's tables deal with the position up to the early part of 1896, but during the past three years the process of transfer has been quickened rather than retarded. It is to be regretted that the name of the town of Maidstone does not figure among recent cases of proposed purchase.

The final section of the report deals with urban districts, and the figures for these as for non-county boroughs are taken from the Local Taxation Accounts, the same general remarks applying in each case. Of the 766 urban district councils which existed at the beginning of 1895-96, 356 appear to have regularly established waterworks for the supply of their districts. A comparison of the work of the councils under this head with the other local government services shows that the receipts and expenditure of the councils in connection with their waterworks form a very large proportion of the total transactions of the councils, and the loans under this head amount to nearly one-fifth of the loans for all purposes. In the great majority of the urban districts in which the local authorities control the water supply the works have been established by the authorities; but a few cases of purchase have occurred. It will readily be understood that in a large number of cases the water supply of urban districts is obtained in bulk from corporations, generally county boroughs. In most cases these districts appear to be outside the compulsory limits of the corporation supplying them, and the system appears to have been adopted as the most convenient means of providing a water supply. We need only say, in conclusion, that Mr. Gomme has prepared a return which has remarkable interests for students of local government and its legitimate developments.

*　　*　　*

**The Dorchester Main Road Arbitration.** We recently made some comments on the subject of the repair of main roads, and took occasion to notice some of the questions which have from time to time arisen in connection with them and some leading legal decisions. We now propose, in continuation of the same topic, to make a brief reference to the Local Government Board award in the recent arbitration between the Dorchester Town Council and the Dorsetshire County Council. From the report of the proceedings before the arbitrator (Colonel Slack, R.E.) it appears that the amount of the contribution by the county council towards the cost incurred by the town council in respect of main roads was in former years regulated by a written agreement, under which the county council agreed to pay for maintenance and repair of the roads a maximum sum of £450 per annum, together with certain fixed sums in respect of scavenging, watering, tools, &c., and half the cost of improvements. This agreement, however, was terminated by the county council by notice expiring in March, 1896, and certain overtures which they afterwards made to renew it on terms slightly more favourable to the town council were declined by the latter, who intimated that they should in future expect payment of the whole of their expenditure as shown by their accounts. In due course the town council sent in their claim for the year ended March, 1897, amounting altogether to £849 4s. 1d., of which the county council disputed items amounting in the aggregate to £197 8s. 9d., leaving £651 15s. 4d. only admitted. The disputed items consisted of charges for siding, cleaning, watering, repair of tools and improvements. Some of these items the county council rejected *in toto*—*viz.*, the improvements of the roadways, as distinct from improvements of footpaths and repair of tools—whilst as to others they offered to pay a portion of the amount expended. The improvements of footpaths were of three kinds—*viz.*, (1) The substitution of brick paving for gravel, (2) the substitution of tar paving for gravel, and (3) the removal of tar paving, the total cost being £166 10s.2d., of which the county council were willing to pay one-half only. For siding and cleaning, out of £113 10s.8d. expended they offered £45, and for watering a like sum out of £69 2s. 6d. expended, while for " establishment charges " £30 was offered out of £40 8s. 9d. charged, the latter sum being something less than 5 per cent. on the total outlay. By his award the arbitrator allowed £821 8s. 2d. out of the £849 4s. 1d. claimed by the town council (or 96¼ per cent. of the total claim), payable as to £163 16s. 8d. by ten annual instalments, and as to the balance forthwith. The award does not, of course, show how these figures were arrived at, but we think it may be assumed that the £163 16s. 8d. ordered to be paid by instalments represented the amount allowed in respect of the claim of £166 10s. 2d. for improvements to footpaths. In the case of *Wiltshire County Council v. Marlborough Borough Council*, referred to in our previous remarks, it was laid down that as to improvements the benefits of which may endure for more than one year the whole of the actual cost for any one year is not necessarily repayable by the council in that year, they being only bound to make such payment towards the sum as may be agreed or settled by arbitration. This case was quoted at the hearing before the arbitrator by Mr. Macmorran, Q.C., on behalf of the county council, and it is evident that it is in pursuance of the principle referred to that the payment of this item has been extended over a period of ten years. The further reductions may probably be regarded as having reference to the items of scavenging and watering, which were very keenly contested. It was contended by the county council that a distinction must be drawn between watering for the purpose of maintenance and watering for the sake of the amenity of the public ; whilst as to the cleaning charges, it was alleged that they were excessive and had been going up from year to year. The reduction comes to a trifle over 15 per cent. on these items, which cannot be regarded as very serious. On the whole the award appears to be quite as satisfactory as could have been expected from the point of view of the town council, and it is to be hoped that the result will tend to restrict future differences between county and district councils

anent this subject to somewhat narrower dimensions, and thus obviate the necessity in many cases of recourse to expensive arbitration or legal proceedings.

\* \* \*

**The Intercepting Trap.** The intercepting trap occasionally meets with condemnation in America, as here. At the last annual meeting of the American Public Health Association, at Ottawa, Mr. J. W. Hughes, Montreal, read a paper entitled " The Intercepting Trap in Private Sewers." In his opinion minute investigation has shown that when a main intercepting trap is used it not only modifies the speed and partly obstructs the flow of sewage, but it prevents any of the air carried down by the soil and other waste-water pipes from discharging into street sewer, " where its aerating functions are so necessary to commence the purification of the sewage in the drains and assist in preventing sewer gases generating in the sewers." He is also of opinion that " when the main intercepting trap is omitted there is a superior and self-cleansing flow of sewage, and that large volumes of air pass forward to the street sewer, creating a healthy atmosphere and circulation of air down the soil pipe through which the fluid is passing, and up other soil pipes that are at the time standing idle." Mr. Hughes added that his observation had led him to believe that in houses in which there is an absence of drain pipes having intercepting traps there is freedom from odours and diseases that could be traced to sewer-gas poisoning, while, on the other hand, those cities which have adopted the principle of intercepting traps have often quite the reverse, and of disease a great deal is found among the inhabitants who happen to live in modern-built houses where the intercepting scheme has been adopted. Mr. Hughes adds that this state of affairs prevails " in spite of the fact that the same towns often spend large sums of money in flushing the drains and artificially ventilating the street sewers, a thing which is never necessary if the sewers are laid down properly and the right, unobstructed system is adopted." Certainly a lot of trouble and expense would be saved if every town and city could be from the first drained and sewered on the most modern principles, but the mischief done in the past is not to be quickly or easily remedied, nor can we hope that the mistakes and carelessness of the past will be completely avoided in the future.

\* \* \*

**The Work of the Coming Year.** As we have announced in our advertising columns, we shall, in the course of the next few weeks, bring out our customary Special Annual Issue, one of the chief features of which will, as in former years, be an exhaustive forecast of works projected for the coming year by municipal authorities throughout the country. We have again to thank engineers and surveyors to local authorities for the gratifying extent to which they have forwarded information in regard to works about to be undertaken. There still remain, however, a number of places, more or less important, in which considerable municipal activity must always prevail, and from which some particulars might naturally be expected. We should therefore be glad if our readers would note that for the purposes of our special issue we can still avail ourselves of any information that may reach us ; but it must come to hand not later than the end of next week. Our new year's number will, as before, provide us with an opportunity of reviewing the progress of municipal engineering during the past year, and of referring to our efforts to assist in that development to the best of our power. In the meantime, having come to the end of another year, we wish to take this opportunity of thanking our readers for the support – more emphatic than ever—accorded during the past twelve months, and to wish them every prosperity during the year on which we are about to enter.

# Municipal Work in Birmingham.

## SOME DETAILS OF PROGRESS.

Not the least interesting part of the programme arranged in connection with the recent Sanitary Institute Congress at Birmingham were the visits to various municipal works of interest in the city. The number of valuable papers in which our readers were likely to be interested was so great that we have not until now been able to refer to the visits, but the illustrations and brief descriptive notes now given will no doubt be interesting.

For those attending the conference of Municipal and County Engineers it was arranged that on the afternoon of Wednesday, September 28th, visits should be paid to the public convenience in course of construction in the Bull Ring; to Saltley to inspect the diversion of the Rea main sewer (7 ft. circular), in course of construction; to the Edward-street depot, in course of completion; to the river Rea improvement works, recently commenced, and to Queen's Ride.

### CONVENIENCES AND DEPOT.

The public convenience in the Bull Ring is being constructed by Mr. George Jennings, of Lambeth Palace-road, London, the amount of the contract being £1,977. A similar structure is being erected in the Old Square by Messrs. Doulton, of Lambeth, the amount of the contract in their case being £1,762 10s. Ample provision is made in each case for both sexes. The walls are 18-in thick, faced on the inside with white glazed bricks; the floors are laid with black and white tiles; and all wood fittings are carried out in polished teak. Mr. George Jennings supplies his "1892" patent radial urinals, and Messrs. Doulton their white glazed semi-circular backed urinals and No. 300 E closets. The Bull Ring convenience is ventilated by means of a water-driven air propeller and the Old Square convenience by air gratings. The refuges above are supported on steel joists on iron columns, the conveniences being lighted by prismatic pavement lights. The drainage is being carried-out as shown on the drawings. The entire work is being executed in accordance with the designs of the city surveyor. Needless to say, they were examined with much interest by the visitors, who then proceeded to inspect the works in connection with the diversion of the Rea main sewer before proceeding to visit the depot at Edward-street, Balsall Heath.

This corporation depot provides houses for a storekeeper and a horsekeeper, and offices for the foreman and sanitary inspector. The stables consist of two twelve-stall buildings, provision being made for a future stable (above to accommodate sixteen horses), which will be reached by the inclined way already provided, the floor of which, together with that of the gallery, is constructed with disused tram rails placed at 2 ft., centres filled in with fine concrete, topped with 4 in. cubes. A combined mess and harness room is provided, on the ground floor adjoining the stables, with hot water, &c., the mess-room above being used in the meantime as a store. There are also two loose boxes, a shoeing-shed and a large cart-shed, together with a two-stall nag stable and coach-house, with loft and store-rooms. The manure pit and men's water-closets and urinals are arranged at the top end of the yard, near to the inclined way, under which is a lock-up store. Protection against fire is insured by the provision of a fire hydrant, placed in a central position in the yard. The bricks for the stables, &c., are best local commons, those for the storekeeper's house being best local face bricks, with Hollington stone dressings. The drainage is carried out on the separate system, as shown on the plan, and the yard is paved with granite setts. Mr. T. Johnson of Great Brook-street, Birmingham, was the builder, the contract price being £3,888, and the buildings have been erected from the designs of the city surveyor, Mr. J. Price, M.I.C.E.

### SALTLEY SEWAGE FARM.

On the following Friday, on the invitation of Alderman Baker (chairman of the Birmingham, Tame and Rea Drainage Board), a party of about 100 members paid a visit to the sewage farm at Saltley. Alderman Baker, who was accompanied by Alderman Barratt, Councillors Nixon and J. Wilkinson, Mr. W. Harris (clerk to the board), and others, conducted the party over the works at Saltley, and thence over the farm to Tyburn, where an inspection of the buildings and the produce grown on the farm was made. In proposing a vote of thanks to Alderman Baker and his colleagues, Dr. Hewitt (Cheshire County Council) said that the farm over which they had been conducted was probably unique in England. They had seen sufficient to impress upon them the great difficulties the board had in dealing with the sewage of Birmingham and the district, and he was glad to know that the operations of the board were successful. Alderman Baker, in replying, said they had been trying to do their best with the difficult question they had to deal with, and had followed the advice of the first experts of the country.

The following account of the sewage question in Birmingham has been given by Mr. Robert K. Dent, in his work entitled "The Making of Birmingham":—

"The first note of a long and tedious discussion on the pollution of the streams into which the sewage of Birmingham was poured was sounded in 1854, when the Earl of Bradford, Lord Leigh and other landowners called attention to the fouling of the river Tame, as the result of the formation of a sewer outlet at Saltley in 1852. This was followed a few years later by still louder complaints from Mr. C. B. Adderley (now Lord Norton), through whose park the river ran, and from the residents on Gravelly Hill, in whose neighbourhood the corporation had made an ineffectual attempt to deal with the sewage matter by irrigation on a plot of land about 200 acres in extent. Injunctions were obtained against the corporation by both parties in 1870, and the question began to assume a serious and perplexing aspect, involving the possibility of a writ of sequestration in case the injunctions were not complied with. An elaborate report was presented to the council by the Public Works Committee, recommending a scheme involving an expenditure of £275,000. The council, however, felt that the subject had not been fully considered by the committee and that their scheme was impracticable, and thereupon a special committee was formed to consider and report on the best mode of dealing with the sewage. The result of the committee's inquiries was published in 1871, in a volume of nearly 300 pages, which has been regarded by engineers and authorities on sanitary subjects as a most important contribution to the question. As a result of the recommendations of the special committee the corporation decided upon the gradual abolition of middens in the town and the substitution of a new privy system, whereby a weekly collection of the contents might be practicable; the acquisition of a larger area of land whereon the sewage matter might be treated by a system of filtration through the soil, so that the liquid before being turned into the stream might be rendered comparatively pure and un-, objectionable; the establishment of a large sewage farm 'converting what was at present a dismal swamp into a thriving market garden;' and the formation of a joint drainage board upon which all the adjacent districts draining into the river Tame might be represented. A Bill was introduced into Parliament during the session of 1872 empowering the corporation to carry its scheme into execution, but it was defeated on the third reading, mainly through the exertions of Sir Charles Adderley and Sir Robert Peel, who objected to it as likely to prove injurious to their property. Matters continued in an unsettled condition until 1877, when a joint drainage board was formed under a provisional order of the Local Government Board, constituting the borough of Birmingham, the urban districts of Aston Manor, Balsall Heath, Handsworth, Harborne, Smethwick and West Bromwich, and the unions of Aston, King's Norton, Solihull and West Bromwich a united drainage district, with eleven representatives from Birmingham, two from Aston, and one each from the other districts. A larger area of land was secured at Tyburn, forming a sewage farm 807 acres in extent, and the necessary designs were prepared by the borough engineer and the farm manager for its utilisation and culture and for conveying and distributing the sewage over the land, the total cost of the estate, of the construction of conduits, and the erection of farm buildings thereon, amounting to £188,000. Thus the corporation in attempting a satisfactory solution of the sewage difficulty entered upon a new department of work as farmers and market gardeners on a large scale, and have been as successful in the one direction as in the other, as well in the raising of satisfactory crops of all kinds as in dealing with one of the greatest difficulties which they have ever been called upon to face."

The points to which special attention was paid during the visit to the sewage farm were the precipitation works and the method of treating the sludge at the outfall, the irrigation lands at Tyburn, the farm buildings, stock, &c., at Tyburn, and the new works at Plant's Brook. The farm occupies an area of 1,240 acres, and is being increased by a further 1,200 acres. It extends from Saltley to below Water Orton, a distance of more than 6 miles. It is held and managed by the Birmingham Tame and Rea District Drainage Board, and deals with the population of 725,000, spread over an area of 47,000 acres. The volume of sewage dealt with daily in dry weather is about 22,000,000 gallons. The process of purification employed is a combination of precipitation in tanks with subsequent irrigation.

### WHITACRE PUMPING STATION AND FILTER-BEDS, AND SHUSTOKE RESERVOIRS.

During the congress visits were also paid to the Whitacre pumping station and filter-beds, and Shustoke reservoir. These works constitute the most important source of the present water supply of the Birmingham Corporation. The small reservoir at Whitacre adjoining the pumping station is for the storage of the waters of the river Blythe, and was constructed by the late Birmingham Waterworks Company in 1872. The two Cornish engines were erected at the same time. This reservoir has a water area of 10½ acres and a total capacity of 32,000,000 gallons. The Cornish engines perform the double duty of (1) raising the water from the reservoir to the filter-beds, and (2) pumping the filtered water on to Birmingham. In addition to the two Cornish engines, there are three small steam pumps available for raising the water from the reservoirs to the filter-beds.

The reservoirs at Shustoke are two in number. They impound the waters of the river Bourne, and together con$_{\text{sti}}$ tute the principal storage of the corporation. Their united area is 98¼ acres, with a total capacity of 443,000,000 gallons, about 300,000,000 gallons of which is available for consumption. The powers for constructing the Shustoke works were obtained by the late waterworks company in 1870, when the powers for the construction of the Whitacre works were granted; but as regards Shustoke, beyond acquiring some of the land, no further steps were taken by the company. The reservoirs were constructed by the corporation immediately after the transfer of the undertakings in 1876. In connection with the Shustoke reservoirs the two compound engines at Whitacre were erected. These engines, in common with the Cornish, are employed in pumping the filtered water through the mains connecting the station with Birmingham. The water flows from the Shustoke reservoirs to the filter-beds by gravitation. The filter-beds have a total area of over 183,000 square feet, and are large enough to allow as much as 10,000,000 gallons per day being pumped from this station. The station is connected with Birmingham by a single line of 36-in. pipes in direct communication with the reservoir at Erdington, giving a pumping head of over 220 ft.

The next four years in Birmingham—that is to say until the first instalment of the Welsh water is available—are expected to be somewhat anxious ones for Birmingham, and especially for the corporation and the Water Committee. Everything tends to show that the Welsh scheme was not undertaken a moment too soon. Every available local source is now drawn upon for all it is worth, and every effort that ingenuity can devise is being put forth to prevent waste and to make the existing supply hold out; but the water consuming constituency has grown and is growing with a rapidity which at certain seasons renders a water famine in Birmingham a danger by no means to be despised. The prolonged drought of last autumn caused an unprecedented drain upon the reserve of water, and a similar danger will not be averted until the Welsh water arrives in 1902. The storage reservoir at Shustoke, which was opened in 1883, and, as we have mentioned above, has a capacity of 400,000,000 gallons of water, derived from the river Bourne, is a beautiful sheet of water 1¾ miles in circumference, and at the time it was formed the Water Committee no doubt flattered themselves that they had provided for the wants of the city for a good many years to come.

The increase of population in the water district, to which reference has been made, has amounted during the last four years to no less than 60,000, or 15,000 a year. Owing to economies in administration and to the steps taken for the prevention of waste, the whole of this additional population have been supplied with water without any augmentation of the aggregate amount of water pumped; their needs have, in short, been met by the use of water that previously was wasted. The waste in question was chiefly due to defective fittings, and has been very sharply looked after by house-to-house visitation and by nocturnal observations. It is felt, however, that all the saving that can be got by administrative measures in these directions has been practically reached, and that any further economy depends entirely upon a perception of the situation by the water consumers as a whole and by their loyal co-operation in the endeavour to keep their consumption of water as low as possible. These considerations, of course, are especially urgent during times of drought, but they are likely to apply more or less forcibly at all seasons until the new supply is poured in from the Elan valley.

SANITARY PROGRESS IN BIRMINGHAM.

In a paper read by Alderman W. Cook, J.P., chairman of the Health Committee of the Birmingham City Council, some interesting details were given of sanitary progress in the city. The sanitary history of Birmingham, Alderman Cook explained, might be said to have commenced with the appointment of a medical officer of health and a health committee in 1873. Until then little attention had been paid to sanitary matters, and the condition of the town was decidedly bad. There were 60 miles of streets and roads unsewered, and only 4 miles of road surface out of a total of 190 miles were properly paved. The drinking water was largely obtained from shallow wells, almost all of which were badly polluted, and a large part of the closet accommodation was on the ash, pit-privy system. In certain parts of the town there was a large number of old and crowded houses, and very little was done to prevent the spread of infectious diseases. In the first five years after the appointment of the Health Committee the death rate was 24·8 per 1,000. In the second live years (1878-82) it was 21·6, and in the succeeding five years it was reduced to 20·7. The zymotic death rates for the same periods were 5·3, 3·8 and 3·2 respectively. At the present time, out of 262 miles of streets, Birmingham had 33 miles paved with granite or wood and 8¼ miles partially so paved. The remaining ash-pits, a large proportion of which were in the recently added parts of the city, were being gradually abolished. The number of water-closets was over 50,000, and of pan-privies over 30,000. A large number of old and

unhealthy houses had been demolished, and extensive provision now existed for the isolation of cases of small-pox and scarlet fever and for the disinfecting of houses and their contents. The refuse disposal in Birmingham was conducted partially on the conservancy system and partially on the water-carriage system, the latter having been for many years past the only system allowed for new buildings. The water supply of the town was at present derived from streams and deep wells, being well filtered before delivery, but the corporation was now engaged in obtaining a more abundant supply from Radnorshire. Practically the whole of the small-pox cases and 80 per cent. of the scarlet fever cases now obtained treatment at the city hospitals. Much remained to be done in Birmingham, as in other places. Evils that had been growing up for generations could not be overtaken in a day. If they could start and plan a town as they did a hospital they might do something fairly satisfactory from a sanitary point of view. But our large towns had grown up without system and without much sanitary control, and they had to take things as they were and make the best of them.

## SEWAGE DISPOSAL AT MANCHESTER.

BACTERIAL SYSTEM APPROVED.

On the 19th inst., at a meeting of the Rivers Committee of the Manchester Corporation, the preliminary report of Messrs. Baldwin Latham, Percy F. Frankland and W. H. Perkin, junr., the experts appointed by the council last spring, was read. It was also announced that the Local Government Board had determined to hold an inquiry into the working of the bacteriological system of sewage treatment in Manchester, when the experts may be expected to give evidence. This inquiry will be held on January 12, 1899. It is proposed that the scope of the inquiry shall be confined to the main principles determining the treatment of the sewage at Davyhulme, and that an adjournment shall then be made for the purpose of preparing plans, estimates, &c. These are to form the subject of a later inquiry. The report is as follows:—

"Knowing that you are desirous of having a preliminary report from us with reference to the purification of the sewage of Manchester, we beg to inform you that since entering upon this inquiry, in June last, we have not only visited a number of sewage works presenting features of novelty in different parts of the country, but we have also instituted experiments of our own, with a view to determining the best mode of dealing with the sewage of Manchester so as to obtain an effluent of sufficient purity to comply with the requirements of the Mersey and Irwell Joint Committee.

"Our inquiry has already reached such a stage that we are able to say without hesitation that from the results obtained with the double-contact beds constructed according to our instructions at Davyhulme by your city surveyor, and the experiments carried on by us, which have been directed to the treatment and purification of settled and crude sewage without the use of any chemicals, we are of opinion that the bacteriological system, notwithstanding the particular nature of the Manchester sewage, will purify that sewage and will yield an effluent which will comply with all the requirements of the Mersey and Irwell Joint Committee, and which, when discharged into the Manchester Ship Canal, will, in our judgment, be the means of greatly improving the waters of the latter.

"We must point out that further time is now required for us to determine as carefully as possible by experiment the precise form and details of the method which will be the most suitable to carry out works on such a large scale as will be required at Manchester, so as to make the proposed works a complete success.

"We should like to say that every request for experimental plant and other facilities which we have made to you has been promptly complied with to our entire satisfaction, and that the large amount of analytical work which our experiments have necessitated has been most efficiently carried out by Mr. Gilbert J. Fowler (your chemist) and his staff of assistants.

"We are anxious to express our sense of the value of the assistance of Sir Henry Roscoe's experimental filters, constructed and worked for some time under the direction of Mr. Scudder, for treating the tank effluent. We also think it desirable that the reports of Mr. Fowler, showing the progress which has been made in the purification of the sewage during the period the experiments have been going on, should be appended to our report."

Carlisle.—Recent minutes of the committee contained the report of the sub-committee upon various systems of electric traction in operation in a number of towns, and also the committee's resolution recommending the adoption of the overhead trolley system, following closely the lines of that in operation at Dover, provided the tramway company undertook to obtain the electric current from the corporation upon terms to be hereafter agreed upon, and subject also to such other conditions as the town clerk might consider necessary in the interests of the city. The council have had a long discussion respecting the trolley system, and the recommendation of the committee has been adopted.

# The Liverpool Municipal Electric Tramways.

As soon as the Liverpool Corporation decided to acquire the somewhat extensive systems of horse tramways in the city they immediately gave careful consideration to the question of adopting mechanical traction, and early last year a special committee was appointed to inquire into and report their recommendations as to the best means of improving the tramway service.

PRELIMINARY INQUIRIES.

The first step of the committee was to place themselves in communication with three of the most eminent engineers having experience of tramway matters, for the purpose of obtaining independent reports. The engineers selected were Mr. Graham Harris; Mr. T. S. Pearson, engineer-in-chief to the largest street traction corporation in New York; and Mr. Granville C. Cunningham, who had had great experience in Canada. It was obvious that in solving the problem as to the system of traction to be applied in Liverpool, involving an early outlay of over £1,000,000, very great care was necessary on the part of the municipality. Very early in the inquiries, however, the committee found a complete unanimity of opinion that electricity appeared to be the best form of motive power, both as regards efficiency and cost. To some extent the committee were guided in their course of procedure by a report from Mr. Pearson, in which he estimated that the cost of operation per car mile would be—on the overhead trolley, 3·68d.; the slotted conduit, 4·00d.; and compressed air, 5·02d. As compared with these figures, Sir David Radcliffe had stated that on the same data the cost at that time of horse traction in Liverpool was 7·19d. per car mile. The recommendations of the engineers were in complete accord as to the overhead wire system being the cheapest and most satisfactory system to adopt.

In addition to the assistance provided by the experts, most exhaustive inquiry was made by a deputation of the committee upon actual systems in use on the Continent, and for that purpose the various systems of mechanical traction at Hamburg, Berlin, Dresden, Vienna, Buda-Pesth, Zurich, Brussels, Milan, Genoa, Turin, Geneva, Vevey and Paris were visited. In selecting the system of mechanical traction for the Liverpool tramways the deputation thought the following conditions should be duly considered:—

(a) The steep gradients that existed in Liverpool.
(b) The exceptionally heavy character of the road traffic.
(c) The necessity of avoiding any system which would be a source of danger to the lighter traffic.

Moreover, it was necessary that they should fulfil the following conditions:—

(a) To have a small time interval between the cars.
(b) The cars to be of such a design as to save time in loading and unloading.

The deputation very speedily came to the conclusion that self-contained cars, whether propelled by steam, compressed air or electric accumulators, would be inconveniently heavy and uneconomical in working. They were considerably impressed with the advantages of the underground conduit system, but their inspection and investigations soon convinced them that the mechanical construction of the conduit was unsuitable for Liverpool roadways, with their heavy and crowded traffic. The evidence collected by the deputation showed conclusively that in no case had an underground system been adopted or continued where an overhead system could be constructed. Even in Buda-Pesth, which is one of the most favourable examples of the underground conduit system, and where the road traffic is exceptionally light, the overhead system had been preferred and adopted where possible. The deputation were more and more convinced, as their tour of inspection proceeded, that as regards good mechanical construction, elasticity of work, freedom from breakdown, facility of repair and economy, the overhead system was without a rival. The report of the deputation also stated that the system had the merit of being much less expensive to construct and maintain than a conduit system, the capital expenditure for a conduit system being at least 50 per cent. greater than for the overhead trolley line.

AN EXPERIMENTAL LINE.

Before embarking upon any large expenditure, or coming to a final conclusion as to the mode of electricity or the character of the rolling stock to be employed, it was desirable that a trial should be made with one part of the tramway system. For that purpose arrangements for laying and equipping a service of electric traction were made, and a line from St. George's Church to The Dingle, viâ Park-lane and St James's-street, on the overhead system was undertaken. This route was selected because it would not interfere with the working of any other lines in the city, and because it was thought that the only fair trial of mechanical power would be on lines which were not used by horse traction. It was thought that by this means the public would have an opportunity of forming an opinion as to the advantages or otherwise of the system. The effect of the overhead wires would then be better appreciated, and at the same time a means be afforded for instructing the staff in the management of mechanically-propelled cars. It is this experimental line which has just been completed, and it is more than usually interesting.

SOME ENGINEERING DETAILS.

That the experiment is being conducted on fairly liberal lines is evident from the fact that the system includes over thirty cars, and it is proposed to have a four minutes' service. The complete length of line, including the branch section now under construction, is a little over 3 miles. As already indicated, the system commences in the centre of the town and passes out to one of the southern suburbs, known as The Dingle. Although not specially difficult, the route traversed is by no means an easy one, and certainly affords a fair test of the capabilities of electric traction. The most conspicuous feature of the system is that which relates to the housing of the electric cars. For this purpose most extensive car-sheds have been erected at the end of the line, which will give accommodation for probably seventy or eighty vehicles. As a matter of fact, they constitute the largest sheds in the country, and it is a point of some importance to mention that the whole of this building has been designed by corporation officials and carried out under their supervision. There are no unusual features in the method of the track. A very heavy type of rail is used, in accordance with the practice commonly adopted in this country, and for the most part 100 lb. rails are bedded on concrete. The rails are bonded together by means of Chicago crown bonds, and it is interesting to mention that a system of continuous rail may be eventually adopted on other portions of the tramways that are equipped for electrical work. One of the most objectionable features of an overhead trolley system is the necessity of employing a complete system of guard wires, which are placed above the trolley wire proper and its supports in such a way as to prevent telephone and telegraph wires coming into contact with the live trolley line. In Liverpool the guard wires have been dispensed with completely, and at places where telegraph and telephone wires cross the streets a light piece of wood has been clipped on to the trolley wire, and it is claimed that this will prevent any wire coming into contact with the live wire, and also permit the trolley passing by in the cleanest possible manner. For the most part the system known as the span-wire suspension has been adopted, although at some portions of the route, where curves are considerable, double-arm bracket posts have been placed in the centre of the track, but, generally speaking, side posts placed on each side of the street, some 40 yards apart, support the trolley wire by means of a span wire. In some of the streets these poles are replaced by rosettes attached to the walls of buildings. It is generally conceded that the overhead work in Liverpool has been most effectively carried out, and we believe the feeling prevailing in the locality is that the wires are less objectionable and noticeable than was supposed.

ROLLING STOCK.

The chief experiment that has been carried out is in the rolling stock. There are two types of cars employed—one that is of purely American design and the other of the German type. So far as electrical details are concerned there is no very wide difference between these, but the German cars are usually run in pairs, one being a motor-car, having a trailer attached to it. The motor-cars are equipped with a series parallel controller and two motors. The controller is in some respects similar to what is employed in the Westinghouse system, and it is possible by operating the controller in the reverse direction to make the motors act as a kind of brake. What really happens is that the motors are short-circuited and act as generators, thus exercising a pulling effect upon the car axles. As a further safeguard, however, the trailer, which can only be used when attached to a motor-car, is also supplied with a special form of break, which can be operated by the man on the motor-car. This is an emergency brake, and consists of electro-magnetic apparatus, which is operated by current from the trolley line. The American car is very similar to the one employed on the Glasgow tramways. It is of the double bogey type, 34 ft. in length. This type of car is divided into two compartments, entrance being obtained from the middle of the car; one portion is reserved exclusively for smokers, and in consequence is not provided with windows. The bodies are mounted on wheel trucks, which have 30-in. driving wheels and 20-in. trailing wheels.

ELECTRICAL EQUIPMENT.

The electrical equipment has been supplied by Messrs. Dick, Kerr & Co., and consists of two four-pole motors, connected to the car axles by a single reduction gearing. The frame of the motor consists of two semi-cylindrical castings, the pole pieces being laminated, thus economising copper on the field coils and reducing the current necessary for exciting the fields. An important improvement has been made in regard to bearings, which are carried outside the cases, and thus waste oil is prevented from getting into the motors. The motors are suspended in a special manner, the end away from the axle being suspended on a cross-bar which is able to rotate on its own axis. At the axle end of the motor spiral springs are used, which, it is claimed, exercise a cushioning effect, and thus prevent a heavy hammer blow affecting the electrical apparatus. It need hardly be added that the series parallel type of controller is employed, and the sparks created between the brushes and the segments are blown out by means of solenoids, which are excited when the controller is in operation. There is also provided a reversing cylinder, which enables the driver to short circuit the motors and thus become an emergency brake. But what is of unusual interest on the American cars is the use of the "Standard" air brake. For this it is necessary to employ an air compressor, which is geared to the axle, and is automatically put in and out of action by the variation of the air pressure.

The committee, in suggesting the introduction of electric tramways into Liverpool, were convinced of the economy of combined stations for supplying electrical energy for lighting and tramway purposes, and being the owners of an extensive lighting system, it was thought desirable to obtain the necessary electrical energy required for the tramways from the existing lighting station, and, as a matter of fact, the whole of the power now required for operating a tramway system is obtained from the Paradise-street electricity works, which have been in existence for some time as a lighting station. For the tramway purposes it has been necessary to erect special plant, which consists of three Willans engines, directly connected to Siemens' dynamos of 250 horse-power each. In addition to these machines, a very large battery has been provided, which will to a great extent serve to meet the sudden fluctuations that are usually encountered in the operation of a tramway service. As a matter of fact, the battery is of unusual size, even for tramway purposes, but it will no doubt prove extremely valuable in meeting the sudden rise and fall in demand. The type of machines and dynamos employed do not differ very materially from the machines that have been already used for lighting purposes in Liverpool, except so far as regards voltage. A special switchboard has been erected, on which are placed the usual measuring instruments and automatic circuit-breakers, to protect the dynamos and battery. An interesting feature is the use that is made of a motor dynamo for raising the pressure of the current at the ends of the system, and this machine serves also the purpose of preventing an extreme drop of potential in the return circuits, thus precluding the possibility of electrolytic troubles.

The work has been carried out to the designs of the late Dr. John Hopkinson, and under the personal supervision of Mr. Talbot, of the city engineer, and of Mr. Bromley Holmes the city electrical engineer. There can be little doubt of the result of this experiment, for already extensions are in hand, and we may shortly be able to announce that the Liverpool Corporation have decided to undertake a very large addition to the present system. It would not be incorrect to say that probably the whole of the future work will be left entirely in the hands of Mr. Brodie, the city engineer, and of Mr. Bromley Holmes, who are in a great measure responsible for some of the excellent features that abound on the recently-opened system.

## ASSOCIATION OF BIRMINGHAM STUDENTS OF THE INSTITUTION OF CIVIL ENGINEERS.

At the Midland Institute, Birmingham, Mr. H. R. Thomas, B.SC., recently read a paper before the above association on "Axles for Road Carriages and Motor-Cars, and their Manufacture."

The first form of axle known was, said Mr. Thomas, without doubt fixed to the wheels, and revolved in a very primitive form of journal. The most primitive axle met with now was used in parts of South America and Australia, and made of wood, whence comes the name of axletree. The simplest form of iron axle in everyday use was found in ordinary carts, and consisted of a short bed or tail, which was bolted to the wooden axletree, and an arm or bearing of conical shape. Better-class axles underwent a process of "steeling," which was done by driving two small pieces of steel, about 2 in. by $1\frac{1}{4}$ in. by $\frac{1}{4}$ in., into the hot iron on the underside of the arm, one near the end and the other near the shoulder, these being the parts which had the most wear. The steel being thus hardened considerably lengthened the life of the axle.

Drabble's patent, Collinge's, the Mail, Longmore and other axles were referred to. Ball bearings were not applicable to cart or carriage axles, as it was very difficult to properly harden the large bearings necessary, and either the ball races or the balls themselves were soon crushed by the excessive weight. Roller bearings had a great future before them, as in this case the rollers ran the whole length of the arm. Axles were manufactured from piled scrap iron, from faggotted bars and common bars. A faggotted axle consisted of from seven to nine pieces of iron welded together under a steam hammer into one solid bar, and then the collar is welded on. The advantage of this was that, should there be a flaw in any one piece of iron, it could not affect the strength of the finished axle to any extent. American axles were not so good as English ones, as they were only made to last one or two seasons, while English axles had to last a lifetime. Before the axles was finished the arm had to be case-hardened, which was done by keeping it at a bright red heat in contact with some carbonaceous substance for about three hours, and then dipping it in potash and quenching it. Of the cast-iron boxes there were two distinct kinds—the case-hardened box and the chilled box. The former were made from haematite pig iron. The annealing process took about twelve hours, the boxes being put into iron pans and kept at a bright red heat, after which they were ready for machining. The hardening was accomplished by filling the boxes with animal charcoal, such as burnt leather, bone dust, &c., the ends being stopped with clay to prevent the charcoal from being consumed in the air. The boxes were then placed in a specially-constructed furnace, and heated to a cherry red, and maintained at that temperature for a considerable time to enable the surface to absorb a certain amount of carbon from the charcoal. The theory advanced to support this method was that in the class of iron used a large proportion of the carbon existed in a free uncombined state as graphite. This left the iron free to combine with the charcoal and form a thin coating of steel on the inner surface of the box, which was hardened by being quenched in cold water.

The best axles were made from grey cold-blast iron. The sand core is replaced by a chill of cast iron, the effect of which was to form an extremely hard surface on the inside of the box, which did not require machining. The chill or core was driven out as soon as the metal was set. The hard lining was caused by the sudden cooling of the grey iron in contact with the chill and its consequent change into granulated white cast iron, which was the hardest variety known. The depth of the hardening can be varied by altering the temperature of the chill, the warmer it was before the metal was poured the thinner being the hardened surface. Case-hardened boxes were weakened somewhat by the repeated heatings; chilled boxes could therefore be made lighter.

Wheels were built conical to resist the strain set up in the spokes in turning corners. The centre line of the axis was bent down until the spokes were vertical to the ground at their point of contact. As an example of the dip required, a wheel 3 ft. in diameter and dished 2 in. (that is the height of the cone, of which the hub is the apex), and having an arm of 8 in. on the axle, the arm should be dipped $\frac{8 \text{ in.} \times 2 \text{ in.}}{36}$ = nearly $\frac{1}{2}$ in. In addition to this, some manufacturers "foregather" the arms, that inclining them forward $\frac{1}{4}$ in. or $\frac{3}{8}$ in. This was supposed to cause the wheels to run against the collar rather than against the nut, but it interfered with the easy running of the vehicle. The method of testing axles was a cantilever. Axles for motor-cars, with special arrangements to facilitate turning corners, and other interesting points were described.

The president, Mr. J. C. Vaudrey, M.I.C.E., occupied the chair, and after the discussion and vote of thanks to the author read a letter he had received from Mr. Henry C. Adams, who tendered his resignation of the post of hon. secretary, after five years' service. The president referred in very complimentary terms to the progress of the association during Mr. Adams' long term of office, and proposed a hearty vote of thanks for his services, stating that it was with much regret that they allowed him to sever his official connection with the association. Mr. W. Bayley Marshall, M.I.C.E., past-president, seconded the vote, which was carried unanimously.

Mr. G. J. de Brissac Phelps, B.A., STUD.INST.C.E., was then appointed hon. secretary in Mr. Adams' place.

## PROPOSED ELECTRIC TRAMWAYS FOR LINCOLN.

Last week, at a meeting of the Lincoln Corporation, it was reported that at a meeting of the whole council in committee the following resolution, adopted by the directors of the Lincoln Tramways Company, had been considered: That the directors, having under consideration the desirability of introducing (as in other towns) electricity as the motive power in working their tramway system, and the necessity of meeting the reasonable demands of the public for an extension of the system, as also the possibility of the tramways being taken over by the local authority, are of opinion that under these circumstances the company would not be justified in incurring the heavy capital expenditure which these improvements and extensions would involve without first conferring with a representative committee of the council on the subject, and the directors accordingly ask the council to appoint such a committee at an early date. The committee had resolved that it was desirable to enter into negotiations with the tramways company with a view to the tramways being taken over by the corporation at an early date, and several members had been appointed as a committee to confer with the directors on the subject. The minutes were confirmed.

**Weston-super-Mare.**—Mr. H. Percy Boulnois, Local Government Board inspector, last week held an inquiry touching an application of the council for sanction to borrow £14,300 for the purpose of erecting a public pavilion, £1,482 for effecting extensions at Knightstone baths, and £131 for additional furniture in connection with public offices. On the termination of the proceedings the inspector intimated that he would visit the sites of the proposed improvements and present his report to the Local Government Board at an early date.

# Comparative Reports of General Practice.

## XXX.—TRAMWAY TRACTION : WEST BROMWICH REPORT.—VII.

PROPOSALS OF THE BRITISH ELECTRIC TRACTION COMPANY.

Early in June the British Electric Traction Company, as arranged at the conference with Major Marindin, of the Board of Trade, submitted a statement of the arrangements entered into with the South Staffordshire Tramways Company and their proposals for the adoption of electric traction. From this statement we quote the following paragraph : " By the agreement with the South Staffordshire Company we are working that section of their tramways which is already electrically equipped, and in consideration of our providing the necessary capital for the purposes specified in the agreement we have the option of taking a lease of the whole of that company's lines, with a view to the adoption of electric traction ; also on that section of the South Staffordshire Company's lines at present worked by steam. We have undertaken, as part of such agreement, to introduce into Parliament, in the name of the South Staffordshire Tramways Company, and to use our best endeavours to secure, the passing of a Bill to confirm the said lease, and to give power to the lessees to reconstruct and convert to electrical working the whole or any part of the tramways. We propose to introduce this Bill in the next session of Parliament, in the hope of being able to facilitate the introduction of an improved tramway service in the district at as early a date as is practicable. Our proposal is to unite the tramways of the South Staffordshire Company with those of other companies in the neighbouring districts, our object being to connect the greater part of the important district known as South Staffordshire and to provide an efficient and uniform service of electric tramways. The scheme is a comprehensive one, and embraces the tramways of the Dudley-Stourbridge Company, Wolverhampton Company, the light railways to Kinver, Kingswinford and Cradley, and its accomplishment cannot fail to prove of great benefit to these thickly-populated districts."

The company then proceeded to refer to the proposed insertion in their Bill of the various clauses inserted in existing Acts for the protection of the local authorities. It was pointed out that the system had been developed at different periods, and that, owing to the variety of Acts and provisional orders, the clauses were so complicated and conflicting as to render their assimilation quite impossible without creating further complications. It was therefore proposed that a new set of clauses, which the company considered adequate, should take the place of all the previous clauses relating to the electrical equipment and working of the lines. Incidentally it was pointed out that the company would be subject to the standard regulations enforced by the Board of Trade in the case of every electric tramway, and that these afford every possible protection to the interests of public and private undertakings. It was also suggested that a conference should be arranged at West Bromwich before the Bill was introduced to obtain the views of each local authority, in order that suitable arrangements might be made, if possible, whereby the Act might be obtained without increasing its cost through opposition in Parliament. The clauses, of course, were to be subject to such modifications as might appear desirable to this conference. The following were the company's proposals in regard to the system of traction to be adopted :—

"The system we propose to adopt for the equipment of the whole of the lines is that known as the overhead system of electric traction, which has been so successfully adopted on the Continent and in America, and has been favourably reported upon by the corporations of Glasgow, Manchester, Liverpool and Belfast. We cannot recommend the adoption of any other system, and although we do not say that other systems of electric traction are impracticable, yet the expense of constructing and maintaining the same, on the conduit system for instance, is entirely incompatible with the character of the district and with the amount of traffic to be served.

"We are prepared to instal the overhead system of electric traction in such manner as to embody all the latest improvements, and in view of the fact that other neighbouring lines, which we hope to run in connection with the tramways of the South Staffordshire Company, are proposed to be equipped on the same system, we trust that our proposal will receive your favourable consideration.

"We propose to abandon cars with top seats as far as possible, and to introduce small cars upon a more frequent service. The delay which is occasioned by passengers leaving the car from the top seats minimises to a great extent the advantages which are to be derived from the use of electric traction."

THE SUB-COMMITTEE'S RECOMMENDATIONS.

The sub-committee having considered the above proposals, and also the question of municipalisation, submitted the following recommendation :—

"Your sub-committee, taking into consideration the fact that the corporation have lately obtained a provisional order to generate and supply electricity within the borough, and that the two schemes—namely, electric lighting and tramways, could be worked to the advantage and benefit of the town, unanimously recommend the town council to purchase the part of the tramway undertaking within the borough of West Bromwich on the expiration of the present lease, under sec. 34 of the Tramways Act, 1870, and to apply for the necessary power to equip and work the said tramways when taken over."

In the event of the corporation not deciding to municipalise the tramways, the sub-committee recommended as follows:—

(1) *Permanent Way.*—That the permanent way of the whole of the existing system within the borough of West Bromwich requires reconstructing, including the setts paving. This work should under any circumstances be carried out by the town and leased to the company on terms to be arranged. The dual control, which causes continual annoyance, would then be done away with.

(2) *Form of Traction Advised.*—As to the form of mechanical traction to be adopted, your sub-committee have given the subject most careful consideration, and have unanimously come to the conclusion that overhead electric traction is the best known system of traction, having due regard to efficiency and cost, for West Bromwich.

(3) *Position of Poles.*—That in adopting this system the poles, which must be of designs to be approved by the corporation, should be placed in the middle of the roads where the width from kerb to kerb is not less than 36 ft., and that the corporation should be allowed to use them for arc lighting of the streets free of charge. In the case of Boar-lane, Leeds, the average width from kerb to kerb is 38 ft. 3 in., and in Euston-road (east of Gower-street), London, which has an immense traffic, centre poles have been adopted for electric street lighting every 240 ft. apart; here the width is from 38 ft. to 40 ft. from kerb to kerb. Your sub-committee have not met with any street more suitable for the adoption of centre poles in the towns visited by them.

(4) *Current.*—That arrangements be made to supply the electric current to the company by the corporation from their proposed electric light station.

(5) *Cars.*—The adoption of small cars of the most modern type, with a gangway inside of at least 2 ft. 8 in. (cars lighted by electricity are far more comfortable and convenient for passengers and a very great improvement to the badly-lighted cars at present in use), and a frequent service at popular prices, which will be a very great benefit to the citizens. Your sub-committee recommend a five minutes' service from the New Inns to Carters Green, with a ten minutes' service from Carters Green to Great Bridge and Hill Top; also that the conductors and drivers should be provided with proper and suitable uniforms.

A conference of local authorities through whose districts the South Staffordshire tramways run was held on June 25th to consider the proposals of the company. The bodies represented were the corporations of West Bromwich, Wednesbury and Dudley, and the urban district councils of Handsworth, Tipton and Darlaston. After a long discussion the following resolution was adopted : " That, having regard to the views expressed by the Midland Electric Traction Company with regard to the acquisition of the tramways undertaking, this meeting be adjourned, to enable the various local authorities to consider the suggestion of municipalisation."

The conference was resumed on July 20th, when the chairman, Councillor Pitt, J.P., mayor of West Bromwich, stated that the matter had come before the West Bromwich Town Council, who referred it to the General Purposes Committee, and after full consideration they had decided to take over the tramways in their own district. They had not decided upon any system, or as to sub-letting their rights to any company, but simply to purchase and leave the working to the future. They had also received a communication from Wednesbury, Darlaston and Tipton, who had held a private conference and had passed a resolution affirming the desirability of taking over the tramways in their respective districts. Ultimately it was resolved : " That in the opinion of this conference it is desirable that all the local authorities within the district of the South Staffordshire Tramways Company should take steps to purchasing the tramway lines within their respective districts, and also to oppose the proposed application to Parliament of the British Electric Traction Company for a Bill to confirm the lease of the tramways to that company, and that a copy of the resolution be sent to each local authority."

When the report of the sub-committee was before the council reference was made to the able manner in which it had been compiled by the borough surveyor.

**Business Announcement.** — In consequence of the retirement of Mr. Fothergill, to-morrow, from the management of the London and Lancashire Fire Insurance Company, we have been informed that the directors have appointed the present sub-manager, Mr. F. W. P. Rutter, to be the manager and secretary as from the 1st prox.

# The Disinfection of Excreta.

By HENRY E. ARMSTRONG, D.SC., Medical Officer of Health, Newcastle-upon-Tyne.*

It has long appeared to the writer that our methods of dealing with the excreta of diseases known to be most readily communicable through the medium of alvine discharges is a weak point of preventive medicine. In one class of ailment the surface of the body is disinfected with the most scrupulous care and prolonged attention. In another the respiratory passages are treated in like manner. The segregation of the sick in all infectious diseases is practised wherever the nature of these diseases is understood. So highly is this mode of preventive treatment valued in one malady—small-pox—that hospitals for its isolation are required by the authorities to be located at a distance of half a mile from human habitations. Infected rooms and clothing, bedding, &c., exposed to infection are each rendered safe by special modes of treatment.

Are we equally careful and certain in our disinfection of the bowel discharges in cholera and enteric fever? In these diseases—whether treated at home or in the hospital—the evacuations, from their offensiveness, are liable to summary treatment. So long as the patient is in bed they are generally voided into a bed-pan containing more or less of some disinfectant solution. More disinfectant is perhaps added, and the contents of the pan are thrown down the closet or slop-sink, or buried in the ground as quickly as possible. The proportion of disinfectant used in such cases is seldom suffi-

at St. Petersburg during the outbreak of cholera in 1894. The evacuations and other infected liquids from the different cholera pavilions were conveyed in pipes to a large general boiler, into which steam was turned after the lid had been closed and fixed. This process had the disadvantage of allowing the liquids to leave a pavilion for disinfection at a considerable distance, thus giving rise to continual infection and fouling of a large amount of pipe. This defect is avoided in the apparatus devised for the cholera hospital of the corporation of Newcastle-upon-Tyne by their city engineer, Mr. W. George Laws, and the writer, in which a small steriliser is provided for each ward. A model of the apparatus was shown in the exhibition of the congress of the Sanitary Institute at Liverpool, and a paper describing the steriliser was read before the congress of the British Medical Association at Newcastle in 1892 by Dr. C. U. Laws.† The appliance having been found fairly to answer its purpose at the cholera hospital, others have lately been fixed in off-shoots of the enteric wards of the city hospital for infectious diseases. The steriliser, a circular cast-iron vessel about 2 ft. 6 in. in diameter and holding 30 gallons, stands on the floor of a chamber containing also a slop-sink for rinsing soiled linen, bed-pans, &c. The waste pipe from this sink is attached by a swivel joint, so that it can be turned up when not in use. When turned down it conveys the slops into the steriliser. The bed-

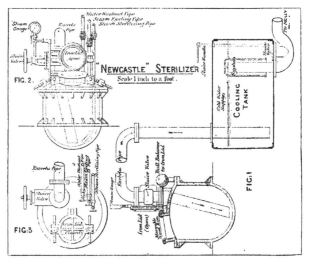

"NEWCASTLE" STERILIZER

Scale 1 inch to a foot.

FIG. 2.

FIG. 1.

COOLING TANK

FIG. 3.

cient. If, for instance, the agent used be perchloride of mercury, an ounce or two of a 1 in 500 solution to, say, 1 lb. of stool, is generally considered ample, whereas the evacuation itself requires for its proper disinfection 1-500th its weight—i.e., 76·80 grains of the dry perchloride, or 500 times the amount of solution (i.e., about 4 pints). The excreta and the disinfectant must of necessity be intimately mixed if the disinfection is to be perfect. But who can rely on this being done, even when the evacuation is liquid? In the solid state such mixture is not to be expected, being indeed hardly practicable. The rinsings of soiled linen, &c., at the slop-sink require disinfection equally with the discharges caught in the bed-pan. But they are too often sent direct into the drain, with a flush of disinfectant thrown in after to overtake them as it may. The infected dejecta of convalescents from either of the diseases in question are commonly voided down the water-closet, often without the pretence of disinfection.

### HOSPITAL ARRANGEMENTS.

Burning the discharges after mixture with sawdust cannot be considered free from danger. The quickest, safest, most thorough and most certain way to disinfect excreta is by boiling them under steam pressure, a method requiring special apparatus not hitherto available for domestic use. Sterilisation of excreta by steam was practised in a hospital

pans from the wards are emptied into the steriliser, the inlet to which is provided with a movable wooden rim, to allow of its also being used as a closet by convalescent patients. When the container is about three parts full the lid is closed and screwed down, and steam is turned on. Disinfection is completed in about twenty minutes, after which the contents are ejected by steam up the discharge pipe and into the tank at the outside of the building, there to cool before going to the drain. After each operation the steriliser is washed out by means of a ¾-in. water pipe, the dirty water being also driven into the cooling tank by the steam ejector. The chamber for the apparatus is shelved, for bed-pans, urinals, &c., and is provided with an opening in an outer wall, beneath which is a truck for the reception of linen which has been rinsed at the sink.

### HOME TREATMENT.

The foregoing observations refer only to the sterilisation of the discharges of patients in hospital. But the necessity for similar disinfection in cases under treatment at home is quite

*A paper read at the Birmingham congress of the Sanitary Institute.
†Our readers may remember that this apparatus was fully described in a paper prepared by Mr. W. George Laws for the annual meeting of the Incorporated Association of Municipal and County Engineers in London in 1894, and reported in our issue of July 5, 1894. We reproduce the illustration there given.

as great as in hospital. In private houses, and still more so in tenement dwellings, the night-soil and slops are apt to be thrown into the ash-pit or down the sink without the addition of a disinfectant. The soiled linen is frequently left lying for days before it is purified. In a household of ten persons, six of whom are at present in hospital at Newcastle with enteric fever, the spread of infection was due to the neglect of instructions to disinfect and purify the bed-clothing.

To prevent the danger from these causes special arrangements for disinfecting the excreta and slops from cases of enteric fever, &c., not removed to hospital are required. This may be done either (1) by receiving the discharges into air-tight vessels and removing them daily to a sterilising station for treatment, or (2) by sterilising them on the premises where they are produced. As in the hospital, the nearer the steriliser to the ward the better; so, *primâ facie*, in private practice, sterilisation on the spot appears preferable to that of removal for treatment at some distance, however small. In this view the idea of a household steriliser first suggested itself, and the writer accordingly applied to Messrs. Goddard, Massey & Warner, of Nottingham, the makers of the hospital steriliser, for plans for a portable apparatus for use on private premises to be worked by an official of the local authority. A capacity of 2 gallons was thought sufficient, and lightness of weight for convenience of transport was a desideratum. It was proposed that steam should be generated by means of a coal fire or a ring of gas burners beneath the receiver. The appliance was to be provided with a seat for the use of convalescents, and suitable means for filling and discharge of contents into a drain.

The impracticability of heating by means of gas in tenement premises, and the length of time required to generate steam, may be difficulties in the way of the satisfactory general working of this appliance. These objections are avoided if the liquids to be disinfected are removed to a central steriliser, a proposal suggested by Mr. Laws and endorsed by the writer. An ordinary 30-gallon steriliser, with small steam boiler, cooling tank, &c., would probably be found enough for the requirements of a district of half-a-mile radius. The number of such stations would, of course, depend on the area of the town. The infected liquids may be received into tin canisters, with hermetically closing lids, and removed daily for disinfection. In cases beyond the radius, or when found preferable for other reasons, the portable household steriliser would be found useful.

## ELECTRIC LIGHT AT POPLAR.

### PROPOSED EXPENDITURE OF £79,000.

At the last meeting of the Poplar District Board of Works the Electric Lighting Committee presented a report in which they stated that they had considered the several reports of Mr. A. Blackburn, the electrical engineer, in reference to the public electricity supply of the district, and had carefully deliberated upon the suggestions contained in them. They submitted the following recommendations for the approval of the board:—

That the low-tension continuous-current three-wire system, with a pressure of 460 volts between the outside wires, and supplying energy to consumers at either 460 or 230 volts pressure, be adopted. That the generating plant, to commence with, consist of two 100-kilowatt and two 200-kilo. watt generating plants, consisting of four high-speed engines, coupled direct to four shunt-wound dynamos, and four boilers, together with a main switchboard, balancing transformers, storage battery, " Booster " dynamos, steam pipes, hot wells, cold water tanks, pumps, economiser, and other necessary adjuncts. That a light iron tramway be constructed from the edge of the Limehouse Cut, across the board's depot and Yeo-street, to the proposed boiler-house. That arrangements be made for taking a supply of cooling water for surface-condensing purposes from the Limehouse Cut. That water-tube boilers be the type of boilers adopted, fitted with mechanical stokers. That a travelling crane, capable of lifting 15 tons, be provided in the engine-room. That the mains be laid in stoneware casing, filled in solid with bitumen or similar compound. That where gas lamps now exist in the roads and streets not to be lighted by arc lamps and through which mains are to be laid, such lamps be utilised for incandescent electric lights. That fifty-four 10-ampere arc lamps and seventy-one 7½-ampere arc lamps be provided, to be replaced at midnight by incandescent electric lamps, and that the existing gas lamp-posts in the streets to be lighted by arc lamps be removed. That the charges to consumers be 5d. per unit for the first hour of the maximum demand per day, 4d. per unit for the second hour, and 3d. per unit for all further consumption for lighting, and 3d. per unit for the first hour of the maximum per day, and 1½d. per unit for all subsequent consumption for power. That the board undertake the wiring of private premises where desired by consumers, payment for the same to be made in one sum or by instalments, at the option of the consumer. That the engineer be instructed to forthwith prepare the necessary specifications, founded on the foregoing, that tenders for the required plant and machinery be invited, and that the necessary application be made to the London County Council for permission to carry out the works, to which the consent of

that authority is required. That it be referred to the Finance Committee to consider the question of applying to the London County Council, or other authorities, for the necessary loans for the undertaking, including the wiring of consumers' premises, the estimated amount being £79,000.

The consideration of the report was adjourned till the next meeting.

## ARBITRATIONS AND AWARDS.

An arbitration of considerable importance to the borough of Brighton has just been settled by agreement, after the proceedings had extended over three days. In order to perfect the water supply, the Brighton Corporation decided to acquire compulsorily 47 acres of land at Shoreham, belonging to Messrs. Bridger. The latter claimed £10,000 for the land, a further sum of £57,000 for a stream of water which traversed it (based on twenty-five years' purchase for royalties on water calculated to be drawn at 1d. per gallon), together with an additional sum of 10 per cent. as compensation for the compulsory purchase. Sir E. Clarke and Mr. Boyle appeared before the under-sheriff on behalf of the claimants, whilst the case for the corporation was argued by Mr. Pember, Q.C., Sir William Marriott and Mr. J. E. Bankes. At the conclusion of Sir Edward Clarke's speech the under-sheriff and jury proceeded to Old Shoreham to view the property. Sir John Whittaker Ellis (Farebrother, Ellis, Clark & Co., London) gave evidence on behalf of the vendors. He valued the land to be compulsorily acquired at £9,500, and the rights in the water at £62,727. Mr. Pember, Q.C., for the corporation, contended that the vendors had no property in the water, but were only entitled to compensation as riparian owners who had rights of using the stream and no more. It was decided, however, as a point of law, that the jury were to assume a property in the water, which might be contested after the verdict; but on the third day of the hearing the arbitration came unexpectedly to a close, a compromise being agreed to under which the Brighton Corporation pay £6,000 for the land compulsorily acquired, and the vendors, Messrs. Bridger, are to receive a royalty of 1d. per 1,000 gallons on all water pumped along the mains to any point outside the Shoreham district of supply.

## THE SANITARY INSTITUTE.

### EXAMINATIONS AT MANCHESTER.

At an examination in practical sanitary science, held at Manchester on the 16th and 17th inst., six candidates presented themselves, and Mr. William John Ball, 17 Wellfield-street, Warrington, was granted a certificate. The following were the questions set for answer in writing: (1) Describe the action of the so-called lift and force pump. From what depth is it theoretically possible—with the barometer standing at 30in.—to raise water with a simple lift pump? (2) What is the average usual rainfall in the North, South, East and West of England respectively? What are the chief geographical conditions modifying the rainfall? (3) How would your define hardness of water? Describe in detail a method suitable for softening water for a general public supply. (4) What methods have been proposed for the treatment of sewage? Upon what principles do they depend? Describe any one method in detail. (5) Contrast the advantages and disadvantages of open fireplaces, and warming by hot air, hot water, and steam. (6) What is the best position for a fresh-air inlet to enter a disconnection chamber as regards the disconnecting trap? Illustrate by sketch and give the size of air inlet in relation to the sectional area of the upcast shafts of the drains. (7) What is meant by an infectious disease? Give two examples and detail the chief precautions to be taken when an infective fever occurs in a house. (8) What weight of water would be discharged per second through a circular orifice of 1-in. diameter, under a pressure of 1,000 lb. per square foot, neglecting friction?

On the same days an examination was held for inspectors of nuisances, at which 121 candidates presented themselves, of which fifty-six were certified, as regards their sanitary knowledge, competent to discharge the duties of inspectors of nuisances. The following were the questions set for answer in writing: (1) The purity of a well water is questioned. What steps should be taken by an inspector in ascertaining whether the suspicions are warranted or not? (2) A person who has purchased from a butcher's stall a pair of kidneys that are obviously diseased, brings them to you as an inspector. Describe in detail how you would act. (3) Describe a good form of waste-water closet, and enumerate the advantages and disadvantages of this form of closet. Under what conditions would you recommend their adoption? (4) In tracing the origin of an outbreak of diphtheria, what would you inquire into and how would you proceed? (5) Describe briefly the structure and drainage of a model slaughter-house. (6) What are the general provisions of the Model By-Laws of the Local Government Board with respect to house drainage? (7) What is the area of a room of the dimensions shown? (8) Describe and draw to scale (1 ft. to 1 in.) the following joints in lead pipes—a " wiped " and a " copper-bit." State which is the stronger joint, and why?

## SEWAGE DISPOSAL IN LEEDS.

THE BACTERIAL EXPERIMENTS AT KNOSTROP.

The details of the experiments carried out at Leeds under the direction of Mr. W. J. Dibdin have been put together in the form of a report compiled by the Lord Mayor (Alderman T. W. Harding) and Mr. T. Hewson, the city engineer. After estimating the population of Leeds at 416,618, the compilers, says *The Yorkshire Post*, point out that the city possesses an abundant supply of good water, the present consumption being at the rate of 15,000,000 gallons per day, 4,000,000 of which are supplied for trade purposes. Almost the whole pours into the sewers. The volume of sewage varies from hour to hour. Apart from rainfall, the maximum flow occurs at about mid-day and the minimum flow at night. The rate of flow rises to over 22,000,000 gallons in the day and falls to below 8,000,000 gallons in the night.

A lengthy description is given of the old works, with details of working expenses. With the increase in the volume of sewage since 1874 the old settlement area was found to be insufficient, and the effluent from the precipitation tanks was generally turbid and unsatisfactory, while as soon as the normal mid-day flow was expanded to more than double by rain it was found impossible to deal with it with the present machinery, and the excess of sewage, diluted by the rain, then flowed untreated into the channel leading to the river. Reference is made to the serious difficulties encountered in connection with the production, storage and removal of sludge. Although a biological scheme to deal effectively with the huge volume of Leeds sewage would involve a large outlay, the committee felt that the expenditure would be much less than that required by broad irrigation, for which, indeed, no suitable land appears to be available within 21 miles of Leeds.

In July, 1897, the committee called in Mr. W. J. Dibdin, the eminent chemist, to advise them, and he undertook to make some laboratory experiments on small-coke filters with samples of average Leeds sewage, and with samples of specific trade effluents, notably effluents from tanneries and the iron liquor from chemical works. He found, in dealing with iron liquor by itself, that there was at first a considerable oxidisation of the iron salts; but this result was obtained at the expense of the efficiency of the beds, which soon became unfit for further work. With samples of average Leeds sewage, containing iron liquor, tan refuse and other trade effluents, diluted with domestic sewage, good results were obtained on the small experimental beds, giving 80 per cent. of purification as the measure of the work of the double beds. In the case of tan liquors alone, undiluted by sewage, it was found that the effect of this double treatment, first on a coarse and then on a fine bed, gave nearly 80 per cent. purification and removed the solids in suspension. Encouraged by this report, the committee decided to proceed to a practical experiment on bacterial treatment at the Knostrop works, and the council having approved, Mr. Dibdin was asked over to Leeds in the beginning of September last year to advise upon the matter. Acting upon his suggestions, a coarse bed and a fine bed were constructed, each of about one-eigth of an acre. The coarse bed was filled with coarse coke not less than 3 in. diameter, and the fine bed with coke not less than ⅛ in. diameter and not more than 1¼ in. diameter. The floors of the beds are paved with old bricks grouted with cement, and are formed with a fall to the outlet end of the beds. Upon them are laid 3 in. agricultural tile drains, 2 ft. apart, connected at their low ends with a brick collecting drain, which conveys the drainage to outlet valves.

The sewage was first turned on to the beds on October 2, 1897. Absolutely crude sewage was used, and the beds were worked in this way for four months. The amount of purification shown by the final effluent after the beds had become established is considered satisfactory, and proves that, notwithstanding iron liquor and other trade effluents mixed with the sewage of Leeds, it can be treated on bacteria-beds so as to produce a really good effluent. The effluents from the fine bed had no smell, except at times a slight earthy odour. The first flow was always cloudy, and in some cases turbid, but it cleared more or less according to the varieties of sewage being treated. The latter part of the flow was always very clear. In order to make a physiological test of the effluent, some carp were put into the effluent basin. More than half died within a month, but this was apparently due to the rush of the effluent carrying them against the outflow grating. Provision was then made to protect the fish from the full pressure of the rush, and the three carp that were living at the time this was done are still alive, having been continuously in the effluents, good and bad, which have passed through the basin for a year.

Good results having been obtained in the final effluent, it remained to consider whether the beds were really digesting the large quantity of suspended matter brought down in the sewage or whether this was accumulating in the beds. The gross capacity of the rough bed is 174,800 gallons, and the nett or liquid capacity, after filling in the cake, is estimated to be 83,300 gallons. When the beds were considered to be in good working order a careful measure of capacity was made, which showed that the rough bed had been reduced to 63,400 gallons. From the analysis of a large number of samples of crude sewage taken daily for two and a half months (October 2 to December 15, 1897) it appears that the average amount of matter in suspension in the crude sewage

of Leeds is 37·2 grains per gallon. The analysis of the effluent from the rough bed during the same period gave 11·9 grains per gallon as the amount of solids in suspension; so that 25·3 grains per gallon were kept back by the rough bed. Chemical changes set up by allowing the beds to remain empty for a fortnight were found beneficial, and the experiment points to the possibility of treating the crude sewage and consuming the sludge if periods of rest are provided, say, two weeks out of five in winter and one week in four in summer.

Experiments with screened sewage were begun on March 4th of the present year. Considerable trouble arose from the large volumes of strong dye which came down pretty regularly at about the time for filling the beds. The dye discolours the whole volume of the sewage, and occasionally astonishing volumes of foul trade effluents have to be dealt with. In one recent instance a large quantity of what was apparently printing ink actually choked up the pumps. It will be necessary, the report continues, to maintain a systematic inspection of the trade effluents flowing into the sewers, with a view to their regulation. It is possible that in some cases the flow is the result of waste unnoticed by the manufacturers themselves. The experiments with screened sewage were carried on for six months, from March 4th to September 8th, with seven days' rest, from April 27th to May 4th, and an enforced rest of thirty-eight days, from June 16th to July 25th. The number of fillings during the whole period was 315. The average of the fillings was 46,000 gallons, and the total passed over the bed during the six months was 14,490,000 gallons; and, after making allowances for the solids screened off, it is estimated that about 51,000 gallons of sludge were retained by the rough bed. The capacity on March 2nd was 52,100 gallons, and on September 8th 41,000 gallons ; nett loss of capacity, 11,100 gallons. Deducting this from the estimated amount of 51,100 gallons retained by the rough bed, we have 40,000, or about 80 per cent., as the amount of sludge consumed in this period by the rough bed. The fine bed retained 16,700 gallons of sludge, the whole of which was consumed, the capacity of the bed not having been decreased. The total consumption by the two beds was 56,700 gallons of sludge. The effluent from the fine bed during the six months, except for the first fortnight after the long rest and during the heavy flow of dye, continued satisfactory.

After referring to experiments with settled sewage, some general observations are made on the biological experiments. It is pointed out that the action of the bacteria beds give something beyond mere filtration—namely, a chemical action upon the organic matters in solution, and evidently a much greater purification than is represented by the mere withdrawal of suspended matters ; and, in addition, it digests the organic solids left behind, a process which, if incomplete, can probably be completed by adequate periods of rest. The effluent from precipitation, with or without lime, is known to give rise to decomposition and putrefaction. The effluent from the bacteria-beds improved on keeping, and in no case did subsequent putrefaction arise. From the experience gained during the year from treating Leeds sewage on bacteria-beds it was found that the effluents were much superior to those from lime precipitation, and superior to those obtained in some cases from land filtration. They were proved capable of sustaining the life of coarse fish for a long period, and showed no signs of putrefaction on keeping. Their chemical analysis gives results which are generally well within the limit of 1 grain per gallon oxygen absorbed in four hours, and 1 grain of albuminoid ammonia, which has in recent years been generally accepted as a provisional standard of purity for effluents going into a stream not used for drinking purposes.

Dealing with the extension of the experiments authorised by the city council in June last, the report states that new beds are being constructed, and clinkers from the destructors are being used instead of coke. It is proposed to make a series of trials with different volumes of sewage, with sewage under different conditions as regards matter in suspension, with different periods of rest, with filtering of material of different sizes, and with varying arrangements as to drainage, &c. The question is raised as to whether an experiment should not be made without delay to ascertain the effect of the septic tank treatment for the destruction of the solids in suspension ; also to see how far an open septic tank, or upward septic filtration through coarse material covered with a layer of sand, would be effective in destroying the sludge, and so far relieving the filter-beds. Experience in Leeds shows that either a first filtration or a septic tank, or both, must precede the fine bacteria-bed. Intermittent flow and intermittent aëration are also necessary.

In concluding, the compilers of the report say : The subject is a complex one, but the whole drift of modern scientific thought in regard to sewage treatment is in the direction of biological treatment. It is, in fact, a return to Nature's methods in disposing of animal and vegetable decay by means of the countless organisms in the upper layers of the soil, the chemical action of which is being year by year increasingly investigated and understood.

---

Limehurst.—A loan of £8,500 has been sanctioned by the Local Government Board for the carrying out of the district council's sewage scheme.

# For Assistants and Pupils.

## THE CONSTRUCTION OF ROADS AND STREETS.—XXIV.

By WILLIAM H. MAXWELL, Assistant Engineer and Surveyor, Leyton Urban District Council.

### BRICK PAVEMENTS.

The paving of carriageways with bricks has received but little attention in this country, although they have been somewhat largely used for footways. In Holland the use of brick for this purpose has prevailed for some 150 years, and in America and other countries "vitrified brick" is also very largely employed for carriageway traffic.

In England the experience derived from the use of brick upon footways shows this class of pavement to be particularly apt to wear unevenly, owing to the varying quality of the bricks. The want of attention of English municipal engineers to the use of this material has been pointed out by Mr. J. T. Eayrs, M.I.C.E., in a very interesting paper, entitled "Brick Paving for Carriageways,"[*] in which he says in America "It is claimed that neither granite, asphalte nor wood can offer so many advantages as vitrified brick as a paving material, and that, if properly laid, it is as noiseless as any other kind of pavement: the surface is smooth without being slippery; it offers a minimum amount of resistance to the passage of traffic, and inflicts a minimum amount of wear and tear on horses and vehicles; it is practically impervious, and therefore perfectly sanitary; is easily cleansed, and requires less scavenging than any other paving; it can be washed without injury or becoming slippery when wet; is readily taken up and relaid; reasonable in first cost and maintenance; and has a life which compares favourably with other materials, such as asphalte, wood, &c."

The city engineer of Chicago says, "Comparing brick pavements with asphalte, I believe that for general use shale brick, properly burned and of the right size, properly laid on a hydraulic cement concrete foundation, is superior to asphalte, as to its first cost, facilities and cheapness for repairs, its sanitary qualities, its ease upon horses, and last, but not least, its durability. . . . Brick can be laid on a grade where it is out of the question to lay asphalt. Brick can be washed continually without injury. . . . Brick when wet is not more slippery than when dry; asphalte is always dangerous, and if wet is more slippery than when dry, and when a horse is down on asphalte it is with difficulty that he regains his feet. Brick is not more noisy than asphalte, and as it can be continually sprinkled it is far less dusty."

In selecting a suitable brick for paving purposes the points to which the attention should be directed are—the nature of the clay from which they are manufactured, the uniformity of shape and size, absorption, specific gravity, transverse and crushing strength and abrasion.

In regard to the quality of the clay, Mr. Eayrs, in the paper above referred to, points out, "The composition of this varies very considerably in different districts, but most bricks are made from a hydrated silica of alumina, generally containing traces of magnesia, iron, lime and potash. Lime in excess is very injurious to paving brick, as it is changed to caustic lime in burning, and a small amount of moisture will cause it to slake and disintegrate the brick. A small amount of magnesia aids in producing vitrification. Iron is not injurious, but in a brick to resist high temperature an excessive quantity would be fatal. Alumina gives elasticity, and renders the material tough and binding. The alkalies act as a flux in chemical combination with the silica and alumina. One writer states that from an analysis of a large number of clays, most of them carboniferous, he finds, after averaging one with another, the alumina, silica and water make up about 85 per cent. of the material, leaving 15 per cent. for lime, potash, soda, iron, and other impurities. Clays with a low percentage of these impurities, and more especially of potash, soda and iron, are fireclays. Alumina and silica are practically infusible alone, but the presence of even 3 per cent. of potash or soda renders the whole mass easily fusible. The presence of these so-called impurities is absolutely essential where vitrification is desired. The ease with which a clay will vitrify depends largely upon the percentage of the respective impurities which act as fluxes. A clay may have so large a percentage of fluxing material as to make it too easily fusible."

In America the sizes of paving bricks vary between 7½ in. by 3½ in. by 2 in. and 9½ in. by 4½ in. by 3½ in., but the size mostly used is 9 in. by 4 in. by 3 in. They are made both with square edges and rounded nosings and with rounded tops. The square edges are mostly used, make better joints, and are more easily scavenged.

Paving bricks should not absorb more than from 1½ to 3½ per cent. of moisture in twenty-four hours. The degree of absorption is an important factor in determining the life of the pavement, as the succession of wet and dry weather, and of frost and thaw, tend to disintegrate the brick. Where the specific gravity of a brick is specified, it is required in

American specifications to be from 2·00 to 2·30. A transverse strength of about 2,000 lb. is also required, and a crushing resistance of from 10,000 to 12,000 lb. per square inch.

The greatest amount of wear on a road surface is caused by the pounding produced by horses' feet, so that paving bricks which will withstand an abrasion test will have the longest life. For this test the bricks are usually placed in a "tumbler" or "rattler," either with or without other materials. The tumbler, consisting of an iron barrel mounted on trunnions, is made to revolve at a certain speed and for a certain time, and in so doing rattles the bricks together with iron castings, or other materials placed inside with the bricks, so as to abrade the surfaces. The bricks under test are weighed before being placed in the tumbler, and again after rattling for a specified time, and the loss is then noted.

In laying brick pavements in America the only foundation adopted in many instances consists of either macadam, broken ballast, slag or gravel rolled down. In some cases the bricks have been laid without foundation, except the rolling of the natural ground and spreading a bed of sand. The necessity of a stronger foundation, however, is now being recognised, and the larger cities are adopting a Portland cement concrete foundation with a cushion, 1 in. to 2 in. in thickness, of clean, dry sand to bed the bricks upon. About seven days are allowed for the concrete to set before the bricks are laid.

The bricks are laid in straight course at right angles to the curb, or diagonally at an angle of 60°. They are usually laid close together, without leaving spaces for joints, the irregularity in shape of the bricks being of itself sufficient for this. In some instances the bricks are even forced up towards the curb with the aid of a lever, and then wedged up with a closer; but this practice seems likely to cause the paving to lift and arch, or to displace the curbs in the event of expansion.

The bricks are next either hand-rammed or rolled with a steam or horse roller drawn by men. In ramming, a plank of 1 in. or more in thickness is frequently placed between the bricks and the rammer.

The pavement is grouted with either cement or pitch and sand. The sand used is clean, sharp river sand. In pitch grouting a semi-elastic watertight joint is aimed at, such as will not crack in winter or "spew" up in the hot season. The cement grout is mixed with sand in the proportion of from one to one and one to one and a half. The pitch or cement grouting is applied by means of a filler or funnel-shaped instrument, so that the grout is not allowed to run over the pavement, but simply to fill the joints. The curvature of cross-section of the pavement varies with the gradient, but is the same as that adopted in wood paving.

The pavement is finally covered with clean, coarse sand (¼ in. to 1 in. in thickness), and allowed to so remain, with traffic passing over it, for about a fortnight, when it is cleared off.

This pavement is usually laid under contract, including maintenance after completion for periods from one up to five years. The life of this pavement in America is given as ranging from fifteen to twenty years under ordinary conditions, and its use for carriageways appears to be rapidly increasing.

The provincial instructor in road-making to the Ontario Department of Agriculture, in his report on "Road and Street Improvement in Ontario" for the year 1896, contains some instructive observations on the question of the use of vitrified brick for street pavements in that province. He says:—

"The only competitor of asphalte is vitrified brick. This pavement has come in a most timely way to take the place of the decayed cedar-block pavements, which are disgracing the streets of so many towns and cities. Vitrified brick is becoming popular, and presents features which tend to cause it to become more so. It offers a better foothold for horses than does asphalte. The surface is not so smooth, and in consequence radiates less heat and light, is quite as sanitary, with less liability to become dusty. Among bicyclists it is much more popular than the asphalte. If the joints are filled with suitable cement brick pavement is but little more noisy than asphalte.

"The majority of failures which have occurred with brick have been traced to defects which the material or better construction could have obviated. Its ease of construction and repair offers a great advantage over asphalte, ordinary labourers being easily taught to do the work. Few repairs are needed if good brick is used, and in the first cost as well as in maintenance brick should be, and generally is, cheaper than asphalte.

"Although brick is one of the oldest paving materials, it has been used on this continent for only about a quarter of a century; and only within the last ten years has it attracted widespread attention. In the United States it has been used

[*] "Proceedings of the Association of Municipal and County Engineers," vol. xxiii.

very extensively, but in Ontario experience with the modern vitrified brick is very limited.

"Of its success as a paving material little remains in question. Brick pavements have been in existence in the United States for eighteen years, remaining in good condition. It was feared that the climate of northern countries, with severe frosts and rapidly-alternating conditions of moisture and temperature, would be unfavourable to its use, but the experience of various northern cities shows that vitrified brick of a good quality is a most valuable addition to our list of paving materials.

"The best vitrified brick is made of shale or clay, or a mixture of the two. It is not "vitrified," as the name indicates, but is raised by intense heat just to the point of fusion. More than this fuses or melts the clay, permits it to run together, and the product is then glassy or vitrified, and brittle in consequence. The process of cooling must be very gradual. A brick if too rapidly cooled or "annealed" will be brittle, but with a thoroughly pulverised and well-mixed shale, brought to the proper temperature and then slowly annealed, the resultant brick should be sufficiently hard and tough to scratch steel. . . . The chief tests used are—that of absorption, representing the probable effect of atmospheric action, the rattler test, showing the effect of impact and abrasion as found in the chipping of horses' hoofs and the grinding of wheels, the transverse strength, showing the power to resist the breaking strain of heavy loads. Other tests are sometimes used, such as to determine the crushing strength, and the depth to which oil will penetrate the surface, &c.

"Where in towns the facilities for performing these experiments are not available, and only short sections of pavement are to be constructed, the experience of cities will generally afford a safe guide in choosing between different makes of brick. A further safeguard may be had by requiring the contractor or manufacturer to maintain the pavement up to a certain standard for at least five years.

"There is a tendency to endeavour to reduce the cost of brick pavements by the use of a weak foundation or no foundation at all. Brick pavements laid on gravel and sand have been successful, but this has been the case only when the subsoil has been of such a kind as to be very porous, easily drained and naturally firm. The experiment in Ontario, in view of Fall and Spring conditions, with alternate freezing and thawing, is a very dangerous one, a lesson which has been strongly impressed by the experience with cedar blocks. While a brick pavement may give satisfaction for a few years on sand and gravel foundation, there is every probability that the brick will settle irregularly, and rendered thereby more susceptible to wear and strain, the bricks will be broken and the life of the pavement very much shortened.

"A concrete foundation should almost invariably be employed. A 4-in. layer will, where a brick surface is suitable, be sufficiently durable. This forms a stiff monolith base, which distributes the weight of the traffic. There cannot be irregular settlements of brick, as is the tendency with yielding materials, such as sand and gravel. It also prevents water percolating beneath the road—not a very important feature in the South, but in freezing climates a matter of considerable importance.

"Between the bed of cement and the surface covering of brick a thin cushion of sand is necessary. By this means the brick can be laid evenly, a certain amount of spring is obtained, which lessens the effect of blows on the brick, and it over. comes the rumbling noise otherwise created. It is a common practice to merely fill the joints of the brick with sand. While this is not at all objectionable, by the use of a cement composed of pitch and sand the pavement becomes less noisy, absorbs less street filth, and renders the edges of the brick are strengthened."

*McDougall's Patent "Combination Set Pavement."*—This consists of a highly vitrified blue paving brick, 10 in. by 4½ in. by 5 in., containing recesses into which square wooden plugs, 2 in. long by 1 in. square, are driven, thus giving it the character of a wood pavement rather than brick. The plugs, which are previously creosoted, are intended to remain always about ⅛ in. above the surface of the brick. The advantages claimed for this type of paving are: That it is not slippery and affords a good foothold for horses, that it is durable, non-absorbent, wears evenly, is cheap, and readily handled and laid. It is laid on a concrete foundation with close joints, and grouted with hot pitch or a bituminous mixture. This pavement has been used at Cheltenham, Oxford, Preston, Manchester, Bootle and elsewhere.

At an annual meeting of municipal engineers, held in London in July, 1897, Mr. J. Hall, borough surveyor, Cheltenham, said : " I have laid several crossings with McDougall's patent bricks, and after two years' experience a motion has been adopted by the council to the effect that no other material is to be used anywhere for street crossings. The first crossing has been under observation by the police, and no record of any horse falling upon it has been made during that time, though previously it was a common experience to have two or three horses down upon a granite sett crossing in the same place in a week. The cost is about the same as granite."

**Largs.**—The commissioners have let the work connected with their new drainage scheme to Mr. Hastie, of Ayr, the price being about £1,200.

## METROPOLITAN IMPROVEMENTS.

### A GROSS EXPENDITURE OF £5,591,800.

Among the local Bills already lodged at the Parliament House are the several measures prepared and approved by the London County Council. These include a measure to empower the council to make a new street from Holborn to the Strand and a widening of Southampton-row, a widening of High-street, Kensington, and to make other street improvements and works in the county of London, involving altogether a gross expenditure of something over £5,591,000.

The works in connection with the proposed new thoroughfare to the Strand are to consist of a new central street, to commence in High Holborn opposite the southern end of Southampton-row, and to terminate at or near the northern corner of the site now occupied by the Olympic Theatre; a curved street to connect the new central street with the Strand at two points, the eastern end of such curved street to form a junction with the Strand, as proposed to be widened, at or near the point where Wych-street and Holywell-street now open on the roadway west of St. Clement Danes Church, and the western end to form a junction with the Strand between Catherine-street and Wellington-street. In connection with these central and curved streets subsidiary streets or junctions are to be made with Little Wild-street, Lincoln's Inn-fields, Great Wild-street, Kemble-street, Clare-street and Clare Market, Houghton-street, and a new street is to be formed on the site of that part of Exeter-street which is situate between Wellington-street and Catherine-street. The widening of Southampton-row is to be on the eastern side thereof, commencing at Vernon-place and Theobald's-road, and terminating at Holborn ; and there is to be a widening of Holborn on the northern side, commencing at the southern end of Southampton-row, and to extend some 50 yards eastward from the centre of that thoroughfare. There are also to be two new streets, one commencing in Kingsgate-street at the western end of Fisher-street and the other at Eagle-street, Kingsgate-street, both to be continued into Southampton-row. The estimated cost of the whole scheme for the new street from Holborn to the Strand is £4,802,500, and of the Southampton-row widening £272,000; but the estimates in these cases and in the case of other improvements included in the Bill are calculated to cover the original cost of purchasing lands and executing the works without any allowance in respect of returns from resale or letting of lands which will be ultimately available for that purpose, and from which there should, indeed, be a very considerable return.

The other improvements proposed in the Bill are of very much less magnitude, though interesting to the localities concerned. High-street, Kensington, for instance, is to be widened on the northern side near St. Mary Abbott's Church, and a new roadway is to be constructed from Clarence-mews to the High-street, the estimated cost in this case being £308,500. Provision is made in the Bill as to accommodation for persons of the labouring classes who may be displaced in effecting the improvements.

## STREET LIGHTING.

Mr. C. R. Bellamy, superintendent of street lighting to the Liverpool Corporation, has presented to the Lighting Committee of that body a report on street incandescent gas lighting. He points out the improvements and economy effected since the corporation gave attention to street lighting in 1894, resulting in a total reduction in cost to the city of £9,600, which enabled the committee to increase the number of lights in the city. Improvements in gas lighting had also been effected in the added areas since 1895. The lighting of the streets by incandescent gas could be extended, and by regulating the illuminating powers between certain hours during the night a saving could be made of 3s. per lamp. He recommends that the system be extended at a rate which the surplus funds at the disposal of the committee would cover, which would provide for the equipment of 2,800 lamps in each year. This would obviate the opening of a capital account and the raising of from £20,000 to £25,000, while the work could be carried out by the present staff, and the entire lighting of the city—apart, of course, from the streets lighted by electricity—with incandescent gas would be completed in four years. At the end of that period the lighting throughout the city would be increased by nearly three times where the single-burner lamp is adopted and by over five times with the double lamp, with a reduction of the permanent charges of between £3,000 and £4,000.

**Bolton.**—It is stated that Mr. Arthur Ellis, the borough electrical engineer, and the electricity works staff are now busily engaged extending the electricity works in order to accommodate two 1,000 horse-power engines and two 500 horse-power ditto, together with two 600 kilowatt and two 300 kilowatt continuous-current generators for tramways and lighting purposes. It is intended to change over portions of the town to continuous current, leaving the present alternating-current plant to supply the residential districts. This will take place during next summer. It is hoped to have the trams running next year (45 miles of truck).

# Law Notes.

## Edited by J. B. REIGNIER CONDER, 11 Old Jewry Chambers, E.C.,

### Solicitor of the Supreme Court.

*The Editor will be pleased to answer any questions affecting the practice of engineers and surveyors to local authorities. Queries (which should be written legibly on foolscap paper, one side only) should be addressed to "The Law Editor," at the Offices of The Surveyor. Where possible, copies of local Acts or documents referred to should be enclosed. All explanatory diagrams must be drawn and lettered in black ink only. Correspondents who do not wish their names published should furnish a nom de plume.*

Street Accident: Liability of Local Authority.—In *Thurrold v. Vestry of St. George's, Hanover-square*' (Queen's Bench Division, Mr. Justice Wills and a special jury, December 6, 1898), the plaintiff, a cab driver, sought to recover damages for injuries to himself and his horse and cab incurred under the following circumstances: He was driving a fare to Hyde Park-gardens on March 8th, about 8 p.m. When in Belgrave-square he passed on the right-hand side of a refuge, with the intention of going along Grosvenor-crescent, but just at that point his fare told him to go by way of Wilton-crescent, whereupon the plaintiff turned sharp to the left, in order to go through Wilton-crescent. In doing so he drove very near the refuge, and the cab was upset by a heap of sand and gravel lying close to the refuge. The gas lamp near the spot was out at the time, and, while it was admitted that the lamp was not under the control of the vestry, the plaintiff contended that if they put this heap in the road they did so at their peril. The cab was thrown over, the shafts were broken, and the horse was cut. The plaintiff, who was driving, was thrown from his seat, and he had his head and wrist injured. Plaintiff admitted that on the refuge there was a notice, "Keep to the left," but he had kept to the right. This notice had been put up by the Commissioner of Police, but it appeared that the place in question was not within the "special limits" defined by the Metropolitan Streets Act, 1867, and that therefore the police had no statutory authority to put up the notice. The sand, which was required for wood paving, was now put in a tin bin on the pavement, and plaintiff said that there would have been no accident if that precaution had been adopted before. For the defendants it was contended that the plaintiff must show that the accident was brought about substantially by the defendants' negligence, and by that alone. Under the Metropolitan Management Acts the vestry had the duty of lighting the streets, and they had made a contract with a gas company to do the lighting, and through no fault of either the vestry or the gas company the lamp went wrong. It was submitted that there was no negligence in a gas lamp being out for an hour, the defect having been remedied as quickly as possible. It was the duty of the vestry to maintain the streets, and they had put the gravel where it could be most easily got at. Mr. Justice Wills, in summing up, said that the question was whether the vestry had taken all reasonab'e precautions to render the heap safe. If the place was not a fit one, there was carelessness. If the place was a fit one, but was not properly lighted, it was a question of negligence. He did not think that the vestry was in any better position by giving the contract for lighting to the gas company. It was the duty of the vestry to light the heap, and want of light was evidence of negligence. The jury must take into account how the traffic was likely to go. Was there any negligence in the way of putting the heap there or in its being unlighted, and, further, was there any contributory negligence by the plaintiff? The jury found that there was negligence on the part of the defendants, and that the plaintiff was not guilty of contributory negligence, and upon these findings judgment was entered for the plaintiff.

### QUERIES AND REPLIES.

The Cleansing of Cesspools: Public Health Act, 1875, sec. 42.—" W. A. F." writes: The owner of eighteen houses, each having a privy and two privies draining into one cesspool, has called on the urban council to empty the cesspools. Our by-law No. 13 seems only to refer to cesspools in connection with buildings to accommodate animals. The above houses, although in the urban district, are more than half a mile from the nearest sewer. There is no contract for the removal of night-soil, and only an ordinary contract for the removal of refuse. There is no sewage rate levied, but a general rate. (1) Are the local authority under any obligation to empty the cesspools? (2) Can you quote a case?

By sec. 42 of the Public Health Act, 1875, it is provided that every local authority may, and when required by order of the Local Government Board shall, themselves undertake or contract for (*inter alia*) the cleansing of cesspools. Unless, however, they have undertaken or been required by the Local Government Board to undertake this work, there appears to be no obligation on their part to perform it. I am not aware of any case on the subject.

Storm-Water Sewer: Public Health Act, 1875, sec. 150.—" Surveyor " writes: Have an urban district council power to enforce the payment for the construction of a storm-water drain or sewer in a private street under the provisions of the Public Health Act, 1875? At present there is a sewer which takes the sewage and storm water in the street, and the council ordered notices to be served upon the owners, under

sec. 150, and to disconnect the storm water from the sewer and to lay a separate drain for storm-water purposes.

This depends upon whether the authority have expressed satisfaction with, or were in fact satisfied with, the existing sewer; and this is a question of fact to be decided on the evidence (*Barrow-in-Furness Corporation v. Dawson*, cited in Lumley's "Public Health Acts," fifth edition, p. 178). And if after a reasonable time after the vesting of sewers in an authority they do nothing, and express no views on the subject, it must be taken to be conclusive as a matter of fact that at the time the sewer was originally constructed they were satisfied with it for the purpose for which it was then used (*Bonella v. Twickenham Local Board*, 18 Q.B.D., 577). And although in *Batty and Codsarton Local Board v. Parry* (The Surveyor, vol. vii., p. 404) it was decided that until a street has been declared to be a highway repairable by the inhabitants at large the powers of sec. 150 may be exercised over and over again, as occasion requires, sewers were expressly excepted from the scope of this decision, as being in a different category from paving, &c., under secs. 13 and 15 of the Act.

Water-Closets: Flushing Apparatus.—" Dubious " writes: A certain owner of a row of old cottages in a rural district has drained the same into a new public sewer recently constructed in my district. Prior to such redrainage the cottages were supplied with pail privies. The owner has now provided, in place of the privies, new water-closets; but without flushing cisterns or the laying on of water for flushing purposes, trusting to the tenants occasionally throwing down water from a pail or other vessel. Water is laid on to the cottages for domestic purposes. The owner refuses to do more and defies the council. Can the rural district council compel the laying on of water for flushing these closets and the provision of flushing cisterns? Would sec. 36 of the Public Health Act, 1875, apply, or could you suggest any better enactment under which to proceed?

Yes, sec. 36 of the Public Health Act, 1875, undoubtedly applies. *Sherborne Local Board v. Bogle* (46 J.P.,676) is a case precisely in point. The defendant was the owner of several houses, each having a water-closet without a flushing apparatus. The surveyor having reported that the water-closet accommodation was insufficient, the local board gave notice to the owner to provide sufficient water-closet accommodation, and on his default executed the necessary works and summoned him for the cost. The magistrate made an order against him, refusing to go into the question of the necessity for the works; and the Queen's Bench Division held that the magistrates were right, as it was for the local board to determine whether the works were sufficient, upon the report of their surveyor, subject only to the right of appeal to the Local Government Board under sec. 268.

Combined Drainage: Local Act.—" Anxious " writes: Enclosed please find copy of sec. 57 of the Edmonton Urban District Council Act, relating to combined drainage, and also a copy of a resolution adopted by the council. (a) Is such a resolution in conformity with the section? (b) Is a separate resolution required for each set of drains to be constructed? The following is a copy of the section referred to: "If it appear to the council that two or more houses, plans for which have been approved after June 1, 1898, may be drained more economically or advantageously in combination than separately, and a sewer of sufficient size already exists or is about to be constructed within 100 ft. of any part of such houses, the council may order that such houses be drained by a combined drain, to be constructed either by the council, if they so decide, or by the owners in such manner as the council shall direct, and the costs and expenses of such combined drain and the repair and maintenance thereof shall be apportioned between the owners or occupiers of such houses in such manner as the council shall determine, and may be recovered by the council from such owners or occupiers in a summary manner." The following is also a copy of the resolution of the council: That in future all combined back drains be constructed by the council in accordance with the Edmonton District Council Act, at the cost and expense of the owners, and that all parties submitting plans be informed at the time that all drains are so to be done.

I think it is doubtful whether the section empowers the council to make a general order applicable to all future cases. It has been held in several cases that a local authority cannot, under sec. 36 of the Public Health Act, lay down a general rule for the conversion of privies into water-closets, but that each individual case must be considered and resolved upon separately (See, *amongst others, Wood v. Carpenter of Widnes*, The Surveyor, vol. xii., page 210). It would be far safer to make a separate order in each case.

Storm-Water Sewer: Public Health Act, 1875, Sec. 150.—" Surveyor " writes: Has an urban district council power to enforce the payment for the construction of a storm-water drain or sewer in a private street under the provisions of the Public Health Act, 1875? At present there is a sewer which takes the sewage and storm water in the street, and the council served notice upon the owners, under sec. 150, to put the street into a proper state of repair, and to disconnect the storm water from the sewer, and to lay a separate storm-water drain so as to discharge into the storm-water system of the town.

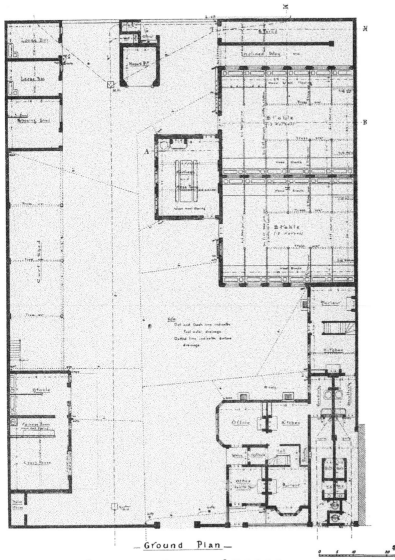

— Ground Plan —

EDWARDES STREET

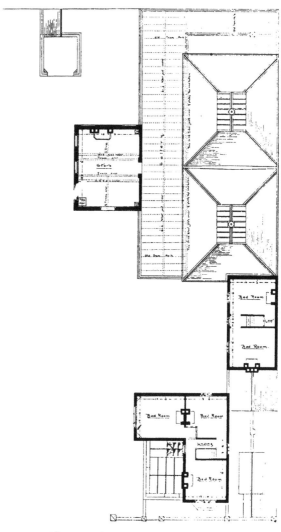

— 1$^{ST}$ Floor Plan —

50 Feet

If the local authority have expressly, or by implication, expressed satisfaction with, or, in fact, been satisfied with, the present sewer (which is a question of fact), they cannot compel the frontagers to bear the expense of any further sewer. If after the lapse of a reasonable time after the vesting of sewers in a corporation they had done nothing and expressed no view on the subject, it must be taken to be conclusive, as a matter of fact, that at the time the sewer was originally constructed they were satisfied with it for the purpose for which it was then used. (*Bonella* v. *Twickenham Local Board*, 18 Q.B.D., 577; *Barrow-in-Furness Corporation* v. *Dawson*, December 4, 1890; *Hornsey Local Board* v. *Davis*, 1893, 1 Q.B., 756.)

BUILDING ON DITCH.—"J. S. P." writes: In roads immediately outside the town there is a ditch on each side of the road. The owners of land abutting on to the road claim 4 ft. from the edge, which includes the ditch. We frequently have plans submitted showing buildings proposed to be erected 4 ft. beyond the hedge, that is over the ditch. The ditch in many cases receives the surface water from the road. Can the council refuse to pass plans where the ditch is shown to be built over? If the council are compelled to pass plans, can they call upon the owners of buildings to substitute a proper drain in lieu of the ditch?

By sec. 67 of the Highway Act, 1835, the council, as highway authority, have power to scour, cleanse and keep open all ditches; and by sec. 68 of the same Act, if any owner, &c., shall alter, obstruct or in any manner interfere with any such ditches after they shall have been made or taken under the charge of the authority without their consent he is chargeable with the cost of reinstating in addition to penalties. In *Rhodes* v. *Thomas* (3 J.P., 117) the appellant, having an orchard opening into a turnpike road, made an access from the orchard to the road across a ditch at the side of the road. He laid pipes in the ditch, which, being insufficient to carry off the water, obstructed the waterflow. It was held that he was properly convicted under the General Turnpike Act, 1862, of obstructing the ditch. Having regard to these enactments and this decision, I think the council would be justified in making the passing of the plans conditional upon proper provision being made for the continued unobstructed passage of water along the ditch, whether by the substitution of a proper drain or otherwise.

## SURVEYORS AND INSPECTORS.

It is generally admitted that in our rural districts the sanitary administration is not so efficient as in the urban districts, and that in the former numerous insanitary conditions abound which in the latter are rarely tolerated. These nuisances, says *The Journal of State Medicine*, are due either to lax supervision or administration, or to both. If the inspectors of nuisances have done their duty these nuisances have been detected and reported, and continue to exist merely because the sanitary authorities have not followed up the inspectors' reports by insisting upon their being abated. Where an inspector is not supported by his authority the supervision naturally becomes lax, since it is useless detecting and reporting nuisances which the district council will not make an effort to have removed. There can be no doubt that in too many cases the inspectors are not encouraged in the discharge of their duties, and an energetic officer often receives a hint, which he cannot mistake, that his energies would be better employed than in detecting what we have heard rural district councillors call "little pottyfogging nuisances."

One of the most effectual ways of preventing sanitary improvements in rural districts is that of constituting the same person "surveyor and inspector." Such an officer soon discovers that so long as he keeps the roads in order and attends to nuisances reported by persons aggrieved, that he is neither expected nor desired to make any other inspections for the discovery of insanitary conditions. This dual appointment, however, is a most economical one from the district councillor's point of view. The apportionment of the salary paid rests with the district council, and as half the salary of the inspector of nuisances is refunded by the county council, naturally a very considerable proportion is alloted for the office of sanitary inspector—in fact, the payment is inversely proportioned to the work which has to be performed. This condition of things is nothing less than a public scandal, and we are glad to hear that the Local Government Board have at length recognised it as such, and are refusing to sanction all fresh appointments to the dual office. Since the formation of rural district councils, the latter have become highway authorities and are responsible for the maintenance of all public roads except the main roads, which are under the charge of county councils. In the great majority of rural districts the charge of these roads fully occupies the time of a surveyor, and as either sanitary matters or the roads must be neglected, the sanitary condition of the district suffers.

There are numerous instances also in which men not only occupy the dual position of surveyor and inspector, but have other duties imposed upon them as well, such as rate-collecting. They may also be required to act as engineers and architects, and as clerks of works whenever any sanitary work is undertaken. This is a condition of things which the Local Government Board should carefully consider, with the object of devising some way in which it can quickly be ended. Reappointments should not be sanctioned in any district in which the district council have control of more than a certain length of road, nor in which the surveyor and inspector is also required or permitted to hold other offices. Until this is done there is very little hope for any improvement in the sanitary condition of our rural districts. The arrangement not only prevents the performance of the duties of the nuisance inspector, but it practically removes that officer from the control of the medical officer of health, and seriously diminishes the usefulness of that official. The reason usually urged for combining the two appointments is that the surveyor has constantly to visit every parish in the district, and that at such times he can always look round and attend to any sanitary matters which come under his notice. However plausible this may be in theory, it is lamentably inaccurate in fact. The duties which now devolve upon an inspector of nuisances are so numerous and varied, and so frequently of such a character as to require immediate attention, that it is utterly impossible for them to be satisfactorily discharged by a surveyor who has a number of labourers under his control and who must do his systematically if he is to do it satisfactorily. The subject is of the greatest importance in the interest of rural sanitation, and whilst the action of the Local Government Board in refusing to sanction fresh dual appointments is to be commended, the board might fairly consider every case of reappointment, and refuse to sanction all such where it appears impossible for both duties to be discharged satisfactorily by the same person.

## NEW LONDON WATER BILLS.

Among the private Bills relating to new water schemes other than those promoted by the London County Council is one promoted by the West Middlesex Waterworks Company. This company have deposited a measure to confer further powers upon themselves with respect to the construction of works, taking of water from the river Thames, raising further capital, and for other purposes. The preamble of this Bill declares it to be expedient that, pending the completion of the works authorised by the Act of 1896 and the Staines Reservoirs Act of 1898, the company should be empowered to draw from the Thames a further quantity of 24,500,000 gallons, which they are now entitled to draw, on any one day. The company may, if the Bill becomes law, raise additional capital, not exceeding in the whole £250,000, by the creation and issue of debenture stock. Another of the measures is the Metropolitan Waterworks Company's Bill. Under this measure it is proposed, "with the view of obviating the possibility of a deficiency in time of drought, or by reason of accident, or in cases of emergency in the quantity of water which any one or more of the metropolitan water companies may be able to supply within their district or districts, that provision should be made for improving and facilitating intercommunication between the mains and works of those companies respectively, and that such obligations shall be imposed upon those companies and such powers given to the Local Government Board, and such provisions made as is in the Act contained." The Local Government Board are to be empowered to sanction such quantity of water to be taken temporarily from the Thames and its tributaries as in the opinion of the board may be necessary for preventing any deficiency in the supply of water within the district of any of the companies. The East London Waterworks Company have deposited a Bill to enable them, with the sanction of the Local Government Board, to take further water from the river Thames in cases of exceptional drought and other emergencies, and another Bill to authorise them to construct additional storage reservoirs and other works, and to enable them to raise further capital by the creation and issue of debenture stock in a sum or sums not exceeding in the whole £1,500,000.

## PROPOSED LONDON MARKETS.

The copy of a Bill which will be introduced into Parliament next session has been deposited for the purpose of incorporating a company with powers to establish markets at Millwall and Shoreditch. The Millwall market, which will adjoin the Millwall dock, is intended to be "for the sale of cattle, horses, sheep, pigs, poultry and other live-stock imported from Ireland," whilst the market at Shoreditch is proposed to be confined to "the sale of British, Irish and colonial butchers' meat, fish, poultry, game, eggs, corn and other cereals, hay, straw, fodder, roots, fruit and vegetables, and other produce." The capital which it is estimated will be required to carry out this scheme is £3,000,000, of which £600,000 will be raised by mortgages on the markets.

Auctioneers' Institute.—The third meeting of the session of the above Institute will be held on Tuesday, January 3, 1899, at 7.45 p.m., when a paper will be read by Mr. Walter Simms, F.S.I., F.S.I., on "The River Thames." The chair will be taken by the president, Mr. Edward Dobson.

Kilsyth.—The police commissioners last week considered a report by Mr. Frew, of Messrs. Kyle, Denison & Frew, Glasgow, on a proposal to increase the present water supply by about 200,000 gallons per day by erecting a reservoir at Corrie, on the Campsie Hills. The scheme is to cost between £7,000 and £8,000, and the principle being adopted, it was remitted to a committee to see what compensation rates would require to be given.

# Municipal Work in Progress and Projected.

Hard and steady work seems to be the order of the day with the majority of the provincial authorities, as will be seen from the paragraphs relating to East Sussex, Lancaster, Barry, Chester, Shrewsbury, Southend-on-Sea and other towns. The metropolitan authorities, too, appear to have their hands full.

## METROPOLITAN AUTHORITIES.
### VESTRIES AND DISTRICT BOARDS.

**Bermondsey.**—The Finance Committee recommended the vestry, at their last meeting, to purchase 800 additional dust-pails, as they were greatly needed. The recommendation was adopted.—The Electric Lighting Committee reported the receipt from the Lee Board of Works of a letter stating that it would be convenient for representatives of the local authorities affected by the application of the County of London and Brush Provincial Electric Lighting Company for a provisional order to meet in conference to consider the proposal. The board pointed out that the authorities concerned by the application were those of Bermondsey, Deptford, St. Paul's and St. Nicholas', Deptford, Lambeth and Lewisham, and they suggested that one of the members and the clerk should attend the proposed conference on the 5th proximo. Having, however, already decided to oppose the company's application, the Electric Lighting Committee announced that they had informed the Lee Board of Works that no benefit would accrue by being represented at the conference.—The General Purposes Committee reported the receipt from the London County Council of a letter announcing that the Parker's-row improvement scheme, together with a number of others in various parts of the metropolis, would be taken into consideration by the Improvements Committee in February next.

**Lambeth.**—The Sanitary Committee reported to the vestry, at their last meeting, that they had reconsidered the proposal of the Public Health Committee of the London County Council in regard to the establishment of public abattoirs, and a letter on the subject from the Clerkenwell Vestry. On the recommendation of the committee the vestry resolved to co-operate with the Clerkenwell Vestry in protesting against the proposal of the county council to abolish private slaughter-houses and erect abattoirs at the expense of the ratepayers.—In a report submitted by the Sewers Committee it was stated that Mr. Spicer, the delegate appointed to represent the vestry at the conference of metropolitan local authorities to consider combined drainage, had informed them that the conference had held their final meeting. It had been decided to promote a Bill in the ensuing session of Parliament to amend the law relating to combined drainage, and a draft of the Bill would be sent to the clerk of each vestry and district board.—On the recommendation of the General Purposes Committee it was decided to pave Electric-avenue with wood as soon as possible, at an estimated cost of £1,020.—The Lighting Committee presented a report in reference to a communication received from the Lee Board of Works drawing attention to the proposal of the County of London and Brush Provincial Electric Lighting Company to obtain a provisional order to lay trunk mains through Bermondsey, Rotherhithe, Deptford, Lambeth and Lewisham. The board pointed out that it would be convenient for representatives of the local authorities to meet in order to consider the proposal, and invited the vestry to nominate delegates to attend the conference. It was decided to postpone the consideration of the question, but in the meantime to object to the company's application.—A further report was submitted by the Lighting Committee in regard to the resolution passed at the previous meeting, desiring to know twenty-five are lamps erected in the positions determined some time ago in accordance with an arrangement made with the South London Electric Supply Corporation. With reference to the cost of the standards for the twenty-five lamps, the committee stated that they intended at the proper time to invite tenders, by advertisement, for the supply of the columns.—After a long delay, the vestry considered the question of appointing a committee to inquire into the statements and charges made on the subject of the transfer of the electric lighting provisional order. Mr. Cooper, who intended to propose the members of the committee, stated that as the Progressive party had declined to serve on the committee, he would not proceed with the motion, which was accordingly dropped.—The following tenders were considered for the construction of a thirteen-stall urinal in the Upper Marsh : McDowell, Stevens & Co., 4 Upper Thames-street, E.C., £84; W. McFarlane & Co., Saracen Foundry, Glasgow, £105; and G. Smith & Co., Sun Foundry, Glasgow, £170. The tender of the first-mentioned firm was accepted.

**Paddington.**—In reference to the letter from the Union of Women's Liberal and Radical Associations of the Metropolitan Counties requesting that a free compartment be provided in all public conveniences for women, the Works Committee announced, at the last meeting of the vestry, that they had informed the associations that a free compartment was provided for women in the Walterton-road lavatory, that being the only public lavatory in the parish constructed for the accommodation of both sexes.—It was resolved, on the

recommendation of the Works Committee, that the existing sewer in Elgin-mews should be reconstructed with 9-in. pipes, at a cost not exceeding £375.—On the recommendation of the Electric Lighting Committee it was decided to concur with the views expressed by the Hammersmith Vestry to the effect that, in the event of legislation being brought forward on the lines indicated in the report of the Joint Committee of both Houses of Parliament upon the subject of electrical energy (generating stations and supply), they had decided to take up a strong position in opposition thereto.

**Poplar.**—At a meeting of the board of works, last week, the Works Committee recommended, and it was agreed, "that the plan of the surveyor for a public convenience for women, in Bow-road, at the rear of the Gladstone statue, be approved, and the work of constructing such convenience be carried out by direct labour, at an estimated cost of £650; and that the consent of the Local Government Board be asked to the necessary borrowing."—It was also decided to inform the London County Council, in reply to their inquiry, that the board were willing to contribute £500 towards the cost of the scheme known as Carpenter's-road improvement, under the conditions named by the council.—The Works Committee recommended the board to carry out the construction of the additional bath, &c., accommodation at Bromley depot by direct labour, at an estimated cost of £99 17s. The recommendation was adopted.—The Electric Lighting Committee submitted an important report in reference to the proposed electric supply scheme for the district, but its consideration was adjourned till next meeting, as was also a report of the Works Committee embracing a long list of carriageways and footways which required to be paved or repaired. The total cost of these latter works was estimated at £43,851, while £79,000 was the estimated total cost of the electric supply scheme. Full particulars of this latter scheme will be found in another column.

**Rotherhithe.**—At the last meeting of the vestry consideration was given to a report of the General Purposes and Works Committee on the subject of the abolition of private slaughter-houses, and it was eventually decided to protest against the proposal which is now before the London County Council in connection with the matter.—A resolution of the same committee, suggesting that the vestry's support should be given to the Bill for the amendment of the law relating to workmen's trains, was adopted, it being at the same time resolved to forward copies of the motion to the Government and the Parliamentary representative of the division.—Consent was refused in the case of a proposed application of the City of London Brush Provincial Electric Lighting Company to the Board of Trade for a provisional order to supply electricity in the parish.—The consideration of various matters relating to London local government was adjourned, it being understood that a special committee would be formed shortly after Christmas to deal with them.—Agreement was expressed with the views of the Hammersmith Vestry in regard to the report of the joint committee of both Houses of Parliament upon the subject of electrical energy.—No decision was arrived at in regard to a proposal to construct an underground convenience in the vicinity of Southwark Park-road, but the clerk and surveyor were directed to give the matter their joint attention and report at an early date.—As the vestry had already signified their approval of the proposed establishment of bacteriological laboratories by the county council, no action was taken respecting a letter on the subject from the secretary of the Clinical Research Association, Limited.

**Shoreditch.**—At the last meeting of the vestry it was decided to apply to the Local Government Board for sanction to borrow £2,025 for the construction of the Hoxton-street underground convenience.—The Finance Committee recommended that application should be made to the London County Council to borrow £14,582 for paving and sewering works and for additions to the Flemming-street depot. This was agreed to.—A letter was read from the clerk to the Holborn Board of Works drawing attention to the draft Bill prepared with a view to an amendment of the law relating to combined drainage, and stating that the principle of the Bill was approved by Parliament in the case of the West Ham Corporation Bill passed last year. The Holborn board asked the vestry to support the Bill, and it was decided to do this and to urge upon the local members of Parliament to render assistance, and, if necessary, to bring forward the Bill in question.—After a consideration of the question of abattoirs and of letters received on the subject from the London Chamber of Commerce and the Butchers' Trade Society, the Public Health Committee recommended the vestry to make representations to the London County Council in opposition to the proposed establishment of public slaughter-houses. It was, however, decided to take no action in the matter.—The Lighting Committee reported that they had considered reports from the vestry clerk and the chief electrical engineer on the question of acquiring a site for the erection of a new electricity generating station. As a result the committee submitted the following recommendations : (1) That it is desirable that an additional site should be acquired, of sufficient size, and in such a situation in regard to railway or canal accommodation, as to be suitable for meeting the increasing demands for electric light and power; (2) that the vestry clerk be instructed to approach the Ironmongers' Company with a view to the purchase of their property known as the Ironmongers' Almshouses; and (3) that a specification be prepared by Messrs. Kincaird, Waller & Manville, in conjunction with the chief electrical engineer, with a view to obtaining tenders for two 750 kilowatt sets of engines and dynamos, with necessary boilers and switch gear, &c., in preparation for the new station. These recommendations were discussed by the vestry in committee.—It was decided to pave Mill-road with asphalte and to improve the sewer in that road, at a cost of £1,145.—The tender of the British Insulated Wire Company, of Prescot, was accepted for the supply of electric cables for the Haggerston district.

**St. Mary, Stoke Newington.**—The vestry met on Tuesday of last week, when the General Purposes Committee brought up a recommendation in reference to the Cheap Trains Bill. They suggested that the vestry, while not agreeing with all the provisions of the Bill, should express their agreement with the opinion that further facilities in relation to workmen's trains were urgently required, and this was agreed to.—Sanction was given to a proposal to appoint four delegates to attend a conference of the various boards affected by the decision of the London County Council to apply to Parliament for the transfer to the local authorities of the duty of maintaining main and disturnpiked roads.—Approval was given to a recommendation that in replying to a letter from the county council in reference to the London Overhead Wires Act, 1891, the vestry should state that nothing had as yet been done in this connection, and that they did not at present consider any action necessary.—It was resolved to oppose an application for an electric lighting provisional order which the County of London and Brush Provincial Electric Lighting Company shortly proposed to make.—The county council, it was stated, had declined, on the ground that the improvement did not appear to be of a character to justify their so doing, to contribute to the suggested widening of Wordsworth-road, but it was decided, in view of its importance, to carry out the work at the sole cost of the parish.—The establishment of public abattoirs was, in the opinion of the Sanitary Committee, both unnecessary and inexpedient, and would not meet the end desired. They further considered that an efficient official inspection of meat could be obtained without such provisions. The vestry concurred.—It was decided to receive a circular letter on the subject of district surveyors from the London County Council.

**St. Pancras.**—At the last meeting of the vestry it was announced by the Baths Committee that Mr. A. H. Tiltman, F.R.I.B.A., had placed before them draft instructions and conditions for the guidance of architects competing for the new baths to be built in the Prince of Wales'-road. The committee had carefully gone into the matter and had finally settled the instructions, which, on the recommendation of the committee, the vestry decided to approve.—On the recommendation of the Electricity and Public Lighting Committee it was decided to apply to the London County Council for a loan of £30,000 for the purposes of extensions at the Regent's Park electric light station. The committee reported that they had been in communication with the Board of Trade respecting the supply of electricity to consumers whose premises were situated on the border line of the parishes of St. Pancras and Islington. The board stated that they had no power to authorise the erection of overhead wires, as suggested by the vestry, and that the question was a matter for arrangement between the two local authorities. The Electricity Committee considered that an arrangement for dealing with that and similar cases that would from time to time arise should be made, and at the suggestion of the committee it was decided to ask the Islington Vestry to appoint a small committee to meet the St. Pancras committee with the object of promoting a reciprocal agreement dealing with cases of the kind incidental to the Brecknock and York roads.—It was resolved to co-operate with the Hammersmith Vestry in opposing any legislation proposing to give effect to certain recommendations of the Parliamentary Joint Committee on the Supply of Electrical Energy, especially in regard to the opening of streets for the laying of mains and the granting of provisional orders.—The chairman of the Health Committee consented to withdraw for further consideration a report relating to the acquisition of additional lands in connection with the Brantome-place and Prospect-terrace improvement schemes.—It was decided, on the recommendation of the committee, to affix the seal of the vestry to petitions to the Local Government Board for the holding of a local inquiry for carrying into effect the Chapel-grove and Eastnor-place improvement schemes.—At the suggestion of the Highways Committee the vestry decided to repave with hard wood the carriageway of Goodge-street from Tottenham-court-road to the parish boundary, at an estimated cost of £1,990.—A long discussion took place on the presentation by the Works Committee of a report dealing with the proposal made by Mr. Hillyard that no more broken granite should be ordered until the whole of the setts now lying at the various depots were disposed of. Although the committee were not prepared to entirely agree with the proposition, they recommended that no further granite should be bought until the stock of granite

had been removed from Bangor Wharf alone. In connection with this matter a letter was read from Mr. W. N. Blair, the engineer to the vestry, stating that if the committee's recommendation was adopted it would mean the discharge of more than half of the macadam labourers. The recommendation was, however, adopted.—It was resolved, in the event of the cargoes not arriving in time, to permit Messrs. Palfreeman, Foster & Co. to supply smaller wood blocks, at a reduction in price, for the paving of Guilford-street, on condition that the company would undertake to defray the extra cost of laying the blocks.—The following tenders were received for alterations to the first-class swimming bath at the Whitfield-street establishment: Messrs. H. M. Dove, 131 Euston-road, £38; E. R. Danes, 137 Albany-street, N.W., £40; W. Titmus & Sons, Grafton-street, W.C., £46 15s.; and F. Bedford Pitch, 6 Fitzroy-street, W., £55. The tender of Mr. H. M. Dove was accepted.

**Strand.**—At last week's meeting of this board a letter was read from the Gas Light and Coke Company in regard to the complaints made of the quality of the gas supplied in the Strand district, respecting which a petition was received from tradespeople and ratepayers in the locality calling attention to the indifferent lighting of Charing Cross-road from Cranbourn-street to Cambridge-circus. The gas company contended that as the inspectors of the London County Council were satisfied with the quality and illuminating power of the gas supply in the Strand that should be sufficient. It was decided to forward the letter to the London County Council.

**St. Saviour's, Southwark.**—The district board of works have accepted the tender of Messrs. E. H. Bayley & Co., Newington-causeway, S.E., for the supply of three slop-vans, at a cost of £40 each.

# PROVINCIAL AND GREATER LONDON AUTHORITIES.

## COUNTY COUNCILS.

**East Sussex.**—Last week, at a special meeting of the county council, the vice-chairman submitted the report of a committee on a new asylum. This recommended that the preliminary plans and estimates should be approved as submitted and as provisionally approved by the Local Government Board, and that the necessary steps be taken to give effect to this resolution, and to authorise the architect, Mr. Hine, to proceed with the preparation of detailed plans, &c. The vice-chairman dealt with the question of expense, and said that it had been put down at £300,000. Allowing £90,000 as the sum to be received from Brighton for the Haywards Heath asylum, that would leave £210,000 to be provided. The report was subsequently adopted unanimously, after which it was resolved to adopt a report of the Finance Committee recommending an application to the Local Government Board for permission to borrow the necessary money.

## MUNICIPAL CORPORATIONS.

**Barnsley.**—The council last week adopted recommendations of the Park and Lighting Committees: That, subject to the consent of the Local Government Board to borrow money for electric lighting being obtained, the following tenders be accepted: For plant, boilers, &c.—Messrs. W. Arnold & Co., £3,260; engines, dynamos, plant, &c.—Messrs. Johnson & Phillips, £8,030; storage batteries, &c.—Messrs. Pritchetts & Gold, £1,319, and £70 per annum for maintenance of batteries; electrical mains—The British Insulated Wire Company, £6,322 4s. 2d., and £110 per annum for maintenance. Buildings: Tall chimney—Messrs. Mellor, £930; bricksetters', masons', &c., work—Messrs. J. K. Taylor & Sons, £1,242; carpenters' and joiners' work—Messrs. Robinson & Son, £385; plasterers' and slaters' work—Messrs. Fleming, £57 and £113; plumbers' and glaziers' work—Mr. S. Rushforth, £87; smiths' and founders' work—Messrs. Newton, Chambers & Co., £466 19s. 3d.; painters' work—Mr. Thomas L. Stephenson, £40.

**Bootle.**—The town council have decided to extend the electric supply mains, at an estimated cost of £1,175.

**Cardiff.**—The purchase by the corporation of Cathays Park from the Marquis of Bute has been completed, a cheque for £160,000 having been paid over. The area of the park is about 60 acres.

**Chester.**—Mr. C. A. Sandford Fawcett, A.M.I.C.E., recently held an inquiry, on behalf of the Local Government Board, in reference to an application of the town council for sanction to borrow £20,000 for electric light extensions.

**Chesterfield.**—Negotiations are proceeding in connection with a proposal to purchase a strip of land and half the river course on the west side of the corporation land at the rear of the slaughter-houses, and the Markets and Public Halls Committee have approved of recommendations of the Cattle Markets Committee that the council purchase certain land adjoining the proposed cattle market, and supported the adoption of the recommendation and instruction of the committee.

**Congleton.**—The corporation are about to erect new technical school premises, and have appointed Messrs. Wm. Sugden & Son, F.R.I.B.A., Leek and Hanley, to be their architects.

**Codmanchester.**—A Local Government Board inquiry was held recently in respect to an application of the corporation for sanction to borrow £1,000 for enlarging and repairing the municipal buildings.

**Gravesend.**—The new borough market, which has been entirely rebuilt, was recently opened by the mayor. The walls of the market inclose a space 135 ft. by 48 ft. It has a floor space of 7,000 ft., in addition to 1,600 square feet available for fish sales. Its main roof is formed by sixteen wrought-iron principals resting on thirty-two iron standards, one long skylight forming a ridge of the roof. The cost of the building, including municipal offices at the side, was £3,000. Accommodation is provided for fifty-nine general, nine meat, and sixteen fish stalls.

**Haslingden.**—The mayor has stated that, if the electric lighting scheme proved a success, it was proposed to extend the use of electricity to the running of the trams. Consequent on the proposal of the Accrington Town Council to buy out the company, there has grown among the Haslingden Town Council a feeling that, inasmuch as the several corporations through whose boroughs the company run have certain powers of purchase, the company ought, when the time comes, to be bought out by the corporations jointly.

**Ipswich.**—The corporation have decided to extend and relay the sewers in various outlying parts of the town, in accordance with plans prepared by the borough surveyor, Mr. E. Beckham, at an estimated cost of £3,000, and also to widen Short-lane, St. Helens and St. Clements, at a further cost of £1,445. A scheme for the widening of the narrow portion of the main thoroughfare known as the Butter Market, at an estimated cost of £8,000, has been referred back to the committee.

**Keighley.**—The town council last week decided to invite competitive plans from architects for the new municipal offices which it is proposed to erect at a cost of £5,000.

**Lancaster.**—At the last monthly meeting of the town council it was resolved to make an application to the Local Government Board for sanction to borrow £30,000 for the purchase of the King's Arms Hotel, £3,500 for alterations thereto so as to provide a vegetable market, and for sanction to sell 2,000 square yards of land to the railway company for new station purposes.

**Leeds.**—The purchase by the corporation of the Yorkshire House-to-House Electricity Company's business was completed on the 15th inst. The total amount of money transferred for the undertaking was £222,987.—The Markets Committee of the corporation have instructed Mr. Thomas Hewson, the city engineer, to prepare a ground plan of the new market hall which it is proposed to erect in Vicar-lane, so as to enable them to advertise for competitive designs from architects.

**Liverpool.**—At a recent meeting of the Baths Committee it was reported that during the present year close upon 1,000,000 persons had availed themselves of the privilege of bathing at either the enclosed or the open-air corporation baths. Of this number upwards of 600,000 had paid admission fees, and it is not surprising that, while the expenditure was about the same as last year, the receipts so far show an excess of £200.

**Newport, Isle of Wight.**—Much interest was manifested at Newport, Isle of Wight, on Wednesday of last week, on the occasion of the opening of new waterworks, constructed at a cost of £21,000. The ceremony of turning on the new supply was performed by the mayoress, in the presence of a large assembly. Princess Henry of Battenberg, the governor of the island, was represented by the deputy-governor. The source of supply is on land belonging to Sir Charles Seely, who has afforded the corporation many facilities. Mr. Baldwin Latham, the engineer of the works, stated that the supply was sufficient for several towns the size of Newport, and the absolute purity of the water was attested by the highest analytical authority.

**Norwich.**—The city council have referred to a special committee the consideration of the desirability of erecting a town hall, the guildhall in the market place now in use, and built five centuries ago, being utterly inadequate for municipal purposes.

**Ripon.**—At the last meeting of the city council the mayor submitted for confirmation the minutes of the Gasworks Committee, which recommended that the tender of Messrs. W. & C. Holmes, of Huddersfield, for a new gasholder and brick and puddle tank be accepted at £3,046, but that if, when the excavation is completed, the foundations be found unsuitable for a brick and puddle tank the same firm's tender for holder and steel tank at £3,499 be adopted instead. The recommendation was unanimously adopted.

**Sheffield.**—Profiting by the experience of Bradford, the Sheffield Tramways Committee has been seriously considering the question of brakes, in order to minimise the difficulties of steep gradients and curves occurring on the Walkley electric line. In addition to the ordinary brakes there will be slipper brakes employed, and these are considered sufficient to overcome all difficulties.

**Shrewsbury.**—Local Government Board sanction has been received by the corporation to the borrowing of £30,463 for the purchase of the Shropshire electric light works.

**Southampton.**—One of the inspectors of the Local Government Board recently held an inquiry respecting an application of the corporation for a provisional order under the Public Health Act to borrow additional money for the purposes of their waterworks undertaking. Mr. W. Matthews, waterworks engineer to the corporation, explained that the £124,500 already sanctioned and borrowed was practically exhausted. During the next five years the corporation would require £25,000 for the purpose of executing additional works in order to meet the increasing demands for water for domestic and sanitary purposes, owing to the continued increase and development of the borough.

**Southend.**—A Local Government Board inquiry has been held by Mr. W. O. E. Meade-King concerning the applications of the council to borrow the following sums—viz., £5,500 for cemetery purposes; £8,200 for a stores depot; £3,230 for new underground conveniences; £1,162 for works in connection with the pier, including the new electric cars; £916 for works of sewerage; and £254 for private street improvements to Clifton-drive.

**Southport.**—The Electricity Committee have decided to recommend the town council to apply to the Local Government Board for power to borrow £3,500 for the provision of a condensing reservoir for the electricity.

**Sunderland.**—It was reported, at a recent meeting of the town council, that the Local Government Board had, after some considerable delay, eventually issued an order confirming the Hat Case area improvement scheme, so that now the corporation would be allowed to erect dwellings for 325 instead of 480 persons, as originally proposed, and to demolish the whole of the buildings before any of the new dwellings were erected.

**Walsall.**—Consideration is being given by the council to the following resolution: "That in the opinion of this council it is desirable that, wherever practicable, works of street-making, sewering and other similar works should be carried out by workmen in the direct employ of the corporation, under the supervision and direction of the staff in the borough surveyor's department; and that the Streets Committee be requested to take the matter into their consideration, and, if practicable, carry out as an experiment a portion of the works in connection with the proposed surface-water drainage scheme."—The tender of Mr. James Atkins, Ryecroft, Walsall, has been accepted by the town council for the construction of surface-water sewers in Field-street and Sandwell-street, at a cost of £99 12s. and £50 10s. 6d. respectively.

**Welshpool.**—The council have decided to proceed with the construction of new filter-beds and other works. They have also instructed Messrs. Beloe & Priest, of Liverpool, to prepare specifications and have further decided to make an application to the Local Government Board for sanction to borrow the necessary money—£2,000.

**Yarmouth.**—The Yarmouth and Gorleston Tramway Company recently wrote asking the corporation to supply current for traction purposes, on the basis of 2d. per unit up to 150,000 units, at 1¼d. between that limit and 200,000 units, and exceeding 200,000 units at 1½d. per unit; and also asking that the time within which the tramways became purchaseable should be extended to twenty-one years, making twenty-seven years from the present time. The Lands Committee recommended the council not to entertain the application. When the matter came before the council, last week, an amendment referring it back to the committee was negatived.

## URBAN DISTRICT COUNCILS.

**Barry.**—The Public Works Committee of the council have decided to borrow £13,000 for new street and other works.—The following new loans have been sanctioned by the Local Government Board: £2,936 for widening Cardiff-road, £541 for Palmerstown-road, £489 for St. Nicholas-road, and £3,298 for roads around Cadoxton Common; but it was decided to defer these works for the present, notwithstanding a protest that the roads were in a disgraceful condition.

**Carshalton.**—The two following tenders were received by the district council for the making-up of Denmark-road in accordance with plans and specifications prepared by Mr. W. Willis Gale, surveyor to the council: Mr. A. Jenner, Sutton, £1,417, and Messrs. Free & Son, Maidenhead, £2,200. The first-named tender has been accepted. The surveyor's estimate for the work was, we may mention, £1,452.

**Epsom.**—A contemporary states that the Lighting Committee of the district council recently visited Harrow for the purpose of obtaining reliable information in regard to electric lighting, as the population of that town is nearly the same as at Epsom, and came to the conclusion that electric lighting was desirable for Epsom. Mr. Hawtayne's 1896 report to the council was looked up. In that report the estimated cost of the undertaking was given as £14,980, and the estimate of the probable receipts £2,178. The plant as arranged would be of ample size to deal with the whole of the public lighting in addition to providing 5,000 private lamps, and room would be left for putting in an additional plant when required. The committee recommended that Mr. Hawtayne be instructed to prepare specifications of the necessary works to be carried out in all the streets mentioned in the compulsory area, and the whole of the district as at present lighted by public lamps that tenders be advertised for. In view of the importance of the matter, a special council meeting was to be held yesterday to consider it.

**Hornsey.**—On the 19th inst. the Works Committee reported that at the last meeting of the committee the tender of Mr. J. A. Dunmore for the construction of a proposed new road through Queen's Wood, for £3,278, had been accepted, subject to approval of sureties and to the execution of the usual contract and bond. The surveyor submitted plans and an estimate, which were approved and passed, for the making-up of Prince's-avenue, Muswell Hill.

**Idle.**—The district council have decided to purchase a plot of land for £2,300 as a site for the proposed Thackley sewage works.

**Kingswood.**—On Thursday last Mr. H. Percy Boulnois held an inquiry, on behalf of the Local Government Board, in reference to an application by the Kingswood Urban District Council for sanction to borrow £2,700 for work of private street improvement and £320 for the purchase of certain sanitary appliances. No objection was raised to the proposed loans.

**Llandudno.**—Upon the recommendation of the Finance Committee it has been decided to apply to the Local Government Board for sanction to borrow a sum of £1,170 for hospital extension purposes.—A long statement was made at the last monthly meeting by Mr. W. Williams, chairman of the Sanitary Committee, as to the sanitary condition of the town. This, he said, was excellent, there being not a single house unfit for human habitation.

**Padiham.**—The contract for the supply and delivery of 530 yards of unclimbable iron hurdle fencing and 760 yards of wire fencing, for the district council, has been let to Mr. James Starkie, of Preston.

**Portishead.**—The contract for the construction of main drains throughout Portishead has just been completed for the district council. Mr. Moss Flower, C.E., late surveyor to the council, designed and superintended the execution of the works, and Messrs. J. & T. Binns were the contractors.

**St. Anne's.**—The Local Government Board have sanctioned the borrowing by the district council of £7,340 for sewerage works in the north-western portion of the district.

**Waterloo.**—At their last meeting the district council resolved to apply to the Local Government Board for sanction to a loan of £550 for electric lighting purposes.

## RURAL DISTRICT COUNCILS.

**Aberystwyth.**—The council have resolved to apply to the Local Government Board for sanction to borrow £692 for the supply of water to the village of Llanbadan, which lies outside the town of Aberystwyth.

**Betts-y-Coed.**—An inspector of the Local Government Board recently conducted an inquiry in reference to the application of the district council for permission to borrow £205 for sewerage works and £91 for water supply works in the parish of Trefriw.

**Bury.**—On the 21st inst., at a meeting of this authority, the clerk drew attention to the two Water Bills which were proposed to be promoted in the next session of Parliament by the Bury and Rawtenstall Corporations respectively. The proposed Rawtenstall waterworks would be partly in the Bury rural district and partly in the Ramsbottom rural district, and Rawtenstall proposed to separate themselves entirely from Bury. The loss of the revenue now derived from Rawtenstall would be a serious loss to Bury, and it was proposed that the Bury Rural District Council should appoint two representatives to a standing committee, consisting of representatives from Radcliffe, Ramsbottom and Whitefield Urban District Councils and the Bury Rural District Council, to watch the progress of both the Bury and Rawtenstall Bills.

**Grimsby.**—The Louth Rural District Council have written to the effect that they agreed to the proposals of the council with regard to certain temporary repairs to the Humberstone and Tetney bridge, and were prepared to pay half the cost. They thought it best to postpone the work of building a new bridge until spring.

**Llandaff.**—The excavations made by the council at Maindy in connection with certain sewerage works have resulted in the unexpected discovery of springs which yield a copious supply of water. The original intention of the council was to make a large cesspit, 40 ft. by 20 ft., to receive the drainage from Pontcanna and to pump from thence to a higher level. The depth of the pit was to be 47 ft. The subsoil was soon cleared out and solid rock reached. When a depth of some 30 ft. had been attained water began to ooze up at one corner of the pit. As the work went on the water accumulated quickly, and by the time the pit had been deepened to 40 ft. three other springs were tapped, and the water flowed in so abundantly that operations had to cease. Since then a powerful pumping engine has been at work almost continuously, but the pit still has nearly 30 ft. of water in it. The water has also flooded the heading along which the Pontcanna sewage was to have been conveyed into the cesspit. The water is beautifully fresh and pure when

the river is low, but after rain it becomes discoloured, the result doubtless of a certain backflow into it from the Taff. The mouth of the largest spring is nearly 2 ft. in diameter, and is at the northern end of the pool.

**Newton.**—At last week's meeting of the council Messrs. C. Isler & Co. reported that in boring for water they had reached limestone, which extended to a considerable depth. They had bored 22 ft., and might have to go to a tremendous depth. The matter was referred to committee.

**Northwich.**—At a meeting of the council on Friday the representatives of the Marston and Wincham district, where the greatest of the Cheshire salt subsidences have occurred, reported that Wincham-lane, which forms part of the main road between Northwich and Warrington, has sunk no less than 2 ft. within the month. So continuous has been the subsidence in this locality that it is feared that it may at any time become imperative to open a new road. Orders were given for the repair of Forge-lane, to serve as an alternative route, and other measures of a protective character are to be taken.

## SCOTLAND AND IRELAND.

**Arbroath.**—At a recent meeting of the Committee of Management of the Gas Corporation a draft of a proposed electric lighting provisional order was submitted. The various schedules were read, and from these it appeared that powers were sought to expend a sum of £9,950 on the works, made up as follows: Buildings and appliances, £1,000; generating plant, £2,900; private lighting, mains, feeders, &c., £4,450; public lighting and mains, £650; legal and expert services and contingencies, £750. The draft order was approved of, and the treasurer was authorised to deposit the requisite sum of £50 with the Board of Trade.

**Limerick.**—For years back the condition of the Irish town and English town has been one of ruin and decay, houses that were once the residences of the nobility and gentry being but in too many instances masses of tottering masonry dangerous to pedestrians. The corporation recently gave the matter their careful consideration, and decided upon an important step. They resolved to clear the sites, and the Local Government Board, approving the scheme submitted, held an inquiry and advanced a loan of £5,000 towards the project, refusing, however, to advance any more until the finances of the corporation were improved. Several of the leading merchants in the city have, however, promised to contribute towards the scheme, which is to include the erection of houses for the working classes.

---

# Some Recent Publications.

AN INQUIRY INTO THE RELATIVE EFFICIENCY OF WATER FILTERS IN THE PREVENTION OF INFECTIOUS DISEASE is a reprint of a special report to *The British Medical Journal* by Dr. G. Sims Woodhead and Dr. C. E. Cartwright Wood, and is issued, at the price of 2s. 6d., from the offices of the British Medical Association. "The investigation," as stated by the authors in their preface, "was undertaken at the desire of the late Mr. Ernest Hart, editor of *The British Medical Journal*;" and they further note that "as in the case of so many other questions affecting the public health, Mr. Hart recognised the danger to which the public were exposed through the use of inefficient filters and knowing that so much attention had not been directed to the question in this country as in France and Germany, he suggested that they should examine and report upon the efficiency of a number of filters in general use in this country and abroad in preventing the spread of water-borne disease." Drs. Woodhead and Wood may be congratulated upon the eminently satisfactory results attending their united inquiries and experiments. These are best summarised in their own words: "As the outcome of this investigation we believe that we are warranted in concluding that we have been able to settle the principle on which must be based the method of testing the efficiency of filters in preventing the transmission of water-borne infective disease. The method had already been suggested by Gruber and his pupils, but we have been able to carry out experiments on so many types of filters, and over such prolonged periods, that we may now hope that this vexed question has been finally set at rest." Want of space precludes us from entering into a detailed review of many important matters treated with skill and judgment in the volume under consideration, but we have no hesitation in recommending it to our numerous readers who are privately or professionally interested in the subject of water purification.

## WATER SUPPLY.

NOTES ON WATER SUPPLY, by J. T. Rodda, A.M.I.C.E. (King, Sell & Railton. Price 5s.), contains references, tables, useful memoranda and detailed advertisements relating to waterworks engineering, and also an illustrated description and prices of apparatus, appliances, tools and materials usually required. These notes and references, originally written for *The Journal of Water Supply*, gave rise to useful discussion at the time of their first appearance, and the author, in now issuing them, with additions, in book form, hopes that they may prove of some benefit to a wider circle of readers. Although Mr. Rodda does not advance any pretensions to having compiled a treatise on the subject, the book is no doubt well adapted to fulfil the design he had in view—viz., "to point out the specialists from whom valuable information may be obtained, and to indicate the best waterworks appliances now in the market, with notes on the same and their usefulness in modern distribution of water supply."

## SOME SHORT NOTICES.

The opening chapter of THE NEW GUIDE TO BRISTOL AND CLIFTON AND THE BRISTOL CHANNEL CIRCUIT, by James Baker, F.R.H.S., F.R.G.S. (J. Baker & Son. Price 2s. 6d.), gives an historical and a descriptive sketch of Bristol and Clifton, and appears to be an expanded reprint of an article contributed to a publication of more general character than the present. In the second chapter Prof. Lloyd Morgan treats of the physical features and local geology in an interesting manner. In the following chapter Mr. J. W. White, F.L.S., deals with the botany of the British district. The remainder of the volume is devoted to topographical descriptions, first of Bristol and Clifton, and afterwards of various places bordering on the Bristol Channel that afford attractions for visitors and tourists. Probably the most unsatisfactory feature of this hand-book is the method of illustration adopted. Many of the views are very indistinct renderings of places referred to in the text, and in several instances their size do not harmonise with the limits of the page. As Mr. Baker claims to have adhered to Baedeker's plan in the arrangement of preliminary matter, we would suggest an improvement also on the lines of Baedeker—namely, the omission of interleaved advertisements in future issues of the book.

A comprehensive and useful manual for all who require a practical knowledge of ornamental lettering is ALPHABETS, OLD AND NEW, by Lewis F. Day (B. T. Batsford. Price 3s. 6d.). The work furnishes a complete series of 120 different examples of alphabetical letters, thirty of numerals, and numerous facsimiles of ancient dates, &c., carefully selected and arranged, with a short preliminary account of alphabets. It thus appeals to a wide circle, among whom we may include architects, designers, sculptors, masons, sign writers, brass and seal engravers, heraldic stationers, draughtsmen, bookbinders, and many others. In the varied succession of alphabets displayed here we find about 100 ancient examples reproduced with such care as to faithfully preserve the spirit of the originals. This selection ranges from the earliest historical period to the eighteenth century, and is arranged in chronological order. The section devoted to the illustration of modern work embraces selections from the highly-artistic productions of Walter Crane, Patten Wilson, the author, and

others, whilst the architectural branch represents designs of lettering by A. Beresford Pitt, J. Cromer Watt and Roland W. Paul.

BLACK'S GUIDE TO CANTERBURY AND THE WATERING PLACES OF EAST KENT (price 1s.) appears in a remodelled and improved form under the editorship of Mr. E. D. Jordan, B.A. Those who indulge in home or foreign travelling, even to a limited degree, are so well acquainted with many of the admirably compiled and eminently practical series of portable hand-books bearing the imprint of Messrs. Black that words of commendation with respect to them appear almost superfluous at this time of day. The volume now before us is entirely new, both as regards text and maps. The latter are well engraved in a clear and intelligible manner, and a special feature of all the section maps, which considerably enhances their utility, is that they are printed in coloured contours, to show the elevations of the different localities above the sea level. The book should be useful to those who have occasion to visit a district not without historical associations or attractive scenery.

THE "COMPLEAT" AND UNIVERSAL GUIDE TO HOTELS, APARTMENTS, BOARDING-HOUSES, &c., 1898 (Simpkin, Marshall & Co. Price 1s.), constitutes one of that extensive series of publications, portable and otherwise, issued at recurring periods with a view of affording all desirable information relative to "the general accommodation which is daily required by travellers, tourists, sportsmen and many others." We must leave our readers to form their own private opinion as to whether a new compilation at present required for this purpose, and will merely add that the editors in a prefatory note state that they "seek to gratify a long-felt want by placing in a complete and accessible form full information where it is known that accommodation at hotel, boarding-house, apartments, school, &c., can be obtained either in town, the seaside, the provinces or abroad."

As may be anticipated from previous editions, the 1899 issue of "THE LIVE STOCK JOURNAL" ALMANAC (Vinton & Co. Price 1s.) is replete with interesting matter for all who are attached to a country life and are fond of rural pursuits. In the abundantly-illustrated annual now lying before us we remark the usual breeders' tables, lists of societies, fairs, statistics, and other particulars of importance in connection with the farm and the country house; and these are followed by forty-eight special articles relating to nearly every variety of British live stock. A prominent feature always appreciated is the annual breed histories, which are invariably contributed by gentlemen well qualified to furnish reliable information.

THE "GLOUCESTER" DIARY AND DIRECTORS' CALENDAR FOR 1899 is published at the instance of the Gloucester Railway Carriage and Waggon Company, Limited, by F. J. Brooke, of that city. In addition to a conveniently-arranged diary, interspersed with well-executed illustrations of the different types of vehicles and miscellaneous articles produced by the company mentioned, it includes brief notes descriptive of such local features as are calculated to interest visitors. A list of mayors and a general calendar are here introduced into the present issue.

TRIGONOMETRY AT A GLANCE, by G. W. Usill, A.M.I.C.E., and F. J. Browne, C.E. (G. Philip & Son. Price 2s.), affords, by means of novel and somewhat ingenious contrivances and simple arrangements, a graphic demonstration of the various functions of an angle and its complement. Precise directions as to the proper use of the diagrams and attached appliances are duly specified, and for purposes of class instruction, as well as of private study, the methods adopted may prove of considerable value in facilitating the solution of numerous complicated calculations.

*Any of the Books noted below will be sent post free if the published price be forwarded to the offices of* THE SURVEYOR.

THE EVOLUTION OF THE ENGLISH HOUSE, by Sydney Oldall Addy, M.A.; 224 pp., 7½ in. by 5 in. Swan, Sonnenschein & Co., Limited. Price 4s. 6d.

CARPENTRY AND JOINERY, by Frederick C. Webber, 320 pp., 7½ in. by 5 in. Methuen & Co. Price 3s. 6d.

PITMAN'S POPULAR GUIDE TO JOURNALISM, by Alfred Kingston, F.R.HIST.S.; 112 pp., 7½ in. by 5 in. Sir I. Pitman & Sons, Limited. Price 1s. 6d.

VINTON'S AGRICULTURAL ALMANAC, 1899; 108 pp., 9½ in. by 7½ in. Price 6d. Vinton & Co.

PRACTICAL MASONRY, by Wm. R. Purchase; 142 pp., 9½ in. by 6½ in. Crosby Lockwood & Son. Price 7s. 6d.

**Watford.**—Local Government Board sanction has been received by the district council to the borrowing of £1,220 for street improvement works.

**The Sanitary Inspectors' Association.**—A general meeting of the above association will be held at Carpenters' Hall, London-wall, E.C., on Saturday, January 7, 1899, at 6 p.m., when the president, Sir John Hutton, L.C.C., J.P., will deliver a "New Year's" address. An election of members and associates will also take place.

# Personal.

Glamorgan County Council have appointed a bacteriologist, at a salary of £250 a year.

Mr. Wm. Beavan, surveyor to the Gelligaer Rural District Council, has been granted an increase of salary.

The appointment is reported, as assistant to the burgh surveyor of Stirling, of Mr. William J. Crawford.

Mr. J. E. Cooke, of the city engineer's department, Coventry, has received an increase of salary and also a bonus.

Mr. H. W. Bowen, surveyor to the Wigmore Rural District Council, has had his salary increased from £120 to £150 per annum.

The salary of Mr. J. T. Robinson, surveyor to the Chesterfield Rural District Council, has been increased by £25 per annum.

Ashton Town Council have adopted a resolution proposing the appointment of an assistant electrical engineer, at a salary of £130.

Mr. C. C. Fowler, superintendent of the electricity mains of the Brighton Corporation, has had his salary increased to £225 per annum.

Mr. G. Balfour recently read a paper before the Edinburgh Architectural Society on electric lighting. Mr. A. R. Scott occupied the chair.

Mr. Wm. Richard Dewey, of Redhill, Surrey, has been appointed gas manager to the Corporation of Newbury, at a salary of £200 per annum.

Wenlock Corporation have appointed Mr. W. E. Woolam, of Whitchurch, as assistant borough surveyor and inspector of nuisances, at a commencing salary of £80 per annum.

Mr. Cecil S. Hodges, of the county surveyor's office, Nottingham, has been appointed main road inspector under the Bedfordshire County Council, at a salary of £100 per annum.

Mr. Andrew Paterson, district surveyor of Acle District Board on the Norfolk County Council, has accepted an appointment as surveyor under the Staffordshire County Council.

Mr. Thomas Nuttall, of Bury, has resigned the surveyorship of the Prestwich Urban District Council, and his son, Mr. William Nuttall, of 20 Market-street, Bury, has been appointed resident surveyor.

The death is announced of Mr. John Paterson, who for many years held the appointment of inspector of lighting and cleansing in Edinburgh. The deceased, who retired some time ago, was in his eightieth year.

Mr. John Rutherford Blackie, of 11 Melville-road, Redlands, Bristol, has been appointed resident engineer at the electricity supply station of the Newington Vestry. There were seventy-seven applications for the post.

Mr. J. Hewett, of the firm of Messrs. Hewett & Duffield, has been appointed consulting engineer to the Chatham Town Council for the electric lighting of the new town hall, now in course of erection on the Military-road.

A memorial tablet to the late Sir Joseph W. Bazalgette is about to be erected by a committee of eminent engineers and Lady Bazalgette. The tablet will be attached to the wall of the Victoria-embankment, at a point facing the end of Northumberland-avenue and near the Charing-cross pier.

The Liverpool Corporation have appointed Mr. Jonathan Roberts Davidson as assistant engineer, in place of the late Mr. R. T. Martin, late superintendent of the Rivington water-works, at a salary of £208 a year, with the use of the corporation's house at Horwich and coal and light free.

Mr. J. C. Melliss, M.I.C.E., has been appointed consulting engineer to the Goole Urban District Council in reference to the carrying out of new waterworks from the designs of Mr. Matt. Dunn, the gas and water engineer to the council, for which Parliamentary powers have been applied for.

At the last meeting of the Middlesex County Council the Highways Committee were authorised to advertise for two assistant surveyors, at a salary of £250 a year each; an assistant surveyor, to take charge under the county surveyor of the duties as to rivers, at £250 per annum; and a draughtsman, at £175 a year.

At the last monthly meeting of the Urmston Urban District Council a letter was read from Mr. C. C. Hooley, resigning his position as surveyor to the council. He thanked them for the courtesy which he had received at their hands. No reason was given for the resignation. The letter was referred to the General Purposes Committee.

Mr. Thomas Blashill, F.R.I.B.A., gave a dinner at the Café Monico, Regent-street, W., last week, to the members of the architectural staff of the London County Council and a few friends. General satisfaction was expressed by those present that Mr. Blashill had acceded to the request of the county council and had postponed his retirement until the 31st March.

Mr. George Stevens, surveyor to the Abercarn Urban District Council, has been commissioned to supervise the carrying out of a new water scheme and cemetery, and to act in the capacity of engineer to the council, at a salary of £300 per annum, for three years, the stipulation being that at the completion of the work his salary will again be considered.

At the last monthly meeting of the Abergele and Pensarn Urban District Council it was mentioned that since the previous meeting, when it was decided to appoint a person to fill the combined offices of surveyor and inspector of nuisances, a large number of ratepayers had expressed their disapproval of the action of the council in the matter. Some two-thirds of the ratepayers were understood to be opposed to the appointment, and the recision of the minutes was therefore proposed. A discussion ensued, but the minutes were eventually confirmed by a large majority.

At a recent meeting of the Sunderland Town Council it was decided to adopt a report of the Tramways Committee recommending the payment of 100 guineas to Mr. Snell for services rendered and to be rendered until the decision of Parliament on the Tramways Bill. Upon the passing of the measure Mr. Snell's present engagement will be terminated, and he will be re-elected borough electrical engineer upon the following terms: First year, £600; second year, £700; third year, £750; fourth year, £800; fifth and last year, £800. The report of the committee included a proposal to also grant the sum of 100 guineas to the borough surveyor for extra services rendered.

We very much regret to record the death of Mrs. John Eldford, wife of the borough surveyor of Poole, which occurred under distressing circumstances on Thursday evening last. Deceased was returning from a visit to some relatives when, while crossing the level foot-crossing on the railway near Poole station, she was knocked down by the Weymouth and London express and killed. At the coroner's inquest, which was held on the following evening, it transpired that while crossing the railway her foot caught between the rails and the wooden platform by the side, and before she could release herself the train cut her down. A verdict of "accidental death" was returned.

The Shrewsbury Corporation received at their last meeting a report from a committee stating that in response to an advertisement for plans for a science and art school, to be erected, at a cost of £3,500, on a site in St. Julian's Friars, given by the Horticultural Society, five sets of plans were sent in, and the committee had selected two. The plan placed first was signed "Daylight," and that placed second "Sphinx." The report was adopted after a discussion consequent on a proposal, which was defeated, to select another site for the school, but the names of the competitors were not stated. The premiums offered were £20 and £10, and the competition was limited to architects practising in Salop.

The special committee of the Manchester Corporation appointed to arrange for the erection of the four fountains presented to the city by the late Alderman Clay have adjudicated upon the designs which have been sent in at the invitation of the committee. There were twenty-four competing architects and sculptors, and the committee selected the two designs submitted by Mr. J. W. Beaumont, architect, of St. James's-place, Manchester, and two fountains of each design will be erected. Each design consists of a canopy covering a basin of water, from the centre of which will spring a jet or jets of water, the basins for drinking purposes being placed on the outside of the base of the canopy. Small drinking troughs for dogs are also provided. The fountains will stand on three steps, and the ground round them is to be laid out for grass and flowers. In both designs the base will be of granite, in one case grey and in the other red, and the superstructure will be of red sandstone from the Corsehill quarries. The fountains are to be erected at a cost of £700 each.

At a recent meeting of the Institution of Junior Engineers, Mr. E. A. Heath read a paper on "British Cable Tramways and their Construction." For towns in hilly districts requiring tramway communication the author claimed that cable haulage had no rival. Being independent of rail adhesion, the steepest gradient could be ascended or descended with absolute safety, provided that for descending an emergency brake was employed which would grip the slot rails. A brake of this description was fitted to the cars on the Douglas tramway, of a gradient of 1 in 10, and on those of the Matlock line, with a gradient of 1 in 4. The system of constructing the track and cable tube was described in detail. A very good lish-joint for track rails was shown, which formed practically a continuous running surface for the car wheels. Approximate figures were given for calculating the horsepower required to haul the cable; to arrive at anything approaching the actual figure mature experience had to be applied of the various conditions under which the tramway was to be operated. The special features in the construction of Highgate tramway, Streatham, Douglas, Matlock and others, were reviewed, particulars being furnished. A discussion followed the reading of the paper.

## VESTRY AND WATER COMPANY.

Last week, at the Lambeth Vestry Hall, Mr. A. A. Hopkins, the magistrate for Lambeth, renewed the hearing of the summons issued by the Lambeth Vestry against the South-wark and Vauxhall Water Company, to revise the price to be paid by the vestry for water supplied by the company for the purpose of watering streets. Mr. Bodkin and Mr. Lindsey Smith appeared for the vestry, and Mr. Claude Baggallay, Q.C., and Mr. Gore Browne for the company. It appeared that in 1883 the price for water supplied was fixed by Mr. Chance, the then magistrate, at 8½d. per 1,000 gallons, the price to continue for five years. The vestry had continued to pay that sum; but, in view of the improved position of the company and the fact that the water was supplied to the public baths of the vestry at 6d. per 1,000 gallons, the vestry now asked that the price should be revised. The magistrate said he would give his decision some day next month.

## INSTITUTION OF CIVIL ENGINEERS.

### ORDINARY MEETING.

An ordinary meeting of the members of the above Institution will be held on Tuesday, the 10th January, 1899, at 8 p.m., when Mr. John Handsley Dales, A.M.I.C.E., will read a paper on "High-speed Engines." At this meeting a ballot for members will be taken.

### STUDENTS' MEETING.

At a meeting for the students of the Institution, on the 13th January, 1899, Dr. Archibald Barr, M.I.C.E. (Professor of Civil Engineering and Mechanics in the University of Glasgow), will deliver an address on "The Application of the Science of Mechanics to Engineering Practice." Dr. Alex. B. W. Kennedy, F.R.S. (member of council), will take the chair at 8 p.m.

## THE SURVEYORS' INSTITUTION.

### ORDINARY GENERAL MEETING.

The next ordinary general meeting of the above Institution will be held on Monday, January 9, 1899, when the adjourned discussion on the paper read by Mr. Wm. Weaver at the last meeting, entitled "The London Building Act and the Official Supervision of Buildings," will be resumed. The chair will be taken at 8 o'clock.

Radcliffe.—The council have adopted a resolution recommending that an application should be made to the Local Government Board for sanction to borrow a sum of £16,000 for the electric lighting of the district.

## DOVER ADMIRALTY HARBOUR.

The first pile of the Admiralty pier extension, forming the western arm of the new national harbour at Dover, was driven on Wednesday of last week. The piles that are being used are the largest employed in any marine work in the kingdom, being 105 ft. long and 20 in. square. All the requisite machinery is in position. On the top of the turret which contains the 80-ton guns a powerful crane, specially constructed for the purpose, is being used in connection with the pile-driving. The works at East Cliff, where the marine railway and reclamation wall are being constructed, are proceeding rapidly, and at the works on the shore near Shakespeare's Cliff good progress is observed. The contractors' new cliff railway from Martin Mill to Dover is also being rapidly constructed.

## NEW PUBLIC PARK FOR EALING.

A special meeting of the Ealing District Council was held on Saturday morning, under the presidency of Sir Montagu Nelson, to consider the advisability of accepting the offer of Sir Spencer Walpole to sell to the council, for the purposes of a public park, the Walpole property, including a mansion, grounds and park, covering in all about 31 acres, for the sum of £40,000. The mansion was for many years the residence of the late Right Hon. S. H. Walpole, who died there a few months ago. Some slight opposition was offered to the purchase, on the ground that Ealing at the present juncture would not be justified in incurring the expenditure; but on a vote being taken a motion in favour of the purchase was carried nem. con., fourteen out of sixteen members being present.

## QUERIES AND REPLIES.

*We cannot undertake to reply to any queries which are not accompanied by the writer's name and address. These are required as a guarantee of good faith and not for publication. Sketches accompanying queries should be made separate on white paper, in plain black ink lines. Lettering or figures should be bold and plain.*

**230. Sewage Farms in the United Kingdom : Particulars Required.**—In this query, which appeared in our last issue (page 806), for the word "soluble" (seventh line down) read "saleable."

**Cwyrfai.**—The district council, at their last meeting, received a letter from the Local Government Board empowering them to borrow £2,000 for the purpose of supplying Portdinorwic with water. Before deciding to advertise for contracts, however, the council decided to consider plans of proposed waterworks for the supply of Saron Bethel, Capel Seion and Portdinorwic, the total cost of which was estimated at £6,600.

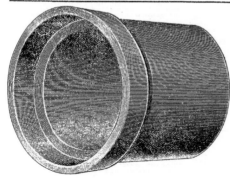

## APPOINTMENTS VACANT.

*Official and all similar advertisements received later than Wednesday evening are too late for classification and cannot therefore be included in these summaries until the following week. No advertisements received after 3 p.m. on Thursday can be inserted until the following week.*

ASSISTANT ENGINEER.—December 31st.—Carlisle Corporation. £130.—Mr. C. D. Burnet, city electrical engineer.

ASSISTANT ENGINEER FOR TRAMWAYS DEPARTMENT.—December 31st.—Manchester Corporation. £200.—Mr. Wm. Henry Talbot, town clerk.

TEMPORARY ENGINEERING ASSISTANT FOR TRAMWAYS DEPARTMENT. — December 31st. — Manchester Corporation. £2 10s.—Mr. Wm. Henry Talbot, town clerk.

TEMPORARY ASSISTANT.—January 2nd.—Morley Corporation. £2 2s.—Mr. W. E. Putman, A.M.I.C.E., borough engineer and surveyor.

SUB-INSPECTORS OF NUISANCES (Two).—January 2nd.—Bradford Corporation. £80.—The Town Clerk.

INSPECTOR OF ROADS.—January 2nd.—Vestry of St. Mary, Islington. £2 10s.—Mr. J. Patten Barber, chief surveyor to the vestry.

SURVEYOR, INSPECTOR OF NUISANCES, &c.—January 4th.—Tarporley (Cheshire) Urban District Council.—Mr. Thomas Cawley, clerk to the council.

BOROUGH SURVEYOR.—January 4th.—Corporation of Penzance. £200.—Mr. T. H. Cornish, town clerk.

DISTRICT ROAD SURVEYOR.—January 5th.—Norfolk County Council. £2.—Mr. T. H. B. Heslop, county surveyor, Norwich.

ASSISTANT COUNTY ROAD SURVEYOR'S CLERK.—January 5th.—Worcestershire County Council. £52.—Mr. S. Thornely, county clerk, Shire Hall, Worcester.

CLERK OF WORKS.—January 5th.—Islington Vestry.—Mr. Wm. F. Dewey, clerk to the vestry.

ROAD FOREMAN.—January 6th.—Axbridge Rural District Council.—Mr. George Cook, district surveyor.

SURVEYOR AND INSPECTOR OF NUISANCES.—January 7th.—Whitworth Urban District Council.—Mr. Owen March, clerk to the council.

WORKING FOREMAN.—January 7th.—Wath-upon-Dearne (Yorks.) Urban District Council. 27s.—Messrs. Saunders & Nicholson, clerks to the council.

ASSISTANT SANITARY INSPECTOR.—January 7th.—Paddington Vestry. £100.—Mr. Frank Dethridge, vestry clerk.

SANITARY INSPECTOR.—January 9th.—Islington Vestry. £150.—Mr. Wm. F. Dewey, clerk to the vestry.

ASSISTANT SANITARY INSPECTOR. — January 9th. — West Bromwich Corporation.—Mr. Alfred Caddick, town clerk.

INSPECTOR OF NUISANCES.—January 9th.—West Bromwich Corporation. £150.—Mr. Alfred Caddick, town clerk.

ROAD INSPECTOR.—January 10th.—Sale Urban District Council.—Mr. D. Hallewell, clerk to the council.

ASSISTANT MARSH BAILIFF.—January 10th.—West Ham Corporation.—Mr. Fred. E. Hilleary, town clerk.

ASSISTANT FIRE BRIGADE OFFICER.—January 11th. London County Council. £300.—Mr. C. J. Stewart, clerk to the council, County Hall, Spring gardens, S.W.

TEMPORARY CLERK OF WORKS.—£3 3s.—Box 95, office of THE SURVEYOR, 24 Bride-lane, Fleet-street, London, E.C.

TEMPORARY ASSISTANT. — Southend-on-Sea Corporation. £3 3s.—Mr. Alfred Fidler, A.M.I.C.E., borough engineer and surveyor.

PUPIL.—Mr. Alfred Fidler, A.M.I.C.E., borough engineer and surveyor, Southend-on-Sea.

RESIDENT ENGINEER.—Mansfield Corporation. £4.—Mr. R. Frank Vallance, borough surveyor.

## MUNICIPAL COMPETITIONS OPEN.

*Official and all similar advertisements received later than Wednesday evening are too late for classification and cannot therefore be included in these summaries until the following week. No advertisements received after 3 p.m. on Thursday can be inserted until the following week.*

HARROGATE.—January 2nd.—Erection of a pump-room, &c., at a cost not exceeding £8,000. £50, £30 and £20.—Mr. Samuel Stead, borough surveyor.

BRADFORD. — February 1st. — Erection of a central fire brigade station. £100, £50 and £30.—Mr. George McGuire, town clerk.

KNUTSFORD.—February 28th.—Laying out of a plot of land at Tabley Hill for a cemetery, and also the erection of a chapel and caretaker's lodge for same, for the urban district council.—Mr. W. J. Downes, surveyor to the council.

LONDON.—February 28th.—Design for a dust-cart and cover for use in connection with the collection and disposal of house refuse. £25.—Mr. C. J. Stewart, clerk to the council, County Hall, Spring-gardens, S.W.

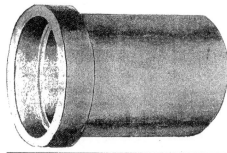

BRADFORD.—April 14th.—Erection of a building for the Cartwright memorial hall and art gallery. £150, £100 and £50.—Mr. George McGuire, town clerk.

## MUNICIPAL CONTRACTS OPEN.

*Official and all similar advertisements received later than Wednesday evening are too late for classification and cannot therefore be included in these summaries until the following week. No advertisements received after 3 p.m. on Thursday can be inserted until the following week.*

HULL.—December 30th.—Supply of steel roof trusses, steel columns, &c., in connection with the erection of car sheds for the electric tramways.—Mr. A. E. White, city engineer.

HULL.—December 30th.—Erection of two car sheds and other buildings (area about 4,000 square yards) in connection with the electric tramways.—Mr. A. E. White, city engineer.

HULL.—December 30th.—Supply of pipes, fittings, &c., for the power station in connection with the electric tramways.—Mr. A. E. White, city engineer.

WILLENHALL (Staffs.).—December 30th.—Erection of a new span-roof greenhouse, 30 ft. by 12 ft., at the new cemetery at Bentley, for the urban district council.—Mr. Chas. J. Jenkin, engineer and surveyor to the council.

ELGIN.—December 30th.—Supply of road metal during the year ending May 15, 1900, for the various divisions of the county highways, for the county council.—Mr. Alexander Hogg, county road surveyor, 24 Academy-street, Elgin.

WEST SUSSEX.—December 31st.—Supply of picked surface flints, pit flints, local stone, and 2-in. broken granite or stone, from April 1, 1899, to March 31, 1900, for the county council.—Mr. W. R. Parker, county surveyor, 31 Bedford-road, Horsham.

DUNDEE.—December 31st.—Supply of 500 2-in., 1,000 4-in., 500 6-in. and 500 8-in. turned and bored cast-iron pipes, for the water commissioners.—Mr. George Baxter, engineer and manager to the commissioners, 93 Commercial-street, Dundee.

ROTHERHAM.—December 31st.—Supply and erection of sludge-pressing plant, boilers, sewage ejectors and sewage lifts, for the corporation.—Mr. R. E. W. Berrington, Bank-buildings, Wolverhampton.

RAMSGATE.—December 31st.—Supply of a compound condensing beam engine at the Whitehall pumping station.—Mr. William A. Valon, gas and water engineer to the corporation.

ST. GEORGE, HANOVER SQUARE.—December 31st.—Supply of various materials for one year from March 15, 1899, for the vestry.—Mr. George Livingstone, surveyor to the vestry.

FOLKESTONE.—December 31st.—Supply of 1,000 to 2,000 yards super. of 2½-in. York stone.—Mr. A. F. Kidson, town clerk.

DARTMOUTH.—December 31st.—Erection of stone boundary walls and public latrines on the reclaimed land, North-parade and Mayor's-avenue, for the urban district council.—Mr. T. O. Veale, surveyor to the council.

PADDINGTON.—January 2nd.—Supply of two dust-tipping vans, three slop-tipping vans and five pairs of wheels, for the vestry.—Mr. Frank Delbridge, clerk to the vestry.

STIRLING.—January 2nd.—Supply of various electric lighting plant, for the commissioners.—Prof. A. B. W. Kennedy, 17 Victoria-street, London, S.W.

LEAMINGTON.—January 2nd.—Erection of an entrance lodge to Victoria Park, for the corporation.—Mr. Fredk. G. Cundall, 41 Parade, Leamington.

EASTBOURNE.—January 2nd.—Relaying of the Tideswell-road district low-level sewer.—Mr. R. M. Gloyne, A.M.I.C.E., borough engineer.

WIMBLEDON.—January 2nd.—Making-up of Malcolm-road, for the urban district council.—Mr. W. H. Whitfeld, clerk to the council.

LIMERICK.—January 2nd.—Relaying the paving of Galt-street and parts of Rhodes-well-road and Belgrave-street, for the district board of works.—Mr. S. G. Ratcliff, clerk to the board.

EDINBURGH.—January 2nd.—Supply and delivery at the electric light works in Macdonald-road of a switch-board and boosters, for the corporation.—Prof. A. B. W. Kennedy, 17 Victoria-street, London, S.W.

BOOTLE (Lancs.).—January 2nd.—Certain private improvement works in College-view and various passages in the borough.—The Borough Engineer.

RYDE (I.W.).—January 3rd.—Supply of two new pumping engines; overhead travelling crane and a Galloway boiler at the Knighton pumping station, near Newchurch.—Mr. C. G. Vincent, town clerk.

GLASGOW.—January 3rd.—Supply and erection of generating plant at one of the new electricity works, for the corporation.—Mr. W. A. Chamen, 75 Waterloo-street, Glasgow.

HANDSWORTH (Staffs.).—January 3rd.—Making-up of part of Putney-road, for the urban district council.—Mr. E. Kenworthy, engineer and surveyor to the council.

EPPING (Essex).—January 3rd.—Construction of about 4 miles of 12-in. and 9-in. iron and stoneware pipe sewers and the preparation of the outfall land, for the rural district council.—Mr. G. J. Creed, clerk to the council.

RHONDDA.—January 3rd.—Erection of three corrugated-iron buildings for use as fire stations, for the urban district council.—Mr. W. J. Jones, surveyor to the council.

ANNAN (Scotland).—January 3rd.—Supply of road metal for one year, for the commissioners.—Mr. Alex. Tweedie, burgh surveyor.

MANCHESTER.—January 4th.—Alterations at Leaf-street baths.—The City Surveyor.

ST. ALBANS.—January 4th.—Extension of the sewers at London Colney, for the rural district council.—Mr. H. H. Scott, borough surveyor to the council.

HOVE.—January 4th.—Road-making and other works in Suffolk-street and Molesworth-street.—Mr. H. H. Scott, borough surveyor.

MIDDLETON (Lancs.).—January 4th.—Sewering and draining of Haworth and Wade streets.—Mr. W. Welburn, borough surveyor.

FEATHERSTONE (Yorks.).—January 5th.—Laying of about 30 yards of cast-iron pipe sewer, for the urban district council.—Mr. W. A. Palliser, engineer and surveyor to the council.

COCKERMOUTH.—January 6th.—Erection of two bridges over Bonk Beck in Brackenthwaite, for the rural district council.—Mr. J. R. Wilson, A.M.I.C.E., surveyor to the council.

JOHANNESBURG, S.A.—January 6th.—Supply of a complete carburetted water-gas plant, for the corporation.—Messrs. Robert Whyte & Co., 22 Bury-street, St. Mary Axe, London, E.C.

EDINBURGH.—January 6th.—Installation of inclined retorts, together with coal and coke elevators and conveyors at the Mill-lane gasworks.—Mr. James Parkinson, town clerk.

WANSTEAD.—January 6th.—Making-up of Morningston-road (northern portion) and Asylum-road (eastern portion), for the urban district council.—Mr. Wm. Blewitt, clerk to the council.

WEST HAM.—January 7th.—Enlargement of the hospital in Southern-road, Plaistow, E.—Mr. Fred. N. Hilleary, town clerk.

CARMARTHEN.—January 7th.—Supply of 11,400 yards of 9-in., 2,100 yards of 6-in., 1,500 yards of 4-in., and 4,500 yards of 3-in. cast-iron water pipes.—Mr. F. J. Finglah, borough surveyor.

SURBITON.—January 7th.—Making-up of St. James', Gladstone and Southborough roads, Southborough, and Orchard-road, Hook, for the urban district council.—Mr. Samuel Mather, A.M.I.C.E., surveyor to the council.

TUNBRIDGE WELLS.—January 9th.—Construction of filter-beds at the waterworks at Pembury.—Mr. W. C. Cripps, town clerk.

WOLVERHAMPTON.—January 9th.—Levelling, paving, channelling, sewering, metalling, kerbing and completion of Raby-street extension (Melbourne-street to All Saints'-road) and Lever-street (Green-lane to Raby-street).—Mr. J. W. Bradley, borough engineer and surveyor·

BECKENHAM.—January 9th.—Making-up of Border-crescent, for the urban district council.—Mr. F. Stevens, clerk to the council.

SOUTHAMPTON.—January 9th.—Construction of certain precipitating tanks, storm-water overflow and other works.—Mr. W. B. G. Bennett, borough engineer.

BECKENHAM.—January 9th.—Paving works in Trinity, Arthur and Croydon-roads, for the urban district council.—Mr. John A. Angell, surveyor to the council].

MALDON (ESSEX).—January 9th.—Supply of about 850 tons of 6-in., 4-in., 3-in. and 2-in. cast-iron water mains and special castings for the Purleigh district waterworks, for the rural district council.—Mr. Horace G. Keywood, engineer to the council.

SOUTHAMPTON.—January 9th.—Private street works in Brighten-road. —Mr. W. B. G. Bennett, borough engineer.

SOUTHEND-ON-SEA.—January 10th.—Reconstruction of the recently damaged portion of the pier.—Mr. Alfred Fidler, A.M.I.C.E., borough engineer.·

BANES.—January 10th.—Erection of a new fire station in High-street, Mortlake, for the urban district council.—Mr. G. Bruce Tomes, M.I.C.E., engineer and surveyor to the council.

BURNLEY.—January 10th.—Supply and delivery at the electricity supply station of underground cables.—Mr. W. R. Wright, borough electrical engineer.

WEST HAM.—January 10th.—Supply of 216 waterproof coats and leggings for roadmen.—Mr. Lewis Angell, borough engineer.

ASHFORD (Kent).—January 10th.—Supply of cast-iron pipes and appendages, for the urban district council.—Mr. J. Creery, clerk to the council.

SWANSEA.—January 10th.—Construction of about 2,360 lineal yards and 2,440 yards of brick and pipe sewers at Morriston.—Mr. R. H. Wynill, borough engineer.

DOVER.—January 10th.—Completion and construction of Beaconsfield-road.—Mr. Henry E. Stilgoe, A.M.I.C.E., borough engineer.

CLACTON-ON-SEA.—January 11th.—Making-up of Ellis-road, Agnis-road, Dudley-road and Hayes-road, for the urban district council.—Mr. A. R. Robinson, surveyor to the council.

SELBY.—January 11th.—Erection of public baths, for the urban district council.—Mr. Jno. Hy. Bastoft, clerk to the council.

HORNSEY.—January 11th.—Alteration and extension of the heating system at the isolation hospital at Muswell Hill, for the urban district council.—Mr. E. J. Lovegrove, engineer to the council.

ISLINGTON.—January 11th.—Demolition of buildings abutting on the site of the electric light station in Eden-grove, Holloway, for the vestry. —Mr. William F. Dewey, clerk to the vestry.

KIDDERMINSTER.—January 11th.—Erection of a fire engine station.— Mr. Arthur Comber, borough surveyor.

ISLE OF WIGHT.—January 14th.—Widening of the road at Haven-street, near the board school, for the rural district council.—Mr. K. Humphries, surveyor to the council, Newchurch.

SOUTHAMPTON.—January 16th.—Construction of concrete founda-tions, erection of brick, steel and concrete superstructures of new infirmary wards, sanitary blocks, boiler-house, tall chimney shaft, and sundry other work at the county lunatic asylum at Knowle, near Fare-ham, for the county council.—Mr. W. J. Taylor, county surveyor, The Castle, Winchester.

BERMONDSEY.—January 16th.—Supply of 60,000 bricks, for the vestry. —Mr. Frank Sumner, surveyor to the vestry.

ROCKDALE.—January 17th.—Erection of buildings required for the proposed electricity works.—Mr. J. Leach, town clerk.

LANCASHIRE.—January 17th.—Erection of a police station, dwelling-houses, &c., at Huyton, for the county council.—Mr. Henry Littler, architect to the Standing Joint Committee, County Offices, Preston.

ECCLES (Lancs.).—January 19th.—Various street works in Back St. Mary's-street, Back New-lane East, Back New-lane West, Back Hampson-street and Barton-grove.—Mr. Geo. Wm. Bailey, town clerk.

BARROW-IN-FURNESS.—January 20th.—Wiring of the free library in Cornwallis-street.—The Borough Electrical Engineer.

BANBURY.—January 21st.—Supply of Hartshill stone during the year ending March 31, 1900.—Mr. N. H. Dawson, borough surveyor.

WITHNELL.—January 31st.—Various works at the sewage works, for the urban district council.—Mr. T. Beaver, surveyor, Brincall.

CHELTENHAM.—January 23rd.—Reconstruction of the retaining wall at the No. 3 reservoir at Hewletts.—Mr. E. T. Brydges, town clerk.

LONDON.—January 24th.—Supply of a 5-ton overhead traveller at the new pumping station now in course of erection at North Woolwich, for the county council.—Mr. C. J. Stewart, clerk to the council, County Hall, Spring-gardens, S.W.

LONDON.—January 24th.—Construction of a tunnel for pedestrian traffic under the river Thames from Greenwich to Poplar, for the county council.—Mr. C. J. Stewart, clerk to the council, County Hall, Spring-gardens, S.W.

SOUTHAMPTON.—January 28th.—Construction and erection of the superstructure of Bresmore bridge over the river Avon, for the county council.—Mr. W. J. Taylor, county surveyor, The Castle, Winchester.

CHIPPING NORTON.—January 31st.—Certain main drainage works.—

SHANGHAI.—March 15th.—Construction and working of about 23 miles of electric tramways on the trolley system, for the municipal council.—Messrs. J. Pook & Co., 8 Jeffery's-square, St. Mary Axe, London, E.C.

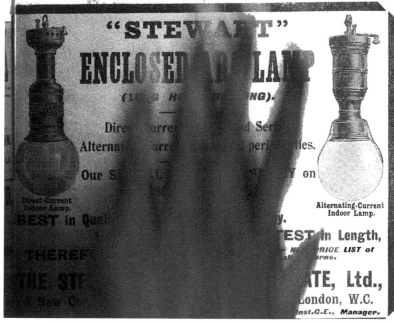

BRADFORD.—April 14th.—Erection of a building for the Cartwright memorial hall and art gallery. £150, £100 and £50.—Mr. George McGuire, town clerk.

## MUNICIPAL CONTRACTS OPEN.

*Official and all similar advertisements received later than Wednesday evening are too late for classification and cannot therefore be included in these summaries until the following week. No advertisements received after 3 p.m. on Thursday can be inserted until the following week.*

HULL.—December 30th.—Supply of steel roof trusses, steel columns, &c., in connection with the erection of car sheds for the electric tramways.—Mr. A. E. White, city engineer.

HULL.—December 30th.—Erection of two car sheds and other buildings (area about 4,000 square yards) in connection with the electric tramways.—Mr. A. E. White, city engineer.

HULL.—December 30th.—Supply of pipes, fittings, &c., for the power station in connection with the electric tramways.—Mr. A. E. White, city engineer.

WILLENHALL (Staffs.).—December 30th.—Erection of a new span-roof greenhouse, 30 ft. by 12 ft., at the new cemetery at Bentley, for the urban district council.—Mr. Chas. J. Jenkin, engineer and surveyor to the council.

ELGIN.—December 30th.—Supply of road metal during the year ending May 15, 1900, for the various divisions of the county highways, for the county council.—Mr. Alexander Hogg, country road surveyor, 24 Academy-street, Elgin.

WEST SUSSEX.—December 31st.—Supply of picked surface flints, pit flints, local stone, and 2-in. broken granite or stone, from April 1, 1899, to March 31, 1900, for the county council.—Mr. W. R. Furber, county surveyor, 31 Bedford-road, Horsham.

DUNDEE.—December 31st.—Supply of 500 2-in., 1,000 4-in., 500 6-in. and 500 8-in. turned and bored cast-iron pipes, for the water commissioners.—Mr. George Baxter, engineer and manager to the commissioners, 93 Commercial-street, Dundee.

ROTHERHAM.—December 31st.—Supply and erection of sludge-pressing plant, boilers, sewage ejectors and sewage lifts, for the corporation.—Mr. R. E. W. Berrington, Bank-buildings, Wolverhampton.

RAMSGATE.—December 31st.—Supply of a compound condensing beam engine at the Whitehall pumping station.—Mr. William A. Valon, gas and water engineer to the corporation.

ST. GEORGE, HANOVER SQUARE.—December 31st.—Supply of various materials for one year from March 25, 1899, for the vestry.—Mr. George Livingstone, surveyor to the vestry.

FOLKESTONE.—December 31st.—Supply of 1,000 to 3,000 yards super. of 2½-in. York stone.—Mr. A. F. Kidson, town clerk.

DARTMOUTH.—December 31st.—Erection of stone boundary walls and public latrines on the reclaimed land, North-parade and Mayor's-avenue, for the urban district council.—Mr. T. O. Veale, surveyor to the council.

PADDINGTON.—January 2nd.—Supply of two dust-tipping vans, three slop-tipping vans and five pairs of wheels, for the vestry.—Mr. Frank Dethridge, clerk to the vestry.

STIRLING.—January 2nd.—Supply of various electric lighting plant, for the commissioners.—Prof. A. B. W. Kennedy, 17 Victoria-street, London, S.W.

LEAMINGTON.—January 2nd.—Erection of an entrance lodge to Victoria Park, for the corporation.—Mr. Fredk. G. Cundall, 41 Parade, Leamington.

EASTBOURNE.—January 2nd.—Relaying of the Tideswell-road district low-level sewer.—Mr. R. M. Gloyne, A.M.I.C.E., borough engineer.

WIMBLEDON.—January 2nd.—Making-up of Malcolm-road, for the urban district council.—Mr. W. H. Whitfield, clerk to the council.

LIMEHOUSE.—January 2nd.—Relaying the paving of Galt-street and parts of Rhodeswell-road and Belgrave-street, for the district board of works.—Mr. S. G. Ratcliff, clerk to the board.

EDINBURGH.—January 2nd.—Supply and delivery at the electric light works in Macdonald-road of a switch-board and boosters, for the corporation.—Prof. A. B. W. Kennedy, 17 Victoria-street, London, S.W.

BOOTLE (Lancs.).—January 2nd.—Certain private improvement works in College-view and various passages in the borough.—The Borough Engineer.

RYDE (I.W.).—January 3rd.—Supply of two new pumping engines, overhead travelling crane and a Galloway boiler at the Knighton pumping station, near Newchurch.—Mr. C. G. Vincent, town clerk.

GLASGOW.—January 3rd.—Supply and erection of generating plant at one of the new electricity works for the corporation.—Mr. W. A. Chamen, 75 Waterloo-street, Glasgow.

HANDSWORTH (Staffs.).—January 3rd.—Making-up of part of Putney-road, for the urban district council.—Mr. E. Kenworthy, engineer and surveyor to the council.

EPPING (Essex).—January 3rd.—Construction of about 4 miles of 12-in. and 9-in. iron and stoneware pipe sewers and the preparation of the outfall land, for the rural district council.—Mr. G. J. Creed, clerk to the council.

RHONDDA.—January 3rd.—Erection of three corrugated-iron buildings for use as fire stations, for the urban district council.—Mr. W. J. Jones, surveyor to the council.

ANNAN (Scotland).—January 3rd.—Supply of road metal for one year, for the commissioners.—Mr. Alex. Tweedie, burgh surveyor.

MANCHESTER.—January 4th.—Alterations at Leaf-street baths.—The City Surveyor.

ST. ALBANS.—January 4th.—Extension of the sewers at London Colney, for the rural district council.—Mr. R. W. Brabant, clerk to the council.

HOVE.—January 4th.—Road-making and other works in Suffolk-street and Molesworth-street.—Mr. H. H. Scott, borough surveyor.

MIDDLETON (Lancs.).—January 4th.—Sewering and draining of Haworth and Wade streets.—Mr. W. Welburn, borough surveyor.

FEATHERSTONE (Yorks.).—January 5th.—Laying of about 30 yards of cast-iron pipe sewer, for the urban district council.—Mr. W. A. Palliser, engineer and surveyor to the council.

COCKERMOUTH.—January 6th.—Erection of two bridges over Hope Beck in Brackenthwaite, for the rural district council.—Mr. J. B. Wilson, A.M.I.C.E., surveyor to the council.

JOHANNESBURG, S.A.—January 6th.—Supply of a complete carburetted water-gas plant, for the corporation.—Messrs. Robert Whyte & Co., 22 Bury-street, St. Mary Axe, London, E.C.

BRIDGNORTH.—January 6th.—Installation of inclined retorts, together with coal and coke elevators and conveyors at the Mill-lane gasworks.—Mr. James Parkinson, town clerk.

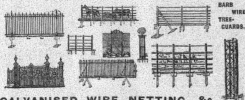

WANSTEAD.—January 9th.—Making-up of Mornington-road (northern portion) and Asylum-road (eastern portion), for the urban district council.—Mr. Wm. Blewitt, clerk to the council.

WEST HAM.—January 7th.—Enlargements of the hospital in Southern-road, Plaistow, E.—Mr. Fred. E. Hilleary, town clerk.

CARMARTHEN.—January 7th.—Supply of 11,400 yards of 9-in., 2,100 yards of 6-in., 1,500 yards of 4-in., and 4,500 yards of 3-in. cast-iron water pipes.—Mr. F. J. Finglah, borough surveyor.

SURBITON.—January 7th.—Making-up of St. James', Gladstone and Southborough roads, Southborough, and Orchard-road, Hook, for the urban district council.—Mr. Samuel Mather, A.M.I.C.E., surveyor to the council.

TUNBRIDGE WELLS.—January 9th.—Construction of filter-beds at the waterworks at Pembury.—Mr. W. C. Cripps, town clerk.

WOLVERHAMPTON.—January 9th.—Levelling, paving, channelling, sewering, metalling, kerbing and completion of Raby-street extension (Melbourne-street to All Saints'-road) and Lever-street (Green-lane to Raby-street).—Mr. J. W. Bradley, borough engineer and surveyor.

BECKENHAM.—January 9th.—Making-up of Border-crescent, for the urban district council.—Mr. F. Stevens, clerk to the council.

SOUTHAMPTON.—January 9th.—Construction of certain precipitating tanks, storm-water overflow and other works.—Mr. W. B. G. Bennett, borough engineer.

DECKENHAM.—January 9th.—Paving works in Trinity, Arthur and Croydon-roads, for the urban district council.—Mr. John A. Angell, surveyor to the council.

MALDON (Essex).—January 9th.—Supply of about 650 tons of 3-in., 4-in., 3-in. and 2-in. cast-iron water mains and special castings for the Purleigh district waterworks, for the rural district council.—Mr. Horace G. Keywood, engineer to the council.

SOUTHAMPTON.—January 9th.—Private street works in Brighton-road.—Mr. W. B. G. Bennett, borough engineer.

SOUTHEND-ON-SEA.—January 10th.—Reconstruction of the recently damaged portion of the pier.—Mr. Alfred Fidler, A.M.I.C.E., borough engineer.

BARNES.—January 10th.—Erection of a new fire station in High-street, Mortlake, for the urban district council.—Mr. G. Bruce Tomes, M.I.C.E., engineer and surveyor to the council.

BURNLEY.—January 10th.—Supply and delivery at the electricity supply station of underground cables.—Mr. W. R. Wright, borough electrical engineer.

WEST HAM.—January 10th.—Supply of 210 waterproof coats and leggings for roadmen.—Mr. Lewis Angell, borough engineer.

ASHFORD (Kent).—January 10th.—Supply of cast-iron pipes and appendages, for the urban district council.—Mr. J. Creery, clerk to the council.

SWANSEA.—January 10th.—Construction of about 2,360 lineal yards and 2,240 yards of brick and pipe sewers at Morriston.—Mr. R. H. Wyrill, borough engineer.

DOVER.—January 10th.—Completion and construction of Beaconsfield-road.—Mr. Henry E. Stilgoe, A.M.I.C.E., borough engineer.

CLACTON-ON-SEA.—January 11th.—Making-up of Ellis-road, Agate-road, Dudley-road and Hayes-road, for the urban district council.—Mr. A. R. Robinson, surveyor to the council.

SELBY.—January 11th.—Erection of public baths, for the urban district council.—Mr. Jno. Hy. Bantoft, clerk to the council.

HORNSEY.—January 11th.—Alteration and extension of the heating system at the isolation hospital at Muswell Hill, for the urban district council.—Mr. E. J. Lovegrove, engineer to the council.

ISLINGTON.—January 11th.—Demolition of buildings abutting on the site of the electric light station in Eden-grove, Holloway, for the vestry.—Mr. William F. Dewey, clerk to the vestry.

KIDDERMINSTER.—January 11th.—Erection of a fire engine station.—Mr. Arthur Comber, borough surveyor.

ISLE OF WIGHT.—January 11th.—Widening of the road at Haven-street, near the board school, for the rural district council.—Mr. E. Humphries, surveyor to the council, Newchurch.

SOUTHAMPTON.—January 13th.—Construction of concrete foundations, erection of brick, steel and concrete superstructure of new infirmary wards, sanitary blocks, boiler-house, tall chimney shaft, and sundry other work at the county lunatic asylum at Knowle, near Fareham, for the county council.—Mr. W. J. Taylor, county surveyor, The Castle, Winchester.

BERMONDSEY.—January 16th.—Supply of 60,000 bricks, for the vestry.—Mr. Frank Sumner, surveyor to the vestry.

ROCHDALE.—January 17th.—Erection of buildings required for the proposed electricity works.—Mr. J. Leach, town clerk.

LANCASHIRE.—January 17th.—Erection of a police station, dwelling-houses, &c., at Huyton, for the county council.—Mr. Henry Littler, architect to the Standing Joint Committee, County Offices, Preston.

ECCLES (Lancs.).—January 19th.—Various street works in Back St. Mary's-street, Back New-lane East, Back New-lane West, Back Hampson-street and Barton-grove.—Mr. Geo. Wm. Bailey, town clerk.

BARROW-IN-FURNESS.—January 20th.—Wiring of the free library in Cornwallis-street.—The Borough Electrical Engineer.

BANBURY.—January 21st.—Supply of Hartshill stone during the year ending March 31, 1900.—Mr. N. H. Dawson, borough surveyor.

WITHNELL.—January 21st.—Various works at the sewage works, for the urban district council.—Mr. T. Beaver, surveyor, Brinscall.

CHELTENHAM.—January 23rd.—Reconstruction of the retaining wall at the No. 3 reservoir at Hewletts.—Mr. E. T. Brydges, town clerk.

LONDON.—January 24th.—Supply of a 5-ton overhead traveller at the new pumping station now in course of erection at North Woolwich, for the county council.—Mr. C. J. Stewart, clerk to the council, County Hall, Spring-gardens, S.W.

LONDON.—January 24th.—Construction of a tunnel for pedestrian traffic under the river Thames from Greenwich to Poplar, for the county council.—Mr. C. J. Stewart, clerk to the council, County Hall, Spring-gardens, S.W.

SOUTHAMPTON.—January 28th.—Construction and erection of the superstructure of Breamore bridge over the river Avon, for the county council.—Mr. W. J. Taylor, county surveyor, The Castle, Winchester.

CHIPPING NORTON.—January 31st.—Certain main drainage works.—Mr. Thomas Mace, town clerk.

SHANGHAI.—March 15th.—Construction and working of about 23 miles of electric tramways on the trolley system, for the municipal council.—Messrs. J. Pook & Co., 8 Jeffery's-square, St. Mary Axe, London, E.C.

## TENDERS FOR MUNICIPAL WORKS OR SUPPLIES.

*ACCEPTED.

BARKING (Essex).—For the erection of eighty-five cottages for the working classes in Creeksmouth-lane, for the urban district council.—Mr. C. J. Dawson, F.R.I.B.A., surveyor to the council :—

| | |
|---|---|
| J. J. Reave, East Ham | £20,500 |
| E. Hughes, Strood Green | 20,543 |
| J. C. Garbett, Barking | 16,300 |
| H. Lane, East Ham† | 12,750 |

† Accepted subject to sanction of Local Government Board.

BARNSLEY.—Accepted for the supply of various plant, &c., for the electricity supply works.—Mr. J. Henry Taylor, A.M.I.C.E., borough surveyor :—

Contract No. 1 ( ).—W. Arnold & Co., £3,260.
Contract No. 2 (engines, dynamos, plant, &c.).—Johnson & Philips £3,030.
Contract No. 3 (storage batteries, &c.).—Pritchetts & Gold, £1,319 and £70 per annum for annual maintenance of batteries.
Contract No. 4 (electrical mains, &c.).—The British Insulated Wire Company, £6,322 and £110 per annum for maintenance.

EAST RETFORD.—For sewerage and sewage disposal works, for the town council.—Mr. J. C. Melliss, M.I.C.E., engineer, 264 Gresham House, Old Broad-street, London, E.C. :—

| | |
|---|---|
| A. Brunton & Son | £52,916 |
| W. Pattinson & Co. | 51,961 |
| J. H. Vickers, Limited | 49,805 |
| J. D. Nowell & Son | 49,500 |
| G. Osenton | 44,765 |
| B. Cooke & Co. | 43,946 |
| G. Bell | 42,887 |
| J. Jackson | 40,100 |
| J. Bentley | 39,353 |
| E. Tempest | 35,171 |
| H. Arnold & Son, Doncaster* | 34,249 |

HACKNEY.—For the supply of Portland cement, for the vestry.—Mr. James Lovegrove, chief surveyor to the vestry :—

| | Per ton. £ s. d. |
|---|---|
| T. Blyth, Kingsland-road, N.E. | 2 6 0 |
| W. Griffiths, Bishopsgate-street Without, E.C. | 2 5 0 |
| L. Sommerfeld, Great Tower-street, E.C. | 2 3 3 |
| J. Bealey, White & Bros., Limited, Lime Street-square, E.C. | 2 1 0 |
| Whincop & Son, Mount Wharf, Leeside-road, Upper Clapton, N.E. | 2 0 11 |
| J. Byford, Moody Wharf, Poplar, E. | 2 0 0 |
| F. Kosher, Kingsland-road, N.E. | 1 19 9 |

COVENTRY.—For the construction of five electric light sub-stations.—Mr. J. E. Swindlehurst, city engineer :—

| | |
|---|---|
| A. Care, Coventry | £868 |
| C. G. Hill, „ | 849 |
| T. G. Golby, „ | 839 |
| R. Wootten, „ | 833 |
| C. H. Barber, „ | 818 |

HACKNEY.—For the laying of about 600 superficial yards of yellow deal wood paving at Northwold-road and about 1,000 superficial yards of hard wood paving in Kingsland-road, for the vestry.—Mr. James Lovegrove, surveyor to the vestry :—

Kingsland-road (jarrah wood blocks, laid on concrete foundation).—Acme Wood Flooring Company, Limited, Gainsborough-road, Hackney Wick, N.E.,* 14s. per super. yard.
Northwold-road (yellow deal blocks, pickled in creosote and laid on concrete foundation).—Acme Wood Flooring Company, Limited, Gainsborough-road, Hackney Wick, N.E.,* 9s. 11d. per super yard.
Extra Concrete (if ordered).—Acme Wood Flooring Company, Limited, Gainsborough-road, Hackney Wick, N.E.,* 15s. 9d. per cubic yard.

HORNSEY.—For the making-up of Rathcoole-gardens (section 1) and Temple-road, for the urban district council.—Mr. E. J. Lovegrove, engineer to the council :—

| | Rathcoole-gardens (section 1). | Temple-road. |
|---|---|---|
| Pedrette & Co., Finsbury Park | £1,467 | £609 |
| Ballard & Co., Childs Hill | 1,180 | 666 |
| Killingback & Co., Camden Town | 1,163 | 536 |
| T. Adams, Wood Green | 1,077 | 497 |
| E. T. Bloomfield, Tottenham | 1,163 | 544 |
| G. Bell, Tottenham | 1,135 | 527 |
| W. Walker, Holloway | 1,328 | 548 |
| H. Clark, Andover-road* | 1,045 | 476 |

LUTON.—For kerbing, channelling, metalling, &c., works in Cranley-road.—Mr. A. J. L. Evans, borough engineer :—

| | |
|---|---|
| G. Powdrill, Luton | £2,032 |
| Free & Sons, Maidenhead | 2,800 |
| Patent Victoria Stone Company, Leicester* | 2,775 |
| S. Kavanagh, Surbiton† | 2,154 |

Surveyor's estimate, £2,800.
† Withdrawn.

MIDDLESBROUGH.—For the reconstruction and repair of Emily-street and the back street between Beaufort and Cook streets and the alterations of the old town hall police station.—Mr. Frank Baker, borough engineer :—

EMILY-STREET.

J. Crombie & Son, Middlesbrough ... £263
J. T. Dixon, Preston-on-Tees* ... 230
(Mr. J. T. Dixon's tender was accepted for the carriageway only, on his schedule of prices.)

BACK STREET BETWEEN BEAUFORT AND COOK STREETS.
J. T. Dixon, Preston-on-Tees* ... £60

WOKING.—For the supply and delivery of one road-sweeping machine, for the urban district council.—Mr. G. J. Woolridge, surveyor to the council :—

| | |
|---|---|
| Gloucester Carriage and Wheel Works, Cannon-street, E.C. | £33 |
| Bristol Waggon and Carriage Works Company, Bristol | 29 |
| W. Smith & Sons, Barnard Castle, Durham | 27 |
| Glover & Sons, Eagle Works, Warwick | 26 |
| H. Wadsworth & Son, Halifax | 25 |
| Barrows & Co., Banbury, Oxon.* | 25 |

WEST HARTLEPOOL.—Accepted for the supply of various materials and goods required during the year ending December 31, 1899.—Mr. J. W. Brown, borough engineer :—
Caithness Flags.—Caithness Quarrying Company, Thurso.
Yorkshire Flags.—W. Bancroft, Denholme.
Concrete Flags.—J. Burn, West Hartlepool.
Kerbstone.—Brunton & Son, North Queensferry (Scotch) and Scotsgate Ash Company, Pateley Bridge (Yorkshire).
Paving Setts.—Brunton & Son (Scotch) and Northumberland Whinstone Company, Newcastle (blue whinstone), and Tees Scoria Company, Middlesbrough (scoria).
Broken and Unbroken Whinstone.—Craddock, Wake & Co., Eaglescliffe.
Pitch.—T. Ness, Darlington.
Tar.—J. A. Jobling, Newcastle-on-Tyne.
Lime.—G. & W. H. Carter, West Hartlepool.
Metal Castings.—F. J. White, West Hartlepool, and Ord & Maddison, Darlington.
Cement.—O. Trechmann and Casebourne & Co., West Hartlepool.
Disinfectants.—Lakin & Co., Pendleton (powder), Calvert & Co., Manchester (fluid), Sanitary Dry Lime Company, Bootle (fluid), and T. Oliver, George Foster and Foster & Armstrong, West Hartlepool.
General Stores.—Booker & Co., Sheffield ; Jameson & Co., Newcastle-on-Tyne; Rogerson & Co., Wolsingham ; R. Hardy, West Hartlepool ; J. Oliver, West Hartlepool ; Barker Brothers, West Hartlepool ; T. Phillips, Middlesbrough ; B. Clarke, Leeds ; Burt, Boulton & Haywood, West Hartlepool; and G. R. Troupe, West Hartlepool.

## MEETINGS.

*Secretaries and others will oblige by sending early notice of dates of forthcoming meetings.*

JANUARY.
9.—The Surveyors' Institution: Discussion on Mr. Weaver's paper on "The London Building Act and the Official Supervision of Buildings." 8 p.m.
10.—Institution of Civil Engineers: Ordinary meeting ; Mr. J. H. Dales, A.M.I.C.E., on "High-speed Engines." 8 p.m.
13.—Institution of Civil Engineers : Students' meeting ; Dr. Archibald Barr, M.I.C.E., on "The Application of the Science of Mechanics to Engineering Practice." 8 p.m.
17.—Liverpool Self-propelled Traffic Association : Mr. S. A. Sparkes on "Motor v. Horse Haulage; An Account of our Nine Months' Experiences." 8 p.m.
26.—Association of the Birmingham Students of the Institution of Civil Engineers : Mr. L. L. Baldwin, A.M.I.C.E., on "Coalville Water Supply ; A few notes on the sinking of a trial bore-hole." 7.30 p.m.

Trowbridge.—The council have been informed that a Local Government Board inquiry will be held shortly with respect to an application for sanction to borrow £2,600 for works of main road paving.

## NOTICES.

THE SURVEYOR AND MUNICIPAL AND COUNTY ENGINEER *may be ordered direct, through any of Messrs. Smith & Son's book-stalls, or of any newsagent in the United Kingdom. Applications to the Offices for single copies by post must in all cases be accompanied by stamps.*

*The Prepaid Subscription (including postage) is as follows :*

| | Twelve Months. | Six Months. | Three Months. |
|---|---|---|---|
| United Kingdom | 14s. | 7s. 6d. | 3s. 9d. |
| Continent, the Colonies, India, | | | |
| United States, &c. | 19s. | 9s. 6d. | 4s. 9d. |

*The International News Company, 83 and 85 Duane-street' New York City ; The Toronto News Company, Toronto ; and The Montreal News Company, Montreal, have been appointed agents in the United States and Canada for the sale of* THE SURVEYOR AND MUNICIPAL AND COUNTY ENGINEER. *A thin paper edition is printed for circulation abroad.*

EDITORIAL OFFICES :—
24 BRIDE-LANE, FLEET-STREET, LONDON, E.C.

ADVERTISEMENT AND PUBLISHING OFFICES :—
13 NEW STREET-HILL, FLEET-STREET, LONDON, E.C.

## APPOINTMENTS OPEN.

BOROUGH OF PENZANCE.
APPOINTMENT OF BOROUGH SURVEYOR.

The Penzance Corporation are prepared to receive applications for the appointment of Borough Surveyor.
Salary, £200 per annum, with residence. List of duties, &c., can be obtained from the undersigned, to whom applications must be addressed, endorsed "Borough Surveyor," and delivered at the Town Clerk's office on or before the 4th January, 1899.

Canvassing members of the Council will be a disqualification.

T. H. CORNISH,
Town Clerk.

Town Clerk's Office, Penzance.
December 14, 1898.

COUNTY BOROUGH OF WEST HAM.
APPOINTMENT OF ASSISTANT MARSH BAILIFF.

The Council require the services of a competent man as Assistant to the Marsh Bailiff in the supervision and maintenance of river walls, wharf, tidal ditches, culverts, penstocks, and other like works under the Borough Engineer.

Application, in candidate's own handwriting, stating age, trade, experience, &c., accompanied by testimonials and references, to be sent to my office not later than 4 p.m. on Tuesday, 10th January, 1899.

(By order of the Council)
FRED. E. HILLEARY,
Town Clerk.

Town Hall, Stratford, E.
December 23, 1898.

URBAN DISTRICT COUNCIL OF WHITWORTH.
SURVEYOR AND SANITARY INSPECTOR.

The Urban District Council of Whitworth invites applications for the offices of Surveyor and Inspector of Nuisances, at a salary of £150 for the two offices (£100 as Surveyor and £50 as Inspector).

The person appointed must have a thorough and practical knowledge of road maintenance, the management of sewers and sewage works, and of the duties appertaining to the office of an inspector of nuisances under the Public Health and Sanitary Acts, and be able to keep the necessary accounts.

He will be expected to devote his whole time to the work of the Council, and to be prepared generally to comply with and abide by their instructions. He will also be required to give a bond in £200 for the due discharge of his duties.

Applications, marked "Surveyor," stating age, present and previous occupation and experience, and accompanied by copies of not less than three recent testimonials, must be sent to me not later than January 7, 1899.

OWEN MARCH,
Clerk to the Council.

Whitworth, near Rochdale.
December 20, 1898.

BOROUGH OF MANSFIELD.

The Town Council require the services of a Resident Engineer or Inspector of Works to superintend, under the direction of the Borough Engineer and Surveyor, the construction of a brick and pipe intercepting sewer and works in connection therewith in the said borough, and also of a sewerage and outfall works at Pleasley Hill, in the said borough. The gentleman appointed must be an accurate leveller and have had previous experience in similar works, and will be required to devote his whole time to the duties of the office.

Salary, £4 per week.

Applications, stating age and previous experience, accompanied by copies of three testimonials of recent date, to be sent to Mr. R. Frank Vallance, Borough Surveyor, Mansfield.

Canvassing members of the Council is prohibited.

J. HARROP WHITE,
Deputy Town Clerk.

December 23, 1898.

CIVIL ENGINEER.—Surveyor to urban district council, 20 miles from London, has a vacancy for well-educated youth as Articled Pupil. Works for 1899 include sewerage and sewage disposal (£55,000). Moderate premium.—Address "LEVEL," office of THE SURVEYOR, 24 Bride-lane, Fleet-street, E.C.

BOROUGH OF SOUTHEND-ON-SEA.

Wanted, a Temporary Assistant; must have had experience in preparing schemes for main sewerage and sewage disposal works. Salary, £3 3s. per week.

Apply to Mr. Alfred Fidler, ASSOC.M.INST.C.E., Borough Engineer and Surveyor, Clarence-road, Southend-on-Sea.

THE Borough Engineer of Southend-on-Sea has a vacancy in his office for a Pupil.—Apply, Mr. Alfred Fidler, ASSOC.M.INST.C.E., Clarence-road, Southend-on-Sea.

## COMPETITIONS.

LONDON COUNTY COUNCIL.
DUST-CART AND COVER.

The London County Council invite designs for a Dust-Cart, for use in connection with the collection and disposal of house refuse.

It is required that the cart shall be so constructed and

Lightning Source UK Ltd.
Milton Keynes UK
UKHW020344090219
336963UK00010B/638/P